Baseball
The Biographical Encyclopedia

Baseball
The Biographical Encyclopedia

EDITED BY
DAVID PIETRUSZA
MATTHEW SILVERMAN
MICHAEL GERSHMAN

INTERIOR ILLUSTRATIONS BY
ANDY NELSON

KINGSTON, NEW YORK TOTAL Sports Illustrated NEW YORK, NEW YORK

Permissions
Total Sports Publishing
100 Enterprise Drive
Kingston, New York 12401

ISBN: 1-892129-34-5
Library of Congress Catalog Card Number: 00-100100

Printed in United States of America
10 9 8 7 6 5 4 3 2 1

Baseball
The Biographical Encyclopedia

Contents

To Mike Gershman,
our departed friend,
still at play in these extra innings

Acknowledgments

As the editorial team that produces *Total Baseball*, the official encyclopedia of the history of the game, we were already quite familiar with the statistical accomplishments of the more than 15,000 players in Major League Baseball history; for *Baseball: The Biographical Encyclopedia*, we came to know them better as individuals. On the way to creating the 2,000 biographies herein, we added to our roster a bunch of talented rookies, grizzled veterans, and semi-glamorous free agents.

Foremost on that list of Total Sports editors is Mikhail Horowitz, who on his first day at Total Sports was hurled headlong into a sea of biographies, formats, and fonts and admirably remained afloat. George Pattison and King Sackett followed this initiation process. Greg Spira, Sean Lahman, and Jed Thorn lent their vast baseball knowledge to the project all along the line. Rob Wilson came on board midway through the project and made sure we stopped debating the selections and actually finished the book.

A sincere thank-you goes to our off-premises copy editors, who accepted each package with a smile and actually met all their tight deadlines. Bob Carroll churned out the material prolifically and promptly, and Beau Riffenburgh surely became the first man on the Antarctic continent to read a biography of Ossie Bluege. Ed Dinger took all the biographies we had to offer and asked for more. Bill Doolittle and Mark Paddock handled their parts professionally and thoroughly. John Day's contribution was invaluable.

Some of the original material for this book was produced in 1994 and 1995, for a remarkable CD-ROM called Microsoft *Complete Baseball*. We knew we had our work cut out for us if we were to match its breadth and quality. We also had to update and verify the information. Fortunately, Peter Haugen had already reviewed most of the material before *Baseball: The Biographical Encyclopedia* got started in earnest.

While the editorial portion of this project was formidable—at last count the text amounted to 1.1 million words—the production component was equally daunting. Dick Perez painted the beautiful art for the book's jacket. Andy Nelson's illustrations appear throughout the interior.

From the end of the World Series to the start of spring training, no one put more effort into this book than Chad Lawrence. Chad took the ideas of the editors and the other designers and made *Baseball: The Biographical Encyclopedia* a beautiful book. Todd Radom's art direction kept this massive project moving forward, too.

Mark Rucker provided most of the photographs of baseball figures both immortal and obscure; tracking down the rest required the sometimes fevered efforts of several people. Dianne Robinson and Donna Harris played vital parts in this process and kept the whole project on schedule. Thanks also go to Bryan Reilly at Photo File, Bill Burdick at the Baseball Hall of Fame, Paula Mirabile Baker (who miraculously provided the photo for D.L. Adams), and our longtime friends and colleagues Fred Ivor-Campbell and Marty Appel. Ann Sullivan and Darryl Litts had the arduous task of sorting the photographs while learning the differences between Bill Lee and Big Bill Lee, George Burns and Tioga George Burns, and Bill Veeck, Sr., and Bill Veeck, Jr.

As always, Stanley Weil at *Sports Illustrated* had a prompt answer to every question. We are also grateful for Amy Schmetterling's assistance.

This book, like every Total Sports baseball research project, could not have been produced without the participation of John Thorn and Pete Palmer. Pete provided all the statistical materials; he had complete career statistics available for all current players before the ink was even dry on the 1999 season. We relied on John, the publisher of Total Sports, for his wisdom and experience in everything from design issues to Doc Cramer's hat size.

Finally, we thank our late colleague Mike Gershman for his fine work on the first incarnation of this material. Some of our best times as friends were spent sitting in the stands at ballgames, arguing about the skills of many of the players included in this book. It is somehow fitting that *Baseball: The Biographical Encyclopedia* continues Mike's argument even after the Umpire shouts "Game Called."

The Editors

Introduction

Total Baseball is not just the name of the publisher's most noted book; it expresses how we view baseball. When the task of selecting the greatest players of the century arose, the editors at *Total Baseball* took it one step further. Several prestigious publications and organizations created lists of the 100 greatest players of the 20th century, but a list of that size tells only part of baseball's story. What it leaves out—most notably, professional baseball's 19th-century origins—is as significant as what it includes.

Just about every player who has put on a major league uniform has a good story to tell. After 130 years, though, there are more than 15,000 players' stories, not to mention the stories of owners, umpires, broadcasters, sportswriters, and promoters. We know a lot about big books—the sixth edition of *Total Baseball* comprises more than 2,500 pages—but a book that chronicles the life of every major leaguer would probably weigh 20 pounds. So, for *Baseball: The Biographical Encyclopedia* we did the most feasible thing: We sought to profile only the 2,000 most significant and influential people in baseball history. Settling on 2,000 entries was not, at the start of the millennium, difficult; deciding which 2,000 to include required a Ruthian effort.

The easy stuff came first. Every Hall of Famer made the list, as did every position player with 2,500 hits and pitcher with 200 wins. Then we included every winner of each league's Most Valuable Player Award and every Cy Young Award winner. Since baseball is a game that is ultimately measured by champions, we included every World Series-winning manager and the winners of the League Championship Series and World Series MVP Awards (plus the Babe Ruth Award). Not surprisingly, the same names came up again and again. That's when the subjective portion of the process took over.

We had the best baseball reference tool at our fingertips, so we opened up *Total Baseball* and started checking each entry. We used traditional measurements such as batting average, on-base percentage, slugging percentage, RBIs, ERA, won-lost record, and strikeout-to-walk ratio. We also used the sabermetric statistics found in *Total Baseball*, such as adjusted production, batting runs, fielding runs, stolen base runs, pitching runs, adjusted ERA, Total Player Rating, and Total Pitcher Index. Minimums were something we shied away from: Why be required to include a certain player just because he played in 1,000 games if another player had superior statistics while playing in only 900? Players deemed even questionable were placed on a list; they had plenty of company.

Lists were created for people fitting similar descriptions; these lists were followed by lists from other lists. Some players were in the final 2,000, then out, then in again. Like college admissions officers, we took our work very seriously. Still, we tried to have fun, too. We added Max Patkin, Eddie Gaedel, Harry Caray—one could argue that these people are as important to the game's history as some members of the Hall of Fame (does Morgan G. Bulkeley ring a bell?). So-called "one-hit wonders" were also included—players who had one grand, memorable moment in the game that outweighed an otherwise mediocre career.

Approximately 1,500 names required no second thought about whether they belonged, but we checked their statistics anyway. The final 500 were a test of argumentation and an illustration of the inherent difficulty of comparing players from different eras. This task would not have been possible without sabermetric numbers to act as a guide. Even with sabermetrics, differences of opinion abounded. This culling process seemed like something that should take a few days. It took months.

Baseball would not have evolved as it did, nor prospered as it has, were it not for the people who changed the game without playing it on the professional level. Every commissioner is included in this book, but the editors have also selected a sampling of the game's most influential owners, executives, agents, lawyers, and umpires. Our choices included several recipients of the J.G. Taylor Spink Award for sportswriters and the Ford Frick Award for broadcasters.

Today's game of baseball is dominated by the National and American Leagues, but their strength is partly a result of the leagues that preceded them (and in most cases, competed with them). The National Association, American Association, Union Association, Players' League, Federal League, and Negro Leagues are all represented. Some of the great career minor leaguers are included, as are a few legendary names from the college game.

Inevitably, the reader may still argue, "How was this fellow left out of the book? He was better than that guy!" Such arguments have helped maintain baseball's popularity through parts of two centuries and now into a third. Every baseball enthusiast has his or her own interpretation of greatness and fame. We think we've touched all the bases, but read on and see if you agree. Just as no fielder could handle 2,000 chances without a bobble, we freely concede that an occasional grounder might have hit us on the chin. Only a game with a history as rich as baseball's could yield a book like this one—and cause a reader to say upon finishing it, "Y'know, they could have used 3,000."

Explanation of Terms

Putting together 2,000 biographies is a massive undertaking, but coming up with a universal system covering each entry proved to be equally difficult. Every position on the diamond is represented in this book—including designated hitter, pinch hitter, pinch runner, closer, setup man, and even the elusive situational lefthander.

Total Baseball is the source for all statistics, as well as for each player's full name; height and weight; birth, death, and debut dates; and whether the player was righthanded or lefthanded. Information is more difficult to come by for those who influenced the game without ever making a major league appearance. Some people never wanted anyone to know how old they were or where they were born, and some tried to hide middle names or given names they found embarrassing; many were successful in these quests, even in death. We have tried to fill the gaps, but the occasional base is left uncovered. Some career totals in the book are incomplete or unverified; such totals are underlined.

Total Baseball provides 24 columns of statistical information on each major league position player and 27 on each pitcher. It lists both annual and career totals. In addition to listing traditional statistics, *Total Baseball* employs sabermetrics, the mathematical and statistical analysis of records coined in honor of the Society for American Baseball Research. Because *Baseball: The Biographical Encyclopedia* lacks the luxury of space afforded to *Total Baseball*, we have condensed the information into nine essential career stat columns for each position player and pitcher. The nine columns for batters are abbreviated as follows:

G Games
AB At Bats
R Runs
H Hits (Bases on balls were counted as hits by scorers in 1887, but in this book they are counted neither as times at bat nor as outs as in 1876.)
HR Home Runs
RBI Runs Batted In
OBP On-Base Percentage (Figured as hits plus walks plus times hit by pitch, divided by at bats plus walks plus times hit by pitch. When OBP was adopted as an official statistic in 1984, the denominator was expanded to include sacrifice flies. In this book, as in *Total Baseball*, OBP is calculated without considering sacrifice flies, which in any event are calculable on a continuing basis only since 1954.)
SLG Slugging Percentage (total bases divided by at bats)
AVG Average (hits divided by at bats)

The columns for pitchers are similarly familiar to the baseball fan. There is one wrinkle, however. The middle column contains shutouts *or* saves, whichever number is higher. Since shutouts (for which 27 outs are generally required) are usually considered more difficult to attain than saves (for which a minimum of one out to end the game is required), shutouts are used in the event of a tie. The abbreviations for pitchers are as follows:

W Wins
L Losses
PCT Win Percentage (wins divided by decisions)
G Games
SH Shutouts (complete-game shutouts only)
SV Saves (employing the definition in force at the time or the 1969 definition for years before 1969)
IP Innings Pitched (fractional innings included)
BB Bases on Balls allowed
SO Strikeouts
ERA Earned Run Average (calculated as earned runs times nine, divided by innings pitched. For a few years after ERA was introduced as an official statistic, in the National League in 1912 and the American League in 1913, runs aided by stolen bases were not counted as earned. For years prior to 1912, ERA has been constructed from raw data, but for some teams in some seasons, earned runs cannot be identified with absolute certainty. For those teams we have used the estimating procedure created by Information Concepts, Inc., of assigning to those runs whose earned/unearned status is unknown the percentage of earned runs to runs that characterizes the team's known runs.)

Most followers of the game are familiar with the abbreviations for player positions (except, perhaps, those used for pinch hitter, pinch runner, and designated hitter, although they are similarly logical). Abbreviations for manager and umpire appear in the entries for players who also served in these capacities in the major leagues:

P Pitcher
C Catcher
1B First Base
2B Second Base
3B Third Base
SS Shortstop
OF Outfield
DH Designated Hitter
PH Pinch Hitter
PR Pinch Runner
M Manager
U Umpire

Only major league totals are included in the statistical lines. The major leagues include the National League (1876 to present), American Association (1882 to 1891), Union Association (1884), Players' League (1890), American League (1901 to present), and Federal League (1914 to 1915). Of the many leagues whose statistics are not included in the stat lines in *Baseball: The Biographical Encyclopedia*, the following three require explanation.

The National Association, the forerunner of the National League, has not received major league status from Major League Baseball as of the publication of this book. Although National Association information is not provided in player stat lines, a player's NA debut year and team are listed.

Records for Negro League players and managers are difficult to re-create and even more difficult to verify. It is also hard to determine from Negro League records when an individual's role changed from player to manager. In all cases we have done our best to represent the years that spanned a man's career.

Japanese League and major league statistics are generally not comparable and can be confusing when presented side by side. In most cases, a player's career in Japan is mentioned in his biography.

Where relevant and reliable, statistics from the above and other leagues are mentioned in the text of many of the player biographies.

While abbreviations are unavoidable in the statistic lines, they can be explained in the text of the biographies. Most organizations and terms dealing with baseball are spelled out upon first reference. Exceptions to this rule are RBIs and ERA, which are standard baseball terms and appear often enough to merit abbreviation throughout this book.

This book differs from *Total Baseball* in that players are listed by popular name rather than given name. In the hypothetical examples below, Chip Baganacho, the outfielder and third baseman, is listed before his grandfather Chuck Baganacho, the pitcher, even though Charles Hurlen Baganacho comes before Joseph Paul Baganacho alphabetically.

Chip Baganacho

Baganacho, Joseph Paul **OF–3B**
1984–89, 1991–* B:2/2/1962, New Rochelle, NY
Deb:4/29/1984, CLE AL BB/TR 5'11", 195

G	AB	R	H	HR	RBI	OBP	SLG	AVG
2088	7370	1124	2182	162	1101	.388	.436	.296

In Chip Baganacho's case, he is still an active player. The second line lists his years playing Major League Baseball, excluding 1990, when he did not play at the big league level. Although still considered an active player at the time of publication, his career statistics extend only through 1999. All players, managers, and owners active as of spring training 2000 are noted with an asterisk. (As a further definition, most players who were invited to spring training 2000 or were otherwise considered active at the time of publication are also noted with an asterisk.) The date and place of birth follow the abbreviation *B*. Next comes the date of the player's major league debut and the team for which he played in that game—in this case, the Cleveland Indians of the American League. This is followed by the player's manner of batting and throwing, abbreviated in the above example to denote a player who bats both ways and throws righthanded. The final figures are height and weight.

Chuck Baganacho

Baganacho, Charles Hurlen **P**
1888–95, 1898–1902 M(1901, 1904–06, 302–302) U(1896–97, 1903) Owner(1906–09) B:4/5/1865, Rome, NY D:3/17/1954, Caracas, Venezuela Deb:5/12/1888, NY NL BR/TL 5'9", 165

W	L	PCT	G	IP	SH	BB	SO	ERA
186	117	.614	470	2593	13	668	1538	3.51

Chuck Baganacho's information line differs from his descendant's in that it includes three additional roles in major league baseball. His years as a player are followed by his managing career, abbreviated M. Listed in parentheses are the years he managed in the major leagues, followed by his career record. The next listing, beginning with the abbreviation U, shows his tenure as a big league umpire. Finally, his term as a major league owner is listed. Owner is not abbreviated, so as to avoid confusion with other positions, such as outfielder. As in the example above, the date and place of death are given for deceased individuals.

Player positions are listed judiciously; that is, with a few exceptions, positions are listed only if a player appeared at the position more than 100 times. Likewise, only a few entries in the book include both pitching and hitting statistics, even though there have been plenty of good-hitting pitchers as well as numerous position players who have taken the mound on occasion. Both sets of career statistics are listed only for individuals who had distinct careers as a position player and a pitcher. There are several 19th-century examples of this phenomenon, including Charley Radbourn and Al Spalding, while 20th-century exceptions include one-time Red Sox teammates Babe Ruth and Smokey Joe Wood.

Hank Aaron

Aaron, Henry Louis **OF-1B-DH**
1954–76 Negro League Player (1952) B:2/5/1934, Mobile, AL Deb:4/13/1954, MIL NL BR/TR 6', 180

G	AB	R	H	HR	RBI	OBP	SLG	AVG
3298	12364	2174	3771	755	2297	.377	.555	.305

One of the greatest hitters ever to touch a bat, Henry Aaron combined exceptional natural physical ability and lightning-quick reflexes with a professorial study of opposing pitchers to break the immortal Babe Ruth's "unbreakable" record of 714 home runs. In fact, he surpassed Ruth's record by 41. The African-American Aaron made waves well beyond baseball.

The fact that he moved almost overnight from a segregated environment into the white major-league baseball world had a deep impact on Aaron. When he realized he could use his talents as a springboard to speak out effectively against racial intolerance and inequality, he became more than just a highly skilled athlete. He became a man with a mission.

Never in a rush, always quiet and dignified, Aaron played without the flash of Willie Mays, the fire of Roberto Clemente, or the haughtiness of Frank Robinson. As a result, he failed to receive his due recognition until his exploits were already of Hall of Fame caliber. His consistently excellent performance and his longevity added up to still-standing records of 755 lifetime home runs, 2,297 RBIs, 1,477 extra-base hits, and 6,856 total bases. He ranks second to Ty Cobb in lifetime runs scored, tied with Ruth's 2,174, and in runs produced. He placed third in lifetime hits. Aaron averaged 33 homers per year, hit more than 20 home runs in 20 consecutive years, and scored more than 100 runs 15 times, including a record 13 consecutive seasons. Not surprisingly, he played in 21 consecutive All-Star Games. For his career he batted .305 and slugged .555.

As a hitter, Aaron's style was unique. Counter to conventional baseball wisdom, he aggressively hit off his front foot. His incredibly strong wrists made this possible. He claimed that his hitting style was the result of batting bottle caps with a broom as a youngster. "A bottle cap will swerve at the last instant," he said. "You've got to go out and get it."

His approach to hitting was scientific but not technical. As Aaron described it, "Ted Williams concentrated on the things he had to do himself. I concentrated on the pitcher. I didn't stay up nights worrying about my weight distribution or the location of my hands or the turn of my hips; I stayed up thinking about the pitcher I was going to face the next day." He connected for 17 home runs, his best against any pitcher, off Dodgers Hall of Famer Don Drysdale.

The success of his relaxed style confounded many observers. Pitcher Robin Roberts once said, "Aaron is the only batter who could fall asleep between pitches and still wake up in time to hit the next one." Some misjudged him as lazy. An article on Aaron in *Time* magazine was titled "The Talented Shuffler." According to *Time*, "Thinking, Aaron likes to imply, is dangerous. But by now everyone knows that Aaron is not as dumb as he looks when he shuffles around the field." As Lonnie Wheeler, Aaron's collaborator on his autobiography, *I Had a Hammer*, reflected, "It was odd that Joe DiMaggio was also quiet and deliberate, and yet in DiMaggio's case these traits were perceived as dignity and grace, which translated into American heroism. In Aaron's case, the same qualities translated into comparative invisibility."

Aaron once explained, "The thing I had on my side was patience. It's something you pick up pretty naturally when you grow up black in Alabama. When you wait all your life for respect and equality and a seat in the front of the bus, it's nothing to wait a little while for the slider inside."

Aaron's rise from Alabama teenager to major league star happened quickly. He signed with the Negro League Indianapolis Clowns in 1952 for $200 a month. A shortstop, he batted cross-handed, but on the Clowns of that time no one bothered with his style, probably thinking it was part of the show. The truly competitive era of the Negro Leagues had ended with the integration of the majors. The Clowns were barnstormers like their basketball counterparts, the Harlem Globetrotters, and featured players with names such as King Tut and Spec Bebop. Why they were called the Indianapolis Clowns was a mystery to Aaron. "We never made it to Indiana the whole time I was with the team."

It was with the Clowns that the young Aaron got a bitter taste of racial hatred. On a northern trip, the team was rained out of a Sunday doubleheader at Griffith Stadium in Washington, D.C. "We had breakfast while we were waiting for the rain to stop, and I can still envision sitting with the Clowns in a restaurant behind Griffith Stadium and hearing them break all the plates in the kitchen after we were finished eating. What a horrible sound. Even as a kid, the irony of it hit me: here we were in the capital in the land of freedom and equality, and they had to destroy the plates that had touched the forks that had been in the mouths of black men. If dogs had eaten off those plates, they'd have washed them."

Aaron was turned down at a Dodgers tryout because he was too skinny, which he later said caused him to reflect on the difficulty of scouting athletes who had rarely seen a square meal. After observing Aaron at the plate, Braves scout Dewey Griggs suggested he uncross his hands to hit. That night, May 25, 1952, Griggs wrote to Braves general manager John Mullen. Five rather ambivalent paragraphs addressed Aaron's skills, but the letter closed with the prophetic words, "This boy could be the answer." Mullen moved quickly to pay Indianapolis $7,500 for the young infielder.

One of Aaron's regrets as a ballplayer was not becoming a switch hitter. "When you bat left-handed, you do put your left hand above your right, and I had a head start doing that," Aaron told Dick Schaap in his 1999 book, *Home Run: My Life in Pictures.* "I tried learning to switch-hit when I was at Eau Claire, but once, when I was taking batting practice hitting lefthanded, the bat flew out of my hands and sailed into a teammate and broke his nose, and I was so upset I never again swung lefthanded."

He played 87 games for Eau Claire in 1952, hitting .336 with nine home runs and 61 RBIs. The following year Aaron, outfielder Horace Garner, and infielder Felix Mantilla were sent to Class A Jacksonville to break the color line in the South Atlantic League, also known as the Sally League, in the Deep South of the early 1950s.

Every day Aaron and his African-American teammates were subjected to the worst kinds of racial epithets and threats. It was there, however, that Aaron's baseball skills began to dent those long-standing barriers. As an infielder Aaron led the league in runs, hits, doubles, RBIs, batting average, putouts, assists, and errors, and was chosen Most Valuable Player.

Aaron was expected to play the 1954 season at either Class AAA Toledo or AA Atlanta. He was hoping he would not have to help integrate another Southern league when his hero, Bobby Thomson, broke a leg in spring training. The next day Aaron started for the Braves in Thomson's place in left field against the Red Sox in Sarasota, Florida. He came to the plate against pitcher Ike Delock, who had given up a prodigious minor league homer to Aaron the year before. Aaron said, "I cracked one over a row of trailers that bordered that outfield fence—hit it so hard that Ted Williams came running out from the clubhouse wanting to know who it was that could make a bat sound that way when it hit a baseball."

On their way north to begin the season, the Braves toured with the Dodgers. The black players from both teams stayed at the same "colored" hotels, and Aaron always made a point of hanging around Jackie Robinson's room, where Don Newcombe, Joe Black, Jim Gilliam, and Roy Campanella would gather to play cards and talk. Aaron paid close attention to what they had to say about everything from pitchers to restaurants to how to handle sensitive racial situations. "Those hotel rooms were my college," Aaron said. "Being around the Dodgers made me realize that I could never be just another major league player. I was a black player, and that meant I would be separate most of the time from most of the players on the team. It meant I'd better be good, or I'd be gone.... And it meant that I had a choice. Either I could forget that I was black and just smile and go along with the program until my time was up, or I could never forget that I was black. After hearing Jackie Robinson and the other Dodgers, there was only one way to make that choice. If there's a single reason why the black players of the '50s and '60s were so much better than the white players in the National League, I believe it's because we had to be. And we knew we had to be."

Aaron's major league debut was typically understated. "My arrival in the major leagues was pretty dull. No drama, no excitement, absolutely none. I just arrived, that's all." The Braves' highlight film of their 1954 season featured only one shot of Aaron, hitting a foul ball.

The next year marked a new era for both Aaron and the Braves. It was the first of 20 years in which he would hit 20 or more home runs. It was also the first season he batted .300, a mark that he would achieve 13 more times, and the first of his 11 seasons of 100-plus RBI totals. In 1955 and 1956 the Braves finished second, and Aaron put up impressive numbers, leading the league in batting average hitting .328 in 1956. But 1957 was the real breakout year for Aaron and the Braves. He delivered a league-leading 44 homers and 132 RBIs, and batted .322, tying for third place in the National League with Frank Robinson.

With St. Louis challenging in a wintry late September, Aaron hit an 11th-inning homer that clinched the pennant for the Braves. "I galloped around the bases, and when I touched home plate the whole team was there to pick me up and carry me off the field.... I had always dreamed about a moment like Bobby Thomson had in '51, and this was it." After Aaron's career ended he said that this had been his most satisfying homer. Milwaukee set a league season attendance record, and Aaron was elected Most Valuable Player.

The Braves were underdogs in that year's World Series, and their opponents, the supposedly invincible Yanks, let them know it. Mickey Mantle referred to Milwaukee as "bush league." But the Braves had the last laugh, winning in seven games as Aaron led all hitters in runs, hits, homers, batting average, and RBIs.

In 1958 Aaron batted .326 with 30 homers and 95 RBIs as the Braves easily won the pennant. The Yankees were out for revenge, however, and despite Aaron's .333 batting average in the Series, he drove in only two runs. The Yanks prevailed in seven games. Aaron won his second batting title in 1959 and slugged for 400 total bases, the most in baseball since 1948 and until 1978. The Braves blew their chance to make it three straight World Series appearances when they lost two games of a best-of-three playoff. Aaron and his team would not see postseason action for 10 more years. Although Aaron maintained his standard of excellence, recording consecutive years of 39, 40, 34, 45, and 44 home runs from 1959 through 1963, Milwaukee's fortunes plummeted. When the team moved to Atlanta in 1966 things changed forever for Aaron.

In his autobiography, Aaron reflected on the move. "Atlanta changed me as a hitter and a person at the same time. The real world made me angrier and hungrier than I had been as a young Milwaukee Brave.... I was tired of being invisible. I was the equal of any ballplayer in the world, damn it, and if nobody was going to give me my due, it was time to grab for it."

He found the southern air of Atlanta to his liking, slugging 44 and 39 homers, respectively, in his first two years there. He was 34 years old and had 481 lifetime home runs, seemingly a universe away from Babe Ruth's mark.

The 1967 season was an unhappy one for Aaron. The Braves had traded away his good friend Eddie Mathews, with whom he had set numerous two-teammate home run records. The pitching-dominated 1968 season didn't make him feel any better. Batting statistics plummeted throughout baseball, and Aaron's 86 RBIs were the fewest since his rookie season.

In spring training the following year the Braves invited Satchel Paige along as a goodwill gesture. Aaron looked around at all the youngsters and felt "as old as Satchel." He began to think of retirement. Then legendary baseball historian Lee Allen pulled him aside. Allen explained the place Aaron was about to create for himself in baseball history. With his second home run that season he would pass Mel Ott. He had a good chance to get more at bats than anyone else in history, and with 2,792 lifetime hits he had an excellent chance to reach the 3,000 level attained by only eight players. Aaron listened and realized he had a chance not only to set records but also to make himself heard. He had always spoken out against the spring training segregation and discriminatory hiring practices of baseball. Now he saw a chance to do even more.

His first objective was to reach 3,000 hits. When Aaron smacked No. 3,000 in 1970 he joined Ty Cobb, Stan Musial, Eddie Collins, Tris Speaker, Honus Wagner, Nap Lajoie, Cap Anson, and Paul Waner. But lack of recognition still plagued him. When he sent the 3,000-hit ball to the Hall of Fame, they put it away in a back room.

The quest to match Ruth became an obsession. The Babe's record still seemed unreachable, and Willie Mays was nearly 100 homers ahead of Aaron. In 1971, at the age of 37, Aaron hit a career-best 47 home runs. At the same time he hit .327 and drove in 118 runs. He signed a two-year contract that made him the first player to earn $200,000 a year, but because of financial problems he felt driven to break Ruth's record. He surpassed Musial for lifetime leadership in total bases in September 1972 and finished the season 41 home runs behind Ruth's magical 714.

A quarter-century later, it is hard to comprehend the enmity that Hank Aaron inspired as he closed in on Ruth's sanctified record. Atlanta police had to assign a bodyguard to him. It was rumored that Aaron's daughter had been kidnapped from her college dorm, and Aaron told sportswriters about the hate mail he'd received. It became big news, and before long Aaron was receiving more supportive letters than threatening ones. At the end of the year he received a plaque from the U.S. Post Office for having received the most mail of any nonpolitician during the year—930,000 letters. Aaron finished 1973 with 40 homers, leaving him at 713, one behind Ruth.

The next year began with a minor brouhaha. The Braves wanted to hold Aaron out of the lineup for their first three road games so he could tie and break Ruth's record in Atlanta. The commissioner's office and many sportswriters felt that such maneuvering was a travesty. Ordered to play at least two of the games, Aaron hit homer No. 714 off Jack Billingham in his first at bat of the season. He sat out the second game, and in the third he struck out twice and grounded out once against Clay Kirby.

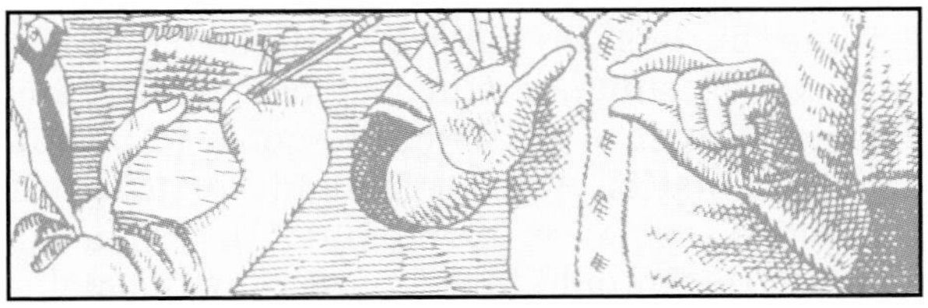

Aaron's tie-breaking home run came at home against Al Downing of the Dodgers. In Aaron's first at bat, Downing had walked him. When Aaron finally came around to score, he broke Mays' NL record for runs. But no one noticed. The Dodgers were ahead, 3-1, in the fourth and Aaron was again at bat. With a man on first, Downing didn't want to walk him again. Aaron deposited a low slider into the Braves' bullpen in left field for home run No. 715. Teammates, fans, and Aaron's mother met him at the plate. The game was halted for a brief ceremony, and the next time Aaron batted the stands had nearly emptied.

Aaron ended the season with 733 homers. He was traded to the American League Milwaukee Brewers, where he added 22 more for a career total of 755 home runs. Aaron once said, "I believed, and I still do, that there was a reason why I was chosen to break the record. It's my task to carry on where Jackie Robinson left off."

Aaron became a vice president of the Braves and a leading spokesman for better opportunities for African-Americans in baseball. He sponsors the Hank Aaron Scholarship Program, and serves on the boards of foundations involved with cystic fibrosis, cancer, leukemia, sickle-cell anemia, the Salvation Army, the Boy Scouts, and Big Brothers/Big Sisters. The last player from the Negro Leagues to play in the white majors, he left a legacy much greater than his remarkable statistics on the field.

Don Aase

Aase, Donald William **P**

1977–82, 1984–90 B:9/8/1954, Orange, CA Deb:7/26/1977, BOS AL BR/TR 6'3", 210

W	L	PCT	G	SV	IP	BB	SO	ERA
66	60	.524	448	82	1109^1	457	641	3.80

At one time Don Aase appeared to be on his way towards a promising career in the starting rotation for the California Angels. By the time he retired, however, he had become an excellent relief pitcher, and he had not started a game in the last nine years of his career.

A sixth-round draft choice of Boston, Aase received a rude awakening early on, going 0–10 with Williamsport of the New York–Penn League in 1972. He didn't fare much better the following season, as he led the Florida State League with 15 losses. Aase stuck to it, however. The next year he rebounded to pace Carolina League hurlers in victories, starts, complete games, and shutouts and was named Carolina League Pitcher of the Year. Promoted to Boston in 1977, one of Aase's highlights in that 6–2 campaign came on September 5, when he blanked the Toronto Blue Jays, 8–0, in the nightcap of a doubleheader, matching a shutout the Sox had recorded in the first game.

The Sox traded Aase to the Angels in December 1977 for second baseman Jerry Remy. He made occasional relief appearances for the Angels in his first two and a half years, but then switched to relief full time. An elbow injury shut down his 95-mph fastball and shelved him from July 1982 until June 1984.

Granted free agency following the 1984 season, Aase joined Baltimore. The Orioles were willing to use him considerably more than the Angels had, and he established himself as one of the AL's more reliable relievers. In 1985 he went 10–6 with 14 saves. The next year he earned a berth on the AL All-Star Team and set a Baltimore record with 34 saves.

But Aase had been overworked in 1986. In August and September of that year his ERA ballooned to 5.32. His arm injuries recurred, costing him most of the 1987 season. Released by the Orioles after the 1988 campaign, he finished his career with the Mets and Dodgers.

Jim Abbott

Abbott, James Anthony **P**

1989–96, 1998–99 B: 9/19/1967, Flint, MI Deb: 4/8/1989, CAL AL BL/TL 6'3", 210

W	L	PCT	G	SH	IP	BB	SO	ERA
87	108	.446	263	6	1674	620	888	4.25

Jim Abbott spent his entire life proving doubters wrong. Born without a right hand, Abbott had always been told he couldn't be a pitcher. He didn't listen. After an outstanding career at the University of Michigan, he won the Sullivan Award as the nation's top amateur athlete. He led the 1988 U.S. Olympic baseball team to the gold medal in South Korea.

Skeptics then questioned whether he could survive in the majors. Abbott, a first-round pick in the 1988 draft, skipped the minor leagues entirely. As a rookie with the California Angels in 1989, he won 12 games. He slipped to 10–14 the following season.

In 1991 he notched a career-best 18 wins. The following year Abbott's ERA dipped to 2.77, the second straight year he was among the American League leaders in that category, but his record was just 7–15. In December 1993 the New York Yankees sent their top prospect, first baseman J.T. Snow, along with two pitchers in exchange for the Angels' lefty. Abbott had a record of 20–22 over two seasons with the Yankees, but his one shutout in pinstripes was a no-hitter against the Cleveland Indians on September 4, 1993.

He signed with the White Sox as a free agent in 1995, but California reacquired him in July of that year. In 1996, having lost much of his velocity, he experienced one of the worst seasons in major league history: a 2–18 mark and a 7.18 ERA. The Angels released him in spring training the following year.

After a year away from baseball, Abbott signed a minor league contract with the Chicago White Sox in 1998. He was called up to the majors in September; he won all five of his starts. Milwaukee signed him as a free agent in 1999. It was his first time in the National League, meaning he would have to bat regularly. Swinging the bat with one hand wasn't his main problem; on the mound he was just 2–8 with a 6.71 ERA. The Brewers released him in July.

Jerry Adair

Adair, Kenneth Jerry **2B–SS**

1958–70 B:12/17/1936, Sand Springs, OK D:5/31/1987, Tulsa, OK Deb:9/2/1958, BAL AL BR/TR 6', 175

G	AB	R	H	HR	RBI	OBP	SLG	AVG
1165	4019	378	1022	57	366	.294	.347	.244

The phrase "good field, no hit" certainly applied to Jerry Adair. A brilliant American League gloveman with the Baltimore Orioles, Adair set major league records in 1964 for the highest fielding percentage (.994) and fewest errors (five) recorded by a second baseman. That same season he handled 458 consecutive chances without a miscue. In 1965 Adair kept up the pace, again leading AL second basemen in fielding.

The Orioles signed Adair in 1958 straight out of Oklahoma State University for a reported $40,000 bonus. He immediately jumped to the major league roster, but his puny .105 batting average proved he wasn't ready. In 1961 he finally made the major league roster for the season, and he remained with Baltimore until 1966. His most successful year was in 1962, when he set personal career highs of 153 hits, 29 doubles, 11 homers, and a .284 batting average.

Adair was sent to Chicago in 1966, but the very next season the White Sox traded him to Boston. There he helped propel the Red Sox to a pennant, although he then hit only .125 in the World Series.

In 1969 the Kansas City Royals selected Adair in the expansion draft. He left major league baseball after the 1970 season and played for the Hankyu Braves in Japan in 1971, posting a .300 average. From 1972 to 1974 he returned to the major leagues as a coach with Oakland, and in 1975 he coached the Angels.

Babe Adams

Adams, Charles Benjamin **P**

1906–07, 1909–16, 1918–26 B:5/18/1882, Tipton, IN D:7/27/1968, Silver Spring, MD Deb:4/18/1906, STL NL BL/TR 5'11 ½", 185

W	L	PCT	G	SH	IP	BB	SO	ERA
194	140	.581	482	44	2995^{1}	430	1036	2.76

Babe Adams' legendary control allowed him to have a long career with the Pittsburgh Pirates. It was his three wins in the 1909 World Series, however, that made him an overnight sensation and a significant figure on the national baseball scene.

Scouted in 1904 by a Pacific Coast League umpire (a practice then still legal), Adams was signed to a contract with the Parsons, Kansas, Preachers of the Class D Missouri Valley League. Two years later the St. Louis Cardinals purchased his contract, but his one start saw him give up nine hits in four innings, and the Cardinals returned him to the minors.

The Pirates acquired Adams near the end of the 1907 season. After a brief spell in Pittsburgh, they dispatched him to the Louisville Colonels, where he went 22–12 in 1908 and acquired the nickname "Babe." Adams was allegedly the first ballplayer to be so christened.

In 1909 Adams split time between starting and relief for the Pirates. He posted a 12–3 record with a sparkling 1.11 ERA for the pennant winners. Before the start of the World Series, National League president John Heydler mentioned to Pirates manager Fred Clarke that the American League champion Detroit Tigers had been ineffective versus Washington's Dolly Gray. He suggested that Adams, with his superior pitching speed, could keep Detroit off balance. Clarke took the tip in Game 1, bypassing 25-game winner Howie Camnitz for Adams. "I'll never forget the look on Adams' face when I told him he was to pitch the opener," recalled teammate Honus Wagner, "He asked me if I wasn't fooling and I told him I wasn't, and he hadn't better fool, either, when he got to the mound." Despite a shaky first frame, Babe was a 4-1 winner. In Game 5 Adams continued his mastery, winning 8–4. For the final game, Clarke went with his new ace, and in 40-degree weather the rookie blanked Detroit, 8–0. In each win Adams pitched a six-hit complete game. He became a national sensation.

The next year, working almost entirely as a starter, Adams recorded an 18–9 mark with a 2.24 ERA. Then came the first of his two 20-

win seasons, when he went 22–12. Two years later he followed that with a 21–10 mark. Adams' record became less impressive as the Pirates gave him less backing through the ensuing years. On May 17, 1914, for example, he lost a 21-inning duel to New York's Rube Marquard. In that contest, Adams didn't walk a single batter—still a major league record.

In 1916 Adams' ERA suddenly soared, from 2.87 to almost double that, 5.72. The next year he found himself pitching in the Western Association. Late in 1918 a second wind sent him back to Pittsburgh, where he remained through 1926. In 1919 and 1920 he won 17 games each year, and he never showed better control the latter year, when he surrendered only 18 walks in 263 innings. His last three years he was mainly a relief pitcher.

Adams' career ended in controversy. In August 1926 the defending world champion Pirates were still in the pennant race, but veteran center fielder Max Carey was mired in a dreadful slump. Fred Clarke was now a Pirates vice president, but he sat on the club's bench in full uniform and was more than free with his opinions.

Clarke pressed manager Bill McKechnie to bench Carey, saying "anybody" could play better than the future Hall of Famer. "Put the batboy in," he growled. Asked what he thought of the situation, Babe Adams backed up McKechnie: "Well, I think the manager should manage, and no one else should interfere." A player revolt demanded that Clarke be removed from the Pittsburgh bench. Clarke, in turn, demanded that the outspoken players be disciplined.

Pirates ownership lashed out in several directions, and player opposition collapsed. Carey was suspended and then peddled to Brooklyn. Adams and outfielder Carson Bigbee drew their unconditional release. The Pirates drifted into third place, and McKechnie was let go at season's end. Clarke soon followed him out the door.

The three exiled players appealed to league president John Heydler. "I am 18 years in baseball without ever opening my mouth, and then when I answer a question, I find myself chucked off the club," explained Adams. Heydler exonerated the trio of "insubordination" but nonetheless upheld the club's untrammeled right to dispose of personnel as it saw fit.

Adams later managed in the minors, farmed, and worked as a sportswriter and a foreign correspondent. In his 1960s he was still known as one of the best marksmen in the country. He died of throat cancer in 1968.

D.L. Adams

Adams, Daniel Lucius, Jr.

Baseball Pioneer B:11/1/1814, Mt. Vernon, NH
D:1/3/1899, New Haven, CT

It is now generally accepted that baseball evolved naturally from the similar English game of rounders. But the question of who invented the American national pastime continues to provoke debate.

To the uninformed, the father of baseball was General Abner Doubleday, a Civil War hero and one-time resident of Cooperstown, New York. Others point to Alexander Cartwright, who is often given credit for organizing the first recorded game. Cartwright staged a match for the New York Knickerbockers club on June 19, 1846, at Elysian Fields in Hoboken, New Jersey.

Finally there is Daniel Lucius Adams, Jr. The second of two sons of Dr. Daniel Adams and Nancy Mulliken Adams, he graduated from Yale in 1835 and obtained his medical degree from Harvard three years later. He moved to New York City and distinguished himself by assisting in the treatment of the city's impoverished underclass. In Manhattan, "Doc" Adams, as he was almost always known, became involved in the up-and-coming game of baseball. This was about the same time that Doubleday was supposedly "inventing" the game in Elihu Phinney's cow pasture in upstate Cooperstown. Doubleday was actually at West Point at this time.

"I was always interested in athletics while in college and afterwards," Adams told an interviewer in 1896, "and soon after going to New York I began to play 'base ball' just for exercise, with a number of other young medical men. Before that, there had been a club called the New York Base Ball Club, but it had no definite organization and did not last long. Some of the younger members of that club got together and formed the Knickerbocker Base Ball Club, September 24, 1845." [Actually it was the preceding day.]

"The players included merchants, lawyers, Union Bank clerks [such as Cartwright], insurance clerks, and others who were at liberty after three o'clock in the afternoon. They went into it just for exercise and enjoyment, and I think they used to get a good deal more solid fun out of it than the players in the big leagues do nowadays. About a month after the organization of this club, several of us medical fellows joined it...The following year I was made president and served as long as I was willing to retain the office."

Adams' account overturns a key assumption of previous baseball historians—that the Knickerbockers were the first organized baseball club. Not only did the New York Base Ball Club precede the

Knickerbockers, but the more aggressive members of that club, such as William Wheaton, James Lee, and Abraham Tucker, launched the supposedly pioneer Knickerbockers.

The Knickerbockers of the 1840s played in the area around 27th Street, at the future site of the earliest incarnation of Madison Square Garden. As the city's population exploded and open land became scarce, the Knickerbockers were forced to board a ferry and head across the Hudson River to Hoboken's Elysian Fields. Sometimes the results were disappointing, and Adams would arrive to find that only two or three other Knickerbockers had shown up for practice. Baseball at the time usually featured anywhere from eight to 11 players per team. There was no such position as shortstop, and infielders practically anchored themselves to their bases. Everybody else, except for the battery, headed for the outfield, which often was quite crowded.

Adams invented the shortstop position around 1850. "I used to play shortstop," he reminisced, "and I believe I was the first one to occupy that place, as it had formerly been left uncovered." He occupied the position not only to handle batted balls but also to take relay throws from the outfielders, for then the ball was so light that it could not be thrown more than 200 feet. Adams played slightly deeper than today's position. As the ball became harder and throws could travel farther, Adams moved forward into the infield.

Adams also had a hand in the design of the ball itself. "We had a great deal of trouble getting balls made," Adams recalled, "and for six or seven years I made all the balls myself, not only for our club but also for other clubs when they were organized.

"I went all over New York to find someone who would undertake this work, but no one could be induced to try it for love or money. Finally I found a saddler who was able to show me a good way to cover the balls with horsehide, such as was used for whiplashes. I used to make the stuffing out of three or four ounces of rubber cuttings, wound with yarn and then covered with the leather. Those balls were, of course, a great deal softer than the balls now in use." Adams turned the bats for all those primitive clubs as well.

Cartwright generally is credited with defining baseball's rules, including abandoning the old rounders or "town ball" concept of hitting a runner with the ball to retire him. He is also credited with drawing foul lines, limiting teams to nine men on the field, and limiting games to nine innings. But it was Adams, not Cartwright, who in 1848 became chairman of the Knickerbocker Club's Committee to Revise the Constitution and By-Laws.

In the early 1850s two strong rivals emerged to challenge the Knickerbockers. The Washington Baseball Club was formed in 1850 and in 1852 was renamed the Gothams. The old Eagles town ball club switched to base ball, becoming the Eagle Base Ball Club. Confusion regarding rules mounted. Adams realized that some sense of cohesion was necessary for the game to continue, let alone prosper.

"The playing rules remained very crude up to that time," said Adams, "but in 1853 the three clubs united in a revision of the rules and regulations. At the close of 1856 there were 12 clubs in existence, and it was decided to hold a convention of delegates from all of these for the purpose of establishing a permanent code of rules. A call was therefore issued, signed by the officers of the Knickerbocker Club as the senior organization, and the result was the assembling of the first convention of 'base ball' players in May 1857. I was elected presiding officer.

"I was chairman of the Committee on Rules and Regulations from the start and so long as I retained membership. I presented the first draft of rules, prepared after much careful study of the matter, and it was in the main adopted. The distance between bases I fixed at 30 yards. The only previous determination of distance being the bases shall be from home to second base 42 paces, from first to third base 42 paces equidistant—which was rather vague.

"In every meeting of the National Association while a member, I advocated the fly-game—that is, not to allow first-bound catches—but I was always defeated on the vote. The change was made, however, soon after I left, as I predicted in my last speech on the subject before the convention. The distance from home to pitcher's base I made 45 feet. Many of the old rules, such as those defining a foul, remain substantially the same today, while others are changed and, of course, many new ones added. I resigned in 1862, but not before thousands were present to witness matches, and any number of outside players standing ready to take a hand on regular playing days."

After 1862 Adams' role in the game quickly diminished. He had wed Cornelia A. Cook in May 1861 and in 1865 the Adamses left New York. Adams took up a medical practice in Ridgefield, Connecticut. He continued his interest in the game, however, playing his last formal contest in 1875 at a specially arranged old-timer's game. He also continued to toss the horsehide around in his backyard until he was in his 80s.

Any of his improvements to baseball would have landed Adams a prominent page in baseball history. Taken together, they earn him the right to be called the true "Father of Baseball."

Sparky Adams

Adams, Earl John **2B-3B-SS**

1922–34 B:8/26/1894, Zerbe, PA D:2/24/1989, Pottsville, PA Deb:9/18/1922, CHI NL BR/TR 5'5 ½", 151

G	AB	R	H	HR	RBI	OBP	SLG	AVG
1424	5557	844	1588	9	394	.343	.353	.286

Sparky Adams was an extremely versatile National League infielder who had a good glove, a useful bat, and a personality that earned him his nickname. He played more than 500 games at second base, once leading the league in fielding percentage, and another 500-plus at third, where twice he led in fielding percentage. He also played shortstop in about 300 games.

Adams first reached the majors with the Chicago Cubs in 1922, and spent most of the next two years sharing shortstop. In 1925 he moved into George Grantham's second base slot after Grantham was traded. In 1928 Adams followed Grantham to the Pirates and pushed his predecessor over to first. Adams was sold to the Cardinals in 1930 and installed at third base just in time to play on a pennant winner. He hit a personal high of .314 and followed with .293 for the 1931 World Series champions. A knee injury in 1932 led to his retirement two years later.

Adams was the leadoff man for much of his career. He was a .286 hitter, with an excellent eye and a small strike zone. He was also fast, and he not only scored more than 90 runs six times in a seven-year period, but stole more than 20 bases four times. Of course, at 151 pounds he had little power. In 13 seasons he produced only nine home runs, and for five full years in mid-career he never once reached the seats.

Joe Adcock

Adcock, Joseph Wilbur **1B-OF**

1950–66 M(1967, 75–87) B:10/30/1927, Coushatta, LA D:5/1/1999, Coushatta, LA Deb:4/23/1950, CIN NL BR/TR 6'4", 220

G	AB	R	H	HR	RBI	OBP	SLG	AVG
1959	6606	823	1832	336	1122	.339	.485	.277

The National League in the Golden Era of the 1950s featured a trio of hard-hitting first basemen—Gil Hodges, Ted Kluszewski, and a soft-spoken Louisiana slugger named Joe Adcock. Signed by the Cincinnati Reds following an impressive stint at Louisiana State University, Adcock advanced rapidly through the Reds' system, but ultimately his progress was blocked by Kluszewski's presence. From 1950 to 1952 Adcock played in Cincinnati but had to be shifted to the outfield. He demanded a trade, and the Reds were happy to oblige him, sending him to the Boston Braves in early 1953.

Soon enough, the Braves packed Adcock up along with the rest of their luggage and set up shop in Milwaukee. His first season with the Braves was impressive, capped by his powering of a homer into the Polo Grounds' center-field bleachers on April 29. Only Henry Aaron and Lou Brock would ever equal his feat.

Adcock's biggest day in baseball came at cozy Ebbets Field on July 31, 1954. In the second inning he homered off Brooklyn's Don Newcombe. The next inning he faced Erv Palica and doubled off the left-center fence. In the fifth he faced Palica again and homered into the upper deck. In the seventh he clipped Pete Wojey for yet another home run. When Adcock came to the plate again, in the ninth, southpaw Johnny Podres' first two pitches were balls. Adcock resolved to swing at anything near the plate. On a pitch over his head, he clubbed the ball into the center field bleachers and put himself into the record books—not only for four homers in a single game but also for most total bases in one contest.

"On my first three home runs," said Adcock, "I was swinging away in a carefree fashion. But on the last one I went to the plate tensed, aiming to poke one. Perhaps the strangest part of the day was I hit four home runs and only swung the bat five times." The next day he doubled in his first at bat. The Dodgers had enough after that. On his next turn at the plate, Adcock was beaned by Clem Labine and was carried off the diamond.

Adcock played on the great Braves teams of the 1950s—clubs that boasted Hank Aaron, Eddie Mathews, Warren Spahn, Lew Burdette, and Del Crandall. During the eight years he and Hammerin' Hank were teammates, Adcock actually out-homered Aaron per at bat. Nonetheless, Adcock paid proper homage to the future home run king. "Trying to sneak a pitch past Hank Aaron is like trying to sneak the sunrise past a rooster," drawled Adcock. On June 8, 1961, Mathews, Aaron, Adcock, and Frank Thomas homered one right after the other.

An Adcock "home run" also took center stage in May 1959. Burdette and the Pirates' Harvey Haddix locked horns in a 12-inning duel of shutout baseball, with Haddix working on a perfect game. In the bottom of the 13th, Felix Mantilla reached on an error, and Aaron walked. Adcock then dispatched a ball through the evening fog and over the fence. In a bizarre twist, however, he would not be officially credited with a homer. Aaron had gotten as far as second. Thinking the ball had gone for a double and the winning run had scored, Aaron trotted, head down, off the field. Adcock—also oblivious to events—continued circling the bases and was called out for passing Aaron. He got credit for a double.

During the course of his career Adcock hit 10 grand slams, had 28 multiple-homer games, and was the first player to homer over the grandstand roof at Ebbets Field. "I was a guess hitter," he once explained, "and anybody who says he isn't just won't admit the truth. It's always better to be lucky than good."

In 1967 club president Gabe Paul hired Adcock to manage the Cleveland Indians. The Tribe finished eighth, and Adcock was not rehired. He managed two more years in the minors before leaving baseball. Adcock then settled down on a 288-acre farm in his hometown of Coushatta, Louisiana, to devote his time to breeding horses.

Tommie Agee

Agee, Tommie Lee **OF**

1962–73 B:8/9/1942, Magnolia, AL Deb:9/14/1962, CLE AL BR/TR 5'11", 195

G	AB	R	H	HR	RBI	OBP	SLG	AVG
1129	3912	558	999	130	433	.321	.412	.255

Chunky Tommie Agee may not have looked like a Gold Glove center fielder, but he certainly played like one, twice leading his league in putouts and winning Gold Glove Awards. Agee grew up in Mobile, Alabama, with future Mets teammate Cleon Jones. The fleet-footed Agee starred at Grambling University and was signed by the Indians to a $60,000 bonus. After three years of occasional appearances, the Tribe gave up on him, however, along with a young pitcher named Tommy John, and dealt both to the White Sox.

In Chicago Agee had an outstanding all-round year and was named 1966 American League Rookie of the Year. Hit by the sophomore jinx, Agee found himself traded with Al Weis to the Mets; his luck turned even worse. On his very first 1968 spring training pitch, Agee was beaned by a Bob Gibson fastball. After that he couldn't buy a hit. From April 15 to May 1 Agee went 0-for-34—the worst Met streak since Don Zimmer's in 1962. When Agee singled to break the skein, the Shea Stadium crowd gave him a standing ovation. Even after that, it was a horrible year. Agee finished the year hitting .217 with a pathetic 17 RBIs.

One of the most miraculous things about the 1969 Miracle Mets was the resuscitation of Agee. He hit 26 homers and won another Gold Glove, helping his club to a world championship. His heroics in Game 3 of the World Series included a homer and two circus catches that saved a combined five runs. "I've seen outfielders make great catches in World Series play before," exclaimed Orioles manager Earl Weaver, "but I've never seen two such great catches by the same player in the same game."

The next two years, Agee had productive seasons, batting over .280 and stealing an average of about 30 bases. In 1970 he put together a 20-game hitting streak, although during that streak Agee was so dissatisfied with his hitting he reportedly employed 22 different bats. He finished his career in 1973 with the Astros and Cardinals. After retiring he operated the Outfielder's Lounge near Shea Stadium.

Rick Aguilera

Aguilera, Richard Warren **P**

1985–* B:12/31/1961, San Gabriel, CA
Deb:6/12/1985, NY NL BR/TR 6'5", 205

W	L	PCT	G	SV	IP	BB	SO	ERA
85	79	.518	678	289	1243²	333	992	3.52

Rick Aguilera arrived at Shea Stadium in June 1985 in the midst of a knockdown, drag-out race for the National League East title. In his second month in the major leagues, he won three times and led NL pitchers with an ERA of 0.89. The rookie's biggest moment came on October 3 in St. Louis. Although he pitched well, the Cards held on for a 4-3 win that ultimately decided the division title.

Aguilera established himself as a pitcher who enjoyed pressure situations. The 10-game winner also batted .278, the best among NL pitchers with at least 20 at bats. His hitting may have surprised the Mets, but the Cardinals had drafted him as a third baseman, in 1980. Aguilera decided to go to Brigham Young University, became a pitcher, and went to the Mets in the third round of the 1983 draft.

On a team that won 108 games in 1986, Aguilera's second straight 10-7 season almost seemed suspect. He bounced back from a terrible start with a six-game winning streak. He did not allow an earned run in five innings of work in the Championship Series against Houston. Despite a dreadful 12.00 ERA in two World Series games against Boston, he got credit for the 6-5 victory in the Mets' legendary comeback in the 10th inning of Game 6.

Injuries dominated his next two seasons, but the Mets started to think about Aguilera as a relief pitcher after he allowed only one earned in seven innings of relief during the 1988 NLCS. He moved to the bullpen the following year, and then the Mets moved him to Minnesota. On July

31, 1989, Aguilera was sent to the Twins with four other young pitchers for southpaw Frank Viola, the reigning American League Cy Young Award winner.

Minnesota manager Tom Kelly moved Aguilera to the starting rotation for the rest of 1989, but switched him to the bullpen the following year. Aguilera earned 32 saves for the 74–88 Twins in 1990. He saved a career-best 42 games the following year to help Minnesota become the first team to go from last place to first place in one season. He earned three saves in the ALCS, then saved the first two games of the World Series against Atlanta. In Game 3 he became the first pitcher to pinch hit in a Series game since Don Drysdale in 1965. Aguilera flied out with two outs and the bases loaded in the top of the 12th inning, and then surrendered the game-winning hit in the bottom of the inning. He earned the win in Game 6, however, and the Twins went on to win in seven games.

Aguilera became a three-time All-Star in Minnesota, as well as the team's all-time leader with 254 saves and 490 appearances. Following a late-season trade to Boston in 1995, he returned to Minnesota the following year and joined the rotation. He went back to the bullpen in 1997.

On May 21, 1999, the Twins, fearful that Aguilera would walk away as a free agent at season's end, sent him to the Cubs along with minor league lefthander Scott Downs for minor league righthanders Kyle Lohse and Jason Ryan. In Chicago he went 6–3 with a 3.69 ERA and eight saves in 44 relief appearances. In November 1999 he re-signed with the Cubs, exercising a $3.5 million player option for 2000.

Willie Aikens

Aikens, Willie Mays **1B–DH**

1977, 1979–85 B:10/14/1954, Seneca, SC Deb:5/17/1977, CAL AL BL/TR 6'3", 220

G	AB	R	H	HR	RBI	OBP	SLG	AVG
774	2492	301	675	110	415	.358	.455	.271

Named after one of baseball's all-time greats, Willie Mays Aikens twice led minor leagues in home runs (Texas League, 1976, with 30, and Pacific Coast League, 1978, with 29). However, in the majors the slow-footed slugger never lived up to his name nor the expectations put upon him.

Aikens first reached the major leagues with the California Angels in 1977, but after hitting only .198 was returned to the minors. His performance in the PCL was rewarded by another shot in the big leagues, and this time, in 1979, Aikens had a successful season, hitting .280 with 21 homers for California. Kansas City obtained him after the 1979 season, and he became a regular. In his first year in Kansas City he set a record by hitting two homers in a game twice in the same World Series. His best regular season came in 1983, when he hit .302 with 23 homers.

After the 1983 season, however, Aikens was arrested along with Willie Wilson and Jerry Martin on drug charges. He plea-bargained a misdemeanor charge and was given the maximum sentence—one year in prison, the last nine months suspended. He was the first major leaguer to be sent to jail on drug charges. Commissioner Bowie Kuhn suspended Aikens and the others from baseball for a year. After his release, Kuhn reinstated Aikens with the proviso that he continue community service and submit to regular urinalysis.

Traded to Toronto in the off-season, Aikens turned in poor numbers in a partial 1984 season. The next year he was out of the major leagues after 12 games.

Then Aikens began a spectacular second career. After hitting .311 with 16 home runs for Syracuse, he played for Puebla in the Mexican League. There he led the league with 202 hits and 154 RBIs. He hit 38 doubles and 46 homers, and his .454 batting average was the highest batting average by a minor league batting champion in the 20th century.

Jack Aker

Aker, Jackie Delane **P**

1964–74 B:7/13/1940, Tulare, CA Deb:5/3/1964, KC AL BR/TR 6'2", 190

W	L	PCT	G	SV	IP	BB	SO	ERA
47	45	.511	495	123	746	274	404	3.28

Jack Aker was a minor league batting champion, but wound up as an effective major league relief pitcher. Originally signed as an outfielder, Aker led the Nebraska State League in hitting in 1959 before he was converted to a pitcher. Brought up by the Kansas City A's in 1964, he soon established himself as a valuable right hander. Aker earned *The Sporting News* American League Fireman of the Year honors in 1966, when he recorded a 1.99 ERA with 32 saves, then a major league record.

Despite his value to the club, volatile A's owner Charles O. Finley soon cut Aker loose. The Athletics' player rep, Aker got caught in the middle of an argument between manager Alvin Dark and first baseman Ken Harrelson regarding drinking while on a team flight. Harrelson was traded; Dark was fired; and Aker was used less and less in the A's bullpen.

The Seattle Pilots selected him in the 1969 expansion draft, but a poor start saw him traded in mid-1969 to the Yankees. He pitched well for New York—finishing with an ERA of 2.06 in consecutive years—despite severe back pain. Only spinal surgery kept his career going.

Aker played for three teams in his final two years. Following his playing career he served as the Indians' pitching coach from 1985 to 1987. Explaining the increase in home runs being hit off his charges, he once remarked, "It's the underground nuclear testing. Because of that, all gravity is leaving the Earth. And so are the baseballs." He went on to manage in the Mets' minor league system, and to operate his own baseball school. He is married to baseball broadcaster and writer Jane Charnin-Aker.

Vic Aldridge

Aldridge, Victor Eddington **P**

1917–18, 1922–28 B:10/25/1893, Indian Springs, IN D:4/17/1973, Terre Haute, IN Deb:4/15/1917, CHI NL BR/TR 5'9 ½", 175

W	L	PCT	G	SH	IP	BB	SO	ERA
97	80	.548	248	8	1600^2	512	526	3.76

Vic Aldridge was a steady contributor for the Chicago Cubs and Pittsburgh Pirates in the 1920s as a second or third starter in their pitching rotations. If he had been a little less hard-headed, he might have continued to pitch in the majors for a number of years more.

Given a trial with the Cubs in 1917, Aldridge split 12 decisions, pitching mostly out of the bullpen. Sent back to the minors, he returned to Chicago in 1922 as a starter. For three seasons the crafty righthander proved remarkably consistent, winning 16, 16, and 15 games with ERAs of 3.52, 3.48, and 3.50, respectively. However, after the 1924 season he was traded to Pittsburgh with infielder George Grantham and first baseman Al Niehaus in exchange for pitcher Wilbur Cooper, first baseman Charlie Grimm, and shortstop Rabbit Maranville.

In Pittsburgh that first season Aldridge won 15 games as the Pirates took the pennant. In the ninth inning of Game 2 of the World Series against the Washington Senators, Aldridge loaded the bases with no outs and then recovered to retire three men in a row, with only one run scoring on a sacrifice fly, as Pittsburgh won, 3–2. He collected a second complete-game victory in Game 5, which the Pirates won, 6–3. He started Game 7, but a slippery mound made his pitching uncharacteristically wild. He was charged with two hits, three walks, and four runs in just one third of an inning, but Pittsburgh rallied to win, 9–7, clinching the title.

Aldridge slumped to 10–13 in 1926 but came back for 15 wins in 1927 as the Pirates again took the pennant. He expected a raise in 1928, but Pittsburgh owner Barney Dreyfuss, noting that his ERA had ballooned to more than four runs a game, traded Aldridge to the New York Giants. Aldridge held out for much of the season, reported out of shape, and then pitched ineffectively. After the season Giants manager John McGraw waived him to Brooklyn. Aldridge now 35 years old, refused to report to the Dodgers and retired.

Dale Alexander

Alexander, David Dale **1B**

1929–33 B:4/26/1903, Greeneville, TN D:3/2/1979, Greeneville, TN Deb:4/16/1929, DET AL BR/TR 6'3", 210

G	AB	R	H	HR	RBI	OBP	SLG	AVG
662	2450	369	811	61	459	.394	.497	.331

A look at Dale Alexander's batting statistics raises the question of why he didn't play longer. Despite a lifetime .331 average, Alexander was in the major leagues for only five seasons. His short career was no mystery to those who saw him field, however. Only his bat kept him in the lineup, and when his average dipped to .281 in 1933 it was back to the minors for "Moose."

Alexander first reached the majors in 1929, when, with the Detroit Tigers, he hit .343, led the AL with 215 hits, and hit 25 homer runs and 137 RBIs. The next year he almost matched those numbers, with a .326 batting average and 135 RBIs.

Early in 1932 Alexander was traded from the Tigers to the Red Sox for Earl Webb. Alexander became almost unstoppable at the plate, hitting .367 for the full year. That was the highest average of any regular in the American League, but since he did not have enough plate appearances the title instead went to Jimmie Foxx, who had a .364 average.

Alexander went on to play in the minors until 1942, appearing in 1,673 minor league contests and hitting as high as .338 in such places as Newark, Nashville, and Chattanooga. He hit four home runs in a single game in Minneapolis on June 14, 1935, for Kansas City of the American Association.

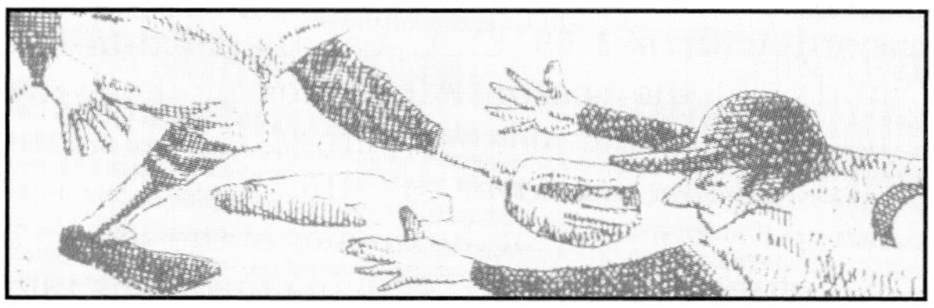

Doyle Alexander

Alexander, Doyle Lafayette **P**

1971–89 B:9/4/1950, Cordova, AL Deb:6/26/1971, LA NL BR/TR 6'3", 205

W	L	PCT	G	SH	IP	BB	SO	ERA
194	174	.527	561	18	3367^{2}	978	1528	3.76

Doyle Alexander made nine team changes in his 19-year major-league career. His overall numbers were average, but he had some outstanding moments and excellent seasons in that time.

The Los Angeles Dodgers' 44th-round draft pick in June 1968, Alexander reached the majors in 1971. The next year he was shipped to the Baltimore Orioles, with whom, in the next four and a half years, he managed only one winning season. In mid-1976, he was dealt to the New York Yankees, and his 10–5 record helped the Bombers to their first pennant in more than a decade. Alexander, who did not pitch at all in New York's dramatic five-game victory over Kansas City in the Championship Series, started and lost Game 1 in the World Series. The Cincinnati Reds went on to sweep the Yankees.

Alexander left New York as a free agent after that campaign, and signed with the Texas Rangers. In 1977 he won a career-best 17 games. However, in each of the next two years he had losing seasons, and he then made stops in Atlanta and San Francisco. In 1982 the Yankees reacquired Alexander, but he posted a 1–9 record in his second tour and earned owner George Steinbrenner's wrath by injuring his hand after angrily punching a wall. Steinbrenner remarked that infielders were afraid to play behind him, but Graig Nettles added to that comment, saying, "If I was in the bleachers, I'd be scared."

Released from the Yankees in June 1983, Alexander signed with Toronto, where everything seemed to come together. In both 1984 and 1985, he won 17 games, including the Blue Jays' AL East clincher over the Yankees on the next-to-last day of the 1985 season. A poor start in 1986, however, saw him traded to the Atlanta Braves. Midway through the next year, the Braves traded Alexander to the contending Detroit Tigers for a 20-year-old pitcher named John Smoltz.

The journeyman junkballer exceeded the Tigers' wildest expectations, compiling a 9–0 record with a 1.53 ERA. On the next-to-last Sunday of the season Alexander pitched 10⅔ innings, allowing just one earned run in a crucial 13-inning win over the Blue Jays. The following Friday he won the opener of the season's final series with Toronto, moving the teams into a first-place tie. When the season ended, the Tigers had won all 11 of Alexander's starts to claim the AL East title.

Alexander's magic faded in the ALCS, however. In the opener against the Twins, he and Mike Henneman lost a 5–4 lead and were torched for four runs in the bottom of the eighth. In Game 5 Minnesota savaged Alexander four runs in less than two innings. He completed his postseason career at 0–5 in six starts with an awful 8.38 ERA.

After two more years with the Tigers—including being selected to his first All-Star Game in 1988—Alexander retired, having become the fourth pitcher to defeat all 26 teams in existence at the time.

Grover Cleveland Alexander

Alexander, Grover Cleveland **P**

1911–30 B:2/26/1887, Elba, NE D:11/4/1950, St. Paul, NE Deb:4/15/1911, PHI NL BR/TR 6'1", 185

W	L	PCT	G	SH	IP	BB	SO	ERA
373	208	.642	696	90	5190	951	2198	2.56

Grover Cleveland Alexander may not have been the only ballplayer named after a seated U.S. president, but he was the only one later to be portrayed in the movies by a future one; Hollywood's Ronald Reagan played him in the 1952 motion picture *The Winning Team*. His life story certainly made for an interesting script.

The Nebraska-born Alexander was one of 13 children, 12 of them boys. He could throw a rock faster and straighter than any of them. After he'd traded rocks for baseballs he played semipro ball. In 1907, at age 22, he received a professional contract for $50 per month with Galesburg, Illinois, of the Central Association.

Alexander posted a fine first season, going 15–8, but his debut was marred by a beaning that may have contributed to the bouts of epilepsy that afflicted him later in life. While trying to break up a double play he took a rival shortstop's relay throw squarely on the head and did not regain consciousness for two days. Although he felt dizzy for the remainder of the season, his condition did not inhibit the top-level American Association Indianapolis Indians from acquiring him. But when his pitch plunked the manager in batting practice and broke three of his ribs, the club sent Alexander packing.

Alexander recovered sufficiently in 1910 to win 29 games and pitch a phenomenal 15 shutouts for the Syracuse Stars of the Class B New York State League. They sold him to the Philadelphia Phillies at the bargain price of $750. Alexander's Philadelphia baptism came that same fall in the postseason City Series, at that time an annual institution, against the cross-town rival Athletics, who had been crowned world champions. "You'll pitch five innings," manager Pat Moran warned. "They'll be murder, but you'll learn something." Moran was half right. There was learning to be done, but the rookie did the schooling, giving up no runs, no walks, and no hits.

His first full season proved the value of the investment, as Alexander broke in like few rookies before or since. He paced the league with 28 wins, 31 complete games, seven shutouts, and 367 innings pitched, while finishing second in strikeouts and fourth in ERA. Four of his shutouts were in succession, including a 12-inning, one-hit, 1–0 victory against Cy Young. Alexander's 28 wins remain the modern rookie record.

He was just getting started. From 1915 to 1917 he enjoyed seasons as good as any ever posted, winning 31, 33, and 30 games, with ERAs of 1.22, 1.55, and 1.83, respectively. He became the only player ever to win the pitching Triple Crown—wins, ERA, and strikeouts—three years running. No one since has pitched more than the 38 complete games Alexander recorded in 1916. No one has since surpassed his 33 wins in 1916. And only Bob Gibson in 1968 has since bettered Alexander's 1.22 ERA of 1915. In 1915 he also led the Phils to their first pennant of the modern era. He threw four one-hitters that year, another record, all the while pitching in the tiny Baker Bowl, with its seemingly miniscule distance between first base and the right-field wall. As if to cap his awesome three-year display, Alexander won a September 1917 Labor Day doubleheader at Ebbets Field, defeating Brooklyn, 5–0 and 7–3.

The Phillies, fearful that Alexander and catcher Bill Killefer would be lost in the military draft, unexpectedly sold them both to the Chicago Cubs after the 1917 season for $60,000. Indeed, Alexander spent most of the 1918 season with General Pershing's American Expeditionary Force in France, where he served as a sergeant in the artillery and suffered from shell shock. He returned home with a partial loss of hearing and ever-worsening seizures.

Epilepsy was just one of Alexander's problems. Drinking was another, and it was even more severe after Armistice Day. "His face looked like a piece of raw meat in the later stages of his career," one observer wrote, "and his managers often had to check with his teammates to see if they thought old Pete could make it that day."

Nonetheless, Alexander was a more than reasonably effective hurler for the Cubs. Twice he won more than 20 games. In 1920 he achieved another Triple Crown, going 27–14 with a 1.91 ERA and 173 strikeouts. And in 1923 he went 22–12. However, on June 22, 1926, the Cubs gave up on him. Manager Joe McCarthy, tired of Alexander's bouts with the bottle and his perceived insubordination, sold him to the Cardinals for the $4,000 waiver price.

In St. Louis Alexander proved he still had some pitching in him. His most dramatic moment came not long after the trade, in the seventh game of the 1926 World Series. He had already pitched complete game victories in Games 2 and 6. In Game 7 at Yankee Stadium the score was 3–2 in favor of the Cardinals when St. Louis starter Jesse Haines developed a blister on his finger and had to be removed from the game in the seventh inning. Cards manager Rogers Hornsby summoned Alexander from the bullpen. True to form, Alexander had not recovered from celebrating his victory of the previous day and had to be shaken awake.

When Alexander took the mound, the bases were loaded with two men out. Tony Lazzeri, who drove in 114 runs as a rookie during the season, lashed a pitch down the left-field line that just missed being a grand slam. Pete then struck him out in one of the greatest confrontations in Series history. Alexander made the score stand the next two innings and the Cardinals had their first world championship.

Alexander won 21 games for the Cards in 1927, but he continued drinking heavily, leading the club to release him at the end of a mediocre 1929 season. He signed with the woeful Phillies, but went 0–3 before being released again. He pitched briefly in the Texas League, then hooked up with the barnstorming House of David, pitching for the bearded wonders until 1938.

After retiring from baseball Alexander lived from hand to mouth, debilitated by even worse bouts of alcoholism and epilepsy. His 1938 induction into Baseball's Hall of Fame and the plaque that came with it brought him little solace. "You know I can't eat tablets or nicely framed awards," he told Fred Lieb. "Neither can my wife. But they don't think of things like that."

Dick Allen

Allen, Richard Anthony **1B-3B-OF**

1963–77 B:3/8/1942, Wampum, PA Deb:9/3/1963, PHI NL BR/TR 5'11", 190

G	AB	R	H	HR	RBI	OBP	SLG	AVG
1749	6332	1099	1848	351	1119	.381	.534	.292

Even in the turbulent 1960s Dick Allen was a league-leader in controversy, feuding with writers, fans, managers, and teammates; earning suspensions; and behaving and fielding erratically. However, he certainly could hit, and, when he wanted to, Dick Allen could carry a team. In an era that favored the men on the mound, pitchers still had to be careful when pitching to Allen.

Allen came from an athletic family. He and four of his brothers were all-state in basketball. Brothers Hank and Ron also played major league baseball. The Phillies recognized Allen's power potential and signed him for a $60,000 bonus. Sent to the minors, protest parades greeted his arrival as the first black ballplayer in barely desegregated Little Rock. Overcoming the racial tension, Allen led the league in total bases and won promotion to Philadelphia, where he soon established himself as a star, winning National League Rookie of the Year honors in 1964 after hitting .318 and leading the circuit in runs and triples.

Despite his ability with the bat, Allen did have a downside on the field. He struck out often, twice fanning five times in a single game and once whiffing seven times in a row. His fielding also left a lot to be desired, although his league-leading total of 38 errors at third base was understandable since he had never played the position before.

Fans and scribes, however, proved unforgiving. Allen bore much of the blame for the Phils' disastrous pennant swoon of 1964, although in fact their principal deficiencies lay in pitching and managing. Nonetheless, Philadelphia sportswriters criticized Allen mercilessly, terming him "a con man with muscles" and a "schizophrenic."

The next year Allen was selected to the first of seven All-Star Games, but a fistfight with veteran Frank Thomas in July led to Thomas' release and did little to boost Allen's standing with the fans. He couldn't be called popular even in 1966, when he hit 40 home runs and drove in 110. Then the next year, on August 24, 1967, a mysterious accident occurred in which Allen gashed his throwing hand by pushing it through a car headlight. The injury necessitated his move to first base. Allen once remarked, "I'll play first, third, left. I'll play anywhere—except Philadelphia."

In June 1969 Allen earned a 26-day suspension after showing up late for a doubleheader at Shea Stadium. He had been at Monmouth Race Track in New Jersey, and, as he tried to get to the game, he was stopped by police for cutting across lanes in the Lincoln Tunnel. The incident culminated a long series of controversies, including fines for missing planes and batting practices, drunkenness, a fight with a barroom owner, and an overall lack of hustle. "I'd been hearing I was a bum for so long that I began to

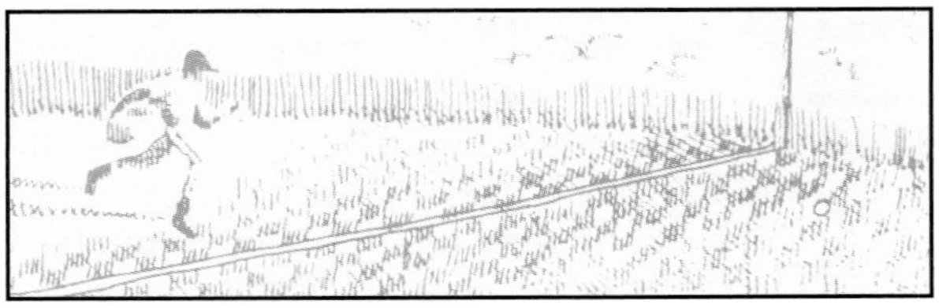

think that's just what I was," he admitted. "I began to hit the sauce pretty good, and I didn't care who knew it."

Then came the great name-change controversy. As a boy, Allen had been known as either "Dick" or "Sleepy." When he came to the majors he was known as "Richie." Now he demanded that he be called Dick. "Richie is a little boy's name," he explained, but few fans understood, and to most it was another sign of his lack of normality.

In 1971 the Phillies shipped Allen and two other players to the Cardinals for Tim McCarver, Curt Flood, and two others from St. Louis. Flood refused to report and sued baseball, paving the way for free agency. Allen couldn't move from team to team freely, but he moved plenty anyway.

Despite 34 homers and 101 RBIs, Allen soon wore out his welcome in St. Louis and went to the Dodgers for Ted Sizemore and Bob Stinson. One year later it was off to the White Sox in exchange for Tommy John and Steve Huntz. At Comiskey Park he finally found a home. Leading the Sox to a division championship in 1972, Allen impressed even his harshest critics. He paced the American League with 37 homers, 113 RBIs, 99 walks, an on-base percentage of .422, and a slugging average of .603. He received 21 out of 24 first-place votes for AL MVP.

"He was on a rampage, a man on a mission," marveled Chicago manager Chuck Tanner, "He could do anything he wanted. Dick Allen picked the White Sox up on his back and carried it all season. It was a powerful thing to watch. He had an incredible mind for baseball. He thought like a manager. He saw the whole field.... In 1972, Dick Allen piloted the Chicago White Sox as much as I did. We were co-managers."

That was 1972. By 1974 Allen became embroiled in a feud with newly acquired third baseman Ron Santo. Leading the league in homers with 32, Allen walked out on the club on September 14. The frustrated Sox sold his contract to the Braves for only $5,000 and a player to be named later, but Allen had no interest in ever playing in Dixie again. The Phillies, led by announcer Richie Ashburn, coaxed him out of retirement; however, he was not the same player he had been. Granted free agency in November 1976, he finished his career in 1977 with Oakland. Again there was an explosion. Faced with the possibility of being reduced to designated-hitter status, Allen stormed off the team. "Cost me about two hundred grand to walk away, but it was worth every penny," he commented.

After leaving baseball as a player, Allen had a run of bad luck. His house, uninsured, burned to the ground in October 1979, his marriage fell apart, and his wife received the rights to his pension. He did work with the Texas Rangers in spring training of 1981 and as a White Sox minor league instructor in 1988. He also authored an autobiography, aptly titled *Crash*. But perhaps his true ability was shown by a comment by Phillies star third baseman Mike Schmidt. "When I was playing Legion ball in Ohio," Schmidt said, "I always pretended I was Dick Allen. He was my idol."

Ethan Allen

Allen, Ethan Nathan **OF**

1926–38 B:1/1/1904, Cincinnati, OH D:9/15/1993, Brookings, OR Deb:6/21/1926, CIN NL BR/TR 6'1", 180

G	AB	R	H	HR	RBI	OBP	SLG	AVG
1281	4418	623	1325	47	501	.336	.410	.300

Ethan Allen was a solid major league outfielder for 13 seasons, a career .300 hitter and a reliable fielder. But his contributions to the game after his playing career far outdistanced anything he did on the field.

Allen never played in the minors. He began his career with the Reds in 1926, appearing in 18 games, mostly as a pinch hitter, and batting .308. The following year he played more or less regularly, hitting .295 in 111 games. The 1928 and 1929 seasons were two of his best seasons. He batted .305 and .292, respectively, and knocked in more than 60 runs each season. In 1929 he led all NL outfielders in fielding percentage.

Traded to the New York Giants in 1930, Allen filled a reserve role for three seasons behind such stars as Mel Ott, Freddy Lindstrom, and Jo-Jo Moore. In 1933 he was sent to the St. Louis Cardinals, and the next year to the Philadelphia Phillies. Given the regular left field position in Philadelphia, he had his best season, tying for the league lead with 42 doubles while hitting .330 with a career-high 85 RBIs. Much of his success stemmed from his ability to slap the ball off Baker Bowl's near right-field wall. Although his other batting stats fell off slightly in 1935, his 46 doubles were second best in the National League.

Allen was traded to the Chicago Cubs in 1936, and then spent the final two seasons of his career with the St. Louis Browns in 1937 and 1938. He hit over .300 each season.

Intelligent, knowledgeable, and articulate, Allen was a better student of the game than he was a player. He is best remembered for a revolutionary tabletop baseball game he developed in the 1930s. It consisted of circular cards representing baseball players. The space around the outside of a card was divided into various hit and out possibilities in accordance with the players' actual batting statistics. The cards were placed on a spinner for each "at-bat." Although anything might happen on an individual at bat, in the course of hundreds of spins, players accrued statistics similar to their actual baseball performance. For many youngsters in the 1940s and 1950s, the game was an important adjunct to "real" baseball. Allen later served as the National League's motion picture director, coached college baseball, and wrote several books on playing techniques.

Johnny Allen

Allen, John Thomas **P**

1932–44 B:9/30/1905, Lenoir, NC D:3/29/1959, St. Petersburg, FL Deb:4/19/1932, NY AL BR/TR 6', 180

W	L	PCT	G	SV	IP	BB	SO	ERA
142	75	.654	352	18	1950[1]	738	1070	3.75

When Johnny Allen was working as a bellhop in a hotel, he was asked to bring some electric fans up to New York Yankees superscout Paul Krichell, who wanted to cool off his sweltering room. The tempestuous, hard-throwing youngster confided to the former catcher that he was a pitcher of sorts, and Krichell gave him a tryout.

Krichell's faith paid off in 1932, when Allen posted a 17–4 rookie record, a mark that gave him the best winning percentage in the American League. The next year Allen won 15 games, but the Yankees soon tired of him. He habitually held out for more money, and when a sore arm threatened to end his career, they packed him off to Cleveland in 1936.

The trade was a huge one for the Indians. Despite a slow start, Allen won 20 games and followed that up in 1937 by winning his first 15 decisions. He came close to tying the AL mark for consecutive victories set by Walter Johnson in 1912, but lost 1–0 on an error by teammate Odell "Bad News" Hale. Nevertheless his 15–1 season mark was the major league record for won-lost percentage until Elroy Face's 18–1 performance in 1959.

One of the first pitchers to throw the slider, Allen won his first 12 decisions and was selected for his first All-Star Game, but he then suffered a mysterious injury during the All-Star break. Some contend he slipped on a bar of soap in a hotel room shower. Whatever the reason, he soon went into a serious decline, only won twice the rest of the year, and never approached his former performances, having six mediocre years before retiring in 1944.

Ironically, despite Allen's notorious temper and numerous run-ins with umpires, he went on to become umpire-in-chief of the Carolina League. He died of a heart attack on March 29, 1959.

Mel Allen

Allen, Melvin

Broadcaster B:2/14/1913, Johns, AL D: 6/16/1996, Greenwich, CT

The single most recognizable—and likable—voice in the history of baseball broadcasting may well have been that of Mel Allen. Although his broadcasting career included stints covering football and other sports, his many years of broadcasting the Yankees, the World Series, and the All-Star Game have forever linked his comfortable style with the Golden Age of Baseball on the air. Later, as the voice of the syndicated television show *This Week in Baseball*, he captured the hearts of a new generation of baseball fans. His easy drawl and signature "How 'bout that, sports fans?" were inextricably connected with the pleasure of baseball.

As a student at the University of Alabama, Allen tried out for football but was too skinny and settled for the job of student manager, which included announcing the tackles and downs over the public address system. At age 20 he landed his first broadcasting job as the voice of the Crimson Tide on CBS's Birmingham affiliate. Although his radio skills were still undeveloped, his voice possessed a special quality.

Pioneer CBS sportscaster Ted Husing heard Allen and suggested he audition. Allen passed the test, but stayed in school to complete his law degree. That completed, he went to New York in 1937 and was hired as a CBS staff announcer for $45 a week. When Larry MacPhail broke the New York baseball radio blackout, Allen was hired as the Yankees' broadcaster for the 1940 season. He and Red Barber did the first of their World Series broadcasts together the following year. Allen proved to be an immediate hit with New York fans. He nicknamed Joe DiMaggio "The Yankee Clipper" and christened Phil Rizzuto "Scooter."

Allen left to serve in the Army during World War II, and, without sponsors, neither the Giants nor the Yankees broadcast in 1943 or 1944. When Allen returned in 1946 the Yankees announced they would be the first team to air all their games live—no studio re-creations of away games.

In 1948 Allen introduced his famous home run call: "It's going, going, gone!" In 1950 Dizzy Dean joined Allen on the Yankees' television broadcasts. With Jim Britt and Russ Hodges, Allen called his first televised World Series in 1951. As author Curt Smith pointed out, this was the beginning of a great era for baseball broadcasting. "In New York, one [could] hear Allen, Barber, Hodges, [Vin] Scully, and [Ernie] Harwell—five of the first six broadcast [recipients of the Ford C. Frick Award] at Baseball's Hall of Fame."

In 1954 Barber and Jim Woods joined Allen in the Yankees broadcast booth. In the 1960 World Series he called a seventh-game home run by Yogi Berra "foul, barely foul." It was written in *Sports Illustrated* that this was the greatest miscall since Clem McCarthy's historic error in the 1947 Preakness.

On NBC-TV Allen covered all the Yankees' World Series games from 1955 through 1963, 12 consecutive All-Star Games from 1952 through 1961, and the Rose Bowl. "One year *Variety* ran a list of the most recognizable voices in the world...Churchill, Roosevelt, people like that," Allen said. "I was the only sports announcer on the list. I guess then I realized I had a special voice."

That voice had a famous breakdown in 1963. On October 6 the Yankees were in an unaccustomed predicament. They were losing the World Series to Sandy Koufax and the Dodgers three games to none, and down 1–0 in Game 4. Mickey Mantle homered in the seventh to tie the game at 1–1. As Allen described it, "The crowd roared, and I started to roar, too. Then I suddenly lost my voice." Allen had to be removed from the air. Barber described the event as "shattering"—and Scully took Allen's place for the final two innings as the Yankees were swept.

Not surprisingly, New York sports pundit Dick Young offered a unique interpretation of the event: "If you have a television set, you know of the emotional crackup that knocked him off the air...They said he had laryngitis, but if it was it was psychosomatic laryngitis. Mel Allen couldn't believe his beloved Yankees were losing four straight to the Dodgers. His voice refused to believe it, and therefore he could not report it." In actuality, Allen had suffered voice problems earlier that season, exacerbated by a nasal condition and his emotional intensity, which Barber had warned him about to no avail.

Ironically, Allen's "roar" after Mantle's homer was the last sound he would make broadcasting a World Series game. He was fired after the next season and replaced by Phil Rizzuto, who had become a personal favorite of bigwigs at Ballantine Beer, the primary sponsor of the Yankees. Allen's firing shocked the broadcasting world. According to Red Barber, Allen was "desolate, stricken." Allen was notorious for not appearing in the broadcast booth until moments before airtime, which didn't sit well with the consummate professional Barber. But the night Allen was fired, Barber got to the booth in Cleveland 15 minutes before airtime, and Mel was already there. "He was sitting in his place. He was staring across the ball field. He didn't speak. I don't think he knew I had come in. I don't think he knew where he was. He was numb. His eyes were bulging out so far they looked like Concord grapes. He was the saddest-looking man I had ever seen. He was in a nightmare. His look was not frantic, not wild—just sad, numb, deserted. He just couldn't believe it...Mel could not believe he wouldn't be on the Series, could not accept he wasn't the Voice of the Yankees."

Team officials never held a press conference or commented on the firing. *Sports Illustrated* commented, "Allen became a victim of rumors. He was supposed to be a drunkard, a drug user. Neither rumor was true, but he couldn't fight them...It was as if he had leprosy."

Allen was reduced to menial work. He announced some TV games for Cleveland in 1966 (during one especially dull game with the Twins he delivered an impromptu recitation of the first 37 lines of Longfellow's "Hiawatha"), a two-minute syndicated radio program, Ballantine Beer commercials, and, in a supreme irony, the 1966 Little League World Series. But he was essentially gone from the national scene.

Curt Smith put it, "By the mid-'60s, Mel Allen's innate enthusiasm and sense of drama had sold more cigars, more cans of beer, more Gillette safety razors, and possibly, more fans on the game of baseball than any broadcaster who had ever lived." However, in 1977, Major League Baseball introduced its first syndicated series, *This Week In Baseball.* Allen was back. Merle Harmon said, "I've never seen a show like it so closely synonymous with one person."

When the Yankees hired Allen to work their cablecasts in 1985, *Sports Illustrated* waxed eloquent. "The Voice is back where it belongs, an old campaigner, a keeper of tradition. If baseball is back, then Mel Allen must be too...When you hear it, it's summer again, a lazy July or August afternoon with sunlight creeping across the infield...Like the game itself, Allen is timeless."

Newt Allen

Allen, Newton Henry **2B-3B-SS-OF-1B**
Negro League Player/Manager 1922–44, 1947
B:5/19/1901, Austin, TX D:6/11/1988, Cincinnati, OH
BR/TR 5'8", 160

As has been proven many times through the history of baseball, a player doesn't have to be big to be a star. At 5 feet 8 inches and just 160 pounds, Newt "Colt" Allen was yet another example of this, playing and managing so well for nearly three decades that he achieved a stature out of all proportion to his size.

Discovered while playing semipro ball by Kansas City Monarchs owner J.L. Wilkinson, Allen signed with the All-Nations in 1922 before going on to play 23 seasons with Wilkinson's Monarchs. He also put in service with the St. Louis Stars, Homestead Grays, and Indianapolis Clowns. Allen batted .301 in 24 games against big league competition. He also played in the Caribbean Leagues and toured Japan and the Philippines.

As a manager Allen led the Monarchs to five pennants, including four in a row from 1939 to 1942. It was Allen who advised Wilkinson about a shortstop the owner was eyeing: "He's a very smart ballplayer, but he can't play shortstop—he can't throw from the hole. Try him at second base." That infielder was Jackie Robinson, and Allen had sized him up pretty well.

Gene Alley

Alley, Leonard Eugene **SS-2B**
1963–73 B:7/10/1940, Richmond, VA Deb:9/4/1963, PIT NL BR/TR 6', 165

G	AB	R	H	HR	RBI	OBP	SLG	AVG
1195	3927	442	999	55	342	.312	.354	.254

Gene Alley arrived in Pittsburgh in 1963 with a reputation as a sensational fielder and an excellent hitter. However, he never quite lived up to the rave reviews, before injuries abbreviated his once-promising career.

Never a slugger, the soft-spoken Alley was a good hit-and-run man and an excellent bunter. His best year was 1966, when he hit .299, won a Gold Glove, and, with second baseman Bill Mazeroski, helped the Pirates log an National League record 216 double plays.

The next two years Alley was selected to the All-Star Game, but a shoulder injury suffered in August 1967, combined with knee problems and a broken left hand, affected both his fielding and his hitting. He never was quite able to match either his hitting or fielding success, although he remained with the Pirates through 1973. He appeared in the 1971 World Series against Baltimore, and started all five games of the 1972 Championship Series against Cincinnati, although he went hitless against the Reds.

Bob Allison

Allison, William Robert **OF-1B**
1958–70 B:7/11/1934, Raytown, MO D:4/9/1995, Rio Verde, AZ Deb:9/16/1958, WAS AL BR/TR 6'4", 220

G	AB	R	H	HR	RBI	OBP	SLG	AVG
1541	5032	811	1281	256	796	.360	.471	.255

American League pitchers had to rethink the way they approached the Washington Senators in 1959. That year both Bob Allison and Harmon Killebrew became regulars, and the fences suddenly seemed to have been drawn in closer.

The husky Allison had played both football and baseball at the University of Missouri before a stint in the minor leagues. Allison's time in the minors gave little indication of the power hitter that he would become. "Hitting was the hardest thing I have ever tried to learn in my life," Allison once admitted.

But in 1959 Allison blossomed, being named American League Rookie of the Year with 30 home runs and a league-leading nine triples. Although he never matched Killebrew's totals of leading the league in homers six times, Allison did finish third in 1963 and sixth in 1964, both years that he was selected for the All-Star Game. All told, he topped 25 homers five times in his first six years.

Unlike many sluggers, Allison was no lumbering behemoth; on the contrary, he was an aggressive, intelligent baserunner. One player said, "He looks like a locomotive when he's coming in to break up a double play. He's gonna slide into somebody and send him to the moon one of these days."

Allison was also capable of excellence in the outfield. His strong arm led him to be shifted to right field early in his career. Calvin Griffith observed that Allison had "the best arm on this club since Jackie Jensen." Allison's diving catch off Dodger Jim Lefebvre's bat in the second game of the 1965 World Series has been called "the best in Twins' history."

His competitive attitude was lauded by teammates and opponents alike. "He wants to win at everything," observed an admiring Killebrew, "cards, ping pong, handball, or baseball. He wants to be the first on the airplane and first on the bus."

It was his home runs that brought Allison his most famous moments. On May 17, 1963, he hit three in a single game and followed that up on July 18 by combining with Killebrew to become the first teammates to clout grand slams in the same inning. On May 2, 1964, he teamed up with Tony Oliva, Jimmie Hall, and Killebrew to hit four consecutive homers.

Billy Martin, who skippered the Twins for a season late in Allison's career (after Allison had been hobbled by injuries in 1966 and 1967), found the outfielder a joy to work with. Allison, he noted, "was my leader on the bench, a beautiful buffer for me. I'd say to him, 'Bob, tell so-and-so about such-and-such when you get a chance,' and coming from Bob they wouldn't resent it as if it came from me....He'd have made somebody an excellent coach."

Instead, Allison became general manager of Coca-Cola's Twin Cities Marketing Division. He later contracted amyotrophic lateral sclerosis (Lou Gehrig's Disease). He died in 1995.

Roberto Alomar

Alomar, Roberto (Velasquez) **2B**
1988–* B:2/5/1968, Ponce, Puerto Rico Deb:4/22/1988, SD NL BB/TR 6',185

G	AB	R	H	HR	RBI	OBP	SLG	AVG
1722	6611	1117	2007	151	829	.378	.446	.304

Roberto Alomar was a hard-working ballplayer with a solid baseball pedigree. He was so dedicated to his craft he lived at the ballpark—well, actually he lived at the hotel attached to the SkyDome in Toronto. He was an everyday major leaguer at 20, won eight Gold Glove Awards, played in 10 straight All-Star Games, stole 20 or more bases eight times, and appeared in six postseasons in his first 12 years in the big leagues. A 1996 spitting incident with an umpire overshadowed many of his on-field achievements, but he remained popular enough to be voted to start the All-Star Game three times following his controversial suspension. He was even selected as Most Valuable Player of the 1998 All-Star Game.

At age 6, Alomar won a spot on his first Little League team after tagging along with older brother Sandy. More than 20 years later, he recalled what he learned from his father, former major leaguer Sandy Alomar, Sr.: "To be the same person when you become a big leaguer. To make sure money does not change your personality. And to play the game hard."

Signed by San Diego at age 17, Robbie was in the majors within three years. He impressed observers with his raw hitting instincts, phenomenal fielding range, and superior baserunning. After the 1990 season Alomar came to Toronto with Joe Carter in a blockbuster trade for Fred McGriff and Tony Fernandez. In his first season as a Blue Jay he batted .295 and won the first of six straight Gold Gloves.

Alomar's Game 4 ninth-inning home run against Dennis Eckersley turned around the 1992 American League Championship Series.

The Blue Jays, who had trailed Game 4 by five runs in the eighth inning, tied it on Alomar's two-run shot and won the game two innings later. He batted .423 to claim Most Valuable Player honors as the Blue Jays beat Oakland in six games. Toronto then beat the Atlanta Braves for their first world championship. A year later John Olerud, Paul Molitor, and Alomar became the first American League teammate trio to finish one-two-three in the batting race. Alomar batted .480 with six RBIs and four steals in Toronto's World Series triumph over Philadelphia.

A free agent after 1995, Alomar left the Blue Jays for the big dollars of division rival Baltimore. The change of scenery seemed to inspire him, as he hit .328 with 22 homers and 94 RBIs for the Orioles. Alomar's heroics, however, were overshadowed by an incident in Toronto on September 27, 1996. He was ejected from a crucial game for arguing balls and strikes, and the furious Alomar spat in the face of umpire John Hirschbeck. After wrangling between AL president Gene Budig, the umpires' union, and the players' union over his punishment, Alomar was suspended for five games at the beginning of the 1997 season. Baltimore was nonetheless bounced from the playoffs in the 1996 ALCS.

Fans turned against Alomar, and injuries limited his playing time in 1997 even as he hit a career-best .333. In November 1998 he signed a four-year deal with Cleveland that reunited him with brother Sandy for the first time since they were both Padres in 1989. The move also paired Robbie with the league's best defensive shortstop in Omar Vizquel. Newly energized, Alomar turned in a bang-up offensive season, batting .323 with 24 homers, 120 RBIs, and 37 steals as the Indians rolled to their fifth straight division crown.

Sandy Alomar, Jr.

Alomar, Santos Jr. (Velazquez) **C**

1988–* B:6/18/1966, Salinas, Puerto Rico
Deb:9/30/1988, SD NL BR/TR 6'5", 215

G	AB	R	H	HR	RBI	OBP	SLG	AVG
896	3073	373	845	86	417	.316	.421	.275

Unlike his father, Sandy Alomar Sr., who played 15 years in the major leagues, or his younger brother Roberto, a perennial All-Star who joined him on the Indians in 1999, Sandy Alomar Jr. spent a good deal of his career on the disabled list. Following 1990, when he played in 132 games and became the first rookie catcher to start the All-Star Game, Alomar had a five-year run in which he failed to play more than 89 games or come to the plate more than 300 times in a season.

After missing most of the first half of the 1995 season, though, he bounced back to hit .300 with 10 home runs in 66 games for Cleveland's American League champions. He finally managed to string together a few years of relative good health in the late 1990s, but missed four months of the 1999 season following knee surgery.

While brother Roberto made the San Diego Padres at age 20, Sandy Jr. had a more difficult road, struggling his first three seasons in the minors. When he finally arrived and was ready for the big leagues, Sandy was stuck behind Benito Santiago, the Rookie of the Year two years earlier and the man considered to be the best catcher in the National League. Alomar had to bide his time in the minors, but he made the most of it. With Las Vegas, the Padres' AAA affiliate, in 1988, Alomar shared Most Valuable Player honors; in 1989 he won the award outright.

Alomar was traded to the Indians along with Carlos Baerga for Joe Carter, who would ironically be packaged off to Toronto with Roberto Alomar the following year. Given the chance he needed, Sandy was the unanimous choice for American League Rookie of the Year in 1990. Five years later he helped end Cleveland's 41-year drought between World Series appearances, although the Tribe lost in six games to the Atlanta Braves.

Sandy had a great year at the plate in 1997, batting .324 with a 30-game hitting streak. He was MVP of the All-Star Game at Cleveland's Jacobs Field, and he broke up Mike Mussina's perfect game with a one-out single in the ninth on May 30 in Baltimore. But he really produced in the 1997 playoffs. In the American League Division Series against the Yankees, Alomar scorched Mariano Rivera for a home run that tied Game 4 in the eighth; the Indians went on to win the game and, the next night, the series. He followed that up in the Championship Series with a game-winning hit in the ninth inning of Game 4, breaking a 7–7 tie with the Orioles. Although the Indians lost to Florida in the World Series, Alomar stayed hot, hitting .367 with 11 hits and two homers. His 1997 postseason exploits earned him a spot on a Wheaties cereal box, and he launched Sandy Alomar Steak Sauce the following year.

After a mediocre season in 1998, Alomar missed most of 1999, appearing in just 37 games and batting .307. In November, the Indians exercised a $2.7 million option on their affable but battle-worn catcher.

Sandy Alomar, Sr.

Alomar, Santos Sr. (Conde) **2B–SS**
1964–78 B:10/19/1943, Salinas, Puerto Rico
Deb:9/15/1964, MIL NL BB/TR 5'9", 155

G	AB	R	H	HR	RBI	OBP	SLG	AVG
1481	4760	558	1168	13	282	.291	.288	.245

Better known now as the father of two All-Stars, catcher Sandy Alomar, Jr. and second baseman Roberto Alomar, Sandy Alomar, Sr. was a respectable journeyman infielder for 15 seasons. He was rarely a regular, but when he was he played well enough to be selected to the All-Star Game himself.

It took Alomar a number of years to earn a position as a starter, and in that time he seldom stayed in one place for long. Starting with the Milwaukee Braves in 1964, he moved with the team to Atlanta and then on to the New York Mets and Chicago White Sox before finding a home with the California Angels. He played five years with the Angels, twice appearing in every game of the season, which earned him the nickname "the Iron Pony." Alomar's value as a defender and baserunner was indicated by his selection to the All-Star Game in 1970 despite hitting only .251 for the season with a pair of triples and a pair of homers. He did, however, steal 35 bases that season, and swiped 227 for his career.

Midway through the 1974 season, the Angels dealt Alomar to the Yankees. In 1976 he saw the only playoff action of his career. He finished with two years in Texas.

After retiring, Alomar operated a gas station in his native Puerto Rico, and helped coach the national team. In 1984 he became a minor league instructor for San Diego. He also managed Santurce in the Puerto Rican winter league and, from 1986 to 1990, coached for the Padres. In 1988 and 1989 he coached both of his sons on that team.

Felipe Alou

Alou, Felipe Rojas **OF–1B**
1958–74 M(1992–*, 603–590) B:5/12/1935, Haina, Dominican Republic Deb:6/8/1958, SF NL BR/TR 6', 195

G	AB	R	H	HR	RBI	OBP	SLG	AVG
2082	7339	985	2101	206	852	.330	.433	.286

Felipe Alou was born into poverty in the Dominican Republic and always dreamed of escaping it by becoming a doctor. Instead, he did so by becoming the first Dominican to play regularly in the major leagues.

Alou was well on his way to attaining his career goal, having gained admission into the University of Santo Domingo, when fate intervened. Slated to compete in the Pan-American Games on the track team, Felipe was switched to the baseball team at the last moment. He excelled as the Dominican team took the Gold Medal, and major league scouts soon besieged him with offers. Despite all the attention, he stuck with his decision to follow a medical career—until a family crisis forced him to sign with the New York Giants in November 1955 for a paltry $200.

The Giants dispatched Alou to their Lake Charles, Louisiana, farm club in the Class C Evangeline League. Faced with hostility and discrimination, the dark-skinned Alou and his roommate were sent packing from the circuit after just five games. After moving to the Florida State League he responded with base hits and dignified courage, becoming a born-again Christian in the bargain. "Guys from the Dominican Republic don't know fear," Alou explained. "People from the Dominican try to cross the Atlantic in boats to get to the United States. The only thing on their mind is to give it all they've got."

Alou arrived in the majors with the newly relocated Giants in 1958. He played more and more, and in 1962 was selected for the All-Star Game in a season that saw him hit .316 with 25 home runs and 98 RBIs. The next year he was joined on the Giants by his brother Jesus, along with brother Matty, who had made the San Francisco club in 1960. All three batted in one inning against the New York Mets' Carlton Willey on September 10, 1963, at the Polo Grounds. Willey retired them in order.

In 1964 Alou was traded to the Braves, with whom he started playing first base. Two years later he had his best season, hitting .327 with 31 homers, while leading the National League with 218 hits and 122 runs. This was an unusual amount of power for a leadoff batter, and Alou hit 20 career home runs as the leadoff batter in a game. He is also one of only a handful of players to hit leadoff homers in two consecutive contests and was the first player to have attained that feat twice.

Alou retired as a player after stints with Oakland, the New York Yankees, Montreal, and the Milwaukee Brewers. Long vocal about the need for Hispanics to enter the administrative and management sides of the game, he became an Expos coach in 1979, alternating between that job and managing in the Montreal farm system. In 1985 the Giants gave him a chance to interview for their managerial post, but he backed away from the chance and stayed with the Expos. "I really didn't care if it was my only opportunity," he explained. "I was glad to stay with the Expos. They have been very good to me and continue to be good to me."

His loyalty paid off in May 1992 when he replaced Tom Runnells as the Expos' manager. Alou responded by bringing the team to a surprising second-place finish, earning praise for his low-key but very effective style. "He brings out the best in his players, just like [Pirates manager] Jim Leyland," said infielder Bret Barberie. In 1994 Alou won Associated Press Major League Manager of the Year. Even as the team's best players were sent elsewhere because of Montreal's fiscal constraints, Alou still produced quality players year after year. The Dodgers tried to hire Alou after the 1998 season, but the Expos signed their manager to a lucrative long-term contract to keep the winningest manager in team history.

Jesus Alou

Alou, Jesus Maria Rojas **OF**

1963–75, 1978–79 B:3/24/1942, Haina, Dominican Republic Deb:9/10/1963, SF NL BR/TR 6'2",195

G	AB	R	H	HR	RBI	OBP	SLG	AVG
1380	4345	448	1216	32	377	.307	.353	.280

Jesus Alou was the youngest of the three ballplaying Alou brothers. Before ending his major league career in 1979 he earned a reputation as one of the most fearsome pinch hitters in the game's history. Between 1963 and 1979 he produced 82 pinch hits, placing him above such notable bench heroes as Enos Slaughter and Bob Skinner.

Although little fanfare had greeted Alou's brothers Felipe and Matty when they joined the San Francisco Giants in 1958 and 1960, that was not the case when Jesus joined the big club on September 10, 1963. The Giants had always considered Jesus a more valuable prospect than his brothers. While Felipe and Matty received signing bonuses of $200 each, Jesus received $4,000. The Giants initially hoped Alou would be a pitcher, but they soon moved him to the outfield. The hoopla surrounding his major league debut stemmed from both the presence of his talented brothers and from his prodigious minor league feats: batting .667 in a few games at Hastings; .352 at Artesia; .350 in a few more contests at Eugene and then .336 in a full season there; .343 at El Paso; and .324 at Tacoma in the Pacific Coast League. Giants manager Alvin Dark pronounced there was no way this kid could miss and predicted a .310 rookie season in 1964.

Fueling the excitement were the circumstances of Alou's major league debut. On September 10, 1963, Jesus, Matty, and Felipe Alou all batted against Mets pitcher Carlton Willey in the same inning—the only time three major league brothers have ever stepped to the plate in the same inning. Five days later all three started in the Giants' outfield. They had to push aside Hall of Famers Willie Mays and Willie McCovey to get playing time.

In his first full year, in 1964, Alou had a hard time living up to the expectations. He hit .274 but came nowhere near Felipe's power figures. He did have his biggest day in baseball that year, however; on July 10, 1964, he went 6-for-6—five singles and a homer—against the Cubs. Each hit came against a different Chicago pitcher.

Alou was productive at the plate, but not at the level Giants management had predicted for him. Like brother Matty, Jesus got some help in adjusting his swing from "Harry the Hat" Walker, who suggested the youngest Alou brother quicken his swing and be more selective in choosing pitches. Jesus was such a wild swinger at one point that he actually homered off a Sandy Koufax fastball meant to brush him back from the plate.

On October 14, 1968, the Giants allowed Montreal to select Alou in the National League expansion draft. The Expos then traded Alou and first baseman Donn Clendenon to the Houston Astros for first baseman Rusty Staub. But Clendenon refused to report to the Astros and threatened to accept an executive position with an Atlanta pen company. "By clear baseball rule and precedent the deal was off," noted the *Official Baseball Guide*. However, the Montreal Expos had been trumpeting the addition of Staub, and Commissioner Bowie Kuhn hoped to see the first Canadian franchise gain early acceptance. For months Alou's career was in limbo. Although he trained with the Astros there was no telling whether he would be ordered to return to Montreal. Finally a deal was reached: Clendenon would report back to Montreal, and the Expos would send Alou, pitchers Jack Billingham and Skip Guinn, and cash to the Astros.

Alou now had a team, but he got off to a miserable start, hovering around .200. On June 10, 1969, he collided with shortstop Hector Torres while hustling after a pop fly. Both were knocked unconscious, and Alou suffered a severe concussion and a broken jaw. After missing six weeks, he finally regained his batting strength and raised his average to .248. The next year was perhaps his best, as Alou hit .306 with a career-high 27 doubles. But after 1971 he became to play less regularly, and midway through the 1973 season he was traded to the Oakland A's. The move was a stroke of luck.

Houston was going nowhere, but with Oakland he got into both the 1973 and 1974 World Series. He played all seven games of the 1973.

Alou was released by the A's in March 1975 with two world championship rings in a little more than a year and a half. He was signed by the Mets, but was released during spring training a year later. He signed on with Cordoba of the AAA Mexican League, where he managed only one homer in a circuit known for inflating hitters' reputations. On June 4, 1976, he was even released by Cordoba.

In 1978 the Astros gave him another chance. Remarkably he came through with flying colors, hitting .324 in part-time action. The Astros made him a player-coach the following year. Alou later became a scout in the Montreal Expos system, evaluating talent in his native Dominican Republic.

Matty Alou

Alou, Mateo Rojas **OF–1B**

1960–74 B:12/22/1938, Haina, Dominican Republic Deb:9/26/1960, SF NL BL/TL 5'9", 160

G	AB	R	H	HR	RBI	OBP	SLG	AVG
1667	5789	780	1777	31	427	.346	.381	.307

Matty Alou was the middle of the three Alou brothers. Although he didn't possess the power of elder brother Felipe or receive the initial publicity of younger brother Jesus, he was statistically the best hitter, and he was the only Alou to capture a major league batting title, with .342 in 1966.

To say Alou was not a textbook hitter would be an understatement. "He violates most of the principles I teach, but somehow he manages to get on base," Ted Williams once commented. His hitting style called to mind such individuals as Luke Appling, Richie Ashburn, Johnny Pesky, and Ferris Fain—players with virtually no power who managed to slap-hit their way to a .300 average year after year.

As a minor league player, Alou was considered better as a fielder than as a hitter, displaying an exceptional arm and twice leading the league in assists. Brought up to the Giants for four games at the close of the 1960 season, he was largely a part-time player for the next three years there and was platooned after that. On May 15, 1961, he and Felipe achieved the rare feat of brothers homering in the same game when they connected against Cubs Joe Schaffernoth and Dick Ellsworth, respectively.

Alou's biggest moment as a Giant came in 1962. His pinch-hit leadoff bunt single in the final game of the three-game playoff against the Dodgers ignited a four-run rally that gave San Francisco its first National League pennant. He continued his clutch hitting in the World Series against the Yankees with a .333 average San Francisco lost in seven games.

Prior to the 1966 season, Alou was traded to the Pittsburgh Pirates, where came under the tutelage of manager "Harry the Hat" Walker, an expert on hitting. Walker persuaded him to exchange his 34-ounce bat for a 38-ounce model. He ordered him to choke up, wait on the pitch, and hit more to left field. The results were dramatic. Finally playing full-time, Alou responded with a league-leading .342 mark. The following two years he was virtually as successful, hitting .338 and .332. Then, in 1969, he hit .331 while setting a major league record (since broken) with 698 at bats; he also paced the NL with 231 hits and 41 doubles.

Following the 1970 season Alou was then traded to St. Louis with pitcher George Brunet for pitcher Nelson Briles and outfielder Vic Davalillo. After recording .315 and .314 seasons for the Cardinals, he was dispatched on June 7, 1972, via waivers to Charlie Finley's Oakland A's. Little more than a spare part for Oakland in 1972, he did see action in all seven games of that fall's World Series. He played for three teams in his last two years before going to Japan in 1974. After playing there for three seasons he managed Cuidad Trujillo in the Dominican Winter League.

Moises Alou

Alou, Moises Rojas **OF**

1990, 1992–98,* B:7/3/1966, Atlanta, GA Deb: 7/26/1990, PIT NL BR/TR 6'3", 190

G	AB	R	H	HR	RBI	OBP	SLG	AVG
919	3271	535	966	145	612	.366	.506	.295

Moises Alou became a major leaguer under his father's watchful eye in Montreal. He was the final piece of the puzzle for the 1997 Florida Marlins; less than a year later he was the first to go in a tragic breakup of the world champions. He helped both Florida and Houston reach the postseason, and may have done the same with the Expos were it not for the 1994 strike.

His grandfather, Jose Rojas, spawned a baseball clan that made the Alous baseball's reigning family in the Dominican Republic. It started with the famed Alou brothers of the 1960s and 1970s—Felipe, Matty, and Jesus—and extended all the way to the 1990s when

Moises, his father Felipe, and cousin Mel Rojas all wore Expos uniforms.

Alou was born during his father's best season in 1966. His parents divorced two years later, and he rarely saw his father. He did not play organized baseball until he attended Canada College in California. After batting a league-leading .447 in 1986, the Pittsburgh Pirates made Alou the second overall pick. He was the player to be named later in a trade to the Expos for pitcher Zane Smith in 1990.

When Felipe became Montreal's manager in 1992, father and son had a series of closed-door meetings regarding playing time. Moises, who had missed the entire 1991 season with a shoulder injury, played a key role down the stretch as the Expos made an unsuccessful run at the Pirates for the National League East title. Felipe benched his son the following year when pitchers figured out he was a first-pitch fastball hitter; Moises adjusted well enough to drive in 85 runs before breaking his leg in September.

The 1994 season was his breakthrough year. Alou batted .339 with 22 home runs, he won the All-Star Game with a 10th-inning double, and his team had the best record in baseball. The season ended abruptly, however, when the strike stopped play on August 11. Alou finished third in Most Valuable Player voting, and his father was named Manager of the Year. It was small consolation. The Expos, convinced they could not afford to keep their star players, started trading their best players for prospects. Alou missed 51 games because of shoulder problems, and Montreal finished last.

The Expos remained in contention until late in the 1996 season, but it was Alou's final season playing for his father. He signed with Florida as a free agent on December 12. He homered in his first at bat as a Marlin on Opening Day. He drove in 115 runs to set a new family record—Felipe had 98 RBIs in 1962. He drove in 15 runs in the postseason, including nine during the World Series. Alou hit three-run homers in both Game 1 and Game 5 against Cleveland. He singled to lead off the bottom of the ninth inning in Game 7, and scored the tying run. The Marlins won in the 11th inning.

Just three weeks later Alou was traded to the Astros. He set career highs in nearly every offensive category in 1998. He finished third in the NL MVP voting behind Sammy Sosa and Mark McGwire. Alou fell off a treadmill before spring training 1999, resulting in major knee surgery. He missed the entire season.

Walter Alston

Alston, Walter Emmons **1B**

1936 M(1953–76, 2040–1613) B:12/1/1911, Venice, OH D:10/1/1984, Oxford, OH Deb: 9/27/1936, STL NL BR/TR 6'2", 195

G	AB	R	H	HR	RBI	OBP	SLG	AVG
1	1	0	0	0	0	.000	.000	.000

When the Brooklyn Dodgers named Walter Alston as their manager on November 24, 1953, skeptics asked, "Who's he?" Alston was replacing the brash Chuck Dressen, who had delivered back-to-back pennants. Dressen, who had demanded a multi-year contract, had been shown the door by an unmoved Walter O'Malley, who then introduced his new hire to the New York media by saying, "This is Walter Alston. I've hired him as my manager to beat the Yankees next season."

Brooklyn had fallen to the Yankees in the World Series each of the five times they had met. "If Alston doesn't win the pennant and beat the Yankees in the World Series," sneered sportswriter John Lardner, "there's a clause in his contract which requires him to refund his entire salary and report immediately to the nearest Federal penitentiary."

Alston didn't beat the Yankees in 1954. He couldn't even best the hated Giants, but O'Malley gave him a second chance. In fact Alston's one-year contract was renewed so many times that when he retired on September 27, 1976, he had managed the Dodgers longer than anyone had ever managed a single team with the exception of legends Connie Mack and John McGraw. Along the way he delivered seven pennants and four world championships. He was named Manager of the Year three times by *The Sporting News*, five times by United Press International, and six times by the Associated Press.

Alston came from a background of rural poverty; his father had been a sharecropper. As a youngster Alston was a hard-throwing pitcher, earning the sobriquet "Smokey" for his fastball. A baseball and basketball star at Miami (Ohio) University, Alston never had the benefit of an athletic scholarship. To support himself and his wife, he drove a laundry truck and played a very sharp game of pool.

The day after Alston received his degree in physical education, Branch Rickey's brother Frank signed him to a Cardinals minor league contract at $125 per month. A power-hitting first baseman, Alston earned a promotion to the big club at the end of the 1936 season. It took Alston some time to get into the lineup, and when he did, he struck out in his only at bat and committed an error on one of his two fielding chances.

Alston never played in the majors again. By 1940 he was a bush league player-manager, but his teams never did any better than fourth; by 1943 he was no longer even managing. The following season he was released as a player. His career appeared over.

Enter Branch Rickey, then with the Dodgers. Rickey offered Alston a chance to manage in the Brooklyn farm system, and by 1947 he was telling people, "Alston is the man we're grooming to manage the Dodgers someday." Soon Alston was managing the Dodgers' high-level farm clubs, and he was ready to run the show by the time Dressen wore out his welcome. "I'd been in the minors a long time," he observed. "I had managed 17 of the 25 players at one time or another in the past at Saint Paul or Montreal. I had the advantage of knowing what to expect of them." One of his stops along the way had been at Nashua of the New England League, where he managed Don Newcombe and Roy Campanella. Alston was the right man to help integrate the Dodgers system. When ejected from games, Alston would turn his club over to Campanella, fresh from the Negro Leagues. He was clearly ahead of his time in recognizing leadership and ability regardless of color.

Although low-key in many ways, Alston had a temper. He was also an incredibly strong man, so strong that many players were afraid of him. He was known to fling chairs, splinter doors, and challenge players to fights. Few ever thought of taking him up on the offer. "When I get mad, I get too mad," Alston once admitted. "I know this but I can't help myself." One such occasion came in 1963, when Alston, at age 51, halted the team bus after players complained about a lack of air conditioning. He dared anyone on the bus to have it out with him. Nobody did.

Yet this was only one side of this usually quiet, complex man. He had a sense of stoic perspective as well. "Look at misfortune," he recommended, "the same way you look at success. Don't panic. Do your best and forget the consequences." Alston knew misfortune, but once in the majors he had more than his share of success. He delivered a long-awaited world championship to Brooklyn in 1955 after wrapping up the pennant on September 8, the earliest clinching of the flag up to that date. Despite increasing friction with Jackie Robinson, who was still loyal to the deposed Dressen and once called the undemonstrative Alston a "wooden Indian," the Dodgers took the pennant again in 1956.

After the 1957 season the "Boys of Summer" broke a million hearts and moved to Los Angeles. They also grew old. Alston had to adjust from managing a power-hitting team to one featuring pitching, defense, and speed. He also had to contend with Dressen, who was with the team as a coach, and another coach, Leo Durocher, who had also been a successful—and controversial—manager of the Dodgers. They undercut his authority and waited in the wings for him to fail. It was not an easy situation, but Alston persisted. He captured another world championship in 1959, took the Dodgers to a tie for the pennant in 1962 before losing to the Giants, and won pennants again in 1963, 1965, 1966, and 1974. By the mid-1960s Alston was so secure that he could sign a blank contract and trust that Walter O'Malley would do right by him.

Although often criticized as overly conservative, Alston helped usher in the coming stolen-base revolution. He employed the bunt regularly, called for the hit-and-run often, and was not afraid to platoon players. All in all, he was an innovator. His public image suffered from his reticence with the press. Alston typically responded to reporters' questions with bland non-answers. He didn't wax eloquent about rookies. He didn't blast erring players. He simply won. In the 1950s Dressen and Durocher were baseball's equivalents of Harry Truman and Joseph McCarthy; Walter Alston was the game's Dwight Eisenhower. "If you weren't inclined to make conversation, he wouldn't make it," explained sportswriter Dick Young. "Some (sportswriters) called him a bad manager because he didn't write their stories for them."

Shortstop Maury Wills said, "I know that as far as handling men, no one is better at it than Walt Alston. He doesn't crack a whip or needle us. He treats us like men, and expects us to act that way. Sometimes we act like boys, but at least he gives us credit for being mature. He doesn't watch over us, and few Dodgers ever have taken advantage of him."

After retirement Alston returned to Ohio, where he occupied his time with woodcarving and trail-bike riding. He won election to the Hall of Fame in 1983.

Joe Altobelli

Altobelli, Joseph Salvatore **1B**

1955, 1957, 1961 M(1977–79, 1983–85, 1991, 437–407) B:5/26/1932, Detroit, MI Deb:4/14/1955, CLE AL BL/TL 6', 185

G	AB	R	H	HR	RBI	OBP	SLG	AVG
166	257	27	54	5	28	.280	.323	.210

As a player, Joe Altobelli was an undistinguished journeyman who appeared sparingly for the Cleveland Indians and Minnesota Twins. As a manager, he won the World Series in his first year with the Baltimore Orioles.

Altobelli guided the San Francisco Giants to fourth place with a 75–87 mark as a rookie manager in 1977. The team improved to 89–73, and Altobelli won Manager of the Year honors. When the Giants sank back to fourth place in 1979, he was fired late in the season and was replaced by Dave Bristol.

He joined the Yankees as a coach in 1981. The team made four managerial changes in two seasons, but Altobelli was not tabbed to manage in New York. His assignment would be even tougher than working for George Steinbrenner; he was hired to replace legendary Earl Weaver in Baltimore.

The 1983 Orioles made Altobelli feel at home. The team cruised to a division title behind solid pitching and a Most Valuable Player season by young shortstop Cal Ripken, Jr. Baltimore then stymied baseball's highest scoring team, the Chicago White Sox, to win the pennant in four games. The O's knocked off the Philadelphia Phillies to win their first World Series since 1970. Stoic first baseman Eddie Murray—who, by Altobelli's own admission, had "maybe five conversations" with the skipper all season—called his manager "one of the smartest baseball men I've ever known."

Two years later, Altobelli was replaced by Weaver after 55 games. He managed just one more game—a loss as interim skipper of the Chicago Cubs—but Altobelli retired with as many world championships as Baltimore's beloved Weaver.

Nick Altrock

Altrock, Nicholas **P**

1898, 1902–09, 1912–15, 1918–19, 1924
B:9/15/1876, Cincinnati, OH D:1/20/1965, Washington, DC Deb:7/14/1898, LOU NL BB/TL 5'10", 197

W	L	PCT	G	SH	IP	BB	SO	ERA
83	75	.525	218	16	1514	272	425	2.67

Nick Altrock became famous for his antics in the coaching box, but he put together three outstanding seasons for the Chicago White Sox, the last one as a pitching ace on the 1906 "Hitless Wonders." From 1904 to 1906 he went 62–39. He won just 21 more games over the rest of his prodigiously extended career, which continued sporadically until a final pinch-hitting appearance in 1933 at age 56.

A stocky lefthander with wild hair, Altrock featured outstanding control. He began his major league career with Louisville in the National League in 1898, then reemerged with Boston in the American League in 1902. After he lost his first start in April 1903, Boston sold him to the White Sox, with whom he compiled a 4–3 record that year (supplemented by an 11-for-33 performance at the plate).

In 1904 Altrock suddenly became a force. He won 19 games that year and a career-best 23 the next season, each year recording 31 complete games. In 1906 he won 20 games for the pennant-winning White Sox. They faced their cross-town rivals, the favored Cubs—winners of a record 116 games—in the first single-city World Series.

With snow flurries marring the opener at the Cubs' West Side Park, Altrock matched Three Finger Brown with a four-hitter, and came out a 2–1 winner. In Game 4 Altrock faced Brown again and threw a seven-hitter. But right fielder Ed Hahn lost Frank Chance's flyball in the sun leading off the seventh to set up the game's only run, as Brown twirled a two-hitter. The White Sox went on to win the World Series in six games, and Altrock's 1.00 ERA was the best among all pitchers.

Altrock injured his arm after the 1906 season and never had another winning record. He was traded to the Washington Senators in May of 1909 with outfielder Gavvy Cravath and first baseman Jiggs Donahue for pitcher Bill Burns, later infamous for his role in the Black Sox Scandal of 1919. Altrock pitched sparingly for Washington, making 23 mound appearances over eight seasons, the last in 1924.

Named as a coach in 1912, Altrock remained on the Senators' staff until 1953. He earned fame for his antics in the coaching box and before games. Germany Schaefer, the man who stole first base, was an early partner in those escapades. Altrock also helped a skinny Senators righthander named Al Schacht break in his act as "the Clown Prince of Baseball."

Red Ames

Ames, Leon Kessling **P**

1903–19 B:8/2/1882, Warren, OH D:10/8/1936, Warren, OH Deb:9/14/1903, NY NL BB/TR 5'10½", 185

W	L	PCT	G	SV	IP	BB	SO	ERA
183	167	.523	533	36	3198	1034	1702	2.63

Hard-throwing Red Ames was only 21 when the New York Giants brought him up from Ilion in the New York State League. In his debut on September 14, 1903, he pitched a five-inning no-hitter against St. Louis in the second game of a doubleheader. In a second start before the end of the season he won again, throwing a five-hit complete game and allowing only two earned runs.

Despite such a promising beginning, Ames made only 16 appearances for the Giants in 1904. The following year, however, manager John McGraw moved him ahead of Hooks

Wiltse and Dummy Taylor in the rotation. Ames had an excellent year with 22 wins, 21 complete games, 198 strikeouts, and a 2.74 ERA. Christy Mathewson and Joe McGinnity remained the aces of the Giants' staff and started every game of New York's World Series victory over Philadelphia. Ames relieved McGinnity in the ninth inning of Game 2, the only game the Giants lost.

Ames never again won more than 15 games in a season. Although the Giants finished in the first division each year from 1906 through 1912, he won only 78 games in that time. He was laid up with a knee injury for part of 1906, and he was ill for part of the 1908 season, but, more importantly, he also tended to be wild and sometimes ran out of gas in the late innings. As a result, he completed less than 60 percent of his starts, well below what better pitchers were doing at the time.

The one area that Ames holds records in is a rather dubious one. He and Walter Johnson share the major league record for career wild pitches with 156, although Johnson worked nearly twice as many innings. In 1905 Ames made 30 wild pitches to set the season record.

In May 1913 the Giants sent Ames, third baseman Heinie Groh, and outfielder Josh Devore to the lowly Cincinnati Reds for pitcher Art Fromme and infielder Eddie Grant. The next year Ames lost 23 games and won only 15, despite a 2.64 ERA and a career-high 297 innings pitched. He was sold to the St. Louis Cardinals in 1915, and had two successful seasons. He had losing seasons after that, however. Ames left the majors following the 1919 season. Despite 533 appearances, his ERA was 2.63

Ames subsequently spent three years with Kansas City of the American Association. He then managed Dayton in the Ohio State League in 1923.

Sandy Amoros

Amoros, Edmundo (Isasi) **OF**

1952, 1954–57, 1959–60 B:1/30/1930, Havana, Cuba
D:6/27/1992, Miami, FL Deb:8/22/1952, BRO NL
BL/TL 5'7 1/2", 170

G	AB	R	H	HR	RBI	OBP	SLG	AVG
517	1311	215	334	43	180	.363	.430	.255

Sandy Amoros will always be remembered for his one spectacular play in the 1955 World Series, perhaps the greatest play ever by a Brooklyn Dodger. It was the bottom of the sixth inning of the seventh game of the World Series. Brooklyn had never won a world championship, and the Dodgers clung to a 2–0 lead against their perennial postseason rivals, the New York Yankees. In the top of the sixth Dodgers manager Walter Alston had inserted a pinch hitter for Don Zimmer, necessitating the shift of left fielder Junior Gilliam to second. In came the little-used Amoros to play left.

With two on and none out, Yogi Berra sliced a ball to the left-field corner; Alston had just adjusted the Brooklyn outfield around to right and Berra's shot looked like a sure double, which would tie the game. From out of nowhere Amoros raced toward the ball and speared it with his right hand just as he neared the foul line. Then he turned and threw to second, nailing Gil McDougald for a double play. The Yankees rally was crushed. A few innings later the Brooklyn Dodgers finally became world champions for the only time in their history.

The next year Amoros—who had played for the Dodgers for three years—had his best season. Seeing part-time action, he hit .260, with 16 home runs and 58 RBIs. Still, he was optioned to Montreal, although he did make brief appearances with the Los Angeles Dodgers in 1959 and 1960 before ending his career with Detroit.

After Fidel Castro took over Cuba, Amoros—a prosperous rancher there—was forced into exile in Miami. In poor health, he lived in poverty for more than three decades.

Larry Andersen

Andersen, Larry Eugene **P**

1975, 1977, 1979, 1981–94 B:5/6/1953, Portland, OR
Deb:9/5/1975, CLE AL BR/TR 6'3", 205

W	L	PCT	G	SV	IP	BB	SO	ERA
40	39	.506	699	49	995[1]	311	758	3.15

A solid relief pitcher throughout his major league career, Larry Andersen will probably be best known as the zany player involved in a historic trade between the Houston Astros and Boston Red Sox. The Red Sox sent prospect Jeff Bagwell to the Astros for Andersen because they were in need of bullpen help for the stretch run in 1990. At the time, it seemed like a decent deal, especially since Andersen pitched magnificently (15 games, 1.23 ERA) and helped Boston reach the playoffs. However, when Bagwell won National League Rookie of the Year honors the next year and followed with subsequent All-Star caliber seasons the trade turned into a major *faux pas* for the Red Sox.

Andersen began his career with the Indians in 1975, bouncing between the major and minor leagues for several seasons. He finally made the bigs to stay starting in 1981 with the Seattle

Mariners. Andersen moved on to Philadelphia for several seasons, followed by stops in Houston, Boston, and San Diego. He spent his final two seasons with the Phillies, calling it quits in 1994. He appeared in the postseason four times, with Philadelphia in 1983 and 1993, with Houston in 1986, and with Boston in 1990.

Andersen's colorful personality made him popular in the clubhouse and with fans. It was perfectly suited to his subsequent broadcasting career, which he began with Philadelphia in 1998. Andersen was offered a spot in the booth for the Astros when the job was left vacant by Larry Dierker's move to manager in 1997, but he chose to stay in the Phillies organization as the pitching coach of Triple A Scranton.

Brady Anderson

Anderson, Brady Kevin **OF**

1988–* B:1/18/1964, Silver Spring, MD Deb:4/4/1988, BOS AL BL/TL 6'1", 185

G	AB	R	H	HR	RBI	OBP	SLG	AVG
1528	5483	919	1431	182	661	.368	.438	.261

Once hailed as a can't-miss outfield prospect, Brady Anderson did not hit above .231 in any of his first four major league seasons. Anderson was "one phone call away from going to Japan" when he decided to change his approach at the plate in August 1991. He adopted a simple hitting philosophy: "swing hard all the time." The result was a breakthrough season. He made the 1992 American League All-Star team, cracked 21 home runs, drove in 80 runs, and stole 53 bases to become the first player ever to post a "20-80-50" season.

The Maryland native's speed and power, as well as his high profile and good looks, made him a fan favorite in Baltimore; but he became something more in 1996. In a year filled with home run accomplishments, none was as startling as Anderson's power explosion. He eclipsed his previous career high of 21 by June, and finished the season with 50 home runs—as a leadoff hitter. Anderson set a major league record with 12 home runs leading off games in 1996. A competitor in the mode of longtime teammate Cal Ripken, Anderson played through appendicitis in 1996 and a cracked rib a year later to lead the Orioles to two straight playoff appearances.

John Anderson

Anderson, John Joseph **OF–1B**

1894–99, 1901–08 B:12/14/1873, Sarpsborg, Norway D:7/23/1949, Worcester, MA Deb:9/18/1894, BRO NL BB/TR 6'2", 180

G	AB	R	H	HR	RBI	OBP	SLG	AVG
1635	6341	870	1841	49	976	.329	.404	.290

John Anderson found himself shuffled between the outfield and first base because of inferior fielding skills. His bat kept "Honest John" in the lineup. He arrived in the National League with Brooklyn in 1894. He started the 1898 season with Brooklyn, was sent to Washington, and then returned to Brooklyn late in the season. The following year Anderson led the NL with 22 triples and a .494 slugging percentage.

In 1901, the inaugural year of the American League, the switch-hitting Anderson had career bests with 99 RBIs and a .330 batting average while playing for the Milwaukee franchise in its only season before the team became the St. Louis Browns the following season. Anderson also played with the New York Highlanders, Washington Senators, and Chicago White Sox.

The Norwegian-born Anderson led the AL with 39 stolen bases in 1906. In 14 seasons he stole 338 bases, including 10 seasons with 20 or more steals.

Sparky Anderson

Anderson, George Lee **2B**

1959 M(1970–95, 2194–1834) B:2/22/1934, Bridgewater, SD Deb:4/10/1959, PHI NL BR/TR, 5'9", 170

G	AB	R	H	HR	RBI	OBP	SLG	AVG
152	477	42	104	0	34	.283	.249	.218

Sparky Anderson was the first manager to win a World Series in both leagues and only the seventh to reach 2,000 career wins. He piloted both the Detroit Tigers and the Cincinnati Reds to more victories than any previous manager. Anderson also was the first manager to have 100-win seasons with two different teams, and was named Manager of the Year twice in each league.

Despite his success, Anderson's ebullient optimism and outrageous hyperbole sometimes overshadowed his managerial abilities. He was not infrequently compared to Casey Stengel for his winning ways and nonstop mouth. Famed for his pregame gab sessions, the pipe-puffing Anderson often made contradictory statements. All the same, most observers agreed that he believed what he said.

Yet after filling out more than 4,000 lineup cards, Anderson still got nervous before every game. Indeed, in 1989 nervous exhaustion led to a three-week midseason absence. "There will never be a day during the season when I don't have that," Anderson said, holding out a slightly trembling right hand. "If you don't have that, you're not in the game. You're not alive."

Nevertheless, Anderson claimed that managers play a limited role in a contest's outcome. "There's never been a good manager in the history of the game," he said, "but there have been some great players." Anderson managed some of the greatest and adapted his managerial style to accommodate those players and keep peace in the clubhouse. He respected players' talents and tried to stay out of their way.

With the Reds from 1970 through 1978, Anderson often consulted with team leaders Johnny Bench, Joe Morgan, Tony Perez, and Pete Rose. But he also earned the nickname "Captain Hook" for his quick removal of struggling starting pitchers.

In the early 1990s Anderson added a new wrinkle to his managerial style with the powerful Tigers. He routinely placed players out of position defensively in order to put his best bats in the lineup. "If they make an error, it's my fault," Anderson said. "If I'd played Johnny Bench at first 40 games a year, it would've added years to his career. There's no telling what he would have done."

Anderson grew up in Los Angeles, near the University of Southern California, and at age 9 met legendary Trojans coach Rod Dedeaux, who made him a USC batboy. Anderson starred along with Billy Consolo, later one of his Detroit coaches, on the 1951 American Legion champions. They won the title in Detroit, at the ballpark then known as Briggs Stadium. Anderson then spent six years as a minor leaguer in the Dodgers organization. "I didn't have a lot of talent, so I tried to make up for it with spit and vinegar," Anderson wrote, explaining the origin of his nickname in his 1990 autobiography, *Sparky!*

Before the 1959 season the Philadelphia Phillies acquired Anderson to be their regular second baseman. In 152 games he batted .218 with 12 extra-base hits and 34 RBIs. He returned to the International League for four seasons with Toronto, never hitting above .257, but studying the moves of manager Chuck Dressen. Still, Anderson assumed he would go into his family's house painting business after his playing days. However, he was asked to manage Toronto in 1964 and brought the team in fifth at 80–72. He won at least a split-season pennant in each of his next four seasons with four different teams, earning a major league coaching job under old Dodgers comrade Preston Gomez for the San Diego Padres' inaugural season of 1969.

Anderson had signed to coach the California Angels in 1970 before he was hired to replace Dave Bristol as manager of the Reds. He immediately led the Reds to 102 wins and a division title. They swept the Pittsburgh Pirates in the National League Championship Series before losing to the Baltimore Orioles in a five-game World Series. After suffering his only losing record in his first 19 years of major league managing, Anderson guided the Big Red Machine back to the World Series in 1972, where they lost to the Oakland A's.

The Reds won the NL West again in 1973 but lost to the underdog New York Mets in the NLCS. Two years later the Reds won 108 games, clinching a division title in the first week of September. Cincinnati then swept the Pirates in the playoffs and beat the Boston Red Sox in a memorable seven-game World Series for the first of Anderson's three world championships.

The 1976 Reds won 102 games, becoming the first club in the league since expansion to post back-to-back 100-win seasons. They swept the Phillies in the NLCS and the New York Yankees in the World Series, the only sweep in the history of the two-tier postseason format. The Reds' consecutive world titles were the first for an NL team since the New York Giants in 1921 and 1922. During those first seven years Anderson averaged 98 wins and collected five pennants. But after trading Perez the Reds finished second in both 1977 and 1978, and Anderson was fired. He went home to Los Angeles and worked briefly as a broadcaster. But that wasn't what he wanted out of his career. "I didn't get nervous anymore," Anderson said. "If you don't have that, you've got nothing. You might as well die."

He took over a renascent Detroit team from Les Moss on June 14, 1979. Under Anderson, youngsters Alan Trammell, Lou Whitaker, Kirk Gibson, Lance Parrish, Jack Morris, and Dan Petry blossomed. The Tigers posted winning records during their first four seasons under Anderson, then exploded in 1984. That year the Tigers won their first nine games and built records of 18–2 and 35–5 on the way to a club record 104 wins, a sweep of the Kansas City Royals in the ALCS, and a five-game World Series victory over the Padres.

After a pair of third-place finishes the Tigers overtook the Toronto Blue Jays in the last week of the 1987 season, sweeping the Jays in Detroit on the final weekend for Anderson's second title with the Tigers. Detroit lost in the playoffs, but Anderson's 34–21 postseason record, a .619

winning percentage, was the best in major league history.

In 1989 the stress of managing his second losing team forced him to take several weeks off. He returned with a lighter schedule of off-field commitments and a healthier approach. Anderson managed the Tigers through 1995, although with limited success.

He went back to Southern California and broadcasting. "It's a marvelous fantasy," Anderson has said of baseball. "There will be 40,000 people in the stands and every one of them wishes they could be down here." In 2000 he was elected to the Hall of Fame

Joaquin Andujar

Andujar, Joaquin **P**

1976–88 B:12/21/1952, San Pedro De Macoris, Dominican Republic Deb:4/8/1976, HOU NL BB/TR 6', 180

W	L	PCT	G	SH	IP	BB	SO	ERA
127	118	.518	405	19	2153	731	1032	3.58

Joaquin Andujar gave new meaning to the word "temperamental" in the 1980s. He was a brilliant pitcher at times, but those times were as off and on as his famous temper. He summed up baseball, and his career, best in *Sports Illustrated* in 1987: "There is one word in America and that says it all, and that one word is, 'You never know.'

Signed to a Cincinnati Reds minor league contract in 1969, Andujar was traded in October 1975 to the Houston Astros for two pitchers. The next year he joined the Astros where he showed flashes of brilliance and periods of remarkable inconsistency. In his five full seasons with Houston, he was twice named to the All-Star Game, but he still managed only one winning record and never recorded an ERA under 3.41.

In June 1981 the "one tough Dominican" (as he liked to call himself) was traded to the Cardinals for outfielder Tony Scott. Andujar's career took off. He finished that season 6–1 with St. Louis and then won all three of his postseason starts, including Game 7 of the World Series. In 1984 he led the league in victories, shutouts, and innings pitched.

In 1985 he again won 20 games, but Andujar became completely unhinged in Game 7 of that year's World Series. The circumstances were enough to excite less colorful personalities, but with Andujar on the mound anything could happen. As the Royals were sitting on a 10–0 lead Andujar twice exploded over ball calls by home plate umpire Don Denkinger, whose miscall at first base the previous night had led to a Royals win. Andujar was ejected and ultimately suspended. After the Series he demanded to be traded to Oakland. St. Louis manager Whitey Herzog was more than happy to oblige, but Andujar was never the same. He finished his major league career back with the Astros in 1988.

Andujar was capricious not only on the mound. If he mistrusted either the control or the motives of the opposing pitcher he would turn around at the plate to protect his pitching arm. (Andujar once injured himself in batting practice, a rarity for an American League pitcher.) He fancied himself a decent hitter, despite a .127 lifetime average.

In 1989 Andujar attempted a comeback with the Fort Myers Sun Sox of the ill-fated Senior League, compiling a 1.31 ERA in five games. He later negotiated a non-guaranteed $1 million contract with the Montreal Expos but failed to make the team.

Cap Anson

Anson, Adrian Constantine **1B-3B-C**

1871–97 M(1875, 1879–98, 1296–947) B:4/11/1852, Marshalltown, IA D:4/14/1922, Chicago, IL Deb:5/6/1871, ROK NA BR/TR 6', 227

G	AB	R	H	HR	RBI	OBP	SLG	AVG
2276	9101	1719	2995	97	1879	.395	.446	.329

Cap Anson was a great hitter, manager, and innovator, one of the men who popularized baseball, and certainly the game's first true superstar. During his 27-year career, he had 24 seasons batting .300, and he topped .380 three times. Yet today his name is most often mentioned only in connection with the debate over the final number of hits that he made in his career as the Chicago White Stockings' first baseman. Many also think of Anson as the man who helped segregate baseball.

Anson was born in what was then the American frontier, Marshalltown, Iowa, a town his father helped found and almost named "Ansonia." In the 1860s young Anson, with his father and uncle, helped earn the local Marshalltown Stars a statewide reputation. In 1869 he attended Notre Dame and helped organize its first baseball nine, which he served as captain and third baseman. In 1871 all three Ansons were invited to turn pro, but only Cap took advantage of the opportunity, signing with the Forest City club of Rockford, Illinois, a member of the National Association, the first major league. His pay was $66 per month. The 19-year-old wasn't known as "Cap" then; he was "Baby" Anson or "the Marshalltown Infant."

Anson joined the Philadelphia Athletics in 1872 and played until 1876, when he jumped to

William Hulbert's Chicago White Stockings for $2,000. Jumping from one club to another was a common practice, but Hulbert and Anson, as well as several other notable players such as Boston pitcher Albert Spalding, had violated league rules by conducting their negotiations while the season was in progress. The White Stockings faced expulsion from the National Association. To forestall this measure Hulbert formed the new National League.

However, by this time Anson met and married a Philadelphia resident, and she was not interested in heading west. Anson tried to buy his release from Hulbert, but the magnate would have none of it. To vent his displeasure Anson actually played a game for Chicago in a Prince Albert coat and formal trousers. Hulbert ignored the display and held Anson to his obligations. Anson planned to re-sign with the Athletics in 1877, but when they were expelled from the National League for failing to complete their 1876 road schedule, he inked another contract with Hulbert's White Stockings. Anson soon warmed up to the Windy City, and by 1879 he was manager, or "captain," hence his nickname "Cap."

Anson was a pioneer in the use of the hit-and-run, signals, platoons, and a pitching rotation. A big man—6 feet, 227 pounds—he was a stiff-backed martinet who marched his men onto the field in military formation and used his fists to enforce his rules, the least popular being his no-drinking edict. Whether the players always liked his style or not, Anson led the White Stockings to five pennants between 1880 and 1886.

He also helped segregate the national pastime. In 1883 the White Stockings showed up for an exhibition game in Toledo, Ohio. The presence of Moses Fleetwood Walker, an African-American ballplayer, in the opposing lineup so upset Anson that he cursed and raged from the dugout and threatened to withdraw his team from the game. Toledo countered with the possibility of withholding Chicago's financial guarantee, and Anson backed down. Both he and Walker took the field.

In July 1888 Anson's club scheduled another exhibition against an integrated squad, the International League's Newark club. The team's ace hurler was George Washington Stovey, an African-American. This time Anson got his way. Apparently, the New York Giants were about to sign Stovey but dropped the idea in the aftermath of the incident. In some quarters Anson is blamed for pushing through the color barrier that was not broken until Jackie Robinson's 1947 arrival in Brooklyn. However, this theory overstates Anson's influence. Baseball historian Bill James noted, "In this climate, it is enormously likely that Jim Crow would have come to baseball even had Cap Anson never been born."

That Anson's impact on the field continued, however, is not in doubt. For 10 years, from 1881 through 1890, the sturdy infielder was out of the lineup in only 12 games. Eight times he led the National League in RBIs, four times in batting average and on-base percentage, five times he was the fielding champ, and he also was the first player to hit three consecutive homers, five homers in two consecutive contests, four doubles in a game, and to make two unassisted double plays in a game. On August 24, 1886, he scored six runs in one game to match Jim Whitney's NL mark. Ten times Anson registered five or more hits in a contest.

It was his powerful hitting that brought him the greatest renown. Observers said he always watched the first pitch sail by. Often he waited until he faced two strikes before swinging at the ball. "As a batsman," historian Robert Smith wrote, "he struck terror to the hearts of pitchers even when he was deemed too old to play. His hits were usually booming drives, streaking on a dead-level course to the outfield. He hit the ball where it was pitched and his line drives might land in any field."

In 1885 Anson's White Stockings engaged the American Association's St. Louis Browns in the World Series, capturing honors by a 3–1 margin. Anson chipped in with a .423 average. The following year both clubs repeated. Al Spalding, now owner of the club following Hulbert's death, and Anson challenged Browns' owner Chris Von der Ahe: "We will play you under only one condition, and that is winner take all, and by all, I mean every penny taken at the gate." Their bravado drew national attention. Unfortunately for Chicago, the Browns won, 4–2, and walked away with all the gate receipts, $14,000.

In 1886 Anson took his club to Hot Springs, Arkansas. That same year, Harry Wright took his Philadelphia club to Charleston, South Carolina. Together, they introduced the practice of spring training.

In 1888 Anson signed a 10-year contract to manage Chicago. It was a smart move on his part. The White Stockings captured no more pennants and new Chicago co-owner James Hart began to second-guess the managerial strategy of Anson, who by then had mellowed enough that the players called him "Pop." In 1897, the last year of Anson's contract, the team finished ninth in the 12-club National League, a whopping 34 games back. Anson made an already bad situation worse by publicly charging that his team was "a bunch of drunkards and loafers" who were pulling him down. Hart let Anson go, and a sympathetic public dubbed his former charges "the Orphans." The following year, volatile Giants owner Andrew Freedman engaged Anson as manager, but the man who had managed Chicago for 19 seasons lasted only two months.

In 1900 Anson tried to get back into baseball by helping organize a new version of the defunct American Association. His criticism of the baseball establishment has a more than modern ring to it. "Baseball as at present conducted is a gigantic monopoly, intolerant of opposition and run on a grab-all-there-is-in-sight policy that is alienating its friends and disgusting the public that has so long and cheerfully given it the support that it has withheld from other forms of amusement."

Anson was named president of this new American Association, but at the first sign of trouble he declared the circuit dissolved, thus scuttling the whole venture. *Sporting Life* editor Francis Richter, a prominent and influential backer of the league, charged Anson had "made an ass of himself...a pitiful ending, indeed, to a brilliant, if meteoric leader of men."

Anson remained in the public eye. Elected Chicago city clerk in 1905, he came under official investigation and was turned out of office in 1907. To make ends meet he managed a semipro team and turned to the vaudeville stage, this time with his two daughters. But all his efforts failed, and Anson declared bankruptcy. The National League attempted to come to his aid, but the proud old first baseman refused all charity. Just before taking a job as manager of a golf club, he had delusions of becoming baseball commissioner in 1921. When he died the next year, the National League paid for his funeral.

Anson died thinking he was the first member of the 3,000-hit club; research by John Tattersall in his review of newspaper boxscores proved that Cap was just shy of this milestone. In 1879 Anson was the beneficiary of 20 extra hits, either by error or through a civic-minded Chicago official scorer. *Total Baseball* lists his final National League hit total at 2,995; this does not count the 423 hits he had in his five National Association season. He was selected the Baseball Hall of Fame by the Old Timers Committee in 1939.

Johnny Antonelli

Antonelli, John August **P**

1948–50, 1953–61 B:4/12/1930, Rochester, NY
Deb:7/4/1948, BOS NL BL/TL 6', 190

W	L	PCT	G	SH	IP	BB	SO	ERA
126	110	.534	377	25	1992[1]	687	1162	3.34

When a baseball fan hears the name of Johnny Antonelli, the phrase "bonus baby" comes to mind. Although Antonelli did draw one of the larger bonuses of his day, there was more to him that: he was also a quality starting pitcher for much of his 12-year career.

The majors showed little interest in Antonelli until he developed his curveball while pitching in the semipro Vermont Hotel League in the summer of 1947. When he returned to Jefferson High School in Rochester, New York, he spun five no-hitters, and suddenly the scouts were interested. "I've never seen a kid with so much equipment," marvelled Giants scout Carl Hubbell. "The most unusual thing is he knows what to do with it."

It was a feeding frenzy for the talent hunters. Antonelli's father rented Rochester's International League ballpark to feature the young southpaw in a game of the area's best semipro squads—staged for the scouts. Not only did they show up, so did 7,000 fans. The Boston Braves' Lou Perini offered Antonelli a $65,000 signing bonus. When Antonelli signed with the Braves on June 2, 1948, his bonus was the largest in baseball history.

Antonelli's story quickly turned sour, however. Because of his big bonus, major league rules prohibited him from being farmed out to the minors, at least until he spent two seasons with the parent club. Boston manager Billy Southworth hated the idea of the 18-year-old kid joining the Braves, and considered Antonelli just about worthless, since the club was fighting for the pennant. Equally disgruntled was pitcher Johnny Sain, who had won 21 games in 1947 and 11 by the 1948 All-Star Game. Sain, justifiably, felt cheated to be receiving a mere $21,000 salary. He stunned the baseball world by threatening a walkout. "I meant it," Sain said later. "I was gonna walk away from the whole thing." Sain forced Perini to grant him a two-year contract worth $30,000 a season. Antonelli, meanwhile, pitched only four innings all year, gaining a save and posting a 2.25 ERA.

He received little work during the next two seasons, and with the outbreak of hostilities in Korea he was drafted into the military in March 1951. When Antonelli emerged from the service in 1953 the Braves were in Milwaukee,

Southworth was long gone, and Antonelli was finally ready to pitch. The results were less than stellar, 12–12 with a 3.18 ERA.

On February 1, 1954, the Braves dispatched Antonelli, catcher Ebba St. Claire, infielder Billy Klaus, pitcher Don Liddle, and $50,000 to the New York Giants in exchange for Polo Grounds immortal Bobby Thomson and catcher Sam Calderone. Most observers initially thought the Braves had gotten the better end of the deal, but Thompson soon fractured his right ankle (opening the door for a young Henry Aaron), while Antonelli set the National League on fire. He posted a 21–7 mark, was selected to the All-Star Game, and led the circuit with six shutouts, a 2.30 ERA, and a .750 won-lost percentage. During a stretch in August in which the Giants dropped seven of nine games, Antonelli provided New York's only two victories.

The Giants won the pennant and faced a Cleveland team that had won an amazing 111 games during the regular season. Antonelli started Game 2 of the 1954 World Series and was tagged for a leadoff homer by Al Smith. That was the only run the Indians would score. Antonelli won the game, 3–1, scattering eight hits and six walks and striking out nine. By Game 4 Leo Durocher's Giants had a three-to-none lead. Before 78,102 subdued Indians fans, the Giants took a 7–4 lead into the eighth inning. Suddenly, reliever Hoyt Wilhelm lost his effectiveness. With men on first and third and only one out, Durocher brought in Antonelli, who had pitched nine innings just two days before. Antonelli mowed down five straight on three strikeouts and two popups, and the Giants had won the title.

After an off year, Antonelli won 20 games again in 1956, and he was selected to the first of four consecutive All-Star Games. But in 1960, a year after going 19–10, things seemed to come apart, and he slipped to just 6–7, with most of his work coming from the bullpen. The Giants shipped Antonelli and outfielder Willie Kirkland to Cleveland in December 1960 for outfielder Harvey Kuenn. On July 4, 1961, the Indians peddled Antonelli back to his original club, the Braves, for cash. On October 11, 1961, the Braves traded Antonelli to the one-day-old New York Mets for cash. Antonelli decided enough was enough and called it quits.

After retiring as a player, Antonelli managed the Memphis Blues of the Texas League from 1969 to 1972 and the International League's Tidewater Tides from 1973 to 1974. Ironically, both were Mets farm clubs. He later owned and operated a chain of tire dealerships in upstate New York.

Luis Aparicio

Aparicio, Luis Ernesto (Montiel) **SS**
1956–73 B:4/29/1934, Maracaibo, Venezuela
Deb:4/17/1956, CHI AL BR/TR 5'9", 160

G	AB	R	H	HR	RBI	OBP	SLG	AVG
2599	10230	1335	2677	83	791	.313	.343	.262

Luis Aparicio helped set the pattern for slick-fielding, spray-hitting, speedy shortstops. An amazingly consistent bundle of defense and speed, each year from 1959 to 1966 he led AL shortstops in fielding percentage, he won nine Gold Gloves, and each year from 1956 to 1964 he led the league in stolen bases.

Aparicio seemed born to play baseball. His father had been an excellent shortstop in Venezuela, playing until he was 41. Luis Sr. and his brother, Ernesto, were owners of the Maracaibo Gavilanes Winter League club, yet 19-year-old Aparicio didn't play for his father. Instead, he performed with the Cardenales in Barquisimeto. Red Kress, a Cleveland Indians coach, managed the Gavilanes and urged young Aparicio to move over to his club. In a full-fledged ceremony on the night of November 18, 1953, the elder Aparicio embraced his son and handed over his glove and position to him.

Soon Aparicio was playing better than his father ever did. Indians owner Cy Slapnicka was interested in signing Aparicio, and he negotiated back and forth with uncle Ernesto. White Sox general manager Frank Lane was also scouting him. Lane, who had received glowing reviews about him from incumbent White Sox shortstop Chico Carrasquel (also a Venezuela native), used a combination of threats plus an offer of $5,000 down and $5,000 in first year's salary to land Aparicio.

Aparicio immediately impressed observers in the minors, hitting respectably in the 3-I and Southern Leagues and fielding and stealing bases with aplomb. "This kid Aparicio down in Memphis—he could make you forget Carrasquel," bragged Lane. Chicago White Sox manager Marty Marion became amenable to the idea of replacing the aging Carrasquel after he saw Aparicio run the bases. "As Paul Richards would say, that kid runs like a scalded dog!" Marion exclaimed.

Aparicio had the regular shortstop job by Opening Day 1956, and after batting .266 with a league-leading 21 stolen bases, he received 22 of 24 first-place votes for American League Rookie of the Year honors.

Aparicio was a puzzle to AL pitchers. "Aparicio doesn't hit a long enough ball to kill you," said Whitey Ford, "but believe me, there is nothing more aggravating than to get past the good hitters and then have a weak hitter come up and brush across a couple of runs. Since it's axiomatic that young hitters can hit the fastball but have to learn to hit the curve, I tested him with the breaking stuff to every conceivable part of the plate. And every time I faced him, he seemed to hit me a little better."

In 1958 Aparicio was selected to the All-Star Game for the first of seven consecutive and 10 overall appearances. The next year he was one of the key figures leading the "Go-Go" White Sox to their first pennant in 40 years (their first since the 1919 Black Sox). Although the Los Angeles Dodgers won the World Series in six games, Aparicio batted .308.

Aparicio was overweight and out of shape in 1962 and suffered an off year, batting only .241 with 22 fewer stolen bases than the previous year. Chicago manager Al Lopez believed that Aparicio was no longer giving 100 percent, and when general manager Ed Short attempted to cut Aparicio's salary, the shortstop's relationship with the club rapidly deteriorated. On January 14, 1963, Short did the unthinkable when he packaged Aparicio and veteran outfielder–third baseman Al Smith to Baltimore for four players, including relief pitcher Hoyt Wilhelm.

Aparicio immediately returned to form with the Orioles, leading the league in stolen bases in 1963. The next year, he led the league in steals for the ninth consecutive year, with a career-high 57; he also had a career highs with 10 home runs. In 1966 Aparicio helped bring the Orioles their first pennant and subsequent World Series title. He finished ninth in MVP balloting.

At the end of the 1967 season the Orioles started playing a younger, slick-fielding shortstop named Mark Belanger. That November Aparicio was traded back to the White Sox, with outfielders Russ Snyder and John Matias, for infielder Don Buford and pitchers Bruce Howard and Roger Nelson. Aparicio continued his remarkable performance, and in 1970 had career highs of 29 doubles and a .313 batting average. That year rumors began to swirl that Aparicio would become the next White Sox manager. Instead he became the next Red Sox shortstop, as Chicago traded him to Boston. Aparicio played three solid seasons in Boston, although he no longer possessed his former speed or range. He retired after the 1973 season.

Aparicio went on to own an insurance agency in Venezuela; he also handled television commentary of baseball in his homeland. In 1984 he became the first Venezuelan elected to the Baseball Hall of Fame. As historian Bill James wrote, "Aparicio's defensive statistics are probably the best of any shortstop before Ozzie Smith...In my own opinion Ozzie is a slightly greater defensive shortstop, but the two men are comparable, and are the two best I have ever seen."

Kevin Appier

Appier, Robert Kevin **P**

1989–* B:12/6/1967, Lancaster, CA Deb:6/14/1989, KC AL BR/TR 6'2", 195

W	L	PCT	SH	IP	BB	SO	ERA
121	94	.563	10	1889^{1}	657	1504	3.54

Mike MacFarlane, Kevin Appier's catcher in both Kansas City and Oakland, once called Appier "one of the most intense people I've ever been around." That intensity caused Appier tremendous frustration. Though Appier won 94 games for Kansas City between 1990 and 1996, the Royals never came close to playoff contention. Worse, in 35 of his 80 career losses through 1998, Kansas City scored one or no runs to support him. Only in 1993, when he went 18–8 with a league-best 2.56 ERA, did his numbers reflect his effectiveness on the field.

Appier signed a long-term contract extension with the Royals in 1996, but in the first year of the deal he went just 9–13 with the league's fifth-best ERA. Shortly after he formally asked the Royals for a trade, an off-season fall at home changed his plans. Appier required surgery to repair a torn labrum in his shoulder, and missed almost all of 1998.

Healthy again in 1999—and still looking to leave Kansas City—the Royals traded him to the contending Oakland Athletics in July. After a brilliant start for Oakland, Appier and the A's both stumbled down the stretch. Appier finished the season with a 16–14 mark.

Luke Appling

Appling, Lucious Benjamin **SS**

1930–43, 1945–50 M(1967, 10–30) B:4/2/1907, High Point, NC D:1/3/1991, Cumming, GA Deb:9/10/1930, CHI AL BR/TR 5'10", 183

G	AB	R	H	HR	RBI	OBP	SLG	AVG
2422	8856	1319	2749	45	1116	.399	.398	.310

Luke Appling played every game of his 20-season major league career with the Chicago White Sox. Since his tenure at Comiskey Park fell precisely in the middle of Chicago's 40-year pennant drought, he belongs in that rare category of Hall of Famers who never played in a World Series.

Appling was a sophomore at Oglethorpe College in 1930 when he signed a professional contract with the Southern Association's Atlanta Crackers. He immediately showed an aptitude for hitting. The Chicago Cubs eyed him but backed off, presumably because of his 42 errors in 104 games.

Undaunted, the White Sox paid $20,000 for Appling's contract, and he appeared for them in six games at the end of the 1930 season, making four errors but collecting twice as many hits. The following two seasons went badly, as his hitting regressed and his fielding didn't improve. The White Sox tried to trade him without success.

In 1933, it all turned around; Appling stopped swinging for Comiskey's fences and started instead to hit to all fields. He finished the season batting .322, the first of nine consecutive .300-plus seasons. His fielding also seemed to improve gradually, although he never became as sure handed as many shortstops. He led American League shortstops in errors five times. However, his range was excellent, leading in assists seven times and in putouts twice. He always insisted that many of his errors were due to the uneven surface at Comiskey Park.

Appling was a notorious complainer. Although he suffered only one serious injury during his long career—a broken leg that kept him out for half of the 1938 season—he never lacked for minor ills. One day he would have a sore back, the next day a weak shoulder, then pinkeye followed by shinsplints. No doubt many of his gripes were simply a means of getting attention, and some said that the more he complained the better he played. Nevertheless, the nickname "Old Aches and Pains" hung on him throughout his career.

Appling was an excellent leadoff hitter, combining a high batting average, good speed, and a facility for drawing walks—three times he had more than 100 free passes in a season. Yet the White Sox's chronic lack of other strong batters often meant he batted third in their order. Although he was anything but a slugger, he still drove in 1,116 runs during his long career.

Only once did Appling top 100 RBIs: during his career year of 1936, when he also set personal highs with 111 runs scored and 204 hits. At one point Appling had a club record 27-game hitting streak. On the season's final day he went 4-for-4 to finish with a .388 batting average and become the first AL shortstop to win a batting title. The mark is also the highest compiled by a shortstop in this century. He won a second batting crown in 1943 with a .328 average.

Of all Appling's skills, the most legendary was his ability to foul off pitches until he got one he liked. According to a popular tale he once fouled off 14 unsatisfactory tosses before bashing a triple. In another story, Appling went to the White Sox business manager to ask for several baseballs to sign for friends. It was the Depression, and the club official turned him down after advising him that baseballs cost $2.75 each. Appling said nothing, but in his first at bat that afternoon he fouled the first 10 pitches into the grandstand. He then turned to the club official sitting in the owner's box and said, "That's $27.50, and I'm just getting started!" Supposedly he was never again refused when he requested baseballs.

Appling was named to play in the All-Star Game seven times, but his White Sox teams seemed jinxed. Something always went wrong to bring them up short of a pennant. In 1938, when they appeared in preseason to have a strong chance of breaking the Yankees' pennant grip, Appling fractured his leg sliding into second in a spring training game; he was out until August, effectively ending any possibilities of a pennant.

Appling was 38 when he returned from military service in late 1945, but he picked up as though he had never been away, hitting .368 in his short season. In 1949, at age 42, he hit .301. But under general manager Frank Lane the White Sox were committed to a youth movement that included installing young and flashy Chico Carrasquel at shortstop. Appling played 50 games as a utility infielder in 1950 and then retired with a lifetime .310 batting average. At the time, he held the league career records for most games played, assists, putouts, and chances accepted by a shortstop, all later eclipsed by Luis Aparicio. Appling was elected to the Hall of Fame in 1964.

Appling managed successfully in the minors for many years, winning pennants for Memphis of the Southern Association and Indianapolis of the American Association. He was named Minor League Manager of the Year in 1952. His only chance with a major league club came in late 1967 when he replaced Alvin Dark at Kansas City and guided the club to a 10–30 record. At age 75 he appeared in the Cracker Jack All-Star Game in Washington, D.C., and hit an improbable home run off Warren Spahn.

Jimmy Archer

Archer, James Patrick **C**

1904, 1907, 1909–18 B:5/13/1883, Dublin, Ireland
D:3/29/1958, Milwaukee, WI Deb:9/6/1904, PIT NL
BR/TR 5'10", 168

G	AB	R	H	HR	RBI	OBP	SLG	AVG
847	2646	246	660	16	296	.288	.333	.249

According to many eyewitnesses, native Irishman Jimmy Archer was the best-throwing catcher in baseball before World War I. New York Giants shortstop Al Bridwell, who had plenty of chances to see him in action, said, "Best arm of any catcher I ever saw. He'd zip it down there to second like a flash. Perfect accuracy, and under a 6-foot bar all the way." Chief Meyers, a fine catcher himself, said of Archer, "He didn't have an arm. He had a rifle."

Archer came by his legendary arm strength in an unusual way: his right arm was severely burned by hot tar in a factory accident. When the burns healed, the muscles in his arm shortened but became particularly strong. Archer's trademark was his ability to fire the ball down to second base without rising from his squat behind the plate.

Weak hitting caused Archer to fail in trials with Pittsburgh in 1904 and Detroit in 1907. The chunky Irishman hit only .119 in 18 regular-season games with the Tigers and went hitless in the World Series. Catcher Johnny Kling of the Chicago Cubs took off the 1909 season to defend his billiards championship, opening up a spot on the roster for Archer. In 80 games, he hit .230 and impressed people with his brilliant throwing. On the other hand, the Cubs had won three consecutive pennants, and some suggested that the absence of Kling, a better all-around player than Archer, was the reason the team failed to repeat in 1909.

Archer shared catching duties with Kling in 1910 and hit .259 as the Cubs won their fourth pennant in five years. In 1911 Kling was dealt to Brooklyn and Archer became the regular catcher, appearing in more than 100 games each season from 1911 through 1913. The 1912 season was his best; he reached personal highs with a batting average of .283 and 58 RBIs. He also led all NL catchers in assists. Archer shared duties with aging Roger Bresnahan, still considered the outstanding catcher of the day, in 1914 and 1915. But his batting performance began to tail off again. Archer retired in 1918, having played briefly for Pittsburgh, Brooklyn, and Cincinnati.

Buzz Arlett

Arlett, Russell Loris **OF**

1931 B:1/3/1899, Elmhurst, CA D:5/16/1964, Minneapolis, MN Deb:4/14/1931, PHI NL BB/TR 6'2", 210

G	AB	R	H	HR	RBI	OBP	SLG	AVG
121	418	65	131	18	72	.387	.538	.313

Buzz Arlett was called the "Babe Ruth of the Minor Leagues," and it was a fitting description. Arlett, like Ruth, was initially a superlative pitcher, then an awesome slugger. The only difference was that, with the exception of one season with the Philadelphia Phillies in 1931, Arlett performed all his heroics in the minors, largely as a member of the Pacific Coast League's Oakland Oaks.

Arlett's start was humble, as a 19-year-old kid hanging around the Oaks' spring training site at Boyes Springs, California, in 1918. Arlett wormed his way onto the diamond and the roster. His ERA as a rookie was 2.70, and from 1919 to 1922 he went 95–71. In 1921 he won 29 games and pitched 427 innings during the Pacific Coast League's extended 200-game season.

After pitching so many innings, it is no surprise that Arlett's pitching skills declined in 1923. When his ERA ballooned to 5.76 he was switched to the Oaks' outfield and proceeded to hit 19 homers, drive in 101 runs, and bat .330. In 1926 he hit a career-high .382, with 25 homers and 140 RBIs, but he still remained a minor leaguer.

With stats like that, why wasn't he in the majors? In that era, high minor league clubs were under no obligation to send talent to the big leagues. Arlett's contemporary, pitcher Lefty Grove, was similarly trapped on Jack Dunn's Baltimore club in the International League (although "trapped" may not be the right word, as high minor league salaries were often comparable to or even higher than those paid in either of the major leagues).

Part of Arlett's problem was his fielding, which wasn't very good. It wasn't until 1930 that a serious bid was made to send the switch-hitting slugger to the majors. A deal with Brooklyn fell through at the last minute after Arlett got into a pushing match with Pacific Coast League umpire Chet Chadwick, who struck Arlett with his mask, cutting him under his eye. The next year, however, Arlett was finally purchased by the Phillies. He did well at first, hitting .324 as late as August 9, and then he went into a brief slump and was benched. He finished the season at .313 with 18 homers and 72 RBIs. As respectable as that was, Philadelphia placed him on waivers; no other major league club was interested, and he became the property of Baltimore.

In 1932 Arlett paced the International League with 49 home runs. Twice he hit four in one game. Several of his homers were noteworthy, but one hit on May 5 caused real damage. The ball soared over the right field fence, crashed a window in a home, and hit 45-year-old Ida Moore on the head. "Mrs. Moore was playing bridge when she was hit," noted one account.

In 1935 Arlett lost part of the ring finger on his left hand during spring training with the Minneapolis Millers, but he still hit .360 with 25 homers and 101 RBIs in 122 games. He retired in 1937 after pinch hitting in a handful of games with the Syracuse Chiefs.

In 1946 he was given a "day" at Oakland and

was proclaimed "the mightiest Oak of all time." Arlett was ecstatic. "The affair made a big man of me in Minneapolis," he noted. "Minneapolis folks, even those who watched me play ball there...figured I must be pretty important if Oakland would give me a civic party and an automobile."

As a minor league hitter Arlett played in 2,390 games, hit 432 homers (the record until it was broken by Hector Espino), and had a .341 lifetime average. When the Society for American Baseball Research (SABR) published its first volume of *Minor League Baseball Stars*, Arlett's picture was on the cover.

Tony Armas

Armas, Antonio Rafael (Machado) **OF**
1976–89 B:7/2/1953, Anzoategui, Venezuela Deb:9/6/1976, PIT NL BR/TR 6'1", 200

G	AB	R	H	HR	RBI	OBP	SLG	AVG
1432	5164	614	1302	251	815	.290	.453	.252

Tony Armas was not a complete player by any means. His batting average was low and his command of the strike zone was atrocious, but he played hard and when he hit the ball he hit it hard—so hard that he twice led the American League in homers.

Armas was one of 14 children. He was signed by Pittsburgh in 1971, but didn't reach the major leagues until 1976, when he played only four games for the Pirates. In March 1977 Armas was traded to Charley Finley's Oakland A's along with pitchers Dave Giusti, Doc Medich, Doug Bair, Rick Langford, and outfielder Mitchell Page for pitcher Chris Batton and infielders Phil Garner, and Tommy Helms. The deal did much to revitalize the ailing Oakland franchise.

Armas spent six years in Oakland, with his most productive being 1980, when he batted a career high .279, hit 35 home runs, and drove in 109 runs. The next year he tied for the league lead with 22 homers in the strike-shortened season and was selected to play in the All-Star Game.

In 1983 Armas moved to Boston and immediately became a major contributor, with 36 homers and 107 RBIs. He topped those figures the next year, when his 43 homers and 123 RBIs led the league. In 1986 Armas helped lead the Red Sox to the pennant with his hitting, strong arm, and aggressive play. Ralph Houk claimed Armas was as tough a player as he had ever managed—high praise indeed. Armas spent the last three years of his career with the California Angels.

Luis Arroyo

Arroyo, Luis Enrique **P**
1955–57 1959–63 B:2/18/1927, Penuelas, Puerto Rico Deb:4/20/1955, STL NL BL/TL 5'8", 190

W	L	PCT	G	SV	IP	BB	SO	ERA
40	32	.556	244	44	531^{1}	208	336	3.93

Luis Arroyo simply exploded onto the National League scene in 1955. The left-handed rookie from Puerto Rico cracked the starting rotation of the St. Louis Cardinals and then was so impressive that he was selected to the All-Star Game. But he faded in the second half of the season and finished with a middling 11–8 mark and a 4.19 ERA.

Arroyo was subsequently dealt to Pittsburgh, where he spent two years in the bullpen. A 3–11 record in 1957 caused the Pirates to trade him to Cincinnati, where he played only briefly between stints in the minors.

In July of 1960 the New York Yankees purchased Arroyo's contract in a transaction that attracted little notice. But baffled American League batters treated Arroyo's screwball like a visiting celebrity—something to be waved at but not touched. He was 5–1 with seven saves down the stretch as the Yanks took another pennant. Arroyo was at his apogee in 1961, going 15–5 and collecting 29 saves, a 2.19 ERA, and a spot in the All-Star Game. He pitched the last inning or more of most of Whitey Ford's victories, while Ford enjoyed his first 20-win season. With Roger Maris and Mickey Mantle homering at a record clip and Arroyo reigning supreme in the bullpen, the Yankees handed manager Ralph Houk his first New York pennant and his first World Series title.

However, the next year Arroyo's sore arm, which had first acted up in 1961, had ballooned his ERA and cut down on his time. An even poorer performance in 1963 meant that he was finished in the majors.

Richie Ashburn

Ashburn, Don Richard **OF**
1948–62 B:3/19/1927, Tilden, NE D:9/9/1997, New York, NY Deb:4/20/1948, PHI NL BL/TR 5'10", 170

G	AB	R	H	HR	RBI	OBP	SLG	AVG
2189	8365	1322	2574	29	586	.397	.382	.308

Fleet outfielder Richie Ashburn twice won the National League batting title, finished second three times, and batted over .300 nine times. He possessed an excellent batting eye, leading the league in walks on four separate occasions. Ashburn's 1958 season marked the only time a leadoff hitter has paced the circuit in both average and bases on balls. Four times he led the NL in on-base percentage.

His fielding was simply incredible. Baseball historian Bill James claimed that Ashburn's defensive statistics were by far the best of any outfielder ever to play major league ball. Ted Williams marveled over Ashburn's ability to cover ground: "That kid has twin motors in his pants."

Baseball researcher Bob Carroll summed up Ashburn's glove work in the Society for American Baseball Research journal, *The National Pastime*: "His career chances-per-game average of three is well ahead of his more celebrated contemporaries of Willie [Mays], Mickey [Mantle] and 'the Duke' [Snider]. Put it this way: Over a 162-game season, Ashburn would catch about 50 balls that Mays wouldn't get to. That's a lot of base hits obliterated."

When the Nebraska-born "Whitey" Ashburn was 16, the Indians offered him a pro contract. Commissioner Kenesaw Mountain Landis voided the agreement and fined the Tribe $500. After Ashburn finished high school, the Cubs signed him to a pact with their Nashville farm club. A technicality voided that contract as well. After two "almosts," it looked like Ashburn just was not meant to be a major league ballplayer. He enrolled at Norfolk Junior College in Nebraska, where he received a degree in elementary education. On graduation day, the Phillies offered him $3,500 to sign with them, and Ashburn finally made it into organized baseball.

The Phils assigned him to the Eastern League's Utica Blue Sox. Manager Eddie Sawyer quickly moved Ashburn, who had been a catcher, to center field. At Utica, Ashburn hit .312 in 1945. After spending a year in the army, he returned to Utica to hit .362 in 1947.

When Ashburn arrived in Philadelphia in 1948, the Phillies already had a center fielder—Harry "the Hat" Walker, the reigning NL batting champion. In 1947 Walker had hit .363, a 46-point margin over his nearest rival, Bob Elliott of the Boston Braves. Walker, however, smashed a pitch off his foot one March day in spring training, an injury that forced the Hat out of the lineup until late May. Ashburn made the most of the opportunity, hitting close to .350 during the first half of the season. He compiled a 23-game hitting streak, which was then a rookie record, and, of course, ran down every flyball in sight. More than a million ballots named Ashburn for the 1948 All-Star Game, the only rookie elected to the squad. He justified the fans' selection by going 2-for-4 and swiping a base.

Ashburn was hitting .333 on August 28, when he fractured a finger sliding into second, missing the remainder of the season. His .333 average, though, was still good enough for second best in the circuit—and good enough to capture *The Sporting News* Rookie of the Year honors.

Notwithstanding his injury as a rookie, Ashburn was a remarkably durable performer. From June 6, 1950, to the end of the 1954 season, Ashburn played in every game, even after injuring his knee in spring training of that year. In 1955 Phils manager Mayo Smith finally decided to rest Ashburn in an effort to prevent any further damage to the star center fielder. At the time, Ashburn was just 91 games short of what was then the NL consecutive-games record held by Gus Suhr.

Ashburn was a sparkplug of the 1950 "Whiz Kids," who brought the Phils their first pennant in 35 years. That season Ashburn broke a million hearts in Brooklyn. The Phils had been atop the league standings for most of the year. As late as September 17, they still held a seven-and-a-half-game lead and a nine-game cushion over the third-place Dodgers. Suddenly the Bums made their move, and the Phillies' seven-game lead was dissipated in nine days. On September 29, the Phils traveled to Ebbets Field, needing to win one of the season's two remaining games to clinch the flag.

Brooklyn took the first game, 7–3. The next day Robin Roberts, making his third start in five days, faced Don Newcombe. In the bottom of the ninth, with the score tied, 1–1, Brooklyn left fielder Cal Abrams led off with a single. Pee Wee Reese fouled off a couple of pitches, then lined a single to left, advancing Abrams to second. Duke Snider batted next, and for some reason Philadelphia manager Eddie Sawyer expected the power-hitting Snider to attempt a bunt. As the Philadelphia infielders crept in, so did Ashburn.

Snider swung away, however, lining a single to center. The Dodger third base coach, Milt Stock, furiously waved Abrams in, but Ashburn quickly scooped up the ball and pegged a perfect strike to catcher Stan Lopata. Abrams was out by 15 feet. The Phils won the game in the 10th, on Dick Sisler's three-run homer, to take the pennant.

The Phils never really contended after 1950, but Ashburn put together fine season after fine season. From 1948 to 1954 he led the NL in putouts. In 1949 and 1951 he recorded more than 500 putouts per year. He led the league in batting in 1955, with .338, and in 1958, with .350. In 1959 Ashburn hit .266, just the second time since 1950 he'd been below .300. The Phillies traded him to the Cubs in January 1960. After two sub-.300 seasons, the New York Mets acquired him for their inaugural 1962 season. He hit .306 for the Mets, was voted Most

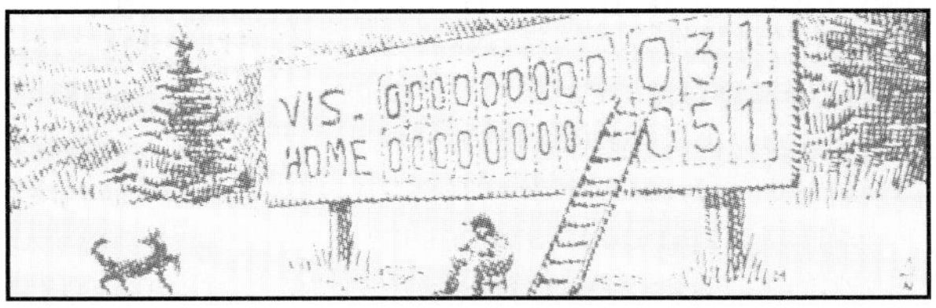

Valuable Player of the worst team in baseball history and won a boat as part of the honor.

Ashburn retired after the 1962 season and broadcast Phillies games until his death at age 70. He won election to the Hall of Fame in 1995.

Alan Ashby

Ashby, Alan Dean **C**

1973–89 B:7/8/1951, Long Beach, CA Deb:7/3/1973, CLE AL BB/TR 6'2", 190

G	AB	R	H	HR	RBI	OBP	SLG	AVG
1370	4123	397	1010	90	513	.323	.361	.245

Alan Ashby is a catcher who is more remembered for his pitchers than for what he did himself. Ashby tied the National League record by catching three no-hitters during his career: the first by the Astros' Ken Forsch, followed by Nolan Ryan, and then Mike Scott's division clincher on September 25, 1986.

Ashby first reached the majors with the Cleveland Indians in 1973. After four years as a light-hitting, part-time performer, he moved to Toronto, where in 1978 he had began to show that he could hit, raising his average to .261.

The switch hitter joined the Astros in 1979. During the early 1980s, he suffered numerous broken bones in his hands and toes—going on the disabled list five times—thanks to constant exposure to Joe Niekro's knuckleballs. He became the first Astro to homer from both sides in the same game on September 27, 1982. Ashby had his most productive year at the plate in 1987, attaining career highs of 14 home runs, 63 RBIs, and a .288 batting average. By 1989, his body finally lost the war with time, and the Astros replaced him with Craig Biggio.

Emmett Ashford

Ashford, Emmett L.

Umpire (1966-70) B:11/11/1914, Los Angeles, CA D:3/1/1980, Marina Del Rey, CA Deb:1966, AL

When Emmett Ashford was named an American League umpire at the advanced age of 51 in 1966, some suggested his promotion was the result of political pressure to finally place a black umpire on the field. Almost two decades had passed since Jackie Robinson joined the majors, and there was agitation for African-Americans to begin filling roles other than as players. Moreover, any quibbles that Ashford was less than deserving of a major league job overlooked his thorough minor league apprenticeship, where he was a fair-minded and competent arbiter.

Ashford had been successful from early on. He became the first African-American student body president of Jefferson High School in Los Angeles as well as the student newspaper editor. He attended Los Angeles City College and graduated from Chapman College with a B.S. degree. During a brief stint playing semipro baseball, he gained his first experience as an umpire. After service in the Navy from 1944 through 1947, he joined the postal service but devoted much of his time to umpiring local high school and semipro baseball games.

In 1951, Ashford became the first African-American umpire in organized baseball when, on the recommendation of major league scout Rosey Gilhousen, he was hired by the Class C Southwest International League. In 1953, he advanced to Class A and the next year jumped to the Triple A Pacific Coast League. He spent 11 seasons in the PCL, serving as umpire-in-chief in his final two years. During off-seasons, he refereed high school and college football games and umpired in the Dominican Republic.

Ashford brought a new and somewhat controversial style to the majors. Whereas umpires had been traditionally faceless, conservative figures in the background, he wore flashy jewelry, including sparkling cuff links, and emphasized his calls with exaggerated gestures. Purists criticized his flamboyance, but he was popular with fans, and his extravagant motions heralded the many individualized styles that distinguish today's umpires. As one of baseball's most visible goodwill ambassadors, he conducted umpiring clinics in Europe and Asia.

Ashford umpired the 15-inning 1967 All-Star Game won by Tony Perez's home run. His final assignment before his mandatory retirement at age 55 was the 1970 World Series. Until his death in 1980, he continued to umpire Pac-10 college games while also filling a role as Commissioner Bowie Kuhn's West Coast public relations representative.

Paul Assenmacher

Assenmacher, Paul Andre **P**

1986–* B:12/10/1960, Detroit, MI Deb:4/12/1986, ATL NL BL/TL 6'3", 200

W	L	PCT	G	SV	IP	BB	SO	ERA
61	44	.581	884	56	855²	315	807	3.53

Paul Assenmacher was converted into a reliever in 1985; he was later converted into a one-out specialist. He rose quickly through Atlanta's system, and got plenty of opportunities to relieve for the cellar-dwelling Braves of the late 1980s. The Cubs acquired him in 1989 in a late-season deal, and he helped Chicago win the National League East. Assenmacher pitched more than 100 innings in both 1990 and 1991, earning double-digit save totals each season. In 1990 the Cubs gave Assenmacher his only start in 884 appearances.

Assenmacher bounced around with the New York Yankees and Chicago White Sox before he signed with the Indians as a free agent in 1995. He was a valuable member of Cleveland's bullpen during its five consecutive American League Central titles. Used almost exclusively as a situational lefty, he was called upon to retire one or two lefthanded hitters with his big curve. Assenmacher had the worst season of his career in 1999. Although he still could get out lefties, righthanded batters hammered him. With 644 games, Assenmacher tied Cleveland teammate Mike Jackson for the most pitching appearances in the 1990s.

Gene Autry

Autry, Gene
Owner (1961–96) B:9/29/1907, Tioga, TX
D:10/2/1998, Studio City, CA

In 1927 in Chelsea, Oklahoma, Will Rogers noticed the singing talent of telegrapher Gene Autry, and before long Autry emerged as one of Hollywood's most famous "singing cowboys." Through ambition and astute business sense, Autry parlayed his singing and acting career into a multimillion-dollar empire, which included ownership of the California Angels for 36 seasons.

Yet his millions were unable to purchase the world championship he coveted. He once said, "I have a lot of money to spend and not a lot of time [to live] and I want a World Series ring." Unfortunately, his team was never able to get him one.

A boyhood friend of Dizzy Dean, Autry was offered a contract to play shortstop for Tulsa, a Cardinals affiliate, when he was 19. But the offer was for $100 a month, and Autry already made half again as much as a telegrapher for the Frisco Line. Money talked; he stayed with the railroad and took correspondence courses in accounting.

Although he owned some stock in the Hollywood Stars of the Pacific Coast League for a time, Autry was not connected with baseball during most of his performing career. He built his fortune through sound investments coupled with business innovations. He was one of the first entertainers to play for a percentage of the gate rather than for a flat fee, and he was also one of the first to merchandise his name, selling Gene Autry guitars. The money he made as a performer enabled him to move into broadcasting. The money he made there opened the door to ownership of the expansion Angels.

By the late 1970s Autry owned, directly or indirectly, six radio stations, two television stations, a TV and motion picture production facility, a 20,000-acre cattle ranch, a Palm Springs resort hotel, and the Gene Autry Western Heritage Museum. Autry himself said, "It has always amused me when people seem surprised by my success in business. Actually, working with numbers was what I did best. What I did less well was sing, act, and play the guitar."

In 1960 Walter O'Malley's Dodgers chose not to renew their radio contract with Autry's radio station, KMPC, and Autry looked for the inside track when the new California American League expansion team was announced. Partners Bill Veeck and Hank Greenberg lost interest in owning the new club when O'Malley demanded $350,000 for "invading his territory." Autry decided the best way to assure the radio business was to buy the team. He came up with $2.1 million to draft 28 players from current rosters, plus O'Malley's fee; Autry said the payment to the Dodgers was "for grazing rights."

The park in which the Angels played their first season (also determined in the O'Malley deal) was Wrigley Field, the former PCL park built in 1925 but unused since 1957. With 345-foot power alleys and a potent wind, Wrigley was made for slugging, and general manager Fred Haney saw that Autry stocked his team with long bombers.

Ted Kluszewski and Bob Cerv were drafted early. That year Steve Bilko, Ken Hunt, Leon Wagner, Earl Averill, and Lee Thomas each belted more than 20 home runs, and 248 homers were hit in all at Wrigley Field, the most in any park in one season. The Angels finished 70–91, the best expansion season ever. The following year, even after moving to O'Malley's new stadium at Chavez Ravine, they finished a respectable third.

The Angels' bad-luck streak was beginning. The club signed University of Wisconsin star outfielder Rick Reichardt as a $200,000 bonus baby, but he came down with a kidney ailment. In 1967 a fatal brain tumor sidelined rookie Dick Wantz. Reliever Minnie Rojas delivered 27 saves in 1968, but after that season a car accident left him paralyzed from the neck down.

The late 1960s did bring some good tidings for Autry, however. Kansas City's Charles Finley had been trying to move his team without success for years, because the stubborn owners always refused his efforts. When Finley sought permission to move to Oakland after the 1967 season, Autry saw the advantages of another American League team in California. Autry reminded Mike Burke, the Yankees president, how much business that team's parent company, CBS, did with Autry's Golden West Broadcasting. Burke switched his position. It was the one vote Finley needed.

In 1976 Autry led the way into big free agent spending. The Angels forked over $5.2 million to Joe Rudi, Don Baylor, and Bobby Grich. Autry noted that he had spent less than half that for 28 players in 1961. A back injury felled Grich, a pitch broke Rudi's hand in late June, and the best the Angels could do was fifth place. The next free agent they signed, Lyman Bostock, was having a terrific year when he was fatally shot in September.

Division titles finally came. In 1979 the Angels won the West by three games but lost the AL Championship Series to Baltimore. California's 1982 division winner became the first team to lose the five-game ALCS after taking a two games to none lead. When the Angels took a three-to-one lead in games in the 1986 ALCS, the curse struck again.

Leading in the top of the ninth, Angels pitcher Donnie Moore gave up a homer to Dave Henderson that put the Red Sox ahead. Boston won that game and the final two. In the aftermath of another loss, manager Gene Mauch reminded the press, "You have to bear in mind that Mr. Autry's favorite horse was named Champion. He ain't ever had one called Runner-Up." The brave talk, however, didn't take.

In 1990 Autry's wife Jackie became operating head of the team, replacing her ailing husband. The Walt Disney Company purchased controlling interest in the Angels, now the Anaheim Angels, in 1996. Autry died in 1998.

Earl Averill

Averill, Howard Earl **OF**

1929–41 B:5/21/1902, Snohomish, WA D:8/16/1983, Everett, WA Deb:4/16/1929, CLE AL BL/TR 5'9 ½", 172

G	AB	R	H	HR	RBI	OBP	SLG	AVG

Ironically for a batter of his stature, Earl Averill's most memorable batted ball wasn't a hit. During the 1937 All-Star Game he smashed a drive that caromed off pitcher Dizzy Dean's toe. Although Averill was thrown out at first, Dean's toe was broken. When Dean returned to pitching before it had completely healed, he altered his motion to favor the foot and eventually ruined his arm.

In a peculiar twist of fate, Averill's own career ended in a similar fashion. In the dugout one day Averill suddenly found himself paralyzed from the waist down. The paralysis was temporary, but an examination revealed a congenital spinal problem that forced him to alter his swing. Although he played for four more seasons, both his batting average and power declined.

Averill had begun playing on amateur teams around Snohomish, Washington, in the early 1920s. His friends and neighbors chipped in to send Averill—jobless at the time and supporting a wife and young child—to try out with Seattle of the Pacific Coast League. He flunked the tryout, but rather than return home, he hooked up with a semipro club in Bellingham, Washington, which eventually led to a full-time job with the PCL's San Francisco Seals.

For three seasons he tore up PCL pitching, but the major leagues didn't pay much attention. Finally, when Cleveland Indians general manager Billy Evans came west to look at outfielder Roy Johnson, who was Averill's teammate, Averill caught his eye. "There was something about the nonchalant Averill that won you over," Evans later explained. "I guess it was the easy, steady manner in which he did his work, without any great show." When Evans learned that the Tigers had already offered $65,000 and two players for Johnson, whereas Averill was available for a flat $50,000, his mind was made up.

On April 16, 1929, the lefthanded-batting Averill stepped up for his first major league at bat. On the mound stood Detroit's ace, lefty Earl Whitehill. A moment later, Averill circled the bases with his first home run. No other American League rookie had ever homered in his first at bat, and only two had done it in the National League. Averill remains one of only two Hall of Famers (relief pitcher Hoyt Wilhelm is the other) to have performed the feat.

Off to a roaring start, Averill had a monster year, batting .332 with 96 RBIs and 18 home runs. Vowing to do better in 1930, he raised his batting average to .339 and his RBI total to 119, but by September 17 he had hit only 14 home runs. When reminded he was four short of the previous year's mark, he said, "Well, I'd better step on it." That day he smashed four home runs in a doubleheader, three in one game. Another drive into the seats went foul at the last moment. He amassed 11 RBIs for the afternoon. On the season's final day he hit his 19th homer to make good on his promise. In each of the next two seasons he upped his homer total to 32.

Despite his long-ball heroics, Averill was no physical giant. But he generated excellent power and pulled the ball consistently, a necessary skill, as he played half his games in Cleveland's League Park with its inviting right-field fence. Although his arm was ordinary, he patrolled center field with a special loping grace that made him appear perpetually relaxed.

Cleveland fans, spoiled by the presence of the fabled Tris Speaker in center only a few years before, nevertheless deemed Averill a worthy successor. Easily the most popular player in town, he earned numerous affectionate nicknames. "The Earl of Snohomish" was his usual sobriquet on the sports pages, but fans and teammates often called him "Rock," or occasionally "Rockhead," "Sloppy," "Popeye," or "Elephant Ears.'

Beginning in 1931 Averill played in 673 straight games. Although that figure pales alongside the marks of Lou Gehrig and Cal Ripken, Jr., it was the fourth-longest consecutive streak on record at the time. It took a mishap with a Fourth of July firecracker in 1935 to knock Averill out of the lineup.

In both 1933 Averill started in center fielder for the American League in the first All-Star Game. He went on to become the only AL outfielder named to the first six All-Star Games, although he bowed out of the 1935 tilt after the firecracker injury to his hand. That accident was responsible for his first sub-.300 season, as he slumped to a still credible .288, with 19 homers.

Averill bounced back in 1936 at age 34 with one of his finest years. His career-high .378 batting average was only 10 points behind league leader Luke Appling's mark. Averill led the league with 232 hits and 15 triples, while hitting 28 homers, scoring 136 runs, and knocking in 126. The following season, after his spine problem was diagnosed, his power nearly disappeared, and his average dropped to .299. In 1938 he hit only 14 home runs but still managed a .330 batting average.

His back problem worsened and early in June 1939 the Indians traded him to Detroit for a second-string pitcher and a cash payment. The Cleveland fans were up in arms, but the trade gave Averill his only chance to play on a pennant winner, albeit as a reserve, when the Tigers won the 1940 flag. In the World Series the Tigers lost to the Cincinnati Reds, and Averill went hitless in three tries as a pinch hitter.

After he played eight games for the Red Sox in 1941, Boston released him, and Averill finished the season in Seattle before returning home to Snohomish. His son, Earl Douglas Averill, grew up and spent seven years in the major leagues himself while his father awaited a call to Cooperstown. In 1975 the Veterans Committee named him to the Hall of Fame, 34 years after his retirement.

Steve Avery

Avery, Steven Thomas **P**

1990–* B:4/14/1970, Trenton, MI Deb:6/13/1990, ATL NL BL/TL 6'4", 190

W	L	PCT	G	SH	IP	BB	SO	ERA
94	83	.531	278	6	1538²	562	974	4.17

Steve Avery was Atlanta's first post-season hero. Before the Braves reeled off eight straight division titles to end the 20th century, the Braves were a last-to-first ballclub in 1991. Part of the reason for the turnaround was the success of a second-year lefthander who had gone 3–11 as a rookie.

Avery led his high school team to the Michigan state championship as a high school senior, and turned down a scholarship to Stanford University to sign with the Braves in 1988. After one year in the minors, the pitching-thin Braves brought the 20-year-old Avery to the majors and let him learn on the go. He went 18–8 in his second season, including a 5–0 mark down the stretch as Atlanta edged the Los Angeles Dodgers for the National League West title. He won back-to-back starts by scores of 1–0 against the Pittsburgh Pirates in the Championship Series. Avery's 16 ⅓ consecutive scoreless innings set an NLCS record and earned him Most Valuable Player honors. He received two no-decisions in Atlanta's seven-game loss to the Minnesota Twins in the World Series.

Avery and the Braves appeared in the post-season from 1991 to 1996, with the exception of the 1994 strike season. Avery won the clinching game of the 1995 NLCS, and earned a victory in Game 4 of that year's World Series. He was injured and ineffective in his final two seasons in Atlanta. He walked in the winning run in Game 4 of the 1996 World Series in his final appearance as a Brave.

He signed with the Boston Red Sox as a free agent in 1997. Despite an injury-marred season, Boston picked up his option the following year. Avery won 10 games as a starter in 1998. He returned to the NL with the Cincinnati Reds.

Bobby Avila

Avila, Roberto Francisco **2B**

1949–59 B:4/2/1924, Vera Cruz, Mexico
Deb:4/30/1949, CLE AL BR/TR 5'10", 175

G	AB	R	H	HR	RBI	OBP	SLG	AVG
1300	4620	725	1296	80	467	.360	.388	.281

Like Bob Lemon, Al Rosen, and Bob Feller, Mexico's Bobby Avila was one of Cleveland's true stars of the 1950s. That status was remarkable considering that Avila was a professional soccer player—and dreamed of being a bullfighter—before he learned how to play baseball from a book authored by former big league pitcher Jack Coombs.

Avila initially signed a contract to play in a winter league called the Vera Cruz State League and then graduated to Puebla of the Mexican League. He gained exposure to American ballplayers in 1946 when Mexican League magnate Jorge Pasquel attempted to convert his circuit into a rival of the major leagues and lured down a number of North Americans. including Sal Maglie, Vern Stephens, and Mickey Owen.

In 1946 and 1947 Avila played winter baseball in Cuba. The Dodgers were interested in him and offered $10,000, but the Indians signed him for $17,500. Avila then spent the 1948 season with Baltimore of the International League, where he hit .220. Bonus rules at the time mandated that Cleveland bring him up in 1949, but Avila merely warmed the bench for the Indians and spent his spare time trying to learn English from pitcher Mike Garcia. Once Avila became a regular, however, he was a hitting machine, topping .300 three times in four years and capturing the American League batting championship in 1954 with a .341 mark.

Traded from Cleveland late in 1958, Avila divided the 1959 season between the Baltimore Orioles, Boston Red Sox, and Milwaukee Braves. After hanging up his uniform at the end of that season, Avila pursued a variety of business interests in Mexico, including ownership of the Vera Cruz Eagles and the presidency of the Mexican League. Eventually he was elected mayor of Vera Cruz.

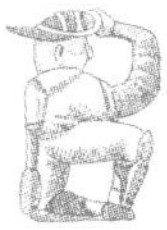

Johnny Babich

Babich, John Charles **P**

1934–36, 1940–41 B:5/14/1913, Albion, CA
Deb:6/19/1934, BRO NL BR/TR 6'1½", 185

W	L	PCT	G	SH	IP	BB	SO	ERA
30	45	.400	112	3	592	220	231	4.93

Johnny Babich was a product of the same San Francisco-area baseball environment that produced Lefty O'Doul, Lefty Gomez, and the DiMaggio brothers. Signed by the San Francisco Seals of the Pacific Coast League in 1931, he was then traded to the cross-town rival Missions in 1933. That year he won 20 games for the seventh-place Missions, and the next year he was 10–3 when Casey Stengel's hapless Brooklyn Dodgers purchased his contract.

Just 21 when he reached the big leagues, Babich still compiled an acceptable 7–11 record and a 4.20 ERA for a sixth-place team. The next year his ERA ballooned to 6.66. Stengel bounced Babich back down the minor league ladder.

Babich returned to the Pacific Coast League and pitched well for the Missions and the Hollywood Stars. He made three appearances for the Boston Bees in 1936 but was sent back down after posting a 10.50 ERA. In 1938, with Hollywood, he was 19–17 with a 3.27 ERA and four shutouts for Wade Killifer's seventh-place squad.

At that point the Yankees took an interest in Babich, and, although he failed to make the majors, the Bronx Bombers assigned him to Kansas City, their American Association farm club. It was a strong team, and Babich ranked third in the league in ERA (behind two teammates). The Yankees, however, still had no room for Babich and peddled him to Connie Mack's threadbare Philadelphia Athletics.

Babich was only 14–13 for the 1940 A's, but he was 5-0 against the Yankees. His fifth win knocked New York out of the pennant race, depriving the club of a fifth straight flag. Yanks manager Joe McCarthy was furious, storming through the locker room, screaming, "Babich...Babich...BABICH! Who in hell ever heard of Babich?" to which Yankees second baseman Joe Gordon drawled, "Well, apparently our scouts didn't."

It was the highlight of his career. The next year Babich disappeared from the big leagues after going only 2–7.

Wally Backman

Backman, Walter Wayne **2B-3B**

1980–93 B:9/22/1959, Hillsboro, OR Deb:9/2/1980, NY NL BB/TR 5'9', 160

G	AB	R	H	HR	RBI	OBP	SLG	AVG
1102	3245	482	893	10	240	.350	.339	.275

Switch-hitting second baseman Wally Backman batted .300 or better three times in nine seasons with the New York Mets, but that statistic is somewhat misleading. Backman was exceptionally vulnerable from the right side of the plate. As the everyday second baseman in 1985, he hit .324 with a .429 slugging percentage from the left side; from the right side he hit an anemic .122 in 131 at bats.

The Mets acquired righthanded-hitting Tim Teufel from the Minnesota Twins in the winter of 1985, and it proved to be a winning platoon. Although the pair made 26 errors in 1986 (17 by Backman), they teamed up for 38 doubles (18 by Backman), 102 runs (67 by Backman), and 193 hits (124 by Backman). On his own, Backman hit .320, was second in the National League with a .346 average on turf, and struck out just 32 times in 387 at bats.

Backman batted only .238 in the National League Championship Series against the Houston Astros, but he made a big contribution as a runner. With the Mets trailing by a run in the ninth inning of Game 3, he bunted up the first base line; he briefly skidded out of the baseline to avoid the tag of Houston first baseman Glenn Davis on the way to safely reaching first. Following an argument by the Astros, Lenny Dykstra homered to win the game. Backman hit .333 in the World Series and scored the tying run in Game 7.

Backman batted .303 in 1988 as the Mets again won the NL East. However, after the season the Mets shipped him to Minnesota, where he struggled against American League pitching. He returned to the senior circuit with the Pirates in 1990, and batted .292 for the NL East champs. Backman played in Philadelphia for two years and ended his career in Seattle in 1993.

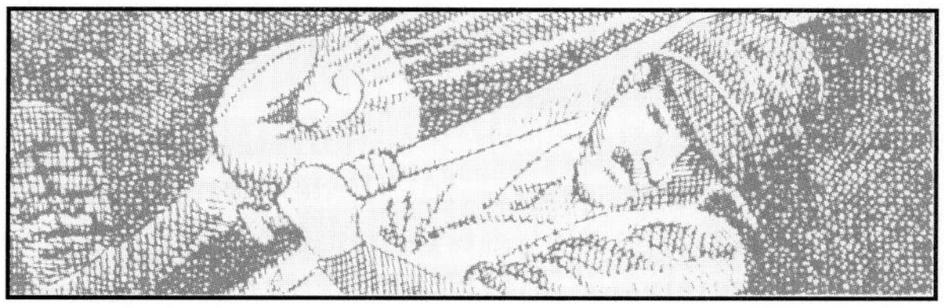

Red Badgro

Badgro, Morris Hiram **OF**

1929–30 B:12/1/1902, Orilla, WA D:7/13/1998, Kent, WA Deb:6/20/1929, STL AL BL/TR 6', 190

G	AB	R	H	HR	RBI	OBP	SLG	AVG
143	382	57	98	2	45	.307	.366	.257

Baseball wasn't Red Badgro's best sport. With the forlorn St. Louis Browns, the outfielder hit just .257 with 30 doubles and a mere three triples and two homers in 143 games spread over 1929 and 1930. Bearing in mind that these were among the best hitting years in baseball history, it makes Badgro's Brownie accomplishments not hugely significant.

That didn't stop Badgro from making the Hall of Fame. No, not at Cooperstown—at Canton, Ohio. The 6-foot, 190-pound Badgro was inducted into the Pro Football Hall of Fame in 1981. An outstanding end at the University of Southern California, Badgro went on to a professional gridiron career for three New York City-based NFL teams in the 1920s and 1930s: the New York Yankees (1927–28), the New York Giants (1930–35), and the Brooklyn Dodgers (1936). He led the NFL in receiving in 1934, a year after having scored the first touchdown in the first regularly scheduled NFL Championship Game.

Carlos Baerga

Baerga, Carlos Obed (Ortiz) **2B–3B**

1990–* B:11/4/1968, Santurce, Puerto Rico Deb:4/14/1990, CLE AL BB/TR 5'11", 200

G	AB	R	H	HR	RBI	OBP	SLG	AVG
1280	4807	659	1400	124	686	.334	.427	.291

Carlos Baerga, who averaged 162 hits per year and batted .305 in his first six major league seasons, was one of the main forces behind Cleveland's resurgence from perennial American League doormat to playoff team. Originally signed by San Diego, he came to the Indians with Sandy Alomar, Jr., in a deal for Joe Carter.

He was moved around the infield in his first two years with the club, but once he became the everyday second baseman his hitting flourished. Baerga put together back-to-back 20-homer, 100-RBI, 200-hit seasons in 1992 and 1993. He played in the All-Star Game three out of four years, and was regarded as the league's best offensive second baseman. Batting in front of Albert Belle in the powerful Tribe lineup, Baerga's career reached its apex in 1995, when the Indians reached the World Series for the first time in 41 years.

Baerga, playing with an injured ankle, had three hits and drove in three runs against Atlanta in Game 3 of the World Series. He started the decisive rally, lining a double off the wall in center field in the 11th inning. Eddie Murray then singled home pinch runner Alvaro Espinoza with the winning run in the first World Series game ever played at Cleveland's Jacobs Field.

Concerns about Baerga's weight, his limited range at second base, and love of the nightlife came to the forefront in 1996. Baerga, a .300 hitter for four straight seasons, was batting only .267 through July. Indians general manager John Hart made a bold move, sending the popular Baerga, along with Espinoza, to the Mets for Jeff Kent and Jose Vizcaino. Hampered by injuries, Baerga hit only .193 in 26 games in New York.

While Baerga rebounded to bat .281 in 1997, he was no longer a serious threat. Surprisingly, his glove work at second base improved, but at the plate the switch hitter was practically an automatic out from the right side. He batted .266 in 1998, and the Mets did not pick up his option at season's end. After failed attempts to make the majors in St. Louis and Cincinnati, he signed with San Diego. He was dealt back to Cleveland in August 1999, only to serve as a back-up third baseman.

Jim Bagby

Bagby, James Charles Jacob, Sr. **P**

1912, 1917–23 B:10/5/1889, Barnett, GA D:7/28/1954, Marietta, GA Deb:4/22/1912, CIN NL BB/TR 6', 170

W	L	PCT	G	SV	IP	BB	SO	ERA
111	72	.607	268	24	1549	391	362	3.20

The titles "world champions" and "30-game winner" don't seem to belong in the same sentence with "Cleveland Indians," given the team's dismal history before recent years. But pitcher Jim Bagby was one player who managed to combine these seemingly incongruent elements.

Bagby's professional baseball career began with Augusta of the South Atlantic League in 1911. In 1912 he appeared briefly with Garry Herrmann's Cincinnati Reds before going to the Southern Association, where he had a lucky break. While subbing in the outfield, 'Sarge' Bagby collided with a fellow outfielder and fractured his forearm. Oddly, the injury improved his curveball.

The desperate Indians purchased his contract, and, beginning in 1917, Bagby responded with 57 wins over the next three seasons. Then came the Indians' magical year of 1920. They won their first-ever American league pennant, edging out the New York Yankees and the rapidly unraveling Chicago "Black Sox." Bagby went 31–12 while pitching 339 innings, leading the league in both categories.

The Indians then defeated the Brooklyn Robins, 5–2, in the World Series. Bagby was 1–1 with a 1.80 ERA, and his win in Game 5 was assisted by one of the most memorable moments in Series history—Bill Wambsganss' unassisted triple play. With runners on first and second, Brooklyn pitcher Clarence Mitchell lined a ball to Wambsganss. He stepped on second base to double Pete Kilduff for the second out and then tagged Otto Miller, who was running toward second.

Bagby's ERA soared almost two points the next year, and he was used less and less. He retired as a player in 1923. His son, Jim Bagby, Jr., became a respectable American League pitcher in his own right, best known for halting Joe DiMaggio's 56-game hitting streak in 1941.

Jeff Bagwell

Bagwell, Jeffery Robert **1B**

1991–* B:5/27/1968, Boston, MA Deb:4/8/1991, HOU NL BL/TL 6', 195

G	AB	R	H	HR	RBI	OBP	SLG	AVG
1317	4759	921	1447	263	961	.422	.545	.304

If losing Babe Ruth wasn't bad enough, Boston Red Sox fans also bitterly lament the 1990 trade that sent Jeff Bagwell to the Houston Astros. In an attempt to bolster their bullpen for a pennant drive, the Sox traded Bagwell for relief pitcher Larry Anderson at the August 31 deadline. Although Anderson helped Boston secure the division title, he only appeared in 15 games for a Boston team that was swept four straight by Oakland in the Championship Series. He went to San Diego as a free agent the next year. Bagwell went on to be National League Rookie of the Year; by 1994 he was the NL Most Valuable Player, a Gold Glove Award winner, and a four-time All-Star.

To make matters worse, Bagwell was born in Boston, grew up not far away in Connecticut, and his family was filled with Red Sox fans. They were thrilled when he was the team's fourth-round choice in the 1989 free agent draft out of the University of Hartford. "I hated leaving, but it was the best move of my career," Bagwell said of the trade that landed him in Houston.

Originally a third baseman, Bagwell found the position already occupied in Houston by an established player, Ken Caminiti. Given the choice of playing third in Triple A or first in the majors he did not hesitate to change positions. He responded to the opportunity by hitting .294 with 15 home runs and 82 RBIs.

Bagwell steadily improved his game, transformed his body with weigh training, and perfected his unique batting stance. Feet planted wide apart, Bagwell would bob in a crouch until the pitch was delivered. Instead of striding forward he shortened his stance while straightening his legs, uncoiling his body to generate a tremendous whip action with the bat. By 1994 Bagwell's swing was machine tooled. In only 110 games of a strike-shortened year he produced an MVP season that included a .368 batting average, 39 home runs, and league-leading totals of 104 runs scored, 116 runs batted in, .461 on-base average, and an incredible .750 slugging percentage. He also won a Gold Glove for his play at first base.

His penchant for crowding the plate, however, cost Bagwell some playing time. Twice he broke his hand on pitched balls, prompting him to wear a padded brick on the back of his batting glove. After the 1995 season, when he appeared in only 114 games, Bagwell proved durable as he continued to improve his power game while leading the Astros to postseason play. He played in 162 games in each of the next two seasons. In 1997 the Astros started a run of three straight division titles, but Bagwell's difficulties in the Division Series led to three straight early exits.

Twice he topped the 40 home run mark and consistently batted in more than 110 runs in a season, topping out with a career-high 135 in 1996. He also showed surprising speed. In 1997 Bagwell became the first Astro to hit 30 home runs and steal 30 bases in a season, the first in a Houston uniform.

Stan Bahnsen

Bahnsen, Stanley Raymond **P**

1966, 1968–82 B:12/15/1944, Council Bluffs, IA Deb:9/9/1966, NY AL BR/TR 6'2", 203

W	L	PCT	G	SV	IP	BB	SO	ERA
146	149	.495	574	20	2529	924	1359	3.60

Stan Bahnsen virtually had two careers. For the Yankees and White Sox he was a big, strong, dependable starter from 1968 through 1974. His 17–12 mark with a 2.05 ERA for the Yanks in 1968 earned him Rookie of the Year honors. He twice won 14 games in the succeeding three seasons in pinstripes.

In the winter of 1971, Bahnsen was traded to Chicago for third baseman Rich McKinney. In 1972 he pitched 252 innings and won 21 games; the following year he virtually turned his record around, losing 21 games. From 1972 through 1974 he posted a 51–52 won-lost record.

Traded to Oakland midway through the 1975 season, he began to spend more and more time in the bullpen. Bahnsen no longer had great stuff, but he still knew how to pitch. Oakland used him five times in relief in 1975, then 21 times (as opposed to 14 starts) in 1976. Traded to Montreal in 1977, he started 22 times in 23 appearances, but his ERA was an unhealthy 4.81. He started only four more games for the rest of his major league career.

During the next three seasons in Montreal, Bahnsen made 155 appearances in relief. Primarily a setup man, he notched 17 saves from 1978 through 1981. His last season consisted of 15 games with California and Philadelphia in 1982.

Bob Bailey

Bailey, Robert Sherwood **3B–OF**

1962–78 B:10/13/1942, Long Beach, CA Deb: 9/14/1962, PIT NL BR/TR 6', 188

G	AB	R	H	HR	RBI	OBP	SLG	AVG
1931	6082	772	1564	189	773	.350	.403	.257

Bob Bailey received a $175,000 Pittsburgh signing bonus back in 1961, but he never quite delivered the goods. The Pirates assigned him to Asheville (Sally League), where he played shortstop and made 27 errors in only 75 games. Shifted to third, he tied for the International League lead in RBIs with 108, hit .299, and was named *The Sporting News* 1962 Minor League Player of the Year. He earned a promotion to Pittsburgh but was never a star. Bailey's teammates were completely baffled as to why such a limited player had received such a large bonus.

"What disturbed me most about Bob was his fielding," wrote Willie Stargell. "He didn't have much range, he had little speed, and his arm was no better than average at best."

In December 1966 Pittsburgh gave up on Bailey, trading him and infielder Gene Michael to the Dodgers for Maury Wills. Bailey didn't cut it in Los Angeles either, hitting .227 in consecutive seasons. The Dodgers sold him to the expansion Expos in October 1968. There, Bailey's offense picked up, although his fielding didn't. "Bailey means wood," said Montreal manager Gene Mauch ruefully. "Bailey doesn't mean leather."

"They called him Beetle, after the comic strip character," said one sneering former opponent. "He fielded like a comic strip character."

In December 1975 the Expos traded Bailey, who was then the last member of the 1969 club still with the team, to the Reds for pitcher Clay Kirby. By the time Bailey left Montreal he led the Expos in nine career offensive categories. Later peddled to the Red Sox for a minor league pitcher and cash, he finished his career in 1978.

Bob Bailor

Bailor, Robert Michael **OF–SS**

1975–85 B:7/10/1951, Connellsville, PA Deb:9/6/1975, BAL AL BR/TR 5'11", 170

G	AB	R	H	HR	RBI	OBP	SLG	AVG
955	2937	339	775	9	222	.312	.325	.264

Bob Bailor was an aggressive competitor whose "all out" style of play left him injured too often to be an everyday player. Although he was a free-swinging hitter he was tough to strike out, and his speed on the basepaths was his main weapon. After demoting him in the spring of 1975, Baltimore skipper Earl Weaver said, "His ticket to the major leagues is his wheels."

Bailor languished in the Orioles farm system for several years, unable to break into a Baltimore infield that featured Gold Glovers like Brooks Robinson, Bobby Grich, and Mark Belanger. After showcasing himself in the instructional league, Bailor was the first player selected by the Toronto Blue Jays in the 1977 expansion draft. Toronto manager Roy Hartsfield moved Bailor to the outfield, hoping that he could avoid the kinds of injuries he'd suffered as a shortstop. By mid-May, Bailor was leading the American League in hitting, finishing the season with a .310 average that was the highest ever for a player with a first-year expansion club.

With little to be excited about in the early days of the Toronto franchise, Bailor became a fan favorite who provided some of their first exciting moments. In 1978 he scored from second on an infield grounder to give the Jays a dramatic 10th inning win over the Royals. He was named the Blue Jays' Player of the Year in 1977 and 1978.

The nagging injuries that cost him a handful of games in his first two seasons caught up with Bailor in 1979, as he struggled at the plate and lost his starting job. By 1980 he was used primarily as a utility infielder, adding three appearances as a mop-up reliever.

Traded to the Mets before the 1981 season, Bailor appeared to have won the starting shortstop job before the strike interrupted the season. When the strike ended, so did Bailor's return to the starting lineup. Over the next few years, he was a key member of New York's bench—playing four positions, pinch hitting, and stealing 38 bases in 44 attempts. Bailor was traded to the Dodgers before the start of the 1984 season for pitcher Sid Fernandez. His role in Los Angeles was greatly reduced, and he retired after two seasons with the Dodgers.

The Blue Jays' first-ever player was back with the club when it won back-to-back World Series in 1992 and 1993. Bailor was the first-base coach from 1992 through 1995 before serving as a manager in the Blue Jays' minor league system.

Harold Baines

Baines, Harold Douglass **DH-OF**

1980-* B:3/15/1959, Easton, MD Deb:4/10/1980, CHI AL BL/TL 6'2", 195

G	AB	R	H	HR	RBI	OBP	SLG	AVG
2702	9541	1270	2783	373	1583	.361	.469	.292

From an early age it was easy to see that Harold Baines could hit. White Sox owner Bill Veeck scouted Baines as a Little Leaguer. In 1977 Veeck made the 18-year-old outfielder the first pick in the country. After a brief minor league apprenticeship, he was in the White Sox lineup for good in 1980. Two decades later Baines was still rapping out hits.

Baines quickly established himself as Chicago's franchise player as he became the youngest player in Sox history to reach 100 RBIs. Along with righthanded sluggers Carlton Fisk, Ron Kittle, and Greg Luzinski, Baines was the lefthanded sock in the Sox batting order in 1983 when Chicago made its first postseason appearance since 1959. Baines even drove in the winning run against Seattle in the game that clinched the division championship. The Baltimore pitching staff held Baines to just two singles in the Championship Series as the Orioles took the pennant.

Baines is already in the Hall of Fame; at least his bat is. He launched a home run in the 25th inning to end the longest game in major league history in 1984. His bat only got hotter as he got older, but in the process injuries took their toll on his knees. While Baines became the only White Sox player to hit 20 or more home runs for six consecutive years, from 1982 to 1987, he also changed from an everyday outfielder to an everyday designated hitter.

Chicago was in shock when Baines was traded to Texas for Wilson Alvarez, Scott Fletcher, and Sammy Sosa. While Sosa was later traded to the Cubs, Alvarez and Fletcher were key members of the rebuilt White Sox team that won the AL West title in 1993.

After stops in Baltimore and Oakland, Baines returned to Chicago in 1996 and responded with the second-highest batting average of his career. He hit .311 while batting behind two-time Most Valuable Player Frank Thomas most of the season. Baines connected for 22 home runs and drove in 95 runs in 143 games for the White Sox. On July 29, 1997, the Sox traded Baines to Baltimore for infielder Juan Bautista. In that year's ALCS Baines batted .353. At the 1999 trading deadline, the moribund Orioles sent Baines to Cleveland. He appeared in his fifth postseason with his fourth different team.

Dusty Baker

Baker, Johnnie B. **OF**

1968–86 M(1993–*, 558–512) B:6/15/1949, Riverside, CA Deb:9/07/1968, ATL NL BR/TR 6'2", 187

G	AB	R	H	HR	RBI	OBP	SLG	AVG
2039	7117	964	1981	242	1013	.351	.432	.278

A mediocre center fielder with the Atlanta Braves, Dusty Baker became an All-Star left fielder for the Los Angeles Dodgers in the late 1970s and early 1980s. His combination of power and speed made him an outstanding player; his timely hitting was crucial in four postseasons for Los Angeles. He later became a well-respected manager for the San Francisco Giants.

Born in southern California and raised near Sacramento, Baker was the Braves' 27th round pick in the June 1967 draft after starring in baseball, basketball, football, and track at Del Campo High School in Carmichael, California. He made brief appearances in the majors each year starting in 1968, but didn't stick until 1972, when he batted a career-best .321, third in the National League; the next year he had a career-high 99 RBIs. However, these numbers were the exception rather than the rule, and after the 1975 season, the Braves tired of waiting for him to realize his potential. Baker was traded him to the Dodgers with infielder Ed Goodson for outfielder Jim Wynn, second baseman Lee Lacy, outfielder Tom Paciorek, and infield prospect Jerry Royster.

Baker had a miserable first season in Los Angeles, but in 1977 he became part of the first 30-homer quartet in baseball history, along with Ron Cey, Reggie Smith, and Steve Garvey. Oddly, after leading NL outfielders in total chances and putouts in 1973, Baker set a major league record for fewest chances by an outfielder in 1977. He won a Gold Glove in 1981, appeared in the 1981 and 1982 All-Star Games, and won the first two NL Silver Slugger Awards in 1980 and 1981.

Baker frequently seemed to play his best during the playoffs, hitting .371 during four National League Championship Series with Los Angeles. During the 1977 playoffs he demonstrated his knack for big postseason hits. In Game 2 he touched Philadelphia starter Jim Lonborg for a fourth-inning grand slam, breaking a 1-1 tie to start a rout. He drove in two runs in the Dodgers' 6–5 Game 3 win. And his second-inning, two-run homer off Steve Carlton in Game 4 put the Dodgers ahead to stay, advancing Los Angeles to the World Series under rookie manager Tom Lasorda. Baker's performance earned him the first Most Valuable Player Award of a Championship Series.

Facing the New York Yankees in Game 1 of the World Series, Baker's single leading off the ninth inning started a game-tying rally, but the Dodgers lost in 12 innings. In Game 2 he bobbled Reggie Jackson's first-inning single, allowing Jackson to take second and eventually to score an unearned run; Baker atoned with a game-tying three-run homer in the bottom of the third. He collected three singles, knocked in two runs, and scored twice in the Dodgers' 10–4 Game 5 rout, although the Dodgers lost the Series in six.

In the 1978 NLCS rematch with Philadelphia (another four-game Los Angeles win) Baker again hit safely in each contest and had four hits in the finale. He tied the NLCS record with a .467 batting average, and the four-game mark with eight RBIs. In a World Series rematch with the Yankees he opened the scoring with a homer and singled twice in an 11–5 Game 1 win, but he hit just two more singles during the rest of the Series, another six-game win for New York.

In the 1981 playoffs against Montreal, with the Dodgers facing elimination in Game 4, Baker singled to lead off the eighth inning of a 1–1 tie. He scored the go-ahead run on Steve Garvey's two-run homer to force a decisive fifth game, which the Dodgers won on Rick Monday's ninth-inning homer. The Dodgers played the Yankees again in the World Series, this time beating New York in six games.

After the 1983 season Baker and the Dodgers became embroiled in a bitter contract dispute that led to his release. He signed with the Giants for the 1984 season and ended his career after two seasons with the Oakland Athletics.

He later returned to the Giants and began a five-year apprenticeship on Roger Craig's coaching staff. Baker got his first taste of managing after the 1992 season in the Arizona Fall League; he took over the Giants on December 16, 1992. In Baker's first year as manager the Giants won 103 games, but only finished second behind Atlanta. Even in defeat, the baseball writers voted Baker NL Manager of the Year. In 1997 San Francisco won the NL West, and *The Sporting News* honored Baker as Manager of the Year. In 1998 Baker's Giants battled back to tie the Cubs for the league Wild Card slot, but lost a one-game playoff. San Francisco finished second in the NL West in 1999.

Frank Baker

Baker, John Franklin **3B**

1908–19, 1921–22 B:3/13/1886, Trappe, MD
D:6/28/1963, Trappe, MD Deb:9/21/1908, PHI AL
BL/TR 5'11", 173

G	AB	R	H	HR	RBI	OBP	SLG	AVG
1575	5984	887	1838	96	987	.363	.442	.307

Frank "Home Run" Baker never hit more than 12 round-trippers in any one season, and his lifetime total was but 96. Nevertheless, his nickname was well deserved. His peak seasons came during baseball's Dead Ball Era, when no one could knock the ball over the fence with any regularity. As home run hitters went at the time, Baker was the best in the American League, using a monstrous 52-ounce bat.

Baker grew up in Maryland and played baseball for local amateur teams. A lefthanded hitter and righthanded thrower, he was a bit awkward in the field, but he could powder the ball. He initially flunked a Baltimore Orioles tryout but in 1908 signed to play with Reading of the Class B Tri-State League, where he hit .299.

When the Philadelphia Athletics' Connie Mack wanted to replace fading Jimmy Collins at third he acquired Baker's contract. An exuberant Baker showed up at the Chicago hotel where the A's were staying and announced, "Mr. Mack, I'm here." The manager eyed Baker's 5-foot 11-inch, 173-pound frame. "I see you are," replied the taciturn Mack, who then continued the conversation Baker had interrupted.

When young Baker got through the last nine games of the season without making an error and hit .290, the job was his. He started at third base for the A's the following year and hit a grand slam on Opening Day, but it took the rest of the season to hit three more homers. He did, however, slug a league-leading 19 triples, bat in 85 runs, and finish with a .305 average. He also led in putouts and assists, despite committing 42 errors to top league third basemen.

In late August 1909 the Athletics traveled to Detroit, holding a one-game lead over the second-place Tigers. In the opener Ty Cobb slid into third base and took a divot out of Baker's right forearm with his spikes. All hell broke loose. Mack called Cobb the dirtiest player in the league and accused him of spiking the young third baseman intentionally (which probably wasn't true—a photograph of the play shows Baker reaching awkwardly across his body, putting his bare arm at risk). The Tigers won the series and went on to take the pennant.

After hitting only two regular-season home runs for the 1910 World Series champions, Baker suddenly became a deep threat in 1911. He learned to pull the ball, upping his homer production to 11, most in the league. That year also saw the A's "$100,000 infield" come together, with Baker joined by first baseman Stuffy McInnis, second baseman Eddie Collins, and shortstop Jack Barry. In the World Series against the Giants, Baker also earned a nickname.

Christy Mathewson downed Philadelphia, 2–1, in the opener. In Game 2 the score was tied in the sixth at 1–1, as Giants lefty Rube Marquard sailed along. Then Eddie Collins doubled. Marquard threw an inside pitch to Baker, who pulled it down the Polo Grounds' short right field foul line for a home run and a 3–1 Phillies win. The next morning a ghost-written newspaper story under Mathewson's byline informed Marquard of the obvious: "Baker should be pitched outside." That afternoon Mathewson faced the Athletics. He held a 1–0 lead going into the ninth and had handled Baker three times without trouble. But the fourth time up Baker grooved one, putting it into the same friendly seats he'd found the day before; Philadelphia won in the 11th. Because two home runs in two days was something to gasp at in that era, the A's third baseman became "Home Run" Baker.

After two championships in a row, Mack's Athletics slipped to third in 1912, although Baker successfully defended his home run title with 10, also leading the league with 130 RBIs. The next year, when the A's returned to the World Series, Baker retained both crowns, with 12 homers and 117 RBIs. Years later he was asked how many home runs he might have hit with a modern, lively baseball. "I'd say 50 anyway," he allowed. "The year I hit 12, I also hit the right-field fence at Shibe Park 38 times."

Baker hit only one home run in the 1913 World Series, but he devastated the Giants even more than he had in 1911. He batted .450 with seven RBIs, as the Athletics won in five games. In 1914 Baker won his final home run title with a mere nine, while the Athletics captured their fourth pennant in five years. In the World Series the surprising Boston Braves took the A's in four straight.

A disappointed Mack decided it was time to tighten his belt and sold off most of his stars. He kept Baker, but, when refused a raise, the third baseman sat out the season. In 1916 Mack sold Baker's contract to the Yankees for $35,000. Baker gave New York four good years.

In 1919 his 10 homers tied him for second place behind Boston's Babe Ruth, who cracked a then-astounding 29. Baker sat out 1920 when his first wife became ill and died, during which time Ruth was sold to the Yankees and, with the help of the new, lively baseball, astonished the sports world with 54 home runs. In 1921 Baker returned as a part-time performer and helped the Yankees win their first two pennants. His last major league at bat was as a pinch hitter in the 1922 Series. His ground out left him with a .363 batting average, 18 RBIs, and three homers in 25 World Series games.

Upon retiring as a player, Baker managed the Easton, Maryland, team of the Eastern Shore League to a pair of last-place finishes. While there, he discovered a muscular young slugger named Jimmie Foxx and urged his old manager Connie Mack to sign him. Later, Baker bought the Easton team but left to raise horses on his Maryland farm. In 1955 he was named to the Hall of Fame.

Lady Baldwin

Baldwin, Charles Busted **P**

1884–88, 1890 B:4/8/1859, Oramel, NY D:3/7/1937, Hastings, MI Deb:9/30/1884, MIL UA BL/TL 5'11", 160

W	L	PCT	G	SH	IP	BB	SO	ERA
73	41	.640	118	9	1017	233	582	2.85

Charles Busted "Lady" Baldwin acquired his unusual nickname back in the 1880s as testimony to his strait-laced demeanor. He did not smoke, drink, or swear. He was a "perfect lady," and he was a 42-game winner in 1886.

Baldwin got his start in the minors in 1884 with Milwaukee of the old Northwest League. Before the season was over he was pitching for the same city's entry in Charles Lucas' ill-fated Union Association. Despite a nondescript 1–1 record, Baldwin was one of the few players to make the transition from that circuit to the established National League when the Union Association folded at the end of the season.

Baldwin's six-year major league record was unremarkable except for one season. In 1886 the Detroit Wolverines made a serious run for the National League pennant, largely propelled by Baldwin's strong right arm. The team eventually finished second, but Baldwin went 42–13, leading the circuit in victories, strikeouts (323), and lowest opponents' batting average (.202). He threw seven shutouts, a one-hitter, five two-hitters, and five three-hitters.

The following season—due largely to fatigue, as well as to a change in the rules regarding pitching delivery—Baldwin lost effectiveness. In fact, at one point he was sent home without pay. However, in the 1887 World Series against Chris Von Der Ahe's St. Louis Browns, Baldwin was deadly, winning four of five starts and limiting the Browns to a measly .155 team batting average. In 1890 Baldwin retired to a farm near Hastings, Michigan.

Mark Baldwin

Baldwin, Marcus Elmore **P**

1887–93 B:10/29/1863, Pittsburgh, PA D:11/10/1929, Pittsburgh, PA Deb:5/2/1887, CHI NL BR/TR 6', 190

W	L	PCT	G	SH	IP	BB	SO	ERA
154	165	.483	346	14	2802^{1}	1307	1349	3.37

Marcus Elmore "Fido" Baldwin of the American Association's Columbus Colts struck out 368 batters in 1889—a total that has since been exceeded only by Sandy Koufax and Nolan Ryan. Mark Baldwin won 39 games in the minors in 1886, then at season's end signed to pitch for the Chicago White Stockings, the National League team later known as the Cubs. When Cap Anson attempted to use Baldwin in the 1886 World Series against the Browns, Charles Comiskey objected and Anson withdrew the idea.

Baldwin spent two years with Chicago before going to Columbus. In 1889 he led the American Association in appearances (63) and innings pitched (513 2/3) as well as strikeouts. Jumping to the Players League in 1890, he led that circuit in victories (33), appearances (58), complete games (53), innings pitched (492), and strikeouts (206).

Back in the National League with Pittsburgh, on September 12, 1891, he pitched two complete games in a doubleheader against Brooklyn, winning 13–3 and 8–4, while allowing a mere 11 hits. The wins gave Baldwin four victories in just six days. That year he won 21 games for a last-place club.

Baldwin repeated the trick of pitching two complete games in one day again on May 30, 1892, defeating Baltimore 11–1 and 4–3. In September of that year Baldwin was arrested in Homestead, Pennsylvania, the site of a bloody Carnegie Steel Company strike. He was charged with helping to foment the labor stoppage and the resulting riots. After posting $2,000 bail Baldwin rejoined Pittsburgh, where he finished the season with 26 victories. Baldwin retired after spending a year with New York of the National League.

Phil Ball

Ball, Philip DeCatesby

Owner (1914–32) B:1864, Keokuk, IA D:10/22/1933, St. Louis, MO

St. Louis Browns owner Philip DeCatesby Ball was not as patrician as his middle name would suggest. His father wanted to name him after Al Catesby, a famous Welshman, but his mother balked and suggested "DeCatesby" as a more genteel, French-sounding alternative.

Interested in baseball from an early age, Ball was a catcher for a club in Shreveport, Louisiana, until a barroom knifing cost him the full use of his left hand. Following that incident he labored as a cowpuncher until he saved $1,000, with which he purchased his first ice manufacturing plant. Before he was through, Ball owned several plants and had become a St. Louis-based millionaire. In 1914 Federal League President "Fighting Jim" Gilmore recruited Ball to replace brewer Otto Stifel as the backer of the St. Louis Terriers.

The Federal League lasted only two years. As part of the league settlement, the Terriers and the American League St. Louis Browns merged with Ball in charge. Once in the AL he became a staunch, bitter supporter of the declining presidency of league founder Ban Johnson. Ball remained the Browns' owner until 1932.

George Bamberger

Bamberger, George Irvin **P**

1951–52, 1959 M(1978–80, 1982–83, 1985–86, 458–478) B:8/1/1925, Staten Island, NY Deb:4/19/1951, NY NL BR/TR 6', 175

W	L	PCT	G	SV	IP	BB	SO	ERA
0	0	—	10	1	14^{1}	10	3	9.42

Victor in 213 games in his minor league pitching career, George Bamberger made only 10 brief appearances in the majors with the New York Giants and Baltimore Orioles. His post-playing major league career, however, was remarkable. In nine years as Baltimore's pitching coach, his pitchers won three Cy Young awards and posted 20 or more wins a total of 18 times. Bamberger's 1971 staff featured four 20-game winners, the only modern team to accomplish that feat.

Bamberger left the Orioles after the 1977 season to take the reins of a struggling Milwaukee Brewers franchise that had never posted a winning record. His positive demeanor and aggressive managing style endeared him to the players and fans. Bambi's Brewers soared to third place in 1978, winning 93 games. The turnaround was keyed by a lineup that led the league in batting and home runs and by the performance of Mike Caldwell. A journeyman pitcher for his first seven seasons, Caldwell won 22 games in his first year under Bamberger.

The Brewers were even better the following year, finishing second and winning 95 games, but it was not a good year for Bamberger. He suffered a midseason heart attack, and although he was able to return, the 54-year-old manager resigned in September to spend more time with his family.

He didn't stay away long, though. Bamberger took over as manager of the New York Mets in

1982. He was not able to duplicate the success he had enjoyed in Milwaukee and failed to turn the Mets around. They finished last, and Bamberger resigned after a 16–30 start in 1983. He returned to Milwaukee for two more seasons, but after finishing sixth in 1985 and 1986, he retired again.

Dave Bancroft

Bancroft, David James **SS**

1915–30 M(1924–1927, 249–363) B:4/20/1891, Sioux City, IA D:10/9/1972, Superior, WI Deb:4/14/1915, PHI NL BB/TR 5'9½", 160

G	AB	R	H	HR	RBI	OBP	SLG	AVG
1913	7182	1048	2004	32	591	.355	.358	.279

Dave "Beauty" Bancroft is less famous than some, but he's one of the three top fielding shortstops ever, along with Ozzie Smith and Art Fletcher. No shortstop ever handled more chances than Bancroft did in 1922 with the Giants—984.

At age 17 Bancroft tried out for Winona of the Class C Minnesota–Wisconsin League. "On the day before the season started, the manager came into the clubhouse and laid brand-new uniforms on a table," Bancroft said later. "I kept looking and I didn't find one for me, so I knew I didn't make the team. I cried all the way home." But he didn't give up, and in 1909 Bancroft caught on with Duluth in the same league. He hit only .210 but led the circuit in putouts and assists. He spent 1910 and 1911 with Superior and then played from 1912 to 1914 with Portland in both the Pacific Coast League and the Northwest League. In 1914 his 453 putouts led the Pacific Coast League.

The Philadelphia Phillies acquired him in 1915, and they promptly leaped from sixth place to their first pennant. Manager Pat Moran claimed it was his slick-fielding rookie shortstop who made the difference. Bancroft played a steady shortstop for Philadelphia for the next four seasons, but the Phillies finished in second place the next two years, slipped to fifth in 1918, and then plummeted to last in 1919. While in Philadelphia, Bancroft has earned his nickname from his habit of yelling "Beauty!" whenever his pitcher made a good pitch.

In 1920 Giants manager John McGraw became convinced Bancroft was just what his team needed to take the pennant. He asked New York owner Charles Stoneham to offer Phils president William Baker $100,000, shortstop Art Fletcher, and pitcher Bill Hubbell for Bancroft. When Stoneham called Baker on June 7, 1920, with the proposition, Baker could hardly contain himself. This was the largest amount of cash that had ever been offered in National League history—and he would have parted with Bancroft for far less. The deal was completed the next day.

With New York, Bancroft quickly established himself as an intelligent player. "Now we'd better go over our signs, young fellow," said Giants catcher Frank "Pancho" Snyder to the new arrival. "They may be new to you, and you've got to know them."

"Have you changed them lately?" asked Bancroft. "No, they're the same, but..." Snyder responded. "Well, never mind," Bancroft replied. "I know them already. I knew them when I was with the Phillies."

Bancroft was immediately named the captain of his new team, and he played a key role in the Giants winning three consecutive league championships from 1921 through 1923. A .260 hitter in Philly, Bancroft found his stroke in New York, hitting .318 in 1921, .321 in 1922, and .304 in 1923. A switch-hitting leadoff man who crowded the plate, Bancroft was not only a fiery team leader, but as tough as they came. In 1923 he showed up for duty with a high fever but insisted on playing. After the game he collapsed in the Polo Grounds clubhouse and a doctor was summoned. "Call an ambulance," said the physician. "The man has pneumonia."

In November 1923, the Giants traded Bancroft to the Braves, and he became Boston's player-manager, replacing Fred Mitchell. His first year Bancroft fined catcher Earl Smith $500 for tossing a chair out of a Philadelphia hotel room window. In July the Braves sold Smith to Pittsburgh, but he didn't forget the fine. He wanted his $500 back, and Bancroft saw no reason to return it. One day in Pittsburgh in 1927, Bancroft was crossing the plate on a run when Smith smashed him in the jaw and knocked him unconscious. Smith was suspended for 30 days and fined another $500. When the Pirates visited Boston, Bancroft attempted to have Smith served with papers for $15,000 in damages. The catcher climbed over the Braves Field fence to avoid the process server, leading to the headline in *The Sporting News*: "Blackguards Always Are Cowards."

Under Bancroft, the Braves finished eighth, fifth, seventh, and seventh. Boston owner Judge Emil Fuchs absolved Bancroft of any blame but replaced him with former catcher Jack Slattery following the 1927 season. And even though Bancroft hit better than .300 two of his four seasons as a player-manager, some felt that his double duties caused too much strain. "I feel that [Bancroft] cared immensely about playing shortstop and about going up there to bat in his turn," contended *Boston Herald* writer Burt Whitman, "but he never did enjoy himself thoroughly as a manager. He was the ballplayer first and last, not the manager."

In 1928 Bancroft went to Brooklyn as a player but was released following the next season. He returned to the Giants as a player-coach in 1930. Bancroft played little, recording a .059 average in 10 games, and retired. He remained with the Giants in a coaching capacity, often filling in for the ailing McGraw until 1932, when McGraw retired, and first baseman Bill Terry became New York's manager.

Bancroft managed second-place Minneapolis in the American Association in 1933, succeeding Donie Bush. Minneapolis sportswriter Charles Johnson said that Bancroft knew "the technical side of the game up and down. Like Bush, he was always a smart, fiery player. As John McGraw's trusted assistant for three years, he rated with the best brains in the game."

In 1936 Bancroft managed Sioux City of the Western League to a fifth-place finish in a six-team circuit. In 1947 he managed St. Cloud of the Class C Northern League and led them to a pennant by 10 full games.

In 1971 the Veterans Committee elected Bancroft to the Hall of Fame. "I was more surprised by my election than anything that ever happened to me," Bancroft said. "But my wife wasn't. She thought it should have come a little sooner." He died in October 1972 after a long illness.

Frank Bancroft

Bancroft, Frank Carter

Manager (1880–85, 1887, 1889, 1902, 375–333)
B:5/9/1846, Lancaster, MA D:3/30/1921, Cincinnati, OH

Frank "Banny" Bancroft never played professional baseball, but as a manager he was an able leader, an astute judge of talent, and a canny businessman, three qualities that served him well in a baseball career spanning 40 years.

Bancroft first managed during the Civil War, arranging baseball games between Union Army regiments. Later he settled in New Bedford, Massachusetts, ran several successful businesses, and in 1878 became manager of New Bedford's entry in the International Association, the first minor league. After the season he took his team barnstorming to Cuba, introducing baseball in the Caribbean. Two years later he was at the helm of Worcester when it entered the National League.

The innovative, independent-minded Bancroft was often at odds with the club owners because of his controversial decisions. He quit the Detroit Wolverines in 1882 over a trifling matter and during his career argued with enough owners to manage a record seven different major league teams. One of them, the Providence Grays, won the NL pennant in 1884 and then beat the New York Metropolitans in the first World Series, the high point of Bancroft's managing career. In 1892 he became business manager of the Cincinnati Reds, a post he held until his death in 1921.

Sal Bando

Bando, Salvatore Leonard **3B**

1966–81 B:2/13/1944, Cleveland, OH Deb:9/3/1966, KC AL BR/TR 6', 205

G	AB	R	H	HR	RBI	OBP	SLG	AVG
2019	7060	982	1790	242	1039	.355	.408	.254

Third baseman Sal Bando captained the feisty Oakland Athletics during their dynasty of the early 1970s, providing his share of punch and leadership to an exciting and talented ballclub. Although he retired third in career home runs by an American League third baseman—with 242, behind only Graig Nettles and Brooks Robinson—his strongest point was neither his hitting nor his fielding, but his drive to succeed.

Bando was a standout third baseman at Arizona State University and was signed by Kansas City Athletics scout Hank Peters in 1965 for a $30,000 bonus. He received brief trials with Kansas City in 1966 and 1967, but not until the A's moved to Oakland in 1968 did he begin to look like a serious major league player. In spring training that year, he hit 10 homers and earned a starting role. That season he played in all 162 A's games and led AL third basemen in putouts. Only 24, the rookie Bando was elected captain. The following season he was named to the AL All-Star team and posted a career-high 31 homers and 113 RBIs. From 1971 to 1975 Bando was a catalyst for Oakland's five straight trips to the postseason, and was three times more named to the All-Star Game.

Bando was at his best in the playoffs. "Playoff games have a different type of life to them because they are very pressure-oriented," he observed. "I think most players would agree with me that they are even more so than those in the World Series."

In Game 2 of the 1973 AL Championship Series against the Baltimore Orioles, Bando hit two of Oakland's four homers. "I could have easily had three home runs," Bando recalled. "In the third inning, with a man on base, I hit a shot to left field that looked like it was going to clear the fence. But Al Bumbry, the left fielder, got back there and leaped up to make the catch. In the photos of the play, it looked like he had reached three feet above the fence to get his glove on the ball."

The following season the Athletics and Orioles faced each other again in the ALCS. In Game 2 Bando homered in the fourth inning to give Oakland a 1–0 lead. In Game 3, with the game scoreless, he led off the fourth inning against Baltimore's Jim Palmer. The count went full and stayed there as Bando fouled off pitch after pitch. Finally, Bando launched a Palmer delivery down the left field line for another homer. It was the only run of the game, and it gave Oakland its third straight pennant.

Following the 1974 season, Bando engaged in a nasty salary arbitration with A's owner Charlie Finley. Bando eventually had to settle for $100,000, the same amount he had received in the previous season. A volley of negative comments went back and forth: Bando claimed the A's had "the worst front office in baseball," and Finley spoke of Bando's "unmitigated gall" and labeled him a "pop-off." All the commotion may have triggered Bando's horrible slump early in the 1975 season. In May of that year, during an embarrassing 10–5 loss, Bando scuffled with teammate Reggie Jackson in the dugout.

As Bando's bat and glove showed no signs of revival, his disposition worsened, particularly when manager Alvin Dark moved him from batting leadoff to eighth. Dark, a born-again Christian, also told Bando he was praying for him. The comment only infuriated the third baseman further. But after Dark's wife gave Bando's wife, Sandy, a religious book, Bando noted a distinct change in her personality. He read the same book, and before long he too had a different outlook.

Coincidentally or not, Bando started hitting, lifting his season average from .190 to .230. "I doubled my home run production, ending up with a respectable 15 for the season," recounted Bando. "I played some part in getting the A's into the league playoffs. These were not terrific accomplishments on the face of them, but they were to a guy who had been in the cellar."

In 1976, Bando played out his option with Oakland and signed with the Milwaukee Brewers. In five seasons with Milwaukee, Bando played third base, shortstop, second base, first base, and designated hitter; he even pitched three innings in a 1979 game. Bando did not resist the move to designated hitter. "I've learned to enjoy it because of the rest it provides," he said at the time. "It enables you to give 100 percent, mentally, to hitting." In 1981, his final season as a player, Bando played only 32 games, but became the regular third baseman in the pennant drive and batted .294 in the postseason.

After his retirement, he became a special assistant to the general manager with the Brewers. In late 1991 he was named Milwaukee's general manager. Bando hired Phil Garner as manager, and the Brewers won 92 games in the first season with the pair overseeing the club. Six and a half losing seasons followed; both Bando and Garner were fired during the summer of 1999.

Dan Bankhead

Bankhead, Daniel Robert **P**

1947, 1950–51 Negro League Player (1940–47)
B:5/3/1920, Empire, AL D:5/2/1976, Houston, TX
Deb:8/26/1947, BRO NL BR/TR 6'1", 184

W	L	PCT	G	SV	IP	BB	SO	ERA
9	5	.643	52	4	153^1	110	111	6.52

Jackie Robinson was the first modern black major leaguer, but it was Brooklyn's Dan Bankhead who, in the same season that Robinson came up, became the first-ever black major league pitcher. Of five Bankhead brothers who all played in the Negro Leagues, Dan was the only one to make it to the desegregated majors.

He had pitched from 1940 until 1947 for the Chicago American Giants, the Birmingham Black Barons, and the Memphis Red Sox. Despite being touted as the "next Satchel Paige" and "the fastest pitcher in baseball, black or white," he didn't enjoy the same level of success with the Dodgers as Rookie of the Year Robinson. True, the righthander did homer off Fritz Ostermueller in his first major league appearance on August 26, 1947, and he appeared in that fall's World Series (as a pinch runner), but those were the only highlights in Bankhead's otherwise mediocre debut year, during which he pitched in just four contests with a 7.20 ERA.

The next season he was farmed out to Nashua of the New England League, where he fired a no-hitter against Springfield. Bankhead returned to Brooklyn in 1950 and went 9–4. His career came to an end in 1951 after he pitched in only seven games that year.

Sam Bankhead

Sam Bankhead **SS-OF-2B-3B-P**

Negro League Player (1930–50) Manager B:9/18/1910, Empire, AL D:7/24/1976, Pittsburgh, PA BR/TR, 5'8", 175

Sam Bankhead was the oldest of five brothers who all played Negro League baseball. He was a powerful hitter, played almost every position at one time or another, and had a reputation for being a strong and accurate thrower. Bankhead started as a pitcher with the Birmingham Black Barons in 1930 and was converted to the field for the Nashville Elite

Giants. During his career he played shortstop, second base, and the outfield, in addition to spending time on the mound.

In 1935 he starred as an infielder for a championship Pittsburgh Crawfords team that also featured Judy Johnson, Josh Gibson, and Buck Leonard. He later played with Satchel Paige for the Homestead Grays and appeared in seven East-West All-Star Games. Like many of his teammates, Bankhead played winter ball in the Puerto Rican and Cuban leagues as well.

Bankhead was serving as player-manager of the Grays when the club disbanded in 1950. His younger brother Dan Bankhead had a brief major league career.

Ernie Banks

Banks, Ernest **SS–1B**

1953–71 Negro League Player (1950, 1953)
B:1/31/1931, Dallas, TX Deb:9/17/1953, CHI NL
BR/TR 6'1", 180

G	AB	R	H	HR	RBI	OBP	SLG	AVG
2528	9421	1305	2583	512	1636	.333	.500	.274

During his distinguished 19-year major league career Ernie "Mr. Cub" Banks never had the satisfaction of playing on a championship team. Yet Banks twice won the National League's Most Valuable Player Award—in 1958 and again in 1959, both seasons in which the Cubs finished in fifth place in an eight-team league.

Banks was a rarity—a durable, power-hitting shortstop. Referring to his performance at the plate, former NL home run king Mel Ott once commented, "How many shortstops can hit you a home run in the clutch?" From August 26, 1956, until June 23, 1961, Banks played in 717 consecutive games. At the time it was the third-longest streak in NL history behind Gus Suhr's 822 and Richie Ashburn's 730. He hit 512 homers during his career, drove in 1636 runs, and hit .274. Rival manager Jimmy Dykes once said, "Without him the Cubs would finish in Albuquerque."

Despite the weaknesses of his teammates, Banks managed consistently high spirits and a positive attitude, as made famous in his remark, "It's a great day for a ballgame. Let's play two." His reputation was known throughout baseball. Discussing the low morale on George Steinbrenner's Yankees, Oscar Gamble once said, "Ernie Banks is the only person who would have been happy to be here." A sunny disposition didn't make Banks any less of a competitor. In 1957 only four pitchers—Don Drysdale, Bob Purkey, Bob Friend, and Jack Sanford—dared to knock Banks down. Each time Mr. Cub got up and hit the next pitch out of the park.

Banks began his career at age 17 with the semi-pro Amarillo Colts, barnstorming in the South and Midwest before graduating to the Negro League Kansas City Monarchs. A two-year hitch in the Army interrupted his stint with the Monarchs. Upon returning he hit .386 with 20 home runs, but hitting baseballs in the Negro Leagues was not a lucrative occupation. "Five, 10, maybe $15,000 a year, and our biggest payday was in Lincoln, Nebraska—$20 for the night," said Banks. But the Chicago Cubs scouted Banks and liked what they saw, paying $10,000 to sign Banks and a pitcher named Bill Dickey. On the first day of batting practice Banks sent the first pitch into Wrigley Field's left-field bleachers.

When Banks was brought up in September 1953, he arrived in Chicago with another black shortstop, Gene Baker. "They felt Gene had more experience and could make the change more easily than I could," said Banks. But Banks adapted quickly to big league play, becoming a regular and soon establishing himself as a star. At one point in his career the St. Louis Cardinals owner August Busch offered Cubs owner P.K. Wrigley $500,000 for Banks' services; Wrigley turned him down.

Banks was moved to first base in 1962 because of knee problems and was already past his prime when Leo Durocher became the manager in 1966. In certain situations Banks had become a liability; for example, with men on base and less than two outs he had a tendency to ground into double plays. Durocher was frustrated because he knew that if he did not play the popular Banks—or even if he rested the player when he was ailing—the Chicago fans and media would be up in arms.

"He was a great player in his time," Durocher later wrote. "Unfortunately his time wasn't my time. He couldn't run, he couldn't field; toward the end he couldn't even hit. There are some players who instinctively do the right thing on the base paths. Ernie had an unfailing instinct for doing the wrong thing."

According to Durocher, these problems were compounded by Banks' inability to read signs and by a bad knee that would periodically swell to twice its normal size. Durocher appreciated Banks' enthusiasm but felt it was no longer an asset. Others felt that the autocratic Durocher resented Banks' unique position with the Cubs. Some alleged that Durocher tried to publicly embarrass the aging Chicago favorite. Banks, for his part, chose not to respond to Durocher's tactics or attitude. Even Durocher admitted that Banks never balked. "Never a troublemaker. He knew I wanted to get rid of him and it didn't affect our personal relationship a bit," said the manager.

The 1969 season was a major disappointment. The Cubs lost a huge lead to the Miracle Mets, and Banks' last chance to play in a World Series evaporated. The next season, on May 12, Banks hit his 500th career home run off Atlanta's Pat Jarvis, becoming only the ninth player to do so. After the game he jumped up on a chair in the clubhouse and shouted, "The riches of the game are in the thrills, not the money."

But Banks learned that fame can have a sinister aspect. In February 1970 a death threat was delivered by an anonymous phone call to Cubs coach Joe Becker at the Chicago training camp in Scottsdale, Arizona. "I've got a rifle and I'm gunning for Ernie Banks," said the caller. The FBI was brought in; Banks later said, "I thought I'd been traded." Shortly thereafter the FBI arrested a young man who had made the call from a Chicago YMCA.

Banks' final game was played with no fanfare at Wrigley Field on September 26, 1971. "I didn't want another year, but I didn't want a big deal either," he said. He stepped down in the off-season, but even before his retirement he had been voted the "Greatest Cub of All Time." Following his trade from the Cubs in 1973, Ferguson Jenkins said, "I don't think those people at Wrigley Field ever saw but two players they liked, Billy Williams and Ernie Banks. Billy never said anything and Ernie always said the right thing." Six years after he left the game, in 1977, Banks was inducted into baseball's Hall of Fame.

After leaving baseball as a player, Banks worked as a Cubs minor league instructor. He later worked as a public relations officer for Chicago's First African Bank and pursued a degree in finance from Northwestern University. In 1983 he pulled up stakes and moved to Los Angeles, where he placed commercial products in motion pictures. Later he worked as an executive with New World Van Lines.

Floyd Bannister

Bannister, Floyd Franklin **P**

1977–89, 1991–92 B:6/10/1955, Pierre, SD
Deb:4/19/1977, HOU NL BL/TL 6'1", 195

W	L	PCT	G	SH	IP	BB	SO	ERA
134	143	.484	431	16	2388	846	1723	4.06

Floyd Bannister was a product of the University of Arizona's powerhouse baseball program. He had great potential but, despite a few flashes of brilliance, failed to live up to advance billing.

The Sporting News honored him in 1976 as the College Player of the Year, and the Houston Astros made him the nation's top amateur draft pick that June. Bannister advanced to Houston the next season but was hampered by a variety of problems, including blisters on his pitching hand. After two seasons Houston dealt him to Seattle where, in 1982, he led the AL with 209 strikeouts. Yet he was never a consistent winner—his ERA never dropped below 3.35—in part because of his reluctance to pitch inside.

Taking advantage of free agency, Bannister signed with the White Sox in 1983. He helped bring a division championship to Chicago that year by going 13-1 after the All-Star break. He struggled after that bright spell, however, going 50–50 in his next four years in Chicago. The Sox traded Bannister and Dave Cochrane to the Royals after the 1987 season for mound prospects Melido Perez, John Davis, and Greg Hibbard. Bannister ended his career as a long reliever with California and Texas. He retired following the 1992 season.

Red Barber

Barber, Walter Lanier

Broadcaster B:2/17/1908, Columbus, MS
D:10/22/1992, Tallahassee, FL

Red Barber's greatest achievement was not so much that he was first in so many broadcasting endeavors, but rather that his influential broadcasting style has had a lasting effect on the sport of baseball. Barber defined for all time what a baseball broadcaster should be. Coupling a homespun, folksy style with a fierce professional discipline, Barber thought of himself as a reporter first and foremost. He was fond of quoting Commissioner Kenesaw Mountain Landis' instructions to the announcers before the first nationally broadcast World Series game in 1935: "I know you're very good and you know your business, but these ballplayers are very good, and I don't want you to try to play ball with them. You are to report what they do. These managers are very good. Don't try to second-guess them, don't try to manage. Just report what they do. The umpires are very efficient. Don't, for heaven's sake, second-guess them. You report what they do. Report everything you can see. Gentlemen, leave your opinions in your hotel room and report."

Barber's commitment to journalistic integrity and completeness and his love for the game offered him many opportunities outside the press box—to put on a Mobil Oil cap; pour a bowl of Wheaties; or say of a Dodgers home run, "That's a Real Old Goldie" (for a cigarette sponsor)—without ever becoming a shill for advertisers or a pitchman for the home team.

Barber was working at college radio station WRUF in Gainesville, Florida, in 1934 when Larry MacPhail invited him to Cincinnati to broadcast the Reds' games. "The Old Redhead" announced the Reds' games when they were at home and did re-creations from the teletype when they were out of town. Unlike broadcasters who tried to make the public believe re-creations were the real thing, Barber made a point of having the sounds of the teletype in the background. When the wire went out, he'd say, 'The wire went out.'

When MacPhail joined the Dodgers in 1938, he lifted the ban of radio broadcasts that the Yankees, Giants, and Dodgers had agreed to impose. He understood that, contrary to popular belief, "giving the games away for free" would boost attendance, not hurt it. Just as dramatically, he proclaimed that the Dodgers would broadcast both home and away games live, with Barber as the announcer.

The soft, friendly rhythms of Barber's voice were just what Brooklyn fans wanted on lazy summer afternoons. "Brooklyn had three million people and needed a voice," he once said, "and the fates made me that voice." Encouraged by fan response, Barber began to plumb his southern heritage for catch phrases that became his signatures: "the bases are FOB" (full of Brooklyns); "oh, doctor!"; "hold the phone"; and "tearin' up the pea patch."

When NBC decided to experiment by televising games in 1939, Barber was chosen as the announcer, making him not just the first radio baseball broadcaster in New York but the first TV baseball broadcaster anywhere. By 1940 he had announced six World Series on national radio; when the Series was televised for the first time in 1948, Barber sat behind the microphone.

During World War II, Barber took pride in using the power of radio for good—he solicited war bond sales and promoted Red Cross blood drives. But then he had his integrity tested in a visceral way. In 1945, when Dodger boss Branch Rickey told Barber he was going to hire a black player, Barber was upset by the news. A southerner, he contemplated resigning but finally concluded that he was a reporter first; nothing else mattered.

Ernie Harwell joined the Dodgers broadcasting team in 1948, and Vin Scully in 1950. Trained by Barber, both went on to become broadcasting legends themselves. Harwell said later, "Probably more than any announcer, we learned from him, every one of us."

Barber left the Dodgers in a salary dispute and joined the Yankees in 1954. With Mel Allen already on board and the addition of Jim Woods, the three may have been the finest broadcasting team ever. When Phil Rizzuto replaced Woods in 1956, the green announcer dismayed the two old hands. Woods said later that because of their different styles, "Allen and Barber had always been cool, aloof, toward each other. But after 1956, their common hostility toward Rizzuto brought them together."

For 10 years Allen and Barber were the voices of the Yankees, but ownership unceremoniously canned Allen in 1964 and dumped Barber two years later. In 1966 the Yankees finished in last place for the first time since 1912, and fans reacted appropriately—only 413 showed up for a game. When Barber asked cameramen to show the thousands of empty seats, he learned that they had been instructed otherwise. In fact, the cameramen were not supposed to show any balls hit down the foul lines, lest the viewing audience realized almost no one was at the stadium. That didn't stop Barber the journalist. "I don't know what the paid attendance is today," he said. "But whatever it is, it's the smallest in the history of the stadium. And this smallest crowd is the story, not the ballgame." After 33 years of play-by-play, the Yankees told Barber he was no longer needed.

After leaving the Yankees, Barber began a new career as a writer and published six books. His study of baseball on the air, *The Broadcasters*, is still the finest book on how life in the booth really works. His history of the signing of Jackie Robinson, *1947: The Year All Hell Broke Loose in Baseball*, is a masterpiece of American history.

In 1978 Barber was chosen as the first recipient of the Ford C. Frick Award with, appropriately, Mel Allen. He was featured for years on National Public Radio every Friday morning, chatting on *Morning Edition* with host Bob Edwards about life, his flower garden, and the game he so dearly loved. He died in 1992.

Steve Barber

Barber, Stephen David **P**
1960–74 B:2/22/1939, Takoma Park, MD
Deb:4/21/1960, BAL AL BL/TL 6', 200

W	L	PCT	G	SH	IP	BB	SO	ERA
121	106	.533	466	21	1999	950	1309	3.36

Flame-throwing lefthander Steve Barber was the first 20-game winner for the modern Baltimore Orioles, but he's best known for losing despite combining with Stu Miller to pitch a no-hitter.

As a rookie in 1960, Barber's fastball clocked at 95.5 miles per hour, the third-fastest mark then on record, trailing only legendary fireballers Walter Johnson and Bob Feller. But more than just the speed, opposing batters remember the movement on his fastball. He never developed an effective breaking ball or a changeup, but his fastball was rarely straight. Out of a stylish windup featuring a pause with his leg cocked, Barber's fastball darted all around the strike zone, and often out of it, leaving hitters guessing and uncomfortable in the batter's box. Barber could also throw a memorable sinker. "It felt like you were hitting a ball made of iron," Elrod Hendricks recalled. "Your hands would remember it the next day. And if you hit it early in the season on a cold day, you'd remember it all year."

As a rookie, Barber led the AL with 113 walks, a harbinger of the control problems that, along with arm trouble, would plague his 15-year career. The next year he tied Camilo Pascual for the league lead with eight shutouts, going 18–12. After spending part of 1962 on the disabled list, he recorded a 20–13 mark in 1963 and was named to his first All-Star team.

In 1966 he was having his best season—he had been selected for his second All-Star squad—when arm trouble shelved him in August and kept him from appearing in Baltimore's World Series sweep of the Los Angeles Dodgers.

In his first start of the 1967 season, Barber appeared to have come all the way back. He held the California Angels hitless until Jim Fregosi doubled with one out in the ninth, giving Barber with his second one-hitter. Two starts later, Barber faced the Detroit Tigers in the opener of a Sunday doubleheader at Baltimore. Through eight innings he held the Tigers hitless while issuing seven walks and hitting a batter. The Orioles made several spectacular plays in the field, perhaps the best by Barber when he stopped Jim Northrup's line drive through the box with his left hip and recovered to throw him out at first base. The Orioles scratched out a run in the bottom of the eighth without a hit, on three walks (one to Barber) and Luis Aparicio's sacrifice fly. Barber issued a pair of walks to start the ninth, and Wilson sacrificed the runners over. Willie Horton fouled out to the catcher for the second out, and Barber got ahead of Mickey Stanley, 1–2. Catcher Larry Haney called for a slider, but Barber shook him off for a changeup. The delivery bounced well in front of the plate, hit Haney on his chest protector, and rolled about 20 feet toward the first base dugout.

Dick Tracewski, the pinch runner on third base, remembers, "We were looking for a wild pitch because he was so wild. He was usually borderline wild, but on this day he was very wild." Tracewski slid home, beating Haney's throw to Barber, and the score was tied.

Barber walked Stanley for his 10th free pass of the game, one short of the AL record for a nine-inning contest, and Stu Miller relieved. Don Wert hit a bouncer up the middle. Shortstop Aparicio raced to his left to flag it down, but rookie second baseman Mark Belanger, who would win eight Gold Gloves at short, dropped Aparicio's throw. A second Tigers run crossed the plate on the play, and they held on for the 2–1 win. Barber had thrown 144 pitches in the first combined nine-inning no-hit loss in major league history. "If you can't get the ball over the plate, you don't deserve to win," he said afterwards.

Barber won only two of his next 10 decisions, and the Orioles traded him to the Yankees in July. In the next seven years he played with six different clubs, going 26–31. His most notable stopover came with the expansion Seattle Pilots in 1969. His constant visits to the trainer's room and his unreliability in the rotation drew severe rebukes from Jim Bouton, another pitcher trying to hang on after arm woes and author of *Ball Four*, in which Barber appears as a principal villain.

Jesse Barfield

Barfield, Jesse Lee **OF**

1981–92 B:10/29/1959, Joliet, IL Deb:9/3/1981, TOR AL BR/TR, 6'1", 205

G	AB	R	H	HR	RBI	OBP	SLG	AVG
1428	4759	715	1219	241	716	.338	.466	.256

Although he made only one All-Star Game appearance, Jesse Barfield was one of the most talented outfielders of the 1980s. He had an outstanding arm and, when he connected, home run power. However, he played the Toronto part of his career before the team rose to AL dominance.

After first playing in the majors in September of 1981, Barfield spent 1982 platooning in the Blue Jays' outfield under new skipper Bobby Cox. He showed a rocket for a right arm and finished second in the league in outfield assists. He also hit 18 home runs. As the Blue Jays began climbing out of the cellar, Barfield became one of their most dependable players. He could not keep an everyday role during his first several years because of his low batting average, but his power—including 27 homers in 1983—made sure that he would see plenty of action.

By 1984 his average was up to .284, and when the 1985 season started Barfield had finally become an everyday player. He gunned down 22 runners from his right field post in 1985, leading the league not only in outfield assists but also in double plays. He also hit

.289 with 27 homers, leading the Jays to their first postseason appearance.

In 1986 Barfield had the best year of his career. He not only won his first Gold Glove while leading American League outfielders in assists and double plays, but also hit .289, with a league-leading 40 homers. He had career highs in hits (170), runs (107), doubles (35), and RBIs (108), and was selected to the All-Star Game.

For the next few years, Barfield was generally considered to be among the game's best outfielders. His batting average, however, began to decline. Problems also developed off the field, when Jimmy Williams replaced Cox as manager. Barfield was a devout Christian, and in 1988 Williams halted clubhouse prayer meetings. The team later banned players from wearing the Blue Jay logo at charitable religious functions, and Barfield became a leading critic of the new policy. On April 30, 1989, Toronto traded him to the New York Yankees for injured pitcher Al Leiter. Barfield left the Jays as their all-time home run leader. Not long after, the team fired Williams and replaced him with Cito Gaston, who led the Blue Jays to the top of the AL East four times in the next five years.

Meanwhile, Barfield performed creditably with the Yankees. His 20 assists in 1989 topped the league, and he won a second Gold Glove. His average, however, slumped to .234. Barfield spent another three years with the Yankees. He later coached for Houston and Seattle.

Len Barker

Barker, Leonard Harold **P**

1976–85, 1987 B:7/7/1955, Fort Knox, KY Deb: 9/14/1976, TEX AL BR/TR 6'5", 225

W	L	PCT	G	SH	IP	BB	SO	ERA
74	76	.493	248	7	1323^2	513	975	4.34

Len Barker's promise was rarely fully realized, as he exhibited a 96-mph fastball but little control. In 1979, after he had spent a couple years primarily as a reliever, Barker was dealt from Texas to Cleveland, where he slowly gained command of his pitches. In 1980 he blossomed into a big winner with a 19–12 mark while leading the AL with 187 strikeouts. He also walked only 92 in 246 innings, a huge improvement over his former wildness, yet his ERA was a suspiciously high 4.17.

Barker began 1981 like gangbusters, firing a perfect game against Toronto on May 15, and he was the starting pitcher for the American League in the All-Star Game that year. Even though a spate of arm trouble limited him to eight wins in the strike-shortened season, he still managed his second strikeout crown.

With his arm seemingly recovered in 1982, Barker posted a 15–11 record and remained among the league strikeout leaders, but everything seemed to come apart in 1983, when his ERA ballooned to 5.11. Late that season, despite his problems, Atlanta traded outfielder Brett Butler, third baseman Brook Jacoby, pitcher Rick Behenna, and $150,000 for Barker. But as soon as Barker arrived in Atlanta his arm went sour. During the next two unfulfilling seasons he spent more time on the disabled list than on the mound and went 9–17. He pitched briefly for the Brewers in 1987 after a year away from the majors.

Al Barlick

Barlick, Albert Joseph

Umpire (1940–43, 1946–55, 1958–71) B:9/29/1907, Tioga, TX D:10/3/1998, Los Angeles, CA

When a labor strike shut down the coal mine where he worked in Springfield, Illinois, young Al Barlick turned to umpiring local sandlot games for $1 per contest. Soon he entered the minor leagues, and in 1940, when famed umpire Bill Klem was sidelined with an injury, Barlick was brought up to the majors. He stayed in the National League for the next 32 years, with time out for military service during World War II. He also took two years off following a heart attack in the mid-1950s.

Barlick worked a record seven All-Star Games and seven World Series. He was universally regarded as strict but fair—unyielding in his demand for respect. He controlled a ballgame as well as any umpire of his generation. Fellow umpire Ed Vargo called him "an umpire's umpire."

Barlick led the walkout of NL umpires in the 1970 Championship Series. The umpires missed the first game of the Cincinnati–Pittsburgh series, but returned for Game 2 with a four-year deal that increased their pay for postseason games as well as All-Star Games. Barlick called his final game the following season. In 1989 he became only the sixth umpire to be named to the Hall of Fame.

Jesse Barnes

Barnes, Jesse Lawrence **P**

1915–27 B:8/26/1892, Perkins, OK D:9/9/1961, Santa Rosa, NM Deb:7/30/1915, BOS NL BL/TR 6', 170

W	L	PCT	G	SH	IP	BB	SO	ERA
152	150	.503	422	26	2569²	515	653	3.22

Jesse Barnes went from big loser to big winner with no trouble at all—he just needed John McGraw's Giants behind him. Barnes started his career with the Boston Braves in 1915. By then they were no longer the "Miracle Braves," and before long they needed a miracle in order to win games. Barnes paced the National League in losses in 1917, but on January 8, 1918, along with second baseman "Laughing Larry" Doyle, he was dealt to the Giants for New York second baseman Buck Herzog.

"Nubby" Barnes spent much of that year in the Armed Services, but in 1919 he led the NL with 25 victories. He won another 20 the following year. In 1921 Barnes won two games in the World Series against the Yankees, and on May 7, 1922, he no-hit the Phillies. Traded back to Boston in June 1923, Barnes reverted to form, pacing the senior circuit in losses with 20.

Barnes' younger brother Virgil also hurled for the Giants. After Jesse Barnes was traded they faced each other 10 times, with Nubby compiling a 5–3 mark against Virgil.

Ross Barnes

Barnes, Roscoe Charles **SS-2B**

1871–79, 1881 B:5/8/1850, Mount Morris, NY D:2/5/1915, Chicago, IL Deb:5/5/1871, BOS NA BR/TR 5'8½", 145

G	AB	R	H	HR	RBI	OBP	SLG	AVG
234	1032	239	329	2	111	.356	.401	.319

The National League's first batting champion and a four-time .400 hitter, diminutive Ross Barnes used speed and a loophole in the rules to make himself a great hitter. He took advantage of a rule that declared any ball that landed in fair territory fair—even if it later rolled onto foul ground—by becoming expert at punching crazily bouncing bunts across the foul line while using his speed to leg out the hit.

In 1871 manager Harry Wright recruited Barnes and pitcher Al Spalding from the Forest City club of Rockford, Illinois, for his Boston Red Stockings of the new National Association of Professional Base Ball Players, the forerunner of the National League. At 5 feet 8 ½ inches tall and about 145 pounds, Barnes became the prototype of the small, speedy second baseman. Teamed with shortstop George Wright, Harry's brother, he helped make Boston's keystone combination the envy of the league. He also scored 459 runs in just 265 career NA games.

On offense, Barnes was an immediate star. In 1871 he squibbed his way to the first of three straight .400-plus seasons and led the league with 66 runs scored in 31 games. According to the records of those early days, Barnes led the league in batting average, slugging percentage, hits, and doubles for each of the next two seasons. Remarkably, for the five years of the National Association, he averaged almost two hits per game. He also scored 459 runs in just 265 career NA games.

Following the Association's final season in 1875, Barnes jumped to William Hulbert's Chicago White Stockings of the new National League, as did Spalding and two other Boston stars. Joined by a young Cap Anson, they formed the foundation of the first NL pennant winner. Barnes was by far the best hitter of the National League's first season, becoming the first player to lead two major leagues in batting, slugging, on-base percentage, runs, hits, doubles, total bases, and walks. He also led NL second basemen in fielding percentage and became the second National Leaguer to go 6-for-6 in a game, accomplishing the feat on July 27, exactly one month after Dave Force had established the standard.

In 1877 the NL pulled the rug out from under Barnes. The league adopted the current rule governing foul balls, decreeing that a groundball had to pass the base in fair territory in order to count as fair. That change eliminated Barnes' primary offensive weapon. His numbers took a monumental dive that season, with his batting average down 157 points, his on-base percentage down 129 points, and his slugging down 307 points. Barnes was a career .396 hitter under the old rules and a .269 hitter thereafter.

His 1877 output also dropped because of an illness that kept him out of action for three months. The White Stockings deducted $1,000 of his $2,500 salary for the season, common practice for that era. Barnes then became the first star player to take his team to court. Beginning a pattern that would last nearly a century, the court ruled in favor of the owners. Barnes played two more seasons in the National League—1879 for Cincinnati and 1881 for Boston—but never recovered his batting stroke.

Rex Barney

Barney, Rex Edward **P**

1943, 1946–50 B:12/19/1924, Omaha, NE
D:8/12/1997, Baltimore, MD Deb:8/18/1943, BRO NL
BR/TR 6'3", 185

W	L	PCT	G	SH	IP	BB	SO	ERA
35	31	.530	155	6	597[2]	410	336	4.31

Rex Barney got his pro start with Durham in the Class B Piedmont League in 1942. Thanks in part to World War II, the hard-throwing 19-year-old was in Ebbets Field before the next season was over. After that it was Barney's turn, and he spent the next two years in the armed service.

Barney pitched with Brooklyn from 1946 to 1950. "The fastest [pitcher I ever faced] might have been Rex Barney," recalled slugger Ralph Kiner, and a lot of his fellow players might have agreed with him. That was the good news. The bad news was Barney's control—or lack of it. Only in 1948 did he fan more batters than he walked. He no-hit the New York Giants on September 9, 1948. For that season—his best—he was 15–13 with a 3.10 ERA.

After his playing career was over, Barney became a broadcaster and a long-time public address announcer for the Baltimore Orioles. In 1993 he authored an autobiography with writer Norman Macht. He was beloved in Baltimore for his good humor and his trademark "thank you" sign-off on even the most mundane public service announcements.

Jim Barr

Barr, James Leland **P**

1971–80, 1982–83 B:2/10/1948, Lynwood, CA
Deb:7/31/1971, SF NL BR/TR 6'3", 205

W	L	PCT	G	SH	IP	BB	SO	ERA
101	112	.474	454	20	2065[1]	469	741	3.56

Although Jim Barr once pitched nearly 14 consecutive perfect innings, he failed to record a perfect game because he performed his feat over two separate starts. On August 23, 1972, he retired the last 21 Pittsburgh batters, and on August 29, he set down the first 20 St. Louis Cardinals who faced him—the major league record for most consecutive batters retired. Not bad for a fellow who began his big league career as a reliever.

Barr was a star at the University of Southern California, where his teammates included Bill Lee, Dave Kingman, and Brent Strom. Drafted by five other clubs (the Angels, Phillies, Yankees, Pirates, and Twins), Barr signed with the Giants in June 1970. They sent him to Amarillo and Phoenix for seasoning before bringing him up in the 1971 season.

As a reliever Barr helped the Giants win the National League West and soon became a member of the starting rotation. Not an overwhelming mound force, he was nevertheless very consistent. From 1973 to 1977 he never won more than 15 or fewer than 11 games.

After the 1978 season he signed with the Angels as a free agent but suffered arm trouble and spent time on the disabled list. California released him in April 1981, and Barr signed a minor league contract with the White Sox's Edmonton farm club. Even they released him, but he returned to the major leagues with San Francisco in 1982 and 1983, where he was reasonably effective in short relief.

Marty Barrett

Barrett, Martin Glenn **2B**

1982–91 B:6/23/1958, Arcadia, CA Deb:9/6/1982,
BOS AL BR/TR 5'10", 176

G	AB	R	H	HR	RBI	OBP	SLG	AVG
941	3378	418	938	18	314	.340	.347	.278

Usually an afterthought in the potent Boston Red Sox lineup, Marty Barrett emerged as its best hitter in the team's valiant, yet ultimately doomed, charge through the 1986 postseason. In the regular season Barrett hit .286 and set career highs in games played, at bats, hits, and RBIs. He also fanned just 31 times in 625 at bats; he had more walks than strikeouts for nine of his 10 seasons.

In the American League Championship Series Barrett paced the Red Sox with 11 hits in 30 at bats, as Boston outlasted the California Angels in seven games. Barrett, the ALCS Most Valuable Player, was just warming up.

Barrett went 13-for-30 in the World Series for a team-high .433 batting average. Barrett posted a .514 on-base percentage for the Series. Ironically, one of the most lasting images of that October was Mets reliever Jesse Orosco striking out Barrett to end the World Series. Barrett's 24 playoff hits remained a postseason record until 1995, when Atlanta's Marquis Grissom collected 25 in three playoff rounds.

Ed Barrow

Barrow, Edward Grant
Executive M(1903–04, 1918–20, 310–320)
B:5/10/1868, Springfield, IL D:12/15/1953, Port Chester, NY

Edward Barrow did just about everything that could be done in baseball except play the game. He discovered Honus Wagner, put Babe Ruth in the outfield, managed a championship team, and finally found his life's work in helping to turn the New York Yankees into baseball's greatest dynasty.

Barrow was born in Springfield, Illinois, but his family moved to Des Moines, Iowa, when he was 9. He quit school at age 16 to work for *The Des Moines Daily News*. He moved on to other local newspapers, in that era when every city had several, serving at *The Blade* and then becoming advertising manager of *The Leader*. But Barrow also managed a Des Moines semipro baseball team, and, after moving to Pittsburgh in 1890 to be assistant manager of the Staley Hotel, he formed a partnership with Harry Stevens, who owned the scorecard and soda pop concession at Exposition Park.

In 1894 the ambitious Barrow decided to get into baseball full time. With Stevens again as a partner, he became manager, general manager, and one-third owner of the Wheeling, West Virginia, club of the fledgling Inter-State League. The league died in midseason, but Barrow and Stevens had a winning team and they shifted it smoothly into another league.

The next year the Atlantic League was formed, and Barrow acquired the Paterson, New Jersey, franchise, where he pioneered night baseball. By 1897 he was also president of the league. One day he noticed a long-armed, bow-legged youngster tossing rocks along the Ohio River. The kid turned out to be Honus Wagner. Even if Barrow had done nothing else in baseball, he would be remembered for discovering the future great. In 1897 Wagner hit .379 in half a season for Paterson before Barrow sold him to Louisville of the National League.

In 1900 Barrow purchased a quarter interest in the Eastern League's Toronto Maple Leafs and installed himself as manager; in 1902 Toronto won the pennant. That brought Barrow the opportunity to manage the Detroit Tigers. He took them from seventh to fifth in 1903, but the Tigers were back in seventh after 84 games in 1904 when Barrow resigned because of a disagreement with team business manager Frank Navin. It was a classic confrontation between a banker's mentality—Navin wanted to keep Detroit's expenditures within its receipts—and a builder's; Barrow wanted to spend money to create a winning team, believing that increased income would follow.

Barrow returned to the minors, managing Indianapolis of the American Association for two years and then returning to Toronto in 1907, where he won another Eastern League pennant. He then managed Montreal of the Eastern League, and before the year was out he was elected league president. During his reign, which lasted until 1918, he renamed the circuit the International League.

In 1914, when the Federal League tried to achieve major league status overnight, it not only raided stars from the American and National Leagues but also from the high minor leagues. Barrow's spirited defense of his league's integrity won the respect of AL President Ban Johnson. When Red Sox manager Jack Barry went into the service during World War I, Johnson recommended Barrow for the position to team owner Harry Frazee.

The team Barrow took over in 1918 retained the nucleus of the championship Red Sox squads of 1915 and 1916. The pitching staff was particularly strong. Outfielder Harry Hooper suggested to Barrow that Babe Ruth, the team's outstanding pitcher, could also hit well and might take a turn in the outfield. Barrow agreed, and Ruth ended up leading the league with 11 home runs, helping Boston to win the pennant and the World Series.

Barrow had some problems corralling Ruth, who always regarded team rules as something for the other guys. One day after Ruth and Barrow exchanged words, Barrow ordered him into the clubhouse and began stripping off his jacket and tie in preparation for a fight. Barrow was 30 years older than the Babe, but when the young player saw that his manager was serious, he backed down.

Ruth was a full-time outfielder in 1919, hitting a record 29 homers. But the Red Sox finished sixth, and Frazee, whose real love was Broadway shows, suffered a string of financial flops and needed cash. On January 2, 1920, Frazee sold Ruth to the Yankees for $125,000 plus a $350,000 mortgage on Fenway Park.

Harry Sparrow, the Yankees' business manager, died that year, and Frazee did Yankees owner Jacob Ruppert another good turn by recommending Barrow for the job. The Yankees that Barrow came to in 1921 had talent, but the team hadn't quite jelled. Part of the problem was that the players refused to abide by manager Miller Huggins' rules, and the front office had let them get away with it.

One of Barrow's first moves was to call a team meeting to declare that Huggins had been elected God and that anyone who didn't follow his commandments was likely to wind up doing penance in an unsavory location. With that settled, the Yankees went out and won their first pennant. Two more followed, along with a world championship in 1923.

Their success was not just a matter of team rules. Barrow was a great judge of baseball talent, and he had Ruppert's money to back him. Frazee was a big help: his string of flops continued and he sold off the best Red Sox players to the Yankees. Barrow's philosophy of spending money to make money worked beautifully in New York. After Yankee Stadium opened in 1923, the cash rolled in. But he did far more than simply buy pennants. He increased the Yankees' emphasis on scouting and development, and eventually the Bombers' farm system became the most productive in baseball.

Barrow was also willing to take a chance. In 1925 Tony Lazzeri was a promising slugger in the Pacific Coast League, but most major league teams shied away from him because he was epileptic. Barrow bought his contract and Lazzeri went on to a Hall of Fame career. Ten years later another West Coast star was considered damaged goods because of a knee injury. Barrow sent a doctor to examine the young outfielder. Pronounced fit, Joe DiMaggio became a star.

When Ruppert died in 1939, Barrow was named club president. He served in that capacity until 1945 when Ruppert's heirs sold the team and he was named chairman of the board. He retired two years later. His Yankees legacy included 14 pennants and 10 world championships. In addition, he left in place the groundwork for a string of pennants in the late 1940s and 1950s. Twice named *The Sporting News* Executive of the Year, Barrow was elected to the Hall of Fame in 1953, six months before his death.

Jack Barry

Barry, John Joseph **SS–2B**

1908–17, 1919 M(1917, 90–62) B:4/26/1887, Meriden, CT D:4/23/1961, Shrewsbury, MA Deb:7/13/1908, PHI AL BR/TR 5'9", 158

G	AB	R	H	HR	RBI	OBP	SLG	AVG
1223	4146	532	1009	10	429	.321	.303	.243

"Black Jack" Barry was the kind of player whose worth cannot be measured by statistics alone. Despite a .243 lifetime average, he was regarded as one of the better clutch hitters of his day. Baseball writer and historian Fred Lieb wrote, "All during Jack Barry's baseball career, his batting average lied. He saved his singles for vital moments when a hit was needed to win a 2–1 or 3–2 game."

Barry was an outstanding fielder who led AL shortstops and second basemen in fielding average once each. But the only statistic that really mattered with Barry was his team's won-lost record. On that count he did well, playing for six pennant winners in 11 seasons.

Connie Mack recruited Barry straight from the Holy Cross campus into the Athletics lineup in July of 1908. As a rookie shortstop he immediately meshed with another college graduate at second base, Eddie Collins. In 1909 the A's were locked in a bitter pennant race with the Tigers. In a late September series that year the Tigers literally mauled Philadelphia. Ty Cobb spiked both Barry and third baseman Frank "Home Run" Baker, and Detroit shortstop Donie Bush slid into Collins' ankle so hard it swelled to twice its normal size. The Tigers went on to win the pennant, but the young Athletics had learned what it took to win. In 1910 they took the pennant by 14 ½ games over the Yankees and went on to humble the Chicago Cubs in the World Series.

A year later slick-fielding John "Stuffy" McInnis replaced aging Harry Davis at first base, completing what came to be known as "the $100,000 Infield." In today's market, four more zeros might be added to the price. First baseman McInnis, second baseman Collins, and Barry would all have been strong Gold Glove Award candidates had that award been in existence at the time. Third baseman Baker was a bit awkward in the field but more than made up for it with his powerful bat and, of course, he and Collins both went on to the Hall of Fame.

The A's won the 1911 pennant easily and then defeated John McGraw's New York Giants in the World Series, four games to two. Most of the credit for the win went to Baker and Philadelphia's excellent pitching staff, but McGraw reserved special praise for the keystone combination of Barry and Collins, claiming they were better than the Cubs' legendary duo of Joe Tinker and Johnny Evers.

One of the most successful Barry–Collins maneuvers soon became standard. Whenever a double steal was attempted with runners on first and third, the man not covering a base would head for the middle of the infield. If the runner on third made a move toward home the throw could be cut off and returned to the catcher for a tag. If the runner stayed on third the throw was allowed to go through in order to nail the runner coming from first.

Barry had his best season at bat in 1913, hitting .275 with 85 RBIs as the A's won the pennant. They then bested McGraw's Giants in the World Series once again. Another pennant followed in 1914, but the "Miracle Braves" shocked Philadelphia in the World Series.

The Federal League formed in 1914 and, by offering higher salaries, lured many players away from the American and National leagues, forcing teams to raise players' salaries in order to keep them. Connie Mack decided to sell off most of his stars and rely instead on younger players. In the middle of the 1915 season he sold Barry to the Boston Red Sox for $8,000. Installed at second base, Barry helped the Red Sox finish first and defeat the Phillies in the World Series. In 1916 Barry played on his sixth pennant winner in seven seasons, but injuries limited him to only 94 games, and he sat out the World Series victory over Brooklyn.

When Boston manager Bill Carrigan retired after the 1916 season Barry was named to replace him. As player-manager he led the league's second basemen in fielding, but his batting average fell to a mere .214. The Red Sox won 90 games—only one fewer than the 1916 champions—but finished second to the Chicago White Sox.

After the 1917 season Barry entered the military. When he returned in 1919, Ed Barrow, who'd taken the club to a pennant the year before, was manager. After 31 games Barry was sold back to the Athletics, but he felt that he was slowing down and decided to retire. He became the baseball coach at Holy Cross, where he served for more than three decades. In 1952 he was named College Coach of the Year.

Dick Bartell

Bartell, Richard William **SS-3B-2B**

1927–43, 1946 B:11/22/1907, Chicago, IL D: 8/4/1995, Alameda, CA Deb:10/2/1927, PIT NL BR/TR 5'9", 160

G	AB	R	H	HR	RBI	OBP	SLG	AVG
2016	7629	1130	2165	79	710	.355	.391	.284

Dick Bartell was a good-hitting, fine-fielding shortstop throughout the 1930s. A two-time All-Star and the key defensive player on three pennant winners, he batted over .300 six times, but his aggressive personality caused him to be traded frequently. Bartell fought tooth and nail for every base hit and every putout, which helped earn him the nickname "Rowdy Richard." Although he brought fire to each new team, he inevitably wore out his welcome after a few years.

He was not the only such player at the time. The fans loved or hated players like Bartell, usually depending on whether they were with the home team or the visitors. In 1937 he led off for the Giants in Brooklyn's first home game of the season. When the first pitch was called a strike, Bartell turned to register his usual complaint. At that moment a large ripe tomato thrown from the stands smashed into his chest.

Upon graduating from Alameda High School in California in 1926, Bartell was offered athletic scholarships to three colleges. Instead he signed with the Pittsburgh Pirates. At the end of his first minor league season with the Eastern League's Bridgeport Bears, the Pirates brought him to the majors for the last game of the 1927 season. Pittsburgh thought so highly of him that it traded away another shortstop prospect, Joe Cronin.

In 1928, substituting often for sore-armed shortstop Glenn Wright, Bartell hit .305. When Wright was traded to Brooklyn after the season, Bartell inherited his job. In 1929 and 1930 he batted .302 and .320, respectively. He then was traded to the Phillies for shortstop Tommy Thevenow and pitcher Claude Willoughby. Thevenow hit .213 and Willoughby went 0–2 for Pittsburgh, while Bartell became an All-Star in Philadelphia, starting for the National League in the first game in 1933.

Following the 1934 season, in which he batted .310, Bartell was traded to the New York Giants for four players and cash. Bartell helped the Giants win pennants in 1936 and 1937. He hit a rousing .381 in the Giants' unsuccessful effort against the Yankees in the 1936 World Series.

In 1937 Bartell was again selected to the All-Star Game, but after a disappointing 1938 he was traded in a six-player swap to the Chicago Cubs. Bartell lasted only one season in Chicago. His predecessor, the popular Billy Jurges, had been the league's finest fielding shortstop, and anyone replacing him suffered by comparison. As one Cubs historian put it, Bartell "specialized in fumbling balls hit to him. He executed many a throw to first base that had dugout denizens and even box-seat patrons scrambling to get out of the way." Moreover, his batting average tumbled to .238.

In December 1939 Bartell was traded to Detroit, and his arrival there coincided with the Tigers' surprise pennant. But in the 1940 World Series against Cincinnati, Bartell's team once more came up a loser. No longer the hitter he had been and slowing in the field, Bartell was released by the Tigers after five games in 1941. He rejoined the Giants and hit .303 in his last season as a regular. For two more seasons he filled a utility role in New York, then spent two years in the service during World War II. After appearing in five games in 1946, he retired as a player.

Bartell spent 10 years as a minor league manager and major league coach before entering the business world in 1957. His autobiography, *Rowdy Richard*, written with Norman Macht, was published to favorable reviews in 1987.

Kevin Bass

Bass, Kevin Charles **OF–DH**
1982–95 B:5/12/1959, Redwood City, CA
Deb:4/9/1982, MIL AL BB/TR 6', 183

G	AB	R	H	HR	RBI	OBP	SLG	AVG
1571	4839	609	1308	118	611	.325	.411	.270

The career of Kevin Bass was all about 1986. That year the slender outfielder played in his only All-Star Game, reached the postseason for the first and last time, and made the final out of what some have called the greatest game of all time.

Bass played in only 18 games with Milwaukee before being shipped to Houston in 1982. The Astros loved his strong outfield arm, terrific speed, and beautiful uppercut swing from both sides of the plate. He earned a full-time job a year before his breakthrough 1986 campaign. In the Astrodome, baseball's toughest hitting park, Bass batted .311 with 20 homers and 22 stolen bases.

Bass enjoyed three two-hit games in the 1986 Championship Series against the Mets before the classic Game 6 affair. Down 7–6 in the bottom of the 16th, he faced Jesse Orosco with two on and two out. On a 3–2 pitch, Bass whiffed at a slider to end the Series.

In 1987 Bass clubbed three extra-inning homers, and drove in a career-high 85 runs. He batted .300 and stole 31 bases the following season. In 1989 he became one of the few batters ever to slug grand slams from both sides of the plate in the same season. Chronic injuries that season, and in the years that followed, kept him from playing every day. Over the last seven years of his career he played with the Giants, Mets, Astros, and Orioles, never exceeding 44 RBIs.

Earl Battey

Battey, Earl Jesse **C**
1955–67 B:1/5/1935, Los Angeles, CA Deb:9/10/1955, CHI AL BR/TR 6'1", 205

G	AB	R	H	HR	RBI	OBP	SLG	AVG
1141	3586	393	969	104	449	.351	.409	.270

Throughout the early 1960s, Earl Battey was one of the superior hitting and throwing (but slower running) catchers in the American League. A goiter problem frequently caused his weight to balloon—which partly accounted for his poor mobility on the basepaths and his unfortunate knack for hitting into double plays—but his other skills made him a four-time All-Star Game selection and a three-time Gold Glove winner.

Battey's big break came on April 4, 1960, when the Chicago White Sox, his original team, traded him and first baseman Don Mincher to Washington for first baseman Roy Sievers. Immediately inserted as the Senators' first-string catcher, Battey appeared in 805 of the first 970 games the club played in Minnesota, starting in 1961. In 1962 Battey hit .280, threw out 24 runners, and picked off 13. After suffering a broken cheekbone, he wore a special helmet after that season. The following season he had a career-high 26 homers and 84 RBIs. He hit for his highest average in 1965 when he batted .297, and that year he topped the voting for the AL All-Star team.

Battey suffered a memorable injury in the third game of the 1965 World Series against Los Angeles when he ran into a neck-high crossbar at Dodger Stadium, attempting to catch a foul popup. Even though he could barely speak or turn his head, he played the remainder of the Series.

Hank Bauer

Bauer, Henry Albert **OF**
1948–61 M(1961–62, 1964–69, 594–544)
B:7/31/1922, East St. Louis, IL Deb:9/6/1948, NY AL BR/TR 6', 192

G	AB	R	H	HR	RBI	OBP	SLG	AVG
1544	5145	833	1424	164	703	.347	.439	.277

Columnist Jim Murray once said that Hank Bauer had a face like a clenched fist, an impression enhanced by Bauer's Marine Corps crew cut. Bauer was the epitome of the hard-nosed ballplayer when he played left field with Casey Stengel's great Yankees teams of the late 1940s and early 1950s. He played on nine pennant winners in a 10-year period and he held his own with the greats of those teams, making the American League All-Star team three times.

Making the World Series was serious business to Bauer. "They had an expression on the Yankees, 'Don't screw with our money,'" Bauer recalled, "because we were going to the bank every October."

Bauer had served with the Marines in the Pacific during World War II, and he had been involved in the invasion and occupation of Okinawa. On his 53rd day on the island, while engaged in digging out Japanese holdouts, he was hit in his left thigh by a piece of shrapnel. "We went in with 64, and six of us came out," he once reminisced. "The only thing they ever told us was to keep your head and your ass down."

After V-J Day, Bauer signed with the Yankees' Kansas City Blues farm club for $175 a month, with the proviso that if he was still playing on Opening Day, 1946, his pay would be raised to $200 with an additional $200 bonus. He spent the 1946 season with the 3-I League's last-place Quincy Gems and then played the next two seasons in Kansas City, where he hit .300 each year.

When Bauer was called up from Kansas City for a brief trial in late 1948 he exhibited his usual hustle. Once, after snaring a ball in deep right-center, he noticed that center fielder Joe DiMaggio was glaring at him. When Bauer asked DiMaggio if he'd done something wrong, DiMaggio replied, 'No, you didn't do anything wrong, but you're the first son of a bitch who ever invaded my territory.'

Bauer began playing regularly for the Yankees in 1949 and became a key component in Casey Stengel's platoon system, usually alternating with either Enos Slaughter or Gene Woodling. "I didn't like it, but there wasn't much I could do about it," Bauer said. "He was the boss...Later on in my career, when I was almost through, I finally realized he probably prolonged my career a couple of years."

At the plate Bauer had a distinct style. "I was a fastball hitter," he explained. "And I could hit the breaking ball from the middle in. I couldn't throw a ball to right field. If I hit a ball that way, it was accidentally. I was a dead-pull hitter."

In December 1959 Bauer, along with Marv Throneberry, outfielder Norm Siebern, and World Series hero Don Larsen, was traded to the Kansas City Athletics for first baseman Kent Hadley, shortstop Joe DeMaestri, and a young Roger Maris.

In 1961 Charlie Finley hired Bauer to manage at Kansas City, and then Finley fired him in 1962. In 1963 Bauer coached for Billy Hitchcock in Baltimore, taking over the club the next year and bringing them in third. In 1966 Bauer's Orioles, augmented by Frank Robinson and Luis Aparicio, won the AL pennant and swept the Dodgers in the World Series. Baltimore coach Earl Weaver replaced Bauer in mid-1968. Bauer recalled that he hadn't wanted Weaver on his staff. "I could see the handwriting on the wall," he said.

Frank Baumholtz

Baumholtz, Frank Conrad **OF**

1947–49, 1951–57 B:10/7/1918, Midvale, OH D:12/14/1997, Winter Springs, FL Deb:4/15/1947, CIN NL BL/TL 5'10½", 175

G	AB	R	H	HR	RBI	OBP	SLG	AVG
1019	3477	450	1010	25	272	.342	.389	.290

Frank Baumholtz may have had the toughest job in baseball in the mid-1950s: playing center field in Wrigley Field between lumbering fellow outfielders Ralph Kiner and Hank Sauer. According to Kiner, the only encouraging words Baumholtz ever received from his comrades were, "You take it!"

As a star basketball guard at Ohio University, Baumholtz was named All-America in 1941 and MVP of that year's National Invitation Tournament. He performed professionally with Youngstown of the ill-fated National Basketball League in 1946–47 and with Cleveland of the National Basketball Association in 1947–48; he was the top scorer in both circuits.

Baumholtz played only one year of minor league baseball, dividing the 1941 season between the California and Pioneer leagues before being drafted into the armed forces in World War II. After his discharge he spent a year at Columbia of the Class A Sally League, and the next year burst onto the major league scene as an outfielder for the Cincinnati Reds. He performed well enough to finish fifth in the 1947 Rookie of the Year balloting, the first year the honor was given. That season Baumholtz played in a career-high 151 games, had a .283 average, and, revealing a powerful arm in right field, cut down 18 opposing base runners; on June 18 of that year he salvaged Ewell "The Whip" Blackwell's no-hitter against the Boston Braves by spearing a liner off the bat of Bama Rowell.

Baumholtz's average rose to .296 in 1948, but was in an extended slump in 1949 when he was traded to the Cubs, along with Sauer, for outfielders "Harry the Hat" Walker and Harry Lowrey. In Chicago, Baumholtz's numbers continued to slide, in 1950 he was dropped back to the minors with the Pacific Coast League's Los Angeles Angels. That dose of reality brought Baumholtz's bat back to life. He hit 15 homers, a circuit-leading 53 doubles, and compiled a .379 batting average. He was the last Coast Leaguer to register more than 250 hits in a season, with 254.

Baumholtz returned to the National League with a vengeance, registering batting averages of .284, .325, .306, .297, and .289 for the Cubs from 1951 to 1955. In 1952 his .325 average would have been second only to Stan Musial's .336 for the league batting crown, but Baumholtz did not have enough at bats to qualify.

Baumholtz began pinch hitting in 1954, and in 1955 he exploded, going 15-for-37. Sold outright to the Phillies, he played only 15 games in their outfield in 1956 but continued pinch-hitting through the 1957 season.

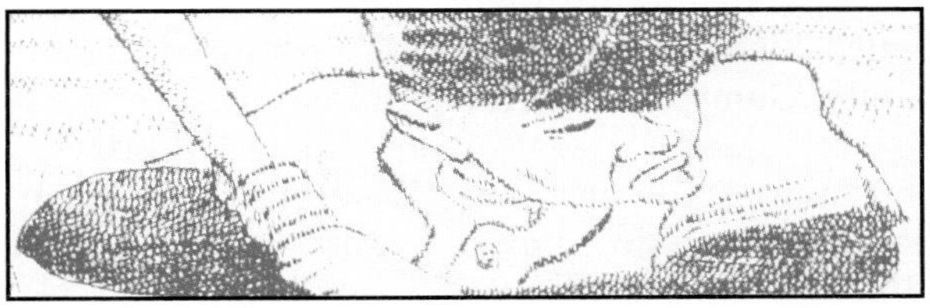

Buzzie Bavasi

Bavasi, Emil Joseph

Executive B:12/12/1915, New York, NY

E.J. "Buzzie" Bavasi's life in baseball began modestly enough, but eventually he became one of the game's most successful executives. He engineered world championships for the Dodgers on both coasts, started the San Diego Padres from scratch, and was instrumental in dozens of former players entering the Hall of Fame through the Veterans Committee.

Bavasi's front office career began in 1939 when Brooklyn Dodgers' executive Larry MacPhail hired him as assistant to the team's traveling secretary and publicity director. The following year Bavasi was named business manager of the Dodgers' Class D minor league team in Georgia. As a $30 per week employee, he even suited up for a few games when the team's roster was reduced to nine men. Bavasi was named general manager of the Triple A Montreal Royals in 1948. After three seasons in Montreal, he earned a promotion to Brooklyn as general manager of the Dodgers.

From 1951 to 1966 the Dodgers won eight National League pennants and four world championships. Four years removed from the team's only world championship in Brooklyn, the relocated Dodgers won the World Series in Los Angeles in 1959. *The Sporting News* honored Bavasi as baseball's top executive that season. He engineered one of his greatest trades the following spring, acquiring bullpen ace Ron Perranoski from the Chicago Cubs for Don Zimmer, a .165 hitter.

One of Bavasi's few mistakes involved Roberto Clemente, whom the Dodgers had signed out of Puerto Rico in 1954. According to a rule of the time, any amateur signing a contract for more than $4,000 had to be placed on the major league roster immediately or risk being taken in a draft of unprotected bonus players. Dodgers scout Al Campanis fought to put Clemente on Brooklyn's roster, but Bavasi assigned him to Montreal. The Dodgers lost Clemente to the Pirates at the end of the season.

In 1968 Bavasi took on a new challenge as part owner of the expansion Padres. He doubled as team president, serving in that role until his resignation in 1977. Almost immediately, Gene Autry hired him as vice president of the California Angels. In 1978 Bavasi became a member of the Veterans Committee, participating in Hall of Fame elections until his retirement in 1999.

Don Baylor

Baylor, Don Edward **DH-OF-1B**

1970–88 M(1993–98, * 439–469) B:6/28/1949, Austin, TX Deb:9/18/1970, BAL AL BR/TR 6'1", 195

G	AB	R	H	HR	RBI	OBP	SLG	AVG
2292	8198	1236	2135	338	1276	.346	.436	.260

Perhaps the classic designated hitter, Don Baylor brought power, speed, desire, and leadership to a half-dozen major league teams. The first of these qualities was shown by his career mark of 338 home runs. The second by his being a feared baserunner who not only stole 285 bases in his career but took great pride in busting up double plays. He indicated his desire to win and his physical toughness by establishing one of baseball's least-coveted records—he was hit by 267 pitches. And even before his playing career ended in 1988, Baylor built on his reputation for leadership by lobbying for a major league managing job, which he received with the Colorado Rockies in 1993, their inaugural season.

A legendary streak hitter, Baylor was nicknamed "Groove," and, appropriately, he shares several streak records. He tied the Opening Day record for hits with four extra-base hits—two doubles, a triple, and a homer—on April 6, 1973, as a member of the Baltimore Orioles. On August 13 and 14 of that season, Baylor had nine hits during two games. On July 1, 1975, he homered in his final at bat and then hit three homers in his first three trips the next day to tie the major league record for homers in consecutive at bats. Baylor also had eight RBIs in a game on August 2, 1979, while playing for the California Angels.

Baylor was an outstanding high school baseball and football player in Austin, Texas. His one shortcoming as a baseball player, a weak throwing arm, resulted from a football injury to his shoulder. He signed with the Orioles in June 1967 and was the minor league Player of the Year in 1970, but couldn't crack the Baltimore lineup until 1972, when he played outfield and first base. Baylor helped the Orioles to AL East titles in 1973 and 1974, but they lost to the Oakland Athletics in the AL Championship Series both years. In 1975 he had a breakthrough season, with 25 homers and 32 steals. He was part of a blockbuster deal just before the 1976 opener. With both Baylor and Reggie Jackson impending free agents, Baylor and pitchers Mike Torrez and Paul Mitchell were traded to Oakland for Jackson, pitcher Ken Holtzman, and a minor leaguer.

Baylor stole a career-high 52 bases with the

A's and then signed as a free agent with California, where he established himself as the top designated hitter in the American League, while continuing as a part-time outfielder and first baseman. In 1979 Baylor led the majors with 120 runs and 139 RBIs, winning AL Most Valuable Player honors plus his only All-Star Game selection. In California's first-ever post-season series, Baylor had two hits, walked, scored once, and knocked in a run against Baltimore in Game 2 as a furious California rally from a 9–1 deficit fell one run short. His homer in Game 3 helped the Angels avoid a sweep. Baylor missed six weeks with a fractured left wrist in 1980, and had an off year during strike-torn 1981 when his role as a member of the executive board of the Players Association may have contributed to his woes.

He rebounded with 24 homers and 93 RBIs for the 1982 Angels, and they advanced to the playoffs against the Milwaukee Brewers. Baylor led all batters with 10 RBIs in the five-game series. In the opener he knocked in the Angels' first run with a sacrifice fly in the first inning, and then put them ahead to stay with a two-run triple in the third. He added two more RBIs with a fourth-inning single, tying the one-game playoff record with five. Baylor doubled in a run in Game 3, and hit a grand slam off Moose Haas in Game 4, but the Brewers won three straight to claim the pennant.

The New York Yankees signed Baylor as a free agent in 1983, and he hit a career-best .303 in his first season in the Bronx. He had at least 85 RBIs for three consecutive seasons with the Yankees and became an acknowledged team leader. Dave Winfield remembered him as a quiet leader, inspiring by example and being available for advice. Mike Pagliarulo, on the other hand, recalled Baylor chewing out a teammate for failing to run out a grounder during the spring training opener. On the field, Baylor won the league's award as outstanding designated hitter in 1985 and again in 1986.

Days before the start of the 1986 season, the Yankees sent Baylor to the Boston Red Sox for designated hitter Mike Easler. Baylor went on to set a league record that year, getting hit by pitches 35 times. He also began a stretch of three consecutive World Series appearances with three different teams. He 31 homers and 94 RBIs helped the Red Sox win the AL East over the Yankees, and he hit .346 in the playoffs against the Angels. In Game 5, he homered to put Boston on the board and, after being hit by a pitch to start the 11th inning, scored the winning run on Dave Henderson's sacrifice fly. Baylor reached twice—on a single and a hit-by-pitch—in Game 6 and scored twice in the Sox's 10–4 win. He singled, doubled, and scored in the 8-1 rout that sent the Sox to the World Series.

The Red Sox dealt Baylor to the Minnesota Twins for a minor league pitcher late in 1987, and, despite playing sparingly down the stretch, he pinch-hit the game-winner in the playoff opener, as the Twins rallied to beat the Detroit Tigers. In the World Series, Baylor singled and scored in the Twins seven-run fourth-inning rally in Game 1, and then knocked in three runs in Game 6, including a two-run homer off John Tudor. In Game 7, Baylor was hit by a pitch and singled, as he won his first world championship ring.

A free agent again, Baylor signed with the A's in February 1988 and split DH duties with Dave Parker, finishing his career by participating in Oakland's upset loss to the Los Angeles Dodgers in the World Series.

After retiring, Baylor served as a batting instructor for the Brewers and the Cardinals, making first baseman Andres Galarraga his prime pupil. When he got a chance to manage the Rockies, he brought Galarraga to Colorado and helped the infielder win a batting title. In 1995 he won BBWAA and *The Sporting News* NL Manager of the Year awards. He was fired by the Rockies after the 1998 season, but he spent the following year as hitting instructor with the Atlanta Braves. He was credited with helping make Chipper Jones a true power threat from both sides of the plate. He was named manager of the Chicago Cubs on November 1, 1999.

Ginger Beaumont

Beaumont, Clarence Howeth **OF**

1899–1910 B:7/23/1876, Rochester, WI D:4/10/1956, Burlington, WI Deb:4/21/1899, PIT NL BL/TR 5'8", 190

G	AB	R	H	HR	RBI	OBP	SLG	AVG
1463	5660	955	1759	39	617	.362	.393	.311

Ginger Beaumont didn't look like the kind of player whose main virtue was speed. Yet, although he carried 190 pounds on his 5'8" frame, he could move as quickly as anyone in baseball. In a game played on his birthday in 1899, he went 6-for-6 and not a hit left the infield. "My fourth time at bat, the third baseman stood 10 feet from the plate, and I still beat my bunt out," he recalled later. His speed made him one of the top leadoff men of baseball's Dead Ball Era.

At Beloit College, Beaumont was primarily a catcher, but he occasionally pitched or played in the outfield. After college he played semipro ball in Wisconsin, where he came to the attention of Connie Mack, then the manager of the Western League's Milwaukee Brewers. When injuries decimated the Brewers' outfield late in 1898, Mack asked Beaumont to join the team. In the season's final 24 games he batted .354 and stole 11 bases. That got the attention of the Pittsburgh Pirates, who purchased his contract.

When Patsy Donovan became the Pirates' skipper he put Beaumont in left field, where his fielding began to improve, and eventually he was switched to center. Opponents jumped on his given name, chanting "Clar-ence!" But after Beaumont finished his rookie year with a .352 batting average and 90 runs scored, he was known to everyone as "Ginger" for his shock of red hair.

Fred Clarke arrived as Pirates manager in 1900, and with a boatload of new talent that included Honus Wagner, the Bucs jumped to second place. Beaumont scored 105 runs, the first of four consecutive 100-plus years, but he was beset by leg injuries that would bother him throughout his career.

The next three seasons were the high point of Beaumont's career. The Pirates won three consecutive pennants, and Beaumont hit over .330 each season. In 1902 he led all NL batters with a .357 average and 193 hits. The next year he upped his league-leading hits to 209, while hitting .341, sixth behind batting champ Wagner.

That fall the Pirates met Boston in the first modern World Series. In Game 4 Beaumont went 3-for-4 with a triple to score twice in a 5–4 Pirate win. Game 6 saw him go 4-for-5, steal two bases, score one run, and drive in another. Despite his efforts, the Pirates lost the game and, a few days later, the series. Although the Pirates slipped in 1904, Beaumont again led the league in base hits, but the next year his leg problems returned. After playing in only 80 games he was traded to Boston. Beaumont gave his new team one good season before his leg problems became more frequent. He was in and out of the lineup for his last three years, the final one with Chicago.

The man who was the first to step to the plate in the modern World Series made his last major league appearance pinch-hitting for the Cubs in the 1910 World Series against the Athletics. After one more season with the American Association's St. Paul Apostles, he retired to his Wisconsin farm, where he maintained a lively interest in baseball until his death in 1956.

Boom-Boom Beck

Beck, Walter William **P**

1924, 1927–28, 1933–34, 1939–45 B:10/16/1904, Decatur, IL D:5/7/1987, Champaign, IL Deb:9/22/1924, STL AL BR/TR 6'2", 200

W	L	PCT	G	SV	IP	BB	SO	ERA
38	69	.355	265	6	1034	342	352	4.30

"Boom-Boom" Beck pitched in the major leagues for all or parts of 12 different seasons over a period of 22 years. That longevity speaks of a certain kind of success; however, he had only two winning seasons. In 1927 he was 1–0 in only three appearances with the Cardinals. In 1945 he was 8–5 with the Reds and Pirates as wartime stripped much of the talent from baseball. Beck's wins reached double figures only once, with 12 victories for Brooklyn in 1933, but he also lost 20 games the same year.

There are multiple versions of how Beck came by his colorful nickname. However, the generally accepted story involves a 1934 game Beck pitched for the Dodgers in Philadelphia's Baker Bowl, famous for its close, steel-covered right-field wall. On that particular hot summer day the combination of Beck's pitches and the wall produced an overabundance of booms. In right field for the Dodgers was slugger Hack Wilson, who was winding down his career but not his carousing excesses, and chasing down the rockets off Philadelphia bats did not improve the after-effects of his previous evening's outing. When Wilson saw Brooklyn manager Casey Stengel head for the mound to remove Beck, he decided to catch a few winks. But as Stengel reached the mound, Beck, in a fit of pique at being removed, turned and heaved the ball against the distant right-field fence, where it bounced audibly off the steel-covered wall. Wilson, suddenly and rudely awakened, knew only that another baseball was coming toward him; he played it neatly on the bounce and fired a perfect throw into second base. Even Stengel laughed.

After leaving the majors for the last time, Beck continued to pitch and coach in the minors. In 1951 he won a 10–2 game with the American Association's Toledo Mud Hens to bring his final professional record to a satisfyingly even 236–236.

Rod Beck

Beck, Rodney Roy **P**

1991–* B:8/3/1968, Burbank, CA Deb: 5/6/1991, SF NL BR/TR 6'1", 235

W	L	PCT	G	SV	IP	BB	SO	ERA
26	37	.413	540	260	587^{1}	131	499	3.20

At 6 feet 1 inch, 235 pounds, Rod Beck never had the physique of the prototypical athlete, yet he managed to do things in baseball that few before him accomplished. In 1998 the stocky Cub became the fifth reliever in major league history to surpass 50 saves, with his 51st coming in a one-game playoff against the Giants to decide the National League Wild Card. It was the fifth time in six seasons that Beck had saved 30 or more games, and his 81 appearances led the league.

The Oakland Athletics drafted Beck in 1986 in the 13th round out of high school in Van Nuys, California. He was traded to the Giants two years later. Beck made his major league debut in 1991.

From 1993 to 1995 only Lee Smith and Randy Myers had more saves than Beck, who notched 109 saves in that span. Beck's 48 saves in 1993 were the most in Giants history. He converted all but four of his save opportunities that season and had a hand in nearly half of the Giants' 103 victories. Although Atlanta overtook the Giants for the NL West title, Beck performed admirably down the stretch. He pitched in eight straight games, earning a win and six saves from September 24 to the end of the season.

Glowering in from the mound with his trademark mutton chops, he certainly looked intimidating; the results were indisputable. He was injured on Opening Day 1994 and missed the first month of the season, yet he still won the NL Rolaids Relief Award. In 1995 he converted 22 of his final 24 opportunities. He helped the Giants win their first division title in nine years in 1997. He joined the Cubs as a free agent that winter,

After his 51-save season in 1998, he underwent surgery for bone spurs and chips in his right elbow during the 1999 season. The disappointing Cubbies dealt Beck to the contending Red Sox at the trade deadline for southpaw Mark Guthrie and minor league third baseman Cole Liniak. Beck filled a void in the Boston bullpen, and helped the Red Sox capture the Wild Card in his first stint in the American League.

Glenn Beckert

Beckert, Glenn Alfred **2B**

1965–75 B:10/12/1940, Pittsburgh, PA Deb:4/12/1965, CHI NL BR/TR 6'1", 190

G	AB	R	H	HR	RBI	OBP	SLG	AVG
1320	5208	685	1473	22	360	.319	.345	.283

After the Cubs' Rookie of the Year second baseman Ken Hubbs died in a plane crash in February 1964, Chicago found a worthy successor in Glenn Beckert. As a minor league shortstop in 1964, Beckert had led the Pacific Coast League in putouts and assists, and during his rookie year with the Cubs he followed that up by pacing the senior circuit in assists with 494—four more than he'd had in the previous year at his natural position. Beckert became known for his aggressiveness defensively. He wouldn't hesitate to body-slam teammates to catch popups, leading catcher Paul Popovich, a minor league teammate, to give him the nickname "Bruno," after pro wrestler Bruno Sammartino.

Beckert was a decent contact hitter, rarely struck out, and was an exceptional hit-and-run man—a necessity for a hitter who usually batted second. For six consecutive years, from 1966 through 1971, he batted at least .280, with a personal high of .342 in 1971. This contributed to his being named to the All-Star team each year from 1969 through 1972. He also won a Gold Glove in 1968.

In November 1973, having slowed down in the field, Beckert was traded to the Padres, along with minor leaguer Bob Fenwick, for outfielder Jerry Morales. Upon retiring from baseball two years later, he became a commodities trader at the Chicago Board of Trade.

Jake Beckley

Beckley, Jacob Peter **1B**

1888–1907 B:8/4/1867, Hannibal, MO D:6/25/1918, Kansas City, MO Deb:6/20/1888, PIT NL BL/TL 5'10", 200

G	AB	R	H	HR	RBI	OBP	SLG	AVG
2386	9526	1600	2930	87	1575	.361	.436	.308

Jake Beckley was called "Eagle Eye" for his ability to discern good pitches, which helped make him baseball's best hitters during a 20-year career. Thirteen times he batted over .300, and he finished with a .308 lifetime batting average. He fell short of 3,000 hits, but he scored 1,600 runs, and accounted for 1,575 RBIs.

Beckley was never a home run hitter—no one hit very many homers in the Dead Ball Era—

but he certainly had power. He ranks fourth all-time with 243 career triples. Unfortunately, Beckley's batting success was squandered on behalf of teams that came up short, often far short, in the pennant race. Like Ernie Banks, he never played on a major league team that finished first.

At 5 feet 10 inches and 200 pounds, the left-handed first baseman was a big man for his time, yet he ran surprisingly well. He was credited with 315 steals for his career, and even when he was nearly 40 years old he could still steal. However, until 1898 runners were credited with a stolen base when they went from first to third on a single or advanced an extra base on an out. Beckley played half his career before 1898 and the records don't reveal how many bases he stole according to the modern definition.

Beckley was both a crowd-pleaser and a smart baseball man. He developed a hidden ball trick that was all his own: he hid the ball under a corner of the base, and when the runner took a lead, Beckley quickly reached under the base, grabbed the ball, and tagged the runner out. One day he reportedly lifted up the wrong corner of the bag, and Honus Wagner zipped down to second, laughing all the way.

Beckley began his career with Leavenworth, Kansas, of the Western League in 1886. He started the 1888 season with Western Association's St. Louis Whites, but after 34 games the National League's Pittsburgh Alleghenys purchased his contract. He joined the team in June and hit .343 the rest of the way, one point less than league batting champion Cap Anson.

After eight and a half years in Pittsburgh—during which he topped 100 RBIs four times and scored more than 100 runs five times—Beckley was dealt to the New York Giants in 1896. The following year he moved on to Cincinnati, and on September 26, 1897, he hit three home runs in the first game of a doubleheader, a feat no NL batter would duplicate until 1922. On May 16 of the following year, he cracked three triples in a game. In seven seasons with the Reds, he batted over .300 six times. His final four major league seasons were spent with the St. Louis Cardinals.

In spite of his prowess at the plate, Beckley's most impressive figures were based on his longevity. He played 2,377 games at first base, more than anyone before or since. He also holds the major league record for putouts by a first baseman, with 23,709.

Beckley did not have a good arm, and his inability to make accurate throws caused one of the strangest plays ever seen in baseball. With Beckley's Cardinals playing Pittsburgh, Pirate Tommy Leach laid down a bunt along the first-base line and took off. In swooped Beckley, who fielded the ball smartly, spun, and threw in the general direction of pitcher Jack Taylor, who was covering first. The throw would have been perfect had Taylor been nine feet tall. Leach rounded first and headed for second while the ball bounded into foul territory. To redeem himself, Beckley chased the ball down and, when he saw Leach head for third under a full head of steam, charged for the plate. The crowd cheered as the two players raced toward home. As Leach slid feet first from one direction, Beckley made a headlong dive from the other. Leach was out and also suffered two broken ribs.

After leaving the majors in 1907, Beckley continued to play in the minor leagues until 1911, often as a player-manager. He tried umpiring in the Federal League in 1913, the year before the circuit went major league. Beckley was named to the Hall of Fame in 1971.

John Beckwith

Beckwith, John **SS-3B-C-OF**

Negro League Player (1916–38), Manager B:1902, Louisville, KY D:1956, New York, NY BR/TR 6'3", 220

"One of the most powerful men, black or white, ever to swing a bat." That's how one expert on the Negro Leagues described the versatile John Beckwith, who turned professional in 1917 with the Chicago Giants.

Beckwith was like a combination of Honus Wagner and Babe Ruth—capable of handling a variety of tough positions but having the added dimension of immense power. He also had a bit of Ty Cobb in him—at least in terms of temperament. In 1925 Beckwith and teammate Jud Wilson slugged an umpire following an argument. Wilson was arrested and Beckwith skipped town until things blew over.

When he was only 19, Beckwith was the first hitter of any league to power a ball over the left field fence at Cincinnati's Redland Field. In 1927, the year that Ruth belted 60 home runs out of AL ballparks, the husky Beckwith was credited with 72. The following year he had 54.

Beckwith played as a shortstop, third baseman, catcher, and outfielder, performing with such clubs as the Baltimore Black Sox, Homestead Grays, Harrisburg Giants, Lincoln Giants, New York Black Yankees, and Newark Dodgers after he left the Chicago Giants. Following his retirement in 1938, he worked briefly as a New York City police officer.

Steve Bedrosian

Bedrosian, Stephen Wayne **P**

1981–91, 1993–95 B:12/6/1957, Methuen, MA Deb:8/14/1981, ATL NL BR/TR 6'3", 200

W	L	PCT	G	SV	IP	BB	SO	ERA
76	79	.490	732	184	1191	518	921	3.38

Mostly a steady pitcher over his 14 seasons, Steve Bedrosian enjoyed one stellar year with Philadelphia in 1987, capturing the National League Cy Young Award. Meticulous about his pitching mechanics, as well as his finely trimmed beard, "Bedrock" pitched his first full major league season in the heat of a tight race in 1982. He won eight games and saved 11 for the National League West champion Braves.

Armed with a 95-mph heater and nasty slider, he averaged 15 saves in both 1983 and 1984. Each season, however, he wore down during the stretch run, prompting Atlanta to obtain relief ace Bruce Sutter.

Bedrosian was converted to a starter, a role he had performed in the minors, but produced a disappointing 7–15 mark with a 3.83 ERA. Bedrosian was shipped to Philadelphia and handed the closer job. Bedrosian saved 29 games for the Phillies in 1986, then saved a league-high 40 games the following season. Pitching for the fifth-place Phillies, Bedrosian won the NL Cy Young Award over Rick Sutcliffe, whose Cubs finished sixth.

Although he missed a month of the 1988 season, he still saved 28 of Philadelphia's 65 victories. After toiling for the San Francisco Giants from 1989–1990 and the world champion Minnesota Twins in 1991, Bedrosian was forced to retire when his fingertips turned cold and white. Two years later the ailment subsided and he made a triumphant return to Atlanta, posting a 1.63 ERA in 49 games in 1993. He pitched two more seasons for the Braves before retiring.

Mark Belanger

Belanger, Mark Henry **SS**

1965–82 B:6/8/1944, Pittsfield, MA D:10/6/98, New York, NY Deb:8/7/1965, BAL AL BR/TR 6'1", 170

G	AB	R	H	HR	RBI	OBP	SLG	AVG
2016	5784	676	1316	20	389	.302	.280	.228

An eight-time Gold Glove winner at shortstop, Mark "Blade" Belanger teamed with Brooks Robinson at third base to give the Earl Weaver-era Baltimore Orioles the best-fielding left side of the infield in American League history. When Bobby Grich joined them as second baseman in 1973, the Orioles may have had the best-fielding infield trio ever, as each player won Gold Gloves from 1973 to 1975.

Rex Barney, a teammate of Pee Wee Reese's who watched great shortstops for decades, called Belanger "as good with the glove as anyone," a common assessment of Belanger. The Baltimore star gained the acclaim using a tiny glove and almost never leaving his feet or deviating from his classic overhand throwing motion. His smoothness masked great speed, hands, and instincts, and he had the ability to make the extraordinarily difficult seem mundane.

Ironically, Belanger first gained national attention for an error. On April 30, 1967, he came in to play second base in the ninth inning of lefthander Steve Barber's very hairy no-hitter in which he walked a total of 10 and hit one batter. After Barber walked two and wild-pitched home the tying run, Don Wert grounded reliever Stu Miller's offering up the middle. Shortstop Luis Aparicio made a nice stop and threw to Belanger at second base, but Belanger dropped the ball for an error, allowing the winning run to score. It was the first no-hit loss in major league history.

Belanger replaced future Hall of Famer Aparicio as the Orioles' shortstop in 1968 and was as miserable at the plate as he was marvelous with the glove. Fortunately, the Orioles had enough power to carry Belanger's glove. He added an element of speed that came in handy when Baltimore's power hitting declined, and they ran to division titles in 1973 and 1974. Although he had a knack for hitting some of the most feared pitchers of his time, notably Nolan Ryan and Ron Guidry, his .228 career average ranks 18th from the bottom among major leaguers with 2,500 or more at bats.

Belanger's best year at the plate was 1969, when he hit .287—with a career-high 50 RBIs and 76 runs scored—and cut his strikeout total from the 114 of his first full season to 54. The Orioles cruised to the AL East title, and Belanger won his first Gold Glove.

After having only two home runs all season, he homered to break a 1–1 tie in the playoff opener against the Minnesota Twins. Then he singled in the 12th inning and scored the winning run on Paul Blair's two-out, suicide-squeeze bunt. Belanger had two more hits and scored twice as Baltimore completed the sweep in Game 3. In the World Series, he singled off Mets ace Tom Seaver and scored in the Orioles' opening-game triumph. But Baltimore lost the next four games, with the other bats on the team falling even more silent than Belanger's .200 average.

Belanger's regular-season production never reached his 1969 level again. He did, however, hit .333 in the playoff sweep of the Twins, including three hits and three runs scored as the leadoff batter in Game 2. In the World Series, Belanger was mired in a 1-for-15 slump when he singled in the tying run in the second inning of Game 5 off reliever Wayne Granger. The Orioles went on to win the game and the world championship.

In 1971 Belanger won his second Gold Glove, but failed to hit a homer in 500 at bats. He repeated the homerless season two years later, when he began a string of six straight Gold Glove-winning seasons. In 1976, he overcame his hitting deficits—batting .270 for the second-best season of his career—to earn his lone selection to the All-Star Game.

By the time the Orioles broke their postseason drought in 1979, Belanger was hitting only .167 and was splitting time at shortstop with Kiko Garcia. He played in three contests of Baltimore's four-game playoff win over the California Angels, extending his playoff records, which included most games, chances, putouts, and assists for a shortstop. He got his last playoff hit off Nolan Ryan, knocking in a run. He started twice and appeared defensively in three other contests as the Orioles blew a three-to-one lead in games to Pittsburgh in the World Series.

In 1982 Belanger played his final season, after signing as a free agent with the Los Angeles Dodgers. He later joined the Major League Baseball Players Association as a special assistant to Don Fehr, remaining in that post until his death from lung cancer at age 54.

Tim Belcher

Belcher, Timothy Wayne **P**

1987–* B:10/19/1961, Mount Gilead, OH
Deb:9/6/1987, LA NL BR/TR 6'3", 220

W	L	PCT	G	SH	IP	BB	SO	ERA
142	135	.513	385	18	2402	838	1497	4.12

Three major league teams selected Tim Belcher before he ever threw a pitch as a professional. Following an All-America season at Mount Vernon Nazarine College in Ohio, the Minnesota Twins made Belcher the number one pick in the country, yet he did not sign. Seven months later the New York Yankees chose him in the first round of the January draft. Again he did not agree to terms. Less than a month later the Oakland Athletics grabbed Belcher in the compensation pool draft for free agents; finally Belcher signed a professional contract.

Plagued by control problems in the minor leagues, Belcher was traded to the Los Angeles Dodgers on September 3, 1987. He made his major league debut in relief three days later and beat the New York Mets. Belcher won three of five starts the rest of the year, earning a shot at a regular spot in the Dodger's rotation. As a rookie he posted a 12–6 record, then added three more wins in the postseason when Los Angeles upset the favored Mets and A's en route to the world championship.

Belcher won 15 games in a season three times, and in 1989 led the National League in complete games and shutouts. He was durable and always much in demand: in his first 13 major league seasons he wore seven different uniforms. Regardless of the which uniform he wore, he hated to lose. Upset over an extra-inning loss in 1989, he challenged umpire Ed Montague to a fight in the Dodgers dugout; with Anaheim 10 years later, he belted Dodgers pitcher Chan Ho Park after a brushback pitch. "Sometimes I fly off the handle too far, get a little too emotional," he said, "but I'd rather be a little off center that way than to be the slightest bit passive."

Bo Belinsky

Belinsky, Robert **P**

1962–67, 1969–70 B:12/7/1936, New York, NY
Deb:4/18/1962, LA AL BL/TL 6'2", 191

W	L	PCT	G	SH	IP	BB	SO	ERA
28	51	.354	146	4	665[1]	333	476	4.10

A sometimes effective pitcher, Bo Belinsky was also an occasional television actor, the hurler of a much-ballyhooed no-hitter, a pool shark, an escort of numerous starlets, and the husband of first a Playboy Playmate of the Year and later an heiress. Belinsky descended upon an unsuspecting baseball world like a bombshell in 1962. Plucked by the Los Angeles Angels from the Baltimore Orioles system in the 1961 expansion draft, the veteran minor leaguer was not good enough to make the team that first year. In 1962, however, he began to make up for lost time. He was off to a 2–0 start when, on the night of May 1, 1962, he joined pitching's elite circle: he threw a no-hitter. Many pitchers had done it before, and many have done it since, but only Belinsky seemed to know how to exploit it properly—although he later claimed, "It actually cost me money. I had to buy drinks for everyone. It was like making a hole in one."

In short order after the no-hitter, he moved deep into the Hollywood scene, shot off scores of quotable quotes for eager reporters, became a personal favorite of Broadway columnist Walter Winchell, and dated the likes of Ann-Margret, Connie Stevens, Doris Duke, Juliet Prowse, Tina Louise, and Mamie Van Doren ("I needed her like Custer needed Indians"), to whom he became engaged in April 1963.

Belinsky knew how to work the media. "These guys didn't want the truth," he said later. "That wasn't as good a story as something I could make up. So I went along with them. When they asked about [women], I built it up. When they asked about pool, I made out to be the best player that ever picked up a cue. When they asked about my contract, I made it sound like I wouldn't sign under any conditions unless [Gene] Autry begged me personally."

Not that a character like Belinsky needed to exaggerate. "He's a handsome son of a bitch," observed Angels publicity director Irv Kaze, analyzing Belinsky's appeal. "He's got that lean and hungry look. You can almost feel the animal sex in him."

After the no-hitter Belinsky lost six of seven decisions. He finished the 1962 season at 10–11 but kept the publicity up anyway. He appeared on such popular TV shows as *77 Sunset Strip*, *Surfside Six*, and *Dakota*, as his record fell and his ERA rose. Traded to Philadelphia in 1965, he blasted that city's notorious fans: "Philadelphia fans would boo funerals, an Easter egg hunt, a parade of armless war vets, and the Liberty Bell." Demoted to the Pacific Coast League's Hawaii Islanders after a season with Houston, Belinsky pitched another no-hitter on August 18, 1968. When no one showed an interest in bringing him back to the majors, he charged that there was a conspiracy to "blackball" him.

Belinsky once revealed that he had been out quite late the night before his celebrated no-hitter (which was hardly news) and had met someone special whom he felt had somehow altered his fate. "I got home at 4 A.M.," he said. "That night I pitched my no-hitter. I tried to find her and never did. She was my good luck charm. When I lost her I lost all my pitching luck." He retired in 1970 after short stints with the Pittsburgh Pirates and the Cincinnati Reds.

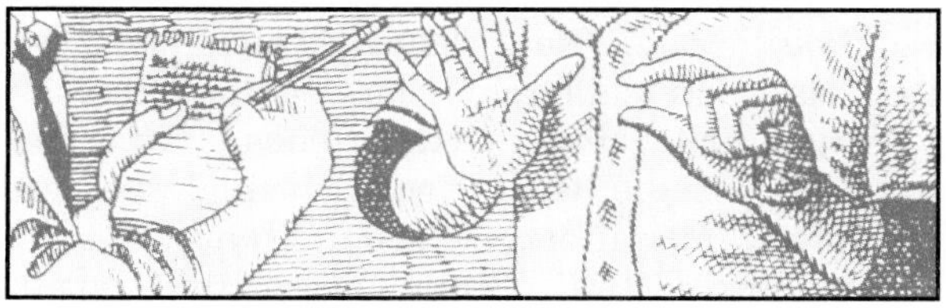

Buddy Bell

Bell, David Gus **3B–OF**

1972–89 M(1996–98, * 185–277) B:8/27/1951, Pittsburgh, PA Deb:4/15/1972, CLE AL BR/TR, 6'2", 185

G	AB	R	H	HR	RBI	OBP	SLG	AVG
2405	8995	1151	2514	201	1106	.343	.406	.279

To observers with long memories, Buddy Bell seemed like a modern version of Harlond Clift: both were third basemen of considerable skill, who tended to be overlooked. Although Bell posted a solid .279 lifetime batting average with 201 homers, the son of former big league outfielder Gus Bell is best remembered for his fielding.

Bell won Gold Glove Awards and made *The Sporting News* All-Star Fielding Team every year from 1979 to 1984. At his peak, Brooks Robinson said of him: "Might be the top player in the league. He plays every day...just write his name in the lineup. A top clutch hitter."

Selected by the Cleveland Indians in the 16th round of the June 1969 free agent draft, Bell started his minor league career at second base but was switched to third while with Sumter of the Western Carolinas League. He played outfield when he first came up to Cleveland in 1972. By the next season he was representing the Indians as a third baseman at the All-Star Game, the first of his five appearances.

Bell was traded to Texas in December 1978 for third baseman Toby Harrah. He responded with one of his finest seasons: a career-high 101 RBIs plus 18 homers and a .299 average. Bell was "one of the game's best at his position," said play-by-play announcer Ned Martin in 1983. "A tough, productive hitter. Very competitive. He deserves to be a winner. He's playing up to his potential and more, because of where he has played. Just hasn't gotten the publicity he deserves."

Starting the next season, Bell was selected to the All-Star Game four times in the next five seasons. This prompted the Cincinnati Reds, who had long coveted Bell, to trade outfielder Duane Walker and pitcher Jeff Russell for him on July 19, 1985. Bell, however, never got up to speed for the Reds that year, hitting just .219 as he struggled to adjust to National League pitching. It was said that he had trouble with high fastballs, with opening up his swing, and with falling behind in the count. His future seemed seriously in doubt.

However, Bell eventually adjusted to the different league, and bounced back with a career-high 20 homers in 1986. He had another successful season in 1987, but the next year he was traded to Houston midseason, and then released in December 1988. Bell rejoined the Rangers in 1989, but he batted a mere .183 in 34 contests before announcing that he was hanging up his spikes.

It was not until after his retirement that Bell revealed that he had played baseball for 15 years while suffering from epilepsy. "One reason I never wanted people to know was just that I didn't want them to worry about me," he said. "I don't think about it every day. I don't think about it every month. I'd be the same way without it."

In 1988 Bell was inducted into the Texas Baseball Hall of Fame. He later served as director of minor league instruction for the White Sox, coached for the Indians, and managed the Detroit Tigers. In 1999 he was field coordinator in the Reds' minor league system. He was hired as manager of the Colorado Rockies following the 1999 season.

Cool Papa Bell

Bell, James **OF–P**

Negro League Player 1922–46 B:5/17/1903, Starkville, MS D:3/7/1991, St. Louis, MO BB/TL 5'11", 150

How fast was Negro League outfielder Cool Papa Bell? Some claimed he was so fast he could flip the light switch and get into bed before the light went out. According to Satchel Paige, Bell once smashed a line drive and was hit by it as he rounded second. His speed was legendary: "I scored from first base on singles lots of time," he said. "If the ball isn't hit straight at the outfielder, I'd score. You have to be heads up and watch those things."

Tall tales seem appropriate for Bell because of both the magnitude of his talent and the limited record-keeping in Negro League games. He once remarked, "I remember one game. I got five hits and stole five bases, but none of it was written down because they forgot to bring the scorebook to the game that day." The information that did find its way into the record books speaks for itself: Bell once circled the bases in 12 seconds (Reds outfielder Evar Swanson, the fastest major leaguer on the basepaths, accomplished the feat in 13.3 seconds in 1931); he stole 175 bases in a 200-game span in 1933; and in 1940, at age 37, he batted .337 for Torreon in the Mexican League. Bell estimated his lifetime average to be around .340 or .350.

Bell began playing baseball for the St. Louis Compton Hill Cubs in 1920, along with his four brothers. At the time he was a pitcher with a strong knuckleball. By 1922 he was making $30 each Sunday pitching semipro ball—good money compared to the $35 to $40 a week he earned in a packinghouse. When the East St. Louis Cubs asked him to fill in and pitch against the St. Louis Stars, a higher level club, he struck out eight while his team went down, 8–1. The manager of the team, Bill Gatewood, was impressed and offered Bell a job. Legend has it that Gatewood was hesitant at first to put Bell in a game before a big crowd, thinking the pitcher might be nervous. But when Bell took the mound he was calm and composed. "Oh that guy, he's taking it cool," his teammates said. "So they started calling me that," Bell remembered. "When I'd go in, they'd yell 'C'mon Cool,' like that. But that didn't sound right. That's not enough of a name, they said, got to put something else on it. They added 'Papa' to it and started calling me 'Cool Papa.' That's where it came from. In 1922."

When the Cuban team he played for in the winter leagues needed an outfielder, Bell made the shift, so that he could exploit his tremendous speed. At first he played left, but when balls were hit over the center fielder's head, Bell habitually rushed over from left to snag them. From then on he played center. "Defensively he was the equal of Tris Speaker, Joe DiMaggio, or Willie Mays," said team owner Bill Veeck.

From 1928 to 1948 Cool Papa Bell proved he could hit against big league competition. One compilation of box scores from 54 games between Negro Leaguers and white barnstorming teams shows that in 193 at bats against such pitchers as Bobo Newsom, Dizzy Dean, Bob Feller, Bob Lemon, and Mike Garcia, Bell hit at a .378 clip, with four homers and 13 stolen bases. During a series in Mexico, Bell made a spectacular catch off the bat of Rogers Hornsby, who shook his head and asked, "That was the hardest ball I ever hit, how'd you catch it?" On the same trip, Connie Mack's son, Earle, said to Bell, "If the door were open, you'd be the first guy I'd hire. I'd pay you $75,000 a year to play ball. You'd be worth it in drawing power alone."

But Bell never came close to earning $75,000 and instead made do with second-class treatment. "We went into a lot of small towns where they'd never seen a colored person," Bell said. "In some of those places we couldn't find anyplace to sleep so we slept on the bus. If we had to, we could convert the seats into beds. We'd just pull over to the side of the road, in a cornfield or someplace, and sleep until the break of day."

On the final day of the 1946 season, Bell led Monte Irvin of the Newark Eagles .402 to .398 for the Negro National League's batting title. Bell had to play in both games of a doubleheader in order to qualify for the title; he got two singles in the first game but sat out the second, and the title went to Irvin. Bell's fans were puzzled, but it came out that, rather than take the title himself, he chose to sit out in order to build up Irvin's chances to make it in the major leagues.

"We would rather pass on something to a young guy to help the future of the black man," Bell said. "And I'm not the only older guy who kept his average down. We didn't have a future. We were too old."

Although Cool Papa Bell never played major league ball, he was inducted into baseball's Hall of Fame in 1974. When asked if arrival at the Hall had been his biggest thrill, he said, "No, it's my biggest honor. My biggest thrill was when they opened the door in the major leagues for the black players."

Gary Bell

Bell, Gary **P**

1958–69 B:11/17/1936, San Antonio, TX D:5/7/1995, Cincinnati, OH Deb:6/1/1958, CLE AL BR/TR 6'1", 198

W	L	PCT	G	SV	IP	BB	SO	ERA
121	117	.508	519	51	2015	842	1378	3.68

Early in his career, Gary Bell looked like he might be a star, but the hard-throwing righthander never really lived up to the promise of his first two seasons. Bell played basketball and baseball at San Antonio Junior College before signing with the Cleveland Indians in 1954. After working his way through the Indians' minor league system, he broke into the majors in 1958, winning 12 games his rookie season and 16 the following year. He remained in the majors through 1969, but he finished his career with a lifetime record of only 121–117.

Bell played for seven different managers with the Indians from 1958 to 1967, and that contributed to his frequently being moved between the starting rotation and long relief. In 1962, he led AL relievers in victories with nine, and in 1965 he recorded 17 saves, but he often expressed his displeasure at having to pitch out of the bullpen, since, at that time, starters usually made more money than relievers did.

The Indians returned him to a starting role in 1966 and he responded with one of his best seasons, 14–15, 3.22 ERA, a career-high 194 strikeouts, and 12 complete games. However, when he got off to a 1–5 start the following season, the Indians traded him on June 4 to the Boston Red Sox in exchange for first baseman Tony Horton and outfielder Don Demeter. Bell went on to win 12 games for the Red Sox in their pennant drive that season. In the 1967 World Series, he had a loss and a save against the St. Louis Cardinals. In 1969, his last season, Bell played for both the expansion Seattle Pilots and the Chicago White Sox.

George Bell

Bell, George Antonio (Mathey) **OF–DH**

1981–93 B:10/21/1959, San Pedro de Macoris, Dominican Republic Deb:4/9/1981, TOR AL BR/TR, 6'1", 190

G	AB	R	H	HR	RBI	OBP	SLG	AVG
1587	6123	814	1702	265	1002	.320	.469	.278

George Bell fans remember him as one of the top sluggers of the mid-1980s, highly competitive and a tough clutch hitter. His critics, however, challenge his 1987 Most Valuable Player Award and say his competitiveness sometimes went too far.

One of the many great players from San Pedro de Macoris, Dominican Republic, Bell earned Toronto's right-field job in 1984 after a torrid spring training. Soon, Blue Jays slugging records began to fall. That season he smashed 26 homers while setting a club record with 39 doubles (a mark he later broke). Bell had a unique batting style: he rocked back before the pitch and then exploded into the ball. Balls exploded out of parks throughout the American League. In 1985 he cleared the roof at Comiskey Park twice in one series. In 1986 he improved to 31 homers, along with 108 RBIs and a .309 average.

In one of the great power seasons of the decade, Bell bashed a career-high 47 home runs and led the American League with 134 RBIs in 1987. Against Detroit in the stretch run, however, his bat fell silent, and the Tigers overtook the Jays in the final weekend of the season for the Eastern Division title. Bell still was still named league MVP, beating out Detroit's Alan Trammell in a controversial vote.

Meanwhile, Bell was also gaining a reputation as a hothead. After a questionable brush-back pitch in 1985, he karate-kicked Boston pitcher Bruce Kison. When Toronto manager Jimy Williams announced Bell would be the designated hitter in 1988 because of his bad knees, George squawked loudly. He became the first big leaguer to belt three homers on Opening Day, but he hit just 21 more homers in 1988 and was blamed for the team's demise.

Bothered by knee and shoulder problems, Bell was shipped to the Chicago Cubs after the 1990 season. He appeared in his third All-Star Game in 1991 but struggled in left field. After the season, the Cubs dealt him back to the American League, to their cross-town rivals for Sammy Sosa—a deal universally hailed as one of the worst in White Sox history. Now almost exclusively a designated hitter, Bell clubbed 38 homers in two seasons with the Sox before his knees forced him to retire.

Gus Bell

Bell, David Russell **OF**

1950–64 B:11/15/1928, Louisville, KY D:5/7/1995, Montgomery, OH Deb:5/30/1950, PIT NL BL/TR 6'2", 196

G	AB	R	H	HR	RBI	OBP	SLG	AVG
1741	6478	865	1823	206	942	.333	.445	.281

Mickey Mantle wasn't the first ballplayer to be named after a catcher by admiring parents. Outfielder David Russell Bell, better known as "Gus," was given his nickname in honor of New York Giants backstop Gus Mancuso.

Bell started playing professionally with the Class C Central Association's Keokuk Pirates in 1947. At Indianapolis in 1950 he was hitting .400 six weeks into the season, when he was called up to the Pittsburgh Pirates. He produced 53 RBIs and a .282 average in 111 games. Another strong year followed as he led the league with 12 triples, and hit for the cycle on June 12, 1951.

Serious trouble developed the next season, however, when Bell insisted that his family travel with him during spring training. Pirates general manager Branch Rickey said Bell should travel alone and by train. "Rickey took a dislike to me because I refused to be one of his hungry ballplayers," said Bell, who was promptly optioned to the Pacific Coast League's Hollywood Stars. After hitting .297 there he was brought back up on May 12.

Rickey didn't take long to get rid of Bell for good, peddling him to the Cincinnati Reds on October 14, 1952, for outfielders Cal Abrams and Gail Henley and catcher Joe Rossi. Bell became a key player for the Reds, making the All-Star team in 1953, 1954, 1956, and 1957. His consistency was amazing: from 1953 to 1957 he never hit less than .292 or more than .308. "He's so remarkably steady," Reds manager Birdie Tebbetts pointed out, that "he sometimes goes unnoticed." Bell drove in more than 100 runs four times and had eight RBIs on three homers in a single game on September 21, 1955.

Bell's career was winding down when the New York Mets selected him in the National League expansion draft. During 1962 spring training Mets manager Casey Stengel filmed a promotional spot in which he went over the Mets' new lineup. He did fine until he got to right field, and his chronic inability to remember names tripped him up. "We got five or six fellas that's doing very good," he bobbed and weaved in classic Stengelese, "and the best played for Hornsby in Cincinnati, bats left-handed, and hit .300, done very good, delighted to have him, is married, has seven kids in the station wagon he drives down here from Cincinnati where he lives." On and on Stengel went, remembering everything except Bell's name. "Yes, sir, he comes down here for spring training with the whole family, and if he can hit for us like he hit for Hornsby, he'd ring the bell—and that's his name, Gus Bell!"

Bell was the starting right fielder for the Mets on Opening Day, April 11, 1962. He singled for the team's first-ever hit, but otherwise Bell got off to a horrible start. He was hitting only .149 on May 21 when the Mets sold him to the Milwaukee Braves. After three seasons in Milwaukee, Bell retired for good in 1964, following which he managed the Minutemen temporary employment service in Cincinnati. His son Buddy became an All-Star third baseman, and a third generation, David, made his major league debut in 1995.

Jay Bell

Bell, Jay Stuart **SS-2B**

1986–* B:12/11/1965, Elgin Air Force Base, FL Deb:9/29/1996, CLE AL BR/TR 6'1", 185

G	AB	R	H	HR	RBI	OBP	SLG	AVG
1681	6240	963	1677	162	732	.346	.420	.269

Jay Bell, a first-round draft pick, was part of a package of four young players traded by Minnesota to Cleveland for established pitcher Bert Blyleven in 1985. Bell's first major league at bat came against Blyleven a year later, when the 21-year-old prospect homered on the first pitch—the record-setting 47th home run of the season allowed by Blyleven.

Although Bell began 1988 as Cleveland's regular shortstop, he was demoted to Double A in midseason and dealt to the Pittsburgh Pirates the following spring. Bell was in the Bucs' Opening Day lineup in April, but was back in the minor leagues by May after going 1-for-20. He worked his way back to Pittsburgh, and his fielding and bat-handling skills soon made him an integral part of the Pirates' three straight division championship teams.

As Pittsburgh's second-place hitter, Bell bunted (twice leading the National League in sacrifices), took pitches, and found ways to get on base. Bell was steady defensively, winning a Gold Glove in 1993 and leading the league in total chances for five consecutive seasons. He started almost every game at shortstop for seven seasons before the Pirates traded him to Kansas City in a salary purge after the 1996 season.

After one successful year as a Royal, Bell signed a lucrative contract with the expansion Arizona franchise for its inaugural season in 1998. The following year he converted to playing second base. He slugged 38 home runs in 1999 and was also among the league leaders in runs scored and RBIs. Bell was selected as a starter on the All-Star team, as he helped lead the Diamondbacks to the earliest-ever postseason berth for an expansion franchise.

Albert Belle

Belle, Albert Jojuan **OF–DH**

1989–* B:8/25/1966, Shreveport, LA Deb:7/15/1989, CLE AL BR/TR, 6'1", 210

G	AB	R	H	HR	RBI	OBP	SLG	AVG
1398	5294	903	1569	358	1136	.377	.573	.296

Arguably one of the greatest hitters of his generation, Albert Belle was saddled with a well-earned reputation as a malcontent, sometimes robbing him of honors bestowed on lesser talents. In 1995 Belle became only the 12th player to hit 50 home runs in a season—and the first to hit 50 home runs and 50 doubles. The outfielder helped the Indians reach the postseason for the first time in 41 years en route to an impressive 100–44 record. He led the league in slugging percentage, doubles, home runs, total bases, and tied for the lead in RBIs and runs scored. He also hit .317 and had a .401 on base percentage.

When the Most Valuable Player votes were tallied, however, Mo Vaughn of the Boston Red Sox was the winner despite Belle's far superior stats. The community-minded Vaughn was certainly well liked by the writers, who vote for the award. Belle was known to yell at the media, when he spoke to them at all. Once he was chastised for throwing a baseball at a photographer; another time he purposely hit a fan with a thrown ball.

In 1996 Belle had a chance to again hit 50 home runs and 50 doubles, but fell two home runs short. He might have succeeded were it not for a two-game suspension incurred for needlessly barreling over Milwaukee Brewers second baseman Fernando Vina on a routine play.

Early in his career, when known as Joey Belle, he had a drinking problem. He went through treatment and was trying to start over again, using his real first name, Albert. On May 10, 1991, a fan named Jeff Pillar yelled to him, "Hey Joey, keg party at my house after the game. C'mon over." Belle picked up a ball and fired it into Pillar's chest at a distance of less than 20 feet. Belle was suspended for seven days, establishing an unsavory reputation in the game.

It also turned out to be the year that Belle established his credentials as a slugger. He hit 28 home runs and drove in 95 runs for the last-place Tribe in 1991. Belle upped those numbers to 34 homers and 112 RBIs in 1992. Belle took over the league lead in RBIs in 1993, and captured his first Silver Slugger Award (others followed in 1994, 1995, 1996, and 1998).

The American League split into three divisions in 1994 and the Indians were only one game out of first place in the Central Division by the middle of August. Belle was only two points off the league lead with a .357 batting average, and had a .714 slugging percentage, .442 on-base percentage, and 36 home runs in 106 games of the strike-shortened season. Even then Belle managed to tarnish a fine season by earning a six-game suspension for using a corked bat.

Following his stellar years in 1995 and 1996, Belle took his services to the highest bidder. His $11 million per year salary from the Chicago White Sox made him the highest-paid player in baseball history at the time. He had a down year in 1997—although he still had 30 home runs and 116 RBIs. He returned to superstar form in 1998, reaching 200 hits for the first time in his career. He led the league in total bases (399) and finished second in home runs (49) and RBIs (152).

When Belle fell out of the top three in major league salaries following the 1998 season, he invoked a free agent clause in his contract and signed a five-year deal with Baltimore. With a number of other big names on its roster, the Orioles were expected to contend in 1999, but the team never jelled and Belle could not avoid controversy. After being pulled in the ninth inning of one game, Belle yelled at manager Ray Miller and was benched for the next game. Belle's hitting didn't seem to suffer, though, as he posted his eighth straight year with at least 30 home runs and 100 RBIs, tying him with Babe Ruth for the third-longest such streak in history.

Johnny Bench

Bench, Johnny Lee **C–3B–1B**

1967–83 B:12/7/1947, Oklahoma City, OK Deb:8/28/1967, CIN NL BR/TR 6'1", 208

G	AB	R	H	HR	RBI	OBP	SLG	AVG
2158	7658	1091	2048	389	1376	.345	.476	.267

Johnny Bench clearly ranked among the greatest catchers ever, even before he was voted to the All-Century team in 1999. Although his numbers do not appear to be particularly remarkable, when viewed in the context of the physically bruising and mentally demanding environment of the catcher, they are among the best recorded. Further, while Bench's batting average reflects the lower marks typical of his era, his major league standing—second among catchers in homers and RBIs—tells the story. It is not surprising that when Ted Williams autographed a ball for Bench, then starting his second season, it was inscribed, "To Johnny Bench, a Hall of Famer for sure."

Bench was poised for success from the beginning. "Failure was the only thing I ever really feared," he once remarked. A straight-A student and the valedictorian of both his junior and senior high school classes, Bench's decision to pursue baseball was influenced by his father. A frustrated ballplayer whose career had been derailed by two hitches in the service and some physical limitations, Ted Bench coached his son in Little League and advised him to become a catcher. Even then Bench had a powerful and accurate throwing arm, enough so that he pitched occasionally. "If he had stuck with pitching he'd have been another Tom Seaver," said Ted Bench. But hitting was Bench's real gift. As a high school star in Binger, Oklahoma, Bench was known as the "Binger Banger."

The Reds' second-round pick in the 1965 amateur draft (behind Bernie Carbo), Bench tore up the minors, winning 1966 Player of Year honors in the Carolina League even after missing half the season with a broken thumb. He was so impressive at Buffalo in 1967 that, despite being promoted to Cincinnati in midseason, he was still named *The Sporting News* Minor League Player of the Year.

Bench's arrival in training camp was widely heralded. "They talk about the Messiah coming back. I'm not sure he hasn't returned already in catcher's clothes," said Reds manager Sparky Anderson. Bench did his best to live up to the grandiose expectations: in 1968 he was named National League Rookie of the Year and set records for doubles by a catcher (40) and most games caught by a rookie (154). He was selected to the first of 13 consecutive All-Star Games.

From the beginning Bench had durability, power, and arm strength—former Reds manager Dave Bristol said, "John has a quicker release than Joe Namath." His overall performance behind the plate, however, needed work; he led the league with 18 passed balls. Although Bench was an innovator with his one-handed style, his catching wouldn't be as respected as his hitting for several years to come.

In 1970 Bench enjoyed what would be the best year of his glorious career. He led the NL with 45 home runs and 148 RBIs, earned the league Most Valuable Player Award, and helped propel the Reds to the World Series. Great things were expected the next year, but Bench never equaled those numbers. The 1971 season was a disaster: his average declined to .238 as the Reds fell to fourth place.

The following year, worried about his mother's poor health, Bench got off to a terrible start, and by the end of April had only five RBIs. Then he caught fire: in one five-game stretch from May 30 to June 3, 1972, he hit seven homers. Bench finished the season with no passed balls, hit homers in all 12 National League parks, led the league with 40 homers and 125 RBIs, and earned his second MVP award.

Although the Big Red Machine beat the Red Sox in seven games in the 1975 World Series, Bench hit a meager .207. A year later, in an interview before the

1976 World Series against the Yankees, Sparky Anderson was asked about Yankees catcher Thurman Munson. He said, "I don't want to embarrass any other catcher by comparing him with Johnny Bench." The remark infuriated Munson, who responded with a .529 batting average for the Series. But Bench topped that, hitting for a .533 average with two homers and six RBIs to earn Series MVP in Cincinnati's sweep.

Despite all the attention Johnny Bench was a quiet hero, well suited to the city in which he played. He said, "Cincinnati is a quiet city, as American as apple pie. I think the club and the fans prefer that I have a wholesome image. I'm not seen at fancy places or parties and I don't date models or glamour types." Bench ate his words when he married Vicki Chesser, a high-profile New York model. Before long Bench was on TV with Johnny Carson, and one writer quipped, "Most of his closest friends didn't set records; they cut them." The marriage ended, and Bench resumed his quiet lifestyle for the remainder of his career.

Bench won 10 straight Gold Glove Awards and was named to 14 All-Star squads overall. He hit .379 in All-Star competition although he never hit .300 in a full season. "My job on the Reds is to drive in runs," Bench reminded critics, "and that's what I'm always trying to do with my bat."

Gifted with huge hands, Bench was one of the first catchers to employ the hinged catcher's mitt. He established a NL record by catching 100 or more games in each of his first 13 complete seasons. Despite being shifted to less strenuous positions late in his career, he established NL records for most putouts and most lifetime chances accepted by a catcher.

Bench suffered plenty of bumps and bruises, so playing other positions was almost like a vacation. "When I'm in the outfield I get more of a chance to think about what the pitchers are throwing and what I should look for when I'm up there batting. You get a chance to concentrate more out there. Catching absorbs all your attention."

Bench slowed down noticeably toward the end of his career. After repeatedly asking management to shift him full-time to first base or the outfield, he was sent to first in 1981. He responded by hitting .328 through May 28, silencing the critics who liked to point out that he had never broken the season .300 barrier. On that date he fractured his ankle and was out until August 22 (his first time on the disabled list), but he finished the year at .309. After recovering from the injury he moved over to third. Bench went back behind the plate for his last major league game in 1983, the year that he was selected for his final All-Star Game.

That autograph from Ted Williams proved prophetic in 1989, when Bench was indeed elected to the Hall of Fame.

Chief Bender

Bender, Charles Albert **P**

1903–17, 1925 B:5/5/1884, Crow Wing County, MN D:5/22/1954, Philadelphia, PA Deb:4/20/1903, PHI AL BR/TR, 6'2", 185

W	L	PCT	G	SH	IP	BB	SO	ERA
212	127	.625	459	40	3017	712	1711	2.46

Chief Bender, a righthanded pitcher who helped Connie Mack's Philadelphia Athletics win five pennants during the early years of the century, was one-quarter Chippewa. The subtle and not-so-subtle prejudices that affected players of Native American descent drove many to misery and some to drink, but Bender was different.

When teammates teased him, he referred to them as "foreigners." When admiring children crowded around him in the street and sought to ingratiate themselves with war whoops and rain dances, he never lost his patience. He was not unaware of the racism around him, but the easygoing Bender weathered the worst while doing his job. At that time teammates, fans, and the media called most baseball players of Native American background "Chief," not exactly a positive epithet. Bender, known as Chief to nearly everyone in baseball, didn't complain, but he always signed autographs "Charles Bender." Connie Mack always called him by his middle name, Albert.

From 1898 to 1901 Bender played baseball and football at Carlisle Indian School in Pennsylvania, the same school later attended by Jim Thorpe. In 1902 he enrolled at Dickinson College and played semipro baseball under the name Charles Albert with the Harrisburg, Pennsylvania, Athletic Club to help pay his tuition. When he beat the Chicago Cubs in an exhibition game, he caught the attention of Athletics scout Jesse Frisinger.

Bender joined the A's during the spring of 1903 and produced a 17–14 record. He started 33 games and pitched 270 innings, two figures he never attained again. Mack believed that Bender lacked the stamina to sustain such a heavy work load, so for the rest of his time with the A's Mack gave him extra rest between starts, usually saving him for must-win games. Mack could afford to be judicious; his staff also included legendary hurlers Eddie Plank and Rube Waddell.

After going 18–11 in 1905, Bender earned Philadelphia's only win in the World Series, as Christy Mathewson of the Giants pitched three shutouts. In Game 2 Bender tossed a four-hit shutout of his own. Despite allowing only five hits, he lost Game 5 to Mathewson, 2–0. All five games of that World Series were shutouts.

Bender relied on a good fastball, a sharp curve, and excellent control. Teammate Eddie Collins believed that neither Walter Johnson nor Amos Rusie "had any more speed when [Bender] was at his best." On May 12, 1910, pitching against Cleveland, Bender had spectacular success with a pitch that was halfway between a fastball and a curve. He had no name for it, but it helped him no-hit the Indians, 4–0. Bender's invention became known as the slider, or "nickel curve," and when he became a coach he taught it to others.

But it was the rangy pitcher's keen intelligence that set him apart from other players. Mack often used him as a third-base coach because of his ability to steal signs. Ty Cobb called him the "brainiest pitcher" he ever faced. In the 1911 World Series, Bender faced Chief Meyers, a righthanded hitter who was known for murdering fastballs. Bender waved his outfield around to the right. Naturally, Meyers expected a curve on the outside corner, but Bender crossed him up with a fastball down the middle for strike three.

Each year from 1908 through 1910 Bender compiled an ERA under 1.80. The 1910 season was probably his best. In addition to pitching a no-hitter, he won 22 other games. He led the AL with an .821 winning percentage, allowed only 182 hits and 47 walks in 250 innings, and had a 1.58 ERA. He won the opening game of the World Series that year, beating the Cubs, 4–1, with a three-hitter. He lost Game 4 in 10 innings, 4–3, but the A's came back to win the series the next day. The next year, after going 17–5 in the regular season, he won two more games in the World Series.

In 1913 the Athletics won another pennant. Illness sidetracked ace Jack Coombs, and Mack was forced to use a number of inexperienced starters, saving Bender for relief work. During the season Bender started only 21 games while relieving in 27. He won six games out of the bullpen and saved a league-high 13, finishing with a record of 21–10. The Athletics defeated the Giants in the World Series, and Bender won two games. In 1914 Bender led the league in winning percentage for the third time with a 17–3 record. He opened the World Series for the A's against the Boston Braves but was knocked out in the sixth inning, the first shock in a series full of surprises, as the lightly regarded Braves swept the A's.

In 1915 the Federal League, which had claimed major league status the year before, was trying to lure American and National League players into its fold with high salaries. Connie Mack was losing money, and he gave aging star pitchers Plank and Bender permission to jump to the rival league. Despite collecting a $5,000 signing bonus and $8,500 in salary, Bender later termed the move "the biggest mistake of my life." He went 4–16 with a terrible Baltimore team. In 1916 and 1917 he pitched with the Phillies, and then he retired from the majors other than for one inning pitched for the Chicago White Sox in 1925.

After his retirement, Bender managed in the minors, coached in the majors, and scouted for various teams while pursuing such interests as oil painting, trapshooting, and billiards. In 1953, the year before he died, he was elected to the Hall of Fame. Mack paid him perhaps the highest compliment. Although he had sent such pitchers as Plank, Waddell, and Lefty Grove to the Hall before Bender, Mack said, "If I had all the men I've ever handled and they were in their prime and there was one game I wanted to win above all others ... Albert would be my man."

Andy Benes

Benes, Andrew Charles **P**

1989–* B:8/20/1967, Evansville, IN Deb:8/11/1989, SD NL BR/TR 6'6", 235

W	L	PCT	G	SH	IP	BB	SO	ERA
131	119	.524	328	9	2135	729	1721	3.79

After a successful collegiate career at Evansville, Andy Benes was the first player drafted in 1988. He reached the majors after spending only part of one season in the minors, and pitched well enough in his first season with the San Diego Padres to be honored by *The Sporting News* as National League Rookie Pitcher of the Year.

Benes reached double-digits in victories in each of his first four seasons, and appeared in the 1993 All-Star Game. He never lived up to expectations that he would become a dominant pitcher in San Diego. The Padres' dwindling fortunes resulted in a trade with Seattle during the pennant-stretch in 1995. Benes helped pitch the Mariners to the postseason for the first time in franchise history. His two postseason starts, however, were not impressive He was much more effective the following year as a Cardinal.

Benes joined his younger brother Alan on the St. Louis pitching staff in 1996, and Andy enjoyed the best season of his career. He won 18 games, including a victory over the Pirates that got the Cardinals into the postseason. Benes signed a contract to stay in St. Louis after the 1997 season, but a technicality voided the deal. Major League Baseball did not grant Benes and agent Scott Boras an exemption to return to the Cardinals, so the righthander joined the expansion Arizona Diamondbacks for their inaugural 1998 season.

He started the first game in Diamondbacks history, and later narrowly missed a no-hitter, surrendering a one-out, ninth-inning single to Cincinnati's Sean Casey on September 13, 1998. His 14 wins tied Tampa Bay's Rolando Arrojo for most ever by a first-year expansion-team pitcher. In 1999 Benes was a key member of a pitching staff that led Arizona to a division title, the quickest postseason appearance ever made by an expansion team. Two seasons after he tried—and failed—to sign with St. Louis, he officially became a Cardinal again as a free agent.

Juan Beniquez

Beniquez, Juan Jose (Torres) **OF–DH**

1971–88 B:5/13/1950, San Sebastian, Puerto Rico Deb:9/4/1971, BOS AL BR/TR 5'11", 165

G	AB	R	H	HR	RBI	OBP	SLG	AVG
1500	4651	610	1274	79	476	.329	.379	.274

Much-traveled Juan Beniquez played for eight American League teams in his 18-season major league career. Signed as a free agent by the Red Sox in October 1968, the native of Puerto Rico started his minor league career as a second baseman with Winter Haven, leading the Florida State League in triples and errors. He played in the minors with Winston-Salem, Pawtucket, and Louisville before reaching Boston. In 1971 he led the International League in triples and in 1973 paced it in batting.

However, Beniquez was never able to equal his minor league batting achievements in the majors. Similarly, early on, his fielding was a question mark. In one of his early stints in the majors, playing at shortstop, Beniquez made six errors in the space of two games on July 13 and 14, 1972. After a couple of seasons with the Red Sox, in November 1975 he was traded to Texas for Ferguson Jenkins. In his second season with the Rangers, Beniquez showed that he had turned his fielding around, earning Gold Glove honors.

Beniquez was dealt to the Yankees in a 10-player transaction in November 1978. Traded to the Mariners at season's end, he signed with California as a free agent in December 1980. After five seasons in Anaheim, he became a free agent again at the close of the 1985 season and signed with Baltimore. With the Orioles, he had his most memorable offensive performance, homering three times in one game on June 12, 1986. Beniquez later played with Kansas City and Toronto.

Charlie Bennett

Bennett, Charles Wesley **C**

1878, 1880–93 B:11/21/1854, New Castle, PA
D:2/24/1927, Detroit, MI Deb:5/1/1878, MIL NL
BR/TR, 5'11", 180

G	AB	R	H	HR	RBI	OBP	SLG	AVG
1062	3821	549	978	55	533	.340	.387	.256

Regarded as the 19th century's finest catcher, Charlie Bennett led National League catchers seven times in fielding percentage and claimed credit for inventing the chest protector. By comparison to today's catchers, he performed under barbaric conditions. Bennett, the *Detroit Free Press* once stated, had been "arrayed in nothing more than a base ball suit, a rubber cork between his teeth, and a thin kid glove on his left hand with the fingers cut out, no mask or protector...No wonder that Charlie Bennett can show a pair of hands with many a kink in them."

Bennett began his baseball career with the semipro Neshannock club of New Castle, Pennsylvania, played briefly for the short-lived Milwaukee Grays of the National League, and was catching for Worcester on June 12, 1880, when J. Lee Richmond recorded the major league's first perfect game. Richmond said Bennett was "the best backstop that ever lived. He went after everything, he knew no fear, and he kept his pitcher from going in the air."

In 1881 Bennett left Worcester to join the new National League entry in Detroit, the Wolverines, where he invented the chest protector—he had his wife rig up a cork-lined vest, which he wore under his uniform. During the following season he signed an option to perform with the American Association's Pittsburgh Alleghenys, but he not only reneged on the deal, he brought pitcher James "Pud" Galvin and third baseman Ned Williamson back to the National League with him. The American Association sued Bennett, but the court permitted him to remain with the Wolverines, ruling he had merely signed an option, not a binding agreement.

In 1887, his seventh year with Detroit, the Wolverines finally won the NL pennant and faced the American Association's St. Louis Browns in the World Series. Bennett hit .262 in the 15-game series, but his primary contribution to the Wolverines' victory was the shutting down of the Browns' running game. Despite a badly injured right thumb, his throwing made the Browns "scared to move a yard away from the sacks."

Following the 1888 season the Detroit franchise collapsed and Bennett was sold to Boston along with first baseman Dan Brouthers and two other players. He played five years for the Beaneaters, and participated in their World Series victory in 1892.

After the 1893 season Bennett went hunting with pitcher John Clarkson. They were on their way from Kansas City to Williamsburgh when Bennett got off the train at Wellsville, Kansas, to speak to an acquaintance. Attempting to reboard the train, he slipped, fell under its wheels, and lost both legs. Fitted with artificial limbs but confined to a wheelchair, Bennett then earned his living running a cigar store.

Detroit fans arranged a day in his honor, and he was given a wheelbarrow full of silver dollars. Later, Detroit's ballpark was named Bennett Park. When it opened on April 28, 1896, he caught the ceremonial first pitch and repeated the feat for every home opener through 1926.

Jack Bentley

Bentley, John Needles **P**

1913–16, 1923–27 B:3/8/1895, Sandy Spring, MD
D:10/24/1969, Olney, MD Deb:9/6/1913, WAS AL
BL/TL 5'11½", 200

W	L	PCT	G	SV	IP	BB	SO	ERA
46	33	.582	138	9	714	263	259	4.01

Babe Ruth was not yet near his prime in 1923 when New York Giants tub-thumpers began hailing Jack Bentley as "the next Babe Ruth." Like the Bambino, Bentley was a fine lefthanded pitcher and a powerful lefthanded slugger. And, like Ruth, Bentley came to the major leagues after creating a stir with Baltimore of the International League: he was 48–9, with a 5–0 mark in the Little World Series from 1916 through 1922. In his last year with the Orioles he even doubled as an outfielder and hit .349.

Not many Giants fans remembered that Bentley had already spent parts of four uneventful seasons—from 1913 to 1916—with the Washington Senators. Bentley's numbers in Washington weren't even worth mentioning except in 1914, when he went 5–7 with four saves, while splitting time between being a starter and a relief pitcher.

With the Giants, Bentley started well enough, winning 13 of 21 decisions for manager John McGraw's 1923 pennant winners. However, he was whacked for a 9.45 ERA in two World Series appearances against Ruth and friends. The next year he improved to 16–5 as the Giants won the pennant again. After losing Game 2 of the World Series, 4–3, he won Game 5 and then lost the finale in relief; two New York errors and a bad bounce cost him the game in the twelfth inning.

Jack Bentley had done some effective pinch hitting in his first two seasons, but as he put on weight his effectiveness both at bat and on the mound faded. The Phillies tried him as a first baseman in 1926, but after 1927 he was out of the majors for good.

Rube Benton

Benton, John Clebon **P**

1910–21, 1923–25 B:6/27/1887, Clinton, NC
D:12/12/1937, Dothan, AL Deb:6/28/1910, CIN NL
BL/TL 6'1", 190

W	L	PCT	G	SH	IP	BB	SO	ERA
150	144	.510	437	23	2517^1	712	950	3.09

Not every player charged with complicity or "guilty knowledge" in the Black Sox scandal was banished from professional baseball—Rube Benton was one who managed to stay in the game. Benton, then a pitcher with John McGraw's Giants, admitted in sworn testimony before a Chicago grand jury that he had been present in a New York City hotel room when fellow Giants hurler Jean Dubuc received a telegram from conspirator "Sleepy Bill" Burns, advising him of the fix. Benton also acknowledged knowing that first baseman Hal Chase had received similar telegrams and that Chase had won $40,000 on the World Series. He further revealed that he had heard from a Cincinnati gambler that Chick Gandil, Happy Felsch, Lefty Williams, and Eddie Cicotte had been involved in the Chicago dive. Benton denied, however, that he had himself won $3,800 on the series.

Shortly thereafter Benton, reputedly a chronic drunkard and womanizer, was demoted to the minors—not banned from the game as was Buck Weaver. After a successful season with the American Association's St. Paul Saints, however, the Cincinnati Reds wanted to bring him up. Both National League president John Heydler and American League president Ban Johnson thundered that there was no place in either big league for him. Commissioner Kenesaw Mountain Landis intervened, however, arguing with some logic that if Benton was eligible to play for St. Paul then he was also eligible to play for Cincinnati, so Benton was allowed to join the Reds.

Benton's move up to Cincinnati was his second stint with the Reds. He had originally entered the majors with them in 1910, being a regular starter for four years before being traded to the Giants in 1915. He played with the Giants in the 1917 World Series, going 1–1 against the White Sox, losing the sixth and final game despite giving up no earned runs. He had some excellent seasons in his first decade in the majors, winning at least 16 games four times, although he lost at least that many four times as well. In his reincarnation in 1923, Benton went 14–10, but after two losing seasons he was sent back to the minors, where he played until 1934.

Moe Berg

Berg, Morris **C**

1923, 1926–39 B:3/2/1902, New York, NY
D:5/29/1972, Belleville, NJ Deb:6/27/1923, BRO NL
BR/TR 6'1", 185

G	AB	R	H	HR	RBI	OBP	SLG	AVG
663	1813	150	441	6	206	.278	.299	.243

Moe Berg may have been the most intelligent man, and perhaps the most eccentric one, ever to don a major league uniform. He read and spoke 12 languages, including Sanskrit. As a shortstop on the Princeton University baseball team, he and the second baseman called who would cover second base on attempted steals—in Latin. As a rookie with the White Sox, he reported late to spring training in order to complete his term at law school. As a third-string major league catcher, he invariably found his locker surrounded after a game by newsmen looking for a dissertation on Urdu, ancient Greek history, or astronomy.

Berg was a panelist on the popular radio program, *Information Please*, with regulars John Kieran, Clifton Fadiman, and the playwright George S. Kaufman. Berg correctly answered questions on Roman mythology, French impressionism, spatial geometry, and the infield fly rule. Kieran later remarked, "Moe wasted his time in baseball. He could have become a Supreme Court justice with that rare brain he possessed." Although a hit on the radio, Berg soon regretted his appearance. He was inundated with letters from listeners who were eager to test his knowledge of trivia, and he finally stopped reading his mail. He also put up with ribbing from opposing players, who would come to the plate, turn to Berg, and utter such taunts as, "Hey, Moe, recite the Book of Leviticus for us!"

Unfortunately, Berg could not do well at what many baseball fans believe is the most difficult task in the game: hit a baseball. He was reportedly the subject of Mike Gonzalez's legendary scouting report, "Good field, no hit." After Berg proved Gonzalez correct, it was said that "Berg can speak 12 different languages and can't hit in any of them."

Berg's shortcomings with the bat became apparent in 1923, his first season in the majors, when he hit .186 as an infielder with the Brooklyn Dodgers; he then returned to the minors. In 1926 the White Sox, undaunted by his weak bat, paid $50,000 for his contract and brought him back to the majors as a utility infielder. Then in 1927, after injuries had decimated the Chicago catching staff, Berg found his true position.

When both the first- and second-string catchers were injured in a game, manager Ray Schalk looked down the bench and asked, "Any of you fellows ever a catcher?" Berg replied, "I thought I was once, but somebody told me I wasn't." Schalk asked, "Who was that?" Berg: "My high school coach in Newark." But Schalk, desperate for a catcher, replied, "Well, as long as he isn't around, how about getting in there and trying it again?" Oddly enough, while wearing the "tools of ignorance," baseball's most intelligent player discovered it was the only position in which he could use his mind. In 1929 he played in 107 games and hit .287. He then hurt his knee, which affected his batting stance, and he never again hit with even minimal authority. Still, he played for 10 more seasons, always as a reserve, and was valued for his defense and handling of pitchers. At one point, he went 133 games without committing an error.

Despite finding his true position, Berg sometimes sat for weeks without playing. On one fiercely hot day in Washington, he was put into the Senators' starting lineup after spending a month lounging in the bullpen. By the seventh inning he was dragging, as "Doc" Cramer came to bat for the Philadelphia A's against Washington's Earl Whitehill. Playing mind games, Cramer kept stepping out of the batter's box just as Whitehill was ready to pitch. When Cramer stepped back in, Whitehill stepped off the rubber. Berg went into his crouch with each false start. Frustrated, the catcher ripped off his mitt, mask, chest protector, and shin guards and stacked them on home plate. "I'll return when those two are ready to play ball," he announced to the startled umpire. "Right now I'm taking a shower."

In 1934, the year he was traded from Washington to Cleveland, a team of American All-Stars, including Babe Ruth, traveled to Japan on a goodwill tour. At the last minute, Berg was added to the squad. His selection made sense when he gave a welcoming speech in perfect Japanese and addressed the legislature in Tokyo. However, instead of playing, Berg spent much of his time taking photographs. By order of the State Department, Berg was to photograph key Japanese military installations and other potential targets. Eight years later, General Jimmy Doolittle used these photographs in making the first American attack on Japan during World War II.

When Berg retired from baseball after the 1939 season, he joined "Wild Bill" Donovan's Office of Strategic Services, the forerunner of the CIA. His primary objective was to determine Germany's nuclear potential. In the course of his work, Berg met Albert Einstein. Berg offered to teach Einstein baseball if the professor taught him mathematics. "I'm sure you'd learn mathematics faster," said Einstein.

Berg undertook several dangerous missions behind enemy lines to keep track of German scientists. His gift for languages served him well, and he always returned home safely. Some of his missions were rumored to involve assassinations, but Berg never discussed them. After the war, he characteristically declined the Medal of Merit.

Before baseball's leading intellectual died in 1972, he received many requests to write his memoirs. After turning down such offers for years, Berg at last agreed, but the project never got off the ground. He quit in a huff after the co-writer assigned to him confused him with Moe Howard of the Three Stooges.

Casey Stengel once called Berg "the strangest man ever to play baseball," but perhaps the best epitaph for him was a comment made by White Sox pitcher Ted Lyons, a college graduate himself. "He was different because he was different," Lyons said. "He made up for all the bores of the world."

Wally Berger

Berger, Walter Antone **OF**

1930–40 B:10/10/1905, Chicago, IL D:11/30/1988, Redondo Beach, CA Deb:4/15/1930, BOS NL BR/TR 6'2", 198

G	AB	R	H	HR	RBI	OBP	SLG	AVG
1350	5163	809	1550	242	898	.359	.522	.300

Until Eddie Mathews and Hank Aaron arrived in the 1950s, Wally Berger was the greatest slugger ever to wear a Braves uniform. From 1930 through 1936 the righthanded outfielder was practically the only home run threat the Braves could muster. In 1935, for example, he hammered 34 homers to lead the National League. Significantly, the second-most prolific home run hitter on the club was Babe Ruth, who hit six before he retired in May.

Chicago-born Berger grew up in San Francisco playing sandlot baseball. In high school he played third base on a team that featured future Hall of Famer Joe Cronin at second. In 1927 he signed his first professional contract with the Class C Utah–Idaho League's Pocatello Bannocks and became an outfielder. When he hit .385 with 24 home runs in 92 games, he was brought back home to play for San Francisco's PCL team. Although Berger tore up PCL pitching for the next two seasons, he was not brought up to the majors for even the traditional "cup of coffee." His rights were owned by the Chicago Cubs, whose 1930 team boasted an outfield of Riggs

Stephenson, Hack Wilson, and Kiki Cuyler, each of whom would hit .300 with more than 100 RBIs that year.

Before the 1930 season opened, Berger was traded to Boston. He rewarded his new employers with one of the best rookie seasons on record, hitting .310 with 38 home runs and 119 RBIs. His home run total as a rookie, although tied by Frank Robinson in 1956, stood as the major league record until Mark McGwire bested it in 1987.

Although he never surpassed his rookie home run total in any other year, Berger hit between 17 and 34 home runs for each of the next six seasons. He also batted over .300 four times with the Braves, with a career-high .323 in 1931. Four times he batted in more than 100 runs, with a league-leading 130 in 1935. He started in center field for the NL in the first three All-Star Games (1933, 1934, 1935) and was also named to the squad in 1936.

In 1933 Berger missed almost three weeks of the season because of illness, but led the Braves into the first division for the first time in a dozen years. He hit .313 with 106 RBIs, and his 27 homers were exactly half his team's total for the season.

Two factors make Berger's record all the more impressive. First, during his entire time with Boston, pitchers could always pitch around him because there was never a longball threat coming up behind him. The second-highest homer total for a Brave during those seven years was 13 by Gene Moore in 1936, and only two other batters had seasons in which they reached double figures. Another factor working against Berger was the Braves' ballpark. Braves Field had the most distant fences in the National League. As a righthanded pull-hitter, Berger was challenged by a distance of 350 feet down the left field line before the fence intruded. Although he hit 105 homers at Braves Field, more than any other player in history, one can only wonder how many he might have hit in more friendly confines.

A shoulder injury in 1936 reduced Berger's hitting ability, and in 1937 he was traded to the New York Giants. Playing only part-time, he helped them win the 1937 NL pennant. In 1938 he was sent on to Cincinnati, where he helped the Reds win a pennant in 1939. Released after two games in 1940, he signed with the Phillies but didn't finish the season.

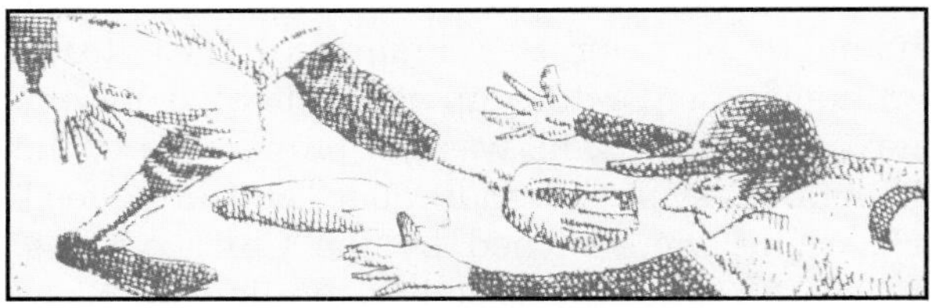

Bill Bernhard

Bernhard, William Henry **P**

1899–1907 B:3/16/1871, Clarence, NY D:3/30/1949, San Diego, CA Deb: 4/24/1899, PHI NL BB/TR 6'1, 205

W	L	PCT	G	SH	IP	BB	SO	ERA
116	81	.589	231	14	1792	365	545	3.04

One of the most effective pitchers of his era, "Strawberry Bill" Bernhard was a key figure in baseball's inter-league war for players and fans that erupted in the first decade of the 20th century. After reaching the majors in 1899 at the age of 28, Bernhard won 15 games for the Philadelphia Phillies in 1900. After the season, Bernhard joined star shortstop Napoleon Lajoie and a handful of other teammates in jumping from the Phillies to the Philadelphia Athletics of the upstart American League.

With organized baseball still in its fledgling stages and no players union to speak of, Bernhard and his fellow jumpers were in a precarious position. The Phillies went to court to invalidate the players' contracts with the Athletics; the ultimate upshot was that Lajoie and Bernhard both left the A's in May 1902 to sign with Cleveland's AL entrant, then called the Blues.

For legal reasons, the National League refugees could not accompany their teammates to Philadelphia until midway through the 1903 campaign. Despite the uncertainty surrounding his contract status, Bernhard thrived in Cleveland. He went 18–5 in 1902, and recorded the franchise's first-ever Opening Day win in 1904 en route to a 23–13 record for the season.

Yogi Berra

Berra, Lawrence Peter **C–OF**

1946–63, 1965 M(1964, 1972–75, 1984–85, 484–444) B:5/12/1925, St. Louis, MO Deb:9/22/1946, NY AL BL/TR 5'8", 194

G	AB	R	H	HR	RBI	OBP	SLG	AVG
2120	7555	1175	2150	358	1430	.350	.482	.285

An entire generation has now grown up knowing Yogi Berra mainly for the malapropisms attributed to him, but the abilities shown during his brilliant 19-year career were such that he was still selected to the All-Century team in 1999. As with Johnny Bench, the straight numbers—although impressive—do not begin to tell the whole story of the three-time American League Most Valuable Player.

Berra's nickname was bestowed upon him during his boyhood by Bobby Hofman, who later played for the New York Giants. After seeing a movie about an Indian snake-charmer, Hofman exclaimed, "That yogi walks like Lawdie [Lawrence] Berra." The name stuck. "Even his wife calls him Yogi," wrote Joe Garagiola. "Carmen still laughs about how, after more than 30 years of marriage, she got an anniversary card signed 'Yogi Berra.' She asked him if he thought he had to sign his last name so she wouldn't think it came from some other Yogi."

Three teams missed signing the future Hall of Famer, who was elected to the shrine in 1972. The Cardinals let Berra go but signed his buddy Garagiola for $500. The Browns offered Berra a contract with no bonus, but Berra insisted on what Garagiola had received. Cardinals general manager Branch Rickey was quoted as saying, "He'll never make anything more than a Triple A ballplayer at best." Garagiola recalled that "Rickey was leaving the Cardinals at the time to go to the Dodgers"; when Rickey arrived in Brooklyn he telegraphed Berra, inviting him to a Dodgers tryout in Bear Mountain, New York. However, Berra had already signed with the Yankees after scout Leo Browne convinced them that he was worth the $500.

Berra was assigned to the Class B Piedmont League Norfolk Tars, but then enlisted in the Navy after turning 18. After the war he played with the New London, Connecticut, club, where Giants manager Mel Ott saw him and was impressed. "He seemed to be doing everything wrong, yet everything came out right. He stopped everything behind the plate and hit everything in front of it."

Ott was determined to pry Berra away from the Yankees and offered general manager Larry MacPhail $50,000 for him. MacPhail had no idea who Berra was but figured that if Ott wanted him that badly he had to be worth keeping. When MacPhail first saw Berra in the flesh he was crestfallen. "The instant I saw him my heart sank, and I wondered why I had been so foolish as to refuse to sell him," he confessed. "He was one of the most unprepossessing fellows I ever set eyes on."

In 1946 Berra was apprenticed to the Newark Bears and responded with a .314 season. The following year was his first with the Yankees, but, until 1949, Berra merely shared the catching duties with Aaron Robinson, Charlie Silvera, and Gus Niarhos. Part of the time he played in Yankee Stadium's left field, which was beset by early evening shadows. "It gets late early out here," he once said of the stadium.

In Berra's first year with the Yankees he was honored at St. Louis' Sportsman's Park with a "Yogi Berra Night," receiving not only good wishes but also a new Nash automobile. He had prepared a two-sentence speech: "I'm a lucky guy and I'm happy to be with the Yankees. I want to thank everyone for making this night possible." But in front of his friends it came out: "I want to thank everyone for making this night necessary."

With his malapropisms, clumsiness behind the plate, and comical appearance, Berra was often the butt of jokes. In 1949 new Yankees manager Casey Stengel made a point of trying to instill confidence in his catcher, whom he saw as one of the great raw talents in the game. "He is a great man," Stengel told reporters. "I am lucky to have him and so are my pitchers. He springs on a bunt like it was another dollar." Stengel also stated that he wouldn't trade Berra, his "assistant manager," for anyone, even Ted Williams.

Berra was a wild swinger, like fellow Hall of Famer Joe Medwick. Yet his swing was balanced and his follow-through never ungainly. He was also tough in the clutch, leading Paul Richards to praise him as "the toughest man in baseball in the last three innings." For all of Berra's wild swinging, he was not easy to strike out. In 1950, for instance, he fanned just 12 times in 597 at bats.

Berra eventually became a skilled receiver and a good handler of pitchers. One of his most unusual practices was to jabber away at opposing batters in order to distract them. During the 1958 World Series Hank Aaron had finally had enough after Berra kept telling him to hit with the label up on the bat. "Yogi, I came up here to hit, not to read," said Aaron.

Among his many accomplishments, Berra's most impressive marks were being selected for the All-Star Game 15 consecutive years, playing on 14 pennant-winning teams and 10 world champion squads, setting the World Series record for most hits (71), and going an entire season (1958) without an error.

In 1964, at the end of his playing career, Stengel's erstwhile "assistant" rose to become the Yankees' manager; he responded to the challenge by winning a pennant. But when New York fell to Johnny Keane's Cardinals in a seven-game Series, Berra was fired amid talk that he had lost control of his players. In a public relations coup, the rival Mets signed him as a player-coach, thereby reuniting him with Stengel. Berra played in only a handful of games, but he once teamed up with Warren Spahn, making for a memorable combination. "I don't know if we're the oldest battery, but we sure are the ugliest," admitted Spahn.

Berra coached the Mets long after Stengel had gone, and, following the death of Gil Hodges in 1971, he was named manager. In 1973 his "Ya Gotta Believe" Mets incredibly came from last place in the final month of the season to capture the National League pennant with the lowest won-lost percentage of any league champion in

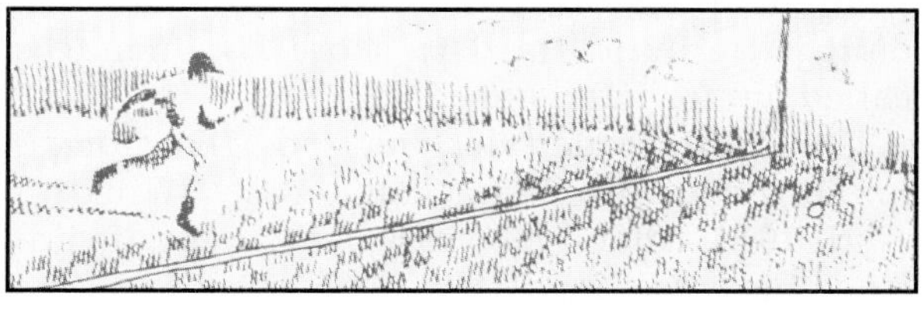

history. That year he coined his famous line, "It ain't over 'til it's over."

Berra was dismissed as Mets manager in 1975 and returned to the Yankees the following year as a coach. In 1984 George Steinbrenner hired him to manage the club and Berra brought New York in third. Twenty-two games into the next season he was fired. Disgusted with Steinbrenner, Berra long refused to participate in any event at Yankee Stadium. The two made amends after the 1998 season, and he threw out the first pitch on Opening Day 1999.

Berra signed on as a coach with the Houston Astros in 1986, and served in that capacity until his retirement in 1992. In 1998 a Yogi Berra Museum opened on the campus of Montclair State College in Upper Montclair, New Jersey.

Bob Bescher

Bescher, Robert Henry **OF**

1908–18 B:2/25/1884, London, OH D:11/29/1942, London, OH Deb:9/5/1908, CHI NL BB/TL 6'1", 200

G	AB	R	H	HR	RBI	OBP	SLG	AVG
1228	4536	749	1171	28	345	.353	.351	.258

When Cincinnati Reds outfielder Bob Bescher set the National League record for stolen bases—with 80 thefts in 1911—it was a mark that would stand for more than half a century. It was not until 1962, when Maury Wills swiped 104, that Bescher's record was finally surpassed.

Bescher first arrived in the major leagues with the Reds in 1908, and the next year, when he became a regular, he recorded the first of four consecutive stolen base titles. One reason that Bescher had so many chances was that he was a very patient batter. Although he did not hit for a high average, he drew a large number of walks, leading the NL in that category with 94 in 1913.

Perhaps the highlight of Bescher's career was when he ruined Nap Rucker's no-hit attempt on July 22, 1911, by singling with two outs in the ninth inning. Rucker ultimately won the game, 1–0.

In December 1913 Bescher was traded to the New York Giants for Buck Herzog. While with New York, on July 17, 1914, he was involved in a truly unusual play. Playing center field, Bescher fielded a ball hit by the Pirates' Jim Viox and, in an attempt to catch runner Honus Wagner, threw it to third baseman Milt Stock. Stock flubbed the catch and the ball disappeared. It was discovered nestled under the arm of Wagner, who had chugged around third to score. Wagner was called out for interference.

The Giants traded Bescher and Mike Gonzalez to the Cardinals for catcher Ivy Wingo in April 1915. After three years in St. Louis, he finished his career in 1918 with Cleveland.

Kurt Bevacqua

Bevacqua, Kurt Anthony **3B-2B-1B**

1971–85 B:1/23/1947, Miami Beach, FL Deb:6/22/1971, CLE AL BR/TR 6'1", 185

G	AB	R	H	HR	RBI	OBP	SLG	AVG
970	2117	214	499	27	275	.309	.327	.236

Supersub Kurt Bevacqua inspired fellow benchwarmers everywhere when San Diego manager Dick Williams selected him as his designated hitter for the 1984 World Series. The critics scoffed; after all, designated hitters were supposed to be imposing sluggers, not mere utility men like the wisecracking Bevacqua, who once won a bubble-gum blowing contest by major league players.

The critics had a field day after Bevacqua committed a baserunning blunder in Game 1, but they had to eat their words when he came through with a game-winning two-run homer in Game 2. He also homered in Game 5.

Bevacqua had already been in the majors more than a decade, initially coming up with the Cleveland Indians in 1971, even though the Mets, Braves, and Reds had drafted him. Rarely staying with any team more than two years, he was bounced to the Royals, Pirates, Royals (again), Brewers, Rangers, Padres, and Pirates (a second time), before finding his final home with the Padres.

Although never hugely successful as a regular, his lifetime off-the-bench batting average was a full 30 points higher than his overall percentage. In 1980 he paced the National League in pinch hits.

Jim Bibby

Bibby, James Blair **P**

1972–81, 1983–84 B:10/29/1944, Franklinton, NC Deb:9/4/1972, STL NL BR/TR 6'5", 235

W	L	PCT	G	SH	IP	BB	SO	ERA
111	101	.524	340	19	1722[2]	723	1079	3.76

Throughout much of his minor-league career, Jim Bibby's greatest claim to fame was being the brother of Henry Bibby, an All-America guard for John Wooden's NCAA champion basketball teams. But although hampered by wildness and inconsistency, once in the majors Bibby ultimately earned a reputation all his own.

Signed by the New York Mets in 1965, Bibby spent two years in the armed forces (including a tour of duty in Vietnam) before reaching the major leagues with the St. Louis Cardinals in 1972. Early the next season, the Cardinals traded him to Texas, leading to Bibby's finest moment. On July 30, 1973, while pitching for the Rangers, he no-hit the defending world champion Oakland Athletics.

In 1975 Bibby was traded to Cleveland mid-season, and in 1978 he ended up in Pittsburgh, where he had his finest years. In 1980 he earned his only selection to the All-Star Game in a season that saw him go 19–6. The next year, while pitching against Atlanta on May 21, 1981, he surrendered a lead-off single to Terry Harper and then calmly mowed down the next 27 batters. Soon afterward Bibby suffered a torn rotator cuff, which eventually would end his career.

After a year of rehabilitation, Bibby returned to the Pirates in 1983 before finishing his career with the Rangers in 1984. In 1999 he coached for the Carolina League's Lynchburg Hillcats.

Dante Bichette

Bichette, Alphonse Dante **OF**

1988–* B:11/18/1963, West Palm Beach, FL
Deb:9/5/1988, CAL AL BR/TR 6'3", 225

G	AB	R	H	HR	RBI	OBP	SLG	AVG
1442	5415	809	1625	239	1002	.339	.504	.300

The thin air of Colorado helped transform Dante Bichette from a part-time player to an All-Star. In his first five major league seasons with California and Milwaukee, the former 17th-round draft choice hit a total of 38 home runs. In the strike-shortened 1995 season, he hit 40 homers for the Rockies.

After hitting just five home runs in 112 games for the Brewers in 1992, Bichette was convinced that Japan would provide his best chance to play regularly. The expansion Rockies, however, were looking for an inexpensive player with good defensive skills and acquired the outfielder in a trade.

Bichette proved to be a steal. Combining tremendous upper-body strength with a calm approach at the plate, Bichette thrived in the high altitude of Denver. He batted over .300 with home runs totals of 21 and 27 in his first two years at Mile High Stadium, and when Coors Field opened in 1995 Bichette began to post superstar numbers. He was a hero from the first night; his three-run homer won the inaugural game in extra innings. He went on to bat .377 at Coors, with 31 homers, 83 RBIs and a staggering .755 slugging percentage. Bichette's road numbers were respectable but more down to earth: .300 average, nine homers, and 45 RBIs. That discrepancy may have cost him the Most Valuable Player Award. Although he led the league in home runs, RBIs, slugging percentage, and hits, Bichette finished second in the MVP balloting to Cincinnati's Barry Larkin.

Still, it was an impressive accomplishment for Bichette. He became the first player since Norm Cash in 1961, and just the 14th player overall, to reach five lofty milestones in one year: .340 average, 40 home runs, 120 RBIs, 100 runs scored, and 350 total bases. Bichette was also one of four Rockies to hit 30 or more home runs in 1995, helping Colorado reach the playoffs after only three years of existence.

While the Rockies did not return to the playoffs for the rest of the decade, Bichette continued to post superior numbers. In 1996 he joined the elite 30–30 club, notching 31 home runs and 31 stolen bases. In 1998 he established a major league record with 47 hits in April. He finished the year with a major league-best 219 hits. In 1999 he finished with 177 hits and 133 RBIs, but was two points shy of his seventh consecutive .300 season. He surpassed 100 RBIs in each of his five seasons at Coors Field. After earning All-Star status four times in his seven years with the Rockies, Bichette was traded to Cincinnati after the 1999 season, shortly before his 36th birthday.

Lou Bierbauer

Bierbauer, Louis W. **2B**

1886–98 B:9/28/1865, Erie, PA D:1/31/1926, Erie, PA
Deb:4/17/1886, PHI AA BL/TR, 5'8", 140

G	AB	R	H	HR	RBI	OBP	SLG	AVG
1383	5706	819	1521	33	835	.301	.354	.267

Lou Bierbauer was a slick fielding and solid hitting second baseman who played in three leagues over a 13-year period. But he is best remembered as the man who—in a manner of speaking—brought the Pirates to Pittsburgh.

The origins of the National League Pittsburgh Pirates can be traced back to the city's Allegheny club, which was founded in 1882. From 1882 through 1886 the Alleghenies competed in the old American Association, before moving over to the NL. The Players' League War of 1890 left personnel issues to be resolved, two of which involved Bierbauer and outfielder Harry Stovey. Both men had played for the Philadelphia Athletics of the American Association but had jumped to the Players' League. When it collapsed after one season, the Athletics, through a clerical error, neglected to reserve Bierbauer's and Stover's services, and Pittsburgh eagerly signed them to contracts. Although an impartial Arbitration Board (which included American Association President Allan Thurman) ruled in Pittsburgh's favor, the Athletics kept squawking that their cross-state rivals were "Pirates." The name stuck, becoming the new nickname for Pittsburgh's ballclub.

The incident also set off a new struggle between the National League and the American Association, which led to the AA's quick demise. On the field, the highlight of Bierbauer's career was making 12 putouts in a single game in 1888.

Carson Bigbee

Bigbee, Carson Lee **OF**

1916–26 B:3/31/1895, Waterloo, OR D:10/17/1964, Portland, OR Deb:8/25/1916, PIT NL BL/TR 5'9", 157

G	AB	R	H	HR	RBI	OBP	SLG	AVG
1147	4192	629	1205	17	324	.345	.369	.287

A journeyman for most of his career, outfielder Carson Bigbee put together two big seasons for the Pittsburgh Pirates. In 1921 and 1922, he hit .323 and .350, respectively, slashing 17 and 15 triples in those seasons.

Reduced to part-time duty with the arrival of Kiki Cuyler in 1924, Bigbee was on the bench in August 1926 when he overheard former Pirates manager and current coach Fred Clarke bad-mouthing star Max Carey. Bigbee repeated the slam to Carey, and asked pitcher Babe Adams for his opinion on Clarke's attitude toward his players.

Adams, Bigbee, and Carey led a revolt (called the "ABC Affair") against the cantankerous Clarke. Owner Barney Dreyfuss was touring Europe at the time, but he still acted decisively: on August 13, Adams and Bigbee were released, and Carey was traded to the Brooklyn Dodgers.

Craig Biggio

Biggio, Craig Alan **2B–C**

1988–* B:12/14/1965, Smithtown, NY Deb:6/26/1988, HOU NL BR/TR 5'11", 180

G	AB	R	H	HR	RBI	OBP	SLG	AVG
1699	6389	1120	1868	152	706	.383	.437	.292

Craig Biggio, the premier National League second baseman of the 1990s, began his career as a catcher. He was All-America at Seton Hall University, playing on the same team as John Valentin and Mo Vaughn. Biggio reached the major leagues as a catcher with the Houston Astros after less than 500 minor league at bats.

In 1989, his first full season in the majors, Biggio won *The Sporting News'* Silver Slugger award as the top offensive player at his position. He averaged 22 steals in his first three seasons—a number that only two catchers had previously reached in a single season. Although Biggio was named to the All-Star team in 1991, there was concern that regular catching duties would diminish his offensive contributions. The following year he switched to second base and didn't miss a beat.

In 1992 Biggio played in all 162 games for the Astros. Although he struggled at times to make the transition defensively, he was again named to the All-Star team, making him the only player to earn the honor as both a catcher and a second baseman. In the strike-shortened 1994 season, Biggio led the NL in doubles, stolen bases, and fielding percentage. He won the first of four consecutive Gold Gloves and established himself as one of the elite all-around players in the major leagues.

Biggio added a new dimension to his offense in 1995. Wearing a baggy jersey and bulky arm pad, and employing a plate-crowding stance, he was hit by pitches a league-leading 22 times. Biggio led the majors in that category the next three seasons; his 34 times hit by a pitch in 1997 was the third highest total in the 20th century. By the end of the 1999 season, Biggio had been hit 153 times, ranking him fifth all-time.

Remarkably, Biggio avoided injuries. He began a consecutive-game playing streak in 1995 that lasted more than three years. It was snapped at 494 on August 5, 1998 when he sat out a game against the Florida Marlins. Biggio was given the day off because of the 92-degree temperature, not because he was unable to play. "I'm not going to say I'm not a little upset about it," Biggio said. His priorities were clear, though: "We're here to win a division. We're not here to keep streaks alive."

Biggio fulfilled that goal, helping to lead the Astros to three consecutive division titles from 1997 to 1999. With Biggio and teammates Derek Bell and Jeff Bagwell at the top of the order, the potent Houston lineup became known as the "Killer B's."

Biggio led the NL in runs scored in 1997 and ranked among the top five the following two years. In 1998 he joined Tris Speaker as the only other 20th-century player to collect 50 doubles and 50 steals in the same season. His total of 56 doubles in 1999 made him the first NL player since Joe Medwick in 1937 to hit that many, and only the sixth player in major league history to hit 50 or more doubles in back-to-back seasons.

Although there were opportunities for him to return to his native New York area, Biggio twice shunned free agency—and likely more money—to remain in Houston. "Not a lot of guys get to play their whole careers with one team because of the economics of the game," Biggio said in 1999. "I can't think of a better time to be wearing an Astros uniform."

Steve Bilko

Bilko, Stephen Thomas **1B**

1949–54, 1958, 1960–62 B:11/13/1928, Nanticoke, PA D:3/7/1978, Wilkes-Barre, PA Deb:9/22/1949, STL NL BR/TR 6'1", 230

G	AB	R	H	HR	RBI	OBP	SLG	AVG
600	1738	220	432	76	276	.339	.444	.249

Steve Bilko was an oversized first baseman with undersized major league statistics. He played off and on in the majors for 10 seasons over 14 years but only twice saw action in more than 78 games. Built like a packing crate for farm machinery, the blond slugger had a fantastic minor league record. The St. Louis Cardinals first brought him up late in 1949 after he smashed 34 homers for the Rochester Red Wings. However, he didn't win a major league job until 1952. When he finally played a full schedule in 1953, he hit 21 homers and batted in 84 runs, but he also struck out 125 times, a huge figure considering Vince DiMaggio held the major league record with 134.

By 1955 Bilko was back in the minors. After smacking 55 and 56 home runs in the Pacific Coast League, he returned to the majors but was unsuccessful in trials with Cincinnati, Los Angeles, and Detroit. In 1961 the expansion Angels gave Bilko one last shot, and he responded by hitting .279, with 20 homers in 114 games, but he also struck out in nearly every third at bat. He played sparingly for the Angels in 1963 before retiring.

Although relatively unsuccessful in the big leagues, Bilko left behind impressive minor league marks of 313 homers and a .312 batting average.

Jack Billingham

Billingham, John Eugene **P**

1968–80 B:2/21/1943, Orlando, FL Deb:4/11/1968, LA NL BR/TR 6'4", 215

W	L	PCT	G	SH	IP	BB	SO	ERA
145	113	.562	476	27	2230^{2}	750	1141	3.83

Cincinnati Reds starter Jack Billingham will always be remembered as the pitcher who served up Henry Aaron's record-tying 714th home run at the start of the 1974 season. After waiting all winter to catch the immortal Babe Ruth, Aaron connected on Billingham's first Opening Day serve. Billingham said, "It wasn't a bad pitch, but it wasn't good enough against Hank Aaron."

Starting with the Los Angeles Dodgers organization in 1961, Billingham labored in such minor league outposts as Orlando, St. Petersburg, Salisbury, Spokane, and Albuquerque before finally making the Dodgers as a reliever in 1968. That fall he was selected by the Expos in the expansion draft, but he never played for Montreal; he was dealt along with pitcher Skip Guinn to Houston in April 1969 to complete the controversial Donn Clendenon non-trade. (Clendenon vetoed the trade and went to the New York Mets instead.) Billingham became a moderately successful starter with the Astros and in 1971 was traded along with Joe Morgan to the Reds.

The distant cousin of Christy Mathewson, Billingham played six years in Cincinnati. He won at least 10 games each season, and twice reached 19 victories. He helped the Big Red Machine make the playoffs four times and was particularly effective in World Series competition: in three series he went 2–0 and surrendered just one earned run in 25 1/3 innings, giving him the World Series record with a glittering 0.36 ERA.

Traded to Detroit in March 1978 for two unknowns, Billingham recorded 15 wins that year. In May 1980 the Tigers sold him to the Boston Red Sox, where he spent his last year in the majors. After retiring, Billingham entered the sporting goods business in Winter Park, Florida. In 1999 he coached for the Florida State League's Kissimmee Cobras.

Max Bishop

Bishop, Max Frederick **2B**

1924–35 B:9/5/1899, Waynesboro, PA D:2/24/1962, Waynesboro, PA Deb:4/15/1924, PHI AL BL/TR 5'8½", 165

G	AB	R	H	HR	RBI	OBP	SLG	AVG
1338	4494	966	1216	41	379	.423	.366	.271

Max Bishop must have listened to his mother when she counseled, "Walk, don't run." Six times in 12 major league seasons he accumulated more bases on balls than hits, and he played in more than 100 games during five of those seasons. No other player batting in that many games has had more walks than hits with that kind of frequency.

Bishop was walked five times during a game twice, and he once received eight free passes in a doubleheader. As teammate Jimmy Dykes explained, "Max had one of the greatest batting eyes in the game. If he didn't swing at a pitch, the umpires just assumed that it didn't catch the plate and called it a ball." That knowledge of the strike zone earned him the nickname "Camera Eye."

From 1918 through 1923, Bishop played for Jack Dunn's Baltimore Orioles, one of the most successful minor league teams of all time.

Because of the team's success, Dunn could afford to keep his stars until major league teams were willing to pay the premium price he demanded for their contracts. Had it not been for Dunn's greed, Bishop might have reached the majors earlier. He was 24 years old when Connie Mack paid a reported $50,000 for his contract in 1924. By that time the Athletics were beginning to emerge from the 10-year pennant drought that had followed the sale of their stars after the 1914 season. With the country's economy growing again, Mack was able to buy potential stars such as future Hall of Fame sluggers Al Simmons, Jimmie Foxx, and Mickey Cochrane as well as Joe Boley, George Earnshaw, and others.

Bishop shared the Athletics' second base duty with Dykes during his rookie season and then took over for nine seasons as the regular. Quiet, unassuming, and completely colorless, Bishop inspired one Philadelphia writer to describe him as "merely a name in the lineup, a workman on the job. Bland, blond, phlegmatic, and no more responsive to the glamour of his game than a dead man to an indictment." Bishop seemed to take no pleasure in his skill, a rarity for ballplayers. Even when he set a record in 1926 with 53 errorless games in a row, he responded to reporters as though it was just another day at the office.

In that 1926 season and again in 1928, Bishop led AL second basemen in fielding average, a prelude to the 1932 season when he set a major league record with a .988 fielding percentage.

Yet, as good as he was in the field, Bishop was more valuable as a leadoff man. From 1925 through 1934 his on-base percentage fell below .400 only once, to .398 in 1929. During that season his .232 batting average was his lowest with the A's, yet he led the American League with 128 walks. He walked more than 100 times during every season from 1926 through 1933 except for 1928, when he fell three short.

In 1929 the A's defeated the Chicago Cubs in the World Series. The next year they topped the St. Louis Cardinals. A third straight flag followed in 1931, but this time the Cardinals triumphed. In the three World Series, Bishop batted a minuscule .182, but he scored 11 runs in the 18 games.

When the Great Depression began to take its toll, Mack was forced once again to sell his stars. In 1934 the Boston Red Sox bought Bishop, along with pitchers Lefty Grove and Rube Walberg. Bishop played for two seasons with Boston as a utility infielder before retiring.

In 1938 Bishop became head baseball coach at the U.S. Naval Academy, a post he held until shortly before his death in 1962. His record in 24 seasons at Annapolis was 306–143.

Bud Black

Black, Harry Ralston **P**

1981–95 B:6/30/1957, San Mateo, CA Deb:9/5/1981, SEA AL BL/TL 6'2",180

W	L	PCT	G	SH	IP	BB	SO	ERA
121	116	.511	398	12	2053^{1}	623	1039	3.84

The son of a professional hockey player, Bud Black once said that he was headed towards a career in sports from an early age. What he didn't know was how many stops he would make on that journey, as the lefthander ultimately played for four minor league and five major league teams.

Previously drafted (but not signed) by both the Giants and the Mets, Black was signed by the Seattle Mariners as their 17th-round selection in the 1979 draft. He reached the Mariners after playing in their system at Bellingham, San Jose, Lynn, and Spokane, but appeared in only two games.

Traded to Kansas City in October 1981, Black became a regular starter in 1983, and the next year he won a career-high 17 games. In 1986 Black became a key reliever for the Royals; this was quite a change, because from 1983 to 1985 he had pitched in 92 games, every single one of them as the starter. In 1986 he appeared in 56 games, but only started four.

In June 1988 the Royals traded Black to Cleveland, where he again became a regular starter. There he pitched 26 consecutive scoreless innings. After being traded to Toronto in September 1990, he achieved free agency and signed a four-year contract with the San Francisco Giants. He finished his career in 1995 with a final year back in Cleveland.

A number of Black's marks were not of the most positive nature. He paced both leagues in balks, and also led the NL with 16 losses in 1991. And in the fourth inning of a July 8, 1988, contest he hit a major league record three Angels batters.

Joe Black

Black, Joseph **P**

1952–57 Negro League Player 1943–50 B:2/8/1924, Plainfield, NJ Deb:5/1/1952, BRO NL BR/TR 6'2", 220

W	L	PCT	G	SV	IP	BB	SO	ERA
30	12	.714	172	25	414	129	222	3.91

Pitcher Joe Black's career serves as an object lesson in how managerial meddling can ruin a promising arm. After serving in World War II, Black graduated from Morgan State College in Baltimore, played with the Negro Leagues' Baltimore Elite Giants, and signed with the Brooklyn Dodgers in 1950. Following short stints in Montreal and St. Paul, he debuted with the Dodgers in 1952 as a reliever and set the league on its ear. Black went 15–4 with 15 saves in an era long before closers were the norm, and he was named National League Rookie of the Year.

Although Black made only two starts in 56 games during the season, he was chosen to pitch the World Series opener for Brooklyn, defeating Allie Reynolds and the Yankees, 4–2, to become the first African-American pitcher to win a World Series game. He subsequently lost Game 4, 2–0, and Game 7, 4–2, although he pitched well in both.

The following spring manager Chuck Dressen, usually noted for his canny handling of players, urged Black to add new pitches to his repertoire. In attempting to do so the reliever lost control of the fastball and curve that had made him an overnight star. Used sparingly for several years, he was traded to the Cincinnati Reds for Bob Borkowski in 1955 and ended his career with the Washington Senators. He later became a vice president for special markets with the Greyhound Corporation.

Lena Blackburne

Blackburne, Russell Aubrey **SS-3B-2B**
1910, 1912, 1914–15, 1918–19, 1927, 1929 M(1928–29, 99–133) B:10/23/1886, Clifton Heights, PA D:2/29/1968, Riverside, NJ Deb:4/14/1910, CHI AL BR/TR 5'11", 160

G	AB	R	H	HR	RBI	OBP	SLG	AVG
550	1807	173	387	4	139	.284	.268	.214

In baseball Lena Blackburne's name is mud—but in his case it's a compliment. It is to Blackburne that umpires owe their thanks for the fact that new baseballs do not unduly shine. Blackburne, a former major league infielder, coach, and manager, discovered near his home in the Delaware Valley a special type of mud that removes gloss from new baseballs without disfiguring or discoloring them. To this day umpires use this mud to rub on baseballs before games.

A Philadelphia sandlot star, Blackburne, also nicknamed "Slats," made it to the big leagues with the Chicago White Sox in 1910, just in time to christen brand-new Comiskey Park with its first base hit on July 1 of that year. He was up and down from the majors for the rest of the decade, mostly playing for the White Sox, but also seeing action with the Reds, Phillies, and Braves.

Most of Blackburne's managing was in the minors, including piloting the Kansas City Blues to a 1923 Junior World Series win, but from July 1928 until the end of the 1929 season he managed the White Sox. He appeared in one game for the Sox in 1929, as he had in 1927. The most notable event of his tenure in Chicago was a knock-down fist fight with contentious White Sox first baseman "Art The Great" Shire, who outweighed his manager by 30 or 40 pounds. Blackburne coached for the White Sox, Browns, and A's and for many years scouted for both the Philadelphia and Kansas City A's.

Ewell Blackwell

Blackwell, Ewell **P**
1942, 1946–53, 1955 B:10/23/1922, Fresno, CA D:10/29/1996, Hendersonville, NC Deb:4/21/1942, CIN NL BR/TR, 6'6", 195

W	L	PCT	G	SH	IP	BB	SO	ERA
82	78	.512	236	15	1321	562	839	3.30

Long-and-lean Ewell "the Whip" Blackwell baffled National League hitters in the late 1940s with a blazing fastball and an unorthodox delivery. He assembled a 16-game winning streak in 1947 that included a no-hitter against the Braves on June 18, 1947. "The toughest pitcher for me to hit," said Pittsburgh's league-leading slugger Ralph Kiner, "was Ewell Blackwell. I wouldn't rate him as the fastest I ever saw, but his delivery was the toughest to fight."

Blackwell's angular body and odd pitching motion prompted a host of colorful descriptions. "He looked like a fly rod with ears," observed columnist Red Smith. Dixie Walker thought he looked like "a man falling out of a tree."

Blackwell's reputation intimidated batters as much as his fastball did. On the morning Pirates catcher Vinnie Smith was married, several of his teammates served as his ushers. They celebrated throughout the day, and when they returned to the ballpark, still in formal wear, pockets filled with high-priced cigars, they learned that Blackwell was scheduled to pitch that night. "It was bad enough to go up against him when you were sober," said Kiner. "In the condition they were in it was frightening." The Pirates made a beeline for the Cincinnati clubhouse, where they found Blackwell, presented him with their fine cigars, and begged him to go easy on them.

"It's hard to believe today," Blackwell told an interviewer in the 1970s, "but ... I wondered if I'd ever be big enough to play ball. When I was a sophomore in high school I was 5-foot-5." By his junior year he'd shot up to 6'3".

Blackwell had been pitching for an aircraft company team in 1941, when he signed a contract to play for the Cincinnati Reds' organization. Why the Reds? "They had a farm club in Ogden, Utah, where my mother was from originally," said Blackwell. "I thought it would be nice if I went to pitch there."

He went to spring training with Ogden, a member of the Class C Pioneer League, but was told by the club that they were tearing up his contract. Instead, he would be going straight up to the Reds. He appeared in two games for Cincinnati in 1942 before being sent to the Syracuse Chiefs, where he was 15–10 with a 2.02 ERA.

Blackwell then enlisted in the Navy, but as he was about to leave home, President Roosevelt announced that all enlistments were canceled. Instead, Blackwell headed for the infantry, to George Patton's Third Army, where his 71st Division would ultimately meet up with advancing Russian forces in Austria. He pitched for the 71st Division, leading them to the Third Army Championship.

Despite Blackwell's limited experience, he made the Reds in 1946, benefiting enormously from the knowledge and tutoring of manager Bill McKechnie. Despite a losing record in his rookie season, Blackwell led the NL in shutouts and was selected for the first of six consecutive All-Star Games.

After going 2–2 at the start of the 1947 season, he began his string of 16 straight wins, all of which were complete games. His biggest victory was the eighth. Before 18,000 fans at Cincinnati's Crosley Field, Blackwell pitched a no-hitter, beating Boston's Ed Wright, 6–0. Speaking on the radio after the game, an exuberant Blackwell audaciously predicted his next start would be another no-hitter. If he fulfilled his prophecy, he'd join Johnny Vander Meer as the only pitchers in major league history to post consecutive no-hitters.

He almost did. On June 22, 1947, he no-hit Brooklyn for eight innings. With one out in the ninth, Eddie Stanky hit a low liner back through the box. Blackwell reached but couldn't handle it, and the no-hitter was gone. "Some observers," said Blackwell, "believe I missed [it] because I am so tall that I couldn't get down low enough to have fielded the ball. That wasn't the case. I had my glove down low enough to have fielded the ball but misjudged its speed and lifted my gloved hand an instant too soon and the ball passed under my glove, through my legs, and on out to center field."

Blackwell started for the National League in the 1947 All-Star Game, and he pitched three shutout innings, striking out Ted Williams, George Kell, Lou Boudreau, and Joe Gordon. His All-Star scoreless streak would eventually reach 11 innings. He finished the 1947 season having led the NL with 22 wins, 23 complete games, and 193 strikeouts.

Blackwell's production was way down the next two years, as in 1948 he developed arm problems, which were compounded in 1949 by the recurrence of a kidney ailment.

In 1950 Blackwell pitched two one-hitters—the first against the Cubs, and the other 10 days later against the Dodgers. But he no longer was consistent in his quality pitching, and his record showed it: he was 17–15 in 1950 and 16–15 the next year.

The Reds traded him to the Yankees on August 28, 1952, for outfielders Jim Greengrass and Bob Marquis, pitchers Johnny Schmitz and Ernie Nevel, and $35,000 cash. Blackwell started Game 5 of the 1952 World Series against the Dodgers and took a no-decision in Brooklyn's 6–5, 11-inning win. He had brief appearances with the Yankees the next year and with Kansas City in 1955 before retiring.

Blackwell finished with a career record of just 82–78. Yet when an elite panel of veteran sportswriters—Grantland Rice, Red Smith, and Frank Graham—discussed who they would pitch "in the biggest ball game" of their lives, their verdict was Ewell Blackwell.

George Blaeholder

Blaeholder, George Franklin **P**

1925, 1927–36 B:1/26/1904, Orange, CA D:12/29/1947, Garden Grove, CA Deb:4/20/1925, STL AL BR/TR 5'11", 175

W	L	PCT	G	SH	IP	BB	SO	ERA
104	125	.454	338	14	1914^{1}	535	572	4.54

A righthanded pitcher who spent most of his 11-year major league career with the St. Louis Browns, George Blaeholder was credited as one of the original practitioners of the slider or "nickel curve." The slider had been used previously by other pitchers, but not nearly as extensively as Blaeholder threw it, because the pitch was said to ruin the throwing arm.

Although Blaeholder won 10 or more games in seven consecutive seasons, he never had a winning record for the perennial second-division Browns. He was a true workhorse, six times during those seven seasons pitching more than 200 innings. However, he was not exactly dominating, as his ERA never dipped below 4.18 in that period. On May 21, 1935, the Browns traded him to another below-average ballclub, the Philadelphia Athletics. Blaeholder finished out that year 6–10 with the A's, then went to the Cleveland Indians in 1936, where his 8–4 record in his final major league season gave him his first winning mark.

Although Blaeholder pitched for first-division teams only twice in his 11-year career, Hall of Famer Jimmie Foxx called him the toughest pitcher to hit in the American League.

Paul Blair

Blair, Paul L.D. **OF**

1964–80 B:2/1/1944, Cushing, OK Deb:9/9/1964, BAL AL BR/TR 6', 171

G	AB	R	H	HR	RBI	OBP	SLG	AVG
1947	6042	776	1513	134	620	.305	.382	.250

A wide-ranging, sure-handed center fielder, Paul Blair collected eight Gold Gloves in his 17-year major league career and was a key figure in the Baltimore Orioles going to the playoffs six times and winning two World Series. Not known foremost for his batting skills, Blair had some of his biggest hits in postseason play.

Blair originally signed with the Mets for a $2,000 bonus after he graduated from Manual Arts High School in Los Angeles. Assigned to the Class C California League's Santa Barbara Rancheros, he hit just .228, but the Mets had enough confidence in him to bring him to their postseason Florida Instructional League. There scouts from competing clubs got a look at Blair and a number became very interested. Instructional League manager Solly Hemus informed scouts who inquired that Blair had a bad ankle and wasn't going to be playing anymore. But the Orioles' Jim Russo didn't buy Hemus' tale, and, on his advice, the Orioles drafted him off the Syracuse Chiefs' roster in November 1962.

Blair played in the California League in 1963—where he earned the nickname "Motormouth"—and with the Elmira Pioneers in 1964, where he led the Eastern League with a .311 batting average, a .981 fielding percentage, and 34 stolen bases. Blair moved onto the Orioles' major league squad in 1965. Through the years, his offensive production was up and down: in 1967, for example, he batted .293 and led the AL with 12 triples; the next season, his batting average dipped to .211 and he tripled only once. He did have his magic moments with a bat, however—on April 29, 1970, he hit three homers in a single game.

Blair was particularly noticeable in postseason play. In Game 3 of the 1966 World Series against the Dodgers, he connected for a 430-foot homer into the left-field bleachers, providing the Orioles' Wally Bunker with a 1–0 victory. In Game 4 his sensational leaping catch robbed Jim Lefebvre of what might have been an inside-the-park homer, preserving the Orioles' 1–0 victory and their sweep of the Dodgers.

In Game 1 of the 1969 Championship Series against Minnesota, Blair's 12th-inning suicide squeeze brought home shortstop Mark Belanger with the winning run, giving the Orioles a 4–3 victory. In Game 3 he collected two singles, two doubles, and a homer in six at bats as Baltimore routed Minnesota, 11–2, and completed a sweep.

In May 1970 a fastball by Ken Tatum hit Blair in the face, and he suffered serious facial and eye injuries. He remained on the disabled list until June 21, and when he returned he was extremely wary at the plate. Eventually, he went to a hypnotist to regain his confidence. The treatment obviously worked, because against the Reds in the 1970 World Series, Blair tied a record for most hits in a five-game series, going 9-for-19.

After hitting only .197 in 1976, Blair was traded to the Yankees. His postseason magic continued in 1977 when his single brought in the winning run in the 12th inning of Game 1 of the World Series. He batted .375 in the 1978 World Series. During the regular season, though, Blair was not as consistent. The Yankees released him after just two games the following year. He signed with Cincinnati in midseason but hit only .150 in 75 games.

In 1980 Blair was hired as the Yankees' minor league base running and fielding instructor. In May general manager Gene Michael called him at the motel at which he was staying and asked him if he wanted to suit up again. It took Blair only three hours to get to the airport and to board the next plane for New York. He played 12 games, mostly as a defensive replacement. After retiring again, Blair served as a minor league instructor for the Houston Astros, and in 1986 he was named commissioner of the North American Baseball League. In 1989 the 45-year-old Blair took his Gold Glove out of retirement and signed up with Earl Weaver's Gold Coast Suns of the Florida-based Senior League.

Sheriff Blake

Blake, John Frederick **P**

1920, 1924–31, 1937 B:9/17/1899, Ansted, WV D:10/31/1982, Beckley, WV Deb:6/29/1920, PIT NL BB/TR 6', 180

W	L	PCT	G	SH	IP	BB	SO	ERA
87	102	.460	304	11	1620	740	621	4.13

Sheriff Blake was a typical hardworking third or fourth starter on the Chicago Cubs' staff during most of his 10-year career, which took off in 1924 after a brief stint with Pittsburgh in 1920. Blake would take his regular turn, relieve half a dozen times, and usually finish just on the downside of .500—no matter where the team ended up.

Blake struggled with his control early, and suffered his worst season in 1925, when he went 10–18 with a 4.86 ERA. Three years later he had improved that to 17–11 and a 2.47 ERA, including a league-leading four shutouts. The next year he went 14–13, helping lead the Cubs to the pennant.

While other Cubs pitchers started the five games in the 1929 World Series against Philadelphia, Blake was dropped to relief, the second time being his best-known major league performance. He was the third of four Cubs pitchers in the nightmare seventh inning of Game 4, when the Athletics entered the bottom of the frame trailing, 8–0, and left it ahead, 10–8. When Blake came in with one out and Mickey Cochrane on first, Chicago still led, 8–7. Blake promptly gave up singles to Al Simmons and Jimmie Foxx, with Cochrane scoring the tying run on Foxx's hit. Then Blake went to the bench and watched Pat Malone hit Bing Miller in the ribs to load the bases. Jimmy Dykes' double scored both Simmons and Foxx to give the A's their lead, and Blake was tagged with the loss.

Traded to the Phillies during the 1931 season, Blake was out from the majors from 1932 to 1936 before ending his playing career with the Cardinals in 1937.

Johnny Blanchard

Blanchard, John Edwin **C-OF**

1955, 1959–65 B:2/26/1933, Minneapolis, MN
Deb:9/25/1955, NY AL BL/TR 6'1", 198

G	AB	R	H	HR	RBI	OBP	SLG	AVG
516	1193	137	285	67	200	.320	.441	.239

Power hitter Johnny Blanchard was in the right place at the wrong time. Not only did he have to play understudy to the feisty Yogi Berra, but Blanchard also had the bad fortune to be a Yankees catcher at a time when the other catcher was All-Star Elston Howard. Consequently Blanchard generally took the field only to catch the second games of doubleheaders or to fill in for short stretches at first base or in the outfield.

When he did make it to the plate Blanchard was a dangerous hitter. In 1961 he hit .305 and delivered 21 homers and 54 RBIs in only 243 at bats. He was also an excellent pinch hitter. Blanchard once boasted, "Yankees have pride. I had to produce when the chips were down." Unfortunately his love of the Yankees turned out to be his undoing. When New York traded him to 10th-place Kansas City in 1965 he was crushed. "Damn, I really started to drink. It was the end of the world," he said.

That was Blanchard's last year in baseball. He later went on to become a successful salesman for a crane manufacturing firm.

Steve Blass

Blass, Stephen Robert **P**

1964, 1966–74 B:4/18/1942, Canaan, CT
Deb:5/10/1964, PIT NL BR/TR 6', 165

W	L	PCT	G	SH	IP	BB	SO	ERA
103	76	.575	282	16	1597'	597	896	3.63

In baseball pitchers sometimes lose their control or confidence for days, weeks, even months at a time. But for a pitcher to spend eight years in the majors; compile a record of 100–67; win 18, 16, 10, 15, and 19 games in consecutive seasons; hurl a 2–1 complete-game victory in the seventh game of a World Series; and then suddenly and totally lose his ability to pitch—with no apparent physical cause—is one of the great puzzles in baseball history. That is the story of Steve Blass, a mystery that has defied the efforts of professional psychologists and of Blass himself to find a solution.

Blass was not a naturally talented pitcher. He worked hard to reach the majors, spending nearly five years in the minors before coming up to the Pittsburgh Pirates for good in 1966. He was a serious student of the game who worked on his pitches until his control was first-rate. Before his fall from grace, his lifetime walks-per-game average was only 1.9.

After two years of swingman duty Blass was given starter status in 1968, and he responded with an 18–6 record and a 2.12 ERA. By 1969 he was the staff ace of a team that had moved up from sixth to third place.

Blass was in the spotlight in 1971 as Pittsburgh won the pennant, going 15–8 and leading the league in shutouts. He pitched two complete-game wins against Baltimore in the World Series, allowing only seven hits and fanning 13. His 2–1 win in Game 7 was a four-hit masterpiece.

The 1972 season was even bigger for Blass. With a 19–8 record and a 2.49 ERA, he was one of the league's best starters and was selected for the All-Star Game. He won Game 1 of the 1972 NLCS, 5–1, and left the fifth and final game with a 3–2 lead that the Bucs were unable to hold.

Respected on the mound, Blass was also a key protagonist in the clubhouse antics of the wacky Pirates of that era. An astute mimic and boyish prankster, Blass was, according to one Pirate, "about 90 percent of the good feelings on this club."

Then Blass' streak abruptly ended. His performance during spring training in 1973 was spotty, but that wasn't unusual, and the entire team was shaken by the death of Roberto Clemente. Blass began the season by struggling to a 3–4 record before manager Bill Virdon suggested a stint in the bullpen in order to work out his problems.

On June 13 Blass was brought in to face Atlanta in the fifth inning. It was a perfect opportunity to rectify matters: the game was all but over with the Bucs down, 8–3. But the first two men Blass faced received free passes. He lasted only one and one-third innings and gave up seven runs on five hits, six walks, and two wild pitches. Blass later described the experience: "You can't imagine the feeling that you suddenly have no idea what you're doing out there! It was kind of scary."

In practice Blass could pitch as well as ever, but everything changed when he entered a game. The drive to succeed, the impetus that pushed him to challenge hitters and beat them, seemed gone. His teammates commented that he seemed not to care on the mound any more. Blass completed that season with a 3–9 mark and a horrendous 9.85 ERA.

The next spring saw more of the same. Blass walked 25 men in 14 exhibition innings. He was hammered in a five-inning relief stint in April and shortly thereafter was demoted to Class AAA. The minors were no solution—in 61 innings at Charleston he walked 103 batters, gave up 60 hits, and achieved an ERA of 9.74.

Blass listened to all the opinions about his sudden decline. He tried every solution he could find—visualization, hypnosis, long throwing, pitching from a kneeling position, psychotherapy, and Transcendental Meditation. After another bad outing in his only spring training appearance in 1975, the Pirates released him. Blass decided not to try to play for another team, but rather to leave baseball.

In an article about Blass for *The New Yorker*, Roger Angell wrote: "Of all the mysteries that surround the Steve Blass story, perhaps the most mysterious is the fact that his collapse is unique. There is no other player in recent baseball history—at least none with Blass' record and credentials—who has lost his form in such a sudden and devastating fashion and been totally unable to recover." (Mark Wohlers' collapse with the Braves in 1998 did, however, bring numerous comparisons to Blass.)

After jobs as a salesman of class rings and as a goodwill ambassador for a large beer distributor, Blass was hired by the Pirates to broadcast their games during the 1983 season. His still-boyish wit and enthusiasm continue to be a source of pleasure.

Buddy Blattner

Blattner, Robert Garnett **2B**

1942, 1946–49 B:2/8/1920, St. Louis, MO
Deb:4/18/1942, STL NL BR/TR 6'½", 180

G	AB	R	H	HR	RBI	OBP	SLG	AVG
272	713	112	176	16	84	.347	.384	.247

After Buddy Blattner's playing career ended, he became a popular broadcaster with the St. Louis Browns, the St. Louis Cardinals, the California Angels, and the Kansas City Royals, handling play-by-play far more ably than he ever handled the curveball.

A natural athlete, Blattner was a table-tennis champion as a boy. He came to the majors with the Cardinals in 1942, sporting the label of a good-field, no-hit infielder, and he did nothing to dispel the rumor in 19 games before serving in the military from 1943 to 1945.

When in 1946 the New York Giants installed him as their second baseman, he played his only full season as a major league regular. He hit .255, with an on-base percentage nearly 100 points higher, and he cracked 11 homers. The following year, however, Bill Rigney replaced him, and Blattner served out the season as a utility man. Despite hitting .261 in 1947, he again was demoted the following year, virtually disappearing from the playing roster.

In 1949 Blattner completed his major league career as a Phillies sub. He began broadcasting St. Louis Browns games the following year. He later teamed up with Dizzy Dean on *Game of the Week*, which broadcast the first nationally televised regular-season games.

Jeff Blauser

Blauser, Jeffrey Michael **SS-2B**

1987–* B:11/8/1965, Los Gatos, CA Deb:7/5/1987,
ATL NL BR/TR, 6', 170

G	AB	R	H	HR	RBI	OBP	SLG	AVG
1407	4522	691	1187	122	513	.356	.406	.262

Jeff Blauser was not flashy, but he blossomed into a steady shortstop with occasional home run power. The native Californian was drafted and signed by Atlanta in 1984, made the big league club in 1987, and cracked the lineup two years later. He was already a major league veteran by the time the Braves began a decade-long run of excellence.

In 1993 he became the first Braves shortstop to hit .300 since Alvin Dark in 1948; he also made the National League All-Star team for the first time. Blauser repeated both feats four years later. Although Blauser posted career highs in 1997 with a .308 average and 17 home runs, he left the

Braves because of prolonged contract negotiations that prompted Atlanta to acquire shortstop Walt Weiss.

Blauser signed with the Chicago Cubs for the 1998 season, but failed to maintain his offensive output. Blauser, who had hit three home runs in a 1992 game at Wrigley Field, had trouble playing there on a regular basis. He was relegated to a part-time role in 1999, going 11-for-44 with three homers as a pinch hitter.

Blauser will be remembered for his years with Atlanta. He hit five postseason home runs for the Braves, including two in the 1993 National League Championship Series. He played in the postseason seven times, and set a record with 18 career runs scored in the Championship Series. He had 10 hits in 48 career World Series at bats.

Curt Blefary

Blefary, Curtis Le Roy **OF-1B**

1965–72 B:7/5/1943, Brooklyn, NY Deb:4/14/1965, BAL AL BL/TR 6'2", 195

G	AB	R	H	HR	RBI	OBP	SLG	AVG
974	2947	394	699	112	382	.345	.400	.237

Curt Blefary was a dangerous power hitter whose poor fielding made him a man without a natural position. His nickname "Clank" was inspired by his "iron glove."

Although Blefary was originally signed by New York for a reported $40,000 bonus, the Yankees nonetheless left him unprotected, and in April 1963 the Orioles claimed him on first-year waivers. Promoted after a 31-homer season in Rochester in 1964, Blefary hit two home runs in his first full major league game and went on to win Rookie of the Year honors in 1965 with 22 home runs, 70 RBIs, and a .260 average for the season.

Blefary's performance in his second season was much like that in his first, and he was a key figure in Baltimore's drive to the World Series. He had the best single day of his career, hitting three homers (including a grand slam) against the California Angels on June 6, 1967.

However, Blefary's continuing fielding woes, in conjunction with his falling batting average, made the Orioles think seriously about whether they could use him. In 1968 they even tried him behind the plate, where he caught Tom Phoebus' no-hitter against the Red Sox on April 27 of that year.

Ultimately the Orioles unloaded him, trading him to Houston in December 1968 for pitcher Mike Cuellar. Blefary's playing time got progressively less during the next three years, during which he played for the Yankees, Oakland A's, and San Diego Padres. After retirement he owned "Curt's Coo Coo Lounge" in Dania, Florida.

Ron Blomberg

Blomberg, Ronald Mark **DH-1B**

1969, 1971–76, 1978 B:8/23/1948, Atlanta, GA Deb:9/10/1969, NY AL BL/TR 6'1', 205

G	AB	R	H	HR	RBI	OBP	SLG	AVG
461	1333	184	391	52	224	.363	.473	.293

Ron Blomberg etched his name into baseball history by becoming the American League's first designated hitter on Opening Day of 1973. With the bases loaded in the top of the first inning, Blomberg drew a walk against Red Sox starter Luis Tiant to drive in a run. Blomberg finished the day with one hit in three at bats.

While much was made about Blomberg's being the first AL designated hitter in 1973, he certainly never let his cult celebrity go to his head. Of his feat, Blomberg joked, "I've been a DH all my life: Designated Hebrew."

He was used to being first—he was the first overall pick in the 1967 June amateur draft. The muscular hitter at DeKalb Junior College in Clarkston, Georgia, was chosen by a no-longer powerful Yankees franchise. He signed for a reported $60,000 bonus, but his flaws soon became grievously apparent. He could not field. He could not hit lefthanders. He could not stay healthy for any amount of time, as various muscle ailments and tears racked his body.

But he could definitely hit righthanded pitching. In 1971, his first extended action in the major leagues, Blomberg finished with a .322 batting average. The next year he shared the job at first base, but he seemed nothing special. "I was quite happy to be the designated hitter," he said several years later. "With Bobby Bonds in right field and three first basemen, I might as well have donated my glove to charity."

Blomberg actually split his time between first and DH, hitting a career high .329. But injuries dogged Blomberg. He played in only 90 games in 1974, when he hit .311. Then his time dropped to 34 games in 1975; he played just once with the Yanks the following year.

In 1978, after missing an entire season, Blomberg tested free agency and signed a multi-year pact with the Chicago White Sox. But he still wasn't healthy, and he hit just .231 in 61 games. He was released the following spring, after which he entered the insurance business in Chicago.

Lu Blue

Blue, Luzerne Atwell **1B**

1921–33 B:3/5/1897, Washington, DC D:7/28/1958, Alexandria, VA Deb:4/14/21, DET AL BB/TL 5'10", 165

G	AB	R	H	HR	RBI	OBP	SLG	AVG
1615	5904	1151	1696	44	695	.402	.401	.287

Lu Blue did not have the power that many consider a requisite of playing first base, but he was a solid percentage hitter and he possessed an outstanding batting eye that made him one of the more successful base-on-balls men in baseball history. Four times in his 13-year career Blue drew more than 100 walks, including seasons of 126 in 1929 and 127 in 1931. Almost 70 years after his last full season, Blue still ranked among the all-time leaders in bases on balls, lifetime on-base percentage, and base-on-balls percentage.

Despite not being a particular favorite of Detroit player-manager Ty Cobb, Blue immediately filled the first base job in 1921. He was a switch-hitter who fielded his position with grace. In four of his first five years, Blue batted at least .300, and on August 22, 1922, he had five hits in a single game.

After seven successful seasons in Detroit, in December 1927 he was traded with Hall of Famer Heinie Manush to the St. Louis Browns for shortstop Chick Galloway, pitcher Elam Vangilder, and outfielder Harry Rice. In his first season in St. Louis, Blue more than doubled his previous high by hitting 14 home runs.

In April 1931 Blue was sold to the White Sox for $15,000. He completed his career with one game for Brooklyn in 1933. Blue, a World War I veteran, is buried in Arlington National Cemetery.

Vida Blue

Blue, Vida Rochelle **P**

1969–83, 1985–86 B:7/28/1949, Mansfield, LA Deb:7/20/1969, OAK AL BB/TL 6', 189

W	L	PCT	G	SH	IP	BB	SO	ERA
209	161	.565	502	37	3343^{1}	1185	2175	3.27

Unlike "Catfish" Hunter or "Blue Moon" Odom, Vida Blue could not be swayed by A's owner Charlie Finley to take a catchy nickname. When Finley asked Blue to assume the name "True Blue," the never-shy pitcher retorted, "How about if you change your name to True Finley?" Blue said, "I like my name. It was my father's name. It's Spanish. It means life."

As a teenager Blue was a top football prospect. In his senior year at DeSoto High School in Mansfield, Georgia, he threw 35 touchdown passes. Twenty-five major colleges offered scholarships, and Blue even signed a letter of intent with the University of Houston. Most baseball teams passed on him in the amateur draft, but Blue needed instant cash to support his family. When the A's heard about Blue's situation, they picked him in the second round. After Finley personally offered him a $25,000 bonus, Blue signed.

Blue joined the A's in 1969, but he was ineffective and was sent down to Iowa in 1970. Blue was called up in midseason, and he went 2–0, including a 6–0 no-hitter against the Minnesota Twins on September 21.

In 1971, his first full season in the majors, Blue was arguably the dominant pitcher in baseball. He posted a 24–8 record and a league-leading 1.82 ERA and won both the Cy Young and Most Valuable Player awards. His eight shutouts were tops in the league, and he was second in the American League in strikeouts and complete games.

In 1972 Blue wanted more green. He had been paid only $14,750 during his Cy Young season, so he staged a holdout, arguing he should receive $115,000 for the upcoming year. Even President Richard M. Nixon commented, "The young man has so much talent. Maybe Finley ought to pay him." Finley countered with $45,000. On May 1 Blue signed for $50,000, plus a retroactive $5,000 bonus and an $8,000 reserve scholarship fund, which he never used.

The money did not improve his pitching, and Blue struggled to a 6–10 record in 1972. He made eight postseason appearances for Oakland, but he made just one start. He did, however, earn two saves in three days: one in clinching Game 5 of the Championship Series, and the other in Game 1 of the World Series. The next year he was back on the top of his game as a starter and went 20–9. The A's won their second straight world championship in 1973, but with little help from Blue. He was 0–1 with a 10.29 ERA in the ALCS and 0–1 with a 4.91 ERA in the World Series. In eight World Series appearances, Blue's lifetime won-lost record was 0–3.

Blue could be independent and brash, traits that were hardly unique on the A's, where players battled each other in the clubhouse before they went out on the field to defeat opponents. Finley once offered his players $300 each to grow mustaches for "Mustache Day." Blue grew some whiskers, but as soon as the afternoon's ceremonies were over, he rushed back to the clubhouse to shave them off, just to spite "Charlie O."

During spring training of 1974 Blue declared that he was mulling over the possibility of leaving baseball to become a quarterback in the new World Football League. "I'm not trying to start a war between the two professions," he commented, "but in my own mind, I'd consider both options. It's good for anybody to have that option." He stayed with baseball, of course, and was in the regular rotation throughout the season as the A's won another World Series title.

Blue won 22 games in 1975 and 18 in 1976. But in 1977 he led the American League in losses with 19, and his ERA ballooned from 2.35 to 3.83. Finley, who was now dismantling the team, attempted to sell Blue to the Yankees for $1.5 million. Later Finley tried to deal Blue to the Reds for $1.75 million and several players. Commissioner Bowie Kuhn vetoed both deals "in the best interests of baseball." Finley finally succeeded in trading Blue to the Giants on March 15, 1978, for seven players and $390,000.

Blue pitched well enough (18–10, 2.79 ERA) his first year with the Giants to be named *The Sporting News* NL Player of the Year. He also started the 1978 All-Star Game, becoming the first pitcher to start for both leagues in the All-Star Game. The next year, however, his ERA soared to 5.01. By April 1982 the Giants had tired of Blue, and they traded him to Kansas City.

In August 1983 authorities revealed that a federal drug probe of the Royals was in progress. On August 5 the club handed Blue (then 0–5) his unconditional release, even though he had a year and a half to go on his guaranteed contract. Four days later confirmation came that Blue was one of the players being investigated for use, distribution, and sale of cocaine. The Royals denied that the investigation and Blue's release were related, but the connection was obvious.

In a plea bargain, along with teammates Willie Mays Aikens, Jerry Martin, and Willie Wilson, Blue pleaded guilty to attempting to purchase cocaine. As part of the deal, the federal government refrained from prosecuting him for intent to distribute the drug. Each player was sentenced to a year in prison, with nine months of each sentence suspended. Blue served his time during the off-season, but he sat out the entire 1984 season anyway.

After completing his suspension, Blue re-signed with San Francisco, where he had two break-even seasons. He then attempted to rejoin the A's, but after he failed a urine test he retired from baseball.

Ossie Bluege

Bluege, Oswald Louis **3B**

1922–39 M(1943–47, 375–394) B:10/24/1900, Chicago, IL D:10/14/1985, Edina, MN Deb:4/24/1922, WAS AL BR/TR 5'11", 162

G	AB	R	H	HR	RBI	OBP	SLG	AVG
1867	6440	883	1751	43	848	.352	.356	.272

Not too many folks have spent half a century in baseball in baseball with the same outfit, but Ossie Bluege did. His best moments were as Washington's third baseman from 1922 to 1939, but he also served the Griffith family in both Washington and Minnesota as coach, manager, secretary, and controller.

Bluege's father wanted him to be an accountant, but he entered pro baseball in 1920 with the Class B 3-I League's Peoria Tractors. After the 1921 season the Senators purchased his contract and the outstanding fielding Bluege was a key component in Washington's pennant years of 1924, 1925, and 1932. Meanwhile, he also built up his accounting business, with clientele including many of the District of Columbia's finest hostelries. Washington owner Clark Griffith ordered Bluege to cease this off-season activity, fearing the eyestrain would hurt Ossie's playing; Bluege nonetheless continued his business.

He retired following the 1939 season, but Bluege stayed on as a coach for Washington for three years. He then took over the managing reins from 1943 to 1947. The Senators twice finished second during Bluege's tenure, including a down-to-wire race with the St. Louis Browns in 1944.

From 1948 to 1956 Bluege served as Washington's farm director. When Clark Griffith received a tip in the early 1950s from U.S. Senator Herman Welker of Idaho, it was Bluege who was sent west to check it out. Bluege liked what he saw in Idaho and signed a strapping young fellow named Harmon Killebrew. From 1958 until his retirement in 1972 Bluege was the Senators/Twins controller.

Bert Blyleven

Blyleven, Rik Aalbert **P**

1970–90, 1992 B:4/6/1951, Zeist, Holland Deb:6/5/1970, MIN AL BR/TR 6'3", 207

W	L	PCT	G	SH	IP	BB	SO	ERA
287	250	.534	692	60	4970	1322	3701	3.31

The two most important aspects of Bert Blyleven's career were his longevity and his wicked curve ball. In 22 years with five teams, Blyleven started 685 games, eighth on the all-time list. He registered 3,701 strikeouts, retiring with third-highest total in history. Many of those strikeouts were due to the tall righthander's trademark—a big breaking pitch described by Dave Winfield as "a bowel-locking, jelly-leg-inducing curveball." Blyleven threw with an easy, fluid motion, and his bender moved sideways sharply.

Blyleven's other credentials include 60 shutouts—the ninth-highest total ever—and 15 wins of 1–0, putting him in a third-place tie with Eddie Plank. Through 1999 he was in 13th place in innings pitched and seventh among expansion-era hurlers with 242 complete games. Before retiring, he was the last active pitcher, along with Nolan Ryan, to hurl 300 innings in a season, throwing 325 for the Minnesota Twins in 1973, his lone 20-win campaign.

The Holland native also allowed 430 career home runs—seventh most on the all-time list—including a major league-record 50 in 1986. But his consistently outstanding control may have contributed to this; he walked fewer than 2.4 batters per game and threw strikes, some of which were hit a long way.

Appropriately, Blyleven gave up a home run to his first big league batter, Lee Maye of the Washington Senators, on June 5, 1970. An injury to Luis Tiant brought Blyleven to the majors after 21 minor league starts, less than a year after the Minnesota Twins had chosen him in the third round of the June 1969 draft. The youngest player in the majors at age 19, Blyleven took the ball for the first-place Twins, threw seven shutout innings following the homer, and bunted the winning run to second base in a 2–1 victory. That September 16 he became the 25th major league teenager to win 10 games in a season when he beat the California Angels. During that game he struck out the first six Angels he faced to tie an AL record for the most consecutive strikeouts at the start of a game.

In 1973 Blyleven became the 13th-youngest 20-game winner of this century and led the American League with nine shutouts, and finished second in the ERA and strikeout races. That year he made the first of his two All-Star Game appearances, allowing two runs and taking the loss.

After a slow start in 1976, the Twins decided Blyleven would never pitch up to his potential and shipped him to Texas. His first win with the Rangers was a 10-inning, 1–0 one-hitter, and his next start was another 1–0, 10-inning win. Late the next year, coming off a groin pull, he threw a no-hitter for the Rangers against the Angels.

Despite these heroics, in the winter of 1977 a three-way deal sent Blyleven and slugger John Milner to Pittsburgh for Al Oliver and Nelson Norman. In his second year in Pittsburgh, Blyleven went 12–5 for the 1979 world champion Pirates. He complained about manager Chuck Tanner's quick hook, but then he went all the way to complete the Pirates' three-game Championship Series sweep of the Cincinnati Reds. In the World Series against Baltimore, Blyleven pitched six innings in Game 2 but let a 2–0 lead slip away in an eventual Pittsburgh 3–2 win. In Game 5, with the Bucs down three games to one, Blyleven relieved in the sixth, trailing 1–0; he tossed four scoreless innings for the win, sparking Pittsburgh's comeback to the title.

After a dissatisfying year in 1980, Blyleven was exiled to Cleveland. His best season as an Indian came in 1984, when a broken bone in his right foot cost him at least four starts and a chance at 20 wins. Blyleven went 19–7 with a team that won only 75 times.

He was traded back to Minnesota on August 1, 1985, for four players, and became the leader of the Twins' staff. He led the league with five shutouts and 24 complete games. After setting the record for most home runs in 1986—although he also won 17 games and tossed a league-leading 271⅔ innings—Blyleven won 15 games the following year for the world champions. Blyleven won Games 2 and 5 of Minnesota's ALCS upset over the Detroit Tigers, and then won Game 2 of the World Series against the Cardinals.

Traded to California after leading the league in losses in 1988, Blyleven collected Comeback Player of the Year honors, winning 17 games. He spent two more years with the Angels before going to the Twins—and then not making their roster—in 1983. The good-humored hurler later went into broadcasting.

Bruce Bochte

Bochte, Bruce Anton **1B–OF**
1974-82, 1984-86 B:11/12/1950, Pasadena, CA
Deb:7/19/1974, CAL AL BL/TL 6'3", 200

G	AB	R	H	HR	RBI	OBP	SLG	AVG
1538	5233	643	1478	100	658	.363	.396	.282

Bruce Bochte was an exceptional hitter, but he walked away from the game for a year in an attempt to make himself a better-rounded person. Bochte anchored the Mariners' lineup from the day he arrived in Seattle in 1978. He was the team's leading hitter three times in five years, and was the Mariners' lone representative when the Kingdome hosted the All-Star Game in 1979. At the end of the 1982 season, however, the 32-year-old first baseman retired.

The business aspects of baseball bothered Bochte, who had served as Seattle's player representative during the 1981 strike. He also became frustrated with the day-to-day aspects of the game. "Unimportant things are amplified," he said, "and you start to believe that everything hinges on one day's performance."

He became increasingly concerned about national and world affairs. Bochte moved his family to Whidbey Island in Puget Sound, Washington, where he enrolled in the Chinook Institute of Learning to "expose myself to a wide variety of progressive thinkers." After sitting out the 1983 season, Bochte thought about playing again. He signed with the Oakland A's in 1984. He played three more seasons, hitting .295 with 14 homers in 1985.

Bruce Bochy

Bochy, Bruce Douglas **C**

1978–80, 1982–87 M(1995-*; 409-383) B:4/16/1955, Landes de Bussac, France Deb:7/18/1978, HOU NL BR/TR 6'4", 210

G	AB	R	H	HR	RBI	OBP	SLG	AVG
358	802	75	192	26	93	.300	.388	.239

Bruce Bochy played in 100 games only once in his 14-year professional playing career. Bochy put his idle time on the bench to good use. He carved out a second career by studying the game and became a player-coach in Triple A in his last season. Managing was the next step, and he excelled at his new profession.

Bochy earned Northwest League Manager of the Year honors in his first season as a skipper in 1989. His teams won their league championships three of his first four campaigns in the San Diego system, earning him a promotion to major leagues as a coach. New Padres owners John Moores and Larry Lucchino picked Bochy as their first manager in 1995. A year later the team captured the National League West title and also won back the fans, who gave their heroes a prolonged standing ovation following a Division Series sweep by the St. Louis Cardinals. Bochy was named National League Manager of the Year.

The Padres slipped below .500 the following year, but the 1998 season was another year of enchantment. Led by Greg Vaughn, Kevin Brown, Trevor Hoffman, and the always reliable Tony Gwynn, San Diego ran away from the NL West. The Padres defeated Houston in the Division Series, then upset Atlanta in the Championship Series. The clock finally struck midnight when the Padres were swept by the Yankees' juggernaut in the World Series.

San Diego's on-field success was crucial in winning voter approval of a controversial measure to subsidize a new baseball-only downtown ballpark for the Padres. Nevertheless, after management let its veteran free agents leave for greener pastures, the 1999 squad quickly slid below .500 again. Despite a sub-.500 season, Bochy became the winningest manager in San Diego history in 1999.

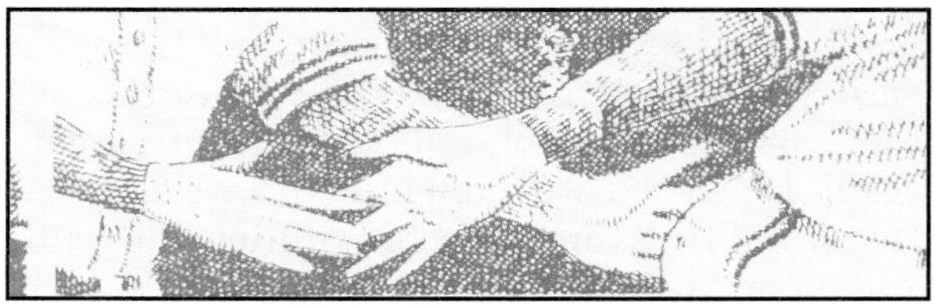

Mike Boddicker

Boddicker, Michael James **P**

1980–93 B:8/23/1957, Cedar Rapids, IA Deb:10/4/1980, BAL AL BR/TR 5'11", 172

W	L	PCT	G	SH	IP	BB	SO	ERA
134	116	.536	342	16	2123^{2}	721	1330	3.80

Through an up-and-down career, Mike Boddicker showed the same thing many other pitchers have: if they have some support, they can finish with a fine record; if not, they finish looking mediocre. Boddicker was a true star with a number of playoff teams, but he wasn't able on his own to make poor teams winners.

Boddicker first joined the Baltimore Orioles late in the 1980 season, but he had only two decisions to show for three partial seasons in the major leagues. However, in 1983 Boddicker finally earned a regular spot in the Orioles' starting rotation. He went 16–8 and led the league with five shutouts. In Game 2 of that year's American League Championship Series, he shut out the White Sox with a then-record 14 strikeouts. Then, in his single World Series start that year he gave up only three hits as the Orioles went on to capture the world championship.

By 1984 Boddicker had matured into a fine pitcher. He was named to the All-Star team, and his 20 wins and 2.79 ERA led the league. By then, however, many of Baltimore's stars were gone, so the club's offensive production slumped. That skid continued through the next four seasons, and Boddicker's record during that time fell to 42–53.

Midway through the Orioles' horrific 1988 season, Boddicker was shipped to Boston, where his 7–3 record and 2.89 ERA helped the Red Sox to the ALCS. He won 15 games in 1989 and 17 in 1990, when his fielding also earned him a Gold Glove and the Sox returned to the playoffs.

Traded to Kansas City in 1991, Boddicker won 12 and lost 12 for a mediocre team. He had relatively unproductive years in 1992 and 1993 for the Royals and Brewers before retiring.

Ping Bodie

Bodie, Frank Stephan **OF**

1911–21 B:10/8/1887, San Francisco, CA D:12/17/1961, San Francisco, CA Deb:4/22/1911, CHI AL BR/TR 5'8", 195

G	AB	R	H	HR	RBI	OBP	SLG	AVG
1050	3670	393	1011	43	516	.335	.396	.275

Ping Bodie, born Francesco Stephano Pezzolo, was among the first Italian-Americans to play in the major leagues. Although a solid player for eight years, he was known almost as much for his wit and bragging as for his playing ability. In fact, it is said that Ring Lardner's popular *You Know Me, Al* stories were partly inspired by Bodie's boastful personality. Lardner certainly appreciated Bodie, and he once wrote about one of his unsuccessful steal attempts, stating, "There was larceny in his heart, but his feet were honest."

Bodie started out in professional baseball in 1908 with Vallejo of the California League. In 1910 he hit 30 homers for the San Francisco Seals of the Pacific Coast League, a remarkable figure for the Dead Ball Era, and was promptly drafted by the White Sox.

Bodie had an excellent rookie season in 1911, driving in 97 runs and hitting 13 triples, just one shy of the American League record set by Socks Seybold in 1901. But after hitting .294 in 1912, his production fell off, and by 1915 he was back with San Francisco. Bodie got a second chance in the majors in 1917 with the woeful Philadelphia Athletics. He had good numbers, but not to the level about which he bragged, stating once, "The Liberty Bell and I are the only attractions in Philadelphia."

The A's dealt him to the Yankees in March 1918 for first baseman George H. Burns, and Bodie played four seasons for Jacob Ruppert's club. When asked during spring training in 1920 whom he roomed with, Bodie responded, "Babe Ruth's suitcase."

After leaving the Yankees in 1921 Bodie played in the minors until 1928. He later worked as an electrician in Hollywood's movie studios.

Wade Boggs

Boggs, Wade Anthony **3B–DH**

1982–99 B:6/15/1958, Omaha, NE Deb:4/10/1982, BOS AL BL/TR 6'2", 197

G	AB	R	H	HR	RBI	OBP	SLG	AVG
2440	9180	1513	3010	118	1014	.419	.443	.328

Wade Boggs lacked speed and power, yet he used a solid hitting stroke and keen eye to climb his way to baseball's elite circle of players with 3,000 hits. The red-haired, mustachioed third baseman batted .300 or better in each of his first 10 seasons, and won five batting titles in six years. He played in 12 consecutive All-Star Games.

As an All-America shortstop out of Tampa, Boggs signed with the Red Sox organization in 1976. Boston soon realized that he lacked the range to play the middle infield, and moved him to third base. Despite hitting over .300 in five straight minor league seasons and winning the International League batting title, Boggs found his ascent to the majors hindered by a lack of home run production (he had never hit more than five in a season) and inconsistent defensive play.

Finally, Boggs earned a promotion to the Red Sox in 1982 and quickly established himself in the league when he batted .349 for the year, the best average by a rookie in American League history, while playing more games at first base than third. The Red Sox were now confident enough in his abilities to make room at third base by trading Carney Lansford to Oakland.

Boggs quickly blossomed into a star, known for his ritual meal of chicken before each game, as well as dedication to his craft. He put in long hours with Boston hitting coach Walt Hrniak to maintain his machine-like swing. In 1983 the effort paid off, as Boggs led the AL with a .361 batting average. Two years later he batted a career-high .368, the best mark in either league.

In 1986 Boggs advanced to the postseason for the first time in his career and batted a solid .290 in Boston's heartbreaking World Series loss to the New York Mets. The following season he led the AL with a .363 average. More surprisingly, he hit 24 home runs, 16 better than his previous high, which for many was proof enough that the ball was "juiced" in 1987.

Boggs won his fourth consecutive batting title in 1988, as well as the fourth time he batted over .360. In 1989 Boggs reached the 200-hit plateau for a record-setting seventh consecutive season. The decade, however, did not end without Boggs becoming mired in scandal, when in 1989 a woman named Margo Adams revealed details of a four-year extramarital affair with Boggs. Adams filed a palimony suit and although Boggs reached an out-of-court settlement, his reputation was tarnished.

As Boggs approached his 32nd birthday in 1990, his hitting began to fall off. He batted .302, by far the poorest mark of his career, and failed to lead the league in any major offensive category for the first time since 1984. He rebounded, however, to hit .332 the following season and play well at third base.

Approaching free agency, Boggs slumped to a .259 batting average in 1992. The Red Sox decided against re-signing the 34-year-old third baseman, whose impressive statistics now became fodder for critics who charged that Boggs was more concerned with his own numbers than the team's record. Boggs eventually signed a three-year deal with the rival Yankees, desperate for a third baseman.

The move to New York rejuvenated Boggs, who proceeded to top the .300 mark in his first four seasons in pinstripes. His defensive play also improved, as he earned back-to-back Gold Gloves—the first of his career. More importantly, Boggs fulfilled a career-long goal in 1996 by playing on his first world champion—and taking a memorable victory lap on horseback at Yankee Stadium.

Boggs' play began to tail off and his game no longer suited the Yankees' needs. He signed with Tampa Bay, his hometown team, following the 1997 season. He batted .280 during the Devil Rays' inaugural season, and achieved one more moment of glory. On August 7, 1999, Boggs became the 23rd player to reach the 3,000-hit plateau—and, ironically, the first to reach the milestone with a home run. After the season Boggs announced his retirement, accepting the team's offer to work in the front office.

Tommy Bond

Bond, Thomas Henry **P**

1874–82, 1884 M(1882, 2–4) B:4/2/1856, Granard, Ireland D:1/24/1941, Boston, MA Deb:5/5/1874, ATL NA BR/TR 5'7½", 160

W	L	PCT	G	SH	IP	BB	SO	ERA
193	115	.627	322	35	2779^{2}	178	860	2.25

Tommy Bond was one of the true ironmen of early baseball. He is best remembered for being the last pitcher to win 40 or more games in three consecutive seasons, but he also was the first to capture pitching's Triple Crown. And he was also one of the early proponents of the curveball, which he had learned from the pitch's reputed inventor, Candy Cummings.

Bond was a workhorse pitcher in the National League's predecessor, the National Association, with the Brooklyn Atlantics and the Hartford Dark Blues. In 1874, he pitched 55 games, all of them complete. He was particularly impressive against the circuit's best club, the Boston Red Stockings, and he was the last pitcher to defeat the NA Boston club at home. After Bond bested them on September 30, 1874, Boston won its last 39 home games before the National Association expired at the end of the 1875 season.

When Hartford moved to the NL in 1876, Bond was part of that shift, but his biggest years came beginning in 1877, when he joined the Red Stockings. That first year in Boston he led the league with 40 victories, 170 strikeouts, and a 2.11 ERA. The next year he again won 40 games, while leading the NL in complete games (57), shutouts (9), and strikeouts (182). He made it three years in a row with 40 wins by picking up 43 in 1879, to go along with a league-best 1.96 ERA.

In 1881 Bond was replaced in Boston's starting rotation. The difference in playing time was vast: he went from 493 innings pitched in 1880 to 25 ⅓ in 1881. After retiring from the mound in 1882, Bond briefly managed Worcester and then umpired in the New England League. In 1884 he pitched for Boston of the Union Association and Indianapolis of the American Association.

Bond also coached at Harvard, where his players included future Hall of Famers John Clarkson and Tim Keefe. Before he died in 1941, Bond was the last surviving member of the National League's inaugural season of 1876.

Barry Bonds

Bonds, Barry Lamar **OF**

1986–* B:7/24/1964, Riverside, CA Deb:5/30/1986, PIT NL BL/TL 6'1", 190

G	AB	R	H	HR	RBI	OBP	SLG	AVG
2000	6976	1455	2010	445	1299	.413	.559	.288

Barry Bonds was one of the best players in the 1990s both defensively and offensively. His baseball pedigree came second to none: he was the son of Bobby Bonds (332 career home runs), the godson of Willie Mays (660 home runs), and, through his mother, the cousin of Reggie Jackson (563 home runs).

San Francisco drafted Bonds out of high school in San Mateo, California, but when the Giants offered $70,000 instead of the $75,000 he wanted, Bonds wound up at Arizona State University. He was an All-America outfielder for the Sun Devils, hitting 23 home runs as a junior. The Pittsburgh Pirates made him the sixth overall pick in the 1985 draft (the Giants took Will Clark with the second pick). Bonds was playing every day in Pittsburgh a year later.

He did not develop quickly with the Pirates. From 1986 to 1989 he did not exceed 59 RBIs and batted higher than .261 only once. The Pirates tried to trade Bonds when his contract demands exceeded his production, but several teams feared his moodiness and lack of production. The Bucs held on to Bonds; in 1990 they were glad they did.

Bonds batted .301 with 33 home runs, and his 114 RBIs nearly doubled his total from the previous season. He also stole 52 bases to become just the second player in baseball history to hit 30 home runs and steal 50 bases in the same season. He was rewarded with his first Most Valuable Player Award, as well as his first Gold Glove. Bonds helped lead the Pirates to the playoffs for the first time in 11 years in 1990. He hit just .167 as Pittsburgh lost to the Reds in six games, the first of four postseason appearances in which Bonds failed to hit and in which his team failed to advance.

The Pirates again went to the National League Championship Series in 1991, but the Braves slipped by the Bucs in seven games. Bonds lost in the MVP chase to Atlanta's Terry Pendleton. Bonds was MVP again in 1992 with a .311 average, 34 homers, 103 RBIs, and 39 stolen bases. Once again, though, the Pirates lost to the Braves in the NLCS—this time on a two-out, two-run single to left as Bonds' throw to the plate was just a shade too late to keep former teammate Sid Bream from scoring the winning run.

In 1993 Bonds returned to his hometown San Francisco. He made the Giants pay handsomely: more than $43 million over seven years. From the first pitch of the season, however, Bonds seemed intent to show that he deserved every penny. He batted .336 with 46 home runs, and he became the first player to lead the league in on-base percentage and slugging percentage since Mike Schmidt in 1981. He also joined Schmidt as a three-time MVP; Bonds was the first player to win the award three times in four years.

The Giants, who missed the NLCS by one game in 1993, were within four games of the NL West lead when the baseball strike wiped out the 1994 season. It also washed away a sluggers' race to see who could approach 61 home runs. Bonds was in the hunt with 37 homers.

After a solid 1995 season, Bonds stepped to the next level the following season. He became the first National League player to hit 40 home runs and steal 40 bases in the same season. Playing on a last-place team, Bonds walked 151 times, including 30 intentional passes.

Seemingly driven to become better and better, Bonds took on an intensive workout schedule after 1996. The result was another 40 home runs and his seventh Silver Slugger Award in 1997. He also led the Giants to the playoffs for the first time in nine years; he batted .250 in a three-game sweep at the hands of the Florida Marlins. The following season he became the first player to reach 400 home runs and steal 400 bases in a career. In some ways, 1999 was his most distinctive year. Despite playing in a career-low 102 games because of injuries, he hit 34 home runs and scored 91 runs.

Bonds captured a Gold Glove in every season of the 1990s except two. Even without the hardware, few could argue about Bonds' place as one of the greatest left fielders of all time. In his first 14 major league seasons, his single-season fielding percentage did not drop below .980, and his accurate arm notched 129 career assists. Added to his incredible production at the plate, it came as little surprise that *The Sporting News* named Bonds the player of the decade.

Bobby Bonds

Bonds, Bobby Lee **OF**

1968–81 B:3/15/1946, Riverside, CA Deb:6/25/1968, SF NL BR/TR 6'1", 190

G	AB	R	H	HR	RBI	OBP	SLG	AVG
1849	7043	1258	1886	332	1024	.356	.471	.268

Prior to Bobby Bonds' arrival in San Francisco in 1968, most major league players—except for rare players like Mickey Mantle and Willie Mays—had either power or speed. If one had both, he rarely used his speed to steal bases because his manager didn't want a key hitter injured on the basepaths. Bobby Bonds changed that. In only his second year in the majors, he became the first player in baseball history to hit 30 home runs and steal 30 bases in a single season. Bonds did it five times in his 14-year career, a record that still stands.

A graduate of Polytechnic High in Riverside, California, Bonds came from an athletic family. In 1965 his brother, Robert V. Bonds, was a 13th-round draft pick of the Kansas City Chiefs. His sister, Rosie, a world-class hurdler, was a member of the 1964 Olympic team. Bobby once threw six touchdowns in only three quarters of a high school football game.

Signed by the Giants in 1965, Bonds moved through the minors until he exploded at Phoenix in the Pacific Coast League in 1968. That year he hit .370, and the Giants promoted him. On June 25, 1968, against Dodgers hurler John Purdin, he hit a grand slam in his first major league game. Only the Phillies' Bill Dugglesby had previously accomplished that feat, back in 1898.

The Giants installed Bonds as leadoff hitter and he responded like no leadoff hitter had before. In 1969, his first full season in the majors, he hit 32 homers, stole 45 bases, drove in 90 runs, and led the National League with 120 runs scored. He would eventually break Eddie Yost's record of leading off games with home runs, and he could also come through in the clutch. Five times he homered to provide the margin of victory in 1–0 games, a feat matched by only Ted Williams.

But being a free swinger also meant that Bonds struck out a lot. In 1969 he fanned a record 187 times, then surpassed that with 189 strikeouts in 1970. He struck out six times in a doubleheader on September 5, 1971. His ratio of one strikeout for every four at bats is one of the worst in major league history. His strikeouts contributed to a perception that he often lacked effort. Another such area was running out ground balls to first. "If you get 200 hits a season," he reasoned, "you're going to hit .333 and you'll still have 400 outs. I don't see why you have to run down to first base every time to make an out."

Bonds twice reached the All-Star Game with the Giants, in 1971 and 1973, the latter year when he led the NL with 131 runs, had a career high 39 home runs, batted .283, stole 43 bases, and drove in 96 runs. After the 1974 season, the Giants traded Bonds to the Yankees for Bobby Murcer. Bonds played well enough in New York to make the 1975 All-Star Game in which he played center field. But during the off-season he was traded to the Angels for outfielder Mickey Rivers and pitcher Ed Figueroa.

After injuring the middle finger on his right hand in an exhibition game, Bonds played the

1976 season without his usual power. But he rebounded in 1977 to hit 37 home runs, with 115 RBIs, 103 runs, and 41 stolen bases. However, prior to the 1978 season, he was traded to the White Sox because he would become a free agent at season's end. The trade was unpopular with Angels fans and even more unpopular with Bonds after he saw the White Sox's new uniforms. "I'm going to retire," he threatened. "No way will I wear those damn hot pants."

He didn't wear them for long. In mid-May he was traded to the Texas Rangers, and in October he went to Cleveland. Despite hitting 25 homers for the Indians, Bonds was criticized by his teammates. "Bobby wouldn't hit the cutoff man if he were King Kong," said Indians teammate Rick Manning. "I thought Bobby was a dumb base stealer. He was the only guy who could steal 34 bases and get thrown out 30 times. Every time we needed a clutch hit he never got it done."

Bonds acknowledged the criticism. "This is by far my toughest year in baseball," he said. At season's end he was traded to the Cardinals and in 1981 was dealt to the Cubs for cash. He retired following the 1981 season after hitting only .215 with Chicago.

Bonds served as first-base coach and hitting instructor for Cleveland from 1984 to 1987. In 1989 he was a player-manager for the St. Lucie Legends of Florida's ill-fated Senior League. He returned to the majors as a coach on Dusty Baker's staff at San Francisco in 1993, when his son Barry joined the club via free agency.

Bobby Bonilla

Bonilla, Roberto Martin Antonio **3B–OF**
1986–* B:2/23/1963, Bronx, NY Deb:4/9/1986, CHI AL
BB/TR 6'3", 240

G	AB	R	H	HR	RBI	OBP	SLG	AVG
1906	6800	1044	1912	277	1124	.363	.477	.281

Bronx native Bobby Bonilla proves the adage that you can't go home again. Or in his case, you can't go home again, *again*. Bonilla came into prominence in Pittsburgh where he was a key player, along with Barry Bonds and Andy Van Slyke, in a lineup that transformed the Pirates from a last-place club to division champions in 1990 and 1991. The Pirates had acquired Bonilla from the Chicago White Sox for Jose DeLeon in 1986.

He hit .300 in his first full season with the Pirates and then drove in 100 runs in three of the next four seasons, earning Silver Slugger Awards in 1988, 1990, and 1991. He hit 32 home runs with 120 RBIs, and finished second to Bonds in the 1990 Most Valuable Player voting. Bonilla finished third in the MVP voting in 1991 with a league-leading 44 doubles and a .302 average. The Pirates made the postseason both years, but lost to Cincinnati in 1990 and Atlanta in 1991. Bonilla batted .304 in the seven-game loss to the Braves.

The Mets won a bidding war to bring Bonilla home to New York. He embraced the challenge, but after hitting two home runs in his first game with the team in 1992, he struggled to meet the expectations of the fans and media. Because of his $27.5 million five-year contract, plus $1.5 million in guaranteed endorsements, Bonilla took the brunt of the blame when the Mets showed no visible improvement, and his dream of playing before hometown fans soured.

Bonilla fared better in his second season with the Mets, collecting 34 homers and 87 RBIs, and earned his fifth All-Star berth. The team, however, stumbled to a 103-loss season. In 1994 he moved from the outfield to third base, where he committed 18 errors in only 107 games before the strike ended the season.

Bonilla returned to form in 1995, but he also returned to the American League; the Mets traded him to Baltimore for two prospects in July. He finished the 1996 season with 116 RBIs, plus 12 assists and six errors (both team highs for outfielders). He hit .200 with two home runs, including a grand slam, in Baltimore's upset of Cleveland in the Division Series. A home run in the American League Championship Series was his only hit in 20 at bats in a five-game loss to the New York Yankees.

Bonilla did not get along with Baltimore manager Davey Johnson, who wanted the heavy-set slugger to be a designated hitter. After the 1996 season, Bonilla signed another lucrative free agent contract, this time with the Florida Marlins, who penned Bonilla to a four-year deal worth $23.3 million.

The surprising Marlins climbed into the 1997 postseason as a Wild Card winner. After sweeping San Francisco in the Division Series, Florida upset Atlanta in six games, helped by Bonilla's .261 average and four RBIs. He struggled against Cleveland in the World Series, but he delivered one of the team's most important hits. In Game 7, trailing 2-0, Bonilla cracked a solo home run in the seventh. Florida tied the score in the ninth and won the Series in the 11th.

The Marlines, forced to dismantle the team because of financial losses, shipped Bonilla to Los Angeles in a blockbuster trade that involved Mike Piazza and Gary Sheffield in May 1998. Bonilla was on the disabled list three times that season. He was traded to the Mets for Mel Rojas in the off-season.

Bonilla savored the chance to redeem himself in New York, but spent most of 1999 on the disabled list and out of favor with manager Bobby Valentine, as well as the media and fans. He played in just 60 games, batted .160, and was reduced to pinch-hitting in New York's first post-season appearance since 1988. He was reportedly playing cards with Ricky Henderson while the Mets were locked in a frustrating 11-inning loss in Game 6 of the NLCS. Two months later the club bought out Bonilla's contract, putting an end to his second career with the Mets.

Zeke Bonura

Bonura, Henry John **1B**

1934–40 B:9/20/1908, New Orleans, LA D:3/9/1987, New Orleans, LA Deb:4/17/1934, CHI AL BR/TR 6', 210

G	AB	R	H	HR	RBI	OBP	SLG	AVG
917	3582	600	1099	119	704	.380	.487	.307

First baseman Zeke Bonura became the Chicago White Sox's first legitimate home run threat when he set a club record (since broken) of 27 homers as a rookie in 1934. Whether keeping his bat in the lineup justified allowing his glove on the field was an ongoing debate around Comiskey Park throughout his years in Chicago. Although he actually led AL first basemen in fielding percentage three times, Bonura's chief liability was his reluctance to make the effort required to be a top-notch fielder. When a ground ball came close enough to require something more than a disdainful stare, Bonura would wave at it with more style than enthusiasm.

Criticism of his fielding did not deter Bonura from the important matter of hitting. In four years with the Sox he clubbed 79 homers, knocked in 440 runs, and never batted below .295. So focused was he on his deeds with a bat that he sometimes overlooked the lesser niceties of the game, such as signs. In one of his greatest moments, he stole home with two outs to score the winning run against the Yankees. After he dusted himself off, manager Jimmy Dykes informed Bonura that the sign he'd been given had actually instructed Bonura to run on any batted ball.

"Banana Nose," as he was affectionately known, was popular with fans for his outspoken personality, heavy hitting, and unique base running, but his annual holdouts infuriated the White Sox front office. In 1938 he was rumored to be romantically involved with the daughter of club owner J. Louis Comiskey, and he was quickly traded to Washington for Joe Kuhel in a deal billed as the "worst-fielding first baseman for the best."

Bonura hit 22 homers with 114 RBIs for the Senators in 1938, after which he was sold to the New York Giants for two players and $20,000. He hit .321 for the Giants, but because his power numbers had begun to slip, he was sold back to Washington. Before the 1940 season ended, he was back in Chicago for his final major league at bats, this time with the Cubs.

Bob Boone

Boone, Robert Raymond **C**

1972–90 M(1995–97, 181–206) B:11/19/1947, San Diego, CA Deb:9/10/1972, PHI NL BR/TR 6'2", 202

G	AB	R	H	HR	RBI	OBP	SLG	AVG
2264	7245	679	1838	105	826	.318	.346	.254

Bob Boone is the middle member of the first three-generation major league family. His father, Ray, was an All-Star infielder, and his son, Bret, reached the majors in 1993 as a second baseman for the Seattle Mariners. At age 33 in 1981, Bob Boone had played nine years in the National League as a regular and had earned two Gold Gloves. That year his batting average fell to .211, and the Philadelphia Phillies thought he was through. But he lasted the rest of the decade after moving to the American League, resurrecting his reputation as a defensive catcher with five more Gold Gloves, and shattering Al Lopez's 30-year-old mark for games caught.

Generally a mediocre hitter, Boone won raves as a defensive catcher during his 19-year career. Among the best at framing borderline pitches to steal strikes, he was a smart, dedicated student of hitters and pitchers. He built a reputation as a great baseball thinker. Known as a superb handler of pitchers, Boone once said, "That term always grated on me. I never handled any pitcher. I had a relationship with them."

Boone played third base at Stanford, where he earned a psychology degree, and in 1969 he was a 20th-round draft selection. In 1971 former Phillies backstop Andy Seminick converted Boone into a catcher. Boone's father had done just the reverse, beginning as a catcher and moving to third base.

In late 1972 Bob Boone joined the Phillies and in 1973 he succeeded Tim McCarver as their regular catcher, placing third in voting for NL Rookie of the Year. Everything was not perfect, however, as Boone did not always see eye-to-eye with ace pitcher Steve Carlton; in 1975 the Phillies re-signed McCarver to be Carlton's personal catcher.

The next year, however, Boone earned the first of five All-Star Game selections, and the Phillies made their first of three straight trips to the playoffs. In 1977 he recorded the fewest errors and passed balls among the league's catchers. The following year he led the league's catchers in fielding percentage and won the first of back-to-back Gold Gloves, breaking Johnny Bench's 10-year monopoly.

Boone's offensive production took a big dive in 1980, but he came through in the clutch, batting a team-high .412 in the Phillies' six-game World Series win over the Kansas City Royals. However, his poor hitting in 1981 and the availability of Keith Moreland to take his place prompted the Phillies to sell Boone to California that winter.

In a new, more appreciative environment in 1982, Boone threw out 63 of 109 runners attempting to steal and won his first AL Gold Glove, while the Angels won the AL West crown. Boone impressed manager Gene Mauch with his defensive wizardry and his physical toughness. Mauch declared, "[Pole vaulter] Billy Owens couldn't jump over Boone's pain threshold."

Boone was selected to his fourth All-Star Game in 1983, and continued to produce in his quiet style. Then he exploded when the Angels went to the 1986 Championship Series against the Red Sox. Boone led all regulars with a .455 batting average and recorded five consecutive hits, both ALCS records. He singled two times, scored twice, and knocked in a run in Game 1, then began his hitting string in Game 4, singling in the ninth inning with the Angels down, 3–1, to knock out Roger Clemens. California won the contest in 11 innings to take a 3–1 lead in games. In Game 5 Boone had three hits, including a solo homer. After outfielder Dave Henderson's two-out, two-run homer in the top of the ninth gave the Red Sox a 6–5 lead, Boone kicked off the Angels' half with a single, sparking the game-tying rally. But Boone left for a pinch runner and the Sox won in 11. In Game 6 Boone's first-inning passed ball allowed one Boston run to score and set up a second that tied the game and helped keep the Sox's momentum going all the way to the World Series.

In 1986 Boone became, at age 38, the oldest non-pitcher to win a Gold Glove, which he snagged again in each of the next three seasons. He surpassed Al Lopez's games-caught record on September 16, 1987, at Kansas City. On June 13, 1988, he produced his 100th career home run, making the Boones the second family with father and son hitting 100 home runs.

Boone batted a career-best .295 in 1988 and, granted "new look" free agency as a result of ownership collusion, signed with the Royals following that season. He played for two years in Kansas City, making his only trip to the disabled list in 1990, and tried unsuccessfully to catch on with the Seattle Mariners in 1991 in hopes of playing with his son.

Boone became the manager of the Oakland A's Class AAA Tacoma Tigers affiliate for two seasons. He accepted a coaching job for 1994 with Cincinnati, where he joined his son, Bret, whom the Reds acquired from the Mariners after the 1993 season. After the 1994 season, Boone replaced Hal McRae as manager of the Kansas City Royals. He guided the Royals to second place in his first year with the club, but was let go midway through the 1997 season. He later joined the Reds as a consultant.

Bret Boone

Boone, Bret Robert **2B**

1992–* B:4/6/1969, El Cajon, CA Deb:8/19/1992, SEA AL BR/TR, 5'10", 180

G	AB	R	H	HR	RBI	OBP	SLG	AVG
945	3448	442	880	106	462	.313	.412	.255

Bret Boone arrived in the major leagues with great baseball bloodlines: his father Bob was a major league catcher for 19 years, and grandfather Ray was an infielder during a 13-year career. Like the Boones before him, Bret became an All-Star at his position, second base, and in 1999 became the third generation in his family to play in the World Series—nabbing the unique honor ahead of brothers Aaron, a Cincinnati third baseman, and Matthew, a Detroit prospect.

Boone's father was still playing when Seattle made Bret its fifth-round draft choice in 1990. The younger Boone and Seattle manager Lou Piniella did not get along, prompting the Mariners to trade the second baseman to Cincinnati following the 1993 season. Boone responded by hitting a career-high .320 in his first year with the Reds. Boone had a career-best 24 homers and 95 RBIs in 1998. That season he just missed becoming the first second baseman to lead both leagues in fielding for four straight seasons. Mickey Morandini of the Chicago Cubs edged him by .005 percentage points.

The Atlanta Braves acquired Boone for the 1999 season. He set career marks with 102 runs and 14 stolen bases while giving the Braves power (20 homers) and defense up the middle. He had a pair of two-homer games, a four-hit game, and a career-best 14-game hitting streak. He was one of the few Braves to hit well in the World Series sweep at the hands of the New York Yankees. He batted .538, including four straight doubles in Games 2 and 3. Despite his productivity with Atlanta, Boone was traded in a multi-player deal to San Diego on December 21, 1999.

Ike Boone

Boone, Isaac Morgan **OF**

1922–25, 1927, 1930–32 B:2/17/1897, Samantha, AL D:8/1/1958, Northport, AL Deb:4/22/1922, NY NL BL/TR 6', 195

G	AB	R	H	HR	RBI	OBP	SLG	AVG
356	1160	177	372	26	194	.394	.475	.321

Like Buzz Arlett and Smead Jolley, his fellow players in the Pacific Coast League of the 1920s, Ike Boone will always be remembered as a great hitter whose lack of speed and fielding skills denied him a lasting career in the major leagues. But as a pure hitter, he was almost unmatchable.

Boone had made a quick trip to the majors with the New York Giants in 1922 and had gone back to the minors. But in 1923 he had a magnificent year with the San Antonio Bears, in which he hit .402 and collected 53 doubles, 26 triples, and 135 RBIs—all league-leading totals.

He was back up in the major leagues with the Boston Red Sox for the end of the 1923 season, and then had two excellent years at the plate for the Red Sox. In 1924 he hit .337 and drove in 98 runs, and the next year he batted .330 with another 68 RBIs. Other than a brief stint with the Chicago White Sox in 1927, he disappeared from the majors again.

Boone had one of the greatest batting seasons in minor league history in 1929 for the PCL's Mission Reds, hitting .407 with 55 homers and 218 RBIs in 198 games. His 553 total bases that season have never been equaled. He was on his way to the all-time single-season minor league batting average in 1930—hitting an astronomical .448—when the Dodgers called him back up to the majors. His playing time was limited despite hitting .297. But in a season when National League hitters averaged .303, Boone's talents weren't looked upon as anything special.

Each of the next two years, Boone made appearances with the Dodgers, but each year the real story was his tearing up of the minor leagues. He led his league in hitting twice more, in 1931 for Newark and in 1934 for Toronto. Boone finished with having hit .350 or more 10 times in the minors, and his lifetime minor league average was an awesome .370. His career major league batting average was .321.

Ray Boone

Boone, Raymond Otis **3B-SS-1B**

1948–60 B:7/27/1923, San Diego, CA Deb:9/3/1948, CLE AL BR/TR 6'1", 188

G	AB	R	H	HR	RBI	OBP	SLG	AVG
1373	4589	645	1260	151	737	.363	.429	.275

Ray Boone essentially had three careers, playing shortstop for five years with the Cleveland Indians, serving primarily as a third baseman for the Detroit Tigers for four years, and then finishing off his career as a first baseman. Boone was batting .355 as a third baseman for Oklahoma City in the Texas League when he was called up to fill in for Cleveland shortstop-manager Lou Boudreau when Boudreau was injured. Boone was so good that Boudreau moved himself to third upon returning to the lineup, and Boone didn't return to his natural position for several years.

Boone was traded to Detroit in June 1953, and his career really took off. He finished the year with 26 home runs—when his previous high had been 12—and his 114 RBIs almost doubled his previous high.

In 1954 he was selected for his first All-Star Game; in 1955 he tied for the AL lead with 116 RBIs; and in 1956 he went to his second All-Star Game. Despite his success, Boone was traded to Chicago during the 1958 season, and then finished out his career with brief stints in Kansas City, Milwaukee, and Boston.

Boone was one of many players who hated to fly, when air travel in the majors was relatively new. On one occasion the Tigers were flying to Kansas City for a weekend series when one of the four engines on their plane conked out. The plane made an emergency landing at Chicago O'Hare Airport and the Tigers were put on another aircraft. On Sunday the Tigers were scheduled to fly out of Kansas City.

At the airport Boone pulled a piece of crumpled paper out of his pocket, scanned it quickly, and then glanced at the plane they were about to board: he'd written down the number of the plane that the Tigers had been forced to abandon in Chicago, and this was the same plane.

"See you later, guys," he said, as he headed for the train station.

Boone's son Bob was later a catcher in the major leagues. Bob became a manager at the end of his 19-year playing career. The Boones became a three-generation major league family in 1993 when Boone's grandson, second baseman Bret, joined the Seattle Mariners. All three generations played in a World Series and were named to an All-Star team.

Scott Boras

Boras, Scott Dean
Agent B:11/2/1952

Few player agents have been more effective for his clients, or hated by management and vilified by the media, than Scott Boras. Boras began his involvement in professional baseball as an infielder/outfielder in the St. Louis organization during the mid-1970s. He never advanced past Double A, retiring in 1977. In the off-season Boras pursued a law degree. He became convinced of the inequity of minor-league contracts. "The deals were unilaterally imposed and the team could get out of them at any time," he said later. "There was never any negotiation."

In his new career as an agent, Boras looked to challenge the system. After drawn-out, confrontational negotiations, he secured ever-larger amounts for top picks Andy Benes, Ben McDonald, and Brien Taylor, the New York Yankees' first selection in 1991 who signed for $1.55 million—and never reached the major leagues. Although Boras improved his major league client roster, it was another amateur, Florida State outfielder J.D. Drew, who gained Boras his greatest notoriety.

In 1996 amateurs Travis Lee and Matt White had escaped the draft through a loophole and commanded deals for over $10 million each; Boras envisioned even bigger numbers for Drew. "When you remove the barrier of the draft, you see what teams are willing to pay for select amateur players," Boras said.

He warned frugally-minded teams not to select his client, but the Philadelphia Phillies called his bluff and tapped Drew with the second overall pick. Drew rejected Philadelphia, demanding $11 million. He spent the season in the independent Northern League, which Boras maintained freed him from the draft. An arbitrator rejected his position, but Drew refused to sign with Philadelphia and went back into the draft. This time, the Cardinals selected him and quickly signed Drew for a record $8 million.

The Philadelphia press lambasted Boras during the course of the Drew affair; the New York media was no less kind during contentious negotiations between the Yankees and Bernie Williams. Kevin Brown, another Boras client, signed baseball's first nine-digit contract following the 1998 season, prompting many to declare that poorer teams could no longer compete in the economic system Boras had helped to define.

Pedro Borbon

Borbon, Pedro (Rodriguez) **P**
1969–80 B:12/2/1946, Valverde, Dominican Republic
Deb:4/9/1969, CAL AL BR/TR 6'2", 185

W	L	PCT	G	SV	IP	BB	SO	ERA
69	39	.639	593	80	1026^{2}	251	409	3.52

Hard-throwing Pedro Borbon was one of the first relief pitchers to really know that he could put on a show for the fans. He specialized in getting ready quickly, and he liked to show off his strong arm by firing strikes to home plate while standing on the warning track in center field.

The St. Louis Cardinals signed the Dominican-born Borbon as a free agent in 1964. Snapped up by the California Angels in the minor league draft in 1968, he was ineffective and was traded to the Cincinnati in 1969. With the Reds he became a star, going 8–3 in 1972, his first year of significant action. The next season, he won 11 times, saved 14 games in a career-best 80 appearances, and had an outstanding 2.16 ERA.

Borbon was especially effective in NLCS competition, where he compiled a lifetime 0.63 ERA and did not yield an earned run in seven games from 1973 to 1976. His most famous playoff moment, however, occurred during the Pete Rose–Bud Harrelson brawl during Game 3 of the 1973 playoffs. Borbon was an active participant in the melee at Shea Stadium, and in his anger he inadvertently picked up a New York Mets hat. When he realized his mistake he took a large bite out of the offending cap. He pitched two scoreless innings later that day.

Borbon was traded from the Reds to San Francisco for outfielder Hector Cruz on June 28, 1979. He pitched briefly for the Cardinals in 1980, before retiring. In 1992 his son, southpaw Pedro Borbon, Jr., debuted with the Atlanta Braves.

Frenchy Bordagaray

Bordagaray, Stanley George **OF–3B**
1934–39, 1941–45 B:1/3/1910, Coalinga, CA
Deb:4/17/1934, CHI AL BR/TR 5'7½", 175

G	AB	R	H	HR	RBI	OBP	SLG	AVG
930	2632	410	745	14	270	.331	.366	.283

Although he never lived up to his supposed potential, Frenchy Bordagaray nonetheless had a marvelous time in the majors. A football star at Fresno State, he arrived at the Brooklyn Dodgers' spring training in 1935 sporting an oversized mustache, such as those worn in that era by movie villains. Forced to shave, he blamed his hair loss for a subsequent batting slump. Fined $500 on another occasion for spitting at an umpire, Bordagaray protested, "Maybe I did wrong, but the penalty was a little more than I expectorated."

He hit .315 playing semiregularly for Brooklyn in 1936 while putting more gray hairs on manager Casey Stengel's head than had any other player. Traded to the Cardinals in 1937, he played washboard in the Gas House Gang's Mudcat Band. Later, after hitting only .197 for the Reds, he was sent back to the minors.

With the American Association's Kansas City Blues in 1940 he hit .358 and led the league in hits, which earned him a trip back to the majors as a utility man with the 1941 Yankees. But when he told manager Joe McCarthy that Stengel would have won 15 pennants with McCarthy's personnel, Bordagaray was traded back to Brooklyn. A good wartime player for the Dodgers, Bordagaray returned to the minors in 1946 for an undistinguished try at managing.

Joe Borden

Borden, Joseph Emley **P**

1875–76 B:5/9/1854, Jacobstown, NJ D:10/14/1929, Yeadon, PA Deb:7/24/1875, PHI NA BR/TR 5'9", 140

W	L	PCT	G	SH	IP	BB	SO	ERA
11	12	.478	29	2	218^{1}	51	34	2.89

Pitcher Joe Borden came from a prominent New Jersey family that disapproved of his playing professional baseball. When he joined Philadelphia of the National Association late in 1875 he played under the pseudonym "Nedrob," then switched to "Joseph E. Josephs." Under any name, he pitched well but without much luck.

Despite a 1.64 ERA in seven appearances, Borden went only 2–4. Both of his victories were shutouts, and one was especially significant: on July 28 he set down the Chicago White Stockings without a hit. The 4–0 victory was the first and only no-hitter in the five-year history of the National Association and therefore the first in major league history. It also earned him a nickname: "Josephus the Phenomenal."

When the National League was formed the next year, the Boston Red Stockings needed a pitcher to replace the great Al Spalding. They made Borden one of the highest-paid players in the league at $2,000 a year for three years. He was the Opening Day pitcher for Boston in the new league's first game, played at Philadelphia on April 22. When the Red Stockings, greatly aided by 13 Philadelphia errors, emerged with a victory, their new hurler became the first NL pitcher to gain a win. By midseason, he went on to win 10 more while losing 12.

One report has it that Borden's arm gave out—not unlikely considering his slender, 140-pound physique. Since he had a guaranteed $2,000-a-year contract, the Boston owners, according to legend, ordered him to fulfill his contract by acting as the team's groundskeeper, hoping in this way to embarrass him into leaving. Instead, Borden went happily on his way, cutting the grass, trimming the hedges, and digging dandelions, and he became the wealthiest groundskeeper in America. After the owners finally bought him off with a lump sum payment, he never pitched again.

Ila Borders

Borders, Ila Jane

Baseball Pioneer B:2/18/1975, Downey, CA

In 1997, as baseball paid homage to Jackie Robinson on the 50th anniversary of his breaking the game's color barrier, a young woman named Ila Borders challenged baseball's last wall of exclusion. That season she became the first woman to pitch in a men's professional game as a member of the St. Paul Saints of the independent Northern League.

Borders had wanted to play professional baseball since the age of 10. She was the only girl in her La Habra (California) Little League, then had to sue for the right to play in junior high. At Whittier College in California, she was the first woman to pitch in and win a game on the college level.

When the 5-foot 10-inch, 150-pound southpaw joined the St. Paul Saints she had to contend with heckling opposing players and team officials. She persevered, and finally, while pitching for the Duluth-Superior Dukes, she picked up her first professional win with six scoreless innings against Sioux Falls on July 26, 1998. Even then the disgruntled manager of the losing team complained that she should not have been allowed in the league.

Borders had her best season in 1999 for the Madison Black Wolf of the Northern League. She went 1-0 with a 1.76 ERA in 15 appearances. She repeatedly said her quest was no publicity stunt, but she got plenty of coverage, anyway. Reporters, photographers, and cameramen followed her every move in the Northern League. Mike Wallace and *Sixty Minutes* even did a piece on her. Fans, in turn, took to Borders with an enthusiasm not generally displayed for struggling pitchers with 80-mph fastballs.

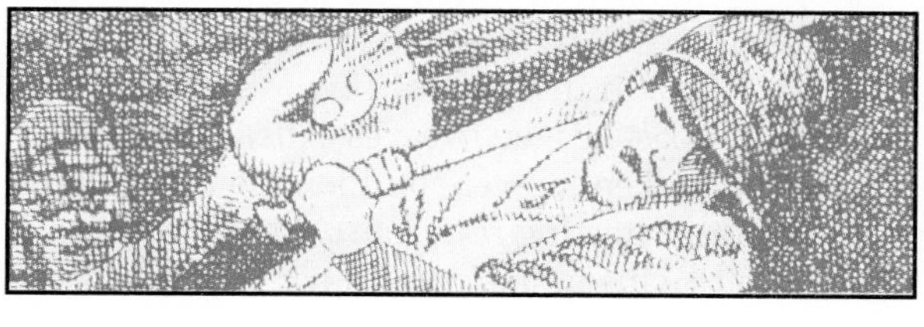

Pat Borders

Borders, Patrick Lance **C**

1988–* B:5/14/1963, Columbus, OH Deb:4/6/1988, TOR AL BR/TR 6'2", 200

G	AB	R	H	HR	RBI	OBP	SLG	AVG
1001	3046	266	779	67	327	.293	.380	.256

Hardly a star player, Toronto Blue Jays catcher Pat Borders briefly grabbed the spotlight when he won the Most Valuable Player Award in the 1992 World Series. Borders had spent seven years in Toronto's minor league system before landing a major-league job in 1989. When veteran Ernie Whitt moved to Atlanta in 1990, Borders became the regular catcher on a team that made the playoffs each year from 1991 to 1993. Borders had a career-high 13 home runs in 1992, but batted just .242. His offensive production, however, would show dramatic improvement come October.

Borders hit .318 in a six-game victory over Oakland in the Championship Series. In the World Series he led both teams with nine hits and three doubles, and his home run off Atlanta's Tom Glavine in Game 4 led the Blue Jays to a 2–1 win. Borders batted .450 and caught every inning as the Jays beat the Braves in six games.

Borders batted .304 in the World Series the following year as the Blue Jays claimed another title, but after a mediocre 1994 season Borders began a tour of the major leagues. He signed with Kansas City as a free agent but was traded to Houston late in 1995. Signing with St. Louis in the off-season, he was promptly traded to California, who then dealt him to the White Sox a month later. He settled into a backup role in Cleveland for two seasons before returning to Toronto late in the 1999 season.

Chris Bosio

Bosio, Christopher Louis **P**

1986–96 B:4/3/1963, Carmichael, CA Deb:8/3/1986, MIL AL BR/TR 6'3", 225

W	L	PCT	G	SH	IP	BB	SO	ERA
94	93	.503	309	9	1710	481	1059	3.96

Chris Bosio's career was characterized by brief moments of dominance, followed by long periods of injury. Bosio reached the major leagues having established himself as both a starter and reliever. He led the Midwest League in wins with a 17–6 record at Class A Beloit in 1984 and two years later led the Pacific Coast League in saves. After starting 1987 in the Milwaukee Brewers bullpen, he finished the season in the starting rotation. A two-hit shutout against the Twins in late August solidified his role. By mid-May 1988 Bosio was 6–3 with a 1.97 ERA. Then he lost 10 straight decisions and was demoted to the minors. When he returned, Bosio found himself in the closer's role and earned six saves in the final month of the season.

Armed with a new split-finger pitch in 1989 Bosio suddenly became one of the top starting pitchers in the American League. He posted a 15–10 record and a 2.95 ERA. A knee injury in 1990 cost him half the season, but he returned with 14 wins in 1991 and followed that with 16 victories in 1992.

Bosio joined Seattle as a free agent in 1993. He threw a 7–0 no-hitter against Boston on April 22, but only a week later a knee injury sent him back to the disabled list. His knee would force two more trips to the DL in 1993, and end his 1994 season at the All-Star break. By 1995, although seemingly healthy, he was no longer as effective a pitcher. He made his first trip to the playoffs that fall, starting the first postseason game in franchise history. He did not get a decision in either start against the Yankees in Seattle's five-game Division Series triumph, but he pitched well in a losing effort against Cleveland in the Championship Series.

Continuing problems with his knee cost Bosio most of the 1996 season, and he sat out all of 1997. He attempted a comeback with the Red Sox in 1998, but decided to retire after suffering a shoulder injury early in spring training.

Dick Bosman

1966–76 B:2/17/1944, Kenosha, WI Deb:6/1/1966, WAS AL BR/TR 6'3", 208

W	L	PCT	G	SH	IP	BB	SO	ERA
82	85	.491	306	10	1591	412	757	3.67

Dick Bosman, second cousin of infielder Duane Kuiper, once threatened a teammate, "If you don't hustle when I'm pitching, I'll kick your ass." He probably meant it. Stuck on such mediocre teams as the Washington Senators, Texas Rangers, and Cleveland Indians between 1966 and 1975, he knew the bitterness of losing.

Despite playing on a losing team, his 2.19 ERA led the American League in 1969. Senators owner Bob Short rewarded Bosman with a raise to $35,000 for the 1970 season. While Bosman had no problems getting along with Short, he did not always get along with Washington Manager Ted Williams. "Dick Bosman was bitter at not being left in games longer, but he could not win the argument with Ted," contended Senators play-by-play announcer Shelby Whitfield.

Bosman moved with the club to Texas in 1972 but was traded to Cleveland the following year. While in Cleveland he shut out the world champion

Oakland A's on July 19, 1974, losing a perfect game on his own throwing error.

To better Oakland's chances in the 1975 AL West race, Charlie Finley acquired Bosman and fellow pitcher Jim Perry on May 20, 1975, for pitcher John "Blue Moon" Odom and cash. "This trade will put us in the playoffs," bragged Finley, and the events that followed proved him right. Bosman, at 31, and Perry, at 38, joined Finley's "Over the Hill Gang" and helped clinch a division title for Oakland. "Winning baseball's beaten me, kept me up nights, got me drunk, and kept me down for years, and now I'm part of it," said Bosman, happy to finally be pitching for a team in a pennant race.

But his happiness was short-lived. Finley rewarded Bosman's good work by releasing the pitcher in the spring of 1977. "Charlie Finley just cut my throat and left it to bleed," charged an angry Bosman. "He didn't can me till the end of spring training when it was too late to catch on anywhere else."

Bosman, who raced and built dragsters as a youth and once finished second in the National Drag Racing Championships, worked at a Chevrolet dealership in northern Virginia after retiring from baseball. He later served as a respected pitching coach for the White Sox, Orioles, and Rangers.

Lyman Bostock

Bostock, Lyman Wesley **OF**

1975–78 B:11/22/1950, Birmingham, AL D:9/23/1978, Gary, IN Deb:4/8/1975, MIN AL BL/TR 6'1", 180

G	AB	R	H	HR	RBI	OBP	SLG	AVG
526	2004	305	624	23	250	.368	.427	.311

Lyman Bostock was one of those rare players who could do it all. Tragically, he never had the chance to demonstrate the full measure of his talents. Bostock's father, Lyman Sr., spent nine years in the Negro Leagues as an outfielder and first baseman for the Birmingham Black Barons, the Chicago American Giants, and the New York Cubans. Bostock Jr. attended California State University, Northridge—one of the most successful small-college baseball programs—before being drafted by the Minnesota Twins in 1972.

After three outstanding seasons in the minors, Bostock made the Twins' lineup as a center fielder in 1975. Although he missed a month of the season with an injury, he hit .282 during his rookie season. However, he was easily outvoted in the Rookie of the Year balloting by Boston's Fred Lynn and Jim Rice.

Bostock became a true star in 1976, hitting .323 for the Twins. On July 24 he hit for the cycle. The following season he proved he was a complete ballplayer. He set a major league record with 12 putouts in a single game in center field, and he finished second in the league batting race to teammate Rod Carew, hitting .336. He also hit for power, with 14 home runs, 12 triples, and 36 doubles, while scoring 104 runs and driving in 90.

A free agent at the end of 1977, Bostock fled penurious Minnesota owner Calvin Griffith for the California Angels, where he signed a multimillion-dollar contract. At age 26, he seemed poised for greatness, but then slumped badly at the beginning of the season. Believing that he wasn't earning his money, Bostock tried to refuse his salary. Angels owner Gene Autry turned down the offer, but the fans appreciated the gesture.

Eventually Bostock started hitting again, and the surprising Angels were locked in a three-way battle for first place. With his average up to .296, it seemed certain that Bostock would top .300. On September 23, with the team in Chicago, Bostock went to visit his uncle in Gary, Indiana. His uncle was driving a car containing Bostock and two women he'd met only a few minutes earlier. Another vehicle pulled alongside and the husband of one of the women fired shots at the car. One of the bullets struck Bostock, and he died three hours later.

Jim Bottomley

Bottomley, James Leroy **1B**

1922–37 M(1937, 21–56) B:4/23/1900, Oglesby, IL D:12/11/1959, St. Louis, MO Deb:8/18/1922, STL NL BL/TL 6', 180

G	AB	R	H	HR	RBI	OBP	SLG	AVG
1991	7471	1177	2313	219	1422	.369	.500	.310

It would be hard to imagine a better day than that which Hall of Famer "Sunny Jim" Bottomley had for St. Louis on September 16, 1924, at Brooklyn's Ebbets Field. In the top of the first, facing starter Rube Ehrhardt with the bases loaded, Bottomley drove in two runs with a single. Then he doubled in another run in the second inning against Bonnie Hollingsworth. With runners on second and third in the fourth inning, Robins manager Wilbert Robinson ordered pitcher Art Decatur to walk Rogers Hornsby (a .424 hitter that season) to get at Bottomley. The strategy backfired; Bottomley delivered a grand slam. Decatur was still on the mound in the sixth, when Bottomley responded with a two-run homer. By then the score was 13–1 and Bottomley had nine RBIs. In the seventh, he drove in two more runners against Tex Wilson to tie Robinson's 32-year-old league record. Hornsby tripled in the ninth, and Bottomley's run-scoring single against Jim Roberts established a new RBI record.

Bottomley grew up in Illinois coal-mining country and went to work as a blacksmith's apprentice at age 16. While playing semipro ball he caught the eye of a Cardinals scout during a game in which he hit two homers and three triples. In 1922, after playing with the Syracuse Stars, he earned a late-season promotion to St. Louis, where he hit .325.

In his first full season, Bottomley batted .371, but it was just the start of a magnificent career. He had more than 110 RBIs in each of the next six years, leading the NL twice in that category, as well as leading it in doubles twice. In 1928 he had the remarkable double of leading the league in both home runs (with 31) and triples (with 20), while on his way to being named the league's MVP. In 1931 he barely missed leading the NL in batting average, finishing with a .3482 mark behind Bill Terry's .3486 and Chick Hafey's .3489 in the closest three-man batting race in baseball history.

Bottomley also enjoyed a number of notable one-game performances. He collected three triples in one game on June 21, 1927; he hit for the cycle on July 15, 1927; he collected six hits on August 5, 1932; and he had five hits in a game three times.

And he could make remarkable fielding plays. During Game 2 of the 1931 World Series, Cardinal starter "Wild Bill" Hallahan was unraveling in the ninth inning against Connie Mack's powerful Philadelphia Athletics. Jimmie Foxx walked, and, after Bing Miller fouled out, Jimmy Dykes also walked. Jim Moore then reached when St. Louis catcher Jimmy Wilson dropped a third strike to load the bases. With two outs, Max Bishop popped one up in foul ground that Bottomley chased down, and then dove over the A's bullpen bench and caught reaching into the stands to end the game.

Bottomley was also a tremendous leader. In one game, after third baseman Les Bell had come up to the Cardinals near the close of the 1923 season, Bell made two throws clean over everything, to some 10 to 20 rows high in the stands behind first base. "When I came into the dugout after that inning I was feeling pretty blue," Bell said. "Who sits down next to me but the regular first baseman, Jim Bottomley. All he did that year was hit .371. Jim put his arm around me and said, 'Now, kid, Old Jim will be out there tomorrow playing first base. So when you throw the ball, you throw it in the direction of first base and Old Jim will get it.' That made me feel better. What a fine gentleman he was."

Traded to the Reds just before the "Gas House Gang" jelled, Bottomley returned to St. Louis for a last hurrah in 1936, this time with the Browns. When Rogers Hornsby was fired in 1937, Bottomley took over as player-manager and ended his playing career with a .310 average.

In 1938 he returned to Syracuse and managed the Chiefs of the International League. He was then out of baseball until 1957 when he signed on as a scout for the Cubs. In midseason he was appointed manager of the Class D Appalachian League's Pulaski Cubs, but he retired after two games. Bottomley died of a heart attack in 1959. He was elected to the Hall of Fame in 1974.

Lou Boudreau

Boudreau, Louis **SS**

1938–52 M(1942–50, 1952–57, 1960, 1,162–1,224)
B:7/17/1917, Harvey, IL Deb:9/9/1938, CLE AL BR/TR
5'11", 185

G	AB	R	H	HR	RBI	OBP	SLG	AVG
1646	6029	861	1779	68	789	.380	.415	.295

Lou Boudreau had a long and highly successful career as both a playing manager and one of the outstanding shortstops of the 1940s. He ranks as one of the best defensive shortstops of all time and was also a sensational hitter—through 1999 he ranked seventh among all shortstops in lifetime batting average and on-base percentage and eighth in slugging percentage. A confident and creative manager, he was elected in 1970 to the Hall of Fame for his talents on and off the field.

A natural athlete, Boudreau captained his high school basketball team to the Illinois state championship and was the captain of the University of Illinois basketball team as a junior. But, while still in school, Boudreau accepted money from Cleveland general manager Cy Slapnicka with the promise that he would sign with the Indians upon graduation. Boudreau's jealous stepfather complained to the Big Ten, and Boudreau was ruled ineligible to play college sports.

Boudreau arrived in Cleveland as a third baseman, but veteran Ken Keltner had a lock on the position, so manager Ossie Vitt shifted the rookie to shortstop. In 1940, his first full season in the majors, Boudreau hit .295 with 101 RBIs, 46 doubles, and 10 triples. He was also named to the All-Star team for the first of eight times.

Following the next season, the confident young Boudreau wrote to owner Alva Bradley about the manager's job, which had come open. Player-managers were not uncommon at the time, and Boudreau felt his experience as captain of his college team would be a plus. In his autobiography he revealed that he had second thoughts about the letter and worried that his brashness might upset the management. One friend counseled, "Don't worry. Bradley'll probably just throw your letter in the wastebasket anyway." But after a two-hour interview, he was named the new manager.

One Cleveland sportswriter was appalled and wrote, "Great! The Indians get a Baby Snooks for a manager and ruin the best shortstop in baseball." But Boudreau quickly hired three experienced baseball men—Burt Shotton, Oscar Melillo, and George Susce—to help him run the team. When the 1942 season opened, Boudreau was, at age 24, the youngest person to start a major league season as a manager.

For the next six years, Boudreau's Indians finished out of the pennant race, but Boudreau was marvelous on the field. In 1944 he led the league with a .327 batting average and 45 doubles. He also set records for shortstops with a .978 fielding percentage and 134 double plays (since broken).

In June 1946, with the Indians in fifth place, Bill Veeck purchased the team. Veeck made it clear to Boudreau that while he had the greatest respect for him as a player, he doubted his ability to manage. The Indians were struggling, and no one was treating them any worse than Red Sox slugger Ted Williams, who'd just returned from the service.

On July 14 the Indians played the Red Sox in a doubleheader. In the first game Boudreau had four doubles and a homer, making him the only American Leaguer to ring up five extra-base hits in one game, a still-standing record, but Williams went 5-for-5, and his three homers drove in eight runs. The Indians lost, 11–10, and Boudreau was boiling. The Indians kept charts that showed Williams hit to right 95 percent of the time. Boudreau decided to play the percentages. He stationed six of his players to the right of second base, leaving only left fielder George Case on the left side, playing a deep shortstop. Boudreau probably didn't know that White Sox manager Jimmy Dykes had tried the same strategy against Williams in 1941. Boudreau's shift had its desired effect only once during that game, as Boudreau threw out Williams on a grounder to the right side. The Sox slugger still walked twice and doubled, scoring two runs in Boston's 6–4 victory, but Boudreau had established himself as a creative thinker.

Boudreau's charts indicated that, through the years, his team was 37 percent more successful against Williams while using the shift. "A psychological, if not always a tactical, victory," he called it. During the same season, he also moved Bob Lemon from the outfield to the pitcher's mound; the Hall of Famer went on to win 207 games and was a seven-time All-Star.

After the Indians finished fourth in 1947, word leaked out that Veeck wanted to swap Boudreau for Vern Stephens of the St. Louis Browns and several other players. Cleveland fans were outraged. Veeck received more than 4,000 letters demanding he keep Boudreau. When the *Cleveland News* ran a front-page ballot to elicit the fans' opinions, 100,000 responded, voting to retain Boudreau by a 10–1 margin. Veeck backed down.

Boudreau was under huge pressure to win the pennant, and during the off-season the Indians made a number of moves. Boudreau turned knuckleball-throwing lefthander Gene Bearden into a starter, and he responded with 20 wins. Veeck signed Satchel Paige, and he rang up a 6–1 record. Larry Doby was made the regular center fielder: he hit .301. Lemon matched Bearden with 20 wins, while Bob Feller won 19.

But the real star was the player-manager himself. Boudreau hit .355, had an on-base percentage of .453, and slugged .534. He hit 18 homers, drove in 106 runs, and scored 116. He also led AL shortstops in fielding percentage for the eighth time in nine years and was the club's emotional leader. A hard collision at second base in early August left him with a shoulder contusion, a bruised right knee, a sore right thumb, and a sprained left ankle.

Icing his wounds, he was on the bench, managing, during an August 8 doubleheader against the Yankees, with whom the Indians were tied for first place. Down, 6–1, in the seventh inning of the first game, the Indians put three runs on the board, then loaded the bases. Lefty relief pitcher Joe Page came in, and Boudreau put himself in the game as a pinch hitter. He singled to right, tying the score. The Indians went on to win both games.

The season ended with the Indians and the Red Sox in a tie for first. Boston won the right to host the first postseason playoff in American League history. Bearden pitched a five-hitter on only two days' rest, and the Indians won, 8–3. Boudreau hit two singles and two home runs. To cap the already incredible season, he hit four doubles as the Indians defeated the Boston Braves in the World Series.

In 1949 the Yankees reasserted themselves and the Indians fell to third. In 1951, after nine years as Cleveland's player-manager, Boudreau joined the Red Sox, ending his playing career there in 1952. As manager from 1952 to 1954, he coaxed the Sox to only one winning season, and he had little success as Kansas City manager from 1955 through 1957.

Boudreau then became the Cubs' broadcaster, and in 1960 he was hired to manage the team, replacing Charlie Grimm, who took Boudreau's place in the radio booth. But after one season, Boudreau was back on radio and remained a WGN broadcaster until 1989. But it was in Cleveland where Boudreau remained a hero. The street next to Cleveland Stadium was renamed Boudreau Boulevard in his honor.

Jim Bouton

Bouton, James Alan **P**

1962–70, 1978 B:3/8/1939, Newark, NJ
Deb:4/22/1962, NY AL BR/TR, 6', 185

W	L	PCT	G	SH	IP	BB	SO	ERA
62	63	.496	304	11	1238^2	435	720	3.57

With the exception of two years with the New York Yankees in 1963 and 1964, Jim Bouton's career as a pitcher consisted primarily of comeback tries. His greatest success actually came when he wrote *Ball Four*, a revealing book about what players in the national pastime said, did, and thought.

Bouton's sometimes hilarious, often disturbing, stories of the sexism and childish high jinks typical of major leaguers shocked the baseball establishment. Commissioner Bowie Kuhn said that the book was "detrimental to baseball." Mickey Mantle vowed he would never appear in an Old Timer's game with Bouton. (The Yankees did not invite Bouton to one until 1998.)

In a sense, Bouton's book was a sequel to the two books written in the 1960s by another bullpen habitué, Jim Brosnan: *The Long Season* and *Pennant Race*. Those books certainly upset the baseball establishment, but *Ball Four* leapt well beyond that. Players taking amphetamines (greenies, in the parlance of the day), playing while hung over, and ogling young women were scattered throughout Bouton's reminiscences of the 1969 season, as he tried to mount a comeback as a knuckleballer with the expansion Seattle Pilots, was sent down to Vancouver for two weeks, then was traded to Houston.

Bouton's irreverence was disarming: "I've been tempted to say into a microphone that I feel I won tonight because I don't believe in God." Or, "Lots of people look up to Billy Martin. That's because he just knocked them down." The close of the book became his most famous quote: "You spend a good part of your life gripping a baseball, and in the end it turns out it was the other way all the time."

In 1962, Bouton's first major league season, he started 16 games and relieved in 20 more, compiling a 7–7 record. The next year, in only his second season, he became a star, going 21–7 with a 2.53 ERA and ranking second in victories and winning percentage behind only fellow Yankee Whitey Ford. His six shutouts trailed only Chicago's Ray Herbert.

The Dodgers swept the Yankees in the 1963 World Series, and Bouton was saddled with an especially tough loss. In the first inning of Game 3, he allowed a run on a walk, a wild pitch, and a single. It was to be the only run scored in a game won by Don Drysdale. Even though Bouton's ERA increased by half a run in 1964, he led the Yankees with 18 wins, and then won Games 3 and 6 of the World Series, a seven-game loss to St. Louis.

Bouton's early-career pitching style was dynamic; he seemed to throw his whole body at the batter along with the ball. His cap frequently wound up in the dirt. His arms and legs flailed. Sportswriter Maury Allen nicknamed him "Bulldog" for his aggressive style. But his all-or-nothing pitching style cost him. In 1965 he hurt his arm and then tried to pitch through it. Throwing 151 innings, he won only four times while losing 15, and his ERA ballooned to 4.82. New manager Johnny Keane felt the pressure and directed many of his acid remarks at the struggling Bouton. The whole team crumbled, falling into sixth place. Bouton said, "It wasn't all my fault. I needed lots of help and I got it."

Bouton had a hard-luck season in 1966, recording an ERA of 2.69, but finishing with a won-loss record of 3–8; the Yankees were a last-place team for the first time since 1912. He made only 29 appearances with the Yankees the next two seasons, and began to work on his knuckleball.

The Yankees traded him to Seattle before the Pilots even had their expansion draft. Bouton began taking notes on what it was like to try to make a comeback, and when the things his teammates and coaches said struck him as funny, he'd write them down, too. Often he would gallop into the bullpen toilet to scribble on a popcorn box what someone had just said. The result became *Ball Four*.

After being traded to Houston, Bouton remained with the Astros for a second season, going 4–6 before retiring. But he had trouble leaving the game behind. In 1975 a minor league comeback didn't secure a major league job. In 1977 he tried again, and in 1978 he was signed by the Braves and went 1–3 in five starts.

After the success of *Ball Four*, Bouton wrote a sequel, *I'm Glad You Didn't Take It Personally*, about the reaction to his first book. He also wrote several other baseball books, and worked as a broadcaster. Bouton is still a free spirit, and he now endorses products with a baseball theme.

Larry Bowa

Bowa, Lawrence Robert **SS**

1970–85 M(1987–88, 81–127) B:12/6/1945, Sacramento, CA Deb:4/7/1970, PHI NL BB/TR 5'10", 155

G	AB	R	H	HR	RBI	OBP	SLG	AVG
2247	8418	987	2191	15	525	.301	.320	.260

Larry Bowa was one of the best shortstops of all time, an All-Star, a Gold Glove winner, and a World Series champion. But Mr. Congeniality he was not. Bowa won six NL fielding titles, a league record until Ozzie Smith came along, and set shortstop records (since broken) for fielding percentage, with .991 in 1979, and for fewest errors, with nine in 1972. He retired with the best career fielding percentagey a shortstop in major league history, at .980.

The son of a minor league infielder and manager, Bowa possessed a strong arm, a sure glove, and good speed. However, he relished playing the role of an underdog making the most of his limited skills. Bowa was twice cut from his high school team and signed with the Phillies as an undrafted free agent in 1965 after playing a season at Sacramento City College. He spent four years in the minors, leading the Pacific Coast League with 48 steals in 1969, before joining the Phillies in 1970.

At first, pitchers knocked the bat out of the switch hitter's hands, especially when he batted lefthanded. One night he fanned four times and wondered if he'd ever hit big league pitching. A teammate consoled him, saying, "That kid out there is something special"; the kid was Nolan Ryan. Bowa eventually became a decent batsman in the second spot in the order. He was selected to five All-Star teams and played in the postseason six times.

In 1972 Bowa earned the first of two Gold Gloves and led the NL in triples and sacrifice bunts. In 1975 he hit a career-high .305. In 1980, Bowa played on his first world championship team. In the World Series against the Kansas City Royals, he hit .375 with a team-high nine hits, collected all three of Philadelphia's steals, and participated in a World Series-record seven double plays.

In Game 1 of the World Series, with the Royals ahead, 4–0, Bowa singled with one out and stole second to ignite a five-run third inning. Bowa's two-out, fifth-inning RBI single in Game 2 upped Philadelphia's lead to 2–0 in a 6–4 triumph. In Game 3 he singled three times, stole second with two outs in the eighth, and scored on Pete Rose's single to tie the game, 3–3, but the Royals won in 10 innings. And in Game 6 he doubled in the sixth and scored on Bob Boone's single for the Phillies' last run as the ballclub captured the world title.

When Philadelphia manager Dallas Green was named general manager of the Chicago Cubs, he traded shortstop Ivan DeJesus to the Phillies for Bowa and minor league infielder Ryne Sandberg. Bowa and Sandberg were the NL's best double-play combination as the Cubs broke their postwar postseason drought, winning the NL East in 1984. The next year Bowa griped about sharing time with rookie Shawon Dunston, and he was released in August. He signed with the New York Mets and retired at the end of the season.

In 1986 Bowa managed the Las Vegas Stars, to a second-half pennant and the Pacific Coast League title. He replaced Padres manager Steve Boros for the 1987 season, but the volatile Bowa and the young Padres were a poor match. San Diego lost 97 games that season, the most losses by the club in 14 years.

After the team got off to a slow start in 1988, Bowa was fired in May. He rejoined the Phillies as their third base coach on August 11, 1988, and remained in that capacity through 1996. He joined the Angels' coaching staff in 1997.

Oil Can Boyd

Boyd, Dennis Ray **P**

1982–91 B:10/6/1959, Meridian, MS Deb:9/13/1982, BOS AL BR/TR 6'1", 155

W	L	PCT	G	SH	IP	BB	SO	ERA
78	77	.503	214	10	1389[2]	368	799	4.04

The dossier on Dennis "Oil Can" Boyd always said he was a talented but troubled righthander. He was one of the American League's top starters in the mid-1980s while pitching for the Boston Red Sox.

Boyd became a part-time starter in 1983, and he displayed fine ability despite his final record of 4–8. The next year he became a member of the regular rotation. In 1985, despite his frail, 6-foot 1-inch, 155-pound frame, Boyd was a 15-game winner. He had 11 wins by midseason of 1986, but he seemed emotionally traumatized after having been left off the All-Star team. Boyd was suspended by the Red Sox soon after and checked himself into a hospital. He won five more games in the second half of the season but was bothered by blood clot problems in his right shoulder for the remainder of his major league career. He pitched for parts of two seasons in Montreal and ended his career in Texas in 1991.

Boyd was well known for his flamboyant style on the mound—especially pumping his fist after a strikeout—which won him few friends around the league. But nothing distinguished Boyd like his nickname. He acquired it in his college days at Jackson State in Mississippi, where beer was called oil.

Clete Boyer

Boyer, Cletis Leroy **3B–SS**

1955–57, 1959–71 B:2/9/1937, Cassville, MO Deb:6/5/1955, KC AL BR/TR 6', 182

G	AB	R	H	HR	RBI	OBP	SLG	AVG
1725	5780	645	1396	162	654	.301	.372	.242

A superb defensive third baseman, Clete Boyer found life as a New York Yankee to be a double-edged sword. He recalled the thrill of playing on star-studded teams and making annual trips to the World Series, but he also said, "I batted eighth, and the park killed me." In fact, after being traded to the Atlanta Braves, Boyer, past his physical prime, still set career highs with 26 homers and 96 RBIs.

Boyer and his older brothers Ken and Cloyd are one of only 16 families to produce three or more major league siblings. Clete and Ken, a third baseman with the St. Louis Cardinals, combined for 444 lifetime home runs.

Boyer's pro career began in 1955 as a bonus baby with the Kansas City Athletics. He never produced with the Athletics, and in 1957 he was traded Boyer to the Yankees' organization in a 12-player deal.

"The fans loved guys like [Mickey] Mantle, [Roger] Maris, [Bill] Skowron, [Yogi] Berra, who could hit the ball a long way," Boyer said. "Me and [Bobby] Richardson and [Tony] Kubek were the guys the pitchers loved." But each year he lost the Gold Glove Award to his nemesis in Baltimore. "Honestly, I think I was as good as Brooks Robinson, or anybody, with the glove," Boyer says, "but he was a much better hitter."

Boyer had difficulty concentrating at the plate. He preferred to play defense, and set a World Series record with 65 assists at third base, a mark later broken by Graig Nettles. He put up his best offensive numbers with the Yankees in 1962, with 18 homers, 68 RBIs, and a .272 batting average. He then hit .318 with four RBIs in the World Series against San Francisco. In Game 1 Boyer's homer leading off the seventh inning broke a 2–2 tie, and then he knocked in what proved to be the decisive run in the Yankees' 3–2 win in Game 3. In Game 4 his sixth-inning RBI single tied the score, 2–2, and his fifth-inning single kept alive a rally that resulted in the only run of Game 7.

The Boyer brothers squared off in the 1964 World Series. "That week was the most fun I ever had," Clete said. "I wanted to win, but I was pulling for Kenny, too." In Game 1, after Ken gave the Cards a 1–0 lead with a sacrifice fly, Clete singled, stole second, and scored in the Yankees' three-run second. In Game 2 Clete's fourth-inning sacrifice fly tied the score, 1–1, and New York went on to win, 8–3. He then doubled in the first run of the Yankees' 2–1 Game 3 win. In Game 7, after Ken went deep in the seventh, Clete homered in the ninth, making the Boyers the first brothers ever to homer in the same World Series game. Clete's blast closed the gap to 7–4, but the Yankees' rally fell short.

Two years later Boyer was traded to the Braves, and he helped Atlanta win the first NL West title in 1969, the year he finally won a Gold Glove, leading NL third basemen in fielding percentage. Released by the Braves in 1971, he played for Hawaii of the Pacific Coast League and was traded to the Taiyo Whales in what is reputed to have been the first trade between American and Japanese pro teams.

After finishing his playing career in Japan, Boyer spent three seasons as a minor league instructor for the Braves. In 1980 he was hired as third base coach and infield instructor for the Oakland Athletics under former Yankees teammate Billy Martin. Boyer outlasted Martin, spending five years with Oakland and making Carney Lansford his star pupil. He left the A's organization after feuding with farm director Karl Kuehl.

In 1987 Boyer rejoined the Yankee organization as a minor league instructor, then coached third base and infielders under Martin in 1988. He managed Class A Fort Lauderdale in 1989 and spent the 1990 and 1991 seasons as third base coach for the Class AAA Columbus Clippers. On November 6, 1991, he was named third base coach for the Yankees, where he remained through the 1994 season.

Ken Boyer

Boyer, Kenton Lloyd **3B–OF**

1955–69 M(1978–1980, 166–190) B:5/20/1931, Liberty, MO D:9/7/1982, St. Louis, MO Deb:4/12/1955, STL NL BR/TR, 6'2", 200

G	AB	R	H	HR	RBI	OBP	SLG	AVG
2034	7455	1104	2143	282	1141	.351	.462	.287

Once likened by Joe Garagiola to Gary Cooper in *High Noon*, the soft-spoken Ken Boyer—who starred with the St. Louis Cardinals from the mid-1950s to the mid-1960s—won five Gold Gloves, earned six straight All-Star selections, and led NL third basemen in double plays five times. At the plate, he hit 23 or more homers and knocked in at least 90 runs in seven straight seasons. He was National League Most Valuable Player in 1964 when the Cardinals won their first world championship in two decades.

Boyer was one of 14 children growing up in Alba, Missouri, and six Boyer brothers actually played professional baseball. Ken, Clete, and Cloyd are one of 16 sets of three or more brothers to have played in the majors. Clete and Ken combined for 444 home runs to tie Lee and Carlos May for third place among brothers, behind the Aarons and the DiMaggios.

Boyer originally signed with the Cardinals for a $6,000 bonus. The Cards first tried him as a pitcher, but when he hit .455, his future was decided. He served in the U.S. Army from 1951 through 1953. The Cardinals traded third baseman Ray Jablonski after the 1954 season to make room for Boyer, who, in 1956 was selected to his first All-Star Game. That year he batted .306, the first of five .300-plus seasons in six years. In 1957 Boyer was shifted to center field to make room for rookie Eddie Kasko, and he led the league's outfielders in fielding percentage. The next year, however, Curt Flood's arrival allowed Boyer to go back to third base.

In 1959, the year he put together a career-best 29-game hitting streak, Boyer was selected to the first of six consecutive All-Star Games. The following season he hit a career-high 32 homers, and in 1961 Boyer batted .329, which ranked third in the league. Boyer culminated his peak years by winning the NL MVP Award in 1964, when he led the league with 119 RBIs and hit for the cycle a second time.

As the Cardinals' team captain he provided quiet leadership during their successful 1964 pennant drive. St. Louis faced the New York Yankees—and Clete Boyer—in the World Series. In the first inning of the opener Ken knocked in the first run with a sacrifice fly, then singled to start the Redbirds' four-run, game-winning rally in the sixth inning of a 9–5 victory. Boyer didn't get another hit until Game 4, but his grand-slam homer into Yankee Stadium's left field stands gave the Cardinals a 4–3 victory and tied the series at two games apiece. In Game 5 he beat out a sacrifice bunt attempt in the 10th inning, helping the Cards to a 5–2 win. In Game 7 he singled and scored the Cardinals' first run in the fourth, doubled in a three-run fifth inning that put St. Louis in command, and homered for their final run.

In 1965 back trouble slowed Boyer down, and following the season he was traded to the New York Mets. The Mets sent Boyer on to the Chicago White Sox in July 1967. He was released in early 1968, then played as a part-timer for the Los Angeles Dodgers before retiring early in 1969.

In 1970 Boyer managed the Cardinals' Arkansas affiliate in the Texas League, then coached with the big league team for two years before returning to minor league managing. In 1978 he replaced Vern Rapp as St. Louis skipper; the Cardinals improved by 17 games in Boyer's first full year at the helm, but he was fired after starting 18–33 in 1980. He returned to managing in the Cardinals organization in 1982, the same year he was diagnosed with inoperable lung cancer. He died that September. The Cardinals retired Boyer's uniform number 14 in 1984.

Bill Bradley

Bradley, William Joseph **3B**

1899–1910, 1914–15 M(1905, 1914, 97–98) B:2/13/1878, Cleveland, OH D:3/11/1954 Cleveland, OH Deb:8/26/1899, CHI NL BR/TR 6', 185

G	AB	R	H	HR	RBI	OBP	SLG	AVG
1461	5430	754	1471	34	552	.317	.371	.271

Until the 1950s, Bill Bradley was commonly ranked with Jimmy Collins and Pie Traynor as one of the best third basemen in baseball history. Collins, asked in 1904 who was tops at the position, said, "Well, if I could field and bat like Bradley, I should lay claim to that title myself."

Bradley began his pro career in 1897, reaching the National League with Chicago two years later. He jumped to the American League in 1901 and spent the next decade in Cleveland. Bradley revolutionized his position, topping AL third baseman in fielding four times. He set a league record with seven putouts in a game in 1901, a feat he matched in 1909.

Bradley could hit, too. In 1902 he homered in four straight games, and finished the year with a .340 average. He topped .300 in each of the next two seasons. In 1906, however, a pitched ball fractured his arm; Bradley then contracted typhoid fever. He was never the same player. Bradley finished his big league career as a player and manager in the Federal League. He later spent decades as a scout for the Indians. He was elected to Cleveland's Hall of Fame shortly after his death.

George Bradley

Bradley, George Washington **P–3B**

1875–77, 1879–84 B:7/13/1852, Reading, PA D:10/2/1931, Philadelphia, PA Deb:5/4/1875, STL NA BR/TR 5'10½", 175

W	L	PCT	G	SH	IP	BB	SO	ERA
138	125	.525	287	28	2404^{1}	179	611	2.50

G	AB	R	H	HR	RBI	OBP	SLG	AVG
509	2004	244	456	3	148	.242	.295	.228

In eight years in the "bigs," George Bradley played for eight teams in four leagues. But the righthander is best remembered not for his mobility, but for his 1876 season with the St. Louis Brown Stockings, when he pitched the National League's first no-hitter.

In 1874 Bradley pitched for the semipro Eastons, considered to be one of the better teams around. The next season he moved up to the National Association's St. Louis Brown Stockings, by whom he was paid $1,200. The highlight of his year came on June 5, when he beat the previously undefeated Boston franchise.

When St. Louis moved into the National League for its inaugural 1876 season, Bradley went with the club as its one-man pitching staff, which was not unusual at that time. St. Louis played 64 games that season, and Bradley started 63 of them. In the one game he did not start, he appeared in relief. His no-hitter came on July 15, 1876, against Hartford's ace, Tommy Bond. Bradley won the game, 2–0, striking out three, walking one, and overcoming three errors. It was his third shutout in the three-game series.

Bradley's numbers for that season are mind-boggling by today's standards. He was 45–19 and pitched 573 innings, walking 38 while striking out 103. He led the NL with a 1.23 ERA, and his league-leading 16 shutouts are still a major league record (matched by Grover Cleveland Alexander for the Philadelphia Phillies in 1916).

Bradley never approached such numbers again. He pitched for Chicago in 1877—replacing Al Spalding, who later made a lot of money selling sporting goods—but was only 18–23. Bradley sat out the next season and then moved to Troy, where he lost a league-leading 40 games for a last-place team. From 1881 to 1883 he was 24–20 for Cleveland and Philadelphia (of the American Association), then went 25–15 for Cincinnati in the Union Association during his last year as a pitcher. A career .228 hitter, he also took occasional turns at third, shortstop, first base, and the outfield.

Bobby Bragan

Bragan, Robert Randall **SS-C**

1940–44, 1947–48 M(1956–58, 1963–66, 443–478) B:10/30/1917, Birmingham, AL Deb:4/16/1940, PHI NL BR/TR 5'10½", 175

G	AB	R	H	HR	RBI	OBP	SLG	AVG
597	1900	136	456	15	172	.282	.309	.240

Although Bobby Bragan is remembered most for his high jinks as an umpire-baiting manager, he built his reputation on intelligence and creative approaches to the game. He was also a versatile major league player who changed positions midway through his career to help his team win.

In 1940 Bragan came up to the Philadelphia Phillies as a shortstop, and in 1941 he played all 154 games, batting .251 and driving in 69 runs. In 1942 the team was strapped for catching help because of injuries and military call-ups, and Bragan offered to learn the job. Dodger general manager Branch Rickey liked the youngster's dedication and obtained him in a trade for Tex Kraus; Bragan was a backup catcher for the Dodgers during the next two seasons.

After spending two years in the military, Bragan returned in time for the 1947 season. Rickey called his players in for one-on-one discussions during spring training about the imminent arrival of Jackie Robinson. Bragan told Rickey he would prefer to be traded rather than play with Robinson. Rickey acknowledged Bragan's forthrightness and agreed to trade him, but Bragan stayed, batting only 36 times all year.

Even as a player, Bragan thought like a manager. He spent his off-field time talking baseball with Dodgers teammates Clyde Sukeforth and Gene Mauch. Bragan, Mickey Owen, and Eddie Stanky were once so deep in discussion on a train that they missed their stop in Indianapolis, where the rest of the team got off for an exhibition game.

Released during the 1948 season, Bragan was offered a job managing the Dodgers' Texas League affiliate, and he guided the Fort Worth Cats to a first-place finish one year and second another. In 1953 the Pirates hired him as manager of their Triple A Hollywood Stars.

Bragan was an unconventional manager during his four years with Hollywood. He once sent a batboy out to coach third, and, on another occasion, stripped off his uniform on the field after being ejected from a game, which earned him a suspension. In a bizarre protest against the umpires' handling of a situation, he once sent up eight consecutive pinch hitters for the same batter, with none staying put long enough to see a pitch. Despite Bragan's outrageousness, in 1953 the Stars won the Pacific Coast League Championship Series, and in 1954 they lost a one-game playoff for the title.

One 1955 play was typical example of Bragan's creativity. With an opposing runner on second and the pitcher at bat in an obvious bunt situation, Bragan brought in right fielder Lee Walls to serve as a fifth infielder. Tempted by the large gap in right, the pitcher tried to hit the ball to right field instead of bunting and popped to center; the Stars won by a run.

Rickey's last official act as general manager of the Pirates was to hire Bragan. As skipper of the hopeless Bucs, Bragan would bat his best hitter first and his pitcher seventh, effectively shifting the lineup around by one third in order to get more at bats for the better hitters. In 1955 Bragan helped the Pirates improve by 13 wins, which moved them out of last place, but he was fired.

Bragan began the 1958 season as Cleveland's manager, but was canned after only 67 games. However, while managing Spokane in the Dodgers' organization that year, Bragan turned righthanded Maury Wills into a switch hitter. Bragan began the 1963 season managing the Milwaukee Braves, where his teams finished sixth once and fifth twice; he was the Braves' first manager in Atlanta. Replaced after 112 games in 1966, Bragan began a third baseball career—in the front office. He served as president of Fort Worth for several years, became president of the Texas League (where, ironically, he was in charge of disciplining managers who mistreated umpires), and ultimately became president of the National Association.

Asa Brainard

Brainard, Asa **P**

1871–74 B:1841, Albany, NY D:12/29/1888, Denver, CO Deb:5/5/1871, OLY NA TR 5'8½ ", 150

When Harry Wright was commissioned in 1869 to form the Cincinnati Red Stockings, baseball's first all-professional team, he imported righthander Asa Brainard from New York and paid him a princely $1,100 for the season.

Only Wright and his brother, shortstop George Wright (the team's star), received more. Brainard pitched most—some sources say all—of the games as the Red Stockings toured from coast to coast, taking on all comers, and going undefeated in 65 games. (One theory has it that Asa, shortened to "Ace," later became the generic nickname for star pitchers.)

Some reports describe Brainard as a "scientific" pitcher who relied on speed changes and sharp control, while other accounts credit him with being the second-fastest pitcher in the country. He probably threw only as hard as was necessary; the Red Stockings supported him by averaging 41 runs a game. There is also evidence that, despite his success, Brainard was a hypochondriac who often tried to beg off from pitching.

When the Red Stockings lost a few games in 1870 the team was broken up. Brainard pitched for four years in the National Association with little success, finishing 24–53. He was managing a pool hall in Denver in 1888 when he became the first of the original Red Stockings to pass away.

Ralph Branca

Branca, Ralph Theodore Joseph **P**

1944–54, 1956 B:1/6/1926, Mt. Vernon, NY
Deb:6/12/1944, BRO NL BR/TR 6'3", 220

W	L	PCT	G	SV	IP	BB	SO	ERA
88	68	.564	322	19	1484	663	829	3.79

Ralph Branca is remembered as the man who threw the pitch that Bobby Thomson hit for the "shot heard 'round the world," the famous home run that capped the New York Giants' historic comeback to win the 1951 National League pennant. With the chips down in the third and deciding game between New York and Brooklyn, the Giants' Bobby Thomson advanced to the plate. Brooklyn manager Chuck Dressen, with two pitchers in the bullpen to choose from, called in Branca rather than Clem Labine, who had struck out Thomson two days before.

A one-time New York University basketball star, Branca started in the Dodger system with the Class D Pony League's Olean Oilers in 1943 for $90 a month. "I got a new glove and a supporter with a cup in it, and I didn't know what to do with it, and that's the truth," said Branca. By 1944 he had reached the wartime Brooklyn roster and roomed with Hall of Famer Paul Waner. In 1947, at the age of only 21, he was selected to the All-Star team for the first of three consecutive years. That season he went 21–12 with an ERA of 2.67. In 1950, Branca began to be used much more extensively as a relief pitcher.

After a slow start in 1953, Branca was sold to Detroit in July. He then went to the New York Yankees in 1954 before returning to Brooklyn for one appearance in 1956.

After his retirement, Branca helped found the Baseball Assistance team, a group that aided former ballplayers and their families in need. Ironically, because of his good humor and many appearances for BAT, he eventually became more recognizable than Thomson to a new generation of New York fans. He is the father-in-law of New York Mets manager Bobby Valentine.

Kitty Bransfield

Bransfield, William Edward **1B**

1898, 1901–11 B:1/7/1875, Worcester, MA
D:5/1/1947, Worcester, MA Deb:8/22/1898, BOS NL
BR/TR 5'11", 207

G	AB	R	H	HR	RBI	OBP	SLG	AVG
1330	4999	529	1351	13	637	.304	.353	.270

Late in the nineteenth century, when William Bransfield first played baseball in his hometown of Worcester, Massachusetts, he was known as "Kid," then "Kiddy." One day a reporter with a bad ear mistakenly tagged him as "Kitty." The name stuck.

Bransfield grew into a stocky first baseman, a better fielder than hitter. The National League's Boston team gave him a five-game trial in 1898, but he had no realistic chance of replacing star Fred Tenney on first base.

In 1901 he joined the Pittsburgh Pirates, one of the greatest teams of the period. With stars such as Honus Wagner, Fred Clarke, Tommy Leach, Ginger Beaumont, Deacon Phillippe, Sam Leever, Jack Chesbro, and Jesse Tannehill, the Pirates were loaded with talent. The Bucs ran away with the NL pennant. Bransfield ranked as a worker bee among his more famous teammates, but his rookie year provided the best offensive numbers of his career, as he hit .295 with 91 RBIs and 92 runs scored.

The Pirates were just getting started. In 1902 they won the pennant by a whopping 27½ games, winning 103 games and losing only 36. Bransfield hit .305 as injuries limited him to 102 games. Pittsburgh took its third straight pennant in 1903, but the Pirates lost to Boston in the first modern World Series; Bransfield hit only .265 during the season. After hitting .223 in 1904, he was swapped to the Philadelphia Phillies with two other players for first baseman Del Howard.

The Pirates had problems at first base for the next 15 years, suffering from what came to be known in Pittsburgh as the "Bransfield Curse." No fewer than 12 men were designated as the regular first baseman during that period, and none of them lasted more than two seasons. Not until Charlie Grimm in 1920 did the curse finally disappear.

In the meantime, Bransfield played a reliable first base for the Phillies through the 1910 season. He batted .304 in 1908 and led all NL first basemen in fielding the next year. He ended his major league career with the Cubs in 1911.

Steve Braun

Braun, Stephen Russell **OF-3B-DH**

1971–85 B:5/8/1948, Trenton, NJ Deb:4/6/1971, MIN AL BL/TR 5'10", 180

G	AB	R	H	HR	RBI	OBP	SLG	AVG
1425	3650	466	989	52	388	.373	.367	.271

Steve Braun played in the same infield as Rod Carew, was in the Seattle Mariners' original starting lineup, and provided a dangerous bat off Whitey Herzog's St. Louis bench for two pennant winners; he also knew how to get a laugh. Late in Braun's career, he was playing with the Triple A Louisville Redbirds. Irascible pitching legend Bob Feller, a relentless critic of modern players, was firing "fastballs" past overweight local radio personalities and volunteers from the crowd. An irritated Braun left batting practice with the Redbirds to change into street clothes. Minutes later, he stepped in against the former Indians great and launched three deep home runs, shocking Feller and causing his teammates to double over with laughter.

Braun was also able to deliver on cue in the major leagues. His 113 career pinch hits stood as the seventh most all-time through 1999. One of the highlights of his playing career was actually a walk he drew as a pinch hitter in Game 2 of the 1982 World Series for the St. Louis Cardinals. The walk forced in the eventual winning run, as the Cards went on to take the title in seven games. His last at bat in the major leagues came as a pinch hitter in the 1985 World Series.

Sid Bream

Bream, Sidney Eugene **1B**

1983–94 B:8/3/1960, Carlisle, PA Deb:9/1/1983, LA NL BL/TL 6'4", 220

G	AB	R	H	HR	RBI	OBP	SLG	AVG
1088	3108	351	819	90	455	.340	.420	.264

Sid Bream proved that a first baseman did not need be a great slugger—or runner—to be a valuable performer. Seldom used in Los Angeles, Bream won the full-time first base job with Pittsburgh in 1986. With his big looping swing, he hit .268 with 37 doubles. Defensively, he charged bunts aggressively, erased lead runners with his a strong arm, and perfected the 3–6–3 double play. The result: a league-record 166 assists.

After solid seasons in 1987 and 1988, Bream endured three knee operations—including a reconstruction. The knee never fully healed, but he was able to hit .270 in 1990 and help the Pirates make their first postseason appearance in a dozen seasons.

In 1991 Bream moved to Atlanta, where he was part of a veteran influx that helped the Braves become the first NL team to go from last place to first place in one season. He tormented his former Pirates teammates in the NLCS the next two years. He batted .300 in 1991 as Atlanta won in seven games. In Game 7 of the 1992 NLCS, Atlanta trailed Pittsburgh, 2–1, with two outs in the bottom of the ninth. Francisco Cabrera singled to left with the bases loaded, and Bream—one of the slowest men in the game—chugged around third, barely beating Barry Bonds' throw to score the series-winning run.

Harry Brecheen

Brecheen, Harry David **P**

1940, 1943–53 B:10/14/1914, Broken Bow, OK Deb:4/22/1940, STL NL BL/TL 5'10", 160

W	L	PCT	G	SH	IP	BB	SO	ERA
133	92	.591	318	25	1907[2]	536	901	2.92

In 1946 Harry Brecheen, nicknamed "the Cat" for his grace on the field, became the first lefthanded pitcher to win three games in a World Series. His career World Series ERA of 0.85 was a record for 30 years.

As a boy Brecheen and his family moved to Ada, Oklahoma, the home of baseball legends Paul and Lloyd Waner. "I used to climb through a hole in the fence to see them play exhibitions after the regular season," Brecheen recalled. But his real hero was pitcher Carl Hubbell, also from Oklahoma.

In 1936 Brecheen pitched for the Class C Western Association's Bartlesville Bucs and was 6–18 for a last-place team. The next season he went 21–6 for the Class B Piedmont League's Portsmouth Cubs, using the pitch that made Hubbell famous, the screwball. The Cardinals were impressed enough to buy Brecheen for $3,000 on the recommendation of Eddie Dyer, a manager in the St. Louis organization who continued to play a key role in Brecheen's career.

In 1938 Dyer managed Brecheen at Houston. After Brecheen went 18–4 with four shutouts, his manager made a promise: "If I ever manage a big league club, kid, you'll get your chance to see whether you can pitch up there." But every year the Cardinals would give Brecheen only a perfunctory look, then ship him back to Columbus of the American Association. In 1942 Branch Rickey even sent the young prospect a letter saying that although he would spend the first part of the year with St. Louis, he really wasn't in the Cardinals' plans.

It wasn't until the middle of World War II that Brecheen, who had been rated 4-F because of a spinal malformation and a childhood ankle injury, finally stuck with the Cards. In 1943 he went 9–6 with a 2.26 ERA as a spot starter. The next year, as a regular, Brecheen went 16–5 and then won Game 4 of the World Series versus the Browns. In 1945 he finished 15–4, and then in 1946, despite a mediocre regular season, he really shone in the World Series against Boston. In Game 2 he beat Mickey Harris on a four-hit shutout. In Game 6 he defeated Harris again, 4–1. In the deciding Game 7 two days later, Manager Dyer sent Brecheen down to the bullpen in the seventh inning to start warming up.

With the Cardinals ahead, 3–1, Brecheen entered the game in the top of the eighth. Two pinch hitters had opened the inning with a single and a double off starter Murry Dickson. Brecheen quickly retired Wally Moses and Johnny Pesky, but center fielder Dom DiMaggio doubled off the wall in right-center, tying the score. In the bottom of the inning Enos Slaughter scored all the way from first on a single to give the Cardinals the lead. In the ninth Brecheen surrendered singles to Rudy York and Bobby Doerr before retiring Pinky Higgins, Roy Partee, and pinch hitter Tom McBride to nail down the win—and the Series.

Brecheen's finest regular season was 1948, when he was named to *The Sporting News* All-Star Team based on a won-lost record of 20–7 and league-leading figures of seven shutouts, a 2.24 ERA, and 149 strikeouts. In October 1952 the Cardinals released him, and he signed with Bill Veeck's Browns. When the Browns moved to Baltimore, Brecheen signed a one-year contract as the Orioles' pitching coach but stayed for 14 seasons.

Ted Breitenstein

Breitenstein, Theodore P. **P**

1891–1901 B:6/1/1869, St. Louis, MO D:5/3/1935, St. Louis, MO Deb:4/28/1891, STL AA BL/TL 5'9", 167

W	L	PCT	G	SH	IP	BB	SO	ERA
160	170	.485	379	12	2964[1]	1203	889	4.04

Ted Breitenstein's first start as a big league pitcher was a memorable one. St. Louis Browns manager Charles Comiskey gave the 22-year-old left-hander the ball on the last day of the 1891 season; Breitenstein responded with a no-hitter against Louisville. He walked only one, and faced the minimum 27 batters. That also turned out to be the last game the Browns ever played as members of the American Association. St. Louis transferred to the National League, where the Browns immediately fell to the bottom of the standings—and stayed there.

From 1892 to 1896 Breitenstein had three 20-loss seasons and one 30-loss campaign sandwiched around a 27–23 season. In 1893 he was involved in 20 one-run games and won only eight. That year he teamed with catcher Heinie Peitz to form the famous "Pretzel Battery."

Despite his losing seasons with St. Louis he was still coveted by other clubs. The Cincinnati Reds purchased him for $10,000 in October 1896. In his first two seasons with the Reds he won 23 and 20 games. On April 22, 1898, Breitenstein pitched the second no-hitter of his career, again walking just one and facing 27 batters.

The Reds returned Breitenstein to St. Louis after the 1900 season. He pitched just three games for the Cardinals, all losses, and was sent to the minor leagues in St. Paul. In 1902 Memphis manager Charlie Frank, a former teammate, persuaded him to pitch in the Southern Association. Breitenstein compiled a 157–89 record in 10 years for the Memphis and New Orleans franchises. He stayed in the league as an umpire for nine more years. After umpiring in the Texas League in 1921 he finally left baseball for good.

Bob Brenly

Brenly, Robert Earl **C**

1981–89 B:2/25/1954, Coshocton, OH Deb:8/14/1981, SF NL BR/TR 6'2", 210

G	AB	R	H	HR	RBI	OBP	SLG	AVG
871	2615	321	647	91	333	.333	.403	.247

Bob Brenly was known for his quick wit, home run power, and solid defense during his eight-year career. The San Francisco Giants catcher also helped mold manager Roger Craig's young pitchers into one of the National League's top staffs of the late 1980s.

In 1984 the Giants' offense led the league in hits, and Brenly had his best season (batting .291 with 20 home runs, and 80 RBIs), but the pitching staff was tops in hits allowed and had the NL's highest ERA; San Francisco posted the worst record in baseball. Then Craig arrived to emphasize pitching and Brenly became more valuable for his defense than his hitting. By 1987 San Francisco had the league's lowest ERA, and, not coincidentally, its first division title in 16 years.

It was while playing a rare game at third base that Brenly tied a dubious major league record, committing four errors in one inning to hand the Atlanta Braves a 4–0 lead. Brenly sat silently on the bench when the inning finally ended. "I had an incredible feeling of calm," he recalled years later. "I never even thought about throwing a tantrum." Perhaps he knew how the story would end. Brenly slugged a solo home run in the fifth inning. He hit a two-out, two-run single in his next at bat to tie the game at 6–6. Finally, in the bottom of the ninth, Brenly hit a two-out solo homer to win the game. Brenly was always an affable player, a trait that would serve him well in his future career as a broadcaster.

Roger Bresnahan

Bresnahan, Roger Philip **C-OF**
1897, 1900–15 M(1909–12, 1915, 328–432)
B:6/11/1879, Toledo, OH D:12/4/1944, Toledo, OH
Deb:8/27/1897, WAS NL BR/TR 5'9", 200

G	AB	R	H	HR	RBI	OBP	SLG	AVG
1446	4481	682	1252	26	530	.386	.377	.279

During the course of his 17-year career, Roger Bresnahan was considered baseball's greatest catcher, and in 1945 he became the first catcher elected to the Hall of Fame. Actually, Bresnahan could play anywhere on the diamond; he served behind the plate for 974 games, about two-thirds of those in which he appeared, while also playing outfield, all four infield positions, and even pitcher.

Although born and raised in Toledo, Ohio, Bresnahan was nicknamed "the Duke of Tralee," as his family originally came from Tralee, County Kerry, Ireland. He debuted as a pitcher in semi-pro ball in Ohio and first appeared in the majors in 1897 with Washington's National League team. He went 4–0 and pitched a shutout, but when he demanded a raise, he was allowed to drift back to the minors. In 1900 he appeared in two games for the Orphans, and in 1901 he found his true calling as a catcher when he joined Baltimore of the new American League.

John McGraw, who became one of Bresnahan's closest friends, managed the Orioles. Both were stocky, pugnacious Irishmen bent on winning at whatever cost, and when McGraw jumped the American League in 1902 to become the New York Giants' manager, he took Bresnahan, ace pitcher Joe McGinnity, and several other players with him. As the Giants were well-stocked with catchers, he played wherever needed. In 1903, as New York's center fielder and leadoff hitter, he stole 34 bases and batted a career-high .350, only five points behind league leader Honus Wagner.

Bresnahan was still primarily an outfielder when the Giants won the 1904 pennant, but in 1905 he became their regular catcher—and soon Christy Mathewson's favorite batterymate. That year the Giants won another pennant, and Bresnahan caught all five games of their World Series triumph over the Philadelphia Athletics, including four shutouts, three from Mathewson and one from McGinnity.

In 1907, tired of taking foul tips off his legs, Bresnahan started using a set of cricket leg pads. When he first appeared wearing them there was great hooting from opponents' dugouts, and Pirates manager Fred Clarke insisted that they posed a danger to sliding baserunners. But during the following winter baseball's brain trust approved them and they soon became standard issue for catchers. Shortly afterward, Bresnahan also improved on the flimsy wire facemask then worn by catchers, inserting padding so that the mask might better absorb the shock of foul balls.

After seven years in New York, McGraw traded Bresnahan to the St. Louis Cardinals. It was a good deal for both clubs: McGraw received three useful players, and Bresnahan got a chance to be a player-manager for a major league team. When he pushed the hapless Cardinals up to fifth place in 1911, team owner Mrs. Schuyler Britton delightedly rewarded him with a five-year contract at $10,000 per season plus a share of the profits. But when the team slipped in 1912 and she asked some pointed questions, Bresnahan replied with language far too salty for her taste and was fired. Bresnahan simply moved on to Chicago, where he played for the Cubs for three years, in 1915—his final year in the majors—serving as player-manager.

After retiring, Bresnahan managed, and for a while owned, Toledo of the American Association. In 1921 he and Jim Thorpe were granted a National Football League franchise, but the team never got off the drawing board. Bresnahan returned to the majors in 1925 and coached for McGraw's Giants through 1928 and for the Detroit Tigers in the early 1930s.

At the age of 64, he once again donned the tools of ignorance and caught for Walter Johnson in an exhibition to raise money for war bonds. Bresnahan died in Toledo in 1944 and was elected to the Hall of Fame the following year.

Rube Bressler

Bressler, Raymond Bloom **OF-1B-P**
1914–32 B:10/23/1894, Coder, PA D:11/7/1966, Cincinnati, OH Deb:4/24/1914, PHI AL BR/TL 6'0", 187

G	AB	R	H	HR	RBI	OBP	SLG	AVG
1305	3881	544	1170	32	586	.378	.413	.301

W	L	PCT	G	SH	IP	BB	SO	ERA
26	32	.448	107	3	540	242	229	3.40

Raymond Bressler won 10 games as a 20-year-old rookie for Connie Mack's 1914 Philadelphia Athletics. Like many promising young lefthanded pitchers of the day he was nicknamed "Rube" after Edward "Rube" Waddell. The presence of Bressler and several other young players convinced Mack that he could sell off most of his team's established stars and still compete. He was wrong. In 1915 the A's plunged to the bottom of the American League, and Bressler went 4–17 with a 5.20 ERA. Thereafter he pitched with little success, usually as one of the last men in the bullpen.

Bressler was picked up by Cincinnati in 1917. After he had fractured an ankle in 1920, he returned too soon, altered his throwing motion to favor the injury and ruined his arm for pitching. Bressler began to take occasional turns in the outfield or at first base and proved to be a solid hitter. In 1921 he batted .307, and three years later hit .347.

Although Bressler lacked power, he had a good eye and seldom struck out. In the spring of 1928 he was traded to Brooklyn, where he played four years before one final season split between the Phillies and Cardinals. After 19 major league seasons, Bressler left the game in 1932 with a .301 career batting average and the distinction of having had three Hall of Famers as roommates: Albert "Chief" Bender, Eppa Rixey, and Arthur "Dazzy" Vance.

George Brett

Brett, George Howard **3B–DH–1B**

1973–93 B:5/15/1953, Glen Dale, WV Deb:8/2/1973, KC AL BL/TR 6', 200

G	AB	R	H	HR	RBI	OBP	SLG	AVG
2707	10349	1583	3154	317	1595	.373	.487	.305

For two decades George Brett was one of the best hitters in the game. The most famous disciple of hitting coach Charlie Lau's techniques, Brett hit .300 or more 11 times during his major league career. He won a batting title in each of three decades—the 1970s, 1980s, and 1990s—a baseball first.

One pitcher offered this advice on facing Brett: "The only way to pitch him is inside, so you force him to pull the ball. That way when he hits his line drive it won't be at you."

In 1974, his first full year in the majors, Brett batted .282 under Lau's tutelage. The next year he increased his average to .308, the first of nine times that he would pass .300 in an 11-year period. He was the league's dominant third baseman in hitting, leading his position in every offensive category except homers, including league-leading totals of 195 hits and 13 triples.

In 1976 Brett was even better. He had six consecutive three-hit games early in the year, led the league with 215 hits and 14 triples, and won his first batting title, hitting .333. He was selected for his first of 11 consecutive All-Star Games and helped lead the Royals to their first division title, before they lost to the Yankees in the American League Championship Series.

Brett was hampered by injuries each of the next two years, and the Royals again lost both times in the ALCS. But in 1979 he led the league in both hits and triples, each for the third time, while batting .329. He also drove in 107 runs, and his 42 doubles and 23 homers made him only the sixth player in history to exceed 20 doubles, triples, and homers in one season.

Somehow, in 1980 he improved his performance yet again. He was close to the .400 mark for most of the year, finishing at .390, the highest average by a third baseman in this century, and the highest by any hitter since Ted Williams in 1941. Despite missing a month with a knee ligament injury that occurred while sliding, along with being sidelined for 10 days because of tendonitis in his wrist, Brett had a 30-game hitting streak during the season. In 117 games he drove in 118 runs, the first year anyone had more RBIs than games played since Walt Dropo's 1950 season. Brett also had fewer strikeouts (22) than home runs (24), a feat not accomplished in 24 years. Not surprisingly, he was AL Most Valuable Player.

When Kansas City took on the Yanks in the ALCS for the fourth time in five years, Brett made sure the tale had a different ending. The Royals took the first two games in Kansas City. They were down 2–1 in the seventh inning of Game 3 when, with two men on, Gossage tried to power his fastball past Brett. He sent it into Yankee Stadium's third tier; the Royals had finally made it to the World Series.

In the World Series, Brett was one of four Royals to hit .375 or better. The Phillies prevailed in six games. For his spectacular season, Kansas City extended Brett's contract for five years for $1 million a year. During the next five season the Royals always contended in the AL West, and Brett always hit .300 or close to it, but a tie for the division in 1981 and a title in 1984 were the best Kansas City could do.

The most famous single event of Brett's career occurred on July 24, 1983. Down 4–3 to the Yankees in the top of the ninth, Brett powered a two-run homer off Gossage. Yankees manager Billy Martin had been tipped off that Brett, who never wore batting gloves, had quite a lot of pine tar on his bat. Major league rules state that pine tar cannot extend more than 18 inches from the bat's handle.

Martin showed the bat to plate umpire Tim McClelland, who measured it against the 17-inch-wide home plate and called Brett out for an illegally batted ball. The usually mild-mannered Brett, celebrating his homer in the dugout, went crazy. He charged McClelland, and it took another umpire and two players to restrain him. The sight of Brett exploding from the dugout to challenge the umpire became one of the highlights of many baseball history videos. "I can still see his bulging eyes and red face," McClelland later recalled.

The Royals filed a protest that was upheld by American League president Lee MacPhail, who stated, "The umpire's interpretation, while technically defensible, is not in accord with the intent or spirit of the rules and the rules do not provide that a hitter be called out for excessive use of pine tar...Games should be won or lost on the playing field." He ordered that the game be completed from the point of Brett's home run. The Yankees tried everything, including a lawsuit, to prevent it.

When the continuation of the game began 25 days later, Martin immediately ordered appeal plays at all the bases because the umpires were not the same crew that worked on July 24. The Yankees' manager contended that the new umpires could not know that Brett had touched all the bags. But the umpires were ready. They presented an affidavit from the previous crew testifying that he had. The event has gone down in baseball lore as "the Pine Tar Incident."

In 1985 Brett was back at the top of his game. He led the Royals to another division title, hitting .335 with a league-leading slugging percentage of .585, which included his career high 30 home runs. He also won his only Gold Glove.

From 1986 through 1989 Brett surpassed .300 only once. In 1987 he moved to first base to make room for rookie Kevin Seitzer and began spending more time as a designated hitter. In 1990 Brett surprised the experts who had written him off by claiming his third batting title. He hit .329 and led the league with 45 doubles, the same total as when he had led it a dozen years before.

On September 30, 1992, Brett needed one hit to become the eighteenth man to reach the 3,000-hit plateau; he got four. Moments after he reached that plateau, the still dazed Brett was picked off first base. It was one of the few embarrassments of his career. In 1999, his first year of eligibility, he was elected to the Hall of Fame.

Ken Brett

Brett, Kenneth Alven **P**

1967–81 B:9/18/1948, Brooklyn, NY Deb:9/27/1967, BOS AL BL/TL 5'11", 195

W	L	PCT	G	SV	IP	BB	SO	ERA
83	85	.494	349	11	1526[1]	562	807	3.93

By the end of his career, Ken Brett was best known as George Brett's older brother, yet the lefthander was a pretty good pitcher—and hitter—in his own right. He reached the majors with Boston in 1967 as a 19 year old. In his first major league win against the New York Yankees, he had three hits, including a home run. That fall he became the youngest pitcher to appear in a World Series game, making two hitless appearances against the St. Louis Cardinals.

Over a 14-year career, Brett pitched for 10 different teams. His greatest success came with Pittsburgh. He made two postseason appearances with the Pirates and was the winning pitcher for the National League in the 1974 All-Star Game. With the White Sox in 1976, Brett lost a no-hitter with two outs in the ninth inning when he gave up a questionable infield hit to the Angels' Jerry Remy. The other "highlight" of his career was surrendering Hank Aaron's 700th home run.

For many, Brett will be remembered as a great hitting pitcher. He once hit home runs in four consecutive starts. He made 36 appearances as a pinch hitter, and finished with a .262 average and 10 homers—43 points and 307 clouts behind brother George, but not bad for a journeyman pitcher.

Perhaps his greatest fame came after his retirement, when Brett appeared in a television commercial for a beer company. The well-traveled player jokingly forgot which town he was in at the moment, with the punch line "Utica?" The response was overwhelming, and the next summer Brett was managing the minor league Utica Blue Sox.

Chet Brewer

Brewer, Charles **P**

Negro League Player 1925–48 B:1/14/1907, Leavenworth, KA D:3/26/1990, Whittier, CA BB/TR 6'4", 187

Chet Brewer's best days were spent in the relative obscurity of the Negro Leagues. From 1925 to 1948, he pitched for the Kansas City Monarchs, Washington Pilots, Chicago American Giants, Philadelphia Stars, New York Cubans, Cleveland Buckeyes, and Tennessee Rats.

A righthander with an above-average fastball—and what was then a legal emery ball—Brewer was 12–1 in his first full season in 1926. He was a part of a rotation that included Satchel Paige and Bullet Joe Rogan. In 1929 Brewer was 16–3, and his .842 winning percentage led the league. At one point, he threw 31 consecutive scoreless innings.

During a 30-win season in 1930, Brewer struck out 19, including 10 in a row, against the Homestead Grays, only to lose, 1–0, in 12 innings on a fluke hit. He also won 16 straight games in 1934 and finished the season with 33 wins. He eventually went on to pitch in Mexico, where, in 1939, he threw two no-hitters. He returned to the United States as a scout for the Pirates, a tenure that spanned from 1957 to 1974, after which he was employed as a major league scout.

Jim Brewer

Brewer, James Thomas **P**

1960–76 B:11/17/1937, Merced, CA D:11/16/1987, Tyler, TX Deb:7/17/1960, CHI NL BL/TL, 6'2", 195

W	L	PCT	G	SV	IP	BB	SO	ERA
69	65	.515	584	132	1040^2	360	810	3.07

Lefthanded pitcher Jim Brewer had a rather rude introduction to the major leagues. While pitching in only his fifth game, on August 4, 1960, the Chicago Cubs rookie was attacked on the mound by hot-headed Cincinnati Reds second baseman Billy Martin for throwing too far inside. A Martin roundhouse broke Brewer's cheekbone, and the Cubs sued Martin for $1 million in damages. Charges were eventually dropped, although Brewer later won $10,000 from Martin in his own lawsuit.

Many people in baseball thought the young hurler's career was over, but Brewer made a successful return from injury. After learning to throw a screwball, allegedly from the great Warren Spahn, Brewer became a top Dodger reliever, exceeding 20 saves in four of the five years from 1969 through 1973.

After his career ended Brewer became a Montreal coach, and was credited with helping Tom House learn the screwball, and Charlie Hough the knuckler. He died one day before his fiftieth birthday from injuries sustained in a car accident.

Jack Brickhouse

Brickhouse, John

Broadcaster B:1/24/1916, Peoria, IL D:8/6/1998, Chicago, IL

Jack Brickhouse became a baseball broadcaster in the earliest days of the profession and developed a loyal following for more than 43 years. He was an exponent of what became known as the "Midwestern style" of announcing—unabashed rooting for the home team. The voice of the Cubs before Harry Caray, Brickhouse broadcast for both the Cubs and White Sox when their games were first aired in Chicago in 1940. He learned at the elbow of the legendary Bob Elson. When Elson joined the Navy to do public relations work during World War II, Brickhouse took over the job by himself.

Brickhouse spent one year as the announcer for the Giants in 1946 before returning to Chicago. In 1948 he was the first Chicago broadcaster to call a game on television when WGN began baseball telecasts. In fact, Brickhouse was the first voice ever heard over WGN, when he called a boxing tournament from Chicago Stadium earlier that year. His legendary "Hey Hey" home run call became a familiar part of Cubs lore.

Brickhouse also was involved in national events. He covered five national political conventions and several World Series, both on radio and on television. When he called the 1950 World Series on television, a remarkable 38 million people watched. The Mutual Radio Network broadcast his calling of the 1952 World Series on more than 700 stations.

For a while, Brickhouse became embroiled in a nasty spat with Cubs manager Leo Durocher, who claimed Brickhouse wanted to run him out of town. Actually, Brickhouse was so closely identified with the team and town that Durocher's paranoia merely identified Brickhouse as the lightning rod.

Brickhouse called 5,060 games before his friend Caray replaced him as Cubs announcer. Named winner of the Ford Frick Award in 1983, he joined broadcasting greats such as Mel Allen, Red Barber, and Vin Scully in this honor given by the Hall of Fame.

In February of 1998 he was hospitalized with a brain tumor and was too ill to attend Caray's funeral. He died August 6, 1998.

Tommy Bridges

Bridges, Thomas Jefferson Davis **P**

1930–43, 1945–46 B:12/28/1906, Gordonsville, TN D:4/19/1968, Nashville, TN Deb:8/13/1930, DET AL BR/TR 5'10½", 155

W	L	PCT	G	SH	IP	BB	SO	ERA
194	138	.584	424	33	2826^1	1192	1674	3.57

Tommy Bridges, son of a Tennessee country doctor, was expected to follow in his father's profession. Instead, despite his lack of size at 5 feet 10 inches and 155 pounds, he became one of the best pitchers in baseball.

Bridges began his pro baseball career in 1929 with the Class C Middle Atlantic League's Wheeling Stogies, where he was 10–3. In 1930 he moved to the 3-I League's Evansville Hubs, where he recorded a 7–8 record. Nonetheless, impressed by his 20 strikeouts in one game, the Detroit Tigers called upon Bridges in midseason, and he went 3–2 for Detroit.

The next year Bridges became a regular for the Tigers. Then, on August 5, 1932, he came within one out of pitching a perfect game against Walter Johnson's Washington club. The Senators trailed Detroit 13–0, but Johnson sent Dave Harris up to hit for pitcher Bobby Burke with two out in the ninth. Harris was a crack pinch hitter, and he smashed a single to left. Bridges got the next batter to finish the game.

In 1934 Bridges started a string of three straight 20-victory years, going 22–11 in 1934, 21–10 in 1935, and 23–11 in 1936. He was selected for the All-Star Game all three years and in 1935 and 1936 he paced the American League with 163 and 175 strikeouts, respectively. "One of the best curveball pitchers I ever saw. I always said I was glad I didn't have to hit against him," teammate Charlie Gehringer said in his praises.

Sometimes, however, Bridges was alleged to have less than sanitary pitches in his repertoire. When arbiter Bill Summers accused him of throwing a wet one, Bridges innocently drawled, "Why Mr. Summers, don't you know the spitter has been outlawed for years? How would I ever learn to throw one?"

The Tigers made it to the World Series in 1934, but had to wait until 1935 to win a world title. That year the Tigers–Cubs World Series went down to the seventh game. With the score tied in the top of the ninth, Chicago's Stan Hack led off with a triple against Bridges. Bridges got Billy Jurges on a strikeout. Then pitcher Larry French—a good hitter—was at the plate. Bridges induced him to tap the ball back to the mound, with Hack still holding third. After that, Augie Galan hit a long fly to left, but it was too late to do any damage. Detroit scored in the bottom of the ninth for the victory.

Bridges remained a key starter for the Tigers through the 1943 season when, at age 37, he was called into the military. He missed the 1944 season and virtually all of the 1945 campaign. When he reported for duty with the Tigers in the spring of 1946 he was told that he was over the hill. But Bridges wanted to play baseball, and he wasn't too proud to go down to the minors. From 1946 to 1949 he pitched for the PCL's Portland Beavers. In 1947, at 42 years old, he not only led the league in ERA (1.64), he also no-hit the San Francisco Seals. In 1950 he moved down the coast and pitched for San Francisco.

Bridges was a combination coach and scout for the Cincinnati Reds in 1958 and scouted for the Tigers from 1958 to 1960 and the Mets from 1963 to 1968. To supplement his income he sold tires in the Detroit area.

Al Bridwell

Bridwell, Albert Henry **SS**

1905–15 B:1/4/1894, Friendship, OH D:1/23/1969, Portsmouth, OH Deb:4/16/1905, CIN NL BL/TR 5'9", 170

G	AB	R	H	HR	RBI	OBP	SLG	AVG
1252	4169	457	1064	2	348	.347	.295	.255

Al Bridwell was considered one of the greatest-fielding shortstops of the Dead Ball Era. He played 11 seasons for five different teams, but his most productive years—and memorable hit—occurred with John McGraw's New York Giants.

On September 23, 1908, Bridwell came to the plate in the bottom of the ninth inning with runners on first and third in a 1–1 game between the Giants and Chicago Cubs. He delivered what he thought was the game-winning base hit, only to see the result overturned because Fred Merkle, the runner on first, failed to touch second base. "Well, all the people were jumping over the railing and running onto the field and yelling, everybody thinking the game was over," Bridwell said of the pandemonium at the Polo Grounds, "so it was a natural reaction, him heading for the clubhouse to get away from the crowd."

The game had to be replayed, and New York lost. "Merkle's Boner" ultimately cost the Giants the National League pennant. Bridwell later regretted his role in one of the most famous plays in baseball history. "I wish I'd never gotten that hit," he said. "I wish I'd struck out instead. If I'd done that, then it would have spared Fred a lot of humiliation."

Johnny Briggs

Briggs, John Edward **OF–1B**

1964–75 B:3/10/1944, Paterson, NJ Deb:4/17/1964, PHI NL BL/TL, 6'1", 195

G	AB	R	H	HR	RBI	OBP	SLG	AVG
1366	4117	601	1041	139	507	.357	.416	.253

Johnny Briggs was a top prospect in the early 1960s who signed a long-term contract with the Philadelphia Phillies and came up to the team quickly. However, although he had longball power, he never lived up to his hitting potential.

Briggs' arrival on the team coincided with a spectacular 1964 season: fellow rookie Dick Allen burst onto the scene, and the Phillies led the NL East by as many as 12 games in August. Largely inexperienced, however, Philadelphia broke under pennant-drive pressure and finished one game behind the St. Louis Cardinals, who went on to win the World Series.

Briggs' lack of consistent hitting never really allowed him to crack the Phillies' starting lineup, and in 1971 Philadelphia traded him to Milwaukee. With the Brewers he finally seemed to get the hang of big league pitching. In his first two seasons with the club, his home run total increased to 21, and his average climbed above .260.

Unfortunately, that was the best he could manage, and after a couple of average seasons the Brewers converted him into a utility man/designated hitter. In 1975 they shipped him to Minnesota, and he retired at season's end.

Nelson Briles

Briles, Nelson Kelley **P**

1965–78 B:8/5/1943, Dorris, CA Deb:4/19/1965, STL NL BR/TR 5'11", 200

W	L	PCT	G	SV	IP	BB	SO	ERA
129	112	.535	452	22	2111^{2}	547	1163	3.44

For three years with the St. Louis Cardinals, Nelson Briles was one of the better pitchers in baseball. Although he was a hard thrower and competitor, he was more a workman than ace over the rest of his 14-year career.

Briles first joined the Cardinals in 1965, and the next year he had a horrendous record of 4–15, mostly in relief. But in 1967 pitching ace Bob Gibson broke his leg on July 15, and Briles was moved into the St. Louis starting rotation. He won nine straight to finish 14–5, as well as pacing the club with a 2.43 ERA. In the World Series, Briles was the only St. Louis pitcher to get a victory other than Gibson, as he won the crucial third game.

The following year, pitching only as a starter, Briles won 19 games with an excellent 2.81 ERA. However, he lost his only decision in the World Series. He won 15 games in 1969, but then things turned sour; his 1970 his ERA climbed to 6.24 and he went back to the bullpen.

In January 1971 Briles was traded along with outfielder Vic Davalillo to the Pirates for outfielder Matty Alou and pitcher George Brunet. That year he went 8–4 and then threw a two-hit shutout against the Orioles in Game 5 of the World Series. But his winning percentage dropped the next year, and his singing of the National Anthem prior to the start of Game 4 was his only World Series appearance in 1972.

Briles finished his career with two years each in Kansas City, Texas, and Baltimore. His final season as a regular starter was 1976, when he won 11 games and hurled 200 innings for the Rangers.

During the off-season, he had sung in nightclubs, and he later became a broadcaster. He seemed to win through force of will rather than great stuff. He took that grit and determination into his later career, championing the cause of retired players who were down on their luck.

Ed Brinkman

Brinkman, Edwin Albert **SS**

1961–75 B:12/8/1941, Cincinnati, OH Deb:9/6/1961, WAS AL BR/TR 6', 170

G	AB	R	H	HR	RBI	OBP	SLG	AVG
1845	6045	550	1355	60	461	.282	.300	.224

No one can take away Ed Brinkman's reputation as a slick-fielding shortstop. He led AL shortstops in double plays twice and set a major league record for fielding. As a hitter, though, he was in a different league. Worse hitters have held a bat, but of any batter with at least 1,700 games played, no one had a record worse than Brinkman.

A graduate of Cincinnati's Western Hills High, which has sent numerous players to the majors—including Pete Rose and Don Zimmer—Brinkman received a reported $65,000 bonus in 1961 to sign with expansion Washington. He went from the Alabama–Florida and Appalachian Leagues to the Senators, where, as a harbinger of things to come, he hit .091. He joined the big league team on a regular basis in 1962 and became a starter in 1963; in the next six years he never hit above .229, and he had back-to-back seasons of .188 and .187 in 1967 and 1968. Ted Williams' arrival as the Senators' manager in 1969 made an immediate and dramatic difference in Brinkman's hitting: his average rose from .187 to .266.

Brinkman was involved in a blockbuster trade after the 1970 season. Along with pitchers Joe Coleman and Jim Hannan and third baseman Aurelio Rodriguez, he was swapped to Detroit for pitchers Denny McLain and Norm McRae, third baseman Don Wert, and outfielder Elliott Maddox. Brinkman learned about the trade when he received a call from pitcher Darold Knowles, who had heard about it on the radio. When he heard the names of the other players involved, Brinkman thought Knowles was playing a practical joke.

Brinkman immediately fit in as a Tiger, and both his fielding and his hitting seemed to improve. From May 21 to August 4, 1972, he had 72 consecutive errorless games, handling 331 chances in that span. That year he played 156 games at shortstop and committed only seven miscues, setting a major league record for fewest errors in a season. He was named as the shortstop on *The Sporting News* AL All-Fielding Team and won a Gold Glove Award.

Following the 1974 season, Brinkman was part of a three-club swap involving Detroit, San Diego, and St. Louis. The Tigers swapped Brinkman to the Padres, who then immediately sent him to the Cardinals. He had played in only

28 contests for the Cards by June 4, 1975, when he and pitcher Tommy Moore went to Texas for outfielder Willie Davis. The well-traveled Brinkman played just one game in a Rangers uniform before being sold to the New York Yankees, where he ended his playing career after the 1975 season.

Brinkman coached for the Tigers in 1979, the San Diego Padres in 1981, and the Chicago White Sox from 1983 to 1988. In 1999 he was a special assignment scout for the Cincinnati Reds.

Lou Brissie

Brissie, Leland Victor **P**

1947–53 B:6/5/1924, Anderson, SC Deb:9/28/1947, PHI AL BL/TL 6'4", 215

W	L	PCT	G	SV	IP	BB	SO	ERA
44	48	.478	234	29	897[2]	451	436	4.07

Pitcher Lou Brissie earned high marks for courage both during and after his World War II combat days. As a corporal in the paratroops, he led a 12-man patrol into battle in Italy. Brissie was the only survivor. One leg was blown off, the other badly shredded. It took two years, 23 operations, a brace, and an artificial leg before he could make a remarkable return to baseball.

In 1947 Brissie went 23–5 with a sparkling 1.91 ERA for Savannah in the South Atlantic League. By season's end he had reported to Connie Mack's Philadelphia Athletics. On Opening Day 1948 Ted Williams smashed a line drive off Brissie's remaining leg. The ball caromed almost to the right field wall, but Brissie continued to play. He finished the year with a 14–10 mark. The next season was Brissie's best. He went 16–13 and was selected to the All-Star Game.

In 1951 Brissie was traded to Cleveland, where he spent most of the next three years as a reliever. On one occasion with the Indians, he entered a game in the fourth inning. He finally surrendered a run in the 19th inning, but he still emerged a winner, as Al Rosen clouted a two-run homer.

Brissie served as national director of the American Legion's baseball program for 16 years. Following that he sold insurance in Greenville, South Carolina.

Lou Brock

Brock, Louis Clark **OF**

1961–79 B:6/18/1939, El Dorado, AK Deb:9/10/1961, CHI NL BL/TL 5'11½", 170

G	AB	R	H	HR	RBI	OBP	SLG	AVG
2616	10332	1610	3023	149	900	.344	.410	.293

When St. Louis general manager Bing Devine acquired outfielder Lou Brock from the Cubs in June 1964 in a trade that sent former 20-game-winner Ernie Broglio to Chicago, baseball fans figured the Cardinals had been taken. Nobody knew much about Brock, a .260 hitter with limited power and negligible fielding ability. As it turned out, however, the deal was one of the best in baseball history.

As much as any other player, Brock revolutionized the art of base stealing. He stole 938 bases in 1245 attempts. He broke Maury Wills' single-season record and Ty Cobb's career mark and transformed the stolen base into an offensive weapon to be used at every opportunity. "Say you've got to exist between 68 and 72 [degrees]," Brock once said. "If I turn it up to 85, you're going to feel it. I turn up the thermostat of the game."

Brock's arrival in the Cardinals clubhouse was not wildly popular. "Everybody loved Ernie," said catcher Tim McCarver, and nobody was particularly eager to see Brock arrive. Sent up to pinch-hit against the Astros in his first appearance as a Cardinal, Brock swung wildly and struck out on three pitches. When he returned to the bench someone loudly remarked, "I guess our next trade will be [first baseman] Bill White for two broken bats."

"We thought we had given up too much," admitted White, a future National League president. He said Brock "was not a good fielder, he struck out too much, and he made a lot of mistakes on the bases."

Manager Johnny Keane, a Brock supporter, realized that Brock had to change his style of play, and fast. "To play regularly on this club," he informed Brock, "you have to steal bases. You go anytime; go anywhere and if anybody asks you about it, you tell them where to go." Brock did just that.

Only a .251 hitter when he arrived, Brock batted .348 for the Cardinals for the rest of the season and helped lead them from seventh place to a world championship. He hit .461 down the stretch as St. Louis caught Gene Mauch's folding Phillies. "Brock changed the entire complexion of the team," said Cardinals infielder Jerry Buchek.

Running the bases was not painless for Brock. "Stealing is not an easy thing to do," he explained.

"You get yourself bruised and beat up in ways the public just doesn't understand. I've had guys tag me so hard that I've seen stars. I'll call time and get my head cleared but it takes something out of you."

Brock's earliest recollection of baseball stems from a minor disciplinary incident in grade school in tiny Colinston, Louisiana. He hit his teacher with a spitball and as punishment was assigned to prepare an oral report on five baseball players: Stan Musial, Jackie Robinson, Roy Campanella, Joe DiMaggio, and Don Newcombe. "The one thing that got my attention," recalled Brock, "was the fact that they got an awful lot for meal money. Money just for eating! That was one of the aspects of baseball that caught my fancy at the age of 10."

Brock played baseball at segregated Union High School "because there was nothing else to do" and later received some work-study assistance at Southern University in Baton Rouge. Once, while working out in the hot sun with the school's baseball team, he collapsed. It came out that the young ballplayer was so poor that he subsisted by dropping in at friends' houses during mealtimes.

After graduation Brock took a bus to St. Louis for a tryout, but the scout he had been in contact with was in Seattle signing pitcher Ray Washburn, and he couldn't get the time of day. Instead, he headed for Chicago and signed with the Cubs for a reported $30,000 bonus.

Chicago sent him to the Northern League's St. Paul Rox. He led the league with 117 runs scored, 181 hits, 33 doubles, 268 total bases, and 277 putouts, and his .361 average was the second best in the minor leagues. At season's end the Cubs promoted Brock all the way from Class C to Wrigley Field. He singled off Robin Roberts in his first at bat but committed a pair of errors in the game and went hitless for the rest of the year, ending up 1-for-11.

Early in his career Brock was recognized more for his power than for his speed. In 1962 he became one of only three players—joining Willie Mays and Joe Adcock—to homer into the center field bleachers at New York's Polo Grounds. But that was one of the few highlights of that season. His average hovered around .260, he struck out a lot, and he rarely walked. His fielding was atrocious. "Brock as in Rock," fans would say.

The came the trade to the Cardinals in 1964 and Brock's new style of play. From 1967 through 1974 he led the NL in stolen bases in all but one season and he was named to four All-Star Games. He also began a string of eight consecutive seasons in which he hit better than .295.

In 1974 Brock stole a major league-record 118 bases, eclipsing Maury Wills' mark of 104 set in 1962. He accomplished the feat despite suffering a severe hand injury in late July that kept him in pain for six weeks. Compounding Brock's difficulties was the brutal heat of a Busch Stadium summer. "I don't think Wills could have stolen as many bases," said Brock, "if he had to play his home games in an area as hot as it is in the Midwest."

Brock tied and broke Wills' record on September 10, 1974, when he twice stole second base against Philadelphia. The tying steal came in the first inning. The new record was recorded in the seventh. Both times he reached base on a single and stole second with an 0–1 count on teammate Ron Hunt. Despite the wear and tear, Brock hit .306, the 10th-best average in the NL, and was named *The Sporting News* Major League Player of the Year.

Brock would go on to break Ty Cobb's lifetime stolen base record on August 29, 1977, when he recorded number 893. Two years later he became the 14th major leaguer to record 3,000 hits. When Brock retired, the only active player with more hits was Pete Rose. "People think of me as a base stealer," said Brock in 1977, "but the thing that keeps me in the major leagues is my ability to hit." Although his stolen base records have since been broken by Rickey Henderson, the trophy awarded to each year's NL stolen base leader is named the Lou Brock Award. He was elected to the Hall of Fame in 1985, his first year of eligibility.

Steve Brodie

Brodie, Walter Scott **OF**

1890–99, 1901–02 B:9/11/1868, Warrenton, VA D:10/30/1935, Baltimore, MD Deb:4/21/1890, BOS NL BL/TR 5'11", 180

G	AB	R	H	HR	RBI	OBP	SLG	AVG
1437	5699	886	1726	25	900	.364	.381	.303

Steve Brodie played two seasons with both Boston and St. Louis before going to Baltimore, where he was the center fielder for the great Orioles teams of the 1890s. A competent player his first four years, as soon as he put on an Orioles uniform, he suddenly became a star.

In his first three years, Brodie hit about .270. His mark went up to .361 when he joined Baltimore late in 1893, and each of the next two years he helped lead the Orioles to the pennant by hitting .366 and .348, respectively, while also driving in more than 100 runs each year.

The Orioles were famous for doing whatever it took to win—even when it meant cheating. One day left fielder Joe Kelley threw a runner out with a ball he had chased into the high outfield grass. Kelley had actually thrown in one of the extra balls the Orioles always hid in the outfield for just such occasions, and no one would have noticed except that Brodie didn't see Kelley's ploy. Brodie ran down the original baseball and threw it back to the infield, and, when the two balls appeared, the runner was awarded the base.

The durable Brodie played in 727 consecutive games, starting in 1891, a 19th-century record. He went to Pittsburgh in 1897, returning to the Orioles midway through the next year. In 1902 he spent his final year with the New York Giants. After he retired as a player, he coached baseball at both Rutgers (1912–14) and the U.S. Naval Academy (1914–22).

Hubie Brooks

Brooks, Hubert **OF-3B-SS**
1980–94 B:9/24/1956, Los Angeles, CA Deb:9/4/1980, NY NL BR/TR 6', 200

G	AB	R	H	HR	RBI	OBP	SLG	AVG
1645	5974	656	1608	149	824	.318	.403	.269

Hubie Brooks and Mookie Wilson both came up from the minor leagues in September 1980, bringing a little life into another disappointing Mets season. Both quickly became fan favorites at Shea Stadium. Wilson had the speed the team lacked, and Brooks looked like the answer to the vacuum at third base that had existed since the Mets inaugural season in 1962.

Brooks batted .307 in his first full season, earning Mets Player of the Year and finishing third in the National League Rookie of the Year voting. His batting average dropped almost 60 points his sophomore year, but his bat showed some life the following season.

Brooks played a major role in the Mets' transformation into a contender in 1984. He went on a prolonged tear in May and put together a club-record 24-game hitting streak. The night his streak ended, fans at Shea littered the field with shoes on "Flip Flop Night" as a tribute to their hero.

The suddenly contending Mets acquired third baseman Ray Knight from the Astros in midseason. Brooks, the 69th and most consistent third baseman in team, immediately shifted to shortstop—a position he had played once previously in the big leagues. On December 10, the Mets sent Brooks to Montreal with catcher Mike Fitzgerald, pitcher Floyd Youmans, and outfielder Herm Winningham, for All-Star catcher Gary Carter.

The Expos made Brooks a full-time shortstop, and in 1985, he became the first to reach 100 RBIs at that position since Ernie Banks in 1960. He played in the All-Star Game for two straight years. By 1990 Brooks had become an outfielder and was playing in his native Los Angeles. He hit 20 home runs and drove in 91 runs in his lone season as Dodger.

Brooks, who had missed the most successful period in Mets history, returned to New York when the club was starting to slip. Plagued by back problems, Brooks still hit 16 home runs and was the only player in the majors to steal home twice in 1991. He returned to California, with the Angels, and finished his career with two seasons as a Royal.

Scott Brosius

Brosius, Scott David **3B**
1991–* B:8/15/1966, Hillsboro, OR Deb:8/7/1991, OAK AL BR/TR 6'1", 185

G	AB	R	H	HR	RBI	OBP	SLG	AVG
891	2991	430	770	112	418	.327	.426	.257

Scott Brosius is living proof that there *are* second acts in American lives. After hitting just .203 for the Oakland Athletics in 1997, more than one scribe was inspired to verse in the sports pages: "Brosius is atrocious." Nonetheless, the New York Yankees were shopping for a full-time third baseman to improve on their Wade Boggs–Charlie Hayes platoon, and shipped Kenny Rogers to Oakland in November 1997 for cash considerations. Ten days later, Brosius, the player to be named later, traveled east.

New York hoped Brosius could approach his 1996 season, when he hit 22 homers and batted. 304, but they got more than they ever hoped for. Brosius knocked in 98 runs, all of them while batting seventh, eighth, or ninth, the best in the majors from those spots in the order. He batted .300 with 19 home runs and played steady defense while appearing in a career-high 152 games. The Yankees cruised to a division title with 114 wins.

In New York's playoff sweep of Texas, Brosius batted .400 and knocked in three runs, two more than the Rangers scored in three games. In the American League Championship Series against Cleveland he hit .300 and led the team with six RBIs. As it turned out, those impressive numbers were just a prelude to a stellar World Series performance.

The Yankees defeated the San Diego Padres in the first two games at home before heading west. With New York trailing 3–0 in Game 3, Brosius led off the seventh inning with a solo homer run. He then hit a three-run homer in the eighth inning off closer San Diego Trevor Hoffman to stun the Padres, 5–4. It was only fitting that the last out of Game 4 was a grounder to Brosius, who, after batting .471 and driving in six runs, was the obvious choice as World Series Most Valuable Player.

The 33-year old Brosius saw his numbers decline in 1999. The reduced playing time was due mostly to his leaving the team to join his ailing father, who died in late September. Despite the turmoil in his personal life, Brosius remained a solid contributor as the Yankees won their 25th world championship.

Jim Brosnan

Brosnan, James Patrick **P**

1954, 1956–63 B:10/24/1929, Cincinnati, OH
Deb:4/15/1954, CHI NL BR/TR, 6'4", 210

W	L	PCT	G	SV	IP	BB	SO	ERA
55	47	.539	385	67	831^{1}	312	507	3.54

Among the many baseball books published each spring there are usually several player autobiographies. Some of these are "diaries" that purport to show what really goes on inside Major League Baseball—"as told to" stories that focus on the titillating aspects of an athlete's life and contribute little to understanding the game.

Two books written by Jim Brosnan were different. *The Long Season* and *Pennant Race* broke new ground in the genre. For one thing, Brosnan wrote the books himself, without the aid of a ghostwriter. And the books delivered on their promise, providing a unique, inside look at Major League Baseball that is intelligent, thoughtful, and enlightening. Some critics have charged that many baseball writers are simply frustrated players. In Brosnan's case, the opposite may have been true.

Brosnan grew up in Cincinnati and signed as a pitcher with the Chicago Cubs for $2,500 in 1946. After two seasons in the minor leagues, he quarreled with his manager and left baseball, returning home with a reputation as a brooding introvert. His baseball career was in jeopardy, and Cubs general manager Jim Gallagher asked club stockholder Arthur Meyerhoff to take Brosnan under his wing. Meyerhoff gave him a job at his ad agency and persuaded him to enter psychoanalysis.

After a two-year break, Brosnan resumed his professional career, entered the Army for two years, and then returned to baseball again. He nearly quit after the 1953 season, when he went 4–17 in Class AAA. But the Cubs were desperate for pitching, and he made the club in 1954. He struggled, however, with a whopping ERA of 9.45.

Brosnan was sent back to the minors before returning to the Cubs in 1956. Appearing mostly in relief, he attained very modest records in the next couple of years with average ERAs. After starting 1958 with a record of 3–4, Brosnan was traded to the St. Louis Cardinals for infielder Alvin Dark. A year later the Cardinals dealt him to the Reds for pitcher Hal Jeffcoat.

Brosnan flourished in his native Cincinnati, going 8–3 in 1959, 7–2 in 1960, and 10–4 in 1961. At the same time, his writing career took off. He'd written an article for *Sports Illustrated* in 1958, and during the 1959 season he kept a diary. He sold his diary to a major publisher, which released it in 1960.

The Long Season was a sensation. Although the honest, articulate description seems tame today, it was a revelation at the time, and the book became a best seller. Brosnan credited the process of writing the book for his new success on the mound. "Writing about pitching actually forced me to recognize how simple it is," he said. His second book, *Pennant Race*, was about the 1961 season. It did not have the runaway success of his first book, but it still managed to rankle the world of baseball. The Reds tried to convince Brosnan to censor his writing. He refused, and they traded him to the Chicago White Sox in 1963.

Brosnan pitched relatively well, but in 1964 the White Sox tried to prohibit him from writing during the baseball season. Brosnan refused to go along with the plan and they released him. No one else offered him a contract, so Brosnan retired. He continued to write but never duplicated his early successes. His influence, however, extended far beyond anything he might have imagined, opening the door to a new era of honesty in books about sports.

Dan Brouthers

Brouthers, Dennis Joseph **1B**

1879–96, 1904 B:5/8/1858, Sylvan Lake, NY
D:8/2/1932, East Orange, NJ Deb:6/23/1879, TRO NL
BL/TL 6'2", 207

G	AB	R	H	HR	RBI	OBP	SLG	AVG
1673	6711	1523	2296	106	1296	.423	.519	.342

First baseman "Big Dan" Brouthers was the first great slugger in baseball. Not only was he a remarkable percentage hitter, leading his league in batting average five times, he also was the a great home run hitter, who hit the then amazing career total of 106 homers.

Brouthers spent two years with the National League's Troy Trojans before moving to the Buffalo Bisons in 1881, and becoming an overnight star. He hit .319 and led the league with eight homers and a .541 slugging average. It was the first of six consecutive times he led the NL in slugging.

In 1882 he won the batting title by hitting .368, and then came back the following year to become the first player in major league history to win back-to-back titles, as he hit .374 and also led the league with 17 triples and 97 RBIs. Bothered by an ankle injury in 1884, Brouthers still managed to hit 14 homers and to lead the league in slugging, at .563. In 1885, his last season with the Bisons, who folded at season's end, he hit .359.

Before the 1886 season, the Detroit Wolverines purchased the entire Bisons roster for $7,000, and Brouthers proceeded to have one of his best years. He hit .370 and topped the league with 11 homers and 40 doubles.

One of his circuit clouts, at Washington's Capitol Park, was widely recognized as the longest home run in the game's short history. Another homer at Boston's Sullivan Towers is reported to have scattered some fans, who were enjoying a free view of the game. Some of his longest home runs were marked by flags at various parks around the league.

Brouthers played two more years in Detroit before the franchise disbanded, and he paced the league in doubles and runs both seasons. His next stop was Boston, and he won his third batting title in 1889 with the Beaneaters, hitting .373 with 118 RBIs.

An early recruit of John Montgomery Ward's Brotherhood of Professional Base Ball Players in 1885, Brouthers joined Ward and Ned Hanlon on the union committee that tried to resolve the differences with the owners. He also served on the league's board of directors. Thus Brouthers didn't hesitate to jump to the Players League in 1890. And when he jumped, he did it noisily. Referring to the three owners of the Beaneaters, he said, "No one would pay a nickel to see Arthur Soden play first, Arthur Conant at second, and [J. L.] Billings at third."

Unfortunately for the new league, not enough fans were interested, and the Players' League folded after one season. Brouthers then signed with the American Association's Boston Red Stockings—with whom he led the league by batting .350—but the AA folded after that season.

Of course, Brouthers had no problem finding a new team. He signed with Brooklyn in the National League for the 1892 season and hit .335 to win his last batting title, as well as again leading the league with 197 hits and 124 RBIs. Injuries limited Brouthers' playing time in 1893, but he was able to crank up one more time in 1894 after he was traded to the Orioles with "Wee Willie" Keeler. At age 36, he hit .347 with 39 doubles, 23 triples, and 128 RBIs, and he also had a career-high 38 stolen bases.

Brouthers played only part-time with Baltimore, Louisville, and Philadelphia during the next two seasons and appeared to have played his last major league game in 1896 with the Phillies. However, he kept playing in the minors, hitting .415 for the Eastern League's Springfield Ponies in 1897. He played two more seasons, sat out for five years, then, at age 46, led the Class D Hudson River League's Poughkeepsie Colts to a pennant, hitting a league-leading .373.

The New York Giants signed Brouthers to a contract in 1904, but he was hitless in five at bats. After he finally retired, he worked at the Polo Grounds as a press attendant for many years. He died in 1932 and was elected to the Hall of Fame in 1945. His lifetime batting average was .342, ninth on the all-time list.

Bobby Brown

Brown, Robert William **3B**

1946–52, 1954 AL President (1984–94) B:10/25/1924, Seattle, WA Deb: 9/22/1946, NY AL BL/TR 6'1", 180

G	AB	R	H	HR	RBI	OBP	SLG	AVG
548	1619	233	452	22	237	.367	.376	.279

Like Yogi Berra, his Newark Bears roommate, Bobby Brown enjoyed spectacular success in several fields. Brown hit .439 in four World Series during his eight years of platooning with the Yankees, became a respected cardiologist, and then in 1984 returned to the game as president of the American League.

As a youngster, Brown was a coveted left-handed-hitting infield prospect who had his first tryout at age 13. At 16, he was brought to Detroit for a tryout with future big leaguers Art Houtteman and Rex Barney. But Brown stayed in school, attending UCLA and Stanford, then enrolling in medical school at Tulane. In 1946 the Yankees offered Brown a deal that would allow him both to continue his education and also to play professional baseball. Brown joined Newark that year and studied medical texts while Berra read comics. When each had closed his book, Berra would ask, "How'd yours come out?"

Brown was a contact hitter with moderate power to all fields (more than 40 percent of his hits went for extra bases) and a good eye, drawing more than two walks for every strikeout. However, Casey Stengel might have had Brown in mind when he said, "I don't like those fellas who drive in two runs and let in three." The Yankees tried to hide Brown at third base, platooning him with Billy Johnson and later Gil McDougald. Brown also occasionally played second, short, third, and the outfield. In 42 career games at shortstop he committed 26 errors, a 95-error pace for a 154-game season.

In his first full year with the Yankees, 1947, Brown batted .300 and helped the team to its first postwar World Series. In four pinch-hitting appearances against the Brooklyn Dodgers, Brown had two doubles, a single, a walk, three RBIs, and three runs scored.

Brown hit .300 again in 1948, and the Yankees returned to the World Series against the Dodgers in 1949, beginning their run of five consecutive crowns. Despite starting just three games of the Series, Brown led all players with four runs, six hits, two triples, and five RBIs. He batted .500 and slugged .917.

In 1950 Brown graduated from medical school. After a solid 1951 season, he batted .357 in the World Series, which the Yankees won in six games over the Giants. He appeared in just 29 games in 1952 before his draft number came up, and he missed the entire 1953 season while serving in the Army. He came back in 1954 but retired after 60 at bats to start his medical internship. He later spent 25 years as a cardiologist in the Dallas–Fort Worth area.

In the early 1980s, Brown was considering other branches of medicine to lighten his workload when Lee MacPhail, a Yankees executive during his playing days, contacted him about succeeding MacPhail as AL president in 1984. Brown said it was "an offer too tempting to turn down." He remained as AL president until 1994.

Gates Brown

Brown, William James **OF**

1963–75 B:5/2/1939, Crestline, OH Deb:6/19/1963, DET AL BL/TR 5'11", 220

G	AB	R	H	HR	RBI	OBP	SLG	AVG
1051	2262	330	582	84	322	.333	.420	.257

Detroit Tigers outfielder Gates Brown was the foremost pinch hitter in American League history, collecting 107 over the course of his career (the previous record being 81 by Fatty Fothergill). Sixteen of his pinch hits were homers, including one in his first major league game on June 19, 1963, and two in consecutive at bats on August 9 and 11, 1968. The following year he went 18-for-39 as a pinch batter, a .461 average.

Some thought his nickname came from prison gates, but that was not the case. "When I was five years old," Brown once explained, "I used to hang out at the gate of the family farm. My mother started calling me Gates."

Brown played for 13 years for the Tigers, but rarely as a regular. His most impressive season was 1968, when he hit .370 and had a slugging percentage of .685 as Detroit won the World Series.

Kevin Brown

Brown, James Kevin **P**

1986, 1988–* B:3/14/1965, Milledgeville, GA Deb:9/30/1986, TEX AL BR/TR, 6'4", 195

W	L	PCT	G	SH	IP	BB	SO	ERA
157	108	.592	349	16	2430^2	683	1701	3.27

Jim Morris, the Georgia Tech baseball coach who helped develop Kevin Brown from a walk-on to the fourth overall pick in the 1986 draft, still is not sure how it happened. "He went from throwing 83, 84 mph to 85, 86," Morris said years later. "Then he suddenly started hitting 93, 94 on the gun, and no one does that. No one increases their velocity that significantly so quickly."

It would not be the last time Brown defied explanation. The Texas Rangers called him up for good in 1989, and Brown won 33 games over the next three seasons while working to harness his dazzling stuff. He seemed to break through in 1992, leading the American League with 21 wins, but went a modest 32–30 over the next three seasons before signing with Florida.

The National League seemed to suit Brown, who won 17 games and posted a league-best 1.89 ERA. After 16 wins in 1997, highlighted by a no-hitter on June 10, Brown led the Marlins into the postseason. In the Championship Series against favored Atlanta, Brown won the series opener, but a stomach virus postponed his next start. Returning for Game 6, he allowed three early runs before stifling the Braves the rest of the way to clinch the pennant. Although Florida went on to defeat the Cleveland Indians in the World Series, Brown played a minor role, with two losses and an ERA of 8.18.

When the Marlins moved to cut payroll after their championship, they traded Brown to San Diego. There, the sinkerballer imparted his competitive fire to the rest of the staff. He went 18–7, and helped to elevate the effectiveness of starters Andy Ashby, Joey Hamilton, and Sterling Hitchcock as the Padres won the division. Brown struck out 21 in two Division Series starts against Houston, then bedeviled the Braves again with a complete-game NLCS win to lead San Diego to the pennant. Once again, however, he contributed little in the World Series, losing one game as the New York Yankees swept the Padres.

A free agent after the season, Brown and agent Scott Boras entertained a half-dozen offers before finally signing a stunning seven-year, $105 million contract with Los Angeles. Despite Brown's consistency, durability, and big-game track record, the deal outraged critics who noted that Brown had never won a Cy

Young Award and had registered just one 20-win season. Though Brown went 18–9 and was as fiery as ever on the mound and in the clubhouse, the pitching staff did not show the overall improvement that Dodgers officials hoped for, and the team finished a disappointing third.

Mace Brown

Brown, Mace Stanley **P**
1935–43, 1946 B:5/21/1909, North English, IA
Deb:5/21/1935, PIT NL BR/TR 6'1", 190

W	L	PCT	G	SV	IP	BB	SO	ERA
76	57	.571	387	48	1075^{1}	388	435	3.46

Strategy-minded managers responded to the advent of longball baseball by introducing the relief specialist. Mace Brown was one of the first pitchers for whom relief was his only job. Strangely, despite a 10-year career and league-leading efforts in both the National and American leagues, Brown's place in baseball history focuses on a home run he gave up that probably cost the Pittsburgh Pirates the 1938 NL pennant.

Acquired by Pittsburgh from the St. Louis Cardinals organization in 1934, Brown arrived in the majors in 1935. The following year he began a string of five years among the top five pitchers in appearances, twice in that time leading the NL in saves.

Unlike today's reliever (more properly called a "closer"), who generally enters the game when his team is ahead, Brown frequently pitched in contests when his team was tied or behind, which was how he won 15 games in 1938, nine in 1939, and 10 in 1940. As he described it, "When you win 15 games relieving like I did, you're darned lucky. Your club's coming from behind and scoring or you go in when the game's tied and they score." That year Brown was the first pure reliever to be chosen for the All-Star Game.

Brown's worst moment happened in 1938, his best year. The Pirates had been in first place since June 12 and enjoyed a seven-game lead on September 1. But the Cubs were red-hot, and by the time the two teams met in Chicago for a three-game series that began on September 27, the Pirates' lead was down to 1½ games. The Pirates dropped the first game to a worn-out Dizzy Dean. The second game was a wild one, including a major brouhaha over an uncalled balk for the Cubs' pitcher. Brown entered the game in the last of the eighth with the score 5–5 and the bases loaded. The first batter he faced grounded into an inning-ending double play. With the skies rapidly darkening, the umpires decided to play just one more inning.

In the last of the ninth, the park nearly dark, Brown retired the first two batters. Two curves to Gabby Hartnett resulted in two strikes. Brown tried a third curve, but he hung it, and Hartnett hit it out of the park. The Pirates never recovered from that defeat and lost the pennant by two games. Hartnett's "Homer in the Gloamin'" became a part of baseball history.

Swapped to the Brooklyn Dodgers in 1941, Brown had an unpleasant season under Leo Durocher before being traded to the Boston Red Sox. In Boston he was 9–3 in 1942 and led the league in appearances the next year. After a stint in the military, he pitched briefly for the 1946 pennant-winning Red Sox before retiring.

Mordecai Brown

Brown, Mordecai Peter Centennial **P**
1903–16 M(1914, 50–63) B:10/19/1876, Nyesville, IN
D:2/14/1948, Terre Haute, IN Deb:4/19/1903, STL NL
BB/TR, 5'10", 175

W	L	PCT	G	SH	IP	BB	SO	ERA
239	130	.648	481	55	3172^{1}	673	1375	2.06

Mordecai Brown was one of the great pitchers of all time, as shown by his career ERA of 2.06, the third best (after Ed Walsh and Addie Joss) in the history of major league baseball. What made the performance of "Three Finger" Brown amazing, however, was that he had to overcome a disability in order to attain his remarkable record.

Brown was a seven-year-old Indiana farmboy when he put his right hand into his uncle's corn grinder. His index finger was so badly damaged that it was amputated just below the knuckle. A few weeks later, his hand still in a cast, he fell while chasing a hog and broke the third and fourth fingers on the same hand. As they healed, each finger bent and twisted unnaturally.

Despite his disability, Brown later played third base for a semipro team in Coxville, Indiana. One day, after the team's pitcher fell and hurt his arm, Brown volunteered for the job. He had good control and a fair fastball, but his curve was a wonder.

Because his index finger was barely a stub, he was forced to exert extra pressure on the ball with his middle finger. A normal curveball thrown in a three-quarter motion by a righthanded pitcher swerves away from a righthanded batter. But lefthanded batters have a good view of the ball as it approaches the plate, so lefties can usually hit better off righthanded pitchers. Because of Brown's unique grip, his curve dropped as if it had rolled off a table, like a modern forkball, and it perplexed batters from both sides of the plate.

That special curveball made Brown one of baseball's most famous pitchers. Newspaper reporters nicknamed him "Three Finger," but his more sensitive teammates called him "Miner" (he had worked in the mines) or "Brownie." One day a reporter asked Brown if pitching with such a misshapen hand was a disadvantage. He replied, "I don't know. I've never done it the other way."

After Brown won 27 games for the Class A Western League's Omaha Indians in 1902, the St. Louis Cardinals bought his contract. In 1903 he went only 9–13 for the last-place Cards. Still, Chicago Cubs manager Frank Selee was impressed and was convinced that Brown could become a great pitcher. He traded 21-game winner Jack Taylor to the Cardinals for Brown in December 1903.

In 1905, when Brown lifted his victory total to 18, Selee resigned due to illness and was replaced by first baseman Frank Chance. Under Chance, the 1906 Cubs set the all-time major league record for victories by winning 116 games, and Brown topped the staff with a 26–6 record. He led the NL with nine shutouts, and posted an ERA of 1.04, the second lowest recorded in the 20th century.

Brown pitched the opening game of the World Series against "the Hitless Wonders"—the Chicago White Sox. He held them to four hits but lost the game, 2–1, after he committed an error in the seventh inning. He recovered to shut out the White Sox in Game 4 with a two-hit, 1–0 win. Entering the sixth game, the underdog White Sox led the Series, three games to two. Chance rushed Brown to the mound on only one day's rest, but the husky righthander didn't have the stamina. He was battered for six runs before leaving the game in the second inning, marking one of the greatest upsets in World Series history.

Brown had another excellent season in 1907, going 20–6 as the Cubs won 107 games and finished 17 games in front of second-place Pittsburgh. He then won the clinching fifth game of the World Series with a 2–0 shutout.

The Cubs won the pennant again in 1908 but faced a stiff challenge from the New York Giants. On September 22 the teams met in a doubleheader at New York's Polo Grounds. Brown was slated to pitch the second game, but when Chicago's first starter ran into trouble in the sixth inning, Brown relieved, and the Cubs rallied to win, 3–1. He stayed on the mound for the second game and won again by the same score. The next day saw one of the most famous contests of all time. New York's young first baseman, Fred Merkle, committed a baserunning error that erased a New York victory, ending the contest with the teams tied. When the two teams finished in a dead heat at season's end, the tie was replayed to decide the pennant.

Christy Mathewson took the mound for the Giants in the makeup game on October 8. Chance decided to pitch Jack Pfiester, called "the Giant Killer" because of his previous success against New York. The first three Giants hit safely and Pfiester walked two more to give the Giants a 2–0 lead. Brown didn't say a word to Chance; he just walked to the mound, took the ball from Pfiester, and, without warming up, shut New York down. The Cubs rallied to win, 4–2, to give Brown his ninth straight win over Mathewson and his 29th victory of the season, to go along with a league-leading five saves. In the anticlimactic World Series, Chicago again beat the Tigers in five games. Brown won twice—once with two scoreless innings of relief and once by pitching a shutout.

The Cubs finished second to Pittsburgh in 1909, but Brown had another remarkable season. He led the NL with 50 appearances, which included not only a league-high 27 victories and 32 complete games, but an NL-best seven saves. The Cubs came back to win the 1910 flag as Brown won 25 games and led the league in complete games, shutouts, and saves. In 1911 Brown's ERA went over 2.00 for the first time in six years, but he still won 21 games and set a major league record with 13 saves.

Brown had arm injuries in 1912, and followed that up with a poor season in 1913. When the Federal League invited him to manage and play for its St. Louis club, he jumped at the chance. Although he soon gave up his managerial duties, he won 31 games for Federal League teams in two seasons.

When the Federal League folded, Brown returned for a last try with the Cubs. On September 4, 1916, he and Mathewson, then the Cincinnati manager, pitched against each other for the last time. The game featured more sentiment than skill as Mathewson staggered to a 10–8 victory.

After Brown left the majors, he pitched and managed in the minors through 1920. From then until his retirement in 1945, he ran a filling station in Terre Haute, Indiana. He died in 1948, the year before he was elected to the Hall of Fame.

Tom Brown

Brown, Thomas Tarlton **OF**

1882–98 M(1897–98, 64–72) B:9/21/1860, Liverpool, England D:10/25/1927, Washington, DC Deb:7/6/1882, BAL AL BL/TR 5'10", 168

G	AB	R	H	HR	RBI	OBP	SLG	AVG
1786	7363	1521	1951	64	736	.337	.361	.265

Tom Brown was a journeyman player in more than the normal sense of the expression. As well as being very average for most of his career, Brown never really laid down any roots in professional baseball, playing for a new club or in a different league 11 times in his 17-year career.

Brown entered pro baseball with Baltimore of the American Association in 1882, but he didn't become a regular until the next year, in his first of two seasons with Columbus. After two years playing with Pittsburgh, he and his team entered the National League together, but midway through the 1887 season he was traded to Indianapolis.

In 1888 Brown moved on to Boston, two years later switching from the Beaneaters to the Boston franchise in the Players League. He made it three Boston teams in a row when he moved to the Red Sox of American Association in 1891. There he had his greatest year, leading the league with 189 hits, 177 runs, 21 triples, and 106 stolen bases. On June 25 of that year, he and Bill Joyce became the first teammates to lead off a game with home runs when they connected off Sadie McMahon in a 13–5 triumph. Brown would finish with 11 lifetime leadoff homers.

Brown saw the most action of his career with Louisville of the National League from 1892 to 1894. In the second of those years, he led the National League with 66 stolen bases . After starting the 1895 season with St. Louis, he finished with three and a bit years in Washington. In June 1897 Brown was hired by the Wagner brothers to replace Washington manager Gus Schmelz, who in 1895 had taken a leave from piloting the club to guide the fortunes of the Wagners' traveling wild west show. After bringing the club home sixth in 1897, Brown was re-hired at season's end and given a bonus in the bargain. When the club fell to 11th place by the following June, however, he was fired and replaced by first baseman "Dirty Jack" Doyle, who lasted only a week.

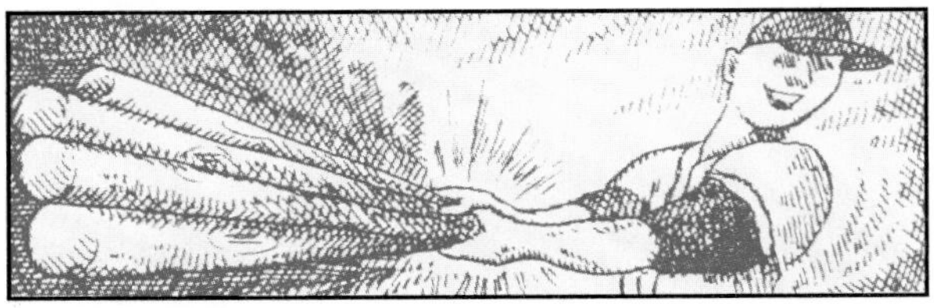

Willard Brown

Brown, Willard Jessie **OF**

1947 Negro League Player (1935–50) B:6/26/1915, Shreveport, LA D:8/8/1996, Houston, TX Deb:7/19/1947, STL AL BR/TR 5'11½", 200

G	AB	R	H	HR	RBI	OBP	SLG	AVG
21	67	4	12	1	6	.179	.269	.179

In 1947, after Major League Baseball finally opened its doors to black players, the St. Louis Browns signed Willard Brown and Hank Thompson. Brown was considered the better prospect, even though he was more than 30 years old.

Brown had starred with the Kansas City Monarchs, winners of six Negro League pennants between 1937 and 1946. He was considered Josh Gibson's chief rival as the greatest home run hitter in black baseball. Brown used an unusually heavy bat and was known as a free swinger (on one occasion he homered on a pitch that bounced in front of the plate). He also won three batting championships and three home run titles playing winter ball in Puerto Rico.

Unfortunately, St. Louis rushed Brown into the lineup without giving him time to adjust to his new and intimidating surroundings. As a result, the husky righthander hit only .179 with one home run in 21 games. Although he later played in the Texas League with success, he never returned to the majors.

Pete Browning

Browning, Louis Rogers **OF-3B**

1882–94 B:6/17/1861, Louisville, KY D:9/10/1905, Louisville, KY Deb:5/2/1882, LOU AA BR/TR 6', 180

G	AB	R	H	HR	RBI	OBP	SLG	AVG
1183	4820	954	1646	46	659	.403	.467	.341

Pete Browning was the original "Louisville Slugger"—the one for whom the famous Hillerich and Bradsby bat was named. One of the most prodigious hitters in history, Browning won three major league batting titles in the 19th century and finished his career with a .341 lifetime batting average to rank 11th all time and fourth among righthanded batters.

Yet Browning had few redeeming qualities beyond his batting average. As one writer commented, he was "tall and ungainly in appearance...personally and professionally eccentric, notoriously illiterate, chronically drunk, and defensively a buffoon in the field."

Unfortunately, the physicians of the day were unable to discover that most of his faults were either caused or exacerbated by a medical condition that was never properly treated and that eventually killed him. Browning suffered from mastoiditis, an infection of the bone behind the ear. As a boy he was completely deaf for a time. Embarrassed, he skipped school regularly, hence his illiteracy.

While he wasn't entirely deaf, Browning's poor hearing affected his play and was at least partially responsible for his atrocious fielding and some of his odd behavior. For example, while playing the infield early in his career he would stand on one leg with his other leg extended toward the base runner. Newspaper reporters commented on this stance and chalked it up to eccentricity. In fact, he was simply trying to protect himself from runners whose footsteps he could not hear.

Switched to the outfield, Browning continued to use his odd stance to ward off teammates in case he could not hear their calls for flyballs, and he was at a further disadvantage because at that distance he was unable to hear the crack of the ball off the bat. Still, even when all allowances are made for his medical condition, the fact remains that Browning had hands of stone. In the 1880s fielding averages under .900 were not unusual, but in 1886 Browning was way down at .791. He was sometimes derisively called "the Gladiator" because of his frequent bouts with balls in the field.

The pain and isolation caused by his condition were probably partially responsible for his alcoholism. He started drinking as a boy and kept it up throughout his life. He was probably not drunk on the field as often as he was reported to be, but no doubt such incidents were common. He was quoted as saying, "I can't hit the ball until I hit the bottle."

Hitting the ball was obviously natural for Browning. In 1882 he broke in with Louisville's first American Association team and as a rookie led the league with a .378 batting average. In 1885 he again led the AA, with a .362 mark. He was only one point off the lead the next year, batting .340. His finest year came in 1887, when he hit .402 but finished second in the batting race to Tip O'Neill, who hit .435. Browning won his last batting title in 1890 with Cleveland of the Players League, hitting .373.

"The Louisville Slugger" collected his nickname one spring day in 1884 when he broke his best bat in a game at Louisville. Seated in the stands was Bud Hillerich, who was taking a day off from his father's woodworking shop. Young Hillerich offered to make a bat for Browning. The two went to his shop, where Hillerich turned a piece of white ash on the lathe until it suited Browning's specifications.

The next day Browning collected three hits with his new bat. As players around the league learned about the bat, they began to descend on the Hillerich shop to have their own bats made. From those beginnings grew the Hillerich and Bradsby Company, the most famous and successful producer of baseball bats. Their most famous model, of course, became the Louisville Slugger.

Browning ultimately had surgery for his mastoiditis. He resumed his career, but the condition worsened again, and he retired in 1894. He then failed in several business endeavors, began to act strangely, and was even committed to a mental hospital. Finally he submitted to another mastoid operation, but his condition was too advanced. He died in 1905 at the age of 44.

Tom Browning

Browning, Thomas Leo **P**

1984-95 B:4/28/1960, Casper, WY Deb:9/9/1984, CIN NL BL/TL 6'1", 190

W	L	PCT	G	SH	IP	BB	SO	ERA
123	90	.577	302	12	1921	511	1000	3.94

In 1985 Tom Browning posted a 20–9 record, becoming the first rookie to reach 20 wins since Bob Grim in 1954. For the next six seasons, the southpaw from Wyoming remained a stalwart of the Cincinnati staff. He compensated for an average fastball with a slider, curve, change, and *two* screwballs—hard and soft. He worked the entire strike zone and confused hitters with an unpredictable and brazen pitch selection. He also excelled in the field and on the basepaths, sometimes entering games as a pinch runner.

On September 16, 1988, Browning pitched the National League's first perfect game in 23 years, defeating the Dodgers while throwing only 102 pitches. He struck out seven men, including pinch hitter Tracy Woodson to end the game.

Browning went 18–5 in 1988 and helped the Reds win the 1990 World Series. In his last healthy season, 1991, he won 14 and lost 14. Then a series of injuries—a knee in 1992, a fractured finger the following year, and a broken arm in 1994—hampered his ability to the point where he was no longer effective. He was forced to retire after making only two appearances with Kansas City in 1995.

Browning will also be remembered for a bizarre episode at Wrigley Field in 1993. He was spotted on top of a residential building across the street from the ballpark, in uniform, watching the Cubs-Reds game with Chicago fans.

Tom Brunansky

Brunansky, Thomas Andrew **OF–DH**

1981–94 B:8/20/1960, Covina, CA Deb:4/9/1981, CAL AL BR/TR 6'4", 211

G	AB	R	H	HR	RBI	OBP	SLG	AVG
1800	6289	804	1543	271	919	.331	.434	.245

When Tom Brunansky broke in with the California Angels in 1981, scouts touted him as a perennial 20-plus homer man. He achieved that feat for eight consecutive seasons. Traded by the Angels to Minnesota, Bruno hit 20 homers as a rookie in 1982. The big righthanded batter with an uppercut swing never surpassed his .272 rookie mark, yet averaged 28 homers from 1983 to 1987, making the All-Star team in 1985. In right field, he possessed a powerful arm, twice leading American League outfielders in double plays.

In the postseason Brunansky had mixed results. He slugged 1.000 during the 1987 Championship Series, pounding out four doubles and two homers in the Twins upset of Detroit. Although he batted only .200 in the World Series against the St. Louis Cardinals, he tied for the Series lead with five runs scored as the Twins won in seven games.

After six productive seasons with the Twins, Brunansky was traded early in the 1988 season to St. Louis and its spacious Busch Stadium, where his homer production dipped. The Boston Red Sox then acquired him in 1990. Brunansky would prove his worth in the final week of the season during an Eastern Division title showdown with Toronto by contributing five home runs.

Although hailed for his intelligence—at the plate, on the bases, and in the outfield—Brunansky began to lose bat speed. After a year in Milwaukee and brief return to Boston, he retired with 271 career home runs.

John T. Brush

Brush, John Tomlinson

Owner (1884–1912) B:6/15/1845, Clintonville, NY D:11/25/1912, Louisiana, MO

Although best known as the owner of John McGraw's New York Giants, John T. Brush played an active role in shaping the game while owning major league clubs in three different cities in two different leagues. His advocacy of salary limitations led almost directly to one of baseball's most explosive insurrections, the Players' League, and his feuding with sportswriter Ban Johnson helped bring about the founding of the American League.

Orphaned at age 4, Brush lived with his grandfather until he ran away at 17 and enrolled at Eastman's Business College, where he excelled at the valuable art of penmanship. In 1863 he enlisted in the First New York Artillery. Returning from the Civil War, he became involved in commercial interests in Albany, Troy, and then Lockport, New York.

In 1875 Brush moved to Indianapolis, where, after numerous delays, he opened a new department store. Brush's daughter recalled, "Finally, my father took a full-page ad in the newspapers with only the word WHEN printed on the page. He rented the roofs of barns all over the state and had WHEN painted on them and he emblazoned WHEN over the front of the still-building store. Naturally, curiosity was aroused. By the time of the opening everyone knew about the WHEN store, and that was the name which was retained."

In the early 1880s Brush became involved in Indianapolis baseball. Why he did so remains unclear. One story claimed Brush acquired some stock in the local club as payment for a bad debt. Another that he spied one of his clerks reading a rulebook, confiscated it, and took to perusing it himself. While thumbing through it, he supposedly saw the possibilities for promoting his store through baseball.

In 1882 Brush built a ballpark in Indianapolis, and two years later he secured an American Association franchise, although he had to retreat to the Western League the following year. When that league collapsed, Brush unsuccessfully attempted to move the Detroit Wolverines to Indianapolis. In 1886 the unsuccessful National League franchise in St. Louis went up or sale, and Brush bought it and moved it to Indianapolis. He refurbished his ballpark, installing modern drainage systems and building a special celebrity box from which such Hoosier dignitaries as Benjamin Harrison, James Whitcomb Riley, and Booth Tarkington viewed games.

Brush proved to be ahead of his time in 1888, when he also gave the distinguished African-American player Bud Fowler, from Crawfordville of the Central Interstate League, a tryout. But resistance to integration was widespread, and Brush dropped the idea. Another of his ideas then caused a great deal of trouble for the national pastime. In an attempt to limit escalating player salaries, Brush devised a Classification Rule that divided players into the following five salary groupings according to their "habits, earnestness, and special qualifications": Class A, $2,500; Class B, $2,250; Class C, $2,000; Class D, $1,750; Class E, $1,500. The players were outraged, and their anger found vent in the Players' Association and, ultimately, in the Players' League.

Indianapolis kept its NL franchise through the 1889 season, after which that city and

Washington were replaced in the National League by Cincinnati and Brooklyn. Brush received $67,000 in cash plus shares in the Giants. Additionally, he retained honorary league membership and was promised the next available franchise.

Brush then picked up Cincinnati's National League franchise after it collapsed in the wake of the Players League war. Most observers expected him to move the team to Indianapolis, but instead he maintained it in the Queen City. He survived an American Association challenge in Cincinnati in 1891 and soon became one of the most influential men in the National League. In Cincinnati, however, he often clashed with *Cincinnati Commercial Gazette* sportswriter Ban Johnson. To get Johnson out of town, Brush supported the writer's successful bid for the presidency of the moribund Western League. Ironically, Brush's stratagem would ultimately lead to Johnson's founding of the American League.

When Johnson finally converted the AL into a rival major league in 1901, Brush was naturally in the thick of the fray. He aligned himself with obstreperous New York Giants owner Andrew Freedman in opposing a more conciliatory National League faction headed by Albert Goodwill Spalding. The rivalry between the two groups resulted in an embarrassing deadlock in choosing a new league president. Brush and Freedman also collaborated on an imaginative bit of sabotage against the American League's Baltimore franchise. By promising managerial positions to John McGraw in New York and Joe Kelley in Cincinnati, they gutted the Orioles and embarrassed Johnson. Shortly thereafter Freedman left baseball, partly to appease Spalding. Brush took over the Giants, selling the Reds.

The American and National leagues made peace following the 1902 season, and in 1903 the respective league champions played the first World Series. In 1904 the Giants captured the NL pennant, but so intense was Brush's hostility toward Johnson that he refused to let the Giants meet the AL champion Boston club.

With McGraw and ace hurler Christy Mathewson on board, Brush's Giants were the powerhouse of baseball, but physical problems prevented Brush from fully enjoying his team's success. For the last decade of his life he suffered from locomotor ataxia, a disease of the nervous system, and was in constant pain. He attended the 1912 World Series between the Giants and the Red Sox, but it seemed that he might expire at any moment. Finally, on doctors' orders Brush set off by train for the warmer climes of California, but he died en route at Louisiana, Missouri.

Bill Bruton

Bruton, William Haron **OF**

1953–64 B:11/9/1925, Panola, AL D:12/5/1995, Marshalltown, DE Deb:4/13/1953, MIL NL BL/TR 6'½", 169

G	AB	R	H	HR	RBI	OBP	SLG	AVG
1610	6056	937	1651	94	545	.329	.393	.273

In the era of Willie Mays, Mickey Mantle, and Duke Snider, Milwaukee's Bill Bruton was still considered one of the finest fielding center fielders in the major leagues. He was also a threat offensively, as he led the NL in stolen bases for each of his first three seasons and twice paced the circuit in triples.

Bruton had his baseball career put on hold by a tour of duty in the army. After his discharge, he played semipro ball in the Wilmington, Delaware, area before signing with the Negro League Philadelphia Stars. Before actually playing for them, however, he was released and hooked up with a Midwestern barnstorming squad. It was while Bruton played with that club that Braves' scout Johnny Ogden signed him to a pro contract.

Bruton became an immediate starter with Milwaukee and was part of the team when it won pennants in 1957 and 1958, although those were not his best playing years. A knee injury in 1957 led to surgery and a long stint on the disabled list. "I didn't even go [to the 1957 World Series] and had kind of an empty feeling about it, but later on I was proud to wear the World Series ring, even though I wasn't there," he recalled.

After leading the National League in runs and triples in 1960, Bruton surprisingly was traded to Detroit. There he hit a career-high 17 homers in 1961 and knocked in 74 runs in 1962. In May 1964 Bruton announced he would retire at season's end. "I felt I could have played a couple of more years, but I would have been platooned and I didn't want to sit around and waste my time."

During the off-season in Milwaukee, Bruton worked in the sports promotion department of Miller Brewing. After being traded to Detroit he spent 23 years with the Chrysler Corporation before retiring in January 1988. Bruton's father-in-law was Hall of Famer Judy Johnson.

Jack Buck

Buck, John Francis
Broadcaster B:1924

"That's a winner" is Jack Buck's signature call and also the title of his 1997 autobiography. A native of Holyoke, Massachusetts, Buck moved to Cleveland at age 15. "His father was dying, his family was poor, and God knows the jobs Jack had as a kid," said Bob Broeg of the *St. Louis Post Dispatch.* "He worked on river boats, assembly lines, selling things on corners, working with cranes—just to support everyone."

Buck served in World War II in Europe and was injured on the same shoulder, in the same battle—Remagen Bridge—as Lindsey Nelson, although the two broadcasters-to-be did not meet until years later. After returning home, Buck attended Ohio State University. He got his start in 1950, doing radio play-by-play for the Columbus Redbirds of the American Association. By 1953 he was making calls for the Cardinals Triple-A affiliate at Red Wing Stadium in Rochester. A year later he joined Harry Caray on KMOX.

Buck's voice became synonymous with Cardinals baseball, but he was nationally well known for his coverage of football. Buck covered the first-ever American Football League game, and was the longtime voice of CBS Radio's NFL coverage. He received the Ford C. Frick Award in 1987, and was later inducted into both the Broadcasters' and Radio halls of fame. The Cardinals honored the legendary broadcaster with a bronze statue of himself behind a microphone at Busch Stadium. He broadcast six pennant-winning clubs in St. Louis, and had the thrill of working with his son, Joe Buck, who started calling Cardinals games at 22.

Buck has few bad things to say about his business—and even fewer bad things to say about the Cardinals—but he admits losing makes it tough. "When you have a bad club and you're out of it in August, baseball can become drudgery because you get spoiled, " he said. "But there's nothing like winning baseball, especially when it engulfs the city and lasts through the winter."

Buck has been in the thick of many events that buoyed him and his listeners. When Ozzie Smith's homer won Game 6 of the National League Championship Series in 1985, Buck yelled, "Go crazy, folks, go crazy." Three years later it was the Kirk Gibson's game-winning home run in Game 1 of the 1988 World Series. As the ball flew over the right-field fence, Buck couldn't contain himself. "Unbelievable! The Dodgers win, 5-4, and I don't believe what I just saw!" Mark McGwire's record-setting homer-spree in 1998 led him to join in the cheerleading-for-the-home-run craze.

Bill Buckner

Buckner, William Joseph **1B–OF–DH**
1969–90 B:12/14/1949, Vallejo, CA Deb:9/21/1969, LA NL BL/TL 6', 185

G	AB	R	H	HR	RBI	OBP	SLG	AVG
2517	9397	1077	2715	174	1208	.324	.408	.289

In his long career Bill Buckner was a speedster in Los Angeles, a batting champion with the Cubs, and had consecutive 100-RBI seasons in Boston, but he will forever be remembered for one error. In Game 6 of the 1986 World Series, the Boston Red Sox led the New York Mets by two runs with two outs in the bottom of the 10th inning, and the Sox were only one out away from their first world championship since 1918. Three straight singles and a wild pitch erased Boston's lead before Mookie Wilson's grounder deep behind first sneaked under Buckner's glove and between his ankles to allow the winning run to score.

It was a tricky play for Buckner, and it is not certain that if he had fielded the ball cleanly he could have beaten the fleet-footed Wilson to the bag. More important was the fact that relievers Calvin Schiraldi and Bob Stanley had already let the Mets back in the game. If the bullpen had done its job, the Sox would have escaped the "curse of the Bambino." Still, Buckner and manager John McNamara, who failed to insert Dave Stapleton as a defensive replacement for Buckner (something he had done throughout the postseason), drew fire, and the controversy endured. In 1993 Buckner left his home in Massachusetts because of harassment over the fateful error.

Buckner was a good player whose 22 years in the major leagues were unjustly overshadowed by the World Series error. After attending the University of Southern California and Arizona State University, he was picked in the second round of the June 1968 draft by the Los Angeles Dodgers. Voted to the Northern California Football Hall of Fame for his exploits as a wide receiver at Napa High School, with the Dodgers Buckner held his own in foot races with the likes of Willie Davis. He made his first major league appearance as a pinch hitter in 1969 and came to the majors to stay in 1971 as a first baseman and outfielder.

Buckner was a lefthanded contact hitter

who rarely struck out, but who produced only middle infielder offensive statistics while playing a primary hitting position. Actually, his most historic accomplishment came on defense, when in 1985 he established a big league record for assists by a first baseman, with 184.

In his six seasons as a regular with the Dodgers, Bucker showed remarkable inconsistency, batting above .300 in even-numbered years, while dropping significantly below that every other year. His initial stint at first base ended in 1973, when Ron Cey moved in at third, bumping Steve Garvey over to first. "Billy Buck" was an outfielder the rest of his time in Los Angeles.

In January 1977 the Dodgers traded Buckner to the Chicago Cubs in a five-player deal that sent Rick Monday to Los Angeles. It proved a new lease on life for Buckner, who was having progressively more problems in the outfield. In 1975 he had injured his left ankle on a slide. That September he underwent surgery to remove a tendon from the ankle, and later he had bone chips taken out, which robbed him of his speed. In Chicago, Buckner moved back to first base, and didn't have to worry so much about his mobility.

Although never considered a power hitter, Buckner did hit at least 10 home runs in six of his seven full seasons in Chicago, something he had never accomplished with the Dodgers. He also hit at least .306 four times in a period of five years, including winning the NL batting title in 1980 with a .324 average. He led the league in doubles in 1981 (his lone All-Star season) and 1983.

Early in the 1984 season Bucker was traded to the Red Sox. The next year he batted .299 and knocked in 110 runs. Then, in 1986, he helped Boston to the World Series by hitting a career high 18 homers as well as 39 doubles and 102 RBIs. His hobbled ankles required him to wear special high-top cleats for the Series. Despite the pain, he played in every game and had the most at bats of any player in the Series; Buckner hit just .188. "I don't think anybody else could have gotten as much out of this body as I did," Buckner later said.

The Red Sox released Buckner in July 1987, but he continued to play for three more seasons. He first migrated to Anaheim and then joined the Kansas City Royals as a part-timer. In 1990 he made the Red Sox as a nonroster player but was released for good on June 5. His 2,715 hits were the most among active players at the time of his retirement. He was later able to pass his knowledge on to others as a batting coach.

Charlie Buffinton

Buffinton, Charles G. **P–OF**

1882–92 B:6/14/1861, Fall River, MA D:9/23/1907, Fall River, MA Deb:5/17/1882, BOS NL BR/TR
6'1", 180

W	L	PCT	G	SH	IP	BB	SO	ERA
233	152	.605	414	30	3404	856	1700	2.96

Charlie Buffinton was one of the great curveballers of the 19th century. A workhorse for most of his 11 years, he won more than 20 games seven times, and his 1884 season was one of the most impressive in baseball history.

Buffinton joined Boston in 1882 and helped them to a pennant the next year by winning 25 games. His money pitch was an overhand curve that dropped straight down. There was no pitching mound at the time, but Buffinton was one of the taller players in the league, which added to the effectiveness of his drop curve. He was also known as a pitcher who elicited a large number of ground balls. This was sometimes a liability; the Boston grounds were said to be the worst-kept in the National League and bad hops were common.

"Big Buff" virtually had a career in a season in 1884. He chalked up a marvelous 48–16 record, having pitched 587 innings and 63 complete games, registered 417 strikeouts, and compiled a sparkling 2.15 ERA. However, he was constantly overshadowed by Charley "Old Hoss" Radbourn of the Providence Grays. On August 9, 1884, the two great righthanders squared off against each other in the middle of a red-hot pennant race. Inning after inning Radbourn and Buffinton held their opponents in check, and the game was scoreless through 10 frames. In the top of the 11th, Arthur Irwin, the Providence shortstop, pulled one of Buffinton's pitches deep to right. The ball hit the fence and disappeared—it had gone through a hole in the ramshackle Boston barrier for a home run. Radbourn retired the Boston batters without a score in the bottom of the inning for a Providence victory.

Buffinton had another big year in 1885, although his results were not as impressive, as he finished 22–27 despite a 2.88 ERA. Late that year he developed arm trouble, and Boston released him in 1886. He joined Philadelphia in 1887, and that year he threw back-to-back one-hitters. His strong comeback saw him win 21 games in 1887, followed by a pair of 28-victory seasons. Buffinton won 19 games for the Philadelphia Players League team in 1890 and then returned to Boston in 1891 to pitch for the American Association's pennant-winning team. His 29–9 season that year gave him the league lead in winning percentage.

When the American Association collapsed after the 1891 season, Buffinton joined the National

League Baltimore Orioles. After a poor start he was ordered to take a pay cut. He quit in a huff and went home to Fall River, Massachusetts, to become a successful businessman.

Don Buford

Buford, Donald Alvin **OF-2B-3B**

1963–72 B:2/2/1937, Linden, TX Deb:9/14/1963, CHI AL BB/TR 5'8", 165

G	AB	R	H	HR	RBI	OBP	SLG	AVG
1286	4553	718	1203	93	418	.364	.379	.264

Don Buford holds the distinction of being the hardest man to double-up in major league history. In 4,553 career at bats, he grounded into only 33 double plays. Speed was his strong suit.

Buford played outfield for the great college coach Rod Dedeaux and was a member of a national championship team at the University Southern California. When he first reached the big leagues in 1963, Chicago White Sox manager Al Lopez said, "He's a terrific athlete. He's got a great arm and can run a hole in the wind." At the time, however, Buford played as an infielder—and not a very good one. He was nicknamed "Stonefingers" and "Iron Glove."

It was only after shifting to Baltimore in 1968 that Buford returned to his natural position in the outfield. And his hitting improved as well. Buford was an ideal leadoff hitter and, after a year of adjustment, scored 99 runs per season in three straight years for the Orioles.

Buford homered against the New York Mets' Tom Seaver to lead off the 1969 World Series. He also helped Baltimore win pennants in 1970 and 1971, the latter year earning his only selection to the All-Star Game. He retired from playing American baseball after the 1972 season, and from 1973 to 1976 he played in Japan for the Nankai Hawks. Buford coached for the San Francisco Giants from 1981 to 1984 and later for Baltimore. His son Damon became an outfielder for the Orioles in 1993, and later played for Mets, Rangers, and Red Sox before being traded to the Cubs in December 1999.

Bob Buhl

Buhl, Robert Ray **P**

1953–67 B:8/12/1928, Saginaw, MI Deb:4/17/1953, MIL NL BR/TR 6'2", 190

W	L	PCT	G	SH	IP	BB	SO	ERA
166	132	.557	457	20	2587	1105	1268	3.55

The third starter in a rotation with Lew Burdette and Warren Spahn, Bob Buhl was a major contributor to the successful Milwaukee Braves teams of the mid and late 1950s, winning 100 games from 1953 through 1960, including successive 18-win seasons. His winning percentage of .720 led the National League in the Braves' championship season of 1957, and he was third in the league in ERA in 1959. Perhaps more importantly, he was the toughest Braves pitcher against the very tough Dodgers: in 1956 he sported an 8–0 record against the league-champions from Brooklyn.

As opposed to his pitching success, Buhl was depressing with a bat, and he was actually a convincing argument for the designated hitter. His lifetime batting average was a paltry .089, and in 1962 he came to bat 70 times and never reached base. No pitcher has ever had a worse year at the plate.

Jay Buhner

Buhner, Jay Campbell **OF**

1987–* B:8/13/1964, Louisville, KY Deb:9/11/1987, NY AL BR/TR 6'3", 205

G	AB	R	H	HR	RBI	OBP	SLG	AVG
1341	4604	744	1171	282	878	.362	.492	.254

Ken Griffey, Jr., and Alex Rodriguez became bigger stars, but Jay Buhner played a crucial role in turning around the fortunes of the Mariners franchise—both on and off the field. As a measure of the slugging outfielder's popularity, in 1994 the Mariners held the first Jay Buhner Haircut Night at the Kingdome (it has since become an annual event). A total of 426 people showed up to get a buzz cut like Buhner's in exchange for a free right-field bleacher seat. "It was crazy," Buhner recalled. "Hair was flying everywhere. I should have collected some in case I need a weave someday." By the end of the decade, more than 3,000 fans were showing up every year to get buzzed.

Seattle can thank George Steinbrenner. In 1988 the Yankees sent Buhner, who had played just 32 major league games, to the Mariners for designated hitter Ken Phelps. Phelps disappeared, but after some additional seasoning in Calgary in 1989 and 1990, Buhner matured into one of the American League's blue chip sluggers. From 1991 to 1997, he crushed 224 home runs, topping 40 homers and 100 RBIs three times. His slugging average was better than .500 four years in a row. Buhner set a major league mark with a .984 RBI-to-hits ratio in 1995, knocking in 121 runs on only 123 hits.

When Griffey went down with a broken wrist early in 1995, everyone thought that Seattle's playoff chances had vanished. But with Buhner hitting home runs in five straight games down the stretch, the Mariners emerged from the shadows of the Kingdome into the national spotlight. Thirteen games behind the Angels, the team forced and won a one-game playoff, then took on the Yankees in the Division Series. Against his old team, Buhner went on a tear, going 11-for-24 (.458) with a home run and throwing out a runner from right field as the Mariners came back from a two games to none deficit to win the best-of-five series.

In the six-game loss to the Indians in the American League Championship Series, Buhner cooled down to .304, but he had his moment. Having muffed a flyball in Game 3 that allowed the Tribe to tie the game, Buhner vindicated himself in the 11th, slamming a game-winning two-run homer off Julian Tavarez. In his only other postseason appearance, he was .231 with two homers in Seattle's four-game Division Series loss to the Orioles in 1997.

Buhner's playing time and productivity dropped off in 1998 and 1999, due to knee and elbow problems that required surgery. The Mariners resigned him as a free agent in December 1999, to a one-year contract covering the 2000 season.

Morgan Bulkeley

Bulkeley, Morgan

NL President (1876) B:12/26/1837, East Haddam, CT D:11/6/1922, Hartford, CT

Try as it may, the Baseball Hall of Fame cannot explain away Morgan Bulkeley. Whenever someone's favorite player is bypassed for enshrinement and apologists try to outline just how and why the candidate fell short, the question can always be raised, "Then what about Morgan Bulkeley?"

Indeed, if all candidates had only to meet criteria equal to those that got Bulkeley enshrined, the Hall would find itself accepting utility infielders who rose no higher than Double A. Bulkeley had an interesting and honorable career, but very little of it had anything to do with baseball.

Bulkeley's father was the first president of the Aetna Life Insurance Company. The younger Bulkeley succeeded him in 1879, and the company grew rapidly. He also served as Hartford's mayor from 1880 to 1888, when he was elected governor of Connecticut. A Republican, he was literally locked out of his office by a Democratic legislature. Undaunted, he pried the door open and was henceforth called "The Crowbar Governor." He went back into business in 1893 and raised horses until he was elected a U.S. Senator in 1905.

In 1875, while still an aspiring politician, Bulkeley became the chief backer of Hartford's National Association team, perhaps in order to get on the good side of the voting public. When William Hulbert decided to dismantle the National Association and form the National League in 1876, he invited a number of association team owners to a February meeting in New York. It was Hulbert's show, and he did the talking, but he was from Chicago, and it was generally felt that someone from the East should be listed at the top of the league. Cards were drawn and Bulkeley's came out of the hat first. He allowed his name to grace the league stationery and then went back to Hartford to practice banking and politics. He may have taken in a few baseball games that summer, but if so, that was the extent of his actions as league president.

In 1937, when the Hall of Fame was being formed, American League founder and first president Ban Johnson was a shoo-in. The electors wanted to give the National League equal time; they figured that the older league's first president must have done something to get it going. Apparently, they didn't bother to look into the matter; because of that lack of intellectual curiosity, Bulkeley was enshrined.

Al Bumbry

Bumbry, Alonzo Benjamin **OF–DH**

1972–85 B:4/21/47, Fredericksburg, VA Deb:9/5/72, BAL AL BL/TR 5'8", 175

G	AB	R	H	HR	RBI	OBP	SLG	AVG
1496	5053	778	1422	54	402	.345	.378	.281

Al Bumbry, born Alonza Benjamin Bumbrey, was very fast, a good hitter, and a distinguished defensive outfielder. After serving in Vietnam, Bumbry made his major league debut with the Baltimore Orioles in 1972. Although he played in only 110 games in his rookie year of 1973, he hit .337 and smacked 11 triples to share the major league lead with Rod Carew. The effort, on an Orioles team that won its division, earned him the American League Rookie of the Year Award.

Bumbry stayed in Baltimore's outfield until 1984. He served as the team's regular leadoff hitter, missing only part of the 1978 campaign because of an injury. Although he never won a Gold Glove, his disciplined style of play ensured that he committed few errors. His speed made him a consistent basestealing threat. He was solid at the plate, hitting above .300 four times.

With Bumbry in the outfield, the Orioles won four division crowns, two pennants, and a World Series. Although he never seemed to be able to hit much in any of Baltimore's postseason outings, Bumbry was undeniably an essential element in the club's continued success. He made his only All-Star appearance in 1980.

He went to San Diego in 1985, leaving as Baltimore's all-time basestealer, with 254 career swipes. His experience and leadership failed to provide the cohesion the Padres required to repeat as National League champs. Bumbry retired after the 1985 season. He returned to the majors as a coach with the Boston Red Sox in 1988. He later served as a coach with the Orioles and Cleveland Indians.

Jim Bunning

Bunning, James Paul David **P**

1955–71 B:10/23/1931, Southgate, KY
Deb:7/20/1955, DET AL BR/TR 6'3", 195

W	L	PCT	G	SH	IP	BB	SO	ERA
224	184	.549	591	40	3760[1]	1000	2855	3.27

The highlight of Jim Bunning's career came—appropriately for a parent of seven—on Father's Day. On June 21, 1964, Bunning, of the Philadelphia Phillies, pitched the first regular-season perfect game since Charlie Robertson of the Chicago White Sox had done it on April 30, 1922. Using a state-of-the-art slider and a sweeping sidearm delivery that contorted his body so that his glove hand dusted the mound, Bunning shut down the New York Mets, 6–0, at Shea Stadium with the first perfect game tossed in the National League since 1880.

With a reputation for a live fastball, Bunning first signed with the Detroit Tigers after earning his degree in economics at Xavier University. In the minors, he toiled with mixed results in Richmond, Davenport, Williamsport, Buffalo, and Little Rock. He made the majors midway through the 1955 season, but compiled just a 3–5 record with a 6.35 ERA that year. Bunning quickly realized that a good fastball was not enough to get big league hitters out. "I think I had to make an adjustment early," he said. "In 1956, I started getting a good breaking ball. That was the winter I went to the Cuban Winter League and pitched for the Marianao club and worked on a slider."

His extra work paid off. In nine years with Detroit, Bunning won 118 games, and in 1957, his first season in the regular rotation, he led the American League in wins, posting a 20–8 mark with a 2.69 ERA. That year he was selected to the first of his seven All-Star Games. On July 20, 1958, Bunning recorded his first no-hitter, against the Boston Red Sox. In 1959 and again in 1960, he led the league in strikeouts, each year with 201.

After the 1963 season, Bunning was traded to Philadelphia, and midway through his first year he recorded his perfect game. The economical Bunning threw only 90 pitches, striking out 10 Mets and issuing as many as three balls to only two batters. The closest New York came to having a baserunner was in the fifth inning when Jesse Gonder lined a ball to right. Second baseman Tony Taylor speared it, dropped it, then picked it up and threw to first to retire the slow-footed catcher. Bunning said, "It was a great play. When he did that, I knew I had something special."

In the ninth inning Bunning called catcher Gus Triandos to the mound. The crowd of more than 32,000 looked on and wondered what strategy the batterymates were hatching. "He said I should tell him a joke, just to get a breather," Triandos related after the game. "I couldn't think of anything. I just laughed at him." Facing rookie pinch hitter John Stephenson as the last batter, Bunning threw five straight curveballs, the last of which ended the game with a strikeout.

Bunning went 19–8 that first season in the National League, the first of three 19-win seasons in four years in Philadelphia. He went on to win more than 100 games in the National league with Philadelphia, Pittsburgh, Los Angeles, and Philadelphia again. He became not only the first modern-era pitcher to win 100 games in both leagues, but the first to record 1,000 strikeouts in both circuits. Bunning was also the first to pitch in All-Star Games for both leagues, being scored on only once in his eight appearances.

Bunning retired after the 1971 season, spent five years managing in the Phillies' minor league system, and later became a player agent and investment broker for athletes. He launched a career in politics by serving in the Kentucky state legislature; later he was elected to Congress, but then lost a bid to become governor of Kentucky. He won election to the Hall of Fame in 1996 and two years later to the U.S. Senate.

Lew Burdette

Burdette, Selva Lewis **P**

1950–67 B:11/22/1926, Nitro, WV Deb:9/26/1950, NY AL BR/TR 6'2", 190

W	L	PCT	G	SH	IP	BB	SO	ERA
203	144	.585	626	33	3067[1]	628	1074	3.66

The New York Yankees certainly must have regretted trading pitcher Lew Burdette. He came back to haunt his first club, defeating the Yanks not once, not twice, but three times in the 1957 World Series to give the Braves a world championship. Two of the games were shutouts, and Burdette's ERA was a remarkable 0.67.

Burdette was initially signed by the Yankees in 1950 and, despite making brief appearances with the parent club that year, spent most of his time the next two seasons in places such as

Norfolk, Amsterdam, Quincy, and Kansas City. On August 30, 1951, New York sent Burdette and $50,000 to the Boston Braves for veteran hurler Johnny Sain. Two seasons later he ended up with the Braves.

Burdette was an extraordinarily consistent hurler with the Braves. In his first year in Milwaukee he went 15–5, and, with one exception, from 1953 to 1961 he never won fewer games than that. In 1956 he topped the National League with a 2.70 ERA. The next year he made the first of two All-Star Game appearances. And in 1959 he tied for the league lead with 21 victories.

However, his greatest success was that historic 1957 World Series. In Game 1 Warren Spahn took a loss, but in Game 2 Burdette shut down Casey Stengel's squad, 4–2. In Game 5 Burdette came back with a 1–0 whitewash, and then was on the mound again with just two days' rest for the deciding Game 7. "I'll be all right," Burdette calmly reassured worried Milwaukee fans. "In 1953 I once relieved in 16 games out of 22. I'm bigger, stronger, and dumber now." Burdette was right on the money. He again shut out the Yankees on just seven hits, becoming the first pitcher to toss two World Series shutouts since Christy Mathewson in 1907.

How did Burdette enjoy such mastery? "I exploit the greed of all hitters," he said. More cynical observers had another theory: the spitter. Although Burdette denied all charges, columnist Jim Murray once quipped that if he ever received a Cy Young Award, the trophy should take the form of a spittoon.

"They talk as if all you had to do to throw a spitter was to crank up and throw one," Burdette retorted. "Don't they know it's the hardest pitch to control? It takes a lot of practice and you just don't throw one when you figure it might get the hitter out. I'd love to use it, if I knew how. Burleigh Grimes told me five years ago not to monkey around with it, but to let them think I threw it. That's what I've done."

The Yankees got their revenge in the 1958 World Series when they beat 20-game winner Burdette in two out of three decisions. The next year he recorded his most famous individual victory, the 1–0, 13-inning win over Pittsburgh's Harvey Haddix after Haddix had hurled 12 perfect innings. On August 18, 1960, Burdette himself approached perfection as he no-hit the Phillies. He faced only 27 batters; after walking Tony Gonzalez in the fifth, he induced the next batter to hit into a double play.

Traded to the Cardinals in 1963, Burdette bounced around the last five years of his career. Upon leaving the game in 1967, he worked as a public relations specialist for an Athens, Georgia, cable television company.

Smoky Burgess

Burgess, Forrest Harrill **C**

1949, 1951–67 B:2/6/1927, Caroleen, NC D:9/15/1991, Asheville, NC Deb:4/19/1949, CHI NL BL/TR, 5'8", 187

G	AB	R	H	HR	RBI	OBP	SLG	AVG
1691	4471	485	1318	126	673	.364	.446	.295

Others may have exceeded his totals, but to many baseball experts the quintessential pinch hitter will always be Smoky Burgess. The rotund Burgess entered the record books when he erased Red Lucas' career pinch hit mark of 114 on the last day of the 1965 season. By the time he retired in 1967, Burgess had accumulated 145 pinch hits.

Burgess got his start in professional baseball in 1944 with the Class D PONY League's Lockport Cubs. He spent most of 1945 and all of 1946 in the military, but returned in 1947 to lead the Tri-State League in batting. He did the same during the following campaign for the Southern League and earned a promotion to the Chicago Cubs in 1949.

After two mediocre trials in the big leagues, Burgess was traded in October 1951 to the Cincinnati Reds, who turned right around and traded him to the Phillies. Burgess had three strong years in Philadelphia, hitting .296, .292, and then, in 1954, batting .368 and making the All-Star Game. Early in 1955, Burdette was dealt back to the Reds, and he responded with a .301 batting average and a career-high 21 homers, including three on July 29 that year.

Even playing most of the time as a regular, Burgess performed some notable pinch-hitting. In 1956 the Reds were closing in on the 1947 Giants' National League team record for most homers in a season. It was the last game of the season, and the Reds needed one homer to tie it. "Birdie Tebbetts sent me up to hit a home run or nuthin," Burgess recalled. "So the one time in 18 years I went up trying to hit one out, I did."

Burgess spent more time with Pittsburgh than he did with any other club. He came to Forbes Field with Harvey Haddix and Don Hoak for Frank Thomas and three other players in January 1959. Later that year it was Burgess who noticed that Hank Aaron had not touched second on Joe Adcock's homer, which had ruined Haddix's 12-inning perfect game. After Burgess motioned to the umpires, Aaron was called out, Adcock's home run became a single, and the score rolled back from 3–0 to 1–0. After being selected to the All-Star Game four times in six years in Pittsburgh, Burgess finished his career with the Chicago White Sox.

After his retirement, Burgess became a hitting instructor for the Atlanta Braves. He also managed in the Atlanta farm system and produced pennants three years in a row. When he once took time out to analyze his pinch-hitting prowess, Burgess stated: "It was a gift from God that I could swing as hard on the first pitch as on the second or third. But the other key was that I studied pitchers. I'd watch what they'd throw to guys who hit similar to me, and then when I went up to the plate I knew what to expect. Most players just watch the whole game and then go up looking for a certain pitch they want."

Tom Burgmeier

Burgmeier, Thomas Henry **P**

1968-84 B:8/2/1943, St. Paul, MN Deb:4/10/1968, CAL AL BL/TL 5'11, 185

W	L	PCT	G	SV	IP	BB	SO	ERA
79	55	.590	745	102	1258²	384	584	3.23

Lefthanded reliever Tom Burgmeier got outs when his team needed them, whether it was a crucial spot in the sixth inning or a save situation in the ninth. His 742 career relief appearances were among the top 10 in that category when he retired.

He was drafted by the expansion Kansas City Royals before his second major league season in 1969. Burgmeier had winning records in his first four seasons with the Royals. In 1971 he pitched in a career-high 67 games and posted nine wins, 17 saves, and a career-low 1.73 ERA. He spent four years with the Minnesota Twins, then joined the Red Sox as a free agent in 1978.

Burgmeier notched 24 saves and had a 2.00 ERA in 1980, earning a spot on the All-Star team. His success with the Red Sox continued even after he suffered a mild stroke during the winter of 1981. "I was in the hospital for about three days undergoing tests, and the next day I was out quail hunting," he said years later.

Burgmeier bounced back to go 7–0 with a 2.29 ERA in 1982, his last season with Boston. He was still effective in his final season at 41; he went 3–0 with a 2.35 ERA for Oakland in 1984.

Tim Burke

Burke, Timothy Philip **P**

1985–92 B:2/19/1959, Omaha, NE Deb:4/8/1985, MON NL BR/TR 6'3", 205

W	L	PCT	G	SV	IP	BB	SO	ERA
49	33	.598	498	102	699¹	219	444	2.72

Tim Burke was a tough sinkerball pitcher who had great stuff, but not tremendous endurance. After a number of years in the minors, he was finally called up to the majors in 1985 at age 25 to serve as a middle reliever for Montreal. New Expos manager Bob Rodgers had coached Burke in the minors and knew the righthander could provide consistent, high-quality work in a fine bullpen that featured closer Jeff Reardon. In Burke's rookie season he led NL pitchers with 78 appearances, all in relief. He gave up a low 2.39 ERA and finished 9–4 with eight saves.

In 1987 the Expos traded Reardon, and Burke became the team's bullpen ace. He left opponents practically hitless, posting an ERA of only 1.19, going 7–0, and recording 18 saves. Although Burke's numbers fell the next year, he was still one of the toughest relievers in the National League. He was selected to the All-Star Game in 1989, a season in which he went 9–3 with a career-high 28 saves.

In midseason 1991, after Rodgers was fired, Burke was traded to the Mets. The next year, his last in the majors, he was sent to the Yankees, where he ended the season 2–2.

Jesse Burkett

Burkett, Jesse Cail **OF**

1890–1905 B:2/4/1868, Wheeling, WV D:5/27/1953, Worcester, MA Deb:4/22/1890, NY NL BL/TL 5'8", 155

G	AB	R	H	HR	RBI	OBP	SLG	AVG
2066	8421	1720	2850	75	952	.415	.446	.338

Outfielder Jesse Burkett was something of a Dr. Jekyll and Mr. Hyde. With a bat in his hands, he was one of the greatest players of the 19th century. However, he was possibly the worst fielder ever enshrined in the Hall of Fame. And on the field, he earned the telling nickname "Crab."

Born in Wheeling, West Virginia, Burkett spent much of his childhood fishing and swimming in the Ohio River. In 1888 he became a professional ballplayer, and he won 27 games for the Central League's Scranton Miners as a lefthanded pitcher. In 1889 he joined Worcester of the Atlantic Association and posted an eye-popping 39–6 mark. He liked Worcester so much that he bought a house, married, and made the city his home for the rest of his life.

Indianapolis of the National League held Burkett's contract, but the club went bankrupt before Burkett ever appeared in uniform. In 1890 he was signed by the New York Giants, who were desperate due to the defection of many NL stars to the new Players' League. But the dilution of talent did not help Burkett. He flopped as a major league pitcher, going 3–10, with an ERA of 5.56. So the Giants tried him in the outfield, where he hit .309, although his fielding average was an atrocious .824.

Cleveland, then an NL member, bought Burkett's contract in 1891 and assigned him to the Western Association's Lincoln Rustlers, with instructions to teach him to field. By August he was hitting .349, and the Spiders decided they could live with his errors and brought him back to Cleveland. By 1893 Burkett's average had soared to .348, but he also set a career high with 46 errors, the worst in the league. To be sure, most outfielders made flocks of errors in those days. Even Hugh Duffy, considered the league's best outfielder, made 20 or more errors three times. Gloves were then ratty pieces of leather used more to protect the hand than to help catch the ball. Outfields were often strewn with rocks and other hazards, and baseballs were kept in play no matter how dirty or discolored they became. But Burkett, who led league outfielders in errors twice more in his career, was most certainly a poor fielder.

However, Burkett was paid to swing the bat. In 1895 he banged out 225 hits, and his .409 average led the league. The next year he topped even that, leading the NL with 240 hits, 160 runs, and a batting average of .410. Only 5 foot 8 inches and 155 pounds, Burkett batted leadoff for Cleveland and scored more than 100 runs in eight consecutive seasons.

Burkett ascribed his hitting to "that old con-fee-dence!" Yet his real secret was his remarkable bunting ability. He once claimed he could have bunted .400, and under the rules of 1890, he might have been right. A foul bunt with two strikes was just another foul ball, and Burkett was particularly adept at bunting pitches foul until he got a pitch he could place where he wanted.

Burkett's Cleveland team was a colorful outfit. Although they habitually finished behind the Boston Red Stockings and the Baltimore Orioles, they were second to none in ability to play hard-nosed baseball. They baited umpires, spiked opponents, beaned batters, circumvented rules, and fought with foes, fans, and even teammates. Historian Lee Allen describes team captain Patsy Tebeau as "the prototype of hooligans."

Although off the field Burkett was a perfect gentleman, neither drinking liquor or smoking, he played down to his teammates' level of sportsmanship. On one occasion he walked to the plate as a pinch hitter. The umpire asked whom he was batting for. "None of yer business," snarled Crab. On another occasion he so infuriated an umpire in Louisville that he was booted from each game of a doubleheader. After the second ejection, the police escorted him off the field. The next day a court fined Burkett $200 for inciting a riot.

In 1899 Cleveland owner Frank Robison, who also controlled the St. Louis franchise, shifted all his best Spiders to the Cardinals. That year he hit .396, just missing becoming one of only three men, along with Ty Cobb and Rogers Hornsby, to reach .400 three times. In 1901 he hit .376 and won his third NL batting championship, again leading the league in hits and runs.

In 1902 Burkett jumped to the American League's St. Louis Browns, and his batting average fell to .306. Burkett was getting older, but he also suffered from a new rule in the majors: with two strikes, a foul bunt was now a strikeout. Some called the change "the Burkett rule." He didn't reach .300 in any of his last three years before leaving the majors after the 1905 season. Returning to Worcester, he continued to play for the city's New England League team, which he owned and managed from 1906 through 1913.

Burkett then scouted and managed in the minors, returning to the major leagues as a coach for the New York Giants in 1921. Proving that time hadn't mellowed him, he annoyed the players with caustic ribbing so often that, when they won the World Series, the players didn't vote Burkett a share of the winnings. He then returned to the minor leagues, where he managed until 1933.

One day when Burkett was well over 70 years old, he watched the Red Sox take batting practice and noticed that most of the players were having trouble bunting. Burkett stripped off his jacket, stepped to the plate with a bat, asked the pitcher to throw as hard as he could, and laid the first pitch deftly down the third-base line. He dropped the next pitch down the first-base line. He then cracked the third pitch for a line drive over second base. Named to the Hall of Fame in 1946, he died in 1953.

John Burkett

Burkett, John David **P**

1987, 1990–* B: 11/28/1964, New Brighton, PA
Deb:9/15/1987, SF NL BR/TR 6'3", 215

W	L	PCT	G	SH	IP	BB	SO	ERA
119	101	.541	319	4	1940	482	1238	4.31

For a while it seemed as if John Burkett would never make it as a major league pitcher, and instead might have to fall back on another sport: bowling. A sixth-round pick by the San Francisco Giants in the 1983 draft, Burkett spent seven years in the minor leagues, including a 17–23 stretch as the number five starter in Triple A. Meanwhile, he honed his bowling game, racking up three perfect (300) games and a 225 average.

When San Francisco plugged him into the starting rotation in 1990, Burkett established himself as a workhorse and a consistent winner. He relied on superb control and a mix of pitches to succeed in the major leagues. His breakout year came in 1993, when he tied for the National League lead with 22 wins. In his only All-Star appearance, he took the loss for the NL in Baltimore. His record slipped to 6–8 in 1994, but he rebounded the next year to win 14 games for the Florida Marlins.

In 1996 the Rangers acquired him for the team's stretch run, and he responded by winning the franchise's first-ever postseason game. Injuries and shoulder fatigue began to limit his effectiveness, but he still managed to win nine games each season from 1997 to 1999.

Ken Burkhart

Burkhardt, Kenneth William **P**

1945–49 U(1957–73) B:11/18/1916, Knoxville, TN
Deb:4/21/1945, STL NL BR/TR 6'1", 190

W	L	PCT	G	SV	IP	BB	SO	ERA
27	20	.574	148	7	519^{2}	165	181	3.84

Kenny Burkhart, long known as one of the better umpires in the National League, was also once one of the most promising, although more unusual, rookie hurlers the St. Louis Cardinals ever unveiled. In the late 1940s he was known as "Frozen Shoulder" Burkhardt (later shortening his name to Burkhart). The nickname came from a malady that offered him not only his draft deferment, but also provided his unusual, shot-put-like delivery.

Burkhart first reached the majors in 1945, due to war-time attrition. That year he split his time between starting and relief, posting an 18–8 record with a 2.90 ERA. As other players began to return from the war in 1946, Burkhart's innings fell to less than half their previous total, and his record dropped to 6–3. That record reversed itself in 1947, and the next July he was sold to the Reds, from where he was soon out of the majors.

Burkhart returned to the National League as an umpire in 1957 and worked until his retirement in 1973 without taking a day off. The only baseball he missed in that span was two innings in Atlanta. "It was so hot that day you'd have thought you were at the equator," recalled fellow umpire Tom Gorman. "Burkhart was felled by heat prostration in the seventh inning of the opener and, with great reluctance, agreed to go into our dressing room. We finished the game without him. The Atlanta team doctor told him to go back to the hotel, but Burkie refused and came back for the second game. He was proud of his streak and didn't want to break it."

Burkhart umpired back-to-back no-hitters, thrown by San Francisco's Gaylord Perry on September 17, 1968, and by Ray Washburn of St. Louis the following day. His most controversial moment came in Game 1 of the 1970 World Series when he got entangled with Baltimore catcher Elrod Hendricks during a play at the plate. Burkhart called the Reds' Bernie Carbo out at home, but replays showed Hendricks had tagged Carbo with an empty mitt. The ball was actually in his throwing hand. Burkhart became NL supervisor of umpires after retiring as an active umpire.

Ellis Burks

Burks, Ellis Rena **OF**

1987–* B: 9/11/1964, Vicksburg, MS Deb:4/30/1987,
BOS AL BR/TR, 6'2", 205

G	AB	R	H	HR	RBI	OBP	SLG	AVG
1550	5651	971	1635	261	916	.362	.503	.289

One of baseball's best clutch hitters, Ellis Burks entered the 2000 season with a career average of .293 with runners in scoring position. The San Francisco Giants outfielder hit .378 in that category in 1999, good for third in the National League. Burks finished with his third 30-homer season even though he was held to 120 games by leg ailments.

Burks, a first-round draft choice by the Boston Red Sox in January 1983, hit 10 career grand slams in his first 13 years in the major leagues. He had 17 career multiple home run games. Burks homered twice in the fourth inning against the Chicago White Sox on August 27, 1990. He tied his personal peak by driving in seven runs on June 29, 1999, against his former team, the Colorado Rockies.

Burks had career bests with the 1996 Rockies when he hit .344 with 40 home runs, 211 hits, 128 RBIs, and 32 stolen bases. He finished third that year in the National League Most Valuable Player voting. Burks joined Hank Aaron as the only players with 40 homers, 200 hits, and 30 steals in the same season.

Rick Burleson

Burleson, Richard Paul **SS-2B**

1974–84, 1986–87 B:4/29/1951, Lynwood, CA
Deb:5/4/1974, BOS AL BR/TR 5'10", 165

G	AB	R	H	HR	RBI	OBP	SLG	AVG
1346	5139	656	1401	50	449	.331	.361	.273

Shortstop Rick "Rooster" Burleson was a hustling, scrappy ballplayer. "He's even-tempered," Joe Garagiola once said. "He comes to the park mad and stays that way." Burleson was a very good defensive shortstop, with a gun for an arm and better than decent range. His defensive talents were the major reason he was named to the All-Star Game four times in a five-year period. He also won a Gold Glove that season.

Burleson first made the majors with the Red Sox in 1974, the same year that Fred Lynn and Jim Rice were both brought up late in the season. He was never a huge contributor with the bat, although he did hit .291 and .293 in 1976 and 1977, respectively. That latter year, on June 17, he and Lynn—batting one-two in the order—tied a major league record by both homering to lead off a game. The victim was Catfish Hunter, and, before the frame was through, Carlton Fisk and George "Boomer" Scott added two more homers, tying another record for most homers in an inning by one team.

In 1979 Burleson won a Gold Glove, and the next season he was credited with 147 double plays, establishing a record for major league shortstops. But he was expendable despite his glove, and, on December 10, 1980, he and Butch Hobson were traded to California for third baseman Carney Lansford, outfielder Rick Miller, and pitcher Mark Clear.

Burleson again made the All-Star team while playing for the Angels in 1981. But in April 1982 he tore his rotator cuff, spending the rest of the year on the disabled list. The comeback process was long, painful, and never really complete. He then missed the 1985 season entirely, but he bounced back to win AL Comeback Player of the Year honors in 1986. Granted free agency at the end of the year, he finished out his career with Baltimore. In 1999 he managed the California League's Lake Elsinore Storm.

Johnny Burnett

Burnett, John Henderson **SS–3B**

1927–35 B:11/1/1904, Bartow, FL D:8/13/1959, Tampa, FL Deb:5/7/1927, CLE AL BL/TR, 5'11", 175

G	AB	R	H	HR	RBI	OBP	SLG	AVG
558	1835	288	521	9	213	.345	.366	.284

Cleveland shortstop Johnny Burnett holds the record for the most hits (nine) in a major league game, a feat he accomplished on July 10, 1932, in an 18-inning game against the Philadelphia Athletics. In 11 at bats he hit two doubles and seven singles, breaking the previous record of six hits. Burnett had two hits the previous day, so his two-game total of 11 hits also set an AL record. (Chicago's Cal McVey set the major league mark of 12 on July 22 and 25, 1876.)

Burnett signed with the Indians shortly after he graduated from the University of Florida in 1927, and he played briefly at Terre Haute and New Orleans before joining the major league club. After three years as a little-used reserve, he hit .312 as a utility infielder in 1930. The next year, splitting his time between shortstop, second, and third, he hit an even .300, including his first major league home run.

Burnett was the Indians' regular shortstop in 1932 before dropping back to his utility role the next season. Traded to the Browns in November 1934, he played for only one season with his new team before retiring from baseball.

Jeromy Burnitz

Burnitz, Jeromy Neal **OF–DH**

1993–* B:4/15/1969, Westminster, CA Deb:6/21/1993, NY NL BL/TR 6', 190

G	AB	R	H	HR	RBI	OBP	SLG	AVG
678	2183	381	580	123	406	.370	.508	.266

Cleveland general manager John Hart helped resurrect the Cleveland Indians through long-term contracts to young players and astute deals. One deal Hart wished he wished he had never made was a 1996 swap of Jeromy Burnitz to Milwaukee for Kevin Seitzer. After years of benchings and demotions in Cleveland and New York, Burnitz became one of the National League's great sluggers in Milwaukee.

A first-round pick of the Mets in 1990, Burnitz bounced between New York and Triple A in 1993 and 1994; he did the same with Cleveland in 1995. Finally, the Brewers—admiring his long-ball potential and fence-crashing intensity on defense—rescued him on August 31, 1996.

In 1997 he became the first Brewer to hit 20 homers and steal 20 bases since 1980. He earned a reputation as a great fastball hitter who went for the downs. In August he homered in five straight games—two as a pinch hitter. In 1998, the year the Brewers switched leagues, Burnitz belted 38 home runs, more than any other lefty hitter in the National League—of course righthanded sluggers Mark McGwire and Sammy Sosa each surpassed 65. Burnitz's 125 RBIs were the second most in Brewers history. Despite missing a month in 1999 with a broken hand, Burnitz left the yard 33 times. He played in his first All-Star Game, and even outlasted Sosa and McGwire in the televised home run hitting contest.

George Burns

Burns, George Joseph **OF**

1911–25 B:11/24/1889, Utica, NY D:8/15/1966, Gloversville, NY Deb:10/3/1911, NY NL BR/TR 5'7", 160

G	AB	R	H	HR	RBI	OBP	SLG	AVG
1853	7241	1188	2077	41	611	.366	.384	.287

George Burns was one of the best leadoff men of his day. His job was to score runs, and from 1911 through 1925 the quiet, modest outfielder "set the table" as well as anyone. Five times in his nine complete seasons with the New York Giants he led the National League in runs, and he helped his solid .287

career batting average enormously by also leading the league in walks five times and in stolen bases twice.

Burns first reached the major leagues in 1911. After a few false starts he became a regular in 1913, helping the Giants to the pennant. The next year he had perhaps his best season, batting .303 while leading the league with 62 stolen bases and 100 runs.

An outstanding fielder, Burns was particularly adept at playing the odd caroms off the wall. To shade his eyes from the notorious sun in left field he wore a cap with an unusually long bill, and he was one of the first players to wear sunglasses onfield. He became so popular with Giants fans that the left field stands at the Polo Grounds were called "Burnsville" in his honor. A righthanded batter with limited power, he was still able on occasion to pull an inside pitch down the Polo Grounds' short left field foul line into those stands.

After he was traded with Mike Gonzalez and $150,000 to Cincinnati for infielder Heinie Groh in 1922, Giants fans gave him a day during the Reds' first trip to New York and presented him with a diamond-studded watch. Burns finished his career with the Philadelphia Phillies in 1925.

Tioga George Burns

Burns, George Henry **1B–OF**

1914–29 B:1/31/1893, Niles, OH D:1/7/1978, Kirkland, WA Deb:4/14/1914, DET AL BR/TR, 6'1½", 180

G	AB	R	H	HR	RBI	OBP	SLG	AVG
1866	6573	901	2018	72	951	.354	.429	.307

First baseman "Tioga George" Burns had a career marked by more ups and downs than the route of a San Francisco cable car. He hit as high as .361 and as low as .224, and scattered his yearly average nearly everywhere in between.

Burns got his start in 1913 with the Class D Central Association's Burlington Pathfinders. He graduated to the Class A Western League later that year, and in 1914 he made the jump to Detroit. In his rookie year with the Tigers, Burns hit .291 and garnered a lot of attention for his glove work. As a fielder, he was good news and bad news: that year Burns led the American League in putouts with 1,576, but he also led the league with 30 errors.

Burns had a down year in 1917, when he batted just .226, and the Tigers shipped him to New York, from where he was traded to Connie Mack's A's for outfielder Ping Bodie. In his first year with Philadelphia, Burns had his best performance yet; in a season shortened by World War I and threatened by the possible shutdown of professional baseball, Burns hit .352 while leading the league with 178 hits and producing 70 RBIs.

In May 1920 Mack sold the again slumping Burns to the Indians. Despite batting only .268, he helped the team win its first pennant. Then in the World Series he hit .300 and, in Game 6, drove in the only run of a 1–0 victory with a sixth-inning double.

Perhaps his most important contribution to that club was his influence on rookie Joe Sewell. The young shortstop came to Cleveland in August to replace Ray Chapman, who had been killed by a pitched ball. As Sewell prepared for his first game, Burns reached into his locker and handed the rookie one of his own 44-ounce black bats. "Here, take this," he said. "It's a good bat. Make sure you take care of it." And Sewell did take care of it. He named the bat "Black Betsy," and it lasted him throughout a career that saw him become known as the hardest batter to fan in the game's history.

Burns hit .361 in part-time action for the Indians in 1921, but he was traded in 1922 with outfielders Elmer Smith and Joe Harris to the Red Sox for first baseman Stuffy McInnis. Boston was a rotten team, but Burns was given a chance to play full time, and he responded with a career-high 12 home runs and 70 RBIs. The next year he hit .328, drove in 82 runs, and got revenge on Cleveland for trading him. Playing first base on September 14, 1923, he snagged the Indians' Frank Brower's line drive, tagged Rube Lutzke off first, and ran to second base to nail Riggs Stephenson for an unassisted triple play.

The Indians reacquired Burns in January 1924, and it was with them in 1926 that Burns set a major league record with 64 doubles. He also hit .358, led the league with 216 hits, drove in 114 runs, and captured the MVP Award that year.

Only two years later, Cleveland released Burns, whose average had dropped to .249. Picked up by the Yankees, he was cut the next season and signed by the A's, with whom he finished his major league career.

From 1932 to 1934 Burns was a player-manager for the Pacific Coast League's Seattle Indians, leading that league with 140 RBIs in 1932. He also managed the Portland Beavers from the bench in 1935.

Oyster Burns

Burns, Thomas P. **OF–SS–P**

1884–95 U(1899) B:9/6/1864, Philadelphia, PA D:11/11/1928, Brooklyn, NY Deb:8/18/1884, WIL UA BR/TR, 5'8", 183

G	AB	R	H	HR	RBI	OBP	SLG	AVG
1187	4637	869	1389	65	832	.368	.446	.300

A versatile player who pitched and played both the infield and outfield early in his career, "Oyster" Burns was named captain of the 1887 Baltimore Orioles in recognition of his boisterous leadership style and offensive accomplishments. With a .519 slugging average (built on 33 doubles and a league-leading 19 triples) and a .341 batting average in 1887, he was one of the league's most feared power hitters in the Dead Ball Era.

For unknown reasons Burns was replaced as Orioles captain in early 1888 and then sold to Brooklyn in August, where he became a full-time outfielder and stayed for more than six years. In 1889 he knocked in the winning runs in two early World Series games and led his team in the series with 11 RBIs. When Brooklyn jumped from the American Association to the National League in 1890, Burns led his new league with 13 homers and 128 RBIs.

Burns ended his major league career in 1895 with the Giants. He then returned to the minors and hit .378 for the Atlantic League's Newark Colts and .324 for the Hartford Bluebirds in his two final seasons as a player. He later umpired briefly in the National League.

Burns' nickname, purportedly given him because of his love of eating oysters, seems to be a relatively recent invention. Writer Ralph Horton pointed out that Burns was called "Tom" or "Tommy" for most of his career, and even his 1928 obituary made no mention of the nickname.

Tom Burns

Burns, Thomas Everett **3B-SS**

1880–92 M(1892, 1898–99, 187–170) U(1892) B:3/30/1857, Honesdale, PA D:3/19/1902, Jersey City, NJ Deb:5/1/1880, CHI NL BR/TR 5'7", 152

G	AB	R	H	HR	RBI	OBP	SLG	AVG
1251	4920	722	1299	39	683	.303	.364	.264

Third baseman Tom Burns made his mark when he hit two doubles and a homer in the seventh inning of a September 6, 1883, game against Detroit—a game in which the White Stockings scored 18 times that inning and won, 26–6. In the three-game series, Chicago outscored Detroit 53–8.

The clean-living Burns started as a professional with independent clubs at Providence in 1876 and Auburn in 1877. In 1878 he played third base for Hornellsville and Albany of the International Association. In 1879 he was signed by the National League White Stockings, for whom he initially played shortstop and second base. Burns ultimately became a fine defensive third baseman.

Burns had a generally unremarkable career. However, in June 1886, he committed a "bonehead" play that presaged Fred Merkle's similar blunder in 1908. When the go-ahead run was driven in during the top of the ninth, Burns thought it was bottom of the inning and ran off the field. New York's Roger Connor called for the ball and forced Burns at second, ultimately costing Chicago a win.

Burns managed Pittsburgh for two stints in 1892, and also briefly as an NL umpire. He piloted Springfield in the Eastern League from 1893 to 1895. Burns returned to the NL with Chicago in 1898 and 1899 (replacing Cap Anson). He went back to Springfield in 1900, and moved on to Buffalo in the Eastern League the following year. Scheduled to manage the Jersey City Skeeters in 1902, he died of a heart attack while visiting Eastern League president Patrick Powers.

Ray Burris

Burris, Bertram Ray **P**

1973-87 B:8/22/1950, Idabel, OK Deb:4/8/1973, CHI NL BR/TR 6'5", 200

W	L	PCT	G	SH	IP	BB	SO	ERA
108	134	.446	480	10	2188[1]	764	1065	4.17

Though almost always on lousy teams during his 15-year career, Ray Burris pitched with guts and intelligence. In his only Championship Series, he yielded just one run in 17 innings.

Burris emerged as the ace of the lowly Chicago Cubs in the mid-1970s, winning 44 games from 1975 to 1977. He complemented his heater with a slider and changeup, and he threw three-quarters, over-the-top, and sidearm to befuddle hitters. In his better years, he saved his best pitches for the toughest situations.

After rocky seasons with the Cubs, Yankees, and Mets, Burris found new life in Montreal. He stepped it up in the 1981 NLCS, shutting out the Dodgers in Game 2. In the decisive Game 5, he kept the score 1–1 through eight innings before L.A.'s Rick Monday homered in the ninth against Steve Rogers in relief.

Burris kept himself in great shape in his later years, reportedly doing 500 sit-ups a day. To keep his arm loose, he pitched in long sleeves—even in the hottest weather. "Your arm is like a woman," he said. "Be good to it and it will be good to you."

Burris enjoyed one more fine season, going 13–10 with Oakland in 1984. His 3.15 ERA that year was the second-lowest of his career. He played out the string with two stints in Milwaukee sandwiched between one season in St. Louis in 1986. He later served as a coach in Milwaukee and Texas.

Jeff Burroughs

Burroughs, Jeffrey Alan **OF–DH**
1970–85 B:3/7/1951, Long Beach, CA Deb:7/20/1970, WAS AL BR/TR 6'1", 200

G	AB	R	H	HR	RBI	OBP	SLG	AVG
1689	5536	720	1443	240	882	.359	.439	.261

Jeff Burroughs was the first overall choice in the June 1969 amateur draft, and Bob Short's Washington Senators tendered him a reported $88,000 bonus. Even Ted Williams, the Senators' manager, was impressed with Burroughs' swing, describing it as "classic." Basically a fastball hitter, Burroughs tended to be especially effective in parks with short power alleys, such as in Seattle and Minnesota, as well as in classic fields such as Fenway Park and Tiger Stadium.

Burroughs made it to the big leagues in 1970, but he didn't become a regular until after the Senators moved to Texas in 1972. That change seemed to agree with Burroughs, who the next year had his breakthrough season with 30 homers and 85 RBIs. The 1974 season was Burroughs' best, however. He batted .301 and hit 25 homers and a league-leading 118 RBIs for Billy Martin's second-place Rangers. He was selected to the All-Star Game and was named AL Most Valuable Player.

Burroughs seemed to respond to Martin's leadership. "He hates to lose and when he does, he lets you know about it," said Burroughs. "He really gets upset when you do stupid things. After a game you lose, he's angry, and you figure if he's going to act like that, let's bust our butts a little more and win. It's all psychological and it's the believability of the manager. Some managers don't mean it. Billy does."

But Martin was fired in midseason 1975 and after the next season the Rangers traded Burroughs to the Braves for five players and an estimated $250,000. In his first season in Atlanta, Burroughs responded with 41 homers and 114 RBIs. The next year Burroughs turned out to be more of a "get-on-base" player, as he not only batted .301 but drew a National League high 117 walks, giving him a league-leading .436 on-base percentage. Strangely, his power continued to evaporate, as Burroughs never again hit more than 16 home runs.

With one year left on his contract, the Braves let Burroughs go to the Mariners in March 1981 for pitcher Carlos Diaz. He followed his year in Seattle with three in Oakland, and eventually finished his career with Toronto in 1985.

In retirement, Burroughs concentrated on helping his son Sean play baseball. With Burroughs as coach, the All-Star team from Long Beach, California, went to consecutive Little League World Series. Sean was selected by the Padres in 1998, making the Burroughs the second father-and-son team to be picked in the first round of the amateur draft (Ben and Tom Grieve were the first).

Jim Busby

Busby, James Franklin **OF**
1950–62 B:1/8/1927, Kenedy, TX D:7/8/1996, Augusta, GA Deb:4/23/1950, CHI AL BR/TR 6'1", 175

G	AB	R	H	HR	RBI	OBP	SLG	AVG
1352	4250	541	1113	48	438	.316	.350	.262

Outfielder Jim Busby distinguished himself in the 1950s as a slick-fielding speed merchant. He led all AL outfielders in putouts for three straight years and once in fielding percentage in the pre-Gold Glove era.

A quarterback on Texas Christian University's 1945 Cotton Bowl team, Busby played baseball at Muskegon (Central League), Waterloo (3-I League), and Sacramento (Pacific Coast League) before reaching the majors with the Chicago White Sox late in 1950. The next year, in his first full season, he was selected for the All-Star Game in a season in which he hit .283, drove in 68 runs, and stole 26 bases. The next year, despite his obvious skills, Busby—a cousin of future Kansas City Royals 20-game winner Steve Busby—was traded to the Washington Senators.

Busby had his most productive years in Washington. In 1953 he batted .312 and drove in 82 runs. The next year he hit .298 and had 80 RBIs. Nevertheless, early in the 1955 season he was traded back to the White Sox. Busby became a regular for the Cleveland Indians in 1956 and, although he hit only .235 for the year, he had his biggest pair of games there. On July 5 and 6, 1956, he followed in the footsteps of Babe Ruth, Bill Dickey, and Jimmie Foxx to become only the fourth American Leaguer to hit grand slams in consecutive games. Despite this awesome display, he was trundled off to Baltimore in 1957 and Boston in 1959, and he ended his career as an original Houston Colt .45s. Busby later coached under his old skipper Paul Richards with the Orioles, Colt .45s, Braves, and White Sox.

Steve Busby

Busby, Steven Lee **P**
1972–76, 1978–80 B:9/29/1949, Burbank, CA Deb:9/8/1972, KC AL BR/TR 6'2", 205

W	L	PCT	G	SH	IP	BB	SO	ERA
70	54	.565	167	7	1060^2	433	659	3.72

In 1972 Steve Busby pitched under "Trader Jack" McKeon at Omaha of the American Association and flirted with no-hitters several times. When Busby groused about his ill fortune, McKeon said prophetically, "Quit worrying. You'll pitch a couple of no-hitters, and they'll be in the big leagues." McKeon was exactly right, and Busby became one of only 25 major league hurlers to pitch two no-hitters.

Busby was a hard luck, often-injured pitcher who might have achieved even more, given the opportunity. By the time he graduated from high school in 1967, he had begun alternating between solid pitching and serious injuries. He was close to signing with San Francisco when his knee gave out; the Giants cut their offer in half. Busby elected instead to accept a scholarship to the University of Southern California. He suffered an injury there as well, missing a season following surgery to fix an ulnar nerve.

Busby recovered and pitched USC to a victory over Southern Illinois in the national championship game at the College World Series in 1971. He signed soon afterwards with Kansas City. Busby got off to a hot start with San Jose of the California League; he pitched a two-hit shutout in his second professional start and posted an 0.68 ERA in his first eight games.

Reaching the majors late in the 1972 season, Busby went 3–1 with the Royals. The next three years he was in the regular rotation for Kansas City. The tall righthander made major league history by posting no-hitters in each of his first two full seasons with the Royals. The first came against the Detroit Tigers on April 27, 1973. In Busby's next start he flirted with matching Johnny Vander Meer's double no-hit feat; however, after five hitless innings against Milwaukee, Busby threw a gopher ball to Dave May.

The next season was Busby's best, and he earned All-Star Game selection for his performance, which included 22 victories. He threw his second no-hitter on June 19, 1974, his wedding anniversary. Pitted against Milwaukee's Clyde Wright, Busby won, 2–0, striking out three and yielding only a second-inning walk to George Scott. Teammate Paul Splittorff, who had pitched a two-hit shutout the night before, said, "I figured Buzz would try to outdo me, so he could heckle me, rub it in." In Busby's next start, against Chicago, he went 5 1/3 innings before giving up a hit. This allowed him to set an AL record by retiring 33 consecutive batters, besting the old mark set by Vic Raschi and equaled by Lindy McDaniel.

Busby again was named to the All-Star Game in 1975, when he went 18–12. However, he began to show signs of wear and tear. He suffered serious knee and rotator cuff injuries and, despite efforts to regain his old effectiveness, was no more than a part-time, .500 pitcher in the next four years. He retired after the 1980 season.

Donie Bush

Bush, Owen Joseph **SS**

1908–23 M(1923, 1927–31, 1933, 497–539)
B:10/8/1887, Indianapolis, IN D:3/28/1972, Indianapolis, IN Deb: 9/18/08, DET AL BB/TR 5'6" 140

G	AB	R	H	HR	RBI	OBP	SLG	AVG
1946	7210	1280	1804	9	436	.356	.300	.250

Donie Bush spent 65 years in organized baseball as a player, manager, scout, and owner. He had just a sixth-grade education, but he was brilliant by baseball standards.

He used his keen knowledge of the strike zone to lead the American League in walks in five of his first six full professional seasons. With Hall of Famers Ty Cobb and Sam Crawford—and later Harry Heilmann—batting behind him, Bush scored 90 or more runs in eight of his first nine full seasons. Bush led the AL with 112 runs in 1917. A skillful basestealer, he finished his career with 404 stolen bases.

Although he had an excellent career as a player, Bush is probably best remembered as a manager. He took over the Washington Senators as a player-manager in 1923; the Senators finished with 75 wins and 78 losses, and he was not retained. Bush received another chance to manage in 1927. He led the Pittsburgh Pirates to the World Series in his first season with the club, but the New York Yankees and their "Murderers Row" swept the Pirates. The disciplinarian Bush benched star outfielder Kiki Cuyler for the entire Series because of a previous altercation. Cuyler was traded to the Chicago Cubs following the sweep.

The Pirates finished the 1928 season in fourth place. Bush was fired 119 games into the next season. He took over the lowly Chicago White Sox in 1930, but two consecutive finishes in the second division led to another firing. He guided the Cincinnati Reds to last place in 1933; it was his final major league managerial post.

Bush continued to manage in Triple A. He became part owner of the Indianapolis Indians and later, the Minneapolis Millers. The lifelong bachelor remained close to the game by scouting for the Boston Red Sox in his later years. He was working with the White Sox when he died at age 84.

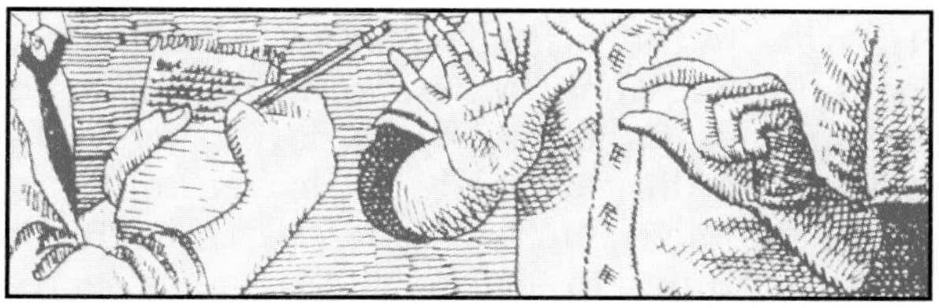

Guy Bush

Bush, Guy Terrell **P**

1923–38, 1945 B:8/23/1901, Aberdeen, MS D:7/2/1985, Shannon, MS Deb:9/17/1923, CHI NL BR/TR 6', 175

W	L	PCT	G	SV	IP	BB	SO	ERA
176	136	.564	542	34	2722	859	850	3.86

Guy Bush, who began his major league career in 1923, is remembered among baseball trivia buffs as the pitcher who gave up Babe Ruth's final two home runs. On May 25, 1935, Ruth, now a Boston Brave, had already homered off Pittsburgh starter Red Lucas. Bush came in to relieve Lucas, and the Babe smacked career homers 713 and 714, the final shot being the first ball ever hit over the right-field roof at Forbes Field. Ruth retired a few days later, and Bush's dubious place in history was secure.

Bush had already made a mark in baseball as both a starter and a reliever for the Cubs. Although a key member of the starting rotation for Chicago, Bush had never held that position exclusively. All told, he started 308 games and relieved in 234. "The Mississippi Mudcat" explained that his unique ability was that he "could warm up on about 10 pitches and do a good job."

Bush had first joined reached the major leagues in 1923, and his role grew in each of the next couple of years. Facing Boston on May 14, 1927, Bush pitched an 18-inning complete-game victory. Only one NL pitcher has had a longer stint since: three days after Bush's feat, Bob Smith of the Braves went 22 innings against the Cubs.

He reached real stardom in 1929, when he led the NL with 50 appearances and eight saves. Then, in the 1929 World Series against the Philadelphia Athletics, Bush was the only Chicago hurler to post a win, beating George Earnshaw, 3–1, in Game 3. His regular-season record of 18–7 that year was the second of a seven-year period in which he never won fewer than 15 games, twice reaching 18, once 19, and, in 1933, 20.

One version of Babe Ruth's famous "called shot" home run in Game 3 of the 1932 World Series claims that Ruth's gestures and shouts were directed at Bush, who was razzing the Bambino from the bench. When Ruth came to bat the next day against Bush, a pitch hit him.

Bush's success was partly psychological. He went to Cubs trainer Andy Lotshaw once, complaining about a twinge in his arm, and Lotshaw obligingly rubbed a dark "secret liniment" on the sore limb; Bush went out and won his next start. From then on, Bush would indulge in a little of Lotshaw's secret cure before every appearance. Only after Bush was traded to Pittsburgh did Lotshaw reveal that he'd been out of liniment on that day long before. Believing the ache was more in Bush's head than in his arm, Lotshaw had substituted another dark liquid: Coca-Cola.

Bush split his final four years between the Pirates, Braves, and Cardinals. His career seemingly ended for good after the 1938 season, but seven years later he came back, at age 44, to pitch four more innings for the Cincinnati Reds.

Joe Bush

Bush, Leslie Ambrose **P**

1912–28 B:11/27/1892, Brainerd, MN D:11/1/1974, Ft. Lauderdale, FL Deb:9/30/1912, PHI AL BR/TR 5'9", 173

W	L	PCT	G	SH	IP	BB	SO	ERA
196	184	.516	489	35	3087[1]	1263	1319	3.51

"Bullet Joe" Bush was a key member of five pennant-winning clubs in three American League cities—Philadelphia, Boston, and New York. A workhorse for all three teams, Bush pitched 200 or more innings 11 times.

After service in the minors, Bush got a break with Connie Mack's Philadelphia Athletics when Jack Coombs became ill. Mack inserted the 20-year-old Bush into the rotation in 1913, and he not only went 15–6 for the season but also posted a five-hit World Series win that fall. As the penny-pinching Mack sold off his champions one by one, Bush's record suffered. On August 26, 1916, he no-hit Cleveland, 5–0.

Eventually Bush also departed, going to the Red Sox in December 1917. There he played for another pennant winner in 1918 before being traded to the Yankees in December 1921. Bush had his finest season in 1922, going 26–7 to lead the league in winning percentage (.788). An excellent hitter, Bush batted .326 that year to become the third AL pitcher to win 20 games and hit .300 in the same year, as had Babe Ruth in 1917 and Carl Mays in 1921.

Bush won 19 games in 1923, dropped to 17 the next year, and then was traded to the St. Louis Browns. After that he hopscotched to the Senators, Pirates, and Giants before ending his career back with the A's in 1928.

The flame-throwing righthander received his nickname for two reasons. First, while playing in Billings, Montana, he was tagged "Joe Bush" after a "bewhiskered character" who hung around the ballclub's office. The "Bullet" part came after he killed a chicken with a stone in Missoula and was fined $25. The local newspaper headlined the event, "Joe Bush Throws Bullets at Sage Hen."

Brett Butler

Butler, Brett Morgan **OF**
1981–97 B: 6/15/1957, Los Angeles, CA
Deb:8/20/1981, ATL NL BL/TL 5'10", 160

G	AB	R	H	HR	RBI	OBP	SLG	AVG
2213	8180	1359	2375	54	578	.379	.376	.290

On May 3, 1996, Brett Butler planned to have his tonsils removed, but instead a lump the size of a plum was discovered in his throat. It was malignant and required two sets of operations to remove. Over the next two months Butler endured radiation treatments, could barely talk, and subsisted on a liquid diet. He was in constant pain, yet he was determined to play baseball again—in 1996.

The 39-year-old center fielder, whose mother had died of cancer just one year earlier, took the field for the first time in four months on September 6. Butler went 1-for-3 and scored the winning run in a 2–1 win over the Pirates at Dodger Stadium. Just four days later Butler's left hand was broken attempting to bunt. He returned for a final season in 1997, retiring with 558 career stolen bases.

Born in Los Angeles and raised in the San Francisco Bay area until age 12, Butler played football, baseball, ran cross-country, and wrestled at Libertyville High School in Illinois. He won All-America honors twice as an outfielder at Southeastern Oklahoma State. The slightly-built Butler lasted until the 23rd round of the 1979 draft.

Butler won International League MVP honors at Richmond in 1981; he opened the following season as the leadoff hitter for the Atlanta Braves. Despite Atlanta's 13–0 start, Butler was rarely on base and was sent back to Richmond. Dale Murphy took over in center field and the Braves captured the National League West title. After a .363 season in Richmond, Butler returned to Atlanta. He appeared in two games off the bench in a three-game sweep by St. Louis in the Championship Series.

Murphy, the 1982 MVP, was shifted to right field to make room for Butler in center. In 1983 Butler led the NL with 13 triples and added 39 stolen bases—and was caught stealing 23 times. After the season the Braves sent Butler and Brook Jacoby to Cleveland to complete the ill-fated deal for Len Barker.

Butler stole a career-high 52 bases in 74 tries in 1984, batted .311, and scored 108 runs, the first of six 100-run seasons in eight years. He led American League outfielders with a .998 fielding percentage in 1985; he later topped that with an errorless 161-game season for the San Francisco Giants in 1991. Butler paced the AL with 14 triples in 1986, becoming the second player to lead each league in three-baggers—Hall of Famer Sam Crawford was the first.

Butler led the NL with 109 runs in 1988, and helped the Giants win the pennant the following year. He had the Giants' only two stolen bases in the World Series and reached base six times in 16 trips to the plate in Oakland's earthquake-interrupted sweep. In 1990 Butler led the NL with 192 hits.

Butler fulfilled a boyhood dream by signing with the Dodgers as a free agent following the 1990 season. The following season he topped the NL with 161 games played, 112 runs, and 108 walks. He was named to his only All-Star team that season.

He was a free agent when the strike ended the 1994 season, and, after the Dodgers showed little interest, he signed with the Mets. The Dodgers traded for him during the stretch-run in 1995. Butler, a players' union spokesman during the strike, was briefly the target for boos by Dodgers fans when he made harsh comments about teammate Mike Busch, a former replacement player. Butler gained the fans' applause back with his play on the field, and won their hearts with his courageous comeback from cancer.

Pee Wee Butts

Butts, Thomas **SS**
Negro League Player 1938–50 B:1919, Sparta, GA
D:1973, Atlanta, GA BR/TR 5'7", 145

Shortstop "Pee Wee" Butts was widely regarded as one of the best Negro Leaguers at that position and is often credited with aiding the career of his keystone partner Junior Gilliam. Butts posted an estimated lifetime batting average of .316, and in 1940 he led the Negro National League with a .391 mark.

"Gilliam went to the majors," recalled Kansas City Monarch Hilton Smith, "but he didn't look anything like the ballplayer that Pee Wee Butts was."

Born in Atlanta in 1919, Butts never carried more than 145 pounds on his 5-foot-7-inch frame. He quit high school to join the Atlanta Black Crackers in 1936 and started with the Baltimore Elite Giants in 1938, rooming with catcher Roy Campanella. In his first game with the club he fired three wild throws into the stands.

Butts, who also played with Monterrey of the Mexican League and in Puerto Rico, performed in six East–West Games. After leaving the Negro Leagues he played in Canada and also for Lincoln of the Western League.

Enos Cabell

Cabell, Enos Milton — 3B-1B-OF

1972–86 B:10/8/1949, Fort Riley, KN Deb:9/17/1972, BAL AL BR/TR 6'5", 185

G	AB	R	H	HR	RBI	OPB	SLG	AVG
1688	5952	753	1647	60	596	.309	.370	.277

Enos Cabell was ready to be either the Orioles' first baseman or third baseman of the 1970s. The trouble was, he had two enormous roadblocks in front of him, namely Boog Powell and Brooks Robinson. So after three underused seasons in Baltimore, in which he barely totaled 200 at bats, Cabell was dealt to the Astros after the 1974 season.

Installed as Houston's third baseman, he began a successful run as a consistent National League performer. Although the angular Cabell was known as a bad-ball hitter, he kept his batting average in the .270-or-better range.

He stole 30 or more bases every year from 1976 through 1979, and it was during this span that he enjoyed his finest overall season. In 1977 he hit .282 with 16 home runs, 68 RBIs, and 42 stolen bases. In 1980 the Astros, and Cabell, made the postseason for the firtst time. He started all five games in Houston's Championship Series loss to Philadelphia.

He went on to play for the Giants, Tigers, and Dodgers, but eventually returned to the Astros for a second tour of duty, this time as a first baseman. Cabell became part of the first trio of Astros to hit three consecutive home runs in one game on June 24, 1984. Cabell, Phil Garner and Jose Cruz all went deep in succession—the only National Leaguers to accomplish the feat that season.

Francisco Cabrera

Cabrera, Francisco (Paulino) — 1B-C

1989–93 B:10/10/1966, Santo Domingo, Dominican Republic Deb:7/24/1989, TOR AL BR/TR, 6'4", 193

G	AB	R	H	HR	RBI	OBP	SLG	AVG
196	351	32	89	17	62	.296	.453	.254

Although he had only a fleeting taste of fame during his short career, Francisco Cabrera will always be a legendary figure in Atlanta sports history. Never more than a backup player, he spent most of the 1992 season at Triple A Richmond but landed a spot on Atlanta's postseason roster because of his ability to catch, play first base, and pinch hit.

In the ninth inning of Game 7 of the National League Championship Series against Pittsburgh, Cabrera delivered a two-out, two-run, pinch-hit single against reliever Stan Belinda. Sid Bream, one of the league's slowest runners, barely beat the throw from left fielder Barry Bonds, giving the Braves a 3–2 win and the NL pennant.

Despite his heroics, Cabrera never escaped his journeyman tag. In five seasons he had only 351 at bats in 196 games. Cabrera's last appearance as a major leaguer came just one year after his greatest moment. It occurred in the postseason, and not surprisingly, he came through with two hits in three at bats in the NLCS.

Leon Cadore

Cadore, Leon Joseph — P

1915–1924 B:11/20/1890, Chicago, IL D:3/16/1958, Spokane, WA Deb:4/28/1915, BRO NL BR/TR 6'1", 190

W	L	PCT	G	SH	IP	BB	SO	ERA
68	72	.486	192	10	1257^{1}	289	445	3.14

Brooklyn righthander Leon Cadore holds the honor of pitching in the longest major league game (by innings) ever played. Facing the Braves' Joe Oeschger on May 1, 1920, both pitchers went the distance in the 26-inning contest that was called on account of darkness. Oeschger allowed one run in the fourth, Cadore one in the fifth. The curveballing Cadore struck out seven, walked five, and surrendered 15 hits. Oeschger allowed just nine hits and four walks. Interestingly, the two pitchers had also squared off in an 11-inning duel in April 1920, which Cadore won, 1–0.

On May 2, the day after the 26-inning marathon, the Dodgers played 13 innings, with starter Burleigh Grimes going all the way to a victory. And the day after that they struggled through 19 innings against the Braves before losing; their starting pitcher, Sherry Smith, went the distance just as Grimes and Cadore had done.

Despite Cadore's career-high 15 wins during the 1920 season, Brooklyn manager Wilbert Robinson dropped him to fourth in the rotation for the World Series against Cleveland. After appearing in relief in Game 1, he started Game 4, surrendered two earned runs in the first inning and was removed. He was charged with the loss.

The Robins waived Cadore to the White Sox on July 6, 1923. He retired after an uneventful season with the Yankees in 1924.

Mike Caldwell

Caldwell, Ralph Michael **P**

1971–1984 B:1/22/1949, Tarboro, NC Deb:9/4/1971, SD NL BR/TL 6', 185

W	L	PCT	G	SH	IP	BB	SO	ERA
137	130	.513	475	23	2408²	597	939	3.81

Mike Caldwell, known as "Iron Mike" and "Mr. Warmth," had the reputation of being a "clubhouse lawyer." Caldwell employed a three-quarter sidearm delivery, dropping at times to nearly a straight sidearm. His most effective pitch was a sinker, although he was dogged by speculation he threw a spitter. Not surprisingly this tough-minded hurler was never afraid to move a batter off the plate.

Selected by the Padres in the 11th round of the June 1971 amateur draft, Caldwell made brief stops at Tri-City and Lodi, both Class A, before reaching San Diego. Mediocre for the Padres in 1972 and 1973, he was traded to the Giants in October 1973 for Willie McCovey and outfielder Bernie Williams. With San Francisco he hit his stride, going 14–5 with a 2.95 ERA in 1974. But after off-season elbow surgery he spent several years trying to recover his former effectiveness.

He arrived in Milwaukee in midseason 1977 and was unspectacular as a starter and reliever. George Bamberger, who had been instrumental in Baltimore's success as pitching coach, was hired as manager for the 1978 season. Caldwell became his prize pupil. His 22–9 performance in 1978 and league-leading 23 complete games helped earn Caldwell American League Comeback Player of the Year. The next year his 16–6 mark gave him the league's best won-lost percentage. In 1982 he won 17 games and helped propel the Brewers into the World Series.

The Angels hammered him in the Championship Series, but he bounced back with a three-hit shutout of St. Louis in Game 1 of the World Series. He also earned a victory in Game 5 despite giving up 15 hits in 8 ⅔ innings. St. Louis eventually took the championship.

Ray Caldwell

Caldwell, Raymond Benjamin **P**

1910–21 B:4/26/1888, Corydon, PA D:8/17/1967, Salamanca, NY Deb:9/9/1910, NY AL BL/TR 6'2", 190

W	L	PCT	G	SH	IP	BB	SO	ERA
134	120	.528	343	21	2242	738	1006	3.22

The year is 1915 and a promising American League hurler is so proficient with the bat that his manager has no compunction at all about using him in the outfield or employing him in key pinch-hitting situations. In fact, he leads the circuit in pinch hits, delivering 15. Against the White Sox on June 10 he smashes a rare pinch hit homer; the next day he does it again—a feat so difficult it would not be repeated for 28 years.

Babe Ruth? No. The hurler is a dipsomaniacal knuckleballer (and sometime spitballer) named Ray Caldwell.

"Slim" or "Rube" Caldwell began his big league career with Yankees in 1910. His best seasons came in 1914 and 1915 when he achieved 17–9 and 19–16 marks, respectively. When he left New York after the 1918 season he held franchise records for most seasons pitched and most bases on balls delivered.

He was a .248 lifetime hitter, who batted as high as .291 in a season with 10 doubles. In 1915 he belted four homers—Braggo Roth paced the American League that year with just seven. Over in Boston, Ruth also had four homers in a situation very similar to Caldwell's, although Ruth delivered his four-baggers in just 92 at bats; Caldwell needed 144. Ruth was first in homers per at bat in the AL in 1915; Caldwell was third. Another pitcher, Smokey Joe Wood, was fifth.

In December 1918 owner Harry Frazee began his fire sale of the once-mighty Red Sox and unloaded outfielder Duffy Lewis and pitchers Ernie Shore and Dutch Leonard to his favorite trading partner, the New York Yankees, in exchange for Caldwell, three minor players, and $15,000 cash. The Red Sox soon tired of Caldwell, and by mid-season 1919 he was in Cleveland, where he began regaining his effectiveness.

During Caldwell's first game for the Tribe at League Park, he was actually hit by lighting, as a thunderstorm quickly advanced from nearby Lake Erie. Perhaps attracted by the metal button on the top of his cap, the lighting passed through Caldwell's body, causing only the damage of a burned chest. He dusted himself off—and pitched a complete game. At the Polo Grounds on September 10, 1919, Caldwell pitched a no-hitter against the Yankees. Inspired by Slim's heroics the Tribe won 10 in a row and 13 of their last 17 in a futile effort to catch the White Sox.

To combat Caldwell's well-known drinking problems Cleveland manager Tris Speaker tried a new tack, inserting this clause into his 1920 contract: "After each game he pitches, Ray Caldwell must get drunk. He is not to report to the park the next day. The second day he is to report to Manager Speaker and run around the park as many times as Manager Speaker stipulates. The third day he is to pitch batting practice, and the fourth day he is to pitch in a championship game." The reverse-psychology strategy pretty much worked, as Caldwell never showed up drunk for Speaker.

Slim responded in 1920 with his only 20-win season. He also tossed 33 complete games out of

34 starts to help propel Cleveland to its first American League pennant. Caldwell started Game 3 of the World Series, but did not survive the first inning. Although the best-of-nine Series with Brooklyn went seven games, Caldwell saw no more action.

Baseball's Rule 8.02 outlawed the spitter after the 1920 season, but Slim was one of eight major league hurlers "grandfathered" by the statute and allowed to continue using the unsanitary and often hard-to-control delivery. Nonetheless, Caldwell went just 6–6 for the Tribe in 1921 and was finished in the big leagues.

Nixey Callahan

Callahan, James Joseph **OF-P-3B**

1894, 1897–1905, 1911–1913 M(1903–04, 1912–14, 1916–17, 394–458) B:3/18/1874, Fitchburg, MA D:10/4/1934, Boston, MA Deb:5/12/1894 PHI NL BR/TR 5'10½", 180

G	AB	R	H	HR	RBI	OBP	SLG	AVG
923	3295	442	901	11	394	.311	.352	.273

W	L	PCT	G	SH	IP	BB	SO	ERA
99	73	.576	195	11	1603	437	445	3.39

Nixey Callahan did a little bit of everything. He won 99 games as a pitcher and produced a .273 lifetime batting average. He played the outfield, the infield—just about every position except catcher. He even stole 45 bases one season after giving up pitching. He made a little history, too; in 1902, Callahan pitched the first American League no-hitter.

He played sparingly with the Phillies in 1894 as a 20-year-old, then spent the next two seasons in the minors, returning for good in 1897 with the Chicago Colts (they didn't become the Cubs until 1902). He went 12–9 that season for a 59-win team, and completed 21 of his 22 starts. Even in an era when the complete game was expected—1,360 of 1,576 games in the National League that season were complete games—Callahan was unusually durable, completing 169 of his 177 career starts. And when he wasn't pitching that season, he played 30 games at second base, 18 at shortstop, two at third base, and 21 in the outfield, while hitting .292.

For the next five seasons Callahan concentrated on pitching. He was 20–10 in 1898 and 21–12 the next season. After slumping to 13–16 in 1900, he jumped ship, moving to the Chicago White Sox of the newly-formed American League. He won 15 games in 1901 and 16 the next year, his last as a pitcher. His no-hitter came against Detroit, by far the league's worst-hitting team, on September 20.

In 1903 Callahan saw the beginning of his managerial career. He succeeded Clark Griffith as the 29-year-old player-manager of the White Sox. Callahan hit .292 in 118 games, 102 of them at third base. His managing numbers were not as impressive; the White Sox went 60–77 and finished seventh.

They improved in 1904, but Fielder Jones replaced Callahan in midseason, even though the White Sox were 42–33. After hitting .272 as an outfielder in 1905 and stealing four bases in a game, Callahan left the majors for six seasons, organizing the famous Logan Squares semipro club of Chicago in 1908.

When Callahan returned to the White Sox in 1911 he was 37, which didn't prevent him from stealing 45 bases and hitting .281 in 120 games. He became player-manager the next season and hit .272 while the Sox finished fourth at 78–76. After a sixth-place finish in 1914, Clarence "Pants" Rowland replaced Callahan. He sat out a year, was hired to manage the Pirates, and lasted less than two seasons.

Johnny Callison

Callison, John Wesley **OF**

1958–73 B:3/12/1939, Qualls, OK Deb:9/9/1958, CHI AL BL/TR 5'10", 175

G	AB	R	H	HR	RBI	OBP	SLG	AVG
1886	6652	926	1757	226	840	.333	.441	.264

In the bottom of the ninth inning in the 1964 All-Star Game at New York's newly christened Shea Stadium, Philadelphia outfielder Johnny Callison sent one into the bleachers for a three-run homer and a 7–4 National League win as 50,850 fans went wild. Callison was rewarded with the first Arch Ward Memorial Trophy as the game's Most Valuable Player. "He can run, throw, field, and hit with power," said Phils manager Gene Mauch. "There's nothing he can't do well on a ballfield."

Traded by the Cubs to the Phils in 1960 for third baseman Gene Freese, Callison hit .300 for the Phils in 1962. He once hit three homers in a game, and twice paced the league in triples and once in doubles. A superb fielder, Callison tied an NL record by leading all outfielders in assists from 1962 to 1965. Despite the Phils' 1964 late-season collapse, Callison finished second in the MVP balloting, and he played errorless outfield ball during the 1968 season.

After slowing down from his peak production years in the 1960s, he was traded back to the Cubs in 1970 and finished his career with the Yankees in 1973. In retirement, Callison sold automobiles in Glenside, Pennsylvania.

Dolph Camilli

Camilli, Adolph Louis **1B**

1933–43, 1945 B:4/23/1907, San Francisco, CA D:10/21/1997, San Mateo, CA Deb:9/9/1933, CHI NL BL/TL 5'10", 185

G	AB	R	H	HR	RBI	OBP	SLG	AVG
1490	5353	936	1482	239	950	.388	.492	.277

The transition from "Daffiness Boys" to "Boys of Summer" at Ebbets Field may be traced without too much exaggeration to Larry MacPhail's acquisition of one class player in March 1938—Dolph Camilli. When he took over the Dodgers, the colorful MacPhail carefully perused the club's roster and came to the conclusion that he needed help, and quickly. He called the Brooklyn Board of Directors together to announce, "We need a first baseman, and I know where I can get one." Then he announced this new, unnamed first sacker would cost $45,000.

The board's enthusiasm waned. "You mean the $45,000 is for the whole team, don't you?" a director asked. So MacPhail borrowed the money from George V. McLaughlin's Brooklyn Trust Company to buy Dolph Camilli from the Phillies. The power-hitting Camilli helped begin the transformation of Brooklyn from an inept franchise of lovable losers into a perennial contender and National League powerhouse. Brooklyn's first pennant in 20 years came in 1941 with Camilli, the leagues' Most Valuable Player, on first.

Adolph Louis Camilli had started playing professional baseball in 1926, and he made stops at Logan and Salt Lake City in the Class C Utah–Idaho League, and with the San Francisco Seals and Sacramento Solons of the Pacific Coast League. He came up to the Cubs in September 1933 for 16 games. The next season he played 32 games for the big club before being traded to the Phils on June 11 for pitcher Don Hurst.

With the woeful Phillies he became a solid performer, hitting at least 25 homers and driving in at least 80 runs in each of his three full seasons in Philadelphia. In 1937 he batted .339 and led the National League in both fielding average (.994), and on-base percentage (.446).

Such a talent was available to the Dodgers because owners at least as far back as Connie Mack in 1915 and Harry Frazee in 1919 have peddled top players for short-term monetary gains. The Phillies' threadbare owner, Gerry Nugent, was no exception. He had wanted $75,000 for Camilli; he settled for $45,000 and first baseman Eddie Morgan.

Once they had Camilli, the Dodgers steadily rose from seventh in 1938 to third in 1939 to second in 1940 and to a long-awaited pennant in 1941. That season Camilli led the league in both homers (34) and RBIs (120) while fielding brilliantly. He garnered 300 votes for league MVP, to teammate and runner-up Pete Reiser's 183.

That year also set the pattern for the next four Ebbets Field pennant winners—humiliation at the hands of the New York Yankees in the World Series. Camilli was no help, hitting a pitiful .167 and striking out a Series-high six times as the Bums fell in five games.

Camilli's batting average dipped to .252 in 1942, but he still slugged 26 homers and drove in 109 runs. The Dodgers lost a heartbreaking pennant race to the Cards, blowing a 10½-game lead over the Redbirds in mid-August. In July 1943 the 36-year-old Camilli, hitting .246 with only six homers and 43 RBIs, was dealt to the Giants in a five-player deal. In those days, team rivalries were taken seriously and Camilli refused to report to the Giants. His major league playing days appeared to be over.

The next year he managed the Pacific Coast League's Oakland Oaks to a fourth-place finish. Rehired for 1945, he left the club on June 12 to suit up as a wartime fill-in for the Boston Red Sox. In 63 games he batted .212 and hit the final two home runs of his major league career.

In the middle of the 1948 season, Camilli took over the Class B Western International League's Spokane club from Buddy Ryan and brought in a pennant. He managed again for the Class A Central League's Dayton Indians in 1950 and for the Class C Pioneer League's Magic Valley Cowboys in 1953. He also scouted for the Yankees from 1960 through 1967 and the Angels from 1969 through 1971.

Ironically, this graceful fielder once committed three errors in a single inning. His son, Doug, was a light-hitting catcher for the Dodgers and Senators in the 1960s. Dolph's brother was a professional boxer who died in the ring fighting heavyweight champ Max Baer.

Ken Caminiti

Caminiti, Kenneth Gene **3B**

1987–* B:4/21/1963, Hanford, CA Deb:7/16/1987, HOU NL BB/TR 6', 200

G	AB	R	H	HR	RBI	OBP	SLG	AVG
1583	5724	816	1566	209	897	.349	.444	.274

Ken Caminiti arrived in the major leagues as a chiseled 6-footer with a classic power-hitter's stance and scowl. The only problem was he hit just 57 home runs in nearly 3,000 major-league at bats for the Houston Astros through 1993. After admitting to a drinking problem, Caminiti checked himself into a rehab clinic.

He rebounded in 1994 with better numbers and a new focus. That winter a 12-player deal sent Caminiti to San Diego, where the switch hitter refined his craft at the plate under the tutelage of

Padres great Tony Gwynn. In 1995 he hit .302 with 26 homers and 94 RBIs. With his sure glove and cannon arm at third base, Caminiti won the first of three consecutive Gold Gloves.

Caminiti hurt his left rotator cuff diving for a ball in April 1996, and soon required cortisone shots to dull the pain as the injury worsened. Instead of shutting him down, his shoulder woes spurred a greater reliance on his lower body at the plate. "I just went up there thinking there was nothing wrong," he said the following spring. "I was just nice and relaxed."

Caminiti's most memorable moment that season occurred in Mexico. Despite suffering from dehydration, he yanked an IV out of his arm, ate a candy bar, and then homered twice against the New York Mets in the final game of a three-game series in Monterrey, Mexico. He finished the year batting .326 with 40 home runs and 130 RBIs and cruised to Most Valuable Players honors. He led the Padres to the National League West title for the first time since 1984.

Injuries plagued Caminiti again in each of the next two seasons, but he still managed 26 and 29 home runs, respectively. San Diego again topped the NL West in 1998. In his last hurrah in a Padres uniform, Caminiti slugged two home runs to help overcome Atlanta in the Championship Series. Groin and back injuries, however, rendered him ineffective in the World Series.

Over the winter, he declined more lucrative offers elsewhere to head back to Houston as a free agent. Injuries limited him to 78 games in 1999, but he hit three home runs and drove in eight runs for the Astros in their Division Series loss to the Atlanta Braves.

William Cammeyer

Cammeyer, William

Park Owner B:3/20/1821, New York, NY D:9/4/1898, Brooklyn, NY

To Brooklyn's William Cammeyer goes the credit of being the first to enclose a ballpark and charge money for admittance. That, as much as anything else, helped create professionalism in baseball.

Cammeyer's father, John E. Cammeyer, ran a tanning yard in New York City and has been described as one of the "largest leather merchants in the United States." In 1849 the Cammeyers moved to the Williamsburgh section in Brooklyn. When his father died, young William inherited the family business.

In 1861 Cammeyer took out a lease on property at the corner of Brooklyn's Lee Avenue and Rutledge Street and proposed developing a skating rink and ballpark on the site. He opened it first as a rink, then enclosed it and used it for baseball. Its opening day as a ballpark was May 15, 1862.

Cammeyer's idea was this: he would allow ballclubs to use the field for free but would charge spectators 10 cents apiece for the privilege of watching and would keep all the money for himself. Amateur clubs such as the Eckfords, the Atlantics, and the Excelsiors were quick to use the park and quick to see the injustice in letting Cammeyer retain all receipts. Before long they were refusing to play unless cut in. "That was really the beginning of professional base ball playing," writer Henry Chadwick contended.

Others knew a good idea when they saw one. Within a year or so, two enterprising capitalists named Weed and Decker converted their ice skating rink at the Capitoline Grounds into a ballpark and they, too, charged admission.

On his Union Grounds, Cammeyer erected clubhouses and a covered grandstand. Originally the grandstand was intended for women. The men still preferred the old-fashioned custom of standing on the lines to watch a game.

"Although a fine park in most respects, Union was built on low swampland below street level and flooded easily," author William Ryczek wrote. "Proprietor Cammeyer, ever mindful of his investment in the property, refused to allow teams to play when he felt the wet field might be further damaged."

Gamblers congregated at the Union Grounds, and in at least one case police had to be called in to settle things when allegations of a fix were made. Prices rose quickly at the park. By 1866 Cammeyer was charging 25 cents to see big games. The next year that was the price for all contests. In 1870 the price for significant games rose to 50 cents.

The park was home to three clubs—the Eckfords, the Mutuals, and the Atlantics—in the new National Association, the first major league. The Mutuals were controlled by New York's infamous Boss Tweed, and in 1875, the league's last year, Cammeyer became president of the club.

He managed the team in 1876 when the Mutuals shifted over to William Hulbert's new National League, but it was a troubled season. The Mutuals failed to make the last western road trip of the year, even though promised $400 by Hulbert and St. Louis Brown Stockings owner Charles Fowle. At the new league's meeting in Cleveland in December 1876 the club was expelled from the infant circuit.

Baseball continued to be played at the Union Grounds for quite some time. In 1877 the Hartford Dark Blues scheduled home games there. As late as May 24, 1889, an American Association contest was held there, although it appears Cammeyer's involvement may have ended prior to that. "He coined money on the Union Grounds," wrote the *Brooklyn Times*. "Then the interest in baseball began to wane and for a while he conducted the grounds at a loss. It is authoritatively stated, however, that he cleared a profit of $20,000 in the venture." He lost much of that, however, in another investment.

Howie Camnitz

Camnitz, Samuel Howard **P**

1904–15 B:8/22/1881, Covington, KY D:3/2/1960, Louisville, KY Deb:4/22/1904, PIT NL BR/TR 5'9", 169

W	L	PCT	G	SH	IP	BB	SO	ERA
133	106	.556	326	20	2085^{1}	656	915	2.75

Howie Camnitz was a 20-game winner three times but is now best remembered as an agent in other ballplayers' fortunes. A pink-cheeked youngster from Covington, Kentucky, Camnitz was dubbed "the Kentucky Rosebud" when he came to the majors. The Rosebud had a few trials with the Pirates before pitching well enough to stay in 1907. He posted a 1.56 ERA with 16 wins in 1908 and then tied the great Christy Mathewson for the league lead in winning percentage with a 25–6 mark in 1909.

Camnitz, sometimes also called "Red," was slated to open the World Series that year against the Tigers, but he came down with an acute inflammation of the tonsils. Instead, young Babe Adams started the opener and won, 4–1. In Game 2 Camnitz was knocked out in the third inning and took the loss, and his only other appearance was in relief in Game 6. Adams emerged as the star of the Series as he went on to win twice more, leading the Pirates to their first championship.

After an off year in 1910 Camnitz came back with 20 and 22 wins in the next two seasons. He was on the mound when a famous incident occurred between the Pirates and the Giants. With no outs in the ninth and a Giants runner on second, New York manager John McGraw signaled for "Red" Murray to bunt. Camnitz, expecting the sacrifice, threw a high, tight fastball, which was Murray's favorite pitch, and the Giants outfielder unloaded a game-winning home run. Despite the result, McGraw was furious that his sign was ignored and fined Murray $100.

In 1913 Camnitz suddenly became ineffective. When his record fell to 6–17 he was dealt to the Phillies, where he split six decisions before the season ended. He jumped to the Federal League's Pittsburgh franchise in 1914, posted another losing record, and retired after the 1915 season.

Roy Campanella

Campanella, Roy **C**

1948–57 Negro League Player (1937–45) B:11/19/1921, Philadelphia, PA D:6/26/1993, Woodland Hills, CA Deb:4/20/1948, BRO NL BR/TR 5'8", 200

G	AB	R	H	HR	RBI	OBP	SLG	AVG
1215	4205	627	1161	242	856	.362	.500	.276

Hall of Famer Roy Campanella was a pioneer in the integration of major league baseball. He was the National League's best catcher during the 1950s and won Most Valuable Player Awards in 1951, 1953, and 1955, before a tragic 1958 auto accident left him a quadriplegic.

A product of the Negro Leagues, Campanella was the son of an Italian father and an African-American mother. He began his career with the Nicetown Giants, a Philadelphia newsboys team, and later graduated to the Bacharach Giants, a local semipro team. After subbing for the aging Raleigh "Biz" Mackey on weekends, Campanella became—at age 16—first-string catcher for the Negro National League's Baltimore Elite Giants.

Catching always attracted the short, squat Campanella. "From the start, catching appealed to me as a chance to be in the thick of the game continuously. I never had to be lonely behind the plate where I could talk to the hitters. I also learned that by engaging them in conversation I could sometimes distract them," he recalled.

He once caught four Elite Giants games on a single Sunday, working a doubleheader in Cincinnati in the afternoon and another in Youngstown, Ohio, that same evening. "You didn't get hurt playing in the Negro Leagues. You played no matter what happened to you, because if you didn't, you didn't get paid."

Before long he was almost as highly regarded in Negro League circles as the legendary Josh Gibson, and was voted MVP of the 1941 Negro League East-West All-Star Game. After becoming embroiled in a contract dispute with Elite Giants owner Tom Wilson, Campanella was fined $250; rather than pay it, he jumped to Jorge Pasquel's Liga Mexicana de Baseball for $100 a week plus expenses. He played in Monterrey, Mexico, in 1942 and 1943, but returned to the Negro Leagues in 1944 after Wilson dropped the fine, added a $300 signing bonus, and raised Campanella's salary to $3,000 a year.

Campanella led the league in doubles in 1944 and RBIs in 1945. In October 1945 he barnstormed against a collection of major leaguers managed by Dodgers coach Charlie Dressen. Impressed with Campanella's performance,

Dressen asked him to meet with Brooklyn general manager Branch Rickey. Campanella declined to play with a new black club, the Brown Dodgers, but after Jackie Robinson's signing was announced Campanella signed with the Brooklyn Dodgers and took a pay cut from $3,000 to $1,107.50.

Originally scheduled to be sent to Danville in the 3-I League, Campanella went instead to Nashua, New Hampshire, of the Class B New England League after the 3-I League refused to accept black players. Campanella hit .290 and was named MVP. He advanced the following season to Montreal, where he again won the MVP Award. Buffalo Bisons manager Paul Richards called him "the best catcher in the business—major or minor leagues."

Rickey asked Campanella to go to St. Paul for the purpose of integrating the American Association. "Mr. Rickey, I'm a ballplayer, not a pioneer," Campanella protested. But Rickey prevailed, partly because he agreed to pay Campanella $6,500—$1,500 more than the major league minimum he would have received at Brooklyn.

Finally called up to the majors in 1948, Campanella quickly established himself as a mainstay of the powerhouse Dodgers team that won pennants in 1949, 1952, 1953, 1955, and 1956. (They lost out in 1950 and 1951 on the last day of the season.) On a team full of future Hall of Famers—Robinson, Pee Wee Reese, and Duke Snider—Campanella stood out enough to win three National League MVP awards, a feat matched only by Stan Musial, Mike Schmidt, and Barry Bonds.

"When you win that Most Valuable Player Award the first time you're real happy, and when you get it a second time you're mighty happy. But when you get it a third time—well, you're just overwhelmed. And that's just what I am," said Campanella.

In the mid-1950s, catching took its toll on Campanella. He endured numerous knee injuries, and a bone chip surfaced in his left hand in 1954 and returned in 1955 despite surgery. After he suffered another serious injury to his left knee, he began preparing for a life outside of baseball and purchased a liquor store in Harlem.

At 1:30 A.M. on January 28, 1958, he finished counting receipts at the store and got into a rented 1957 Chevy sedan. Campanella wasn't driving fast, but his car skidded on an icy patch of roadway, hit a telephone pole, and flipped over. The accident left Campanella paralyzed in both his arms and legs.

On his birthday, May 7, 1959, the Dodgers held a special tribute night for Campanella at the Los Angeles Coliseum. The largest crowd in major league history, over 93,000 fans, showed up to honor the catcher at an exhibition game. "I thank God that I'm living to be here," said an emotional Campanella. As he finished speaking the lights went out, and every person present lit a match. He later wrote, "The Coliseum burst into a mass of twinkling stars. It was a gesture, for my benefit, in the form of a huge birthday cake. I've never seen anything like it." Campanella was inducted to the Hall of Fame in 1969

Bert Campaneris

Campaneris, Dagoberto (Blanco) SS-3B-2B

1964–83 B:3/9/1942, Pueblo Nuevo, Cuba
Deb:7/23/1964, KC AL BR/TR 5'10", 160

G	AB	R	H	HR	RBI	OBP	SLG	AVG
2328	8684	1181	2249	79	646	.313	.342	.259

Bert Campaneris was the everyday shortstop for the powerful Oakland A's dynasty of the 1970s, but many fans remember him as a "supersub." He made major league history on September 8, 1965, when he played every position in a single game. That was when the A's were based in Kansas City, and Charlie Finley worked overtime to come up with crazy, and sometimes not-so-crazy, stunts. Although it was the first time a major leaguer had ever performed that feat, it was hardly the first instance that Campaneris had shown what he could do at positions other than shortstop.

The speedy Campaneris, aptly nicknamed "Road Runner," started in the Athletics' system as a catcher. He wasn't too impressive behind the plate and switched to the infield to take advantage of his speed. In the minors he also dabbled in pitching, although he did it somewhat differently than most. With Daytona Beach he pitched to righthanded batters righthanded and threw southpaw to lefthanded batters.

Born and raised in a tiny village in the Matanzas region of Cuba, where his father made lariats, Dagoberto Campaneris y Blanco (his full Spanish name) was an early Finley find—and one of his cheaper ones. A's scout Felix Delgado signed young Campaneris for just $500. "Campy" was tearing up the Southern League in 1964, batting at a .325 clip, when the Athletics called him up. He responded on July 23 by belting a home run on the first major league pitch he saw. He added a second homer later in the game off Jim Kaat.

During his sophomore season, Campaneris led the league with 12 triples. On August 29, 1967, he tied a league record with three triples in one game. By the time the A's moved to Oakland in 1968, Campy was an established star. His blazing speed allowed him not only to capture stolen base titles in 1965, 1966, 1967, 1968, and 1970, but to even to advance two bases on a sacrifice bunt. In 1968 Campaneris led the league with 177 hits. Two years later he smacked a career-high 22 homers.

The A's won the American League West title in 1971 but lost the Championship Series to Baltimore. The next year Campy was picked for the All-Star Game but was snubbed by AL manager Earl Weaver, who played Bobby Grich the entire game and kept Campy on the bench. Campaneris maintained a stoic silence, but for the rest of his career he performed with extra intensity against Weaver's Orioles.

Oakland returned to the ALCS in 1972, this time playing Billy Martin's Detroit Tigers. Campy ripped the Tigers apart in the first two games of the Series, with a .429 average and two stolen bases. In the sixth inning of Game 2 Martin decided he had enough and instructed rookie reliever Lerrin LaGrow to throw at Campy's legs. The pitch hit Campaneris just above the left ankle. Instead of limping to first or charging the mound, Campaneris let his bat fly directly at LaGrow's head. Luckily, LaGrow threw himself to the ground as the projectile missed his head by inches. The fiery Martin rushed out to attack Campy but was restrained by three team members. Before the melee ended, both LaGrow and Campaneris were ejected.

"The man's got no guts," fumed Martin. "He should be suspended. There shouldn't be any place in baseball for anybody dumb enough to throw a bat. The man's an idiot. If he had come out and taken a punch at my pitcher, I could respect him. But a bat? The next thing he ought to do is carry a knife." AL president Joe Cronin fined Campaneris—who was still hobbling—$500, and suspended him from the rest of the playoffs. Oakland won the ALCS anyway.

Before the World Series opened, Commissioner Bowie Kuhn ruled that Campaneris could play against Cincinnati, but that he would be ineligible for the first seven contests of the 1973 season. In the Series Campy hit only .179 and scored just a single run, but the A's won in seven games.

Campaneris was named to the 1973 and 1974 *Sporting News* All-Star teams, and was a key performer in the postseason both years. In the 1973 ALCS against the Orioles, Campy homered in Oakland's Game 2 victory and then led off the bottom of the 11th inning of Game 3 with a homer to give the A's a 2–1 win. He was also Mr. Clutch in the World Series against the Mets, driving in the winning run in Game 3 and hitting a two-run homer in Game 7. He also had the only three stolen bases by either team in the Series.

Two-time world champion Oakland made it three straight titles in 1974. Campaneris hit .353 in the World Series as the A's downed the Dodgers in five games. But Campy's batting average dropped from a career-high .290 in 1974 to .265 in 1975 and to .256 in 1976. In November 1976 he signed as a free agent with Texas. After his numbers continued declining with the Rangers, he was dealt to the Angels in May 1979 for third baseman Dave Chalk. In 1983 he finished his career with the Yankees—oddly enough, after receiving a tryout from none other than Billy Martin.

Through 1999 Campaneris ranked 14th all-time with 649 stolen bases—more career swipes than either Maury Wills or Davey Lopes accumulated. On May 24, 1976, Campaneris stole five bases in one game. His speed also allowed him to finish his career as one of the toughest players to double up.

Al Campanis

Campanis, Alexander Sebastian **SS**

1943 Executive B:11/2/1916, Kos, Dodecanese Islands D:6/21/1998, Fullerton, CA Deb:9/23/43, BRO NL BB/TR 6', 185

G	AB	R	H	HR	RBI	OBP	SLG	AVG
7	20	3	2	0	0	.250	.100	.100

Seventy-year-old Al Campanis was fired from his job as Los Angeles Dodgers vice president of player personnel because of racist remarks he made on national television. Campanis had been a member of the Dodgers family for more than 40 years as a player, scout, and scouting director. He had scouted and signed Roberto Clemente. He had played short when Jackie Robinson played second for Montreal in 1946, the year before Robinson integrated the major leagues. Campanis' son, Jim, had been a big-league catcher for parts of six seasons. His reputable baseball record was undone on April 5, 1987 on ABC's *Nightline*.

The day before the Dodgers were to open the season, Ted Koppel, the host of the show, wanted to do a tribute commemorating the 40th anniversary of Robinson's first major league year. Koppel had planned to have Don Newcombe and Dodgers historian Roger Kahn as his guests to talk about Robinson. But Newcombe missed a plane connection and couldn't make it to New York on time. So Koppel contacted Campanis, who had briefly roomed with Robinson.

Koppel asked Campanis why there were no black managers or general managers in the majors, and Campanis replied, "I can't answer that question directly. The only thing I can say is you have to pay your dues to become a manager. Generally you have to go to the minor leagues. There's not very much pay involved, and some of the better-known black players have been able to get into other fields and make a pretty good living that way."

Koppel dismissed that as "baloney," and questioned whether there was still prejudice in baseball. Campanis answered, "No, I don't believe it's prejudice. It's just that they [blacks] may not have some of the necessities to be, let's say, a field manager or perhaps a general manager."

Shocked by Campanis' response, Koppel tried to let him off the hook. "Do you really believe that?" he asked. Campanis proceeded to hang himself. "Well, I don't say that about all of them," he remarked, "but they certainly are short. How many quarterbacks do you have? How many pitchers do you have that are black?"

The national response was amazement followed by outrage. The comments weren't just inappropriate and insensitive, they were incongruous—Campanis held a high position with a team noted for its forward thinking on racial matters.

Campanis issued an official apology the next day, but the Dodgers asked for his resignation anyway. His comment, several years later: "If Jackie Robinson had been alive to see what happened to me, he would have been irate."

Count Campau

Campau, Charles Columbus **OF**

1888, 1890, 1894 M(1890, 42–27) B:10/17/1863, Detroit, MI D:4/3/1938, New Orleans, LA
Deb:7/7/1888, DET NL BL/TR 5'11", 160

G	AB	R	H	HR	RBI	OBP	SLG	AVG
147	572	97	153	10	93	.322	.397	.267

Count Campau, perhaps the premier minor leaguer of the 19th century, capped his career with an unusual feat: in 1890, he led both a minor and a major league in home runs. After hitting three homers in 39 games for Detroit of the International League, the outfielder moved up to the St. Louis Browns, where he also led the American Association with nine round-trippers. He became the Browns' player-manager later that year.

Campau, a member of one of Detroit's founding families, inherited the nickname "Count" from his father, a Union Army captain who had been given the honorific by Napoleon III of France. The young Campau began his career in 1885 with Erie of the Interstate League and went on to play in 20 different cities. He performed for Detroit clubs in three different circuits—the National, International, and Western Leagues.

After retiring as a player, Campau umpired briefly in the Eastern and Southern Leagues. He resigned on August 23, 1906, after fleeing from a mob of angry fans in Shreveport, Louisiana. Later he worked as a scales clerk and a placing judge at a New Orleans race track.

Bill Campbell

Campbell, William Richard **P**

1973–87 B:8/9/1948, Highland Park, MI
Deb:7/14/1973, MIN AL BR/TR 6'3", 190

W	L	PCT	G	SV	IP	BB	SO	ERA
83	68	.550	700	126	1229^{1}	495	864	3.54

Few relief pitchers have experienced a two-year period like Bill Campbell had in 1976 and 1977. He put together a 30–14 record and saved 51 games for two teams in that span. Campbell, nicknamed "Soup," became one of the first free agents to cash in on his success.

Coming off a 20-save season in 1975 for the Minnesota Twins, Campbell was the first free agent to sign with the Boston Red Sox. Campbell, who had been in combat as a U.S. Army radio operator in Vietnam just a few years earlier, received a five-year, $1.075 million contract on November 6, 1976. He responded with a 13–9 mark and a league-high 31 saves in 1977. Injuries and ineffectiveness cost Campbell his closer's role the following season. By the time he returned to full health, he was a middle reliever for the Chicago Cubs.

After two seasons in Chicago and one with Philadelphia, Campbell landed with St. Louis in 1985 and reached the postseason for the only time in his career. He held the Dodgers scoreless in three National League Championship Series appearances, and allowed just one run in four World Series innings against Kansas City. He retired in 1987 after short stints in Detroit and Montreal (his fourth and fifth teams in a five-year span). Campbell subsequently began a second career as a pitching coach.

John Candelaria

Candelaria, John Robert **P**

1975–93 B:11/6/1953, New York, NY Deb:6/8/1975, PIT NL BL/TL 6'7", 232

W	L	PCT	G	SV	IP	BB	SO	ERA
177	122	.592	600	29	2525^{2}	592	1673	3.33

At age 21, the towering lefty did his part both during the season and playoffs. He posted an 8–6 year that included a shutout and a 2.76 ERA. And with his team down two games in a best-of-five NLCS, he threw more than seven innings of Game 3, whiffing 14 Reds batters. The juggernaut Reds won the game, and the pennant, in the 10th inning.

The next year the young lefty exhibited good speed, excellent control, and, at 6-feet-7 inches, an intimidating style. He went 16–7, including the first no-hitter at home by a Pirates pitcher in the club's history. In 1977 Candelaria hurled 20 victories, posted the lowest ERA in the National League at 2.34, and led the league in winning percentage, with .800. He was also named to the All-Star team. In only three seasons Candelaria had become one of the best pitchers in the league. Although the Pirates finished second to the Phillies for the second straight year, the team expected to soon realize the championship promise it had held for most of the decade.

In 1979, when the Pirates finally climbed to their second World Series victory of the decade, Candelaria's 14 wins led the staff. After being knocked out of the box in the fourth inning of Game 3 by five Baltimore runs, Candelaria came back in Game 6 to hurl seven shutout innings and force a seventh game against the Orioles.

The 1980s were a money decade, and Candelaria remained a well-paid member of the Pirates rotation until 1985. An arm injury sidelined him for most of the 1981 season, and the Pirates sank into lean years. The "Candy Man" recovered from his injuries but was never again able to hurl many innings. Still, he won a total of 39 games from 1982 to 1984.

In 1985 the Pirates switched Candelaria to a relief role. After earning nine saves in 37 appearances, the Pirates traded him to the California Angels, who were in the midst of a close division race. Back to a starting role and with a decent team behind him, Candelaria went 7–3, hurling a shutout—although the Angels still finished one game behind the division champion Royals. The next year he was again California's "money" pitcher, reclaiming his old glory with a 10–2 record and helping the club to a division championship. In the playoffs he won Game 3 but was clobbered in Game 7 as the Angels lost.

In 1987 Candelaria publicly criticized Angels skipper Gene Mauch. Although the manager stepped down at the end of the year, California sold Candelaria to the Mets. In New York, the Candy Man won two of his three starts and pitched a no-decision in the other; the Mets finished three games behind the Cardinals in second place. Candelaria was twice arrested for drunk driving that year, and in the off-season he spent three weeks in an alcohol treatment center, although he denied that he was either dependent on alcohol or a had an abuse problem.

When the 1988 season started, Candelaria was with the Yankees. He was still reliable, and he won 16 games in a year and a half, mostly as a starter. But his ERA was slowly creeping up on him. In 1989 he went to Montreal as a full-time reliever. In 1990 he started the year with the Twins but ended the season with Toronto. He signed with the Dodgers in 1991, where he stayed as a reliever for 1991 and 1992. In 1993 he ended his career back with the Pirates, posting three losses and a save in 24 appearances.

Tom Candiotti

Candiotti, Thomas Caesar **P**

1983–* B:8/31/1957, Walnut Creek, CA Deb:8/8/1983, MIL AL BR/TR 6'2", 200

W	L	PCT	G	SH	IP	BB	SO	ERA
151	164	.479	451	11	2725	883	1735	3.73

That Tom Candiotti ever pitched in the major leagues at all was a minor miracle of medicine. In 1981, while pitching in the Milwaukee Brewers farm system, Candiotti underwent complete elbow reconstruction by Dr. Frank Jobe, the pioneer of "Tommy John" surgery. Candiotti recovered to make his major league debut in 1983, but his career seemed to be going nowhere until he turned to the pitch that would become his trademark: the knuckleball.

Candiotti had experimented with the knuckleball since Little League, but Milwaukee management first noticed him throwing it in spring training 1985. The Brewers sent him back to the minors to develop it further. Years later, Candiotti credited the trick pitch with saving his career. "Throwing the knuckler got me off the bubble, made me a starting pitcher, and made my career take off," he said.

Candiotti signed with Cleveland in 1986, and the Indians brought in future Hall of Famer Phil Niekro to complete Candiotti's knuckleball education. Candiotti spotted his knuckler with a breaking pitch and a fastball he threw at different speeds. He won 16 games in 1986, and posted between 11 and 15 victories each season between 1988 and 1992. By then he was with the Los Angeles Dodgers, where he stayed through the 1997 season. He signed with Oakland in 1998 and briefly returned to Cleveland during the 1999 season.

Jose Canseco

Canseco, Jose (Capas) **OF–DH**

1985–* B:7/2/1964, Havana, Cuba Deb:9/2/1985, OAK AL BR/TR 6'4", 240

G	AB	R	H	HR	RBI	OBP	SLG	AVG
1713	6472	1093	1728	431	1309	.354	.520	.267

In the late 1980s, Oakland slugger Jose Canseco appeared poised for one of the greatest careers in baseball history: Rookie of the Year in 1986; charter member of the "40–40 Club" with 42 home runs and 40 steals; 1988 American League Most Valuable Player; plus 128 career homers and a World Series ring at age 25. Canseco's biggest problem was handling the demands and pressures of fame.

He returned from a March 1989 hand injury to crack 17 home runs in 65 games and hit .357 with a homer in Oakland's World Series sweep of San Francisco. Batting back-to-back with Mark McGwire to form one of the most feared slugging tandems in history, Canseco added 81 homers and 223 RBIs over the next two seasons. But Canseco's name also appeared in the news for speeding tickets, an intentional car collision with his first wife, an arrest on weapons charges, a 900-number for his fans, and a reported liaison with Madonna.

On August 31, 1992, Canseco was traded by the Athletics to the Rangers for three players. His tenure with Texas was marked by farce. After having a flyball bounce off his head for a home run early in the 1993 season, Canseco made his first and only appearance as a pitcher on May 29. Days later, he felt soreness in his arm and shoulder. Within a month, Canseco was out for the season with a torn ligament in his elbow. After one more year in Texas, Canseco spent two seasons in Boston. He averaged less than 100 games per season with the Red Sox, but still provided "protection" for Mo Vaughn in the middle of the order. He returned to the A's in 1997, but hit just 23 homers in another injury-marred campaign.

Signed for a relative pittance by Toronto in 1998, Canseco exploded for a career-high 46 home runs. Toronto looked at his .237 average and 159 strikeouts, and let the itinerant slugger walk away during the winter. He joined the second-year Tampa Bay Devil Rays, who needed a slugger almost as badly as they needed a marquee name. Canseco started the season 103 home runs shy of the 500 mark that, he figured, would land him in the Hall of Fame. He got off to another fine start with the Rays until a midseason back injury disabled him once again—and put his ultimate goal in jeopardy. He finished the year with 34 home runs in 113 games.

Harry Caray

Carabina, Harry

Broadcaster B:3/1/1920 *, St. Louis, MO D:2/18/1998, Rancho Mirage, CA

(* The year is disputed. Some accounts put it as early as 1915.)

When young Harry Carabina decided he wanted to be a baseball announcer, he conned his way into an audition with Merle Jones, owner of KMOX, St. Louis' largest radio station. After the audition Jones commented, "Your voice has an exciting timbre." He helped Carabina land his first broadcasting job, in Joliet, Illinois, and the voice of the renamed Harry Caray went on to excite fans well over half a century.

Caray always described himself as the fan's man in the booth, and his unabashed delight at his team's victories resonates with any baseball devotee. While working at his second professional job, for WKZO in Kalamazoo, Michigan, he invented his famous home run call—"It might be...it could be...it *is* a home run!"—while announcing play-by-play for a semipro tournament.

Caray's first major league job was with his hometown Cardinals, for whom he was the play-by-play man at home games for one of the three stations broadcasting the Cards. His sponsor was Griesedieck beer, and his first partner was former big league catcher Charles "Gabby" Street. Their fun-loving style captured the imaginations of Cardinals fans, and before long their station and sponsor were given exclusive rights to the broadcasts. Caray stayed there for 25 years, from 1945 to 1969, working with four different owners—Sam Breadon, Fred Saigh, Bob Hannegan, and August Busch.

When Busch took over, there was concern that the man so long associated with Griesedieck Beer couldn't switch allegiance to Budweiser. But a survey of 100 Bud wholesalers found that they wanted Caray to promote their product. In his autobiography Caray points out that when Busch bought the Cardinals in 1953, Bud was the No. 2 beer in national sales. By 1957 Bud was No.1 and "has never looked back."

The Cardinals fired Caray in 1969 amid damaging rumors concerning his romantic liaisons. Caray's comment: "If you were me, would you have gone around denying rumors like that?" The local fans protested his dismissal vigorously, but to no avail.

He went on to work for Charlie Finley in Oakland, but after one season with the A's he returned to the Midwest. The struggling Chicago White Sox hired him in 1971 and promised a bonus if attendance improved. That incentive made Caray a wealthy man as the Sox, who had won only 56 games in 1970, improved dramatically under aggressive new manager Chuck Tanner.

Caray stayed on when the White Sox were sold to Bill Veeck in 1976. On Opening Day that year, when the crowd began singing "Take Me out to the Ball Game" during the seventh-inning stretch, Veeck noticed that Caray was singing along in the broadcasters' booth.

Without the announcer's knowledge Veeck had a microphone set up in the booth, and Caray's raspy singing voice was soon booming throughout the stadium. Confronted by Caray, Veeck explained, "Anybody in the ballpark hearing you sing that song knows he can sing as well as you can. Probably better than you can. So he or she sings along." From that day on Caray's enthusiastic rendering of the song was a Chicago tradition. When he died before the 1998 season, celebrities took turns singing "Take Me Out to the Ballgame" during all home games. The Cubs wore a patch on their uniform sleeve with a caricature of Caray.

When Jerry Reinsdorf and Eddie Einhorn bought the White Sox from Veeck, they announced their grand plans for a sports pay-TV channel. Caray felt that it wouldn't work, and moved to the North Side. He broadcast Cubs games from then on, taking his seventh-inning singalong with him. In fact, he became a Wrigley Field institution, so closely identified with Chicago's National League club that many latecomers would have been surprised to learn he'd ever been associated with another team. In 1989 Caray was honored at the Hall of Fame when he received the Ford C. Frick Award, given to broadcasters for "major contributions to baseball."

The secret to his success? "I have always contended that if you put a microphone in front of anyone in the bleachers and told him to start talking about the game he was watching, he would sound very much the way I do."

Bernie Carbo

Carbo, Bernardo **OF–DH**

1969–80 B:8/5/1947, Detroit MI Deb:9/2/1969, CIN NL BL/TR 6', 175

G	AB	R	H	HR	RBI	OBP	SLG	AVG
1010	2733	372	722	96	358	.389	.427	.264

Although his team didn't defeat the Reds in the 1975 World Series, journeyman outfielder Bernie Carbo emerged as one of the Series' unlikeliest stars. Carbo achieved greatness on the field in the legendary 1975 Series, equaling Chuck Essegian's feat of blasting two pinch homers in a Fall Classic. In Game 3 he socked one into Riverfront Stadium's left lower deck. In fabled Game 6, with the Sox down 6–3, Carbo came up with two on and two out in the eighth and delivered a dramatic game-tying, three-run homer into the center field bleachers. Although the Sox lost in seven games, Carbo batted .429.

Ironically, Carbo was a cast-off from the same Reds he pummeled in the postseason. Moreover, he had not started out as just another journeyman, but rather as a top Cincinnati prospect, the team's first-round pick in the 1965 amateur draft—ahead of even Johnny Bench. After stints in the lower minors, he hit .359 at Indianapolis and was named to *The Sporting News* Minor League All-Star Team. He became a regular with the Reds in 1970, batted .310 with 21 homers, and won *The Sporting News* National League Rookie of the Year honors.

Unfortunately that was the peak of Carbo's regular-season career. In 1972 he was traded to St. Louis for first baseman Joe Hague and then had a minor resurgence after becoming a regular again with the Red Sox in October 1973. When he was sold to Cleveland in June 1978, his pal, Bill "Spaceman" Lee, walked out on the Red Sox, charging that the move was ridiculous because Carbo was "the best 10th man in baseball."

On or off the field, Carbo earned a reputation as an eccentric. First, he was probably the only big leaguer who was also a hairdresser. Secondly, Carbo traveled with a giant stuffed gorilla, "Mighty Joe Young," and would actually pay for an extra ticket so he could go in style with his simian companion.

Jose Cardenal

Cardenal, Jose Roberto Domec **OF**

1963–80 B:10/7/1943, Matanzas, Cuba
Deb:4/14/1963, SF NL BR/TR 5'10", 150

G	AB	R	H	HR	RBI	OBP	SLG	AVG
2017	6964	936	1913	138	775	.335	.395	.275

Jose Cardenal may have been a fleet-footed Cuban, but for most of his major league career he must have felt more like the Flying Dutchman. Playing for nine teams—the Giants, Angels, Indians, Cardinals, Brewers, Cubs, Phillies, Mets, and Royals—in 18 seasons, Cardenal combined impressive speed with a somewhat moody personality. His speed made him a valuable asset, but his temperament prevented him from staying with a team for very long.

In one typical incident, Cardenal was on the field at Dodger Stadium on April 25, 1976, when his Cubs teammate, center fielder Rick Monday, rescued an American flag from the hands of two war-protesting flag burners. Cardenal observed tartly, "Now we have three great patriots: Lincoln, Washington, and Monday."

Signed by the Giants organization in September 1960—just as dictator Fidel Castro was slamming the door shut on Cuba—the lanky Cardenal displayed flashes of talent, but clearly not enough to rank him with teammates Willie Mays, Willie McCovey, or any of the Alous. In November 1964 San Francisco traded him to the Angels for catcher Jack Hiatt.

Cardenal, the cousin of A's shortstop Bert Campaneris, became a regular in Anaheim. After three seasons he was traded to Cleveland, where he tied a major league record by recording two unassisted outfield double plays in the same season.

He enjoyed his longest major league tenure with the Cubs, playing in the Chicago outfield from 1972 to 1977. Cardenal found his niche at Wrigley Field and in 1973 bettered .300 for the first time in his career. That year he paced the club in batting, doubles, and steals, and local sportswriters named him Player of the Year. On May 2, 1976, he went 6-for-7 in a single 14-inning game.

Released by the Mets in August 1980, Cardenal moved on to the Royals and helped propel them into postseason play, batting .340 down the stretch and seeing action in his first World Series. Following his retirement as a player he became a broadcaster with the Cubs' Spanish-speaking network and later a coach for the Reds, Cards, and Yanks. He joined the Devil Rays as a coach in 2000.

Leo Cardenas

Cardenas, Leonardo Lazaro **SS–3B**

1960–75 B:12/17/1938, Matanzas, Cuba
Deb:7/25/1960, CIN NL BR/TR 5'10", 163

G	AB	R	H	HR	RBI	OBP	SLG	AVG
1941	6707	662	1725	118	689	.313	.367	.257

Cuban-born Leo Cardenas was irritable and depressed back in 1957 while playing shortstop for Savannah in the Class A South Atlantic League. According to teammate Curt Flood, none of Cardenas' many letters home to the Pearl of the Antilles were being answered. When his teammates noticed that the Spanish-speaking Cardenas (son of outstanding Cuban shortstop Rafael Cardenas) was depositing his missives not into an official U.S. Post Office mailbox, but rather into a similar-looking trash can, the problem was solved.

Cardenas solved a lot of problems himself as shortstop for the Cincinnati Reds in the 1960s. A Gold Glove winner in 1965, Cardenas twice topped the National League in fielding and putouts and once in turning double plays. In 1971 with Minnesota he broke the American League record for fewest miscues in a season (11), a mark that lasted just a single season before being broken by Eddie Brinkman.

Cardenas was also potent with a bat, hitting a career-high 20 homers in 1966—the last time an NL shortstop hit 20 or more homers until Houston's Dickie Thon slammed 20 in 1983. When Cardenas retired in 1975, he was third on the all-time list for homers by NL shortstops with 118, behind only Ernie Banks and Pee Wee Reese.

After hanging up his glove Cardenas was employed in the automotive industry in Cincinnati. His son, Leo Jr., was selected by Minnesota in the 1983 amateur draft.

Rod Carew

Carew, Rodney Cline **2B–1B–DH**

1967-1985 B:10/1/1945 Gatun, Canal Zone
Deb:4/11/1967, MIN AL BL/TR 6', 182

G	AB	R	H	HR	RBI	OBP	SLG	AVG
2469	9315	1424	3053	92	1015	.395	.429	.328

Rod Carew was arguably the finest hitter for average of his era. He batted .300 or better for 15 consecutive years, a feat that, upon Carew's retirement, only five players had matched: Ty Cobb, Cap Anson, Honus Wagner, Stan Musial, and Ted Williams.

Even jaded major leaguers had a tendency to wax poetic about Carew's hitting. Pitcher Ken Holtzman once said, "He has an uncanny ability to move the ball around as if the bat were some kind of magic wand." White Sox infielder Alan Bannister contended, "He's the only guy I know who can go 4-for-3."

A Panamanian national, Carew was born on a train in the Canal Zone while his mother was traveling to a hospital in Colon. He was named after the physician who delivered him, Dr. Rodney Kline, who was riding at the time in one of the segregated train's whites-only cars. After a childhood of poverty, Carew emigrated to New York City at age 16 and was spotted on the sandlots by Twins scout Herb Stein. Carew passed a tryout and was given a $5,000 bonus with an additional $7,500 if he made the Twins. He made the grade in 1967.

Carew spent six years in the minors, and established himself as a hitter the moment he arrived in the majors. His first hit came April 11, 1967, against the Orioles' Dave McNally. "Your first hit in the majors—that's tops. It means you're on your way. When you get the first hit, then you can get the rest," said Carew. He collected 150 hits in his first year, hit .292, and was named American League Rookie of the Year.

Early in his career Carew was also an effective, aggressive baserunner who stole home 17 times—seven in 1969 alone. "I taught him how to steal home. That's all I ever taught him. As for hitting, he knew how to do that all by himself," said Billy Martin, Carew's manager in 1969.

Pitchers vainly schemed—legally or otherwise—to stop this human base-hit machine. Gaylord Perry once complained, "Greaseball, greaseball, greaseball. That's all I throw him, and he still hits them. He's the only player in baseball who consistently hits my grease. He sees the ball so well, I guess he can pick out the dry side." He hit *so* consistently that the only thing that stopped him was a torn ligament in his left knee that sidelined him for three months in 1970.

Carew enjoyed his finest year in 1977, flirting with .400 and finally catching national media attention—*after* he'd already won five of his seven career batting titles. He finished the year with a .388 average, the highest since Ted Williams registered the same mark in 1950. His league-leading total of 239 hits was the greatest since Bill Terry's 254 in 1930. He also led the league in runs, triples, and on-base percentage. Carew drove in a career-high 100 runs.

A loner, who never really enjoyed good relations with the press, Carew won the American League MVP Award. "There was a point at which I thought I'd never get the MVP, especially the years I played at Minnesota. We never won a pennant there, we were far away from the big media centers of Los Angeles and New York, and I wasn't a flashy power hitter but a guy who hit to spots, who bunted and stole bases," he said.

Carew felt that his most memorable game came June 26, 1977, against the White Sox, as he was striving to hit .400. It was T-Shirt Day, and the then-largest regular-season crowd in Twins history jammed Metropolitan Stadium. As a gesture to Carew, the shirts all featured his number "29" on them.

"I was really pumped up for that game and the crowd was on my side, like it never had been before," recalled Carew. "Every time I came to bat they cheered for me. Every time I got a hit, they gave me a standing ovation." Carew went 4-for-5, collecting two singles, a double, and a homer; he drove in six runs and raised his average to .403.

By then Carew had become a defensive liability, so he was moved from second to first base. In 1983 one especially harsh critic wrote, "He will not dive for a ball and his range is limited, even for a first baseman. He has difficulty in catching a throw from another infielder unless it is directly to him. He will not stretch for a throw. Fielding is not his strong point." Nevertheless, Carew was chosen for the All-Star team in every season from his rookie year of 1967 to his penultimate season in 1984.

In the late 1970s Carew became upset with the fiscal policies of Twins owner Calvin Griffith: "Griffith is horse spit. They [the Twins] are penny pinchers. They take everything they can get and give nothing in return." He demanded a trade, and in fact a deal with San Francisco was pending, but Carew vetoed it to stay in the AL. Finally Minnesota sent him to the Angels on February 3, 1979, for four players. Granted free agency on November 7, 1983, he re-signed with California and collected his 3,000th hit off Twins southpaw Frank Viola on August 4, 1985.

When his contract expired after the 1985 season, Carew's defensive skills had eroded to such an extent that no other club would sign him. Still, Carew's seven batting titles earned him a first-ballot election to the Hall of Fame in 1991. A roving hitting instructor after his retirement, he became an Angels coach in 1992.

Max Carey

Carey, Max George **OF**

1910–29 M(1932–33, 146–161) B:1/11/1890, Terre Haute, IN D:5/30/1976, Miami, FL Deb:10/3/1910, PIT NL BB/TR 5'11½", 170

G	AB	R	H	HR	RBI	OBP	SLG	AVG
2476	9363	1545	2665	70	800	.361	.386	.285

Max Carey, born Maximilian George Carnarius, gave up the ministry to become a thief—of bases. In 1909 he completed a six-year ministerial program at Concordia College in Fort Wayne, Indiana, and was about to embark on a religious career when he and a friend attended a Terre Haute Hottentots Central League game in Terre Haute. The South Bend shortstop didn't meet Carnarius' standards. When Carnarius told the South Bend Greens manager that he was much better, he got a tryout and the job. To protect his amateur status, he played as Max Carey.

In 48 games he batted only .158, but he fielded well enough to be invited back the next year. That fall he enrolled at Concordia Seminary in St. Louis. When he returned to his team in the spring, he found an even better shortstop in place. Undaunted, he moved to the outfield, lifted his batting average to .293, and fielded brilliantly. Late in the season the Pittsburgh Pirates purchased his contract. In two October games he collected three hits in six at bats and gave up all thoughts of the ministry.

In 1911 Carey won the Pirates' center field job. Pittsburgh was only two years removed from a world championship, and shortstop Honus Wagner and player-manager Fred Clarke were still on the squad. But the team was slipping in the standings. Carey, a 5-foot-11-inch, 170-pound switch hitter, batted only .258. Nevertheless, his ability to track down flyballs in spacious Forbes Field was more important than anything he did with a bat, and with his speed he was an exceptional fielder.

Nicknamed "Scoops" for his ability to dash in and turn line drives into outs, Carey was simply the National League's best outfielder for more than a dozen years. He led the league outfielders in putouts nine times, and trails only Willie Mays and Tris Speaker in career outfield putouts, with 6,363. Carey also knew what to do with the ball once he caught it. He led the league in assists four times and in double plays five times.

To many Pirates fans, Carey's basepath exploits were of even greater consequence than his fielding. He led the league in stolen bases 10 times. He took his first crown in 1913, when he swiped 61, his last in 1925, with 46. He stole 50 or more bases in six seasons, and his 738 career steals was the league record until Lou Brock surpassed it. During Carey's career the National League did not keep track of the number of times a player was caught stealing, but records show that in 1922 he stole 51 bases and was thrown out only twice.

Through 1919 Carey averaged only .273. Not an exceptional batter, he hit above .300 only twice during that span: .302 in 1912 and .307 in 1919 when illness limited him to 66 games. But his ability to draw walks kept his on-base average at an acceptable level for a leadoff man. Although he led the league in triples in 1914, with 17, he seldom hit home runs. Even more surprising for a player with his speed whose home park was Forbes Field, Carey never hit more than 26 doubles per season during the Dead Ball Era.

With the coming of the lively ball his performance at the plate improved dramatically. He averaged .304 from 1920 through 1926. He scored more than 100 runs in each season from 1922 through 1925, scored at least one run in 15 consecutive games in 1924, and led the league in triples a second time in 1923, with 19.

In 1924 the Pirates played the Tigers in an exhibition game, and Carey saw Ty Cobb play for the first time. Cobb held his bat with his hands spread 6 inches apart, and he would either slide his top hand down to pull the ball or move his bottom hand up to slap it to the opposite field, depending on the pitch. Honus Wagner, Carey's teammate for many years, had used the same style, and Carey decided to try it himself. In 1925 at age 35 he responded with his greatest year, hitting .343 and helping the Pirates win the pennant.

Pittsburgh squared off against the Washington Senators in the World Series. Carey doubled three times and stole a base in the seventh game to key a comeback against Walter Johnson. He batted .458 for the Series and scored six runs.

Bothered by sinus trouble, Carey started slowly in 1926. One day he overheard Fred Clarke, then an adviser to manager Bill McKechnie, tell McKechnie to bench Carey in favor of anyone, "even the batboy." Stung, Carey called a team meeting and complained about playing for "two managers."

Surprisingly, the players voted to let Clarke stay. Pirates owner Barney Dreyfuss heard about the dissension and also supported his old friend Clarke. He suspended Carey without pay, then sold him to Brooklyn. Carey gave the Dodgers a couple of fair years, but after appearing in 19 games in 1929, he retired as a player.

He returned to the Pirates as a coach in 1930, managed the Dodgers in 1932 and 1933, then managed in the minors and scouted intermittently through 1956. Carey was named to the Hall of Fame in 1961.

Tex Carleton

Carleton, James Otto **P**

1932–40 B:8/19/1906, Comanche, TX D:1/11/1977, Fort Worth, TX Deb:4/17/1932, STL NL BB/TR 6'1½", 180

W	L	PCT	G	SH	IP	BB	SO	ERA
100	76	.568	293	16	1607^{1}	561	808	3.91

In 1940, the rebuilt Brooklyn Dodgers launched their season with eight straight wins. In the ninth game manager Leo Durocher started a pitcher who was clearly over the hill, veteran National League righthander Tex Carleton. Carleton had not even pitched in the previous season, yet he responded by no-hitting Cincinnati to defeat the Reds' Jim Turner, 3–0.

Tex Carleton—the nickname was given to him by writer Ernest Lanigan—was born in Comanche, Texas. He pitched minor league ball in Texarkana, Austin, and Houston before moving up to the International League's Rochester Cardinals, where he no-hit the Toronto Maple Leafs. Returning to the Houston Buffs in 1931, Carleton went 20–7 with a 1.83 ERA but was overshadowed by Dizzy Dean, who posted a 26–10 season with a 1.53 ERA.

The two were promoted together to the Cardinals, and Carleton was again outpitched by Hall of Famer Dean. In 1934 Carleton went 16–11 and saved two games in relief; Dean went 30–7, to become the last NL pitcher to win 30 games in a season.

The Cards traded Carleton to the Chicago Cubs after the season, where Dean joined him again in 1938. Even near the end of his career Dean bettered Carleton, Dean going 7–1 to Carleton's 10–9.

Carleton did not play in 1939, but he resurfaced with Brooklyn in 1940. After his no-hitter, he appeared in 33 more games, and retired from baseball.

Steve Carlton

Carlton, Steve Norman **P**

1965–88 B:12/22/1944, Miami, FL Deb:4/12/1965, STL NL BL/TL 6'4", 210

W	L	PCT	G	SH	IP	BB	SO	ERA
329	244	.574	741	55	5217^{1}	1833	4136	3.22

With his devastating slider, Steve "Lefty" Carlton struck out more batters than any other southpaw in history, won more games than any lefthander except Warren Spahn, and collected four National League Cy Young Awards—even after he'd alienated the writers on the election committee.

His gangly build won Carlton the childhood nickname "Ichabod," after the fictional beanpole Ichabod Crane. But from the time scouts first told him he didn't throw hard enough to be a major leaguer, Carlton battled to improve his strength. First he used weights, even though weight lifting was then considered taboo for ballplayers, especially pitchers. Working with fitness guru Gus Hoefling in the mid-1970s, Carlton helped revolutionize baseball's approach to conditioning. Interestingly, the other pitcher most responsible for changing ideas about conditioning was Nolan Ryan, with whom Carlton swapped the career strikeout lead in 1983, after both had passed Walter Johnson.

Carlton's best-known routine involved working his pitching hand down to the bottom of a 3-foot barrel of rice. He also squeezed metal balls to build strength in his forearm, regularly deforming the balls with the imprint of his grip. Under Hoefling's guidance Carlton practiced a variety of martial arts workouts lasting up to two hours and also delved into Eastern philosophy. He even performed a pregame meditation routine in the trainer's room, visualizing the "fertile lanes" on the inside and outside of the plate, according to Tim McCarver, his batterymate for more than four seasons.

Carlton played Little League and American Legion ball and pitched for North Miami High School before signing with the St. Louis Cardinals for a $5,000 bonus in October 1963 while at Miami-Dade Community College. He began his professional career by blazing through the Class A West Carolinas League, going 10–1 with a 1.03 ERA in 11 starts. He was promoted twice, finishing the year in the Class AA Texas League, and spent all of 1965 with the Cardinals, seeing limited NL action.

After 19 Class AAA starts he came to the majors to stay in late 1966 and took a regular place in the Redbirds' rotation. He was second in wins, ERA, and innings pitched for the pennant-winning 1967 Cardinals, beginning a string of 18 straight seasons with double-figure wins, 161 or more strikeouts, and at least 190 innings.

Yet he lacked confidence during his first seasons and didn't believe in his own strength and stamina, or in his better-than-average fastball and shaky curve. Teammate Curt Flood recalled the young Carlton habitually returning to the bench between innings complaining he was exhausted, only to have the veterans convince him to try one more inning.

Carlton earned a start in Game 5 of the 1967 World Series, allowed only one unearned run but was eventually tagged with the loss. In the 1968 Series Carlton made a pair of relief appearances in the Cards' seven-game Series loss to Detroit.

After the Series, Carlton joined his team on a trip to Japan where he began experimenting with the slider that became his signature pitch. It broke down and in late to righthanded batters. In 1969, his first year using the pitch, his ERA dropped by 0.82, his strikeout total jumped by 48 compared to 1968 in roughly the same number of innings, and his win total climbed from 13 to 17. On September 15 he struck out 19 New York Mets, although he lost the game on two Ron Swoboda home runs.

Carlton held out because of a contract dispute and missed spring training in 1970, then lost 19 games. He turned around and won 20 in 1971, the first of six 20-win seasons, then held out again for a raise to $60,000. The Cardinals wouldn't budge from $55,000 and traded Carlton to Philadelphia for pitcher Rick Wise on February 25, 1972. The trade may have inspired revenge in Carlton: from then on he beat the Cardinals handily, compiling a 38–14 mark against his old club.

In 1972 Carlton became the fifth pitcher ever to win 20 games for a last-place team, collecting 27 of the Phillies' 59 victories, a record 45.8 percent. Carlton's 27–10 record included a 15-game winning streak, eight shutouts, and 30 complete games, which was the highest completion total since the 1940s. He won the pitching Triple Crown, leading the NL in wins, ERA, and strikeouts with 310, becoming the second NL pitcher to top 300. His 346$\frac{1}{3}$ innings were the most by a National Leaguer since 1953.

He was a unanimous choice for the Cy Young Award, and finished fifth in MVP voting. His 27 wins were the 12th-most this century for a pitcher and the most by any lefty since Hal Newhouser's first MVP year, 1944.

Carlton followed with 20 losses in 1973, and after two more mediocre seasons he returned to Cy Young form, thanks in part to his work with

Hoefling and his reunion with Tim McCarver. Carlton and McCarver had first met as Cardinals in 1965 and became friends, hunting together during the off-season and sharing a love of fine wine. Carlton continued to seek McCarver's advice even when they were on opposing teams, sometimes meeting him surreptitiously. When the Red Sox released McCarver in June 1975, Carlton encouraged the Phillies to sign him. Although Bob Boone was the Phillies' regular catcher, McCarver became Carlton's personal mask man for the rest of the decade. "We'll be buried 60 feet 6 inches apart," McCarver joked.

McCarver acknowledged that he helped Carlton with mechanics and confidence, but his biggest contribution may have been letting Carlton relax, thereby allowing the pitcher to exercise his extraordinary powers of concentration. "When Carlton was pitching," Phillies broadcaster Richie Ashburn once said, "you could have run a herd of elephants across the field and he wouldn't have seen them."

The Carlton–McCarver partnership worked. In 1976 and 1977, Carlton had a pair of 20-win seasons, and the Phillies won back-to-back NL East crowns, their first titles of any kind since 1950. Carlton started the 1976 playoff opener against Cincinnati but lost 6–3, beginning the Reds' postseason sweep.

Carlton's league-leading 23 victories in 1977 brought his second Cy Young Award, and he faced Dodgers southpaw and Cy Young runner-up Tommy John in the playoff opener at Los Angeles. Carlton took a 5–1 lead into the bottom of the seventh. But two walks and a single loaded the bases, and with two out, Ron Cey fouled off three 3–2 pitches before slugging a game-tying grand slam to knock Carlton from the game. The Dodgers eliminated the Phillies in Game 4 as John outdueled Carlton.

In 1978, the year Carlton completely stopped talking to the media because of some items in the Philadelphia newspapers, his record fell to 16–13, but the Phils won a third straight NL East title to earn a rematch against the Dodgers. He started Game 3 of the playoffs and went the distance on an eight-hitter, beating Don Sutton, 9–4. Carlton, a .201 career hitter who finished in the top 10 in hits and RBIs among 20th-century pitchers, knocked in four runs with a three-run homer and an RBI single in the Phils' only win of the playoffs.

Carlton won 24 games in 1980, earning his third Cy Young Award, and Philadelphia returned to postseason play. He won the playoff opener over the Houston Astros but left Game 4 trailing, 2–0, in the sixth. The Phillies went on to win in 10 innings and took Game 5—the fourth straight extra-inning contest of the NLCS—to face the Kansas City Royals in the World Series. He started Game 2 but was not credited with the win. However, he went seven innings in the Game 6 clincher, as the Phillies won their first-ever world championship.

The Phillies got back into postseason play in 1981, but after a fine regular season, Carlton lost both division playoff starts to the Montreal Expos as they bounced the Phillies. In 1982 Carlton had his final great year, leading the league with 23 wins and topping the circuit in complete games, shutouts, innings, and strikeouts. He was also chosen for his 10th All-Star Game and collected his fourth Cy Young Award.

At age 38 Carlton fell to 15–16 in 1983 for the Phillies, who were called the "Wheeze Kids" because a number of the players were past the usual age for retirement. Nevertheless, he collected his fifth NL innings and strikeout crowns and his 300th victory, on September 24, over the Cardinals. Carlton started the playoff opener at Los Angeles and shut out the Dodgers for 7⅔ innings for the win. In Game 4 he gave up only one run in six innings as the Phillies cruised to a 7–2 win, sending them on to the World Series against the Baltimore Orioles. He started Game 3 but was a loser in his final Series appearance.

Going on 40, Carlton worked less but more effectively in 1984, slugging his first grand slam (and 12th of 13 career homers) off Fernando Valenzuela, his successor as the league's best lefty. In 1985 Carlton suffered his first serious injury, a strained left rotator cuff, and was on the disabled list for more than two months. He came back in 1986, but the Phillies tried to get him to retire after his 16 starts resulted in an ERA of over 6.00.

Carlton refused to leave and broke his public silence to explain his reasons and thank his supporters. The Phillies released him in late June. He struggled with the Giants, White Sox, Indians, and Twins before finally retiring in May 1988.

At the end of his career, Carlton ranked second in strikeouts to only Nolan Ryan. In 1989 the Phillies retired Carlton's No. 32, reestablishing the warm relationship between the franchise, the fans, and the greatest pitcher in the team's history, the owner of virtually every Phillies pitching mark. He was elected to the Hall of Fame in 1994, his first year of eligibility.

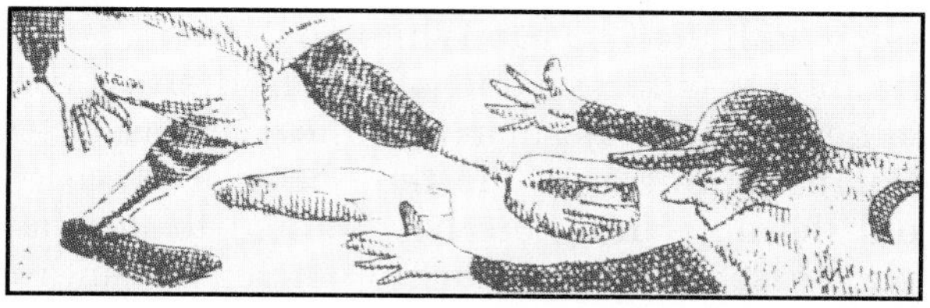

Hick Carpenter

Carpenter, Warren William **3B**
1879–92 B:8/16/1855, Grafton, MA D:4/18/1937, San Diego, CA Deb:5/1/1879, SYR NL BR/TL 5'11", 186

G	AB	R	H	HR	RBI	OBP	SLG	AVG
1118	4637	720	1202	18	543	.281	.322	.259

Hick Carpenter holds the major league record for games played at third base by a lefthanded fielder. Although other southpaws have also played the position, none have approached Carpenter's total of 1,059 games. He was notable not only for his durability but also for his fielding ability; historian Lee Allen called him "the most skillful of the lefthanded infielders of the last century."

Originally a first baseman, Carpenter moved to third base with Cincinnati in 1880. Given the irregularities of early playing fields, it is not surprising that Carpenter averaged nearly 60 errors a year, recording as many as 70 in 1887 and 69 in 1888. Except in his first year, Carpenter's fielding average never rose above .881.

When the Reds released him in 1889 the *Cincinnati Enquirer* wrote, "It is often that a man's nickname is a detriment to his success. People have called Carpenter 'Old Hick' for so long that people think he has been around forever." After retiring as a player, Carpenter became a Pullman conductor and a deputy customs collector.

Chico Carrasquel

Carrasquel, Alfonso (Colon) **SS-3B**
1950–59 B:1/23/1928, Caracas, Venezuela Deb:4/23/1950, CHI AL BR/TR 6', 170

G	AB	R	H	HR	RBI	OBP	SLG	AVG
1325	4644	568	1199	55	474	.334	.342	.258

Chico Carrasquel was the first of a long line of shortstops from Venezuela who made their marks in the major leagues. He was followed by Dave Concepcion, Luis Aparicio, and Ozzie Guillen, among others.

Carrasquel was a smooth and graceful fielder with a strong throwing arm. A four-time All-Star, he led American League shortstops in fielding percentage three times. He was a solid hitter who compiled a .258 lifetime batting average for 10 major league seasons, most of them with the Chicago White Sox.

Chico was the second of 10 children whose father was a salesman for the Caracas Beer Company. But from the time he was 11 years old the only thing the boy wanted to do was play baseball. His maternal uncle, Alejandro "Alex" Carrasquel, had pitched in the major leagues with the Washington Senators from 1939 through 1945. Young Alfonso looked so good on the field and had such a strong arm that by age 11 he was playing in a league reserved for 16-year-olds. He started as a third baseman and even pitched part of the time before switching to shortstop. For part of one season he played for three amateur teams at the same time. At 15 he quit school to play for the General Tire Company in Caracas. He reported to work for the company once in a while, but basically he was hired to play baseball.

In 1946 Carrasquel turned professional at age 18, signing with the Venezuelan Winter League. He became Venezuela's Rookie of the Year and two years later signed with the Brooklyn Dodgers. They assigned him to Montreal but because he couldn't speak English, Royals manager Clay Hopper refused to play him. The Dodgers reassigned him to Fort Worth of the Texas League where teammates first gave him the nickname "Chico." He batted .315 in his first season of U.S. baseball and compiled the second-best fielding average among regular shortstops in the Texas League.

The Dodgers, though, had no intention of replacing Pee Wee Reese at short, so they finally agreed to sell Carrasquel to the Chicago White Sox. He joined the team in 1950 and was voted the third-best rookie in the American League that year. In 141 games he hit .282 with 72 runs scored and 46 RBIs.

But all was not rosy for the Venezuelan youngster. Although he had no problem adjusting to the game on the major league level, the language barrier was another matter. He knew little more than "yes," "no," and "thank you" in English. "Every time I order coffee, they bring me Coca Cola," Carrasquel once said.

Fortunately for Carrasquel, the White Sox had a pitcher on the team named Luis Aloma, who hailed from Havana, Cuba, and could converse with Carrasquel in Spanish. Another supporter was Luke Appling, whom Carrasquel succeeded at shortstop for the White Sox. Appling became a coach with the team, and his main project was turning Carrasquel into a big league shortstop.

Appling was a patient teacher and Carrasquel a willing pupil. In explaining what he wanted his student to practice, Appling would talk slowly, using gestures. The results were almost always pleasing. Carrasquel played the game hard and loved it as much as Appling.

Carrasquel had a career-best 24-game hitting streak as a rookie and was a standout at shortstop. When asked how he was able to play so well despite his linguistic shortcomings,

Carrasquel flashed his winning smile and said, "The ball, she speak no English and the bat, she speak no English."

In 1954 the White Sox won 94 games and finished 17 games back of the pennant-winning Indians. Carrasquel led AL shortstops in double plays, hit a career-high 12 homers, and scored 106 runs. He hit .256 for the White Sox the following season before being traded to Cleveland. Replacing him as Chicago's shortstop was fellow Venezuelan Luis Aparicio, who went on to a Hall of Fame career.

Carrasquel was the Indians' starting shortstop in 1956 and 1957. In June 1958 he was traded to Kansas City for infielder Billy Hunter. Four months later he was swapped to Baltimore for future major league manager Dick Williams. After hitting .223 for the Orioles in 1959, Carrasquel retired from the game.

He returned to Venezuela and became a coach and later manager for the Caracas Lions. He also scouted in Venezuela for the Royals and the Mets. He then spent 10 years as a radio and TV analyst in the Venezuelan Winter League. In 1990 he joined the Spanish-language broadcasting team of the White Sox.

Bill Carrigan

Carrigan, William Francis **C**

1906–16 M(1913–16, 1927–29, 489–500)
B:10/22/1883, Lewiston, ME D:7/8/1969, Lewiston, ME
Deb:7/7/1906, BOS AL BR/TR, 5'9", 175

G	AB	R	H	HR	RBI	OBP	SLG	AVG
709	1970	194	506	6	235	.334	.314	.257

Never much of a hitter, lantern-jawed Bill Carrigan was a competent catcher for the Boston Red Sox, but he had greater success later as their manager. In an age when a backstop needed courage, durability, and aggressiveness as much as playing ability, "Rough" Carrigan handled about half of the team's catching chores each season beginning in 1906. Only in 1910 did he appear in more than 100 games. Although the Sox won the 1912 pennant and World Series, petty jealousies and injuries brought them down the next season.

Midway through the 1913 season Carrigan was named player-manager, and the team responded to his firm leadership by nudging back into the first division. After raising the team to second in 1914, he led the Sox to the American League pennant and the World Series the next two years. The 1916 win was particularly noteworthy because Boston had traded their best player, Tris Speaker, before the season.

At the peak of his success, Carrigan retired to become a banker. In 1927, after the Red Sox had fallen to arguably their lowest point in history, Carrigan was lured back. The Sox finished a well-deserved last each year during the next three seasons. It is probable that no manager could have won with Boston's personnel, but the game had changed; the lively ball had made baseball a free-swinging game, and Carrigan was still rooted in the Dead Ball Era. He retired for the second time after the 1929 season.

Clay Carroll

Carroll, Clay Palmer **P**

1964–1978 B:5/2/1941, Clanton, AL Deb:9/2/1964,
MIL NL BR/TR 6'1", 200

W	L	PCT	G	SV	IP	BB	SO	ERA
96	73	.568	731	143	1353^1	442	681	2.94

When Sparky Anderson was nicknamed "Captain Hook," because he replaced starting pitchers with such glee, one of the relievers he called for most was Clay Carroll, who piled up 143 career saves.

Carroll was at his best in the postseason, winning four, losing two, saving two, and chalking up a stingy 1.39 ERA. A two-time All-Star, the fastballing Carroll tried to get by on stuff rather than smarts. He posted a career record of 96–73 and was known for being able to withstand pressure under fire. Johnny Bench said of him, "Clay tells you he can do the job, then he goes out and does it."

Nicknamed "Hawk" because of his sharp nose, Carroll started in the Braves organization in 1961 with Davenport of the Midwest League. A country boy from Clanton, Alabama, he starred at Boise in 1962, leading the Pioneer League with 14 wins and 16 complete games. He also played with Austin of the Texas League and with Denver of the Pacific Coast League.

He began in the big leagues with Milwaukee, moved with the Braves to Atlanta, and led the National League with 73 appearances in 1966. Traded to the Reds in June 1968, he led the league in saves in 1972 with a since-broken league record of 37; he tied for the lead in appearances and was named NL Fireman of the Year.

He slumped to 14 saves in 1973, and Anderson tried him as a starter five times. Then, back on track, he went 12–5 in 1974 and came up big in the 1975 World Series, winning Game 7.

His reward: a trade to the White Sox in December. Injured for part of 1976, he was traded to the Cardinals in March 1977, was traded back to the White Sox for three players that August, and spent most of 1978 in the minors before returning to the major leagues with the Pirates for just two games.

Fred Carroll

Carroll, Frederick Herbert **C–OF**

1884–91 B:7/2/1864, Sacramento, CA D:11/7/1904, San Rafael, CA Deb:5/1/1884, COL AA BR/TR 5'11" 185

G	AB	R	H	HR	RBI	OBP	SLG	AVG
754	2892	546	820	27	366	.370	.408	.284

The handsome Fred Carroll was one of the first and most famous ballplayers to come from California. He came East with Ed "Cannonball" Morris in 1883 to play with the Reading Actives. Primarily known as Morris' batterymate, the two friends made the big leagues the next year with Columbus of the American Association. They played together until 1890.

Seven of Carroll's eight big league years were spent in Pittsburgh. He was a versatile player who played several positions throughout his career. He predominantly caught and played the outfield, but he also played first base, and could fill in at shortstop and third base. One of the highlights of Carroll's career was playing for the "All-American" team that joined the Chicago White Stockings for a global tour in 1888–89.

In 1890 both Carroll and Morris played for Pittsburgh's entry in the Player's League. After the season, Pittsburgh's Player's League club merged with the National League Allegheny team to form what is now the Pittsburgh Pirates. Carroll's last major league season was in 1891, after which he returned to the west to play ball. He played for several years in the California League, followed by two seasons in the Western League. Carroll showed exceptional power in the Western League, belting 43 home runs in those last two years.

After his playing days Carroll ran a successful freight business. He was only 40 years old when he died of heart disease in San Rafael, California.

Gary Carter

Carter, Gary Edmund **C–OF–1B**

1974–92 B:4/8/1954, Culver City, CA Deb:9/16/1974, MON NL BR/TR 6'2", 215

G	AB	R	H	HR	RBI	OBP	SLG	AVG
2296	7971	1025	2092	324	1225	.338	.439	.262

Gary Carter succeeded Johnny Bench as the National League's best catcher in the late 1970s. He had a short, powerful stroke that resembled a logger swinging an ax. He hit off a stiff front leg and generated enough power with his upper body to hit 20 or more homers nine times and collect 100 or more RBIs four times.

A three-time Gold Glover, "the Kid" set the league career record for games caught (2,056), and is, according to one study, the fifth-best catcher ever, behind Gabby Hartnett, Yogi Berra, Bill Dickey, and Mickey Cochrane.

A high school All-America quarterback in Fullerton, California, two-year captain of the baseball, basketball, and football teams, and a National Honor Society member, Carter signed a letter of intent to play football at UCLA. Instead he opted for a professional baseball career after the Montreal Expos selected him in the third round of the June 1972 draft.

In the minors, Carter played the outfield, the infield corners, and behind the plate. Promoted to the Expos in September 1974, he played mostly in right field his first two years in the majors. His bat was good enough to win him a spot on the 1975 NL All-Star team, the first of his 10 All-Star Game appearances, and Rookie of the Year honors from *The Sporting News*.

Carter missed 55 games with two hand injuries during his sophomore season. He recovered to hit three home runs off Jim Rooker at Olympic Stadium on April 20, 1977, and finished with a, then club-record 31 homers that season. On June 15, 1977, the Expos traded Barry Foote to Philadelphia, making Carter their regular catcher.

Under the tutelage of former Dodger Norm Sherry, Carter became one of the best defensive catchers in the game. In 1978 he established a major league record with just one passed ball in 152 games behind the plate. Over the course of his career, he led NL catchers in fielding percentage twice, assists four times, double plays five times, games played a league-record six consecutive years, total chances a league-record eight times, and putouts a league-record eight times.

Carter played in his second All-Star Game in 1979 in Seattle. He recorded the Expos' first All-Star Game hit, and in the eighth inning took Dave Parker's throw to nail Brian Downing at the plate and preserve a 6–6 tie. The Expos led the NL East in the final week of the season, when Carter tore ligaments in his thumb. Without him, Montreal lost four of its last five games and was overtaken by the Pittsburgh Pirates.

In 1980 Carter topped 100 RBIs for the first time in his career, finishing second in the NL Most Valuable Player voting to Mike Schmidt. The Expos also ended second to the Philadelphia Phillies by a game in the NL East race. The following season Carter made his first All-Star start behind the plate and smacked two homers to win the game's MVP award.

The Expos won the split season's second-half title and beat first-half winner Philadelphia in the division playoff. In Game 2 against Philadelphia, Carter's two-run homer was the difference in a 3–1 win; he hit safely in all five games, adding the Expos' only other homer in

Game 4, and leading all Montreal batters with a .421 average, three doubles, and six RBIs.

Montreal met Los Angeles in the Championship Series, and Carter extended his postseason hitting streak to 10 games, leading the Expos with a .438 batting average. However, Montreal fell in five, losing two of the final three games in their home park.

Carter signed an eight-year contract prior to the 1982 season and collected the most votes for the that year's All-Star Game at Montreal. But his popularity with the fans, won with natural ebullience and a camera-mugging attitude, drew resentment from other players. Carter once overheard a teammate complaining about the clubhouse stools, so he bought a new set of chairs for the players. Some teammates thought Carter was flaunting his wealth and assuming team leadership.

In 1984 he tied for the league's most RBIs with 106, hit a career-best .294, and won his second All-Star MVP award with a tie-breaking homer off Dave Stieb. But after the Winter Meetings, Montreal traded Carter to the New York Mets for infielder Hubie Brooks, catcher Mike Fitzgerald, pitcher Floyd Youmans, and outfielder Herm Winningham.

Although he was recovering from surgery on his right knee, Carter batted cleanup in 1985 and hit a career-high 32 homers, including a game-winning 10th-inning shot off Neil Allen in his first game as a Met. He had the second three-homer game of his career in San Diego on September 3, and then clubbed two more the following day to tie the major league record for home runs in consecutive games. He finished with 100 RBIs, and New York stayed in the pennant race until the final weekend.

In 1986 Carter drove in 105 runs—his third straight season in triple figures—and hit 24 homers despite missing two weeks with torn thumb ligaments as the Mets coasted to the NL East crown. He stroked a double, scoring the game-winning tally in Game 2 to even the NLCS against the Houston Astros, but that was his only hit in 21 at bats until his single off Charlie Kerfeld in the 12th inning of Game 5 gave the Mets a 2–1 win. In Game 6 he added two hits, including a 14th-inning single that ignited a rally that put the Mets temporarily ahead. New York eventually won that game in 16 innings, advancing to the World Series against the Boston Red Sox.

The Kid had two hits and drove in a run as the Mets lost the first two games. In Game 3 at Fenway Park, Carter doubled in a run in the first inning, singled in two more in the seventh, and then hit two homers and a double in Game 4 as the Mets evened the Series. In Game 6 Carter's eighth-inning sacrifice fly tied the score, 3–3, forcing extra innings. Then, with two out in the 10th and the Mets down, 5–3, Carter's two-out single started the Mets' miracle rally. In Game 7 Carter's bloop to right knocked in the tying run as the Mets overcame a 3–0 deficit to win the world championship.

Carter's skills began to decline in 1987, and the Mets dropped him from the cleanup spot to sixth in the order. In 1988, named Mets co-captain with Keith Hernandez, he won his eighth straight, and final, nod as the league's starting All-Star catcher. He hit his 299th career homer on May 10 and then went more than 230 at bats before homering again. On August 11 he blasted No. 300 at Wrigley Field. He also broke a 10-year, 0-for-27 pinch-hitting drought, going 4-for-7 off the bench.

In the 1988 NLCS opener against the Dodgers, Carter's bloop double scored two runs in the ninth off Jay Howell, giving New York a 3–2 win. He had five more hits, including a triple, and knocked in two runs in the Mets' seven-game playoff loss. In 1989 he batted .183 in 50 games, ending his streak of 12 years with 100 games caught, one shy of the record held by Bill Dickey and Johnny Bench.

Carter became a free agent at season's end and signed with the Giants. He saw limited action, and in 1991 he played 101 games with the Dodgers. In 1992 he returned to the Expos and retired at season's end.

Carter finished with 298 home runs as a catcher, the fourth-best total among receivers, and second only to Bench among National League backstops. Upon his retirement he joined the Florida Marlins television team as an analyst. In 1993 Montreal retired his uniform No. 8.

Joe Carter

Carter, Joseph Chris **OF–1B–DH**

1983–98 B:3/7/60, Oklahoma City, OK Deb:7/30/83, CHI NL BR/TR 6'3" 215

G	AB	R	H	HR	RBI	OBP	SLG	AVG
2189	8422	1170	2184	396	1445	.310	.464	.259

Despite a long and impressive career, Joe Carter retired to little fanfare after the 1998 season. Carter, who played for six teams in his 16-year career, owns a distinction shared by only eight other players in baseball history. And he owns one more mark that is shared by no one.

When Carter plated his 100th run for Toronto in 1997, he became only the ninth player in baseball history to reach 100 RBIs in 10 separate seasons. Several days after achieving the feat, he was still unaware that he was part of this select club. When handed a piece of paper in the clubhouse listing the other eight, he smiled broadly, humbled to be among company of Goose Goslin, Babe Ruth, Lou Gehrig, Jimmie Foxx, Al Simmons, Stan Musial, Willie Mays, and Hank Aaron—all members of the Hall of Fame.

Carter's greatest glory, however, was not statistical but historic. Playing at Toronto in Game 6 of the 1993 World Series, he came up to face Philadelphia closer Mitch Williams. With the Blue Jays trailing, 6–5, Carter got the bat head under a low fastball and golfed it down the left-field line, just over the 328-foot marker in the SkyDome. Carter's Series-ending homer was only the second walk-off home run to clinch a World Series, joining Bill Mazeroski in Game 7 of the 1960 Series. His game-ending blast had an added distinction: it was the first walk-off home run in which the batting team was trailing. The blow gave Toronto back-to-back world championships.

The five-time All-Star was involved in three historic trades during his career: in 1984 he was traded from the Chicago Cubs to the Cleveland Indians in the mid-season deal for eventual National League Cy Young winner Rick Sutcliffe; in 1989 he was traded by the Indians to the San Diego Padres for Carlos Baerga and Sandy Alomar, Jr.; and after one year in San Diego he was shipped to Toronto with Roberto Alomar in a blockbuster deal for Tony Fernandez and Fred McGriff.

Carter ended his career as he began it—in the National League. He hit seven home runs in limited action with San Francisco after being traded from Baltimore in mid-season. Carter was named to the "Level of Excellence" at SkyDome in 1999 along with former Blue Jays manager Cito Gaston.

Alexander Cartwright

Cartwright, Alexander Joy, Jr.

Baseball Pioneer B:4/17/1820, New York, NY
D:9/9/1892, Hawaii

Alexander Cartwright's Hall of Fame plaque reads: "Alexander Joy Cartwright Jr. 'Father of Modern Base Ball.' Set bases 90 feet apart. Established nine innings a game and 9 players a team. Organized the Knickerbocker Baseball Club of N.Y. in 1845. Carried baseball to Pacific Coast and Hawaii in pioneer days."

According to legend, Abner Doubleday invented baseball in 1839 at Cooperstown, New York, but this story has since been thoroughly disproved. Baseball was never really "invented"; it evolved. Young Americans had played the old English game of rounders and several similar games since the 1700s. Those games gradually metamorphosed into baseball as we know it today, and Cartwright had an important role in that evolution.

Born in New York in 1820, Cartwright left school at age 16 and entered the business world, as was common in those days. Bright and ambitious, he started as a clerk and soon advanced to a position of responsibility.

After work, Cartwright joined other young New Yorkers to play a version of rounders. The group included merchants, lawyers, and clerks whose professional status allowed them to leave work in midafternoon to enjoy healthy recreation. Common laborers usually had to work until dusk.

According to one participant, Dr. Daniel L. Adams, the group's game was called "base ball" rather than rounders. Adams began playing after 1839, when he set up his medical practice in New York. His group was preceded by an earlier association, "the New York Base Ball Club," but according to Adams it had "no definite organization" and did not last long.

Several members of the New York Base Ball Club joined other young men in a new assembly that included Cartwright. In his diary, Cartwright claims to be one of the group's better players. The jovial and gregarious clerk was a leader of the group when it wrote a formal constitution that named it "the Knickerbocker Base Ball Club of September 23, 1845." Cartwright served as secretary and vice president.

Cartwright may have been the first to suggest to his fellow Knickerbockers that they write down the rules of baseball, thereby codifying the regulations members had been following for years. He and three other members defined 14 rules, only three of which differed markedly from the rules of rounders.

They laid out the field in a diamond shape rather than a square, introduced the concept of foul territory, and discarded the practice of retiring a runner by hitting him with a thrown ball ("plunking"). These rules were created out of necessity: the diamond and foul territory were suggested by the dimensions of Madison Square, where the Knickerbockers played until 1846, and plunking was eliminated as ungentlemanly and potentially hazardous.

Perhaps more interesting is what the new rules did not include. The bases were not set at 90 feet apart. The length of the game was not set at nine innings, nor were the number of players mandated as nine. All three features are falsely credited to Cartwright on his Hall of Fame plaque.

Other equally important rules that led to the modern game were also not included by the Knickerbockers. The distance from the pitcher's mound to the plate was not mentioned; the rules did not state that a ball had to be caught on fly to record an out (the first bounce was considered good enough); and there was no system of balls and strikes.

The only fixed dimension was the 42 paces from home to second base and from third base to first.

For many years this was interpreted as placing the bases 90 feet apart. However, the size of a "pace" in 1845 was 2 to 3 feet depending on which authority is consulted. The Knickerbockers' bases were only about 75 feet apart if the smaller measurement is used.

With their rules in hand, the Knickerbockers advertised for opponents. On June 19, 1846, they met the New York Nine at the Elysian Fields in Hoboken, New Jersey, in what is often called the first modern baseball game. The Nine won, 23–1. The score indicates that the game followed the rules of rounders, ending after a specific number of runs rather than innings. Although Cartwright was supposedly one of the best Knickerbockers, he umpired the game and enforced a 6-cent fine, payable on the spot, for swearing.

Over the next few years the Knickerbockers rarely played with nine men on a side. More often they had eight men—three outfielders, three infielders, the pitcher, and the catcher—although 10 and sometimes as many as 12 players were also used.

Cartwright went to California during the great gold rush of 1849. As he made his way across the Great Plains, he supposedly taught baseball to anyone willing to play. By August, he and another Knickerbocker arrived in San Francisco, where they introduced the game to the West Coast. Arriving too late to strike gold, after only six weeks they gave up and booked passage for New York on a boat taking the Pacific route.

Cartwright became ill and put ashore on the Sandwich Islands, now known as Hawaii. He fell in love with the tropical islands and sent for his family, who joined him in 1851. His interest in baseball continued, and he established leagues throughout the islands. He prospered in business and died a wealthy man in 1892.

The game continued to evolve in New York. In 1849 and 1850 the position of shortstop was created to facilitate relaying outfield throws. D.L. Adams was one of the first to play at that position. Initially, the position was set between the outfield and the infield, for at that time the ball was so light that few outfielders could throw it all the way to the infield.

As the ball was eventually wound tighter, becoming heavier and thus easier to throw, the shortstop drifted closer to the infield and helped to greatly reduce the number of base hits. In 1857 the bases were set at 90 feet apart. As the size of the diamond increased, so too did the importance of the new position.

In May 1857, Adams presided over a convention of ballplayers who decided that the winner of a game was the team that was ahead after nine innings rather than the first team to score 21 runs. The following year the group adopted the name "the National Association of Ball Players." Adams pushed for a rule requiring that the batter be called out if the ball was caught on the fly, not on the first bounce. This provoked intense argument, and in 1860 it was finally decided that the "fly ball rule could be used if both teams agreed beforehand," but it was not made an official rule.

Alexander Cartwright's contributions to baseball would have been overshadowed by Adams' more substantive role in the game's development had it not been for Abner Doubleday. In 1938 the Hall of Fame in Cooperstown, New York, was nearly ready to open, and a great deal of the publicity named Doubleday as one of the game's inventors.

This grated on the Cartwright family. Cartwright's grandson Bruce presented the Hall with his grandfather's diaries, clippings, and other paraphernalia that showed how Cartwright and the Knickerbockers had codified the transformation of rounders into baseball, thus rendering the Doubleday tale a fairy tale. But by that time publicity surrounding the Doubleday legend was too widespread for the founders of the Hall to admit their mistake. After all, the general's supposed brainstorm was the reason for building the Hall of Fame in Cooperstown in the first place.

Fortunately, no one had to call the Civil War hero a liar. He never claimed to have invented baseball and had been dead for a decade before anyone else asserted that he had. The Hall of Fame wisely chose to downplay the myth, and Doubleday was never elected as Cartwright was in 1939—a de facto rejection of the Doubleday claim. However, the far more significant Adams was overlooked.

Cartwright's role in developing the early game in New York and in spreading it across the continent to Hawaii is certainly important. But it is more accurate to view him as a symbol of all those who helped to change the game from an old English diversion into the American national pastime.

Rico Carty

Carty, Ricardo Adolfo Jacobo **DH-OF-1B**
1963–1979 B:9/1/1939, San Pedro de Macoris, Dominican Republic Deb:9/15/1963, MIL NL BR/TR 6'3", 200

G	AB	R	H	HR	RBI	OBP	SLG	AVG
1651	5606	712	1677	204	890	.372	.464	.299

Rico Carty once homered twice in the same at bat, with Toronto of the International League in 1963. The first four-bagger was disallowed because time had been called. Carty returned to the batter's box and promptly hit another ball into the seats. That incident prefigured the rest of Rico Carty's career. If something bad could happen to him, it would—but after it did, Carty, a lifetime

.299 hitter, would usually go right on hitting as if nothing had ever happened.

Carty was born Ricardo Adolfo Jacobo in San Pedro de Macoris, a region of the Dominican Republic famous for producing exceptional ballplayers. Originally a boxer, he switched to baseball, became a catcher, and was so impressive that 10 clubs signed him—not scouted, but signed. Because Carty hadn't actually accepted money from any of the 10 teams, National Association president George Trautman ruled that Carty could go with whomever he wanted. He chose the Braves, hung up his catcher's gear, and became an outfielder.

After two at bats with the Braves at the end of the 1963 season, Carty went to spring training with the big club in 1964. He struggled initially, but on the advice of hitting coach Dixie Walker began waiting on pitches "until the last second." As a result Carty enjoyed a freshman year that he felt should have earned him Rookie of the Year honors over Dick Allen. That year Carty hit .330 with 28 doubles, four triples, 22 homers, and 88 RBIs in 455 at bats for the highest-scoring team in the league. Allen, meanwhile, hit .318 with 38 doubles, a league-leading 13 triples, 29 homers, and 91 RBIs in 632 at bats; Allen, however, committed an embarrassing 41 errors at third base.

In 1965 Carty suffered chronic back problems and missed half the season. A specially designed shoe helped to correct the situation, and he hit .326 the following year as a regular player. In 1967, however, Carty missed 18 games with an injured shoulder after a baseline collision with Ron Hunt. He hit only .255.

Once, during spring training in 1968, Carty jokingly pretended that he didn't feel well. The team physician, taking Carty seriously, found that the ballplayer had a slight fever and that his appetite was abnormal. As it turned out, Carty was in the early stages of tuberculosis and missed the entire season. He came back as strong as ever in 1969—except for his shoulder, which he dislocated seven times. Atlanta won the National League West in the first year of division play, and Carty hit .342 in 104 games, driving in 58 runs in only 304 at bats.

Carty avoided mishap in 1970 and won the NL batting crown with a whopping .366 average, 25 homers, and 101 RBIs in only 478 at bats. That winter while playing in the Dominican Winter League, Carty collided with Matty Alou and fractured his kneecap. He missed all of 1971. To compound matters, his newly opened Atlanta restaurant, the "Rico Carty Open Pit Barbecue," burned down, and the better part of Carty's losses were not covered by fire insurance.

As if Carty hadn't endured enough misfortune, he was stopped and attacked by Atlanta police officers in August 1971 while driving his Dominican brother-in-law home. The officers kept beating and kicking him until they realized who he was. Fortunately, fears that Carty's vision might be damaged were unfounded.

True to form, he came back in 1972, although not as strong as before, hitting .277 in 86 games. He failed to get along with manager Eddie Mathews and was traded to Texas right after the season. In Texas he was injured again, and again he didn't see eye to eye with his manager, in this case Whitey Herzog. Carty was sold to the Cubs in August, and a month later was shipped off to Oakland.

Oakland released him in December, and Carty played with Cordoba of the Mexican League in 1974, batting .354. On August 17, 1974, he made it back to the majors with Cleveland and revived his career. As the Tribe's designated hitter he batted .363 in 33 games that season and then .308 and .310 in the next two seasons. In March 1978 he was traded to Toronto, who dealt him back to Oakland in August. He returned to the Blue Jays that October on waivers, and his last year was 1979, when he hit .256 as a 40-year-old.

"I never gave up when things were bad," Carty said. "Not one moment. I think that's what helped me. My positive thinking."

Since leaving the major leagues Carty has been associated with the Dominican League. Also, he holds the honorary rank of general in the Dominican Army.

Bob Caruthers

Caruthers, Robert Lee **P–OF**

1884–93 M(1892, 16–32) U(1902–03) B:1/5/1864, Memphis, TN D:8/5/1911, Peoria, IL Deb:9/7/1884, STL AA BL/TR 5'7", 138

W	L	PCT	G	SH	IP	BB	SO	ERA
218	99	.688	340	24	2828^{2}	597	900	2.83

G	AB	R	H	HR	RBI	OBP	SLG	AVG
705	2465	508	695	29	359	.391	.400	.282

At 5 feet 7 inches and 138 pounds, Bob Caruthers may not have seemed like much of a dual pitching and hitting threat. Yet in both the National League and its 19th-century rival, the ill-fated American Association, "Parisian Bob" was an athlete of great stature. His won-lost percentage of .688 on a record of 218–99 is one of the best ever, and his lifetime batting average was a respectable .282 in nearly 2,500 at bats.

Caruthers was best known as a pitcher. From 1885 through 1890 his hurling helped propel two different clubs to five pennants. From 1885 through 1889 he never won fewer than 29 games, and he won 40 in both 1885 and 1889. He combined a deceptive delivery with what was then known as "headwork," the ability to outguess an opposing batter.

He had a sickly childhood. A Memphis doctor recommended outdoor exercise to improve his chances for survival, and Caruthers developed a compact but muscular physique. By 1883 he was an outfielder with Grand Rapids of the Northwestern League. He became a pitcher the next season with Minneapolis in the same circuit, and when that club folded he signed for $250 per month with Chris Von der Ahe's St. Louis Browns of the American Association. In 1885 Caruthers recorded 40 of the pennant-winning team's 79 victories.

He earned his unusual nickname in the off-season after he and a teammate, catcher Doc Bushong, vacationed in the French capital. While nibbling on croissants, Caruthers conducted a long-distance contract negotiation with the colorful, but sometimes frugal, Von der Ahe. Parisian Bob ended up inking a pact for $3,200.

Caruthers became the first of three pitchers ever to record four extra-base hits in a single game when he smashed two homers, a double, and a triple on August 16, 1886. Parisian Bob also hit 29 home runs in his career, including eight in 1887. That year he hit .357, although at the time his batting percentage was calculated as .459. In that single season walks were counted as hits.

Von der Ahe wanted to showcase his champions and scheduled the 1887 World Series for 15 games in a variety of cities. He promised to pitch Caruthers in every game, but the pitcher went 4–4 as the Browns took only five games. Von der Ahe blamed Caruthers for the defeat and sold him to the rival Brooklyn Bridegrooms for $8,250, nearly a $5,000 profit for Von der Ahe.

Caruthers' new club was more than glad to have him and rewarded him with a $5,000 contract, making him the American Association's highest paid performer. Caruthers helped lead Brooklyn to consecutive pennants—in two different leagues. In 1889 the Bridegrooms took the American Association title; in 1890 they moved over to the National League and captured another flag. The club eventually became the Brooklyn Dodgers.

In 1892 Caruthers returned to St. Louis, playing primarily right field. After leaving the National League in 1893, the year the pitching distance grew to 60 feet 6 inches, Caruthers pitched in the Western League and the Western Association until 1898. Caruthers, who had been a substitute umpire during his playing days, umpired in the early days of the American League. He was umpiring in the 3-I League in 1911 when he died.

George Case

Case, George Washington **OF**

1937–47 B:11/11/1915, Trenton, NJ D:1/23/1989, Trenton, NJ Deb:9/8/1937, WAS AL BR/TR 6', 183

G	AB	R	H	HR	RBI	OBP	SLG	AVG
1226	5016	785	1415	21	377	.341	.358	.282

Between the end of the Dead Ball Era and the appearances of Luis Aparicio and Maury Wills, American League outfielder George Case was arguably the fastest man in baseball. There can be no arguments about his base stealing accomplishments. From 1930 to 1960 his 349 stolen bases led all other major leaguers. Case was also the hardest man to double up—he averaged only one double play in every 94 at bats—until his record was bettered by Don Buford, Don Blasingame, and Joe Morgan.

He led the AL in stolen bases six times within an eight-year span. There was only one way to stop him: wait him out. "I'm licked when that pitcher takes the ball to his chest and just holds it there, just staring at you. You're tense out there on your toes, and this drains you and kills your speed. Not all pitchers know that, though."

Evidently, few hurlers figured this out—otherwise Case wouldn't have been able to put together an excellent 76.2 stolen base percentage during his 10-year major league career. Case's peak stolen base total was 61, amassed for Washington in 1943 when base stealing was not in fashion. "If I were running today the way they're playing it, there's no doubt in my mind I'd be stealing a hundred bases," he told an interviewer in the 1970s.

Few would dispute this. "One year I stole 44 bases and was caught only six times," Case recalled, "and three of those times I was thrown out of the game for arguing the decision. Were they that close? Hell, no, they weren't close—that's why I was arguing. They were bad calls. I had the damned base stolen, and I told the umpire so, which was why I was run out of there."

It was not unusual for Case to give pregame exhibitions of his blazing speed. In Washington, owner Clark Griffith staged one show to prove that Case could eclipse Hans Lobert's mark of circling the bases in 13.8 seconds, and perhaps even Cincinnati outfielder Evar Swanson's unofficial record of 13.2 seconds. (Although the mark is deemed unofficial because of the informal way in which Swanson was timed, it has gained credence over the years.) Case registered 13.5 seconds and said,

"I feel I hold the record and ought to be given credit for it, because I had three AAU people behind me."

Case was traded to Cleveland on December 14, 1945, for heavy-hitting outfielder Jeff Heath. Although he still managed to lead the league in steals in 1946, with 28, Case was traded back to Washington, this time for washed-up knuckleballer Roger Wolff. Case saw part-time service and then retired.

He managed the Oneonta Yankees to two New York–Penn League pennants before becoming a roving batting instructor for the Yankees and, later, for the Seattle Mariners.

Dan Casey

Casey, Daniel Maurice **P**

1884–90 B:11/20/1862, Binghamton, NY D:2/8/1943, Washington, DC Deb:8/18/1884, WIL UA BR/TL, 6', 180

W	L	PCT	G	SH	IP	BB	SO	ERA
96	90	.516	201	14	1680^{1}	543	743	3.18

Baseball's battle between labor and management did not begin with Marvin Miller; 19th century pitcher Dan Casey is proof of that. His first pro season was 1884, when he played sparingly with Wilmington of the Union Association. When that club folded he moved to the Detroit Wolverines of the National League, and was 4–8 in 12 games. He blossomed in 1886 as he moved to the Phillies and went 24–18 with a 2.41 ERA and four shutouts.

His best year was 1887, when he was 28–13 and led the NL with a 2.86 ERA and four shutouts. Casey completed 43 of 45 starts.

Casey was 14–18 in 1888. Then at the end of the 1889 season he and outfielder George Wood were released for union activity. They were part of the Brotherhood of Professional Base Ball Players, the driving force behind the Players' League, which began play in 1890 (and folded after one season).

Casey pitched his last season in 1890 for Syracuse of the American Association. He was 19–22 for a team that finished 17 games under .500. He claimed to have been the inspiration for Ernest L. Thayer's poem, "Casey At the Bat," although there is no credence to his claim. Casey was a career .162 hitter.

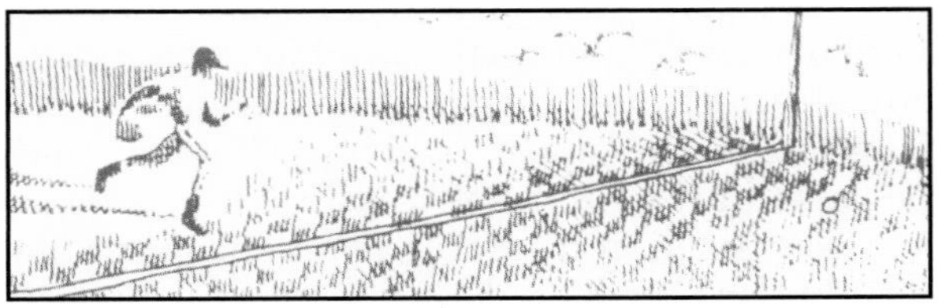

Hugh Casey

Casey, Hugh Thomas **P**

1935–49 B:10/14/1913, Atlanta, GA D:7/3/1951, Atlanta, GA Deb:4/29/1935, CHI NL BR/TR 6'1", 207

W	L	PCT	G	SV	IP	BB	SO	ERA
75	42	.641	343	55	939^{2}	321	349	3.45

Brooklyn's ace reliever Hugh Casey threw the strike that should have ended Game 4 of the 1941 World Series, but a heartbreaking passed ball by catcher Mickey Owen cost Casey the game and the Dodgers the Series. Although Brooklyn entered Game 4 down two games to one in the Series, the Dodgers held a 4–3 lead on the Yankees heading to the ninth inning. Casey ran the count full on first baseman Johnny Sturm before getting him to ground out to Pete Coscarart at second. The next batter, third baseman Red Rolfe, bounced back meekly to Casey. Then, with two outs, New York left fielder Tommy "Old Reliable" Henrich came to the plate. With the count at 3–2, Henrich swung and missed, seemingly giving the Dodgers the victory. But the ball bounded away from catcher Owen, allowing Henrich to race safely to first.

Then it all unraveled for Casey, who had previously surrendered only one hit in four innings. Joe DiMaggio singled to left, and Charlie "King Kong" Keller unloaded a double off the right-field wall, scoring Henrich and DiMaggio and putting New York ahead, 5–4. But the carnage wasn't over yet. Casey walked Bill Dickey, Joe Gordon doubled over left fielder Jimmy Wasdell's head, and two more runs scored. Casey then walked Phil Rizzuto before reliever Johnny "Grandma" Murphy tapped a ball harmlessly to Pee Wee Reese at short for the third out. Brooklyn lost the game, 7–4, and ultimately the Series, one of the most memorable in baseball history.

Rumors surfaced that the sharp-breaking pitch that had sailed past Owen had been a spitball, but it was actually just a curve. "What's odd about that play was the three people involved," said Owen in 1989. "Hugh Casey holds the record for the highest winning percentage among relief pitchers, .709. He lost the game. One of the most reliable clutch hitters ever—Henrich—struck out. And the catcher in the midst of setting the league record for consecutive chances without an error, made an error. All three failed miserably in doing what they were best at doing."

Casey signed his first professional contract in 1932 and appeared briefly with the Cubs in 1935. While pitching at Charlotte in 1937 he led the Southern Association in ERA with a 2.56 mark. Casey started 25 games for the Dodgers in

1939, but had become a full-time reliever by the time Owen dropped his third strike in the 1941 Series. In his remaining 201 games Casey started just three times.

Casey was well known for his escapades, particularly during a notorious 1942 spring training trip to Havana. When the Dodgers hired detectives to shadow their ballplayers, Casey and pitcher Kirby Higbe would, in Higbe's words, "climb out the window and go our merry way. Then about three or four in the morning, we'd come back and climb back through the window."

One of Casey's more violent episodes in Havana involved author Ernest Hemingway. According to some observers, the novelist sucker-punched Casey, precipitating a knock-down, drag-out brawl. "Ernest would belt Case one and down he would go. Case would belt old Ernest and down he would go. The furniture really took a beating," said Higbe.

Following his release from the Dodgers after the 1948 season, Casey pitched for the Pirates and later won a game for the Yankees in 1949. He retired with a lifetime record of 75–42, but tallied only 55 career saves, even though he twice led the league in saves. Allegedly upset over the breakup of his marriage, Casey took his own life when he was only 37.

Dave Cash

Cash, David **2B**

1969–80 B:6/11/1948, Utica, NY Deb:9/13/1969, PIT NL BR/TR 5'11", 175

G	AB	R	H	HR	RBI	OBP	SLG	AVG
1422	5554	732	1571	21	426	.336	.358	.283

Dave Cash, a durable National League second baseman in the 1970s, set a record of 699 at bats in 1975 (later broken by Willie Wilson with 705 in 1980). When Cash led the major leagues in at bats for three consecutive years he set another record. He also established a National League mark when he played 443 consecutive games at second base.

The Pirates selected Cash in the fifth round of the June 1966 free agent draft and sent him to Salem in the Appalachian League. The next season, playing shortstop, he led the Western Carolinas League in hits, putouts, and batting average.

Back at second base, Cash was promoted to Columbus in the International League before joining Pittsburgh late in the 1969 season. He hit .314 in part-time duty in 1970, and by 1971 he had succeeded all-time Pirates great Bill Mazeroski at second. With Pittsburgh he played in three League Championship Series—1970, 1971, and 1972—hitting .421 in the 1971 playoff, the only year of the three the Pirates reached the World Series.

The Pirates traded Cash to the Phillies in October 1973 for pitcher Ken Brett. Given a chance to play every day with Philadelphia, he made the All-Star team each year from 1974 through 1976.

Granted free agency in November 1976, Cash signed a five-year, $1.5 million contract with the Montreal Expos. But while Cash's bat remained potent—in 1977 he smacked 42 doubles—his foot speed and agility declined. In 1979 Expos manager Dick Williams replaced Cash at second with newly acquired Rodney Scott. "Oddly enough," recalled Williams, "Scott came into my office and told me I should move him to shortstop, let Cash play second, and bench shortstop Chris Speier."

Traded to the Padres in November 1979 for Bill Almon and Dan Briggs, he retired from baseball after the 1980 season. He later became a coach serving in that role for the International League's Rochester Red Wings in 1999.

Norm Cash

Cash, Norman Dalton **1B**

1958–74 B:11/10/1934, Justiceburg, TX D:10/12/1986, Beaver Island, MI Deb:6/18/1958, CHI AL BL/TL 6', 190

G	AB	R	H	HR	RBI	OBP	SLG	AVG
2089	6705	1046	1820	377	1103	.377	.488	.271

In 1961 Tigers first baseman Norm Cash had a season to remember. With American League expansion and 20 more pitchers in the big leagues who otherwise would have been in the minors, Roger Maris hit 61 home runs, Mickey Mantle hit 54, and four other players hit 40 or more. None of them, however, could match Norm Cash's year. He hit .361 in 1961 to lead the league by 37 points, with an on-base percentage of .488 and a slugging average of .662. Along with his 41 homers, his 193 hits led the league, and he drove in 132 runs, scored 119, and walked 124 times.

Much later in his career, Cash attributed his success to a corked bat and went so far as to doctor a bat for *Sports Illustrated*. He drilled a small hole 8 inches deep in the barrel of the bat, filled it with a mixture of glue, cork, and sawdust, and then sealed it. As a result, his 36-ounce bat felt like a 34-ounce model, providing extra power.

When Cash finished college, he wasn't a carpenter but a running back. Drafted by football's Chicago Bears, he signed with the White Sox instead. After a year with Indianapolis, the White Sox brought him up in 1958, and then traded him to Cleveland after the 1959 season. The Indians promptly swapped him to the Tigers in 1960 for Steve Demeter. In his first season in Detroit, Cash hit 18 homers, batted .286, and quickly became one of the Detroit fans' all-time favorites.

After his stellar 1961 season, Cash's batting average fell to .243 in 1962, the largest drop in history by a batting champion, so cork alone couldn't have caused his big year. Cash never again hit above .283 in 13 more seasons in the big leagues. It was his consistent power, solid fielding, and fun-loving personality that kept him in the majors.

When Nolan Ryan was looking for his second no-hitter on July 15, 1973, Cash came to the plate with two outs in the bottom of the ninth. He felt powerless against Ryan and, to the fans' amusement, carried a table leg to the plate instead of a bat.

Cash led AL first basemen in fielding percentage in both 1964 and 1967, tied for the lead in assists for first basemen in 1965, and then led the league in assists the next two years. He was named Comeback Player of the Year in 1965 after increasing his home run total from 23 to 30. Cash belted 25 homers for the Tigers in their 1968 championship year and was their leading batsman in the World Series, hitting .385. He also tied a Series record with two hits in the third inning of Game 6. In the seventh inning of Game 7 he started a three-run rally that won the Series for Detroit with a two-out single.

After failing to hit 20 or more home runs in 1970 for the first time in 10 years, he belted 32 in 1971 and was once again named AL Comeback Player of the Year. Cash's power wasn't just plentiful, it was occasionally prodigious. He hit four balls over the right-field roof in Tiger Stadium, one more than anyone else ever did. His 377 home runs, including eight grand slams, puts him third among all AL first basemen. When he retired in 1974, he ranked among the Tigers top 10 in numerous batting categories.

After briefly playing professional softball, Cash worked as a Tigers announcer on cable television for several years. He died in 1986 in a drowning accident.

Vinny Castilla

Castilla, Vinicio (Soria) **3B**

1991–* B:7/4/1967, Oaxaca, Mexico Deb:9/1/1991, ATL NL BR/TR, 6'1", 185

G	AB	R	H	HR	RBI	OBP	SLG	AVG
956	3516	518	1049	203	611	.345	.528	.298

Originally a shortstop in the Atlanta Braves organization, Vinny Castilla came to Colorado in the 1992 expansion draft. The thin air of Denver did wonders for his game. He spent two years as a backup at second and short before moving to third in 1995, where he made the National League All-Star squad.

The next year, Castilla started a string of three-straight seasons with at least 40 home runs and a .300 batting average—a feat performed by only five other players in baseball history. The streak started in 1996, when Castilla homered in his last at bat of the year to join Andres Galarraga and Ellis Burks at the 40-homer plateau and give the Rockies baseball's second trio of 40-homer teammates—matching the 1973 Braves.

In 1997 Castilla reproduced his numbers from the previous year in all three Triple Crown categories: a .304 average, 40 homers, and 113 RBIs. Then in 1998 he went on a tear. Castilla played in every game of the 162-game schedule and reached personal peaks with a .319 average, 46 homers, and 144 RBIs. The latter was the highest RBI total ever produced by a National League third baseman and was just one short of Al Rosen's 1953 major league mark of 145 for the position.

Castilla's production fell in 1999, even though he enjoyed his fourth straight 100-RBI season. In a game played in Mexico, fans at Monterrey Stadium greeted Castilla as a returning hero when the Mexican native's Rockies beat the San Diego Padres on April 4. It was the first Opening Day game ever played outside the United States or Canada.

Castilla enjoyed the first three home run game of his career on June 5. His third homer of that game capped a four-run rally in the eighth to give the Rockies a 12–11 win over the Milwaukee Brewers at Coors Field. Castilla signed with the Tampa Bay for the 2000 season, joining sluggers Jose Canseco, Fred McGriff, and Greg Vaughn.

Danny Cater

Cater, Danny Anderson **1B-OF-3B**

1964–75 B:2/25/1940, Austin, TX Deb:4/14/1964, PHI NL BR/TR 5'11½", 180

G	AB	R	H	HR	RBI	OBP	SLG	AVG
1289	4451	491	1229	66	519	.318	.377	.276

Danny Cater is most remembered for being traded in March 1972 for reliever Sparky Lyle in one of the worst transactions in Red Sox history. Lyle dominated out of the Yankees bullpen; Cater was a part-timer with Boston.

He started professionally with Johnson City in 1958, where he led the Appalachian League in home runs, RBIs, and total bases. He also performed with Bakersfield, Williamsport, Buffalo, and Arkansas before reaching the Phillies, leading the Eastern League with 33 doubles in 1960 and 193 hits in 1961.

Brought up to Philadelphia in 1964, he spent five weeks on the disabled list and was traded to the White Sox that December. Dealt to the Kansas City Athletics in May 1966, he moved with the club to Oakland and led American League outfielders in fielding in 1968; he finished second to Carl Yastrzemski among the circuit's batters. In December 1969, the A's sent Cater to the Yankees in a trade that saw Al Downing leave New York.

Cater ended his career with the Cardinals after being traded from Boston in March 1975. That club featured substantial turnover. "So many guys come and go here that if we won the pennant, our shares would be $50 apiece," quipped Cater. He served as comptroller of public accounts for the state of Texas after his retirement from baseball.

Bill Caudill

Caudill, William Holland **P**

1979–87 B:7/13/1956, Santa Monica, CA
Deb:5/12/1979, CHI NL BR/TR 6'1", 210

W	L	PCT	G	SV	IP	BB	SO	ERA
35	52	.402	445	106	667	288	620	3.68

Although Bill Caudill's 90 mph fastball and good control earned him 106 saves in nine seasons, he is more often remembered for his outlandish sense of humor. Caudill had two nicknames: "Cuffs," for his habit of handcuffing unsuspecting teammates to bullpen fences, and "The Inspector," for the routine he began as a Seattle Mariner, in which he would arrive in the clubhouse sporting a deerstalker cap and meerschaum pipe (like Sherlock Holmes) and begin inspecting the Mariners' bats in search of "missing" hits.

After consecutive 26-save seasons with Seattle, Caudill was dealt to Oakland, where he registered 36 saves in 1984. The A's swapped him to Toronto in a major trade for Alfredo Griffin and Dave Collins. Caudill arrived at spring training overweight, and the Jays told the public address announcer to identify him as "Sid," as in Fernandez, the Mets' portly lefthander.

When the season started, Caudill lost the closer's job to Tom Henke. Caudill saved only 14 games in 1985 and two the following year, when he compiled a disappointing 6.19 ERA. He pitched only eight innings for Oakland in 1987, his last year in the majors.

Phil Cavarretta

Cavarretta, Philip Joseph **1B-OF**

1934–55 M(1951–53, 169–213) B:7/19/1916, Chicago
IL Deb:9/16/1934, CHI NL, BL/TL 5'11½", 175

G	AB	R	H	HR	RBI	OBP	SLG	AVG
2030	6754	990	1977	95	920	.372	.416	.293

Phil Cavarretta, Cubs hero for two decades, capped his career with triple honors in the wartime year of 1945: a National League batting championship, a Most Valuable Player Award, and a trip to the World Series. He later managed the club, but his honesty cost him the job.

He signed with Peoria, Illinois, of the Central League before he graduated from high school. He hit for the cycle in his first professional game, went on to hit .308 at Reading in the New York–Penn League, and was promoted to the Cubs before the season's end. Cavarretta said, "Talk about going up the ladder in a hurry! The year before I was one of the kids waiting outside for them to come out after the game."

In 1935, at age 19, he was the regular first baseman on a pennant-winning team. "In September we put on a real drive. We won 21 straight games. You ever go 75 miles an hour on the highway while everyone else is doing 55? That's how we felt," recalled Cavarretta.

In the World Series, however, the Cubs developed engine trouble as they lost to Detroit in six games; Cavarretta got just three hits in 24 at bats. In 1938 the Cubs again won the pennant, but Cavarretta moved to the outfield to make room for Rip Collins at first. The Cubs lost to the Yankees in four straight, but this time Cavarretta hit .462.

Exempt from military service because of an ear problem, Cavarretta had his best years during World War II when the general caliber of play had eroded. In Game 2 of the 1945 World Series Cavarretta hit a flyball between Detroit outfielders Doc Cramer and Roy Cullenbine, who stood like statues as the ball fell between them for a double. "I could have caught the ball but Cullenbine kept shouting, 'all right, all right.' When I heard that, I stopped and then the ball plopped to the ground. I asked Cullenbine why he didn't make the catch, and he told me, 'When I called all right, all right, I meant all right, you catch it,'" explained the 40-year-old Cramer. Even with help of this kind the Cubs lost, although Cavarretta excelled with 11 hits and a .423 average.

He was made Cubs player-manager on June 21, 1951, replacing Frankie Frisch, and held the job through 1953. "Cavarretta should get a bonus for watching the Cubs every day," wrote Chicago sportswriter Warren Brown. On March 29, 1954, Cavarretta gave the Cubs' owner an honest assessment of the team's chances and was fired for his "defeatist attitude," making him the first modern manager to be canned during spring training. Cavarretta played part-time during the next two years with the White Sox.

He managed the International League's Buffalo Bisons from 1956 to 1958, and from 1961 to 1963 coached at Detroit. He scouted for the Tigers in 1964 and then managed in the minors from 1965 to 1972 with stops at Salinas, Reno, Waterbury, and Birmingham. He later became the New York Mets' minor league batting instructor.

Cesar Cedeno

Cedeno, Cesar (Encarnacion) **OF–1B**
1970–86 B:2/25/51, Santo Domingo, Dominican Republic Deb:6/20/1970, HOU NL BR/TR 6'2", 195

G	AB	R	H	HR	RBI	OBP	SLG	AVG
2006	7310	1084	2087	199	976	.350	.443	.285

In hindsight, it's obvious that Astros star Cesar Cedeno suffered from too many favorable comparisons to the game's superstars as a 19-year-old rookie. Astros manager Leo Durocher deserves most of the blame for his oft-quoted remark that Cedeno was "better than Willie Mays at the same age." But Durocher had plenty of accomplices.

Take Harry "The Hat" Walker, for example, who said, "I had Roberto Clemente in Pittsburgh. He was the best. But Cesar could have had a better record after four years than Roberto ever did." Or Mets skipper Yogi Berra, who predicted, "You'll remember his name. He's the one that will lead Houston into a World Series one of these days." Added John McMullen, Astros assistant general manager, "Hank Aaron and Cedeno came up at the same age, 19 years old, and I'd have to say they are very similar. But if I give an edge to one of them, I'd have to give it to Cedeno."

When Cedeno came through with a .320, 22-homer season in 1972 and followed with another campaign of .320 and 25 homers, those glowing predictions seemed to be right on the money. Cedeno could not only hit, but also he won Gold Glove Awards in both seasons. He was an All-Star. The Astrodome was dubbed "Cesar's Palace," and after the 1973 season the Astros signed him to a then-phenomenal 10-year, $3.5-million contract.

His rise to the spotlight was like a dream for Cedeno, who had come far. Like so many youngsters in his native Dominican Republic, he had taken to baseball with a vengeance. "When I was 11 I used to run away from school and play ball all day. When my father caught me he would whip me. But my mother bought me a new glove," he said.

The Astros signed Cedeno when he was only 16. Although that may seem premature, the Cardinals had already arranged for Cedeno to try a two-week stint with a local pro team. "I was scared but I hit .400. The Cardinals offered me $500 to sign, then $700, then $1,000. After that the scout had to go back to the States for a week, and, by the time he got back, Pat Gillick of the Astros had signed me for $3,000," Cedeno remembered.

Following Cedeno's 1973 season and the signing of his 10-year pact, tragedy struck. At 2 A.M. on December 11, 1973, Cedeno checked into a bungalow at a Santo Domingo motel. With him was his 19-year-old girlfriend, Altagracia de la Cruz.

Cedeno had been drinking. He carried a .38-caliber revolver, and de la Cruz wanted to look at it. As Cedeno attempted to get it back, they struggled, and the gun went off. De la Cruz was killed. Cedeno told authorities, "She asked for my revolver because she found it pretty. I answered 'no' because it was loaded and very dangerous. I tried to stand up to drink a glass of beer while she insisted that I let her hold it."

Cedeno insisted that it was de la Cruz who had pulled the trigger, but he was charged with voluntary manslaughter. While he was in jail, a paraffin test revealed powder burns on de la Cruz's right hand, indicating that she had fired the gun. Charges were reduced to involuntary manslaughter, an offense that in the Dominican Republic carries a maximum three-year sentence. But Cedeno paid a 100-peso fine and walked out of jail.

Cedeno's ballplaying was never the same after that day, with the exception of one hot stretch in 1985 that helped propel the St. Louis Cardinals to a pennant. He was dogged by taunts of "killer." Once in Atlanta in 1981 he charged into the stands to get at an abusive fan and was fined $5,000. His baseball career ended in Los Angeles after the 1986 season. He had a lifetime .285 average with 199 homers and 976 RBIs. Not bad, but not a Clemente, an Aaron, or a Mays.

Perhaps he had a better perspective on his talent—or on his fate—than any of those who had predicted greatness for him. Said a young Cedeno, "Harry (Walker) told me I might be Clemente someday. So I told him, 'That might be hard to do. I know Clemente. I might be something like him, but, ha, not like him. There is only one Clemente.'"

Orlando Cepeda

Cepeda, Orlando Manuel (Penne) 1B-OF-DH
1958–74 B:9/17/1937, Ponce, Puerto Rico
Deb:4/15/1958, SF NL BR/TR 6'2", 210

G	AB	R	H	HR	RBI	OBP	SLG	AVG
2124	7927	1131	2351	379	1365	.353	.499	.297

Orlando Cepeda was the darling of San Francisco fans when Horace Stoneham's Giants moved west in 1958. Named National League Rookie of the Year, at age 20 Cepeda had already arrived. While teammate Willie Mays was considered a holdover from the club's New York days, Cepeda, San Franciscans felt, was "theirs."

Before Cepeda was through as a ballplayer he would compile an impressive record: 379 homers, 1,365 RBIs, and a .297 lifetime average. But after he was through playing he would have a record of a different sort—a prison record stemming from his 1975 conviction for importing marijuana. The first record earned him admission into the Hall of Fame; the second kept him out until 1999.

Cepeda was the son of Pedro Cepeda, a fearsome Puerto Rican slugger who was called the "Babe Ruth of the Caribbean"; he was also nicknamed "Perucho" (The Bull). The younger Cepeda, seeing his father play against such visiting big leaguers as Vic Raschi and Allie Reynolds, resolved that he, too, would be a ballplayer. Inevitably the teenager was compared to his father, and the comparisons were not favorable. "I said to hell with baseball," Orlando remembered. "They kept saying, 'You'll never be as good as your father.' So I stopped playing."

At 13 Cepeda turned to basketball but suffered torn cartilage in his right knee that required surgery and kept him out of athletics for a year. During his recuperation Cepeda grew, becoming truly a "Baby Bull" at 170 pounds. Once recovered, he was asked to play in a sandlot baseball game, and everything came together as he hit liner after liner. "The kids were standing around with their mouths open," said Cepeda.

Cepeda was soon asked to join one of the region's top amateur teams and helped lead the club to the Commonwealth championship. During an exhibition against a Dominican team featuring Julian Javier and Jesus Alou, New York Giants scout Pedro Zorilla spotted the 17-year-old Cepeda and signed him for $500.

The Giants had difficulty finding a place for Cepeda in their farm system and were about to release him when Zorilla assigned him to an independent club in Salem, Virginia. Before his first at bat Cepeda had to race back to Puerto Rico to be at his dying father's side; the entire $500 bonus went for his father's funeral. Cepeda's mother persuaded him to go back to the Giants. "There was nothing for me in Puerto Rico. She reminded me that it was Perucho's dream to see me play professional baseball."

Cepeda quickly tore through the Giants' farm system, logging a .393 year at Kokomo in 1955 and winning the Northern League Triple Crown in 1956. He came to San Francisco in 1958, where manager Bill Rigney described him as "the best young righthanded power hitter" he'd seen. In 1962 he helped lead the Giants to a playoff win against the Dodgers for the franchise's first pennant in San Francisco.

In 1963 Cepeda skipped playing in the Puerto Rican Winter League to concentrate on getting into shape. While weightlifting, he dropped an 80-pound weight on the same knee he'd injured as a teenager. Afraid to tell manager Alvin Dark about his problem, he played the next two seasons despite serious damage.

Accused of malingering, Cepeda opted for surgery in 1965, but the rehabilitation process ruined his season. In May 1966 the Giants, who now preferred Willie McCovey as their first baseman, dealt Cepeda to the Cardinals for pitcher Ray Sadecki. "I even had been hoping it would happen, but it hurt," Cepeda said.

St. Louis was happy to have him and rescinded a pay cut Cepeda had taken before leaving San Francisco. The next year Cepeda led the NL with 111 RBIs and helped send the Cardinals to the World Series and a world championship. He was the unanimous selection as Most Valuable Player, the first National Leaguer to be so honored since Carl Hubbell in 1936. Cepeda was now nicknamed "Cha Cha" for the Latin music he played in the clubhouse. "We were one of the loosest teams ever. We'd play around until five minutes before the game," Cepeda recalled.

Even though the Cards brought home another pennant in 1968, Cepeda slumped to .248 and was traded after the season to Atlanta for catcher-first baseman Joe Torre. The Braves won the NL West in 1969, but in mid-1972 a rapidly declining Cepeda went to the A's for cash and Denny McLain (then at Birmingham in the Southern League). He played just three games for Oakland and was released, but had his last hurrah with the Red Sox as a designated hitter in 1973, hitting 20 homers for the 12th time in his career.

His playing career ended with the 1974 Royals. A year later federal agents found 160 pounds of marijuana in the trunk of his car at the San Juan airport. He served a 10-month sentence at Florida's Elgin Air Force Base. "The isolation, the disgrace, the feelings of numbness, they were horrible," he recalled. After rehabilitation, Cepeda coached for the White Sox in 1980. He later served as a Giants Community Representative. Cepeda was elected to the Hall of Fame in March 1999.

Rick Cerone

Cerone, Richard Aldo **C**

1975–92 B:5/19/1954, Newark, NJ Deb:8/17/1975, CLE AL BR/TR 5'11", 192

G	AB	R	H	HR	RBI	OBP	SLG	AVG
1329	4069	393	998	59	436	.304	.343	.245

Filling Thurman Munson's shoes was a tall order, but catcher Rick Cerone met the challenge with the best season of his career. Three months after Munson died piloting his own plane in a tragic crash on August 2, 1979, the Yankees acquired Newark-born Cerone from Toronto in a postseason trade. As if replacing perennial All-Star Munson hadn't put enough pressure on Cerone, the trade also sent away the popular Chris Chambliss.

Although Cerone's season high as a Jays regular had been only .239 with seven home runs, he came through with a 14-homer, 85-RBI, .277 season and helped lead the Yankees to the 1980 American League East title. He was named to *The Sporting News* AL All-Star team.

Signed originally by Cleveland as the Indians' first-round pick in the 1975 amateur draft, Richard Aldo Cerone had excelled in baseball, football, and fencing at Newark's Essex Catholic High. A standout at local Seton Hall University, the strong-throwing catcher had played in the 1974 and 1975 College World Series and was named the NCAA All-American backstop in both years.

After hitches with Atlanta and Milwaukee Cerone returned to the Yankees in 1987 and led the league's catchers in fielding average; he repeated the feat in 1988 with the Red Sox. He finished his playing career with single seasons with the Yanks, Mets, and Expos from 1990 to 1992. He became an advance scout for the Yankees in January 1993. He later served as a broadcaster and became owner of the independent Newark Bears.

Bob Cerv

Cerv, Robert Henry **OF**

1951–62 B:5/5/1926, Weston, NE Deb:8/1/1951, NY AL BR/TR 6', 202

G	AB	R	H	HR	RBI	OBP	SLG	AVG
829	2261	320	624	105	374	.343	.481	.276

Outfielder Bob Cerv had three separate stints with the New York Yankees. A product of the club's farm system, Cerv came up with New York in 1951 and for five years played primarily off the bench. One day in 1956 manager Casey Stengel announced, to no one in particular, "Nobody knows this yet but one of us has been sold to Kansas City." When Cerv realized that he and Stengel were the only two people present, he got the message.

With newfound motivation, Cerv had a career year in 1958, hitting 38 homers and collecting 104 RBIs; he was even chosen for the All-Star Game over American League batting champion Ted Williams. Even a broken jaw couldn't slow him down—Cerv played the last month of the season with his jaw wired shut.

Cerv went back to the Yankees in May 1960 in exchange for third baseman Andy Carey. His single off the bench in that year's World Series gave him a perfect 3-for-3 pinch-hitting record in Series play. Even so, the Yanks made him available in the December 1960 AL expansion draft, and he was picked up by the Angels. In midseason 1961 he went back to New York for the third time in a deal that sent hard-throwing reliever Ryne Duren to Los Angeles. Cerv finished his playing career with Houston in 1962. After retiring, Cerv coached baseball at Sioux-Empire College in Iowa.

Ron Cey

Cey, Ronald Charles **3B**

1971–87 B:2/15/1948, Tacoma, WA Deb:9/3/1971, LA NL BR/TR 5'10", 185

G	AB	R	H	HR	RBI	OBP	SLG	AVG
2073	7162	977	1868	316	1139	.357	.445	.261

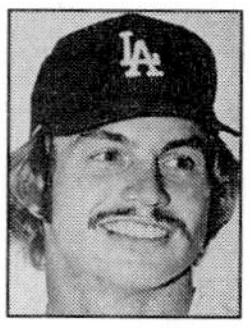

From 1974 to 1981, the always dangerous Los Angeles Dodgers featured the longest-running set infield in history—Steve Garvey at first, Davey Lopes at second, Bill Russell at short, and a fellow nicknamed "The Penguin" at third, power-hitting and oddly-proportioned Ron Cey. Although the foursome was not always graceful afield, they more than got the job done, helping the Dodgers capture pennants in 1974, 1977, 1978, and 1981. Cey twice led the National League in fielding and once each in assists and putouts.

Drafted originally by the Mets in 1966, he waited until 1968 to sign with the Dodgers, after being taken in the third round of the June amateur draft. He saw service at Tri-Cities, Bakersfield, Albuquerque, and Spokane before reaching Dodger Stadium late in the 1971 season.

Power was Cey's forte. From 1975 to 1985 (with the exception of the strike-shortened 1981 season) he hit at least 22 homers, including a high of 30 in 1977. Although overshadowed by Mike Schmidt, Cey still managed to play in six All-Star Games. When he retired in 1987, Cey's 316 lifetime home runs placed him fifth among third basemen, behind only Schmidt, Eddie Mathews, Graig Nettles, and Ron Santo.

Cey's greatest moment came in the 1981 World Series when he shared Series Most Valuable Player honors with teammates Steve Yeager and Pedro Guerrero. Cey came back from a frightening Game 5 beaning by Rich Gossage to drive in the winning run in the sixth and final contest. He had also delivered a three-run homer and a sparkling diving catch of Bobby Murcer's bunt in Game 3. It was sweet redemption against the Yankees, who had beaten the Dodgers in both the 1977 and 1978 World Series.

"The most important thing to me Sunday morning was winning Game 5. But by the time I got home that night, the most important thing was being alive, sitting with my kids. I'm glad they aren't going to present that award to me posthumously," joked Cey.

After a 1982 season in which he still hit 24 homers, Cey was traded (almost given away) to the Chicago Cubs for outfielder Dan Cataline and pitcher Vance Lovelace. "With the Dodgers, it's time to move on when you reach a certain salary figure. That's just the way they operate," said a bitter Cey.

Not everyone in Chicago approved either. "Cey and (shortstop Larry) Bowa are old enough to be dead," wrote columnist John Schulian. But by 1984 the Cubs had reached the Championship Series. It was the team's first postseason appearance in 39 years.

That season Cey had to battle back from a horrible start that saw him hitting only .212 in late July. "I had to denounce everything I had done to that point," Cey said. "I had to say, 'I can't be hitting .212,' and start over."

He started over, batting .281 with 12 homers and 45 RBIs in his last 59 games as the Cubs edged out the Mets for the NL East crown. Cey played while injured, with both hands heavily padded; his right hand was hit with a pitch in June, and the left hand suffered a strained ligament. During the NLCS against San Diego, Cey, by now a medical textbook case, hurt his elbow while lifting baggage and had only three hits in his 19 at bats. After four years with the Cubs, Cey ended his career in 1987 in Oakland as a designated hitter and utility infielder.

Henry Chadwick

Chadwick, Henry

Baseball Pioneer B:10/5/1824, Exeter, England D:4/29/1908, Brooklyn, NY

Known as "Father Chadwick" and "the Father of Baseball," Henry Chadwick greatly influenced the direction of the game. Without his efforts the sport might never have adopted the infield fly rule, games might be scored differently, and even extra innings might be unknown. He also sounded a loud alarm by reporting on gambling in the game.

Chadwick's family moved from his native England to Brooklyn, New York, in 1837, when the boy was 13. He began playing baseball around 1847 and started writing about the game in 1858 as a sportswriter for the New York *Clipper*.

When Father Chadwick took up the cause of the infield fly rule, he may have saved baseball from thousands of rally-ending double and triple plays. As chairman of the National Association of Base Ball Players (NABBP), Chadwick supported the rule and chided the association's members in the paper when they did not adopt it immediately.

He is also credited with creating the form for scoring a game, a version of which is still used today. He borrowed many aspects of the system from fellow sportswriter M.J. Kelly.

On June 14, 1859, a single decision by Father Chadwick changed baseball forever. After the ninth inning of a 5–5 game in Brooklyn, with 9,000 paying customers in the park, the home team was content with the tie and walked off the field. Harry Wright, the visiting team's captain, protested, arguing that play should continue until the tie was broken. The argument was taken to Chadwick, there in his capacity as chairman of the NABBP's Committee on Rules. Chadwick ruled in favor of Wright, thus setting the precedent eliminating tie games.

As early as 1858 Chadwick was writing about problems associated with gambling in baseball. Once he wrote, "Two Brooklyn cranks had a wager of $100 a side on John Holden's making a home run. One was an Atlantic rooter, the other an Excelsior fan. In this game I noticed that when Holden went to bat he was very particular in selecting his bat. It appears that the man who had bet on him went to him and told him he would give him $25 of his bet if he made the hit; so Jack was very anxious. Matt O'Brien was pitching and Jack, after waiting for a good ball, got one to suit him, and sent it flying over Harry Wright's head at right-center and made the round of the bases before the ball was returned, thus winning the $25."

Chadwick did not win all his battles. He opposed the National Association when it decided to pay umpires. He opposed creation of both the Players' League and the National League, writing that the latter was "a sad blunder." He took on owners and players with equal gusto. He also traced baseball's origins to the English game of rounders instead of the popular myth of its invention by Abner Doubleday.

During Chadwick's career his byline appeared in many local papers and national sports magazines including *The Sporting News* and *Sporting Life*. When he returned from his duties as a Civil War correspondent he edited several baseball books in addition to *Ball Players*

Chronicles, the country's first weekly baseball magazine. He was employed as editor of the *Spalding Guide* from 1881 until his death in 1908. Elected to Cooperstown in 1938, Chadwick remains the only writer honored not in a separate exhibit, but in the Hall of Fame itself.

Elton Chamberlain

Chamberlain, Elton P. **P**

1886–94, 1896 B:11/5/1867, Buffalo, NY D:9/22/29 Baltimore, MD Deb: 9/13/1886, LOU AA BR/TR 5'9" 168

W	L	PCT	G	SH	IP	BB	SO	ERA
157	120	.567	321	16	2521^{2}	1065	1133	3.57

Elton Chamberlain pitched for six teams in a 10-year career, but is best remembered today for pitching ambidextrously in a game. On May 9, 1888, Chamberlain went seven innings throwing from his normal righthanded side, then pitched the final two innings lefthanded to lead Louisville in an 18–6 rout of Kansas City, in an American Association game. (Larry Corcoran, Tony Mullane, and Greg A. Harris also accomplished this trick.)

Chamberlain was commonly called by the nickname "Icebox," and some of teammates took that a bit farther to refer to him as "The Cool One." Chamberlain won 18 games for Louisville in 1887, and was 14–9 (including the ambidextrous victory) in 1888 when traded in August to the St. Louis Browns. He won 11 of 13 decisions in the final six weeks of the season, leading the Browns to the AA championship. Chamberlain pitched five complete games in the postseason championship against the Giants, but he went 2–3 as St. Louis lost to New York six games to four. One of his victories was a six-hit shutout in Game 2.

In 1889 "Icebox" won a career-high 32 games for the Browns. After the season, his 1889 manager, Charlie Comiskey, had taken over the Chicago team. Comiskey offered Chamberlain an $800 salary increase. The Browns caught wind of the situation and matched the offer. The Browns would regret that decision; Chamberlain showed up out of shape and compiled a miserable 5.91 ERA in five games. Disgusted with his performance, the Browns sold Chamberlain to Columbus, where he went 12–6. The next season he was 22–23 for Philadelphia.

When the American Association folded, Chamberlain jumped to the National League with Cincinnati. He won 45 games over three years, but his most memorable distinction was serving up four gopher balls in one game to Boston's Bobby Lowe on May 30, 1894.

Chris Chambliss

Chambliss, Carroll Christopher **1B**

1971–88 B:12/26/1948, Dayton, OH Deb:5/28/1971, CLE AL BL/TR 6'1", 215

G	AB	R	H	HR	RBI	OBP	SLG	AVG
2175	7571	912	2109	185	972	.336	.415	.279

Known during the early years of his career for steady defense and only occasional power, the Yankees' Chris Chambliss became a slugger with one swing of his bat against Royals hurler Mark Littell in the final game of the 1976 Championship Series. New York had taken a 6–3 lead into the top of the eighth, only to lose it on a three-run homer by George Brett. But in the last of the ninth, leadoff hitter Chambliss, who already had 10 hits and seven RBIs in the Series, slugged Littell's first pitch over the right-field fence, just over the outstretched glove of right fielder Al Cowens.

Hometown fans, who hadn't seen the Yanks reach the World Series in a dozen years, rioted as soon as the ball reached the stands. Chambliss had to touch second with his hand as a fan ran off with the base; third base was long gone by the time he got there, and his teammates had to bring him back out of the dugout to make sure he touched the field where home plate had been. Despite the fact that the exhausted Yanks were then swept by Cincinnati in the World Series, Chambliss remained a hero. WPIX, the station that carried the team's games, endlessly ran highlights of his hit on its commercials for the next year.

After winning the Triple A and American League Rookie of the Year awards in consecutive years (1970–71), Chambliss failed to live up to home run expectations in Cleveland and was traded to New York in 1974. Aiming at the close right field porch in Yankee Stadium, he hit a total of 64 home runs between 1976 and 1979; he knocked in 90 or more runs in three of those years.

A trade to Toronto, which then sent him to Atlanta, didn't affect his home run stroke. In 1980 he belted 18, and in 1982 his 20 homers helped the Braves to a division championship. In 1985 he was relegated to the role of pinch hitter and in 1986 led the NL with 20 pinch hits. After a single at bat with the Yankees in 1988, he became a coach for the Bronx Bombers, the St. Louis Cardinals, and a minor league manager.

Dean Chance

Chance, Wilmer Dean **P**

1961–71 B:6/1/1941, Wayne, OH Deb:9/11/1961, LA AL BR/TR 6'3", 200

W	L	PCT	G	SH	IP	BB	SO	ERA
128	115	.527	406	33	2147^{1}	739	1534	2.92

A lifetime .066 hitter, Dean Chance has the all-time worst batting average of any player with more than 500 at bats. During one stretch he went 73 at bats without a hit. "Batting's flower child," joked one writer. To say the least, Chance was no magician with the bat.

Fortunately he could pitch. The big righthander might be described as Bo Belinsky with talent. Belinsky's claim to fame rested largely on his womanizing and a highly publicized no-hitter, but Chance won a Cy Young Award, once pitched 11 shutouts in a year, had two 20-win seasons, and recorded both a nine-inning no-hitter and a rain-shortened five-inning perfect game.

The Baltimore Orioles originally signed Chance to a professional contract after he spun a 51–1 record in high school. Twelve of his victories were no-hitters. Yet Chance advanced only as far as Fox Cities of the 3-I League before the Angels grabbed him in the American League expansion draft. He spent most of the 1961 season at Dallas–Fort Worth, making just five appearances with the big league club. He won 14 games for the Angels in 1962 and 13 games in 1963 before exploding in 1964 Chance's Cy Young Award–winning season. That year he led the AL with 20 victories, 11 shutouts, and an eye-popping 1.65 ERA. When the Cy Young Award was still given to one pitcher for both leagues, Chance beat out National Leaguers Larry Jackson and Sandy Koufax for the honor. Koufax, who won the honor in 1963, went on to win the Cy Young in 1965 and 1966.

Despite his attraction to Los Angeles nightlife, Chance was not happy with the Angels, for beneath the devil-may-care attitude, he deeply wanted to win. He schemed to get himself traded to contenders, often concocting rumors having him exchanged for the game's biggest stars. In December 1966 Chance got his wish and was sent to the Twins for outfielder Jimmie Hall, first baseman Don Mincher, and pitcher Pete Cimino.

Chance, whose record had been only 12–17 for the 1966 Angels, responded well to the change of scene. He won 20 games in 1967 and topped the AL in both complete games and innings pitched. He had two very special nights that August. On August 5 Chance pitched a rain-shortened, five-inning 2–0 perfect game against the Red Sox. In Cleveland on August 25 he tossed a nine-inning no-hitter, beating the Indians, 2–1. In that game, six batters reached base against Chance—five on walks, one on an error.

"I knew I had a no-hitter all along, and I'm glad my parents were there," Chance said. "I don't want to say I've got ice water in my veins, but I've been through too much in this business to get steamed up over a no-hitter. It was nice. But the World Series, that's what I want! Now you're talking thrills."

Chance never made it to the Series, but with Minnesota he did get as far as the 1969 Championship Series, the first division playoffs in major league history. Yet the season was a sour one for Chance. That spring he had held out for more money. When he finally settled with Twins owner Calvin Griffith, Chance rushed his training, hurt his arm, and appeared in only 20 games.

After the ALCS, Chance was traded with Graig Nettles, pitcher Robert Miller, and outfielder Ted Uhlaender for Indians pitchers Luis Tiant and Stan Williams. Chance was never the same. "One day you can throw tomatoes through brick walls. The next day you can't dent a pane of glass with a rock. It hurts, but you hang on hoping it'll come back. Oh, well, it's a helluva ride, the one on the way up," Chance said.

He bounced from the Indians to the Mets to the Tigers before retiring in 1971. After his baseball career ended, the unpredictable Chance managed boxer Ernie Shavers, farmed, and even traveled with a carnival.

Frank Chance

Chance, Frank Leroy **1B–C**

1898–1914 M(1905–1914,1923, 946–648) B:9/9/1877, Fresno, CA D:9/15/1924, Los Angeles, CA Deb:4/29/1898, CHI NL BR/TR 6', 190

G	AB	R	H	HR	RBI	OBP	SLG	AVG
1287	4297	797	1273	20	596	.394	.394	.296

Frank Chance might have stolen baseball's most expensive base. The Chicago Cubs and the Cincinnati Reds were tied in a late inning when Cubs player-manager Chance singled and stole second. He then gave the bunt sign, and even before the ball hit the dirt he rounded third and sprinted home, barely beating the throw. In gratitude for Chance's hustle and quick thinking, Cubs owner Charles Murphy rewarded him with a 10 percent interest in the Cubs, which the player later sold for $150,000.

Although Chance doesn't rank among the all-time great first basemen, he was a very good player when healthy. His career statistics, which include a .296 batting average and 401 stolen bases, match or exceed those of any National League first baseman of the Dead Ball Era, when batting averages were generally low and home runs were rare.

His real talents were as a manager and a leader. Called "the Peerless Leader," the manager compiled a lifetime 946–648 record for a .593 winning percentage. In eight years as Cubs' skipper he won two world championships and four pennants and never brought the team in below third.

Chance attended the University of California, preparing for a career in dentistry, but he left Berkeley and transferred to Washington College in Irvington, California. Chicago Cubs' star outfielder Bill Lange was playing for a local independent team when he spotted Chance. Lange urged the club to sign the Californian. Chance joined the Cubs in April 1898 as a reserve catcher and outfielder, batting .279 in 53 games.

Nicknamed "Husk" because of his husky build and aggressive play, Chance continued as a backup catcher, outfielder, and first baseman through 1902. As a backstop, he had trouble catching foul tips and was frequently sidelined with broken fingers. On the Cubs' trip back from spring training in 1903, the regular first baseman, Bill Hanlon, abruptly left the team. Manager Frank Selee asked Chance to take over until he could find a regular.

Chance was an excellent first baseman, and his hitting improved markedly. He batted .327 in 1903 (the first time he exceeded .300), scored 83 runs, and knocked in 81. In his first year as a full-time first baseman he led the NL with 67 stolen bases.

In August 1905 Selee became ill and resigned. Owner Jim Hart was in the process of selling the team to Charles Webb Murphy, and one of his last decisions was to name Chance manager. Selee had built a strong team, but it was languishing in the middle of the standings. Under Chance's driving leadership the Cubs moved up to third by season's end.

In 1906 Chance pushed the Cubs to the top. The team won a major league-record 116 games against only 36 losses, outdistancing second-place New York by 20 games. Although modern schedules include 10 more games than were played in that era, no major league in the 20th century won that many games in a season.

Chance himself had his finest year, batting .319 and leading the league with 103 runs and 57 stolen bases. The Cubs were heavily favored in the World Series, but the crosstown White Sox pulled off one of the greatest upsets in Series history, winning in six games.

The Cubs ran away with the pennant again in 1907. This time they made short work of the Detroit Tigers in the Series to become world champions. In 1908 Chance won his third straight pennant. The Cubs finished the season tied with the Giants and were forced to replay an earlier game that had ended in a tie after Giant Fred Merkle made a crucial base running mistake. Chance's Cubs won the tiebreaker, 4–2, and once again went on to defeat Detroit in the Series.

The 1908 season was Chance's last as a regular first baseman. He was only 31 years old and still a good player, but his health was slipping. When at bat he often crowded the plate and was hit in the head a number of times. By 1909 the beanings had started taking their toll. His hearing was impaired, and he experienced blinding headaches that left him all but incapacitated, making it impossible for him to play regularly.

In addition to losing Chance as a regular in 1909, the Cubs also lost ace catcher Johnny Kling, who sat out the season for contractual reasons. The team finished third. When Kling returned in 1910, Chance led the Cubs to their fourth pennant in five years. In the World Series, Connie Mack's young Philadelphia Athletics won in five games.

Chance drove his talented team with an iron hand, making his players perform better than they thought they could. He brought the aging Cubs to second in 1911 and to third in 1912, better than owner Murphy had any right to expect.

In 1912 Chance quarreled with Murphy over the owner's refusal to spend the money necessary to acquire good players. Chance thought his team would fail to contend, and he was released at season's end.

That winter he underwent surgery to alleviate the blood clots that were thought to cause his headaches, and in 1913 he accepted a job as New York Yankees player-manager. In two seasons, Chance couldn't move the Yanks out of seventh place. He returned to California and grew oranges. For a time he was part owner and manager of a Pacific Coast League team in Los Angeles.

In 1923 he returned to the majors as Red Sox manager; however, most of Boston's talent had been sold off to pay the owner's debts. This hopeless team finished a well-deserved last. Chance was slated to take over the Chicago White Sox when his health gave out, and he died in September 1924. In 1946 he was elected to the Hall of Fame with Joe Tinker and Johnny Evers, his partners in the Chicago infield and forever linked with Chance in F.P Adams' brief poem in the *New York Globe*, "Baseball's Sad Lexicon."

Albert Chandler

Chandler, Albert B.

Commissioner (1945–1951) B:7/14/1907, Corydon, KY D:6/15/1991, Versailles, KY

Albert B. "Happy" Chandler's tenure in office as baseball's second commissioner was marked by contradictions: his favoritism toward his friends and his outmaneuvering of his enemies. He was often vilified, sometimes with good reason, by the press, yet he was inducted into the Hall of Fame along with the immortals of the game. He was no Kenesaw Mountain Landis, essentially because it didn't suit the owners to have a commissioner as dominant as Landis had been.

By the age of 30, the hardworking, Kentucky-born lawyer had already realized his future lay in politics. He served as governor of his home state and, later, as a U.S. senator. While in the Senate he was a frequent visitor to Washington's Griffith Stadium, and during World War II he spoke out about his belief that baseball should remain in operation through the war years. This public stand, along with his friendship with Yankees owner Larry MacPhail, won him the commissioner's job in 1945.

Chandler's personal style made for an interesting relationship with the anxious millionaires who owned the game. As Lee Lowenfish and Tony Lupien put it in *The Imperfect Diamond*, "A commissioner willing to sing 'My Old Kentucky Home' at a moment's notice embarrassed the urbanites…(but) in Commissioner Chandler (the owners) had a leader of no great force or distinction, which suited them perfectly."

His early decisions seemed to favor neither players nor owners. In one case, he gave 10 Tiger farmhands their freedom because of signing irregularities, a common major league ploy of "hiding" players on minor league rosters. But when 18 big leaguers, known as "the Mexican Jumping Beans," signed contracts to play for the Mexican League's Pasquel brothers in 1946, Chandler immediately suspended them for five years. One such "Jumping Bean," Mickey Owen, asked for clemency and was refused, although Chandler eventually backed down and granted the players amnesty.

When Robert Murphy tried to establish a players' union in 1946, Chandler presented a gold watch to Pirates pitcher Rip Sewell, one of the players who opposed the guild. Yet when the owners voted 15 to 1 against allowing Dodgers president Branch Rickey to integrate professional baseball, Chandler disagreed, and his support made Jackie Robinson's appearance in the big leagues possible.

But Chandler did not always think so clearly. The day he publicly blasted the players and officials who patronized racetracks, newspapers published photos of Chandler's wife and daughter at Churchill Downs. When Larry MacPhail pulled a shady waiver deal, Chandler conveniently failed to launch an investigation. Newspaper columnist Red Smith commented that Chandler was "the most relentlessly affable employee, most tireless handshaker, most indefatigable signer of autographs baseball has ever known. When he makes a speech, he cites poetry of the Edgar Guest stripe. When he makes a decision, his friends do not get the worst of it."

Perhaps the most striking example of Chandler's favoritism was one regarding Leo Durocher in 1947. Durocher, manager of the Brooklyn Dodgers, was hounded by rumors he fraternized with gamblers and other unsavory types. Yet at the same time that Chandler was conducting an investigation into Durocher's character, photos were taken showing two known gamblers in Larry MacPhail's box at an exhibition in Havana, Cuba. Little evidence existed Durocher had done anything very wrong, but Chandler still suspended him for a year for "conduct detrimental to baseball."

In his ruling, Chandler included a clause that said, "All parties to this controversy are hereby silenced from the time this order is issued." Chandler never kept his part of the bargain; he was once quoted as saying, "If I ever opened my private files on Durocher, the American people would say I acted too leniently."

Durocher fought back the only way he could, with nasty phone calls. Every time he saw something in the press about a "confidential file," he'd call Chandler and vex him. "Oh, we had long, intimate talks for a while, Happy and I," said Durocher years later.

Because MacPhail was never reprimanded for his association with gamblers, Rickey once said, "Are there two sets of rules, one for the owners, the other for managers and players?" When Red Smith criticized Chandler's handling of the controversy, the commissioner exploded and charged that Smith was at the center of a conspiracy to run him out of baseball. Smith replied by calling Chandler a "clown and a mountebank."

Chandler did help put the players' pension fund on a sound financial footing when he sold a six-year contract for the radio and television rights to the World Series and All-Star Game to Gillette. The rights turned out to be worth a lot more than the $1 million Chandler negotiated. Some insisted he could have received more from a beer company, but his Baptist background made that alternative unacceptable.

Five years into his seven-year contract Chandler asked for an extension and was refused; he resigned a year early. "I always regarded baseball as our national game that belongs to 150 million men, women, and children," he said, "not to 16 special people who happen to own big league teams." He went on to call the owners "semi-bandits."

After leaving baseball he was again elected governor of Kentucky, and in 1982 he was elected to baseball's Hall of Fame. Perhaps the clearest assessment of him came from J.G. Taylor Spink of *The Sporting News*: "Chandler," he said, "insisted on being himself."

Spud Chandler

Chandler, Spurgeon Ferdinand **P**

1937–1947 B:9/12/1907, Commerce, GA D:1/9/1990, South Pasadena, FL Deb:5/6/1937, NY AL BR/TR 6', 181

W	L	PCT	G	SH	IP	BB	SO	ERA
109	43	.717	211	26	1485	463	614	2.84

Chandler was a gem of consistency during his 11-year major league career with the New York Yankees. A righthanded control pitcher who debuted as a 29-year-old rookie with the powerful 1937 Yankees, Chandler never had a losing season.

He went 10–4 in 1941 and 16–5 in 1942, but his luck turned sour in the World Series both seasons. In 1941 he started, and lost, Game 2. In the 1942 Series he picked up a save in Game 1, but lost a 2–0 decision in Game 3 despite yielding only one earned run.

As Yankees ace at age 35 in 1943, Chandler was spectacular. He finished with a 20–4 record and led the AL in victories, winning percentage (.833), complete games (20), shutouts (five), and earned run average (1.64), the lowest mark in the circuit in 24 years. On July 26, 1940, he tied a league record for pitchers when he hit two homers in a game, including a grand slam off Chicago's Pete Appleton.

But Chandler wasn't finished. He hurled two complete-game victories in the 1943 World Series, tossing a 2–0 shutout against the St. Louis Cardinals in the Game 5 clincher. It came as no surprise when Chandler was named the league's Most Valuable Player.

After spending most of the next two years in the military, Chandler returned to the Bronx for the 1946 season in top form. He finished with a 20 wins and a 2.10 ERA, second only to Hal Newhouser's 1.94. The following season, at age 39, Chandler was 9–5 with a 2.46 ERA. He appeared in one game as a reliever in the 1947 World Series, but was shelled in two innings of work. That was the last major league game Chandler pitched in. He left with a lifetime record of 109-43 and a 2.84 ERA.

Ben Chapman

Chapman, William Benjamin **OF–3B**

1930–41, 1944–46 M(1946–48, 196–276)
B:12/25/1908, Nashville, TN Deb:4/15/1930, NY AL
BR/TR 6', 190

G	AB	R	H	HR	RBI	OBP	SLG	AVG
1717	6478	1144	1958	90	977	.383	.440	.302

The Yankees dynasty of the 1920s ended when its mastermind, Miller Huggins, died in 1929. In 1930 the team was in a rebuilding era under new skipper Joe McCarthy. Although Babe Ruth, Lou Gehrig, Earle Combs, and Bill Dickey—all immortals—still all pounded the ball, and Lefty Gomez and Herb Pennock still pitched strongly, the much-respected club fell to third. One of the brightest stars who would help pull them back to the top of the American League in the early McCarthy years was young Ben Chapman.

Chapman was a capable hitter and a speedy, smart-running outfielder who would go on to 15 major league seasons. He was always tough at the plate and on the basepaths, but he would never join the Yankees immortals.

He started in the team's infield in 1930, but his speed and good arm made him a natural outfielder, and McCarthy moved him to left in 1931 beside Combs in center and Ruth in right. He played as much a champion's game as either of them. From 1931 to 1933 he hit .309 and led the AL in stolen bases each year. He was instrumental in bringing the aging Yankees back to contention and in helping secure their single world championship during his time with the team, in 1932.

In 1933 the Yankees and the Washington Senators battled for the AL pennant all year long. Chapman's aggressive base running started the season's biggest on-field fracas and kept the Yankees in contention until the end, when they finished second. Chapman was the first batter in that year's first-ever All-Star Game. He also led all AL outfielders in assists.

In the 1935 season, from which Yankees Combs and Ruth were absent, Chapman again led the league in assists. But his average declined, and after the season McCarthy traded him to the Senators for Jake Powell, a ball-crusher who could fill in the now depleted Yankee batting order. Joe DiMaggio, who was just coming up from the San Francisco Seals, had already been pegged as the next legendary Yankees outfielder. Powell hit .455 in the 1936

World Series for the Yankees and played on the 1937 and 1938 world champion teams.

Chapman, who had played on the AL All-Star team in each of its first three assemblies, continued to hit well and steal bases. He led the league in swipes in 1937, with 35, and became a key ingredient in deals between the Senators, the Red Sox, and the Indians, shuttling among those teams for the next five years. None could ever overpower the dominant Yankees.

Chapman went to the White Sox in 1941 and, after returning from military service in 1944, still had enough strength in his arm to sign as a pitcher with the Brooklyn Dodgers. He was little used in his two years there but posted a respectable record.

In 1945 he took over as utility man for the Phillies and was manager by the end of that year. He retired from play in 1946 but stayed on as skipper. His virulent and profane hostility to Jackie Robinson's debut with Brooklyn was widely criticized. His anger towards Robinson, and his team's 37–42 record, led to his firing in 1948.

Ray Chapman

Chapman, Raymond Johnson **SS**

1912–20 B:1/15/1891, Beaver Dam, KY D:8/17/1920, New York, NY Deb:8/30/1912, CLE AL BR/TR 5'10", 170

G	AB	R	H	HR	RBI	OBP	SLG	AVG
1051	3785	671	1053	17	364	.358	.377	.278

On August 17, 1920, Cleveland shortstop Ray Chapman stepped to the plate at New York's Polo Grounds against the Yankees' Carl Mays. A pitch barely outside the strike zone struck Chapman on the left temple and he was carried from the field on a stretcher. He never regained consciousness, dying 12 hours later in a New York City hospital, the first major leaguer to die as a result of an on-field accident.

Chapman's unfortunate death eventually had far-reaching implications for baseball. Some baseball scholars feel that this incident had perhaps as much influence in sparking the batting revolution of the 1920s as did Babe Ruth and the introduction of the "lively ball."

Prior to 1912, baseballs hit into the stands were thrown back into play, and it was not unusual to use a single ball for an entire game. Even after 1912 it was still rare to discard a scuffed or worn-out ball. This naturally gave an advantage to pitchers. Owners didn't allow fans to keep balls hit into the stands until April 29, 1916, when Cubs owner "Lucky Charlie" Weeghman set precedent by letting fans have the balls as souvenirs.

The spitball, shineball, and all other dubious pitches had been outlawed on February 9, 1920, six months before Chapman's death. After Chapman died, balls hit into the stands stayed there, and umpires tossed out nicked or scuffed balls with greater frequency. In 1919 the National League went through 22,095 baseballs; in 1924 that figure had grown to 54,030. Batters now got to swing at baseballs that were more visible and less apt to "sail." Batting averages rose accordingly.

One change that surprisingly did not occur for another three decades was the introduction of batting helmets. The *Spalding Guide* advocated their use immediately after the Chapman tragedy, saying, "A head helmet for the batter is not to be despised. There is nothing 'sissy' about it." Yet nothing was done until the Pittsburgh Pirates introduced protective headgear in the early 1950s.

Chapman was born on his father's small farm in Kentucky; the family moved to Herrin, Illinois, when Ray was 14. He began working in the mines soon thereafter and held a United Mine Workers card for the rest of his life.

He also played semipro ball, and in the spring of 1910 "Sinister Dick" Kinsella, a famous scout and minor league club owner, signed him for his Springfield Senators of the 3-I League. Chapman played little but ingratiated himself wherever he went. His manager, Dick Smith, told him, "You know, kid, even if you never played a game, you'd earn your pay just by sitting on the bench and being such a cheerleader."

In 1911 Kinsella sold Chapman to the rival Davenport Prodigals and the shortstop responded with a .293 average and 75 stolen bases. Spotted by Bill Armour, who had discovered Ty Cobb, Chapman was sold to Armour's Toledo Mud Hens and became a star. "Chappie" hit .310 with 49 stolen bases and 101 runs scored and was called up to Cleveland. He became a solid player with the Indians, and his 52 stolen bases in 1917 remained a club record until broken by Miguel Dilone's 61 in 1980.

The 1920 Indians, who featured seven .300 hitters, were engaged in a three-way pennant race with the Yankees and the defending league champion White Sox. When Chapman came to the plate on August 17 he faced Carl Mays, who had a reputation as a headhunter who scuffed the ball. (In 1917 Mays led the AL with 14 hit batsmen.)

As was his custom, Chapman crouched toward the plate. Catcher Herold "Muddy" Ruel had trouble seeing the ball, which was headed straight at Chapman. One witness said Chapman seemed "hypnotized." There was an "explosive sound" and the ball came bounding back at Mays, who fielded it and flipped it to first baseman Wally Pipp for what he thought was the inning's first out. Pipp caught the ball and started to toss it around the infield, when suddenly he became aware something was wrong with Chapman.

"We need a doctor," home plate umpire Tom Connolly shouted. "Is there a doctor in the house?" The Indians gathered around Chapman, who at first could not speak, as the Yankees team physician applied ice to his injury. After a few minutes Chapman was able to stand, to the immense relief of the crowd. With the assistance of two teammates Chapman began walking off the field toward the center field clubhouse. At second base he crumpled to the ground; he died 12 hours later at St. Lawrence Hospital.

Mays pitched the rest of that game, losing to Stanley Coveleski, 4–0. The public reaction was one of sadness mixed with shock and anger. An incensed Browns club voted unanimously that Mays "must be removed from baseball," and a widespread player boycott of the pitcher was rumored.

In response Mays said, "It is terrible to consider the case at all, but when any man, however ignorant, illiterate or malicious, even hints that a white man in his normal mind would stand out there on the field of sport and try to kill another, the man making the assertion is inhuman, uncivilized, bestial."

Other fingers were pointed at AL umpires, citing their failure to toss out scuffed balls. Umpires Billy Evans and Bill Dinneen issued a statement that blamed Mays and that read in part: "No pitcher in the American League resorted more to trickery than Carl Mays in attempting to rough a ball to get a break on it."

Evans and Dinneen also addressed the issue of throwing balls out of a game, and placed the blame squarely on team owners. "A short time ago," they alleged, "the club owners complained to President [Ban] Johnson that too many balls were being thrown out. President Johnson sent out a bulletin telling the umpires to keep the balls in the games as much as possible except those which were dangerous."

Ray Chapman was buried at Cleveland's St. John's Cathedral on August 20, 1920. His place at shortstop was taken by a rookie named Joe Sewell who would wind up in the Hall of Fame. The 1920 Indians went on to win the pennant after the eight "Black Sox" were suspended in late September, and Cleveland subsequently defeated the Brooklyn Robins in the World Series.

Joe Charboneau

Charboneau, Joseph **OF**

1980–82 B:6/17/1955, Belvidere, IL Deb:4/11/1980, CLE AL BR/TR 6'2", 205

G	AB	R	H	HR	RBI	OBP	SLG	AVG
201	647	97	172	29	114	.333	.453	.266

Joe Charboneau, the 1980 American League Rookie of the Year, is better known for his startling antics off the field than for solid play on it. "Super Joe" had a fine season, with 23 homers, 87 RBIs, and a .289 average to win the award, but that was hardly the whole story. His many dubious achievements include opening beer bottles with his eye socket; shaving his head a decade before it became fashionable; cutting off a tattoo with a razor blade; eating cigarettes; and fighting in boxcars for $25 a match.

Originally signed by the Phillies, Joseph Charboneau quit baseball in only his second minor league season after fighting with management. He retreated into slow-pitch softball until the Phillies gave him another shot. Charboneau responded by leading the California League in batting in 1978, but after some barroom brawling he was traded to Cleveland that December.

He paced the Southern League in batting in 1979 with a .352 mark but was not expected to make the 1980 Indians until a knee injury felled Andre Thornton. Even then it was not an easy transition. During an Indians trip to Mexico, a local fan shoved a pen knife 4 inches into Charboneau's side and said he would do it again. "The amazing thing was that the police listened to what this guy said about wanting to get me again, and they fined him 50 pesos. That's $2.27 for stabbing a person," said Charboneau.

Charboneau's rookie season was his career year. By midseason 1981 he was back in the minors, and he developed a bad back that was never cured despite two operations. His farewell to baseball came with Buffalo in 1983. Super Joe, hitting just .200 after 11 games, gave Buffalo fans an "obscene salute" and was released summarily by the Indians. Now active in sports management in Cleveland, Charboneau has also hosted a radio show.

Oscar Charleston

Charleston, Oscar **OF-1B**

Negro League Player (1915–41) M(1942–54)
B:10/14/1896, Indianapolis, IN D:10/61954, Philadelphia, PA BL/TL 6', 190

Many players have been compared to a great one—to Babe Ruth, Tris Speaker, Willie Mays, or Ty Cobb. But only one player was compared to all four. He was Oscar Charleston. Among the men who played Negro Leagues ball, he is often called the greatest of all. Like Speaker, Charleston played a shallow center field to grab short line drives and flares. And like Speaker, he broke with the crack of the bat to run down the deepest drives.

"Oscar was the only player I've ever seen who could turn twice while chasing a fly and then take it over his shoulder," remembered second baseman Bingo DeMoss, himself a great player. "He had an uncanny knowledge of judging fly-balls." Another Hall of Fame center fielder, James "Cool Papa" Bell, compared Charleston with Willie Mays and pointed out that although Charleston's arm was weak, he had better range than Mays.

Like Cobb, Charleston was a consummate base stealer with blinding speed. "He was so fast," a publicity release said, "that he makes Ty Cobb look like Ham Hyatt." (Hyatt was a notoriously slow first baseman.) Charleston also shared Cobb's aggressive reputation and was known to come in spikes high. "See that scar?" Newt Allen once asked an interviewer. "Oscar Charleston jumped at me at third base, cut my glove off my hand. I had him out, but he hit me, he jumped high, knocked my glove and the ball."

Like Ruth, Charleston hit the ball far and often. Built along the same lines as the Babe, he was a big, barrel-chested man, standing 6 feet tall and weighing close to 200 pounds, with spindly legs and delicate ankles. As Charleston put on weight his legs gave out, and he switched to first base.

Slowing down didn't affect his hitting, however. "Charleston could hit that ball a mile," said Dizzy Dean, who barnstormed against him in the 1930s. "He didn't have a weakness. When he came up, we just threw and hoped like hell he wouldn't get a hold of one and send it out of the park." In a 1921 exhibition game against the St. Louis Cardinals, Charleston hit four home runs.

Born the seventh of 11 children, he ran away from home at 15, lied about his age, and joined the army. Shipped to the Philippines, Charleston was the only African-American player in the Manila League. On his return home in 1915 he became the center fielder for the Indianapolis ABC's, and his powerful lefthanded bat helped them win a championship the next year.

During the 1920s he moved around the top teams of the Negro National League, the Eastern Colored League, and the American Negro League. Among his stops were stints with the New York Lincoln Stars, Chicago American Giants, St. Louis Giants, Harrisburg Giants, and Philadelphia Hilldales. Although complete statistics are lacking, he is believed to have batted .430 in 1921, .399 in 1922, and .418 in 1925. He led his league in homers four times.

In winter Charleston often played in the Cuban League, where he became a great hero. Off the field he was fun-loving, popular, warm, and friendly, with an underlying edge of danger. On the field he developed a reputation as a brawler, and several of his fights became legend. Teammate Ted Page once remarked that Charleston had "vicious eyes. Steel-gray, like a cat. You could see cold-bloodedness. You would say, 'I sure would hate to tangle with this guy.'"

In 1930 Charleston joined Smoky Joe Williams and Josh Gibson on Cum Posey's great Homestead Grays. That season the team won a 10-game Eastern Championship Series against the New York Lincoln Giants. In 1932 Charleston jumped to Gus Greenlee's Pittsburgh Crawfords as player-manager. Gibson and several other Grays joined him; other teammates included pitcher Satchel Paige and third baseman Judy Johnson. That year Charleston hit .363, second on the club to Gibson, as the Crawfords went 99–36 playing an independent schedule. Many observers consider it the strongest black baseball team of all time.

When the Negro National Association was formed in 1933, the Crawfords joined and became the dominant team, and although he was nearing 40, Charleston started at first base in the first three Negro All-Star Games, from 1933 through 1935.

He stayed with the Crawfords through 1940 as the team moved first to Toledo and then to Indianapolis. His career batting average is usually given as .376 in the Negro Leagues,.326 in exhibitions against white teams, and .361 in the Cuban League. In the 1940s, when Branch Rickey began the integration of major league ball, he asked Charleston to scout and evaluate black players.

Charleston continued to manage and in 1954 led the Indianapolis Clowns to the Negro American League championship. Shortly after the season he died of a heart attack. In 1976 the Committee on Negro League Baseball named him to the Hall of Fame.

Norm Charlton

Charlton, Norman Wood **P**

1988–* B:1/6/1963, Fort Polk, LA Deb:8/19/1988, CIN NL BB/TL 6'3", 205

W	L	PCT	G	SV	IP	BB	SO	ERA
47	52	.475	559	96	848^2	392	759	3.67

Norm Charlton pitched as a starter, middle reliever, set-up man, and closer. He changed teams six times and endured the dreaded "Tommy John" surgery. Nevertheless, the crafty lefty enjoyed a remarkable stretch of consistency, posting ERAs under 3.00 for five straight years.

Charlton began his professional career in 1988 in Cincinnati as a starter, but he shined when he was moved to middle relief in 1989. Charlton attacked hitters with his low-90 mph fastball and a repertoire of breaking pitches. One of those hooks was a curveball that he "backdoored" to righthanded hitters.

Though a spot starter in 1990 and 1991, Charlton also teamed with Rob Dibble and Randy Myers to form the team's "Nasty Boys" relief corps. Charlton lost Game 1 of the Championship Series in relief, but he did not allow a run in four subsequent postseason appearances. He won Game 6 of the NLCS in relief as Cincinnati won its first pennant in 15 seasons. The Reds shocked Oakland with a four-game World Series sweep.

In 1992 Charlton (26) and Dibble (25) became the first teammates ever to save 25 games apiece. Charlton starred with Seattle in 1993 until leaving the team in August. He underwent major surgery on his ulnar collateral ligament, wiping out his 1994 season. His reconstructed elbow did not adjust well to Philadelphia. He had a 7.36 ERA in 25 games before the Phillies released him in July.

Lou Piniella, who had managed Charlton in Cincinnati and Seattle, gave the southpaw another chance with the Mariners. Amazingly, he registered a 1.51 ERA and was named the American League Pitcher of the Month for September. In that year's postseason, Charlton went 2–0 with two saves. He was not the same pitcher after that, however, and closed the decade with stints in Baltimore, Atlanta, and Tampa Bay.

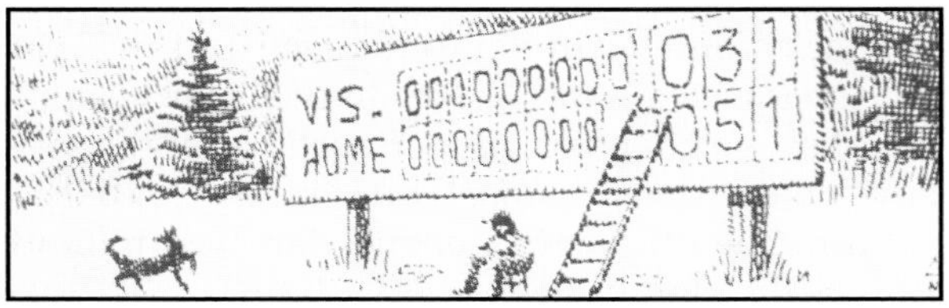

Hal Chase

Chase, Harold Homer **1B**

1905–19 M(1910–11, 86–80) B:2/13/1883, Los Gatos, CA D:5/18/1947, Colusa, CA Deb:4/14/1905, NY AL BR/TL 6', 175

G	AB	R	H	HR	RBI	OBP	SLG	AVG
1919	7417	980	2158	57	941	.319	.391	.291

An article in *The Sporting News* in June 1913 said of Hal Chase, "That he can play first as it never was and perhaps never will be played is a well known truth. That he will is a different matter." The story intimated what many baseball followers had known for years: Hal Chase did not always play to win.

He wasn't lazy; he was crooked. Yet each time he was charged with corruption, "Prince Hal" wiggled off the hook. At the time, baseball officials believed that the game was best served by sweeping its dirt under the rug. But by protecting Chase, these leaders opened the door to an even greater scandal that nearly ruined the game.

Chase starred for Santa Clara University in 1903 and played for Los Angeles of the Pacific Coast League in 1904 before the New York Highlanders purchased his contract for a reported $2,700. With a shock of red hair and sparkling blue eyes he immediately became the team's most popular player. In 1907 *Sporting Life* called him "perhaps the biggest drawing card in baseball."

He also rapidly became baseball's biggest pain in the neck. In 1908 Prince Hal threatened to jump to the outlaw California League if not paid the then-princely salary of $4,000 per year. The club gave in, but Chase jumped anyway. The Highlanders suspended him and then reinstated him when it appeared he might really stay out west. He earned the respect of his New York teammates by standing up to management, and they presented him with a silver loving cup upon his return.

Two years later, New York manager George Stallings accused Chase of throwing games. Chase went to the team owner, bad-mouthed Stallings, and was named the new manager. Under his less-than-inspiring leadership the club sank from second place to sixth.

Although Chase threw lefthanded, he batted from the right side, a fairly unusual arrangement. A line drive hitter, he was dangerous but erratic, batting .249 as a rookie and .323 as a sophomore before slumping to .257 two years later. Some of the fluctuation may be attributed to the opposing pitchers, but much of Chase's inconsistency might also have been due to his attempts to influence the game according to how he bet.

He was regarded as a much better hitter than his .291 career average indicates. Even in his best seasons, his runs and RBI totals were suspiciously low:

he never knocked in more than 89 runs in a year and never scored more than 85.

In the field, however, Chase was magic, blessed with great range and remarkable hands. Most observers, including such slick first basemen as George Sisler and Stuffy McInnis, grudgingly ranked Chase as the best fielder in the game. He apparently invented the tactic of charging a bunt, often catching the ball on the fly and turning it into an easy double play.

Yet this paragon of fielders led his league in putouts only once in 15 seasons. He never led in fielding percentage or assists, although he led the league's first basemen in errors six times. Chase played only 10 seasons in the American League, but he still holds the AL career record for most errors by a first-sacker, with 285 miscues.

Granted, a fielder with exceptional range usually makes a fair number of errors because he gets to so many balls that other players would only wave at. Even the great Sisler led the league in errors six times. What is most suspicious about Chase's fielding record is his tiny number of assists.

When Chase bet money on his opponent, he was too savvy to blow the play and cause the loss. One writer said Chase had "a corkscrew mind." Chase always managed to look his best while doing his worst. He often dived for a ball just out of his reach, but he hesitated a second too long before diving.

Sometimes he made a fantastic stop but then ended up in an awkward position, unable to make the throw to first. When he did make the play, his throws to first often arrived in such a way that the poor pitcher who couldn't handle the ball would be charged with an error. The crowd would cheer Chase for his effort, and the miscue would allow him to collect on his bet. To the casual fan, he looked like a hero. Only those who watched him day after day, as Stallings did, caught on.

Frank Chance, a former first baseman himself, took over as New York manager in 1913. After 39 games he traded Chase to the Chicago White Sox. Midway through the next season, the first baseman jumped to the Federal League.

When that league folded, Chase's career appeared to be over. Rumors of his involvement in fixing games were so rampant that American league president Ban Johnson decreed that Chase would never again play in the junior circuit. But the charges were never proved, and baseball's rulers feared the fans might lose confidence in the game if they found out what Chase was up to. The Cincinnati Reds signed him for 1916.

Chase might have played the 1916 season straight. He led the National League in batting, with a .339 average and 184 hits. But by 1917 he was back to his old ways. When he tried to bribe Cincinnati pitcher Jimmy Ring to throw a game, Ring reported him to manager Christy Mathewson. At midseason, Mathewson suspended Chase for "indifferent play."

Chase had the guts of a burglar and knew that baseball's leaders lacked his nerve. He appealed to National League president John Heydler to force Cincinnati to pay the salary he lost during his suspension. Chase appeared at the hearing with two lawyers and a stenographer. Heydler had Mathewson's affidavit, but Christy was in France with the army in the closing months of World War I. Ring's story was not substantiated by any other witnesses, and Chase threatened to sue and make the entire mess public. Heydler cleared Chase of all charges and ordered the Reds to pay him.

In perhaps the most bizarre twist of all, New York Giants manager John McGraw traded two players to the Reds for Chase and installed him at first base in 1919, and then he hired Mathewson as a coach. McGraw, who knew every rumor circulated about Chase, apparently believed he could turn the talented player into an honest man.

Chase lasted until August, when the Giants sent him to California with the admonition never to return to the major leagues. Shortly thereafter, members of the White Sox conspired to throw the 1919 World Series. Chase was rumored to have played a role in the fix, but nothing was proven. In California he managed to get suspended from three separate leagues for attempting to bribe players.

Before the 1920 season the Chicago Cubs released an infielder named Lee Magee. Because his contract ran through the end of the season, he sued the team for his pay. But times had changed. Testimony in court proved that Magee and another player, as Cincinnati teammates in 1918, had thrown a number of games to collect on bets against their own team. The other player, of course, was Hal Chase.

Chase became an alcoholic and drifted in and out of California mining camps, playing ball until he was well past 50 years old in return for a night's lodging or a drink. He never admitted to any wrongdoing and died of beriberi in 1947.

Larry Cheney

Cheney, Lawrence Russell **P**

1911–19 B:5/2/1886, Bellevillle, KS D:1/6/1969, Daytona Beach, FL Deb:9/9/1911, CHI NL BR/TR 6'1½", 185

W	L	PCT	G	SH	IP	BB	SO	ERA
116	100	.537	313	20	1881[1]	733	926	2.70

A broken thumb was the best thing that ever happened to Larry Cheney. In September 1911 Cheney had just been brought up from Indianapolis to the Chicago Cubs and was pitching in his first game. In the bottom of the ninth, the Dodgers' Zack Wheat hit a line drive right back at Cheney's head. Cheney raised his pitching hand to protect his face just as the ball struck. The force of it pushed his thumb up Cheney's nose, breaking both.

After the injury Cheney found he could no longer grip the ball as he had before. To compensate he started digging his fingers harder into the ball. Within a short period of time he had developed an effective knuckleball. With that pitch, Cheney won 20 or more games his first three full seasons with the Cubs. Later he learned a spitball from Ed Walsh.

On September 14, 1913, he shut out the Giants while surrendering a major league record 14 hits. Relying as he did on trick, hard-to-control pitches Cheney led the National league in wild pitches six times. He won 18 games for pennant-winning Brooklyn in 1916, and held opponents to a league-low .198 average. He also allowed an NL-low 6.33 hits per game and had a 1.92 ERA. It was Cheney's last winning season.

Tom Cheney

Cheney, Thomas Edgar **P**

1957–66 B:10/14/1934, Morgan, GA Deb:4/21/1957, STL NL BR/TR 6', 180

W	L	PCT	G	SH	IP	BB	SO	ERA
19	29	.396	115	8	466	245	345	3.77

Washington Senators hurler Tom Cheney holds the major league record for most strikeouts in an extra-inning game. On September 12, 1962, he whiffed 21 batters in a 16-inning game at Baltimore's Memorial Stadium. The righthander threw 228 pitches that night, striking out every Oriole except Boog Powell at least once.

The old extra-inning strikeout record was 18 in 15 innings, set by Jim Whitney in 1884; it was equaled by Jack Coombs in 1906 in 24 innings and by Warren Spahn in 1952 in 15 innings. Cheney got his record-breaking strikeout No. 19 in the 14th inning, fanning opposing pitcher Dick Hall. Future major league manager Dick Williams was his 21st and final victim, and Cheney won the contest, 2–1, on Bud Zipfel's solo homer.

"I had no idea it was a record until they announced it over the PA," he said. "The fans gave me an ovation. It was the farthest thing from my mind. I just wanted to win the ballgame. I was kind of surprised. It took me a couple of pitches to get my concentration back," said Cheney.

Jack Chesbro

Chesbro, John Dwight **P**

1899–1909 B:6/5/1874, North Adams, MA D:11/6/1931, Conway, MA Deb:7/12/1899, PIT NL BR/TR 5'9", 180

W	L	PCT	G	SH	IP	BB	SO	ERA
198	132	.600	392	35	2896^{2}	690	1265	2.68

In 1904 Jack Chesbro put together the biggest season of any pitcher in the 20th century when he won 41 games. But when it was over, all anybody remembered was one pitch.

On October 10, 1904, Chesbro took the mound for the New York Highlanders, the future Yankees, in the first game of a do-or-die doubleheader against the Boston Pilgrims. New York had led the American League throughout most of the season, but Boston surged at the end to move in front by a game and a half. To win the pennant the Highlanders needed to win both ends of the doubleheader. The second game appeared to be up for grabs, but the 30,000 New York fans were confident of victory in the first game. Chesbro was matched against Boston's Bill Dinneen, a 20-game winner but no Chesbro.

The two men pitched scoreless baseball until the fifth inning, when New York plated a pair of runs. Chesbro lined a single off Dinneen's little finger and came around to score the second run. In the seventh, Boston tied the game with two unearned runs on a pair of errors by New York second baseman Jimmy Williams. With the score even in the ninth, Boston catcher Lou Criger, a .217 hitter and slow on his feet, legged out a roller to New York shortstop Norman "Kid" Elberfeld. Dinneen sacrificed Criger to second. When Kip Selbach grounded out, Criger moved to third base. Freddy Parent, a dangerous .296 hitter, stepped to the plate.

Chesbro worked the count to one ball and two strikes. Then the spitball soared out of his hand and over the head of catcher Red Kleinow, allowing Criger to trot in with the go-ahead run. New York failed to score in the bottom of the inning, so the pennant went to the Boston Pilgrims. New York came back to win the nightcap, 1–0, in 10 innings, but it meant nothing.

Chesbro's pleasant disposition won him the nickname "Happy Jack" while he worked as an attendant at the state mental hospital in Middletown, New York, and pitched for the hospital team. In 1895 he turned pro with Albany of the New York State League.

For the first few years he appeared jinxed, as leagues folded around him. The Atlantic League finally remained in operation long enough for Chesbro to post a couple of good seasons with

Richmond and attract some attention. When Pittsburgh brought him up in the middle of 1899 he went a disappointing 6–9.

That winter the Louisville and Pittsburgh franchises were to be merged as a part of National League reorganization, with Louisville owner Barney Dreyfuss taking over the Pirates. Dreyfuss wanted to bring his better players, such as Honus Wagner, Fred Clarke, Deacon Phillippe, and Rube Waddell, to Pittsburgh. But other owners wanted a shot at the Louisville ballplayers and complained. So, just before the merger, Dreyfuss traded Wagner and his other Louisville stars to Pittsburgh for Chesbro and five other players no one cared about. When the merger became official, there were no players of value left on the Louisville roster. Chesbro was back in Pittsburgh without ever having left it.

He became a useful pitcher in 1900, finishing 15–13, and he improved even more in 1901, going 21–10 and leading the league with a .677 winning percentage and six shutouts. He began throwing a spitball in 1902, and the new pitch helped him post a league-high 28 wins. His .824 winning percentage and eight shutouts were also league bests.

Chesbro was a full-fledged star on a team full of stars. With players such as Wagner, Clarke, Ginger Beaumont, and Tommy Leach behind him, he had it easy. The Pirates hardly worked up a sweat to win pennants in 1901 and 1902.

The American League proclaimed itself a major league in 1901 and tried to prove it by luring some of the better players away from the National League. The new league's money was attractive, and Jack Chesbro was one of the many players who jumped. He signed with New York and won 20 games for the third straight season in 1903. His spitball was getting better, and the stocky Chesbro, only 5 feet 9 inches but weighing 180 pounds, was proving to be durable as well as talented.

In 1904 he completed 48 of 51 starts and pitched in relief in another four games. In 454 ⅔ innings he allowed only 338 hits. His earned run average was a terrific 1.82, and his season record was a phenomenal 41–12. From May 14 to July 4 he won 14 straight games. From his last eight innings on June 26 through his first six innings on July 16 he threw 40 consecutive scoreless innings. He led the AL in wins, winning percentage, games pitched, complete games, and innings pitched. Were it not for that final wild pitch, his season would have been nearly perfect.

Chesbro never duplicated his 41 wins, but neither has anyone else. He slumped to 19 wins in 1905, won 23 in 1906, and then faded, finishing with only 198 career victories. Many observers ascribed his collapse to too much work in 1904. Others blamed that disastrous wild pitch for his demise.

After retiring as a player in 1909, Chesbro coached at Amherst College for a year, then got involved in running a sawmill and raising chickens. Clark Griffith, who had been Chesbro's manager in 1904, brought him back as a coach with the Washington Senators in 1924, but he was soon let go in a cost-cutting measure.

The wild pitch haunted Chesbro for the rest of his life. New acquaintances always asked him about it. Anytime a wild pitch lost a game, someone was certain to remember Chesbro's toss. His friends even tried to get the official scoring on the throw changed to a passed ball to get the pitcher off the hook, but they were unsuccessful.

Chesbro died in 1931 and was elected to the Hall of Fame in 1946. His plaque wrongly credits him with only 192 victories; mercifully, it does not mention the wild pitch.

Cupid Childs

Childs, Clarence Algernon **2B**

1888–1901 B:8/14/1867, Calvert County, MD
D:11/8/1912, Baltimore, MD Deb:4/23/1888, PHI NL
BL/TR 5'8", 185

G	AB	R	H	HR	RBI	OBP	SLG	AVG
1456	5618	1214	1720	20	743	.416	.389	.306

Clarence Algernon Childs was known as "Cupid," but exactly why remains a mystery. Some say he received the moniker because he was lovable; others claim it was because he was unlovable. A third theory suggests that he possessed cherubic features. A regular National League second baseman for 10 years at the end of the 19th century, Childs was a career .306 hitter and an infielder with impressive range. He always seemed to get on base, either via hits or walks, and had good speed on the bases.

Childs made the Phillies in 1888 as a 20-year-old rookie. But after playing only two games and going hitless in four at bats he was traded to Washington on May 5 for Gid Gardner. Childs refused to report and the trade was nullified.

In 1890 he moved to Syracuse of the American Association and hit .345, led the league with 33 doubles, and scored 109 runs. It was the first of seven 100-run seasons for Childs. On June 1 he handled 18 chances at second base, still a major league record for a nine-inning game.

Beginning in 1891 he spent eight seasons with the Cleveland Spiders, hitting over .300 five times, including .353 in 1894 and a career-high .355 in 1896. He led the National League in runs in 1892 with 136, and he also had four seasons with at least 100 walks, reaching a high of 120 in 1893. Defensively, he led the league twice in putouts and assists, once in double plays, and four times in chances per game, the best gauge of range. He also led the league in errors four times, including 1891 when he committed 82.

In 1895 the Spiders finished second to the NL Baltimore Orioles of John McGraw and "Wee Willie" Keeler. Cleveland advanced to the Temple Cup, the World Series of that time, where they met the Orioles. After Game 4 in Baltimore, a 5–0 victory for the Orioles, a riot broke out. Police escorted the Spiders out of the park, but the mob hurled anything they could get their hands on at the players, including fruit, potatoes, rocks, and bricks. One of the rocks hit Childs in the head.

In 1896 he was involved in another violent episode. In a game on July 26, with Cincinnati ahead, 10–1, in the eighth inning, Eddie Burke stole second and collided with Childs. The two started to duke it out, and soon both teams joined the melee. Fifty policemen were needed to clear the field.

Harry Chiti

Chiti, Harry **C**

1950–1962 B:1/16/1932, Kincaid, IL Deb:9/27/1950, CHI NL BR/TR 6'3", 225

G	AB	R	H	HR	RBI	OBP	SLG	AVG
502	1495	135	356	41	179	.296	.365	.238

Harry Chiti was the first major leaguer traded for himself. When the Mets came into being in 1962 they purchased Chiti from the Indians, and general manager George Weiss announced, "We have purchased Harry Chiti for a player to be named later." When Chiti failed to make the grade in Flushing, Weiss completed the trade by sending him back to Cleveland.

Considered a *wunderkind* when he debuted with the Chicago Cubs late in 1950, Chiti was only 17 and seemed headed for greatness. However, his development was almost exclusively defensive, and while he became an adequate backstop with a fine knack for handling knuckleballs, his offensive contributions never came close to those expected of someone 6 feet 3 inches tall and weighing 225 pounds.

The Cubs waited for Chiti to complete two years in the military before handing him a starting job in 1955, but his .231 batting average was disappointing. Kansas City gave him a shot in 1958, but a .268 average wasn't enough to keep him in the lineup. In 1960 he was dealt to the Tigers, where he hit only .163 in 37 games. After he was sent back to Cleveland by the 1962 Mets, who went on to lose a 20th-century worst 120 games, he never appeared in another major league game.

Nestor Chylak

Chylak, Nestor

Umpire (1954–78) B:5/11/1922, Olyphant, PA D:2/17/82, Dunmore, PA

Nestor Chylak was one of the premier umpires of his day, serving in the American League from 1954 through 1978. He officiated in five World Series (1957, 1960, 1966, 1971, and 1977), three AL Championship Series (1969, 1972, and 1973) and four All-Star Games (1957, both games in 1960, 1964, and 1973).

At several points in his life, umpiring seemed like the least likely profession Chylak would follow. In high school he was only 5 feet 2 inches. Eventually he sprouted to a full 6 feet and weighed 200 pounds. During World War II he served in the European theater, and in 1945 was blinded by a German shell. For a full 10 days Chylak was sightless. He received both the Purple Heart and a Silver Star.

Chylak started his umpiring career in the Class D PONY league in 1947. He moved up to the Class C Canadian–American League in 1948, the Class B New England League in 1949, the Class A Eastern League in 1950–51, and spent the next two years in the Triple A International League.

Chylak was behind the plate when Bill Mazeroski homered to end the 1960 World Series, but his most memorable umpiring outing may have been at Cleveland's Municipal Stadium on the evening of June 14, 1974—the infamous "Beer Night" that saw suds offered at 10 cents a cup. In the bottom of the ninth, the Indians rallied to score two runs and tie the score 5–5, the crowd of 25,134 was out of control. The Tribe had the winning run on third with two out, but then several hundred fans swarmed onto the field. Chylak, who had earlier suffered a cut wrist when fans had previously invaded the field, declared the game forfeited to the visiting Texas Rangers.

That same season the Players Association conducted a secret poll of players regarding who the best and worst major league umpires were. Nestor Chylak and Ron Luciano were the only American League umpires rated as excellent. After retiring as an active umpire following the 1978 season, Chylak served as the American League's assistant supervisor of umpires.

"He was an umpire's umpire," Yogi Berra said in 1999, "He kept the game under control, but he would listen to you if you had a beef...Nestor would let you have your piece, and then he'd say, 'Fine, let's play.'"

"For every bad call Chylak made, he made 499 good ones," National League umpire Tom

Gorman once observed. "He was one of the great umpires."

He died of a heart attack in his sleep at Dunmore, Pennsylvania. The Veterans Committee elected Chylak to the Hall of Fame in 1999.

Eddie Cicotte

Cicotte, Edward Victor **P**

1905–20 B:6/19/1884, Detroit, MI D:5/5/1969, Detroit, MI Deb:9/3/1905, DET AL BB/TR 5'9", 175

W	L	PCT	G	SH	IP	BB	SO	ERA
209	148	.585	502	35	3226	827	1374	2.38

On October 1, 1919, Cincinnati Reds second baseman Morrie Rath stepped to the plate in the bottom of the first inning of Game 1 of the World Series. On the mound, Chicago White Sox righthander Eddie Cicotte wound up and delivered a strike. Cicotte took a sign from catcher Ray Schalk and then went into his windup again. The pitch was inside and hit Rath in the middle of his back. In various seats at Redland Field gamblers relaxed and smiled. The signal they'd been waiting for had just been delivered. The fix was on.

A year later on September 29, 1920, The *New York Times* headline read, "Eight White Sox Players Are Indicted on Charge of Fixing 1919 World Series; Cicotte Got $10,000 and Jackson $5,000." Cicotte, outfielders Joe Jackson and Happy Felsch, pitcher Lefty Williams, first baseman Chick Gandil, shortstop Swede Risberg, and utility infielder Fred McMullin were named in the conspiracy.

Third baseman Buck Weaver was not accused of throwing games, but he knew about the plot and kept silent. Although rumors of a fix had circulated throughout the year following the Reds' Series win, many baseball fans found the charges hard to believe. Yet two players, Jackson and Cicotte, had confessed.

At the time, Cicotte was one of baseball's most respected pitchers. The first hurler to truly master the knuckleball, his nickname was "Knuckles." His pitching arsenal also included the spitball and the shineball. If a trick pitch existed, Eddie knew how to throw it. Only 5 feet 9 inches and 175 pounds, he used any pitch he could get away with to make up for what he lacked in power.

Although he won more than 200 games during his career, Cicotte had been no instant sensation. In 1905 he pitched well enough in a three-game trial with the Detroit Tigers, but manager Bill Armour liked big pitchers and thought Cicotte was too small. The hurler was sent back to the minors.

In 1908 Cicotte resurfaced with the Red Sox, and during the next four years he won 51 games and lost 46. He was sold to the White Sox in the middle of the 1912 season. He won 18 games for Chicago in 1913 and then had several mediocre years while he learned to control his knuckleball and other trick pitches.

In 1916 he went 15–7, leading the league with a .682 winning percentage and dropping his ERA below 2.00. His new success aroused suspicion. "I do not see how he could have so much speed without doctoring the ball," Connie Mack said. Cleveland players sneaked into his locker, stole his glove and uniform, and sent them to a laboratory, but scientists found nothing illegal.

In 1917 he went 28–12 and led the American League with 346 innings pitched and an earned run average of 1.53. In 1919 he played his greatest season, finishing with a 29-7 record and a sparkling 1.82 ERA. He topped the American League in wins, winning percentage, complete games, and innings pitched. By the time he was indicted in 1920, he had won 21 games for the year and 208 lifetime.

Cicotte was popular with fans and with most of his teammates—no small accomplishment among the dissension-ridden White Sox. He was sportswriter Ring Lardner's favorite player. Lardner liked Cicotte's occasional pranks and wisecracks and the way he handled the banter of locker rooms and hotel lobbies. But Cicotte was a crook, by his own admission.

In Game 1 of the 1919 World Series the Sox hurler grooved enough pitches for the Reds to score five runs in the fourth inning on their way to a 9–1 win. Co-conspirator Lefty Williams gave away Game 2. Embarrassed by the way he let the Reds tattoo him in Game 1, Cicotte planned to be less obvious in Game 4. But the Reds weren't much help.

The game was still scoreless in the fifth inning. Taking matters into his own hands—or, more precisely, out of them—he threw wildly to first on one play and then cut off and fumbled a throw from the outfield that might have caught a runner at the plate. Cicotte was regarded as the best-fielding pitcher in the American League, but his two errors gave Cincinnati a pair of runs and they won, 2–0.

The gamblers then stiffed the players. Cicotte received $10,000 before the first game, Jackson had $5,000 in hand, and some of the other players received a few dollars. But no one had received what they had been promised. The cheaters, outraged at having been cheated themselves, decided to play the rest of the Series on the square.

Cicotte took his turn in Game 7. Pitching to win for the first time in the Series, he held the Reds to seven hits for a 4–1 victory. The Sox still trailed, three games to four, but the gamblers were nervous. Lefty Williams was quietly informed that if he won Game 8, it would be the last victory of his career. He obediently let himself get knocked out in the first inning, and the Reds went on to win, 10–5.

The "Black Sox" were willing to go into the tank because they felt they had been underpaid by Sox owner Charles Comiskey. Cicotte, for example, was paid only $7,000 after his glorious 1918 season; lesser pitchers were making a good deal more. In 1919 he was 35 years old, his career was almost over, and he was worried about the heavy mortgage payments due on his farm. "I did it for the wife and kiddies," he later said.

During the trial, both Cicotte's and Jackson's confessions mysteriously disappeared. Gambler Arnold Rothstein, known as "the Big Bankroll," ensured that disappearance with a bribe. The judge told jury members that they could convict the players only if they believed the players had intentionally set out to defraud the public, an impossible matter to prove.

The Black Sox were guilty as sin—except in a court of law. Judge Kenesaw Mountain Landis, baseball's new commissioner, banned all eight Black Sox from the game forever.

Cicotte appeared to feel his guilt more deeply than the others and took an assumed name to protect his family. For many years he worked for the Ford Motor Company in Detroit. In 1965, four years before his death, he told a reporter, "I admit I did wrong, but I've paid for it. I've tried to make up for it by living as clean a life as I could. Nobody can hurt me anymore."

Galen Cisco

Cisco, Galen Bernard **P**

1961–69 B:3/7/1936, St. Mary's, OH Deb:6/11/1961, BOS AL BR/TR 5'11", 215

W	L	PCT	G	SH	IP	BB	SO	ERA
25	56	.309	192	3	659	281	325	4.56

Righthander Galen Cisco, the sixth Mets pitcher employed by manager Casey Stengel in baseball's longest uninterrupted game, pitched the final nine innings of a seven-hour, 23-inning marathon between the Mets and the Giants on Sunday, June 23, 1964. Cisco provided eight innings of shutout relief, but ultimately surrendered two runs on Del Crandall's ground-rule double, giving the Giants an 8–6 win.

When the CBS-TV show, *What's My Line?* came on that night, host John Charles Daly remarked that he had been backstage watching "the most fantastic baseball game I've ever seen." Thousands of New York area viewers switched away from his show, and network officials later admitted that their ratings had dropped as a result of Daly's offhand comment.

Cisco had been a co-captain and fullback for the Ohio State team that defeated Oregon in the 1958 Rose Bowl. Signed by the Red Sox in 1957, he pitched at Raleigh, Corning, Allentown, Waterloo, Minneapolis, and Seattle before joining Boston in 1961. He was released to the Mets on waivers on September 7, 1962. In 1963 he won seven games for the Mets, posting a career-high 51 appearances.

After pitching briefly for the Red Sox and Royals, Cisco retired and later became a well-traveled but respected pitching coach with the Royals, Expos, Padres, Blue Jays, and Phillies.

Jim Clancy

Clancy, James **P**

1977–91 B:12/18/1955 Chicago, IL Deb:7/26/1977, TOR AL BR/TR 6'4", 220

W	L	PCT	G	SH	IP	BB	SO	ERA
140	167	.456	472	11	2517[1]	947	1422	4.23

Jim Clancy was an expansion-team pitcher who blossomed into an All-Star. He began his career in 1977 with the first-year Toronto Blue Jays. After five losing seasons, he got over the hump in 1982 with a 16–14 record and a career-best 266 innings pitched. He registered 15–11 marks for the Jays in both 1983 and 1987.

Clancy moved to Houston in 1989. He made a gradual transition from workhorse to relief pitcher. After making just 10 starts in 1990, Clancy appeared in a career-high 54 games—all in relief—the following year. He notched eight saves while splitting the year between Houston and Atlanta.

Clancy helped two teams reach the postseason: the 1985 Blue Jays and the 1991 Braves. His final decision in the major leagues came in Game 3 of the 1991 World Series, a 12-inning, 5–4 victory over the Minnesota Twins. It was the Braves' first win in a World Series game since the franchise was located in Milwaukee in 1958.

Jack Clark

Clark, Jack Anthony **OF-1B-DH**

1975–92 B:11/10/1955, New Brighton, PA Deb:9/12/1975, SF NL BR/TR 6'2", 205

G	AB	R	H	HR	RBI	OBP	SLG	AVG
1994	6847	1118	1826	340	1180	.383	.476	.267

Despite an 18-year major league career in which he slammed 340 home runs, appeared in four All-Star Games, and hit a dramatic, ninth-inning home run to win the 1985 National League Championship Series for St. Louis, Jack Clark is widely remembered as one of baseball's spoiled free agents, a player who wore out his welcome on every team he played for before falling into financial ruin. For a time Clark was a fine ballplayer whose working-class background should have endeared him to fans. But he always seemed to play with a chip on his shoulder.

Clark spent his teenage nights cruising around Southern California with his low-rider buddies and indulging in petty crime, but he was also an excellent athlete. As a high school senior Clark was named to the All-City basketball team, and on the baseball team he went 11–3 as a pitcher and hit .517. College beckoned, but Clark signed with the San Francisco Giants in 1973 for $10,000. He began his minor league career as a third baseman, but after leading both the California and Texas leagues in errors, he was moved to the outfield. Called up to San Francisco late in 1976, he never returned to the minors.

The young Clark was a complete ballplayer. A slashing, line drive hitter with good power, he rarely struck out and was initially a good base runner and a fine defensive outfielder with a particularly strong throwing arm. He made the All-Star team in 1978, his second full year in the major leagues, and tied for the NL lead in double plays for an outfielder, with five, the first of three times he would do so. He hit a career-high .306 in 1978, with a career-best 46 doubles, eight triples, 25 home runs, and 98 RBIs.

Clark played in San Francisco through 1984, a steady if not spectacular performer. Bothered by a number of minor injuries, he rarely played a full season, and his speed and defensive skills began to erode. Then Clark got into a dispute with the Giants front office when, following knee surgery, he refused to play the last month of the 1984 season. On February 1, 1985, the Giants traded him to St. Louis for four players.

In 1985 he led the Cardinals to the division championship. In the NLCS the Dodgers trailed St. Louis, three games to two, but the Dodgers held a 5–4 lead in the top of the ninth inning of Game 6. When Dodgers manager Tommy Lasorda chose to pitch to Clark with two men on base, "the Ripper" hit a dramatic home run that sent St. Louis to the World Series—where they fell to Kansas City in seven games. St. Louis made it to the Series again in 1987, but Clark had torn ligaments in his ankle and did not play.

Clark clashed with a number of teammates in 1987; he left the Cardinals as a free agent and signed with the Yankees. That year, Clark changed as a hitter. Almost overnight both his stats for walks and strikeouts doubled, leading some to charge that he was only concerned about hitting home runs. Clark griped about not appearing in the field, and the Yankees traded him to San Diego in 1989.

He lasted in San Diego for two seasons, but before he left he blasted the Padres organization. He signed a three-year contract for $8.5 million in Boston and had one productive year before slumping in 1992, hitting only .210 with five home runs and 33 RBIs. Just after the All-Star break, word leaked out that Clark was in serious financial trouble. Despite the huge contract, Clark was $6.7 million in debt. He had sponsored a drag racing enterprise, which lost $1 million a year, built a multimillion-dollar mansion that he was forced to sell, owned a restaurant that was losing money, picked up tabs and tipped big no matter where he went, and owned 18 automobiles. Clark filed for bankruptcy. When the season ended, the Red Sox released him.

Forced to sell nearly everything he owned, Clark was expected to do everything possible to return to the major leagues. In the spring of 1993, he finally signed a minor league contract with Montreal. Pleading personal problems, Clark reported to the team one month late and 40 pounds overweight. After working out for only a couple of weeks, he was released again.

Will Clark

Clark, William Nuschler **1B**

1986–* B:3/13/1964, New Orleans, LA Deb:4/8/86, SF NL BL/TL 6'2", 190

G	AB	R	H	HR	RBI	OBP	SLG	AVG
1846	6746	1108	2040	263	1135	.386	.493	.302

"Will Clark," said catcher Terry Kennedy in 1989, "is the best baseball player I've ever seen."

He earned such high praise offensively and defensively. In 1991 Clark became only the 16th player to win both a Gold Glove and lead a major league in slugging in a single year. The company Clark was keeping included Mays, Aaron, Joe Morgan, Al Kaline, Carl Yastrzemski, and George Brett. In his first six years he had a .317 average with men on base; with runners in scoring position it was .315.

Clark became a first baseman through an act of dog. Flash, the Clark family's retriever, returned from his neighborhood rounds one day with a beat-up lefthanded first baseman's mitt in his mouth. The Clarks tried to find out who it belonged to and even put an ad in the lost-and-founds. No luck. Then Flash brought back a second—this time brand-new—first baseman's glove (probably the property of the same family; after all they had to replace their missing mitt). Again no luck in returning it.

Taking advantage of fate, young Clark put his new gloves to use; becoming a first baseman and employing them through high school. He was a high school All-America at New Orleans' Jesuit High and went to Mississippi State instead of signing with the Royals, who drafted him as their fourth-round pick in the June 1982 amateur draft. "The money was fair," commented Clark, "but it was a question of maturity. I didn't think I was ready mentally and physically for pro ball."

He prepared himself well at MSU. Clark anchored a Bulldogs lineup that also included future major leaguers Rafael Palmeiro and Bobby Thigpen. Clark was an integral part of the 1984 U.S. Olympic Team that included such future stars as Mark McGwire and B.J. Surhoff. The following year he won the Golden Spikes Award as the best college player in the country.

Selected as the second overall pick in the June 1985 draft (Surhoff was selected by Milwaukee with the first choice), Clark was signed by Giants scout Ken Parker. Assigned to Fresno in the California League he homered on his first swing in pro ball—and homered again later in the game. He finished with a .309 average and 10 homers in 65 contests. In the Arizona Instructional League that fall he hit .487 in 10 games.

The 1986 Giants didn't have a lot to lose by giving him a chance in spring training 1986. They had dropped 100 games the year before; from 1980 to 1985 the club had employed six different Opening Day first basemen; in 1986 Clark became No. 7 by impressing everybody who saw him that spring. It was then he gained the nickname "Will the Thrill." Giants catcher Bob Brenly came up with it: "It was just one of those things that seemed to roll off the tongue."

Just as Clark had homered in his first pro at bat in Fresno, he homered off Houston's Nolan Ryan in his first major league swing becoming only the 65th individual to accomplish that feat. "I wasn't nervous," said Clark, "To tell you the truth, I was kind of loose, He was Nolan Ryan and I didn't have a durn thing to lose."

Clark could surely hit but his aggressive style hardly endeared him to all of his new teammates. His high-pitched, emotional outbursts grated on some, particularly outfielder Jeff Leonard who greeted Clark by spray-painting his new lizard-skin cowboy boots a day-glow orange. Later when Clark went on the disabled list with a hyper extended elbow, Leonard tossed all his bats in the garbage. "You won't be needing these for awhile," jeered the outfielder.

Eventually the two scuffled, after the African American Leonard called Clark an obscenity and Clark responded with a racial epithet. Clark did the same with often-injured Giants infielder Chris Brown, also African American, although he apologized. Understandably, Clark was labeled a racist, a charge he denied. "I've been branded a racist," he said. "That's so far from the truth to be unbelievable." Defenders point out that his best friend is African American.

Eventually his teammates became used to Clark's in-your-face approach to baseball and life in general. The Giants even built a 1990 advertising program around it: "I've Got A Giant Attitude."

"He [Clark] hits a grounder awhile ago," catcher Bob Brenly was quoted as saying in 1987, "comes back to the dugout and screams in that squeaky voice of his, 'Why don't they mow the damned grass?' He reacts to an out like it's the end of the world. But if he keeps hitting like this, I'll keep him supplied with batting helmets to throw."

One thing that everyone mentions about Clark is his swing, often described as the best in the game. It's a big factor in "Will the Thrill's" second nickname, "The Natural."

"Everyone thinks my swing just kind of came naturally and that I was born and blessed with it," explains Clark, "That's true but it's also taken a lot of hard work. Until you are around, you don't know how hard it is to get it that way every day."

In 1989 Clark helped lead the Giants into their first World Series since 1962. In 1987 the Giants had won the NL West and Clark had hit .360 in the Championship Series. In 1989 he outdid himself, batting .650, with two homers and eight RBIs and winning the Most Valuable Player Award in the five-game victory over the Cubs. In the World Series, however, he hit just .250 as Oakland humiliated San Francisco in what started out as the BART (Bay Area Rapid Transit) Series and ended up as the Earthquake Series.

"I knew something was wrong when the ground was moving faster than I was," said Clark. "When it first happened I thought it was the fans rocking the stadium. I didn't immediately catch the magnitude of it. It really put baseball in perspective. We're not as worried about baseball as about people's health and their property. We'll worry about baseball in time."

With two years before he became eligible for free agency, Clark signed a $15-million, four-year contract near the end of the 1989 season; it temporarily made him the game's highest paid player. "This is where the money makes a big difference," said Clark, "What happened is I played for years for fun. That part of the game will never change. The fun part will never change. Playing for money has allowed me to take care of my family better."

When his contract expired, Clark opted for free agency. He signed with the Rangers on November 22, 1993, replacing former college teammate Rafael Palmeiro as the Texas first baseman. Clark helped propel the team into the postseason in both 1996 and 1998—but hit badly in the playoffs both years, .125 in 1996 and .091 in 1998.

In 1998 he topped the 100-RBI mark for the first time since 1989 and once again declared free agency. On December 5, 1998, he signed with the Baltimore Orioles—ironically, once again replacing Rafael Palmeiro as first baseman.

Fred Clarke

Clarke, Fred Clifford **OF**

1894–1915 M(1897–1915, 1,602–1,181) B:10/3/1872, Winterset, IA D:8/14/1960, Winfield, KS
Deb:6/30/1894, LOU NL BL/TR 5'10½", 165

G	AB	R	H	HR	RBI	OBP	SLG	AVG
2242	8568	1619	2672	67	1015	.386	.429	.312

On June 30, 1894, a young outfielder named Fred Clarke sat stubbornly in his street clothes in the Louisville Colonels' clubhouse as his teammates dressed for the game. He was scheduled to start his first major league game in left field that afternoon, but he balked at the opportunity. He had been promised $100 upon his arrival from Savannah, Georgia, and he refused to play until the money was in his hands. The Colonels' owner, Barney Dreyfuss, peeled off the bills and handed them to the recalcitrant newcomer, who then changed into his uniform. By the end of the game, the youngster had cracked out four singles and a triple, going 5-for-5. Fred Clarke retired 21 years later with 2,672 major league hits.

Born in Iowa in 1872, he delivered newspapers as a boy in Des Moines. When he was 19 he spotted an ad in *The Sporting News* seeking players for the Hastings team of the Nebraska State League. He answered the ad, won a job, and became a professional ballplayer. Two years later he was hitting .311 for the Southern League's Savannah Modocs when Dreyfuss came to the club's rescue.

Clarke stood 5 feet 10 inches tall and weighed 165 pounds. A lefthanded line drive hitter, he used his speed to collect 220 career triples and 506 stolen bases and bat .312. He was also valuable in the clutch, amassing 1,015 RBIs, although he never had more than 82 in a year. His real forte was scoring runs. During 10 of his seasons he scored 95 runs or more for a lifetime total of 1,619.

In 1897, with Louisville mired in the depths of the 12-team National League, Dreyfuss named Clarke, not yet 25 years old, his new manager. The responsibilities of both playing and managing often turned stars into ordinary players, but Clarke responded with his best season, batting .390 to finish second in the league to "Wee Willie" Keeler's .424. Unfortunately, Louisville's winning percentage was only 10 points higher than Clarke's batting average, and the team finished next to last. But Dreyfuss stuck with the manager through several ninth-place finishes during the next few years.

In 1900, when the National League decided to cast out the perennial losers and strip down to a more manageable eight teams, Dreyfuss merged his Louisville club with Pittsburgh and became half owner of the Pirates. The beauty of the deal was that he could bring his best players with him from Louisville.

A poor team overall, the Colonels nevertheless had several superior young players on the verge of stardom. They included Clarke, who became manager in Pittsburgh, eccentric lefthanded hurler Rube Waddell, pitching control artist Deacon Phillippe, young third baseman Tommy Leach, and, best of all, Honus Wagner, perhaps the greatest player in the history of the league. Armed with this influx of talent, the Pirates fought Brooklyn down to the wire for the 1900 pennant, only to finish a close second.

In 1901 Dreyfuss became sole owner of the Pirates, and the team won its first pennant, claiming the world championship, although that title was disputed by the upstart American League. In 1902 Clarke's Pirates turned the NL pennant race into a shambles, winning 103 games against only 36 losses and winning the flag by 27½ games over second-place Brooklyn. Wagner led the league in runs, doubles, RBIs, and stolen bases; Leach led in triples and home runs; and center fielder Ginger Beaumont led in hits and batting average. Clarke himself contributed a .316 batting average and scored 103 runs.

Clarke had a unique ability to produce 20-game winners; his pitchers enjoyed 25 seasons of 20 or more wins during his 19 years of managing. Only Al Lopez, who produced 16 such pitchers in 17 seasons, comes close to matching Clarke's record.

In 1903 Clarke lost several pitchers to the American League, but the Pirates still managed to win their third straight flag. Dreyfuss arranged a "world's series" with AL winner Boston. Unfortunately, by the time the games were played, injuries and illness had decimated Clarke's pitching staff. Phillippe, the only one in good form, won three games before exhaustion set in, and Boston stormed back to win the best-of-nine series in eight games.

Clarke led the Pirates to the thick of the pennant race for the next few years, but they didn't capture another flag until 1909, when the Pirates moved into spacious Forbes Field. Although he was approaching age 40, Clarke patrolled the vast expanse of left field, and he still led all the league's outfielders in fielding percentage that season.

In the World Series the Pirates knocked off the Detroit Tigers in seven games. Wagner outplayed Ty Cobb, batting .333 to the Tiger star's .231, and Clarke hit a pair of home runs.

Clarke retired to his Kansas farm after the 1915 season. In 1925 Dreyfuss brought him back as a coach under manager Bill McKechnie. That year the Pirates won their first pennant since 1909 and defeated Washington in the World Series. He was gruff and plain in his language, and several players called for Clarke's removal from the bench, thinking it undermined McKechnie. Within days of the arguments being made public, the three players—pitcher Babe Adams and outfielders Carson Bigbee and Max Carey—were released or traded away. In 1945 Clarke was named to the Hall of Fame.

John Clarkson

Clarkson, John Gibson **P**

1882–94 B:7/1/1861, Cambridge, MA D:2/4/1909, Belmont, MA. Deb:5/2/1882, WOR NL BR/TR
5'10", 155

W	L	PCT	G	SH	IP	BB	SO	ERA
328	178	.648	531	37	4536^{1}	1191	1978	2.81

John Clarkson's "rubber arm" produced 328 wins in 12 major league seasons, including five consecutive 30-plus win seasons. In 1885 he won 53 games for the Chicago White Sox, the second highest season win total in major league history after Providence hurler Charley Radbourn's 59 in 1884.

"John Clarkson never had a superior as a pitcher and never will," infielder Fred Pfeffer said of his former teammate. "He was a master of control. I believe he could put a ball where he wanted it nine times out of 10. He had everything any pitcher ever had as well. His speed was something terrific, and he could throw any curve. However, his favorite pitch was a drop something like the spitball today, although he delivered it without the ointment necessary nowadays."

Clarkson's father was a jeweler. His two pitcher brothers, Arthur "Dad" Clarkson and Walter Clarkson, also distinguished themselves on major league diamonds.

John started the 1884 season playing for Saginaw of the Northwestern League where White Sox player-manager Adrian "Cap" Anson discovered him. Anson quickly learned how to handle his young star, "Scold him, find fault with him and he could not pitch at all. Praise him, and he was unbeatable. In knowing exactly what kind of ball a batter could not hit and in his ability to serve up just that kind of ball, I don't think I have ever seen the equal of Clarkson." The righthander, who had already recorded 10 shutouts in 40 starts for Saginaw, won 10 games more for Chicago.

Although he had several excellent seasons, Clarkson's 1885 numbers are almost superhuman. In addition to his 53–16 record and 1.85 ERA, he completed 68 games, pitched 623 innings, struck out 308, and tossed 10 shutouts and one no-hitter. In a battle of future Hall of Famers, Clarkson no-hit Providence and Charley Radbourn, 4–0, on July 27. He gave up no walks and was denied a perfect game only because five batters reached base on five errors.

The White Sox moundsman also had a sense of humor. One afternoon, as the skies darkened and the umpire refused to stop the game on account of darkness, Clarkson wound up and threw a lemon to the plate. When his catcher showed the umpire that the batters were no longer facing a ball, the ump relented and called the game.

After the 1887 season Clarkson demanded to be sold to Boston in order to be closer to home. The Boston Red Stockings bought Clarkson that winter from Chicago for $10,000. After winning 33 games in 1888, Clarkson was dazzling in 1889, winning pitching's Triple Crown by leading the league with 49 wins, 284 strikeouts, a 2.73 ERA, 620 innings pitched, eight shutouts, and 68 complete games. He was sent to Cleveland in the middle of the 1892 season, and ended the year by facing his old teammates in the World Series. Clarkson lost both his starts to Boston, as did Cy Young. Clarkson pitched his last game for the Spiders two years later.

He died of pneumonia on February 4, 1909. He was inducted into the Hall of Fame in 1963.

Roger Clemens

Clemens, William Roger **P**

1984–* B:8/4/1962, Dayton, OH Deb:5/15/1984, BOS AL BR/TR 6'4", 220

W	L	PCT	G	SH	IP	BB	SO	ERA
247	134	.648	480	45	3462[1]	1102	3316	3.04

In addition to his record five Cy Young Awards, Roger Clemens enjoys a distinction that practically no one knows about. Through 1999 Clemens won 247 games and lost just 134; a .648 percentage accumulated for teams (mostly the Boston Red Sox) with a combined winning percentage of .522. The .126 differential is the greatest pitcher-team differential in history for any player with 100 or more wins.

What is better known about Clemens is the blazing fastball that earned him the nickname "The Rocket." The heralded fireballer from the University of Texas won a total of 16 games in his first two years with the Boston Red Sox. Then he exploded. In 1986 Clemens led the American League with 24 wins, a startling .857 winning percentage, and a 2.48 ERA. He became the first pitcher in history to fan 20 batters in a nine-inning game, a feat he matched 10 years later. He walked away with the Cy Young and Most Valuable Player Award, and left Game 6 of the 1986 World Series with a lead. It did not hold up, as the Red Sox bowed to the New York Mets.

Clemens captured the Cy Young again the following year and won it for a third time in 1990. He won five strikeout crowns, six ERA titles, and was invited to seven All-Star Games.

After four mediocre seasons from 1993 through 1996—in which he still struck out nearly a batter per inning—Clemens left the Red Sox to sign with Toronto as a free agent in December 1996. No one expected what followed. On a team that finished 76–86 in 1997 and 88–74 in 1998, Clemens was 21–7 and 20–6. In the process, he became only the second pitcher ever to reach 3,000 strikeouts before issuing 1,000 walks (Ferguson Jenkins was the first). He also won the pitching Triple Crown both years and walked away with his fourth and fifth Cy Young trophies.

All that remained was for "The Rocket" to pitch for a World Series winner. He requested a trade from Toronto and seemed likely to go near his home in Texas or Houston. But neither of those teams was willing to meet his contract demands. He was eventually traded in February 1999 to the New York Yankees. In return, Toronto received David Wells, who had turned in a career best 18-4 in 1998, as well as Homer Bush and Graeme Lloyd. Wells was a guy who loved being a Yankee and fans loved him in turn. Clemens had always been a dangerous enemy.

Although his 1999 season was hardly a Rocket launch—he finished 14–10 with an ERA of 4.60—his goal of pitching for a World Series champion was realized. He won the deciding Game 4 of the World Series as the Yankees swept the Atlanta Braves.

A panel selected Clemens for Major League Baseball's "All Century Team," as one of the 100 greatest players. He was then chosen by fans as one of the six greatest pitchers of all time.

Roberto Clemente

Clemente, Roberto (Walker) **OF**

1955–1972 B:8/18/1934, Carolina, Puerto Rico D:12/31/1972, San Juan, Puerto Rico Deb:4/17/1955, PIT NL BR/TR 5'11", 175

G	AB	R	H	HR	RBI	OBP	SLG	AVG
2433	9454	1416	3000	240	1305	.362	.475	.317

Roberto Clemente was one of the true heroes American baseball has produced. His dedication on the field was unequaled, and his concern for his fellow human beings was that of a saint. In today's world, where a visit to a hospital by an athlete is usually a photo opportunity, Clemente's day-in, day-out commitment to helping needy people seems unbelievable.

More than once, filmmakers have tried to tell his story and have given up. The way Clemente lived and played was grander, more touching, and more passionate than any screen treatment could convey. Commissioner Bowie Kuhn said of Clemente, "He had about him a touch of royalty." Filmmaker John Sayles noted, "Most of what I know about style I learned from Roberto Clemente."

Clemente played the game as if it were his and his alone. His haughty stance at the plate, the way he snared flyballs, and the way he used his marvelous arm were all unique. Next to Clemente, any other batter would look uncomfortable, any other outfielder would appear clumsy, and anyone else trying to throw as he did would seem ineffectual; but that was the only way that Clemente knew how to play.

He won four batting titles and set a National League record for most years leading the league in outfield assists, with five. He won 12 Gold Gloves, tying him with Willie Mays for the most awarded an outfielder, and was the all-time Pirates leader in games played, at bats, hits, singles, and total bases.

As a youth in Puerto Rico, Clemente sneaked peeks at his favorite player, Monte Irvin, through the outfield fence. By age 14 he was playing against Negro Leaguers and major leaguers. As a teenager Clemente played in the same Puerto Rico winter league outfield with Willie Mays, an experience he never forgot. It was his first brush with greatness.

The Dodgers signed him for $10,000, although he received offers nearly three times that after agreeing to the contract. A rule at the time stated that Clemente could be drafted by any team for $4,000 if he wasn't brought up to the majors. The Dodgers sent him to Triple A.

Playing his first professional season with the Dodgers' farm club in Montreal, Clemente felt he was treated oddly. The Dodgers were trying to hide him from the Giants, but this was never explained to him, and he was so hurt and confused by the way he was handled that he thought of quitting. He recalled, "If I struck out I stayed in the lineup. If I played well I was benched. One day I hit three triples and was benched the next day. Another game I was taken out for a pinch hitter in the first inning with the bases loaded."

After this disappointing first season Clemente returned to Puerto Rico. While he was visiting his brother, who was dying of a brain tumor, a drunk driver plowed into his car. The crash damaged three spinal discs, an injury that would plague Clemente for the rest of his career.

When the last-place Pirates met after the 1954 season to discuss who they—should draft first, Clyde Sukeforth said to Pittsburgh general manager Branch Rickey, who had also been his boss in Brooklyn, "You will never live long enough to draft a boy with this kind of ability for $4,000 again."

During his first two seasons as the Pirates' right fielder Roberto Clemente gunned down 18 and 20 runners, respectively, on the bases. In his second year he hit .311 but wouldn't top .300 again until 1960. Because he was a free swinger, according to Bucs batting coach George Sisler, Clemente's head "bobbed when he swung." In 1958 he led the league in outfield assists for the first time with 22.

Clemente, and all of Pittsburgh, had a terrific year in 1960. He hit 16 homers and batted .314, and his 94 RBIs led the team as they won the NL pennant and shocked baseball by upsetting the powerful Yankees in the World Series. Clemente hit .310 for the Series, batting safely in all seven games and driving in three runs.

One play in Game 7 epitomized his inimitable style. The Pirates were down 7–5 and batting in the bottom of the eighth when Clemente came to the plate with runners on second and third

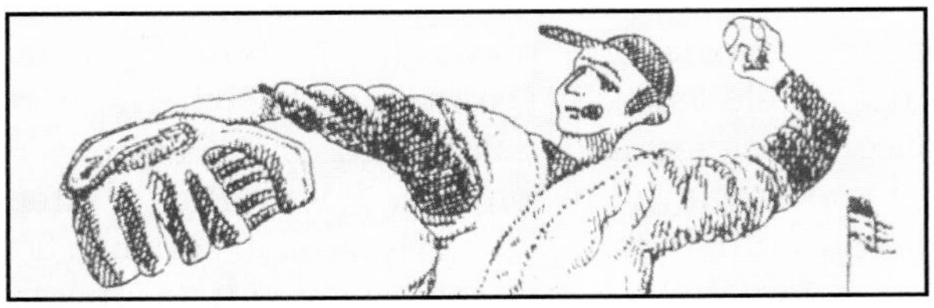

and two out. He hit a feeble bouncer toward first baseman Bill Skowron. Yankees hurler Jim Coates dawdled over to the bag, but Clemente hustled. He beat Coates to first base, another run scored, and Hal Smith followed Clemente with a three-run homer that gave the Pirates the lead. The Yankees tied it in the ninth inning, but Bill Mazeroski's home run in the bottom of the inning ended the Series.

Always a proud man, Clemente took it hard when he got the news that he had only finished eighth in the 1960 Most Valuable Player voting. It pushed him to try even harder. The next season Clemente changed his bat. To avoid over swinging on bad balls he began to use heavier lumber and went on to enjoy 11 .300-plus seasons in the next 12 years. He won his first batting title in 1961, hitting .351 with 23 homers, 10 triples, and 89 RBIs.

Clemente put on a show in that season's first All-Star Game, too. He tripled for the first hit off Whitey Ford in the second inning and later scored the game's first run. He drove in the second run with a sacrifice fly, and in the bottom of the 10th his single brought home Mays with the winning run. From then on he wore his 1961 All-Star Game ring, not his 1960 World Series ring.

That year Clemente missed the last five games of the season because a Don Drysdale fastball had chipped a bone in his right elbow, requiring off-season surgery. Because of the aggressive way he played, he suffered numerous other injuries. Unlike other players who declined to speak about their physical problems, Clemente discussed his aches and pains with anyone who asked. ("My bad shoulder feels good, but my good shoulder feels bad," he once said.) According to a biographer, he suffered from "backaches, flu attacks, a nervous stomach, spasms of diarrhea, infected tonsils, headaches, and bone chips in his throwing elbow." He even contracted malaria in 1965.

To deal with his physical problems Clemente relied on a Puerto Rican chiropractor, Arturo Garcia, who "rubs on a potent orange ointment called Atomic Balm, 'cauterizes' tendons with a black plastic cylinder that emits crackling blue sparks, and heats aching muscles with a small infrared lamp." Several times Clemente infuriated Pirates management by shunning medical experts in Pittsburgh, instead relying on Dr. Garcia and his methods.

Clemente learned how to crack his troublesome neck by himself and gave chiropractic and massage treatments to teammates, friends, and acquaintances. His constant complaining about aches and pains didn't sit well with Pittsburgh sportswriters, who accused him of being a hypochondriac, overlooking the fact that Clemente played more than 140 games for eight seasons in a row.

In 1964 and 1965 he won batting titles again, but the Pirates felt he wasn't providing as much power as he could. Manager Harry "The Hat" Walker asked him to swing for the fences more often. Clemente responded by belting 29 homers and driving in 119 runs in 1966, although his batting average fell a dozen points to .317. That year he had 15-game and 17-game hitting streaks and four four-hit games.

His defensive abilities never suffered. In one game, in a bases-loaded situation, a batter lined an apparent single to right. The runner on third didn't see any need to hustle home; Clemente fired a strike to the catcher for a stunning force-out. Clemente won the league's Most Valuable Player Award in 1966, and he felt that the injustice of 1960 had been rectified.

He suddenly became more open, eagerly taking the reins of leadership in the clubhouse. If a young Pirate had a problem, Clemente discussed it quietly. Manager Walker failed to get new Pirate Matty Alou to quit pulling every pitch and use a heavier bat, but Clemente spoke to Alou. The newcomer responded with a 111-point increase in his batting average and won the league batting title.

Clemente hit .357 in 1967 to win his fourth batting title, adding 23 homers and 110 RBIs for good measure. When he hit three homers and drove in all seven of his team's runs in an 8–7 loss to Cincinnati that year, he agreed it was his "biggest" game ever. "But not my best. My best game is when I drive in the winning run. I don't count this one. We lost."

An off-field incident gave a clue to his fierce pride. While the Pirates were playing the Mets in Shea Stadium, filmmakers were shooting scenes for the movie comedy *The Odd Couple*. Clemente was offered $100 to appear in it. Although the film was based on Neil Simon's hit Broadway play of the same title, Clemente thought he had been asked to be in an instructional film for children. When he learned it was a commercial venture, he became upset at how little money he had been offered. And when he found out the screenplay had him hitting into a triple play, Clemente refused to participate at all.

With the arrival of rookies Manny Sanguillen, Richie Hebner, and Al Oliver in 1969, Clemente's role as a leader became even more valuable. From 1969 through 1971 Clemente hit .345, .352, and .341. The Pirates honored him in 1970 at their new Three Rivers Stadium. Puerto Rican fans, who by now viewed him as a demigod, delivered a scroll signed by 300,000 people in Puerto Rico (roughly 10 percent of the island's population).

More than 43,000 fans showed up for the festivities and game, which the Bucs won, 11–0. Clemente obligingly had two hits and made a great catch of a Joe Morgan line drive. He also made a running, diving grab of a foul popup by Denis Menke that meant absolutely nothing to the outcome of the game and tore his knee open in the process. "It's the only way I know how to play baseball," he explained.

His intensity and skill received their finest showcase in 1971. The Pirates knocked off the Giants in the 1971 National League Championship Series, with Clemente hitting .333 and driving in four runs. As the team prepared for the World Series, the consensus was that the young Bucs, despite their great hitting, would be no match for the pitching-rich Orioles, who were armed with Jim Palmer, Dave McNally, and Mike Cuellar.

Cuellar and Clemente also had a more personal score to settle. In the previous off-season Cuellar had quit a winter league team that Clemente was managing. The pitcher grandly announced, "I've pitched too long now for Clemente to be telling me how."

Cuellar's haughtiness reflected Baltimore's overconfidence. The Orioles had won their last 11 games in the regular season and had swept Oakland in the ALCS. In Clemente's first at bat in the World Series, he doubled off McNally; he added another single, and had two hits in Game 2, but the Bucs lost both.

Events would show that the Series turned on a single play in Game 3, and Clemente's hustle against Cuellar made the difference. Clemente had driven in the first Pirates run, and the Bucs were ahead 2–1 as he led off the seventh and topped a pitch back to the mound. Cuellar prepared for a leisurely toss to first, but when he saw Clemente running full speed, he reacted with a wild throw that pulled Boog Powell off the bag. Rattled, Cuellar then walked Willie Stargell, and Bob Robertson sealed the issue with a three-run homer.

Clemente had four hits as the Pirates won Games 4 and 5. In Game 6 he tripled and homered, and his heroic throw from deep right held Mark Belanger at third in the ninth inning to keep the game tied. But the Orioles won in 10 innings on Brooks Robinson's sacrifice fly.

Game 7 began with Cuellar pitching against Steve Blass, and the Orioles hurler retired the first 11 Pirates he faced. When Clemente went to

the plate against him in the fourth, however, he jumped on Cuellar's first pitch and homered deep to left field. The Pirates went on to win, 2–1, on Blass' stellar pitching performance, and Clemente was the Series MVP. When a writer told Pirates general manager Joe L. Brown that Clemente was overachieving, Brown explained, "You don't understand. He always plays this way."

For the Series, Clemente hit in all seven games, batting .414 and slugging .759. Writer Roger Angell said, "Clemente played a kind of baseball that none of us had ever seen before—throwing and running and hitting at something close to the level of absolute perfection."

Clemente would never scale such heights again. Injuries allowed him to play in only 102 games in 1972, but he still hit .312. His double off the Mets' Jon Matlack on September 30 was his 3,000th hit. The Pirates again made it to the NLCS but lost on Bob Moose's wild pitch in the ninth inning of the final game.

In late December of that year a devastating earthquake struck Nicaragua. More than 6,000 people were killed, 20,000 injured, and tens of thousands left homeless. Clemente raised money and other contributions to help the survivors. As always, he was tireless, pleading for donations personally, negotiating discounts with airlines for transporting the materials, and packing and loading boxes for shipment. While Puerto Rico celebrated the holidays, Clemente was working 16-hour days to see that earthquake victims received what they needed.

After hearing that some of the supplies they had sent to Nicaragua were not getting to the right people, Clemente decided to take matters into his own hands. He decided to fly to Nicaragua in a cargo plane and make sure that distribution was carried out properly. On New Year's Eve he boarded an overloaded DC-7 that he had rented for $4,000 to fly to Nicaragua. The plane crashed into the ocean shortly after takeoff.

New Year's Day was to have been a day of great celebration in Puerto Rico, with a new governor being inaugurated. Instead, the inaugural festivities were canceled, and the entire Pirates team flew to Puerto Rico for the funeral.

The Hall of Fame waived the five-year wait between last playing appearance and eligibility for Clemente, as it had done earlier for Lou Gehrig. Ninety-three percent of the votes favored Clemente's induction; those who voted against it explained that they felt the five-year rule should be adhered to despite the tragedy. The first Latin player so honored, he was inducted into the Hall of Fame on the same day as his boyhood idol, Monte Irvin. In 1971 the Commissioner's Office had started an annual award to the player who best exemplified baseball on and off the field; in 1973 it was renamed the Roberto Clemente Award.

More than 20 years after his death, a video about Clemente on the Three Rivers Stadium scoreboard produced instant, awestruck silence, followed by respectful applause and cheers touched with sadness. A statue of him was unveiled at Three Rivers Stadium at the 1994 All-Star Game. He said in the late 1960s, "If you have an opportunity to make things better and you don't, then you are wasting your time on this earth."

Jack Clements

Clements, John J. **C**

1884–1900 M(1890, 13–6) B:7/24/1864, Philadelphia, PA D:5/23/1941, Norristown, PA Deb:4/22/1884, PHI UA BL/TL 5'8½", 204

G	AB	R	H	HR	RBI	OBP	SLG	AVG
1157	4283	619	1226	77	687	.347	.421	.286

Jack Clements remains the last regular major league backstop to catch lefthanded. He was a curiosity even in the 19th century, but observers said he handled himself well, with no hint of awkwardness. If a batter got in Clements' way, that was the batter's problem; Clements would flatten the batter with a throw.

Described as a "wide shouldered, grim-lipped man with the stature of a growing oak," Clements stood 5 feet 8½ inches and weighed 204 pounds, a key to his home run production; he never led the league in circuit clouts but he finished second in 1893 and third in 1895. He was also one of the first catchers to wear a chest protector, strapping one on as early as 1884.

Clements had a 17-year major league career, mostly with the Phillies. His .303 average in the 1890s was second only to Mike Grady's among catchers. Clements remained a baseball man to the end. After ending his playing days, he worked in A.J. Reach's baseball factory in Philadelphia. When that operation closed its doors, he found employment in another ball manufacturing firm in Perkasie, Pennsylvania.

Donn Clendenon

Clendenon, Donn Alvin **1B–OF**

1961–72 B:7/15/1935, Neosho, MO Deb:9/22/1961, PIT NL BR/TR 6'3½", 210

G	AB	R	H	HR	RBI	OBP	SLG	AVG
1362	4648	594	1273	159	682	.331	.442	.274

Donn Clendenon was a college-educated athlete whose talents earned him professional offers in basketball, football, and baseball. After joining the Pirates in 1961, Clendenon developed a powerful stroke that peaked with 28 home runs and 98 RBIs in 1966. He also fanned frequently, setting a short-lived record for season whiffs with 163 in 1968. As a fielder he was smooth and fast, and he led the league in double plays five times.

Selected by Montreal in the 1969 expansion draft, the first baseman was swapped to Houston that January for Rusty Staub. Clendenon refused to report, officially retired, and threw baseball into a quandary. The rules seemed to indicate that the deal was void, but rookie Commissioner Bowie Kuhn decided he "had the broad power to override the rules and do what is best for the game." Kuhn ordered that the two teams restructure the deal. Clendenon then "unretired" and was dealt to the Mets in June.

Platooning with Ed Kranepool, Clendenon hit 12 home runs in 200 at bats and helped spark the Mets' stretch drive for the pennant. In the 1969 World Series against the Orioles, he homered to give the Mets the lead in Games 2 and 4—both ultimate victories—and his two-run shot in the last of the sixth inning of Game 5 brought the Mets to within one run. They tied the game later that inning and went on to win the game and the Series. Despite the many Met heroes in the Series, Clendenon was named Most Valuable Player of the Series.

Harlond Clift

Clift, Harlond Benton **3B**

1934–45 B:8/12/1912, El Reno, OK D:4/27/1992, Yakima, WA Deb:4/17/34, STL AL BR/TR, 5'11", 180

G	AB	R	H	HR	RBI	OBP	SLG	AVG
1582	5730	1070	1558	178	829	.390	.441	.272

The St. Louis Browns' Harlond Clift gets the nod from many baseball historians as the major leagues' most underrated third baseman. He was, for instance, the first third baseman to hit at least 30 homers in a season, a feat he accomplished in 1938 with 34 dingers, to break his own previous high of 29 in 1937. He drove in 118 runs in both seasons, scored 100 or more runs seven times, drew more than 100 bases on balls in a season six times, and broke up three no-hitters. Clift led all American League third basemen in fielding in 1938 and 1940 and was the first third baseman to start 50 double plays in a season—the record until Graig Nettles' 54 in 1974.

In 1940 the Tigers offered the Browns $200,000 for Clift along with first baseman George McQuinn and pitcher Emil "Hill Billy" Bildilli, but Browns owner Donald Barnes refused the offer. Three years later, however, Clift's power had disappeared almost completely, and he was traded to Washington with knuckleballer Johnny Niggeling for pitchers Ellis Clary and Ox Miller and $35,000.

A bout of mumps in 1943 and a fall from a horse in 1944, resulting in an injured right shoulder, limited Clift's effectiveness with the Senators, and he retired after the 1945 season.

Tony Cloninger

Cloninger, Tony Lee **P**

1961–72 B:8/13/1940, Lincoln, NC Deb:6/15/1961, MIL NL BR/TR, 6', 210

W	L	PCT	G	SH	IP	BB	SO	ERA
113	97	.538	352	13	1767^{2}	798	1120	4.07

From 1964 through 1966 Tony Cloninger was the top starter on the Braves' staff, notching 19, 24, and 14 victories. Although Cloninger was a tough, uncompromising hurler, his major claim to fame came with his bat during a two-week period in June and July 1966, the Braves' first year in Atlanta. On July 3 he hit two grand slam homers and added a single to drive in another run for a total of nine RBIs. No National Leaguer, pitcher or otherwise, had ever hit two grand slams in a game before (it has since been matched).

Two weeks earlier Cloninger had also slugged two homers in a game, giving him a total of 18 RBIs in four games. The power surge was as remarkable as it was unexpected: Cloninger finished his career a lifetime .192 hitter. Beyond the two hot games, he hit only seven other homers and drove in 39 other runs in 12 major league seasons. He later became a coach of the New York Yankees.

Ty Cobb

Cobb, Tyrus Raymond **OF**

1905–28 M(1921–26, 479-444) B:2/18/1886, Narrows, GA D:7/17/1961, Atlanta, GA Deb:8/30/1905, DET AL BL/TR 6'1", 175

G	AB	R	H	HR	RBI	OBP	SLG	AVG
3035	11434	2246	4189	117	1937	.433	.512	.366

Ty Cobb, "the Georgia Peach," was a man possessed. Every game, every play, and every at bat was a war to him. And he refused to be second in anything. In baseball legend he is the antithesis of Babe Ruth. Ruth was the lazy, overweight hero to whom baseball excellence came easily and for whom life was fun. Cobb was the trickster for whom nothing came easily, and he had to sharpen his spikes and his wits in equal degrees to carry himself to the Hall of Fame.

Probably no other athlete has ever matched Cobb's furious desire to excel. He was egotistical, brash, rude, thin-skinned, a racist, and a bully. In short, he was a great player and a terrible person. While Cobb was certainly blessed with physical skills, he far exceeded what anyone could have expected from him. And because of his unique personality, he was right in the middle of some of the game's noisiest controversies.

"When I began playing the game, baseball was about as gentlemanly as a kick in the crotch," Cobb once said. "I was like a steel spring with a growing and dangerous flaw in it. If it is wound too tight or has the slightest weak point, the spring will fly apart, then it is done for."

Longtime teammate Davy Jones recalled, "When Cobb got into a slump you couldn't talk to him. He got meaner than the devil himself."

Another teammate, Sam Crawford, said, "It wasn't that he was so fast on his feet, although he was fast enough. There were others who were faster.... It was that Cobb was so fast in his thinking. He didn't outhit the opposition and he didn't outrun them. He outthought them."

Cobb's fierce pride lasted him until long after he had retired. The story is told that a 70-year-old Cobb once sat next to a former big league catcher at an old-timers' luncheon. During casual conversation the catcher mentioned a trick he had used on plays with two outs, whereby he would tag a runner trying to score and then throw off his glove, indicating the third out, even when the runner was safe. "I must have caught you seven or eight times with that, Ty," he told Cobb. "Seven or eight times the ump called you out when you were really safe."

Suddenly Cobb began screaming, and he wrapped his fingers around the former catcher's throat. "You cost me eight runs!" he bellowed. "Eight runs I earned!"

Eight more runs wouldn't have made a significant difference in Cobb's statistics. His career runs stood as the major league record through the end of the 20th century. Among his other big league marks are highest lifetime batting average, with .366; most years leading the league in both batting average and hits; and most games with five or more hits, with 14. His record of 4,189 hits stood for 56 years. He ranks among the top five players of all time in games, runs, hits, total bases, doubles, triples, RBIs, and stolen bases.

When it comes to batting records Cobb and Ruth stand together. When Cobb retired in 1928 he was the leader in 90 major league or American League offensive categories. Even some 70 years later, he still holds more than 30 records, including one for most consecutive years leading the league in RBIs,

a record he shares with Ruth and a future Tiger, Cecil Fielder. Seven times Cobb had consecutive-game hitting streaks of 20 or more games.

Many baseball fans believe that Cobb's batting average was high partly because the players of his era tended to have better percentages. However, current league-wide averages are regularly around the .260 mark, and a batter usually wins the batting title hitting 80 to 90 points higher than that. In eight of Cobb's first 11 years in the majors, the AL average was less than .250, yet Cobb put up marks of .324 to .383, typically batting 100 to 140 points higher than the league.

Cobb was also an expert on the basepaths. Since he knew exactly how long it took him to run to first, to second, and to third, he would often try to stretch a single into a double in an unimportant game. The fielder might throw him out, but the next time Cobb tried it, when more was at stake, the same fielder could be pressured into a bobble or a bad throw. Cobb's single-season record of 96 stolen bases in 1915 wasn't broken until 1962. His 20th-century lifetime stolen base mark of 891 stood until 1977.

Cobb was famous for sharpening his spikes in the dugout in clear view of the opposition, but this was more of a psychological ploy than a real physical threat. Cobb was smart; he knew that intentional spiking would cause more trouble than it was worth, a fact he learned in 1909. He preferred to slide away from the bag with a hook slide, offering just his toe to be tagged. But if the defense blocked the base or the baseline, he had no qualms about dumping a player on his backside. The fear Cobb could command from his opponents gave him the edge he desperately wanted.

Cobb used the same intelligence in the field that he did at bat and on the bases. He had 30 assists his first full major league season, then led the league with 23 the next year. He had 18 or more assists 13 times during his career.

The key to his fanatical drive to succeed lies in his youth and his relationship to his father. Cobb grew up in Royston, Georgia. His father, a respected local schoolteacher, demanded educational excellence from him, but the boy preferred bats to books. "I felt guilty," Cobb said later, "that some great, vaulting ambition hadn't seized me beyond handling hard hoppers and line drives."

When Cobb left Royston to play pro ball, his father's final words were, "Don't come home a failure." In 1905, during Cobb's second year as a professional player, his father was accidentally shot and killed by his mother, who thought he was a prowler. Some claim that the loss of the man to whom he desperately wanted to prove himself was the source of Cobb's fiery determination to excel for the rest of his life.

Cobb came to the Tigers during the middle of the 1905 season. Subjected to the razzing that all rookies receive, Cobb didn't take it the way most youngsters did. As Davy Jones said, "What would usually be an innocent enough wisecrack became cause for a fist fight if Ty was involved." Cobb batted just .240 in 41 games his first season.

In 1906 the 19-year-old Cobb became ill and appeared in just 98 games. But he knew what to do with the bat, hitting .316. The next season he began his string of batting titles with a .350 average and never hit below .323 again for his entire 24-year career.

In 1907 Cobb began using a black bat he described as having magical powers. After that season he never used the bat in a game but always had it with him in the on-deck circle. In fact, the "magical" bat even appeared in a photograph of the cake-cutting ceremony when Cobb got married in 1908.

On September 30, 1907, Cobb's Tigers held a slim lead over the Philadelphia Athletics in the AL standings. In a matchup between the clubs going into the top of the ninth, Philadelphia had a two-run lead. Then Cobb slugged a two-run homer. The teams played to a 17-inning, 9–9 tie that eliminated the A's from the race. Cobb said later that the game was one of the most satisfying moments of his career. The 20-year-old Georgian had driven the Tigers to their first World Series, against the Cubs.

The first Series game that year was declared a tie after 12 innings because of darkness—the closest Detroit would get to a win. The Tigers failed to score more than one run in any game thereafter, and Cobb hit just .200.

Despite his prowess at the plate, Cobb's unpleasant disposition presented an ongoing problem for manager Hughie Jennings. Before the 1908 season the Tigers offered Cobb in a straight-up deal to Cleveland for outfielder Elmer Flick. Flick was no slouch; he had won the 1905 batting title and had a lifetime average of .317 at the time. He would eventually be elected to the Hall of Fame.

However, Cleveland player-manager Nap Lajoie, even though he had had a personal brawl with Flick several years earlier, still preferred his 31-year-old veteran to the irascible, 21-year-old Cobb. Flick managed only 78 more hits in the three seasons remaining in his career. Cobb, meanwhile, had no trouble winning his second straight batting title in 1908, beating out teammate Sam Crawford by 13 points.

That year's pennant race was furious, with the Tigers ultimately winning by one-half game. (The rules of the time did not require Detroit to make up an earlier rainout.)

In the World Series the Tigers found Chicago pitchers Orval Overall and Mordecai Brown nearly unhittable. In four games the two held Detroit to 13 hits, and the Cubs won four of the five games. But because Cobb had three hits in Game 3, he finished with a .368 average in the Series.

In 1909 Cobb's label as a dirty player received its greatest play. That August the A's led the Tigers by one-half game when they began a series in Detroit's Bennett Park. In the first inning of the first game, Cobb walked and stole second base. On a ball four thrown to Sam Crawford, Cobb sprinted to third.

The throw to A's third baseman Frank Baker was in plenty of time. As Cobb dodged the tag with a hook slide to his left, Baker reached down and tagged him with the ball in his bare hand. Cobb's right shoe scraped Baker's arm, drawing blood.

The A's went wild, demanding Cobb be ejected for a deliberate spiking. Cobb later said it was the only time he tried to spike a player in his life. Baker wasn't seriously hurt; he wrapped a bandage around the cut and continued to play. Later in the game Cobb doubled in the tying run and knocked A's second baseman Eddie Collins off his feet with a hard slide. Before Collins could pick himself up, the lead run had scored. The Tigers and A's were tied for first, and Cobb led Detroit to two more wins for a series sweep.

The uproar over Cobb's "dirty play" extended nationwide. The A's manager, the usually ministerial Connie Mack, screamed for Cobb's banishment from the game. Even league president Ban Johnson threatened Cobb with expulsion. But when Johnson saw a photograph of the play (action shots during a game were rare at that time), he saw that Baker was clearly off the base and leaning down toward Cobb. Johnson officially reversed his earlier statements.

Despite the reversal, the atmosphere remained charged when Cobb and the Tigers went to brand-new Shibe Park in Philadelphia the next month. A mind-boggling 120,000 people showed up for the four-game set. The police were out in force. Cobb, who had received death threats, had a motorcycle cop escort him to and from the games. According to historian Bruce Kuklick, "Officials scattered several dozen plainclothesmen in the stands and stationed a solid line of bluecoats in right field between Cobb and those fans behind ropes on the outfield grass."

In the second game of the series Cobb stole third base. Baker offered his hand, and Cobb took it. The tension broke. Later in the game Cobb dove into the roped-off crowd to snag a foul fly,

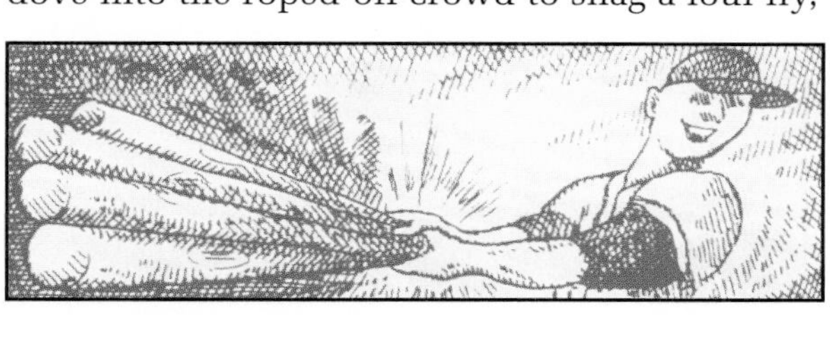

and the Philadelphia fans cheered his effort. When Cobb returned to his position in the next inning, he handed a $5 bill to a man whose hat he had crushed previously, and the fans cheered even louder.

After Detroit had won the 1907 and 1908 pennants by a total of two games, their 3½-game cushion in 1909 must have seemed like a runaway. Cobb had his best season to date, not only leading the league with his .377 batting average but also topping the circuit in runs scored, RBIs, hits, on-base percentage, and slugging average. His nine homers also led the league, making him the second Triple Crown winner in the AL's young history.

That year the Tigers played the Pirates in the World Series—one of the roughest ever. Three men were knocked out during the Series, four others were injured, and there were plenty of spikings. According to sportswriter Fred Lieb, Game 6 ended with Pirates outfielder Chief Wilson and Tigers infielder George Moriarty "on the ground, kicking at each other with their spikes." Behind the pitching of young Babe Adams—who won three games in the Series, including an 8–0 shutout in Game 7—the Pirates prevailed.

Cobb hit only .231 in the Series and was outplayed by the legendary shortstop Honus Wagner, who had won that year's National League batting title and hit .333 in the Series. Despite the fury on the field, there was no violence between Cobb and Wagner. The often-told story that Cobb called Wagner "Krauthead," announced he would steal on the next pitch, then was tagged out by Wagner so viciously that Cobb lost several teeth appears to have never happened.

The young Cobb admired and respected the older Wagner, and he said as much in his biography, claiming that only a foolhardy man would challenge Wagner. And Cobb was not a foolhardy man. In fact, even after Cobb's poor performance in the Series, *Sporting Life* reported, "Hans Wagner graciously declares that Ty Cobb is the most finished player in the game today." Nevertheless, Cobb had played in his last World Series and had been on the losing end every time the Tigers had competed for the championship title.

In 1910 there was no close pennant race, as Philadelphia outdistanced third-place Detroit by 18 games. But there was a furious battle between Cobb and Nap Lajoie for the league batting title. And for the first time ever, a new car awaited the

winner. Prior to the start of the season, the president of the Chalmers Motor Company had announced that the batting champ would receive a new Chalmers auto.

At the end of August the likeable Lajoie and Cobb, his unsympathetic counterpart, were only three points apart. Fans loved it. "Adding to the excitement and the frustration," historian Jim Murphy related, "was the fact that there was no unanimity on exactly what the averages were at any one time." Believing that he had the car in his garage already, Cobb sat out his team's last two games. Lajoie went 1-for-4 in his third-to-last game of the year, then prepared to face the St. Louis Browns in a doubleheader to close the 1910 season.

After Lajoie tripled in his first at bat in the first game, Browns manager Jack O'Connor told his rookie third baseman to play deep, ostensibly to avoid being hurt by one of Lajoie's wicked line drives. Lajoie bunted to third base six straight times for hits. The seventh time he tried it, a play was made on a runner going to third, so he was awarded a sacrifice-fielder's choice.

Some speculated O'Connor was out to rob Cobb of the batting title. When St. Louis owner Robert Hedges asked O'Connor to explain, he was told, "Lajoie outguessed us." O'Connor was fired. Ban Johnson announced that new data indicated Cobb had won the batting title anyway. Chalmers decided to give cars to both men. (Seventy years later historian Paul MacFarlane declared that Cobb had been credited with two imaginary hits, so Lajoie really was the winner.)

In 1911 Cobb batted over .400 for the first of three times. Only outfielder Jesse Burkett and infielder Rogers Hornsby achieved that mark as often. In addition, Cobb hit safely in 40 consecutive games to set an AL record and finished with a .420 average, the highest in league history. His 248 hits were a major league record, and he unanimously won the Chalmers Award as Most Valuable Player.

In 1912 Cobb hit .409, but his wicked temper led to one of the most embarrassing incidents of his life. After a fan behind the Tigers dugout heckled him for two innings of a May 15 game in New York's Hilltop Park, Cobb leaped into the stands and started punching the man.

Ban Johnson suspended Cobb indefinitely for his actions. After the Tigers played their next game at Shibe Park, the entire team refused to continue unless Cobb was reinstated. On May 18 not one of them showed up, and a pickup team made up of former coaches and collegians took the field wearing Detroit uniforms. The A's beat them 24–2. When Johnson threatened the legitimate Tigers with lifetime banishment from the game, they relented, with Cobb's approval and thanks. Cobb was suspended for 10 days and fined $50.

In 1914 Cobb sat out several weeks with a broken rib and also missed nearly two months with a broken right thumb that, according to baseball historian Bill James, "he had suffered in a fight with a butcher's clerk." Cobb finished the season with a .368 average, 22 points higher than Eddie Collins' mark, and was awarded the batting title again, even though his 345 at bats were almost 200 fewer than Collins had.

When Cobb's .369 average led the league in 1915, it was the ninth year in a row that he had won the batting title, though the 1910 and 1914 awards have been shown to be less than legitimate. In 1916 Cleveland player-manager Tris Speaker snapped his string, but Cobb won the title again in 1917, 1918, and 1919.

Cobb's penchant for trouble continued as well. He was named player-manager of the Tigers in 1921, but new responsibilities didn't calm him down. That year he nearly came to blows with Babe Ruth three times in one game, and he also slugged it out with an umpire. Cobb was furious when arbiter George Hildebrand called him out trying to steal home against the Senators. The next inning umpire Billy Evans called Cobb out after an attempted swipe of second base, and Cobb got even angrier. After the game he challenged Evans to a fight, and the two went at it under the stands in front of an audience of players and Cobb's son, Ty Jr.

According to Cobb biographer Charles Alexander, "Cobb split Evans' left eyebrow and right cheek. Evans got in a few punches before the two wrestled to the ground. Cobb was banging Evans' head into the cinders when a burly groundskeeper pulled him off and ended the fray. After stanching his wounds and showering and getting dressed, Evans came over to the Detroit locker room and shook Cobb's hand."

Cobb's managerial style was not to the team's liking. Although Cobb was respected around the league for his knowledge of the game, Detroit didn't finish any better than second place, 16 games back, with Cobb managing. Cobb continued, however, to better his personal record, racking up the tallies in runs scored. On May 25, 1923, Cobb scored the run that put him ahead of Wagner on the all-time list.

Before a game in 1925 a reporter asked Cobb about Ruth and the art of the home run. Cobb said hitting homer was no big deal. To prove it, he brought his hands together and quit choking up on the bat and slugged three homers that day. He added a double and two singles to set the AL record, since broken, for total bases in one game. The next day he hit two more homers, just to prove his performance was no fluke.

In 1926 Cobb gave more playing time to outfielders Heinie Manush and Al Wingo than to himself. He batted .339 in 79 games, but miserable pitching doomed the Tigers to a sixth-place finish.

When Cobb announced his resignation on November 2, 1926, fans were shocked. And when Cleveland manager Tris Speaker resigned one month later, rumors began to spread.

A letter was made public from Hubert "Dutch" Leonard, a 33-year-old pitcher whom Cobb had cut from the Tigers after an 11–4 season. In the letter Leonard claimed that seven years earlier he had met with Cleveland outfielder Smokey Joe Wood, Cobb, and Speaker between September 24 and 25. At that meeting, Leonard claimed, Cobb and Speaker discussed how badly Cobb wanted to finish in third place and land a World Series share. (The fourth-place team received nothing at the time.)

The White Sox had the pennant nailed down, and Speaker's Indians were assured of second place. Speaker allegedly said to Cobb, "Don't worry. You'll win tomorrow." Leonard suggested that because it was a done deal, they should make some money on it. Wood, Leonard, and Cobb agreed to bet on the game.

In 1926 baseball fans were still recovering from the 1919 World Series scandal, in which seven White Sox players had conspired to throw the Series. All seven, and an eighth who had known about the fix but who had not participated, were banned from baseball for life. Seven years later, the notion that two of the game's greatest players would have agreed to throw a game and to wager on it was almost too much to bear. It appeared that Cobb and Speaker had retired to avoid investigation of the incident. Because they were no longer on major league payrolls, they were not under the baseball commissioner's power. But that didn't stop Commissioner Kenesaw Mountain Landis.

Landis interviewed Cobb and Speaker, released a 100-page report to the press on December 20, and on January 27 acquitted the two stars with this simple notice: "This is the Cobb-Speaker case. These players have not been, nor are they now, found guilty of fixing a ball game. By no decent system of justice could such finding be made. Therefore, they were not placed on the ineligible list. As they desire to rescind their withdrawal from baseball, the releases which the

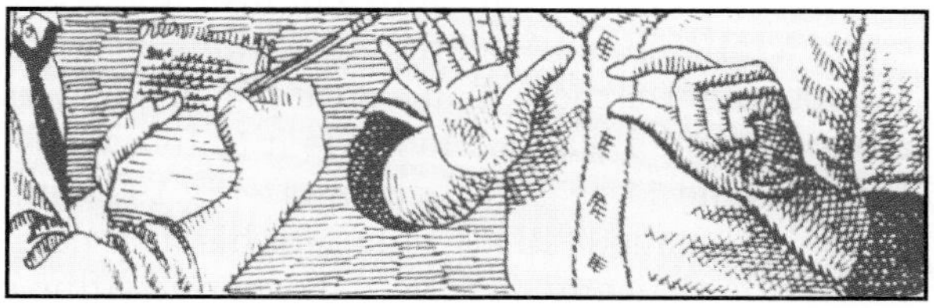

Detroit and Cleveland clubs granted at their requests, in the circumstances detailed above, are canceled and the players' names are restored to the reserve lists of those clubs."

Some fans claimed that Speaker and Cobb were found not guilty because of their status in the game. But that hadn't stopped Landis from handing down the "death penalty" to outfielder Joe Jackson, pitcher Ed Cicotte, and the other stars of the so-called Black Sox. Again, Cobb's personality provides the clearest clue to the truth. Gambling was not his nature; winning was. He never believed in getting something for nothing.

Both Cobb and Speaker were allowed to make a deal with any team that wanted them. After spirited bidding by every club in the American League, Cobb joined Connie Mack in Philadelphia and Speaker went to the Washington Senators.

In 1927 the 40-year-old Cobb played 134 games for the A's, batting .357 and stealing 22 bases, which ranked third in the league. He was one of seven future Hall of Famers on the A's roster. In his final year he hit .323. The next season Philadelphia won the World Series, but Cobb had retired.

Cobb was the first man elected to the Hall of Fame when it opened in 1936. He was also the game's first playing millionaire. While his teammates had been squandering their money, Cobb had been investing. He was an early stockholder in both Coca-Cola and General Motors. Before Cobb died in 1961 he endowed a medical center in his home town with $100,000 and started an educational fund.

Mickey Cochrane

Cochrane, Gordon Stanley **C**

1925–37 M(1934–38, 348–250) B:4/6/1903, Bridgewater, MA D:6/28/1962, Lake Forest, IL Deb:4/14/1925, PHI AL BL/TR 5'10½", 180

G	AB	R	H	HR	RBI	OBP	SLG	AVG
1482	5169	1041	1652	119	832	.419	.478	.320

Mickey Cochrane was one of the greatest catcher in major league history. His .320 lifetime batting average is a record for catchers. His keen batting eye helped him to only 217 strikeouts in 5,169 at bats, and he hit third in the batting lineup at a time when catchers were expected to bat eighth. Defensively, he could do it all—make the plays, call a game, and get the most out of his pitchers. The only catcher to handle more 20-game winners than Cochrane was Jim Hegan.

Cochrane was more than a great player—he was a winner and a leader. He made it to five World Series in the 11 seasons encompassing 1925 and 1935. Nicknamed "Black Mike" for his fiery competitive spirit and for his surly mood after a defeat, Cochrane was twice the American League's Most Valuable Player, and after the A's sold him to Detroit he became the Tigers' player-manager at only 31.

Cochrane starred in several sports at Boston University. He ran track, played basketball, and boxed for the varsity. As captain of the football team he once drop-kicked a 53-yard field goal. Although he didn't make the baseball team until his junior year, when he did, he starred there, too.

When Cochrane signed a professional contract with the Eastern Shore League's Dover Senators, he was an outfielder, but the only position open on the team was catcher, so he made the switch and batted .322. Unfortunately, his defensive play was miserable.

After Cochrane batted .333 for the Pacific Coast League's Portland Beavers the following year, Philadelphia A's manager Connie Mack came looking for him. Portland wanted $50,000 for the talented slugger. Mack balked, but then he discovered that the whole team could be had for about $200,000. He purchased the club and sold the players he didn't want for a tidy profit.

When Cochrane reported to spring training in 1925, Mack was dismayed. His prize catch was no prize catcher—in fact, he was a disaster behind the plate. Mack decided to try him at third, but, as Cochrane told it, "Even he didn't think my chest would stand up under the wear and tear of stopping ground balls with it." It was back to catching, with a vengeance.

The determined backstop caught two hours of batting practice every day. He showed up early, stayed late, and studied with veteran catcher Cy Perkins. Mack later said that "Cochrane was a misfit in February, but a star in April."

He hit his way into the A's lineup early in the season and went on to catch 134 games and hit .331. In one memorable game he swatted three homers. Cochrane's influence on the pitching staff also became apparent as the team ERA dropped by nearly half a run. The A's, who had been second-division chumps since Mack had sold off his stars 10 years earlier, jumped into second place. With other young standouts such as outfielder Al Simmons and pitcher Lefty Grove coming into their own, Philadelphia was on the way back.

Cochrane knew what made each of his pitchers tick. Once, when he felt that Rube Walberg was not putting forth enough effort, Cochrane charged the mound, spun the pitcher around, and kicked him solidly in his posterior. With Lefty Grove it was different; they had an intuitive understanding of each other. Grove once said, "It's funny, even before I looked at him I had in mind what I was going to pitch and I'd look up and there'd be Mickey's signal, just what I was thinking." Grove would compile a 16-game winning streak with Cochrane catching, and later the Tigers' Lynwood "Schoolboy" Rowe would accomplish the same feat, again with Cochrane as his partner.

By 1929 the A's were back on top. Cochrane hit .331, 22-year-old infielder Jimmie Foxx had his first big season, and the A's won their first pennant since 1914, finishing 14 games ahead of the Yankees. The Mackmen beat the Cubs in five games in a World Series marked by mutual animosity. As Cochrane put it, "We had started the Series with a fine appreciation of invective and were hurling it from bench to bench across the infield until the air around home plate was blue."

Commissioner Kenesaw Mountain Landis, offended by the inappropriate language, told both managers that a substantial fine would be levied against any player who used profanity during the rest of the Series. Cochrane did his best to comply. Before the final game he hollered over to the Cubs bench, "Hurry up, sweethearts. Tea will be served at four o'clock." Everyone, including Landis, heard him. After the Series was over, Landis joined the A's victory celebration and congratulated each player—except Cochrane. He ignored the catcher until just before he left, when Landis said slyly, "Hello, sweetheart. I came by for tea."

The turning point in the Series was Game 4. The hard-hitting A's, down 8–0 in the last of the seventh, slammed 10 hits and scored 10 runs in the most famous comeback in World Series history. Cochrane led AL catchers in fielding average in 1930, and the powerhouse A's grabbed another pennant and roared into the Series against St. Louis. This time it took them six games to nail down the world championship. In Game 1 Lefty Grove beat Burleigh Grimes, 5–2, even though the A's could manage only five hits; however, all were for extra bases, and one was a home run by Cochrane.

In 1931 the A's won their third consecutive pennant as Cochrane hit .349, but the Series was a different story. The Cardinals had a rookie named John "Pepper" Martin who ran away with the Series—literally. Martin hit .500 and stole five bases, while Cochrane batted only .160. The Cardinals won in seven games.

After second- and third-place finishes the next two years, Mack did what he had done in 1915: he dismantled the A's for financial reasons. Cochrane was sold to the Tigers. Recognizing his leadership abilities, the Detroit team made the 31-year-old their manager, and in 1934 the Tigers won their first pennant in 25 years.

Cochrane hit .320 and once again worked his magic on a pitching staff. According to baseball historian David Voigt, "Overnight he made stars of Tommy Bridges and Schoolboy Rowe." The duo had won 21 games between them in 1933. In 1934, Bridges won 22 and Rowe 24. It helped, of course, that their team scored 958 runs, the most ever by the Tigers.

In the World Series, Cochrane and his men found themselves up against the pesky Cardinals—"the Gas House Gang." In batting practice before Game 1, Cards pitcher Dizzy Dean snatched the bat from Tigers first baseman Hank Greenberg's hands and walloped two balls over the wall. "Remember," Dean said, "I'm the weakest hitter on this team." Cochrane was so worn out by his combined catching and managerial duties that he spent all of his spare time in bed. He hit only .214 in the Series, which the Cardinals won when Dean shut out the Tigers, 11–0, in Game 7.

Led by Hank Greenberg's bat and 40 more wins from Bridges and Rowe, Cochrane's team was back in the World Series in 1935. This time their opponents were the Cubs, and Cochrane experienced what he called his "greatest thrill in baseball."

The Tigers won three of the first four games, but the Cubs won Game 5 and the action moved back to Wrigley Field. In Game 6 the teams were tied, 3–3, going into the ninth inning. In the top of the ninth the Cubs' Stan Hack led off with a triple against Tommy Bridges.

Cochrane went to work. The first pitch to the next batter, Billy Jurges, was one of Bridges' famous "jug-handle" curves. It broke into the dirt a couple of feet in front of the plate, and Cochrane had to make a great play to prevent the lead run from scoring. Bridges then fanned Jurges, and with Cochrane nursing him along, he nailed down the last two outs.

In the bottom of the ninth, Cochrane singled with one out and eventually scored the winning run on outfielder Goose Goslin's single to right. The Tigers were world champions for the first time. According to sportswriter Fred Lieb, Detroit went berserk. "The screeching at the ballpark did not stop until the sun came out over the downtown streets the following morning. No town was ever more deliriously happy over a baseball triumph."

Weary of the pressures of managing, Cochrane left baseball for a while to savor his triumphs. In 1936 the *Reach Guide* reported that "he broke down in health in midseason and had to go to

Wyoming to recuperate." He returned after two months, but his career ended on a tragic note in 1937. Early in the season he homered against the Yankees' Bump Hadley. The next time Cochrane came to the plate, Hadley's beanball fractured his skull in three places.

Cochrane lay unconscious for 10 days. He tried to return to the game as a nonplaying manager, but that wasn't his style. After the 1938 season Cochrane left professional baseball, and Ty Cobb supposedly sent him checks to help him deal with his financial problems. Cochrane was one of only three players at Cobb's funeral in 1961.

During World War II, Cochrane ran the athletic program at the Great Lakes Naval Training Station. With his eye for talent, he made sure that his team was well stocked. During the first three war years his record as a playing manager was 116–26.

Elected to the Hall of Fame in 1947, Cochrane coached the A's in 1955 and later scouted for both the Yankees and the Tigers. Detroit made him a vice president, a position he retained until his death in 1962.

Bill Curran, in his book *Mitts*, remembers a photograph in a New York newspaper during the 1930s that showed the hands of some major league catchers without identifying whose they were. Most looked like bags of bones—shattered, twisted, and torn. But one pair, Curran said, "displayed long slim fingers that might have belonged to Vladimir Horowitz." They belonged to Mickey Cochrane.

Rocky Colavito

Colavito, Rocco Domenico **OF**

1955–68 B:8/10/1933, New York, NY Deb:9/10/1955, CLE AL BR/TR 6'3", 190

G	AB	R	H	HR	RBI	OBP	SLG	AVG
1841	6503	971	1730	374	1159	.362	.489	.266

When Cleveland general manager Frank "Trader" Lane traded Indians idol and American League home run champ Rocky Colavito to the Detroit Tigers for league batting champion Harvey Kuenn, he had no idea what a firestorm of protest he would unleash. "They wanted to lynch me," said Lane. "I went back to my hotel that day and there was this dummy hanging in effigy from a lamp post. 'Frank Lane,' it said on the dummy. They must have thought, 'here's our handsome Rocky gone and all we've got is an ugly slob of a general manager.'"

Hordes of fans, many of them young girls who adored the personable young slugger, picketed Cleveland Stadium, carrying signs with such slogans as, "Don't Knock the Rock," "We love you, Rocky," and "You'll always be ours, Rocky." Rarely has a trade generated such genuine outrage, and Lane added fuel to the fire when he asked, "What's all the fuss about? All I did was trade hamburger for steak."

It's difficult to imagine now how popular Colavito was in Cleveland. Aside from his slugging abilities and good looks, Indians fans had a personal love affair with this Bronx import and overlooked his lack of speed and ungainliness. (He was literally flat-footed.) But Colavito never stopped hustling, and his right arm was like a rocket launcher, the strongest of any AL outfielder. In 1958 he led league outfielders with six double plays and at one point put together a streak of 241 errorless games.

The clean-living right fielder always had time for his public. Hundreds of fans would gather at the stadium gates after each game for his autograph, and Colavito would oblige them all. "I'll tell you what," he would shout to each day's crowd, "if you'll do me a favor and line up, I'll sign for all of you." The fans did—they knew Colavito would keep his word, even if it took hours.

Colavito grew up in the Crotona Park section of the Bronx and had himself been a kid waiting outside the ballpark with pencil in hand. "I made up my mind that if I ever became a big league player I'd never pass the kids by," he recalled.

Colavito had resolved to be a big leaguer from the beginning. By the age of 9 he was playing on local semipro clubs, and at age 16 he dropped out of Theodore Roosevelt High School to concentrate on baseball. Because of a rule stipulating that a player could not be signed before his high school class graduated, it took a special appeal to the Commissioner's Office—plus a year's waiting period—before Colavito was eligible to sign.

He worshipped the Yankees' Joe DiMaggio and would have preferred to go with New York; however, the Yankees had little interest in him and offered Colavito a mere $500 bonus—but only if he survived spring training. The Philadelphia Athletics were more interested, offering a first-year salary of $5,000 plus a $6,000 bonus. But at the last minute they backed off, crying poverty. In fact, they had just mortgaged Shibe Park to meet expenses.

That left the Indians. They offered Colavito $1,000 on signing, $1,000 more if he lasted 30 days, and an additional $1,000 if he survived 30 days after that. His base salary was to be $150 per month. There was some haggling over whether the $3,000 should be paid all at once, but then Rocco Domenico Colavito, Sr., put his foot down, telling his son in Italian, "Sign before you don't get nothing." The next morning the Colavitos received a call from the

Phillies, who were interested in topping the Indians' bid, but it was too late.

When Colavito reported to the Indians' spring training camp in 1950 he reminded everyone of DiMaggio, and he reinforced the comparison by altering the "255" on his uniform to read "5"—DiMaggio's number. As he moved up through the Indians' system, however, Colavito's DiMaggio fixation became a hindrance. Manager after manager warned the outfielder to be himself and not a poor copy of someone else.

In 1956 Colavito thought he had made the club, but Cleveland manager Al Lopez instead shipped him to San Diego in the Pacific Coast League. Colavito tore the cover off the ball and amused himself with showcasing his strong arm by standing at home plate and firing the ball over the center-field fence. His longest throw was 436 feet—just shy of the all-time mark of 443 set by Chattanooga's Don Grate in 1953.

Five weeks and several phone calls to Indians general manager Hank Greenberg later, Colavito was back in Cleveland. He made no real progress until 1958 when he hit 41 homers, losing the league title by just one home run to Mickey Mantle. On June 10, 1959, Colavito hit four homers in one game, and did it in consecutive at bats, a feat accomplished only three times before in history.

After being traded to Detroit in April 1960 Colavito had a poor season, but in 1961 he came through with 45 homers and 140 RBIs. Frank Lane's remarks about Colavito being hamburger seemed a poor choice of words in retrospect. "I like hamburger," chortled Tigers GM Bill DeWitt.

But Detroit did not take to Colavito as Cleveland had. In fact, many fans resented his replacing the solid, if less spectacular, Harvey Kuenn. Once Colavito got so angry at the razzing he was receiving from the right-field stands that he threw a ball over the Briggs Stadium roof.

Colavito's problems in Detroit were exacerbated by influential *Detroit News* columnist Joe Falls. "Rocky Colavito will play left field for the Tigers, and he has the feet for it," announced Falls, who thought Colavito was "a self-ordained deity." He initiated a *News* feature that chronicled Colavito's "RNBIs"—Runs Not Batted In. The animosity peaked when Falls, in his capacity as official scorer, gave Colavito an error on a disputed play, and Colavito responded by trying to attack the columnist.

After Colavito's banner 1961 season he held out for more money than the Tigers were paying established local hero Al Kaline (Kaline was getting $52,000; Colavito wanted $57,500). Again publicity was negative. Colavito went to the A's in November 1963, then returned to the Indians in January 1965, where he led the league in RBIs that year. He ended his career with the Yankees, the team he had once longed to play for. In 1976 Colavito was voted the most memorable personality in Cleveland Indians history.

Nate Colbert

Colbert, Nathan **1B**

1966–76 B:4/9/1946, St. Louis, MO Deb:4/14/1966, HOU NL BR/TR 6'2", 209

G	AB	R	H	HR	RBI	OBP	SLG	AVG
1004	3422	481	833	173	520	.324	.451	.243

Power-hitting Padres first baseman Nate Colbert had the biggest night of his career in Atlanta on August 1, 1972. During a doubleheader he drove in 13 runs, the twin bill record that broke the old mark of 11 set by Earl Averill in 1930 and tied by Jim Tabor, Phil Weintraub, and Boog Powell. He also hit five home runs that day, tying the record set almost 20 years earlier by Stan Musial. Colbert had been an 8-year-old in the stands at Sportsman's Park on May 2, 1954, the day Musial hit those five homers in a doubleheader against the New York Giants.

A three-time National League All-Star, Colbert was susceptible to slumps and strikeouts. During one stretch in 1970 he struck out seven consecutive times. But he could also carry a club: in 1972 Colbert drove in 111 of the 488 runs the Padres scored, as he equaled his career high of 38 homers.

Originally signed by the Cardinals in 1964, Colbert got as far as Cedar Rapids in the Midwest League before being drafted by Houston. Colbert showed his first glimpse of power with Amarillo in 1967, when he led the Texas League with 28 home runs. The Padres selected him as their ninth choice in the NL expansion draft on October 14, 1968.

After Colbert's power stats took a nosedive in 1974, the Padres traded him to Detroit for Gold Glove shortstop Eddie Brinkman and two other players. Detroit sold Colbert to the Montreal Expos, and he finished his playing career with the Oakland A's in 1976.

Jerry Coleman

Coleman, Gerald Francis **2B–SS**

1949–57 M(1980, 73–89) B:9/14/1924, San Jose, CA D:4/9/1998, Fort Myers, FL Deb:4/20/1949, NY AL BR/TR 6', 170

G	AB	R	H	HR	RBI	OBP	SLG	AVG
723	2119	267	558	16	217	.341	.339	.263

Jerry Coleman may be best known for his use of language throughout his years as an announcer for the Padres: "Winfield goes back to the wall. He hits his head on the wall, and it rolls off! It's rolling all the way back to second base! This is a terrible thing for the Padres!"

But prior to confusing, amusing, and amazing listeners, Gerald Francis Coleman played a solid second base for six Yankees pennant winners. And in 1950 he was chosen as World Series Most Valuable Player. Coleman signed with the Yankees in 1942 and started with the Class D PONY League's Wellsville Yankees before World War II interrupted his career. He flew 57 bombing missions in the Solomon Islands.

Despite his low minor league batting averages, Coleman beat out regular second baseman George Stirnweiss to win a regular job with the Yankees in the spring of 1949. During the conflict in Korea he rejoined the military. He flew 120 missions and won two Distinguished Flying Crosses.

Coleman served as the Yankees' play-by-play announcer from 1963 to 1969. He earned a reputation for his zany "Colemanisms" as the announcer for the San Diego Padres, where he's worked since 1972, with the exception of a stint in 1980 as manager of the club. He also broadcast games nationally on CBS radio.

Some of his more famous Colemanisms:

"McCovey swings and misses, and it's fouled back."

"Rich Folkers is throwing up in the bullpen."

"Pete Rose has 3,000 hits and 3,014 overall."

"He slides into second base with a standup double."

"Grubb goes back, back. He's under the warning track."

Joe Coleman

Coleman, Joseph Howard **P**

1965–79 B:2/3/1947, Boston, MA Deb:9/28/1965, WAS AL BR/TR 6'3", 195

W	L	PCT	G	SH	IP	BB	SO	ERA
142	135	.513	484	18	2569^{1}	1003	1728	3.70

Trades don't often drastically change careers, but one swap made a 20-game winner out of pitcher Joe Coleman. The first-round choice of the expansion Washington Senators in the inaugural free-agent amateur draft in 1965, Coleman signed for a $75,000 bonus but never finished a full season with a record above .500. Then an October 1970 trade sent him to the Tigers, and Coleman was suddenly transformed from a mediocre pitcher into a 20-game winner. In his first Detroit season, Coleman went 20–9.

In 1972 he made the All-Star team and helped lead the Tigers to the division championship. In Game 3 of the Championship Series against Oakland he set what was then a playoff record with 14 strikeouts. "Here you have a lot more confidence and a better defense than we did in Washington," Coleman said of pitching in Detroit. "In Washington they didn't score that many runs. Here you get to stay around longer."

Even as a successful pitcher Coleman had to battle a tendency to nibble around the edges of the plate rather than challenge hitters with his fastball and his forkball, a precursor of the split-finger fastball.

Coleman came from a baseball family: his father, former American League pitcher Joseph Patrick Coleman, appeared in the 1948 All-Star Game. "My dad helped me a lot. The only thing he didn't do, which I'm grateful for, is he never pushed the game on me. He let me make my own mistakes, and helped me whenever I asked for it."

Vince Coleman

Coleman, Vincent Maurice **OF**

1985–97 B:9/22/1961, Jacksonville, FL Deb:4/18/1985, STL NL BB/TR 6', 185

G	AB	R	H	HR	RBI	OBP	SLG	AVG
1371	5406	849	1425	28	346	.325	.345	.264

Baseball's fastest man enjoyed six record-setting seasons with the St. Louis Cardinals, where he set the style as the leadoff hitter for an offense that featured speed on the basepaths. When he joined the Mets in 1991, however, things turned ugly fast. He hit his low point in 1993 with the infamous "firecracker incident."

The buzz about Coleman's world-class speed began in 1983, when he set a pro baseball record with 145 steals for Class A Macon of the South Atlantic League. He stole 110 bases as a rookie in 1985—the third most in the 20th century. He also ran away with the National League Rookie of the Year Award. The only thing that stopped him was a slow-moving automatic tarpaulin.

While doing his pre-game stretching at Busch Stadium before Game 4 of the Championship Series, his foot became caught underneath the automatic tarp as it unrolled across the infield. He was trapped for 30 seconds and had to be removed from the field in a stretcher. Without Coleman, the Cards beat the Dodgers for the pennant, but lost to Kansas City in a seven-game World Series.

Besides his sprinter's speed, Coleman took enormous leads at first base—sometimes getting both feet on the rug at Busch Stadium. He also claimed that third base was easier to steal than second, and he often swiped both in the same inning. (In Triple A ball with the Louisville Redbirds, Coleman had even devised a special play in which he would streak from first to third on a bunt fielded by the third baseman.)

Coleman stole 107 bases in 1986 and 109 in 1987. Though a light-hitting switchhitter, he managed to bat .289 with 121 runs in 1987—his best offensive season. He topped the National League in steals the next three years as well, earning All-Star berths in 1988 and 1989. His 50 consecutive steals without being caught in 1989 set a major league record.

Coleman's success did not transfer to New York. He signed a lucrative contract with the Mets after the 1990 season, but hamstring and rib injuries kept him out of the lineup. He complained that Shea Stadium's dirt infield was keeping him "out of the Hall of Fame," and he had nasty run-ins with coach Mike Cubbage and manager Jeff Torborg. The team suspended him for two games for insubordination. Coleman, who led the NL in steals in each of his first six years in the major leagues, stole 99 bases in three seasons as a Met.

On July 24, 1993, in Los Angeles, autograph seekers approached Coleman in his car. He responded by throwing a lit firecracker at the fans, injuring two children and a woman. Coleman was charged with a felony and received three years probation. The Mets said he would never play for them again, but he continued his career elsewhere. The Royals, Mariners, Reds, and Tigers all took him in. Coleman's 752 career steals ranked sixth on the all-time list through the 1999 season.

Dave Collins

Collins, David S. **OF-1B-DH**

1975–90 B:10/20/1952, Rapid City, SD Deb:6/7/1975, CAL AL BB/TL 5'11", 175

G	AB	R	H	HR	RBI	OBP	SLG	AVG
1701	4907	667	1335	32	373	.340	.351	.272

The switch-hitting outfielder from Rapid City, South Dakota, became one of the fastest men in baseball. Dave Collins stole 375 bases in his 16-year, seven-team career. His 79 steals in 1980 were a career high, but that was only good for third in the National League in a year when 10 of the league's 12 teams had triple-digit steal totals. Although Collins never led the league in stolen bases, he surpassed 20 steals nine times.

In high school, Collins was all-state in track, football, and basketball. After two years in junior college, he quickly climbed the minor league ladder, winning the Texas League batting title in 1974. He joined the Angels the following season. He went from California to Seattle to Cincinnati over the next four years, batting just .232 in reserve roles.

Injuries to Reds outfielders George Foster and Ken Griffey finally gave Collins a shot at a regular job in 1979. He responded with a .318 average, helping Cincinnati to a division title. He followed that up with a .303 mark and the 79 steals. The Reds liked his tenacious style on the field, but not at the bargaining table.

Collins went on to play for the Yankees, Blue Jays, A's, Reds again, and Cardinals over the next decade. In Toronto he batted .308, stole 60 bases, and led the league with 15 triples in 1984. After retiring as a player, Collins coached for the Cardinals and Reds.

Eddie Collins

Collins, Edward Trowbridge, Sr. **2B**

1906–30 M(1924–26, 174–160) B:5/2/1887, Millerton, NY D:3/25/1951, Boston, MA Deb:9/17/1906, PHI AL BL/TR 5'9", 175

G	AB	R	H	HR	RBI	OBP	SLG	AVG
2826	9949	1821	3315	47	1300	.424	.429	.333

As a member of four world championship teams, Eddie "Cocky" Collins had earned the right to be confident about his abilities. He built an impressive .333 lifetime average and batted .300 or better every year from 1909 through 1916 and from 1919 through 1928.

Had his contemporary Ty Cobb not been so dominant, Collins might have enjoyed even greater recognition. As it was, Collins hit .372, .365, and .360 without ever winning a batting title. He did lead the league in stolen bases four times, winding up with 743 career steals, seventh all-time.

Defensively, Collins played more games (2,826) and had more putouts (6,526), assists (7,630), and total chances (14,591) than any other second baseman. He won eight fielding titles, and with the exception of 1918, when he missed 57 games because of injuries, he led the league in one fielding category or another from 1909 through 1922. He is usually listed among the top three second basemen to play the game. His career stretched from the last half of Nap Lajoie's into the prime of Rogers Hornsby's. Connie Mack, who managed Collins and Lajoie and managed against Hornsby, ranked Eddie as the best.

His reputation for intelligence matched his reputation as a player. A reporter was therefore surprised that Collins apparently had a superstition. Before each at bat, he'd take his gum out of his mouth and afix it to the button on the top of his cap. The reporter asked him about it. Collins explained he wasn't superstitious; he just thought it was "unlucky not to get base hits."

In 1906, debuted professionally under the alias "Edward T. Sullivan" and played until it was revealed that he was Columbia University's junior quarterback and infielder. He was allowed to continue for Columbia as nonplaying captain and joined the A's after graduation. Collins quickly became the keystone of the A's infield. When shortstop Jack Barry, third baseman Frank "Home Run" Baker, and first baseman John "Stuffy" McInnis joined the A's in 1909, together with Collins they became known as the "$100,000 infield," because Connie Mack "wouldn't take that sum for all of them." The A's proceeded to win four pennants in the next six years.

He was sold to the White Sox in 1915 the year after winning the Chalmers Award as Most Valuable Player. Collins hit .409 in the 1917 World Series and scored the deciding run by slipping out of a rundown between third and home to beat Heinie Zimmerman to the plate.

Reportedly, Collins was the highest paid player on the White Sox, and jealousy over his salary may have contributed to the decision by some Chicago players to take bribes from gamblers to throw the 1919 World Series. Dispirited by the play of his "Black Sox" teammates , Collins batted only .226 against the Reds but still stole one base, which gave him 14 career World Series thefts.

In 1925 he became a manager, piloting the White Sox for two seasons before returning to the Athletics as a pinch hitter and leading the league with 12 pinch hits in 34 pinch-hit at bats. Elected to the Hall of Fame in 1939, he served as a Red Sox executive from 1932 until his death in 1951. His son, Edward Trowbridge Collins, Jr., had a three-year major league career with the A's, from 1939 to 1942.

Jimmy Collins

Collins, James Joseph **3B–OF**

1895–1908 M(1901–06, 455–376) B:1/16/1870, Buffalo, N.Y. D:3/6/1943, Buffalo, NY Deb:4/19/1895, BOS NL BR/TR, 5'9", 178

G	AB	R	H	HR	RBI	OBP	SLG	AVG
1725	6795	1055	1999	65	983	.343	.409	.294

During an 1895 matchup between the Baltimore Orioles and the Louisville Colonels, seven consecutive Orioles bunted the ball toward third baseman Walter Preston. And seven times Preston clumsily played the ball into a base hit.

After the seventh bunt, Louisville manager John J. McCloskey called Fred Clarke in from left field and offered him $50 more a month to play third base. Clarke balked. He had played shortstop early in his career and knew he belonged in the outfield. "Why don't you move that fellow Collins from center field?" he asked. "I understand he played third base at Buffalo."

Jimmy Collins was hastily summoned to the infield. As he later recalled, "McGraw bunted and I came in as fast as I dared, picked up the ball, and threw it underhanded to first base. He was out. Keeler tried it and I nailed him by a step. I had to throw out four bunters in a row before the Orioles quit bunting." The barehanded pickup and underhand throw are standard today; a third baseman who cannot make the play will not keep his position for long. But in 1895 it was revolutionary.

Collins completely recast the position of third base with that play and with other innovations. Before he came along, third basemen stood close to the base; some even kept one foot on the bag. Collins noticed that most balls were hit to the third baseman's left, so he moved away from the foul line to lessen the gap between himself and the shortstop, realizing that he was quick enough to grab balls hit down the third-base line. He also played in close on bunting situations, trusting that his reflexes were fast enough to stop the ball should the batter suddenly swing out.

Collins began his career with the Eastern League's Buffalo Bisons in 1893. A solid 5 feet 9 inches tall and 178 pounds, he played a little third base but was mainly an outfielder. He hit .353 in 1894, and in 1895 Boston purchased his contract and brought him to the National League.

The veteran club had no place for him to play, however, and after appearing in 11 games and batting only .211 he was sold to Louisville for $1,500. There Collins hit a respectable .273, but his third base play was the talk of the league. When he rapped out four hits and handled 16 fielding chances faultlessly in a game against his old team, the Boston fans howled about the one that got away.

Collins didn't get away for long, however. The deal that sent him to Louisville included a provision that gave Boston the right to buy back his contract at the end of the season for the same price. Boston exercised its option and demonstrated its faith in Collins by dealing Billy Nash, the third baseman for 10 seasons, to Philadelphia.

Along with Collins, Boston featured three other future Hall of Famers: pitcher Kid Nichols and outfielders Hugh Duffy and Billy Hamilton. The club's infield was perhaps the best ever up to that time. Collins played third, acrobatic Herman Long played shortstop, reliable Bobby Lowe covered second, and slick-fielding Fred Tenney played first. Collins hit a career-high .346 in his second season back in Boston and finished second in the league in RBIs with 132.

In the close 1897 pennant race the Beaneaters wrested the NL championship from the Orioles by two games, and they repeated as pennant winners in 1898, widening their margin over Baltimore to six games. Collins again excelled, batting .328, leading the league with 15 home runs, and finishing second in RBIs with 111.

Boston might have won a third consecutive pennant in 1899 except for a maneuver that is now illegal: the Orioles' owner purchased the Brooklyn club, combined the two squads in Brooklyn, and produced a powerhouse. Boston finished second.

Despite Boston's success on the field and at the gate, its owners were notoriously cheap. Their ballpark was falling apart, and their players were underpaid. In 1901 the American League declared itself a major league and began waving money at the older league's players. Many Beaneaters leapt at the chance, including Collins. His brilliant third base play was not lost to the fans, though; he signed with the city's AL team as player-manager for $5,500 a year. Within a few seasons he earned $10,000 a year plus 10 percent of the gate, which was nearly $18,000 one year.

It was a fabulous salary for the time, and Collins earned it. In his first two AL seasons he hit .332 and .322, and Boston finished second and third. This early success, combined with the NL Beaneaters' fall to the second division, made the AL club Boston's more popular team. In 1903 Collins' men won the AL pennant.

That season, following two years of bitter acrimony, the two leagues were at peace. Barney Dreyfuss, owner of the NL champion Pirates, and Boston owner Henry Killea agreed to a postseason "world's series" to settle the championship of baseball. Pittsburgh had won three straight pennants and was a slight favorite, but by the time the World Series was played, illness and injuries had left the Pirates with only one reliable pitcher, righthander Deacon Phillippe.

In the best-of-nine affair Phillippe won three of the first four games before he tired. Boston pitchers Cy Young and Bill Dinneen took over, and Boston won in eight games to become the first true world champions.

In 1904 Boston successfully defended its AL title in a close race with the New York Highlanders. However, the NL champion New York Giants owner John T. Brush and manager John McGraw refused to play in a second World Series.

The Boston club aged rapidly after 1904, and Collins wasn't immune to the rigors of time. After the team tumbled in the standings for two straight seasons, he was replaced as manager, although he began the 1907 season as the regular third baseman. In July he was traded to Connie Mack's Philadelphia Athletics where he completed his major league career. In 1945, the Old Timer's Committee named him to the Hall of Fame, the first third baseman to be inducted.

Rip Collins

Collins, Harry Warren **P**

1920–31 B:2/26/1896, Weatherford, TX D:5/27/1968, Bryan, TX Deb:4/19/1920, NY AL BR/TR 6'1", 205

W	L	PCT	G	SH	IP	BB	SO	ERA
108	82	.568	311	15	1712^{1}	674	569	3.99

Nicknamed "Rip" after a pre-Prohibition brand of whiskey, righthander Harry Warren Collins was described as a man with a million-dollar arm and 25 cents' worth of enthusiasm. He never became the pitcher he might have been, but Collins expressed no regrets.

After a four-sport career at Texas A&M, he joined the Yankees in 1920, just before Babe Ruth arrived to turn the team into a dynasty. Although Collins won 25 games over two seasons, it was far short of what the Yankees had expected. After the 1921 season, he went to the Red Sox as part of a package that brought New York Everett Scott, Joe Bush, and Sad Sam Jones.

Collins spent his remaining nine years in the majors pitching for the Red Sox, Tigers, and Browns. At each stop he produced at least one double-digit-win season but never blossomed into a star. Nonetheless, he finished with an impressive lifetime 108–82 record. After retiring from the game in 1931, he eventually became a law enforcement officer in Texas.

Shano Collins

Collins, John Francis **OF–1B**

1910–25 M(1931–32 73–134) B:12/4/1885, Charlestown, MA D:9/10/1955, Newton, MA Deb:4/21/1910, CHI AL BR/TR 6', 185

G	AB	R	H	HR	RBI	OBP	SLG	AVG
1799	6390	747	1687	22	709	.306	.364	.264

Shano Collins spent most of his career with the Chicago White Sox and was one of the players who played it straight during the 1919 World Series. He usually patrolled the outfield, where his speed and strong arm made him an excellent defender; however, during player absences he sometimes played first base, where he was merely adequate. After he hit .197 as a rookie in 1910, he cut down his swing and became a fair offensive player.

When the Sox won the 1917 and 1919 American League pennants, Collins was platooned in left field with Nemo Leibold. In 1920 Shano (a play on Sean, the Gaelic version of John) played first while regular first baseman Chick Gandil decided to sit out the season after apparently pocketing $35,000 for throwing the 1919 World Series. Collins responded with his best year and hit .303, the only time he ever topped .300 for a full season.

The next year he and Leibold went to the Red Sox for outfielder Harry Hooper. Collins' career ended with the Red Sox in 1925, and he became their manager in 1931. The Sox finished sixth that year, and when they fell to last place in 1932, Collins was fired.

Earle Combs

Combs, Earle Bryan **OF**

1924–1935 B:5/14/1899, Pebworth, KY D:7/21/1976, Richmond, KY Deb:4/16/1924, NY AL BL/TR 6', 185

G	AB	R	H	HR	RBI	OBP	SLG	AVG
1455	5746	1186	1866	58	632	.397	.462	.325

Hall of Famer Earle Combs was an exceptional all-around ballplayer who made key contributions to the mighty Yankees of the 1920s and 1930s. He originally hoped to be a teacher, attending Eastern Kentucky State Normal School in Richmond. He played basketball, ran track, and starred on the baseball field, hitting .591 in his final year. During the summer he taught in one-room schools, but he soon learned that he could make more money and have more fun playing semipro ball. When he hit .444 for the Harlan team, the American Association's Louisville Colonels signed him.

His first professional game was a total disaster. Installed in center field, he soon made two errors on groundballs. The Colonels overcame those miscues to lead by a run in the ninth. With two opposing runners on base, another ball bounced toward Combs and rolled between his legs. Before he could run it down and send it back to the infield, both runners, and the batter, had joyfully circled the bases to win the game. Afterward, he sat in front of his locker, bleakly contemplating life as a Kentucky schoolteacher. Colonels manager Joe McCarthy approached the disconsolate rookie. "Look," he said, "if I didn't think you belonged in center field on this club, I wouldn't put you there. And I'm going to keep you there."

Combs soon became an excellent outfielder, outrunning flyballs and snagging tricky grounders. He finished his first season at Louisville with a .344 batting average. In 1923 he upped his average to .380, and the Yankees bought his contract for $50,000 and two players.

When spring came around, however, he refused to report to New York's training camp. He had been promised a percentage of his purchase price by the Colonels but had received nothing. "I am not a dumb animal to be browbeaten, cowed, lashed, coerced, or goaded into anything I do not think is right," he announced. The Colonels paid him.

Combs had been such an accomplished basestealer in the minor leagues that Louisville fans called him "the Mail Carrier." When he became New York's leadoff hitter, though, manager Miller Huggins took him aside and explained that times had changed. With sluggers such as Babe Ruth, Lou Gehrig, and Bob Meusel in the lineup, the Yankees needed little help in scoring runs. Stealing bases made no sense when the next batter was likely to hit one into the seats. "Up here," Huggins said, "we'll call you 'the Waiter.'"

As a result, Combs never stole more than 16 bases in a major league season. Had he played for any other team he might have doubled or tripled that figure. Nevertheless, his scoring record shows the wisdom of Huggins' strategy. Despite missing most of three seasons due to injury, the Waiter scored more than 100 runs in eight of his 12 seasons for a total of 1,186 runs, an average of 99 a season.

The American League's best leadoff man, Combs collected at least 190 hits five times on his way to a .325 career batting average. While Ruth, Gehrig, and others hit home runs, the left-handed-batting Combs' specialty was hitting line drives to all fields, although he collected more than his share of extra-base hits. When one of his drives sliced between the outfielders, he was a good bet to wind up on third base. He led the league in triples three times and finished with a career total of 154, averaging more than one three-bagger for every 10 games he played.

A skillful bunter, Combs was especially good at drawing walks, the last thing a pitcher wanted before facing Ruth or Gehrig. His career on-base percentage was .397.

The 6-foot, 185-pound speedster broke in quickly with the Yankees in 1924, hitting .400 in his first 24 games before fracturing his ankle and missing the rest of the season. Combs' injury probably cost the Yankees the pennant. After winning flags in 1921, 1922, and 1923, New York finished second to Washington by two games.

In 1925 Combs, fully recovered, showed that his great start the previous year had been no fluke. He lashed out 203 hits, batted .342, and scored 117 runs. But Ruth was out of the lineup for much of the year, and several other players had disappointing seasons. The Yankees plummeted to seventh.

In 1926 Ruth returned to form, Gehrig blossomed at first base, and second baseman Tony Lazzeri added another powerful bat to the lineup. The Yankees clinched the pennant with a victory in St. Louis.

The next day they clowned their way through a doubleheader with the hapless Browns. Among other hijinks, Combs performed a burlesque strikeout. Perhaps he should have played with more dedication; he finished the year with a .299 batting average, the only time he failed to hit .300 until his final major league season. The exciting 1926 World Series was highlighted by Pete Alexander's clutch strikeout of Tony Lazzeri with the bases loaded in the final game. The St. Louis Cardinals beat the Yankees in seven.

The next year featured the New York club that many experts consider to be the greatest team of all time, the 1927 Yankees. The Bronx Bombers cruised to the pennant and demolished the Pirates in the World Series in four straight games. During the regular season Ruth slugged his then-record 60 home runs, and Combs set a club record with 231 hits. In 1986 Don Mattingly topped Combs' mark with 238.

Gehrig was a favorite of Yankee fans, and Ruth was of course the most popular figure in baseball. But Combs also rated high with both fans and reporters. In appreciation of his fine season in 1927, the fans in Yankee Stadium's right field took up a collection and bought him a gold watch. In 1931 sportswriter Fred Lieb wrote, "I believe if a vote were taken of the sportswriters on who is the most popular player in New York, I think the vote would go to Combs."

The Yanks won another pennant and swept another World Series in 1928 but fell short the next three seasons. Huggins, whose two favorites had been Gehrig and Combs, died suddenly in 1929. Following a third-place finish by Bob Shawkey, Joe McCarthy, Combs' original manager at Louisville, became the Yankees skipper in 1931. The next year New York was back in the Series, toppling the Chicago Cubs in four games.

Combs never played in another Series. On July 24, 1934, he ran into the center field wall at Sportsman's Park in St. Louis while chasing a fly-ball and suffered a fractured skull as well as shoulder and knee injuries. In 1935 he appeared in 89 games as a player-coach before retiring as a player to coach full time. His first coaching assignment was to teach a young prospect named Joe DiMaggio the intricacies of playing center field at Yankee Stadium.

Combs coached with the Yankees and several other teams through 1954 and then settled down on his 400-acre farm in Kentucky. He was named to the Hall of Fame in 1970, six years before his death. "I thought the Hall of Fame was for super-stars," the modest center fielder said, "not just average players like I was."

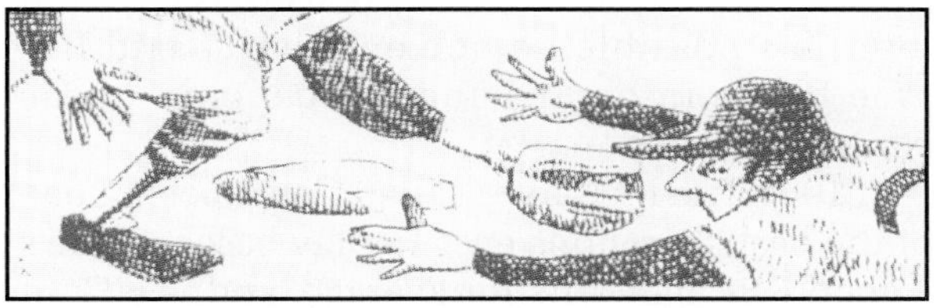

Charles Comiskey

Comiskey, Charles Albert **1B**

1882–94 M(839–542) Owner(1901–31) B:8/15/1859, Chicago, IL D:10/26/1931, Eagle River, WI Deb:5/2/1882, STL AA BR/TR 6', 180

G	AB	R	H	HR	RBI	OBP	SLG	AVG
1390	5796	994	1530	29	883	.293	.338	.264

The image of Charles Comiskey, "the Noble Roman," has shifted dramatically over the years: from star player and pioneer defensive strategist to manager and virtual cofounder of the American League, to farsighted magnate, to the unfortunate victim of a conspiracy of ungrateful players, to a tightwad owner whose ill treatment of his personnel helped bring on the Black Sox Scandal of 1919. All are valid.

Comiskey was playing with an independent club, the Dubuque Rabbits, in 1882 when he answered a letter from Al Spink, secretary of Chris Von der Ahe's St. Louis Browns of the new American Association. Spink wrote, "They are paying players from $90 to $125 a month. Make your terms as low as possible so I can clinch one of the jobs for you."

Comiskey later recalled, "So there could be no possible chance for an argument, I put my figure at $90. I got that, however, for only one month. The second, Vondy raised it to $150."

That Comiskey survived at all was remarkable because he reported to the Browns as a pitcher, and almost immediately his arm gave out. He convinced manager Ted Sullivan to put him at first and then proceeded to revolutionize the position. First basemen had traditionally played practically bolted to the bag. According to contemporary accounts, Comiskey ranged far and wide to cut off numerous base hits. He also changed how pitchers operated, forcing them to cover first base on balls hit to him.

"He taught the first baseman how to play the position," said longtime New York Giants manager John McGraw. "He furnished the rest of the infielders with new strategy. He gave you the impression, wherever you happened to meet him, that he was always thinking. There was hardly a game he didn't spring something new."

By his second season with St. Louis, Comiskey, at age 23, was the playing manager, and every year from 1885 to 1888 the Browns won the American Association pennant.

Brooklyn Dodgers owner Charles Ebbets recalled the time Comiskey had switched around his powerful Browns lineup, putting himself at second, second baseman Yank Robinson on first, third baseman Arlie Latham behind the plate, and catcher Doc Bushong at third. "Needless to say," Ebbets concluded, "St. Louis beat Brooklyn just the same, but I thought it was kind of Commy to give us a chance."

In 1890 Comiskey jumped to the upstart Players' League, but when it collapsed after one season, he returned to St. Louis. The AA also folded after the 1891 season, and Comiskey moved on to manage John T. Brush's Cincinnati club. There he met a man who would not only change his life but also would alter baseball history, *Commercial-Gazette* sportswriter Ban Johnson.

Johnson soon became president of the Western League, and in 1894 Comiskey became the owner of its Sioux City franchise, which he quickly transferred to St. Paul. Baseball lore has it that the two men hatched the idea of a rival to the National League at a Cincinnati tavern called the Ten-Minute Club (so named because patrons had to order new drinks every 10 minutes or vacate the premises).

In 1900 the Western League became the American League, and St. Paul was dropped. In its stead Comiskey was given the AL's new Chicago franchise. He dubbed his team the White Stockings, in honor of the Windy City's original National League club. A year later the league declared itself major. In 1906 Comiskey's "Hitless Wonders" (they hit .230 in 151 games) surprised everyone by winning the pennant and then defeating their crosstown rivals, Frank Chance's Cubs, in the World Series.

In 1910 the visionary Comiskey constructed "the Baseball Palace of the World," Comiskey Park, which hosted its last game in 1990. The concrete and steel structure, costing $750,000 ($150,000 for the site alone), opened on July 1, 1910. Any reputable Chicago organization could use the park free of charge. "The fans built it, didn't they?" the Noble Roman reasoned.

That was his generous side. Comiskey would invite a hundred guests to his Wisconsin estate, pay the Notre Dame tuition for the sons of pitcher Ed Walsh and catcher Billy Sullivan, and even tithe his revenues to the Red Cross during World War I.

With his players, however, he was an absolute tightwad. The White Sox played in the league's filthiest uniforms; Comiskey had given orders to cut down on laundry bills. Most clubs received $4 per day for meals; Comiskey gave his men $3. Stars such as outfielders Joe Jackson and Happy Felsch, pitchers Lefty Williams and Ed Cicotte, and infielder Buck Weaver were grievously underpaid. In 1917 Comiskey promised the club a bonus for winning the pennant: all he delivered was a case of cheap champagne at the team's victory party.

In 1919 Fall Classic the White Sox were overwhelming favored to beat the Reds. But seven of Comiskey's players, including Jackson and Cicotte, were part of a conspiracy to throw the Series. An eighth player, Weaver, knew of the plot but didn't participate. When the White Sox lost the first two contests to Cincinnati, rumors of a fix spread, and by Series' end they were everywhere. Publicly, Comiskey dismissed them as "made of whole cloth and grown out of bitterness due to losing wagers," but he also offered $20,000 "to anyone unearthing information to that effect."

It wasn't until the end of the 1920 season that the rumors were proved true, but, typically, Comiskey did not pay the reward because a Chicago jury found his players not guilty. It didn't matter to Kenesaw Mountain Landis, the new baseball commissioner. He permanently banned all eight men from the game. The White Sox settled into the second division for the rest of Comiskey's life.

"I blame Ban Johnson for allowing the Series to continue," a tearful Comiskey once said. "If ever a league president blundered in a crisis, Ban did." It was the continuation of a feud long in the making. Just a year before the 1919 Series, the two old friends had permanently fallen out. "I made you, and by God I'll break you!" Comiskey often threatened Johnson.

In January 1927 Comiskey finally saw Johnson tossed out of the AL presidency. Still heartbroken from the 1919 scandal he helped create, Comiskey died in 1931, at age 72, at his Wisconsin summer home.

Dave Concepcion

Concepcion, David Ismael (Benitez) SS-2B-3B
1970–88 B:6/17/1948, Aragua, Venezuela
Deb:4/6/1970, CIN NL BR/TR 6'1", 180

G	AB	R	H	HR	RBI	OBP	SLG	AVG
2488	8723	993	2326	101	950	.325	.357	.267

When the "Big Red Machine" rolled over the National League in the 1970s the focus was on hitting, but the glue holding the Cincinnati defense together was shortstop Dave Concepcion. Concepcion won Gold Gloves every year from 1974 to 1977 and again in 1979, and probably would have won several more had it not been for the advent of superstar Ozzie Smith.

"Mark Belanger may be a little smoother. Larry Bowa is very quick. Rick Burleson is a leader type. Bill Russell has an accurate arm. But no one does everything as well as Concepcion. It's possible no one ever has," said Pee Wee Reese in comparing Concepcion to his contemporaries.

In 1983 Tim McCarver called Concepcion "one of the best shortstops ever to play baseball. He's a good RBI man, hits for average, and is a Gold

Glove fielder. He has good speed and can steal bases. There's not much left."

He learned to play ball in his native Venezuela. The Reds signed him in September 1967 and assigned him to Tampa of the Florida State League, where he battled homesickness and an inability to speak English. He started out as a second baseman, but manager George Scherger shifted him over to short. "He looked like a shortstop to me. He had a whip arm and the good fluid motion of a shortstop. Any infielder can play second base, but not everyone can play shortstop," Scherger said.

After stints at Asheville and Indianapolis, Concepcion came to the Reds spring training camp in 1970 and made the team. It was there that the shortstop adopted his trademark uniform number 13. "The players tell me not to take 13, that it's a bad number. But 13 is my lucky number. I think it funny most hotels don't have 13th floors. I wear 13 on my uniform ever since I first play with the Reds. I wear it on my uniform in Venezuela. My mother, she was born in 1913. Joe Tinker, he hit .315 in 1913."

Concepcion hit .260 in his rookie year, then fell to .205 and .209, but later became a competent hitter (he had three .300 seasons) by paying attention in the dugout. "I've always been around good hitters. They were always talking about hitting in the dugout. They talked about what guys were doing wrong. You can learn by listening," Concepcion said.

Toward the end of his Reds tenure Concepcion seemed to wear down mentally. "I think if (Reds manager) Pete Rose has one major project," said announcer Dave Campbell in 1983, "it's Davey Concepcion. Davey can do just about anything he wants in this game. The trouble, however, is making him want to play every day." As his hitting slumped, his defense also suffered. He bounced back a bit in 1987, hitting a career-high .319, but he played in only 104 games as Barry Larkin became the regular shortstop.

David Cone

Cone, David Brian **P**

1986–* B:1/2/1963, Kansas City, MO Deb:6/8/1986, KC AL BL/TR 6'1" 190

W	L	PCT	G	SH	IP	BB	SO	ERA
180	102	.638	390	22	2590	985	2420	3.19

David Cone's arrival in New York was like a gift from above—both when he arrived for the Mets and later when he arrived with the Yankees. He first arrived in New York in one of the greatest trades in Mets history: New York got Cone and Chris Jelic from the Kansas City Royals for Ed Hearn, Rick Anderson, and Mauro Gozzo on March 27, 1987. With the Mets staff decimated by injuries, Cone quickly worked his way into the starting rotation. The righthander earned his first major league victory on May 12 with a complete-game victory against the Reds, and he was 2–2 when he broke the pinky of his right hand while attempting to bunt. He missed two months with the injury.

In 1988 Cone became the fifth Mets pitcher to win 20 games, and his three losses were the fewest in the National League by a 20-game winner since Preacher Roe went 22–3 in 1951. Spurred on by an unbelievable month of May (5–0, 0.72 ERA), Cone made the All-Star team, finished second in the National League in ERA (2.22), and was second in strikeouts (213). The league hit .213 against him, with righthanders managing only a microscopic .165 average. Cone finished third in the voting for the 1988 Cy Young Award, behind Orel Hershiser and Danny Jackson. Cone split two decisions in the NL Championship Series against the Dodgers, as the Mets fell in seven games.

Cone won 14 games in each of the next three seasons and led the league in strikeouts in 1990 and 1991. The lefthanded hitter led the league in hits by a pitcher in 1989, and, in 1990, he became the first Mets pitcher to get a pinch hit.

In 1991 Cone struck out 13 batters in a game twice and he struck out the side in the fifth inning in Cincinnati on nine pitches on August 30. He tied the NL record with 19 strikeouts in Philadelphia on October 6.

Cone was the Opening Day pitcher for the Mets as well an All-Star in 1992. He compiled a 13–7 record with a 2.88 ERA in 27 starts. With free agency looming at season's end, Cone was traded to Toronto for infielder Jeff Kent and outfielder Ryan Thompson on August 27. Cone became the first pitcher to lead the major leagues in strikeouts (261) for three straight years since Nolan Ryan (1972–1974). Because he spent the final five weeks of 1992 in the American League, he did not win the NL strikeout title. But he only missed by one whiff. Cone went 1–1 for the Blue Jays in the ALCS, and, although he did not get a decision in two World Series starts, Toronto won both games and the Series.

Cone became a free agent in November 1992 and returned to Kansas City. After an 11–14 campaign in 1993, Cone was masterful in 1994 at 16–5 with a 2.94 ERA. He became the first Cy Young Award winner to capture the award without either leading the league in any statistical category or pitching for a first-place club.

In 1995 Cone was sent back to Toronto and then returned to New York—this time with the Yankees. He was 9–2 for the Yankees down the stretch (18–8 overall), and he won Game 1 of the

Division Series against Seattle. In Game 5, however, he walked in the tying run in the eighth inning and the Mariners won the series in 11 innings.

An aneurysm in his pitching shoulder was operated on during the 1996 season, but Cone returned to action with seven innings of no-hit ball in his first major league start since the surgery. A prescribed pitch count kept Cone from finishing the game, but Jose Herrera's infield hit off reliever Mariano Rivera was Oakland's only hit. Cone pitched well in the Division Series, ALCS, and World Series as the Yankees won their first world championship in 18 years.

Cone progressed to 12–6 in 1997, despite a late-season stint on the disabled list and leading the AL with 14 wild pitches. On June 23 of that season he struck out 16.

Cone bounced back fully in 1998, leading the league in victories with 20. He won the deciding games of both the Division Series against Texas and the ALCS against Cleveland, but had no decision in that year's World Series sweep of San Diego.

Cone jumped off to 9–4 start with a 2.86 ERA in the first half of the 1999 season, then began the second half with a perfect game against Montreal on July 17. Fittingly, the Yankees honored Don Larsen, pitcher of New York's first perfect game that day; also on hand was Yogi Berra, Larsen's catcher in his 1956 World Series perfecto.

Despite such an incredible performance, Cone slumped to 3–5 with a 4.28 ERA in the second half of the season. In the postseason, however, he rebounded to All-Star form, allowing two runs and seven hits in seven innings against the Red Sox in the ALCS and just a single hit in seven shutout innings against the Braves to lead the Yanks to another World Series sweep.

Tony Conigliaro

Conigliaro, Anthony Richard **OF**

1964–75 B:1/7/1945, Revere, MA D:2/24/1990, Salem, MA Deb:4/16/1964, BOS AL BR/TR 6'3", 185

G	AB	R	H	HR	RBI	OBP	SLG	AVG
876	3221	464	849	166	516	.330	.476	.264

A graduate of nearby Swampscott High School, Tony Conigliaro was a Boston favorite with unlimited potential—the youngest player ever to lead a league in homers and among the youngest to reach 100 homers. "He might have been the guy to break Ruth's and Aaron's records. With his swing, in that ballpark, there's no telling how many he would have hit," mused Jim Palmer.

A single pitch in the fourth inning of an August 18, 1967, game at Fenway Park undid Conigliaro's career. With the game scoreless and two men out, "Tony C." stepped in against Angels righthander Jack Hamilton. Boston, battling for the pennant, was just 3½ games out. Up to that point Conigliaro had 20 homers, 67 RBIs, and a .287 average. Hamilton let loose with his pitch. It smashed into Conigliaro's face.

Conigliaro later wrote in his autobiography, "When the ball was about four feet from my head I knew it was going to hit me. And I knew it was going to hurt." Manager Dick Williams said, "My heart nearly stopped. I raced to the plate and saw a man motionless, with blood rushing from his nose and a left eye already beginning to blacken and swell as we watched. In a few minutes he started flipping his legs around in agony and we could no longer watch."

Several teammates carried the stretcher off the field. Jose Tartabull replaced Conigliaro and the Red Sox won the game. They won the pennant that year too, but without Conigliaro. He spent the rest of the season in the hospital, upset that his teammates didn't visit and unaware that owner Tom Yawkey had asked them to stay away for his own good.

Conigliaro missed the entire 1968 season. When he returned in 1969 he was blind in his left eye, a fact that neither he nor the club made public. It's remarkable that Conigliaro returned at all. That he slammed 20 homers with 82 RBIs and won the AL Comeback Player of the Year Award was all the more incredible, but 1969 paled in comparison to his 36-homer, 116-RBI season in 1970.

That performance verified the potential Boston had seen when it first signed him for a reported $25,000 bonus. Sent to Wellsville in 1963, Conigliaro hit .363 and was both Rookie of the Year and Most Valuable Player of the New York–Penn League, jumping all the way to the big club the following season. In his first Fenway Park appearance he gave long-suffering Boston fans reason for hope by homering off Joel Horlen in his initial at bat.

Despite missing six weeks due to injuries, he hit 24 home runs in 1964, the most by any teenager in major league history. The next year he topped the AL with 32 to become the youngest player ever to capture a home run crown. Only Mel Ott and Eddie Mathews had hit more homers by age 22 than Conigliaro's 102.

Yet his home runs weren't the whole story. Injury-prone, he suffered a broken finger, thumb, wrist, hand, and shoulder blade in addition to his beaning. He also attracted attention by dating Bo Belinsky's old flame, Mamie Van Doren, performing a duet with singer Dionne Warwick, releasing his own solo version of "Little Red Rooster," and appearing on *The Merv Griffin Show*.

After the 1970 season the Red Sox traded Conigliaro to the Angels, where his eye problems intensified. He conferred with management and, at a hastily called press conference, announced his retirement. He tried coming back with the Red Sox in 1975 but was embarrassingly bad, striking out five times in his last game.

Tragedy continued to stalk Conigliaro. In January 1982 he had just auditioned for a Red Sox broadcasting job when he suffered an incapacitating heart attack that left him in need of around-the-clock care. He died in February 1990 at age 45.

In the end, everything came back to that one pitch, and the way Conigliaro wouldn't give an inch to a hurler. Dick Williams said, "He loved to crowd the plate and force a pitcher to give him something good to hit. Hamilton threw the ball where it wouldn't have touched most batters."

Jeff Conine

Conine, Jeffrey Guy **1B–OF**

1990, 1992–* B:6/27/1966, Tacoma, WA Deb:9/16/1990, KC AL BR/TR, 6'1", 220

G	AB	R	H	HR	RBI	OBP	SLG	AVG
987	3395	434	973	119	551	.355	.457	.287

Jeff Conine, a former pitcher at UCLA, was taken in the 58th round of the 1987 free agent draft. Most players drafted that far down the line don't last more than a couple of years as a professional. But three years after the draft Conine made his major league debut with the Kansas City Royals.

Conine became an everyday player after the Florida Marlins selected him in the first round of the 1992 expansion draft. He played all 162 games of his rookie season and batted .292. He went on to become the franchise leader in hits, doubles, RBIs, and average.

Named to the 1995 All-Star team, Conine homered in his first All-Star at bat, helping the National League to a 3–2 victory in Texas. He was named the game's Most Valuable Player. Two years later Conine was a key man on the world champion Florida Marlins. He batted .364 in the Division Series and played in all but one postseason game during Florida's run to the title. But like many of his teammates, Conine did not last long in Miami after the championship was won. He was traded to the Royals in November 1997.

Conine spent most of 1999 with the Baltimore Orioles, who acquired him for a minor league player on April 1. He hit .375 with two homers as a pinch hitter and had three four-hit games, giving him a dozen in his career. Usually used as a first baseman or outfielder, Conine also played a new position—third base—for the first time.

Jocko Conlan

Conlan, John Bertrand **OF**

1934–1935 U(1941–64) B:12/6/1899, Chicago, IL D:4/16/1989, Scottsdale, AZ Deb:7/6/1934, CHI AL BL/TL 5'7", 165

G	AB	R	H	HR	RBI	OBP	SLG	AVG
128	365	55	96	0	31	.327	.334	.263

Jocko Conlan was a National League umpire for 24 years. If a manager came to Jocko with a beef, he was likely to take an earful back to the dugout. Not surprisingly, Conlan had his most volatile relationships with managers who shared his feistiness, men like Leo Durocher and Frankie Frisch. In Conlan's first year as a major league umpire he performed 26 ejections.

One Durocher–Conlan battle has become legendary. Durocher had been out of baseball for five years when the Dodgers hired him as coach in 1961. Leo was back only a week or so when he and Jocko Conlan had a disagreement over a play and Jocko tossed him. Leo thought it would be amusing to kick some dirt on Conlan's clean trousers before he left the field. Jocko tried to return the compliment in kind, but since umpires don't wear spikes his shoe slipped and he kicked Durocher in the shin. Durocher kicked back. Conlan retaliated. Durocher did the same. Since umpires wear shin guards under their trousers as protection against foul balls and also wear toe plates on their shoes, the Dodger manager took a beating. As Durocher described it, "Every time Jocko kicked me, he raised a lump on my shins; every time I kicked him, I bruised my toes. All at once it occurred to me that these were the lousiest odds I'd ever come up against."

Conlan, a utility outfielder with the White Sox, was drafted into umpiring off the Chicago bench during a 1935 game when regular ump Red Ormsby became sick. Already a licensed boxing referee, he took over, and began umpiring in the minors the next year. From 1941 through 1964 he umpired five World Series and six All-Star Games. He was also an arbiter for the 1951, 1959, and 1962 National League playoff series. He was elected to the Hall of Fame in 1974. Conlan was the last NL umpire to use the outside chest protector. The league gave him a grandfather clause when the rest of the umpires switched to the inside version.

A scrappy Irishman whose trademarks were a polka-dot bow tie and a big grin, Conlan personified the best spirit of the game. Responding to Richie Ashburn's bellyaching over a call, he said, "All right. You be the umpire. You call the next pitch." When the pitch came in, Conlan said nothing. Ashburn looked back and said, "Strike?" Conlan rang up the strike, then said, "Richie, you just had the only chance in the world to hit and ump at the same time. And you blew it."

Gene Conley

Conley, Donald Eugene **P**

1952–63 B:11/10/1930, Muskogee, OK
Deb:4/17/1952, BOS NL BR/TR 6'8", 225

W	L	PCT	G	SH	IP	BB	SO	ERA
91	96	.487	276	13	1588²	511	888	3.82

One of the most successful two-sport stars in history, Gene Conley pitched in baseball's All-Star Game and World Series and played on three championship NBA basketball teams. After starring in both sports in high school and at Washington State University, the 6-foot 8-inch Donald Eugene Conley signed with the Boston Braves and was an immediate success in the minors. *The Sporting News* named him Minor League Player of the Year in 1951 when he went 20–9 for Class A Hartford. The Braves tried to rush him into their starting rotation in 1952, but he wasn't ready and returned to the minors after an 0–3 start. That winter he played the last half of the pro basketball season with the Boston Celtics.

After again being named Minor League Player of the Year in 1953, Conley was back with the now-Milwaukee Braves for the 1954 season. He won 14 games and was third in Rookie of the Year balloting behind Wally Moon and Ernie Banks (and ahead of Hank Aaron). That summer he pitched in his first All-Star Game—as the losing pitcher in an 11–9 slugfest.

Off to a good start in 1955, he was again named to the All-Star squad. The game was played in Milwaukee, and Conley delighted the home crowd by striking out the side in the top of the 12th inning. When Stan Musial homered in the bottom half of the inning Conley became the winning pitcher.

Unfortunately, he had strained his arm in spring training and could only pitch with cortisone injections. Conley became less and less effective as a starter and was moved back to middle relief. When Milwaukee won the 1957 World Series he pitched only briefly in relief in Game 3; Conley didn't pitch at all in the 1958 World Series.

Although he hadn't played basketball for five years, Conley returned to the Boston Celtics after the 1958 baseball season. He became one of the team's most effective rebounders and defensive players as the Celts went on to win three straight NBA titles.

In the meantime Conley was traded to the Philadelphia Phillies, where he found that his arm had recovered. He won a dozen games for the Phillies in 1959 and was named to his third All-Star squad. In 1961 he was traded again, this time to the Red Sox.

By 1962 the strain of constant professional sports competition began to tell. Conley had not had an off-season in five years. One day Conley walked away from the Red Sox team bus and disappeared for three days. He was finally discovered at the airport trying to purchase a ticket for Israel. Acutely embarrassed, he returned to the Red Sox and worked harder than ever before. His 241 innings pitched and 15 victories were career highs, but he ruined his arm in the process. After nine games in 1963 Conley's major league baseball career was over, but he played with the New York Knicks in the NBA through 1964.

Tom Connolly

Connolly, Thomas Francis

Umpire (1898–31) B:1870, England D:4/28/1961, Natick, MA Deb:1898 NL

Umpiring in the early part of the 1900s was no job for wimps. Usually, only a single arbiter took the field, made all the calls, and took all the abuse. He was fair game for both teams and fans. American League umpire Tom Connolly believed in the quiet, dignified approach to umpiring, consciously foregoing grandstanding and controversy. He could be tough when necessary, but he was more likely to win his points through fairness and an encyclopedic knowledge of the rules. Over one 10-year span, he did not eject a single player.

Connolly never actually played baseball, but because he was so well-informed on its rules he was often called on to umpire local games in Natick, Massachusetts. New England League President Tim Hurst recommended that Connolly umpire professionally, and Connolly worked in that circuit from 1894 to 1897.

From 1898 to 1900 he worked in the National League but found that the NL president Nicholas E. Young would not enforce his rulings. Believing Ban Johnson's promises of better support for umpires, he went over to the new American League in 1901. Connolly umpired the first AL game in Chicago on April 24, 1901. (All the other scheduled contests had been rained out.) He also worked the first World Series in 1903.

The English-born umpire officiated in the AL from 1901 until June 1931, when he was appointed the league's umpire-in-chief by

William Harridge. He held that position until January 1954.

He was elected to the Hall of Fame in 1953. Connolly and Bill Klem were the first two umpires to be enshrined.

Roger Connor

Connor, Roger **1B–3B**
1880–97 M(1896, 8–37) B:7/1/1857, Waterbury, CT
D:1/4/1931, Waterbury, CT Deb:5/1/1880, TRO NL
BL/TL 6'3", 220

G	AB	R	H	HR	RBI	OBP	SLG	AVG
1997	7794	1620	2467	138	1322	.397	.486	.317

Roger Connor was the most prolific home run hitter of the 19th century, and his 138 career long balls stood as the major league record until that mark was eclipsed by Babe Ruth. Oddly, he only once led his league in homers which may explain in part why he was not named to the Hall of Fame until 1976, 45 years after his death.

Born in 1857 to Irish immigrants in Waterbury, Connecticut, Connor began his professional career in 1876 with the Waterbury Monitors of the Eastern League. At 6 feet 3 inches and 220 pounds, he was a giant for his time and required an oversize uniform. Although he threw left-handed, Connor played third base for Waterbury. He switched to first base, a more appropriate position for a man his size, only after he hurt his arm in 1881.

In 1878 and 1879 Connor played for the Holyoke, Massachusetts, team of the Eastern League. His hitting so impressed Bob Ferguson, the manager at rival Springfield, that in 1880 when Ferguson was named manager of the National League's Troy Trojans, he signed Connor. Ferguson brought in 16 additional new players, including pitchers Tim Keefe and Mickey Welch and catcher Buck Ewing. Those three, along with Connor, were eventually enshrined in the Hall of Fame.

Connor committed 60 errors in only 83 games during his rookie year at third, but he batted .332 and helped Troy leap from last to fourth place. Connor's fielding improved markedly, however, after he shifted to first base. Although he was limited in range, he presented infielders with a big target. He also had sure hands and was particularly adept at digging low throws out of the dirt. He eventually led the league's first basemen in fielding average four times.

On September 10, 1881, Connor blasted the first major league grand slam. In 1882 he began to show consistent longball power, hitting four home runs and leading the NL with 18 triples. When Troy was expelled from the league that year, manufacturer John B. Day purchased the players, including Welch, Ewing, and Connor for his New York National League franchise. A few other players, including Keefe, were added to the Metropolitans, an American Association team in New York, also owned by Day.

Connor received a new contract for $1,800 with bonuses that increased his take to $2,100, one of the best salaries in the league. In his first season in New York, he earned the money by hitting .357, including one monstrous home run that so impressed the crowd they took up a collection and bought him a $500 gold watch. The big first baseman was one of the Gothams' most popular players; the fans referred to him as "Dear Old Roger."

Despite the presence of three future Hall of Famers in the Gothams' lineup, New York finished only fifth in the league in 1884. Connor played second base, outfield, and third base that season because manager Jim Price had installed rookie Alex McKinnon at first base. Connor committed 96 errors and moved back to first base the following year.

Day realized that there was more prestige and money available in the National League, so he shifted some of the Metropolitans' best players, including Keefe, plus manager Jim Mutrie, to the Gothams. The team's roster included an unusual number of tall players, Connor among them, and Mutrie referred to them as "my giants." The name stuck and eventually became the official team name.

The 1885 New York Giants battled Chicago down to the final days of the season before finishing two games behind. Connor led the National League with 169 hits, a batting average of .371, and an on-base average of .435. In 1886 he paced the league in triples for the second time with 20 and batted .355. In 1887 he smacked 17 home runs. Chicago's Ned Williamson had set the major league home run record with 27 a few years before, but he had played in a tiny ballpark with 180-foot foul lines. Four of Williamson's teammates had also topped 20 homers that year. Apart from that single season, no other NL player had smacked more than 14 home runs before 1887. But Connor missed out on the 1887 crown because Billy O'Brien of Washington hit 19. Connor also finished second in RBIs, with 104.

The Giants won their first pennant in 1888. Connor contributed 14 home runs, three of them in a May 9 game at Indianapolis. At season's end, the Giants defeated the AA champion, St. Louis, in a 10-game "World Series."

New York won the pennant again in 1889 after a close race with Boston. Connor slammed 13 home runs and led the league with 130 RBIs.

The Giants took on the AA's Brooklyn club in the Series. Down three victories to one, the Giants rallied to win the next five games to secure their second consecutive world championship. Connor hit .343 and drove in 12 runs in the Series. That hard-fought playoff marked the beginning of the Giants-Dodgers rivalry that lives to this day.

Brooklyn left the American Association in 1890 to join the National League. Then known as the Bridegrooms, they won a tainted pennant in 1890, when most stars deserted to the Players' League. The Giants were hit particularly hard and fell to sixth place. Deeply involved in the Brotherhood of Professional Base Ball Players, which sponsored the new league, Connor led the Players' League with 14 homers, his only home run crown, and hit .349 with 103 RBIs.

The Players' League folded after one season. Connor returned to the Giants, who moved into the Players' League park, calling it the Polo Grounds, after their former home. It remained their home park for 67 years. Connor, however, was dealt to Philadelphia in 1892. He returned to the Giants the next year and had his final 100-RBI season. Early in 1894 he was sent to St. Louis, where he completed his major league career in 1897. On June 1, 1895, he went 6-for-6 against his old New York team, with two doubles and a triple.

Chuck Connors

Connors, Kevin Joseph Aloysius **1B**

1949–51 B:4/10/1921, Brooklyn, NY D:11/10/1992, Los Angeles, CA Deb:5/1/1949, BRO NL BL/TL 6'5", 190

G	AB	R	H	HR	RBI	OBP	SLG	AVG
67	202	16	48	2	18	.280	.302	.238

First baseman Chuck Connors never achieved his major league ambitions, but after being sent down to the Pacific Coast League's Hollywood Stars he literally became a Hollywood star, most prominently in the 1950s television western *The Rifleman*.

Connors, who also played in the National Basketball Association with the Boston Celtics, was a contentious member of the Dodgers organization, always battling with Brooklyn management over his salary. Once Chuck wrote—in red ink—to Dodger executive Buzzy Bavasi: "You want my blood, please send contract with more money as you can see I am running out of bl . . . ."

His problem wasn't with Bavasi, however, but with Bavasi's boss, Branch Rickey. Connors observed, "It was easy to figure out Mr. Rickey's thinking about contracts. He had players and money and just didn't like to see the two of them mix."

After only one at bat as a Dodger Connors was traded to the Cubs. He retired as a ballplayer when he became a bit player in the 1952 film *Pat and Mike*. After *The Rifleman* he starred in another TV series, *Branded*, and also had a featured role in the groundbreaking miniseries *Roots*.

Wid Conroy

Conroy, William Edward **3B-OF-SS**

1901–11 B:4/5/1877, Camden, NJ D:12/6/1959, Mt. Holly, NJ Deb:4/25/1901, MIL AL BR/TR 5'9", 158

G	AB	R	H	HR	RBI	OBP	SLG	AVG
1374	5061	605	1257	22	452	.301	.329	.248

Bill Conroy was called "Wid"—short for Widow—because of his "motherly" concern for younger ballplayers in the sandlot leagues. The compassionate infielder enjoyed an 11-year career as a shortstop and third baseman with the Milwaukee Brewers (American League precursor to the St. Louis Browns), Pittsburgh Pirates, New York Highlanders, and Washington Senators. He owed it to his glove.

He started out as a shortstop, replacing Honus Wagner with the Paterson, New Jersey, team in the Atlantic League, but caught malaria and was forced to miss the season. In 1900 Connie Mack invited Conroy to try out for his Milwaukee team that would transfer to Philadelphia when the American League was born. Conroy earned the final spot on the roster.

He played for the National League champion 1902 Pirates as their shortstop, but became a third baseman in 1903 for the Highlanders, the team later renamed the "Yankees." Conroy twice led AL third basemen in total chances per game. He played until 1911, ending his career with the Senators. After his retirement, Conroy became a coach with the Phillies.

Duff Cooley

Cooley, Duff Gordon **OF-1B**

1893–1905 B:3/29/1873, Leavenworth, KS D:8/9/1937, Dallas, TX Deb:7/27/1893, STL NL BL/TR 5'11", 158

G	AB	R	H	HR	RBI	OBP	SLG	AVG
1316	5364	847	1576	26	557	.341	.380	.294

Duff Cooley was a versatile player as well as an accomplished slap hitter—1,268 of his 1,576 hits were singles. Cooley, a .294 career hitter while playing for five different teams, was an outfielder who also filled in at all four infield positions, in addition to catching 11 games. A good baserunner, he was credited with 224 stolen bases in his 13-year career.

Like Rumplestiltskin, the most interesting part of Cooley is his name. Contrary to what just about everyone thinks when they first see it, "Duff" is no nickname. Cooley's actual nickname was "Sir Richard," perhaps for an aristocratic manner, but nobody knows for sure. Sometime it was shortened to "Dick" which is head and shoulders above shortening Duff to "Duh." After his retirement, he owned minor league clubs in Topeka and Salt Lake City.

Jack Coombs

Coombs, John Wesley **P**

1906–20 M(1919, 18–44) B:11/18/1882, Le Grand, IA D:4/15/1957, Palestine, TX Deb:7/5/1906, PHI AL BB/TR 6', 185

W	L	PCT	G	SH	IP	BB	SO	ERA
158	110	.590	354	35	2320	841	1052	2.78

On September 24, 1906, two rookie pitchers facing each other delivered complete games—of 24 innings. Jack Coombs of the Philadelphia Athletics defeated Joe Harris and the Boston Americans, 4–1. The young pitchers paths diverged afterwards—Harris ended the season with a 2–21 record and was soon out of the game with a career record of 3–30; Coombs pitched for 14 years in the majors with a 158–110 record and won three games in the 1910 World Series.

Born in Iowa in 1882, Coombs moved to Maine with his family and attended Colby College, where he pitched and batted the school baseball team to the New England championship. Connie Mack signed the righthander for $2,400 and got plenty of value out of "Colby Jack" by occasionally using him in the outfield.

If the Cy Young Award had existed in 1910, Coombs would have won it, hands down. He won 31 games and also topped the league with 13 shutouts to lead the A's to a pennant. If anything, Coombs was even better in that year's World Series, winning all three games he pitched against the Chicago Cubs and batting .385.

Less than two years after a 28-win season in 1911, Colby Jack's career seemed over in 1913 when he was stricken with typhoid during spring training. The disease settled in his spine and nearly killed him. He missed virtually all of the following two seasons before making a comeback with Brooklyn in 1915. During the next two seasons he went 28–18 for Brooklyn and ended his career with the Detroit Tigers in 1920.

Coombs went on to coach baseball at Williams College, Princeton, and Duke University. He also conducted a traveling baseball clinic and wrote a highly regarded instructional book on baseball.

Johnny Cooney

Cooney, John Walter **OF-1B**

1921–30, 1935–44 M(1949, 18–44) B:3/18/1901, Cranston, RI D:7/8/1986, Sarasota, FL Deb:4/19/1921, BOS NL BR/TL 5'10", 165

W	L	PCT	G	SH	IP	BB	SO	ERA
34	44	.436	159	7	795^1	223	224	3.72

G	AB	R	H	HR	RBI	OBP	SLG	AVG
1172	3372	408	965	2	219	.329	.342	.286

After his left arm went dead when he was only 24, pitcher Johnny Cooney refashioned himself into an outfielder and returned to the majors for a long run. The son and brother of major league shortstops—his father, James Joseph, played in the 1890s, and his brother, James Edward, played in the 1920s—Cooney signed with the Boston Braves in 1921 for a $500 bonus and $400 a month. By 1925 he was in the Braves rotation in 1925 with a 14–14 record. Then his arm went dead.

He had an operation that left his pitching arm three inches shorter than his right arm. He tried to come back but could only manage 59 games over the next five years. He had always been a good hitter, so starting in 1930 he converted to the outfield. He spent almost all of the next six seasons in the minors, largely with Indianapolis of the American Association. And after he hit .371 with 224 hits in 1935 he got his chance the majors again.

Casey Stengel brought him up to the Brooklyn Dodgers and he hit .282 in 1936 at the age of 35 and .293 in 1937. He was traded to Cardinals after the 1937 season in the deal that sent Leo Durocher to Brooklyn, but he was released before the season started. No matter. Stengel was managing the Braves by then and he installed Cooney as a semiregular for the next four years. He hit .318 in 1940 and .319 in 1941 and after that season he was *The Sporting News* Veteran of the Year, chosen in a vote of fans.

His playing time soon dwindled and he finished up with the Yankees in 1944. He had a .286 lifetime batting average and all of two homers in 3,372 at bats. They came on consecutive days: September 24 and 25, 1939.

Cooney became a Braves coach in 1946 and was the interim manager for the last 45 games of 1949. He also umpired once, when the boat carrying the regular umpires from New York to Boston failed to arrive in time.

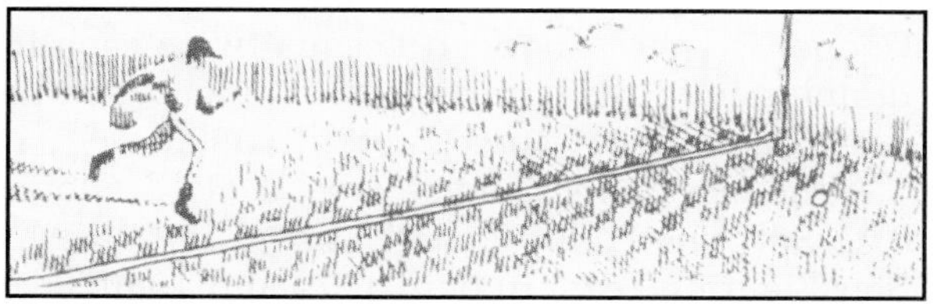

Cecil Cooper

Cooper, Cecil Celester **1B–DH**
1971–87 B:12/20/1949, Brenham, TX Deb:9/8/1971, BOS AL BL/TL 6'2", 190

G	AB	R	H	HR	RBI	OBP	SLG	AVG
1896	7349	1012	2192	241	1125	.340	.466	.298

In 1982 first baseman Cecil Cooper delivered the biggest hit in Brewers history—a two-run single that gave Milwaukee a 4–3 victory in the deciding game of the American League Championship Series against the Angels, putting the Brewers in their first World Series. Despite that moment of glory, he remains one of the most under-appreciated players of his era.

Manager Buck Rodgers offered this analysis of Cooper: "People don't notice him because he's so steady. He really doesn't have many highs or lows. He just goes out day after day and does the same thing." The same thing, in Cooper's case, included chalking up 200 or more hits three times and eight full seasons of hitting .300 or better.

In 1970 he led the Midwest League with a .336 average and was named Player of the Year, but then he bounced between Boston and its farm clubs from 1971 through 1973. Even when up to stay in 1974 Cooper was not perceived as a player destined to be a regular in the Red Sox lineup. Boston wanted more of a power hitter at first base and needed a position for slowing Red Sox legend Carl Yastrzemski.

Additionally, Cooper still had flaws in his swing and his attitude. "I saw him at Boston when he first came up. He was a wild swinger, not disciplined at all," Rodgers said.

Moreover, Cooper chafed at being a spare part. "Yaz was playing first base. I think he struck out. He came back and threw the bat and hurt his hand. Naturally, they came over and asked me to go into the game. I don't know, I'd been upset for a few days about not playing. At the time, I didn't know what to do and I just said, 'No,'" Cooper explained.

After going 1-for-19 in the 1975 World Series, Cooper was sent to Milwaukee for George "Boomer" Scott and Bernie Carbo. Cooper thrived in a Midwestern environment and became an integral part of "Harvey's Wallbangers," manager Harvey Kuenn's group of heavy hitters that included Cooper, Robin Yount, Paul Molitor, and Gorman Thomas. Cooper led the American League twice each in doubles and RBIs but never in batting. When he hit .352 in 1980, George Brett hit .390.

Although Cooper never won a Gold Glove, *The Sporting News* named him to its AL All-Star Fielding Team in both 1979 and 1980.

Mort Cooper

Cooper, Morton Cecil **P**
1938–49 B:3/2/1913, Atherton, MO D:11/17/1958, Little Rock, AR Deb:9/14/1938, STL NL BR/TR 6'2", 210

W	L	PCT	G	SH	IP	BB	SO	ERA
128	75	.631	295	33	1840[2]	571	913	2.97

For three brief years during World War II Mort Cooper was the best righthander in the National League. Before arm problems got the better of him, he helped the Cardinals win three pennants while garnering a host of honors for himself.

In 1939 he was one of the top rookies in the National League—12–6 as both a starter and reliever. Cooper continued pitching effectively during the next two years, although his record was a middling 24–21. In 1941, when the Cardinals fought Brooklyn down to the wire for the pennant, his brother Walker, a catcher, joined him on the club.

During the next three seasons the Coopers became one of the outstanding sibling batteries in baseball history. Had they stayed healthy, St. Louis might well have edged out the Dodgers in 1941. As it turned out, Walker Cooper played in only 68 games due to a broken collarbone, Mort Cooper lost six weeks because of elbow surgery, and the Cards narrowly lost to the Dodgers.

The next year he won a league-leading 22 games in 29 decisions as the Cardinals seized the pennant. Cooper started in the All-Star Game (but lost), led the league with 10 shutouts and a 1.78 earned run average, and at season's end won league Most Valuable Player honors. He lost the opening game of the World Series against the Yankees, but the Cards won the next four games to become world champions.

The 1943 season was almost a carbon copy of 1942. Cooper led the league in victories with 21 and started the All-Star Game (he lost again). St. Louis won the pennant a second time and once more faced the Yankees in the Series. Cooper won Game 2, 4–3, pitching a six-hitter. In the do-or-die fifth game he allowed only five hits in seven innings, but New York's Bill Dickey hammered a two-run homer in the sixth inning, which was all Yankee Spud Chandler needed to win, 2–0.

In 1944 Cooper had his third terrific season in a row—22–7 with a league-leading seven shutouts—as the Cardinals took their third pennant in three years. Cooper lost the World Series opener against the St. Louis Browns, a 2–1 heartbreaker, despite giving up only two hits; unfortunately, the hits came back-to-back in the fourth inning, a single followed by George McQuinn's home run. With the Series tied at two games apiece, Cooper pitched Game 5 and scattered seven hits to win, 2–0. A day later the Cardinals won again to take the championship.

In 1945 both Coopers held out for more money. After finally re-signing, a disgruntled Mort Cooper won his first two decisions for St. Louis, then was suspended for leaving the team in a further dispute over money. In May the Cards abruptly traded him to the Boston Braves for journeyman righthander Charles "Red" Barrett and $60,000.

Although Barrett surprised everyone by winning 21 games for St. Louis, Cooper was a disappointment in Boston. He had pitched with bone chips in his elbow for years, saying, "When my arm feels free of pain, I rarely win; when it hurts like a toothache with every pitch, I do okay." Nevertheless, he often took aspirin tablets while pitching to ease the pain. In Boston the pain became worse, and after winning seven games he submitted to a second elbow operation. In 1946 he came back to go 13–11 and make the All-Star squad for the third time.

Walker Cooper

Cooper, William Walker **C**

1940–57 B:1/8/1915, Atherton, MO D: 4/11/1991, Scottsdale, AZ Deb:9/25/1940, STL NL BR/TR
6'3", 210

G	AB	R	H	HR	RBI	OBP	SLG	AVG
1473	4702	573	1341	173	812	.332	.464	.285

In his heyday Walker Cooper was regarded as the strongest man in baseball and the game's best catcher. Standing 6 feet 3 inches and weighing 210 pounds, he intimidated any base runner foolhardy enough to risk colliding with him at the plate. His arm was among the strongest and most accurate in the league, and his bat was a powerful instrument of destruction he could hit for power as well as for high average.

Had he started with any team except the St. Louis Cardinals, Cooper might have reached the majors several years earlier. But the Cardinals of the late 1930s had developed baseball's largest and best farm system, and many superior players bided their time while other good prospects got their chances. Before he received a September call-up to St. Louis in 1940, Walker was 25 years old and had completed back-to-back .300 seasons in the high minors.

Cooper reportedly complained to veteran umpire John "Beans" Reardon about the first pitch thrown to him in the majors. "Turn around, busher," Reardon ordered. "You haven't been here long enough to get a cup of coffee."

Undaunted, Walker shot back, "If this is a sample of your work, you've been here too long."

As part of one of baseball's best sibling batteries with his older brother, Cardinals pitcher Mort Cooper, William Walker Cooper came into his own in 1942, hitting .281 and appearing in 125 games. He was named to the National League All-Star squad, an honor he would receive each year through 1950 (except in 1945, when no All-Star game was played). Cooper ended the season by clinching the Cards' victory over the Yankees in the World Series, picking Joe Gordon off second base to extinguish a ninth-inning Yankee threat in the deciding game.

"Walk" Cooper finished second to teammate Stan Musial in 1943's Most Valuable Player voting on the strength of his .318 batting average and 81 RBIs. The Cardinals won the pennant again, but this time lost to the Yankees in the World Series. In 1944, with Cooper hitting .317, the Redbirds took their third straight flag, then beat the Browns in the only all–St. Louis World Series. In the 16 World Series games he played from 1942 through 1944, Cooper averaged .300 and collected six RBIs.

Cooper was in the Navy for all but four games in 1945, and while he was in the service the Giants paid $175,000 for his contract. He returned in 1946 and in 1947 had his best season with the New Yorkers, batting .305 with 122 RBIs. Despite his strength, Cooper was not known as a home run hitter, but in 1947 he smashed 35 homers (15 more than he would collect in any other season) as the Giants set a major league club record with 221 round-trippers.

In 1948 Leo Durocher became the Giants manager and began rebuilding the club to put more speed into the lineup. Slow power hitters were jettisoned, and Cooper went to Cincinnati in June 1949. He rewarded his new employers on July 6 by driving in 10 runs in a single game. The trade to the Reds began an odyssey that saw him play for six teams in nine years: from the Reds he went to the Braves, Pirates, and Cubs, and finally back to St. Louis.

As Cooper approached 40 and became too old and beefy to take a regular turn behind the plate, he was still valuable as a backup and pinch hitter. However, when his daughter Sara married Cardinals second baseman Don Blasingame, Cooper quipped, "It's time to quit when you've got a daughter old enough to marry a teammate."

Wilbur Cooper

Cooper, Arley Wilbur **P**

1912–26 B:2/24/1892, Bearsville, WV D:8/7/1973, Encino, CA Deb:8/29/1912, PIT NL BR/TL 5'11" 175

W	L	PCT	G	SH	IP	BB	SO	ERA
216	178	.548	517	35	3480	853	1252	2.89

Wilbur Cooper used a devastating sinkerball to earn a club-record 202 wins with the Pittsburgh Pirates. He won 20 games four times, and had 19 victories on two other occasions. He arrived in Pittsburgh late in the 1912 season, going 3–0 with a sparkling 1.66 ERA in 38 innings, and remained a Pirate for 12 more seasons.

Cooper won at least 17 games each season from 1917 to 1924. He led the National League in wins and innings pitched in 1921. Cooper usually finished what he started. He led the National League in complete games in 1919 and 1922. He tossed a club-record 263 complete games as a Pirate.

Cooper also fielded his position exceptionally well. He was especially skillful at picking runners off third base. He had seven pickoffs in 1924. His partner in crime, Pie Traynor, would dive towards third base as Cooper whipped a sidearm throw. Another advantage Cooper enjoyed was his ability to work fast, not allowing batters to settle in too comfortably at the plate. Catcher Walter Schmidt was Cooper's batterymate during most of the lefty's career. Schmidt knew Cooper so well that they wasted little time on signals, which also helped Cooper work swiftly.

The native of Bearsville, West Virginia, was no easy out at the plate, either. He owned a .239 career batting average. In 1922 Cooper slugged four home runs while winning 23 games, and in 1924 he batted .346 while winning 20. Cooper left Pittsburgh after the 1924 season. He won 12 games for the Chicago Cubs in 1925. His last major league appearance came in 1926 with the Detroit Tigers.

Larry Corcoran

Corcoran, Lawrence J. **P–OF**

1880–1887 B:8/10/1859, Brooklyn, NY D:10/14/1891, Newark, NJ Deb:5/1/1880, CHI NL BL/TR

W	L	PCT	G	SH	IP	BB	SO	ERA
177	89	.665	277	22	2392^{1}	496	1103	2.36

In the words of one historian, Larry Corcoran "possessed all the attributes of greatness except durability." For five years—1880 to 1884—he was supreme in the art of pitching, with his many outstanding feats including three no-hitters. And then, suddenly, his glory vanished.

Corcoran had begun pitching for semipro clubs in his native Brooklyn in 1877 before joining Buffalo's first professional team. In 1880 the diminutive righthander joined the National League's Chicago White Stockings. Corcoran's fastball and Fred Goldsmith's slow curves gave pennant-winning Chicago the league's most effective one-two pitching punch.

Corcoran's 43–14 season mark is the third-highest win total for a rookie pitcher. Only Al Spalding, with 47, and George Bradley, with 45, two veterans of the National Association enjoying their "rookie" seasons in the National League's initial year, ever exceeded Corcoran's first-year win total. He led the league in strikeouts with 268 and posted a 1.95 ERA in 536 innings. At one point he ran off 13 consecutive wins, and on Aug. 19 no-hit Boston, 6–0.

Corcoran's only flaw was a tendency to tire in the late innings, hardly surprising considering he weighed just 120 pounds. Chicago manager Cap Anson grumbled that he had "the endurance of an Indian pony." Nevertheless, on days that he wasn't pitching, Corcoran often played shortstop or in the outfield because of his excellent fielding.

He "slumped" to a 31–14 record in 1881 but tied for the league leadership in wins, and Chicago again won the pennant. In 1882 Corcoran led the NL in winning percentage with his 27–12 record; his 1.95 ERA also topped the league. On September 20 he became the first National League pitcher to throw two no-hitters as he downed Worcester, 5–0. Although Chicago failed to win a fourth straight pennant in 1883, Corcoran turned in a strong 34–20 season.

He and catcher Silver Flint are sometimes credited with developing the first set of pitching signs. Corcoran always had a huge chaw of tobacco in his cheek. Flint (or possibly Michael "King" Kelly) suggested he park his chaw on one side for a fastball and the other side for a curve to let the catcher know which pitch was coming.

The outlaw Union Association, formed in 1884, courted most of the NL's stars with offers of higher salaries, and many players jumped to the new league. Corcoran was willing, but threats of blacklisting finally convinced him to re-sign with the White Stockings for $2,100, considerably less than he could have earned with the Unions.

Facing Buffalo in early June with a sore finger on his pitching hand, Corcoran attempted to ease the pain by pitching at times with his left arm. After four poor innings, he was moved to shortstop. Yet 11 days later, on June 27, he pitched his third no-hitter, besting Providence, 6–0. For the fourth time he topped the 30-victory plateau with a 35–23 mark, and for the second time he surpassed 500 innings pitched with 516.

In five seasons Corcoran had won 170 games and lost only 83. He began 1885 by winning five of seven decisions, but he strained his shoulder so badly he was unable to pitch. When the condition persisted, Chicago released him. By July he sufficiently recovered to sign with New York but pitched only three games, winning two. In early October he sprained his ankle in what turned out to be his final major league victory.

Over the next few seasons Corcoran appeared in four major league games and also pitched in the minors, but his arm was gone for good. He turned to umpiring in 1890 and died of Bright's disease a year later.

Tommy Corcoran

Corcoran, Thomas William **SS-2B**

1890–1907 U(1915) B:1/4/1869, New Haven, CT D:6/25/1960, Plainfield, CT Deb:4/19/1890, PIT PL BR/TR 5'9", 164

G	AB	R	H	HR	RBI	OBP	SLG	AVG
2200	8804	1184	2252	34	1135	.289	.335	.256

At a Baker Bowl doubleheader on September 17, 1900, it was Cincinnati Reds shortstop Tommy Corcoran who literally uncovered one of baseball's most blatant attempts at sign stealing. While coaching third for the Reds, Corcoran came upon a buried wire leading from the coaching box to the Phillies clubhouse in center field. In the clubhouse Philadelphia catcher Morgan Murphy (aided by binoculars) was stealing opposing catchers' signs and relaying them to utility player Pearce Chiles who was coaching for the Phils at third. Corcoran, the Reds captain, uncovered a small wooden box that delivered electric signals to Chiles' feet. Chiles would then verbally cue Phillies batters to what sort of pitch was coming. The Phillies groundskeeper rushed out in a futile effort to keep Corcoran from discovering the dirty little secret, but the truth was out.

Corcoran started as a barehanded shortstop but eventually converted to the use of a glove. In 1890 "Corky" began his major league career with the Players' League and was in the Pittsburgh club's Opening Day lineup. After that circuit's collapse, he joined the A's of the American Association. The next year he was with Brooklyn of the National League. A trade sent him to Cincinnati in 1897.

A better fielder than hitter, Corcoran set a major league record with the Reds on August 7, 1903 with 14 assists in a nine-inning game. Four times he led the league in fielding percentage, twice in assists and errors, and once each in games played at that position and in putouts. At shortstop he is among the major league career leaders for games played and total chances accepted per game at short.

After the 1906 season he went to the New York Giants where he shifted to second base. Manager John McGraw deemed him a liability and then paid a record $4,500 to Springfield of the 3-I League for Corcoran's replacement, Larry Doyle. Corcoran later umpired in several circuits, including the Federal League.

Pop Corkhill

Corkhill, John Stewart **OF**

1883–92 B:4/11/1858, Parkesburg, PA D:4/4/1921, Pennsauken, NJ Deb:5/1/1883, CIN AA BL/TR 5'10", 180

G	AB	R	H	HR	RBI	OBP	SLG	AVG
1086	4404	650	1120	31	631	.288	.337	.254

Nineteenth-century outfielder John "Pop" Corkhill compensated for a relatively weak bat with speed and defense. He joined the Cincinnati Reds in 1883, the team's second season in the American Association. At a time when most players still fielded barehanded, Corkhill was adept at catching flyballs and in cutting off hits. He led league outfielders in fielding average in 1883 (his rookie year), 1884, 1887, and 1889 while accumulating an impressive number of putouts and assists. In 1885 he led the league with 35 assists. The Reds occasionally employed him as a pitcher

Stockily built, Corkhill threw righthanded and batted lefthanded. Although he hit only .216 as a rookie, he hit as high as .311 in 1887. That year, bases on balls were counted as hits. Under those rules, Corkhill, who seldom walked, was actually credited with a .328 batting average, which was not that great among the swollen marks of the year. Late in 1888 the Reds decided he was slowing down and traded him to Brooklyn. Although he batted only .250, he helped his new club win the 1889 American Association pennant with a league-leading .949 fielding average.

Clint Courtney

Courtney, Clinton Dawson **C**

1951–61 B:3/16/1927, Hall Summit, LA D:6/16/1975, Rochester, NY Deb:9/29/1951, NY AL BL/TR 5'8", 180

G	AB	R	H	HR	RBI	OBP	SLG	AVG
946	2796	260	750	38	313	.341	.366	.268

"Scrap Iron" Courtney lived up to his nickname as a battler in every sense of the word. Satchel Paige, his teammate on the St. Louis Browns, once said, "He's the meanest man I ever met. I'm glad he's on my side."

The belligerent catcher earned his nickname in 1952 as a Browns rookie. Sportswriter Milton Richman had been needling Browns players about their lack of speed, so he and Courtney met in an impromptu train station foot race to decide the issue. Courtney not only lost but also crashed into a baggage car, ripping his clothes and sustaining numerous bruises. St. Louis manager Rogers Hornsby made him catch nine innings the next day, but Courtney never complained.

The first catcher to wear glasses, Courtney was named *The Sporting News* American League Rookie of the Year in 1952. But in 1953 it was his brawling that established his name in baseball history after his famous scrape against the Yankees. First Courtney duked it out with Billy Martin, Phil Rizzuto, and Allie Reynolds over a close play at second. A 15-minute bench-clearing melee followed. The Yankees left their dugout armed with Louisville Sluggers, but the police had to protect them from the Sportsman's Park crowd. Courtney was fined a then-AL record $850, Martin $150, and five other Yanks $100 each.

Courtney battled at everything—foot races, fisticuffs, Ping-Pong, cards—and lost at nearly everything, but he never stopped competing. Since he bet wildly at cards but hardly ever won, teammate Cookie Lavagetto put a nickel limit on games to protect Courtney from himself.

"Clint had total confidence in his ability to do anything," Whitey Herzog recalled. "You had to like him because he came to play. He wasn't quite as good as he thought he was, but you couldn't tell him. He always came back for more."

Harry Coveleski

Coveleski, Harry Frank **P**

1907–18 B:4/23/1886, Shamokin, PA D:8/4/1950, Shamokin, PA Deb:9/10/1907, PHI NL BB/TL 6', 180

W	L	PCT	G	SH	IP	BB	SO	ERA
81	55	.596	198	13	1248	376	511	2.39

Harry Coveleski was one of four brothers who came out of the coal fields of Pennsylvania to play professional baseball. Born as Harry Frank Kowalewski, he was less famous than younger brother and Hall of Famer Stan Coveleski; Harry nonetheless had his moments, particularly against the New York Giants.

In 1908 Coveleski took a 1–1 record to the mound against the Giants in the second game of a doubleheader at the Polo Grounds on September 29. New York was locked in a three-way pennant race with the Cubs and Pirates, which had been compounded by the famous tie with Chicago that occurred when Fred Merkle failed to touch second base, costing New York a crucial win. The Giants hoped to use the Phillies as a springboard to the pennant.

Christy Mathewson won the opening game for New York, but young Coveleski frustrated the Giants in the nightcap, defeating James "Doc" Crandall with a six-hit shutout. Two days later the clubs traveled to Philadelphia for another doubleheader. Again Mathewson won the first game, and again Coveleski befuddled the New Yorkers in the second game, this time with a four-hit, 6–2 victory over George "Hooks" Wiltse.

The Giants won the next day, but the day after that Coveleski returned to the mound for his third appearance in five days; this time opposed by the great Mathewson. The Big Six made no difference, however; Coveleski pitched a six-hit, 3–2 victory and became known as "the Giant Killer." His performance earned him a $50 bonus from Phillies manager Billy Murray. When the Giants lost the playoff game to make up the earlier tie, fans blamed Fred Merkle for losing the pennant, but Coveleski was far more responsible.

Unfortunately, Coveleski lost his ability to beat the Giants or anyone else the next season due to a sore arm. Dealt to Cincinnati in 1910 and then sent to the minors, he recovered, going 28–9 for Chattanooga, and the Detroit Tigers purchased his contract.

For three years he was a sensation, winning 22, 22, and 21 games for the Tigers while pitching more than 300 innings each season. Then, suddenly, his arm went out again, and this time it did not improve.

Stan Coveleski

Coveleski, Stanley Anthony **P**

1912, 1916–1928 B:7/13/1889, Shamokin, PA D:3/20/1984, South Bend, IN Deb:9/10/1912, PHI AL BR/TR 5'11", 166

W	L	PCT	G	SH	IP	BB	SO	ERA
215	142	.602	450	38	3082	802	981	2.89

Most players start at the bottom and work their way up. Stan Coveleski came further; he started from the bottom of a mine. A Pennsylvania coal miner at age 12, Coveleski, born Stanislaus Kowalewski, escaped from the mines to become a Hall of Fame pitcher with legendary control. In the 1920 World Series, he pitched three brilliant complete-game victories.

Stan came from a family of ballplayers. All his brothers played, and older brother Harry was a three-time 20-game winner who in 1908 helped derail John McGraw's pennant hopes by defeating the Giants three times in the last week of the season.

Harry and Stanley Coveleski never faced each other in the majors—and only once during their professional careers. "I was with Lancaster of the Tri-State League and Harry was already in the majors," said Stan Coveleski. "We faced each other in an exhibition game and when neither team scored in five innings our managers took us out. Harry refused to pitch against me in the majors. He told the Detroit manager never to use him when I was pitching. He explained to me, 'Win or lose, it would take something away from us. If I lose, they'll say I was laying down on purpose so you could win. If I win, they'll say you were laying down.'"

As a youngster, Stanley didn't play much baseball. He worked 12-hour days in the anthracite mines. "There was nothing strange in those days," Coveleski said, "about a 12-year-old Polish kid in the mines for 72 hours a week at a nickel an hour. What was strange was that I ever got out."

About the only form of recreation left open to Coveleski was throwing stones at tin cans. He would tie cans to tree limbs and just fire away until dark. After a few years of this he "could hit one of those things blindfolded," he said.

The local semipro team, Shamokin of the independent Atlantic League, heard about his talent and offered him a tryout. Before long he was signed to a contract with Lancaster of the Class B Tri-State League. The Philadelphia Athletics eventually gave Coveleski a trial in 1912. In his major league debut, he pitched a three-hitter but was not good enough to crack Connie Mack's ace staff.

Back in the minors, he picked up a new weapon—the spitball. He saw another pitcher working on the pitch and thought he too would experiment with it. Said Coveleski: "I started working on the spitter, and before long I had that thing down pat. Had never thrown it before in my life. But before that season was over it was my main pitch.... I got so I had as good control over the spitter as I did over my other pitches. I could make it break any of three ways: down, out, or down and out."

The pitch took Coveleski back to the majors, and he became a consistent winner for Cleveland. From 1918 to 1921 he won at least 22 games a year. In 1920 he walked an average of less than two batters per nine innings. In one game he went the first seven innings without throwing a single ball.

That 1920 season was Coveleski's best—24–14 for the world champion Indians, with an AL-best 133 strikeouts. In the World Series against Brooklyn, he tossed five-hit complete game victories in Games 1, 4, and 7. The last game was a 3–0 shutout, and he finished the Series with a remarkable 0.67 ERA. "I figured it was my job and I done it and that's all," said the man often referred to as the "Silent Pole."

Yet, on a personal level, 1920 was a year of tragedy for Coveleski. He lost teammate Ray Chapman, who was killed by a Carl Mays pitch. In May 1920 Coveleski's wife, who had been ill for three years, died unexpectedly back in Shamokin.

In 1921 Coveleski won 23 games, in 1922 he was 17–14, and in 1923 he led the AL with a 2.76 ERA. Traded to the Washington Senators in December 1924, Covaleski pitched in the 1925 World Series, losing two games to Pittsburgh. Unconditionally released by Washington in June 1927, he signed with the Yankees that December.

Coveleski appeared in only 12 games for the Yankees, posting a 5–1 record. He retired at season's end. He led the league in K's just once, but one of the great Covaleski stories deals with strikeouts. Like most of his contemporaries, Coveleski, one of the last of the legal spitballers, did not consciously try for strikeouts, but once while facing Washington he did.

Sam Rice had led off the inning with a triple. Recalled Coveleski: "I threw spitballs to the next three batters and they struck out. Steve O'Neill was our catcher, the greatest I ever played with, and those balls were breaking so much he didn't catch a single one. But he did block them and we got out of the inning without them scoring."

He was inducted into the hall of Fame by the Veterans Committee in 1969.

Wes Covington

Covington, John Wesley **OF**

1956–66 B:3/27/1932, Laurinburg, NC Deb:4/19/1956, MIL NL BL/TR 6'1", 205

G	AB	R	H	HR	RBI	OBP	SLG	AVG
1075	2978	355	832	131	499	.339	.466	.279

Covington was a platoon player with a good bat and suspect glove, but he made critical circus catches off the Yankees in the 1957 World Series. With the score 1–1 in the second inning of Game 2 his backhand grab of a Bobby Schantz liner ended the inning and saved a run. In the fourth inning of Game 5 he snagged Gil McDougald's fly while bouncing off the left-field fence. The next two Yankees reached base but didn't score, preserving Lew Burdette's 1–0 victory.

He hit 45 home runs for the Braves in their pennant-winning seasons of 1957–58, but when his hitting fell off he was waived. From 1961 through 1966, he played for four different teams with his longest spell as a Phillie.

Billy Cox

Cox, William Richard **3B-SS-2B**

1941–55 B:8/29/1919, Newport, PA D:3/30/1978, Harrisburg, PA Deb:9/20/1941, PIT NL BR/TR 5'10", 150

G	AB	R	H	HR	RBI	OBP	SLG	AVG
1058	3712	470	974	66	351	.318	.380	.262

For seven years Billy Cox held down the hot corner for a Brooklyn team that won three National League championships. Some feel that this was the best fielding unit ever assembled, and although more recent writers place Cox behind Brooks Robinson, Mike Schmidt, Aurelio Rodriguez, and Buddy Bell, Cox had no peer during his era.

After two years as the Pirates' full-time shortstop in 1946 and 1947, Cox went to the Dodgers in one of the most lopsided deals of all time. Along with Preacher Roe and Gene Mauch, Cox was swapped for an aged Dixie Walker, a rapidly aging Hal Gregg, and Vic Lombardi; it was no secret that Walker's hostility toward Jackie Robinson motivated the transaction.

Pee Wee Reese was locked in as the Brooklyn shortstop, so Cox moved quietly to third, led the league in fielding in 1950, and established himself as one of the great glovemen of all time. Casey Stengel once told Brooks Robinson that he could field as well as Cox, but that his arm was no match for the stocky little guy from south central Pennsylvania.

Bobby Cox

Cox, Robert Joseph **3B-Manager**

1968–69 M(1978–85, 1990–*, 1521–1204) B:5/21/1941, Tulsa, OK Deb:4/14/1968, NY AL BR/TR 5'11", 180

G	AB	R	H	HR	RBI	OBP	SLG	AVG
220	628	50	141	9	58	.313	.309	.225

A $40,000 "bonus baby" out of California's San Joaquin Valley, Robert Joseph "Bobby" Cox never made much of a dent in the major leagues as a player, but he became baseball's most successful manager of the 1990s. An able fielder who spent nearly a decade in the minor leagues, he hit a paltry .229 in 1968 with the Yankees, his only season as a big league regular.

Eventually he became a coach in the Yankees organization. In 1977 he coached for Billy Martin on a Yankees club that won the World Series. That led to a chance to manage the Atlanta Braves in 1978. Although considered an able skipper, he failed to bring Atlanta in better than fourth during his four seasons at the helm. In 1982 he took the manager's job with the Blue Jays.

Under Cox the talented Jays advanced steadily. From last in the American League East in 1981, they climbed to sixth the next year. In 1983 they finished fourth and in 1984 moved to second. The following year Cox guided Toronto to the first division championship ever won by a team from outside the United States. Although the club lost the AL Championship Series to the Royals in seven agonizing games, the Braves recognized Cox's accomplishments. After the season Cox moved back to Atlanta to head up the Braves' front office. When the team didn't live up to expectations, Cox moved back to the dugout in 1990. The next season the Braves were National League champions.

From 1991 through 1999, Cox's Braves won eight division titles and played in five World Series. On the debit side, only in 1995 did Cox bring a world championship to Atlanta, defeating the Indians in the Fall Classic in six games.

Danny Cox

Cox, Danny Bradford **P**

1983–88, 1991–95 B:9/21/1959, Northampton, England Deb:8/6/1983, STL NL BR/TR 6'4", 235

W	L	PCT	G	SV	IP	BB	SO	ERA
74	75	.497	278	8	1298	432	723	3.64

Though he recorded more than 12 wins only once in his career, Danny Cox often found himself on the mound in crucial games. His breakthrough came in his third major league season, when he went 18–9 with St. Louis in 1985. Though an intimidating presence on the mound, at 6-feet-4 inches, 235 pounds, Cox threw just an average over-the-top fastball. It was his fine curve and outstanding changeup that baffled hitters.

Cox followed a win in the 1985 National League Championship Series with two strong outings in the World Series. In Game 6, with the Cards one win away from the title, he blanked Kansas City through seven innings before a controversial umpiring call in the ninth inning helped the Royals rally to tie the Series against the St. Louis bullpen. Kansas City went on to win in seven games. In 1987 Cox won the division clincher and shut out San Francisco in Game 7 of the NLCS.

He missed all of 1989 and 1990 due to a blown elbow, but Cox made an extraordinary comeback following ligament transfer surgery. He shined in relief in the 1992 NLCS for Pittsburgh and the 1993 ALCS for Toronto.

Harry Coyle

Television Director B:1/6/1922, Ridgewood, NJ

Harry Coyle always had the angles figured. Baseball's foremost television director gave us Pete Rose's slide into Ray Fosse in the 1970 All-Star Game (from the home plate camera), Carlton Fisk's body-English homer in Game 6 of the 1975 World Series (left-field camera), and Kirk Gibson's echo of *The Natural* to win the opener of the 1988 World Series (the low center-field camera).

Coyle introduced the center-field shot in 1957, and says he came up with this new angle because, "I was never happy with the pitcher-batter shot from behind home plate." Coyle grew up in Paterson, New Jersey, next to a playground that was the preferred site for local softball games. "We only had one umpire," said Coyle. "He stood behind the pitcher and had a clear shot of home plate. I never forgot that shot."

What was clear in Coyle's mind was not technologically possible for a very long time. "We had to wait until telescopic lenses were developed and television cable was improved," Coyle explained. "There's resistance in the distance (from camera to control room). We couldn't get enough signal through, so we were limited to 100 or 200 feet."

Finally, by using amplifiers, broadcast engineers could use as much as 900 feet of cable. At that point, there was only one obstacle: getting the cooperation of the parks' owners to build a space for the cameramen. "The tower in left field has to be high enough to get over the head of the second baseman." Coyle said. The director called the angles for his last event in 1992, and then moved to Iowa.

Roger Craig

Craig, Roger Lee **P**

1955–66 M(1978–79,1985–1990, 738–737)
B:2/17/1930, Durham, NC Deb:7/17/1955, BRO NL
BR/TR, 6'4", 191

W	L	PCT	G	SV	IP	BB	SO	ERA
74	98	.430	368	19	1536[1]	522	803	3.83

Roger Craig found more success as a coach and manager than as a pitcher. A product of the Brooklyn Dodgers' deep farm system, he helped the team win its 1955 world championship with a victory over the Yankees in Game 5 of the World Series. He went to the New York Mets in the expansion draft following the 1961 season. He became baseball's losingest pitcher as the anchor of New York's pitching rotation for the first two years of the club's existence. Craig lost on Opening Day 1962 and then lost 23 more for the woefully inept Mets that year.

The next year things got worse. On May 4, 1963, Craig lost a game to the San Francisco Giants, then continued losing until he had dropped 18 in a row. During that streak his teammates scored just 29 runs for him, and he lost twice to the Phillies on ninth-inning homers by Roy Sievers. Fans showered him with good-luck charms. On the night of August 9 he drove to the Polo Grounds and changed his uniform from his usual "38" to "13." The game went into the bottom of the ninth inning with the Mets and Cubs tied, 3–3. With two outs, light-hitting shortstop Al Moran doubled, sending a runner to third. Tim Harkness then batted for Craig. "I wouldn't care if he was my uncle. He was out of the game," said Casey Stengel.

Harkness walked to load the bases, and then Jim Hickman hit Lindy McDaniel's next pitch to left field. Billy Williams settled back to make the catch, but the ball ticked off the roof's overhang and dropped onto the field. The umpires signaled a grand slam, and Craig's luckless streak was over. Craig held the major league record for most consecutive losses until another unfortunate Mets pitcher, Anthony Young, broke it in 1993.

In 1963 Craig lost five 1–0 decisions, and the Mets mercifully traded him to the Cardinals. He went from last place to the pennant, and he won Game 4 of the World Series by pitching 4⅔ scoreless innings of relief. After pitching briefly for the Reds and Phillies he finished his pitching career with Seattle in the Pacific Coast League.

He managed at Albuquerque, then returned to the big leagues as a pitching coach for San Diego and then the Astros. In March 1978 he replaced Alvin Dark as San Diego's manager. Fired at end of the 1979 season, he became Sparky Anderson's pitching coach and played a pivotal role in Detroit's 1984 world championship. Craig's meal ticket was the split-finger fastball, and he used it to transform the careers of Detroit pitcher Jack Morris as well as non-Tiger hurlers such as Mike Scott. After picking up pointers from Craig, Scott, formerly a journeyman, became the 1986 National League Cy Young Award winner.

Craig retired from coaching after the 1984 season, but kept busy as a Tigers scout. He returned to managing that December when he replaced Jim Davenport as San Francisco Giants manager. He led the Giants to the 1987 NL West title and the 1989 pennant, but lost to Tony La Russa's A's in the earthquake-racked Bay Area World Series.

Doc Cramer

Cramer, Roger Maxwell **OF**

1929–48 B:7/22/1905, Beach Haven, NJ D:9/9/1990, Manahawkin, NJ Deb:9/18/1929, PHI AL BL/TR 6'2", 185

G	AB	R	H	HR	RBI	OBP	SLG	AVG
2239	9140	1357	2705	37	842	.340	.375	.296

At 6 feet 2 inches and 185 pounds, Doc Cramer looked like a power hitter, but he hit only 37 home runs in 20 major league seasons. He once went four straight years as a regular without a homer. His game depended on speed and on his ability to hit the ball to all fields. He usually batted leadoff and led the American League seven times in at bats and once in hits, with an even 200 in 1940. He also set a league record and tied the major league mark by going 6-for-6 in two different games (June 20, 1932, and July 13, 1935). In center field he was such certain death on flies that a sportswriter nicknamed him "Flit," for the insecticide. Through 1999 Cramer still ranked among the top 10 outfielders in career putouts.

Discovered by former Philadelphia Athletics catcher Cy Perkins, Cramer signed with the A's in 1929 and was sent to the Class D Blue Ridge League's Martinsburg Blue Sox. Originally a pitcher, he soon shifted to center. On the last day of his first season he led the league in hitting, and only future major leaguer Joe Vosmik was in a position to catch him. Cramer returned to the mound for the final game and walked Vosmik four times to win the title with a .404 average. "Only three were intentional," Cramer said later.

He played in two games for the A's at the end of 1929 and remained in the majors through 1948, with the exception of a half-season demotion to Portland of the Pacific Coast League in 1930, ostensibly because he had missed signs. In 1933 he became the Athletics' regular center fielder and hit .295. Even though he made the All-Star team in 1935, he was traded to the Boston Red Sox in 1936 and had his best years there, being named to the All-Star teams from 1937 through 1940.

After spending 1941 with Washington he went to Detroit, where he finished his career. Although the A's won three straight pennant from 1929 to 1931, when he was a substitute, Cramer had to wait until 1945, when he was 40 years old, to play regularly on a pennant winner. He starred in the Tigers' victory over the Cubs in the 1945 World Series, smacking 11 singles and hitting .379 with seven runs scored and four RBIs.

After retiring as a player, Cramer coached for several years. With the White Sox from 1951 through 1953, he received much of the credit for developing Nellie Fox as a hitter.

Del Crandall

Crandall, Delmar Wesley **C**

1949–66 M(1972–75, 1983–84, 364–469) B:3/5/1930, Ontario, CA Deb:6/17/1949, BOS NL BR/TR 6'1", 195

G	AB	R	H	HR	RBI	OBP	SLG	AVG
1573	5026	585	1276	179	657	.315	.404	.254

On a club featuring Hall of Famers Hank Aaron, Eddie Mathews, and Warren Spahn, Del Crandall helped turn the Milwaukee Braves into a National League power with his hitting and receiving skills. He was one of the league's top catchers of his era.

From 1953 through 1960, the team's first eight seasons in Milwaukee, the Braves went to the World Series twice, took second five times, and finished third once. Significantly, Crandall was in his prime during that period. He went to the All-Star Game seven times, missing only in 1957. Named to *The Sporting News* Major League All-Star Team in 1958 and 1960, he captured Gold Gloves in 1958, 1959, and 1960 while averaging 70 RBIs and more than 19 home runs per season.

In 1960, at age 30, Crandall batted .294 with a career-high 77 RBIs. He also caught the second and third no-hitters of his career. On August 18 Crandall was behind the plate when Lew Burdette no-hit Philadelphia. Less than a month later Warren Spahn pitched the first of his two career no-no's, shutting down the Phillies, 4–0. After an arm injury limited Crandall to only 15 games in 1961, he delivered one more standout season in 1962. He won his eighth and final All-Star berth, captured his fourth Gold Glove, and was again named to *The Sporting News* NL All-Star team.

He later served as a manager in Milwaukee—with the Brewers—but he did not enjoy the success he had seen in that city with the Braves. Things were not much better in Seattle, where he managed the Mariners for parts of two years.

Doc Crandall

Crandall, James Otis **P**

1908–18 B:10/8/1887, Wadena, IN D:8/17/1951, Bell, CA Deb:4/24/1908, NY NL BR/TR 5'10½", 180

W	L	PCT	G	SV	IP	BB	SO	ERA
102	62	.622	302	25	1546²	379	606	2.92

Doc Crandall was one of the game's first relief specialists, or what passed for a relief specialist in the first two decades of the 20th century. He got his nickname from Damon Runyon, a baseball writer of the time. "Crandall is the Giants' ambulance corps," wrote Runyon. "He is first aid to the injured. He is the physician of the pitching emergency. The doctor of ballgames. He is without an equal as an extinguisher of batting rallies and run riots. He is the greatest relief pitcher in baseball."

A spitballing righthander, he was 12–12 as a Giants rookie in 1908, and 24 of his 32 games were starts. He became a "reliever" the next season, finishing second in the National League with four saves. In 1910 he had his best season, going 17–4 with 18 starts and 13 complete games. He also worked 24 times in relief, winning a league-high seven games while saving four others. In 1911 he was 15–5 for John McGraw's pennant winners. He again led NL relievers with seven wins and was second in saves with five.

Not only did he get the win in Game 5 of the World Series, he also drove in a run in the two-run rally in the ninth that tied the game. That RBI was no fluke. Crandall had a lifetime .285 batting average and 126 RBIs in 887 at bats. Also considered an excellent fielder, he made occasional appearances in the field (70 games at second base, 16 at first base, eight at shortstop and four in the outfield).

By August 1913 he was only 2–4 in 24 starts and McGraw shipped him to the Cardinals for backup catcher Larry McLean. But the trade proved so unpopular with Giants fans that McGraw bought him back exactly one week later.

Sentiment, however, did not keep Crandall from jumping to the St. Louis Terriers of the Federal League in 1914. He won 13 games as a starter that season and 21 in 1915, starting 33 times. He moved to the St. Louis Browns in 1916 when the Federal League folded, but his major league career was near its end. His final stop came with the Boston Braves in 1918.

Ed Crane

Crane, Edward Nicholas **P-C-OF**

1884–1893 B:5/27/1862, Boston, MA D:9/20/1896, Rochester, NY Deb:4/17/1884, BOS UA BR/TR 5'10½", 204

G	AB	R	H	HR	RBI	OBP	SLG	AVG
391	1409	199	335	18	84	.283	.329	.238

W	L	PCT	G	SH	IP	BB	SO	ERA
72	96	.429	204	7	1550[1]	885	719	3.99

As a rookie catcher with Boston of the Union Association in 1884, Ed Crane hit 12 home runs to finish second in the league. When that league collapsed after the 1884 season, he jumped to the National League and found himself facing stronger pitching. His home run total and batting average dropped significantly and he was tried at pitcher.

"Cannon-Ball" Crane had a strong right arm but was extremely wild. In his first season with the Washington Statesmen he finished 1–7 with a 7.20 ERA and in 1890, while pitching for New York's Players' League team, he walked 208 batters in 330 innings. His only winning season was 1889, when he went 14–10 with the champion New York Giants. In that fall's "World Series" against Brooklyn's American Association champs, a best-of-11 affair, he won four games and lost one.

When the Players League collapsed after the 1890 season, Crane played for Cincinnati of the AA, going 14–14 and leading the league with a 2.45 ERA. In 1892 he returned to the Giants with a 16–24 record. Four years later he committed suicide by drinking acid.

Gavvy Cravath

Cravath, Clifford Carlton **OF**

1908–09, 1912–20 M(1919–20, 91–137) B:3/23/1881, Escondido, CA D:5/23/1963, Laguna Beach, CA Deb:4/18/1908, BOS AL BR/TR 5'10½", 186

G	AB	R	H	HR	RBI	OBP	SLG	AVG
1220	3951	575	1134	119	719	.380	.478	.287

Gavvy Cravath was baseball's leading home run hitter during the Dead Ball Era. Pitchers dominated the game during the first two decades of the 20th century, and even the greatest hitters seldom reached double figures in home runs. But in one season Cravath slugged a remarkable 24 homers and in two others hit 19.

Although his record soon paled in comparison to Babe Ruth's exploits, Cravath played with a much different ball than Ruth did during his greatest seasons. Cravath retired just as a livelier ball was introduced in 1920. Cravath stood only 5 feet 10 inches and weighed 186 pounds, yet he could still knock a baseball that had the resilience of a rock out of the ballpark. He was not strictly a pull-hitter, which he used to his advantage in the intimate confines of the Philadelphia Phillies' Baker Bowl, where a ball hit down the right-field line could travel only 272 feet.

He failed his first big league trial with three different team over parts of two seasons, but after several strong minor league seasons he was purchased by the Phillies for $9,000 in 1912. He was 31 years old when he played his first full major league season. In 1913 he blossomed into the league's most feared power hitter, leading the circuit with 19 homers, 179 hits, and a remarkable 128 RBIs, 33 more than anyone else. His .341 average, a career high, was second only to league-leader Jake Daubert.

Sometimes called "Cactus" because of an abrasive and gruff personality, he could also be congenial and modest. He enjoyed practical jokes and clubhouse banter. One of his favorite targets was tall lefthander Eppa Rixey, a Southerner, whom he constantly twitted with references to the Civil War.

In 1915 he and first baseman Fred Luderus provided enough power to let a strong pitching staff led by Grover Alexander take the Phillies to their first National League pennant. Cravath hit 24 home runs and drove in 115, both league highs. His 89 runs scored, 86 walks, and .393 on-base average also led the league. On August 8 he tied a still-standing big league record by smacking four doubles in one game.

Alexander won the opening game of the 1915 World Series, 3–1, scattering eight Boston hits. The Red Sox then took four straight one-run decisions to win the world championship. In the first inning of the fifth and final game, Philadelphia's first three batters reached base. Cravath had worked the count to 3–2 when manager Pat Moran inexplicably flashed him the bunt sign. His roller to the pitcher turned into a double play, ruining what could have been a big Phils inning.

Philadelphia finished second the next two seasons and then began spiraling downward in the standings. Cravath tied for the league lead in home runs in 1917 with 12, then won the title the next two years with eight in 1918 and 12 in 1919, when he played in only 83 games.

Sam Crawford

Crawford, Samuel Earl **OF–1B**

1899–1917 B:4/18/1880, Wahoo, NE D:6/15/1968, Hollywood, CA Deb:9/10/1899, CIN NL BL/TL 6', 190

G	AB	R	H	HR	RBI	OBP	SLG	AVG
2517	9570	1391	2961	97	1525	.362	.452	.309

Outfielder Sam Crawford was one of the greatest all-around players of the dead-ball era. Although overshadowed in the public eye by teammate Ty Cobb, "Wahoo Sam" was more than respectable on offense and vastly superior to Cobb on defense.

Crawford's 309 career triples are a record that will stand forever unless baseball undergoes a revolutionary change. With today's ball and in today's ballparks, the triple is the rarest of all hits. Now only 2 percent of all major league hits are triples. Batters are four times more likely to hit a home run than a triple. In 1914, however, when Crawford cracked 26 three-base hits, nearly 6 percent of all hits in the majors were triples and batters were three times more likely to triple than to hit a home run. Even allowing for the relative prevalence of triples at the time, it is remarkable that Crawford reached double figures in triples in 17 consecutive seasons and led his league in the category six times.

Nicknamed for his hometown of Wahoo, Nebraska, Crawford left school after fifth grade to learn the barbering trade, playing for several semipro Nebraska teams, and beginning his professional career in 1899 with the Canadian League's Chatham Reds. Before the year was out he moved up to the Western League, hit .333 in 60 games, and was purchased by the National League's Cincinnati Reds, for whom he hit .307 in 31 games and batted in 20 runs.

Crawford's hitting fell off sharply in his sophomore season, although he did bang out 15 triples to begin his streak. Back on track in 1901, he hit .330 with 104 RBIs and 16 home runs, a career high and league-best. When he hit .333 with a league-leading 22 triples in 1902, he was established as one of the NL's best young hitters.

The American League had declared itself a major league in 1901, and set about luring National League stars into its fold with the promise of higher salaries. A contract offer of $3,500, considerably more than the Reds were paying, convinced Crawford to become a Detroit Tiger, although he had unwisely signed a contract with Cincinnati as well. In the ensuing settlement reached by the two leagues, Crawford was awarded to the Tigers over the bitter objections of the Reds. He proved a bargain in 1903 as he hit .335, knocked in 89 RBIs, and smacked 25 triples—an AL record for nearly a decade.

Ty Cobb arrived in Detroit in 1905 and soon eclipsed Crawford at the plate. By 1907 many regarded Cobb as the preeminent player in the American League, but he was a troubled and difficult individual. For years Detroit manager Hughie Jennings played Crawford, a natural right fielder with a powerful arm, in center. Jennings assigned Cobb to right field because Cobb and left fielder Matty McIntyre hated each other, and neither would call for a flyball hit between them.

Cobb didn't dislike Crawford—no one did—but Cobb was so jealous of him that it led to an enmity of sorts. Crawford seemed to do things naturally that Cobb worked hard to accomplish. Most of all, Cobb envied Crawford's popularity, which nothing short of a total makeover of Cobb's personality could help him attain.

Nevertheless, Cobb and Crawford soon became the league's most potent one-two batting punch. In 1907 they led the Tigers to their first pennant. Crawford hit .323 and led the league in runs scored. Cobb led in hits, total bases, RBIs, batting average, and stolen bases. Detroit lost the World Series to the Chicago Cubs in five games.

The Tigers repeated as league champions in 1908, but again fell to the Cubs in the Fall Classic. Crawford led the league that year with seven home runs and finished second to Cobb with 184 hits, 270 total bases, 80 RBIs, a .311 batting average, and a .457 slugging average.

Detroit won its third straight pennant in 1909. Crawford led the league with 35 doubles and finished second to Cobb with 266 total bases, 97 RBIs, and a slugging average of .452.

After the 1909 season Cleveland owner Ernest S. Barnard built a 40-foot right-field wall at League Park, announcing, "I'm going to stop Crawford from hitting home runs in our park." Crawford accepted the challenge, telling reporters that he would indeed smack one over the barrier. On one of the Tigers' first visits to Cleveland in 1910 he proved to be as good as his word.

From 1910 through 1915 Crawford led the league in triples four times. He led in RBIs three times, topping 100 in five of the six years. But despite the best efforts of Crawford and Cobb, the Tigers' poor pitching prevented them from winning another pennant. Ty Cobb campaigned to have him enshrined in the Hall of Fame, and succeeded in 1957.

Jim Creighton

Creighton, James

Baseball Pioneer B:4/15/1841, New York, NY
D:10/18/1862, New York, NY

Jim Creighton was baseball's first national star, probably its first professional, and its first martyr. He was the greatest hitter of his time, and his pitching revolutionized the game. Remarkably, he accomplished all this by the age of 21.

Creighton grew to more than 6 feet tall, with long arms and a muscular physique. In 1857 he helped to organize a neighborhood baseball club, the Young America Base Ball Club. The next year, he and his friend George Flanley founded the Niagara Club. Creighton played either second or third base. In the ninth inning of a game between the Niagaras and the Brooklyn Stars, perhaps the best junior team in the area, he took over the pitching duties with his team well behind. From that moment on, baseball was never the same.

According to the existing rules, the ball was supposed to be "pitched"—that is, delivered with a stiff-armed, locked-wrist, underhand motion, much like a bowler's delivery. Throwing the ball was illegal, the calling of balls and strikes was still in the future, and the pitcher's task was simply to deliver the ball to the batter so that he could hit it. A kind of partnership developed between the pitcher and the batter. The best pitchers delivered pitches that were easily hit. As the game grew more competitive, pitchers tried to make batters hit the ball to a location where it would produce an out. But the rules of the day, which limited pitchers to pitching underhanded, left them with few options. Most pitchers tried to keep the ball away from the batter, hoping that frustration would lead to a swing at a "bad" pitch. Consequently, with no bases on balls awarded to limit an at bat, some batters stayed at the plate for up to 15 minutes.

That changed when Creighton became a pitcher. According to an eyewitness account, "When Creighton got to work something new was seen in base ball—a low, swift delivery, the ball rising from the ground past the shoulder to the catcher. The Stars soon saw they could not cope with such pitching." Creighton was responsible for several important innovations. He threw much faster than other pitchers did, and because there was no mound the ball's trajectory was nearly horizontal, as opposed to the arcing lobs batters expected. Also, he put spin on the ball in such a way that his fast pitches "hopped" as they approached the plate. These inventions changed the face of baseball.

As Creighton's reputation grew, some claimed that he could make the ball dip, rise, or sail at will. A few historians have even suggested that he was the first man to throw a curveball, but if he did it was probably not intentional.

How did Creighton come up with such a revolutionary pitching style? He cheated. As he brought his long right arm around he imparted an almost imperceptible, and completely illegal, wrist snap. Although the ball was still being hurled underhand, Creighton was throwing it instead of pitching it like a horseshoe.

The new style sparked a great deal of controversy. Purists correctly insisted that Creighton's tosses were illegal. Other pitchers studied Creighton, trying to imitate him. Fans were excited by the way he threw. The game moved faster and was more interesting. Umpires maintained that they saw nothing illegal. When Henry Chadwick, the era's most influential baseball writer, commended Creighton for his "head work," the battle was over and the groundwork laid for the game, as we know it today.

After his pitching performance against the Stars, Creighton was recruited for their team. In 1859 he joined the Brooklyn Excelsiors, regarded as baseball's national champions, and traveled with them throughout the East in 1860 and 1861. With Creighton as their star they regularly won games by such inflated margins as 51–6 and 45–16. Not only did Creighton pitch and usually win every game, he reportedly went the entire 1860 season without making an out at bat. He was also an excellent fielder; while playing left field one day, he made a remarkable catch and reportedly started baseball's first triple play.

Batters eventually learned how to hit Creighton's offerings, and it soon became clear that mere speed on the pitch was not enough. Even though the balls were delivered from only 45 feet away, the best batters managed to get around on the pitches. To counter this Creighton developed the ability to change speeds, probably by varying the degree of his wrist snap.

No one knows how much the Excelsiors secretly paid their "amateur" pitching star, but today Creighton is generally considered to have been the first professional ballplayer. He became famous, and large crowds turned out to see him perform. Young players tried to duplicate his style. Teams even adopted his name. Decades later, fans who had seen him pitch would remark that while stars such as Charley Radbourn and Tim Keefe were good pitchers, they weren't Creightons.

In late 1862, in a game between the Excelsiors and the Unions of Morrisiana, a New York City team, Creighton smashed a home run. As he swung, he heard something pop. Circling the bases, he remarked to George Flanley as he crossed the plate, "I must have snapped my belt." Then he collapsed with a ruptured bladder. After several days of internal hemorrhaging he died on October 18, 1862, five months shy of his 22nd birthday.

Creighton's grief-stricken teammates erected a tall granite monument over his grave in Brooklyn's Greenwood Cemetery. Carved on it are crossed bats, a base, a cap, and a scorebook. A large stone baseball rests on top.

Lou Criger

Criger, Louis **C**

1896–1910,1912 B:2/3/1872, Elkhart, IN D:5/14/1934, Tucson, AZ Deb:9/21/1896, CLE NL BR/TR 5'10", 165

G	AB	R	H	HR	RBI	OBP	SLG	AVG
1012	3202	337	709	11	342	.295	.290	.221

Cy Young's batterymate and Ty Cobb's nemesis: Lou Criger's claim to fame was built on those two noteworthy pillars. Criger caught most of Young's 511 major league victories, beginning in 1896 with Cleveland and continuing in St. Louis. When Young jumped to Boston's American League team in 1901 he took Criger along with him. Although he hit just .221 for his career, Criger ranks high as one of the all-time defensive specialists. Third in career assists per game by catchers, he trails only Bill Bergen and Duke Farrell.

Cobb and Criger were great rivals, and Criger stated that after several years of unsuccessful attempts to steal against him, Cobb gave up and never tried again. Both claimed greater success against each other than was probably deserved, but Criger was one of the best catchers of his era at throwing out base stealers, Cobb included.

Long after his career ended Criger made headlines during the O'Connell–Dolan scandal of 1924. AL president Ban Johnson produced a previously secret affidavit in which Criger admitted that he had been approached by a gambler and offered $12,000 to throw the 1903 World Series. Criger refused, told no one but Cy Young of the offer, and, incidentally, caught every inning of the eight-game Series and drove in four runs as Boston beat Pittsburgh.

Hughie Critz

Critz, Hugh Melville **2B**

1924–35 B:9/17/1900, Starkville, MS D:1/10/1980, Greenwood, MS Deb:5/31/1924, CIN NL BR/TR 5'8", 147

G	AB	R	H	HR	RBI	OBP	SLG	AVG
1478	5930	832	1591	38	531	.303	.352	.268

Hugh Melville "Hughie" Critz was an outstanding defensive second baseman who spent 12 years in the National League. Although never a ball-crushing hitter, he may have been his era's most sure-handed second baseman.

In his first game with the Cincinnati Reds, in 1924 the talented former college star smacked two hits off Grover Cleveland Alexander. Critz finished the season with a .322 average. He never again hit as well, but in the field he sparkled. In 1926 and 1927 Critz led the league in double plays, and in 1926 he also won his first fielding average crown. A reliable batter, he remained a regular in the Reds' infield until 1930, when he was sold to the New York Giants because of a salary dispute.

Manager John McGraw liked his new player's heads-up defensive play and made him the Giants' regular second baseman. In 1933, although McGraw had been replaced by Bill Terry, Critz was still playing as well as ever. He again posted the best fielding average of any National League player at his position, and the Giants took both the league crown and the World Series. Although his hitting declined further, Critz led the league in fielding average for the fifth time in 1934, and for the third time he turned more double plays than any other player at his position.

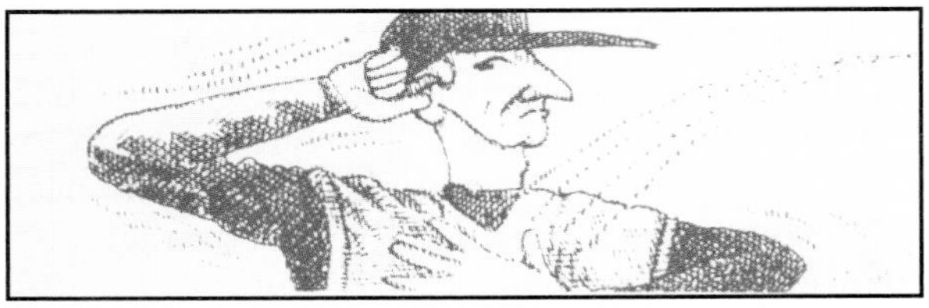

Warren Cromartie

Cromartie, Warren Livingston **OF–1B**
1974–83,1991 B:9/29/1953, Miami Beach, FL
Deb:9/6/1974, MON NL BL/TL 6', 192

G	AB	R	H	HR	RBI	OBP	SLG	AVG
1107	3927	459	1104	61	391	.339	.402	.281

In the late 1970s the Expos believed they had the best young outfield in the league—future stars Warren Cromartie, Andre Dawson, and Ellis Valentine—a trio that was supposed to lead a resurrection in Montreal. But Cromartie and the Expos never exploded the way the experts predicted, and by 1984 he was playing in Japan.

In his freshman 1977 season, Cromartie hit 41 doubles, good for fourth on the all-time rookie list. He hit the Expos' only grand slam in 1978 and had the NL's longest hitting streak—21 games—in 1979. In 1980 Cromartie batted .288, with 14 home runs and 70 RBIs.

A gifted athlete prone to slumps, he had his best season in 1981, when the Expos won their first division title. Cromartie batted .304 in the strike-shortened season but hit only .167 in the Championship Series as the Expos lost to the Dodgers. After his defection to the Yomiuri Giants in 1984, Cromartie hit 30 or more home runs in each of his first three seasons in Japan. He collaborated with Robert Whiting to write an entertaining book, *Slugging It Out In Japan: An American Major Leaguer In The Tokyo Outfield.* He put together a fitting ending by returning to the majors in 1991. He batted .313 in 69 games for Kansas City.

Joe Cronin

Cronin, Joseph Edward **SS–3B**
1926–45 M(1933–1947, 1,236–1,055) AL President (1959–73) B:10/12/1906, San Francisco, CA D:9/7/1984, Osterville, MA Deb:4/29/1926, PIT NL BR/TR 5'11½", 180

G	AB	R	H	HR	RBI	OBP	SLG	AVG
2124	7579	1233	2285	170	1424	.390	.468	.301

Few other figures in baseball have ascended the ladder of success as Joe Cronin did. In a career that spanned decades, he rose from backup shortstop to Most Valuable Player, pennant-winning manager, general manager, Hall of Famer, and finally president of the American League.

Raised in San Francisco's Mission District, Cronin won the city's junior tennis championship when he was 15. Talented on the diamond as well, he was offered a scholarship to play baseball in college but turned it down. It was the right decision. In 1925 Pittsburgh scout Joe Devine signed Cronin and sent him to the Class C Middle Atlantic League's Johnstown Johnnies. Despite weighing only 152 pounds, the 19-year-old Cronin hit .313, and by the next season he was a big league shortstop.

After playing 50 games for the Pirates in 1926 and 1927 he was sold to the American Association's Kansas City Blues. Kansas City owner George Muehlebach sold him to Washington for $7,500 in midseason.

Initially Cronin did little to impress Senators owner Clark Griffith, who ordered manager Bucky Harris to play Bobby Reeves at short instead. Griffith soon noticed that Harris was continuing to start Cronin on the road. "Reeves will never learn to play shortstop if you don't play him," Griffith complained. "Neither will Cronin," replied Harris, whose judgment eventually prevailed.

Cronin hit .281 with 61 RBIs in 1929. He exploded the next season, hitting .346, driving in 126 runs, and leading AL shortstops in putouts, assists, double plays, and chances per game.

After the 1932 season Cronin replaced Walter Johnson as the Senators' manager. Determined to deliver a pennant at the age of 26, Cronin sat down with Griffith to rebuild the team Over the next few months the Senators acquired catcher Luke Sewell from the Indians, pitcher Lefty Stewart and outfielders Goose Goslin and Fred Schulte from the Browns, and pitchers Earl Whitehill and Jack Russell from the Tigers.

The strategy worked. "Our team just gathered momentum that year," said Cronin, who contributed his fourth straight 100-RBI season (he had eight in his career). "And I guess because of the way we played, it seemed the breaks fell our way." The Senators won their last pennant as a Washington franchise that year before losing to the New York Giants in five games in the World Series.

Cronin's defensive skills began to slip, and his marriage to Griffith's adopted daughter, Mildred Robertson, was the high point of his year. Meanwhile, new Boston Red Sox owner Tom Yawkey ordered general manager Eddie Collins to buy up the best talent available, and Collins suggested that the Sox obtain Cronin as player-manager. Aside from family considerations, Griffith had philosophical objections to selling off players. But as the bidding escalated his resolve weakened, and when offered $250,000 plus shortstop Lyn Lary for Cronin, Griffith capitulated. Even Cronin approved. "Make the deal, you can't afford not to," he told his new father-in-law.

Griffith secured a five-year, $30,000-a-year contract for Cronin, and the new manager soon became popular with Boston's large Irish population. "His smile and his manner place him rightfully in the blood royal of the Irish race," said one paper, but Cronin's teammates weren't so enthusiastic.

Although he continued to be a strong hitter, by the time Cronin reached Boston, he was no longer a capable shortstop. He inaugurated his Red Sox career with a series of embarrassing errors. Even worse, he seemed to lose his nerve in the field, developing a case of "groundball jitters." He would drop to one knee to block balls—and still flub them. Cronin's exasperated double-play partner, Oscar Melillo, once shouted, "Joe, if you're going to miss 'em, you might as well stand up and miss 'em like a big leaguer."

Cronin wasn't Yawkey's only big-ticket player. Lefty Grove and Jimmie Foxx had come to Boston from Connie Mack's disintegrating Philadelphia Athletics franchise. Neither admired their new skipper. "I can't recall one of the Philly players that he took to," remembered former A's outfielder Doc Cramer. "Once during a game I heard Grove tell [Cronin] that he couldn't play shortstop on a high school team. And Joe didn't like Foxx. He didn't like me. I didn't care much for him, either."

Pitchers especially disliked Cronin. Apart from his defensive shortcomings, he annoyed them by calling pitches from the bench. "If we had a shortstop, we'd win the pennant," Wes Ferrell complained. "Cronin has lost me four games already." In August 1936, Ferrell stormed out of a game in the middle of an inning to protest Cronin's managing. He was suspended and fined $1,000, although the fine was later rescinded.

Compounding these on-the-field problems was the fact that Cronin often negotiated contracts with his players—and usually won. Perhaps the only Red Sox player who liked Cronin was Ted Williams. "Joe was the easiest man in the world to play for," Williams once said of his former skipper. "He was a hitter's manager."

Cronin's last year as a regular player was 1941. He appeared in only 183 games during the next four seasons before a broken leg in 1945 brought his playing days to an end. "I used to send myself up to pinch-hit whenever the wind was blowing out from home plate," he would joke. It must have been blowing at gale force in 1943 when he pinch-hit five homers, including two grand slams.

Cronin hadn't brought the Red Sox a pennant since his arrival in 1935, and by 1946 criticism of his managing was mounting. But that season he silenced his detractors when Boston captured the AL flag, although they lost the World Series to St. Louis on Enos Slaughter's famous dash home in Game 7.

Cronin's last day in uniform was September 30, 1947. In 1948 he became Red Sox general manager, replacing Eddie Collins. Perhaps his greatest blunder in that job was his failure to sign Willie Mays in 1947.

The 16-year-old Mays was playing for the Birmingham Black Barons, a Red Sox farm team. According to David Halberstam in *Summer of Forty-Nine*, Barons general manager Eddie Glennon called Cronin to rave about Mays, but Cronin didn't even send a scout. Glennon convinced the area scout to take a look. The scout called Cronin at home to report that a sensational young ballplayer could be had for $5,000. Cronin reacted coolly. Finally he sent a scout—who didn't sign Mays. The Red Sox were the last major league team to integrate, and wouldn't even hire African-American ushers until threatened with a lawsuit in the 1970s.

In 1956 Cronin was elected to the Hall of Fame. Three years later he became AL president, a post he held until 1974, when he was named chairman of the league, an honorary title.

Frankie Crosetti

Crosetti, Frank Peter Joseph **SS–3B**
1932–48 B:10/4/1910, San Francisco, CA
Deb:4/12/1932, NY AL BR/TR 5'10", 165

G	AB	R	H	HR	RBI	OBP	SLG	AVG
1683	6277	1006	1541	98	649	.341	.354	.245

Frankie Crosetti acquired so many World Series rings in his long career with the Yankees he eventually began asking for, and receiving, shotguns instead. Crosetti came to the team the year Babe Ruth made his legendary "called shot" and remained with them until Mickey Mantle hit his final homer. The 37 consecutive years he wore the pinstripes—his first 17 years as a player and the next 20 years as third-base coach—represent the longest continuous service in uniform in the New York club's history.

Unlike such powerful teammates as Ruth, Lou Gehrig, and Joe DiMaggio, "the Crow" was more valuable for his glove than for his bat. In 1932 the 21-year-old Crosetti replaced Lyn Lary as the Yankees' regular shortstop. That fall Crosetti enjoyed his first of seven World Series as a player, when New York swept the Chicago Cubs in four games.

Part of the American League All-Star squad in 1936 and 1939, he remained the Yankees' shortstop through 1940, when he was supplanted by Phil Rizzuto. When Rizzuto served in the navy during World War II, Crosetti returned to the starting lineup.

Never a high-average hitter, Crosetti's personal best was a .288 mark in 1936, but he usually hit much lower. In 1940 he played in 145 games and batted .194, but he had a knack for drawing bases on balls and led the league in being hit by pitches eight times. These factors, along with the backing of his powerful teammates, enabled him to score more than 100 runs in four consecutive seasons (1936–39).

Despite his spindly, 165-pound frame, he hit with occasional power, reaching double figures in home runs four times. In Game 2 of the 1938 World Series against the Cubs, sore-armed Dizzy Dean held the Yanks at bay for seven innings with his "nothing ball." But in the eighth, with New York trailing, 3–2, Crosetti slammed a two-run homer to give the Yankees the lead. DiMaggio iced the game in the ninth with another two-run shot.

The Crow was usually at or near the top in most fielding categories. He led AL shortstops in assists and fielding percentage once each and in putouts and double plays twice each. When Rizzuto became the starter Crosetti remained as a utility player, filling in at third, short, or second through 1948. As New York's third-base coach he took part in 15 more World Series, making him a participant in 22 Series in the same uniform.

Lave Cross

Cross, Lafayette Napoleon **3B-C-OF**
1887–1907 M(1899, 8–30) B:5/12/1866, Milwaukee, WI D:9/6/1927, Toledo, OH Deb:4/23/1887, LOU AA
BR/TR 5'8½", 155

G	AB	R	H	HR	RBI	OBP	SLG	AVG
2275	9072	1333	2645	47	1371	.328	.382	.292

Other catchers since "Lave" Cross have moved from the back of the plate to other positions, but none since have taken their catcher's mitt with them. When Cross would switch to various infield positions, he would take his mitt along. Although the rules were amended in 1895 to restrict the size of mitts for players other than catchers and first basemen, they were not stringently enforced. Accordingly, Cross was employing his catcher's mitt on August 5, 1897, when he set a major league record for most assists by a second baseman (15) in an extra-inning game.

A career .292 hitter in more than 9,000 at bats, Cross mostly played third base, with a brief stint as player-manager. Frank Robison, owner of the Cleveland Spiders, bought the competing St. Louis Browns after the 1898 season. On April 3, 1899, Robison stocked the St. Louis with Cleveland players—including Cy Young and Jesse Burkett—and brought Cross in as Cleveland manager. He was dismissed and sent to the Browns after an 8–30 start, but the record was no reflection on Cross' managerial skills. The 1899 Cleveland team won only 20 games and their 134 losses set a major league record for ineptitude.

In 1901 Cross jumped to the Philadelphia Athletics in Ban Johnson's new American League. From April 23, 1902, to May 8, 1905, Cross appeared in 447 consecutive games, mostly at third base. In January 1905 he was sold to Washington. Cross retired after the 1907 season, the last of three brothers (along with Amos and Frank) to play major league ball.

Monte Cross

Cross, Montford Montgomery **SS**
1892–1907 B:8/31/1869, Philadelphia, PA D:6/21/1934, Philadelphia, PA Deb:9/27/1892, BAL NL
BR/TR 5'8½", 148

G	AB	R	H	HR	RBI	OBP	SLG	AVG
1682	5821	718	1364	31	621	.316	.314	.234

There are distinctions, and then there are distinctions. Monte Cross, an everyday big league shortstop for 11 seasons, has this: his .234 career batting average over 5,817 at bats is the second lowest average for a shortstop with that many at bats. Only Eddie Brinkman, who hit .224 in 6,045 at bats, was worse.

Cross played briefly for the Baltimore Orioles in 1892 and the Pittsburgh Pirates in 1894. He hit .257 in 108 games for the Pirates in 1895. He moved to the St. Louis Browns the following year, and hit a career-high .286 in 1897. He moved to the Phillies the next season and stayed in Philadelphia for the rest of his career. After he hit only .197 for the Phillies in 1901, he jumped crosstown to the American League Athletics. In 1904, he hit a career-low .189.

He set one career high in his first season with the Phillies by making 93 errors. Amazingly, that figure, which led the National League in 1898, is not a record. Washington's Joe Sullivan had 102 errors in 1893, and Cleveland's John Gochnauer had 98 errors in 1903. In 1899 Cross again led the league in errors with 90, but he also set a major league record for putouts by a shortstop in an extra-inning game that still stands—14.

He cut down on his errors dramatically after 1899, though he led the league for a third straight season with 62 in 1900. But for six straight seasons between 1898 and 1903 Cross led his league in putouts. He also led the NL in assists in 1897 and 1899 and the AL in double plays in 1902. In other words, he came by his errors honestly by covering a lot of ground.

Alvin Crowder

Crowder, Alvin Floyd **P**

1926–36 B:1/11/1899, Winston-Salem, NC D:4/3/1972, Winston-Salem, NC Deb:7/24/1926, WAS AL BL/TR 5'10", 170

W	L	PCT	G	SV	IP	BB	SO	ERA
167	115	.592	402	22	2344^{1}	800	799	4.12

Despite a rather high earned run average and a tendency to walk as many batters as he struck out, Alvin "General" Crowder was an effective American League pitcher for three different teams. The secret of Crowder's success was a slow, almost lazy delivery that made his fastball "sneaky" fast. He also excelled at holding runners on base, although he seldom threw to first except when he had a runner cold. He explained, "I just take a look over there at any runner who's on first. When I look, I cock my head the same way every time and just shift my eyes. If I see the runner, I don't worry. He's not far enough off the bag to hurt me.... But when I look and I can't see him, he's too far off and he's mine."

He was nicknamed after Gen. Enoch Crowder, who originated the draft lottery during World War I. Alvin Crowder had also been an army man, too, serving in the Philippines; he rose to sergeant before returning to the minors. He was 27 when he made his debut with Washington in 1926. He finished the year 7–4, but when he got off to a rocky start the next year, he was traded to the St. Louis Browns for lefthander Tom Zachary.

It was a terrible deal for the Senators. In 1928 Crowder blossomed with a 21–5 mark to lead the AL in winning percentage. The next year he won 17 games and tied for the league lead with four shutouts. When the General started slowly in 1930, Washington owner Clark Griffith worked a deal that brought outfielder Heinie Manush and Crowder to the Senators in exchange for Goose Goslin.

Crowder won 15 games for the Senators in the remainder of the 1930 season and 18 the next year. In 1932 he led the AL in victories with a 26–13 mark that included 15 wins in a row. Although he was no control artist, he once went a league-high 327 innings without hitting a batter.

Crowder was selected in 1933 as one of the American League pitchers for the first All-Star Game. He delivered three shutout innings in the inaugural game. His 24–15 record that year again put him on top of the league in victories, and the Senators won the pennant. He started Games 2 and 5 of the World Series but was kayoed in the sixth inning each time.

He was also kayoed verbally on one occasion by Senators manager Joe Cronin. When Cronin came to the mound to relieve him, Crowder fired his glove all the way to the dugout. Informed it would cost him $25, he told Cronin it was a "bush league fine." Cronin rejoined that it was for a "bush league trick."

Crowder also objected in 1934 when Cronin played rookie Cecil Travis at third instead of the veteran Ossie Bluege. Fed up with Crowder, the pitcher was sent to Detroit, where he arrived in time to help the Tigers win the pennant with a 5–1 mark down the stretch.

Again he opened the World Series for his team, and again he lost. In 1935, his last good season, Crowder won 16 games to help the Tigers win another pennant. He pitched a five-hitter against the Cubs in Game 4 of the 1935 World Series to defeat Tex Carleton, 2–1, and finally pick up a Series win. His team captured the world championship two games later.

George Crowe

Crowe, George Daniel **1B**

1952–61 Negro League Player (1947–49) B:3/2/1923, Whiteland, IN Deb:4/16/1952, BOS NL BL/TL 6'2", 212

G	AB	R	H	HR	RBI	OBP	SLG	AVG
702	1727	215	467	81	299	.335	.466	.270

George Crowe always had trouble cracking the starting lineup, stuck as he was behind such stars as Joe Adcock, Ted Kluszewski, and Stan Musial. Instead he became a skilled pinch hitter, delivering four pinch-homers in both 1958 and 1959. Of his 56 career pinch hits, perhaps the most dramatic came in 1956 when Crowe's ninth inning performance frustrated a no-hit bid by the Chicago Cubs' Warren Hacker.

Crowe's finest season came with the Reds in 1957 when he was Cincinnati's regular first baseman. He collected 31 homers and 92 RBIs. Ironically, he was the only member of the Reds regular lineup *not* to be voted to the All Star Game that year as Cincinnati fans stuffed the ballot box. (Two other Reds were kept from the All-Star Game by a disgusted Commissioner Ford Frick.)

The Braves traded "Big George" to the Reds in April 1956 for outfielder Bob "Hurricane" Hazle and pitcher Corky Valentine. The Reds traded him to the Cardinals along with pitcher Alex Kellner and infielder Alex Grammas in October 1958 for pitcher Bob Mabe, infielder Eddie Kasko and outfielder Del Ennis.

Crowe led two minor leagues in RBIs, the New England League with 106 in 1949 and the American Association with 119 in 1951 and again with 128 in 1954. He paced the Eastern League with a .353 average in 1950.

Terry Crowley

Crowley, Terrence Michael **DH–OF**
1969-83 B:2/16/1947, Staten Island, NY
Deb:9/4/1969, BAL AL BL/TL 6', 180

G	AB	R	H	HR	RBI	OBP	SLG	AVG
865	1518	174	379	42	229	.348	.375	.250

Lefthanded batter Terry Crowley was one of the players who prompted Baltimore manager Earl Weaver to say, "Our depth is deep." Crowley posted a career .258 pinch-hitting average; when he retired, he was sixth on the all-time list with 108 pinch hits and 419 at bats as a pinch hitter. His ninth-inning pinch-hit grand slam on August 8, 1982, broke open a 6–6 tie against Kansas City.

A 15th-round draft choice of the Orioles in June 1966, Crowley never had a major league season in which he played in 100 games or accumulated 250 at bats. Yet he lasted 15 years in the big leagues as a specialist among specialists, and he played for four pennant winners.

The Orioles sent him to Texas in December 1973 for $100,000, but he never wore a Rangers uniform. Texas passed Crowley on to Cincinnati the following March. Following his release by the Atlanta Braves in 1976 after only six at bats, he was re-signed by the Orioles organization. Sent down to Rochester in 1977 to regain his batting stroke, he poled 30 homers to lead the International League.

After a final season with Montreal in 1983, Crowley worked as a highly respected batting coach, first for Baltimore, and then for Minnesota.

Jimmie Crutchfield

Crutchfield, Jimmie **OF**
Negro League Player (1930-42) B:3/15/1910, Ardmore, MO D:3/31/1993, Chicago, IL BL/TL 5'7", 150

Outfielder Jimmie Crutchfield played in the Negro Leagues in the 1930s and 1940s. His story is typical of life in baseball's era of segregation.

Crutchfield batted .286 as a rookie for the 1930 Birmingham Black Barons. He was hitting .330 in 1931 for the Indianapolis ABC's, but when the ABC's couldn't pay him he jumped to the Pittsburgh Crawfords. "We weren't being paid," he recalled. "That would go on maybe for two months, till we had a good gate. Then, perhaps, you got some of your back pay. Maybe one or two of the fellows would be getting something under the table, but most of us weren't being paid. So we were going to Pittsburgh to play, and when we got there the Crawfords gave me $25 or $50, so I stayed. That's how I went to the Pittsburgh Crawfords."

He moved to Effa Manley's Newark Eagles in 1937 and made the East-West Game in 1941 as a member of the Chicago American Giants. Crutchfield retired after the 1942 season. "I have no ill feelings about never having had the opportunity to play in the big leagues," said Crutchfield. "There have been times...you know, they used to call me the Black Paul Waner [and] I used to think about that a lot. He was on the other side of town in Pittsburgh making $12,000 a year and I didn't have enough money to go home on. I had to borrow bus fare to come home.

"It seemed like there was something wrong there. But that was yesterday. There's no use in me having bitterness in my heart this late in life about what's gone by." After leaving baseball he worked for the U.S. Post Office for 26 years.

Jose Cruz

Cruz, Jose (Dilan) **OF**
1970–88 B:8/8/1947, Arroyo, Puerto Rico
Deb:9/19/1970, STL NL BL/TL 6', 175

G	AB	R	H	HR	RBI	OBP	SLG	AVG
2353	7917	1036	2251	165	1077	.358	.420	.284

Houston Astros outfielder Jose Cruz is a good example of the way a player's home field can distort his statistics. Cruz put up solid numbers playing in the cavernous Astrodome; however, they were nowhere near as impressive as they might have been had he played elsewhere. For example, he hit just 40 home runs at home from 1975 to 1987. Yet in the same time period he hit 97—more than twice as many—on the road.

He started with the Cardinals in 1970 and was sold to the Astros in October 1974. Despite the home-field disadvantage, he blossomed in Houston, topping .300 six times, and was the Astros Most Valuable Player in 1977, 1980, 1983, and 1984. In 1983 he led the league in hits.

Although not regarded as a defensive standout, Cruz had an explanation: "I want so much to do good. And I am fast. Sometimes I was too quick getting to the ball, and it got past me."

Originally a dead-pull hitter, Cruz was taught by Astros batting coach Deacon Jones to change his approach, adapt to the ballpark, and take advantage of his speed. The man Houston fans always greeted with an affectionate "Cruuuuuuz" retired with more career at bats, hits, triples, and RBIs than any other Astro.

In 1997 he returned to the field as an Astros coach when former teammate Larry Dierker took over as manager. His son, Jose Cruz, Jr., was a highly-touted prospect, but struggled to live up to his father's reputation.

Julio Cruz

Cruz, Julio Louis **2B**

1977–86 B:12/2/1954, Brooklyn, NY Deb:7/4/1977, SEA AL BB/TR 5'9", 165

G	AB	R	H	HR	RBI	OBP	SLG	AVG
1156	3859	557	916	23	279	.324	.299	.237

Slick-fielding second baseman Julio Cruz, with the range and arm of a shortstop, set acrobatic standards for his position while playing with the Seattle Mariners and the Chicago White Sox from 1977 to 1986. On June 7, 1981, Cruz set an American League mark for second basemen (and tied a major league one) with 18 total chances without an error in nine innings. Combining his defensive skills with blinding speed (he once had 32 successful steals in a row), Cruz was a double threat to rival AL teams. He stole 343 bases in just 10 seasons, averaging almost 50 steals a year during his peak.

Yet he could have been better. Had he been able to bunt he could have taken far better advantage of his speed. Had he been able to lay off the high fastball his base on balls totals might have matched those of a successful leadoff hitter. When in a slump, Cruz would fiddle endlessly with his stance, sometimes even during the same at bat.

Selected by Seattle from the California Angels in the expansion draft, Cruz was traded even-up to the White Sox in June 1983 for second baseman Tony Bernazard. He drove in 40 runs, scored 47, and stole 24 bases in 99 games following the trade to help the White Sox reach the postseason for the first time since 1959. His last season in the majors was 1986. Cruz's brothers, Hector and Tommy, were also major leaguers, both of whom later played in Japan.

Tony Cuccinello

Cuccinello, Anthony Francis **2B–3B**

1930–45 B:11/8/1907, Long Island City, NY D:9/21/1995, Tampa, FL Deb:4/15/1930, CIN NL BR/TR 5'7", 160

G	AB	R	H	HR	RBI	OBP	SLG	AVG
1704	6184	730	1729	94	884	.343	.394	.280

Even though Tony Cuccinello was an All-Star second baseman in the 1930s, he is often remembered for an oddity. Playing for the White Sox in 1945, he finished second in the race for the American League batting title, only a point behind Snuffy Stirnweiss' .309. And then he was released.

When Chicago released him, "Cooch" was 38-years-old, and many younger players were returning to the major leagues after World War II. As a result, his 15-year career ended on a historically rare high note. Cuccinello's .308 average in his final season was later topped by two Hall of Fame players, Ted Williams' .316 in 1960 and Roberto Clemente's .312 in 1972.

Cuccinello began his career in 1930 with the Reds, batting .312. He played with the Dodgers from 1932 to 1935 and then joined the Boston Braves in 1936. He batted over .300 four times in the decade and was named to the National League's All-Star team in 1933 and 1938. His younger brother, Al, played with the Giants for one season in 1935, and the two Cuccinellos joined a small fraternity of brothers who homered in the same game. On July 5, 1935, while the Dodgers were playing the Giants, Tony hit a homer in the eighth inning, followed by Al's in the ninth.

Mike Cuellar

Cueller, Miguel Angel (Santana) **P**

1959–1977 B:5/8/1937, Las Villas, Cuba Deb:4/18/1959, CIN NL BL/TL 5'11", 175

W	L	PCT	G	SH	IP	BB	SO	ERA
185	130	.587	453	36	2808	822	1632	3.14

Lefthander Mike Cuellar served as the quiet linchpin of Earl Weaver's Baltimore rotation in the late 1960s and early 1970s. What was surprising about Cuellar was that a pitcher of such limited speed could win 20 or more games for three straight seasons. (A sportswriter once said his "swiftest offering could be caught barehanded.") Forced to rely on variety rather than velocity, his assortment included a palm ball and breaking pitches of different speeds and different arcs.

Necessity forced him to become a thinking man's pitcher. Orioles catcher Elrod Hendricks said, "Mike always thinks two pitches ahead. When they make an out on one of his 'set-up' pitches, he looks like they've spoiled his fun."

He impressed scouts by pitching a no-hitter while serving in the army of Cuban dictator Fulgencio Batista, and he began his professional baseball career with the International League's Havana Sugar Kings in 1957. Given a brief trial with the Cincinnati Reds in 1959, he was sent back to the minors, then released to Monterrey of the Mexican League.

Acquired by the Cardinals, Cuellar developed a screwball in the spring of 1964. Traded to the Astros in June 1965, Cuellar became an effective starter but didn't blossom until a December 1968 trade sent him to the Orioles. He won 20 games or more four times and—with Denny McLain—was co-winner of the 1969 American League Cy Young Award. In 1969 and 1974 *The Sporting News* named him as left-handed pitcher on their AL All-Star Team.

In the 1970 World Series he won Game 5 against Sparky Anderson's Reds after surviving a three-run Cincinnati first inning. "Mike wanted to throw his screwball and two of the four hits were off the screwball," said Andy Etchebarren, the catcher. "Between innings we [pitching coach George Bamberger, Cuellar, and Etchebarren] huddled in the runway behind the dugout and decided to forget the screwball and rely more on the curve and slider." Cuellar shut the Reds out the rest of the way to win, 9–3.

He pitched in five postseasons for the Orioles between 1969 and 1974; he went 4–4 in 12 postseason starts. By 1976, however, the four-time All-Star was no longer effective but hadn't fully accepted it. "Weaver buried me. I have him to thank for a lousy season. I don't think he wants me to win."

Weaver, noting the fact that Cuellar had been knocked out of 13 straight starts, replied, "I've given him more chances than I gave my first wife." In December 1976 the Orioles released Cuellar, who finished his major league career with the California Angels in 1977.

Three years later he attempted an abortive comeback in the Inter-American and Mexican leagues and later became a minor league pitching instructor for Peninsula in the Carolina League.

Roy Cullenbine

Cullenbine, Roy Joseph **OF-1B**
1938–47 B:10/18/1913, Nashville, TN D:5/28/1991, Mt. Clemens, MI Deb:4/19/1938, DET AL BB/TR 6'1", 190

G	AB	R	H	HR	RBI	OBP	SLG	AVG
1181	3879	627	1072	110	599	.408	.432	.276

Switch-hitting outfielder Roy Cullenbine had Kenesaw Mountain Landis to thank for his big break. Cullenbine, going nowhere in the Detroit system, was set free by the commissioner with more than 20 other farmhands after Landis ruled the Tigers were playing fast and loose with the roster rules.

Cullenbine spent 25 games with the Tigers in 1938 and 75 in 1939 and was cut loose by Landis in January 1940 when he was 26. He signed with Brooklyn for $25,000, was traded to the Browns after 22 games and hit .220 with 40 RBIs in 108 games. But 1941 was a different story. Cullenbine hit .317, with 98 RBIs (despite a mere nine homers), and walked 121 times, second in the American League. Cullenbine was quite the walking man, in fact, finishing with 853 in 1,181 games, including a league-leading 112 in 1945 and 137 in 1947, his final season.

He was quite the moving man as well. In 1942, for example, he went from the Browns to the Senators to the World Series-bound Yankees. He was waived to New York in August and took over left field for Tommy Henrich, who left to enter the armed service.

The Yankees then traded him to the Indians in December where he stayed put for two years before being traded to the Tigers early in 1945. Back where he started, Cullenbine hit .272 with 18 homers and 93 RBIs in 1945 and a career-best .335 in 113 games in 1946. He hit 24 home runs as the Tigers' first baseman in 1947—he had slowed down too much to play the outfield anymore—yet he batted only .224. Cullenbine then retired with a .276 career average.

Candy Cummings

Cummings, William Arthur **P**
1872–1877 B:10/18/1848, Ware, MA D:5/16/1924, Toledo, OH Deb:4/22/1872, MUT NA BR/TR 5'9", 120

W	L	PCT	G	SH	IP	BB	SO	ERA
21	22	.488	43	5	371²	27	37	2.78

William "Candy" Cummings is the probable inventor of the curveball. A few years after his retirement, he described how the idea came to him. "It was in the 1860s that I discovered the curve ball, and strange to say, it was the idle throwing of half a clam shell that gave birth to such an idea. As I watched the shells sail through their irregular course, the theory developed in my mind that I might apply it in baseball," Cummings said.

"I decided that I would try to see if I could throw a ball in a similar manner. I was laughed at by scientific men and experts, but I finally proved to them that the stunt could be done, and for a long time I was known as the 'boy wonder.'"

While it may never be proven conclusively that Cummings invented the curve, his claim was backed by such 19th-century notables as George Wright, Albert Spalding, National League president Nick Young, and Chicago manager Cap Anson.

The 5-foot 9-inch, 120-pound Cummings used his newly invented pitch to work his way up from semipro teams in Brooklyn to five ballclubs in the National Association and the National League from 1872 to 1877. He led the NA in ERA, shutouts, and innings pitched in 1873, and he won 35 games in 1875.

Cummings moved to the newly created International Association and served as president of the league and of his team, the Lynn Live Oaks. By midseason he was 1–7, and the Live Oaks dropped out of the league. Cummings then returned to the National League and completed a thoroughly dismal 1877 season, going 5–14 for Cincinnati.

If only his NL totals of 21–22 are counted, he is, along with Rollie Fingers and Leroy "Satchel" Paige, one of only three Hall of Fame pitchers with losing lifetime major league won-lost records. He had a 124–72 mark in the NA for a very respectable .633 winning percentage. He failed to complete only five of his 199 career NA starts and had an impressive 2.31 ERA in the league.

After Cummings retired from the majors, he opened a paint and wallpaper business in Athol, Massachusetts. He continued to play semipro ball until one afternoon in 1884, when he lost both ends of a doubleheader, 14–2 and 21–2.

Joe Cunningham

Cunningham, Joseph Robert **1B-OF**
1954–66 B:8/27/1931, Paterson, NJ Deb:6/30/1954, STL NL BL/TL 6'1", 190

G	AB	R	H	HR	RBI	OBP	SLG	AVG
1141	3362	525	980	64	436	.406	.417	.291

Joe Cunningham was a slick-fielding, line-drive hitting Cardinals first baseman at a time when St. Louis already had a pretty good first sacker: Stan Musial. Musial shifted from outfield to first baseman shortly after Cunningham began his major league career in 1954. After two years in the minors, Cunningham, now a part-time outfielder and fill-in first baseman, batted .318 in 1957 (including three pinch-hit home runs). He followed that by batted .312 in 1958. The next year he batted .345, second to Hank Aaron in the batting race, led the National League in on-base percentage, and was named to the All-Star Game.

Despite his commendable performances, his lack of either base-stealing speed or home run power made him only a marginal offensive threat. He was swapped to the White Sox for Minnie Minoso after the 1961 season. Cunningham hit .295 for the White Sox in 149 games in 1962, but was benched the following season to make room for Tommy McCraw. Cunningham finished his career with the expansion Senators in 1966. After retiring, he worked for the Cardinals in their Speakers' Bureau and sales department.

Nig Cuppy

Cuppy, George Joseph **P**
1892-1901 B:7/3/1869, Logansport, IN D:7/27/1922, Elkhart, IN Deb:4/16/1892, CLE NL BR/TR 5'7", 160

W	L	PCT	G	SH	IP	BB	SO	ERA
162	98	.623	302	9	2283	609	504	3.48

While Cy Young was winning 159 games for the Cleveland Spiders of the National League between 1892 and 1896, he had a teammate called Nig Cuppy who was winning 120 games. They were a serious one-two punch. Unfortunately for Cuppy, his arm blew out and he was history by 1901, while Young kept pitching and winning big-time until 1909.

Cuppy's nickname was what it sounds like, short for the racial epithet considered highly offensive today. Those were different times and the man who was born George Koppe in Logansport, Indiana, had a dark complexion.

He started with the Spiders in 1892, which turned out to be his best year. He went 28–13 with a 2.51 ERA in 376 innings. Cuppy, one of the first pitchers to wear a glove, went 17–10 in 1893 when an injury limited him to 243⅔ innings, but he followed with three straight 20-win seasons.

But 1897 marked the beginning of the end for Cuppy. After just 19 total wins over two-year span, he was traded to the St. Louis Browns in 1899, the Boston Beaneaters in 1900, and the Boston Somersets in 1901.

Before Game 3 of the Spiders-Orioles Temple Cup in 1895 Cuppy was presented by Spiders fans with a shotgun. According to the *Cleveland Plain Dealer*, Cuppy "brought the gun to his shoulder and pulled both triggers. A moment later, a boy ran out of the crowd from the direction in which he fired and placed a dead pigeon in the pitcher's hand."

George Cutshaw

Cutshaw, George William **2B**
1912–23 B:7/27/1887, Wilmington, IL D:8/22/1973, San Diego, CA Deb:4/25/1912, BRO NL BR/TR 5'9", 160

G	AB	R	H	HR	RBI	OBP	SLG	AVG
1516	5621	629	1487	25	653	.305	.344	.265

Second baseman George "Clancy" Cutshaw was about as colorful as a glass of spring water. Words such as "steady," "reliable," and "dependable" best describe his 12-season major league career.

His lack of panache was all the more noticeable because he played alongside so many characters. For example, he arrived in the major leagues with Brooklyn in 1912, the same year a loquacious rookie outfielder named Casey Stengel debuted with the team. Cutshaw became a regular immediately; it took Stengel a while to win a starting spot, but he was the rookie who inspired anecdotes. That Brooklyn team also included such strong personalities as shortstop Ivy Olson, first baseman Jake Daubert, outfielders Hy Myers and Zack Wheat, and pitcher Nap Rucker. Former Oriole Wilbert "Uncle Robby" Robinson managed the circus.

As a young ballplayer Cutshaw was known primarily for his defensive skills. More solid than spectacular, the 5-foot 9-inch, 160-pound Cutshaw led all National League second basemen in putouts from 1913 through 1916 and again in 1918. He added assist titles in 1914, 1915, 1916, and 1918, and led the league in double plays in 1913 and 1914.

In 1915 his .971 fielding average topped the National League, and his .980 average in 1919 set a new major league record, breaking a mark set in 1896. Although improved glove design and better fields soon wiped out all the fielding records before 1920, a later poll conducted by the Society for American Baseball Research voted Cutshaw the top defensive second baseman of the 1910–19 period.

On August 9, 1915, Cutshaw collected six singles in six trips to the plate. But offensively, Cutshaw was best known for his base running. He finished among the league's top 10 basestealers in seven consecutive seasons from 1913 through 1919, including a personal high of 39 in 1913. In 12 seasons he totaled 271 steals.

When Cutshaw arrived in Brooklyn the team was improving after a decade of poor finishes. He was in the Opening Day lineup when Ebbets Field opened in 1913. The Dodgers, then called the Robins in honor of Robinson, won the 1916 pennant. Daubert and Wheat supplied most of the batting punch, and "Uncle Robby" was given credit for squeezing good seasons out of supposedly washed-up pitchers such as Jack Coombs.

In 1916 Cutshaw hit .260, drove in 63 runs, and stole 27 bases. He batted fifth in the order in the World Series against the Boston Red Sox, but contributed little to Brooklyn's attack, hitting only .105 while scoring one run and batting in a pair. His error in the opening game allowed a run to score in what turned out to be a one-run loss. He never played in another World Series.

In 1918 Brooklyn traded Cutshaw and Stengel to Pittsburgh, where Cutshaw played between first baseman and banjo player Charlie Grimm and shortstop Rabbit Maranville, one of baseball's greatest pranksters.

In 1921, platooning with Cotton Tierney, Cutshaw hit a career-high .340 for Pittsburgh. He was always a difficult batter to strike out, fanning only 242 times in 5,621 at bats. He finished his career in 1923 with the Detroit Tigers under manager Ty Cobb.

Kiki Cuyler

Cuyler, Hazen Shirley **OF**

1921–38 B:8/30/1898, Harrisville, MI D:2/11/1950, Ann Arbor, MI Deb:9/29/1921, PIT NL BR/TR 5'10½", 180

G	AB	R	H	HR	RBI	OBP	SLG	AVG
1879	7161	1305	2299	128	1065	.386	.474	.321

Gifted with blazing speed and a powerful bat, Hazen "Kiki" Cuyler was a gentleman off the field who never gave an inch while on it. Although he won no batting titles, his lifetime .321 average ranks him in the top 45 of all time.

A key to his success was his speed and grace. The grace was evident when he won several waltz trophies; the speed was well documented—he led the NL in stolen bases four times and finished second twice. Triples were another specialty, and his 26 three-baggers in 1925 were not reached again for the rest of the 20th century. The 369 total bases he piled up that same year are still a Pirates record.

The teenage Cuyler had a good job in a Michigan auto assembly plant and played ball for the company team. When an economic downturn caused layoffs, he signed with Class B Michigan-Ontario League's Bay City Wolves for 1920. The Pirates brought him up after he hit .340 for the Southern Association's Nashville Volunteers in 1923 and was named Most Valuable Player there.

His nickname was not pronounced, "kee-kee," as many readers assume today. It was based on a shortened version of his last name. Nashville infielders liked to back off and let the speedy Cuyler take whatever got past them. Their cries of "Cuy! Cuy!" led local sportswriters to dub the young ballplayer "Kiki."

Cuyler exploded onto the scene in Pittsburgh in 1924, finishing fourth in batting average (.354) and triples (16) and second in stolen bases (32) behind teammate Max Carey. In 1925 the Pirates won the pennant, thanks largely to Cuyler. His .357 average was fourth in the league; he finished second in doubles, total bases, runs produced, slugging average, and stolen bases; and he led the league in runs scored and in triples. In the heat of the pennant race he put together a string of 10 consecutive hits in September, tying the record. With fellow outfielders Carey and Clyde Barnhart hitting .343 and .325, respectively, the potent Pittsburgh offense won the flag by more than eight games.

Before the World Series against hurler Walter Johnson and the Washington Senators, hometown admirers gave Cuyler a gold ball and bat. The symbolism was prophetic: Cuyler hit a home run to turn the tide in Game 2 and had two singles, a walk, and a run scored in the Game 5 Bucs victory.

In the cold drizzle of Game 7, Johnson was battling for another championship for the Senators, but the aging superstar couldn't hold leads of 4–0 and 6–3 on the slippery mound. Cuyler's fifth-inning double brought the score to 6-4, and his sacrifice bunt in the last of the seventh helped bring the Bucs to within a run. Down 7–6 in the bottom of the eighth, the Pirates mounted a two-out rally. With two men on and a run in, Senators shortstop and that year's AL MVP Roger Peckinpaugh flubbed a play on the wet ground for his eighth error of the Series. After hitting two vicious line drives foul, Cuyler smashed a dramatic hit down the right-field line. Some thought it had cleared the fence for a grand slam; Senators outfielder

Goose Goslin claimed he had seen the ball land two feet foul and stick in the mud. The umpires conferred and awarded Cuyler a two-run double and the Bucs a 9–7 lead. Pitcher Red Oldham preserved the lead in the top of the ninth for the first Pirates world championship since 1909.

In 1926 the Pirates brought up outfielder Paul Waner, who promptly hit .336, and it looked as if the Pittsburghers were building a dynasty. But dissension struck when Bucs coach and legend Fred Clarke locked horns with three Pirates—pitcher Babe Adams and outfielders Carson Bigbee and Max Carey—in a confrontation known as "The A-B-C Incident." Within days of the arguments being made public, the three were released or traded away. The team stumbled to third place despite Cuyler's .321 average and league-leading 113 runs.

In 1927 Lloyd Waner joined the Pirates outfield and outpaced all National Leaguers in runs scored, while brother Paul Waner led the league with his .380 average and the team captured the pennant. But Cuyler was nowhere to be found.

About midway through the season Cuyler was battling a minor slump. New manager Donie Bush decided it was time to make some changes in his lineup. He moved Cuyler from his accustomed spot as the Bucs' third batter to second in the order.

Cuyler balked. He felt he was much more valuable as the No. 3 hitter, had more opportunity to drive in runs in that slot, and wasn't the true contact hitter the No. 2 position called for. In fact, Cuyler offered to bat anywhere but second. Bush began to fume, and Cuyler talked himself into being a miserable second-slot batter—although he still batted .309 for the year.

In one game against the Giants, Cuyler was on first when a teammate hit a perfect double-play ball. Instead of sliding into second, Cuyler came in standing up in an effort to break up the twin killing. But the Giants infielder fumbled the ball and easily tagged Cuyler out. Although some Giants and most Pirates agreed that Cuyler had made the right play, Bush was adamant. He benched Cuyler for the rest of the season, putting Barnhart in left and moving Lloyd Waner to center. He didn't let the slugging star bat once in the World Series. The Yankees swept the Pirates as if brushing off a fly.

Backing his manager, Pirates owner Barney Dreyfuss traded Cuyler after the Series. What might have been one of the all-time classic outfields—Cuyler and the Waners—was broken up. Cuyler, who had hit .336 in three and a half seasons as a Pirate, was sent to the Cubs for infielder Sparky Adams and outfielder Pete Scott. Adams was 33 years old, and Scott played only 60 games that year before leaving the majors. The Pirates didn't see another World Series for 33 years.

Cuyler enjoyed life as a Cub. Although he slumped below .300 in his first season in Chicago, he led the league in stolen bases, then roared back in 1929 with a .360 average and another stolen base crown as the Cubs took the pennant. Cuyler drove in six runs and hit .300 in the Series, but the Cubs were conquered by Connie Mack's Philadelphia Athletics.

In 1930 and 1931, Cuyler's .355 and .330 seasons weren't enough to push the Cubs above second, and a broken foot limited his effectiveness in 1932. Still, he drove in the run that clinched the 1932 pennant with a bases-loaded triple against his old team, the Pirates. But the Yankees, featuring Babe Ruth and Lou Gehrig, swept the Cubs as they had dismissed the Pirates five years earlier.

In 1933 a broken ankle limited Cuyler to only 70 games for Chicago, but he came back in 1934 to bat .338 and lead the league with 42 doubles. Even though he hit over .300 in five of his seven Chicago years, the team released him during the 1935 season. The Reds picked him up, and in 1936 Cuyler came back again, this time with a .326 average, leading Cincinnati in average, doubles, runs, RBIs, and stolen bases—all at age 37. He ended his career with the Dodgers in 1938.

Cuyler successfully managed in the minors around a major league coaching stint with the Cubs during World War II. He was a Red Sox coach in 1950 when he suffered a heart attack at age 51. The Veterans Committee of the Hall of Fame elected him to the Shrine posthumously in 1968.

Bill Dahlen

Dahlen, William Frederick **SS-3B**

1891–1911 M(1910–1913, 251–355) B:1/5/1870, Nelliston, NY D:12/5/1950, Brooklyn, NY Deb:4/22/1891, CHI NL BR/TR 5'9", 180

G	AB	R	H	HR	RBI	OBP	SLG	AVG
2443	9031	1589	2457	84	1233	.358	.382	.272

Playing in an era when infields were littered with stones and pitted with craters, when scorekeepers regarded any ball touched as playable, and when gloves afforded hand protection but little help in spearing a ball, "Bad Bill" Dahlen made 975 errors at shortstop, more than any other player in history. Ironically, this proved that he was a wonderful fielder—had he not been so good at covering the toughest position on the diamond, his managers would never have penciled him in at shortstop 2,132 times.

In Dahlen's day, the batted ball sometimes arrived lopsided and was often covered with some slippery foreign substance that the pitcher had added. Dahlen got to more of these than most shortstops and, naturally, made more errors; however, he led the league in errors only once (in 1895), and that year was one of the four in which he led in assists. In fact, he ranks among the top three shortstops of all time in both putouts and assists. His nickname had nothing to do with his playing ability—it reflected the vehemence with which he argued.

He and Cap Anson, who managed Dahlen for his first seven years in the National League, constantly squabbled. But his most common foes were umpires. Any time a call was close, the umpire could expect a bad time from Bad Bill. He was often ejected and more than once suspended. His intensity caused even many teammates to dislike him.

Dahlen came to the NL with the Chicago White Stockings in 1891, and Anson put him at third base to get his bat into the lineup. He usually batted fifth or sixth for Chicago, hit less than .290 only once from 1892 through 1898, and hit .357 with 107 RBIs in 1894 and .352 in 1896. In 1894 he set a record by hitting safely in 42 consecutive games, a mark surpassed only by Willie Keeler, Pete Rose, and Joe DiMaggio.

Once he left the White Stockings after the 1898 season Dahlen's batting average tumbled. He was fortunate to be dealt to Brooklyn in time to play shortstop for pennant winners in 1899 and 1900. Brooklyn had built a powerhouse team by acquiring most of the stars of the old Baltimore Orioles, renowned for their rough, no-holds-barred play, and Dahlen fit right in.

In 1904 former Oriole John McGraw brought Dahlen to the Giants, where he led the league in RBIs with the astonishingly low total of 80. Dahlen's statistics for the 1905 World Series were indicative of the way he played the game late in his career: he went hitless in 15 at bats, yet drew three walks, stole three bases, scored a run, knocked in another, and handled 28 fielding chances flawlessly. Dahlen finished his playing career with Boston in 1909, although he made a few pinch-hitting appearances while managing the Dodgers from 1910 through 1913.

As a manager, his sharp tongue and irascible temper made him unpopular with his players and with reporters, but Brooklyn owner Charlie Ebbets liked him enough to keep him as skipper for four seasons, even though the club never finished higher than sixth.

Babe Dahlgren

Dahlgren, Ellsworth Tenney **1B**

1935–46 B:6/15/1912, San Francisco, CA D:9/4/1996, Arcadia, CA Deb:4/16/1935, BOS AL BR/TR 6', 190

G	AB	R	H	HR	RBI	OBP	SLG	AVG
1137	4045	470	1056	82	569	.329	.383	.261

Nicknamed "Babe" by his grandfather, Ellsworth Tenney Dahlgren played a total of 12 years with eight different major league teams, but his most notable brush with baseball fame came on May 2, 1939, when he replaced a failing Lou Gehrig at first base for the New York Yankees, ending Gehrig's streak of 2,130 consecutive games. Dahlgren had himself achieved an iron man reputation in the minors, compiling a streak of over 600 consecutive games at first base, including 188 in 1932 and 189 in 1933, in the Pacific Coast League before being called up to the Boston Red Sox in 1935.

Standing in for Gehrig that historic day, Dahlgren homered, and after the game, he had the foresight to ask Gehrig for his glove (even though Gehrig was lefthanded). "Sure, go ahead and take it, I won't be needing it anymore," Gehrig replied. Years later, Dahlgren traded the valuable glove to renowned collector Barry Halper for some keepsakes of his own career.

Dahlgren remained the Yankees first baseman for two more seasons. With the Pittsburgh Pirates in 1944 he enjoyed his finest overall season, batting .289 with 12 homers and 101 RBIs.

Hugh Daily

Daily, Hugh Ignatius **P**

1882–87 B:1857, Baltimore,MD D:Unknown
Deb:5/01/1882, BUF NL BR/TR 6'2", 180

W	L	PCT	G	SH	IP	BB	SO	ERA
73	87	.456	165	10	1415	369	846	2.92

Hugh Daily lacked a hand and a personality. He lost his left hand in an accident and was surly and uncommunicative and had no friends among teammates or fans. When he left baseball he disappeared completely. What he did, where he lived, and when he died remain a mystery.

Although nicknamed "One Arm" in the insensitive manner of the day, Daily was actually missing only his hand. As a young man he and a companion were playing around in a Baltimore theater when an English flintlock musket went off in his friend's hands; Daily's left hand was so badly injured it had to be amputated at the wrist. To play baseball, Daily fashioned a leather pad that he wore at the end of his left arm. When a ball was hit or thrown to him he would block it with the pad and then grab it. Missing a hand proved to be no disadvantage in batting: in his short career, he knocked out 88 hits.

Daily won 23 games for Cleveland in 1883, including a 1–0 no-hit victory over Philadelphia on September 23. The next year he jumped to the upstart Union Association, a wannabe rival of the National League. He led the new league with 483 strikeouts, the third-highest total ever. His accomplishment is somewhat vitiated by the second-rate quality of the competition and by the rules of the time, which included seven balls for a walk and a pitching distance of only 45 feet.

When the Union Association collapsed after one season, Daily paid a $500 fine to be allowed back in the National League. It proved hardly worth it. During the next three seasons he pitched 33 games for three different teams, lost 26 of them, and then walked out of baseball, never to be heard from again.

Steve Dalkowski

Dalkowski, Steven Louis

Minor League Phenomenon B:6/3/1939, New Britain, CT BL/BL 5'10", 170

Steve Dalkowski may have been the fastest pitcher in baseball history, but terminal wildness kept the fireballing lefthander in the minor leagues. In a nine-year pro career that occurred in towns like Kingsport, Aberdeen, Pensacola, Kennewick, Elmira, and Rochester, he established records—and fear.

"Hearing him warm up on the sideline was like hearing a gun go off," marveled Dalton Jones. "I kept thinking, if this guy ever hits me, he'll kill me. I batted against Nolan Ryan and 'Sudden Sam' McDowell, but Dalkowski was noticeably faster." One manager estimated that Dalkowski could throw 120 miles per hour.

When he was only 18, he struck out 129 batters in just 62 innings in the Appalachian League. His career record was only 46–80 with a 5.59 ERA. He struck out 1,396 in 995 career innings—and walked 1,354. One Dalkowski fastball actually ripped an earlobe off a batter. Another shattered umpire Doug Harvey's mask in three places and propelled him back 18 feet. In one game in 1957, Dalkowski struck out 24—and walked 18. He once hit a batter *kneeling in the on-deck circle.* On another occasion he threw six consecutive wild pitches. Beset by arm and drinking problems, Dalkowski pitched his last game in 1965 with San Jose in the California League.

Abner Dalrymple

Dalrymple, Abner Frank **OF**

1878–91 B:9/9/1857, Warren, IL D:1/25/1939, Warren, IL Deb:5/1/1878, MIL NL BL/TR 5'10½", 175

G	AB	R	H	HR	RBI	OBP	SLG	AVG
951	4172	813	1202	43	407	.323	.410	.288

Abner Dalrymple "lost" a batting championship more than 20 years after his death. His .354 average in 1878 as a rookie with the Milwaukee Grays was credited as the league's leading batting mark. However, research in the 1960s revealed that Providence's Paul Hines had actually batted .358, dropping Dalrymple to second. The good news for all those Dalrymple fans out there is that Abner still qualifies as the official champ because that's how they called it in 1878.

In 1879 the Chicago White Stockings paid a reported $2,500 for the lefthanded-batting speedster. Dalrymple later insisted that, at $300 a month, he was the team's highest-paid player. Although he never matched his rookie hitting performance, he was a consistent left fielder and solid batsman for eight seasons, during which time Chicago won five pennants. Dalrymple led the league in hits and runs in 1880 and in home runs in 1885 with 11; the 1885 mark came after he had hit 22 round-trippers in 1884, when the White Stockings played in a tiny ballpark with a 300-foot center field and foul lines under 200 feet.

Tom Daly

Daly, Thomas Peter **2B–C**

1887–1903 B:2/7/1866, Philadelphia, PA D:10/29/1938, Brooklyn, NY Deb:4/23/1887, CHI NL BB/TR 5'7", 170

G	AB	R	H	HR	RBI	OBP	SLG	AVG
1564	5684	1024	1582	49	811	.361	.387	.278

Tom Daly started out as a catcher but had to switch positions when his arm was deemed inadequate. After a few years as a utility player he ended up as a second baseman, a second baseman who could hit. Daly, who spent most of his career with Brooklyn, hit .308 between 1893 and 1901.

"Tido," as he was known, debuted in the majors in 1887 with the National League's Chicago White Stockings. He batted only .207 in 74 games as a rookie and .192 in 65 games in 1888. Traded to the Washington Statesmen, his fortunes changed. He batted .300 in 1889, but was traded again, this time to Brooklyn. He spent two seasons trying to find a position. When he settled in at second base in 1893 his hitting improved dramatically.

In 1894 Daly hit a career-high .341 with 82 RBIs and a career-high 135 runs, but he also led NL second basemen with 68 errors. His stay in Brooklyn was interrupted in 1897, when he jumped to the Western League to play for Connie Mack's Milwaukee team.

He returned to the Dodgers at the end of the 1898 season. In 1899 he hit .313 with 88 RBIs and led the league in double plays, chances per game, and errors. He had his last big season in 1901, batting .315 with career-highs of 90 RBIs and 38 doubles as a 35-year-old. He also led the league in putouts and chances per game.

Daly then jumped to the American League's Chicago White Sox as the NL and the year-old AL waged war over franchises and players. The White Sox, ended up with a player who was fading; he retired after two subpar seasons. He later managed in the high minors and scouted for the Indians and Yankees. Daly's brother Joe played 23 major league games as an outfielder in the 1890s.

Ray Dandridge

Dandridge, Ray **3B- 2B- SS- OF**

Negro League Player (1933–49) B:8/31/1913, Richmond, VA BR/TR 5'7", 170

Ray Dandridge has been called the best third baseman that the Negro Leagues ever produced, and he very well may be the most popular American ever to play in Cuba and Mexico. He came tantalizingly close to playing in the major leagues, but first discrimination and then his own age stymied him.

"There was never a smoother-functioning master at third than Ray Dandridge, and he can hit that apple too," raved Cum Posey, who owned the highly respected black baseball club the Homestead Grays.

"Ray Dandridge was fantastic," marveled Hall of Famer Monte Irvin, one of the first blacks signed by the Giants. "Best I've ever seen at third. I saw all the greats—Brooks (Robinson), (Graig) Nettles—but I've never seen a better third baseman than Dandridge. He had the best hands. In a season he seldom made more than two errors. If the ball took a bad hop, his glove took a bad hop."

The son of a textile worker crippled in an industrial accident, young Dandridge was the 19-year-old captain of a local baseball team in Richmond, Virginia. A Negro League squad called the Detroit Stars came to Richmond and easily disposed of the locals. But Detroit manager "Candy Jim" Taylor couldn't take his eyes off of Dandridge, who not only homered but also fielded brilliantly.

Taylor recruited Dandridge for the Detroit ballclub. Once Dandridge joined the Stars, Taylor taught him to hit line drives rather than to try for home runs. During his career Dandridge hit few homers but compiled an estimated .321 average in the Negro Leagues and .347 against white major league competition.

Dandridge started his career with the Stars as an outfielder but was soon converted to third base. The next year he moved over to the Newark Dodgers, the predecessors of the famed Newark Eagles. Later he starred for the Eagles themselves.

In 1939 Dandridge received an offer to play in the Mexican League. He approached Eagles owner Mrs. Effa Manley, saying that if she matched the Mexicans' offer he would stay. "At that time we were having such a bad time financially, I decided not to give it to him," said Manley. "But I thought it showed a nice attitude, because he had a family to support." Dandridge took the bonus money he received from the Mexican team and bought a small house in Newark.

Wherever he played, he hit well over .300. In 1946 Mexican League owner Jorge Pasquel started importing major leaguers such as Max Lanier, Sal Maglie, Danny Gardella, Vern Stephens, and Mickey Owen. He compensated them handsomely, fostering resentment among the circuit's poorly paid Latinos and blacks. Dandridge, making just $350 a month, demanded more money from the wealthy Pasquel. He got $10,000 a year.

In 1949 he returned to the United States to manage Alexander Pompez's New York Cubans, whose home field was the Polo Grounds. New York Giants farm director Carl Hubbell then purchased Dandridge and pitcher Dave Barnhill from Pompez. Dandridge, 35 at the time, gave his age to the Giants as 30.

Except for segregated accommodations in Louisville and Kansas City, Dandridge and Barnhill faced little discrimination. With Minneapolis Dandridge hit .362 in 1949. Despite his age he was voted the American Association Rookie of the Year. In 1950 he led the league with 627 at bats and 195 hits, batted .311, and was named the circuit's Most Valuable Player.

In 1950 the parent New York Giants were battling for the pennant. Giants hurler Sal Maglie, who had seen Dandridge play in Mexico, begged them to promote Dandridge. He was told Dandridge was too old. "But we could have won the pennant," insisted Maglie. "I know damn well with Dandridge playing third, we'd have won that pennant in '50."

In 1951 Dandridge continued to play well for Minneapolis, hitting .324. That year he roomed with a young Willie Mays, who had been promoted from the Giants' farm club at Trenton. Mays hit .477 and was called up to New York. Dandridge stayed behind again. The Philadelphia Athletics were interested in purchasing him, but "Minneapolis wouldn't sell him for no money," said William "Judy" Johnson, then a scout for the A's.

After his retirement, Dandridge once complained to Giants owner Horace Stoneham about never having the chance to play in the majors. "I just wanted to get my left foot in there," Dandridge explained. "I just would have liked to have been up there one day, even if it was only to get a cup of coffee."

Eventually Dandridge did better than that. He was voted into the Baseball Hall of Fame in March 1987. When informed of his induction over the phone, Dandridge at first thought it was some sort of a cruel hoax. Then he grew quiet, mumbled a thank you, and began to cry.

Dave Danforth

Danforth, David Charles **P**

1911–25 B:3/7/1890, Granger, TX 9/19/1970, Baltimore, MD Deb:8/1/1911, PHI AL BL/TL 6', 167

W	L	PCT	G	SV	IP	BB	SO	ERA
71	66	.518	286	23	1186	455	484	3.89

Lefthander Dave Danforth was best known for his unusual ability to grip a baseball so hard he could loosen the seams on it and improve his curveball. Danforth was also accused of using an illegal "shine ball," developed when he was with Louisville in 1915. He was in the minors with Columbus when certain pitchers were "grandfathered" and allowed to use trick pitchers, so he was not allowed to employ his "shine ball" in 1922, when he returned to the majors with the Browns. Umpires were constantly watching to prevent him from scuffing the ball. In one contest umpire Billy Evans used 58 balls with Danforth on the mound.

The nickname "Dauntless Dave" referred either to his ability to work out of a jam or the courage he showed by pitching in pain—maybe both. David Charles Danforth attended Baylor University and received a degree in dentistry from the University of Maryland in 1915. After retiring from baseball Danforth practiced that profession in Baltimore.

Harry Danning

Danning, Harry **C**

1933–42 B:9/6/1911, Los Angeles, CA Deb:7/30/1933, NY NL BR/TR 6'1", 190

G	AB	R	H	HR	RBI	OBP	SLG	AVG
890	2971	363	847	57	397	.330	.415	.285

Up on Coogan's Bluff back in the 1930s New York Giants fans fell in love with a funny-looking guy they called "Harry the Horse." Harry Danning, who stood 6 feet 1 inch and weighed 190 pounds, was a backup catcher for the first half of his career until Giants manager Bill Terry elevated him to a starting role in 1938.

Given his opportunity, Danning didn't disappoint. He became an All-Star. In 120 games that year, he batted .306, the first of three consecutive .300 seasons. A contact hitter with a little bit of pop in his bat, Harry the Horse had the best year of his career the following season when he hit .313, drove in 74 runs and smashed 16 home runs. And he handled the great Carl Hubbell to boot.

Giants fans were wild about Harry, maybe because he represented the underdog, the guy who waited patiently for his big chance and then delivered when his turn in the spotlight came. In his brightest World Series moment, his single plated the first run of a six-run rally against the Yankees in Game 4 of the 1937 Series.

Alvin Dark

Dark, Alvin Ralph **SS–3B**

1946–60 M(1961–64, 1966–71, 1974–75, 1977, 994–954) B:1/7/1922, Comanche, OK Deb:7/14/1946, BOS NL BR/TR 5'11", 185

G	AB	R	H	HR	RBI	OBP	SLG	AVG
1828	7219	1064	2089	126	757	.334	.411	.289

Alvin Dark was a three-time All-Star who helped his teams win three pennants as a player, and then reached the postseason three more times as a manager. Beset by a series of major controversies in the mid-1960s—charges of racism, an adulterous affair, and a highly publicized firing by Charlie Finley—Dark overcame adversity to manage the Oakland A's to a world championship in 1974.

A shortstop with the Boston Braves in 1948, Dark was a vital cog on three pennant-winning teams. Always a student of the game, he hung up his glove in 1960 and immediately made the transition to major league manager. In 1962, his second year as a manager, he steered the San Francisco Giants to a pennant.

In July 1964, however, Dark became involved in serious controversy. A story by Stan Isaacs in *Newsday* had him saying: "We (the Giants) have trouble because we have so many Negro and Spanish-speaking players on this team. They are just not able to perform up to the white player when it comes to mental alertness. You can't make most Negroes and Spanish players have the pride in their team that you can get from white players. You couldn't name three colored players in our league who are always mentally alert to take advantage of situations."

Dark claimed he had been "gravely misquoted" and that the quotes were "deformed." Once praised by the NAACP for making Willie Mays the Giants' team captain, he was faced with a player revolt and speculation that he would be immediately fired. Mays talked his black teammates out of rebellion, and Jackie Robinson commented: "I have found Dark to be a gentleman and, above all, unbiased. Our relationship has not only been on the ballfield but off it."

As things turned out, Dark was fired anyway, but not for his comments. Giants owner Horace Stoneham found out that the Bible-quoting Dark was having an affair with an airline stewardess, whom he later married. The romance eroded Stoneham's trust in Dark and, when the Giants finished fourth at season's end, Dark was gone.

In July 1965 Charlie Finley hired Dark as his "administrative assistant" for the Kansas City A's. By the start of the 1966 season he was the team's manager. Dark met with the usual frustrations in dealing with Finley, but the big blowup came in August 1967. Pitcher Lew Krausse was accused of rowdy behavior on a team flight, and Finley fined him $500 and suspended him indefinitely. The A's revolted. Finley summoned Dark and ordered the manager to defend him, but Dark refused. The A's players issued a statement that read in part: "If Mr. Finley would give his excellent manager and fine coaching staff the authority they deserve, these problems (of discipline) would not exist."

The incensed Finley not only fired Dark on the spot; he also gave first baseman Ken Harrelson (whom Finley called "a menace to baseball") his unconditional release. Harrelson subsequently signed with the Red Sox for a $62,000 bonus and helped lead them to the 1967 pennant.

Dark (nicknamed "Blackie" because of his jet-black hair) had starred in football at Louisiana State University and was drafted by the Philadelphia Eagles. He passed on professional football and took a $50,000 bonus from the Boston Braves. Dark batted.322 as a rookie and helped the Braves win the world championship. He was voted Rookie of the Year in 1948, the last time that one award was given for both leagues. Dark also finished third in the National League Most Valuable Player balloting.

In December 1949 Dark and Eddie "the Brat" Stanky were traded to the New York Giants, and Dark was promptly named team captain by manager Leo Durocher. With Dark at short the Giants won pennants in 1951 and 1954. In the 1951 World Series against the Yankees Dark hit .417; against Cleveland in postseason play in 1954 the steady Dark hit .412.

Adequate in the field and a dangerous hitter, Dark was traded to the Cardinals, Cubs, Phillies, and a second tour with the Braves, this time in Milwaukee. Meanwhile, the Giants had moved to San Francisco and were looking for a new manager. In October 1960 they sent infielder Andre Rodgers to the Braves to acquire Dark—not to play, but to manage.

The second-guessing that often came with the job frustrated him. "There are surprisingly few real students of the game of baseball, partly because everybody, my 83-year-old mother included, thinks they learned all there was to know about it at puberty," Dark said. "Baseball is very beguiling that way."

After being fired by Charlie Finley in 1967, he was hired to manage the Indians and lasted until August 1971. He then made his living at golf tournaments until Finley gave him a second chance in 1974. Dark won a world championship that year, Oakland's third in a row, and then was fired despite another first-place finish in 1975. Signed to manage the Padres in 1977, he lasted just one season.

Ron Darling

Darling, Ronald Maurice **P**

1983–95 B:8/19/60 Honolulu, HA Deb:9/6/83, NY NL
BR/TR 6'3", 195

W	L	PCT	G	SH	IP	BB	SO	ERA
136	116	.540	382	13	2360^{1}	906	1590	3.87

In his glory days with the New York Mets, Ron Darling was a darling of the Shea Stadium faithful. In New York's championship year of 1986, he teamed with Bob Ojeda, Sid Fernandez, and Dwight Gooden to provide the Mets with the best starting rotation in the National League. In the World Series against Boston, he pitched heroically in Game 1 only to lose, 1–0, on an error, but got his revenge in Game 4, earning the win in a 6–2 victory. He extended his scoreless streak against the Red Sox to 18 innings in Game 7 before giving up a couple of home runs, although the Mets rallied to win the game and the Series.

After a standout career at Yale, Darling arrived in Queens by way of Texas. He came to the Mets in a swap with the Rangers (along with Walt Terrell) for Lee Mazzilli on April 1, 1982. He won a dozen in 1984, his first full season, and followed that by going 16–6 with a 2.90 ERA and a place on the NL All-Star squad. He won a career-best 17 games for the Mets in 1988, pitching into the seventh inning in 24 of his 34 starts and throwing four shutouts. In Game 7 of the NLCS against the Dodgers, however, Darling took the loss, yielding six runs (four earned) on six hits in a single inning.

Darling slipped to 14–14 in 1989, but looked good with the bat and glove. He belted home runs in back-to-back starts in June, and became the first Gold Glove pitcher in Mets history. But his great days at Shea were over. For the next season-and-a-half he was used as a starter and a reliever, with mixed success, and on July 15, 1991, he was dealt to Montreal. After starting three games for the Expos and posting a ghastly 7.41 ERA, Darling was sent to Oakland on July 31. His first American League win—and his 100th career victory—came against Seattle on August 5.

The change of scenery seemed to revitalize Darling, and his 1992 season seemed like old times. He took a no-hitter into the seventh inning five times for the A's, and flirted with a no-hitter as late as the eighth in two games. He won 15, and his brilliant performance after the All-Star break—7–3, 2.90 ERA—was a key factor in the A's winning the AL West. It proved to be his last hurrah. Darling retired in 1995, after registering a career-worst 6.23 ERA as the A's finished last.

Danny Darwin

Darwin, Daniel Wayne **P**

1978–98 B:10/25/1955, Bonham, TX Deb: 9/8/1978, TEX AL BR/TR 6'3", 190

W	L	PCT	G	SV	IP	BB	SO	ERA
171	182	.484	716	32	3016^{2}	874	1942	3.84

Danny Darwin was one of the best pitchers with a losing record in major league history. Despite a lifetime 171-182 record, he pitched in the majors for 21 seasons, led the National League in ERA in 1990, and twice led that league with the lowest on-base percentage by opposing batters.

Signed as a free agent by the Texas Rangers organization in 1976, Darwin pitched at Asheville, Tulsa, and Tucson before reaching Arlington. He posted his best season with Texas in 1980 when he went 134. In 1985 Darwin went to Milwaukee as part of a complicated four-team deal. Darwin sunk to 818 with Brewers that year, allowing an AL-high 34 homers.

Milwaukee traded Darwin to Houston in August 1986, and he seemed to do much better in his native state. Darwin's 2.21 ERA was best in the National League in 1990. At season's end he signed as a free agent with Boston, but he spent most of the next season on the disabled list. Darwin won a career-high 15 games in 1993, leaving the club after the 1994 season to sign as a free agent with Toronto. When the Jays released him in July 1995, he signed with Texas. Unsigned by the Rangers at season's end, he hooked up with Pittsburgh, who traded him back to Houston for pitcher Rich Loiselle in July 1996.

Darwin signed with the White Sox in February 1997. He had the opportunity to pitch on the same team with younger brother Jeff, but it did not last long. That July Danny Darwin, and fellow pitchers Roberto Hernandez, and Wilson Alvarez went to the Giants in a trade that helped give San Francisco the NL West championship. At age 42 he started 25 games for the Giants in 1998.

Jake Daubert

Daubert, Jacob Ellsworth **1B**

1910–24 B:4/7/1884, Shamokin, PA D:10/9/1924, Cincinnati Deb:4/14/1910, BRO NL BL/TL 5'10½", 160

G	AB	R	H	HR	RBI	OBP	SLG	AVG
2014	7673	1117	2326	56	722	.360	.401	.303

The National League's best first baseman between 1910 and 1920, Jake Daubert played 15 seasons as a regular and helped two different teams win pennants. Talented, modest, and a bit colorless, he was often described as "nearly" as good defensively as Hal Chase. But Daubert was a better hitter and, unlike Chase, always played the game on the square. A quiet man, who led by example, Daubert captained the Cincinnati Reds from 1919 until his death in 1924.

Born into a coal mining family, at age 11 he started working in the mines but played baseball on weekends, beginning as a pitcher before settling at first base. The Cleveland Indians drafted him in 1908, but he failed to hit enough to make the team. He was sold to Brooklyn after the 1910 season..

As a rookie, Daubert hit only .264 but was impressive defensively. A wiry 5 feet 10 inches and 160 pounds, he was sure-handed and mobile, and had an accurate arm. On May 6,1910, he made 21 putouts in a nine-inning game, one shy of the major league record. He led the league in fielding average three times.

Daubert started to hit in 1911, finishing the year at .307. He went on to hit above .300 in 10 big league seasons. A lefthanded hitter with good speed and bat control, he normally batted second in the lineup. He stole 251 bases during his career, with a high of 32 in 1911, and often gave himself up for the team. An excellent bunter, he set a record with four sacrifices in one game in 1914 and finished his career with 392.

In 1913 Daubert won the league batting crown with a .350 mark. Although he neither scored nor knocked in many runs, he still won the Chalmers Award as Most Valuable Player. He repeated as batting champion in 1914 with a .329 mark.

After many years in the second division, Brooklyn climbed to third place in 1915 and won a surprise pennant in 1916. Daubert batted .316 that season but slumped to only .176 in the World Series as Brooklyn lost to the Boston Red Sox.

When Organized Baseball's battle with the Federal League led to rising salaries, Daubert's annual take jumped from $5,000 to $9,000 per year. After the new league collapsed, many salaries were cut, but Brooklyn president Charles Ebbets continued to pay Daubert the higher wage.

In 1918 World War I shortened the major league season, and owners attempted to prorate salaries. Daubert sued and recovered most of the unpaid balance of $2,150. An irate Ebbets thought Daubert disloyal and traded him to Cincinnati in March 1919 for strong-armed outfielder Tommy Griffith.

Although Daubert hit only .276 in 1919, he helped key the Reds' unexpected pennant win. In Cincinnati's shocking World Series victory over the Chicago White Sox, he batted .241 and scored four runs. Officials later discovered that eight White Sox players had conspired to throw the Series.

Daubert's best season was 1922, when he was 38 years old. He batted .336, scored 114 runs, drove in 66, and led the NL with 22 triples. For the only time in his career, he reached double figures in home runs, with 12. Two years later he was still an effective player, but toward the end of the season he became ill. On October 9, 1924, he died in Cincinnati from complications following an appendectomy.

Rich Dauer

Dauer, Richard Fremont **2B–3B**
1976–85 B:7/27/1952, San Bernardino, CA
Deb:9/11/1976, BAL AL BR/TR 6', 180

G	AB	R	H	HR	RBI	OBP	SLG	AVG
1140	3829	448	984	43	372	.313	.343	.257

Rich Dauer's first task was to make the Orioles forget about All-Star second baseman Bobby Grich, who had departed to California in 1976. Dauer never hit up to expectations, although he was solid defensively. He arrived in Baltimore after having led the International League with a .336 average, and hit .103 in a brief trial with the Orioles. Dauer eventually settled in at the .250 range.

He hit a home run in the seventh game of the 1979 World Series to give the Orioles a brief lead over the Pirates, but Pittsburgh came back to take the Series. Dauer struggled in the 1983 postseason. He was 0-for-14 in the Championship Series, and 4-for-19 in the World Series against the Phillies, although Baltimore won in five games. Dauer had an unusual penchant for hitting into double plays. He ranked among the all-time easiest to double up, hitting into 128 double plays in 3,829 total at bats, a ratio of one every 29.9 at bats.

He was reliable in the field, however. In 1978 he set major league records by playing in 86 straight errorless games and handling 425 chances without an error.

Darren Daulton

Daulton, Darren Arthur **C–OF**
1983–97 B:1/3/1962, Arkansas City, KS
Deb:9/25/1983, PHI NL BL/TR 6'2", 190

G	AB	R	H	HR	RBI	OBP	SLG	AVG
1161	3630	511	891	137	588	.360	.427	.245

Darren Daulton came to the major leagues in 1985 as Philadelphia's top catching prospect, but he struggled at the plate and was constantly hampered by injuries. At the same time, the Phillies descended into last place in the National League East. By 1992 Daulton was an All-Star performer, and in 1993 the Phillies won the pennant. In the final year of his career, after injuries had slowed him to a virtual walk for several seasons, Daulton was picked up by the Marlins in midseason of 1997; he was instrumental in leading Florida to a World Series victory.

In his first five seasons, however, Daulton never batted higher than .225. He landed on the disabled list in four of those seasons, undergoing two major knee surgeries in 1986. Daulton improved to .268 with 12 home runs in 1990, but 1992 was his true breakout year: 27 homers, a league-leading 109 RBIs, and the first of three All-Star appearances.

With Daulton as their unquestioned leader, the Phillies erupted for 97 wins and the National League pennant in 1993. Physical ailments made it his last 100-game season in Philadelphia. In 1995 he tore his right anterior cruciate ligament in August. After eight operations on his left knee, the right was now just as bad; his catching days were over. Daulton opened the 1996 season in left field, but his knees forced him out after just five games. Many thought his career was finished.

After nine months of rest and rehabilitation, Daulton returned for the 1997 campaign. With Rico Brogna at first base, Daulton again went to the Philadelphia outfield. He played regularly until a July trade sent him to Florida. Platooned at first base, Daulton added clutch hitting and veteran moxie to the Marlins. After underdog Florida won the NL pennant, Daulton hit .389 in the World Series, including a homer and two doubles, to end his career with a ring.

Hooks Dauss

Dauss, George August **P**

1912–26 B:9/22/1889, Indianapolis, IN D:7/27/1963, St. Louis, MO Deb:9/28/1912, DET AL BR/TR 5'10½", 168

W	L	PCT	G	SV	IP	BB	SO	ERA
223	182	.551	538	39	3390^{2}	1067	1201	3.30

Ask baseball historians to name the all-time Detroit Tigers leader in victories, and they're likely to guess Jim Bunning, Mickey Lolich, Hal Newhouser, Denny McLain, or Jack Morris. The correct answer is Hooks Dauss, who pitched for the club for 15 seasons.

The righthander, born George August Daus, won in double figures for 14 consecutive seasons, even though the Tigers finished higher than third only twice. Three times he reached the 20-victory plateau with a high of 24 in 1915, and on another occasion he won 19.

A willing worker, Dauss once went 11 straight years without making fewer than 25 starts. As was the custom of the day, he also pitched in relief and compiled 40 career saves. And, in a bit of trivia, Dauss was the winning pitcher in the most lopsided loss ever hung on the Yankees in Yankee Stadium—a 19-1 decision in 1925.

He relied heavily on a big curveball, a pitch that not only served him on the mound but gave him his nickname as well. People called him "Hookey," or "Hooks." When a pitch is distinctive or effective enough to give the pitcher a nickname, he's got something special.

Vic Davalillo

Davalillo, Victor Jose (Romero) **OF–1B**

1963–74, 1977–1980 B:7/31/1936, Cabimas, Venezuela Deb:4/9/1963, CLE AL BL/TL 5'7", 155

G	AB	R	H	HR	RBI	OBP	SLG	AVG
1458	4017	509	1122	36	329	.317	.364	.279

Although he never became the major star some predicted, Vic Davalillo captured a Gold Glove in 1964, played in the 1965 All-Star Game, and appeared in five postseasons. Generously listed as 5 feet 7 inches, Davalillo was at his best in clutch situations off the bench.

In 1970 with St. Louis the diminutive Venezuelan led the National League with 24 pinch hits in 73 at bats, while setting major league records for most pinch-hit doubles, with eight, and triples, with three. After the season he was traded with pitcher Nelson Briles to Pittsburgh for Matty Alou and George Brunet. He batted .333 as a pinch hitter for a club that became the 1971 world champions. Davalillo spent nearly three years in the Mexican League, but returned to the major leagues in August 1977.

He became a key pinch hitter for the Dodgers in their pennant drive and made a major contribution in Game 3 of that year's Championship Series. With the Dodgers and Phils tied at a game apiece, Philadelphia held a 5–3 lead with two outs in the bottom of the ninth inning. Davalillo came through with a drag bunt, beating the throw to first. Manny Mota drove him home, and two more singles gave Los Angeles a 6–5 win. When Davalillo retired after the 1980 season, his 95 career pinch hits ranked sixth on the all-time list.

Jim Davenport

Davenport, James Houston **3B–SS–2B**

1958–70 M(1985, 56–88) B:8/17/1933, Siluria, AL Deb:4/15/1958, SF NL BR/TR 5'11", 175

G	AB	R	H	HR	RBI	OBP	SLG	AVG
1501	4427	552	1142	77	456	.320	.367	.258

When Jim Davenport first arrived in the majors in 1958, San Francisco manager Bill Rigney called him "the greatest third baseman I ever saw—at least the only one I'd compare to Billy Cox." That was a bit of an overstatement, and Davenport never hit enough to rank with the third base greats. Nevertheless, he was a popular and reliable player throughout his career.

The steady third baseman led the National League in fielding percentage in 1960 and 1961; he repeated the feat in 1962 and also won a Gold Glove in helping the Giants capture the pennant. Davenport tied a World Series record by turning four double plays in a seven-game Series. San Francisco, however, lost the Series.

Davenport was one of the original San Francisco Giants, manning third base as a rookie on Opening Day 1958. As a result, he—like Orlando Cepeda and the other Giants rookies—was a great fan favorite. Davenport received an even warmer welcome from Bay Area fans than did star Willie Mays.

Alvin Davis

Davis, Alvin Glenn **1B–DH**

1984–92 B:9/9/1960 Riverside, CA Deb:4/11/1984, SEA AL BL/TR 6'1", 195

G	AB	R	H	HR	RBI	OBP	SLG	AVG
1206	4240	568	1189	160	683	.384	.450	.280

Alvin Davis was one of the most promising rookies ever to set foot in Seattle. Called up to play first base for the hapless Mariners in 1984, he hit the first of his 27 home runs that season off Dennis Eckersley. He finished the season at .284 with 116 RBIs to claim American League Rookie of the Year honors.

The M's tried to build a team around Davis, but he never quite matched his rookie season. When Seattle moved him to designated hitter in 1990 his batting average dropped sharply. At the end of 1991 he left the Mariners for the Angels, departing with more games played, hits, home runs, doubles, RBIs, and total bases than any player in the young franchise's history; he has since been surpassed in every category. He played a few games in 1992 for the Angels before finishing the season, and his career, in Japan.

Chili Davis

Davis, Charles Theodore **OF–DH**
1981–99 B:1/17/1960, Kingston, Jamaica
Deb:4/10/1981, SF NL BB/TR 6'3", 210

G	AB	R	H	HR	RBI	OBP	SLG	AVG
2436	8673	1240	2380	350	1372	.363	.451	.274

Charles Theodore Davis got a bad haircut in sixth grade, and it never stopped following him around. His haircut made a friend howl because he thought the barber had used a chili bowl to do the cutting. The name "Chili" stuck through Dorsey High School in Los Angeles, four stops in the minor leagues, 19 major league seasons, three All-Star Games, and three world championships.

Chili Davis displayed speed and power in seven years as a San Francisco Giants outfielder. He moved to the American League and remade himself into a durable and consistent designated hitter good for at least 20 home runs and 85-plus RBIs per season. Along the way, he earned a reputation as a clubhouse leader admired by teammates and fans.

Davis signed with the California Angels as a free agent after the 1987 season. He worked closely with batting coach Rod Carew to refine his hitting skills, but injuries marred his final season in California in 1990.

Davis landed next in Minnesota, where he brought a stabilizing presence to a veteran group. With the new DH contributing 29 home runs, Minnesota won a division title and knocked off Toronto for the pennant. Davis batted .286 in both the Championship Series and World Series, homering twice in the Twins' seven-game triumph over the Atlanta Braves.

Davis established a career high with 112 RBIs with the Angels in 1993. But the 1994 strike robbed him of what might have been his best season: Davis was hitting .311 with 26 homers and 84 RBIs when play stopped in early August.

In 1997 Davis signed with rebuilding Kansas City, and set another career best with 30 home runs at age 37. The desire for another championship drove him to sign with the New York Yankees after the season. Davis missed most of 1998 with an ankle injury he suffered in the second game of the year, but was back in time for the playoffs. He hit a homer and collected seven RBIs in postseason action as the Bronx Bombers won three rounds of playoffs in just 14 games.

Back to full health in 1999, Davis turned in another solid campaign for the repeating-champion Yankees. But with four players sharing time at the DH spot for New York, Chili retired after the World Series to pursue acting, restaurateuring, and clothes merchandising—all of which he had dabbled in during his baseball career.

Curt Davis

Davis, Curtis Benton **P**
1934–46 B:9/7/1903, Greenfield, MO D:10/13/1965, Covina, CA Deb:4/21/1934, PHI NL BR/TR 6'2", 185

W	L	PCT	G	SV	IP	BB	SO	ERA
158	131	.547	429	33	2325	479	684	3.42

Curt Davis was an avid hunter and a dead shot, earning him the nickname "Coonskin." He also had great aim with the baseball; he walked only 479 batters in 2,325 innings, or 1.8 walks every nine innings.

The sidearmer began his baseball career while working in a logging camp. On a day off, Davis went to watch a semipro game. Seeing that the pitching was inadequate, he sauntered over to one of the teams, said "I can do better than that," then went out to the mound and backed up his boast. Davis worked in the logging camp and pitched semipro ball for $15 a game until age 24, when he was discovered by a scout.

It took him six years of beating the bushes before he finally made it to the Phillies as a 30-year-old rookie in 1934. He became an immediate success, going 19–17 with a 2.95 ERA for a seventh-place team. He went on to pitch successfully with the Cubs, Cardinals, and Dodgers, remaining in the major leagues for 13 seasons. His best year came in 1939 with St. Louis, when at age 36 he went 22–16 with seven saves and also hit .381 with one homer. For his career, Davis hit .203 with 11 homers, including a grand slam in 1938.

Eric Davis

Davis, Eric Keith **OF**
1984–94, 1996–* B:5/29/1962, Los Angeles, CA
Deb:5/19/1984, CIN NL BR/TR 6'3", 185

G	AB	R	H	HR	RBI	OBP	SLG	AVG
1460	4911	883	1321	272	872	.363	.489	.269

Three years after he retired, and one year after he was diagnosed with colon cancer, Eric Davis batted a career-high .327. Injuries had kept him from becoming a superstar—and even forced him to retire for one season—but he used the knowledge gained from adversity to get through chemotherapy. "My situation with cancer didn't make me look at life differently; my retirement did," Davis told *Baseball Weekly.* "Being home, not being part of the game for the first time in 15 years, people treated me different. They forgot about me."

In Baltimore, they did not forget. Davis received a minute-long standing ovation at Camden Yards upon his return to the lineup on September 15, 1997. He was named to Baltimore's postseason roster and played in nine games, homering in Game 5 of the Championship Series. In 1998 Davis set an Orioles record with a 30-game hitting streak, generating 10 homers and 35 RBIs in that span.

The Cincinnati Reds drafted Davis out of Fremont High in Los Angeles in 1980, and by 1986 he was a fixture in center field at Riverfront Stadium. In an era of 20–20 and 30–30 clubs, Davis in 1986 became the first National Leaguer to crack 20 home runs and steal 80 bases. The next season he socked 37 home runs and stole 50 bases. He also set a league record by stroking three grand slam home runs in May of that season.

Davis won three consecutive Gold Glove Awards and played in two All-Star Games as Cincinnati's best slugger and most proficient basestealer. In 1990 "Eric the Red" led the Reds to the world championship. He started the World Series with a home run in his first at bat, but finished the Series in the hospital. He suffered a lacerated kidney diving for a ball in Game 4.

Davis played just 89 games for the Reds in 1991, and went to the Los Angeles Dodgers in 1992. Injuries ruined what Davis had hoped would be a happy California reunion with childhood friend Darryl Strawberry. After batting just .232 as a Dodger, Davis was traded to the Detroit Tigers in August 1993. He barely played in 1994 because of a herniated disk in his neck. After his ninth trip to the disabled list in an 11-year career, Davis retired.

He returned to baseball and to Cincinnati in 1996, batting .287 with 26 home runs and 23 stolen bases. That season he was named NL Comeback Player of the Year by *The Sporting News.* But his greatest comeback was from cancer a year later.

George Davis

Davis, George Stacey **SS-3B-OF-2B**

1890–1909 M(1895, 1900–01, 107–139) B:8/23/1870, Cohoes, NY D:10/17/1940, Philadelphia, PA Deb:4/19/1890, CLE NL BB/TR 5'9", 180

G	AB	R	H	HR	RBI	OBP	SLG	AVG
2368	9031	1539	2660	72	1437	.361	.404	.295

Stocky, powerful switch hitter George Davis began his career as a slightly erratic outfielder and went on to become a league-leading shortstop. In 20 major league seasons he hit nearly .300, and ranks high in such lifetime statistics as hits, runs, and RBIs. He was a hero in one of the greatest upsets in World Series history. Yet it took nearly 90 years after his final at bat before he was finally elected to the Hall of Fame.

Davis came to the major leagues with the National League's Cleveland Spiders in 1890. After three ordinary seasons as an outfielder and third baseman, he was traded to the New York Giants for Buck Ewing, considered one of the great players of the age. Davis' arrival in New York coincided with an increase in the pitching distance from 50 feet to 60 feet 6 inches. His batting average jumped more than 100 points, to .355. He played with the Giants for nine seasons, hitting more than .300 each year. In each of four seasons he scored more than 100 runs and in three seasons collected more than 100 RBIs.

Davis' best year offensively was 1897, when he batted .353, stole 65 bases, scored 112 runs, hit 31 doubles, 10 triples, and 10 home runs, and led the league with 136 RBIs. He also became New York's regular shortstop after several years of utility play. Two years later he led NL shortstops in fielding, a feat he repeated in 1900.

Despite his outstanding play and the efforts of a few teammates, the 1890s Giants represented a low point in the club's history between the pennant-winning clubs of the 1880s and John McGraw's teams of the early 1900s. After finishing a close second to the Baltimore Orioles in 1894 and sweeping them in the postseason Temple Cup, the Giants were sold to Tammany Hall politician Andrew Freedman.

Freedman soon became the most hated owner in baseball. Tightfisted, abrasive, and untrustworthy, he blamed everyone but himself as the club's fortunes fell. He changed managers on a whim. Davis twice took charge, once for 33 games in 1895 and again from mid-1900 through the 1901 season. The team stayed near the bottom of the standings.

The war between the National League and the new American League gave Davis his chance to escape Freedman, and in 1902 he became one of many National Leaguers to jump to the AL, joining the Chicago White Sox. He hit .299 that year and led all shortstops in the league in fielding.

The situation changed drastically when the leagues reached agreement after the 1902 season. John T. Brush bought the Giants and made John McGraw manager. Davis wanted to return to the Giants, despite being bound to the White Sox for another year. He played four games for New York in 1903 before being declared the property of Chicago. Davis took his case to court but lost.

Davis returned to the White Sox in 1904. His average dropped to .252, still respectable in the Dead Ball Era, when batting averages plummeted throughout baseball. The American League averaged .244 in 1904, and only four regular players reached .300. A better measure of Davis' value was that the White Sox jumped from seventh place to third with him back at shortstop. In 1905 they moved up to second as the 35-year-old Davis again led league shortstops in fielding.

The 1906 season capped his career. Chicago was engaged in a real dogfight for the pennant with Cleveland and New York when a 19-game winning streak in August put the White Sox on top. New York caught them twice in September, but the Sox pulled away at the end. Even in the Dead Ball Era the White Sox, aptly dubbed "the Hitless Wonders," were poor batters. The team average was .230, worst in the league. Second baseman Frank Isbell, the team's leading hitter, batted .279. Davis hit .277, and no one else hit as high as .260. Davis led the team with 80 RBIs. The team's strengths were pitching and defense.

Few experts gave the Hitless Wonders a chance in the World Series. The Cubs had taken the NL pennant with an all-time regular-season record 116 victories, but Sox pitching bested them in six games. Big Ed Walsh, the Sox's famous spitballer, won two games. Davis hit .308 with three doubles and a Series-leading six RBIs. The Veterans Committee elected Davis to the Hall of Fall in 1998.

Glenn Davis

Davis, Glenn Earle **1B–DH**

1984–93 B:3/28/61, Jacksonville, FL Deb:9/2/1984, HOU NL BR/TR, 6'3", 210

G	AB	R	H	HR	RBI	OBP	SLG	AVG
1015	3719	510	965	190	603	.335	.467	.259

In his day, Glenn Davis was one of the National League's top sluggers. But he had the misfortune to play in one of the league's worst parks for hitting. When he finally got a chance to swing the bat in a hitter's park, he was unable to play.

The two-time All-Star was the first Astro to hit 30 home runs three times. From 1985 to 1990 he hit 164 homers, with less than half that total coming at home in the expansive Astrodome. His best home run output was 34 in 1989. In 1986 he knocked in a career-high 101 runs, and helped the Astros win the NL West title. He homered for the only run in Houston's 1–0 win over the New York Mets in Game 1 of the Championship Series.

On the eve of spring training in 1991, Houston dealt Davis to the Baltimore Orioles for Steve Finley, Pete Harnisch, and Curt Schilling. While Finley and Harnisch found success in Houston and Schilling moved on to stardom in Philadelphia, neck and rib cage injuries forced Davis to miss an estimated 300 games in three seasons in Baltimore. He hit only 24 home runs as an Oriole, despite playing his last two seasons at hitter-friendly Camden Yards. Davis was out of baseball at age 32.

Harry Davis

Davis, Harry H. **1B–OF**

1895–99,1901–17 M(1912, 54–71) B:7/19/1873, Philadelphia, PA D:8/11/1947, Philadelphia, PA Deb:9/21/1895, NY NL BR/TR 5'10", 180

G	AB	R	H	HR	RBI	OBP	SLG	AVG
1755	6653	1001	1841	75	951	.335	.408	.277

Slugging first baseman Harry "Jasper" Davis was the first major leaguer to pace his circuit in homers four consecutive seasons, a feat equaled or surpassed by only Frank "Home Run" Baker, Babe Ruth, and Ralph Kiner.

Davis played five years in the National League during the 1890s without making much of a stir, despite leading the league in triples with 28 in 1897. In 1900 he left baseball and took a job with the railroad in Philadelphia. But Connie Mack, who was building the Philadelphia Athletics franchise in the new American League, remembered Davis from the days when they were both with Pittsburgh.

Mack recruited him to the A's. Davis became a premier power hitter in the young circuit, hitting for the cycle his first season in Philadelphia. Not only did he win four consecutive home run titles from 1904 through 1907, he led the league twice in RBIs, three times in doubles, and once in runs scored. Once when New York Highlanders hurler "Buffalo Bill" Hogg was attempting to intentionally walk him, Davis reportedly reached across the plate and launched a three-run homer, giving Philadelphia a 4–3 victory.

Following the 1905 season and the sale of team captain Lave Cross to the Senators, Mack appointed Davis to the A's captaincy and would often leave the team in Davis' hands during his absence. "Davis at once became far more valuable to Mack's team than the average captain," wrote Fred Leib a few years later. "Harry's duties were not so much to attend to the kicking—the White Jumbos do very little of that—but to steady down the inside work, and to attend to the field strategy, at which he had always been a past…master."

By 1910 Davis' power stroke was history. He hit only one homer and batted .248. But in the World Series his bat came alive. He hit .353 with three doubles, five runs scored, and two RBIs. Philadelphia won the world championship over the Cubs in five games.

In the 1911 World Series, the A's beat the Giants in six games, and Davis' sign stealing played a big part in the victory. "They're getting our signs from someplace," Giants catcher Chief Meyers informed manager John McGraw. "That coach on third base, Harry Davis, is calling our pitches. When he yells, 'It's all right,' it's a fastball."

McGraw thought Davis was getting them from Meyers' signals, so to foil Davis, Meyers went to

Giants pitchers Rube Marquard and Christy Mathewson and said, "Pitch whatever you want to pitch. I'll catch you without signals." Meyers marveled, "And still the guy (Davis) was hollering 'It's all right' for the fastball. He knew something. I never did find out how he did it."

Davis left the Athletics following the 1911 Series, and for part of the 1912 season he managed Cleveland. He then returned to the A's as a coach from 1913 to 1919. In 1915 Davis, a skilled trapshooter, undertook a national tour with former A's pitchers Chief Bender and Eddie Plank to promote the sport.

Jody Davis

Davis, Jody Richard **C**

1981–90 B:11/12/1956, Gainesville, GA Deb:4/21/1981, CHI NL BR/TR 6'3", 210

G	AB	R	H	HR	RBI	OBP	SLG	AVG
1082	3585	364	877	127	490	.310	.403	.245

Jody Davis, a fine defensive catcher and star slugger, earned the Chicago Cubs' starting catcher spot in 1982. The next year the big redhead walloped 24 home runs and hit .271.

In 1984 Davis emerged as one of the most popular Cubs players, earning an All-Star berth and becoming a key offensive weapon in Chicago's National League East title. It was the Cubs' first championship of any kind since 1945, and Davis became a local hero. In the playoffs Davis was the team's most prolific hitter, crushing two home runs and seven hits in the team's eventual loss to the San Diego Padres.

Davis' popularity inspired Cubs fans to create a theme song for him, which they sang whenever he stepped to the plate. Between 1984 and 1986 he caught almost every game for the Cubs, who couldn't afford to have him missing from their lineup. He made the All-Star team again in 1986. After that, however, the grueling schedule began to take its toll, and his hitting declined. The singing stopped. In the middle of the 1988 season, Damon Berryhill emerged to become their regular catcher, and the Cubs traded Davis to Atlanta.

Davis played part-time for Atlanta until 1990. When he retired, the Braves searched for another catcher and found a familiar replacement for Davis by making a deal with the Cubs for Damon Berryhill.

Mark Davis

Davis, Mark William **P**

1980–81, 1983–94, 1997 B:10/19/1960, Livermore, CA Deb:9/12/1980, PHI NL BL/TL 6'4", 205

W	L	PCT	G	SV	IP	BB	SO	ERA
51	84	.378	624	96	1145	534	1007	4.17

Closer Mark Davis spent his first eight years in the major leagues working toward his stellar 1989 season with the San Diego Padres. But a year later he was back where he started. As the saying goes, "He went from Cy Young to sayonara."

Davis' big year was highlighted by 44 saves and a 1.85 ERA. But those glittering numbers and his National League Cy Young Award were put out to bid after the 1989 season. The Kansas City Royals opened their checkbook and signed Davis to a $13 million deal over four seasons.

Davis never again saved more than six games in a season. First he lost his location, then his confidence, and finally his closer's job. "I dwell on it inside," he said. "I'd get out on the mound and I'd want to stay, so I think I tried too hard."

The Royals released Davis midway through the 1992 season. The Braves, Phillies, and Padres were successively unable to influence a turnaround, and Davis retired in 1994. The expansion Arizona Diamondbacks, still a year away from their first major league game, gave him a shot in their minor league system in 1997. Davis was sent to the Milwaukee Brewers in a trade, appearing in what likely were the final 19 games of his star-crossed career.

Piper Davis

Davis, Lorenzo **2B-1B-SS**

Negro League Player 1942–50 M(1947–50) B:7/3/1917, Piper, AL BR/TR 6'3", 186

When Branch Rickey decided to integrate the major leagues after World War II, he had his scouts search the Negro Leagues for the right player. One who was just a bit too old to be considered was Lorenzo "Piper" Davis, a talented infielder for the Birmingham Black Barons.

He started playing "professionally" in the late 1930s for the American Cast Iron and Pipe Company; he didn't get paid for playing baseball, but he got a job at $3.36 a day, plus time off to play.

In 1942, he joined the Black Barons for $5 a game, and—playing shortstop—he teamed with Artie Wilson to form one of the Negro Leagues' top double-play combinations. Davis also played winter ball in Cuba, as did many Negro League players; once after he won a big game with a home run, the fans passed the hat. He netted $200, equal to his original salary for 40 games with the Black Barons.

In July 1947, the Browns signed him, along with fellow Negro League stars Willard Brown and Hank Thompson. Brown and Thompson were brought up to St. Louis that season but Davis was kept on option with Birmingham. When he refused to go to the minors in August, the Browns dropped their option.

In 1948 he became the Black Barons' player-manager—a dual job he kept through 1950—which meant he was Willie Mays' first pro manager. That season Davis hit .353 and led the Negro League in RBIs.

In 1950, at the age of 33, Davis became the first black player to be signed by the Red Sox (who had passed on Mays in 1948). Some feel that Boston deliberately chose an older player to make it easier not to bring him up. The Red Sox were the last team to integrate on the major league level. They paid the Black Barons $7,500 for Davis, with the promise of $7,500 more if he was with any Boston club on May 15.

The spring in Florida was difficult: Davis had to eat and room with one of the waiters at the team hotel. He hoped to play for Triple A Louisville but was sent, instead, to Class AA Scranton. As May 15 approached, he was hitting well over .300 and leading the team in home runs and RBIs, but he was released. All his manager, Jack Burns, could say was, "It's orders."

A marvelous all-around athlete, Davis also played with the Harlem Globetrotters and stayed in baseball as well, spending one year in the Mexican League and five with Oakland in the Pacific Coast League. He later served as player-manager for the Fort Worth Cats and was a scout for the Tigers, Cardinals, and Expos.

Storm Davis

Davis, George Earl **P**

1982–94 B:12/26/1961, Dallas, TX Deb:4/29/1982, BAL AL BR/TR 6'4" 207

W	L	PCT	G	SV	IP	BB	SO	ERA
113	96	.541	442	11	1780^{2}	687	1048	4.02

Storm Davis enjoyed some fine seasons with Baltimore, but it was his second wind with the Oakland Athletics in the late 1980s that earned him the 1988 *Sporting News* AL Comeback Player of the Year Award. Davis was part of two world championship pitching staffs.

Selected by the Orioles in the June 1979 amateur draft, Storm (a nickname bestowed upon him by his mother in honor of a fictional character, "Dr. Storm") toiled at Bluefield, Miami, Charlotte, and Rochester before reaching the big club. He helped lead the team to the 1983 world championship, starting and winning Game 4 in that year's World Series. Traded to San Diego in October 1986 for catcher Terry Kennedy and pitcher Mark Williamson, his career was already beginning a downward spiral. The Padres let Davis go to Oakland in August 1987 for two players to be named later.

Davis won 16 games with the 1988 A's (despite throwing a league-leading 16 wild pitches), but lost two games in that fall's World Series against Los Angeles. He won 19 games for the 1989 world champion A's, and declared free agency at season's end. Davis signed with Kansas City, but fell to 7–10 in 1990. The Royals traded him to Baltimore in December 1991 for catcher Bob Melvin. After a 7–3 season with the Orioles, Davis returned to Oakland as a free agent. He finished out his career with Detroit.

Tommy Davis

Davis, Herman Thomas **OF-DH-3B**

1959–76 B:3/21/1939, Brooklyn, NY Deb:9/22/1959, LA NL BR/TR 6'2", 205

G	AB	R	H	HR	RBI	OBP	SLG	AVG
1999	7223	811	2121	153	1052	.332	.405	.294

Two-time National League batting champion Tommy Davis eventually wore 10 different uniforms. "When Tommy left for an evening at the ballpark, his wife never knew whether to pack him a lunch or a suitcase," wrote Art Spander.

Along the way, Davis accumulated the highest lifetime pinch-batting average in history, .320, based on 63 pinch hits in 197 at bats. He broke the old mark of .312 set by another one-time Dodger, Frenchy Bordagaray.

In the minors Davis led the Midwest and Pacific Coast leagues in hitting and never batted less than .304. His two great years were 1962 and 1963, when he led National League batters with .346 and .326 averages, respectively. In 1962 he paced the league with 230 hits and 153 RBIs, totals that he never came close to approaching again. Even then Davis' relaxed approach to the game drew criticism. Years later he commented: "They used to call me lazy or lackadaisical, but the lazier I felt the better I hit."

Nonetheless, those were glory days for Davis. "When there are men on base and I'm at bat, all I can see are dollar signs," Davis remarked in 1963.

On May 1, 1965, Davis suffered an injury that would affect the balance of his career. In a night game against the Giants, he was attempting to break up a double play at second base. His spikes caught on the base, and he not only fractured but dislocated his ankle. The injury put Davis in the hospital for six weeks and in a cast for more than three months.

"Naturally, it affected my speed and subconsciously I didn't put weight on my back foot, which is the way most batters hit, for a number of years," Davis said. "I learned to hit off my front foot."

Davis bounded back to hit .313 in 1966, but was

traded that December to the Mets, beginning an odyssey which would see him playing for nine different clubs in the last decade of his career. Once asked to respond to all the trades and releases he endured, he snapped: "I'm very bitter, bitter as hell. Why do I keep getting released? Don't ask me no reason why."

With Baltimore in 1973, the often-hobbled Davis had become a designated hitter. "I've found it's important to keep busy and loose when you're a designated hitter," he commented. "There were times...when I would go back in the clubhouse and read or maybe even shave. I used to come to the park with a real heavy beard. Fortunately I made every time at bat."

Willie Davis

Davis, William Henry **OF**

1960–76, 1979 B:4/15/1940, Mineral Springs, AR
Deb:9/8/1960, LA NL BL/TL 6'2½", 181

G	AB	R	H	HR	RBI	OBP	SLG	AVG
2429	9174	1217	2561	182	1053	.314	.412	.279

Fleet-footed Willie Davis was an integral part of the Dodgers' pitching-speed-and-defense strategy that rewarded Los Angeles fans with National League pennants in 1963, 1965, and 1966. Yet Davis could be a frustrating player. Three times in a row he won the Gold Glove Award, but twice he paced the league in errors.

His worst moment came in the fifth inning of Game 2 of the 1966 World Series, when he committed a Series-record three errors. His first was on Paul Blair's flyball, which Davis lost in the sun and dropped for a two-base error. The next batter, Andy Etchebarren, lifted a short fly to center, which Davis again flubbed. Picking up the ball, Davis saw Blair heading for third and overthrew the base, allowing Blair to score and Etchebarren to take second.

Such ineptitude might rattle the average player, but there was nothing average about Davis. "I consider myself better adjusted than anyone else in this game," Davis once contended. "That's because nothing can make me unhappy. If we win, I am happy for myself. If we lose, I am happy because of the happiness it has brought the other guy. There is no way baseball can upset me."

Management did not properly appreciate such a noble fellow. "He can run, hit, and throw. The only thing Davis has never been able to do is think," Dodgers vice president Buzzie Bavasi once commented.

The Sporting News Minor League Player of the Year, Davis joined the Dodgers at the end of the 1960 season. Often considered the fastest man in baseball, he twice led the National League in triples. But he was at his worst in World Series competition. In the 1963 Series he hit .167 and struck out six times in the Dodgers' four-game sweep of the Yankees. Two years later, when Los Angeles defeated Minnesota in seven games, Davis batted only .231 and did not drive in a run. And not only did he commit three errors in one inning of the 1966 Series, he also finished with only one hit in 16 at bats.

In 1969 Davis hit in 31 consecutive games, the longest streak in the National League since Tommy Holmes' skein of 37 in 1945. Davis hit .311 that season and followed with a .305 showing in 1970, when he led the league with a career-high 16 triples.

In 1971 Davis became a member of the Soka Gakkai, a Nicheren Buddhist sect. Before each game Davis would fervently chant, *"Nam-myoho-renge-kyo,"* he explained that the phrase had a lengthy translation. "It's important to say it and chant it, not what it means," he said. "It's the key to find out all the things you can accomplish."

In 1973 Davis set a goal of 50 homers and 50 stolen bases. Instead he collected 16 home runs and 17 stolen bases, though he did record six hits in a game on May 24. In December he was traded to the Montreal Expos for reliever Mike Marshall, beginning a four-year period during which Davis performed for five different clubs.

In 1977 and 1978 Davis played in Japan. With the Chunichi Dragons in 1977 he batted .306 and hit 25 homers in just 73 games. In 1978 with the Crown Lighter Lions he hit 18 homers and .293 in 127 games. As a practicing Buddhist, Davis thought he, of all visiting Americans, would fit in well in Japan.

But he overdid it. Davis continued to finger his prayer beads and go into Buddhist chants prior to each game. "It gave the others the feeling they were at a Buddhist funeral," Chunichi manager Wally Yonamine said. Davis broke his wrist, and the Dragons proceeded to go into a winning streak. He was traded to the Lions during the off-season.

In 1979 Davis returned to the big leagues and signed a contract with the California Angels. In 43 games he hit .250 but his power and speed had deserted him. He hit no homers and stole only one base. California won the American League West by three games and advanced to the ALCS against the Orioles. Davis went 1-for-2 with a double and run scored, but the Angels were defeated in four games. He retired at season's end.

In 1970 Davis had played a featured role in the Jerry Lewis film *Which Way to the Front?* Davis, who was then earning $20,000 a year with the Dodgers, admitted, "It's a lot of fun. A lot more fun than facing Jerry Koosman."

Andre Dawson

Dawson, Andre Nolan **OF**

1976–96 B:7/10/1954, Miami, FL Deb:9/11/1976, MON NL BR/TR 6'3", 195

G	AB	R	H	HR	RBI	OBP	SLG	AVG
2627	9927	1373	2774	438	1591	.327	.482	.279

Andre Dawson, an 11th-round draft pick, started his career at tiny Jarry Park in Montreal in 1976. The 22-year-old outfielder played in only 24 late-season games for the last-place Expos, but it was apparent that both Dawson—and his team—were headed for better things.

The Expos began the 1977 season in a new ballpark with Dawson as a fixture in center field. Dawson batted .282, hit 19 home runs, and stole 21 bases to earn National League Rookie of the Year honors. In the years that followed, his numbers only got better.

After two narrow misses for the NL East title in 1979 and 1980, the Expos captured the second-half division championship in the 1981 strike-interrupted season. Dawson batted .300 as Montreal beat the Phillies in five games in the special divisional playoffs, but he batted just .150 as the Expos lost to the Dodgers in five games in the NL Championship Series.

Dawson's best season in Montreal came in 1983, when he socked 32 home runs, drove in 113 runs, and had an NL-leading 189 hits. By 1986 he already held the franchise records for hits, doubles, triples, home runs, and RBIs.

Meanwhile, Dawson was missing up to 30 games each year, mostly due to knee problems exacerbated by playing on the artificial surface at Olympic Stadium. Desperate to play on natural grass, and unable to find any takers because of possible collusion between the owners, Dawson asked the Chicago Cubs for a contract with the dollar amount left blank. Thus, his 1987 salary of $500,000 was far below market value—and his performance was far above anything the Cubs could have expected.

"The Hawk" thrived on the grass and daylight at Wrigley Field. He accumulated 49 home runs and 137 RBIs while batting .287 to earn NL MVP honors. He batted .332 in home games in the last full season before lights were installed at Wrigley Field, and he started in center field in the All-Star Game. He was named Player of the Month for August, collecting 15 home runs and 28 RBIs.

Dawson had another phenomenal season in 1988, batting .303 (third best in the NL) while leading the league with 57 multihit games. His 12 stolen bases gave him 12 consecutive years with at least 10 home runs and 10 stolen bases, making him the first to accomplish the feat. His fielding skills were recognized with his eighth Gold Glove Award.

At age 36 in 1990, Dawson set a career high with a .310 batting average, and finished with 27 home runs and 100 RBIs. The 1991 season was his 15th consecutive season with at least 45 extra-base hits, putting him in a class with Hank Aaron, Stan Musial, Willie Mays, Mel Ott, and Honus Wagner.

After the 1992 season he became a free agent and joined the Boston Red Sox—another organization that plays a lot of day games in a historic grass ballpark. But things did not work out as well as they had in Chicago. Dawson battled injuries for two seasons in Boston and then opted to finish his career in his native Miami. Florida Marlins fans already loved Dawson—he had a street named after him in South Miami while still a member of the Cubs—and they cheered wildly whenever the eight-time All-Star was healthy enough to play. He hit .257 in 1995, but he finished his career strong in part-time duty in 1996, including a .429 clip in his final week in the major leagues. In 1997 the Expos made Dawson just the third player in club history to have his number retired.

John B. Day

Day, John B.

Owner (1882–92) M(1899, 29–35) B:9/23/1847, Colchester, MA D:1/25/1926, Cliffside, NJ

John B. Day once owned both the Mets of the American Association and the National League Giants, two 19th-century clubs based in New York City. A millionaire Connecticut tobacco magnate who relocated to New York to establish a new cigar factory on the city's Lower East Side, Day enjoyed playing baseball for relaxation. One afternoon in 1880 while he was on the mound for an amateur Manhattan club, his team was taking a pasting. Observing with some amusement was James Mutrie, former manager of the Fall River and Brockton clubs.

Mutrie challenged Day: "If you will furnish the money, I'll get you a team that can beat the other nine." Day accepted Mutrie's invitation. In September 1880 the two men formed the "Metropolitans," filling the team's roster with players largely from the Unions of Brooklyn and from the disbanded Rochester Hop Bitters. They did well against all clubs they faced, even those belonging to the National League.

The following year they entered the new minor league Eastern Championship Association and played at the original Polo Grounds, just north of Central Park in New York. In 1882 the Mets moved into the American Association, a new major league that would successfully rival the National League in the 1880s.

The NL at that time had no club in New York, having expelled the Gothams following the 1876 season. In 1883 Day was given a franchise for New York, but, under the loose requirements of the day, still continued to operate the Mets through the 1884 season. The Mets won that year's AA pennant but, much to Day's chagrin, lost the "World Series" to the NL. Day stripped the club of talent and sold it in 1885 to Frank Rhouer.

Day's Giants featured such stars as John Montgomery Ward, Mickey Welch, Buck Ewing, Roger Connor, and Tim Keefe, all future Hall of Famers. The Giants won both the NL pennant and the "World Series" in 1888 and 1889, the last against rival Brooklyn. Although his team beat Brooklyn, Day fumed about his opponent's dirty tactics and poor umpiring: "I don't mind losing games on their merit, but I do mind being robbed of them."

The next season the club fell apart with massive defections to the new Players' League. The National League was in grave trouble, and Day mortgaged himself heavily to keep both his ballclub and the league itself operating. Following the collapse of the Players' League after one season, Day's finances continued to decline. He sold part of the club to Edward Talcott, and with the Giants' financial difficulties growing, Day sold more and more stock to the newcomer. Finally, Day was out in the cold; C.C. Van Cott succeeded him as Giants president in late 1892.

In 1899 Day returned to the Giants as, of all things, field manager. In worse financial shape than ever—he no longer had his cigar factory—Day lasted until July 5, when the Giants were ninth in the 12-club league.

Day's bad luck continued. The National League helped him by giving him the position of inspector of umpires, but by the 1920s he was too ill to remain even in that job. "I raised $50 on my sewing machine," said Day's wife, "and sold a few pieces of furniture—I guess it will all go. Many a time I washed roomers' clothes to help out. I didn't let John know, for he was a great man, once."

Leon Day

Day, Leon **P-2B-OF**

Negro League Player (1934–50) B:10/1/1916, Alexandria, VA D:3/13/1995, Baltimore, MD BR/TR 5'9", 170

Although not as well known as Satchel Paige, pitcher Leon Day rivaled him as one of the Negro Leagues' most outstanding pitchers in the 1930s and 1940s, particularly when Day was pitching for Effa and Abe Manley's Newark Eagles. Day was playing for a local Baltimore team, the Silver Moons, when the Baltimore Black Sox's Rap Dixon spotted him. Only 17, Day had to ask his father's permission to go with the team. His father said he could "if that's what you really want to do." Day responded, "It's the only thing I want to do."

A good hitter and baserunner, Day often played second base when he wasn't pitching. In 1937 he was 13–0 for the Eagles on the mound while batting .320. He performed in a record seven East-West Negro League All-Star Games, and set a Negro League record of 18 strikeouts in one game.

World War II interrupted his career. Day went ashore at Normandy shortly after D-day, pitched for integrated service clubs in Europe, then returned home to pitch a no-hitter on Opening Day in 1946. He entered Organized Baseball with Toronto in 1951 and Scranton in 1952.

"He was like Bob Gibson," said his Eagles teammate Monte Irvin. "In fact he was better than Bob Gibson." He died one week after being named to the Hall of Fame in 1995.

Dizzy Dean

Dean, Jay Hanna **P**

1930–47 B:1/16/1910, Lucas, AR D:7/17/1974, Reno, NV Deb:9/28/1930, STL NL BR/TR 6'2", 182

W	L	PCT	G	SV	IP	BB	SO	ERA
150	83	.644	317	30	1967^{1}	453	1163	3.02

Dizzy Dean was a man of many accomplishments and even more words, some of which actually were standard English. The National League's last 30-game winner and a card-carrying member of St. Louis' "Gas House Gang," Dean often made good on his outrageous boasts. As he put it, "It ain't bragging if you can do it."

To some reporters he gave his actual name as Jay Hanna Dean; to others, Jerome Herman Dean. He also provided them with a "dizzying" choice of birthplaces and birthdays. When confronted with the inconsistencies, he explained, "I was helpin' these writers out. Them ain't lies; them's scoops."

Dean came by his hillbilly image honestly. He grew up poor, the son of a sharecropper. "The boys used to pick cotton for me at Purcell, Oklahoma," Dizzy's father recalled in 1934. "Jay used to scheme about how to make money from his great right arm and used to think a lot." According to the elder Dean, Dizzy's brother Paul "would pick as much as 500 pounds a day, but Jay never went over 400 pounds a day. And I was only able to pick about 200 pounds cuz I had to watch Jay."

Diz dropped out of school in the fourth grade and enlisted in the army at age 16 for $21 a month. He pitched well for an army-camp team—sharpening his control by hurling spuds during KP duty—but soon tired of military life. Brother Paul bought Dizzy's way out of the service for $120, approximately one-fourth of his annual wages from picking cotton.

On May 29, 1929, Cardinals scout Don Curtis signed Dizzy Dean—but offered no bonus. In 1930 the Cardinals organization assigned the pitcher to the last-place St. Joseph Saints of the Class A Western League, where he compiled a 17–8 record. Promoted in midseason to the Texas League's Houston

Buffaloes, Dean went 8–2 and earned a late-season call-up to St. Louis. On the last day of the 1930 season he three-hit Pittsburgh in his major league debut.

The Cardinals had a strong pitching staff, and Dean was sent back to Houston. Once there he got on the phone to a rival Texas League manager, "Say, this is Dizzy Dean. Yep, back in town and I can hear you gnashing your teeth, brother. Just thought I would call and tell you that I am gonna pitch against your ballclub this afternoon and hold them to two or three hits."

He did indeed surrender just two hits. Dean led the Texas League with 26 victories, 303 strikeouts, and a 1.57 ERA in 1931. He returned to the Cardinals in 1932 and paced the National League in innings pitched, strikeouts, and shutouts.

In 1933 Dean won 20 games and again led the league in strikeouts. In the first game of a July 30, 1933, doubleheader, Dean struck out 17 Chicago Cubs to set a now-broken modern major league record. That same year Paul Dean, soon to be christened "Daffy" by the sportswriters, was pitching in the Cardinals system with the Columbus Red Birds and leading the American Association with 197 strikeouts to post a 22–7 record.

In January 1934 Dizzy boldly predicted a league championship for St. Louis. "How are they going to stop us?," Dean boasted. "Paul's going to be a sensation. He'll win 18 or 20 games. I'll count 20 to 25 for myself. I won 20 last season, and I know I'll pass that figure."

Pass it he did. In 1934 the Cardinals won the pennant and rookie Paul Dean contributed 19 wins. Dizzy went 30–7. But both could have won more. They each missed two starts after being suspended for skipping an exhibition game in a salary dispute.

On September 21, 1934, the Dean brothers took the mound at Ebbets Field for a doubleheader against the Dodgers. In the first game Dizzy carried a no-hitter into the eighth inning and beat Brooklyn, 13–0, settling for a three-hitter. In the nightcap Paul pitched a no-hitter, allowing only a first-inning walk. "If I'd a known what Paul was gonna do, I would have pitched one, too," Dizzy said.

The brothers were so overpowering the Dodgers could only gawk in admiration. "If there is such a thing as getting a kick out of losing, I got it today," Brooklyn catcher Al Lopez said. "I think we were all up there with our mouths open in admiration of the stuff those two were throwing."

The Deans were even better in the postseason. As the Cardinals prepared for the World Series against the Detroit Tigers, Dizzy predicted, "Me and Paul'll win two games apiece."

That's exactly what happened. Dizzy won Games 1 and 7, pitching a six-hit shutout on one day's rest in the clincher. Paul won Game 3, singled in the tie-breaking run in Game 6, and went on to win that game, too.

During that Series Dizzy also proved he could generate headlines simply by running the bases. Pinch-running for Virgil "Spud" Davis in Game 4, Dean went barreling into second base. As Billy Rogell relayed the ball to first, Dean forgot to duck. The ball caromed off his forehead and landed more than 100 feet away in right field.

"The blow that floored Dizzy would have knocked down two elephants," wrote beloved sportswriter and poet Grantland Rice. Dean was carried off the field and taken to a hospital. Later he proudly announced, "The doctors x-rayed my head and found nothing."

After his dazzling 1934 season Dean, of course, wanted more money. Brother Paul said, "I think all the other players on this club ought to volunteer to take a cut so's Diz can get the salary he wants."

Dizzy Dean's career began to unravel in July 1937. After being chosen for the All-Star team, Dean didn't want to attend; he wanted to go fishing over the extended baseball holiday. His wife, however, insisted he participate, arguing he owed it to the game. Dean played, but in the third inning Earl Averill lined the ball off Dean's left little toe, fracturing it. "Fractured, hell! The damned thing's broken!" Dean said.

Two weeks after the incident Dean was pitching in Boston, he said, with "splints on my foot, and a shoe two sizes too big for me." To compensate, Dean placed all his weight on one foot. "Pain is stabbin' up through my hip," he said in describing the scene later. "Because of this, I change my natural style and don't follow through with my body on the delivery, so's I don't have to tromp down on my hurt foot.... As the ball left my hand, there was a loud crack in my shoulder, and my arm went numb down to my fingers."

During the off-season Branch Rickey traded Dean to the Cubs for three journeyman players and $185,000. "Jeez, $185,000.... If I'd a had a good arm wonder what I'd a brought," Dean joked.

Dean went 7–1 in 13 games in his first season in Chicago, and even pitched twice in a sweep at the hands of the Yankees in the World Series. Dean lasted with the Cubs as both a player and a coach until June 1941, when he started broadcasting Cardinals and Browns games for Falstaff beer. Dean's disregard for correct grammar caught the attention of the St. Louis Board of Education, which demanded that he be taken off the air. Dean stood his ground. "Let the teachers teach English, and I will teach baseball." As for his use of "ain't," he said, "There is a lot of people in the United States who say isn't, and they ain't eatin'."

When another critic asked if he knew the King's English, he answered, "Yes sir, I do, and I know the Queen's English too." Aside from avoiding such nuisances as correct grammar and pronunciation, Dean also disdained statistical analysis, or "statics" as he put it. "I hate statics. What I know I keep in my haid," he explained.

When the Cincinnati Reds loaded the bases with Ted Kluszewski on first, Bob Borkowski on second, and Fred Baczewski on third, Dean told listeners, "I was hopin' no one'd get a hit so I didn't have to pronounce them names." When the next Cincinnati batter sent a drive in the direction of left-center, Dean announced, "There's a long drive—and here's Gene Kirby to tell you all about it."

Elected to the Hall of Fame in 1953, Dean informed his Cooperstown audience, "The good Lord was good to me. He gave me a strong body, a good right arm, and a weak mind."

Paul Dean

Dean, Paul Dee **P**

1934–41, 1943 B:8/14/1913, Lucas, AR D:3/17/1981, Springdale, AR Deb:4/18/1934, STL NL BR/TR 6', 175

W	L	PCT	G	SH	IP	BB	SO	ERA
50	34	.595	159	8	787^{1}	179	387	3.75

Paul Dean came up with the St. Louis Cardinals in 1934. His older brother Dizzy was at the height of his career and bragged that the pair would win as many as 45 games. He was too modest. They won 49, as Dizzy collected 30 victories and rookie Paul chipped in 19. In the 1934 World Series against the Tigers, Dizzy predicted, "Me and Paul'll win two games apiece." Paul won Games 3 and 6, while Dizzy won the opener and the final game.

Paul Dean first pitched with Houston of the Texas League at age 17 when Dizzy, two years older, was just about to burst onto the Cardinals' roster. By Paul's rookie year, the Cards were one of the most colorful teams in baseball history. In addition to Dizzy, they included such unusual personalities as Leo Durocher, Frankie Frisch, Ducky Medwick, and Pepper Martin. Although the press called him "Daffy" as a gimmick to echo his brother's nickname, Paul was shy, quiet, and serious, unlike the fun-loving, loquacious Dizzy.

Never quite the pitcher his brother was, Paul nevertheless won 19 games in each of his first two seasons with the Cardinals. During the heat of the 1934 pennant race, Dizzy three-hit Brooklyn in the first game of a September 21 doubleheader. Paul came back in the nightcap, throwing a no-hitter to win, 3–0. "If I'd known Paul was going to pitch a no-hitter," Dizzy said afterward, "I'd have pitched one too."

In 1936 Paul held out for a better contract. When he finally reported, he tried to pitch too soon and hurt his arm. His fastball was gone. Although Paul pitched off and on until 1943, he never again won more than five games in a season. Like his brother Dizzy, who also hurt his arm, he was essentially finished as a major leaguer by the time he was 30.

Doug DeCinces

DeCinces, Douglas Vernon **3B**

1973–87 B:8/29/1950, Burbank, CA Deb:9/9/1973, BAL AL BR/TR 6'2", 194

G	AB	R	H	HR	RBI	OBP	SLG	AVG
1649	5809	778	1505	237	879	.333	.445	.259

Doug DeCinces was a talented utility infielder, groomed by the Baltimore Orioles in the mid-1970s to take over for aging third sacker Brooks Robinson. He played virtually full-time during the 1976 and 1977 seasons and seemed to have the potential to fill the shoes of the future Hall of Famer.

In 1977 DeCinces led American League third basemen in assists and double plays. When Robinson finally left the team in 1978, DeCinces became official owner of the hot corner. Finally playing every day, he smashed 28 homers while hitting .286.

In 1979 he continued to play good defense, but his hitting dropped off considerably. Nevertheless, the Orioles were solid all around and won the AL East title. In the Championship Series DeCinces exhibited his defensive prowess with a spectacular catch that turned a potential bases-loaded California rally into a double play. It immediately evoked memories of the exceptional postseason play of his predecessor. DeCinces also batted .308 as the O's took the Angels, but Baltimore was eventually outhit and outpitched by the Pittsburgh Pirates team in the World Series.

In 1980 DeCinces again had trouble fulfilling the legacy. He led AL third basemen in putouts and double plays but had another mediocre year at the plate. In 1981, when a young infielding prospect came along who was not only talented but also happened to be the son of Orioles coach Cal Ripken, DeCinces was phased out. In the last year of his contract, he was traded to the Angels.

The move to his native California invigorated DeCinces' hitting. In 1982 he hit .301 and once again led league third basemen in assists. His bat didn't fail him in the 1982 ALCS either—among position players only Fred Lynn's amazing hitting performance was better. But as the Brewers pounded California pitching in the last three games, DeCinces chalked up three errors to contribute to the Angels' demise.

DeCinces had proven himself, however, and in 1983, his 11th year in the league, he became an All-Star for the first time. When the Angels again went to the ALCS in 1986 he was still covering third. That season he slugged 26 homers, and in yet another postseason loss for the club he batted .281. DeCinces had a chance to give the Angels their first pennant when he came to bat in the ninth inning of Game 5 with the game tied, the bases loaded, and one out. Thinking a sacrifice fly would win the game, he swung at the first pitch—and popped up.

"If I could take that swing back, I would have gone back to my aggressive style of hitting," he said in Mike Sowell's book *One Pitch Away*. "I could drive in the run by being aggressive." The Angels lost Game 5 in extra innings, and then dropped the final two games of the series to the Red Sox.

The World Series–bound St. Louis Cardinals purchased him as insurance late in the 1987 season, but he saw action in only four games and was unused during the postseason. In 1989 he played a single season of Japanese baseball.

Rod Dedeaux

Dedeaux, Raoul Martial **SS**

1935 College Coach(1942–86) B:2/17/1915, New Orleans, LA Deb:9/28/1935, BRO NL BR/TR 5'11", 160

G	AB	R	H	HR	RBI	BB	OBP	SLG	AVG.
2	4	0	1	0	1	0	.250	.250	.250

By almost any standard, Rod Dedeaux was the greatest coach in college baseball history. In his 45 years at the University of Southern California he led the Trojans to 11 national championships, 28 conference titles, and an overall record of 1332–571–11, a winning percentage of .699. His victory total was an NCAA Division I record until surpassed in 1994 by Cliff Gustafson of Texas.

Dedeaux was a three-time letterman at USC (1933-35), and then joined the Brooklyn Dodgers organization. He appeared in his only two major league games as a September rookie. Seven years later, in a highly unusual move, Dedeaux was named co-head coach at USC, joining the incumbent—and his own former coach—Sam Barry. The next year, when Barry entered the Navy for World War II, Dedeaux took over on his own.

Barry returned in 1946, and he and Dedeaux again shared the job for five years, winning the Trojans' first national title in 1948. When Barry died in the fall of 1950, Dedeaux became the sole man at the helm. He led USC to 11 consecutive conference titles, capturing national championships in 1958, 1961, and 1963.

After priming themselves with another national title in 1968, the Trojans dominated college baseball in the early 1970s. Dedeaux led USC to five consecutive national championships (1970–74). His final NCAA crown came in 1978.

As impressive as Dedeaux's victory records and titles is the list of young men he helped guide into outstanding major league careers, including Ron Fairly, Don Buford, Tom Seaver, Bill Lee, Dave Kingman, Mark McGwire, and Randy Johnson. Perhaps his greatest team was the 1973 national championship squad that included future major leaguers Fred Lynn, Roy Smalley, Steve Kemp, Rich Dauer, Randy Scarbery, Pete Redfern, Dennis Littlejohn, and Ed Putnam (each of the first five was named All-America at least once). This collection of talent allowed the 1973 Trojans to stage perhaps the most amazing comeback in the history of the College World Series. Trailing Minnesota and its all-star pitcher Dave Winfield 7–0 going into the bottom of the ninth in an NCAA semifinal game, USC parlayed eight singles, a stolen base, a sacrifice fly, and several Minnesota errors into a stunning 8–7 victory that propelled the Trojans into the championship game.

Dedeaux was voted national coach of the year six times, was inducted into the College Baseball Coaches Association Hall of Fame, and was named the head coach of the all-time College World Series team. In 1984 he was selected as head coach of the U.S. Olympic baseball team, and in 1998 he fittingly was named college Coach of the Century by *Collegiate Baseball*.

Rob Deer

Deer, Robert George **OF**

1984–93, 1996 B:9/29/1960, Orange, CA Deb:9/4/1984, SF NL BR/TR, 6'3", 210

G	AB	R	H	HR	RBI	OBP	SLG	AVG
1155	3881	578	853	230	600	.325	.442	.220

Like Dave Kingman, Rob Deer carried a well-deserved reputation as an all-or-nothing slugger. In 11 major league seasons, he hit 230 home runs but struck out 1,409 times, including 175 or more whiffs in a season three times. Although a talented right fielder with a strong arm, it was Deer's longball power that kept him in the lineup. He hit 20 or more home runs for eight straight seasons.

Deer's best season was 1986, his first in Milwaukee. He had career peaks with 33 home runs and 86 RBIs. With the 1991 Detroit Tigers, Deer batted just .179, but 25 of his 80 hits were home runs. A year later, he batted .247—the second highest mark of his career—following a winter of workouts with White Sox hitting coach Walt Hriniak.

On June 12, 1992, Deer hit a ball that bounced on the roof of Tiger Stadium, an area cleared previously only by Cecil Fielder, Frank Howard, and Harmon Killebrew. By July 19 he had hit two home runs in a game five times. By the end of the next season, however, he was out of the major leagues. He did not return until 1996, when he emerged with the Padres and batted .180. But, true to form, four of his nine hits were home runs.

Ivan DeJesus

DeJesus, Ivan (Alvarez) **SS**
1974–88 B:1/9/1953, Santurce, Puerto Rico
Deb:9/13/1974, LA NL BR/TR 5'11", 175

G	AB	R	H	HR	RBI	OBP	SLG	AVG
1371	4602	595	1167	21	324	.324	.326	.254

Ivan DeJesus was a capable and durable shortstop for the Cubs and Phillies, but he is best known for being traded for Larry Bowa and Ryne Sandberg in what has to be one of baseball's most lopsided deals. DeJesus was the Cubs' everyday shortstop for five seasons and the Phillies' for three. He had an excellent arm and above-average range. No great shakes as a hitter, he nevertheless led the National League in runs scored in 1978.

When his batting average dropped to .194 in 1981, the Cubs looked to move him. They settled for Bowa, who was on the downside of his long career. Sandberg came along in the deal.

Only 29, DeJesus continued slipping with the Phillies. His hitting was unproductive and his range declined each season. His error in the top of the seventh inning of Game 3 of the 1983 World Series allowed the winning run to score. Baltimore won the Series in five games. DeJesus had only two singles in 16 at bats.

He remained in Philadelphia for one more season before becoming a utility player. He ended his career with one year apiece with the Cardinals, Yankees, Giants, and Tigers.

Ed Delahanty

Delahanty, Edward James **OF–1B–2B**
1888–1903 B:10/30/1867, Cleveland, OH D:7/2/1903, Niagara Falls, NY Deb:5/22/1888, PHI NL BR/TR 6'1", 170

G	AB	R	H	HR	RBI	OBP	SLG	AVG
1835	7505	1599	2596	101	1464	.411	.505	.346

Big Ed Delahanty was one of the greatest hitters in baseball history, but his accomplishments have been overshadowed by the circumstances of his unusual death. Today, few fans are aware that he had a .346 career batting average, that he once hit four home runs in a single game, or that he is the only man ever to be credited with batting titles in both the National and American leagues. If they have heard of Delahanty at all, it is because he died by being swept over Niagara Falls.

In the summer of 1903, Delahanty, the defending AL batting champion, was in his 16th major league season—hitting a solid .333 for Washington but hitting the bottle even harder. John McGraw had recently offered him $4,500, which was $500 more than he was being paid by Washington, to jump back to the NL and join the New York Giants. But the two leagues made peace before the season began and locked Delahanty into his Washington contract, leaving him to sulk and drink.

At the end of June, with the team in the middle of a western road trip, Delahanty failed to show up for a game in Cleveland. Manager Tom Loftus suspended him, but Delahanty continued to travel with the team.

On July 2 the slugger boarded a train in Detroit, apparently going to New York. While drinking on the train, he brandished a razor at several other passengers and caused a disturbance. The conductor tried to quiet him but failed, and Delahanty was put off the train at Niagara Falls, Ontario. Under Canadian law, he should have been put into the charge of a constable as a drunk and disorderly person, but the conductor, perhaps pressed to keep on schedule, simply kicked him off. When the train left the station to cross the bridge into the United States, Delahanty pushed past a guard and followed across the bridge on foot, ignoring the bridge tender's warning that the draw was open. Delahanty was never again seen alive.

One week later his body was discovered in the Niagara River some 20 miles below the falls. He apparently had fallen from the bridge and been swept over the falls. His money and jewelry were missing, leading some to suspect that he had been robbed and killed by an assailant. But the turbulence of the water below the falls is more likely responsible for his death.

Historian Bill James speculated that a mystery developed around the circumstances of Delahanty's death because "some of the press of the time and many of the writers of kids' books after that time did not wish to come right out and say that one of the game's greatest stars had died of damned foolishness, drunk and disorderly. They preferred, instead, to throw a cloak of mystery over it."

Big Ed certainly was one of the game's finest hitters. He had four younger brothers who followed him to the major leagues. Jim Delahanty, 12 years younger than Ed, played for 13 seasons.

Ed began his professional career in 1887, when he hit .355 and played second base for Mansfield of the Ohio State League. He hit .408 in 21 games with Wheeling of the Tri-State League in 1888 before the Philadelphia Phillies purchased his contract. He hit only .228 for the remainder of the season and played second base miserably. His hitting improved during the next three seasons, including one year with the Players' League in 1890, but Delahanty struggled in the field until 1891, when Philadelphia stationed him permanently in the outfield.

In a preview of what was to come, he hit .306 in 1892 and led the NL with 21 triples. From 1893 through 1896 he hit .368, .407, .404, and .397. In an era of high batting averages, this performance was only second best in the league in 1895 and third best the other three years. Delahanty led the league in doubles with 49 in 1895 and 44 in 1896, and in home runs and RBIs in 1893 and 1896. In a game on June 16, 1894, he went 6-for-6, a feat he had already achieved in the Players' League on June 2, 1890. In a loss to Chicago on July 13, 1896, Delahanty became the second man to hit four consecutive home runs in a single game, all inside the park.

During this period the Philadelphia outfield was one of the greatest ever assembled. Delahanty played left, "Sliding Billy" Hamilton patrolled center, and Sam Thompson held down right. All three were eventually enshrined in the Hall of Fame. In 1894 each man batted more than .400. But Philadelphia's poor pitching prevented the club from winning a pennant.

In 1899, after several close calls, Delahanty finally topped the league in hitting with a .410 batting average, his third time over .400. Only Ty Cobb and Rogers Hornsby have since matched this record. Also that season, Delahanty led the league with 238 hits, 55 doubles, and 137 RBIs. He hit well for the Phillies the next two seasons, leading the league in doubles for the fourth time in 1901 with 38.

The National League's maximum salary was only $2,500, and when Washington of the upstart American League offered him $4,000, Delahanty jumped. Although the dead ball pushed down averages, he hit .376 in 1902 to lead the league. However, later research by Information Concepts Inc. showed that runner-up Napoleon Lajoie should have been credited with four extra hits than he was originally given. The Cleveland second baseman's resulting average was two points higher than Delahanty's.

At the time of Delahanty's death in 1903, when he was only 35, his batting average was the fourth best of all time. Those marks proved more than enough for his election to the Hall of Fame in 1945.

Jim Delahanty

Delahanty, James Christopher **2B-3B-OF**
1901–15 B:6/20/1879, Cleveland, OH D:10/17/1953, Cleveland, OH Deb:4/19/1901, CHI NL BR/TR, 5'10½", 170

G	AB	R	H	HR	RBI	OBP	SLG	AVG
1186	4091	520	1159	19	489	.357	.373	.283

Among five brothers to reach the majors, James Christopher Delahanty's accomplishments were exceeded only by those of the eldest, "Big Ed," a Hall of Fame hitter. When Jim, 12 years younger, played his first major league game with Chicago in 1901, Ed was nearing the end of his career and his life. (He drowned in 1903.) By 1909, Jim Delahanty had played for the New York Highlanders, Boston Beaneaters, Cincinnati Reds, St. Louis Browns, and Washington Senators. He had performed at every position except catcher.

Midway through the 1909 season, he was traded to the Detroit Tigers, who needed a strong bat in the lineup and could survive his so-so play at second base. Delahanty helped the Tigers win their third straight pennant. In the World Series that fall he was the leading hitter, with a .346 batting average, as the Tigers lost to Pittsburgh in seven games. The 1911 season was the best of his career. He hit .339 with 94 RBIs and 83 runs scored, all personal highs.

Carlos Delgado

Delgado, Carlos Juan (Hernandez) **1B**
1993–* B:6/25/1972, Mayaguez, Puerto Rico Deb:10/1/1993, TOR AL BL/TR, 6'3", 220

G	AB	R	H	HR	RBI	OBP	SLG	AVG
667	2332	378	622	149	467	.365	.531	.267

It did not take long for Carlos Delgado to become one of the most potent hitters in Toronto Blue Jays history. In 1999, his fourth season as a regular, he joined Joe Carter and Fred McGriff as the only Blue Jays to produce at least 30 home runs for three straight seasons. His 82 home runs in 1998–99 set a Toronto club record. And his 44 homers in 1999 fell just three shy of Jose Gonzalez's mark for most home runs by a Puerto Rican.

Delgado also reached career highs in 1999 with 134 RBIs, 113 runs scored, and 156 hits. His numbers would have been better had his season not ended with an injury on September 22.

Like many power hitters, Delgado often does his damage in streaks. In 1998 he went on a 19-game hitting tear, and in August blasted three home runs in a game. In 1999, the lefthanded swinger had a four-hit game, a five-RBI game, and six multi-homer games.

Signed as a catcher in 1988, Delgado won two minor league Most Valuable Player awards at that position. But he became a major league regular only after moving to first base in 1996. While several teammates asked out of Toronto before and after the 1999 season, Delgado happily signed a contract extension with the Blue Jays.

Al Demaree

Demaree, Albert Wentworth **P**
1912–19 B:9/8/1884, Quincy, IL D:4/30/1962, Los Angeles, CA Deb:9/26/1912, NY NL BL/TR 6', 170

W	L	PCT	G	SH	IP	BB	SO	ERA
80	72	.526	232	9	1424	337	514	2.77

Perhaps no major league player has ever made a more unusual career change after his retirement than Al Demaree. Following his last game in the 1919 season, Demaree became a sports cartoonist and was syndicated in over 200 newspapers. His work appeared in *The Sporting News* for more than 30 years.

Demaree went 13–4 for the pennant-winning 1913 Giants and won another 14 games for the Phillies when they took the pennant two years later. In 1916, still with the Phillies, he won 19 games, including both ends of a September 20 doubleheader against the Pirates. Only 12 NL pitchers have ever won two complete games in one day, and no one has accomplished the feat since 1924. Demaree also earned a spot in the record books by throwing a shutout in his first major league start—a 4–0 blanking of the Boston Braves on September 26, 1912, while pitching for the Giants.

Frank Demaree

Demaree, Joseph Franklin **OF**

1932–34, 1935–44 B:6/10/1910, Winters, CA D:8/30/1958, Los Angeles, CA Deb:7/22/1932, CHI NL BR/TR 5'11½", 185

G	AB	R	H	HR	RBI	OBP	SLG	AVG
1155	4144	578	1241	72	591	.357	.415	.299

Frank Demaree went from star in the 1930s to journeyman in the 1940s. He appeared in four World Series, but his team lost each time.

Born Joseph Franklin Dimaria, he got his first significant playing time in 1933 when future Hall of Famer Kiki Cuyler broke a leg in spring training. The Cubs started Demaree in Cuyler's spot in center field, and the rookie responded by hitting .272 in 134 games.

Still, in 1934 the Cubs sent him back to Triple A Los Angeles for more seasoning. There he won Pacific Coast League Most Valuable Player honors, hitting .385 with 40 homers, 45 stolen bases, and 190 RBIs in 186 games.

The performance earned him a second promotion to the Cubs, and from 1935 to 1937, he hit .325, .350, and .324 respectively. In 1937, he also had a career-high 17 homers, 104 runs, and 115 RBIs. Demaree was the starting center fielder for the NL in both the 1936 and 1937 All-Star Games. On December 6, 1938, the Cubs traded him, shortstop Billy Jurges, and catcher Ken O'Dea to the New York Giants for shortstop Dick Bartell, pitcher Hank Leiber, and catcher Gus Mancuso.

For the Giants in 1939 Demaree hit .304 with 11 homers and 79 RBIs. Two years later, however, he was waived in July to the Boston Braves. After playing sparingly for the Braves as a reserve outfielder and pinch hitter in 1942, Demaree was sold to the St. Louis Cardinals, with whom he finished out his career in 1944.

Don Demeter

Demeter, Donald Lee **OF-1B-3B**

1956–67 B:6/25/1935, Oklahoma City, OK Deb:9/18/1956, BRO NL BR/TR 6'4", 190

G	AB	R	H	HR	RBI	OBP	SLG	AVG
1109	3443	467	912	163	563	.309	.459	.265

Hard-hitting outfielder Don Demeter, a solid, if unspectacular glove man, enjoyed two three-homer days in his major league career. He also set a big league record for consecutive errorless games by an outfielder (266), since broken by Darren Lewis of the Giants. Demeter's span extended from September 1962, while he was with the Phils, through July 1965, while he performed for Detroit.

He hit 41 homers in 1956 for the Dodgers' Dallas Eagles farm club, and then he hit 18 for the Dodgers in 1959. Traded to the Phillies in May 1961, he and pitcher Jack Hamilton became Tigers in December 1963 in a swap for pitcher Jim Bunning and catcher Gus Triandos.

An early member of the Fellowship of Christian Athletes, Donald Lee Demeter took his faith seriously. During his tenure with the Phillies he roomed with Bobby Malkmus, also a devout Christian; together they brought recordings of church organ music on the road.

His teammates often probed Demeter's religious beliefs by using hypothetical situations. If, for instance, Demeter knew an umpire had made an incorrect decision in his favor, would he correct him or let it stand? "I think it is my duty to play within the rules of the game," Demeter responded. "The rules call for the umpire to make the decision. I respect the decision whatever it is." After retiring from baseball Demeter became a minister.

Gene DeMontreville

DeMontreville, Eugene Napoleon **2B-SS**

1894–1904 B:3/26/1874, St. Paul, MN D:2/18/1935, Memphis, TN Deb:8/20/1894, PIT NL BR/TR 5'8", 165

G	AB	R	H	HR	RBI	OBP	SLG	AVG
922	3615	537	1096	17	497	.340	.373	.303

Gene DeMontreville, a handsome French Canadian from St. Paul, Minnesota, hopscotched across baseball's playing fields around the turn of the 20th century. His whistle-stop tour took him to seven different cities—Pittsburgh, Washington, Baltimore, Chicago, Brooklyn, Boston, and St. Louis—in 11 major league seasons. Club owners no doubt tired of watching him hopelessly trying to catch the baseball.

In his first two full seasons with Washington of the National League, DeMontreville proved to be a potent hitter, batting .343 in 1896 and .341 in 1897. However, he led the league in errors both years, with an astounding 97 miscues in 133 games one season and 91 in the same number of games the next.

The following season DeMontreville signed with the Baltimore Orioles and played second base. The position shift didn't seem to make much of a difference; in 1898 he committed 60 errors.

His best all-around season may have been 1901 with Boston, when he batted .300 and drove in 72 runs. He assembled a career-best 23-game hitting streak, and even more impressive, committed only 43 errors. He retired in 1904 with nearly as many career errors (439) as RBIs (497).

Bingo DeMoss

DeMoss, Elwood **2B–SS–OF–P**

Negro League Player (1910–30) Manager B:3/5/1889, Topeka, KS D:1/26/1965, Chicago IL BR/TR 6'2", 175

DeMoss played for or managed 10 different Negro League teams from 1905 through 1943 and was regarded as the best second baseman in black baseball. A smart player, daring baserunner, and consummate bat handler, Elwood "Bingo" DeMoss was most valuable in the field, where his sure hands and speed made him a star. Although he could make all the defensive moves, he was particularly renowned for his ability in turning double plays. In 1917, when he and legendary shortstop John Henry "Pop" Lloyd formed the keystone combination for the Chicago American Giants, they made up one of the greatest infield duos in baseball history.

A righthanded batter, DeMoss made contact often (hence his nickname), which made him a valuable man in the lineup, even though he usually hit below .300. To take advantage of his bunting and hit-and-run skills he ordinarily batted second. He was regarded as the best bunter in black baseball. As the pitch was delivered, he'd remain in his normal stance; then, at the last second, he'd drop the bat and place the ball with precision. he'd Some observers insisted he could even put a reverse spin on the ball to draw it back from a charging infielder.

An astute student of the game, he helped I. C. Taylor's Indianapolis ABCs win the 1916 championship. He captained Rube Foster's Chicago American Giants to championship seasons in 1917 and from 1920 through 1922.

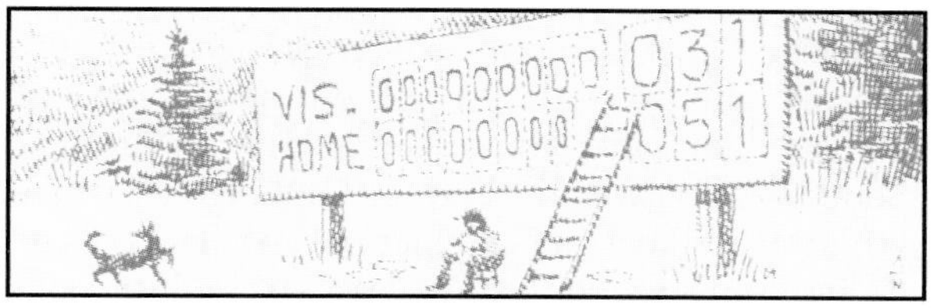

Rick Dempsey

Dempsey, John Rikard **C**

1969–92 B:9/13/1949, Fayetteville, TN Deb:9/23/1969, MIN AL BR/TR 6', 190

G	AB	R	H	HR	RBI	OBP	SLG	AVG
1766	4692	525	1093	96	471	.321	.347	.233

A gutsy leader behind the plate, Rick Dempsey ranks among the top 15 major leaguers in games caught. A career .234 hitter, he batted .303 in the postseason and won World Series Most Valuable Player honors in 1983 with the Baltimore Orioles.

Dempsey also won renown for his rain-delay performances of "Baseball Soliloquy in Pantomime," featuring parodies of Babe Ruth (complete with stomach padding) and Robin Yount, as well as lengthy belly-flop slides across the tarp. He inherited a bit of ham from his actor father. John Rikard Dempsey is his full name, the "Rikard" for a role his father had played.

After stints with the Minnesota Twins and New York Yankees, Dempsey was sent to Baltimore in a 10-player deal on June 15, 1976. The Orioles gave up established pitchers Ken Holtzman, Doyle Alexander, and Grant Jackson in return for young lefthanders Scott MacGregor and Tippy Martinez, plus a catcher who helped anchor the Orioles staff for the next decade.

Dempsey did his best work in the postseason. He finished the 1979 World Series batting .286 with six hits and three runs scored, and was MVP of the 1983 Series when he batted .385 with five extra-base hits. When Dodgers regular catcher Mike Scioscia was injured during the 1988 Series, Dempsey filled in admirably. Dempsey later became a minor league manager and major league coach.

Jerry Denny

Denny, Jeremiah Dennis **3B–SS**

1881–94 B:3/16/1859, New York, NY D:8/16/1927, Houston, TX Deb:5/2/1881, PRO NL BR/TR 5'11½", 180

G	AB	R	H	HR	RBI	OBP	SLG	AVG
1237	4946	714	1286	74	667	.287	.384	.260

Nineteenth-century third baseman Jerry Denny usually played without a glove, but that did not keep him from being described as the "most wide-ranging third baseman in history." More than a century after his final game Denny remained the leader in chances per game and putouts per game among major leaguers with 1,000 or more games at third. Denny remains the leader in chances per game and putouts per game. On August 17, 1882, he accepted 16 chances in an 18-inning game.

Raised in California orphanages, Denny played from 1878 to 1880 for three San Francisco teams: the Eagles, Stars, and Athletics. Hooking up with the National League's Providence Grays, he played third base in their 1884 championship season.

On October 24, 1884 he hit the first home run in World Series competition, homering at the Polo Grounds against the New York Metropolitans' Tim Keefe; his three-run blast won Game 2 for Charles "Ol' Hoss" Radbourn. After the Grays swept the Mets, Providence claimed to be "champions of the world," and the World Series was born.

John Denny

Denny, John Allen **P**

1974–86 B:11/8/1952, Prescott, AZ Deb:9/12/1974, STL NL BR/TR 6'3", 190

W	L	PCT	G	SH	IP	BB	SO	ERA
123	108	.532	325	18	2148^{2}	778	1146	3.59

John Denny was a control pitcher with an excellent curveball who struggled to attain the success predicted for him, finally achieved it, and then faded. He came up with the Cardinals, earned 10 wins in 1975, and posted the lowest ERA in the National League in 1976.

Unfortunately, his control was affected by a recurring injury, and he failed to live up to the Cardinals' hopes. In 1980 he was traded to the Indians, who passed him on to the Phillies two years later. He arrived with a reputation for unfulfilled potential and nine mostly mediocre seasons under his belt. It was exactly the right moment for him.

In 1983 Denny and the "Wheeze Kids," a team full of players past 30, collectively produced a summer full of outstanding individual performances that brought Philadelphia to the top of the National League. Abetted by his aging but still dominant teammates Mike Schmidt, Steve Carlton, Pete Rose, Joe Morgan, and Tony Perez slugging out runs and quashing opponents, Denny fashioned 19 wins and a career-best 2.37 ERA. The effort gave him not only his best year, but also earned him the NL Cy Young Award. After a decade he finally became the ace of a championship staff.

He won the World Series opener against Baltimore, but the Phillies lost the next four games. Denny stayed with the Phillies for three more seasons. Although he continued to post respectable strikeout totals, his ERA slowly rose. He retired after spending the 1986 season with the Reds.

Bucky Dent

Dent, Russell Earl **SS**

1973–84 M(1989–90, 36–53) B:11/25/1951, Savannah, GA Deb:6/1/1973, CHI AL BR/TR 5'11", 181

G	AB	R	H	HR	RBI	OBP	SLG	AVG
1392	4512	451	1114	40	423	.300	.321	.247

Bucky Dent is loved in New York and reviled in Boston for the home run he hit off Mike Torrez at Fenway Park on October 2, 1978. The seventh-inning blow to left field overcame a 2–0 Red Sox lead; the Yankees held on for a 5–4 win in the one-game playoff for the American League East championship. The home run was heroic, historic, and totally out of character for the light-hitting, smooth-fielding shortstop.

Buoyed by his game-winning homer, Dent kept hitting in the postseason. He drove in the first run in the Yankees' Game 1 Championship Series victory over the Royals and then added three more RBIs in their 10–4 win in Game 2. In the World Series Dent was even better. The Yankees were down, two games to none, and were clinging to a 2–1 lead in Game 3. Dent led off the seventh with a single. The Yankees added three more runs and held on for the win. A 10th-inning win in Game 4 evened the Series, and Dent went 6-for-8 with four RBIs in the final two games to stake New York to a world championship. He batted .417 in the World Series—only double-play partner Brian Doyle hit higher for the Yankees—and Dent was named Series Most Valuable Player.

It is ironic that Dent is best known for the homer he hit in 1978, because for a dozen years he was a smart and exceptionally sure-handed shortstop. He led AL shortstops in fielding three times. Originally drafted by the Cardinals, Dent was plucked out of the St. Louis system by the White Sox, who groomed him in the minors for three years. He became Chicago's starting shortstop in 1974, batting .275, and finishing second in Rookie of the Year voting.

During spring training in 1977, the White Sox sent Dent to the Yankees, where he and second baseman Willie Randolph formed one of the smoothest double-play combos the Bronx had seen in years. Dent was named to the AL All-Star team for the third time in 1981, but when he slumped in 1982, he was dealt to Texas. Dent led AL shortstops in fielding percentage again but finished his playing career the next season.

Dent managed in the Yankees system, and replaced Dallas Green in New York late in the 1989 season. The team lost 11 of the first 13 games he managed, but after a nine-game winning streak in September he was rehired for 1990. He was fired with the Yankees in last place after an 18–31 start. He became a coach for the Cardinals and Rangers.

Bob Dernier

Dernier, Robert Eugene **OF**

1980–89 B:1/5/1957, Kansas City, MO Deb:9/7/1980, PHI NL BR/TR, 6', 165

G	AB	R	H	HR	RBI	OBP	SLG	AVG
904	2483	374	634	23	152	.318	.333	.255

Outfielder Bob Dernier's speed made him doubly valuable to a major league club—he could cover great distances in center field and could also steal 40 bases in a season. Originally drafted by the Reds, Dernier signed as an amateur free agent with the Phillies and then went to the Cubs in March 1984.

"We need Bobby for his extraordinary defense, and he gives us a leadoff man who can steal bases," Cubs manager Jim Frey said. "He's probably as good as anybody in baseball in running down fly-balls. We appreciated him more, maybe, when he wasn't there."

Cubs coach Jimmy Piersall put it less delicately: "Keith Moreland and Gary Matthews really want Bobby to get to the balls in the outfield because they can't get to a lot of them themselves." In 1984 Dernier helped the Cubs win the National League East title, Chicago's first postseason berth since 1945. *The Sporting News* named Dernier to its National League All-Fielding Team.

Dernier had his liabilities, too, namely a lack of power and a tendency to spend time on the disabled list. On July 17, 1985, for example, he had a bursa sac and a ganglion removed from the top of his left foot. When he came off the DL he was still not healthy. "Toward the end of the year I got pretty frustrated. I couldn't bunt as much because I lost a half step. I couldn't cut corners on the bases. I was just treading water," Dernier said.

Toward the end of his Cubs tenure Dernier bunted less and seemed to swing for the fences more. A shoulder injury in 1986 lessened Dernier's value to the club even more. Granted free agency on November 9, 1987, he re-signed with the Phillies and then retired after the 1989 season.

Paul Derringer

Derringer, Samuel Paul **P**

1931–45 B:10/17/1906, Springfield, KY D:11/17/1987, Sarasota, FL Deb:4/16/1931, STL NL BR/TR 6'3½", 205

W	L	PCT	G	SH	IP	BB	SO	ERA
223	212	.513	579	32	3645	761	1507	3.46

In 1933 Paul Derringer lost two games for the Cardinals and 25 more after being traded to the Reds. In the process he came close to breaking Vic Willis' dismal major league record of 29 losses. Nevertheless Cincinnati's Larry MacPhail gave Derringer a $1,500 raise.

During that season the Reds were shut out in seven of Derringer's losses. In fact, his mates were blanked in 36 of the 212 games he lost in his career. Given some runs, Derringer won 20 games in each of four seasons and 223 in his career, teaming with Bucky Walters to lead the Reds to pennants in 1939 and 1940.

Nicknamed "Duke" or "Dude" because of his elegant wardrobe, Derringer became a pitcher in some pretty "fishy" circumstances. Originally a catcher, Derringer watched his teammates get lambasted one day while his friends waited in the car to take him on a fishing trip. Duke asked his manager, "Lemme pitch, will ya? I can get this game over with." He was as good as his word.

Derringer signed with the Cardinals and led the International League in strikeouts. When faced with promoting Derringer or Dizzy Dean in 1931, Branch Rickey chose Derringer. He was 18–8 and led the league in winning percentage (.692).

The rookie got tattooed in the first game of the 1931 World Series by Philadelphia Athletics batters Jimmie Foxx, Al Simmons, and Mickey Cochrane and was also bombed in Game 6. His confidence gone, Derringer was 11–14 in 1932. He began squabbling with the St. Louis front office and was traded to Cincinnati, where he played for the equally fiery MacPhail.

MacPhail once fined Derringer $250 for not sliding when he should have, suspended him, and lectured the pitcher for an hour. Furious, the rangy righthander flung an inkwell at MacPhail, missing him by inches. MacPhail gasped, "You might have killed me!", to which Duke replied, "That's what I was meaning to do." MacPhail reached into his desk, grabbed his checkbook, and gave Derringer a check for $750. Derringer asked, "What's this for?" MacPhail replied, "That's a bonus for missing me."

MacPhail gave Derringer the honor of pitching in the first night game in major league history, and he beat the Phils, 2–1. But he had more World Series trouble in 1939. Facing the Yanks in Game 1, he lost, 2–1, when Ival Goodman misplayed a long fly into a triple. Derringer left Game 4 after seven innings, winning 4–2. But the Reds' errors gave the Yanks the championship in extra innings.

Derringer also lost the 1940 World Series opener against Detroit, but he ended his Series jinx by winning Game 4 to tie the Tigers at two games apiece. Locked in a classic pitching duel with Bobo Newsom in Game 7, Derringer allowed no earned runs and won, 2–1, giving Cincinnati the championship.

Delino DeShields

DeShields, Delino Lamont **2B**
1990–* B:1/15/1969, Seaford, DE Deb:4/9/1990, MON NL BL/TR, 6'1", 170

G	AB	R	H	HR	RBI	OBP	SLG	AVG
1271	4721	713	1272	62	428	.355	.373	.269

Fleet second baseman Delino DeShields stole more than 50 bases three times in his first 10 seasons. He topped 40 steals three other times, for a career total of 393. DeShields also led the National League with 14 triples in 1997 while playing for the St. Louis Cardinals.

A first-round draft pick out of Villanova University in 1987, DeShields reached the majors with the Montreal Expos in 1990. His tendency to strike out frequently—he led the NL with 151 whiffs in 1991—hurt his average and interfered with his ability to become a distraction on the basepaths. The converted shortstop also led NL second basemen with 27 errors in 1991.

On November 19, 1993, the Expos dealt DeShields to the Los Angeles Dodgers in a trade that brought the Expos pitcher Pedro Martinez. Martinez moved into Montreal's rotation and won the NL's Cy Young Award four years later. DeShields spent three years in Los Angeles, moved to St. Louis in 1998 via free agency, then signed with Baltimore in 1999 when Roberto Alomar jumped to Cleveland as a free agent. DeShields' first season as an Oriole began slowly after he fractured his left thumb during spring training. He later went on the disabled list with hamstring and thigh problems. Still, he managed to hit .301 in his last 74 games with the Orioles.

Mike Devereaux

Devereaux, Michael **OF**
1987–98 B:4/10/1963, Casper, WY Deb:9/2/1987, LA NL BR/TR, 6'1", 195

G	AB	R	H	HR	RBI	OBP	SLG	AVG
1086	3740	491	949	105	480	.311	.401	.254

Mike Devereaux was an Atlanta Brave only briefly, but enjoyed the greatest moment of his career while wearing a Braves uniform. Acquired by Atlanta for the 1995 stretch run, Devereaux wound up as the Most Valuable Player of the 1995 National League Championship Series.

The little-used outfielder delivered the game-winning single that beat the Cincinnati Reds in the 11th inning of Game 1 of the NLCS. His three-run, seventh-inning homer was the big blow of Game 4, a 6–0 victory that climaxed Atlanta's sweep. He went 4-for-13 (.308) with a team-best five RBIs. Like Francisco Cabrera three years earlier, Devereaux was an unlikely postseason hero. He played in only 29 games after arriving in Atlanta in a waiver deal with the Chicago White Sox. Devereaux moved on to Baltimore after the Braves won the World Series.

Early in his career, Devereaux was an acrobatic center fielder, robbing hitters of home runs by leaping above outfield walls. He had proven his jumping ability by setting the Wyoming state high school high jump record at 6 feet, 8 inches. Devereaux broke in with the Los Angeles Dodgers in 1987, but came into his own in his first tour with the Orioles two years later. He reached career peaks in 1992 with 24 home runs and 107 RBIs.

Art Devlin

Devlin, Arthur McArthur **3B**
1904–13 B:10/16/1879, Washington, DC D:9/18/1948, Jersey City, NJ Deb:4/14/1904, NY NL BR/TR 6', 175

G	AB	R	H	HR	RBI	OBP	SLG	AVG
1313	4412	603	1185	10	505	.364	.338	.269

For eight years in the early 1900s, Art Devlin played third base for John McGraw's New York Giants. The Giants won four pennants and finished second three times in those eight seasons.

Devlin was a regular in his rookie season of 1904, hitting .281 with 33 stolen bases and 66 RBIs—and smacking a grand slam in his first major league at bat. His batting average fell to .246 in 1905—his lowest average as a regular—but he led the National League with 59 steals. Devlin also led NL third basemen in assists, a feat he achieved three times. Devlin's bat bounced back in 1906, when he hit a career-best .299 and stole 54 bases, third best in the league. His best year with the glove was 1908, when he led NL third basemen in putouts, assists, and fielding.

In 1910, Devlin was involved in the kind of incident that was not that uncommon in baseball's early days. On June 23, 1910, in a game with the Brooklyn Superbas (they wouldn't be the Dodgers until 1912) at Washington Park, Devlin was arrested with two teammates after a brawl with some Brooklyn fans. The festivities began after the Giants had beaten the Superbas, 8–2. Devlin walked over to a Brooklyn fan, Bernard J. Roesler, who had been heckling the third baseman throughout the game, and smashed him in the jaw. Roesler lay unconscious for seven minutes.

Some nearby fans began shouting that Roesler had not been the heckler, and a free-for-all erupted when two of Devlin's teammates, Larry Doyle and Josh Devore, came to his defense. As

Dodgers owner Charles Ebbets started arguing with McGraw, Devlin was escorted to the police station, but was released when Roesler failed to bring any witnesses with him. When Roesler returned with a witness and swore out a warrant, Wee Willie Keeler, McGraw's teammate with the old Baltimore Orioles, posted Devlin's bail. The case never went to trial, but NL president Thomas Lynch suspended Devlin for five days. He fined Devore and Doyle $50 each.

Grantland Rice named Devlin the third baseman on his Giants all-time team, and his colleague, Frank Graham, called him "the greatest third baseman ever to wear a Giant uniform."

Jim Devlin

Devlin, James Alexander **P-1B**

1873–77 B:1849, Philadelphia, PA D:10/10/1883, Philadelphia, PA Deb:4/21/1873, PHI NA BR/TR 5'11", 175

W	L	PCT	G	SH	IP	BB	SO	ERA
65	60	.520	129	9	1181	78	263	1.89

Louisville pitcher James Alexander Devlin was a key figure in baseball's biggest gambling-related disgrace prior to the infamous Black Sox scandal. In 1877 the Louisville Grays were on the verge of winning the National League pennant when Jim Devlin, the Grays' only pitcher, suddenly lost his effectiveness, as did several other key players. As the pennant slipped away, rumors arose that the Grays were "hippodroming," or throwing games. Newspapers ran huge headlines about the abrupt turnaround, and a mysterious telegram to Grays management implied that gamblers were laying big money against the team.

The season ended with the Grays in second place. Devlin, who had been a first baseman in the National Association before becoming a pitcher, suddenly regained his effectiveness during a series of postseason exhibitions that followed the Grays' collapse. This only fueled suspicions: "The Celt has completely given himself away," was one sportswriter's assertion.

Louisville president Charles E. Chase confronted Devlin, demanded that he come clean, and gave him a deadline to confess by. Meanwhile, Devlin's co-conspirator George Hall thought Devlin had cracked and so admitted to Chase that he had been throwing games. Hall further implicated infielder Albert H. Nichols, who he said was the club's contact with gambling elements.

Informed that Hall had confessed, Devlin admitted his guilt. The story was that Hall and Nichols had approached Devlin and offered him $100 to throw an exhibition game against Lowell. Once Devlin had complied he was virtually blackmailed into hippodroming regular season games.

Devlin, Hall, Nichols, and team captain Bill Craver were expelled from the National League in December 1877 for "conduct in contravention of the objects of this League." The scandal led not only to the collapse of the Louisville franchise but also to that of St. Louis, which had been counting on signing Devlin for the 1878 season.

Devlin repeatedly but unsuccessfully petitioned the National League for reinstatement. Ironically, he later became a policeman in Philadelphia.

Josh Devore

Devore, Joshua D. **OF**

1908–14 B:11/13/1887, Murray City, OH D:10/6/1954, Chillicothe, OH Deb: 9/25/1908, NY NL BL/TL 5'6", 160

G	AB	R	H	HR	RBI	OBP	SLG	AVG
601	1874	331	520	11	149	.361	.359	.277

Speed demon Josh Devore was one of the few National Leaguers with the speed to equal Ty Cobb. After swiping 61 bases in 1911, he had one of the great innings in running history. On June 20, 1912, he reached base twice in the ninth inning and, both times, stole second and third off pitcher Bradley Hogg and catcher Gilbert Whitehouse in a 20–12 victory over the Braves.

Devore got a chance to try out for the Class D Cotton States League's Meridian White Ribbons only after his brother posted a $100 bond for his expenses—manager Sy Sample thought Devore too small to look at. He was purchased from Meridian in 1908 and came to the Giants at the end of the season.

Despite a relatively short, seven-year career, Devore played in three World Series. In Game 3 of the 1912 World Series, the Giants led the Red Sox, 2–1, with two out and the tying and winning runs on second and third. Catcher Hick Cady hit a drive deep to right-center field, but Devore ran it down to end the game and save the victory for New York. Tris Speaker called it "one of the greatest catches I've ever seen."

Lou Dials

Dials, Lou **1B-OF**

Negro League Player (1925–1936) Manager B:1/10/1904, Little Rock, AR BL/TL 5'10", 185

Lou Dials figured in early efforts to integrate baseball. A few years before Branch Rickey launched his plan to break the color barrier, Oakland Oaks owner Vince DeVicenzi wanted to sign Dials and another black player, but it never happened. The Oaks were independent, but that didn't mean DeVicenzi could overcome the racism of the day.

"There was nothing he [DeVicenzi] could do," Dials said later. "That was the way it was then."

That same year, general manager Pants Rowland of the minor league Los Angeles Angels announced tryouts for three black players. Rowland had to back down two weeks later when Philip K. Wrigley, whose Cubs owned the franchise, told him, "The other owners would crucify me."

Born in Little Rock, Dials moved to Los Angeles when he was a child. In 1925 Negro League pioneer Rube Foster signed Dials to his Chicago American Giants. He spent 13 years in the Negro Leagues, playing for Chicago, the Detroit Stars, the Philadelphia Hilldales, and the New York Black Yankees. Dials then spent four years in the Mexican League before returning to Los Angeles when World War II broke out.

Dials was a 39-year-old veteran of the Negro Leagues, but still a capable player, when he almost got that chance to make history. In 1950, at the age of 46 he finally played in Organized Baseball, for the Class C Sunset League's Tijuana Potros. "And I was hitting about .300," he said. "But my legs were hurting so bad. I was just too old." Dials later scouted for Houston and Cleveland.

Bo Diaz

Diaz, Baudillo Jose (Seijas) **C**

1977–89 B:3/23/1953, Cua, Venezuela D:11/23/1990, Caracas, Venezuela Deb:9/6/1977, BOS AL BR/TR 5'11", 190

G	AB	R	H	HR	RBI	OBP	SLG	AVG
993	3274	327	834	87	452	.300	.387	.255

A part-time catcher for most of his career, Diaz showed enough power at the plate and a tough enough attitude behind it to stay in the majors for 13 years. Late in his career, former teammate Mike LaValliere said of Diaz, "I've seen his knees. They're scarred and swollen and every time he squats to catch, it makes me hurt just watching him."

In 1981 Diaz, filling in for Cleveland's injured Ron Hassey, belted the ball hard for the first half of the strike-shortened season. He made the All-Star team, but was injured and finished the season at .313 with seven homers and 38 RBIs. In November he was swapped to the Phillies in a three-team deal.

In 1982 Diaz had his biggest year, with 18 home runs, 85 RBIs, and a .288 average. He was traded to the Reds and became their starter. In 1987 Diaz hit 15 homers and drove in 82 runs and enjoyed another All-Star year. In November 1990 Diaz died when he was struck by lightning while trying to install a satellite dish at his home in Venezuela.

Rob Dibble

Dibble, Robert Keith **P**

1988–95 B:1/24/1964, Bridgeport, CT Deb:6/29/1988, CIN NL BL/TR 6'4", 230

W	L	PCT	G	SV	IP	BB	SO	ERA
27	25	.519	385	89	477	238	645	2.98

Regularly clocked on the radar at over 100 mph, Rob Dibble emerged as one of baseball's most dominating and intimidating relievers in the early 1990s. Coaches loved his heat, but wondered about his unorthodox delivery. In the end, the delivery proved fine. It was Dibble's fiery temper that proved to be his greatest obstacle. Frequently suspended for throwing at batters, Dibble felt he was just being an effective pitcher. "I'm a firm believer in Bob Gibson's philosophy," Dibble explained "The pitcher owns the inside and outside two inches of the plate."

Unlike most overpowering pitchers, Dibble did not struggle with his control, regularly striking out four or five batters for every one he walked. In his first four years in the majors he struck out 511 and walked 129 in 350 innings.

Along with Randy Myers and Norm Charlton, Dibble was one of Cincinnati's self-proclaimed "Nasty Boys" who helped lead the Reds to a World Series sweep of Oakland in 1990. Dibble worked primarily as a setup man for John Franco and then Myers before assuming the closer duties in 1991. He was named to the National League All-Star team twice.

Shoulder injuries sidelined Dibble for parts of the next two seasons, and he missed the 1994 season completely. After his attempted comeback failed in 1995, Dibble launched a career as a sports radio personality.

Bill Dickey

Dickey, William Malcolm **C**

1928–43, 1946 M(1946, 57–48) B:6/6/1907, Bastrop, LA D:11/12/1993, Little Rock, AR Deb:8/15/1928, NY AL BL/TR 6'1½", 185

G	AB	R	H	HR	RBI	OBP	SLG	AVG
1789	6300	930	1969	202	1209	.382	.486	.313

One of the greatest catchers of all time, Bill Dickey batted .300 or better 11 times, and was an important part of why the Yankees won eight pennants and seven World Series during his tenure in pinstripes. "Dickey isn't just a catcher, he's a ballclub," Dan Daniels wrote. "He isn't just a player, he's an influence."

He was originally signed in 1926 by Little Rock of the Southern Association. A number of major league clubs began to show an interest in Dickey, as did Yankees scout Johnny Nee, who wired his general manager, Ed Barrow, "If this boy doesn't make it, I'll quit scouting."

The Yankees purchased Dickey's contract on the condition that he start the 1928 season with Little Rock. He hit .300 in 60 games there and was promoted to New York, where he batted only .200 in 10 contests. "I have a hunch about this kid because every other club is trying to make a deal for him," Yankees manager Miller Huggins told reporters in spring 1928. "We bought him from Little Rock for $12,500. Today we could sell him for $35,000."

In training camp with the Yankees, Dickey tried to emulate the slugging feats of Ruth and Gehrig, but all he could manage were "the highest pop flies you ever saw." Finally Huggins took him aside and said, "Young man, choke up on the bat and stop unbuttoning your shirt on every pitch. That way you'll be around here longer."

Dickey had an impressive first season even though he was soon put to the test by the opposition. "They saw he was a new man and they figured they'd try him out. They tried, and they found out," recalled outfielder Earle Combs.

Dickey had a reputation as a gentleman but could play rough. One day, Washington outfielder Carl Reynolds slid hard into Dickey at home plate. When the dust settled, both players scrambled to their feet. Dickey, who thought Reynolds was coming at him, swung first and broke his opponent's jaw. He was fined $1,000 and suspended for 30 days. "It was hot, and the games had been close, and I had been banged around for days," Dickey explained later. "When Reynolds came at me high, I just had to hit somebody."

"Sure, Bill shouldn't have hit the fellow," manager Joe McCarthy said, "but I can tell you, after that they were a bit more polite when sliding in on him."

Dickey enjoyed well-earned praise for his pitch selection. The story is that after the last game of the 1943 World Series, a serviceman spoke to him in the hotel elevator, "I bet you don't remember me." Dickey responded, "I don't recall your name, but I remember we pitched you high and tight." The serviceman was Joe Gantenbein, who at one time had spent two years with the A's—and who had been pitched to in just that fashion.

Dickey's career had several singular highlights: hitting three homers in one game on July 6, 1939; catching 125 games without a passed ball during the 1931 season; being the first player to catch 100 or more games for 13 seasons; and being selected for 11 All-Star Games.

His biggest day in baseball, however, came in Game 5 of the 1943 World Series. With no score in the bottom of the sixth, left fielder Charlie "King Kong" Keller singled between first and second. Dickey, batting sixth, came to the plate against the Cardinals' Mort Cooper.

"I wasn't trying to outguess Cooper," Dickey recalled. "I wasn't trying to hit the ball out of the park either. I wanted a fastball and I only wanted to meet it, just so it would go safe. Well, I got it...and hit it good but not hard." At least he didn't think he'd hit it hard. But as he was running to first he saw the ball heading for the roof. The Yankees' first-base coach, Earle Combs, yelled at him, "You got one, Bill." The only thing Dickey remembered thinking was, "We'll get a run, anyway, for 'Spud' [Chandler] and maybe it'll be enough." Then Dickey saw third-base coach Art Fletcher waving his cap and knew he'd hit a home run.

Dickey spent the 1944 and 1945 seasons in the Navy. Returning to the Yankees in 1946, he replaced McCarthy as manager in late May. The team never played well under him, and Dickey was let go on September 12. He later scouted and coached for the Yankees and was a sound judge of baseball talent.

"You guys got to see this kid we have in camp," he told skeptical reporters in 1951. "Out of Class C ball, hits both ways, 500 feet both ways. You got to see him." The prospect was Mickey Mantle. And of course Dickey helped turn the raw catching prospect Yogi Berra into a Hall of Fame receiver.

Dickey was elected to the Hall of Fame in 1954. Some people believe he was the greatest catcher of all time. Often the choice narrows down to either Dickey or Mickey Cochrane. Cochrane's teammate Charlie Gehringer once said, "You might be inclined to pick Cochrane over Dickey because of Mickey's aggressiveness. But Dickey certainly made catching look easy."

Murry Dickson

Dickson, Murry Monroe **P**

1939–40,1942–43,1946–59 B:8/21/1916, Tracy, MO D:9/21/1989, Kansas City, KS Deb:9/30/1939, STL NL BR/TR, 5'10½", 157

W	L	PCT	G	SH	IP	BB	SO	ERA
172	181	.487	625	27	3052[1]	1058	1281	3.66

Joe Garagiola used to joke on NBC about those dreadful Pirates teams he caught for in the early 1950s. The best pitcher on those Pirates staffs was Murry Dickson, a hurler who got a late start in the majors but made up for lost time once he established himself.

Dickson, a durable righthander who pitched at least 200 innings for 10 straight seasons (even though he only weighed 157 pounds) lasted in the majors until he was 43, and just missed being a four-decade player. Garagiola said, "We used to call him Thomas Edison because he had so many pitches. He even had a good knuckleball. And another thing about him was, even if the batter knew what pitch was coming, he still had to figure out if it was going to be sidearm or three-quarter or overhand. But the big thing about him was that he was one of those guys that always wanted the ball and it was more than having a rubber arm. He was the kind of guy you wanted out there when things were tight."

After leading the American Association with 21 wins in 1941, he was 6–3 with a 2.91 ERA for the Cardinals in 1942 as a 26-year-old rookie. He was 8–2 in 31 games the next season as St. Louis won its second straight pennant. Drafted into the army just as the season was ending, Dickson was given a 10-day pass from Fort Riley, Kansas, so he could pitch in the World Series against the Yankees, who won in five games.

When he returned to baseball in 1946 Dickson's career took off. He was 15–6 with a career-low 2.88 ERA and led the National League in winning percentage. He pitched well in the World Series when the Cardinals beat the Red Sox in seven games. Dickson started Game 3 and allowed a three-run homer to Rudy York in the first inning, but Dave "Boo" Ferriss shut out the Cards that day. Dickson also started Game 7 and left the mound with a 3–1 lead, two on, and no one out in the eighth inning. But Harry "the Cat" Brecheen blew the save, only to earn his third win of the Series an inning later on Enos Slaughter's mad dash around the bases. So Brecheen became the hero, the first pitcher in 26 years to win three games in a Series, all because he blew the win for Dickson.

Dickson was 25–32 over the next two seasons and was sold to the Pirates for a reported $125,000 in January 1949. He was 22–29 in his first two years in Pittsburgh, then had his best season in 1951, going 20–16 and pitching a career-high 288⅔ innings for a 64–94 team. It was his only 20-win season. Dickson's ERA dropped from 4.02 to 3.57 in 1952. Unfortunately, the Pirates dropped too—to a horrific 42–112 as Dickson led league pitchers with 21 losses. He fell one defeat short of 20 losses the following year, but still tied for the NL in that category.

Traded to the Phillies in January 1954, for two warm bodies and $70,000, Dickson led the league in losses all by himself this time, going 10–20 with a respectable 3.78 ERA for a team that finished only four games under .500. After going 12–11 in 1955, Dickson went to St. Louis in May 1956, with Herm Wehmeier for Harvey Haddix, Stu Miller, and Ben Flowers. At age 40 Dickson went 13–8 for St. Louis in 28 starts. He lasted one more season with the Cards and then hung on for two more years with the Yankees and the A's before retiring in 1959, one season short of four decades.

Larry Dierker

Dierker, Lawrence Edward **P**

1964–77 M(1997–*, 270–189) B:9/22/46, Hollywood, CA Deb:9/22/64, HOU NL BR/TR 6'4", 215

W	L	PCT	G	SH	IP	BB	SO	ERA
139	123	.531	356	25	2333²	711	1493	3.31

Larry Dierker has personified baseball in Houston. He made his major league debut with the Colt .45s, precursor of the Astros, on his 18th birthday in 1964, striking out Willie Mays in the first inning. During his 14-year career, he set nearly every pitching record for the club. In 1969 Dierker became the Astros' first 20-game winner, and was twice named as their representative in the All-Star Game. After four near misses, he threw a no-hitter in 1976 against the Montreal Expos.

After spending the final season of his playing career with the Cardinals, Dierker returned to Houston in 1977 and joined the Astros front office. In 1979 he became a commentator for the club's television and radio broadcasts. His insightful commentary and his willingness to question traditional strategies made him very popular. Dierker downplayed the emphasis on batting average and RBIs as indicators of playing ability, espousing instead the work of researchers like Bill James and Pete Palmer.

In 1997 Dierker was given an opportunity to put his theories to the test when the Astros summoned him from the broadcast booth to assume the club's managerial duties. Critics howled at the thought of a first-time manager coming from the booth, citing the failed experiment in San Diego by Jerry Coleman (73–89). Dierker made Houston general manager Jerry Hunsicker look like a genius.

In his first year at the helm, he guided the Astros to their first division title in 11 years. It marked only the sixth time in history that a rookie manager had guided his team to a first-place finish. Dierker was named National League Manager of the Year in 1998 when the Astros won a second division title. Dierker managed more by feel than by the book, letting his starters pitch late into games with success while opponents floundered with suspect middle relievers. He had confidence in his hitters, allowing them to bat when others would have been tempted to double switch. Dierker's endearing qualities made what happened in the Astrodome dugout in the middle of a game even that much more disturbing.

On June 13, 1999, Dierker suffered a grand mal seizure during a game, collapsing in the dugout; he was removed on a stretcher and the game was suspended. He returned a month later and the Astros won a third consecutive division title, but once again did not advance past the Division Series.

Martin Dihigo

Martin Dihigo **OF–P–1B–3B**

Negro League Player(1923–45) Manager B:5/25/1905, Matanzas, Cuba D:5/22/1971, Cienfuegos, Cuba BR/TR 6'3", 190

Only Martin Dihigo has been elected to the Cuban, Mexican, and United States Baseball Halls of Fame. His speed, size, and strong throwing arm made him one of the most versatile players in baseball history. During his 30-year career Dihigo played every position on the field—sometimes more than one in the same game—and played each of them exceptionally well. A superb pitcher, Dihigo is credited with the first no-hitter in Mexican League history.

Dihigo was arguably the greatest Cuban ballplayer of all time. Among Cuban-born players, only Cristobal Torriente was considered his peer at the plate. Johnny Mize, who played for a team Dihigo managed in the Dominican Republic winter league in 1943, said Dihigo was the greatest player he'd ever seen. Negro League great Buck Leonard shared Mize's opinion: "He could run, hit, throw, think, pitch, and manage."

Known as "El Maestro" in Mexico and "El Immortal" in Cuba, Dihigo began his U.S. career as an 18-year-old second baseman for the Cuban Stars. After five years he moved on to the Homestead Grays, and had short stints with the Philadelphia Hilldales, the Baltimore Black Sox, and the New York Cubans. Dihigo won three Negro League home run crowns and tied Josh Gibson for another. As a pitcher, he racked up more than 200 wins in American and Mexican ball.

Dihigo was an affable, fun-loving man. Once, while safely on third base, he screamed at the pitcher, "You balked! You balked!" He continued to holler as he strolled toward home. Everyone stared as if Dihigo had suddenly gone mad. But when he crossed the plate and walked slyly into the dugout, the fans laughed and cheered in appreciation of the stunt.

In September 1938 Dihigo met Satchel Paige in a much-anticipated pitching matchup that has become a Mexican League legend. Paige, hindered by a sore arm and relying on underhand and trick pitches, battled Dihigo for six scoreless innings. In the seventh, Paige's control faltered. After two walks and a single loaded the bases, he uncorked a wild pitch, giving Dihigo's team the lead. Paige left for a pinch hitter, and his team later tied the game, 1–1. Dihigo took matters into his own hands in the ninth and homered to win the game.

He played sparingly as player-manager for the New York Cubans in 1945 and continued to play and manage in Cuba and Mexico until the early 1950s, when he returned to Cuba to stay. Dihigo served as Cuba's minister of sports until his death in 1971. In 1977 he became the first Cuban to be elected to the National Baseball Hall of Fame.

Dom DiMaggio

DiMaggio, Dominic Paul **OF**

1940–42, 1946–53 B:2/12/1917, San Francisco, CA Deb:4/16/1940, BOS AL BR/TR 5'9", 168

G	AB	R	H	HR	RBI	OBP	SLG	AVG
1399	5640	1046	1680	87	618	.383	.419	.298

In an 11-year career with the Red Sox, Dom DiMaggio proved to be a superb center fielder and excellent leadoff man. The two roles were vital for the team. The Sox sluggers in the middle of the batting order needed someone on base to drive in, and Ted Williams needed a good center fielder next to him to compensate for his defensive shortcomings.

Dom was the youngest of the professional—baseball-playing DiMaggio boys—and the smallest, standing only 5 feet 9 inches and weighing 168 pounds. Because of his quiet demeanor and spectacles, some wag nicknamed him "the Little Professor."

And "the Prof" could play. Seven times in his 10 full seasons in the majors he was named to the All-Star team, where he occasionally played next to brother Joe in the outfield. In the 1941 game, brother Dom drove in Joe with a single.

In Dom's 11 big league seasons he never batted below .283. Five times he pushed past the .300 mark, including a .328 performance in 1950. On June 30, 1950, Dom and Joe each homered in the same game, becoming the fourth brother tandem to accomplish that feat in major league history.

Dom DiMaggio batted safely in 34 straight games in 1949, only to have the streak snapped when his brother Joe made a super catch to rob him of a hit in the 35th game. In 1951 Dom hit in 27 straight games.

His leadoff skills were demonstrated by his 90 or more walks in three different seasons. The Red Sox sluggers knocked him in often enough in 1950 and 1951 that he led the American League in runs scored. He also led the league in triples and stolen bases once each.

But as a fielder he truly shone. Some called him "Jesse James without the horse" because of his frequent robberies of potential hits. His 503 putouts in 1948 set the AL record, which wouldn't be broken until Chet Lemon did it 29 years later.

In 1946 Dom batted .316 as the Red Sox returned to World Series action for the first time since Babe Ruth's trade to New York in 1920. The youngest DiMaggio's double in the seventh inning of Game 5 sparked a three-run rally that put the Sox up, three games to two. And when he doubled in the eighth inning of Game 7 to tie the game, 3–3, it looked as though he might wear a hero's medal.

But in a twist of fate, DiMaggio turned his ankle running out the double. The man who replaced him in center, Leon Culberson, was no match for DiMaggio in either outfield speed or throwing capability. When Cardinals outfielder Harry Walker ripped a hit into center field in the last of the eighth, Enos Slaughter, the man on first, didn't have to fear DiMaggio's speed or his arm. "Slaughter's Mad Dash," as it has become known, won the Series for St. Louis.

Joe DiMaggio

DiMaggio, Joseph Paul **OF**
1936–42, 1946–51 B:11/25/1914, Martinez, CA
D: 3/8/1999, Hollywood, FL Deb:5/03/1936, NY AL
BR/TR 6'2", 193

G	AB	R	H	HR	RBI	OBP	SLG	AVG
1736	6821	1390	2214	361	1537	.398	.579	.325

Of the great players in baseball history, only a handful have possessed a unique, inimitable style. Joe DiMaggio was one of those players. His grace and almost princely elegance truly set him apart.

His 1941 record of hitting safely in 56 consecutive games might be called a freak statistic, but in some ways it is the perfect Joe DiMaggio stat. DiMaggio's creed was excellence, and he did whatever was needed for his team to win, without pomp or showmanship. Although another ballplayer might be better at one skill or another, it is difficult to imagine a player who would be better in a lineup on offense and defense every day than DiMaggio.

DiMaggio was both "the Yankee Clipper," a quiet, effortless batter who moved like a graceful sailing ship, and "Joltin' Joe," the potent slugger. But it was as a fielder and baserunner that DiMaggio's intelligent style of play was most obvious. Manager Joe McCarthy said simply, "He was the best baserunner I ever saw."

In 1932 Joe's older brother Vince was playing for the minor league San Francisco Seals in the DiMaggios' hometown, and the team needed a new shortstop. "Why don't you try my brother Joe?" Vince suggested. "He's pretty good." The 17-year-old Joe played just three games for the Seals that year, but in 1933 he tore up the Pacific Coast League, hitting .340 with 28 homers and a league-leading 169 RBIs. He also hit safely in 61 consecutive games, foreshadowing his 1941 major league feat.

His strong season sparked the interest of major league scouts. But the Seals stalled. The team needed cash, like so many others during the Great Depression, and management figured DiMaggio would be worth even more, perhaps as much as $100,000, if he played another season for the Seals.

After DiMaggio broke his knee getting out of a cab in 1934, the scouts stopped calling for a while. But prior to the 1935 season the wealthy Yankees offered the Seals $25,000 and five minor leaguers for DiMaggio. San Francisco agreed, on condition that DiMaggio play one more season on the coast. DiMaggio's performance indicated that the Yanks had gotten a bargain: he batted .398 and led the league in RBIs and outfield assists.

DiMaggio's big league debut with the Yankees came on May 3, 1936. He set American League rookie records that season with 132 runs scored and 15 triples. He hit .323, belted 29 homers, and drove in 125 runs. His 22 assists led all AL outfielders. He had 21 assists the next season and had managed another 20 in 1938 before runners wised up.

Like many Americans, DiMaggio served during World War II. He missed three full seasons, from age 28 to 31. Before the war he had been the model of consistency, from 1936 through 1942 batting over .300 every year and bettering .350 three times. He had more than 100 RBIs each season, including 167 in 1937. Only during the 1942 season, before he joined the military, did he fail to hit at least 29 home runs. He hit 15 triples twice and 13 twice.

DiMaggio won two batting titles and led the league in triples, runs scored, home runs, RBIs, and slugging percentage once each. His 46 home runs in 1937 are still the record for a Yankee righthanded hitter. He was the AL's Most Valuable Player in 1939 and in 1941. For the first seven years of DiMaggio's career, his Yankees only once failed to make the World Series—and they won the world championship five times.

After his stellar 1937 season DiMaggio made what was probably the only public relations gaffe of his career. After reminding team management that his 151 runs scored, 46 homers, and .673 slugging percentage led the league, he asked for a substantial raise, from $15,000 to $45,000. When his bosses told him that all-time great Lou Gehrig was making only $41,000, DiMaggio's answer was terse and to the point: "Gehrig is underpaid."

DiMaggio held out for more money until late that April, but the fans didn't like it. He got nasty letters and was booed when he returned to play after signing for $25,000. But he earned his raise. DiMaggio won back-to-back batting championships in 1939 and 1940, and he hit more than 30 home runs and drove in more than 125 runs both years.

On May 15, 1941, DiMaggio started his streak of hitting safely in 56 consecutive games, during which he batted .408. The streak came to an end in Cleveland on July 17 in front of 67,468 fans, when Ken Keltner made two great plays and Lou Boudreau made another to keep DiMaggio off the bases. DiMaggio's streak had lasted 15 games longer than George Sisler's 1922 mark and 12 games longer than Willie Keeler's 19th-century effort.

The next day DiMaggio hit safely again, and continued for 16 more games. His record-breaking hitting streak helped him win his second MVP Award. He finished the season with a .357 average and 125 RBIs. Ted Williams' outstanding .406 average that year earned him a mere second place in MVP balloting.

DiMaggio batted "only".305 in 1942, and was out of baseball for the next three seasons because of the war. After he returned to play, a series of injuries hampered his effectiveness. He never won another batting title and only twice reached the 30-homer, 100-RBI level that he had topped in five of his first seven years.

Prior to the 1947 season DiMaggio underwent surgery on his left heel and on his right elbow to remove bone chips. Despite the surgery, he was voted the American League MVP that year. In 1948 his 39 home runs and 155 RBIs led the league, and he almost single-handedly dragged the Yankees closer to the World Series, but they finished 2½ games behind Cleveland.

In November 1948 he once again underwent surgery to remove a bone spur on his right heel. This time DiMaggio's comeback was slow and painful, and he missed the first 65 games of the 1948 season. Reports came in that fans were praying for him all across the country, and one day in June the pain suddenly and miraculously disappeared. He began an intense period of rehabilitation.

He rejoined the lineup for a series in Fenway Park. The Yanks were locked in a tight battle for first place with the Red Sox after Boston had won nine of their last 10 games. Back to his old tricks, DiMaggio belted four homers and drove in nine runs in the three-game Yankee sweep. He finished the season with a .346 batting average with 14 homers and 67 RBIs in only 76 games. The Yankees went on to take the 1949 world championship against Brooklyn, four games to one.

In 1950 DiMaggio's average fell to .301, second-lowest in his career, but he still swatted 32 homers, drove in 122 runs, and led the league in slugging average. That year he became the first player ever to homer three times in one game in Washington's mammoth Griffith Stadium.

With the new decade, DiMaggio's physical problems returned; his body was wearing out. He struggled to play 116 games and batted only .263 in 1951. He decided to retire. The Yankees offered him a full $100,000 salary if he would play in only home games during the 1952 season, but the great DiMaggio declined.

DiMaggio never left the American consciousness, even in retirement. In 1954 he married movie star Marilyn Monroe. Their marriage didn't last long, but the couple remained close friends for the rest of Monroe's life. For decades after her death, fresh flowers appeared at her grave each day, and many speculated that they came from DiMaggio.

The man who had been celebrated in song throughout his career was once again honored in songwriter Paul Simon's ballad "Mrs. Robinson" in the late '60s. And in the 1970s and '80s Joe DiMaggio showed up on television screens across the country as a spokesman for a coffeemaker in TV ads.

DiMaggio worked as a coach and front office executive for Charlie Finley's Oakland A's in 1968 and 1969. In 1969 he was honored during baseball's centennial celebration as the greatest living ballplayer.

Any attempt to summarize Joe DiMaggio's baseball career must take into account the three years of prime playing time that he lost to World War II. Also worth consideration is that he played half of his major league games in a park especially detrimental to righthanded power, with fences in left and center field more than 400 feet from the plate. Of DiMaggio's 361 lifetime homers, 213 were hit on the road.

Gifted with an incredible batting eye, DiMaggio struck out only 369 times in his career. His rookie year was his worst for whiffs, with 39. In his sensational 1941 season he hit 30 homers and struck out only 13 times. Baseball historian Bill James said, "As great as DiMaggio was, he likely would have been greater at most other times and in many other places."

But historical perspective aside, the grace and personal elegance of Joe DiMaggio is the stuff of legend. Some say his calm and quiet style was a result of his shyness; some claim he was cold and aloof. It doesn't matter. On the ballfield Joe DiMaggio was Fred Astaire: all class, all the way.

Vince DiMaggio

DiMaggio, Vincent Paul **OF**

1937–46 B:9/6/1912, Martinez, CA D:10/3/1986, North Hollywood, CA Deb:4/19/1937, BOS NL BR/TR 5'11", 183

G	AB	R	H	HR	RBI	OBP	SLG	AVG
1110	3849	491	959	125	584	.324	.413	.249

It was never difficult to tell the DiMaggio brothers apart. Joe was the best hitter, Dom the best fielder, and Vince the best singer. The eldest, Vince started his big league career as a strikeout threat at the plate, but enjoyed two All-Star years with the Pittsburgh Pirates. Clashes with management and inconsistent hitting shortened a career that took him back to the minor leagues before he was done.

While playing for his hometown San Francisco Seals of the Pacific Coast League, Vince recommended his younger brother Joe to the team's owner.

"I could play the outfield better than him," Vince later recalled, "but when it came to batting, forget it.... I just didn't have his eye."

With Boston in his second year as a major leaguer, Vince DiMaggio broke Dolph Camilli's record for strikeouts in a season by 31. His 134 whiffs made this the second of six years that Vince led his league in fanning. Boston sent him down and the Cincinnati Reds picked him up for only 14 at bats in 1939.

He suddenly found his power stroke after being traded to Pittsburgh in early 1940. He hit 19 homers that year and 21 the next, driving in 100 runs in that 1941 season. He was an All-Star in 1943 and 1944.

It was an off-the-field incident that prompted the Pirates to trade him. Late in the 1944 season, DiMaggio and some teammates enjoyed a late dinner after a game in Philadelphia. The hotel's restaurant-nightclub featured a floor show. Despite the 20-percent entertainment surcharge, DiMaggio signed his entire bill over to the team. The ballclub refused to pay, he made a fuss, and they sent him to Philadelphia in 1945.

Luckily for the Phillies, DiMaggio hit four grand slams that year and his defense remained more than adequate. Yet splashes of power hitting could not keep him in the major leagues. He returned to the Seals in 1946 and served as a minor league player-manager from 1947 through 1951.

Bill Dinneen

Dinneen, William Henry **P**

1898–1909 U(1909–37) B:4/5/1876, Syracuse, NY
D:1/13/1955, Syracuse, NY Deb:4/22/1898, WAS NL
BR/TR 6'1", 190

W	L	PCT	G	SH	IP	BB	SO	ERA
170	177	.490	391	24	3074^{2}	829	1127	3.01

Bill Dinneen was the only person to both pitch a major league no-hitter and umpire one. In fact, he umpired six no-hitters in the big leagues, second only to Silk O'Loughlin's seven.

As a pitcher in the days of four- and five-man pitching staffs, Dinneen had his first good year as a member of the Boston Nationals in 1900. He won 20 and lost 14. He jumped to Boston's American League Pilgrims in 1902, where he became the second starter behind Cy Young and joined the exclusive 20–20 club, with 21 victories and 21 defeats.

In 1903 the Boston Pilgrims won the pennant handily by 14½ games over Connie Mack's Philadelphia Athletics. Dinneen was 21–13 and had two saves, the most in the league. But his greatest moments of pitching glory came in that year's World Series, the first held in the 20th century. Dinneen pitched four complete games, winning three and striking out 28 batters—a Series record until Bob Gibson fanned 31 in 1964. Dinneen's four-hit shutout in Game 8 gave the Pilgrims the first modern world championship.

The following year he started 37 times, pitched 37 complete games totaling 335⅔ innings, and went 23–14. On October 10, he was the winning pitcher when New York Highlander Jack Chesbro, a 41-game winner, made his infamous wild pitch that cost New York its last shot at the pennant.

Because of arm problems and the arrival of moundsman Jesse Tannehill, Dinneen pitched less often and less effectively in 1905, although he pitched a no-hitter on September 27. He continued to slump; 1909 was his final season as a pitcher.

Less than two weeks after he was released as a player, the league hired Dinneen as an umpire. Even though he had no formal umpire training and was a known umpire-baiter as a player, he did an excellent job as an American League arbiter for 29 years. During his tenure the AL offered a cash prize to the umpire whose games were the shortest. Dinneen won, hands down.

Illness forced Dinneen to retire from umpiring at age 61. AL president Will Harridge said, "If there ever was a finer umpire, especially on balls and strikes, than Dinneen, I don't know who he was."

Bill Doak

Doak, William Leopold **P**

1912–24,1927–29 B:1/28/1891, Pittsburgh, PA
D:11/26/1954, Bradenton, FL Deb:9/1/1912, CIN NL
BR/TR 6'½", 165

W	L	PCT	G	SH	IP	BB	SO	ERA
169	157	.518	453	34	2782^{2}	851	1014	2.98

"Spittin' Bill" Doak may have been responsible for causing more batters to be retired than any other pitcher in the history of baseball. He did so not with his pitching, fine though it was, but by inventing a baseball glove so superior to any used earlier that he earned royalties from it for nearly 35 years.

Before Doak came along, fielders' mitts were nothing but small leather pillows. They helped protect the hand but did not help the fielder make a catch, particularly before they were broken in. Players often spent several seasons pounding out a satisfactory pocket; some even cut the palm out of the glove to form a pocket.

Around 1920 Doak sketched a glove with a pocket already formed. He inserted a lace of leather strips between the thumb and first finger, which were previously connected with a single slab of leather. He took his sketches to the Rawlings Sporting Goods Company, and within a few years the Doak Glove was the most popular mitt on the market. It still protected the hand but for the first time helped the player snag the ball. Fielding improved dramatically in the 1920s, and, with continued improvement in glove design based on Doak's breakthrough, new records continue to be set today.

A slim, 6-foot righthander, Doak relied on two pitches: a good, stiff-wristed, overhand spitball and what he called his "slow drop." Other pitches were just decoration, but he had good control of everything he threw. A good fielder but not much of a hitter, in 905 at bats he struck out 332 times.

In the first two decades of the 20th century, the St. Louis Cardinals were confirmed losers, seldom venturing into the first division; Doak managed to win 20 games twice with the Cards. In 1914, his second year with the club, he went 20–6 and led the National League in earned run average, with 1.72. His effort helped the last-place Cards of 1913 climb to third place. St. Louis regressed after that, though, and Doak's record reflected the team's weak support.

From 1915 through 1921 Doak's ERA was between 2.59 and 3.11. Yet he had losing seasons four times during that span, including a 20-loss campaign in 1917. Two of his 16 wins that year came on September 18, when he pitched and won both ends of a doubleheader over Brooklyn, 2–0 and 12–4.

In 1920 various trick pitches were made illegal. Doak was one of 17 major league pitchers for whom the spitball was considered a basic part of their repertoire, and he was allowed to continue throwing it. He responded with his second 20-win season. He followed with a 15–6 record in 1921, when he led the league in winning percentage and ERA.

Joe Dobson

Dobson, Joseph Gordon **P**

1939–54 B:1/20/1917, Durant, OK D:6/23/94, Jacksonville, FL Deb:4/26/39, CLE AL BR/TR 6'2", 197

W	L	PCT	G	SH	IP	BB	SO	ERA
137	103	.571	414	22	2170	851	992	3.62

Those who faced him will tell you that Joe Dobson had a great curveball. According to one Boston writer, it "started out somewhere around the dugout and wound up clipping the outside corner of the plate. There are curveballs, and there are curveballs."

Dobson spent most of his career with the Red Sox, a mainstay of their starting rotation from 1940 to 1950. His best season was 1947, when he won 18 games. His magic moment, however, came a year earlier when he appeared in three games for Boston in the 1946 World Series against the Cardinals. With the Series tied at two games apiece, Dobson delivered a complete-game victory, allowing just four hits and no earned runs. He also made two scoreless relief appearances in the Series, but the Cards still beat the Red Sox in seven games.

Nicknamed "Burrhead," Dobson credited teammate Ted Williams for helping him become a successful pitcher. "My first year in Boston was 1941," said Dobson. "I would pitch to Williams in practice, maybe for 45 minutes. I learned a lot from that man."

Pat Dobson

Dobson, Patrick Edward **P**

1967–77 B:2/12/1942, Depew, NY Deb:5/31/1967, DET AL BR/TR 6'3", 190

W	L	PCT	G	SV	IP	BB	SO	ERA
122	129	.486	414	19	2120^{1}	665	1301	3.54

Righthander Pat Dobson's finest season came in 1971 when he was one of four 20-game winners on Earl Weaver's Baltimore Orioles staff. The only other team in modern history to produce four 20-game winners was the 1920 White Sox.

Weaver helped Dobson by simplifying the pitcher's repertoire. Ray Miller, an Orioles minor leaguer at the time and a future pitching coach, recalled, "Dobson joined us with four or five pitches which [he] threw from two or three different windups. Earl would ask why [he] needed all those pitches and windups. Didn't [he] have a couple of pitches that worked well? He wants pitchers to simplify things."

Originally signed by Detroit for a $35,000 bonus, Dobson had a losing record in his first five seasons in the majors. In 1971, his first season with the Orioles, Dobson went 20–8 with a 2.90 ERA. Dave McNally, Jim Palmer, and Mike Cuellar also won at least 20 games for the Birds. At one point during the season Dobson won 12 consecutive games. He appeared in three games of the 1971 World Series against Pittsburgh, but did not receive a decision.

Dobson was an All-Star in 1972, and although he reduced his ERA to 2.65, he lost a league-leading 18 games. In 1972 he was traded to Atlanta. He went on to win 19 games for the Yankees in 1974 and 16 games for the Indians in 1976.

Larry Doby

Doby, Lawrence Eugene **OF**

1947–59 Negro League Player (1942–43, 1946–47) M(1978, 37–50) B:12/13/1924, Camden, SC Deb:7/5/1947, CLE AL BL/TR 6'1", 182

G	AB	R	H	HR	RBI	OBP	SLG	AVG
1533	5348	960	1515	253	970	.387	.490	.283

Larry Doby broke the color barrier in the American League on July 5, 1947—the same season Jackie Robinson became the first modern African-American player in the National League. On the road, Doby was often denied entrance to hotels and restaurants frequented to by his teammates; on the field, opposing players were sometimes downright hostile.

"Once, as I slid into second base, the guy playing shortstop spit on me. But I walked away from it," Doby related. "I knew the racial remarks were from people who were prejudiced or who wanted to disturb me. I wasn't going to let them upset my play, so I didn't think too much about them."

Doby was an excellent all-around athlete. As a standout running back he led his East Side High team to the South Carolina state football championship. The team was then invited to play a bowl game in Florida, but only on the condition that Doby not participate. The team voted not to go.

From 1942 through part of the 1947 season Doby played second base for the Negro League Newark Eagles until Cleveland Indians owner Bill Veeck bought his contract for $15,000 and made him a major league outfielder. A seven-time AL All-Star, Doby averaged 27 homers and 77 RBIs in nearly a decade in Cleveland. He led the league twice in homers and once in RBIs. After leaving Cleveland Doby played a year in Japan for the Chunichi Dragons.

Doby went into business in New Jersey for 10 years before returning to baseball as a coach for the Montreal Expos and later for the Indians. Many thought he would be named Major League Baseball's first African-American manager, but that distinction went to Frank Robinson instead. Doby became the second African-American to hold that position when he replaced Bob Lemon as manager of the White Sox in the middle of the 1978 season. Don Kessinger took over the helm the following season.

Doby later became director of community affairs for the New Jersey Nets. He was elected to the Hall of Fame in 1998.

Bobby Doerr

Doerr, Robert Pershing **2B**

1937–44, 1946–51 B:4/7/1918, Los Angeles, CA
Deb:4/20/1937, BOS AL BR/TR 5'11", 175

G	AB	R	H	HR	RBI	OBP	SLG	AVG
1865	7093	1094	2042	223	1247	.362	.461	.288

Bobby Doerr played every one of his 1,865 games at second base, and he was named to the All-Star team nine times. Baseball historian Bill James accurately summed up his career, calling him "an excellent offensive and defensive player from the day he reached the majors until the day that he left."

Red Sox scout Eddie Collins signed both Doerr and Ted Williams out of San Diego on the same trip west. Coincidentally, Williams and Doerr were both born in the same year, 1918, the last time the Red Sox had won a World Series.

Installed as the regular Sox second baseman in 1938, Doerr hit well but without much power. He soon learned to pull the ball and take advantage of Fenway Park's left-field wall, the Green Monster. He was the American League Most Valuable Player in 1944, when he led the league in slugging average, with .528, and was second in batting average, at .325. Doerr knocked in more than 100 runs six times in his career and ranks among the top second basemen in lifetime batting average, on-base percentage, slugging average, runs produced, fewest strikeouts, and home runs per season.

Doerr was also an exceptional fielder, especially adept at double plays. In 1950 he set a record by participating in eight double plays in a doubleheader. He led league second basemen in fielding average four times and tied for the lead on two other occasions. One of his many errorless strings deserves special notice. During the sizzling pennant race of 1948, Doerr handled 414 chances between June 24 and September 19 without an error.

Doerr was definitely a Fenway Park hitter. Lifetime, he batted .315 with 145 homers in the oddly shaped park, but only .261 with 78 home runs on the road. In his only postseason appearance, the 1946 World Series, he hit .409, drove in three runs, and handled 49 chances without an error as the Sox fell to the Cardinals in seven games.

He retired because of back trouble after the 1951 season but later coached for the Sox and Toronto. Doerr, who wore No. 1 for the Red Sox, was only the third player in team history to have his number retired. He was elected to the Hall of Fame in 1986.

Red Donahue

Donahue, Francis Rostell **P**

1893,1895–1906 B:1/23/1873, Waterbury, CT
D:8/25/1913, Philadelphia, PA Deb:5/06/1893, NY NL
BR/TR 6', 187

W	L	PCT	G	SH	IP	BB	SO	ERA
165	175	.485	367	25	2966^1	689	787	3.61

Few pitchers accumulated a record as poor as Francis "Red" Donahue did in his first couple of major league seasons. Fewer still turned their career around and became a star.

After only a brief trial with the New York Giants in 1893, at age 20, Donahue returned to the National League for a couple of games with St. Louis in 1895. In 1896, the righthander became an unimpressive regular starter. His record was 7–24, fitting numbers for his team, which finished 11th in a 12-team league. However, Donahue's 5.80 ERA indicates that most of the losses came on merit. The situation worsened in 1897. St. Louis dropped to last place with a horrendous 29–102 record. Donahue led the league with 46 appearances and 38 complete games but went 10–35, and his ERA climbed to 6.13.

Donahue did not have a great fastball. He relied on curves, changes of speed, and control. Unfortunately, his control was not so good, and his curves didn't fool enough batters. In 1897 Donahue allowed 106 walks and 484 hits in 348 innings.

In 1898 the Philadelphia Phillies acquired him. With a new team, some strong bats to support him, and improved control, he turned his career around. On July 8, 1898, he no-hit Boston, the league's championship team. After 1898 his ERA never went above 3.60 in a full season again. He won 21 games in both 1899 and 1901. Although he continued to surrender more hits than innings pitched, he brought the difference within manageable proportions.

In 1902 Donahue joined the second wave of National League players to jump to the American League. He returned to St. Louis with the new AL Browns and collected the third 20-win season of his career. Sold to Cleveland in 1903, he helped the Indians make a run for the pennant in 1904 with a 19–14 season. He completed his 13-season major league career with Detroit in 1906.

During his years with the dreadful Cardinals, Donahue had a 17–60 record. Following his trade to the Phillies in 1898, and in three subsequent stops, he compiled a 148–115 mark.

John Donaldson

Donaldson, John **P**

Negro League Player (1913–34) B:2/20/1892, Glasgow, MO D:4/141970, Chicago, IL BL/TL 6', 185

John Donaldson was considered one of the finest and most feared pitchers in the Negro Leagues. During a 20-year career that began in 1912 he was with a number of teams, including the much-heralded All-Nations squad that boasted black players as well as whites, Latinos, Japanese, Hawaiians, and Native Americans. During a 12-game span in 1916, Donaldson—a lefthander who relied on a sharp-breaking curveball—reportedly struck out 240 batters. In one 18-inning game, Donaldson struck out 35. In a subsequent 12-inning game, he struck out 27.

Thanks to Donaldson's heroics, the All-Nations team defeated that year's black world champions, the Indianapolis ABC's, three games to one. In that same season, All-Nations defeated Chicago's American Giants, two games to one, with Donaldson earning both victories. All-Nations was forced to disband during World War I, but after the war's conclusion, Donaldson rejoined the team, which was then called the Kansas City Monarchs. Playing center field as well as pitching, Donaldson helped comprise the mighty starting rotation that included Bullet Joe Rogan, Jose Mendez, and Rube Currie.

After leaving the Monarchs in 1923, Donaldson formed his own team, the John Donaldson All-Stars, and toured the Midwest, playing local and semipro teams. He eventually went on to scout for the Chicago White Sox.

Mike Donlin

Donlin, Michael Joseph **OF-1B**

1899–1906, 1908, 1911–12, 1914 B:5/30/1878, Peoria, IL D:9/24/1933, Hollywood, CA Deb:7/19/1899, STL NL BL/TL 5'9", 170

G	AB	R	H	HR	RBI	OBP	SLG	AVG
1049	3854	669	1282	51	543	.386	.468	.333

Had Mike Donlin been less of an actor, he might be remembered as one of the great hitters in baseball history. Not that his time on the stage was his only limiting factor. Donlin also managed to absent himself from baseball for significant periods because of injury, a holdout, and a jail sentence. In a career that stretched more than 16 seasons, he played in only 12.

The future actor made it to Hollywood well before the movies even arrived in California. His first job in professional baseball was as a pitcher with Los Angeles of the California League. His lack of control dictated a move to the outfield. In 1899 he began the season with the California League's Santa Cruz Sandcrabs but by July, when he was hitting .402, St. Louis of the National League snapped him up. He hit .323 for the remainder of the season.

In 1900 John McGraw moved over from Baltimore and became the St. Louis third baseman. He and Donlin, both pugnacious Irishmen, became fast friends. Donlin once said of McGraw, "He's a wonder. He can start more fights, and win fewer, than anybody I ever saw." When McGraw jumped to the new American League to manage the Baltimore Orioles in 1901, Donlin went with him, and batted .347 for the Orioles. Donlin finished second in the AL batting race to Nap Lajoie, who hit .422; the .075 differential remains the widest margin in baseball history. On June 24, 1901, Donlin went 6-for-6 with two singles, two doubles, two triples, and five runs; the four extra-base hits and five runs in one game remained AL records for 45 years.

In March of the following year, Donlin was arrested for assaulting an actress on a Baltimore street. Sentenced to six months in jail and fined

$250, he signed a contract to play for Cincinnati while still incarcerated. In the meantime, McGraw jumped back to the National League to manage the New York Giants. In August Donlin was released from jail after his friends and teammates paid his fine. He worked out for a few days with the Baltimore team, then joined the Reds and hit .294 in 34 games. He lifted his average to .351 in 1903, playing more than 100 games for only the second time in his major league career.

In July 1904 McGraw brought Donlin to New York in exchange for Moose McCormick, and Donlin helped his old friend win his first of 10 pennants. But the Giants refused to meet Boston, the AL champion, in a postseason World Series.

The 1905 season was Donlin's best, as he hit .356 with 80 RBIs and a league-leading 124 runs scored. New York won its second consecutive pennant and faced the Philadelphia Athletics in the World Series. All five games were shutouts, four of which were hurled by New York, three by Christy Mathewson alone. Donlin tied for the Series lead in hits with five and led in runs scored with four.

One nickname, "Turkey Mike," referred to his strutting walk. A handsome man, he had a strong profile and winning smile, both of which he risked in numerous fights. Donlin dated a number of actresses and in 1906 married Mabel Hite, who at the time had more name recognition than he did. "Oh, you Mabel's Mike!" screamed fans after a good play.

At the top of his game, Donlin suffered a broken ankle, which kept him out of all but 37 contests in 1906. The next year he and McGraw clashed over Donlin's demand for a $6,000 contract. McGraw did not budge, and Donlin became one of the first players to hold out for a full season. He returned in 1908 and hit .334 with 198 hits and 106 RBIs, second in the league in all three categories. He also put together a 24-game hitting streak, a career best.

Later that fall when Donlin and his wife appeared in a New York vaudeville production with an act called "Stealing Home," Donlin received glowing reviews. One critic wrote that his dancing "brought down the house," and *Variety* gushed, "If you haven't already attended *The Big 42nd Street Ovation*, by all means beg off from the office and do so without delay. Mike Donlin as a polite comedian is quite the most delightful vaudeville surprise you ever enjoyed, and if you miss him you do yourself an injustice."

Buoyed by such praise—and that he and Mabel were earning $1,500 a week in New York, $2,000 in other cities—Donlin made his decision to leave baseball. The Giants fans mourned, and he turned down a contract for the 1909 season. He and Mabel took their act on the road for two years, making much more money than Donlin would have earned in baseball.

When Donlin's wife died, he returned to the game midway through the 1911 season. In August McGraw sold him to Boston; Donlin hit .316 in 68 games. Boston traded him to Pittsburgh in 1912, where he played only part-time and again hit .316. In December the Pirates waived him to the Philadelphia Phillies, but he refused to report and returned to vaudeville.

Donlin managed to squeeze in 36 games with the International League's last-place Jersey City Skeeters in 1913, but baseball was now no more than a hobby. McGraw used him as a pinch hitter for a time in 1914, after which Donlin retired from the game for good. He finished with a .333 career batting average and unanswered questions about what might have been.

The year he left baseball he married Rita Ross, another actress, and turned his thoughts toward Hollywood and the movies. He never became a star but he appeared in numerous supporting roles. When he died in 1933, the *New York Times* gave him his final review, summing up his theatrical career with the comment, "He was never the actor he thought he was."

Pete Donohue

Donohue, Peter Joseph **P**

1921–32 B:11/5/1900, Athens, TX D:2/23/1988, Fort Worth, TX Deb:7/1/1921, CIN NL BR/TR 6'2", 185

W	L	PCT	G	SH	IP	BB	SO	ERA
134	118	.532	344	16	2112^1	422	571	3.87

Finesse was Pete Donohue's game. Donohue, who had five terrific seasons for the Reds in the 1920s before he blew out his arm, had one of the great changeups of his day. His other weapon was his pinpoint control—he walked only one batter every five innings in his career. It was a lot easier to hit him—he allowed more hits than innings pitched every year of his career except the first—than it was to beat him.

Donohue pitched for Texas Christian University before joining the Reds in 1921 and going 7–6 in 21 games. Moved into the Reds' rotation in 1922, he went 18–9 to lead National League pitchers in winning percentage. He had the first of his three 20-win seasons in 1923 when he went 21–15, then followed that with a 16-win season in 1924.

Donohue was 21–14 in 1925, and led the league with 27 complete games and 301 innings (walking only 49). His ERA was a career-low 3.08. He won 20 games again in 1926, leading the league in wins, shutouts, and innings pitched. That gave him a 103–67 career record. He was not even 26 and the future seemed bright.

Unfortunately Donohue's arm was gone from the overwork of those last two seasons. He was 6–16 in 1927, and he labored through the next five seasons—with the Reds, Giants, Indians, and Red Sox—before leaving the majors for good. His record after 1926 was 31–51.

Bill Donovan

Donovan, William Edward **P**

1898–1912, 1915–16, 1918 M(1915–17, 1921, 245–301) B:10/13/1876, Lawrence, MA D:12/9/1923, Forsyth, NY Deb:4/19/1942, WAS AL BR/TR 5'11", 190

W	L	PCT	G	SH	IP	BB	SO	ERA
185	139	.571	378	35	2964[2]	1059	1552	2.69

In 1923, while on his way to attend baseball's annual winter meeting, "Wild Bill" Donovan died in a train wreck in Forsyth, New York. George Weiss, later the architect of the Yankee dynasty, was in a nearby berth but escaped with injuries. At the time of his death, Donovan was managing the Class A Eastern League's New Haven Indians (he had won the 1922 EL pennant by 15½ games), and was headed to the meetings in Chicago to shore up the club. As a pitcher, Donovan had twice won 25 games, and from 1901 through 1908 he won at least 17 games in seven out of eight seasons. He also featured two managerial stints on his resume.

Blessed with good looks and plenty of personality, Donovan broke into the major leagues in 1898 with Washington of the National League. Nothing in Donovan's first three seasons, during which he went a combined 3–10, suggested what was to come. But in 1901 with Brooklyn he blossomed into the best pitcher in the league, posting 25 wins with a 2.77 ERA. He moved to Detroit of the American League in 1903. In 1907 Donovan posted a 25–4 mark, for a league-leading winning percentage of .862; that percentage stood as the American League record until Lefty Grove bettered it in 1931. Ed Killian's 25 wins and George Mullin's 20 gave the Tigers three 20-game winners in 1907, and Detroit won the pennant by four games.

In the World Series against the Chicago Cubs, Donovan was winless despite allowing only four earned runs in 21 innings. Chicago won the Series in five games.

In 1908 Donovan won 18 games and Detroit captured its second straight pennant. In a rematch against the Cubs, Donovan again made two starts, and again he failed to win a game. He held the Cubs to one hit in the first seven innings of Game 2, but Joe Tinker's homer sparked a six-run, eighth-inning rally. With the Tigers trailing in the Series, three games to one, Game 5 took place in Detroit before a crowd of 6,120, the smallest in World Series history. Donovan pitched another complete game but lost, 2–0.

Donovan finally won a World Series game in 1909, as the Tigers made their third consecutive appearance in the Series. He downed Pittsburgh's Howie Camnitz, 7–2, in Game 2, but he was shelled in the seventh and deciding game, 8–0.

Donovan followed with two winning seasons, but his arm gave way in 1912. Though he made brief appearances in subsequent years, his vocation was now manager. He worked in the minor leagues in 1913 and 1914, and then got a chance to manage in the majors. Colonel Jacob Ruppert and Colonel Tillinghast Huston bought the American League's New York franchise in January 1915, and Donovan got the managing job. He finished fifth, fourth, and sixth. Donovan's final big league managing job came when he replaced Gavvy Cravath at the Phillies helm in 1921. But he was replaced himself before the end of the season.

Dick Donovan

Donovan, Richard Edward **P**

1950–52,1954–65 B:12/7/1927, Boston MA D:1/6/1997, Weymouth, MA Deb: 4/24/1950, BOS NL BL/TR 6'3", 205

W	L	PCT	G	SH	IP	BB	SO	ERA
122	99	.552	345	25	2017[1]	495	880	3.67

It took Dick Donovan four years in the big leagues before he won his first game. By then, the 6-foot-3-inch righthander was 28 years old and full of impatience and self-doubt. Between 1950 and 1954, pitching for the Red Sox and Tigers, Donovan had gone winless in four decisions.

Donovan's slider finally matured while he was with the White Sox, and he posted a 15–9 record in 1955. He was named to the All-Star team, which he later achieved twice more. Donovan posted double figures in wins for four straight years from 1955 through 1958, and led the American League in winning percentage with his 16–6 record in 1957. He won 15 games the next year for the White Sox before ending up with the expansion Washington Senators in 1961.

That year Donovan led the league with a 2.40 ERA, despite a 10–10 record. Nevertheless, the Senators traded Donovan to the Indians the following season, where he became a 20-game winner. That was also Donovan's most successful season as a hitter. Of his 16 hits, four were home runs, which he swatted in a pair of two-homer games. Donovan went deep twice on May 30, 1962, and repeated his accomplishment on August 31.

Patsy Donovan

Donovan, Patrick Joseph **OF**

1890–1904,1906–07 M(1897, 1899, 1901–04, 1906–08, 1910–11, 684–879) B:3/16/1865, County Cork, Ireland D:12/25/1953, Lawrence, MA Deb:4/19/1890, BOS NL BL/TL 5'11½", 175

G	AB	R	H	HR	RBI	OBP	SLG	AVG
1821	7496	1318	2253	16	736	.347	.355	.301

Patsy Donovan, a well-traveled baseball man who spent 17 years patrolling major league outfields, managed in the big leagues for 11 years, eight of them as player-manager. He also put in extensive time in the minor leagues, where he won a couple of pennants.

Despite this impressive resume, however, Donovan's biggest contribution to baseball may have come off the field, when well after his playing days he had a role in bringing Babe Ruth to the majors. Donovan was acquainted with one of the Xaverian brothers who coached Ruth at a Baltimore orphanage. In 1914 this connection led to Boston's acquiring the man who would become the towering figure in the history of the game.

Donovan broke into the majors in 1890 with Boston of the National League. No doubt the presence of the Players' League that season, creating a need for more players, helped get Donovan to the big leagues, but once he arrived, he stayed. Donovan batted .300 as a regular 10 times in an 11-season span from 1893 to 1903. He was a fine baserunner, accumulating 518 stolen bases and 1,318 runs scored. His record as a manager was 684–879, and he never finished higher than fourth

Red Dooin

Dooin, Charles Sebastian **C**

1902–16 M(1910–14, 392–370) B:6/12/1879, Cincinnati, OH D:5/14/1952, Rochester, NY Deb:4/18/1902, PHI NL BR/TR 5'9½", 165

G	AB	R	H	HR	RBI	OBP	SLG	AVG
1290	4004	333	961	10	344	.272	.298	.240

An excellent defensive catcher—but not much of a hitter—Red Dooin spent the first 13 years of his 15-year career with the Phillies, including five years as their player-manager. Claiming a spot in the history of the game's equipment, Dooin is credited with trying to invent a shin guard. Before Roger Bresnahan came up with the first shin guards in 1907, Dooin experimented with some of his own—made out of papier-mache.

Dooin hit .231 in 94 games as a rookie. He became the Phillies' semiregular catcher in 1904 when he batted .242 in 108 games and, inexplicably, hit six of his 10 career home runs, tying for third in the league. When the Phillies finished second by a game to the Giants in 1908, gamblers tried to bribe Dooin to dump a series against the Giants. The plan was foiled when Dooin reported the offer.

After catching 140 games in 1909, Dooin took over as player-manager in 1910 and promptly broke his ankle. He broke his leg in 1911 (when he hit .328 in 74 games) and was never a regular again. He managed through 1914 and his best team was the 1913 edition that went 88–63 and finished second, 13 games behind the Giants. He spent 1915 and 1916 as a backup with the Reds and Giants.

Mickey Doolan

Doolan, Michael Joseph **SS**

1905–16,1918 B:5/7/1880, Ashland, PA D:11/1/1951, Orlando, FL Deb:4/14/1905, PHI NL BR/TR 5'10½", 170

G	AB	R	H	HR	RBI	OBP	SLG	AVG
1728	5977	513	1376	15	554	.279	.306	.230

Mickey Doolan could not hit very well, but for a number of years in the beginning of the 20th century, he was one of the best-fielding shortstops around. Born Michael Joseph Doolittle, he arrived with the Phillies in 1906 after two years in Jersey City of the Eastern League. He spent the first nine years of his 13-year career with Philadelphia. His best years at the plate were 1910, when he hit a career-high .263 with 57 RBIs, and 1912, when he hit .258 with a career-high 62 RBIs. He usually ranked high in defensive categories such as putouts, assists, and double plays.

In 1914 Doolan jumped to the Federal League under strange circumstances. He had gone on a postseason barnstorming tour—called the "World Tour"—with Charles Comiskey and John McGraw, and when the ship sailed into New York harbor, representatives of the new league were waiting on the dock. Doolan and the Cardinals' Steve Evans were the only two players to sign up on the spot.

Doolan played for the Baltimore Terrapins in 1914 and was traded to the Chicago Whales late in the 1915 season. When the Federal League folded, he moved to the Cubs, but by then he was 36 and nearly washed up. He later coached for the Cubs and Reds.

Bill Doran

Doran, William Donald **2B**

1982–93 B:5/28/1958, Cincinnati, OH Deb:9/06/1982, HOU NL BB/TR 5'11", 175

G	AB	R	H	HR	RBI	OBP	SLG	AVG
1453	5131	727	1366	84	497	.356	.373	.266

Bill Doran was a rock-solid contributor both at second base and with the bat on Houston's 1986 division-winning team and a key late-season addition to Cincinnati's 1990 championship squad. Doran earned his shot in the majors after an impressive year in Triple A in 1982. The following season he was Houston's full-time second baseman, rapping out 145 hits in 154 games for a .271 average.

Doran's talent, grit, and determination helped boost the Astros out of their perennial also-ran position. In 1985 he earned team most valuable player honors by finishing with a .287 batting average, 14 home runs, and 31 doubles. The following year the Astros enjoyed their most successful season since the team came into the National League—96 wins and the NL West crown. Doran hit safely in four of six Championship Series games, with one home run, but the Mets came away with the pennant following a 16-inning victory in Game 6.

In 1987 Doran ranked as one of the game's best second basemen. He played in a league-high 162 games and led NL second basemen with a .992 fielding average, committing only six errors all season. He set personal highs for hits (177), home runs (16), and RBIs (79).

Beginning in 1988, however, injuries took their toll on Doran. He again led league second basemen in fielding but was sidelined because of problems with his left shoulder, left hamstring, and back. He fought off the pain for much of the season and ended July with a .273 batting average, but swooned the final two months of the season to finish at .248. Doran underwent surgery to repair damage to the rotator cuff in his left shoulder at season's end.

Continued physical problems ruined his 1988 season; Doran finished the year with a .219 batting average. "I wanted to crawl in a hole," Doran told the *Houston Post* the following season. "People in all walks of life go through their own kinds of adversities, but I don't think anybody in America did their job as badly as I did mine last year."

Doran put together a good first half for Houston in 1990, then broke his left big toe and missed half of July. On August 30 he was traded to Cincinnati in exchange for Terry McGriff, Butch Henry, and Keith Kaiser. When Doran left Houston, he ranked in the top 10 in franchise history in games, at bats, runs, hits, doubles, triples, home runs, RBIs, steals, walks, and total bases.

Doran hit .373 in 17 games as a Red, and he was named Player of the Week for September 10–16. His average reached the .300 mark for the first time in his career. However, on the day Cincinnati clinched the NL West, Doran wound up in the hospital with back spasms from an infected disc. The injury required surgery and Doran was flat on his back as he watched the Reds win the World Series.

Doran served as a utility player with the Reds for the next two seasons. He signed with the Milwaukee Brewers for 1993 but spent almost the entire year on the disabled list and retired following the season.

Richard Dotson

Dotson, Richard Elliott **P**

1979–90 B:1/10/1959, Cincinnati, OH Deb: 9/4/1979, CHI AL BR/TR 6', 204

W	L	PCT	G	SH	IP	BB	SO	ERA
111	113	.496	305	11	1857^{1}	740	973	4.23

Richard Dotson was one of a trio of promising starters for the Chicago White Sox in the early 1980s. LaMarr Hoyt, Britt Burns, and Dotson quickly went from rookies in 1980 to heroes in 1983. That year the trio combined for 56 wins as the White Sox qualified for the postseason for the first time since 1959.

Dotson first opened eyes with a shutout during a brief call-up in September 1979. He joined the Sox rotation full-time the following spring, but after three seasons his career record was just 34–33. That changed dramatically in 1983.

In 1983 he went 22–7 and would have led the American League in victories if not for 24 wins by teammate Hoyt. Dotson's 137 strikeouts and 3.23 ERA were also career bests.

He made the All-Star team the following season, but the Sox, the defending AL West Champions, faded to fifth place. He suffered a 14–15 record despite a 3.59 ERA; worse, his heavy workload seemed to be catching up with him. After throwing a combined 495 innings in 1983–84, Dotson was limited to just nine starts in 1985 by a circulatory problem in his upper chest near the right shoulder. He had only one more winning season in his career.

Dotson became a Yankee in 1982, but rejoined the White Sox in the middle of the following season. He ended his career in Kansas City in 1990.

Abner Doubleday

Doubleday, Abner
"Baseball Pioneer" B:6/26/1819, Ballston Spa, NY
D:1/26/1893, Mendham, NJ

Only small children believe in Santa Claus, the Easter Bunny, or the Tooth Fairy. Yet millions of adult American baseball fans still believe that on a fine spring day in 1839 Abner Doubleday spontaneously invented baseball at Cooperstown, New York. He didn't. It is even unlikely that he ever played the game, although it's possible he may have watched an inning or two. Yet the myth persists, despite the earnest efforts of baseball historians who have labored for more than half a century to set the record straight.

Some facts about Doubleday are not disputed. After graduating from West Point he fought heroically in the Mexican War. In 1861 he was at Fort Sumter, South Carolina, and commanded the first Union gun to answer the Confederate shelling that began the Civil War. Later he fought at Gettysburg and eventually rose to the rank of major general. General Doubleday is a legitimate American hero. Nevertheless, he did not do the one thing for which he is most famous today.

When Doubleday allegedly invented baseball on the green at Cooperstown, he was in fact at West Point. Had he been in Cooperstown he would have been AWOL, an offense serious enough to have put his graduation and military career in doubt. At no time did Doubleday himself ever maintain, suggest, hint, or intimate that he conceived, invented, transformed, adapted, or improvised a game called baseball.

After his death in 1893, not even his closest friends recollected that the general ever uttered a word about baseball. Recalling his own youth, Doubleday had written, "I was fond of poetry and art and much interested in mathematical studies. In my outdoor sports, I was addicted to topographical work and even as a boy amused myself by making maps of the country around my father's residence." The real question is not whether Doubleday invented baseball, but how his name ever got tied to the game in the first place.

Henry Chadwick, the greatest baseball writer of the 19th century, knew the truth about the game's origins and wrote on the subject long before Doubleday was known as anything other than a military man. Born in England in 1824, Chadwick moved to the United States with his parents 13 years later. He vividly recalled seeing English boys playing a bat-and-ball game called rounders, which he correctly recognized as the ancestor of baseball. Chadwick thought it was obvious that in America rounders had evolved naturally into baseball. He explained this to his readers on more than one occasion.

But Chadwick's explanation was not very popular. By the 1880s, when people began to wonder how this popular pastime had begun, Americans had become aware of their own place in history. The West had nearly been won, industry was booming, and American nationalism was on the rise. This American chauvinism was decidedly Anglophobic, so Chadwick's suggestion that the American sport was in any way beholden to the English bordered on heresy.

In 1888 John Montgomery Ward, a shortstop, lawyer, and president of the Brotherhood of Professional Base Ball Players, wrote a fine pamphlet, *Base Ball, How to Become a Player with the Origin, History, and Explanation of the Game*. He dismissed Chadwick's notion and stated his belief that baseball stemmed from a game called "one old cat," which had been played by boys in the American colonies.

A number of Ward's "facts" were wrong, and he neatly sidestepped the likelihood that one old cat probably had originated in England as well, another apparent offshoot of rounders. In reality, one old cat resembled baseball far less than did the English game that Chadwick had identified. Although Ward's thesis was seriously flawed, most readers didn't care. Ward had given baseball an American genealogy, and that was what people wanted to believe.

Albert Spalding organized a banquet at Delmonico's in New York in 1889 to welcome home a group of ballplayers from a world tour. The question of the game's origins was put forth to the gathering, which included Theodore Roosevelt and Mark Twain. The master of ceremonies was former National League president Abraham G. Mills. As the champagne flowed, Mills offered his strong, if not totally coherent, belief that baseball's sources were strictly American. The crowd chanted, "No rounders! No rounders!" The argument continued for years. Chadwick championed rounders, while Spalding insisted on an American origin. Ironically, Chadwick was the editor of *Spalding's Official Baseball Guide*, a yearly compendium of the game. In the 1903 edition he traced the journey of rounders from England via "town ball," which was sometimes called the "Massachusetts game"

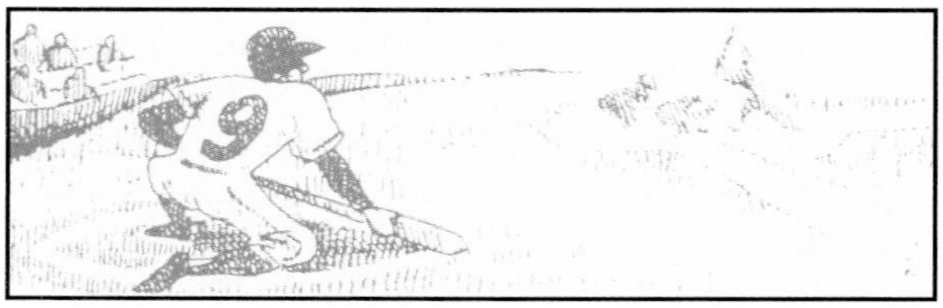

and was once played in New England. The game evolved, he explained, into the "New York game," a variant that became baseball during the 1840s and 1850s after the Knickerbocker Base Ball Club of New York City instituted a number of rule changes developed by Alexander Cartwright and others. Chadwick was essentially correct, but that didn't pacify Spalding.

In the 1905 *Guide*, Spalding himself wrote an article ridiculing the rounders theory and calling for a blue-ribbon commission to investigate the origin of the game. He then loaded the commission with his supporters, and Abraham Mills was named chairman. During the next few years the Mills Commission reported that it was "deluged" with letters and manuscripts on the subject. It finally threw its support behind a single letter—which just happened to have Spalding's approval.

Abner Graves, a mining engineer in Denver, had written the letter. Graves had been born and raised in Cooperstown, New York. He claimed to have been present on the day in 1839 when Abner Doubleday "outlined with a stick in the dirt the present diamond-shaped Base Ball field, indicating the location of the players in the field, and (I) afterward saw him make a diagram of the field on paper, with a crude pencil memorandum of the rules for his new game, which he named 'Base Ball.'"

With that short paragraph, all the evidence supporting rounders, town ball, and the Knickerbockers went out the window. In its final report in 1907, the Mills Commission stated that Abner Doubleday invented baseball at Cooperstown. This conclusion was such a popular, simple, and "American" answer that nearly everyone accepted it as gospel.

Twenty-seven years later, so-called proof was discovered in a musty trunk in an attic near Cooperstown. The trunk, allegedly once belonging to Graves, contained an old, misshapen baseball that was immediately dubbed "the Doubleday baseball." When the Baseball Hall of Fame was established, its location at Cooperstown was a foregone conclusion.

Someone would undoubtedly have conducted a serious investigation of the Doubleday myth eventually, but the publicity surrounding the opening of the Hall of Fame sparked renewed interest in the story. First Alexander Cartwright's descendants presented his diary and papers to demonstrate the importance of the Knickerbockers in baseball's development. Then in 1940, Robert W. Henderson's *Baseball: Notes and Materials on Its Origin* showed that the rules for rounders and baseball were at first identical.

Other researchers chipped in and soon the Doubleday legend was totally discredited. In the words of historian Harold Peterson, "Abner Doubleday didn't invent baseball. Baseball invented Abner Doubleday."

Patsy Dougherty

Dougherty, Patrick Henry **OF**

1902–11 B:10/27/1876, Andover, NY D:4/30/1940, Bolivar, NY Deb: 4/19/1902, BOS AL BL/TR 6'2", 190

G	AB	R	H	HR	RBI	OBP	SLG	AVG
1233	4558	678	1294	17	413	.346	.360	.284

Boston Pilgrims left fielder Patsy Dougherty became the first player to hit two homers in one World Series as he connected in the very first Fall Classic, in 1903. He hit both in Game 2 to help give Bill Dinneen a 3–0 victory. The first was a leadoff, inside-the-park blast to deep right center off starter Sam Leever; after being hit by a pitch his next time up, Dougherty knocked the second over the left-field fence off Bucky Veil. They were the only two World Series homers Dougherty would hit in 14 postseason contests, but few others had much luck hitting home runs in the World Series, either. After Dougherty's two blasts, no one homered in the World Series until 1908, when Joe Tinker of the Cubs hit one against Detroit in Game 2—a span of 23 Series games.

Dougherty was the first batter ever at New York's Hilltop Park, stepping in against the Highlanders on April 30, 1903. He became a Highlander the following June. Despite leading the American League in runs in 1903 and 1904, he was unable to get along with manager Clark Griffith. After a June 1906 fistfight with Griffith, New York placed Dougherty on waivers. He was claimed by Fielder Jones' "Hitless Wonders" White Sox, and ended the season with his second world championship.

Four times in his career Dougherty ruined no-hitters—his last victim being Detroit's Ed Sommers on July 29, 1910. The fleet-footed lefthanded batter led the AL in stolen bases in 1907, and swiped 261 bags in his 10-year career.

Phil Douglas

Douglas, Phillip Brooks **P**

1912,1914–15,1917–22 B:6/17/1890, Cedartown, GA D:8/1/1952, Sequatchie Valley, TN Deb:8/30/1912, CHI AL BR/TR 6'3", 190

W	L	PCT	G	SH	IP	BB	SO	ERA
94	93	.503	299	20	1708¹	411	683	2.80

Phil Douglas was a bear of a righthander with a wicked spitball and an unquenchable thirst for the hard stuff. His bizarre off-field behavior eventually earned him permanent banishment from the game.

The 6-foot-3-inch, 190-pound Georgia native was called "Shufflin' Phil" because of his slow walk. But the nickname could have come just as easily from his habit of shufflin' off to parts unknown on weeklong benders that he called "vacations." His many midseason vacations got him bounced off one team after another.

Douglas first arrived in the majors in 1912 with the White Sox. By the time he was traded to the New York Giants in 1919, he'd worn out his welcome with the Reds, Dodgers, and Cubs. When sober, Douglas was a fine pitcher, but managers never knew whether he'd show up at all, let alone without a hangover.

His first full season in the majors was 1914, when he went 11–18 with a 2.56 ERA for Cincinnati. Sold to Brooklyn in June 1915, he was sent on to the Cubs just three months later. After missing the entire 1916 season, Douglas lost 20 games in 1917, appearing as both a starter and a reliever.

Chicago won the pennant in 1918 and Douglas appeared in Game 4 of the World Series against Boston. With the score tied, 2–2, in the eighth inning, Douglas' wild throw allowed the winning run to score. Boston won the Series in six games.

On July 25, 1919, the Cubs traded Douglas to the Giants for outfielder Dave Robertson. Douglas was 10–6 in midseason when he was acquired by New York. Manager John McGraw prided himself on his ability to reclaim such lost souls through a combination of threats, intimidation, fines, humiliation, detectives, and drugs. He did reform a few drunks but often failed. When one of his projects slipped, McGraw tended to turn surly and take revenge.

At first his methods seemed to work for Douglas. At age 30 in 1920, Douglas was one of 16 pitchers still allowed to throw the spitball legally. He went 14–10 for the Giants, the best season of his career to that point. The next year his 15 wins helped the Giants win the pennant. He pitched the opening game of the World Series against the New York Yankees, losing to Carl Mays, 3–0. He bounced back to strike out Babe Ruth four times and win two more starts, 4–2 and 2–1. The Giants won the best-of-nine Series, five games to three.

In 1922 Douglas was 11–4 record with a 2.63 ERA when McGraw bawled him out after a loss to Pittsburgh at the Polo Grounds. Douglas decided it was time for a vacation. After several days, McGraw sent detectives to look for the pitcher; they found him passed out in an apartment near his home. They hauled the half-naked player to the police station, where he passed out again. Douglas entered a sanitarium and was sedated and held against his will for five days. When finally released, he immediately got drunk again.

His life then spun out of control. The Giants billed Douglas $224.30 for his stay in the sanitarium. Then, when he finally arrived at the ballpark on the day of a rainout, McGraw bawled him out again, fined him $100, and docked him five days' salary. His head reeling, Douglas left McGraw's office and wrote the letter that ended his career. He addressed it to Les Mann, an outfielder with the St. Louis Cardinals, who were then involved in the pennant race with the Giants.

Though the wording was somewhat ambiguous, in essence Douglas offered to take a vacation for the rest of the season if the Cardinals chipped in and gave him an inducement. This was only three years after the Black Sox scandal shook the baseball establishment.

Douglas later claimed he had second thoughts about the letter from the moment he sent it, and said he called Mann the next day to ask him to destroy it. Mann said he never got such a call. He knew that George "Buck" Weaver of the White Sox had recently been suspended for life, not for taking part in the World Series fix, but for knowing about it and not reporting it.

Mann waited a day and then showed the letter to Cardinals manager Branch Rickey. Rickey sent Mann to Commissioner Kenesaw Mountain Landis, who in turn went immediately to Pittsburgh, where the Giants were to play the Pirates. He met with McGraw, then called Douglas in and suspended him for life. McGraw called Douglas "without exception...the dirtiest ballplayer I have ever seen."

The *New York Times* called the incident "the biggest scandal in the history of baseball." Douglas returned to Georgia and later worked as a laborer for the Tennessee Highway Department. In 1936 he applied to the commissioner for reinstatement and was turned down. He died in 1952. In 1990 some of his friends petitioned Commissioner Fay Vincent to overturn Landis' decision. Vincent refused.

Taylor Douthit

Douthit, Taylor Lee **OF**

1923–33 B:4/22/1901, Little Rock, AR D:5/28/1986, Fremont, CA Deb:9/14/1923, STL NL BR/TR
5'11½", 175

G	AB	R	H	HR	RBI	OBP	SLG	AVG
1074	4127	665	1201	29	396	.364	.384	.291

In 1931 Branch Rickey, ever the accountant, was determined to trade Taylor Douthit, his center fielder. Douthit was making $14,000, pretty good money in 1931, and Rickey had Pepper Martin waiting in the wings. Martin was making only $4,000.

There was a reason Douthit was making good money. Douthit, a fine outfielder and hitter, had hit .303 the previous season with a career-high 93 RBIs (31 more than his previous career best). All the same, Rickey made his deal to send Douthit to the Reds on a Saturday, a deal not to be made public until Monday (June 15). In response Douthit he got hits in his last two at bats, and in the Sunday doubleheader he reeled off seven more to make it nine in a row, one short of the major league record at the time. His performance made no difference. On Monday morning, a heartbroken Douthit was gone.

Douthit graduated from the University of California, majoring in agriculture and specializing in bacteriology. He first came up to the Cardinals in 1923, but after shuttling between the minors and the majors for three seasons, he thought about quitting. Rickey actually offered him more money to stay.

Douthit hit .308 in 139 games in 1926 with 23 stolen bases; he slumped to .262 the next season, but rebounded in 1928 to hit .295. He then batted a career-high .336 in 1929. He played for three St. Louis pennant winners in five years.

Defensively, he had an unusual technique for catching fly balls—he held his hands much higher than anyone else and kept his palms up. His reason? "If I juggled it I would have a second chance to grab it."

Douthit's career nose-dived after the trade. He was only 30 but a victim of arthritis. "I was depressed [over the trade]," he said about his decline, "but mainly I was hurt and began playing 'safety first' baseball. You can't win that way." He hit .280 in 1931 and was out of baseball two years later, finishing with a career .291 average.

Tommy Dowd

Dowd, Thomas Jefferson **OF–2B**

1891–99,1901 B:4/20/1869, Holyoke, MA D:7/2/1933, Holyoke, MA Deb:4/8/1891, BOS AA BR/TR 5'8", 173

G	AB	R	H	HR	RBI	OBP	SLG	AVG
1320	5511	903	1492	24	501	.319	.345	.271

"Buttermilk" Tommy Dowd was a good-fielding outfielder and poor hitter in the 1890s. His main strengths on offense were his ability to draw walks and his speed on the basepaths. In 10 major league seasons he had 366 stolen bases, with a high of 59 in 1893. However, during most of that time, runners were credited with a stolen base when they took an extra base on a hit or an out.

Dowd started his major league career with Boston's American Association team in 1891, but after four games he went to Washington and became their regular second baseman. He switched to the outfield in 1892, when Washington switched to the National League. His most productive seasons were spent with St. Louis, beginning in 1893. He hit an uncharacteristic .323 in 1895, his best season to that point.

In 1896 Dowd managed St. Louis for the last half of the season. When the team started 6–25 the next season, he was fired and dealt to Philadelphia. He returned to St. Louis in 1898. The next year the Cleveland owners acquired the St. Louis franchise, put all their best players there, and sent the leftovers to Cleveland. Dowd, one of the leftovers, was a regular with the infamous Spiders team of 1899, which won only 20 of 154 games. He completed his major league career with Boston of the new American League in 1901.

Al Downing

Downing, Alphonse Erwin **P**

1961–77 B:6/28/1941, Trenton, NJ Deb:7/19/1961, NY AL BR/TL 5'11", 177

W	L	PCT	G	SH	IP	BB	SO	ERA
123	107	.535	405	24	2268[1]	933	1639	3.22

Lefthander Al Downing is best remembered for two things: as the victim of Hank Aaron's record-breaking 715th homer while pitching for Los Angeles, and as the first African-American starting pitcher in Yankees history. In between these two moments, Downing put together a solid major league career.

Signed by the Yankees out of Rider College, Downing needed just two seasons of minor league apprenticeship. After being recalled from the minors in 1963 by the Yankees, Downing was quickly dubbed the "Black Sandy Koufax" because of his exploding fastball and dancing curve. But while he did lead the American League in strikeouts with 217 in 1964, he never could live up to that billing because of control problems and a series of arm miseries.

Downing's best year with the Yankees was 1967 when, aided by a perfected changeup, he was 14–10 with a 2.63 ERA. He also pitched two perfect innings in the 1967 All-Star Game. In 1968, however, something snapped in his left elbow and for the next three years he never matched the level of play of his first four seasons with New York. Finally, on December 5, 1969, the Yankees traded Downing and catcher Frank Fernandez to the Oakland A's for outfielder Danny Cater and utility man Ossie Chavarria.

His stay in Oakland was brief. The following June he was traded again, this time to the Milwaukee Brewers. There he finished out the 1970 season with a 2–10 record. Then in 1971, the Dodgers got him from Milwaukee in a trade for outfielder Andy Kosco. His career revived. Asked to take a $2,000 cut, to $29,000, with the Dodgers, Downing responded with 20 wins and a 2.68 ERA in 1971. Along with that, he tied for the National League lead with five shutouts. He was named Comeback Player of the Year.

While he remained with the Dodgers for six more seasons, he never came close to equaling his 1971 performance. Early in 1974 Aaron tagged Downing for the slugger's record-breaking 715th home run, eternally making Downing the answer to a trivia question.

Brian Downing

Downing, Brian Jay **DH–OF–C**

1973–92 B:10/9/1950, Los Angeles, CA
Deb:5/31/1973, CHI AL BR/TR 5'10", 194

G	AB	R	H	HR	RBI	OBP	SLG	AVG
2344	7853	1188	2099	275	1073	.373	.425	.267

Though injuries marred his career, Brian Downing played 20 major league seasons. At various times a catcher, an outfielder, and a designated hitter, the Southern California native played with the Angels for 13 seasons and became their all-time leader in home runs, runs batted in, runs scored, extra-base hits, total bases, hits, doubles, and games played.

Downing's career was foreshadowed on the first pitch of the first game he ever played in the big leagues. He made his debut starting at third base for the Chicago White Sox in 1973. On that first play, Downing dove into the stands pursuing a foul ball. He made the catch, but bruised his leg and was out of action for six weeks. During his second game off the disabled list, he got his first major league hit, an inside-the-park home run off the Detroit Tigers' Mickey Lolich. By 1975 he was Chicago's everyday catcher.

After the 1977 season, Downing was traded to the California Angels. Named to the All-Star team in 1979, he had his best offensive year to that point: a .326 batting average, 12 home runs and 75 RBIs, as the Angels won the American League West title for the first time. Like the rest of the team, Downing did not have a good Championship Series, batting only .200 as the Angels lost to Baltimore in four games.

Downing broke his ankle in 1980, leading to his permanent shift to the outfield. In 1982, he established an AL record for most consecutive errorless outfield chances (330). In 1986 Downing set a career high total for RBIs, 95, to match a .267 average and 20 home runs. Club owner Gene Autry named Downing left fielder on the franchise's 25th-anniversary team.

In the 1986 ALCS against the Boston Red Sox season, Downing hit only .222, but his seven RBIs led both teams. In Game 4 a Calvin Schiraldi pitch with the bases loaded hit Downing to tie the game in the bottom of the ninth inning. The Angels went on to win in extra innings, but the Red Sox ultimately won the series in seven games.

Downing, an extremely patient batter, often batted leadoff despite his lack of speed (he had only 50 career stolen bases). In 1987 he led the league in walks with 106 while batting .272 with 77 RBIs and a career-high 29 homers. He ended his career as a designated hitter for the Texas Rangers in 1991 and 1992, hitting .278 each season.

Brian Downing had an unusually wide, open stance at home plate, facing the pitcher while holding the bat high over his head. He was one of the first ballplayers to devote himself to bodybuilding year-round, building both a batting cage and a special workout gym at his Southern California home. His impressive physique earned him the nickname "the Incredible Hulk."

Jack Doyle

Doyle, John Joseph **1B–C–OF–2B**

1889–1905 M(1895, 1898, 40–40) U(1911)
B:10/25/1869, Killorglin, Ireland D:12/31/1958,
Holyoke, MA Deb:8/27/1889, COL AA BR/TR 5'9", 155

G	AB	R	H	HR	RBI	OBP	SLG	AVG
1564	6039	971	1806	25	967	.351	.385	.299

It is now generally agreed that baseball's first pinch hit occurred in April 1892. However, for many years it was believed that "Dirty Jack" Doyle became baseball's first pinch hitter on June 7, 1892, when Cleveland Spiders manager Patsy Tebeau installed him in a game against John Montgomery Ward's Brooklyn team.

The strategy worked—Doyle singled, sending teammate Jack O'Connor to third. Later in the season Tebeau again sent Doyle in as a pinch hitter. In that same year, Washington used Connie Mack as a pinch hitter, and the following season Chicago player-manager Cap Anson started employing himself regularly in that role. Before long the practice was commonplace.

Primarily a first baseman and catcher, Doyle is one of only 20 major leaguers to play 100 or more games at four different positions. He started in baseball as a catcher in 1888 with Lynn of the New England League and served as player-manager in 1895 with the Giants and in 1898 with the Senators. The feisty Doyle earned his nickname by using every tactic in the book—some of them highly questionable—to win ballgames. Ironically, six years after retiring as a player, he became an umpire.

Larry Doyle

Doyle, Lawrence Joseph **2B**

1907–20 B:7/31/1886, Caseyville, IL D:3/1/1974, Saranac Lake, NY Deb:7/22/1907, NY NL BL/TR 5'10", 165

G	AB	R	H	HR	RBI	OBP	SLG	AVG
1766	6509	960	1887	74	793	.357	.408	.290

"Laughing Larry" Doyle once remarked, "Gee, it's great to be young and a Giant." Considering his Giants won three straight pennants from 1911 through 1913, his enthusiasm was justified.

Nicknamed for his cheerful disposition, Doyle was hitting .290 and playing third base at Springfield of the 3-I League when he was purchased by New York for $4,500, then a record price for a minor leaguer. So nervous about joining the Giants, Doyle took the wrong ferry across the Hudson River and was late for his major league debut. Even though he delivered a single and a double, his agitation stayed with him throughout the contest, causing him to make a crucial ninth-inning error at second base that cost New York the game.

Manager John McGraw called him into his office afterwards, and Doyle thought he was headed back to Springfield. "I know you were playing a strange position. When you learn more about playing second you won't make those mistakes. The main thing is that probably you have learned, and you can hit," said McGraw. Much relieved, Doyle went on to a solid career and ultimately became the team captain.

Although he earned a reputation as a heads-up player, Doyle did commit a potentially costly blunder against the Philadelphia Athletics in Game 5 of the 1911 World Series. On third base in the bottom of the 10th inning when Fred Merkle hit a long fly to Danny Murphy in right field, Doyle scored the winning run, but umpire Bill Klem later stated that had the A's tagged Doyle, he would have been out, as he never touched home plate. The A's wrapped up the World Series the next day. The Giants lost the Series in both 1912 and 1913.

In 1915 Doyle won the National League batting crown on the last day of the season; he collected four hits in a 15–8 pasting of the Boston Braves to end up with a .320 average, five points higher than the mark of the Phillies' Fred Luderus. He also led the league in hits (189) and doubles (40). Traded to the Cubs in 1916, Doyle returned to the Giants in 1918 and retired after the 1920 season.

Doug Drabek

Drabek, Douglas Dean **P**

1986–98 B:7/25/62, Victoria, TX Deb:5/30/86, NY AL BR/TR 6'1", 185

W	L	PCT	G	SH	IP	BB	SO	ERA
155	134	.536	398	21	2535	704	1594	3.73

Doug Drabek rose to fame as the ace of the Pittsburgh Pirates from 1988 to 1992. In that five-year stretch, Drabek won 81 games to help Pittsburgh capture three division titles. Boasting a deadly sinker and a moving fastball and slider, Drabek won the 1990 National League Cy Young Award with a 22–6 record and 2.76 ERA.

Although he had a 2–5 mark in seven career starts in the Championship Series, his postseason ERA was just 2.05. He took a 2–0 lead into the bottom of the ninth inning of Game 7 of the 1992 NLCS, but an error and a blown save cost Pittsburgh the pennant. It was Drabek's final game as a Pirate.

That winter the University of Houston alum signed with the Astros as a free agent for four years and $19.5 million. Drabek lost a league-high 18 games in his first season back in Texas, but he bounced back in 1994 with a 12–6 record, and made his only All-Star appearance.

By the time his contract ran out, however, Drabek had compiled just a 38–42 record as an Astro. The final two years of his career, he pitched in the American League, for Chicago in 1996 and Baltimore in 1997.

Moe Drabowsky

Drabowsky, Myron Walter **P**

1956–72 B:7/21/1935, Ozanna, Poland Deb:8/7/1956, CHI NL BR/TR 6'2", 200

W	L	PCT	G	SV	IP	BB	SO	ERA
88	105	.456	589	55	1641	702	1162	3.71

Polish-born righthander Moe Drabowsky was a fair pitcher in his 17-year major league career, operating mostly out of the bullpen, but he was best known for his practical jokes and wild sense of humor.

Jay Johnstone, a flake in his own right, said, "The first time I met Moe Drabowsky was at one of Larry McTague's restaurants in New York. Larry said, 'Jay, I'd like you to meet Moe Drabowsky.' With that Moe dropped his cocktail glass and reached out to shake my hand. I mean, it shattered all over the floor, and he didn't blink an eye. I knew right away that this was my kind of guy."

Myron Walter Drabowsky could also pitch. Entering Game 1 of the 1966 World Series in relief for the Orioles, he one-hit the Dodgers for 6⅔ innings, striking out 11 and setting the tone for the rest of the Series. After getting two runs off starter Dave McNally, the Dodgers never scored again.

Off the mound Drabowsky was the sort of guy who would set off cherry bombs in Chief Nok-a-Homa's Atlanta teepee, change everyone's room keys at a Shriners convention, or dress up like a gorilla and toss rocks and assorted debris at opposing relievers. He once hired a skywriter to send greetings to his former Orioles teammates during the 1969 World Series and then had a 6-foot boa constrictor delivered to their clubhouse. The Miracle Mets took the Series.

"Gee, I didn't want it to work out that way even though they traded me away. They never won a game after getting my gift. I guess you could say they were 'snakebit,'" Drabowsky quipped.

Sometimes there was a method to his madness. Once, when he was still with the Orioles, Drabowsky called up the Oakland bullpen, impersonating A's manager Alvin Dark, and barked out orders to get a pitcher up and throwing. A's pitcher Jim Nash, working on an easy two-hitter, became incensed, unraveled, and lost the game. "I think my stats should include another win," said a grinning Drabowsky.

Dave Dravecky

Dravecky, David Francis **P**

1982–89 B:2/14/1956, Youngstown, OH
Deb:6/15/1982, SD NL BR/TL 6'1", 195

W	L	PCT	G	SV	IP	BB	SO	ERA
64	57	.529	226	10	1062^{2}	315	558	3.13

In one of baseball's more tragic tales, Dave Dravecky came back from surgery to remove a cancerous tumor on his pitching arm only to have the arm amputated despite his indomitable courage and deep religious faith. The most enduring image of Dravecky is of him writhing on the mound in pain after throwing the last pitch of his career.

After three years in the Pirates organization, the lefthanded Dravecky was swapped to the Padres in a minor league deal. He went 14–10 and pitched in the All-Star Game in 1983, his first full year in the majors. The following year the Padres made it to the World Series, and their biggest heroes were neither their hitters nor their starters but rather their middle relievers, such as Dravecky. In 10⅔ postseason innings he allowed only five hits and no runs.

In 1985 and 1986 Dravecky worked primarily as a starter, winning a total of 22 games in that span. He was dealt along with Kevin Mitchell and Craig Lefferts to the Giants for four players in 1987. Dravecky fired a two-hit shutout against the Cardinals in Game 2 of the Championship Series. In the second inning of Game 6, Giants outfielder Candy Maldonado lost Tony Pena's flyball in the lights. Pena wound up on third and scored the game's only run, beating Dravecky, 1–0.

Dravecky underwent arthroscopic surgery on his pitching arm in 1988, and a biopsy revealed a cancerous growth that required surgery. On October 7 doctors removed the tumor along with half of his deltoid muscle, freezing part of the humerus bone to kill any remaining cancer. After intensive rehabilitation, Dravecky pitched again in less than a year. In late July of 1989 he pitched three complete games in the minor leagues and returned to the majors on August 10.

Giants manager Roger Craig later said, "The day he pitched that comeback game is a day I'll never forget as long as I live. As many games as I've seen—and I was there when Don Larsen pitched that perfect game in the 1956 World Series—this was even more incredible." Dravecky had a one-hit shutout through the seventh inning. Tired in the eighth, he allowed a three-run homer and was taken out with a 4–3 lead. The Giants held on to win and deliver the victory to Dravecky.

In his next start, against Montreal, he allowed only three hits and no runs through five innings. Then he noticed that his left arm was tingling. His physician had cautioned him against pitching if he felt any pain in his arm because the freezing process had weakened the bone. But Dravecky ignored the warning and, with the Giants leading 3–0, took the mound in the last of the sixth.

On the first pitch to the third Montreal batter he broke his arm. "It sounded as though someone had snapped a heavy tree branch," he said later. Out for the rest of the season, he joined the celebration on the mound after the Giants defeated the Cubs in the NLCS. In the midst of all the carousing, someone fell on his left arm and broke it yet again.

Dravecky's doctors discovered that the cancer had returned. They later amputated his arm. Dravecky told the story of his trials in two books, *Comeback* and *What to Do When You Can't Come Back.*

Chuck Dressen

Dressen, Charles Walter **3B**
1925–31,1933 M(1934–37,1951–53,1955–57, 1960–61,1964–66, 1,008–973) B:9/20/1898, Decatur, IL D:8/10/1966, Detroit, MI Deb:4/17/1925, CIN NL BR/TR 5'5½", 146

G	AB	R	H	HR	RBI	OBP	SLG	AVG
646	2215	313	603	11	221	.343	.369	.272

Chuck Dressen's keen study of the game and his brash spirit made him a successful coach and manager. Baseball savvy was second nature to him. Dressen's career is best summed up in his advice to the teams he managed: "Keep 'em close, boys. I'll think of something."

For a time, Dressen played both baseball and football. While he was an infielder in the minor leagues he also played quarterback for two early National Football League franchises. Later, he put in seven years, characterized by mediocre statistics but heady play, as a Cincinnati third baseman. A career .272 hitter, he hit his only grand slam on August 27, 1926, and scored five runs in a game on July 4, 1928.

Dressen ended up back in the minors in 1931. A born gambler, he landed his first managing job on a bet. In 1932 he wanted to pilot the Southern Association's Nashville Volunteers, but the Depression-era ownership felt that his salary demand was too high. So Dressen made a wager: his team would finish above .500 or the owners would owe him nothing. The club won its final game of the season to finish at 39–38 under Dressen.

Late in the 1933 season the pennant-bound New York Giants needed help at third base and called Dressen to the big leagues. He played in only 16 games, but his unsolicited advice helped the Giants pull out a crucial World Series victory. In Game 4 the Giants were clinging to a one-run lead with the bases loaded and one out in the 11th inning. Dressen advised manager Bill Terry to play back against Senators pinch hitter Cliff Bolton. Terry followed Dressen's advice, and pitcher Carl Hubbell induced Bolton to bounce into a game-ending double play. New York won the Series the next day.

Dressen spent the next four years managing in Cincinnati, where he moved a last-place club up to sixth, then fifth. When the Reds fell back into the cellar during the 1937 season, Dressen was replaced with 25 games left to play. He joined Leo Durocher and Babe Ruth on the 1938 Dodgers coaching staff.

A clever sign stealer, Dressen coached third for Dodgers manager Durocher in 1941, and during one game was watching Bob Bowman pitch for St. Louis. Whenever Dressen saw Bowman wrap his fingers around the ball to throw a curve, the coach would let out a whistle to tip off the hitter. The Cardinals catcher suggested that Bowman grip the ball like a curve but throw a fastball instead. Bowman complied, Dressen whistled, and Joe Medwick strode into a Bowman fastball, taking it in the head. The 30-year-old Medwick was never the same again.

When Durocher left to manage the Giants in 1951, Dressen took over his job. After completing a three-game sweep of Durocher's team on August 9, the first-place Dodgers had a 12½-game lead over the Giants. Dressen taunted Durocher and the Giants through the clubhouse walls. It was a bad idea; the Giants came back to tie the Bums for the pennant and force a three-game playoff.

The Dodgers took a 4–1 lead into the last of the ninth of the third game of the playoff, but starter Don Newcombe was losing his velocity. Two singles and a double pushed over a run and put men on second and third with one out. Dressen brought in Ralph Branca to pitch to Bobby Thomson, who had beaten Branca with a home run two days earlier. Although first base was unoccupied, Dressen decided against an intentional pass to Thomson, which would have brought a rookie named Willie Mays to the plate. Thomson answered with a three-run homer—the "Shot Heard 'round the World."

Dressen had a spectacular team playing for him in Brooklyn. His lineup included Roy Campanella, Gil Hodges, Pee Wee Reese, Duke Snider, Carl Furillo, and Jackie Robinson. The Dodgers won pennants in 1952 and 1953, but the Yankees denied them the world championship both times. Dressen, confident of his position, demanded a multi-year contract. Owner Walter O'Malley refused, replacing Dressen with Walter Alston, who managed under one-year contracts for 23 years.

Dressen later managed the Senators, Braves, and Tigers, but the best he could accomplish was a second-place finish by Milwaukee in 1960. When Dressen was managing in the minors with Toronto in 1962, a young infielder named George "Sparky" Anderson studied Dressen's managerial style. In 1966 Dressen was in his fourth season of managing the Tigers when he became sick in May. He checked into a hospital and died three months later.

J.D. Drew

Drew, David J. **OF**

1998–* B:11/20/1975, Tallahassee, FL Deb:9/8/1998, STL NL BL/TR 5'11", 190

G	AB	R	H	HR	RBI	OBP	SLG	AVG
118	404	81	104	18	52	.353	.473	.257

Few young players have come to the major leagues enveloped in as much controversy as J.D. Drew. At Florida State he won the Golden Spikes Award, and drew comparisons to Barry Bonds because of his five-tool skills. Drew was the second player selected in the 1997 draft; he would have been the first if not for his well-publicized bonus demands. The Philadelphia Phillies, desperately in need of a power-hitting outfielder, picked him. His brother Tim was a first-round pick out of high school by Cleveland in the 1997 draft, the first time two brothers had been taken in the first round of the draft. Tim signed with the Indians without great fanfare.

J.D. Drew's signing situation set off a titanic clash of wills immediately after the draft. Both the Phillies and Drew claimed they were acting on principle, though it was easy to see that both were acting in their own pecuniary self-interest. The Phillies steadfastly refused to give Drew anywhere near what he wanted, offering him a record bonus of about $3 million for a player subject to the draft. Scott Boras, Drew's agent, demanded more than $10 million—the amount given to unrestricted amateur free agents Travis Lee and Matt White the previous year. The negotiating battle quickly went public.

Drew signed with the independent St. Paul Saints of the Northern League in 1997. Since he was now a professional, he claimed that he was no longer bound by the draft restrictions. Major League Baseball, of course, saw it differently. It changed the name of its annual June draft to the "First Year Player Draft," removing the key word *amateur*.

The unbelievably rancorous matter came to a head in the spring of 1998. On behalf of Drew, who had returned to play in St. Paul for a second year, the Players Association filed a grievance claiming that MLB had no right to change the amateur draft rules without the union's consent. The Players Association also asserted that Drew should be declared an unrestricted free agent. The arbitrator ruled that Drew was not a free agent and was still subject to the major league draft, but the ruling also affirmed that MLB had no right to unilaterally change the rules under which the annual June draft was conducted.

Drew was then selected by St. Louis as the fifth pick in the first round of the 1998 draft. He and Boras came to an agreement with the Cardinals that kept his bonus to approximately $3 million, but Drew was ensured a minimum of $7 million when combined with his annual salaries in the guaranteed contract. He moved quickly through the minors after signing.

He made his major league debut on national television, but no one noticed; it was the game in which Mark McGwire broke Roger Maris' single-season home run record. Drew's .417 average and five home runs in 14 September games showed everyone why he could command a record contract. His 1999 encore was, however, much less impressive. A combination of injuries and poor play resulted in his demotion to Triple A in midseason. Drew survived his toughest test of all: a packed Veterans Stadium crowd showering him with abuse in his first series in Philadelphia.

Barney Dreyfuss

Dreyfuss, Barney

Owner (1889–1932) B:2/23/1865, Freiburg, Baden, Germany D:1/5/1932, New York, NY

In many ways, Barney Dreyfuss typified the "benevolent despots" who ran baseball in the early 1900s. Although sometimes more benevolent than most owners, occasionally putting the good of the game ahead of profits, he was often dictatorial, impulsive, and hard-headed. He owned a National League franchise for 40 years, and for much of that time was one of the league's foremost builders and shapers.

Educated at the Karlsruhe Gymnasium (a school, not a sports facility), Dreyfuss worked in a German bank until 1881. He then moved to Paducah, Kentucky, reportedly to escape military conscription. He worked as a laborer with the Bernheim Brothers distillery but within six years became one of the company's officers.

In the meantime, from 1884 until 1888, he ran a semiprofessional baseball team. He then moved to Louisville with the company and, in 1889, purchased an interest in the Louisville Colonels of the American Association. The team won the AA pennant in 1890, but the league collapsed the following season. Louisville and three other AA clubs were taken into the National League.

Although the Colonels were among the NL's weakest teams in the 1890s, toward the end of the decade they acquired a few outstanding players. Dreyfuss purchased full control of the team in 1899 for a reported $50,000. At season's end, the NL scaled back to eight teams by closing down four franchises, including Louisville. Dreyfuss received only $10,000 for his franchise but received the right to sell his players on the open market and to purchase an interest in the Pittsburgh Pirates. Instead of taking a large profit by selling such players as Honus Wagner, Tommy Leach, Fred Clarke, Deacon Phillippe, and Jack Chesbro, Dreyfuss traded them to Pittsburgh and sold off his lesser players. In so doing, he built a powerhouse Pirates team that won three straight pennants from 1901 through 1903. At the same time, he bought sole interest in the Pirates in 1901.

In 1903 Dreyfuss challenged the owner of Boston's American League champions to play a "world's series." Although his Pirates lost, the Pittsburgh players actually made more money from the Series than the Boston players when Dreyfuss contributed his share of the profits to his men.

In 1909, when the Pirates won another pennant and their first World Series, he opened Forbes Field, a modern steel-and-concrete structure that remained the team's home until 1970. Always true to his principles, Dreyfuss did not allow advertising on the fences. During his 32 years as head of the Pirates, the team finished in the second division only four times. They won pennants in 1925 and 1927; the 1925 team won the World Series.

Generous to players who remained loyal to him, Dreyfuss could be stern when crossed or when players did not mirror his somewhat puritanical standards. Such longtime Pirates heroes as Babe Adams and Max Carey were unceremoniously dropped when Dreyfuss felt they helped ferment a rebellion against his old friend Fred Clarke. It was said he refused to sign Tris Speaker after he learned Speaker smoked cigarettes.

Although Dreyfuss was active in the Pittsburgh community, his principal business was his baseball team. Influential in league circles, beginning in 1902 he chaired the committee that coordinated the National League and American League schedules. He was also one of the men who successfully opposed the potentially disastrous move to "syndicate baseball" advocated by another group of owners. In 1920 Dreyfuss helped get the National Commission replaced by a single commissioner in the wake of the Black Sox scandal. On the other hand, he was unsuccessful in his opposition to the "lively ball" and to the spread of farm systems.

In 1930, he put his son Samuel in charge of the team's daily operation but resumed the role when Samuel died in February 1931. Dreyfuss died one year later.

Dan Driessen

Driessen, Daniel **1B–3B**

1973–87 B:7/29/1951, Hilton Head, SC Deb:6/9/1973, CIN NL BL/TR 5'11", 190

G	AB	R	H	HR	RBI	OBP	SLG	AVG
1732	5479	746	1464	153	763	.359	.411	.267

Dan Driessen became the National League's first designated hitter when he filled that role for Cincinnati in the 1976 World Series. A low-key member of Sparky Anderson's "Big Red Machine," Driessen broke in at third base, a position at which he struggled mightily. Then, when Tony Perez left the club, Driessen shifted over to first and proceeded to lead the league in fielding three times.

Signed by the Reds as a free agent in August 1968, Driessen was hitting .409 at Indianapolis when Cincinnati called him up in 1973. For the remainder of his rookie year he hit an impressive .301. Although he topped the .300 mark only once more in what would ultimately be a 15-year major league career, Driessen was a productive player with fair power, a good batting eye, and exceptional basestealing ability for a first baseman.

The Reds traded Driessen to the Expos in July 1984. After that Driessen moved around the league, performing for the Giants, the Astros, and finally the NL champion Cardinals in 1987.

Part of a sports-oriented family, Driessen is the uncle of former first baseman–outfielder Gerald Perry and the cousin of Reggie Kinlaw, a noseguard in the National Football League from 1979 to 1986.

Walt Dropo

Dropo, Walter **1B**

1949–61 B:1/30/1923, Moosup, CT Deb:4/19/1949, BOS AL BR/TR 6'5", 220

G	AB	R	H	HR	RBI	OBP	SLG	AVG
1288	4124	478	1113	152	704	.327	.432	.270

Walt Dropo exploded into major league baseball in 1950. Playing first base for the Boston Red Sox, he hit .322, slugged 34 homers, and tied teammate Vern Stephens for the American League lead with 144 runs batted in—one short of the all-time rookie record, set by teammate Ted Williams. Dropo was the AL starting first baseman in that year's All-Star Game, and delivered a triple in three at bats. He was voted AL Rookie of the Year over Whitey Ford. Unfortunately his career went downhill from there.

No one is quite sure whether the 6-foot 5-inch, 220-pound slugger's nickname "Moose" was due to his demeanor, his hometown of Moosup, Connecticut, or his impressive physique. His mother once said, "Walter was born big. When he was 5, I had to buy men's clothes to fit him." Before his baseball career, the Chicago Bears drafted him to play football.

Dropo's play did not keep pace with his rookie performance. He slumped to .239 the following season. His homer output plummeted to 11, and he drove in only 57 runs. He was part of a nine-player deal with the Tigers in June 1952.

A month later he was in the record books. Over three games on July 14 and 15 Dropo delivered hits in 12 consecutive at bats. Unlike Mike "Pinky" Higgins, who had set the record but walked twice during his streak, Walt never saw a free pass. He just banged out a dozen straight hits. Finally lefty Lou Sleater of the Senators got Dropo to pop up to the catcher. The next day Dropo had three hits to tie Joe Cronin and John K. Lewis for the AL record of 15 hits in four consecutive games.

The 1952 season was as close as Dropo ever got to his astonishing rookie year. He finished with 29 homers (23 after being traded to the Tigers) and 97 RBIs, batting .276. Although he played into the 1961 season, only once more would he top 15 home runs in a season. He never hit above .281 after 1953.

Don Drysdale

Drysdale, Donald Scott **P**

1956–69 B:7/23/1936, Van Nuys, CA D:7/3/1993, Montreal, Quebec, Canada Deb:4/17/1956, BRO NL BR/TR 6'6", 216

W	L	PCT	G	SH	IP	BB	SO	ERA
209	166	.557	518	49	3432	855	2486	2.95

Dodger righthander Don Drysdale combined a great arm with an ability to intimidate batters. Not only did Drysdale knock down opposing batters, but he also plunked them with regularity. He led the National League in hit batsmen each year from 1958 through 1961. He set the National League career mark at 154.

Frank Robinson, another tough cookie, said, "He was mean enough to do it, and he did it continuously. You could count on him doing it. And when he did it, he just stood there on the mound and glared at you to let you know he meant it."

Drysdale had learned from a master of aggressive pitching, Sal "the Barber" Maglie. Convinced of the value of keeping hitters off balance, Drysdale hung around the veteran Maglie in Brooklyn when he was just starting.

"What being around Maglie did for me," Drysdale explained, "was to confirm this idea in my mind and refine it. It was part of the game. I watched Maglie, I listened to Maglie, and it all sunk in. It just sort of clicked." Drysdale even developed some personal ground rules. "My own little rule was two for one. If one of my teammates got knocked down, then I knocked down two on the other team."

Drysdale had never pitched until his senior year at Van Nuys High in California, but he showed so much promise that the Dodgers signed him right out of high school in 1954. He reported to Bakersfield of the Class C California League. Drysdale spent spring training in 1955 with the Dodgers, and by 1956 he was in the majors. "For a kid like me, just pulling up a seat next to the Sniders and Robinsons and Campanella and tuning in was a thrill," he said. "Plus, I had the added benefit of having Gil Hodges as my first roommate on the road. When you roomed with Gil, it was like rooming with a saint."

Drysdale was 5–5 in 99 innings in 1956 and moved into the rotation the next season, going 17–9 in the Dodgers' last year in Brooklyn. In 1959 he led the league in strikeouts, and repeated in 1960 and 1962. But it was in 1962 that Drysdale firmly established himself as a star. That year an injury to Sandy Koufax probably cost the Dodgers the pennant. The Giants beat them in a three-game playoff, but the series gave Drysdale a clear path to the Cy Young Award. He won 25 games with a 2.83 ERA in 314 innings. In fact, he averaged 315 innings a season from 1962 through 1965.

In 1965 Drysdale also enjoyed his career year as a hitter. Normally a .186 batter with some power—29 lifetime homers—he was Los Angeles' sole .300 hitter and delivered seven homers. Only Lou Johnson and Jim Lefebvre, with 12 home runs, outperformed him in that category.

After the Dodgers won the 1965 World Series Drysdale and Koufax staged a well-publicized joint holdout. Each wanted a $500,000 three-year contract. In 1965 Koufax, with 382 strikeouts, and Drysdale, with 210, had set the all-time NL record for strikeouts by two teammates.

Dodgers vice president Buzzie Bavasi said, "You players are entitled to all you can get. That's the history of baseball. But I'm going to stick to our club's policy of one-year contracts."

Tension mounted as the days dragged on. With the Dodgers at spring training in Vero Beach, Florida, Koufax and Drysdale remained in Los Angeles and strengthened their hand by signing a contract with Paramount Studios to appear in a now-forgotten David Janssen film, *Warning Shot*. Koufax also obtained a reported $110,000 advance from Viking Press for his autobiography. In late March the impasse broke. Both pitchers signed one-year contracts, Koufax for $130,000, Drysdale for $105,000.

"Sandy and I did give in on our original request of three-year contracts," Drysdale admitted, "but we never really expected them anyway." The duo led the Dodgers to another pennant in 1966.

Drysdale's last full season was 1968. He broke Carl Hubbell's NL consecutive scoreless innings streak of 46, set back in 1933, and Walter Johnson's 1913 major league mark of 56. In a game against the Phils on June 8, Howie Bedell finally drove in a run with a sacrifice fly, snapping Drysdale's streak of 56⅔ consecutive scoreless innings. Along the way he had six straight shutouts.

Arm problems ended Drysdale's career in mid-1969. "A torn rotator cuff is cancer for a pitcher. And if a pitcher gets a badly torn one, he has to face the facts: it's all over baby," he admitted.

Drysdale was elected to the Hall of Fame in 1984, and the Dodgers retired his uniform number, 53, on July 1 of that year. He enjoyed great success as a broadcaster, working the mike for ABC for a decade. He announced for the Dodgers from 1988, when he broadcast the end of Orel Hershiser's scoreless streak, until his death in 1993. His wife, Ann Meyers Drysdale, a former All-America basketball star with UCLA, was elected to the Basketball Hall of Fame in February 1993, several months before Drysdale died while in Montreal to announce a game.

Hugh Duffy

Duffy, Hugh **OF**

1888–1901,1904–06 M(1901,1904–06,1910–11, 1921–22, 535–671) B:11/26/1866, Cranston, RI D:10/19/1954, Boston, MA Deb:6/23/1888, CHI NL BR/TR 5'7", 168

G	AB	R	H	HR	RBI	OBP	SLG	AVG
1737	7042	1552	2282	106	1302	.384	.449	.324

Diminutive Boston outfielder Hugh Duffy holds the all-time record for the best single-season batting average, .440 in 1894—a year for exceptional averages. The Phillies had a .400-hitting outfield, and the National League maintained a batting mark of .309, also the highest ever.

For his efforts Duffy received a raise of $12.50 per month, to $2,700 annually. "No one thought much of averages in those days. I didn't realize I had hit that much until the official averages were published months later," he recalled a half century later.

Originally a mill worker who supplemented his income by playing ball on Saturdays and Sundays, Duffy joined the Eastern (International) League's Hartford Dark Blues in 1886 and then split the 1887 season between Springfield of the Eastern League and Salem-Lowell of the New England League.

By 1888 he was with Cap Anson's Chicago White Stockings, although Anson was not impressed with Duffy's 5-foot 7-inch frame. "Where's the rest of you?" sneered Anson.

"This is all there is," Duffy coolly replied. Anson kept him but wouldn't speak to him for the next two months.

In 1890 Duffy jumped to the Players' League, along with many other National League stars. When it disbanded he signed with Boston's American Association franchise. After the 1891 season the AA also folded, and Duffy joined Boston's NL club, where he teamed with future Hall of Fame outfielder Tommy McCarthy to form the best defensive duo of the era. Boston fans called them the "Heavenly Twins." Frustrated batters called them less printable things.

Duffy had his career year in 1894. Not only did he bat .440, but he also went hitless in only 17 games that season, had 12 four-hit games, and got five hits in a game twice, a feat he accomplished five other times in his career. Hitting just .260 in early May, Duffy got hot and stayed that way for the rest of the season. He led the league in home runs (18) and did so again in 1897 (11).

Duffy played for Milwaukee in 1901, its first year as an American League franchise. The following year the club moved to St. Louis and became the Browns, but Duffy remained behind and served as player-manager for Milwaukee's entry in a new Western League. He returned to the National League in 1904 as the Phillies' player-manager, a position he held through 1906.

In 1910 and 1911 he managed the White Sox; he then went back to manage Milwaukee (now in the minor league American Association) before returning to the NL as a scout for the Braves in 1917. In 1920 he managed Toronto of the International League, and in 1921 and 1922 he managed in the majors for the last time when he took charge of the Red Sox. He stayed with Boston as a scout and coach until his death in 1954. He served as a tutor to the young Ted Williams, and helped him play Fenway's "Green Monster." Duffy was elected to the Hall of Fame in 1945.

Joe Dugan

Dugan, Joseph Anthony **3B-SS-2B**
1917–29, 1931 B:5/12/1897, Mahanoy City, PA
D:7/7/1982, Norwood, MA Deb:7/05/1917, PHI AL
BR/TR 5'11", 160

G	AB	R	H	HR	RBI	OBP	SLG	AVG
1447	5410	665	1516	42	571	.317	.372	.280

"Jumping" Joe Dugan's acquisition by the New York Yankees in the middle of the 1922 pennant race was so controversial it helped establish the June 15 trading deadline. Dugan was traded along with one other player for four men and $50,000. This transaction continued the dismantling of Harry Frazee's Boston Red Sox and the consolidation of the Yankee Dynasty.

Joseph Anthony Dugan acquired his nickname not from any acrobatic skills (although he was a fine fielder), but rather from his habit of taking unauthorized leave from various clubs. In 1917, while still at Holy Cross College, Dugan was signed by Connie Mack for a $500 bonus and went directly to the Philadelphia Athletics. Dugan remembered the signing: "My father looked at the money, then glanced at my seven brothers and sisters. He couldn't contain himself. He said, 'For five hundred dollars you can take the whole family.'"

In January 1922 Dugan was traded to Boston as part of a three-club deal with Washington. Then he went to New York, where he played on ,five pennant winners. Dugan played in all but one of the Yankees' World Series in that time. He batted .333 in the 1926 Series.

Of teammate Babe Ruth he commented: "Born? Hell, Babe Ruth wasn't born. He fell from a tree."

Dugan, like most ballplayers, had his share of superstitions. One involved throwing the ball back to the pitcher—unless it was to obtain an out, Dugan simply wouldn't do it. On occasion during infield practice when Dugan had the ball, his fellow infielders would turn their backs on him, hoping to force a toss back to the pitcher. Resolute, Dugan would simply walk over to the mound and hand the ball to his pitcher rather than throw it to him. He later played for the Braves and Tigers before retiring in 1931.

Dave Duncan

Duncan, David Edwin **C**
1964,1967–76 B:9/26/1945, Dallas, TX
Deb:5/06/1964, KC AL BR/TR 6'2", 200

G	AB	R	H	HR	RBI	OBP	SLG	AVG
929	2885	274	617	109	341	.280	.357	.214

An 11-year big league catcher, Dave Duncan has the worst batting average of any major leaguer with 2,500 at bats since World War I. But he must have learned something about pitching, for he became one of the most respected pitching coaches of the 1980s and 1990s, teaming with manager Tony La Russa to win six division titles in Chicago, Oakland, and St. Louis.

A tall, muscular, righthanded pull-hitter, Duncan didn't even hit his weight in the majors until 1970, when he batted a career-high .259. From then on he showed significant power, banging at least 10 home runs for six consecutive seasons.

During the early 1970s Duncan caught some of the American League's premier pitchers, including Jim "Catfish" Hunter, Vida Blue, Rollie Fingers, and Ken Holtzman. In 1971 he was named to the AL All-Star squad. Later that season the Athletics met the Baltimore Orioles in the playoffs. Duncan batted .500, going 3-for-6 in the three-game sweep by Baltimore.

In 1972 he registered career bests with 19 homers and 59 RBIs. The A's returned to postseason play, defeating Detroit in five games in the ALCS and then edging Cincinnati in seven games to win the world championship.

In 1978 he began his coaching career in the Indians' bullpen under manager Jeff Torborg. Duncan was promoted to pitching coach under manager Dave Garcia, and remained with the Tribe through the 1981 season. He later coached for the Mariners before hooking up with La Russa with the White Sox in 1983. Chicago's young pitching staff helped the club reach the postseason that year for the first time since 1959. La Russa and Duncan teamed to win four division titles, including the 1989 world championship, in a decade in Oakland. In the coaching staff's first year in the National League, the Cardinals won the Central Division title in 1996.

La Russa calls Duncan the "absolute complete pitching coach," knowledgeable about strategy as well as mechanics, conditioning, and psychology. Although Duncan is noted for teaching the split-finger fastball, his real strength is his ability to adapt his approach to each case.

"I believe in all the basic things that all successful pitchers do—pitch ahead in the count, don't walk guys, keep the ball down," Duncan said. "I try to realistically recognize what the ability of the individual is and help develop a style that [suits] his abilities."

Fred Dunlap

Dunlap, Frederick C. **2B**
1880–1891 M(1882,1884–85,1889, 145–102)
B:5/21/1859, Philadelphia, PA D:12/1/1902, Philadelphia, PA Deb:5/1/1880, CLE NL BR/TR 5'8", 165

G	AB	R	H	HR	RBI	OBP	SLG	AVG
965	3974	759	1159	41	366	.340	.406	.292

Fred "Sure Shot" Dunlap's reputation as a great second baseman—some say the best player—of the 1880s seems overblown in light of his statistics. Yet there's no denying that observers of the time regarded him as exceptional and continued to praise him long after he left baseball.

Uncaring foster parents raised Fred Dunlap, an orphan at age 10. He fled to the fields around Philadelphia, playing baseball at every opportunity, and by his mid-teens had become an excellent player, turning professional in 1876 at age 17.

In 1880 Dunlap came to the National League with Cleveland, and for the next four years he and exceptional shortstop Jack Glasscock formed the best-fielding keystone combination in baseball. Dunlap possessed excellent range. He had small but extremely sure hands—playing without a glove, he was able to make circus grabs with either hand. His arm, from which he derived his nickname, was legendary for both strength and accuracy. Dunlap led the league's second basemen twice in assists, and three times each in putouts, double plays, and fielding average. His .924 career fielding average was unusually high for those gloveless days.

In 1884 millionaire Henry Lucas formed the Union Association to compete with the established National League and American Association. Lucas made "Sure Shot" baseball's highest-paid player by paying him $3,400 to jump to the new league—and to Lucas' own St. Louis Maroons. Dunlap, as Maroons player-manager, led the league in batting (.412), home runs, hits, runs, slugging average, and on-base percentage. St. Louis finished 35½ games in front of the second-place team.

After the Union Association folded a year later, the NL fined Dunlap $500 for his dalliance with the outlaw league. When St. Louis replaced Cleveland in the National League, Dunlap returned to his former team once again, but in 1885 the club finished last. During the next season Detroit bought Dunlap's contract, and he helped the Wolverines win the NL pennant the following year.

Dunlap and Detroit center fielder Ned Hanlon did not get along. The second baseman was sold again in 1888, this time to Pittsburgh. He shocked baseball by holding out for a percentage of the purchase price. Eventually he received $6,000 in salary and bonus, a staggering amount for the time, but the holdout cost him half of the 1888 season. In 1889 he batted a mere .235 for Pittsburgh, and he was released early the following season.

His once-exceptional range in the field gone, Dunlap played one game for New York in the Players' League in 1890 and ended a comeback attempt with Washington in 1891 after suffering a broken leg. Although he left baseball a wealthy man, Dunlap was reportedly in poverty when he died a dozen years later.

Jack Dunn

Dunn, John Joseph **P-3B-SS**
1897–1904 B:10/6/1872, Meadville, PA D:10/22/1928, Towson, MD Deb:5/06/1897, BRO NL BR/TR 5'9"

W	L	PCT	G	SH	IP	BB	SO	ERA
64	59	.520	142	3	1076²	334	171	4.11

G	AB	R	H	HR	RBI	OBP	SLG	AVG
490	1622	197	397	1	164	.287	.292	.245

Jack Dunn had three baseball careers. He was a major league pitcher, a major league infielder, and a minor league manager and club owner. Although he did well at his first two careers, his final performance was what stamped him as an important figure in baseball history. In fact, he had a far greater impact on baseball in his minor league days than he ever did while playing in the majors.

No power pitcher, Dunn relied on an assortment of curves and good control. In 1899 the merger of the Brooklyn and Baltimore franchises combined his talents with those of hitting stars Willie Keeler and Joe Kelley. He responded with his best season—a 23–13 record—and Brooklyn won the NL pennant.

But his arm then went dead, and Brooklyn passed him on to the Philadelphia Phillies at midseason. A good hitter for a pitcher, Dunn had occasionally taken a turn in the field during his first five years in the majors. In 1901 he jumped to Baltimore of the new American League, and when player-manager John McGraw was injured, Dunn took over at third base and hit .249 in 96 games. *The Reach Guide* described him as a "clever infielder."

Clever he may have been, but he was a poor hitter for a position player. In 1902 he returned to the National League, joining McGraw on the New York Giants. Despite his weak bat, Dunn's hustle and intelligence kept him with the club as a utility infielder for two more seasons. In his final major league season the Giants won the 1904 pennant. In 64 games Dunn hit an uncharacteristic .309 and connected for his only big league home run. He retired with a .245 major league average.

In 1905 Dunn became player-manager for the International League's Providence Clamdiggers, leading them to a pennant. Two years later Ned Hanlon hired him to manage the league's Baltimore franchise. In 1908, Dunn's second year as the Orioles manager, the team won the pennant. Dunn still played full-time at second base. *The Spalding Guide* noted that he had a fine team and "kept the team together and got out of it the full limit of its individual and collective capabilities." The next year he purchased the Orioles from Hanlon for $70,000.

Although Dunn didn't win a pennant during his first few seasons as owner-manager, he fielded a competitive team made up of youngsters on their way up and veterans on their way down. He paid top salaries to get good players and had an eye for talent.

In February 1914 he discovered his greatest gem. At Baltimore's St. Mary's Industrial Home for Boys was an incorrigible teenager named George Herman Ruth, who, according to Dunn, had "all the earmarks of a great ballplayer. He hits like a fiend, and he seems to be at home at any position, even though he's lefthanded. He's the most promising young ballplayer I've ever seen."

Ruth was paroled to Dunn, who signed him to a contract for $100 a month. Some of the older players resented Dunn's protective attitude toward the naive youngster. "Here comes Dunnie's new babe," they ragged. The name stuck.

Ruth was such a success that Dunn soon upped his salary to $200 and then $300 a month. At the same time, the Orioles faced tremendous competition from the Federal League team that played across the street from them. The Baltimore fans weren't excited about Dunn's minor league team and chose instead to root for the Federal League Terrapins. Ernie Shore, one of Dunn's pitchers, later recalled a day early in the season when the first-place Orioles played before only 19 fans while, across the street, the Terrapins drew more than 10,000.

The Orioles were in first place in June 1914 but Dunn was forced to sell many of his players to make ends meet. Ruth, Shore, and catcher Ben Egan went to Boston in exchange for $8,900. Nine additional players were sold to other teams at bargain prices, and the Orioles finished sixth. In 1915 Dunn didn't even try to compete with the Feds. He moved his team to Richmond, Virginia, and paid a fine of $12,500 for invading the home of Richmond's Class C minor league club.

Better days were ahead. The Federal League collapsed after the 1915 season, and Dunn purchased Terrapin Park for $25,000. During the next three years he built the Orioles into the greatest minor league club in baseball history.

Dunn found it easy to assemble his team because the International League was not party to the agreement that allowed the major league teams to draft players from minor league clubs for a nominal price. Therefore, he could hold on to his best players until a major league team was willing to pay his price. Because Dunn often paid his players more than they could earn in the majors, they were happy with the arrangement.

Among his stars during the next few years were Max Bishop, Joe Boley, George Earnshaw, Jack Bentley, Lefty Grove, Dick Porter, and Tommy Thomas, all of whom eventually went on to excellent major league careers.

In 1919 the Orioles trailed Toronto in the final month of the season and then won their last 25 games to take the pennant. Early in 1920 they put together a 27-game winning streak and turned the pennant race into a romp. The 1921 team won 119 games. Dunn's Orioles captured seven consecutive International League pennants, an unprecedented dynasty. When they finally slipped to second in 1926, they still won 101 games.

Eventually, the International League agreed to allow its players to be drafted, but Dunn could still exact large sums from major league teams. Grove, for example, brought Dunn $100,600 from the Philadelphia Athletics. The last $600 was added so that the price would be more than the amount the Yankees reportedly paid Boston for Babe Ruth.

In 1923 Dunn's son, who had been expected to succeed his father as owner of the Orioles, died suddenly of pneumonia. Dunn took several years to recover. For a while he didn't even come to the bench, leaving most of the managing to the players.

Dunn turned down several offers to manage major league teams. In October 1928 he twice refused to take over the Boston Braves. Later that month while watching field trials for his prize hunting dogs, he suffered a fatal heart attack. Dunn left an estate reportedly worth $1 million.

Shawon Dunston

Dunston, Shawon Donnell **SS**

1985–* B:3/21/63, Brooklyn, NY Deb:4/9/85, CHI NL
BR/TR 6'1", 175

G	AB	R	H	HR	RBI	OBP	SLG	AVG
1556	5378	675	1457	128	591	.300	.413	.271

A free-swinging phenom out of Brooklyn, Shawon Dunston was selected by the Chicago Cubs as the first pick overall in the 1982 amateur draft. His career was marked by flashes of promise punctuated by a succession of injuries that have limited his playing time and kept him from realizing his potential.

Dunston was the Cubs' Opening Day shortstop in 1985, but he returned to the minors in May with a .194 batting average and nine errors. Recalled in August, he batted .320 in his last 40 games. Dunston spent his first full season in the majors in 1986 and led NL shortstops with 17 homers; both his home run and RBI totals were the most for a Cubs shortstop since Ernie Banks in 1961. He made his first trip to the All-Star Game in 1988, the first Cubs shortstop to make the squad since Don Kessinger in 1974.

Dunston made his second All-Star appearance in front of the home fans at Wrigley Field in 1990. That season he equaled his career high of 17 home runs and combined with teammate Ryne Sandberg to hit 57 homers, which at that time tied a major league record for a middle-infield combo. From 1992 through 1994, however, he suffered a herniated disc in his lower back and was limited to appearing in 113 games. He made an excellent comeback in 1995, putting together one of his best seasons. The next year he signed with the San Francisco Giants because the Cubs wanted to move him to third base.

Dunston returned to the Cubs in 1997 and put together another solid season before being traded to the contending Pittsburgh Pirates on August 31. He collected hits in his first 10 games with the Pirates, and finished the year at .300 with 22 doubles and 57 RBIs. He started a second career as a utility player, successively signing with the Indians, Giants, Cardinals, and Mets.

It was with the 1999 Mets that Dunston had perhaps his most heroic moment, in the 15th inning of rainy Game 5 of the Championship Series against the Braves. Notorious as a first-ball hitter throughout his career, Dunston took Kevin McGlinchy to 12 pitches (fouling off six) before singling to start what proved to be the winning rally.

Ryne Duren

Duren, Rinold George **P**

1954,1957–65 B:2/22/1929, Cazenovia, WI
Deb:9/25/1954, BAL AL BR/TR 6'1", 195

W	L	PCT	G	SV	IP	BB	SO	ERA
27	44	.380	311	57	589[1]	392	630	3.83

When reliever Ryne Duren shot his 95 mph fastball over batters' heads in the 1950s, they blamed his poor eyesight (20/70 and 20/200 uncorrected) for the wild throws. But his famous pop-bottle glasses weren't the problem—a chronic alcoholic, Duren rarely had just cola in his glass.

"I would not admire hitting against Duren because if he ever hit you in the head you might be past tense," Casey Stengel once said. Duren was certainly an intimidating reliever, and, at his peak, an effective one. In 1958 he led the American League in saves, but he soon went into a decline.

The atmosphere surrounding the Yankees club only exacerbated Duren's drinking problem. He estimated that 13 of his 25 teammates were alcoholics. "Some of the most wonderful players I performed with were downing a fifth of scotch a day."

Traded to the Angels in May 1961 along with two other players in a deal that brought outfielder Bob Cerv and pitcher Tex Clevenger to New York, Duren brought his habit with him to California. He crashed into the room of sportswriter Dan Hafner and overturned the mattress Hafner was sleeping on. One morning at 5:30 he kept busy by chipping golf balls off the window of Angels pitching coach Marv Grissom. Grissom opened the door and calmly asked, "Got kind of an early starting time, don't you, Ryne?"

On another occasion he got an unaccustomed starting assignment at Cleveland and came through with a 1–0 shutout. That called for a postgame celebration—including wading through the fountains of a local Polynesian restaurant. The restaurant's owner called Angels manager Bill Rigney and informed him, "Mr. Rigney, I've got one of your players." Rigney interjected, "Don't tell me, I know exactly which one. I'll be right down."

Duren did have his moments with the Angels. On June 9, 1961, he fanned seven consecutive batters for a then major league record.

After his Angels stint, Duren bounced from club to club. Unmercifully pounded by his old Yankees teammates in August 1965 while pitching for Washington, he had eight beers in the clubhouse and followed that with martinis back at the hotel. He then walked to a bridge and tried to jump off it, but manager Gil Hodges talked him down.

Released by the Senators, Duren continued on his path of self-destruction. He fell asleep while smoking in bed and burned his house down. He passed out at the wheel of his car. Finally his wife left him, and he attempted suicide again by parking his car on the railroad tracks in San Antonio, Texas.

Eventually he went in for treatment at the San Antonio Mental Hospital but fell off the wagon 11 months later. Another attempt at treatment failed and again he tried suicide. "I realized that as a human being I was one big mess but I felt powerless to do anything about it," he admitted.

In May 1968 Duren underwent rehabilitation again, and this time it worked. He went on to become director of Stoughton Community Hospital in his native Wisconsin and worked to control alcohol advertising through a program called SMART (Stop Marketing Alcohol on Radio and Television).

"I'm no prohibitionist," explained Duren. "I'm an educator who wants to communicate the right image for alcohol. When I was a drunk, I was just as bad as a drug addict, which I told myself I'd never be."

Leon Durham

Durham, Leon **1B-OF**

1980–89 B:7/31/1957, Cincinnati, OH Deb: 5/27/1980, STL NL BL/TL 6'2", 210

G	AB	R	H	HR	RBI	OBP	SLG	AVG
1067	3587	522	992	147	530	.358	.475	.277

Leon "Bull" Durham broke in with the St. Louis Cardinals in 1980, but the Chicago Cubs so coveted Durham's exciting mix of power and speed that the Cubs traded star reliever Bruce Sutter for Durham and Ken Reitz after Durham's rookie season. A lefthanded hitter, Durham could drill anything low in the strike zone—even sliders and sinkers. He ran the bases with smarts and aggressiveness, showing no mercy on middle infielders trying to turn double plays. In 1982 he became the first Cub in 71 years to tally 20 homers and 20 steals. He also batted .312—third best in the league—and was named a NL All-Star.

After four years in the Cubs outfield, Durham replaced Bill Buckner at first base in 1984. That year Durham produced his greatest power numbers, stroking 23 home runs and 96 RBIs as Chicago reached postseason play for the first time in 39 years. Though he belted a homer in the decisive Game 5 of the Championship Series, Durham let a routine grounder shoot through his legs in the seventh inning. That leak through the wickets opened the floodgates for the Padres, who rallied for four runs and a 6–3 victory to claim the pennant.

Durham remained a home run threat for three years, launching two-thirds of his bombs at Wrigley Field. He also donated money to charity for each long ball he hit, an uncommon practice at the time. His career nosedived in 1988, when he missed most of the year while undergoing drug rehabilitation. He was suspended for drug use again in 1989, his final season.

Leo Durocher

Durocher, Leo Ernest **SS-2B**

1925,1928–41,1943,1945 M(1939–55,1966–73, 2,008–1,709) B:7/27/1905, West Springfield, MA D:10/7/1991, Palm Springs, CA Deb10/2/1925, NY AL BR/TR 5'10", 160

G	AB	R	H	HR	RBI	OBP	SLG	AVG
1637	5350	575	1320	24	567	.299	.320	.247

Leo "Lippy" Durocher was a nasty battler who would do anything to win a game. He dressed like a dandy and mingled comfortably with the show business and high society crowd. He was an excellent shortstop but a poor hitter. Above all, he was a gambler, at the poker tables, at the racetrack, and on the field as a manager. Once he sent Dusty Rhodes up to hit for a catcher even though he had no one left to catch. His coaches screamed at Durocher, but Rhodes drove in the winning run. The manager commented, "I'd rather be in the 10th inning with no catcher than in the clubhouse with a loss."

Branch Rickey once explained that Durocher "had an infinite capacity for immediately making a bad thing worse." Durocher was at the center of some of the most exciting, controversial events in the history of the game. He's even in *Bartlett's Familiar Quotations.*

Signed by legendary Yankees scout Paul Krichell, Durocher batted once in the 1925 major league season before returning to the minors for further training. When he came back in 1928 he was ragged mercilessly by the veterans of Murderers Row. Babe Ruth called him "the All-American Out." Manager Miller Huggins, a small man himself, stuck by the kid, and from then on Durocher was Huggins' boy. Durocher kept a notebook handy and dutifully studied Huggins' managerial moves.

By 1930 the high life and fashion pleasures of New York City had become major temptations for the fun-loving Durocher, and he was rolling up debts in big league proportions. Before the 1930 season he asked for a $1,000 raise to be paid in advance so he could pay a large hotel bill. Yankees general manager Ed Barrow wouldn't agree to the raise and Durocher cursed him. The next morning Barrow traded him to the Reds. Durocher continued spending in Cincinnati. "It is possible to spend money anywhere in the world if you put your mind to it," he explained.

He loved playing for Cincinnati owner Sidney Weil and was becoming recognized as an excellent glove man as well as a leader on the field. When Branch Rickey needed a shortstop for the Cardinals in 1933, he made a deal for Durocher.

Thus began one of the most unlikely working relationships baseball has ever seen—the God-fearing, Bible-quoting, and sometimes pompous and penurious Rickey against the smart-aleck, skirt-chasing, and profligate gambler Durocher. The two battled over everything but worked together for nearly 20 years.

Rickey had his own approach to keeping his high-living shortstop solvent. At the end of every year Durocher would be in hock to the team for $2,000 or $3,000 in advances. Rickey would say, "Forget it, we'll call it a raise. But we'll leave the contract the same, and while we're at it we'll sign for the next year at the same salary." So Durocher got a "bonus" every year, but never a raise.

He soon became one of the most valued members of this highly talented and hell-raising Cardinals team. Durocher dubbed them the "Gas House Gang." They had a ball, on and off the field. If they went on a winning streak, they refused to change their mud-caked uniforms. "We looked horrible, we knew it, and we gloried in it," Durocher said.

The daring speed of outfielder Pepper Martin, the power and grit of outfielder Joe Medwick, the no-nonsense play of infielder Frankie Frisch, and the outrageous pitching ability and behavior of Dizzy Dean matched Durocher's sensibilities exactly. They got thrown out of hotels, dropped water balloons out of windows, and fought with the opposing teams and among themselves.

The Cardinals placed fifth in 1933 but finished strong after Frisch took over as player-manager. In 1934, with Dizzy Dean winning 30 games and his brother Paul winning 19, St. Louis survived a late charge from the Giants and won the pennant by two games.

Durocher had developed a stratagem to help Ol' Diz on the mound. Durocher sharpened a point on his belt buckle. When Dean needed one pitch for a big out, he'd throw to Durocher, who would grind the ball on his buckle and hand it back to the pitcher saying, "It's on the bottom, pal." Dean would then throw a wicked slider.

In the World Series the Cards faced the powerful Tigers. Dean was hit in the head by a double-play throw, Medwick was removed from the seventh game because the Tigers' fans showered him with garbage, and Pepper Martin stole bases all over the lot. The "Gang" won in seven.

After finishing second in 1935 and 1936 the Cards fell to fourth place. Frisch theorized Durocher wanted his job and demanded Rickey trade the Lip. Into Durocher's life came "the Roaring Redhead," eccentric, erratic Dodgers GM Larry MacPhail, another character Durocher would battle for years.

One MacPhail innovation was to install lights for night baseball in Ebbets Field. In the first night game there the Reds' Johnny Vander Meer threw the second of his two consecutive no-hitters. Durocher hit a loud, foul fly into the right-field seats before looping a liner to center field for the final out.

When Burleigh Grimes learned that MacPhail planned to fire him as manager before the 1939 season, he told Durocher to ask for the job. MacPhail at first made fun of the idea, but then changed his mind. Durocher's initial assignment was a preseason warm-up session in Hot Springs, Arkansas, for the pitchers and catchers.

One night Durocher and his coaches went to a country club for dinner, and after the meal the tables were cleared for a bingo party. Durocher was the big winner, taking in the grand prize of $660, which he promptly spent buying champagne for the house. The next morning MacPhail woke him with a phone call to announce that Durocher was fired. "You're a gambler!" the Redhead shouted. In fact, MacPhail "fired" Durocher a number of times—and then rehired him a few hours later. After he was rehired in 1939, Durocher's team finished a surprising third and he was named Manager of the Year.

MacPhail was free with advice to his manager, who usually ignored his boss. The one time Durocher relented, it cost him. One day he saw MacPhail talking to outfielder Pete Reiser between innings. So when Reiser handed Durocher a piece of paper that said, "Get [Hugh] Casey hot, [Whit] Wyatt's losing it," Durocher changed pitchers. Casey got belted around, and the manager took it out on Reiser. "Don't ever give me a piece of paper from MacPhail again!" That was when Durocher found out the note had come from Brooklyn superfan Hilda Chester.

In 1941 Durocher's managerial genius resulted in Brooklyn's first pennant in 21 years. He realized that something special had happened with the team. "They know I had hunches all the time, that I did things that went against the book. Enough of them worked out so that over the last two months of the season the kind of situation had developed that a manager dreams of and almost never gets—25 men who had absolute belief that any decision I made was the right one."

One decision backfired, however, and it became part of the Durocher-MacPhail legend. After the Dodgers' pennant win Durocher was told that the train home would stop at 125th Street so the players could get off and avoid the large crowd waiting for them at Grand Central Station. Durocher believed his players deserved a hero's welcome, so he told the conductor not to stop at 125th Street. What Durocher didn't know was that MacPhail, also eager to join the celebration, was waiting on the 125th Street platform to board the train. MacPhail "fired" Durocher again the next morning.

The Dodgers lost the 1941 World Series to the Yankees, and years later Durocher took some of the blame. The turning point of the Series was catcher Mickey Owen's infamous dropped third strike with two outs in the ninth inning of Game 4. The Yankees rallied for four runs to win and go ahead, three games to one. Instead of a deadlocked Series, New York won it all in the next game. In his autobiography, Durocher took responsibility for the loss because he hadn't gone out to the mound to help calm down the emotional Hugh Casey after the catcher's mistake.

During the next five years Durocher solidified his reputation as a smart manager and an umpire-baiter. Stories of his scraps with the men in blue abound. During a heated debate with oversized George Magerkurth, the large ump looked down at the smaller Durocher and said, "I'm going to reach down and bite your head off." Durocher shot back, "If you do, you'll have more brains in your stomach than you do in your head."

When Rickey decided to bring African-American Jackie Robinson to the majors in 1947, Durocher was all for the idea. In fact, a few years earlier Durocher had been quoted as saying he had seen "a million good colored players" and would have them on his team if they "weren't barred by the owners." Commissioner Kenesaw Mountain Landis denied any such agreement existed.

Early in the spring of 1947, while playing an exhibition series in Panama, Durocher got wind of the plan of several of his players—outfielder Dixie Walker leading the pack—to refuse to play if Robinson were promoted to the majors. Rickey was not traveling with the team but Durocher couldn't keep quiet about what he had heard. He got his players out of bed and held a team meeting in a large, empty kitchen.

Durocher told them, "I'm the manager of this ball club and I'm interested in one thing: Winning. I'll play an elephant if he can do the job, and to make room for him I'll send my own brother home. This fellow is a great ballplayer. He's going to win pennants for us. He's going to put money in your pockets and money in mine. I don't want to see your petition, and I don't want to hear anything more about it."

Ironically, Durocher didn't get to manage Robinson in the player's rookie year. In one of the most controversial decisions by *any* commissioner, A.B. "Happy" Chandler suspended Durocher for a year. The charges were vague and implied moral turpitude on Durocher's part for associating with gamblers and for marrying actress Laraine Day in Mexico before her California divorce was final.

At the center of the battle was a hidden agenda: the war between Rickey and former accountant Walter O'Malley for control of the team. MacPhail, now the Yankees general manager, was involved as well. Some people believed Chandler let himself be maneuvered into suspending Durocher.

The next year Durocher took center stage in an event that shocked the baseball world even more. By then Rickey had decided that it was time for a new Dodgers manager. When Giants owner Horace Stoneham asked for permission to talk to Burt Shotton, a Dodgers coach, about succeeding Mel Ott, Rickey offered Durocher instead. Overnight, Durocher, hero of an entire borough, was the new manager of the detested Giants.

New York was stunned. The Dodgers-Giants rivalry was baseball's fiercest, and Brooklyn fans could not believe that one of theirs would so quickly leap to the opposition. Giants fans were aghast. Durocher was one of their greatest villains. Now he was their manager. When Durocher joined the team, Stoneham asked him to evaluate the personnel. Durocher replied that he'd need time to fully analyze the team. After that season he filed his four-word report: "Back up the truck."

Stoneham was shocked initially, but then the two of them began putting together a team that suited Durocher's managerial style, including Eddie Stanky, a longtime Durocher favorite. "He can't hit, he can't run, he can't field, he can't throw. He can't do a goddamn thing—except beat you."

The Giants moved up to third place in 1950, and then came 1951 and the "Miracle of Coogan's Bluff." Willie Mays had joined the Giants early in the season, but he wasn't yet a superstar. By the middle of August the Dodgers were 13½ games in front.

A couple of weeks earlier Durocher made a move that would prove crucial—switching Bobby Thomson from the outfield to third base. The Giants started winning almost every day while the Dodgers settled into a win-one, lose-one pattern. All the while Durocher kept up the heat. To this day, Giants outfielder Monte Irvin claims Durocher deserved personal credit for six or seven wins down the stretch. "I never will forget it," Irvin said years later. "We won 16 in a row and we beat everybody in the seventh, eighth, and ninth innings."

When the regular season was over these bitter rivals were tied for first place. A three-game playoff followed, and Hollywood couldn't have written it better. The Giants won the first game, and the Dodgers won the second game. In Game 3 Sal Maglie and Don Newcombe, a couple of 20-game winners, were the starters in what was arguably the most dramatic contest in baseball history.

According to Irvin, "Durocher told us if you could stay close to Don you could beat him in the eighth or ninth. But he was blinding us for eight innings." And when the Dodgers scored three runs off Maglie in the top of the eighth to take a 4–1 lead, it looked like Durocher had run out of magic. Then Newcombe weakened in the ninth, Ralph Branca relieved him, and the rest is history. Thomson hit the "Shot Heard 'round the World," a three-run, game-winning homer, and the Giants were the NL champs.

They lost the 1951 World Series to the Yankees in six games, along with any chance to repeat in 1952 when Mays was drafted into the Army early in the season. They were 4½ games ahead when he left, and they finished second to the Dodgers—by 4½ games. The following year was disastrous. The Giants finished 35 games out.

When Mays returned in 1954, so did the magic. The Giants won the pennant by five games as the slugger burst into stardom with 41 home runs, 110 RBIs, and a league-leading .345 batting average. But that was only the beginning. In the World Series, New York faced Cleveland—a team that had won 111 games and dethroned the mighty Yankees. It didn't matter.

The Giants became world champs with a shocking four-game sweep. Mays made his fabulous catch off Vic Wertz about 425 feet from home plate to save Game 1. Dusty Rhodes contributed two home runs and seven RBIs in six times at bat, including the game-winning pinch homer in the opener.

Durocher didn't stay on top long. The Giants were a distant third to the Dodgers in 1955, and Stoneham fired his manager. Durocher became a broadcaster for NBC and stayed for five years. He made cameos on television programs, including hitting fungoes to Fred Gwynne in *The Munsters*. But he couldn't resist the chance to wear a uniform again and became a Dodgers coach under Walter Alston, a job that lasted until 1965.

In typical Durocher style, he bristled under Alston's rule, and frequently let people know how he would have done things differently. So when the Cubs offered him the job as manager in 1966 he leaped at the opportunity. At his inaugural press conference he announced that the Cubs were not an eighth-place team. He proved prophetic—they finished 10th in his first year at the helm. But some young talent was on the way, and the Cubs finished third the next two seasons.

It was all a prelude to 1969, when the National League found itself in another magical pennant race. Only this time Durocher wasn't the one waving the wand. On August 7 the Cubs were in first place by 9½ games when the "Miracle Mets" caught fire and passed them a month later. In a memorable series at Shea Stadium, a black cat that lived under the stands paraded in front of the Cubs dugout. The Mets swept the Cubs.

After a major clubhouse blowup between Durocher and Cubs third baseman Ron Santo in 1970, the team considered a vote to demand that Durocher be fired. But owner Phil Wrigley took out a full-page newspaper ad to announce that Durocher was there to stay. Controversy continued to follow Durocher. In the 1971 off-season Commissioner Bowie Kuhn presided over hearings that addressed Durocher's alleged gambling, but charges didn't stick.

One hundred games into the 1972 season Durocher retired. He was 67. A few weeks later he resurfaced and replaced Harry Walker as Houston's manager. The Lip was tiring of the game, of the new breed of players, and of what he saw as interference by such people as Marvin Miller, head of the Major League Baseball Players Association. While Miller met on the field with the Houston players one day during spring training, Durocher told his coaches to hit fungoes in their direction.

Houston had an 82–80 record in 1973, Durocher's last year as a manager. He retired again, this time for good. In 24 years of managing, Durocher had a 2,008–1,709 record for a .540 winning percentage. After retiring, he wrote his autobiography, *Nice Guys Finish Last*. The book's title is a fitting one for the Durocher story.

One day while Durocher was still managing the Dodgers, he was holding court with sportswriters before a game at the Polo Grounds. The topic was Eddie Stanky, and Durocher was explaining how "the Brat" overcame his physical limitations with a ferocious will to win.

Just then the Giants came out for batting practice led by player-manager Mel Ott. "Nicer guy never drew a breath," Durocher proclaimed. He began calling off the names of other Giants. "All nice guys," he said. "They'll finish last. Nice guys. Finish last." Durocher was elected to the Hall of Fame posthumously in 1994.

Frank Dwyer

Dwyer, John Francis **P**
1888–99 M(1902, 52–83) U(1899, 1901, 1904)
B:3/25/1868, Lee, MA D:2/4/1943, Pittsfield, MA
Deb:9/20/1888, CHI NL BR/TR 5'8", 145

W	L	PCT	G	SH	IP	BB	SO	ERA
177	151	.540	366	12	2819	764	565	3.84

Although Frank Dwyer is remembered chiefly as a pitcher, there weren't too many jobs in baseball he didn't try. He played every position except catcher, and also served as an umpire, manager, coach, and scout.

Dwyer pitched Hobart College to the New York State college championship in 1886–87, and earned a professional contract in the Northwestern League. He made his big league debut with Cap Anson's Chicago Colts in 1888. Dwyer toiled for six different teams in three leagues during his first five years in the majors. He finally found his niche in

Cincinnati. With the Redlegs, he won 16 or more games each season between 1892 and 1898.

After losing all five of his starts in 1899, Dwyer embarked on a new career, as an umpire. He umpired in both the American League and National League between 1899 and 1904, with a one-year stint as the Detroit Tigers' manager in between. He later coached and scouted for the New York Giants.

Dwyer spent several years as New York State Boxing Commissioner, but his biggest success outside baseball was as a businessman. He entered the coal industry in Geneva, New York, and established a business that stayed in the family for more than 60 years.

Jim Dwyer

Dwyer, James Edward **OF–DH**

1973–1990 B:1/3/1950, Evergreen Park, IL
Deb:6/10/1973, STL NL BL/TL 5'10", 175

G	AB	R	H	HR	RBI	OBP	SLG	AVG
1328	2761	409	719	77	349	.357	.398	.260

Although he never had over 260 at bats in a season, Jim "Pig Pen" Dwyer enjoyed 18 years in the majors as a classic platoon player, pinch hitter, and reserve outfielder. His most successful seasons were with Baltimore from 1981 to 1988 as he set the Orioles club record with nine career pinch homers.

Inserted into the starting lineup for Game 1 of the 1983 World Series, Dwyer homered in his first at bat, off Philadelphia's John Denny in the first inning. Dwyer made his only Series a memorable one by hitting .375.

Selected by the Cardinals in the 11th round of the June 1971 amateur draft, Dwyer earned a reputation as an accomplished hitter in the minors, leading the American Association in 1973 with a .387 batting average. He finished the year with the Cardinals, beginning a journey that took him to seven major league clubs, including two stops each in St. Louis, Montreal, and Minnesota.

Eddie Dyer

Dyer, Edwin Hawley **P**

1922–27 M(1946–50, 446–325) B:10/11/1900, Morgan City, LA D:4/20/64, Houston, TX Deb: 7/8/22, STL NL BL/TL 5'11½", 168

W	L	PCT	G	SV	IP	BB	SO	ERA
15	15	.500	69	3	256	96	63	4.75

The St. Louis Cardinals surprised baseball fans when they selected Eddie Dyer as their manager for the 1946 season. Both the fans—and the Cards—were even more surprised when Dyer brought home the world championship.

Dyer's association with baseball began in college at Rice Institute, where he threw a no-hitter at rival Baylor University and earned 10 varsity sports letters. Despite a devastating knee injury in football, Dyer tried his hand at professional baseball. As a pitcher, he was totally unspectacular. The lefthander won 15 and lost 15 before a sore arm ended a six-year career with St. Louis in 1927. But, Dyer's skills as a manager proved excellent.

Dyer won nine pennants in various cities in 15 years managing in the Cardinals farm system. He became known as a keen handler of young players, and earned *The Sporting News'* Minor League Manager of the Year Award with Columbus in 1942. After a two-year stint as the Cardinals' farm director, Dyer quit baseball to enter the oil and insurance businesses in Houston.

When the popular and successful Billy Southworth defected from the Cards to join the Boston Braves, Dyer was the surprise choice to succeed him for the 1946 season. Dyer became the second manager in history to win a world championship as a rookie. The Cards followed with three straight second-place finishes. When St. Louis stumbled home a disappointing fifth in 1950, Dyer resigned to concentrate on his business ventures.

Jimmy Dykes

Dykes, James Joseph **3B–2B–SS–1B**

1918–1939 M(1934–46, 1951–54, 1958–61, 1,406–1,541) B:11/10/1896, Philadelphia, PA D:6/15/1976, Philadelphia, PA Deb:5/06/1918, PHI AL BR/TR 5'9", 185

G	AB	R	H	HR	RBI	OBP	SLG	AVG
2282	8046	1108	2256	108	1071	.365	.399	.280

Fun-loving Jimmy Dykes remained in baseball for over four decades, first as a favorite of Philadelphia Athletics manager Connie Mack and later as a manager in his own right.

He set a (since broken) record for seasons managed without a pennant. In fact, Dykes had trouble leading the league in anything. "I almost led the league in strikeouts," he once said, "I had 98 and Babe Ruth had 99. I'd always said, 'Someday I'll lead this league in something.' But

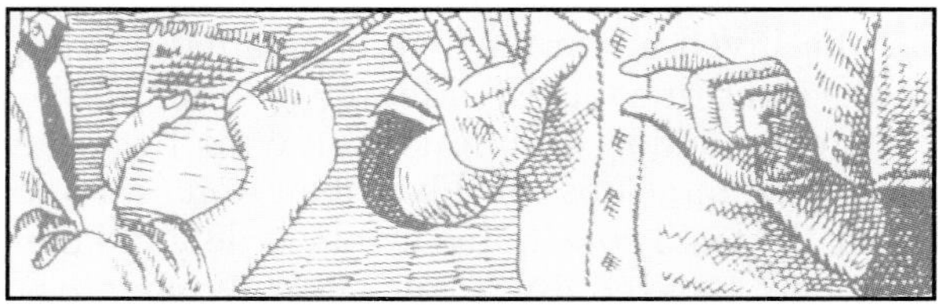

all I could do was be the runner-up in the strikeout department."

Dykes could be self-deprecating, but he could also be tough. When he came up to the majors he was playing second, and Ty Cobb decided to test the rookie. The first time Cobb got on he stole second, nearly cutting Dykes with his spikes, and in choice Cobbian language let the newcomer know what he thought of him. The next time Cobb got on he headed for second again. Dykes ignored the throw, but pushed down on Cobb's knee with his spikes. "I'll give you one more chance," warned Dykes. "But the next time you flash your spikes at me, you're a cripple!"

Dykes was one of the first players to go when Mack broke up the A's. In 1932 Mack sold him along with outfielders Al Simmons and Mule Haas to the White Sox for $100,000. In the first-ever All-Star Game Dykes collected two hits and scored two runs.

He took over as White Sox manager in 1934 and lasted until 1946. Still a favorite of Mack, he returned to the A's as a coach in 1949. In 1951 he replaced the legendary manager when Mack retired after a half-century on the bench. Dykes also managed the Orioles, Reds, Tigers, and Indians. In the first trade of managers, in August 1960 Dykes was traded from the Tigers to the Indians for manager Joe Gordon. Dykes managed more than 2,900 games without ever finishing higher than third.

Lenny Dykstra

Dykstra, Leonard Kyle **OF**

1985–96 B:2/10/1963, Santa Ana, CA Deb:5/3/1985, NY NL BL/TL 5'10", 167

G	AB	R	H	HR	RBI	OBP	SLG	AVG
1278	4559	802	1298	81	404	.376	.419	.285

Lenny Dykstra made his mark in baseball as a gutsy ballplayer—a kind of throwback to another time—with a hot bat and a perpetually dirty uniform. He was a timely hitter, a daring baserunner, and above all, a winner. Injuries brought a difficult end to an exciting career.

Dykstra tore through the New York Mets farm system on his way to the big leagues. He stole 105 bases at Lynchburg as the Carolina League's Most Valuable Player in 1983, and by 1985 the Mets could no longer keep him in the minors. He arrived in the majors with a bang, homering in his second at bat. The rookie platooned in center field with veteran Mookie Wilson. On days Dykstra led off, the Mets were 21 games over .500.

The outfielder nicknamed "Nails" excelled at key times. He was a career .323 hitter in the Championship Series, and batted .320 in two World Series. In the 1986 NLCS he was New York's leading hitter—and its most clutch performer. His two-run home run in the bottom of the ninth inning gave the Mets a 6–5 win in Game 3. His pinch-hit triple leading off the ninth in Game 6 sparked a three-run rally to tie the game, and his RBI-single in the 16th inning helped the Mets win the pennant. With the Mets down two games to none in the World Series, Dykstra led off Game 3 at Fenway Park with a home run, and eventually cracked four hits to lead his team to a 7–1 victory. The Mets beat the Red Sox in seven games.

Dykstra's numbers for the Mets were good over the next three seasons, but he yearned to play every day. That chance came in 1989, when the Mets traded Dykstra and pitchers Roger McDowell and Tom Edens to Philadelphia for outfielder Juan Samuel. The deal was a steal for the Phillies.

As the everyday center fielder in Philadelphia in 1990, Dykstra played in 149 games and hit .325. His 192 hits tied for the league lead, and he was selected for the All-Star team. Not only was Dykstra popular with his new hometown fans, he was establishing himself as a favorite with fans throughout baseball.

But a dark cloud always seemed to follow clear skies for Lenny Dykstra. A car accident after he had been drinking put Dykstra on the disabled list for the first time in his career in May 1991. In August he crashed into the outfield wall in Cincinnati, fracturing his shoulder for the second time that season. The next year brought more physical problems for Dykstra. An Opening Day pitch from Greg Maddux fractured a styloid bone in his left arm. With Dykstra playing in just 85 games, the Phillies finished last in the NL East in 1992.

Dykstra responded with his finest season in 1993, and led his team from last place to the pennant. He led the National League in hits and walks, and his 143 runs scored were the most in the league in 61 years—since Chuck Klein scored 152 for the Phillies in 1932. Dykstra finished second in the MVP voting. He batted .348 with four home runs in the World Series, but Joe Carter's dramatic seventh-game, Series-ending home run lifted the Toronto Blue Jays to the championship. Dogged again by injuries, Dykstra played only 186 more games over the next three years. A spinal condition ended the three-time All-Star's career in 1998.

George Earnshaw

Earnshaw, George Livingston **P**

1928–36 B:2/15/1900, New York, NY D:12/1/1976, Little Rock, AR Deb:6/3/1928, PHI AL BR/TR 6'4", 210

W	L	PCT	G	SH	IP	BB	SO	ERA
127	93	.577	319	18	1915^1	809	1002	4.38

George Earnshaw did not make it to the majors until he was 28, but from 1929 through 1932 he teamed with Lefty Grove to give Connie Mack a terrific left-right pitching combination. Relying on a blazing fastball, Earnshaw won 86 games during those four seasons to help the Philadelphia Athletics to three World Series appearances. In the 1930 Series against the Cardinals he pitched 22 scoreless innings.

Yet Earnshaw, a man born into wealth, cared little for baseball achievements. Writer Ira Smith described him as "sociable, [a] fine dresser, good storyteller and a hand at playing practical jokes. Proficient at billiards, tennis and golf. All in all, a type of man rarely encountered in a sport which he took very lightly at first but which brought him fame and success when he fully applied his brain and talents to it."

Born on New York's Riverside Drive and listed in the *Social Register*, Earnshaw attended Swarthmore and excelled in baseball, basketball, and football, serving as the school's basketball captain in 1923 and 1924. A large man at 6 feet 4 inches and 210 pounds, he was given the nickname "Moose." Although he signed a contract with Jack Dunn's International League Baltimore Orioles as a sophomore, he did not join them until two years later, in 1924. He simply didn't need the money.

After several outstanding seasons with Baltimore, Earnshaw was purchased by the Athletics in 1928. In 1929 he went 24–8 for the world champion A's, leading the league in wins. The A's repeated in 1930, with Earnshaw going 22–13 and winning two games against the St. Louis Cardinals in that year's Series. Had he not been removed for a pinch hitter in the ninth inning of Game 5 he might have recorded three victories.

In 1931 Earnshaw was 21–7, but the A's lost the Series to the Cards, this time in seven games. He had one big season left, going 19–13 in 1932, but his arm was gone and he fell to 5–10 in 1933. Moose was among the first to go the following season when Mack once again broke up a championship club to pay his bills.

In World War II, despite being 41, Earnshaw served in the Navy, rising to lieutenant commander. Admiral Chester Nimitz awarded him the Commendation Ribbon for his actions during a carrier strike on Truk on April 29, 1944.

Mike Easler

Easler, Michael Anthony **OF–DH**

1973–77, 1979–87 B:11/29/1950, Cleveland, OH Deb:9/5/1973, HOU NL BL/TR 6'1", 196

G	AB	R	H	HR	RBI	OBP	SLG	AVG
1151	3677	465	1078	118	522	.353	.454	.293

Known as "the Hit Man" for his batting skills, Mike Easler was selected by the Astros in the sixth round of the June 1969 amateur draft. It was but because of his defensive shortcoming, however, that he didn't reach the majors for good until nearly a decade later.

Easler led the American Association with a .352 average in 1976 and the International League with a .330 mark in 1978. He saw service in the Houston, St. Louis, California, Pittsburgh, and Boston organizations before settling in with the Pirates in 1979. He hit .338 for Pittsburgh in his first full season as a major league regular and made the National League All-Star team the following year.

In December 1983 the Pirates traded him to Boston for pitcher John Tudor. Easler found a niche as the Red Sox designated hitter, hitting 27 homers and driving in 91 runs in 1984. Boston and the Yankees swapped designated hitters in March 1986, with Don Baylor going to Fenway and Easler to Yankee Stadium.

After one season New York sent him to Philadelphia for pitcher Charles Hudson; that same year the Yankees reacquired Easler and then released him. The Hit Man went down swinging, batting .282 in his final big league season. He later coached for the Brewers and Red Sox.

Luke Easter

Easter, Luscious Luke **1B**

1949–54 B:8/4/1915, Jonestown, MS D:3/29/1979, Euclid, OH Deb:8/11/1949, CLE AL BL/TR 6'4½", 240

G	AB	R	H	HR	RBI	OBP	SLG	AVG
491	1725	256	472	93	340	.350	.481	.274

Luscious "Luke" Easter was known for his tape-measure home runs wherever he played, whether it was in the Negro Leagues, the majors, or in his lengthy minor league career. "I just hit 'em and forget 'em," he once commented.

In the Negro Leagues, Easter played for the Cincinnati Crescents in 1946 and the Homestead

Grays in 1947 and 1948. In 1947 he hit an estimated 75 homers. He also performed in the Puerto Rican Winter League in 1948. Following the 1948 season the Grays sold Easter's contract to the Cleveland Indians for $5,000. In his brief tenure with Cleveland, he hit 31 homers in 1952 and twice drove in more than 100 runs in a season. On June 23, 1950, Easter hit a ball 477 feet into the upper deck at Municipal Stadium.

Bad knees cut short his major league stay, but starting with Indianapolis in 1952 Easter began the third phase of his career—minor league legend. In 1956, the International League's Buffalo Bisons acquired Easter for $7,500 from the Charleston Senators, and he soon became noted in western New York for his enormous shots. In 1956 he led the International League in homers (35) and RBIs (106). On August 6 Easter hit a 550-foot blast that went clear out of Buffalo's Offermann Stadium and landed two streets beyond the ballpark. In 1957 he led the International League in homers (40), total bases (300), and RBIs (128).

Released by Buffalo in May 1959, he spent six more seasons with the International League's Rochester Red Wings as a player and a coach and enjoyed a popularity akin to what he had enjoyed in Buffalo.

Easter's life ended tragically. After leaving baseball he found employment at TRW, Inc., in Cleveland, where he became a shop steward. He was in the habit of taking his fellow workers' checks each payday and cashing them at a local bank. On March 29, 1979, as Easter was leaving the bank, two men accosted him and demanded the cash. He refused to give it up and was hit above the heart by a shotgun blast.

Rawly Eastwick

Eastwick, Rawlins Jackson **P**

1974–81 B:10/24/1950, Camden, NJ Deb:9/12/1974, CIN NL BR/TR 6'3", 180

W	L	PCT	G	SV	IP	BB	SO	ERA
28	27	.509	326	68	525^1	156	295	3.31

The bullpen was the secret weapon for Cincinnati's "Big Red Machine." While most attention was focused on the Reds' famous hitters and basestealers, Cincinnati's relief pitching was also excellent. Cherub-faced Rawly Eastwick was the most effective member of a superb relief corps that helped the Reds take back-to-back world championships in 1975 and 1976.

Eastwick tied for the National League lead with 22 saves as a rookie for the Reds in '75. He tallied a win and a save in Cincinnati's three-game sweep of the Pirates in the NL Championship Series, and he won twice and added a save while pitching five times in the Reds' memorable seven-game World Series triumph over the Boston Red Sox.

The hard-throwing righthander posted even better numbers in 1976: an 11–5 record, 2.09 ERA, and a league-best 26 saves. Eastwick, however, saw little action in October—the Reds were on fire, and hardly needed relief pitching as they swept the NLCS and the World Series.

By 1977 Eastwick was at odds with Cincinnati management, whom he called "a bunch of backstabbers." He was traded to St. Louis midway through the 1977 season; it set him on a wandering path beset by injuries and ineffectiveness. Eastwick split the 1978 season between the Yankees and Phillies, and moved on to the Royals and Cubs before retiring in 1981.

Charles Ebbets

Ebbets, Charles Hercules

Owner(1898–1925) M(1898, 38–68) B:10/29/1859, Greenwich Village, NY D:4/18/1925, Brooklyn, NY

The namesake of fabled Ebbets Field, Brooklyn's Charles Ebbets spent more than four decades in the game, rising from ticket taker to club owner. He is credited with many innovations, including the rain check and regularly scheduled batting and fielding practice. He advanced the idea that teams should draft new players in inverse relation to their season records, and advocated fixed dates for World Series play. He also helped institute Sunday baseball in Brooklyn.

Ebbets trained as a draftsman and architect but soon found those occupations too constricting for his entrepreneurial spirit. He turned to publishing novels, which he actually sold door to door. His baseball career began on May 12, 1883, at the opening of Brooklyn's new Washington Park at Fifth Avenue and 3rd Street. Ebbets sold tickets that day but also handled a variety of tasks for club President Charles H. Byrne.

Slowly, he worked his way up the organizational ladder. Using borrowed funds, by late 1897 he made public his purchase of co-owner George W. Chauncey's shares for $25,000. Shortly thereafter he took an option on Ferdinand A. Abell's shares. On January 1, 1898, Ebbets announced to reporters that he now controlled 85 percent of the franchise. Three days later Charles Byrne died, and Ebbets assumed the presidency. But his announced purchases had fallen through. He failed to exercise his option to purchase the Abell block of stock and did not pick up all of Chauncey's share. As late as the summer of 1898 Ebbets owned only 18 percent of the club.

That season, however, brought two significant changes for the Dodgers. First, they relocated to "New Washington Park," a facility they rented for $5,000 per year. Second, Ebbets and company entered into a syndicate baseball scheme with Harry Von der Horst, owner of the Baltimore Orioles. The two ownership groups merged, and a number of talented players including Wee Willie Keeler shifted from Baltimore to more populous Brooklyn. Orioles manager Ned Hanlon also moved over to Brooklyn, and the club was renamed the Superbas after a then-popular vaudeville act. In 1899 Brooklyn won the NL pennant.

In 1905, with funds provided by Brooklyn furniture manufacturer Henry W. Medicus, Ebbets bought Von der Horst's shares. Finally, in 1907, Ebbets actually had control of the club. He held 60 percent; his son, Charles, Jr., owned 10 percent, and Medicus held 30 percent.

Ebbets made a speech in 1909 in which he argued that baseball was still in its infancy. Most people found the contention ridiculous, and he was laughed off the podium. One of the topics of Ebbets' speech was the ramshackle condition of baseball's wooden grandstands. He was prepared to erect a new park in Brooklyn.

Ebbets first considered building on the site of Washington Park, but soon abandoned the idea. Instead he settled on a site called "Pigtown," described by author Frank Graham as "a huddle of ramshackle houses surrounding a hole in the ground partly filled with steaming and odorous garbage."

Friends thought Ebbets had lost his mind, but he followed through with his plans, and Ebbets Field was unveiled on April 11, 1912. The Dodgers played there for 46 seasons.

"I am a firm believer in the future of baseball," wrote Ebbets in *Leslie's Weekly*, "both in Brooklyn and in the country at large. Otherwise I would not invest close to three-quarters of a million dollars in this new park. It will contain every convenience that we can devise and will be absolutely safe. I will no longer have to worry about fires, collapsing stands and other dangers that menace the spectators and of which they seldom give thought."

Ebbets originally planned to name the facility Washington Park, but was dissuaded by reporters who said the name would mean nothing in the new location. Len Wooster of *The New York Times* suggested: "Why don't you call it Ebbets Field? It was your idea and nobody else's, and you've put yourself in hock to build it. It's going to be your monument, whether you think about it or not."

Wooster was right—not only about the name, but also about Ebbets being in hock. The magnate solved that problem in August 1912 by buying out Medicus and then selling 50 percent of his stock to his friends, Edward J. and Stephen W. McKeever, for $100,000. Two corporations were formed: the Ebbets-McKeever Exhibition Company, which owned the land and the ballpark itself, and the Brooklyn National League Club, which owned the franchise.

Although the Dodgers won only two pennants during Ebbets' reign, in 1916 and 1920, the years were good to Ebbets. When he died on April 18, 1925, he left an estate estimated at $1.25 million, principally in the ballclub. The Giants were scheduled to play the Dodgers at Ebbets Field on the afternoon of his death, and Brooklyn manager Wilbert Robinson was asked if the game should be canceled. "No," he responded. "Charley wouldn't want anyone to miss a Dodger-Giant game just because he died!"

The 1926 *Reach Guide* eulogized: "The late Mr. Ebbets gave baseball his best service for all of 40 years, was always a constructive force in the game, bravely fought its battles in Brooklyn, through good and ill fortune, until final success crowned his efforts in the closing stages of his life, and withal was always the soul of honor. He never played baseball 'politics,' was without guile, and [was] so universally popular that he may be truly said to have been the best loved man, not only in his own league, but throughout the entire realm of baseball. Ebbets was one of the comparatively few old time magnates whose interest in the affairs of the game never faltered. His counsel and efforts toward the improvement of the game were always wise and practical."

Dennis Eckersley

Eckersley, Dennis Lee **P**

1975–98 B:10/3/1954, Oakland, CA Deb:4/12/1975, CLE AL BR/TR 6'2", 190

W	L	PCT	G	SV	IP	BB	SO	ERA
197	171	.535	1071	390	3285[2]	738	2401	3.50

Fading starter Dennis Eckersley was virtually given away by the Chicago Cubs, who had to agree to pay part of his future $3 million-a-year salary, to the Oakland A's. But Eckersley blossomed into the most effective reliever in history, capped by an unprecedented 1992 season: Reliever of the Year, Cy Young Award, and American League Most Valuable Player Award.

Eckersley accomplished this transformation by using his two main pitches, a fastball and a fearsome slider, and simply getting them over the plate with amazing consistency. From 1988 to

1992 he converted 89 percent of his save opportunities. In 1992 he became only the second pitcher in history to save 50 or more games in a season. He became the first pitcher to record 40 or more saves in four different years.

Eckersley arrived in Cleveland as a starting pitcher in 1975. In his first major league start he shut out the A's, 2–0. He went on to be named *The Sporting News* American League Rookie Pitcher of the Year. On May 30, 1977, he tossed a no-hitter against the Angels. But the next year the Indians traded Eckersley to the Red Sox. When Eckersley called to tell his wife they were moving to Boston, she refused to go, then asked for a divorce. He poured his efforts into baseball and became the first Red Sox pitcher in seven years to win 20 games. In Boston he charmed the media with his unique vocabulary: bridgepiece (homer), walk-off piece (game winning homer), cheese (fastball), yakker (curve), and Bogart (a big game).

His career, however, began to sour, and the fans turned on him. "I used to have a car with THE ECK license plates," he said about that period, "but I came out of a bar one night and the tires were slashed." By 1983, suffering from arm problems, he was traded to the Cubs. He helped Chicago to win its division in 1984 and was off to a flying start the next year when he developed tendinitis in his right shoulder. His problems continued into the following season, exacerbated by his heavy drinking.

Finally, Eckersley sought help. He quietly checked himself into the Edgehill Newport treatment center in Newport, Rhode Island, and emerged six weeks later with a handle on his problems. This was all unknown to Cubs management, however, which traded him to Oakland on April 3, 1987, for three unknowns.

When Oakland relief ace Jay Howell came down with a sore arm, a place opened up in the bullpen for Eckersley. His tenure with the A's was one of almost uninterrupted success, except for giving up Kirk Gibson's dramatic ninth-inning homer in Game 1 of the 1988 World Series. But Eckersley earned new respect from the media as he answered question after question about his fatal pitch, which NBC was interspersing with footage from *The Natural*. "It got so I began thinking I had given up a home run to Robert Redford," he said.

Traded to the Cardinals in February 1996, Eckersley posted 30 saves that year and 36 the next. He signed as a free agent with Boston in December 1997 and finished his career with the Sox in 1998. When he left the game Eckersley was third on the all-time saves list with 390—behind only Lee Smith and John Franco. Following his retirement he helped broadcast A's games.

Eckersley was one player generally liked by his fellow professionals. "I always root for him," said his former Red Sox manager Don Zimmer in 1992. "I still check the box scores for his name. Of all the people I've managed in this game he's the one kid I'll always remember, because he always approached the game like it was supposed to be approached. He had fun, he was competitive, and he loved it."

William Eckert

Eckert, William D.

Commissioner 1965–68 B:1/20/1909, Freeport, IL D:4/16/1971, Grand Bahama, Bahamas

They called him the "Unknown Soldier," and decades after his death, baseball's fourth commissioner, Gen. William D. "Spike" Eckert, remains an unknown to most baseball fans.

When Commissioner Ford C. Frick retired in 1965, no clear successor emerged, although such familiar names as Lee MacPhail, Joe Cronin, Gabe Paul, and Gen. Curtis LeMay were bandied about for the job. Eckert's name was never publicly mentioned, so the November 17, 1965, announcement of his unanimous election to a seven-year term at $65,000 a year caught observers by surprise.

Eckert graduated from West Point in 1930, and subsequently graduated from the Army-Navy Staff College and the Harvard Graduate School of Business. During World War II, he commanded the 432nd Bomb Group of the 8th Army Air Force. Later he moved over to the field of defense procurement, where he specialized in negotiating defense contracts for the Air Force. Eckert reached the rank of lieutenant general before suffering a heart attack and retiring from the service in 1961.

As commissioner, Eckert was assisted by Lee MacPhail, who was given a three-year appointment as baseball's administrator at $40,000 per year. In his first year, Eckert smoothed over relations with Japanese baseball and ruled that Tom Seaver's contract with Atlanta was void. However, Eckert was handicapped not only by his previous lack of a public image, but by his colorless demeanor and inexperience in the inner—or even outer—workings of baseball. Prior to his election as commissioner, he had not seen a game in 10 years.

Eckert vanished from the baseball scene just as quickly as he had appeared. On December 6, 1968, the club owners, concerned about upcoming labor troubles, requested his resignation. Dutifully, he complied, making it effective February 4, 1969. "He could not give the illusion of vigorous leadership, the illusion the owners wanted, and when he did involve himself in a few problems of substance, the owners considered his honest efforts to be meddling," wrote Leonard Koppett. Eckert died of a heart attack while playing tennis on Grand Bahama on April 16, 1971.

Ox Eckhardt

Eckhardt, Oscar George **OF**

1932,1936 B:12/23/1901, Yorktown, TX D:4/22/1951, Yorktown, TX Deb:4/16/1932, BOS NL BL/TR 6'1", 185

G	AB	R	H	HR	RBI	OBP	SLG	AVG
24	52	6	10	1	7	.263	.269	.192

Outfielder Oscar "Ox" Eckhardt was one of the greatest hitters in minor league history. The big Texan enjoyed only a brief moment in the majors, but his .367 lifetime minor league average ranks second only to Ike Boone's .370.

Eckhardt, Boone, and Smead Jolley comprised the minor league "Murderers Row." And much like Boone and Jolley, Ox was a "character," according to historian Lee Allen, who also noted that Eckhardt's "bulk made him as durable as his nickname would imply." In 1932, the first of his two big league seasons, Eckhardt came to spring training and requested a double room; he needed the extra space for his dog, a Saint Bernard.

A University of Texas athlete, Eckhardt spent the 1928 football season as a fullback with the New York Giants of the NFL. When his hitting advanced him through the minor leagues he gave up the gridiron.

He won his first batting championship with a .379 average for the Texas League's Beaumont Exporters in 1930, also leading all other batsmen in hits with 217 and doubles with 55. Purchased by San Francisco's Mission club in 1931—to replace Ike Boone—he won the first of four PCL batting titles with a .369 mark. After a brief stint with the big league Braves, Eckhardt returned to the Missions, where he again led the league, this time batting .371.

The next season was his greatest, as Eckhardt recorded the highest batting average in PCL history, .414, and collected 315 base hits—the third-highest total in Organized Baseball annals. After "slumping" to .378 in 1934, Eckhardt again led the league in 1935 (his last season with the Missions and in the Pacific Coast League) with a .399 average.

His hitting earned him a tryout with the hapless Dodgers in 1936. Eckhardt was barely adequate in the outfield, however, and soon returned to the minors. He spent his last professional season with the Texas League's Dallas Rebels in 1940.

Jim Edmonds

Edmonds, James Patrick **OF**

1993–* B:6/27/1970, Fullerton, CA Deb:9/9/1993, CAL AL BL/TL 6'1", 190

G	AB	R	H	HR	RBI	OBP	SLG	AVG
709	2644	464	768	121	408	.360	.498	.290

In 1992, when minor league outfielder Jim Edmonds was at Double A Midland, Angels farm director Bill Bavasi issued a word of caution about the standout prospect: "His body language will drive you nuts." Throughout his career in Anaheim, Edmonds emoted too much or too little for some tastes, showing satisfaction from a home run or great catch, looking around during at bats, smiling after chasing a bad pitch. These mannerisms, and his unusual candor with the media, sparked some resentment among teammates and coaches despite his success on the field.

Edmonds hit at least 25 home runs every season between 1995 and 1998, set a club record with 120 runs scored in 1995, and twice batted over .300. He played through assorted injuries in 1997 and 1998, winning two Gold Gloves and turning in highlight-reel performances with several unbelievable catches in center field.

Edmonds batted a career-high .307 in 1998 after two off-season knee surgeries, including a .340 mark with 20 RBIs in September. As the Angels imploded in 1999, Edmonds could only watch: he underwent surgery to repair a shoulder tear in April, and didn't make it back to active duty until August.

Johnny Edwards

Edwards, John Alban **C**

1961–74 B:6/10/1938, Columbus, OH Deb:6/27/1961, CIN NL BL/TR 6'4", 220

G	AB	R	H	HR	RBI	OBP	SLG	AVG
1470	4577	430	1106	81	524	.314	.353	.242

Johnny Edwards, one of the game's best defensive catchers in the 1960s, won Gold Gloves in 1963 and 1964, and later set the National League record for catchers with 138 consecutive errorless games from July 11, 1970, to August 20, 1971. During that stretch he handled 805 chances, another league record.

A Columbus, Ohio, native, Edwards was not considered the city's best high school catcher; that honor went to a fellow at Upper Arlington High School: Jack Nicklaus. After attending Ohio State University, Edwards signed with the Reds in 1959, moving up to the majors in 1961. Despite a miserable .186 batting average and trouble fielding balls in the dirt, he became the Reds' regular catcher as they held off the Dodgers to win their first pennant since 1940.

Edwards' defensive skills developed rapidly, but his hitting left much to be desired. His offensive production did improve, but not much. Edwards had the advantage of being a lefthanded-hitting catcher, a rarity in baseball. But although he hit .254 in 1962 and a career-high .281 in 1964, his lifetime average after 14 years was only .242. Still, his defensive play earned him a place on the NL All-Star team in 1963, 1964, and 1965. Edwards also caught his first no-hitter in 1965, courtesy of Jim Maloney. The second, thrown by Ray Washburn, came three years later. His career with the Reds ended abruptly before the 1968 season, thanks to the appearance of a young catcher named Johnny Bench.

Wish Egan

Egan, Aloysius Jerome **P**

1902,1905–06 B:6/16/1881, Evart, MI D:4/13/1951, Detroit, MI Deb:9/3/1902, DET AL BR/TR 6'3", 185

W	L	PCT	G	SV	IP	BB	SO	ERA
8	26	.235	42	0	279^2	72	52	3.83

Wish Egan scouted for the Tigers for 40 years, from 1910 to 1950, sometimes filling in as a coach. His unusual nickname came from his first name, Aloysius.

Among those signed by Aloysius Jerome Egan were Hal Newhouser, Paul "Dizzy" Trout, and Walter "Hoot" Evers. Legend has it that, on Wish's insistence, Detroit traded Barney McCosky for George Kell in 1946.

Egan's reputation as a scout was so widespread that it eclipsed his earlier career as a pitcher. A 6-foot-3 righthander, Egan was 6–15 for the St. Louis Cardinals in 1905. At the age of 24, he might have had a future, but he hurt his arm that season and his career ended after the 1906 campaign, in which he was 2–9 with a 4.59 ERA for St. Louis. Out of baseball for three years, he returned as a 29-year-old rookie scout for the Tigers in 1910.

Howard Ehmke

Ehmke, Howard Jonathan **P**

1915–17,1919–30 B:4/24/1894, Silver Creek, NY D:3/17/1959, Philadelphia, PA Deb:4/12 /1915, BUF FL BR/TR 6'3", 190

W	L	PCT	G	SH	IP	BB	SO	ERA
166	166	.500	427	20	2820^2	1042	1030	3.75

Shock waves swept Wrigley Field on October 7, 1929, when 35-year-old Howard Ehmke took the mound for the Philadelphia A's. The Game 1 starter in the World Series against the Chicago Cubs was not the most likely choice. The A's had a starting rotation that included Lefty Grove and George Earnshaw. As recently as September 12, manager Connie Mack had called the rarely used Ehmke into his office to discuss the pitcher's release.

"All right, Mr. Mack," Ehmke had replied. "But I've always had the ambition to pitch in a World Series. My arm is not what it once was, but I honestly feel there's one more good game left in it. I'd like a chance to prove it to you."

An idea took shape in Mack's mind. He told Ehmke to go home and not report back to the team until the day before the Series. But as the Cubs arrived in town to play a late-season series with the Phillies, Mack told Ehmke to attend the games anonymously in the stands and study the Chicago hitters. "You're going to pitch the first game," he told the hurler, "but don't tell anybody."

Mack's secret weapon had begun his big league career in 1915 in the Federal League. When that circuit folded, his contract was sold to Detroit, where he remained for six years. During his tenure Ehmke won 17 games twice for the Tigers.

In October 1922 he was traded to Boston. On September 7, 1923, he pitched a no-hitter against Philadelphia, following that up with a one-hitter four days later. Ehmke finished the year at 20–17, making him one of only five pitchers in American League history to win 20 games for a last-place team.

Ehmke won 19 games the following season, but his record dipped to 9–20 in 1925. During the 1926 season he joined the A's as part of a four-player deal with Boston. After two 12-win seasons for the A's, Ehmke saw his starts diminish in 1928 and 1929. In September 1929 he didn't tell anyone of Mack's World Series plans, not even his wife. Before Game 1, he approached his manager, inquiring, "Have you changed your mind, Mr. Mack?"

"Should I?" Mack asked.

"Why, no," the pitcher replied. "I'm ready."

The old righthander took his place on the mound, and for six innings he matched zeroes with Cubs starter Charlie Root. What Mack had realized was that the center-field bleachers at Wrigley Field would be filled with white-shirted fans. Ehmke's sidearm delivery would make the baseball almost impossible for Cubs batters to see against that background.

In the seventh A's slugger Jimmie Foxx homered, giving the A's a 1–0 lead. By the eighth inning Ehmke had tied Ed Walsh's 1906 record of 12 strikeouts in a Series game. In the ninth the A's added two runs. Then, with two outs in the last of the ninth, the Cubs came back, putting the tying runs on base. Mack left Ehmke in to face pinch hitter Chick Tolson. On a 3–2 pitch, Tolson swung—and missed. Ehmke not only had his win, but he had set a new World Series strikeout record.

As it turned out, Ehmke's World Series win was his last in the major leagues. In 1930 he was hit hard in three games and released by the A's.

Mark Eichhorn

Eichhorn, Mark Anthony **P**
1982–94, 1996 B:11/21/60, San Jose, CA
Deb:8/30/82, TOR AL BR/TR 6'3", 210

W	L	PCT	G	SV	IP	BB	SO	ERA
48	43	.527	563	32	885^{2}	270	640	3.00

When the Blue Jays drafted Mark Eichhorn in 1979, they immediately converted him from shortstop to pitcher. By the age of 21 he was widely regarded as the best pitching prospect in Toronto's organization. Shortly thereafter, pain in his right shoulder threatened to completely derail his breakthrough to the major leagues.

Two Toronto coaches, Al Widmar and John Sullivan, suggested Eichhorn attempt to come back from his shoulder strain by using a new delivery. Eichhorn abandoned the three-quarter motion he had used previously and adopted a submarine style that Dan Quisenberry had used with success in Kansas City. Eichhorn said the new sidearm delivery "was like I was resting my arm."

Pitching exclusively in relief, Eichhorn was named *The Sporting News* American League Rookie Pitcher of the Year in 1986. He came within five innings of winning the league's ERA title, an almost unheard-of accomplishment for a full-time reliever. Eichhorn won a combined 24 games in his first two full seasons and became arguably the best set-up man in the AL, a perfect complement to Toronto's hard-throwing closer, Tom Henke.

A heavy workload of pitching in 1986 and 1987, however, seemed to take a toll on Eichhorn. After making a league-leading 89 appearances in 1987, his effectiveness waned, resulting in a trade to the Atlanta Braves. After a disappointing year in Atlanta, Eichhorn returned to the AL with the California Angels. He pitched well over the next two and a half seasons, but California traded him back to Toronto in midseason. Eichhorn pitched successfully for the Blue Jays through 1993, for Baltimore in 1994, and, following a one-year hiatus, for one additional season with the Angels in 1996.

Jim Eisenreich

Eisenreich, James Michael **OF**
1982–84, 1987–98 B:4/18/1959, St. Cloud, MN
Deb:4/6/1982, MIN AL BL/TL 5'11", 195

G	AB	R	H	HR	RBI	OBP	SLG	AVG
1422	3995	492	1160	52	477	.345	.404	.290

Jim Eisenreich's major league story began as a seemingly normal variation on the "hometown boy makes good" theme. The St. Cloud, Minnesota, native with the sweet lefthanded swing landed a spot in the Minnesota Twins outfield in 1982. He batted .303 in 99 at bats as a rookie, but it did not take long to see that something was wrong.

Eisenreich shook, twitched, and gave off other visible signs of discomfort during games, once even running off the field tearing at his uniform and yelling, "I can't breathe!" He had been mocked and teased for these behaviors since childhood; doctors had declared him hyperactive. In his mid-20s, with a promising baseball career hanging in the balance, Eisenreich was diagnosed with Tourette's syndrome, a genetic disorder that often causes rapid physical and verbal actions and is usually accompanied by obsessive-compulsive or attention-deficit disorders. The illness limited Eisenreich to a total of 39 at bats over the next two seasons, then finally forced him out of baseball altogether in 1984.

With the help of medication and regular attention from doctors, Eisenreich returned to the majors in 1987 with Kansas City. He spent six years as a regular with the Royals, posting a career-high 33 doubles and 59 RBIs in 1989. Eisenreich signed with Philadelphia before the 1993 season, and batted .318 as the Phillies won the National League pennant. He added a home run and seven RBIs in the World Series. Eisenreich batted .300 or better in each of his four seasons with the Phillies, including a .361 mark in 113 games in 1996.

Eisenreich moved on to the Florida Marlins in 1997. After a solid regular season, he again shone in the World Series, batting .500 with a home run as the Marlins won the title in seven games. Eisenreich used his heightened visibility to spread the message of understanding for Tourette's sufferers across the country.

In May 1998 Eisenreich was part of the deal that sent Bobby Bonilla, Gary Sheffield, and Charles Johnson to the Los Angeles Dodgers for Mike Piazza and Todd Zeile. But in contrast to previous changes of venue, he did not prosper in Los Angeles. He hit just .215 for the year and retired—with a .290 lifetime batting average, and a legion of admiring fans.

Kid Elberfeld

Elberfeld, Norman Arthur **SS–3B**
1898–99,1901–11,1914 M(1908, 27–71) B:4/13/1875, Pomeroy, OH D:1/13/1944, Chattanooga, TN
Deb:5/30/1898, PHI NL BR/TR 5'7", 158

G	AB	R	H	HR	RBI	OBP	SLG	AVG
1292	4561	647	1235	10	535	.355	.339	.271

Norman Elberfeld, an outstanding shortstop at the beginning of the 20th century, earned the nickname "the Tabasco Kid" for his fiery play. Standing only 5 feet 7 inches and weighing 158 pounds, he played hard and received similar treatment from opposing teams. Playing in the style of the day, he was spiked often, and when cut, he'd go to the bench, roll down his sock, cauterize the wound with whiskey, and then return to the field.

After trials with the Phillies and Reds, Elberfeld became Detroit's regular shortstop in 1901, the American League's first season as a major League. Hardly a "kid" at 26 years old, he hit .308 and led the league's shortstops in putouts and double plays. Although he edged his batting average over .300 in two other seasons during his 14-season career, he was generally an ordinary hitter at best, with a .271 career batting average. In the field, he played with more fire than finesse, never leading his league in any particular defensive category after 1901 but simply getting the job done.

Traded in June 1903 to the New York Highlanders (Yankees), Elberfeld was their regular shortstop through 1907. He was at short in 1904 when the team came within Jack Chesbro's wild pitch of winning the American League pennant. In 1908 he suffered a serious leg injury. While recovering, he replaced Clark Griffith as the Highlanders manager. The team went 27–71 under Kid and finished dead last. His leg never quite returned to normal, and in his remaining years in the majors, Elberfeld usually played third base.

Elberfeld spent many years as a volatile yet successful minor league manager, but he was never again given a chance to manage in the majors.

Bob Elliott

Elliott, Robert Irving **3B–OF**

1939–53 M(1960,58–96) B:11/26/1916, San Francisco, CA D:5/4/1966, San Diego, CA
Deb:9/2/1939, PIT NL BR/TR 6', 185

G	AB	R	H	HR	RBI	OBP	SLG	AVG
1978	7141	1064	2061	170	1195	.375	.440	.289

Besides being a Hall of Fame player and a successful manager, Frank Frisch was a good enough salesman to move Bob Elliott from the outfield to third base. Elliott came up to the majors with the Pittsburgh Pirates in 1939. A good hitter, he was named to the 1941 National League All-Star team, but he was something less than a gazelle in the outfield.

In 1942 manager Frisch moved the awkward-fielding Elliott to third base and told him, "It's an easy position to play, Bob. I even played it myself. All you need is a strong arm and a strong chest. Whatever I couldn't stop with my glove I stopped with my chest. Playing the outfield wears out your legs. You can play third base on a dime, no running or nothing. It will add five years to your playing career."

Frisch tirelessly hit grounders to Elliott during practice. One day a ball hit Elliott squarely between the eyes and knocked him out. As he regained consciousness Elliott muttered, "Hey, Frank, remember what you told me about third base adding five years to my career? Well, I think I lost three of those five extra years already." Elliott survived and went on to have a long and fruitful major league career. Along the way he spoiled three no-hitters, mastered third base well enough to lead the league in fielding one year, and was named to seven All-Star teams.

The Pirates traded Elliott to the Boston Braves after the 1946 season for Billy Herman, who became their manager. The swap became known as one of the worst in Bucs history when, in 1947, the righty-swinging third baseman hit 22 home runs, had 113 RBIs, batted .317 with a .517 slugging percentage, and won the Most Valuable Player Award. The next year he led the Braves to a pennant. Elliott was so valuable to his mates that they nicknamed him "Mr. Team."

He was traded to the New York Giants for the 1952 season and split 1953, his last season as a player, between the Browns and White Sox. Elliott later managed in the minors, and in 1960 he took the reins of the awful Kansas City Athletics.

Dock Ellis

Ellis, Dock Phillip **P**

1968–79 B:3/11/1945, Los Angeles, CA
Deb:6/18/1968, PIT NL BB/TR 6'3", 210

W	L	PCT	G	SH	IP	BB	SO	ERA
138	119	.537	345	14	2127²	674	1136	3.46

An outspoken African-American playing for a team in a racially polarized city, pitcher Dock Ellis was one of the most outrageous characters ever to put on a Pittsburgh Pirates uniform. Whether pitching well or poorly, he found himself in constant hot water with team management, demanding simultaneously that he not be treated differently from other players and that he be allowed to march only to his own drummer. As he put it, "I pitch. I win. I'm free."

In 1976 Dick Young, a reporter for the *New York Daily News*, wrote: "There is nothing wrong with Dock Ellis' arm. What's wrong is with his head. It's not screwed on properly. He is, to put it tastefully, a pain in the butt. He is profane, even bigoted, churlish, troublesome and irreverent."

Ellis' eccentricities included wearing curlers in his hair before the game to keep his Afro hairdo first-rate. He pitched a no-hitter against San Diego in 1970 while allegedly on LSD. To his mind, it wasn't unusual. Describing the 1973 Pirates he said, "Whole team is on pills. I have taken about 15 at one time."

One of his most notorious displays occurred before the 1971 All-Star Game. Ellis, 14–3 at the time, announced to the Associated Press that he wouldn't be chosen as the starter for the National League because "they'll never start a brother against a brother." (Vida Blue was certain to start for the American League.) Newspaper columnists across the country pilloried Ellis, who later confessed that he made his announcement just to make sure that he got the start. But his performance wasn't impressive; in the third inning Luis Aparicio singled and Reggie Jackson slugged one of the longest home runs anyone had ever seen. Two outs later, Frank Robinson lined another two-run homer, and Ellis took the loss.

In 1974, upset at the way the Reds had spoken about the Pirates, Ellis devised a plan to wake up his "sleeping" teammates. Beginning in spring training, Ellis apparently decided to hit as many Cincinnati batters as possible when he pitched against them, and he even notified some teammates of his idea. On May 1 of that year he started against the Reds. In the pregame meeting to review Cincinnati's lineup, he told catcher Manny Sanguillen that the discussion was unnecessary. "I'm just going to mow them down," he announced.

He hit Pete Rose, Joe Morgan, and Dan Driessen on five pitches; threw two pitches behind Tony Perez's head before walking him; and threw two balls at Johnny Bench (one at his jaw and one at the back of his head). Manager Danny Murtaugh brought in a reliever. Sanguillen said he had never seen a pitcher so wild. "I was trying to convey a message," Ellis said. "Leave my hitters alone."

The city didn't like him, management didn't like him, and the press didn't like him. Every year the experts on the sports pages announced that Ellis wasn't long for Pittsburgh. "Ellis Probably Most Unpopular Buc of All Time," one article was headlined. But Ellis' teammates did like him; they liked his brash humor and his pitching competitiveness. He was a solid starter with 13, 19, and 15 wins in three Pittsburgh divisional championships from 1970 to 1972. Eventually, however, injuries and further difficulties with management reduced his playing time and he was swapped to the Yankees along with Willie Randolph and Ken Brett for Doc Medich.

Ellis thrived as a Yankee under the fiery leadership of Billy Martin. According to his biographer, Donald Hall, "Dock relished Billy Martin and the violent competitiveness of this Yankee club." His 17–8 record and Game 3 ALCS win over the Royals earned him Comeback Player of the Year honors. In 1977 he was traded to Oakland and then to Texas, where he finished with a 10–6 mark for the Rangers. His career ended where it began, in Pittsburgh, in 1979 as the team sought help from the stretch-drive pitcher.

After his final season, Ellis was encouraged to seek help for drug and alcohol problems, and the flamboyant righthander changed his life dramatically. He later worked as a counselor to help others fight addiction. He offered advice and assistance to major leaguers who seem to have sought advice for their problems, but preferred to work with young street addicts in his position as the head of a drug rehabilitation clinic.

Dick Ellsworth

Ellsworth, Richard Clark **P**
1958,1960–71 B:3/22/1940, Lusk, WY
Deb:6/22/1958, CHI NL BL/TL 6'4", 195

W	L	PCT	G	SH	IP	BB	SO	ERA
115	137	.456	407	9	2155^{2}	595	1140	3.72

The Chicago Cubs signed 18-year-old lefthander Dick Ellsworth for a $50,000 bonus in 1958, and by 1960 he had a regular spot in the rotation, along with fellow phenoms Dick Drott, Glen Hobbie, and Don Cardwell. While Ellsworth surrendered more than his share of homers, including a league-leading 34 in 1964, he developed into a decent pitcher. In 1963, his peak year, he posted a record of 22–10.

Ellsworth, who attended the same high school in Fresno, California, that produced Tom Seaver and Jim Maloney, did not always find the Cub experience rewarding. "Playing with the Cubs, you felt like everybody was waiting for the other team to win. In the late innings, especially, we'd figure out a way to lose somehow or other," he said.

Ellsworth was selected for the 1964 NL All-Star squad but did not pitch. After he led the league in losses in 1966, the Cubs traded him to the Phillies, and he soon moved on to the Red Sox. With Boston he regained his effectiveness, going 16–7 in 1968.

In 1969 he was dealt to the Indians in a controversial deal that also sent popular Red Sox first baseman Ken "Hawk" Harrelson to Cleveland. Ellsworth never posted a winning record after the trade and ended his career with the Milwaukee Brewers in 1971.

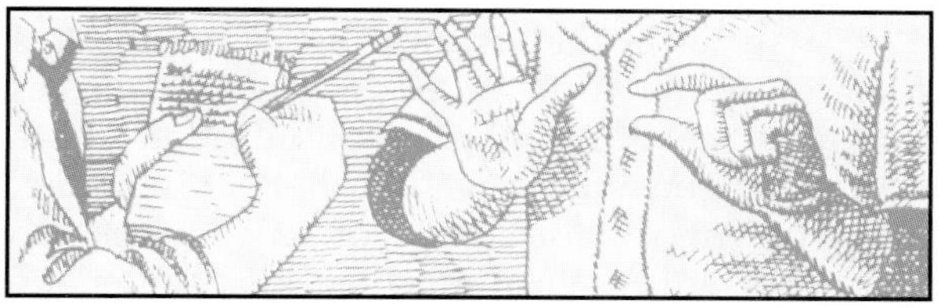

Bob Emslie

Emslie, Robert Daniel **P**

1883–85, U(1891–1924) B:1/27/1859, Guelph, Ontario, Canada D:4/26/1943, St. Thomas, Ontario, Canada Deb:7/25/1883, BAL AA BR/TR 5'11"

W	L	PCT	G	SH	IP	BB	SO	ERA
44	44	.500	91	5	792¹	165	362	3.19

National League umpire "Blind Bob" Emslie was working the bases in 1908 when the famous "Merkle Boner" occurred. Because Emslie had not seen the play ("I had to fall to the ground to keep [Al Bridwell's batted] ball from hitting me," as he later wrote in his report to NL president Harry Pulliam), home plate umpire Hank O'Day took charge and called Merkle out—a decision that ultimately cost New York the pennant.

The duties of umpiring weighed so heavily on Emslie that he went completely bald and on umpired wearing a hairpiece, which earned him another uncomplimentary nickname, "Wig." Because Emslie's nerves were so shaky, his partner, the younger Bill Klem, took over the duties of home plate umpire full-time—a practice he continued after Emslie retired.

As on American Association pitcher, Robert Daniel Emslie went 32–17 with a 2.75 ERA for the 1884 Baltimore Orioles. He started the following season by going 3–10, then signed with the AA Philadelphia Athletics in midseason and went 0–4. That spelled the end of one career and the beginning of another. He made his debut as an umpire in 1891.

Emslie was an expert rifle shot and once bet John McGraw $500 that he could outshoot him firing at apples placed at second base. The scrappy manager refused the dare. "Maybe you can see the apples, but you can't see baseballs," huffed McGraw.

Joe Engel

Engel, Joseph William **P**

1912–15,1917,1919–20 B:3/12/1893, Washington, DC D:6/12/1969, Chattanooga, TN Deb:5/30/1912, WAS AL BR/TL 6'1½", 183

W	L	PCT	G	SV	IP	BB	SO	ERA
17	23	.425	102	4	407¹	242	151	3.38

Before there was a Bill Veeck, there was Chattanooga's Joe Engel. Known as the "Barnum of Baseball," Engel enlivened games with such stunts as bringing in a female pitcher to face Babe Ruth, raffling off a house (car in the garage included) at a minor league stadium that bore his name, and trading shortstop Johnny Jones to Charlotte for a 25-pound turkey. Later he invited reporters over for a turkey dinner. "I still think I got the worst of that deal," Engel said. "That was a mighty tough turkey."

Engel started as a pitcher for the Senators in his native Washington, D.C., but his career never took flight. He made brief stops at Cincinnati and Cleveland. Earlier, he had performed in vaudeville and once led an elephant down Pennsylvania Avenue.

Following Engel's playing days, he was hired by Clark Griffith as Washington's one-man scouting bureau. Among his finds were Bucky Harris, Ossie Bluege, Goose Goslin, and Joe Cronin. He also scouted Cronin for Griffith's niece. "Tall and handsome, so be dolled up to meet him," advised Engel. The two eventually married.

In 1929, Engel became president of the Southern Association's Chattanooga Lookouts, remaining with the club until his death in 1969. Early in his tenure he constructed Engel Stadium, long considered one of the finest and best-maintained minor league facilities.

Clyde Engle

Engle, Arthur Clyde **OF-1B-3B**

1909–16 B:3/19/1884, Dayton, OH D:12/26/1939, Boston, MA Deb:4/12/1909, NY AL BR/TR 5'10", 190

G	AB	R	H	HR	RBI	OBP	SLG	AVG
836	2822	373	748	12	318	.335	.341	.265

Clyde Engle is best known for hitting a flyball that should have been an easy out but was not. In the 10th inning of the deciding eighth game of the 1912 World Series, Boston utility man Engle led off against the Giants' Christy Mathewson, pinch-hitting for Smokey Joe Wood, a good-hitting pitcher, who had injured his hand in the top of the inning. The Red Sox were down 2–1 as Engle lifted an easy fly to center fielder Fred Snodgrass. Snodgrass settled under it—and dropped it.

"Any high schooler could have caught it with ease," commented Fred Lieb. "The only possible excuse... was that he'd had too much time to think while the ball was in the air." Engle scored on Tris Speaker's single. Minutes later Larry Gardner's long sacrifice to right brought home Steve Yerkes with the winning run—and Snodgrass' error became his "$12,000 Muff."

Engle, nicknamed "Hack" because his strength reminded observers of the powerful wrestler Hackenschmidt, was a teammate of Ty Cobb and Nap Rucker on the 1905 Augusta Tourists. Detroit was originally considering Engle's purchase (the Tigers had an option to buy any player they wished off the Augusta roster for $700), but Sally League umpire Bill "Lord" Byron advised Detroit that Cobb was the better bet.

Woody English

English, Elwood George **SS-3B**

1927–38 B:3/2/1907, Fredonia, OH D:9/26/1997, Newark, OH Deb:4/26/1927, CHI NL BR/TR 5'10", 155

G	AB	R	H	HR	RBI	OBP	SLG	AVG
1261	4746	801	1356	32	422	.366	.378	.286

The Chicago Cubs paid $50,000 for English's contract in 1927, and he helped them win a pennant in 1929. He did not have a good World Series. Batting second, he hit just .190 and made an error that led to three Philadelphia runs.

Nevertheless, English was a good defensive player. He lacked power at the plate, but made up for it with a knack for drawing walks. In a game on August 19, 1930, he scored five runs. His combined total of 314 walks and hits in 1930 is among the best in National League history. He scored more than 100 runs three times, with a personal high of 152 in 1930.

Woody's Cubs again won the pennant in 1932, and again his performance was less than memorable, as he batted just .176. English played in the first All-Star Game in 1933 and unsuccessfully pinch-hit for Cub teammate Lon Warneke in the seventh inning.

Del Ennis

Ennis, Delmer **OF**

1946–59 B:6/8/1925, Philadelphia, PA D: 2/8/1996, Huntingdon Valley, PA Deb:4/28/1946, PHI NL BR/TR 6', 195

G	AB	R	H	HR	RBI	OBP	SLG	AVG
1903	7254	985	2063	288	1284	.341	.472	.284

A year before Jackie Robinson won the first Baseball Writers Association of America Rookie of the Year Award in 1947, Phillies outfielder Del Ennis captured the first-ever *Sporting News* Rookie of the Year honor. He was among the top five in the National League that year in home runs, slugging percentage, total bases, and batting average (a career-high .313).

For a decade Ennis was one of the top run producers in the league. From 1948 through 1957 he drove in fewer than 95 runs only once and topped the 100 mark seven times. He reached personal peaks with 31 homers and a league-leading 126 RBIs in 1950 as the Phillies won their first pennant since 1915. On July 23, 1955, Ennis hit three homers in one game.

Ennis was an all-time favorite of Philadelphia fans, an eternal "Whiz Kid." In 1983, he was chosen as a member of the Phillies' Centennial Team on the occasion of upon the club's 100th anniversary.

Mike Epstein

Epstein, Michael Peter **1B**

1966–74 B:4/4/1943, Bronx, NY Deb:9/16/1966, BAL AL BL/TL 6'3½", 230

G	AB	R	H	HR	RBI	OBP	SLG	AVG
907	2854	362	695	130	380	.360	.424	.244

In 1966, Epstein, a former University of California fullback, was named the International League Player of the Year and *The Sporting News* Minor League Player of the Year. Unfortunately, he performed his feats for the Rochester Red Wings, a farm team of the Baltimore Orioles, who already had a massive power-hitting first baseman in John "Boog" Powell.

Unable to find a place in Baltimore's starting lineup, Epstein jumped from the team in May 1967. That helped get him traded to the Washington Senators. In his first at bat against Baltimore, he unloaded a grand slam.

Epstein's big league career spanned nine seasons, and he enjoyed some success with the Ted Williams–managed Senators, for whom he slugged 30 homers in 1969, and with Oakland, batting .270 with 26 home runs for the A's in 1972. But "Superjew," as Epstein was affectionately known, never lived up his hype as "the next Hank Greenberg" or to the expectations that his minor league record and impressive physique had prompted.

Scott Erickson

Erickson, Scott Gavin **P**

1990–* B:2/2/1968, Long Beach, CA Deb:6/25/1990, MIN AL BR/TR 6'4, 224

W	L	PCT	G	SH	IP	BB	SO	ERA
130	108	.546	310	16	2013^2	697	1111	4.27

Scott Erickson's durability and superior sinking fastball made him a highly sought-after prospect. The New York Mets, Houston Astros, and Toronto Blue Jays each drafted the big Californian, but Erickson turned them all down. In 1989 the Minnesota Twins drafted him after he set a University of Arizona record with 18 wins. He signed and was in the major leagues just a year later. In half a season he posted an 8–4 record with a sparkling 2.87 ERA.

Erickson's first full season was the best year of his career. He won 12 consecutive games, including back-to-back shutouts. He led the American League with 20 wins and finished second to Roger Clemens in the 1991 Cy Young Award balloting. The upstart Twins advanced to the World Series, ultimately winning the title from the St. Louis Cardinals in seven games.

After a solid campaign in 1992, disaster struck Erickson a year later: an 8–19 record and an unsightly .305 opponents' batting average. He tossed a no-hitter against the Milwaukee Brewers on April 27, 1994, but his final mark that year was 8–11 and a career-worst 5.44 ERA. In the Minnesota clubhouse, teammates were tiring of the pitcher's list of excuses for his struggles—from the Metrodome turf that turned groundouts into singles, to the departure of slick-fielding shortstop Greg Gagne, to poor pitch-calling by Twins catchers. On July 7, 1995, the Twins dealt Erickson to the Baltimore Orioles for two minor leaguers.

After a slow start with his new club, Erickson reeled off five straight wins to close the '95 season. The natural grass at Camden Yards, plus an exceptional defensive infield, helped the groundball specialist win a combined 60 games in his first four full seasons in Baltimore. He led the league in starts, innings pitched, and complete games in 1998. Despite an ERA of 4.81, Erickson won 15 games for the O's in 1999.

Carl Erskine

Erskine, Carl Daniel **P**

1948–59 B:12/13/1926, Anderson, IN Deb:7/25/1948, BRO NL BR/TR 5'10", 165

W	L	PCT	G	SH	IP	BB	SO	ERA
122	78	.610	335	14	1718^{2}	646	981	4.00

"Oisk" was an integral part of Brooklyn's powerful "Boys of Summer" teams that won six pennants in 10 years. He also pitched two no-hitters in that bandbox known as Ebbets Field. Long after his playing days were over, Erskine still treasured the Brooklyn experience. "When we started to win with Jackie Robinson as a superstar, it lifted the whole borough," he recalled. "The memory of the Dodgers is bright, young, and vital, like when a young person dies. People won't surrender that memory, and have sustained it for years."

Erskine pitched almost his entire career in pain. His problems began almost as soon as he was called up from Fort Worth in 1948. He won two games in relief and then was given a starting assignment by manager Burt Shotton. "In the seventh inning, I threw my fastball to Bill Nicholson and I felt a sharp, hot twinge in my right shoulder," Erskine recalled. "I finished the game in extreme discomfort, and we won, 6–4. For two days, I couldn't raise my right arm."

He was afraid to mention it to anyone, but four days later, when he was defeating the Phils, 1–0, in the seventh inning, the pain became so intense that he had to tell Shotton. "Why, son, you're pitching a shutout," was all the manager said, and he left him in to finish. Four days later Erskine started again. "I did some real damage," he admitted. "I pulled a muscle away from the bone in my right shoulder and I scarred the muscles up around the area of the tear."

By 1951 Erskine was part of the starting rotation, going 16–12. He also played a small part in the legend of the "Shot Heard 'round the World." Dodgers manager Chuck Dressen decided to pull Don Newcombe in the ninth inning of the third and deciding game against the Giants. Erskine and Ralph Branca were warming up. When Dressen asked bullpen coach Clyde Sukeforth if both pitchers were ready, he supposedly answered, "Erskine just bounced a curve." Branca surrendered Bobby Thomson's legendary homer, and the rest is history.

Erskine went 14–6 the next season and split two decisions as the Yankees beat the Dodgers in the Series. Then came his career year. In 1953 he was 20–6 but made his biggest headlines in the World Series. Although he had been knocked out early in the Series opener, Dressen asked Erskine if he could pitch Game 3 in front of the home folks. Erskine broke Howard Ehmke's record of 13 strikeouts in a World Series game by fanning 15 in a 3–2 win. He finished dramatically, striking out the side—Don Bollweg, Johnny Mize, and Joe Collins—in the ninth.

Erskine pitched his first no-hitter on June 19, 1952, against the Cubs. The gem helped boost his already substantial popularity in Brooklyn. "When we would ride on the subway, everybody would know Pee Wee Reese and the Duke [Snider]," Erskine said. "After the no-hitter in '52, it put me in the scene. It was the door that opened for me to become established with that great team." His second no-hitter came on May 12, 1956, against the Giants.

After 1956 Erskine was used sparingly as his arm problems grew worse. The Dodgers released him in June 1959. "The day I retired they brought up Maury Wills, Larry Sherry, and Frank Howard, and that was the pennant," he said.

Nick Esasky

Esasky, Nicholas Andrew **1B–3B**

1983–90 B:2/24/1960, Hialeah, FL Deb:6/19/1983, CIN NL BR/TR 6'3", 205

G	AB	R	H	HR	RBI	OBP	SLG	AVG
810	2703	336	677	122	427	.332	.446	.250

Promising careers have come to an end for a multitude of reasons, ranging from wars to devastating diseases to beanball injuries. For Nick Esasky, it was a strange case of vertigo.

A first-round draft pick out of Miami, Esasky emerged as a highly touted third baseman in the Cincinnati organization. In 1983 the Reds brought him up to replace Johnny Bench, whose shot knees forced him to end his career at the hot corner.

The strikeout-prone Esasky never reached his potential with Cincinnati. The Reds moved him to first base, a more comfortable position for him defensively, but he fell into manager Pete Rose's doghouse. Rose preferred fiery players. Esasky was soft-spoken and gentlemanly. First base was also player-manager Rose's position. In his mid-40s, Rose batted .264 in 119 games in 1985 as he chased Ty Cobb's record for most career hits. Esasky, nearly 20 years younger, batted .262 in 125 games that season, but he hit 21 home runs.

A trade to the Red Sox after the 1988 season—and with it the opportunity to play in hitter-friendly Fenway Park—proved a godsend for the righthanded-hitting slugger. Esasky batted .277 with 30 home runs and 108 RBIs in his new surroundings. The career season came at the right time, allowing Esasky to sign a lucrative free agent contract with Atlanta, not far from his home in Marietta, Georgia. Unfortunately, the great career move soon turned into disaster. Bothered by dizziness, Esasky struck out 14 times in his first 35 at bats and committed five errors in nine games before leaving the lineup.

Esasky underwent a battery of tests before doctors determined that he was suffering from vertigo, caused by an ear infection. He tried medication, experimented with glasses, and performed balancing exercises to allay his problem, but none provided a long-term solution. The prolonged bout with vertigo kept Esasky out of action until 1992, when he attempted a comeback with the Braves' affiliate at Richmond. Esasky hit well in his minor league trial, but the dizziness did not fully dissipate, precluding a return to the major leagues.

Chuck Essegian

Essegian, Charles Abraham **OF**

1958–63 B:8/9/1931, Boston, MA Deb:4/15/1958, PHI NL BR/TR 5'11", 202

G	AB	R	H	HR	RBI	OBP	SLG	AVG
404	1018	139	260	47	150	.326	.446	.255

In the 1959 World Series Chuck Essegian did what no major leaguer had done before in Series play. The Los Angeles Dodgers outfielder belted two pinch-hit homers. Only Bernie Carbo has since matched Essegian's feat.

Essegian's first homer tied the score, 2–2, in the seventh inning of Game 2 against the Chicago White Sox. His second blast, while batting for Duke Snider in the ninth inning of the final game, came when the Dodgers were already up, 8–3. The Dodgers went on to win the world championship, four games to two.

Essegian's power was his primary virtue. He played for eight minor league clubs in seven years, hitting 139 homers, and for seven teams in six years of major league duty, smacking 47 homers, including 21 for Cleveland in 1962.

A 1954 graduate of Stanford, Essegian also played football for the university. He was a member of its 1952 Rose Bowl team.

Andy Etchebarren

Etchebarren, Andrew Auguste **C**

1962,1965–78 B:6/20/1943, Whittier, CA Deb:9/26/1962, BAL AL BR/TR 6'1", 197

G	AB	R	H	HR	RBI	OBP	SLG	AVG
948	2618	245	615	49	309	.308	.343	.235

Andy Etchebarren was a talented defensive catcher who, despite mediocre hitting, became an integral part of Earl Weaver's championship Baltimore Orioles in the late 1960s and early 1970s. Breaking in with the O's in 1966 he hit 11 home runs, collected 50 RBIs, and proved sufficiently adept at handling the fine Orioles pitching staff (and opposing base runners) to be named to the American League All-Star team. The O's won their first World Series at the conclusion of that 1966 season.

The next year Etchebarren was again an All-Star, although his hitting dropped to .215. Weaver began platooning him with catcher Ellie Hendricks. Neither was a strong hitter, and they were almost equally matched in other respects, too. Between them they helped the Orioles become American League champions in 1969, 1970, and 1971, and world champions in 1970.

In 1972 the club kept Etchebarren and traded away Hendricks to the White Sox, but the Orioles failed to win their division and the next year Hendricks rejoined Etchebarren in their dual role. The O's went to the playoffs again in 1973 and 1974. Never as an Orioles duo did Etchebarren an Hendricks both hit above .270 in the same season, but somehow their platoon worked well.

Traded to the California Angels in 1975, Etchebarren served as their regular catcher in 1976.

Nick Etten

Etten, Nicholas Raymond Thomas **1B**

1938–39,1941–47 B:9/19/1913, Spring Grove, IL D:10/18/1990, Hinsdale, IL Deb:9/8/1938, PHI AL BL/TL 6'2", 198

G	AB	R	H	HR	RBI	OBP	SLG	AVG
937	3320	426	921	89	526	.371	.423	.277

For players like Nick Etten, the World War II era was their only chance to shine. Etten spent eight years in the minors before he made it to the majors for good. He was the Phillies' first baseman in 1941 and 1942, although some will claim that in those years the Phillies were only masquerading as a major league team. Etten was traded to the Yankees. He commented, "Imagine a man in that environment hearing that he had been traded to the Yankees."

Etten played baseball at Villanova before the Great Depression forced him to drop out of school. He turned pro in 1933, and although he had a number of fine seasons in the minors and a trial with the Philadelphia Athletics, he was going nowhere when the Phillies acquired him before the 1941 season. At the age of 27, he found himself the starting first baseman for Philadelphia.

To everyone's surprise, he hit .311 with 14 homers and 79 RBIs as the Phillies finished eighth with a 43–111 record. Etten did lead the league in one category: errors by a first baseman (23), a feat he kept up for the next two years. He was last in the National League in chances per game in 1941 and 1942, and never finished higher than fifth in this category in his three years as the Yankees' everyday first baseman.

The Yankees acquired Etten for $12,000 and four marginal players. The war was on—players were hard to come by—and the Yankees had never really found an acceptable first baseman to replace Lou Gehrig. Enter Etten, a bit too old to be prime draft material, he was the perfect stopgap.

In fact, Etten outperformed his job description, In 1943, he had 14 home runs and 107 RBIs, second best in the American League. He still wasn't much of a fielder; after his 17 errors led the league's first basemen that year, he finished second in errors the next two seasons.

In 1944 Etten led the league with 22 homers. although his total was the lowest by a league leader since the lively ball came into use in 1920. Etten also drove in 91 runs and led the league with 97 walks. In 1945 he led the AL with 111 RBIs while hitting 18 homers. In a span of 15 games between July 30 and August 15, he had five homers and nine doubles, but not one single.

Then his tour with the Yankees was over; the troops were coming home. Etten hit .232 with nine homers and 49 RBIs in 108 games in 1946 and was waived back to the Phillies. He was out of the majors a year later.

Billy Evans

Evans, Williams G.

Umpire(1906–27)B:2/10/1884, Chicago, IL
D:1/23/1956, Miami, FL Deb:1906 AL

Billy Evans, people said, was the Bill Klem of American League umpires. He was the youngest major league ump ever and perhaps the only one to make the jump from Class C ball directly to the majors. When most umpires of the day would have used bluster and vitriol to settle an argument, Evans employed diplomacy. He felt fans were there to see a game, not him.

Evans was working as a sportswriter for the *Youngstown Vindicator* in 1903 when the umpire assigned to officiate a local baseball game failed to appear. Evans was pressed into service and did such a fine job that he was soon umpiring elsewhere. By 1905 he was a professional umpire in the Ohio-Pennsylvania League. At one point during the season, St. Louis Browns manager Jimmy McAleer observed his skills. McAleer liked what he saw and recommended Evans to American League president Ban Johnson. In 1906 at just 22 years of age, Evans became a major league umpire.

Evans' role in a 1909 incident during the Pittsburgh-Detroit World Series brought about today's four-umpire system. At this time only two umpires were used, but since 1908 two extra umps had been kept in reserve in the stands. The Series crowds at Pittsburgh were so large that temporary stands had been erected. Ground rules stated that a ball hit or even bouncing into the permanent stands would be a homer; into the temporary ones, a double.

In the third inning Pittsburgh's Dots Miller hit a line drive near the right-field foul pole that bounced into the stands. Evans could see the ball was fair but had no idea where it had bounded. Neither had his co-umpire Bill Klem. Evans marched to the outfield to determine where the ball had finally landed.

Evans asked the crowd, "Was the ball fair or foul?" They roared, "Fair!" Then one fan in the temporary bleachers stood up, shouting, "I caught it right here." Evans ruled it a double. But he was not yet out of the woods. Ban Johnson contended that it was inappropriate for a professional umpire to need any assistance from the fans. Evans pleaded guilty of needing assistance, but then suggested it would be better if, instead of sitting in a box, the two extra umpires were out on the field watching the foul lines. On October 12, 1909, the four-umpire system was employed for the first time. It became a standard World Series procedure in 1910.

On one occasion Evans made an umpiring decision far too soon. A dribbler bounded across the foul line and Evans instantly shouted, "Foul ball!" Then the ball hit a pebble, kicked back into fair ground, and came to a halt. Since this occurred in front of the first base bag, the ball was obviously fair. The call outraged the team at bat, but Evans calmly stated, "It certainly looks fair. It would have been a fair ball yesterday and it will be a fair ball tomorrow and for all the years to come. But right now, unfortunately, it's foul because that's the way I called it."

In Washington in September 1921, Evans and the fiery Ty Cobb met under the stands in what became one of baseball's more celebrated fights. Evans had called Cobb out on an attempted steal of second; the umpire had at one time boxed in the ring, but this fight had no rules and Cobb beat him mercilessly. After the brawl ended, Evans walked into the Tigers' clubhouse and shook Cobb's hand.

"As a matter of fact I was probably wrong," he said. "I challenged Cobb and there was nothing else he could do but accept."

Evans wore many hats. Even during his umpiring career he wrote a syndicated column, authoring *Billy Evans Says* from 1920 through 1927. Later he became a sports editor with the Newspaper Enterprise Association. He wrote a book called *Umpiring from the Inside* and helped on the first *Knotty Problems of Baseball*.

Following the 1927 season, Indians owner Alva Bradley offered Evans the newly created post of general manager, a position he accepted and held until November 1935. When, in a Depression-era economy move, Bradley tried to cut the general manager's salary from $30,000 to $12,000 Evans quit.

The next year he became farm director of Tom Yawkey's Boston Red Sox. In 1938 Evans saw a player he liked so much that he advocated buying the entire Louisville franchise just to obtain him—Pee Wee Reese. When Boston sold Reese to Brooklyn, relations between the club and Evans deteriorated. He quit the Red Sox in the autumn of 1940.

Evans temporarily left baseball, becoming general manager of the National Football League's Cleveland Rams until accepting the presidency of baseball's Southern League in December 1942. On December 14, 1946, he signed a five-year contract with the Detroit Tigers to be club vice president and general manager. During his tenure, lights were finally installed at Tiger Stadium. After his contract expired, Evans retired in August 1951.

Darrell Evans

Evans, Darrell Wayne **3B-1B-DH**
1969–89 B:5/26/1947, Pasadena, CA Deb:4/20/1969, ATL NL BL/TR 6'2", 205

G	AB	R	H	HR	RBI	OBP	SLG	AVG
2687	8973	1344	2223	414	1354	.364	.431	.248

Like fine wine, third baseman Darrell Evans seemed to get better with age. He became, at 38, the oldest player to win a home run title and the second oldest to hit 40 homers in a season. When he retired, only three players had exceeded his homer total (414) and had not yet been inducted into the Hall of Fame—Mike Schmidt (selected in 1995), Dave Kingman, and Reggie Jackson (selected in 1993).

Oddly enough, as a youth Evans was not a home run hitter. The Braves drafted him after the 1968 season, and they concentrated on changing his batting style. "I was strong enough but I didn't know how to pull the ball," he said. "(Eddie) Mathews taught me how to do it. He was a hitting instructor in the Braves system and he showed me how to turn my body, how to shift my weight, how to lay back on the ball, how to be patient—and how to pull it. He did more for me than anyone else in my career."

With Atlanta in 1973, Evans hit 41 home runs, while Hank Aaron slugged 40 and Davey Johnson added 43. It was the first time in major league history that three teammates hit 40 or more.

Evans hit for power but not for average, so he could easily be stereotyped as a free-swinging slugger. Actually, he was quite selective at the plate, and during the course of his career walked more times than he struck out, 1,605 versus 1,410. Twice he led the National League in bases on balls.

Atlanta traded him to San Francisco in June 1976. Although the terms of his Giants contract were lucrative, Candlestick Park hurt Evans' home run and RBI totals. In 8½ years in San Francisco, he hit more than 20 homers in a season only once; that was in 1983, his final year with the Giants. (Evans has attributed his resurgence at the plate in that and subsequent years to his sighting of a UFO in the summer of 1982.) When his second Giants contract expired in 1983, rights to negotiate with Evans were sought by 18 clubs, and he signed with the Tigers in December. With Detroit beginning in 1984, he shifted between first base and designated hitter, and he eventually regained his Atlanta-style power. In 1985 he rebounded, hitting a league-leading 40 homers.

Evans' renewed power continued. At age 40 in 1987 he hit 34 homers, topping Hank Sauer's previous record of 26 at that age. He hit 22 homers in 1988, his penultimate season.

Dwight Evans

Evans, Dwight Michael **OF-DH**
1972–91 B:11/3/1951, Santa Monica, CA Deb:9/16/1972, BOS AL BR/TR 6'2", 205

G	AB	R	H	HR	RBI	OBP	SLG	AVG
2606	8996	1470	2446	385	1384	.373	.470	.272

Despite a ballyhooed arrival, Red Sox right fielder Dwight "Dewey" Evans was often overshadowed by more spectacular teammates, such as Carl Yastrzemski, Jim Rice, Fred Lynn, Wade Boggs, and Roger Clemens. By the time he finally retired, however, the eight-time Gold Glove winner was among the most respected of all Red Sox alumni, with 2,446 hits, 385 homers, and 1,384 RBIs in 20 big league seasons.

Great things were predicted when Evans arrived in Boston. His scouting report in *Baseball Digest* was glowing: "Hits, fields and runs. Has chance to be top American League rookie in 1973." But eight years passed before Evans finally harnessed his talents and became a star. He took over right field full-time in 1974. Although his fielding was as good as advertised, and his powerful throwing arm was so respected that runners were simply afraid to challenge him, his hitting lagged. Evans never drove in more than 70 runs in any of those first eight seasons. The highlight of those years came with his glove, when Evans made a memorable catch of Joe Morgan's would-be homer in Game 6 of the 1975 World Series between the Red Sox and the Reds.

In 1980 Evans was off to his worst start ever. Just before the All-Star break, his average was a feeble .192. Red Sox hitting coach Walt Hriniak urged him to stop aiming at Fenway's inviting left field wall on every pitch. Before Hriniak stepped in, Evans was notorious for tinkering with his stance. "They called me the man of many stances; I had about 300 of them," he joked. But he vowed never to change his stance again and the improvement was immediate. Evans finished the season at .266, and in the strike-shortened 1981 season he led the league with 22 homers and 85 walks in 108 games. He also drove in 71 runs, the fourth best in the league. Evans had four 100-RBI seasons between 1984 and 1989 and averaged 32 homers in those years.

In the 1986 World Series against the Mets, Evans contributed two homers and nine RBIs, including a homer, a double, and three RBIs in the Game 7 loss. He finally began to slow down in 1990 at age 38 and was used exclusively as a designated hitter that year. The Red Sox then exercised their option to buy out the last year of his contract—it cost them $200,000. Evans spent the final year of his career with Baltimore.

Hoot Evers

Evers, Walter Arthur **OF**
1941,1946–56 B:2/8/1921, St. Louis, MO
D:1/25/1991, Houston, TX Deb:9/16/1941, DET AL
BR/TR 6'2", 185

G	AB	R	H	HR	RBI	OBP	SLG	AVG
1142	3801	556	1055	98	565	.353	.426	.278

For three seasons, Tigers left fielder Walter "Hoot" Evers was one of the better outfielders in the American League. Then for no apparent reason, his performance declined and he was just another player. Evers claimed he picked up his nickname because he "hooted" as a baby, although some said it was because he was a big fan of Hollywood cowboy star Hoot Gibson.

After spending three years in the service, Evers made the Tigers in 1946 and hit .266 in 81 games. He was a semi regular in 1947, hitting .296 with 10 home runs and 67 RBIs, and moved into the American League's upper echelon in 1948 when he hit .314 with 103 RBIs, striking out only 31 times in 538 at bats. Evers hit .303 the next season but drove in only 72 runs, then rebounded in 1950 with career-high numbers in batting average (.323), doubles (35), triples (a league-leading 11), and homers (21). He had 103 RBIs, and hit for the cycle on September 7, something no Tiger did again until Travis Fryman pulled it off in 1993.

The 1950 Tigers were 95–59, finishing three games behind the Yankees, but they collapsed the next season, going 73–81. The same thing happened to Evers, who hit .224 with 11 homers and 46 RBIs. The rest of his career, five seasons with seven address changes, wasn't much better. He was traded to the Red Sox in June 1952 in a nine-player deal. One of the ideas behind the trade: Evers was supposed to replace Ted Williams, who was in Korea. Instead, he broke a finger and hit .264 with 14 homers. He didn't come close to those numbers the last four seasons of his career.

Johnny Evers

Evers, John Joseph **2B**
1902–17,1922,1929 M(1913,1921,1924, 180–192)
B:7/21/1881, Troy, NY D:3/28/1947, Albany, NY
Deb:9/1/1902, CHI NL BL/TR 5'9", 125

G	AB	R	H	HR	RBI	OBP	SLG	AVG
1784	6137	919	1659	12	538	.356	.334	.270

A Hall of Fame second baseman, Johnny Evers is remembered in lore and legend. He was immortalized long before he made it to Cooperstown by Franklin P. Adams, whose poem beginning, "These are the saddest of possible words: Tinker to Evers to Chance" enshrined the old Chicago Cubs double-play combination in the popular mind. Evers is also credited as the man who used the rule book to wrest the 1908 National League pennant from the Giants. But for those who saw him play, "the Crab" was a baseball maniac who had no concern for other players, umpires, reporters, or fans.

Tinker and Evers had a fight early in their careers and played side by side for many years without speaking to each other. Tinker may have considered himself lucky because when Evers spoke, he rarely had anything nice to say. Of sportswriters Evers commented, "A ballplayer has two reputations, one with the players and one with the fans. The first is based on ability. The second the newspapers give him." Of fans Evers said, "The spectators take for granted really wonderful catches and unless the outfielder is compelled to climb a tree, turn a double somersault, leap over a 10-foot bleacher fence, or do something equally sensational, he scarcely attracts attention."

But Evers saved his worst vitriol for umpires and suffered numerous suspensions. Cubs owner Charles Murphy offered Evers a new suit if he would go two weeks without being ejected from a game. Evers won the suit but was expelled the day after collecting his prize.

His worst arguments were with Bill Klem, and in late 1909 he got into a real doozy with the umpire. Evers said he would leave the settlement of the issue to the league office. "That suits me," Klem replied. "I'll bet you five bucks you don't show up," challenged Evers. "You're on," Klem replied. Evers showed up but Klem did not. After that, whenever Klem umpired a Cubs game, Evers would scream about the five dollars Klem owed him and draw the figure "5" in the dirt with his bat at home plate. Finally the two met on a car of a train between Chicago and Pittsburgh and Klem paid off. He made Evers write out a receipt, which he then proceeded to tear into pieces in front of Evers.

Evers' nightly habit was to curl up in bed with the rule book, *The Sporting News*, and two candy bars. In 1908 his research paid off when he played a key role in the "Merkle Boner." On September 4 he complained to umpire Hank O'Day after Warren Gill of the Pirates ran off the field without touching second base in a force situation when the winning run had scored—the common practice of the time. O'Day said that if the play happened again he would call it. On September 23 the Giants' Fred Merkle failed to touch second base, and Evers secured a ball and made the force. Merkle was called out, and the play eventually cost the Giants the pennant.

Evers came from Troy, New York, and his hometown brought him the nickname "Trojan." He played minor league ball there before coming to the Cubs in 1902. The lefthanded hitter is generously listed at 5 feet 9 inches and 125 pounds; when he reported to the Cubs the team did not have a uniform small enough for him.

A career .270 hitter, Evers was known more for his glove than his bat. Yet he did have his moments at the plate. He hit .350 in the 1907 World Series, and became a better hitter in 1908 when he began to use his size to draw walks and better pitches. His .300 in 1908 was a career high to that point, and he again hit .350 in the 1908 World Series, with five runs scored.

Evers was a thief on the bases early in his career. In 1906 he and Frank Chance combined for 106, and they still rank among the best NL stolen base duos in a single season. On June 16, 1907, Evers stole four bases in one game.

A series of personal tragedies enveloped Evers in 1910. Late in the season he was the driver in an accident that killed his best friend. A few weeks later he lost his life savings when his business partner invested in two shoe stores that went belly-up. During the off-season Evers had a nervous breakdown, and soon after he caught pneumonia. Then his daughter died.

He played sparingly in 1911 and hit only .226. He came back in 1912 to have the best offensive season of his career, batting .341 with a league-leading .431 on-base percentage. Appointed player-manager of the Cubs in 1913, he batted .284 and led the team to a third-place finish, but was traded to the Braves in February 1914. Evers responded by leading the "Miracle Braves" to an unlikely pennant and an even more unlikely sweep of the favored Athletics in the World Series. He was voted the NL's Most Valuable Player that year.

After retiring from major league baseball, Evers operated a sporting goods store in Albany, New York, and was hired as superintendent of the city's Bleeker Stadium. In 1938 he was to appear on a radio program and did not know that Tinker was also scheduled to be there. When the two former combatants met, they fell into each other's arms. "Both of us could hardly keep from crying," Evers remembered.

Buck Ewing

Ewing, William Buckingham **C–1B**

1880–97 M(1890, 1895–1900, 489–395)
B:10/17/1859, Hoagland, OH D:10/20/1906, Cincinnati, OH Deb:9/9/1880, TRO NL BR/TR
5'10", 188

G	AB	R	H	HR	RBI	OBP	SLG	AVG
1315	5363	1129	1625	71	883	.351	.456	.303

"Buck" Ewing is widely considered the best all-around player of the 19th century. In 1919, more than 20 years after his final game, sportswriter Francis Richter wrote in the annual *Reach Guide*: "We have always been inclined to consider Ewing in his prime as the greatest player of the game from the standpoint of supreme excellence in all departments—batting, catching, fielding, baserunning, throwing, and Baseball brains—a player without a weakness of any kind, physical, mental, or temperamental."

Ewing's accomplishments are even more impressive considering the rigors of the catcher's role in the 1880s. The facemask (introduced in 1875) was barely padded, and a foul tip to the mask was the equivalent of a punch in the face. The catcher's mitt offered only marginal protection. The invention of shin guards was 20 years in the future. To compound matters, the pitching distance was only 45 feet, allowing a catcher almost no reaction time on a poorly thrown pitch.

With no runners on base, many catchers moved back from the plate to catch the ball on one bounce, but as soon as a man was on base the backstop had to move closer to the plate and take his chances. Bunting and basestealing were integral elements of the game, and consequently the 19th-century catcher did more running and throwing than his modern counterpart. It was such an exhausting job that no catcher was expected to play every game. Ewing, who some believe was the first to adopt the now-traditional catcher's squat, was considered a workhorse, but even he never caught more than 97 games in a season.

A consistently good hitter, Ewing bettered .300 in 11 of his 18 seasons but was valued more for his leadership and defensive ability. His throwing arm was legendary. Reports say he often threw out runners without rising from his squatting position behind the plate. An outstanding leader on the field throughout his playing career, he gained further respect when he later turned to managing.

Ewing began his playing career in 1878 with the independent Mohawk Browns and Buckeyes. In 1880 he played for Rochester of the National Association. After playing only 13 games and hitting .148 he signed with the Troy Haymakers, then in their second season in the National League. In 13 September games, he gave little indication of his hitting ability, batting only .178. But his strong arm impressed everyone. As his hitting improved, he spent the next two seasons as Troy's regular catcher.

The Troy Haymakers were expelled from the National League after the 1882 season. When John B. Day was awarded franchises for New York City in both the National League and the American Association, he purchased the Troy club and divided its players between the two teams. Ewing joined the National League club, the Gothams.

In his first season in New York Ewing lifted his batting average to .303 and led the league with 10 home runs. In 1884 he led the league in triples, with 20. When he topped the .300 mark in 1885 he began a string of nine straight .300-plus seasons.

Ewing was not especially fast, but he studied pitchers carefully and became a feared base runner. Until 1898 a stolen base was credited to a runner who took an extra base on a hit or an out, so it is difficult to interpret Ewing's 354 career stolen bases in modern terms. When compared to his contemporaries, however, his record is more than respectable.

Day's American Association team outperformed the Gothams in its first few seasons. But when the owner realized that there was more money to be made in the National League, he gutted the other club and transferred most of its better players to the Gothams. Manager Jim Mutrie, noting that many of his players were unusually tall, began calling them his "giants." The Gotham name was soon abandoned and the franchise has been known as the Giants ever since.

They won their first National League pennant in 1888. Ewing batted .306, contributed his usual exceptional defense, and helped ace pitchers Tim Keefe and Mickey Welch win 61 of New York's 84 victories. In the World Series between the Giants and the American Association champion St. Louis Browns, he hit .346 with two triples and a home run to pace New York's victory.

The Giants repeated as champions in 1889, but were unable to defend their crown in 1890 because of the Brotherhood War. In 1885 Ewing helped found the Brotherhood, a benevolent association and protective organization for players. By 1889 the group was engaged in an all-out fight with the club owners. The immediate cause of the conflict was the owners' plan to rank all players, paying them between $2,500 and $1,500 according to criteria established by the owners. The players, with few bargaining rights to begin with, now found themselves with none.

In a daring move, they started their own Players' League in 1890. Ewing was named player-manager of the New York entry, which finished in third place. Although most of baseball's stars played in the new league, it failed after a single season. The players couldn't get along with the investors, and the fans grew disgusted with the whole situation. Most of the teams in all three leagues lost money in 1890, but only the established National League teams were in a position to absorb the losses. The American Association folded two years later.

Ewing went back to the Giants in 1891, but an arm injury limited him to 14 games. His arm, once the marvel of baseball, never recovered, and Ewing played his final seasons at first base or in the outfield. Traded to Cleveland in 1893 for infielder George Davis, he responded with perhaps his best year at the plate, hitting .344 with 122 RBIs.

Cincinnati, one of the league's weaker teams, acquired him as its manager in 1895; the club finished above .500 for five straight seasons, coming in third twice. In 1900 Ewing became the manager of the New York Giants, but the team had so deteriorated under owner Andrew Freedman that he was helpless. He retired at midseason.

Ewing closed his career with a .303 lifetime average and 1,129 runs scored in only 1,315 games. He became reasonably wealthy, thanks to some real estate investments in the West, but he developed diabetes and died in 1906. His reputation survived, however. In 1932, when Mickey Cochrane was at his peak, many old-timers still insisted that Buck Ewing was the greatest catcher of all time. In 1939 he became the first catcher elected to the Hall of Fame.

Red Faber

Faber, Urban Charles **P**

1914–33 B:9/6/1888, Cascade, IA D:9/25/1976, Chicago, IL Deb:4/17/1914, CHI AL BB/TR 6'2", 180

W	L	PCT	G	SH	IP	BB	SO	ERA
254	213	.544	669	29	4086^{2}	1213	1471	3.15

Hall of Famer Urban "Red" Faber, a four-time 20-game winner, was the last of Chicago's 1919 "Black Sox" to remain active. He was also one of the last legal spitballers. Even when Faber was in his mid-40s, AL batters considered him a tough pitcher. "A batter can't guess with Faber," Goose Goslin said. "His only chance is to close the eyes and hope bat meets ball."

With the 3-I League's Dubuque Dubs, Faber pitched the first perfect game in minor league history on August 18, 1910. The next day Pittsburgh purchased his contract. The club sent him to Minneapolis, where he injured his arm and was released to Pueblo in the Class A Western League. There he experimented with a spitball. Faber said, "I never resorted to the spitter until I was obliged to. I nearly ruined my arm throwing curves." After winning 20 games with the Western League's last-place Des Moines club, he was purchased by Chicago for $3,500. But he earned his ticket to the big leagues by traveling around the world pitching against his own team.

Charles Comiskey's White Sox and John McGraw's Giants had scheduled a globe-circling baseball tour, and invited the rookie to accompany them as far as Seattle. As the teams were about to embark for the Orient, however, several Giants, including Christy Mathewson, decided not to go. Chicago manager Nixey Callahan suggested Faber pitch for New York, so the hurler dutifully boarded the ship. Only in the middle of the Pacific did he realize that he had no passport.

Faber won 24 games in 1915. Comiskey was so impressed that he named a moose at his Wisconsin hunting preserve after the spitballer. In September 1916 the moose escaped and startled a couple of farm lads, one of whom was carrying a rifle. The local paper headlined its story: "Red Faber Killed in Self-Defense."

Faber performed magnificently in 1917. When the Giants and White Sox faced each other in the World Series, he posted four decisions, losing Game 4 but winning Games 2, 5, and 6.

The White Sox went to the World Series again in 1919—the infamous Black Sox debacle—but Faber missed it because of a sore ankle. Catcher Ray Schalk once said, "If Red had been able to pitch, I'm sure there would have been no Black Sox scandal."

Faber rebounded the next year and won 20 or more games for three straight seasons. In 1921 and 1922 he led the AL in ERA, but after that was hampered by the sluggish White Sox. "We were a lousy team in those years," Schalk said. "Otherwise Red would have won 300 games easily." Faber was elected to the Hall of Fame in 1964.

Roy Face

Face, Elroy Leon **P**

1953,1955–69 B:2/20/1928, Stephentown, NY Deb:4/16/1953, PIT NL BR/TR 5'8", 155

W	L	PCT	G	SV	IP	BB	SO	ERA
104	95	.523	848	193	1375	362	877	3.48

At 5 feet 8 inches and 155 pounds, the diminutive Roy Face relied on one pitch, his forkball, to dominate National League hitters for years. He learned the forkball, today called a split-finger fastball, from Yankees reliever Joe Page. Later in his career Face threw the forkball 75 to 80 percent of the time. Gripped between the first two fingers, "it would come in hard and break whichever way it wanted to," he said. "Sometimes in, sometimes out, mostly down."

In 1959 Face had one of the most remarkable seasons ever enjoyed by a pitcher. He won 17 games before recording a loss, his first in 90 appearances. Combined with his five consecutive wins to end the 1958 season, he had 22 victories in a row and pitched an entire month, June 11 to July 12, without giving up a run. More than a few times he entered games in save situations and blew the lead, but he saw the Bucs rally behind him for the victory. On several occasions first baseman Dick Stuart made critical fielding errors that robbed Face of saves, only to follow with clutch home runs to give Face wins. By the end of the year, Face had registered 10 saves and finished at 18–1, setting records for winning percentage and relief wins in a season.

When Pittsburgh reached the World Series in 1960, Face saved the first three games; the Pirates went on to beat the Yankees in seven on Bill Mazeroski's ninth-inning homer. With the different utilization of relief pitchers in his day, Face saved 193 games in his 16-year career. He won 96 games in relief and eight more as a starter. He was at his peak in 1962, leading the league with 28 saves and posting a spectacular 1.88 ERA.

Ferris Fain

Fain, Ferris Roy **1B**
1947–55 B:5/29/1921, San Antonio, TX
Deb:4/15/1947, PHI AL BL/TL 5'11", 186

G	AB	R	H	HR	RBI	OBP	SLG	AVG
1151	3930	595	1139	48	570	.425	.396	.290

Ferris Fain had a curious career. He came up to the Philadelphia A's in 1947 and after four seasons was a .282 career hitter. Throw in an average of 80 RBIs and 119 walks a season, and the result is a pretty good first baseman.

Then Fain won the AL batting title in both 1951 and 1952—no easy task. Only five of the league's players have won consecutive titles since Fain: Ted Williams, Tony Oliva, Carl Yastrzemski, Rod Carew, and Wade Boggs. His marks were .344 in 1951 and .327 in '52, when he also led the AL in doubles, with 43, and on-base percentage, at .438. Starting in 1950, he made the All-Star team for five straight seasons. And even though he led the league's first basemen in errors in five of the six seasons between 1947 and 1952, Fain is third on the all-time list of assists per game.

Known as an uncompromising, brawling competitor, Fain hated to lose and hated making an out. He once said, "Some fellows can shrug off a slump. I can't. Baseball is a serious business to me. If I'm not going well, I can't make jokes about it." Once in a fit of anger Fain kicked the first-base bag and broke his foot. He was out for 37 days. His career declined dramatically after his second batting title because of knee injuries, and he was out of baseball by 1956.

On September 24, 1985, El Dorado County deputies arrested the 64-year-old Fain for growing marijuana at his Georgetown, California, farm. They confiscated 25 pounds of dried plants. An official report noted that Fain "claimed adamantly that he grew it for his own personal use, for medical reasons, and only occasionally would he share it with friends."

On December 9, 1985, he pled no contest and was sentenced to four months of house arrest while the district attorney's office argued that Fain was a "big-time dealer." In March 1988 Fain was arrested again and charged with possessing more than 400 marijuana plants.

Ron Fairly

Fairly, Ronald Ray **1B–OF**
1958–78 B:7/12/1938, Macon, GA Deb:9/9/1958,
LA NL BL/TL 5'10", 181

G	AB	R	H	HR	RBI	OBP	SLG	AVG
2442	7184	931	1913	215	1044	.363	.408	.266

Ron Fairly never hit 20 home runs. He never drove in more than 77 runs. He never had more than 28 doubles. He never won a Gold Glove Award at first base or in the outfield. But he was able to play in the majors for 19 full seasons and parts of two others because he was smart, because he always hustled, and because he never complained when he didn't play regularly.

Fairly was an All-American at Southern Cal. He signed with the Dodgers in 1958. In 1961, he hit a career-high .322 in 111 games, and over the next four seasons he played regularly and averaged 11 homers and 73 RBIs. When the Dodgers beat the Twins in the 1965 World Series, Fairly hit .379 and led both teams in RBIs, with six.

He was traded to the expansion Expos in June 1969. From there on he became a journeyman, doing stints with the Montreal Expos, the St. Louis Cardinals, the Oakland A's, the Toronto Blue Jays, and the California Angels.

Bibb Falk

Falk, Bibb August **OF**
1920–31 M(1933, 1–0) B:1/27/1899, Austin, TX
D:6/8/1989, Austin, TX Deb:9/17/1920, CHI AL BL/TL
6', 175

G	AB	R	H	HR	RBI	OBP	SLG	AVG
1353	4652	655	1463	69	784	.372	.449	.314

Bibb Falk earned his ticket to the major leagues by impressing the Chicago White Sox with his hitting and pitching in an exhibition game against his alma mater, the University of Texas. In three varsity seasons there he had been undefeated as a pitcher while batting over .400, and also starring as a tackle on the football team.

Falk arrived in Chicago in 1920 just as the 1919 World Series fix was coming to light. Without benefit of any minor league experience, he replaced Joe Jackson in left field for the last few games of the 1920 season and stayed there for eight years, hitting over .300 five times. Traded to Cleveland in 1929, Falk—who was known as "Jockey" for the riding his sharp tongue gave opposing players—produced three more .300-plus seasons, the last two primarily as a pinch hitter.

He managed in the minors in 1932 and then became a major league coach. In 1940 Falk became baseball coach at the University of Texas and, with the exception of three years spent in the service during World War II, remained there until 1967. He compiled a 468–176 record and led the Longhorns to win or share 20 Southwest Conference titles as well as NCAA championships in 1949 and 1950.

Cy Falkenberg

Falkenberg, Frederick Peter **P**

1903, 1905–11, 1913–15, 1917 B:12/17/1880, Chicago, IL D:4/14/1961, San Francisco, CA Deb:4/21/1903, PIT NL BR/TR 6'5, 180

W	L	PCT	G	SH	IP	BB	SO	ERA
130	123	.514	330	27	2275	690	1164	2.68

At one time, the rules allowed pitchers to doctor baseballs, and few were more practiced at the art than Cy Falkenberg. One of the few college-educated players to make the major leagues in the early 20th century, Falkenberg began his pro career with Worcester of the Eastern League after attending the University of Illinois. An 18-win season earned the tall righthander a shot with Pittsburgh in 1903.

Falkenberg struggled with Pittsburgh, which sent him back to the minors after he lost five of six decisions. In 1905 he returned to the majors, this time with the Washington Nationals. Although Falkenberg pitched creditably, he lost 37 games over a two-year span and was sold to the Cleveland Naps. He won a respectable 14 games in the American League in 1910, but would not achieve his greatest success until three years later.

Falkenberg peaked when he refined his practice of throwing the "emery ball." He rubbed the ball against a piece of emery board (similar to sandpaper), which he kept hidden in the heel of his glove. "All you needed," he explained, "was a spot less than the size of a 25-cent piece to make the ball sink or sail, depending on how you held it." By scuffing the ball in such a way—a perfectly legal practice at the time—Falkenberg's pitches moved unpredictably within the strike zone. He won his first 12 decisions to start the 1913 season, on the way to a 23–10 record.

Taking advantage of his career-best season, Falkenberg jumped from Cleveland to the Federal League, where he signed with the Indianapolis Hoosiers. Although he lost 16 decisions, he won 25 games and led the league in games, shutouts, innings pitched, and strikeouts.

Falkenberg struggled the following year, which he split between Federal League rivals Newark and Brooklyn. When the Federal League folded, he found himself back in the minors, where he won 16 games in the American Association. Falkenberg returned to the major leagues in 1917, but was no longer the same pitcher. He finished out his pro career by toiling in the minors over the next two seasons.

Duke Farrell

Farrell, Charles Andrew **C–3B–OF**

1888–1905 B:8/31/1866, Oakdale, MA D:2/15/1925, Boston, MA Deb:4/21/1888, CHI NL BB/TR 6'1", 208

G	AB	R	H	HR	RBI	OBP	SLG	AVG
1563	5679	826	1564	51	912	.337	.383	.275

Duke Farrell had an 18-year career as a major league catcher around the turn of the century, and has an entry in the record books more than 100 years old. He made his mark on May 11, 1897, playing for the NL Washington Senators. Nine Baltimore Orioles—John McGraw, Wee Willie Keeler, and others—tried to steal on Farrell that day, but only one—Joe Corbett—made it. And those eight caught stealing in one game gave Farrell a major league record that still stands. (Through the end of the 20th century, Brooklyn's Bill Bergen held the NL record, with seven, and the Athletics' Wally Schang the AL record, with six.)

Farrell could hit, too. A switch hitter, he finished with a .275 career average, had four seasons hitting .300 or better, and led the American Association in RBIs in 1891 with 110. It was while playing for the Boston Reds that season that he picked up his nickname. Before an exhibition game he was introduced as "the Duke of Marlborough" because he came from nearby Marlborough, Massachusetts.

Cap Anson bought Farrell for his National League Chicago Colts in 1888. Farrell never stayed with any team for more than three seasons, and his travels took him from the Colts to the Chicago Pirates of the Players, League, Boston in the American Association, the Pirates, the Giants, the Senators, the Brooklyn Superbas, and finally the hometown Boston Americans for his last three seasons (1903 through 1905).

Jeff Fassero

Fassero, Jeffrey Joseph **P**

1991–* B:1/5/1963, Springfield, IL Deb:5/4/1991, MON NL BL/TL 6'1", 195

W	L	PCT	G	SV	IP	BB	SO	ERA
92	83	.526	366	10	1465^{1}	507	1229	3.81

After eight years refining his pitching in the minors, Jeff Fassero made his major league debut with Montreal in 1991. The lefthanded groundball specialist notched eight saves for Felipe Alou's club that season. Fassero moved to a setup role a year later, and was a member of the starting rotation by 1993. He posted a 12–5 record and a sterling 2.29 ERA in his first year as a starter. He opened the 1994 season as the third starter on an Expos team that had the best record in baseball when the August strike halted the season.

Fassero spent two more seasons in Montreal. He went 15–11 with a career-high 222 strikeouts in 1996 despite minimal run support. Dealt to the hard-hitting Seattle Mariners in 1997, Fassero was pegged by many as a likely 20-game winner. He won 16, but the porous Mariners bullpen cost him six more victories with blown saves. Fassero registered his first postseason victory with an eight-inning, three-hit gem against Baltimore in the playoffs.

After Randy Johnson was traded in July 1998, Fassero opened the following season as Seattle's ace. The previously reliable lefty was inexplicably off his game. He lost 14 decisions and was banished to the bullpen before a late-summer trade to Texas.

Charles Faust

Faust, Charles Victor **P**

1911 B:10/9/1880, Marion, KS D:6/18/1915, Fort Steilacoom, WA Deb:10/7/1911, NY NL BR/TR 6'2"

W	L	PCT	G	SV	IP	BB	SO	ERA
0	0	—	2	0	2	0	0	4.50

Charles Victor "Victory" Faust shows up in the record books as a New York Giants pitcher who appeared in two games in 1911, pitched two innings, and gave up two hits for a lifetime ERA of 4.50 and a record of 0–0. In legend, though, he's the jinx-breaker who won two pennants for manager John McGraw and the Giants.

Faust was either an incredibly naive farm boy whose capers provided an amusing diversion during the 1911 and 1912 seasons or a shrewd, skillful self-promoter who was cannier than his simple, gap-toothed smile suggested. Perhaps he was a little of each.

According to Faust, one day in the early spring of 1911 he left his family farm near Marion, Kansas, to travel all the way to Wichita, the nearest city, to see the sights. He chanced upon a fortune-teller there, who, for a small sum, told him that he would join the New York Giants, become the greatest pitcher of all time, and lead his team to the pennant.

After returning to the farm and mulling over his destiny, Faust either set out determinedly to save the Giants or fell for a telegram sent by some practical jokers offering him a job on the team. He arrived at the Planter's Hotel in St. Louis on the morning of July 28, 1911, and asked to see John McGraw, for the Giants were in town on a western road trip. Directed to the Giants' skipper, the articulate Faust introduced himself and explained his mission. Surprisingly, McGraw listened to him and offered to let him try out during a game that afternoon.

Faust, 30 years old, 6 feet 2 inches, and skinny as a cornstalk, arrived wearing a bowler hat and dressed in his Sunday best. McGraw himself warmed up the newcomer. After arranging his signals with the manager, Faust went into a windmill windup like a man fighting a swarm of bees and delivered his best fastball. It arrived several moments later. That settled, McGraw told Faust to take batting practice and gave the boys on the team a wink. Faust bumped a grounder to short. The shortstop promptly and purposely booted it and threw wildly to second as Faust slid into the base, soiling his suit. He raced to third on another overthrow and then ran to home, where his trip mercifully ended in a final swirl of dust. The crowd in the stands loved it.

The Giants let Faust sit on the bench that day while they lost to the Cardinals, 5–2. When he showed up the next day, the Giants gave Faust a uniform, albeit one for a man about half his size. This time New York won.

Faust missed the Giants' train out of town when he went back to the hotel for a ticket that somehow wasn't waiting for him at the front desk. But he showed up in Boston a few days later, having made his way by hopping freight trains. Again he was allowed to sit on the bench, and that day the Giants began a winning streak that carried them into first place.

The superstitious ballplayers soon got the notion that Faust was a good luck charm. Exactly what McGraw thought is open to surmise, but he was enough of a psychologist to decide that if his team believed it could win with an oddball on the bench, Faust would stay on the bench. The Giants began paying Faust's traveling expenses. Sometimes when New York fell behind, McGraw would have Faust warm up in the bullpen, an act that almost always sparked a rally.

When the secret of Faust became known, a vaudeville promoter offered him $200 a day to go onstage and relate his baseball experiences. Only a few days into his run the Giants began losing. Faust believed the team needed him, so he jumped his contract. Whether it was luck, coincidence, magic, or some combination thereof, the Giants subsequently won the pennant. After it was clinched McGraw let Faust pitch in a couple of games, and in his brief career he acquitted himself better than many genuine ballplayers. He also came to bat a couple of times, though unofficially—his turns at the plate were essentially entertainments for the fans, and came after the third out of the inning had been made.

Unfortunately, whatever powers Faust possessed he lost during the 1911 World Series. The Giants fell to the Philadelphia Athletics. And once a charm is broken, say the experts in such matters, it remains broken.

So when Faust showed up again in 1912, McGraw refused him a uniform. He was, however, allowed on the bench. By the end of the season, the Giants won another pennant. Faust, however, couldn't take as much credit for the second one.

After failing yet again to persuade McGraw to return him to uniform, Faust complained to league president Garry Herrmann, who said he had no authority in the matter. At last Faust gave up. He was in California when the Giants lost the 1912 World Series to the Red Sox.

For the next few years Faust tried in vain to be reinstated. In December 1914 he was admitted to a mental hospital in Fort Steilacoom, Washington, and he died six months later of pulmonary tuberculosis. Whether it was a trick of fate or blind destiny, Faust had been a member of what was the best team in the National League in 1911, and he received some kudos for its success. In his autobiography McGraw wrote, "Wherever Charley Faust is today, I want him to know that I give him full credit for winning the National League pennant for the Giants in 1911."

Chub Feeney

Feeney, Charles Stoneham

NL President (1970–86) B:1921, South Orange, NJ D:1/10/1994

As president of the National League, Chub Feeney believed in maintaining traditional rules, which meant eschewing the designated hitter. But Feeney also broke with tradition at times, especially when it came to the idea of divisional play.

Feeney was the grandson of New York Giants owner Charles Stoneham and grew up as a baseball fan. As a youth, he worked as batboy for the Jersey Giants, a minor league team near his hometown. Realizing he did not have the ability to become a major league player, he decided to pursue a career as an executive.

He began working for Stoneham's Giants in 1946, eventually working his way up to the position of president as the team relocated to San Francisco. As the Giants' de facto general manager, Feeney engineered trades for key pitchers like Sam Jones and Billy Pierce, helping San Francisco win the pennant in 1962. He also played a role in the team's aggressive approach to signing black and Latin players.

Feeney held his position with the Giants until 1970, when he became president of the National League. Almost immediately, he had to deal with a strike by the umpires. Although Feeney officially succeeded Warren Giles in 1970, he had actually played an important role in the league's decision-making process the previous year. With the NL expanding from 10 to 12 teams, he supported the idea of splitting the league into two divisions. "A lot of clubs wanted to keep a 12-club league," Feeney said years later, "but with that many clubs, it just didn't make sense to have that many teams in one league." At Feeney's behest, the NL joined the American League in adopting a two-division format, with the winners of each division meeting in the Championship Series.

Four years later, Feeney took a different approach when it came to departing from tradition and implementing a controversial new rule: the designated hitter. Although the AL would adopt the rule, Feeney staunchly opposed the idea. National League owners soon voted down the DH, not even deigning to use it on a trial basis.

Feeney retired as league president in 1986, turning over the reins to A. Bartlett Giamatti. He made a brief return to the game as the president of the San Diego Padres, but soon opted for retirement. In 1992 Feeney suffered a heart attack six months after experiencing a stroke. Following a second heart attack, he died in 1994 at age 72.

Don Fehr

Fehr, Donald Martin

Executive B:7/18/1948, Marion, IN

As executive director of the Major League Baseball Players Association, Don Fehr guided the players' union through some of baseball's most turbulent times. His first involvement with baseball came when he worked on the Andy Messersmith case as a young attorney in Missouri.

Messersmith and fellow pitcher Dave McNally challenged the reserve clause, which the owners claimed gave them the right to unilaterally renew player contracts in perpetuity. The players argued that that the reserve clause bound them to their teams for only one year, and in December of 1975 an arbitrator agreed, making Messersmith and McNally free agents. Fehr was hired to oppose the owners' appeal of that decision in federal court, and he succeeded. It was the most significant victory to date for the players' union, and it set into motion a series of events that would dramatically change baseball over the next 25 years.

Fehr became the Players Association general counsel in 1977 working alongside Marvin Miller. Over the next few years, Fehr helped Miller make continued progress on behalf of the players, even through a 50-day strike in 1981. He became the union's executive director in 1984, two years after Miller retired. Where Miller was a fiery union leader, Fehr was more stoical—a colorless labor lawyer who didn't give the media the type of meaty quotes they were accustomed to getting from Miller. Fehr once said, "I'm not at ease in social situations where I have to make small talk." Although his public persona was very different from that of his predecessor, Fehr was mostly effective in continuing in Miller's footsteps.

There were problems, however, every time the players and owners had to negotiate a new collective bargaining agreement. In August 1985 Fehr led players on a two-day strike over the issues of salary arbitration. In 1990 players were locked out of spring training, with the season starting a week late as a result. Fehr steadfastly defended the gains the players had made and fought the owners' attempts to limit salaries and change the rules for salary arbitration and free agency.

Player salaries rose dramatically during the 1990s, and Fehr stood his ground as the owners proposed a plan to implement a salary cap in 1994, which they claimed was vital to baseball's survival. Fearing that the owners would implement their own plan unilaterally, Fehr led the players in a walkout on August 12, 1994. The strike lasted until the following April, forcing the cancellation of the 1994 World Series and delaying the start of the 1995 season. In the end, Fehr blocked the owners' attempt to implement a salary cap but agreed to a "luxury tax" on teams with the highest payrolls.

The strike alienated many fans and prompted congressional hearings, but perhaps something positive ensued as a result. Despite the fact that many serious financial issues remained unresolved, Fehr felt that in the years immediately following the strike, a much better rapport came to exist between the Players Association and the Commissioner's Office. With better communication, a relatively less adversarial relationship emerged, and Fehr felt somewhat optimistic that this might help resolve issues without having to resort to another work stoppage.

In 1999 Fehr said, "We don't always agree, we don't always get it done, but there is a much higher level of joint commitment to trying to avoid difficulties than we've had in the past, and what I hope will turn out to be very valuable working relationships are being developed. I would like to think that everybody will remember what we went through in '94 and do their level best to avoid it."

Bob Feller

Feller, Robert William Andrew **P**

1936–41,1945–56 B:11/3/1918, Van Meter, IA
Deb:7/19/1936, CLE AL BR/TR 6', 185

W	L	PCT	G	SH	IP	BB	SO	ERA
266	162	.621	570	44	3827	1764	2581	3.25

In the gathering gloom of one late afternoon game, Bob Feller took the mound. Opposing pitcher Vernon "Lefty" Gomez walked up to the plate and lit a match. "D'ya think that match'll help you see Feller's fastball?" sneered the umpire. "No," said Lefty. "I just want to make sure he can see me!"

While the yarn may be apocryphal, Feller's fastball was not. Observers said Feller was faster than Walter Johnson, Lefty Grove, or anyone who ever lived. After World War II the Army studied his fastball with a device that supposedly measured the speed of a moving projectile. The result, 98.6 mph, disappointed a few people. But the experiment was conducted just after Feller had spent nearly four years in the Navy, and he probably wasn't throwing as fast as he had been before the war.

Since then, several pitchers' fastballs, notably Nolan Ryan's, have been calibrated as faster, and the fastballs of old-timers such as Johnson and Grove were never measured with modern devices. But comparisons between one era and the next are pointless. Suffice it to say that Bob Feller was probably the fastest pitcher of his time.

He was certainly the most frightening. In his windup he pivoted away, turned his back on the batter, then exploded toward the plate. If the batter was lucky the ball zipped through the strike zone in a third of a second. But Feller could be wild, "pleasingly wild," as Hall of Famer Wilbert Robinson once said. Feller could never guarantee that his next pitch wouldn't drill the batter right in the side of his head. Batters went up against Feller with their hearts already safely back on the bench.

Feller grew up on a farm just west of Des Moines, Iowa, in the small town of Van Meter. Farm chores made him strong, and his father made him a pitcher. According to Feller, his father "made a home plate in the yard, and I'd throw to him over it. He even built me a pitching rubber. When I was 12, we built a ballfield on our farm. We fenced the pasture, put up the chicken wire and the benches and even a little grandstand behind first base. We formed our own team and played other teams from around the community on weekends."

Feller pitched five no-hitters at Van Meter High School. The Cleveland Indians took note and signed him to a contract with Fargo-Moorhead of the Northern League. But major league teams were forbidden to sign free agents still in high school, a condition the Indians had violated. Feller was advised to retire voluntarily in 1936 while his contract was transferred to New Orleans of the Southern Association.

When these contract maneuvers came to light, Commissioner Kenesaw Mountain Landis declared Feller a free agent. Feller and his parents then insisted that the young prospect preferred Cleveland, and he was allowed to sign again with the Indians, who paid a $7,500 fine.

In July 1936 the 17-year-old Feller made his debut for Cleveland in an exhibition game, striking out eight St. Louis Cardinals in three innings. From that moment on, he was major league news. After several relief appearances, he made his first start in mid-August and struck out 15 St. Louis Browns in a 4–1 victory. In September he struck out 17 Philadelphia Athletics, tying the major league mark and setting a new AL record. In 14 appearances in 1936, Feller completed five of eight starts, won five of eight, and struck out 76 batters in 62 innings. Then he went home to finish high school.

His windup, featuring a high leg kick and a unique pivot, launched the ball with tremendous speed. Yet many felt that his most devastating pitch was his big, fast-breaking curve. After two or three Feller fastballs, few batters could adjust to the bender.

In 1937, while still only 18 years old, "Rapid Robert" went 9–7 for the Indians, with 150 strikeouts in 149 innings. The next year he was named to the AL All-Star team for the first of eight times. He won 17 games and led the league with 240 strikeouts. On the last day of the season he struck out 18 Detroit Tigers, a major league record at the time. But he was also wild, walking 208 batters in 278 innings.

Feller put together three remarkable seasons starting in 1939. During those three years he won 76 games—an *average* of 25 wins a season! He led the league in victories, innings pitched, and strikeouts all three years, in complete games and shutouts twice, and in earned run average once. Yet despite finishing 24–9 in 1939 with 246 strikeouts, he couldn't lift Cleveland out of third place.

On April 16, 1940, Feller hurled a 1–0 no-hitter against the Chicago White Sox, the first Opening Day no-hitter in baseball history. The Indians were steadily improving and now boasted the crackerjack double-play combination of Lou Boudreau and Ray Mack and sluggers Ken Keltner, Hal Trosky, and Jeff Heath.

The Yankees limped out of the blocks, and by midsummer the pennant race was between Cleveland and Detroit. All was not well in Cleveland. Manager Ossie Vitt demoralized the team with his constant complaints to the press about the players' shortcomings. Tired of being humiliated in print, most of the Cleveland players signed a petition demanding Vitt's ouster and delivered it to the team owner. When word of the rebellion got out, the Indians were castigated as "crybabies" in every AL city. Meanwhile, the owner refused to remove Vitt.

Nevertheless, Cleveland remained in the race. On the season's final weekend Detroit played a three-game series in Cleveland. In need of a sweep, the Indians started 27-game winner Feller in the first game. The Tigers' staff was tired. Floyd Giebell was their sacrificial lamb and made only his second appearance of the season. Feller pitched brilliantly and made only one mistake, giving up a home run to Rudy York with a runner on base. But Giebell pitched a shutout to clinch the pennant for Detroit. Ironically, he never won another major league game.

In 1941 Feller went 25–13 with 260 strikeouts but missed more than a month of the season. The day after Japan bombed Pearl Harbor he enlisted in the Navy. While some baseball stars spent the war playing exhibition baseball games to build the troops' morale, Feller served as a chief specialist on the battleship Alabama, winning five campaign ribbons and eight battle stars.

Feller came back from the war better than ever. He learned to throw a slider, which, when added to his fastball and curve, made him even harder to hit than before. On April 30, 1946, he fired his second no-hitter, beating the Yankees, 1–0. He went on to win 26 games for the sixth-place Indians. Ten of his victories were shutouts.

Even more impressive was Feller's torrid strikeout pace. The Wheaties cereal company offered him $5,000 if he broke the existing strikeout record. Feller learned that the record was 343, set by Rube Waddell. Feller finished the season with 348 strikeouts, and then was told that Waddell's record was actually 349. Had he known the correct figure, he would doubtless have pitched another inning or two to pick up a few more whiffs.

In 1947 he led the league with 20 wins, 299 innings pitched, five shutouts, and 196 strikeouts. His total income, including his salary, endorsements, and a postseason barnstorming tour with other major leaguers against black all-stars, was estimated at $150,000, an enormous figure at the time. He incorporated himself as Bo-Fel Inc.

Feller began the 1948 season out of kilter. Ironically, with their ace pitching poorly, the Indians made a strong run at the pennant. Feller finally got hot during the second half and finished 19–15, nailing down his seventh strikeout crown. Meanwhile, Bob Lemon and Gene Bearden each

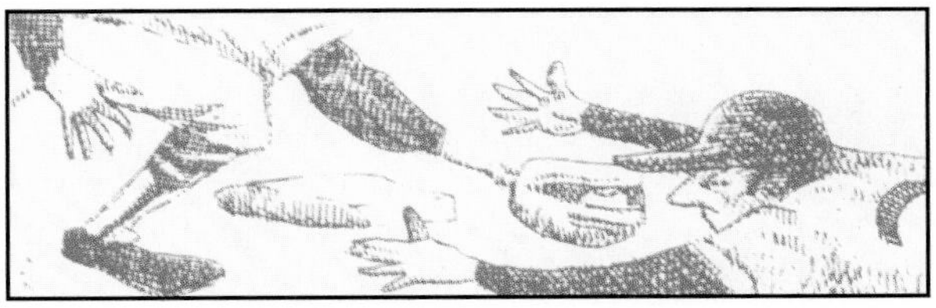

won 20 games for the Tribe. They beat the Red Sox, 8–3, in a one-game playoff, and Cleveland won its first flag since 1920.

Feller opposed the Braves' Johnny Sain in Boston to open the World Series. Both pitched shutout ball until the bottom of the eighth. Feller walked a batter, who was in turn sacrificed to second. Then, in the most controversial play of the Series, Feller seemed to pick Boston's Phil Masi off second base. Later, photos clearly showed that Masi was out, but the umpire had called him safe. Tommy Holmes followed with only the second Boston hit of the day and drove the run home. Feller lost the two-hitter, 1–0. He started Game 5 but was battered for eight hits and seven runs. Ironically, those were the only games Cleveland lost in the Series.

Although he no longer possessed a 98-mph fastball, Feller won 31 games in the next two seasons. In 1951 he compiled a 22–8 record, again led the league in wins, and for the first time also led in winning percentage. On July 1, against Detroit, he threw his third no-hitter, winning 2–1. At the time he was one of only three pitchers to throw three no-hitters (Cy Young and Larry Corcoran were the others). Sandy Koufax, with four, and Nolan Ryan, with seven, have since surpassed Feller.

In the mid-1950s Feller became a spot starter for Cleveland. He was 13–3 for the pennant-winning 1954 team, but didn't pitch as the Tribe lost the World Series to the New York Giants in four straight. He retired after the 1956 season, working in the insurance business and as an unofficial baseball ambassador who never feared to speak his mind.

Named to the Hall of Fame in 1962, his first year of eligibility, Feller was bothered by his Hall of Fame plaque, which lists his baseball career as spanning "1936 to 1941" and "1945 to 1956" with no explanation. He once suggested to Commissioner Peter Ueberroth that the plaque might be changed to reflect the facts. The commissioner answered that such a change would be "inconvenient." "Well," said Feller, "it was inconvenient to get shot at." In 1996 the Society for American Baseball Research helped make amends, as Feller became the first recipient of SABR's Hero of Baseball Award. Still throwing every day in his 80s, Feller claimed to have thrown a baseball more often than any man in history.

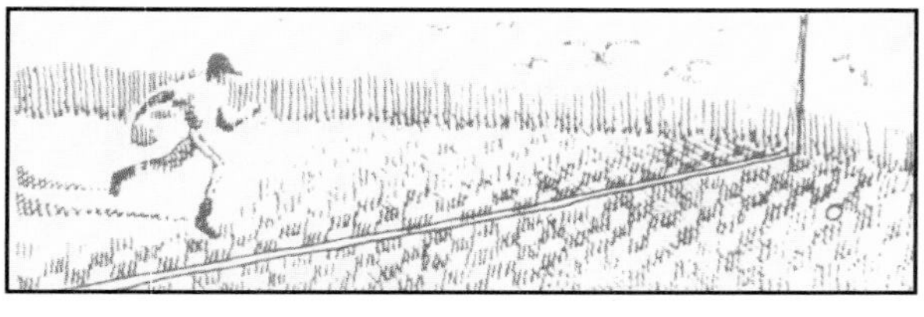

Happy Felsch

Felsch, Oscar Emil **OF**

1915–20 B:8/22/1891, Milwaukee, WI D:8/17/1964, Milwaukee, WI Deb:4/14/1915, CHI AL BR/TR 5'11", 175

G	AB	R	H	HR	RBI	OBP	SLG	AVG
749	2812	385	825	38	446	.347	.427	.293

Happy Felsch was one of eight members of the Chicago White Sox banned from Organized Baseball for life by Commissioner Kenesaw Mountain Landis for their role in the tainted 1919 World Series. A Chicago grand jury had actually acquitted the group—a "hometown decision" supported by the convenient loss of players' confessions. The commissioner held absolute power in those days, and the eight men never played another professional game. Although their case has been reexamined and treated in books and motion pictures such as *Eight Men Out* and *Field of Dreams*, Felsch and the other seven remain consigned to baseball infamy.

Felsch's personality was described as easygoing, which may account for his nickname. He never finished elementary school but had speed to burn and a good aptitude for batting. In 1917 he was at the top of the baseball world. He hit .308 with 102 RBIs to lead Chicago to the pennant, its first since 1906. In the World Series, Felsch batted .273 as the White Sox beat the New York Giants in six games. His home run in the fourth inning of Game 1 gave Chicago a 2–0 lead, and moundsman Eddie Cicotte made it stand up for a 2–1 victory.

At that point, Felsch was 26 years old, a center fielder with an arm that could cut down base runners and a .300 hitter for the best team in baseball. It all disappeared very quickly. In 1919 Chicago won the pennant by 3½ games over the second-place Cleveland Indians. It was the worst thing that ever happened to Felsch. The White Sox were heavily favored to defeat the Cincinnati Reds in the World Series, but they lost it, five games to three, amid rumors of involvement by gamblers. Felsch played in all eight games, batted .192, and made two errors.

He played one season after the 1919 Series and ironically produced one of the greatest campaigns ever turned in by a White Sox player. Chicago's record book still gives eloquent testimony to his monster of a summer. Felsch's 69 extra-base hits, 115 RBIs, .540 slugging average, and 300 total bases still rank among the top marks in franchise history. Hitting a career-high .338, with 14 homers, Felsch was in the prime of what could have been a brilliant career.

In September 1920, the story broke. A grand jury convened and made indictments. Felsch told his part of the episode and is said to have commented, "I'm going to hell, I guess. The beans are all spilled and I think that I am through with baseball. I got my $5,000, and I guess the others got theirs, too."

On August 2, 1921, a friendly jury, denied much of the evidence such as the confessions of Joe Jackson and Eddie Cicotte, acquitted the players of conspiracy to defraud the public. The spectators in the courtroom applauded. Even Judge Hugo M. Friend said he believed the jury had reached a just verdict. But acquittal or no, Landis made the decision to bar them from the game.

Afterward, Felsch continued to play ball for a decade on the sandlots of Milwaukee. He and reputed fellow conspirators Swede Risberg and Joe Jackson later sued the White Sox for back pay. On February 9, 1925, Felsch was awarded $661 plus interest that brought the sum to $1,166.

Bob Ferguson

Ferguson, Robert Vavasour **2B-3B**

1871–84 M(1871–87, 417–516) B:1/31/1845, Brooklyn, NY D:5/3/1894, Brooklyn, NY Deb:5/18/1871, NY NA BB/TR 5'9½", 149

G	AB	R	H	HR	RBI	OBP	SLG	AVG
562	2306	346	625	1	226	.305	.323	.271

When Bob Ferguson is mentioned today it's usually in reference to his odd nickname, "Death to Flying Things." Ironically, the descriptive phrase was originally and most commonly applied to his one-time teammate, Jack Chapman. Ferguson himself was better known as "Old Fergy."

Ferguson's career included service as a player, manager, umpire, and league president. Ferguson was probably the first switch hitter to play for an important team, in his case the Atlantics of Brooklyn in 1866. His batting was little better than ordinary, but he excelled in the field, on the bases, and as a team leader, serving as captain or manager of nearly every team he played on. Revered for his forthrightness, integrity, competitive spirit, and intelligence, Ferguson managed for 16 seasons, though none of his teams finished higher than third.

In 1870, when the Atlantics broke the Cincinnati Red Stockings' two-year winning streak, Ferguson drove in the tying run and scored the winning run. When the National Association formed in 1871 he joined the New York Mutuals for a season before returning to the Atlantics. A tireless campaigner for honest baseball, he became president of the National Association in 1872 and served through 1875 while continuing as a player and manager.

He remained active as a player through 1884, seeing action with both Hartford teams (in the NA and National League), and with Chicago, Troy, Philadelphia, and Pittsburgh. Ferguson umpired for a year in the National League in 1885 and then managed New York's American Association team in 1886 and 1887.

In 1888 he returned to umpiring, where his honesty, complete impartiality, and ability to make quick, firm decisions made him an outstanding arbiter. He put in two years in the American Association and one with the Players' League before physical infirmities forced his retirement from baseball.

Charlie Ferguson

Ferguson, Charles J. **P-OF-2B**

1884–87 B:4/17/1863, Charlottesville, VA D:4/29/1888, Philadelphia, PA Deb:5/1/1884, PHI NL BB/TR 6', 165

W	L	PCT	G	SH	IP	BB	SO	ERA
99	64	.607	183	13	1514^{2}	290	728	2.67

Had he lived longer, Charles J. "Charlie" Ferguson might have been remembered as the greatest player of his day, and perhaps of all time. In later generations only Babe Ruth would ever combine such marvelous hitting and fielding abilities with such magnificent pitching skills. Moreover, Ferguson hadn't even reached his peak when his life was suddenly cut short.

While pitching for the independent Richmond, Virginia, club, Ferguson attracted attention when he shut out Boston's major league team on four singles. In 1884 he signed with Philadelphia's National League team and produced a 21–25 record, creditable enough for a sixth-place club. But Ferguson was just getting started: he followed up with seasons of 26–20, 30–9, and 22–10. His ERA was a minuscule 1.98 in 1886, and he finished the season with 11 straight victories.

Yet pitching was only one of his talents. Each year Ferguson played more games in the field to take advantage of his batting, fielding, and baserunning skills. Twice he batted over .300 with good power. His long, loping strides made him a deceptively fast center fielder. On one occasion a race around the bases was set up between Ferguson and one of the league's fastest runners; Ferguson won easily.

Toward the end of the 1887 season Philadelphia had a chance to finish second, so for the final 17 games of the season Ferguson played second base when he wasn't pitching. During that span he hit .361, fielded .963—an exceptional mark at that time—and pitched seven games without a loss. Philadelphia won 16 games and tied one to reach second place.

The modest Ferguson was extremely popular with teammates and also won plaudits coaching Princeton's baseball team during the off-season.

There seemed to be no limit to his virtues, but his end came all too suddenly. In the spring of 1888 he contracted typhoid fever and died 12 days after his 25th birthday.

Joe Ferguson

Ferguson, Joseph Vance **C-OF**
1970–83 B:9/19/1946, San Francisco, CA
Deb:9/12/1970, LA NL BR/TR 6'2",200

G	AB	R	H	HR	RBI	OBP	SLG	AVG
1013	3001	407	719	122	445	.361	.409	.240

During his first three years of professional baseball, Joe Ferguson bounced back and forth between the Dodgers and their farm teams as a backup catcher. He finally thrived as a regular in 1973.

Given the starting catcher's job for the Dodgers, Ferguson put together a solid season both offensively and defensively, leading NL backstops by committing only three errors in 757 chances. He also hit 25 homers and 26 doubles, drove in 88 runs, scored 84 more, and walked 87 times.

The next year, however, Steve Yeager started behind the plate in Los Angeles, and Ferguson spent more time in the outfield. He slugged 16 homers in 1974, and his home run in Game 2 of the 1974 Fall Classic gave the Dodgers their only win in the Series.

Traded in 1976 to St. Louis and then to Houston, Ferguson caught 122 games and hit 16 home runs for the Astros in 1977. Reacquired by Los Angeles in 1978, he put together another power year in 1979 with 20 home runs. But subsequently his abilities declined, and he ended his career as a part-time player with the Angels in 1983.

Alex Fernandez

Fernandez, Alexander **P**
1990–* B:8/13/1969, Miami Beach, FL Deb:8/2/1990, CHI AL BR/TR 6'1", 215

W	L	PCT	G	SH	IP	BB	SO	ERA
103	83	.544	255	10	1708	536	1225	3.73

After just eight minor league starts, Alex Fernandez was pitching in a major league pennant race at the tender age of 20. At 22, he became the third-youngest pitcher in White Sox history to start at least 20 games.

Fernandez was drafted in the first round of the 1988 draft, but opted to attend the University of Miami. *Baseball America* named him Freshman of the Year after he put together a 15–2 record, 2.01 ERA, and 177 strikeouts in 148 innings with the Hurricanes, including a no-hitter against Maine. He transferred to Miami–Dade South Community College and fashioned a 12–2 mark with a school-best 1.19 ERA as a sophomore. Named National Junior College Player of the Year, Fernandez also won the Golden Spikes Award and the Dick Howser Award.

The White Sox selected Fernandez with the fourth overall pick of the 1990 draft. After eight minor league starts—the last one a 17-strikeout performance at Double-A Birmingham—he was pitching at Comiskey Park. With the White Sox battling the A's in the AL West, Fernandez went 5–5 with a 3.80 ERA in 13 starts. For the year—in college, minor and major leagues—he was a combined 23–8 with a 2.19 ERA in 258 innings pitched.

In his first two seasons, the hard-throwing righthander tried to blow the ball past hitters whenever he got into trouble. Many times, that got Fernandez into more trouble. Sent back to the minors briefly in 1991, he was back in the big leagues for good after giving up just three earned runs in 28⅔ innings at Vancouver.

Fernandez made believers out of everyone in the American League in his breakthrough year in 1993. He went 18–9 with a 3.13 ERA and 169 strikeouts in 247 innings—all career highs. He pitched well in the AL Championship Series, but lost both his starts despite a stingy 1.80 ERA in 15 innings against the eventual world champion Blue Jays.

Fernandez followed that with a solid 1994 campaign. He put together an 11–7 record with a 3.86 ERA and a career-high three shutouts in 24 starts before the baseball strike wiped away Chicago's chances of making the postseason for the second consecutive year. The White Sox stumbled to a distant third-place finish in 1995, but Fernandez again came through with a solid season. In 30 starts, he went 12–8 with a 3.80 ERA, pitching 203 innings and completing a career-best five games.

In the 1996 offseason Fernandez signed with the Florida Marlins, and in 1997 helped the fledgling franchise to its surprising world championship. A highlight of that season was a 1–0, one-hit, complete-game win over the Cubs on April 10. After being on the disabled list for the entire 1998 season, Fernandez returned to action in 1999 with a 7–8 record and a respectable 3.38 ERA.

Sid Fernandez

Fernandez, Charles Sidney **P**
1983–97 B:10/12/1962, Honolulu, HI Deb:9/20/1983, LA NL BL/TL 6'1", 230

W	L	PCT	G	SH	IP	BB	SO	ERA
114	96	.543	307	9	1866²	715	1743	3.36

Sid Fernandez made 249 starts with the Mets, but a relief appearance in the 1986 World Series may have been his greatest moment in New York. The Mets trailed the Red Sox 3–0 in the fourth inning of Game 7 when manager Davey Johnson called Fernandez in from the bullpen with a runner at second and two out. Fernandez, who had been denied a World Series start by Johnson, walked the first batter he faced, Wade Boggs, but then retired the next seven, four of them on strikeouts. The Mets came back, and Roger McDowell got the victory, but if it hadn't been for "El Sid," the Red Sox's 68-year championship drought might have ended at Shea Stadium.

Fernandez was not brought to New York to pitch out of the bullpen. The Mets plucked the stocky southpaw from the Dodgers along with Ross Jones for Carlos Diaz and Bob Bailor on December 8, 1983. Fernandez was pitching in New York midway through 1984 and, after starting the 1985 season in Class AAA Tidewater, he joined the Mets rotation for good.

He was a .500 pitcher his first two seasons, but blossomed to 16–6 in 1986 with 200 strikeouts in 204⅓ innings. Fernandez became the first native Hawaiian to play in an All-Star Game and struck out three American League batters—Brook Jacoby, Jim Rice, and Don Mattingly—in one inning (he also walked two). He fanned 14 hitters at Shea on September 1 and boasted the NL's second-best ERA at home (2.17).

Fernandez won 12 games each of the next two seasons. He was the team's best pitcher in 1989, putting together a 2.51 ERA over his final 24 starts, running up three double-figure strikeout games in a row, and fanning 16 in one outing. For the season, Fernandez recorded 198 strikeouts and missed the league lead by three Ks.

Fernandez limited batters to a .200 average in 1990, but finished with a 9–14 record, mostly because of a poor 1–9 road record. Injuries limited him to eight starts in 1991, but he bounced back with a fine campaign (14–11, 2.73 ERA, 193 strikeouts) in 1992. The next year, however, he was plagued by injuries, and left for Baltimore as a free agent after the season.

In nine years in the NL, Fernandez had never posted an ERA higher than 3.81, but he finished his first year in the American League with a 5.15 ERA, with two stints on the disabled list. In 1995, he had a 7.39 ERA in eight games and was released by the Orioles on July 10. But Fernandez found new life with the Philadelphia Phillies, posting a 6–1 record over the rest of the season, with a 3.34 ERA and 79 strikeouts in 64⅔ innings.

Injuries cut into his playing time again in 1996. Fernandez signed with Houston for 1997, but pitched just one game for the Astros before ending his career.

Tony Fernandez

Fernandez, Octavio Antonio (Castro) SS-2B-3B
1983–95,1996–* B:6/30/1962, San Pedro de Macoris, Dominican Republic Deb:9/2/1983, TOR AL BB/TR 6'2", 175

G	AB	R	H	HR	RBI	OBP	SLG	AVG
2082	7788	1046	2240	92	829	.350	.399	.288

Once the American League's best shortstop, Tony Fernandez was able to move to second base and third base without missing a beat. And his bat got better with each position change.

After posting a .321 batting average mainly as a second baseman in 1998, Fernandez moved to third base and flirted with .400 for the first three months of the 1999 season. He made his fifth All-Star appearance, and finished the year with a .328 average and 75 RBIs, both career bests. It marked the fifth time in his three tours of duty with the Blue Jays that he batted over .300. The native of the Dominican Republic spent 11 of his first 16 seasons as a mainstay of the Canadian team's infield.

Despite four Gold Gloves and a .980 career fielding percentage as a shortstop, Fernandez will unfortunately be remembered for a rare defensive lapse committed in Game 7 of the 1997 World Series. Playing second base for the Cleveland Indians, he committed a key error in the 11th inning that prolonged Florida's turn at bat. Minutes later, Edgar Renteria singled in Craig Counsell for the Series-winning run. It was only Fernandez's fifth error in 177 career postseason chances. The miscue soured an otherwise brilliant Series for Fernandez, who batted .471 and drove in both of Cleveland's runs in Game 7. He had helped the Indians reach the World Series with a home run in the 11th inning in Game 6 of the American League Championship Series.

Fernandez was the linchpin in the infield and at the top of the order when Toronto had its first success. He batted .333 in Toronto's first postseason appearance, a seven-game loss in the 1985 ALCS. Four years later he hit .350 with five steals in a five-game loss to the Oakland A's in the ALCS. After a season-plus stint in the National League, where he made the 1992 NL All-Star team with the San Diego Padres, the Blue Jays obtained Fernandez from the New York Mets during the 1993 season. His nine RBIs led all batters in the 1993 World Series as Toronto defeated Philadelphia in six games.

Fernandez signed with Cincinnati for the 1994 season, continuing to hit well, this time playing third base. He also made brief stops with the Yankees and Indians before heading back "home" to Toronto in 1998. After his stellar 1999 season with the Blue Jays, Fernandez signed a contract with the Seibu Lions of the Japanese Pacific League in January 2000.

Rick Ferrell

Ferrell, Richard Benjamin **C**
1929–45,1947 B:10/12/1905, Durham, NC D:7/27/1995, Bloomfield Hills, MI Deb:4/19/1929, STL AL BR/TR 5'10", 160

G	AB	R	H	HR	RBI	OBP	SLG	AVG
1884	6028	687	1692	28	734	.378	.363	.281

Rick Ferrell's 1984 election to the Hall of Fame by the Veterans Committee proved that hard work and longevity might someday be rewarded, even though Ferrell was the No. 3 AL catcher of his day, behind Bill Dickey and Mickey Cochrane. In addition, although his pitching brother, Wes, attracted more attention, Rick Ferrell's admittance to Cooperstown proved that it is ultimately possible to get out from under the shadow of a flashier brother, even one who has matinee idol looks and hits more home runs.

Ferrell began his baseball career with the Detroit organization, signing for a $1,500 bonus. In 1928 he batted .333 for the American Association's Columbus Senators but was not promoted. The Tigers appeared to be concealing him. Baseball Commissioner Kenesaw Mountain Landis, no supporter of the farm system, declared Ferrell a free agent, causing a bidding war for his services. The threadbare St. Louis Browns signed Ferrell, scraping together a $25,000 bonus and paying him a $12,500 salary. Ferrell joined St. Louis in 1929.

In 1932 Ferrell batted a career-high .315. But in May 1933 the Browns unloaded him to the Red Sox in Boston's first deal under Tom Yawkey's ownership. That season, Ferrell was the American League's catcher in the premiere All-Star Game and caught the full nine innings. Two weeks later, in a memorable game on July 19, 1933, both Ferrells hit home runs: Wes, off Boston's Hank Johnson; and Rick, off Wes.

On May 25, 1934, Ferrell reunited with his younger brother when the Red Sox traded for Wes. The siblings formed a successful battery, although they did not always get along. In one game, Wes shook off his brother's signals until finally the backstop shouted, "Throw anything you please. You can't fool me." Wes became incensed and tried to "powder that ball by him." Rick Ferrell, for his part, caught his brother's fastballs nonchalantly, as if they were changeups. The hurler became even more upset, but the result was a two-hit shutout. "Well, you pitched a pretty good ballgame," said Rick after the contest. "But if you'd listened to me, you would have pitched a no-hitter!"

In June 1937 the Red Sox sent the Ferrell brothers, along with outfielder Mel Almada, to Washington for pitcher Bobo Newsom and outfielder Ben Chapman. In May 1941 Washington sent Rick back to the Browns for pitcher Vern Kennedy. On June 8, 1942, against Washington, Ferrell got his revenge, pulling off one of the rarest feats in baseball, an unassisted double play by a catcher. In March 1944 the Browns traded him back to the Senators, where he finished his career in 1947.

Ferrell was a fine and durable receiver, but some have pointed out that this defensive specialist actually led the AL in passed balls in 1931, 1939, 1940, 1944, and 1945. The statistics don't show that he spent the last four years with the Senators, however. Ferrell was a good enough receiver at age 39 for Washington to buy his contract and have him catch their four knuckleballers—Mickey Haefner, Dutch Leonard, Roger Wolff, and Johnny Niggeling.

Dependable rather than charismatic, Ferrell was one of baseball's finest defensive catchers. He once held the record for most games caught in the American League (1,806), and although his brother Wes hit 10 more homers than he did in nearly 5,000 fewer at bats, there's only one Ferrell in the Hall of Fame.

Wes Ferrell

Ferrell, Wesley Cheek **P**
1927–41 B:2/2/1908, Greensboro, NC D:12/9/1976, Sarasota, FL Deb:9/9/1927, CLE AL BR/TR 6'2", 195

W	L	PCT	G	SH	IP	BB	SO	ERA
193	128	.601	374	17	2623	1040	985	4.04

Unlike his brother Rick, Wes Ferrell never was elected to the Hall of Fame. But in his day, Wes was the bigger star. He won 20 or more games in each of his first four big league seasons and hit more home runs than any pitcher in major league history.

Ferrell started the 1928 season with Cleveland, but except for two appearances, all he did was toss batting practice. One day, he'd had enough and didn't take his accustomed pregame position. Someone shouted at him to get to the mound. "The hell with you," the brash youngster responded. "I didn't come up here for that." His outburst got him quickly demoted to the 3-I League's Terre Haute Tots. Ferrell made the most of it by going 20–8 with a 2.74 ERA. By 1929 Ferrell was back in Cleveland, where he started his string of four straight 20-game seasons. In 1931 he won 13 straight games.

But in 1934, the cash-strapped Cleveland club sent Ferrell to the Red Sox, along with outfielder Dick Porter, for pitcher Bob Weiland, outfielder Bob Seeds, and $25,000. There he was united with his brother Rick, whom Boston had acquired in 1933 from the St. Louis Browns.

The two brothers had previously shared one memorable moment as opponents. At League Park on April 29, 1931, Wes had hurled a no-hitter against Rick's Browns, striking out eight and walking three. The Brown who had come closest to getting a hit was Rick, who rapped a ball to shortstop Bill Hunnefield that was ruled an error.

As batterymates, the Ferrell brothers worked well together. Although they did not always see eye to eye on pitch selection, Wes gave Rick high marks as a receiver. "You never saw him lunge for the ball," said Wes. "He never took a strike away from you."

Perhaps the greatest difference between the two brothers was their temperament. Rick was low-key and quiet; Wes was volatile and combative. In 1932 Cleveland manager Roger Peckinpaugh fined Wes for refusing to leave the mound. In 1936 Red Sox player-manager Joe Cronin fined him for leaving a game without permission. While managing in the minors after his major league days were over, Ferrell once hit an umpire and pulled his men off the diamond, earning a suspension.

Ferrell won a league-best 25 games for the Red Sox in 1935, leading the AL in games started, complete games, and innings pitched. A 20-game winner the next season, he led the league with 28 complete games.

But arm trouble eventually took its toll, and Ferrell, a power pitcher early in his career, had to become a junkball pitcher. He continued to be a dangerous hitter, though. His lifetime batting average was .280, and he holds records for most home runs by a pitcher in a season, with nine, and in a career, with 37. He hit one more as a pinch hitter and slammed two homers in a game five times. His 38 homers are 10 more than brother Rick hit in his 17-season career.

In June 1937 both Rick and Wes were traded to Washington in a deal involving colorful pitcher Bobo Newsom. In August 1938 Wes was given his unconditional release, despite a 13–8 record. During the next three seasons he had brief stints with the Yankees, Dodgers, and Braves before leaving the majors.

Dave Ferriss

Ferriss, David Meadow **P**

1945–50 B:12/5/1921, Shaw, MS Deb:4/29/1945, BOS AL BL/TR 6'2", 208

W	L	PCT	G	SH	IP	BB	SO	ERA
65	30	.684	144	12	880	314	296	3.64

Dave "Boo" Ferriss got his nickname in childhood, from his inability to pronounce "brother." He blazed briefly at Fenway Park and then became another of the disappointments Red Sox fans so enjoy bemoaning.

A former Mississippi State athlete, the 6-foot-2-inch righthander didn't set the minors on fire, registering a mediocre 7–7 mark in the Piedmont League. Asthma forced his early release from military service in February 1945, and Ferriss was ordered to report to Boston's Louisville farm club. When the Red Sox got off to one of their patented staggering starts, losing eight of their first nine games, "Boo" was called up to the majors.

Given a start by manager Joe Cronin, Ferriss responded with a two-hit, 2–0 win over Philadelphia. A week later he whitewashed the Yankees, 7–0. He went on to win his first 10 starts, four of which were shutouts, and he still holds the record for scoreless innings pitched from the start of a pitcher's career, with 22. At midseason he was on a 30-win pace, but asthma got the better of him and he settled for a 21–10 mark with the seventh-place Sox.

By 1946 the stars had returned from the war. Ferriss again won his first 10 decisions to jump-start Boston toward a pennant. With Ferriss, Tex Hughson, Mickey Harris, and Joe Dopson, Boston had the AL's best starting staff. Ferriss finished 25–6 to lead all AL pitchers in winning percentage, with .806.

When the Red Sox faced the Cardinals in the 1946 World Series, Ferriss shut out the Redbirds, 4–0, in Game 3. In the seventh and deciding game, however, he was knocked out after giving up three runs in $4\frac{1}{3}$ innings. Although the Red Sox rallied to tie the game, St. Louis eventually won it and the Series.

The Red Sox were favored to repeat in 1947, but during the season Ferriss, Hughson, and Harris all developed sore arms, and none of them ever fully recovered. Ferriss was 12–11 in 1947 with an ERA over 4.00. In 1948 he was 7–3 in only 115 innings as his ERA zoomed to 5.23. He tried to come back several times over the next few seasons, but his arm was gone.

John Fetzer

Fetzer, John
Owner (1961–89) B:3/25/1901, Decatur, IL
D:2/20/1991, Honolulu, HI

A successful pioneer in radio, John Fetzer eventually branched out into films, oil, mining, manufacturing, and real estate. As owner of the Detroit Tigers, he personified low-key but effective ownership by leaving day-to-day control of the club in the hands of baseball professionals.

In 1956 Fetzer headed a syndicate that purchased the Tigers from the estate of Walter O. Briggs. He became two-thirds owner and president of the Tigers in 1960, and sole owner two years later. One of his first moves as sole owner was to hire Jim Campbell as general manager. "Not once did Mr. Fetzer ever interfere with the operation of the ballclub," Campbell said. "He had his input but he let me make the decisions." Involved in selling major league baseball to television, Fetzer helped negotiate a two-year, $12.2 million dollar deal with ABC-TV in 1964.

Fetzer's Tigers won the world championship in 1968 and a division championship in 1972. In the fall of 1983 he sold the club for $53 million to Domino's Pizza magnate Tom Monaghan, who requested that Fetzer stay on as Tigers chairman of the board.

Mark Fidrych

Fidrych, Mark Steven **P**
1976–80 B:8/14/1954, Worcester, MA Deb:4/20/1976,
DET AL BR/TR 6'3", 175

W	L	PCT	G	SH	IP	BB	SO	ERA
29	19	.604	58	5	412^{1}	99	170	3.10

A beloved phenom, gawky right-hander Mark "the Bird" Fidrych pitched less than one full season for the Detroit Tigers before injuring his arm. A true innocent who exuberantly congratulated his infielders on good plays and gave pep talks to baseballs before he threw them, Fidrych was a breath of fresh air.

In 1976 Fidrych was not on the Tigers' spring training roster and didn't make his first start for Detroit until May 1. Nevertheless, by July he had established his ability to throw a hard strike at the knees. He started the All-Star Game for the AL and won the Rookie of the Year Award with a 19–9 record and a league-leading 2.34 ERA. At age 22, Fidrych had completed a season, leading the league in ERA and complete games despite his late start.

Nicknamed "The Bird" for his wide-eyed resemblance to Big Bird, the popular Sesame Street character, Fidrych became a fan favorite. The media wanted to know everything about him, and Fidrych was an open book with a flair for language in the tradition of Casey Stengel and Yogi Berra. When asked about his living quarters he told a reporter, "Sometimes I get lazy and let the dishes stack up. But they don't stack too high, I've only got four dishes."

The young pitcher became a national sensation, filling ballparks in cities that usually had poor attendance. At Anaheim the Angels held a Mark Fidrych Autograph Day, and the Bird patiently signed autographs for thousands of fans.

When Tigers broadcaster Ernie Harwell got wind that a network was considering a television series starring Fidrych, Harwell went straight to the Bird's beak to see if it was true. Fidrych told him, "I don't know [the details]. Maybe my agent will be making the deal. But I'll tell you this, Ernie. No matter what happens, I will have the last hearsay."

Fidrych also became a favorite of teammates, although they did not always understand him. "Some of the older players, we try to protect him, just keep the sharks from getting to him, the guys with the fast deals," teammate Rusty Staub said at the time. "But nothing bothers him. When it got out that he was only making $16,000 a year, somebody started a drive: 'Send a buck to the Bird.' But Mark stopped it. You have to know how he talks. He said, 'Hey, I'm making more money now than I need. If they gave me a raise, I'd probably get cocky and pitch lousy.' He drives a subcompact, and if he really could live the way he wanted, he'd drive a truck, work in a garage, and drink beer all day."

Fidrych believed that the baseball was an equal partner in his performance. He was sensitive to the karma of each ball. If a batter got a hit Fidrych would often ask for a new ball, explaining to umpires that the ball still had hits in it and needed to mix with other balls to "get right" again.

During 1977 spring training Fidrych injured his arm chasing a flyball and was on the disabled list for most of the next three seasons. After the injury, the Bird lost his effectiveness, and the Tigers released him after the 1981 season. He spent the next three years in the Red Sox minor league system and then retired from baseball. "I got no regrets," Fidrych philosophized. "I got memories. I'll always keep them alive. Grab it while you can, 'cause you never know when it's gonna disappear."

Cecil Fielder

Fielder, Cecil Grant **1B–DH**
1985–88, 1990–98 B:9/21/1963, Los Angeles, CA
Deb:7/20/1985, TOR AL BR/TR 6'3", 240

G	AB	R	H	HR	RBI	OBP	SLG	AVG
1470	5157	744	1313	319	1008	.348	.482	.255

Though Mark McGwire and Sammy Sosa will be remembered as the premier power hitters of the 1990s, Cecil Fielder began the decade as the personification of home run heroism. "Big Daddy" averaged 36 home runs and 113 RBIs from 1990 to 1996. All his success came after he swapped the uniform of the Hanshin (Japan) Tigers for that of the Detroit Tigers. And make that uniform extra, extra large.

Fielder broke into the majors with the Toronto Blue Jays in 1985, but failed to establish himself in four seasons. In 1989 he left the States to play in Japan, hitting 38 home runs in just 106 games for Hanshin. Although few players had ever returned from Japan and excelled in the major leagues, power-deprived Detroit signed the slugger. All he did was drive in 132 runs (for the first of three straight RBI titles) and slug 51 homers—the most in the majors since Cincinnati's George Foster hit 52 in 1977, and the most in the American League since Roger Maris' 61 and Mickey Mantle's 54 in 1961.

Fielder led the AL again with 44 homers and 133 RBIs in 1991. He was runner-up in the balloting for Most Valuable Player for the second consecutive year, and the Tigers rewarded him with the richest contract in baseball history to that point. As Detroit's record sunk below .500, however, Fielder publicly called for a change of scenery. In July 1996 the Tigers dealt him to the New York Yankees, then in a tight battle for first place in the AL East. Fielder hit 13 homers down the stretch for New York. He batted .308 in the postseason—including a .391 mark in the World Series—as the Yankees claimed their first championship since 1978.

In 1997 Fielder slumped on the field and squabbled off it. A return to his native southern California in 1998 did not work out as planned; the Angels released him in midseason. After a short stint with Cleveland, Fielder was out of baseball at age 35.

Ed Figueroa

Figueroa, Eduardo (Padilla) **P**
1974–81 B:10/14/1948, Ciales, Puerto Rico
Deb:4/9/1974, CAL AL BR/TR 6'1", 190

W	L	PCT	G	SH	IP	BB	SO	ERA
80	67	.544	200	12	1309^{2}	443	571	3.51

In 1974 Eduardo Figueroa was a strong-armed rookie with the last-place Angels. Since he was one of their few tradable assets, the California club sent Figueroa and teammate Mickey Rivers to the Yankees for Bobby Bonds at the end of 1975.

When the New York Yankees returned to American League domination the following year, Figueroa established himself as their most dependable starter. He won 19 games in 1976, 16 in 1977, and 20 in 1978—more than any other Yankee hurler during their three straight league championship seasons and 1977 world championship year.

Figueroa injured his elbow in 1979, just as he seemed to be maturing into a consistently effective moundsman. Although he tried comebacks with Texas and Oakland, he never recovered, and he retired in 1981. He was the first Puerto Rican-born 20-game winner in major league history.

Rollie Fingers

Fingers, Roland Glen **P**
1968–82,1984–85 B:8/25/1946, Steubenville, OH
Deb:9/15/1968, OAK AL BR/TR 6'4", 195

W	L	PCT	G	SV	IP	BB	SO	ERA
114	118	.491	944	341	1701^{1}	492	1299	2.90

If Roland Glen Fingers hadn't been such a worrier, he might have been only an average starting pitcher. Instead, he fretted himself right into the bullpen and became baseball's leading fireman with 341 career saves, the major league record at the time he retired.

An American Legion Player of the Year, Fingers became part of the A's regular five-man pitching rotation in 1969 but psyched himself out of a starting role. He explained, "I would plan my pitches days in advance of my start and get so wound up I couldn't sleep the night before my turn."

Relegated to mop-up duty in 1971 after finishing only 4 of 35 starts, he took immediately to the relief role. Rollie was the main man out of the Oakland bullpen in the early 1970s when the A's won five division titles, three pennants, and three world championships.

He saved Game 2 of the 1972 World Series with one of the most daring plays in Series history. In the top of the eighth inning, with runners on first and third and one out, Fingers faced feared Cincinnati slugger Johnny Bench. The count went to 2-2, and on ball three the runner on first, Bobby Tolan, stole second. Dick Williams went to the mound and signaled for an intentional walk to load the bases. But as Fingers went into his windup, catcher Gene Tenace shifted back toward the plate. Fingers delivered a hard slider over the outside corner as an amazed Bench stood frozen and took strike three. "After that," Fingers said, "everything was ho-hum."

In the 1974 World Series, his one win and two saves earned Fingers the MVP nod. His six saves in three Series is a record. When Fingers and penurious A's owner Charlie Finley reached an impasse in contract talks, Finley sold the pitcher to Boston for $1 million on June 15, 1976. But Commissioner Bowie Kuhn voided the sale. This only delayed Fingers' departure; he signed in 1977 with San Diego. Fingers pitched for San Diego from 1977 to 1980 and had his two top save seasons there, with 35 in 1977 and 37 the following year. Both marks led the NL, and in both seasons he was named Rolaids Relief Man of the Year and *The Sporting News* Fireman of the Year. San Diego broadcaster Lon Simmons said, "Fingers has 35 saves, a better record than John the Baptist."

Returning to the AL with Milwaukee in 1981, Fingers led the AL in saves with 28 in a strike-shortened season. He was named both MVP and Cy Young Award winner. An arm injury in 1982 kept him out of the World Series and caused him to miss the 1983 season. He came back to notch 23 saves by July 1984, when a herniated disk ended his season. He was released in November 1985. Fingers was voted into the Hall of Fame in 1992.

Charlie Finley

Finley, Charles O.

Owner (1961–80) B:2/22/1919, Ensley, AL D:2/19/1996, Chicago, IL

Charlie Finley made millions of dollars selling insurance and then spent as few of them as possible on his baseball team. A promoter who specialized in self-promotion, Finley brought numerous controversial innovations to the game during the 20 years he owned the A's, which he moved from Kansas City to Oakland after the 1967 season. Though he publicly berated his players and managers, he nonetheless assembled a club that did what no team other than the Yankees has ever done—win three consecutive World Series.

Before becoming a big league owner, Finley's involvement with baseball had been limited to a single meeting with his boyhood hero Connie Mack and a stint as player-manager of a semipro team while moonlighting at a U.S. Steel plant. When he contracted tuberculosis and had to quit playing ball, he began selling insurance. With one sale, a group disability policy to the American College of Surgeons, Finley made a fortune.

He tried to buy the Tigers, the White Sox, and the Philadelphia A's in the 1950s. Outbid by Arnold Johnson for the Kansas City A's in 1960, Finley picked up 52 percent of the stock when Johnson died a few months later, and bought the remainder of the shares within a few weeks.

Finley's first edict was to halt the flow of players between Kansas City and the Yankees. Throughout the 1950s the A's had supplied the Yanks with a wealth of talent for almost nothing, serving as a glorified farm team for the New Yorkers. Finley intended to hold on to valuable players.

Finley also revamped right field in Kansas City to match Yankee Stadium's short porch. When the league made him tear down the modification before Opening Day, he ordered his announcers to say of any ball that fell into the former short porch area, "That would have been a home run in Yankee Stadium." But public reaction turned negative, and Finley put up a 40-foot fence in right so that no one could homer out there.

On Opening Days he had all his players ride onto the field on mules, and "hired" a mule (named Charlie O., of course) as team mascot. Finley even asked announcer Harry Caray to change his famous home run call of "Holy cow!" to "Holy mule!"

During his career Finley advocated World Series night games and the adoption of the designated-hitter rule, both of which later became part of baseball. He also tried unsuccessfully to introduce the designated runner and orange baseballs. He dressed his players in gaudy uniforms resembling those of softball teams and staged outrageous giveaways. When the A's all grew mustaches during spring training to make fun of Reggie Jackson, Finley offered mustachioed players a bonus, and held a Mustache Night at the ballpark. In 1976 he hired an astrologer to prepare daily charts on his players, which manager Chuck Tanner promptly threw into the wastebasket.

Challenged on innovations that went counter to baseball tradition, Finley argued, "The day Custer lost at the Little Big Horn, the Chicago White Sox beat the Cincinnati Red Legs, 3–2. Both teams wore knickers. And they're still wearing them today."

The power struggles between Finley and Commissioner Bowie Kuhn are the stuff of baseball legend. The egomaniacal Finley and the pompous Kuhn were perfect comic foils for each other.

Their first major spat was over young slugger Reggie Jackson. After Jackson's third year, in which he hit 47 home runs at age 23, he and Charlie O. had a bitter contract dispute. Having accepted Finley's terms, Jackson sulked, then slumped. Finley announced that he was sending Jackson back to the minors. In stepped Kuhn to block the move, saying it was "motivated by personal reasons unrelated to Jackson's ability."

After Vida Blue's sensational 24–8 year in 1971—his pitching appearances accounted for 43 percent of Oakland's home attendance—Finley wouldn't budge on his contract offer. The season started without Blue. Kuhn, Finley, Blue, and their lawyers negotiated until Finley consented to a few bonuses. At one point Finley tried to get Vida to change his name to "True" for $2,000. "If it's such a good name," Vida asked, "why isn't yours True O. Finley?"

During the 1973 World Series, A's second baseman Mike Andrews made two errors in the 10th inning of Game 2, which helped the Mets to a 10–7 win. Finley demanded that Andrews sign a letter agreeing to the team doctor's phony diagnosis that he had a shoulder injury and could no longer participate in the Series. Then Finley activated Manny Trillo in Andrews' place. Kuhn halted the move, which was clearly meant to embarrass Andrews and get a better fielder on the team. The commissioner fined Finley $5,000, then tacked on an extra $1,000 because Finley had ordered a public address announcement saying the Mets were "forcing the Oakland club to play with 24 men."

But Finley's most costly actions were yet to come. When he failed to pay an insurance annuity that was part of Jim "Catfish" Hunter's 1974 salary, arbitrator Peter Seitz declared Hunter a free agent. The same arbitrator ruled a year later that the players' Basic Agreement did not bind them to one team forever, and players began to consider the possibilities of free agency.

Finley realized that his budget wouldn't be enough to keep his terrific young team together, so he began to maneuver. He dealt Reggie Jackson and Ken Holtzman to Baltimore, knowing they would be gone in a year anyway. He also sold Vida Blue to the Yankees for $1.5 million and peddled Joe Rudi and Rollie Fingers to the Red Sox for $1 million each.

Kuhn wouldn't stand for it. To Finley, it was a way of getting something back for his players rather than having them leave without compensation. To Kuhn, Finley was setting a dangerous precedent. The commissioner thought the moves would upset the competitive balance of the league, even though Finley's maneuvers basically would have the same effect as free agency. Worse, Kuhn feared that putting a value on the players would encourage others to beef up their own free-agent demands. Finley publicly called Kuhn "the village idiot."

Then Finley sold Paul Lindblad for $400,000. When Kuhn approved that deal he added a rider stipulating that $400,000 was the limit for the sale of any player. Finley next announced that he had "traded" Blue to the Reds for minor leaguer Dave Revering and $1.75 million, but Kuhn blocked that transaction, too. Finally Finley traded Blue to the Giants for seven players and $390,000. Kuhn became Finley's enemy for life.

Making enemies was a way of life for Charlie Finley. Somewhat unexpectedly, after two years as his manager Dick Williams was still praising Finley, saying, "He has been wonderful to me. I have nothing but the highest regard for him." Williams, however, quit the next season, in the middle of the A's' third World Series celebration, conceding, "A man can take just so much of Charlie." Finley went through 10 managers in 16 years, ranging from the fiery Williams to the meek Alvin Dark to the popular Chuck Tanner.

Finley branched out into other sports as well, and owned both American Basketball Association and National Hockey League franchises. Despite a typical flurry of claims and counterclaims, his sale of the A's to the Haas family in 1980 brought his baseball career to an atypically quiet end. Explaining his decision, he said, "It's no longer a battle of wits, but how much you have on the hip. I can no longer compete."

Chuck Finley

Finley, Charles Edward **P**

1986–* B:11/26/1962, Monroe, LA Deb:5/29/1986, CAL AL BL/TL 6'6", 214

W	L	PCT	G	SH	IP	BB	SO	ERA
165	140	.541	436	14	2675	1118	2151	3.72

Chuck Finley was one of the American League's most consistent pitchers in the 1990s. In the eight-year span between 1989 and 1996, Finley made four All-Star teams while winning 18 games twice, 16 games twice, and 15 games twice. He logged over 200 innings each season in that span, except 1989, when he threw 199⅔, and 1994, when the strike stopped him at a league-high 183⅓.

A fitness enthusiast who managed to keep his left arm healthy through a variety of odd injuries, Finley increased his strikeout totals in the later stages of his career through greater reliance on his forkball and split-finger fastball. He was especially tough on lefthanded hitters. They batted just .234 against him in 1999.

Finley surpassed Nolan Ryan as the Angels' all-time leader in victories, games, starts, and innings pitched. He reeled off a club-record 14-game winning streak between July 1997 and May 1998. "When he doesn't have his good stuff, he finds a way to compete," Angels catcher Matt Walbeck said of Finley. "And when he does have his good stuff, it's lights out."

Known as one of the game's tougher competitors on the field, Finley also gained a reputation as one of baseball's premier practical jokers. Two of his better pranks: dipping the uniform of teammate Brian Anderson in water, hanging it in a freezer overnight and then displaying it in the clubhouse, and jacking up reliever Mark Holzemer's car, removing all four tires, and placing them in Holzemer's locker.

Steve Finley

Finley, Steven Allen **OF**

1989–* B:3/12/1965, Paducah, KY Deb:4/3/1989, BAL AL BL/TL 6'2", 180

G	AB	R	H	HR	RBI	OBP	SLG	AVG
1538	5788	905	1586	153	649	.332	.430	.274

In 1990 the Baltimore Orioles believed the franchise was just one player away from contending for the American League East title. Their attempt to obtain that franchise player resulted in one of the worst trades in club history. The Orioles sent prospects Pete Harnisch, Curt Schilling, and Steve Finley to Houston for veteran slugger Glenn Davis. Over the next decade Harnisch and Schilling each became All-Star pitchers, while Davis hit 24 homers in three miserable seasons for Baltimore. Finley surpassed 24 homers three times, stole 242 bases, and became one of the National League's finest defensive center fielders.

As an Astro, Finley stole 44 bases in 1992, led the NL with 13 triples in 1993, and showed newfound power with 11 homers in strike-shortened 1994. The next year he was traded to San Diego in a big, 12-player deal. Finley batted .297 and won the first of two-straight Gold Gloves in 1995. He helped the Padres win the National League West title the following year with a .298 average and 30 home runs—19 more homers than his previous best.

Finley was an All-Star in 1997, and helped the Padres win another division title the following season. His average declined significantly each year, however, and the Padres let him leave when his contract expired. He signed with the Arizona Diamondbacks in 1999, and for the third time in four years helped a team win the NL West. Finley reached career highs with 34 homers and 103 RBIs. In the division series, he drove in five runs and batted .385.

Lou Finney

Finney, Louis Klopsche **OF–1B**

1931,1933–42,1944–47 B:8/13/1910, Buffalo, AL D:4/22/1966, Lafayette, AL Deb:9/12/1931, PHI AL BL/TR 6', 180

G	AB	R	H	HR	RBI	OBP	SLG	AVG
1270	4631	643	1329	31	494	.336	.388	.287

Connie Mack wanted a successor to Al Simmons. Instead, he got Lou Finney. Finney wasn't a poor player. He was just ordinary—an outfielder-first baseman who finished with a .287 career batting average and only 31 homers in 4,631 at bats.

The brother of Pirates catcher Hal Finney had a nine-game tour of duty with the A's in 1931. In 1933 he hit .267 in 74 games with three homers and 32 RBIs. In 1936 he got his first chance to play every day and hit .302—with one home run and 42 RBIs in 653 at bats. Mack sold him to the Red Sox in May 1939, and he hit .325 in 95 games for Boston (.310 overall) while leading the AL in pinch hitting, going 13-for-40 (.325) with 15 RBIs. He had his best season in 1940, with career highs in average (.320), triples (15), and RBIs (73).

Eddie Fisher

Fisher, Eddie Gene **P**

1959–73 B:7/16/1936, Shreveport, LA Deb:6/22 /1959, SF NL BR/TR 6'2½", 200

W	L	PCT	G	SV	IP	BB	SO	ERA
85	70	.548	690	81	1538^2	438	812	3.41

He was never married to Elizabeth Taylor, but this Eddie Fisher made headlines of his own in 1965, winning Fireman of the Year honors from *The Sporting News* as the best reliever in Major League Baseball. The righthanded knuckleballer appeared in 82 games for the Chicago White Sox, an AL record at the time. He would have set a major league record had Ted Abernathy not pitched in 84 games that same season across town with the Cubs. Fisher recorded 24 saves and 15 wins in relief.

Fisher began his professional career as a starting pitcher. He joined the White Sox in November 1961 and went 9–5 in 1962, pitching mostly as a reliever. After his record-setting 1965 season, he led the league in appearances again in 1966 with 67, splitting time between Chicago and Baltimore. In November 1967 he was traded to Cleveland, and in October 1968 he was dealt to California. Pitching for the Angels in 1970, Fisher appeared in his 571st career game, surpassing Hoyt Wilhelm as the busiest reliever in AL history—a record since bettered by several pitchers.

Jack Fisher

Fisher, John Howard **P**

1959–69 B:3/4/1939, Frostburg, MD Deb:4/14/1959, BAL AL BR/TR 6'2", 215

W	L	PCT	G	SH	IP	BB	SO	ERA
86	139	.382	400	9	1975^{2}	605	1017	4.06

Certain pitchers are doomed to be forever remembered for their mistakes. Journeyman hurler Jack Fisher's 193 home runs allowed doesn't even make the top 100 in that ignominious category, but he served up two significant gopher balls less than a year apart.

On September 28, 1960, the husky hurler, nicknamed "Fat Jack," faced soon-to-retire Boston Red Sox legend Ted Williams at Fenway Park. In his final at bat, Williams, 42, belted his 521st career home run off the 21-year-old Fisher.

Fisher again found himself in the path of history at Yankee Stadium on September 26, 1961. New York's Roger Maris entered the game one home run shy of tying Babe Ruth's record of 60 in a season. Maris smashed Fisher's hanging curveball down the right-field line. The ball stayed fair by about three feet, and Maris trotted into history, dragging Fisher with him.

After going 12–11 in 1960, Fisher endured eight consecutive losing seasons, hitting bottom with an 8–24 record for the 1965 New York Mets (his eight victories, however, tied Al Jackson for the most on the staff). He finished up with a 4–4 record for Cincinnati in 1969.

Ray Fisher

Fisher, Ray Lyle **P**

1910–17,1919–20 B:10/4/1887, Middlebury, VT D:11/3/1982, Ann Arbor, MI Deb:7/2/1910, NY AL BR/TR 5'11½", 180

W	L	PCT	G	SH	IP	BB	SO	ERA
100	94	.515	278	19	1755^{2}	481	680	2.82

Cincinnati Reds righthander Ray Fisher started Game 3 of the infamous 1919 World Series. Opposed by Dickie Kerr, one of the few White Sox players trying to win, he lost, 3–0. The game's key hit was a two-run double by Chick Gandil—one of the Black Sox—that scored Shoeless Joe Jackson and Happy Felsch, two more who were in on the fix.

Fisher received a B.A. from Middlebury College in 1910, and soon thereafter joined the New York Highlanders (who were to become the Yankees in 1913). He moved into the starting rotation in 1913, when he went 12–16 with a 3.18 ERA for a 57–94 team. He had his best season in 1915, when he went 18–11 in a career-high 247⅔ innings with a 2.11 ERA, for a team that finished 14 games under .500. After missing the 1918 season because of World War I, Fisher was waived to the Reds in May 1919.

Finally pitching for a talented team, Fisher was 14–5 with a 2.17 ERA as a spot starter. But he lost his start in the Series and went 10–11 with a 2.73 ERA the next season. When the Reds decided to cut his pay by $1,000, Fisher asked for his release so he could coach baseball at Michigan State. Instead, he was placed on the ineligible list, which meant he was blacklisted.

Fisher coached baseball and freshman football at the University of Michigan instead (one of Fisher's freshman footballers was Gerald R. Ford). He lasted 38 years as baseball coach and won nine Big 10 championships and the NCAA title in 1953. He returned to Organized Baseball in 1960 as a spring training instructor for the Braves and had the same job with the Tigers from 1963 through 1965. Commissioner Bowie Kuhn officially reinstated Fisher as "a retired player in good standing" in 1980.

Carlton Fisk

Fisk, Carlton Ernest **C–DH**

1969,1971–93 B:12/26/1947, Bellows Falls, VT Deb:9/18/1969, BOS AL BR/TR 6'2", 220

G	AB	R	H	HR	RBI	OBP	SLG	AVG
2499	8756	1276	2356	376	1330	.343	.457	.269

"What I really wanted to be was a power forward for the Boston Celtics," Carlton Fisk once admitted. A good enough basketball player to win a scholarship to the University of New Hampshire, Fisk was too good a baseball player to refuse the call when the only baseball team he wanted to play for made him the fourth pick in the nation in the January 1967 draft.

By the time his career was over, some four decades later, Fisk had caught more games than anyone in history, had hit one of the most dramatic home runs in World Series annals, and had played professional baseball as hard as the New England winters that had shaped his character.

Fisk won Boston's regular receiving job in 1972. That year he became the first unanimous choice as AL Rookie of the Year. He batted .293 and tied for the league lead in triples, giving fans many opportunities to observe his distinctive upright, hands-bobbing running style. He slugged 22 home runs with a short, ugly swing that hitting guru Walt Hriniak tried to refine during two decades in two different cities. Also in 1972 Fisk led AL catchers in putouts, assists, and errors, won the only Gold Glove of his career, and was named to his first of 11 All-Star teams.

Fisk, whose nickname was "Pudge," lost nearly 30 pounds during the 1973 season, and his batting average dipped from a June high of .320 to a final figure of .246. The contentious backstop accused Bill Singer of delivering a spitball in the All-Star Game, and in August he got into a home-plate fistfight with Thurman Munson and Gene Michael of the Yankees. That season Fisk also fought with "Dirty Al" Gallagher of the California Angels after a home-plate collision, and with Gallagher's teammate, Frank Robinson, after a brushback pitch. In the fall of 1973 Fisk almost lost a fingertip in a scrap with a garage door.

During spring training in 1974 Fisk took a foul tip in the groin and missed the start of the regular season. That June he tore knee ligaments while trying to block the plate, and subsequently underwent reconstructive surgery. "Doctors gave me no hope of ever coming back," he recalled. With intensive rehabilitation Fisk recovered in time for spring training in 1975. In his second exhibition game a pitch hit his forearm and broke it, but Fisk was around at season's end to help the Red Sox hold off the Baltimore Orioles for the AL East flag, batting .331 with 52 RBIs in 79 games.

The Reds led the World Series three games to two when Game 6 unfolded at Fenway. Cincinnati tied the score in the fifth and then built a 6–3 lead. In the bottom of the eighth Bernie Carbo's three-run home run, his second pinch homer of the Series, brought the Sox even. The game eventually went to extra innings, setting the stage for one of the most dramatic moments in Series history.

Before leading off the 12th inning Fisk had "one of those feelings you get that something is afoot." In the on-deck circle he turned to Fred Lynn and declared, "Fred, I'm going to hit one off the wall. Drive me in." Then, on a 1–0 pitch, Fisk outdid his prediction, driving the ball high and deep down the left-field line. Fisk knew it was either gone or foul, and a few steps down the first-base line he began to jump and wave his arms frantically, as if to guide the ball into fair territory. The ball hit the net attached to the foul pole for a game-winning home run. Fisk leaped high, arms raised in exultation. But the joy in Beantown was short-lived. After seizing a 3–0 lead in Game 7 the Red Sox lost the Series.

Fisk finally had two consecutive healthy seasons in 1977 and 1978, catching a total of 309 games, one short of the highest back-to-back total in AL history. In 1977 he became the fifth major league catcher to score 100 runs and drive in 100 in one season. Prior to the 1981 season Fisk signed with the White Sox and swapped his old No. 27 for No. 72 because, as he said, "it was a turning point in my life."

Playing home games in much less accommodating Comiskey Park, Fisk still matched his career high with 26 homers during Chicago's 1983 division championship season. Batting second in the order, he scored the run that clinched the AL West title. However, the White Sox lost to the Orioles in the ALCS.

In 1985 Fisk set career highs with 37 homers and 107 RBIs. He hit 33 of his homers as a catcher, establishing a league record. In 1987, at age 39, he became the oldest catcher to hit 20 home runs. He broke his right hand in 1988, but came back to catch his 1,807th game, breaking Rick Ferrell's league record. With Ferrell in attendance in Detroit, Fisk celebrated with a five-hit game, his first since high school.

Fisk broke the same hand in 1989, but returned to the lineup and hit his 307th home run as a catcher. Fittingly, it came at Yankee Stadium, breaking former Yankee Yogi Berra's AL record. Then, in 1990, Fisk hit No. 328 off Charlie Hough at Texas to break Johnny Bench's major league catcher's mark. That homer was also his 155th as a member of the White Sox, which made him the franchise's all-time home run leader (his eventual total of 214 has since been surpassed by Harold Baines and Frank Thomas). In 1991 Fisk became the oldest player to get a hit in the All-Star Game. Before retiring, he also set the record for homers after age 40, finishing with 70.

Fisk caught game No. 2,226 to break the major league record on June 22, 1993. Six days later he got his release papers. In 2000, he was elected to the Hall of Fame.

Freddie Fitzsimmons

Fitzsimmons, Frederick Landis **P**

1925–43 M(1943–45, 105–181) B:7/28/1901, Mishawaka, IN D:11/18/1979, Yucca Valley, CA Deb:8/12 /1925, NY NL BR/TR 5'11", 185

W	L	PCT	G	SH	IP	BB	SO	ERA
217	146	.598	513	29	3233^{2}	846	870	3.51

A 20-game winner only once, Freddie Fitzsimmons nonetheless won at least 14 games in nine different seasons. Nicknamed "Fat Freddie," he explained his weight problem with, "Maybe I just eat too much." Despite his bulk, he was an unusually good hitter and fielder.

Fitzsimmons came up to the Giants in 1925 and went 6–3. During spring training with the club in 1927, he fell victim to one of baseball's more unusual accidents. Having fallen asleep in a rocking chair on the veranda of a Sarasota, Florida, hotel, Fitzsimmons rocked over the fingers of his pitching hand. He was out of action for three weeks but sustained no permanent damage.

In 1928 Fitzsimmons went 20–9 with a 3.68 ERA. He won 15 the following season, and his 19–7 record led the NL in winning percentage in

1930. On May 10, 1931, Fitzsimmons hit a grand slam off Chicago's Pat Malone; he wound up with 14 career homers. However, he had less luck pitching in World Series contests.

In the 1933 Fall Classic against Washington, Fitzsimmons lost to Earl Whitehill in Game 3, allowing four runs in seven innings. In the 1936 Series against the Yankees, he lost Game 3, to Bump Hadley, and Game 6, to Lefty Gomez.

In June 1937 the Giants traded Fitzsimmons to Brooklyn for pitcher Tommy Baker in what turned out to be an extremely one-sided deal. Fitzsimmons became a valuable addition to the Dodgers staff, while Baker won only one game for New York. Brooklyn's Leo Durocher said, "I wish we had nine guys like Fitz. We'd never lose."

In 1940 Fitzsimmons again led the league in winning percentage, going 16–2 with a 2.81 ERA. Bad luck, however, was in the offing. During Game 3 of the 1941 World Series against the Yankees, with two out in the seventh inning and the score tied, 0–0, a line drive off the bat of opposing pitcher Marius Russo hit Fitzsimmons in the kneecap. He was forced to leave the game. "I guess I should have learned to duck long ago," ruminated Fitzsimmons, who later developed arthritis in the injured knee.

In July 1943 the Dodgers released Fitzsimmons so he could manage the second-division Phillies, replacing Bucky Harris. He lasted until June 29, 1945, when he was replaced in turn by Ben Chapman.

Aside from being active in baseball, for two seasons Fitzsimmons also served as general manager of the All-America Football Conference Brooklyn Dodgers—a franchise run by Fitzsimmons' boss at Philadelphia, William D. Cox.

Max Flack

Flack, Max John **OF**

1914–25 B:2/5/1890, Belleville, IL D:7/31/1975, Belleville, IL Deb:4/16/1914, CHI FL BL/TL 5'7", 148

G	AB	R	H	HR	RBI	OBP	SLG	AVG
1411	5252	783	1461	35	391	.342	.366	.278

When Max Flack retired in 1925 he had the highest fielding percentage of any outfielder in major league history. It's ironic, then, that such an excellent glove man is best known for an error he made that cost the Cubs the 1918 World Series. In Game 6 Flack dropped a liner by Red Sox left fielder George Whiteman in the third inning. The error allowed two unearned runs to score, giving Boston a 2–1 victory and the Series.

Flack started his big league career in 1914, with Chicago of the Federal League. When that league folded in 1916, the NL Cubs purchased the entire Chicago team. Flack was a fixture in the Chicago outfield for six-plus seasons. His best years at the plate were 1920 and 1921, when he batted .302 and .301, respectively.

On Memorial Day 1922, Flack walked the three blocks home between games of a morning-afternoon doubleheader with St. Louis. Upon returning to the Chicago locker room he was informed by manager Bill Killefer, "Maxie, boy, you're in the wrong clubhouse!"

"And I was," said Flack. "They had traded me to the Cardinals for Cliff Heathcote. So he played for the Cubs that afternoon and I was in right field for the Cardinals. The fans were astonished when they saw us in different uniforms."

Mike Flanagan

Flanagan, Michael Kendall **P**

1975–92 B:12/16/1951, Manchester, NH Deb:9/5/1975, BAL AL BL/TL 6', 195

W	L	PCT	G	SH	IP	BB	SO	ERA
167	143	.539	526	19	2770	890	1491	3.90

Gritty lefthander Mike Flanagan won the 1979 Cy Young Award as a workhorse starter. Twelve years later, he battled back from a variety of injuries and diminished velocity to throw the Orioles' last pitch at Memorial Stadium.

A third-generation professional baseball player, Flanagan's lineage includes his grandfather, Ed "Sleepy" Flanagan, who came up to the big leagues in 1887, and his father, also named Ed, who pitched in the Boston Red Sox organization from 1947 through 1952.

Joining the Orioles' starting rotation in 1977, Flanagan went 15–10. He lost a bid for 20 victories in 1978 when Detroit beat him, 5–4, on the final day of the season. In 1979, on the way to a career-best record of 23–9, Flanagan went 13–3 with 10 complete games down the stretch. He led the AL in wins, tied for the lead with five shutouts, and added a career-best 190 strikeouts. He received 26 of 28 first-place ballots in the AL Cy Young voting.

A tired arm troubled Flanagan in 1980, but he didn't miss a start. However, a torn muscle in his left forearm sidelined him for 26 days in 1981. After a healthy 1982, he was 6–0 when he injured ligaments in his left knee fielding a groundball on May 17, 1983—an ironic turn for this fine fielder—and he missed almost three months. He rebounded, however, to go 6–1 during the Orioles' sizzling 34–10 stretch run to win the AL East.

In 1984 Flanagan topped 200 innings for the sixth time in eight seasons. During that span he pitched more innings and made more starts than any AL hurler, winning 122 games, a figure topped only by Yankee southpaw Ron Guidry.

In January 1985 Flanagan injured his Achilles tendon in a charity basketball game and was out until July 20. He had a losing record after his return, and another in 1986. On May 18, 1987, Flanagan went on the disabled list with elbow trouble, returning to the Orioles on July 17 after a minor league rehabilitation assignment.

Baltimore traded Flanagan to Toronto on August 31, 1987. From 1987 through 1990 Flanagan went 26–27 with the Blue Jays. In 1991 he came to the Orioles camp as a nonroster invitee and wound up with 64 appearances. Flanagan entered the final game played at Memorial Stadium with one out in the ninth inning and the Orioles trailing, 7–1. He struck out Detroit's Dave Bergman and Travis Fryman, and an emotional standing ovation from the 50,700 fans in attendance followed.

Art Fletcher

Fletcher, Arthur **SS**

1909–20, 1922 M(1923–26, 1929, 237–383)
B:1/5/1885, Collinsville, IL D:2/6/50, Los Angeles, CA
Deb:4/15/1909, NY NL BR/TR 5'10½", 170

G	AB	R	H	HR	RBI	OBP	SLG	AVG
1533	5541	684	1534	32	675	.319	.365	.277

Art Fletcher was a spark plug on four pennant winners for John McGraw's New York Giants. He never won a world championship as a player, but he won nine titles as a coach with the New York Yankees.

While Fletcher was playing for Dallas of the Texas League, McGraw scouted him during a spring exhibition game against the Giants in 1908. The Giants manager purchased the option to buy Fletcher for $1,500. Beginning in 1909, Fletcher was New York's shortstop for 11 years, and was team captain for his final three seasons. Many attributed his abrasive and belligerent demeanor during games to McGraw. Off the field, Fletcher was a churchgoing family man.

The Giants made the World Series in 1911, 1912, 1913, and 1917, but lost each time. Fletcher batted just .191 in the 25 Series games. McGraw traded him to the Philadelphia Phillies early in the 1920 season, with pitcher Wilbur Hubbell and $100,000, for shortstop Dave Bancroft. Fletcher missed all of 1921 because of several deaths in his family. He finished his playing career with the Phillies in 1922.

The following year Fletcher took over as manager of the Phillies. His teams finished no better than sixth in four years in Philadelphia. He became a coach for Miller Huggins and the New York Yankees in 1927, and took over the Yankees as interim manager after Huggins died in 1929. Fletcher turned down offers to manage the Yankees, White Sox, Indians, Browns, and Tigers, preferring the fewer responsibilities of a coach. He remained a coach with the Yankees until 1945.

Scott Fletcher

Fletcher, Scott Brian **SS–2B**

1981–95 B:7/30/1958, Fort Walton Beach, FL
Deb:4/25/1981,CHI NL BR/TR 5'11, 173

G	AB	R	H	HR	RBI	OBP	SLG	AVG
1612	5258	688	1376	34	510	.334	.342	.262

Scott Fletcher had little power, hit .300 only once, and bounced around with six different teams. He still managed to put together a respectable 15-year career in the major leagues.

Fletcher started out in the Cubs' organization, where he impressed scouts by winning the New York–Penn League's Most Valuable Player Award in 1979. He arrived in the major leagues two years later. The Cubs liked Fletcher's hustle and his fielding skills, yet they soon acquired Bump Wills and Larry Bowa to play the middle infield, leaving Fletcher as odd man out. The Cubs included him in a six-player deal with the crosstown White Sox.

In the spring of 1983, Fletcher surprisingly emerged as Chicago's starting shortstop, bumping incumbent Vance Law to third base. He helped lead Chicago to its first postseason berth since 1959. But the Sox were looking for more punch from their middle infielders, and they traded Fletcher to Texas as part of a five-player deal after the 1985 season. Fletcher became the Rangers' regular shortstop the following season, batting a career high .300.

The fiery Fletcher continued to hit well over the next two seasons before struggling in 1989. Midway through the season, the Rangers packaged Fletcher with outfield prospect Sammy Sosa and traded him back to the White Sox for Harold Baines. With Ozzie Guillen now at shortstop, the Sox moved Fletcher to second base. He developed a pattern of hitting well one season and then bottoming out the following year. He batted .285 with 16 steals after signing with the Red Sox as a free agent in 1993; the next year he managed just .227. Fletcher finished his career with Detroit in 1995.

Elmer Flick

Flick, Elmer Harrison **OF**

1898–1910 B:1/11/1876, Bedford, OH D:1/9/1971, Bedford, OH Deb:5/2/1898, PHI NL BL/TR 5'9", 168

G	AB	R	H	HR	RBI	OBP	SLG	AVG
1483	5597	950	1752	48	756	.389	.445	.313

Fans today may find it amusing, but when Detroit Tigers manager Hughie Jennings offered to swap Ty Cobb to Cleveland for Elmer Flick after the 1907 season, the deal made sense. Although Cobb, at 22, was nine years younger than Flick and fresh from a batting championship for the pennant-winning Tigers, he was an erratic outfielder, despised by his teammates, and a negative factor in the clubhouse. Moreover, with his no-holds-barred playing style he seemed destined for a short career.

Flick was everything that Cobb wasn't—modest, a team player, and well liked by both teammates and opponents. His fielding was smooth and sure. Cobb was the reigning basestealing champ with 49 thefts, but Flick had won the title twice before. And his 41 steals in 1907 ranked second only to Cobb's total. Although Flick's 1907 batting average of .302 was well below Cobb's .350, the Cleveland outfielder was a consistent .300 hitter. After much deliberation Cleveland owner Charles Somers decided Cobb was too much of a risk. Flick stayed in Cleveland.

Only in hindsight does Somers' decision seem like a mistake. Cobb went on to win batting and basestealing titles for another two decades, but in the spring of 1908 Flick developed a mysterious stomach ailment that soon caused him to retire. The trade that never was helped Detroit win two more pennants and kept Cleveland out of the winner's circle, yet indirectly it may have helped to land Flick in the Hall of Fame.

Elmer Flick became a semipro ballplayer literally by accident. A large crowd turned out one day at the Bedford, Ohio railroad station to see the local team off to a game. At the last minute team members discovered that one of the players was missing. In desperation the team captain asked 15-year-old Flick to join the team. The barefoot lad happily climbed aboard.

After several years of semipro ball the young Flick joined Youngstown of the Inter-State League as an outfielder in 1896 and hit an amazing .438 in 31 games. The following year, in a full season with Dayton of the International League, he hit .386 and attracted the attention of the Phillies.

Unfortunately, Philadelphia, with an All-Star outfield of Ed Delahanty, Duff Cooley, and Sam Thompson, had little room for Flick. And it looked as though Flick was going to provide comic relief when he showed up at spring training carrying a canvas suitcase and a thick-handled bat he'd turned on a lathe himself. The Phillies veterans snickered at the hayseed—until he started knocking the ball all over the park with his odd bat.

At 5 feet 9 inches and 168 pounds, Flick was built for speed rather than power. Pitchers tried to jam him inside, but his thick bat handle allowed him to get good wood on inside slants and drive them over the infield. One reporter described the new kid as the "fastest and most promising youngster the Phillies ever had." Promising as he was, Flick rode the bench as the season opened. But when Thompson developed back trouble, Flick entered the lineup and began hitting. He finished the season with a .302 average, 81 RBIs, and 84 runs scored.

Flick kept improving. In 1899 he upped his average to .342, with 98 RBIs and 98 runs scored. One day in Pittsburgh he made a leaping, one-handed grab that the local press called the most spectacular ever seen in the city. The bleacher fans were so taken with the likable Flick that they showered him with silver—even after he robbed a Pirate of extra bases.

In 1900, Flick's best season, he batted .367, second only to Honus Wagner. That year he scored 106 runs, led the National League with 110 RBIs, and was third in the league with 32 doubles, fifth with 16 triples, and second with 11 home runs.

In 1901 the National League was at war with the upstart American League, which had declared itself a major circuit. Several of Flick's teammates, including the great Napoleon Lajoie, jumped to the new league for higher wages. But Flick and left fielder Ed Delahanty stayed on, and their hitting lifted the Phillies to second place in the National League.

The money was too tempting, however, and in 1902 Delahanty jumped to Washington and Flick to Connie Mack's Philadelphia Athletics. Flick played only 11 games with the A's before the Phillies secured an injunction preventing him from playing baseball in Pennsylvania for anyone but the NL team. They had used the same strategy with Lajoie the previous year. In order to keep these valuable players in the American League, Connie Mack sold both to Cleveland.

For the next six years Lajoie and Flick gave the Indians a potent one-two batting punch. On the surface, Flick's performance seemed to suffer in Cleveland, but this had nothing to do with his ability. Pitchers were learning to use such trick deliveries as the spitball and emeryball, and the so-called dead ball came into play. Mighty swings that once produced screaming line drives now yielded soft popups to the infield, and batting averages plummeted throughout baseball.

In 1905 Flick was the American League's leading hitter with a .308 mark, the lowest for a batting champion until Carl Yastrzemski's .301 in 1968. His .302 in 1907 was 48 points below

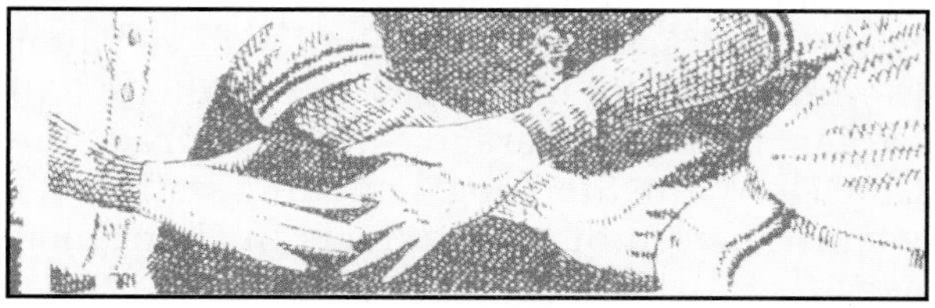

Cobb's average, but was still the fourth highest in the league.

Flick led the league in runs scored in 1906 with 98, but his real talent was hitting triples. Shortly after his arrival in Cleveland he hit three in one game. From 1905 through 1907 he led the AL in triples each season, smacking 18, 22, and then 18 again.

At spring training in New Orleans in 1908, Flick developed an unexplained stomach problem. Some suspected contaminated water, but no other players had been affected. His weight dropped to 135 pounds and he appeared in only nine games all season. When he tried to come back in 1909 he was only a shadow of his former self. After playing 24 games for Cleveland in 1910 he left the major leagues. During the next two seasons he attempted a comeback with Toledo in the American Association, but failed.

After retiring from baseball Flick was virtually forgotten. In the flood of stories and anecdotes precipitated by Ty Cobb's death in 1961, the tale of Cobb's near-trade for Flick came up often. That probably led the Hall of Fame's Veterans Committee to reexamine Flick's career, and he was named to the Hall in 1963. At his induction ceremony the 87-year-old Flick said, "This is a bigger day than I've ever had before."

Silver Flint

Flint, Frank Sylvester **C–OF**

1875,1878–89 M(1879, 5–12) B:8/3/1855, Philadelphia, PA D:1/14/1892, Chicago, IL Deb:5/4/1875, RS NA BR/TR 6', 180

G	AB	R	H	HR	RBI	OBP	SLG	AVG
743	2852	376	682	21	294	.253	.330	.239

Eddie Cuthbert, one of baseball's early outfielders, described Frank "Silver" Flint as the greatest worker he'd ever seen behind the bat, and perhaps the greatest catcher. Nicknamed "Silver" for his light blond hair (and possibly also for his middle name, "Sylvester"), Flint worked with pitchers John Clarkson, Larry Corcoran, Fred Goldsmith, and Jim McCormick. McCormick credited Flint with being the best developer of pitchers around.

Known for his exceptional arm and ability to block errant pitches, Flint played 12 years in the majors, catching barehanded even after the introduction of the glove. Despite a .239 career batting average, he anchored the Chicago White Stockings' pitching staff for 11 years. He died of tuberculosis in Chicago at age 36.

Curt Flood

Flood, Curtis Charles **OF**

1956–69,1971 B:1/18/1938, Houston, TX D:1/20/1997, Los Angeles, CA Deb:9/9/1956, CIN NL BR/TR 5'9", 165

G	AB	R	H	HR	RBI	OBP	SLG	AVG
1759	6357	851	1861	85	636	.344	.389	.293

Every time a major leaguer collects a huge paycheck, he should thank Curt Flood. In 1970 the St. Louis Cardinals center fielder sued Major League Baseball in an effort to eliminate the reserve clause that had, since 1879, bound a player to his team forever. Although Flood lost the battle, the players ultimately won the war. Flood's suit paved the way for arbitration, free agency, and million-dollar salaries.

After two short trials with Cincinnati, Flood was traded to St. Louis. He came to the majors to stay in 1958 at age 20. Flood played sparingly until the middle of 1961, when Johnny Keane replaced Solly Hemus as the Cardinals skipper. In 1961 he batted .322, up 85 points from the previous year. It was the first of six .300-plus seasons in his remaining nine years with the Cardinals.

Flood's real gift was playing the outfield. He won the first of seven straight Gold Glove Awards in 1963. By the middle of the decade it was widely acknowledged that he'd surpassed Willie Mays as baseball's best center fielder. He had other talents, too: a 1968 *Sports Illustrated* cover featured a self-portrait by Flood the painter.

From September 3, 1965, through June 2, 1967, Flood played 226 errorless games in the outfield for a National League record and handled 568 consecutive chances, a record in the majors. The string ended when he muffed his third chance of a game on June 4, 1967. His streak included playing a record 159 errorless games in 1966, in which he flawlessly accepted 396 chances. On June 19, 1967, Flood completed the first unassisted double play by an NL outfielder in 34 years, the first in the majors since 1945.

Surprisingly, Flood's most memorable moment in three World Series appearances occurred when he misjudged a fly ball in the 1968 Series. With two out in the seventh inning of a scoreless Game 7, Jim Northrup drove a Bob Gibson pitch deep into center field. Flood took a step in and then could not catch up to the drive, which fell for a triple, scoring both runners. Northrup later scored, and Detroit held on to win the Series.

Flood was a co-captain, with Tim McCarver, of those St. Louis pennant winners. When the Cards failed to win a third straight flag in 1969, the front office set about remaking the squad. Late in the season Flood complained publicly about management throwing in the towel while the team still had a slim chance to win. He was among the first to go.

On October 7, 1969, the Cardinals traded Flood, McCarver, pitcher Joe Hoerner, and outfielder Byron Browne to Philadelphia for first baseman Dick Allen, second baseman Cookie Rojas, and pitcher Jerry Johnson. Flood found out about the trade from a reporter who called to ask for a comment. After 12 years with the Cardinals, he felt he had earned more consideration. "If I had been a foot-shuffling porter, they might have at least given me a pocket watch," Flood wrote. Moreover, he said, the trade "violated the logic and integrity of my existence. I was not a consignment of goods."

He declared he would retire rather than report to Philadelphia, a standard ploy for a traded veteran player. He disliked the Philadelphia organization's reputation and the city's treatment of black players. But as the hurt of the trade faded, its injustice remained. Flood began to think about suing baseball over the reserve clause, which bound him either to play for Philadelphia or retire. He consulted a local attorney, who endorsed the possibility of a successful lawsuit.

Flood met with Marvin Miller, executive director of the Major League Baseball Players Association (MLBPA), who had been trying to reform the game's archaic labor-relations policies ever since he had taken over as head of the union in 1966. Miller warned that the suit could end Flood's career and cost him hundreds of thousands of dollars in lost salary as well as legal fees. Flood declared, "I want to go out like a man instead of disappearing like a bottle cap."

Still, Flood took Miller's advice to think the suit through carefully. He dined with Philadelphia general manager John Quinn, who thought at the time that he'd convinced Flood to join the Phillies. Flood decided to proceed with the suit anyway, and in mid-December he met with MLBPA representatives, who voted unanimously to pay legal fees and other expenses related to Flood's suit.

On December 24, 1969, Flood, with help from Miller and former U.S. Supreme Court Justice Arthur Goldberg, drafted the following letter to baseball Commissioner Bowie Kuhn:

"After twelve years in the major leagues, I do not feel I am a piece of property to be bought and sold irrespective of my wishes. I believe that any system which produces that result violates my basic rights as a citizen and is inconsistent with the laws of the United States and of the several States.

"It is my desire to play baseball in 1970, and I am capable of playing. I have received a contract offer from the Philadelphia club, but I believe I have the right to consider offers from other clubs before making any decision. I, therefore, request that you make known to all Major League clubs my feelings in this matter, and advise them of my availability for the 1970 season."

Kuhn's reply reaffirmed Organized Baseball's intention to hold Flood to the provisions of his 1969 contract, which included the right of the Cardinals to assign it wherever they pleased. In April, Philadelphia acquired first baseman Willie Montanez and minor league pitcher Bob Browning from St. Louis as substitutes for Flood. In January 1970, the case of Flood vs. Kuhn was filed in U.S. District Court in New York. Judge Irving Ben Cooper denied Flood's request for an injunction voiding the trade and recommended the issue be settled in a trial, which began in May.

Hall of Famers Jackie Robinson and Hank Greenberg testified for Flood, along with former club owner Bill Veeck and former pitcher and author Jim Brosnan. No active players testified for Flood, nor did any show up to give moral support. Despite the MLBPA representatives' vote, rank-and-file players were divided, some believing Organized Baseball's dire predictions that eliminating the reserve clause would destroy the game.

Sitting out the 1970 season to avoid prejudicing his case, Flood went to Copenhagen after the trial to paint and to pursue plans to open a restaurant. In August, Judge Cooper decided against Flood without touching on the merits of the reserve clause. His ruling simply upheld the 1922 U.S. Supreme Court decision exempting Organized Baseball from antitrust laws because it was sport, not interstate commerce. A federal appeals court upheld Cooper's ruling, but the U.S. Supreme Court agreed to hear Flood's appeal.

On June 12, 1972, the Supreme Court ruled in a 5–3 decision against Flood, with Justice Lewis Powell abstaining because he held stock in Anheuser-Busch, which owned the Cardinals. However, the majority opinion hoisted a warning flag for baseball, calling its antitrust exemption an "aberration" and an "anomaly." Flood's suit had exposed the vulnerability of Organized Baseball's legal position, as well as its immorality, and had begun the march toward the modification of the reserve rules, which culminated in arbitrator Peter Seitz's 1976 ruling establishing free agency.

Flood reaped little from shaking the game to its roots. With his U.S. business interests going sour, he accepted owner Bob Short's offer to play for the Washington Senators for the 1971 season, after securing an agreement that Major League Baseball's attorneys would not use it against him in court. Short had to send Philadelphia a player for the right to negotiate with Flood, and two more after signing him. However, after batting .200 in 13 games, Flood left the team, saying that age and rust had robbed him of his skills.

Flood went back to Europe, landing in Spain, but ultimately returned to the Bay Area, where he worked as a broadcaster for the Oakland Athletics in 1978, painted, and headed Oakland's Little League. In a final irony, the man who had sued a commissioner of Organized Baseball ultimately became one himself. Flood headed the short-lived Senior League, which played its single season in the winter of 1989–90.

Tim Foli

Foli, Timothy John **SS**
1970–85 B:2/8/1950, Culver City, CA Deb:9/11/1970, NY NL BR/TR 6', 179

G	AB	R	H	HR	RBI	OBP	SLG	AVG
1696	6047	576	1515	25	501	.286	.309	.251

A major league shortstop for 16 seasons, Tim Foli didn't get the nickname "Crazy Horse" for nothing. A ferocious competitor, too often he would lose his cool. He never met an umpire with whom he couldn't argue. So contentious was his temperament that he frequently fought his own teammates.

Gene Mauch, who managed him in Montreal and California, said Foli's tantrums reflected his "constant search for perfection." Other people said he had the annoying habit of trying to tell everybody else how to play the game. As for the umpires, a teammate acknowledged, "It's like he had some psychological problem with them. He'd get upset over some meaningless ball-and-strike call in the second inning and he'd still be angry in the ninth inning. You know, maybe he swung at the first or second pitch so often because he didn't want to let the umpire call him out."

Timothy John Foli signed with the Mets for $75,000 out of high school as the first player picked in the June 1968 amateur draft. He made the Mets as a utility infielder in 1971, the year he got into a fight with teammate Ed Kranepool, who cleaned his clock. Foli got a chance to play for Mauch when the Mets sent him to Montreal in the Rusty Staub trade just before the start of the 1972 season. Foli had his moments with the Expos, enjoying the best season of his career with them in 1976. He hit .264 that year with career highs in homers (6) and doubles (36), but the Expos tired of his act and sent him to San Francisco the next April for shortstop Chris Speier.

In San Francisco the Giants and some of the team's beat writers took to calling Foli "Rubber Room" behind his back; San Francisco sold him to the Mets after one season. He got the break of his career when Pittsburgh swapped shortstops with New York on April 19, 1979. The Pirates needed a second-place hitter and a reliable shortstop. On a team of strong personalities, including Chuck Tanner and his positive thinking, Foli had to behave.

The Pirates beat the Orioles in the 1979 World Series after losing three of the first four games. After hitting a career-best .288 in the regular season with a career-high 65 RBIs, Foli hit .333 in the Series. In 1980, he led NL shortstops in fielding and hit .265. He was reunited with Mauch in Anaheim for the 1982 season, his last as a regular. He hit .252 in 150 games and led the league in fielding as the Angels won their division and just missed making the World Series.

Lew Fonseca

Fonseca, Lewis Albert **1B-2B-OF**
1921–25,1927–33 M(1932–34, 120–196) B:1/21/1899, Oakland, CA D:11/26/1989, Ely, IA Deb:4/13/1921, CIN NL BR/TR 5'10½", 180

G	AB	R	H	HR	RBI	OBP	SLG	AVG
937	3404	518	1075	31	485	.355	.432	.316

Lew Fonseca was a fine ballplayer in his day, playing many positions gracefully and winning a batting title. But his accomplishments after his retirement in 1932 were of greater importance, for he pioneered the use of motion pictures in professional baseball.

While playing a small part in the 1927 Joe E. Brown film *Slide, Kelly, Slide*, Fonseca became interested in motion picture technology. A few years later, while managing the Chicago White Sox, he used films of his players to study and improve their techniques. Appointed director of motion picture promotion for the American League in 1939, Fonseca eventually became director for both major leagues.

His pioneering work with film tends to overshadow the fact that Lewis Albert Fonseca was an outstanding, although unlucky, player. Quite versatile, he played second or first base most of the time but also saw action at third, short, and in the outfield. Plagued by injuries in his first four major league seasons with Cincinnati, he was traded to the Phillies in 1925. Fonseca played regularly with Philadelphia and hit .319, but when he held out the following year, he was unceremoniously sold to Newark of the International League.

Cleveland brought him back to the majors in 1927, when he hit .311. A broken leg in 1928 and a broken arm in 1930 ruined those seasons, but in 1929 he led the AL in batting with .369 and had 103 RBIs. He hit .312 between the Indians and the White Sox in 1931. Named player-manager a year later, Fonseca tore a ligament in his leg, effectively ending his days on the field.

Davy Force

Force, David W. **SS-3B**

1871–77,1879–86 B:7/27/1849, New York, NY
D:6/21/1918, Englewood, NJ Deb:5/5/1871, OLY NA
BR/TR 5'4", 130

G	AB	R	H	HR	RBI	OBP	SLG	AVG
768	2950	323	623	1	209	.245	.249	.211

The "Force Case" of 1875 was more catalyst than cause; nevertheless, the battle over the rights to shortstop Davy Force sparked the collapse of the National Association. Dissatisfaction with the league already ran deep among thoughtful men who cared about the future of baseball. All that was needed to dissolve the National Association was lighting the right fuse. Force had no idea what the consequences would be when he signed a contract in 1874; he just wanted to make more money.

At age 18 Force attracted favorable attention as a catcher for the Unknowns of Harlem, and Abraham G. Mills, future president of the National League, convinced him to move to Washington, D.C., and play for the Olympics. Like many other teams at the time, the Olympics claimed to be amateurs, but historians assume their players received some sort of payment. Force may have been paid cash under the table, or he may have been given a token job, freeing him to play ball.

Force remained with the Olympics through 1871 and built a reputation as a shortstop with talents second only to Harry Wright, the legendary shortstop who played for the Nationals of Washington. The 5-foot-4-inch, 130-pound Force was called "Wee Davy" or "Tom Thumb." In 1871 the National Association of Professional Base Ball Players formed the first professional league. As part of the nine-team circuit, the Olympics finished in the middle of the pack with a 15–15 record. Force hit .278, some 214 points lower than league-leader Levi Meyerle, but his strength was fielding.

In 1872 Force became a "gypsy," a player who annually changed teams in search of a better deal. He started the season with Troy, but when the team dropped out of the league after only 25 games, he switched allegiance to Baltimore. He hit .406 for the season, third best in the league.

The National Association was financially weak and poorly organized. Any team with nine players and $10 was able to join, so the league was filled with poor teams on the brink of financial collapse. After a bad start or when a team started losing money, it had little incentive to try to complete the season, so teams disappeared with regularity.

Not until their teams folded were players permitted to change clubs during the season. They could, however, sign with any team after the season. Force played with Baltimore through 1873 and then moved on to Chicago in 1874.

The Boston Red Stockings dominated the league at that time. The team was managed by Harry Wright and featured his brother, George, at shortstop. The Red Stockings finished third in 1871, but collected their first pennant the following year. In each of the subsequent three seasons, their margin over the other league teams increased. The National Association was becoming a one-team league, with the remaining teams fighting for second place.

William Hulbert, president of the Chicago White Stockings, decided to change the situation. He wasn't quite sure how to do it, but he knew he needed a shortstop if his team hoped to challenge Boston. Force performed well for Hulbert in 1874 and was signed again for the following season. According to some accounts, Hulbert signed Force for 1875 before the 1874 season ended, a direct violation of league rules, which were routinely ignored.

However, Force then signed another contract, with the Philadelphia Athletics. Hulbert protested to the league offices, claiming that Force belonged to the White Stockings. The National Association judiciary committee initially upheld Hulbert's claim. But when league officials met in Philadelphia, they determined that the Chicago contract had indeed been signed too soon and awarded Force to Philadelphia. Hulbert was incensed. Harry Wright, perhaps the man most critical of the National Association's laxity toward its rules, took umbrage and accused the Athletics of some underhanded dealing of their own. During the summer of 1875, Hulbert blatantly violated NA rules, signing four of Wright's stars and one Philadelphia player for the 1876 season.

Before league officials could respond, Hulbert devised a plan to form a new association, to be called the National League. He lined up four teams, including his own White Stockings, and headed east for a showdown with the National Association. Although Wright had lost some of his best players to Chicago, he joined Hulbert's league, seeing the new affiliation as a huge improvement over the poorly run and untrustworthy National Association. The Philadelphia Athletics joined for similar reasons.

Several teams were excluded from the new league, which was limited to only eight clubs, and the price of membership was raised. Only one team per city was allowed, creating a monopoly for each franchise.

In the National League's first game, in 1876, Boston played the Athletics at Philadelphia. When the first batter, Boston's George Wright, bounced to short, Davy Force threw him out to make the first assist in league history. Force played for both Philadelphia and the New York Mutuals that year, then moved to St. Louis in 1877, where he led league shortstops in fielding.

In 1878 he accepted a $1,200 deal with Buffalo of the International Association. The National League may well have been the only true major league at the time, but a number of other organizations, including the International League, considered themselves equals. In 1879 Buffalo decided to join the NL, and Force wrote to the team's president, advising against it and cautioning him, "I have heard we are going to join the league. I hope and pray not, for if we do, we are gone financially."

Force stayed with Buffalo through 1885. Only once did his batting average rise above .225, but he led the circuit in fielding three times. After playing for Washington in 1886, he spent several seasons in the minor leagues and then retired as a player. He umpired for one season in the Western Association before taking a job with the Otis Elevator Company. His boss was Abraham G. Mills, the man who had brought him to the Olympics in 1867.

In 10 National League seasons Force hit only .211, but veteran sportswriter Francis Richter ranked him as the second-best shortstop of his era, after George Wright. Four fielding titles appear to support that view.

Dan Ford

Ford, Darrell Glenn **OF**

1975–85 B:5/19/1952, Los Angeles, CA
Deb:4/12/1975, MIN AL BR/TR 6'1", 185

G	AB	R	H	HR	RBI	OBP	SLG	AVG
1153	4163	598	1123	121	566	.326	.427	.270

"Disco Dan" Ford could hit. Before his bum knees prematurely ended his career in 1985, he had 21 homers and 101 RBIs for the Angels in 1979 and two home runs against the Orioles in the 1979 ALCS. He drove in 86 runs in 1976 and 82 in 1978 for the Twins. Ford is best remembered, however, for a couple of baserunning escapades that bordered on theater of the absurd.

In a 1978 game, Ford was on third with the bases loaded. A teammate singled. Ford started running home—backwards. It seems he was encouraging the runner on second to hurry in with another run. But Ford never scored. He stopped before reaching home, and the runner from second passed him. Manager Gene Mauch dismissed him from the game on the spot.

In a contest against the Tigers, Ford was steaming from first to third on a single to right. A wild throw from the right fielder sent third baseman Aurelio Rodriguez about 15 feet up the third-base line. Ford would have made it easily—if he had slid into the base. Instead, he slid into Rodriguez.

More? On another occasion, Ford had to change his spikes in the middle of the game. The ones he had on were illegal. Somehow it comes as no surprise that he was also ejected from a game in 1981 for using a corked bat.

Hod Ford

Ford, Horace Hills **SS–2B**

1919–33 B:7/23/1897, New Haven, CT D:1/29/1977, Winchester, MA Deb:9/8/1919, BOS NL BR/TR 5'10", 165

G	AB	R	H	HR	RBI	OBP	SLG	AVG
1446	4833	484	1269	16	494	.316	.337	.263

Hod Ford was an outstanding middle infielder and respectable hitter who helped form one of the best double-play combinations of the 1920s. He went straight from Tufts University to the Boston Braves in 1919, and after a midseason stint in the minors, he returned to the major leagues to stay in 1920.

Although Ford became an everyday player for the Braves, he shuttled between shortstop and second base. In 1921 he led second basemen in fielding percentage, but he was switched to shortstop the following season. Ford also switched teams frequently. He spent 1924 with the Philadelphia Phillies, and the next year with the Brooklyn Dodgers. Ford found a home in Cincinnati in 1926.

As the Reds shortstop, Ford teamed with second baseman Hughie Critz to form one of the National League's most effective middle-infield combinations. In 1928 Ford and Critz helped the Reds set a major league record for most double plays in one season, breaking a mark established by Washington in 1923. Ford also set an individual record for starting the most double plays in a season, surpassing a mark held jointly by Rabbit Maranville and Glenn Wright.

A disagreement with Reds management in 1931 resulted in Ford holding out in spring training. After batting only .229 after his holdout, he was sold to St. Louis. Ford played one game for the Cardinals and then finished his career where it had started, with the Braves. After his retirement, he remained in the Boston area, operating a successful restaurant in Winchester, Massachusetts.

Whitey Ford

Ford, Edward Charles **P**

1950,1953–67 B:10/21/1928, New York, NY
Deb:7/1/1950, NY AL BL/TL 5'10", 181

W	L	PCT	G	SH	IP	BB	SO	ERA
236	106	.690	498	45	3170^{1}	1086	1956	2.75

Columnist Russell Baker once observed that the Yankees' Whitey Ford was "to left-handed pitching what Edward G. Robinson was to the .45-caliber automatic." Ford's manager, Casey Stengel, put it another way: "If you had one game to win and your life depended on it, you'd want him to pitch it."

Ford—backed, of course, by an awesome Yankee lineup—was the toughest pitcher to beat in modern history. He enjoyed the highest winning percentage of the 20th century—.690, with 236 victories against only 106 losses. He was a dominant postseason pitcher, too; his 32 consecutive scoreless innings in Fall Classic play broke Babe Ruth's mark of 29⅔ innings. Ford also holds World Series records for most victories (10), strikeouts (94), and innings pitched (146).

Ford started compiling his October records in his rookie season, 1950, winning the last game of the Yankees-Phillies World Series. After missing the next two Series because of military duty, he won Game 7 of the 1953 Fall Classic, holding Brooklyn to just one run in seven innings. In 1955 he beat the Dodgers in Games 1 and 6. In 1956, with the Yankees down two games to none, Ford won Game 3, and New York rallied to win the Series.

In Game 5 of the 1957 Series Ford five-hit Milwaukee, and in Game 6 of the 1960 Series he shut out Pittsburgh on just three hits. He was World Series MVP in 1969 when the Yankees bested the Reds.

Ford led the AL in wins, innings pitched, and won-lost percentage in the same season twice, in 1961 and 1963. In '63 he also won the Cy Young Award by posting 24 victories, including eight in the month of June. Catcher Elston Howard nicknamed Ford "the Chairman of the Board" in recognition of Whitey's masterly fashion of controlling a game and all the fielders around him. And Stengel called him "Slick" after the manager caught Ford and his drinking buddy Mickey Mantle staying out late. He labeled them "a couple of whiskey slicks," and the name stuck.

Ford signed a Yankee contract in early 1947. Called up to the majors in 1950, he won nine consecutive games for the team. That October, pitching in Game 4 of the World Series against the Phillies, he came within one out of a 5–2 complete game as the Yankees capped a sweep of the "Whiz Kids." He spent the next two seasons as a private in the Army signal corps. "Army life was rough," he once remarked. "Would you believe it, they actually wanted me to pitch three times a week?" In fact, Ford developed some bad work habits in the Army, and when he returned to the Yankees in 1953 he was overweight. "I didn't lose my stuff, but I didn't improve it either," he said.

Ford still won 18 games in 1953, the first of 13 straight seasons of at least 11 victories. He didn't record a losing record until the 1966 and 1967 seasons, his last two in the majors. Even then, his ERAs were 2.47 and 1.64, respectively.

"Stick a baseball in his hand and he became the most arrogant guy in the world," said Mickey Mantle. "Off the field he was as smooth as butter. If you tried to rile him, he'd give you one of those rosy-cheeked smiles and walk away. He hated arguments. To him, they were a total waste of time."

Toward the end of his career Ford was dogged by accusations of doctoring the baseball. "I didn't begin cheating until late in my career, when I needed it to survive," he admitted. "I didn't cheat when I won the 25 games in 1961. I don't want anyone to get any ideas and take my Cy Young Award away. And I didn't cheat in 1963 when I won 24 games. Well, maybe just a little."

One of the "little" ways involved his hiding a rasp on his wedding ring to nick the ball. "It was a ring with a sharp edge, just right to cut up the ball a bit," Ford explained. "This pitch wasn't like the spitter or the mudball; it just sank slightly more than my ordinary pitches." He got away with it until rival manager Alvin Dark collected a bushel of balls Ford had used and noticed they were all scuffed in exactly the same way. Umpire Hank Soar made Ford get rid of his ring.

"I know men are not supposed to talk about love for other men, especially so-called macho athletes," Mantle said in the introduction to Ford's book, *Slick*, "but I don't mind telling you that I love Whitey Ford. I couldn't love him more if he was my own brother."

Ford was elected to the Baseball Hall of Fame in 1974, in his second year of eligibility. His pal Mantle was inducted the same year

Bob Forsch

Forsch, Robert Herbert **P**

1974–89 B:1/13/1950, Sacramento, CA Deb:7/7/1974, STL NL BR/TR 6'4", 200

W	L	PCT	G	SH	IP	BB	SO	ERA
168	136	.553	498	19	2794^{2}	832	1133	3.76

Bob Forsch and his brother Ken are the only brothers to each pitch a no-hitter in the majors. Bob added a second no-hitter in St. Louis, albeit a disputed one, when a generous official scorer called a line drive by the Phillies' Garry Maddox past Cardinals third baseman Ken Reitz an error.

The younger of the two brothers, Bob Forsch was a dependable starter for the Cardinals for more than 14 years. He pitched 200 or more innings seven times, and once won 20 games. His 15 wins tied for the team lead in the Cardinals' 1982 championship season. Forsch added a three-hit shutout of the Braves in Game 1 of the NLCS but lost both of his World Series starts against the Milwaukee Brewers. When Forsch retired he ranked third among Cardinals pitchers in wins and innings pitched, behind Hall of Famers Bob Gibson and Jesse Haines.

The righthander twice won NL Silver Slugger awards as the league's best-hitting pitcher. He joined the Astros in August 1988, and in 1989 had a night he'd rather forget. Houston starter Jim Clancy had given up six hits and a walk to the first seven Reds to bat when Forsch was brought in. He endured seven long innings of relief, allowing 18 hits and 10 runs in an 18–2 Houston loss. He retired at the end of the season.

Ken Forsch

Forsch, Kenneth Roth **P**

1970–84,1986 B:9/8/1946, Sacramento, CA Deb:9/7/1970, HOU NL BR/TR 6'4", 210

W	L	PCT	G	SV	IP	BB	SO	ERA
114	113	.502	521	51	2127^{1}	586	1047	3.37

The elder of two big league pitching brothers, Ken Forsch entered the majors in 1970. The lanky 6-foot-4-inch righthander was one of a slew of promising youngsters who came up with the Astros in the late 1960s and early 1970s. Others included Joe Morgan, Mike Cuellar, Cesar Geronimo, and Mike Marshall. Astros fans looked to them to bring the team into contention. All but Forsch were traded.

Although faith in Forsch remained strong, he developed slowly as a starter and didn't have a winning season until the Astros switched him to a relief role in 1974. He became their relief workhorse and developed a forkball that earned him 19 saves in 1976 and a spot on the NL All-Star team that year.

Forsch remained with the Astros and in 1979 was moved back into the starting rotation. With Forsch, J.R. Richard, Joe Niekro, and Joaquin Andujar, the Astros featured one of the strongest pitching staffs in the league. Forsch no-hit the Atlanta Braves on April 7, 1979, making him and brother Bob, who had performed the feat a year earlier, the only brothers to each pitch a major league no-hitter.

With the acquisition of Nolan Ryan in 1980, the Astros went to the NLCS for the second time in Forsch's career. The following year Forsch was traded to the California Angels for shortstop Dickie Thon. He remained with the Angels as a starter until 1986.

Terry Forster

Forster, Terry Jay **P**

1971–86 B:1/14/1952, Sioux Falls, SD Deb:4/11/1971, CHI AL BL/TL 6'3", 210

W	L	PCT	G	SV	IP	BB	SO	ERA
54	65	.454	614	127	1105^{2}	457	791	3.23

Terry Forster was only a year out of high school when he made the Chicago White Sox in 1972. He earned 29 saves in 62 outings, second in the AL only to Sparky Lyle. Two years later he led the AL in saves, with 24, and took the Fireman of the Year Award. He injured himself the following season, perhaps from overwork, and at the end of 1976 was traded with Rich Gossage to Pittsburgh for outfielder Richie Zisk.

In 1978 Forster went to the Dodgers as a free agent, becoming the first free agent signed to a Dodgers contract. During the next four years his play was sometimes effective, but he had become prone to weight problems and injury. Nevertheless, he saw World Series action in both 1978 and 1981. He was a good hitter for a pitcher and often pinch-hit.

By 1985 Forster had moved on to the Braves and added a few more pounds to his frame. Late-night talk show host David Letterman called him "a fat tub of goo...the fattest man in professional baseball." The running joke once again brought him national recognition.

Tony Fossas

Fossas, Emilio Antonio (Morejon) **P**

1988–99 B:9/23/1957, Havana, Cuba Deb:5/15/1988, TEX AL BL/TL 6', 187

W	L	PCT	G	SV	IP	BB	SO	ERA
17	24	.415	567	7	415^{2}	180	324	3.90

Tony Fossas is a baseball purist's bugaboo. In 567 career games, he never started, had only one at bat, and had just two seasons with more innings than appearances. Fossas spent 11 years in the minor leagues before reaching the majors with the Texas Rangers in 1988. He appeared in just five games, getting scorched for a .423 batting average by his opponents. Fossas and the Rangers parted ways, and to many it looked as if the 31-year-old journeyman was near the end of his baseball career.

But as a lefty reliever in baseball's age of specialization, Fossas was in luck. He caught on with the Brewers, and later moved on to Boston. He found his niche with St. Louis in 1995. Pitching almost exclusively against lefthanded hitters, Fossas posted a 1.47 ERA in 58 appearances. He pitched even more often when Tony LaRussa arrived as manager in 1996, but the southpaw's ERA went up a full run in each of the next two years. At age 40 he was released by the Cardinals, but still found work with the Mariners, Cubs, and Rangers in 1998. The peripatetic southpaw signed with the Yankees in 1999. Typically, he made five appearances for a grand total of one inning.

Ray Fosse

Fosse, Raymond Earl **C**

1967–77,1979 B:4/4/1947, Marion, IL Deb:9/8/1967, CLE AL BR/TR 6'2", 215

G	AB	R	H	HR	RBI	OBP	SLG	AVG
924	2957	299	758	61	324	.308	.367	.256

One of the defining moments in Pete Rose's career came at Ray Fosse's expense. In the bottom of the 12th inning of the 1970 All-Star Game, with the Riverfront Stadium crowd screaming, Rose tore around third base with the potential winning run. A one-bounce throw to Cleveland catcher Fosse arrived just as Rose got to the plate and initiated a brutal, jarring collision. The ball squirted loose and the crowd roared even louder.

Ironically, the night before the game, Rose had entertained Fosse and Sam McDowell, his Cleveland batterymate, for dinner.

For Fosse, the game was also a defining moment. He was on his way to becoming a star ballplayer. After the collision that night, his arm was never the same. "When I got back to Cleveland to start the second half I could not lift my left arm above my head," said Fosse, who never went on the disabled list that season. "It limited my power. I got my strength back in my shoulder but I never regained my home run power. My swing had changed."

Fosse was a top prospect coming out of high school, the Indians' No. 1 choice in the very first amateur draft, in 1965. He got his chance to be the regular catcher in 1970 and was an immediate hit, making the All-Star team as a backup catcher. Thurman Munson would go on to be the Rookie of the Year in 1970, after Fosse's injury in the All-Star Game cut his production dramatically. Fosse, however, was the Gold Glove winner that year, and again in 1971.

Rose's take on the crash at the plate was predictable: "Fosse was playing to win and so was I. He stood up there and tried to make a tough tag, tried to make a good play, and I suppose I just made a better play, and that's the way it is."

Fosse ended up hitting .307 with 18 home runs that season, both career highs. He hit .276 the next year, with 12 homers and 62 RBIs, and was traded to Oakland after falling to .241 in 1972, with 41 RBIs in 457 at bats. Fosse was a regular catcher for one more year, but after 1973 he was a platoon player who kept getting injured. Traded to Cleveland in 1976, he hit .301 in 90 games, but spent all of 1978 on the disabled list and retired after hitting .231 in 19 games for the Brewers in 1979.

Bill Foster

Foster, Bill **P**

Negro League Player M(1923–38) B:6/12/1904, Calvert, TX D:9/16/1978, Lorman, MS BB/TL 6'1", 195

Big Bill Foster, who was elected to the Hall of Fame in 1996, was the Cy Young of the Negro Leagues—he won more games than anyone, and that includes Satchel Paige. In fact, Foster was probably the best black lefthander of all time. Among the moderns only Vida Blue can challenge him, but Blue's claim pales before Foster's record.

Foster was two years older than the illustrious Paige. Their careers in the abbreviated Negro League seasons (40–90 games a year) look like this:

	Years	W	L	Pct.
Foster	1923–37	137	62	.688
Paige	1927–48	129	79	.620

Foster's teammate on the Chicago American Giants, outfielder Nat Rogers, recalled a doubleheader when the two great pitchers were scheduled to face each other in game one. "Paige pulled out at the last minute, but Bill pitched anyway and won. When Satchel went out to pitch the second game, Bill said, 'Shucks, give me the ball, I want to beat him.' " Smiled Rogers: "When the game ended, Bill had him, 6–2."

"As near as I can remember," Foster said, "Satchel and I faced each other around 13 or 14 times. And I think I got the edge on him when I beat him a doubleheader in Pittsburgh one Saturday, 5–0 and 1–0."

Foster would have won more games were it not for the Depression. He was 29 years old in 1933, his last regular season, when he won eight and lost four with the Chicago American Giants. Thereafter he barnstormed to make a living, eventually retiring to sell insurance and manage the Harlem Globetrotters. Paige went on to pitch another decade before going into the white major leagues.

In 1923 the 19-year-old Bill joined his older half-brother, Hall of Famer Andrew "Rube" Foster, who was with the Chicago American Giants. Bill went on to become the American Giants' money pitcher, with a career postseason record of 11–5. The year 1926 was typical. The Giants went into the final doubleheader against the archrival Kansas City Monarchs, trailing by one game. Foster (9–4) faced the great Bullet Joe Rogan (12–2) in game one and beat him, 1–0, to throw the race into a tie. It all hinged on the second game.

In the clubhouse Chicago manager Dave Malarcher asked the players who they wanted to pitch game two. "Foster," they chorused. So he went back out to warm up.

Rogan saw him. "You gonna pitch?" he demanded.

"Yeah, I'm gonna pitch," Bill replied.

"Well, I'm coming back," Rogan growled, grabbing a ball.

"I think in the first inning we made four or five runs off him," Foster recalled. "But that was all. He closed the door, but I think it was 5–0 we beat him."

The Giants hurriedly caught a train for Atlantic City and the Negro Leagues World Series against the Bacharach Giants. Two days after his iron-man stint, Foster was on the mound again, against Arthur "Rats" Henderson (7–3). The two dueled to a 3–3 tie in 10 innings. Big Bill started two more games and won them both, including the clincher, 1–0.

Foster's best season was 1927, when he posted a 21–4 mark to lead the American Giants to their second straight pennant. Bill won two more in the playoff that year over Paige's Birmingham Black Barons and two more in the black World Series.

In seven decisions against some of the best white stars in the country, Foster won six and lost one. In October 1929 he faced an All-Star team of Charlie Gehringer, Heinie Manush, and Harry Heilmann, all future Hall of Famers. He beat them, 10–1, on a three-hitter. "The major league stars just didn't beat those Negro League teams," he said.

The next year the Depression hit. Foster retired from the game to sell insurance and manage the Harlem Globetrotters, who bumped around the country in a bus. He later became dean of men and baseball coach at Alcorn College in Mississippi.

He vividly remembered the hard times. "One week I lived on 36 cents," he recalled. "And out of that 36 cents I had to take three cents for a stamp to send back home to my mother to send me some money so I could come home."

George Foster

Foster, George Arthur **OF**

1969–86 B:12/1/1948, Tuscaloosa, AL Deb:9/10/1969, SF NL BR/TR 6'1", 185

G	AB	R	H	HR	RBI	OBP	SLG	AVG
1977	7023	986	1925	348	1239	.341	.480	.274

George Foster had several terrific seasons at the plate as a member of Cincinnati's potent "Big Red Machine," hitting for both power and average. Dealt to the Mets in 1982, he was briefly the richest man in baseball but in the long run a disappointment to the team.

Foster was arguably baseball's best power hitter during the late 1970s. Named to the All-Star team in 1976, he upped his homer output to 29 and drove in a league-best 121 runs while hitting .306. The Reds won all seven of their postseason games, sweeping the Yankees for a second consecutive world championship. Foster hit .429 in the Series and was named NL Player of the Year by *The Sporting News.*

Foster's 1977 season was the greatest ever by a Cincinnati batter. He hit .320 and led the league in homers, runs scored, RBIs, and slugging. *The Sporting News* again named him NL Player of the Year, and this time baseball writers also chose him as NL Most Valuable Player. His 52 home runs made him the sixth National Leaguer to hit 50 homers in a season and the only major leaguer to reach the 50-homer mark in the 1970s. However, 1977 was the year the Rawlings Company supplied the major leagues with inferior baseballs, made in Haiti. As Roger Angell put it, the balls may have been "secretly polished there with applications of Haitian ju-ju oil." Whatever voodoo was involved, a record number of home runs were hit in the majors that year—a 32 percent jump in National League home run output over 1976.

Foster ruled again as the power king of the National League in 1978, slugging 40 home runs and driving in 120 to lead the league in both categories. A leg injury reduced his playing time in 1979, but he still hit 30 homers and contributed 98 RBIs. While he slumped to only 25 home runs in 1980, in the strike season of 1981 he hit 22 dingers and drove in 90 runs in only 108 games.

The Mets decided they needed a bat like Foster's to complement Dave Kingman in their lineup. In 1981 Kingman had belted 22 homers while no other Met had hit more than six. The Mets sent three players to the Reds for Foster, and then signed him to the richest contract in baseball, $10 million for five years.

Mets fans were elated, but in retrospect, it seems New York's largesse was nothing but foolishness. Foster needed the protection he enjoyed in the middle of the Cincinnati lineup, something the woeful Mets couldn't offer. Moreover, Foster was never a "gamer." Former teammate Pete Rose said, "I never once saw him get his uniform dirty. He doesn't dive for balls and will never go to the wall if it means crashing into it."

Foster's first-half stats for the Mets in 1982 weren't terrible, but fans expected more. And they began to vent their displeasure—loudly. Asked to carry the team by his lonesome, he couldn't do it. He never hit better than .270 or smacked more than 29 home runs again. He was branded, perhaps unfairly, as a man who'd lost his edge and gave up once he signed for the big money.

In 1986 Mets manager Davey Johnson benched Foster in favor of a platoon of Mookie Wilson and Kevin Mitchell. The big slugger who some called "the Destroyer" did not live up to Johnson's expectations and was released in August. Picked up by the Chicago White Sox, he played 15 games, hitting one home run—his 348th—before retiring.

Rube Foster

Foster, Andrew **P**

Negro League Player-Manager, League Executive (1902–1926) B: 9/17/1878, Calvert, TX D:12/9/1930, Kankakee, IL BR/TR 6'2", 200

No man merits the title of "the father of black baseball" more than Andrew "Rube" Foster. After beginning his career as a superb pitcher, he became an exceedingly shrewd and talented manager and an executive whose powerful will created the first real organization for the black game.

Without the organization Foster imposed upon black baseball, the Negro Leagues could never have prospered to become the initial source of players when the white majors integrated. One of the most important contributions Foster made to baseball was to bring respectability to the black leagues. As one sportswriter wrote, "Rube Foster was a creative personality. Way back in the darkest years he walked in and looked bankers in the eye and walked out with a $20,000 loan. That's quite an accomplishment."

The son of a minister in Calvert, Texas, Foster was an asthmatic child. He dropped out of school after the eighth grade. By age 18, though, he was a big, strong, successful pitcher for the semipro Fort Worth Yellow Jackets.

In 1902 Foster won 44 games in a row for the Cuban Giants. The next year he was easily the best pitcher in black baseball. Playing for the Cuban X Giants, he won four games in the best-of-seven championship series against Sol White's Philadelphia Giants. When he bested Rube Waddell of the Philadelphia Athletics in an exhibition that year, fans called him "the Black Rube," and the nickname stuck.

In 1905 Foster joined White's Athletics and posted an amazing 51–5 record. He would use any trick to win, and was a master of the psychological edge. "I have often smiled," he said, "with the bases full and two strikes and three balls on the hitter. This seems to unnerve them."

After the 1906 season Foster was upset by the size of the players' cut of the team's postseason winnings, and he quit the Athletics, basically taking the whole team with him. In Chicago, after meeting with businessman Frank Leland, Foster managed and pitched the new Leland Giants to a 110–10 record in 1907.

As a manager Foster built his team on speed and smarts. Every player had to be able to bunt and hit-and-run. Arthur Hardy, a pitcher for Foster, once said, "Rube wasn't harsh but he was strict. His dictums were not unreasonable, but if you broke one he'd clamp down on you." When a player tripled after Foster had given him the bunt sign, the player got rapped over the head with Rube's pipe.

Foster's Giants won 64 of 86 games in 1908. The following season he challenged the Chicago Cubs to a series. The Giants lost to the white major leaguers in three tight games. After that season Foster broke off ties with Leland and took his players to form a new team. In the legal wrangles that ensued, Foster was allowed to use Leland's name.

Before the 1911 season started, Foster formed a partnership with Chicago tavern owner (and son-in-law of Charles Comiskey) John C. Schorling and created the Chicago American Giants, one of the greatest black clubs of all time. They played their home games in old South Side Park, which Schorling had purchased and renovated to seat 9,000 fans. The American Giants won Negro League championships in 1914 and 1917. They shared the title with the New York Lincoln Stars in 1915.

Foster began to formulate plans to build a true league, to control costs, to eliminate frequent player raiding and jumping, and most importantly, to gain respectability. In 1919, he joined a number of club owners and started the Negro National League the (NNL). Not surprisingly,

Foster was elected president and secretary. The slogan on the NNL letterhead read, "We are the ship, all else the sea."

One of Foster's first acts as president was to return his star player, Oscar Charleston, to Indianapolis, the team from which Charleston had jumped to the Giants. Throughout the NNL's history Foster often sent his players to other clubs to help balance the league. Foster put a lot of his own money behind the league; he virtually bankrolled the Dayton club by himself.

He took no salary but received 5 percent of all gate receipts off the top, which probably earned him considerably more than a salary would have. His dictatorial style caused problems with some teams. Three times in 1921 he pulled his team off the field because of disputes. Opposing managers saw the futility of protesting. As one writer explained, "Each manager would have to file a complaint against Manager Foster, mail it to Secretary Foster, and then President Foster would have to decide." Foster's teams got away with more rule infractions than others because Foster paid the umpires.

It is indisputable that formation of the Negro National League saved the black game. Foster's players became the highest paid in black baseball—by 1930 players earned an average salary of $2,000. The Negro National League's success spawned imitators. A Southern Negro League soon formed, as did the Eastern Colored League. The first real Negro League World Series took place from 1924 through 1927.

The last official baseball meeting Foster attended was in 1926, with longtime associates Ban Johnson and John McGraw. Foster was supposedly trying to schedule more games with white teams. But his behavior had taken a serious turn for the worse. As he became more and more bizarre and erratic, Rube Foster, the control freak who almost single-handedly built black baseball, lost control. Finally committed to the Kankakee State Hospital, he died there in 1930. In 1981 Foster was elected to the Baseball Hall of Fame.

Fatty Fothergill

Fothergill, Robert Roy **OF**

1922–33 B:8/16/1897, Massillon, OH D:3/20/1938, Detroit, MI Deb:4/18/1922, DET AL BR/TR 5'10½", 230

G	AB	R	H	HR	RBI	OBP	SLG	AVG
1106	3269	453	1064	36	582	.368	.459	.325

A player as large as Bob "Fatty" Fothergill had to have been a good hitter to last 12 major league seasons. From 1922 through 1933 Fothergill hit .325, ranking 14th among all American Leaguers with more than 1,000 at bats during that span. Of the other 13 ballplayers, 10 are in the Hall of Fame.

An accomplished pinch hitter, in 1929 Fothergill collected 19 pinch hits, a since-broken AL record. Overall, he had 76 pinch hits in 253 at bats for a lifetime .300 average. Only four other major leaguers have career .300 averages as pinch hitters.

Fothergill made his major league debut with the Detroit Tigers in 1922, but he didn't appear in more than 101 games in a season until 1926, when he hit a career-high .367, with 31 doubles and 73 RBIs. He led the AL in batting until August, when he went into a late-season swoon and was benched, without collecting enough at bats to qualify for the title. In both that year and 1928, Fothergill was a part of all-.300-hitting outfields for Detroit.

His best all-around season was 1927, when he batted .359 and established career highs in hits (189), doubles (38), home runs (9), runs scored (93), RBIs (114), and stolen bases (9). But that was the only time Fothergill played more than 116 games in a season.

The 5-foot-10½-inch Fothergill merited his nickname because he tipped the scales at 230 pounds, but he was insecure about his size. He was the subject of innumerable insensitive fat jokes by sportswriters and ballplayers alike.

Jack Fournier

Fournier, John Frank **1B**

1912–18,1920–27 B:9/28/1889, AuSable, MI D:9/5/1973, Tacoma, WA Deb:4/13/1912, CHI AL BL/TL 6', 195

G	AB	R	H	HR	RBI	OBP	SLG	AVG
1530	5208	822	1631	136	859	.392	.483	.313

Known for his bat, Jack Fournier led the American League in slugging percentage in 1915 and the National League in homers in 1924. But his best day came on June 29, 1923, when the lefty-hitting first baseman went 6-for-6 with two doubles and a home run.

Fournier played high school football in Tacoma, Washington, and said he preferred the gridiron action to baseball as a boy. But in 1912, at age, 19 he broke into the major leagues as a member of the Chicago White Sox. Although a threat with the bat, he was a miserable fielder, twice leading the National League in errors.

After 15 years with five clubs Fournier retired, and began a long career as a football coach. He also scouted for several clubs and once signed Roy Sievers to a contract with the St. Louis Browns for a pair of spikes.

Dave Foutz

Foutz, David Luther **P-1B-OF**
1884–96 M(1893–96, 264–257) B:9/7/1856, Carroll County, MD D:3/5/1897, Waverly, MD Deb:7/29/1884, STL AA BR/TR 6'2", 161

W	L	PCT	G	SH	IP	BB	SO	ERA
147	66	.690	251	16	1997¹	510	790	2.84

G	AB	R	H	HR	RBI	OBP	SLG	AVG
1135	4533	784	1253	31	749	.323	.378	.276

Dave Foutz was a very busy man in 1886. Pitching for the St. Louis Browns of the American Association, he was 41–16 and led the league in wins and ERA, with 2.11, while pitching 504 innings and completing 55 of 57 starts. He also played 34 games in the outfield and 11 at first base, and hit .280 in 414 at bats. The next season Foutz went 25–12 and hit .357.

Foutz went to Colorado to prospect for gold as a young man but had more success pitching for the local team. When his minor league team folded in midseason, he signed with the Browns and struck out 13 batters in 13 innings in his major league debut. He missed part of the 1884 season when he contracted malaria. After the season, he reportedly lost heavily betting on the presidential election when Grover Cleveland defeated James G. Blaine.

In 1885 Foutz made $5,000 and went 33–14 as St. Louis won the AA pennant with Charles Comiskey managing. After posting 11 shutouts in 1886, the pitcher's career derailed the next season when a line drive broke his thumb. After that, Foutz couldn't control his curve properly.

The Browns won the AA pennant that season nonetheless and met the National League champion Detroit Wolverines in the pre-1903 equivalent of the World Series. Foutz, 0–3 in the Series, wasn't happy with the players' cut of the gate. "If we won this Series from the best baseball club in the world outside ourselves, we would get our little $100. If we lost, we wouldn't get a blank cent." After the season, Browns owner Chris Von der Ahe, who felt he had to cut the team's $40,000 payroll, sold Foutz and Bob Caruthers to Brooklyn.

In 1889 Foutz, who rarely took the mound during his last six years in the majors, was second in the American Association with 113 RBIs as a first baseman. Brooklyn won the pennant, and Foutz was voted a gold medal as best player in the league. In 1890, Brooklyn moved to the National League. The 35-year-old Foutz hit .303 with 98 RBIs for another pennant winner, his fifth in six seasons.

Foutz's health began to fail after that season. He went 13–8 as a starter in 1892, and belted a career-high seven homers in 1893, the year he became the Bridegrooms' manager. Brooklyn never finished higher than fifth in the four years Foust managed the club, although he posted a winning record.

Bud Fowler

Fowler, John W. **2B-P-SS-3B-OF-C**
Early Black Player (1877–99) B:3/16/1858, Fort Plain, NY D:2/26/1913, Frankfort, NY BR/TR 5'7", 155

John "Bud" Fowler, a versatile player reared in Cooperstown, New York, was the first African-American in the ranks of professional baseball. Born John W. Jackson, Fowler first played in a pro league in 1878. His appearance with the Lynn, Massachusetts, Live Oaks of the International Association that year represents the first record of a black player in Organized Baseball.

According to some historians, Fowler was also the first African-American in the major leagues. Although most consider the International Association the first minor league, at the time there was little distinction between major and minor operations, and International Association clubs commonly defeated National League teams in exhibition games.

The much-traveled Fowler could pitch or play any position with skill, once working five different positions in five consecutive games. In 1886, when Topeka won a Western League championship, Fowler led the circuit in triples, with 12, and hit .309 while playing second base and the outfield. But despite his talents, he had difficulty finding a permanent niche in the pro ranks because of racism. He played for nearly 20 teams from 1878 through 1895.

By 1887 at least six other black players were named on International League rosters, but Fowler's tenure with Binghamton was controversial. Reporting yet another instance of teammates' refusing to take the field with Fowler, *The Newark Daily Journal* revealed that the directors of the Binghamton club had fined the players $50 each. Nevertheless, Fowler was eventually asked to leave the team, although he had batted .350 in 34 games.

In 1894 Fowler tried his hand at organizing a club. His creation, the Page Fence Giants, was one of the first great black barnstorming outfits. Sponsored by barbed wire manufacturers, the team was based in Adrian, Michigan, where Fowler plied his off-season trade of barbering. The club toured through six Midwestern states before Fowler left in July 1895 to play for Lansing, his last minor league team. At age 37, he batted .331 in 31 games.

Fowler died of pernicious anemia in 1913. He ended his days in distressed circumstances and lay buried in an unmarked grave at Oak View Cemetery in Frankfort, New York, until July 25, 1987. That was the day the Northeast New York chapter of the Society for American Baseball Research, in a ceremony featuring several Hall of Famers and Negro League veterans, placed a suitable marker on the site.

Nellie Fox

Fox, Jacob Nelson **2B**

1947–65 B:12/25/1927, St. Thomas, PA D:12/1/1975, Baltimore, MD Deb:6/8/1947, PHI AL BL/TR 5'9", 150

G	AB	R	H	HR	RBI	OBP	SLG	AVG
2367	9232	1279	2663	35	790	.349	.363	.288

A 12-time American League All-Star, Nellie Fox led the league in fewest strikeouts 11 times. With the 150-pound "Mighty Mite" Fox at second, the White Sox ranked first or second in team fielding for 10 straight years. Fox also hit .300 or better six times and led or tied for the league lead in hits four times.

When he was 16, Nellie talked his parents into letting him try out at the Philadelphia A's wartime spring training camp. Connie Mack spotted the youngster's drive and talent, and Fox spent the next two summers playing first base and the outfield in the A's system. After a year in the military, the A's brought him up in 1949, and he played 88 games at second behind Pete Suder, struggling to hit .255. Swapped to the White Sox for catcher Joe Tipton, Fox started a 14-year career in Chicago, establishing himself as the top AL second baseman of his era.

His success was partly due to his insistent drive to excel. Thirty-year baseball veteran Paul Richards, who managed the White Sox in the early 1950s, said, "I've never seen anybody who wanted to play more than Fox did. In spring training you had to run him off the field to get him to rest. I mean literally run him off the field."

Fox set the record for consecutive games played at second base, 798. Only two players in history have played more games at the keystone, and only Bill Mazeroski turned more double plays at second base than Fox. He holds major league records for the most years leading the league in singles, with eight, and the most years doing it consecutively, with seven. He rarely whiffed; only Joe Sewell and Lloyd Waner have bested his strikeout–at bat ratio.

Fox paired in keystone duty with two of the best: Chico Carrasquel and Luis Aparicio. No other AL second baseman ever led the league more frequently in double plays. He also routinely led the league in fielding average. Fox's league-leading marks in chances (eight times) and putouts (10 times) are records for second basemen. He was elected to the Hall of Fame in 1997.

The high point of Fox's career was 1959, when he and Aparicio led the Sox to their first World Series since the "Black Sox" team of 1919. Although Fox didn't top the league in a single offensive category, he was voted Most Valuable Player by the Baseball Writers Association. Teammates Aparicio and Early Wynn finished second and third. The "Go-Go Sox" batted only .250, and five of the other seven teams in the league scored more runs, but they led the league in triples and stolen bases and got the runs when they needed them.

Pete Fox

Fox, Ervin **OF**

1933–45 B:3/8/1909, Evansville, IN D:7/5/1966, Detroit, MI Deb:4/12/1933, DET AL BR/TR 5'11", 165

G	AB	R	H	HR	RBI	OBP	SLG	AVG
1461	5636	895	1678	65	694	.347	.415	.298

Right fielder Ervin "Pete" Fox, a solid lifetime .298 hitter over his 13-year career, was also an excellent outfielder with a strong, accurate arm, and he could steal a base when necessary. He hit .288 in 1933 as a Tiger rookie outfielder with a career-high 13 triples in 128 games, and .285 the next season, scoring 101 runs in the first of three 100-run seasons. He also stole 25 bases, fourth best in the AL. Fox then set a World Series record that still stands when he smacked six doubles (out of eight hits) as the Tigers lost to the Cardinals in seven games.

Fox had his breakthrough season in 1935, when he hit .321 with 38 doubles, 73 RBIs, 116 runs, and a career-best 15 homers. This time around, the Tigers won the Series, beating the Cubs in six games. Fox hit .385 (10-for-26) to lead all Detroit batters, and his four RBIs tied Charlie Gehringer for the team lead.

Fox started to slip at the end of the decade, although he finished second in the AL in steals in 1939 with 23. Sold to the Red Sox on December 12, 1940, he was a part-timer in 1941. Too old for the draft, in 1942 he became a regular for a couple of seasons, as the war took many of baseball's best players. He hit .315 in 1944.

Jimmie Foxx

Foxx, James Emory **1B–3B**

1925–42,1944–45 B:10/22/1907, Sudlersville, MD D:7/21/1967, Miami, FL Deb:5/1/1925, PHI AL BR/TR 6', 195

G	AB	R	H	HR	RBI	OBP	SLG	AVG
2317	8134	1751	2646	534	1922	.428	.609	.325

The true successor to Babe Ruth as baseball's preeminent slugger in the 1930s was not Lou Gehrig but Jimmie Foxx. Gehrig never hit more than 47 homers in a season, while Foxx hit 58 in 1932, two shy of Ruth's then record. Foxx, also known as "the Beast" and "Old Double-X,"

ranked second in career homers behind Ruth until 1966, when Willie Mays passed his total of 534. Foxx hit 415 homers in the 1930s, more than anyone else during that decade, and won the Triple Crown in 1933 after missing the batting title by only three percentage points the previous year. He also led the AL in homers four times, in RBIs three times, and in batting twice, not to mention his three Most Valuable Player Awards.

Foxx began as a catcher for Frank "Home Run" Baker, who was then managing Easton of the Class D Eastern Shore League. In his first professional game, he batted eighth and hit a home run; he went on to hit .296 for the season in 76 games—at age 15. Both the Yankees and the A's were interested, but out of loyalty to his old boss, Connie Mack, Baker sold Foxx to the A's for only $2,000.

The 17-year-old Foxx had nine at bats and six hits with the A's in 1925. The following year he was up 32 times. Future Hall of Famer Mickey Cochrane became the A's regular catcher while Foxx tried several positions, backing Cochrane and playing third or first base. As a 20-year-old in 1928 he started to mature, hitting .328 with 13 homers and 79 RBIs in 400 at bats while playing 61 games at third, 30 at first, and 20 behind the plate.

People started to notice. According to one baseball writer, "Already, the wise men of the sport are predicting that this 6-foot, 180-pound youngster is swinging a bat over the wondrous achievements of mighty Babe Ruth." But Mack appreciated Foxx for more than his slugging. "He is the easiest boy on the team to handle... does whatever I ask...plays any position and never complains," said Mack.

In 1929 Foxx finally became the A's regular first baseman. At age 21, he hit .354 with 33 homers and 118 RBIs for the world champion A's. He was even better the next season. The A's repeated as Foxx hit .335, smacked 37 homers, and drove in 156 runs.

Foxx's career hit a speed bump in 1931. His average fell to .291, his home run total to 30, and his RBIs to 120—an excellent season by almost any other player's standards. But his walk total fell from 93 to 73, and he led the league in strikeouts for the third straight season; ultimately, he led the AL seven times in that category. He decided to cut down on his swing. Five years after Ruth had hit 60 home runs, Foxx hit 58, and lost two more to rainouts. His league-leading slugging percentage was a phenomenal .749, and he led the league with 169 RBIs and 151 runs scored.

People were impressed not only by the number of homers that Foxx hit but also by how he hit them. One time Double-X hit a homer off Yankee ace Lefty Gomez that sailed into the distant upper deck in Yankee Stadium; another 20 feet and it would have gone out of the park altogether. Gomez decided to investigate the force of the blow. He climbed all the way up to where Foxx's homer had touched down. When he got there he saw that the seat it had landed on had been shattered by the impact. "It's impossible," marveled Gomez, "but old Double-X did it." Many baseball people agreed with Gomez when he joked about Foxx, "He has muscles in his hair."

Although the media portrayed this new superstar as a wholesome farm boy, he was hardly a role model. "[Foxx] never made any bones about his love for Scotch," recalled Ted Williams. "He used to say that he could drink 15 of those little bottles of Scotch, those miniatures, and not be affected. Of course nobody could do that and stay healthy, and it got to Jimmie later on."

Foxx was also famous for his profligate spending. As Bobby Doerr recalled, "Jimmie was a big spender! He would always be the one to pick up the tab whenever we went out for steaks at Durgin Park or wherever. It was not unusual for him to call out, 'The drinks are on the house—Old Double-X is here!'"

While Foxx was throwing his money around, his boss was desperately counting pennies in the wake of the Great Depression. Connie Mack could no longer afford to maintain his stable of stars. In fact, after Foxx won the 1933 Triple Crown, Mack actually tried to cut his salary from $16,333 to $12,000. Foxx balked, but eventually took a token cut to $16,000.

Mack finally sold him after the 1935 season, sending Foxx and 17-game winner Johnny Marcum to Tom Yawkey's Red Sox for $150,000 and two no-name pitchers. Yawkey, who had some of the deepest pockets in baseball, doubled Foxx's salary. Foxx hit 41 homers with 143 RBIs in his first season in Boston but slumped in 1937, hitting a mere .285 with 36 homers and 127 RBIs. His last heroic season came in 1938, when he drove in a career-best 175 runs (one every 3.2 at bats) and hit 50 homers to win his third MVP Award.

Injuries limited Foxx to 124 games the next season, but he still led the AL with 35 homers. Predictably, his drinking was catching up with

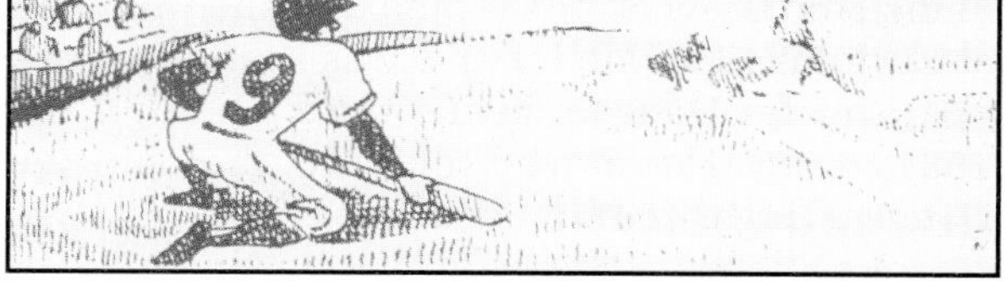

him. He still had enough vigor left to produce 100-RBI seasons in 1940 and 1941, but he hit only 19 homers in 1941 and was waived to the Cubs on June 1, 1942. The fading slugger finished that season with a decidedly unheroic .226 average and eight homers at the relatively youthful age of 34.

He left baseball at the season's end, worked briefly for a Philadelphia oil company, then returned to the Cubs in 1944 for 20 at bats, with only one hit. He managed Portsmouth of the Piedmont League at the end of that season before returning to the big leagues as a part-timer for the Phillies in 1945, where he hit .268 with seven homers.

So desperate was wartime baseball for manpower that on August 19 Phillies manager Ben Chapman called on Foxx to pitch against the Cincinnati Reds. Foxx pitched six innings of no-hit ball. In the seventh inning his arm gave out, but it was nonetheless a remarkable accomplishment. He ended up going 1–0 with a 1.59 ERA in his final year in the majors.

Although Foxx had serious financial troubles after his playing career ended, they never affected his outlook. "His personality was one of the gentlest in the game," said sportswriter Al Hirshberg. "Foxx hated no one and no one hated him. From the day he first went into the major leagues, he was pleasant to everyone, never impatient with fans or admirers, always, always accessible to anybody who appreciated him." He was elected to the Hall of Fame in 1951.

John Franco

Franco, John Anthony **P**

1984–* B:9/17/1960, Brooklyn, NY Deb:4/24/1984, CIN NL BL/TL 5'10", 185

W	L	PCT	G	SV	IP	BB	SO	ERA
77	70	.524	878	416	1041^{1}	404	801	2.64

Tug McGraw, Jesse Orosco, Randy Myers, John Franco—the best relief pitchers in Mets history have all been lefthanded. But Franco had more saves than any of them. In fact, at the end of the 1999 season, he had more saves than any lefthander in major league history.

Franco always wanted to play in New York. He grew up in Brooklyn and graduated from Lafayette High School, the school that produced Mets president Fred Wilpon and Hall of Fame southpaw Sandy Koufax. Franco pitched at St. John's University and was drafted by the Los Angeles Dodgers in the third round of the 1981 draft. He moved quickly through the Dodgers organization, spending his first two seasons almost exclusively as a starting pitcher.

Franco began 1983 as a reliever at Class AAA Albuquerque and finished it as a starter in Cincinnati's minor league system. He started the 1984 season as a reliever at Wichita and was called up to the major leagues a few weeks later. Franco picked up his first save on April 29, and his first win two days later against Houston. The total of 54 games he logged as a rookie was Franco's lowest in five years in Cincinnati, and his four saves constituted the only time in his major league career he was not in double digits.

He won 11 straight games pitching in relief in 1985, finishing with a glittering 12–3 record. The following season he recorded 29 saves and made his first appearance on the All-Star team. The good work continued into 1987 as Franco began the season with a "reliever's no-hitter"—no hits or walks in his first nine innings pitched. He retired 31 of the first 32 batters he faced; the lone baserunner reached on an error.

That season Franco also started a streak of five straight 30-save seasons, to tie Jeff Reardon's major league record. In 1988, his league-leading and career-high 39 saves broke Clay Carroll's single-season and career save records in Cincinnati. He started out hot in 1989 but had trouble down the stretch, finishing the campaign with an ERA over 3.00 for his first time as a Red. Two months later he was a Met.

In a trade of big relievers, the Mets got Franco from Cincinnati in exchange for muscular Randy Myers. Franco returned to the top of the heap in the National League with 33 saves in 1990 to become the first Met to lead the league in saves. He set a club record, won his second Rolaids Relief Man Award (just ahead of Myers), and had the NL's best save percentage: 33 in 39 opportunities (85 percent).

Franco notched 30 more saves in 1991, and allowed no earned runs in May and August. Injuries limited the lefty to 15 saves in 1992, and 10 in 1993, but his 30 saves in 1994 were the best in the league. He broke Dave Righetti's all-time southpaw save record (254), as well as Jesse Orosco's Mets team record of 107 saves. His success helped bring the Mets back from a 103-loss season the year before to three games below .500 when a strike ended the season.

Franco experienced an uncharacteristically slow start in 1995, and his team tumbled through the standings as well. But he put together an 11-game scoreless streak in August, and ended the season by converting his last nine save opportunities as the Mets had a solid second half to finish tied for second place.

On April 29, 1996, Franco recorded his 300th career save against Montreal—12 years to the day after recording his first one. He also became the first southpaw to surpass the 300-save barrier. He did not allow a run in 17 straight games from May 16 to July 14; after allowing one in the first game of the July 14 doubleheader against Houston, he went another 11 games before he was scored upon again.

Franco finished 1996 with 28 saves and a 1.83 ERA. A poll conducted by Rolaids voted him the top lefthanded relief pitcher in the major leagues from 1976 to 1996. He posted 36 and 38 saves in 1997 and 1998, respectively, but fell prey to injuries in 1999. The Mets won the NL Wild Card berth, however, and Franco saw postseason action for the first time. With flame-throwing Juan Benitez also on their roster, Franco remarked after the 1999 season that he wanted to stay with the team—even if limited appearances kept him from breaking Lee Smith's all-time save mark of 486.

Julio Franco

Franco, Julio Caesar **SS-2B-DH**
1982–97,1999 B:8/23/1958, Hato Mayor, Dominican Republic Deb:4/23/1982, PHIL NL BR/TR 6'1", 165

G	AB	R	H	HR	RBI	OBP	SLG	AVG
1891	7244	1104	2177	141	981	.369	.418	.301

Julio Franco was a batting champion, a three-time All-Star, and a career .300 hitter during his 15 years in the majors. But after leading the AL with a .341 batting average while with Texas in 1991, the Dominican shortstop and second baseman fell upon hard times.

Disabled on three occasions with knee problems, Franco played only 35 games in 1992. The Rangers tried him as a designated hitter, and then decided he could play left field—a position where the strain on his knees would be minimized. But he logged only four games in left before becoming a full-time DH. Only in 1996, when he got into 97 games as a first baseman in his second tenure with Cleveland, did Franco deviate from the DH role.

But hitting got Franco to the major leagues and hitting is what kept him there long enough to surpass 2,000 hits. He broke in with Philadelphia in 1982 but became an everyday player when the Indians made him their shortstop a year later. Franco was the key man in a pre-Christmas 1988 trade in which Cleveland swapped him to the Texas Rangers for Oddibe McDowell, Jerry Browne, and Pete O'Brien. The Indians had moved him to second, where he was less of a liability, the year before.

Franco hit .316 in 1989, his first year in Texas, and was an All-Star for the first time. In 1990 he won All-Star MVP honors when his double off Rob Dibble drove in the game's only runs. In 1991 he became the first AL player since Paul Molitor in 1982 to produce 100 runs, 200 hits, and 30 stolen bases. In 1994 he cracked 20 homers and 98 RBIs.

Even though Franco turned 40 in 1998, the eight-time .300-hitter continued to play. He hit .290 with 18 home runs for Chiba Lotte, a Japanese team, and earned an invitation to spring training with Tampa Bay in 1999. He struck out in his one regular-season appearance, as a pinch hitter, and joined a Mexican League team.

Tito Francona

Francona, John Patsy **OF-1B**
1956–70 B:11/4/1933, Aliquippa, PA Deb:4/17/1956, BAL AL BL/TL 5'11", 190

G	AB	R	H	HR	RBI	OBP	SLG	AVG
1719	5121	650	1395	125	656	.346	.403	.272

A contact-hitting outfielder, Tito Francona came up with the Baltimore Orioles in 1956, was shipped to the White Sox and then the Tigers in 1958, and finally landed an everyday role with the Cleveland Indians in 1959. With regular playing time he began to hit regularly and even showed some home run power.

In 1959 Francona batted .363 in 399 at bats and posted an exceptional .566 slugging percentage. He led the AL in doubles the following year, hitting .292. In 1961 he hit .301 and was named to the AL All-Star team. In 1965 the Tribe sent him to the St. Louis Cardinals.

The Cards used Francona as a backup in the outfield and at first base. Although his numbers weren't exceptional, he provided solid play and decent fielding. He remained one of the top utility men in baseball for the remainder of the decade, playing for the Phillies, the Braves, the A's, and the Brewers before retiring after the 1970 season. His son, Terry Francona, played for the Expos, Cubs, Reds, Indians, and Brewers during the 1980s and then became the Phillies' manager.

Fred Frankhouse

Frankhouse, Frederick Meloy **P**
1927–39 B:4/9/1904, Port Royal, PA D:8/17/1989, Port Royal, PA Deb:9/11/1927, STL NL BR/TR 5'11", 175

W	L	PCT	G	SV	IP	BB	SO	ERA
106	97	.522	402	12	1888	701	622	3.92

Fred Frankhouse, a curveballing righthander who pitched for the Cardinals, the Braves, and the Dodgers between 1927 and 1939, won 106 games in the majors. His most famous win came on May 27, 1937, when he beat Carl Hubbell, ending Hubbell's 24-game winning streak, the longest in major league history.

Frankhouse didn't stick in the majors until 1929, when he went 7–2 for the Cardinals in 30 games. He was traded in the middle of the next season to the Braves for Hall of Famer Burleigh Grimes, who was 37 years old at the time. Frankhouse's first three years in Boston were rather uneventful, as he went 19–20, averaging only 122 innings a season.

He moved into the Braves' rotation in 1933, however, and was 16–15 with a career-low 3.16 ERA. The next year his ERA was 3.20, and almost all his other numbers were similar to those of 1933, except one—his won-lost record of 17–9.

He never regained that height. Traded to the Dodgers after slumping to 11–15 in 1935, Frankhouse was 13–10 and 10–13 his first two Brooklyn seasons. After going 3–5 in 1938, he moved back to the Braves for 38 innings in 1939, his last season in the majors.

Chick Fraser

Fraser, Charles Carrolton **P**

1896–1909 B:3/17/1871, Chicago, IL D:5/8/1940, Wendell, ID Deb:4/19/1896, LOU NL BR/TR 5'10½", 188

W	L	PCT	G	SH	IP	BB	SO	ERA
175	212	.452	433	22	3356	1332	1098	3.68

Two-time 20-game winner Charles Carrolton "Chick" Fraser was not noted for his control. Not only did he walk more batters than he struck out over the course of his career (three times leading the circuit in bases on balls), but he also plunked 217 batters, or one for every 15.2 innings he worked.

The hawk-nosed hurler started in the majors with Louisville and narrowly missed a no-hitter with that club on May 22, 1898, when Brooklyn's Fielder Jones beat out an infield hit in the ninth inning. Fraser still won, 3–0. Along with Nap Lajoie, Fraser jumped to the A's in 1901 (causing a messy legal battle) but returned to the Phillies the following year. He finally got his no-hitter on September 18, 1903, for the Phillies, defeating the Cubs' Peaches Graham, 10–0. Fraser struck out four and walked five while four errors were made behind him.

Harry Frazee

Frazee, Harry

Owner 1916–23 B:1881, Peoria, IL D:1929

Boston Red Sox owner Harry Frazee may have produced the hit Broadway show *No, No, Nanette* and brought the Red Sox a World Series title in 1918, but he will be forever Boston's greatest sports villain. He sold Babe Ruth to the Yankees.

Peoria-born Frazee got his start as a bellhop in his hometown, and then served as ticket taker in a local theater. By age 16 he was an advance man for a stage show called *Uncle Josh Perkins,* and for a short period was general manager of Peoria's second-division entry in the Class A Western League.

Frazee then returned to show business. He built his first theater in Chicago in 1907. In 1913 he opened the Longacre Theater on Broadway in New York, gained control of Boston's Arlington Theater, and made money with a string of hits, including *The Kissing Girl, Leave It to Jane,* and *Ready Money.* Frazee also helped promote the controversial Jack Johnson–Jess Willard heavyweight bout in Havana in 1915, a fight whose credibility was considered highly questionable.

Soon afterward Frazee scored big on Broadway with a show called *Nothing But the Truth.* With his profits, he bought the Red Sox on November 1, 1916, from Joseph Lannin for $675,000, in partnership with Hugh Ward and G.M. Anderson. "I had intended to sell out, and these gentlemen had the cash," Lannin said. Actually they didn't have the cash. A large portion of the sale price was in the form of notes from Frazee to Lannin.

"I have always enjoyed the game," Frazee announced, "and now I think that I shall have a chance to show what I know about handling a baseball club. I think that by giving the public a first-class article, I am bound to hold their support. And this goes double for Boston, by all odds the greatest balltown on earth."

One of Frazee's first moves was to sound out Washington Senators owner Clark Griffith regarding hearsay that pitcher Walter Johnson was available for $50,000. Frazee offered Griffith $60,000 but was turned down.

Frazee's Red Sox, with Babe Ruth as the pitching hero, won the World Series in 1918. World War I had caused major league schedules to end on Labor Day, and the loss of a month of games translated into a month of lost revenue. In addition, Frazee began to suffer a string of reverses on Broadway.

Something had to give, and he decided it was

the Red Sox. Outfielder Duffy Lewis and pitchers Ernie Shore and Dutch Leonard were exchanged to Colonel Jacob Ruppert's Yankees for four players and $50,000. Then on December 26, 1919, Frazee sold Ruth to the Yankees for $25,000 in cash, three promissory notes of $25,000 each, and a $300,000 loan secured by a mortgage on Fenway Park.

Frazee continued to unload players on Ruppert. Wally Schang, Everett Scott, Bullet Joe Bush, Joe Dugan, Sad Sam Jones, Herb Pennock, and Waite Hoyt all headed for New York, where they began the greatest dynasty in American sports. Not surprisingly, Frazee became the most hated man in Boston. On one occasion he hired a carriage to take him to Fenway Park, and when the cabby learned the identity of his passenger he punched him in the mouth.

On July 11, 1923, Frazee finally sold the Red Sox, by now a last-place team, for $1.25 million to a partnership headed by Bob Quinn. The sale was delayed pending a lawsuit for overdue bills filed by concessionaire Harry M. Stevens. In September 1925, Frazee brought *No, No, Nanette* to Broadway. It was his biggest hit, earning him $2.5 million.

Bill Freehan

Freehan, William Ashley **C-1B**
1961,1963–76 B:11/29/1941, Detroit, MI
Deb:9/26/1961, DET AL BR/TR 6'2", 205

G	AB	R	H	HR	RBI	OBP	SLG	AVG
1774	6073	706	1591	200	758	.342	.412	.262

Bill Freehan was the catcher many other American League receivers measured themselves against during the late 1960s. An 11-time All-Star, he shares the highest lifetime fielding percentage of any catcher in history, .993, with Elston Howard. Freehan was responsible for handling what developed into an outstanding Detroit pitching staff that included Denny McLain and Mickey Lolich.

In 1961 the Tigers gave William Ashley Freehan a $100,000 signing bonus. "My deal with my dad was, I didn't see a dime of my bonus until I got my degree," Freehan said. The catcher went to the University of Michigan during the off-season and graduated in 1966. "Now I tell parents, 'Make that same deal with your kid.'"

Far from a natural, the 20-year-old backstop led the American Association in passed balls in 1962. When Freehan came to the majors to stay in 1963, Hall of Famer Rick Ferrell worked with him on defense and made him an ace catcher.

Freehan was the consummate team player. A righthanded hitter, he played through leg injuries and back trouble and in 1968 set a new league record by getting hit with pitches 24 times. That year the Tigers won the pennant by 12 games as McLain won 31 games and Freehan contributed 25 home runs.

In the World Series it was Lolich who excelled, beating the Cardinals three times. In Game 5 Freehan, despite hitting only .083 for the Series, made a key play at the plate during the fifth inning when Lou Brock tried to score from second on Julian Javier's single to left. Willie Horton threw in to Freehan. Brock came in standing up to try to jar the ball loose, but umpire Doug Harvey signaled him out. The Tigers won that game and the next to even the Series. Then, in Game 7, they defeated Bob Gibson to become world champions. Freehan caught Tim McCarver's foul pop to end the game.

Freehan's controversial book, *Behind the Mask*, records the events of the 1968 season. In it he alleges Tigers manager Mayo Smith allowed Denny McLain special privileges, which may have contributed to decisions to fire Smith and trade McLain. Freehan later served as baseball coach at the University of Michigan.

Buck Freeman

Freeman, John Frank **OF-1B**
1891,1898–1907 B:10/30/1871, Catasauqua, PA
D:6/25/1949, Wilkes-Barre, PA Deb:6/27/1891,
WAS AA BL/TL 5'9", 169

G	AB	R	H	HR	RBI	OBP	SLG	AVG
1126	4208	588	1235	82	713	.346	.462	.293

Washington outfielder John Frank "Buck" Freeman collected 25 homers in 1899, just missing Ned Williamson's then major league mark of 27. Freeman's total went unmatched until Babe Ruth slugged 29 in 1919, ushering in the era of the lively ball. For his slugging heroics that season Freeman was paid just $225 a month.

Freeman started as a pitcher with Washington of the American Association in 1891, but later played in the minors before returning to the majors in 1898. Although he had a good arm in right field, his throwing was not accurate, and he was occasionally tried at first base. In 1901, along with Chick Stahl, Parson Lewis, and Jimmy Collins, he jumped from the NL's Boston Beaneaters to the crosstown Boston Pilgrims in the new American League. Freeman became the first player to lead both leagues in homers when he hit 13 for the 1903 Pilgrims.

Freeman batted fifth and played first base in the Pilgrims' first game ever on April 26, 1901. He led the AL in RBIs in 1902 and 1903, and batted .281 in the 1903 World Series. His highest salary with the Red Sox (Pilgrims) was $3,500.

Jim Fregosi

Fregosi, James Louis **SS-3B-1B**

1961–78 M(1978–81,1986–88,1991–96, *, 945–1006)
B:4/4/1942, San Francisco, CA Deb:9/14/1961,
LA AL BR/TR 6'1", 190

G	AB	R	H	HR	RBI	OBP	SLG	AVG
1902	6523	844	1726	151	706	.340	.398	.265

One of the few bright spots for the expansion Los Angeles Angels in their dreary first decade was a hard-hitting shortstop named Jim Fregosi. As a rookie in 1962, the Angels' second season, the 20-year-old Fregosi hit .291. He was fast and accurate in the field, a team player, and was liked and respected by club management. He soon became a favorite of the fans and a regular member of the AL All-Star team—named to the squad every year from 1964 through 1970, save for 1965. In 1966 he and fellow infielder Bobby Knoop led the league in double plays, and Fregosi led in assists. The following year he earned the Gold Glove.

Every year Fregosi's fielding got better. By the end of the decade he was easily the best position player on the hapless squad. But in mid-1971, with the Angels again having a terrible season, Fregosi developed a tumor in his foot that required surgery.

Uncertain as to Fregosi's ability to recover from his injury, the Angels sent him to the New York Mets in what proved to be the most historic trade in the Angels history. For Fregosi they got four players, including a promising but unproven fastballer named Nolan Ryan.

Fregosi never regained his previous form. He broke his thumb and filled a utility role for the Mets until being traded in mid-1973 to the Rangers. He spent 3½ years in a similar role with Texas before being dealt to the Pirates. When Angels' owner Gene Autry offered Fregosi the team's managerial job in June 1978, the Pirates did not stand in his way.

Fregosi was named manager of a California club that had not finished better than fourth since 1969. By the end of the 1978 season the Angels had moved up to third. In Fregosi's first full year at the helm—and the Angels' last with Nolan Ryan in their rotation—the team finished atop the AL West for the first time in its history. Fregosi remained the Angels' skipper until 1981, when Gene Mauch replaced him. In 1986 he resurfaced as manager of the White Sox, but after three seasons with no improvement by the team Fregosi was out of a job.

In 1991 Fregosi took over as skipper of the Philadelphia Phillies, and under his leadership and motivation the team finished third. The 1992 season was one of change for the Phillies and they finished sixth, but by the next year Fregosi had cultivated a posse of sluggers and a carefree team attitude that took the Phils to the NLCS and brought them wide popularity. They demolished the favored Atlanta Braves to take the NL flag, but dropped the 1993 World Series to the defending world champion Toronto Blue Jays in six games. Fregosi later served in the Giants front office and in 1999 replaced Tim Johnson as manager of the Blue Jays.

Larry French

French, Lawrence Herbert **P**

1929–42 B:11/1/1907, Visalia, CA D:2/9/1987, San Diego, CA Deb:4/18/1929, PIT NL BR/TL 6'1", 195

W	L	PCT	G	SH	IP	BB	SO	ERA
197	171	.535	570	40	3152	819	1187	3.44

Larry French wanted the ball. He averaged 276 innings a season in his five years in the Pirates rotation, and after being traded to the Cubs he averaged 254 innings a season in his first three years in Chicago. He was also a winner—197 times, against 171 losses—in a big league career that lasted 14 seasons. He reached double figures in wins 11 consecutive years, but he was unable to hit that winning pitching number: a 20-game season.

Earle Mack, Connie's son, discovered French in a semipro game in Oregon. Scouting another player, he changed his mind when he saw French pitch a no-hitter. The native Californian's first stop as a pro was with Ogden in the Class C Utah-Idaho League in 1926. He spent the next two seasons with Portland of the Pacific Coast League, and learned the screwball from former major leaguer Hub Pruett. Sold to the Pirates for $55,000 and five players, French went 7–5 as a spot starter in 1929 and moved into the Pirates rotation in 1930, going 17–18 and leading the league in losses.

French also allowed 325 hits in 274⅔ innings, a pattern he followed throughout his career. It wasn't until 1933 that he allowed fewer hits than innings pitched. In fact, he led NL pitchers in hits allowed for three straight seasons, beginning in 1931.

After winning 18 games in 1932 and 1933 (with ERAs of 3.02 and a career-low 2.72), French slumped to 12–18 in 1934. The Pirates decided to trade him, which turned out to be a big mistake. They sent 27-year-old French and a fading Freddie Lindstrom to the Cubs for Babe Herman and Joe Bush, both nearing the end of their careers, and 31-year-old righthander Jim Weaver, who had won 28 games his first two years in Pittsburgh before slumping badly. Throwing for the Cubs,

French went 90–70 over the next six seasons as a mainstay of the rotation.

French found himself in the World Series in 1935, his first year in Chicago, after he went 17–10 and tied for the league lead with four shutouts. (He had four shutouts in 1936, and again tied for the league lead.) But he lost Game 3 of the Series to the Tigers in relief on Jo-Jo White's 11th-inning single, and he started and lost the sixth and deciding game, 4–3, when Goose Goslin singled home Mickey Cochrane with two outs in the ninth. In a move that sparked criticism, Cubs manager Charlie Grimm had let French, a weak hitter, bat in the top of the ninth. French had a terrible season in 1941, going 5–14, and was waived to Brooklyn on August 20.

He bounced back as a spot starter in 1942, going 15–4 with a 1.83 ERA; seven of his wins came in relief. He also just missed a perfect game against the hapless Phillies on September 22 at Ebbets Field, when Nick Etten dinked a single inches over Pee Wee Reese's glove in the second inning. Etten was the only baserunner French allowed.

French joined the Navy after the season and got a commission, but while stationed at the Brooklyn Navy Yard he unsuccessfully petitioned the Navy to let him pitch long enough to get the three wins he needed to reach 200. He had been willing to donate $8,000 in salary to the Naval Relief Society if his request was approved. French served through the end of the war but was too old to come back as a player. He stayed in the reserves, went back on active service during the Korean War, and retired as a captain in the reserves in 1969.

Lonny Frey

Frey, Linus Reinhard **2B-SS**

1933–43, 1946–48 B:8/23/1910, St. Louis, MO
Deb:8/29/1933, BRO NL BL/TR 5'10", 160

G	AB	R	H	HR	RBI	OBP	SLG	AVG
1535	5517	848	1482	61	549	.359	.374	.269

Lonny "Junior" Frey was willing to work to get what he wanted—and he started working early. Frey grew up poor in St. Louis, and went to work immediately after graduating from grammar school. He played sandlot ball at night and on weekends. When he was suddenly out of work at the height of the Depression, Frey decided to pursue a career in professional baseball. It was an excellent choice.

Frey signed a minor league contract in 1932, and a year later he was a Brooklyn Dodger. He was hit in the head by a pitch the following spring, but the incident set him back only temporarily. The gritty Frey battled back from a concussion and a one-week hospital stay to hit .284 in 125 games.

Frey played two more years for the Dodgers, who traded him to the Chicago Cubs after the 1936 season. Stuck behind the likes of Billy Herman, Billy Jurges, and Stan Hack, Frey played in only 78 games. But his career took a sudden turn for the better when he was sold to the Cincinnati Reds in 1938.

The first thing the Reds did was move him from shortstop, where he had twice led the National League in errors, to second base. Frey exhibited terrific range on ground balls, especially those hit to his left. He also used his speed to become a dangerous basestealer, leading the National League with 22 thefts in 1940. He was named to the All-Star team three times in five years. Frey helped the Reds win back-to-back pennants in 1939 and 1940. In the World Series, though, he wasn't much help, going hitless in 20 career Series at bats.

After serving two years in World War II, Frey returned to the Reds in 1946. He also made brief appearances with the Cubs, Yankees, and Giants before retiring in 1948.

Ford Frick

Frick, Ford

Commissioner (1951–65) NL President (1934–51)
B:12/19/1895, Wawaka, IN D:4/8/1978, Bronxville, NY

The third commissioner of baseball, Ford Frick was both praised and vilified for his laissez-faire style of governing. Regarded by many as merely a "tool" of the owners, his 14 years as the game's czar (1951–65) were largely uneventful.

The most controversial decision Frick made was to order that an asterisk be applied to Roger Maris' record 61 homers in 1961, because the mark had been accomplished in a 162-game season as opposed to Babe Ruth's record 60, slugged over a 154-game season in 1927. Maris supporters felt the real motive for the asterisk decision lay in Frick's connection to the "Sultan of Swat" back in his sportswriting days, when he had been a close friend of Ruth and had "ghosted" numerous articles under the Babe's byline.

In every other respect, Frick's benign stewardship had little or no impact on the game. Though there was no labor strife, no Marvin Miller to cope with under his tenure, Frick presided over the beginning of major change in baseball's geography after nearly 50 years of status quo. Not surprisingly, given his style and performance, he regarded franchise shifts and expansion as a "league matter," deferring to the clubs.

Prior to succeeding Happy Chandler as commissioner in 1951, Frick served as president of the National League from 1935 until 1951. His most notable decision in that position was his stance against the St. Louis players who threatened to strike after Jackie Robinson broke baseball's color barrier in 1947. "If you strike, you're through," Frick told the St. Louis players. "I don't care if it wrecks the league for 10 years." No strike materialized, and after Robinson many other African-American and Hispanic players followed.

A moving force behind establishing the Baseball Hall of Fame, Frick was elected to it in 1970.

Bob Friend

Friend, Robert Bartmess **P**

1951–66 B:11/24/1930, Lafayette, IN Deb:4/28/1951, PIT NL BR/TR 6', 190

W	L	PCT	G	SH	IP	BB	SO	ERA
197	230	.461	602	36	3611	894	1734	3.58

In the old days of baseball, he would have been called the "staff workhorse"—the reliable pitcher who would take his turn every time his name was on the schedule and, moreover, take the game into late innings. In today's language, the manager would describe him as "a guy who'll give me a lot of innings."

In Pittsburgh, pitcher Bob Friend was that guy. Like many others who wore the workhorse badge, Friend was strong, large, and perhaps a little beefy, with a smooth and uncomplicated pitching motion and a demeanor at once quietly intense and unflappable. He seldom walked batters and never issued more than 85 free passes in a season, although he hurled more than 200 innings for 11 consecutive seasons and led the league twice in innings pitched—in 1956 with 314 and 1957 with 277.

Friend did most of that pitching on the miserable Pittsburgh teams of the early 1950s. After only one year in the minors, he appeared in 34 games for the Pirates in 1951. For the abyssmal 1952 Bucs he was 7–17. In 1955 Friend earned the distinction of being the only pitcher in history to lead his league in ERA while his team finished last. Because he pitched for a losing team, he finished his career 197–230, the only pitcher to lose at least 200 games in the majors without winning 200.

However, like others in the workhorse category, when his team played well, Friend reaped the benefits. While serving on the young Pirates team that came to life suddenly in 1958, he led the league with 22 wins. For the 1960 world championship team he went 18–12, although his unaffected pitching style was no challenge for the hard-hitting Yankees.

In that World Series, Friend started two games and appeared in relief in a third, yet he lasted only six innings in all. The Yankees pounded him for 13 hits and 10 runs. Called in to pitch the top of the ninth in Game 7, with the Bucs winning 9–7 after Hal Smith's home run in the last of the eighth, Friend was clipped for two quick singles. Both of those Yankees came in to score, tying the game, and setting the stage for Bill Mazeroski's heroic homer that won the game for Pittsburgh and delivered the team's first championship in 35 years.

Friend was also a businessman and politician. He proved himself savvy in Pittsburgh's political and business communities after retiring from baseball. A staunch Republican, Friend ran for local office, won, and served for years in Allegheny County.

Frankie Frisch

Frisch, Frank Francis **2B–3B**

1919–37 M(1933–38,1940–46,1949–51, 1,138–1,078) B:9/9/1898, Bronx, NY D:3/12/1973, Wilmington, DE Deb:6/14/1919, NY NL BB/TR 5'11", 165

G	AB	R	H	HR	RBI	OBP	SLG	AVG
2311	9112	1532	2880	105	1244	.369	.432	.316

Second baseman Frankie "the Fordham Flash" Frisch faced intense pressure as the 1927 National League season began. In December the Giants had traded him to the Cardinals for second baseman Rogers Hornsby, who had not only proven himself the greatest righthanded hitter in history but also had just managed St. Louis to its first pennant. Frisch had to fill his shoes. St. Louis fans were ready to eat him alive.

Frisch responded magnificently. Even though St. Louis did not win the pennant that year, the Cards did win three more games than they had under Hornsby. And Frisch proved to be a demon on the field, setting NL records with 1,037 total chances and 641 assists. Despite playing with a swollen hand late in the season, Frisch batted .337 and led the league with 48 stolen bases. The switch hitter finished just one vote behind Paul Waner of the pennant-winning Pirates in Most Valuable Player balloting. "The greatest player I ever saw in one season was Frankie Frisch in 1927," Cardinals catcher and manager Bob O'Farrell said.

Frisch went to Fordham University in the Bronx and "flashed" not only in baseball but also in track, basketball, and football. Named halfback on Walter Camp's second All-America team, he captained the baseball, football, and basketball squads. His Fordham coach, former New York Giant Art Devlin, secured a tryout for Frisch at the Polo Grounds. Giants manager John McGraw was impressed and wanted to sign Frisch. "Only for the summer," young Frisch's father told him reluctantly.

"I signed for what was then a satisfactory bonus of $200 and a salary of $400 a month during the baseball season," Frisch recalled. "There was an unusual clause in the contract, though. It said that if I failed to make good with the Giants after two years, I would be given my unconditional release. That was pretty good thinking for a dopey college kid."

At first McGraw was almost a father figure to Frisch, repeating a role he had played for young Christy Mathewson two decades before. Yet "Little Napoleon" could be a harsh taskmaster, even to those he liked. Once, with a runner on first, the righthanded Frisch doubled to left on an inside pitch. McGraw upbraided Frisch for not hitting to right and fined him $100. "Next time when there's a man on first base, maybe you'll hit to right," McGraw told him.

McGraw's combination of kindness and cruelty apparently paid off; the Giants earned pennants in 1921, 1922, 1923, and 1924. Frisch felt little pressure playing in the World Series year after year. "I never fretted about anything. Slept like a baby... A young squirt isn't afraid of anything," he said.

Frisch eventually was named New York's team captain. All signs from McGraw were relayed through him, and if McGraw felt like leaving a game early or not showing up at all, which was not an unusual circumstance, Frisch took charge. McGraw was obviously grooming Frisch as his heir apparent.

Then in the heat of the 1926 pennant race Frisch and McGraw's relationship unraveled. Giants third baseman Freddy Lindstrom recalled: "There was constant squabbling between them, and they became terrible enemies ....The problem lay, I think, in a similarity of personalities. They were both fighting types, aggressive and outspoken. McGraw had simply formed a dislike for Frisch, and you could feel it whenever they came together."

On December 20, 1926, Frisch and pitcher Jimmy Ring were traded to St. Louis for Hornsby. With Frisch at second base, the Cardinals won pennants in 1928 and 1931. In the latter year Frisch was the league's Most Valuable Player. Adding to his pleasure was the fact that, of the two teams the Cardinals beat out for the flag, McGraw managed one and Hornsby the other.

In 1933 Frisch replaced Gabby Street as St. Louis manager. The next season, player-manager Frisch and his rambunctious crew, known as the "Gas House Gang," won a world championship. "They drove me nuts," he later admitted, "but if I could have a bunch like that every year, I'd be quite content to stay nuts."

The arguments between manager Frisch and umpires are legendary. Once he feigned a swoon when jawing with Bill Klem. "Frisch, if you ain't dead, you're out of the game," Klem rasped. On another occasion he came to the plate under an open umbrella to argue that a game should be called on account of rain. Not surprisingly, he was ejected.

Frisch never won another pennant after 1934. Replaced as manager in late 1938 by Mike Gonzalez, he spent the 1939 season as a Braves broadcaster. "I didn't know how much I could miss the game until I began broadcasting in Boston," he said. He left after just one season to manage Pittsburgh. He eventually returned to broadcasting, serving as the Giants radio man from 1947 to 1949. The Fordham Flash was inducted into the Hall of Fame in 1947.

Travis Fryman

Fryman, David Travis **3B–SS**

1990–* B:3/25/1969, Lexington, KY Deb:7/7/1990, DET AL BR/TR 6'1" 194

G	AB	R	H	HR	RBI	OBP	SLG	AVG
1327	5176	726	1418	187	823	.337	.449	.274

An All-American high school ballplayer, Travis Fryman began his professional career when the Detroit Tigers selected him as the 30th pick overall in the 1987 draft. The young Floridian started out as a shortstop with no power, but he ripened into a slugging third baseman in the major leagues.

Fryman started showing some power in the high minors and was promoted to Detroit in the middle of the 1990 season. With Tigers legend Alan Trammell as the incumbent shortstop, the rookie had to learn to play third base in the majors. Fryman struggled defensively at first, though his hitting kept him in the lineup.

For the next three seasons Fryman played both short and third for the Tigers, who signed him to a lucrative five-year contract after 1993. Although he made the All-Star team four times, he never matured into the franchise-caliber player the team expected. Detroit traded Fryman to Arizona during the 1997 expansion draft, and two weeks later the Diamondbacks dealt him to Cleveland for another power-hitting veteran third baseman, Matt Williams. Fryman hit a career-best 28 homers in his first season with the Indians, but suffered through an injury-shortened 1999.

Woodie Fryman

Fryman, Woodrow Thompson **P**

1966–83 B:4/15/1940, Ewing, KY Deb:4/15/1966, PIT NL BR/TL 6'2", 205

W	L	PCT	G	SV	IP	BB	SO	ERA
141	155	.476	625	58	2411[1]	890	1587	3.77

Few major leaguers got such a late start in baseball as Woodie Fryman. Until he was signed at age 25, the lefthander was a Kentucky tobacco farmer. But Fryman quickly found success in a career that spanned 18 years, mostly in the National League. He got off to a blazing start, beginning the 1966 season with the Pirates by throwing three consecutive shutouts—that, despite pitching in only 12 minor league games the year before.

A hard thrower, Fryman fired four one-hitters in his career and struck out 15 Phillies on September 1, 1967. Traded to Philadelphia in 1972, he was 4–10 before being dealt to the Tigers in midseason; he promptly won 10 of 13 decisions to help Detroit to a division title.

Fryman went on to pitch for the Expos, the Reds, and the Cubs before returning to Montreal in 1979, where he became an effective reliever. In four seasons with Montreal, Fryman totaled 24 wins and 46 saves.

Hugh Fullerton

Fullerton, Hugh S.

Sportswriter B:1873, Hillsboro, OH D:12/27/1945, Dunedin, FL

Sportswriter Hugh Fullerton was renowned for his amazingly accurate World Series forecasts. His greatest fame, however, came as the result of a Series that didn't go as predicted.

Fullerton began his career in journalism at age 16, working his way through Hillsboro (Ohio) High School and Ohio State University at the *Cincinnati Enquirer.* He later moved on to Chicago, New York, Columbus, and Philadelphia. Along the way he helped found the Baseball Writers' Association of America in 1908.

He became a nationally known prognosticator with his pick of the 3–1 underdog Chicago White Sox to beat the Chicago Cubs (who had finished an astounding 116–36 during the regular season) in the 1906 Series. He followed with detailed forecasts each year—right down to the scores of games—based on the statistical "dope" he had compiled. He was rarely far off the mark, and when he saw the Cincinnati Reds beating the heavily favored White Sox in 1919, he knew something was amiss. Fullerton took the leading role in breaking what came to be known as the "Black Sox Scandal."

The well-liked, hard-drinking Fullerton also wrote for syndicates, magazines, and books. He was noted for his "Ten Commandments of Sports," and his Tenth Commandment was, "Honor the game thou playest, for he who plays the game straight and hard wins even when he loses."

Fullerton received several prestigious honors after his death. In 1956 he was inducted into the Ohio State University Hall of Fame. In 1965 he became just the third recipient of the J.G. Taylor Spink Award, presented annually "for meritorious contributions to baseball writing." His son, Hugh IV, also became a noted sportswriter.

Carl Furillo

Furillo, Carl Anthony **OF**

1946–60 B:3/8/1922, Stony Creek Mills, PA D:1/21/1989, Stony Creek Mills, PA Deb:4/16/1946, BRO NL BR/TR 6', 190

G	AB	R	H	HR	RBI	OBP	SLG	AVG
1806	6378	895	1910	192	1058	.356	.458	.299

The right fielder on the great Brooklyn Dodgers teams of the 1950s, Carl Furillo won the 1953 National League batting title and posted a .299 lifetime average. He was best known, however, for his powerful throwing arm and his prickly personality.

Signed by Reading in the Interstate League, he so impressed Brooklyn talent hunters they purchased the entire franchise—team bus and all—to obtain Furillo. He hit .284 as a 24-year-old rookie in 1946, improving to .295 and .297 the next two seasons. Furillo blossomed in 1949 when he hit .322 and drove in 106 runs. He remained a key member of the Brooklyn team for the next eight years.

After slumping to .247 in 1952, Furillo learned he was suffering from cataracts. An operation corrected the problem, and he won the NL batting title the next season, when he hit .344. As he put it, "I look at the ball and I see dollar signs instead of stitches."

Capturing that title was not without its drama. On September 6, Furillo came to bat against the Giants' Ruben Gomez. Giants manager Leo Durocher began riding Furillo, finally ordering Gomez to "stick it in his ear." The pitcher proceeded to plunk Furillo in the side. In retaliation Furillo ignored the pitcher and headed straight for Durocher, grabbing him around the neck and choking him. New York third baseman Monte Irvin, trying to break up the fight, fractured a knuckle on the little finger of Furillo's left hand and put him out for the rest of the season.

Defensively, Furillo was outstanding. In 1950 and 1951 he led NL outfielders in assists, and base runners stopped testing his arm. He once picked up a base hit by Pirates pitcher Mel Queen and threw him out at first by two feet. He played the tricky caroms off Ebbets Field's right-field wall masterfully.

Despite his contributions to six Brooklyn pennants, Furillo never really fit in with the "Boys of Summer." He hadn't gone past eighth grade, and "he may have felt some of the other players were aloof because they had a better education," teammate Clem Labine said. "And he wouldn't socialize. Very, very seldom did he socialize with the Sniders, the Erskines. He just wouldn't do it."

Furillo had three nicknames: "Skoonj," "the Reading Rifle," and "Rock." "Skoonj" derived from *scungilli*, the Italian word for squid. "The Reading Rifle" was a tribute to Furillo's first pro club and his throwing arm. "Rock" was short for "Rock-Headed," a snide reference to his lack of education.

Released by the Dodgers on May 17, 1960, Furillo contended that he was injured and that the club should pay his medical expenses. He sued and collected $21,000. "I won. I got my money," he noted. "Then, all of a sudden, I was blackballed. Nobody wanted me to coach, to pinch hit, not even in the minors."

Eddie Gaedel

Gaedel, Edward Carl **PH**

1951 B:6/8/1925, Chicago, IL D:6/18/1961, Chicago, IL Deb:8/19/1951, STL AL BR/TL 3'7", 65

G	AB	R	H	HR	RBI	OBP	SLG	AVG
1	0	0	0	0	0	1.000	—	—

Eddie Gaedel's career consisted of just one major league appearance, but the four-pitch walk he drew in 1951 made him a baseball immortal. A 3-foot 7-inch, 65-pound midget, Gaedel was the principal in the most famous publicity stunt in baseball history. On August 19, 1951, at Sportsman's Park in St. Louis, he emerged out of a birthday cake and pinch hit for Frank Saucier of the Browns against the Detroit Tigers. Gadel's uniform number was ⅛.

Innovative owner Bill Veeck conceived the stunt to boost Browns attendance and to celebrate the 50th anniversaries of the American League and the Falstaff Brewing Company, the sponsor of Browns' games. Veeck paid Gaedel $100 and insured him for $1,000 for his pinch-hitting performance. Detroit lefthander Bob Cain did not come close to throwing a strike to Gaedel. Gaedel was immediately removed for a pinch runner.

When home plate umpire Ed Hurley initially objected to Gaedel pinch-hitting, Browns manager Zack Taylor presented him with a signed contract and the notification papers to the league office. Afterward, AL president William Harridge was furious over the stunt and threatened to have Gaedel's name erased from the record books. Harridge had no recourse, however, because Veeck had managed to get approval of Gaedel's contract from officials in the league office the day before.

An unusually large crowd (for the Browns) of 18,369 was at Sportsman's Park that day, mostly because Veeck had promised them something special. Gaedel made out on the stunt too, garnering enough bookings off his renown to make a decent living until his death in 1961.

Upon returning to baseball as owner of the Chicago White Sox in 1959, Veeck arranged for a helicopter to land in the infield of Comiskey Park whereupon a group of midgets, dressed as Martians, popped out, and "kidnapped" Chicago's diminutive double play combo, Nellie Fox and Luis Aparicio. Naturally, Gaedel was one of the midgets.

Gary Gaetti

Gaetti, Gary Joseph **3B**

1981–* B:8/19/1958, Centralia, IL Deb:9/20/1981, MIN AL BR/TR 6', 200

G	AB	R	H	HR	RBI	OBP	SLG	AVG
2502	8941	1128	2280	360	1340	.311	.434	.255

In his first full season in the major leagues, in 1982, Gary Gaetti hit 25 home runs—but he batted just .230. His defense and power potential kept him in the lineup over the next three seasons, while Minnesota waited for the rest of his game to develop.

The wait ended in 1986. Gaetti came through with a .287 average, 34 homers, and 108 RBIs, and won his first of four consecutive Gold Gloves at third base. The following year, he helped propel the Twins to the American League West title with 31 homers and 109 RBIs.

In the 1987 Championship Series against Detroit, Gaetti's .300 average and two home runs won him the series' Most Valuable Player honors as Minnesota advanced to the World Series. Facing the St. Louis Cardinals, Gaetti helped win Game 2 with a homer and collected seven hits, four for extra bases, in the Twins' seven-game triumph.

As Minnesota's fortunes declined over the next three seasons, Gaetti's star began to fade. An August 1988 conversion to Christianity alienated some teammates, and journalists snickered that the formerly rambunctious Gaetti had found God, but lost his power stroke. Gaetti went from 65 home runs in 1986–87, to just 35 in the next two years. Minnesota manager Tom Kelly criticized him during a 1990 slump, and when the California Angels offered a large free agent contract the following winter, Gaetti left Minnesota.

The move proved a disaster. While the Twins rebounded from a last-place finish to win their second world championship, Gaetti quickly became a target of ire from fans in Anaheim. Things got worse in 1992, when Gaetti hit just .226 and ran afoul of new Angels manager Buck Rodgers. Thinking his career was over, California released Gaetti in June 1993, eating $5 million of his contract.

Quickly signed by Kansas City, the supposedly washed-up Gaetti hit 14 homers in 82 games and looked revitalized. In 1995 he slammed 35 home runs for the Royals, then signed as a free agent with the Cardinals, the favorite team of his childhood. Gaetti hit .273 with 23 home runs as St. Louis won its division in 1996. He blasted a dramatic grand slam off Atlanta ace Greg Maddux in Game 2 of the NLCS.

He spent another season and a half with the Cards before joining the Cubs for the 1998 stretch drive, batting .320 with eight homers in 37 games to help Chicago secure the Wild Card. In 1999 Gaetti became one of only 40 players ever to appear in 2,500 games.

Greg Gagne

Gagne, Gregory Carpenter **SS**

1983–97 B:11/12/1961, Fall River, MA Deb:6/5/1983, MIN AL BR/TR 5'11", 172

G	AB	R	H	HR	RBI	OBP	SLG	AVG
1798	5673	712	1440	111	604	.304	.382	.254

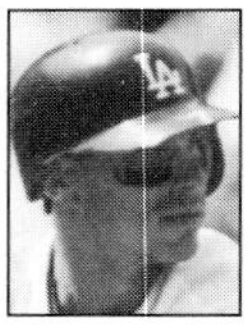

Greg Gagne was a consistent shortstop with a knack for getting hits at key times. Gagne was a fixture in the lineup wherever he played, playing 100 games in each of his 13 full seasons with the Minnesota Twins, Kansas City Royals, and Los Angeles Dodgers. Gagne never batted higher than .280, hit more than 14 home runs, or had more than 59 RBIs, but he was a major factor in Minnesota's two world championship teams.

"Gags" tied an American League record with two inside-the-park home runs in one game on October 4, 1986. A year later, in the first playoff action of his career, Gagne hit two home runs in the 1987 Championship Series against Detroit. The second proved to be the winning run in Game 4, with the Twins winning the series in five games. He added a homer and tied for the team lead with five runs scored in Minnesota's thrilling World Series win over St. Louis.

Gagne again rose to the occasion when the Twins returned to the postseason four years later. His three-run home run sparked a 5–2 victory over the Atlanta Braves in the Series opener. As in 1987, Minnesota took the title in seven games.

Augie Galan

Galan, August John **OF–1B**

1934–49 B:5/25/1912, Berkeley, CA D:12/28/1993, Fairfield, CA Deb:4/29/1934, CHI NL BB/TR 6', 175

G	AB	R	H	HR	RBI	OBP	SLG	AVG
1742	5937	1004	1706	100	830	.390	.419	.287

As a boy Augie Galan broke his elbow playing baseball. While the accident left him with a permanently deformed arm, neither that nor a host of later injuries prevented him from having a fine major league career as a switch-hitting outfielder.

Galan reached the major leagues in 1934, spending that season as an infield sub. He became the regular left fielder for the pennant-winning Cubs in 1935, hitting .314 and leading the National League with 133 runs scored and 22 stolen bases. He also became the first full-time player to complete a season without hitting into a double play, although, strangely enough, he did hit into a triple play.

Galan's batting fell off during the next couple of years, in part because of injuries. However, he did have some bright spots. In 1936 he was chosen for the All-Star Game and became the first Cubs player to homer in it. The next year, on June 15, he became the first National League player to homer from both sides of the plate in the same game.

In 1940 a broken knee threatened to end Galan's career, and the next year the Cubs dealt him to the Dodgers. He arrived in time to help in Brooklyn's successful stretch drive to the pennant. He seemed to improve with age with the Dodgers, hitting above .300 three years in a row, leading the National League in walks in 1943 and 1944, and being selected to the All-Star Game each of those years.

In 1947 he joined Cincinnati and continued his outstanding play, hitting .314 and leading the league in on-base percentage. He retired after the 1949 season, which he spent with the New York Giants and the Philadelphia A's.

Andres Galarraga

Galarraga, Andres Jose **1B**

1985–98, * B:6/18/1961, Caracas, Venezuela Deb:8/23/1985, MON NL BR/TR, 6'3", 235

G	AB	R	H	HR	RBI	OBG	SLG	AVG
1774	6629	1011	1921	332	1172	.349	.504	.290

Andres Galarraga won all three components of the Triple Crown over a five-year span: he led the National League in batting at .370 in 1993, slammed a league-leading 47 home runs in 1996, and produced consecutive RBI crowns in 1996 (150) and 1997 (140). He was a quiet clubhouse leader with remarkable quick reflexes for a big man—or as his teammates called him, "The Big Cat."

Signed as a nondrafted free agent by the Montreal Expos in 1979, Galarraga reached the majors six years later. Although he had two .300 seasons and won two Gold Gloves during his Montreal tenure, Galarraga struck out with alarming frequency. He led the NL in strikeouts from 1988 to 1990. After his average slipped to .219 during an injury-riddled 1991 campaign, the Expos traded him to St. Louis for pitcher Ken Hill.

Cardinals hitting coach Don Baylor helped save Galarraga's career, then signed the first baseman shortly after being named the first manager of the Colorado Rockies. Galarraga thrived in his new surroundings. He raised his average 127 points in 1993 to win the batting title as well as *The Sporting News* Comeback Player of the Year Award. When the Rockies moved from Mile High Stadium to more intimate Coors Field in 1995, Galarraga's already impressive power numbers became astronomical.

"The Big Cat" hit more home runs (172) than any other Rockie. He also enjoyed a three-homer game and a six-hit game, both in 1995, as he led the Rockies to the postseason in just their third season. Galarraga left Colorado via free agency to sign a three-year contract with the Atlanta Braves on November 20, 1997.

Although skeptics charged his numbers would decline without the help of Denver's thin atmosphere, Galarraga responded with 44 home runs and 121 RBIs in Atlanta's pitcher-friendly ballpark. He not only set franchise records for home runs and RBIs by a first baseman, but also became the first player in baseball history to hit at least 40 homers in consecutive seasons for different teams. It marked his fourth consecutive season with at least 100 RBIs. Galarraga was named to the All-Star team for the fourth time.

He added a grand slam in the seventh inning of Game 5 of the Championship Series, but Atlanta lost that series to San Diego in part because Galarraga hit .095 with an uncharacteristic four errors in six games. Although he complained of lower-back pain at the time, he was not diagnosed with cancer until February. The Venezuelan slugger missed the 1999 campaign while undergoing radiation and chemotherapy treatments.

Denny Galehouse

Galehouse, Dennis Ward **P**

1934–44, 1946–49 B:12/7/1911, Marshallville, OH
Deb:4/30/1934, CLE AL BR/TR 6'1", 195

W	L	PCT	G	SH	IP	BB	SO	ERA
109	118	.480	375	17	2004	735	851	3.97

Denny Galehouse won 109 games in his career, and was the winner of the first World Series game in St. Louis Browns history. Say his name to any Boston Red Sox fan from the 1940s, however, and the response will most likely be a groan.

The Red Sox and Cleveland Indians were tied atop the American League at the end of the 1948 season, forcing a one-game playoff. Galehouse was Boston skipper Joe McCarthy's surprise choice to start the game that would decide the pennant. Galehouse had never won more than 12 games in a season during his 14-year career with the Indians, Browns, and Red Sox.

The 37-year-old righthander had spent most of 1948 in the bullpen, while rookie lefty Mel Parnell, a 15-game winner, was rested and ready to make the start. McCarthy, however, was swayed by the memory of a game against Cleveland earlier in the season, when the Indians had chased Parnell in the first inning and Galehouse had pitched two-hit relief the rest of the game. Cleveland had, however, hit Galehouse hard in two subsequent appearances, and with the pennant on the line, the Indians did so again. Galehouse took the loss in an 8–3 decision. He pitched just two more games in his career.

Jim Galvin

Galvin, James Francis **P**

1875, 1879–92 M(1885, 7–17) U(1895–96)
B:12/25/1856, St. Louis, MO D:3/7/1902, Pittsburgh, PA
Deb:5/22/1875, STL NA BR/TR 5'8", 190

W	L	PCT	G	SH	IP	BB	SO	ERA
361	308	.540	697	57	5941¹	744	1799	2.87

Except for Cy Young, no major league pitcher ever hurled more innings than Jim "Pud" Galvin, a 19th-century workhorse. One observer noted, "In those days it was work for a pitcher, and hard work at that. The team that had two pitchers was lucky; it was a case of go in and do the pitching day after day. That was what Galvin was called on to do, and his record shows he did it well."

A native of Kerry Patch, the Irish district of St. Louis, Galvin began in baseball in 1875 with the St. Louis Brown Stockings of the National Association and spent the following year with the independent St. Louis Red Stockings. He pitched two no-hitters that year, on July 4 against Philadelphia and on August 17 against the Cass Club of Detroit. The latter was a perfect game, perhaps the first ever by a professional.

Galvin joined Buffalo of the National League in 1879 and immediately became the heavy-duty pitcher of the team, throwing 65 complete games in his 66 starts, and winning 37 of them. The next year his record dropped to 20–35, but he did throw his first National League no-hitter on August 20, 1880, defeating Worcester, 1–0, despite six Buffalo errors.

The next two years were remarkably similar for Galvin, as he won 28 games in both 1881 and 1882, each season throwing 48 complete games. It was all a build-up to 1883, however, when he put together one of the most amazing seasons in history. That year he led the league with 76 appearances, including 75 starts and a league-leading 72 complete games. He threw a remarkable 656⅓ innings, striking out 279, while walking only 50. He finished with a 46–29 record.

In 1884 Galvin was even better, going 46–22 with a 1.99 ERA, 71 complete games, and a league high 12 shutouts. Even more remarkable was his streak against Detroit midway through the season. On Saturday, August 2, he yielded only a fifth-inning single to Charlie Bennett and struck out seven. On Monday, August 4, he pitched a no-hitter, striking out nine. He threw a third straight shutout on Thursday, August 7, three-hitting

Detroit, 9–0. And the next day, in the second game of a morning-afternoon doubleheader, Galvin pitched shutout ball for 11 innings, losing in the 12th on an unearned run. In four games, he had pitched 39 innings, allowed 12 hits, walked none, struck out 36, and surrendered only one unearned run.

Galvin was also a fine fielder; he often played in the outfield and had an excellent pickoff move. "If I had Galvin to catch, no one would ever steal a base off me," observed catcher Buck Ewing. "That fellow keeps 'em glued to the base, and he also has the best control of any pitcher in the league."

From mid-1885 until 1890 Galvin pitched for Pittsburgh teams in three different leagues: the American Association (1885–86), the National League (1887–89, and 1891–92), and the Players' League (1890). He finished his career in the NL with St. Louis. He retired after an ill-fated comeback attempt with Buffalo's entry in the Eastern (International) League in 1894, when he went lost twice in three appearances. The next year he unsuccessfully tried his hand at National League umpiring.

Galvin had a large family of 11 children. He often joked about organizing his own ballclub, to be called the Galvinized Nine. He died in a rooming house in Pittsburgh without even enough money to pay for his funeral. Six decades later, however, he was inducted into the Hall of Fame, and two of his children were still alive to enjoy the moment.

Oscar Gamble

Gamble, Oscar Charles **OF-DH**
1969–85 B:12/20/1949, Ramer, AL Deb:8/27/1969, CHI NL BL/TR 5'11", 165

G	AB	R	H	HR	RBI	OBP	SLG	AVG
1584	4502	656	1195	200	666	.358	.454	.265

There was no figuring out Oscar Gamble. For 17 years, his performance was up and down and all over the place. He batted .358 one year and .184 another. He hit 31 home runs one season and also had three one-homer seasons. He was a terror to righthanded pitching, but he never quite solved southpaws.

The Chicago Cubs drafted Gamble in the 16th round of the June 1968 amateur draft, and he was in the majors by the end of the 1969 season at the age of 19. But he was a work in progress, and after that season he and pitcher Dick Selma were traded to Philadelphia. He spent the next three years bouncing up and down between the Phillies and their Triple A farm team in Eugene, Oregon.

Gamble got a chance to play more regularly when he was traded to Cleveland for Del Unser. Gamble responded by hitting .267 with 20 homers in 1973. After two more productive seasons with the Indians, he went to the Yankees for Pat Dobson. Gamble loved New York, and seemed made for Yankee Stadium's short right-field porch. He even enjoyed the give and take with the press, and would start sentences with a phrase like: "A man of my ability..." He fit right in with the crew that breezed to the American League East title in 1976. But the Yankees needed a shortstop for 1977, so they sent Gamble, La Marr Hoyt, and $200,000 to the White Sox for Bucky Dent.

Gamble thrived as one of Bill Veeck's rent-a-players, reaching career-highs with 31 homers and 83 RBIs. Ray Kroc, the CEO of McDonalds and the Padres' owner, wanted to spend his hamburger dollars on a superstar like Reggie Jackson, but kept getting turned down. So he offered Gamble $2.2 million for six years, then sweetened the offer to $2.8 million a few days later even though no one had come close to his first offer. But Jack Murphy Stadium was a big park where the ball didn't carry well, and Gamble dropped to seven home runs and only 47 RBIs. The Padres traded him to the Rangers that winter, and Kroc told the writers, "I got Oscar Gamble on the advice of my lawyer. I no longer have my lawyer, and I no longer have Oscar Gamble."

For his part, Gamble responded with a terrific 1979, although part of it was played in New York after he was traded back to the Yankees in mid-season. He hit .358 with 19 homers and 64 RBIs. He spent another five years with the Yankees, although he did not reach that level of production again. He then signed as a bargain-basement free agent with the White Sox for 1985. He retired after that season, having slumped to .203 with four homers.

Chick Gandil

Gandil, Arnold **1B**
1910, 1912–19 B:1/19/1887, St. Paul, MN D:12/13/1970, Calistoga, CA Deb:4/14/1910, CHI AL BR/TR 6'1½", 190

G	AB	R	H	HR	RBI	OBP	SLG	AVG
1147	4245	449	1176	11	557	.327	.362	.277

Chick Gandil was the ringleader of the infamous Black Sox. He instigated the fix of the 1919 World Series by letting gambling friends know that games could be thrown for a price, usually thought to be either $80,000 or $100,000. He recruited the other conspirators from the Chicago White Sox—shortstop Swede Risberg, pitchers Eddie Cicotte and Lefty Williams, and outfielders Joe Jackson and Happy Felsch. Utility infielder Fred McMullin forced his way into the group when he learned of the conspiracy, while third baseman Buck Weaver knew of the plans but refused to take part.

Gandil ran away from home at age 17 to play baseball in mining towns along the Arizona–Mexico border. He played part of the 1910 season with the Chicago White Sox, hit only .193, and, after returning to the minors for 1911, was sold to Washington in 1912. A better fielder than hitter, he led the American League in fielding average among first basemen four times. Although he hit .305 and .318 for the Senators in 1912 and 1913, Gandil lacked power and never reached .300 again.

Sold in 1916 to Cleveland for $7,500, a year later he was passed on to Chicago for $3,500. The White Sox won the pennant in 1917 and 1919 with Gandil on first, but he was never one of the team's stars. Gandil was the leader of a clique that included Risberg and Weaver, and he and his cohorts disliked the more educated and dedicated players on the team, such as Eddie Collins and Ray Schalk, who garnered a larger portion of owner Charles Comiskey's meager payroll.

Gandil used the players' complaints about Comiskey and their teammates to bring them into the plot to throw the World Series. Although none of the conspirators received as much as they were promised, Gandil apparently pocketed $35,000 and did not report to the White Sox the following spring.

When the story of the fix came out near the end of the 1920 season, Gandil returned to Chicago for the trial along with the other Black Sox. Confessions by Jackson and Cicotte mysteriously disappeared, and the judge ruled that it had to be proved that the players had set out to defraud the public. Under the circumstances, conviction was impossible. However, new baseball Commissioner Kenesaw Mountain Landis still suspended the conspirators for life. Gandil returned to the west and became a plumber.

Ron Gant

Gant, Ronald Edwin **OF-2B**

1987–93, 1995–* B:3/2/1965, Victoria, TX
Deb:9/6/1987, ATL NL BR/TR 6', 192

G	AB	R	H	HR	RBI	OBP	SLG	AVG
1497	5422	903	1393	266	856	.339	.467	.257

While 1994 was a lost season for most major leaguers because of the strike, it truly was a lost campaign for Ron Gant. A week after agreeing to a $5.5 million salary, the largest one-year contract in major league history at the time, Gant broke his right leg in a dirt bike accident on February 3, 1994. He got just 16 percent of his salary in termination pay from the Braves.

"At the time, I was more disappointed than bitter," he said. "But after the morphine wore off, I got angry." The Reds took a chance on Gant—and also paid him $2 million less than Atlanta would have in the process. In his first series against Atlanta, he twice beat his former team with extra-inning home runs. He wound up hitting 29 homers with 88 RBIs to win National League Comeback Player of the Year Award. Coming off a broken leg, Gant had his lowest stolen base total since 1989, but he still managed to swipe 23 bases.

Signed as a free agent in the fourth round of the 1983 draft out of Victoria High School in Texas Gant came up through the Braves' system as a slick-fielding middle infielder. He was the top fielding second baseman in the Southern League with Greenville in 1987.

Atlanta made him the regular second baseman the following year. Although Gant surprised the Braves' brass by belting 19 home runs, he also disappointed them by committing 26 errors. He was the team's third baseman to start the 1989 season, but a .172 average and 16 errors sent Gant all the way down to Class A Sumter to learn to play the outfield.

Gant rose along with the Braves. In 1990 he put together his first 30-homer, 30-stolen base season. The following year he joined Willie Mays (1956–57) as the second National Leaguer to have back-to-back 30–30 seasons. Gant stole a record seven bases against Pittsburgh in the Championship Series and then hit .267 in the World Series as Minnesota won in seven games.

Gant slumped in 1992, and even lost his position to Deion Sanders in the postseason, but he rebounded the following year with career highs in home runs (36) and RBIs (117) as the Braves rallied to take the NL West title from the Giants on the final day of the 1993 season.

After his broken leg, and his subsequent comeback, Gant landed with his third team in three years in 1996. He hit for power, but not for average, in three St. Louis seasons—although he did bat .400 in the 1996 NL Division Series win over San Diego. In November 1998 the Cards sent Gant and pitchers Jeff Brantley and Cliff Politte and cash to Philadelphia for pitchers Ricky Bottalico and Garrett Stephenson. Gant batted .260, his highest average since 1994, and scored 107 runs.

Jim Gantner

Gantner, James Elmer **2B–3B**

1976–92 B:1/5/1953, Fond Du Lac, WI Deb:9/3/1976, MIL AL BL/TR 6', 180

G	AB	R	H	HR	RBI	OBP	SLG	AVG
1801	6189	726	1696	47	568	.322	.351	.274

There were those who thought that Jim Gantner was the weak link of the Milwaukee Brewers' infield in their playoff years of the early 1980s. Despite his detractors, Gantner still played 17 years in Milwaukee, most of them as the regular second baseman.

Gantner first came to the Brewers as a third basemen, but he saw limited action there in his first three years in the majors. In 1979 his role as a utility infielder increased dramatically, and the next year he started some 130 games, splitting his time between second and third. In 1981 Gantner became the team's regular second baseman, and, with Robin Yount, led the American League in double plays for the first of two straight seasons.

Gantner hit .295 in 1982, and then took his game up a notch when the Brewers reached the playoffs that year. In the decisive Game 5 of the Championship Series, Gantner singled, and then he sprinted home on Cecil Cooper's single, scoring the winning run in a come-from-behind 4–3 victory over California. In the World Series, he hit .333 and led all Series participants with 33 assists. In Game 4 his two-out double in the seventh drove in the first of six runs in a 7–5 comeback win, tying the Series. In Game 7 Gantner led off the sixth inning with a double and scored, giving Milwaukee a short-lived lead.

The next year was probably Gantner's best. He batted .282 with career highs in runs, triples, homers, and RBIs. The gritty lefthanded batter continued to play at a solid level, rebounding from reconstructive knee surgery in 1989 to continue his career He finally retired in the spring of 1993 at age 40.

Joe Garagiola

Garagiola, Joseph Henry **C**

1946–54 B:2/12/1926, St. Louis, MO Deb:5/26/1946, STL NL BL/TR 6', 190

G	AB	R	H	HR	RBI	OBP	SLG	AVG
676	1872	198	481	42	255	.355	.385	.257

Joe Garagiola was one of the first baseball players to make a successful career out of what he did *not* do on the field. A platoon player or a backup for most of his years in the major leagues, Garagiola once said of his career, "I went through life as a player to be named later."

Garagiola actually had some of his most successful moments in 1946, his first year in the majors. That year he shared time at catcher for St. Louis with Del Rice and Clyde Kluttz, as the Cardinals finished in a dead heat for the pennant with Brooklyn. In the three-game playoff and the subsequent World Series, Garagiola became a major contributor. In the first playoff game, he had three singles in four at bats and drove in two runs in a 4–2 victory. His eighth-inning double in Game 1 of the World Series put St. Louis ahead, although the team lost in the 10th. In Game 4 he had four hits and three RBIs as the Cardinals walloped the Red Sox, 12–3. For the Series he batted .316.

In 1947 Garagiola had about equal time behind the plate with Rice, hitting .257 for the second-place Cardinals. Demoted after a poor start in 1948, he returned to share the job again in 1949. The following year he suffered a shoulder separation while he was hitting .347, and he never neared that season's average again.

Although he didn't know it at the time, getting traded to the Pirates early in the 1951 season would be a boon to his later career. The miserable Bucs, losers of 112 games in 1952, became an endless source of wacky stories for Garagiola. He made his fame telling those tales and adding a healthy dollop of Yogi-isms from his close boyhood friend. In 1953 the Bucs sent Garagiola and outfielder Ralph Kiner to the Chicago Cubs, and, despite performing very well in the Windy City, Garagiola's playing career was over in a year.

However, he soon landed a job with Harry Caray announcing the Cardinals' games, and his new career was under way. In fact, the Cardinals fired Milo Hamilton and replaced him with their former catcher. Garagiola worked hard to improve his on-air skills, but his special combination of insider's feel for the game, boyish exuberance, and humor made him an immediate standout.

He worked with Caray for seven years, and by 1961 he was an announcer for the All-Star Game. Two years later he was calling the World Series. He became a frequent visitor on *The Tonight Show*, regaling the audience with his yarns, short and long. Garagiola later announced for the Yankees, replacing Mel Allen; was a co-host of NBC's *Today Show*; and hosted syndicated talk and game shows. His television program *The Baseball World of Joe Garagiola* won a Peabody Award for broadcasting excellence. Garagiola and Tony Kubek became one of the best-liked announcing duos ever when they worked together on the *Game of the Week* from 1975 through 1983. Their relentless disagreements were great fun as well as a great education for baseball fans. In 1991 Garagiola received the Ford Frick Award

As an announcer, Garagiola liked doing things his own way. When asked if he would mention on the air that a no-hitter was in progress, he replied, "I believe in telling the people. In fact, I'll try to build up the audience by saying, 'If you've got any friends not listening, call them up. We might have a no-hitter here tonight.' "

Garagiola also was successful as a writer. His book *Baseball Is a Funny Game* became one of the best-selling baseball books ever. His feel for baseball lore engaged fans and humanized the game, paving the way for other media personalities such as former umpire Ron Luciano and former catcher Bob Uecker. Garagiola worked tirelessly to help former ballplayers in need as a spokesman for the Baseball Assistance Team; he also attended spring training each year in an attempt to warn players about the health hazards of chewing tobacco. His son, Joe Jr., was selected as the first general manager of the Arizona Diamondbacks.

Gene Garber

Garber, Henry Eugene **P**

1969–70, 1972–88 B:11/13/1947, Lancaster, PA Deb:6/17/1969, PIT NL BR/TR 5'10", 175

W	L	PCT	G	SV	IP	BB	SO	ERA
96	113	.459	931	218	1510	445	940	3.34

Gene Garber had one of the longest careers of any relief pitcher in major league history. In 19 years he appeared in 931 games, and right up until the end his righthanded, sidearm delivery made him a nightmare for many hitters.

Garber signed with the Pittsburgh Pirates in 1965 as a 13th-round draft choice. He did not throw especially hard, and he kicked around the minors for most of the next eight years. He made three brief visits to the majors (for a total of 20 games) but it was not until he was traded to the Royals for Jim Rooker after the 1972 season that he got his chance.

By then Garber had mastered his changeup, which became his out pitch. His changeup had a lot of motion, like Stu Miller's, and the bottom dropped out as it crossed the plate. He was 9–9 for the Royals in 1973 in 48 games, eight of them starts, something he never did again in the majors after that season. Despite his success with the Royals, he was sold to the Philadelphia Phillies in July 1974. It was then that his career really took off.

The Phillies were serious about using Garber, and in 1975 he went 10–12 with 14 saves while leading the National League with 71 appearances. The next year he was 9–3 with a 2.82 ERA and 11 saves as the Phillies won the NL East. Garber improved to 19 saves in 1977, but he was on the mound for the Dodgers' dramatic three-run, two-out, none-on rally in Game 3 of the Championship Series that turned the series around.

In June 1978 Garber was traded to Atlanta for starter Dick Ruthven, a deal that helped both teams. Garber saved 25 games in both 1978 (with a career-low 2.15 ERA) and 1979. On August 1, 1978, he earned his most lasting fame by striking out Pete Rose to end "Charlie Hustle's" 44-game hitting streak. He had his problems that following year, however, as his 16 losses set the major league record for a reliever. After two poor years Garber returned in splendid fashion in 1982 when the Braves won the NL West. That year he finished second in the league with 30 saves and had a 2.34 ERA.

A sore elbow hampered Garber in 1983 and he lost his job as the Braves' primary closer. After a couple of years of seeing more action in middle relief, he reclaimed the position as closer in 1986 when he saved 24 games. That was his last hurrah. He was traded the next year to Kansas City, and he retired following the 1988 season. Through the 1999 season his total of 922 games in relief puts him third on the all-time career list, and his 931 games overall are good for fifth place all time.

Mike Garcia

Garcia, Edward Miguel **P**

1948–61 B:11/17/1923, San Gabriel, CA D:1/13/1986, Fairview Park, OH Deb:10/3/1948, CLE AL BR/TR 6'1", 200

W	L	PCT	G	SH	IP	BB	SO	ERA
142	97	.594	428	27	2174²	719	1117	3.27

Mike Garcia was an integral part of the 1954 Cleveland Indians pitching staff, regarded as one of baseball's finest rotations. Garcia, Bob Lemon, Early Wynn, Ray Narleski, and Bob Feller propelled the Indians to an American League-record 111 victories and a trip to the World Series.

Garcia's professional career had started in 1942 with the Class D Wisconsin State League's Appleton Papermakers, where he went 10–10. After spending 1943 through 1945 in the service, he returned to baseball in 1946 with Bakersfield of the California League. That season he led the league in games and ERA. Playing with the Wilkes-Barre Barons in 1947, Garcia led the Eastern League with 17 victories. He spent most of 1948 at Oklahoma City of the Texas League, where he was 19–16, with a 3.09 ERA. Late in the season he was called up to Cleveland.

"From the beginning Mike was a sneaky quick pitcher," said Feller. "For a big guy, he was certainly mobile."

Garcia won 14 games with five shutouts and a league-leading 2.36 ERA during his 1949 rookie season. He posted back-to-back 20-win seasons in

1951 and 1952 and followed with 18 victories in 1953. Then in 1954 he went 19–8, again leading the league with five shutouts and with a 2.64 ERA. He was not as successful in his one post-season appearance, lasting only three innings while allowing four runs in Game 3 of the World Series. The New York Giants swept the Series the next day.

The 1954 season was the last real highlight for Garcia. He followed it with two losing seasons before going 12–8 in 1957. He played in 1960 with the Chicago White Sox and 1961 with the Washington Senators but did not win a game his final two seasons.

After retiring in 1961, Garcia operated a dry cleaning establishment in Parma, Ohio. "I love Cleveland," he said at the time. "I'm going to stay here the rest of my life." In the 1970s Garcia became disabled from diabetes and kidney failure and required frequent dialysis treatments. He was forced to sell his business to pay his mounting medical bills.

A month before his death, in January 1986, his former teammates organized a benefit to help Garcia. "He did more than his share," said Lemon, "and I hope the Cleveland fans remember that."

Nomar Garciaparra

Garciaparra, Anthony Nomar **SS**
1996–* B:7/23/1973, Whittier, CA Deb:8/31/96, BOS AL
BR/TR 6', 165

G	AB	R	H	HR	RBI	OBP	SLG	AVG
455	1907	347	615	96	340	.370	.566	.322

In his first three full seasons in the major leagues, Nomar Garciaparra was compared to some of baseball's greatest shortstops. Most of it was news to Garciaparra, who spent his time playing baseball as opposed to following it.

"I never had a baseball hero or anything like that," Garciaparra told *Sports Illustrated*. "I loved the game just for the sake of playing it. I'd tell my dad from the time I was 5 or 6: 'Teach me that. Don't tell me about who plays the game in the majors. Tell me *how* to play it.' I wanted to learn as much as I could about every position."

Ramon Garciaparra gave his eldest son his love for baseball and a unique middle name by spelling his own name backwards. Anthony Nomar Garciaparra became a standout athlete at baseball, soccer, and football at St. John Bosco High School in Bellflower, California.

Although he weighed just 135 pounds in high school, prompting the nickname "Glass," Garciaparra played catcher and pitcher before settling in as a shortstop. The University of Arkansas recruited him as a placekicker—he once kicked a 60-yard field goal in practice. UCLA said he could take his pick of football, soccer, or baseball. The Milwaukee Brewers drafted him in the fifth round of the 1991 draft. In the end, however, Garciaparra decided to go to Georgia Tech. He became just the fourth Yellow Jacket to reach 100 hits in a season, he was an academic All-America, and he was the first freshman to walk on and make the U.S. Olympic team.

The Red Sox took Garciaparra in the first round of the 1994 draft with the 12th pick. He was in a Boston uniform after less than 200 minor league games. In his first major league start on September 1, 1996, he homered for his first major league hit and added two more hits in an 8–3 win in Oakland.

Despite Garciaparra's presence, the Red Sox already had one of the better-hitting shortstops in the game in John Valentin. New manager Jimy Williams could have put Garciaparra at second base, but it would have diminished the rookie's outstanding talents and, in turn, hurt an already suspect defense. Instead, Williams upset the veteran Valentin and moved him to second base. Valentin briefly walked out on the team in spring training, but it turned out to be the best move the Red Sox made all year.

Garciaparra became the first rookie to bat .300 with 30 home runs, 90 RBIs, and 20 stolen bases—prior to the 1997 season only 13 players had ever accomplished the feat. Garciaparra also led the American League in hits, multi-hit games, and triples while finishing second in runs scored. His 98 RBIs were a record for a lead-off hitter.

He set an AL rookie record with a 30-game hitting streak and won the AL Silver Slugger Award. Garciaparra was the first Boston player since Fred Lynn in 1975 to earn AL Rookie of the Year and the first Red Sox since Carlton Fisk in 1972 to earn the honor unanimously.

Despite a two-week stint on the disabled list, Garciaparra's sophomore 1998 season was even stronger than his rookie campaign. He collected 35 homers and 122 RBIs, while raising his average to .323—finishing second in AL Most Valuable Player balloting. His homer total made him just the fifth in history to surpass 30 home runs in each of his first two seasons. Perhaps more significantly, Garciaparra sliced his strikeout total from 92 to 62.

In 1999 he led the Red Sox to the AL Wild Card berth for the second straight year. He batted an AL-best .357 with 27 homers and 104 RBIs, while reducing his strikeouts to just 39. Garciaparra batted .400 in the stormy Championship Series against the Yankees. In addition, he did it while taking over the role as team leader and chief power source following Mo Vaughn's departure to the Angels.

Danny Gardella

Gardella, Daniel Lewis **OF**

1944–45, 1950 B:2/26/1920, New York, NY
Deb:5/14/1944, NY NL BL/TL 5'7½" 160

G	AB	R	H	HR	RBI	OBP	SLG	AVG
169	543	74	145	24	85	.343	.433	.267

Danny Gardella of the New York Giants had a brief career that hardly merited attention for what he did on the field. However, he came close to starting a baseball revolution in the late 1940s when his lawsuit challenging baseball's reserve clause seemed headed for the U.S. Supreme Court.

A minor leaguer from 1939 to 1942, Gardella worked in shipyards in 1943. The next year, however, he returned to baseball, earning a place on the Giants' roster as a reserve outfielder. In 1945, his only season as a regular, Gardella hit .272 with 18 homers.

The end of the war signaled the return of more talented ballplayers, so Gardella jumped to Jorge Pasquel's Mexican League in 1946. When that scheme collapsed, he and the other players who had jumped leagues were barred from Organized Baseball for five years by Commissioner Happy Chandler. Gardella tried to play semipro baseball for a while, but he found that the blacklist stretched quite far; he wound up working as a hospital orderly on the outskirts of New York City.

Aided by New York attorney Frederic Johnson, Gardella sued Organized Baseball in 1947. He sought $100,000 in damages, which under the antitrust laws would translate into $300,000. Johnson further called the entire system of reserving players in perpetuity into question. It was, he said, used "contrary to settled principles of equity and to further a conspiracy in restraint of trade and commerce." This last point made Organized Baseball particularly nervous, for it knew it stood on extremely shaky legal ground.

On February 10, 1949, a panel of three federal judges voted two to one that Gardella's suit merited a trial. Judge Learned Hand ruled that the nation's antitrust laws banned "all restraints of trade which were unlawful at common law, and one of the oldest and best established of these is a contract which unreasonably forbids anyone to practice his calling." The reserve clause, he reasoned, fell into this category.

The trial was scheduled for November 1949. Branch Rickey charged that persons with "avowed Communist tendencies" were challenging the reserve clause. One congressman stated that "a Gardella victory could well sound the death knell for the sport that has kindled the fires and ambitions in the breasts of so many thousands of young Americans."

The trial never took place, however, because on July 5 Chandler granted amnesty to all who had jumped to the Mexican League. While players like Sal Maglie, Fred Martin, and Max Lanier immediately returned to the majors, Gardella played with Trois Rivieres of the Provincial League. He hit .286, with 14 homers and 53 RBIs.

At season's end Gardella returned to New York, where he and his attorney decided to settle out of court. On October 8, 1949, Chandler announced the settlement. No monetary terms were cited, but years later Gardella admitted that Organized Baseball had paid $60,000 to kill Gardella v. Chandler. Half went to Johnson. "I feel so relieved," crowed Chandler. "If I were a drinking man, I'd get drunk."

Soon thereafter Gardella was sold to the St. Louis Cardinals. He flied out in his one big league at bat in 1950. That April he was sent to minor league Houston, where he batted .211 before being released in June. In 1951 he played for the semipro Brooklyn Bushwicks.

Larry Gardner

Gardner, William Lawrence **3B-2B**

1908–24 B:5/13/1886, Enosburg Falls, VT D:3/11/1976,
St. George, VT Deb:6/25/1908, BOS AL BL/TR 5'8", 165

G	AB	R	H	HR	RBI	OBP	SLG	AVG
1923	6688	866	1931	27	934	.355	.384	.289

Although not normally remembered as a great hitter, Larry Gardner was a key figure at the plate in the World Series victories of the Boston Red Sox in 1912, 1915, and 1916. He also helped get the Cleveland Indians to the Series in 1920.

Gardner attended the University of Vermont. He had a brief stay with the Red Sox in 1908, but came up to stay late in the summer of 1909. He was Boston's regular second baseman in 1910 and was shifted from there to third midway through 1911, replacing the incumbent, Bill Purtell.

In 1912 the Red Sox won the pennant, and Gardner's improvement was a significant reason. He hit .315 and doubled his RBIs and triples from the previous year. Then in the World Series against the New York Giants he led the Red Sox in runs and RBIs. The Series came down to an eighth game (Game 2 had been a 6–6 tie). In the second inning of the finale he booted a grounder to let Chief Meyers reach first base. Later in the inning he dropped a throw, allowing Meyers to reach third.

But in the bottom of the 10th inning, with Boston behind 2–1, Fred Snodgrass made his "$30,000 Muff" in center field, igniting a Red Sox rally. Boston battled back, and with the score tied, the bases loaded, and one out, Gardner hit a long sacrifice fly to score second baseman Steve Yerkes with the winning run. Gardner came back with more heroics in the 1916 World Series, when he hit the only two home runs the Red Sox could manage in their five-game victory over the Brooklyn Robins.

In January 1918 Gardner was traded to the Philadelphia Athletics, and the next year he was traded again, this time to Cleveland. In 1920 he helped propel the Indians to the AL pennant by hitting .310 with 118 RBIs. The next year Gardner was even better, batting .319 with career highs in hits, runs, RBIs, and doubles. After he retired in 1924 Gardner served as baseball coach and athletic director at the University of Vermont.

Debs Garms

Garms, Debs C. **OF-3B**

1932–35, 1937–41, 1943–45 B:6/26/1908, Bangs, TX D:12/16/1984, Glen Rose, TX Deb:8/10/1932, STL AL BL/TR 5'8 ½", 165

G	AB	R	H	HR	RBI	OBP	SLG	AVG
1010	3111	438	910	17	328	.355	.379	.293

Outfielder Debs Garms was rarely more than a part-time player in his dozen years with four major league teams. Nevertheless, he managed to win the 1940 National League batting title with a .355 average.

A graduate of Howard Payne College, Garms first played pro baseball for the Class D West Texas League's Abilene Aces in 1928. He reached the major leagues at the end of the 1932 season, when he hit .284 for the St. Louis Browns. Garms batted .317 and .293 the next two seasons as a part-timer but spent most of 1935 and 1936 with the San Antonio Missions of the Texas League.

Garms returned to the majors with the Boston Braves in 1937, splitting his time between outfield and third base, but he had a relatively mediocre year. For some reason, he was a different hitter the next season, as he improved his average more than 50 points, to .315. The highlight of the year undoubtedly was when he broke Johnny Vander Meer's hitless string at 21⅓ innings. After hitting .298 in 1939, Garms was sold to the Pirates and again he had a huge improvement in his batting average. He played in only 103 games, and had just 358 at bats, but his .355 average beat out teammate Spud Davis as the NL's top hitter.

The rules under which the batting title is decided have been changed three times since, and Garms would not have qualified under any of the newer standards. Current rules require that a batter must have 3.1 plate appearances for each of his team's games, or 502 plate appearances. If a batter has the highest average without enough appearances, he can still win the title if his average would be the highest if he is charged with the additional number of appearances necessary to qualify.

Garms' career went quickly downhill after his sizzling season. He hit .264 in 1941 and then was sold to the Cardinals. In 1942 he played with the Sacramento Solons of the Pacific Coast League but, being too old to be drafted into the armed services, he was brought back to St. Louis during World War II. By that time, Garms was strictly a backup. Garms appeared in both the 1943 and 1944 World Series, but failed to get a hit in either. He batted .336 in 74 games in 1945, but once the war was over, his career was too.

Phil Garner

Garner, Philip Mason **2B-3B-SS**

1973–88 M(1992–*, 563–617) B:4/30/1949, Jefferson City, TN Deb:9/10/1973, OAK AL BR/TR 5'10", 177

G	AB	R	H	HR	RBI	OBP	SLG	AVG
1860	6136	780	1594	109	738	.326	.389	.260

Phil Garner has the rare distinction of representing one team in the All-Star Game and another team in the playoffs in the same year. He also split his time almost evenly between second base and third base during his 16-year career. Garner had led the NCAA in home runs in 1969 at the University of Tennessee. Although he never developed into a slugger at the major league level, Garner hit grand slams in back-to-back games on September 14 and 15, 1978.

"Old Scrap Iron" was a tough everyday player with good speed and a solid glove, who got the most out of his ability. He broke into the major leagues during the closing days of the Oakland A's powerhouse. In his first full season in 1975, Garner played in a league-high 160 games at second base, helping Oakland to a fifth straight American League West title.

In 1976 Garner was selected to the All-Star Game, but the next spring he was shipped to Pittsburgh in a nine-player deal. Although the Pirates initially moved him to third base, Garner moved back to second base following a 1979 mid-season trade for Bill Madlock. The trade solidified the infield and the Pirates held off Montreal to win their sixth division title of the 1970s. Garner sparkled in the postseason, homering for Pittsburgh's first run in a three-game playoff sweep of Cincinnati and tying World Series records by batting .500 and collecting at least one hit in all seven games of the Bucs' comeback victory over Baltimore.

Garner was selected to the All-Star Game in 1980 and 1981. But after that second NL appearance, he was traded to Houston, helping the Astros win National League West titles in 1981 and 1986. A good baserunner, Garner stole

235 career bases, including five seasons of 20 or more. He stole 35 bases in 1976, the year the A's swiped 341.

After retiring as a player in 1988, Garner spent three seasons as an Astros coach. In 1992 he was named manager of the Milwaukee Brewers. There he taught the same classic brand of counterclockwise baseball that manager Alvin Dark had drilled him in at Oakland. Milwaukee responded well enough to finish second in the American League East, earning Garner second place in Manager of the Year voting. The Brewers never finished .500 again during Garner's tenure with the team. He was fired midway through his seventh season with the club, but was hired to manage the Detroit Tigers shortly after the 1999 season ended.

Ralph Garr

Garr, Ralph Allen **OF-DH**

1968–80 B:12/12/1945, Monroe, LA Deb:9/3/1968, ATL NL BL/TR 5'11", 197

G	AB	R	H	HR	RBI	OBP	SLG	AVG
1317	5108	717	1562	75	408	.340	.416	.306

Ralph Garr, who won the National League batting title in 1974 with a .353 average, had no doubt from where his natural hitting talents came—his mother. "She played softball when she was growing up, and, man, could she hit it!" Garr said. "She never did any running or anything. All she did was hit the long ball. I just know I inherited my ability to hit from her."

Garr starred in football at Grambling State University, where he received a degree in physical education. He also hit .582, the highest average at that point in the history of the National Intercollegiate Athletic Association. The Atlanta Braves selected him in the third round of the June 1967 draft, and his stops on the way to the majors included Austin, Shreveport, and Richmond. With Austin in 1967, he paced the Texas League with 32 stolen bases. With Richmond, he led the International League with a .329 average and 63 stolen bases in 1969, and a .386 mark with 39 steals in 1970.

After parts of three seasons with the Braves, that 1970 season helped earn him a regular job in the big leagues in 1971. As soon as he began playing regularly, Garr was an immediate hit. He batted .343 with 219 hits, and also stole 30 bases. Reds scout Ray Shore commented, "Garr is the fastest player in the game between home and first. I don't care who you name. Garr is a step faster."

After two more excellent seasons, he had his career year in 1974, when he not only led the National League in batting but his 214 hits and 17 triples also topped the circuit. He was also selected to the All-Star Game. The next year he again led the league with 11 triples. "They claim Mantle was fast, but Ralph gets down to first faster than anybody I ever saw," said his teammate Hank Aaron. Despite his speed, Garr had only two seasons with 30 or more steals.

Traded to the White Sox after the 1975 season, Garr had two .300 batting years before being traded to the Angels, with whom he finished his career. Following his playing days, he became a minor league baserunning and batting instructor, and was thus able to pass on his training and beliefs to a younger generation. "People think I swing wild and crazy," he once said. "I do. But I look for certain pitches in certain spots and try to hit that way. I'm a guess hitter. I try to think some up there, but I don't think it's good to think too much."

Wayne Garrett

Garrett, Ronald Wayne **3B-2B**

1969–78 B:12/3/1947, Brooksville, FL Deb:4/12/1969, NY NL BL/TR 5'11", 183

G	AB	R	H	HR	RBI	OBP	SLG	AVG
1092	3285	438	786	61	340	.352	.341	.239

Drafted out of the Atlanta organization for only $25,000 in December 1968, Garrett played second base, third base, and a bit of shortstop as a rookie for the Miracle Mets of 1969. He had curly red hair, boyish looks, and a positive attitude that prompted sportswriters to dub him "Huckleberry Finn," all of which contributed to make Garrett an immediate fan favorite. He hit only .218 with just one home run in the regular season that year, but came through in the first National League Championship Series with a .385 average and a two-run homer in Game 3 that gave the Mets the lead for good against the Braves.

For the next three years Garrett continued to play part time at third and second. Then, in 1973, he won the regular third base job and responded with 16 homers and 20 doubles. But in that year's World Series he was dismal, fanning 11 times to tie a record. He was the regular third baseman again in 1974, but then he dropped back to platooning there again.

In 1976 Garrett was dealt to the Expos. He finished his career with the Cardinals in 1978.

Ned Garver

Garver, Ned Franklin **P**

1948–61 B:2/25/1925, Ney, OH Deb:4/28/1948, STL AL
BR/TR 5'10½", 180

W	L	PCT	G	SH	IP	BB	SO	ERA
129	157	.451	402	18	2477^{1}	881	881	3.73

Only seven pitchers in the 20th century—Ned Garver, Noodles Hahn, Scott Perry, Howard Ehmke, Sloppy Thurston, Steve Carlton, and Nolan Ryan—won 20 games for a last-place club. But only Garver won 20 *and* hit better than .300 for a club that lost 100 or more games.

Garver pitched for the woeful St. Louis Browns from 1948 through 1952, their final, pitiful years before relocating to Baltimore. In 1951 he won 20 of the Browns' 52 victories, while losing only 12.

Garver had been with the Browns' organization since 1943. He began his professional career after impressing three club scouts with his pitching at a national amateur tournament in Youngstown, Ohio. In 1944 he went to spring training with the Browns, but he was optioned to their Toledo Mud Hens farm club. Not sure of his chances, he asked to be sent to a club nearer his home in eastern Ohio. The Browns obliged and transferred him to the Class D Ohio State League's Newark Moundsmen. Garver led the circuit with 21 wins, 221 strikeouts, and 245 innings pitched, and his 1.21 ERA was the lowest in Organized Baseball. "I pinch-hit and played the outfield," Garver says, "and, believe it or not, drove in more runs than our catcher."

In 1946 and 1947 Garver pitched for San Antonio of the Texas League and got some practice winning for a second-division club. In 1947 he went 17–14 for a San Antonio team that finished seventh. The next year he joined the Browns, with whom he started his career with three seasons below .500, including 18 losses in 1950, when he also led the league with 22 complete games.

In 1951 Garver got off to a fast start and had won 11 games by the All-Star Game—for which he was the American League starter—although the Browns were already 23½ games back. At that point he got a boost from new Browns owner Bill Veeck, who never left a publicity stone unturned. To boost attendance, Veeck instructed manager Rogers Hornsby to give Garver every opportunity to win 20 for what was certain to be an eighth-place club.

"It was easy to do with Ned," admitted Veeck in his autobiography, "because he was also the best hitter on the team and there was never any reason to take him out for a pinch hitter in the late innings. There was almost nothing Ned could do to get knocked out of a game."

Veeck was not exaggerating about Garver's batting. He often batted sixth in the lineup, and in 1951 he hit .400 as a pinch hitter and .305 for the entire season. Garver won 38.5 percent of the Browns' games that year, the highest percentage of any pitcher between 1922 and 1972. He also led the league with 24 complete games, and finished second in AL Most Valuable Player balloting behind Yogi Berra.

Garver's sensational season made him the highest-paid player in Browns history, with a salary of $25,000. But in 1952 his effectiveness began to diminish. In April he suffered a herniated disk while shagging flies in the outfield, and his elbow stiffened up as a result. In August Veeck traded him to Detroit.

After four-plus seasons in Detroit, the Tigers sent Garver to Kansas City in 1957 as part of an eight-player deal. Following the 1960 season, the Athletics made him available in the first American League expansion draft. The Angels drafted him but released him after he had appeared in only 12 games. Garver then retired from the major leagues.

Steve Garvey

Garvey, Steven Patrick **1B–3B**

1969–87 B:12/22/1948, Tampa, FL Deb:9/1/1969,
LA NL BR/TR 5'10", 192

G	AB	R	H	HR	RBI	OBP	SLG	AVG
2332	8835	1143	2599	272	1308	.333	.446	.294

Steve Garvey had a brilliant career on the field—six 200-hit seasons in seven years, five 100-RBI seasons, seven .300-plus seasons, and the longest consecutive-game streak in National League history. He was not the "Mr. Perfect" that he was made out to be, but he helped his teams win five pennants and was the leader of the longest-running infield in baseball history.

Although born in Tampa, Garvey was the grandson of a Brooklyn native who was a serious Dodgers fan. His father even drove the Dodgers' team bus in Florida every spring. Young Garvey sometimes came along for the ride. "The time [I] spent with the Dodgers made baseball seem very wonderful to me," Garvey once said. "I sincerely think I was born to be a Dodger."

He went to Michigan State, where he played defensive back on the football team, was an All-America third baseman, and earned a B.S. in education. Garvey was the Dodgers' first choice in the secondary phase of the June 1968 draft. He signed for a $40,000 bonus and showed up in Ogden, Utah, for the Rookie League in a suit and tie, while the rest of his teammates showed up in jeans and sneakers. He signed every autograph request and kissed grandmothers and babies.

Garvey's manager was Tommy Lasorda. "Steve Garvey," Lasorda once said, "is as fine a young man as I've ever seen in my life." Garvey explained, "All that autograph signing and handshaking and cheek kissing, that's how I am and always have been. I did it in Ogden when nobody cared. I do it because I'm convinced it can make a difference. You sign a baseball for a kid and you've done something he's going to carry with him for years."

"Nobody can question that Garv came to play and that he gave 100 percent every single day, no matter how he felt," said Davey Lopes, who came up through the minors with Garvey and played with him in Los Angeles. "It was all the other stuff. It created a tension that never went away, that never eased."

By the end of 1970 Garvey was in the majors, hitting .269 in 34 games as a third baseman. He was not an instant star, playing fewer than 100 games and hitting below .270 in each of his first three seasons. He was vulnerable to the inside fastball, and in 1972 he spent hour after hour working on the flaws in his swing. But he also had defensive problems—committing 28 errors in only 85 games in 1972.

The 1973 season saw the start of the turnaround of Garvey's career. His biggest problem at third had been his arm. But he moved to first base in 1973 and hugely reduced his errors by avoiding throwing to second on forceout attempts. He went on to win four Gold Gloves and to set a major league record when he went the entire 1984 season without committing an error in 160 games. He set another record when he went 193 straight games without an error. His .996 career fielding average is yet another major league record.

The 1973 season also saw Garvey's bat came alive, as he hit .304. The next year, he arrived at star level as he finally learned how to get around consistently on a fastball. He hit .312 with 200 hits, 21 homers and 111 RBIs. That year he became the first player to start an All-Star Game as a write-in choice. He responded by being named the game's Most Valuable Player. He then led the Dodgers in hits in both the Championship Series against Pittsburgh and the World Series with Oakland. He finished the season by being named the league's MVP.

Between 1974 and 1980 Garvey averaged 201 hits, 104 RBIs, and 23 home runs per season. He was selected to the All-Star Game eight years in a row; he won his second All-Star MVP trophy in 1978. But many of his teammates felt Garvey tried too hard to be Mr. Perfect. They thought he played up to the press to further his image. They scoffed at his "perfect marriage" to a beautiful blonde named Cyndy. Once, when Don Sutton insulted Garvey's wife in the clubhouse, Garvey jumped on him and started choking him.

The Dodgers, meanwhile, supplanted the Reds in 1977 as the power in the NL West, and the Garvey–Lopes–Bill Russell–Ron Cey infield was a big reason why. They played as a unit for more than seven seasons—the longest run any infield combination has ever had in the majors—as the Dodgers won four pennants and the 1981 World Series. Meanwhile, Garvey began a streak of his own, not missing a game from 1975 until he broke his thumb while playing for the San Diego Padres in 1983. All told, he set the NL record with 1,207 consecutive games played.

Garvey left the Dodgers for San Diego as a free agent after the 1982 season. He was 34 years old and his production was slipping. In 1984 he hit only eight homers, but he drove in 84 runs and led the Padres to their first World Series. He contributed some heroics in Game 4 of the NLCS against the Cubs, driving in five runs to stave off elimination, including a game-winning, two-run homer in the ninth against Lee Smith. He was selected to the All-Star Game twice more with the Padres.

Garvey retired in 1987. He had been divorced and his reputation as Mr. Perfect was further stained by revelations of numerous trysts that put his name in the gossip tabloids as well as the sports pages. Still, as a player, Garvey was one of the premier performers at his position in the 1970s and 1980s.

In 2000 Garvey was awarded $3 million when the U.S. Circuit Court of Appeals overruled a previous arbitration decision. More than a dozen years after major league owners were penalized for collusion, Garvey got his slice of the pie.

Cito Gaston

Gaston, Clarence Edwin **OF**

1967, 1969–78 M(1989–97, 683–616) B:3/17/1944, San Antonio, TX Deb:9/14/1967, ATL NL BR/TR 6'4", 210

G	AB	R	H	HR	RBI	OBP	SLG	AVG
1026	3120	314	799	91	387	.300	.397	.256

Cito Gaston was a power-hitting outfielder for several clubs before accepting a job as batting coach for the Toronto Blue Jays. By 1993, he had not only become the first manager to win back-to-back world championships since Sparky Anderson in 1975–76, but Gaston had also become the first African-American manager to win the World Series and the first to lead a Canadian team to the Series.

Gaston succeeded Jimy Williams as Toronto manager in May 1989, when the club was floundering with a 12–24 record, and engineered a reversal that led to a surprise American League East title. But the Jays lost to the Oakland Athletics in the Championship Series.

Gaston's club finished a close second in 1990, then took another divisional title the following year before losing the ALCS again, this time to the Minnesota Twins. In 1992, however, Toronto would not be denied.

The Blue Jays won the first World Series played outside the United States by stopping the favored

Atlanta Braves in six games in 1992. Toronto repeated its six-game dominance against the Philadelphia Phillies in the 1993 Series.

Even though his record showed four first-place finishes, Gaston's low-key style did not work as well when the club tried to substitute young players for veterans who had departed as free agents. After three straight losing seasons, Toronto fired Gaston late in the 1997 campaign. Although there were some bitter feelings between Gaston, ownership, and the media, he was added to the "Level of Excellence" at SkyDome in 1999 along with Joe Carter, whose home run won the Toronto's second World Series in 1993. After the 1999 season Gaston was welcomed back to Toronto as a coach under manager Jim Fregosi.

As a player, Gaston got his big break when the San Diego Padres picked him from the Braves in the expansion draft that followed the 1968 season. In his second San Diego season, he not only made his only All-Star Game appearance but finished with a .318 average, 29 home runs, and 93 runs batted in—all career peaks.

In four more seasons with the Padres, Gaston never reached 20 homers again. He returned to the Braves as a backup outfielder and pinch-hitter in 1975, lasting three-plus seasons before finishing his career with the Pittsburgh Pirates.

Rich Gedman

Gedman, Richard Leo **C**

1980–92 B:9/26/1959, Worcester, MA Deb:9/7/1980, BOS AL BL/TR 6', 215

G	AB	R	H	HR	RBI	OBP	SLG	AVG
1033	3159	331	795	88	382	.307	.399	.252

Rich Gedman was a slugging catcher who grew up in New England watching Boston Red Sox legend Carlton Fisk. Like Fisk, Gedman is remembered for something that happened in Game 6 of the World Series. Unfortunately, Gedman's moment is the polar opposite of Fisk's dramatic home run in 1975.

Boston was one out away from winning the 1986 World Series against the New York Mets. With runners on first and third in the bottom of the 10th, reliever Bob Stanley's inside pitch to Mookie Wilson tailed away from Gedman. The wild pitch, which many later claimed was a catchable ball, allowed the tying run to score. The Mets won the game minutes later when Bill Buckner missed Wilson's grounder. Although Gedman homered in Game 7, the Mets rallied to win that game and the Series.

A two-time All-Star, Gedman used his power to win the everyday catching job in Boston. The left-handed hitter smacked 24 home runs and 26 doubles in 449 at bats in 1984. He batted .295 with 80 RBIs the following year. He drove in 65 runs in 1986, but it was his skillful handling of the young Red Sox pitching staff that helped ensure the division title for Boston. Gedman batted .357 and drove in six runs in the Championship Series as the Red Sox rallied to beat the California Angels in seven games.

Gedman's career went downhill after 1986. He never played in 100 games nor batted higher than .231 in his final seven seasons.

Lou Gehrig

Gehrig, Henry Louis **1B**

1923–39 B:6/19/1903, New York, NY D:6/2/1941, Riverdale, NY Deb:6/15/1923, NY AL BL/TL 6', 200

G	AB	R	H	HR	RBI	OBP	SLG	AVG
2164	8001	1888	2721	493	1995	.447	.632	.340

His accomplishments on the field made him an authentic American hero, but Lou Gehrig's tragic early death made him a legend. He emerged from the shadow of Babe Ruth to be everything one could want out of a superstar. Historian Fred Lieb once asked Gehrig about playing in Ruth's shadow, and the answer by "The Iron Horse" was true to form: "It's a pretty big shadow. It gives me lots of room to spread myself."

When actor Edward Herrmann was hired to play Gehrig in a TV movie, he had trouble getting into the role. "What made it so tough is I could find no 'key' to his character. There was no strangeness, nothing spectacular about him. As Eleanor Gehrig told me, he was just a square, honest guy." Sportswriter Jim Murray described the tall, strong Gehrig as "Gibraltar in cleats."

Gehrig's numbers are almost too impressive to believe. He was a tireless worker, with a record for consecutive games played that would last more than half a century before Baltimore's Cal Ripken, Jr. finally surpassed it. His lifetime batting average was .340, and he amassed more than 400 total bases on five occasions. Only 15 men have achieved that level in a season; Ruth did it twice, and Chuck Klein did it three times. Gehrig is also one of only two players with more than 100 extra-base hits in more than one season.

In his 13 full seasons, Gehrig averaged 147 RBIs. No player was to reach the 147 mark in a single season again until George Foster did four decades later. He finished with three of the top six RBI marks of all time. And, as historian Bill Curran pointed out, Gehrig accomplished it "while batting immediately behind two of history's greatest base-cleaners, Ruth and DiMaggio."

His other phenomenal marks include having stolen home 15 times, holding the record for career grand slams at 23, and having batted .361

in 34 World Series games with 10 homers, eight doubles, and 35 RBIs.

The son of German immigrants, Gehrig was the only one of four children to survive to adulthood. Shortly before he entered Columbia University he was advised by New York Giants manager John McGraw to play summer professional baseball under an assumed name ("Henry Lewis"). "Everyone does it," McGraw explained, even though the illegal ballplaying could have jeopardized Gehrig's collegiate sports career. The gullible Gehrig was found out after playing a dozen games for Hartford of the Eastern League. As a result, he was banned from intercollegiate sports during his freshman year, 1921–22.

Gehrig returned to play fullback during Columbia's 1922 football season, and then pitched and played first for the Columbia baseball team in 1923. Signed by Yankees scout Paul Krichell in 1923, Gehrig returned to Hartford and hit .304. Called up to the majors in September, he hit .423 in 26 at bats.

Manager Miller Huggins petitioned McGraw to permit Gehrig to replace the ailing Wally Pipp on the Yankees' roster for the World Series. McGraw, always looking for an edge, exercised his prerogative and refused. The Yankees won anyway. After a full season at Hartford, where he hit .369, Gehrig became a Yankee for good in 1925.

The first reports on Gehrig as a first baseman were not promising. Called a "tanglefoot," he begged coach Charley O'Leary to give him extra fielding practice and sat next to Huggins, who lectured him on the proper positioning for different hitters. On May 31 he pinch-hit for Pee Wee Wanninger. The next day, Pipp, who had been a reliable and productive first baseman, took the day off with a headache. Gehrig's streak of consecutive games played began and wouldn't end until 1939, after he'd played 2,130 straight games.

Gehrig's streak didn't come easily. He played every game for more than 13 years despite a broken thumb, a broken toe, and back spasms. Late in his career his hands were x-rayed, and doctors were able to spot 17 different fractures that had "healed" while Gehrig continued to play. Despite having pain from lumbago one day, he was listed as the shortstop and leadoff hitter. He singled and was promptly replaced, but kept the streak intact. In fact, Gehrig didn't just move in and stay there initially. On three occasions in June 1925, a pinch hitter batted for him, and he didn't start the July 5 game that year, although he did appear later as a pinch hitter. But the Yanks were stumbling in seventh place, so Huggins stayed with the youngster.

After batting .295 in 1925, Gehrig exploded onto the national scene in 1926. He hit .313—the first of 12 consecutive years he would top .300—drove in 112 runs, and led the league with 20 triples. The Yanks won the pennant; Gehrig hit .348 in the World Series, but the Yankees lost to Rogers Hornsby's Cardinals in seven games.

Ruth and Gehrig began dominating the baseball headlines in 1927 in a way two players had never done before. That year Ruth hit 60 homers, breaking his old record of 59, and Gehrig clouted 47, more than anyone other than Ruth had ever hit. As late as August 10 Gehrig had more homers than the Babe, but Ruth's closing kick was spectacular. Together they outhomered every team in baseball except one. But homers were not Gehrig's only contributions. He hit .373 and led the league with 52 doubles and 175 RBIs. He was also named the AL's Most Valuable Player.

Gehrig continued his performance in 1928. He hit .374, again led the league with 47 doubles, and tied Ruth for the RBIs lead with 142. In the World Series, despite being walked six times, he hit .545 and slugged a stunning 1.727.

By Gehrig's standard, 1929 was an off year. But he still finished second in the league in home runs, third in runs, and fourth in RBIs. During that season Paul Krichell brought 18-year-old Hank Greenberg to watch the Yankees play. "See that guy at first?" Krichell allegedly said. "He's washed up. You can replace him." Greenberg saw that Gehrig wouldn't be dislodged for many years, and signed with Detroit instead.

Gehrig bounced back to bat .379 and lead the league with 174 RBIs in 1930. The next year he led the AL in hits, runs, and RBIs, and tied Ruth for the lead with 46 home runs, even though he lost one on a curious play. With teammate Lyn Lary on second against the Senators, Gehrig smashed a home run so hard it bounced out of the stands and back into the arms of the center fielder. Lary misread the signals of the coach, who was trying to tell him to slow down, and he stopped running. Gehrig passed him, was declared out, and the Yanks lost two runs. They also lost the game by a two-run margin.

On June 3, 1932, Gehrig became the first American Leaguer to hit four home runs in a game. After his third homer to right field in a game against Philadelphia, an upset Connie Mack removed pitcher George Earnshaw and demanded that Earnshaw stay with him to watch reliever Roy Mahaffey pitch to Gehrig. Gehrig's fourth homer was to left field, and only a great catch by Al Simmons kept him from hitting his fifth.

Ruth's dominance as a power hitter was slipping, and Gehrig was taking his place. The Yanks missed the postseason three years in a row (1933–35). During an off-season barnstorming trip to Japan, the civil relationship between the two slugging stars boiled over, apparently over a comment Mrs. Gehrig

made about how Ruth's daughter dressed. Ruth got word to Gehrig that he never wanted to speak to him again off the field. And the two did not trade words for the next six years.

Gehrig won the Triple Crown in 1934, with 49 home runs, 165 RBIs, and a .363 batting average. He came close to repeating two years later, when he led the American League in home runs, runs, RBIs, and on-base and slugging percentages, while batting .354. He was named the league's Most Valuable Player after the Yankees regained the World Series title. For the next two years DiMaggio and Gehrig dominated the league the way Gehrig and Ruth had, with the Yankees in the midst of a four-season dynasty that included winning four straight World Series.

In 1938 Gehrig's batting average fell below .300 for the first time since 1925, and it was clear that there was something wrong. He lacked his usual strength. Pitches he would have hit for home runs were only flyouts. Doctors diagnosed a gall bladder problem, and they put him on a bland diet, which only made him weaker. Wes Ferrell noticed that on the golf course, instead of wearing golf cleats, Gehrig was wearing tennis shoes and was sliding his feet along the ground. Ferrell was frightened. When asked if he would remove Gehrig from the lineup, manager Joe McCarthy said, "That's Lou's decision."

Gehrig played the first eight games of the 1939 season, but he managed only four hits. On a ball hit back to pitcher Johnny Murphy, Gehrig had trouble getting to first in time for the throw. When he returned to the dugout, his teammates complimented him on the "good play." Gehrig knew when his fellow Yanks had to congratulate him for stumbling into an average catch it was time to leave. He took himself out of the game.

The next day, as Yankee captain, he took the lineup card to the umpires, as usual. But his name was not on the card. Babe Dahlgren was stationed at first. The game announcer stated, "Ladies and gentlemen, Lou Gehrig's consecutive streak of 2,130 games played has ended." Doctors at the Mayo Clinic diagnosed Gehrig as having a very rare degenerative disease: amyotrophic lateral sclerosis. There was no chance he would ever play baseball again.

New York writer Paul Gallico suggested the team have a recognition day to honor Gehrig on July 4, 1939. With more than 62,000 fans in attendance, Gehrig spoke his immortal words of thanks:

"Fans, for the past two weeks you have been reading about the bad break I got. Yet today I consider myself the luckiest man on the face of the Earth. I have been in ballparks for 17 years, and have never received anything but kindness and encouragement from you fans. Look at these grand men. Which of you wouldn't consider it the highlight of his career just to associate with them for even one day?

"Sure I'm lucky. Who wouldn't consider it an honor to have known Jacob Ruppert? Also, the builder of baseball's greatest empire, Ed Barrow? To have spent six years with that wonderful little fellow, Miller Huggins? Then to have spent the next nine years with the best manager in baseball today, Joe McCarthy?

"Sure I'm lucky. When the New York Giants, a team you would give your right arm to beat, and vice versa, send you a gift...that's something. When everybody down to the groundskeepers and those boys in white coats remember you with trophies...that's something. So I close in saying that I may have had a tough break, but I have an awful lot to live for."

At the close of Gehrig's speech, Babe Ruth walked up, put his arm around his former teammate, and spoke in his ear the first words they had shared since 1934. Gehrig was elected to the Hall of Fame that December. He worked on youth projects for New York Mayor Fiorello LaGuardia until he was unable to walk. He died in 1941 at age 38, 16 years almost to the day after he had replaced Wally Pipp at first base for the Yanks.

Charlie Gehringer

Gehringer, Charles Leonard **2B**

1924–42 B:5/11/1903, Fowlerville, MI D:1/21/1993, Bloomfield Hills, MI Deb:9/22/1924, DET AL BL/TR 5'11", 180

G	AB	R	H	HR	RBI	OBP	SLG	AVG
2323	8860	1774	2839	184	1427	.404	.480	.320

They called second baseman Charlie Gehringer "the Mechanical Man" because of the quiet, methodical way he went about his business. "Charlie was not exactly a gabby fellow," wrote teammate Mickey Cochrane. "He never told anybody how good he was and never thanked anybody for flattery." Outfielder Doc Cramer remarked, "You wind him up on opening day and forget about him."

Gehringer played in the All-Star Game the first six times it was held, hit .320 lifetime, collected more than 200 hits in a season seven times, led the AL in fielding seven times, and twice had consecutive-game streaks that exceeded 500. During one 14-season span he fell under .300 only once, when he dropped to .298. According to Gehringer, "That was the year I was going to be Babe Ruth. I think I had eight (home runs) before he had any, and I began going for the fences. I wound up getting not many homers—and not many hits either."

Prior to his major league career, Gehringer played baseball in rural Fowlerville, Michigan. Tigers outfielder Bobby Veach hunted in the vicinity and discovered Gehringer there. On Veach's recommendation, the Tigers gave Gehringer a tryout, presided over by manager Ty Cobb. Cobb was extremely impressed, but, not wishing to rush into any decisions, kept the youngster around for a week before signing him. Gehringer recalled, "No bonus. But I did get a lot of tips on the stock market."

In 1925 Gehringer drove in 108 runs and led the International League in fielding while with Toronto. He came up to Detroit late in the season and stayed with the Tigers until 1942. Cobb made Gehringer his protégé, but the Georgia Peach could be tough. In Gehringer's rookie year, Cobb got into a snit over something Gehringer had done and wouldn't speak to him for weeks. "The only way I managed to get into the lineup was because our second baseman, Frank O'Rourke, got the measles," recalled Gehringer. "Cobb had no other choice but to put me in. But even then he wouldn't tell me to bunt or to hit or to do this or that. He'd tell the coaches to tell me what to do."

When 500 Fowlerville admirers honored him with his own "Day," which, according to longstanding baseball tradition, jinxed a player, he hit the first pitch he saw for a home run, collected three other hits, and stole home to win the game. There was one glitch in the proceedings. Gehringer's friends had purchased a regular set of golf clubs for the southpaw-swinging second baseman. Not wishing to embarrass anyone, Gehringer merely shifted around and golfed righthanded for the rest of his life.

Gehringer's first great season was 1929, when he batted .339 and led the American League in hits, runs, doubles, and triples. He later led the league again in the first three categories. However, his best year statistically was 1937, when he led the AL with a .371 average and won league Most Valuable Player honors. "There's some luck involved in hitting .371," he admitted. "I hit the ball a lot better in years when I hit 20 points lower, but more of the balls were getting caught then. In that good year the hits were falling in."

One of Gehringer's most embarrassing moments came when batting against the St. Louis Browns. He grounded out for the second putout in the inning, but he thought he had made the third out and headed over to his position, picked up his glove, and absent-mindedly stood next to St. Louis second baseman Oscar Mellilo. Mellilo said, "Charlie, thanks all the same, but I don't need any help."

Gehringer far preferred batting to fielding. "I always did look at the fielding part of it as being very mechanical," he said. "You just get that part done so you can go back and hit. I think hitting is the thing people remember most vividly, the home run or the base hit that wins the game. You can make the greatest fielding play in the world, and they probably won't remember it the next day."

Gehringer played his last season in 1942, spending most of it on the bench. He played service ball during the war, and when he wasn't swinging a bat rose to the rank of lieutenant commander in the Navy. Returning to civilian life he got involved in the sale of parts to the automobile industry and became a partner in the firm of Gehringer and Forsyth.

Gehringer was named to the Hall of Fame in 1949. "I wasn't a rabble rouser," he said. "I wasn't a big noisemaker in the infield, which a lot of managers think you've got to be or you're not showing interest. But I don't think it contributes much. You can't talk your way into a batting championship." On August 10, 1951, the Tigers appointed him as their general manager and vice president. He held the GM post until October 1953 and retained the vice presidency through 1959.

Jim Gentile

Gentile, James Edward **1B**

1957–58, 1960–66 B:6/3/1934, San Francisco, CA
Deb:9/10/1957, BRO NL BL/TL 6'4", 215

G	AB	R	H	HR	RBI	OBP	SLG	AVG
936	2922	434	759	179	549	.372	.486	.260

As a young, lefthanded first baseman in the Brooklyn farm system, "Diamond Jim" Gentile had the promise of greatness. Roy Campanella saw star slugger potential in Gentile and gave him his nickname. The Dodgers, however, decided he didn't have enough polish to replace Gil Hodges, and in 1960—after he had had two short stops with the major league club—traded Gentile to the Baltimore Orioles.

With the Orioles, Gentile became an instant All-Star, batting .292 with 21 home runs in his rookie year and finishing behind two teammates for American League Rookie of the Year honors. In 1961 he drove in 141 runs and hit 46 home runs, including a new AL season record of five grand slams. The most unforgettable moment of that incredible season came on May 9, when Gentile hit grand slams in consecutive innings of a single game. His season-long effort landed him third in the MVP balloting, behind Roger Maris and Mickey Mantle.

In 1962 Gentile hit 33 homers and was selected to his third straight All-Star Game. The next year his hitting dropped off some, but he led AL first basemen in fielding percentage.

Traded in 1964 to Kansas City for Norm Siebern, Gentile hit 28 homers for the A's that season, but at age 30 his luster was already fading. In mid-1965 the A's sent him to Houston, who dealt him to Cleveland a year later. He retired at the end of the 1966 season.

Joe Gerhardt

Gerhardt, John Joseph **2B**

1873–79, 1881, 1883–87, 1890–91 M(1883, 1890, 72–61) B:2/14/1855, Washington, DC D:3/11/1922, Middletown, NY Deb:9/1/1873, WAS NA BR/TR 6', 160

G	AB	R	H	HR	RBI	OBP	SLG	AVG
986	3770	448	854	7	347	.261	.289	.227

More than 115 years after he set a major league record, in 1885, Joe Gerhardt still holds it. Unfortunately that record is for the lowest batting average in a season, at .155.

Gerhardt played three years in the old National Association before joining the National League in 1876, its first year, as the first baseman for the Louisville Grays. The next he moved to second base, where he immediately had the two best seasons of his career. He hit .304 and .297, the latter for the Cincinnati Reds. When his batting average dipped below .200 in 1879, Gerhardt's slick fielding saved his major league career. Although his lifetime .913 fielding percentage may not be impressive by today's standards, he was consistently one of the best fielders in an era when many players did not wear gloves.

In 1885 Gerhardt joined the New York Giants, whose managements must have wondered what happened, because his batting average dropped 65 points to .155. The next year it only improved to .190, and Gerhardt was gone at the beginning of the 1887 season. He finished his career with Louisville of the American Association.

Gerhardt helped form the first baseball union, The Brotherhood of Professional Base Ball Players, which included Hall of Famers John Montgomery Ward, Roger Connor, and Buck Ewing. He had better success as a manager.

Cesar Geronimo

Geronimo, Cesar Francisco (Zorrilla) **OF**

1969–83 B:3/11/1948, El Seibo, Dominican Republic Deb:4/16/1969, HOU NL BL/TL 6'2", 170

G	AB	R	H	HR	RBI	OBP	SLG	AVG
1522	3780	460	977	51	392	.327	.368	.258

Three-time Gold Glove center fielder Cesar Geronimo was, along with Davey Concepcion, one of the two defensive stars of Cincinnati's "Big Red Machine," a team best known for its hitting. He reached the postseason five times in nine years with the Reds.

The New York Yankees signed Geronimo as a free agent in February 1967. From the start he was an outstanding fielder, but he hit poorly even in the minors, posting averages of only .100, .071, and .194. The Astros drafted him in December 1968, and he spent parts of three seasons on the their bench. Then, in November 1971, Houston traded him, with Joe Morgan, to the Reds.

Geronimo found a home in Cincinnati and quickly became the Reds' center fielder. He won his first Gold Glove in 1974 and the next year led NL outfielders in putouts, total chances, and double plays.

Geronimo was basically a slap hitter, and in 1976 it all came together for him at the plate. That year he was part of a .300 outfield for the Reds; he batted .307—the only time he topped .300—and Ken Griffey hit .336 and George Foster .306. However, he didn't come within 40 points of that average again. On July 4, 1980 he made a minor footnote in the record books when he became the 3,000th strikeout victim of Nolan Ryan; he already had been number 3,000 for Bob Gibson, on July 17, 1974. "I was just at the right place at the right time," he said.

Traded to Kansas City in January 1981, Geronimo was granted free agency at season's end but stayed with the Royals. He retired after the 1983 season.

Charlie Getzien

Getzien, Charles H. **P**

1884–92 B:2/14/1864, Germany D:6/19/1932, Chicago, IL Deb:8/13/1884, DET NL BR/TR 5'10", 172

W	L	PCT	G	SH	IP	BB	SO	ERA
145	139	.511	296	11	2539^{2}	602	1070	3.46

Charlie "Pretzels" Getzien made one of the most remarkable pitching turnarounds in major league history. He went from being 12–25 in 1885 to 30–11 the next year. Then, in 1887, he was the ace of the world champion Detroit Wolverines.

Getzien was born in Germany on Valentine's Day in 1864. Late in his career he and catcher Charlie Ganzel would form Boston's famous "Pretzel Battery," an allusion to their German heritage.

Getzien started professionally with Grand Rapids of the Northwest League in 1883, going 14–12, then followed with a 27–4 mark in 1884. He made his major league debut for Detroit late that year, a 1–0 defeat at the hands of former Grand Rapids teammate John Henry, who was also making his first major league appearance. On October 1, 1884, Getzien hurled a six-inning no-hitter against Philadelphia.

Getzien finished an unremarkable 5–12 for in 1884, and he began the next year 3–15. But the Wolverines were a weak team, and once they brought in some talented new players from the minor league Indianapolis club, Getzien's record approached respectability. Then, in September of 1885, the Wolverines bought out Buffalo's National League club for $7,000, and Getzien finally became a big winner.

The 1886 season showed what some support could mean. That year he won 30 games with a 3.03 ERA, the exact same as it had been the year before when he lost 25. The next year he was just as good, going 29–13 and leading the NL with a .690 winning percentage. He also showed a lot more than pitching skill, as demonstrated when he pulled off one of the craftiest plays in big league annals.

With Chicago runner Fred Pfeffer on second and Marty Sullivan on third, Getzien was facing Ned Williamson. He called catcher Charlie Bennett out to the mound for a conference. They spoke in hushed tones and were seen glancing at Sullivan. Getzien's next pitch was at Williamson's head. The second was low and away. It had little speed on it, but it bounced off Bennett's mitt, rolling about 10 feet away. This was no accident; Bennett had let the ball get past him on purpose. As soon as Getzien released the pitch, he came racing toward the plate. Sullivan, concentrating on the action at home, broke for the plate when he saw the ball scoot away. He did not see Getzien, who was waiting for him with the ball when he arrived.

"Then, as the Detroiters started in for their bench," noted one account, "and the White Stockings went to the field, the nature of Bennett and Getzien's little consultation dawned upon the spectators and a roar of mingled laughs and cheers went up from the big crowd."

In the pre-1903 equivalent of the World Series that year, a 15-game contest, Getzien won four games and lost two as Detroit won the title. His fortunes changed the following year, and he dropped to 19–25.

Detroit sold him to Indianapolis' new National League franchise following the 1888 season, but Getzien's ERA soared by one and a half points, and then he was out of action the last six weeks of the season with arm trouble. In 1890 he won 23 games for Boston, but for the final two years of his career he was a part-timer.

Getzien later worked as a typesetter with *The Chicago Tribune*, and he pitched for the company team. He died after suffering a heart attack at his Chicago home in 1932.

Bart Giamatti

Giamatti, A. Bartlett

NL President (1986–89), Commissioner (1989)
B:4/4/1938, Boston, MA D:9/1/1989, Edgartown, MA

When Renaissance literature scholar A. Bartlett Giamatti was named president of Yale University at age 40, he commented, "All I ever wanted to be was president of the American League." He didn't exactly get his wish, but he did serve as president of the National League for three years and as Commissioner of baseball for 154 days.

Bart Giamatti's eloquent sense of what baseball truly meant to America brightened the hopes of fans who shared his profound love for the game. He spoke in a voice of historical perspective, of wisdom and poetry, that seemed to promise to lift the game above the greedy manipulations of owners, agents, and players.

In his essay "The Green Fields of the Mind," Giamatti wrote of baseball, "It breaks your heart. It is designed to break your heart. The game begins in the spring, when everything else begins again, and it blossoms in the summer, filling the afternoons and evenings, and then as soon as the chill rains come, it stops and leaves you to face the fall alone." But destiny did not intend that Giamatti become the poet laureate of baseball.

Giamatti broke into the public baseball consciousness with an op-ed piece in *The New York Times* during the strike of 1981. He wrote, "Call it what you will, the strike is utter foolishness. It is an act of defiance against the American people, and the only summer God made for 1981, and I appeal for it to cease. I do so as a citizen...The people of America care about baseball, not your squalid little squabbles. Resume your dignity and remember that you are the temporary custodians of an enduring public trust."

To the narrow mind of Marvin Miller, head of the players' union, Giamatti's essay was "sucking up to management," and Miller lambasted Giamatti as a "pseudophilosopher." Adhering to the theory that anyone Miller didn't like bore consideration, baseball owners began keeping tabs on Giamatti. His tough line on unionization at Yale further endeared him to the lords of baseball, and his name surfaced as a replacement possibility for Commissioner Bowie Kuhn as early as 1983. But Giamatti was busy at Yale, and Peter Ueberroth got the job instead.

By 1986, ready for a change, Giamatti was named president of the National League. His strong edict against beanballs after Chicago Cubs outfielder Andre Dawson was severely injured by one in 1987 "had a quick, positive effect," according to *The Sporting News Baseball Guide*.

When Pete Rose got into a shoving match with umpire Dave Pallone and almost caused a fan riot on April 30, 1988, Giamatti fined Rose $10,000 and suspended him for 30 days, the longest suspension since Commissioner Happy Chandler kicked Leo Durocher out of the game for a full year.

When Giamatti replaced Ueberroth as commissioner on April 1, 1989, he continued to speak out against what he called "the NFL-ization of baseball." Mascots, dot races, and rock music trivia at baseball games didn't sit well with him, but soon there was little time for philosophizing. Sex scandals involving Wade Boggs and Steve Garvey rocked baseball, and an investigation into gambling on baseball games by Cincinnati player-manager Rose got under way.

Giamatti's baseball career was marred by a series of bad decisions. He fired David Pallone without a hearing after the umpire's homosexuality came to light, and he apparently supported Major League Baseball's attempts to keep Pam Postema from being the first woman to umpire in the majors, without hearing her side of the argument.

However, his biggest blunder occurred during the Rose investigation. He signed a letter to a judge in another case asserting that one of the people being questioned about Rose's gambling had been "truthful" in discussions with the commissioner. Rose's lawyers tried to have Giamatti disqualified from ruling on Rose because the letter indicated the commissioner had prejudged the case. Giamatti prevented the case from coming to court. Because a court fight seemed unlikely, Rose's lawyers advised him to sign an agreement to a suspension. In the statement, Rose did not admit to gambling, but he said that the commissioner had "reason" to recommend suspension.

The agreement promised that no court actions would be taken. After Giamatti read the statement, one of the first questions from a reporter was, "Do you think Pete Rose bet on baseball?" Giamatti responded, "In the absence of a hearing and therefore in the absence of any evidence to the contrary, I am confronted by the factual record of the Dowd report, and on the basis of that, yes, I have concluded that he bet on baseball." Another question: "And on the Reds?" Giamatti replied, "Yes."

A week after the announcement of the Rose decision, Giamatti had a mammoth heart attack at his summer home on Martha's Vineyard and died. One of Giamatti's own quotes serves as a bitter epitaph: "There is nothing bad that accrues from baseball. [Realizing] that has been the most rewarding part of all this."

Bob Gibson

Gibson, Robert **P**

1959–75 B:11/9/1935, Omaha, NE Deb:4/15/1959, STL NL BR/TR 6'1$\frac{1}{2}$", 195

W	L	PCT	G	SH	IP	BB	SO	ERA
251	174	.591	528	56	3884[1]	1336	3117	2.91

To the hitters of the National League in the 1960s and 1970s, Bob Gibson of the St. Louis Cardinals is remembered as being aggressive and sometimes downright mean. To historians of baseball, he is remembered as having enjoyed one of the greatest seasons any pitcher has ever recorded. "I'd like to avoid using words like outstanding, awesome, and great, but they are accurate," former teammate Dal Maxvill said of that 1968 season. "I don't know how to describe it."

Gibson's 1.12 ERA in 1968 was the best since the introduction of the lively ball and the third best of the twentieth century, behind only Dutch Leonard's 0.96 in 1914 and Mordecai "Three Finger" Brown's 1.04 in 1906. During his sensational season Gibson pitched 13 shutouts. In two other games he went seven and 12 innings, respectively, without surrendering an earned run. Five of his shutouts came consecutively—against the Astros, Braves, Reds, Cubs, and Pirates. He lasted less than eight innings only twice and recorded 28 complete games in 34 starts. At one point Gibson pitched $47\frac{2}{3}$ scoreless innings, ending his skein on a wild pitch against the Dodgers. He then pitched another $17\frac{1}{3}$ scoreless innings. In one 95-inning stretch he surrendered a mere two earned runs.

Gibson won 22 games in 1968, including 15 in a row. The string would have been 16, except for an 11-inning no-decision against the Pirates. It was not egotism that caused Gibson to exclaim, "I'm amazed that I lost nine ballgames." In three of Gibson's defeats the Cardinals were shut out. Gibson pitched a four-hitter against the Giants on September 17, but Gaylord Perry pitched a no-hitter and Gibson lost, 1–0.

Of course, 1968 was "the Year of the Pitcher." Seven pitchers that year had ERAs under 2.00, and the general lack of offense triggered a number of rule changes designed to help hitters. Still, Gibson's figures were nothing short of amazing.

During the course of Gibson's 17-year career, his success was based on hard work, a fierce determination to win, control, and a willingness to back hitters off the plate. Although Gibson struck out more than 200 batters in a season nine times and led the league in strikeouts in 1968, he was not obsessed with striking batters out. "Believe me," he once contended, "I would much rather get three outs on three pitches than three outs on nine pitches, because that's going to make me that much stronger at the end of the game. My pitching philosophy is simple. I believe in throwing the ball over the plate and not walking a lot of men."

Most controversial was his habit of brushing hitters back from the plate. "He broke Jim Ray Hart's collarbone," Willie Mays recalled. "But he rarely hit me. I got out of there fast." Batterymate Tim McCarver confirmed: "Far and away, the meanest, nastiest pitcher I ever saw. There is no second place on this list."

Gibson's reputation was so bad that throughout his years in the National League only one pitcher, the Mets' Tom Seaver, dared to challenge him. In 1973, after Gibson had knocked down the Mets' John Milner, Seaver waited until Gibson came to the plate. He got ahead on the count, 0–2, then gave Gibson, not one, but two chin-high fastballs. Gibson strode toward the mound, shouting, "You're not that wild." Seaver retorted, "Neither were you when you were pitching to Milner." McCarver observed, "Tom was the only guy who ever had the guts to do that."

Gibson saw the brush-back pitch as just part of his job. "I don't like the idea that pitchers can't knock hitters down," he once explained. "It gives batters a false sense of security. And obviously they think pitchers have better control than they do, because sometimes a ball is going to get away."

Gibson claimed that he had another reason for pitching the way he did: he was defending one of his own. "Lou Brock was basically the reason I knocked guys down," he said. "Teams didn't like Brock stealing on them when we were up, 5–0 or 6–0. They knocked him down. So I'd knock them down. And I'd get blamed for it."

Although opposing hitters despised him, his teammates held Gibson and his style in the highest regard. "When I first came up, he was the meanest man alive," said Vada Pinson. "I didn't like him, but I really didn't know him. When I joined him with the Cardinals, I really learned to appreciate the man, playing behind him. He's a man of men—all business on the field. He's in a class by himself. If hard work pays off, there's the perfect example."

Gibson came from a life of harsh poverty in Omaha, Nebraska, as he told in his autobiography *From Ghetto to Glory*. His father died three months before he was born, leaving his mother and six other children. She worked in a laundry and cleaned houses to make ends meet.

Gibson was a sickly child who was bothered by wheezing and coughing. For a time, it looked as if he might not survive his illnesses. His older brother, Leroy, was a major influence on him. Leroy helped care for Bob and promised him a bat and ball if he pulled through.

As a teenager Gibson grew so quickly that he suffered a temporary heart murmur. Still, he was a switch-hitting catcher and shortstop for a local YMCA team and also starred at basketball. He had planned to attend college at the University of Indiana until he was told that the school had already filled its "quota" of African-Americans. At that point Cardinals scout Runt Marr offered a $3,000 bonus to play baseball. But Leroy Gibson insisted that his brother attend college. Bob enrolled at Creighton and became the first African-American on its basketball team.

In 1957, with just a few credit hours to go at Creighton, Gibson signed with the Cardinals. He spent two years in the minors, with Columbus, Omaha, and Rochester. In Omaha he first came under the tutelage of manager Johnny Keane. Initially, he also played basketball with the Harlem Globetrotters during the off-season.

In 1959 Gibson was promoted to the Cardinals. His major league debut was hardly impressive: the first batter to face him, the Dodgers' Jim Baxes, homered. Gibson returned to Rochester in the middle of the 1960 season. The rap on him, oddly enough, was that he lacked the nerve to pitch in the late innings. Another flaw was his lack of control.

Gibson was recalled by the Cardinals in 1961 and never looked back. In July of that year manager Solly Hemus was replaced by Keane; the new manager inserted Gibson into the starting rotation. Gibson responded with not only a shutout but also a home run. He finished 13–12, from which he would improve his win total each season for the next five years.

In 1962 Gibson was selected to the first of eight All-Star Games. Three years later, when he went to his second, he was on his way to winning 20 games for the first time. The next year it was 21.

Gibson missed a third of the 1967 season with a broken leg, finishing only 13–7. But then he turned it on in the World Series. In leading the Cardinals to a title over the Boston Red Sox, he went 3–0, pitching three complete games and recording an ERA of 1.00. After his phenomenal season the next year, he took up where he left off in the Series. In Game 1 he shut out Detroit, 4–0, while striking out a World Series record 17 batters. He came back in Game 4 to beat Denny McLain a second time, 10–1. But then the postseason magic ended, as it was Mickey Lolich who won a third time, beating Gibson, 4–1, in Game 7.

Gibson then rolled off two more 20-win seasons, including a 23–7 mark in 1970. He contin-

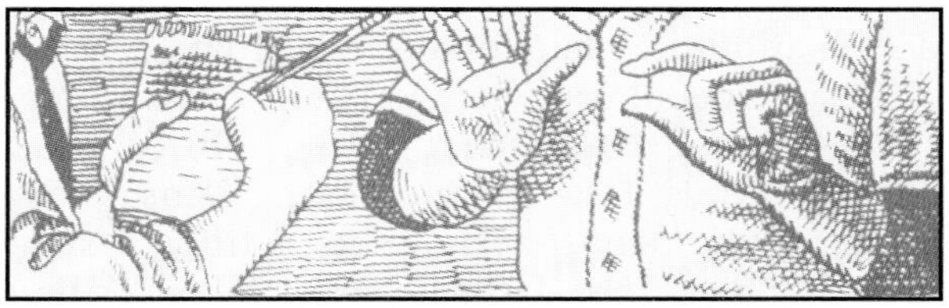

ued to be dominating much of the time, but in 1975 he had the worst year of his career. When he surrendered a grand slam to light-hitting Pete LaCock in early September, he knew his time was over, and he retired before the season was over. In 1981 he became only the 11th man to be inducted into the Hall of Fame on the first ballot.

As outstanding as Gibson was, he was a complete athlete and offered more than his pitching. An excellent fielder, he won nine consecutive Gold Glove Awards from 1965 to 1973. A lifetime .206 hitter, with 24 homers and 13 stolen bases, he hit five home runs in a season twice, and in 1963 he had 20 RBIs.

"I've always thought that you only really enjoy baseball when you're good at it," he once told Roger Angell of *The New Yorker*. "For someone who isn't at the top of his game—who's just hanging on somewhere on down the totem pole—it's a real tough job, every day. But when I was playing I never wished I was doing anything else. I think being a professional athlete is the finest thing a man can do."

Josh Gibson

Gibson, Joshua Jr. **C-OF-3B-1B**

Negro League Player (1929–46) B:12/21/1911, Buena Vista, GA D:1/20/1947, Pittsburgh, PA BR/TR 6'1", 210

Josh Gibson was clearly the most outstanding position player and the most dominating power hitter in the history of the Negro Leagues. In fact, there are those who feel his overall skills were so great and his slugging so prodigious that he may have been the best ballplayer of all time. Because of the paucity of reliable statistics, aficionados may never know how Gibson compared to other players in the Negro Leagues, much less to those in the majors. But records do show that he hit nearly 800 home runs, including a high of 75 in one season. Unlike Babe Ruth's home runs, Gibson's were not arching flyballs but wicked line drives that never seemed to drop.

"When I broke in with the Baltimore Elite Giants in 1937," Dodgers catcher Roy Campanella once said, "there were already a hundred legends about him. Once you saw him play, you knew they were all true. I couldn't carry his bat or glove. The stories of his 500-foot home runs are all true, because I saw them. And he was one of those sluggers that seldom struck out. You couldn't fool him; he was too quick with the bat. And he could do it behind the plate, including throw."

Gibson's debut with Cumberland Posey's Homestead Grays in 1930 was the stuff of Hollywood legend. In July 1930 the pioneering Kansas City Monarchs brought their portable lighting system to Forbes Field to play the Grays in the park's first night game. Despite the lights, the field still had many shadowed areas.

Grays catcher Buck Ewing split his finger open when he tried to catch a ball in the shadows, leaving the team without a catcher. The Grays called out to the big crowd to see if there was a catcher in the stands. Gibson, just 18 years old, stepped forward and became at that moment a member of the Grays.

Almost immediately his hitting caused jaws to drop. "Samson Gibson is green," noted a correspondent with the *Philadelphia Independent*, "but a terrific threat when crouching over the plate with a bat." Gibson pressed his teammates for advice and distracted opposing batters with his banter at the plate. Even in 1930 he was quoted as saying: "A homer a day will boost my pay." In 1931 he hit 75.

Gibson's most legendary homer, however, was probably just that, a legend. The story goes that in 1934 Gibson hit the only home run ever to clear the Yankee Stadium roof. His biographer, William Brashler, having studied all the accounts of the Grays' games at Yankee Stadium that season, found no documentation of this feat. In fact, in a 1943 interview in the *Pittsburgh Courier*, Gibson cited a 1930 blast against the Lincoln Giants in Monessen, Pennsylvania, measured by the town's mayor at 512 feet, as his longest shot.

Gibson's catching took a while to catch up with his hitting. "I can remember when he couldn't catch this building if you threw it at him," said outfielder Jimmie Crutchfield. "He was only behind the plate because of his hitting. And I watched him develop into a very good defensive catcher."

Gibson was not only the subject of legends, he also helped create one. It was Gibson who first told the tale about outfielder Cool Papa Bell being so fast that he could get out of bed, turn off the light switch across the room, and be back in bed under the covers before the lights went out.

In 1932 Gibson jumped from the Grays to Gus Greenlee's Pittsburgh Crawfords. The Grays belonged to the Negro National League, and the Crawfords were an independent barnstorming club. Gibson teamed up with pitcher Satchel Paige, and often the two were teamed in game advertisements, a typical ad reading, "Josh Gibson will hit a home run and Satchel Paige will strike out the side on nine pitches."

The records are sketchy, but the Crawfords' statistics show that in 1933 Gibson batted 512 times, drove in 239 runs, and hit 55 homers. His salary was $250 to $400 per month. Negro Leagues finances, however, were so thin that in January 1937 the Grays offered $2,500 and two journeyman players for Gibson and aging Hall of Fame third baseman Judy Johnson. It was a terrible trade for Pittsburgh, but since Gibson was about to jump to a third team, leaving the Crawfords with no compensation, the deal was consummated.

Gibson, like most Negro Leaguers, performed with some regularity against white major leaguers, and he impressed all comers. Washington Senators pitcher Walter Johnson once observed, "There is a catcher that any big league club would like to buy for $200,000. His name is Gibson. He can do everything. He hits the ball a mile. And he catches so easy, he might as well be in a rocking chair. Throws like a rifle. Bill Dickey isn't as good a catcher."

There were rumors that Washington manager Clark Griffith was interested in signing Gibson and that in 1943 Pirates owner William Benswanger was about to offer Gibson and Buck Leonard contracts. Shortly thereafter, when Branch Rickey considered integrating the Dodgers, Gibson was one of the players he considered for the role of pioneer. "For sheer talent alone," Rickey later said, "Gibson would have been the obvious choice. You know what I feel about Campanella; but whatever Roy can do, Josh could do better." Yet for a number of reasons, including temperament and Gibson's declining health, Jackie Robinson became Rickey's choice for breaking the color barrier.

During his career Gibson performed not only in the United States but in the Caribbean, playing his first season in Puerto Rico in 1933. In mid-1937 he went to the Dominican Republic but returned in time to help the Grays win their first Negro National League championship. In 1941 he was chosen as the Puerto Rican winter league's Most Valuable Player, and he jumped from the Homestead Grays to Vera Cruz of the Mexican League, for $6,000 per year.

Gibson returned to the Grays in 1942, but he didn't seem to be the same player. He spoke incoherently at times, and manager Vic Harris occasionally benched him. Sometimes Harris would find him drinking beer in the Grays' bullpen. The puzzled Harris chalked Gibson's unusual behavior up to stress.

In January 1943 Gibson's year-round ballplaying and hard living caught up with him. He suffered from horrendous headaches and sought medical advice. "Gibson", wrote Cum Posey, "was worried about his batting and overworked himself in an effort to hit his usual playing stride. He was ordered to take a rest by his physician at the close of the season but did not follow the doctor's orders until he was completely run down. He is not the same Josh who never knew the candle had both ends."

Posey did not know Gibson had been diagnosed with a brain tumor. An operation was ordered, but Gibson vetoed it. As his sister said, "He figured if they operated, he'd be like a vegetable."

He continued to play and, incredibly, continued to post big numbers. He captured the National Negro League batting title in 1945 with a .393 average, but to careful observers his performance was slipping badly. In 1946 he still paced the league with a .331 average, but he drank more and more. His weight ballooned to 230 pounds.

In January 1947 Gibson met some friends on a Pittsburgh street corner. They stopped off for a drink, but Gibson complained of a headache and went home to bed. The next morning he felt no better. A doctor came and gave him an injection. He fell asleep and never awoke.

For nearly three decades Gibson lay in an unmarked grave in Pittsburgh's Allegheny Cemetery. In 1972 he was elected to the Hall of Fame. Two years later, Pedro Zorilla, the former owner of the Santurce ballclub in Puerto Rico, came to Pittsburgh for the All-Star Game. Visiting Gibson's grave, he was shocked to see its condition. He began seeking contributions for a suitable gravestone, but when officials in Commissioner Bowie Kuhn's office learned of the project, they announced that Major League Baseball would bear all costs.

Fifty years later fans still wonder what kind of numbers Gibson would have produced had he played in the big leagues, but to Satchel Paige there was no question. "Josh Gibson was the greatest hitter who ever lived," claimed Paige. "He couldn't play in those ballparks with the roof on 'em. He would have hit 'em through the roof."

Kirk Gibson

Gibson, Kirk Harold **OF–DH**

1979–95 B:5/28/1957, Pontiac, MI Deb:9/8/1979, DET AL, BL/TL 6'3", 215

G	AB	R	H	HR	RBI	OBP	SLG	AVG
1635	5798	985	1553	255	870	.355	.463	.268

Kirk Gibson began Game 1 of the 1988 World Series in street clothes. With a severely pulled left hamstring and strained ligaments in his right knee, Gibson could barely walk. But when the Los Angeles Dodgers fell behind Oakland, Gibson pulled on his uniform and limped to a batting cage beneath the stands.

With a man on and two outs in the ninth, and the Dodgers down, 4–3, manager Tommy Lasorda summoned Gibson to pinch hit. Relief ace Dennis Eckersley blew two fastballs by him. On the next pitch, Gibson—with a one-legged swing—muscled the ball over the right field-fence. Though it was Gibson's only appearance in the Series, it helped inspire the Dodgers to an upset triumph in five games. A panel of local sports experts later declared Gibson's homer and subsequent limp around the bases as the greatest moment in Los Angeles sports history.

The Michigan native was an All-America wide receiver at Michigan State, but he signed to play baseball with his hometown Detroit Tigers. By the early 1980s "Gibbie" was reviving the dormant franchise with his ferocious enthusiasm, sprinter speed, and roof-top power. In 1984 Gibson slugged 27 homers with 91 RBIs as Detroit won 104 games. He earned Most Valuable Player honors in a Championship Series sweep of Kansas City. Gibson smashed two homers in the decisive Game 5 of the World Series against San Diego. His three-run clout in the eighth helped insure Detroit's first world championship since 1968.

Over the next three seasons with Detroit, Gibson belted 29, 28, and 24 homers—and stole 30, 34, and 26 bases. He moved to Los Angeles as a free agent, and was named Most Valuable Player in his first season in the National League, despite his relatively low total of 76 RBIs. Gibson proved his value to the team by leading the undermanned Dodgers past the heavily-favored New York Mets in the NLCS and then turning the World Series upside-down with one plate appearance.

Injuries plagued Gibson in his next two years in Los Angeles. He spent single seasons in Kansas City and Pittsburgh before returning to Detroit in 1993. He revived his career with the Tigers with 23 home runs in just 98 games in strike-shortened 1994. He retired after the 1995 season, but later joined the club's broadcast team.

Warren Giles

Giles, Warren
NL President (1951–69) B:5/28/1896 Tiskilwa, IL
D:2/7/1979, Cincinnati, OH

Warren Giles presided over an era of unprecedented change during his 18 years as National League president. While in office professional baseball experienced the first franchise shifts in more than half a century, two different league expansions, and the building of numerous new stadiums.

As a young man Giles served in France during World War I. Shortly after the war, he was working in his father's paint business in Moline, Illinois, when he first became involved in baseball. He was invited to a meeting to discuss the town's community-owned franchise in the Class B 3-I League. Once there, Giles was free with his opinions—actually, a little too free.

"In effect," Giles recalled, "they told me that if I knew so much, why didn't I run the club. They elected me president and there I was, suddenly, totally, and happily, in baseball for life." One of his ideas was to hire Connie Mack's son, Earle, as manager of the club. Not only did Moline win the pennant that year (1920), but through the Mack family Giles made some excellent contacts in Organized Baseball.

In 1923 Giles moved up to the St. Joseph club of the Class A Western League. At one point during his tenure with the Saints, Branch Rickey's Cardinals optioned outfielder Taylor Douthit to the club but neglected to file the necessary paperwork to reserve him. Technically, the talented Douthit now belonged to Giles. The Pirates offered Giles $10,000 for Douthit.

"I know it was an honest oversight," Giles told Rickey, "and you can have Douthit for nothing." Rickey appreciated such honesty and shortly thereafter rewarded Giles by installing him as general manager of the Cardinals' Syracuse Stars farm club.

Giles joined the Cincinnati Reds in 1936, when they were $700,000 in debt. The following year he became their general manager. By the time he left, in 1951, they had won two pennants, were completely solvent, and had become a model of stability.

In 1951 Giles gathered up a great deal of support for his bid to replace Happy Chandler as commissioner. However, when he and NL president Ford Frick deadlocked, Giles withdrew, declaring that "my first interest in baseball is the welfare of baseball itself."

Eventually named to succeed Frick as league president, he held the post until 1969. One change he had to make as the league's chief executive was to support instead of condemn its umpiring staff. "You know," he quipped, shortly after taking over the job, "it's amazing how much better the umpiring looks than it did when I was with the Reds."

On retiring from the game in 1969, Giles said, "We are a game of tradition. The right kind of tradition has made baseball what it is, but blindly following tradition may lead into a rut. Baseball must always keep pace with the times." The Veterans Committee elected him to the Hall of Fame in 1979.

Bernard Gilkey

Gilkey, Otis Bernard **OF**
1990–* B:9/24/1966, St.Louis, MO Deb:9/4/1990,
STL NL BR/TR 6', 190

G	AB	R	H	HR	RBI	OBP	SLG	AVG
1096	3791	581	1057	113	517	.359	.442	.279

St. Louis native Bernard Gilkey had spent his 12-year career with the Cardinals when he was sent to the New York Mets for three minor leaguers in 1996. Gilkey responded with the season of his life in his first year at Shea Stadium.

The 30-year-old outfielder pounded his way through the club's record book: his 44 doubles broke Howard Johnson's 1991 record, and his 117 RBIs tied Johnson's mark set that same year. He and another Johnson—Lance—became the first two Mets to score 100 runs in the same season, and Gilkey and Todd Hundley became the first pair of Mets to drive in 100 runs in a season. Gilkey finished among the leaders in 10 other offensive categories, and he also paced National League outfielders with 18 assists.

These were numbers that he never reached in St. Louis, although his career with the Cards started with a lot of promise. In 1991 he became the first Cardinals rookie since Red Schoendienst in 1945 to start on Opening Day. Gilkey reached base in 19 of his first 21 games, and was developing into a deluxe leadoff hitter when he broke his right thumb on June 14. He slumped after the injury, but he hit for high average over the next few years. Gilkey did not, however, produce the power number the Cards were looking for in a left fielder and he was traded to the Mets.

He signed a large contract after his superb 1996 season, but his numbers skidded. He batted just .248 in 1997, then was dumped on the Arizona Diamondbacks in July 1998 for pitcher Willie Blair and catcher George Fabregas. He rebounded to a .294 average in part-time action in 1999.

Jim Gilliam

Gilliam, James William **2B-3B-OF**

1953–66 B:10/17/1928, Nashville, TN D:10/8/1978, Inglewood, CA Deb:4/14/1953, BRO NL BB/TR 5'10½", 175

G	AB	R	H	HR	RBI	OBP	SLG	AVG
1956	7119	1163	1889	65	558	.361	.355	.265

Jim Gilliam, a valued utility infielder for the Brooklyn and Los Angeles Dodgers for 14 seasons, was one of the first black coaches in the major leagues. "Father, friend, and locker room inspiration that will never be forgotten," is how former Dodgers second baseman Davey Lopes phrased it.

"He didn't hit with power, he had no arm, and he couldn't run," Dodgers manager Walter Alston said of Gilliam. "But he did the little things to win ballgames. He never griped or complained. He was one of the most unselfish ballplayers I know."

"You might say I was born on the ballfield," Gilliam recounted in Jackie Robinson's book, *Baseball Has Done It*. "There was one on the block where I lived in Nashville and another right beside the school I went to. I was playing softball at 7, and hardball on a semipro team, the Crawfords, when I was 14. I never did anything but play ball, except one time I worked as a porter in a five-and-ten."

Gilliam dropped out of high school during his senior year to become a professional ballplayer, joining the Nashville Black Vols of the Negro Southern League for $150 a month. The Baltimore Elite Giants soon offered him a better contract. While he was with Baltimore, veteran second baseman George Scales taught him to switch hit, and he picked up the nickname "Junior" because he was the youngest player on the club.

After Gilliam was named to the Negro National League East All-Star team three straight years, from 1948 through 1950, the Dodgers signed him and the following year sent him to Montreal. He would have gone to Fort Worth of the Texas League, but blacks still weren't allowed to play in that circuit.

In his first two years in the International League Gilliam topped the circuit in RBIs, with 117 in 1951 and 111 in 1952. When he joined the Dodgers in 1953 he replaced Jackie Robinson at second base, led the league in triples, set a rookie record with 100 walks, and won the NL Rookie of the Year Award.

Gilliam was a fixture in the Dodgers infield for all of his 14 major league seasons, playing both second and third. He also had stints in the outfield. Perhaps his best season was 1956, when he hit .300 and was selected for the All-Star Game. That season he scored at least 100 runs for the fourth straight year, drove in 95 runs, and stole 21 bases. On July 21 he tied a major league record for second basemen by recording 12 assists in a nine-inning game.

When Gilliam was first named as a coach in 1964, a reporter inquired, "What would you have done if the Dodgers hadn't made you a coach?" Gilliam answered, "Why I would have kept on playing. I was good for four more years."

He wasn't kidding. When the Dodgers needed him, Gilliam came out of retirement in 1965 and again in 1966 to fill in at third base. In 1965 he batted .280 and helped the club win a world championship. Gilliam, first baseman Wes Parker, second baseman Jim Lefebvre, and shortstop Maury Wills formed the major league's first all-switch-hitting infield.

The well-respected Gilliam was considered a likely candidate to be the major leagues' first black manager, but he never received a managerial appointment. Asked if he felt bypassed or bitter, he responded, "I think baseball people know a man by his ability. Like I have always said, I don't care about being a pioneer, just so I don't get left out."

Gilliam died of a brain hemorrhage shortly before the start of the 1978 World Series. The Dodgers placed his uniform in the casket with him and retired his number, 19.

Jim Gilmore

Gilmore, James A.

Federal League President (1914–15) B:3/2/1870, Portsmouth, OH D:not known

The baseball establishment faced one of its most difficult challenges in 1914 and 1915, when its legal underpinnings were shaken to their very foundation. The threat came from an unlikely source—a Chicago coal dealer and machinery manufacturer who became better known as Federal League president "Fighting Jim" Gilmore.

The Federal League had started in 1913 as an outlaw minor league. Gilmore quickly upped the stakes and declared war on Organized Baseball. The infant Federal League, he vowed, would become a major league. "It came about in August 1913," Gilmore once explained. "I was on my way to the Chicago Golf Club. In my company was E.C. Racey, then treasurer of the Federal League. Now, at this time my baseball experience was limited in the extreme. I was a fan of White Sox convictions. Like most fans, I considered myself wise in the game. That day for the first time I learned of the Federal League."

With 22 games left in the schedule, Gilmore and a friend, Charlie Williams, became backers of the new league's Chicago franchise. They lost $14,000 before the season ended. In August, when league founder and chief John T. Powers was deposed as the infant enterprise prepared to become a major circuit, Gilmore became Federal League president.

Gilmore had been a "change pitcher" on Chicago's West Side. His first job was as a messenger at three dollars a week. Then he landed a seven-dollar-a-week position at a nearby coal company. During the Spanish–American War he enlisted in the Illinois National Guard and was sent to Manila and Santiago de Cuba. In Cuba he contracted malaria and lost 70 pounds in 46 days. Mustered out with the rank of commissary sergeant, he returned to the coal business, becoming a salesman. By 1910 he was president of the Kerchner Company, which manufactured machinery.

Gilmore was particularly good at attracting well-to-do backers to the Federal League, and his investors included restaurant magnate Charles Weeghman in Chicago, banker Robert B. Ward in Brooklyn, oil tycoon Harry Sinclair in Newark, and ice machine king Philip De Catesby Ball in St. Louis.

Gilmore's ability did not go unnoticed. "I believe that man Gilmore," said National League president John K. Tener with a mixture of admiration and frustration, "not only can convince a millionaire the moon is made of green cheese, but he can induce him to invest money in a cheese factory on the moon."

Gilmore lured major league players such as shortstop Joe Tinker; second baseman Otto Knabe; pitchers Claude Hendrix, Mordecai Brown, Russ Ford, and Cy Falkenberg; first baseman George Stovall; and outfielder Rebel Oakes to sign with the Federal League. However, unlike American League president Ban Johnson in 1901 and 1902, Gilmore never attracted the superstars. He came close with Walter Johnson, but the pitcher soon jumped back to Washington.

In January 1915 the Federal League sued Major League Baseball for violating the Sherman Antitrust Act. The Federal League hoped to secure relief from Judge Kenesaw Mountain Landis, who enjoyed a widespread reputation as a trustbuster. Instead, Landis allowed the case to drag on, and the Federal League to twist slowly in the wind. "Both sides must understand that any blows at the thing called baseball would be regarded by this court as a blow to a national institution," Landis said.

When Brooklyn's Robert Ward died in October 1915, a major portion of the league's war chest went with him. In December a complicated settlement was reached between the Federal League and Organized Baseball. The Federal League went out of business, but Phil Ball was allowed to buy the St. Louis Browns, and Charles Weeghman to purchase the Chicago Cubs. Chicago's Federal League park eventually became Wrigley Field.

"There is no room for three major leagues," Gilmore admitted in 1916. "There is no public demand for more than two. But I wouldn't trade the experience for a fortune. That surely was the life."

Al Gionfriddo

Gionfriddo, Albert Francis **OF**

1944–47 B:3/8/1922, Dysart, PA Deb:9/23/1944, PIT NL BL/TL 5'6", 165

G	AB	R	H	HR	RBI	OBP	SLG	AVG
228	580	95	154	2	58	.366	.355	.266

Every moment in a World Series is magnified. Al Gionfriddo's time in the majors was brief, but a single catch made in the World Series spotlight brought him far more fame than many other players received for longer and much more productive major league careers. His catch, Red Barber's radio call, and a famous photograph of what turned out to be his final game as a major leaguer, made Gionfriddo one of the most memorable defensive replacement in baseball history.

Gionfriddo arrived in the majors with the Pittsburgh Pirates in September 1944, a war year in which most major league clubs were happy to put nine able-bodied players on the field. Gionfriddo had no power, but he was rabbit-quick and could run down anything in the outfield.

In 1945 Gionfriddo became a real contributor as, playing regularly, he hit .284 while scoring 74 runs. However, his meager two home runs doomed him to the bench once more players returned in 1946. Relegated to the role of occasional pinch hitter and late-inning defensive replacement, he saw little action for a Pirates team that seldom had a lead to protect. In a deal for five players early in 1947, the Brooklyn Dodgers got $100,000 and, as an afterthought, Gionfriddo.

The Dodgers won the pennant in 1947, although Gionfriddo's .177 batting average in 37 games was a minor contribution. However, he came to the fore in the World Series against the New York Yankees. In Game 4 Gionfriddo was sent in to run for Carl Furillo, who had walked with one out in the bottom of the ninth. Walks were all the offense the Dodgers had been able to muster as the Yankees' pitcher, Bill Bevens, closed in on the first World Series no-hitter with a 2–1 lead.

Bevens got Spider Jorgensen to pop up for the second out and worked the count to 2–1 on pinch hitter Pete Reiser. Then on ball three, Gionfriddo stole second. With the count now favoring Reiser and with first base empty, New York manager Bucky Harris ordered him intentionally passed, putting the Dodgers' potential winning run on first. The next batter, pinch hitter Cookie Lavagetto, broke up the no-hitter and the ballgame by pounding a pitch off the right-field wall to score both runners.

Despite the dramatic win, New York took a 3–2 lead in the Series after five games. In Game 6 Brooklyn took an 8–5 lead into the bottom of the sixth, and manager Burt Shotton inserted Gionfriddo into left field for defensive purposes.

Dodgers pitcher Joe Hatten walked one batter and then, with two outs, gave up a single to Yogi Berra. Joe DiMaggio strode to the plate, swung at Hatten's first offering, and sent it screaming toward deepest left. At the 415-foot mark he turned, reached up, and grabbed the ball just as it was about to disappear over the bullpen fence. DiMaggio, by then nearing second base, could only kick the ground in frustration. Many at the time called it the greatest catch ever. Broadcaster Red Barber made it one of radio's most memorable calls: "...Gionfriddo, back, back, back, back ... he makes a one-handed catch against the bullpen. Oh, doctor!"

Saved for a day, the Brooklyn Dodgers lost Game 7 while Gionfriddo rode the bench. By the next season he was back in the minors—the game of his life turned out to be his final game in the majors. He later opened a cafe in California and prominently displayed a photo of his catch.

Dave Giusti

Giusti, David John **P**

1962, 1964–77 B:11/27/1939, Seneca Falls, NY Deb:4/13/1962, HOU NL BR/TR 5'11", 195

W	L	PCT	G	SV	IP	BB	SO	ERA
100	93	.518	668	145	1716^2	570	1103	3.60

The bullpen ace of the great Pittsburgh clubs of the early 1970s, Dave Giusti is unfortunately most remembered for a save he never made: the final game of the 1972 Championship Series. Giusti was on the mound to protect a 3–2 lead in the bottom of the ninth in Game 5. The 1972 Pirates, ranked by many as the best Pittsburgh team of all time, were hoping to play in their second consecutive World Series. However, Johnny Bench, the first Cincinnati batter in the ninth, got hold of a high Giusti fastball and powered it over the right-field fence to tie the game. After the next two batters singled, Bob Moose replaced Giusti and threw a wild pitch that put the Reds in the Series. It was also Pittsburgh outfielder Roberto Clemente's last game; he was killed in a plane crash less than three months later.

In Giusti's first seven years in the majors—six with Houston and one with St. Louis—he was a workhorse starter, although hardly a star. After he came to Pittsburgh in 1970 in exchange for Carl Taylor, Pirates manager Danny Murtaugh gave him bullpen duty. Giusti responded with 26 saves his first year (along with nine relief wins), 30 saves and a Fireman of the Year Award in 1971, and then 22 and 20 saves in the following two seasons. In seven appearances totaling 10⅔ innings against the Giants and Orioles in the 1971 postseason, he registered four saves and didn't allow a run. Giusti played for Pittsburgh through the 1976 season. In 1977 he was traded to Oakland, and then to the Chicago Cubs, for his last season in the major leagues.

Dan Gladden

Gladden, Clinton Daniel **OF**

1983–93 B:7/7/1957, San Jose, CA Deb:9/5/1983, SF NL BR/TR 5'11", 180

G	AB	R	H	HR	RBI	OBP	SLG	AVG
1197	4501	663	1215	74	446	.327	.382	.270

After a long minor-league career, Dan Gladden burst into prominence in 1984, when he hit .351 with 31 steals in a half-season with the Giants. But after he failed to live up to that promise in two subsequent seasons, San Francisco traded Gladden to Minnesota. The move proved fortuitous for the outfielder, whose good looks and hell-bent playing style endeared him to the Metrodome faithful.

After an unspectacular regular season, Gladden took center stage in October, batting .350 with five RBIs as Minnesota dispatched the Tigers in five games to claim the pennant. In the World Series against St. Louis, he batted .291 and paced the Twins with seven RBIs, with four coming on a grand slam in Minnesota's opening 10–1 win.

Four years later, Gladden returned to the postseason when Minnesota rose from the ashes of a last-place finish in 1990 to face the Atlanta Braves in the 1991 World Series. After splitting the first six games, the teams were scoreless in Game 7 heading into the bottom of the 10th inning. Gladden doubled off Atlanta reliever Alejandro Pena to open the inning. After a sacrifice and two intentional walks loaded the bases, pinch hitter Gene Larkin smacked a hit over the drawn-in outfield, and Gladden came home with the Series-winning run.

Jack Glasscock

Glasscock, John Wesley **SS–2B**

1879–95 M(1889, 1892, 35–35) B:7/22/1859, Wheeling, WV D:2/24/1947, Wheeling, WV Deb:5/1/1879, CLE NL BR/TR 5'8", 160

G	AB	R	H	HR	RBI	OBP	SLG	AVG
1736	7030	1163	2040	27	825	.337	.374	.290

Jack Glasscock was the outstanding defensive shortstop of the 1880s and an above-average hitter. The major obstacle between Glasscock and the wider fame that some of his contemporaries enjoyed was that he never played for a championship team in his 17 major league seasons.

A second drawback to greater recognition was his low-key personality. Glasscock was a team leader, but not a particularly fiery one. He was not averse to a drink or two after a game, but he was never a carouser. He would argue vehemently with an umpire, but so did everyone else. When batting, he had a routine that included pounding his bat on the plate, but it was nothing worth imitating on the vaudeville circuit. He was neither illiterate nor particularly quotable. He showed up, he fielded, he hit, and after the season he went back to his wife and four children in Wheeling, West Virginia, and practiced carpentry.

Glasscock's one verifiable idiosyncrasy was his penchant for landscaping his position. Critics said he found pebbles to throw away where none existed. Perhaps so, but "Pebbly Jack," playing without a glove until 1890, led league shortstops in putouts twice, in double plays four times, and in fielding percentage and assists six times each. Meanwhile, less fastidious shortstops earned no nicknames and were charged with countless bad-hop errors.

Glasscock arrived in the National League with Cleveland in 1879 as a good-field, no-hit third baseman. The next year he switched to shortstop, where he stayed for the rest of his career. His hitting improved from awful to adequate to outstanding. In 1879 he hit .209, by 1883 it was up to .287, and in 1889 he led the league with 205 hits and batted a career-high .352. He doubled as the Indianapolis manager for part of the 1889 season and some accounts say he discovered pitcher Amos Rusie.

He intended to jump to the Players' League in 1890 but ended up instead with the NL's New York Giants. That year he again led the league in hits and also in batting average, at .336. In a game on September 27, he went 6-for-6.

Glasscock played for four teams in his final three years, hitting .341 with Pittsburgh in 1893 and .338 with Louisville in 1895, his last year in the majors. After he left the majors, he played five more seasons in the minors, mostly as a first baseman. He hit .431 for St. Paul one year, but after 1900 he returned to carpentry.

Tom Glavine

Glavine, Thomas Michael **P**

1987–* B:3/25/1966, Concord, MA Deb:8/17/1987, ATL NL BL/TL 6' 1", 190

W	L	PCT	G	SH	IP	BB	SO	ERA
187	116	.617	399	18	2659^{2}	900	1659	3.38

Tom Glavine was the link between the dismal Atlanta Braves of the late 1980s and the perennial division champions of the 1990s. When the young left-hander arrived in Atlanta the city's feeling for the team, and sports in general, could be summed up by a crude banner: "Go Braves—and take the Falcons with you."

Growing up in Concord, Massachusetts, Glavine's favorite sport was hockey, and his major league career began like a slam into the boards. He had 17 losses and a .292 winning percentage in his first full season in the big leagues for 54–106 Atlanta in 1988. It was a very different story seven years later. Still six months shy of his 30th birthday, Glavine was nothing short of brilliant in the sixth game of the 1995 World Series; he combined with Mark Wohlers on a 1–0 one-hitter against the Cleveland Indians to clinch the first title in Atlanta history and won the Series Most Valuable Player award to boot.

"I've seen Tommy throw a lot of great games, but given the circumstances and the pressure on us all, he was about as good as I've ever seen him," Atlanta pitching coach Leo Mazzone said of Glavine's Game 6 performance. "What he did was put the stamp on five years of great pitching."

Glavine's great seasons, not coincidentally, began about the same time the Braves became contenders in 1991. After consecutive 97-loss seasons, Atlanta turned the tables on the National

League West. The Braves pursued, caught, and overtook the Dodgers in the final week of the season to win the division by one game.

Glavine provided the guiding light for a young and talented pitching staff. He was among the league leaders in almost every category, tying for the league lead with 20 wins and nine complete games, while posting a 2.52 ERA. He easily claimed the NL Cy Young Award.

Glavine actually had a better year in 1992. He started the season with a two-hitter, and went on to win 20 games. He allowed only six home runs and tossed a league-best five shutouts. Greg Maddux was also having quite a year in Chicago, so Glavine finished second in the Cy Young voting.

The Braves, who had lost back-to-back World Series, made the best pitching staff in baseball better. Maddux signed as a free agent, and Glavine (22–6) nearly beat him out for the Cy Young. Atlanta, however, could not get past the Philadelphia Phillies in the Championship Series.

The following season Glavine's record slipped to 13–9, his ERA ballooned to 3.97, and Montreal ran away with the newly configured National League East. Then the baseball strike hit and Glavine shifted to a visible role with the Players' Union.

Despite the shortened 1995 season, Glavine won 16 games and returned his name to its rightful spot among league leaders in ERA (3.08) and innings pitched (198). The Braves also returned to first place, winning the NL East by 21 games. Atlanta beat both the Colorado Rockies and Cincinnati Reds in four games to get back to the World Series.

Maddux started the Series with a two-hitter, and Glavine allowed three hits in six innings in Game 2 as the Braves beat the Indians for the second straight night. When Maddux lost Game 5 to send the series back to Atlanta, the ball was in Glavine's hand. All Glavine did was drive Cleveland crazy, carrying a no-hitter into the sixth inning before allowing a bloop single.

He followed that with 15 wins and a 2.98 ERA in 1996. In the postseason he won the clinching game of both the Division Series and the Championship Series—and his first-inning, bases-clearing triple in Game 7 against the Cardinals all but sewed up the pennant. He lost his only start in the World Series as the Yankees won in six games.

After just 14 wins in 1997, he returned to the Cy Young level the following year. Glavine went 20–6 with a sparkling 2.47 ERA, capturing his second Cy Young Award. In 1999 Glavine's record plummeted to 14–11 and an ERA of 4.12, his highest since 1990. He remained a clutch postseason competitor, however, winning games in both the Division Series and the Championship Series to give him an 11–11 career postseason mark.

Kid Gleason

Gleason, William J. **2B–OF–P**

1888–1908, 1912 M(1919–23, 392–364) B:10/26/1866, Camden, NJ D:1/2/1933, Philadelphia, PA Deb:4/20/1888, PHI NL BB/TR 5'7", 158

G	AB	R	H	HR	RBI	OBP	SLG	AVG
1966	7452	1020	1944	15	823	.311	.317	.261

W	L	PCT	G	SH	IP	BB	SO	ERA
138	131	.513	299	10	2389[1]	906	744	3.79

Kid Gleason achieved an unenviable form of immortality as the manager of the 1919 Black Sox. With eight of his Chicago players conspiring to throw the World Series to the Cincinnati Reds, Gleason was forced to watch the sorry tragedy unfold—and there was precious little he could do to prevent it.

Gleason, like everyone else, had his suspicions. After one loss, he spied pitcher Eddie Cicotte and shortstop Swede Risberg in the lobby of Cincinnati's Hotel Sinton. The two were oddly cheerful, even laughing. The sight infuriated Gleason. Angry over their behavior, and by what it suggested, he berated them until Chicago sportswriter Hugh Fullerton led him away.

As a player, Gleason had enjoyed a 22-year career. He began as a pitcher with the Philadelphia Phillies, and was the ace of their staff in 1890, going 38–17 in the year the National League was weakened by massive desertions to the Players' League. He had three more 20-win seasons—two with St. Louis—but after the pitching distance was moved back to its present 60 feet 6 inches in 1894, the diminutive Gleason lost much of his effectiveness.

He moved over to second base and helped the Orioles to the pennant in 1895, hitting .309 with 74 RBIs. The following year he was traded to the Giants, where he was named team captain and played for five years. After jumping to the Tigers of the new American League in 1901, he was sold back to the Phillies in 1903.

Gleason managed the White Sox from 1919 to 1923. He led them to the pennant in 1919, second place in 1920 (amid suspicions that some of his players had dumped the pennant race to the Indians), and then—beset by the scandal and resulting banishments—to three second-division finishes.

In *Eight Men Out,* Eliot Asinof wrote of Gleason: "He was tough, single-minded, always fair. The ballplayers had to respect him whether they liked him or not. No one ever spoke harshly about him; they knew no one would believe them if they did."

Dave Goltz

Goltz, David Allan **P**

1972–83 B:6/23/1949, Pelican Rapids, MN
Deb:7/18/1972, MIN AL BR/TR 6'4", 215

W	L	PCT	G	SH	IP	BB	SO	ERA
113	109	.509	353	13	2039²	646	1105	3.69

The first Minnesota native signed by the Twins, Dave Goltz endured arm problems and a tour in Vietnam before he finally landed in the Twin Cities. Once he got there, he spent his first eight seasons in the major leagues in the club's starting rotation.

Goltz posted .500 records in four of his first five seasons, he had a career year in 1977 with a 20–11 record and 3.36 ERA in 330 innings pitched. He finished tied for the American League lead in starts and victories, including a one-hitter against the Boston Red Sox. Goltz won 15 games with a personal-best 2.49 ERA a year later, but then reverted to his previous .500 form.

The Los Angeles Dodgers gambled and lost when they signed Goltz to a large free agent contract after the 1979 campaign. He made 27 starts the following year, but pitched so poorly he was demoted to relief work. Goltz went 9–19 in three seasons for the Dodgers but made two relief appearances against the New York Yankees in the 1981 World Series.

A return to the AL in 1982 helped the righthander. Although he was hampered by a finger injury, Goltz went 8–5 with three saves as a relief pitcher to help the California Angels win the AL West title. Goltz finished his career with the Angels the following season.

Lefty Gomez

Gomez, Vernon Louis **P**

1930–43 B:11/26/1908, Rodeo, CA D:2/17/1989,
Greenbrae, CA Deb:4/29/1930, NY AL BL/TL 6'2", 173

W	L	PCT	G	SH	IP	BB	SO	ERA
189	102	.649	368	28	2503	1095	1468	3.34

Lefty Gomez ranks as one of the premier pitchers in New York Yankees history. Through 1999 he ranked third in career victories, with 189, and fourth in strikeouts, with 1,468. Yet his quips and antics are probably better remembered than his statistics. Indeed, "Lefty" wasn't his only nickname; to his teammates he was more frequently known as "Goofy," such as when he proposed a revolving bowl for tired goldfish because it would "save them the trouble of swimming around."

Gomez hated pitching to Jimmie Foxx, a batter who simply owned him. In fact, it was Gomez who originally observed that Foxx had "muscles in his hair" and that "he was wasn't scouted, he was trapped." During one game Gomez shook off every pitch to Foxx that catcher Bill Dickey called. Finally Dickey strode to the mound to find out just what his pitcher wanted to throw. "Nothing," replied Gomez. "Let's just stall around and maybe he'll get mad and go away." Foxx slugged the next pitch for a home run.

Notoriously poor at the plate, Gomez longed to be a great hitter. One time, after advancing to the plate, he adjusted his cap, tugged at his belt, and did all the things a real hitter would, including swinging his bat to knock the mud from his spikes. Unfortunately, he smashed himself in the ankle and spent the next three days in the hospital.

Gomez began as a player in 1928 for the Class C Utah–Idaho League's Salt Lake City Bees, where he went 12–14 but led the league with 172 strikeouts. The following year he moved up to the Pacific Coast League's San Francisco Seals. His first game with the Seals was on a Sunday, when the Pittsburgh Pirates were visiting San Francisco's old Recreation Park for an exhibition. The Seals' starting pitcher had loaded the bases and had retired only one Pittsburgh batter when manager Nick Williams summoned the 19-year-old Gomez from the bullpen. He threw a three-hitter.

By year's end Gomez was a hot commodity. He had gone 18–11 and led the league with a 3.43 ERA. The Yankees purchased him for $35,000, expecting him to step into their rotation with little or no effort in 1930. However, at midseason of his first year in the majors, he was sent down to the St. Paul Saints of the American Association. In his first game in St. Paul, Gomez was summoned from the bullpen into a bases-loaded, no-out jam. "Gomez," recalled trainer Bob Bauman, "came up the foul line whistling 'Marching Through Georgia.' He was so wild, but so powerfully fast, that he scared 'em into three straight strikeouts."

In 1931 the Yankees recalled him, and he responded with 21 victories. The following year he was a 24-game winner. In that fall's World Series against the Cubs, he had what he called his greatest game ever. He struck out eight and walked one, and the Yankees won the game, 5–2. "It wasn't any closeness of score or suspense that made it my biggest day," he explained. "It was simply my first World Series game, and I won it."

After the Series, Gomez signed up for 12 weeks in vaudeville, delivering a baseball monologue. It was not a great success. "I lasted three weeks," he confessed, "but the audiences didn't."

After the 1932 season Gomez was advised to gain weight. He was painfully thin, and general manager Ed Barrow felt that he could be more effective if he were heavier. "About 25 years ago we had a pitcher here named Jack Chesbro," Barrow informed Gomez, "the first pitcher ever to win 16 straight games in the

American League. If you'd only put on more weight, you could make the fans forget Chesbro."

The next season, Gomez came back 23 pounds heavier but dropped to only 16 wins. "Listen, Barrow told me that if I put on 20 pounds, I'd make the fans forget Chesbro," he explained to reporters. "I go Barrow three better with 23 pounds and almost make the fans forget about Gomez." The fans didn't forget about Gomez, though. He was picked to start the first All-Star Game on July 6, 1933. Gomez recorded the first RBI in All-Star history when he singled in a run, and earned the historic victory.

In 1934 he recorded a league-best 26–5 record while leading the AL in complete games, shutouts, innings pitcher, strikeouts, and ERA. In 1937 he led the league in wins and ERA for a second time. That year Gomez also started his fourth All-Star Game in a five-year period, winning it for the third time.

Gomez continued to pitch for the Yankees through the 1942 season and threw one game for Washington in 1943 before retiring. After leaving baseball, Gomez answered an employment questionnaire from the sales promotion department of a sporting goods company. When he came to the question, "Why did you leave your last job?" he wrote, "I couldn't get anybody out." He was elected to the Hall of Fame in 1972.

Juan Gonzalez

Gonzalez, Juan Alberto (Vazquez) **OF–DH**
1989–* B:10/20/1969, Arecibo, Puerto Rico
Deb:9/1/1989, TEX AL BR/TR 6'3", 210

G	AB	R	H	HR	RBI	OBP	SLG	AVG
1248	4831	791	1421	340	1075	.347	.572	.294

Juan Gonzalez and Sammy Sosa began their professional careers side-by-side in the outfield; between them they had four home runs (none by Gonzalez) and 64 RBIs over a full season. Thirteen seasons removed from the Gulf Coast Rookie League, the pair combined for 111 home runs and 315 RBIs in the same season. Gonzalez and Sosa, playing in different leagues in 1998, both earned Most Valuable Player Awards. For Gonzalez it was his second MVP trophy.

While Sosa earned worldwide adoration for his home run prowess, Gonzalez was slower to achieve fame. Success, however, was something that had come steadily. Gonzalez made his pro baseball debut at 16, played in his first major league game at 19, captured his first home run crown at 22, won his first MVP Award at 27, and reached 300 home runs at 29.

Gonzalez started to hit with power after his third minor league season. He became a regular in the Texas outfield in 1991. He led the team in home runs in his first full season, and led the American League in homers in his second. Gonzalez led the AL again in homers in 1993, and also topped the league in slugging percentage. The 1994 season began with the death of his brother and ended with the players' strike. Injuries limited him to 90 games the following season.

Gonzalez spent most of May 1996 on the disabled list, but he still finished with 47 home runs, 144 RBIs, and a .314 average in 134 games. He helped the Rangers reach the postseason for the first time in franchise history. He batted .438 with five home runs in the Division Series, but the Rangers lost to the New York Yankees in four games. Gonzalez beat out Seattle's Alex Rodriguez for the AL MVP in one of the closest races in history. In 1997 Gonzalez reached 40 home runs for the fourth time and 100 RBIs for the fifth time, but he also went on the disabled list for the fifth time in his career. Gonzalez showed the kind of numbers he could put up over a full season in 1998.

He drove in 35 runs in April, drove in 22 in 12 games in May, and the RBIs kept piling up. His 101 RBIs at the All-Star break were the second-most in history. He had 26 RBIs solely against the Kansas City Royals. Gonzalez finished with 157 RBIs, the most in the AL since 1949. After the season he became the 15th player in history to win two MVP Awards. Gonzalez batted a career-high .326 in 1999, but he gained more notoriety for what he didn't do. When the fans did not vote him to start the All-Star Game, he selfishly stayed home. He helped the Rangers win the AL West title for the third time in four years, yet Texas lost to the Yankees for the third time. Gonzalez drove in the team's only run in a three-game sweep.

Gonzalez was involved in the first blockbuster trade of the 1999 off-season. Gonzalez, about to enter the final year of his contract, was sent to Detroit in a nine-player deal.

Dwight Gooden

Gooden, Dwight Eugene **P**
1984–94, 1996–* B:11/16/1964, Tampa, FL
Deb:4/7/1984, NY NL BR/TR 6'3" 210

W	L	PCT	G	SH	IP	BB	SO	ERA
188	107	.637	403	24	2695²	910	2238	3.46

At the start of the 1984 season few people had heard of Dwight Gooden; less than two years later he was considered the best pitcher in baseball. His blazing fastball and devastating curve made the young Mets righthander a household name.

At age 19, Dwight Gooden was the youngest player ever to be named Rookie of the Year, and also the youngest to play in an All-Star Game. He fanned 276 batters in 1984 to become the first teenager to lead the major leagues in strikeouts. He set an all-time strikeout record for rookies, shattering Herb Score's 29-year-old record and established another major league record with 43 strikeouts in three consecutive starts in September.

Gooden was quickly dubbed "Dr. K," and fans at Shea Stadium—and sometimes on the road—hung "K" signs every time the rookie struck out a batter. The Mets, who had their best record since 1969, finished second to the Cubs, and Gooden finished second to Chicago's Rick Sutcliffe in the National League Cy Young Award voting.

In 1985 he became the youngest Cy Young Award winner at age 20. He captured pitching's Triple Crown with a league-leading 24–4 mark, 1.53 ERA, and 268 strikeouts. Gooden's ERA was the lowest registered since Bob Gibson's 1.12 in 1968.

"Doc" was the ninth player ever to capture the Cy Young unanimously, and he finished fourth in the NL Most Valuable Player voting. He hurled 16 complete games and eight shutouts. He won 14 consecutive games and had a scoreless streak of 31 innings. To cap it all, he was named Associated Press Male Athlete of the Year.

A seasoned veteran at 21, Gooden was merely great in 1986, compared with his phenomenal first two seasons. He became the first pitcher in major league history to strike out at least 200 batters in each of his first three years. He went 17–6 for the runaway NL East champions, and was again unflinching in tight situations: batters hit just .048 against him with runners in scoring position in late innings. He had a 1.06 ERA in the Championship Series, with a 1–0 loss to Houston in Game 1 and then he went 10 innings without a decision in New York's eventual 2–1 victory in Game 5. In the World Series, however, he lost both starts and had an 8.00 ERA.

Gooden's string of record-breaking seasons was interrupted in 1987 due to an admitted drug problem. He did not pitch until June, but he still put together a 15–7 record. In 1988 he won 18 games as the Mets won another division title. He set a record with 20 strikeouts in three NLCS games, but New York lost to the Dodgers in seven games.

Injuries limited Gooden to 17 starts and a 9–4 record in 1989, but he continued to find his way into the record book. Gooden became the first player in 90 years to pitch above .500 in each of his first six years and he was also the third youngest pitcher in the modern era to score 100 wins. His 37 losses at the 100-win mark were second to Whitey Ford's 36.

In 1990 he bounced back from injuries to surpass 200 strikeouts for the first time since 1986. Early in the year he dipped below .500 for the first time in his career, and he was 3–5 with a 4.37 ERA on June 2. But he regained his form and plowed through the league for a 16–2 record the rest of the season.

The 1990 campaign, however, was his last injury-free year with the Mets. After a 13–7 season in 1991, Gooden's record fell below .500 each of the next three years. In 1994 he won on Opening Day, but was back on the disabled list by April 22. When he returned, he wasn't the same pitcher. On June 28, with an ERA of 6.31, more than three runs above his career mark, Gooden was suspended for 60 days for violating his drug treatment program. He ultimately was granted free agency after the season.

He returned to baseball in 1996 with the Yankees. After a rocky start, he no-hit the Mariners on May 14 and was given the key to the city by the mayor's office. Gooden finished the season with 11 wins, and was 9–5 with a 4.91 ERA for New York in 1997. He made his first postseason appearance since 1988, and left Game 4 of the Division Series with a lead against the Indians; Cleveland rallied to win the game and the series.

The next year Gooden was in an Indians uniform, but his season ended sadly when he was ejected for arguing in the first inning of a Division Series game. He won just three times with the Indians in 1999, and was lopped off the team's postseason roster. Hoping for yet another comeback, Gooden signed with Houston after the season.

Billy Goodman

Goodman, William Dale **2B-1B-3B-OF**

1947–62 B:3/22/1926, Concord, NC D:10/1/1984, Sarasota, FL Deb:4/19/1947, BOS AL BL/TR 5'11", 165

G	AB	R	H	HR	RBI	OBP	SLG	AVG
1623	5644	807	1691	19	591	.377	.378	.300

In 16 seasons Billy Goodman played every position except pitcher and catcher. A lifetime .300 batter, he was the ultimate slap hitter. He won the American League batting championship in 1950, the same year he tied a career-high with four home runs. Four times he did not hit a home run all season despite more than 400 at bats.

Goodman was brought up on a North Carolina dairy farm and assisted in the usual variety of chores—duties, he later said, that served him in good stead in his later role as a utility man. Farming, however, held little appeal compared to baseball. "I just never thought of doing anything else except playing baseball," he said. "It was an ambition of mine right from the very beginning."

Signed by a scout for the Atlanta Crackers, an independent Southern Association club, Goodman tore up the league: he hit .336, led the circuit in runs scored, and tied for the lead in triples. After serving a year in the military, he returned to Atlanta in 1946, hit .389, and was bought by the Red Sox.

Goodman became Boston's starting first baseman in 1948, when he hit .310. The next year he led AL first basemen in fielding average and was selected to the first of his two All-Star Games.

In 1950 Goodman was bounced all over defensively, starting at every infield and outfield position. The novelty seemed to do him good: he won the AL batting title with a .354 average. Two years later, he began to settle down as the regular second baseman, filling the shoes of Boston legend Bobby Doerr. That was the first of three consecutive years that he hit over .300.

After a 1-for-16 start in 1957, Goodman was traded to the Baltimore Orioles. He bounced back to finish the season at .308. That December he was traded to the Chicago White Sox. Twelve years into his career, Goodman finally made it to a World Series with the "Go Go Sox" of 1959. "We had a good bunch of boys there," he said. "They played together, as a unit, better than any club I ever played on. We were a fine defensive team and we had phenomenal pitching."

After two years spent mainly on the bench, Goodman was granted his unconditional release by Chicago in May 1962, and finished his major league career with the expansion Houston Colt .45s. He later scouted for the Red Sox, managed in the Houston system, coached for Atlanta, and served in the Kansas City organization.

Ival Goodman

Goodman, Ival Richard **OF**

1935–44 B:7/23/1908, Northview, MO D:11/25/1984, Cincinnati, OH Deb:4/16/1935, CIN NL BL/TR 5'11", 170

G	AB	R	H	HR	RBI	OBP	SLG	AVG
1107	3928	609	1104	95	525	.352	.445	.281

Johnny Bench, Pete Rose, and Joe Morgan may generally be thought of as the great Cincinnati Reds hitters of the past, but right fielder Ival Goodman had some impressively productive years in the late 1930s. He won two triples titles, hit a then club-record 30 homers, and made two trips to the World Series.

Goodman didn't begin playing pro ball until 1930 when he surfaced with Shawnee of the Western Association. He made it to the majors with the Reds in 1935 and hit .269 that first year, driving in 72 runs and leading the National League with 18 triples. In 1936 he hit .284 with 17 homers and again led the league in triples, with 14.

In 1938 Goodman was selected to the first of two All-Star Games. That year he surprised a lot of people by hitting 30 homers, after having had hit only 41 in his three previous seasons. That was good for second in the league behind Mel Ott's 36, and it set a Reds record that lasted until Ted Kluszewski hit 40 in 1953. Goodman's 92 RBIs were also a career high, as were his 103 runs.

The next year his home run production was down, but Goodman hit a career-best .323, and his 37 doubles were also a career high. The Reds won the pennant that season and faced the Yankees in the World Series. In the ninth inning of Game 1, with the score tied 1–1, Charlie Keller led off with a fly to right. Goodman tried for a lunging catch but missed as the ball rolled past him for a triple. A few moments later Bill Dickey hit a game-winning single. The Yankees went on to sweep the Series.

The Reds won the National League pennant again the next year, but Goodman, who was 32, was already slipping. He did contribute in a major way in the World Series, however, with five runs and five RBIs, as the Reds beat the Tigers in seven games. That was Goodman's last season as a regular, and he retired after hitting .262 in 62 games in 1944. He subsequently managed in the minor leagues and scouted for the Cubs.

Joe Gordon

Gordon, Joseph Lowell **2B**

1938–43, 1946–50 M(1958–61, 1969, 305–308) B:2/18/1915, Los Angeles, CA D:4/14/1978, Sacramento, CA Deb:4/18/1938, NY AL BR/TR 5'10", 180

G	AB	R	H	HR	RBI	OBP	SLG	AVG
1566	5707	914	1530	253	975	.357	.466	.268

Joe Gordon was a slick-fielding second baseman with home run power. He was named to nine All-Star Games and appeared in six World Series. He also had another claim to fame. In 1960, while managing the Indians, Gordon was traded for Tigers manager Jimmy Dykes. It marked the first time that managers were traded for each other.

Gordon is remembered first and foremost, however, as a great player. "The greatest all-around ballplayer I ever saw, and I don't bar any of them, is Joe Gordon," Joe McCarthy remarked after Gordon's spectacular performance in the 1941 World Series.

Gordon set the American League single-season record for most home runs by a second baseman, with 32 for Cleveland in 1948, as well as the Yankees' record, with 30 in 1940. His 246 career homers established an AL record for a second baseman. But batting was not his favorite pastime. "Hitting? What is there to it?" he once said. "You swing, and if you hit the ball, there it goes. Ah, but fielding. There's rhythm, finesse, teamwork, and balance!"

While a student at the University of Oregon, Gordon not only played baseball but was also a fine gymnast, long jumper, soccer player, and halfback on the football team. He even played the violin. "He played in the school orchestra when he wasn't on an athletic field," recalled Bobby Grayson, a three-time All-America in football, "and later, when he managed Sacramento after World War II, he and Tommy Heath used to get together in a combo."

After hitting .418 as a sophomore at Oregon, Gordon was signed by Yankees scout Bill Essick, who had summed up the kid up in this report back to the Bronx: "At his best when it meant the most and the going was toughest."

In 1937 he played second base with the legendary Newark Bears, often heralded as the greatest minor league team of all time. Gordon hit only .280 at Newark but professed not to be concerned. "I hit a lot of hard luck," he said, "and with a little better fortune, I might even increase those figures in the American League."

Gordon made it across the Hudson in 1938 and was an immediate success, hitting 25 home runs with 97 RBIs in his rookie season. He averaged 25 homers and 101 RBIs during the next four seasons and was selected to the All-Star Game each year. In 1942 he was named the AL's Most Valuable Player over Ted Williams, who had won the Triple Crown.

Following a disappointing season in 1943, Gordon spent the next two years in the military. He had a dreadful season when he returned in 1946, hitting only .210, and subsequently was traded to Cleveland for Allie Reynolds.

Reynolds anchored the Yankees' pitching staff for the next eight years, but the Indians didn't do badly out of the deal either. Gordon immediately revived his career in Cleveland. He hit 29 homers and drove in 93 runs during his first season there and followed that with 32 homers and 124 RBIs for the 1948 world champs. He had two more solid years before retiring after the 1950 season.

Gordon's next stop was Sacramento in the Pacific Coast League, where he managed in 1951 and 1952. From 1953 through July 1956, he served as a scout for Detroit. At that point he became manager of the PCL's San Francisco Seals. He directed them to a first-place showing in 1957, and was then hired to manage Cleveland.

It wasn't a happy marriage. Shortly after Gordon was hired, Frank "Trader" Lane was installed as Cleveland's new general manager. Gordon and Lane did not get along, and late in the 1959 season their feud heated up. Gordon was annoyed by Lane publicly questioning his strategy, and on September 18, 1959, Gordon announced he would not return in 1960. The next day Lane went to Pittsburgh to ask Leo Durocher, then an NBC broadcaster, if he was interested in taking over the Indians.

Lane also announced that Gordon would be terminated as soon as the club was mathematically eliminated from the pennant race. When Al Lopez's White Sox clinched the pennant on September 22, Lane said that Gordon was out "as of now" and that pitching coach Mel Harder would be taking over the club. The next day Lane backpedaled. Suddenly disenchanted with Durocher and his demands, Lane announced not only that Gordon was back, but also that he had a two-year contract and a raise. "I made a mistake," said Lane, "and I decided I didn't have to live with it, so I tried to correct it."

Yet relations between and Lane and Gordon did not improve. So when Detroit general manager Bill DeWitt suggested trading managers, Lane went for it. On August 3, 1960, Gordon was swapped for Jimmy Dykes. Gordon was probably relieved to finally be free of Lane and graciously remarked, "I have always been appreciative of the Cleveland club for hiring me in the first place." He lasted only two months with Detroit. Wrote sportswriter Joe Falls, "Gordon took one long look at the Tigers and shook his head. When the remainder of the season was over, he barricaded himself in his apartment and refused to talk to anyone. He quit."

On October 5, 1960, Charles O. Finley, the new owner of the Kansas City A's, hired Gordon as manager—but fired him in midseason. Gordon then worked as a scout and minor league batting instructor for the Angels from October 1961 through 1968. In 1969 he became the first manager of the expansion Kansas City Royals. Finishing fourth, he was let go after the season. After leaving baseball, Gordon sold real estate. He died of a heart attack in 1978.

Sid Gordon

Gordon, Sidney **OF–3B**

1941–55 B:8/13/1917, Brooklyn, NY D:6/17/1975, New York, NY Deb:9/11/1941, NY NL BR/TR 5'10", 185

G	AB	R	H	HR	RBI	OBP	SLG	AVG
1475	4992	735	1415	202	805	.377	.466	.283

Leo Durocher was a Sid Gordon fan, but when he took over the Giants in 1948, the team was top-heavy with power hitters who couldn't run and couldn't cover a lot of ground in the field. He knew that wholesale changes were needed. Gordon, a left fielder-third baseman who hit with power, was on the block.

Durocher made his move after the 1949 season. He wanted Alvin Dark of the Braves, the 1948 NL Rookie of the Year, to play shortstop, and he also wanted a second baseman that could turn double plays with Dark. He thought he was going to have to settle for Sibby Sisti and was astounded to learn he could also get Eddie Stanky, one of his all-time favorite players—with one catch: Gordon would have to be part of the trade. Durocher called Gordon "a man I hated to lose." But he lost him, and the reconstituted Giants were on their way to making history in 1951.

Gordon was born in Brooklyn's Brownsville section. Although he desperately wanted to play for the Dodgers, he had to settle for the Giants when he failed a tryout at Ebbets Field. He began his pro career in 1938 with Milford of the Class D Eastern Shore League and he spent the next three years with Jersey City. He made the Giants for good as a 26-year-old rookie in 1943 and had a decent season, hitting .251 with 63 RBIs. He spent the next two years in the Coast Guard, and when he returned in 1946 he hit .293, but with only five homers and 45 RBIs.

In 1948 Gordon's career seemed to turn around. He hit .299 with 30 homers and 107 RBIs, beginning a stretch of four seasons—two with the Giants, two with the Braves—that saw him average 28 homers and 102 RBIs (with two homers in one inning in 1949, four grand slams in 1950, and a career-high 109 RBIs in 1951). He also was selected to the All-Star Game in 1948 and 1949.

Gordon hit 25 home runs in 1952, and he had eight straight hits at one point, but his RBIs dropped. The next season was a little less successful for him, and, seeing his age catching up to him, the Braves traded him to the Pittsburgh Pirates before the 1954 season. He played a year and a half with the Pirates before finishing his career back with the Giants.

Tom Gordon

Gordon, Thomas **P**

1988–* B:11/18/1967, Sebring, FL Deb:9/8/1988, KC AL BR/TR 5'9", 180

W	L	PCT	G	SV	IP	BB	SO	ERA
104	96	.520	444	71	1645	807	1431	4.15

When your last name is Gordon, you have to expect the nickname "Flash." Tom Gordon earned that sobriquet with a spectacular rookie season in 1989, winning 17 games for the Kansas City Royals and being named American League Rookie Pitcher of the Year by *The Sporting News*. Things went downhill pretty quickly, though. The diminutive Gordon struggled in 1990, and spent the next three seasons bouncing between the starting rotation and bullpen in Kansas City.

Gordon regained enough consistency to pitch solely as a starter in 1994 and 1995, but he was never able to recapture the level of success as a starter that he'd reached as a rookie. Following the 1995 season, Gordon left the Royals as a free agent and signed with the Boston Red Sox.

After struggling through another season as a starter, Gordon found his niche in Boston's bullpen. Given a chance in late 1997 to take over the closer's role, he seized the opportunity and made the job his own. After nine unspectacular seasons, he suddenly set the league on fire in 1998. Gordon set a major league record by recording 43 consecutive saves, and his 46 total saves set a Boston club record. He was named to the All-Star team and won the Rolaids award as best reliever in the American League. A shoulder injury cost him most of the 1999 season, and there were concerns not only about the proper treatment for the injury, but also whether or not he would be able to return.

Gordon was memorialized in an odd way when the popular novelist Stephen King used him in his book, *The Girl Who Loved Tom Gordon*.

George Gore

Gore, George F. **OF**

1879–92 M(1892, 6–9) B:5/3/1857, Saccarappa, ME D:9/16/1933, Utica, NY Deb:5/1/1879, CHI NL BL/TR 5'11", 195

G	AB	R	H	HR	RBI	OBP	SLG	AVG
1310	5357	1327	1612	46	618	.386	.411	.301

George Gore was one of the swiftest baseball players of his day, and his speed made him a top player at bat, on base, and in center field. He had a knack for winning—he starred on seven pennant-winning teams during the 1880s—but his love for wine, women, and song often kept him in the managerial doghouse.

Gore joined Cap Anson's Chicago White Stockings in 1879, and in his second season helped the team to a pennant by leading the National League with a .360 batting average. Gore led the league in runs scored in both 1881 and 1882. With the number of games in a season increasing during the 1880s, he enjoyed a string of four straight seasons with more than 100 runs scored, registering 150 in 1886. That year he collected 102 bases on balls despite the requisite nine balls for a walk.

Chicago won pennants in 1885 and 1886, but the straight-laced Anson became fed up with Gore's after-hours activities. Anson bundled him off to New York, where Gore helped the Giants win the pennant in both 1888 and 1889. In 1890 he hit .318 for New York of the Players' League, before returning to the Giants for the last two years of his career. Despite his reputation as a carouser, Gore lived to the ripe old age of 76.

Goose Goslin

Goslin, Leon Allen **OF**

1921–38 B:10/16/1900, Salem, NJ D:5/15/1971, Bridgeton, NJ Deb:9/16/1921, WAS AL BL/TR 5'11½", 185

G	AB	R	H	HR	RBI	OBP	SLG	AVG
2287	8656	1483	2735	248	1609	.387	.500	.316

Some said outfielder Leon Goslin acquired the alliterative nickname "Goose" because he flapped his arms while running after flyballs. But his long neck and prominent nose lent a certain gooselike quality to his profile, and ballplayers have never been afraid to make fun of a teammate's physical features.

Born on a southern New Jersey farm, Goslin wanted to play baseball from a young age. At 16 he began pitching for the semipro Salem, New Jersey, All-Stars for $3 per game. Goslin was pitching in an industrial league when umpire Bill McGowan told him he was good enough to play professionally. Goslin joined the Class C Sally League's Columbia Comers in 1920 and was switched to the outfield because of his power at bat.

Years later Goslin said, "I could always swing that bat real quick, just natural. Never had to train or practice a whole lot. Good eyes, quick reflexes, strong arms—oh, did I ever love to get up there and hit! And most of all I truly loved those fastballs. They were right down my alley. Zip, they'd come in, and whack—right back out they'd go. I never could wait for spring to come so I could get out there and swat those baseballs!"

In 1921 he hit a league-leading .390 for Columbia. Jack Dunn, owner of the minor league Baltimore Orioles, planned to offer $5,000 for Goslin's contract, but Washington owner Clark Griffith, notoriously careful with his pennies, beat him to it with an offer of $6,000. After joining the Senators, Goslin asked Griffith to use his influence to have umpire McGowan promoted from the minor leagues. McGowan eventually became a top American League umpire and was elected to the Hall of Fame in 1992.

Goslin was remarkably naive at the beginning of his career. In his first major league game he smacked a bases-loaded triple to help Washington defeat Chicago. When a teammate remarked that he never expected the Senators to beat famous pitcher Red Faber that day, Goslin asked, "Was that Faber?" When American League pitchers threw at him, he was slow to realize that they were doing so deliberately. He once asked teammate Sam Rice, "Gee, Sam, how come those pitchers are never wild when you're at bat?"

In 1922, his first full season with the Senators, Goslin hit .324, his first of seven straight seasons over .300, all but one of them over .320. His second year he led the AL in triples, feat he repeated in 1925.

Like Babe Ruth, Goslin put everything he had into his swing. When he missed, he often ended up on the ground. Still, he never admitted that he'd hit a pitch as well as he wanted to. Once, after hitting a ball into the center-field bleachers at Fenway Park, Goslin remarked, "I wish I had really gotten hold of that ball. It really would have gone places."

Goslin was a huge driving force as the Senators won their first pennant in 1924. He hit .344, led the league with 129 RBIs, and was second in the AL in triples. He continued his outstanding performance in the World Series against the New York Giants. In Game 2 he hit a two-run homer to spark the Senators' 4–3 win. In Game 4 he went 4-for-4 with a three-run homer and a run-scoring single in a 7–4 victory. He hit his third home run of the Series in a Game 5 losing effort. The Senators won a thrilling seventh game to become world champions. Washington repeated as the pennant winner in 1925 with Goslin scoring 116 runs, driving in 113, and leading the league in triples. Although Goslin again hit three home runs in the Series, the Senators lost to Pittsburgh.

In 1928 spring training Goslin tried to throw a 16-pound shot like a baseball and hurt his arm. Throughout the following season, the Senators' shortstop was forced to race deep into left field to relay Goslin's weak throws. Despite his bad arm, Goslin remained in the lineup; Washington needed his bat, and he was having a banner year at the plate.

On the last day of the 1928 season Goslin and Heinie Manush of St. Louis were virtually tied for the batting title, and Washington and St. Louis faced each other in the final game. Goslin got hits in his first two trips to the plate and knew he had the title if he didn't bat again. But teammate Joe Judge shamed him into going to the plate a third time. After collecting two quick strikes, Goslin saw his batting title slipping away.

He quickly hatched an idea. He realized that if he were thrown out of the game, the at bat would be credited to whoever finished it. He started an argument with the umpire and even stood on the umpire's shoes. But the umpire refused to be baited, and a reluctant Goslin stepped back into the batter's box. He promptly singled to clinch the title.

Early in the 1930 season Goslin was traded to St. Louis for Manush and pitcher Alvin Crowder. He celebrated his new, friendlier surroundings by hitting 37 home runs, more than twice as many as he had ever had before. Two years later Goslin started to use a zebra-striped bat to confuse the opposition. When the other teams complained, league president Will Harridge ruled the bat illegal.

After three strong seasons with the Browns,

Goslin was traded back to Washington. He reminded Clark Griffith that the Senators had never won a pennant without him in the lineup. Although Goslin had an off year, Washington won its third (and final) pennant. And while the New York Giants beat the Senators in five games, Goslin hit his seventh World Series homer in Game 2.

Griffith traded Goslin to Detroit at the end of the 1933 season, just in time for him to help the Tigers win pennants in 1934 and 1935 by driving in more than 100 runs each year. Detroit lost the 1934 World Series to the Cardinals but defeated the Cubs in six games in 1935. With two out in the bottom of the ninth inning of the final game, Goslin singled in Mickey Cochrane with the winning run. In 1936 Goslin put together one of his finest seasons, hitting .315 with 24 homers and 125 RBIs. He was also selected to his only All-Star Game.

Goslin left the majors after the 1938 season to serve as player-manager of the Class C Inter-State League's Trenton Senators. When he retired from baseball, he ran a boat and fishing tackle business in New Jersey. In 1968, three years before his death, he was named to the Hall of Fame.

He once told writer Lawrence Ritter, "I was just a big ol' country boy havin' the time of my life. It was all a lark to me, just a joy ride...They didn't have to pay me. I'd have paid them to let me play. Listen, the truth is it was more than fun. It was heaven."

Rich Gossage

Gossage, Richard Michael **P**
1972–89, 1991–94 B:7/5/1951, Colorado Springs, CO
Deb:4/16/1972, CHI AL BR/TR 6'3", 217

W	L	PCT	G	SV	IP	BB	SO	ERA
124	107	.537	1002	310	1809[1]	732	1502	3.01

In Rich Gossage's heyday, the big, mustachioed righthander glowered at the hitters, then blew his fastball right by them. "Goose" didn't have a whole lot more than heat and intimidation, but for an inning or two he threw the hottest heat and was the most intimidating pitcher in baseball.

He led the American League in saves with the fifth-place Chicago White Sox in 1975. The next year, desperate for starters, the Sox put him into the rotation. He struggled to a 9–17 record and was traded to Pittsburgh. Returned to his natural habitat, the bullpen, he saved 26, won 11, and set a National League record for relievers with 151 strikeouts.

In 1978 Goose signed with the New York Yankees as a free agent. He displaced reigning American League Cy Young winner Sparky Lyle as the top closer on the team—and in the league. Gossage led the circuit with 27 saves and won 10 as New York caught Boston late in the season. The Yanks then won the AL East in a one-game playoff that Gossage saved.

Gossage spent six seasons in New York, earning a reputation as one of the top relievers in the game. He had a small but notable role in the "Bronx Zoo" clubhouse of the late 1970s, breaking his thumb in a scuffle with teammate Cliff Johnson in 1979. The loss of Gossage in the middle of the season put an end to the Yankees' hopes for a fourth straight pennant.

He returned the following year to lead the AL in saves, but his most memorable moment from the 1980 season was surrendering a mammoth home run to George Brett that resulted in Kansas City's sweep of the Yankees in the American League Championship Series. Gossage also allowed Brett's famous "Pine Tar" home run in 1983. Manager Billy Martin argued that Brett had too much pine tar on the bat. The umpires agreed and called Brett out to end the game. Gossage went from taking the loss to getting the save—though the loss was eventually returned to his record when AL president Lee MacPhail overruled the umps.

Gossage's 151 saves as a Yankee were the most in club history when he left the team following the 1983 season. Dave Righetti later surpassed that mark.

Gossage moved on to San Diego as a free agent in 1984, and helped the Padres to their first pennant. The following year he made the All-Star team for the ninth time in 14 years. He later moved into a setup role and logged time in the bullpens of six different teams from 1988 to 1994. Gossage pitched until he was 43, appearing in more than 1,000 games. He finished his career with 310 career saves. His 115 wins as a reliever ranked third on the all-time list behind Hoyt Wilhelm and Lindy McDaniel.

Curt Gowdy

Broadcaster B:July 31, 1919, Green River, WY

"Cowboy Curt" Gowdy rode a rich, clear, friendly voice to fame in broadcasting, charming baseball, football and basketball fans alike with his graceful and astute commentary. Best known as the "Voice of the Boston Red Sox" for 15 years, the Wyoming native called some of the signature moments in baseball history: Ted Williams' home run in his last at bat for Boston, Mickey Mantle's 10th-inning blast that won Game 3 of the 1964 World Series, Hank Aaron's 715th home run to break the Babe's record, and Game 6 of the 1975 World Series between the Cincinnati Reds and the Red Sox, arguably the greatest game in Fall Classic annals.

Gowdy graduated from the University of Wyoming in 1938, having lettered in baseball and basketball. His got his first major break in broadcasting in 1948, when Russ Hodges left the New York Yankees' booth for the Polo Grounds across the Harlem River. Gowdy pulled up stakes from Oklahoma City, where he was calling games for the Oklahoma Indians of the Texas League, and joined the voice of the Yankees, Mel Allen. "Allen showed me, by example, how bad I was in comparison at baseball," said Gowdy. "Under him, I found out quickly how far from a hot shot I was. Timing, organization, reading a commercial—I had so many bad habits, but Mel's polish helped me to learn. He had that wonderful attention to detail and he knew how to weave in the commercial naturally, which was done all the time back then."

His baseball apprenticeship under Allen led to another opportunity. "I wanted to be some club's top announcer," Gowdy recalled, "and I knew Mel would be at Yankee Stadium forever." Though he had a year left in his contract with New York, the Yankees let Gowdy go to Boston, where he wound up doing play-by-play on the 50-outlet network of WHDH from 1951 through 1965. Gowdy became an institution among the Red Sox faithful, his voice carrying over six New England states. Before long, his TV work drew praise from another legend. "In my measured opinion," Red Barber wrote, "the greatest TV sports announcer is Curt Gowdy. He has amazing versatility and authority and knows his business."

In 1966 Gowdy got the assignment from NBC for the network's new *Game of the Week*, working with, among others, Pee Wee Reese, Sandy Koufax, Maury Wills, Mickey Mantle, and Joe Garagiola before settling in with Tony Kubek. From 1966 through 1975 he seemed to be everywhere. He did play-by-play for every All-Star Game, every World Series game, and most every regular season network game.

The final ledger shows that Gowdy did 12 World Series and 15 All-Star Games, more than even his mentor Mel Allen. He also presided over seven Super Bowls, seven Olympic games, 12 NCAA basketball championships, 13 Rose Bowls, and an assortment of Sugar, Cotton, and Orange bowls. Add to that 20 years of his Emmy award-winning TV show, *The American Sportsman.* His greatest thrill, however, according to a 1999 article in the *Palm Beach Post,* was reciting "Casey at the Bat" with the Boston Pops at Tanglewood in 1988.

"He concentrated on the game and never confused his own importance with that of the event he was covering," said Hall of Fame president Ed Stack, upon announcing Gowdy as recipient of the Ford Frick Award in 1984. "He was always interesting, yet restrained; smooth and calm, yet newsy and knowledgeable." Ironically, Gowdy's omnipresence and versatility may have contributed to his being dropped by NBC in 1975 and two years later by CBS. But chronic pain resulting from trigeminal neuralgia, a nerve malfunction in the jaw, was the deciding factor in making him give up live broadcasting in the late 1980s.

Hank Gowdy

Gowdy, Henry Morgan **C–1B**
1910–17, 1919–25, 1929–30 M(1946, 3–1)
B:8/24/1889, Columbus, OH D:8/1/1966, Columbus, OH
Deb:9/13/1910, NY NL BR/TR 6'2", 182

G	AB	R	H	HR	RBI	OBP	SLG	AVG
1050	2735	270	738	21	322	.351	.358	.270

Hank Gowdy was one of the better catchers of the first half of the 20th century. He finished 10th in Hall of Fame balloting for 1955 and 1956; every player who finished above him in those years was later enshrined.

Gowdy came to the majors in 1910 with the New York Giants but was traded to Boston the next year. He did not become a regular until 1914, when he batted .243 for the "Miracle Braves." Always a better defensive catcher than a batter, Gowdy nonetheless was a hitting star in Boston's shocking 1914 World Series sweep of the Philadelphia Athletics, when he batted .545 with one home run and three RBIs.

The first major league player to enlist during World War I, Gowdy missed the 1918 season while fighting in France. When he returned, he was platooned at catcher, During the 1923 season, Gowdy was traded back to New York, and he helped the Giants win pennants in that year and the next. He was the goat of the 1924 World Series against Washington. In the 12th inning of Game 7, he stepped on his mask while pursuing a foul popup hit by Senators catcher Muddy Ruel. The ball dropped safely. Given a second chance, Ruel doubled and eventually came around to score the winning run.

Gowdy was a backup catcher in 1925. After three years out of the majors, he played for the Braves in 1929 and 1930.

Mark Grace

Grace, Mark Eugene **1B**

1988–* B:6/28/1964, Winston-Salem, NC Deb:5/2/1988, CHI NL BL/TL 6'2", 190

G	AB	R	H	HR	RBI	OBP	SLG	AVG
1767	6646	982	2058	137	922	.390	.447	.310

Mark Grace pummeled National League pitching for 1,854 hits and 364 doubles in the 1990s, totals topping those of any other player in either league for the decade. Moreover, he achieved something that eluded such Cubs as Ernie Banks, Billy Williams, and Ron Santo in all their years with Chicago: playing in the playoffs in October.

Grace made the most of his first postseason opportunity. In the 1989 National League Championship Series against the Giants, his .647 batting average—including a homer his first time up—has become the stuff of legend in Wrigley Field. Grace had six singles, five extra-base hits and eight RBIs, but the Cubs lost to the Giants in five games. He cooled off considerably in the 1998 Division Series against the Braves, managing only one hit in 12 trips to the plate as the Cubs were swept by the Braves.

Although not a home run hitter, Grace has averaged 34 doubles a year; his high was a league-leading 51 in 1995, the most in the NL since Pete Rose had the same total in 1978. Grace goes against the grain, a lefthanded hitter who hits both righties and southpaws with equal zest. His .331 average in 1996 was the highest by a Cub in 20 years, and he has been especially productive in the friendly confines of Wrigley Field, as demonstrated by his .330 batting average at home in 1999.

Grace has earned the sobriquet of "Amazing" for his dexterity with a glove around first base, a skill that fetches comparisons to Keith Hernandez, an 11-time Gold Glove winner with the Cardinals and Mets. "He's all business," Hernandez said of Grace. "He doesn't do anything fancy, but any ball he gets to, he handles flawlessly."

Grace picked up his third Gold Glove in 1995 with a .995 fielding percentage. He also won the award in 1992 and 1993. On three occasions he has led the league in assists and total chances. His 180 assists in 1990 set an NL record.

Had Grace gone after the first offer that came his way, he might have been the slickest-fielding first baseman in the American League. The Twins drafted Grace in the 15th round of the free agent draft in 1984, but he didn't sign and remained at San Diego State University. The Cubs came calling a year later and picked him in the 24th round of the 1985 draft.

Grace led the Midwest League in hitting during his first professional season and topped the Eastern League with 101 RBIs in his second. He only appeared in 24 games at Triple A in 1988 before the Cubs called him up for good. Grace hit .296 in 134 games that year and finished second to the Reds' Chris Sabo in the Rookie of the Year voting.

Grace considered moving crosstown to the White Sox in 1995, but was wooed back to the North Side when he saw that the Cubs were committed to contend for the postseason. In 1999, with the Cubs out of the running, he did some radio color commentary for the NL Division Series between Atlanta and Houston.

Jack Graney

Graney, John Gladstone **OF**

1908, 1910–22 B:6/10/1886, St. Thomas, Ontario, Canada D:4/20/1978, Louisiana, MO Deb:4/30/1908, CLE AL BL/TL 5'9", 180

G	AB	R	H	HR	RBI	OBP	SLG	AVG
1402	4705	706	1178	18	420	.354	.342	.250

Jack Graney wasn't the biggest or fastest or best player, but in a number of areas he was the first. In 1914 he was the first man to bat, hit, and score against rookie Red Sox pitcher Babe Ruth. Two years later he was the first player to wear a uniform number, a small insignia attached to his sleeve. He was also the first former ballplayer to become a broadcaster. And, because of his lifelong connection with Cleveland baseball, he was the first ballplayer to have a Society for American Baseball Research regional organization named after him.

In 1908 Graney showed up at Cleveland's spring camp in Macon, Georgia, convinced he was a pitcher. Facing the legendary Nap Lajoie, who was also the team's manager, Graney decided to prove he could be tough. He hit Lajoie with his first pitch. Shortly thereafter he received a note from the skipper: "All wild men belong in the wild west. So you're going to Portland, Oregon."

Graney became an outfielder in the minors, returning to Cleveland in 1910 as a leadoff hitter who offset limited batting skills by working pitchers for bases on balls. His propensity for not swinging earned him the nickname "Three-and-Two Jack."

Graney improved considerably his second year, batting .269, but then he had a miserable year in 1912. In Chicago, pitcher Bill Dinneen stepped on his stomach. He got ptomaine poisoning in Boston, and in Detroit he broke his right collarbone while catching a line drive. Graney decided he needed a good luck charm for the 1913 season, so he brought a bull terrier named "Tige" to spring training that year. Within days, the team had adopted the playful pup and rechristened it "Larry." It would be the team's mascot for the next five years.

Perhaps Graney's best year was 1916. That season he hit only .241, but he led the American League with 41 doubles and established personal career highs in runs, hits, triples, and home runs.

Graney was a close friend and roommate of second baseman Ray Chapman. The two sang together in a group made up of Cleveland players called "the Quartette." When Chapman was fatally injured by a Carl Mays pitch in 1920, Graney helped his injured friend off the field and then continued to play in a daze.

The year Chapman lost his life Graney lost his job as the regular left fielder. The younger and harder-hitting Charlie Jamieson was ready to step into Graney's spot in the lineup when tonsillitis knocked Graney out. Jamieson replaced him for good on Memorial Day. Graney had only three at bats in Cleveland's 1920 World Series victory over Brooklyn.

Graney batted only 167 times during the next two years before leaving baseball. He stayed in Cleveland and sold cars, but when Ford closed down for a year to retool the Model T into the Model A, Graney was out of work. He lived on his stock market investments until the crash of 1929 all but wiped him out.

Stuck for a radio announcer in 1932, the Indians asked Graney to try out, and he became an immediate success. His enthusiastic style, clear voice, and logical sentences made him a favorite, even when he was forced to re-create the games from ticker-tape reports. Jimmy Dudley, Graney's sixth and last partner in 25 years behind the mike, said that Graney had "an extremely high-pitched voice which generated more excitement than anyone else's." The former major leaguer's final broadcasting job was calling the Giants' 1954 World Series sweep of the Indians.

Charlie Grant

Grant, Charles **2B**

Negro League Player (1896–1916) B:1879, Cincinnati, OH D:7/1932, Chicago, IL BR/TR 5'8", 160

In 1901, Organized Baseball had been segregated for more than a decade. But John McGraw and Charlie Grant were at the heart of a scheme to circumvent the color line barrier. It didn't work, and Grant continued on for many years in the Negro Leagues.

Grant, the son of a horse trainer, had first played as a pro in 1896 for the Page Fence Giants. In 1899 and 1900 he had been with the Chicago-area Columbia Giants. Then, in March 1901, while McGraw's Baltimore Orioles were in spring training in Hot Springs, Arkansas, McGraw saw Grant, a bellboy at the Eastland Hotel, playing second base. McGraw liked what he saw. To avoid the color line issue, he decided to claim the light-skinned Grant was Cherokee, since Native Americans were not prohibited from playing on teams with white players. McGraw allegedly took the name of a creek from a map and dubbed Grant "Charlie Tokohama."

The scheme quickly unraveled. A black team was in town for an exhibition, and to celebrate, the club presented Grant with an alligator bag and cheered him on by calling out, "Our boy, Charlie Grant." When White Sox owner Charles Comiskey got wind of this, he recognized Grant as the Columbia Giants' second baseman. McGraw was forced to end the charade.

Grant later played with the Cuban X Giants, who won the unofficial championship of black baseball in 1903, and the Philadelphia Giants, who won the same championship in 1904. He went on to play with the New York Black Sox and the Lincoln Giants. He retired in 1916.

In July 1932 Grant was on the sidewalk of the Chicago apartment building where he worked as a janitor when a passing car blew a tire. The car spun out of control, jumped the curb, and struck and killed him. He is buried in Cincinnati's Spring Grove Cemetery near the grave of another second baseman, Miller Huggins.

Eddie Grant

Grant, Edward Leslie **3B–SS**

1905, 1907–15 B:5/21/1883, Franklin, MA D:10/5/1918, Argonne Forest, France Deb:8/4/1905, CLE AL BL/TR 5'11½", 168

G	AB	R	H	HR	RBI	OBP	SLG	AVG
990	3385	399	844	5	277	.300	.295	.249

"Harvard Eddie" Grant owns the sad distinction of being the only major leaguer killed in World War I. Grant graduated from Harvard in 1905 and played two games at season's end for Cleveland, getting three hits in the first one.

He spent 1906 with Jersey City of the Eastern League and returned to the majors with the Philadelphia Phillies in 1907 as a utility infielder. He became the regular third baseman and leadoff hitter the next year, batting .244 and leading the league in errors and double plays. After hitting .269 and .268 the next two seasons, he was traded to the Reds and hit only .223 in 1911, his last season as a regular. Traded to the Giants in the middle of the next season, he stayed with them through the 1915 season before retiring and becoming a lawyer.

When the United States entered World War I in 1917, Grant was among the first to enlist. He served as a captain with the 77th Infantry Division and, after all the superior officers in his regiment had been killed or wounded, he led his troops at the Battle of the Meuse-Argonne. During a four-day search for the "Lost Battalion," he was killed by an exploding shell on October 5, 1918. The war ended 37 days later. The Giants later honored Grant with a plaque in center field at the Polo Grounds.

Frank Grant

Grant, Frank **2B-SS-P-OF**

Baseball Pioneer 1886–1905 B:8/1/1868, Pittsfield, MA D:5/27/1937, New York, NY BR/TR 5'7½", 155

Most experts agree that Frank Grant, a superb fielder and a powerful hitter, was the greatest black player of the 19th century. He was the only black player to play three consecutive seasons with the same team in a white minor league, with Buffalo from 1886 to 1888.

Pioneer black baseball historian Sol White, a contemporary of Grant's, said of the second baseman-outfielder, "In hitting he ranked with the best, and his fielding bordered on the impossible." He was called "the Black Dunlap," a reference to Fred Dunlap, whom Albert Spink called the greatest second baseman who ever lived. A Buffalo writer said that Grant was the best player of any race ever to play in that city, ranking him ahead of Jim Galvin, Dan Brouthers, Jim O'Rourke, and Hoss Radbourn, all Hall of Famers.

Grant faced the most vicious racial bigotry, with beanballs hurled at him as often as racial slurs. He had to create a crude shin guard to wear as protection against the opposition's spikes, and he was finally moved to the outfield in 1888 for his own safety. But the malice didn't deter him: in his three Buffalo seasons he batted .344, .353, and .346 and slugged over .520 each year. Unfortunately racism got the upper hand and, by 1889, the International League effectively banned black players.

Grant played in 1889 for the Cuban Giants, the era's dominant black team, then returned to the minor leagues in 1890, beginning the season with Harrisburg of the Eastern League. When the team jumped to the Atlantic Association, it was on condition that they could bring Grant with them. A court battle over the rights to his contract delayed his appearance, but he finally came to town, and *The Harrisburg Patriot* reported, "Everyone was anxious to see him come, and there was a general stretch of necks toward the new bridge, all being eager to get a sight of the most famous colored ball player in the business."

Grant played for barnstorming black teams in the 1890s. His final two seasons, 1902 and 1903, were spent with the Philadelphia Giants.

Mudcat Grant

Grant, James Timothy **P**

1958–71 B:8/13/1935, Lacoochee, FL Deb:4/17/1958, CLE AL BR/TR 6'1", 186

W	L	PCT	G	SV	IP	BB	SO	ERA
145	119	.549	571	53	2441²	849	1267	3.63

Jim "Mudcat" Grant enjoyed a long and productive career as a righthanded pitcher for six major league teams. He had many solid years, but 1965 was his year to remember, a year in which he earned the undying affection of all Twins fans.

Florida-born Grant was nicknamed by a minor league teammate in 1954 who mistakenly thought he was from Mississippi, which is sometimes referred to as the "Mudcat State." The name followed him through his entire major league career, which began in 1958 as a part-time starter for the Cleveland Indians. In six-plus years in Cleveland, Grant compiled very average numbers, with his best year 1961, when he went 15–9 with a 3.86 ERA. Two years later he was selected to his first All-Star Game, although a weak finish saw his final record at 13–14.

In 1964 Grant was traded to Minnesota for pitcher Lee Stange and outfielder George Banks. He went 11–9 for the Twins that year, but he really turned it on the following season. In 1965 Grant led the American League with 21 victories and a .750 winning percentage, as well as with six shutouts. His pitching helped Minnesota to a franchise-record 102 wins and the AL pennant.

Grant opened the 1965 World Series with an 8–2 win over Don Drysdale and the Los Angeles Dodgers. Drysdale returned the favor in Game 4, but Grant bounced back on two day's rest to beat the Dodgers in do-or-die Game 6. Grant helped his own cause by hitting a three-run homer while allowing only six hits. Sandy Koufax blanked the Twins the next day to win the world championship.

After a 13–13 season in 1966, he was moved into a long relief role with the Twins, and in late 1967 he was traded to the Dodgers. For the remainder of his career Grant was primarily a reliever—and a well-traveled one at that. He pitched for both the Expos and Cardinals in 1969, compiling an 8–11 record with seven saves.

Sold to Oakland for the 1970 season, he saved 24 games for the A's before being traded again, this time to the Pittsburgh Pirates for outfielder Angel Mangual in September. The 1971 season, in which he traded back to the A's, was his final one. After his retirement, Grant performed as the lead singer in a band called "Mudcat and the Kittens."

George Grantham

Grantham, George Farley **2B-1B**
1922–34 B:5/20/1900, Galena, KS D:3/16/1954, Kingman, AZ Deb:9/20/1922, CHI NL BL/TR 5'10", 170

G	AB	R	H	HR	RBI	OBP	SLG	AVG
1444	4989	912	1508	105	712	.392	.461	.302

It is lucky for George Grantham that he could hit. The sometimes first baseman, sometimes second baseman had eight consecutive seasons batting over .300. But his fielding was some of the worst seen in the major leagues.

Grantham picked up the nickname "Boots" as a Cubs rookie in 1923. That year he committed 55 errors, 25 more than any other second baseman in the National League, and finished last in fielding. Although he hit .281 that year, he also led the league with 92 strikeouts.

The next year Grantham's batting average rose to .316, but he again led the league in strikeouts, with 63, and in errors (48), while finishing last in fielding. After the season, he went to the Pirates in a six-player deal and moved to first base. As Pittsburgh rolled to the pennant, Grantham hit a career-high .326. But two years later when the Pirates had the not-so-bright idea of returning him to second base, he finished seventh in fielding at his position, although he hit .305 for another pennant winner.

The story continued for the next several years. As a first baseman in 1928 he finished last in fielding, but he hit .323 with 85 RBIs. He had his best offensive year in 1930 when he batted .324 with career-bests in home runs (18) and RBIs (99), but he again led NL second basemen with 35 errors.

Grantham was sold to the Cincinnati Reds in 1931 and spent two years with them before one final season with the Giants in 1934.

Pete Gray

Gray, Peter J. **OF**
1945 B:3/6/1915, Nanticoke, PA Deb:4/17/1945, STL AL BL/TL 6'1", 169

G	AB	R	H	HR	RBI	OBP	SLG	AVG
77	234	26	51	0	13	.259	.261	.218

In 1945, with the wartime player shortage at its height, Pete Gray became the major league's only one-armed outfielder. Gray had lost his right arm after falling off a moving wagon at age 6. Determined to play professional baseball anyway, Gray taught himself to bat lefthanded and dropped out of high school to pursue his dream.

A shoemaker made him a special glove. Gray explained, "He'd take out most of the padding, and I'd use it like a first baseman's glove, keeping my pinky inside. It helped me get rid of the glove quicker. I'd catch the ball, stick the glove under my stump, roll the ball across my chest, and throw it back in. No big deal. It was just grounders that gave me some trouble."

Gray was only 15 years old when he watched Game 3 of the 1932 World Series at Wrigley Field in Chicago. That day Gray witnessed Babe Ruth's famous "called shot" home run against Charlie Root. It inspired the teenager. He later said, "That was an important turning point. I realized that if I was sure I would do it, I would do it."

He played for two years with the semipro Bushwicks of Brooklyn and in 1942 moved to Trois Rivieres, Quebec, which had been admitted to the Class C Canadian–American League. "They signed me by telephone," said Gray. "When I got up to Montreal, the manager met my train. I had a coat draped over my stump, and when I took it off, the guy almost passed out. But he figured I already had a contract and he might as well give me a chance."

Gray's first pro game went like a Hollywood movie. With two out in the bottom of the ninth, he delivered a game-winning hit. "The next thing I remember, everyone was throwing money at me. By the time I finished stooping, I'd collected over $700. I figured this game was made for me." Gray broke his collarbone early in the season but came back to hit .381 in 42 games. In 160 at bats he struck out only three times and was nicknamed "the Wonder Boy."

A 1943 tryout with Toronto of the International League ended when Gray didn't get along with manager Burleigh Grimes. He joined the Southern Association's Memphis Chicks, where he hit .299, fielded 1.000, and began attracting national attention. In 1944 he hit .333, stole 63 bases to tie a league record, and was named the league's Most Valuable Player.

The Browns bought him for $20,000, but St. Louis manager Luke Sewell was skeptical. "Gray is just another player to me. He has to stand on what he has." Gray, however, hit well in spring training and went north with the club. Sewell started him in left field on Opening Day and batted him second, but he still wasn't convinced. "When I got him, I knew he couldn't make it," Sewell contended years later. "He didn't belong in the majors, and he knew he was being exploited."

Gray fanned only 11 times in 234 American League at bats but hit only .218 for the season. In the book *Even the Browns*, St. Louis third baseman Mark Christman wrote, "He cost us the pennant in 1945. We finished third, only six games out." Christman contended that hitters singling to center "could keep on going and wind up at second base. I know that cost us eight or ten ballgames."

That was Gray's only big league season. The following year, other ballplayers were returning from the war, and Gray was optioned to the American Association. "I figured they were going to send me to Toledo, and that's the way it worked out," he said. "All I wanted to do was play one game in the big leagues, and that was it."

With the Mud Hens in 1946, Gray hit .250 in 48 games. In 1947 he voluntarily retired but returned the following year to Elmira of the Eastern League, a pitcher's league. Elmira hit only .236 as a team, but Gray batted .290. In 1949 he moved to the Texas League's Dallas Eagles, slumped to .214, and retired from baseball.

Dallas Green

Green, George Dallas **P**

1960–67 M(1979–81, 1989, 1993–96, 454–478)
B:8/4/1934, Newport, DE Deb:6/18/1960, PHI NL
BL/TR 6'5", 210

W	L	PCT	G	SV	IP	BB	SO	ERA
20	22	.476	185	4	562¹	197	268	4.26

Dallas Green was not a man to try to push around. The 6-foot 5-inch, 210-pound Green was known for his nasty temperament when he pitched for three big league clubs in the 1960s. After his playing career ended, he took his temper into the clubhouse. Green managed a full 162-game schedule just once—baseball strikes and midseason changes occurred in his seven other seasons as a skipper—and that 1980 campaign produced Philadelphia's first world championship in 97 seasons in the National League.

Green pitched six years for the Phillies, despite arm problems. His most memorable episode as a player occurred when he gave up Jimmy Piersall's 100th career homer in 1963, and the eccentric Piersall circled the bases backwards. The 28-year-old pitcher glowered at Piersall as he made his reverse circuit of the bases.

When Green retired as a player, he managed in the Phillies' organization and worked in their front office. He became their manager with 30 games remaining in the 1979 season, and the following year led them to their first World Series appearance in 30 years.

The obstreperous Green seemed to be what the Phillies needed. Philadelphia beat out Montreal by one game for the division title, then outlasted the Astros in a tight five-game Championship Series. The Phillies came from behind to beat the Royals three times in the World Series, and Tug McGraw pitched out of two bases-loaded jams in Game 6 to give the franchise its first world championship.

The Phillies responded with a first-place finish in the first half of the 1981 strike season, although they lost to Montreal in the East Division Series. Disappointed with himself, Green quit after the season.

The Cubs immediately hired him as their general manager, and he wisely picked up talent he knew from the Phillies—most notably Ryne Sandberg—to help Chicago to its first postseason appearance since 1945. He was instrumental in developing the young talent that won for the Cubs again in 1989, even though he had left two years earlier.

George Steinbrenner hired Green to manage his Yankees in 1989, but the two strong personalities didn't mesh. Green was dumped late in the season for griping about the owner's meddling. The Mets, beset by bad play, brought Green aboard to manage in 1993, but he wasn't able to make a difference as New York lost 103 games. Although the Mets showed some improvement the next two seasons, he never posted a winning record with the club. He was fired late in the 1996 season. He retired to his farm in Pennsylvania, where he served as an advisor to the Phillies.

Dick Green

Green, Richard Larry **2B**

1963–74 B:4/21/1941, Sioux City, IA Deb:9/9/1963, KC AL BR/TR 5'10", 180

G	AB	R	H	HR	RBI	OBP	SLG	AVG
1288	4007	427	960	80	422	.305	.347	.240

When the Oakland A's won their third straight World Series in 1974, the Series Most Valuable Player was Rollie Fingers, who had a win and three saves. But there were some people who thought that Dick Green, the A's second baseman, was equally deserving. He put on a brilliant defensive exhibition throughout the five-game Series even though he went 0-for-13 at the plate. "If he'd got one hit," Catfish Hunter said, "he would've been the MVP. A lot of people told me that."

Green signed with the Kansas City A's after attending Black Hills State College in Spearfish, South Dakota. After a four-year apprenticeship in the minors, he took over as the A's second baseman in 1964. In his first season in the majors he hit .264 with 11 homers, and committed only six errors while fielding a brilliant .990.

The next year Green hit 15 homers, but his average fell to .232 and he struck out 110 times. The A's soon tired of his strikeouts—he fanned once every 5.1 times at bat in his career—and started platooning him with John Donaldson. After two seasons of sharing duty, Green reclaimed the job in 1969, the team's second season in Oakland. That year he hit a career-high .275, collected 64 RBIs, and led AL second basemen in fielding. However, the next year his batting collapsed to a nightmarish .190.

Green played only 26 games in 1972 as a herniated disk kept him on the disabled list most of the season, but when the World Series started he was ready. Back problems made him a semiregular the next two seasons, but, again, when October rolled around, his defense made him an everyday player.

The 1974 World Series was all about defense and pitching—only 27 runs were scored in the five games—and Green made one brilliant play after another against the Dodgers. He set a World Series record for five games by participating in six double plays, including three in the pivotal Game 3.

Green was 33 years old, and his back wasn't going to get any better. He decided—correctly—that Oakland's finest days were over once Hunter turned free agent after Charlie Finley breached his contract. So Green asked Finley for a $20,000 raise he knew he wouldn't get and retired when Finley turned him down. Green headed home to South Dakota and went into the moving van business with his father in Rapid City.

Hank Greenberg

Greenberg, Henry Benjamin **1B–OF**

1930, 1933–41, 1945–47 B:1/1/1911, New York, NY D:9/4/1986, Beverly Hills, CA Deb:9/14/1930, DET AL BR/TR 6'3½", 210

G	AB	R	H	HR	RBI	OBP	SLG	AVG
1394	5193	1051	1628	331	1276	.412	.605	.313

"Hammerin' Hank" Greenberg is remembered as the classic slugger—big, strong, and powerful. His lifetime rate of .92 RBIs per game is matched only by Lou Gehrig and Sam Crawford, and his career slugging percentage of .605 is the fifth highest of all time. When he retired in 1947, his 331 homers were the fifth-best total in major league history.

Yet Greenberg's career numbers could have been even better had he not missed four and a half seasons in the armed services. The second baseball player to join the military during World War II (Hugh Mulcahy was the first), Greenberg received his discharge on December 5, 1941. Two days later the Japanese attacked Pearl Harbor, and he reenlisted.

Greenberg was 30 years old when he entered the military. He had just led the American League with 50 doubles, 41 homers, 150 RBIs, and a .670 slugging percentage. When he returned in 1945 he was not the same player. Historian Bill James projects that if Greenberg hadn't lost so much time to the war and to injuries and had he not retired early, he easily could have hit more than 600 home runs.

Born to Rumanian Jewish immigrants, Greenberg developed quickly. By age 13 he was 6 feet 3 inches tall. Three years later he had muscled up to 200 pounds. But he was no natural athlete; with flat feet and a poor complexion, the oversized youngster didn't look like a future sports star. But according to his high school coach, Greenberg's fear of looking foolish drove him to practice constantly. Hard work became the center of his athletic philosophy, and by his senior year he had led his baseball, basketball, and soccer teams to city championships.

Giants manager John McGraw had his eyes out for a Jewish player to entice New York's large Jewish community to the ballpark. But his scouts saw Greenberg play high school baseball and reported that he was too clumsy. Greenberg graduated from high school and enrolled, at his parents' request, at New York University. The Yankees came after him, offering him $10,000 to sign.

In 1929 Yankee scout Paul Krichell took Greenberg to see his first major league game. The two sat in the dugout beforehand to watch warmups. Krichell pointed at Lou Gehrig, the 26-year-old superstar, and whispered to Greenberg, "He's all washed up. In a few years you'll be the Yankee first baseman." Greenberg took another look at Gehrig and turned down the club's offer. A similar scenario took place when the Senators offered Greenberg $12,000. They had Joe Judge entrenched at first base, and Greenberg declined again.

The Tigers offered him a $9,000 bonus, but they understood that the family wanted Greenberg to get his degree, so the bonus was set up to be $3,000 on signing, $6,000 more when he graduated. That pleased Greenberg's parents, but after one semester at NYU, he wanted to play baseball. He left college and joined the Tiger organization for the 1930 season.

In the minors Greenberg was always taking extra batting and fielding practice. "What else was there to do in most of those minor league towns anyway?" he later said. In his third minor league season Greenberg clubbed 39 homers and drove in 131 runs. His play at first base was consistently improving, too. The Tigers promoted him to the majors for the 1933 season, and by June he had replaced Harry Davis at first base.

In 1933 Greenberg hit 12 homers and 87 RBIs while batting .301, the first of eight consecutive times he hit better than .300. And that winter he had the first of his frequent contract squabbles. Having made $3,300 in 1932, he wanted a raise to $5,500. Tigers owner Frank Navin read him the riot act. "If you don't want to play for us you can just stay home. I told Ty Cobb that he could stay home." Greenberg didn't budge. No further negotiating took place until February, when Navin called and gave Greenberg another earful.

However, at the end of the conversation, the owner said, "I'll give you $5,000, and if we finish one-two-three, I'll give you the $500 as a bonus."

The likelihood of the Tigers, a perennial fifth-place team, making the top three in the league was slim, but Greenberg signed. Detroit hired catcher Mickey Cochrane as its player-manager, and the Tigers finished first for the first time since 1909.

That 1934 Tigers team was a powerful crew, featuring four future Hall of Famers—Cochrane, Greenberg, second baseman Charlie Gehringer, and outfielder Goose Goslin. Greenberg batted .339, drove in 139 runs, and had 26 homers and 63 doubles, the fourth most doubles in history. But the St. Louis Gas House Gang toppled the Tigers in a crazy, seven-game World Series. Greenberg hit .321 in the Series but fanned nine times.

In 1935 the Tigers returned to the World Series as Greenberg was chosen AL Most Valuable Player. He led the league with 36 homers and 170 RBIs, while finishing second in doubles, third in triples and runs, an fourth in hits. In Game 2 of that year's Series against the Cubs, a pitch by Fabian Kowalik broke Greenberg's wrist. He stayed in the game and even tried to score from first on a two-out single the same inning. But on the train trip to Chicago that night the swollen wrist signaled the end of the Series for Greenberg; Detroit won in six.

As he was throughout his early playing days, Greenberg was subjected to ethnic taunts by the Cubs because he was Jewish. He never retaliated, claiming that the slurs only motivated him to play better.

Greenberg started the 1936 season on fire. He had a remarkable total of 16 RBIs by April 17, but a collision at first base with Washington outfielder Jake Powell broke the same wrist again, and his season was over. But he returned with a vengeances the next year. Along with 49 doubles, 40 homers, and a .337 average, Greenberg knocked home 183 runs, only one off Gehrig's all-time AL record.

The next year it was Babe Ruth's record that he fell just short of, as he equaled Jimmie Foxx's record for homers by a righthanded batter, with 58, with five games to go in the season. He needed two to tie Ruth's record, and he had already set the major league record with 11 multiple-homer games. But Greenberg wouldn't hit another. The last game of the season was called after six innings because of darkness.

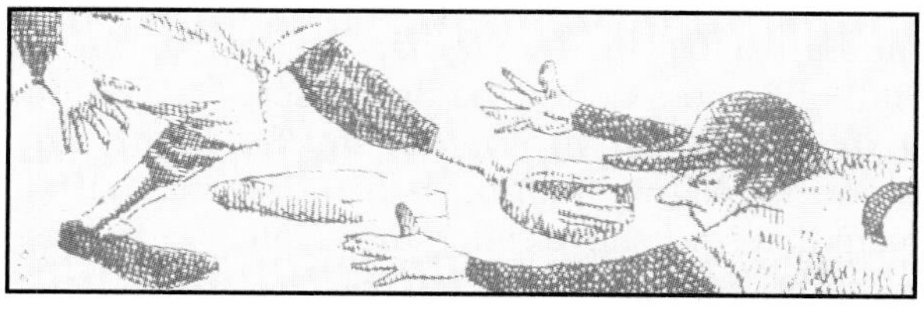

In 1939 Detroit slipped to fifth despite Greenberg's 33 homers. But the next season saw two important changes. First the Tigers' front office asked Greenberg to take a $5,000 cut from his $40,000 salary. Management really wanted Greenberg to move to the outfield in order to open a spot for the lively bat but glum glove of Rudy York. The Tigers offered a $35,000 salary and a $5,000 bonus if Greenberg changed his position. Greenberg didn't like the idea. He had worked hard to become a major league first baseman. He had led his position in putouts and assists twice and in fielding percentage once.

Greenberg gave the matter careful consideration and returned a counterproposal. "I want the same salary as last year. But if you want me to go to the outfield, I'll buy a fielder's glove and go down to spring training and work my tail off and give you all spring to make up your mind what you want to do. I won't even put on a first baseman's mitt. I'll practice in the outfield as hard as I can. Then on opening day, if you want me to stay in the outfield, you have to give me a $10,000 bonus. I'm taking all the risk in this experiment. I have the most to lose, so I deserve some compensation for it." He got his wish, his $10,000, and the Tigers again took the pennant.

In the second significant development that season, manager Del Baker began to use his sign-stealing skills to help Greenberg and York. From the third base coaching box he could tell from a pitcher's motion what was coming, and he let the batters know. Greenberg loved it. He had his best season ever and led the AL with 50 doubles, 41 homers, 150 RBIs, and a .670 slugging percentage—and won his second MVP Award.

"I was the greatest hitter in the world when I knew what was coming," he said later. However, as the season wore on and the Tigers kept winning, Greenberg recalled, "Baker started taking credit for the hitting. If he called a pitch correctly and I hit a home run he thought it was his home run. There's a big difference between knowing what's coming and hitting it." Late in the season the Tigers enhanced their sign-stealing by stationing a player or a coach in the upper deck with binoculars to spot the catcher's signals.

The Tigers squeezed by both the Indians and Yankees to recapture the AL pennant, and they met Cincinnati in the World Series. Greenberg batted .357 and drove in six runs, but the Tigers' 3–2 Series lead evaporated when Bucky Walters shut them out in Game 6. Then Paul Derringer outpitched Bobo Newsom for a 2–1 Reds win in Game 7.

Nineteen games into the 1941 season Greenberg began a stint in the armed forces. He spent much of the war on active duty in India and China, unlike some ballplayers who spent their service years on military base ballclubs. He had barely swung a bat in more than four years when he returned to his team in front of nearly 50,000 delirious Detroit fans on July 1, 1945. He obligingly slugged a homer to lead the Tigers to a win.

On the final day of the 1945 season Greenberg delivered his most dramatic homer ever, a grand slam under darkening skies that gave Detroit a ninth-inning 6–3 win, clinching the pennant. He also homered to win Game 2 of the World Series against the Cubs, driving in seven runs in the seven games as the Tigers got revenge for their 1935 defeat to Chicago.

In 1946 Greenberg hit 44 home runs and drove in 127, both league-leading figures, but batted.277, becoming the first player to hit more than 40 homers without batting .300. The Tigers figured he wasn't worth the $20,000 raise he wanted (boosting his salary to $75,000), and put him on waivers. The Tigers didn't bother to notify Greenberg of their decision; he heard about it on the radio.

No AL team claimed him. The Pirates paid the Tigers $40,000 for Greenberg, but he refused to report to Pittsburgh. He wanted to retire. The Pirates wanted to create a wall-banging duo of Greenberg and young Ralph Kiner, and they seduced Greenberg by upping the ante to $100,000 and adding a race horse from Pittsburgh owner John Galbreath's stables worth thousands of dollars.

Management also volunteered to bring in the left-field fence by 35 feet, thereby creating the home run paradise known as "Greenberg Gardens"; to let him fly to games instead of taking the train; to let him live without a roommate; and to give him his unconditional release at the end of the season. It was an offer Greenberg couldn't refuse. The deal made him the first $100,000 National Leaguer. (It took 11 more years for Stan Musial to become the second.)

Hampered by back ailments, Greenberg wasn't an overwhelming offensive force for the Pirates. He homered 25 times, but batted only .249. His patience at the plate became an object lesson for the free-swinging Kiner, as Greenberg led the league with 104 walks. When the Pirates decided to return Kiner to the minors early in the season, Greenberg talked them out of it. Kiner responded by walking 25 more times, striking out 28 fewer times, and adding 28 home runs to his previous season's total. The Pirates tied for last place but set a club home attendance record with 1,283,611 fans. More than a million people came to see them on the road as well.

Greenberg did retire after the 1947 season, and the next year Cleveland's Bill Veeck hired him as farm director. In 1950 he was promoted to general manager. A major force in building the 1954 Cleveland pennant-winners, Greenberg also became part-owner of the team. He was elected to the Hall of Fame in 1956, and two years later he followed Veeck to the White Sox as a partner and vice president. In 1959 the Sox won their first pennant in 40 years. Greenberg had a chance to buy the team from Veeck in 1961 but declined.

In 1963 Greenberg left baseball for good and began amassing wealth through the investment business. He died in 1986. A long-planned documentary film on his career and influence on the public, *The Life and Times of Hank Greenberg*, was released in 1999.

Gus Greenlee

Greenlee, William Augustus

Negro League Team Owner (1931–38) B:1897 D:1952

Gus Greenlee was known as "Mr. Big" and "Big Red" in Pittsbugh's black culture, both for his 200-plus pound frame and his similarly large impact on sporting ventures like the Negro Leagues. Many historians, in fact, claim he may have been the chief person responsible for keeping black baseball alive during the Depression.

Greenlee performed a variety of jobs as a teenager, from shining shoes to driving a taxi cab. When he returned from service in World War I, he began running several nightclubs and a bootleg liquor operation. He later ran a numbers game and became a successful promoter of boxing matches. Greenlee gained most of his notoriety for his eventual involvement in another sport.

In 1931 an area sandlot team called the Pittsburgh Crawfords asked Greenlee to become their owner. In the past, the Crawfords had used mostly local amateur talent to fill out their roster, but that philosophy changed under Greenlee. The new owner began recruiting and paying the best available out-of-town talent. Greenlee also sought to raise the level of competition by forming the second Negro National League and by funding and renovating Greenlee Field, the Crawfords' home.

Greenlee declared his Crawfords champions of the league in 1933, although the Chicago American Giants disputed the title. There was no dispute in 1935. The Crawfords, anchored by future Hall of Famers Cool Papa Bell, Oscar Charleston, Josh Gibson, Judy Johnson, and Satchel Paige, won the league championship outright with a team that some have called the greatest in the history of the Negro Leagues.

Greenlee also played a large part in the league's success. In addition to owning the Negro National League's elite franchise, he served as league president for five seasons and helped create the popular East-West All-Star Game. After several of the Crawfords' top players left the team in 1937, lured to the tropics by Dominican Republic dictator Rafael Trujillo, Greenlee disbanded the franchise. He remained out of baseball until 1945, when he formed the USL, a rival black league that lasted for two seasons. He died in 1952 following a long illness.

Mike Greenwell

Greenwell, Michael Lewis **OF**

1985–96 B:7/18/1963, Louisville, KY Deb:9/5/1985, BOS AL BL/TR 6', 200

G	AB	R	H	HR	RBI	OBP	SLG	AVG
1269	4623	657	1400	130	726	.371	.463	.303

Mike Greenwell was the successor in a line of great left fielders in Red Sox history: Jim Rice, Carl Yastrzemski, and Ted Williams. Although Greenwell never played to the lofty level of his predecessors, he enjoyed a solid major league career and was a favorite of the Boston fans.

As a youngster, Greenwell emulated the swing of George Brett, whom he often watched during visits to spring training in Fort Myers, Florida. A few years later Greenwell returned to spring training as an unproven big league hopeful with the Red Sox. He apprenticed in Boston as a pinch hitter and late-inning replacement. Greenwell went 1-for-5 in the 1986 postseason against the Angels and Mets, then became Boston's regular left fielder the following spring.

He batted .328 in his first full major league season, and batted over .300 in three of the next five campaigns. In 1988 Greenwell reached career highs with 22 home runs and 119 RBIs, placing a distant second to Oakland's Jose Canseco in the Most Valuable Player voting. Greenwell played in the All-Star Game in both 1988 and 1989.

Although some predicted that he would reach the same heights of success enjoyed by Rice and Yaz, those forecasts proved overly optimistic. Although he played hard and well, Greenwell was more of a slashing, line-drive hitter than the slugger Boston had come to expect out of the left field position.

In 1996 Greenwell drove in all of Boston's runs in a 9–8 win, one of the few bright spots of an injury-scarred season. He refused to return to the Red Sox as a free agent, in part because of his dislike of general manager Dan Duquette. Greenwell signed a lucrative contract with the Hanshin Tigers, but he soon broke his foot, ending his Japanese career after seven games.

Rusty Greer

Greer, Thurman Clyde **OF**

1994–* B:1/21/1969, Fort Rucker, AL Deb:5/16/1994, TEX AL BL/TL 6', 190

G	AB	R	H	HR	RBI	OBP	SLG	AVG
809	2991	516	923	103	503	.397	.489	.309

Considered a marginal prospect coming out of Alabama's tiny University of Montevallo, Rusty Greer established himself as one of the game's more consistent hitters. The former 10th-round pick spent four years in the minors and burst upon the major league scene with the Texas Rangers in 1994. He posted a .314 average and finished third in American League Rookie of the Year voting. On July 28, 1994, he showed his flair for the dramatic by making a diving catch in the ninth inning to save Kenny Rogers' perfect game.

Greer also earned a reputation as one of the best clutch hitters in baseball. From 1995 through 1998, he had 37 game-winning RBI, and 13 times he drove in the winning run in his team's last at bat. Greer and teammate Ivan Rodriguez were the first Rangers to bat .300 for four consecutive years. Greer batted .300 or better in five of his first six seasons. His .309 batting average through 1999 was the second-best in club history.

Bobby Grich

Grich, Robert Anthony **2B–SS**

1970–86 B:1/15/1949, Muskegon, MI Deb:6/29/1970, BAL AL BR/TR 6'2", 190

G	AB	R	H	HR	RBI	OBP	SLG	AVG
2008	6890	1033	1833	224	864	.373	.424	.266

Until he hurt his back picking up an air conditioner, Bobby Grich was one of the best-fielding second basemen the game has ever seen. What made him even more special, however, was his bat. During his career he hit 224 homers, not a typical mark for Gold Glove second basemen. Grich's career didn't fall apart after he injured his back. He was still a fine fielder, and he could still pop the baseball. His greatness in the field, however, vanished forever.

Grich grew up in Southern California wanting to play for the Angels, the team he played for during the last 10 years of his career. His hero was infielder Jim Fregosi, who eventually became his manager in Anaheim. Instead the Orioles made Grich their top draft choice in the June 1967 amateur draft, signing him for $40,000. In 1971 *The Sporting News* named him Minor League Player of the Year after he batted .336, with 32 home runs, at Rochester.

After two brief stints with the Orioles, he came up to Baltimore fulltime in 1972. Putting in time at short, second, first, and third, he fielded well, hit .278, and drove in 50 runs. He showed enough potential that the Orioles traded Davey Johnson after the season and made Grich their regular second baseman.

Then followed four years of brilliance that would be hard to equal. Grich won four Gold Gloves and led the league in putouts, assists, double plays, and chances per game in 1973, 1974, and 1975. In 1973 he committed only five errors and set a major league record with a .995 fielding percentage. While Jose Oquendo of the St. Louis Cardinals subsequently topped that mark, Oquendo set it on an AstroTurf home field in a league filled with artificial surface infields. When Grich set his record, all 12 AL fields were grass, with far-less accommodating bounces.

During Grich's Gold Glove years he teamed with shortstop Mark Belanger to give the Orioles one of the greatest double play combinations the game has ever seen. At no time was their teamwork more important that in Baltimore's second-to-last game of the 1974 season, at which point the Orioles were one game ahead of the Yankees. The Orioles were clinging to a one-run lead in the bottom of the ninth, with the bases loaded, one out, and Detroit's Aurelio Rodriguez at bat. Rodriguez hit a one-hop bullet up the middle that could have been a game-winning single. In a play still remembered with more than a little disbelief, Grich came out of nowhere to make a diving stop and somehow flipped the ball to Belanger to start the game-ending double play.

Meanwhile, at the plate, Grich averaged 14 homers, 87 runs, and 98 walks a season. When free agency dawned after the 1976 season, Grich was one of the hottest commodities. His status gave him the chance to live out his boyhood fantasy. He signed a five-year contract with the Angels for $1.69 million as club owner Gene Autry, trying to buy a pennant, signed Joe Rudi and Don Baylor as well.

On Valentine's Day, 1977, however, Grich hurt his back trying to lift an air conditioner. He played only 52 games before undergoing surgery on July 1 for a herniated disk. When he struggled in 1978, hitting only six homers, he worried that it might be time to get out of baseball and pursue a career in college coaching or real estate.

However, he came back healthy in 1979 and had career highs with 30 homers, 101 RBIs, and 30 doubles as the Angels won their first division title. It was "a dream come true," Grich said, before the team fell to the Orioles in the American league Championship Series. Two years later, in the strike-shortened 1981 season, Grich hit a career best .304 and led the AL with 22 homers. The next year, in which Grich was selected for his sixth All-Star Game, his third as an Angel, the California club won the AL West a second time. The Angels even won the first two games of the ALCS against the Brewers before giving up three straight.

That loss was nothing compared to the heartbreak of the 1986 ALCS, however. In Game 5 the Angels were one out away from the World Series, only to have the Red Sox score four runs in the ninth and eventually win in extra innings. Grich, 37 years old and in his last season, had a chance to be the greatest hero in Angels' history. With two outs in the bottom of the ninth, the score tied and the bases loaded, he came to the plate against Joe Sambito. Grich broke his bat, ending the inning with a weak, humpbacked liner that Sambito caught. Grich retired after the season with a career .984 fielding percentage, at the time a major league record.

Ken Griffey Jr.

Griffey, George Kenneth, Jr. **OF**

1989–* B:11/21/1969, Donora, PA Deb:4/3/1989, SEA AL BL/TL 6'3", 205

G	AB	R	H	HR	RBI	OBP	SLG	AVG
1535	5832	1063	1742	398	1152	.383	.569	.299

Those too young to have seen Willie Mays in his prime can see in Ken Griffey, Jr. the player nearest to Mays in ability. The 6-foot 3-inch slugger commonly known as "Junior" is the embodiment of the five-tool player that Leo Durocher referred to when speaking of Mays. Griffey can hit, hit with power, run, field, and throw. Just 30 years old, and finishing the 1999 season with 398 career home runs, Griffey has already placed himself in elite company.

Like Stan Musial—and Ken Griffey, Sr.—Junior was born in Donora, Pennsylvania. His grandfather, Buddy Griffey, was a teammate of Musial's at Donora High School. His dad, Ken Sr., played 19 seasons in the major leagues, including two as a right fielder with the world champion Cincinnati Reds in 1975 and 1976. Griffey Sr. finished with the Seattle Mariners in 1991, playing 51 games over his last two seasons with his son. They became the first father-son tandem to play in the same outfield in September 1990.

As good a player as his father was, the feats of Griffey Jr. have far surpassed those of the father. Junior led the American League in homers four times in his first 11 years, including back-to-back seasons with a league-leading 56 homers. Indeed, Griffey is the player that Hank Aaron thinks has the best chance of breaking his record of 755 career home runs. While Griffey belts them with enough frequency (one per every 14.9 at bats, eighth place on the all-time list through 1999) and has youth on his side, he still needs 358 homers to pass Aaron. Aaron never hit 50 or more home runs in a season as Griffey has, but he hit 40 home runs at the age of 39 and clubbed 245 homers after the age of 35. Griffey would need to play eight more seasons after 2000 and average nearly 40 home runs per year.

Griffey, the 1997 American League Most Valuable Player, also proved himself an outstanding fielder and baserunner. He won 10 consecutive Gold Gloves and made numerous leaping catches in center field to rob opponents of home runs. His arm was also one of the best at his position. Though not a prolific basestealer, he was a swift baserunner. He flew from first to home to score the most important run in Mariners history, crossing the plate on Edgar Martinez's double in Game 5 of the 1995 Division Series to top the Yankees in 11 innings.

Elected by experts to the "All Century Team" announced in July 1999, Griffey Jr. was then voted by fans as one of the top 25 players of the 20th Century. He finished in eighth place in the outfield voting with 645,389 votes. One of the game's most popular players, Junior was voted to start the All-Star Game 10 consecutive times—in 1992 he joined his dad as an All-Star MVP, making them the first father-son due to turn that trick.

At the end of the 1999 season Griffey publicly announced that he wanted to be traded from Seattle so he could spend more time with his family in Florida. He turned down one trade to the Mets, saying that he only wanted to go to Cincinnati, where he grew up and where his dad was a coach. After a month of on-again, off-again talks, Seattle and Cincinnati finalized a deal that brought Griffey to the Reds for Brett Tomko, Mike Cameron, Antonio Perez, and Jake Meyer. Griffey then signed a nine-year, $116.5 million deal, with much of the money deferred.

Ken Griffey Sr.

Griffey, George Kenneth, Sr. **OF–1B**
1973–91 B:4/10/1950, Donora, PA Deb:8/25/1973, CIN NL BL/TL 6', 200

G	AB	R	H	HR	RBI	OBP	SLG	AVG
2097	7229	1129	2143	152	859	.361	.431	.296

Until his son came along, Ken Griffey, Sr. was the second-best lefthanded hitter from Donora, Pennsylvania, also the hometown of Stan Musial. Griffey was an unsung star on Cincinnati's "Big Red Machine" of the 1970s. He and his son Ken Jr. became the first father and son to play simultaneously in the major leagues in 1989, and they were Seattle Mariners teammates in 1990 and 1991. He said that playing ball with his son was his greatest thrill.

Griffey starred in football, basketball, baseball, and track at Donora High School, and he was already starting a family with his high school sweetheart when the Reds drafted him in the 29th round in June 1969. He fit the Reds' preferred player profile with his great speed and family responsibilities. In his first pro season, Griffey led Gulf Coast League hitters in doubles and outfielders in errors, and he would struggle with his defense and his loneliness throughout his apprenticeship. "I was out on the streets of Sioux Falls, South Dakota, and I survived," Griffey said. "I had to learn everything on my own."

After hitting .244 for Sioux Falls in 1970, Griffey put together three straight .300 campaigns, led the International League in stolen bases in 1973, and grew from a skinny teenager into a barrel-chested adult who could reach first base in 3.5 seconds. He earned a promotion to the majors in August 1973 and hit a blistering .384 in 25 games to help the Reds win the National League West title. He started two games in right field and doubled in the Reds' Championship Series loss to the New York Mets.

But Griffey began 1974 back in the minors. He returned to Cincinnati after 43 games, then hit only .251 and was a defensive liability. With coach Ted Kluszewski tutoring him at the plate and George Scherger working on his defense, Griffey turned it around after that year. He became a competent outfielder and hit .300 or better in five of the next seven seasons.

Griffey became a regular in Cincinnati in 1975 after Pete Rose shifted from outfield to third base. On that star-studded squad, he says, "I just did my job and kept my mouth shut." The Reds clinched the division on September 7, and in their playoff sweep of the Pirates, Griffey knocked in three runs with a double in the opener and stole three bases in Game 2. He also started the winning rally in the 10th inning of Game 3, bunting with two strikes against Ramon Hernandez, and later scoring the winning run.

Griffey was also a key factor in the classic 1975 World Series against the Red Sox. In Game 2 he doubled in the winning run in the ninth; he doubled Rose home with the first run of Game 4; and he had two hits and a walk in Game 6. In the fifth inning of Game 6, with the Reds down 3–0, Griffey tripled in two runs and scored the tying run on Johnny Bench's single. In the seventh inning of Game 7, he walked and stole second, then scored the tying run on Rose's single. In the ninth inning Griffey drew a leadoff walk and scored the winning run on Joe Morgan's single, giving the Reds their first world championship since 1940.

In 1976 Griffey had his best season in the majors. He hit a career-best .336, but was edged out for the batting title by Bill Madlock on the final day of the season. He also stole a career-high 34 bases. He was selected to the All-Star Game for the first of three times.

Griffey tripled in the opener of that year's NLCS against the Phillies, had a key single in the Reds' Game 2 comeback win, and scored the go-ahead run. In Game 3 he had two hits, and his high chopper in the ninth inning glanced off the glove of first baseman Bobby Tolan to win the game and complete a sweep.

The Reds also swept the New York Yankees in the World Series. In the opener he stole second and scored an insurance run in a 5–1 win. In Game 2 he chipped in with a sacrifice fly in a three-run second inning; then with the score tied 3–3 and two out in the ninth, Griffey's speed forced Fred Stanley to rush his throw on a slow roller to short. The throw went into the dugout, Griffey wound up on second, and he scored the winning run on a single by Tony Perez.

Knee trouble caused Griffey to miss much of the 1979 season, including the NLCS, but he rebounded in 1980. In that year's All-Star Game, he homered off Tommy John, singled to begin a rally in the NL's comeback victory, and was a unanimous selection as the game's Most Valuable Player. (Twelve years later his son also won the award, making them the first father-son combination to be named All-Star Game MVPs.)

Following the 1981 season Griffey was traded to the Yankees for two minor league pitchers. In the next four and a half years, he twice batted above .300. During an August 1985 pennant race game against the Boston Red Sox, Griffey made one of the most spectacular catches ever at Yankee Stadium. He sprinted into the left-field corner, leapt high above the fence, snagged Marty Barrett's potential game-tying homer, and landed in a somersault.

On June 30, 1986, he was traded to the Atlanta Braves. He enjoyed a revival in Atlanta, where, in only 80 games, he hit 12 homers for a combined career-best total of 21 and stole a dozen bases. In 1987 he started most of the time but was also the league's top pinch hitter, going 11-for-18.

In 1988 he was released after a slow start and rejoined the Reds as a part-time first baseman and outfielder. Then in 1990, at the club's urging, rather than being handed his release, Griffey was placed on the voluntarily retired list to allow Cincinnati to add pitcher Chris Hammond to its roster.

It was widely speculated that Griffey would join the Mariners to play with his son, but his status precluded that move. With high-level paper shuffling, and some embarrassment to the Reds, Griffey was granted his release and signed with the Mariners on August 29, 1990. The Griffeys started side-by-side in left and center fields for the Mariners on August 31 and singled back-to-back in their first at bats.

Griffey Sr. hit .472 with 14 RBIs in his first 10 games with the Mariners, and he won the first Player of the Week award of his career in September, when he batted .632 with seven RBIs and started a 12-game hitting streak. That streak included back-to-back father and son homers off California's Kirk McCaskill on September 14.

After hitting .377 for the Mariners in 1990, he earned a place on the 1991 squad but suffered a neck injury during spring training that eventually required surgery. He played only 30 games before going on the disabled list in June, and he announced his retirement in November. "I surprised myself being in the game for 19 years," Griffey said. "I hung around long enough for Junior."

Griffey was a Mariners minor league instructor in 1992 and became the batting coach under Lou Piniella, his one-time teammate and two-time manager, in 1993. He joined Colorado's coaching staff in 1996, but returned to Cincinnati as a coach the following year.

Mike Griffin

Griffin, Michael Joseph **OF**

1887–98 M(1898,1–3) B:3/20/1865, Utica, NY D:4/10/1908, Utica, NY Deb:4/16/1887, BAL AA BL/TR 5'7", 160

G	AB	R	H	HR	RBI	OBP	SLG	AVG
1511	5914	1405	1753	42	719	.388	.407	.296

Slick center fielder Mike Griffin was the first player to homer in his first major league at bat, which he did on April 16, 1887. That first-inning homer was one of three extra-base hits he collected that day.

Griffin began his career with Utica of the New York State League and was signed by Orioles manager Billy Barnie, who had confused him with Sandy Griffin, also of Utica. He played three years with the Orioles before joining Philadelphia of the Players' League in 1890. There he led all outfielders with 10 double plays.

The next year Grffin joined the National League with Brooklyn. He led the league with 36 doubles and scored 106 runs, going over the 100 mark for the fifth consecutive year. Griffin's best two seasons were 1894, when he batted .358, and 1895, when he hit .333 with 38 doubles. He left baseball in 1898 after a contract dispute resulting from the merger of the Brooklyn and Baltimore teams. He died of pneumonia in 1908.

Clark Griffith

Griffith, Clark Calvin **P**

1891, 1893–1907, 1909–10, 1912–14 M(1901–20, 1491–1367) Owner (1920–55) B:11/20/1869, Clear Creek, MO D:10/27/1955, Washington, DC Deb:4/11/1891, STL AL BR/TR 5'6½", 156

W	L	PCT	G	SH	IP	BB	SO	ERA
237	146	.619	453	22	3385^{2}	774	955	3.31

Clark Griffith, nicknamed "the Old Fox," excelled as a pitcher, manager, and club owner in a distinguished baseball career that spanned nearly seven decades. After his playing and managing days were over, he became one of baseball's true power-brokers.

The son of a Missouri fur trapper, Griffith was born in a Missouri log cabin. The Griffiths then moved to Bloomington, Illinois, where young Clark caught the baseball bug. His first paid performance was for a team in nearby Hoopeston, receiving $10 to pitch a game against Danville.

On the strength of that performance, the diminutive Griffith began his professional pitching career in 1888 with Bloomington in the Central-Interstate League, where he earned $50 a month before being sold for $700 to the Western League's Milwaukee Brewers. "His fine play and genial disposition have made him a general favorite with the baseball cranks," noted one Milwaukee newspaper. In 1891 he reached the majors with St. Louis and then moved to Boston in the last year of the American Association.

After the AA expired Griffith found work in the Pacific Coast League, where he went 30–18 with Oakland in 1893. While at Oakland, Griffith helped organize a players' strike when paychecks lagged. To survive during the work stoppage, Griffith and several teammates moonlighted on the vaudeville stage in San Francisco.

Griffith soon returned to the mound and to the majors, this time with Cap Anson's Chicago Colts. Each year from 1894 to 1899, Griffith collected at least 21 victories for Chicago, reaching a high of 26 in 1895. His well-rounded arsenal of pitches featured a sneaky and effective quick pitch and six different deliveries in which he mixed in spitters and screwballs, a pitch he claimed to have invented. He also took credit for the scuffball, proudly hacking the ball with his spikes.

"No brainier pitcher ever lived," wrote Chicago sportswriter Hugh Fullerton. Some said Griffith could sit in the dugout, or even in the stands, and accurately predict 97 percent of the pitches that would be thrown.

During one game in the 1890s the Orioles' often-obnoxious John McGraw reached first base against Griffith. McGraw immediately began insulting not only Griffith but also base umpire Joe Cantillon, positioned just behind Griffith.

"Pick him off," Cantillon hissed to Griffith. Griffith wanted to know how, since McGraw was only a couple feet off the bag. "Balk him off," advised Cantillon. And that's what Griffith did. McGraw became so upset by the shenanigans that he was thrown out of the game. The next Baltimore batter also reached first, and Griffith tried the same trick. "Balk!" roared Cantillon. When Griffith questioned the call, Cantillon replied, "Balks only work against McGraw."

Another noteworthy Griffith run-in involved Kip Selbach. Griffith's Chicago club was ahead by a run, with runners on second and third. Up came Selbach to the plate. Griffith immediately went to work on Selbach's psyche. "You big stiff, you couldn't hit this one with a board," Griffith yelled. Although he purposely placed his offerings slightly off the plate, he enticed the high-strung Selbach to swing at a couple of them and worked the count full. Then Griffith screamed, "Here, hit this you big bloat." Pitching underhand, he floated the ball as slowly as he could. By now, Selbach was so flustered that he swung long before the ball reached him. So emphatic was the swing that he collapsed to the ground.

In 1901 Ban Johnson declared his upstart American League a major circuit and needed help to force the National League to accept his league as an equal. That year Griffith moved to Charles Comiskey's Chicago franchise as a player-manager, won 24 games as the team's top pitcher, led the new league in shutouts, and batted .303 to boot. He also directed the White Sox to an AL pennant.

Johnson needed a franchise in New York City to compete with John T. Brush's Giants. So Johnson, who had almost dictatorial authority in the new league, moved the Baltimore club to New York, and in 1903 installed Griffith to manage the new Highlanders. Griffith delivered respectable second-place finishes in 1904 and 1906, but soon animosity erupted between him and club ownership. He lasted until midseason 1908, when he returned to the National League to become playing-manager for Garry Hermann's Cincinnati Reds.

Griffith bounced back to the American League in 1912 as manager of the Washington Senators. He remained as bench manager until 1920, but the best he could do was second-place finishes in 1912 and 1913. In addition to managing the club, Griffith bought 10 percent of the team stock for $27,000.

When Griffith's managerial tenure ended in 1920, he bought out Washington's old ownership. He and Philadelphia grain exporter William Richardson purchased 80 percent of the team for $290,000. Washington's reputation as "First in War, First in Peace, and Last in the American League" didn't ring true during Griffith's tenure. The Senators were a first-division club in almost half of the 45 seasons in which Griffith was either manager or president. In fact, during those 45 seasons Washington ended in the cellar only three times.

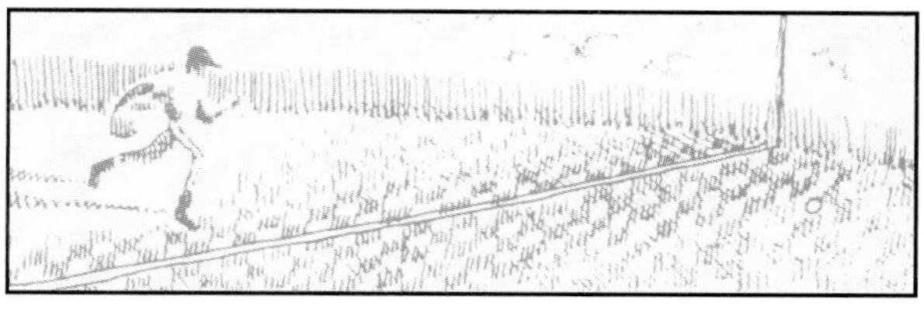

Griffith is often portrayed as a hidebound reactionary. Critics often quote his 1935 remarks on night baseball: "There is no chance night baseball ever will become popular in the major leagues. The game was meant to be played in the Lord's own sunshine." Yet once he saw how profitable major league night ball could be, Griffith vigorously advocated removing all restrictions on evening play.

During World War II, Commissioner Kenesaw Mountain Landis used Griffith to approach President Franklin Roosevelt with a plea to keep baseball alive. It was also Griffith who used wartime conditions as an excuse to hold down ballplayers' salaries. "In these war times, with conditions as they are, anybody ought to welcome the same salary they received last year," he informed 18-game winner Dutch Leonard in early 1942.

The highlights of Griffith's Washington ownership include back-to-back pennants in 1924 and 1925 and a world championship in 1924 under manager Bucky Harris. The team won another pennant under player-manager Joe Cronin in 1933. In 1934 Griffith sold Cronin, his own son-in-law, to Tom Yawkey's Boston Red Sox.

The Old Timer's Committee named Griffith to the Baseball Hall of Fame in 1946. He died of a massive stomach hemorrhage in Washington on October 27, 1955. Griffith's adopted son, Calvin, took over the club's reins and moved the team to Minnesota following the 1960 season, and the club changed its name to the Twins. After 65 seasons of family ownership, the franchise was sold in 1984.

Burleigh Grimes

Grimes, Burleigh Arland **P**

1916–34 M (1937–38, 131–171) B:8/9/1893, Emerald, WI D:12/6/1985, Clear Lake, WI Deb:9/10/1916, PIT NL BR/TR 5'10", 175

W	L	PCT	G	SH	IP	BB	SO	ERA
270	212	.560	616	35	4179^2	1295	1512	3.53

Burleigh Grimes was the last of the legal spitball pitchers. It's the peg upon which most people hang his career, but in reality Grimes was a lot more than that. He was a fierce competitor who pitched for seven teams during a career that spanned 19 years and had five 20-win seasons.

When Grimes was 16 years old, his father, who managed a semipro ballclub, gave him $25 and told him, "Son, go out into the world and make something of yourself." Grimes started his baseball career in 1912 with the Eau Claire Commissioners of the Class D Minnesota–Wisconsin League. Unfortunately, the league disbanded on July 1, and he didn't get his salary.

He was a spitballer from the beginning, with slippery elm his lubrication of choice. At the end of 1916, after five years in the minors, Grimes made it to the Pittsburgh Pirates and went 2–3 in six games. The next season he pitched for the Pirates the entire season, losing 13 straight en route to a 3–16 record. His career turned around in January 1918 when he was traded to the Brooklyn Dodgers in a deal that sent outfielder Casey Stengel to Pittsburgh.

It was a steal for the Dodgers. Grimes was 19–9 his first year in Brooklyn. In the five years between 1920 and 1924, he won at least 21 games four times and led the National League in complete games three times.

After the 1920 season the spitter, along with all other pitches aided by an illegal substance or defacement, was banned in the wake of the beaning death of Cleveland second baseman Ray Chapman. Grimes was one of only 17 major leaguers who were allowed to continue to doctor the ball. At one point in Grimes' career Philadelphia Phillies shortstop Art Fletcher noticed that when Grimes threw a spitter his cap would move on his head. Grimes eventually caught on to this and solved his problem by wearing a larger cap.

Grimes was not only the Dodgers' ace but was a fiery competitor. Before a game against the Giants late in the 1924 season, he called a team meeting and announced, "Anyone who doesn't want to play today's game to win, let me know right now." Grimes then went out and knocked down the first New York batter on the first pitch of the game.

In 1926, after Grimes fell to 12–13, Brooklyn traded him to New York; he went 19–8 the following season as a Giant. Despite that record, in February 1928 the Giants traded him to Pittsburgh. Grimes responded with his last big season, going 25–14 and leading the league in wins, complete games, innings pitched, and shutouts.

During the next three seasons Grimes was 50–27 for Pittsburgh, the Boston Braves, and the St. Louis Cardinals. He won both his starts for the Cardinals in the 1931 World Series against the Philadelphia Athletics, including Game 7. He got two outs in the ninth in that game but had to leave when he dislocated a vertebra while trying to get the last out. He could barely walk back to the bench. From 1932 through 1934 he played with the Cubs, Cardinals, Pirates, and Yankees before finally retiring at age 41.

Grimes managed in the minors before succeeding Casey Stengel as Dodgers manager. Grimes finished sixth in 1937, and seventh in 1938. He returned to the minors, managed for several years, and then turned to scouting for the Yankees, A's, and Orioles. Elected to the Hall of Fame in 1964, he died in 1985 at age 92.

Charlie Grimm

Grimm, Charles John **1B**

1916, 1918–36 M(1932–38, 1944–49, 1952–56, 1960, 1287–1067) B:8/28/1898, St. Louis, MO D:11/15/1983, Scottsdale, AZ Deb:7/30/1916, PHI AL BL/TL 5'11½", 173

G	AB	R	H	HR	RBI	OBP	SLG	AVG
2166	7917	908	2299	79	1078	.341	.397	.290

When Pittsburgh traded Charlie Grimm and two other players to the Chicago Cubs after the 1924 season, Pirates owner Barney Dreyfuss announced, "I got rid of my banjo players."

The perception that "Jolly Cholly" was more interested in strumming his banjo and having a good time than in playing first base or winning baseball games followed him all his life. Admittedly, Grimm was a virtuoso on the instrument, and enough humorous incidents occurred in his proximity to fill several books. But he was also a good hitter, a superior fielder, and an outstanding manager, facts that are sometimes overlooked.

As a boy, Grimm served as a batboy at Sportsman's Park. Signed by the Philadelphia Athletics in 1916, he hit .091 in a dozen games. He spent 1917 with Durham of the Class D North Carolina League and was signed by the St. Louis Cardinals in 1918. The Cardinals brought him up for 50 games in 1918, but Grimm hit only .220, and St. Louis sent him to Little Rock of the Southern Association to learn to play first base. He was hitting .285 and leading the league's first basemen in fielding when the Pittsburgh Pirates acquired him late in 1919.

Installed as the regular first baseman in 1920, he hit only .227 but led National League in fielding at his position. During the next few years his hitting showed significant improvement. The left-handed Grimm was nearly 6-feet tall and weighed a solid 173 pounds, but he seldom hit home runs, instead spraying line drives to all fields. In 1923 he had his best season, leading the league in fielding again while batting .345 with 99 RBIs.

The following year he formed a quartet of dubious musical talent with Rabbit Maranville, George Whitted, and Cotton Tierney. Grimm starred on banjo. The Pirates put on a rush in August and got within a game of the league-leading New York Giants by September 1. When they slipped back at season's end, Dreyfuss blamed the team's lighthearted spirit. However, Grimm's slump, to a .288 batting average and only 63 RBIs, had as much to do with him being traded as did his banjo playing.

Maranville accompanied Grimm to Chicago. During spring training a photographer arranged a gag photo involving the two pranksters. Grimm lay on his back with a golf tee holding a ball clenched between his teeth. Poised above him was Maranville, a golf club at the ready. The picture was snapped, and suddenly Maranville swung the club and knocked the ball down the course.

Grimm hit .308 and a career-high 10 home runs for the 1925 Cubs, but the team fell apart when the happy-go-lucky Maranville was named manager. When Joe McCarthy became Cubs manager the next year, the team began moving up in the standings. McCarthy had few run-ins with Grimm, who was, in fact, one of the easier personalities McCarthy had to deal with. Prickly Rogers Hornsby and party-loving Hack Wilson were far more trouble. Grimm hit .298 and knocked in 91 runs when the Cubs won the 1929 pennant. He batted .389 in a losing World Series effort against the Philadelphia Athletics.

When the Cubs failed to repeat in 1930, Hornsby replaced McCarthy. Where McCarthy had used persuasion and psychology, Hornsby used criticism and sarcasm. Wilson proved particularly unresponsive to Hornsby's acid tongue, but he nevertheless batted .331, including a career-high 11 triples. The Cubs dropped to third, 17 games out of first.

During the first part of 1932, Chicago was in and out of first place. But the team appeared to be well out of the pennant race by August when Hornsby and club president William Veeck got into an argument. Hornsby was canned. Grimm, a surprise replacement, was the perfect selection. Under his relaxed hand, Chicago steamed past the Pirates to win the pennant by four games. Although Grimm hit .333, New York swept Chicago in the World Series.

Because of his managerial duties, Grimm played only part-time in 1933 and 1934. After finishing in third place for two straight seasons, new owner Phil K. Wrigley announced before the 1935 season that nothing short of a pennant would be satisfactory. Grimm's Cubs took off on a 21-game winning streak in September to catch and pass the New York Giants for the title. But once again Chicago came up short in the World Series, losing to the Detroit Tigers in six games.

Although he continued to make occasional appearances through 1936, Grimm's active playing career was essentially over. He would always clown around for a camera but ran a tighter ship than most fans realized. He didn't browbeat or humiliate his players, but he could enforce discipline when necessary. In July 1938 Wrigley decided to replace Grimm with Gabby Hartnett, much to the consternation of the fans. All was forgiven when Chicago put on another September spurt to win the pennant. Grimm, in the meantime, moved into the broadcasting booth and called the pennant drive.

After more than two years as a broadcaster, he returned to the Cubs as a coach. Next he managed Milwaukee of the American Association, which was owned by Bill Veeck, son of the former Cubs president. One day in 1943 Veeck asked Grimm what he wanted for his birthday. "A good lefthanded pitcher," Grimm replied. When Grimm's birthday was celebrated with a ceremony on the field, newly acquired lefthanded pitcher Juan Acosta hopped out of a cake. With the improved pitching, Grimm's club won the AA pennant and the Little World Series.

In 1944 Grimm returned to manage the Cubs, and he won his third NL pennant in 1945 before losing another World Series to the Tigers. During the war years, when good players were hard to find, Grimm often told the story of a fellow who claimed, "I'm 4-F and I can throw like Dizzy Dean, hit like Ted Williams, and play the outfield like Joe DiMaggio." A skeptical Grimm replied, "You must be nuts." The fellow nodded. "That's why I'm 4-F."

In 1949 Grimm moved to the Cubs' front office but soon quit after a dispute with the business manager. He managed Dallas in the Texas League in 1950 and won another AA pennant and Little World Series with Milwaukee in 1951. The next year he was named manager of the Boston Braves early in the season. The team finished seventh, but Grimm was retained as manager after the club moved to Milwaukee in 1953. The revitalized Braves finished a surprising second, and Grimm kept them in contention each year until he was fired in mid-1956.

He returned to his beloved Cubs, and at different times he served as a vice president, a consultant, a broadcaster, and a scout until his death in 1983. He even took one last fling as a manager, for 17 games in 1960. His major league record during 19 seasons as a manager was 1,287–1,067, with three pennants.

Ross Grimsley

Grimsley, Ross Albert **P**

1971–80, 1982 B:1/7/1950, Topeka, KS Deb:5/16/1971, CIN NL BL/TL 6'3", 200

W	L	PCT	G	SH	IP	BB	SO	ERA
124	99	.556	345	15	2039[1]	559	750	3.81

Free-spirited lefthander Ross Grimsley was one of those pitchers who had three speeds: slow, slower, and slowest. Some suspected that he occasionally aided the flight of the baseball with a foreign substance. Tom Boswell of *The Washington Post* once wrote about Grimsley's alleged chicanery: "He is said to have enough greasy kid stuff in his ultra-long curly hair to give A.J. Foyt a lube job and oil change." That aside, Grimsley's still won 124 games in 11 years in the big leagues and a couple of games in the 1972 World Series.

Grimsley signed with the Reds in 1969 and was in the big leagues two years later. He won 10 games during his rookie season, then improved that to 14 wins with a 3.05 ERA in 1972. He then came up big in the postseason. With the Reds trailing two games to one in the Championship Series, Grimsley beat the Pirates, 7–1, on a complete-game two-hitter. Then, after losing Game 2 of the World Series as a starter against the A's, he picked up relief wins in Games 5 and 6.

But the Reds were perhaps the most conservative team in baseball, and Grimsley, a child of the 1960s, did not fit in. After going 13–10 in 1973 he was traded to the Orioles for Merv Rettenmund. Grimsley responded to the change with a terrific 1974 season, going 18–13 with a 3.07 ERA, four shutouts, and 17 complete games.

The next two seasons were not as successful, but he rebounded in 1977, going 14–10 with 11 complete games. His timing was perfect; he was a free agent after the season. Grimsley signed with the Montreal Expos and had his best season in 1978, going 20–11 with a career-high 19 complete games. He retired in 1982, having returned to the Orioles for his final season. In 1999 he coached for the Texas League's Shreveport Captains.

Marquis Grissom

Grissom, Marquis Deon **OF**

1989–* B:4/17/1967, Atlanta, GA Deb:8/22/1989, MON NL BR/TR 5'11", 190

G	AB	R	H	HR	RBI	OBP	SLG	AVG
1435	5603	839	1550	131	601	.329	.410	.277

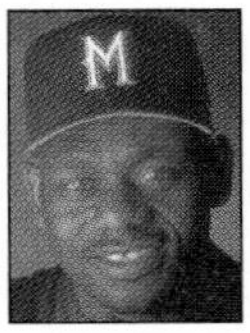

One of 15 children, Marquis Grissom was a fine hitting and pitching prospect at Florida A&M. His blazing speed and .448 batting average as a junior ensured that his quickest route to the major leagues was as an outfielder. The Expos drafted him in the third round of the 1988 draft, and less than two seasons later he was in the major leagues.

Grissom swiped 76 bases in 1991 and followed it with a career-best 78 steals. He led the National League in stolen bases both years while being thrown out just 30 times in 182 attempts. Although he was not as active on the basepaths later in his career, Grissom still had 380 stolen bases in his first 10 full major league seasons.

After back-to-back All-Star seasons in 1993 and 1994, the cost-conscious Expos traded Grissom to the Atlanta Braves. The native Georgian had a poor season in 1995, but he had a fine October.

He batted .360 with three steals in his first World Series as Atlanta defeated the Cleveland Indians in six games. In 1996 Grissom reached career highs with 10 triples, 23 homers, a .308 average, and a 25-game hitting streak for the Braves. He also won his fourth consecutive Gold Glove Award that season.

A fine clutch player, Grissom enjoyed a career .390 World Series average, a .320 Division Series mark, and a .273 average in three League Championship Series. He was Most Valuable Player of the 1997 ALCS while playing for the Cleveland Indians. Grissom was traded to Milwaukee following Cleveland's seven-game loss to Florida in the 1997 World Series. In 1999 he joined Tommy Harper, Robin Yount, and Jeromy Burnitz as the only Brewers ever to have 20 homers and 20 steals in the same season.

Dick Groat

Groat, Richard Morrow **SS**
1952, 1955–67 B:11/4/1930, Wilkinsburg, PA
Deb:6/19/1952, PIT NL BR/TR 5'11½", 180

G	AB	R	H	HR	RBI	OBP	SLG	AVG
1929	7484	829	2138	39	707	.332	.366	.286

When Pittsburgh signed Dick Groat in 1952, a few days after he graduated from Duke University, it was the finishing touch on Branch Rickey's efforts to make the Pirates respectable again. As *Pittsburgh Post-Gazette* sportswriter Al Abrams wrote, "Branch Rickey told me one day last year, 'If I can sign Dick Groat to a Pirate contract, we can win the pennant.'"

Groat was an All-America basketball player in his junior and senior years at Duke and set the NCAA all-time single-season scoring record (since broken), with 831 points. But he was also a baseball All-America, and both Cardinals manager Eddie Stanky and Giants boss Leo Durocher wanted the intelligent, hard-working Groat. He was a Pittsburgh boy, born and raised only a few miles from Forbes Field, and he had always wanted to play for his home team.

Groat was not a natural athlete in the conventional sense. He lacked great running speed and a powerful arm, but he had an instinct for the rhythms of the game, intelligence, and a burning desire to excel—qualities that led to his being rated third in all-time shortstop fielding range by A.W. Laird.

After hitting .284 in 95 games with the Pirates in 1952, Groat played one season of professional basketball for the Fort Wayne Pistons. He then spent two years in the Army at Fort Belvoir, Virginia, where he led his baseball and basketball teams to the worldwide Army championships, the first time a single Army base won both titles the same year. Groat batted .362 and .377 and averaged 35 points a game in basketball.

He returned to the Pirates lineup in 1955 and proved particularly adept at the hit-and-run. Bill Virdon commented, "In the seven years he and I batted one-two in the order, I could probably count on one hand the number of times that Groat failed to advance me with one out."

Groat also rapidly improved his fielding. Roy Face said, "Groat wasn't a player that had a lot of range, but he knew the hitters and was always in position." Before the 1960 season, it was rumored that the Pirates were ready to trade Groat for Roger Maris, but Pittsburgh skipper Danny Murtaugh nixed the deal. Groat responded with his greatest season in one of Pittsburgh's most memorable years. He led the league in hitting with a .325 average, was the acknowledged team leader, and won the league Most Valuable Player Award, the first Pirates player to do so since the team had last reached the World Series in 1927.

A pitch by Lew Burdette fractured Groat's wrist on September 6, but Groat's substitute, Dick Schofield, hit .403 during the captain's absence. Although Groat batted only .214 during the World Series, his RBI single helped key the Pirates' five-run comeback in the eighth inning of Game 7.

All the Pirates seemed to slump in 1961, and Groat's batting average tumbled 50 points. He was back up to .294 in 1962 when he was selected to his third All-Star Game, but Pittsburgh general manager Joe L. Brown was on the hunt for more pitching. He dealt Groat to the St. Louis Cardinals for Don Cardwell.

Pirates fans couldn't understand the trade. No one was more closely identified with the team than Groat, who had hoped to become a coach and manager there after retiring as a player. However, even though he continued to live in the area, Groat refused to have any formal contact with the Pirates until, at the request of his ailing wife, he joined his teammates for a reunion of the 1960 team in 1990.

Groat became a leader on the Cardinals in 1963. He batted .319, led the league with 43 doubles, and had a career-high 201 hits. The next year the Cardinals won it all, and Groat played a large part in that success. He had brief stints with Philadelphia and San Francisco before retiring in 1967. He later ran a golf course outside Pittsburgh and announced Duquesne University basketball.

Heinie Groh

Groh, Henry Knight **3B-2B**

1912–27 M(1918, 7–3) B:9/18/1889, Rochester, NY D:8/22/1968, Cincinnati, OH Deb:4/12/1912, NY NL BR/TR 5'8", 158

G	AB	R	H	HR	RBI	OBP	SLG	AVG
1676	6074	918	1774	26	566	.373	.384	.292

Once upon a time, there was something called a bottle bat. Before the ball was juiced up in 1920, the basic offense in baseball was to choke up on the bat, scratch a run here, and scratch a run there. And the bottle bat, with its ultra-thick handle, was the weapon of choice for more than a few players. Third baseman Heinie Groh was one of them, and he used it for 16 productive big league seasons.

Groh started his pro career in 1908 as a shortstop at Oshkosh in the Wisconsin–Illinois League. The Giants bought him in 1911 and he spent 27 games with them the next year, hitting .271 as a utility infielder. He was almost 23 years old, but only 5 feet 8 inches and 158 pounds, and he still had a baby face. In Groh's first at bat, umpire Bill Klem thought Giants manager John McGraw had sent up a batboy to pinch-hit. Unfazed, Groh singled.

Groh began using the bottle bat after McGraw suggested he use a heavier bat. He made one modification—he whittled down the handle a bit. "You couldn't hold that bottle bat down at the knob end," he said, "because the way the weight was distributed the ball would knock it right out of your hands. But I always choked up and chopped at the ball."

He got a chance to play regularly after the Giants traded him to the Cincinnati Reds on May 22, 1913, in a five-player deal. He hit .282 for the Reds that season as their regular second baseman and made the move to third two yeas later. He then led NL third basemen in double plays four of the next five seasons. He also led the league in fielding percentage five times (1917, 1918, 1922, 1923, and 1924).

Groh began a streak of outstanding hitting years in 1917, when he batted .304 and paced the league with 182 hits and 39 doubles. He led the league with 28 doubles the next season and hit .320 as he established himself as one of the game's top third basemen. He also managed the Reds for the last 10 games of that war-shortened 1918 season when Christy Mathewson left to enlist.

In 1919 Cincinnati won the pennant, and Groh played a major part by hitting .310 with a career-high 63 RBIs. He led the Reds with six runs in the World Series against a Chicago opponent that later became known as the "Black Sox" for throwing the Series.

After hitting .331 in an injury-plagued 1921, Groh was traded back to the Giants for backup catcher Mike Gonzalez, outfielder George Burns, and $150,000. He was on the downside of his career at that point and didn't hit over .290 in his five seasons in New York. He did, however, revive in the World Series, hitting .474 as the Giants swept the Yankees in 1922. "I had the Yankees' signs in that 1922 World Series," Groh admitted later. "Not their pitching signs, their hitting signs. I knew when they were going to bunt and when they were going to hit away. Which is a very nice thing for a third baseman to know."

He finished with the Pirates in 1927. He went on to manage in the minors before scouting for the Giants, Dodgers, and Phillies.

Steve Gromek

Gromek, Stephen Joseph **P**

1941–57 B:1/15/1920, Hamtramck, MI Deb:8/18/1941, CLE AL BB/TR 6'2", 180

W	L	PCT	G	SV	IP	BB	SO	ERA
123	108	.532	447	23	2064²	630	904	3.41

Wartime in the mid-1940s brought uncertainty and uneasiness to most Americans, but for players like Steve Gromek it brought opportunity for stardom. During his first three seasons with the Cleveland Indians, Gromek was used sparingly, appearing in only 26 games. But in 1944, as hundreds of major leaguers were on active duty, Gromek became the club's workhorse. He led the staff with 204 innings pitched, posted a 10–9 record, and showed signs that he was ready for greatness.

He reached that level in the 1945 season, compiling a 19–9 record and a 2.55 ERA and being selected for the All-Star Game. With his pinpoint control, he shot ahead of everyone else on the Tribe's pitching staff, including highly touted Allie Reynolds.

The following season, however, the big righthander lost 15 of 20 decisions as his ERA skyrocketed to 4.33. Gromek became a reliever over the next six years, and made only occasional starts. His record was not outstanding except in 1948, when he went 9–3 for the world champion Indians. Gromek played a key role in that Series, pitching a complete-game 2–1 victory in Game 4 against Boston Braves' star pitcher Johnny Sain.

In 1953 Gromek was traded to the Detroit Tigers. Seemingly inspired by the move back to his native state, in his first full season with the Tigers Gromek rang up 18 victories with a 2.74 earned run average. It proved to be his last All-Star caliber season. He finished his career three years later as a mop-up man out of the bullpen.

Kevin Gross

Gross, Kevin Frank **P**

1983–97 B:6/8/1961, Downey, CA Deb:6/25/1983, PHI NL BR/TR 6'5", 215

W	L	PCT	G	SH	IP	BB	SO	ERA
142	158	.473	474	14	2487^2	986	1727	4.11

Kevin Gross had a journeyman's career, but his name evokes memories of sandpaper, first and foremost. Signed by the Philadelphia Phillies, he emerged as one of the organization's top prospects and led the staff with 15 wins in 1985. Liking his size and moving fastball, the Phillies believed they had found in Kevin Gross their ace of the future.

Unfortunately, Gross never developed into that ace. Struggling with wildness in 1986, he finished a mediocre 12–12. The following spring, Gross suffered a herniated disc, which caused discomfort in his leg. After umpires found sandpaper glued to his glove in a game on August 10, the National League suspended him for 10 days. Gross later revealed that he had resorted to scuffing his pitches with sandpaper because continuing pain in his leg had slowed his fastball. A year later, however, Gross made the All-Star team for the only time in his career,

Gross never played for a playoff team and always seemed to pitch just well enough to lose, but he had one moment of glory. On August 17, 1992, Gross pitched a no-hitter—a 99-pitch masterpiece for the Dodgers against San Francisco. The postgame comments of Giants manager Roger Craig seemed appropriate in summarizing Gross' career. "I told my coaches before the game I've never understood why this guy didn't win more ballgames," said Craig. "He's a big, strong guy and he's got outstanding stuff." Prior to the no-hitter, the enigmatic Gross had lost 12 of 17 decisions.

After the 1994 season, Gross signed as a free agent with Texas. He won just one of his first seven decisions and posted a 9.89 ERA before recovering in the second half. In 1996 his ERA rose above 5.00 for the second straight year. The following spring, the Rangers sent him to the minor leagues before releasing him. Gross signed with the Angels, but struggled in 12 appearances before his season—and career—came to an end.

Jerry Grote

Grote, Gerald Wayne **C**

1963–64, 1966–78, 1981 B:10/6/1942, San Antonio, TX Deb:9/21/1963, HOU NL BR/TR 5'10", 190

G	AB	R	H	HR	RBI	OBP	SLG	AVG
1421	4339	352	1092	39	404	.318	.326	.252

Jerry Grote was a fine defensive catcher for the New York Mets in their pennant-winning seasons of 1969 and 1973. Although never an overpowering hitter, his skill in catching and calling pitches made him a key contributor to those title teams.

Originally signed by the Houston Colt .45s, Grote was made the club's first-string catcher in 1964 at age 21. However, the Colt .45s were convinced that Grote would never learn to hit after he batted only .181 that season and traded him to the Mets in October 1965 for pitcher Tom Parsons.

"I was glad to come over to the Mets from Houston," Grote once said. "I knew that team would never win. They had too many old players, and they had no defense. It was different with the Mets. You could see the young talent."

Grote handled much of that young pitching talent. In his 13 seasons in New York he caught Tom Seaver, Jerry Koosman, Nolan Ryan, and Jon Matlack. Grote played in the All-Star Games of 1968 and 1974. His best statistical year was probably 1975, when he batted .295 with 39 RBIs.

Grote was traded to Los Angeles in 1977. After playing there for two years he retired, but came back in 1981, playing for Kansas City and then returning to Los Angeles. He briefly coached for the Tigers' Lakeland and Birmingham farm clubs and later became the sales manager for development with a San Antonio firm.

Lefty Grove

Grove, Robert Moses **P**

1925–41 B:3/6/1900, Lonaconing, MD D:5/22/1975, Norwalk, OH Deb:4/14/1925, PHI AL BL/TL 6'3", 190

W	L	PCT	G	SV	IP	BB	SO	ERA
300	141	.680	616	55	3940^2	1187	2266	3.06

Lefty Grove combined raw talent and sheer determination as few other pitchers ever have. Walter Johnson or Christy Mathewson may have been more talented, but they didn't come close to Grove in terms of competitiveness. Grove was as intense, and had as much pop on the ball, as any pitcher who ever took the mound.

Grove once struck out Babe Ruth, Lou Gehrig, and Tony Lazzeri on only 10 pitches. He equaled that 10-pitch, three-strikeout performance later in his career against Chicago. Baseball analyst Bill James called Lefty Grove "the greatest pitcher of all time, period."

He hated losing, and his opponents feared his temper. But he denied ever trying to hurt another player. "I never threw at a hitter," he contended. "If I ever hit a guy on the head with my fastball, he'd be through. I knew it, and the hitters knew it. However, I was naturally wild enough to give them something to think about."

He also gave his teammates plenty to think about. In 1931 rookie outfielder Jimmy Moore, playing in place of an injured Al Simmons, made an error that cost Grove a chance at his 17th straight victory. The livid southpaw tore the entire locker room apart. "Threw everything I could get my hands on, giving Al Simmons hell all the time," he admitted.

Ted Williams once said of Grove, "He was a moody guy, a tantrum thrower like me, but when he punched a locker or something he always did it with his right hand. He was a careful tantrum thrower."

A descendant of Betsy Ross, Grove was the son of a Maryland coal miner. He secured his first job in a glass factory for $5.25 a day, and started playing baseball seriously in 1919 as a first baseman in Midland, Maryland. "Sort of amateur ball," Grove said. "We got $20 apiece at the end of the season."

In 1920 he signed with Martinsburg, West Virginia, of the Class D Blue Ridge League for $125 a month. The club needed funds to put a fence around its park, however, and Grove, then 3–3, seemed to be its only marketable commodity. Jack Dunn of the Baltimore Orioles was approached, and Dunn offered $3,500. "I was the only major leaguer ever traded for a fence," Grove later said.

Dunn's Orioles were an independent team without any ties to a big league club. Because Dunn was free to keep a player as long as he wanted him, the Orioles dominated the International League, winning seven straight pennants. Staying with the Orioles wasn't a bad deal for Grove. "We were getting bigger salaries in Baltimore than lots of clubs were paying in the big leagues," Grove said. "We couldn't get $750 to $1,000 a month in the big leagues in those days." Dunn's players also received a cut of the profits from every exhibition game they played.

Grove joined the Baltimore club in June of 1920 and went 12–2 that season. He did it with one pitch, the fastball. When he later developed a curve, he became virtually unbeatable. From 1921 to 1924 Grove compiled a 109–36 record. Four times he led the International League in strikeouts.

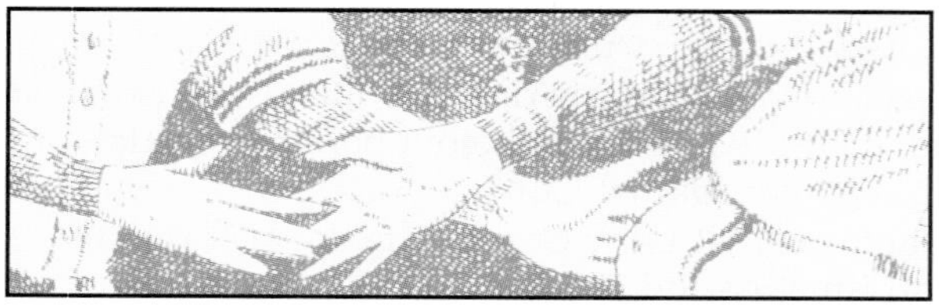

Twice he won 27 games. At one point the Giants offered $75,000 for Grove, but Dunn wouldn't accept anything less than $100,000. Grove stayed in the International League until Connie Mack offered $100,600. The extra $600 was to ensure that Grove's purchase price would be a new record.

If Grove had one flaw when he joined the Athletics, it was his lack of control. Mack and A's catcher Cy Perkins were convinced that the solution lay in merely slowing him down on the mound. To do so, they instructed Grove to count to 10 before releasing each delivery. The strategy worked until opposing batters deciphered what Grove was doing, observing that he moved his lips while counting. They started counting along with him. At about six they would step out of the box and ask for time in order to break his rhythm.

By 1927 Grove's problems were solved, and his counting began more frequently to be in the victory column. He rattled off seven straight seasons of 20 or more victories. During four of those years he led the league in wins, and five times he led the American League in won-lost percentage. No other pitcher, before or since, has ever led the league in won-lost percentage more than three times. Nine times in career Grove's ERA was the lowest in the league. No other pitcher has accomplished that feat more than five times. And in his first seven seasons he also led the league in strikeouts.

Legend has it that Satchel Paige was known to call in his outfielders and then strike out the side. A similar incident once occurred with Grove. The A's were in Syracuse playing an exhibition game against the Marksons, a decent semipro club. The crowd pleaded for Grove to pitch, and Mack brought in his lefty for the bottom of the ninth. When he completed his warm-ups, Grove looked back to make sure his outfielders were in place. Each one was standing just behind the infield, grinning broadly. Grove proceeded to strike out the three batters who faced him, preserving a 10–4 Philadelphia victory.

Grove had a number of idiosyncrasies, including avoiding sportswriters and photographers. Once he explained why. "I was with the Athletics in spring training at Fort Meyers, Florida. A writer who represented a Philadelphia newspaper spent three hours with me in connection with a story he was going to write. And what a story he wrote! It didn't contain anything I told him, but plenty of things I never talked about. From that time on I decided I'd do very little talking."

Writers knew to keep away from Grove after games, especially ones he lost. "Let me tell you," Grove said, "I was a TOUGH loser. It burned me up worse than a fever to get beat. There are fellows who can laugh and take a loss as a joke, but I'm not one of them. I would get angry with myself, for I considered it my fault when I lost."

First baseman Tony Lupien admitted he was "scared to death" of Grove. On one occasion Lupien recalled seeing a little kid ask Grove for an autograph outside the Red Sox clubhouse. Grove was carrying a rolled-up copy of the *St. Louis Post-Dispatch*. "He hit that kid across the puss with that paper, and the kid went flying," said Lupien.

Grove's two biggest years came in 1930 and 1931, years in which Mack's Athletics went to the World Series. In 1930 he went 28–5 while leading the league not only in victories, but in saves, strikeouts, and ERA. Grove won two World Series games as the A's knocked off the St. Louis Cardinals in six games.

His 1931 season was one of the finest in baseball annals. He finished at 31–4 with an ERA of only 2.06, in a year when the league's average was 4.38. He led the AL in wins, complete games, shutouts, strikeouts, and ERA. He also won the AL Most Valuable Player Award over teammate Al Simmons, who batted .390; Babe Ruth, who slugged 45 home runs and drove in 163 runs; and Lou Gehrig, who batted .341, hit 46 homers, and had 184 RBIs. Grove then went 2–1 in the seven-game World Series loss to the Cardinals.

With the onset of the Depression, Connie Mack broke up his Athletics. In December 1933 Grove was sent to the Boston Red Sox in a five-player trade that netted Mack $125,000. In spring training of 1934 Grove injured his arm. He was so discouraged that he openly talked of retiring and going home to Maryland. But by season's end Grove discovered that his arm hurt less when he threw his curve, so he relied on that pitch more and more.

Grove's control was also far better than it had been when he first arrived in the majors. "I remember the opening game of the 1937 season in Washington," recalled catcher Gene Desautels. "Every pitch I called, I would move my glove a little bit—wherever I wanted him to throw it. And I could have caught the ball with my eyes closed. His control was that good."

Grove spent eight productive years in Boston, once winning 20 games, once leading the league in winning percentage, four times leading in ERA, and five times being selected to the All-Star Game.

He retired after the 1941 season, having recorded exactly 300 victories and having set the mark for highest winning percentage by any pitcher with that many wins. He was particularly proud of his 300 victories. "Durn right I'd made up my mind to get that. I wanted that," he said. He often insisted that had he been pitching in an earlier era with a deader baseball and trick deliveries, he could have won 500 games. He was elected to the Hall of Fame in 1947.

After his career was over, Grove coached Little League and owned and managed three bowling alleys in Ohio. "I loved baseball," he said. "If I had to do it all over, I'd do the same thing. If they said, 'Come on, here's a steak dinner,' and I had a chance to go out and play a game of ball, I'd go out and play a game of ball and let the steak sit there. I would."

Kelly Gruber

Gruber, Kelly Wayne **3B**

1984–93 B:2/26/1962, Houston, TX Deb:4/20/1984, TOR AL BR/TR 6',185

G	AB	R	H	HR	RBI	OBP	SLG	AVG
939	3159	431	818	117	443	.310	.432	.259

Kelly Gruber, a golden-haired favorite in his early days in Toronto, ended his Blue Jays career under a cloud of whispers and allegations. From 1989 to 1991 he slugged 69 home runs and made the All-Star team twice. He hit 31 homers and drove in 118 in 1990, finishing fourth in the American League Most Valuable Player voting. The best year in team history, though, turned out to be the third baseman's worst.

On April 25, 1992, Gruber heard his neck pop during an at bat against Kansas City. He tried to play through the pain, but unsympathetic teammates referred to him as "Mrs. Gruber." Rumors circulated about wild off-field behavior even as his first marriage was breaking up. He returned to the everyday lineup in August, but Gruber's .229 average was his lowest since his rookie season.

Gruber delivered two clutch home runs in the postseason, but batted just .105 in the World Series against the Atlanta Braves. Toronto traded him to the California Angels over the winter. When the pain continued in the early weeks of the season, Gruber retired after 18 games. In 1995 he underwent major surgery to have a bone spur removed and repair a herniated disc from his neck. He mounted an unsuccessful comeback try with Baltimore in 1998 before retiring for good.

Mark Gubicza

Gubicza, Mark Steven **P**

1984–97 B:8/14/1962, Philadelphia, PA Deb:4/6/1984, KC AL BR/TR 6'5", 220

W	L	PCT	G	SH	IP	BB	SO	ERA
132	136	.493	384	16	2223[1]	786	1371	3.96

Mark Gubicza posted victory totals in double figures for the Kansas City Royals seven times. Although hampered by wildness early in his career, Gubicza finished his Royals career as the all-time Kansas City leader in strikeouts, with 1,366.

The Royals selected Gubicza in the second round of the June 1981 free agent amateur draft, as compensation for losing free agent catcher Darrell Porter to the St. Louis Cardinals. In the minors he led the Gulf Coast Rookie League in victories in 1981 and led the Southern League in strikeouts two years later.

Gubicza used his fastball and slider to beat Toronto in Game 6 of the 1985 Championship Series. He did not appear in the World Series against St. Louis. A shoulder injury eventually cost him velocity and effectiveness.

In his career year of 1988 he won 20 games, posted a 2.70 ERA, and pitched four shutouts. The following year he led the American League with 36 starts. In both seasons he appeared in the All-Star Game. In October 1996 the Royals traded Gubicza and righthander Mike Bovee to the Angels in exchange for designated hitter Chili Davis. He pitched just twice for the Angels before injuries eventually forced him to retire.

Pedro Guerrero

Guerrero, Pedro **1B-OF-3B**

1978–92 B:6/29/1956, San Pedro de Macoris, Dominican Republic Deb:9/22/1978, LA NL BR/TR 6', 195

G	AB	R	H	HR	RBI	OBP	SLG	AVG
1536	5392	730	1618	215	898	.374	.480	.300

When he was healthy, Pedro Guerrero was one of the best hitters in baseball. A career .300 hitter with excellent power, he had enough talent for a Hall of Fame plaque. Baseball analyst Bill James once wrote that Guerrero "was the best hitter that God has made in a long time." But since Guerrero suffered one injury after another in his 15 years with the Dodgers and Cardinals, he never really quite hit his stride.

Guerrero had only four seasons in which he played 150 or more games. He was on the disabled list nine different times during his career, not counting the times he played while injured or missed bunches of games without going on the DL.

Born in the Dominican Republic's hotbed of baseball, San Pedro de Macoris, Guerrero signed with the Cleveland Indians in 1973 as a skinny 16-year-old shortstop. He hit .255 with just two homers in his first year in the minors at Sarasota. So when the Indians had a chance to get lefty Bruce Ellingsen at the beginning of the 1974 season, they had no qualms about sending Guerrero to the Dodgers in a trade that haunted the Tribe for years.

By the time Guerrero had grown up and filled out, the injury jinx struck him. In 1977, after hitting .403 in his first 32 games for Triple A Albuquerque, he broke his ankle and missed the rest of the season. After brief appearances with the Dodgers over the next two seasons, he stuck in 1980, hitting .322 while filling in at first, second, and third base and in the outfield. But he went on the disabled list for the first time when he hurt his knee while sliding in August of 1980.

Guerrero became the everyday right fielder in 1981, hitting .300 with 12 homers and 48 RBIs in that strike-shortened season and being selected to the first of his four All-Star Games. In the 1981 World Series against the Yankees, he hit two homers and drove in seven runs, five in the final game. He shared the Series Most Valuable Player Award with Ron Cey and Steve Yeager as the Dodgers won in six games.

Healthy the next two years, Guerrero became one of the National League's most feared hitters, hitting .304 with 32 homers and 100 RBIs in 1982, and practically matching those numbers the following year. It marked the last time he was to be healthy in back-to-back seasons.

He missed 18 games in 1984 with a bum shoulder that bothered him most of the season and reduced his offensive output. He had some brilliant moments in 1985, hitting .320, leading the NL in slugging at .577, and belting a career-high 33 homers, but he missed 25 games with back spasms and a sprained wrist. Guerrero hit 15 homers that June to tie the major league record (Babe Ruth, Roger Maris, and Bob Johnson). He also reached base 14 times in a row on two homers, three doubles, two singles, six walks, and a hit-by-pitch.

A ruptured tendon in his knee limited Guerrero to 31 games in 1986, but he rebounded in 1987 to hit a career-best .338 with 27 homers. He was back on the DL in 1988 with a pinched nerve, and in August was traded to St. Louis for lefty John Tudor.

Guerrero had one more big season left. In 1989 he batted .311 and recorded career highs in games (162), RBIs (117), and doubles (42, to lead the NL). He also showed his adaptability as a hitter at spacious Busch Stadium, he cut down his swing and was content to hit for a high average. The Cardinals released him after a poor start in 1992. Guerrero spent 1993 in the Mexican League, hoping for one more shot in the majors, which never came.

Vladimir Guerrero

Guerrero, Vladimir **OF**

1996–* B:2/9/1976, Nizao Bani, Dominican Republic Deb:9/19/1996, MON NL BR/TR 6'2", 158

G	AB	R	H	HR	RBI	OBP	SLG	AVG
418	1585	256	498	92	281	.369	.567	.314

When Vladimir Guerrero arrived in the major leagues in 1997, he was already considered one of the best players to ever come out of the productive Montreal farm system. An Expos scout signed the 16-year-old Guerrero after seeing him play just once, and the youngster had little trouble jumping from the sandlots of his native Dominican Republic to the professional ranks.

Guerrero was tapped as *The Sporting News* Minor League Player of the Year in 1996. After winning back-to-back batting titles in the minors, he skipped Triple A and was brought directly to Montreal. The young man with braces on his teeth evoked comparisons to Hall of Famer Roberto Clemente.

Favored to win the National League Rookie of the Year Award in 1997, Guerrero made three trips to the disabled list and was limited to just 90 games. In 1998, however, the 22-year-old displayed his talents in full. He set six franchise records and finished among the major league leaders in 10 offensive categories. The low-budget Expos, who even traded for his older brother Wilton to entice Vladimir to stay in Montreal, uncharacteristically signed the young superstar to a five-year, $28 million contract late in the 1998 season.

The cannon-armed right fielder committed nine errors in the first 21 games in 1999, but he rewarded the team for its patience. He set new career highs with 42 homers and 131 RBIs, and also notched a 31-game hitting streak, the longest of any player in the 1990s.

Ron Guidry

Guidry, Ronald Ames **P**

1975–88 B:8/28/1950, Lafayette, LA Deb:7/27/1975, NY AL BL/TL 5'11", 162

W	L	PCT	G	SH	IP	BB	SO	ERA
170	91	.651	368	26	2392	633	1778	3.29

Ron Guidry first appeared on the scene as a Yankees regular in 1977—seemingly out of nowhere—and started throwing 95 mph fastballs and one of the most explosive sliders that baseball had ever seen. Then, in 1978, Guidry had one of the greatest seasons ever by a pitcher. He went 25–3 and led New York to a second straight world title.

Born in Lafayette, Louisiana, Guidry was Cajun through and through. While with the Yankees he was nicknamed "Gator" because of his background. An ardent hunter and fisherman Guidry often spoke of the virtues of squirrel stew. But he only killed what he planned to eat, and he refused to kill deer because, he said, they were too beautiful. Pitcher Dick Tidrow, his teammate on the Yankees, recalls the time Guidry shot a squirrel that got stuck in the top branches of a tree. As Tidrow watched in amazement, Guidry climbed more than 30 feet to knock the squirrel loose. Guidry's rationale? "If I respected it enough to kill it, I respected it enough to not leave it there."

Guidry signed with New York in 1971 while at the University of Southwestern Louisiana, where he majored in architecture. He then began a long, slow climb to the majors. Although he always had a great fastball, he couldn't master a breaking ball, so the Yankees converted him to short relief. Called up to the Yankees from Syracuse in 1975, his first outing was a disaster. He sat in the bullpen for the next 46 days.

While he sat, however, he watched reliever Sparky Lyle throw his slider. Lyle didn't throw the usual slider, the pitch that used to be a called a nickel curve because it slid across a corner of the plate with much less of a break than would a curveball. Lyle threw his slider over the top of the plate, and the ball broke straight down at the last second. And since the ball's spin resembled that of a pitched fastball, hitters were constantly fooled.

Guidry might not have had much bulk on his 5-foot 11-inch, 160-pound frame, but he was strong and wiry, not skinny and weak, and he was a remarkable athlete to boot. One of the fastest Yankees, he could have been an outstanding defensive outfielder. From 1982 through 1986 he won five straight Gold Gloves, and was amazingly fast at covering the third-base line.

Guidry quickly picked up the slider from Lyle, but hearing he was about to be sent to Syracuse, he decided to quit and started driving back to Louisiana. His wife, Bonnie, talked him out of it, and he made a U-turn and headed back to Syracuse. By July he was virtually unhittable, allowing only 16 hits in 40 innings.

The next spring owner George Steinbrenner almost traded Guidry but backed down after Gabe Paul, general manager of the Yankees, told the owner he would have to issue a public statement that the deal was made over Paul's objections. As Paul later recounted, he told Steinbrenner he would hold him responsible when Guidry became an outstanding major league pitcher for another team.

Guidry finally got his chance in late April 1977 when the Yankees needed an emergency starter. He pitched so well that a month later he became a permanent member of the rotation. He finished the season 16–7 in 25 starts with five shutouts and a 2.82 ERA. Guidry was that rarest of successful starters—a winner with only two pitches in his repertoire.

In 1978 he won his first 13 games, including an 18-strikeout contest against the California Angels on June 17, a feat Guidry called his "greatest single thrill." His accomplishment set an American League record for lefties (later broken by Randy Johnson). Guidry lost his first game of the season to the Milwaukee Brewers on July 7, his second to the Baltimore Orioles on August 4, and his third to the Toronto Blue Jays on September 20.

Guidry virtually kept the Yankees from collapse as the team endured a succession of injuries and friction between Reggie Jackson and manager

Billy Martin. When the season came down to one playoff game against the Boston Red Sox at Fenway Park, Guidry went 6⅔ innings on three days' rest and got his 25th win, putting the Yankees in the playoffs and capping one of the greatest team comebacks in baseball history. He topped that off by winning a start in both the Championship Series and World Series; he had a 1.06 postseason ERA as the Yanks won their second straight world championship.

That year his 1.74 ERA led the American League, and his .893 winning percentage set a major league record for 20-game winners. His nine shutouts set a team record, topped the circuit, and tied Babe Ruth's AL record for lefties. And his 248 strikeouts broke Jack Chesbro's 74-year-old team record. The unanimous choice for the Cy Young Award, Guidry finished second to Boston's Jim Rice in Most Valuable Player balloting.

Although Guidry did not again approach the brilliance of the 1978 season, he remained a key figure in the Yankees' successes in the next decade. From 1977 through 1985 his 154 wins led the majors. In 1979 was selected to his second successive All-Star Game and earned his second ERA title. In 1983 he went 21–9 and led the league with 21 complete games. In 1985, having added a curve and a changeup to his repertoire, he recorded a 22–6 mark.

The following year his arm blew out, and he went only 16–23 his last three seasons. He retired after an abbreviated 1988 season.

Ozzie Guillen

Guillen, Oswaldo Jose (Barrios) **SS**

1985–* B:1/20/1964, Oculare Del Tuy, Venezuela Deb:4/9/1985, CHI AL BL/TR 5'11", 150

G	AB	R	H	HR	RBI	OBP	SLG	AVG
1930	6579	751	1738	26	607	.290	.338	.264

Although not as flashy as some other shortstops, Ozzie Guillen made the tough plays look routine. Guillen, a native of Venezuela, followed the lead of his fellow countrymen—Luis Aparicio, Dave Concepcion, and Manny Trillo—by making a career out of being a strong-fielding, and timely-hitting, middle infielder.

Guillen was named American League Rookie of the Year for the White Sox in 1985 after he hit .273 with 71 runs scored and a franchise record-low 12 errors at shortstop. He had at least 13 steals each season from 1987 through 1991, with a career-high 36 swipes in 1989. In 1995 he fanned only 25 times in 415 at bats.

Fielding, however, was Guillen's most valuable asset. He won the 1990 Gold Glove award after committing just 17 errors and turning 100 double plays in a career-high 159 games. Guillen twice exceeded 800 total chances.

Guillen came up in the San Diego Padres system, but became the second slick-fielding shortstop named Ozzie that the Padres traded away in a two-year period. In 1984, two years after the Padres dealt Ozzie Smith, San Diego sent Guillen, a minor leaguer, to Chicago. With the White Sox, Guillen never played a day in the minors and was in the team's Opening Day lineup of 1985.

Guillen filed for free agency after the 1997 season and signed with Baltimore, but was released after appearing in just 12 games. He hooked on with Atlanta, where he served as a valuable infield reserve in both 1998 and 1999. In the 1998 Championship Series he batted .417. In Game 6 of the 1999 NLCS his ninth-inning, pinch-hit single tied the score against the Mets and helped lead Atlanta to the pennant.

Don Gullett

Gullett, Donald Edward **P**

1970–78 B:1/6/1951, Lynn, KY Deb:4/10/1970, CIN NL BR/TL, 6', 190

W	L	PCT	G	SH	IP	BB	SO	ERA
109	50	.686	266	14	1390	501	921	3.11

When Don Gullett showed up in Tampa in 1970 for spring training with the Reds, he had only 78 innings of Class A ball on his resume. When asked about the powerful 19-year-old lefthander, Pete Rose said, "Gullett's the only guy who can throw a baseball through a car wash and not get the ball wet."

Gullett made the Reds that spring, and for a while he was arguably the National League's best lefthander. He had a tragic flaw: he threw across his body instead of driving toward home plate with his right shoulder leading. Some pitchers—Tommy John, for example—could get away with that delivery, but not Gullett. He retired in 1978 at the age of 27 with a rotator cuff that was damaged beyond repair.

Born in rural Lynn, Kentucky, Gullett was a legendary three-sport star at Southshore McKell High School. Among his accomplishments were scoring 47 points in a basketball game, scoring 72 points in a football game, and striking out 20 of 21 batters in a baseball game.

The Reds' first pick in the June 1969 amateur draft, Gullett went 7–2 with a 1.96 ERA for Sioux Falls of the Northern League. He pitched almost entirely in relief for Cincinnati as a rookie, going 5–2 with a 2.43 ERA and 76 strikeouts. His season highlight came on August 23, when he struck out the first six Mets he faced. He then picked up two saves in the Championship Series sweep of the Pittsburgh Pirates.

Gullett moved into the starting rotation in 1971

with a new and improved curveball. He was an instant star, going 16–6 with a league-leading .727 winning percentage. He contracted hepatitis the following year and struggled much of the season, although he pitched well in a World Series start against Oakland.

Healthy again in 1973, Gullett went 18–8, starting 30 times and picking up five wins in 15 relief appearances. As a full-time starter in 1974, he won 17 games in 35 starts, working a career-high 243 innings despite some back problems. A broken thumb limited him to 22 starts in 1975, but he still finished with a 15–4 record, a career-low 2.42 ERA, and led the league with a .789 winning percentage. He then won a game in both the NLCS and the World Series.

In 1976 Gullett was limited to 23 starts because of a pinched nerve in his neck and the beginning of his rotator cuff problems. Nonetheless, he was 11–3 and started and won Game 1 in the World Series sweep of the Yankees.

That winter, Gullett was in the first class of free agents. He jumped to the Yankees for a six-year deal worth almost $2 million. The Yankees won their second straight pennant and Gullett was 14–4, but his shoulder limited him to 158⅓ innings. He started the Series opener for the third straight season and saw Sparky Lyle blow the win for him in the ninth. He took a battering and the loss in Game 5, but his team still won the world championship for the third straight year.

Gullett's shoulder worsened the next season, and he made only limited appearances. Dr. Frank Jobe, the man who rebuilt Tommy John's elbow in 1974, operated on Gullett's shoulder that winter, but it was too late. He retired to his farm in Kentucky, finishing with an incredible .686 winning percentage. He has been Reds' pitching coach since 1993.

Bill Gullickson

Gullickson, William Lee **P**

1979–87, 1990–94 B:2/20/1959, Marshall, MN
Deb:9/26/1979, MON NL BR/TR 6'3", 215

W	L	PCT	G	SH	IP	BB	SO	ERA
162	136	.544	398	11	2560	622	1279	3.93

Bill Gullickson was one of the National League's best young hurlers in the early 1980s. A mid-career slump sent him overseas to play in Japan, but he re-emerged as a 20-game winner in the American League.

As a 21-year-old rookie with Montreal in 1980, Gullickson struck out 18 Cubs on September 10—a still-standing Expos record and an NL rookie mark until Kerry Wood broke it in 1998. Gullickson finished the year 10–5 and was the NL Rookie of the Year runner-up.

After winning seven games in the strike-shortened 1981 season (plus a 1–2 postseason mark), Gullickson earned double-digit victories in each of the next six seasons with the Expos and Reds. But he also threw over 200 innings in each of those seasons except 1985, when he tossed 181⅔ innings. Ineffective with the Reds and Yankees in 1987, Gullickson opted to cross the Pacific, where he pitched for the next two seasons.

Gullickson returned with the Houston Astros in 1990, going 10–14 and prompting most observers to believe that his sabbatical hadn't halted his career slide. But a year later with the Detroit Tigers, Gullickson tied for the AL lead with 20 wins. He showed it wasn't a fluke in the two subsequent seasons, putting up 14 and 13 wins, respectively. Gullickson's career ended with the 1994 strike, which halted a season in which he posted a career-worst 5.93 ERA.

Harry Gumbert

Gumbert, Harry Edward **P**

1935–44, 1946–50 B:11/5/1909, Elizabeth, PA
D:1/4/1995, Wimberley, TX Deb:9/12/1835, NY NL BR/TR
6'2, 185

W	L	PCT	G	SV	IP	BB	SO	ERA
143	113	.559	508	48	2156	721	709	3.68

Harry "Gunboat" Gumbert was one of the best fielding pitchers of his era and an important part of pennant-winning teams with the New York Giants and St. Louis Cardinals. After joining the Giants in 1935, Gumbert filled in as both a starter and reliever. Although Carl Hubbell was clearly the ace of the staff, Gumbert contributed by reaching double figures in wins in both 1936 and 1937, as the Giants claimed the National League pennant each time.

Never a hard thrower, the crafty Gumbert led the Giants' staff with 15 victories in 1938. On May 23, he displayed his fielding brilliance by recording 10 assists, a National League record for a pitcher. By 1939, he had started to replace a declining Hubbell as the anchor of the Giants' mound corps. The durable Gumbert did not succumb to the pressure, winning a career-high 18 games.

In the middle of the 1941 season, the Giants traded an aging Gumbert to the Cardinals, but the wily righthander wasn't finished winning big games for pennant contenders. He won 30 games over the next two and a half seasons, helping the Redbirds to a pair of pennants and the world championship in 1942.

Gumbert missed all of 1945 due to World War II, but returned to the major leagues the following season. By 1947, he had become a full-time reliever. Pitching for Cincinnati in 1948, he led the National League with 17 saves and

61 appearances. His career ended two years later, after a one-game stint with the Pirates.

Gumbert capped off a long run for a successful baseball family. Two of his great uncles, Ad and Billy, had pitched in the National League during the 19th century.

Larry Gura

Gura, Lawrence Cyril **P**

1970–85 B:11/26/1947, Joliet, IL Deb:4/30/1970, CHI NL BB/TL 6'1", 185

W	L	PCT	G	SH	IP	BB	SO	ERA
126	97	.565	403	16	2047	600	801	3.76

Larry Gura is a testament to the virtue of patience. Neither the Cubs nor the Yankees had much use for him during his first five years in the majors. But Gura, a highly disciplined fitness enthusiast when such players were rare, didn't give up.

Swapped to Kansas City for Fran Healy in May of 1976, Gura went 4–0 in 18 relief appearances and two starts for the division-winning Royals. The following year his 10 saves were third on the club as Kansas City again took its division.

Moved into the starting rotation in 1978, Gura immediately became a star. His 16–4 record gave him the third-best winning percentage in the AL. He then recorded the Royals' only victory in the ALCS.

Two years later, Gura won 18 games and was selected to the All-Star Game. He then recorded a complete-game 7–2 victory over Ron Guidry, as the Royals swept the Yankees in the ALCS. He didn't get a decision in two starts in the World Series.

His win total was 18 again in 1982, leading the staff in victories. Only LaMarr Hoyt won more games in the AL that season. After two more years with the Royals, Gura ended his career where it had begun, with the Cubs.

Cliff Gustafson

Gustafson, Clifford

College coach (1968–94, 1427–373–2) B:2/17/1931, New Orleans, LA 5'11", 160

Cliff Gustafson was already the most successful baseball coach in Texas high school history when he was named to replace the legendary Bibb Falk at the University of Texas following the 1967 season. Gustafson was nearly as successful in Austin as he had been in the college ranks. He was named national coach-of-the-year three times, and was later inducted into both the College Baseball Coaches Association Hall of Fame and the Texas Sports Hall of Fame.

Gustafson had lettered as an infielder at the University of Texas in 1952, and played for a short while in the minor leagues. As a coach he emphasized sound pitching and defense, and that formula led to 12 division titles and seven state championships in 13 years at South San Antonio High School. His record at Texas was just as impressive.

In 29 years, his Longhorns won 22 Southwest Conference titles, made a record 17 appearances in the College World Series, and won two NCAA national championships. His career mark of 1427–373–2 not only included the NCAA record for victories, but his .793 winning percentage was the third best in the history of college baseball. In both 1975 and 1982 Gustafson's teams won more than 90 percent of their games. His 1977 squad won an NCAA-record 34 consecutive games to open the season.

Gustafson tutored the only three three-time All-America pitchers in college baseball history: Burt Hooton (1969–71), Greg Swindell (1983–85), and Kirk Dressendorfer (1988–90). Gustafson's other first-team All-America pitchers included Ron Roznovsky, Jim Gideon (twice), Richard Wortham, Jerry Don Gleaton, Tony Arnold, Calvin Schiraldi, and Kurt Krippner. Schiraldi, the national pitcher-of-the-year in 1983, overshadowed another Longhorns hurler who went on to the most successful major league career of any of Gustafson's big arms of Texas—Roger Clemens.

Tony Gwynn

Gwynn, Anthony Keith **OF**

1982–* B:5/9/1960, Los Angeles, CA Deb:7/19/82, SD NL BL/TL 5'11", 200

G	AB	R	H	HR	RBI	OBP	SLG	AVG
2333	9059	1361	3067	133	1104	.392	.459	.339

Tony Gwynn was one of the game's best pure hitters in two different decades. The likeable Padre won four batting titles each in the 1980s and 1990s; Gwynn and Honus Wagner shared the National League record for most batting titles with eight apiece. A true rarity for a modern athlete, Gwynn spent his career in one uniform and established himself as San Diego's all-time leader in nearly every offensive category except home runs.

He was selected by the Padres in the third round of the 1981 amateur draft out of San Diego State, where he lettered in both baseball and basketball. Gwynn, who set the all-time assists record for the Aztecs, even considered a career in basketball after being drafted by the San Diego Clippers (now in Los Angeles) in the 10th round of the 1981 NBA draft. Instead he chose a career in baseball.

Gwynn failed to hit .300 in 1982, a feat he managed each of the next 17 seasons. Despite missing almost the first three months of the 1983 season with an injury, Gwynn batted .309 and also had a 25-game hitting streak. The 1984 season was a breakout year for both Gwynn and his team. Gwynn won his first batting title with a .351 average and helped lead the Padres to the National League pennant. He also made the first of his 14 All-Star Game appearances.

Gwynn batted .368 in the 1984 National League Championship Series, scoring a series-best six runs to lead the Padres to a come-from-behind win over the Cubs. Chicago was originally scheduled to host the final three games of the best-of-five series, but because Wrigley Field had no lights, Major League Baseball switched sites to accommodate the television schedule. Chicago dominated the first two afternoon games at Wrigley Field and the Padres limped back to San Diego facing elimination. The Padres won the next two games, both at night, and trailed 3–2 in the seventh inning of the Sunday matinee. A grounder went through Leon Durham's legs at first base to bring in the tying run, and Gwynn followed with a double for the go-ahead run. Tigers pitching held Gwynn to a 5-for-19 performance in the World Series as Detroit topped San Diego in five games.

Gwynn won the first of his five Gold Glove Awards in 1986. Despite his stocky build, Gwynn stole at least 10 bases in 11 seasons, including four seasons of 30 or more. In 1987 he stole 56 bases to finish second in the league.

One year after he won his second batting title with a .370 mark, Gwynn's .313 average set an NL record for lowest batting average by a leader in 1988. He won his third consecutive batting title the following year. Gwynn showed some signs of slowing down in the early 1990s because of nagging injuries. He was back to his usual form in 1993, but expansion to the mile-high elevation of Denver provided some of his toughest competition for the batting title. The only three batting titles Gwynn did not win from 1993 to 1999 were won by Colorado Rockies—Andres Galarraga (1993) and Larry Walker (1998–99).

Gwynn topped even himself in 1994. His .394 average was the highest in the major leagues since Ted Williams hit .406 in 1941, and the highest in the NL since Bill Terry of the New York Giants hit .401 in 1930. Gwynn batted .433 (26-for-60) over his last 15 games when the baseball strike ended the season on August 11.

Gwynn had the opportunity to be teammates with his brother Chris in 1996; the brothers ended the year in the postseason. Tony won the batting title with a .353 average, and Chris singled in the winning run to clinch the NL West title on the final day of the season. The Cardinals eliminated the Padres in the Division Series.

In 1997 Gwynn won his fourth consecutive batting title, joining Ty Cobb, Rogers Hornsby, Rod Carew, and Wade Boggs as the only players to win four or more consecutive batting titles. Gwynn tied Honus Wagner for the most NL batting titles; only Cobb, who won 12 American League titles, won more. Gwynn, sometimes maligned for his lack of production, also set a career highs that season with 17 home runs, 119 RBIs, 220 hits, and 49 doubles. He appeared in his second World Series the following year, but San Diego's dream season ended with a sweep by the Yankees.

Gwynn became the 22nd member of the 3,000-hit club with a single against Montreal's Dan Smith on August 6, 1999. It was part of a "milestone weekend" for baseball—Gwynn and the Padres had surrendered Mark McGwire's 500th home run the previous night in St. Louis; Boggs notched his 3000th hit the night after Gwynn's milestone. Gwynn finished the 1999 season with 3,067 career hits, good for 18th on the all-time list. Long known for his charitable nature and big heart, Gwynn was honored in 1999 with the Roberto Clemente Award as the player who best exemplified baseball on and off the field.

Mule Haas

Haas, George William **OF**

1925, 1928–38 B:10/15/1903, Montclair, NJ D:6/30/1974, New Orleans, LA Deb:8/15/1925, PIT NL BL/TR 6'1", 175

G	AB	R	H	HR	RBI	OBP	SLG	AVG
1168	4303	706	1257	43	496	.359	.402	.292

George "Mule" Haas compiled a .292 career batting average in a dozen major league seasons, and was a key participant in the greatest World Series comeback ever. Nicknamed by a sportswriter who wrote that his bat "packed the kick of a mule," Haas knocked around the minors for five years before coming up to Pittsburgh for only three at bats. He moved to the Philadelphia Athletics in 1928, where he saw part-time duty.

He developed his fielding skills under the tutelage of Tris Speaker, then winding up his illustrious career with the A's. Haas became an excellent outfielder, adopting Speaker's strategy of playing shallow and going back on the ball.

In 1929 Haas became the middleman in a hard-hitting outfield that included Al Simmons and Bing Miller; he batted .313 to help Philadelphia win the pennant. In the World Series, Haas, with a little help from the sun, hammered out the pivotal line drive in the Series' most legendary rally.

On October 12, 1929, the Chicago Cubs seemed on their way to tying the World Series at two games apiece; the Cubs led the Athletics, 8–0, entering the bottom of the seventh inning. Few of the 29,921 spectators in Shibe Park got excited when Simmons blasted a Charlie Root fastball onto the left field roof. But then Jimmie Foxx singled and Miller received a gift base hit when Chicago center fielder Hack Wilson lost the ball in the sun.

Jimmy Dykes and Joe Boley followed with singles to make the score 8–3. The next batter, pinch hitter George Burns, popped up for the first out of the inning, but Max Bishop singled to score Dykes, and Chicago's seemingly insurmountable lead had suddenly been cut in half.

Manager Joe McCarthy brought in lefty Art Nehf to pitch to the lefthanded Haas, who laced the first pitch toward center field for what became the turning point of the Series. Wilson, who had already lost one ball in the sun, compounded his crime by losing another. By the time the ball was returned to the infield the speedy Haas had circled the bases for an inside-the-park home run, the score was 8–7, and the Cubs were in full retreat.

Mickey Cochrane then walked. Sheriff Blake was brought in from the bullpen, but Simmons, in his second appearance of the inning, singled, and then Foxx singled to tie the score. Blake went to the showers and Pat Malone came in to try to stop the avalanche; he promptly struck Bing Miller in the ribs to load the bases. After that, Dykes doubled to left to put the A's up, 10–8, completing the greatest rally in World Series history.

The Cubs held a 2–0 lead entering the ninth inning of Game 5 when Haas came to the plate a man on. Haas smacked a home run to tie the score. Malone allowed the winning hit for the second straight game when Miller doubled to score Simmons with the Series-ending run.

Haas hit .299 and .323 as the A's repeated as American League champs in 1930 and 1931. Batting second behind Max Bishop, ahead of Simmons and Foxx, he was expected to move Bishop along for the big bats to follow. He more than lived up to expectations, leading the league in sacrifice bunts from 1930 through 1934 and again in 1936.

The Depression forced A's manager Connie Mack to break up his great team. After the 1932 season, he sold Haas, Simmons, and Dykes to the Chicago White Sox for $100,000. Although his hitting fell off in Chicago, Haas remained an effective player for several more years. In 1938 he returned briefly to the A's and then retired. He served as a White Sox coach from 1940 through 1946.

Stan Hack

Hack, Stanley Camfield **3B**

1932–47 M(1954–58, 199–272) B:12/6/1909, Sacramento, CA D:12/15/1979, Dixon, IL Deb:4/12/1932, CHI NL BL/TR 6', 170

G	AB	R	H	HR	RBI	OBP	SLG	AVG
1938	7278	1239	2193	57	642	.394	.397	.301

"Smiling Stan" Hack was one of the National League's outstanding third basemen in the 1930s and one of its most popular players. As one observer quipped, "He has more friends than Leo Durocher has enemies."

Not a traditional power-hitting third baseman, Hack was rather a lefthanded-hitting leadoff man who compiled a .301 career batting average and rarely struck out. He also hit .348 in four World Series and .400 in All-Star competition.

The son of a former semipro player, Hack was pursued by both Oakland and Sacramento of the Pacific Coast League after he graduated from high school in Sacramento. He took a job at a branch of the Bank of Italy (later renamed Bank of America) instead, playing semipro ball on weekends. In 1931 he took two weeks off from his job to try out with Sacramento. Not only did he make the club, but also he went on to collect 232 hits and hit .352 for the season. The Cubs were so impressed with Hack's performance that they purchased him for $40,000.

He hit only .236 in 178 at bats for the Cubs in 1932 and spent most of the next season with Albany in the International League, where he batted .299. Back with the big team to stay in 1934, he hit .289 in 109 games at third. But he produced only 21 RBIs in 402 at bats. His breakthrough season came in 1935, when he hit .311, drove in 64 runs, struck out only 17 times in 427 at bats, and stole 14 bases, fourth best in the National League.

Most of his hits went to the opposite field. "I watch the ball more than most hitters," he admitted. "I let it get right up on me—maybe I even swing a little late." This explains why he struck out only 466 times in 7,278 at bats, one strikeout for every 15.6 at bats. Like all good leadoff hitters, he knew how to draw walks, receiving 1,092 free passes in his career. Hack was also a good base stealer for his time, leading the NL in steals in 1938 with 16 and tying for the lead the following year with 17. He scored 100 or more runs in six straight seasons from 1936 to 1941.

Hack was an excellent fielder as well. He led the league in assists, chances per game, and fielding percentage twice each, in double plays three times, and in putouts five times. The durable third baseman averaged 152 games a season—in a time of 154-game seasons—between 1936 and 1941, despite his propensity for late-night socializing.

The likable Hack soon became popular with the fans. In 1935, the year that Hack established himself, Bill Veeck came up with one of his more unusual promotional gimmicks: the "Smile with Stan Hack" mirror. Veeck, then 21 years old and working for his father, the team president, sold the contraptions to fans in the bleachers. But before long the league office prohibited the practice.

William Curran, who authored a study about fielding, had this to say about "Smiling Stan": "Hack came closest to an earthly manifestation of the ideal third baseman of the day. Tall, slender, handsome, confident—Hack was the idol of every sandlot urchin playing third base in a pair of torn knickers."

In 1935 the Cubs lost the World Series to the Tigers in six games. In the top of the ninth inning of the final game, with Detroit ahead by a run, Hack led off with a triple but was stranded on base as Tommy Bridges got three easy outs. Ten years later Hack returned to Briggs Stadium for another Series against the Tigers. He walked over to third base and announced, "I just wanted to see if I was still there."

Hack's two best seasons were 1940 and 1941. He hit .317 and led the league in hits both seasons. In 1940 he struck out a mere 24 times in 603 at bats—once in every 25 at bats. Hack retired as a player in 1943 following a series of disagreements with Cubs manager Jimmie Wilson, even though Hack was only 33 and coming off a strong season. When Charlie Grimm replaced Wilson in the middle of 1944 Hack returned. In 1945 he went 54 straight errorless games at third with 138 chances, hit .323, and scored 110 runs as the Cubs won the pennant. Hack hit .367 in the Series, but the Cubs lost in seven to the Tigers.

After two more seasons as a part-time player, Hack managed Des Moines in 1948 and 1949, Springfield in 1950, and Los Angeles from 1951 through 1953 before taking over as the Cubs' skipper in 1954. Hack's new responsibilities didn't suppress his sense of humor. In 1954 pitcher Bob Zick showed up. "Hi, I'm Zick," said the righthander. Hack responded, "I haven't been feeling so well myself."

As Cubs manager, Hack developed the odd habit of coaching third base for the first inning, then spending the rest of the game in the dugout. It didn't seem to help. The Cubs finished sixth in 1955 and last in 1956. Hack was fired and then served as an infield coach and a batting coach for the Cardinals in 1957 and 1958. In 1959 he managed Denver. He also managed Salt Lake City in 1965 and Dallas-Fort Worth for most of the 1966 season.

Harvey Haddix

Haddix, Harvey **P**

1952–65 B:9/18/1925, Medway, OH D:1/8/1994, Springfield, OH Deb:8/20/1952, STL NL BL/TL 5'9½", 170

W	L	PCT	G	SV	IP	BB	SO	ERA
136	113	.546	453	21	2235	601	1575	3.63

Harvey Haddix was short and slight, and he didn't make his major league debut until he was a month shy of 27 years old. But at age 33 he turned in the greatest pitching that baseball has ever seen—12 perfect innings, with no batter reaching first, against the powerful defending National League champion Milwaukee Braves.

In 1947, Haddix's first professional season, he was voted the Most Valuable Player of the Carolina League. He won 19 games and struck out 268 batters in 204 innings. After leading the American Association in both wins and strikeouts in 1950, he had earned the chance to pitch for the big league St. Louis Cardinals, but he was drafted into the military and spent all of 1951 and most of 1952 in the service.

In 1953 Haddix had another brilliant rookie season, this time as a major leaguer with St. Louis. He compiled a 20–9 record that featured a league-leading six shutouts and earned his nickname, "the Kitten," because of his resemblance to fellow

St. Louis southpaw "Harry the Cat" Brecheen in size and intensity of style. Unfortunately, that season Haddix also lost a no-hitter in the ninth inning. In Rookie of the Year voting he finished second to Dodgers second baseman Jim Gilliam.

Haddix followed up his sensational freshman season with another solid performance, going 18–13; but his ERA jumped up more than half a run. The next year it increased nearly a whole run as he won only 12 games while losing 16.

In May 1956 the Cards dealt Haddix to Philadelphia, where he put together 12–8 and 10–13 records. Then the Cincinnati Reds wanted him, and in December 1957 the Phillies traded him, but he managed to win only eight games the next year.

After that season he became a key player in one of the most important trades in Pittsburgh Pirates history. Along with catcher Smoky Burgess and third baseman Don Hoak, Haddix joined the Bucs in exchange for slugger Frank Thomas and three unknowns. The brash young Pirates, who had surprised the baseball world with a second-place finish in 1958, now had a proven field leader in Hoak, a hard-hitting catcher and pinch hitter in Burgess, and a reliable lefty in Haddix.

On May 26, 1959, under a sky filled with lightning and thunder, Haddix did what no pitcher has done before or since—he retired 36 consecutive batters in a single game. However, while Haddix was flawless, his mound opponent, Braves hurler Lew Burdette, was just good enough.

The Pirates rapped 12 singles off Burdette. In the third inning they had three hits but didn't score because Bucs outfielder Roman Mejias was nailed trying to scamper from first to third on an infield out. When Haddix retired Burdette in the last of the ninth, he had done what no National league pitcher had done in 79 years—he had pitched a perfect nine-inning game. But his night's work wasn't over.

The Braves went up and down in order the next three innings, but Burdette was still holding the Pirates scoreless. Burgess, the Pirates catcher, said the key was Haddix's control: "He was pinpointing every pitch."

The situation deteriorated in the 13th. Milwaukee infielder Felix Mantilla, the first batter, took an 0–2 pitch that Haddix and Burgess thought was strike three, but the umpire disagreed. Then Mantilla grounded to third-sacker Don Hoak, whose low throw eluded first baseman Rocky Nelson. Burgess, backing up the play, grabbed the ball and put a hasty tag on Mantilla. But the umpires didn't buy Burgess' tag. The next batter, third baseman Eddie Mathews, bunted successfully, and Mantilla was at second. Outfielder Hank Aaron was intentionally walked.

Then Braves fielder Joe Adcock, who had twice struck out on Haddix's sliders inside, got one out over the plate, and he rapped it over the centerfield fence. Bucs center fielder Bill Virdon made a leaping try, but Aaron thought the ball had hit the wall, so he touched second and headed across the pitcher's mound to the dugout. Adcock continued to run, and when he reached third, Aaron was called out for being passed on the bases.

The final score, which wasn't clear until NL president Warren Giles ruled the next day, went into the books as 1–0. Haddix had lost his perfect game, no-hitter, and shutout. And he also lost the game. In the clubhouse afterward, an eager young journalist asked Haddix if it was the best game he had ever pitched, but the answer was obvious. It was simply the best game anyone had ever pitched.

Haddix finished the season with a 12–12 record, although he won his second of three consecutive Gold Gloves. The following season he was 11–10 for the world champion Pirates, and he won Game 5 as a starter and the incredible Game 7 in relief.

His pitching skills, however, were deteriorating. In 1964 Pittsburgh traded him to Baltimore, where he spent his final two seasons.

Haddix then served as pitching coach for several teams: the New York Mets in 1966 and 1967, the Reds in 1969, the Boston Red Sox in 1971, the Cleveland Indians from 1975 through 1978, and the Pirates from 1979 through 1984. In his last year as a Bucs coach his staff won the league ERA title while the team finished last.

In a final twist for the unlucky Haddix, in 1991 an ad hoc committee clarified the official rules for a no-hitter. They decreed that the pitcher must pitch the entire game without allowing a hit. So Harvey Haddix doesn't get credit for 12 innings of perfect pitching. Instead, his name is in the record books for pitching the longest one-hitter.

Bump Hadley

Hadley, Irving Darius **P**

1926–41 B:7/5/1904, Lynn, MA D:2/15/1963, Lynn, MA
Deb:4/20/1926, WAS AL BR/TR 5'11", 190

W	L	PCT	G	SV	IP	BB	SO	ERA
161	165	.494	528	25	2945[2]	1442	1318	4.24

Irving Darius "Bump" Hadley was a hard-throwing but wild American League righthander from 1926 through 1941. Saddled with losing teams for most of his career, he generally pitched better than his won-lost record indicates, but he is best remembered for one pitch—the one that nearly killed Mickey Cochrane.

Bump—a nickname he acquired as a youngster because his short, chunky build was similar to that of Bumpus, a storybook character—pitched his first full major league season in 1927 for the

Washington Senators. Although he had a 14–6 record and a 2.85 ERA, he walked 86 batters in fewer than 200 innings.

He would remain a "wild man" his entire career. Hadley led the American League in bases on balls in 1932 and 1933 and topped 100 walks six times; he finished his career in 1941 with 1,442 free passes, at the time the third highest total ever. In 16 seasons he averaged 4.4 walks per nine innings, placing him on a tier just below such consummate wild pitchers as Tommy Byrne, Rex Barney, and Ryne Duren.

Hadley won 15 games for the Senators in 1930, but a trade in 1932 to the lowly St. Louis Browns resulted in two straight 20-loss seasons. In 1936 he was dealt to the Yankees. With a winning team at last, he responded with his finest won-lost record, 14–4. In Game 3 of the World Series that fall, he scattered 11 hits to defeat the Giants, 2–1.

On May 27, 1937, he faced Detroit at Yankee Stadium with the Tigers' catcher and manager, Mickey Cochrane, at the plate. Hadley fired a high, tight fastball. (Cochrane later admitted he lost track of the pitch as soon as it left the pitcher's hand.) The ball hit Cochrane squarely in the forehead and bounced all the way back to the mound. Cochrane was carried from the field with a fractured skull, and for several days doctors feared for his life. Although he eventually recovered, he never played again.

Hadley won 32 more games for the Yankees during the next three seasons. Knocked out of Game 4 of the 1937 World Series during the Giants' six-run second inning, he made up for it in Game 3 of the 1939 Series against Cincinnati. Relieving Lefty Gomez in the second inning, he went the rest of the way for a 7–3 win.

He spent his final year in the major leagues with the Philadelphia Athletics. Despite his success with the Yankees, Hadley's earlier seasons with the Browns and Senators left him with a losing career record of 161–165.

Chick Hafey

Hafey, Charles James **OF**

1924–35, 1937 B:2/12/1903, Berkeley, CA D:7/2/1973, Calistoga, CA Deb:8/28/1924, STL NL BR/TR 6', 185

G	AB	R	H	HR	RBI	OBP	SLG	AVG
1283	4625	777	1466	164	833	.372	.526	.317

Giants manager John McGraw once said, "If Chick Hafey had two good eyes, he'd be the best ballplayer anybody ever saw." Cardinals skipper Branch Rickey, who discovered Hafey, was only slightly less enthusiastic. "If Hafey had had good eyesight and good health," Rickey said, "he might have been the finest righthanded hitter baseball has ever known."

The same "if only" theme is repeated in the comments of almost everyone who saw Hafey play. While no one, not even Rickey or McGraw, can accurately estimate his level of performance under different circumstances, Hafey was still a great player despite his bad eyesight and other health handicaps.

Charles James Hafey was one of eight children. After he hurt his right arm as a youth, doctors inserted a steel plate, the muscles regenerated, and the arm became extremely strong. Hafey was pitching semipro ball when the St. Louis Cardinals took notice. He signed with the Cards as a pitcher when just 17 years old—although he claimed to be 18, thinking it would improve his chances. He pitched batting practice for the Cardinals in 1922, but Rickey decided he was too erratic to become a successful pitcher, so he was moved to the outfield.

In 1923 he hit .284 with 16 home runs for Fort Smith of the Class C Western Association. After being promoted to Houston of the Texas League in 1924, he hit .360 with 90 RBIs and a league-leading 20 triples. The Cardinals called him up in August, and he hit .253 in 24 games. He started the 1925 season with Syracuse of the International League, but after 21 games he returned to St. Louis for good. In 93 games he hit .302 with 57 RBIs.

In one 1926 game, Hafey was hit twice by pitches. While examining him in the locker room, Dr. Robert Hyland discovered that Hafey couldn't see the doctor's hand when he held it above Hafey's locker. The doctor prescribed a fish diet, but Hafey's eyesight failed to improve. Hafey was then told to wear glasses on the field. Although they are now common in baseball, few players wore spectacles at the time. Hafey's sight varied daily, and he required three different pairs of glasses.

In 1926, under player-manager Rogers Hornsby, the Cardinals won the first pennant in the team's history. Hornsby and first baseman Jim Bottomley were the team's big hitters, but each starter in the outfield—Ray Blades, Taylor Douthit, and Billy Southworth—batted over .300. Hafey, a reserve outfielder and pinch hitter, batted .271 in 78 games. He started all seven games of the World Series for the victorious Cards in place of the injured Blades but hit only .185.

By 1927 Hafey had adjusted to his eyewear and hit .329, beginning a string of five straight outstanding seasons for the Cardinals. He was a remarkable outfielder who had both speed and a powerful arm. In the early 1950s, when Willie Mays arrived in the major leagues, Ernie Lombardi and Paul Waner described him as "another Hafey."

In 1928 the Cardinals, under manager Bill

McKechnie, were looking for another pennant and led the Giants by two games with only three to play. Playing in Boston, the Cardinals were tied, 3–3, with the Braves up in the bottom of the 12th inning when Boston's Jack Smith tried to score from second on a single. Hafey cut him down at the plate, and the Cardinals went on to win in the 15th inning. Two days later they clinched the pennant.

Hafey was a major contributor to the St. Louis offense in 1928, batting .337, with 27 home runs, 111 RBIs, and 101 runs scored. During one stretch he had eight consecutive hits. On July 28, 1928, he set a major league record with six extra-base hits in a doubleheader when he stroked two doubles and a pair of homers. The Yankees made short work of the Cardinals in the World Series, though, sweeping them in four games. Hafey had only three singles in 15 at bats.

In 1929 Hafey had perhaps his best all-around season, hitting .338, with 29 homers, 125 RBIs, and 101 runs scored. During one stretch he tied the NL record with 10 straight hits. On July 6 he hit two grand slams in the same game. On September 9 he had four extra-base hits in one game. The outfield trio of Hafey, Taylor Douthit, and Ernie Orsatti all batted over .300.

Nevertheless, the Cardinals failed to repeat as NL champions. The loss of the 1928 World Series so upset Cardinals management McKechnie was replaced with Billy Southworth. Although he eventually became an outstanding manager, Southworth wasn't ready for the task in 1929, and the Cardinals were a .500 club most of the year. By midseason McKechnie was back in charge.

When Hafey went to spring training in 1930, Gabby Street was the Cardinals' fifth manager in five seasons. Such disruptions did not bother Hafey. He hit .336, with 26 homers, 107 RBIs, and 108 runs scored. On May 17, 1930, Hafey had five RBIs in one inning, one short of the then major league record. On August 21, 1930, he hit for the cycle.

The Cardinals won the pennant and faced the Philadelphia Athletics in the World Series. Hafey had a good Series, hitting .273 with a Series-record five doubles, but the A's won in six games.

Hafey had power but was primarily a line drive hitter. Teammate Bottomley compared Hafey to Hornsby, but he added, "Hafey hit harder than Rogers. He hit with his arms and wrists. He used a long-handled bat, and when he leaned on the ball you could hear the seams crack."

On one occasion Hafey ripped a ball off the shins of Phillies third baseman Fresco Thompson. In his next at bat, he bunted safely down the third-base line. When he returned to the dugout, a vendor handed him a Popsicle, saying, "Compliments of Mr. Thompson. He says if you bunt again, he'll send over another one."

Street was retained as manager for the 1931 season, and the Cardinals won another pennant. Hafey slipped to 16 homers and 95 RBIs, but he won the NL batting title in a close race with New York's Bill Terry and teammate Bottomley. Hafey finished at .3489, Terry at .3486, and Bottomley at .3482. Hafey's best game of the season occurred August 23, when he drove in eight runs.

Hafey was held to a mere .167 batting average in the 1931 World Series, but Pepper Martin led the Cardinals to victory over the Athletics. However, it was Hafey's last appearance in a Series. Overall he hit only .205 in Series play, with 18 hits in 88 at bats.

Hafey was shy and quiet with a good sense of humor, but he refused to be steamrolled in contract negotiations. After the 1930 season, he had asked for a raise, from $9,000 to $15,000. He held out until Opening Day and finally signed for $12,500. Rickey inserted a clause that stated Hafey would not be paid until he was "ready to play." He then kept Hafey on the bench and deducted $2,100 from his pay. In 1931 Hafey demanded $15,000 plus restoration of the $2,100. On April 11, 1932, Rickey traded him to last-place Cincinnati for two players and $45,000.

The Reds met Hafey's contract demands, but the fielder missed nearly half the season while undergoing two sinus operations and spending a month on the sidelines with the flu. He still hit .344 in 83 games, but his power stats were down. He hit .303 and .293 during the next two seasons and played for the National League in the first All-Star Game in 1933. But his sinus condition grew worse, and he retired after 15 games in 1935. A comeback in 1937 was unsuccessful.

Because of his physical limitations, Hafey played in only 1,283 games in 13 seasons. He hit 164 home runs with 833 RBIs and had a .317 career batting average. After his retirement, he raised sheep and cattle but continued to suffer from ill health. In 1971, two years before his death, the Veterans Committee named Hafey to the Hall of Fame.

Noodles Hahn

Hahn, Frank George **P**

1899–1906 B:4/29/1879, Nashville, TN D:2/6/1960, Candler, NC Deb:4/18/1899, CIN NL BL/TL 5'9, 160

W	L	PCT	G	SH	IP	BB	SO	ERA
130	94	.580	243	25	2029[1]	381	917	2.55

A hard-working, durable lefthander, Noodles Hahn starred at the turn of the 20th century before a sore arm ended his career all too quickly. As a youngster, Hahn picked up his nickname thanks to an oft-declared love for his mother's noodle soup. More significantly, he pitched exceptionally for several amateur teams. At the age of 15, he hurled a three-hit shutout against Nashville of the Southern League. The following season, Hahn signed his first pro contract with Mobile, one of Nashville's rivals. After two years with Mobile and two more with Detroit of the Western League, he earned a promotion to the National League.

At the age of 20, Hahn made an impressive major league debut with Cincinnati. Featuring an imposing fastball and fine control, he dominated National League hitters to the tune of a 23–8 record. Hahn slumped to 16–20 in 1900, but he did become the first pitcher to throw a no-hitter in the 20th century. In 1901, Hahn completed a league-leading 41 of 42 starts and won the National League's strikeout crown for a third consecutive season. He won 22 games in spite of the Reds' last-place standing.

Hahn's effectiveness continued over the next two seasons, as he posted a combined 45 wins. In 1904 he fell to a 16–18 despite a 2.06 ERA and soon encountered arm trouble. The Reds released Hahn in the midst of the 1905 season because he had lost his imposing fastball. He later attempted an abbreviated comeback with the New York Highlanders before calling it quits in 1906.

After retiring, Hahn returned to Cincinnati and worked as a government meat inspector for more than 30 years. He also helped out the Reds, in an unpaid capacity, by assisting Cincinnati's coaches in running batting practice at Crosley Field.

Jesse Haines

Haines, Jesse Joseph **P**

1918, 1920–37 B:7/22/1893, Clayton, OH D:8/5/1978, Dayton, OH Deb:7/20/1918, CIN NL BR/TR 6', 190

W	L	PCT	G	SH	IP	BB	SO	ERA
210	158	.571	555	24	3208^2	871	981	3.64

Jesse Haines, a righthander who pitched more than 18 years in the majors, had a long and successful career with the St. Louis Cardinals. He won 210 games with the club, including three 20-win seasons, and pitched in the Cards' first four World Series. He picked up the nickname "Pop" late in his career when his hair was gray and the youngest Cardinals had been in diapers when he made his major league debut.

Haines entered pro ball as a teenager with Dayton in 1913. He was bought by the Tigers in 1917 but was cut, although Ty Cobb told him, "Some day they're going to be reading about you." He made it to the majors with the Reds in 1918, pitched one game, was released, signed with Tulsa, was ineffective, and was traded to Kansas City, where he went 21–5 in 1919.

The Cardinals bought Haines for $10,000, and he spent the rest of his career in St. Louis. He went 13–20 with a 2.98 ERA as a 27-year-old rookie in 1920, leading the National League in games and pitching 301 ⅔ innings. He was 18–12 the next season and led the league with three shutouts, but he fell to 11–9 in 1922. His career was at a crossroads.

Haines, never overpowering, added a knuckleball—learned from Philadelphia Athletics' hurler Eddie Rommel—and went 20–13 in 1923 with a 3.11 ERA. "I threw a hard knuckler, a lot harder than they throw it today. It broke sharper, too" Haines said after he retired. Kidding about his age, he remarked, "Every time I read about Hoyt Wilhelm pitching into his 40s, I think I quit too soon." Haines pitched until he was 44.

He slumped badly in 1924, his worst season in the majors, going 8–19 with a 4.41 ERA despite pitching a no-hitter against Boston on July 17. After a 13–14 season in 1925, Haines was 13–4 in 1926 as the Cardinals won their first pennant. He beat the Yankees with a five-hit shutout in Game 3 of the Series. He had to leave Game 7 of the World Series when he developed a blister on his hand in the seventh inning with the bases loaded and two outs. A hungover Grover Cleveland Alexander, who had beaten the Yankees the previous day, relieved Haines and struck out Tony Lazzeri in an unforgettable confrontation. Haines got the win, but Alexander was the hero. In the film *The Winning Team*, future President Ronald Reagan played Alexander; future Hall of Famer Bob Lemon played Haines.

The 1927 season was Haines' best, with career highs in wins, shutouts and complete games. He led the NL with 25 complete games and six shutouts. His 2.72 ERA was a career low for a full season. The next season the 35-year-old Haines again won 20 games.

He pitched another nine seasons in the majors, but after 1928 he never worked more than 182 innings or won more than 13 games in a season. He remained a very determined competitor. Terry Moore, who joined the Cardinals in 1935 when Haines was 42, once said. "I never forgot how much Haines expected of himself and others."

After he retired in 1937, he managed Dayton in the Middle Atlantic League and coached for the Dodgers before working as the Montgomery County (Ohio) Auditor for 28 years. Haines was elected to the Hall of Fame in 1970.

Jerry Hairston

Hairston, Jerry Wayne, Sr. **OF–DH**

1973–77, 1981–89 B:2/16/1952, Birmingham, AL Deb:7/26/1973, CHI AL BB/TR 5'10", 180

G	AB	R	H	HR	RBI	OBP	SLG	AVG
859	1699	216	438	30	205	.366	.371	.258

Outfielder Jerry Wayne Hairston was the son of Sam Hairston, the first black player signed by the White Sox, and the brother of John Hairston, who played four games for the Cubs in 1969. Another brother, Sam Jr., played in the minors for the White Sox. Sam Sr., a 40-year scout and coach for the White Sox organization, signed his son Jerry as a fourth-round selection in the June 1970 draft.

Jerry Hairston reached the majors with the 1973 White Sox but spent that season and the next three shuttling between the majors and Triple A. In 1977 he was sold to the Pirates and the next spring was sold to Durango of the Mexican League.

For most players, that would have meant a permanent *adios*. But Hairston rode the buses in Mexico for four seasons and returned to the White Sox at the tail end of 1981. He spent the next six seasons in various roles: designated hitter, outfielder, first baseman, and pinch hitter. He was only 10-for-55 (.182) as a pinch hitter before he went to Mexico, but after he came back he was 84-for-306 (.275) and led the American League in pinch hits for three straight seasons.

Switch-hitting Hairston, much better from the left side than the right, led AL pinch hitters from 1983 to 1985, batting .281 (49-for-174) off the bench in that span. On April 15, 1983, he ruined Milt Wilcox's no-hit bid with a pinch-hit single with two outs in the ninth. He retired with a .258 career batting average. As a pinch hitter, he was 94-for-361 (.260). His son, Jerry Jr., became the third generation to play major league baseball when he debuted with the Orioles in 1998.

Dick Hall

Hall, Richard Wallace **P–OF**

1952–71 B:9/27/1930, St. Louis, MO Deb:4/15/1952, PIT NL BR/TR 6'6", 200

G	AB	R	H	HR	RBI	OBP	SLG	AVG
669	714	79	150	4	56	.274	.259	.210

W	L	PCT	G	SH	IP	BB	SO	ERA
93	75	.554	495	68	1259^{2}	236	741	3.32

Dick Hall was a 6-foot 6-inch, gangly Swarthmore student in 1952 when Branch Rickey signed him to the Pirates for a $25,000 bonus. Brought immediately to the big leagues, it took only 80 at bats at a .138 average to prove he couldn't hit. He returned from the minors to platoon in the Bucs outfield for 1954 and hit all of .239 with two home runs and 27 RBIs in 310 at bats.

It was time for a change. Hall turned pitcher and after leading the Pacific Coast League in wins and ERA in 1957, the Pirates traded him with pitcher Ken Hamlin to Kansas City for Hal Smith. After one season at 8–13 and 4.05, Hall was dealt to the Orioles and converted into a reliever. He spent the next 11 years as a star in the bullpen.

The college-educated Hall was always teased by his rough, tough teammates. John Boozer taught him how to eat bugs, and Moe Drabowsky taught him the art of the hotfoot. But Hall used his intelligence to his advantage. He learned the slip pitch from Paul Richards, the changeup from Stu Miller, and the knuckler from Hoyt Wilhelm. As he put it, "I couldn't throw any of them very well, but I learned them all from the best."

Given Hall's lanky build and jerky motion, batters had trouble picking up his deliveries. They said he "threw like a girl," but he won a total of 93 major league games and saved another 68. His control was exceptional: 236 walks in 1,259 innings and, remarkably, only one wild pitch in his entire career. He was also the first pitcher to get the win in an American League Championship Series game, as an Oriole in 1969.

Bill Hallahan

Hallahan, William Anthony **P**

1925–38 B:8/4/1902, Binghamton, NY D:7/8/1981, Binghamton, NY Deb:4/16/1925, STL NL BR/TL 5'10½", 170

W	L	PCT	G	SH	IP	BB	SO	ERA
102	94	.520	324	14	1740^{1}	779	856	4.03

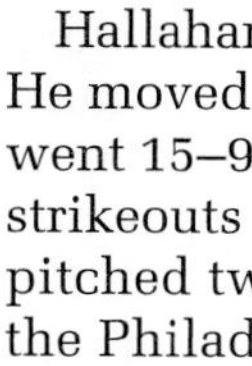

Hard-throwing righthander William Anthony Hallahan wasn't known as "Wild Bill" because of any off-field carousing with the Gas House Gang—he got his nickname because he had trouble throwing strikes. Still, Hallahan had a nice run with the Cardinals between 1930 and 1935 when he went 85–58.

Hallahan reached the majors for good in 1929. He moved into the rotation the following season, went 15–9, and led the National League with 177 strikeouts and 126 walks (both career highs). He pitched twice in the Cards' World Series loss to the Philadelphia Athletics, pitching a seven-hit shutout in Game 3 but lasting only two innings as the loser in decisive Game 6.

Hallahan again paced his league in strikeouts and walks in 1931, when he went 19–9 and led the league in wins. He also had a career-high 16 complete games. In an era when pitchers regularly finished what they started, Hallahan completed only 90 of 224 career starts due to the high number of pitches he invariably threw.

This time the Cards beat the A's in a seven-game World Series and Hallahan was the hero, winning Game 2 with a three-hit shutout and Game 5 with a complete-game nine-hitter. In Game 7 he came out of the bullpen to relieve Burleigh Grimes with two outs in the ninth. He retired Max Bishop to earn the save and give St. Louis its second world championship.

Hallahan never matched that season. Dizzy Dean became the Card's ace in 1932 as injuries limited Hallahan to 22 starts. He was 16–13 in 1933, yet led the league in walks for the third and final time. He was only 8–12 in 1934, but pitched well in his only Series start for the world champions. After rebounding for 15 wins in 1935 at age 33, Hallahan quickly faded. He was 11–28 over the next three seasons for the Cards, Reds, and Phils.

Tom Haller

Haller, Thomas Frank **C**

1961–72 B:6/23/1937, Lockport, IL Deb:4/1/1961, SF NL BL/TR 6'4", 195

G	AB	R	H	HR	RBI	OBP	SLG	AVG
1294	3935	461	1011	134	504	.342	.414	.257

Tom Haller, one of the 1960s better receivers, was a rare bird—a left-handed-hitting catcher with power. The younger brother of American League umpire Bill Haller, Thomas Frank Haller played quarterback for the University of Illinois and signed with the Giants in 1958 as a $54,000 bonus baby. After more than three seasons apprenticing in the minors, he platooned with veteran Ed Bailey in 1962 and 1963.

As a rookie, Haller hit .261 with 18 homers and 55 RBIs in only 272 at bats. His workload only increased. He became the Giants' undisputed starter in 1965, when he hit .251 with 16 homers. From 1965 through 1969 he caught an average of 135 games a season. He also averaged 17 homers a season from 1962 through 1967, peaking in 1966 when he blasted a career-high 27 with a career-high 67 RBIs. He was an All-Star for three straight years.

Haller was dealt to the Dodgers in February 1968 for Ron Hunt and Nate Oliver, the first transaction between the Dodgers and Giants since they moved to the West Coast and the first by the two clubs since the Jackie Robinson trade in 1956 (which was cancelled when Robinson promptly retired). In his first year as a Dodger, Haller batted .285 (37 points above his career average to that point) but hit only four homers. He was 31, around the age when catchers' bodies often start to break down. Nevertheless, that season he caught a career-high 139 games and set a National League record for catchers with 23 double plays.

He spent two more years as the Dodgers' regular catcher, splitting the job with Duke Sims in 1971. In 1972, his final season, he backed up Bill Freehan in Detroit. Haller retired with 134 homers and a .257 career average. He returned to the Giants' organization after his retirement and was the Giants' vice president of baseball operations from the middle of the 1981 season until September 1986.

Billy Hamilton

Hamilton, William Robert **OF**

1888–1901 B:2/16/1866, Newark, NJ D:12/16/1940, Worcester, MA Deb:7/31/1888, KC AA BL/TR 5'6", 165

G	AB	R	H	HR	RBI	OBP	SLG	AVG
1591	6269	1691	2159	40	739	.455	.432	.344

Using the rare combination of the ability to get on base and the speed to steal once there, Billy Hamilton scored a major league-record 192 runs for the 1894 Philadelphia Phillies. It was one of four seasons in which he led the National League in runs scored.

During his 14-year career Hamilton led the NL five times in bases on balls, five times in on-base percentage, and twice in batting average. With a record augmented by 912 career stolen bases, including five base stealing titles and three consecutive 100-plus steal seasons, he compiled the highest ratio of runs scored to games played (1.06) in major league history. Hamilton also holds the fourth-highest career-total average in major league history behind John McGraw, Ted Williams, and Babe Ruth.

Nicknamed "Sliding Billy," the slight, 5-foot 6-inch outfielder was fearless on the basepaths, often colliding with larger men. Playing for the Phillies against the Baltimore Orioles in September 1894, he collided with particular force against the opposing catcher, 250-pound Wilbert Robinson. An account of the incident stated that "after being trampled upon and severely stunned by Hughie Jennings at second base, Hamilton made a grand run for home on Bobby Lowe's single, collided with Baltimore's fleshy backstop, and falling heavily, pluckily crawled toward the base, almost fainting as he touched it."

He finished the 1894 season with a .404 batting average after hitting in 46 consecutive games. His league-leading .523 on-base percentage is the sixth-best single-season percentage on record. Traded to the Boston Beaneaters after the 1895 season for Billy Nash, Hamilton rejected a large contract offer to skip to the American League Boston team and remained with the Beaneaters through 1901.

After he retired from the majors Hamilton played in both the New England and the Tri-State Leagues through 1910. In 1909, at age 45, he led the New England League in batting with a .332 average. He went on to manage in Fall River, Springfield, and Worcester (where he owned a piece of the team) and also scouted for the Red Sox.

In 1937 Hamilton contacted *The Sporting News* after he had been mentioned in an article. "I'll have you know sir," he wrote, "that I was and will be the greatest stealer of all times. I did stole [sic] over 100 bases on [sic] many years and if they ever re-count the record I would get my just reward." He was elected to the Hall of Fame in 1961.

Milo Hamilton

Broadcaster B:9/2/1927 Fairfield, IA

Despite nearly five decades of experience as a major league broadcaster, Milo Hamilton is remembered for one at bat: Hank Aaron's record-breaking 715th home run. Hamilton was the lead announcer for the Atlanta Braves and at the mike when Aaron connected against Al Downing of the Los Angeles Dodgers in the fourth inning in Atlanta-Fulton County Stadium on April 8, 1974.

As Aaron circled the bases, Hamilton stated the facts simply, and triumphantly: "There's a new home run champion of all time and it's Henry Aaron!"

After leaving the Atlanta broadcast booth, Hamilton worked for the Houston Astros. In 1992 a panel of baseball executives and media voted him the Ford C. Frick Award, given annually to a broadcaster for "major contributions to baseball." His name appears on the list of winners in the "Scribes and Mikemen" section of the Baseball Hall of Fame.

Hamilton, who called his first major league game in 1953, completed his 15th year with the Astros in 1999. He previously worked for the Cubs, White Sox, Cardinals, and Pirates. He broadcasted nine no-hitters, five homers in a doubleheader (Stan Musial), five grand slams in a season (Ernie Banks), and another famous home run that broke a Babe Ruth record—Roger Maris' 61st in 1961.

Steve Hamilton

Hamilton, Steven Absher **P**

1961–72 B:11/30/1935, Columbia, KY D:12/2/1997, Morehead, KY Deb:4/23/1961, CLE AL BL/TL 6'7", 195

W	L	PCT	G	SV	IP	BB	SO	ERA
40	31	.563	421	42	663	214	531	3.05

Lefty Steve Hamilton was a college basketball star who played in the National Basketball Association with the Los Angeles Lakers. In 12 major league seasons, most of which spent with the Yankees, he was a reliable reliever who was tough on lefthanded hitters. Yet what everyone remembers about Hamilton is the "Folly Floater."

Hamilton, with his 6-foot-7-inch frame and 195 pounds, would lob the baseball, up, up, up, up, and it would float ever-so-slowly, down, down, down, down. Hamilton would never throw it with runners on base in a clutch situation, although he would throw it in a close game if no one were on base. Most of the time, hitters would just watch; they wanted no part of the floater. After all, how can you hit a pitch going 32 miles per hour when you spend all your time trying to time 90-mph fastballs?

Hamilton graduated from Morehead State in 1958 after leading his basketball team to NCAA appearances in 1956 and 1957. Following college, he spent four seasons starting with the Indians in the minors, during the winters coming off the bench for the Lakers. Feeling stymied in the Indians organization, he asked Gabe Paul to trade him and Paul obliged, sending him with Don Rudolph to the expansion Senators in May 1962 for Willie Tasby. "My Washington experience taught me I could play in the major leagues," Hamilton once said. "I didn't know if the team could play in the big leagues, though."

A year later he lucked out, getting traded to the Yankees for Jim Coates. "The first time I played in Yankee Stadium I got goose bumps all over," he said. And what was his reaction to pitching in the 1963 Series? "It was like walking down the aisle to get married," Hamilton said. "It was something I always wanted to do but I didn't know how it was going to come out."

He was 34–20 in his eight seasons with the Yankees and had a career-high 11 saves in 1968. He later coached baseball at Morehead State.

Granny Hamner

Hamner, Granville Wilbur **SS-2B**

1944–59, 1962 B:4/26/1927, Richmond, VA D:9/12/1993, Philadelphia, PA Deb:9/14/1944, PHI NL BR/TR 5'10", 163

G	AB	R	H	HR	RBI	OBP	SLG	AVG
1531	5839	711	1529	104	708	.304	.383	.262

One of the National League's most durable shortstops in the 1940s and 1950s, Granny Hamner owned the position while with the Phillies from 1948 to 1958. Between 1949 and 1954 he played in no fewer than 150 games a season, and he led the league in 1949 with 662 at bats. A clutch hitter, Hamner hit at least 30 doubles in a season four times during his career, although his best all-around offensive year came when he switched to second base. That came in 1954, when Hamner hit .299 with 13 home runs, 89 RBIs, and 39 doubles.

Hamner, whose brother Garvin had played infield for the Phillies in 1945, was known for his strong arm as well as his bat, and he appeared from time to time as a pitcher in 1956 and 1957. When his career as an infielder ended after 27 games with the Indians in 1959, he joined the Kansas City A's as a minor league manager. There he learned a knuckleball and perfected it well enough to pitch for the A's in 1962 in three relief appearances.

Fred Haney

Haney, Fred Girard **3B**

1922–27, 1929 M(1939–41, 1953–59, 629–757) B:4/25/1898, Albuquerque, NM D:11/9/1977, Beverly Hills, CA Deb:4/18/1922, DET AA BR/TR 5'6", 170

G	AB	R	H	HR	RBI	OBP	SLG	AVG
622	1977	338	544	8	228	.368	.342	.275

Although Fred Haney was a third baseman for the Tigers, Red Sox, Cubs, and Cardinals, he is best known for his managerial career. Three of his teams lost 100 games, but in his final three years as a manager he won two pennants, one World Series, and finished another year tied for first—only to lose in a playoff.

Haney began managing in 1936 at Toledo, then a member of the American Association, and in 1939 won promotion to the St. Louis Browns. Haney found little success there, as the Browns lost a franchise-record 111 games, and early in 1941 he was demoted back to Toledo. Between 1943 and 1948 Haney changed careers, broadcasting games for Hollywood in the Pacific Coast League. But his ties to his former profession weren't entirely severed, and Haney returned to manage Hollywood to two pennants in four years.

Major league teams took notice, and in 1953 Haney was hired to manage the Pirates. He finished last three years in a row. Nevertheless, the Milwaukee Braves hired him in June of 1956, where he began the most successful streak of his career.

The Braves were in fifth place when Haney took over, but he brought the club home second, just one game behind Brooklyn. In 1957 the Braves were the highest-scoring and most prolific home run-hitting team in baseball. The Braves won the pennant by eight games and faced the juggernaut New York Yankees in the World Series. Lew Burdette earned two of Milwaukee's first three wins in the Series, and Haney brought him back for Game 7 on two days' rest. Burdette pitched a shutout at Yankee Stadium.

The Yanks and Braves met in rematch the following year as New York battled back from a three-games-to-one deficit to tie the Series. Again Haney pitched Burdette with two days' rest in Game 7, but the Yankees scored four times in the eighth inning to win the title. In 1959 the Dodgers and Braves finished in a tie for first place. The Dodgers, now located in Los Angeles, won the best-of-three playoff in two games, although both were decided by one run.

Despite his success, he was fired after the 1959 season. Haney returned to the broadcast booth, this time working NBC's *Game of the Week*. He later served as general manager of the expansion Los Angeles Angels.

Ned Hanlon

Hanlon, Edward Hugh **OF**

1880–92 M(1889–1907, 1,313–1,164) B:8/22/1857, Montville, CT D:4/14/1937, Baltimore, MD Deb:5/1/1880, CLE NL BL/TR 5'9½", 170

G	AB	R	H	HR	RBI	OBP	SLG	AVG
1267	5074	930	1317	30	517	.325	.340	.260

Although Ned Hanlon began his career as a player and eventually became a clubowner, he is best remembered as the manager of the most famous—and infamous—team of the 19th century. His rough-and-ready Baltimore Orioles of the 1890s are the stuff of baseball legend. Their reputation for playing down-and-dirty, no-holds-barred baseball has never been matched.

More importantly, many of his team's strategic innovations are still in use today, and a number of players who first learned the intricacies of the game under Hanlon's direction eventually became managers themselves, extending his influence far into the 20th century. Former Orioles Hughie Jennings, Wilbert Robinson, and most significantly, John McGraw all followed in Hanlon's shoes and won more than 1,000 games apiece as managers; the trio captured 15 pennants all told.

Edward Hugh Hanlon began professionally in 1876 pitching for an independent Providence team. He soon switched to the infield, playing the next few years in Fall River, Rochester, and Albany. Quick on the bases, Hanlon was erratic both in the field and at bat. In 1880 he played left field for the National League Cleveland Blues but batted only .246 and made a league-leading 35 errors.

Before the 1881 season he was sold to the Detroit Wolverines in their first NL season. Hanlon played center field, where his speed was put to use in running down flyballs, and he soon became a fine fielder. In 1882 and 1884 he led league outfielders in putouts.

A lefthanded batter, he stood just over 5 feet 9 inches, and weighed 170 pounds, about average for a player of his era. Never a power-hitter Hanlon's few extra-base hits resulted from his speed. Although he batted .302 in 1885, he averaged only .260 in his career. He did, however, have a knack for reaching base through walks or errors, and he twice scored more than 100 runs in a season.

Although no star, he was a leader. At age 24 he was named captain and found himself leading a team of luminaries when in 1887 Detroit bought the entire Buffalo club for $7,000, just to obtain their famous "Big Four"—Dan Brouthers, Deacon White, Jack Rowe, and Hardy Richardson. The Wolverines also added Fred Dunlap, considered the best second baseman of the 1880s and roared to the NL pennant. They then defeated the American Association champion St. Louis Browns in the World Series.

Sold to Pittsburgh in 1889, Hanlon was named manager the following August. A dispute between clubowners and players over a plan to rank players as a basis for limiting their salaries resulted in the formation of the renegade Players' League. Hanlon became center fielder, captain, manager, stockholder, and board member of that league's Pittsburgh franchise.

He returned to the National League club in 1891 after the new league folded but was fired as manager in July after his attempts to discipline some players failed. He finished the season in center field. In 1892 he suffered a serious injury in spring training. While recovering, he received an offer to manage the Baltimore Orioles, a team that had been absorbed into the NL when the American Association disbanded after the 1891 season.

The Orioles were awful. They finished 1892 dead last, 54 games out of first. Hanlon built a new team by gambling on young, unproven players. In 1893 he acquired third baseman John McGraw, outfielder Joe Kelley, and catcher Wilbert Robinson. The next year he added outfielder Willie Keeler, shortstop Hughie Jennings, and veteran first baseman Dan Brouthers. All six were eventually named to the Hall of Fame.

By 1894 Hanlon's club was fully established, and the Orioles won the pennant by three games over the New York Giants. The demise of the American Association had left baseball with only one major league, so in lieu of a World Series, another competition, the Temple Cup Series, was held, pitting the first-place National League team against the second-place club. The Orioles did not take the playoff seriously and fell prey to the Giants.

In 1895 the Orioles took their second straight pennant but again lost the Temple Cup, this time to Cleveland. A third pennant followed in 1896. Baltimore, stung by criticism of their lackadaisical postseason play, set out to prove their critics wrong and routed Cleveland in four straight games.

Hanlon's Orioles have often been cited for their pioneering use of "scientific" baseball tactics, including such innovations as the hit-and-run play, the platooning of lefthanded batters against righthanded pitchers, and the clever use of bunting. They have also been criticized for such questionable practices as having baserunners cut across the infield behind the umpire's back, holding up rival players by surreptitiously grabbing their belts, and concealing extra balls in the outfield so that long hits could be quickly returned to the infield. They were infamous for viciously baiting umpires and opponents and for their willingness to spike, slug, kick, or otherwise attack anyone who got in their way.

In truth, they did all these things, but so did every other team. Boston was every bit as adept at scientific play, and Cleveland was even more brutal than the Orioles were. Baltimore was successful not only because they resorted to trickery and aggressive play but also because the team hit more and played better defense. Although Hanlon never developed a genuine pitching star, his staff was more than respectable.

Attendance fell off as the Orioles finished second in 1897 and 1898. In 1899 the team merged with Brooklyn, and Hanlon received 10 percent of Brooklyn's stock. He was now both president of the Orioles and manager of Brooklyn. He shifted most of Baltimore's best players to Brooklyn, creating a powerhouse that was christened "Hanlon's Superbas," after a vaudeville act of the same name. The Superbas won pennants in 1899 and 1900, giving Hanlon five flags and two second-place finishes in his seven years as a manager.

The AL declared itself a major league in 1901 and set about luring players away from the National League with the promise of higher salaries. The Superbas lost many players to the American League and tumbled in the standings. At the same time, Hanlon was embroiled in a power struggle with Brooklyn club president Charles Ebbets. In 1903 Hanlon purchased the Baltimore ballpark and organized a team to play in the Eastern League, causing further conflicts with Ebbets. Brooklyn finished last in 1905 as Ebbets gained control of the team. Hanlon's salary was slashed from $12,000 to $6,500 a year. In 1906 Hanlon quit to manage Cincinnati, but the Reds were hopeless. After two sixth-place finishes he was fired.

But Hanlon no longer needed to work. After he sold the Baltimore team to Jack Dunn in November 1909, his net worth was more than half a million dollars, most of it in real estate. He remained interested in baseball, however, and briefly held a position with Baltimore's Federal League team in 1914. Later he served as president of the Baltimore City Park Board.

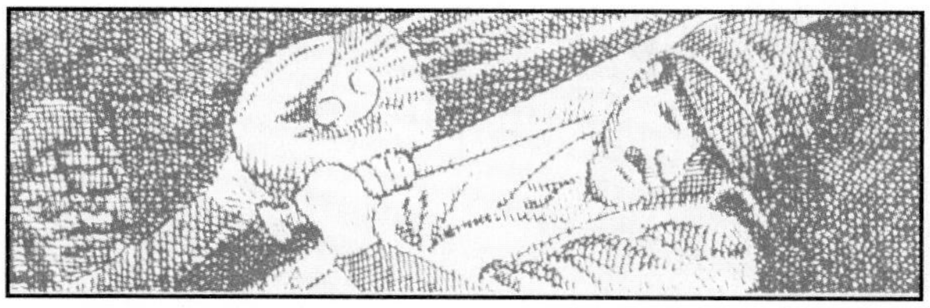

Hanlon's greatest legacy is not his string of pennants but the success of the managers he influenced. Joe Kelley managed in the majors for five years and produced four winning records. Hughie Jennings managed for 18 years, won more than 1,000 games, and captured three pennants. Wilbert Robinson managed for 19 seasons, winning 1,399 games and two pennants. And John McGraw, regarded by some as the greatest manager of all time, won 2,738 games, 10 pennants, and three World Series during 33 seasons. Hanlon joined his disciples in the Hall of Fame in 1996.

Ron Hansen

Hansen, Ronald Lavern **SS**

1958–72 B:4/5/1938, Oxford, NE Deb:4/15/1958, BAL AL BR/TR 6'3", 200

G	AB	R	H	HR	RBI	OBP	SLG	AVG
1384	4311	446	1007	106	501	.323	.351	.234

Ron Hansen covered acres of ground with his long strides, and had some pop in his bat. He had the tools for a wonderful career. Unfortunately, he also had a bad back that essentially ruined his career by the time he was 28.

Hansen signed with the Orioles in 1956 and played for Stockton of the California League. His back problems started the next season, all of which he missed due to a slipped disk. He recovered and won the Orioles' shortstop job in 1960 at age 22. He had a productive rookie season, hitting .255 with 22 homers and 86 RBIs, leading American League shortstops in putouts, and finishing second to Luis Aparicio in total chances. It earned him the AL Rookie of the Year Award.

Hansen slumped in 1961, hitting .248 with 12 homers and 51 RBIs (and leading the league in double plays). And he had a disastrous season in 1962 after his Marines reserve unit was called up during the Cuban Missile Crisis. He didn't return until April 20 and never got on track, hitting .173 in 71 games. After the season he was traded to the White Sox in the deal that sent Luis Aparicio to the Orioles, and he put together three straight solid seasons in Chicago.

From 1963 through 1965 he averaged 15 homers and 67 RBIs, leading the AL in assists in 1963 and 1965 and in putouts, assists, chances, double plays, and chances per game in 1964. Then, disaster struck. Hansen ruptured a spinal disk early in 1966 and missed the rest of the season. He came back in 1967 to play 157 games and to lead the league in assists and double plays, but he hit only eight homers.

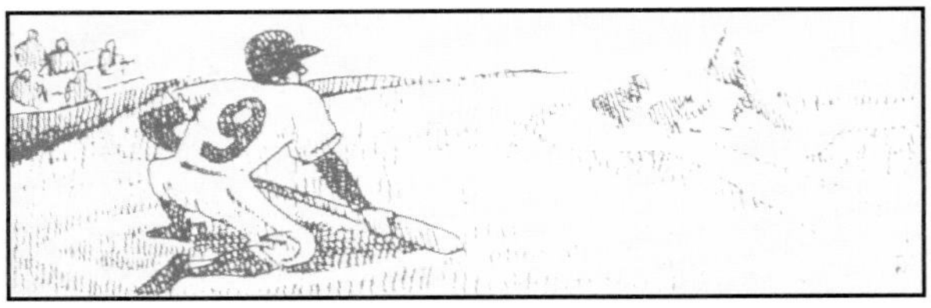

Hansen hung on for five more seasons with the White Sox, Senators, Yankees, and Royals. He pulled off an unassisted triple play on July 29, 1968—the first in the major leagues since 1927. Nevertheless, Hansen was only a shell of the bright young Rookie of the Year in 1960. He retired after hitting .133 in 16 games for the Royals in 1972.

Mel Harder

Harder, Melvin Leroy **P**

1928–47 M(1961–62, 3–3) B:10/15/1909, Beemer, NE Deb:4/24/1928, CLE AL BR/TR 6'1", 195

W	L	PCT	G	SH	IP	BB	SO	ERA
223	186	.545	582	25	3426^{1}	1118	1160	3.80

In the 1930s, when the ball was lively and every team had a gang of great sluggers, dependable Mel Harder feared no one. The quiet, bespectacled righthander from Beemer, Nebraska, set longevity records for Cleveland pitchers, appearing in 582 games in 20 seasons and compiling a lifetime record of 223–186. Only Bob Feller won more games with the Indians, and only Walter Johnson and Ted Lyons had longer pitching careers with one team than Harder.

In 1927, his first season in the minors, the 18-year-old won 17 games with two teams. Harder saw action in 23 games in 1928 with Cleveland. Sent back to New Orleans for further seasoning, he returned in 1930 to take his spot as fourth starter in a rotation that included Wes Ferrell, Willis Hudlin, and Clint Brown. Harder, at age 20, won 11 and lost 10 for the fourth-place Tribe. His ERA was 4.22—but this was 1930, after all, and the league ERA was 4.65.

Harder quietly improved his win totals to 13 in 1931 and 15 in both 1932 and 1933. He pitched the first game played in Cleveland's Municipal Stadium, on July 31, 1932, losing, 1–0, to Lefty Grove and the Philadelphia Athletics in front of 76,979 fans.

From 1932 through 1935, Harder was among the top hurlers in the American League. His ERA in 1933 was the second lowest in the league; the following season he tied Lefty Gomez for most shutouts in the league, with six. He ranked among the AL's top five pitchers in fewest walks per game every season from 1932 to 1935; in ERA in 1933 and 1934; in opponents' on-base average in 1933, 1934, and 1935; in innings pitched in 1935; and in wins in both 1934 and 1935. He even homered twice in one game, on July 31, 1935.

In 1934 Harder was the winning pitcher in the

second All-Star Game, although most baseball fans remember only Carl Hubbell's feat of striking out five in a row of the game's greatest sluggers. Harder pitched in the 1935 All-Star Game (at home in Cleveland) and again in 1936 and 1937. He is the only pitcher to have never allowed a run in more than 10 innings of All-Star Game competition.

After consecutive 20-win seasons in 1934 and 1935, Harder had shoulder and elbow problems, but he gamely delivered more than 220 innings in each of the next two years. Despite having ERAs that were a run or more higher than any of his past five seasons, he won 15 games each year. He then posted a 17-victory season in 1938 and a 15–9 record in 1939.

On June 12, 1940, Harder was knocked from a game against the Red Sox in Boston. As he approached the bench his manager, Ossie Vitt, challenged him: "It's about time you won one, with all the money you're making." The soft-spoken, sore-armed Harder answered truthfully, "I gave you the best I had."

The remark was just another example of Vitt's crude and insensitive managerial style. The team rebelled. The cautious, conservative Harder led a group of players who met with owner Alva Bradley to complain about Vitt's behavior. But word leaked out about their meeting, and they were branded "the Cleveland Crybabies" throughout the AL. They would find diapers hanging over their dugout. Baby bottles were thrown at them. Vitt calmed down, and the Tribe actually came within one game of winning the pennant.

But that was as close as Harder came to appearing in the postseason. Only five men played more seasons than Harder without appearing in a World Series. Ironically, the Indians won the world championship in 1948, the year after Harder retired.

The Indians released Harder in 1941 but gave him a second chance the next year after he responded well to elbow surgery. Using his experience and smarts, he continued on the Tribe staff for six more years, winning 13 games in 1942 and 12 in 1944. When his playing career was over, he was hired as the team's first base coach, but he quickly became entrusted solely with the task of working with the pitchers. He was one of baseball's first exclusive pitching coaches.

He coached in Cleveland for 16 years, and many Indians hurlers gave him credit for improving their games. Early Wynn had been a hard thrower for Washington before going to Cleveland, but Harder taught him a breaking ball and changeup. Wynn won 300 games in the majors. Herb Score said Harder showed him how to throw a good curve. Even Bob Feller went to school with Harder. It was said that Harder "had a camera in his head, and could spot any pitching flaw immediately."

After leaving the Indians, Harder spent several more seasons with the Mets, Cubs, Reds, and Royals. His number, 18, was retired by the Indians in 1990.

Carroll Hardy

Hardy, Carroll William **OF**

1958–67 B:5/18/1933, Sturgis, SD Deb:4/15/1958, CLE AL BR/TR 6', 185

G	AB	R	H	HR	RBI	OBP	SLG	AVG
433	1117	172	251	17	113	.304	.330	.225

He was the only player to pinch-hit for Ted Williams. Of course, the only reason Carroll Hardy got a chance to do it was because Williams had to leave a game in 1960 after he fouled a pitch off his foot. That fluke of an at bat is about the only reason anyone remembers Hardy's eight-year career as an outfielder for the Indians, Red Sox, Astros, and Twins. Hardy also pinch-hit for Carl Yastrzemski in Yaz's rookie season of 1961, and in 1958, when he was with the Indians, Hardy hit a pinch homer batting for Roger Maris.

Hardy had one other distinction. In 1955 he played defensive back for the San Francisco 49ers, after starring in football, baseball, and track at the University of Colorado. He had started in pro baseball that year with the Indians, missing the 1957 season while in the service. He then played a total of 59 games with the Indians in 1958 and 1959, spending most of those two seasons in Triple A at San Diego and Seattle.

Traded to the Red Sox in 1960, he was a semiregular in Boston. In 1962 Hardy played in a career-high 115 games, hitting .215 with eight homers and 36 RBIs. He hung on for three more seasons with the Astros and Twins and then retired with a .225 career batting average. Hardy later became the assistant general manager of the NFL's Denver Broncos.

Bubbles Hargrave

Hargrave, Eugene Franklin **C**

1913–30 B:7/15/1892, New Haven, IN D:2/23/1969, Cincinnati, OH Deb:9/18/1913, CHI NL BR/TR 5'10½", 174

G	AB	R	H	HR	RBI	OBP	SLG	AVG
852	2533	314	786	29	376	.372	.452	.310

Eugene "Bubbles" Hargrave was the first catcher ever to be recognized as a batting champion. In 1926, when the qualification requirement was 100 games, Hargrave took home the award after hitting .353 in just 326 at bats with the Chicago Cubs.

Hargrave, who got his unusual nickname because of a stammer and a particular difficulty with the "B" sounds, caught 93 games in 1926 and pinch-hit in 12 others. As a result, he was able to break a streak of six straight NL batting titles by the immortal Rogers Hornsby.

The Cincinnati Reds bought Hargrave's contract from the St. Paul Saints for $10,000 in 1921. Hargrave hit over .300 for six straight seasons from 1922 through 1927 with the Reds. His best overall season was 1923, when he hit .333 and achieved career highs with 10 homers and 78 RBIs. In 1927 he led NL catchers in fielding percentage.

After sitting out the 1929 season, Hargrave came back for one final season in 1930 with Yankees. Hargrave had a younger brother, William "Pinky" Hargrave, who also caught for 10 years, mostly with Washington.

Mike Hargrove

Hargrove, Dudley Michael **1B–OF**

1974–85 M(1991–*, 721–591) B:10/26/1949, Perryton, TX Deb:4/7/1974, TEX AL BL/TL 6', 195

G	AB	R	H	HR	RBI	OBP	SLG	AVG
1666	5564	783	1614	80	686	.400	.391	.290

In 1974 Texas Ranger Mike Hargrove hit .323 with 66 RBIs to earn the American League Rookie of the Year Award. He also attracted attention and drove opposing pitchers crazy with his long and involved batting ritual in which he often stepped out of the box to analyze his situation. The tactic earned him the nickname, "the Human Rain Delay." The move worked, because pitchers often had a hard time throwing strikes to the patient, if not deliberate, first baseman. His patience later paid dividends as a successful major league manager.

An All-Star in 1975, Hargrove led the AL in bases on balls in 1976 and 1978. In October 1978 he was sent to the Padres, where he performed miserably. He was traded to the Cleveland Indians in June 1979. Hargrove's intimidation of opposing pitchers continued to earn him bases on balls, and in 1981 his .432 on-base percentage led the AL. His .317 batting average that year was a career high. Despite his output, the Tribe remained in the cellar. Although he continued to play, his ability soon began to decline.

Hargrove retired in 1985 with one of the 40 best career on-base percentage marks of all time, an even .400. He took a job as a minor league manager with the Indians, and in July 1991 he became skipper of the big league club. In 1995 he led Cleveland to its first World Series since 1954, although the Tribe fell to Atlanta in six games. The following year the Indians repeated in the AL Central Division but lost to Baltimore in the first round of the playoffs.

"Grover" and the Indians returned to the World Series in 1997, but lost to the upstart Florida Marlins in seven games. After delivering another AL Central title the following year, the Tribe fell to Joe Torre's powerhouse Yankees in the Championship Series. Cleveland won 97 games and its fifth straight division title in 1999, yet Hargrove was fired after the team lost to Boston in the Division Series. He landed on his feet; the Orioles selected him as manager just a few weeks after his dismissal.

Pete Harnisch

Harnisch, Peter Thomas **P**

1988–* B:9/23/66, Commack, NY Deb:9/13/88, BAL AL BB/TR 6', 207

W	L	PCT	G	SH	IP	BB	SO	ERA
102	94	.520	292	8	1793	653	277	3.77

Baltimore's supplemental first-round draft pick in 1987, Pete Harnisch got his first look at major league hitters near the end of the following campaign. After splitting 22 decisions in 1990 he was traded to the Houston Astros, along with Curt Schilling and Steve Finley, for Glenn Davis. Harnisch won 12 games with a 2.70 ERA for the Astros that year, while Davis managed only 10 homers to go with a .227 batting average for Baltimore.

The gregarious Fordham graduate had several strong seasons in the National League, even leading the circuit with four shutouts during a 16–9 campaign in 1993. Injuries often interfered, however, sending Harnisch to the disabled list four times in four seasons. In 1998 he successfully rebounded from a bout with clinical depression.

Harnisch bounced from Houston to the Mets and Brewers before the pitching-poor Reds inked him as a free agent on January 21, 1998. A healthy Harnisch responded with a two-year record of 30–17, the highest win total for a Reds pitcher since Jose Rijo went 30–16 in 1991–92. Harnsich led the team in starts, shutouts, and innings while tying his career high in wins. After enduring a nearly six-hour rain delay, Harnisch earned a 7–1 victory at Milwaukee in the season finale to force a Wild Card playoff against the Mets. Cincinnati lost the one-game playoff.

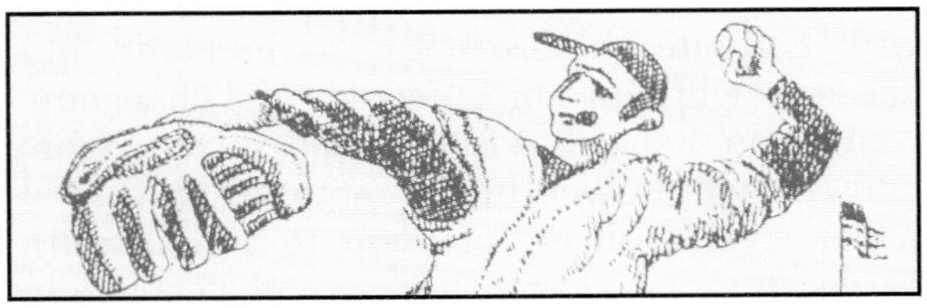

Tommy Harper

Harper, Tommy **OF-3B-DH**

1962–76 B:10/14/1940, Oak Grove, LA Deb:4/09/1962, CIN NL BR/TR 5'10", 168

G	AB	R	H	HR	RBI	OBP	SLG	AVG
1810	6269	972	1609	146	567	.340	.379	.257

Tommy Harper set a modern American League record with 73 stolen bases (since broken) during the 1969 season for the Seattle Pilots. He compiled 408 stolen bases during parts of 15 seasons in the major leagues.

The righthanded hitter started his major league career with the Cincinnati Reds in 1962, and three years later led the NL with 126 runs scored. Though only a career .257 hitter, Harper knew how to draw a walk and compiled a lifetime .340 on-base percentage.

In 1966 Harper assembled a career-best 24-game hitting streak. But the following season his average dipped to .225, and on November 21, 1967, he was traded to Cleveland for first baseman Fred Whitfield, pitcher George Culver, and outfielder Bob Raudman. Harper played 130 games for Cleveland in 1968, but hit only .217 with 11 stolen bases.

He spent most of the off-season in the Air Force. When he was discharged, the Air Force offered to promote him to staff sergeant if he re-upped. Harper told his superiors, "I wouldn't re-up if you made me a general."

On October 15, 1968, the Seattle Pilots selected Harper in the AL expansion draft. The following season he led the league with 73 steals, most in the league since Ty Cobb swiped 96 in 1915. On August 22 the club held a "Tommy Harper Night" but only about 6,000 fans showed up. The Seattle franchise moved to Milwaukee and became the Brewers prior to the 1970 season.

Harper made the move to Milwaukee and had a dream season. Playing third base, second base, and several games in the outfield, Harper posted a .296 batting average and became the first infielder and the fifth player overall to hit at least 30 homers and steal at least 30 bases in the same season. He hit six home runs to lead off games that year to tie an AL record. He also appeared in the All-Star Game and finished sixth in Most Valuable Player voting.

The following season Harper posted more typical numbers—a .258 average, 14 homers, and 25 stolen bases. On October 11, 1971, he was dealt to Boston in a 10-player trade. Harper set a Red Sox club record and led the AL for a second time in 1973 with 54 stolen bases.

In December 1974 Harper was traded to California for infielder Bob Heise. On August 13, 1975, the Angels sold him to Oakland, where Harper saw his only postseason action of his playing career. He had one at bat and walked in the Championship Series, was won by Boston. In April 1976 he signed as a free agent with Baltimore and retired at the end of the season.

Harper's first baseball assignment after his retirement was as a minor league instructor with the Yankees from 1978 through 1979. He joined the Red Sox organization in the same role in 1980 and was appointed to their major league staff as a coach for four seasons. In 1985 he was named as special assistant to the general manager with duties in player relations and as a minor league instructor, before leaving the organization in 1986.

After working for the City of Boston Parks Department, Harper was hired by the Expos on November 20, 1987, as the club's base running instructor. In his first two seasons as an instructor, the Expos organization went from a pre-Harper total of 842 stolen bases to 1,060 steals in 1988.

Toby Harrah

Harrah, Colbert Dale **3B-SS-2B**

1969–86 M(1992, 32–44) B:10/26/1948, Sissonville, WV Deb:9/5/1969, WAS AL BR/TR 6', 180

G	AB	R	H	HR	RBI	OBP	SLG	AVG
2155	7402	1115	1954	195	918	.368	.395	.264

If you look at the numbers, Toby Harrah had a notable career in his 16 years with the Senators, Rangers, Indians, and Yankees. He played 2,155 games and accumulated 1,954 hits, 195 homers, 918 RBIs, 1,115 runs, 238 stolen bases, and 1,153 walks—but he never played on a winner. The two major league records he did set were unfortunately negative. In 1977 he had no assists in a 17-inning game at third base, and in 1976 he had no chances in a doubleheader as a shortstop.

Colbert Dale Harrah played one year on a football scholarship at Ohio Northern University and then signed with the Phillies as a free agent in 1966. The Senators drafted him in 1967 after he hit .256 with three homers in 207 at bats in the Northern League.

By 1971 Harrah was the Senators' shortstop. During his rookie year he hit .230, with two homers. In 1972 (the year the Senators became the Texas Rangers), Harrah started to show some power with a .259 average. He hit 10 homers in 1973, despite missing five weeks with a broken finger. He enjoyed his breakout year in 1974 when he hit .260, with 21 homers and 74 RBIs.

The following year he averaged .293, with 20 homers and a career-high 93 RBIs; he also tallied 98 walks and 23 stolen bases. In 1977 Harrah slugged a career-high 27 homers and led the AL in bases on balls with 109. During this season he moved to third base—he was only 28, but he had lost too much range to handle shortstop.

In 1978 Harrah slumped badly, hitting .229 with 12 homers and 59 RBIs. After the season he was traded to the Indians for Buddy Bell, another third baseman. Harrah spent five years with the Indians. During this time Cleveland finished sixth three times, seventh once, and tied for fifth once. He had only nine homers in his last season and was traded to the Yankees in February 1984. After one year in New York, platooning at third with Mike Pagliarulo, he was traded back to the Rangers.

Harrah retired in 1986 after hitting .218 in 95 games. He managed the Rangers' Triple A Oklahoma City farm club in 1987 and 1988 and then coached for the Rangers from 1989 through 1992. He replaced Bobby Valentine as the Rangers' manager for the second-half of the 1992 season, and later replaced Valentine again as manager of the Mets' Triple A affiliate. He returned to the major league coaching list for the 1996 season with Cleveland.

Bud Harrelson

Harrelson, Derrel McKinley **SS**

1965–80 M(1990–91, 145–129) B:6/6/1944 Niles, CA
Deb:9/2/1965, NY NL BB/TR 5'11", 160

G	AB	R	H	HR	RBI	OBP	SLG	AVG
1533	4744	539	1120	7	267	.329	.288	.236

Bud Harrelson served as the Mets' shortstop during their miracle season in 1969 and for much of the 1970s as well. But he is probably best known for his fight with Pete Rose during the 1973 Championship Series.

Harrelson was small and skinny—barely 160 pounds—but still able to threaten opposing teams, especially on the bases. In one September week in 1966, Harrelson stole home against the Giants and then victimized the Pirates in the same fashion a few days later. Both teams were in the hunt for the pennant, and both were hurt by losses to the lowly Mets and Harrelson's aggressiveness. The Giants finished 1½ games out of first place that year, and the Pirates finished two out.

In 1969 expectations for the Mets were slim. The previous season they had finished ninth in the 10-team National League; in fact, since entering the league in 1962 the club had never risen above ninth place. But by early July 1969 New York found itself in second place, trailing only Chicago. The Mets slumped for a few weeks and dropped nine games back of the Cubs before catching fire in early August.

Harrelson, Cleon Jones, and Tommie Agee were the only regulars in the Mets' lineup; manager Gil Hodges skillfully platooned at every other position. The Mets moved into first place for good on September 10, eventually winning 100 games and claiming the first NL East flag. Harrelson hit only .182 in the NLCS and .176 in New York's five-game World Series win over the Orioles, but he was getting paid for his glove, not his bat.

Named to the All-Star team in 1970 and 1971, Harrelson won the Gold Glove Award in 1971. His best year offensively was 1970, when he reached career highs in five categories and tied the since-broken NL record of 54 consecutive games without an error.

The Mets returned to the postseason in 1973 after posting the lowest winning percentage of any pennant-winner in baseball history. New York and Cincinnati split the first two games of the NLCS, setting up the Game 3 fireworks. The Mets led, 8–2, in the top of the fifth when Rose slid hard into Harrelson at second. They exchanged words—and then blows as both benches emptied. When Rose returned to his left field position fans bombarded him with whatever they could find to throw.

"Me sliding hard into Harrelson trying to break up a double play was baseball the way it's supposed to be played," Rose explained without apology. "I'm no damn little girl out there. I'm supposed to give the fans their money's worth and play hard and try to bust up double plays—and shortstops."

When a liquor bottle sailed down at Rose, Reds manager Sparky Anderson pulled his team off the field. Order wasn't restored until several Mets players, including Willie Mays and Tom Seaver, pleaded with fans to settle down. Hostilities continued throughout the Series, which the Mets won in five games.

Harrelson hit .250 in the World Series, with six hits, five walks, and two runs scored. New York won three of the first five Series games, but the Oakland A's stormed back to take the final two and win the world championship.

In 1977 Harrelson committed only six errors in 98 games at shortstop, but his batting average slipped to a career-worst .178. On March 24, 1978, he was traded to Philadelphia for infielder Fred Andrews and cash. He played his last season with Texas in 1980 and retired with a .236 average. However, he was one of the toughest players to double up in major league history, grounding into a double play once every 89.5 at bats.

After retiring as a player, Harrelson returned to the Mets as a coach and minor league manager. He worked his way up the organizational ladder, and in 1990 Harrelson's wish came true—he was named Davey Johnson's replacement to manage the Mets. Harrelson's tenure lasted less than two full seasons, and he was dismissed in September 1991.

Ken Harrelson

Harrelson, Kenneth Smith **1B–OF**

1963–74 B:9/4/1941, Woodruff, SC Deb:6/9/1963, KC AL BR/TR 6'2", 190

G	AB	R	H	HR	RBI	OBP	SLG	AVG
900	2941	374	703	131	421	.328	.414	.239

Ken "Hawk" Harrelson (so named by catcher Duke Sims for his aquiline nose) is credited with bringing the batting glove to the major leagues. But he's probably best known for exercising his right of free speech in the summer of 1967. In response, Kansas City A's owner Charles O. Finley gave him his right to free agency.

It all began on August 3, on a flight from Boston to Kansas City. Rather than chartering a plane, the Athletics took regularly scheduled airliners. On this particular trip, A's pitcher Lew Krausse had allegedly harassed a stewardess, which Krausse vehemently denied. Finley fined the pitcher $500 and topped things off with a patronizing memo to the entire team, warning them against further "shenanigans."

The team revolted. Manager Alvin Dark refused to support Finley's actions, and Finley fired him. At this point Harrelson stepped prominently into the picture. Harrelson was quoted as saying, "Charles Finley is a menace to baseball." Finley went ballistic and, in effect, fired Harrelson, giving him his unconditional release. Finley's action was unprecedented; Harrelson was still a quality, frontline player. Had Finley placed Harrelson on waivers, he could have received $50,000 for him.

Given pre-Curt Flood free agency, Harrelson shopped his talents around. Seven major league clubs bid for his services, and the Red Sox won with a $73,000 offer. In 1967 the high-living Hawk helped the Red Sox win their first pennant since 1946. The following season he hit 35 home runs and drove in a league-leading 109 runs. The following year he was to Cleveland—one of several change of addresses Harrelson made in his career.

Harrelson, who had signed with the Athletics at age 18, became Kansas City's regular first baseman in 1965. Despite hitting 23 homers, his batting average was only .238.

In June 1966 Harrelson was hitting only .224 and was traded to Washington for pitcher Jim Duckworth. He was with the Senators less than a year before he was sold back to Kansas City. But his second stint with the A's lasted only 61 games, thanks to his choice words toward Finley.

Because of the Flight 85 incident and his booming bat, Harrelson became a popular player in Boston—in one 1968 game he hit three consecutive home runs. When traded to Cleveland in April 1969 (with pitchers Dick Ellsworth and Juan Pizarro for catcher Joe Azcue and pitchers Sonny Siebert and Vicente Romo), fans picketed Fenway Park.

Harrelson hit 27 homers for the Indians in 1969 (plus three for Boston), but he was not happy in Cleveland. "Where else in the AL," he asked, "is the lake brown and the river a fire hazard?" With Cleveland, Harrelson's always erratic fielding came under criticism. Chastised for making one-handed catches, he responded: "When you have hands as bad as mine, one hand is better than two."

In March 1970 Harrelson broke his leg and was out of action until Labor Day. Following the 1971 season he carried out his long-voiced threat to leave baseball for a life on the professional golf tour. With Harrelson's production slipping, management no longer sympathized with his nonconformist behavior.

"When you're hitting home runs, you can get away with anything," he said. "But when you're not delivering, it won't work. They don't buy your act."

Harrelson was not the success in golf that he thought he would be; he returned to baseball as a broadcaster in 1982. On October 2, 1985, he left the booth and joined the White Sox, where he was named the club's executive vice president for baseball operations. But after a series of controversial moves, he was fired.

He served as play-by-play man for the Yankees in 1987 and 1988 before returning to the White Sox broadcast booth in 1990. His exuberant "Yes" call became a fan favorite in Chicago.

Will Harridge

Harridge, William

AL President (1931–58) B:10/16/1885, Chicago, IL D:4/9/1971, Evanston, IL

The third president of the American League, Will Harridge served in the position for a quarter of a century, longer than anyone else. Born on Chicago's South Side, Harridge—who never played a game of baseball in his life—attended business college, taking courses in typewriting and stenography. He secured employment as a passenger agent for the Wabash Railroad Company. Harridge so impressed AL president and founder Byron "Ban" Johnson that, on the resignation of Robert McRoy in December 1911, he was hired as Johnson's private secretary. He had to take a pay cut, though—from $90 a month with the railroad to $50 a week with Johnson.

"McRoy had promised to stay on and teach me the ropes," said Harridge. "He left the day I arrived."

Johnson was forced out of leadership of the American League in January 1927, replaced by

Ernest S. Barnard. Harridge was elected league secretary the following November. He was re-elected to a five-year term in December 1930. Barnard, however, died unexpectedly in March 1931, and on May 27, 1931, Harridge was unanimously chosen as his replacement. Harridge assumed the duties of treasurer of the circuit and retained his post as secretary.

Never a firebrand, Harridge announced on taking office, "I do not propose nor look for any radical changes, although I will always be open to suggestions from any one." He was cool to the introduction of night baseball but instrumental in the creation of the first All-Star Game in 1933.

The decision that Harridge found most vexing involved Yankees catcher Bill Dickey. On July 4, 1932, Dickey punched Washington's Carl Reynolds and broke his jaw. Harridge fined him $1,000 and suspended him for 30 days.

Other noteworthy Harridge decisions involved the 1932 suspension of umpire George Moriarty for punching pitcher Milt Gaston following the conclusion of a game. Moriarty had hit Gaston so hard he broke his own hand.

Harridge resigned on December 3, 1958, but served as AL chairman of the board until his death in an Evanston, Illinois, nursing home on April 9, 1971.

Bucky Harris

Harris, Stanley Raymond **2B**

1919–31 M(1924–43, 1947–48, 1950–56, 2,157–2,218)
B:11/8/1896, Port Jervis, NY D:11/8/1977, Bethesda, MD Deb:8/28/1919, WAS AL BR/TR 5'9½", 156

G	AB	R	H	HR	RBI	OBP	SLG	AVG
1263	4736	722	1297	9	506	.352	.354	.274

Bucky Harris was a good second baseman and a great manager, though in neither occupation was he ever able to match his performance during his first year on the job. The son of a Pennsylvania coal miner, 13-year-old Stanley Raymond Harris dropped out of school to work in a nearby colliery. He played baseball for several amateur teams around Pittston, Pennsylvania. Former Orioles shortstop and Tigers manager Hughie Jennings, who was also from Pittston, discovered him.

In 1915 Jennings got Harris his first minor league job, and in 1919, after he enjoyed a good season at Buffalo, the Washington Senators brought the young infielder to the majors to play eight games. The following year he became the club's regular second baseman.

In 1920, his rookie season, Harris hit an even .300, a mark he would never duplicate. Fielding was always his strong suit. He led American League second basemen in fielding percentage once, putouts four times, and double plays five times, and his 483 putouts in 1922 set a league record not surpassed until 1974.

The Senators, despite the efforts of the great pitcher Walter Johnson and some other good players, had not finished above fourth place since 1918, and as the 1924 season approached it was no surprise when team owner Clark Griffith fired manager Donie Bush. But it was a shock when Griffith offered the job to the 27-year-old Harris.

After some hesitation, Harris accepted. Several Senators veterans felt that they, more than Harris, deserved to hold the reins, but Harris eventually won them over by frankly admitting his inexperience and asking for their help. The team rallied around "the Boy Manager" to win the AL pennant, nosing out the three-time champion Yankees by two games.

In the World Series, Washington faced John McGraw's New York Giants, then making their fourth consecutive trip to the Fall Classic. Even though Johnson lost his first two starts, Washington tied the Series at three wins apiece, and Harris used a clever strategy to begin Game 7. He started righthander Warren "Curly" Ogden, who faced only two batters and collected a strikeout and a walk before Harris replaced him with lefthander George Mogridge, who had been warming up secretly under the stands. The move forced McGraw to take hard-hitting Bill Terry, a left-handed batter he'd been platooning at first base, out of the lineup.

The Senators trailed, 3–1, in the bottom of the eighth inning but tied the game with the help of a ball that took a bad bounce over Giants third baseman Freddie Lindstrom. Walter Johnson came on in relief, and the game remained tied into the last of the 12th inning. Once more the Giants were the victims of poor fielding as Giants catcher Hank Gowdy stepped on his own mask and missed a foul popup. With runners on first and second, a bad bounce on a grounder that again kangarooed over Lindstrom allowed the winning run to score. Harris, who hit two home runs in the World Series (and only nine regular-season homers during his entire career), was a world champion in his first year as manager.

In 1925 the Senators repeated as American League champs. In one of the most exciting World Series of all time, Washington lost to the Pittsburgh Pirates in seven games. Harris, who brought in Walter Johnson in relief in Game 7 the previous year with a positive conclusion, stayed with a tired Johnson in Game 7 of the 1925 Series as Pittsburgh rallied to win.

As the team aged during the next few seasons, Washington slipped in the standings. When they finished fourth in 1928, Harris was traded to Detroit for outfielder Jack Warner and was immediately installed as the Tigers' manager.

Harris became baseball's "available man," a smart manager who could always be counted on to get the most out of the talent available. Unfortunately, he rarely had the players he needed to compete. He went on to manage for four years with Detroit (1929–33) and one year with the Boston Red Sox (1934) before returning to Washington for eight years (1935–42) and spending one year with the Philadelphia Phillies (1943) without winning another pennant.

His low-key approach and solid baseball knowledge won him the players' loyalty and the respect of his peers. When he was fired 92 games into the Phillies' 1943 season, he hadn't finished above fourth with a team since 1927. Nevertheless, the players threatened to strike to protest his axing.

After managing in the minors for a few years, Harris returned to the major leagues as skipper of the 1947 New York Yankees. For only the second time he was at the helm of a good club, and he led the Yankees to the pennant and a World Series victory. Though the team's performance was not as surprising as the Senators' finish in 1924, *The Sporting News* named Harris Manager of the Year. The following year, when the Yankees finished third with a 94–60 record, Harris was let go.

In 1950 he was back for a five-year run with the woebegone Senators, then finished his managerial career with a two-year hitch as Detroit's skipper in 1955 and 1956. In 29 seasons he collected two world championships, three pennants, 2,157 victories, and 2,218 losses—a standard of managerial futility exceeded only by Philadelphia Athletics Manager Connie Mack's 3,948 losses.

Harris served as an assistant with the Red Sox and scouted for the White Sox and the Senators through 1971, completing 57 years in baseball. The Veterans Committee elected him to the Hall of Fame in 1975, two years before his death.

Greg A. Harris

Harris, Greg Allen **P**

1981–95 B:11/2/1955, Lynwood, CA Deb:5/20/1981, NY NL BB/TB 6', 175

W	L	PCT	G	SV	IP	BB	SO	ERA
74	90	.451	703	54	1467	652	1141	3.69

On September 28, 1995, Greg A. Harris pitched with both his left and right arms in a major league ball game—the first time the feat had been accomplished since 1888, when the Louisville Colonels' Elton "Ice Box" Chamberlain won an American Association game.

Despite 703 career appearances, he still needed his middle initial to distinguish him from fellow reliever Greg W. Harris. The ambidextrous Harris had spent 15 unremarkable years as a relief pitcher (all righthanded) with eight different teams. He first considered the idea of pitching from both sides in the same game in 1986, when he saved 20 games for novelty-loving skipper Bobby Valentine of the Texas Rangers. As a lefty, Harris could throw a respectable fastball and spot his curve for strikes, but the proper situation never arose with Texas. Later, he didn't feel secure enough to ask for a chance. "It's not the kind of thing you bring up when you're the ninth or tenth man on a staff," he said.

Harris got his opportunity in the final days of his career. Montreal Expos manager Felipe Alou allowed Harris to toss an inning of two-handed, scoreless relief against Cincinnati. He subsequently donated his specially designed six-finger, two-thumb glove to the Baseball Hall of Fame.

Jim Ray Hart

Hart, James Ray **3B–OF–DH**

1963–74 B:10/30/1941, Hookerton, NC Deb:7/7/1963, SF NL BR/TR 5'11", 185

G	AB	R	H	HR	RBI	OBP	SLG	AVG
1125	3783	518	1052	170	578	.348	.467	.278

Giants third baseman Jim Ray Hart was one of the top sluggers in the National League in the mid-1960s. Yet he had received an unpleasant welcome to the big leagues when he showed up in the middle of the 1963 season.

After a promotion from the Giants' Triple A team in Tacoma, Hart faced Bob Gibson in his second game in the majors on July 7. Gibson was never afraid to push a batter out of the box, but this time he pitched inside and broke Hart's left shoulder with a fastball. Hart returned from the disabled list on August 12 and four days later was once again batting against the Cardinals when Curt Simmons beaned him with a fastball to finish his season.

"There was no bad blood between the teams or anything like that," Gibson said. "He was just unlucky. The thing is, he had a real closed stance, his left foot was almost on the plate, and he had trouble getting out of the way of the inside pitch."

In 1964 he came back from the two injuries and hit .286 with 31 homers, a Giants rookie record that was also good enough for third in the National League. His homer total fell to 23 the next season, but he batted .299, a career-high, and drove in 96 runs.

Hart, who had picked cotton as a youth, never had an easy time handling ground balls. He began his pro career as a second baseman before being shifted to third base. Hart was meant to be a designated hitter, except that he was born 10 years too early. He committed a league-high 32 errors in 1967, and his fielding percentage was a league-low .918. Hart even admitted he didn't like playing third: "Too damn close to the hitters," he said.

In 1966 Hart hit a career-high 33 homers, and the following season he had his best RBI season with 99 as he alternated between third and the outfield. His offensive numbers those first four years were impressive—he averaged 29 homers and 92 RBIs while batting .291.

The rest of his career took a slide, helped by a fondness for alcohol. He slumped to .258 in 1968, with 23 homers and 78 RBIs, when the injuries started coming. Mostly it was his shoulder; he needed surgery after playing only 95 games in 1969. He revived a bit in 1970, but it was only a temporary respite as he shuttled between Triple A and the majors for the next two years. He was dealt to the Yankees early in the 1973 season. The only bright spot during that time came on September 9, 1970, when Hart hit for the cycle and drove in six runs in the fifth inning.

He finished the first year of the designated hitter with 13 homers and 53 RBIs in 342 at bats. Released early in 1974, he never made it back to the majors.

Gabby Hartnett

Hartnett, Charles Leo **C**

1922–41 M(1938–40, 203–176) B:12/20/1900, Woonsocket, RI D:12/20/1972, Park Ridge, IL Deb:4/12/1922, CHI NL BR/TR 6'1", 195

G	AB	R	H	HR	RBI	OBP	SLG	AVG
1990	6432	867	1912	236	1179	.370	.489	.297

Back in the days when players had great nicknames, Charles Leo Hartnett had two of the best: "Gabby," bestowed upon him by sportswriters during his rookie year when the catcher wouldn't say a word to them, and "Old Tomato Face," a testament to his ruddy Irish complexion. Hartnett, along with Mickey Cochrane and Bill Dickey, ushered in a new era of backstops who could hit, often with power. When Hartnett left the game in 1941, he was the first catcher to have reached the 200-homer and 1,000-RBI marks.

He was first-rate behind the plate, too. Despite his small hands, which led one scout to proclaim he could never catch in the big leagues, Hartnett shares the NL record for most consecutive years leading league catchers in fielding percentage, from 1934 through 1937. He won six fielding titles overall and four putout crowns. He also shares the major league record for most years leading the league in assists, with six. No other NL catcher participated in more double plays.

Most experts list Hartnett as the league's greatest catcher until Johnny Bench. Pitchers appreciated Gabby's catching smarts. Dizzy Dean once said of him, "If I had that guy to pitch to all the time, I'd never lose me a game."

Hartnett may have inherited his legendary throwing arm. His father and three brothers, and three of his five sisters, were all known for having "guns." One sister toured state fairs for years demonstrating her baseball skills.

Gabby spent only one season in the minors before the Cubs picked him up for $2,500 in 1922. After a year and a half he couldn't unseat established backstop Bob O'Farrell. But O'Farrell suffered a fractured skull in 1924, and Hartnett moved in and took charge. O'Farrell was swapped to St. Louis the next year, and Hartnett held the post of No. 1 Cubs catcher for the next 15 years, with the exception of 1929, when early in spring training he damaged his arm and sat out most of the season.

Hartnett showed flashes of power during his first few years in the majors. He slugged 16 homers in 1924 and 24 in 1925; he then broke the .300 mark in 1928. But when major league hitters went for a crazy ride in 1930, Gabby went along and took a front seat, batting .339 with 37 homers and 122 RBIs.

Hartnett won his second pennant with the Cubs in 1932. (When they won in 1929, he was limited to pinch-hitting duties.) And he was calling the pitches during Babe Ruth's raucous at bat in Game 3 of the World Series when "the Sultan of Swat" allegedly called his shot, tipping his bat to show that he was going to homer off Charlie Root on the next pitch. But Hartnett claimed that Ruth was merely indicating that he had one strike left.

Hartnett was also behind the plate for the National League in the first All-Star Game in 1933, and he was starting catcher for the next four All-Star teams as well. He was also named to the team in 1938, but he didn't play. Hartnett was catching Carl Hubbell in the 1934 All-Star Game when the first two American Leaguers reached base. Hartnett went to the mound and advised "King Carl" to stick to his screwball. "Nobody in our league can hit it—why should they?" he said. Hubbell proceeded to fan Ruth, Lou Gehrig, Jimmie Foxx, Al Simmons, and Joe Cronin in order. Unable to restrain himself, Hartnett yapped at the American League bench, "We gotta look at that all season!"

Batting .344 in 1935 and leading his team to another NL flag, Hartnett was chosen NL Most Valuable Player. The Cubs came up short in the Series again, this time to the Tigers.

Hartnett batted a career-high .354 in 1937, and he put together a 26-game hitting streak. In the 1937 All-Star Game, Dean was pitching with Hartnett catching and Gehrig up. Dean shook off Hartnett's call for a curve, and Gehrig homered. Diz tried the heat on the next batter as well, but Earl Averill smashed a liner off Dean's left foot. Dean's big toe was broken, and his glory days as one of the best pitchers in the game were over.

During the 1938 season Cubs management ousted "Jolly Cholly" Grimm as the team's manager when they were in third place. The 37-year-old Hartnett was given the job. Under the new manager, the Cubs went on a tear to challenge the league-leading Pirates. The Cubs pitching staff was wearing thin by September 18, with the Pirates holding onto a 3½-game lead. But a hurricane struck the East Coast, and three Chicago games were rained out.

The rested hurlers were able to narrow the gap to 1½ games by September 27, when the Pirates came to Chicago for a three-game set. Stuck for a starter, Hartnett pulled one out of his hat. Dean, who had been used fewer than a dozen times since being obtained from the Cards in April, started and held the Bucs in check for a vital 2–1 Cubs win.

The next day the Pirates had a 5–3 lead over Chicago when the Cubs struck back to tie the game in the last of the eighth. Pittsburgh ace reliever Mace Brown came in to douse the fire. In the growing darkness, the umpires decided to play one more inning before calling the game. The Pirates failed to cross the plate in the top of the ninth. Hartnett led off the bottom half. Brown threw two tricky curves, one for a called strike, the other a foul ball. The count was 0–2, but Brown didn't want to waste one. He came back with his curve, and when he hung it, Hartnett slugged it. "The home run in the gloamin' "put the Cubs in first place, where they stayed for good.

Despite winning a pennant as a rookie manager, Hartnett couldn't repeat his magic in the World Series. The Yankees swept the Cubs in four games to become the first team to win three straight world championships.

Hartnett was still able to catch 86 games in 1939, but his Cubs finished in fourth place that season and fifth the next. Released prior to the 1941 season, he signed on with the Giants as a playing coach that year and hit an even .300 in his final professional season. He managed in the minors for Indianapolis, Jersey City, and Buffalo through 1946.

The Kansas City A's brought him back to the majors as a coach and scout in 1965, but Gabby clashed with manager Alvin Dark the following year. After being moved into a public relations position, he left the game for good. Hartnett retired with the highest career slugging average by a catcher and the fifth-best batting average at his position. He was elected to the Hall of Fame in 1955.

Clint Hartung

Hartung, Clinton Clarence **P–OF**

1947–50 B:8/10/1922, Hondo, TX Deb:4/15/1947, NY NL BR/TR 6'4", 215

W	L	PCT	G	SH	IP	BB	SO	ERA
29	29	.500	112	3	511[1]	271	167	5.02

G	AB	R	H	HR	RBI	OBP	SLG	AVG
196	378	42	90	14	43	.285	.407	.238

Some people thought Clint Hartung was going to be a great hitter. Others thought he would be a great pitcher. He achieved neither. He is remembered for being a pinch runner in the third game of the 1951 Dodgers-Giants playoff.

With the New York Giants rallying in the ninth inning, Don Mueller slid hard into third base and broke his ankle; he had to be carried off the field. At the same time Ralph Branca was summoned from the Brooklyn bullpen, Hartung emerged from the New York dugout as a pinch runner. Hartung crossed home plate minutes later on Bobby Thomson's famous home run to win the pennant.

Hartung was born in 1922 in Hondo, Texas, which is why he was called "The Hondo Hurricane." He spent two years in the minor leagues until he went into the armed services, where he continued to play ball. In Hawaii he looked very impressive—he went 25–0 as a pitcher with an average of 15 strikeouts per game; at the plate he hit .567 with 30 homers in 67 games.

After another season in the minors he was sold to the Giants in 1946 for $25,000 and four players. The ballyhoo began the following year in spring training. He was 6 feet 4 inches, weighed 210 pounds, threw very hard, and hit some long home runs. Hartung didn't have an effective curveball, and his home runs were too infrequent. He needed more time in the minors to learn his craft, but he didn't get it.

In 1947 Hartung was 9–7 with a 4.57 ERA in 23 games as a rookie. He went 8–8 the next season and 9–11 in 1949 with a 5.00 ERA. After another poor season as a pitcher, he became an outfielder, albeit an infrequently used one. Hartung drifted back to the minors and then retired to work for Marathon Oil.

Bryan Harvey

Harvey, Bryan Stanley **P**

1987–95 B:6/2/1963, Soddy-Daisy, TN Deb:5/16/1987, CAL AL BR/TR, 6'2", 212

W	L	PCT	G	SV	IP	BB	SO	ERA
17	25	.405	322	177	387	144	448	2.49

Though injuries often interrupted his career, Bryan Harvey was a brilliant relief pitcher who made All-Star teams in both leagues. At his peak, he was widely considered baseball's best closer. Throwing a high number of split-fingered fastballs, however, put too much strain on his elbow and shortened his career.

After consecutive 25-save seasons for the California Angels in 1989 and 1990, Harvey led the American League with a career-high 46 saves in 1991. He had 101 strikeouts in only 78 innings.

Hampered by elbow problems a year later, the Angels left him unprotected in the expansion draft. The Florida Marlins surprised many by claiming Harvey in the first round. Healthy again, he recorded 45 saves, which, added to his one win, set a record for playing a hand in 71.9 percent of his team's 64 victories.

Unfortunately, physical problems returned a year later. Harvey earned only six saves in his final two years with the Marlins before an unsuccessful comeback attempt with the Atlanta Braves.

Doug Harvey

Harvey, H. Douglas

Umpire (1962–92) B:3/13/1930, Southgate, CA

His license plate read simply "NL UMP." Players, managers, and even fellow umpires called Doug Harvey "God." But umpiring was hardly a lifelong ambition for Harvey. By his own count, he held 53 different jobs by age 32. He finally found his calling as a baseball umpire, something he had first tried at age 16, yet he never attended umpire school. "I was the last of the umpires in the National League that didn't go to school," Harvey said in John C. Skipper's book, *Umpires*.

Harvey quickly ascended through the minors. After four years with the California State League and Pacific Coast League, Harvey joined the National League in 1962. Over the next 31 seasons Harvey umpired 4,888 games, plus eight National League Championship Series, five World Series, and four All-Star Games. He was named the league's best umpire in a 1974 poll, and served as crew chief from 1975 to 1992.

Harvey was known for his delayed, decisive calls, making sure he got the play right before announcing his verdict. "I introduced timing to umpiring," he said. "That's my gift to baseball."

Harvey became the first umpire to command a $100,000 salary. It was over $200,000 by the time he left the field. "I will not embarrass myself or this great game by my inability to do the job any more," Harvey said in announcing his retirement.

Ernie Harwell

Harwell, Ernest

Broadcaster B:1/25/1918, Washington, GA

What Bob Prince was to Pittsburgh, Mel Allen and Red Barber were to New York, and Jack Brickhouse was to Chicago, Ernie Harwell was to Detroit. He brought a deep love of the game and a calm, intelligent style to the Tigers broadcast booth. On summer evenings his voice could be heard over thousands of radios in hundreds of Michigan towns.

While Harwell knew the game inside and out, he never lorded his knowledge over his listeners. Every Harwell broadcast was a mini-course in the ins and outs, details, and rhythms of the game. Harwell began his professional career as a writer, and his use of the language was always precise and firm, never overstated, never windy, never intellectualized. He is a successful writer of songs and lyrics, with more than 50 recorded efforts, having penned tunes for artists as diverse as Merrilee Rush, Barbara Lewis, Tommy Overstreet, and B.J. Thomas.

Harwell, whose first job was as a staff writer for *The Atlanta Constitution*, had been selling articles to national magazines such as *The Saturday Evening Post*, *Collier's*, and *The Sporting News* for more than a dozen years when Branch Rickey heard him call an Atlanta Crackers game. Rickey brought him to New York to join Vin Scully in the Dodgers broadcast booth. To get Harwell, Rickey had to "trade" Cliff Dapper to the Crackers. Harwell stayed with the Dodgers until 1950, when he became a Giants announcer. In 1954 he began a six-year stint broadcasting the Orioles.

In 1960 he settled in Detroit and stayed there through 1991, when new management fired him in a move that outraged many of the Michiganders who had grown up on his warm style. When Detroit native Mike Ilitch purchased the club from Tom Monaghan in the summer of 1992, he invited Harwell to return to the Tigers. He handled television broadcasts through 1997. He went back to Tigers radio the following year and, fittingly, called the final game at Tiger Stadium in 1999. His signature home run call of "long gone" carried across the country as a postseason announcer for the CBS Radio Network.

According to Curt Smith, author of *Voices of the Game*, a history of baseball on the air, Harwell "wore more durably than any other" baseball announcer. Writer John Steadman, who worked the Baltimore broadcasts with Harwell for several years, said that Harwell "had more authenticity as an announcer than anyone [he'd] ever heard."

Harwell was the first active announcer honored with the Ford C. Frick Award, displayed in the Hall of Fame's "Scribes and Mike-Men" exhibit. There you will also find a sample of his writing that is one of the most eloquent descriptions of baseball ever written. It is called "The Game for All America." It has been translated into six languages. Among the passages is this:

> *Baseball is President Eisenhower tossing out the first ball of the season; and a pudgy schoolboy playing catch with his dad on a Mississippi farm. It's America, this baseball. A re-issued newsreel of boyhood dreams. Dreams lost somewhere between boy and man. It's the Bronx cheer and the Baltimore farewell. The left field screen in Boston, the right field dump at Nashville's Sulphur Dell, the open stands in San Francisco, the dusty, wind-swept diamond at Albuquerque. And a rock home plate and chicken wire backstop—anywhere.*
>
> *Baseball is the cool, clear eyes of Rogers Hornsby, the flashing spikes of Ty Cobb, an overaged pixie named Rabbit Maranville, and Jackie Robinson testifying before a Congressional hearing.*
>
> *Baseball is Tradition in flannel knickerbockers. And Chagrin at being picked off base. It is Dignity in the blue serge of an umpire running the game by rule of thumb. It is Humor, holding its sides when an errant puppy eludes two groundskeepers and the fastest outfielder. And Pathos, dragging itself off the field after being knocked from the box....*
>
> *Baseball is cigar smoke, hot-roasted peanuts,* The Sporting News, *winter trades, "Down in front," and the Seventh-Inning Stretch. Sore arms, broken bats, a no-hitter, and the strains of "The Star-Spangled Banner."*

Ron Hassey

Hassey, Ronald William **C**

1978–91 B:2/27/1953, Tucson, AZ Deb:4/23/1978, CLE AL BL/TR 6'2", 200

G	AB	R	H	HR	RBI	OBP	SLG	AVG
1192	3440	348	914	71	438	.343	.382	.266

Ron Hassey could hit a little—a .266 career average—and pitchers liked working with him. He spent 14 years in the big leagues, including three pennant-winning years with Oakland, 1988, 1989 and 1990. But the most interesting part of his career centered around his time with the Yankees in 1985 and 1986. And the attention had nothing to do with Hassey. It had everything to do with the circus that Yankees owner George Steinbrenner was running out of the Bronx.

Hassey, the son of a former Yankees minor leaguer, was All-America on the 1976 NCAA champion University of Arizona. He signed with the Indians that June as an 18th-round draft choice. Coming up to stay with the Indians in the middle of 1979, he hit .287 in 75 games and followed with his best season in 1980. He led all major league catchers with a .318 average and had career-highs with 130 games, 124 hits, 390 at bats, and 65 RBIs.

He was part of a June 1984 trade that sent Rick Sutcliffe to the Cubs, but soon after Hassey arrived in Chicago he hurt his knee and after the season was traded to the Yankees. Hassey loved the short porch in Yankee Stadium right field. He hit .296 in 1985 with a career-high 13 homers in 267 at bats. His teammates started calling him "Babe." Hassey also led the American League with 15 passed balls in only 69 games behind the plate.

That winter Steinbrenner wanted Chicago lefty Britt Burns even though Burns had a very suspect hip. But the White Sox wouldn't make the deal unless Hassey was part of it. Finally on December 12 the Yankees relented. Steinbrenner immediately began plotting to bring Hassey back.

Steinbrenner had once feuded with Chicago owner Jerry Reinsdorf, calling Reinsdorf and minority partner Eddie Einhorn baseball's equivalent of the Katzenjammer Kids. Now Steinbrenner and Reinsdorf had become best buddies. And on February 13, just 63 days after he had been traded to the White Sox, Chicago traded Hassey back to the Yankees for three minor leaguers.

In midseason Hassey was hitting .298, and Burns was recovering from hip surgery (he never pitched again). The Yankees needed a shortstop, a righty designated hitter, and a backup catcher. Reinsdorf was only too anxious to accommodate. He sent Wayne Tolleson, Ron Kittle, and Joel Skinner to the Yankees for Hassey, Carlos Martinez, and a player to be named later.

That player was supposed to be Doug Drabek, a promising rookie. But under Organized Baseball rules a player on a team's major league roster cannot be the player "to be named later." Yet neither Reinsdorf nor rookie general manager Ken "Hawk" Harrelson complained, settling for a minor league pitcher named Bill Lindsey, who never made the majors. Steinbrenner traded Drabek that winter for Rick Rhoden, in one of the many deals that contributed to the Yankees' collapse later in the decade.

As for Hassey, he batted .353 in 49 games for the White Sox and .323 for the season, including an astounding 10-for-18 pinch-hitting. He wound up in Oakland the next season and played on three consecutive pennant winners. A favorite of manager Tony La Russa, Hassey appeared in nearly

100 games each season despite a low batting average and the presence of All-Star catcher Terry Steinbach. After batting .227 for the Expos in 1991, he retired.

Billy Hatcher

Hatcher, William Augustus **OF**
1984–95 B:10/4/1960 Williams, AZ Deb:9/10/1984, CHI NL BR/TR 5'9", 175

G	AB	R	H	HR	RBI	OBP	SLG	AVG
1233	4339	586	1146	54	399	.315	.364	.264

For one three-game stretch, Billy Hatcher was the hottest hitter in World Series history. He batted .750 to lead the Cincinnati Reds to a sweep of the Oakland A's in 1990—the most unlikely sweep since the 1954 New York Giants shocked the Cleveland Indians.

Hatcher was always at his best in October. He had a .404 career average in 14 postseason games. Although in a losing effort, he homered in the 14th inning for the Houston Astros to tie Game 6 of the 1986 National League Championship Series.

As in 1986, Hatcher had an ordinary season in 1990, then exploded in the postseason. He batted .333 with a home run as the Reds defeated the Pittsburgh Pirates in six games in the NLCS. The Oakland pitching staff did not retire Hatcher until Game 3 of the World Series; by then he had already set a Series record with seven straight hits. Although a Dave Stewart pitch struck Hatcher in the hand, forcing him to the bench in the first inning of Game 4, the Reds were able to complete the sweep. Hatcher received the Babe Ruth Award for the Series.

He was good on the bases (218 steals), and good at unpacking his bags (seven teams in 12 seasons); excuses, however, weren't his strong suit. In 1987 his broken bat revealed an illegal cork center. Even though he claimed the bat belonged to relief pitcher Dave Smith, Hatcher he was suspended for 10 days. Hatcher joined the Tampa Bay Devil Rays as a coach after his playing days ended.

Mickey Hatcher

Hatcher, Michael Vaughn **OF-DH-3B-1B**
1979–90 B:3/15/1955, Cleveland, OH Deb:8/3/1979, LA NL BR/TR 6'2", 200

G	AB	R	H	HR	RBI	OBP	SLG	AVG
1130	3377	348	946	38	375	.316	.377	.280

Mickey Hatcher left two world champions just before they climbed to the top. Late in his career, however, the little-used veteran got a chance to play a key role in an unlikely championship run.

Hatcher's major league career began in Los Angeles, where the club experimented with him in the outfield and at third base. After two years they sent him and two minor leaguers to the Minnesota Twins for outfielder Ken Landreaux.

Landreaux provided the Dodgers with more hitting power than Hatcher had and quickly earned a regular spot in Tommy Lasorda's outfield. In the same year the Dodgers won the World Series. In Minnesota, Hatcher was pegged with championship potential by the hopeful club and was weaned away from third base. Speedy but not blindingly fast, he platooned as both an outfielder and a designated hitter.

As his playing time increased his hitting improved, and by 1983 he had developed a spray-hitting style that earned him 119 hits, 47 RBIs, and a .317 average. His easygoing nature also made him a natural team leader, and in 1984 he became a regular in the Twins' outfield. That year he hit .302, and Minnesota went from three straight cellar finishes to third in the American League West.

When the Twins fell in the standings the next season and were back in last place again in 1986, Tom Kelly replaced Ray Miller as manager. Hatcher, who had developed a reputation as a clubhouse comic, returned to the Dodgers, who had finished the 1986 season barely out of the cellar.

In 1987 the Dodgers used him in a utility infield role and finished fourth, but his former team, the Twins, climbed to the top of the AL West and won the World Series in seven games.

He hit .293 in 1988, filling in at first base and in the outfield. With a strong team effort including the slugging of Kirk Gibson and the pitching of Orel Hershiser, the Dodgers made it to the National League Championship Series against the Mets. Hatcher started the NLCS at first base, contributed two RBIs to Los Angeles' Game 2 win, and remained at first for six games.

In Game 7 Kirk Gibson reinjured an already hampered hamstring, and Hatcher moved into left field as the Dodgers won the pennant on a brilliant Hershiser mound effort. Hatcher started the World Series in left field. Although he had managed only one home run all season, he slammed a two-run homer that started the Dodgers on the road to victory. Gibson won the game in his only Series at bat in the ninth inning. Grimacing in pain, he came off the bench to hit a dramatic game-winning two-run homer.

Hatcher continued to fill the hobbled Gibson's shoes. He started Game 5 with another homer. When the Dodgers finished the game as world champions, Hatcher was the team's leading hitter, with a .368 average. He remained with the Dodgers in a backup role for two more seasons before retiring. Hatcher went into coaching, and was on the staff of the Albuquerque Dukes in the Pacific Coast League in 1999.

Joe Hauser

Hauser, Joseph John **1B**

1922–29 B:1/12/1899, Milwaukee, WI D:7/11/1997, Sheboygan, WI Deb:4/18/1922, PHI AL BL/TL 5'10½", 175

G	AB	R	H	HR	RBI	OBP	SLG	AVG
629	2044	351	580	80	356	.368	.479	.284

First baseman Joe Hauser's career was divided by a broken kneecap: in the three years prior to the injury, 1922–24, he was a budding star; in the years following the mishap he never lived up to his early promise and he left the majors for the minor leagues, where he played until 1942. He hit 399 homers as a minor leaguer, and earned the distinction of being the first professional baseball player to have two 60-home run seasons.

Hauser, nicknamed "Unser Choe"—or "Uncle Joe" in German—started with Providence in the Eastern League in 1918, hit .323 in 111 games as a Philadelphia Athletics rookie in 1922, then hit .307 the next season with 16 homers and 94 RBIs. Even better in 1924, he hit .288 with 27 homers and 115 RBIs.

Hauser missed the entire 1925 season with his injury, and when he returned was not the same player. He hit .192 in 91 games in 1926, hit .353 for Kansas City of the American Association in 1927, and returned to the A's in 1928, hitting .260 with 16 homers in 95 games. But after hitting .250 in 37 games for Cleveland in 1929, Hauser's major league career was over.

He played for Baltimore the next season and hit 63 home runs. He drove in 175 runs in 1931, moved to Minneapolis and hit 49 homers in 1932, and then hit 63 home runs for Minneapolis in 1933. Of course, 50 of those round-trippers came at home in cozy Nicollet Park, which was 279 feet down the right field line and 328 feet to the power alley in right-center. Hauser stayed at Minneapolis through 1936 and hung on in the lower minors until 1942, when he was the player-manager for Sheboygan of the Wisconsin State League.

Pink Hawley

Hawley, Emerson P. **P**

1892–1901 B:12/5/1872 Beaver Dam, WI D:9/19/1938, Beaver Dam, WI Deb:8/13/1892, STL AL BL/TR 5'10", 185

W	L	PCT	G	SH	IP	BB	SO	ERA
167	179	.483	393	11	3012^{2}	974	868	3.96

Emerson P. "Pink" Hawley got his nickname at a very young age. He was one of a set of twins so identical that a nurse pinned different colored ribbons on their diapers to tell them apart—his brother got the blue ribbon.

When Hawley came to the National League with St. Louis in 1892, he threw hard, but seldom knew where his pitches were going. After three losing seasons he was sold to Pittsburgh, then managed by Connie Mack. Under the former catcher's care, Hawley developed enough control to become a 31-game winner in 1895.

Although he had two other 20-win seasons, he never became a control artist. In nine NL seasons he hit an astonishing 195 batters. He opened one 1894 game by hitting the first three men he faced, and he topped that by popping five batsmen in a single game in 1896. Off the field, Hawley was quiet and polite, and he was sometimes known to ask players he met on the street to forgive him for hitting them. After topping the league in complete games in 1900, he ended his career with the brand-new Brewers of the equally new American League.

Charlie Hayes

Hayes, Charles Dewayne **3B**

1988–* B: 5/29/1965, Hattiesburg, MS Deb:9/11/1988, SF NL BR/TR 6', 207

G	AB	R	H	HR	RBI	OBP	SLG	AVG
1395	4842	530	1276	135	690	.317	.402	.264

Charlie Hayes was one of the first major leaguers to truly benefit from the mile-high atmosphere in Denver. In 1993, two years before Vinny Castilla displaced him as third baseman of the Rockies, Hayes hit .305 with 25 homers, 98 RBIs, a team-leading 175 hits, and a league-leading 45 doubles for the first-year expansion team.

His career began in 1988 with the Giants, who had drafted him in the fourth round four years earlier. He had two stints each with the Phillies and Yankees as well as the Giants; he also made stops in Pittsburgh and Colorado.

The three-sport high school star from Hattiesburg, Mississippi, had three hits and scored two runs in his only World Series, with the 1996 world champion Yankees. He made the last putout of that Series, smiling broadly as he pulled in the pop foul from the bat of Atlanta's Mark Lemke. Hayes also reached postseason play with the 1997 Yankees. He batted .333 while playing in all five games of the Division Series loss to Cleveland. He spent the next two years with the Giants, fand signed a minor league contract with the Mets after the 1999 season.

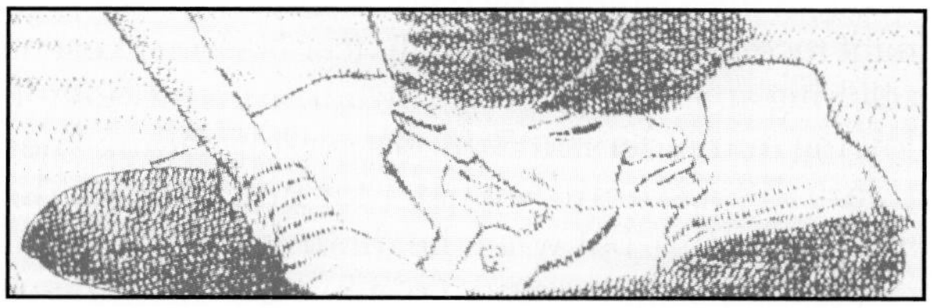

Von Hayes

Hayes, Von Francis **OF–1B**

1981–92 B:8/31/1958, Stockton, CA Deb:4/14/1981, CLE AL BL/TR 6'5", 185

G	AB	R	H	HR	RBI	OBP	SLG	AVG
1495	5249	767	1402	143	696	.357	.416	.267

Outfielder Von Hayes is best remembered for going from Cleveland to Philadelphia in a controversial December 1982 trade that cost the Phils five players: Manny Trillo, George Vukovich, Julio Franco, Jay Baller, and Jerry Willard. He helped the Phillies reach the World Series in his first year with the team, but his best years occurred after the team slid in the standings.

Hayes attended St. Mary's College in California and was a seventh-round draft choice in June 1979. He did not begin playing professionally until 1980, when he batted a league-leading .329 at Waterloo and was named Midwest League Most Valuable Player. He batted over .300 at Charleston in the International League before settling in at Cleveland.

A versatile performer who could play all three outfield positions as well as first and third, Hayes faced tremendous pressure in Philadelphia after his controversial trade. He led the National League in runs and doubles in 1986, while batting a career-high .305. Hayes clouted two homers in the first inning of a 26-7 whipping of the Mets on June 11, 1985. As an All-Star in 1989 he hit 26 home runs, including three in one game on August 29.

Hobbled by injuries in 1990 and 1991, Hayes was traded to the Angels in December 1991. California tendered him his unconditional release on August 21, 1992.

Bob Hazle

Hazle, Robert Sidney **OF**

1955–58 B:12/9/1930, Laurens, SC D:4/25/1992, Columbia, SC Deb:9/8/1955, CIN NL BL/TR 6', 190

G	AB	R	H	HR	RBI	OBP	SLG	AVG
110	261	37	81	9	37	.390	.467	.310

The Broadway hit *Damn Yankees* told the tale of Joe Hardy, a long-suffering, middle-aged Washington Senators fan who sold his soul to the Devil, was transformed into a young phenom, and helped his club win a pennant. In 1957 Milwaukee Braves fans might have thought the script had been rewritten for Bob "Hurricane" Hazle.

The Braves called up Hazle in the midst of a pennant race, and he proceeded to tear National League pitching apart. He joined Milwaukee on July 28 following outfielder Bill Bruton's season-ending knee injury. It took until August 4 for him to crack the starting lineup, but when he did he collected a single, a double, and scored a run in a 9–7 Milwaukee win over Brooklyn. It was the beginning of a 10-game Braves winning streak.

During that streak the Braves, holding a 2½-game lead over the Cardinals, traveled to St. Louis for a three-game series. When the series ended, Milwaukee had a 5½-game lead over the Cardinals. Hazle, who had four hits in the series opener, batted .700 in the three games. During the 10-game winning streak Hazle batted .545 (18-for-33) with 11 RBIs. He finished the season hitting .403 with seven homers in 41 games. The result was Milwaukee's first pennant.

Like Joe Hardy, Robert Sidney Hazle came out of nowhere. He had signed with Cincinnati in 1950, and appeared in six games with the Reds in 1955, when he hit .231 (all singles). The following spring Hazle was traded to the Braves, who farmed him out to Wichita where he soon hurt his knee. At season's end he was about ready to quit, but he decided to stick it out. In 1957 he started slowly, hitting about .220, and then went on a hot streak to drive his average up to .279. That was when Bruton got hurt.

Hazle disappeared from the scene almost as quickly as he had arrived. In the 1957 World Series he went just 2-for-13. The following May he was hitting just .179 when Milwaukee sold him to Detroit. Before Hazle knew it, he was gone from the majors. After playing at Charleston in the Class A South Atlantic League in 1959, he retired from the game.

Hazle's nickname, incidentally, was inspired by Hurricane Hazel, which wrecked Myrtle Beach in 1954. I'll tell you what," he told a writer years later. "If some ballplayer comes along in the next couple years and his name is Hugo, you'd better believe he's gonna be called Hurricane too."

Jeff Heath

Heath, John Geoffrey **OF**

1936–49 B:4/1/1915, Fort William, Ontario, Canada D:12/9/1975, Seattle, WA Deb:9/13/1936, CLE AL BL/TR 5'11½", 200

G	AB	R	H	HR	RBI	OBP	SLG	AVG
1383	4937	777	1447	194	887	.370	.509	.293

Canadian by birth, John Geoffrey "Jeff" Heath made his mark in the United States with Cleveland during the 1930s and 1940s. In 1938 the outfielder got the baseball world's attention with a bang.

During his first full season as a starter for the Indians, Jeff Heath put on a dazzling offensive show, smashing 21 home runs, 31 doubles, and a league-leading 18 triples, while registering 112 RBIs and an eye-popping .343 batting average, second only to American League Most Valuable Player Jimmie Foxx, who hit .349. Heath's slugging percentage was .602, third in the league behind Foxx and Hank Greenberg and ahead of Joe DiMaggio.

Although Heath never again matched his awesome numbers of 1938, he went on to have a solid major league career. He spent 10 years with the Indians before playing for the Washington Senators, St. Louis Browns, and Boston Braves.

During the 1948 season with the Braves, Heath suffered a broken ankle that forced him to miss the World Series and end his career the following season. He finished with 194 home runs, 102 triples, 279 doubles and 887 RBIs. His lifetime batting average during 14 seasons was a robust .293.

Cliff Heathcote

Heathcote, Clifton Earl **OF**

1918–32 B:1/24/1898, Glen Rock, PA Deb:6/4/1918, STL NL BL/TL 5'10½", 160

G	AB	R	H	HR	RBI	OBP	SLG	AVG
1415	4443	653	1222	42	448	.333	.375	.275

Cliff Heathcote and Max Flack were the first players to perform for two major league clubs on the same day. Between games of a Memorial Day 1922 morning-afternoon doubleheader Heathcote went from the Cardinals to the Cubs for Flack. Heathcote took the trade hard, weeping as St. Louis general manager Branch Rickey broke the news to him.

An unusually speedy player Heathcote often beat out infield hits. He led National League outfielders in fielding and assists one and twice in doubles plays. Despite his fielding skills, his nickname "Rubberhead" derived from a notable mistake—when a flyball bounced off his cranium at Sportsman's Park.

Heathcote had played at Penn State before turning professional in 1918. He spent part of that season at Houston where he batted .181 in 20 games.

Heathcote, who hit for the cycle on June 13, 1918, homered and doubled in the same inning on June 21, 1918. He scored five runs on August 25, 1922, going 5-for-5 with four RBIs as the Cubs beat the Phils 26–23. Along with Hack Wilson, Charlie Grimm, and Claude Beck he homered in the seventh inning of a May 12, 1930 contest.

Richie Hebner

Hebner, Richard Joseph **3B-1B**

1968–85 B:11/26/1947, Boston, MA Deb:9/23/1968, PIT NL BL/TR 6'1", 197

G	AB	R	H	HR	RBI	OBP	SLG	AVG
1908	6144	865	1694	203	890	.356	.438	.276

Richie Hebner spent 18 years in the major leagues and later became a coach, but he was probably best known for his offseason occupation as a player—working with his father as a Boston-area gravedigger. "I'm good at this," he once remarked. "In 10 years, no one's ever dug themselves out of one of my graves yet."

Hebner was a winner, appearing in eight National League Championship Series. He batted .284 in 27 NLCS games for three different teams, but he only played in one World Series, as a member of 1971 world champion Pittsburgh.

Hebner was an outstanding high school hockey player, but he chose baseball when the Pirates gave him a $40,000 bonus as a June 1966 first-round draft choice. He performed in the minors with Salem, Raleigh, and Columbus. His early major league career was often interrupted by military obligations, and in 1974 he led NL third basemen in errors.

After five postseason appearances with Pittsburgh, he signed with the Phillies as a free agent after the 1976 season. With Mike Schmidt already at third, Hebner became a first baseman and helped the Phils capture two division titles. When Philadelphia acquired Pete Rose, however, Hebner was dealt to the Mets in 1979. Although he led his new club in RBIs, he was unhappy in New York and was traded to the Tigers after one season. After driving in a career-high 82 runs in his first season in Detroit, Hebner's productivity declined and was traded back to Pittsburgh for a player to be named later. He finished his career with the Cubs, but not before he appeared in one final NLCS in 1984.

Hebner was not a fan of modern ballparks. "My father's cemetery has more life in it than this ballpark," he once said of Three Rivers Stadium. He derided Montreal's Olympic Stadium as "the world's largest toilet bowl." He made an obscene gesture to fans at Shea Stadium. Fittingly, he finished his career with stops in classic Tiger Stadium and Wrigley Field, sandwiched between another stint at Three Rivers Stadium.

Guy Hecker

Hecker, Guy Jackson **P-1B-OF**

1882–90 M(1890, 23–113) B:4/3/1856, Youngsville, PA D:12/3/1938, Wooster, OH Deb:5/2/1882, LOU AA BR/TR 6', 190

W	L	PCT	G	SH	IP	BB	SO	ERA
175	146	.545	336	15	2924	492	1110	2.93

G	AB	R	H	HR	RBI	OBP	SLG	AVG
705	2876	504	812	19	278	.324	.376	.282

Guy Hecker could quite literally do it all—both as a championship pitcher and league-leading batter during his short nine-year career. Hired by Louisville of the American Association in 1882 on the recommendation of star pitcher Tony Mullane, the tall, blond righthander pitched on Mullane's days off, but spent most of the season at first base, hitting .276. When Mullane moved on to St. Louis the next year, Hecker, a power pitcher with a baffling drop, became the club's regular pitcher, winning 26 games.

In 1884 he had his greatest year. He led the league with 670 innings pitched, 72 complete games, 385 strikeouts, and 52 victories, but the strain of pitching so many innings took its toll on his arm. By 1886 he had switched to a finesse style. Rule changes in 1887 limited the number of steps a pitcher could take before delivering the ball; the new rules greatly affected Hecker, and he seldom pitched successfully after that.

When not pitching Hecker often played first base or the outfield. His batting average of .341 topped the AA in 1886 (although under modern standards he didn't have enough at bats to qualify for the batting title). His batting eye began to fade, along with his pitching. In 1890, his final major league season, he batted .226 and went 2–9 on the mound.

Jim Hegan

Hegan, James Edward **C**

1941–60 B:8/3/1920 Lynn, MA D:6/17/1984, Swampscott, MA Deb:9/9/1941, CLE AL BR/TR 6'2", 195

G	AB	R	H	HR	RBI	OBP	SLG	AVG
1666	4772	550	1087	92	525	.296	.344	.228

Jim Hegan, a major league catcher for more than 16 seasons, never hit over .250, yet he was a five-time All-Star. As Hall of Fame catcher Bill Dickey once said, "When you can catch like Hegan you don't have to hit."

He took over the Indians' regular catching job in 1947, when he hit a career-high .249, and he kept the job for the next 10 years and made five All-Star teams. For much of that time he was catching one of the best starting staffs that the majors have ever seen: Bob Feller, Early Wynn, Bob Lemon, and Mike Garcia.

In 1949, the durable Hegan caught 152 games. His most productive seasons with the bat were 1948, when hit .248 with 14 homers and 61 RBIs, and 1950, when he hit .219 with 14 homers and 58 RBIs.

Blessed with an outstanding arm, he led American League catchers in double plays four times (including an unassisted double play in 1949), in putouts three times, in assists twice, and in fielding percentage three times. He also caught three no-hitters: Don Black, 1947; Lemon, 1948; and Feller, 1951.

According to Feller, "Jim Hegan became the best catcher I ever had. He didn't hit as well as the others, but nobody was his equal as a catcher, especially with his arm."

After catching 118 games in 1956 at age 36, he became a backup in 1957 before making the rounds: he played for the Tigers, Phillies, Giants, and Cubs the next three seasons. He retired in 1960 and joined the Yankees as a coach. He spent 20 years as a coach for New York and Detroit. His son Mike was a slick-fielding first baseman; he also had trouble with the bat, batting .242 in 12 seasons.

Harry Heilmann

Heilmann, Harry Edwin **OF–1B**

1914–32 B:8/3/1894, San Francisco, CA D:7/9/1951, Southfield, MI Deb:5/16/1914, DET AL BR/TR 6'1", 195

G	AB	R	H	HR	RBI	OBP	SLG	AVG
2148	7787	1291	2660	183	1539	.410	.520	.342

In 1913 Harry Heilmann was a 19-year-old bookkeeper for a San Francisco biscuit company. One Saturday, as the noon whistle blew, Heilmann left his office wondering how to spend the rest of the day. He walked only a few blocks before realizing he'd forgotten his topcoat.

Retracing his steps, he ran into an old friend who had a problem. His buddy was the manager of the Hanford team of the San Joaquin Valley League, and he needed a third baseman to fill in for a sick player the next day in Bakersfield. He offered Heilmann $10 to play. On Sunday Heilmann doubled in the 11th inning to win the game for Hanford, 4–2. When the happy Hanford fans showered the field with money, Heilmann was shocked to discover he'd made $150, more than a month's salary as a bookkeeper.

In the crowd was a scout from the Class B Northwestern League's Portland Colts. On Monday he signed Heilmann to a professional contract and threw in a spaghetti dinner as a bonus. Thanks to a forgotten topcoat, a Hall of Fame career was under way.

He hit .305 as an outfielder-first baseman for Portland in 1913, and Detroit purchased his contract for $1,500 at the end of the season. It was too much, too fast, for Heilmann. He hit only .225 in 69 games in 1914, fielded abysmally, and was sent to San Francisco of the Pacific Coast League for the 1915 season. After he hit .364 Detroit brought him back up for good in 1916.

At 6-foot-1 and 195 pounds, the righthanded Heilmann was a slow runner and awkward fielder. His teammates nicknamed him "Slug." The Tigers were well stocked in the outfield so he often played first base. In 1919 and 1920, the only two seasons in which he played first base in more than 100 games, Heilmann led AL first sackers in errors. But he also hit better than .300 each season, driving in 95 runs in 1919 and 89 in 1920.

When Ty Cobb became the Tigers' manager in 1921, Heilmann's fortunes improved dramatically. Cobb shifted Heilmann permanently to the outfield and began tinkering with his stance and hitting style. As Heilmann later explained, before the self-absorbed Cobb was named manager of the Tigers, he "didn't care whether I hit or not, (he) just figured it wasn't any of his business, I guess."

But when Heilmann's batting affected Cobb's performance as a manager, things changed. "Cobb got me to crouch more to shorten my strike zone and taught me how to use my wrists to drive the ball," said Heilmann. Cobb also taught him to study pitchers and to distribute his weight while batting, "with a little more weight on the front foot."

Almost overnight Heilmann became a great hitter, and line drives rained off his bat. In 1921 he rapped out a league-leading 237 hits, scored 114 runs, drove in 139, and put together a career-best 23-game hitting streak. His .394 batting average edged Cobb by five points for the batting title and made him the first righthanded hitter to lead the American League in batting since Nap Lajoie in 1905.

A broken collarbone in 1922 hurt Heilmann's general output, but he still had a .356 average. He also came close to setting a league record with 10 consecutive hits. In 1923 he won his second batting crown with a .403 average that included 211 hits, 121 runs, and 115 RBIs. Babe Ruth finished second in the batting race at .393.

In 1924 Ruth won his only batting title when Heilmann slipped to .346. Nevertheless, Heilmann finished among the top five in the league in runs, triples, total bases, RBIs, and batting average while tying Cleveland's Joe Sewell for the most doubles with 45.

Heilmann entered the final month of the 1925 season nearly 50 points behind league-leader Tris Speaker in the race for the batting title. But Heilmann went on a tear. On the morning of the final day of the season, he trailed Speaker by a slim margin—.38927 to .38826. While Speaker sat out his game with leg pains, Heilmann went 3-for-6 in the first game of a doubleheader to forge into the lead at .38947. His teammates urged him to sit out the second game and collect his title, but he refused. In three trips to the plate he cracked out three hits, including a home run, to win the crown at .393.

In 1926 Heilmann hit .367 to finish third in the AL behind teammate Heinie Manush (.378) and Ruth (.372). But his curious pattern of winning batting titles only in odd-numbered years continued into 1927. That year, Heilmann and Al Simmons battled down to the wire. According to today's rules, Simmons, who was sidelined for part of the season and batted only 406 times, wouldn't be eligible for the crown. In 1927 he was not only eligible but took the lead on the final day of the season when he went 2-for-5 against Washington to raise his average to .392.

Heilmann, playing in a later time zone in St. Louis, began the day at .391. In a repeat of the 1925 season, the Tigers played a season-ending doubleheader. Heilmann collected four hits in the first game and edged past Simmons. Once more, Heilmann was urged to sit out the nightcap, and once more he refused. He banged out three hits and finished at .398.

Throughout his career with the Tigers, Heilmann was surrounded by great-hitting outfielders. When he arrived in Detroit the outfield was patrolled by Cobb, Sam Crawford, and Bobby Veach. Later, Manush and Bob Fothergill provided the punch. But Detroit lacked pitching, forestalling any chance Heilmann had of playing for a pennant winner. Few men played as many as Heilmann's 17 seasons without appearing in a World Series.

Heilmann hit .328 in 1928, and on July 26 he drove in eight runs in one game. Opposing teams often tried to pitch around Heilmann—on May 16, 1928, he was walked twice in the same inning. His usual odd-year batting title failed to materialize in 1929, although he still hit .344 with 120 RBIs.

After the season he was waived to the Cincinnati Reds. Heilmann gave them one good year, but arthritis in his wrists forced him to sit out the 1931 season. He tried to comeback in 1932, but after only 15 games he retired as a player and finished out the year as a coach.

In 17 major league seasons, Heilmann delivered 2,660 hits, including 542 doubles, 151 triples, and 183 home runs. He scored 1,291 runs and drove in 1,539. His career .342 batting average is second only to Rogers Hornsby's among righthanded hitters in this century.

Heilmann was a big loser in the stock market crash of 1929, and in 1933 he took a job broadcasting Tigers games for WXYZ radio. His low-key approach and endless supply of droll stories made him a hit for 17 years. When the 1951 All-Star Game was played in Detroit, Heilmann was Commissioner A.B. "Happy" Chandler's first choice as broadcaster, but Heilmann was gravely ill with lung cancer and had to decline.

Ty Cobb led an effort to induct Heilmann into the Hall of Fame in a special election so that he could present Heilmann with the bronze plaque at the All-Star Game. Thinking the campaign had been successful, Cobb told Heilmann of his plan. Heilmann died the day before the game, believing he had been elected to the Hall. In fact, he was not chosen until the regular election in 1952.

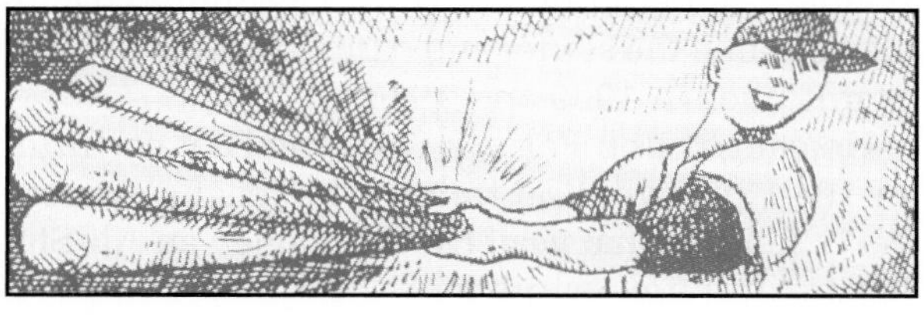

Woodie Held

Held, Woodson George **SS-OF-3B-2B**

1954, 1957–69 B:3/25/1932, Sacramento, CA Deb:9/5/1954, NY AL BR/TR 5'11", 180

G	AB	R	H	HR	RBI	OBP	SLG	AVG
1390	4019	524	963	179	559	.333	.421	.240

Although he made a less than impressive debut as an outfielder with Kansas City in 1957, Woodson George "Woodie" Held evolved into the Indians' starting shortstop in 1959. He became such a fixture between 1959 and 1962 that he averaged 136 games a year in the infield.

While dominating Cleveland's defense, Held retained surprising skill as a longball hitter. He smashed a career-high 29 home runs in 1959 and averaged 21 home runs a year in his six seasons with the Indians. His finest season at the plate was 1961, when he batted .267 with 23 home runs and a career-best 78 RBIs. He had a long swing, however, and was prone to strikeouts—he fanned more than 100 times in three different seasons.

Nevertheless, Held's athleticism allowed him to prolong his career after leaving the Indians in 1965 for the Senators. By then he was 33, but he remained in the big leagues until 1969, bouncing from the Orioles to the Angels to the White Sox as a reliable, sure-handed utility player.

Rollie Hemsley

Hemsley, Ralston Burdett **C**

1928–47 B:6/24/1907, Syracuse, OH D:7/31/1972, Washington, DC Deb:4/13/1928, PIT NL BR/TR 5'10", 170

G	AB	R	H	HR	RBI	OBP	SLG	AVG
1593	5047	562	1321	31	555	.311	.360	.262

Ralston "Rollie" Hemsley was a talented catcher with a long career. He came up with Pittsburgh in 1928 and became the regular catcher in 1929. The Pirates traded him to the Chicago Cubs in 1931, and he backed up Gabby Hartnett.

In 1933 he went to Cincinnati as a backup to Ernie Lombardi, and that August was waived to those perennial losers, the St. Louis Browns, where he not only regained a regular position, but was named to AL All-Star teams in 1935 and 1936.

He hit only .222 in 1937, but Cleveland traded four players to St. Louis to acquire him. When regular catcher Frankie Pytlak was injured, Hemsley became the starter and earned trips to the All-Star Games in 1939 and 1940.

He caught Bob Feller's Opening Day no-hitter in 1940 and went on to lead the league's catchers in fielding that year. He was named an All-Star for the fifth time while with the Yankees in 1944.

In 19 major league seasons, Hemsley appeared in 1,593 games and batted .262. Retiring as a player, he became a successful minor league manager, winning *The Sporting News Minor League* Manager of the Year Award in 1950 and 1963.

Dave Henderson

Henderson, David Lee **OF-DH**

1981–94 B:7/21/58, Merced, CA Deb:4/9/81, SEA AL BR/TR 6'2, 220

G	AB	R	H	HR	RBI	OBP	SLG	AVG
1538	5130	710	1324	197	708	.322	.436	.258

Sports Illustrated once called him "The Fans' Man." Indeed, few players have ever performed with the sheer enthusiasm displayed by Dave Henderson throughout his 14-year career. The Seattle Mariners selected Henderson with the franchise's first-ever pick in the 1977 draft. After mulling a career in football, Henderson opted to sign with Seattle. Four years later, he was the club's Opening Day center fielder. Although Henderson remained with Seattle for six seasons, he did not reach his potential until he was traded to Boston during the 1986 season.

He only played 36 games for the Red Sox that year, but he got into Game 5 of the American League Championship Series when Tony Armas left because of an injury. With Boston facing elimination against the Angels, Henderson hit a two-out, ninth-inning home run against Donnie Moore. The Red Sox eventually won the game and the pennant. His home run in Game 6 of the World Series gave the Red Sox a 10th-inning lead over the Mets, but this time Boston lost the lead and the Series

When the Red Sox fell out of contention in 1987, they dealt the struggling Henderson to the Giants. He finished out the year in San Francisco before signing a free agent contract with Oakland. It turned out to be a perfect career move for Henderson, who preferred playing out of the spotlight. With teammates like Rickey Henderson and Jose Canseco drawing most of the media's attention, the California native felt relatively anonymous. He played on three straight pennant winners and appeared in the 1991 All-Star Game.

Although Henderson didn't like talking to the media, he remained polite and cordial. He also became popular with Bay Area fans, who enjoyed all aspects of the boyishly enthusiastic way he played: his high-stepping approach on flyballs, his elongated home run trots, and his ever-present smile. "Playing professional baseball brings a smile to my face," Henderson told *Sports Illustrated*. "I don't need much else to have a good time."

After the 1991 season, Henderson's production fell way off. Hampered by injuries, he managed 20 homers in 107 games in 1993. He concluded his career the following year in Kansas City.

Ken Henderson

Henderson, Kenneth Joseph **OF**

1965–80 B:6/15/1946, Carroll, IA Deb:4/23/1965, SF NL BB/TR 6'2", 180

G	AB	R	H	HR	RBI	OBP	SLG	AVG
1444	4553	595	1168	122	576	.346	.396	.257

Touted as the San Francisco Giants' successor to Willie Mays in center field, Ken Henderson fell short. While he proved to have one of the strongest and most reliable outfield arms of his era, Henderson never hit more than 20 home runs, never drove in 100 runs, and never hit .300 in a full season.

In 1964 the Giants signed the 18-year-old switch hitter out of West Valley College in Campbell, California, for a large bonus. Before becoming a regular in 1969, Kenneth Joseph Henderson played in Fresno, Magic Valley, Tacoma, and Phoenix, although he was promoted to San Francisco for parts of four seasons.

In 1970, when he recorded a .294 batting average and a .460 slugging percentage, he appeared to be redeeming his promise. But he played with a broken thumb for much of 1971, and Henderson's numbers trailed off. He did hit .313 during the Championship Series loss to Pittsburgh. After more injuries the outfielder was traded to the White Sox following the 1972 season.

Henderson's best season was 1974 when he hit 20 homers, putting him in the company of Mickey Mantle, Tom Tresh, Reggie Smith, and Roy White, the only switch hitters to have accomplished the feat to that point in the American League. That year Henderson also recorded a .467 slugging percentage, drove in 95 runs, and led league outfielders with 462 putouts.

On August 29, 1975, Henderson switch-hit homers in the same game, but he could not duplicate his previous season and was traded to the Braves. Trailed by injury, Henderson was on and off the disabled list for the rest of his career with five other clubs. He retired in 1980 and went into the office furniture business in Saratoga, California.

Rickey Henderson

Henderson, Rickey Henley **OF**

1979–* B:12/25/1958, Chicago, IL Deb: 6/24/1979, OAK AL BR/TL 5'10", 195

G	AB	R	H	HR	RBI	OBP	SLG	AVG
2773	9911	2103	2816	278	1020	.407	.428	.284

It has become commonplace to say that Rickey Henderson is the greatest leadoff hitter who ever lived. Indeed, Henderson's leadoff ability is the key to assessing his career. He sets the table with walks and hits, advances with stolen bases, scores runs, and is better at doing this than any player in the history of the game.

Henderson stole 100 bases in his first full year in the American League, he broke Lou Brock's single season stolen base record in his third full year, and he snapped Brock's career stolen base mark in his 13th season in the major leagues; Henderson stole his 1,000th career base the following year. Meanwhile, Henderson played in 10 All-Star Games, seven postseasons, and hit more home runs to start a game than any player in history. And, his critics would say, he'd be the first one to tell you about all these achievements. When he set the career mark in 1991, he declared to the crowd: "Today, I am the greatest of all time." That night Nolan Ryan hurled his seventh career no-hitter, pushing Henderson's story off the front page of many sports sections.

The emergence of Henderson—and manager Billy Martin—transformed the A's into one of the American League's top running clubs. Oakland won just 54 games in Henderson's rookie year; two years later the team played the Yankees in the American League Championship Series. By 1985 Henderson was a Yankee.

He was not a fan favorite at Yankee Stadium, where he feuded with manager Lou Piniella over the severity of injuries. Despite the equivalent of four healthy seasons with the Yankees—averaging 149 games, 82 stolen bases, 128 runs during that tenure—the insinuation was that Henderson was responsible for the Yankees not winning. In 1988 Henderson hit .305 and set a team record by stealing 93 bases; New York missed the AL East title by two games.

In June 1989, the Yankees, now without a pennant for nine years, traded him back to the A's. With Henderson leading the league in stolen bases and runs, Oakland won its second straight division title. Rickey was devastating throughout the postseason, especially against Toronto. In five game he hit two homers, knocked in five runs, and stole eight bases while batting .400 in one of the most dominant playoff performances ever. He batted .474 in the earthquake-interrupted World Series, including a leadoff home run in Game 4 in San Francisco.

In 1990 Henderson was named the league's Most Valuable Player, hitting .325, scoring 119 runs (his fifth league-leading total), and leading the AL in stolen bases for a record 10th time. He was acquired by the Toronto Blue Jays for their pennant drive in 1993 and played for another World Series winner, although this time he didn't sparkle in postseason play. Henderson returned to Oakland in 1994, and two years later made his National League debut with San Diego. He went to Anaheim late in 1997, and made a fourth visit to Oakland the following year.

Although his batting average was slipping, Henderson, batting in his crouched style with his left leg extended straight out, continued to draw walks—and steal bases. At age 39 he led the AL in both categories with the A's in 1998.

Henderson signed with the Mets just shy of his 40th birthday and set his sights on Ty Cobb's record for runs (2,246) and Babe Ruth's mark for walks (2,056). Henderson hit .315 and was instrumental in New York's first postseason appearance in 12 years. While his antics—snatch catches, talking to fans during games, and going into home run trots on balls that hit the wall—aggravated some, he was still one of the game's clutch performers. He batted .400 and stole six bases in the Mets' four-game victory over Arizona in the Division Series. Mets manager Bobby Valentine summed up Henderson's season and career: "Every time someone thought we have seen it all, he turns it up and gives us more."

Steve Henderson

Henderson, Stephen Curtis **OF**

1977–88 B:11/18/1952, Houston, TX Deb:6/16/1977, NY NL BR/TR 6'2", 190

G	AB	R	H	HR	RBI	OBP	SLG	AVG
1085	3484	459	976	68	428	.354	.413	.280

Steve Henderson was a promising minor league outfielder in the Reds farm system with little chance of breaking into Cincinnati lineup, but he instantly became a major leaguer after the "Midnight Massacre." At the trading deadline on June 15, 1977, the Mets traded Hall of Famer Tom Seaver to the Reds for infielder Doug Flynn, pitcher Pat Zachry, outfielder Dan Norman, and Henderson. It marked the end of a brief era of championship baseball at Shea Stadium and the start of seven years of bad luck.

"Hendu," however, was an immediate success. In just 99 games he tied for the club lead with 12 home runs and led the Mets with 65 RBIs. He finished one vote behind Montreal's Andre Dawson for National League Rookie of the Year. The Mets finished last in each of his first three years despite Henderson's solid numbers.

The Mets were actually in the NL East race for the first half of the 1980 season. Henderson was leading the league in batting at .349 on June 8, and he capped a dramatic seven-run ninth inning comeback with a three-run home run. The Mets faded to fifth in August, and after the season Henderson was sent to Chicago along with $100,000 for Dave Kingman.

Henderson spent two years with the Cubs, two more in Seattle, and three seasons in Oakland before ending his career in his native Houston in 1988. He spent four years as a minor league instructor with the Pirates and three years as a coach with the Astros. He was a coach during Tampa Bay's inaugural season in 1998.

George Hendrick

Hendrick, George Andrew **OF**

1971–88 B:10/18/1949, Los Angeles, CA Deb:6/4/1971, OAK AL BR/TR 6'3", 195

G	AB	R	H	HR	RBI	OBP	SLG	AVG
2048	7129	941	1980	267	1111	.333	.446	.278

An excellent fielder, George Hendrick played for six teams during 18 seasons, hit 267 home runs, and was on two world championship teams. More than anything else, however, the four-time All-Star is remembered for his eerie quietness. "I don't think he even talks to his wife," said teammate Clint Hurdle. Writer Furman Bisher mused, "Hendrick's is the quaint case of a player who has been in the big leagues 10 years and hasn't said anything yet. I see no reason to condemn a man for that. Maybe he can't think of anything to say."

In January 1968 Oakland made Hendrick the top draft pick in baseball. He batted just .182 for the A's in 1972 and didn't hit much better in the postseason. The following spring the A's traded the 23-year-old to Cleveland and he blossomed as an everyday player. On June 19, 1973, Hendrick hit three home runs in a game against the Tigers.

After the 1976 season the Indians traded him to San Diego. Another trade early in the 1978 season brought Hendrick to St. Louis, where twice he drove in more than 100 runs and in 1982 helped the Cardinals win the World Series. In December 1984 the Cards traded Hendrick to the Pirates, and during the 1985 season he went to the Angels, where he spent the final three years of his career. He coached for St. Louis in 1996 and 1997. In 1998 he was named a coach for the Angels.

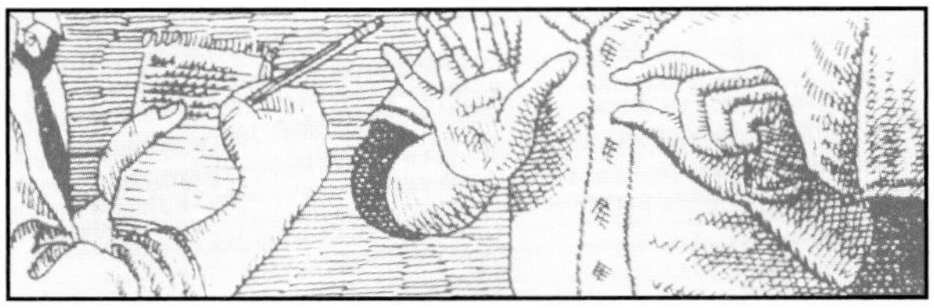

Claude Hendrix

Hendrix, Claude Raymond **P**

1911–20 B:4/13/1889, Olathe, KS D:3/22/1944, Allentown, PA Deb:6/7/1911, PIT NL BR/TR 6', 195

W	L	PCT	G	SH	IP	BB	SO	ERA
144	116	.554	360	27	2371^{1}	697	1092	2.65

Arguably the best pitcher in the short-lived history of the Federal League, Claude Hendrix also won 20 games in the National League both before and after his stint with the Feds. His affinity for trouble and alleged involvement with gamblers, however, shortened his career.

After attending St. Mary's and Fremont colleges, Hendrix joined the Nebraska State League in 1908. He earned a roster spot with the Pittsburgh Pirates in 1911, but he found controversy in his major league debut. A minor league team in Salina, Kansas, claimed that it still had Hendrix under contract. He remained with the Pirates, winning 24 games and leading the league with a .727 winning percentage in his second season.

In 1914 Hendrix gained more notoriety when bolted the Pirates and signed a three-year contract with the Chicago Whales of the Federal League. He led the new league in wins, games, and complete games, while allowing batters to hit just .203. On May 15, 1915, he pitched a no-hitter against the Pittsburgh Rebels. His two years in the league resulted in 45 wins and 60 complete games.

Hendrix returned to the National League when the Whales merged with the Chicago Cubs in 1916. Two years later he won 20 of 27 decisions, leading the NL in winning percentage for the second time. He continued to pitch for the Cubs until he was suddenly released in February 1921.

Although he had slumped to 9–12 in 1920, the decision to cut the 31-year-old righthander had little to do with his ability. Rather, it stemmed from the events of August 31, 1920. Gamblers had placed large sums of money on Philadelphia to beat Chicago that day, even though the Cubs appeared to be the superior team. Rumors began to swirl that several players, including Hendrix, had agreed to throw the game. At the last moment, manager Fred Mitchell pulled Hendrix from his scheduled start and replaced him with Grover Cleveland Alexander. According to some reports, Hendrix had bet $5,000 on his Cubs to lose to the Phillies. Both the National League and Cubs president William L. Veeck, Sr. launched investigations but found no conclusive evidence.

Nonetheless, Veeck considered Hendrix "on the take," and no other team offered him a contract. He was also called to testify in front of a Chicago grand jury about the tainted 1919 World Series. Unofficially blacklisted by organized baseball, Hendrix died from tuberculosis in 1944.

Tom Henke

Henke, Tomas Anthony **P**

1982–95 B:12/21/1957, Kansas City, MO Deb:9/10/1982, TEX AL BR/TR 6'5", 215

W	L	PCT	G	SV	IP	BB	SO	ERA
41	42	.494	642	311	789^{2}	255	861	2.67

Reliever Tom Henke learned to throw strikes through fear—fear of not playing. Despite his overpowering fastball, the young pitcher did not feel he had the confidence of Rangers manager Doug Rader. Henke recalled, "I'd be on the mound knowing if I walked too many guys I was headed for the minors. I'd throw a ball to someone and see the manager throwing things across the dugout."

Texas let Henke go to Toronto in the compensation pool in January 1985, as recompense for the acquisition of free agent Cliff Johnson. The Blue Jays optioned Henke to Syracuse where opponents hit just .081 against him. He led the league in saves and was International League Pitcher of the Year.

He employed four pitches: fastball, splitfinger, curve, and change, but relied mostly on his fastball. He teamed with breaking ball reliever Mark Eichhorn for a highly effective relief operation in Toronto. He was named the 1987 Relief Pitcher of the Year on the *Baseball America* and United Press International AL All-Star teams. That season he was 0–6 but led the league in saves and had most appearances ever in a winless season.

His success at Toronto gave him a chance to do an aftershave lotion commercial. "George [Bell] kept saying he thought you had to be handsome to be the Aqua Velva man," said Henke.

Henke, the 1989 Toronto Pitcher of the Year, in 1991 combined with Duane Ward to become the fourth 20-save duo in history. Henke was granted free agency following the Blue Jays' World Series victory in 1992. With Rader long gone, he signed with Texas, which had originally selected the Junior College All-America in the fourth round of the 1980 draft.

Henke saved 40 games with the Rangers in 1993. Following the 1994 baseball strike, the Missouri native headed to St. Louis. He saved 36 games with the Cardinals, and became the fifth pitcher to save 300 games. He pitched in the All-Star season for the second time, and Henke's 1.82 ERA was his lowest over a full season. At 37 years old and on top of his game, Henke announced his retirement.

Tommy Henrich

Henrich, Thomas David **OF-1B**

1937–50 B:2/20/1913, Massillon, OH Deb:5/11/1937, NY AL BL/TL 6', 180

G	AB	R	H	HR	RBI	OBP	SLG	AVG
1284	4603	901	1297	183	795	.382	.491	.282

Broadcaster Mel Allen nicknamed Tommy Henrich "Old Reliable" after a railroad train that ran from Cincinnati through his home state of Alabama. The train was always on time, and Henrich eventually became known throughout baseball for his steady fielding, heady play, and clutch hitting.

Henrich's father tried to steer him away from baseball because he felt the sport was too dangerous. The youngster played with the Acme Dairies, a local semipro club. During one game not long after Henrich joined the team, a scout came over to him in the eighth inning and asked, "How would you like to play pro ball?"

That September he signed with Cleveland. He played briefly for Zanesville, batted .346 for New Orleans in 1936, and was sold to Milwaukee of the American Association. Henrich felt he was being shunted aside in favor of fellow Indians prospect Jeff Heath and read reports that the club might peddle him to either the Browns or Braves.

Henrich and his father wrote to Commissioner Kenesaw Landis, alleging that the Cleveland organization was illegally "covering up" the young player. Landis presided over a hearing at which Henrich and Cleveland's Cy Slapnicka presented their cases. Henrich said, "The judge could have let it go, but because he didn't like Slapnicka, and because I think he got a kick out of me writing to him and standing up for my rights, he declared me a free agent."

Eight clubs bid for his services. Henrich, despite growing up near Cleveland, had always been a Yankees fan. He signed with New York for a reported $25,000 bonus. The Yankees brought him up briefly but optioned him to Newark after a few weeks. With the Bears he hit .440 and was quickly brought back up to stay.

As things turned out, Henrich's most famous moment came when he struck out. In Game 4 of the 1941 World Series, the Dodgers were ahead, 4–3, in the bottom of the ninth, and were only one out away from knotting the Series at two games apiece when Henrich came to the plate. With a 3–2 count, Brooklyn's Hugh Casey let go with a sharp-breaking curve that, Henrich said, "exploded." It sank and would have been ball four, but Henrich couldn't hold back from swinging.

Umpire Larry Goetz called strike three. But the ball broke so sharply that catcher Mickey Owen had trouble with it. Henrich, reacting quickly, instinctively moved toward first base. When he looked back and saw the ball skipping past Owen, he raced to first, igniting a Yankees rally that buried the demoralized Dodgers, 7–4.

Henrich played on five pennant winners in his first six New York seasons. He spent 1943 through 1945 in the Coast Guard, but the three-year absence did little to erode his skills. In 1946 he made only two errors in the outfield. Henrich led the AL once in runs scored and twice in triples, and he made the All-Star squad in each of his last four seasons.

Henrich had to adjust when Casey Stengel came to manage the Yankees in 1949. The ever-watchful Stengel decided that Henrich wasn't selective enough of pitches when at bat and was susceptible to breaking balls on the outside part of the plate. He warned Henrich several times gently to no avail, then intoned: "Tommy, I told you to lay off of that outside curve. Now you lay off it, or you'll learn to hit it in Newark." Said Henrich, "When he put it that way, you listened."

The pennant race went down to the wire that year, and when Joe DiMaggio was lost to a bad heel at the beginning of the season, Henrich carried the club. With two games left, the Yanks faced the Red Sox, who needed only one win to take the pennant. The Yankees won the first game on Johnny Lindell's homer. In the final game Henrich drove in the first run with a first-inning grounder, led off the eighth with a home run, and—playing first base—made the final putout as the Yankees won, 5–3.

Henrich's ninth-inning homer off Brooklyn's Don Newcombe won Game 1 of the World Series; Henrich sat on a 2–0 pitch and sent it into the lower right field stands. "I knew he wasn't gonna go 3-and-0 and risk walking me [with Berra and DiMaggio on deck], so I dug in," recalled Henrich. "He threw it right where I expected him to throw it, right smack over the middle of the plate."

Henrich retired after the 1950 season. He later coached the Yankees and the Tigers.

Bill Henry

Henry, William Rodman **P**

1952–69 B:10/15/1927, Alice, TX Deb:4/17/1952, BOS AL BL/TL 6'2", 180

W	L	PCT	G	SV	IP	BB	SO	ERA
46	50	.479	527	90	913	296	621	3.26

Relievers Bill Henry and Don Elston inspired Chicago sportswriter Jerome Holtzman in 1959 to develop a formula for determining what constitutes a save. Holtzman mused that the numbers of the Cubs duo would be comparable to those of the Pirates' Roy Face—although the Cubs relievers could hardly match his flashy 18–1 record. "So on a bus ride from Chicago to St. Louis I worked out the formula for the save," recalled Holtzman.

Nicknamed "Gabby" because of his terseness, William Rodman Henry started his baseball career in 1948 with Clarksdale of the Class C Cotton States League. He also performed in the minors with Greenville, Shreveport, San Diego, Louisville, Charleston, Memphis, and Portland.

In 1952 he finally made it to "The Show" with the Boston Red Sox. After four mediocre seasons, Henry returned to the minors. The Cubs brought him back as a reliever in 1958, and he led the National League with 65 appearances in 1959. Traded to Cincinnati before the 1960 season, he responded with a career-best 17 saves.

He performed in the 1960 All-Star Game and, with fellow reliever Jim Brosnan, aided the Reds to their 1961 pennant. Traded to San Francisco in May 1965, he later scouted for the Astros.

Pat Hentgen

Hentgen, Patrick George **P**

1991–* B:11/13/1968, Detroit, MI Deb:9/3/1991, TOR AL BR/TR 6'2", 200

W	L	PCT	G	SH	IP	BB	SO	ERA
105	76	.580	252	9	1555^{2}	557	995	4.14

Pat Hentgen won at least 10 games for the Toronto Blue Jays each year from 1993 to 1999. Drafted and signed by the Jays in 1986, he joined the major league club late in 1991, then served as a set-up reliever in 1992. The following season Hentgen became a starter and earned an impressive total of 19 victories. He also won a game against the Philadelphia Phillies in the 1993 World Series.

Three years later, the Detroit native won his 20th game on the last day of the season to help secure the 1996 American League Cy Young Award. In his 35 starts that year Hentgen posted a 20–10 record, 3.22 ERA, and 10 complete games—three of them shutouts.

A durable worker and three-time All-Star, Hentgen twice led or tied for the league lead in complete games, shutouts, and innings pitched. From 1996 to 1999, however, his victory total slipped each year. In 1999 he compiled a 5.17 ERA, the second worst of his career and highest since he became a starter. He still managed a 3.20 ERA on the road, second only to the 1.90 mark posted by Cy Young Award winner Pedro Martinez. After the season the Blue Jays traded Hentgen to the Cardinals.

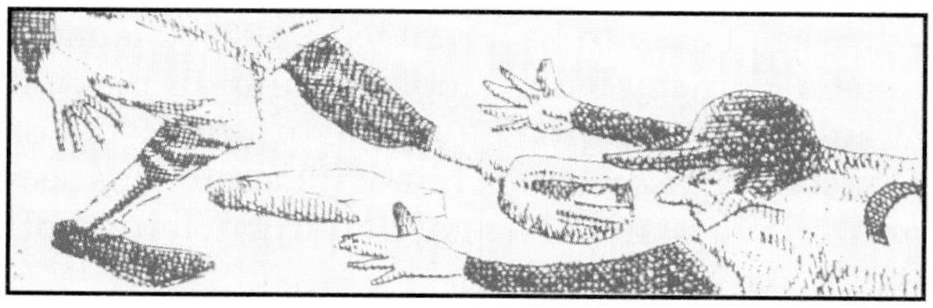

Babe Herman

Herman, Floyd Caves **OF–1B**

1926–37, 1945 B:6/26/1903, Buffalo, NY D:11/27/1987, Glendale, CA Deb:4/14/1926, BRO NL BL/TL 6'4", 190

G	AB	R	H	HR	RBI	OBP	SLG	AVG
1552	5603	882	1818	181	997	.383	.532	.324

Did Floyd Caves "Babe" Herman really triple into a triple play while playing for Wilbert Robinson's Brooklyn Dodgers? Or was he just a fellow who got hit in the head by occasional flyballs and somehow got transformed into a legend?

He didn't exactly triple into a triple play, but it was close. Herman, a fine hitter with a penchant for bizarre behavior, came to bat with the bases loaded and one out. He hit a line drive off the right field wall, and Hank DeBerry, the runner on third, scored easily. Dazzy Vance, the runner on second, rounded third, but put on the breaks 30 feet past the bag and headed back. Chick Fewster, the runner on first, was coming full tilt around second. Soon, both Vance and Fewster were occupying third.

Herman, oblivious to all of this, was charging around the bases. Seconds later, he also arrived at third. Both Fewster and Herman were tagged out and the inning ended. Therefore, technically, Herman merely doubled into a double play. "Everybody," Herman once complained, "overlooks the fact that the run I knocked in on that play was the winning run."

Herman was a career .324 batter who had consecutive seasons of .340, .381, and .393—and he was fast. He ranked among the league's top five in stolen bases from 1929 to 1931. Then there was the matter of his fielding. Fresco Thompson, a weak-hitting Brooklyn infielder who later became a vice president of the Dodgers, said this about Herman: "He wore a glove for one reason: because it was a league custom."

Even Herman knew where his weakness lay. At one point in his Brooklyn career, Herman was called aside in a downtown bank and told that someone was passing himself off as the famous outfielder and cashing several bogus checks per week. Herman had a solution. "Hit him a few flyballs," he advised. "If he catches any it ain't me."

In 1921 Herman signed his first professional contract—for $175 a month—to play for Edmonton of the Western Canada League. It was there that he got his nickname "Babe," supposedly after a champion flyweight prizefighter also named Babe Herman.

In 1922 Herman went to spring training with the Detroit Tigers at Augusta, Georgia. The story goes that Herman pinch-hit for Ty Cobb with the bases loaded and delivered a grand slam. Actually (as is so often the case with the Herman legend) the facts are a little different. Only two runners were on, and Herman responded with a mere single. But he did pinch-hit for the immortal "Georgia Peach."

Nonetheless, there was no room for Herman in Detroit's overcrowded outfield, and player-manager Cobb optioned him to Omaha. "Doubtless the Tigers have made many mistakes, but this is their worst one," Herman modestly commented. He hit .416 in 92 games; his roommate Heinie Manush hit .376.

Another Herman myth claims that after hitting .416 he was released. Not true. Actually, in October 1922 the Tigers packed Herman, along with pitchers Howard Ehmke and Carl Holling, infielder Danny Clark, and $25,000 to the Red Sox for second baseman Del Pratt and pitcher Rip Collins.

While with Boston, Herman was consigned to the bench and informed that, if he wished, he would be sent to the minors instead of being left to rust away as a reserve. He ended up in Atlanta in 1923 and in San Antonio in 1924. In 1925 he was sold to Seattle of the Pacific Coast League, where a Dodgers scout saw him and arranged for Brooklyn to purchase his contract.

Already a sixth-place team, Brooklyn never finished higher than fourth during his stay. The club was led by Wilbert "Uncle Robbie" Robinson, a manager of declining energy and powers, and its players were soon to be known as the "Daffiness Boys."

"They were not normally of a clownish nature," explained writer Frank Graham, "and some of them were very good ballplayers, indeed, but they were overcome by the atmosphere in which they found themselves as soon as they had put on Brooklyn uniforms."

Adding a lot to the atmosphere was Herman. On one occasion he begged a sportswriter, "I wish you would lay off'n me," referring to news articles that depicted him as an oddball. "I don't mind so much on my account, but the missus has funny ideas." Just as the writer was feeling some sympathy for the outfielder, Herman reached into his pocket and pulled out a cigar. "Got a match?" Herman interjected. Then as he started to puff on the stogie he said, "Never mind. It's already lit."

Although Herman had a powerful throwing arm and was capable of some fine plays, he did little to discourage tales of his slipshod fielding. On one occasion, when asked why he held out each spring he replied, "I don't do it for money. The longer I stay away from training camp, the less chance I have of being hit by a flyball."

Despite his theatrics in the field, Herman put up some amazing numbers at the plate. In 1926 he rapped nine consecutive hits. On June 5, 1929, he had four extra-base hits (two doubles and two triples), one short of the National League record. His 241 hits in 1930 are the ninth-most in league history. He hit for the cycle twice during the 1931 season and once more during the 1933 season. No player has hit for the cycle more times.

In 1932 Herman was traded to the Reds along with catcher Ernie Lombardi. He hit .326 in 1932, but the Reds soon traded him to the Cubs for catcher Rollie Hemsley and three other players. Herman had eight RBIs in a game on April 20, 1933, and he belted three home runs on July 20. He finished the season with a team-leading 16 homers and 93 RBIs.

Soon on the trading block again, he went from Chicago to Pittsburgh, back to Cincinnati, and then to Detroit. On June 26, 1936, Herman tied what was then a NL record when he grounded into three double plays in a game against Pittsburgh.

In 1945, eight years after the Tigers dismissed him, Herman came out of retirement to play once again for Brooklyn. In his first at bat he was met with overwhelming applause from the fans in Ebbets Field. He promptly singled sharply to right field—and proceeded to trip over first base.

Wherever he played, Babe Herman was always quotable. Once a salesman tried to sell him an encyclopedia, arguing it "will help your children get their education." But Herman said firmly, "Nothing doing. My kids can walk to school."

Billy Herman

Herman, William Jennings Bryan **2B–3B**
1931–43, 1946–47 M(1947, 1964–66, 189–274)
B:7/7/1909, New Albany, IN D:9/5/1992, West Palm Beach, FL Deb:8/29/1931, CHI NL BR/TR 5'11", 180

G	AB	R	H	HR	RBI	OBP	SLG	AVG
1922	7707	1163	2345	47	839	.367	.407	.304

Billy Herman was one of the game's most intelligent players. Casey Stengel characterized Herman as "one of the two or three smartest players ever to come into the National League." Giants pitcher Carl Hubbell said, "His first two years in the league he couldn't get a hit off me. So he set out methodically to figure me out. From 1933 on I couldn't get him out."

Herman played second base on four pennant-winning teams, posted a lifetime .304 average, and played in 10 All-Star Games. He led the National League in both fielding and assists three times; double plays four times; and games played and putouts seven times.

William Jennings Bryan Herman, named after the great American orator and politician, signed with the Louisville Colonels at age 19 and in three seasons never batted less than .305. After Yankees manager John McGraw dismissed him as too small at 5 feet 11 inches, Herman fetched $30,000 from the Cubs.

It wasn't easy to be a rookie in 1931. Manager Rogers Hornsby barely spoke to him. In his first at bat Herman rapped a single off the Reds' Si Johnson. Johnson struck him with a pitch his second time up, and Herman had to be helped off the field.

The Cubs won the pennant in 1932, Herman's first full season, and repeated in 1935, when Herman led the NL in hits and doubles, and in 1938. He was at his best in All-Star competition, posting a .433 average—the NL All-Star record—in 10 games. He is the only All-Star to have been taken out of a game and then reinserted. In the seventh inning of the 1934 All-Star Game second baseman Frankie Frisch was sidelined with a charley horse, and Herman reentered the contest with the permission of AL manager Joe Cronin.

By 1941 Herman's days in Chicago were numbered. New manager Jimmie Wilson was afraid that Herman might replace him at the job if he failed, and the Cubs were expecting great things from a Los Angeles second baseman named Lou Stringer. Brooklyn Dodgers general manager Larry MacPhail sent two players and $65,000 to Chicago for Herman and then bragged to reporters, "I've just bought the pennant."

Indeed, Herman helped the Dodgers win the 1941 pennant, their first in 21 seasons. In Game 3 of the World Series, however, Herman tore a rib cage muscle and was out for the rest of the Series. He said, "I could hardly breathe.... I came up to bat in the bottom of the first inning and hit the ball well, but I almost collapsed from the pain." Had the heady Herman been on the field when catcher Mickey Owen dropped Tommy Henrich's third strike to lose Game 4 and spoil pitcher Hugh Casey's shutout, Herman might have been able to calm down the explosive pitcher.

In 1943 Herman drove in a career-high 100 runs and was named second baseman on *The Sporting News* Major League All-Star Team. He spent two years in the navy, returned to the Dodgers in 1946, but left under somewhat mysterious circumstances. A disagreement arose over a bill for damages resulting from a wild party in Herman's hotel room. Herman agreed that it was his room but claimed that he had switched accommodations with another player whom he wouldn't name. Nevertheless, Herman was sent packing to the Boston Braves over a $30 hotel bill.

The Braves dealt him to Pittsburgh that September. He played briefly and then finished the 1947 season as the Pirates' manager. He sat out for several years and then returned to play with Oakland in the Pacific Coast League in 1950 and hit .307. He later was a coach for pennant winners in Brooklyn and Milwaukee. Herman managed the Red Sox in 1965 and 1966, taking them to ninth-place finishes before Dick Williams came in to lead them to first.

He later served as a coach for the Angels and Padres. Herman retired from baseball in 1979, four years after the Veterans Committee voted him into the Hall of Fame.

Keith Hernandez

Hernandez, Keith **1B**
1974–90 B:10/20/1953, San Francisco, CA
Deb:8/30/1974, STL NL BL/TL 6', 195

G	AB	R	H	HR	RBI	OBP	SLG	AVG
2088	7370	1124	2182	162	1071	.388	.436	.296

One of the best defensive first basemen in major league history, Keith Hernandez was also a savvy line drive hitter who won a batting title and world championships with two different teams. Co-winner of the National League Most Valuable Player Award in 1979 as a St. Louis Cardinal, Hernandez became a leader of the New York Mets following a shocking 1983 trade.

Neither a classic big target nor a hulking slugger at first base, the 6-foot, 200-pound Hernandez was a career .300 hitter until his two final injury-plagued seasons. He had a great eye at the plate, was consistently among the league leaders in doubles, and won 11 consecutive Gold Gloves. When Hernandez retired only third baseman Brooks Robinson, pitcher Jim Kaat, shortstop Ozzie smith, and outfielders Willie Mays and Roberto Clemente had exceeded his Gold Glove total.

Hernandez displayed nimble footwork around the bag, exceptional range in both directions, and smooth, sure hands. His strong and accurate arm enabled him to gamble, usually successfully, on force plays. He led the league in assists five times and set a career record for assists, which was broken by Eddie Murray in 1993. Despite his high-risk play, he led the league in errors only once, while leading in fielding percentage twice and total chances four times.

"Mex," as he was known in the clubhouse, also led the NL in double plays a record six times, mastering the 3–6–3 twin killing. Quickly and fearlessly charging bunts, Hernandez occasionally fielded sacrifice attempts on the third base side of home plate, duplicating the feats of famed fielders Ferris Fain and Hal Chase. With his glove on his right hand, Hernandez held runners on with his feet in foul ground to make tags as close to the bag as possible, yet was quick enough to get into fielding position after the delivery.

Named captain of the Mets along with catcher Gary Carter, Hernandez also played the role of field general, anticipating plays, signaling infielders, and advising his battery. In the bottom of the 16th inning of a 1986 playoff game at Houston, after pitcher Jesse Orosco had given up two runs to allow the Astros to draw within one run of tying the game, Hernandez approached the mound and told Carter, "If you call one more fastball, we're going to fight." Carter went with Orosco's slider for the final out.

Hernandez drew much of his baseball sense from his father, John, a minor league infielder for 10 years and Hernandez's unofficial batting coach. Keith's brother, Gary, also played in the Cardinals organization for four years. Raised in the San Francisco Bay area, Hernandez was the first Capucino High School student to receive all-league honors in basketball, football, and baseball, and set a league record with a .500 batting average.

Hernandez quit the baseball team during his senior year in a dispute with the coach, a move that pushed him down to the fortieth round of the June 1971 draft. He reached Triple A in his first season, and he won the American Association batting title in 1974. In mid-1975 he became the Cardinals' regular first baseman and led his NL counterparts in assists despite playing only 129 games. In 1977 he batted .291 and registered 41 doubles, 91 RBIs, and 15 homers—including three grand slams, with a record-tying two in September.

After slumping to a full-season low .255 in 1978, Hernandez won the 1979 NL batting crown at .344 and topped the circuit with 116 runs, 48 doubles, and a .421 on-base percentage. Hernandez set career highs with 11 triples and 105 RBIs. He finished the season tied with Willie Stargell in the league MVP voting.

In 1980 he led the league with 111 runs scored and a .410 on-base percentage. He also knocked in 99 runs, batted .321, and went 2-for-2 in his second All-Star Game. He had his third straight season with a .300 average and a .400 on-base percentage in 1981, and he missed a fourth by batting .299 in 1982, the year the Cardinals appeared in the World Series for the first time since 1968.

Batting cleanup in the NLCS that season against the Atlanta Braves, Hernandez singled and scored in each of the Cardinals' first two wins. He then started a four-run rally in Game 3, as the Redbirds advanced to the World Series against the Milwaukee Brewers. Batting third, Hernandez went 0-for-15 and committed two errors before singling in the first inning of Game 5. By the time the Cardinals had completed their seven-game victory, Hernandez had recovered to lead all participants with eight RBIs.

At the June 15 trading deadline in 1983, the Cardinals sent Hernandez to the New York Mets, a team that hadn't had a winning season since 1976, for pitchers Neil Allen and Rick Ownbey. St. Louis Manager Whitey Herzog claimed the trade was made strictly on baseball merits, but he hinted that Hernandez was using cocaine. The 1985 Pittsburgh drug trials proved those suspicions correct, as Hernandez testified to heavy drug use and called cocaine "the devil on this earth." He received a standing ovation from Shea Stadium fans after his testimony and averted a one-year suspension by donating 10 percent of his $1.6-million salary to drug rehabilitation programs, performing 100 hours of community service, and submitting to periodic drug tests.

At first Hernandez disliked playing for the Mets, but he eventually came to enjoy living in Manhattan; he and teammate Ron Darling occasionally rode the subway to Shea Stadium. Hernandez was the Mets' best all-around batter, and on July 4, 1985, he hit for the cycle off four different pitchers in a bizarre 19-inning, 16–13 win over Atlanta.

Hernandez was a disciplined hitter. He holds the season and career records in the short-lived game-winning RBI statistic because of his first-inning successes, and he was most dangerous after he'd batted a couple of times and could dissect a pitcher. As unofficial team leader, he held court for reporters at his corner locker, a bucket of beers at his feet and a cigarette in his hand (a habit he kept only during the season).

After finishing second in 1984 and 1985, the Mets stormed to the NL East title by 21½ games in 1986. Hernandez contributed his third straight .300 average and walked a league-leading 94 times from the third spot in the order. In the playoffs against Houston, Hernandez tied for the team lead with seven hits. In Game 6 he doubled home a run and scored the tying tally in the ninth as the Mets rallied from a 3–0 deficit to force extra innings and win in 16, advancing to the World Series against the Boston Red Sox.

In the Series, Hernandez had only two hits until Game 7. He made the second out of the 10th inning of Game 6, before the Mets' miracle rally. In the finale, his bases-loaded single in the sixth drove in two runs that cut the Mets' deficit to 3–2, and his sacrifice fly in the seventh extended their lead to 6–3 in an eventual 8–5 win to give him his second World Series ring.

In 1987 Hernandez slugged 18 homers and fanned 104 times, both career highs, while gaining his fifth All-Star berth. In 1988 he missed nearly two months with a pulled hamstring, his first time on the disabled list in the majors, while the Mets won the NL East. In the playoffs against the Los Angeles Dodgers, Hernandez homered and singled for three RBIs in a Game 2 loss, but he drove in only two more runs as the favored Mets lost in seven games. The following season he missed two months with a broken kneecap, and after an unproductive season the Mets let him go as a free agent.

Hernandez signed a two-year contract with the Cleveland Indians, who thought his veteran leadership could help the team mature. But he was on the disabled list three times with a pulled calf muscle in 1990, and he missed all of 1991 because of back surgery. He declared himself ready to try a comeback in 1992 at age 38, but he found no takers.

Hernandez pursued outside interests, but maintained his tied with the Mets. He served as a spring training coach and fill-in broadcaster in 1997 and 1998. Despite all his exploits on the field, Hernandez gained lasting fame through an appearance on the television show *Seinfeld*.

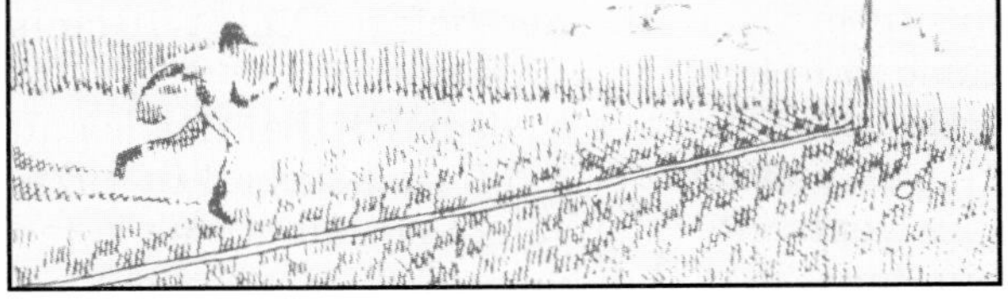

Livan Hernandez

Hernandez, Eisler Livan **P**
1996–* B:2/20/1975, Villa Clara, Cuba Deb:9/24/1996, FLA NL BR/TR 6'2", 220

W	L	PCT	G	SH	IP	BB	SO	ERA
27	27	.500	81	0	533^{2}	220	380	4.38

Livan Hernandez's brief career with the Florida Marlins was a paradigm of the franchise. A Cuban refugee, Livan was signed by Florida as part of the ballclub's effort to market the team to South Florida's large Hispanic community. A few short years later, he was traded to the San Francisco Giants in the Marlins' ongoing purge of veterans and their salaries.

Hernandez, a star member of the world-renowned Cuban National Team, defected in 1995. He signed with Florida as a free agent a year later. After only 30 minor league games, the durable righthander established himself as a major leaguer with a nine-game winning streak in 1997.

Hernandez became an overnight sensation by virtue of his performance in October 1997. He was chosen the Most Valuable Player of the Championship Series after beating Atlanta twice. He earned his first win in relief of injured Alex Fernandez; two days later he hurled a complete-game victory that included an NLCS-record 15 strikeouts, aided by umpire Eric Gregg's very wide strike zone.

After dramatic negotiations between the U.S. and Fidel Castro's government allowed Livan's mother to leave Cuba to attend the final game of the World Series, Hernandez became only the second rookie to win a World Series MVP Award. It was an obviously sentimental vote by baseball writers: Hernandez won two games, but he also posted a 5.27 ERA. His brother Orlando fled Cuba and joined Livan in the major leagues with the New York Yankees in 1998. Like Livan, Orlando was a postseason MVP, earning the award in the 1999 ALCS.

Orlando Hernandez

Hernandez, Orlando P. **P**
1998–* B:10/11/1965, Villa Clara, Cuba Deb:6/3/1998, NY AL BT/TR 6'2" 210

W	L	PCT	G	SH	IP	BB	SO	ERA
29	13	.690	54	2	355^{1}	139	288	3.72

Although Orlando Hernandez compiled the best won–lost record in Cuban amateur history at 129–47, he was removed from the Cuban National team in 1996 over concern that he would follow his half-brother, Livan Hernandez, and defect to the United States. Cuban officials' concerns were realized when Orlando fled the island in December 1997, although how he left the island—as well as his actual age—remained in dispute.

Hernandez said he took a raft with eight other individuals from Cuba. *Sports Illustrated* later told the story of a boat captain who took Hernandez to Costa Rica on a motorized boat. Regardless of how he got there, because he was in Costa Rica he was not subject to U.S. amateur player draft and he could sign with any major league team. The New York Yankees signed him on March 6, 1998. Claiming to be 29 years old when he signed, a birth certificate that surfaced in 1999 confirmed his real age to be four years older. As long as "El Duque" baffled hitters with his whip-like motion and hard breaking stuff, the Yankees seemed to be unconcerned.

Hernandez made his major league debut on June 3, 1998, notching a win against the Tampa Bay Devil Rays. Six days later he threw his first complete game against the Montreal Expos. On September 14, against the Boston Red Sox, Hernandez tossed his first major league shutout. He finished the season with 12 victories and a 3.13 ERA. In the postseason, Hernandez continued to shine.

With the Yankees trailing Cleveland two games to one in the Championship Series, Hernandez combined with Mike Stanton and Mariano Rivera on a shutout to even the series. He also did his part in New York's four-game World Series sweep by beating the San Diego Padres in Game 2.

Hernandez led the Yankees with 17 victories in 1999. Once again he was stellar in the postseason. He allowed just two hits in eight innings in a victory over Texas in Game 1 of the Division Series. He captured the ALCS Most Valuable Player Award by pitching two solid games, including the Game 5 clincher over Boston. He joined his half-brother Livan as a postseason MVP—Livan was named MVP for both the 1997 NLCS and World Series as a rookie with the Florida Marlins.

Orlando climaxed his second year in the major leagues by allowing just one hit in seven innings and struck out 10 in Game 1 of the World Series. New York went onto sweep Atlanta. In six postseason starts, "El Duque" had a mark of 50 with a 1.02 ERA.

Roberto Hernandez

Hernandez, Roberto Manuel (Rodriguez) **P**
1991–* B:11/11/1964, Santurce, Puerto Rico Deb:9/2/1991, CHI AL BR/TR 6'4", 235

W	L	PCT	G	SV	IP	BB	SO	ERA
38	35	.521	512	234	582	244	570	3.02

Roberto Hernandez spent five years in the minor leagues with two organizations, but he quickly became a top of the line closer once he made it to the major leagues. A first-round pick by the California Angels in the 1986 draft, he was traded to the Chicago White Sox with Mark Doran for Mark Davis in 1989. He pitched in nine games as a September call-up in 1991, including the only three starts of his career. Bobby Thigpen, who just two years earlier had set an all-time single season saves record with 57 saves, was unreliable in key moments in 1992. Hernandez moved from set-up man to closer and notched 12 saves with a 1.65 ERA as a rookie.

In 1993, his first full season as the White Sox closer, Hernandez saved 38 games. Hernandez saved 30 or more games in three of the next four seasons. His fame grew; his alma mater, the University of South Carolina at Aikens, named their refurbished stadium after the reliever in 1993. In 1996 Hernandez was named to the All-Star team. He pitched a scoreless inning at Philadelphia, but he made more of an impact before the game when he broke Cal Ripken's nose during the photo session. After slipping on the rafters, he accidentally backhanded Ripken in the nose while trying to regain his balance. Not surprisingly, "Iron Man" Ripken did not miss the start.

Hernandez was sent to San Francisco in a controversial trade on July 31, 1997. Hernandez and soon-to-be free agents Wilson Alvarez and Danny Darwin were traded to the Giants for seven minor leaguers. Owner Jerry Reinsdorf, whose White Sox were just 3½ games behind Cleveland in the American League Central, defended the trade by stating that his club had no realistic shot at the Indians. Hernandez helped the Giants claim the National League West title as both a set-up man and closer. In the Division Series, however, he surrendered the winning hit in the first two games of a three-game sweep by Florida.

Hernandez signed as a free agent with the Tampa Bay Devil Rays on the day of expansion draft in 1997. He was one of the few bright spots in the club's first two seasons. He had a career-high 43 saves and was an AL All-Star for the second time in 1999.

Willie Hernandez

Hernandez, Guillermo **P**

1977–89 B:11/14/1954, Aguada, Puerto Rico
Deb:4/9/1977, CHI NL BL/TL 6'3", 180

W	L	PCT	G	SV	IP	BB	SO	ERA
70	63	.526	744	147	1044^{2}	349	788	3.38

Willie Hernandez made the transformation from a rather ordinary setup man in 1983 to an all-around relief ace in 1984, when he helped pitch Sparky Anderson's Detroit Tigers to a world championship. Throwing screwballs, sinking fastballs, and quick-breaking curves, Hernandez baffled American League hitters. At one point he converted a then-record 32 consecutive save opportunities.

"I said he'd be a good acquisition," boasted Tigers pitching coach Roger Craig, "but I never knew he'd be this good."

As an amateur in Puerto Rico, Hernandez was an outfielder-first baseman—and a pretty good one. It was only when his team needed a pitcher that he took the mound. In his first start, he pitched a seven-inning shutout, with, as he recalls, "a 100-mile-per-hour fastball and an 85-mile-per-hour breaking ball." He went on to pitch for the Puerto Rican national team and defeated the United States—the first Puerto Rican win ever over the U.S.

In September 1973, just two months after Hernandez had first tried pitching, Philadelphia Phillies scout Ruben Amaro signed him to a contract. The Phillies assigned Hernandez to Spartanburg of the Western Carolinas League, and he continued his rapid progress, leading that circuit with 179 strikeouts, 190 innings pitched, 26 starts, and 13 complete games. He split 1975 between Reading of the Eastern League and Toledo of the International League. After his worst minor league season, with Oklahoma City in 1976, the Chicago Cubs drafted Hernandez from the Phillies organization.

The Cubs converted Hernandez into a reliever, using him in both long and short situations. He was 8–2 with a 3.75 ERA in 1978, but lost 13 of his next 18 decisions during the following two seasons. Chicago optioned him to Iowa in 1981. He returned to the Cubs in midseason, but got caught in the players strike that year, unable to pitch in either the majors or the minors. When the strike ended he was sent down again. "My attitude was real bad," said Hernandez. "They were (messing) with me. I said, 'No. You give me my release. I don't want to go nowhere.'"

In 1982 Hernandez made 75 appearances for the Cubs and was credited with 10 saves. On May 22, 1983, he was traded back to the Phillies for pitchers Dick Ruthven and Bill Johnson. Hernandez went 8–4 the rest of the season for the Phils, was unscored on in three appearances in the 1983 World Series, and was rewarded with a three-year, $1.7 million contract.

Yet he still was not in the stopper's role, a niche which Al Holland had carved out for himself in the Philadelphia bullpen. Hernandez was tired of being the setup man and let it be known. During spring training 1984 he was traded to Detroit with Dave Bergman for Glenn Wilson and John Wockenfuss.

Hernandez was an expert at confusing batters. "Sometimes I wonder about those who say that Willie doesn't throw hard," Brooks Robinson once observed. "To me, it seems that he throws much harder than is the popular opinion. The hitters are always looking for a curve or the screwball, but Willie just seems to throw the fastball right by them."

American League hitters were no match for Hernandez's nasty stuff in 1984. Detroit won 35 of its first 40 games, and Hernandez played a role in many of the victories. He went 9–3 with a 1.92 ERA, led the league in appearances with 80, and won both the Most Valuable Player and Cy Young Awards. The Tigers swept the Royals in the ALCS, and Hernandez pitched in all three games, converting a save in the clincher.

Detroit was a heavy favorite in the World Series against San Diego, and the Tigers didn't take long to dispose of the Padres. Hernandez pitched in three of the five games and saved two of them. In 1985 Hernandez became the first Tiger to record back-to-back 30-save seasons. The following season he saved 24 games.

By 1987 he had returned to his given name, Guillermo, but he was no longer Detroit's stopper. Mike Henneman took over the role and helped Detroit sneak past the Blue Jays in the final weekend of the season for a division title. Hernandez saved 10 games in 1988 and 15 in 1989, then was released at the end of the season. He retired shortly thereafter.

Larry Herndon

Herndon, Larry Darnlee **OF–DH**

1974, 1976–88 B:11/3/1953, Sunflower, MS Deb:9/4/1974, STL NL BR/TR 6'3", 195

G	AB	R	H	HR	RBI	OBP	SLG	AVG
1537	4877	605	1334	107	550	.325	.409	.274

Outfielder Larry Darnell Herndon captured the 1976 *Sporting News* National League Rookie of the Year award while playing for San Francisco. Herndon attended Tennessee State University and Skyline College. A third-round draft choice of the Cardinals in June 1971, he started with Sarasota in the Gulf Coast League. He later played with St. Petersburg, Cedar Rapids, Arkansas, Tulsa, and Phoenix. In 1974 he led the Texas League with 50 stolen bases.

Traded to San Francisco in May 1975, he used his speed to capture a spot in the Giants' outfield. He was on the disabled list twice in 1977 and was traded to the Tigers in December 1981. There he enjoyed success until American league pitchers learned to pitch him inside, and his knee problems grew worse.

His high point as a Tiger came during his first season with the club. He homered in his last at bat of a game on May 16, 1982. Then he hit three homers in a game on May 18, giving him four straight four-baggers.

A member of the world champion Tigers in 1984, he homered in the first inning of Game 1 of the World Series. Herndon played in all five Series games and batted .333 against San Diego. He hit a Detroit club-record three homers and 12 RBIs as a pinch hitter in 1986.

Tommy Herr

Herr, Thomas Mitchell **2B**

1979–91 B:4/4/1956, Lancaster, PA Deb:8/13/1979, STL NL BB/TR 6', 185

G	AB	R	H	HR	RBI	OBP	SLG	AVG
1514	5349	676	1450	28	574	.350	.350	.271

An excellent fielder, Tommy Herr debuted with the Cardinals in 1979. His play was good enough in mid-1980 for the Cards to dump third baseman Ken Reitz to the Cubs, move Ken Oberkfell over from second base to replace Reitz, and install Herr at second.

Herr provided the Cardinals with the missing piece. In 1981 he played the best defensive second base in the National League, and he and Ozzie Smith recorded more double plays than any other twin-kill combo in the league. With Gold Glove winner Keith Hernandez at first base and Oberkfell at third, the Cards had the NL's top infield. The Cards had the best NL East record that year but didn't make the playoffs because of the players' strike.

In 1982 the Cardinals got their world championship. Herr provided consistent hitting, excellent baserunning, and steady fielding. For the next five years Herr remained a fixture in the St. Louis infield. In 1984 he and Smith racked up 106 double plays to lead the league again.

In 1985 the clutch-hitting Herr had the best year of his career, batting .302, amassing 110 RBIs, finishing third in the RBI race, and producing more runs than any other batter in the league—an especially impressive feat given that he hit only eight home runs. His performance propelled the talented St. Louis team back to the top of the NL. But his hitting slumped in the World Series, as did that of most of his teammates, and the Cards surrendered the championship to the Royals.

In 1986 Herr and Smith led the league in double plays for the third time, with 121, and in 1987 the Cards were back in the World Series again. This time they lost to the Minnesota Twins in seven games.

After 15 games for St. Louis in 1988, Herr joined the same Twins who had handed him defeat the previous fall. As a utility infielder and designated hitter, he failed to add the same spark to Minnesota as he once had to the Cardinals.

The Philadelphia Phillies, the New York Mets, and the San Francisco Giants all used the experienced Herr as a utility infielder from 1989 through 1991, when he retired from play.

Garry Herrmann

Herrmann, August

Club President (1902–27) B:1859, Cincinnati, OH
D:4/251931, Cincinnati, OH

For nearly 20 years at the beginning of the 20th century Garry Herrmann was probably the second-most powerful executive in baseball. As president of the Cincinnati Reds, his warm, eminently likable personality inspired trust and friendship among the other clubowners. In return, year after year they elected him to one of the three seats on the National Commission, Organized Baseball's ruling authority from 1903 until the adoption of the commissioner system in 1920. The other two seats belonged to the presidents of the National and American Leagues.

While the National League presidency was often under the thumb of the team owners and changed several times, American League president Ban Johnson held full power in his league. Herrmann was sometimes accused of being too ready to side with his friend Johnson when casting a deciding vote, but his basic fairness and honesty were rarely questioned.

When he was 11 years old, his father died, and Herrmann and his older brother went to work to support the family. August found a job in a type foundry and eventually became a proud member of the typesetters' union. He carried his union card for the duration of his life. One day a grizzled foreman dubbed him "Garibaldi" after Italy's national hero, a champion of the masses. Shortened to "Garry," the nickname stuck.

Herrmann eventually entered politics. He was elected to the Cincinnati Board of Education in 1882 and became assistant clerk of the Police Court in 1887. In 1891 he was named to the Board of Administration. A staunch baseball fan, he was the Water Works commissioner when he joined political boss George B. Cox and members of the Fleischmann family of yeast fame in a coalition that purchased the Cincinnati Reds.

Cox persuaded John T. Brush to sell the team by threatening to build a streetcar line through the center of the baseball field. Although his actual financial interest was small, the personable Herrmann was elected club president to inspire trust in the club's stockholders.

The National Commission was established in 1903 as part of the agreement between the American and National Leagues to work together. Herrmann was named chairman. The following year a crisis developed when Brush, now owner of the New York Giants, refused to take part in a World Series. Although the first "modern" Series had been played in 1903, it had taken place under a private agreement between Pittsburgh and Boston.

Despite harsh press criticism, Brush stood firm on his decision, stating that contending for a crown with a "minor league" would jeopardize the National League's prestige. NL president Harry Pulliam supported Brush, claiming that the 1903 Series had been a voluntary arrangement and that no obligatory agreement had ever been reached.

Herrmann and Ban Johnson, whom Herrmann had known since Johnson's days as a Cincinnati newspaperman, were eventually able to establish the World Series as a permanent institution. For his efforts, Herrmann is sometimes called the Father of the World Series.

Herrmann loved nothing more than holding sumptuous parties for his friends, and he had friends everywhere. According to historian Lee Allen, "Garry was a walking delicatessen. A connoisseur of sausage, he carried his own wherever he went. When he presided at a hotel suite or in a bar, his party sat around one or more tables that were piled high with roast chickens, boiled hams, cheeses of every description, Thuringian blood pudding, liver sausage, baked beans, radishes, coleslaw, potato salad, green onions, and every type of fermented drink that was known to Bacchus."

His proudest and happiest moment came when the Reds won the 1919 pennant and World Series. Ironically, it was the revelation that the World Series had been fixed by eight members of the Chicago White Sox that brought about the end of the National Commission.

Herrmann resigned as president of the Reds in 1927 because of ill health. Although he had received little salary as president, he was awarded a substantial pension and bonuses. He died in 1931, just four weeks after the death of Ban Johnson.

Orel Hershiser

Hershiser, Orel Leonard Quinton IV **P**

1983–* B:9/16/1958, Buffalo, NY Deb:9/1/1983, LA NL
BR/TR 6'3", 192

W	L	PCT	G	IP	SH	BB	SO	ERA
203	145	.583	500	3105^2	25	993	2001	3.41

Dodgers Hall of Fame pitcher Sandy Koufax was an early fan of Orel Hershiser's. "The key to Orel's success is his constant striving for perfection," Koufax said. "Perfectionists are usually given a bad name, but there's nothing wrong with trying to be better than you are, the best you can be."

To get close to perfection, Hershiser first had to persevere. Undrafted out of East High School in Cherry Hill, New Jersey, he attended Bowling Green University. He won All-Metro Athletic Conference honors and pitched for the All-American Amateur Baseball Association national champions in the summer of 1979. Despite looking more like an future accountant than a Cy Young Award winner, Hershiser excelled in many sports growing up as he moved from city to city because of his father's printing business.

He was good enough to play hockey for the Philadelphia Flyers' Junior A team. He even chose Bowling Green because it had strong programs in both baseball and hockey. Discouraged from playing hockey by his baseball coach, Hershiser was despondent when he failed to make the traveling baseball team as a freshman. He was also having trouble academically and left school in the middle of a semester to visit high school friends for a couple of days. After hitchhiking back, he was a new man.

He grew three inches his sophomore year and added five miles an hour to his fastball. He not only made the traveling team, he was drafted in the 17th round after his junior year. He quickly moved through the Dodgers farm system, working mostly as a reliever. He caught the eye of manager Tommy Lasorda in spring training of 1983, winning the Jim and Dearie Mulvey Award as the outstanding rookie in Dodgertown. He was sent back to Triple A, but was called up to Los Angeles at year's end. Hershiser started 20 games and tied for the National League lead in shutouts with teammate Alejandro Pena, a starter who went on to become a top reliever.

Soon there was no stopping "the Bulldog"—a nickname given to Hershiser by Lasorda because of the pitcher's tenacious demeanor on the mound. He led the league in at least one category for four of the next five years. In 1985 it was winning percentage, and in 1987 and 1989 it was innings pitched. In 1988 there weren't many categories that he *didn't* lead the league in.

Hershiser tied or shared for the National League lead in wins, complete games, shutouts, and innings. Surprisingly, his 2.26 ERA was third in the league; surprising because Hershiser ended the season by breaking Don Drysdale's once seemingly unbreakable record of 58 consecutive scoreless innings. Hershiser began his streak in the final four innings of an August 30 win at Montreal. He then pitched five straight shutout victories, and went 10 scoreless innings in his final regular season start at San Diego on September 28. During the streak he allowed 31 hits, walked only 11, and fanned 38.

In the National League Championship Series Hershiser started three games, earned a save in another, and tossed a shutout in the seventh game as the underdog Dodgers defeated the New York Mets for the pennant. Against the favored Oakland Athletics in Game 2 of the World Series, Hershiser tossed a three-hit shutout and struck out eight. In Game 5 he completed the upset with a four-hitter.

In the 1988 postseason he pitched 42⅔ innings, went 3–0 with two shutouts, and posted a 1.05 ERA. Always a good hitter, he also batted .250 with two doubles and two RBIs. Needless to say, he walked away with the Most Valuable Player trophies for both the NLCS and World Series.

Injuries and age eventually caught up with Hershiser. He had just one winning season over his final six years with the Dodgers. He signed with Cleveland as a free agent before the 1995 season, and responded with 45 wins in his three seasons with the club. Hershiser also pitched in three postseasons for the Indians, including two World Series. He earned MVP honors for beating Seattle in both his starts in the 1995 ALCS.

In 1998 he signed with San Francisco, where he was 11–10. The 40-year-old hurler then joined the Mets, and at times during the 1999 season was New York's most consistent starter. He earned his 200th career win and his 2,000th strikeout as a Met. His yeoman effort in relief in Games 5 and 6 of the Championship Series brought back memories of a younger Bulldog. The Dodgers possibly thought so; Los Angeles, still searching for its first postseason win since Hershiser's heroics in 1988, signed the pitcher after the season.

Buck Herzog

Herzog, Charles Lincoln **2B-3B-SS**

1908–20 M(1914–16, 165–226) B:7/9/1885, Baltimore, MD D:9/4/1953, Baltimore, MD Deb:4/17/1908, NY NL BR/TR 5'11", 160

G	AB	R	H	HR	RBI	OBP	SLG	AVG
1493	5284	705	1370	20	445	.329	.335	.259

The spotlight always found Buck Herzog. The infielder and manager appeared in four World Series with the New York Giants and made a crucial error in one of them; he was once traded for three Hall of Famers; and Herzog was knifed by an irate fan after being publicly accused of bribing an opposing player to throw a game.

Herzog broke into the National League with the Giants in 1908. He was an aggressive runner with 312 career steals—including 10 of home plate. On September 9, 1908, he stole second, third, and home in the same game. Despite his derring-do, he was traded to Boston after the 1909 season.

On July 17, 1911, Herzog and teammate Doc Miller decided to skip the scheduled game and take the afternoon off. Days later the Braves traded Herzog back to the Giants, where he played in three consecutive World Series. He had 23 hits in 25 career World Series contests, but he is often remembered for his 11th-inning error that caused the winning run to score in Game 3 of the 1911 Series. In 1912 Herzog had his best World Series as he hammered 12 hits for a .400 average.

He was traded to Cincinnati after the 1913 season, and the Reds made the 28-year-old Herzog shortstop-manager. His team never finished higher than seventh place, and on July 20, 1916, the Reds traded their shortstop and manager back to the Giants in a deal that sent future Hall of

Famers Christy Mathewson, Bill McKechnie, and Edd Roush to Cincinnati. He got in one more World Series with the Giants in 1917, but his team lost for the fourth time.

He was later traded back to the Braves and then to the Cubs, where in 1920 he ended his major league career. That same year Giants pitcher Rube Benton testified that in September 1919 Herzog and Hal Chase had offered him $800 to throw a game against the Cubs. Nothing came of the accusation. Herzog denied the charge and said Benton made it because he had held a grudge against Herzog since 1915 when Herzog managed him at Cincinnati.

Later in 1920, while Herzog was in Joliet, Illinois, for an exhibition game, a fan jumped toward the car in which he was riding and shouted, "Here are some of those crooked ballplayers from Chicago. Let's get 'em!" Herzog pushed the fan off and then they fought in the dirt. Another fan slashed Herzog with a penknife several times before other fans rescued him.

Whitey Herzog

Herzog, Dorrel Norman Elvert **OF–1B**

1956–63 M(1973–90, 1,281–1,125) B:11/9/1931, New Athens, IL Deb:4/17/1956, WAS AL BL/TL 5'11", 182

G	AB	R	H	HR	RBI	OBP	SLG	AVG
634	1614	213	414	25	172	.356	.365	.257

Whitey Herzog changed the face of managerial strategy in the 1970s and 1980s as he transformed lackluster franchises in Kansas City and St. Louis into AstroTurf-exploiting, speed-dominated division champions and pennant winners. Stolen bases, defense, and relief pitching were at the heart of "Whitey Ball."

Herzog was signed by the Yankees in 1949, immediately after his graduation from New Athens High School in Illinois. He got his nickname, "White Rat," from sportscaster Bill Speith while he was playing for the McAlester Rockets in the Class D Sooner State League.

During his first year in the minors, Herzog learned to keep his expectations to a minimum. After hitting six doubles in a doubleheader and boosting his average to .446, he was called into manager Vern Hoscheit's office, thinking he was being promoted to a higher classification. Herzog recalled, "But all he did was flip me the keys to the bus and say, 'Drive the boys into town tonight. I've got a social engagement.'"

Herzog lost the 1953 and 1954 season to the military, and he got as far as Kansas City and Denver before the Yankees traded him to Washington in April 1956. He played 117 games for the Senators in 1958, batting .245 with 35 RBIs. He hit only .167 in 36 games the following season, and eight games into 1958 he was sent to Kansas City for cash.

His career as a ballplayer was undistinguished and marred by injuries. Having been traded to Baltimore at the start of the 1961 season, he missed Opening Day after being hit in the nose by a ball coming through the back of a batting cage. Herzog was dealt to Detroit in 1962, and in early 1963 he was beset by an ear infection that hastened his retirement. Summed up one sportswriter: "Whitey Herzog was one of those journeyman players you always heard of but were never sure where. You knew he was either a baseball player or the emcee of a kiddies' TV program."

Hired as a $7,500-a-year scout for the Kansas City Athletics, he signed seven future major leaguers, including pitcher Chuck Dobson. He tried convincing owner Charlie Finley that young Don Sutton was worth a $16,000 bonus, but his persuasive powers failed him. In 1965 he became a Kansas City coach and lasted until getting into a shouting match with Finley regarding traveling expenses.

In 1966 Herzog was named a coach for the New York Mets. He later became director of player personnel for the team, lasting in the organization until a falling out with part-owner M. Donald Grant. Hostilities were so nasty that Grant ordered Herzog to stay away from the funeral of Mets manager Gil Hodges in 1972.

In 1973 Herzog replaced Ted Williams as the Texas Rangers' manager. The Rangers were not a good ballclub. "We need just two players to be a contender," remarked Herzog. "Just Babe Ruth and Sandy Koufax will do it."

After the team finished with a 47–91 record Herzog was fired. His next stop was California as a coach; he even filled in as manager between the time Bobby Winkles and Dick Williams arrived as a replacement. In July 1975, however, Jack McKeon was fired at Kansas City, and Herzog was offered the managerial post. "I said, 'hell, yes, I'll take the job,'" recalled Herzog. "The park here in Kansas City is only two miles from my house."

It was with the Royals that "Whitey Ball," a sort of run-and-gun AstroTurf-defined strategy, first took shape. Herzog replaced Vada Pinson in right field with Al Cowens and dumped aging second baseman Cookie Rojas for Frank White. "Cowens and White had speed, and they could play defense, and that's what we needed," explained Herzog.

Speed and defense were the essence of a Herzog club. And with Kansas City it paid off with three successive American League West titles, but each time the Royals lost to the Yankees in the Championship Series. After Herzog finished second in 1979, he was gone. Squabbles over player John Mayberry and the role of hitting coach Charlie Lau helped speed Herzog's banishment.

"I thought I did my greatest job of managing that year, and yet I got fired," said Herzog. "I never did get along with the owner and his wife, let's put it that way. As a manager, you're always sitting on a keg of dynamite. It's amazing how fast you can get dumb in this game."

Yet as one door closed, another opened. In June 1980 Herzog was got a job across the state with the Cardinals. He switched from manager to general manager in August, and in October he accepted the dual role of general manager-field manager. Herzog wasted little time in ripping apart the disappointing ballclub. He disposed of popular players such as Ted Simmons, Ken Reitz, and Leon "Bull" Durham and imported Darrell Porter and Bruce Sutter. A year later he traded Garry Templeton for light-hitting glove man Ozzie Smith.

By April 1982 Herzog had constructed the club that he wanted and turned the general manager's duties over to Joe McDonald. "Hell, I hated having to work in the off-season anyway," admitted Herzog. "I just wanted to ski and hunt and fish. I hated to come to the park and have five different guys waiting for me."

Herzog's strategies for the Cardinals included speed and defense. He wanted to get rid of players who wouldn't hustle. The results of his efforts were a world championship in 1982 and pennants in 1985 and 1987. Joked Herzog, "The only thing bad about winning the pennant is that you have to manage the All-Star Game the next year. I'd rather go fishing for three days."

Herzog collected a slew of managerial honors with the Royals and the Cardinals: 1976 United Press International Manager of the Year, 1981 and 1982 UPI Executive of the Year, 1982 UPI and *Sporting News* Manager of the Year, 1982 *Sporting News* Man of the Year, Baseball Writers Association of America 1985 Manager of the Year, and *Sports Illustrated* Manager of the Decade for the 1980s.

Herzog resigned as Cardinals manager on July 6, 1990, and remained with the club the rest of the year as a vice president. The California Angels hired him on September 16, 1991, as their senior vice president. He authored two books *White Rat: A Life in Baseball* and *You're Missin' a Great Game : From Casey to Ozzie, the Magic of Baseball and How to Get It Back.*

John Heydler

Heydler, John A.
NL President (1909, 1918–34) U(1898) B:1869
D:4/18/1956, San Diego, CA

John Heydler twice served as National League president, but he didn't leave much of a stamp on the league. He was working as a government printer in Washington when his interest in baseball led him to an umpire's job in the National League in 1898. He then became a sportswriter and served as secretary to league president Harry Pulliam, eventually taking over the duties of secretary-treasurer.

After Pulliam committed suicide in 1909, Heydler served as interim president until Thomas J. Lynch was named to the post in July 30, 1909. Heydler once again became secretary-treasurer until after John K. Tener resigned in December 1918. Named president for the second time, Heydler served until he resigned in December 1934. He was National League chairman until his death in 1956.

Heydler was too much the bureaucrat to oppose the will of the league owners or to actively investigate scandals. He did support the election of Judge Kenesaw Mountain Landis as commissioner in 1920 and helped establish the Hall of Fame. In 1929 he advocated a rule for establishing the designated hitter; that rule would not see the light of day on the field until 17 years after his death.

Jim Hickman

Hickman, James Lucius **OF–1B**
1962–74 B:5/10/1937, Henning, TN Deb:4/14/1962, NY NL BR/TR 6'4", 205

G	AB	R	H	HR	RBI	OBP	SLG	AVG
1421	3974	518	1002	159	560	.337	.426	.252

Jim Hickman was the last of the original Mets to be drafted and, therefore, came at a bargain price—only $50,000. "Premium" picks—Jay Hook and Don Zimmer—were $125,000 each.

Premium or not, James Lucius Hickman demonstrated enough power to put his initials on Mets history. He was the first Met to hit for the cycle and the first to belt three homers in one game. A ninth-inning Hickman grand slam also ended Roger Craig's string of 18 consecutive losses.

Unfortunately, Hickman's pickiness at the plate often exasperated management. Sportswriter Jack Lang said, "It is not recorded officially, but it is generally conceded that Jim Hickman took more third strikes with his bat on his shoulder than any other Met."

After a broken wrist reduced his playing time to 160 at bats in 1966, the Mets swapped him to the Dodgers, where he appeared in only 65 games, one as a pitcher. The Dodgers sent him to the Cubs, where he had a banner year in 1970. Hitting .315, nearly 60 points higher than he had ever hit before, he slugged 32 homers, drove in 115 runs, and belted 33 doubles. (He had never before hit more than 21 homers or doubles in a season.) He also drove in the winning run for the National League in that year's All-Star Game.

Hickman returned to Met-like statistics for 1971 and 1972 with 19 and 17 homers and 60 and 64 RBIs, but his numbers plummeted rapidly thereafter, and he was out of baseball after the 1974 season.

Kirby Higbe

Higbe, Walter Kirby **P**

1937–50 B:4/8/1915, Columbia, SC D:5/6/1985, Columbia, SC Deb:10/03/1937, CHI NL BR/TR 5'11", 190

W	L	PCT	G	SV	IP	BB	SO	ERA
118	101	.539	418	24	1952^{1}	979	971	3.69

Kirby Higbe was a big-time talent ready to blossom when the Philadelphia Phillies traded him to the Brooklyn Dodgers on November 11, 1940. He was the National League's strikeout king, with 137, when he was swapped for Vito Tamulis, Bill Crouch, Mickey Livingston, and $100,000. The deal proved to be a steal for the Bums of Brooklyn.

With the vocal Brooklyn fans at Ebbets Field cheering him on, Higbe rode his incredible stuff during the 1941 season to a 22–9 record, sparking the Dodgers to their first pennant in 21 years. Higbe tied teammate Whit Wyatt for the NL lead in wins; Higbe also led the league with 48 games pitched. He struck out 121 batters and finished with a 3.14 ERA.

Higbe won 46 games for Brooklyn over the next three seasons before the Dodgers sent him packing to the Pittsburgh Pirates on May 3, 1947. With his better days behind him, Higbe could manage only a 19–26 record in two seasons with the Bucs before being sent back to New York—this time with the Giants, who used him sparingly during his final two seasons.

Pinky Higgins

Higgins, Michael Franklin **3B**

1937–46 M(1955–62, 560–556) B:5/27/1909, Red Oak, TX D:3/21/1969, Dallas, TX Deb:6/25/1930, PHI AL BR/TR 6'1", 185

G	AB	R	H	HR	RBI	OBP	SLG	AVG
1802	6636	930	1941	140	1075	.370	.428	.292

Michael "Pinky" Higgins, a career .292 hitter, holds the major league record of 12 consecutive hits. He was named *The Sporting News* Manager of the Year in his first season as Red Sox skipper. He also served as the team's general manager, and in that capacity obstinately continued the team's Jim Crow policy until 1958.

He graduated from the University of Texas and tried out with the A's in 1930. He played 14 games for Philadelphia that season but was sent down for seasoning until 1933. In four full seasons at third base for the A's the righthanded Higgins hit over .300 two times and twice recorded slugging averages of over .500. He led third basemen in double plays in 1934 and hit three home runs in a game on June 27, 1935. In 1934 and 1936 he was named to *The Sporting News* All-Star Teams.

In December 1936 he was traded to the Red Sox, where he hit .300 and drove in more than 100 runs in consecutive seasons. In one game on May 2, 1938, Higgins committed four errors. During his career he would lead the American League in errors at his position three times.

In June 1938 Higgins set the major league record with 12 straight hits. Unlike many record-setters of the day, Higgins was aware of the record. After his 10th straight hit, the field announcer at Deroit's Briggs Stadium announced he could tie Tris Speaker's record his next time up. Higgins did just that, and then set the record with a single off Tommy Bridges in his next at bat. Red Sox first baseman Walt Dropo later tied the mark in 1952.

After the 1938 season Higgins was traded with Archie McKain to Detroit for three players. Though he never again hit .300 or had 90 RBIs, in the 1940 World Series he batted .333 with a home run. He spent 1945 in the army and was sold back to the Red Sox in 1946 in time to play his last games in another World Series.

From 1947 through 1954 Higgins managed at Roanoke, Birmingham, and Louisville. In 1955 he was hired to manage the Red Sox, compiling a 560–556 record in eight seasons. As general manager he resisted racial integration for more than a decade after the Brooklyn Dodgers did away with the color line.

On February 27, 1968, an intoxicated Higgins ran over and killed a Louisiana state highway workman at Ruston, Louisiana, and injured three others. He was found guilty of negligent homicide and sentenced to four years of hard labor but was paroled after serving two months. He died of a heart attack in 1969, two days after being released from jail.

Dick Higham

Higham, Richard **OF-C-2B**

1871–80 M(1874, 29–11) U(1881–82) B:1852, Ipswich, England D:3/18/1905, Chicago, IL Deb:6/1/1871, NY NA BL/TR 5'8½", 171

G	AB	R	H	HR	RBI	OBP	SLG	AVG
130	598	120	193	1	64	.331	.410	.323

Dick Higham was the only major league umpire ever banned from baseball for fixing games. The English-born Higham was a fine player of American baseball in the 1860s and spent five years in the National Association, from 1871 through 1875. An outfielder and occasional catcher, he was a better hitter than fielder. His batting average for five NA seasons was .302, but his defensive lapses occasionally raised eyebrows. He was only one of many NA players suspected of throwing games for a price.

In 1876, while playing for Hartford, he led the National League with 21 doubles. With Providence in 1878, he led the league with 22 doubles and 60 runs. In 1881 he became a National League umpire. Early in 1882 he handled many games played by the Detroit Wolverines. William Thompson, mayor of Detroit and Wolverines owner, became suspicious of some of Higham's calls and had him tailed by a private detective. Sure enough, Higham was placing bets with a well-known gambler on the same games he worked as an umpire. Banished for life but undaunted, Higham became a Chicago bookie.

Pete Hill

Hill, J. Preston **OF-1B-2B**

Negro League Player (1899–1925) B:1880 D:1951, Buffalo, NY BL/TR 6'1", 215

Negro Leagues outfielder J. Preston "Pete" Hill was described by Cum Posey as "the most consistent hitter of his time, and while a lefthanded batter, he hit both lefthanders and righthanders equally well. He was the backbone, year in and year out, of great clubs."

Hill played with the Philadelphia Giants from 1904 to 1908, including service on the 1906 team that some claim was the greatest black club ever. "A gamer gang of ball players never stepped on a diamond," wrote Sol White, "More or less crippled throughout the season, they played the hardest games with the same spirit as the weak ones."

As Cuba opened its winter league to foreigners in 1907, Hill was one of the first black players to take advantage of the opportunity and batted .350 in the 1909 Cuban Winter League season.

When the Leland Giants' Rube Foster raided the Philadelphia Giants in 1909 he lured Hill, Pete Booker, Mike Moore, Nate Harris, Tacky Payne, and George Wright to Chicago, effectively wrecking the Philadelphia team.

Hill went with Foster again in 1911 to the American Giants and once more in 1919 when he formed the Detroit Stars, becoming manager of that club. He also piloted the Madison Stars of Philadelphia, the Milwaukee Bears, and the Baltimore Black Sox. Additionally, he served as business manager of the Baltimore club.

John Hiller

Hiller, John Frederick **P**

1965–70, 1972–80 B:4/8/1943, Toronto, Ontario, Canada Deb:9/6/1965, DET AL BR/TL 6', 195

W	L	PCT	G	SV	IP	BB	SO	ERA
87	76	.534	545	125	1242	535	1036	2.83

John Hiller was a reliable reliever during his first six years with Detroit, and when he suffered a massive stroke in 1971 most people assumed his career ended there. The Tigers, who released him, certainly thought so.

Determined to return to the game, in 1972 Hiller took a job as the Tigers' batting-practice pitcher. Management was impressed enough to place him back on the active roster on July 8, 1972. In 1973 he recorded 38 saves, a major league record at the time, and won Fireman of the Year as well as American League Comeback Player of the Year.

The Canadian-born pitcher was discovered on the sandlots of Toronto, and in June 1962 Detroit signed him as a free agent. He started in Jamestown of the New York–Penn League and went on to Knoxville, Montgomery, Syracuse, and Toledo before sticking with the Tigers in 1967.

A bullpen pitcher who made an occasional start, Hiller was 23–19 with 13 saves in four full seasons before his stroke. He returned in 1972 at age 29 to save three games and win one with a 2.03 ERA. He topped the season off with a Championship Series victory in relief over Oakland, although the A's took the ALCS in five games.

During the next seven post-stroke seasons he went 63–55 with 109 saves for Detroit. He retired in 1980 and later went into the insurance business in Duluth, Minnesota.

Paul Hines

Hines, Paul A. **OF-1B-2B**

1872–91 B:3/1/1852, Washington, DC D:7/10/1935, Hyattsville, MD Deb:4/20/1872, WAS NA BR/TR 5'9½", 173

G	AB	R	H	HR	RBI	OBP	SLG	AVG
1481	6253	1083	1881	56	751	.343	.413	.301

In 1878 Paul Hines won the National League Triple Crown while playing for Providence despite hitting only four homers that season. During the Dead Ball Era home runs were a relatively unimportant statistic, and it was many years before researchers discovered that Hines had actually accomplished what modern-day sluggers dream of; Hines was actually the first player to do it.

After starting his career in 1872 with the National Association, the slick-fielding outfielder signed with Chicago of the National League in 1874. In 1878 Hines moved on to Providence, where he was credited with the first unassisted triple play in major league history.

One contemporary account reads, "As an outfielder Paul Hines has few if any equals, and the wonderful and brilliant running catches made by him are too numerous to mention." In the Providence-Boston game on May 4, 1878, the Boston team wanted one run to tie the score, and they had men on the second and third, with none out and Jack Burdock at the bat.

The account read: "He made a seemingly sure hit just over the shortstop's head, which was caught on the fly close to the ground by Hines after running at terrific speeds for more than 50 yards; and, keeping straight on, he touched third base and threw the ball to second before the respective occupants could return, thus making one of the most brilliant of the triple plays yet chronicled." (Modern scholarship shows that the throw to second was unnecessary. Both runners, according to contemporary rules, were out when Hines touched the bag because both had already rounded third.)

In 1886 Hines came home to Washington, D.C., to play for the city's National League club. Jim Whitney of the Kansas City Grasshoppers beaned him that season, causing Hines to lose his hearing. After retiring from the majors in 1891 with a .301 career average, he played and managed for several minor league clubs.

He left baseball when U.S. President William McKinley appointed him Postmaster in the Department of Agriculture in Washington. In 1935 Hines died at the Sacred Heart Home in the Washington suburbs at the age of 83.

Larry Hisle

Hisle, Larry Eugene **OF–DH**

1968–71, 1973–82 B:5/5/1947, Portsmouth, OH Deb:4/10/1968, PHI NL BR/TR 6'2", 195

G	AB	R	H	HR	RBI	OBP	SLG	AVG
1197	4205	652	1146	166	674	.350	.452	.273

Although Larry Hisle had a solid rookie year, it took several years before he became consistent power hitter in the major leagues. In his rookie year of 1969 he hit .266, swatted 20 home runs, and chalked up 56 RBIs. Although he received Rookie of the Year votes, he finished far behind winner Ted Sizemore.

The sophomore jinx struck Hisle the next year, and even though he managed 10 home runs his hitting slumped to .205. When he failed to improve by mid-1971 he was shipped to the minor leagues.

He got another try in 1973 with the Minnesota Twins. This time Hisle began to connect more regularly. During the next five years he steadily improved his average to .298 and was gradually converted to a designated hitter. In 1977 he finally had his first year above .300. He also regularly swatted homers, knocking 28 out of the park that year and batting in a league-best 119 runs. That season he represented Minnesota at the All-Star Game.

Never on the best terms with thrifty Twins owner Calvin Griffith, Hisle, now at the top of his game, left Minnesota as a free agent and signed a multimillion-dollar deal with the Milwaukee Brewers in 1978. Hisle had another All-Star year, hitting .290, with 34 home runs and 115 RBIs. He finished third in Most Valuable Player balloting.

The next year it was all over. Hisle was injured early in the season and never really recovered. He stayed with the Brewers as a DH but saw limited action. After riding the bench for most of 1982 while his Brewer teammates won the AL championship, Hisle retired from play. As a coach with the Blue Jays, Hisle helped Toronto win back-to-back world championships in 1992 and 1993.

Don Hoak

Hoak, Donald Albert **3B**

1954–64 B:2/5/1928, Roulette, PA D:10/9/1969, Pittsburgh, PA Deb:4/18/1954, BRO NL BR/TR 6', 175

G	AB	R	H	HR	RBI	OBP	SLG	AVG
1263	4322	598	1144	89	498	.347	.396	.265

Don Hoak boxed professionally as a teenager, but not successfully—seven straight knockouts hastened his arrival in the big leagues. Still, Hoak remained combative. When he played for the Brooklyn Dodgers, Clem Labine nicknamed him "Tiger" because he always started fights.

The fiery third baseman became the spiritual leader of the 1960 Pirates, the team that sunned the Yankees in the World Series. Before arriving in Pittsburgh, Hoak made his mark with the Reds, peaking in 1957.

That year he was named to the All-Star team and led the league with 39 doubles. Hoak batted .293 with a career-high 19 home runs and 89 RBIs. The year before, however, Hoak had made an inglorious entrance into the record books, setting a league record by striking out six times in a 17-inning game.

Traded to the Pirates in 1959, he batted .294. In 1960 he hit .282 with 16 home runs and 79 RBIs and led the National League with 97 runs scored. He had two doubles and drove in three runs in the World Series. He remained with the Pirates through the 1962 season, finishing his career with the Phillies in 1964. Hoak then took to managing in the Pirates' farm system. He died of a heart attack on October 9, 1969.

Butch Hobson

Hobson, Clell Lavern **3B–DH**

1975–82 M(1992–94, 207–232) B:8/17/1951, Tuscaloosa, AL Deb:9/7/1975, BOS AL BR/TR 6'1", 193

G	AB	R	H	HR	RBI	OBP	SLG	AVG
738	2556	314	634	98	397	.300	.423	.248

A former football standout under Paul "Bear" Bryant at the University of Alabama, Butch Hobson was a powerful Red Sox third baseman whose slugging never quite reached its potential. He was a part of one of the best hitting lineups of the 1970s, and was among the American League's top run producers while batting ninth.

His first full-time year in Boston, in 1977, was his career-best as he slugged 30 home runs, collected 112 RBIs, and hit .265. He also made 23 errors. The next year he led the AL with 43 errors, and posted a fielding percentage of .899 while hitting 17 homers and managing to hit only .250.

Hobson's aggressive style of play helped him remain a bright prospect, however, and in 1979 he seemed to regain his ability. He swatted 28 homers and amassed 93 RBIs while hitting .261. In the field he committed "only" 25 errors. In 1980, however, he was hampered with injuries and played only half the season.

By the end of 1980 the Red Sox had decided Hobson would be better off elsewhere. He became part of a series of player exchanges between the Red Sox and the Angels, which sent Rick Burleson and Hobson to California for Rick Miller, Mark Clear, and Carney Lansford. In 1982 Hobson injured himself again and went to the New York Yankees, where he hit .172 in 30 games and finished his major league career.

From 1992 to 1994, Hobson managed the Red Sox. He later managed in the Red Sox farm system. Allegations of cocaine possession marred his time as manager of the Pawtucket Red Sox.

Gil Hodges

Hodges, Gilbert Raymond **1B**

1943–63 M(1963–71, 660–753) B:4/4/1924, Princeton, IN D:4/2/1972, West Palm Beach, FL Deb:10/03/1943, BRO NL BR/TR 6'1½", 200

G	AB	R	H	HR	RBI	OBP	SLG	AVG
2071	7030	1105	1921	370	1274	.361	.487	.273

The Dodgers first baseman throughout the 1950s, Gil Hodges was a powerful hitter and a graceful fielder. At 6-foot 1-inch and 200 pounds, he was far from being the largest player in the game, but he was routinely referred to as the strongest.

His immense hands helped him become a fine first baseman. Teammate Pee Wee Reese once said that with his huge hands Hodges didn't really need to use a first sacker's glove: "He just wears one to be fashionable." A soft-spoken man, Hodges could still communicate fierceness. His glare could cow the toughest player. As manager of the Mets in the late 1960s and early 1970s, he even intimidated the New York press corps.

With seven consecutive All-Star Game selections and seven appearances in postseason play, Hodges was an excellent player for one of the best teams of all time. Compared to a ballet dancer for his grace around the bag, Hodges led National League first basemen four times in double plays, and for 15 years he held the single-season record for double plays by an NL first baseman. He led the league in fielding percentage and assists three times each. He was the first winner of the Gold Glove at his position, and won the award two more times.

While playing in Ebbets Field, Hodges drove in more than 100 runs in seven consecutive years. He belted between 23 and 42 homers every year except his first and last as a Dodger for a career total of 370.

Signed by the Dodgers in 1943, Hodges played only one game at third base, where he made two errors in five chances, struck out twice, and walked once in three plate appearances. He joined the Marines and served through 1945, taking part in the battles at Okinawa.

After he returned to baseball the Dodgers wanted him to become a catcher. He went down to the minors to learn the new job and led the Piedmont League in putouts, assists, and fielding percentage. Called up to Brooklyn in 1947, he and Bobby Bragan took turns backing up Bruce Edwards.

In 1948 Roy Campanella arrived, and manager Leo Durocher immediately installed the rookie as the team's catcher. Durocher suggested that Hodges try first base. With his giant paws and quick feet, Hodges took to the position like a duck to water. He handled nearly 100 chances before making an error, and the Dodgers were set with slugging stars at catcher and first base for the next 10 years.

On August 31, 1950, Hodges became the sixth major leaguer to slug four homers in one game. He finished that game against the Phillies 5-for-6, with nine RBIs. After a 40-homer year in 1951 Hodges dipped to 32 the following season. It wasn't just his power that was off. He failed to get a hit in his last nine regular-season games and then had one of the worst World Series on record. He came to the plate 26 times during his team's seven games, walked five times, fanned six, and did not produce a single base hit.

Hodges began the next season where he had left off in 1952. He managed only 14 hits in his first 75 at bats, only one for extra bases. Brooklyn fans showed their love and concern for their first baseman with an outpouring of letters, prayers, rosaries, and good luck charms. Manager Chuck Dressen sat with Hodges and applied both comfort and science to try to help him. Dressen showed Hodges films that clearly demonstrated how Hodges was bailing out of the box.

The slugger looked and learned. He finished the season with 122 RBIs and batted .364 in the 1953 World Series. He came back with 42 homers and 130 RBIs in 1954, and when the Dodgers finally ended their streak of seven consecutive Series appearances without a championship in 1955, Hodges hit .292 in the Series with five RBIs, including both runs in a 2–0 win over the Yankees in Game 7.

When the Dodgers left Brooklyn after the 1957 season Hodges didn't seem to notice. He hit 22 and 25 home runs in the new park on the new coast, and he drove in three runs in the team's two playoff wins in 1959. In the World Series that year, his eighth-inning home run broke a Game 4 tie, and the Dodgers went on to win the Series in six games.

The 36-year-old Hodges was only a part-timer for the Dodgers in 1960 and 1961, but, hoping to connect to some long-lost New York glory, the expansion Mets drafted him. He hit the team's first-ever homer, although knee problems severely limited his playing time. Manager Casey Stengel commented, "He fields better on one leg than anybody else I got on two."

In early 1963 the expansion Senators asked the Mets to release Hodges so that he could become their manager. Hodges squeezed the Senators out of the cellar after his first season there, and in 1967 they won 76 games and tied for sixth. Hodges' character showed through when pitcher Ryne Duren, drunk and disconsolate, walked onto a bridge with ideas of suicide. Hodges talked him down.

When it became clear in New York that Wes Westrum was not the man to turn the Mets into winners, they dealt pitcher Bill Denehy to Washington along with $100,000 for Hodges. Hodges immediately started doing things his way. He reduced the number of players bouncing back and forth from Triple A and recommended that the Mets pick up J.C. Martin, Art Shamsky, Tommy Agee, and Al Weis, all players he knew from the American League. He managed spring training as though he was a drill sergeant at his own personal Marine boot camp. The young Mets got the message.

In 1968, with Jerry Koosman joining Tom Seaver on the pitching staff, the Mets won a dozen more games under Hodges than they'd won the year before. The following year the "Miracle" Mets surprised the universe as Hodges made several excellent managerial moves. He gave Tug McGraw a last chance to make the team—in the bullpen. With platoons in right field and third base, the team was playing well when Donn Clendenon was obtained and installed in a platoon with Ed Kranepool at first. Clendenon put together an excellent season and won Most Valuable Player honors in the World Series.

Hodges' most savvy managerial move, though, came in Game 5 of the 1969 World Series. The Mets needed only one victory to defeat the heavily-favored Orioles. Down 3–0 in the last of the sixth, a pitch from Dave McNally came close to Cleon Jones' foot. Jones claimed he had been hit by the pitch, and Hodges appeared from the dugout with a ball marked with shoe polish.

In a play resembling the famous Nippy Jones shoeshine ball of 1957, Cleon Jones was awarded first. In 1957 Nippy Jones took the ball from the catcher and showed the mark to the umpire. But the ball Hodges presented could have been any ball with anybody's polish. Nevertheless, umpire Lou DiMuro allowed the manager's evidence. Clendenon followed with a two-run homer, and the Mets scored once in the seventh and twice in the eighth to win the Series.

The Mets won 83 games in 1970 and 1971, and near the end of spring training in 1972 the players went on strike. Before heading north for the season Hodges had just finished playing a round of golf when he died from a massive heart attack—two days before his 48th birthday.

Russ Hodges

Hodges, Russell

Broadcaster B:1910, Dayton, KY D:4/19/1971, Mill Valley, CA

"The Giants win the pennant! The Giants win the pennant! The Giants win the pennant!" Russ Hodges' radio call of Bobby Thomson's ninth-inning home run off the Dodgers' Ralph Branca on October 3, 1951, still echoes through the annals of baseball history.

Hodges, whose trademark home run call was "bye, bye, baby," attended the University of Kentucky and played halfback on the football team until he broke an ankle. When he lost his athletic scholarship, he went into broadcasting, and although he later earned a law degree he never practiced. "In those days, lawyers were jumping out of windows," he explained.

He got his start as a baseball announcer by recreating games on radio in Charlotte, North Carolina. He later broadcast for the Cubs and White Sox, and from 1938 through 1945 he announced for the Senators with partner Arch McDonald. Mel Allen first heard Hodges covering games for the Armed Forces Radio Network during World War II, and in 1946 the two teamed up to broadcast Yankee contests. In 1948 Hodges moved to the Giants and announced games on WMCA radio and WPIX television.

The last game of the 1951 playoff was broadcast on television by Ernie Harwell and on radio by Hodges. Ironically, the famous recording of Hodges' gleeful reaction to beating the Dodgers only exists today because a Dodgers fan taped it and sent it to the studio.

When the Giants moved to San Francisco in 1958, Hodges went too. He died of a heart attack in Mill Valley, California, on April 19, 1971. In 1980 he was selected as the third recipient of the Ford Frick Award.

Joe Hoerner

Hoerner, Joseph Walter **P**

1963–64, 1966–77 B:11/12/1936, Dubuque, IA Deb:9/27/1963, HOU NL BR/TL 6'1", 200

W	L	PCT	G	SV	IP	BB	SO	ERA
39	34	.534	493	99	562^2	181	412	2.99

Using a sidearm delivery, lefty reliever Joe Hoerner appeared in nearly 500 games, even though he was 29 when he pitched in his first full season in the major leagues. In the early 1960s, after doctors told him that he had a weak heart, he developed a sidearm motion that was suggested by former hurler Ira Hutchinson to reduce the strain on his vascular system.

Although Hoerner pitched during parts of 1963 and 1964 with the Houston Colt .45s, general manager Paul Richards stated that Hoerner could not strike out righthanders in the major leagues. "In those days when Paul Richards opened his mouth it was like God speaking. People believed it even if it wasn't true," Hoerner said.

The Cardinals drafted Hoerner off the Colt .45s' minor league roster after the 1965 season and gave him a chance to pitch in the majors. Hoerner was a hard thrower who successfully kept the ball down and away from righthanded hitters. He recorded a 19–10 record with 60 saves during four years with the Cardinals. He had a 1.54 ERA in 1966 and lowered it to 1.48 in 1968, and, despite Richards' comments, Hoerner proved very effective against righthanders. Slugger Hank Aaron never got a hit off Hoerner in 22 at bats.

Hoerner saved Game 3 of the 1968 World Series but lost Game 5 in relief of Nelson Briles, when he gave up two runs in less than an inning's work. The Tigers came back to win the final game of the Series.

Traded to the Phillies after the 1969 season, he played for four other clubs before retiring in 1977. Hoerner later served as vice president of a St. Louis travel agency.

Trevor Hoffman

Hoffman, Trevor William **P**

1993–* B:10/13/1967 Bellflower, CA Deb:4/6/1993, FLA NL BR/TR 6', 215

W	L	PCT	G	SV	IP	BB	SO	ERA
36	28	.563	439	228	509	164	580	2.69

Whenever the hard-throwing Trevor Hoffman was summoned from the bullpen at San Diego home games in the late 1990s, the song that accompanied his entrance on the public address system was AC/DC's "Hell's Bells." His heat generated 226 saves in just over six years, putting him ahead of Rollie Fingers as the Padres' career leader. Hoffman's 1999 season propelled him into the top 25 on the all-time major league saves list. His 53 saves in 1998 tied the National League single-season record set by Randy Myers.

Drafted as an infielder out of Arizona College by the Cincinnati Reds in 1989, Hoffman was converted to pitcher in 1991. The Florida Marlins took him in the expansion draft in 1993, and traded him to San Diego in a deal for Gary Sheffield in June of that year. After posting solid years with the Padres from 1994 to 1997, Hoffman established himself as one of the most dominating closers in history in 1998.

He converted all but one of his 54 save opportunities, establishing a record for the highest-ever single season save percentage at .981, to go with a minuscule 1.48 ERA. He was the main reason that San Diego was 85–0 when leading after eight innings. Hoffman was also a key factor in the club's march to the World Series, nailing down two saves against the Houston Astros in the Division Series and a win and a save against the Atlanta Braves in the Championship Series.

The Yankees, however, brought Hoffman down to earth in the World Series when Scott Brosius torched him for the winning homer in Game 3 of New York's Series sweep. Although the Padres made some cost-cutting moves in 1999, they signed Hoffman to a lucrative contract.

Roy Hofheinz

Hofheinz, Roy

Owner1962–71B:1912, Beaumont, TX D:11/21/1982, Houston, TX

Some baseball purists hate artificial turf, luxury boxes, ballparks that double as football stadiums, and domes. They can blame former Houston clubowner Roy Hofheinz; he started it all. The Astrodome was his brainchild, and his legacy lives on in a number of other stadiums that have adopted many of the features first seen in the

Astrodome. To some, Hofheinz was an archetypal Texan, a larger-than-life character who made things happen. To others, he was a tyrant and a crook.

The son of a laundry truck driver, Hofheinz attended Houston's Rice University, the University of Houston, and the Houston Law School, earning his law degree at age 19. At age 22 he was elected to the Texas Legislature. At age 25 he was elected as a judge in Harris County.

Hofheinz acted as Lyndon Johnson's campaign manager in the 1940s, was elected to (and was booted out of) office in 1944, and was elected mayor of Houston in 1952. He ruled with an autocratic hand: when the city council refused to do his bidding in 1955, he had the council arrested. He was then impeached. When he refused to step down, he was censured; Hofheinz then rammed through a piece of legislation that called for new elections. Tired of his bullying, the public finally pulled the plug on Hofheinz's aspirations for public office.

In the meantime, Hofheinz used his position to become a wealthy developer. On a visit to Rome, he learned that the Coliseum once featured an awning to protect spectators from the sun. He approached famous thinker Buckminster Fuller, the creator of the geodesic dome, and asked him to design a dome to cover a shopping mall. The project was never built, but Hofheinz remained intrigued by the concept of domes.

Houston offered a perfect laboratory for his experiment. It was too hot, too humid, and too wet, and there were too many mosquitoes in Houston to enjoy being outside. Using his political influence, in January 1961 Hofheinz got Harris County voters to approve an $18 million general obligation bond to build a domed stadium, to which he gave himself a 40-year lease. The project, including off-site improvements, land acquisition, engineering fees, site roads, and parking lot paving, cost $31.6 million.

Hofheinz took over the expansion Houston Colt .45s in 1963. He hoped to start the club in the new stadium, but construction delays forced the team into temporary quarters until 1965. Hofheinz later dubbed the team the Astros and called their new home the Astrodome. Apart from the dome itself, the stadium itself was part of a larger complex that included a convention center and exhibition halls. Baseball was no longer the centerpiece, and the ballpark had become a stadium with a number of brand-new features, including luxury boxes, air conditioning, and padded seats—amenities that had nothing to do with baseball.

Commenting on what Hofheinz had wrought, sportswriter Wells Twombly said, "God is still the only one who can make a tree, but Judge Roy Hofheinz bears close watching."

Touted as "the eighth wonder of the world," the ballpark had problems from the beginning. The glare from more than 4,700 clear glass panels in the roof turned catching flyballs into a nightmare. And grass simply didn't want to grow indoors. By the end of season, vast areas of the field were dying.

Before the start of the 1966 season, Hofheinz installed artificial grass—AstroTurf. The clear panels were replaced by opaque glass. Although the new surface turned groundballs into singles and bounced soft line drives to the wall, the players eventually adjusted. At a time when anything new was considered better, in less than a decade a number of other teams had followed suit. Astroturf was here to stay.

Hofheinz controlled the team until 1971, when he suffered financial troubles and was forced out. He particularly bemoaned the fact that he was booted from the luxury apartment he had built for himself inside the stadium. He died of a heart attack in 1982.

Walter Holke

Holke, Walter Henry **1B**

1914–25 B:12/25/1892, St. Louis, MO D:10/12/1954, St. Louis, MO Deb:10/06/1914, NY NL BB/TL 6'1½", 185

G	AB	R	H	HR	RBI	OBP	SLG	AVG
1212	4456	464	1278	24	487	.318	.363	.287

Boston Braves first baseman Walter "Union Man" Holke had more putouts than a chain smoker on May 1, 1920. On that day he made a major league record 42 putouts in the 26-inning game between Boston and Brooklyn, which ended in a 1–1 tie.

The record would have been 43, but Holke gave away one of his putouts to catcher Hank Gowdy. In the 17th inning, Boston pitcher Joe Oeschger fielded a grounder and threw home for a forceout. Gowdy threw to first to get a double play, but Holke dropped the ball. The runner from second tried to score, so Holke threw home and nailed him at the plate.

A career .287 hitter, Holke was a switch hitter who threw lefthanded. He was a defensive standout, leading the National League in double plays three times and fielding percentage and putouts once. He played for four NL teams—New York, Boston, Philadelphia, and the Reds, where he finished his career in 1925.

Al Holland

Holland, Alfred Willis **P**

1977, 1979–87 B:8/16/1952, Roanoke, VA Deb:9/5/1977, PIT NL BR/TL 5'11", 207

W	L	PCT	G	SV	IP	BB	SO	ERA
34	30	.531	384	78	646	232	513	2.98

Al Holland broke the 20-save plateau just twice in his career, but his wicked moving fastball marked him as an ideal closer. After long years honing his control in the minors, Holland reached the major leagues to stay with the San Francisco Giants in 1980. His 1.75 ERA and stingy .233 opponent batting average established him as an integral part of the club's bullpen. With Greg Minton as San Francisco's closer, Holland remained in a setup role.

That changed when Holland was traded to the Philadelphia Phillies prior to the 1983 season. A relative youngster on a veteran team known as the "Wheeze Kids," Holland set a team record with 25 saves and struck out 100 batters in 91 innings. The Phillies won their division and advanced to the World Series. In four postseason appearances, Holland did not allow a run and saved two games.

He broke his own club record with 29 saves in 1984; Steve Bedrosian broke that mark three years later. Holland earned a trip to the 1984 All-Star Game, but he lost 10 games and his ERA rose by more than a run to 3.39. Days into the 1985 season, Philadelphia traded Holland to Pittsburgh; within two seasons he suited up for the Angels and New York Yankees. He was released after three ineffective appearances in 1987.

Dave Hollins

Hollins, David Michael **3B–1B**
1990–* B:5/25/1966, Buffalo, NY Deb:4/12/1990, PHI NL BB/TR 6'1", 207

G	AB	R	H	HR	RBI	OBP	SLG	AVG
967	3324	577	867	112	482	.362	.422	.261

Throughout his career, Dave Hollins battled through diabetes and chronic injuries—and the doubts of others. Seven teams gave up on him. When healthy, however, he hammered the ball and inspired his mates with his hard-nosed play.

The Phillies took Hollins away from San Diego in the Rule V draft in 1989. Despite a chronically sore shoulder, he won Philadelphia's third base job in 1992 and finished in the National League's top seven in runs, homers, and RBIs. Hollins was also hit by 19 pitches—a major league-record for a switch-hitter—and became one of the best in the game at taking extra bases. His outstanding play earned him a trip to the All-Star Game where he cracked a double. Despite a broken hand in 1993, he reached 104 runs and 93 RBIs for the second straight year and clubbed a key homer in Game 6 of the Championship Series.

Defensively, however, Hollins racked up the errors with his erratic arm—his throws sometimes landing in the seats. After two separate hand fractures in 1994, he was dealt to Boston, where he broke his wrist after five games. He struggled with the Twins in 1996 before batting .351 during the stretch run for Seattle. Hollins then batted .288 and scored 101 runs for the Angels in a fine comeback year, only to be hampered with more hand, wrist, and shoulder woes in the 1998 season, leading to rotator cuff surgery.

Charlie Hollocher

Hollocher, Charles Jacob **SS**
1918–24 B:6/11/1896, St. Louis, MO D:8/14/1940, Fontenac, MO Deb:4/16/1918, CHI NL BL/TR 5'7", 154

G	AB	R	H	HR	RBI	OBP	SLG	AVG
760	2936	411	894	14	241	.370	.392	.304

Cubs rookie shortstop Charlie Hollocher exhibited great promise as he led the National League in at bats and hits in the war-shortened 1918 season. But his career faltered as stomach pains often kept him out of the lineup and ultimately shortened his playing days.

The only .300 hitter in the lineup for either club in the 1918 World Series, Hollocher hit just .190—although he went 3-for-3 against Sad Sam Jones in Game 5.

Usually batting second in the Chicago order, he was a difficult batter to fan. In 1922 did not strike out until a Memorial Day morning-afternoon doubleheader when he fanned on a spitball thrown by the Cardinals Bill Doak. It was in that doubleheader that Max Flack and Cliff Heathcote switched teams between games.

Between 1918 and 1923 Hollocher had the sixth best batting average of any NL player with 1,500 or more at bats, and his .340 average in 1922 was the best by a shortstop since Honus Wagner's .354 in 1908. Hollocher, who participated in two triple plays, twice led NL shortstops in fielding. He committed suicide by shooting himself in throat at age 44.

Ducky Holmes

Holmes, James William **OF**
1895–99, 1901–05 B:1/28/1869, Des Moines, IA D:8/6/1932, Truro, IA Deb:8/8/1895, LOU NL BL/TR 5'6", 170

G	AB	R	H	HR	RBI	OBP	SLG	AVG
932	3601	539	1014	17	374	.337	.367	.282

Baltimore Orioles outfielder James William "Ducky" Holmes was striking out one day in July 1898 at the old Polo Grounds when he was berated by a local fan: "Oh Ducky, you're a lobster. That's what you left here for." Holmes, a former Giant, responded, "Well, I'm glad I'm not working for a sheeny anymore," an anti-Semitic remark clearly aimed at highly-unpopular Giants owner Andrew Freedman.

Freedman heard the insult, attempted to have Holmes arrested and when umpire Tom Lynch refused to oust Holmes from the game (he claimed he didn't hear the offensive remark), forfeited the contest to the Orioles. That caused the 3,000 customers in the stands to riot, threatening Freedman unless they received their money back.

Holmes jumped to the Tigers on the founding of the American League and was sold to Washington in February 1903. In June of that year he was traded to the White Sox.

In June 1905 Holmes caused more controversy—this time of a more lasting nature. His suspension by AL president Ban Johnson for cursing umpire Silk O'Loughlin resulted in a temporary shortage of Sox outfielders and a permanently strained relationship between Johnson and Chicago owner Charles Comiskey.

Tommy Holmes

Holmes, Thomas Francis **OF**

1942–52 M(1951–52, 61–69) B:3/29/1917, Brooklyn, NY Deb:4/14/1942, BOS NL BL/TL 5'10", 180

G	AB	R	H	HR	RBI	OBP	SLG	AVG
1320	4992	698	1507	88	581	.366	.432	.302

When Pete Rose broke Tommy Holmes' modern National League hitting streak in 1978, an appreciative and tearful Holmes came onto the field and thanked him for "making people remember me." But how could they have forgotten him?

During the 1945 season, when Holmes hit safely in 37 consecutive games, his performance was truly remarkable. The Braves outfielder hit .352 with 117 RBIs, 125 runs scored, and 15 stolen bases. He led the league with 47 doubles, 224 hits, a .577 slugging average, and 28 home runs. In 636 at bats, he struck out only nine times.

Holmes was born and reared in Brooklyn. His father, once a boxer, envisioned Tommy as a future boxing champion. While still in elementary school, the youngster gave boxing exhibitions at neighborhood schools and clubs. When he turned to baseball, he credited his batting success to his boxing training. "It helped develop my arms and wrists, which figure in batting," Holmes later claimed. "Punching the bag also develops coordination, another factor in hitting."

A lefthanded hitter, Holmes played first base at Brooklyn Technical High School. The Dodgers ignored him, and after graduation he played for the semipro Brooklyn Bay Parkways. Finally, Yankees scout Paul Krichell spotted him, and Holmes signed with New York in 1937.

Holmes made the jump to professional baseball look easy. He hit .320 with 25 home runs and 111 RBIs during his rookie season with Norfolk of the Piedmont League. In 1938 with Binghamton, he led the Eastern League with a .368 batting average before moving up to Newark.

In Newark Holmes' career stalled. Although he hit better than .300 in three seasons with the Bears, twice leading the IL in hits, he was a victim of the numbers game. The Yankees' outfielders included Joe DiMaggio, Tommy Henrich, Charlie Keller, and George Selkirk. There simply wasn't any room for Holmes on the talent-rich Yankees.

In the winter of 1941 he was traded to the Boston Braves for infielder Buddy Hassett and cash. Holmes quickly became a fixture in the outfield and a particular favorite of the fans in the Braves Field right field "Jury Box."

After three productive seasons, Holmes broke out in 1945. Between June 6 and July 8 he hit safely in 37 consecutive games, then the third-longest streak in National League history, behind Wee Willie Keeler's 44 and Bill Dahlen's 42. Despite accumulating the league's best offensive statistics, and the best of his career, Holmes was beaten out for the Most Valuable Player Award by the Cubs' Phil Cavarretta. *The Sporting News* selected Holmes as its NL Most Valuable Player; he was second to Phil Cavaretta in the NL MVP vote by the baseball writers.

Although he followed with three consecutive seasons hitting above .300, Holmes never again approached the heights of 1945. After banging out 28 home runs in 1945, he never reached double digits in any other season, and he never came close to 100 RBIs. However, he did have 20-game hitting streaks in 1946 and 1949.

Holmes hit .325 when the Braves won the National League pennant in 1948 and was part of an all-.300 outfield. (Jeff Heath hit .319 and Mike McCormick batted .303.) But Holmes slumped in the World Series against Cleveland, managing only five hits in 26 at bats. As the Braves declined in the next few seasons, so did Holmes' average. He never hit better than .300 again in his career.

In 1951 the Braves offered him a managerial job at Hartford in the Eastern League. For the first two months of the season, the 34-year-old Holmes led Hartford into the first division and hit .319 as a part-time outfielder. Then the Braves fired manager Billy Southworth and convinced Holmes to take over. He directed the Braves to a surprising fourth-place finish, and he appeared in 27 games, mostly as a pinch hitter. But when the club dropped to seventh the next year, he was replaced in midseason by Charlie Grimm.

Holmes signed with Brooklyn as a pinch hitter and finished his career in the 1952 World Series. Retiring as a player, he took a series of minor league managerial jobs and appeared in 24 games for Elmira in 1954. He became a scout for the Dodgers in 1958, then took over as director of the Greater New York Sandlot Baseball Foundation and became a salesman for various metal products. In 1973 the Mets hired Holmes as the community relations director for their own youth baseball program, which sent an astounding 65 players to the major leagues. He also worked as an executive in a sporting goods company before retiring.

In 11 big league seasons, Holmes hit .302 with 1,507 hits. He struck out only 122 times in 4,992 at bats, retiring with the fourth-best ratio of all time. On three separate occasions he robbed pitchers of no-hitters: Chicago's Bill Fleming on June 13, 1942; Pittsburgh's Rip Sewell on August 25, 1942; and New York's Van Lingle Mungo on August 28, 1943.

Jerome Holtzman

Holtzman, Jerome

Sportswriter, Historian B:7/12/1926, Chicago, IL

Winner of the 1989 J.G. Taylor Spink Award, Chicago sportswriter Jerome Holtzman became Major League Baseball's first official historian. Holtzman's career began in 1943, three weeks before his 17th birthday, when he became a sports department copy boy for the *Chicago Daily Times*. A two-year Marine Corps stint interrupted his career, but when World War II ended he returned to the *Times* and served with the paper and its successor, the *Chicago Sun-Times,* for 38 years. In 1981 Holtzman moved to the *Chicago Tribune* where he served for 18 years, resigning on June 1, 1999, to join the commissioner's office. He also served as a weekly contributor to *The Sporting News* for over 30 seasons. His byline appeared in over 1,000 consecutive issues of *The Sporting News.*

Holtzman edited *No Cheering in the Press Box*, a widely respected anthology of baseball sportswriting, and *Fielder's Choice*, an anthology of baseball fiction. With George Vass he co-authored *The Chicago Cubs Encyclopedia*. He also co-authored *Three-and-Two* with Tom Gorman, a National League umpire for more than a quarter of a century. In 1998 Holtzman published *The Commissioners: Baseball's Midlife Crisis*. In 1999 he collaborated with Henry Aaron on *Home Run: My Life in Pictures.*

In 1960 Holtzman developed the formula for relief saves. Major League Baseball's Official Rules Committee later adopted his formula, thus instituting the game's first new major statistic since the RBI in 1920.

Joe Falls of the *The Detroit News* once said of Holtzman: "There is no better baseball writer around, certainly none more knowledgeable." In 1996 Holtzman won the Red Smith Award for outstanding contributions to sports journalism.

Ken Holtzman

Holtzman, Kenneth Dale **P**

1965–79 B:11/3/1945, St. Louis, MO Deb:9/4/1965, CHI NL BR/TL 6'2", 175

W	L	PCT	G	SH	IP	BB	SO	ERA
174	150	.537	451	31	2867¹	910	1601	3.49

Winner of three World Series rings and author of two no-hitters, lefthander Ken Holtzman went from being a thrower with the Chicago Cubs to being a pitcher with the Oakland A's to being in the doghouse with the New York Yankees. He was dubbed the next Sandy Koufax in Chicago, in part because he was lefthanded and Jewish. On September 25, 1966, Holtzman furthered the comparison in his only meeting with Koufax, carrying a no-hitter into the ninth inning and winning, 2–1.

In 1967, while completing his military obligation and pitching when he could get a pass, Holtzman went 9–0, the fourth-best victory total for an undefeated season. He rejoined the Cubs' rotation full-time in 1968 but endured another losing season.

Holtzman became a 17-game winner in 1969 and threw a no-hitter against the Atlanta Braves at Wrigley Field. His 3–0 victory included no strikeouts, the first major league no-hitter without a whiff since 1892. Holtzman threw a more conventional no-hitter over the Cincinnati Reds at Riverfront Stadium on June 3, 1971. In between, he fanned a career-high 202 batters in 1970.

After a 74–69 record in six years with the Cubs, Holtzman was dealt to Oakland in November 1971 for center fielder Rick Monday. Holtzman provided more depth to the AL West champions' already formidable pitching rotation of Catfish Hunter, Blue Moon Odom, and 1971 Cy Young Award-winner Vida Blue. Holtzman helped push the A's from division winners to three-time world champions. With 19 wins, 265⅓ innings, and a career-best 2.51 ERA in 1972, Holtzman was second on the staff to Hunter in each category, as the A's won the AL West by six games.

Holtzman started and lost Game 3 of the American League Championship Series against the Detroit Tigers, thanks to Joe Coleman's record-setting 14-strikeout performance. But Odom and Blue combined on a five-hitter to win Game 5, and the A's advanced to the World Series. Holtzman pitched the Series opener against the Cincinnati Reds and got the win, despite pitching just five innings. He started Game 4 at Oakland, and he took a 1–0 lead into the eighth inning but wound up with a no-decision. Holtzman also relieved briefly in a wild Game 7, won by the A's to secure the franchise's first World Series triumph since 1930, when they were in Philadelphia.

In 1973 Holtzman led the Oakland starters with a 2.97 ERA and career highs of 297⅓ innings, 16 complete games, and 40 games started. He won 21 games, and along with Hunter, with 21 wins, and Blue, with 20, he was part of the last American League staff in the 20th century to feature three 20-game winners. The A's again won the AL West title by six games.

With the ALCS between Baltimore and Oakland tied at one win apiece, Holtzman and Mike Cuellar locked up in one of the best pitching duels in playoff annals. Holtzman gave up a solo home run to Earl Williams in the second inning and limited the O's to three hits and a walk in 11 innings, tying Dave McNally's record for the longest outing in a playoff game. The A's tied the game in the eighth, and Bert Campaneris won it with a homer leading off the bottom of the 11th.

The A's took the playoffs in five games and advanced to the World Series as heavy favorites against the New York Mets, whose record had been an unimpressive 82–79 during the regular season. Holtzman pitched the Series opener at Oakland, contributed a double, and scored on an error. He went five innings and allowed four hits and a run before leaving the mound for a pinch hitter, with a 2–1 lead that held up.

In Game 4 Holtzman lasted just a third of an inning, allowing a three-run homer to left-handed hitter Rusty Staub and absorbing the loss. In Game 7 Holtzman once again helped with his bat, starting a four-run rally with a one-out double in the third inning. On the mound, he limited the Mets to a run on five hits before leaving with one out in the sixth. Rollie Fingers and Darold Knowles finished the A's 5–2 victory for their second straight world championship.

In 1974 Holtzman lost a career-high 17 games, but he also won 19 and recorded three shutouts. The A's won the AL West for the fourth straight season and in the ALCS faced an Orioles team that had dashed to the pennant with 28 wins in their last 34 games. Baltimore routed Catfish Hunter in the playoff opener at Oakland. Holtzman stopped their momentum with a five-hit shutout, and the A's won the next two to secure a World Series berth against the Los Angeles Dodgers.

Holtzman pitched the opener at Dodger Stadium and started another rally with a fifth-inning double, scoring on Bert Campaneris' squeeze bunt for a 2–0 A's lead. But Holtzman ran into trouble in the bottom of the fifth after a one-out error by Campaneris and another by Reggie Jackson allowed a run to score. After issuing a walk, Holtzman was relieved by Fingers, who got the win in the A's 3–2 victory.

The starter in Game 4, Holtzman put the A's on the board with a homer in the third, then allowed the Dodgers to take a 2–1 lead. But the A's bounced back for four runs in the sixth, and Holtzman protected the lead until putting on a pair of runners on with two out in the eighth. He departed for Fingers, but got credit for the 5–2 win. The A's won their third straight world title in five games.

In 1975 Holtzman held opponents to a .222 batting average, matching his career best, but issued a career-high 108 walks on his way to a record of 18–14 and a 3.14 ERA. The A's won their fifth straight AL West crown, even though they'd lost free agent Catfish Hunter to the Yankees. Holtzman lost the ALCS opener to Boston, and then came back to pitch Game 3 on two day's rest. The Red Sox knocked out the tired Holtzman in the fifth inning and swept the series.

Anticipating free agency, Finley traded Holtzman, Reggie Jackson, and minor league pitcher Bill Van Bommell to Baltimore for outfielder Don Baylor and pitchers Mike Torrez and Paul Mitchell at the start of the 1976 season. Holtzman went 5–4 in 13 starts for the Birds, who made him part of a 10-player deal with the Yankees in June.

In 21 games with New York, Holtzman went 9–7, with a 4.17 ERA. He re-signed with New York, and wound up in the Yankee doghouse. Holtzman was lost in the Bronx, where he worked less than 90 innings in 23 games during the next year and a half. The Yankees finally traded him to the Cubs for reliever Ron Davis in 1978. Whatever ability Holtzman had left was soon gone, and he retired in 1979 at age 33.

Rick Honeycutt

Honeycutt, Frederick Wayne **P**

1977–97 B:6/29/1954, Chattanooga, TN

Deb:8/24/1977, SEA AL BL/TL, 5'11", 190

W	L	PCT	G	SV	IP	BB	SO	ERA
109	143	.433	797	38	2160	657	1038	3.72

Rick Honeycutt had a knack for being in the right place at the right time. During his 21-year career, the lefthander pitched for seven first-place teams, including three straight pennant winners in Oakland from 1988 to 1990.

A former All-America first baseman at the University of Tennessee, Honeycutt became a two-time American League All-Star as a starter with the Seattle Mariners before going to the Texas Rangers in an 11-player swap prior to the 1981 season. Following a poor season in 1982, he won AL Comeback of the Year honors as well as the league's ERA title—even though he finished the season with the Dodgers.

Honeycutt increased his longevity by becoming a full-time middle reliever in 1988. He did not start a game for the last decade of his career. Under the guidance of Oakland manager Tony La Russa and pitching coach Dave Duncan, Honeycutt evolved into a situational southpaw, often deployed to face only one or two left-handed hitters per outing. Still, it kept him employed—and busy. He pitched in at least 40 games for nine consecutive years, and had more appearances than innings pitched each season from 1991 to 1996. Honeycutt was reunited with La Russa in St. Louis, where he ended his career in 1997.

Harry Hooper

Hooper, Harry Bartholomew **OF**

1909–25 B:8/24/1887, Bell Station, CA D:12/18/1974, Santa Cruz, CA Deb:4/16/1909, BOS AL BL/TR
5'10", 168

G	AB	R	H	HR	RBI	OBP	SLG	AVG
2309	8785	1429	2466	75	817	.368	.387	.281

Harry Hooper will always be linked with teammates Tris Speaker and Duffy Lewis as the great outfield trio of the Boston Red Sox from 1910 through 1915. They were considered the best of their time and one of the greatest outfields ever assembled.

Brilliant as a unit, each starred in his own right. Lewis was an exceptional clutch hitter who averaged .284 in 11 major league seasons. His defensive work before the incline in left field at Fenway Park caused visiting outfielders to call the slope "Duffy's Cliff."

Speaker is still regarded by many as baseball's best center fielder. His ability to play shallow and to cut off short, over-the-infield flares, yet still go back and flag down the deepest flyballs, is legendary. The best hitter of the three outfielders, Speaker averaged .345 in 22 seasons and ranks high in most career offensive categories.

Hooper's speed and powerful arm made him the best defensive right fielder of his day. At the plate he was a dependable leadoff man and an excellent base runner. Most teams would have been fortunate to have a single outfielder of his caliber. The fact that all three outfielders played together is extraordinary.

Hooper was born and reared in the farming community of Bell Station, California. After graduating from Oakland's St. Mary's College with a degree in civil engineering, he took a job as a surveyor for the Western Pacific Railroad while playing baseball in the outlaw California State League. When he hit .344 for Sacramento in 1908, he aroused the interest of Boston owner John I. Taylor. The Red Sox originally offered Hooper $2,500. When he balked, the Red Sox sweetened the pot and promised him a job working on their new ballpark. Hooper signed for $2,850 but later admitted, "I never did get the engineering job."

Speaker was already an established star in center field when Hooper joined the club in 1909. Playing only part-time, Hooper hit a respectable .282. Lewis joined the Sox in 1910 to complete the "Golden Outfield."

Although he threw righthanded, Hooper batted from the left side. At 5-feet 10 inches and 168 pounds, he had fair power for a leadoff man and was particularly adept at drawing walks. He walked 70 or more times in seven seasons, including a career-high 88 in 1915. Waiting out the pitcher undoubtedly cost him points on his batting average. He hit above .300 five times, but his average also dipped below .260 several times. Once on base, Hooper was a threat to steal. He finished his career with 375 stolen bases, having reached a high of 40 in 1910. He also stole home 11 times in his career.

He was the first outfielder to use the sliding catch, sometimes called the "rump slide," which enables a player to slide into a flyball, then pop to his feet in position to throw, rather than risk a shoestring catch and chance throwing off balance. Base runners seldom tested his arm, but Hooper still accumulated 344 assists.

In 1911, Hooper's second full season in the major leagues, he was part of Boston's .300-hitting outfield. Hooper hit .311, Speaker batted .327, and Lewis finished at .307. But Boston finished in fifth place, 23 games behind the pennant-winning Philadelphia Athletics.

The Red Sox won the pennant in 1912 and faced John McGraw's New York Giants in the World Series. In the fifth inning of the final game, the Giants led, 1–0, when New York's Larry Doyle blasted a drive to deep right-center field at Fenway Park. Hooper later recalled that he "took off when the ball was hit, turned, saw it coming over my shoulder, and stuck out my bare hand. I had the ball, but the fence was there. I jumped over it and the crowd opened up. I can still see that instant."

His remarkable catch allowed Boston to tie the game in the seventh and win in the 10th. The Series lasted eight games, due to a tie, before Boston prevailed. Hooper hit .290 for the Series and reached base 13 times.

On May 30, 1913, Hooper became the first player in American League history to lead off consecutive games with a home run. He finished his career with 10 leadoff homers. On July 14, 1913, Hooper had Boston's only hit in a loss to Reb Russell of the White Sox. He would rob pitchers of no-hitters two other times in his career.

Hooper hit only .235 in 1915, but he tied what was then an AL record when he scored five runs in a game on June 24. Boston was back in the World Series in 1915, when they defeated the Philadelphia Phillies in five games. All five games were close, and again Hooper starred. He scored the winning run in top of the ninth of Game 3, a 2–1 Red Sox victory over Grover Alexander.

In the third inning of the final game, he homered over the center field fence at Philadelphia's Baker Bowl to tie the game; then he homered again into the center field bleachers in the top of the ninth to win the game, 5–4. He was the first player to hit two home runs in a World Series game since Patsy Dougherty, another Boston outfielder, hit a pair in 1903. Hooper hit .350 for the Series.

The Golden Outfield broke up in 1916 when Speaker was traded to Cleveland. Nevertheless, the Red Sox took another pennant and beat Brooklyn in five games in the 1916 Series. Once more Hooper swung a hot bat, hitting .333 and leading all participants with seven hits and six runs scored.

Two years later Boston took the pennant and again won the World Series, their fourth of the decade. Due to World War I, Duffy Lewis spent the 1918 season in the army, making Hooper the only man ever to play on four Red Sox championship teams.

During that 1918 season, Hooper served as manager Ed Barrow's coach on the field; he also hit .289. In spring training the Red Sox had been short several players due to the war, and Babe Ruth filled in at first base and in the outfield, wowing the fans with his bat. With the Red Sox mired in an early batting slump, Hooper convinced Barrow to let Ruth take a regular turn in the outfield. Ruth hit .300, swatted 11 home runs, and the Red Sox won the pennant.

Hooper hit only .200 in the 1918 Series as the Red Sox defeated the Cubs in six games. Just before the Series, baseball's ruling National Commission—Ban Johnson, John Heydler, and Garry Herrmann—informed the players that their share of the Series receipts would be cut that year. On the train to Boston after the first three games in Chicago, players from both teams met and decided to challenge the decision. Hooper and Chicago's Leslie Mann were selected to press their case.

The players lobbied for a meeting before Game 4 but were rebuffed. Before Game 5, they refused to take the field unless the commission agreed to see them. Johnson, Herrmann, and Heydler were rousted from a hotel bar and met with Hooper and Mann in the umpires' room at the park, and the game was delayed while the players argued their case in vain. They finally agreed to play, but only after extracting a promise that there would be no retribution by the National Commission.

One week before Christmas, the winning Red Sox received a letter stating that, due to the aborted "strike," the players would not receive their World Series emblems—diamond stickpins, the equivalent of today's rings. The players protested. Hooper petitioned every commissioner through Bowie Kuhn to award the emblems but was refused. Finally, on September 4, 1993, 75 years after that Series was played, through the combined efforts of *New England Sport* magazine, the Red Sox, and some descendants of the 1918 players, Major League Baseball finally relented and awarded the emblems to the players' families.

The 1918 season marked the end of Boston's remarkable championship run. Owner Harry Frazee started selling off ballplayers to finance his Broadway shows. Ruth was sold to the New York Yankees for $125,000, and a number of other players soon joined him. After hitting .312 and knocking in 88 runs in 1921, Hooper was dealt to the White Sox.

His five seasons with Chicago were among the best of Hooper's career. He hit better than .300 three times and twice scored more than 100 runs. In 1924 the White Sox outfield all hit over .300: Hooper hit .328, Bibb Falk hit .352, and Johnny Mostil hit .325.

John McGraw, no admirer of Babe Ruth, named Hooper to his all-time AL outfield (instead of the Babe), along with Ty Cobb and Tris Speaker. Ruth himself made perhaps the most accurate assessment of Hooper's career when he called Hooper "the greatest defensive right fielder."

Hooper later coached baseball at Princeton University. After a protracted campaign led by his friends and family, he was named to the Hall of Fame in 1971, three years before his death at the age of 87.

Burt Hooton

Hooton, Burt Carlton **P**

1971–85 B:2/17/1950, Greenville, TX Deb:6/17/1971, CHI NL BR/TR 6'1", 210

W	L	PCT	G	SH	IP	BB	SO	ERA
151	136	.526	480	29	2652	799	1491	3.38

Burt Hooton showed flashes of brilliance in a Cubs uniform but like most of the club's best pitchers of his era, his best years came after he left. A college phenom at Texas, Hooton signed for a large bonus and played in the Cubs' minor league system for most of 1971. After tying a Pacific Coast League record by striking out 19 batters in a single game, Hooton started three games for the Cubs late that season in 1971 and pitched two complete-game wins, earning himself a spot in the starting rotation for 1972.

In the first start of his rookie season, on April 16, 1972, Hooton no-hit the Phillies. The no-hitter sent Chicago fans into ecstasy. Hooton's rifle arm seemed to make the off-season loss of Ken Holtzman to the Oakland A's almost insignificant. The Cubs still had Ferguson Jenkins, the reigning National League Cy Young Award winner, and now they had Hooton and a promising rookie named Rick Reuschel.

Hooton finished his first year with a losing record. He posted a losing season again in 1973, as did Jenkins and Reuschel. In 1974 Jenkins went to the Rangers, and Hooton threw only three complete games and won just seven times in 21 starts. When Hooton started the 1975 season with two losses and a no-decision, the Cubs dealt him to the Dodgers.

Hooton responded immediately to being traded. He posted 18 victories and four shutouts for the Dodgers in the remainder of 1975. During the next few years he perfected his knuckle curve, and though he never had a 20-win season, he remained a tough-to-hit starter on the NL's best pitching staff. In 1977 the Dodgers took the pennant. In 1978 Hooton led the rotation with 19 wins as Los Angeles went to the World Series again.

In 1981 the reliable righthander was named to the All-Star team, and his 11 wins, four shutouts, and 2.28 ERA in the strike-shortened season helped the Dodgers to the World Series once more. In the Series, Hooton finally vindicated himself against the Yankees, who had defeated the Dodgers in six games in both 1977 and 1978. He pitched six innings of shutout ball in Game 2 and took the final victory in Game 6 as the Dodgers won the world championship.

After 1981 Hooton's skills gradually declined. He remained with the Dodgers until 1985, when he signed with the Texas Rangers, hoping to recapture his spark. He finished the season with a 5–8 mark before retiring.

Johnny Hopp

Hopp, John Leonard **OF–1B**

1939–52 B:7/18/1916, Hastings, NE Deb:9/18/1939, STL NL BL/TL 5'10", 175

G	AB	R	H	HR	RBI	OBP	SLG	AVG
1393	4260	698	1262	46	458	.368	.414	.296

John Leonard Hopp went by "Johnny," but there were other nicknames: "Cotney"—for the cotton-colored hair—and "Hippity" because of the pleasing alliteration. Whatever Hopp was called, he was a lefthanded-hitting first baseman who batted .303 in his first season as a regular with the Cardinals in 1941. Still, Hopp's career didn't begin in earnest until 1944, after the Cardinals traded Johnny Mize to the New York Giants. Converted to center field, Hopp hit .336 as the Cardinals went on to win the World Series. He also showed his grace in the field, leading NL outfielders with a .997 fielding percentage.

The Boston Braves acquired Hopp in 1946 and he batted .333. Hopp did even better in 1950. Playing for the Pirates and briefly for the Yankees, he batted a career-high .339. He placed himself among baseball's elite that season by getting eight straight hits at one point, four shy of the mark set by Pinky Higgins in 1938. Hopp also distinguished himself by going 6-for-6 in a game on May 14, 1950. His career ended after the 1952 season, which he split between the Yankees and Tigers.

Joe Horlen

Horlen, Joel Edward **P**

1961–72 B:8/14/1937, San Antonio, TX Deb:9/4/1961,CHI AL BR/TR 6', 175

W	L	PCT	G	SH	IP	BB	SO	ERA
116	117	.498	361	18	2002	554	1065	3.11

On former pitcher Ted Lyons' recommendation, the White Sox signed Joe Horlen for a $50,000 bonus after helping Oklahoma State to the 1959 NCAA championship. In the minors Horlen pitched for Lincoln, Charleston, and San Diego.

On July 29, 1963, Horlen had taken a no-hitter into the ninth against Washington. With one out, Chuck Hinton beat out an infield hit. Then Don Lock homered and Horlen lost, 2–1. In 1964 he posted the second-best ERA in the AL.

Horlen led the league in ERA, shutouts, and winning percentage in 1967 for a fourth-place club, but the Cy Young Award still went to Boston's Jim Lonborg. Horlen pitched a no-hitter against Detroit in the first game of a doubleheader on September 10, 1967. He struck out four and walked none but did not record a perfect game because he hit one Detroit batter, and White Sox first baseman Ken Boyer committed an error on a ball hit by Eddie Mathews. Horlen led the league with 14 wild pitches in 1968.

Released by the White Sox in 1972, he signed with the A's and performed on their world championship club. Despite respectable numbers, he was released again at season's end. In both cases he was the club's player representative to the Major League Baseball Players Association, leading to speculation that his involvement in the MLBPA was the real cause of his departure from baseball.

He later served as golf coach at the University of Texas. In 1999 he was coaching for the Pacific Coast League's Fresno Grizzlies.

Bob Horner

Horner, James Robert **3B-1B**
1978–88 B:8/6/1957, Junction City, KS Deb:6/16/1978, ATL NL BR/TR 6'1", 210

G	AB	R	H	HR	RBI	OBP	SLG	AVG
1020	3777	560	1047	218	685	.344	.499	.277

Power-hitting Bob Horner appeared to be on the verge of greatness when he came off a college campus to hit 23 homers and won the 1978 National League Rookie of the Year Award. Although he never quite lived up to his spectacular entrance into the major leagues, Horner slugged 218 homers in just 10 seasons, including four in a single game on July 6, 1986. He retired with a better home run ratio than Hall of Famers Reggie Jackson, Ernie Banks, and Mel Ott.

Horner, who set state home run records at Apollo High School in Glendale, Arizona, was drafted in the 15th round of the June 1975 draft by the Oakland Athletics, but instead elected to attend Arizona State. As a sophomore in 1977, Horner led the Sun Devils to the College World Series, where he was named Most Valuable Player. He was also honored as an All-America second baseman. The following season he collected an NCAA-record 25 homers and was named *The Sporting News* College Player of the Year.

Atlanta rewarded that performance by making Horner the first choice in the June 1978 draft. The Braves originally planned on sending the slugging infielder to Savannah of the Southern League, but once Horner visited Fulton County Stadium, he thought he could start swinging in the majors. "When you see guys like Johnny Bench or George Foster on *Monday Night Baseball*, they look like supermen," said Horner. "Unreal. Down there I saw for myself how they look and what they do. They looked just like me."

Horner and his agent, Bucky Hoy, persuaded Atlanta to start him with the big club—and to give him a signing bonus of $175,000. Horner homered off Bert Blyleven in his first major league game. He played 89 games at third base and ended the season with one homer for every 14.04 at bats, the best ever by a Rookie of the Year. "Another Harmon Killebrew," said Montreal manager Dick Williams—and he was not alone in his opinion.

In 1979 Horner tangled with Braves owner Ted Turner over his salary. When Horner and agent Hoy pointed out that Horner's huge signing bonus should be counted as part of his 1978 base salary—and that Turner could not cut that salary by more than 20 percent—they won a huge victory. But in the process they alienated Turner (who even hinted that the controversy helped speed the death of Braves vice president Bill Lucas). Horner followed up the fracas by breaking an ankle on Opening Day. Nonetheless, he responded with a solid year and signed a new three-year, $1-million contract.

When Horner got off to an .059 start in the first 10 days of the 1980 season, Turner tried to demote the third baseman to Richmond. Horner refused to go and was suspended, knocking three weeks out of his season. Nonetheless, Horner finished the year with a .268 batting average and a career-high 35 homers.

Horner and Dale Murphy combined for 68 homers and 206 RBIs in 1982. The Braves won the NL West on the final day of the season. The Cardinals swept Atlanta in the three-game Championship Series, and Horner hit only .091.

Horner, known to some teammates as "Piggy," battled weight problems throughout his career. In January 1983, when he signed a four-year, $6-million Braves contract, it contained $400,000 in weight clauses. He was also susceptible to injury. In August 1983 he broke a bone in his right wrist. He missed most of the 1984 season when he broke the navicular bone in that same wrist.

In 1985 Horner played 40 games at first base. The following season he made a permanent move across the diamond and led NL first basemen in putouts, double plays, and total chances. At the plate he hit 27 homers and drove in a team-leading 87 runs.

Following the 1986 campaign, Horner was offered a two-year, $3-million contract from Atlanta—which represented a $300,000 cut in salary. When no other club bettered the Braves' offer, the 30-year-old Horner signed a one-year, $2.4-million pact with the Yakult Swallows of the Japan Central League. Swallows ownership prophesied that Horner would deliver 50 homers, and when six of his first seven hits left the park (including three homers in one game), the prediction seemed justified.

But Horner was uncomfortable in Japan. "I don't have any funny anecdotes. Life last year was not amusing," he said after the season. Despite batting .327 and delivering 31 homers in 99 games, he was more than willing to return to the United States—despite a three-year, $10-million offer to stay.

When first baseman Jack Clark left St. Louis for the Yankees prior to the 1988 season, Horner saw his chance and made overtures to Cardinals management. Manager Whitey Herzog's initial response was, "I don't want Horner." But the Cards tendered him a contract calling for a $950,000 base salary with a $500,000 bonus if he played in at least 135 games. Horner, in part hampered by the spacious dimensions of Busch Stadium, never got untracked and retired after appearing in only 60 games.

Rogers Hornsby

Hornsby, Rogers **2B-SS-3B**
1915–37 M(1925–28, 1930–37, 1952–53, 701–812)
B:4/27/1896, Winters, TX D:1/5/1963, Chicago, IL
Deb:9/10/1915, STL NL BR/TR 5'11", 175

G	AB	R	H	HR	RBI	OBP	SLG	AVG
2259	8173	1579	2930	301	1584	.434	.577	.358

Rogers Hornsby was nasty, rude, and mean. He insulted teammates, owners, his own players when he managed, and even the commissioner of baseball. Someone said once that Hornsby thought diplomacy was a respiratory disease.

Despite his uncivil tongue, Rogers Hornsby was a man for whom words such as "dedication," "commitment," and "drive" are inadequate. His specialty was hitting, and there was no better righthanded batter in the history of the game. Standing straight up, deep in the batter's box, he would stride into the pitch to smash line drives all around the park with his perfectly level swing. In Les Bell's words, Hornsby "just didn't think anyone could get him out," and he was usually right.

Hornsby had the highest lifetime batting average and slugging percentage of any National Leaguer. He set the NL record for the highest single-season batting average in the 20th century at.424. He led the league in slugging 10 times, more often than anyone else. Only Ted Williams also won two Triple Crowns, and only Babe Ruth ever had more total bases in a season than Hornsby's 450 in 1922.

Remarkably, Hornsby played second base, one of the least offense-oriented positions, and played it well, leading the league in putouts and assists twice each and double plays three times. His only weakness was pop flies hit over his head, because looking up could make him lose his balance.

Hornsby was fanatical about staying in shape. He believed in the merits of red meat in the diet, and often ate a blood-red steak at all three meals. He never smoked or drank, and he even refused to read books or newspapers or go to the movies for fear of damaging his eyes. His only hobby was playing the horses.

Although he played the ponies as badly as any other two-dollar bettor, Hornsby took immense pride in his knowledge of the strike zone. Once, when a young pitcher was complaining to an umpire about not calling strikes on Hornsby, the umpire informed the youngster, "Son, when you throw a strike, Mr. Hornsby will let you know."

Casey Stengel talked about one specific Hornsby at bat in Robert Creamer's *Stengel: His Life and Times*. The situation called for an intentional walk, but pitcher Lee Meadows sneaked the first pitch over for a strike. The next pitch went for Hornsby's head and he had to hit the dirt. After strike two, Meadows threw two more at Hornsby. With the count full, Hornsby hit what Stengel called "the damnedest line drive I ever saw. After all those fastballs thrown behind his head, instead of falling away on that last curveball, he stepped in and hit a tremendous line drive."

Although scouting reports said Hornsby "couldn't hit a lick" as a minor league infielder, the Cardinals liked his glove and bought him from a Texas minor league team for $500. In 1915 he played in 18 games for St. Louis and batted only .246 as a "crouch and choke" hitter. Cardinals coach Bob Connery thought Hornsby could take advantage f his size and strength if he stood up straight. The next year he hit .313, and he would dip below .300 only once in the next 15 years.

From 1920 through 1925 Hornsby compiled the greatest six-year hitting streak in history. He averaged .397 for the six years; won batting titles every year, setting a league record; and added the on-base and slugging titles every year for good measure. He led the league in homers twice, in runs scored three times, and in hits, doubles, and RBIs four times during that span. In 1922 he chalked up 450 total bases with 42 home runs, 14 triples, 46 doubles, and a .401 average, and won the Triple Crown.

In 1924 he batted .424, tacking on 43 doubles, 14 triples, and 25 homers that year. He hit .400 against five teams in the league, but the Cubs "held" him to .387. Only two pitchers kept him hitless in more than two games. He played in 143 games, hit safely in 119 of them, and batted almost 50 points higher than the player who finished second that year.

Amazingly, he was not chosen 1924 Most Valuable Player. He finished eight points behind Brooklyn's Dazzy Vance, who had won 28 games with a 2.16 ERA. One voter, the *Cincinnati Enquirer*'s Jack Ryder, did not list Hornsby at all among the 10 names he submitted on his ballot. His rationale: "How can you call a guy an MVP whose team finishes sixth?"

MVP or not, the Cards decided to make him their manager. With 115 games left in the 1925 season, they fired Branch Rickey and gave the job to Hornsby. The team was in last when he took over, and they climbed up to fourth, largely because manager Hornsby had player Hornsby deliver a .403 average, 39 homers, and 143 RBIs. Hornsby decided that he should also have a financial stake in the team, and he bought out Branch Rickey's stock in the club, more than 1,000 shares, for $45 a share.

He was not one for team meetings—preferring to insult his players one at a time—but before the 1926 season he called the team together on the first day of spring training. "If there's anyone in this room who doesn't think we're going to win the pennant," he told them, "go upstairs now and get your money and go on home, because we don't want you around here."

Although Hornsby "slumped" to .317, the Cards won the pennant, and then beat the Yankees in the World Series, catching Babe Ruth on an attempted steal to give St. Louis its first championship. Years later Hornsby said his greatest thrill in baseball was "taking O'Farrell's throw, putting down the ball and letting that big monkey tag himself out, so we were world champions."

When Hornsby sat down to negotiate his contract for 1927, he asked for a five-year deal at $50,000 a year, a substantial raise. Cardinals owner Sam Breadon offered him five years at $40,000, or one at $50,000, but the two stubborn men couldn't come to terms. Breadon traded Hornsby to the New York Giants for Frank Frisch and Jimmy Ring.

St. Louis fans didn't take well to the news. How could Breadon trade away the manager who had brought the Cardinals their greatest glory, and the man who had hit .400 three times in the past five years? The mayor and the chamber of commerce filed official protests, and fans talked about a boycott of the team's games.

There was another problem, however: the thousand-plus shares of stock in the club that Hornsby owned. Breadon offered Hornsby the $45 per share he had originally paid for them; Hornsby felt they were worth something in the neighborhood of $100 per share. Commissioner Kenesaw Mountain Landis logically ruled that no one could play for one team while owning stock in another, thereby putting Breadon and Hornsby at an impasse. Hornsby eventually received $100,000 plus $12,000 to cover his legal fees, and all the National League owners had to kick in cash to buy him out.

After the 1927 season Hornsby's horse-playing "partner" filed suit against the ballplayer, claiming that Hornsby had borrowed $92,000 from him and had lost it on the ponies. Court testimony indicated that Hornsby had bet $327,995 at racetracks in the previous two years. When Landis called him on the carpet, Hornsby was not contrite. He said, "At least I'm not gambling other people's money away in the stock market," referring to Landis' investing of Organized Baseball's money in the market. Landis—and baseball—lost a bundle.

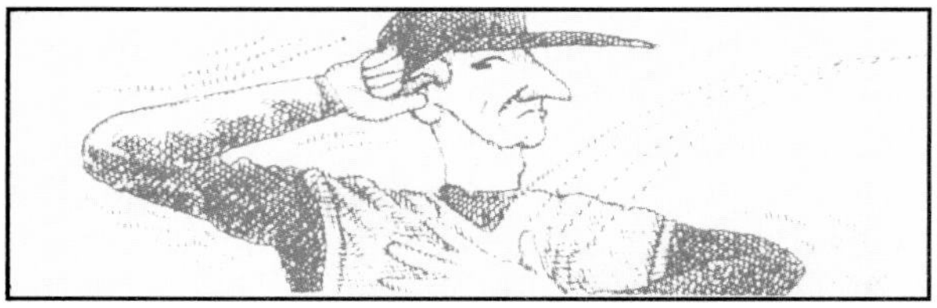

After single seasons with the Giants and Braves, the Cubs, smelling a chance for a pennant, made Hornsby the centerpiece of one of the largest deals ever up to that time. In November 1928 "the Rajah" went to Chicago for five players and $200,000. Hornsby had his last superlative season with the Cubs in 1929, and the North Siders won their first pennant in 11 years. Once again, however, Hornsby failed to shine in the postseason, hitting only .238 and striking out eight times as the Philadelphia Athletics won in five games.

Hornsby broke his ankle sliding during the 1930 season, greatly limiting his playing time. Still bothered by the ankle, he played in only 100 games in 1931. The Cubs finished third, complaining all the while about his rude managing style. Monstrous slugger Hack Wilson said that Hornsby "took the bat out of my hands," referring to Hornsby's consistent giving of the "take" sign when the count was 2–0, 3–0, or 3–1.

Hornsby was too strict for many of his players. His rules included no eating, smoking, or playing cards in the clubhouse. By the middle of the 1932 season he was replaced by easygoing Charlie "Jolly Cholly" Grimm, and the Cubs responded by winning the pennant by four games. The Cubs voted that Hornsby not receive one cent of World Series money. Hornsby protested to Landis and not surprisingly received an unsympathetic response.

Hornsby's playing career was effectively over. He was fired after managing the Browns for a little more than three years, never finishing higher than sixth. The next 14 years saw him manage in the minors and run a baseball school. He was named Minor League Manager of the Year in 1941, and led his team to league championships in 1950 and 1951. The Browns called him back to manage, but after only 51 games owner Bill Veeck let him go, saying, "It's easier to fire one manager than 25 players."

The Reds hired him for the last 51 games of the 1952 season. In 1953 he applied some typical Hornsby logic when he told his pitcher, Clyde King, to knock down Stan Musial. King felt it was a bad idea, but he obeyed, and after getting up Musial smacked a tremendous homer. "That knockdown's for you, Hornsby," King said when he returned to the bench. Hornsby lasted only one full season in Cincinnati, and later scouted and coached for the Cubs and Mets.

Although not known as a dirty player, Hornsby's self-image as a tough guy was so important to him that his ghost-written autobiography, *My Fight with Baseball*, contains this credo: "I've 'cheated' or watched someone else on my team 'cheat' in practically every game. When I played second base I used to trip, kick, elbow, or spike anybody I could. If a big league ballplayer doesn't like cutting the corners or playing with 'cheaters,' then he's as much out of place as a missionary in Russia." Hornsby took his place in the Hall of Fame in 1942 and died in Chicago in 1963.

Joe Hornung

Hornung, Michael Joseph **OF**
1879–90 U(1893, 1896) B:6/12/1857 Carthage, NY D:10/30/1931, Howard Beach, NY Deb:5/1/1879, BUF NL BR/TR 5'8½", 164

G	AB	R	H	HR	RBI	OBP	SLG	AVG
1123	4784	788	1230	31	564	.277	.350	.257

One of the better outfielders of the 1880s, Joe "Ubbo Ubbo" Hornung led the National League in fielding five times. He did not use a glove until near the end of his career. Records show that in 1884, even without a glove, he did not drop one flyball.

Hornung would yell, "Ubbo Ubbo!" whenever he delivered a hit or made a particularly good fielding play. "It started out as a sort of self-satisfied grunt," noted baseball nicknames expert James Skipper, "and later became a loud habit with him."

Although Hornung was not particularly outgoing, he tried his hand at vaudeville while still a player, an experiment lasting until his teammates pelted him with assorted produce from the audience. After his playing days ended with Atlanta of the Southern League in 1895, Hornung umpired in the Eastern (International) League, the Connecticut State League, and the National League. He also worked as a policeman at the Polo Grounds.

Willie Horton

Horton, Willie Watterson **OF–DH**
1963–80 B:10/18/1942, Arno, VA Deb:9/10/1963, DET AL BR/TR 5'11", 209

G	AB	R	H	HR	RBI	OBP	SLG	AVG
2028	7298	873	1993	325	1163	.335	.457	.273

Outfielder Willie Horton was a long-time fan favorite in Detroit, rewarding their affection by being one of the team's leading sluggers as well as a four-time All-Star. Horton also performed off the field. During the 1967 Detroit riots, Horton did his part to help restore order, climbing onto a truck to exhort fellow African-Americans to desist from looting and violence.

Reared in inner-city Detroit, Horton was a highly-scouted high school prospect, particularly after he launched a homer into Tiger Stadium's right field stands as a 16-year-old. He signed with the Tigers for a reported $50,000 bonus in August 1961, and the following year spent his first professional season with Duluth–Superior, where he batted .295 and led the Northern League with 203 total bases.

He began the next season with the International League's Syracuse Chiefs, but was demoted to Knoxville of the South Atlantic League, where a teammate was Denny McLain. Tossed out of one game in Lynchburg, Horton displayed his tremendous strength by ripping the lock off a chain-link fence. "The two strongest men I ever met in baseball were Frank Howard and Willie Horton," said McLain.

Brought up to Detroit at the end of the 1963 season, he singled as a pinch hitter in his first major league at bat. Then he smacked a pinch homer off Robin Roberts his second time up. In 15 games he hit .326 but spent most of the 1964 season at Syracuse, where he hit 28 homers and drove in 99 runs.

Horton became a regular in the Tigers outfield in 1965, hitting 29 homers and driving in 104 runs. On June 22, 1966, he hit his first major league grand slam, and he finished the season with 27 round-trippers and 100 RBIs. Hampered in 1967 by ankle problems that required surgery, Horton bounced back the following year to slug a career-high 36 homers.

The 1968 World Series was billed as a duel between McLain (a 30-game winner during the season) and Cardinals ace Bob Gibson. Gibson twice beat McLain, but the St. Louis fireballer was bested in Game 7 by Mickey Lolich, who won three Series games. Horton batted .304 during the Series, and hit a Game 2 home run off starter Nelson Briles into the left-field bleachers at Busch Stadium.

In Game 5, however, it was Horton's fielding that loomed large. In the fifth inning, with the Cardinals ahead, 3–2, and Lou Brock on second, Julian Javier singled to left. Horton's throw to catcher Bill Freehan was waiting for Brock, who inexplicably chose not to slide. Coming in standing up, he was an easy out. The play kept the Tigers in the game, which they eventually won, 5–3.

Horton battled weight problems—and superstitions—throughout his major league tenure. He used one batting helmet throughout his entire career, repainting it as he went from team to team. He took similar care with his spikes, tenderly placing them in shoe trees after each game to ensure years of wear.

During a two-month stretch in 1969, Horton hit three grand slams. On June 9, 1970, he collected three homers in one game against Milwaukee. In 1972 he hit only .231 with 11 homers, and made his last postseason appearance. He was 1-for-10 in the Championship Series, which the Oakland A's won in five games.

The following season Horton rebounded to hit .300 for the last time in his career. His final days in the outfield were in 1974, a season that also featured one of the strangest plays of Horton's career. Predating the Dave Winfield seagull incident in Toronto, one of Horton's pop flies killed a pigeon at Boston's Fenway Park.

In 1975 Horton hit 25 homers and drove in 92 runs as a full-time designated hitter. He was traded to the Rangers in April 1977 for pitcher Steve Foucault. On May 15, 1977, he again hit three homers in a game, this time against Kansas City. However, he also led the league's designated hitters in strikeouts.

Horton was traded to Cleveland the following February. Released that July, he signed with the A's but was traded to Toronto a month later in a deal that sent Rico Carty to Oakland.

Granted free agency at season's end, he signed with Seattle in January 1979. Used exclusively as a DH by Mariners manager Darrell Johnson, Horton tied for the league lead in games played. At age 37, he hit 29 homers and drove in 106 runs. In one game he missed his 300th homer when he hit a ball that ricocheted off a Kingdome speaker and back onto the field. His efforts earned him honors as *The Sporting News* AL Comeback Player of the Year. He re-signed with the club that December and played one more season in the big leagues.

He later performed in the Pacific Coast League and in Mexico. Horton also served as a Tigers minor league batting instructor and as a Yankees and White Sox coach.

Pete Hotaling

Hotaling, Peter James **OF**

1879–88 B:12/16/1856, Mohawk, NY D:7/3/1928, Cleveland, OH Deb:5/1/1879, CIN NL BL/TR 5'8", 166

G	AB	R	H	HR	RBI	OBP	SLG	AVG
840	3492	590	931	9	371	.314	.353	.267

Pete Hotaling plays a sensible, if ignominious, role in baseball mythology. As the story goes, the fleet-footed outfielder was called to catch for Syracuse in a minor league game in 1877. After he got behind the plate, a batter tipped back a pitch into Hotaling's eye. A month later the bruised outfielder was again asked to catch. Hotaling was taunted as a coward as he took his place behind the plate—wearing the first catcher's mask. He'd had it manufactured at the Remington Arms plant at Ilion, New York.

The idea that it took an outfielder to invent the catcher's mask bespeaks the notoriously stubborn pride of catchers. "Monkey," as he was known, played just a handful of games behind the plate as a major leaguer.

A righthanded hitter with a career .267 average, Hotaling collected six hits in a nine-inning game on June 6, 1888. He was also a fast runner and a good fielder. He played parts of eight seasons in the major leagues with Cincinnati, Cleveland, Worcester, and Boston in the National League and with Brooklyn and Cleveland in the American Association.

Hotaling finished his career with St. Joseph in the Western Association in 1889. He attended Eastman Business College in Poughkeepsie, New York. and later worked as a grocer and machinist in Cleveland.

Charlie Hough

Hough, Charles Oliver **P**

1970–94 B:1/5/1948, Honolulu, HI Deb:8/12/1970, LA NL BR/TR 6'2", 190

W	L	PCT	G	SV	IP	BB	SO	ERA
216	216	.500	858	61	3801^{1}	1665	2362	3.75

In his first major league pitching appearance, with the Los Angeles Dodgers on August 12, 1970, Charlie Hough struck out the Pittsburgh Pirates' Willie Stargell with the bases loaded. A quarter of a century later the oldest man in professional sports closed out his career in a less glorious fashion. When Florida Marlins manager Rene Lachemann yanked Hough with one out in the first inning of a game against the Philadelphia Phillies on July 25, 1994, the 46-year-old righthander had already given up five runs.

"It was the toughest visit to the mound in my career," sighed Lachemann. Hough left the field slowly, a slight limp testifying to the arthritic hip that had finally caught up with him. "If I could do something to fix it, I would," said Hough about the degenerative condition. "But I can't and it's getting worse." Hough underwent hip surgery that winter. "The hip will be replaced," wrote *Miami Herald* sportswriter Greg Cote. "Charlie Hough won't be."

He was a favorite among Miami sportswriters, teammates, and fans alike. Hough came to the Marlins from the Chicago White Sox in the 1992 expansion draft. For Hough, who spent off-seasons in Hialeah, Florida, it was like coming home. Rene Lachemann penciled the veteran knuckleballer into the lineup as his starting pitcher for the Marlins' Opening Day game against the Dodgers, and the first-ever pitch thrown by a Florida Marlin was a Charlie Hough knuckleball, which floated and darted and danced and finally dropped across the plate for a called strike one. The sellout crowd at Joe Robbie Stadium roared its approval, and the veteran on the mound pumped his fist into the air. "The Marlins are born," crowed Cote, "delivered by Charlie Hough." Florida, behind Hough, went on to win the opener.

Hough put up workhorse numbers. He led the team in games started, innings pitched, strikeouts, and his 4.27 ERA was the lowest among Florida starters that first season. Equally important for the expansion club was his easy, friendly style. Hough was the rarest of pitchers, a guy who would chat with reporters in the locker room before he took the mound. "Hey, it's just pitching," he said. "I've been doing this awhile." Hough had a sense of humor too. His first base hit as a Marlin came exactly 13 years after his previous big league hit. "Been in a slump," he shrugged. Asked if he was always so self-deprecating he replied, "Maybe I would be if I knew what that meant."

A third baseman and sometime outfielder, Hough signed with the Los Angeles Dodgers in 1966 at age 18. Tommy Lasorda decided to turn Hough into a pitcher. When the 21-year-old pitching prospect hurt his throwing arm in 1969 while playing in Triple A, Dodgers scout Gordie Holt showed Hough how to throw the knuckler in the Arizona Instructional League. The next season, Hough's first as a knuckleball specialist, he went 12–8 with a 1.95 ERA for the Dodgers' Spokane farm team. (That was the same year he made a quick trip to the bigs to fan Stargell.) From then on, the name Charlie Hough, like Hoyt Wilhelm, became synonymous with that most maddening of all pitches, the knuckleball. Hough later joined Wilhelm as the second pitcher to toss 400 games in each league; Jesse Orosco eventually followed.

Hough enjoyed several brilliant seasons in his journeyman career. In 1973, his first full season in the majors, he went 4–2 for the Dodgers with a 2.75 ERA. In 1976, working as a reliever, his 12 wins were tops among NL relief pitchers, and he led the Dodgers' staff with 18 saves. In addition to being durable, Hough proved to be one of the most versatile pitchers in the history of the game. He could start or come in for long or short relief. He showcased his skills for seven full seasons with the Dodgers before being traded to the Texas Rangers during the 1980 season.

In 1982 Hough returned to the starting rotation for good. He led the Rangers in wins, complete games, strikeouts, and innings pitched that season. In 1984 he paced all AL pitchers with 17 complete games. A broken finger kept him on the bench for the first month of the 1986 season, but he came back strong, and for the first and only time in his career he won a berth on the All-Star team. In 1987 Hough notched a career-high 18 victories. He was traded to the White Sox after the 1990 season and spent two years in the Chicago rotation.

Because the knuckler is such a fickle pitch, he often ranked among the league leaders in hit batsmen. However, he was the first pitcher in big league history to log 400 starts and 400 relief appearances.

The Marlins placed Hough on the disabled list rather than forcing him to retire. The move allowed the veteran to keep his locker and to remain a part of the club for the remainder of his final season. "This is my team," said Hough, stretching out his arms. After recuperating from hip replacement surgery, Hough was pegged to return to the Marlins as a pitching coach but never did. He later served, however, as Dodgers pitching coach, being dismissed early in the 1999 season.

Ralph Houk

Houk, Ralph George **C**

1947–54 M(1961–63, 1968–78, 1981–84, 1,619–1,531)
B:8/9/1919, Lawrence, KS Deb:4/26/1947, NY AL
BR/TR 5'11", 193

G	AB	R	H	HR	RBI	OBP	SLG	AVG
91	158	12	43	0	20	.327	.323	.272

Ralph Houk spent 20 years managing in the American League with the Yankees, Tigers, and Red Sox. Houk was a patient man who, during games, used to stand with one foot up on the dugout steps as he casually played with the pebbles. His first three teams won pennants, but he never reached the postseason again and served as general manager when the Yankees slid off their pedestal in the mid-1960s.

Ralph George Houk was nicknamed "Major" for his rank while he served in World War II. A catcher in his playing days, Houk had the misfortune of playing with the Yankees in the late 1940s and early 1950s when the team boasted Yogi Berra and Charlie Silvera. As a result Houk's career as a Yankee consisted of a series of cups of coffee as he sat in the dugout.

He was a career .272 hitter in a total of 91 games, and he had 158 at bats during his eight seasons with the Yankees. At least the team took the man to two World Series. He got one chance at bat in each Series and delivered a hit in 1947 against Brooklyn.

Houk retired as a player after the 1954 season. He managed the Denver Bears of the American Association from 1955 to 1957. He then returned to New York as a coach, and at age 41 he replaced Casey Stengel as manager after the 1960 World Series. Houk took the Yankees to three consecutive pennants and two world championships. He was then named general manager of the Yankees, and he named Berra team manager.

Berra took New York to another pennant in 1964, but they lost the World Series to the Cardinals. The Yankees fired Berra and hired Cardinals manager Johnny Keane. Keane took an aging team to a sixth place finish in 1965. After the Yanks got off to a slow start in 1966, Houk fired Keane and returned to manage the team.

He oversaw the reconstruction of the Yankees that brought the team back to contention in 1970. But when CBS sold the Yankees to a group that included George Steinbrenner in 1973, Houk quit the team. He managed the Detroit Tigers from 1974 through 1978 and the Red Sox from 1981 through 1984. He was never fired as a manager. Houk was a consultant for the Minnesota Twins in the late 1980s.

Elston Howard

Howard, Elston Gene **C-OF-1B**

1955–68 Negro Leaguer Player (1948–50) B:2/23/1929, St. Louis, MO D:12/14/1980, New York, NY Deb:4/14/1955, NY AL BR/TR 6'2", 200

G	AB	R	H	HR	RBI	OBP	SLG	AVG
1605	5363	619	1471	167	762	.325	.427	.274

Elston Howard was a member of four American League All-Star teams before he earned a regular job. For a good part of his career with the Yankees, Howard was a man without a fixed position, owing to the dominating presence of teammate Yogi Berra. Nevertheless, Howard could hit with power and could field adequately at several positions, and as a catcher he ranked among the greats.

His performance in the 1958 World Series was typical. The Yankees trailed the Milwaukee Braves three games to one and had lost Game 4, partly because Norm Siebern had misjudged a pair of flyballs in left field. Howard started Game 5 in left, and, with New York leading 1–0 in the sixth, caught Red Schoendienst's looper and nailed the speedy Bill Bruton off first for the double play. In Game 6 he threw out a second runner and scored the winning run. He got another pair of hits and stole a base in Game 7 to win the Babe Ruth Award as the outstanding player in the Series.

Howard grew up in St. Louis, an only child whose father taught in a segregated high school. At Cashon High School, four-sport letterman Howard excelled at basketball, football, baseball, and track, but he declined scholarship offers from Big Ten schools, opting to sign with the Kansas City Monarchs of the Negro American League.

He roomed with Ernie Banks and hit well as a catcher-outfielder for the Monarchs. Howard expected an offer from the Cardinals after spending four days at a Cardinals tryout camp, but the club never bothered to write him. Instead, scouts Johnny Neun and Tom Greenwade, the man who brought Mickey Mantle and Bobby Murcer to New York, signed Howard to the Yankees organization for $15,000 in 1950.

After a stint with Muskegon of the Class A Central League and another in the army, Howard went on to play for Toronto, where he was the International League's Most Valuable Player in 1954, hitting .330 with 22 homers. By then he was primarily a catcher, and he led the circuit with 588 putouts and 16 triples. But there were still two serious obstacles to his progress—race and Berra, who had just won the second of his three American League Most Valuable Player Awards behind the plate for New York.

No African-American had ever played for the Yankees, one of the last major league clubs to integrate. Vic Power had been targeted to break the color barrier in the Bronx, but management found him too controversial, so Howard became the pioneer by default. "The Yankees claimed they were waiting for the right man," commented Siebern. "In retrospect, you'd have to say that they couldn't have done better. He had great morals, personality, and character. He was just an outstanding individual."

When Howard faced segregation during spring training in St. Petersburg, the Yankees moved to more liberal Fort Lauderdale and canceled most of their barnstorming in the segregated South. Howard had no complaints about the Yankees, saying, "No one in the Yankee organization made me conscious of my color."

In 1955 Howard homered in his first World Series at bat. Two years later he was selected—for the first of nine straight years—to the AL All-Star team, and in 1961 he won the J.G. Taylor Spink Award as the St. Louis Baseball Man of the Year. On August 19, 1962, he drove in eight runs in one game.

As a catcher, Howard was a pitchers' favorite. "Unless you pitched to him," said Yankees reliever Hal Reniff, "you didn't know how good he was, how agile behind the plate." Hurler Bobby Shantz once said, "He got more strikes for his pitcher than any other catcher I saw. When the ball hit his glove, it didn't move. His glove stayed right there. Most catchers give a little....The umpires can tell the difference between great ones and the not-so-greats. They gave him the call. He was a pitcher's best friend."

In 1963 Howard hit a career-high 28 homers and was voted the league's MVP—the first black to win the honor in the AL. Despite the many years that had passed since Jackie Robinson integrated Major League Baseball, the MVP announcement provoked hate mail and a racist backlash. Howard's wife said, "It makes me proud, him being the first. I tried to explain to Elston Jr. what it meant if his father got the award....I told him winning the MVP was like getting the Nobel Prize of baseball."

In August 1967 Howard was traded to Boston and helped the Red Sox to their first pennant in

21 years. "I don't think I ever saw a pitcher shake off one of his signs. They had too much respect for him," said Boston teammate Tony Conigliaro.

Retiring midway through the 1968 season, Howard returned to the Yankees as a coach, continuing in that capacity until just before his death from heart disease in 1980. Baseball commentator Red Barber said of Howard's death, "The Yankees lost more class on the weekend than George Steinbrenner could buy in 10 years."

Frank Howard

Howard, Frank Oliver **OF–1B**

1958–73 M(1981, 1983, 93–133) B:8/8/1936, Columbus, OH Deb:9/10/1958, LA NL BR/TR 6'7", 255

G	AB	R	H	HR	RBI	OBP	SLG	AVG
1895	6488	864	1774	382	1119	.355	.499	.273

The 6-foot 7-inch, 260-pound Frank Howard looked as if he could bunt the ball over the fence. Ted Williams, Howard's manager late in his career, once called him the strongest man ever to play major league baseball.

Other legendary strongmen of baseball are known for their towering home runs, but Howard's most ferocious hit might well have been a single. He once smashed a screaming line drive 390 feet against Fenway Park's center field fence; the ball rebounded so quickly that it was in outfielder Reggie Smith's glove before Howard could reach first base.

Howard was named All-America in both basketball and baseball at Ohio State. On the court, he set a tournament record with 32 rebounds in a single game, and his baseball ability earned him a $108,000 contract with the Los Angeles Dodgers.

He started out in pro ball with Green Bay of the Class B 3-I League in 1958 and slammed 37 homers. Called up briefly by the Dodgers at the end of the season, he hit his first major league home run. In 1959 *The Sporting News* named him Minor League Player of the Year after he hit 43 homers and batted in 126 runs splitting his season between Victoria of the Texas League and Spokane of the Pacific Coast League.

He began the 1960 season with Spokane but was soon brought up by the Dodgers. That year he was named National League Rookie of the Year Award with 23 home runs and 77 RBIs. Nicknamed "Hondo" after the John Wayne movie, Howard struggled as a sophomore but rebounded in 1962 with 31 homers and 119 RBIs. His production fell sharply in the next two years, and in December 1964 the Dodgers traded him to the Washington Senators in a seven-player deal that brought pitcher Claude Osteen to Los Angeles.

Senators manager Jim Lemon, a former American League slugger himself, got Howard to shorten his swing and use a heavier bat. His batting average improved, but his home run production dipped to 21 in 1965 and 18 in 1966. Howard remained consistent only in strikeouts, as he whiffed more than 100 times each season.

In 1967 Howard's fortunes began to change for the better. He hit 36 home runs, and his 89 RBIs were his best showing since 1962. On May 12, 1968, he began a home run streak in which he hit at least one homer in six consecutive games for a total of 10. The streak set several records, including the most homers in six games. At last Howard was front-page news, and dubbed "the Capital Punisher" by the Washington press, he gained some much-needed confidence. He went on to lead the AL with 44 homers and topped 100 RBIs.

In 1969 Ted Williams became Washington's manager. Under Williams' tutelage Hondo improved to 48 homers (although Minnesota's Harmon Killebrew edged him for the AL crown by a single home run) and he nearly doubled his number of walks, for the first time finishing with more free passes (102) than strikeouts (96). The next year Howard regained the AL home run crown, with 44, while leading in RBIs, with 126, and walks, with 132.

Howard retired as a player after three more seasons and became a major league coach. He managed the Padres in 1981 and the Mets in 1983, but spent nearly 20 years as a coach with the Brewers, Yankees, Mariners, Mets, and Devil Rays.

Art Howe

Howe, Arthur Henry **3B–2B**

1974–82, 1984–85 M(1989–93, 1996–* 696–762) B:12/15/1946, Pittsburgh, PA Deb:7/10/1974, PIT NL BR/TR 6'2", 190

G	AB	R	H	HR	RBI	OBP	SLG	AVG
891	2626	268	682	43	293	.332	.379	.260

Art Howe's managerial career was characterized by the same qualities that marked his playing days: patience and perspective. He led the unproven Houston Astros to three finishes above .500 in five years, but he was dismissed before he could finish the job. The same thing nearly happened in Oakland.

He watched the A's develop from divisional doormat to playoff contender. Like Oakland dugout predecessors Billy Martin and Tony La Russa, Howe favored an aggressive strategy. Howe's comparatively placid dugout demeanor, however, led some to criticize his style as too relaxed. "We're a young ballclub that makes a lot of mistakes," first baseman Jason Giambi said before the 1999 season. "Yelling and screaming are not going to change that....If guys do get out of line, he lets them know, but he's very quiet about it."

One reason why the A's elected to retain Howe was the support of his players, who lobbied general manager Billy Beane to keep Howe after Oakland's second consecutive last-place finish in 1998. The A's responded with their best season since 1992. The club battled the Boston Red Sox for the Wild Card spot until the final week of the 1999 season despite one of the league's lower payrolls.

Steve Howe

Howe, Steven Roy

1980–83, 1985, 1987, 1991–96 B:3/10/1958, Pontiac, MI Deb:4/11/1980, LA NL BL/TL, 6'1", 180

W	L	PCT	G	SV	IP	BB	SO	ERA
47	41	.534	497	91	606	139	328	3.03

Steve Howe was a University of Michigan standout when the Los Angeles Dodgers made him their top choice in the 1979 amateur draft. He was National League Rookie of the Year a year later, when he had 17 saves to go with seven wins and a 2.65 earned run average. A year later, he had a career-best 18 saves and made his only All-Star appearance. Had substance abuse problems not intervened, he might have gone on to an exceptional career.

The Dodgers, tired of waiting for him to clear up his personal problems, sent him to the Minnesota Twins in 1985. He sat out 1986, then resurfaced with the Texas Rangers a year later. Howe did not pitch in the majors from 1988 to 1990. Then the New York Yankees, desperate to replace departed lefty closer Dave Righetti, invited Howe to their spring training camp. He earned a Triple A contract, notched five saves with Columbus, and returned to the majors in May. He immediately became the club's most effective relief pitcher, finishing the season with a sparkling 1.68 ERA.

After his off-season arrest on a cocaine charge in Montana, Howe was handed his seventh suspension, a one-year ban, on June 8, 1992. On appeal, arbitrator George Nicolau overruled Commissioner Fay Vincent but included a proviso that another violation would lead to a lifetime suspension.

Though Howe twice topped 50 outings with the Yankees, he did not approach his 1982 career peak of 66 games. In six years in pinstripes, Howe had only 31 saves. The Yankees released him before reaching the 1996 World Series.

On the mound, Howe was a man in motion, always fussing and fidgeting even before delivering a pitch. Howe mixed a 92 mph fastball with a slider, changeup, and curve. He got stale with long layoffs and thrived when given a heavy workload. In 1994 he was the Yankees' most effective reliever, converting 15 of 19 saves and stranding 68 percent of the runners he inherited.

Harry Howell

Howell, Henry Harry **P**

1898–1910 U(1915) B:11/14/1876, New Jersey D:5/22/1956, Spokane, WA Deb:10/10/1898, BRO NL BR/TR 5'9"

W	L	PCT	G	SH	IP	BB	SO	ERA
131	146	.473	340	20	2567^2	677	986	2.74

"Handsome Harry" Howell was one of the hard luck pitchers of all time. Based on the 1,103 runs he surrendered and the 1,186 that were scored on his behalf, Howell should have expected at little batter fate. His bad luck matched that of the clubs he played for in his 13-year career. Later as a coach for the still luckless St. Louis Browns, he tried to do a favor for a player on another team; it cost him his job.

Howell, one of baseball's first spitballers, spent one year with Brooklyn before transferring to Baltimore. In January 1900 he returned to Brooklyn with Joe McGinnity and four other players as Baltimore vanished from the league. The following year he was back in Baltimore with the new American League; 1903 found him in New York when the Orioles became the Highlanders. Traded to the Browns in January 1904, Howell became a mainstay of the St. Louis staff, three times recording an ERA under 2.00. In 1905 he led the AL with 35 complete games.

On the last day of the 1910 season Howell, then a Browns coach, offered official scorer E.V. Parrish a suit of clothes if he would award Nap Lajoie a base hit—which would give Lajoie the American League batting crown (and a Chalmers "30" automobile) over widely disliked Ty Cobb. When this was discovered, Howell was fired, and Ban Johnson used all of his influence to keep Howell from finding another job in Organized Baseball. Despite Johnson's efforts, Howell later umpired in the minors—as well as in the Federal League in 1915.

Jay Howell

Howell, Jay Canfield **P**

1980–1994 B:11/26/1955 Miami, FL Deb:8/10/1980, CIN NL BR/TR 6'3", 205

W	L	PCT	G	SV	IP	BB	SO	ERA
58	53	.523	568	155	844^2	291	666	3.34

Jay Howell was a hard-throwing reliever for six clubs during his 15-year career. After breaking in with the 1980 Reds, he made all but one of his 21 career starts in the next three seasons, primarily with the Yankees. Before leaving the Bronx, Howell found his niche in the bullpen.

In 1984, his first as a full-time reliever, Howell went 9–4 with seven saves and a 2.69 ERA in 61 games, mostly as a set-up man. Given a chance to close by Oakland a year later, he responded with a career-best 29 saves. Howell topped 20 saves in two other seasons and made three All-Star teams.

After three seasons in Oakland, he was traded to the Dodgers in December 1987. He saved 21 games for Los Angeles in 1988, but that fall was suspended for two games after pine tar was discovered on his glove in Game 3 of the Championship Series against the Mets. Howell, who had not yielded a run for the last six weeks of the regular season, lost Game 1 of the NLCS and Game 3 of the World Series, then bounced back to earn the save in Game 4 against Oakland.

Howell topped 20 saves in his first two seasons as the Dodgers' closer, but suffered shoulder problems that cost him the job. He also suffered periodic elbow, knee, and back ailments. He finished his career with a year each in Atlanta and Texas.

Dick Howser

Howser, Richard Dalton **SS-2B**
1961–68 M(1978, 1980–86, 507–425) B:5/14/1936, Miami, FL D:6/17/1987, Kansas City, MO Deb:4/11/1961, KC AL BR/TR 5'8", 155

G	AB	R	H	HR	RBI	OBP	SLG	AVG
789	2483	398	617	16	165	.348	.318	.248

Dick Howser saw a potentially brilliant managerial career cut short by a fatal brain tumor. With the Yankees in 1980, Howser became only the fourth manager to win more than 100 games in his first full season as New York won the American League East with a 103–59 record. How did George Steinbrenner repay him? A forced resignation after the Royals swept the Yankees in the Championship Series was his reward.

Richard Dalton Howser was an All-America shortstop at Florida State University (and a friend of a Seminole halfback named Burt Reynolds) before signing with the Kansas City Athletics for a reported $21,000 bonus. In 1961 he hit .280 for the A's, made the All-Star team, and was named *The Sporting News* AL Rookie of the Year.

Injuries kept him from ever performing at that level again. Traded to Cleveland in 1963, he moved over to New York in 1966, and retired, at age 32, after playing 85 games for the Yankees in 1968. He stayed on as a coach for the next 10 seasons and spent a year as head coach at Florida State before returning to manage the Yankees in 1980.

Steinbrenner ordered Howser to fire his third base coach, Mike Ferraro, after New York was beaten in the 1980 ALCS. Ferraro had made the mistake of sending home Willie Randolph as the potential tying run late in Game 2 of the series. Randolph was out, and so was Howser when he wouldn't fire his friend.

Steinbrenner concocted the story that Howser was resigning in order to get back into real estate in Florida, but no one really believed it. Howser refused to get into a public sparring contest with Steinbrenner.

At one point Steinbrenner attempted to rescind the firing, but Howser refused to return. On August 31, 1981, he rejoined the managerial ranks, replacing Jim Frey as Royals manager. Kansas City won the second-half AL West title that strike-shortened year, but lost to the A's in the division playoffs.

After second-place finishes in 1982 and 1983, the Royals won the AL West in 1984. Sparky Anderson's Detroit Tigers swept them in the ALCS. In 1985 the Royals overcame three games to one deficits to win the pennant and World Series. After overtaking the Blue Jays in the first seven-game ALCS, Kansas City lost three of the first four World Series games to St. Louis before winning the last three games to claim the world championship.

In July 1986 Howser began to get painful headaches and a stiff neck. At the All-Star Game, as manager of the AL squad, he was "totally out of it," according to one friend. By the time the All-Star break ended, Howser was in a hospital undergoing tests. The results showed a tumor the size of a golf ball in the left frontal lobe of his brain, the area controlling speech and emotion.

Mike Ferraro, who had become a Royals coach, took over his friend's team. Howser had surgery in Kansas City on July 22. It revealed that the tumor, which was malignant, could not be entirely removed without endangering his ability to speak, so intensive radiation treatments were prescribed. On August 12 Howser was able to visit the Royals clubhouse.

That October general manager John Schuerholz announced that the Royals expected Howser to return in 1987. However, in December the doctors discovered that the tumor had grown, and a largely experimental operation, which involved the injection of millions of "killer cells," was performed.

On February 23, after two days back on the job, a weakened Howser retired again. After all the radiation and surgery, he weighed only 150 pounds. He was operated on again on March 20 and felt well enough to attend a few games, but he returned to St. Luke's Hospital on June 3 and died there on June 17. On July 10, 1987, Howser's No. 10 was permanently retired by the Royals.

Dummy Hoy

Hoy, William Ellsworth OF

1888–1902 B:5/23/1862, Houckstown, OH D:12/15/1961, Cincinnati, OH Deb:4/20/1888, WAS NL BL/TR 5'4", 144

G	AB	R	H	HR	RBI	OBP	SLG	AVG
1796	7112	1426	2044	40	726	.386	.373	.287

A deaf mute, William Ellsworth Hoy was called "Dummy," the usual nickname for such a person around the turn of the century—it was a crueler time. Hoy lost his hearing to meningitis as a baby. He attended the Ohio State School for the Deaf, completed grade school and high school in six years, and graduated as class valedictorian. He operated a small shoe repair shop in Houckstown, Ohio, until his weekend baseball play earned him a professional contract with Oshkosh in 1886. Two years later, he was in the major leagues.

Hoy played with a number of major league teams, spending his best seasons in Cincinnati. Only 5 feet 4 inches and 144 pounds, he was an extremely fast center fielder known for playing shallow. Offensively, he hit from the left side with little power. Most of his 40 career home runs were inside-the-park "tweeners." However, Hoy was a consistent .280 hitter, and his lack of size gave him a difficult strike zone. He led the American Association in walks in 1891 and the American League in the same category in 1901. In 14 major league seasons, he amassed 1,004 bases on balls.

His greatest weapon was his speed. As a rookie in 1888, Hoy led the National League in stolen bases (82) on his way to a career total of 594; many of them were recorded before 1898, when runners were credited with a steal whenever they took an extra base on a hit or an out. His career total can't be compared to modern records, but it does indicate his excellent baserunning. He scored 1,426 runs in 1,796 games.

According to some historians, umpires began using hand signals on balls and strikes for Hoy's benefit, but other evidence suggests that the practice began independently. After retiring from baseball, Hoy and his wife, a teacher of the deaf, lived on an Ohio farm. Their son, Carson, became a prominent Cincinnati jurist. In 1961, at age 99, the elder Hoy threw out the first ball in Game 3 of the World Series. He died later that year.

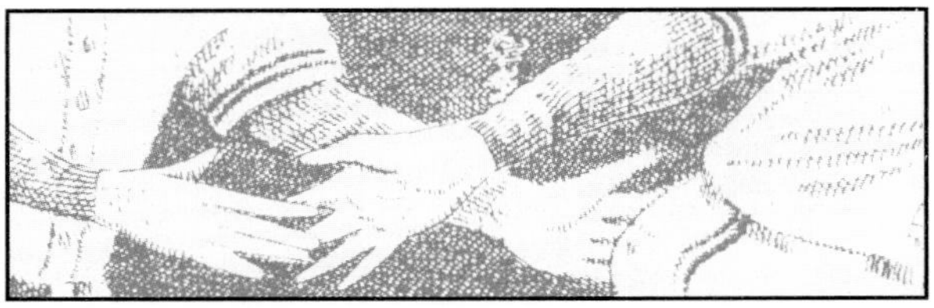

La Marr Hoyt

Hoyt, Dewey La Marr P

1979–86 B:1/1/1955, Columbia, SC Deb:9/14/1979, CHI AL BR/TR 6'1", 222

W	L	PCT	G	SV	IP	BB	SO	ERA
98	68	.590	244	10	1311^{1}	279	681	3.99

La Marr Hoyt was 28 when he won the American League Cy Young Award in 1983. He was supposedly in his prime, but three years later he was through, his career blown apart by alcohol and a flurry of drug-related incidents that landed him in federal prison.

Hoyt, a product of the Yankees farm system, went to the White Sox in April 1976 in the deal that sent Bucky Dent to the Bronx Bombers. It was not until 1980 that Hoyt joined the big league club on a permanent basis, and he went 9–3 that year as a starter. The next season, the righthander moved to the bullpen and went 9–3 with 10 saves. Inserted into the White Sox rotation in 1982, he won his first nine decisions, equaling the franchise record. He led the AL in victories with 19 and walked only 48 in 239⅔ innings.

The following season Hoyt was 24–10, including a 15–2 mark after the All-Star break, as the White Sox won the AL West. He issued only 31 walks in 260⅔ innings, approaching Cy Young's 1906 record of 25 in 287⅔ innings. In the ALCS he defeated Baltimore on a five-hitter in Game 1, although Chicago dropped the next three games. Hoyt outpointed Dan Quisenberry and Jack Morris for that year's Cy Young Award.

His decline was immediate. In 1984 he went 13–18 and surrendered 31 homers (second highest in the league), then was traded to San Diego for resilient shortstop Ozzie Guillen. Hoyt revived his career in 1985, going 16–8 and starting and winning the All-Star Game for the National League.

The next season everything came crashing down. On February 10, 1986, he was arrested by customs officials at the Mexican border for the possession of marijuana, Valium, and a knife; he was fined $620. On February 18 San Diego police stopped his car at 12:50 a.m. and found a switchblade and a small quantity (less than an ounce) of marijuana. In late February Hoyt left the Padres spring training camp to enter an alcohol rehab program. He returned in March, and in April was fined $375 and given three years' probation for the February 18 incident.

He pitched just 159 innings that season, going 8–11 with a 5.15 ERA. On October 28 he was again arrested at the Mexican border. This time he was carrying 500 sleeping pills and a small quantity of marijuana.

In December he was convicted of federal drug violations. He was sentenced to 45 days in jail and $5,025 fine. The court also seized his Porsche. Upon his release from prison, Commissioner Peter Ueberroth suspended Hoyt for one year, but the Padres raised the stakes by giving him his unconditional release, contending he had violated the terms of his contract. (The contract still had three years remaining and was worth $3.2 million.)

The Players Association disputed the Padres' decision, and on June 16, 1987, arbitrator George Nicolau ruled that the team's actions were illegal. He also reduced Hoyt's suspension to 60 days, writing: "There is not a sliver of evidence that he sold, distributed, or facilitated the distribution of drugs at any time." He contended that Hoyt was suffering from a sleep disorder and had to go to Mexico to obtain pills for it.

Even though they had to honor his contract, the Padres didn't want Hoyt back. The White Sox signed him to a minor league contract but soon discovered he had a bum shoulder.

In December 1987 Hoyt was arrested again and charged with possession of cocaine with intent to distribute. In January 1988 Hoyt was sentenced to one year in prison for violating the terms of his parole. A month later he was given a second sentence for the drug possession, to be served concurrently with the first. He entered Allenwood Federal Prison on February 22, 1988, at age 33.

Waite Hoyt

Hoyt, Waite Charles **P**

1918–38 B:9/9/1899, Brooklyn, NY D:8/25/1984, Cincinnati, OH Deb:7/24/1918, NY NL BR/TR 6', 180

W	L	PCT	G	SV	IP	BB	SO	ERA
237	182	.566	674	52	3762¹	1003	1206	3.59

From 1921 to 1928, when the Yankees won half a dozen pennants and three world championships, righthanded pitcher Waite Hoyt won 145 of their 750 regular-season victories and six of their 18 World Series games. He won 157 games in nine years as a Yankee and 237 during his 20-year Hall of Fame career.

The son of a professional minstrel, Hoyt threw three no-hitters at Brooklyn's Erasmus Hall High School and was pitching batting practice at the Polo Grounds at age 15. Growing weary of the long subway ride to the ballpark each day, Hoyt asked for compensation, and Giants manager John McGraw snapped, "Get this boy a contract," making Hoyt one of the youngest players ever to turn professional. There was no talk of a bonus, but after Hoyt's father signed the contract for the minor, he was handed a $5 bill.

The Giants sent Hoyt to Mount Carmel of the Pennsylvania State League, and later that same season he pitched for Hartford and Lynn of the Eastern League. After bouncing from Memphis and Montreal to Nashville and Newark, he made his major league debut in 1918. He struck out two of the three batters he faced and was dubbed "the Schoolboy Wonder."

The Giants, unimpressed, peddled him to Rochester for outfielder Ross Youngs and infielder George Kelly. Hoyt refused to report, however, and instead pitched with the Baltimore Dry Docks in a shipyard semipro league. After he shut out the Cincinnati Reds in an exhibition game, the Red Sox acquired his contract. Following two unremarkable seasons in Boston he was traded to the Yankees in an eight-player transaction that reunited him with former Red Sox teammate Babe Ruth.

Hoyt could carouse with the notoriously libertine Babe, but he always admired what the Bambino had done for baseball. "Babe Ruth found baseball lying in the gutter as a result of the Chicago White Sox World Series scandal in 1919," Hoyt said. "He reached down with his bat and lifted it to the status of America's national pastime."

Together they helped make the Yankees the most successful sports franchise in America. Hoyt pitched 27 innings without allowing an earned run in the 1921 World Series, winning two and losing one. In 1927 he led the AL in victories and in win percentage and followed that with a 23-win season in which he also paced the league in saves with eight.

Hoyt was reasonably well paid for his labors, with a salary of $16,000 (plus a bonus) in 1927 and $17,500 (plus a $2,500 bonus) in 1928, but he augmented his income in unusual ways. In the late 1920s he appeared in vaudeville, dancing and singing in a fine baritone voice. He also went into business as a mortician and once said of his two off-season careers, "I'm knocking 'em dead on Seventh Avenue while my partner is laying 'em out up in Westchester."

"The Merry Mortician" left New York after a disagreement with manager Bob Shawkey over how to pitch to Al Simmons. In 1931 Hoyt joined Simmons on the Philadelphia Athletics. He pitched his final World Series game that year, losing Game 5 to the Cardinals. Hoyt worked for several other big league clubs, ending up back in Brooklyn with the Dodgers, and was finally released in May 1938. He spent the rest of that year with the semipro Brooklyn Bushwicks.

When Babe Ruth passed away in 1948, Hoyt was one of 56 honorary pallbearers at St. Patrick's Cathedral. It was a sweltering summer day, and "Jumping Joe" Dugan whispered to Hoyt, "I'd give anything for a cold beer."

Hoyt responded, "So would the Babe."

By then Hoyt had become a successful broadcaster. As early as September 1927 he had his own program on NBC in New York and in 1938 landed a show called *Grandstand and Bandstand* on New York's WNEW. His big break came in January 1942, when Cincinnati's Burger Brewing Company signed him to broadcast Reds games. He stayed there for a quarter century and became a Cincinnati legend, particularly for his fabled rain-delay tales.

"Waite Hoyt is authoritative," Russ Hodges said of his colleague's broadcasting style. "When he makes a statement there is no doubt as to its accuracy. When Hoyt says it's so, the Cincinnati public goes by what he says."

When he received the news that he was to be inducted into the Hall of Fame in 1969, Hoyt was "shaking all over, and crying at the same time."

Al Hrabosky

Hrabosky, Alan Thomas **P**

1970–82 B:7/21/1949, Oakland, CA Deb:6/16/1970, STL NL BR/TL 5'11", 185

W	L	PCT	G	SV	IP	BB	SO	ERA
64	35	.646	545	97	722	315	548	3.10

Al Hrabosky, alias "the Mad Hungarian," was a power pitcher who did major psyche jobs—on opposing hitters and on himself. Before facing each batter the stone-faced relief pitcher with the threatening Fu Manchu mustache would stand at the back of the mound and meditate for a few seconds, then he would pound his glove, turn around, ascend the mound, and almost always blow fastballs past the hitters. He pitched for 13 years in the major leagues, compiling a 64–35 record, with 97 saves.

Hrabosky made his major league debut in 1970 with the Cardinals, but it wasn't until 1974 that he took on the persona of "the Mad Hungarian." He explained, "When I was in a jam, I'd walk off the mound and I'd say to myself, strictly to myself, something like, 'One, two, three, let's get this next guy,' and very often that would generate enough energy to get the ball past the hitter."

In response to these meditations, Cardinals public relations director Jerry Lovelace gave Hrabosky his famed nickname. "That new approach did wonders for me," Hrabosky admitted. "I ended up 8–1 with an ERA of 2.95 and I had a stretch where I gave up only one run in 47 innings."

While most pitchers like the support of the fans at home, Hrabosky relished road appearances. "When I'm on the road, my greatest ambition is to get a standing boo," Hrabosky said. In 1975 Hrabosky went 13–3 with a league-leading 22 saves, a 1.66 ERA, and a league-leading 21 pitching runs. He was named NL Fireman of the Year.

In 1977 he balked when manager Vern Rapp banned facial hair. "How can I intimidate batters if I look like a goddamn golf pro?" he asked. After the season, the Cardinals traded him to Kansas City for Mark Littell and Buck Martinez. In 1978 Hrabosky contributed 20 saves to help the Royals to an American League West title.

In November 1979 he signed a contract with Ted Turner's Braves for $1.7 million that would pay him over a 30-year span: the gimmick assured him of a job after his playing days ended. He later became a clean-shaven broadcaster for the Cardinals.

Kent Hrbek

Hrbek, Kent Alan **1B–DH**

1981–94 B:5/21/1960, Minneapolis, MN Deb:8/24/1981, MIN AL BL/TR 6'4", 235

G	AB	R	H	HR	RBI	OBP	SLG	AVG
1747	6192	903	1749	293	1086	.370	.481	.282

In December 1989, during contract negotiations with Minnesota Twins general manager Andy MacPhail, Kent Hrbek said he had an offer from the Detroit Tigers for approximately $1.5 million above the $14 million MacPhail was willing to pay. Hrbek wound up signing a five-year contract with the Twins for $15 million.

Immensely popular with his home-state fans, Hrbek finished his career second in Twins history behind the immortal Harmon Killebrew. An intense competitor who balanced a career in baseball with a passion for hunting and fishing, Hrbek was an integral part of the Minnesota teams that captured two World Series crowns. He was runner-up to the Detroit Tigers' Willie Hernandez for American League Most Valuable Player in 1984, and he finished his career as the most prolific indoor home run hitter in major league history.

Hrbek also left the game with some disappointments and one dubious record. Despite twice leading major league first basemen in fielding percentage, Hrbek never won a Gold Glove Award, and his only All-Star Game appearance came in his rookie season. His postseason play never matched his regular-season prowess; his combined batting average for the playoffs and the World Series was .154, the lowest on record for a player with at least 75 at bats. He did, however, hit a World Series grand slam.

An outstanding all-around athlete at Kennedy High in Bloomington, Minnesota, Hrbek appeared to be headed for a baseball scholarship with the University of Minnesota in 1978. Instead, he was drafted by the Twins in the 17th round—a nod to a local hero. Ron Simon, Hrbek's agent throughout his career, wanted $30,000 for Hrbek to sign; Twins scouts doubted that the chunky first baseman was worth that much, but someone convinced the team's owner, spendthrift Calvin Griffith, to take a look at Hrbek in an American Legion contest. Hrbek put on a clinic at the plate and signed with the Twins the next day.

Hrbek's minor league career was undistinguished until 1981, when he hit .379 for Visalia in the California League and was called up to the parent club in August. His major league debut set the tone for his career: after singling off New York Yankees' Tommy John in the fifth inning, he homered off of George Frazier in the 12th to give the Twins a 3–2 victory.

In his first year in the majors Hrbek hit .301 with 23 homers and finished second to Baltimore's Cal Ripken in Rookie of the Year voting. He was the only rookie named to the 1982 AL All-Star team. That same year, Hrbek's father, Ed, died of amyotrophic lateral sclerosis (Lou Gehrig's Disease). Kent later said that his only regret was that his father never saw him play in the World Series.

After hitting a career-high five triples and 41 doubles in 1983, Hrbek signed a six-year, $5.9-million contract during the off-season. The Twins had struggled to a fifth-place finish in the AL West that year, but with the addition of Kirby Puckett the following season, they had assembled the squad that would capture the World Series crown three years later.

Hrbek hit consistently throughout the mid-1980s. He had a career year in 1984, when he recorded a .311 average, 27 home runs, and 107 RBIs. His sole 100-RBI season made him the first Twins player in seven years to achieve that plateau. He belted his 100th career home run in 1986 against Bret Saberhagen of the Kansas City Royals, one day after the only five-hit game of his career.

The 1987 season was a tumultuous one for Minnesota, culminating in the Twins' seven-game triumph over the St. Louis Cardinals in the World Series. In July, Hrbek, angered at being left off the All-Star team, vowed never to play in an All-Star Game. He finished the season with a career-best 34 homers. In October Hrbek batted just .167 in 48 postseason at bats, but he belted a grand slam in the sixth inning to capture Game 6 and send the Series to a seventh game.

In 1988 Hrbek led all major league first basemen with a .997 fielding percentage and hit .312, sixth best in the league. The following year he reached 200 career homers, becoming the fourth Twin ever to do so. He also suffered the first of several shoulder injuries when he dislocated his left shoulder while diving for a grounder. He nevertheless managed to hit 25 homers and collect 84 RBIs. In 1990 he again led league first basemen in fielding percentage. That season he also fractured his ankle in "clubhouse horseplay"—typical of the ebullient Hrbek. Luckily, the mishap occurred in the closing weeks of the season.

The 1991 campaign was Hrbek's last big season, and it ended with one of the most thrilling World Series in history. Hitting well in the clutch all season, Hrbek posted the best average in the majors (.377) with two outs and runners on base. However, his production plummeted again in the playoffs, as he went only 3-for-21 (.143) against the Toronto Blue Jays in the Championship Series and 3-for-26 (.115) with six strikeouts in seven games against the Atlanta Braves in the World Series. In a Series packed with unforgettable moments, Hrbek doubled (some said "shoved") Ron Gant off first in Game 2. Minnesota took the championship with a gripping 1–0, 10-inning victory at home in Game 7.

Shoulder injuries again shortened Hrbek's season in 1992, and he struggled through the season. He injured his right shoulder in August and underwent arthroscopic surgery a month later. By the following year it had become clear that time was running out for the local boy. Although Hrbek rebounded to hit 25 home runs with 83 RBIs in 1993, he also posted the lowest batting average of his career.

After becoming the second Twins player ever to reach 1,000 career RBIs in 1993, Hrbek began dropping hints that 1994 would be his last year. Before the strike ended his last season, Hrbek upped his career home run mark to 293, moved past Rod Carew into third place on the Twins' all-time list for doubles, and advanced to second place in games played for Minnesota.

For a 17th-round draft pick, Hrbek's achievements had far surpassed the scout's predictions, but his postseason slumps and his unsung fielding skills left a sense of might-have-been about his 13-year career, as Twins manager Tom Kelly acknowledged on his radio program on the day of Hrbek's retirement. "Injuries have kept him from winning a Gold Glove," Kelly claimed, "and from going to the Hall of Fame."

In 1998 future Minnesota Governor Jesse Ventura asked Hrbek to be his running mate. Hrbek declined, saying that holding the Lieutenant Governor's post would have taken too much time away from hunting, fishing, and bowling.

Walt Hriniak

Hriniak, Walter John **C**

1968–69 B:5/22/1943, Natick, MA Deb:9/10/68, ATL NL
BL/TR 5'11", 180

G	AB	R	H	HR	RBI	OBP	SLG	AVG
47	99	4	25	0	4	.333	.253	.253

Walt Hriniak had only 25 big league hits, but was responsible for thousands more during his career as a hitting coach. A promising shortstop before an auto accident derailed his career, Hriniak finally made it the major leagues as a catcher for limited action in 1968 and 1969.

Hriniak returned to the majors as a coach with the Montreal Expos in 1974, then joined the Boston Red Sox as bullpen coach in 1977. He became known for his knowledge of hitting, serving as "unofficial batting coach" to Carl Yastrzemski and Carlton Fisk. Hriniak espoused theories taught by legendary Charlie Lau, and worked tirelessly with willing pupils. His efforts with Dwight Evans and Wade Boggs helped turn them into two of the best hitters of the 1980s. When Hriniak moved to the Chicago White Sox in 1989 he tutored another star hitter in Frank Thomas.

Hitting greats such as Ted Williams and Ralph Kiner criticized Hriniak for his theories, and many players didn't appreciate his taskmaster approach. "All he wants is hard work," Boggs said. "That's where he gets the bad rap: from the guys who don't want to work."

Cal Hubbard

Hubbard, Robert Calvin
Umpire (1936–51) B:10/31/1900, Keyteville, MO
D:10/17/1970, St. Petersburg, FL 6'2½", 265

Cal Hubbard was the first person to hold simultaneous membership in three shrines: the National College Football Hall of Fame, the Pro Football Hall of Fame, and the Baseball Hall of Fame. The 6-foot 2½-inch, 265-pound giant first achieved national prominence as a tackle, end, and linebacker under coach Alvin "Bo" McMillin at tiny Centenary College. When McMillin moved on to equally small Geneva in 1925, Hubbard went with him and, in his senior year, the little school upset Harvard.

Hubbard, who graduated in 1927 with a bachelor of arts degree, signed to play with the New York Giants of the National Football League. As a rookie, he spearheaded a rock-ribbed defense that took New York to its first National Football League championship; he later helped the Green Bay Packers win three titles.

He began umpiring baseball games with the Piedmont League in 1928, then advanced through the Western Association and International League before joining the American League staff in 1936. His consummate knowledge of the rule book and commanding presence led several veteran AL umpires to term him the best freshman umpire they had ever seen.

Hubbard umpired four World Series—1938, 1942, 1946, and 1949—and three All-Star Games—1939, 1944, and 1949. He was forced to retire as an active umpire in 1951 when a shotgun pellet ricocheted off a rock and into his left eye, causing blurred vision. He became assistant supervisor of AL umpires and, when Tom Connolly retired in 1954, he was promoted to supervisor, a post he held until 1970.

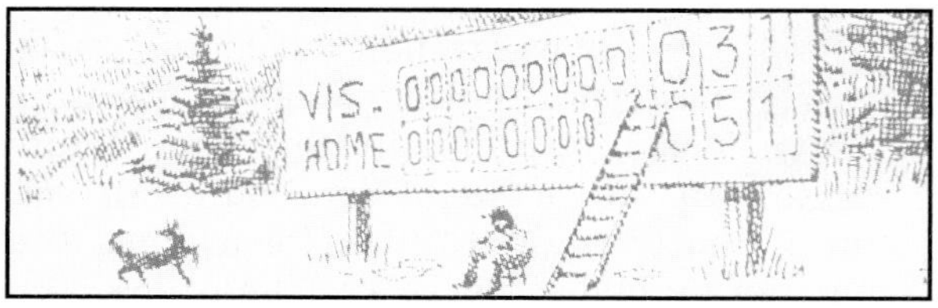

Hubbard had a unique umpiring style. When Yogi Berra complained about big Cal's ball-and-strike calls, Hubbard leaned close to his ear and said, "There's just no sense in both of us umpiring this game. The unfortunate part of the situation, from your standpoint, is that I'm being paid to stand behind the plate and umpire. You're not. You're only being paid to catch. One of us is obviously unnecessary and has to go. It breaks my heart to say so, but the guy who's gonna go is you."

Hubbard was in the inaugural class in the Pro Football Hall of Fame in 1963. He was enshrined in the Baseball Hall of Fame six years after his death in 1976.

Glenn Hubbard

Hubbard, Glenn Dee **2B**
1978–89 B:9/25/1957, Hahn Air Force Base, Germany
Deb:7/14/1978, ATL NL BR/TR 5'7", 180

G	AB	R	H	HR	RBI	OBP	SLG	AVG
1354	4441	545	1084	70	448	.330	.349	.244

A slick-fielding second baseman in his prime, Hubbard played most of his 12-year career with the Atlanta Braves. Hubbard had a career .983 fielding percentage and led National League second basemen in double plays three times and in assists twice.

Hubbard had his best overall season in 1983 when he batted .263 with a career-high 12 homers and 70 RBIs and was selected to the league All-Star team. A throwback to the old era, Hubbard wore a beard much of his career and was regarded as a gritty, aggressive player not afraid to hold his ground at second base while turning a double play. On April 14, 1985, he tied the nine-inning record for most assists in a game by a second baseman, with 12. He was also a proficient bunter and led the majors in sacrifices in 1982.

After his All-Star 1983 season, however, Hubbard's skills seemed to decline significantly as he failed to hit above .235 in any of the next three seasons. He enjoyed a comeback season of sorts in 1987 when he batted a career-high .264. In January 1988 Hubbard left the Braves and signed with the Oakland A's as a free agent. He started at second for the 1988 American League champion A's and was 3-for-12 in the World Series against the Los Angeles Dodgers. The next year, relegated to backup status, he hit just .198 in 53 games and subsequently retired.

Carl Hubbell

Hubbell, Carl Owen **P**

1928–43 B:6/22/1903, Carthage, MO D:11/21/1988, Scottsdale, AZ Deb:7/26/1928, NY NL BR/TL 6', 170

W	L	PCT	G	SH	IP	BB	SO	ERA
253	154	.622	535	36	3590^1	725	1677	2.98

Carl Hubbell was nicknamed "the Meal Ticket" because that's what he was to the New York Giants and manager John McGraw during his career. Hubbell earned two Most Valuable Player Awards on the strength of a screwball that was supposed to be a sinker. He is best remembered for the 1934 All-Star Game during which he struck out future Hall of Fame sluggers Babe Ruth, Lou Gehrig, Jimmie Foxx, Al Simmons, and Joe Cronin in succession.

Hubbell didn't throw a screwball in high school, and the rest of his arsenal didn't interest baseball scouts, but Hubbell refused to give up. Persistence paid off, and he caught on with the Class D Oklahoma State League's Cushing Refiners. In June 1924 the circuit collapsed, and by season's end Hubbell was with the Class A Western League's Oklahoma City Indians. There Hubbell met an older pitcher named Lefty Thomas who worked with him on developing a sinker. As Hubbell tinkered with the new delivery he kept turning his wrist farther and farther over, and as he did he developed an entirely new pitch—the screwball.

The Detroit Tigers purchased him at the close of the 1925 season. "You talk about somebody that was up in the clouds!" said Hubbell. "I couldn't wait until next spring when I'd go into training with Detroit." Then the Tigers told him not to throw the screwball and never put him in a game. "I never pitched one inning of an exhibition game for Detroit in three years! Three years!" said Hubbell. "I pitched batting practice a lot of the time, and they held on to me, farming me out every year."

Hubbell was about ready to leave Organized Baseball and take a job in the oil business. "Financially, I would have been just as well off working for the oil company, and I just felt that I had no future with the Tigers," he explained. "I told Claude Robinson, the Beaumont manager, that I wouldn't go back to the Detroit club and that unless I could be sold to some other major league club I would quit baseball at the end of the year. It was then Dick Kinsella came along and arranged for the New York Giants to buy me."

Kinsella was a longtime scout for John McGraw and was in Houston for the 1928 Democratic National Convention with orders to cast his ballot for New York Governor Alfred E. Smith. One afternoon though, the speeches were even duller than usual, so Kinsella went out to the Houston ballpark. There he witnessed a terrific duel between Hubbell and the ace of the Houston staff, "Wild Bill" Hallahan.

Hubbell's performance so excited Kinsella that he got on the phone to McGraw, telling him, "This afternoon I saw another Art Nehf. Fellow pitching for Beaumont. He worked against Hallahan and beat him, 1–0, in 11 innings." McGraw answered, "Send him along immediately." On July 16, 1928, the Giants purchased Hubbell from the Beaumont Exporters.

Promoted to New York, Hubbell didn't use the screwball until a game against the Cardinals. "I was in a jam with men on base and Chick Hafey at bat, and when the count got to three and one on him, I was plenty worried," said Hubbell. "Shanty Hogan was catching and he signaled for a fastball. I threw Chick a screwball and it fooled him. Shanty gave me the fastball sign again and I threw another screwball and struck Hafey out."

Hogan encouraged Hubbell to stick with the pitch, and Hubbell became "King Carl," eventually leading the National League in ERA and victories three times and in won-lost percentage twice. He registered five consecutive 20-game seasons, and with his excellent control he walked less than two batters per nine innings of work. For seven seasons he enjoyed the lowest opponent on-base percentage in the league. He was named to nine All-Star teams. His success all came from the screwball, which Hubbell threw at the same speed as his fastball, thus giving him a real advantage over batters. He threw it so often that his left arm turned inward.

On May 8, 1929, Hubbell no-hit the Pittsburgh Pirates. In 1933 he helped pitch the Giants to the pennant by leading the league in both victories and ERA. From July 13 to August 1 of that year he recorded $46\frac{1}{3}$ consecutive scoreless innings, a 20th century achievement topped in the NL only by Don Drysdale and Orel Hershiser. At the Polo Grounds on July 6, 1933, Hubbell defeated St. Louis, 1–0, in 18 innings and struck out 12. That year he was named the NL's Most Valuable Player.

In the 1933 World Series, Hubbell was awesome. He struck out the first three Washington Senators to face him and pitched 20 consecutive innings without allowing an earned run. He won Game 1, 4–2, and the 11-inning Game 4, 2–1.

A year later Hubbell was selected to start the All-Star Game, and as great a pitcher as he was, he was nervous about the assignment. "You wait around, and sit on the bench, and then you walk up and down," recalled Hubbell, "and you finally get out there, and naturally you have nervous energy built up, and you try to throw the ball harder than you usually do."

He began by surrendering a hit to Charlie Gehringer and walking Heinie Manush. Then Hubbell bore down and struck out Babe Ruth, Lou Gehrig, and Jimmie Foxx to end the inning. In the next inning Hubbell started off by fanning Al Simmons and Joe Cronin. Bill Dickey broke the skein of five straight strikeouts by singling, but Hubbell's dominance of the game's greats remains remarkable. "I got every one of them on a screwball," said Hubbell. "I figured they'd hit better fastballs than mine and better curves. If they were going to hit me, it would have to be my best. Oh, I showed them the other pitches, but not where they could get a good swing at them. The third strike on every one of them was a screwball."

Yet that may not have been his most remarkable feat in baseball. From July 18, 1936, through the end of the season Hubbell recorded 16 straight victories and captured his second MVP Award. He then started off 1937 by notching eight more consecutive wins before losing to the Dodgers in the first game of a Memorial Day doubleheader.

During the late 1930s Hubbell began to wear down, beset by bone chips probably caused by the screwball's unnatural motion, but he still had one more remarkable game left in him. The game that Carl Hubbell regarded as his best was not his no-hitter but a one-hitter he recorded at Ebbets Field on Memorial Day, 1940.

The only hit he allowed was a looper batted just over his head in the sixth by John "Mr. Chips" Hudson. Hudson was erased when the next batter hit into a double play. "Control made that the most memorable game for me," said Hubbell. "Every pitch went where I wanted it to go. I never had such control before or afterward. I can't explain it. I made only 81 pitches. I faced only 27 batters and only three balls were hit to the outfield."

In December 1943 Giants owner Horace Stoneham named Hubbell farm director of the club, a post Hubbell held until 1977, when he became a scout for San Francisco. In 1947 King Carl Hubbell was elected to the Hall of Fame.

Ken Hubbs

Hubbs, Kenneth Douglas **2B**
1961–63 B:12/23/1941, Riverside, CA D:2/13/1964, Provo, UT Deb:9/10/1961, CHI NL BR/TR 6'2", 175

G	AB	R	H	HR	RBI	OBP	SLG	AVG
324	1255	148	310	14	98	.292	.336	.247

In 1962 Cubs rookie second baseman Ken Hubbs got the attention of the baseball world when he handled 148 consecutive chances in the field without an error, led the National League in fielding at his position, hit a solid .260, and was named Rookie of the Year.

Hubbs signed as an outfielder and switched to third base in his second minor league season. In 1961 he was moved to second, where he was instantly impressive, earning a late-season call-up to the Cubs. His batting average fell off to .235 in 1963 when he suffered from the sophomore jinx, but his fielding continued to impress. The Cubs picked up a remarkable 23 games in the standings to finish at 82–80, their first season above .500 since 1946.

The youthful Cubs, whose lineup included such emerging stars as Ron Santo, Billy Williams, Lou Brock, and pitcher Dick Ellsworth, seemed ready to make a run for the pennant.

At the end of the season, Hubbs began to take flying lessons. He received his license in February 1964 and soon flew with his friend Dennis Doyle from California to Provo, Utah, to visit Doyle's in-laws. On February 15, only a week before spring training, Hubbs and Doyle took off in a snowstorm to return home. They never made it. Five miles into the flight the plane crashed into Utah Lake, killing both men. Hubbs was only 22 years old.

Willis Hudlin

Hudlin, George Willis **P**
1926–40, 1944 B:5/23/1906, Wagoner, OK Deb:8/15/1926, CLE AL BR/TR 6', 190

W	L	PCT	G	SV	IP	BB	SO	ERA
158	156	.503	491	31	2613^{1}	846	677	4.41

Willis "Ace" Hudlin employed a sidearm sinkerball as a workhorse on Cleveland's staff for 15 seasons. Never a 20-game winner, he nonetheless won 18 in his rookie season of 1927 for a sixth-place club.

Because he had excelled in baseball, track, and football in high school, George Willis Hudlin was offered four college scholarships. Instead, in 1926 he signed with the Texas League's last-place Waco Cubs, going 16–11 with a 4.32 ERA, before earning a promotion to Cleveland. From 1927 to 1929 he was especially effective against the Yankees, winning 14 games against the club.

Hudlin was once walked twice in the same inning. He accomplished that feat in the sixth inning of a July 6, 1931, contest. Through 1999 he remained high in several Indians club career categories: third in games, third in losses, fourth in innings pitched, sixth in walks, and seventh in victories. Hudlin, who pitched for four clubs in 1940, spent 1942 through 1944 in the armed service. He attempted a comeback with the St. Louis Browns in late 1944, but it proved fruitless.

He coached for the Tigers from 1957 to 1959. He later scouted for the White Sox, operating out of Little Rock.

Miller Huggins

Huggins, Miller James **2B**

1904–16 M(1913–29, 1,413–1,134) B:3/27/1879, Cincinnati, OH D:9/25/1929, New York, NY Deb:4/15/1904, CIN NL BB/TR 5'6½", 140

G	AB	R	H	HR	RBI	OBP	SLG	AVG
1586	5558	948	1474	9	318	.382	.314	.265

The casual baseball fan might figure the Yankees of the 1920s were a snap to manage. How could you lose if you put Babe Ruth, Lou Gehrig, Tony Lazzeri, Earle Combs, and Bob Meusel on the field every day? But the casual fan may not realize that when Miller Huggins was named the team's manager in 1918, the Bronx club had never won an American League pennant.

From the time the franchise moved from Baltimore to New York in 1903 until Huggins arrived, the club had gone through three names—Orioles to Highlanders to Yankees—and had only two second-place finishes to show for it. Their more likely position was in the second division, where they had been 10 times. Even after Huggins arrived in New York, he had to wrestle with players who sported huge egos and lived the high life. His method of dominating this talented, but unruly, cast of characters is what earned him a place in the Hall of Fame.

The petite Huggins, called "the Mighty Mite" on occasion and "Rabbit" on others, was not a particularly likable man. He suffered from a variety of annoying ailments for most of his life. He was famous for trying to scream his players into better play; his temper tantrums were legendary. He was an uncanny analyst of baseball talent, however, and when that knowledge met the deep pockets of Colonels Tillinghast L'Hommedieu Huston and Jacob Ruppert, they were able to construct one of the greatest teams in the game's history.

Huggins maximized the value of his limited skills through intelligence. As writer George Will noted, five major league managers have had law degrees, and four of them (Huggins, Hughie Jennings, John Ward, and Branch Rickey) are in the Hall of Fame. The fifth, Tony La Russa, had six division titles and remained active through 1999.

In addition to brains, Huggins had good hands. As a second baseman, he led the National League in putouts, assists, and fielding percentage for second baggers once each during his 13 playing seasons. Biographer A.D. Suehsdorf notes: "His record is dotted with games in which he handled 15 chances or figured in three double plays." Although not a strong hitter, passing the .300 mark only once, he used his 5 feet 6½ inches to his advantage and coaxed walks from opposing pitchers. He led the NL in walks four times and in on-base percentage once. He was referred to as the perfect leadoff man. And when he got on he could steal; he pilfered 30 sacks or more six times.

After six years with the Cincinnati Reds, studying the game under legendary manager Ned Hanlon, Huggins moved to the Cardinals in 1910. That year he set a record by making six plate appearances without recording an official at bat—he walked four times and sacrificed twice. Huggins was widely considered one of the smartest players in the game; some say he invented the delayed steal. Cardinals owner Helene Hathaway Robison Britton didn't like the brash antics of her manager, Roger Bresnahan, and replaced him with Huggins as player-manager in 1913.

Huggins was quick with a trick. While stationed in the third base coaching box during a 1915 game against the Dodgers, with a Cardinal on third and one out, he hollered to rookie hurler Ed Appleton, "Hey you! Let me see that ball." The Dodger obligingly made a soft toss in Huggins' direction. Huggins ducked the throw, and the runner scored for the Cardinals. Since then the rules have been changed to prevent a repeat of such an occurrence, but it worked in 1915.

In 1917 Rogers Hornsby showed up in St. Louis. Huggins had farmed him out for lack of hitting two years earlier, but Hornsby, 25 pounds heavier, hit like crazy. Huggins wisely turned over his second base spot to the rookie to become a full-time bench manager.

Huggins' intelligence showed in other ways. He was a prudent investor in the stock market. When St. Louis owner Britton wanted out, Huggins put together a group to buy the team. Other owners were fearful of "absentee ownership" or that Huggins might want to move the team, so they found a local group to make the purchase. Huggins resigned as manager.

At that time Ruppert and Huston were looking for a new skipper to turn the Yankees around. AL president Ban Johnson recommended Huggins, but, fearful of reprisals, he solicited the new editor of *The Sporting News*, J.G. Taylor Spink, to sound him out. The story goes that "the Mite" showed up for an interview with the Yankees wearing a cloth cap, which offended the New Yorkers' highfalutin sensibilities. But his baseball knowledge was so prodigious that he was given the job, chapeau notwithstanding.

The Yanks moved up from sixth to fourth in their first year under Huggins. In 1919 they advanced to third. Huggins was active in seeking out the players he wanted, and his ownership was happy to obtain the talent for him. A key acquisition that season was notorious submarine pitcher Carl Mays, one of several former Boston players who came to New York.

Late in 1919 Huggins recommended that the Yankees try to get Babe Ruth from Boston. When

Sox owner Harry Frazee requested $100,000 for Ruth, Ruppert told Huggins that Frazee was "crazy." Huggins agreed: "He's crazy all right, for letting you have him for that little amount of money." When the Ruth deal was made late in 1919, it was not announced until Huggins could travel to California to meet with the superstar.

Huggins wanted to give Ruth a speech about the merits of moral life in the big city; all Ruth wanted to know was how much money the colonels were willing to pay. The animosity between Ruth and Huggins had begun. The Babe couldn't see how such a small man had become so powerful in baseball; Huggins saw the star as a super talent totally devoid of discipline. In 1920 Ruth slugged 54 homers, but the Yanks finished three games back of the Indians, in third place.

Seeing a need for pitching, Huggins landed Waite Hoyt for the 1921 season. Ruth hit 59 homers and the Yankees won their first pennant. By that year only four men remained from the 1918 aggregation that Huggins had taken over. The Yanks' first World Series experience was not a happy one. Mays, after tossing a shutout in Game 1, was defeated twice in subsequent outings by the New York Giants. John McGraw's club, the landlord of the Polo Grounds, defeated the tenant Yankees in five of eight games. Huggins never forgave Mays for his two losses. Years later Huggins told writer Fred Lieb, "Any ballplayer that played for me...could come to me if he were in need and I would give him a helping hand...with two exceptions, Carl Mays and Joe Bush. If they were in the gutter, I'd kick them." Bush's crime was to disobey Huggins' orders during the 1922 World Series, which the Yanks also lost to the Giants.

During that off-season Huggins suggested that 28-year-old Ruth's career might be over; fast-and-free living had gotten the better of "the Bambino," Huggins hypothesized. The embarrassed Ruth worked himself into shape and came back strong in 1923.

The simmering dispute between Mays and Huggins boiled over in 1923. Although Mays was the team's highest-paid pitcher, the unforgiving Huggins saw fit to use him only 23 times that year. During one game he kept Mays in for a complete-game 13–0 drubbing by the Indians. The Yankees opened their new stadium that year, and they extracted revenge from the Giants in the World Series, finally taking McGraw's men in six games. Mays did not pitch in the World Series and was released before the 1924 season began.

The Yankees finished 1924 two games behind Walter Johnson and the Senators, but they led the league in parties, with Ruth the head celebrator. Babe's excesses in 1925 spring training led to his hospitalization. Huggins berated him during a train trip that July, but Ruth responded by dangling his manager by the heels over the railing. On August 29, Ruth, then batting only .245, was late for batting practice again; Huggins stopped him from going out on the field. The manager called in the rest of the players and announced that Ruth was being fined $5,000 (10 times more than any team had ever fined a player) and suspended indefinitely.

Ruth was furious, and vowed to get Huggins fired. Ruppert would have none of it. He announced that Huggins, not Ruth, was running the team. Ruth snarled and whined, but he finally gave in and apologized. (The $5,000 was returned to him after Huggins' death four years later.) Ruth, always in character, told a reporter: "Confidentially—and you can print this—Miller Huggins is dumb."

With his brazen power play, Huggins had finally established control of the team. He would continue to quarrel and quibble with Ruth almost daily, but there was no longer any doubt about who was in charge.

In 1926 the Yankees began a three-year reign over baseball. They won pennants every year and took the 1927 and 1928 World Series without losing a game. Writer John Kieran explained Huggins' contribution to the 1926 team: "Six of the eight regulars on that team were men who had never played on any other major league team. Except for Ruth in right field and [Joe] Dugan at third base, the players were men who had been picked from the minors by Yankee scouts and developed into a championship array by a Yankee manager. In winning his first three pennants, Huggins had shown he knew how to buy. Now he showed he knew how to build."

In 1926 Mark Koenig and Tony Lazzeri joined the team. In 1928 Huggins scouted and signed Bill Dickey. The manager demanded that Dickey quit trying to be Ruth and Gehrig, shorten his swing, and hit line drives. Dickey obeyed and finished his major league career 17 years later with the second-highest lifetime average of any catcher. Huggins also brought along a scrappy young shortstop and showed him how a "little guy" could be a winner. The shortstop, Leo Durocher, never forgot what Huggins had to say.

Huggins' poor health was noticeably worse in 1929, and it wasn't helped when friends took his advice about investing in a land deal, only to have it turn sour. The pasty-faced Huggins entered the hospital on September 22. At first he was diagnosed as having influenza, but closer observation indicated he was suffering from erysipelas, a nasty skin disease that can cause dangerous swelling under the skin. Huggins died three days later.

Huggins finished with a managerial record of 1,413–1,134. His .555 winning percentage is better than Durocher's, Casey Stengel's, and Connie Mack's.

Only five managers won more pennants than Huggins' six. In 1964 Huggins was elected into the Hall of Fame.

Tom Hughes

Hughes, Thomas James **P**

1900–13 B:11/29/1878, Chicago, IL D:2/8/1956, Chicago, IL Deb:9/7/1900, CHI AL BR/TR 6'1", 175

W	L	PCT	G	SH	IP	BB	SO	ERA
132	174	.431	399	25	2644	853	1368	3.09

"Long Tom" Hughes' best season came in 1903 when, while pitching on a Boston Americans staff that included Bill Dinneen and Cy Young, Hughes recorded a 20–7 record with a 2.57 ERA. Boston went to the first modern World Series that season and beat Pittsburgh, five games to three.

The righthander began his major league career with his hometown Chicago White Sox in 1900. Although he was 10–23 in 1901, the season was punctuated by two noteworthy performances. On August 21 he struck out 15 in a 14-inning game against Cincinnati. A month later Hughes went 17 innings against the Beaneaters' Dinneen. The game was scoreless until the 17th inning, when an error, a hit batter, a force play, and a single gave Hughes the win.

Hughes jumped to the American League the next season splitting 1902 between Baltimore and Boston. He started 1904 with New York before moving on to Washington. On August 2, 1906, Hughes had a pitcher's dream outing. In a scoreless extra-inning duel with the Browns he became the first pitcher to hit a game-winning homer. The feat was not repeated until August 13, 1932, when Yankee Red Ruffing did it.

Tex Hughson

Hughson, Cecil Carlton **P**

1941–49 B:2/9/1916, Buda, TX D:8/6/1993, Austin, TX Deb:4/16/1941, BOS AL BR/TR 6'3", 198

W	L	PCT	G	SH	IP	BB	SO	ERA
96	54	.640	225	19	1375^2	372	693	2.94

Tex Hughson could fire the baseball and he had excellent control. He quickly became the ace of the Boston Red Sox staff in the early 1940s, blazing to a career best year in 1942. Hughson, who finished with a 22–6 record and 2.59 ERA, led the American League in wins, complete games (22), strikeouts (113) and innings pitched (281). A dominating pitcher during the pre-war years, he registered a league-best 20 complete games in 1943 and compiled an 18–5 record and 2.26 ERA in 1944. he was named to three straight All-Star teams.

Called into military service in 1945, Hughson missed the entire season. He returned in 1946 and won 20 games, helping the Red Sox win the American League pennant. Hughson was named by manager Joe Cronin to start the World Series opener against Howie Pollet and the St. Louis Cardinals. The Red Sox won, 3–2, in 10 innings. Hughson pitched into the ninth inning before being relieved by eventual winner Earl Johnson.

He developed arm trouble during the 1947 season and became relatively ineffective for the remainder of his career. In just eight seasons, five as a regular starter, Hughson put up some big numbers: 96 wins, 99 complete games, and a 2.94 lifetime ERA.

William Hulbert

Hulbert, William A.

Owner (1875–81) NL President (1877–82)
B:10/23/1832, Burlington Flats, NY D:4/10/1882, Chicago, IL

In 1871 the National Association of Professional Base Ball Players was created to give stature and credibility to an idea that this "game" might be a "career" worthy of grown men. But the fledgling pro circuit operated with mixed success; disorganized and chaotic, it was run by the players, some of whom received monthly salaries while others preferred to share gate receipts.

Following the 1875 season, marked by the fourth consecutive pennant won by the Boston Red Stockings, the National Association was in ruin, brought down by a combination of noncompetitive play, rampant gambling, and drunkenness—on the field and off. But most of all, the death of the NA was caused by the birth of a bigger idea. That great notion was the National League of Professional Base Ball Clubs—a capitalist consortium of stock companies dreamed up by William A. Hulbert, the game's largely unknown hero.

If baseball players go to bed at night with prayers of thanks for John Ward and Curt Flood (they don't, but they ought to), the owners should hit their pillows with hosannas to Hulbert. For in addition to creating professional baseball as we know it today, his accomplishments include the institution of league-scheduled play; the hiring of a staff of professional umpires; the protection of the new league's principles in its very first year, when he boldly expelled two clubs rather than compromise his vision; and the rescue of the game's reputation after the scandal of the "Louisville Four," who conspired to toss away the 1877 pennant.

Hulbert also created the reserve clause, which for nearly a century defined the owner-player relationship. While he lived, Hulbert was known in the press as "the Savior of the Game." Today he is known by historians and a handful of fans as one of the most important men in baseball history and for decades as the most mystifying oversight by the electors of the Baseball Hall of Fame.

Ironically, Hulbert was born only a few miles from Cooperstown—in Burlington Flats, New York. His parents moved to Chicago two years later, and in 1847 they sent their son to Beloit College in Wisconsin, where he prepared for a life in commerce. After returning to Chicago, he married the daughter of a prosperous grocer and extended that business into a coal dealership.

A man of imposing physique for the period—he stood 6 feet tall and weighed 215 pounds—he was soon one of the proudest young magnates in the West. He was fond of telling people, "I'd rather be a lamppost in Chicago than a millionaire elsewhere." In 1871 Hulbert became a booster of Chicago's professional baseball club, the White Stockings, a charter member of the National Association.

On October 7 of that year, Chicago went up in flames, including the White Stockings' Lake Park. For the next two years the city had to withdraw from the National Association. When the White Stockings returned to competition in 1874 Hulbert became one of the club's officers. By the next year he was its president.

An incident that occurred in 1874 provided the spark to Hulbert's National League of Professional Base Ball Clubs. This was a time of rampant "revolving," or contract jumping, and the White Stockings were nervous that their diminutive shortstop, Davy Force, would desert them at season's end, as he had done with several other clubs. In September 1874 they signed him to a renewal contract for 1875; then they learned that, because the season was still in progress, the contract was invalid by Association rules. Chicago signed Force to another contract in November, but the organization blundered by backdating the contract to September, thus voiding it once again. In December the Philadelphia Athletics offered Force a contract, and he signed it. The Association Council, led by a Philadelphia official, upheld Force's deal with the Athletics.

Albert Goodwill Spalding, the great pitcher of the Boston Red Stockings, met with a distressed Hulbert in 1875. Years later Spalding would write of the wounded civic pride and, by modern standards, paranoia that afflicted Hulbert: "It was borne to him one day that the reason why Chicago—whose phenomenal achievements on other lines were attracting the wonder of all the world—could make no better showing on the diamond was because the East was in league against her; that certain Base Ball magnates in the Atlantic States were in control of the game; were manipulating things to the detriment of Chicago and all Western cities; that if the Chicago Club signed an exceptionally strong player he was sure to be stolen from her; that contracts had no force, because the fellows down East would and did offer players increased salaries and date new contracts back to suit their own ends."

Hulbert reminded Spalding that he had made his name as a pitcher in the 1860s through his exploits with the Forest City club of Rockford, Illinois. "Spalding, you've no business playing in Boston; you're a Western boy, and you belong right here." Within a few months, Hulbert proceeded to give the Easterners, who had, in his view, rustled his prize shortstop, a taste of their own medicine. He not only raided Boston for Spalding but also snatched three other Red Stocking heroes—Ross Barnes, Deacon White, and Cal McVey. From the hated Philadelphia Athletics he took Cap Anson and Ezra Sutton, although Sutton later reneged on his commitment and returned to Philly.

When word leaked in the summer of 1875 that Chicago had denuded Boston of its stars for the following season, a columnist for the *Worcester Spy* wrote of Boston's loss: "Like Rachel weeping for her children, she refuses to be comforted because the famous baseball nine, the perennial champion, the city's most cherished possession, has been captured by Chicago."

Now Hulbert had real cause for worry. Because his club's contracts had been signed, yet again, in midseason, the association council could invalidate them and, perhaps, expel Chicago for gross misconduct. Then he came up with a brainstorm. "Spalding," he said to his ally in revolution, "I have a new scheme. Let us anticipate the Eastern cusses and organize a new association before the March [1876] meeting, and then see who does the expelling."

On February 2, 1876, at New York's Grand Central Hotel, Hulbert met with other large-city magnates and persuaded even the Eastern faction that a new circuit should be founded: the National League of Professional Base Ball Clubs. Straws were drawn for the presidency of the new organization, and Morgan Bulkeley, president of the Hartford entry, selected the short straw. (In his year in office he did nothing of note; when he failed to attend the 1877 National League meeting, the other club owners put a halt to the charade and insisted Hulbert assume the role of president.)

The National League was to be founded on principles of square dealing, recognition of contracts, and business integrity. These lofty principles would be reflected on the playing field—no drinking, no gambling, no play on Sunday. With the strongest National Association franchises signed up for the new National League, the palace revolt was complete. Hulbert's eight-team league commenced play in 1876, and the National Association simply gave up the ghost.

The entrants for the league's two largest cities—the Mutuals of New York and the Athletics of Philadelphia—were used to determining their own fortunes. Once they were eliminated from consideration for the 1876 pennant by Hulbert's new powerhouse White Stockings, their concluding Western swing of the season portended nothing but losses at the gate.

Fearing no consequence of their action, the Mutuals and the Athletics declined to fulfill their remaining schedule; after all, in the National Association such conduct had been tolerated. But not in the National League. Hulbert expelled the two franchises, and NL baseball would not return to those cities for six years.

In 1877, chastened by the Mutuals and Athletics, he instituted the practice of determining the clubs' schedules through the league rather than through club secretaries, as had long been the custom. He also hired umpires to strengthen the public's confidence in the integrity of the game. Then, with only 15 games left in the season, he met perhaps the greatest challenge of the National League's formative years: the game-fixing by four Louisville Gray players—Al Nichols, George Hall, Bill Craver, and most notably, star pitcher Jim Devlin.

Hulbert swiftly meted out justice, expelling the four for life. The result was to drive Louisville out of the league; when St. Louis and Hartford also dropped out, Hulbert scrambled to place franchises in such marginal outposts as Indianapolis, Milwaukee, and Providence. Still the National League survived.

In the winter following his banishment, the distraught Devlin made his way north to Chicago to plead with Hulbert. Spalding, present in the adjoining office of the suite he shared with Hulbert, recalled the meeting: "The situation, as he kneeled there in abject humiliation, was beyond the realm of pathos. It was a scene of heartrending tragedy. Devlin was in tears, Hulbert was in tears.…I heard Devlin's plea to have the stigma removed from his name. I heard him entreat, not on his own account—he acknowledged himself unworthy of consideration—but for the sake of his wife and child. I beheld the agony of humiliation depicted on his features as he confessed his guilt and begged for mercy.

"I saw the great bulk of Hulbert's frame tremble with the emotion he vainly sought to stifle. I saw the president's hand steal into his pocket as if seeking to conceal his intended act from the other hand. I saw him take a $50 bill and press it into the palm of the prostrate player. And then I heard him say, as he fairly writhed with the pain his own words caused him, 'That's what I think of you, personally; but, damn you, Devlin, you are dishonest; you have sold a game, and I can't trust you. Now go; and let me never see your face again; for your act will not be condoned so long as I live.'"

In 1879, hearkening back to the Davy Force case, Hulbert commenced the practice of reserving the services of key players for the season following. This, Hulbert thought, would assure the fans and, not insignificantly, the management, that the business of baseball would be characterized by continuity. At first the reserve clause applied to only five players per club, who by and large were pleased to be so designated. To be reserved meant to be assured of a job for the next season. Soon thereafter, of course, the reserve clause came to apply to all players, binding them to one employer for life.

After the 1879 season Hulbert, in his continuing capacity as owner of the Chicago White Stockings, snatched two star players from the Cincinnati Reds: King Kelly and Fred Goldsmith. Then he expelled the Cincinnati franchise from the National League for selling "spirituous and malt liquors" on the grounds, which violated his sensibilities though not, in truth, league statute. In so doing, Hulbert sparked an insurrection of his own: a rival league. The American Association, centered in the fun-loving, hard-drinking city of Cincinnati, started play in 1882. The AA soon became known as the "Beer-and-Whiskey League," and it gave the National League a run for its money during the next decade.

Hulbert was not around to observe its debut. On April 10, 1882, at the age of 49, baseball's great architect died of a heart attack. Spalding later wrote, "I ask all living professional Base Ball players to join me in raising our hats to the memory of William A. Hulbert, the man who saved the game!"

He was inducted into the Hall of Fame in 1995.

Randy Hundley

Hundley, Cecil Randolph **C**

1964–77 B:6/1/1942, Martinsville, VA Deb:9/27/1964, SF NL BR/TR 6', 175

G	AB	R	H	HR	RBI	OBP	SLG	AVG
1061	3442	311	813	82	381	.294	.350	.236

Randy Hundley was a smooth-fielding catcher in the 1960s and 1970s, whose claim to fame is that he helped popularize the technique of catching pitches one-handed. Hundley got his style from his father, Cecil, a former semipro catcher.

"The only thing my dad knew was that his hands were all broken up from foul balls," said

Hundley. "He kept telling me, 'What good are you with busted-up hands? You can't play, you can't hit, you can't do anything.' So he taught me to catch one-handed." (Cecil Hundley even threatened to storm onto the field and remove his son from a game if he ever caught a ball with two hands.)

Added Randy, "He'd make me sit there with my back hand on my right leg and catch every ball with my glove hand, backhanding just like an infielder. I never missed a game because of a foul ball on my bare hand."

Signed straight out of high school by the Giants, Randy received a $110,000 bonus. He immediately wrote out a check to his father for $55,000 for his instruction. In time, Hundley was audited by the Internal Revenue Service for deducting the amount as a business expense. He sued, and when the case went to court he demonstrated his receiving technique before the judge—and won.

Hundley's innovation soon caught on. He recalls one game in 1967 in which Reds rookie Johnny Bench broke a finger. "That did it," says Hundley. "Now he's in the dugout, blood dripping down his arm, watching me catch 'em one-handed, and that was it. He was back in 1968 as a one-handed catcher."

Hundley, who played only eight games in two seasons for the Giants before being traded to the Cubs after the 1965 season, quickly established himself as one of the National League's finest defensive catchers. "Having Hundley catch for you was like sitting down to a steak dinner with a steak knife," said Ferguson Jenkins in 1970. "Without Hundley, all you had was a fork."

In 1967 Hundley committed only four errors in 928 total chances, which stood as the record for fewest errors by a catcher for 30 years. Florida's Charles Johnson made no errors in 937 chances in 1997.

In 1968 Hundley set a major league record for most games caught in a season, with 160. This time he committed five errors in 971 total chances. From 1966 through 1969 Hundley averaged 153 games behind the plate.

Hundley's wizardry left him when he grabbed a bat. He hit for the cycle during his rookie season, but never batted better than .267. Hundley had his best offensive season in 1969. He batted .255, with 18 homers and 64 RBIs, but Chicago stumbled late in the season and was eventually passed by the "Miracle" Mets.

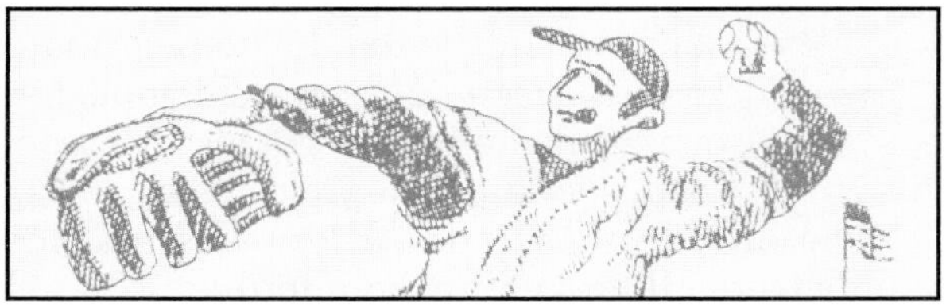

In 1972 Hundley caught two no-hitters, the first by Burt Hooton on April 16 against the Phillies, the second by Milt Pappas on September 2 against the Padres. In 1973 he caught 122 games and hit 10 homers, but his days as a regular catcher were over. He spent his last three years with three different teams, moving from the Twins to the Padres, and back to the Cubs in 1976.

At one point Hundley was the Cubs' player representative, but he was hardly a fire-breathing radical. "If all the owners had been as fair to the players as Mr. Wrigley was, we wouldn't have needed a Players Association," he once remarked. Leo Durocher contended that Hundley quit as the player rep after the executive director of the Players Association, Marvin Miller, drove him "crazy with his daily bulletins and phone calls."

Leaving the majors, Hundley managed in the minor leagues at Midland of the Texas League and Iowa of the American Association. He scouted for the Cubs but was swept out of the organization when Dallas Green arrived in 1981. He turned to running Randy Hundley's Official Big League Baseball Camps, originating the idea of "fantasy camps." Hundley's son, Todd, followed his father into the majors, catching for the Mets and Dodgers.

Todd Hundley

Hundley, Todd Randolph **C**

1990–* B:5/27/1969, Martinsville, VA Deb:5/18/1990, NY NL BB/TR 5'11", 170

G	AB	R	H	HR	RBI	OBP	SLG	AVG
944	2925	389	690	148	452	.321	.438	.236

Catching was in Todd Hundley's blood; hitting came to him after years of hard work. After 10 years in the major leagues, Todd had the same .236 career average as his father, Randy, but the son had power his father could only imagine.

In 1996 Todd Hundley broke Roy Campanella's 43-year-old single-season record for home runs by a catcher. He became only the third switch hitter in major league history to hit 40 home runs (joining Mickey Mantle and Ken Caminiti), made the All-Star team for the first time, and set team records for most home runs and games caught. Hundley's 112 RBI were more than double his previous high, and he also had a .550 slugging percentage. Although never confused defensively with his Gold Glove dad, Todd made just eight errors in 150 games behind the plate.

The Mets drafted the 17-year-old, 150-pound Hundley out of suburban Chicago's William Fremd High School in 1987. He did not even hit his weight his first year as a professional, but he slowly improved as he started to fill out physically. Hundley got a chance to play regularly with the Mets in 1992. He committed only three errors all year, including 37 games without an error to start the year and 61 straight errorless games to end the season. The following year he showed some power, clubbing 11 home runs (all from the left side). He set a record for Mets catchers with 113 consecutive errorless games before committing a miscue on June 18 in Pittsburgh.

Hundley hit the ball better than he ever had in 1995, despite wrist injuries that kept him on the disabled list for six weeks. The following year he displayed power that exceeded everyone's expectations. Former Mets general manager Joe McIlvaine, who scouted Hundley in high school, admitted, "If you had told me that someday Todd would hit 20 home runs in the big leagues, I'd have said you were crazy."

Hundley hit 30 homers in 1997, but the slide after that was dramatic. Beset with injuries, he appeared in just 53 games in 1998. His relations with manager Bobby Valentine deteriorated—and in May the Mets acquired superstar backstop Mike Piazza from the Marlins, making things difficult even for a healthy Hundley. He shifted to left field to fill a void on the team, but it proved to be a disaster—as did his .161 average.

That off-season New York traded Hundley and pitcher Arnold Gooch to the Dodgers for outfielder Roger Cedeno and catcher Charles Johnson (Johnson was immediately traded to Baltimore for Armando Benitez). Hundley hit 24 home runs in 1999, but he batted just .207 and struggled mightily in throwing out runners with his surgically repaired elbow.

Ron Hunt

Hunt, Ronald Kenneth **2B–3B**

1963–74 B:2/23/1941, St. Louis, MO Deb:4/16/1963, NY NL BR/TR 6', 186

G	AB	R	H	HR	RBI	OBP	SLG	AVG
1483	5235	745	1429	39	370	.369	.347	.273

Scrappy second baseman Ron Hunt proved the hard way that he would do anything it took to reach first base. "Some people give their bodies to science," Hunt once joked. "I gave mine to baseball."

Hunt set the major league record for the most times hit by a pitch in a season: he was plunked an astonishing 50 times with Montreal in 1971. For a while he also held the career record for being hit, with 243, but Don Baylor, who played 19 years to Hunt's 12, eventually overtook him, finishing with 267.

"Actually, a player who lacks something should try to compensate for his shortcoming; that's me with HBPs," Hunt said. "If I start bailing out, I don't hit. If the ball is coming on the inside, I roll around but don't fall back. I don't have to. Then it's a judgment call by the umpire." Hunt knew when to draw the line: "As for pitched balls coming at my head, well, there's a difference between courage and stupidity."

Hunt came from a broken home and was reared in both urban St. Louis and on a Missouri farm. He signed for a $20,000 bonus with the Milwaukee Braves and made stops at their McCook, Cedar Rapids, and Austin farm clubs. At McCook of the Class D Nebraska State League, he was a teammate of future author Pat Jordan, and was mentioned in Jordan's classic tale of minor league life, *A False Spring*.

Hunt started as a third baseman, but when the Braves realized that Red Schoendienst was winding down, they moved Hunt to second base. However, before he could make the grade, Milwaukee gave up on him and offered him to the Mets. New York sent coach Solly Hemus down to Austin to scout him.

Hemus liked what he saw, and the Mets purchased Hunt on a conditional basis; they had until May 9, 1963, to decide whether to retain him. Not only did they keep him, but he was also voted the Mets' Most Valuable Player that year. His prize was something called the Aqua-Car, which could maneuver either on land or in water.

"After the game," noted former Mets executive Joe McDonald, "he drove it to the foot of Dyckman Street and took it in the water. He drove it across the Hudson River and then drove it up the Palisades to the place where he lives in Fort Lee. Saved the George Washington Bridge toll."

Hunt, who hit .272 and slugged a career-high 10 homers, was narrowly beaten in the 1963 National League Rookie of the Year voting by another second baseman who played the game with everything he had—Pete Rose. Only Rose and Hunt received first-place ballots for the award.

In 1964 Hunt became the first Met voted to the All-Star Game on his own merits (not as the token representative of a bad ballclub). The game was played at brand-new Shea Stadium, and Mets fans were thrilled to see their hero start at second for the NL. He left the Mets after the 1966 season when manager Wes Westrum mistakenly believed the injury- and allergy-plagued Hunt was no longer giving his all. New York packed him off with outfielder Jim Hickman to Los Angeles for former two-time NL batting champion Tommy Davis.

Hunt played one season with the Dodgers, three with the Giants, and four with Montreal. He played for 12 years in all, batting .273 and striking out only 382 times in 5,235 at bats.

Hunt retired and went into ranching in Missouri. He later operated a highly regarded baseball school.

Catfish Hunter

Hunter, James Augustus **P**

1965–79 B:4/8/1946, Hertford, NC D:9/9/1999, Hertford, NC Deb:5/13/1965, KC AL BR/TR 6', 195

W	L	PCT	G	SH	IP	BB	SO	ERA
224	166	.574	500	42	3449^{1}	954	2012	3.26

As spectacular as Catfish Hunter's achievements on the mound were—and they included a perfect game, a Cy Young Award, and five consecutive 20-win seasons—they paled in comparison to the shake-up of baseball's establishment he launched in 1974 when he set off the first free-agent bidding war.

In a prelude to the free agency revolution, Hunter jumped from the frying pan of Charlie Finley's Oakland A's into the fire of George Steinbrenner's "Bronx Zoo" Yankees. In the process he became known as baseball's "$3 Million Man."

Three million dollars meant a lot to a guy like James Augustus Hunter, born into a North Carolina sharecropping family. But so did baseball. "We were always playing ball even when it rained. When it rained, we'd go in the barn and break up corncobs and hit them with a stick," recalled Hunter's older brother, Pete. "We didn't have much money, but we always had baseball."

Jim Hunter starred in high school and American Legion competition, tossing a slew of no-hitters. His numbers on the mound attracted the attention of numerous scouts, but when his brother accidentally shot Jim in the foot while duck hunting, it looked like his pitching career was over. Thirty shotgun pellets were lodged in his foot and his little toe was gone.

The local newspaper's headline proclaimed, "Hunter's Baseball Career at End," which did little to keep the scouts coming. Hunter was determined to prove them wrong. As soon as he could stand he was attempting to pitch, even though his foot was still numbed by anesthesia.

In no time at all Hunter fully recovered, yet most teams now shied away from him. But at the urging of scout Clyde Kluttz, Kansas City A's owner Charles O. Finley decided to take a gamble and in June 1964 signed Hunter for a $75,000 bonus—he threw in a new identity.

"After we signed the contract, I told him we had to have a good nickname for him," said Finley. "Looking around this country setting, I came upon 'Catfish.' I told him that we would tell the press he had been missing one night and that his folks found him down by the stream with one catfish lying beside him and another on his pole. He looked at me and smiled and said in the drawl of his, 'Whatever you say, Mr. Finley, it's OK with me.'"

Hunter didn't pitch professionally in 1964. In 1965, because of Major League Baseball's rule regarding "bonus babies," Finley had to keep Hunter on the Kansas City roster or risk losing him. Hunter did not appear until mid-May, when he pitched two innings of shutout relief. Before long he was starting for the A's. "With the stuff he's got," marveled Athletics relief ace John Wyatt, "there's no reason he should ever pitch in the minors." Hunter never did.

By 1966 he was an All-Star. On May 8, 1968, Hunter pitched the AL's first regular-season perfect game since White Sox righthander Charlie Robertson turned the trick in 1922. Facing the Minnesota Twins, Hunter no-hit Dave Boswell, 4–0, and struck out 11. Hunter threw 107 pitches, and there wasn't one difficult play made behind him, although he went to a three-ball count seven times. "I went with fastballs and sliders. I threw only three changeups and one curveball all night," said Hunter.

After the game Hunter received a call from Charlie Finley, who congratulated the young man and then said cryptically, "But you cost me $5,000."

"I'm sorry. Who got it?" Hunter wanted to know.

"You did," responded Finley. "It'll be in your next contract."

Soon after the A's moved to Oakland in 1968 both Hunter and the team became regular winners. "He's a great pitcher. Every time he goes out there, I expect him to throw a shutout," raved manager Alvin Dark. Oakland captured world championships every year from 1972 through 1974. In 1974 Hunter won the AL Cy Young Award, but it was Hunter's last season in Oakland.

Hunter's Oakland contract called for Finley to pay half of the pitcher's $100,000 salary into a life insurance fund in what was essentially a deferred compensation agreement. In October 1974, as the World Series was about to begin, Hunter charged that because Finley had failed to honor this portion of the agreement the entire contract was void, including the reserve clause. Hunter therefore claimed he was a free agent.

Finley, alarmed, attempted to make restitution. He went so far as to personally hand Hunter a check for $50,000, but Hunter wouldn't take it. After all, Hunter reasoned, Section 7A of the Standard Player Contract stated that "the Player may terminate this contract upon written notice to the Club, if the Club shall default in the payments to the player provided for…and if the Club shall fail to remedy such a default within 10 days after the receipt by the Club of written notice of such defaults."

The case went to arbitration, and on December 13, 1974, arbitrator Peter Seitz ruled that Hunter's contract was void. Hunter was now a free agent, and an unprecedented bidding war soon erupted. "Go on, Cat! Get it all, man," advised Oakland teammate Reggie Jackson.

The bidding period lasted 13 days, and it was truly an amazing scene. Representatives from 15 major league clubs sent emissaries to Hunter's agent, the rural law firm of Cherry, Cherry, and Flythe in tiny Ahoskie, North Carolina. Six major league owners (Gene Autry, Ted Bonda, Brad Corbett, Dan Galbreath, Ewing Kauffman, and Bud Selig) showed up in person.

Before long the bidding had reached more than $1 million. People speculated about whether Hunter would simply go for the most cash or take other factors into consideration. "You must remember this boy was raised on a farm," attorney Carlton Cherry said at the time. "He's lived in the country all his life. He's a good Christian young man. He doesn't dissipate. He doesn't carouse. He just sits home with his family. The area—housing, schools, tax shelter benefits for him and his family in future life—those will be the deciding factors."

Rumor had it that the Mets dropped out at $1.8 million. Everyone else went higher and the Padres and Royals were allegedly offering $3.5 to $4 million. The Indians were also over the $3-million mark. Yet as Cherry indicated, dollars and cents were not Hunter's sole criteria. He eventually signed a five-year contract with George Steinbrenner's Yankees worth an estimated $3.75 million, including a $1 million signing bonus.

"It could ruin Hunter as a pitcher, rob him of his desire," huffed White Sox owner Arthur Allyn. "No player is worth that kind of money." But despite the big bucks, Hunter kept his head on straight for the Yankees, producing a 23-victory season in 1975 and contributing to pennants in 1976, 1977, and 1978. Hunter found Oakland and New York very similar, with the "same crazy stuff on each team," he said. "But in Oakland there weren't as many reporters to write about it."

In New York Hunter and former Oakland teammate Reggie Jackson were reunited. Hunter provided some interesting observations on Mr. October. "He'd give you the shirt off his back. Of course, he'd call a press conference to announce it," Hunter once remarked. On another occasion Hunter said about the new "Reggie Bar," named after Jackson: "When you unwrap a Reggie Bar, it tells you how good it is."

In March 1978 Hunter was diagnosed with diabetes, but he still won 12 games and was the winning pitcher in New York's 7–2 World Series-clinching victory over the Los Angeles Dodgers in Game 6. However, following through on his original plan, Hunter, only 33, retired when his pact with Steinbrenner expired. Some said he was hampered by shoulder problems—even his Hall of Fame plaque stated he retired because of arm problems. Explained Hunter in 1987, "I wanted to start spending time with my family, and I told the Yankees when I signed that I would only play for five years....I had no arm problems when I retired."

Hunter went back to farming in North Carolina, even though he received several lucrative offers to stay in New York. "Heck, one corporation said I could live in one of those Park Avenue co-ops rent-free in exchange for publicity, and acting as a company spokesman," Catfish recalled.

In 1987 Hunter, in his third year of eligibility, was elected to the Hall of Fame. "I didn't think I would make it," he admitted. "I figured I wasn't good enough. I figured the people in there were like gods." But as Peter Ueberroth observed, "Catfish Hunter had the distinction of playing for both Charlie Finley and George Steinbrenner, which is enough to put a player in the Hall of Fame." Rather than choose to have the insignia of either team on his cap on his plaque, Hunter opted to go into the Hall of Fame without a team designation.

A decade after his election, Hunter was duck hunting when he found he couldn't lift his shotgun. Soon he had other alarming symptoms. "I was kinda hopin' it was a tick bite," he told Steve Wilstein of the Associated Press. "I'm always around dogs and stuff." It was not a tick bite.

After many medical tests in 1998, Hunter was diagnosed with amyotrophic lateral sclerosis, better known as Lou Gehrig's Disease, the incurable, paralyzing malady that ended the career and life of the great first baseman. In 1999 it took Hunter's life as well.

Bruce Hurst

Hurst, Bruce Vee **P**

1980–94 B:3/24/1958, St. George, UT Deb:4/12/1980, BOS AL BL/TL 6'3", 215

W	L	PCT	G	SH	IP	BB	SO	ERA
145	113	.562	379	23	2417^{1}	740	1689	3.92

Bruce Hurst, a devout and abstemious Mormon from tiny St. George, Utah, dreamed of playing basketball for Brigham Young University but instead became one of the top pitchers of his era, winning two World Series games and topping 10 wins for 10 straight years. He was the only active hurler to have done so before his retirement in June 1994.

Hurst spent 13 years in the Boston Red Sox organization before finishing his career with the San Diego Padres. (He made brief comeback attempts with both the Rockies and Rangers.) Never a dominant fastballer like Red Sox teammate Roger Clemens, Hurst was a steady southpaw with a deadly pickoff move. He was selected to the All-Star Game in 1987, and he starred in one of the most famous World Series of all time—the Red Sox–New York Mets imbroglio of 1986.

Throughout his career, Hurst remained true to his Mormon beliefs, which sometimes made him something of a loner in the clubhouse. "I'm not a big clubhouse guy," he told the *Los Angeles Times* in 1991. "I just don't feel real comfortable in there. My life is not going to be consumed by the game."

Hurst was a two-sport star at Dixie High in St. George. At 6 feet 3 inches and 219 pounds, he was a powerful guard on the court, and basketball was his first love. "I remember one day a scout came into our house and compared him to Koufax and Frank Tanana," Bruce's brother Ross recalled. "You know what Bruce did? He kind of shrugged his shoulders and went out and played basketball."

Eventually Boston made Hurst its first selection in the 1976 draft, and his brothers Buck and Ross convinced him to sign. Hurst was on the verge of giving up baseball several times during those early years, on one occasion staying away for three days after a coach for Boston's Pawtucket affiliate cursed at him.

Instead, Hurst pitched for a dozen more years. He entered the Boston lineup in 1980, posting two wins in 12 outings despite an astronomic 9.10 ERA. Back in Triple A Pawtucket for much of 1981, he compiled a 12–7 record, including seven shutouts. He also earned a footnote in baseball history by pitching five innings of two-hit relief in the longest game ever, a 33-inning marathon against the Rochester Red Wings. With Boston, he was 2–0 with an improved ERA of 4.30.

In 1983 Hurst launched the first of 10 consecutive seasons in which he posted at least 10 victories. He posted a 12–12 record, hurled two shutouts, and, for the first of many times, he led the team in pickoffs with nine. Hurst continued to improve over the next three seasons.

He posted a spectacular September in 1986, going 5–0 with four complete games and a 1.07 ERA. His postseason performance was thrilling. After going 1–0 against the California Angels in the American League Championship Series, he won Game 1 and Game 5 of the World Series against the Mets. Starting Game 7 on three days' rest, he threw one-hit, shutout ball for the first five innings before the Mets rallied to tie the game in the sixth inning. Unfortunately, the Mets' improbable comeback overshadowed Hurst's memorable Series performance: 2–0 in three starts, a 1.96 ERA, and 17 strikeouts.

Hurst appeared to be headed for a 20-win year in 1987 when a dismal September dropped him to 15–13. He fanned 190 batters, bettering his own mark for strikeouts in a season by a Boston left-hander. The following year his career-high 18 wins helped Boston to its second AL East championship in three years, but Hurst lost both his starts against the Oakland Athletics in the ALCS. That December he signed with the San Diego Padres as a free agent.

Hurst notched another solid year in 1989, winning 15 games, posting a career-best 2.69 ERA, and tying for the league lead in complete games with 10. In his second NL start he tossed a one-hitter with 13 strikeouts. After finishing second in 1989, the Padres stumbled out of the gate in 1990 on their way to a 75–87 record and a tie for fourth place in the NL West. Hurst once again considered quitting the game, but he came back in the second half to pull out an 11–9 season.

He pitched three more years, logging over 200 innings in 1991 and 1992, posting back-to-back shutouts of the Mets in 1992, and throwing two more shutouts that year for a career total of 23. Hurst underwent shoulder surgery to repair his rotator cuff after the 1992 season, and although he launched a valiant comeback in 1993, it was his last full season in the majors. He had two horrendous starts for San Diego before being traded to the Colorado Rockies, for whom he pitched briefly. His comeback effort with the Texas Rangers in 1994 also fell short.

Fred Hutchinson

Hutchinson, Frederick Charles **P**

1939–40, 1946–53 M(1952–54, 1956–64, 830–827)
B:8/12/1919, Seattle, WA D:11/12/1964, Bradenton, FL
Deb:5/02/1939, DET AL BL/TR 6'2", 200

W	L	PCT	G	SH	IP	BB	SO	ERA
95	71	.572	242	13	1464	388	591	3.73

They called him "Stone Face" and marveled over his mean temper and his tendency to smash anything within sight when his team lost. But when Cincinnati manager Fred Hutchinson was dying of cancer in 1964, the entire baseball world mourned and showed their admiration for a man who was always tough but always fair. "He showed us how to live, now he's showing us how to die," said Gene Mauch, who was managing the Phillies at the time.

There is no denying that Hutchinson did have a bit of a temper. In the 1950s, when the Yankees followed Hutchinson's Tigers into a town, Yogi Berra could always tell if Detroit had won or lost by a quick look at the visitors' changing room. "If we got stools in the clubhouse, I knew he'd won. Otherwise we got kindling," observed Berra. "Hutch doesn't throw furniture. He throws rooms," quipped Philadelphia sportswriter Larry Merchant.

One day an infuriated Hutchinson destroyed every light bulb (reportedly 26) in the tunnel leading from the dugout to the clubhouse in Milwaukee's County Stadium. Then when he got to the clubhouse he overturned the Reds' buffet table and left the place in shambles. Another time he hurled a ball bag through a window. On occasions too numerous to mention, he punched out nearby walls and columns. He explained: "I take it out on inanimate objects. I don't get mad at my friends or family."

Oddly enough, that was true. Despite his rather dour expression and his savage after-loss behavior, he was a popular figure in the game. Joe Garagiola said, "Hutch laughs. The only trouble is his face doesn't know it."

In the 1930s Frederick Charles Hutchinson was an all-around star at Seattle's Franklin High School, where he played the outfield and first base and pitched. Both Detroit and Cleveland wanted to sign him, but instead he opted for the local Rainiers of the Pacific Coast League. By the end of July 1938 he was 17–5. On his 19th birthday, August 12, 1938, an overflow crowd of 16,000 fans turned out to watch him defeat San Francisco, 3–2. At season's end he was 25–7 with a 2.48 ERA. He led the Pacific Coast League in victories and was *The Sporting News* Minor League Player of the Year. It was rumored that he would be sold for as much as $100,000, but instead he went to Detroit for $35,000 and four players.

Hutchinson never developed as the Tigers had hoped. He shuttled back and forth between the majors and the minors. He made one appearance in the 1940 World Series that was won by Cincinnati in seven games. In 1941 he finally appeared ready to break through. Then came Pearl Harbor. He missed 1942 through 1945 while he served in the Coast Guard.

In 1946 he returned to the Tigers and went 14–11. He won a career-high 18 games in 1947 and posted double-figure victory totals during the next four seasons. He could also swing the bat. A career .263 hitter, he drove in 83 runs during his career. He also stole home on August 29, 1949.

By 1952 Hutchinson was pitching primarily in a reliever's role, and in midseason he was a surprise choice to succeed Red Rolfe as Detroit's manager. The club failed to improve significantly under Hutchinson, and he was let go after the 1954 season.

Hutchinson returned to Seattle and managed the Rainiers to a PCL pennant. In 1956 he was hired by Cardinals general manager Frank "Trader" Lane to manage St. Louis. "When I was general manager of the White Sox and Hutch was at Detroit, I went looking for him in Chicago to talk to him about something," Lane later explained. "I found him in a hotel room with several players, explaining the cutoff play on a blackboard. He was the first manager I ever knew who believed in night school."

Hutchinson was named *The Sporting News* Major League Manager of the Year in 1957 after leading the Cardinals to 87 wins and a second-place finish in the NL. Nonetheless, he was let go in the closing weeks of the 1958 season. Once more he returned to Seattle to manage the Rainiers. The following season the Rainiers were struggling in eighth place, but when Cincinnati Reds manager Mayo Smith was let go that July, Hutchinson was named as his replacement.

The Reds at that time were not a particularly strong club, and after a few seasons it didn't look like they were getting any better. Yet their poor play wasn't because they didn't respect Hutchinson. Said Gordy Coleman: "I guess the best compliment you can pay to Hutch is to say he was a man's man. When I first met him, I remember saying to myself, 'Man if you put this guy in a cage with a bear, you'd have to bet on him.'"

As the 1961 season opened the Reds were uniformly picked for the second division. One rival club official called the Reds "a conglomeration of castoffs who banded together for one last stand." In spring training of 1961 the Reds were worse than their critics had made them out to be. "Hutch called a meeting and he laid down the law to the club," recalled Dick Sisler. "He didn't shout or yell or bawl anybody out. He just said the club hadn't looked as good as he thought it should, that he expected more out of the players, and he wouldn't be satisfied until they produced. He was matter of fact about it, but everybody got the idea."

After the season opened the Reds didn't improve. Hutchinson called another meeting, and he was tougher than he'd been in the first. The Reds got the message and headed toward an unexpected pennant. United Press International named Hutchinson its National League Manager of the Year.

In late 1963 Hutchinson, a heavy smoker, was diagnosed with lung cancer. Yet he continued to battle, suiting up to manage the Reds every day. On one occasion he remarked to Cincinnati sportswriter Earl Lawson, "Dammit, Earl. I'm so skinny it hurts just sitting down." Said Lawson, "It was about the closest thing I heard to a complaint during his long siege."

Hutchinson managed the Reds through August 13 of that year, when he took a leave of absence, turning the club over to Dick Sisler. On October 19, 1964, he formally resigned. He died less than a month later. Hutchinson's record in 12 years as a manager was 830–827. The Reds retired his uniform No. 1 after his death, the first number to be retired in club history.

His older brother, Dr. William B. Hutchinson, and a host of friends raised the money to build the Fred Hutchinson Cancer Research Center in Seattle. It was incorporated in 1972 and has become internationally known.

Bill Hutchison

Hutchison, William Forrest **P**

1884–95, 1897 B:12/17/1859, New Haven, CT D:3/19/1926, Kansas City, MO Deb:6/10/1884, KC UA BR/TR 5'9", 175

W	L	PCT	G	SH	IP	BB	SO	ERA
183	163	.529	375	21	3078	1132	1234	3.59

A rules change helped turn Bill Hutchison from the best pitcher in baseball into just another pitcher out of baseball. Hutchison was a Yale man, son of a widely-known minister. After a couple of years in pro ball, Hutchison entered the railroad and lumber businesses in the Midwest. Following some business setbacks, he returned to baseball, soon becoming the highest-paid player and—though in his late 20s—one of the most sought-after pitching prospects in the minor leagues. "Wild Bill" joined Cap Anson's Chicago Colts in 1889. Reporters marveled at Hutchison, a baseball player who actually trained during the off-season.

He led the National League in games pitched, games started, innings, and victories from 1890 to 1892. He amassed 122 wins in those three seasons—more than half of his team's total. He led the NL with 314 strikeouts in 1892; granted it was in a career-high 622 innings.

In 1893 the pitcher's box was moved back to 60 feet 6 inches. Some pitchers were affected more by this change than others, but evidently none more than Hutchison. He struggled through three losing seasons in Chicago and one in St. Louis. By the end of the century, he was back in the railroad business.

Pete Incaviglia

Incaviglia, Peter Joseph **OF-DH**

1986–94, 1996–98 B:4/2/1964, Pebble Beach, CA Deb:4/8/1986, TEX AL BR/TR 6'1", 225

G	AB	R	H	HR	RBI	OBP	SLG	AVG
1284	4233	546	1043	206	655	.312	.448	.246

Pete Incaviglia rocketed straight from college ranks to big leagues, tied a team record for home runs in his rookie season—and saw his career go straight downhill shortly thereafter. Incaviglia was the prospect everyone wanted; the Oklahoma State slugger was *Baseball America*'s NCAA College Player of the Year in 1985. The Montreal Expos drafted Incaviglia in the first round, but he refused to sign and forced a trade to the Texas Rangers.

He made the Rangers as a starter without any minor league experience. Incaviglia hit 30 homers as a rookie in 1986, but he struck out an American League-high 185 times (four short of the major league record), and tied outfielders for the league lead in errors. Despite his deficiencies, some thought he was the next great power hitter.

They were wrong. Incaviglia's home run totals steadily declined, while his strikeout totals remained prodigious. In March 1991 the Rangers released him and he signed with Detroit.

He bounced to Houston and Philadelphia before going to play for the Chiba Lotte Marines in the Japanese Pacific League in 1995. Incaviglia hit a meager .181 in Japan, but returned to the Phillies the following year and helped the team claim the National League pennant. Strictly a part-time player, he was traded to Baltimore in August 1996 along with Todd Zeile. When the Orioles released him in July 1997, he signed with the Yankees. That year Incaviglia finally appeared in the minors, playing three games for the Yankees' Columbus farm team. He split 1998 between Detroit and Houston, and pinch-hit for the Astros in the Division Series.

Garth Iorg

Iorg, Garth Ray **3B-2B**

1978, 1980–87 B:10/12/1954 Arcata, CA Deb: 4/9/1978, TOR AL BR/TR 5'11", 170

G	AB	R	H	HR	RBI	OBP	SLG	AVG
931	2450	251	633	20	238	.294	.347	.258

Garth Iorg was not only the righthanded part of Toronto's third base platoon, he was also the righthanded portion of the Iorg brothers. His brother Dane was older, batted lefthanded, and had the winning hit for the Kansas City Royals in controversial Game 6 of the 1985 World Series. Garth, selected by Toronto from the New York Yankees in the fourth round of the 1977 expansion draft, was a Blue Jay for his entire major league career. He also got a taste of the franchise's first success.

"Those years were just a blast," he said of Toronto's emergence as contenders. "When those guys talk about those years, very few will talk about personal stats. They talk about team references."

Platooned at third base with lefty-hitting Rance Mulliniks, Iorg turned in the best season of his career as Toronto edged the Yankees for the division title in 1985. The platoon, dubbed "Mullinorg" by writers and fans, combined for a .302 average, 198 hits, 17 homers, and 93 RBIs. Dane's Royals, however, beat Garth's Blue Jays in the first seven-game American League Championship Series.

Because he didn't start every game, Garth Iorg was a weapon off the bench; he retired as the club's career leader in pinch hits. Iorg later returned to the Toronto organization as a minor league coach and manager.

Monte Irvin

Irvin, Monford Merrill **OF**

1949–56 Negro League Player (1937–48) B:2/25/1919, Columbia, AL Deb:7/8/1949, NY NL BR/TR 6'1", 195

G	AB	R	H	HR	RBI	OBP	SLG	AVG
764	2499	366	731	99	443	.385	.475	.293

When Monte Irvin finally reached the major leagues at age 30, he said, "This should have happened to me 10 years ago. I'm not half the ballplayer I was then." Who knows what might have happened if he had entered the majors in his 20s, when he hit .400 or better three times in the Negro National League? The *Pittsburgh Courier* selected him as the left fielder on its all-time African-American All-Star team in 1952.

A complete ballplayer, Irvin hit both for average and with power, caught everything hit his way at either shortstop or in the outfield, and had an outstanding arm. Even though he had only limited, "past-his-prime" exposure in the major leagues, he had a lifetime batting average of .293, hit .300 or better three times, and played for two pennant winners in five full seasons.

Alabama born, he and his family moved to New Jersey while he was still a youngster. He won 16 letters in four years at Orange High School. An all-state athlete in baseball, basketball, and football, Irvin was offered a football scholarship to Michigan, but when he asked for $100 in expenses to get to Ann Arbor he was turned down.

Instead Irvin went to Lincoln University in Pennsylvania, where he studied to become a history teacher. Carl Siebert, his baseball coach, tried to interest the Yanks and the Giants in him, but to no avail. In 1937, while still in college, Irvin signed with Abe and Effa Manley's Newark Eagles. To protect his college eligibility, he played under the pseudonym "Jimmy Nelson."

Even though the word on Irvin was that he "looked a little like Josh Gibson at the plate," he was offered no bonus. Abe Manley believed, "Bonuses only spoil players; if you work yourself up to a good salary you'll appreciate it more." After his sophomore year Irvin left Lincoln to play full-time with the Eagles. In 1940 he hit .422, followed by .393 in 1941.

Like many other African-American stars, Irvin performed in Jorge Pasquel's Mexican League. Once he was at bat with two outs and the bases loaded in the bottom of the ninth. Pasquel called the slugger over to his private box and offered him $200 if his team won. Irvin returned to the batter's box and made a deal with rival catcher Roy Campanella: "Give me a fastball, and I'll give you half." Campanella agreed but promptly double-crossed Irvin. Expecting the betrayal, Irvin sat on the curveball and crushed it for a grand slam.

After a three-year hitch in the army during World War II, Irvin returned to the Eagles where he continued to star. After the Dodgers signed Jackie Robinson, Irvin nearly signed with the Dodgers' farm team in St. Paul. However, Effa Manley contended that Irvin was still under contract to the Eagles and refused Brooklyn's offer of $2,500. A year later she offered Irvin to Bill Veeck for $1,000 in a package with Larry Doby, but Veeck declined. The Giants finally signed Irvin in 1949 on the recommendation of executive Chub Feeney, who had gone to high school with Irvin.

The rangy 6-foot 1-inch, 195-pound slugger adjusted slowly to major league pitching and did not hit his stride until June 1951. He credited the improvement to his adapting Ralph Kiner's technique of hitting high outside pitches to right field. That year Irvin hit .312, belted 24 homers, and led the league in RBIs with 121.

With Irvin and Bobby Thomson supplying the power, the Giants won 54 of their last 66 games to take the pennant. Deprived of the major league spotlight in his prime, Irvin made the most of his first World Series game, getting four hits and stealing home in the first inning. He led both teams in hits for the Series, stole the Giants' only two bases, and batted .458 in a losing cause.

On April 2, 1952, Irvin broke his leg in a spring training game slide. Although he came back to hit 21 homers in 1953 and 19 in 1954, his best days were behind him. After finishing his career with the Cubs, he worked in the commissioner's office for many years. He was elected to the Hall of Fame in 1973.

Frank Isbell

Isbell, William Frank **1B-2B**

1898, 1901–09 B:8/21/1875, Delevan, NY
D:7/15/1941, Wichita, KS Deb:5/1/1898, CHI AL
BL/TR 5'11", 190

G	AB	R	H	HR	RBI	OBP	SLG	AVG
1119	4219	501	1056	13	455	.289	.326	.250

On April 24, 1901, Frank Isbell played first base for Charles Comiskey's Chicago White Sox in the first game of the new major circuit, the American League. Five years later, with a .279 average, he was the leading hitter on the world champion White Sox of 1906.

The 1906 Sox were known as "the Hitless Wonders" because they won the pennant despite finishing last in the league in batting average, with a team mark of .230. The pitching-rich team upset the heavily favored crosstown Cubs in the only all-Chicago World Series, four games to two, with a team batting average of only .198.

Isbell was far from "hitless" in the Series; he batted .308. His seven hits were the most ever in two consecutive Series games, and his four doubles were both the most two-baggers and the most extra-base hits achieved in a single Series contest. He balanced that feat by setting a Series record for most errors by a second baseman, which stood until the Los Angeles Dodgers' Davey Lopes broke it in 1981.

Nicknamed "Bald Eagle," Isbell was sensitive about his lack of hair and rarely removed his cap on the field. He was upset when team photos were taken with all the players bareheaded. The lefthanded hitter and righthanded fielder began his major league career playing half a season with the National League Chicago White Stockings in 1898. He then played for Comiskey at St. Paul of the Western League and was with Chicago in the minor American League in 1900.

In 1901, after the league's self-declared rise to major status, Isbell led the circuit with 52 stolen bases. A true utility player, he was used at every position, including pitcher.

On October 2, 1908, Isbell cost teammate Big Ed Walsh a 1–0 game in one of the greatest pitching duels ever. Cleveland's Addie Joss pitched a perfect game, and Walsh gave up four hits and struck out 15. The only run scored because of Isbell's error.

Mike Ivie

Ivie, Michael Wilson **1B**

1971, 1974–83 B:8/8/1952, Atlanta, GA Deb:9/4/1971, SD NL BR/TR 6'3", 205

G	AB	R	H	HR	RBI	OPB	SLG	AVG
857	2694	309	724	81	411	.326	.421	.269

Mike Ivie looked like a golden boy with his bulging muscles and his mane of long blond hair. If he'd had a sunny disposition to match his locks, he might have been a warmly remembered power hitter; instead, he was just another troubled young man unable to live up to his potential.

Taken by the Padres in the first round of the 1970 amateur draft, he hit 79 homers in four minor league seasons, and although he was hurt in 1975, he still won a place on the Topps All-Rookie Team. The next year he led San Diego in batting average and RBIs but didn't show the home run power the team had expected. In 1977 he complained about sharing first base with Gene Tenace. The Padres moved Ivie to third. He sulked, then left the team for several days.

Dealt to the Giants because of his carping, he had a terrific season off the bench in 1978. He batted .387 as a pinch hitter with 20 RBIs in just 31 at bats for San Francisco. Ivie slugged four pinch-hit homers in 1978, including two grand slams to tie the season record set by Gene Freese and equaled by Davey Johnson. Given more playing time, in 1979 he responded with 27 homers, 89 RBIs—his best season ever.

Given that success, he might have gone on to stardom, but during the off-season he accidentally cut a tendon in his hand with a hunting knife. *The Sporting News Guide* said, "The sensitive first baseman couldn't cope with the long rehabilitation process, and the injury also affected his brittle confidence." He retired in midseason, changed his mind, and returned. Dealt to Houston, and then to Detroit in 1982, he later hit 14 home runs as a part-time player with the Tigers. In 1983 after playing in just 12 games, he retired.

Bo Jackson

Jackson, Vincent Edward **OF–DH**

1986–91, 1993–94 B:11/30/1962, Bessemer, AL Deb:9/2/1986, KC AL BR/TR 6'1", 225

G	AB	R	H	HR	RBI	OBP	SLG	AVG
694	2393	341	598	141	415	.311	.474	.250

Howard Johnson once said of Bo Jackson, "Maybe they should see if his body is corked." Jackson had a rare combination of strength, speed, and agility. He was, to be sure, a phenomenon—an athlete who could speak of himself in the third person with the same ease as he hit a baseball or rushed for a touchdown.

"The key was Bo wants to play baseball," Jackson declared when he decided to embark on a professional baseball career. "I want to see what Bo wants to do. Let me state a fact: Bo Jackson can play baseball."

A star running back at the University of Auburn, where he won the 1985 Heisman Trophy, Jackson also played a little college baseball. Though a raw talent, he was projected by scouts to have major league potential, and the Kansas City Royals were willing to take the chance that Bo would find a way to fit baseball into his busy schedule (he was a budding National Football League star with the Los Angeles Raiders). The result was a career filled with moments of tantalizing brilliance that culminated in the disappointment of unrealized potential.

Although the best numbers he would post were 32 homers and 105 RBIs in only 135 games in 1989, Jackson will be best remembered for individual moments of glory. The 1989 All-Star Game when he crushed a Rick Reuschel offering far over the center-field fence in Anaheim as the leadoff hitter for the American League; the catch in which he ran up the wall *ala* Fred Astaire in order to slow his momentum; the one-hand catch of a carom off the left-field wall and throw to the plate to nail a runner. Even after a freak injury ended his football career, Jackson had one final highlight to share. After undergoing hip replacement surgery and sitting out an entire season, Jackson returned to hit a home run in his first at bat.

While he had untold potential, in truth Jackson struck out far too much, walked too little, and was hurt too often. With only 515 at bats in 1989, he struck out 172 times, while walking only 39 times. In his career he struck out more than one of every three times up—841 times in 2,393 at bats. But questions about the career of Bo Jackson will forever linger: What if he had dedicated himself solely to baseball? What if he hadn't hurt his hip? What if...

Grant Jackson

Jackson, Grant Dwight **P**

1965–82 B:9/28/1942, Fostoria, OH Deb:9/3/1965, PHI NL BB/TL 6', 190

W	L	PCT	G	SV	IP	BB	SO	ERA
86	75	.534	692	79	1358^{2}	511	889	3.46

Grant Jackson was the No. 2 man in Pittsburgh's bullpen in the late 1970s and early 1980s, behind angular Kent Tekulve. Particularly effective in 1979 postseason play, he allowed no runs in six appearances.

Jackson, nicknamed "Buck" by a teammate who thought he ambled about like a cowboy, came up to the Phillies in 1965 and won a spot in the rotation in 1967. In 1969 Jackson recorded major league career highs in both wins (14) and losses (18) with the Phils. Traded to Baltimore in December 1970, Jackson went 8–0 with the 1973 Orioles, and that fall he won Game 4 of the ALCS against the A's.

In June 1976 Jackson went to the Yankees in a 10-player deal. That fall the Mariners selected him in the expansion draft, but he never appeared for Seattle. Instead, he was traded in December to Pittsburgh for two infielders.

Jackson appeared in World Series competition with three different clubs—the Orioles, the Yankees, and the Pirates. Only outfielders Andy Pafko and Vic Davalillo and second baseman Eddie Stanky had done so previously.

Joe Jackson

Jackson, Joseph Jefferson **OF**

1908–20 B:7/16/1889, Pickens County, SC D:12/5/1951, Greenville, SC Deb:8/25/1908 PHI AL BL/TR 6'1", 200

G	AB	R	H	HR	RBI	OBP	SLG	AVG
1332	4981	873	1772	54	785	.423	.517	.356

"Say it ain't so, Joe," cried a small boy to "Shoeless Joe" Jackson in September 1920 as news of the 1919 "Black Sox" scandal broke. The kid voiced the desperate hope of an entire nation of fans, but Jackson, described as baseball's greatest natural hitter, let the boy down—as he let down every fan in America.

Jackson, who recorded a lifetime .356 batting average, twice led the AL in hits and three times led the league in triples. Even Babe Ruth admired and copied his batting stance. Jackson fielded flawlessly and had a powerful throwing arm. That a star of his magnitude could sell out the World Series was incomprehensible. But it was true.

Jackson came from a hard life of Southern poverty. Illiterate and possessing no extraordinary mental or social skills, Joe worked in a textile mill just outside of Greenville, South Carolina. He attracted attention playing for the mill's baseball team and was offered a $75 a month contract by the local Class D team. There he picked up the nickname "Shoeless Joe." A new pair of spikes caused blisters on his feet, so he played a game in his stocking feet. No one paid much attention until late in the game, when Jackson slid into third with a triple. A fan of the opposing team screamed, "You shoeless bastard, you!"

When Jackson batted .346 for Greenville, Connie Mack of the Philadelphia Athletics purchased his contract foe $325 near the 1908 season's end. The thought of going to the big city of Philadelphia terrified Jackson. He jumped the train taking him north. Mack finally got him to Philadelphia. Jackson got three hits in his major league debut, then jumped the team again because his teammates ridiculed his hayseed ways.

Mack let his difficult prospect begin the 1909 season with Augusta of the Class C South Atlantic League where he led the league in batting. Philadelphia brought him back up, and he again failed to get along with his teammates. When Jackson spent one afternoon at a burlesque house instead of showing up at brand-new Shibe Park for a game, Mack's patience was at the breaking point. Jackson played only five games for the Athletics that season.

In 1910 Jackson was back in the minors. He hit well in New Orleans but in July Mack traded him to Cleveland for outfielder Bris Lord, with the proviso that Jackson was not to report to Cleveland until after the Southern Association season was over. "I knew exactly what I was doing when I let Jackson go to Cleveland," Mack later explained. "Lord, of course, helped me at the time. I knew our players didn't like Jackson, but that isn't why I traded him. I also knew Joe had great possibilities as a hitter. But at the same time things were going none too well for [owner] Charlie Somers in Cleveland, and I was anxious to do him a good turn in appreciation for the way he had helped us out in Philadelphia in the early days of the league. So I let him have Jackson."

Jackson hit well for Cleveland at the end of the 1910 season. In 1911 he batted .408, but did not win the batting title as Ty Cobb registered a .420 average. The Cleveland ballclub, however, had fallen on hard times—and the emergence of the rival Federal League merely complicated matters. At one point Somers was $1.75 million in debt. In August 1915 he traded Jackson to the White Sox for three players and $31,500. With Chicago Jackson began to develop a reputation for spending large amounts of money on clothes and furnishings. He bought a Greenville poolroom that failed and a farm outside of Greenville that also lost money.

If a ballplayer wanted money, Charles Comiskey's club was the wrong team to be on. Comiskey was generous with the public and with sportswriters, but with his own ballplayers he was a tightwad. Salaries were low, and even meal money was less than what most teams gave players. By 1919 Jackson was making only $6,000 a year for the White Sox.

During World War I Jackson, classified 1-A for the military draft, left the White Sox and took draft-exempt employment at the Bethlehem Steel shipyards near Wilmington, Delaware. While there he continued to play ball, in a Bethlehem Steel League, and took considerable criticism for being a "slacker." "There is no room on my club for players who wish to evade the army draft by entering the employ of shipbuilders," said an angry Comiskey, but after Armistice Day he was all too happy to have Jackson back.

The talented White Sox won the 1917 World Series and the 1919 pennant, but bitter factionalism split the team. In one corner stood Eddie Collins, Ray Schalk, Red Faber, and Dickie Kerr. In the other were rougher and less sophisticated players such as Jackson, Lefty Williams, Happy Felsch, Chick Gandil, and Swede Risberg.

Chicago was a heavy favorite to beat Cincinnati in the 1919 World Series, but they lost the best-of-nine Series in eight games under extremely suspicious circumstances. Rumors of a fix floated openly, and ugly outbursts between Chicago teammates punctuated the Series.

In 1920 Chicago battled the Indians and the Yankees for another pennant, but as the season drew to a close the scandal burst wide open. Faced with evidence of a fix, Jackson and pitcher Eddie Cicotte confessed. Appearing before a Chicago grand jury, Jackson acknowledged having been promised $20,000 to help throw the Series but contended that he had received only $5,000 of that amount. Jackson had batted .375 during the 1919 Series, but admitted he had failed to hustle after balls hit to left field, had made several weak throws, and had struck out in key situations. "I got a big load off my chest!" he concluded.

Leaving the courthouse, Jackson said he was "through with baseball," and admitted to feeling pressure from his fellow conspirators. "Risberg threatens to bump me off if I squawk." According to the *Chicago Herald and Examiner*, a small boy grabbed Jackson's arm and followed him down the street. "Say it ain't so, Joe. Say it ain't so," he pleaded.

Jackson, Risberg, Gandil, Williams, Cicotte, Felsch, Buck Weaver, and Fred McMullin were suspended from the game and in June 1921, with the exception of McMullin, were brought to trial regarding the fix. The trial ended on August 2, and within a few hours the jury brought back acquittals for all defendants.

It was a hollow victory. The next day, newly installed Commissioner Kenesaw Mountain Landis ruled that "Regardless of the verdict of juries, no player that throws a ballgame will ever play professional baseball." Jackson and the other seven "Black Sox" were banned from baseball for life.

In 1924 Jackson sued Comiskey for back pay on the three-year contract he had signed in February 1920. A jury ruled in Jackson's favor, finding that he had not conspired to throw the World Series and that the White Sox had misled him on the terms of the contract. They awarded Jackson more than $16,700. But the judge ordered Jackson jailed for perjury because his testimony denying the fix was at variance with his previous confession, and the jury's verdict was overturned. Jackson and Comiskey later settled out of court.

In 1933 several individuals in Greenville were attempting to place a franchise in Organized Baseball, and proposed that Jackson be its player-manager. Judge Landis, not surprisingly, ruled against the move. "There are not, and cannot be, two standards of eligibility...one for the major leagues, and one for the minors," he stated.

After his banishment Jackson played some semipro ball. Despite reports that he had to support himself as a pants presser, that was hardly the case. Although his earlier business ventures had failed, he successfully ran a fairly large dry-cleaning establishment and a liquor store.

In February 1951 the South Carolina Legislature petitioned for Jackson's reinstatement, but its request was ignored. In December 1951 Jackson suffered his fourth heart attack and died at age 62.

Larry Jackson

Jackson, Lawrence Curtis **P**

1955–68 B:6/2/1931, Nampa, ID D:8/28/1990, Boise, ID Deb:4/17/1955, STL NL BR/TR 6'2", 190

W	L	PCT	G	SH	IP	BB	SO	ERA
194	183	.515	558	37	3262^{2}	824	1709	3.40

Four-time All-Star Larry Jackson led the National League with 24 wins in 1964 and tied for the lead in shutouts in 1966, with five. In 1960 he led the National League in innings pitched, but in spring training 1961 he was hit by a liner off Duke Snider's bat and suffered a broken jaw. In October 1962, St. Louis traded him in a six-player deal to the Cubs. By 1964 he led the league in wins, and that season he also had 109 consecutive errorless chances.

In 1966 Jackson went to the Phils in a deal that sent pitcher Ferguson Jenkins to the Cubs. He remained with Philadelphia through 1968, then retired rather than play for the expansion Expos.

Jackson, who had earned a bachelor's degree from the University of Idaho, returned home after his playing days to pursue a number of occupations. While he worked for a time as a Boise sportswriter and also operated his own insurance agency, he also found employment as a lobbyist for paper and pulp manufacturers and served four terms in the Idaho legislature. In 1978 Jackson, who at one time was executive director of the Idaho Republican State Committee, unsuccessfully sought the GOP nomination for governor.

Mike Jackson

Jackson, Michael Ray **P**

1986–* B:12/22/1964, Houston, TX Deb:8/11/1986, PHI NL BR/TR 6', 200

W	L	PCT	G	SV	IP	BB	SO	ERA
53	61	465	835	138	1017	414	905	3.26

After spending more than a decade as a set-up man, Mike Jackson blossomed into one of baseball's best closers with the Cleveland Indians in 1997. Jackson saved 15 games that season as the Indians won the American League pennant. He followed that with a 40-save year that also featured a 1.55 earned run average, second best of his 14-year career. His 1999 season included a career-best 24 successive save conversions before blowing his first chance on June 4.

Jackson broke into the majors with the 1986 Philadelphia Phillies. He also pitched in San Francisco and Cincinnati, plus two separate stints in Seattle. He was a busy man; Jackson and Indians teammate Paul Assenmacher tied for the most appearances in the 1990s with 644 games apiece. Jackson returned to Philadelphia after the 1999 season, signing as a free agent.

Randy Jackson

Jackson, Ransom Joseph **3B**

1950–59 B:2/10/1926, Little Rock, AR Deb:5/2/1950, CHI NL BR/TR 6'1½", 180

G	AB	R	H	HR	RBI	OBP	SLG	AVG
955	3203	412	835	103	415	.322	.421	.261

A third baseman known for his range, Randy Jackson led National League third sackers in assists and putouts as a rookie in 1951 and tied for the lead in errors. From 1953 through 1955, the righthanded hitter blasted 59 homers for the Cubs, but a knee injury in 1957 permanently limited his range and power.

Nicknamed "Handsome Ransom," Jackson played in the Cotton Bowl for Texas Christian University in 1945. He began his baseball career in 1948 at age 22, with Des Moines, debuting in the majors in 1950 with the Cubs.

His best single game came on April 17, 1954, when he collected four hits (including a homer) in a 23–13 pasting of the Cards. His mammoth four-bagger hit an apartment house across Waveland Avenue, which borders the Cubs' Wrigley Field.

In 1955 Jackson led NL third basemen in double plays, and was named to two All-Star teams. Traded to Brooklyn in 1956, he played in that year's World Series, and hit the last home run in Ebbets Field in 1957.

Reggie Jackson

Jackson, Reginald Martinez **OF–DH**

1967–87 B:5/18/1946, Wyncote, PA Deb:6/9/1967, KC AL BL/TL 6', 200

G	AB	R	H	HR	RBI	OBP	SLG	AVG
2820	9864	1551	2584	563	1702	.358	.490	.262

Any athlete who is recognized by his first name alone is in select company. In the minds of baseball fans, the names Ted, Joe, Mickey, and Willie refer unmistakably to Williams, DiMaggio, Mantle, and Mays, and Reggie refers unmistakably to one Reginald Martinez Jackson, "Mr. October."

His father, Martinez, had briefly played for the Negro League Newark Eagles in the late 1920s and early 1930s. The younger Jackson starred for Wyncote High as a running back and as a pitcher-first baseman in baseball. He received a football scholarship to Arizona State University. Once there, he tried out for the Arizona State baseball team on a five-dollar bet and had an immediate impact on coach Bobby Winkles' ASU powerhouse. During Jackson's sophomore year Arizona State went 41–11. Named to the college All-America team and drafted by the Kansas City Athletics in the first round of the 1966 free-agent draft, the second player chosen overall, he signed for $85,000. By 1967, he was called up to Kansas City. Despite hitting only .178 in 118 at bats, he was installed in the Athletics' outfield in 1968, the team's first season in Oakland.

Owner Charlie Finley's A's were both young and talented. The team moved from 10th to sixth place in 1968 as Jackson, despite a then-record 171 strikeouts, hit 29 home runs in his rookie year.

In 1969, baseball's first year of division play, the A's finished second to Minnesota. Jackson chased Ruth's and Maris' single-season home run records for much of the season, hitting 45 homers by September before slumping and finishing with 47 for the year. Oakland finished second again in 1970 as Jackson batted only .237 with 23 homers.

In 1971 the A's started to put it all together. Pitcher Vida Blue earned American League Cy Young honors with 24 wins, Catfish Hunter chipped in with 21, and reliever Rollie Fingers led a deep and experienced bullpen. On offense, the A's had both power and speed, and Jackson's 32 home runs led the club. Jackson wowed the baseball world in that year's All-Star Game when he socked a home run off the light tower on the right-field roof at Tiger Stadium.

The young, brash, and intimidating A's sported mustaches and white shoes, wore gaudy green and gold uniforms, fought one another and Charlie Finley, and then proceeded to romp through the AL West before falling to Baltimore in the ALCS. The following season the A's won the pennant and defeated the Reds in the World Series in seven games. Jackson, however, missed the Series because he tore a hamstring scoring the winning run in the Athletics' five-game win over Detroit in the Championship Series.

Jackson was named AL MVP in 1973, when he led the league in runs, home runs, and RBIs. He slumped in the playoffs before hitting .310 and leading the A's with six RBIs against the Mets in the World Series. Oakland won in seven games.

The A's won their third straight world championship in 1974, beating Los Angeles in five games. But Charlie Finley lost pitcher Catfish Hunter to free agency in 1975 because of a contract snafu. The A's still won the West, but fell to the Red Sox in the ALCS in three straight games despite Jackson's .417 batting average.

In 1976 free agency was in full swing. Finley took a page from former Athletics owner Connie Mack by trying to sell off or trade away the heart of his ballclub. Jackson was dealt to the Baltimore Orioles for pitcher Mike Torrez and outfielder Don Baylor. Both the A's and the Orioles finished second. Jackson responded with one of his best all-around seasons, hitting .277 with 27 home runs, 91 RBIs, and a career-high 28 stolen bases. In 1977 Jackson filed for free agency and eventually signed with the New York Yankees for a then-record $2.96 million over five years. He bragged that they would name a candy bar after him in New York. They did.

Jackson and New York were made for each other. Jackson craved the spotlight, and New York responded by giving him its full attention. But he was not prepared for the glare. Comments and quips that went unnoticed in Oakland became back-page headlines in New York's tabloids.

Before ever playing a game for New York, Jackson managed to alienate his new teammates in a

Sport magazine interview in which he allegedly stated, "I'm the straw that stirs the drink." Although Jackson later claimed he had been misquoted, Yankees stars Thurman Munson, Sparky Lyle, Graig Nettles, and Chris Chambliss took umbrage. Manager Billy Martin resented Jackson's close relationship with owner George Steinbrenner, and the war was on.

Nevertheless, Jackson earned his salary, hitting 32 home runs and leading the club with 110 RBIs. But his 1977 season is best typified by a single two-day period. During a nationally televised Saturday afternoon game in Boston, Martin thought Jackson second-guessed his call for shortstop Bucky Dent to bunt. Later in the game Jackson misplayed a flyball in right field. Livid, Martin sent outfielder Paul Blair into the game in the middle of the inning to replace Jackson. When Jackson returned to the dugout Martin challenged him to a fight, in front of a national television audience, and had to be restrained.

During the next 48 hours the incident swelled out of proportion. Jackson and Martin met with Yankees general manager Gabe Paul and Steinbrenner, and eventually they reached a tentative peace. Back on the playing field, Jackson went on a tear, and the controversy between Jackson, Martin, and Steinbrenner temporarily subsided.

In the fifth game of the 1977 ALCS against Kansas City, Martin benched Jackson, who bit his tongue, then returned to hit a key single in the comeback victory. Munson sarcastically dubbed Jackson "Mr. October." Jackson soon made the name fit.

In the World Series, the Yankees led the Dodgers three games to one before falling, 10–4, in Game 5. In his last at bat Jackson hit a meaningless home run off Don Sutton. The teams returned to New York for Game 6. Pitcher Burt Hooton walked Jackson on four pitches his first time up. In his next at bat, with New York trailing, 3–2 in the fourth and Munson on first, Jackson hit Hooton's first pitch over the right-field wall for a 4–3 Yankee lead. He came up again in the fifth against pitcher Elias Sosa. On the first pitch, with the crowd chanting "Reg-gie, Reggie!" he hit another home run. In the eighth, with the Yankees leading, 7–4, he came to the plate against knuckleballer Charlie Hough and hit the first pitch into the center-field bleachers. Two games, four pitches, four swings, four consecutive home runs.

Things returned to normal in 1978, which meant that Martin, Jackson, and Steinbrenner squared off again. The Red Sox raced to a huge first-half lead as Jackson slumped. When Martin removed him from the cleanup spot and pulled him from the outfield, Jackson went over Martin's head to Steinbrenner. One night in Kansas City, Martin ordered Jackson to bunt, then changed his mind. Jackson tried to bunt anyway and struck out. Martin again tried to fight him.

Jackson was suspended for five days. When he returned, Martin refused to play him, then griped to Murray Chass of *The New York Times* that "one's a born liar and the other's convicted," referring to Jackson and to Steinbrenner, who had made an illegal contribution to the 1972 Nixon campaign. The comment got Martin fired. He was replaced by Bob Lemon who inserted Jackson back into the cleanup position. The Red Sox collapsed and the Yankees won the division title in a playoff game with Boston. Jackson hit .462 with two home runs and six RBIs in a four-game win in the ALCS, then followed with two more home runs and eight RBIs in the Series as the Yankees again defeated Los Angeles.

The Yankees fell apart in 1979 after the death of Thurman Munson in a plane crash. Martin returned in midseason, only to be fired again in October. The Yankees slumped to third.

The team rebounded in 1980 under new manager Dick Howser. Jackson hit .300 for the only time in his career and slammed 41 homers. The Yankees won the AL East but fell to Kansas City in three straight games in the ALCS. Jackson slumped again in the strike-shortened 1981 season, but the Yankees managed to limp into the World Series on the basis of their first-half finish. This time they fell to the Dodgers in six games in the Series. When Jackson again filed for free agency, Steinbrenner thought he was washed up and let him go.

Jackson surprised everyone by hitting 39 home runs for the Angels, tying for the league lead. On April 27, 1982, in his first game back in New York, he hit a home run. Jackson spent five productive seasons with California, helping them win a division championship in 1982, before signing as a free agent with Oakland in 1987. He retired at the end of that season.

Jackson finished his career with 563 home runs, 1,702 RBIs, and a major league-record 2,597 strikeouts. His performance in postseason play was truly extraordinary. In 27 World Series games he hit .357 with 10 home runs and 24 RBIs. He added six more home runs in the ALCS, and another in the playoff game against Boston. His five Series home runs and 25 total bases in 1977 are major league records. In his 21-year career Jackson was named to the All-Star team 14 times.

Appropriately enough, Jackson, who rarely shared center stage on the field, was the only selection to the Hall of Fame in 1993. Despite his battles with George Steinbrenner, he wore a Yankee cap on his plaque. Ironically, in 1993 he rejoined the Yankees as a special assistant to Steinbrenner. Not surprisingly the two later split on disharmonious terms.

Travis Jackson

Jackson, Travis Calvin **SS-3B**

1922–36 B:11/2/1903, Waldo, AR D:7/27/1987, Waldo, AR Deb:9/27/1922 NY NL BR/TR 5'10½", 160

G	AB	R	H	HR	RBI	OBP	SLG	AVG
1656	6086	833	1768	135	929	.337	.433	.291

Rogers Hornsby, a man known to have been sparing with praise, said of Travis Jackson, "In all the years I watched him, playing with him and against him, I never saw him make a mistake."

Jackson was nicknamed "Stonewall" for his defense at shortstop. He led the National League twice in fielding percentage and four times in assists, and Joe Cronin once said that Jackson was "as good a shortstop as ever lived." As a batter "Stoney" topped .300 six times, once hit game-winning homers in both halves of a doubleheader, and in 1930, a year when batting averages reached new heights, was part of the best-hitting infield in history.

Jackson almost made history in his first major league game. With runners on first and second, a Cincinnati batter hit a liner just to his left. Instead of catching it in the air, Jackson said, "I had to take it on the pickup and so we got a double play. If I had caught it, we would have had a triple play. Imagine, on the first ball hit to me in the majors!"

Jackson was a utility player in 1923, first filling in for Heinie Groh when the third baseman injured his knee and then for regular Dave "Beauty" Bancroft when the shortstop contracted pneumonia in June. The rookie so impressed McGraw that he traded future Hall of Famer Bancroft to the Braves. Giants fans howled over the decision, but soon Jackson was just as good as Bancroft.

From 1925 to 1927, in fact, the Giants boasted a complete Hall of Fame infield: George Kelly at either first or second, Bill Terry at first, Frankie Frisch and Hornsby at second, Jackson at short, and Freddie Lindstrom at third. In 1927, 1928, and 1929 Jackson was named to *The Sporting News* Major League All-Star Team.

Beset by problems with his right knee for a good part of his career, in 1932 he also injured his left knee, and that winter in Memphis had operations on both. Although he went to 1933 spring training, it took him until late in the season to get back into the lineup. By the next season, however, he was named to the All-Star team. In 1982 the Veterans Committee voted him into the Hall of Fame.

Baby Doll Jacobson

Jacobson, William Chester **OF-1B**

1915, 1917, 1919–27 B:8/16/1890, Cable, IL D:1/16/1977, Orion, IL Deb:4/14/1915 DET AL BR/TR 6'3", 215

G	AB	R	H	HR	RBI	OBP	SLG	AVG
1472	5507	787	1714	83	819	.357	.450	.311

Baby Doll Jacobson was a member of a St. Louis Browns outfield that was as good as any in baseball. While the Browns generally finished at the bottom of the American League, for a brief period during the early 1920s they were one of the best teams in the junior circuit. First baseman George Sisler was the star of the club, but he was ably backed by a sensational outfield of left fielder Ken Williams, right fielder Jack Tobin, and Jacobson. From 1919 through 1923, each outfielder hit better than .300.

While playing with Mobile, he received the nickname that stayed with him for the rest of his career. On Opening Day a band in the grandstand played "Oh, You Baby Doll," a popular tune of the day, after Jacobson hit a home run. The next day the newspaper captioned his photo "Baby Doll."

Jacobson spent three seasons in the Southern Association before a chance arose to play in the majors with Detroit in 1915. When he failed to hit, the club traded him to the Browns. By 1916 he was back in the Southern Association. After hitting a league-leading .346, he earned another shot with St. Louis in 1917. Because the 6-foot 3-inch, 215-pound Jacobson was a superior outfielder he won a regular job, despite continuing troubles at the plate. He then missed the entire 1918 season because of military service.

At age 28, Jacobson returned to the Browns and suddenly became a first-rate hitter. In 1919, when the Williams-Tobin-Jacobson outfield first played together, Jacobson hit .323. The next year his 122 RBIs tied Sisler's mark for second in the league, and he batted .355. He followed in 1921 with a .352 mark and 90 RBIs.

In 1922 Jacobson played for the strongest team in Browns history. That season Sisler hit .420, and Williams led the league with 39 home runs. Williams, Sisler, and Tobin each scored more than 120 runs, and second baseman Marty McManus batted in more than 100. As a team the Browns batted .313 and led the league in runs scored. They battled the Yankees for the pennant all season, but New York took a slender lead in August and eventually, with superior pitching, edged St. Louis by one game.

Sisler missed the entire 1923 season with an eye ailment and wasn't the same player after he recovered. Without him, the Browns dropped back to the second division. The outfield continued to produce for several more seasons, but age and injuries torpedoed their pennant hopes.

Not until 1924 did Jacobson, one of the biggest players in the league, hit more than nine home runs in a season. That year he blasted 19, and the next year the righthander hit 15. At one time he held 13 different fielding records, and his 484 putouts in 1924 stood as the record for 24 seasons.

Brook Jacoby

Jacoby, Brook Wallace **3B–1B**

1981, 1983–92 B:11/23/1959, Philadelphia, PA Deb:9/13/1981 ATL NL BR/TR 5'11", 195

G	AB	R	H	HR	RBI	OBP	SLG	AVG
1311	4520	535	1220	120	545	.337	.405	.270

Brook Jacoby, who attended Ventura College, was selected by Atlanta as a seventh-round draft choice in January 1979. The Braves traded Jacoby to Cleveland in October 1983. After a few years of seeing Jacoby perform, Brooks Robinson commented, "Brook is turning out to be a better player than I originally thought. I wasn't the only one who was surprised though; a lot of AL pitchers got caught off guard as well."

Jacoby, who hit three homers in one game on July 3, 1987, tied for the AL lead in both putouts and errors that year. Traded to Oakland in July 1991, he became a free agent in November 1991 and signed with Cleveland in January 1992. At season's end he signed with the Chunichi Dragons of the Japan Central League.

Bill James

James, William Lawrence **P**

1913–15, 1919 B:3/12/1892, Iowa Hill, CA D:3/10/1971, Croville, CA Deb: 4/17/1913 BOS NL BR/TR 6'3", 196

W	L	PCT	G	SH	IP	BB	SO	ERA
37	21	.638	84	5	541²	199	253	2.28

"Seattle" Bill James is one pitcher who can truly say he had a career year. In 1914 his 26–7 record with a 1.90 ERA led Boston's "Miracle Braves" to a world championship. James won just six games before his brilliant season and five games after it.

In 1912 James dropped out of high school and used his fastball and excellent spitball to go 26–8 for Seattle, where he earned his nickname and helped the team claim the Class B Northwestern League pennant. After a mediocre rookie season with the National League Braves, everything fell into place in 1914 for both James and the club, even though James had problems with his veteran second baseman Johnny Evers.

James later explained the feud: "Because of my delivery, batters frequently hit to the opposite field. During one game, in Chicago, I motioned for Evers to move over a bit. He was furious. Here I was, a 22-year-old second-year man, telling the great Evers how to play. He didn't pay any attention to me and the batter hit one right through the spot where I had asked Evers to play. He never liked me after that."

But the Braves and James had more pressing problems during the first half of the 1914 season. On July 4 they were in last place, 15 games behind the New York Giants. Three days later the International League Buffalo Bisons trounced them, 10–2, in an exhibition game. Embarrassed by his club's wretched showing against a team he'd managed for seven years, manager George Stallings screamed, "By God, I'll get you out of last place if I have to break your necks!"

On July 18 the Braves beat the Reds with three ninth-inning runs to escape last place and improve their record to 36–43. By August 1 the Braves had surged to fourth. By August 23, after Dick Rudolph, George "Lefty" Tyler, and James had won 20 straight decisions among them, Boston was tied for first with New York. The Braves went on to take the pennant handily, and James won two World Series games, hurling a two-hitter in Game 2 as the Braves swept Connie Mack's heavily favored Philadelphia Athletics. The next year an arm injury cut short James' promising career.

Vic Janowicz

Janowicz, Victor Felix **C–3B–OF**

1953–54 B:2/26/1930, Elyria, OH D:2/27/1996, Columbus, OH Deb:5/31/1953, PIT NL BR/TR 5'9", 185

G	AB	R	H	HR	RBI	OBP	SLG	AVG
83	196	20	42	2	10	.267	.286	.214

The case of Victor Felix Janowicz is that of a highly skilled athlete who was not a highly skilled baseball player. The 1950 Heisman Trophy winner from Rose Bowl champion Ohio State, Vic Janowicz passed up a contract with the Washington Redskins to play baseball for the Pirates.

The righthanded hitter played catcher, third base, and in the outfield in 1953 and 1954. In 196 major league at bats in his only professional seasons, Janowicz hit .214. After the 1954 season, at age 24, he returned to the gridiron with the Redskins, where, playing halfback, he finished second in the NFL in scoring in 1955. Janowicz's career was cut short in 1956 by a disabling automobile accident.

Larry Jansen

Jansen, Lawrence Joseph **P**

1947–54, 1956 B:7/16/1920, Verboort, OR
Deb:4/17/1947, NY NL BR/TR 6'2", 190

W	L	PCT	G	SH	IP	BB	SO	ERA
122	89	.578	291	17	1765^2	410	842	3.58

New York Giant Larry Jansen had no problem winning 20 games for Leo Durocher, even though he had a league-wide reputation as a "nice guy." In fact, his reputation was so well established that National League president Warren Giles once refused to fine him after he had plunked an enemy batter, noting Jansen had "an excellent conduct record."

After Jansen achieved a 30–6 mark to lead the Pacific Coast League in wins, winning percentage (.833), and ERA (1.57), Giants scout Hank DeBerry heartily recommended that his club purchase the righthander. In 1947, his rookie season, Jansen led the NL in won-lost percentage while winning 21 games. In the 1950 All-Star Game, Jansen struck out six. The next year the Giants came from behind to win the pennant over the Dodgers, and Jansen tied for the league lead in victories with 23. Jansen, however, lost both his World Series starts.

He later served as a longtime Giants pitching coach. Alvin Dark gave him great credit for San Francisco's 1962 pennant. In 1998 he authored an instructional book *The Craft of Pitching.*

Julian Javier

Javier, Manuel Julian (Liranzo) **2B**

1960–72 B: 8/9/1936, San Francisco de Macoris, Dominican Republic Deb:5/28/1960, STL NL BR/TR 6'1", 175

G	AB	R	H	HR	RBI	OBP	SLG	AVG
1622	5722	722	1469	78	506	.298	.355	.257

Julian Javier was a principal in one of those trades that proved invaluable to both teams. When the Pittsburgh Pirates went looking for lefthanded starting pitchers in 1960, they swapped reliever Ed Bauta and Javier, then a minor league second baseman, to the Cards for Wilmer "Vinegar Bend" Mizell and infielder Dick Gray. Mizell helped the Bucs win the world championship that year, but with Javier's artful play at second, the Cards won three NL titles and two Series titles between 1964 and 1968.

A sterling glove man, Javier fit in well with the Cardinals' long tradition of good defense. In 1963 Javier and infield teammates Ken Boyer, Dick Groat, and Bill White all started in that year's All-Star Game.

Javier's three-run homer in Game 7 of the 1967 World Series helped lock it up for the Cards. In four World Series he batted .333. The father of today's major leaguer Stan Javier, the elder Javier started the 1968 All-Star Game, was traded to the Reds in 1972, and retired after the season.

Stan Javier

Javier, Stanley Julian Antonio (de Javier) **OF**

1984–* B: 1/9/1964, San Francisco De Macoris, Dominican Republic Deb:4/15/1984, NY AL BB/TR 6', 185

G	AB	R	H	HR	RBI	OBP	SLG	AVG
1569	4424	676	1182	48	430	.345	.359	.267

Stan Javier came from good baseball bloodlines: His father, Julian, was a star second baseman for the St. Louis Cardinals from 1960 to 1971. Named after Cardinals Hall of Famer Stan Musial, switch-hitting Stan Javier turned pro in 1981 after the Cards signed him as a nondrafted free agent. He broke into the majors three years later with the Yankees, who had acquired him in a five-player trade.

Never a power hitter, Javier was highly regarded for his speed, defense, and versatility. He played all three outfield positions and filled in at all three bases. Javier went to the World Series twice with the Oakland Athletics, earning a ring with the team that won the earthquake-interrupted Series of 1989. The Houston Astros, decimated by injuries to their outfielders, acquired him from San Francisco on August 31, 1999. His .326 average in 20 games helped Houston edge the Reds for the National League Central crown. Javier went 15-for-39 in his final 10 Houston starts. He signed with Seattle after the season as a free agent.

Joey Jay

Jay, Joseph Richard **P**

1953–55,1957–66 B: 8/15/1935, Middletown, CT Deb: 7/21/1953, MIL NL BB/TR 6'4", 228

W	L	PCT	G	SH	IP	BB	SO	ERA
99	91	.521	310	16	1546^1	607	999	3.77

Joey Jay won 21 games in both 1961 and 1962, was once named to the National League All-Star team, and defeated the New York Yankees in the World Series. But, in the end, Jay is remembered principally for his accomplishments as a youngster and for the way baseball took advantage of his youth.

At age 12, Jay enrolled in the newly established Little League program in Middletown, Connecticut. Joey was tall for his age—so tall that the parents of other children unsuccessfully petitioned to bar him from competition because of his size. Ironically, Jay's talent at that age did not equal his stature; not until he reached high school did he show he was destined for the majors. In fact, Jay became the first Little League graduate to hit the big time.

Although he always vowed that his own experience with Organized Baseball for kids was a positive one, Jay was appalled at the abuses he saw in Little League programs everywhere. He went so far as to write a sensitive and sensible magazine article, "Don't Trap Your Son in Little League Madness." Although it was published some 30 years ago, its message still hits home. "I didn't want my son trapped in this Little League madness," Jay wrote. "I discouraged him from joining this year. Instead, he'll be riding his bike, going on camping trips, and occasionally playing pickup ball like anyone his age."

At age 17, Jay himself signed a $40,000 contract with the Milwaukee Braves, thus becoming a "bonus baby." Under the game's rules in the 1950s that meant he had to spend two years on a major league roster rather than with the club's farm team, where he could have developed properly. The ill-conceived rule was designed to stop wealthy clubs from signing up all the good young talent, but it penalized the players in terms of experience. Jay said, "That was a terrible rule, that bonus rule. I got none of the experience I needed, and I took up a spot on the roster someone more deserving should have had. And what a drag I was on the ballclub."

In Jay's case, the bonus signing resulted in seven years in a Braves uniform with only two wins in the first four years and 22 thereafter. Actually, he was beginning to deliver on his promise in 1958, when he was a veteran but still only 22 years old. Until he broke a finger on his pitching hand in midseason, Jay was 7–5 and had a sparkling 2.14 ERA.

When he seemed to be treading water the next two seasons, the Braves traded him to Cincinnati. Jay became a new pitcher overnight. Given a regular spot in the rotation, he led the NL in wins, with 21, and in shutouts, with four. He became the ace of a surprising Reds staff that also boasted significant contributions from Bob Purkey and Jim O'Toole. Cincinnati won the pennant handily only to fall to the Yankees in the World Series in five games. Jay was the only Reds pitcher to win a game, four-hitting the Bronx Bombers, 6–2, in Game 2.

The Reds made a run for a second pennant in 1962. On August 25, Cincinnati won for the 18th time in 21 tries, and Jay won his 20th to put his club within three games of first place. The Reds eventually faded, and the Dodgers and Giants, tied at season's end, played a three-game playoff that San Francisco won.

The Dodgers' unsuccessful run for the pennant had been based largely on the base stealing of shortstop Maury Wills and outfielder Willie Davis. After Jay lost a game to Los Angeles, 3–2, because of their running game, he began varying his windup. Sometimes he would come to a full stop at his waist; sometimes he would hurry his windup; other times, particularly with speedy runners aboard, he would use no windup at all. Jay foiled the Dodgers on occasion, but NL managers complained. The following year the rules committee mandated a complete stop at the belt. Jay suffered one of the worst turnarounds in big league pitching history. From 21–14, he fell to 7–18.

After that, Jay took control of his career again but was barely a .500 pitcher for the balance of his stay with Cincinnati. Joey Jay, the first little leaguer to make the big leagues, is not enshrined at the Little League Museum in Williamsport, Pennsylvania (former U.S. Vice President Dan Quayle, ironically, is).

Hal Jeffcoat

Jeffcoat, Harold Bentley **OF–P**
1948–59 B:9/6/1924, West Columbia, SC
Deb:4/20/1948, CHI NL BR/TR 5'10½", 185

G	AB	R	H	HR	RBI	OBP	SLG	AVG
918	1963	249	487	26	188	.291	.355	.248

W	L	PCT	G	SV	IP	BB	SO	ERA
39	37	.513	245	25	697	257	239	4.22

Outfielder-pitcher Harold Jeffcoat started with Shelby of the Class B Tri-State League in 1946, performing that same year for the Southern Association's Nashville Vols. With Nashville in 1947 he batted .346, drove in 118 runs, and led the league with 630 at bats and 218 hits.

Coming to the majors as an outfielder, he hit two doubles in one inning on May 2, 1948. He injured himself while in the field in 1950. "I was in combat two and a half years as a paratrooper," he remarked. "I made 13 jumps out of an airplane and never got a scratch. Now I get busted up for two months just chasing a little white ball."

Converted to pitching in 1954, he was traded to the Cincinnati Reds in November 1955. He won a dozen games as a starter in 1957, then moved to the bullpen where he saved nine games in 1958. He retired after the season. Jeffcoat's older brother Mike also pitched in the National League.

Gregg Jefferies

Jefferies, Gregory Scott **OF–1B–2B–3B**

1987–* B:8/1/1967, Burlingame, CA Deb:9/6/1987, NY NL BB/TR 5'10", 185

G	AB	R	H	HR	RBI	OBP	SLG	AVG
1424	5378	743	1554	124	649	.347	.422	.289

Gregg Jefferies seemed destined for greatness. Even before his big league debut he was featured in *Sports Illustrated* for his fanatical training regime that included swinging a bat in a swimming pool. The advanced billing seemed prophetic when the 21-year-old third baseman batted .321 in 29 games and knocked veteran Howard Johnson out of the New York Mets' lineup in September 1988. He helped the Mets reach the National League Championship Series, but his costly error in Game 7 was a portent of things to come.

In 1989 Jefferies hit just .258 and antagonized veteran teammates in a clubhouse dominated by superstar egos. When Jefferies faxed a written apology about his performance and behavior that was read with laughter over the radio, his days in New York were clearly numbered. A subsequent trade to Kansas City resulted in a slightly better performance on the field.

A 1993 trade to St. Louis and a move to first base seemed to revive him. Jefferies hit .342 and .325 in two seasons with the Cardinals, leading to a four-year, $20 million free-agent contract with Philadelphia.

Relocated to left field—his fourth big league position—Jefferies batted .306 for the Phillies in 1995, but provided little power and his defense continued to be a liability. The Philadelphia fans soon turned on Jefferies, and nagging injuries and disappointing offensive production marked the remainder of his tenure with the Phillies. He signed with Detroit in 1999, and as a part-time player turned in his worst season.

Fergie Jenkins

Jenkins, Ferguson Arthur **P**

1965–83 B: 12/13/1943, Chatham, Ontario, Canada Deb:9/10/1965, PHI NL BR/TR 6'5", 210

W	L	PCT	G	SH	IP	BB	SO	ERA
284	226	.557	664	49	4500[2]	997	3192	3.34

Ferguson Jenkins became one of the best pitchers in the major leagues in the mid-1960s, but he played in an era that included many other great pitchers, such as Sandy Koufax, Juan Marichal, Bob Gibson, Tom Seaver, and Jim Palmer. As a result, the fans and media often overlooked Jenkins. Nor did he ever appear in a World Series to focus attention on him. Only a handful of players played longer than Jenkins' 19 seasons in the majors without appearing in a World Series. Jenkins lost 13 career 1–0 games (the third most in major league history) and absorbed 45 shutout losses (the sixth most ever).

His personal life fared no better. While pitching for Texas in 1980, he was arrested at a Canadian airport and charged with drug possession; although he denied the charges, believing he had been set up, he was probably kept out of the Hall of Fame for several seasons because of the incident. And the year he finally was elected to the Hall, 1991, his wife died of injuries from an automobile accident. Two years later, Jenkins' girlfriend and daughter were killed. To his credit, Jenkins persevered and in his own quiet way flourished despite such adversity.

Jenkins excelled at baseball, hockey, and basketball in high school. In 1967, after Jenkins was established as a major league pitcher, he played for the Harlem Globetrotters. Despite having played only 15–20 high school baseball games each year due to the short Canadian summer, Jenkins signed with the Philadelphia Phillies for $7,500 after graduating.

Jenkins threw hard, had a good curveball, and demonstrated exceptional control for a young pitcher. The Phillies turned him into a reliever, and he received a late-season call-up in 1965. He started the next season in the bullpen. The Phillies, still smarting from losing the pennant in the last week of the 1964 season, figured they needed some veteran arms to win the pennant in 1966. So on April 21 they packaged Jenkins with outfielder Adolfo Phillips and outfielder-first baseman John Herrnstein and traded them to the Chicago Cubs for veteran pitchers Bob Buhl and Larry Jackson.

In his first appearance for the Cubs, Jenkins cracked a home run and picked up a win in relief. By late summer he had been pushed into the Cubs starting rotation and was on his way to winning 284 games during his career. The Phillies, meanwhile, finished in fourth place in 1966.

For six years Jenkins won 20 or more games each season, averaging about 300 innings, and finishing nearly 75 percent of his starts. In 1968 he lost five 1–0 games on his way to a 20–15 mark. In 1969 he led the NL in strikeouts, with 273. In 1971 his 24 wins finally earned him the Cy Young Award. His pitching performance is all the more remarkable considering that he pitched half his games in hitter-friendly Wrigley Field.

He could also hit. In 1971 Jenkins helped his own cause with six home runs and 20 RBIs. On September 21, 1971, he hit two homers in one game. His 13 career home runs are among the most for a pitcher in major league history.

Each season the Cubs challenged for the pennant early and then faded. Finally, in 1973, Jenkins' streak of six consecutive 20-win seasons ended. He went 14–16 and was traded to the Texas Rangers. He bounced back in 1974 with a career-best 25–12 record, earning Comeback Player of the Year honors from *The Sporting News*. But when he slumped the following season to 17–18, he was dealt to the Red Sox.

It appeared Jenkins might finally get to play on a pennant winner, but the Sox disappointed him. Jenkins pitched fairly well, winning 22 games in two seasons, but the Sox were dissatisfied with his performance. Jenkins was aligned with a group of players headed by pitcher Bill Lee who called themselves "the Loyal Order of the Buffalo Heads," and he fell out of favor with Boston's conservative front office. After the 1977 season he was dumped to Texas. Again he bounced back to win 51 games in four seasons in Texas before finishing up with two seasons with the Cubs, ending as one of baseball's best control pitchers ever, averaging just 1.99 walks per game.

Hughie Jennings

Jennings, Hugh Ambrose **SS–1B**

1891–1903, 1907, 1909, 1912, 1918 M(1907–20, 1924–25, 1,184–995) B:4/2/1869, Pittston, PA D:2/1/1928, Scranton, PA Deb:6/1/1891 LOU AA BR/TR 5'8½", 165

G	AB	R	H	HR	RBI	OBP	SLG	AVG
1285	4904	994	1527	18	840	.390	.406	.311

The most commonly reprinted photo of Jennings shows the freckle-faced redhead in mid-stamp—eyes ablaze, mouth twisted in a snarl. If photos could talk, that one would scream a baffling "Ee-yah!"

Some say Jennings' distinctive yell evolved from "That's the way!" to "Way-yah!" and thence to its final form. Another theory holds that a Hawaiian pitcher once told him it meant "Watch out!" However it originated, the call shattered eardrums on major league diamonds for more than 30 seasons. Even today, 70-plus years after the yell last echoed, baseball buffs who know about Hughie Jennings know "Ee-Yah!"

But there was much more to "Hustling" Hughie Jennings. He managed three pennant winners, played on five championship teams, and for a time was arguably the best player in baseball.

Jennings' father was a coal miner. The young Jennings worked as a breaker boy in the mines for 90 cents a day, but when he discovered he could make $5 a game playing semipro ball on Sundays, his future was determined. In 1890 he turned professional with Allentown of the Eastern Interstate League.

The next season Jennings played shortstop for Louisville of the then-major American Association. His original uniform reportedly was made from three pillowcases. With his bright red hair, Jennings was described as looking "like a flaming red peony in a field of white chrysanthemums." He hit a strong .292 in 90 games as a rookie, but the league was in its final year and its on-field integrity was suspect. The Colonels moved to the National League in 1892, and the improved pitching sent Jennings' batting average into a nosedive. He hit a mere .136 in 23 games in 1893, and Louisville was happy to send him to Baltimore.

Orioles manager Ned Hanlon was amassing a collection of young players about to blossom. By 1894 he had gathered such future immortals as John McGraw, Joe Kelley, and Willie Keeler. Jennings was Hanlon's choice for the key position of shortstop. In spring training Hanlon drilled his young birds in scientific baseball—the bunt, the hit-and-run play, and the stolen base. He also encouraged his players to intimidate the opponent with interminable arguing, intentional spiking, raw bullying, and vicious bench jockeying. Finally, he taught the Orioles dirty baseball. Hanlon's questionable methods included base runners cutting across the infield when the umpire turned his back, outfielders hiding extra balls in tall grass to throw in on long hits, and infielders grasping enemy base runners by the belt to delay their progress.

Jennings, who was named team captain, and McGraw were Hanlon's prize pupils. Both men were ready to fight at the slightest provocation, both were more intelligent than most of their teammates or opponents, and both were driven by a boundless desire to win. They became fast friends and even attended classes together at St. Bonaventure University, but there was nothing saintly about the way they played baseball. The heart of the Orioles, they quickly became the two most detested players in the league. Umpires cringed when either zeroed in for an argument. Some shed tears as McGraw and Jennings took turns screaming hideous obscenities, spraying mists of tobacco juice into the arbiters' eyes and grinding their spikes into the umpires' toes.

The Orioles played ugly, dirty, dishonest baseball, as did several other clubs, and took three consecutive pennants from 1894 through 1896. During this period Jennings was their best player. Starting in 1894 he led league shortstops in fielding for four straight seasons. He also was tops in assists and double plays twice and putouts once. A terror at the plate, he drove in more than 100 runs and scored at least 125 in each pennant season. After hitting .335 in 1894, he jumped up to .386 in 1895 and .401 in 1896.

Because of his aggressive attitude Jennings was a master at getting hit by pitches, and NL pitchers were only too happy to oblige. In 1896 they plunked him 49 times, a record that lasted until 1971 when Ron Hunt became an even better target. In 1897 an Amos Rusie fastball fractured Jennings' skull, and the shortstop missed the last month of the season. Without him the Orioles finished second. He bounced back for another outstanding season in 1898, but Baltimore's best days were over, and the team finished second again. Jennings later suffered two more skull fractures after driving a car off a cliff and diving into an empty swimming pool.

In 1899 Hanlon and Baltimore owner Harry Von der Horst bought a controlling interest in the Brooklyn team while retaining their Orioles stock. Hanlon became Brooklyn's manager and moved Jennings, Keeler, and Kelley, along with pitchers Jim Hughes and Doc McJames, to his new club. After Jennings' arm went bad, Hanlon tried to palm the shortstop off on Pittsburgh. But Jennings, no matter how much he bent the rules on the field, was an honest man. He wrote to the Pittsburgh owner and admitted he was damaged goods.

Hanlon then sent Jennings to Baltimore, but the player was back in Brooklyn after two games. Playing part-time at first base, he helped Brooklyn win two straight pennants but was only a shadow of his former self. After spending 1901 and 1902 as a utility man, he all but retired as a player and turned to managing.

His major league playing career is listed as 17 seasons, but in the last five Jennings appeared in only seven games total. His finest years were with Baltimore from 1894 through 1898, when he played the bulk of his 1,285 games. During that period he was probably the best player on baseball's best team. He finished with a .311 career average, 994 runs, and 840 RBIs.

From 1903 through 1906 he managed Baltimore of the Eastern League, playing whenever his bad arm permitted. Four straight first-division finishes earned him a job as skipper of the Detroit Tigers in 1907. He inherited a team that had finished sixth in 1906. Its assets were a couple of good pitchers, a great outfielder in Sam Crawford, and a 20-year-old firebrand named Ty Cobb.

In his third major league season Cobb exploded, becoming the best player in the American League and leading the circuit in batting, hits, RBIs, and stolen bases. Jennings' Tigers fought off Philadelphia and brought a pennant home to Detroit. But in the World Series the Chicago Cubs of Tinker-to-Evers-to-Chance fame proved too strong and defeated Detroit in five games.

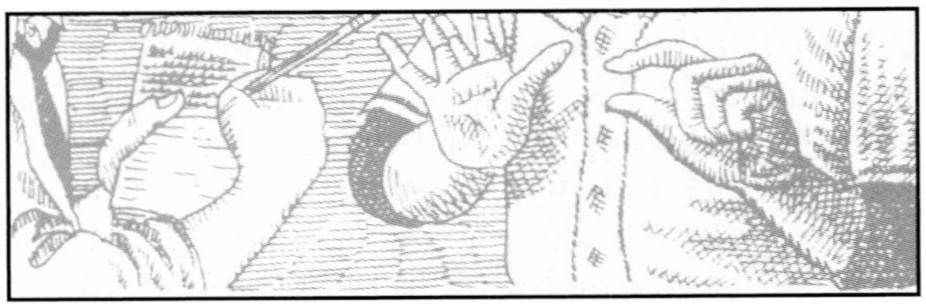

The next two seasons followed a similar script. Cobb, assisted by Crawford, terrorized American League pitchers, and the Tigers won close pennant races followed by World Series losses. In 1908 Detroit edged Cleveland by half a game, then fell to the Cubs. In 1909 the Tigers held off a surprise challenge by Philadelphia to take the flag, then lost to Pittsburgh in the Series.

Despite the Series failures, Jennings became the first manager to win pennants in his first three seasons at the helm. He ran a stern ship, often goading his men with ridicule and sarcasm. But Cobb received special treatment. In his playing days Jennings had been a fighter hated by opponents and their fans. Cobb went even further. He fought not only with his opponents and their fans, but also with his own teammates and the Tigers' fans. Yet the same fury that drove Cobb to attack anyone who crossed him probably made him a great ballplayer.

Jennings let Cobb set his own training rules. Reportedly, Jennings suggested to Cobb that he sit in the dugout and sharpen his spikes to intimidate enemy infielders. For several years Jennings played Crawford, a natural right fielder, in center field and Cobb, who had a weak arm, in right field because Cobb and left fielder Matty McIntyre hated each other so much that they refused to speak, even to call for fly balls.

After 1909 Cobb continued to win batting titles but Jennings won no more pennants. During the next 11 years he finished second twice, third twice, and fourth three times, but he never had effective pitching. When he finished seventh in 1920, Cobb replaced him as manager.

Jennings had earned a law degree at Cornell, but his old friend, John McGraw, asked him to join the New York Giants as third base coach. "Ee-Yah!" echoed through the Polo Grounds. Although the Giants won the pennant and World Series, they may have been the most browbeaten team of all time. Not only did they receive tongue-lashings from McGraw, but also they were the objects of Jennings' sarcastic barbs, along with those of coach Jesse Burkett. Burkett was so hated for his venomous tongue that the players refused to vote him a share of their World Series money.

Jennings helped McGraw win four straight pennants. In 1925, when McGraw became ill, Jennings guided the team for much of the season. But the strain was too much. After the season he suffered a nervous breakdown. While recovering he learned that he was suffering from tuberculosis. Jennings died in 1928. In 1945 the Veterans Committee named him to the Hall of Fame. His plaque cites both his play as a shortstop and the pennants he won as a manager.

Jackie Jensen

Jensen, Jack Eugene **OF**

1950–59,1961 B:3/9/1927, San Francisco, CA
D:7/14/1982, Charlottesville, VA Deb:4/18/1950, NY AL
BR/TR 5'11", 190

G	AB	R	H	HR	RBI	OBP	SLG	AVG
1438	5236	810	1463	199	929	.372	.460	.279

To say that a man who had won three American League RBI titles and was league Most Valuable Player never reached his potential may seem unfair. But that's how the baseball world remembers Jackie Jensen, who retired at age 32 because of his fear of flying, and because baseball was interfering with his family life.

Jensen had an unstable childhood. His parents divorced when he was five and his mother, a warehouse worker, moved the family "every time the rent came due." An accomplished athlete and a fast and deceptive runner, Jensen became an All-America fullback for the University of California. Known as "the Golden Boy," he set a school record by running for 1,080 yards in 1948.

The Pacific Coast League Oakland Oaks signed Jensen for $75,000 before the 1949 season, outbidding several major league clubs. He and Billy Martin were sold to the New York Yankees for $100,000 the next year. When Jensen married Olympic diving medalist Zoë Ann Olson in 1949, the *San Francisco Chronicle* called them "the world's most famous sweethearts."

Jensen had trouble breaking into the potent Yankees lineup and was shuttled to the minors, and in 1952 he was traded to the Washington Senators. In December 1953 he was traded again, this time to the Red Sox for two players. Terrified of flying and missing his home life in California, Jensen talked about not reporting to the Sox. Red Sox GM Joe Cronin gave him an extra $1,000 to continue playing.

Jensen followed with six excellent years in Boston. He hit 20 or more homers each year and only once missed the 100-RBI mark. In 1958, his MVP year, Jensen slammed 35 home runs and drove in 122. Then he quit after the 1959 season. "I have only one life to live," he said, "and I'll be happier when I can spend it with my family. Being away from home with a baseball team for seven months a year doesn't represent the kind of life I want or the kind of life my wife and children want."

Jensen changed his mind after a year and came back to the Red Sox. But unable to control his panic at airports he jumped the team on April 29, 1961, and hired a nightclub hypnotist to help him with his problem. The hypnotist later theorized that the fear of flying was "merely a subterfuge. Jackie needed the fear as an excuse to get home and patch up his marriage. Subconsciously, it developed as a good reason to leave the Red Sox and go home."

Frustrated from a disappointing year in which he drove in only 66 runs and still feared flying, he retired for good at the end of the season. The world's most famous sweethearts divorced soon after.

Sam Jethroe

Jethroe, Samuel **OF**

1950–52, 1954 B:1/20/1922, East St. Louis, IL
Deb:4/18/1950, BOS NL BB/TR 6'1", 178

G	AB	R	H	HR	RBI	OBP	SLG	AVG
442	1763	280	460	49	181	.337	.418	.261

Sam Jethroe is one of baseball's desegregation pioneers, often overlooked amid the contributions of Jackie Robinson, the first African-American to take the field in the modern major leagues, and Larry Doby, the first in the American League. Jethroe was the first African-American to play for a Boston team. As had many black stars in those early days of integrating the majors, Jethroe arrived well past his prime, but he still showed enough ability to win NL Rookie of the Year honors.

Jethroe, who spent seven seasons with the Cleveland Buckeyes, was nicknamed "Jet" for running at speeds so overwhelming that opponents worked on special strategies to contain him. He batted better than .300 during his stint in Cleveland and led the Negro Leagues in hitting in 1942, 1944, and 1945.

Meanwhile, social forces were building for blacks to play in the majors, although most teams lacked the will or courage to make the move. In 1945, a Boston councilman put pressure on the Red Sox to grant black players a tryout. It took place on April 16, with Red Sox coaches Hugh Duffy and Larry Woodall taking a look at Jethroe, Jackie Robinson, and Philadelphia Stars keystoner Marvin Williams. The tryout was a charade, as the Red Sox never had any intention of integrating their team at that time, a view reinforced by the fact that general manager Eddie Collins did not even attend.

In 1947, Brooklyn Dodgers executive Branch Rickey made the move, enlisting Robinson to break the color line. With the initial step having been taken, blacks slowly began to appear in the minor leagues with more frequency. The Dodgers added Jethroe to the roster of their Montreal club in the International League. As the leadoff man for the Royals, he created such havoc that opposing manager Paul Richards sometimes intentionally walked the batter in front of him just to prevent Jethroe from tearing around the bases.

Jethroe's statistics compared favorably to those posted by Robinson in 1946. He finished the 1949 Montreal campaign with 207 hits, including 19 triples, and scored 154 runs. Following the 1949 season, the Boston Braves acquired Jethroe from the Dodgers for $100,000. In 1950 Jethroe finally got his chance to play in the major leagues and was one of the big stories in the Braves' camp. Despite his speed and ability to hit, however, he was not judged to be a complete ballplayer. His throwing was not up to par for a center fielder, and his defensive instincts left something to be desired. For one thing, he played too deep, preferring, as many ballplayers do, to come in on a ball rather than go back.

Despite these flaws, and the fact that the social climate was not always comfortable for black athletes, Jethroe became one of the better players in the National League. He won the basestealing crown with 35, scored 100 runs, and batted .273, with 18 homers and 58 RBIs. In those early days of the Rookie of the Year Award, he was the third African-American to capture the honor in four years, following Robinson and pitcher Don Newcombe.

Even better in 1951, Jethroe repeated his stolen base crown and batted .280, with 101 runs scored, 29 doubles, 10 triples, 18 homers, and 65 RBIs. In 1952 his performance fell off, as he hit only .232 and struck out 112 times. After spending 1953 in the minors, Jethroe went to Pittsburgh during the off-season as part of a blockbuster deal in which the Braves sent six players, plus money, to the Pirates for infielder Danny O'Connell. Jethroe played only two games for Pittsburgh, and his career was over.

Derek Jeter

Jeter, Derek Sanderson **SS**

1995–* B:6/26/1974, Pequannock, NJ Deb:5/29/1995, NY AL BR/TR 6'3", 175

G	AB	R	H	HR	RBI	OBP	SLG	AVG
638	2537	486	807	63	341	.392	.465	.318

At just 25, Derek Jeter is already being talked about as the greatest shortstop in the history of the New York Yankees, a franchise that requires winning multiple world championships before a player can even be considered as one of its best. With three rings in his first four years in the majors, Jeter has already passed the first hurdle.

Jeter's abilities were recognized early. The American Baseball Coaches Association named him High School Player of the Year in 1992. The Yankees made him their first-round draft pick that June, and Sally League managers voted Jeter the "Most Outstanding Major League Prospect" at Class-A Greensboro. In 1994 he was everybody's choice—*Baseball America, The Sporting News, USA TODAY Baseball Weekly*—as Minor League Player of the Year after hitting .344 at Triple-A Columbus, Double-A Albany, and Class-A Tampa. He was called up to the Yankees in May 1995 when Tony Fernandez went on the disabled list. He hit just .250 in his 15-game stint with the Yankees, but it proved to be just a prelude to stardom.

In 1996 Jeter became the first Yankees rookie since Tom Tresh in 1962 to start at shortstop on Opening Day. He played 157 games, hit .314, and followed up with a .361 postseason average as the Yankees won their 23rd world championship. He was also named American League Rookie of the Year.

Jeter's hits, home runs, RBIs, and batting average rose steadily from 1997 to 1999. In 1998 he played in his first All-Star Game. In 1999 he batted .348 and posted his best power numbers—24 home runs, 102 RBIs, and a .552 slugging average. Jeter also averaged 116 strikeouts a season since 1996, considered far too many for a No. 2 hitter, but few shortstops have ever been able to provide such offensive punch.

Tommy John

John, Thomas Edward **P**

1963–74, 1976–89 B:5/22/1943, Terre Haute, IN Deb:9/6/1963, CLE AL BR/TL 6'3", 185

W	L	PCT	G	SH	IP	BB	SO	ERA
288	231	.555	760	46	4710^{1}	1259	2245	3.34

In baseball's happiest medical fairy tale, lefthander Tommy John was the first pitcher to undergo ligament transplant surgery in his pitching elbow and return to his pre-injury form. John recovered to hurl a record-setting 26 seasons in the majors (a record since broken by Nolan Ryan), finishing with 288 wins, 21st on the all-time list.

John pitched for the Indians and White Sox with modest success before being traded to the Dodgers for Dick Allen in 1971. With Los Angeles, the lefthander was 25 games over .500 in his first three seasons, and led the NL in winning percentage with a 16–7 record in 1973. The league's top winner at 13–3 on July 17, 1974, John heard a crunch inside his left elbow while pitching in Montreal. He tried throwing batting practice three weeks later and couldn't throw, confirming he'd torn elbow ligaments.

Until he underwent surgery, doctors didn't know how bad a tear it was. Dodgers orthopedist Dr. Frank Jobe warned John of the worst-case scenario—a ruptured ligament that would require a transplant from his right wrist. A ligament transplant had never been done on a pitcher and Jobe estimated the odds of returning to the mound for the 31-year-old John at 100–1. John had the surgery on September 25, 1974, and woke up with his right forearm bandaged, knowing the worst case had occurred.

The Dodgers won the National League West in 1974 and invited John to throw out the first pitch of the first playoff game at Dodger Stadium, which he did righthanded, believing he'd thrown his last pitch at a big league park. In addition to the transplant, doctors had repaired muscle and nerve damage. But that December John needed a second operation to reroute the nerve because his left hand had gone numb and contracted into a full-time fist. John spent all of 1975 in rehabilitation, lobbing balls against a wall to rebuild his arm strength and squeezing silly putty and golf club grips to return feeling and movement to his hand.

The odds were against a comeback, particularly when the 1976 spring training lockout by the owners gave John little opportunity to work back into pitching shape or to demonstrate his soundness. The Dodgers were also concerned about his pitching speed of 85 miles per hour, although John realized he hadn't thrown any harder before the operation. He was told the Dodgers were ready to release him if he didn't do well in his second start, but he threw seven shutout innings for a reprieve and went 10–10 with a 3.09 ERA and 207 innings pitched for the season. John won Comeback Player of the Year honors from *The Sporting News* and a spot in the 1977 Dodger rotation.

In 1977 John went 20–7, winning 14 of his last 17 decisions, as the Dodgers unseated the two-time world champion Cincinnati Reds in the National League West. He ranked fifth in the league with a 2.78 ERA and finished second to Steve Carlton in Cy Young voting.

An All-Star and 17-game winner in 1978, John became a free agent during the off-season. He signed with the Yankees and had his best year in 1979 when he won 21 games with a 2.96 ERA. He then went 22–9 for the AL East champions in 1980, posting a league-high six shutouts.

In August 1981 John's 3-year-old son, Travis, was critically injured in a fall from a third-story window. After spending 14 days in a coma, Travis made a complete recovery. John and his wife, Sally, wrote a book describing how their Christian faith helped them survive the ordeal. John tossed five straight complete games in September as Travis healed.

The Yankees traded John to the California Angels on August 31, 1982, and he went on to help the Angels win the AL West. But after two losing seasons and escalating ERAs, he was released in June 1985. Prior to the 1987 season, John announced his retirement to become pitching coach at the University of North Carolina, but he resigned after one month on the job and returned to the Yankees to go 13–6. At age 44 John noted that it was his arm's bar mitzvah year, the 13th anniversary of his historic surgery. He pitched for two more seasons, finishing with 51 wins after age 40, eighth on the all-time list.

Alex Johnson

Johnson, Alexander **OF–DH**

1964–76 B:12/7/1942, Helena, AR Deb:7/25/1964, PHI NL BR/TR 6', 205

G	AB	R	H	HR	RBI	OBP	SLG	AVG
1322	4623	550	1331	78	525	.329	.392	.288

Alex Johnson won the American League batting crown in 1970, but he is remembered most for the trouble he caused in clubhouses.

Johnson broke into the majors in 1964 at age 21 and hit .303 in 109 at bats with Philadelphia. The righthanded outfielder was both platooned and employed as a pinch hitter through two seasons in Philadelphia and two dismal years in St. Louis. In 1968 Johnson got the chance to play regularly for the Reds and hit .312; *The Sporting News* named him NL Comeback Player of the Year. He followed with a .315 mark in 1969.

In November 1969 Johnson and infielder Chico Ruiz were traded to the Angels, and Johnson did not take it well. "I'd rather play in hell than for the Angels," he contended. Nevertheless, in 1970 Johnson led the AL with a .329 average while playing in California, edging out Carl Yastrzemski, .3289 to .3286.

Johnson's behavior was unstable. He and Ruiz once brawled at the Angels' batting cage, and Johnson developed a special dislike for reporters, once dumping coffee grounds into the typewriter of *Los Angeles Herald-Examiner* journalist Dick Miller. Johnson's behavior toward reporters became so objectionable that they filed a formal complaint against him. He responded with telegrams that promised, "In the future I will not talk with you in any manner, offensive or otherwise."

In 1971 the Angels benched Johnson four times and fined him on 29 occasions, and on June 26 they suspended him "for failure to give his best efforts to the winning of games." Charges of gunplay in the Angels' clubhouse filled the air as Johnson alleged that Ruiz had pulled a gun on him. The Players Association filed a grievance, arguing that Johnson was suffering from emotional stress and should be reinstated. "He's got a problem deep inside him that he won't talk about," said teammate Tony Conigliaro. "He's so hurt inside it's terrifying." On September 28, 1971, arbitrator Lewis Gill ruled in Johnson's favor, restoring to him $29,970 in back pay and establishing the baseball precedent that emotional incapacitation is akin to physical injury. Johnson played five more years for four teams, but he never again hit .300.

Ban Johnson

Johnson, Byron Bancroft
AL President (1901–27) B:1/5/1864 Norwalk, OH D:3/28/1931, St. Louis, MO

In the first two decades of the 20th century the most powerful and most important man in baseball was not a player, manager, or owner. American League President Ban Johnson held sway over not only his own circuit but also over all of baseball. If his power was not absolute, it nonetheless exceeded that of any other individual. Overall, his reign was beneficial to the game. The tragedy was that it lasted too long.

Johnson was born in Cincinnati, where his father was a prominent school administrator. The young Johnson played baseball as a boy and later as a student at Marietta College. A big fellow with a square jaw, he was regarded as a steady and fearless catcher who worked without a glove, mask, or chest protector. Although his family wanted him to enter the ministry, Johnson wanted to practice law, and after a year at Marietta he entered the University of Cincinnati Law School. Soon after leaving school, however, he joined the *Cincinnati Commercial-Gazette*, specializing in sportswriting, for $25 a week. In 1887 he became sports editor.

His strong opinions won Johnson both friends and foes in the Cincinnati baseball establishment. One of his closest friends was Charles Comiskey, who became manager of Cincinnati's National League ballclub in 1892 after winning four pennants in the American Association. The two men spent many hours discussing how to improve baseball. In particular, they decried the "rowdyism" often found on the playing field. Ironically, Johnson was a bitter enemy of John T. Brush, the owner of the Cincinnati team and Comiskey's employer. While Comiskey loyally defended his boss, Johnson attacked him in the newspaper. He believed Brush didn't spend enough money on the Reds and was allied with other owners who were more interested in making a profit than in ensuring the long-term good of the game. Johnson called him the "past master of parsimony" and a "representative of interests best divorced from baseball."

In 1894 the recently founded Western League, a minor circuit, was looking for a president. Comiskey told Brush that Johnson might make an excellent administrator. Brush got Johnson the job, thereby silencing his sternest critic. The Western League had teams in Indianapolis, Kansas City, Milwaukee, Minneapolis, Toledo, Grand Rapids, Detroit, and Sioux City. When Comiskey's contract at Cincinnati expired he purchased the Sioux City franchise and moved it to St. Paul. Then he and Johnson began planning for further expansion.

Soon Johnson's Western League had a reputation as the best-run minor circuit in the country. Johnson insisted that his umpires crack down on rowdy play. As a result Western League games now were considered family entertainment because sensitive fans would not witness violent behavior or hear bad language there. Attendance increased dramatically. As the Western League was improving its image, the 12-team National League was falling into disrepute. The Cleveland Spiders and Baltimore Orioles raised rowdyism to an art form, and squabbles among the owners, disregard for the public, and the ill treatment of players outraged the fans.

Johnson and Brush continued to cross swords. Brush owned stock in the Western League's Indianapolis franchise. He would draft Western League players presumably to play for Cincinnati, but in fact he deposited them back in the Western League with Indianapolis. He then brought players from Indianapolis to Cincinnati and sold them at a profit. Outraged, Johnson eventually used his growing influence to force Brush to dispose of his Indianapolis stock.

Johnson ran his league as a dictator. Vain, forceful, and stubborn, he drafted schedules, arranged travel contracts, signed players, and shifted franchises at will. The team owners, happy with their profits, gave him a free hand. In 1899 when the National League pared back to eight teams, lopping off Cleveland, Washington, Louisville, and Baltimore, Johnson saw an opportunity to expand. At a meeting of Western League officials that October, its name was changed to the American League to give it a more national character. Johnson then announced that the league would expand by placing one franchise in Cleveland and moving Comiskey's St. Paul club to Chicago.

The Cubs (then called "Orphans") were entrenched in Chicago, and their owner agreed to the invasion of Comiskey's team only because the league feared a revival of the old American Association. By giving Johnson the south side of Chicago, the league thought it was blocking the defunct league. But plans for a new American

Association never materialized, and by the time the National League figured that out, Johnson had turned the American League into a national entity. In 1901 Johnson, armed with a 10-year contract as American League president, placed clubs in Philadelphia, Boston, Baltimore, and Washington, and retained franchises in Cleveland, Chicago, Detroit, and Milwaukee. The following year St. Louis replaced Milwaukee, and in 1903 New York replaced Baltimore.

Few National League owners realized that a second league would spur interest among the fans, increase their attendance, and make a postseason contest possible. Most of them preferred to crush their new rivals. For two years a "war" raged between the two leagues, but the NL never had a chance. Johnson shored up weak franchises by finding financial backers and moving star players to struggling teams, while the older league foolishly capped salaries at $2,400. As a result, 87 NL players jumped to the new league for more money, and by 1902 American League attendance surpassed that in the National League.

The two leagues eventually reached an agreement, establishing a three-man National Commission, composed of both league presidents and a third member elected from among the owners, to rule baseball. The third man was Garry Herrmann, president of the Cincinnati Reds and Johnson's old friend. Although Herrmann was not quite a rubber stamp, he generally sided with the American League president. Johnson was dubbed "the Czar of Baseball," only a slight exaggeration.

Between 1903 and 1920 baseball reached new heights of popularity and prosperity, and truly became the national pastime. Much of the credit goes to Johnson and his firm leadership. He barred liquor from his ballparks, upgraded the umpiring, and continued his crackdown on violence among players and fans. When a new Federal League tried to become a major player in 1914 and 1915, Johnson led the charge to keep it out of the major leagues.

But Johnson's best days were behind him. Beginning in 1916 he antagonized owners in both leagues with several of his decisions concerning players. One person he angered was his old friend, Comiskey, and the two became bitter enemies. During World War I Johnson groveled before politicians to ensure the completion of the 1918 season, upsetting many patriotic fans. His atrocious handling of player unrest in the World Series that year almost resulted in Major League Baseball's suspension. In 1919 Johnson vetoed the sale of Boston Red Sox pitcher Carl Mays to the New York Yankees, but was overruled by the New York Supreme Court.

Johnson's influence was on the wane by the 1919 World Series. After the White Sox lost the first two games, Comiskey reportedly sent Johnson word in the middle of the night that a fix might be under way. Johnson allegedly responded, "That's the yelp of a beaten cur!" and went back to bed. Later when he became convinced that the Series had not been played on the up-and-up, Johnson launched a full investigation.

When the details of the scandal came to light, the triumvirate was replaced by a single man, Judge Kenesaw Mountain Landis. Johnson clashed often with Landis but seldom received any support from American League owners. At last, in July 1927, Johnson resigned as league president, refusing to accept any compensation for the eight years remaining on his $40,000-a-year contract. Already ill, his health continued to decline in retirement. Johnson died of diabetes in 1931 at age 67. In 1937 he was named to the Hall of Fame.

Most of Johnson's successes and failures can be traced to his own personality. Johnson was an utterly humorless autocrat devoted to his work. Unwilling to compromise, he lacked the political dexterity to influence those he couldn't bend to his will. At the same time he was completely fearless and an excellent organizer, and Major League Baseball would not be what it is today without Johnson. The American League was his creation, his life's work, and ultimately his monument.

Bob Johnson

Johnson, Robert Lee **OF**

1933–45 B:11/26/1906, Pryor, OK D:7/6/1982, Tacoma, WA Deb:4/12/1933, PHI AL BR/TR 6', 180

G	AB	R	H	HR	RBI	OBP	SLG	AVG
1863	6920	1239	2051	288	1283	.393	.506	.296

Bob Johnson was a seven-time All-Star outfielder with second-division American League clubs in the 1930s and early 1940s. Because he was part Cherokee, he was called "Indian Bob." Columnist Red Smith noted that "Bob was a first-rate outfielder with a powerful and accurate throwing arm. He was right-handed all the way, a flatfooted hitter with power."

Although he led the league with a .431 on-base percentage in 1944 and tied the American League record of six RBIs in a single inning, Johnson should be remembered for one of the most consistent careers on record. During 13 seasons, Johnson hit more than 20 homers nine times, drove in more than 100 runs eight times, and earned more than 75 bases on balls 10 times.

In 1933 Philadelphia sold veteran Al Simmons to the White Sox, and Johnson beat out Lou Finney for the center field job. In his rookie season, Johnson collected 69 extra-base hits, including 44 doubles. On June 16, 1934, he had his best single day at the plate. He went 6-for-6, with a double and two homers.

During a series of poor seasons for the Athletics it seemed that on some days Johnson alone constituted the offense. On June 12, 1938, he drove in all eight runs in an A's win over the Browns.

After the 1942 season, Johnson thought Philadelphia was underpaying him and demanded a trade. Owner Connie Mack complied and sent the valuable outfielder to Washington for another flyhawk and cash. Johnson was still a valuable player but no longer the power threat he was in his youth. After hitting only seven homers for Washington in 1943 he was sold to the Red Sox at the end of the season.

Aided by Fenway Park's short left-field wall, Johnson had his best overall season in 1944. Although he hit only 17 homers, he smashed 40 doubles and led the American League in on-base percentage.

Charles Johnson

Johnson, Charles Edward **C**

1994–* B:7/20/1971, Fort Pierce, FL Deb:5/6/1994, FLA NL BR/TR 6'2", 215

G	AB	R	H	HR	RBI	OBP	SLG	AVG
613	2013	224	479	79	255	.325	.405	.238

Charles Johnson was one of the few catchers of the 1990s who could dominate a game defensively. Blessed with a rifle arm, he won four consecutive National League Gold Gloves from 1995 through 1998, and set major league records for most consecutive errorless games by a catcher (159) and most consecutive errorless chances by a catcher (1,294). He also tied a major league record with a 1.000 fielding percentage.

Johnson was the starting catcher on the 1992 U.S. Olympic team and became a first-round draft choice by the Florida Marlins out of the University of Miami. He made his debut in the majors less than two years later.

Although he did not hit for a high average and struck out frequently, Johnson showed decent power for a catcher. He hit 19 homers and 26 doubles in 124 games during his All-Star season of 1997. Johnson then hit .357 in the World Series, including a mammoth home run in Game 1 for the world champion Marlins. He actually made two errors during the 1997 postseason after committing none during the regular season.

Johnson became swept up in the salary purge that followed Florida's championship season. He was dealt to the Los Angeles Dodgers in May 1998 in a seven-player deal that included Mike Piazza. After the season Johnson was dealt to the New York Mets, who immediately sent him to Baltimore for Armando Benitez. Johnson batted .251 in his first season in the American League.

Cliff Johnson

Johnson, Clifford **DH–1B–C**

1972–86 B:7/22/1947, San Antonio, TX Deb:9/13/1972, HOU NL BR/TR 6'4", 225

G	AB	R	H	HR	RBI	OBP	SLG	AVG
1369	3945	539	1016	196	699	.358	.459	.258

Slugger Cliff Johnson was born to be a designated hitter, since he never found a position in the field he could master. Although he caught only 66 games for Houston in 1976, he led the NL in passed balls. Not much better at first base or in the outfield, Johnson's value to the Astros was chiefly as a pinch hitter. In 1974, his first full season, Johnson hit five homers off the bench. He finished his career with 20 pinch-hit home runs, more than any other player.

In 1977 Johnson was traded to the Yankees, where as designated hitter he could concentrate on offense. In three years with the Yanks he hit 20 home runs in only 380 at bats, but in 1979 he got into a scuffle with Yank relief ace Rich "Goose" Gossage, fractured the pitcher's thumb, and was quickly traded to Cleveland.

He continued to hit for power, going on to play for the Cubs, A's, Rangers, and Blue Jays. In 1983 he had the best season of his career, hitting 22 home runs for Toronto and reaching career highs in games, at bats, doubles, and RBIs. In 1984 he posted a .304 batting average, his best ever, and 16 more four-baggers. Johnson retired after the 1986 season with 196 career home runs.

Darrell Johnson

Johnson, Darrell Dean **C**

1952, 1957–58, 1960–62 M(1974–80, 1982 472–590) B:8/25/1928 Horace, NE Deb:4/20/1952 STL AL BR/TR 6'1", 180

G	AB	R	H	HR	RBI	OBP	SLG	AVG
134	320	24	75	2	28	.296	.278	.234

Darrell Johnson managed the Boston Red Sox in 1975, taking the team to a thrilling seven-game World Series showdown with the Cincinnati Reds.

The Nebraska native spent most of his playing career in the minors, getting a major league cup of coffee here and there. By 1962 the 32-year-old catcher had played baseball for a dozen years and had only gotten into 134 major league games with seven clubs; but after he retired as a player, he resurfaced as a successful minor league manager.

In 1974, Johnson was named skipper of the Red Sox. Known as a players' manager, Johnson once said, "I've always felt 'My Door Is Always Open' is a lousy expression. I feel I should take the initiative to meet them, rather than sitting back and waiting for them to come to me. When we win, I won't spend a lot of time in the clubhouse. I don't want to take any credit for what they've done. But when we lose, I'll be out there with them. I want them to know they can talk with me anytime."

Some criticized Johnson for a lack of discipline, but his relaxed attitude did bring Boston a pennant in his second year. Pitcher Bill "Spaceman" Lee remembered, "I called Darrell Johnson 'the cat' because he kept falling out of trees and landing on his feet. When you have a ballclub like he had, it didn't matter who he put in. He wasn't going to make a bad move. Great ballclubs make great managers. Let me put it this way: He was a nice guy and he drank, so I liked him."

Johnson was criticized when, in Game 7 of the 1975 World Series, he pinch-hit slumping Cecil Cooper for pitcher Jim Willoughby with the score tied 3–3, two outs, and nobody on in the bottom of the eighth. Cooper popped up to Pete Rose. Then Johnson replaced Willoughby on the mound with rookie Jim Burton, who allowed the winning run to score. Despite the controversy, Johnson won the 1975 American League manager of the Year Award.

Owner Tom Yawkey, a supporter of Johnson, died in 1976, leaving general manager Dick O'Connell in complete charge. O'Connell did not like reports that Johnson was out drinking with his players. After a 41–45 start and rumors of Boston players having a wild party in a Kansas City hotel, O'Connell fired the manager.

Willoughby explained, "In 1976, Darrell's drinking got in the way of his management. And yet when Darrell drank in '75 no one seemed to mind. What happened was that the team didn't do as well in '76, and so the drinking was more obvious. In baseball when you're on top, you make your own rules."

Johnson managed the Seattle Mariners from 1977 through most of 1980 and the Texas Rangers for part of the 1982 season.

Davey Johnson

Johnson, David Allen **2B–3B**

1965–75, 1977–78 M(1984–90, 1993–97, * 1,062–812)
B:1/30/1943, Orlando, FL Deb:4/13/1965, BAL AL
BR/TR 6'1", 180

G	AB	R	H	HR	RBI	OBP	SLG	AVG
1435	4797	564	1252	136	609	.343	.404	.261

Two of the New York Mets' greatest triumphs occurred with Davey Johnson in uniform at Shea Stadium. Unfortunately for Johnson, he was on the winning side for only one of them. As a player with the Baltimore Orioles, Johnson flied out to left fielder Cleon Jones to end the 1969 World Series and seal the Mets' upset victory. As a manager with the Mets, Johnson presided as the New Yorkers steamrolled the National League East, then proceeded to win the playoffs and the World Series in thrilling fashion in 1986.

Johnson was capable of startling power, especially for a second baseman. More than competent in the field, he earned three consecutive Gold Gloves. He played for winners in two cities and spent some time as a player in Japan.

After a brief stint with the Orioles in 1965, Johnson stepped into a regular job as the double-play partner of future Hall of Famer Luis Aparicio. The Orioles won the AL pennant by nine games over Minnesota. Johnson batted .257, with seven homers and 56 RBIs, while making a league-high 19 errors. He batted .286 in the World Series as the Orioles swept Los Angeles, allowing only two runs.

In 1969 Baltimore assembled a monster season, with Johnson hitting .280 and earning the first of three Gold Gloves. The Orioles won 109 games, beating out Detroit by 19 lengths. They then squashed Minnesota in three straight playoff games but lost the World Series to the Mets. A year later the Orioles made no mistakes, again manhandling the division and breezing past the Twins. In the AL Championship Series, Johnson batted .364, with two home runs and four RBIs. He kept his hot bat going in the Fall Classic, hitting .313 as Baltimore downed Cincinnati in five games.

After one more year in Baltimore, the Orioles dispatched Johnson to Atlanta, where he didn't win any pennants but did go down in history. Playing in Atlanta-Fulton County Stadium, "the Launching Pad," Johnson hit 43 home runs in 1973. His next-highest season home run total was 18, then 15. His 1973 mark also represents the most home runs ever hit by a major league second baseman, breaking the previous record of 42 set by Rogers Hornsby. Johnson played three years in Atlanta, then spent some time in Japan, and was in Philadelphia in time to appear in the playoffs for the Phillies in 1977. He finished his playing career with the Cubs in 1978.

His baseball career was not over, however. After winning titles on three levels in the minor leagues as a manager, Johnson returned in the same capacity to the big leagues. In 1984 he took over the Mets and led them to their best season in years. A year later, he brought them within three games of the top, but they lost out to St. Louis. Before the 1986 season, Johnson announced that he wanted to do more than just win the division. He wanted to dominate it. And that's what his ballclub did. Winning 108 games, the Mets put away the division with a style that many resented as arrogant. They topped the Astros in a six-game playoff, then rebounded from a 3–2 deficit to win the World Series in seven games over Boston.

Johnson led the Mets to another division title in 1988, but the club lost to the Dodgers in the playoffs. Johnson was second-guessed for leaving Dwight Gooden in Game 4 long enough to pitch to Mike Scioscia, who homered. The Dodgers' win in extra innings proved to be the series' turning point.

Johnson was fired in 1990. He remained without a managing job until 1993, when he replaced the Reds' Tony Perez. He finished first in the NL Central in both 1994 and 1995 but was replaced at the end of the 1995 season as owner Marge Schott had indicated even before the season began that Ray Knight would manage the Reds in 1996.

He moved over to the Orioles in 1996 and led the team to an American League Wild Card berth. In 1997 Baltimore posted an impressive 98–64 record and won the American League East as they became only the third club in American League history to spend every day of the season in first place. But Johnson—who won both *The Sporting News* and BBWAA American League Manager of the Year honors—feuded with Orioles owner Peter Angelos and was fired at season's end. In 1999 Johnson was hired to manage the Dodgers.

Deron Johnson

Johnson, Deron Roger **1B-3B-DH-OF**
1960–62, 1964–76 B:7/17/1938, San Diego, CA D:4/23/1992, Poway, CA Deb:9/20/1960, NY AL BR/TR 6'2", 209

G	AB	R	H	HR	RBI	OBP	SLG	AVG
1765	5941	706	1447	245	923	.313	.420	.244

Although touted as a second Mickey Mantle, muscular Deron Johnson took his time reaching the majors. Once there, he delivered 245 homers and led the National League in RBIs in 1965 with 130, but he never quite qualified as any team's long-term solution.

Johnson tore through the Yankees' farm system, but the big club decided Tom Tresh was the next Mantle and traded Johnson to the A's in June 1961. He spent much of 1962 in the military and was sold by Kansas City to the Reds in April 1963. In 1965 *The Sporting News* named him to its National League All-Star Team. Two years later, the Reds traded him to the Braves who passed him on to the Phillies after one season.

On July 10 and 11, 1971, he homered in four straight at bats, hitting three on the latter date against the Expos. In May 1973, he was traded to the A's and became the first player to collect 20 homers in a season split between both leagues. Before retiring, he put in time with the Brewers, Red Sox, and White Sox.

Howard Johnson

Johnson, Howard Michael **3B-SS-OF**
1982–95 B:11/29/1960, Clearwater, FL Deb:4/14/1982, DET AL BB/TR 5'11", 178

G	AB	R	H	HR	RBI	OBP	SLG	AVG
1531	4940	760	1229	228	760	.343	.446	.249

Howard Johnson was a power-hitting switch hitter with surprising speed. Although he would become known for his years with the New York Mets, "HoJo" already had a World Series ring when he arrived at Shea Stadium at the age of 24. A part-time contributor for the 1984 Tigers, he was traded to the Mets for pitcher Walt Terrell.

Johnson was not an everyday player in his first two years in New York, but was a power threat off the bench. His pinch-hit home run in the ninth inning in April 1986 in St. Louis served notice that the Mets would challenge the National League champions that year. Johnson went hitless in seven postseason at bats in 1986—he only went 1-for-26 in his postseason career—but the Mets thought enough of him to let World Series Most Valuable Player Ray Knight leave after the season.

Johnson displayed both speed and power in his first year as an everyday third baseman in 1987; he and Darryl Strawberry became the first Mets to hit 30 home runs and steal 30 bases in the same season. Johnson would be a 30–30 man three times in his career. He slumped in 1988, and ended the season watching rookie Gregg Jefferies take over at third base. When Jefferies was moved to second base the following year, Johnson responded with 36 home runs, 101 RBIs, 41 stolen bases, and a career-high .285 average. Johnson made the first of two starts at third base in the All-Star Game.

After an injury-filled 1990 season, Johnson led the National League in home runs and RBIs in 1991. It also marked Johnson's last full season. Further injuries and a shift to the outfield made 1992 a difficult season; 1993 was even worse. He signed with Colorado as a free agent in 1994, reaching double figures in home runs, including a pinch grand slam. Johnson retired the following year after batting .195 with the Cubs. A 1998 spring training comeback with the Mets failed, although Johnson signed with the club as a scout.

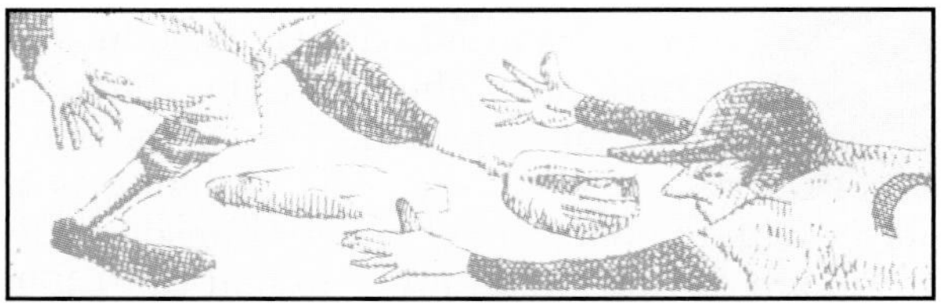

Judy Johnson

Johnson, William Julius **3B–SS**
Negro League Player (1918–37) Manager
B:10/26/1900, Snow Hill, MD D:6/15/1989, Wilmington, MD BR/TR 5'11", 150

When the Negro Leagues Committee made its first nominations for the Baseball Hall of Fame, the third baseman chosen was "Judy" Johnson. Although other Negro League third sackers had better stats in one area or another, Johnson was selected for his professionalism and his intelligent, dedicated style. A superb fielder and line drive hitter, he was noted more for his clutch hits than for high averages.

His father wanted him to become a prizefighter, but young Johnson preferred baseball. In 1918, he signed with the Hilldales of Philadelphia and became their regular third baseman through the 1920s. He was given the nickname "Judy" because he resembled Chicago player Judy Gans.

After hitting .327 in 1924 Johnson played for the Hilldales in the first Negro World Series against the Kansas City Monarchs. His clutch inside-the-park home run won Game 5. His team eventually lost the Series, but he led all batters with a .364 average, six doubles, a triple, and the home run. The following season Johnson batted .392, and his team defeated Kansas City in the Series. Johnson was also a prolific hitter in the Cuban leagues. During six seasons there he batted a hefty .334. As it did for the major leaguers, the ball got livelier in the late 1920s for Negro Leaguers. Johnson's .416 average was only sixth in the league in 1929.

In 1930, when the Great Depression knocked the Hilldales temporarily out of business, Johnson joined the Homestead Grays and was named player-manager at age 29. His intelligence, ability to steal signs, and various methods of trickery helped him win the position. One trick: While the pitcher waved his arms to change the fielders' positioning, third baseman Judy quietly applied sandpaper to the ball.

In a 1930 night game at Pittsburgh's Forbes Field, Johnson's catcher hurt his hand because he couldn't see the ball under the primitive lights. The frightened second stringer refused to catch. Johnson pulled a youngster he'd seen catch on the sandlots out of the stands. Thus began the career of Josh Gibson. Johnson and Gibson were to work together for many years to come. They developed a special closeness. Gibson was eager to learn the game, and Johnson was his mentor. After every game, Gibson would ask, "How'd I look today?" and his lesson would begin.

Johnson returned to Philadelphia in 1931, and in 1932 Pittsburgh numbers boss Gus Greenlee set out to buy himself the best team in the Negro Leagues. Johnson was one of several marquee players to join Greenlee's Pittsburgh Crawfords.

The 1932 Crawfords have been compared to the 1927 Yankees; they were probably the greatest Negro League team ever assembled. Along with Johnson, they boasted Gibson, Oscar Charleston, Chet Williams, Satchel Paige, Vic Harris, and "Cool Papa" Bell.

In 1935 the Crawfords won the pennant in dramatic fashion. They had won the first half of the season but finished behind the Cuban Giants in the second half. A seven-game playoff was set to determine the title. Pittsburgh was losing the seventh and final game, 7–4, in the last of the ninth, with two on and two out when Johnson stepped to the plate. The Giants brought in Martin Dihigo to nail down the championship, but the 36-year-old Johnson beat out an infield hit, and Charleston cracked a grand slam to win the game. Johnson played only one more season with the Crawfords. His final game was a 6–6 tie against a team of white all-stars after the 1936 season.

After Jackie Robinson broke the color barrier, Johnson worked as a scout for several big league teams, including the A's, Phillies, and Dodgers. He once told the story of how he could have kept the A's in Philadelphia. "I could have gotten Hank Aaron for them for $3,500 when he was playing for the Indianapolis Clowns," Johnson said. "I got my boss out of bed and told him I had a good prospect and he wouldn't cost too much, and he cussed me out for waking him up at one o'clock in the morning. He said, 'Thirty-five hundred! That's too much money.' Too much for a man like that! I could have gotten Larry Doby and Minnie Minoso, too, and the A's would still be playing in Philadelphia, because that would be all the outfield they'd have needed."

As a Phillies scout Johnson helped sign future All-Star Dick Allen. Johnson's understanding of the game was utilized every year in spring training as the Phillies brought him south to coach their young players. He continued in that role through 1974. At his Hall of Fame induction in 1975, Johnson broke down in tears during his acceptance speech and could not continue.

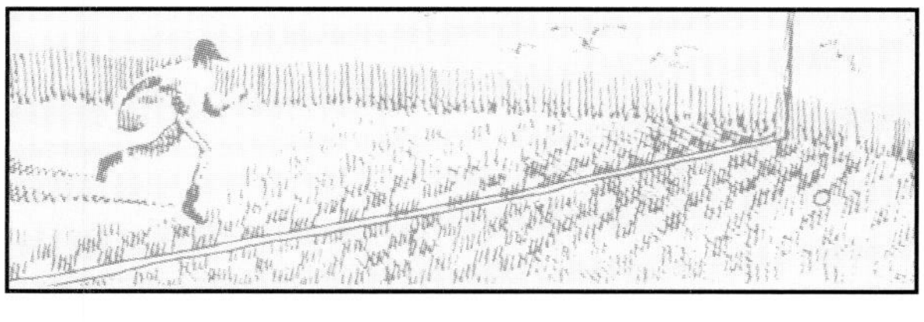

Lance Johnson

Johnson, Kenneth Lance **OF**

1987–* B:7/6/1963, Cincinnati, OH Deb:7/10/1987, STL NL BL/TL 5'11", 160

G	AB	R	H	HR	RBI	OBP	SLG	AVG
1492	5349	761	1556	34	484	.335	.386	.291

Lance Johnson was a master of hitting triples. He tied for the league lead with 13 in 1991, and led the American League four straight seasons.

Johnson went undrafted out of high school because his frame was considered too frail and his arm too weak. He opted for Triton Junior College in Illinois, where fellow outfielders Kirby Puckett and Larry Jackson became first-round draft picks in 1982. Again, Johnson was not selected. Finally, in 1984 the Cardinals picked him in the sixth round. He made his major league debut in St. Louis in 1987, but was traded to the White Sox the following season.

White Sox manager Jeff Torborg had to talk Johnson out of quitting baseball when he was sent down to the minor leagues at the end of 1989 spring training. Johnson worked on his game, eventually made the team and became one of the major reasons the White Sox battled for the American League West title in 1990. Twice he batted over .300 in Chicago—including a .311 season for the 1993 AL West champions.

After joining the Mets as a free agent in 1996, he became the first player to lead both leagues in hits—and Johnson did it in consecutive years. His 227 hits were the most in the National League since Pete Rose's 230 in 1973. His 21 triples were the most in the National League since Adam Comorsky's 23 in 1930. He had at least two hits in a game 75 times, the most since Don Mattingly's 79 in 1986.

Nonetheless, by August of 1997 he was gone, traded back to Chicago, this time to the Cubs. He finished the season hitting .307, but due to six weeks on the disabled list appeared in only 111 games.

Injuries the next two seasons limited his playing time even further, but in 1998 he had the distinction of becoming the first player to appear in the postseason for both the Cubs and White Sox since Vance Law did it for the 1983 Sox and 1989 Cubs.

Johnson, who had the most triples of any major leaguer during the 1990s, signed with the Indians as a free agent after the 1999 season.

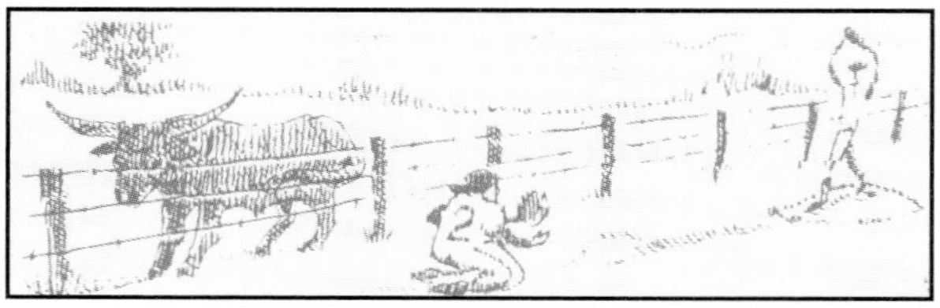

Lou Johnson

Johnson, Louis Brown **OF**

1960–62, 1965–69 B:9/22/1934, Lexington, KY Deb:4/17/1960, CHI NL BR/TR 5'11", 175

G	AB	R	H	HR	RBI	OBP	SLG	AVG
677	2049	244	529	48	232	.313	.389	.258

Traded from organization to organization, Lou Johnson spent eight years in the minors and had only a brief stay with the Cubs to show for it. Then in 1965 after Tommy Davis broke his ankle, he got a chance to play regularly with the Dodgers and helped them win the pennant with a sizzling performance. In the World Series against the Twins, he launched two home runs and batted .296. His fourth-inning homer off the left-field foul pole in Game 7 put Sandy Koufax and the Dodgers ahead 1–0, on their way to a 2–0 clincher.

A .258 career hitter who never achieved consistency in the majors, Johnson once again got hot during the pennant drive in 1966 when he slammed six homers. Dodgers devotees greeted the southern-born Johnson, a fan favorite, with a chant of "All the Way with LBJ" borrowed from President Lyndon Johnson's election campaign. The Dodgers hit only .142 in the 1966 World Series against an excellent Oriole pitching staff that gave up only two runs in the four-game sweep. Johnson led all the regular Dodgers with a .267 average. Los Angeles traded Johnson to the Cubs after the 1967 season. His major league career ended with the Angels in 1969 at age 35—only months after the other LBJ left office.

Randy Johnson

Johnson, Randall David **P**

1988–* B:9/10/63, Walnut Creek, CA Deb:9/15/88, MON NL BR/TL 6'10", 225

W	L	PCT	G	SH	IP	BB	SO	ERA
160	88	.645	331	25	2250	1013	2693	3.26

No pitcher in major league history stood taller than Randy Johnson. At 6'10", the "Big Unit" was an intimidating figure throughout the 1990s, terrorizing lefthanded hitters with a sidearm fastball that approached 100 mph, a biting slider, and sweeping curve. Righthanded hitters fared little better. Johnson led the American League in strikeouts from 1992 to 1995, again in 1997, then paced the National League in 1999.

Johnson spent five years in the Montreal farm system before gaining enough control to pitch in the majors. His Expos career, however, was brief. Following a September call-up, Johnson was traded the following May to the Seattle Mariners, where he quickly established himself as a wild but effective starting pitcher.

Johnson threw a no-hitter against Detroit on June 2, 1990. In 1993 he struck out 300 in a season for the first time, lowered his walks under 100, and won 19 games. He won the 1995 American League Cy Young Award, leading the league in ERA and strikeouts with a record of 18–2 that included a victory in a one-game playoff to clinch the Mariners' first postseason berth. He then won one game as a starter and another in relief in the Division Series against the Yankees.

Although Johnson missed most of the 1996 season with a herniated disk in his back, he rebounded in 1997. He won 20 games for the first time while posting a 2.28 ERA and leading the American League with an .833 won-lost percentage. Twice that season he struck out 19 in a game.

Rumors of an impending trade before the season may have contributed to an inconsistent first half performance for Johnson in 1998. After Houston acquired him at the July 31 trading deadline he became virtually unhittable, going 10–1 with a 1.28 ERA. In the Division Series, however, he twice matched up against Kevin Brown of the Padres and lost.

Johnson then signed with the Arizona Diamondbacks as a free agent and helped lead the team to 100 wins and an NL West title in 1999. His 17–9 record on the way to a second Cy Young Award was not a true indication of his dominance. Johnson posted a 2.48 ERA, with 12 complete games. He fanned 364 in 271 ⅔ innings pitched—19 shy of Nolan Ryan's all-time record. On 23 occasions he struck out 10 or more, matching Ryan's 1973 record. Johnson joined Gaylord Perry and Pedro Martinez as the only pitchers to win the Cy Young Award in both leagues.

"The one thing that was the least in his control was the wins and losses," Arizona manager Buck Showalter said of Johnson, who at one point lost three games while allowing four total runs. "Scoring runs and catching the baseball, that's the thing he couldn't control. Thank goodness people realized that."

Walter Johnson

Johnson, Walter Perry **P**

1907–27 M(1929–35, 529–432) B:11/6/1887, Humboldt, KS D:12/10/1946, Washington, DC Deb:8/2/1907, WAS AL BR/TR 6'1", 200

W	L	PCT	G	SH	IP	BB	SO	ERA
417	279	.599	802	110	5914^{2}	1363	3509	2.17

The Washington Senators' Walter "Barney" Johnson was called the "Big Train." When his fastball came roaring down the tracks, American League batters knew they were facing the fastest pitcher they would ever hear. As Frank "Ping" Bodie once said about Johnson's fastball, "You can't hit what you can't see."

In truth, Johnson may not have been quite as fast as he seemed. He had unusually long arms and threw with an easy sidearm motion. His arm movement seemed suited to easy lobs, but then his fastball exploded past batters. Even if some of his speed was illusory, it sparked a round of most of the well-worn "fast pitcher" stories. Some said that if a batter started swinging at strike two, he had a decent chance of making contact on Johnson's next pitch. During one game Cleveland shortstop Ray Chapman didn't even want to try that. After Johnson had pitched two strikes, Chapman walked away from the plate, not wishing to put off the inevitable. After another Johnson pitch, Joe Gedeon asked umpire Billy Evans if it had been a fastball or a curve, remarking "I never saw it, I had to close my eyes." Said Evans later: "I knew the ballplayers couldn't second-guess me if they were closing their eyes too."

During his career, which ran from 1907 through 1927, Johnson provided plenty of numbers to go with anecdotes. He won 30 or more games in consecutive seasons, including 36 in 1913. He won 20 or more games 12 times, including every season from 1910 through 1919 and in 1924 and 1925. He pitched a major league record 110 shutouts, including 11 in 1913 when his ERA was 1.09. He also lost a record 65 shutouts, 26 of them by the score of 1–0. He won 416 games with the Senators, but his teammates played so poorly they were whitewashed in nearly a quarter of his defeats.

His all-time strikeout record has now been surpassed, but in his day and long after it Johnson was regarded as indisputably the finest strikeout artist in baseball history. Relying solely on his fastball, Johnson led the American League in strikeouts 12 times. Twice in his career with the bases loaded and none out he struck out the side on just nine pitches: against Detroit's Ty Cobb, Sam Crawford, and Bobby Veach and against Cleveland's Tris Speaker, Chick Gandil, and Elmer Smith.

In 1906 Johnson signed his first professional contract, but the Class B club cut him before he pitched a single inning. He signed on with the Weiser Telephone Company in Weiser, Idaho, where he dug postholes and pitched for the company team for $75 a month.

The following season Senators manager "Pongo Joe" Cantillon received a tip and instructed injured catcher Cliff Blankenship and outfielder Clyde Milan to check out the kid when he played in Wichita. After Johnson displayed blazing stuff in a 1–0, 12-inning loss, Blankenship offered him $350 a month salary plus a $100 bonus to sign with Washington. Johnson lost his first game in the majors, a 3–2 decision to Detroit. But Ty Cobb recognized talent when he saw it. "I knew that day that here was a fellow who couldn't miss being a great pitcher," Cobb said. "I asked the Detroit club to buy him, even if they had to offer Washington $25,000. They just stared at me."

In 1908 Johnson had an up-and-down season, going 14–14 for seventh-place Washington. He was at his best at season's end, when in early September he pitched three shutouts in a four-day period against the New York Highlanders. On September 4 he whitewashed them, 3–0, on four hits. The next day he three-hit them to win, 6–0. He might have pitched the next day, but Sunday baseball was still illegal in New York. On Monday, in the first game of a doubleheader, he delivered a two-hitter and won, 4–0.

The following season Johnson was dogged by a fever he contracted during spring training, and he lost a career-high 25 games. In 1910, however, he began the first of 10 consecutive 20-win seasons. That season he pitched 373 innings, hurled 38 complete games, and struck out 313 batters—all career highs.

From July 3 through August 23, 1912, Johnson won 16 straight games before losing in relief to the Browns. No American League pitcher has since won more consecutive games in a single season, although three pitchers have tied the mark

Johnson was at his best in 1913, when he was named American League MVP. Few pitchers have put up similar numbers. His 1.09 ERA, 36 victories (against only seven losses), and 11 shutouts led the league. Johnson issued less than a walk an inning, recorded five one-hitters, and had streaks of 10, 11, and 14 consecutive wins. From the second inning on April 10 through the third inning on May 14 the Big Train did not surrender a single run. Those 56⅔ consecutive scoreless innings remain a league record.

Johnson pitched his entire career for Washington, but he nearly left the Senators during the Federal League "war." Johnson had been approached with a lucrative offer from a Federal League owner, but he was leaning toward signing with Washington until he received an insulting and threatening letter from Washington president Harry Minor. Johnson subsequently agreed to a three-year contract with the outlaw circuit's Chicago Whales for $17,500 a season, but a personal appeal from manager Clark Griffith prompted Johnson to return to Washington.

Johnson's string of 20-win seasons was snapped in 1920 when he suffered from a sore arm. He had pitched 11 straight seasons of 290 or more innings and had also tossed the ball around on preseason barnstorming tours. Yet it was on July 1, 1920, that Johnson recorded his only no-hitter, a 1–0, 10-strikeout victory over the Red Sox in Boston. It would have been a perfect game had it not been for a booted grounder by second baseman Bucky Harris. Ironically, Johnson had not expected to pitch that day, having been away from the ballclub until just before game time because his five-year-old son was ill.

Despite his dominance on the mound, it appeared that the Big Train would never appear in a World Series. But late in his career he pitched in two straight. In the 1924 Series against New York he went to the mound twice as a starter and lost both times. But in Game 7, manager Bucky Harris brought Johnson in as a reliever.

In the 12th inning with the score tied, 3–3, Washington catcher Muddy Ruel came to the plate with one out and would have been retired on a foul pop had Giants catcher Hank Gowdy not tripped over his own mask. Given a second chance, Ruel doubled to left. Johnson then reached on Travis Jackson's error.

The next batter, center fielder Earl McNeely, hit a routine grounder to third baseman Freddy Lindstrom. The ball hit a pebble and bounded high over Lindstrom's head for a hit, and Ruel raced home with the winning run. Johnson, who pitched four scoreless innings, picked up the victory as Washington captured its first and only world championship.

Johnson reversed his record in the following year's Fall Classic, going 2–1. He won Games 1 and 4 but lost Game 7 to Pittsburgh's Ray Kremer. Johnson won 15 games the next season, slipped to 5–6 in 1927, and then retired. He went on to manage the Newark Bears of the International League for the second half of the 1928 season, and from 1929 to 1932 he piloted the Senators but failed to win a pennant. Some said he was just too easy going to get the best from his players.

In June 1933 Johnson was named manager of the Indians but lasted only until August 1935 after becoming embroiled in a controversy over the disciplining of third baseman Willie Kamm. In 1936 he was elected to the Baseball Hall of Fame, and in 1938 Johnson, who owned a 55-acre Maryland farm, was elected to the Rockville County Board of Commissioners.

In 1939 he was a Senators broadcaster. The following year he ran a strong but unsuccessful race for Congress. In April 1946 Johnson suffered a stroke and died that December in Washington, D.C.

Jimmy Johnston

Johnston, James Harle **3B-OF-SS-2B**
1911, 1914, 1916–26 B:12/10/1889, Cleveland, TN
D:2/14/1967, Chattanooga, TN Deb:5/3/1911, CHI AL
BR/TR 5'10", 160

G	AB	R	H	HR	RBI	OBP	SLG	AVG
1377	5070	754	1493	22	410	.347	.374	.294

Minor league phenom Jimmy Johnston stole a record-breaking 124 bases with San Francisco in 1913 and went on to have a successful major league career with the Brooklyn Robins. But he never fulfilled expectations as a basestealer. Blessed with only fair speed, Johnston found that he couldn't get as good a jump off major league pitchers. He never stole more than 28 bases in a season in the majors and had a total of 169 stolen bases in 13 years.

In 1916 Brooklyn purchased Johnston's contract, and the Dodgers won the pennant both that year and in 1920. Johnston and his brother Wheeler "Doc" Johnston, who played for the Indians, became in 1920 the first siblings to oppose each other in a World Series. A career .294 hitter, Jimmy Johnston had his best season in 1921 when he hit .325 with 41 doubles and 28 stolen bases.

Jay Johnstone

Johnstone, John William **OF**
1966–85 B:11/20/1945, Manchester, CT
Deb:7/30/1966, CAL AL BL/TR 6'1", 175

G	AB	R	H	HR	RBI	OBP	SLG	AVG
1748	4703	578	1254	102	531	.331	.394	.267

Jay Johnstone was a solid hitter in the clutch, but his personality made him one of baseball's biggest flakes in the 1970s. "What makes him unusual," explained Danny Ozark, "is that he thinks he's normal and everyone else is nuts."

"The most amazing thing I've ever seen was Jay Johnstone, in uniform, in line at a concession stand in Dodger Stadium after the game had already started," recalled Los Angeles Dodgers vice president Fred Claire.

Johnstone played for eight major league teams and five division winners. In his only World Series appearance—as a pinch hitter in 1981—he had two hits in three at bats including a home run and three RBIs. Johnstone has since become a television show host, baseball broadcaster, and author.

Charley Jones

Jones, Charles Wesley **OF**
1875–80, 1883–88 B:4/30/1850, Alamance County, NC
D:Unknown Deb:5/4/1875, KEO NA BR/TR
5'11½", 202

G	AB	R	H	HR	RBI	OBP	SLG	AVG
881	3687	728	1101	56	542	.347	.443	.299

Charley Jones earned his place in baseball history as the first man to slug two homers in a single inning. Both four-baggers came off Buffalo's Tom Poorman in the eighth inning of a June 10, 1880, 19–3 rout of the Bisons.

Jones was born with the surname Rippay but raised by a relative named Jones. He started with Keokuk of the National Association. When that club folded in midseason, he transferred to Hartford. And when the National Association also failed after the 1875 season, Jones transferred to Cincinnati and played right field in their first National League contest. Mistakenly thinking that club was about to go under, he signed a pact with the White Stockings but had to return to Cincinnati.

In 1879 "Long Charley" Jones signed a three-year contract with Boston and led the league in home runs, RBIs, and runs scored. The often-carousing Jones had serious salary issues with the Red Stockings and sued them in an Ohio court for back pay; he even got the local sheriff to attach Boston's share of the gate at Cleveland on May 14, 1881. In return the club blacklisted him for 1881 and 1882.

On July 20, 1884, Jones slugged three triples against Indianapolis in an American Association contest, as Cincinnati defeated the Blues 17–5.

He later played for New York and Kansas City in the American Association

Chipper Jones

Jones, Larry Wayne **3B**
1993, 1995–* B:4/24/1972, DeLand, FL Deb:9/11/1993,
ATL NL BB/TR 6'3", 185

G	AB	R	H	HR	RBI	OBP	SLG	AVG
779	2890	542	871	153	524	.398	.529	.301

Switch-hitting third baseman Chipper Jones finally found power from the right side of the plate in 1999. The result was the National League's Most Valuable Player Award.

Jones posted impressive numbers: .319 batting average, 45 home runs, 110 RBIs, 116 runs scored, and a .633 slugging percentage. Jones was by far the most potent offensive weapon on the pitching-rich Braves. His performance was even more impressive—and important—given that slugger Andres Galarraga missed all of

1999 and hard-hitting catcher Javy Lopez missed more than half the season.

Larry Wayne Jones became known as Chipper while growing up in Pierson, Florida, where his father was the high school baseball coach. Everyone thought Jones was a chip off the old block, but junior turned out to be an even better player than senior. He became the top overall pick in the 1990 amateur draft.

His rapid ascent to the Braves was interrupted by a knee injury that forced him to sit out the 1994 season, but the following year he made the club and worked his way into the third slot in a batting order that included David Justice and Fred McGriff. Against Colorado in the 1995 Division Series, he hit .389, upping that to .438 in Atlanta's four-game sweep of Cincinnati in the National League Championship Series. He then batted .286 in Atlanta's triumph over the Cleveland Indians in the World Series.

Jones had another great NLCS against St. Louis in 1996, batting .440 with 11 hits, but wasn't much of a presence in Atlanta's subsequent loss to the Yankees in the World Series. In his next Series appearance in 1999, Jones was even more of a no-show, as the Braves lost to the Yankees in four straight games. Nevertheless, Jones had the distinction of appearing in the postseason in each of his five full years in the majors.

Cleon Jones

Jones, Cleon Joseph **OF**

1963, 1965–76 B:8/4/1942, Plateau, AL Deb:9/14/1963, NY NL BR/TL 6', 200

G	AB	R	H	HR	RBI	OBP	SLG	AVG
1213	4263	565	1196	93	524	.342	.404	.281

Cleon Jones is one of those rare birds, a lefty-throwing, righty-batting ballplayer. When he started playing baseball as a child, he did what came naturally—he batted lefthanded. But as a teenager he had to bat righthanded because the field that he and his friends used had a porch jutting into right.

Jones came up to the majors with the Mets in 1963 but didn't play fulltime until 1966. The Mets' "miracle" 1969 season was also Jones' career year: He hit .340 to go with 12 homers, 75 RBIs, and 16 stolen bases. But the one incident everyone remembers from that season was when manager Gil Hodges walked ever-so-slowly out to left field and removed Jones from the game because he wasn't hustling. That sparked the Mets to buckle down, and their renewed determination landed them in the World Series.

Jones batted .429 during the Mets' NLCS sweep of the Braves that year, and although he hit only .158 in the Fall Classic, he was a key participant in two critical plays in the fifth and final game. The Mets were down, 3–0, when Jones, at the plate, claimed that a pitch that had eluded the Braves' catcher and rolled into the Mets dugout had hit him on the foot. Hodges produced a ball with shoe polish on it, Jones was awarded first, and then Donn Clendenon homered to begin the Mets' comeback. In the last of the eighth, with the score tied, 3–3, Jones led off with a double and scored the winning run. A few minutes later he caught Davey Johnson's fly for the final out.

In 1973 the Mets conjured up some more magic to win again. Although Jones was frequently out of the lineup with an injured wrist, he played well down the stretch and contributed 48 RBIs in 92 games and a great throw from center field in the 13th inning of a key game in late September. He batted .300 in the NLCS and .286 in the World Series, scoring the winning run in Game 5.

On July 18, 1975, angered because of his lack of playing time, Jones refused to go to the outfield as a defensive replacement. Manager Yogi Berra demanded that the team suspend him. The Mets stalled for eight days before finally disciplining Jones. Berra was fired soon thereafter, and Jones spent the next season, his last in the majors, with the Chicago White Sox.

Davy Jones

Jones, David Jefferson **OF**

1901–04, 1906–15 B:6/30/1880, Cambria, WI D:3/31/1972, Mankato, MN Deb:9/15/1901, MIL AL BL/TR 5'10", 165

G	AB	R	H	HR	RBI	OBP	SLG	AVG
1089	3772	643	1020	9	289	.356	.325	.270

According to Davy Jones, the great Ty Cobb had "such a rotten disposition that it was damn hard to be his friend. I was probably the best friend he had on the club." Jones, a Detroit outfielder from 1906 through 1912, was a speedy leadoff man and a good fielder on Tigers teams that won three pennants. However, his most valuable contribution may have been his serving as a buffer between the vitriolic "Georgia Peach" and the rest of the team. "I used to stick up for him, sit and talk with him on long train trips, try to understand the man," said Jones.

Even Jones wasn't immune to Cobb's venom. One time, when Cobb was in the midst of a batting slump, he stomped off the field, declaring that Jones had missed a hit-and-run sign. In truth, Cobb never flashed the sign and was simply looking for some time out of the lineup. He even went so far as to declare he would not play unless Jones was benched. Management threatened Cobb with suspension without pay. Of course, as soon as he started hitting again, he stopped complaining about Jones and the phantom hit-and-run sign.

His original ambition was to become a lawyer, and he received an athletic scholarship to Dixon College in Illinois. Although he played baseball at Dixon, track was his specialty. On several occasions he outraced Archie Hahn, the 1904 Olympic champion.

Jones graduated in 1901 but never went into law; an offer of $85 a month from the Rockford Red Sox of the 3-I League convinced him to try baseball. Near the end of the season, the 5-foot-10, 165-pound Jones was hitting better than .300 when he was sold to the Chicago Cubs, but he decided to join Milwaukee in the premier season of the American League. The next year the franchise was shifted to St. Louis. After playing 15 games with the Browns, Jones jumped to the Cubs, who gave him a $1,200 raise plus a $500 bonus. His repeated jumps from club to club earned him the nickname "Kangaroo."

Jones played regularly for the Cubs for several years, but an injury late in the 1904 season nearly ended his career. Chicago sent him to Minneapolis of the American Association, and then Detroit acquired his contract.

In 1907 Detroit won the AL pennant. Cobb and slugger Sam Crawford were the best players on the team. Jones, who usually batted leadoff due to his speed and keen eye at the plate, contributed the best season of his career, batting .273 and scoring 101 runs. In the World Series, which Detroit lost to the Cubs, he hit .353.

The Tigers won two more pennants in 1908 and 1909. Each time, they were defeated in the Fall Classic. In 1913 the Tigers sold Jones to the Chicago White Sox. The next season he jumped to Pittsburgh of the Federal League, then retired in 1915.

While still with the Tigers, Jones set up a partnership in a drugstore with his brother, a pharmacist, and after games he jerked sodas and talked to the fans. The Jones brothers soon owned five stores. Upon retiring from baseball, Jones earned a degree in pharmacy and worked in his business for 35 years.

Doug Jones

Jones, Douglas Reid **P**

1982, 1986–* B:6/24/1957, Lebanon, IN Deb:4/9/1982, MIL AL BR/TR 6'2", 195

W	L	PCT	G	SV	IP	BB	SO	ERA
65	77	.458	792	301	1055	229	855	3.26

Doug Jones proves that you don't have to be young and possess overpowering stuff to be an effective closer. Jones spent a decade in the minor leagues before establishing himself with the Cleveland Indians as a consistent stopper. Less arm strain likely contributed to his remarkable longevity. During his 1999 season with Oakland, Jones turned 42 years old yet appeared more than 70 times, pitching over 100 innings.

Although Jones changed teams often (seven times in his 15 years), he was generally effective wherever he pitched. Jones spread out his 792 appearances, all but four in relief, in Houston, Philadelphia, Baltimore, Chicago (Cubs), Oakland, and two tours each with Cleveland and Milwaukee. He earned five invitations to the All-Star Game and saved 301 games, 10th on the all-time list.

Fielder Jones

Jones, Fielder Allison **OF**

1896–1908, 1914–15 M(1904–08, 1914–18, 683–582) B:8/13/1871, Shinglehouse, PA D:3/13/1934, Portland, OR Deb:4/18/1896 BRO NL BL/TR 5'11", 180

G	AB	R	H	HR	RBI	OBP	SLG	AVG
1788	6747	1180	1920	21	631	.368	.347	.285

Fielder Jones was the player-manager of the 1906 world champion Chicago White Sox—"the Hitless Wonders." And while his given name was indeed Fielder, he was a good enough fly chaser to have picked it up as a nickname.

He earned a degree in engineering from Alfred University, but given the poor economic conditions in the early 1890s, he turned to baseball. He played in the Oregon State League and with Corning, Birmingham, and Springfield before Brooklyn drafted him in 1895. The lefthanded batter hit .353 as a 24-year-old rookie in 1896.

In 1900 Jones led Brooklyn with four RBIs in the *Chronicle-Telegraph* Cup series, the pre-1903 equivalent of the Fall Classic, against Pittsburgh. After the season, Jones jumped to the White Sox in the brand-new American League. He hit better than .300 in 1901 and 1902 and twice led the league in fielding.

In 1904 Jones replaced Jimmie Callahan as White Sox manager. In 1906, Chicago combined defense, pitching, and all-around heady play to win the pennant despite being last in the majors with a .230 team average, and last in team home runs, with seven. The White Sox took the crosstown Cubs in the World Series that year, four games to two. Staying true to their formula for success, the Wonders batted only .198, and Jones himself hit an anemic .095 in the Series. Nevertheless, the pitching of White Sox starters Nick Altrock, Ed Walsh, and Guy "Doc" White prevailed.

Jones later said, "They were a club that a manager could depend upon. Called 'the Hitless Wonders,' it is true that their batting was light. But they hit at the right time as you will notice if you look up their record. Every man knew his business. Baseball was at their fingertips. They won games because they were good ballplayers, and a good ballplayer can't be manufactured out of batting averages."

Connie Mack was more inclined to credit Jones, given the material Jones had to work with. Mack said, "He was a fiery competitor and imparted his tremendous enthusiasm to his men," also noting that "he was the highly strung type but as cool as a lime rickey in a tight spot."

Frustrated by his team's failure to win another pennant and by Comiskey's penurious ways, Jones retired to the lumber business in the Pacific Northwest after the 1908 season. In 1912 he returned to baseball as president of the Class B Pacific Northwest League. Three years later, with the St. Louis Terriers of the Federal League, he took up managing again. His team finished second that season. In 1916 the Federal League was dismantled. Jones replaced Branch Rickey as manager of the Browns after St. Louis owner Phil Ball bought the Terriers and combined the two rosters as part of the league settlement. That season the Browns won 14 straight but finished fourth. Jones resigned one afternoon that summer after the Browns blew a 5–1 lead to Washington in the ninth inning.

A practitioner of reverse superstition, Jones believed in "lucky 13." He was born on August 13 and, on trains, would always travel in berth "lower 13."

Mack Jones

Jones, Mack **OF**

1961–63, 1965–71 B:11/6/1938, Atlanta, GA Deb:7/13/1961, MIL NL BL/TR 6'1", 180

G	AB	R	H	HR	RBI	OBP	SLG	AVG
1002	3091	485	778	133	415	.349	.444	.252

"Mack the Knife" Jones collected four hits in his first major league game on July 13, 1961—tying the modern NL mark set by Casey Stengel, Ed Freed, and Willie McCovey. Despite his multi-hit debut, Jones, who attended Atlanta's Morris Brown College, did not enjoy a full major league season until 1965 when he hit 31 homers for the Braves during their final season in Milwaukee.

Traded to the Reds on October 10, 1967, Jones was selected by Montreal as their second choice in the October 14, 1968, expansion draft. Unlike some other players, Jones enjoyed his experience in French-speaking Canada. "Being able to play in Montreal was the highlight of my career," he contended, and he backed up his words. Off the Cardinals' Nelson Briles on April 14, 1969, he hit the first major league homer in Canada.

Nippy Jones

Jones, Vernal LeRoy **1B**

1946–52, 1957 B:6/29/1925, Los Angeles, CA D:10/3/1995, Sacramento, CA Deb:6/8/1946, STL NL BR/TR 6'1", 185

G	AB	R	H	HR	RBI	OBP	SLG	AVG
412	1381	146	369	25	209	.304	.382	.267

Neatness counts, or at least it did for Braves pinch hitter Nippy Jones in Game 4 of the 1957 World Series. The Yankees led the Series, two games to one. In Game 4 the Braves trailed, 5–4, in the bottom of the 10th inning when Milwaukee Braves manager Fred Haney pinch-hit Jones for starting pitcher Warren Spahn.

Tommy Byrne's first pitch was low and eluded catcher Yogi Berra. Home plate umpire Augie Donatelli called the pitch a ball, but Jones retrieved it and tried to convince Donatelli that the ball had hit him in the foot. The umpire was skeptical, but when he saw black shoe polish on the ball, he awarded Jones first base. The Braves tied the score on Johnny Logan's double, then won the game on Eddie Mathews' two-run homer off Bob Grim. The incident sparked Milwaukee, who won the Series in seven games.

Vernal Leroy Jones inherited his nickname from his father. He said, "My Dad's nickname was 'Nip.' When I was born they called me 'Little Nippy.'" Young Nip played in the majors only eight seasons after his initial appearance in 1946.

Hampered by back problems, he had made his first appearance in the major leagues in five years in 1957. And ironically, his "shoe polish at bat" was his last major league plate appearance.

Randy Jones

Jones, Randall Leo **P**

1973–82 B:1/12/1950, Fullerton, CA Deb:6/16/1973, SD NL BR/TL 6', 178

W	L	PCT	G	SH	IP	BB	SO	ERA
100	123	.448	305	19	1933	503	735	3.42

Were it not for two brilliant, back-to-back seasons in his 10-year major league career, Randy Jones would be a little-remembered lefthanded pitcher. From 1975 to 1976, however, he was as effective as anyone in baseball, winning 20 and 22 games. In 1976 he pitched 315⅓ innings with 25 complete games on his way to winning the National League Cy Young Award. All this with a fastball clocked in the low 70s.

As an amateur, Jones threw hard, but a serious elbow injury taxed much of his speed. Still, Jones was able to make the major leagues with the lowly San Diego Padres. In 1974 he suffered the rare indignity of losing more than 20 games in a season. His pitching coach Tom Morgan then suggested he throw across his body, making it tougher for hitters to pick up his pitches. Jones also improved his sinker, which now began to drop five to 10 inches. Combining these changes with already exquisite control, Jones became an instant winner. Just one year removed from losing 22 games, Jones led the National League with a 2.24 ERA while winning 20.

His soft tosses and effectiveness allowed him to pitch long into games. *Newsweek* featured Jones in its June 21, 1976, edition. "He looks so easy to hit," Joe Torre of the Mets told *Newsweek*, "and that's probably his biggest asset."

In late September of 1976 Jones felt something tear in his arm. Dr. Frank Jobe cut open his left arm to find a severed nerve that could not be repaired. When Jones returned to the mound, he was no longer the same pitcher. He won only six of 18 decisions in 1977, marking the start of six consecutive sub-.500 seasons.

In 1980 problems with a pinched nerve in his shoulder resurfaced and the Padres traded their one-time ace to the Mets. Jones continued to suffer injury problems. He sprained his ankle badly and made a career-low 13 starts, winning just one of nine decisions. Although Jones rebounded to pitch better in 1982, the Mets released him, ending his career at the age of 32. In 1997 the Padres honored Jones by retiring his uniform number, 35.

Ruppert Jones

Jones, Ruppert Sanderson **OF**

1976–87 B:3/12/1955, Dallas, TX Deb:8/1/1976, KC AL BL/TL 5'10", 175

G	AB	R	H	HR	RBI	OBP	SLG	AVG
1331	4415	643	1103	147	579	.332	.416	.250

Ruppert Jones was the first player selected by Seattle in the 1976 expansion draft. Plucked off the Kansas City roster, he hit a career-high 24 homers for the Mariners in 1977 and made the All-Star team. He hit 21 homers in 1979. During a 16-inning game against Detroit on May 16, 1978, he recorded 12 putouts, tying a major league record. His combination of power and defense made him a fan favorite. Long after his departure from the team, Seattle would greet his appearance with a visiting club by yelling "Rupe! Rupe!"

The Yankees, intrigued by his skills, traded four players to Seattle for Jones and pitcher Jim Lewis in November of 1979. But Jones spent much of the 1980 season on the disabled list, and New York gave up on him. When the season ended, he was traded to San Diego. In 1982 Jones again made the All-Star team before a foot injury curtailed his playing time. On July 16 and 17 that year, he tied a major league record by striking out eight times in two consecutive games. Jones was signed as a free agent by Detroit in 1984, and helped the Tigers to their World Series win over San Diego. He played his final two seasons with the Padres.

Sam Jones

Jones, Samuel Pond **P**

1914–35 B:7/26/1892, Woodsfield, OH D:7/6/1966, Barnesville, OH Deb:6/13/1914, CLE AL BR/TR 6' 170

W	L	PCT	G	SH	IP	BB	SO	ERA
229	217	.513	647	36	3883	1396	1223	3.84

Sam Jones pitched 22 consecutive years in the American League, a record he shares with Hall of Famers Herb Pennock, Red Ruffing, and Early Wynn. (Steve Carlton equaled the feat in the National League.) Although he received only one vote for the Hall of Fame on three occasions, Jones earned more victories than several Hall of Fame pitchers, including Jim Bunning, Hal Newhouser, Bob Lemon, and contemporary Jesse Haines. Jones also appeared in four World Series, although he never won a Series game.

Jones, who was known as "Sad Sam" for his downcast demeanor and "Horsewhips" for the sharp crack of his breaking ball, started out with Cleveland in 1914. He was sent to the Red Sox two years later in the trade that brought Tris Speaker to the Indians. Jones posted a record of 16–5 for Boston in 1918, leading the American League with a winning percentage of .762. The following year, he lost 20, but he turned it around in 1921 with 23 wins for the Red Sox, including a league-high five shutouts.

Sad Sam's best year, however, was with the Yankees in 1923. As ace of the club's first world championship team, he went 21–8, a record highlighted by a no-hitter against the Philadelphia Athletics. In the World Series against the crosstown New York Giants, he saved the sixth and deciding game in relief of Pennock.

Jones never reached that pinnacle again in his 12 remaining seasons, but he did enjoy two excellent years with the Washington Senators, going 17–7 in 1928 and 15–7 in 1930. He finished his career with the Chicago White Sox in 1935.

Willie Jones

Jones, Willie Edward **3B**

1947–61 B:8/16/1925, Dillon, SC D:10/18/1983, Cincinnati, OH Deb:9/10/1947, PHI NL BR/TR 6'1", 192

G	AB	R	H	HR	RBI	OBP	SLG	AVG
1691	5826	786	1502	190	812	.345	.410	.258

The cleft-chinned third baseman for the Phillies' "Whiz Kids" team of 1950, Willie "Puddin' Head" Jones hit 25 homers, drove in 88 runs, and scored 100 times despite slumping badly in the second half of the season. Though 1950 proved to be his career year at the plate, Jones, whose nickname comes from a 1933 song entitled "Wooden Head, Puddin' Head Jones," went on to set the National League record for most consecutive seasons leading third basemen in fielding percentage.

After spending three years in the Navy, Jones signed with the Phillies in 1946. He became the club's starting third sacker in 1949. During one game against the Braves, the 23-year-old hit four doubles, and in a later game he homered and tripled in the same inning.

In 1950, after a fast start from Jones yielded a slew of dramatic home runs, including a game-winning three-run job to beat the Dodgers in the ninth of one contest, he was named to the All-Star team. Then he slumped, and his performance reflected the team's as the Whiz Kids turned into "the Fizz Kids" and almost gave away a huge lead in the standings. The Phillies finally clinched the pennant on the last day of the season, and Jones hit .286 in what would be his only World Series. The next season he hit a career high .285 and reprised his All-Star Game appearance.

In each year from 1953 through 1958 Jones led National League third basemen in fielding percentage, and seven times during his 12 full seasons he led the circuit in putouts. In one game in 1958 he knocked in eight runs, but his hitting continued to slide. In 1959 he was traded to Cleveland, and after 11 games on to Cincinnati.

Eddie Joost

Joost, Edwin David **SS-2B-3B**

1936–37, 1939–43, 1945, 1947–55 M(1954, 42–54) B:6/5/1916, San Francisco, CA Deb:9/11/1936, CIN NL BR/TR 6', 175

G	AB	R	H	HR	RBI	OBP	SLG	AVG
1574	5606	874	1339	134	601	.361	.366	.239

Eddie Joost did not mince words. As a result, trouble followed him around for more than a decade until the shortstop found a home with the Philadelphia Athletics in 1947. There, he became a specialist in drawing bases on balls and walked more than 100 times in six consecutive seasons, including 149 passes in 1949 for Connie Mack's A's.

Joost was up and down with Cincinnati during the 1930s, in part because he didn't get along with manager Bill McKechnie. "I was always an outspoken fellow," he explained. "I put up a beef for what I believed I had coming to me. When I broke into pro baseball I didn't change. I called things as I saw them and that frequently got me into hot water with the management."

He finally became a regular in 1940 as the Reds won the NL pennant and defeated Detroit in the World Series. But after he led the league with 45 errors in 1942, the Reds traded him to Boston. In 1943 Joost was so disappointed by his .185 batting average—one of the worst performances ever for a player with more than 400 at bats—that he quit baseball. He returned to the Braves in 1945 and then asked for a raise. The Braves, fed up with Joost's salary demands and embarrassed after the player was charged with creating a disturbance outside a nightclub one evening, sold him to Rochester of the International League.

Suddenly, Joost developed a power stroke. He hit 19 homers and drove in 101 runs for Rochester in 1946. Athletics owner/manager Connie Mack sent scout Harry O'Donnell to check on Joost and purchased him at season's end. Joost formed a good relationship with his boss. "Mr. Mack has just been wonderful to me. He treats you like a man. It's a privilege to hustle for him and any player who wouldn't is crazy."

After joining the Athletics, Joost wore glasses. "My eyes bothered me considerably the season at Rochester. But I was afraid if I wore glasses scouts wouldn't show any interest at all in me. Mr. Mack gave me a go-ahead on wearing them after I came to him." Joost became an offensive threat in Philadelphia, where he learned to take a walk. The result was a high on-base percentage and improved power numbers because pitchers needed to throw strikes. In 1947 and 1949 Joost had more walks than hits. He led the AL in putouts four times and in double plays once.

Bobby Brown, a Yankees infielder who later became AL president, said of Joost, "He was simply a great shortstop who, because of the multitude of great shortstops of that time, never got the credit he deserved.... He transformed the A's from a second-division team into a contender by his exceptional play." Joost remains popular with fans in Philadelphia, where 1,500 lined up at a trading card show in 1990 to get his autograph.

Brian Jordan

Jordan, Brian O'Neal **OF**

1992–* B: 3/29/1967, Baltimore, MD Deb:4/8/1992, STL NL BR/TR 6'1", 205

G	AB	R	H	HR	RBI	OBP	SLG	AVG
796	2882	446	834	107	482	.344	.472	.289

Brian Jordan is one of the few modern athletes to play both major league baseball and professional football. Jordan played defensive back with the Atlanta Falcons for three seasons, 1989 to 1991, while employed in the minors for St. Louis. After he joined the Cardinals in 1992 he decided to quit the National Football League to concentrate on baseball.

Jordan spent seven productive years with the Cardinals before signing with the Atlanta Braves as a free agent on November 23, 1998, but neither he nor the club expected him to become the cleanup man in the Braves' lineup. When the incumbent, Andres Galarraga, was diagnosed with cancer of the lower back just before spring training, Jordan was forced into the role. He responded with a career-best 115 RBIs, tied a previous high with 100 runs scored, and made the All-Star team for the first time—while playing the last two months of the season with an injured wrist.

Always a clutch performer, Jordan led the 1999 Braves by hitting .317 with runners in scoring position. In Game 3 of the Division Series at Houston, he erased a 2–0 deficit with a three-run, sixth-inning homer against Astros ace Mike Hampton; he subsequently won the game with a two-run double in the 12th. In the Championship Series against the Mets, both his homers tied games—a two-run shot against Kenny Rogers in Game 2 and a solo effort off Rick Reed in Game 4.

Jordan's response to pressure was not surprising. With St. Louis in 1996, his diving catch in the eighth, followed by a two-run homer in the ninth, completed a three-game Division Series sweep of San Diego. Jordan then beat his future club, the Braves, with an eighth-inning homer in Game 4 of the NLCS.

Addie Joss

Joss, Adrian **P**

1902–10 B:4/12/1880, Woodland, WI D:4/14/1911, Toledo, OH Deb:4/26/1902, CLE AL BR/TR 6'3", 185

W	L	PCT	G	SH	IP	BB	SO	ERA
160	97	.623	286	45	2327	364	920	1.89

Of all the clutch-pitching performances in the history of baseball, none measure up to the one Addie Joss turned in on October 2, 1908. With a week left in the season, three AL teams—the Detroit Tigers, Chicago White Sox, and Cleveland Indians (then called the Naps after second baseman Nap Lajoie)—were separated by only a game and a half. Every game was critical. Some 11,000 fans filed into Cleveland's League Park expecting a well-pitched game from Joss, seeking his 24th win of the season. But his opponent, "Big Ed" Walsh of the White Sox, had been almost unstoppable. Master of the spitball, Walsh eventually won 40 games that season and pitched 464 innings.

Cleveland managed only four hits off Walsh all day, but one of them—a single in the third—was turned into an unearned run, thanks to a stolen base with an error on the throw, followed by a wild pitch. Meanwhile, in the heat of a torrid pennant race, against one of the game's best pitchers having his greatest season, Joss pitched a perfect game. It didn't bring the pennant to Cleveland—the team finished a half game behind Detroit—but that didn't take any luster off Joss' effort. In 1955 Arthur Daley of *The New York Times* called it "the most astonishing clutch job baseball has had." Certainly, it was the supreme moment of a glittering but tragically short career.

Tall and gangly at 6-foot-3 and 185 pounds, Joss pitched with an exaggerated pinwheel motion that earned him the nickname "the Human Hairpin." He threw a good fastball and a fast-breaking curve with exceptional control. During his career he averaged only 1.43 walks per game, the third-best ratio in major league history.

On April 26, 1902, Joss made a memorable debut with Cleveland. Pitching against the St. Louis Browns, Joss pitched a one-hitter (a disputed line drive by Jesse Burkett) and won, 3–0. Cleveland's right fielder claimed he'd caught Burkett's drive three inches off the ground, and most of his teammates agreed. Umpire Bill Carruthers, with the only vote that counted, ruled the catch a trap.

Joss won 17 games, including a league-leading five shutouts, in his rookie year, then followed with 18 victories in 1903. He slumped to 14 wins in 1904 but led the AL with a 1.59 earned run average. From 1905 through 1908, his numbers were 20–12 with a 2.01 ERA, 21–9 with a 1.72 ERA, 27–11 with a 1.83 ERA, and 24–11 with a 1.16 ERA. His 1908 ERA led the league, as did his 27 victories in 1907, when he won 10 straight.

During the off-season Joss was a sportswriter for *The Toledo News-Bee*. Another Toledo newspaper, *The Blade*, later said of him: "Baseball was a profession, as severe as that of any other.... In taking his vocation seriously he was, in return, taken seriously by the people, who recognized in him a man of more than usual intelligence and one who would have adorned any profession in which he had elected to engage."

Joss was often either ill or injured. In 1903 he missed the last month of the season with a high fever. He suffered with malaria in 1904. Then in 1905 he was sidelined for a while with a back problem. In 1909 his won-lost record slipped to 14–13, and his strikeout total fell to only half that of the previous season. Nevertheless, his 1.71 ERA certainly did not signal any loss of ability.

Joss began the 1910 season with four straight victories. On April 20 he threw his second no-hitter against the White Sox, but it was a questionable call. Early in the game, the Sox's Freddy Parent beat out a slow roller to Bill Bradley at third. Most writers scoring the game marked it as a hit, but as the hitless innings piled up they began to have second thoughts. Some of them sought out the official scorekeeper, only to discover that the penny-wise White Sox owner, Charles Comiskey, had not bothered to hire one. That left the decision up to the writers. They spoke with Bradley, who said he should have had the ball. When Joss went the rest of the way without allowing a hit, the writers agreed to change Parent's hit to an error on Bradley and give Joss his second no-hitter.

When Joss developed a sore arm his record slipped to 5–5, and he was sent home for the rest of the season. The layoff seemed to work. He pitched six innings in a postseason exhibition, with encouraging results. The following spring he seemed ready for a comeback, although several teammates noted he had lost considerable weight. During an exhibition game at Chattanooga, Tennessee, he fainted on the bench. Although he dismissed it as nothing, by the time the team reached Cincinnati he was obviously ill.

Diagnosed with pleurisy, he was ordered to return home to Toledo. On April 14, two days after the season began, Joss died of tubercular meningitis. He was 31 years old. His funeral, presided over by Billy Sunday, the ballplayer-turned-evangelist, drew a huge crowd of people. Later that summer, American Leaguers played an all-star game to raise money for Joss' family. Cy Young, who pitched for one side, said, "He was a great man. I feel sure he never made an enemy."

Joss played in the major leagues for only nine seasons, with a record of 160–97. His career ERA of 1.88 is the second lowest of all time. He completed 90 percent of his starts and threw 46 shutouts. He gave up only 19 home runs, and Ty Cobb batted just .071 in 28 at bats against him. He allowed fewer baserunners per nine innings (8.73) than any pitcher in major league history. In 1978 the Veterans Committee decided to bend its 10-year rule and elected Joss to the Hall of Fame.

Bill Joyce

Joyce, William Michael **3B–1B**

1890–92, 1894–98 M(1896–98, 179–122)
B:9/21/1865, St. Louis, MO D:5/8/1941, St. Louis, MO
Deb:4/19/1890, BRO PL BL/TR 5'11", 185

G	AB	R	H	HR	RBI	OBP	SLG	AVG
904	3304	820	970	70	607	.435	.467	.294

Power-hitting third baseman Bill Joyce was one of the game's most colorful figures of the late 19th century. Known as "Scrappy Bill" for his aggressive, sometimes violent style of play, he was constantly on base; Joyce compiled a .435 career on-base percentage, and stole 264 bases.

His career began in 1885 with the semi-pro St. Louis Standards. He then joined a Western League team in Leavenworth, Kansas, where he quickly showed his ability to hit with power. Joyce clubbed more than 20 home runs at a time when few players reached double figures.

The Players' League gave Joyce his chance to play major league baseball in 1890. He drew a league-leading 123 walks in 133 games for the Brooklyn Wonders managed by John Montgomery Ward. When the Players' League folded after one season, Joyce moved on to Boston of the American Association. He made his National League debut in Brooklyn in 1892.

Unhappy with attempts to cut his salary after his second broken leg in two years, Joyce held out for the entire 1893 season. A trade sent Joyce to Washington, where as team captain he batted .312 or better over the next three seasons. He hit with power, stole bases fearlessly, and contributed solid defense at third base. He also showed a willingness to fight opponents and umpires, which made him popular with hometown fans. In his first game with Washington, Joyce threw his bat at home plate umpire Tim Hurst.

Washington sold Joyce to the New York Giants in the middle of the 1896 season. He was named player-manager, guiding the team to a .595 winning percentage in 316 games at the helm, but the club rarely caught a whiff of the first division. Under Joyce's guidance, however, the Giants became the most physically intimidating team in the league.

In 1896 he batted .333, drove in 94 runs, and led the NL with 13 home runs. The following season he set a record with four triples in a game.

Joyce switched to first base in 1898, and slumped to a .258 average. He left the team that season after management tried to fine several of his players, and retired from major league play.

Wally Joyner

Joyner, Wallace Keith **1B**

1986–* B:6/16/1962, Atlanta, GA Deb:4/8/1986, CAL AL BL/TL 6'2" 203

G	AB	R	H	HR	RBI	OBP	SLG	AVG
1861	6755	935	1961	196	1060	.368	.443	.290

Wally Joyner enjoyed a storybook rookie year in 1986—except for the happy ending. Playing first base for the California Angels, Joyner batted .290 with 22 home runs and 100 RBIs, played in the All-Star Game, and was Rookie of the Year runner-up as the Angels won their division. Thousands of fans waved "Wally World" signs at home games as a salute to the young first baseman. Three games into California's Championship Series match-up with Boston, however, Joyner was hospitalized with an infection stemming from a foul ball. The Angels lost in seven gut-wrenching games.

After his second season, when he set career highs with 34 homers and 117 RBIs, Joyner began to struggle under the weight of high expectations. He never again topped 21 home runs in four more seasons in Anaheim. He joined Kansas City as a free agent in 1992.

As his power numbers declined, Joyner hit for higher average, batting over .300 four times after 1991. Traded to San Diego in 1996, Joyner again became a crowd favorite as he twice contributed to Padres playoff clubs. He hit a career-high .327 in 1997 while providing excellent defense at first base. He was traded to the Braves in a six-player deal on December 21, 1999.

Joe Judge

Judge, Joseph Ignatius **1B**

1915–34 B:5/25/1894, Brooklyn, NY D:3/11/1963, Washington, DC Deb:9/20/1915, WAS AL BL/TL 5'8½", 155

G	AB	R	H	HR	RBI	OBP	SLG	AVG
2171	7898	1184	2352	71	1034	.378	.420	.298

Joe Judge had one of the longest tenures with one team in major league history, playing first base for the Washington Senators from 1915 through 1932. He and Hall of Famer Sam Rice (a Senator from 1915 through 1933) hold the all-time record for most career hits by two teammates.

Small for a first baseman, Judge was extremely agile around the bag and led AL first basemen in fielding five times (1923, 1925, 1927, 1929, and 1930). His lifetime fielding average of .993 was an American League record for more than 30 years after his retirement in 1934. In addition, he held career records for American League first basemen for games played, putouts, double plays, and chances at the time of his retirement.

His 131 double plays at first base in 1922 were a major league record. Indeed, the Senators' infield of 1924, featuring Judge at first base, Bucky Harris at second, Roger Peckinpaugh at short, and Ossie Bluege at third, was regarded by baseball historians of the period as one of the best defensive units ever.

Judge batted over .300 nine times and is one of 19 players in history to stroke three triples in one game. Primarily a singles hitter, Judge hit for double digits in homers only twice in his career—in 1922 and 1930, when he hit 10. His highest batting average was .333 in 1920, a year in which he also scored a career-high 103 runs. His best RBI year was 1926, when he drove in 92.

On June 28, 1930, Senators owner Clark Griffith staged a "day" in Judge's honor. An agreement was made with Detroit Tigers owner Frank Navin prior to the game that Judge would receive a cash tribute if more than 9,000 people turned out for the game. More than 18,000 Washingtonians attended to honor Judge for his long and distinguished career as a Senator, creating an unexpected bonanza—$10,500—for the popular first baseman.

Judge, an integral part of the Senators' pennant-winning teams of 1924 and 1925, was released prior to the 1933 season when the Senators captured their third and last pennant. In his two World Series he hit .286 with one homer and four RBIs. After retiring as a player, Judge coached baseball at Georgetown University.

Billy Jurges

Jurges, William Frederick **SS–3B**

1931–47 M(1959–60, 59–63) B:5/9/1908, Bronx, NY D:3/3/1997, Clearwater, FL Deb:5/4/1931, CHI NL BR/TR 5'11", 175

G	AB	R	H	HR	RBI	OBP	SLG	AVG
1816	6253	721	1613	43	656	.325	.335	.258

To say that Billy Jurges had an interesting career is an understatement. The fiery shortstop played 17 seasons in the major leagues and participated in three World Series and as many All-Star Games. He also coached and managed in the majors, punched an umpire, fought a teammate in the dugout before a packed house, and was shot in a hotel room.

Jurges came up to the Chicago Cubs from Louisville in 1931 and, despite his anemic .201

batting average, pushed veteran Woody English over to third base with his glove. Late in the season another rookie, second baseman Billy Herman, joined him, and together they formed the defensive backbone of three pennant-winning Cubs teams.

By 1932, with the Cubs in a hot race for the pennant, older Cubs fans were comparing the Jurges–Herman combination to the revered Tinker–Evers duo of bygone years. Jurges was batting respectably and was on his way to leading National League shortstops in fielding average when a distraught female fan interrupted his career. After Jurges let her enter his hotel room she pulled a gun and attempted to shoot herself. He wrestled the gun away but was wounded in the hand and ribs.

Fearing that Jurges might be lost for the season, the Cubs called up former Yankees shortstop Mark Koenig from the minors. Although Jurges returned in only three weeks, Koenig went on a hitting tear that helped push the Cubs to the pennant. Koenig's former teammates were outraged when the Cubs players voted him only a partial share of their World Series money and, fueled by indignation, the New Yorkers took the Series in four straight.

The Cubs were on their way to another pennant in 1935 when, in midseason, Jurges, a Brooklyn native, teased North Carolina-born third-string catcher Walter Stephenson about the South's loss in the Civil War. After an insensitive remark by Jurges the two went at it in full view of the Pittsburgh crowd, which enjoyed the show far more than the ensuing 9–6 Pirate loss. The Cubs, who were third in early September, ran off 21 straight wins to win the pennant, only to lose the World Series against Detroit.

In 1937 Jurges led the league in fielding average for the third time, hit a career-high .298, and was selected to his first National League All-Star squad. The Cubs won the 1938 pennant but lost another World Series, continuing a three-year pattern they'd begun in 1929.

In an effort to strengthen the club's offense, the Cubs traded Jurges to the Giants in a six-player had deal that brought shortstop Dick Bartell to Chicago. Cubs fans mourned the loss, which rankled even more when Jurges enjoyed another All-Star season while Bartell had a terrible year. Jurges led the league in fielding for the fourth time and, surprisingly, outhit Bartell with a solid .285 to a weak .238.

Equally surprising, considering Bartell's reputation for fighting, was that Jurges was the one who took part in the season's most celebrated fracas. During an argument over another umpire's call, Jurges and arbiter George Magerkurth came to blows. Magerkurth was four inches taller and 50 pounds heavier, and Jurges won points from the fans for courage if not for common sense. He was fined and suspended for only 10 games when Magerkurth insisted on taking equal blame.

Jurges' 1940 play was shortened by a broken leg before midseason. It cost him an All-Star Game appearance, and prompted questions about whether he would end his career. He came back to give the Giants three more solid years before settling into a utility infielder's role. He returned to the Cubs in 1946 and ended his playing career the next season.

Jurges coached for the Cubs and Senators after retiring as a player. In 1959 he became manager of the Boston Red Sox, replacing Pinky Higgins in midseason and turning the club around to climb within one game of the first division. In 1960 the Sox slumped, and Jurges was let go at midseason. Pinky Higgins replaced him.

David Justice

Justice, David Christopher **OF–DH**

1989–* B:4/14/1966, Cincinnati, OH Deb:5/24/1989, ATL NL BL/TL 6'3", 200

G	AB	R	H	HR	RBI	OBP	SLG	AVG
1235	4322	728	1223	235	799	.385	.505	.283

David Justice came to Atlanta as a first baseman, but when the Braves traded two-time Most Valuable Player Dale Murphy to Philadelphia during the 1990 season Justice moved to right field. He responded by hitting 10 home runs in a 12-game stretch in August in a Rookie of the Year performance: .282 average, 28 home runs, 78 RBIs, and a .535 slugging percentage.

The 1990s were a great decade for both Justice and whatever club he was representing. Following Atlanta's last-place finish in 1990, Justice finished each season (with the exception of strike-aborted 1994) on a division champion.

The 1991 Braves added veterans Terry Pendleton, Sid Bream, and Otis Nixon to a lineup of developing players. At the same time, the promising pitching staff came to maturity. The Braves, a team that had lost 97 games the previous year, passed the Dodgers in the final week of the season to claim the National League West title by one game.

The 1993 season was Justice's best year as a Brave. He crushed a career-high 40 home runs along with 120 RBIs, and played in his first All-Star Game. The Braves overtook the San Francisco Giants for the NL West title the last week of the 1993 season, but Justice batted a meek .143 as the Phillies took the pennant in six games.

The Braves, twice losers in the World Series during Justice's career, made it back to the Series for the third time in 1995. The Braves had a chance to win the Series in five games, but Cleveland bounced back to force a sixth game in Atlanta. "If we don't win, they'll probably burn our houses down," the outspoken outfielder said of Braves fans. "If we get down 1–0 tonight, they'll probably boo us out of the stadium."

The crowd loudly booed Justice when he stepped to the plate in a scoreless game in the sixth inning. Justice crushed a fastball high and deep into the Atlanta night against Cleveland southpaw Jim Poole. It proved to be the only run in a 1–0, one-hit masterpiece by Braves pitchers Tom Glavine and Mark Wohlers. Justice, who led all hitters with five RBIs for the Series, was now wildly cheered for helping bring the Braves their first world championship since 1957—when the team was in Milwaukee.

Justice never really had a chance for an encore. He missed all but 40 games of the 1996 season with injuries, then was sent to Cleveland in a spring training deal the following year. Justice immediately took to his new surroundings. He batted a career-best .329, was voted to start the All-Star Game (although he missed the game with an injury), won his second Silver Slugger Award, and captured American League Comeback Player of the Year honors from *The Sporting News*. He also appeared in his fourth World Series. He walked six times and drove in four runs, but batted just .185 in Cleveland's seven-game loss to Florida. Although his next two seasons with the Indians were not as productive as his first, his club again won division titles in 1998 and 1999.

Jim Kaat

Kaat, James Lee **P**

1959–83 B:11/7/1938, Zeeland, MI Deb:8/2/1959, WAS AL BL TL, 6'4", 217

W	L	PCT	G	SH	IP	BB	SO	ERA
283	237	.544	898	31	4530^1	1083	2461	3.45

At the time he retired, lefthander Jim Kaat had pitched for more years than anyone in baseball history. Commenting on his 25 seasons in the major leagues, Kaat said, "I'll never be considered one of the all-time greats, maybe not even one of the all-time goods. But I'm one of the all-time survivors."

Kaat owed his lengthy career to his ability to adapt and become valuable in every conceivable way. Known as "Kitty," Kaat hit well for a pitcher, enabling him to stay in games when other pitchers might have been removed. He hit 16 home runs in his career, and his 134 sacrifice hits set the record for pitchers. He also won 14 consecutive Gold Gloves, second to only Brooks Robinson's 16. Many experts list him as the best-fielding pitcher of all time.

Oddly enough, the 6-foot-4 Kaat's boyhood idol was 5-foot-6 Bobby Shantz, and Kaat learned to field like his smaller counterpart. No pitcher could match Kaat's speed in getting off the mound to cover first or snag bunts. "No one noticed my fielding," Kaat recalled, "until a sharp bouncer knocked out six of my teeth." In his next outing he fielded two hard grounders up the middle, and people began paying attention. His quick move to the plate also stalled would-be basestealers, and although some critics believed Kaat delivered illegal "quick pitches," he was called for only six balks in his long career.

Kaat had a 1–7 record over parts of two seasons as a Washington Senator before the team moved to Minnesota in 1961, and he was the last Senator to play in the major leagues. After going 9–17 in his first year with the Twins, he won 18, 10, and 17 games in the next three seasons, and won 18 again in 1965 when the Twins took the pennant.

In the World Series Kaat threw a seven-hitter to outdo Dodger Sandy Koufax in Game 2, but the Minnesota pitcher lasted less than three innings against Koufax in Game 5. Kaat also took the loss in Game 7, leaving in the fourth inning after giving up the only two runs the Dodgers would score.

In 1966 Kaat had his best year, leading the American League with 25 wins, 19 complete games, 304 innings pitched, and the fewest walks per nine innings. Only one Cy Young Award was given at the time, and Koufax swept the voting with his 27–9, 317-strikeout season. Kaat, however, was named American League Pitcher of the Year by *The Sporting News*.

During the next five years he was a 14-game winner three times, and he won 16 and 13 once each. Kaat was off to his best start ever (10–2) in 1972 when he broke his wrist sliding. Ineffective in 1973, the 34-year-old pitcher was shipped to the White Sox. In Chicago Kaat was again paired with legendary pitching coach Johnny Sain, who had worked with him during his best seasons in Minnesota. Kaat shortened his delivery and won 41 games in the next two years.

After one year starting with Philadelphia, Kaat spent the final five years of his career as a reliever with the Phils, Yankees, and Cardinals. Less than a month before his 44th birthday he appeared in the 1982 World Series for the Cards. Kaat followers say he began his 25th year in the majors seeking to develop a new pitch, an underhand sinking fastball, to add to his repertoire. After a year as a pitching coach for the Reds, Kaat became a broadcaster, winning many fans with his direct, intelligent commentary.

Al Kaline

Kaline, Albert William **OF-1B-DH**

1953–74 B:12/19/1934, Baltimore, MD Deb:6/25/1953, DET AL BR/TR, 6'2", 180

G	AB	R	H	HR	RBI	OBP	SLG	AVG
2834	10116	1622	3007	399	1583	.379	.480	.297

Al Kaline never spent a minute in the minor leagues. And after an ominous debut, he enjoyed a prosperous career that earned him a plaque in the Baseball Hall of Fame.

Kaline, a Baltimore native, was signed by the Detroit Tigers out of high school for $30,000 in 1953 and went straight to the majors. He joined the club in Philadelphia, entered the lineup on June 25, 1953, as a defensive replacement, and popped out to center field in his first at bat. In the same game he let a line drive get past him in the outfield, an error that cost Detroit the game. While he appeared in only a handful of games during the season, primarily as a late-inning replacement or pinch hitter, the Tigers were patient and didn't give up on him.

The following season, at age 19, Kaline joined the starting lineup and hit .276. He was blessed with all the tools a good ballplayer needed, and Detroit fans felt it was merely a matter of time before he became one of the game's great stars.

It didn't take Kaline long. In 1955 he opened the season with a bang on April 17, hitting three home runs in one game, including two in one inning. He was only the fourth player in American League history to hit two homers in a single inning, and the first since Joe DiMaggio did it 19 years earlier. At age 20, Kaline became the youngest player to win a batting title when he hit .340, belted 27 home runs, and knocked in 102. In the outfield he was also superb. Kaline quickly mastered the tricky caroms and bounces along the right-field wall at Tiger Stadium, and baserunners soon learned not to challenge Kaline's arm.

Kaline looked as if he were Detroit's answer to Willie Mays or Mickey Mantle, and for a few years he was. From 1955 to 1963 he hit at least .300 in all but two seasons. In 1959 Harvey Kuenn and Kaline finished 1-2 in the American League batting race, becoming just the seventh pair of teammates in the league's history to do so.

Unfortunately, Kaline was continually dogged by injuries that kept him out of the lineup for 10 or 15 games a season. He never quite had the protection in the lineup of his counterparts, or their physical ability. Kaline once said of Mantle, "I wish I was half the ballplayer he is."

In a typical season, Kaline hit around 20 home runs, knocked in 80 or 90 runs, and threw out the occasional brazen baserunner. His performance was usually good enough to put him on the All-Star team and earn him a Gold Glove. But he never won another batting title, and he never led the league in home runs or RBIs.

In another city Kaline's performance might have disappointed the fans, but the loyal Detroit followers appreciated his work ethic and modesty. Like many in the city, Kaline did his job, did it well, and did it without grumbling. The Yankees won the pennant almost every season anyway, so Kaline gave Detroit something to cheer.

In 1962 Kaline appeared to be on his way to a career year. But on May 26 in Yankee Stadium he did a somersault to make a game-ending catch and broke his collarbone. Despite missing nearly two months of play, Kaline finished with a career-high 29 home runs, with 94 RBIs in only 398 at bats.

Kaline hit only 17 home runs in 1964 and 18 the following season. But he rebounded to tie his career high with 29 homers in 1966, and was on pace to break that mark in 1967. With Detroit finally challenging for the pennant, however, Kaline broke his hand and missed a month of the season. He finished with 28 homers, the Tigers lost the pennant to Boston on the final day of the season, and it appeared as if he might never get a chance to appear in a World Series.

In 1968 the Tigers got off to a fast start and surprisingly coasted to the pennant, defeating Baltimore by 12 games. Kaline was hit in May by a pitch that broke his arm, and he was out of the lineup for a month. When he returned, he didn't hit well and saw only part-time duty the rest of the season.

Entering the World Series against the Cardinals, Tigers manager Mayo Smith faced a dilemma. He wanted Kaline in the lineup but had no place to put him. Jim Northrup had taken over in right field and responded with a team-leading 90 RBIs. Left fielder Willie Horton had hit 36 home runs during the 1968 season. Kaline didn't have enough range to play center, and besides, center fielder Mickey Stanley was one of the best defensive outfielders in the American League.

Then Smith had an idea. Three different Tigers had shared the shortstop position during the season, and while all three could field, none could hit. In the last few weeks of the season, Smith had experimented with center fielder Stanley at short. He continued the experiment in the Series, moving Northrup from right to center and installing Kaline in right.

The strategy paid off and helped Detroit win the Series. Although pitcher Denny McLain stumbled against Cardinals ace Bob Gibson, Mickey Lolich was magnificent and won three games. Kaline hit .379 for the Series, including two home runs, led both teams with eight RBIs, and made several sparkling plays in the field. Both Northrup and Stanley were also superb defensively, and Detroit won in seven games.

Kaline's performance dropped off during the next three seasons, and he started to see time at first base in addition to the outfield. In 1972 he became a part-time player, and in 1973 he hit a career-low .255 in only 91 at bats. Many thought he should retire, yet he needed only 139 more hits to reach 3,000.

In 1974 he accepted his new role as Detroit's designated hitter better than did most Detroit fans. Manager Ralph Houk was excoriated for his decision to remove Kaline from right field. Said one fan, "He is taking from me—all of us in Detroit—one of the great joys of our life. We don't have too much in Detroit—one good theater, one London Chop House, one Windsor Tunnel, one right fielder. He is taking our right fielder away from us, and summer in the city may never be the same again."

Kaline's move to designated hitter paid off for Detroit, though. In 1974 he went to the plate 558 times, his highest total since 1961. He hit a respectable .262, with 13 home runs, and his 64 RBIs were his best since 1970. On September 24, 1974, facing Baltimore's Dave McNally, Kaline stroked a double for his 3,000th career hit.

Kaline retired at the end of the season with 3,007 hits, 399 home runs, and a .297 batting average in 22 major league seasons, all with Detroit. He ranks third in major league history for the longest career spent with one team. Kaline was a member of 15 All-Star teams and won 11 Gold Gloves. He was elected to the Hall of Fame in 1980, one of 23 players to be inducted in their first year of eligibility. On August 17, 1980, the Tigers retired his uniform No. 6.

Willie Kamm

Kamm, William Edward **3B**

1923–35 B:2/2/1900, San Francisco, CA D:12/21/1988, Belmont, CA Deb:4/18/1923, CHI AL BR/TR, 5'10½", 170

G	AB	R	H	HR	RBI	OBP	SLG	AVG
1693	5851	802	1643	29	826	.372	.384	.281

In 1922, after four years with the San Francisco Seals of the Pacific Coast League, Willie Kamm was purchased by the Chicago White Sox for the amazing price of $100,000—the most any team had ever paid for a minor leaguer. But Charles Comiskey had been desperate; he had been unable to find anyone to replace Buck Weaver, banned because of the Black Sox scandal.

The story goes that Kamm didn't take the news well. After hearing that he'd been traded, Kamm panicked and ran to a movie house for sanctuary.

Kamm had nothing to worry about. He would lead American League third basemen in fielding percentage eight times, including six in a row. His .978 fielding percentage in 1926 was the league record until the late 1940s. Kamm still holds the league record for most putouts in a season at third base, with 243. That same season he was the first major leaguer in history to handle 200 consecutive chances at third without making an error. He was also famous for the hidden ball trick and would use it for one or two outs every year.

Kamm was more than just sure-handed. As a batter he led the league in walks in 1925; he routinely hit between .280 and .290, with one season of .308. He earned a reputation as a clutch hitter, five times driving in more than 80 runs in a season.

After eight years with the White Sox, Kamm in 1931 began to hear rumors that he would soon be traded. No Chicago official said a word to him, even after he saw the trade to Cleveland announced in the newspapers. He felt he had been treated poorly. A letter from Comiskey a few days later didn't help, even though "the Old Roman" apologized for not saying good-bye and closed with, "It is a pleasure to me to have young men of your class and character."

Kamm's style of play didn't change. From 1931 to 1933 he batted between .282 and .295 with the Indians and landed two more fielding crowns. But after a .269 season in 1934, and a spat with manager Walter Johnson, he was eased into a scouting job. Kamm returned to the Pacific Coast League to manage for two more seasons and then retired on wise investments that had survived the stock market crash of 1929.

Eric Karros

Karros, Eric Peter **1B**

1991–* B: 11/4/1967, Hackensack, NJ Deb: 9/1/1991, LA NL BR/TR 6'4", 216

G	AB	R	H	HR	RBI	OBP	SLG	AVG
1183	4456	574	1217	211	734	.332	.470	.273

Eric Karros' career went pretty well for a player who was once "fired" by the fans in the Venezuelan winter league. Batting .113 that season, Karros lasted three weeks before the fans decided he had to go—they let him know by throwing bottle caps at him. He received a much better reception in Los Angeles.

His first major league season began by platooning with Kal Daniels and Todd Benzinger, but the job was all his by mid-May 1992. Karros led the last-place Dodgers with 20 home runs and also drove in 88 runs while starting the final 124 games of the season. He was voted the 12th NL Rookie of the Year in Dodgers history, the most by any club.

With Mike Piazza—and later Raul Mondesi—flanking Karros in the lineup, the Dodgers' fortunes changed. In 1993 Karros became the first player in franchise history to smack 20 or more homers in his first two major league seasons (later matched by Piazza). Defensively, Karros led the league in assists by a first baseman (147) and took part in 118 double plays.

In 1995 Karros raised his batting average 32 points while surpassing 30 home runs and 100 RBIs for the first time. The first baseman hit .500 with two home runs against Cincinnati in the NL Division Series. Unfortunately, Karros couldn't pitch. The normally steady Los Angeles pitching staff surrendered 22 runs in a three-game sweep by the Reds.

Karros surpassed those numbers in 1996, but the Dodgers were once again swept in the Division Series—this time by Atlanta. It was the last playoff appearance of the decade for the Dodgers, but Karros did not decline in the ensuing years. He drove in 104 runs in 1997 and reached .300 for the first time in 1999.

Benny Kauff

Kauff, Benjamin Michael **OF**

1912–20 B:1/5/1890, Pomeroy, OH D:11/17/1961, Columbus, OH Deb:4/20/1912, NY AL BL/TL, 5'8", 157

G	AB	R	H	HR	RBI	OBP	SLG	AVG
859	3094	521	961	49	454	.389	.450	.311

Dubbed "the Ty Cobb of the Federal League," Benny Kauff failed to live up to the grandiose comparison. He was nonetheless a talented player who might have had a long and successful career had he not thrown it all away.

Although Kauff hit with some power, his main asset was speed. After a brief five-game trial with New York in 1912, Kauff returned to the minors. In 1914 he resurfaced as a star with Indianapolis of the new Federal League.

The three enduring legacies of the Federal League, which existed for only two years, are Weeghman Field in Chicago, later renamed Wrigley Field; baseball's appreciation of Judge Kenesaw Mountain Landis, who was rewarded for his partiality in the interleague conflict by being named baseball commissioner in 1920; and those few players such as Kauff who went on to enjoy significant careers in the American and National Leagues following their experience in the renegade circuit.

In 1914 Kauff led Indianapolis to the championship. His .370 batting average, 120 runs, 211 hits, 44 doubles, 305 total bases, .447 on-base percentage, .509 slugging average, and 75 stolen bases were all league highs. Kauff moved on to Brooklyn in 1915, and despite improved pitching he again led the league with a .342 batting average, .446 on-base percentage, .509 slugging average, and 55 stolen bases.

Following the Federal League's collapse the New York Giants acquired Kauff, outfielder Edd Roush, and infielder Bill McKechnie. Although McKechnie later became a great manager, he was only an average player. And many observers felt, correctly as it turned out, that Roush, acquired at the bargain price of $7,500, would become a better player than Kauff. Yet Giants manager John McGraw traded Roush to Cincinnati and kept Kauff, who cost New York $30,000.

Kauff, who lived life in the fast lane, arrived at his first Giants training camp wearing a loud striped shirt, an expensive suit, patent leather shoes, a fur-collared overcoat, and a derby. A diamond stickpin secured his tie, a diamond ring weighed down one finger, and a diamond-encrusted watch sat in his pocket, along with $7,500 in cash. He carried a cane and brought trunks and trunks of clothes.

Kauff struggled during his first year with the Giants. He hit only .264 in 1916, and his other statistics also suffered, although he did manage to finish second in the league in stolen bases, with 40, and tie for second in triples, with 15.

In 1917 Kauff was much improved. His .308 batting average was third best in the league, as were his 30 stolen bases. The Giants won the pennant that year but lost to the White Sox in the World Series. Kauff hit only .160 in the Series but smacked two home runs in Game 4 and led his team in RBIs.

Although in 1918 Kauff hit .315, he spent much of the season in the Army and played in only 67 games. In 1919 both Kauff and the Giants disappointed. New York finished behind Cincinnati, and Kauff hit only .277. Midway through the 1920 season the Giants abruptly sent him down to the minors. He had hit .311 in eight major league seasons, but most of his success had come during the Federal League years.

Kauff had an unsavory reputation and was implicated in several gambling scandals during his career. He allegedly turned down an offer of $500 from teammates Heinie Zimmerman and Hal Chase to fix some games in 1919, and his name came up several times during the Black Sox investigation, but nothing was ever proven.

In 1921 Kauff and his brother were arrested for stealing a car. A jury acquitted Kauff, but Judge Landis banned him from baseball. Kauff sued Landis but lost.

Ewing Kauffman

Kaufman, Ewing

Owner (1969–93) B:9/21/1916, Garden City, MO D:8/1/1993, Kansas City, MO

The original owner of the Kansas City Royals, Ewing Kauffman acquired the club as an expansion franchise in 1968 after the Kansas City Athletics moved to Oakland. He had made his fortune in pharmaceuticals after founding Marion Laboratories in his mother's basement and building it into a diversified health care company worth billions.

The Royals quickly developed into one of baseball's most successful organizations, winning six Western Division titles, two pennants, and a world championship. Even though the Royals were a small-market team, Kauffman supplied the funding for a strong scouting department, paid for the occasional high-priced free agent, and supported such innovative ideas as the Academy—a model for player development.

Hall of Famer George Brett was one of the many young stars signed and developed under Kauffman's ownership. With Bret Saberhagen, Dan

Quisenberry, and Brett leading the way, the Royals won the World Series in 1985, defeating the St. Louis Cardinals in seven games. Royals Stadium was changed to Kauffman Stadium in a special ceremony on July 2, 1993, shortly before Kauffman's death.

Johnny Keane

Keane, John Joseph

Manager (1961–66, 398–350) B:11/3/1911, St. Louis, MO D:1/6/1967, Houston, TX

After two sixth-place finishes under manager Johnny Keane, the St. Louis Cardinals showed major improvement in 1963, contending for most of the following season to finish second in the National League with 93 wins. Expectations in St. Louis ran high going into the 1964 season, but after the Philadelphia Phillies led the National League race for most of the summer and held a commanding lead with less than two weeks to go, Cardinals owner August Busch prepared to fire Keane. Suddenly, the Cardinals surged and overtook the collapsing Phillies. Keane's Cards won the pennant on the final day of the season, then defeated the Yankees in seven games in the World Series.

Naturally, Busch changed his mind about firing Keane. Instead, Keane, who had been with the Cardinal organization since 1938, quit the day after his World Series triumph. Four days later the Yankees announced that he would replace Yogi Berra as manager. Unfortunately, Keane had little success with an aging Yankees team that was past its glory years. He lasted fewer than two seasons in New York before being fired. Less than a year later he died of a heart attack.

Tim Keefe

Keefe, Timothy John **P**

1880–93 B:1/1/1857, Cambridge, MA D:4/23/1933, Cambridge, MA Deb:8/6/1880, TRO NL BR/TR, 5'10½", 185

W	L	PCT	G	SH	IP	BB	SO	ERA
342	225	.603	599	39	5047¹	1236	2560	2.62

Pitchers who worked prior to 1893 had an advantage over their successors, for that year the pitching distance was lengthened to 60 feet 6 inches. Previously the ball had traveled a distance of only 50 feet. The shorter distance had allowed some fastball pitchers to rack up a huge number of strikeouts, making it difficult to judge the best pitchers of the 1880s by modern standards. But one star pitcher of the era undoubtedly could have made the adjustment. Indeed, righthander Tim Keefe might have been even more successful had he pitched a decade or so later.

Most pitchers of the time relied on a fastball. Although a few also included a curve in their repertoires, Keefe was a master of three pitches: a fastball, a curve, and a devastating changeup. He was perhaps the first pitcher to use the changeup as a major weapon; adding an extra 10 feet to the pitch may well have increased his effectiveness.

Mickey Welch, Keefe's teammate and himself a great pitcher, once said, "I never saw a pitcher better than Keefe. It is true that he did his greatest work at the old distance of 50 feet. But if he had been a modern pitcher at 60 feet 6 inches, he would have had no superior. He was a master strategist who knew the weakness of every batter in the league."

As a boy Keefe played baseball on the sandlots of Cambridge despite his family's objections and by his teens was pitching for several semipro teams. He then turned professional, pitching in 1878 and 1879 with Utica, New Bedford, and Albany. In 1880 he joined the Troy Haymakers of the National League and compiled a 6–6 mark in 12 games.

Although the Haymakers had several future stars on their roster, they were still a weak team. Keefe lost 53 games during the next two seasons while winning only 35. After the 1882 season the league canceled the Troy franchise. John Day, who had been granted franchises in both the National League and the American Association for New York City, purchased the Haymakers and divided the players between his two teams. Keefe was assigned to the AA's Metropolitans, the original "Mets."

Day had placed most of his better players with his NL team, but Keefe's pitching made the Mets more successful. In 1883 he led the AA with 68 complete games and 619 innings pitched, compiling a 41–27 record. The following year he finished at 37–17 to account for more than half of the pennant-winning Mets' victories. In a series of postseason games regarded as the first World Series, the Mets faced the NL champion Providence Grays, led by sensational pitcher Charley "Old Hoss" Radbourn. Keefe lost the first two games to Radbourn, then umpired as Old Hoss defeated the Mets a third time to win the Series.

Although Day was pleased with the Mets, he knew that a top National League team would bring him more prestige and larger profits, so he transferred Keefe, several other players, and Manager Jim Mutrie to his National League Gothams. Noting that many members of the Gothams were unusually tall, Day began calling them "my giants." The name caught on, and by 1886 they were known officially as the Giants.

The 5-foot-10, 185-pound Keefe was a big man for his time, but on the mound he seemed immense. He and Mickey Welch gave the Giants the most effective one-two pitching punch of the period. Keefe went 32–13 in his first season with the new club and led the league with an ERA of 1.58. In 1886 he led the league with 42 wins, 64 games pitched, 62 complete games, and 535 innings pitched.

"Sir Timothy," as he was often called because of his stylish clothing, was one of the more intelligent players of his day. He both designed and sold the Giants their tight black uniforms, and between pitching assignments he studied shorthand in preparation for a career after baseball. As a result the Brotherhood of Professional Base Ball Players, a benevolent association formed in 1885, made him its secretary.

Keefe missed several weeks of the 1887 season when one of his pitches hit a batter in the temple and nearly killed him. Keefe agonized over the incident and may have suffered a nervous breakdown. He eventually recovered and won 35 games for the year.

During the 1880s the pitching rules changed frequently. One important change allowed hurlers to deliver the ball overhand instead of underhand, which they had been restricted to earlier. Keefe reportedly continued to use the same submarine delivery as before, although one photograph shows him throwing sidearm.

In 1888, his best season, his 35 victories led the National League, as did his .745 winning percentage. He also threw a league-high eight shutouts, finished with a league-leading 1.74 ERA, and reeled off a string of 19 straight wins. Keefe's streak remains the all-time single-season record, although Rube Marquard later matched it.

Some dispute Keefe's accomplishment, however. After winning eight games in a row, Keefe started a game in which the Giants led, 9–0, after the second inning. To save Keefe's arm, the New York manager let a lesser pitcher finish the game. Under the rules of the time Keefe was credited with the win, but today's rules require that a starting pitcher go five innings to qualify for a win. Some modernists argue that, according to the new rules, the victory should be taken away. But most historians generally agree that the rules of the day should govern the statistics of the day.

The Giants won the 1888 pennant and disposed of the AA's St. Louis Browns in an extended 10-game World Series; Keefe won four games while allowing only two earned runs. When the season ended he demanded and received a contract for $4,500, making him the highest-paid Giants player. In 1889 New York took its second consecutive pennant and World Series, but Keefe slipped to only 28 regular-season wins and was 0–1 in two World Series appearances.

In 1890 baseball's club owners, in a dangerous miscalculation, planned to rank players according to ability and pay set wages of between $1,500 and $2,500 according to their ranking. The Brotherhood strongly opposed the plan and decided to set up its own league. Ever the entrepreneur, Keefe designed the Players League baseball and sold it through his own sporting goods company. Pitching for the New York Players League team, he went 17–11. At age 33, he was obviously no longer the pitcher he had once been.

Keefe returned to the Giants when the Players League folded and was soon dealt to Philadelphia. He pitched for two more years, then retired. During his 14 seasons he compiled a 342–225 record with 554 complete games and a 2.62 earned run average.

He tried umpiring in 1894 and 1895, but after taking abuse one day at the Polo Grounds, where he'd once been cheered, Keefe went home and wrote out his resignation. Later, as a college baseball coach, he put in time with Harvard, Tufts, and Princeton. He died in 1933 and in 1964 was named to the Hall of Fame.

Wee Willie Keeler

Keeler, William Henry **OF**

1892–10 B:3/3/1872, Brooklyn, NY D:1/1/1923, Brooklyn, N.Y. Deb:9/30/1892, NY AL BL/TL, 5'4½", 140

G	AB	R	H	HR	RBI	OBP	SLG	AVG
2123	8591	1719	2932	33	810	.388	.415	.341

"Wee Willie" Keeler was one of the smallest men ever to play major league baseball, but he was often the most important man on the field. Standing only 5-foot-4 and weighing a scant 140 pounds, he nevertheless compiled baseball's 12th-highest career batting average. But statistics were not important to Keeler. He played to win, and he was a master at that. In one seven-year period he was a major contributor to five championship teams and two second-place finishers.

Keeler was born in 1872, the son of a conductor of a Brooklyn horse-drawn trolley car. As a boy he was interested in little but baseball, and his teachers told him he'd never amount to anything. Although he was a lefthanded thrower and batter, he played shortstop and third base for semipro teams around Brooklyn.

In 1892 an injury to the regular third baseman for Binghamton of the Eastern League gave Keeler his professional start. He hit .373 in 93 games and was acquired by the New York Giants for $800. He batted .321 for them in 14 late-season games. Seven games into the 1893 season he fractured his ankle. Giants manager John Montgomery Ward decided Keeler was too small to stand up to major league competition and sold him to Brooklyn for another $800.

When Keeler recovered he split the remainder of the season between Binghamton and Brooklyn, failing to make much of an impression with either team. That winter he and veteran first baseman Dan Brouthers were traded to Baltimore, then considered the Siberia of the league.

The rest of the National League hadn't noticed that Baltimore manager Ned Hanlon was slowly turning a team of unknown ballplayers into a powerhouse. In 1892 he had taken over a last-place team whose only stellar players were veteran catcher Wilbert Robinson and fiery young third baseman John McGraw. He added second baseman Heinie Reitz at the start of 1893. Late in the season he acquired left fielder Joe Kelley from Pittsburgh, center fielder Steve Brodie from St. Louis, and shortstop Hugh Jennings from Louisville. Hanlon saw the potential in each of them, and in 1894 the youngsters all blossomed. Suddenly, the Orioles were contenders.

Of all his discoveries and reclamation projects, Keeler was Hanlon's greatest success. He moved the lefthanded third baseman to right field and made him a star. Despite his small size, Keeler had a strong arm and terrific speed and excelled defensively. Theodore P. Sullivan, who managed in both the National League and the American Association, once called Keeler "the greatest right fielder in the history of baseball."

But it was his offensive skills that drew most of the raves. Keeler stood at the plate flat-footed, choking so far up on the bat that Sam Crawford, a Hall of Fame hitter himself, once commented, "He only used half of his bat." And it wasn't much to begin with. Keeler used the smallest bat in major league history, a 29-ounce, 30-inch matchstick. He never swung for the fences; as Crawford noted, he just "pecked at the ball."

Exercising perfect bat control, time and time again, Keeler pecked the ball just over an infielder's head. If the defender moved back, Keeler simply dropped a bunt. It was a simple strategy that worked over and over again. Occasionally one of Willie's pecks would skip between two outfielders, and Keeler would race to second or third. Nearly all of his 34 career home runs were such inside-the-park "tweeners."

The Baltimore infield became hard as a brick under the summer sun. Keeler discovered that if he chopped down on a pitch the ball would bounce high into the air and he could zip to first base while the frustrated fielders waited for the ball to come down. Such hits, now common on today's artificial surfaces, are still called "Baltimore chops."

Keeler and McGraw hit first and second in the Orioles lineup and together developed the hit-and-run play. While there is some argument as to precisely which team and players first came up with the maneuver, there is no question that McGraw and Keeler brought it to perfection.

Prior to the 1894 season Manager Hanlon drilled the Orioles on bunts, steals, chops, and hit-and-runs. Suddenly, the eighth-place team of the year before was the talk of the league. Their pitching was never better than ordinary, but their offense carried them to a pennant, three games in front of the New York Giants.

Their style also made enemies, because Hanlon's Orioles played a rough game. They were more than willing to use their spikes on any infielder who got in the way, and the stream of profanity that poured from their bench reduced anyone more sensitive than a stone to tears. McGraw and Jennings were particularly abusive, and when they disputed an umpire's decision they turned vicious. A favorite ploy was to stand so close to the umpire that their spikes cut into the arbiter's toes.

Although Keeler was considered a practical joker off the field, on the field, in stark contrast to his teammates, he was one of the quietest players in the league. Apart from the occasional "I've got it," his voice was almost never heard. And while other Orioles swaggered to the plate, trying to intimidate the opposing pitcher with their bravado, Keeler appeared almost apologetic as he stepped into the batter's box. In 1894 he quietly hit .371 to begin a string of eight consecutive seasons in which he amassed 200 or more hits. He also scored an amazing 165 runs and batted in 94 in 1894.

The Orioles won two more pennants with Keeler batting .377 and .386. In 1897 the team slipped to second, but Keeler won the NL batting crown with a .424 average, the third highest ever compiled in a full major league season. His 239 hits also led the league. He got off to a great start, hitting safely in his first 44 games—a major league record until Joe DiMaggio hit in 56 consecutive games in 1941. Pete Rose later tied Keeler's batting streak, and it remains the league record.

In 1898 Keeler won his second batting title, hitting .385 and again leading the league in hits, with 216. Although the Orioles finished second again, attendance in Baltimore fell off. Hanlon and Baltimore owner Harry Von der Horst were able to buy control of the Brooklyn team while retaining control of the Orioles.

Although the practice was legal at the time, such dual control would never be allowed today because the owners could favor one franchise over another. That is precisely what happened. Hanlon became Brooklyn's manager and took Keeler, Joe Kelley, and several others with him. Baltimore named McGraw manager and was left to wither on the vine.

In Brooklyn, Hanlon's combination of Baltimore and Brooklyn stars, known as the Superbas and later the Dodgers, sailed to pennants in 1899 and 1900. Keeler contributed batting averages of .379 and .362 to the attack. He led the league with 140 runs scored in 1899 and 204 hits in 1900. When *Brooklyn Eagle* newspaperman Abe Yager asked Keeler to explain how he hit, he responded with one of baseball's most famous quotes: "Keep a clear eye, and hit 'em where they ain't."

In 1901 a new rule determined that foul balls were strikes if the batter had fewer than two strikes already. The rule hurt "scientific" hitters such as Keeler, who often fouled off pitch after pitch until he saw one he liked. In 1902 another rule change made a foul bunt with two strikes an out, taking away another favorite Keeler strategy. In addition, pitchers began to use a number of trick pitches, such as the spitball. Batting averages fell throughout baseball, and Keeler's was no exception. In 1901 he hit .339, his lowest mark since becoming a regular. By 1902 he was down to .333.

At the same time, the upstart American League declared itself a major organization before the 1901 season. The National League had a salary cap of $2,400, and the AL was able to lure many National League stars into the fold by offering better pay. Keeler initially remained loyal to the NL.

In 1903 the new league established a franchise in New York. The Highlanders (later the Yankees) badly needed a drawing card and offered Keeler $10,000 a year, the highest salary in baseball. Keeler signed, earning his money as he hit better than .300 for four more seasons. Then age began to catch up with him. He played with New York through 1909, appeared in 19 games with the NL Giants in 1910, then retired in 1911 after a final season with Toronto of the International League.

In 19 major league seasons Keeler had 2,932 hits, 86 percent of them singles. Had he known that 3,000 hits would later become such a benchmark, he'd probably have continued to play until he reached it. Keeler's lifetime batting average is .341, and he scored 1,719 runs. Surprisingly, given the nature of most of his hits, he still managed to drive in 810 runs.

After retiring as a player, Keeler coached for a while and lived on his real estate holdings. Eventually he became nearly destitute, and he died in 1923. In 1939 he was one of the first two dozen men named to the Hall of Fame.

George Kell

Kell, George Clyde **1B–3B**

1943–57 B:8/23/1922, Swifton, AK Deb:9/28/1943, PHI AL BR/TR, 5'9", 175

G	AB	R	H	HR	RBI	OBP	SLG	AVG
1795	6702	881	2054	78	870	.368	.414	.306

What George Kell lacked in talent he more than compensated for with hard work and a no-nonsense, quiet professionalism that made him one of the best third basemen in the game.

Both an excellent fielder and a solid hitter, his lifetime .306 average is third best (behind Pie Traynor and George Brett) among all third basemen. A.W. Laird's ranking system for fielding places him sixth all time at his position. He led the AL in assists and total chances four times and in fielding percentage seven times, ranks third lifetime in fielding percentage, and still ranks in the top 20 in assists and putouts.

Historian Jim Kaplan relates a story that illustrates Kell's style of play. In 1948 "Kell had his jaw broken by a Joe DiMaggio smash. Reacting instinctively, Kell picked up the ball, crawled to third for the forceout, then fainted."

Bad knees kept young Kell out of military service, and he spent 1940 through 1943 learning his trade in the minor leagues. In 1943, playing for Lancaster in the Class B Inter-State League, Kell had a mammoth season, leading all hitters in Organized Baseball with a .396 average. His 120 runs, 220 hits, and 23 triples also led his league and, foreshadowing his major league career, he was also the league leader in putouts, assists, and fielding percentage.

When Kell arrived at Connie Mack's spring training camp with the Philadelphia A's in 1944 he fancied himself a power hitter. Mack admired the 21-year-old's glove, but predicted Kell would never be much of a batter. Mack suggested Kell switch to a lighter bat and try to hit line drives using the whole field instead of just pulling the ball.

Kell hit .268 and .272 in his first two years as the Philadelphia third baseman and won his first fielding percentage title in 1945. In May of 1946, with Kell hitting .299, Mack traded him to Detroit for outfielder Barney McCosky. McCosky hit well for Mack, but Kell blossomed into a major star in Detroit.

Kell hit .327 for the Tigers for the remainder of the 1946 season and began a string of nine years of hitting .296 or better. In 1947 he led the AL in assists for the third straight year and was named a starter in his first All-Star Game, an honor he held for the next four years (although a broken wrist and the DiMaggio line drive kept him out of the 1948 contest).

After hitting .320 in 1947 he tailed off to .304 in 1948, although he played in only 92 games because of the broken bones. In 1949 Kell won the AL batting title by the slimmest of margins: his .342911 figure topped Ted Williams' .342756, preventing Williams from winning his third Triple Crown. Kell was in the on-deck circle in the last inning of the final game of the season, knowing that he was ahead of Williams. Manager Red Rolfe told him he didn't have to bat if he wanted to safeguard the title. Kell decided to hit anyway, but he never reached the plate, as the batter ahead of him hit into a game-ending double play.

In his batting championship season Kell struck out only 13 times. No batting champion has ever fanned so few times since strikeout totals were first counted in 1910. Only Ernie Lombardi and Paul Waner came close: Each struck out 14 times in a batting title year. Kell was also the first third baseman to win a batting title since Heinie Zimmerman in 1912, and would be the last to accomplish the feat until Bill Madlock in 1975.

The following season may actually have been an even better all-around hitting year for Kell: He batted .340, almost three points less than the year before, but he hit 56 doubles and had 218 hits, both league-leading totals. Kell, however, lost the batting title to Billy Goodman, who hit 14 points higher, albeit in 217 fewer at bats.

While Kell was enjoying sensational seasons, the Tigers were not. On their way to their worst record ever (50–104) in 1952, they swapped Kell to the Red Sox as part of a nine-player transaction. With the Red Sox, Kell batted .319 for the rest of the year to finish at .311 for the season.

In 1953 Kell batted .307 for Boston and played in his fifth All-Star Game. An early-season swap to the White Sox in 1954 put him on his third team in four years, and he fell below .300 for only the second time since 1946. Kell finished his playing career in Baltimore in 1957, starting in his sixth All-Star Game and ending the season with a .297 average. While he was there he helped tutor a young Baltimore third baseman, Brooks Robinson, who, coincidentally, would be inducted into the Hall of Fame on the same day as Kell.

After Mel Ott's death in a November 1958 car accident, Kell replaced him as a broadcaster for the Tigers. For years Kell's friendly southern drawl was famous throughout the Midwest. He announced several World Series, and had as his partners such notables as Al Kaline and Ernie Harwell. Writer Rebecca Stowe once said, "I thought George Kell-and-Ernie Harwell was one word."

Charlie Keller

Keller, Charles Ernest **OF**

1939–43, 1945–52 B:9/12/1916, Middletown, MD D:5/23/1990, Frederick, MD Deb:4/22/1939, NY AL BL/TR, 5'10", 190

G	AB	R	H	HR	RBI	OBP	SLG	AVG
1170	3790	725	1085	189	760	.410	.518	.286

Charlie Keller, a slugger for the New York Yankees of the Joe DiMaggio era, ranks among the top longball threats in big league history. During his 13-year career he averaged a home run every 20.5 at bats. He could have accomplished more: World War II robbed him of nearly two seasons and back troubles curtailed his career. (The same congenital back disorder ended his son's career after Charlie Jr. led the Eastern League with a .349 batting average in 1961.)

Despite winning the International League batting crown and Minor League Player of the Year honors from *The Sporting News* in 1937, Keller didn't secure a place on the Yankees until 1939. With the Yankees he moved into right field, joining an outfield of DiMaggio in center and George Selkirk in left. Together they formed the majors' only all-.300-hitting outfield that year. Keller batted .334, fifth best in the league, and tied for the fourth-best rookie batting average in American League history.

It would be Keller's only full-season .300 batting average, as Yankee coaches urged him to pull the ball more to take advantage of Yankee Stadium's short right-field porch. In the 1939 World Series Keller developed a reputation as New York's "Mr. October" before Reggie Jackson was even born.

Keller led the Yankees to a four-game sweep of the Cincinnati Reds. In the opener, with the score tied 1–1 in the bottom of the ninth, Keller tripled and scored the winning run. He hit a pair of two-run homers in Game 3 and produced the first run of Game 4 with a homer to lead off the seventh inning. The game went into extra innings and featured one of the most bizarre plays in World Series history.

Frank Crosetti walked to start the 10th and moved to second on Red Rolfe's sacrifice. Keller reached on an error, and Crosetti took third. DiMaggio singled to right, scoring Crosetti with the go-ahead run, and Keller came steaming around third base as outfielder Ival Goodman fumbled the ball.

Goodman's strong throw reached catcher Ernie "Schnozz" Lombardi on one bounce; but Lombardi caught the ball in the groin just as Keller lowered his shoulder and leveled him. Lombardi lay stunned as DiMaggio rounded the bases with another insurance run during "Schnozz's

Snooze." The Yankees won their fourth straight Series, with Keller's .438 batting average, 1.188 slugging percentage, eight runs, seven hits, three homers, and six RBIs leading all players.

In 1940 Keller, now known as "King Kong," increased his home run total to 21, from 11 as a rookie, and hit three in one game. He led the league with 106 walks and ranked second with a career-high 15 triples. He was selected to the All-Star team in 1940 and again in 1941 when he reached career bests with 33 homers and 122 RBIs. He also finished fourth in the American League with a career-best .580 slugging percentage.

That season Keller moved to left field to make room for Tommy Henrich in right, and the three outfielders all reached the 30-home run mark. New York was the first AL team and the second major league team ever to boast three sluggers with 30 homers each.

The Yankees won the pennant by 17 games and faced the Brooklyn Dodgers in the 1941 World Series. Again Keller starred, batting .389 with five RBIs, which tied him with Joe Gordon for tops in the Series. Keller's five runs scored, seven hits, and two doubles led the Yankee squad.

In Game 4 Keller took part in another immortal moment. With the Yankees trailing 4–3 in the ninth, Henrich reached first after catcher Mickey Owen failed to hold strike three from reliever Hugh Casey for what would have been the game-ending out. DiMaggio singled and Keller doubled, scoring both runners for a 5–4 Yankee lead. The Yankees went on to win the game, 7–4, and the Series in five games.

In 1942 Keller reached career highs with 106 runs and 114 walks, adding 26 homers and 108 RBIs as the Yankees won the pennant by nine games. Keller finished second to Triple Crown-winner Ted Williams in slugging and was third in homers, RBIs, home run ratio, and total bases.

The Yankees advanced to face the St. Louis Cardinals, the last team to beat them in a World Series. Keller hit a two-run homer in Game 2 and a three-run homer in Game 4, and Enos Slaughter robbed him of a homer in Game 3. The Cardinals took the Series in five games.

Keller joined the Navy after the 1943 season and returned late in 1945. He had his last big major league year in 1946 when he reached the 30-homer and 100-RBI marks for the third time. In the All-Star Game Keller's first-inning homer off Claude Passeau ignited the American League's 12–0 rout.

Back problems limited him to part-time duty after 1946, but in 1948 he became a dangerous pinch hitter who slugged home runs in consecutive at bats on September 12 and 14, his only two hits of the season in that role. Released by the Yankees in 1949, he spent 1950 and 1951 with Detroit, where he led the league with 38 pinch-hit at bats and nine hits in 1951. He returned to the Yankees for two games in 1952 and struck out in his only at bat.

Keller's brother, Hal, a major league catcher, appeared in 25 games with the Washington Senators from 1949 through 1952. He hit one home run, giving the brothers a total of 190 homers to rank No. 19 on the siblings list.

After his playing career ended, Keller retired to his native Maryland to raise horses on his farm, Yankeeland.

Joe Kelley

Kelly, Joseph James **OF–1B**

1891–08 M(1902–08, 338–321) B:12/9/1871, Cambridge, MA D:8/14/1943, Baltimore, MD Deb:7/27/1891, BOS NL BR/TR, 5'11", 190

G	AB	R	H	HR	RBI	OBP	SLG	AVG
1853	7006	1421	2220	65	1194	.402	.451	.317

Colorful, popular Joe Kelley was a key member of Manager Ned Hanlon's legendary Baltimore Orioles clubs of the 1890s. A powerful hitter and daring baserunner, Kelley teamed with third baseman John McGraw to help bring Baltimore a winner. A few years later he teamed with "Mugsy" McGraw again, this time to wreck baseball in Baltimore.

In 1891 Kelley, at that time a pitcher who hoped to join the staff of the Boston Beaneaters, signed with the Lowell Lowells of the New England League. He went 10–3, but he also hit .331 and stole 21 bases in 61 games. By season's end he was with Boston—but as an outfielder.

He started the 1892 season with the Western League Omaha Omahogs and batted .330 in 49 games. In June he was brought up to Pittsburgh, and in September the Pirates sent Kelley and $2,000 to Baltimore for outfielder George Van Haltren, who had been a disciplinary problem for Manager Hanlon.

The Orioles had finished last in the 12-team National League in 1892, but Hanlon was in the process of rebuilding the club. In 1893 he put Kelley in center field, then shifted him to left in 1894 as the Orioles, featuring such greats as McGraw, outfielder Willie Keeler, and shortstop Hughie Jennings, began a streak of three consecutive NL pennant wins.

Kelley batted .393 in 1894 and scored 165 runs, the fifth-best single-season total in history. From 1893, Kelley's first full season with Baltimore, through 1898, his last season with the club, he hit .352.

On September 3, 1894, Kelley had one of the best days in the history of the game, going nine-for-nine in a doubleheader. In the first game he collected three singles and a triple. In the nightcap he added four doubles and a single.

Kelley was popular with Baltimore fans not only for his proficient hitting, aggressive baserunning, and graceful fielding, but also for his colorful habits. Slightly vain, Kelley would carry a small mirror with him, and when there was little action in the outfield he would take it out and carefully inspect his handsome features.

One of Kelley's tricks with the Orioles was to hide an extra baseball in the high grass in left field for occasions when he might need one on short notice. One day a line drive was hit into the gap between Kelley in left and Steve Brodie in center. Kelley hustled over to his reserve ball and fired it in, but at roughly the same time Brodie retrieved the legitimate game ball and threw it in. Kelley didn't use that ruse again.

Kelley played during the age of syndicate baseball, and the Baltimore and Brooklyn Dodger clubs were under the same ownership. With greater profits to be made in more populous Brooklyn, the Orioles dispatched several players, including Kelley, to the Dodgers following the 1898 season.

At the turn of the century there were also schemes afloat to revive the defunct American Association. In 1900 John K. Mahon, Kelley's father-in-law, planned to back a franchise in Baltimore that was to be managed by McGraw, and one in Philadelphia to be managed by Kelley, but nothing came of the idea.

In February 1902, however, Mahon made a large purchase of stock in the new Baltimore American League franchise. Kelley also bought some and announced that he was leaving Brooklyn to return to Baltimore to play under McGraw, who was in charge of the reconstituted Orioles.

As the season progressed, rumor had it that the following year the franchise would move to New York, but McGraw believed he would be left behind when that happened. Together, McGraw, Kelley, and Mahon hatched a scheme to protect their interests—even if baseball in Baltimore suffered as a result.

First McGraw and Kelley attempted to assume the role of martyrs. On the afternoon of June 28, 1902, the duo went at it hammer and tongs with the umpiring crew of Tom Connolly and Jimmy Johnston. In the eighth inning Connolly finally ejected McGraw, but Mugsy refused to leave the diamond. Kelley rushed to his chief's defense, and he too was summarily ejected.

Both were suspended indefinitely by American League President Ban Johnson, and McGraw sputtered, "No man likes to be ordered off the earth like a dog in the presence of his friends. Ballplayers are not a lot of cattle to have the whip cracked over them."

After conferring with Kelley and Mahon, McGraw obtained his release from the Orioles and engineered the club's takeover by Giants owner Andrew Freedman and Reds owner John T. Brush, who was soon to supplant Freedman as owner of the Giants. The Orioles released two future Hall of Famers, pitcher Joe McGinnity and catcher Roger Bresnahan, both of whom promptly signed with the New York Giants.

Baltimore also released Kelley. He then met with Brush, who was registered under an assumed name at Baltimore's Stafford Hotel. Kelley agreed to manage the Cincinnati Reds. Soon the Orioles' Cy Seymour and Mike Donlin would join him in Cincinnati.

Kelley never enjoyed the success in Cincinnati that McGraw did in New York. Kelley never finished higher than third before being replaced by Ned Hanlon at the close of the 1905 season. Kelley remained as a player with the Reds through 1906.

As a manager he had a few interesting moments. In 1903 he released catcher Branch Rickey, the future St. Louis Cardinals skipper and Dodgers owner, for refusing to play Sunday baseball. "Listen, busher, beat it over to the owner's office and get your release!" he informed Rickey. The next year Kelley pronounced, "I've got a second baseman who'll make you forget Bid McPhee—Miller Huggins." McPhee was considered the best second baseman of all time, while Huggins, though he became a first-rate fielder, became more famous later for managing the Yankees to six pennants and three World Series titles.

In 1907 Kelley managed Toronto of the Eastern League, brought home a pennant winner, and was hired to manage the Boston Doves the following year. It was not a good career move. The Doves, dubbed by sportswriters "the Nine of Least Resistance," were a poor team, and controversy marked the close of their 1908 season. They lost their last three games to New York, forcing a showdown between the Giants and the Cubs, and it was alleged in some quarters that Kelley and several former Giants on the Dove team had gone easy on the New York club.

After the season, Dove catcher Frank Bowerman informed owner George Dovey, who did not like Kelley, that unless he was made the Doves' manager, he would return to farming in Michigan. Dovey put Bowerman in charge, and Kelley managed at Toronto the following year. Ironically, Kelley had pressed for Boston to obtain the unruly catcher.

Kelley won another pennant with Toronto in 1912 and remained there through the 1914 season. He scouted for the 1915–16 New York Yankees, and during the course of an entire season he failed to recommend the purchase of a single

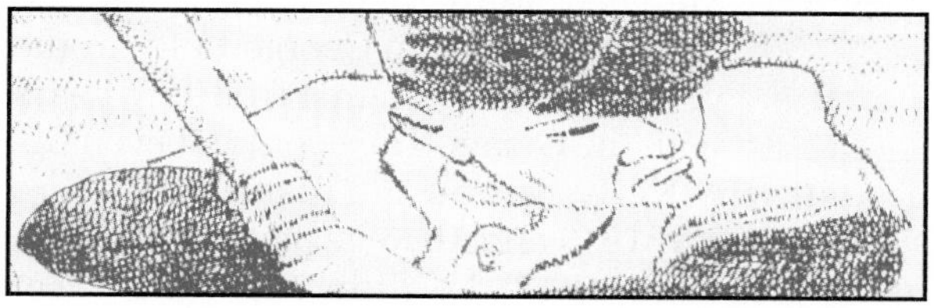

player, thus earning the gratitude of parsimonious New York co-owner Tillinghast Huston.

Following his scouting days Kelley worked for the Maryland Racing Commission, and in 1926 he returned to baseball as a coach for Brooklyn. The Veterans Committee named him to the Hall of Fame in 1971.

Alex Kellner

Kellner, Alexander Raymond **P**

1948–59 B:8/26/1924, Tucson, AZ D:5/3/1996, Tucson, AZ Deb:4/29/1948, PHI AL BR/TL, 6', 200

W	L	PCT	G	SH	IP	BB	SO	ERA
101	112	.474	321	9	1849[1]	747	816	4.41

There was nothing ordinary about righthander Alex Kellner. In his rookie season with the Philadelphia Athletics in 1949, he won 20 games. The next year he lost 20. In the off-season, he hunted fish with a bow and arrow and augmented his income by trapping mountain lions for circuses and zoos.

Kellner, who relied on a roundhouse curve, started with Tucson in the Class C Arizona-Texas League in 1941 and appeared with Muskogee in the Class C Western Association the following year. After serving in the military he returned to the minors with stays at Birmingham and Savannah, pitching a no-hitter on July 21, 1948.

Kellner led the American League in losses, runs, and earned runs in 1950, tied for the lead in losses in 1951, and runs allowed in 1952, and led in earned runs (and tied for the lead in runs) that same year and in wild pitches (10) in 1953.

Transferred with the franchise to Kansas City in 1955, he was sold to the Redlegs on June 23, 1958, and was sent in a six-player deal to the Cardinals on October 3 of that year. Never a control pitcher, Kellner was bothered by chronic shoulder problems toward the end of his career and retired after the 1959 season.

George Kelly

Kelly, George Lange **1B-2B-OF**

1915–32 B:9/10/1895, San Francisco, CA D:10/13/1984, Burlingame, CA Deb:8/18/1915, NY NL BR/TR, 6'4", 190

G	AB	R	H	HR	RBI	OBP	SLG	AVG
1622	5993	819	1778	148	1020	.342	.452	.297

New York fans didn't understand why Manager John McGraw lavished so much attention on George Kelly in the young first baseman's first few years with the Giants. They couldn't even figure out why Kelly was on the roster. In 66 rare appearances in 1915 and 1916 he batted only .158. In 11 games in 1917, he didn't get a hit. Yet McGraw often sat next to him in the dugout, and allowed Kelly to sit on the bench in the 1917 World Series even though he wasn't eligible to play.

Years later, when Kelly was a coach with Oakland of the Pacific Coast League (PCL), a fan called him over and said he had seen him play at the Polo Grounds. Then, according to Kelly, the fan "asked how my aunt was. I said, 'Who?' He said, 'Your aunt. Mrs. McGraw.' That's how lousy I was when I first got there. They wondered why McGraw would keep me around and figured I must be related to him."

Perhaps McGraw was impressed because the youngster was first recommended by Bill "Little Eva" Lange, Kelly's uncle and one of the greatest players of the 1890s. Or maybe McGraw put stock in the glowing report he'd received from scout Dick Kinsella, unaware that Kinsella had fallen asleep in his hotel room and had based his report on hearsay. More likely, he simply recognized Kelly's sharp mind and potential. As in so many other instances, McGraw was right.

One of nine children of a police captain, Kelly left high school in 1914, his senior year, when his uncle arranged for him to play professionally for the Class B Northwestern League's Victoria Bees. Although Kelly was not particularly outstanding with a bat, he showed a strong arm. The Giants acquired him in August, and McGraw took over his baseball education.

"Those first two years I was with the Giants," Kelly later recalled, "McGraw kept me on the bench alongside him, much as he was later to do with another teenager, Mel Ott. He talked to me about what was going on out there on the field, and I never learned so much about baseball. I was always by his side in those days, and sometimes I got a good ribbing about it, too. But I didn't care. It was worth it."

McGraw couldn't teach Kelly to hit a curve, however. Only playing time could do that. The Giants sent Kelly to Pittsburgh for a look-see during 1917, but after he produced only two hits in 23 at bats, the Pirates returned him to New York. Eventually the club farmed him to Rochester of the International League, where he showed some improvement, but before he could solidify the gain, Kelly lost 1918 to the service.

When he returned to Rochester in 1919, his bat really came alive. After 103 games he had 15 home runs and a .356 batting average. The Giants called him back up, and he replaced Hal Chase at first base in the last month of the season. Although he hit .290 during that time, he couldn't duplicate Chase's graceful fielding. The Giants fans booed Kelly. They didn't know Chase had been replaced because McGraw was convinced he was throwing games.

In 1920 Kelly took over as the regular Giants first baseman, earning the nickname "Highpockets" because of his 6-foot-4, 190-pound frame. He became a powerful righthanded batter, blasting 11 home runs and 11 triples in his first full season. Although he batted only .266 and struck out 92 times, he led the NL with 94 RBIs.

Kelly began the 1921 season with seven home runs in April. The New York newspapers began printing daily comparisons between Kelly and Babe Ruth, who had socked a record 54 homers the year before. The comparisons soon stopped. Ruth went on to slug 59 round-trippers, although Kelly's more modest total of 23 was still enough to lead the National League.

Kelly's best years were from 1921 through 1924, when the Giants won four consecutive pennants. In those seasons, Kelly hit 77 home runs and batted in 468, putting up batting averages of .308, .328, .307, and .324. His 136 RBIs in 1924 led the league.

Perhaps his most important home run came on August 17, 1921. The Giants trailed the front-running Pirates by 7 ½ games when they opened a five-game series with the Bucs. Pittsburgh jumped off to a three-run lead, but the Giants loaded the bases in the seventh inning. The first three pitches to Kelly were balls. McGraw flashed him the hit sign, and Kelly creamed the pitch for a grand slam. New York swept the series and went on to win the pennant.

McGraw always said that Kelly got more "important" hits for him during these years than any other player, but Kelly's World Series average was only .248, with one homer and 10 RBIs. His best play in the Series was on defense. In 1921 the Giants won four games in the best-of-nine Series and led 1–0 in the ninth inning of Game 8.

Infielder Aaron Ward was on first for the Yanks with one out when third baseman Frank Baker lashed an apparent hit to right. Giants infielder Johnny Rawlings made a brilliant diving stop and just nipped Baker at first. In the meantime Ward, carrying the tying run, tried to take third. Kelly alertly fired the ball across the infield, and gunned down Ward to end the Series.

His arm was a source of wonder. When Kelly first joined the Giants, McGraw considered making him into a pitcher but decided that he would learn to hit curves long before he'd learn to throw them. In 1917 Kelly was given a chance to pitch. He threw five shutout innings and was credited with a win, but McGraw still believed there was no future for a pitcher with only a fastball. The canny skipper eventually found good use for Kelly's arm. Highpockets made all the cutoffs on throws from the outfield, even those from left field.

Kelly set single-season league records for putouts, assists, double plays, and total chances. His putout record was still standing after the 1999 season. Much of the credit, of course, goes to the other infielders, particularly shortstop Dave Bancroft, who himself set a record for assists.

In 1925 McGraw decided to insert first baseman Bill Terry, a lefthander, into his lineup. "I fought Terry off for two years, trying to keep him on the bench," Kelly said later. "I played with split fingers and everything else to keep him out of the lineup. I didn't want to be another Wally Pipp."

Pipp, of course, was the Yankee first baseman who gave up his position to Lou Gehrig one day and never got back into the lineup. Since Terry played only first, Kelly shifted to his right and became baseball's tallest second baseman. Contrary to some predictions, he acquitted himself quite well, but when the club acquired Rogers Hornsby in 1927, Kelly was out of a job. New York traded him to Cincinnati, where, ironically, he shared first base with Pipp.

Kelly took over as the regular in 1928 and enjoyed two productive seasons with the Reds. Early in 1930 the franchise abruptly released him for financial reasons, although he was playing well. He earned $15,000, a good salary at the time, and the Reds were going to finish last with or without him.

He joined Minneapolis, but the Chicago Cubs acquired him in August to help with their pennant drive. When they fell short, Kelly was released, despite his .331 batting average. He returned to Minneapolis for 1931. After a short time with the Brooklyn Dodgers in 1932, he left the majors for good. In 16 seasons, he batted .297 with 148 home runs and 1,020 RBIs.

Kelly coached for the Reds and Braves from 1935 through 1948, then returned to California to scout and coach for Oakland's PCL team. The Veterans Committee named him to the Hall of Fame in 1973.

King Kelly

Kelly, Michael Joseph **OF-C-3B-SS**

1878–93 M(1887–91, 173–148) B:12/31/1857, Troy, NY D:11/8/1894, Boston, MA Deb:5/1/1878, CIN NL BR/TR, 5'10", 170

G	AB	R	H	HR	RBI	OBP	SLG	AVG
1455	5894	1357	1813	69	950	.368	.438	.308

During a game in the late 19th century while managing Boston, King Kelly saw an opposing batter lift a foul ball toward his bench and realized that it would fall in front of his fielders. Thinking quickly, he leapt off the bench, yelled, "Kelly now catching for Boston," and caught the ball for out number three.

Kelly often outwitted the opposition, usually by twisting the rules in some clever way. In another instance, the score was tied in extra innings as darkness fell on a National League field. With two outs in the bottom of the 12th the batter scorched a drive to right field. Kelly, the right fielder, raced over, jumped, and clasped both hands together, apparently making a remarkable catch. As Kelly ran off the field the umpire called the game because of darkness. Later, a teammate asked Kelly how far the ball was hit. "How the hell would I know?" he said. "It was a mile over my head."

Kelly was born in Troy, New York, on New Year's Eve, 1857. He went on to spend most of his life celebrating the New Year. When asked once if he drank on the field, he answered that it depended on the length of the game.

At age 15 he began playing baseball professionally for the independent Troy Haymakers. A versatile athlete, Kelly could play any position. In 1876 he joined the Paterson Olympics of New Jersey. The next year he moved to Ohio and played for the Columbus Buckeyes. The Cincinnati Red Stockings of the National League signed him in 1878. Playing primarily in the outfield, he hit .283. The following season he batted .348 and scored 78 runs in 77 games.

In 1880 Chicago manager Cap Anson induced Kelly to join the White Stockings. Kelly's arrival and the team's sudden success were no coincidence. In the seven seasons Kelly played for the White Stockings they won five pennants. Anson assembled some excellent players during this time—men such as George Gore, Tom Burns, Ned Williamson, Abner Dalrymple, Silver Flint, John Clarkson, Larry Corcoran, and Fred Goldsmith. Anson himself was the best player on the team, but Kelly ran a close second.

At 5-foot-10 and 170 pounds, Kelly was strikingly handsome, the quintessential "man about town." He wore the latest fashions, carried a cane, twiddled his mustache at the Chicago ladies, and captivated all with his Irish wit and his willingness to buy a round for the house. He played baseball by day, partied by night, and seldom slept in his own bed. The only thing he consumed faster and in greater quantity than alcohol was Cap Anson's patience. The manager was not complimenting Kelly when he said, "There's not a man alive who can drink Mike Kelly under the table."

Yet, Anson knew that Kelly would always show up to play. He led the National League in doubles in 1881 and 1882, in runs scored from 1884

through 1886, and in batting average in 1884 and 1886. It was his knack for winning games with intelligent and sometimes outrageous play, however, that was his claim to fame.

Although Kelly usually played in the outfield, Anson often put him behind the plate in important games so he could be closer to the action. On one occasion Kelly was behind the plate with two outs and a runner on third base. The batter grounded to the shortstop, who threw to first for a bang-bang play. Coming in from third, the runner saw Kelly drop his mitt, apparently indicating the end of the inning, and he slowed down. But the batter at first was in fact safe. The infielder whipped the ball to Kelly, who caught it barehanded and tagged the runner for the third out.

Because of his reputation for cleverness Kelly was later credited with originating signs between the catcher and pitcher and with inventing the hit-and-run play. Other players probably developed both ideas, but Kelly was certainly among the first to use them.

Kelly's baserunning alone was worth the price of admission. He knew just when to run, and he perfected a hook slide that often allowed him to elude tags. He also wouldn't hesitate to kick the ball out of an infielder's glove. During one game umpire "Honest" John Kelly called the King out on a close play. Kelly plucked the loose baseball from beneath his body, looked up, and said "If I'm out, John, what's this?"

The fans yelled, "Slide, Kelly, slide!" as soon as he reached base. An enterprising songwriter eventually turned the cheer into a song that enjoyed great popularity, particularly in Chicago.

During Kelly's 16 years in the majors he played 758 games in the outfield, 583 as catcher, 96 at third base, 90 at shortstop, 53 at second base, and 25 at first base. He even made 12 pitching appearances, compiling a record of 2–2. Fans not only didn't know where to expect Kelly on the diamond, they also didn't know what to expect from him at the plate.

He hit only .255 in 1883, but in 1884 his average jumped 99 points and he led the league. In 1885 it dropped to .288, but the following season he raised it by 100 points and again led the league. Whenever one of his clever plays didn't work or he made an error, he was still cheered. Kelly was king.

After hitting .388 in 1886 and leading the White Sox to another pennant, Kelly was sold to Boston. The city of Chicago was stunned. Anson was certainly fed up with Kelly's drinking, but it was Boston who had instigated the deal. Player contracts had often been peddled before, but no player of Kelly's stature had ever been sold.

Before the deal was made White Stockings President A. G. Spalding asked Kelly if he would consent to the sale. "Horses are sold," said Kelly, "not ballplayers." His contract with Chicago was for $3,000 a year, minus numerous fines levied by Anson. Spalding told him he'd make more money with Boston. Responded Kelly, "If you can get me $5,000, I don't care a damn if you sell me for a hundred thousand."

The deal was made, but when Kelly met with the Boston owners he was offered only $2,000, the limit imposed by the club. After a number of negotiations Kelly finally signed for $2,000 in salary and a $3,000 fee that allowed Boston to use his photograph. The $10,000 sale price was unprecedented for a single player, but the Chicago fans couldn't cheer for greenbacks. In 1887 they virtually boycotted the White Stockings games, turning out in full force only when Boston was in town.

In 1887 Kelly played well, batting .322 and scoring 120 runs. But his presence brought dissension to the Boston team. "Honest" John Morrill had been a member of the club since 1876 and its manager and captain since 1882. He was retained as manager, but Kelly was named the field captain, a more prestigious position at the time. This division of authority led to rancor, and Morrill no more approved of Kelly's lifestyle than had Anson. The team finished a disappointing fifth.

In 1888 Morrill was named captain and the Boston owners sent another $10,000 to Chicago for pitcher John Clarkson. The $20,000 battery of Clarkson and Kelly only edged Boston to fourth place, although Clarkson won 33 games and Kelly hit .318 to lead the club.

Before the 1889 season Boston played an exhibition game with local semipro stars. Kelly led the Boston pros, while poor Morrill was designated captain of the semipros. Morrill was outraged, made a fuss about it, and was sold to Washington. James A. Hart was named manager and Kelly was reinstated as captain. Many Boston rooters blamed Kelly for driving away the popular Morrill, although he won back some support by leading the league in doubles and batting .294. Clarkson won 49 games and the team jumped to second.

After years of unresolved grievances, the National League players revolted and formed their own league in 1890. Kelly, one of the established league's most famous players, was offered a small fortune to stay, but his loyalty was with the upstart players. He managed Boston's Players League team to a pennant and hit .326. It was the only Players League pennant ever awarded, for the league collapsed after a single season.

At the same time, Kelly's indulgent lifestyle was beginning to catch up with him. His body, which once looked like that of a Greek god, began to look like a Grecian vase. Although he played in the majors for three more seasons and appeared intermittently on two more Boston pennant winners, Kelly was only a bloated shadow of his former self.

He played briefly in the minor leagues and later opened a saloon in New York, but it didn't prosper. He also appeared on the stage, reciting Ernest L. Thayer's "Casey at the Bat." He was on his way to Boston to appear at the Palace Theater in November 1894 when he was stricken with pneumonia. As they carried his stretcher into the hospital, the attendants tripped and dumped Kelly on the floor. "That's my last slide," he said. A few days later he died.

As a representative of baseball's misty past, Kelly is often regarded as a lovable scamp. Nonetheless, there remains his .308 career batting average, 1,357 runs scored, 1,813 hits in 1,455 games, five pennants with the White Stockings and another in the Players League, and the recognition of his contemporaries that he was one of the greatest players of his age. In 1945 Kelly was inducted into the Hall of Fame.

Pat Kelly

Kelly, Harold Patrick **OF–DH**

1967–81 B:7/30/1944, Philadelphia, PA Deb:9/06/1967, MIN AL BL/TL, 6'1", 185

G	AB	R	H	HR	RBI	OBP	SLG	AVG
1385	4338	620	1147	76	418	.356	.377	.264

Pat Kelly—brother of star National Football League running back LeRoy Kelly and brother-in-law of first baseman Andre Thornton—made a name for himself as a reliable outfielder. Later in his career he became one of Baltimore manager Earl Weaver's favorite weapons off the bench.

Kelly attended Morgan State College and signed with the Twins as a free agent in September 1962. He made six stops in the minor leagues and had two brief call-ups with Minnesota before expansion helped him become an everyday player.

Kelly was selected by the Kansas City Royals in the October 1968 AL expansion draft. He stole 40 bases as a rookie in 1969, but he slumped the following year and was traded to the White Sox in October 1970. Although Kelly was demoted to Tucson at the beginning of the 1971 season, he became a regular in the Chicago outfield. In 1973 he appeared in the All-Star Game. He led the league in outfield assists two years later.

Traded to Baltimore in November 1976, he hit .364 (including a three-run homer in the last contest) against the Angels in the 1979 Championship Series. He pinch-hit in five games (with one hit and one walk) in that fall's World Series loss to Pittsburgh. In December 1980 he signed with Cleveland, where he ended his career. Kelly later entered divinity school.

Tom Kelly

Kelly, Jay Thomas **1B**

1975 M(1986–99, 986–1074) B:8/15/1950, Graceville, MN Deb:5/11/1975, MIN AL BL/TL, 5'11", 188

G	AB	R	H	HR	RBI	OBP	SLG	AVG
49	127	11	23	1	11	.268	.244	.181

Tom Kelly managed the Minnesota Twins to two unlikely world championships in 1987 and 1991. A skilled game manager as well as teacher, he brought Minnesota its first—and through 1999, its only—world championships in any of the four major sports.

The 1991 World Series against Atlanta is considered one of the most exciting World Series ever. The Twins came back from a three games to two deficit, winning the final two games in extra innings. Many questioned Kelly's wisdom when he allowed Jack Morris, his aging ace, to pitch the 10th inning of a Game 7 scoreless tie instead of bringing in Rick Aguilera, who had saved 42 games for the team during the season. Morris blanked the Braves in the 10th and the Twins scored the Series' winning run in the bottom of the inning.

A baseball brat whose father, Joe Kelly, had pitched in the Giants organization, Tom Kelly was the Seattle Pilots' fifth-round pick in the June 1968 draft. He started in Newark and made stops in Clinton, Jacksonville, Charlotte, Rochester, Toledo, Visalia, and Tacoma. In 1971, while with Tacoma, he was named Most Popular Player.

A career minor leaguer, the lefthanded outfielder-first baseman played 49 games for the Twins in 1975 and hit only .181. In the late 1970s and early 1980s the unassuming Kelly became a phenomenally successful minor league manager. In 1979–80 season he was voted the California League Manager of the Year. In 1981, with Orlando, he won the Southern League Championship and the Manager of the Year Award in that circuit.

Kelly, a Minnesota native, became the Twins' third base coach in 1983 and replaced Ray Miller as manager on September 12, 1986. The team, which finished that season 71–91, made a remarkable turnaround in 1987. They won the AL West with an 85–77 record and defeated the Tigers, four games to one, in the American League Championship Series. At age 37, Kelly was the youngest manager to lead a team into the ALCS. The Twins, who had the worst road record ever for a division champion, did their best work at home against favored St. Louis. While the speedy Cardinals had the advantage at spacious Busch Stadium, the powerful Twins outscored, the Twins used a combination of power and pitching to outscore the Cards at the noisy Metrodome. The Twins overcame a 2–0 deficit in Game 7 to win the Series. Kelly was named the UPI AL Manager of the Year.

In 1988 the Twins bettered their record to 91–71 but lost the division to Oakland. After a disappointing last-place finish in 1990, the Twins obtained veterans Morris, Chili Davis, and Steve Bedrosian and received a Rookie of the Year performance from second baseman Chuck Knoblauch. The 1991 team won 95 games and beat the Blue Jays, four games to one, in the ALCS.

World Series opponents Atlanta and Minnesota became the first teams in major league history to go from last place to first place in a single season. Kelly was voted the 1991 Baseball Writers Association AL Manager of the Year.

Although his teams finished below .500 nine other times in his first 14 years as a manager, he remained one of baseball's most respected—and loyal—managers. When the Dodgers asked if he was interested in coming to Los Angeles after the 1998 season, he politely declined. Through the 1999 season he had the longest continuous tenure of any active manager.

Ken Keltner

Keltner, Kenneth Frederick **3B**

1937–50 B:10/31/1916, Milwaukee, WI D:12/12/1991, New Berlin, WI Deb:10/2/1937, CLE AL BR/TR, 6', 190

G	AB	R	H	HR	RBI	OBP	SLG	AVG
1526	5683	737	1570	163	852	.338	.441	.276

Sometimes a single game can overshadow a player's entire career. On the night of July 17, 1941, Ken Keltner, the Indians' third baseman, took the field in front of more than 67,000 Cleveland fans for a game that would forever etch his name in baseball history.

The man of the moment was New York Yankees star Joe DiMaggio, who had hit safely in a record 56 straight games. Everyone wondered if he could keep the streak alive. His adversary on the mound was Cleveland lefthander Al Smith, a 15-game winner for the Indians the year before.

For a moment in the first inning it looked as if the streak would continue. DiMaggio hit a rocket down the third-base line, but Keltner, playing deep, lunged for the bouncing ball and gloved it. Although his momentum sent him into foul territory, he recovered and threw perfectly to first to retire DiMaggio.

DiMaggio walked in the fourth inning, and in the seventh he sent another screaming drive down the third-base line; Keltner executed a virtual replay of the first inning and again threw out DiMaggio. When reliever Al Milnar got "Joltin' Joe" to hit a bouncer to shortstop with the bases loaded in the eighth, starting a double play,

DiMaggio's streak was history. Keltner became forever known as the man who stopped DiMaggio's streak. That he was one of the best third basemen of his generation is all but ignored.

Installed as the Indians' regular third baseman in 1938, Keltner hit 26 home runs with 113 RBIs as a rookie. In 1939 his RBI total slipped to 97 and his homers dropped to 13, but he batted a career-high .325 and led AL third basemen in fielding for the first time. Although Keltner's offensive numbers continued to fall in 1940, he was chosen for his first All-Star Game.

While his plays against DiMaggio earned him more headlines in 1941, Keltner had one of his best all-around years, cracking 23 homers and again leading the league in fielding. He made his second All-Star Game appearance, collecting a scratch single in the ninth inning that set up Ted Williams' game-winning home run. Selected to five more All-Star teams, Keltner led the American League once in putouts, three times in fielding, four times in assists, and five times in double plays.

In 1948 Cleveland won its first pennant in 28 years, and Keltner, along with several other Indians, had a career year. He hit .297, with 31 home runs and 119 RBIs. In the playoff made necessary after the Indians and Red Sox ended the season tied for first, Keltner hit a towering three-run homer over Fenway Park's Green Monster in the fourth inning to put the Indians ahead to stay. Cleveland went on to win the World Series over the Boston Braves, four games to two.

Injuries limited Keltner to 80 games in 1949, and he played briefly for the Red Sox in 1950 before retiring. Cleveland fans chose him as the Indians' all-time third baseman in 1969, but the efforts of fans in his native Milwaukee to get him elected to the Baseball Hall of Fame failed. However, he was later named to both the Ohio State Baseball Hall of Fame and the Wisconsin Athletic Hall of Fame.

Steve Kemp

Kemp, Steven F. **OF–DH**

1977–88 B:8/7/1954, San Angelo, TX Deb:4/7/1977, DET AL BL/TL, 6', 195

G	AB	R	H	HR	RBI	OBP	SLG	AVG
1168	4058	581	1128	130	634	.370	.431	.278

Lefthanded power hitter Steve Kemp cashed in on his talents after the 1982 season and signed a five-year, $5.5 million free-agent contract with the Yankees. Injuries and high expectations contributed to a performance that most New Yorkers thought should have closed out of town.

A star at the University of Southern California, Kemp was the Tigers' first choice in the January 1976 draft. Sent to the minors for a season, he then started in the Detroit outfield in 1977.

Kemp's power-alley stroke was ideal for Tiger Stadium. He was named to the All-Star team in 1979 after he hit 26 homers and drove in 105 runs with a .543 slugging average. After Kemp drove in 101 runs in 1980, the Tigers traded him to the White Sox for Chet Lemon.

Granted free agency in November 1982, he signed with the Yankees. Owner George Steinbrenner did not pay so much money simply for Kemp's home runs. Steinbrenner explained, "He runs to first base every time like he's running a hundred-yard dash. I like guys like that."

It was soon apparent that Kemp's swing was not suited to Yankee Stadium. And in April 1983 his overzealous hustle in the outfield caused a collision with second baseman Willie Randolph that permanently injured Kemp's shoulder. In two seasons with the Yankees Kemp hit only 19 home runs.

After the 1984 season Kemp was traded to Pittsburgh where eye problems further debilitated him. He played his last major league game while with the Rangers in 1988 and finished his career in the minor leagues with Oklahoma City. In 1993 Kemp barnstormed with the Hollywood Legends.

Jason Kendall

Kendall, Jason Daniel **C**

1996–* B:6/26/1974, San Diego, CA Deb:4/1/1996, PIT NL BR/TR 6', 180

G	AB	R	H	HR	RBI	OBP	SLG	AVG
501	1715	281	535	31	207	.403	.451	.312

The son of a journeyman catcher, Jason Kendall once played with the sons of star ballplayers in the deserted upper deck of San Diego's Jack Murphy Stadium. Two decades later, he was playing against many of them on the field: Barry Bonds, Moises Alou, Bret Boone, and Todd Stottlemyre.

Kendall grew up playing middle infield in Torrance, California. He only took up catching when his high school's regular catcher was injured. After he tied a national record with a 43-game hitting streak over his last two years of high school, the Pittsburgh Pirates selected Kendall in the first round of the 1992 draft. By 1996 he was the club's Opening Day catcher and the first Pittsburgh rookie to make the All-Star team. Despite a poor final month of the season, he still batted .300 for the year.

In 1997 Kendall was a major reason why the inexperienced Pirates surprised baseball by challenging for the National League Central crown until the final week of the season. His defense improved significantly; he threw out 21 more basestealers than the previous year and was more than up to the task of handling a talented young pitching staff.

Kendall's offensive production rose to a new level in 1998. He batted .327 with an impressive .411 on-base percentage. His 26 stolen bases set a record for the most steals by a National League catcher. Kendall was trying to beat out a bunt on July 4, 1999, when he fractured his leg in a horrific misstep while crossing the first-base bag. The result was a premature end to what was promising to be his best season yet.

Bob Kennedy

Kennedy, Robert Daniel **OF-3B**

1939–57 M(1963–68, 264–278) B:8/18/1920, Chicago, IL Deb:9/14/1939, CHI AL BR/TR, 6'2", 193

G	AB	R	H	HR	RBI	OBP	SLG	AVG
1483	4624	514	1176	63	514	.310	.355	.254

Bob Kennedy was a versatile third baseman and outfielder who spent most of his 16-year career in the American League with the Chicago White Sox and Cleveland Indians. He broke into the majors in 1939 with the White Sox and remained with them until June 1948 when he was traded to the Indians. The move proved to be the biggest break of his career as he appeared in his only World Series that year and also befriended Al Rosen, the Indians' All-Star third baseman with whom he had a close relationship long after their playing days.

Prior to signing with the White Sox in 1937, Kennedy worked as a popcorn vendor in Comiskey Park for the Joe Louis–Jim Braddock heavyweight fight. By 1940 he was the starting third baseman for Chicago, committing a league-leading 33 errors. In 1950 he played right field for the Indians and hit a career-high .291. He remained with Cleveland until April 1954 when he was traded to the Baltimore Orioles for outfielder-third baseman Jim Dyck. During the next three seasons Kennedy changed teams four times, including two more brief stints with the White Sox, before ending his career with the Brooklyn Dodgers in 1957.

Kennedy went on to manage the Chicago Cubs from 1963 to 1965, and the Oakland A's in 1968. In later years he worked for Rosen as a special scout and assistant general manager with the Houston Astros and San Francisco Giants.

Kennedy's son, Terry, followed in his father's footsteps as a catcher for the St. Louis Cardinals and San Diego Padres in the 1970s and 1980s.

Brickyard Kennedy

Kennedy, William Park **P**

1892–03 B:10/7/1867, Bellaire, OH D:9/23/1915, Bellaire, OH Deb:4/26/1892, BRO NL BR/TR, 5'11", 160

W	L	PCT	G	SH	IP	BB	SO	ERA
187	159	.540	405	13	3021	1201	797	3.96

In the 1890s William "Brickyard" Kennedy was a workhorse on the mound for Brooklyn. From 1893 to 1900 he averaged more than 300 innings pitched. He pitched both halves of a doubleheader on May 30, 1893, surrendering only eight hits in defeating Louisville, 3–0 and 6–2.

Kennedy was considered a rube by many teammates. Being illiterate, he could not read menus in restaurants and always ordered what the other person had. Once, when trying to find his way from Brooklyn to the Polo Grounds, he was misdirected by a policeman who thought Kennedy was asking him how to go home to Ohio. On August 1, 1897, Manager Billy Barnie fined Kennedy for "stupid work" in a loss to the Giants.

Kennedy hailed from Bellaire, Ohio, home base for a large brick manufacturer—hence his nickname. Some sportswriters also called the righthander "Wild Bill" or "Roaring Bill" because he spoke extremely loudly.

Although Kennedy won 20 or more games four times, his best season was 1899 when he had a record of 22–9 with a 2.79 ERA. Brooklyn sold Kennedy to Pittsburgh after the 1902 season where he played in the first World Series in 1903. Kennedy started Game 5 against Boston's Cy Young; errors hurt him and he lost, 11–2. It was his last major league game. Kennedy finished his 12-year career with a 187–159 record.

Terry Kennedy

Kennedy, Terry **C**

1978–91 B:6/4/1956, Euclid, OH Deb:9/4/1978, STL NL BL/TR, 6'3", 220

G	AB	R	H	HR	RBI	OBP	SLG	AVG
1491	4979	474	1313	113	628	.316	.386	.264

Catcher Terry Kennedy, son of player and executive Bob Kennedy, was named to both the 1976 and 1977 *The Sporting News* College All-American teams and was designated *The Sporting News* College Player of the Year in 1977. In the June 1977 free-agent draft, the Cardinals selected Kennedy in the first round with the sixth overall pick and signed him for a $100,000 bonus.

Kennedy performed in the minors at Johnson City, St. Petersburg, Springfield, and Arkansas. Although he played partial seasons for the big club from 1978 through 1980, he was stuck behind Ted Simmons, the team's regular catcher. In December 1980 the Cardinals dealt Kennedy to San Diego in an 11-player trade, a transaction that sent pitcher Rollie Fingers to St. Louis.

In 1982 Kennedy tied Johnny Bench's NL record for doubles by a catcher, with 40, and in 1983 he earned honors on *The Sporting News* NL Silver Slugger Team. But despite his abilities, Kennedy was hardly a favorite of Padres manager Dick Williams, who dubbed him "our catcher-in-the-cry."

Dealt to Baltimore in October 1986, the next season he became the second catcher to start All-Star Games for both leagues. He returned to the National League in a January 1989 trade to San Francisco, where his father was vice president for baseball operations. He achieved free agency that November and re-signed with the Giants the following month. He retired after the 1991 season.

Jeff Kent

Kent, Jeffrey Franklin **2B-3B**

1992–* B:3/7/1968, Bellflower, CA Deb:4/12/1992, TOR AL BR/TR 6'1", 185

G	AB	R	H	HR	RBI	OBP	SLG	AVG
1032	3742	566	1032	161	668	.339	.477	.276

After being traded by three clubs, Jeff Kent finally realized his potential in San Francisco. As a Giant he became one of the National League's most productive second basemen in history. He posted three straight 100-RBI campaigns, and joined Hall of Famer Rogers Hornsby as the only second basemen ever to produce at least 120 RBIs in multiple seasons.

Kent started his career as one of the bright spots in the Toronto farm system, but he was traded with Ryan Thompson for David Cone late in his rookie season in 1992. After nearly five up-and-down seasons with the Mets, he was traded twice within a few months for Carlos Baerga (to Cleveland) and Matt Williams (to the Giants). He drove in 121 runs in his first season as a Giant, protecting Barry Bonds in the lineup and helping the club win a division title. In 1998 Kent hit career peaks with a .297 average and 31 home runs. His 128 RBIs topped Hornsby's franchise mark for second basemen.

A year later Kent became San Francisco's first righthanded hitter with three straight 100-RBI years since Willie Mays did it from 1959 to 1966. Because he drove in five of those runs while playing first base, Kent just missed joining Charlie Gehringer and Bobby Doerr as the only second basemen in the 20th century with three straight years in triple digits. Kent had 96 RBIs while playing second in 1999.

Though slowed by toe and foot injuries in 1999, Kent produced a pair of 5-for-5 games—one of them while hitting for the cycle at Pittsburgh on May 3. Two months later he played in his first All-Star Game. Kent joined Mays, Willie McCovey, Mel Ott, and Barry Bonds as the only Giants with three straight 20-homer, 100-RBI years.

Jim Kern

Kern, James Lester **P**

1974–86 B:3/15/1949, Gladwin, MI Deb:9/06/1974, CLE AL BR/TR, 6'5", 205

W	L	PCT	G	SV	IP	BB	SO	ERA
53	57	.482	416	88	7931	444	651	3.32

Jim Kern was an effective and even intimidating American League relief pitcher from 1976 to 1979. In 1979, with the Texas Rangers, he shared Rolaids Reliever of the Year honors with Minnesota's Mike Marshall. He was an All-Star in 1977, 1978, and 1979.

Longhaired, lanky, and bearded, Kern was nicknamed "Emu" because he resembled the large bird. Signed by the Indians in September 1967 as an undrafted free agent, he did not reach the major leagues until 1975. Though he lost some time to military service, he was a league leader in wild pitches in 1970 and in 1974. But 1974 was his breakthrough year. His 17 victories with Oklahoma City led the American Association, and he was named that circuit's Pitcher of the Year.

Kern won 10 games and posted 15 saves for Cleveland in 1976. In 1977 he had eight wins and 18 saves, and in 1978 10 wins and 13 saves. His best season was 1979, when he was 13–5 with 29 saves for Texas.

While with the Rangers in 1980, Kern was hit in the mouth on a throw back to the mound by his catcher. He was knocked unconscious and suffered temporary amnesia. That year he also injured his elbow, and was never again the same pitcher. He moved to Cincinnati in 1982 but forced the Reds to trade him in August by regrowing his trademark scruffy beard in violation of team policy. He went to the White Sox, and later to the Phillies, the

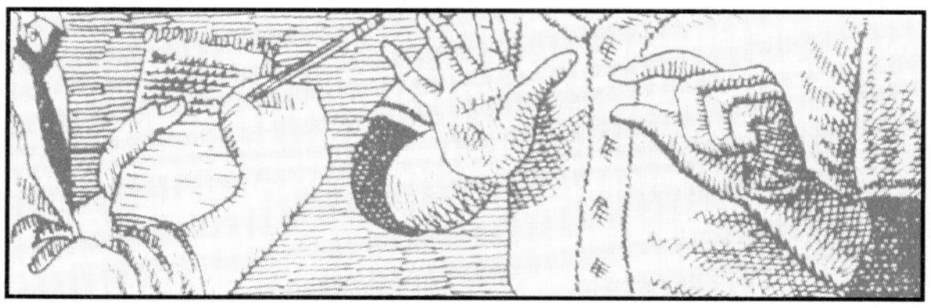

Brewers, and back to the Indians for brief stints, before leaving the game in 1986.

Buddy Kerr

Kerr, John Joseph **SS**

1943–51 B:11/6/1922, Astoria, NY D:10/19/1993, Long Beach, CA Deb:9/8/1943, NY AL BR/TR, 6'2", 180

G	AB	R	H	HR	RBI	OBP	SLG	AVG
1067	3631	378	903	25	333	.312	.328	.249

John "Buddy" Kerr was a slick-fielding, record-setting shortstop for the New York Giants during the 1940s. After retiring as a player he began another equally successful career as a longtime scout for the Giants and the Mets.

One of 10 children, Kerr was a New Yorker, born in Astoria but raised in Washington Heights. A big Giants fan, Kerr received a Polo Grounds tryout when he was only 16 years old and was signed to a contract the following year by New York scout John Shinkoff.

"When he told me I had a chance to play professional baseball I just jumped at it," said Kerr. "He gave me five hundred dollars as a bonus and sent me off to Fort Smith, Arkansas, in the spring of 1940. It was all I ever wanted to do."

With World War II, many players were lost to military service, and Kerr's promotion through the ranks of Organized Baseball was rapid. He came up to New York in midseason 1943. In his first major league at bat, on September 8, 1943, the normally light-hitting Kerr homered.

With the Giants, Kerr established a number of fielding records for a shortstop. From July 28, 1946, through May 24, 1947, he went 68 consecutive contests without an error, a record that would stand until 1989 when Mets shortstop Kevin Elster strung together 88 error-free games. During Kerr's streak he handled a record 383 straight chances cleanly, still the NL record. Kerr also holds the NL mark for consecutive errorless chances in a season, with 286, accomplished in 53 games from July 28 through Sept. 29, 1946.

Kerr participated in streaks in more ways than one. When Cincinnati's Ewell Blackwell was trying for his 10th win in a row in 1947, Kerr came up to bat in the 10th inning with the score tied. "I got two strikes on him, then threw a pitch that, so help me, cut the middle of the plate belt-high," said Blackwell. "Swear I never threw a cleaner strike. But the umpire missed it. So I had to try it again, and this time Buddy looped it over short for a base hit and that beat me, 5–4."

Although he was not much of a hitter, Kerr became part of the trade that broke up the great New York homer-hitting squad of the late 1940s. In 1947 the Giants as a team had belted an NL-record 221 homers, but finished only fourth in the standings. When Leo Durocher moved over from Brooklyn to manage the club, he sent Kerr, outfielder Willard Marshall, and two other players to the Boston Braves for shortstop Alvin Dark and second baseman Eddie Stanky. The trade helped build the foundation for the Giants' 1951 pennant.

Kerr's hitting declined precipitously with Boston and he was released at the end of the 1951 season. He played a few more seasons in the minors before becoming a manager in the Giants system for 10 years, supplementing his income by working as a liquor salesman in the off-season.

In 1964 Kerr became a special-assignment scout for San Francisco, and was able to work out of his own home in New York. "I could see a lot of players in Yankee Stadium or at Shea or in Philadelphia," he said. "Most of the time I slept in my own bed. That was a wonderful change after all those years in hotel rooms. I enjoyed working on reports and I enjoyed being with the other scouts. It is a very tight fraternity."

When club owner Horace Stoneham finally sold the Giants in 1976 to Bob Lurie, the wholesale firing of Stoneham's favorites followed. Kerr was among those who got the ax. He signed on with the Mets, concentrating on special assignments. One even got him a look at a young fellow named Dwight Gooden, who would become an ace righthander for the club. "It's just wonderful being part of the game, even a very small part," Kerr observed.

Dickie Kerr

Kerr, Richard Henry **P**

1919–25 B:7/3/1893, St. Louis, MO D:5/4/1963, Houston, TX Deb:4/25/1919, CHI AL BL/TL, 5'7", 155

W	L	PCT	G	SH	IP	BB	SO	ERA
53	34	.609	140	7	811^{1}	250	235	3.84

In 1920, when 5-foot-7, 150-pound Dickie Kerr won 21 games for the White Sox, baseball's most popular pun was "Little pitchers have big years." That was about as funny as it got around Comiskey Park that season, when every day headlines screamed fresh revelations about the 1919 World Series scandal.

The news that eight White Sox players had conspired to throw the previous year's Fall Classic broke the hearts of baseball fans in Chicago and throughout the country. But the pint-size lefty Kerr had played the Series straight. As one of the club's "Clean Sox," he won deserved cheers after Chicago's "Black Sox" were banned. Ironically, a couple of years later Kerr himself was also banned from the sport.

Because most managers preferred pitchers who were tall, his progress through the minor leagues was slow, and he didn't win a spot with the White Sox until the ill-fated 1919 season.

The Chicago ballclub was divided into various cliques. Kerr hung around with second baseman Eddie Collins, catcher Ray Schalk, and pitcher Urban "Red" Faber, three future Hall of Famers. Another clique included first baseman Chick Gandil and shortstop Swede Risberg, who were antagonistic toward Collins and his friends. In their parlance, Kerr became "the busher." But despite the team's interpersonal turmoil, the Sox were talented and easily won the pennant.

Most of the Sox were underpaid in comparison with others of similar talent and experience elsewhere in the league. This led the Gandil gang to hatch a plan to solicit bribes from gamblers to fix the Series. The group included Gandil, Risberg, outfielders Joe Jackson and Happy Felsch, pitchers Eddie Cicotte and Lefty Williams, and substitute Fred McMullin. Third baseman Buck Weaver declined to enter the plot when he learned about it but did nothing to prevent it.

After Cicotte and Williams tossed away the first two games to Cincinnati, Kerr pitched in Game 3. He possessed good control and a sneaky fastball, and when his curve was working Kerr was particularly tough. Although he was the Sox' fourth starter in 1919 and finished 13–8, he worked Game 3 because Faber was hurt. Kerr pitched one of the best games in Series history, shutting out the Reds, 3–0, on a three-hitter. Cicotte and Williams promptly lost two more games, leaving the White Sox down four games to one in the best-of-nine affair.

In Game 6 Kerr held off the inevitable, winning 5–4 in a gutsy 10-inning performance. Cicotte, apparently pitching on the square because he hadn't received the money he'd been promised, won Game 7, but Williams handed Game 8 to the Reds with four first-inning runs.

The White Sox were in the pennant race until the last week of the 1920 season when word of the fix finally came out along with news of the suspensions of those involved. Cicotte, Williams, Faber, and Kerr had each won 20 or more games; Kerr was 21–9.

In 1921 penny-pinching White Sox owner Charles Comiskey offered Kerr an extremely skimpy contract. Kerr held out for a better deal, then pitched more than 300 innings for the seventh-place White Sox and finished 19–17. When he asked for a $500 raise, Comiskey refused, and Kerr went home to Texas.

As a holdout, Kerr was not allowed to play against any team in Organized Baseball. After he pitched for an independent team in a game against a club that employed a couple of the Black Soxers, Kerr was suspended for a year.

In 1925 he returned to the White Sox but went only 0–1 in 12 games. Kerr then worked for a number of years as a minor league manager and was responsible for switching future Cardinals star Stan Musial from the pitching mound to the outfield.

Don Kessinger

Kessinger, Donald Eulon **SS–2B**

1964–79 M(1979, 46–60) B:7/17/1942, Forrest City, AK Deb:9/7/1964, CHI NL BB/TR, 6'1", 175

G	AB	R	H	HR	RBI	OBP	SLG	AVG
2078	7651	899	1931	14	527	.316	.312	.252

Don Kessinger was an All-Star shortstop with the Chicago Cubs for 12 years. During that time he led the league in assists and double plays four times, putouts three times, and fielding percentage and total chances per game once each.

While at the University of Mississippi, Kessinger was an All-Southeastern Conference player in both baseball and basketball. In 1964 the Cubs gave him a $25,000 signing bonus.

During his tenure with Chicago, Kessinger was named to the NL All-Star team six times, from 1968 through 1972 and again in 1974. *The Sporting News* also honored him, naming Kessinger its NL All-Star shortstop from 1968 through 1970. In 1969 he played 54 straight errorless games. On July 17, 1971, Kessinger went 6-for-6 in a 10-inning game, becoming the first Cub with six hits in a contest since Frank DeMaree did it in on July 5, 1937.

A member of the ill-fated 1969 Cubs, Kessinger had his own theory as to why the Mets were that year's team of destiny. "The heat, day after day, drains your energy," he said. "By August, the regulars were tired, but Leo [Durocher] kept us in there without an occasional day off. When the Mets made their move, we had nothing left."

In 1979, his final season, Kessinger served as player-manager for the White Sox.

Jimmy Key

Key, James Edward **P**

1984–98 B:4/22/1961, Huntsville, AL Deb:4/6/1984, TOR AL BR/TL 6'1", 190

W	L	PCT	G	SH	IP	BB	SO	ERA
186	117	.614	470	13	2591^{2}	668	1538	3.51

Jimmy Key was the first successful left-handed pitcher produced by the Toronto Blue Jays, but he became better known for helping the New York Yankees become winners again in the mid-1990s. He was the victor in Game 6 of the 1996 World Series, beating Greg Maddux and the Atlanta Braves to win the first world championship for the storied franchise in almost 20 years.

Signed out of Clemson University, Key began his major league career in the bullpen. When the Jays acquired veteran lefthanded reliever Gary Lavelle, they moved Key to his more accustomed starting role. He quickly blossomed with his sinking fastball and sharp curveball. With Key, Doyle Alexander, and Dave Stieb anchoring Toronto's rotation, the Blue Jays made the postseason for the first time in franchise history.

After a second straight 14-win season in 1986, Key enjoyed his best season in 1987. He led the league with a 2.76 ERA and held opponents to a league-low .221 batting average. Key never matched those numbers again, but remained an effective starter. Despite undergoing elbow and shoulder surgery, he never won fewer than 12 games over the next five seasons with Toronto and posted only one ERA higher than 4.00.

After the 1989 season, Key underwent arthroscopic surgery to repair a torn rotator cuff, an injury that had previously ended pitching careers. Advancements in arthroscopic procedures, coupled with Key's own work ethic, allowed the determined lefthander to resume his career practically unimpeded.

When Key became eligible for free agency after the 1992 season, the rebuilding Yankees signed him to a four-year, $17 million contract. Key proved to be a bargain. Emerging as a much-needed staff ace, he won a career-high 18 games in 1993. He led the league with 17 victories the following (strike-shortened) season in just 25 starts.

In 1995 Key underwent a more serious rotator cuff surgery, yet rebounded to win 12 games during the Yankees' championship run in 1996. His victory in the clinching game of the World Series, however, turned out to be his final game in pinstripes. The Yankees opted for free agent David Wells, while Key replaced Wells in Baltimore's rotation. The four-time All-Star won 16 games in his first season as an Oriole. Plagued by shoulder problems in 1998, he was forced to retire after 15 seasons.

Harmon Killebrew

Killebrew, Harmon Clayton **3B–1B**

1954–79 B:6/29/1936, Payette, ID Deb:6/23/1954, WAS AL BR/TR, 5'11", 213

G	AB	R	H	HR	RBI	OBP	SLG	AVG
2435	8147	1283	2086	573	1584	.379	.509	.256

Harmon Killebrew, the muscular, slugging outfielder for the Washington Senators and Minnesota Twins for 22 seasons, was a one-dimensional player. But what a dimension it was.

Killebrew, a career .256 hitter, an adequate fielder, and one of the most strikeout-prone players in baseball history, could do one thing exceptionally well: hit home runs. His lifetime home run ratio of 14.2 ranks him behind only Babe Ruth, Ralph Kiner, and Mark McGwire, and his 573 career home runs ranks fifth on the all-time list.

There's no question about where Killebrew got his strength. His grandfather was reputed to have been the strongest man in the Union Army during the Civil War. His father was a collegiate fullback and professional wrestler. Killebrew was born in Payette, Idaho, in 1936, the youngest of four children. While growing up he helped his father paint houses and with farm chores, which included carrying 10-gallon pails of milk. "That will put muscles on you even if you don't try," Killebrew once said.

At Payette High School, Killebrew starred in baseball, basketball, and football. He enrolled at the College of Idaho in Caldwell, but was then offered a scholarship at the University of Oregon. Killebrew had planned on accepting that offer until he batted .847 for the local semipro baseball team of the Idaho-Oregon Border League.

United States Senator Herman Welker, also a resident of Payette, tipped off Clark Griffith, owner of the Washington Senators, about this strong kid back home. Griffith dispatched a scout named Ossie Bluege to Payette, and after Killebrew hit four home runs and three triples and collected four other hits in four semipro games, Bluege wired back to Griffith, "The sky's the limit."

The Senators offered Killebrew a three-year deal worth $30,000 in salary and bonuses, but Killebrew had also caught the attention of the Boston Red Sox, and he had promised Sox scout Earl Johnson over golf that Boston would be given a chance to match any offer. Johnson, however, couldn't convince his bosses to matching the Washington offer, and Killebrew signed with the Senators.

Later, Killebrew remembered what had gone through his head the first time he visited Fenway Park. "I took one look at that green wall and right away it occurred to me that maybe I'd signed with the wrong club. I mean that left field was so close it looked as though you could reach out and touch it."

In 1954 Killebrew was only 18, and because of major league rules at the time, he had to stay on the Washington major league roster for two full years. He hit his first home run on June 24, 1955, off Billy Hoeft. Initially tried at second base, before stints at third, first, and in the outfield later in his career, Killebrew's production was poor enough to get him farmed out as soon as the rules permitted. With Chattanooga in 1956 he led the Southern Association with 27 home runs while driving in 101, but he also committed a league-high 31 errors.

In 1957 and 1958 Killebrew appeared in a combined 22 games for the Senators. He hit .194

in 13 games for Washington in 1958, and many in the Senators organization were ready to write him off—but not Griffith. He ordered Eddie Yost traded to make room at third, and then instructed Manager Cookie Lavagetto to play Killebrew there.

In 1959 Killebrew responded by hitting 42 home runs, tying for the league lead with Rocky Colavito. In one 17-game stretch he had five two-homer games. Many more were on the way—his career total of 46 multi-homer games ranks eighth in major league history.

"It took me five years to catch up with major league pitching," Killebrew once said. When he did, he was a terror to American League hurlers. Killebrew connected for more than 40 home runs eight times in his career, and led the league six times. He drove in better than 100 runs nine times, leading the AL three times. He was named to the All-Star Game 11 times, at three different positions.

In 1961 the Senators left Washington for Minnesota to become the Twins. In 1962 Killebrew blasted 48 homers and drove in 142 runs to win two legs of the Triple Crown, a feat he repeated in 1969. On July 18, 1962, Killebrew and outfielder Bob Allison both connected for grand slams in the first inning of a game against Cleveland, the first time that had been done since 1890. Later in the game Killebrew hit another grand slam.

The following season Killebrew hit 45 home runs, including four in one doubleheader, an American League record. He led the league with 49 homers in 1964, and after falling off to 25 in 1965 he went deep 39 times in 1966 and an AL-high 44 times in 1967.

At the 1968 All-Star Game Killebrew tore a hamstring muscle. He also suffered from a bum knee, and batted only .210 in 100 games that season, leading many to believe that his career was over. But he worked out with weights during the winter to rehabilitate his knee and came back to play a full 162-game season despite much pain. In 1969 he led the American League with 49 homers and 140 RBIs, and was named AL Most Valuable Player.

"I still think Killebrew is the single most dangerous hitter in the league," observed Tommy John, who pitched in the AL in the '60s. "He's got the perfect batting stance. You look down at him and there's no place to throw the ball."

Despite his success in one of the more glamorous aspects of the game, Killebrew was a blue-collar player and one of the most respected men in baseball. "He is a quiet man, and a true gentleman," noted former teammate Rod Carew. "He commands respect. He always went out and did his job and never complained. Harmon never argued with an umpire. It just wasn't his nature."

During Killebrew's years in Minnesota the Twins advanced to postseason play twice. Both campaigns ended in disappointment. In 1965 the Twins, led by Killebrew, Allison, and pitchers Mudcat Grant, Camilo Pascual, and Jim Kaat, won the AL pennant. They took the Los Angeles Dodgers to seven games in the World Series, but were stopped in Game 7 on a three-hitter crafted by Sandy Koufax.

In 1969, under manager Billy Martin, the Twins won the AL West title in the first year of division play, but were swept in three games by the Orioles in the ALCS. Killebrew had three hits in that series, two of them home runs, and drove in four runs.

Killebrew hit 41 homers in 1970, and drove home a league-leading 119 runs in 1971. But eventually the years and the changes in the game caught up with him. "The artificial turf took it out of my legs and I wanted no more of it," Killebrew said. He was released by the Twins in January 1975, and signed with the Kansas City Royals for $125,000—$15,000 more than his best Twins salary. Killebrew hit 14 more home runs at age 39 to finish his career with 573.

After his retirement he broadcast Twins games on TV from 1976 through 1978 and formed an insurance and securities firm in Boise. His uniform No. 3 was retired by the Twins, and he was elected to the Hall of Fame in 1984.

Bill Killefer

Killefer, William Lavier **C**

1909–21 M(1921–33, 524–622) B:10/10/1887, Bloomingdale, MI D:7/3/1960, Elsmere, DE Deb:9/13/1909, STL AL BR/TR, 5'10½", 200

G	AB	R	H	HR	RBI	OBP	SLG	AVG
1035	3150	237	751	4	240	.273	.283	.238

Catcher Bill Killefer's name remains linked with batterymate Grover Cleveland Alexander. Together they helped the Phillies to a pennant in 1915, and on December 11, 1917, both were traded to the Cubs.

Known as "Reindeer Bill," the slow-footed Killefer started in the Class D Southern Michigan League in 1907 with Jackson, a club that folded in midseason. The next year he played for San Francisco, reaching the majors with the Browns in 1909. Demoted to Buffalo of the Eastern (International) League in 1911, he hit .251 in 103 contests before the Phillies picked him up.

After 12 years as a player, Killefer turned to managing. As the skipper for the Cubs, and later the Browns, he managed the teams almost exclusively to second-division finishes. In 1926, Cardinals owner Sam Breadon offered him the job of manager, a post formerly occupied by Rogers

Hornsby, but Killefer declined. Ironically, when Killefer was fired from the Browns in 1933, Hornsby replaced him.

Killefer later managed in the high minors and scouted.

Frank Killen

Killen, Frank Bissell **P**

1891–1900 B:11/30/1870, Pittsburgh, PA D:12/3/1939, Pittsburgh, PA Deb:8/27/1891, MIL AA BL/TL, 6'1", 200

W	L	PCT	G	SH	IP	BB	SO	ERA
164	131	.556	321	13	2511^{1}	822	725	3.78

On July 31, 1896, Frank Killen disputed a call with umpire Daniel Lally and punched him in the face. The lefty pitcher was arrested and charged with disorderly conduct. Nevertheless, he went on to record a 30–18 season for Pittsburgh that year, in 432 innings pitched.

In 1890 Killen posted a 10–0 record with Manistee of the Michigan State League and a 17–7 record with Minneapolis of the Western League. He then spent a year with Milwaukee of the American Association and a year with Washington. Killen arrived in Pittsburgh in 1893. In his first season with the club he went 36–14 in 415 innings.

Killen was badly spiked while covering the plate in a game in Baltimore on June 11, 1895. The injury was so serious that the pitcher had to be hospitalized for 49 days and missed most of the season.

He came back in 1896 and had more trouble against Baltimore. On June 3 he lost a game in the bottom of the ninth when, with the bases loaded, his pitch hit Hughie Jennings. It was Baltimore's 10th win in a row over Pittsburgh.

In 1898 the Pirates sold Killen to Washington. He later played briefly for Boston and Chicago before leaving the majors in 1900 with a lifetime 164–131 record.

Killen later pitched for Wheeling of the Western Association, Indianapolis of the American Association, and Atlanta of the Southern Association. He became a minor league umpire in 1906.

Ed Killian

Killian, Edwin Henry **P**

1903–10 B:11/12/1876, Racine, WI D:7/18/1928, Detroit, MI Deb:8/25/1903, CLE AL BL/TL, 5'11", 170

W	L	PCT	G	SH	IP	BB	SO	ERA
103	78	.569	214	22	1598^{1}	482	516	2.38

For every 178 innings Ed Killian pitched, opponents averaged only one home run, making him the hardest pitcher to homer against in major league history. In his day Killian was appreciated for his outstanding 1907 season when he led Detroit to the World Series.

Known as "Twilight Ed" because he pitched an unusual number of extra-inning games, Killian surrendered only nine homers over an eight-year career, and he once pitched a stretch of 1,001 innings without giving up a home run. Because he pitched in the dead ball era it is difficult to compare today's players with Killian. And because of the current lively ball, Killian's record may never be broken.

The lefthander started his major league career with Cleveland in 1903, then was traded to Detroit in January 1904. In 1905 Killian went 23–14 and led the league in shutouts, with eight. In 1906 he had grievances with Tigers management over money as well as lack of support in the field and at the plate. One day Killian came to Bennett Park drunk, took a bat, and tore up the clubhouse. He was fined and left behind on the next road trip.

Killian was 25–13 in 1907, with a 1.78 ERA. He also helped the team by hitting .320 that year, though he was a lifetime .209 hitter. On Sept. 29 Killian won both ends of a doubleheader to clinch a first-place tie in the race for the American League pennant.

For reasons now unknown, Killian was limited to just one relief appearance in the World Series and gave up one run in four innings. The Cubs won the Series four games to one with one tie. The Tigers won the pennant again in 1908, but Killian was less of a factor, with a 12–9 record. He started one game in the 1908 World Series but lasted just 2⅓ innings.

Matt Kilroy

Kilroy, Matthew Aloysius **P**

1886–98 B:6/21/1866, Philadelphia, PA D:3/2/1940, Philadelphia, PA Deb:4/17/1886, BAL AA BL/TL, 5'9", 175

W	L	PCT	G	SH	IP	BB	SO	ERA
141	133	.515	303	19	2435^{2}	754	1170	3.47

Imagine a pitcher who could strike out 513 men in a season. Matt Kilroy did it in 1886, causing baseball to temporarily require four strikes to retire a batter. The record strikeout performance was aided by the fact that Kilroy logged 583 innings that season and by the 50-foot pitching distance of the time.

The rookie lefthander's feat was tempered somewhat by a 29–34 record for Baltimore of the American Association. Nevertheless, he pitched three one-hitters that season and a no-hitter on August 6, defeating Pittsburgh's Ed Morris, 6–0.

Nicknamed "Matches," probably as a play on his name and a tribute to his blazing fastball, Kilroy was 46–19 in 1887. His 589 innings pitched, 66 complete games, and 80 pitching runs led the league, but the extra-strike rule did cut his strikeout total by more than half from the year before.

Baltimore signed Kilroy to an impressive $2,500 contract for the 1888 season, but an injured shoulder limited him to "just" 321 innings. He came back in 1889 to post a 29–25 record in 480 innings. Kilroy pitched a seven-inning no-hitter against St. Louis on July 29 that ended in a tie.

In 1890 Matches jumped to Boston of the new Players League and went 9–15. During the next five seasons he pitched sparingly for four major league clubs and also took the mound for Syracuse and Hartford of the Eastern League.

After retiring, Kilroy ran a restaurant near Philadelphia's Shibe Park and worked with the Athletics' pitchers.

Ellis Kinder

Kinder, Ellis **P**

1946–57 B:7/26/1914, Atkins, AK D:10/16/1968, Jackson, TN Deb:4/30/1946, STL AL BR/TR, 6', 195

W	L	PCT	G	SV	IP	BB	SO	ERA
102	71	.590	484	102	1479[2]	539	749	3.43

Righthander Ellis "Old Folks" Kinder didn't get his start in the majors until he was over 30, but in 1949 he nearly pitched the Red Sox to the pennant. Kinder compiled a 23–6 record and led the AL in won-lost percentage and shutouts.

By 1951 Kinder had become a relief pitcher and paced the American League in appearances with 63. Two seasons later he established a since-surpassed AL record of 69 appearances. During the 1953 season he also led the AL with 27 saves, a major league record at the time.

Ralph Kiner

Kiner, Ralph McPherran **OF**

1946–55 B:10/27/1922, Santa Rita, NM Deb:4/16/1946, PIT NL BR/TR, 6'2", 195

G	AB	R	H	HR	RBI	OBP	SLG	AVG
1472	5205	971	1451	369	1015	.398	.548	.279

Home-run hitter Ralph Kiner never uttered the famous words, "Home-run hitters drive Cadillacs, singles hitters drive Fords." The author was actually Pirates pitcher Fritz Ostermueller. It was Kiner who declared, "Cadillacs are down at the end of the bat."

Kiner was an expert on hitting homers, and he ranked second to Babe Ruth on the all-time list for the highest number of homers per at bat. Besides that, Kiner set a record that neither Ruth nor even Hank Aaron could top—he led or tied for the lead in homers in the first seven seasons of his career.

Despite his 1975 election to the Hall of Fame, Kiner has often been denigrated as a one-dimensional player whose home run totals profited when Pittsburgh shortened the left-field fences at Forbes Field to create "Greenberg's Gardens"—later known as "Kiner's Korner." Yet Kiner hit better than .300 three times in his 10-year career and finished with a .279 lifetime average.

Each season from 1947 through 1951 Kiner was selected to *The Sporting News* Major League All-Star team. Other outfielders to be named during those years were Ted Williams, Joe DiMaggio, Stan Musial, and Larry Doby. Only Kiner was selected all five years.

Kiner's lifetime offensive statistics place him in pretty good company. He ranks 13th in lifetime slugging average, 44th in on-base percentage, 18th in total average, 16th in bases on balls percentage, and 12th in offensive production.

Kiner was born in New Mexico but reared in Alhambra, California, and in early childhood was a fan of all sports. At age 13 he seriously set his sights on becoming a baseball player. While playing in high school Kiner attracted the attention of major league scouts, particularly representatives of the Yankees and the Pirates.

The Yankees, with their huge farm system, proposed to start Kiner in Class D. Pittsburgh scout Hollis "Sloppy" Thurston offered Kiner a contract that called for $3,000 on signing and another $5,000 if Kiner reached the majors. More importantly, Pittsburgh would start him with the Albany Senators of the Class A Eastern League. Kiner felt that the Yankees route to the majors might take six or seven years. Starting in Class A, however, he estimated he could do it in four. He signed with the Pirates, although he had second thoughts when he first set eyes on huge Forbes Field.

In 1941 the newly signed Kiner went to spring training with Pittsburgh. In his first game against major league pitching he hit homers off White Sox pitchers Bill Dietrich and Thornton Lee. Later that spring Pirates manager Frankie Frisch spotted Kiner loafing in the bullpen instead of running laps in the outfield.

Frisch wanted to know why Kiner wasn't running. "Mr. Frisch, I have only one pair of baseball shoes, and if I wear them out running, I won't have any for the games," Kiner replied. "Well, that's fine," Frisch fumed. "You can take those shoes to Barnwell, South Carolina," the Pirates' minor league camp, "because that's where you'll be playing your next game."

In 1942 Kiner played center field and led the pitcher-friendly Eastern League with 14 homers and 338 putouts. He started 1943 with Toronto in the International League, but five weeks into the season he enlisted in the Navy for a relatively uneventful service hitch.

After being released from the military in December 1945, Kiner worked himself into shape for 1946 spring training. While in the service he had bulked up, from 165 to 195 pounds. That spring he ran into Cleveland pitcher Bob Lemon, who had played against Kiner five years before in the Eastern League. "I remember you," Lemon told Kiner. "I used to have to guard against the bunt when you batted. Now you can't run a lick."

Nevertheless Kiner had a tremendous spring in 1946. "I think I even surprised myself," he recalled. "I hit at least a dozen home runs, some of them for real distance, knocked in a ton of runs, and won a job that nobody expected me to win."

Although Kiner led the National League in homers during his rookie season, he was hardly a polished performer. He swung at virtually everything, and his 109 strikeouts topped the NL. But with help from veteran Hank Greenberg, Kiner soon corrected that problem. He never struck out more than 90 times in a season for the remainder of his career.

"In 1946 I was afraid that when the pitcher got two strikes on me, the next pitch would come at me," Kiner said. "I'd bite at the pitch and strike out. With Hank's coaching, I learned to swing only when the ball was over the plate."

Aside from getting hitting tips from Greenberg, Kiner considered "Hammerin' Hank" a great friend and a great man. "When I married Nancy Chaffee, I asked him to be the best man at our wedding. In fact, he served as best man at my first two weddings. When I mentioned my plans to marry my present wife, DiAnn, he said he wasn't going to be held responsible a third time."

Kiner called Greenberg "the biggest influence in my life." He taught Kiner how to dress ("No brown shoes with a tuxedo, Mr. Kiner.") and how to have fun, taking him to such places as New York's Copacabana. "And going with Hank, that was big league. He knew how to do it right," Kiner said.

Actually, Greenberg probably did his best teaching during Kiner's sophomore season. Kiner was off to a horrible start, with just three home runs by Memorial Day. In one game the Cubs' Hank Borowy struck out Kiner four times, and Pittsburgh management was ready to ship the young slugger back to the minors.

Greenberg, however, approached Pirates owner Frank McKinney, begging him, "Don't send this boy out. He's going to make it. He's got a great swing, he's very determined, and he's going to make it."

Kiner eventually caught fire and hit 48 home runs the rest of the way to tie New York's Johnny Mize for the league lead with 51. He was named *The Sporting News* Major League Player of the Year in 1950, when he slugged 47 homers and drove in 122 runs. That season, Kiner's ninth-inning solo homer tied the All-Star Game, allowing Red Schoendienst a chance to win it for the National League with a leadoff home run in the 14th.

During the course of his career Kiner hit 13 grand slams, collected two or more homers in a game 34 times, and hit three homers three different times. To counteract Kiner's power, opposing teams often employed a righthanded version of the "Williams Shift." The Cleveland Indians had developed the Williams Shift, moving as many as six fielders into his hitting zone to counteract Ted Williams's powerful pull-hitting. Like Williams, Kiner refused to alter his swing in response. "It probably cost me a .300 lifetime average. I lost a lot of base hits," Kiner said.

Because Hollywood crooner Bing Crosby had become part owner of the Pirates in 1946, Kiner had a passport into Hollywood circles and dated such starlets as Elizabeth Taylor and Esther Williams. He had many fans, but Pirates general manager Branch Rickey was not one of them. "Ralph Kiner has so many other weaknesses that if you had eight Ralph Kiners on an American Association team, it would finish last," Rickey once said. After Kiner had just secured his seventh consecutive home run championship, Rickey attempted to cut his salary by 25 percent. "We could have finished last without you," Rickey coldly informed Kiner.

Pittsburgh traded Kiner to the Cubs on June 4, 1953, with three other Pirates for six players and an estimated $100,000. In November 1954 he was sent to Cleveland in a deal bringing two Indians and $60,000 to Chicago. Engineering the Cleveland side of the deal was Kiner's mentor, Greenberg, now the Indians' general manager. At the time, Kiner's chronic sciatica was seriously troubling him. He played only part-time, and according to Greenberg, "He really wasn't happy about the situation." Kiner retired at the close of the 1955 season.

Kiner went on to serve as general manager of the minor league San Diego Padres and briefly broadcast Chicago White Sox games with Bob Elson. One of the original broadcasters for the New York Mets, with Bob Murphy and Lindsey Nelson, Kiner became known for his mispronunciations and "Kinerisms"—for instance, "We'll be back after this word from Manufacturers Hangover." But he also unfailingly displayed a strong grasp of baseball strategy and history. "His fine voice and gentle sense of humor gave the Mets broadcasting crew a touch of class," Nelson said.

In 1987 the Pittsburgh Pirates retired Kiner's uniform No. 4. Kiner was down to his final strike in January 1975 when it came to Hall of Fame balloting. It was his last year of eligibility. A total of 272 votes was needed for election. Kiner received 273 and took his place in Cooperstown.

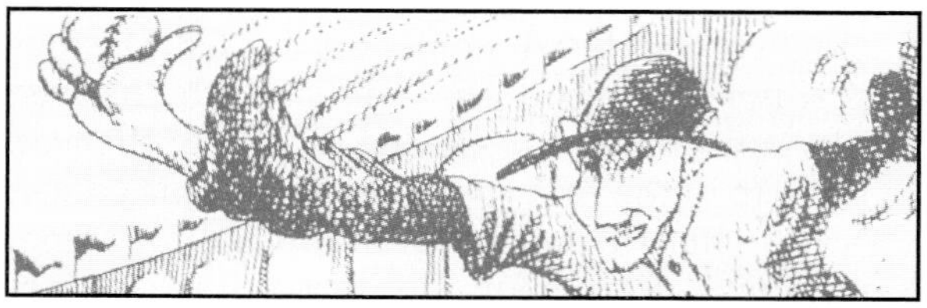

Jeff King

King, Jeffrey Wayne **3B-1B-2B**

1989–99 B:12/26/1964, Marion, IN Deb:6/2/1989, PIT NL BR/TR 6'1", 180

G	AB	R	H	HR	RBI	OBP	SLG	AVG
1201	4262	600	1091	154	709	.329	.425	.256

The first overall pick in the 1986 amateur draft, Jeff King was labeled a failure six years later. By reinventing himself as a hitter, not once but twice, the University of Arkansas All-America developed into a feared run producer in the major leagues.

After posting disappointing numbers his four years with the Pittsburgh Pirates, King found his game in 1993 when he improved his plate discipline and learned to use all fields. He hit .295 with 98 RBIs, while leading National League third baseman in assists. In 1995 King topped the Pirates in RBIs and homers, including two in one inning on August 8. Amazingly, he repeated the feat on April 30, 1996.

After establishing himself as an intelligent, patient contact hitter, King consciously added lift to his swing in 1996. He hit 30 home runs, a dozen more than his previous best. Traded to Kansas City in 1997, King hit 28 home runs and drove in a career-high 112 runs. Back problems plagued him in 1998, and he played only 21 games the following year before retiring at age 34.

Silver King

King, Charles Frederick **P**

1886–97 B:1/11/1868, St. Louis, MO D:5/21/1938, St. Louis, MO Deb:9/28/1886, KC NL BR/TR, 6', 170

W	L	PCT	G	SH	IP	BB	SO	ERA
204	153	.570	397	19	3181^{2}	967	1222	3.18

Charles "Silver" King is thought to be the first sidearm pitcher in baseball. The righthander helped pitch the St. Louis Browns to American Association pennants in 1887 and 1888, and he starred in the ill-fated Players League of 1890. Over a four-season span King won 142 games, and Pittsburgh signed him to the highest salary in baseball in 1891.

We might have known him as Koenig, but King used an English translation of his German surname and picked up "Silver" for his very light blond hair. He started with St. Joseph of the Western League in 1886 then moved to Kansas City of the National League the same season. The franchise folded, still owing King $200 in salary. In 1887 he moved to St. Louis of the American Association and went 32–12 for the first-place team. King was 1–3 with a 2.03 ERA in the 15-game "World Series" of 1887 against the NL champion Detroit Wolverines.

King had one of the best seasons on record in 1888 to help the Browns return to the World Series. He went 45–21 with a 1.64 ERA and 64 complete games in more than 585 innings. In the Series he had a 2.31 ERA and again posted a 1–3 record. After a 35–16 season in 1889 for St. Louis, King jumped to Chicago in the newly formed Players League, notched a 30–22 record, and led the circuit with a 2.69 ERA in 1890.

The new National League Pittsburgh Pirates signed King to an unprecedented $5,000 contract. He went on to pitch for New York and Cincinnati before his first retirement after the 1893 season. Baseball introduced the pitching rubber in that season, and King was said to have had problems getting used to pitching from it.

King joined his father's bricklaying business, but he made a comeback with Washington from 1896 through 1897 before going back to brick contracting.

Dave Kingman

Kingman, David Arthur **OF-1B-3B-DH**

1971–86 B:12/21/1948, Pendleton, OR Deb:7/30/1971, SF NL BR/TR, 6'6", 210

G	AB	R	H	HR	RBI	OBP	SLG	AVG
1941	6677	901	1575	442	1210	.305	.478	.236

Ralph Kiner said of Dave Kingman, "He can hit them out of any park—including Yellowstone." A defensive liability who struck out too much, Kingman had a career .236 average and a personality that many found abrasive, yet his lifetime home run mark of 442 stands as the highest total by a retired player not in the Hall of Fame.

A pitcher in high school, Kingman turned down contracts with the California Angels and Baltimore Orioles so he could play for Rod Dedeaux at the University of Southern California. Kingman went 11–4 with a 1.38 ERA and hit .353 with eight homers and 26 RBIs in 32 games. Noting that "Dave could have been a great pitcher in the majors, but I knew he could be a superstar as a slugger," Dedeaux made him an outfielder.

The 6-foot 6-inch righthanded slugger signed with the San Francisco Giants in 1967, joined the big league club in July 1971, and hit 17 home runs despite going on the disabled list in September with an emergency appendectomy. Kingman recovered quickly and homered against the San Diego Padres to clinch the Western Division title that season.

Although he had an exceptional throwing arm, Kingman was a lousy fielder. When he tore the webbing of his glove during a game once and time was called for the trainer to sew it up, Phils announcer Richie Ashburn commented that "they should have called a welder."

Unhappy in San Francisco, Kingman requested a trade and was sold to the Mets in 1975 for $125,000. He crushed 72 home runs in his first two seasons as a Met and was voted to start the 1976 All-Star Game, yet he was unhappy in New York as well. He requested another trade and was shipped to San Diego for Bobby Valentine during the Mets' "Midnight Massacre" trading frenzy on June 15, 1977. After being swapped three times that season, Dave Kingman became a free agent, and in 1978 the Chicago Cubs signed him. The next season he led the league in home runs with 48, and slugging average with .613.

Traded back to the Mets in 1981, he paced the National League in homers with 37 in 1982. Cub Bill Caudill said of the trade, "It's like going to get a tooth pulled. It's a great pain to lose a bat like that, but eventually the pain goes away, and you feel a whole lot better."

Again a free agent in 1983, Kingman signed as a designated hitter with the Oakland Athletics. In a rare moment of humor he said, "My defensive days are pretty much over." His 35 home runs in 1986 at age 37 stands as the highest final-season total in history.

Jay Kirke

Kirke, Judson Fabian **OF–1B–2B**

1910–18 B:6/16/1888, Fleischmanns, NY D:8/31/1968, New Orleans, LA Deb:9/28/1910, DET AL BL/TR, 6', 195

G	AB	R	H	HR	RBI	OBP	SLG	AVG
320	1148	122	346	7	148	.328	.385	.301

Jay Kirke's major league career was short, but his minor league career stretched from 1906 to 1935. During that time, he played in 2,617 games; batted 10,005 times; scored 1,297 runs; collected 3,165 hits, 557 doubles, 131 triples, and 111 homers; drove in 997 runs; and stole 246 bases in the bushes.

An erratic fielder, Kirke began at short in 1906 with the Class C Hudson River League and played with Poughkeepsie, Wilmington, Binghamton, Wilkes-Barre, and Scranton before reaching Detroit in 1910.

He failed to stick with the Tigers and was sent to New Orleans before returning to the majors with the Braves. Demoted to Toledo in 1913, he transferred with that club to Cleveland, when it was moved there in 1914 to counter the Federal League threat. In both 1914 and 1915 he played for major and minor league clubs in the same city in the same season.

Traded from the Milwaukee Brewers to the Louisville Colonels in early 1916, he lasted with Louisville through 1922. In both 1916 and 1917 he led the American Association in doubles. In 1921 he won the league batting title with a .386 mark and set the all-time American Association record for hits in a season with 282.

Sold to Minneapolis in 1923, he batted just .250 and was dealt to Minneapolis where he hit .326 in 1924. He performed for Fort Worth, Beaumont, and Shreveport in the Texas League and Decatur in the 3-I League before retiring in 1927. Kirke was out of Organized Baseball from 1928 to 1934, but returned to Opelousas in the Evangeline League in 1935 and—at age 47—batted .281 in 60 games.

Bruce Kison

Kison, Bruce Eugene **P**

1971–85 B:2/18/1950, Pasco, WA Deb:7/04/1971, PIT NL BR/TR, 6'4", 178

W	L	PCT	G	SH	IP	BB	SO	ERA
115	88	.567	380	8	1809^{2}	662	1073	3.66

Widearmer Bruce Kison was a member of five NL East champion Pirates teams in the 1970s, but he will be remembered for his postseason work in his rookie year, 1971. The 21-year-old righthander pitched brilliant long relief and won games in both the NLCS and the World Series that season. The Pirates won Game 7 of the Series in Baltimore, but Kison left the celebration early to get married that evening in Pittsburgh.

He signed with the Pirates in June 1968 and played with Bradenton, Geneva, Salem, Waterbury, and Charleston, all Pittsburgh farm clubs. An independent thinker with a youthful naiveté, Kison signed with the Pirates and insisted on a contract provision allowing him to finish his spring semester college courses before reporting to his minor league assignment each season. Understandably, he balked when the team asked him to play winter ball.

On the mound Kison believed in pitching inside. In his first three seasons he led three minor leagues in hit batters.

Kison joined the Pirates in 1971, taking the place of Bob Moose, who had to serve military duty. He finished the season 6–5, then Moose returned to the club, and it looked as though Kison would see little, if any, postseason action.

In the best-of-five NLCS the Pirates led the Giants two games to one. Bucs hurler Steve Blass started Game 4 but was ineffective. Kison was

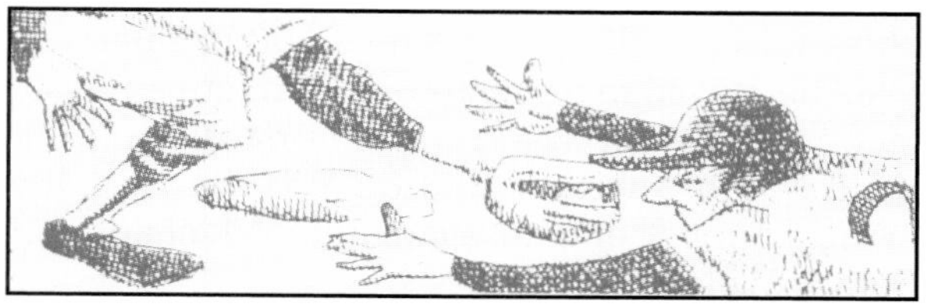

brought in to pitch the third inning, and Manager Danny Murtaugh stayed with the rookie who gave the team 4 2/3 innings of scoreless relief. Kison got credit for the win.

He duplicated the feat in Game 4 of the Fall Classic and won the first Series night game. In relief of Luke Walker he pitched 6 1/3 innings and gave up no runs on one hit to even the Series with Baltimore at two wins apiece.

Kison had planned to get married on October 17 and refused to let the scheduling of Game 7 of the World Series for the same day change those plans. The Pirates won Game 7 in Baltimore by the score of 2–1. Pirates broadcaster Bob Prince had arranged for a helicopter to take Kison and best man Moose to the Baltimore airport where they would board a private jet to fly to Pittsburgh. Kison arrived, a little late, and was married to Ann Marie Orlando, a student nurse, that evening.

Kison pitched a consistent nine seasons for Pittsburgh but never won more than 14 games in a season. He continued to excel in the postseason, compiling a 4–0 record and giving up only one run in 15 2/3 innings of NLCS competition. He was also 1–1 in the World Series.

Before the 1980 season, the Angels signed Kison as a free agent. In 1982, pitching predominantly in relief, he had a 10–5 record as the team won the Western Division. In the AL Championship Series against Milwaukee Kison started two games, with a 1–0 record and a 1.93 ERA in 14 innings of work.

Frank Kitson

Kitson, Frank R. **P**

1898–1907 B:9/11/1869, Hopkins, MI D:4/14/30, Allegan, MI Deb:5/19/1898, BAL NL BL/TR 5'11" 165

W	L	PCT	G	SH	IP	BB	SO	ERA
129	118	.522	304	19	2221^2	491	731	3.18

Frank Kitson was the top lefthanded pitcher during Baltimore's final season in the National League. He won 22 games with a 2.78 ERA for the Orioles in 1899. When the NL cut back from a dozen to eight teams that winter, Kitson joined many other former Orioles in Brooklyn. The influx of talent helped the Brooklyn Superbas reach the 1900 championship series, the Chronicle-Telegraph Cup. Kitson did his part by winning Game 2, as the Superbas took the Cup Series over Honus Wagner and the Pittsburgh Pirates, three games to one.

Kitson won 19 games in each of his next two seasons in Brooklyn. He then moved to the American League where he pitched for the Detroit Tigers, Washington Senators, and New York Highlanders before ending his major league career after the 1907 season.

Ron Kittle

Kittle, Ronald Dale **OF-DH-1B**

1982–91 B:1/5/1958, Gary, IN Deb:9/02/1982, CHI AL BR/TR, 6'4", 220

G	AB	R	H	HR	RBI	OBP	SLG	AVG
843	2708	356	648	176	460	.309	.473	.239

It was hard to give up on Ron Kittle—because he never gave up on himself. The righthanded power hitter won the Rookie of the Year Award with the White Sox in 1983. Five years earlier he had been released by the Dodgers after having part of his spine fused, one of several injuries that limited Kittle to only two full seasons in a 10-year major league career.

The Dodgers signed Kittle in 1977, and he played at Clinton and Lethbridge before his back operation in 1978. He did ironwork until he could arrange a tryout at Comiskey Park. The White Sox signed the 6-foot-4 outfielder, and he played at Knoxville, Appleton, Glens Falls, and Edmonton before joining the big club.

With Glens Falls in 1981 he won Eastern League Player of the Year honors, leading the league with 40 homers, 103 RBIs, and a .694 slugging average. The next season, with Edmonton, Kittle paced the Pacific Coast League (PCL) with 50 homers, 144 RBIs, and a .752 slugging percentage. He was named the league's Most Valuable Player and *The Sporting News* Minor League Player of the Year.

In 1983, his first year as a regular with Chicago, he set the White Sox rookie home run record, with 35, and drove in 100 runs, with a .504 slugging average. That season Kittle won AL Rookie of the Year honors from both the Baseball Writers Association of America and *The Sporting News*.

In 1984 Kittle hit 32 homers, but hit only .215 and demonstrated limited range in the outfield. In 1985 he made only 379 plate appearances because of injuries, yet managed to hit 26 home runs.

Kittle was traded to the Yankees during the 1986 season. The next year injuries limited him to 159 at bats. In the following four seasons he bounced back and forth, returning twice to Chicago after stints in Cleveland and Baltimore, although he spent much of his time on the disabled list. The bespectacled slugger, a tireless worker with a sweet swing, retired in 1991 with 176 career home runs.

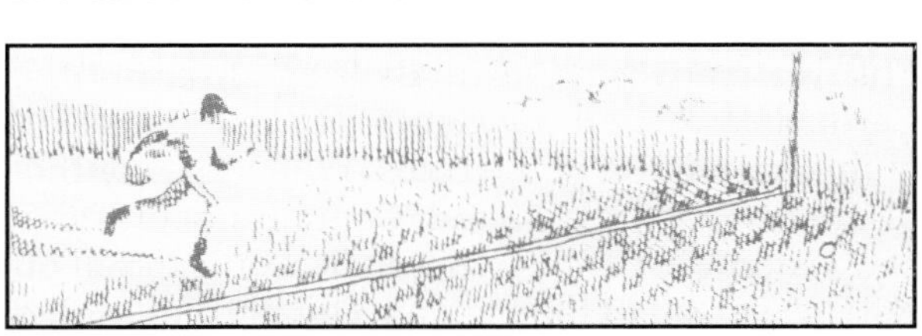

Chuck Klein

Klein, Charles Herbert **OF**

1928–44 B:10/7/1904, Indianapolis, IN D:3/28/1958, Indianapolis, IN Deb:7/30/1928, PHI NL BL/TR, 6', 185

G	AB	R	H	HR	RBI	OBP	SLG	AVG
1753	6486	1168	2076	300	1201	.379	.543	.320

Phillies outfielder Chuck Klein. had five spectacular years in what was essentially a 12½-year career, but his numbers from his last seven seasons don't come close to those of his previous years. Playing in the cozy Baker Bowl, where the plate-to-fence distance was a mere 280 feet down the right-field line, Klein averaged 36 homers, 139 RBIs, and a .359 batting mark. He led the NL in batting once; in doubles, hits, and RBIs twice; in runs and slugging three times; and four times in homers. Named Most Valuable Player in 1932, he won the Triple Crown in 1933. Quite simply, he was the best hitter in the league from 1929 through 1933.

His best year was 1930, when he had career highs with a .386 batting average, a .687 slugging average, 59 doubles, 158 runs, and 170 RBIs. That same season Klein, also an excellent defensive outfielder, set a modern major league record with 44 assists, and he led the NL by taking part in 10 double plays, aided by the Baker Bowl's cozy right field. In all, he led the league in assists three times.

Klein was raised on an Indiana farm and worked on a state road crew before getting a job in a steel mill, where he tossed 200-pound white-hot ingots into blast furnaces and worked eight-hour shifts without even stopping for lunch. When he wasn't working in the mills, he was playing semipro ball for a number of teams. While playing with Indianapolis's Keystone Athletic Club he was spotted by a Prohibition agent, who recommended him to Evansville of the 3-I League.

In 1927 Klein was let go after spending a 13-day training period with the club. On Opening Day his manager told him, "Kid, you can't time the ball right. You hit too many fouls." Then he handed Klein his unconditional release. Several Evansville players were injured later in the season, however, and Klein returned to hit .327 in 14 games before breaking his leg sliding into second base.

In 1928 his contract was sold to Fort Wayne of the Central League for only $200. He hit .331 there with 26 homers after 88 games. At that point he should have been on his way to St. Louis, because Fort Wayne was a Cardinals farm club. But the Cards also owned the Central League's Dayton club, in violation of the rules. When this conflict of interest was discovered, Commissioner Kenesaw Mountain Landis ordered St. Louis to sell off Fort Wayne and all its talent. The Phillies outbid the Yankees and got Klein for $7,500.

When he came to Philadelphia in the middle of the 1928 season Klein introduced himself to Manager Burt Shotton. "All right, Klein," Shotton responded. "Get into uniform. They tell me you can hit. Goodness knows we need hitters." Then he paused and added, "We need everything."

The Phillies did need everything, but after acquiring Klein they didn't need a right fielder for several years. A long-running joke in Philadelphia was that each of the City of Brotherly Love's newspapers kept a headline set in type reading, "KLEIN HITS TWO AS PHILLIES LOSE."

When he hit .360 with 11 homers in 64 games in 1928 he was only getting started. In 1929, his first full year in the majors, Klein led the league with 43 homers and batted .356. He had some help winning the home run title, however. Going into the last game of the season, Klein led the Giants' Mel Ott by one homer. Phils pitchers proceeded to walk "Master Melvin" five straight times, including once with the bases loaded.

In November 1933 Klein, who had just turned 29 and was coming off his Triple Crown season, was traded to the Cubs for $65,000 and three players, two of them veterans on the way out and the other a minor leaguer who never made it to the majors. The Phillies must have known something. Whether it was the move away from the Baker Bowl or injuries, his career started to decline. After averaging 152 games a season during five years, he averaged only 117 games in his two full seasons in Wrigley Field. In 1934 he hit .301 with 20 homers and 80 RBIs, and the next season, despite hitting 21 homers, he slipped to .293 with 73 RBIs. In May 1936 he was sent back to the Phillies along with $50,000 for Ethan Allen, a slap-hitting first baseman near the end of his career, and Curt Davis, a capable starting pitcher.

Back with the Phillies, Klein had one final burst of glory. Against the Pirates on July 10, 1936, he became the first modern National Leaguer to hit four homers in a game. For once his critics could not say he did it with the help of the Baker Bowl; Klein performed his feat in spacious Forbes Field. His first homer was a three-run shot in the first inning. In the second inning he sent Paul Waner to the fence for the out. In the fifth, seventh, and 10th innings he hit solo homers. He finished with 25 homers and 104 RBIs that season, but he never came close to equaling those numbers again.

Unconditionally released by the Phillies on June 7, 1939, Klein signed the same day with Pittsburgh; but the next March, after being dropped by the Pirates, he signed with Philadelphia for a third tour of duty. He served as a player-coach from 1941 through 1945, batting a total of 114 times during those four years.

After leaving baseball he operated a bar in the Kensington neighborhood of Philadelphia until 1947. In rapidly deteriorating health due to heavy drinking, Klein neglected his diet and suffered from malnutrition. As a consequence, his nervous system was heavily damaged and one leg partially paralyzed. He died in 1958 of a cerebral hemorrhage.

The baseball writers passed on Klein for Cooperstown for 15 straight years, but his stats (disregarding his last four seasons, when he was more coach than player) show he averaged 15 homers and 67 RBIs between 1934 and 1940. In 1980, after a lobbying campaign pointed out the similarity of the 10 years of Klein's prime to those of such contemporary Hall of Famers as Earl Averill and Chick Hafey, the Veterans Committee inducted Klein into the Hall of Fame.

Bill Klem

Klem, William J.

Umpire (1905–41) B:2/22/1874, Rochester, NY D:9/11951, Miami, FL Deb:1905, NL 5'7½", 157

Bill Klem, considered the greatest umpire in baseball history, was supposed to have said, "I never missed one in my life." Although that's not exactly what he said, more than 50 years after he arbitrated his last game he is still considered the Babe Ruth of umpires.

Klem, whose family name was actually Klimm, was born and raised in the Dutchtown section of Rochester, NewYork. He got his start in baseball in 1890 as a ticket-taker at the local park. In the spring of 1896 he joined the Canadian League's Hamilton club as a catcher; but his arm went dead and he was quickly released. He bounced around after that, playing with a local team in nearby Palmyra, working as a painter in Springfield, Massachusetts, and doing construction work in Connecticut. Then he tried baseball again. Springfield of the International League signed him to play for Augusta of the Maine State League, where he again washed out.

He drifted in and out of construction jobs and in 1902 was working in Berwick, Pennsylvania, and playing a little baseball on the side when he saw a newspaper headline concerning an old Rochester friend, Silk O'Loughlin, who was umpiring in the National League.

Klem had never thought much of the umpiring profession, but figured that if it could make an old pal such as O'Loughlin famous then there must be something to it. Klem promptly got $5 for a game between the local team and the Cuban Giants and decided to make umpiring his profession.

His first job was in the Class D Connecticut League. Early in the season he got into an argument with the league's secretary and asked him to leave the premises. Klem thought his new career was over, but officials rearranged his schedule so that he could avoid his antagonist, and he was kept on.

"Incidentally," Klem recalled, "I was getting $7.50 per game and no expenses. The fee for doubleheaders was $10.50, you collected after each game, and you umpired alone. And if the home team lost you got an awful lot of abuse with your money."

The next year Klem advanced to the Class B New York State League and was the only umpire to work the entire season. The league wanted him back for the following year, but Klem moved up to the American Association, where he began developing a distinctive style. Once when an outfielder named Frank Hemphill charged after Klem following a disputed call, Klem drew a line in the dirt and turned his back on him. It was a gamble, but it worked. Hemphill jawed away at Klem but was afraid to cross the barrier. From that incident grew Klem's famous habit—often punctuated with the remark, "Don't cross the Rio Grande!"—of drawing a line in the dirt. Any player who crossed the line got thrown out of the game.

While umpiring in the American Association Klem picked up the nickname "Catfish." The epithet became a verbal line in the dirt; he hated the name so much that anyone who used it was guaranteed ejection.

Klem had so distinguished himself during his three years of minor league umpiring that both the American and National Leagues were after him prior to the 1905 season. Both leagues offered him $2,100 for the season, and though the American League pursued him more aggressively, Klem preferred to go with the more established National League. He was soon recognized as the top umpire in baseball. For the first 16 years that Klem umpired he worked exclusively behind home plate because of his superior ability in calling balls and strikes.

The "never missed one" line had its genesis in an incident in 1912 at the Polo Grounds. The Cubs and the Giants were playing at the recently rebuilt ballpark, and in the eighth inning one of John McGraw's Giants hit a long drive off the scoreboard that straddled the foul line in left field. Klem called it foul.

The decision cost McGraw the game, and the disgruntled manager sent the Polo Grounds' architect, Jim Foster, on an errand. Two days after the foul call Foster approached Klem and told him that McGraw had made him climb up on the scoreboard to find the dent the ball had put in it. "Then I measured it," Foster told Klem, "and do you know that ball was foul by three inches?" Klem responded, "You're not telling me a thing, Mr. Foster. I never missed one of those in my life."

According to Klem, he had simply meant that he had never muffed a foul ball call, and he claimed that somewhere along the line his statement had become exaggerated. Whether he said it or not, the more emphatic version of the quote quickly got around the league and all of baseball. "I credit the tag line as the difference between me and all other umpires," admitted Klem. He later revised his remark, but only slightly. "I never missed one in my heart," he said.

Once, on a close play, Klem did not immediately signal his decision. As players crowded around, one asked, "Well, what is it, safe or out?" Klem replied, "It ain't nothing till I call it." Klem's remark sums up the importance of the umpire to the game and is also a subtle reminder to umpires to make sure they've made the right call.

Following his retirement as an umpire in 1940 after 36 years of arbitrating and 18 World Series assignments, he became chief of NL umpires. He took that job as seriously as he did calling balls and strikes. Klem once said, "Baseball is more than a game to me. It's a religion."

Ryan Klesko

Klesko, Ryan Anthony **OF–1B**

1992–* B:6/12/1971, Westminster, CA Deb:9/12/1992, ATL NL BL/TL 6'3", 220

G	AB	R	H	HR	RBI	OBP	SLG	AVG
792	2431	374	684	139	450	.364	.525	.281

Ryan Klesko became the first player in World Series history to homer in three straight road games when he accomplished the feat in 1995 for the Braves. He also boasted a .875 slugging average in the six-game triumph over the Indians.

Despite being a power threat, the lefthanded-hitting Klesko was often removed late in games for defense, or for a pinch hitter when a southpaw was called in from the bullpen. Klesko, whose swing matched his size, struggled so much against lefties that Braves manager Bobby Cox routinely platooned him.

Nevertheless, Klesko was capable of posting impressive numbers. He had 34 homers and 93 RBIs for the 1996 Braves team that returned to the World Series. Klesko hit nine career home runs in postseason play, three each in the Division Series, Championship Series, and World Series.

Klesko showed unexpected versatility in 1999 by playing 50 games in left field and 66 at first base, to help fill the void created by the loss of Andres Galarraga, who missed the entire season while undergoing cancer treatments. Only a late-season slide prevented Klesko from finishing with the second .300 year of his eight-year career. Although he hit .324 with a .402 on-base percentage against righthanded pitchers, he again struggled against lefthanders, hitting only .102 (5-for-49). Klesko, often the subject of trade rumors, was finally dealt on December 21, 1999, to the San Diego Padres.

Ron Kline

Kline, Ronald Lee **P**

1952–70 B:3/9/1932, Callery, PA Deb:4/21/1952, PIT NL BR/TR 6'3", 205

W	L	PCT	G	SH	IP	BB	SO	ERA
114	144	.442	736	108	2078	731	989	3.75

Ron Kline struggled as a starting pitcher with Pittsburgh in the 1950s before he became an excellent reliever with the Senators in the mid-1960s. A colorful performer, he habitually touched his cap, belt, and shirt before each pitch.

A 6-foot 3-inch righthander, Kline started with Bartlesville of the Class D K-O-M League in 1950, and the next season tied for the league lead in wins, with 18, and topped the circuit in strikeouts, with 208. He later played for New Orleans and Burlington.

Kline pitched poorly for a sorry Pittsburgh team in 1952 and took an 0–7 rookie-year record into military service in 1953 and 1954. Things did not get much better from 1955 through 1959, when he led the NL in losses twice and compiled a 53–76 record. On May 31, 1958, Kline surrendered consecutive homers to Milwaukee's Hank Aaron, Eddie Mathews, and Wes Covington and lost the game, 8–3.

In December 1959 Kline was traded to the Cardinals. Without him, the Pirates won the world championship in 1960.

After stops with the Angels and the Tigers, Kline was sold to Washington in March 1963. The Senators made the 30-year-old pitcher a full-time reliever. In four seasons he saved 83 games for the club, and in 1965 he led the American League in saves, with 29. In 1967, pitching in relief for Minnesota, Kline went 7–1 with five saves, and as a reliever back in Pittsburgh in 1968 he went 12–5, with seven saves. He then pitched for San Francisco, Boston, and Atlanta before retiring in 1970 with a 114–144 record and 108 saves.

Johnny Kling

Kling, John **C**

1900–13 M(1912, 52–101) B:2/25/1875, Kansas City, MO D:1/31/1947, Kansas City, MO Deb:9/11/1900, CHI AL BR/TR, 5'9½", 160

G	AB	R	H	HR	RBI	OBP	SLG	AVG
1260	4241	474	1151	20	513	.318	.357	.271

Johnny Kling ranks with Hall of Famer Roger Bresnahan as an outstanding catcher of his era. He was a mainstay of baseball's first 20th-century dynasty, the Chicago Cubs of 1906 through 1910.

Known primarily for his defense and hustle, Kling's constant stream of chatter earned him the nickname "Noisy." He led NL catchers in assists once, fielding percentage twice, and putouts six times. He had a strong and accurate arm, once throwing out all four would-be basestealers in a game against the St. Louis Cardinals. Kling was also a reliable hitter at a time when few catchers contributed to their team's offense.

He began his career as a pitcher with the semipro Kansas City Schmeltzers in the early 1890s, exhibiting enough leadership to be named manager. By the latter part of the decade he had switched to catcher and was performing for St. Joseph, Missouri, of the Western League when the Cubs discovered him and brought him to the National League. In September 1900 he hit .294 in 15 games for Chicago, and the following year he shared catching duties with several others, including a hard-hitting youngster named Frank Chance.

Twenty years earlier the Cubs (then called the White Stockings) had been the National League's most successful franchise, but during the 1890s the team had steadily deteriorated. The slide ended in 1902 when Frank Selee, who'd won five pennants in Boston, was brought to manage. One of his first moves was to station Chance on first base and make Kling his regular catcher. From 1902 through 1908 Kling caught in at least 104 games each year while occasionally filling in at first base or in the outfield.

By 1905 most of the major pieces were in place for the Cubs team that Selee had built so carefully: the legendary double-play trio of Joe Tinker, Johnny Evers, and Chance; several fast outfielders; a pitching staff anchored by Mordecai "Three Finger" Brown and Ed Reulbach; and Kling at catcher. Unfortunately, ill health forced Selee to resign in midseason. Chance took over as manager and brought the team in third.

Selee had built the machine, and Chance ran it magnificently. In 1906 the Cubs won 116 games and lost only 36, the modern record for both victories and winning percentage, to sweep to the NL pennant by 20 games. Kling's .312 was the third-highest batting average on a team that won with pitching, speed, and defense. In the all-Chicago World Series that fall, the Cubs ran into the White Sox' "Hitless Wonders" and were upset, four games to two.

The Cubs came back to win the 1907 and 1908 pennants and defeat the Detroit Tigers, led by Ty Cobb, in both World Series. Detroit won only a single game, largely because of Kling's arm; he cut down seven of 14 Tiger stolen base attempts in 1907 and never allowed the great Cobb to steal.

In 1909 the Cubs won 104 games, yet finished second to the Pittsburgh Pirates, perhaps due to Kling's absence. During the winter of 1909 Kling had won the world pocket billiards championship, at that time a lucrative opportunity, and he had decided to retire from baseball to defend his championship. Many believed his absence from the lineup cost Chicago the pennant.

In 1910, after losing his next billiards championship, Kling returned to the Cubs, and the team won the pennant again but was opposed in the Series by another dynasty just beginning its reign, Connie Mack's Philadelphia Athletics. Hurler Jack Coombs defeated Chicago three times and Chief Bender won once to take the Series for Mack, four games to one.

Early in the 1911 season Kling was traded to the Boston Braves, the NL's weakest team, and was named player-manager in 1912. Although he hit a personal high of .317, Kling couldn't lift the dreadful Braves out of last place. Kling's final major league season came in 1913 with the Cincinnati Reds, where his old teammate Joe Tinker was managing another bad ballclub.

After leaving baseball, John Kling became a successful entrepreneur in Kansas City and ran several businesses, including a billiards hall. From 1934 to 1937 he owned the Kansas City baseball team of the American Association and integrated its ballpark.

Ted Kluszewski

Kluszewski, Theodore Bernard **1B**

1947–61 B:9/10/1924, Argo, IL D:3/29/1988, Cincinnati, OH Deb:4/18/1947, CIN NL BL/TL, 6'2", 225

G	AB	R	H	HR	RBI	OBP	SLG	AVG
1718	5929	848	1766	279	1028	.354	.498	.298

In 1954 Ted Kluszewski, practically a synonym for raw strength, led the NL in home runs with 49, and in RBIs with 141. The 6-foot-2, 225-pound, lefthanded slugger had a career batting average of .298 and a slugging average of .498. In the 1959 World Series, he drove in 10 runs for the White Sox while hitting .391.

If not for World War II, Kluszewski might never have been a professional ballplayer. During the war years teams trained in the north to save on expenses, and the Cincinnati Reds used the Indiana University campus. Groundskeeper Lenny Schwab was sent ahead to prepare the field. Kluszewski, an All-American end on the school's football team, volunteered to help the groundskeeper get the field in shape. When the team arrived for batting practice they let Kluszewski take some swings—he hit balls over an embankment that none of the Reds could reach. He signed with Cincinnati and made the major league club in 1947.

Kluszewski wore uniforms with raggedly cut-off sleeves, which became his trademark. "At first, I did it because the sleeves were restricting me from swinging. They could never make a uniform for me that would give me enough room. These new double-knit uniforms give. But the old flannel ones didn't. I'd get hung up. So I asked them to shorten the sleeves on my uniforms, but they gave me a lot of flak. So one day, I just took a pair of scissors out and cut 'em off. After a while it became kind of a symbol. And it would have to get pretty cold before I'd put a long sleeve shirt on after that."

When Leo Durocher once contended that Gil Hodges was the strongest man in baseball, someone asked, "What about Kluszewski?" Durocher replied, "Kluszewski isn't human."

"Big Klu" was cut down to a mortal scale in 1956 after he suffered a slipped disc during a clubhouse fight. Although he continued to hit for average, he only reached double figures in homers in one other season. After finishing his career with the expansion Angels in 1961, Kluszewski became a hitting coach in the Reds organization. He died of a heart attack in 1988 at age 63.

Bob Knepper

Knepper, Robert Wesley **P**

1976–90 B:5/25/1954, Akron, OH Deb:9/10/1976, SF NL BL/TL 6'2", 200

W	L	PCT	G	SH	IP	BB	SO	ERA
146	155	.485	445	30	2708	857	1473	3.68

Originally signed by the San Francisco Giants in 1976 and traded to the Houston Astros after the 1980 season, Bob Knepper twice led the NL in shutouts and made two All-Star teams. The left-handed junkballer also had 5.00-plus ERAs two years, and his won-lost record came within four games of .500 just three times in 12 full seasons.

Knepper was also known to hold conservative opinions and was unafraid to share them. During 1988 spring training Knepper said of Triple-A umpire Pam Postema, then vying for a major league assignment: "This is not an occupation a woman should be in. In God's society, woman was created in the role of submission to the husband. It's not that the woman is inferior, but I don't believe women should be in a leadership role." The National Organization for Women picketed him.

He was winless in three postseason starts, but Astros relievers blew two of his leads in the 1986 playoffs. Knepper had a one-run lead through seven innings in Game 3, but Dave Smith allowed Lenny Dykstra's two-run homer in the bottom of the ninth. In Game 6, Knepper threw eight shutout innings, leaving with one out, one on, and a one-run lead in the ninth. Smith allowed the tying run to score, and Houston was eliminated in 16 innings. Knepper rejoined the Giants in 1989 and retired after the 1990 season.

Ray Knight

Knight, Charles Ray **3B–1B**

1974–88 M(1996–97, 124–137) B:12/28/1952, Albany, GA Deb:9/10/1974, CIN NL BR/TR, 6'2", 190

G	AB	R	H	HR	RBI	OBP	SLG	AVG
1495	4829	490	1311	84	595	.325	.390	.271

The husband of golf great Nancy Lopez and the hero of the 1986 World Series, Ray Knight seemed to have the world in the palm of his hand after the 1986 season. But either Knight dropped it or the Mets knocked it from his hands, perhaps short-circuiting their dynasty hopes by letting one of their team leaders walk away.

Knight began in the Cincinnati organization. In 1979 he was Pete Rose's replacement at third base and picked up the slack nicely, batting .318 in his first season as a starter. When his hitting fell off during the next two seasons, the Reds dealt Knight to Houston, where he responded with seasons of .294 and .304. In 1984 he was sent to the Mets and suffered through an abbreviated 1985 season, batting only .218 in 90 games.

Knight was almost abandoned during 1986 spring training. The Mets hoped to make room for newcomer Howard Johnson. Responding to advice from batting coach Bill Robinson, Knight switched his batting stance from a crouch to a more upright position.

The result was a .298, 11-homer, 76-RBI season that won him NL Comeback Player of the Year honors. He also emerged as one of the young team's clubhouse leaders, along with first baseman Keith Hernandez and catcher Gary Carter.

That season the Mets coasted to an NL East title and overcame the Houston Astros to win the NLCS. In Game 6 of the World Series against the Red Sox, Knight committed a costly error, and it appeared responsibility for the Mets' loss would be on his shoulders. Fate intervened, however, in the form of teammate Mookie Wilson's ninth-inning groundball through Bill Buckner's legs, and Knight scored the winning run that forced a seventh game.

In Game 7 the Mets fell behind early, but Knight's seventh-inning solo homer off reliever Calvin Schiraldi gave New York the lead for good. "It was probably my greatest thrill in baseball," said Knight, and an amazing finish to what had begun as such a gloomy season. "I went in hearing things like they were going to eat my contract. I've lived with pressure all season, so this didn't seem like that much pressure to me. I was dealing with the fact my career might be over."

Knight had hit .391 for the Series with one home run and five RBIs, and he won the Series Most Valuable Player Award. He was hoping to parlay his honors into a two-year contract in the $1.5-to-2-million range, but the Mets offered the 34-year-old third baseman only one year at $800,000.

Knight decided not to take it. "They didn't want me back," said Knight. "I'm not blaming Davey (manager Davey Johnson). I'm talking about the front office. They tried to get rid of me in spring training.... I'd rather play somewhere else for less than come back to where I'm obviously not wanted."

As Met general manager Frank Cashen explained, "The fact is, Ray is coming off one good year that followed two bad years." Other clubs agreed. Knight had to sign with Baltimore for a price comparable to the figure New York had offered him. The Mets, meanwhile, went their underachieving way for the rest of the decade.

After retiring from the field, Knight went to work for ESPN. When Johnson took over as manager of the Reds in 1992, Knight returned to the game as a Cincinnati coach. He succeeded Johnson in 1996 and brought the Reds in third in the NL Central. He was fired the following year after the team posted a 43–56 record through July. Knight returned to ESPN as a broadcaster.

Chuck Knoblauch

Knoblauch, Edward Charles **2B**

1991–* B:7/7/1968, Houston, TX Deb:4/9/1991, MIN AL BR/TR 5'9", 181

G	AB	R	H	HR	RBI	OBP	SLG	AVG
1313	5145	950	1533	78	523	.391	.419	.298

Second baseman Chuck Knoblauch came to prominence with the Minnesota Twins in 1991 when he was named the American League's Rookie of the Year. He batted .281 with 25 steals as the Twins became the first team to go from last place to a world championship in one year. Knoblauch contributed to Minnesota's thrilling World Series win over Atlanta with a .308 Series average.

While the Twins sank in the standings as age, trades, and injuries broke up their veteran lineup, Knoblauch entered the prime of his own career. He hit .297 and made his first of four All-Star appearances in 1992, batted .312 with a league-high 45 doubles in 1994, and scored a club-record 140 runs in 1996.

Knoblauch signed a long-term contract with the Twins, but soon wanted out of Minnesota. In February 1998 he got his wish; Knoblauch was traded to the Yankees for four prospects and cash. He struggled through his first year in New York, batting a career-low .265 and suffering occasional defensive lapses. His most glaring gaffe came in Game 2 of the Championship Series when he failed to chase down a throw and argued for an interference call as the go-ahead run crossed the plate. The matter was glossed over, however, when the Yankees came back to win the ALCS. Knoblauch batted .375 in the World Series, including a game-tying home run in Game 1.

Knoblauch rebounded offensively in his second year in New York, batting .292 with 18 homers and 120 runs scored. He stole 28 bases, giving him 335 in nine seasons. His defensive play, however, continued to mystify. He seemed to have lost control over his throws, reduced to lobbing overhand rainbows to first base on easy plays. Just two years after winning a Gold Glove, Knoblauch committed 26 errors—the most of his professional career.

Bobby Knoop

Knoop, Robert Frank **2B**

1964–72 M(1994, 1–1) B:10/18/1938, Sioux City, IA Deb:4/13/1964, LA AL BR/TR, 6'1", 170

G	AB	R	H	HR	RBI	OBP	SLG	AVG
1153	3622	337	856	56	331	.298	.334	.236

Sportswriters of his time couldn't say enough about the fielding of Angels second baseman Bobby Knoop. From 1966 through 1968 he dominated the position in the American League and won the Gold Glove. He led the league in assists three times, and in 1966 set the major league record for putouts by a second baseman in one game with 12, and most double plays with six.

His career batting average, however, was only .236, the lowest lifetime average ever for a second baseman with more than 3,000 at bats. In addition, he struck out an inordinate 833 times in 3,622 at bats, including five straight 100-plus seasons. His best offensive year was in 1966 when he had career highs with 17 homers and 72 RBIs (and 144 Ks), as well as a league-leading 11 triples.

Knoop retired as a player in 1972. In 1977 and 1978 he coached for the White Sox, then spent several seasons coaching for the Angels.

Darold Knowles

Knowles, Darold Duane **P**
1965–80 B:12/9/1941, Brunswick, MO Deb:4/18/1965, BAL AL BL/TL, 6', 190

W	L	PCT	G	SV	IP	BB	SO	ERA
66	74	.471	765	143	1092	480	681	3.12

Though Darold Knowles pitched for eight major league clubs, he is best remembered for his relief role with Oakland in the early 1970s. The left-handed bookend to Rollie Fingers, Knowles set a record that can never be broken under current rules by pitching in all seven games of the 1973 World Series.

Knowles came up with Baltimore in 1965, played with Philadelphia for a year, pitched for Washington for four and a half more, and registered 27 saves in 1970. In May 1971 he was traded to Oakland.

In three-plus years with the A's, during which time the team won three division titles, he won 19 games and saved 30. His value to the team was even greater than his numbers. Knowles often served as a set-up man for Fingers; they each saved two games in the 1973 World Series. Knowles pitched in all seven games, threw 6 ⅓ innings, gave up no earned runs, and saved the deciding game.

After the 1974 season Knowles was traded to the Cubs for Billy Williams. Knowles later pitched for Texas, Montreal, and St. Louis before retiring at age 38 with a career total of 143 saves and a 66–74 record. He later became a pitching coach in the Cardinals organization.

Mark Koenig

Koenig, Mark Anthony **SS-3B-2B**
1925–36 B:7/19/1904, San Francisco, CA D:4/22/1993, Willows, CA Deb:9/8/1925 NY AL BB/TR 6', 180

G	AB	R	H	HR	RBI	OBP	SLG	AVG
1162	4271	572	1190	28	443	.316	.367	.279

Because so many experts regard the 1927 Yankees as the greatest baseball team of all time, fans tend to assume that every player on the team was a star. Certainly Babe Ruth, Lou Gehrig, Tony Lazzeri, Bob Meusel, Earle Combs, Herb Pennock, and Waite Hoyt—all members of the Hall of Fame—qualify. The team's shortstop, however, was at best, a journeyman.

Mark Koenig had no illusions about his contribution to the Bombers' success. "I was ordinary, a small cog in a big machine," he told an interviewer after he retired. "The Yankees could have had a midget at shortstop."

In fact, Koenig was a good hitter for a shortstop. In his first three full seasons with the Yankees, starting in 1926, he hit .271, .285, and .319. Usually batting second, he drove in 62 runs in each of his first two seasons and 63 in his third. Had his job been strictly to hit, he would have been a fine player. But shortstops are usually paid to field. Despite good range, he led all American League shortstops with 52 errors in 1926 and maintained the distinction with 47 the next year.

Ralph "Red" Kress, no Gold Glover either, wrested the error title from Koenig in 1928, primarily by playing in 25 more games, but Koenig put up a stout defense of his defenselessness by committing 49 miscues. In each of those seasons, the Yankees won pennants.

Koenig fielded no better in October. He committed four errors in the 1926 World Series loss to the Cardinals and two in the four-game Series sweep of the Redbirds in 1928; however, he got through the 1927 sweep of the Pirates without a bobble and hit .500 as well.

When the Yankees' bats began to show some age in 1929, Koenig's days in pinstripes were numbered. He hit .292, but Leo Durocher had become the regular shortstop. In 1930 Koenig was dealt to Detroit, where he tried several positions, including pitcher. By the beginning of 1932 he was playing in the Pacific Coast League.

That July, the Cubs were vying for a pennant when shortstop Billy Jurges was accidentally shot and wounded while preventing a fan's suicide. Chicago brought Koenig back up to substitute. In 33 games he batted .353, contributing mightily to the Cubs' successful drive for the flag. However, when it came time to divide the World Series money in a vote taken before the Series, the Cubs voted him only a half share.

In that year's World Series against New York, some of Koenig's old friends with the Yankees made snide observations about Chicago miserliness. Retaliatory comments ensued, and the verbal war escalated. Some believe that Babe Ruth's legendary "called shot" home run was in response to these salvos. Others, of course, deny that Ruth ever predicted his homer. Whatever the truth, Koenig appeared in two games and had one hit, a triple.

Despite the World Series brouhaha and subsequent sweep by the Yankees, Koenig remained a Cub the next season. He moved to the Reds in 1934 and spent his final two seasons with the New York Giants. His last appearance came in the 1936 World Series against the Yankees. Although much less controversial than the 1932 Series, it also ended with a Yankees win.

Ed Konetchy

Konetchy, Edward Joseph **1B**

1907–21 B:9/3/1885, La Crosse, WI D:5/27/1947, Ft. Worth, TX Deb:6/29/1907, STL NL BR/TR, 6'2½", 195

G	AB	R	H	HR	RBI	OBP	SLG	AVG
2085	7649	972	2150	75	992	.346	.403	.281

Ed Konetchy broke in with the St. Louis Cardinals in 1907, and in 1911 led the NL in doubles with 38 while batting .289. The year before he had a 20-game hitting streak and hit .302. He was also one of the few players ever to hit a ball out of old Robison Field in St. Louis.

In 1913 the Cardinals sent Konetchy to the Pittsburgh Pirates as part of an eight-player trade, and in 1915 he jumped to the Federal League where he had his best overall season, batting .314 with 10 homers and 93 RBIs for the rival Pittsburgh club. Back in the National League with the Brooklyn Dodgers in 1919, Konetchy became the third of eight NL players to achieve 10 consecutive hits. The following season he had the distinction of playing first base for the entire record-setting 26-inning game between the Dodgers and the Boston Braves.

In all, Konetchy batted over .300 four times and broke up four no-hitters. But Konetchy also made his mark in baseball with his defense. From 1910 until 1919 he led NL first basemen in fielding eight times.

Konetchy retired with a lifetime .281 average and a .990 fielding percentage in 2,085 games. He managed in the minors at both La Crosse, Wisconsin, and Fort Worth, and died in his sleep at age 61.

Jim Konstanty

Konstanty, Casimir James **P**

1944–56 B:3/2/1917, Strykersville, NY D:6/11/1976, Oneonta, NY Deb:6/18/1944, CIN NL BR/TR, 6'1½", 202

W	L	PCT	G	SV	IP	BB	SO	ERA
66	48	.579	433	74	945²	269	268	3.46

Jim Konstanty's major accomplishment was to bring the relief pitcher into the limelight. Although essentially a one-year wonder, his one year was so spectacular that it legitimized the reliever's role and set the stage for the glorification of the "closer."

A number of successful relievers came before Konstanty, such as Firpo Marberry, Johnny Murphy, Clint Brown, and Joe Page, but even the best ones were generally regarded as failed starters until Konstanty demonstrated the incalculable value of a reliable fireman. After his success the baseball establishment began to see the wisdom in training certain pitchers as relievers from the beginning.

The bespectacled Konstanty lettered in four sports at Syracuse University, graduating in 1939 with a degree in physical education. For several seasons he combined a minor league pitching career with duties as a high school coach. In 1944 he logged a 6–4 record as a starter with the Cincinnati Reds before entering the Navy, and in 1946 he pitched a few games for the Boston Braves. Yet, Konstanty was still essentially a minor league pitcher—neither his fastball nor his curve was of major league caliber.

Konstanty finally began to achieve some success after he mastered the palmball that he had learned at Syracuse from former major leaguer Ted Kleinhans. The addition of an effective slider completed his pitching repertoire.

He impressed Phillies manager Eddie Sawyer while pitching for Toronto of the International League. After Sawyer became Philadelphia manager in mid-1948, he called up the 31-year-old Konstanty late in the season to work out of the bullpen. In six appearances the 6-foot-2, 200-pound righthander won one game and saved two others. In 1949, as the Phillies' main fireman, he won nine and saved seven—a fine record for the time, as Ted Wilks of the Cardinals led the NL in saves with nine.

In 1950 the Phillies captured the NL pennant, only the second in their history. Called "the Whiz Kids" because of the number of young players on the team, their 33-year-old reliever was perhaps the most important contributor to their success. In 1950 Konstanty had a 16–7 record and 22 saves in 74 appearances. Although several modern relievers have since bettered these numbers, his wins and appearances set new major league records at the time, and his saves set a new league record. His 2.66 ERA for 152 innings was the second lowest in the league. At one point he pitched 23 consecutive scoreless innings before giving up a solo homer to Ralph Kiner, then went on to shut out the opposition for another 15 innings in a row. Named NL Most Valuable Player in 1950, he was the first relief pitcher to be so honored.

When injuries, overwork, and military call-ups left the Phillies short of starters, "Big Jim" was named the surprise starter for the first game of the 1950 World Series against the Yankees. Although he hadn't started a game in four years, he held the powerful Yankees to four hits and one run, only to lose as New York's Vic Raschi shut out Philadelphia.

Konstanty's performance during the next few seasons was relatively mediocre. In 1953 the 36-year-old veteran returned to the starter's role with some success, going 10–7 and 4–3 in relief. Back in the bullpen fulltime in 1954, he pitched reasonably well, but late in the season he was dealt to the Yankees. Konstanty made a bit of a comeback in 1955 as he won seven and collected 11 saves, but the Yankees decided to go with younger pitchers in 1956. Konstanty finished out that season with the St. Louis Cardinals, then retired.

Jerry Koosman

Koosman, Jerome Martin **P**

1967–85 B:12/23/1942, Appleton, MN Deb:4/14/1967, NY NL BR/TL, 6'2", 208

W	L	PCT	G	SH	IP	BB	SO	ERA
222	209	.515	612	33	3839[1]	1198	2556	3.36

The Mets discovered Jerry Koosman while he was pitching for the U.S. Army. He left the service in 1964 and signed with the team.

Koosman spent three years in the minors. In 1967, after he led the International League in strikeouts, he was brought up to hurl 22 innings for the big club. Despite two losses in his three starts, the Mets liked what they saw in the 26-year-old lefthander, and next spring he was in the starting rotation.

In his rookie year he caught fire, surpassing even sophomore Tom Seaver to become the winningest pitcher on the Mets staff. He won 19 games, tied an NL rookie record with seven shutouts, and posted an ERA of 2.08. He and Seaver both played in that year's All-Star Game, the first held indoors, and Koosman finished second to Johnny Bench in Rookie of the Year balloting.

The next season Koosman was again an All-Star. His 17 wins coupled with Seaver's 25 added up to a surprising NL pennant for the "Miracle Mets." In the World Series, Koosman hurled two of the team's four victories (to Seaver's single win) and posted a 2.04 ERA (to Seaver's 3.00).

For the next four years Koosman and Seaver formed the core of a pitching staff that kept the otherwise mediocre Mets in contention. In both 1970 and 1971 Koosman suffered serious injuries, but he was back in form by 1973, when the Mets took a very close NL East. In the postseason Koosman pitched a complete-game win against the Cincinnati Reds, and a Mets club that might have been even more miraculous than the 1969 team took the NL flag.

In Game 5 of the 1973 World Series, Koosman threw seven innings of shutout ball at the Oakland A's to take the win and give the Mets a 3–2 Series edge. By the end of the week, however, the A's had taken their second straight world championship. Nevertheless, Koosman had helped the Mets to the top once more.

From 1974 through 1976, with sluggers such as Rusty Staub and Dave Kingman providing offense, Koosman again posted winning numbers for the Mets. His 21 wins in 1976 marked his first 20-win season and tied Don Sutton of the Dodgers for second on the league's victory list.

In 1977 Seaver left for the Reds, Kingman and Staub were already gone, and the Mets weren't contenders. Koosman suffered, producing a miserable 8–20 record. The next year he won only three games. In 1979 Koosman was sent to the Minnesota Twins for Jesse Orosco. The new atmosphere brought him the second 20-win season of his career. At age 37 he still seemed to have the magic.

He pitched with the Twins until mid-1981, when he was traded to the Chicago White Sox. Again the change did him good, and he had two winning seasons as both a starter and middle reliever. Back in a starting role in 1983, Koosman helped the White Sox take the AL West, but saw limited action in their postseason defeat.

He finished his career with the Philadelphia Phillies, where in 1984 he had the honor of surrendering hit number 4,000 to Pete Rose. The Phillies released Koosman after the 1985 season. He later served as a Mets minor league pitching coach.

Sandy Koufax

Koufax, Sanford **P**

1955–66 B:12/30/1935, Brooklyn, NY Deb:6/24/1955, BRO NL BR/TL, 6'2", 210

W	L	PCT	G	SH	IP	BB	SO	ERA
165	87	.655	397	40	2324[1]	817	2396	2.76

If a manager today could pick any pitcher in his prime to win a game, Sandy Koufax might be the best choice. Armed with an explosive, rising fastball and a hard, sharp curve, Koufax was for five years the most overpowering southpaw since Lefty Grove. Hall of Famer Harry Hooper, who saw them both play, said that Koufax was the best ever. Teammate Claude Osteen once said, "You know how a guy fouls a ball straight back and you gasp, because he just missed it and is going to get the next one? With Koufax, they never got that next one."

From 1962 through 1966 Koufax went 111–34, winning a record five straight ERA crowns, setting numerous strikeout marks, and pitching four no-hitters. He retired at age 30 rather than risk a crippling injury to his arthritic pitching elbow, a condition that might have been alleviated today with arthroscopic surgery. Five years later Koufax became the youngest inductee into the Hall of Fame and only the fifth player selected in his first year of eligibility.

Born Sanford Braun in Brooklyn, Koufax took the name of his mother's second husband, an attorney she married before Sandy's third birthday. Koufax grew up playing ball in Jewish community clubs and school yards in postwar Brooklyn, where the neighborhood kids included future comedian Buddy Hackett and talk show host Larry King. Tall, with long arms and big hands, Koufax's first interest was basketball; he played baseball mainly to be with his basketball teammates during the off-season. He speculates that his arthritis may have been caused by banging his elbow against the metal basket supports on playground courts.

A light-hitting first baseman at Lafayette High School, where future New York Mets owner Fred Wilpon was the ace lefty, Koufax defends his coach for not making him a pitcher: "I wasn't one."

Former semipro pitcher Milt Laurie admired Koufax's whipping the ball around the infield as a sophomore and recruited him for his sandlot teams, which rode to games in Laurie's newspaper delivery truck. But Koufax went to the University of Cincinnati on a basketball scholarship, planning to become an architect. His freshman basketball coach doubled as the baseball coach, and Koufax volunteered for the squad when he learned that the team planned a spring trip to New Orleans. He fanned 51 batters in 32 innings and was scouted by major league teams when he was pitching for Laurie back in Brooklyn that summer.

Ambivalent about leaving college, Koufax insisted on a signing bonus equal to the remaining value of his scholarship. Under the prevailing rules Koufax would then have to remain on the major league active roster for two seasons rather than gain needed experience in the minors. After Al "Rube" Walker saw Koufax at an Ebbets Field workout he advised Dodgers management, "Whatever he wants, give it to him. I wouldn't let him get out of the clubhouse."

The Dodgers signed Koufax to a $14,000 bonus in December 1954 and put the 19-year-old on their 1955 roster. He did little more than mop up and practice "throwing to the strings," an outline of the strike zone invented to tame another Dodgers fireballer, Rex Barney. Koufax's return from a sprained ankle forced the Dodgers to demote another southpaw to the minors named Tom Lasorda. The future Dodgers manager would later brag, "It took the greatest lefthanded pitcher in the history of baseball to get me out of the majors."

Koufax didn't appear to be ready for the majors either. In his first Dodgers start he walked eight men in 4 ⅔ innings. The next time he started, however, he threw a complete-game two-hit shutout with 14 strikeouts. Koufax made history twice in Brooklyn, first with his dubious achievement of fanning 12 times in 12 consecutive plate appearances in 1955, a record that still stands. He was also the last pitcher to throw a pitch for Brooklyn, on September 29, 1957, before the team relocated to Los Angeles.

His career in Los Angeles began with three more years of inconsistency. Intimations of greatness solidified in 1959 when Koufax fanned 18 Giants at the Coliseum on August 31, tying Bob Feller's major league record. Added to the 13 he had struck out in his previous outing, this gave him the major league record for strikeouts in consecutive starts.

He fanned 10 Cubs in 10 innings in his following start, a loss, thus setting a major league record for strikeouts in three games. More significantly, perhaps, Koufax hurled three straight complete games for the first time. Earning a start in the World Series against the Chicago White Sox, he allowed just one run over seven innings, but took the 1–0 loss.

Koufax felt he'd made the transition from mere thrower to pitcher in 1960 when he posted the lowest opponents batting average in the league, a category he led for six straight seasons, and struck out more batters than innings pitched for the third time in four years. On the other hand, he was so frustrated by his 8–13 record that he nearly quit baseball to sell lighting fixtures. He also asked the Dodgers to trade him, but general manager Buzzy Bavasi shrugged it off, saying, "We stayed with you this long, we might as well keep you."

Koufax owed his breakthrough in 1961 to the benevolent intervention of several individuals. In one workout, when catcher Norm Sherry and part-time scout Kenny Meyers asked the pitcher to throw to a spot, they realized that his motion obstructed his vision. Together with pitching coach Joe Becker, they convinced Koufax to adopt a more compact, deliberate motion, improving his control and shaping the classic Koufax delivery pose: back knee about to scrape the mound and front knee flexed, planted straight toward the batter; torso fully upright and twisted; arm held high and cocked at the elbow.

Koufax cites a number of other reasons for his remarkable transformation: changing his grip on his curve to get it to break away from lefthanded hitters, studying pitching strategies with pioneer Dodgers statistician Allan Roth, and even a bout with tonsillitis that changed his conditioning routine. Or, the impetus may simply have been that three straight years of pitching regularly and nearly 700 major league innings gave Koufax the experience necessary to become successful.

In 1961 Koufax won six consecutive complete games starting in late May, and was named to the first of six straight All-Star teams. He also closed his second Dodger ballpark, the Los Angeles Coliseum, with a 13-inning, 205-pitch, seven-hit complete game, fanning 15 in a 3–2 win over the Cubs. After an early knockout four days later, he went the distance in his final outing of the sea-

son, a 2–1 loss at Philadelphia, but accumulated seven strikeouts to break Christy Mathewson's 58-year-old NL record with 269 for the season.

The next year Koufax tied the single-game strikeout record with 18 against the Cubs on April 24, but in his next start he began to suffer from circulatory problems in the index finger of his left hand. As the finger became swollen, blue, numb, and infected, Koufax inexplicably pitched even better, going 6–2 with four earned runs in eight starts covering 67 ⅓ innings on his way to the first of five straight NL ERA titles.

One of the season's highlights was Koufax's first no-hitter, on June 30 at Dodger Stadium, a 13-strikeout, 5–0 win over the Mets. Koufax fanned the side on nine pitches in the first inning, the first time that had been done in the National League since 1924. But the sore finger eventually knocked him out of action from mid-July to mid-September, and the Dodgers' comfortable lead over the Giants dwindled. The teams finished the regular season tied for first. After three brief tune-ups, Koufax lasted only two batters into the second inning of the playoff opener against the Giants, giving up the first three runs in an 8–0 loss.

Koufax rebounded in 1963 with his first of three pitching Triple Crowns, leading the National League in wins, ERA, and strikeouts. The triumphant season culminated in the first-ever World Series celebration at Dodger Stadium. No NL pitcher has posted more wins with a better winning percentage than his 25–5, .833 log in that year. He set a modern major league record for southpaws with 11 shutouts, the most in the majors since Grover Alexander's 16 in 1916; Koufax's last whitewash was an 87-pitch four-hitter at St. Louis.

Without his best stuff, at least according to Koufax, he no-hit the Giants in Los Angeles on May 11. The Dodgers' anemic offense generally allowed little margin for error. Informed that Koufax had pitched a no-hitter, fellow Dodgers pitcher Don Drysdale cracked, "Did he win?" That year Koufax became the first National Leaguer to fan 300 batters, and allowed a league-low eight baserunners per nine innings.

Matched against Whitey Ford at Yankee Stadium in the opener of the first bicoastal Yankees-Dodgers World Series, Koufax fanned the first five Yankees hitters. One Yankee admitted, "After I saw him strike out Bobby Richardson (New York's second batter), I knew we were in trouble." "Koo," as the New York tabloids christened him, struck out 15 that day, breaking the World Series record set by Carl Erskine 10 years earlier to the day, and went all the way in a six-hit win.

Four days later he threw another six-hitter with eight strikeouts, downing Ford, 2–1, to complete the Dodgers' sweep. Koufax was the first unanimous choice for the Cy Young Award (at that time there was only one award for both major leagues) and was also voted NL Most Valuable Player.

Now established as the dominant lefthander in baseball, Koufax started his first Dodgers opener in 1964, a six-hit shutout of the Cardinals. In his second start, on April 18, he fanned three Reds on nine pitches in the third inning. On June 4 he tied Bob Feller's record with his third no-hitter in as many seasons, a 27-up, 27-down gem at Philadelphia with 12 strikeouts. The only base runner, Richie Allen, reached on a walk and was caught stealing. The no-hitter was the second victory in a two-month, 11-game win streak that was broken only by four unearned runs in the ninth inning of the 12th game.

After winning six straight starts Koufax took a no decision in a nine-inning effort against the Giants, fanning 10 to break another Feller record with his 55th 10-strikeout game. He had a 19–5 season by August 16, including seven shutouts, but he banged his left elbow on the ground when diving back into second base and did not pitch again that year. The jolt triggered his arthritis.

Koufax and his doctors had no idea what to expect in 1965. The original plan had been to use Koufax every seventh day, but he resisted becoming a "Sunday pitcher." He abandoned his slider and his sidearm deliveries to lefthanders. Neither had been prominent in his pitching arsenal because they aggravated his elbow. But he continued to experiment with a forkball, a natural fit for his enormous fingers. He also stopped throwing between starts but returned to the habit later in the season, even making a pair of late-season relief appearances on his throwing day.

The result was a 26–8 record and a second unanimous Cy Young selection. Koufax again won the pitching Triple Crown, setting new major league strikeout records with 382, as well as twenty-one 10-strikeout games (both surpassed by Nolan Ryan in 1973). Koufax completed a league-best 27 games, including eight shutouts, and ran off another 11-game winning streak.

On September 9 at Los Angeles he threw his record fourth no-hitter, a 14-strikeout perfect game over the Cubs in the middle of a pennant race, besting Bob Hendley's one-hitter. The punchless Dodgers got their run without a hit: Lou Johnson

walked, was sacrificed to second, stole third, and continued home on a wild throw. Koufax capped his season with the pennant clincher, a four-hit, 13-strikeout complete game over the Braves on the next-to-the-last day of the season.

The World Series against the Minnesota Twins was scheduled to begin on October 6, which was also Yom Kippur, the most important day on the Jewish calendar. Koufax spent the day at services in St. Paul while the Dodgers lost, 8–2, behind Drysdale. Koufax started and lost Game 2, with a two-base error by third baseman Jim Gilliam setting up a two-run sixth inning for the Twins.

But in Game 5 Koufax threw a four-hit shutout and drove in a run with a single, his only World Series hit. Writer Dick Young lost a box of cigars on a bet when manager Walt Alston pitched Koufax on two days' rest instead of Drysdale in Game 7, and the Dodgers won their second World Series crown in three years. Koufax shut out the Twins on three hits, fanning 10 in a 2–0 win.

That year Koufax and Drysdale had combined for 50 wins including the Series and had set a new NL teammate strikeout record, breaking their own figure set in 1963. They followed up their performance by hiring an agent and staging a joint holdout before the 1966 season. Buzzy Bavasi long regretted not throwing the agent out of his office, but the maneuver proved successful, winning Koufax a record $130,000 contract and a six-figure paycheck for Drysdale as well.

Koufax earned his money in 1966 with a second straight Triple Crown, another unanimous Cy Young selection, and another second place in MVP voting. His 27 wins set an NL record for southpaws, matched by Steve Carlton in 1972, and included the pennant clincher on the final day of the season. Koufax again led the league in innings pitched, complete games, and shutouts. He added 16 more 10-strikeout games for a career total of 98, surpassed only by Nolan Ryan. Koufax and Ryan are also the only pitchers to average better than one strikeout an inning with more than 1,500 innings pitched.

Koufax started Game 2 of the 1966 World Series against the Baltimore Orioles and fell behind on center fielder Willie Davis's three fifth-inning errors, leading to three unearned runs. Jim Palmer threw a shutout against the Dodgers. The loss to Palmer was Koufax's final outing; he announced his retirement in November. Koufax retired with a 0.95 World Series ERA, the best for any pitcher with 50 or more innings.

He stayed in the game as a broadcaster for six seasons and continues to instruct Dodger hopefuls every year at spring training in Vero Beach, Florida. To this day people still refer to fireballing pitching phenoms as having a "Koufax fastball."

Ed Kranepool

Kranepool, Edward Emil **1B-OF**

1962–79 B:11/8/1944, New York, NY Deb:9/22/1962, NY NL BL/TL, 6'3", 215

G	AB	R	H	HR	RBI	OBP	SLG	AVG
1853	5436	536	1418	118	614	.319	.377	.261

An original New York Met, Ed Kranepool signed with New York's expansion team out of James Madison High in the Bronx for $85,000 in 1962 and wound up playing for them at the end of their maiden season. He proceeded to play parts of every Mets season through 1979, after which he retired with a career .261 average and 118 homers in 1,853 games.

Kranepool's best season was 1971 when he batted .280 with a career-high 14 homers and 58 RBIs and led NL first basemen in fielding (.998). Although his signing as a 17-year-old was a much-ballyhooed event in New York, Kranepool never quite lived up to his high school press clippings.

When he hadn't yet developed into a major league star by the age of 19, he was the subject of an absurd New York newspaper headline that asked: "Is Kranepool over the hill?"

After his first six years as a pro, including the Mets' championship season of 1969, Kranepool was briefly sent to the minors and considered retiring. But he came back to have his best season in 1971, then embarked on a second career as a pinch-hitting specialist. From 1974 through 1978, he batted .396 as a pinch hitter, including a major league-leading .486 (17 pinch hits in all) in 1974. He was the last original Met on the team when he retired in 1979. "Steady Eddie" walked away from Shea Stadium as the leader in several club records, including most games (1,853). Upon retiring, Kranepool remained a part of the New York scene as a stockbroker.

Lew Krausse

Krausse, Lewis Bernard, Jr. **P**

1961, 1964–74 B:4/25/1943, Media, PA Deb:6/16/1961, KAN AL BR/TR 5'11", 186

W	L	PCT	G	SH	IP	BB	SO	ERA
68	91	.434	321	5	1283²	493	721	4.00

After several years struggling to make the major leagues, Lew Krausse, whose father had pitched briefly for Connie Mack's Philadelphia Athletics in the 1930s, finally proved himself on the mound when he won 14 games for the Kansas City Athletics in 1966. During the following season, however, Krausse found himself in the center of a controversy away from the field. After an early August road game in Boston, the team caught a flight back to Kansas City. When the plane landed, one of the flight attendants claimed that Krausse had harassed her, a charge he vehemently denied.

When the story reached A's owner Charlie Finley a few weeks later, he suspended the pitcher. Several players as well as manager Alvin Dark spoke out in defense of Krausse. Finley responded by firing Dark, which prompted a full-fledged revolt by the players. Veteran outfielder Ken Harrelson called Finley a "menace to baseball." Finley, who served as his own general manager, promptly gave Harrelson his release.

With Krausse's eventual reinstatement, the furor died down. He went on to an unspectacular pitching career, highlighted by the distinction in 1970 of starting the first game in Milwaukee Brewers history. He lost, 12–0, the first of 97 losses by the team that season.

Mike Kreevich

Kreevich, Michael Andreas **OF**

1931–45 B:6/10/1908, Mt. Olive, IL D:4/25/1994, Pana, IL Deb:9/7/1931, CHI NL BR/TR, 5'7½", 168

G	AB	R	H	HR	RBI	OBP	SLG	AVG
1241	4676	676	1321	45	514	.346	.391	.283

Diminutive outfielder Mike Kreevich was a promising rookie in 1936 and an All-Star in 1938. He is most noted for his fine defensive skills—as well as for two records he holds.

Kreevich shares the record with several other players for most doubles in a game. On September 4, 1937, he collected four while with the White Sox. Unfortunately, he also shares the major league record for grounding into the most double plays in a game. Still with the White Sox on August 4, 1939, Kreevich hit into four, tying the record set by Goose Goslin and later equaled by Joe Torre.

Because he had two children born before Pearl Harbor, Kreevich was draft-exempt and able to continue his baseball career during World War II. Nonetheless, a drinking problem caused him to be released by the A's following the 1942 season. Picked up as a rehabilitation project by St. Louis Browns manager Luke Sewell, he was a key component of 1944's pennant-winning club. In 1945, Kreevich lost playing time to Pete Gray, the fabled one-armed outfielder. He was waived to Washington and retired soon after.

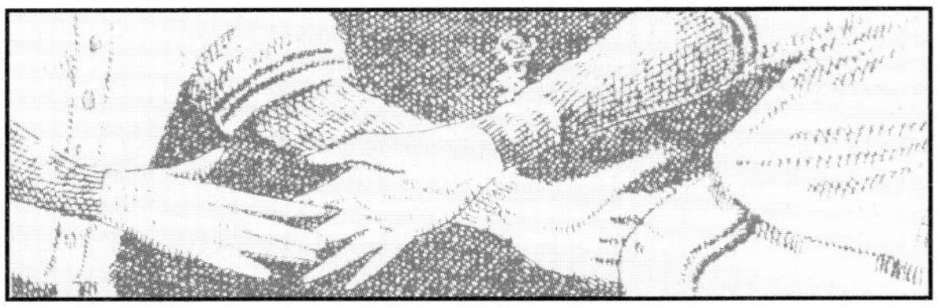

Ray Kremer

Kremer, Remy Peter **P**

1924–33 B:3/23/1893, Oakland, CA D:2/8/1965, Pinole, CA Deb:4/18/1924, PIT NL BR/TR, 6'1", 190

W	L	PCT	G	SH	IP	BB	SO	ERA
143	85	.627	308	14	1954[2]	483	516	3.76

Ray "Wiz" Kremer won Games 6 and 7 of the 1925 World Series for the Pirates. The righthander had a lifetime record of 143–85 and twice led the NL in both wins and ERA.

Kremer spent seven seasons with Oakland in the Pacific Coast League before moving up to the majors. In one of those years he went to spring training with the Giants but did not make the club.

Late in the 1923 season Pirates owner Barney Dreyfuss sent Manager Bill McKechnie to the West Coast to look at Willie Kamm. Kamm was in the process of being sold to the White Sox, however, and McKechnie recommended that the Pirates sign Kremer. The Pirates bought him from Oakland for two players and $15,000.

A heavy drinker, Kremer looked older than his 31 years. Management told McKechnie he had made a mistake in signing a 50-year-old.

"If he's 60, he's still a good pitcher," McKechnie shot back. Kremer was 18–10 in his first season.

In 1925, after going 17–8, Kremer started and completed two games in the World Series against Washington. He lost Game 3 by the score of 4–3 and won Game 6, 3–2. In the seventh contest he was called on to pitch in the fifth inning with Washington ahead, 6–4. Kremer held the Senators to one run the rest of the way, and Roger Peckinpaugh, the Washington shortstop, made two errors that the Pirates turned into five runs to win the championship. In both 1926 and 1927 Kremer led the league in ERA. He lost the opening game of the 1927 World Series to the Yankees, 5–4, as New York scored three unearned runs in the third inning.

Off the field Kremer was a volatile personality who, in an intoxicated state, once wrecked a Pullman car and threw teammates' shoes out the window. Twice a 20-game winner, he achieved a 3.76 lifetime ERA.

Red Kress

Kress, Ralph **SS-1B-3B-OF**

1927–46 B:1/2/1907, Columbia, CA D:11/29/1962, Los Angeles, CA Deb:9/24/1927, STL AL BR/TR, 5'11½", 165

G	AB	R	H	HR	RBI	OBP	SLG	AVG
1391	5087	691	1454	89	799	.347	.420	.286

In his prime, Ralph "Red" Kress was a wide-ranging fielder who hit unusually well for a shortstop.

Kress began his professional career in 1927 with Tulsa, where he was dubbed "the Boy Wonder of the Western League." By season's end he had replaced Jim Levey as the

St. Louis Browns' shortstop. In 1928 the 21-year-old Kress hit .273 and led the league in both assists and errors.

In 1929 Kress came into his own, hitting .305 with 107 RBIs and leading all shortstops in fielding percentage. In 1930 he batted .313 with 16 homers and 112 RBIs and again led the league in errors. Moved to third base in 1931, he hit .311 with 114 RBIs and slammed another 16 home runs.

The following season Kress was traded to the White Sox and played a variety of positions. In 1934 he was swapped to the Senators, but he never matched his early offensive performance and was farmed out to the minor leagues after the 1936 season. Kress spent 1937 in Minneapolis, where he led the American Association with 157 RBIs.

The Red Sox drafted Kress but traded him back to St. Louis before the 1938 season. He hit .302 that year but in 1939 was dealt to Detroit. After being released by the Tigers in 1940, Kress returned to the minors and began a new career as a pitcher. On September 22, 1945, he pitched 8⅓ innings of no-hit ball for Baltimore in the International League playoffs, but lost, 1–0, in the ninth inning. Kress went on to manage in Sacramento, Superior, El Centro, Juarez, and Daytona Beach before coaching for the Giants, Indians, and Mets.

Ray Kroc

Kroc, Ray A.

Owner (1974–83)B:10/2/1902, Chicago, IL D:1/14/1984, San Diego, CA

Ray Kroc, multimillionaire chief of the McDonald's hamburger chain, didn't take long to make his presence felt in baseball after he became the new owner of the San Diego Padres. Watching the Opening Day game in 1974, he became increasingly frustrated by the exhibition his new team was putting on. His patience disappeared when he saw a Padres runner doubled off first base on a foul popup.

Kroc was headed for the public-address system microphone to convey a few ill-chosen words to the Jack Murphy Stadium crowd when suddenly a streaker sped across the outfield grass. Now Kroc was really incensed. "Get that streaker out of here!" he screamed into the microphone. "Arrest that man! Get the police!"

Kroc then got down to business. "This is Ray Kroc speaking," he began. First he told the fans that he had some good news: The crowd at Jack Murphy Stadium was larger than the one in Los Angeles the night before. Then he laid it on his team. "The bad news is that we are putting on a lousy show for you. I apologize for it. I'm disgusted with it. This is the most stupid baseball playing I've ever seen!"

Kroc's performance was widely denounced. "Who does he think he's talking to," complained Astros third baseman Doug Rader, "a bunch of short-order cooks?" Not one to miss a promotional opportunity, Kroc retaliated by saying that Rader had insulted all short-order cooks and announced that all fans wearing chef's hats to the next evening's game would be admitted free. Thousands showed up in that headgear, and at home plate before game time Rader was presented with one.

Kroc was a high school dropout who took over the McDonald Brothers hamburger stand in San Bernardino, California, and made it into a billion-dollar-a-year business. In 1974 Kroc purchased the Padres from banker C. Arnholt Smith for $11 million. He gave all front-office employees raises and over the years invested heavily in such free agents as pitcher Rollie Fingers, outfielder-designated hitter Oscar Gamble, and catcher-infielder Gene Tenace, but the Padres invariably finished in the second division. Kroc continued to criticize his players, categorizing them as "idiots" when they did not produce. In 1977 he succeeded Buzzy Bavasi as Padres president.

In 1979 Commissioner Bowie Kuhn fined Kroc $100,000 for tampering after he had publicly vowed to pursue Graig Nettles and Joe Morgan in the free-agent market. "They can shove it," said Kroc. "I've been disillusioned by everyone I've met [in baseball]. There's a lot more future in hamburgers than baseball." The incident caused Kroc to distance himself from the baseball business and put the Padres in the hands of son-in-law Ballard Smith Jr.

In November 1980 Kroc and his wife Joan conducted an alcoholism seminar for Major League Baseball at their ranch in the Santa Ynez Mountains and created an organization called CORK to battle the problem of alcohol abuse in professional baseball. Kroc died of heart failure in San Diego on January 14, 1984. Only 10 months later, his team won its first NL championship.

John Kruk

Kruk, John Martin **1B–OF**

1986–95 B:2/9/1961, Charleston, WV Deb:4/7/1986, SD NL BL/TL 5'10", 204

G	AB	R	H	HR	RBI	OBP	SLG	AVG
1200	3897	582	1170	100	592	.400	.446	.300

John Kruk's autobiography was titled *I Ain't an Athlete, Lady.* One writer claimed that "Kruk's body looks like a third helping of mashed potatoes." The burly West Virginia native encouraged all the jokes, yet despite appearances he was quite athletic. He played point guard on his high school basketball team, albeit a few pounds lighter, and proved more than adequate playing first base or the outfield in the major leagues. Kruk prided himself on being a throwback—aggressive on the field, irreverent off.

Batting over .300 in his first two seasons with the San Diego Padres, Kruk gained immediate notice. When he struggled mightily in his third season, Kruk blamed it on the temperate San Diego weather. When his batting average continued to slide the following year, he was traded to the Phillies. The fans in Philadelphia loved his attitude, and he returned the compliment by recovering his hitting stroke. Kruk became a key member of the 1993 team that won the National League pennant. He batted .348 in the World Series, although the Phillies lost to Toronto in six games.

Kruk was selected to play in the All-Star Game three times, and will be long remembered for his three token swings at the same number of Randy Johnson fastballs in the 1993 game. The 6-foot 10-inch pitcher was overpowering, and after Kruk struck out he turned to Johnson and made a grand bow of respect. Afterwards Kruk said, "I wasn't going to let him hit me while I was stationary. It would be embarrassing to die on national TV."

Prior to the 1994 season, Kruk underwent surgery for testicular cancer. He made a full recovery, but it was his aching knees that forced him to retire a year later. Consistent to the end, Kruk went out on his own terms, retiring in the middle of a game after fulfilling his desire to get one more hit.

Mike Krukow

Krukow, Michael Edward **P**

1976–89 B:1/21/1952, Long Beach, CA Deb:9/6/1976, CHI NL BR/TR 6'5", 205

W	L	PCT	G	SH	IP	BB	SO	ERA
124	117	.515	369	10	2190^{1}	763	1478	3.90

Mike Krukow had the classic build of a power pitcher; unfortunately, he lacked the classic blazing fastball that went with it. Control, not power, led Krukow to five double-digit-victory seasons in his 14-year career. In 1986, his only 20-win season, Krukow struck out more than three batters for every walk he issued. In later years, however, the ratio was closer to two to one, and his record was closer to .500.

Krukow was .500 or worse in four of his five seasons with the Chicago Cubs. Dealt to Philadelphia in 1982, he responded with 13 wins and a 3.12 ERA. He was traded again over the winter, this time to San Francisco. Krukow posted an unremarkable 30–34 mark in his first three years as a Giant, but responded with a 20–9 record in 1986. His numbers plummeted the following year, even as the Giants raced to a division title. Given an opportunity for redemption in the playoffs, he delivered a complete-game win in Game 4 of the Championship Series against the St. Louis Cardinals. San Francisco ultimately lost the series in seven games. Following his retirement, Krukow became a broadcaster for the Giants.

Tony Kubek

Kubek, Anthony Christopher **SS–OF**

1957–65 B:10/12/1936, Milwaukee, WI Deb:4/20/1957, NY AL BL/TR, 6'3", 191

G	AB	R	H	HR	RBI	OBP	SLG	AVG
1092	4167	522	1109	57	373	.305	.364	.266

As a player, Tony Kubek is best remembered for a bad-hop groundball that hit him in the throat during a World Series game. When his playing career ended, he used that throat to become one of the better announcers in the game.

The son of Tony Kubek Sr., who played for the Milwaukee Brewers of the American Association, the younger Kubek was talented enough with the glove to play short, second, third, and the outfield. Master strategist Casey Stengel enjoyed moving him around the diamond, often during the same game, yet it didn't have an adverse effect on Kubek's career. An immediate star with the Yankees, in 1957 he hit .297 to help the team win the pennant and was named Rookie of the Year.

Playing against the Braves in the first World Series game played in his hometown, Kubek crushed two homers in Game 3 to lead the Yanks to a 12–3 win. He started games at third base, left, and center as the Bronx Bombers lost in seven. A year later Kubek was the starting shortstop as the Yankees won in seven games, again versus the Braves.

Kubek's most infamous World Series moment happened in Game 7 of the 1960 Fall Classic. With the Yankees up 7–4 in the last of the eighth, Gino Cimoli was on first when Bucs outfielder Bill Virdon slapped a double play groundball at Kubek. Kubek may have been tentative because the day before he had fumbled a Cimoli grounder for his third error of the Series. He moved in toward the ball just as it took a bad hop off the notoriously rocky Forbes Field infield and struck him in the Adam's apple. He went down, coughing blood, and the Pirates took advantage of their good fortune to score five runs and went on to win on Bill Mazeroski's home run.

Kubek recovered to start his second All-Star

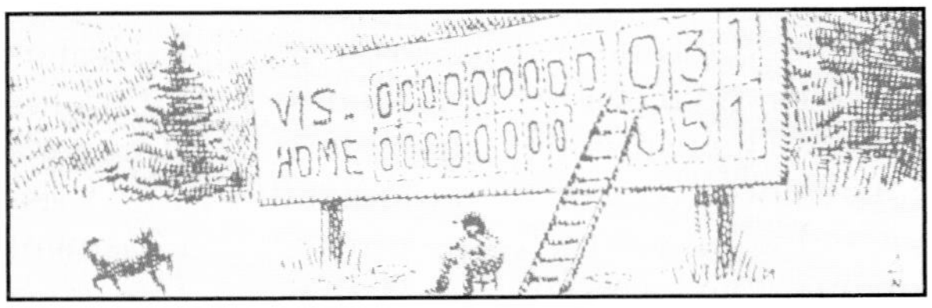

Game in 1961, and in 1962 he topped .300 for the only time in his career. Dissatisfied with his play in 1965, he went to the Mayo Clinic and was told he had three fused vertebrae in his back. Whether it was from an army injury, touch football, or the Virdon grounder, no one could say for sure, but Kubek was told that a collision might result in paralysis. The day he announced his retirement, an NBC executive asked him to audition for a job as a broadcaster.

Behind the mike, Kubek's love for the game, his player's sensibility, and his willingness to express strong opinions shone through. After three years of working the network backup Game of the Week, Kubek replaced Pee Wee Reese as Curt Gowdy's partner for the primary game. With future partners such as Joe Garagiola and Bob Costas, he become a network and fan favorite, and later announced for the Yankees and Brewers.

Harvey Kuenn

Kuenn, Harvey Edward **OF-SS-3B**

1952–1966 M(1975–1983, 160–118) B:12/4/1930, West Allis, WI D:2/28/1988, Peoria, AZ Deb:9/6/1952, DET AL BR/TR 6'2", 190

G	AB	R	H	HR	RBI	OBP	SLG	AVG
1833	6913	951	2092	87	671	.359	.408	.303

An aggressive player capable of making the spectacular play and muffing the easy one, Harvey Kuenn won Rookie of the Year honors in the American League in 1953 and played on six All-Star teams. The righthanded batter led the league in hits four times and doubles three times, and in 1959 was tops in batting when he hit .353. He returned to his native Milwaukee as a coach and manager and in 1982 led the Brewers to the World Series.

Baseball was in his blood. Kuenn's father, a shipping clerk, was city batting champion in 1945 when Kuenn was 14 years old. Detroit scouts spotted the younger Kuenn after he transferred from a Lutheran college to the University of Wisconsin. Tigers farm director John McHale explained later, "One of the big things we liked about him when we were scouting him in college was his aggressiveness. He was captain of the team, and he was always on top of the game."

Signed for a $55,000 bonus, Kuenn muffed a ball in the 11th inning of his first major league start to lose the game, but he quickly recovered and was on his way to earning his Rookie of the Year Award in 1953. Tigers owner Walter O. Briggs Jr. liked Kuenn's spunk. "In his rookie year Kuenn made one of the darnedest plays I ever saw," Briggs recalled. "It was a diving catch of a low line drive over second base. He actually stood on his head to make it. When he bounced back on his feet, the only part of his uniform that had any dirt on it was the top of his cap."

An adventurer at shortstop, Kuenn was also a natural hitter with the ability to think at the plate. "He's the only hitter I know who can change his mind three or four times while the ball is on its way to the plate," said former Brewers pitcher Don McMahon.

In April 1960 the Tigers traded batting champ Kuenn to Cleveland for slugger Rocky Colavito; Kuenn later played for the Giants and the Cubs and was converted to the outfield. He has the dubious distinction of making the last out in two of Sandy Koufax's no-hitters.

Kuenn retired after the 1966 season and suffered through a series of medical procedures including a heart bypass, colon removal, and the amputation of a leg in 1980 after doctors discovered that he had a blood clot. In 1971 he returned to Milwaukee as a coach, and in June 1982 he replaced Buck Rodgers as Milwaukee manager. Kuenn's team went 72–43 the rest of the way and beat California in the AL Championship Series, but they lost a seven-game World Series to the Cardinals. Kuenn was fired at the end of the 1983 season after the Brewers finished fifth.

Joe Kuhel

Kuhel, Joseph Anthony **1B**

1930–47 M(1948–49, 106–201) B:6/25/1906, Cleveland, OH D:2/26/1984, Kansas City, KS Deb:7/31/1930, WAS AL BL/TL, 6', 180

G	AB	R	H	HR	RBI	OBP	SLG	AVG
2104	7984	1236	2212	131	1049	.359	.406	.277

When the Chicago White Sox traded first baseman Zeke Bonura to the Washington Senators for Joe Kuhel in 1938, Sox fans were up in arms.

The popular, flamboyant Bonura hit from the right side and held the Sox' home run record, but he fielded like an innocent bystander who didn't want to become involved. By contrast, the quiet, hard-working Kuhel was a lefthanded singles hitter who was also the best-fielding first baseman in the American League. Although the debate over which team got the better deal raged on Chicago's South Side for years, it was really no contest. Bonura lasted only one season in Washington before being packed off to another team. Kuhel, meanwhile, gave the White Sox the slickest first base play they had ever seen and hit with surprising power.

Kuhel spent three seasons with Kansas City of the American Association, hitting better than .300 each year. He was in the middle of a .372 season in 1930 when the Senators decided to give him a try. In 18 games he hit .286, not a high average for that era, and he began the 1931 season back in the minors. He soon returned to Washington, where he replaced Joe Judge, the Senators' first baseman since 1916. Kuhel's smooth glovework made up for an ordinary bat, and by his second season as a regular his batting average began to rise.

In 1933 Kuhel had perhaps his best season, batting .322, driving home 107 runs, and leading the league's first basemen in fielding percentage. Washington won the AL pennant but lost the World Series to the New York Giants in five games.

During the next several seasons Kuhel's fielding continued to sparkle, although his batting performance fluctuated wildly. In 1935 Kuhel hit only .261, but he rebounded in 1936 to hit .321 with 118 RBIs. In 1938 he took another tumble as his RBI total fell off to 61. He was never chosen for the All-Star Game, an understandable omission in a league that included first basemen such as Lou Gehrig, Jimmie Foxx, and Hank Greenberg.

Despite White Sox fans' initial animosity, Kuhel eventually won them over. His fielding was a revelation to spectators used to Bonura's indifference. He also improved his hitting during his first three years in a Chicago uniform, batting .300 and hitting 15 home runs in 1939. The next year he tied Bonura's club record with 27 home runs, the highest total of his career.

After that his hitting went into steady decline. In 1944 he was sold back to Washington, where he finished out the war years. He then returned to the White Sox in 1946, made only three appearances in 1947, and became manager of the White Sox farm club in Hot Springs, Arkansas, of the Cotton States League.

In 1948 Kuhel was named manager of the Washington Senators, who had finished a well deserved seventh the year before. They again finished seventh in Kuhel's first year and then lost 104 games and dropped to eighth. After Kuhel was fired in 1949, he philosophically remarked, "You can't make chicken salad out of chicken feathers." He managed the Kansas City Blues of the American Association for a year, then went into sales in Kansas City.

Bowie Kuhn

Kuhn, Bowie K.

Commissioner (1968–84) B:10/28/1926, Washington, D.C.

Despite his many mistakes in office, history may well remember Bowie Kuhn as the last true commissioner of baseball in the Judge Kenesaw Landis tradition. His solemn oath to return Major League Baseball to Washington was politically motivated and didn't hold water. The logic behind his voiding of deals "in the best interests of the game" seemed specious at times. Kuhn's banning of Mickey Mantle and Willie Mays from Organized Baseball because of their work as gladhanders at casinos was an overreaction, and he underestimated the impact of Major League Baseball Players Association (MLBPA) head Marvin Miller on the future of the game until it was far too late.

Whatever else may be said of Kuhn, he was a true fan of the game. As a youth he worked at Washington's Griffith Stadium, changing the numbers on the scoreboard during Senators games; he later said that it was the best job of his life. In his first job as a lawyer, with Wilkie Farr & Gallagher, he asked to work on the Major League Baseball account and went on to spend 19 years defending baseball against antitrust suits.

When the owners threw General William "Spike" Eckert out of the commissioner's post in 1968, they were stuck for a replacement. A 19-ballot marathon meeting left them hopelessly deadlocked between Yankees president Mike Burke and future NL president Charles Feeney. Kuhn was offered the job on a one-year interim basis; he would be responsible for restructuring the way baseball conducted its business while the owners continued to seek a real commissioner. Kuhn stayed for 15 years.

Even though Kuhn was never a players' commissioner, as Landis had been and A.B. "Happy" Chandler had tried to be, he certainly didn't back down from fights with owners. Kuhn took on A's owner Charlie Finley dozens of times. Kuhn stepped in when Finley tried to embarrass young talents Reggie Jackson and Vida Blue.

But Finley's most grievous public offense was his attempt to fire Mike Andrews during the 1973 World Series. After the second baseman made two errors that helped the Mets to a victory, Finley fabricated a story that Andrews was injured. Finley cowed the player into signing a letter in which the team doctor asserted he had a "cronic" (sic) shoulder problem, and then Finley sent him packing. Kuhn reinstated Andrews and fined Finley.

When arbitrator Peter Seitz ruled that the Basic Agreement did not bind a player to one team forever, thereby opening the door to free agency, Finley tried to exploit his superstars before they left town. He sold Vida Blue to the Yankees for $1.5 million and Joe Rudi and Rollie Fingers to the Red Sox for $1 million each. Kuhn put a halt to that and to a subsequent Finley "trade" of Blue to the Reds for Dave Revering and $1.75 million. Finley called Kuhn "the village idiot," later modifying the epithet to "the global idiot."

Kuhn was not afraid to pick on more powerful owners, either. After Yankee boss George

Steinbrenner pleaded guilty to felony charges of illegal contributions to Richard Nixon, Kuhn suspended him for two years and then reinstated him 16 months later. Braves owner Ted Turner was suspended for a year for twice tampering with potential free agent Gary Matthews.

In one way or another Kuhn managed to offend a lot of owners, including Nelson Doubleday of the Mets, Jerry Hoffberger of the Orioles, and August Busch of the Cardinals. He survived one "Dump Bowie" movement after his first term, but the owners voted not to renew his contract after his second term ended in August 1983. No one else wanted the job, however, and Kuhn was asked to stay on for another year or until a new commissioner could be found. Peter Ueberroth replaced him in March 1984.

Kuhn's major failure during his term of office was in his dealings with Marvin Miller and the MLBPA. Twice the union went on strike, once in 1981 for nearly two months. The calculating Miller was no baseball fan, but the players loved him. Kuhn and the owners erred by underestimating Miller's power and his ability to rouse public sentiment by painting the owners as stupid, greedy, un-American, or all of the above.

To protect the owners' interests, Kuhn testified in the Supreme Court against Curt Flood when Flood attempted to challenge Organized Baseball's reserve clause. In his book, *Hardball: The Education of a Baseball Commissioner*, Kuhn defended his position on the strikes, saying that it was never his job to side with the players or the owners, but rather to try to bring the two together.

The 6-foot 5-inch Kuhn never came across well in the media. Trained as a lawyer, he gave answers to sportswriters' questions that sounded evasive or even stupid when they were in fact politically tactful. As a result, even his behind-the-scenes successes were often portrayed in the press as failures.

To the public, Kuhn looked his worst when baseball began playing postseason games at night. During cold and rainy League Championship Series or World Series games, the TV cameras couldn't resist panning to the tall, imperious commissioner, sitting in his box at field level, wearing no overcoat, as though he felt the weather was lovely.

After leaving baseball Kuhn formed a law partnership with Harvey Meyerson. The law firm failed in December 1989, and Kuhn sold his home in Ridgewood, New Jersey, and moved to Florida. In 1998 Kuhn contributed a chapter to the book *Why I Am Still a Catholic* in which he compared his feelings for the Roman Catholic Church with his long-held belief in "team loyalty."

Clem Labine

Labine, Clement Walter **P**

1950–62 B:8/6/1926, Lincoln, RI Deb:4/18/1950, BRO
NL BR/TR 6', 180

W	L	PCT	G	SV	IP	BB	SO	ERA
77	56	.579	513	96	1079^{2}	396	551	3.63

Primarily a reliever and only occasionally a starter throughout his career, Brooklyn pitcher Clem Labine threw but three shutouts in his 13 years in the majors. However, it is for two of those that he is still remembered.

Labine became a member of the Dodgers in an unusual way. One day in 1946 he was scheduled to have a tryout with the Boston Braves at Braves Field, but he couldn't get into the team's dressing room to change. Coach Chuck Dressen of the visiting Dodgers suddenly appeared, and Labine tried out for Dressen instead. Shortly thereafter he got a call from Branch Rickey Jr. and a $500 bonus to sign with Brooklyn.

Labine's professional career started in Newport News in 1946, but he was soon demoted to Asheville. He worked his way up through Pueblo and St. Paul before advancing to Brooklyn for one game in 1950.

In 1951 Labine split his time between starting and relief, while going 5–1 with a 2.20 ERA. He had six starts; five of them complete games and two of them shutouts. The most significant was the shutout of the New York Giants in Game 2 of the 1951 three-game playoff. Two years later, Labine went 11–6 with a 2.77 ERA and became the Dodgers' ace reliever. However, he had a World Series to forget, as he appeared in three games and lost to the Yankees twice.

Labine prospered in his role as a reliever and led the National League in appearances in 1955. That year he recorded a 13–5 mark and had his most productive offensive season; although he was only 3 for 31 at the plate, all three hits were homers. Labine also redeemed himself in the 1955 World Series against the Yankees. In Game 4 he pitched 4⅓ innings of relief to record the win, then hurled three innings the following day to save Game 5 for Roger Craig. The Dodgers went on to win their first World Series.

In both 1956 and 1957 Labine led the league and saves and was selected to the All-Star Game. After a 10–6 record in 1956, he had perhaps his biggest moment in that year's World Series. Brooklyn was trailing the Yankees, three games to two. The Dodgers needed a win to stay alive, and turned the ball over to Labine. He responded with a 10-inning, 1–0 shutout. The Dodgers lost Game 7, but Labine had erased fans' memories of his two losses in the 1953 Series.

In 1958 Labine followed the Dodgers to Los Angeles, but his best years were behind him. He lost 10 games in 1959 and pitched only one inning in the Dodgers' World Series triumph over Chicago. Traded to Detroit in 1960, by season's end Labine was with Pittsburgh, where his 3–0 record with a 1.48 ERA helped the Pirates to the pennant. He won his third World Series ring when Bill Mazeroski hit his dramatic Game 7 homer against the Yankees.

Following the 1961 season the Pirates made Labine available in the National League expansion draft, and the New York Mets chose him. In 1962 Labine pitched only four innings for the Mets before being released and retiring from baseball.

Even before his playing days were over Labine had become a partner in a firm that manufactured golf wear and rain suits. Around 1979 he entered banking. He stayed in touch with baseball by participating in numerous fantasy camps.

Lee Lacy

Lacy, Leondaus **OF–2B**

1972–87 B:4/10/1948, Longview, TX Deb:6/30/1972, LA
NL BR/TR 6'1", 175

G	AB	R	H	HR	RBI	OBP	SLG	AVG
1523	4549	650	1303	91	458	.342	.410	.286

While with the Los Angeles Dodgers for seven years, sure-handed outfielder Lee Lacy was always regarded as having outstanding potential. It wasn't until he went to the Pittsburgh Pirates, however, that Lacy prospered as an exceptional major league hitter.

Los Angeles picked Lacy in the second round of the February 1969 free-agent draft. He put in stints at Ogden, Bakersfield, Albuquerque, and El Paso before being promoted to the Dodgers in 1972. As a second baseman in the heyday of Davey Lopes, Lacy never became more than an occasional player. In 1975, as a backup for Lopes and part-time outfielder, he hit .314. Nevertheless, at the end of the season he was traded to Atlanta. In June 1976 the Braves swapped him back to Los Angeles, where for three years he saw part-time duty in the outfield. In 1978 he pinch-hit five home runs, three of them in consecutive appearances. But after hitting only .143 in the 1978 World Series he became a free agent and signed with the Pirates.

Lacy topped .300 in four of his six seasons in Pittsburgh, including a high of .335 in 1980. That same year, at an age when most players slow down, Lacy sped up and started stealing bases. In 1982 he swiped 40. The 1984 season was perhaps his finest. Lacy hit .321 with career highs in hits, doubles, and RBIs, while making only one error and leading National League outfielders with a .996 fielding percentage.

That year Lacy became a free agent again and signed with Baltimore. In 1986 he was named in the Pittsburgh drug trials for alleged cocaine use while with the Pirates. In March of that year Commissioner Peter Ueberroth threatened to suspend him for 60 days unless he donated part of his salary to drug-abuse programs. He concluded his career with the Orioles in 1987.

Nap Lajoie

Lajoie, Napoleon **2B-1B**

1896–1916 M(1905–09, 377–309) B:9/5/1874, Woonsocket, RI D:2/7/1959, Daytona Beach, FL Deb:8/12/1896, PHI AL BR/TR 6'1", 195

G	AB	R	H	HR	RBI	OBP	SLG	AVG
2480	9589	1504	3242	82	1599	.380	.466	.338

When fans debate the question of who was baseball's best hitter in the first decade of the 20th century, the two names most often mentioned are Honus Wagner and Nap Lajoie. Fellow Hall of Famer Kid Nichols called Lajoie "the hardest hitter I ever pitched to."

Hitting .338 for his career, Lajoie amassed three batting titles, four 200-hit seasons, and four 100-RBI seasons. He led the American League in double plays and putouts five times each. He was tops in fielding seven times, and six times he paced the league in chances per game, the best gauge of range. He was a virtual artist at second base—smooth, with sure hands. The word most often used to describe Lajoie is "graceful." It even appears on his Hall of Fame plaque.

Working as a teamster for City Lumber in Woonsocket, Rhode Island, the 21-year-old Lajoie was making $7.50 a week in 1895 when the Fall River, Massachusetts team of the New England League fell short a player. Lajoie signed for $100 a month and played his first game on May 1.

Before long, word of his talent had spread, and several big league clubs began bidding for him in 1896. Boston, Chicago, Pittsburgh, and New York all had discussions with Fall River's management. When Philadelphia made an offer for Lajoie's teammate Phil Geier, Fall River manager Charlie Marston asked for $1,500, and the Phillies refused. Marston then offered to include Lajoie in the deal, and the trade was made. Lajoie was quickly promoted to the majors.

He started his career at first base and hit .326 that first year. The Phillies finished 32½ games out of first place in 1897, but their new star player was right at the top of the league. He batted .361, hit 40 doubles and 23 triples, drove in 127 runs, and led the league with a .569 slugging percentage. He also set a record with 13 total bases in a game.

The next season Phillies manager George Stallings moved Lajoie to second base, where he would stay for most of his career. He batted .324 and led the National League with 43 doubles and 127 RBIs. In July 1899 Lajoie collided viciously at second base with the Reds' Harry Steinfeldt. Steinfeldt was knocked unconscious, and Lajoie was out for two months. Except for a handful of pinch-hitting appearances Lajoie didn't play until the last five games of the season. He still hit .378 with 70 RBIs—in only 312 at bats.

Lajoie injured himself again in 1900, but it didn't happen on the field. In late May, with the Phillies in first place, he and teammate Elmer Flick got into a fight, supposedly over a bat. The most damaging punch was one that missed its mark. Lajoie threw it, Flick ducked, and Lajoie's fist hit a concrete wall. His thumb was broken and he missed five weeks of play.

That year the league had reduced its membership to eight teams by expelling four from the league. That gave Ban Johnson, commissioner of the Western League, the impetus to compete, and he began to solicit players to join his new organization, now called the American League. Lajoie was one of the first to jump to the new circuit.

By then Lajoie had become recognized as one of the top talents in the game. "He glides around the infield with the grace of a tiger," one competitor said. Lajoie was making the maximum salary for a player, $2,400; the average salary was $525. Under-the-table payments raised that by another $200 or so, but the proud Lajoie wanted to make as much as his roommate, Ed Delahanty. Lajoie had seen checks written to Delahanty for $600 extra, so when Connie Mack offered $24,000 for four years, Lajoie became an American Leaguer. When the Phillies' owner learned of the signing, he offered Lajoie $25,000 for two years, but the player refused it.

In the new league, where talent was thin, Lajoie dominated. In 1901 he led the American League in hits, runs, doubles, homers, runs scored, RBIs, batting average, on-base percentage, and slugging average. His batting average of .426 was the best achieved in the 20th century, and the fourth highest ever recorded. In the Dead Ball Era, when seven or eight homers might top the league, he belted 14, the third-highest total of the century's first decade.

A lawsuit had been filed to keep Lajoie from leaving the National League, and a lower court had rejected it. In February 1902 an appeal was finally heard before the Pennsylvania Supreme Court. Lajoie became, in effect, the first person to challenge baseball's reserve clause. He testified that he had not damaged the Phillies by leaving and that they could easily find someone to replace him because his services were "not of a unique or extraordinary character." The judges disagreed, ruling that he be prohibited from playing for any club other than the Phillies for the term of his contract—in other words, forever.

The decision threw Organized Baseball into a tumult. The hopes for a peaceful resolution of the conflict between the two leagues seemed shattered. The Athletics defiantly began the season with Lajoie at second base against Baltimore. But in the ninth inning Mack received a telegram informing him of a temporary injunction forbidding Lajoie to play.

For two months Lajoie was inactive while lawyers and club owners tried to resolve the issue. Someone suggested that the injunction was effective only in Pennsylvania, so the American League devised a solution. Although Mack would have preferred otherwise, he sent Lajoie to Cleveland because the sagging franchise there was in deep trouble. Owner Charles Somers had been a financial bulwark in the first years of the new league, even putting money in Mack's pocket when necessary. Thus Lajoie became a member of the Blues, but whenever his team played in Philadelphia, he was nowhere to be found.

Lajoie was an immediate hit in Cleveland. On June 4 he made his debut, and 10,000 fans turned out to see him. His presence and play rescued the club, which otherwise might have moved to Pittsburgh or Cincinnati. Later research showed that Lajoie hit .378, two points higher than Ed Delahanty, but Major League Baseball maintained that Delahanty should retain his batting crown.

During 1903 spring training Cleveland newspapers ran a contest to find the team a better name than the Blues. The winning moniker was the Naps, after the team's new captain. Only two other teams have been named after a player: the Brooklyn Robins, after their manager, Wilbert Robinson, and Cleveland again, when it took on the Indians name in tribute to its Penobscot Indian superstar, Louis "Chief" Sockalexis. Lajoie responded to the honor by leading the league in batting and slugging averages.

Late in the 1904 season, with the Naps struggling, manager Bill Armour resigned. Lajoie, at age 30, took Armour's place and kept the job for five years. Later Lajoie would say that trying to manage and play was too much for him. One wouldn't have been able to tell from his performance, because he led the league in hits, doubles, RBIs, batting average, and slugging percentage.

Blood poisoning ruined his 1905 season. A spike wound became infected by the dye in his socks, and Lajoie played in only 65 games. His team, nine games in front at the time of the injury, was nine games behind when he returned. Because of his experience, the players began to wear white "sanitary" socks with colored stirrups over them.

Another spiking injury cost Lajoie five weeks in 1907, and that same season George Stovall hit Lajoie over the head with a chair to show his displeasure about being lowered in the batting order. The next year Cleveland seriously contended for the pennant. After a July swoon that dropped the Naps nine games back, they won 15 of 18. By September 21 Detroit, Cleveland, and Chicago were only one game apart.

The Naps were half a game back when they hosted the White Sox on October 3. Lajoie committed an error that led to two runs, and he took an Ed Walsh fastball for a third strike with two outs and the bases loaded in the seventh. The Naps trailed by 1½ games going into the season's final series. Again, Lajoie failed. Cleveland and St. Louis played a tie in the first game, and in the sixth inning of the second game Lajoie's error led to the winning run. He later said, "I honestly believe that the 1908 race took more out of me than three ordinary seasons." He never had a lower batting average (.289) in a full season of play.

That disappointing finish did nothing to quell the grousers on his team, and in the 1909 season Lajoie decided he'd had enough. With the Naps in third place, at 57–57, he quit as manager. The fans were happy with his decision, but when the Cleveland press ran another contest to rename the team, the Naps won again.

In 1910 Philadelphia took the lead early in the pennant race and held it. With no other excitement, Cleveland fans focused on the battle for the 1910 batting title between Ty Cobb and Lajoie. It became the most scandalous batting race in baseball history.

The champion was due to receive a sparkling new Chalmers 30 automobile, so the fans came to call the contest "the automobile race." At the end of August, Lajoie and Cobb were only three points apart. "Adding to the excitement—and the frustration," Jim Murphy wrote, "was the fact that there was no unanimity on exactly what the averages were at any one time. There were repeated statements about 'official' and 'unofficial' figures." On October 6 one set of numbers said Cobb had an eight-point lead; another claimed Lajoie was out front, but only by a point or so.

Cobb, believing he'd already won the car, sat out his team's last two games. Lajoie, meanwhile, prepared to face the Browns in a doubleheader to

close the season. No one wanted Cobb to win; Lajoie, on the other hand, was well respected, even adored. In his final two games Lajoie went 8 for 8.

After Lajoie had tripled his first time up, Browns manager "Peach Pie" Jack O'Connor "recommended" that his rookie third baseman play deep, ostensibly to avoid being hurt by one of Lajoie's wicked line drives.

Lajoie bunted to the left side six straight times for hits. The seventh time he tried it, a play was made on a runner going to third, so he was given a sacrifice instead of an official at bat. His final time up, he grounded to short and Bobby Wallace threw wildly to first. The official scorer decided that Lajoie would have beaten the play anyway and awarded him a hit.

When pressed by his owner, O'Connor said, "Lajoie outguessed us." O'Connor was promptly fired. And after all the collusion Cobb won the title by .0007. Chalmers decided to give cars to both men, but the fiasco prompted a policy change for awarding cars and prizes to battling titlists.

More than 70 years later, *The Sporting News* historian Paul MacFarlane discovered that two hits had been mistakenly credited to Cobb. An attempt to have the "official" data changed and the title given to Lajoie, thereby breaking Cobb's incredible string of nine consecutive batting titles, was taken to Commissioner Bowie Kuhn. But he ruled against Lajoie, and the records stood.

Losing the batting title didn't diminish Lajoie's popularity. In 1912 Cleveland threw a "Nap Lajoie Day" that featured a 9-foot floral horseshoe decorated with 1,009 silver dollars. In 1914 Lajoie reached 3,000 hits, joining Honus Wagner as the second player in the 20th century to reach the milestone. But he was having problems with his new manager, Joe Birmingham, and was sold to the A's before the 1915 season.

Lajoie had two mediocre years in Philadelphia. In 1915 he set the American League record for most errors by a second baseman in a game, with five, and the next year he left the majors after hitting .246 in 113 games. At age 42 he became player-manager for the Toronto Maple Leafs and hit .380 to lead the league. He was managing the Indianapolis club in the American Association when World War I forced the league to close down for the season. Lajoie then left baseball for good.

It's difficult to argue his place among baseball's greats: Lajoie's records speak volumes, and he was immensely popular. As Tommy Leach said, "Even when the son of a gun was blocking you off the base, he was smiling and kidding with you." Lajoie was elected to the Hall of Fame in 1937.

Dennis Lamp

Lamp, Dennis Patrick **P**

1977–92 B:9/23/1952, Los Angeles, CA Deb:8/21/1977, CHI NL BR/TR 6'3", 210

W	L	PCT	G	SV	IP	BB	SO	ERA
96	96	.500	639	35	1830^2	549	857	3.93

The January 1984 free agent signing of White Sox pitcher Dennis Lamp by the Blue Jays caused shock waves in New York. As compensation for losing Lamp, Chicago chose Tom Seaver, whom the Mets had left unprotected, from the free-agent compensation pool. The move nearly caused a fan revolt at Shea Stadium, but it also opened up a slot in the New York rotation for teenaged Dwight Gooden.

The Cubs had originally picked Lamp in the third round of the June 1971 draft. He performed with six different teams in the minors, and in 1977 he paced the American Association with a .733 won-lost percentage. Late in that year he was brought up to the Cubs, but after three uninspiring seasons at Wrigley Field, he was traded across town to the White Sox in 1981. For the Chisox, Lamp started working regularly out of the bullpen. In 1983 he pitched in three of four ALCS games, and did not surrender an earned run.

With Toronto, Lamp became a middle reliever. As such, he had his career year in 1985, appearing in 53 games and posting an 11–0 record. He then appeared in three more ALCS contests, again not giving up an earned run. It was a different case the next year, however, as Lamp's ERA went up by more than a point and a half, and his record dropped to 2–6. Toronto released him in October 1986.

Signed by the A's organization in April 1987, Lamp went first to Tacoma and in midseason was promoted to Oakland. Granted free agency that October, he made the Red Sox staff as a nonroster, spring training invitee. He spent four years in Boston before finishing his career with one season in Pittsburgh.

Jim Landis

Landis, James Henry **OF**

1957–67 B:3/9/1934, Fresno, CA Deb:4/16/1957, CHI AL BR/TR 6'1", 180

G	AB	R	H	HR	RBI	OBP	SLG	AVG
1346	4288	625	1061	93	467	.346	.375	.247

Chicago White Sox center fielder Jim Landis made up for a weak bat—he once struck out five times in one game—with fielding that earned him Gold Gloves each year from 1960 through 1964 and selection to the 1962 All-Star Game. "It may sound a little cocky, but you had to feel this way—there was no ball I couldn't catch," Landis said later. "That to me was real determination, and if you haven't got that, you're not a good outfielder."

While attending Contra Costa College in northern California, Landis was signed by White Sox scout Bobby Mattick. In his first season, 1953, he played third base for the Wisconsin Rapids of the Wisconsin State League, but he was shifted to the outfield by former White Sox center fielder Johnny Mostil. Landis continued his minor league career at Colorado Springs, Memphis, and Indianapolis, and spent 1954 and 1955 in the military.

He reached the major leagues in 1957 and became a regular with the Sox the next year. In Chicago's 1959 World Series appearance, Landis hit .292 and led the team with six runs. The 1961 season was his best, as he hit .283 with eight triples, 22 homers, and 85 RBIs, each figure a career high.

In January 1965 Landis was sent to the Kansas City Athletics in a three-club deal that saw Rocky Colavito return to Cleveland. He played in Kansas City, Cleveland, Detroit, Boston, and Houston before retiring after the 1967 season. His son Craig was a first-round draft pick of the Giants in 1977.

Kenesaw Mountain Landis

Landis, Kenesaw Mountain

Commissioner (1920–44) B:11/20/1866, Millville, OH D:11/25/1944, Chicago, IL 5'6", 135

Baseball's first commissioner, the flinty, colorful, and often arbitrary Judge Kenesaw Mountain Landis took control of the game when its integrity was in question. When he died nearly a quarter of a century later, baseball's name had long since been restored.

Landis was the son of Dr. Abraham Landis, who had lost the use of his leg in the Civil War battle of Kennesaw Mountain in northwest Georgia. At his son's birth, Dr. Landis suggested they call him "Kenesaw Mountain." The name and the misspelling stuck.

His early career gave little indication of the heights Landis would later reach. A high school dropout, his first ambition was to be a brakeman on the Vandalia and Southern Railroad, but the company's officials rejected his application. The diminutive Landis won some fame as a bicycle racer at various Indiana fairgrounds and operated a roller skating rink before moving to journalism. While covering court cases for Indiana's *Logansport Journal*, he decided to become a lawyer and enrolled in the YMCA Law School of Cincinnati. In 1891 Landis obtained his degree from Chicago's Union Law School.

Two of his brothers, Charles and Frederick, were Indiana congressmen. In part through their auspices, while still in his 20s Landis sat in on cabinet meetings representing the State Department. Appointed to the federal judiciary by Theodore Roosevelt, Landis quickly earned a reputation for quirky and newsworthy justice.

He fined Standard Oil $29,240,000, a record penalty at that time. He jailed Industrial Workers of the World members and Socialist Congressman Victor Berger for antiwar activities during World War I. Those cases and others placed him squarely in the public eye, even though his decisions were often overturned.

In one fiery wartime speech Landis demanded that Kaiser Wilhelm II, his six sons, and 5,000 German militarists be "lined up against a wall and shot down in justice to the world and to Germany." Many thought him a mere grandstander. "His career typifies the heights to which dramatic talent may carry a man in America if only he has the foresight not to go on the stage," said Heywood Broun.

But Organized Baseball had a high opinion of Landis. During the Federal League war he had done the baseball establishment a great service. The existing major leagues had faced a stiff challenge from the Federal League, both on the field and in the courts, as the upstart circuit sought to overturn baseball's reserve clause. Landis heard the case within a month, and the owners of the established leagues held their breath.

But then Landis firmly sat on the case. Months passed and he issued no decision. It was obvious he didn't want to issue one, because he knew what a flimsy legal structure baseball was built upon. "Both sides must understand that any blows at this thing called baseball would be regarded by this court as a blow to a national institution," Landis had warned from the bench.

Finally, the Federal League threw in the towel, getting the best deal they could from Organized Baseball. Landis' inaction had been the key. "Many persons felt that Landis had saved baseball in 1915," wrote J.G. Taylor Spink of *The Sporting News*. "Had he ruled Organized Baseball to be a gigantic trust, the Federal League contention, he could have thrown the whole game into chaos. There would have been no sanctity of baseball territory. Had he decided against the legality of the reserve and 10-day clauses, the effect would have been free agencies for all the great players of the time."

Landis had saved the owners' hides and they knew it. When the 1919 World Series fix became public knowledge in September 1920, they needed someone to restore confidence in the badly shaken institution. Landis was an obvious choice. On November 12, 1920, every major league owner except the intransigent Phil Ball of the Browns paid a visit to Landis' Chicago court. They stood in the rear of the room while Landis continued hearing cases. When he finished, Landis called them into his chambers. There, they offered him chairmanship of a new three-member "Board of Control" over Major League Baseball. Landis demanded absolute power and got it.

"At their request and in accordance with my own earnest wishes I am to remain on the bench and continue my work here," announced Landis. "The opportunities for real service are limitless. I have been devoted for nearly 40 years. On the question of policy, all I have to say is this: 'The only thing in anybody's mind now is to make and keep baseball what the millions of fans throughout the United States want it to be.'"

Will Rogers once remarked, "The game needed a touch of class and distinction, and somebody said, 'Get that old guy who sits behind first base all the time. He's out here every day anyway.' So they offered him a season pass and he grabbed it."

In the summer of 1921 the accused "Black Sox" were acquitted under highly questionable circumstances. Long used to having his decisions overturned by higher courts, Landis, as commissioner of baseball, returned the favor and reversed the jury's decision. "Regardless of the outcome of juries," he said, "no player that throws a ball game, no player that entertains proposals or promises to throw a game, no player that sits in a conference with a bunch of crooked players where the ways and means of throwing games are discussed, and does not promptly tell his club about it, will ever again play professional baseball."

Old and new scandals continued to plague baseball for the first few years of Landis' tenure. Youthful Giants outfielder Jimmy O'Connell and Giants coach Cozy Dolan were banned from the game following a failed bribe attempt. Frankie Frisch, Ross Youngs, and George Kelly were implicated but cleared by Landis. Phil Douglas was also banned after offering to throw a game. Outfielder Benny Kauff was blacklisted for implication in an auto-theft ring. As in the Black Sox scandal, Landis ignored the verdict of a jury, this time with what many critics felt was far less justification.

Landis was a headstrong, autocratic czar. *Current Biography* termed him "the only successful dictator in United States history." But Organized Baseball already had a dictator in American League president Ban Johnson. Johnson was by no means ready to relinquish the hold he had on the game. Throughout the early 1920s Landis consolidated power at the expense of his rival. The proud Johnson was left humiliated and stripped of real authority.

The last great scandal of Landis' tenure involved the biggest names in baseball—Ty Cobb and Tris Speaker. In 1926 pitcher Dutch Leonard accused the two stars of conspiring to fix the last game of the 1919 season. Leonard also accused Smokey Joe Wood of placing bets on the contest for Cobb and Speaker. Landis' verdict exonerating the accused trio has come under heavy criticism from some historians.

Landis was a staunch opponent of Branch Rickey's minor league farm system and fought it tooth and nail. "It will be the ruination of the individual minor league club owners," he declared. He liberated numerous minor league players during his term in office. In one 1938 case, the commissioner freed 91 Cardinals farmhands, including Pete Reiser and Skeeter Webb. In January 1940 he hit the Detroit system, freeing scores of players and costing the Tigers an estimated $500,000.

One of Landis' most important personnel decisions came on December 10, 1936, when he awarded young Bob Feller's contract to Cleveland. Another significant decision involved the freeing of Tommy Henrich from the Indians' system in April 1937. Henrich was able to sign with the Yankees for a $25,000 bonus.

Landis' assumption of control over all World Series decisions, his well-publicized disciplining and suspension of Babe Ruth after the 1921 Series, and his removal of Cardinals outfielder Joe Medwick from the field in the riotous seventh game of the 1934 World Series all created headlines.

World War II threatened to interrupt Major League Baseball, but Landis indirectly obtained President Franklin Roosevelt's green light to continue the national pastime. His last major move was in 1943 when he banned Phillies owner William D. Cox from the game for gambling.

It was not until Landis died that major league club owners finally integrated their teams. Many have contended that this was no coincidence. One oft-told tale contended that Landis scuttled Bill Veeck's plan to buy and integrate the Phillies. Recent scholarship by members of the Society for American Baseball Research has largely debunked that story.

Just before Landis died in November 1944, his contract was extended to January 1953, when he would have been 86 years old. Such was the hold of Judge Landis on baseball that, even as frail as he was, no one dared oppose him.

Shortly after he died, Landis was voted into the Hall of Fame. Despite his faults, he was passionately devoted to baseball and to preserving its integrity. "Baseball is something more than a game to an American boy," he declared. "It is his training field for life work. Destroy his faith in its squareness and honesty and you have destroyed something more; you have planted suspicion of all things in his heart."

Frank Lane

Lane, Frank

Executive B:2/1/1896 D:3/19/1981, Richardson, TX

Few trades ever shook a city as much as Frank "Trader" Lane's 1960 expulsion of Rocky Colavito from Cleveland to Detroit. But the natives of Cleveland should hardly have been surprised at Lane's banishment of their beloved slugger. After all, they didn't call him "Trader" for nothing: he had made 241 deals involving 353 players while running the White Sox.

Born on February 1, 1896, Lane played for Marion of the Class D Ohio State League when future President Warren G. Harding still owned a share of the club. Later, he officiated in both football and basketball and ran a semipro baseball league. In 1933 Larry MacPhail hired Lane as business manager of the Cincinnati Reds, and Lane held the same position with Durham of the Piedmont League before returning to Cincinnati as an assistant to Warren Giles.

Lane was the first baseball executive to enlist for service in World War II. When he returned, MacPhail, now with the Yankees, put him in charge of New York's Kansas City farm team. From 1947 through 1948 Lane served as president of the American Association. In 1948 the Comiskey family hired him to run the White Sox. The team had lost 101 games the previous season and was virtually bankrupt.

He was warned not to take the job. "There are only so many major league general managers," he reasoned. "If it were a perfect job, it wouldn't be open. Maybe nobody else wants it, but I want it."

Charles Comiskey II had told Lane that the club had a good nucleus. Lane took one look and quickly placed every player on the White Sox roster on waivers. Only two received any offers whatsoever. "So if we had a good nucleus, it was news to the other clubs," said Lane. He started trading and kept on trading as long as he was in the game.

An early swap was one of his best—catcher Aaron Robinson for Detroit's Billy Pierce and $10,000 cash. In October 1949 Lane stole Nellie Fox from the A's for catcher Joe Tipton. In April 1951 he pried Minnie Minoso away from Cleveland, and he even talked Branch Rickey out of shortstop Chico Carrasquel for two nobodies and $25,000.

It took a while, but the franchise turned around. The White Sox challenged for the pennant in 1955 and eventually won it in 1959, but Lane wasn't there to enjoy it. Bad blood between Lane and Comiskey forced the general manager to move on to the St. Louis Cardinals in October 1955, where he ruffled feathers by trading away local hero Red Schoendienst. He even tried to swap Stan Musial, but was prevented from doing so by Cardinals owner August A. Busch.

At a banquet prior to the start of the 1957 season Busch announced, "If Frank Lane doesn't win the pennant this year, I'm going to fire his ass!" The Cardinals didn't win, and Lane decided to jump before he was pushed.

In November 1957 Lane took over the Cleveland organization. He publicly squabbled with manager Joe Gordon, fired him, rehired him, and then traded him to Detroit for manager Jimmie Dykes. In June 1958 he traded away Roger Maris. But the biggest blow came in April 1960 when Lane sent Cleveland icon Colavito to the Tigers for American League batting champion Harvey Kuenn.

"When I traded him, they wanted to lynch me," Lane recalled. "I went back to my hotel that day and there was this dummy hanging in effigy from a lamp post. 'Frank Lane,' it said on the dummy. I guess they wanted it to be reality instead of effigy."

After leaving Cleveland, Lane was hired by Kansas City A's owner Charles O. Finley, but lasted only eight months with the club before being dismissed. In the ensuing lawsuit Lane received an estimated $113,000 from Finley in an out-of-court settlement. He later worked for the Orioles, Brewers, and Angels. He died in 1981, after a lengthy illness.

Bill Lange

Lange, William Alexander **OF**

1893–99 B:6/6/1871, San Francisco, CA D:7/23/1950, San Francisco, CA Deb:4/27/1893, CHI NL BR/TR 6'1½, 190

G	AB	R	H	HR	RBI	OBP	SLG	AVG
811	3195	689	1055	39	578	.401	.459	.330

Bill Lange ranks as one of the foremost players of the 1890s. He would almost certainly be listed among the greatest of all time on an appropriate plaque in Cooperstown had his career not been prematurely ended by love.

A.H. Spink, the founder and editor of *The Sporting News*, described Lange as "Ty Cobb enlarged, fully as great in speed, batting skill, and base running." Tim Murnane of the *Boston Globe*, when listing baseball's greatest outfielders up to 1914, skipped such immortals as Willie Keeler, Ed Delahanty, and Boston's own Hugh Duffy in favor of Cobb, Joe Jackson, and Lange.

Lange was so exceptional that in later years numerous legends grew in which he was credited with nearly superhuman accomplishments. In perhaps the most famous story Lange was playing for Chicago against the Washington Senators in the nation's capital. He pursued a flyball back to a wooden fence, crashed through the fence, and caught the ball on the far side.

Accounts of this remarkable catch were written well into the next century and cited as proof of Lange's unparalleled fielding prowess. However, a careful check of newspaper accounts of Chicago's games showed that no such catch ever took place. The story probably started after a Washington player used a ladder as a battering ram to break through the fence, to quickly move an injured player to a hospital just behind the barrier.

Standing nearly 6 feet 2 inches tall and weighing 190 pounds, Lange was a giant for his time. His size belied his nickname, "Little Eva," but by all accounts he was one of the fastest players of his day. He also had a strong and accurate arm, and hit with both power and consistency. After playing two seasons with Seattle of the Pacific Coast League, Lange debuted with Chicago in 1893, batting .281—the only time he failed to hit at least .319.

Immensely popular for his outstanding play, pleasant smile, and outgoing personality, Lange was also known as a member of the Dawn Patrol, a group of Chicago players who outraged their stern manager, Cap Anson, by regularly staying out till the wee hours enjoying Chicago's nightlife. The carousing did not affect Lange's play. In 1895 he hit .389—still the team record—with 98 RBIs, 120 runs and 67 stolen bases.

The next year Lange bolstered his .326-batting average with 92 RBIs, 114 runs, and 84 stolen bases. His total for steals was for many years thought to be over 100, but further research has brought it down to a still-exceptional 84. Lange led all National League basestealers with 72 in 1897 and had a career total of 399.

Lange was only 28 years old, with a seven-year batting average of .330, when he abruptly retired after the 1899 season. He had fallen in love with the daughter of a wealthy San Francisco real estate tycoon who had declared that no daughter of his could marry a mere ballplayer; so Lange gave up baseball.

During the next few years he received many financially attractive offers to return to the game, but he refused them all while pursuing a career in real estate and insurance. He eventually scouted for the Cincinnati Reds and coached baseball at Stanford. Ironically, the marriage that terminated his playing career ended in divorce. His nephew, George Lange Kelly, became a Hall of Famer.

Rick Langford

Langford, James Rick **P**

1976–86 B:3/20/1952, Farmville, VA Deb:6/13/1976, PIT NL BR/TR 6', 180

W	L	PCT	G	SH	IP	BB	SO	ERA
73	106	.408	260	10	1491	416	671	4.01

In 1980 Oakland righthander Rick Langford, under the tutelage of manager Billy Martin, led the American League in complete games and innings pitched. In 1981 he again paced the circuit in complete games, but later, like so many members of the Oakland starting rotation, Langford developed arm (specifically elbow) problems and saw his career terminated after several stints on the disabled list.

Selected by the Cardinals in 1971 and the Indians in 1972, Langford did not sign. In 1973 no one drafted him, however, and he signed as a free agent with Pittsburgh. The Pirates started Langford with Bradenton in the Gulf Coast League. He advanced through the Pittsburgh farm system, with stops in Salem, Shreveport, and Charleston. Playing for Shreveport on May 30, 1976, Langford no-hit Memphis 11–0. Later that year he made his major league debut, finishing the season with no wins and one loss in 12 appearances.

In March 1977, Langford was sent with Tony Armas to Oakland in a nine-player deal. In his first year with the A's he led the American League with 19 losses. He improved his record in each of the next three years, culminating with a 19–12 mark in 1980. On October 2 of that year Langford committed an error, his first in the major leagues after an all-time record for a pitcher of 230 consecutive errorless chances (in 142 games).

After winning 12 games and then a playoff contest in the strike-shortened 1981 season, Langford never again equaled his previous success. He lost 16 games in 1982, didn't win for the next two years, and went 1–10 with a 7.36 ERA in 1986, his last year in the majors. In 1999 he coached for the International League's Syracuse SkyChiefs.

Mark Langston

Langston, Mark Edward **P**

1984–* B:8/20/1960, San Diego, CA Deb:4/7/1984, SEA AL BR/TL 6'2", 190

W	L	PCT	G	SH	IP	BB	SO	ERA
179	158	.531	457	18	2962^2	1289	2464	3.97

Mark Langston joined the pitching-starved Seattle Mariners in 1984 and made an immediate impact, winning 17 games in his rookie year. In his first four seasons the hard-throwing left-hander won three AL strikeout crowns, topping out at 262 in 1987 when he also became an All-

Star, won a career-high 19 games and earned the first of seven Gold Gloves.

In May 1989 the Montreal Expos, in a move to bolster their playoff chances, traded righthanded pitchers Brian Holman and Gene Harris, and a 6-foot 10-inch lefthander named Randy Johnson, to get Seattle's ace. Langston left Seattle as the team's all-time leader in wins, shutouts, strikeouts, and walks—all marks that Johnson later surpassed. Langston was excited to finally play for a contender, but Montreal faltered down the stretch.

As a prized free agent Langston signed with California in 1990. In his first start as an Angel, and in his first appearance against his original team, Langston combined with Mike Witt to no-hit Seattle. Continuing his strong pitching, Langston went to the All-Star Game each year from 1991 through 1993.

Injuries, however, began to affect his game. Elbow problems limited Langston to nine starts in 1997. In 1998, as a Padres reliever, the 15-year veteran finally made the postseason. Unfortunately, in his first-ever World Series appearance, he surrendered a grand slam to Tino Martinez. Langston mulled retirement, but worked as a reliever and spot starter for the Cleveland Indians in 1999.

Hal Lanier

Lanier, Harold Clifton **SS-2B**

1964–73 M(1986–88, 254–232) B:7/4/1942,
Denton, NC Deb:6/18/1964, SF NL BR/TR 6'2", 180

G	AB	R	H	HR	RBI	OBP	SLG	AVG
1196	3703	297	843	8	273	.256	.275	.228

Hal Lanier landed a good deal when he signed with the San Francisco Giants in 1961. Not only did he pocket a $50,000 bonus, but he also got his father, Max, a former major league pitcher, a three-year contract as a Giants scout.

Lanier began his major league career in 1964 as a second baseman, but moved to shortstop three years later when the Giants obtained Ron Hunt. No matter where he played, he hit poorly, batting .274 his rookie year but never going above .233 after that. He suffered from epilepsy, but that did not interfere with his duties as the Giants' regular shortstop for five seasons.

In 1972 Lanier went to the New York Yankees, doing service as a utility infielder with the team for two seasons. After ending his playing career, he took on managerial duties in the minors. In 1986, his first year as a big league manager, he led the Astros to the NL West title, but their dream season ended when the Mets won a thrilling Championship Series. Lanier finished sixth in 1988 and the Astros replaced him with Art Howe. He coached with the Phillies in 1990 and 1991.

Max Lanier

Lanier, Hubert Max **P**

1938–46, 1949–53 B:8/18/1915, Denton, NC
Deb:4/20/1938, STL NL BR/TL 5'10", 187

W	L	PCT	G	SH	IP	BB	SO	ERA
108	82	.568	327	21	1619^{1}	611	821	3.01

Lefthanded pitcher Max Lanier is best remembered for having jumped to the Mexican League after a brilliant 6–0 start in 1946. The move resulted in his suspension from Organized Baseball for nearly three seasons.

Born a righthander, Lanier converted to southpaw pitching after breaking his right arm twice as a child. That didn't stop him from becoming an outstanding pitcher and from reaching the majors with the St. Louis Cardinals in 1938. Two years later he made the major league club for good, slowly progressing from relief work to more starts to a key member of the starting rotation.

After reaching double-figure wins in 1941 and 1942, Lanier hit the star level in 1943. That year he went 15–7 with a 1.90 ERA and was selected to the All-Star Game. The next season was his finest, as evidenced by 17 wins—including five shutouts—and a 2.65 ERA, along with another All-Star selection. Lanier started the 1946 season phenomenally, winning each of his first six starts with complete-game performances and posting a 1.93 ERA. Seemingly on the verge of his greatest success in the big leagues, he left for Mexico.

South of the border, Lanier was a star in 1946 and 1947. At one point, he organized a Mexican League barnstorming team—featuring such former major leaguers as Sal Maglie, Danny Gardella, and George Hausmann—to tour the United States. Lanier put up his own money for the venture, even purchasing a bus for the team to travel in, but the tour was a financial flop.

Lanier was eventually reinstated in 1949, and he went 11–9 for the Cardinals in both 1950 and 1951. He seemed to lose his touch the next year with the New York Giants, however, as he went only 7–12. That year he placed himself among a group of dubious record holders by walking 11 batters in one game. His career ended after the following season. Lanier's son, Hal later became a major league player, coach, and manager.

Ray Lankford

Lankford, Raymond Lewis **OF**

1990–* B:6/5/1967, Los Angeles, CA Deb:8/21/1990, STL NL BL/TL 5'11", 198

G	AB	R	H	HR	RBI	OBP	SLG	AVG
1269	4561	781	1267	181	703	.369	.480	.278

Tagged as a "can't miss" player in the minor leagues, St. Louis center fielder Ray Lankford required several seasons before he lived up to expectations. In his first full season in St. Louis in 1991, Lankford impressed the Cardinals with his 44 stolen bases and National League-high 15 triples, plus his smooth fielding. The next season he showed off his power, hitting 20 home runs. His mix of speed and power enabled the Cards to use him as both a leadoff and a cleanup hitter—although his annual triple-digit strikeout totals made him a less-than-ideal first place batter.

Shoulder injuries in 1993 caused Lankford's average to plummet to .238. His numbers improved in the next two seasons, but he was still dogged by inconsistency; painful slumps seemed as common as torrid hitting streaks. In 1996, however, he helped the Cards to their first division title in a decade.

After a sensational start in 1997, Lankford was invited to his first All-Star Game; at the age of 30, he finally seemed to be living up to his potential. As he continued to put up big numbers in both 1997 and 1998, he became more outspoken, often challenging teammates to step up their play and criticizing management for its failure to shore up the team's weaknesses.

Carney Lansford

Lansford, Carney Ray **3B-1B**

1978–92 B:2/7/1957, San Jose, CA Deb:4/8/1978, CAL AL BR/TR 6'2", 195

G	AB	R	H	HR	RBI	OBP	SLG	AVG
1862	7158	1007	2074	151	874	.346	.411	.290

Carney Lansford never drew attention to himself, and he remains one of the unsung stars of the 1980s. He batted over .300 five times in his 15-year career. He won the American League batting title in 1981 and finished second in 1989, both times hitting .336. A sure-handed third baseman, he had the best fielding percentage at his position four times.

Lansford reached the majors in 1978 with the California Angels and was third in voting for AL Rookie of the Year after hitting .294. The next year Lansford was a key contributor as the Angels won their first division title. He hit .287 with 30 doubles, 79 RBIs, and a career-best 19 home runs.

Dealt to Boston before the 1981 season, Lansford made an amazing transformation when he quit trying to be a power hitter. He cut his strikeouts down from 93 to 28, and led the league in hitting. It was the first of four consecutive seasons batting over .300.

In December of 1982, the Sox swapped him to Oakland for Tony Armas. Originally slated to move to first base, Lansford stayed at third after Oakland discovered Mark McGwire couldn't handle the position. After his first couple of years in Oakland, his home runs crept up again and his batting average dipped. In 1989 Lansford made another adjustment and his home runs dropped to two, but his batting average again rose to .336.

While a mainstay of the Oakland pennant winners from 1988 through 1990, Lansford began to concentrate on using his base-stealing skills to optimum advantage. He swiped 27 bases in 1987, 29 the following year, and 37 in 1989. Following injury in 1991, he returned for a final season, in which he drove in 75 runs. In 1999 he managed the Pacific Coast League's Edmonton Trappers.

Frank LaPorte

LaPorte, Frank Breyfogle **2B-3B-OF**

1905–15 B:2/6/1880, Uhrichsville, OH D:9/25/1939, Newcomerstown, OH Deb:9/29/1905, NY AL BR/TR 5'8", 175

G	AB	R	H	HR	RBI	OBP	SLG	AVG
1194	4212	501	1185	15	560	.331	.377	.281

Some parks seemed to agree with Frank LaPorte, and some didn't. LaPorte was an up-and-down hitter who batted very well in St. Louis and Indianapolis—where he led the Federal League with 107 RBIs in 1914—but not so well in the other cities in which he played.

LaPorte initially reached the major leagues with the New York Highlanders in 1905. Sold to the Boston Red Sox in December 1907, he was dealt back to New York in July 1908. There he continued a solid, if uninspiring, career. When Hal Chase became the Highlanders' manager, he traded LaPorte and Jimmy Austin—who had been favorites of previous manager George Stallings—to the St. Louis Browns in January 1911.

The move to St. Louis did wonders for LaPorte. That year he batted a career-high .314, hit 37 doubles, and drove in 82 runs. He also led American League second basemen in games played, assists, and double plays. He started the next season well, but was sold to Washington in July after he lost his position to Del Pratt.

After a season split between second, third, and outfield in Washington, LaPorte jumped to the Federal League Hoosiers in 1914, hitting .311 for the pennant-winning club. When the Hoosiers relocated to Newark in 1915 and became the Peppers, LaPorte's offensive production dropped, but he still led league second basemen putouts, assists, and double plays. It was his final season.

Ring Lardner

Lardner, Ringgold Wilmer

Sportswriter, Author B:3/6/1885, Niles, MI D:9/25/1933, East Hampton, NY

Few writers (James Reston, Damon Runyon, and Paul Gallico) have graduated from the sports pages to higher callings, but the most celebrated of them all was Ring Lardner. Lardner was the sportswriter who became as well known for his literary efforts as his newspaper work.

Using as his protagonist a fictional green-as-grass rookie named Jack Keefe, Lardner was able to investigate the world of baseball in a way unrivaled until the appearance of *Ball Four.* Keefe starred in a series of vignettes, written in the form of letters to a friend back home, that were combined in book form as *You Know Me, Al.* Keefe bragged about his pitching exploits as well as encounters with baseball greats. Much of the humor was derived from the difference between what Jack said and the truth Lardner implied. The stories caught on so well that they ran in the *Chicago Tribune* in comic strip form for years.

Famous for other baseball stories like "Alibi Ike," about a busher who has an excuse for everything, Lardner also had his dark side, evidenced in gothic non-baseball stories like "Haircut." His literary fiction became standard reading in college English courses.

Lardner began covering baseball in 1905 for a paper in South Bend, Indiana; one of his duties was keeping score for the local Class B Central League team. In 1908 he secured a position with the *Chicago Inter-Ocean.* He later wrote for that city's *Tribune*, becoming a syndicated columnist in 1919. He suspected the White Sox of throwing the 1919 World Series after seeing them lose the first two games. While others turned a blind eye, he walked through a railroad car during the ride back from Cincinnati to Chicago parodying "I'm Forever Blowing Bubbles," a popular song of the day, by singing, "I'm Forever Blowing Ballgames."

His baseball fiction translated to a variety of media. A Lardner baseball sketch starring Will Rogers appeared in the 1922 Ziegfeld Follies. In 1928 Walter Huston appeared in a theatrical adaptation of Lardner's *Elmer the Great.* The 1933 film version starred Joe E. Brown; two years later Brown was showcased in Lardner's *Alibi Ike.* In 1963 Lardner became the second writer to reccive the J.G. Taylor Spink Award.

Barry Larkin

Larkin, Barry Louis SS

1986–* B:4/28/1964 Cincinnati, OH Deb:8/13/1986, CIN NL BR/TR 6'0", 190

G	AB	R	H	HR	RBI	OBP	SLG	AVG
1707	6291	1063	1884	168	793	.379	.454	.299

In 1995 Barry Larkin batted .319, stole 51 bases, hit 15 home runs and knocked in 66 runs for the Reds—good numbers, but trifling compared to the league leaders. Yet the Cincinnati shortstop was named the National League's Most Valuable Player because of a quality not measured by statistics—leadership. When the Reds began 1995 with a 1–8 record, Larkin held a closed-door meeting. The team responded by going on a 19–3 streak. Every time the Reds showed signs of a relapse, Larkin intervened on the field and, more importantly, in the dugout, leading the club to a division title.

The Reds coveted the Cincinnati native from the time he was teenager. He was chosen by the club in the second round of the 1982 free agent draft out of Cincinnati's breeding ground for hometown talent, Moeller High School; Larkin opted for the University of Michigan. After he became the Big Ten's first two-time MVP and played for the 1984 U.S. Olympic team, the Reds again drafted Larkin, this time with the fourth overall pick. He spent only two years in the minors, winning MVP honors in the American Association for the Denver Zephyrs in 1986. Already he exhibited leadership skills: Larkin learned Spanish so he could build a better rapport with his Hispanic teammates.

Cincinnati quickly became dependent on Larkin, its success often hinging upon his health. After only one brief stint on the disabled list his first two years with the Reds, he missed nearly two months of the 1989 season; the team stumbled to fifth place. The following year, when he established a career high with 185 hits while batting .301, his team won the World Series. Larkin batted .353 in the Series sweep of the heavily favored Oakland Athletics.

A consummate team player, Larkin was no stranger to individual honors. He was selected to 10 All-Star Games and won three Gold Gloves. He became the first shortstop to hit 30 home runs and steal 30 bases in the same season, adding 96 walks and 89 RBIs. Statistically, it was a better year than his MVP season.

In 1997 Larkin was named the first Reds captain since 1988, but he only played 73 games because of calf and Achilles tendon injuries. He returned to health in 1998, belting 166 hits and recording a .309 average. Larkin, however, grew disillusioned with the course the franchise was taking. After Lenny Harris was traded, Larkin temporarily removed his "C" in protest. During and after the season, he requested a trade, believing that the team's long-term rebuilding would prevent him from reaching another World Series. The Reds found no suitable takers, and Larkin was in the lineup for 1999.

As efficient as ever, he walked 93 times and recorded 171 hits, leading the surprising Reds into playoff contention. The team missed the postseason by one game, but it was the club's finest year since Larkin's MVP campaign.

Gene Larkin

Larkin, Eugene Thomas **1B–DH–OF**

1987–93 B:10/24/1962, Flushing, NY Deb:5/21/1987, MIN AL BB/TR 6'3", 205

G	AB	R	H	HR	RBI	BB	SO	AVG
758	2321	275	618	32	266	268	278	.266

Gene Larkin gained notice when he broke all of Lou Gehrig's records at Columbia University. He gained fame when he delivered the hit that ended the 1991 World Series. Larkin's pinch single over the drawn-in Atlanta Braves outfield scored Dan Gladden in the bottom of the 10th inning of Game 7. The epic 1–0 victory gave the Minnesota Twins their second world championship in five years.

As a rookie Larkin played a minor role in the Twins' 1987 world championship. He made five late-inning appearances in Minnesota's seven-game World Series victory over the St. Louis Cardinals.

He was a patient and selective hitter, albeit one with relatively little power. After playing regularly for three years, Larkin batted a career-high .286 in a reserve role for the 1991 champions. Just two seasons later he played his final major league game in what would have been an unmemorable career, had it not been for that fateful moment when he stepped to the plate with a World Series on the line.

Henry Larkin

Larkin, Henry E. **1B–OF**

1884–93 B:1/12/1860, Reading, PA D:1/31/1942, Reading, PA Deb:5/1/1884, PHI AA BR/TR 5'10", 175

G	AB	R	H	HR	RBI	OBP	SLG	AVG
1184	4718	925	1429	53	836	.380	.440	.303

First baseman–outfielder Henry Larkin was a career .303-hitter who possessed both speed and power. He had several exceptional days at the plate, twice collecting six hits in a single game. It is interesting to speculate what Larkin might have achieved if he had played during the Live Ball Era, when many of his doubles might well have become home runs.

Larkin began playing professionally at age 23 with Reading of the Inter-State League. In 1884 he moved up to the majors with Philadelphia of the American Association. He had his finest seasons in 1885 and 1886, leading the league in doubles both years and hitting .329 and .319.

On June 16, 1885, Larkin not only went 6 for 6 but also hit for the cycle, collecting a home run, a triple, two doubles, and two singles while scoring four runs. Six weeks later he hit four doubles in a game. In 1886 Larkin led the league with a .390 on-base percentage.

In 1890 Larkin jumped to the rebel Players' League and hit .330 as player-manager of the Cleveland Infants. The next year he returned to Philadelphia, where, on June 7, he again collected six hits, including a triple, in a lopsided 20–2 win over Cincinnati. Larkin finished his big league career with the National League Washington Senators in 1892 and 1893.

Larkin left the majors late in the 1893 season and went to Reading of the Pennsylvania State League, where he batted .338 in 16 games. In 1894 he hit .339 with Allentown and Altoona of the Pennsylvania State League. In 1895, splitting time between Allentown and Reading, he posted an impressive .358 average.

Terry Larkin

Larkin, Frank S. **P–2B**

1876–80, 1884 D:9/16/1894, Brooklyn, NY Deb:5/20/1876, NY NL BR/TR

W	L	PCT	G	SH	IP	BB	SO	ERA
89	80	.527	176	9	1567[1]	124	406	2.43

G	AB	R	H	HR	RBI	OBP	SLG	AVG
240	915	116	215	1	69	.274	.303	.235

Terry Larkin won 89 games over a three-year span, and never won again. He pitched 500 innings each season from 1877 to 1879 in the early days of the National League. The constant work ruined his arm, but he made a brief return as an infielder.

Larkin started and lost one game for the New York Giants in 1877. In Hartford the next year he won 29 games with a 2.14 ERA. He joined Chicago in 1878 and became the team's most consistent pitcher, winning 29 games and posting a 2.24 ERA. The following season Larkin increased his wins to 31 to go with a 2.44 ERA. He was the first Chicago pitcher to strike out more than 100 batters in a season with 163 in 1878. He also was the first pitcher in club history to accumulate 1,000 innings in a career; remarkably, he accomplished this in only two years.

Larkin lost all five of his starts with Troy in 1880 to end his career as a pitcher. After a four-year hiatus, he returned to professional baseball—as a third baseman. A .235 career hitter, he landed with Washington of the Union Association. Larkin switched teams, leagues, and positions in midseason, taking over at second base for Richmond in the American Association and batting .201 in 40 games.

Don Larsen

Larsen, Don James **P**
1953–65, 1967 B:8/7/1929, Michigan City, IN
Deb:4/18/1953, STL AL BR/TR 6'4", 227

W	L	PCT	G	SV	IP	BB	SO	ERA
81	91	.471	412	26	1548	725	849	3.78

Don Larsen never won more than 11 games in any one season, and his career statistics are very ordinary. But on October 8, 1956, Larsen had perhaps the most famous pitching day in the history of baseball, when he threw a 2–0 perfect game in the World Series.

The Brooklyn Dodgers had knocked him out in the second inning of Game 2, but Game 5 was Larsen's from the start. Pitching at Yankee Stadium, the righthander used a no-windup delivery that made pitching look like a game of catch. He needed only 97 pitches that day and only once threw as many as three balls to a hitter.

Two excellent plays preserved the perfect game. In the second inning Jackie Robinson hit a grounder in the hole, which third baseman Andy Carey touched with his glove and deflected to shortstop Gil McDougald, who threw Robinson out. In the fifth inning Gil Hodges hit a line drive into left-center field. Mickey Mantle made a fine running catch on the warning track.

The Yankees followed tradition and said nothing to Larsen. But the pitcher cornered Mantle in the runway late in the game and asked him, "Do you think I'll make it?" Mantle ignored him. In the ninth inning Larsen retired Carl Furillo and Roy Campanella before facing pinch hitter Dale Mitchell. The pitcher threw a ball, a called strike, and a foul ball before painting the outside corner with a fastball. Umpire Babe Pinelli, officiating in his last game at home plate before retirement, called strike three. In what is now a legendary moment, catcher Yogi Berra jumped into his pitcher's arms, and the 6-foot 4-inch Larsen carried him off the field as if he were a small child.

Larsen started in the minors with Aberdeen in the Northern League in 1947 and 1948, and then played in Springfield, Globe-Miami, Wichita, and Wichita Falls. He spent 1951 and 1952 in the military and was brought up to the St. Louis Browns in 1953. The next year he moved with the club to Baltimore, where he had a 3–21 record.

Larsen was traded to the Yankees in an 18-player deal in December 1954 and spent part of 1955 in Denver, where he went 9–1 and earned another chance in the majors. After joining the Yankees midway through 1955, he turned around his previous year's record by going 9–2.

The fun-loving Larsen fit in well on a team with such other carousers as Mantle, Billy Martin, and Whitey Ford. One spring training after he ran his car into a mailbox at 5:30 in the morning, manager Casey Stengel responded, "The man was either out too early or too late."

In 1956 Larsen was 11–5, and the next year he went 10–4, the only two times he would win as many as 10 games. In the 1957 World Series he won Game 2 but then lost Game 7. Overall, he pitched in four World Series for the Yankees with a 4–2 record. He pitched another two years with the Yankees before going to Kansas City in December 1959 in the deal that sent Roger Maris to New York.

After a 1–10 season in Kansas City—in which he pitched so poorly that the Athletics sent him back to the minor leagues—Larsen was changed to a relief pitcher. He reached the World Series again in 1962 with the Giants and, at Yankee Stadium on October 8, 1962, on the sixth anniversary of his perfect game he defeated the Yankees in relief.

Larsen hit well for a pitcher, with a lifetime .242 average and 14 career home runs. In fact, he was used a pinch hitter 66 times, and collected 12 hits. He retired in 1967, after a brief stint with the Chicago Cubs.

Tony La Russa

La Russa, Anthony **2B–SS**
1963, 1968–71, 1973 M(1979–*, 1639–1511)
B:10/4/1944, Tampa, FL Deb:5/10/1963, KC AL BR/TR
6'1", 190

G	AB	R	H	HR	RBI	OBP	SLG	AVG
132	176	15	35	0	7	.295	.250	.199

Writer George Will called him a genius. Outfielder Jose Canseco's wife Esther called him a punk. There's an element of truth in each assessment of Tony La Russa. Winner of five American League West titles, three pennants, and one world championship, La Russa was named American League Manager of the Year three times. He was also the primary architect of the Oakland Athletics' four division winners in five years beginning in 1988. La Russa's hallmarks were preparedness, game control, and an us-against-them mentality.

La Russa signed as a shortstop with the Kansas City A's organization for a $50,000 bonus in 1962 after graduating from Jefferson High School in

Tampa, Florida. He played 16 seasons of pro ball, mainly as a second baseman, with six different organizations. However, he spent parts of only six seasons in the majors, and hit only .199 in 176 at bats.

Throughout his playing career La Russa continued his education. He attended the University of Tampa and the University of South Florida during off-seasons and obtained a degree in industrial engineering. He went to law school at Florida State University, graduated in 1978, and passed the bar in 1979. Only four lawyers managed in the big leagues before him; all four—Monte Ward, Hughie Jennings, Miller Huggins, and Branch Rickey—reached the Hall of Fame.

In 1977, his final active season in the minor leagues, La Russa was a player-coach in the St. Louis Cardinals organization. Paul Richards, who had met La Russa when they both were in the Atlanta Braves' chain, was working for the Chicago White Sox and gave La Russa a chance to manage their Class AA Knoxville farm team in 1978. La Russa joined the White Sox as a major league coach later that year, went back to manage their Class AAA Iowa affiliate at the start of 1979, and took over the 46–60 White Sox from Don Kessinger on August 2.

The Sox played .500-ball for the rest of the year under La Russa, finishing fifth. In 1980 they finished fifth again. During the strike-interrupted 1981 season Chicago had an overall winning record, and in 1982 the team placed third, at 87–75. The next season they arrived, going 99–63 and winning the AL West by 20 games. La Russa won his first Manager of the Year Award.

Although the Sox led the league in runs scored in 1983, their real strength was pitching. Coach Dave Duncan guided a staff led by Cy Young Award-winner La Marr Hoyt. Duncan and La Russa went on to enjoy a long and fruitful partnership. It was no accident that pitchers such as Dave Stewart, Dennis Eckersley, Storm Davis, and Jeff Parrett revived their careers under La Russa and Duncan, thanks to a combination of teaching and psychology. Together, La Russa and Duncan also fully developed the concept of clearly defined roles for all pitchers, an approach they readily admitted works best for pitchers of average talent. The manager and coach believed that when pitchers knew exactly what was expected of them, they become more relaxed and better prepared.

The downside of this approach is that developing roles obliges the manager to use the players only in appropriate situations, leading to what some consider excessive pitching changes. Call it over-managing,

aggressive managing, or defensive managing—it prevents second-guessing by creating the match-up that looks best on paper.

The White Sox lost in the playoffs in 1983, fell to a sixth-place finish in 1984, and rebounded to third in 1985. After the 1985 season broadcaster Ken Harrelson, La Russa's polar opposite in personality, was appointed general manager. On June 19, 1986, La Russa was fired.

The next month La Russa joined the Athletics. They were 31–52 when he arrived and went 45–34 for the rest of 1986. In 1987 the team played .500 ball for the first time in five years. In 1988 they won the AL West with a 104–58 record, the first of three straight pennant-winning seasons, and La Russa captured his second Manager of the Year honor. After a bitter defeat to the Los Angeles Dodgers in the 1989 World Series, the A's swept the San Francisco Giants in the earthquake-interrupted 1989 Series. The 1990 pennant was soured by a shocking sweep at the hands of the Cincinnati Reds. After finishing fourth in 1991, the A's took their fourth AL West title in 1992. La Russa guided the team through numerous injuries and impending transition, with at least a dozen potential free agents looming, and received his third Manager of the Year Award.

In Oakland, La Russa won with both pitching and power. In either case, he believed in playing aggressively. Although pitching moves at times were carefully scripted, La Russa conducted other aspects of the game less predictably. He pushed the frontiers of computerizing reports and charts. He occasionally played a hunch, but many of his clever moves resulted from careful research.

La Russa's system demanded a lot from players, and he tailored his approaches to each individual in order to win the player's cooperation. For example, he gave A's outfielder Jose Canseco plenty of room to act like a superstar as long as he did his work. He benched Canseco, however, in Game 4 of the 1990 World Series after he had bungled a pair of flyballs in Game 3. Although La Russa wouldn't say so, the message of the benching was not directed at Canseco but at the rest of the team. It was La Russa's way of saying that if any player failed to give his utmost he was letting the whole team down.

The concept of team unity was a key concern for La Russa. Whatever may have gone on in the clubhouse, his teams presented a united front against the rest of baseball. The manager was passionate about his team, just as he was about animal rights and other issues.

When Canseco left Oakland he drew chuckles by saying he preferred Texas because in Oakland, "All they cared about is winning." Few people in any field could match La Russa's day-in, day-out intensity. After the 1995 season, when the A's fell to last place with a 67–77 record and the team's ownership changed, La Russa departed. He landed in St. Louis, where he piloted the Cardinals as far as the National League Central championship in 1996. The Cards won the Division Series and held a three-games-to-one lead in the NLCS before Atlanta rallied to win.

Despite the record-setting home-run bat of Mark McGwire, La Russa's Cardinals finished out of the running for the playoffs in 1997, 1998, and 1999. At the end of the 1999 season, La Russa's 1,639 wins were the most of any active manager in the majors.

Frank Lary

Lary, Frank Strong **P**

1954–65 B:4/10/1930, Northport, AL Deb:9/14/1954, DET AL BR/TR 5'11", 180

W	L	PCT	G	SH	IP	BB	SO	ERA
128	116	.525	350	21	2162^1	616	1099	3.49

Detroit righthander Frank Lary earned the reputation as the 1950s' premier "Yankee killer," going 5–1 against New York in 1956 and 7–0 in 1958. The latter year was the first time since 1916 that a hurler had done that to the Yankees. Lifetime, Lary was 27–13 against the Yanks, including one victory in which he beat them himself with a squeeze bunt.

Lary was one of seven brothers who played baseball at the University of Alabama, all but one of whom pitched. (His older brother Al eventually reached the Cubs.) He started with Thomasville in the Georgia–Florida League in 1950 before spending 1951 and 1952 in the military. Returning to pitch for the International League's Buffalo Bisons in 1953–54, he went 17–11 and 15–11, respectively.

Lary joined the Tigers for his first full season in 1955. By the next year he was their ace, winning a league-high 21 games, throwing 20 complete games, and pitching a league-leading 294 innings. Lary led the Al in complete games and innings pitched in 1958 and again in 1960. That second year he was chosen to his first of two All-Star Games, in neither of which he allowed an earned run.

The 1961 season was Lary's finest. He went 23–9 with an AL-high 22 complete games. He also won a Gold Glove. However, that was Lary's last top-notch season. He missed the last half of the 1962 season on the disabled list with a sore arm, and then saw limited action in 1963.

He was sold to the New York Mets in May 1964 and then traded to the Milwaukee Braves that August. Sold back to the Mets in March 1965, he was traded to the White Sox that July. It was his final season, although as late as the 1970s Lary was contending he was capable of a major league comeback.

Lyn Lary

Lary, Lynford Hobart **SS**

1929–40 B:1/28/1906, Armona, CA D:1/9/1973, Downey, CA Deb:5/11/1929, NY AL BR/TR 6', 165

G	AB	R	H	HR	RBI	OBP	SLG	AVG
1302	4603	805	1239	38	526	.369	.372	.269

The New York Yankees' shortstop at the tail end of the Babe Ruth era, Lyn Lary is chiefly remembered for the company he kept. The Yankees purchased Lary and his double-play partner, second baseman Jimmy Reese, from the Oakland Acorns of the Pacific Coast League in 1928. In May 1929 he made his Yankees debut, playing part-time at third base and batting .309, the only .300 season of his 12-year career. That winter the Yankees sold Leo Durocher to make room for Lary, and in 1930 he shared shortstop duties with Mark Koenig.

In 1931 Lary became New York's regular shortstop when the Yankees sent Koenig and pitcher Waite Hoyt to the Detroit Tigers. In his only full-time season with New York, Lary recorded 54 extra-base hits, scored 100 runs, and ranked fifth in the league with 88 walks. He also drove in 107 runs, giving the Yankees four players with more than 100 RBIs—Lou Gehrig with an AL-record 184, Ruth with 163, Ben Chapman with 122, and Lary. That tied a major league record, which was later broken by the 1936 Yankees, who had five men with triple figures.

In that 1931 campaign a base-running error by Lary cost Gehrig sole possession of the home run title. Late in the season Gehrig's long, high drive left the park. This would have given him a total of 47 round-trippers for the year, one more than Ruth. But Lary, thinking the ball had been caught, returned to his base and passed Gehrig, who was called out.

In 1932 Lary's batting average dropped to .232, and he began to lose his job to rookie Frank Crosetti. But on July 3 Lary did something that neither Ruth nor Gehrig ever accomplished: he stroked two doubles in the same inning. By the next season he had become a rarely used utility man.

In May 1934 Lary was traded to the Red Sox, where he led AL shortstops in fielding, the high point of a competent career with the glove. After that season he was shipped to Washington along with $225,000 for shortstop Joe Cronin, the son-in-law of cash-strapped Senators owner Clark Griffith.

Lary's travels continued, as in June 1935 he was sent to the St. Louis Browns. In 1936, his only full season with the Browns, he hit .289 with 117 walks and 112 runs. He also was the league's most effective base-stealer, with a total of 37. Traded to the Cleveland Indians before the next season, Lary responded with a .290 average and 46 doubles,

110 runs, and 77 RBIs. After one more solid year, he was sold to Brooklyn in May 1939. Three months later he was dealt to the St. Louis Cardinals. He batted only .176 for the season and retired the next year after hitting an anemic .054.

Despite his five years in the Bronx with some great teams, Lary never played in the postseason. Crosetti replaced him at shortstop in all four games of the Yankees' 1932 World Series sweep of the Cubs.

Tommy Lasorda

Lasorda, Thomas Charles **P**

1954–56 M(1976–96, 1599–1439) B:9/22/1927, Norristown, PA Deb:8/5/1954, BRO NL BL/TL 5'10", 175

W	L	PCT	G	SV	IP	BB	SO	ERA
0	4	.000	26	1	58^{1}	56	37	6.48

"I bleed Dodger blue, and when I die, I'm going to the Big Dodger in the sky." So said longtime team manager Tommy Lasorda, who led the Dodgers to six division titles, four National League pennants, and two World Series championships.

Lasorda's dedication to the Dodgers was well known. So was his cheerleader style of management. "I motivate players through communication, being honest with them, having them respect and appreciate your ability and your help," he explained in 1982. "I started in the minor leagues. I used to hug my players when they did something well. That's my enthusiasm. That's my personality. I jump with joy when we win. I try to be on a close basis with my players. People say you can't go out and eat with your players. I say, why not?"

Originally a lefthanded pitcher, Lasorda was only 16 years old when he signed with the Philadelphia Phillies for $100 a month. "If you'd waited five minutes more, I would've offered you $200 a month to let me play professional baseball," Lasorda later informed the scout.

Philadelphia sent Lasorda to Concord of the Class D North Carolina State League. He lost his first game when a ground ball went through the Concord shortstop's legs. After the game Lasorda roughed his teammate up in the clubhouse. Manager "Pappy" Lehman warned him, "You can't go around fighting with your own teammates. Let me tell you something: you win as a team and you lose as a team, and you better learn that quick if you want to stay in baseball."

In 1948 Lasorda played for Schenectady of the Class C Canadian–American League. Against the Amsterdam Rugmakers on May 31, 1948, he struck out 25 batters in 15 innings. He also walked 12. Control problems dogged him for his entire playing career. He led the Can–Am League in wild pitches, with 20, and, despite striking out 195, he issued 153 bases on balls.

At season's end the Dodgers' organization drafted Lasorda and assigned him to Greenville of the Class A South Atlantic League. They then promoted him to the International League's Montreal Royals, their top farm club, where he met future Dodgers manager Walter Alston. Lasorda went 9–4 for Alston, exhibited his usual wildness, and began a decade at the Class AAA level.

He had several stints with the Dodgers, and after a short stay with the Kansas City Athletics he shifted over to the American Association's Denver Bears and later the Los Angeles Angels of the Pacific Coast League. In 1958 Lasorda returned to the Royals. He went 12–8 in 1959 and was still pitching effectively when he was released on July 9, 1960, following an altercation with Montreal manager Clay Bryant.

The Dodgers and Lasorda patched up their differences, and the club made him a scout. In 1965 he returned to the minor leagues, managing the Dodgers' Pioneer League farm team at Pocatello, Idaho. Pocatello finished second that year and the next, and the organization transferred Lasorda to Ogden, Utah.

His players approved of him. "In many ways, Lasorda was the perfect manager for us," said former infielder Steve Garvey, who had come under the skipper's tutelage as a farmhand. "He was a big, good-natured uncle. He knew baseball and he taught baseball, but he also understood the situation. Maybe that was even more important."

When Ogden captured three consecutive championships the Dodgers promoted Lasorda to manager of the PCL's Spokane Indians. Again Lasorda finished second in his first campaign with a new club. The next season, the team won the PCL's Northern Division by 26 games.

In 1972 the club shifted to Albuquerque. Again Lasorda captured the pennant and the playoffs, and the Dodgers promoted him to the big club's coaching ranks. He served as Alston's heir apparent until September 29, 1976, when Lasorda assumed the team's leadership.

It was a natural succession. Lasorda had molded many of his new charges in the minors, including Garvey, third baseman Ron Cey, second baseman Davey Lopes, shortstop Bill Russell, utility fielder Bobby Valentine, and outfielder Bill Buckner.

Late in his managing career the overweight Lasorda became nationally known as spokesman for a diet program, the result of his losing 30 pounds after being goaded into the program by pitcher Orel Hershiser. It wasn't easy for Lasorda, who was long known for his love of Italian cuisine. "I was so elated that we had finally won the world championship that I spent the entire winter eating," Lasorda said after the 1981 World Series. "Of course, had we lost, I would have been so unhappy I would have spent the entire winter eating."

After suffering a midseason heart attack in 1996, Lasorda turned the managing job over to Bill Russell. He was inducted into the Baseball Hall of Fame in 1997. The next year Lasorda replaced Fred Claire as Dodgers general manager. He retained the title senior vice president in 1999.

Arlie Latham

Latham, Walter Arlington **3B**

1880, 1883–96, 1899, 1909 M (1896, 0–3) B:3/15/1860, West Lebanon, NH D:11/29/1952, Garden City, NY Deb:7/5/1880, BUF NL BR/TR 5'8", 150

G	AB	R	H	HR	RBI	OBP	SLG	AVG
1627	6822	1478	1833	27	563	.334	.341	.269

Arlie Latham was called "the Freshest Man on Earth" after a popular song of the 1880s. The song is long forgotten, but Latham lives on in stories still told by baseball enthusiasts.

The lively third baseman was always ready with a wisecrack, prank, or some kind of physical humor to make the fans roar. The spiritual father of Al Schacht, Nick Altrock, and Max Patkin, the happy-go-lucky Latham charmed his way through a long playing career and even longer post-playing career that totaled 76 years of involvement with the national pastime in one way or another.

Latham began as a semipro player in Stoneham, Massachusetts, when he was 15. He had a brief trial with Buffalo's National League team in 1880, but didn't stay in the major leagues until he joined the St. Louis Browns of the American Association in 1883. After Charlie Comiskey became their manager, the Browns ran off four straight AA championships from 1885 through 1888 with Latham as third baseman, leadoff man, and team clown.

Although he batted above .300 four times in his career, Latham was not considered an outstanding hitter. He excelled mostly on defense, exhibiting one of the strongest arms in baseball, and on the basepaths. Because the rules at that time credited a player with a stolen base whenever he took an extra 90 feet on a teammate's hit, it is impossible to accurately reconstruct Latham's record in modern terms. However, under the rules of his day, he was credited with 129 steals in 1887, and he led the league the next year with 109. His career total, with some years unavailable, is 739.

With his speed and baserunning prowess, it is not surprising that Latham was usually among the league leaders in scoring runs. He scored more than 100 runs in nine different seasons, topped the American Association with 152 in 1886, and had a career total of 1,478.

He was also an adept tumbler. One day Latham bunted down to Chicago's Cap Anson at first. The large first baseman waited with the ball as Latham ran toward him. Suddenly, the 150-pound Latham catapulted into the air, somersaulted over the astonished Anson, and came down on the base—safe!

Latham played part of the 1890 season in the Players' League, and then joined Cincinnati of the National League where he starred through 1895, his last full season. His baseball popularity led him to pursue a stage career, and he appeared on Broadway in a play called *Fashions*. He then spent three years as an umpire before joining the New York Giants in 1909.

That year, at a time when players took turns coaching base runners at first and third, John McGraw hired Latham to be baseball's first professional coach. Some say that his habit of roaming the length of the foul line inspired the creation of the coaches' boxes that bracket the diamond today. Latham also played in four games and, although he went hitless, became, at the age of 49, the oldest player to steal a base.

After World War I, Latham moved to England as administrator of baseball, a post that allowed him to become friendly with the Prince of Wales, England's future King Edward VIII. When he returned to America, he became custodian of the New York Yankees' press box.

Charlie Lau

Lau, Charles Richard **C–PH**

1956, 1958–67 B:4/12/1933, Romulus, MI D:3/18/1984, Key Colony Beach, FL Deb:9/12/1956, DET AL BL/TR 6', 190

G	AB	R	H	HR	RBI	OBP	SLG	AVG
527	1170	105	298	16	140	.321	.365	.255

During his 11-year major league career, catcher Charlie Lau hit only .255. That didn't prevent him from becoming one of the game's best-known hitting coaches. During 15 years as a major league coach Lau was credited with helping the careers of a host of players, among them Reggie Jackson, Harold Baines, Hal McRae, and batting champions Willie Wilson and George Brett.

Lau had been a good hitter in the minors. In his second year in professional baseball, 1955, he hit .293 with 18 home runs and 75 RBIs with Durham of the Carolina League. In 1956 he made a late-season appearance with the Detroit Tigers, then spent several years shuttling between the Tigers and their Class AAA Charleston farm club. In 1959 he flirted with stardom after hitting .292 with 20 home runs for Charleston.

Detroit then traded him to the Milwaukee Braves, with whom he appeared in a backup role in 1960 and 1961 before resuming the Class AAA shuttle. Lau simply couldn't consistently hit big league pitching, but his defense and the fact that he hit from the left side still made him a valuable commodity. Milwaukee sold Lau to Baltimore, where he found some success as a platoon player. He continued the pattern with the Kansas City Athletics, who purchased him from the Orioles in 1963. Baltimore got him back the following year in a trade for pitcher Wes Stock.

After Lau hurt his right elbow in 1966 he never appeared behind the plate again. He struggled through nearly two years as a pinch hitter with the Orioles before being sold to Atlanta in midseason 1967. He appeared in 52 games and retired at the end of the season.

The next year Lau managed Shreveport of the Texas League before returning to coach for the Orioles in 1969. When he was credited with helping light-hitting shortstop Mark Belanger hit a lifetime-high .287, Lau's career as a hitting coach took off.

He moved on to the Oakland A's in 1971, and then to the Kansas City Royals in 1972. In Kansas City he developed his unique theories about hitting, and as both a major league coach and a minor league hitting instructor during the next eight seasons he worked with a number of the Royals' fine young hitters.

Under Lau's tutelage, power hitters often hit for a higher average and singles hitters flourished. Because the artificial turf in Royals Stadium put a premium on speed, Lau convinced many of the Royals' swifter players to hit the ball on the ground and take advantage of their natural talents.

Lau's instruction combined sound biomechanical principles with constant repetition and analysis. He favored an approach in which the hitter remained balanced and used the whole field, hitting down and through the ball to prevent hitting weak pop flies and then finishing "high," pulling the lead arm up and through the ball. Lau's graduates were often easy to spot, as their front arms followed through in an exaggerated "helicopter" arc.

The method had its critics, however, including Hall of Fame outfielder and batting legend Ted Williams. Some complained that the approach was too complicated, and rejected its focus on the batter's front arm. Lau's teachings ran counter to established theories, and some veterans found it difficult to adopt his method, often struggling through one or two terrible seasons before either finding success or returning to their former styles.

Yet as Lau's disciples became more successful, his reputation grew. The coach taught his methods to other hitters and coaches in off-season clinics, and his converts spread the word. Lau moved on to the New York Yankees in 1979 and then to the Chicago White Sox in 1981, signing under what were considered extremely generous terms for a hitting coach. He was officially a "teaching coach," in recognition of his unique talents.

Lau's success continued in Chicago, where Harold Baines flourished under his influence, and his teaching method spread throughout baseball. He published two books, *The Art of Hitting .300* and *The Winning Hitter*, two of the most successful and influential books about hitting since Ted Williams' *Science of Hitting*. Lau died of cancer on March 18, 1984. A decade later, his theories continue to influence an entire generation of professional baseball players.

Cookie Lavagetto

Lavagetto, Harry Arthur **3B–2B**

1934–41, 1946–47 M(1957–61, 271–384) B:12/1/1912, Oakland, CA D:8/10/1990, Orinda, CA Deb:4/17/1934, PIT NL BR/TR 6', 170

G	AB	R	H	HR	RBI	OBP	SLG	AVG
1043	3509	487	945	40	486	.360	.377	.269

Brooklyn Dodgers fan favorite Cookie Lavagetto had only two hits in 17 World Series at bats. But his second one, which also was his last hit as a major leaguer, broke up the no-hit bid by New York Yankees pitcher Bill Bevens with two outs in the ninth inning of Game 4 of the 1947 World Series.

He broke into the majors with the Pittsburgh Pirates in 1934. After three years as a utility infielder, Lavagetto went to the Dodgers with pitcher Ralph Birkofer for pitcher Ed Brandt on December 4, 1936. He became a regular in 1937, playing mostly at second base. He was a coarse-looking player who often had tobacco juice stains on his uniform, and his whole persona helped inspire the chant, "Lookie, lookie, here comes Cookie," among the Dodgers' faithful.

Lavagetto switched to third base in 1938. For the next four seasons he was selected to the National League All-Star team. He also began a streak of six straight seasons with at least twice as many walks as strikeouts. In 1939 he batted an even .300, the only season he reached that mark, and set career bests with 10 homers, 93 runs scored, and 87 RBIs. He had six hits in one game on September 23. But when the Dodgers reached the World Series against the Yankees in 1941, he had just one hit in 10 at bats and was benched for the final two games as Brooklyn fell in five.

Lavagetto joined the armed forces in 1942 and didn't return to major league baseball until 1946. On his return he shared third base with Billy Herman. Teammate Rex Barney remembers him as a steadying veteran influence on the team, but Lavagetto was also one of the first signers of the clubhouse petition against Jackie Robinson.

In 1947 Lavagetto played in just 41 games, nearly half as a pinch hitter, going 4-for-17 in that role. There was little suggestion that Lavagetto would deliver one of the biggest pinch hits in World Series history as the Dodgers faced the Yankees again. In Game 1 of the Series, Lavagetto popped out as a pinch hitter, remained in the game at third, and struck out in the ninth as the Dodgers lost, 5–3. He didn't play in Game 2, a Yankee rout, or Game 3, when the Dodgers jumped to a 6–0 lead in the second inning and hung on for a 9–8 victory.

In Game 4 Brooklyn faced Bevens, the Yankees' fast and wild righthander who had gone 7–13 that season. The Dodgers managed a run on two walks, a sacrifice bunt, and a groundout in the fifth, but they trailed, 2–1, and still didn't have a hit by the ninth. With one out, Carl Furillo drew a walk, but Spider Jorgensen fouled out to first for the second out, leaving Bevens one out short of the first no-hitter in World Series history. Brooklyn manager Burt Shotton sent Al Gionfriddo in as pinch runner for Furillo, and he stole second with pinch hitter Pete Reiser at the plate.

Yankees manager Bucky Harris chose to walk Reiser intentionally, going against the book, which says, "Never put the winning run on base." Eddie Miksis pinch-ran for Reiser. Shotton then called for Lavagetto to pinch-hit for Eddie Stanky. But Lavagetto wasn't on the bench. "When Shotton yelled for Cookie to get a bat, he was sitting in the runway with his socks off and his sore feet up on a chair," Barney recalls. "Arky Vaughan and I had to dress him and get him out on the field."

The Yankees' scouting report said Lavagetto could be beaten with hard stuff away, but it also said he was a pull-hitter, so right fielder Tommy Henrich shaded him toward center field. With the count 0–1, Lavagetto cracked a line drive toward the right-field corner. Henrich had a little trouble seeing the ball against the crowd and then sprinted toward the wall. He jumped feebly, trying to make the catch, but the ball hit high off Ebbets Field's concrete wall. Henrich was too close to the wall to handle the carom cleanly. Gionfriddo scored the tying run, and the relay throw was too late to get Miksis, who slid across the plate with the winning run. Reporters wrote that Lavagetto's double had ended the greatest game ever, as well as tied the World Series at two games apiece.

The next day, with two outs in the ninth, with the Dodgers trailing 2–1 and the tying run on second, Lavagetto was summoned to pinch-hit again. He struck out, and then failed in two more pinch-hit attempts as the Dodgers lost in seven games. He never batted in the majors again.

Lavagetto returned to his hometown to play for the Oakland Oaks under Casey Stengel, and then coached for Brooklyn for three years, starting in 1951, under Chuck Dressen. When Dressen managed the Washington Senators in 1955, Lavagetto coached for him again, and replaced him as manager early in the 1957 season.

After three last-place finishes, Lavagetto's Senators rose to fifth in 1960, and he moved to Minnesota with the team for the 1961 season. But Sam Mele replaced Lavagetto less than halfway through the team's 1961 debut as the Twins. Cookie coached for Stengel's New York Mets for two years, and then returned home to the Bay Area, coaching with the Giants from 1964 through 1967.

Gary Lavelle

Lavelle, Gary Robert **P**

1974–85, 1987 B:1/3/1949, Scranton, PA
Deb:9/10/1974, SF NL BB/TL 6'1", 200

W	L	PCT	G	SV	IP	BB	SO	ERA
80	77	.510	745	136	1085	440	769	2.93

Gary Lavelle did not look the part of an intimidating closer. As Giants broadcaster and former teammate Mike Krukow described him, "Gary Lavelle looked like a barrel-chested coal miner. He was six feet tall, weighed about 240 pounds, was losing his hair, had a scraggly beard that he always kept shaved, ran like he was a Willie Mays bobblehead doll, had one of the best beer bellies in the league (unique because he didn't drink beer), wore glasses as thick as the first base bag, and only had a frozen game face if you told him chapel was canceled on Sunday morning."

What Lavelle lacked in demeanor he overcame with a blazing fastball. The two-time All-Star saved 20 games three times: in 1977 and 1979 while splitting time in the bullpen with Randy Moffitt, and again in 1983 after Greg Minton replaced Moffitt as the team's righthanded closer. Lavelle moved on to Toronto after the 1984 season, and returned to the Bay Area to finish out his career with Oakland in 1987.

Lavelle established the Giants' franchise record with 647 games pitched. He also set the mark for most saves by a Giant, which was later topped by Rod Beck.

Vern Law

Law, Vernon Sanders **P**

1950–51, 1954–67 B:3/12/1930, Meridian, ID
Deb:6/11/1950, PIT NL BR/TR 6'2", 195

W	L	PCT	G	SH	IP	BB	SO	ERA
162	147	.524	483	28	2672	597	1092	3.77

His Pirates teammates called Vernon Law "the Deacon," not only because of his status as an elder of the Mormon church but also because of his solid, stable presence on the mound and in the clubhouse. On a team with such emotional leaders as infielder Don Hoak and outfielder Roberto Clemente, Law was a steadying influence. He was also a workhorse; Law hurled 38 complete games in 68 starts over two seasons

The Pirates signed Law in 1948 when Senator Herman Welker of Idaho recommended him to Pirates vice president Bing Crosby. Although Law did not better a .500 won-loss record during his first five years in the majors, his faith in his ability enabled him to keep going, and he finally cracked the ranks of the top pitchers in the league when he went 18–9 with a 2.98 ERA in 1959.

Law became a true star in the Pirates' 1960 championship season. He went 20–9, led the league with 18 complete games, and was selected to the All-Star Game. More importantly, he was the stopper on the mound. Only twice that same year did the Pirates lose four games in a row; Law put them back on track both times. At the end of the season, he won the Cy Young Award, garnering twice as many votes as runner-up Warren Spahn.

In the clubhouse celebration after the Pirates clinched the pennant, Law injured his ankle. Some said it occurred when raucous outfielder Gino Cimoli tried to wrench off the Deacon's shoe in order to use it as a champagne glass. But Law's performance in the World Series against the Yankees didn't indicate any severe problem. He won Games 1 and 4, although he failed to last six innings in Game 7.

The next year the ankle bothered him, and pitching with it caused him to injure his rotator cuff. He appeared in only 11 games. In 1962 Law fought back to sport a 10–7 record, and two of his losses were by only one run. Other physical problems pushed him to voluntary retirement early in the 1963 season.

Law's religious faith and stoicism served him well, however. He refused to let his injuries keep him out of basball, and in 1964 he came back and recorded 12 wins. The next year he went 17–9, and his ERA was a sensational 2.15 as he helped the Pirates to a third-place finish. That performance earned him Comeback Player of the Year honors.

In 1966 Law recorded another 12-win season, although he was still pestered by a hip injury. His last year as a player was 1967, but he stayed with the team as pitching coach in 1968 and 1969. His son Vance was a major league infielder with five teams from 1980 to 1991.

Tony Lazzeri

Lazzeri, Anthony Michael **2B-3B**

1926–39 B:12/6/1903, San Francisco, CA D:8/6/1946, San Francisco, CA Deb:4/13/1926, NY AL BR/TR 5'11½", 170

G	AB	R	H	HR	RBI	OBP	SLG	AVG
1740	6297	986	1840	178	1191	.380	.467	.292

Tony Lazzeri's most famous moment in baseball came when he struck out during the 1926 World Series. Throughout his Hall of Fame career, however, this talented, intelligent second baseman combined sound defense with power hitting.

Lazzeri's professional career began in 1922 with the Pacific Coast League's Salt Lake City Bees. After brief stops in Peoria and Lincoln he returned to Salt Lake City, where he had one of the greatest minor league seasons of all time in 1925, hitting 60 home runs and driving in 222, to complement a .355-batting average. Of course Lazzeri was helped by the PCL's 197-game extended schedule and by Salt Lake City's compact Bonneville Park; nonetheless, no one in either the minors or the majors had ever hit 60 homers in a season before.

Impressed, the New York Yankees surrendered $55,000 and five players to obtain Lazzeri. The investment paid off immediately as he delivered 18 homers and 114 RBIs in his rookie season. "Tony is a great natural player," said Yankees manager Miller Huggins. "Make no mistake about that. This is his first year in the majors, but he's no flash in the pan. He should improve."

Huggins was right. From 1926 through 1937 Lazzeri, who was nicknamed "Poosh 'Em Up," ranked seventh among American League home run hitters, behind only Babe Ruth, Lou Gehrig, Jimmie Foxx, Al Simmons, Earl Averill, and Goose Goslin. During that same period Lazzeri was sixth in RBIs, behind Gehrig, Simmons, Foxx, Ruth, and Goslin.

In Lazzeri's rookie season, the World Series between the St. Louis Cardinals and the Yanks went down to Game 7, and the key moment occurred with two outs in the bottom of the seventh. The Cardinals were leading 3–2. With Gehrig, Earle Combs, and Bob Meusel on base, Lazzeri was due up. St. Louis manager Rogers Hornsby walked to the mound to take out Pop Haines, who was no longer effective because of a blister on his pitching hand. Hornsby motioned to the bullpen for reliever Grover Cleveland Alexander.

Only the day before Lazzeri had gone 0-for-4 against Alexander, who had defeated the Yankees in a complete-game laugher, 10–2. The Cardinals pitcher took his time as he faced Lazzeri again, hoping to unnerve the rookie. The first pitch was a ball. The next was a low fastball for a called strike. Then came a ball that was high and near Lazzeri's head. Alexander got the next pitch over the plate, and

Lazzeri hit it hard and deep toward the left field stands. The crowd gasped but it landed foul.

Lazzeri swung at Alexander's next pitch—and missed. The soon-to-be world champion Cardinals were out of their toughest jam of the game. "Less than a foot made the difference between a hero and a bum," commented Alexander, referring to how lucky he was that Lazzeri's blow had gone foul.

Throughout his career Lazzeri enjoyed a reputation as one of the smartest infielders in baseball. He was also a natural team leader. Not long after he had joined the Yankees, veteran umpire Tommy Connolly remarked, "When things get tough out there, the others don't look to Ruth or any of the veterans. They look to (Lazzeri), and he never fails them."

Lazzeri improved throughout each of his first four years. After hitting .275 as a rookie, he hit .309 the next year as a member of the Yankee's fabled "Murderer's Row." He followed that with .332 and then .354, the latter mark fourth best in the league. His hitting then tailed off, and he never again topped .303.

On May 24, 1936, Lazzeri became the first player in major league history to record two grand slams in a single game, setting an AL record in the process with 11 RBIs. In Game 2 of that year's World Series he greeted Giants hurler Dick Coffman with another grand slam—only the second in Series competition.

Lazzeri moved to the Chicago Cubs in 1938. He retired as a player following the 1939 season, when he appeared with the Brooklyn Dodgers and the New York Giants. He managed Toronto from 1939 through 1940, and failed in a comeback as player with San Francisco in 1941, hitting only .248. In 1942 Lazzeri managed Portsmouth of the Piedmont League, and the next year he skippered Wilkes-Barre of the Eastern League.

Lazzeri was epileptic, and he died in 1946 after falling down the stairway of his San Francisco home; the accident was probably the result of a seizure. The Veterans Committee elected him to the Hall of Fame in 1991.

Tommy Leach

Leach, Thomas William **OF–3B**

1898–1915, 1918 B:11/4/1877, French Creek, NY D:9/29/1969, Haines City, FL Deb:9/28/1898, LOU NL BR/TR 5'6½", 150

G	AB	R	H	HR	RBI	OBP	SLG	AVG
2156	7959	1355	2143	63	810	.340	.370	.269

At the beginning of his career, Tommy Leach hoped to join a team that needed a third baseman. He was told not to bother with the Washington Senators, because they were already set at third with a player named Wagner. Leach signed with Louisville instead.

"I hardly had time to get settled before it hit me that this guy the Louisville club had at third base was practically doing the impossible," he later told writer Lawrence Ritter. Leach was on the bench when the big Louisville third sacker made an unbelievable stop to throw out a runner. "My eyes are popping out," said Leach.

He asked who was playing third and was told that it was "Wagner... the best third baseman in the league." As it turned out, the Washington Wagner was Al Wagner, a fair player. The Louisville Wagner was his brother Honus, one of the greatest players of all time.

Fortunately for Leach, Wagner could play any position and much preferred the outfield, so Leach was soon installed at third. A few years later manager Fred Clarke wanted Wagner to play shortstop. Wagner didn't believe he could play that position, but Clarke finally talked him into trying third again and shifted third baseman Leach over to short.

Then, Clarke told Leach to complain to Wagner that he hated playing shortstop and that he felt he was hurting the team. After several weeks of this, Wagner agreed to switch positions with Leach. As a result, Wagner became, in the opinion of many, the best shortstop the game has ever known. Leach spent most of his career in Wagner's shadow, but he managed to carve out a reputation of his own.

Leach grew up in Cleveland, where he played ball with the Delahanty brothers, who sent five of their clan to the majors. He began his professional career in 1896 with Petersburg of the Virginia League and during the next few seasons played with several other minor league teams.

The New York Giants expressed some interest in him, but when owner Andrew Freedman noted that Leach was only 5 feet 6 inches, he sent him back to the minors. "Tommy the Wee," as the fans called him, eventually joined Louisville of the National League at the end of the 1898 season.

Louisville was dropped from the National League after the 1899 season, but owner Barney Dreyfuss was allowed to buy into the Pittsburgh Pirates. He switched his best Louisville players—among them Wagner, Clarke, and Leach—to the Pirates, creating a powerhouse. Pittsburgh narrowly missed capturing the 1900 pennant, and then won it the next three years.

Leach hit .305 for the 1901 champions. In 1902 he led the league with six home runs—the lowest league-leading total of the 20th century—and 22 triples. Leach later claimed he weighed only 135 pounds during that season, undoubtedly making him the smallest home run champion in major league history.

After winning the 1903 pennant the Pirates faced Boston's American League champions in the first modern World Series. But illness and injury had decimated Pittsburgh's pitching staff, and Boston upset the Pirates to claim the world championship. Leach was outstanding in the Series, hitting four triples and leading both teams with seven RBIs. He hit two triples in the opening game—still a record—but he benefited from the fact that, because each hit went into overflow outfield crowds, he was awarded third according to prevailing ground rules.

In 1905 Leach injured his hip in a collision at home plate, forcing him to play primarily in the outfield for the rest of his career. He found outfield duty easy after his years in the infield, and after only a couple of games he quipped, "Outfielders ought to pay to get in." At age 35 he led NL outfielders with a .990 fielding percentage

In 1909 Pittsburgh won 110 games and the pennant, and Leach led the National League with 126 runs scored. In the World Series he was again outstanding, hitting .320 in seven games to lead all players. Leach also led all participants with eight runs scored. He also saved the day during the opener, when, with two out and two on in the seventh, he made a spectacular barehanded catch of a long drive by Ty Cobb.

Leach remained with the Pirates until 1912, when he was traded to the Cubs along with pitcher Lefty Leifield for outfielder Solly Hofman and pitcher King Cole. All four were fading veterans, and only Leach was much help to his new club. The next year he again led the league in runs, with 99, and hit .289. After 1915 he left the majors, spending 1916, 1917, and part of 1918 in the minor leagues with Rochester, Kansas City, and Chattanooga. Late in 1918, when a number of major leaguers were serving in the armed forces, he returned to play 30 games with the Pirates.

After leaving the majors Leach helped organize the Florida State League and was player-manager of its Tampa club from 1920 through 1922, before finally hanging up his spikes at age 46. He later managed Lakeland and St. Petersburg, and in a second stint at Tampa he helped develop catcher Al Lopez. In 1935 and 1936 he scouted for the Boston Braves.

One of the amazing statistics about Leach is that of his 63 career home runs, 49 were hit inside the park. He died in 1969 at age 91, the last man alive who had played in that historic 1903 World Series.

Big Bill Lee

Lee, William Crutcher **P**

1934–47 B:10/21/1909, Plaquemine, LA D:6/15/1977, Plaquemine, LA Deb:4/29/1934, CHI NL BR/TR 6'3", 195

W	L	PCT	G	SH	IP	BB	SO	ERA
169	157	.518	462	29	2864	893	998	3.54

"Big Bill" Lee was one of the aces of the Chicago Cubs pitching staff in the 1930s, and he helped them win two pennants with a tremendous overhand curve. Standing 6-foot-3 and weighing nearly 200 pounds, the burly righthander was as durable as he was big, hurling more than 200 innings in nine different seasons, including each of his first seven with the Cubs.

Louisiana-born Lee remained a Southerner by inclination to his dying day. After gaining prominence as a high school athlete in his hometown of Plaquemine, he attended Louisiana State University in 1928 and 1929. After his sophomore year, Branch Rickey of the St. Louis Cardinals signed him to a minor league contract.

At that time, the Cardinals had the biggest farm system in baseball. Lee progressed steadily and reached Columbus of the American Association, St. Louis' top farm club, in 1932. He went 71–31 in his four minor league seasons, but the Cardinals preferred Paul Dean, the brother of Dizzy. In 1934 the Cards sold Lee to the Cubs for $25,000.

Although he shut out the Philadelphia Phillies in his first start for Chicago on May 7, 1934, Lee struggled that year, finishing 13–14. The next year, however, he went 20–6 and led the league in winning percentage. The Cubs roared to the pennant on the strength of a 21-game winning streak down the stretch. Lee collected four victories during the streak and defeated the Cardinals and Dizzy Dean, 6–2, to clinch the pennant.

In that fall's World Series, Lee started Game 3 against Detroit. He held the Tigers to one run through seven innings, but was knocked out in the eighth when Detroit scored four times. The Cubs took the game to extra innings before losing. Two days later, Lee relieved Lon Warneke in the seventh inning and saved a 3–1 Cubs win in Game 5. Detroit won the sixth and deciding game the next day.

After going 18–11 with a league-leading four shutouts in 1936, Lee slumped to 14–15 in 1937. The Cubs of this period won pennants in three-year intervals—in 1929, 1932, 1935, and 1938. In that last championship season, Lee led the league with 22 victories, a 2.66 ERA, and nine shutouts. Earlier in the season, he pitched in his first All-Star Game and blanked the AL for three innings. He pitched four of his shutouts sandwiched around a relief appearance to accumulate 37 consecutive scoreless innings.

The Cubs lost the World Series, however, as the Yankees polished them off in four straight. Lee lost Games 1 and 4, despite allowing only three earned runs in 11 innings.

The next year Lee won 19 games and was again named to the All-Star Game. But in 1940 he began to have trouble with his eyes. He could no longer read the catcher's signs or pitch with confidence, and his record fell to 9–17. In 1942 he started wearing glasses and improved to 13–13, but he never returned to his former dominance.

During the war Lee pitched for the Phillies and Braves. In 1947 he returned to the Cubs for 14 games and then retired. He returned to Louisiana and underwent eye surgery, but eventually lost his sight.

Bill Lee

Lee, William Francis **P**

1969–82 B:12/28/1946, Burbank, CA Deb:6/25/1969, BOS AL BL/TL 6'3", 210

W	L	PCT	G	SH	IP	BB	SO	ERA
119	90	.569	416	19	1944^{1}	531	713	3.62

"In baseball, you're supposed to sit [around], spit tobacco, and nod at stupid things." So said Bill Lee, the "Spaceman," who did none of those three things and eventually paid for it. He was never a great pitcher, although he was one of the more consistent lefthanders in the American League in the mid-1970s, when he won 17 games for the Red Sox three seasons in a row. However, he was without a doubt one of the funniest and most entertaining pitchers ever to play the game. Long after he last pitched for Boston, he remained a hero to many Red Sox fans, not so much for the way he pitched as for the things he said.

Lee grew up in Terra Linda, California, and attended USC on a baseball scholarship. His college teammates included future major league pitchers Jim Barr, Brent Strom, and Tom Seaver. The Trojans won the College World Series in 1968. Lee later quipped, "That was real baseball. We weren't playing for money. They gave us Mickey Mouse watches that ran backwards."

Drafted by the Red Sox in the 22nd round, Lee quickly moved up through the minor leagues, pitching more with his head than with his arm, and made it to Boston for good in 1971. The city was made for Bill Lee. It was full of students who responded to his iconoclastic commentary and unorthodox style, and he became a cult hero before anyone knew what a cult hero was. Lee was in tune with his times, and his personal explorations of Eastern religions, pacifism, drugs, and rock 'n' roll endeared him to his young fans.

Lee also made life easy on the younger members of Boston's press corps. He held court at a bar near Fenway Park, the Eliot Lounge, and delivered equal doses of wisdom and what passed for personal philosophy. The writers ate it up. But Lee also performed an important function for the Red Sox. His presence kept the writers off the backs of other players, which they appreciated—even if management didn't.

Lee never got along with the Red Sox front office. He was tolerated as long as he won but took the blame for everyone when the team lost. After going 9–2 and 7–4 in his first two years as a reliever, he made the starting rotation in 1973. He was 12–4 at the break and was named to the All-Star Game, before finishing 17–11. Lee followed that with a 17–15 record in 1974, and a 17–9 mark in 1975 as the Red Sox won the pennant.

In the World Series against Cincinnati, Lee started Game 2 and took a 2–1 lead into the ninth. Johnny Bench led off the inning with a double, resulting in Lee's replacement by Dick Drago. Drago retired two batters, but Dave Concepcion singled home Bench, stole second, and scored on Ken Griffey's double.

After Cincinnati won Game 5 to go ahead, three games to two, Lee was slated to pitch Game 6. When asked what he'd do if he won, Lee said that he'd declare an automatic 48 hours of darkness so that Luis Tiant could have another day's rest before Game 7. "That's what Zeus did when he raped Europa," said Lee. "He asked the sun god, Apollo, to stay away for a few days."

It rained for the next three days, and Red Sox manager Darrell Johnson passed over Lee and pitched Tiant in a game won by catcher Carlton Fisk's 12th-inning home run. Lee started Game 7 and led, 3–0, through six innings, then gave up a home run to Tony Perez on a blooper pitch. The Red Sox lost, 4–3, and the management and fans never forgave Lee for throwing the blooper.

In 1976 Lee hurt his shoulder when Yankees third baseman Graig Nettles threw him to the ground during a brawl on the field. Don Zimmer was named manager in midseason, and Lee began an extended stay in the doghouse. He called Zimmer "the designated gerbil."

Lee, pitchers Ferguson Jenkins and Jim Willoughby, and outfielder Bernie Carbo formed the Loyal Order of the Buffalo Heads in 1977 and drove Zimmer to distraction. The Spaceman pitched well during the first half of the 1978 season, but when Carbo, his best friend, was sold on June 15 to Cleveland, Lee briefly jumped the club.

The Red Sox slumped miserably in the second half. Zimmer stopped pitching Lee, and it became clear the lefthander's days as a Red Sox player were numbered. Lee summed up the team's dismal performance in the pennant race against the Yankees: "They have positive momentum. We have negative momentum." The Yankees beat the

Sox, and Lee was traded to Montreal for Stan Papi, an infielder who was soon released.

Lee found a measure of happiness in Montreal, going 16–10 his first season and reveling in the French-Canadian culture. He got in some trouble early in the year when he admitted to using marijuana, but when investigated by Commissioner Bowie Kuhn's office, Lee said he used marijuana in his tea. The investigator supposedly fell for the story, and Lee was exonerated.

But Lee soon clashed with Montreal management as well, and as soon as his pitching tapered off, it became clear that his dismissal was imminent. On one occasion Lee offered an explanation for the cause of strife between managers and pitchers. "Most of the managers are lifetime .220 hitters," he said. "For years, pitchers have been getting these managers out 75 percent of the time, and that's why they don't like us."

When teammate Rodney Scott was traded in 1982, Lee again jumped the club. He was released, and no other major league club offered him a contract. He contemplated filing suit but finally retired.

He then played semipro baseball, first in Quebec and later near his home in Vermont. Lee continued to make regular forays into Boston, where many fans considered him a sort of demigod. He later organized a team of Red Sox not-so-oldtimers, the Gray Sox, to make regular appearances in the Boston area for charity.

Thornton Lee

Lee, Thornton Starr **P**

1933–48 B:9/13/1906, Sonoma, CA D:6/9/97, Tucson, AZ Deb:9/19/1933, CLE AL BL/TL 6'3", 205

W	L	PCT	G	SH	IP	BB	SO	ERA
117	124	.485	374	14	2331[1]	838	937	3.56

Thornton Lee took his time reaching the majors and was saddled with poor support once he got there. However, he enjoyed a career year for the Chicago White Sox in 1941, as he led the American League in both complete games and ERA.

Lee began his professional career with Salt Lake City of the Utah–Idaho League in 1928, two years after graduating from California Polytechnic College at San Luis Obispo. He also performed with half a dozen other minor league teams. With Tampa in 1930, he threw a no-hitter versus Montgomery, winning 1–0. In another game that season he fanned 17 Pensacola batters.

He reached Cleveland at age 27 and spent two of the next three years working mainly from the bullpen. The one season in which he started more often than relieved was 1935, when he went 7–10 with a 4.04 ERA.

Traded to the White Sox in December 1936, Lee was aided there by the guidance of former catcher Muddy Ruel. He was immediately made a starter, and his initial year in Chicago was his first with a winning record, 12–10. Fours years later he went 22–11, with 30 complete games and a 2.37 ERA. For his performance he was selected to the All-Star Game and collected a $2,500 bonus.

But following that 1941 season, due to bone chips and an injured neck (both of which required operations), Lee's career headed into a quick tailspin. He neither completed more than seven games nor won more than five in the next three years. On July 9, 1944, he sustained a broken left arm on the last play of the second game of a doubleheader.

Lee made a dramatic comeback in 1945. He went 15–12 with a 2.44 ERA, completed 19 games, and was selected for his second All-Star appearance. After two years of limited action, he was traded to the New York Giants for the 1948 season, after which he retired.

Lee's son Don later pitched in the American League. The pair had the dubious honor of both having surrendered home runs to Ted Williams.

Sam Leever

Leever, Samuel **P**

1898–1910 B:12/23/1871, Goshen, OH D:5/19/1953, Goshen, OH Deb:5/26/1898, PIT NL BR/TR 5'10½", 175

W	L	PCT	G	SH	IP	BB	SO	ERA
194	100	.660	388	39	2660[2]	587	847	2.47

Sam Leever was a quiet, sober righthander with a big, sharp-breaking curveball. He pitched all of his 13 big league seasons with Pittsburgh and produced a winning record 12 times. He won 20 games four times and finished with a .660 winning percentage, still among the top 10 of all time.

Leever was a teacher in the off-season, hence his nickname "the Goshen Schoolmaster." After pitching a few games for the Pirates in 1898, he became the team's workhorse the next season and led the National League with 51 appearances, 379 innings pitched, and (retroactively) three saves. His record was 21–23, his only losing season.

A mainstay on the pennant-winning Pirates teams of 1901 through 1903, Leever enjoyed his finest season in 1903, going 25–7 while leading the league with a .781 winning percentage, seven shutouts, and a 2.06 earned run average. However, he was also a skeet-shooting champion, and that activity gave him a sore arm at the end of the season, so he was ineffective in two appearances in Pittsburgh's World Series loss to Boston.

Leever led the National League in winning percentage again in 1905, when he went 20–5, and followed that with a 22–7 mark in 1906. In 1908 he increased his load in the bullpen, and the next year he began to work almost exclusively in relief. When the Pirates won another pennant in 1909, the 38-year-old contributed an 8–1 record. He was not called upon to pitch in the Pirates' World Series victory that year.

Ron LeFlore

LeFlore, Ronald **OF**

1974–82 B:6/16/1948, Detroit, MI Deb:8/1/1974, DET AL BR/TR 6', 200

G	AB	R	H	HR	RBI	OBP	SLG	AVG
1099	4458	731	1283	59	353	.344	.392	.288

Few major leaguers traveled as hard a road as Ron LeFlore. When the Tigers first scouted him, LeFlore was in a maximum-security prison for armed robbery. A year later he was Detroit's starting center fielder. Perhaps the fastest man in baseball in the mid-1970s, LeFlore led both leagues in stolen bases, hit better than .300 three times, and once collected more than 200 hits in a season.

LeFlore had exhibited unsatisfactory behavior from an early age. To cover his frequent absences from school, he would have a friend steal blank report cards, then fill them in to show to his mother. The real report card would be returned with a forged signature. At age 15 he was convicted of robbing a supermarket and placed on probation. Six months later, he was convicted again for safecracking at a wholesale tobacco company and was sentenced to two-to-five years at the Michigan Training Unit at Ion, Michigan.

It was basically a reformatory for underage youth, but LeFlore came out unreformed. "I was a snot-nosed brat who didn't give a damn about anything or anybody," he later said. "When I got out of the reformatory after 19 months my attitude was worse than ever."

On release, LeFlore sold drugs on the street and continued to get into trouble. Convicted of armed robbery, on April 28, 1970, he was sent to the State Prison of Southern Michigan in Jackson. "Only the worst criminals get sent to Jackson—the murderers, the rapists, the armed robbers," noted LeFlore.

At first his weight ballooned in prison, eventually tipping the scales at 230 pounds, but LeFlore soon turned to athletics. Incredibly, he had never played baseball until May 1971. Nicknamed "Twinkle Toes Bosco" for his speed and his old weight problem, LeFlore established himself as a penitentiary star, both in baseball and football.

That would have counted for little except that a fellow prisoner, Jimmy Karalla, was a friend of Jimmy Butsicaris, a Detroit bar owner who knew Tigers manager Billy Martin. Karalla prodded Butsicaris to convince Martin to give LeFlore a tryout. Martin visited the prison and agreed to give LeFlore a chance.

On a 48-hour furlough in June 1973, LeFlore was given a tryout at Tiger Stadium. He hit balls into the upper deck and impressed observers with his speed and his arm. He returned to prison but was soon eligible for parole. "As soon as I knew I was going home I became obsessed with the idea of playing baseball," he recalled. Three days after his July 2, 1973, release, LeFlore was playing for the Tigers' Midwest League farm club, the Clinton Pilots. A year later he was with Detroit.

LeFlore became a starter in 1975 and made immediate improvement. The next year he hit .316, swiped 58 bases, scored 93 runs, and put together a 30-game hitting streak, the longest in the AL since Joe DiMaggio's 34-game streak in 1949. He also was selected to his only All-Star Game.

In 1977 LeFlore has his best season, batting .325 with 212 hits, 30 doubles, and 16 home runs. He scored 100 runs for the first of three straight seasons, and assembled a 27-game hitting streak. The next season he led the American League with 68 stolen bases and with 126 runs scored.

At age 31 in 1979, LeFlore batted .300 and stole 78 bases, but on December 7 of that year he was traded to the Montreal Expos for pitcher Dan Schatzeder. The following season LeFlore's league-leading 97 steals combined with 63 from fellow Expo Rodney Scott to set a major league record for teammates with 160 stolen bases.

LeFlore signed with the Chicago White Sox the following season as a free agent. As a part-timer his offensive production dropped, but he stole 36 bases in 1981 and 28 in 1982. He retired at the end of the season.

LeFlore's story was published as *Breakout: From Prison to the Big Leagues*, and was later made into a motion picture called *One in a Million*. In 1999 he was coaching for the Cook County Cheetahs in the independent Frontier League.

Charlie Leibrandt

Leibrandt, Charles Louis **P**

1979–82, 1984–93 B:10/4/1956, Chicago, IL Deb:9/17/1979, CIN NL BR/TL 6'3", 200

W	L	PCT	G	SH	IP	BB	SO	ERA
140	119	.541	394	18	2308	656	1121	3.71

Although he didn't throw hard, Charlie Leibrandt was still successful for 14 major league seasons. He won in double figures eight times and pitched in three World Series.

The Cincinnati Reds selected Leibrandt out of Miami University of Ohio in the 1978 amateur draft. He earned a call-up to the Reds the following season and, despite appearing in only three regular season games, made the postseason roster and pitched in the National League Championship Series. He won 10 games as a starter for the Reds in 1980, but mostly pitched out of the bullpen for the next two years. In 1983 the Reds traded the young lefthander to the Royals. The trade turned out to be a steal for Kansas City.

Leibrandt used his best pitch—a changeup—along with a slow curve to win a career-best 17 games for the Royals in 1985. The Royals won the American League West title, but Leibrandt pitched poorly in two ALCS starts. In Game 7, however, he appeared in relief to shut down the Toronto Blue Jays for the pennant-clinching victory. He allowed just 10 hits in 16 ⅓ World Series innings as the Royals won their first world championship.

Traded to the Atlanta Braves in 1990, Leibrandt won 15 games for the 1991 Braves, who became the first NL team to go from last place to first place in one year. Pitching out of the bullpen, Leibrandt allowed a game-winning home run to Kirby Puckett in the sixth game of the World Series. He was branded as one of the goats of the Series, and the Braves lost in seven games.

Leibrandt went 15–7 in 1992, but he again lost Game 6 of the World Series, giving up the double to Dave Winfield that scored the deciding runs for the Toronto Blue Jays in the 10th inning. The Braves traded Leibrandt to the Texas Rangers, with whom he finished out his career with a 9–10 record in 1993.

Lefty Leifield

Leifield, Albert Peter **P**

1905–13, 1918–20 B:9/5/1883, Trenton, IL D:10/10/1970, Alexandria, VA Deb:9/3/1905, PIT NL BL/TL 6'1", 165

W	L	PCT	G	SH	IP	BB	SO	ERA
124	97	.561	296	32	1838	554	616	2.47

Lefty Leifield began his Pittsburgh Pirates career with a shutout, and ended it as part of a blockbuster trade. In between, he was the team's winningest pitcher, posting 103 victories between 1906 and 1911. He won 20 in 1907, and followed that by helping the Pirates to the world championship with a 19–8 record in 1909. His most memorable game, however, was a loss.

On July 4, 1906, Leifield held the Chicago Cubs hitless through eight innings, but legendary mound opponent Mordecai "Three Finger" Brown had surrendered only a single by Leifield. Chicago strung together a single, sacrifice, error, and infield out to score the game's only run in the final inning.

Leifield was sent to the Cubs in a four-player deal on June 22, 1912. He was in the minor leagues a year later. He revived his career in San Francisco and St. Paul, resurfacing with the St. Louis Browns in 1918. He remained with the team as a coach after his pitching days ended, then served in the same capacity with the Boston Red Sox and Detroit Tigers.

Leifield returned to the minors as a manager from 1929 to 1932. He later worked for City Hall in St. Louis, where he had previously operated a grocery/saloon business.

Al Leiter

Leiter, Alois Terry **P**

1987–* B:10/23/1965, Toms River, NJ Deb:9/15/1987, NY AL BL/TL 6'3" 215

W	L	PCT	G	SH	IP	BB	SO	ERA
90	71	.559	233	6	1294²	683	1107	3.82

Two factors prevented Al Leiter from reaching his true potential as a pitcher: injuries and walks. The affable, animated lefthander made numerous trips to the disabled list, and in 1994 and 1995 he led the league in free passes.

The brother of righthander Mark Leiter, Al originally signed with the Yankees. He made only a handful of appearances for the team before being traded to Toronto for outfielder Jesse Barfield in April 1989. His Blue Jays career was unremarkable and filled with injuries, although he picked up a win in the 1993 World Series.

In December 1995 Leiter signed as a free agent with Florida. The change of leagues served him well. On May 11, 1996, he pitched a no-hitter against the Colorado Rockies. He won 16 games that season and got the final out in the All-Star Game. Leiter won just 11 games the following year, but started Game 7 of the World Series, a game he said completely changed the way he approached pitching. Buoyed by his solid performance, Florida won the world championship in 11 innings.

When owner Wayne Huizenga dismantled the Marlins, Leiter was traded to the Mets. The pitcher, who grew up a Mets fan, posted career bests in wins (17) and ERA (2.47) and finished sixth in Cy Young Award balloting. He signed a large contract to remain with the team, and immediately donated $1 million to charity.

Leiter won the New York Baseball Writers Association's Joan W. Payson Award for his humanitarian achievements in 1999. He also received the Branch Rickey Award for outstanding community service. He struggled for most of that season, but his two-hit shutout in a one-game playoff at Cincinnati decided the National League Wild Card.

Frank Leland

Leland, Frank
Negro League Owner B:1868, Memphis, TN
D:Not known

Chicago's Frank C. Leland organized the windy city's Leland Giants, one of the pioneer powerhouse black teams. From the time he arrived in Chicago after graduating from Fisk University in Nashville, Tennessee, Leland was engaged in organizing black baseball clubs.

His first project was to form, along with manager Abe Jones, the Black Union Baseball Club, which became the Chicago Unions in 1888. Leland played outfield for three seasons with the Unions and also served as an umpire and traveling secretary for the club. The Unions had their home grounds at 37th and Butler streets in Chicago, until Charles Comiskey's White Sox moved in just a few blocks away, at 39th and Wentworth.

In 1899 the Chicago Unions played the Columbia Giants for the Western black championship. In 1900 both clubs claimed the title, but, in the absence of a playoff, the issue was never settled

The two clubs merged under Leland's ownership and management in 1901, with their home field at Chicago's Auburn Park. In 1903 these "Chicago Union Giants" faced the Algona Brownies for the Western championship and lost. By 1905 the club was known as "Leland's Giants." That season they played 122 games and lost just 10 with a winning streak of 48 consecutive contests.

In 1907, while retaining ownership, Leland turned managerial duties over to pitcher Rube Foster. Two years later, hampered by Foster's absence due to a broken leg, the club lost the Western championship to the St. Paul Colored Gophers. In the postseason the Leland Giants challenged the Chicago Cubs to a three-game series. They again lost but gave a good account of themselves.

Soon afterwards, Leland and Foster parted company. Both men fielded separate teams and wished to retain use of the name "Leland." Although Leland held onto the bulk of the personnel from the 1909 team, and obviously had a distinct claim to the use of his name, a court decision gave Foster the right to call his squad the "Leland Giants" (sometimes called the "Chicago Leland Giants") while Frank Leland's team was to be called "Leland's Chicago Giants."

Leland remained active in black baseball until 1912. He was busy in Chicago politics, working as a clerk in the Criminal Court and Circuit Court, as clerk of the Board of Review, and as a deputy sheriff. He also served as a member of the Cook County Board of County Commissioners.

Leland's Chicago Giants remained active after he severed his involvement with them. Between 1920 and 1921 they joined the Negro National League where they survived as an independent team until the late 1920s.

Bob Lemon

Lemon, Robert Granville **P**
1941–42, 1946–58 M(1970–72, 1977–79, 1981–82, 430–403) B:9/22/1920, San Bernardino, CA
D:1/11/2000, Long Beach, CA Deb:9/9/1941, CLE AL
BL/TR 6', 185

W	L	PCT	G	SH	IP	BB	SO	ERA
207	128	.618	460	31	2850	1251	1277	3.23

Bob Lemon did something in baseball that may never be equaled: he appeared tieless at his own induction into the Hall of Fame. An independent thinker, Lemon was responsible for uttering two famous pearls of baseball wisdom. He declared, "Baseball is a kids' game adults just screw up," and also noted, more personally, that "I had my bad days on the field, but I didn't take them home with me. I left them in a bar along the way."

Although he never meant to be a pitcher, Lemon became a 20-game winner seven times and led the league lead in wins three times. On a pitching staff that featured such star aces as Bob Feller, Mike Garcia, and Early Wynn, Lemon led the league numerous times in innings pitched and complete games. An all-around talent, his 37 career homers rank him second on the all-time list for pitchers, behind only Wes Ferrell.

Lemon, whose father had played in the Pacific Coast League, got his start as an infielder with an American Legion team. When he was 17, he was signed to a $100-a-month contract with the Cleveland Indians' organization by scout John Engel. The young prospect advanced steadily through the Indians' system, leading the Eastern League in runs scored and tying for the lead in hits at Wilkes-Barre in 1941.

In 1943 Lemon entered the Navy and joined a service team in Aiea, Hawaii. When pitchers Fred Hutchinson and Lou Ciola became injured, manager Billy Herman, aware that Lemon had a pretty good curve, started him. He did well enough to make an American League–National League All-Star series in Hawaii.

After the war Lemon got off to a shaky start. He was shifted to the outfield and was on the verge of being farmed out when the comments of his fellow war veterans saved him. Detroit catcher Birdie Tebbetts said, "You may think he's a third baseman, but I know he's a pitcher. I hit against him during the war in the Pacific, and if I never have to bat against him again it will be too soon."

Aware that Ted Williams, Johnny Pesky, and Bill Dickey felt the same way, Indians manager Lou Boudreau decided it was worth a shot. Lemon, convinced he was a major league hitter, fought the change every step of the way. For his first two seasons as a member of the Indians he refused to wear a toe plate, thinking he would return to being a position player at any time.

After two years mainly working as a reliever, Lemon moved into the regular rotation in 1948. On June 30, he pitched a no-hitter against the Detroit Tigers. That year he was named to the All-Star Game for the first of seven straight seasons, as he went on to win 20 games and lead the league in complete games, innings pitched, and shutouts. He also won Games 2 and 6 of the World Series against the Boston Braves.

Lemon won at least 20 games in five of the next six seasons, including leading the American League with 23 in 1950 and again in 1954. The latter year he helped the Indians to a 111-win season and another World Series. In the Series, however, Lemon lost in Game 1 and Game 4, as Leo Durocher's New York Giants swept the Tribe.

Lemon again led the American League with 18 wins in 1955, although he completed only five—the only time in a nine-year period he had fewer than 17 complete games. The next year was his last 20-win season.

After injuring his leg in 1957, Lemon ended his playing days in the minors with San Diego the following year. He went on to scout for the Indians, Royals, and Yankees, manage in the International and Pacific Coast leagues, coach in the majors, and manage the Royals, White Sox, and Yankees.

In July 1978 he replaced Billy Martin as manager of the dissension-ridden Yankees. Lemon's low-key style played a large role in New York's remarkable rally from fourth place in July to first place in October. The Yankees beat Boston in a one-game playoff for the AL East title, defeated the Kansas City Royals in four games in the Championship Series, and took the Los Angeles Dodgers in six games in the World Series.

Replaced in June 1979 by Martin, he was brought in to manage the Yankees again in September 1981. Because of the strike, the Yankees had to navigate through two rounds of playoffs to claim the pennant. The Yankees beat Milwaukee and Oakland before falling to the Dodgers in six games in the World Series. After being promised another full season, "win or lose," he was dismissed on April 25.

Lemon, who was inducted into the Hall of Fame in 1976, remained on the Yankees' payroll for the rest of his life as a scout and adviser to owner George Steinbrenner. When he died in January 2000, Steinbrenner, who grew up in Cleveland, fondly remembered his old friend. "He was an idol of mine when he pitched for the Cleveland Indians and he has been a true friend of mine for many, many years."

Chet Lemon

Lemon, Chester Earl **OF**

1975–90 B:2/12/1955, Jackson, MS Deb:9/9/1975, CHI AL BR/TR 6', 195

G	AB	R	H	HR	RBI	OBP	SLG	AVG
1988	6868	973	1875	215	884	.357	.442	.273

Outfielder Chet Lemon played in the American League for 16 seasons. He was known primarily for his defense, but he did have three seasons batting .300.

A first-round draft choice of the Oakland Athletics in 1972, Lemon was traded while still a minor leaguer to the Chicago White Sox for pitcher Stan Bahnsen. He first reached the majors in 1975, and the next year he joined the White Sox full time. Although he was a third baseman in the minor leagues, the White Sox shifted him to center field where he became the regular from 1976 through 1981.

In 1977 Lemon set American League records for most putouts by an outfielder, with 512, and for most chances, with 524. He played the field with aplomb, becoming a fan favorite as he patrolled the vast stretches of Comiskey Park. He improved each year early in his career, batting .246 in 1976, .273 the next year, and .300 in 1978, when he was selected to play in his first All-Star Game.

Lemon enjoyed his best offensive season in 1979, when he was again chosen for the All-Star Game. He batted .318 with 17 home runs and 86 RBIs, and he tied for the league lead with 44 doubles. He was a crowd pleaser on the bases, too, occasionally sliding headfirst into the bag while running out a grounder. Lemon also had a knack for getting hit by pitches, and ranks among the all-time top five in that category.

Despite hitting .302 in 1981, Lemon was traded after the season to the Detroit Tigers for outfielder Steve Kemp. His power numbers rose in Tiger Stadium, where the power alleys were smaller than Comiskey Park's, but his batting average slipped. Lemon's best year in Detroit was the Tigers' dream season of 1984 when the team was in first place every day of the campaign, swept the playoffs, and won the World Series.

Accommodating Kirk Gibson by moving to right field, Lemon enjoyed another season in which he made the All-Star Game, hitting .287 with 20 home runs and 76 RBIs. Although he went 0-for-13 in the ALCS, he scored the only run in Game 3 as the Tigers swept Kansas City. In Detroit's five-game victory over the San Diego Padres in the World Series, Lemon went 5-for-17 (.294) and fielded flawlessly.

In 1988 Lemon played 144 games in the outfield, hit 17 home runs, drove in 64 runs, and batted .264. But injuries and lack of production cut down his playing time over the next two years, and he retired after the 1990 season.

Jim Lemon

Lemon, James Robert **OF**

1950, 1953–63 M(1968, 65–96) B:3/23/1928, Covington, VA Deb:8/20/1950, CLE AL BR/TR 6'4", 200

G	AB	R	H	HR	RBI	OBP	SLG	AVG
1010	3445	446	901	164	529	.335	.460	.262

In the 1950s the Washington Senators promoted Jim Lemon as their answer to Mickey Mantle. Both possessed power, but Mantle also had speed, agility, and the Yankees lineup around him to propel him to greatness. Lemon had the Senators.

Lemon started with Pittsfield in the Class C Canadian-American League in 1948. Over the next few years he played with six minor league teams and did two brief stints with the Cleveland Indians before being sold to Washington in 1954.

He developed slowly, remaining a bench player until 1956 when he broke into the Senators' lineup and hit .271 with 27 homers, 96 RBIs, and an American League-leading 11 triples. On August 31 he hit three straight homers—the first player to do so in cavernous Griffith Stadium.

After two solid seasons, Lemon had probably his best year in 1959. He batted .279, hit 33 homers, and had 100 RBIs. On September 5, he hit two homers in one inning to drive in six runs. The next year Lemon chased Mantle for the home run crown, finishing second with 38, and also contributing another 100 RBIs. He was selected for his only All-Star Game.

Lemon followed the Senators' move to Minnesota (as the Twins) with two disappointing seasons and was released early in 1963. He played briefly with the Philadelphia Phillies and the Chicago White Sox before retiring at the end of the 1963 season. He later managed York in the Eastern League and managed the Senators in 1968.

Buck Leonard

Leonard, Walter Fenner **1B-OF**

Negro League Player 1933–50 B:9/8/1907, Rocky Mount, NC D:11/27/1997, Rocky Mount, NC BL/TL 5'10", 185

First baseman Buck Leonard was called "the Lou Gehrig of the Negro Leagues." Just as Gehrig teamed up with Babe Ruth, Leonard and catcher Josh Gibson, "the Babe Ruth of the Negro Leagues," formed the most potent one-two punch in black baseball.

From 1937 through 1945 Leonard's Homestead Grays won Negro National League titles year after year. Negro League records are notoriously incomplete, but those available show Leonard with a lifetime .355 average. In 11 games against big league pitchers he hit .382. Catcher Roy Campanella said, "If [Leonard] batted fourth, behind Gibson, we could pitch around him and make him hit an outside off-speed pitch. He had a real quick bat, and you couldn't get a fastball by him. He was strictly a pull hitter with tremendous power."

Leonard left school at age 14 to work in a textile mill and shine shoes at the railroad station. The following year he hooked up with the Atlantic Coast Rail Road Line and played semipro ball locally. After he lost his railroad job he signed on with the Portsmouth, Virginia, Firefighters club for $15 a week plus room and board.

When Ben Taylor's Baltimore Stars invited Leonard to tour with them, his Portsmouth teammates warned him that barnstorming was no bed of roses. He wouldn't listen, but he later acknowledged it was just as tough as he had been told. The Stars were staying at the Hotel Dumas and were behind in their bills. Accordingly, the hotel management auctioned off the team's transportation—a Buick and a Ford—right in front of the hotel.

Penniless, Leonard was lucky to join the Brooklyn Royal Giants under manager Dick "Cannonball" Redding. The Royal Giants had transportation (a Cadillac and a copper-covered Pierce Arrow), but they were focused more on amusing crowds with stunts and comedy routines than on playing serious ball.

Finally, former Homestead Grays pitcher Smokey Joe Williams urged Leonard to try out for the Grays. Leonard was skeptical about his ability, but Williams talked club owner Cum Posey into giving Buck the money for a train ticket to the Grays' spring training camp in Wheeling, West Virginia. Leonard made the Pittsburgh-based team but announced, "I don't like it out here in this steel mining town. I'm going to finish the season here, then I'm not coming back." He stayed for 17 more seasons.

Actually, Leonard didn't have to spend all his time in Pittsburgh; from 1937 on, the Grays had two homes, Pittsburgh and Washington, D.C. In Washington they played in Griffith Stadium, often outdrawing the big league Senators. At one point Washington club owner Clark Griffith approached Leonard and Josh Gibson about playing in the major leagues, but he never followed up on his proposal.

When Leonard joined the Grays in 1934, he received $125 per month and 60 cents a day in meal money during the four-month playing season. By 1941 he was up to $500 per month plus 75 cents a day for meals, which doubled after he and Gibson received an offer from the Mexican League. In 1948, when he played winter ball in addition to the regular Negro League season, Leonard earned a peak of $10,000. He was probably the third-highest-paid player in the Negro Leagues, behind only Gibson and pitcher Satchel Paige.

Leonard once offered a bit of advice on how to survive in the Negro Leagues: "The thing to do was to borrow enough money from the club so you'd be in debt at the end of the season. Then you could be sure they'd have you back next season. But they got wise to that too, so after a while it didn't work."

When Branch Rickey of the Dodgers signed Jackie Robinson in 1946, there was a hope that Leonard would be among those to join Robinson in integrating the majors. However, he and the older black stars were passed over in favor of younger prospects.

In 1952 St. Louis Browns owner Bill Veeck offered Leonard a chance to play in the major leagues. Then 45 years old, Leonard realized his time was past and turned Veeck down. In 1953, however, Leonard played 10 games for the Portsmouth Merrimacks of the Class B Piedmont League and hit .333.

Upon leaving baseball Leonard worked as a truant officer and physical education instructor in his hometown of Rocky Mount. He also served as a vice president and board member of the Rocky Mount entry in the Carolina League.

In 1972 the Negro Leagues Committee elected Leonard to the Hall of Fame. As the only Negro League first baseman in Cooperstown, he often attended the annual induction ceremonies despite needing a wheelchair to get around. He died in 1997.

Dennis Leonard

Leonard, Dennis Patrick **P**

1974–83, 1985–86 B: 5/8/1951, Brooklyn, NY
Deb:9/4/1974, KAN AL BR/TR 6'1", 190

W	L	PCT	G	SH	IP	BB	SO	ERA
144	106	.576	312	23	2187	622	1323	3.70

From 1975 to 1981, no righthander won more games in the major leagues than did Dennis Leonard for the Kansas City Royals. Despite a disastrous call-up late in 1974, when he went 0–4 with a 5.32 ERA, the red-haired rookie with mud chops made the starting rotation the following spring. He responded with a 15–7 record, the first of eight straight seasons of double-digit win totals.

Leonard won an American League-best 20 games in 1977 and bettered that with 21 in 1978. He went just 1–3, however, in six playoff appearances from 1976 to 1978 as the Royals won three straight division titles, only to lose three straight times to the New York Yankees in the AL Championship Series. In 1980 Leonard cracked the 20-win plateau for the third time in four years, and Kansas City breezed to another AL West crown. Leonard won his lone ALCS start as the Royals finally defeated the Yankees. He squandered a 4–0 lead in Game 1 of the World Series against Philadelphia and took the loss. He rebounded to win Game 4, but the Royals lost the Series in six games.

Leonard was the only pitcher in the major leagues to pitch 200 innings during the strike-marred 1981 season. A year later a severe knee injury put him on the disabled list; he made only 12 appearances over the next three years. Leonard returned to the rotation in 1986, posting an 8–13 record for his first losing season since 1974. He retired the following February as the franchise career leader in complete games, strikeouts, and shutouts.

Dutch Leonard

Leonard, Emil John **P**

1933–36, 1938–53 B:3/25/1909, Auburn, IL
D:4/17/1983, Springfield, IL Deb:8/31/1933, BRO NL
BR/TR 6', 175

W	L	PCT	G	SV	IP	BB	SO	ERA
191	181	.513	640	44	3218^{1}	737	1170	3.25

Emil "Dutch" Leonard was unrelated to the Dutch Leonard who played in the early decades of the 20th century, but both were fine pitchers. Although he rarely played for a winning team in 20 years in the big leagues, Leonard compiled a 3.25 ERA and won 191 games.

Leonard reached the majors with the Dodgers in 1933 and developed rapidly, winning 14 games in 1934. But he then deteriorated just as rapidly, going 2–9 in 1935 and being sent down to the minors in 1936. He returned to the big leagues two years later as a strong knuckleballer.

Playing for the Senators in 1938, Leonard allowed fewer runners on base per game than any other American League pitcher. The next year he had his best season, going 20–8 with 21 complete games. Despite the Senators' generally poor performance, Leonard earned a spot on four All-Star teams in his nine years in Washington, kept his ERA low, and tallied win totals in the teens. He won 18 games in 1941 and 17 in 1945. His continued success even helped boost the popularity of the knuckleball, which previously had been considered a trick pitch. In fact, from 1944–46, the Senators had four knuckleballers in their starting rotation—Leonard, Roger Wolff, Mickey Haefner, and Johnny Niggeling.

In 1947 Leonard was sent to Philadelphia, where he won 17 games for the Phillies. Two years later, the Phillies traded him to the Chicago Cubs, where he had a single miserable season as a starter. Undaunted, the Cubs turned him into a reliever. The move extended Leonard's career by four years and brought him a fifth All-Star selection. He retired in 1953.

Dutch Leonard

Leonard, Hubert Benjamin **P**

1913–21, 1924–25 B:4/16/1892, Birmingham, OH D:7/11/1952, Fresno, CA Deb:4/12/1913, BOS AL BL/TL 5'10½", 185

W	L	PCT	G	SH	IP	BB	SO	ERA
139	112	.552	331	33	2192	664	1160	2.76

Hubert "Dutch" Leonard, the first Dutch Leonard to play in the big leagues, posted the lowest ERA in history—0.96—in 1914. He is also remembered for his controversial game-fixing charges against Ty Cobb and Tris Speaker.

The southpaw began his professional career with the Philadelphia Athletics in 1911, although he did not appear in any games. Sent in 1912 to Denver of the Western League, he went 22–9 with a 2.43 ERA. In 1913 he returned to the American League with the Red Sox. In 1914, his career year, Leonard not only set the all-time ERA mark but went 19–5 with seven shutouts.

Leonard won games in both the 1915 and 1916 World Series. He also pitched two no-hitters, the first against the St. Louis Browns on August 30, 1916, when he struck out five and walked two. The second was at the expense of the Detroit Tigers on June 3, 1918, when he bested Hooks Dauss, 5–0, fanning four and walking one.

Traded to the Yankees in 1918, Leonard refused to report and was instead sent to Detroit. After three years with the Tigers he retired, but he returned to Detroit in 1924, and went 14–6 his last year and a half. He eventually ended his career with Vernon of the Pacific Coast League.

In 1927 Leonard dropped a bombshell on the baseball world, charging Cobb and Speaker with throwing a September 25, 1919, contest. The case collapsed, however, when Leonard refused to leave California to testify before Commissioner Kenesaw Mountain Landis.

Jeffrey Leonard

Leonard, Jeffrey **OF–DH**

1977–90 B:9/22/1955, Philadelphia, PA Deb:9/22/1977, LA NL BR/TR 6'2", 200

G	AB	R	H	HR	RBI	OBP	SLG	AVG
1415	5045	614	1342	144	723	.316	.411	.266

Just as he was known by two different names, Jeffrey Leonard had two different careers. As Jeff he was a punchless, singles hitter; later in his career, as Jeffrey, he became a feared home run hitter.

A product of the Dodgers' heralded farm system in the 1970s, Jeff Leonard was soon traded to the Astros, where he batted .385 during an eight-game audition in 1978. He moved into Houston's starting outfield the following summer. Leonard batted .290 and stole 23 bases as *The Sporting News* NL Rookie of the Year. However, he hit no homers and drew few walks, which made him an offensive liability.

Early in 1981, the Astros traded Leonard to the Giants, where he developed a reputation for arguing with reporters and shouting at teammates. Leonard later admitted to drug use at the infamous Pittsburgh drug trial of 1985.

In San Francisco he began calling himself Jeffrey Leonard, and in 1983 exploded for 21 home runs and 87 RBIs, almost double his previous bests. He put up solid power numbers in three of the next four seasons, helping the Giants win the Western Division title in 1987.

Now known by the nicknames "Hac-Man" (for his free swinging approach at the plate) and "Penitentiary Face" (for his perpetual scowl), Leonard homered in each of the first four Championship Series games. He infuriated the Cardinals with his "one-flap-down" home run trot. He did not go deep in the final three games of the series, including shutouts by St. Louis in Game 6 and 7. Leonard, who batted .417, was named NLCS Most Valuable Player despite the Giants' loss.

After slumping in 1988, Leonard was traded to Milwaukee. He eventually signed with Seattle and proved to be a good influence on young Mariners like Ken Griffey, Jr. "I had one of the great teachers: Jeffrey Leonard," Griffey told *USA Today.* Despite a respectable season in 1990, Leonard's career came to an end when no team offered him a contract.

Buddy Lewis

Lewis, John Kelly **3B–OF**
1935–41, 1945–47, 1949 B:8/10/1916, Gastonia, NC
Deb:9/16/1935, WAS AL BL/TR 6'1", 175

G	AB	R	H	HR	RBI	OBP	SLG	AVG
1349	5261	830	1563	71	607	.368	.420	.297

For a decade of play, interrupted by World War II, Buddy Lewis of the Washington Senators was one of the best third basemen in the American League. Four times he hit above .310, and his fielding range matched that of any of his contemporaries.

Lewis, who attended Wake Forest, started his professional career with Chattanooga of the Southern Association in 1934. The following year he batted .303 with 85 RBIs, and then joined the Senators as an 18-year-old at season's end. With the Senators he came under the tutelage of Buddy Myer, and it was for that reason that Lewis, too, became known as "Buddy."

Lewis made an immediate contribution, hitting .291 with 67 RBIs his first full year, in 1936. The next year he increased his batting average to .314, hit 32 doubles, and scored 107 runs. He collected 15 hits in four consecutive games on July 25–28, 1937, and later committed four errors in the first game of an August 19, 1937, doubleheader against the A's. He was selected to his first All-Star Game in 1938, when he had career-highs with 122 runs, 12 homers, and 91 RBIs. The next year Lewis led the league in triples while batting .319.

Lewis entered the Army in November 1941 and was awarded the Distinguished Flying Cross on December 28, 1944, for flying in the Burmese Theater. Discharged on July 23, 1945, he was in the Washington lineup just four days later, picking up his career as an outfielder. He led AL outfielders in assists in 1946 and was chosen to his second All-Star Game in 1947. Lewis retired at the end of that season and attempted a short-lived comeback in 1949.

Duffy Lewis

Lewis, George Edward **OF**
1910–17, 1919–21 B:4/18/1888, San Francisco, CA
D:6/17/1979, Salem, NH Deb:4/16/1910, BOS AL BL/TL
5'10½", 165

G	AB	R	H	HR	RBI	OBP	SLG	AVG
1459	5351	612	1518	38	793	.333	.384	.284

Duffy Lewis was part of the renowned "Golden Outfield" for the Boston Red Sox, along with future Hall of Famers Harry Hooper and Tris Speaker, in the years just prior to World War I. Known for his fielding abilities, Lewis became adept at patrolling what came to be called "Duffy's Cliff"—a 15-foot incline in Boston's old Fenway Park left field. "I experimented with every angle of approach up the cliff until I learned to play the slope correctly," he said. "Sometimes it would be tougher coming back down the slope than coming up. With runners on base, you had to come down the cliff running."

Of the lefthander's distinctive clothesline throws, sportswriter Joe Cashman wrote, "If you ever got hit by one of Lewis' throws... you'd get killed. Lewis never bounced the ball. It was in the air all the way."

Lewis joined the Red Sox in 1910, and the next year hit a career-high .307. He was a member of three pennant-winning Red Sox teams and hit .444 in the 1915 Series. He was the first player to pinch-hit for Babe Ruth when the Bambino was a pitcher with the Red Sox. In 1917 he hit .302, but was traded the next year to the New York Yankees in a seven-player deal. After playing with the Yankees in 1919 and 1920, he was traded to Washington, where he finished his career.

After leaving the majors Lewis played and managed in the Pacific Coast League, and from 1935 to 1961 he served as traveling secretary for the Boston Braves.

Jim Leyland

Leyland, James Richard
Manager(1986–99, 1069–1131) B:12/15/1944,
Toledo, OH

Before 1997, when he led the Florida Marlins to the quickest world championship ever won by an expansion team, manager Jim Leyland took the Pittsburgh Pirates to three consecutive National League East titles starting in 1990. Almost without exception, players declare Leyland to be the best manager they have played under, and the one they love most.

Leyland's personal warmth and affection for his players are summed up in a story he recounted for *Sports Illustrated* about releasing a player from the low minors, most likely ending the man's professional baseball career. "If I could play baseball for anyone, I'd play for you," the player said. He and Leyland wound up weeping in the manager's office.

Leyland helped rebuild a losing Pittsburgh team that had been embarrassed by drug scandals and was threatening to leave the city for financial reasons. With the Pirates being outbid for many of their own stars due to free agency or choosing to trade big-ticket players in order to cut the payroll, Leyland became the symbol of the resurgent franchise. He helped recast the Pirates as a blue-collar team, an image that suited the town as well as the manager.

One of seven children of a factory foreman, Leyland grew up in Perrysburg, Ohio. After attending his first major league game with his father at Cleveland in 1954, the 10-year-old promptly decided he wanted to have a career in baseball. He signed with the Detroit Tigers' organization in 1963 after he graduated from Perrysburg High School, where he had played basketball and football as well as baseball. But upon entering pro ball, Leyland soon realized he'd never play in the major leagues. "I really had no ability whatsoever," he said.

He spent six years as a catcher in the Tigers' organization, never rising above the Class AA level or batting above .243. Leyland wanted to stay in the game, however, so he planned to return to Perrysburg, attend college, and look for a baseball coaching position. But in 1970 the Tigers offered him a coaching job with their Montgomery affiliate.

The next season, at age 26, Leyland got his first managing assignment, at Bristol, Virginia, of the rookie-level Appalachian League. In 1973 he managed his first title team, winning a second-half crown with Clinton of the Midwest League.

In 1977 his Lakeland team won the Florida State League title and was runner-up the following year, gaining Leyland a promotion to the Class AAA American Association. There his Evansville team finished first twice in three years, and in 1979 the club won the American Association championship and Leyland copped his third straight minor league Manager of the Year Award.

In 1982 Leyland finally reached the big leagues, becoming third base coach with the Chicago White Sox under manager Tony La Russa. On La Russa's staff, Leyland absorbed the administrative side of big league managing, learning how to make the best use of resources on and off the field, how to use statistics to help make decisions, and how to delegate authority to coaches.

Much of his skill in handling people came naturally, although Leyland had learned a few things from watching manager Sparky Anderson during Tigers spring training. La Russa touted Leyland as a potential big league manager, and after an interview with Pirates general manager Syd Thrift, Leyland was hired on the spot on November 20, 1985.

Leyland took over a Pirates franchise that had lost 104 games in 1985. With an infusion of young talent, thanks to clever trading by Thrift, the team improved to 80–82 in 1987. The next season, at 85–75, the Bucs finished second to the New York Mets. Equally important, the club broke the franchise attendance record.

The Sporting News named Leyland its 1988 Manager of the Year in recognition of his role in developing the team. With Thrift remaking the ballclub by trading veterans for young players, Leyland helped make stars out of players such as Bobby Bonilla, Barry Bonds, Andy Van Slyke, Jay Bell, Sid Bream, and Doug Drabek. "I've never seen anybody better at handling pitchers," said Pirates pitching coach Ray Miller.

In 1990 the Pirates won the NL East title, their first division win since 1979, and Leyland won Manager of the Year honors from both *The Sporting News* and the Baseball Writers Association of America. However, the Bucs lost the Championship Series in six games to the Cincinnati Reds.

In 1991 the Pirates again won their division—by 14 games—and then took the Atlanta Braves to seven games in the playoff before being shut out in the final game. The 1992 season was tumultuous. Bonilla left the team as a free agent after 1991, and a shouting match between Leyland and Bonds marred the usually quiet, relaxed atmosphere of spring training. In addition, cost cutting by the front office resulted in the trade of 20-game-winner John Smiley and the release of closer Bill Landrum.

Nevertheless, the club won the NL East for a third time, becoming only the second NL team to win three straight division titles and helping Leyland sweep Manager of the Year honors yet again. All that was a prelude for the Pirates' heartbreaking seven-game playoff rematch against the Braves. "It's the toughest loss I've ever had," Leyland said, "and it is difficult to handle."

That winter the Pirates lost free agents Drabek and Bonds, among others, and the following season they slumped to fifth, at 75–85, as Leyland started over with another young team. By 1995, financial problems had led to a further-slashed payroll, a last-place finish, and a change of owners when Sacramento newspaper heir Kevin McClatchy bought the team. After finishing in the basement for the second year in a row, Leyland resigned at the end of the 1996 season.

Before the next season began, the Florida Marlins signed not only Leyland but free agents Moises Alou, Alex Fernandez, Jim Eisenreich, John Cangelosi, Dennis Cook, and Bonilla. Suddenly one of the best teams in baseball, the Leyland-led Marlins failed to win the NL East title in 1997, but took the Wild Card spot, swept the San Francisco Giants for the division title, and then took the pennant by astonishing the Atlanta Braves in six games. Fueled by rookie pitcher Livan Hernandez's MVP performance, they triumphed in the World Series over Cleveland, when Edgar Renteria's single drove in Craig Counsel for the winning run in the 11th inning of Game 7. Leyland had managed the first Wild Card team ever to win the World Series.

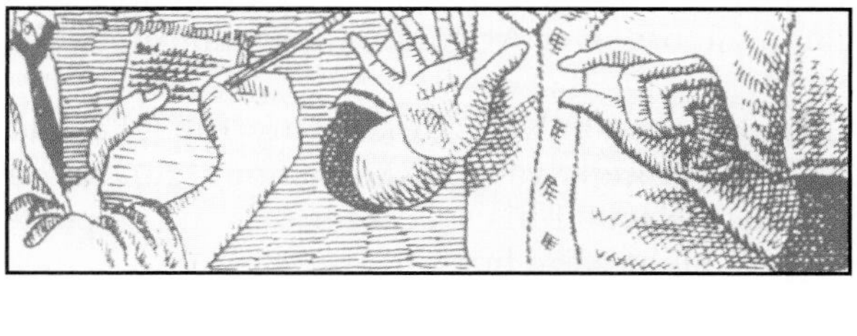

That accomplished, owner H. Wayne Huizenga promptly sold off the pricey nucleus of his championship club, including Hernandez, and then sold the team itself. Leyland resigned after the 1998 season and became manager of the Colorado Rockies. There he found the one place where the pitching staff was in worse shape than Florida's crew of castoffs; Colorado's 6.01 ERA was by far the worst in baseball. Even before the team stumbled home last with a 70–92 record, Leyland had announced that he was set to retire at the end of the 1999 season.

Jim Leyritz

Leyritz, James Joseph **C-DH-1B**

1990–* B:12/27/1963 Lakewood, OH Deb:6/8/1990, NY AL BR/TR 6', 195

G	AB	R	H	HR	RBI	OBP	SLG	AVG
838	2412	320	643	88	375	.368	.422	.267

In the first half of the 1990s Jim Leyritz made a name for himself as a power-hitting utility man. In the second half, he evolved into a postseason slugger with the ability to change a series with one crucial swing.

An excellent athlete with a powerful arm, Leyritz played every position except pitcher and shortstop in his first three years with the Yankees. He also became known for his brash style, annoying opponents with his bat twirling at the plate, and teammates with a self-assurance that earned him the nickname "The King." Eventually Leyritz would prove he deserved the title.

When finally afforded the opportunity, Leyritz thrived in the postseason. In the 1995 Division Series he beat Seattle in Game 2 with a 15th-inning homer. In Game 4 of the 1996 World Series he hit a home run in the eighth against Atlanta closer Mark Wohlers. It was the turning point as New York won that game to tie the Series, and went on to win the world championship in six games.

Despite his success in the big games, Leyritz was passed around both leagues over the next three seasons. He played in Anaheim, Texas, Boston, and San Diego in a span of 18 months. In the 1998 Division Series the King met the challenge again, going deep against Houston three times, including a two-out, game-tying homer in the ninth inning of Game 2. For good measure, he added a home run in the Padres' six-game victory over Atlanta in the Championship Series.

Traded back to New York in July 1999, Leyritz played sparingly yet smashed a home run in the World Series. Of his 13 career hits in the postseason, eight were home runs.

Sixto Lezcano

Lezcano, Sixto Joaquin (Curras) **OF**

1974–85 B:11/28/1953, Arecibo, Puerto Rico Deb:9/10/1974, MIL AL BR/TR 5'11", 175

G	AB	R	H	HR	RBI	OBP	SLG	AVG
1291	4134	560	1122	148	591	.363	.410	.271

Sixto Lezcano was a ballplayer's ballplayer. The versatile 175-pound outfielder could catch, throw, and hit for power. He took his talents to five major league teams in his 12-year career.

A native of Puerto Rico, Lezcano was signed as a free agent by Milwaukee in 1970. He began his career with Newark of the New York-Penn League in 1971, and moved on to Danville, Shreveport, and Sacramento before being promoted to the Brewers in 1974 at age 20.

Lezcano started slowly, hitting only .247 in his first full season in 1975. His average was up to .285 the next year, however, and by 1977 he began to hit with power and authority, accounting for 21 doubles and 21 homers that season. In 1978 he led all American League outfielders in assists.

Lezcano had his best season in 1979. He sizzled both in the field, where he won a Gold Glove, and at the plate, where he hit .321 with 28 home runs, 29 doubles, 101 RBIs, and a .573 slugging percentage. From July 19 to July 22, he homered in four straight games to set a Brewers record (since broken by Jeromy Burnitz). The next year, however, despite a memorable ninth-inning grand slam that beat the Boston Red Sox on Opening Day, his batting average dropped by almost 100 points, with his home runs, doubles, and RBIs also declining. As a result, Lezcano was traded to the St. Louis Cardinals in a deal that brought Ted Simmons, Pete Vuckovich, and Rollie Fingers to Milwaukee in December 1980.

Playing in spacious Busch Stadium on a part-time basis, Lezcano hit only five home runs in 1981 and was traded to the San Diego Padres along with Garry Templeton for Ozzie Smith. In 1982 Lezcano batted .289 with 16 homers, led NL outfielders in double plays, and tied for the lead in assists, with 16.

Late in the 1983 season Lezcano was traded to Philadelphia, where he homered in the final game of the 1983 National League Championship Series to help propel the Phillies to a 7–2 win. After finishing his big league career with Pittsburgh in 1985, he played a season with the Yokohama Bay Stars of the Japanese Central League. In 1999 Lezcano served as roving outfield instructor in the Kansas City Royals system.

Omar Linares

Linares, Omar **3B**

Cuban League Player (1985-*) B:Pinar del Rio, Cuba BR/TR

Until 1996, the prowess of Cuba's Omar Linares was only a rumor to baseball fans in the United States. But when the slugging third baseman led the Cuban National Team to a gold medal in that summer's Olympics in Atlanta, his prodigious performance made converts out of everyone who witnessed it. Linares blasted eight home runs in the tournament, including a first-inning homer against Team USA and three against Japan in the championship game.

Cuba was the uncontested giant of international amateur baseball in the 1990s, and Linares was the country's brightest star. At age 14, he hit better than .500 in his first appearance in world amateur championship play. Linares was Most Valuable Player of the 1987 Intercontinental Cup Tourney in Havana, and he carried Cuba to victory in the first official Olympic medal baseball competition in Barcelona in 1992. He was also MVP of the 1993 IBA World All-Star Game at the Tokyo Dome. In 15 seasons of Cuban League play through 1999, Linares won five batting titles and had a career average in the vicinity of .375.

Omar's father, Fidel Linares, led the Cuban League in base hits while playing for Occidentales in 1963. His brother, Juan Carlos, played alongside Linares for their hometown Pinar del Rio club. Although several of his countrymen defected to play in the major leagues, Linares entertained no such notions. He "has repeatedly expressed his interest in playing nowhere but on the soil of his cherished homeland," Peter C. Bjarkman wrote in *Smoke: The Romance and Lore of Cuban Baseball.* Political realities have made Linares, in Bjarkman's words, "indisputably major league baseball's greatest loss" of the 1990s.

Paul Lindblad

Lindblad, Paul Aaron **P**

1965–78 B:8/9/1941, Chanute, KA Deb:9/15/1965, KC AL BL/TL 6'1", 195

W	L	PCT	G	SV	IP	BB	SO	ERA
68	63	.519	655	64	1213^2	384	671	3.29

Lefthanders Paul Lindblad and Darold Knowles were Oakland's principal middle-relief specialists during the 1970s. Opposing managers frequently opted to remove their lefthanded batters for pinch hitters when either of the two southpaws took the mound, but then righthander Rollie Fingers would come in to save the game.

Lindblad joined the Kansas City A's in 1965 at age 24. In 1968 he moved with the team to Oakland, where he compiled 9–6 and 8–2 records the next two seasons. Shortly before the A's clinched the division in 1971 Lindblad was traded to Washington.

The Senators moved to Texas and became the Rangers before the 1972 season. That year Lindblad led the league with 66 appearances. The A's then reacquired him in an off-season trade, and in 1973 he won Game 3 of the World Series.

Lindblad was an excellent fielder. From August 1966 to April 1974 he recorded a remarkable streak of 385 appearances without an error. The 1975 season was perhaps his best, as he went 9–1 with seven saves and a 2.72 ERA. On September 28 of that year he combined with Vida Blue, Glenn Abbott, and Rollie Fingers to pitch the first multi-pitcher no-hit, no-run game in major league history.

Lindblad played for Texas again in 1977 and 1978 before ending his career with a brief stint for the Yankees at the end of 1978. He later became a building contractor in Arlington, Texas.

Freddie Lindstrom

Lindstrom, Frederick Charles **3B–OF**

1924–36 B:11/21/1905, Chicago, IL D:10/4/1981, Chicago, IL Deb:4/15/1924, NY NL BR/TR 5'11", 170

G	AB	R	H	HR	RBI	OBP	SLG	AVG
1438	5611	895	1747	103	779	.351	.449	.311

When baseball fans discuss who does or doesn't belong in the Hall of Fame, Freddie Lindstrom, who was inducted in 1976, is frequently one of the first names mentioned as a player who doesn't deserve it. Lindstrom was an excellent third baseman until a back injury forced him to move to the outfield in 1931. He hit .300 or better seven times, including six consecutive seasons, and twice rapped 231 hits. But his career was short—only seven seasons as a regular in 13 big league years. And he had his two best batting seasons in 1928 and 1930, when almost every player was pounding the ball.

While it's true he was not a superstar, Lindstrom was a very good player on a very good team. Ironically, he earned a place in baseball history because of two plays that he didn't make in the 1924 World Series.

Lindstrom grew up on the south side of Chicago, and he was an avid White Sox fan. Signed by the New York Giants after graduating from high school, he played a season and a half for Toledo in the American Association before being brought up to the big club when he was only 18 years old. He spent most of the 1924 season as a backup to second baseman Frankie Frisch and third baseman Heinie Groh.

When Groh injured his knee late in the year, Lindstrom was given the job at third base and was the Giants' leadoff hitter against Walter Johnson and the Senators in the 1924 World Series. At 18 years, 10 months, and 13 days old, Lindstrom set the major league record as the youngest player to appear in a World Series game.

Lindstrom played third flawlessly during the Series. In Game 4, facing George Mogridge and Firpo Marberry, his bat came to life, and he stroked three singles, drove in a run, and scored another. However, the Giants lost the game, and the Series was tied at 2–2.

Lindstrom faced Johnson again in Game 5 and rapped out four more singles, knocking home two runs to help New York to a 6–2 win. When the Giants lost Game 6, 2–1, on Bucky Harris' fifth-inning, two-out single, the stage was set for the dramatic events of Game 7, one of the craziest games in Series history.

The Senators had a 1–0 lead when the Giants knocked across three runs against Mogridge and Marberry in the sixth. In the last half of the eighth, pinch hitter Nemo Leibold swatted a one-out double past Lindstrom. After a single, a walk, and a flyout, Harris rapped a grounder to third that hit something and bounced. Was it a pebble? A divot? No one can say for sure, but the ball took a weird hop over Lindstrom's head, and two runs scored to tie the game, 3–3. Johnson came in to face the Giants, and held them scorelss for four innings. Art Nehf, Hugh McQuillan, and Jack Bentley, meanwhile, held the Senators at bay.

In the last of the 12th Muddy Ruel hit a foul pop that appeared to be an easy play for Giants catcher Hank Gowdy. But the wind blew the ball back toward the plate, and Gowdy stepped into his facemask, which he had tossed off to chase the fly. Unable to shake the mask off his foot—"It held me like a bear trap," he later said—Gowdy missed the foul pop, and Ruel delivered a double.

Johnson then reached on an error by Travis Jackson. The next batter, Earl McNeely, was a rookie with fewer than 50 games of big league experience. He swatted a grounder toward Lindstrom and the impossible happened again. The ball took a bizarre hop, and the Senators won their first World Series ever. Despite a .333 average for the Series with 10 hits, Lindstrom will always be remembered as the man who watched two ground balls bounce over hi head.

Despite his rough luck in the Series, Lindstrom's hot bat and normally smooth fielding made him a fan favorite in New York, where he was called "the Boy Wonder." He first attained a .300 average in 1926, and he continued to bat above it through 1931.

Lindstrom's two great years were 1928 and 1930. In the former, he hit .358—third best in the National League—scored 99 runs, hit 39 doubles, and drove in 107 runs. The latter year he finished fifth in the NL with a .379 batting average, again had 231 hits and 39 doubles, scored 127 runs, hit 22 homers, and had 106 RBIs.

Lindstrom openly talked back to John McGraw, something no one would have done years earlier. In 1931 he was told by both club president Charles Stoneham and traveling secretary Jim Tierney that McGraw was on his way out and that Lindstrom would be his successor.

Once he was privy to that information, Lindstrom saw even less reason to heed McGraw's stern talk. But when the 1931 season ended, Bill Terry was named manager. Apparently McGraw, upset at Lindstrom's subversive behavior, had talked the owners out of hiring him. An upset Lindstrom asked to be traded, although a three-way swap with the Pirates and Phillies wasn't worked out until December of 1932.

After two seasons in Pittsburgh, Lindstrom was swapped to the Cubs. In Chicago he played a critical role in one of the most amazing winning streaks that any team has ever enjoyed. Three and a half games out of first place on September 3, 1935, the Cubs won 18 straight games at home and then took three more on the road. During that streak Lindstrom scored or drove in the winning run seven times. So shocking was the Cubs' comeback that there wasn't time to print World Series tickets, and the Series had to begin in Detroit although it was the National League's turn to open.

Lindstrom moved to the Dodgers for the 1936 season but played in only 26 games. He called it quits after a particularly disappointing loss. With two Giants on and Brooklyn up by a run in the last of the ninth, a pop fly to left dropped in after the shortstop, left fielder Lindstrom, and the center fielder miscommunicated. Both runs scored and the Dodgers lost.

Lindstrom finally got his wish to manage a team, albeit in the minors, from 1940 through 1942. He' also spent two years announcing a radio sports program in Chicago. In 1976 the Veterans Committee voted Lindstrom into the Hall of Fame.

Phil Linz

Linz, Philip Francis **SS-2B**

1962–68 B:6/4/1939, Baltimore, MD Deb:4/13/1962, NY AL BR/TR 6'1", 180

G	AB	R	H	HR	RBI	OBP	SLG	AVG
519	1372	185	322	11	96	.296	.311	.235

Phil Linz was a light-hitting but free-spirited player for the New York Yankees who once said, "You can't get rich sitting on a bench—but I'm giving it a try." The utility infielder's harmonica-playing antics in August 1964 probably cost Yogi Berra his job as the team's manager.

Linz first joined the Yankees in 1963, filling the role as utility infielder that year and the next. In 1964 he played much more regularly. That year, the Yankees were stuck in third place and had lost four straight games to the White Sox at Comiskey Park. On the team bus to the airport Linz started playing "Mary Had a Little Lamb" on his harmonica, infuriating rookie manager Berra. The skipper ordered Linz to stop. When Linz asked what his manager had said, Mickey Mantle reportedly told the infielder that Berra had said, "Play louder." When Linz did, Berra stormed to the back of the bus and swatted the harmonica out of the infielder's hands. The incident was widely interpreted as proof of Berra's inability to control the club.

The Yankees won the pennant, but Berra was fired at the close of the seven-game World Series loss to the St. Louis Cardinals. A year later, after hitting only .207, Linz was traded to the Philadelphia Phillies for infielder Ruben Amaro. He spent three years as a little-used reserve for the Phillies and the New York Mets. After his retirement Linz went into the restaurant business in New York.

Danny Litwhiler

Litwhiler, Daniel Webster **OF**

1940–44, 1946–51 B:8/31/1916, Ringtown, PA Deb:4/25/1940, PHI AL BR/TR 5'10½", 198

G	AB	R	H	HR	RBI	OBP	SLG	AVG
1057	3494	428	982	107	451	.342	.438	.281

Danny Litwhiler was an outstanding outfielder for several National League clubs in the 1940s. He appeared in two World Series and went on to coach the Michigan State University baseball team for many years.

Litwhiler started with Charleroi of the Pennsylvania State League in 1936. In 1939 he injured his knee playing at Alexandria and missed the entire season. Nevertheless, the Pittsburgh Pirates called him up at the beginning of 1940, and, although not playing a great deal, Litwhiler responded with a 21-game hitting streak.

In 1941 Litwhiler had what would prove to be his best year offensively. He had career highs with a .305 average, 18 home runs—reaching the seats in every park in the National League—29 doubles, and 66 RBIs. He also had a very curious season in the field, leading NL outfielders in putouts while, on the downside, tallying a league-leading 15 errors.

The following year, 1942, Litwhiler played 151 games without an error. Midway through the next season he was traded to the St. Louis Cardinals, for whom he played in consecutive World Series. In the 1944 showdown with the crosstown Browns, Litwhiler hit a home run to help win Game 5.

In 1945 Litwhiler was reclassified and spent the year in the military after having been previously rejected because of an injured knee. The next year he was sold to the Boston Braves; two years later he was sent to the Cincinnati Reds. In 1951 he served as player-coach for the Reds, before retiring at the end of the season.

Litwhiler continued to coach with the Reds in 1952 and later became head coach for the Michigan State Spartans. He retired from coaching baseball in 1982.

Pop Lloyd

Lloyd, John Henry **SS-2B-1B**

Negro League Player (1906–32) Manager B:4/25/1884 D:3/19/1964 BL/TR 5'11", 180

Pop Lloyd was one of the most feared hitters and most respected men ever to play Negro League baseball. Although he never stayed long with one team, preferring instead to "go where the money was," he was the dominating shortstop of his era, and, according to eyewitnesses, possibly the greatest player of all time in any league. In reference to the completeness of his skills, the 1910 *Indianapolis Freeman* stated, "he contains a ball team within himself." When Honus Wagner heard that Lloyd was being called "the Black Wagner," he said that he considered the comparison with Lloyd an honor.

Lloyd played for 12 different teams in a 26-year career. He ran with long, smooth strides, batted with lefthanded line-drive power, and had "hands as big as a telephone book," according to fellow Negro League star Ted Page. He never went in for showboating, preferring instead to remain aloof and professional. A role model for younger players, he managed for years and was considered an excellent teacher.

Lloyd turned professional in 1905 when he took over as catcher for the Macon (Georgia) Acmes. Unfortunately, his team could not afford catcher's gear, so he played without a facemask. After feeling the effect of foul balls on his face, Lloyd bought a wire wastebasket and wore it over his head while he caught. After a year at second base with the Cuban X Giants, he joined the Philadelphia Giants, where Negro League pioneer Sol White taught him how to play shortstop.

Lloyd had some of his greatest moments in the Cuban Winter League, where he played against teams that included many white major leaguers. In five successive seasons in Cuba he hit .388, .393 (winning the batting title), .367, .371, and .362. The Cuban fans loved him, calling him "La Cuchara," "the Spoon," referring to his large hands.

In 1910 the Detroit Tigers came to Cuba for an exhibition series against Lloyd's Havana Reds and another team. Ty Cobb hit well (.369), but Grant Johnson and Bruce Petway outhit Cobb, and Lloyd batted an even .500. Three times Cobb tried to steal second base and three times Petway threw him out, with Lloyd dancing away from Cobb's spikes in order to make the tags.

Lloyd spent 1914 through 1917 as cleanup hitter for Rube Foster's Chicago American Giants, who won four Western League crowns and were twice Negro League world champions. In 1917 he and youngster Bingo DeMoss teamed up as a legendary double-play combo; then Lloyd took the job as player-manager for the Brooklyn Royal Giants, moved to the Columbus Buckeyes as a first baseman, and then on to the Philadelphia Hilldale Club.

One of his most spectacular seasons came in 1928 with the New York Black Yankees. In a 37-game schedule, the 44-year-old Lloyd demolished league pitching with a league-leading .564 average, 11 home runs, and 10 stolen bases. In 1930 he played a major role in getting Yankee Stadium opened to black baseball when he sponsored a benefit game there for the black Pullman porters' union. When Babe Ruth was interviewed by Graham McNamee and asked to name the greatest ballplayer of all time, he reputedly answered, "John Henry Lloyd."

Lloyd's lifetime .368 batting average was the highest in Negro League competition. In 29 games against major leaguers he batted .321. He "retired" at age 48, but played semipro ball with Atlantic City in 1942, when he was 58 years old. Although Lloyd had no children of his own, he loved to play ball with kids and served for years as commissioner of the Little League in Atlantic City, where, in 1949, the John Henry Lloyd Baseball Park was dedicated. In 1977 he was inducted into the Baseball Hall of Fame.

Hans Lobert

Lobert, John Bernard **3B–SS**

1903, 1905–17 M(1938, 1942, 42–111) B:10/18/1881, Wilmington, DE D:9/14/1968, Philadelphia, PA Deb:9/21/1903, PIT NL BR/TR 5'9", 170

G	AB	R	H	HR	RBI	OBP	SLG	AVG
1317	4563	640	1252	32	482	.337	.366	.274

Hans Lobert would race anyone or anything. The speedster once won a sizable sum in Havana by racing against two horses, two autos, two motorcycles, and one professional runner. His racing became quite a baseball sideshow. In Cincinnati on October 12, 1910, he circled the bases in only 13.8 seconds.

Lobert was known as "Honus No. 2" because of his resemblance to Honus Wagner (who gave him the nickname). The bowlegged Lobert twice led National League third basemen in fielding percentage and putouts.

He started his career with the semipro Pittsburgh ACs. In 1903 Pittsburgh owner Barney Dreyfuss gave him a short trial, but Lobert hit only .077 and spent 1904 in Des Moines of the Western League. After hitting .337 and stealing 57 bases at Johnstown of the Tri-State League in 1905, he played briefly with the Chicago Cubs.

After that season the Cincinnati Reds traded Harry Steinfeldt for the 24-year-old Lobert and pitcher Jake Weimer. Lobert immediately turned on his hitting, batting .310 in 1906. He also became a dangerous base-stealing threat, and during his five seasons in Cincinnati he stole a total of 168 bases. On September 27, 1908, he stole second, third, and home.

Lobert was traded to the Phillies before the 1911 season and played four years in Philadelphia, twice averaging over .300, including a career-high .327 in 1912. During the winter of 1913–14 he participated in a historic world tour with members of the Giants and the White Sox. The Giants acquired him before the 1915 season. But Lobert had slowed considerably by then, and in 1915 he was thrown out 15 times in 29 steal attempts.

He retired after the 1917 season and became a coach at West Point from 1918 through 1925. He then coached for the Giants and managed in Bridgeport and Jersey City before coaching for the Philadelphia Phillies from 1934 through 1941. In Philadelphia Lobert helped convert Bucky Walters from an infielder into a pitcher.

In 1942 Lobert managed the Phillies to a dismal 42–109 finish. He coached for the Reds in 1943 and 1944 and scouted for the Giants from 1945 through 1967. In 1953 Edward G. Robinson portrayed a fictionalized version of Lobert in the film *Big Leaguer*.

Kenny Lofton

Lofton, Kenneth **OF**

1991–* B:5/31/1967, E. Chicago, IN Deb:9/14/1991, HOU NL BL/TL 6', 180

G	AB	R	H	HR	RBI	OBP	SLG	AVG
1096	4379	852	1356	63	412	.387	.429	.310

A superior basestealer, a fine leadoff hitter, and a swift center fielder, Kenny Lofton contributed heavily to five straight playoff teams in the 1990s. From 1992 to 1996, Lofton was the king of the basepaths in the American League. His stolen base totals for those years—66, 70, 60, 54 and 75—were the best in the league each season. His former manager Mike Hargrove commented that Lofton was one of the few who could "distort" a game with his speed. In eight full seasons through 1999, the six-time All-Star had 433 stolen bases.

Many colleges pursued Lofton out of high school—as a basketball player. He finally chose Arizona, and assumed he would become an NBA player. Lofton was a point guard for a team that made it to the Final Four in 1988 and was the top-ranked school in the nation for much of 1989, but he found that college offense was too preplanned for his taste. Eventually, he turned to baseball, which he had played as a teenager. He walked on and made Arizona's varsity team late as a junior. Even though he hardly played, the Houston Astros took him in the 17th round of the 1988 draft.

Hitting only .203 in his first 20 games with the Astros in 1991, and with Steve Finley established as the team's center fielder, Lofton was traded to Cleveland, where he quickly prospered with the developing Indians. He reduced his strikeouts to become a fine contact hitter. In 1993 he batted .325 with 185 hits; his 160 hits led the league in the strike-shortened 1994 season. Lofton hit over .300 the following two years, reaching rare heights in 1996 with 210 hits and 132 runs scored. He also captured a Gold Glove from 1993 through 1996. His finest year in the field came in 1994, when he had two errors in 112 games and a .993 fielding percentage. Not blessed with a strong arm, Lofton compensated with accuracy and consistency.

Meanwhile, the Indians won the American League pennant in 1995. In the final game of the Championship Series, Lofton scored from second base on a passed ball against Seattle. The Atlanta Braves, however, completely shut down Lofton and Cleveland's offense to take the World Series. The Tribe fell in the Division Series the following year, and Lofton was traded to Atlanta in March 1997.

Despite suffering a groin injury that severely damaged his base-running ability, Lofton batted .333 for the Braves. He missed the Division Series against Houston, and then returned to bat .185 as Florida stunned Atlanta in the NLCS. Re-signed by Cleveland as a free agent, Lofton returned to form in 1998: 54 stolen bases, 87 walks, 101 runs scored. Once again, the Tribe faltered, defeated by the powerful New York Yankees in a six-game ALCS.

Injuries again slowed Lofton in 1999; this time, it was a hamstring problem. Still, he batted .301 in 120 games. The season came to another frustrating end for him and the Indians: he batted .125 in a Division Series collapse to Boston and left Game 5 with a dislocated shoulder.

Johnny Logan

Logan, John **SS**

1951–63 B:3/23/1927, Endicott, NY Deb:4/17/1951, BOS NL BR/TR 5'11", 175

G	AB	R	H	HR	RBI	OBP	SLG	AVG
1503	5244	651	1407	93	547	.331	.378	.268

Johnny Logan was the shortstop for the Milwaukee Braves during their back-to-back pennant winning years of 1957 and 1958. He had a gift for both baseball and malapropisms. Asked to name the greatest player of all time, Logan responded, "I'd have to go with the immoral Babe Ruth."

Logan was a four-time All-Star and a scrapper at shortstop, carrying on in the tradition of tough-guy middle infielders such as Leo Durocher, Dick Bartell, and Eddie Stanky. Angered over being hit by a pitch, the 5-foot 11-inch, 175-pound Logan once took on Don Drysdale, giving away seven inches and 40 pounds.

Logan starred with the Milwaukee Brewers of the American Association and gained the nickname "Yatcha" (Ukrainian for John) from the local ethnic populace. Promoted to the Boston Braves in 1951, he played behind Buddy Kerr for a season and then took over most of the playing time at short in 1952, leading National League shortstops in fielding percentage in his first full season .

His prowess in the field began with quick, sure hands and decent range, which made up for an average arm. Logan led NL shortstops in fielding three consecutive years. He also topped the league in assists four times, in total chances per game three times, and in putouts once.

He was picked for his first All-Star Game in 1955, and, in front of the hometown fans, singled in his first at bat, driving in the first run of a comeback from a 5–0 deficit to a 12-inning, 6–5 win. That season Logan set career highs with 83 RBIs, a league-leading 37 doubles, 58 walks, and a .297 batting average. He also hit one of the Braves' league-record-setting eight home runs against the Pittsburgh Pirates on August 30.

The Braves won their first pennant in Milwaukee in 1957 and met the New York Yankees in the World Series. Logan handled 38 chances flawlessly in the Series and delivered a solo home run in the third inning of Game 2, giving Milwaukee a 2–1 lead in Lew Burdette's 4–2 win. Batting second in the lineup between double-play partner Red Schoendienst and Eddie Mathews, Logan had two hits in Game 3.

In Game 4 Logan scored in the fourth and then set a new World Series shortstop assist record in the 10th. The Yankees scored once that inning to go on top, 5–4. In the bottom of the 10th, Yankees pitcher Tommy Byrne hit pinch hitter Vernal Jones, putting the tying run on first.

Logan doubled into the left-field corner to drive home the tying run. Mathews then homered to right for a 7–5 Milwaukee win. In Game 7 Logan reached base three times and scored once in Burdette's third win of the Series.

The Braves and the Yankees met again in the 1958 World Series, and Logan doubled in his first at bat. Dropped to eighth in the order in Game 2, he singled in a run and scored on Burdette's homer in Milwaukee's seven-run first, as the Braves took a 2–0 lead in the Series. In Game 4, batting second again, he drove Schoendienst home from third, and later doubled and scored in the eighth, backing Warren Spahn's two-hit, 3–0 win. However, Logan went hitless in the final three games, won by the Yankees.

In 1959 the Braves nearly made it three pennants in a row, finishing in a tie with the Los Angeles Dodgers. Logan's walk in the second inning of the playoff opener sparked a two-run rally, but the Dodgers came back to win, 3–2. In Game 2 Logan had two hits and scored once as the Braves built a 4–2 lead, but he left the game after getting flattened by Norm Larker while completing a double play. The Dodgers rallied from a 5–2 ninth-inning deficit to tie the score. In the bottom of the 12th, Logan's replacement at short, Felix Mantilla, threw late and wild to first, allowing the winning run to score.

Logan remained the Braves' regular at shortstop through the 1960 season. Then, replaced by Roy McMillan, he was traded to Pittsburgh for outfielder Gino Cimoli on June 15, 1961. He finished up as a backup player for three seasons with the Pirates, and later became a Brewers scout.

Logan never shook his tendency to say the right thing in the wrong way. Once he commented about an acquaintance, "I know the name but I can't replace the face." Informed that a box score depriving him of a hit was a typographical error, Logan responded, "The hell it was. That was a clean base hit."

Mickey Lolich

Lolich, Michael Stephen **P**

1963–76, 1978–79 B:9/12/1940, Portland, OR
Deb:5/12/1963, DET AL BB/TL 6', 210

W	L	PCT	G	SH	IP	BB	SO	ERA
217	191	.532	586	41	3638[1]	1099	2832	3.44

Lefthanded Detroit Tigers pitcher Mickey Lolich used the national arena of the 1968 World Series to upstage Denny McLain and Bob Gibson in their greatest seasons by winning three games. Lolich had gone 17–9 with 197 strikeouts for the year, but teammate McLain had earned the Cy Young Award, going 31–6 with 280 strikeouts and a 1.96 ERA. Gibson, the National League Cy Young winner, had been 22–9 for the Cardinals with 268 strikeouts and an amazing 1.12 ERA.

In the World Series, Gibson beat McLain in Games 1 and 4, but Lolich pitched complete-game wins in Games 2 and 5. Detroit manager Mayo Smith, down three games to two, brought McLain back to pitch Game 6 and gave Lolich the Game 7 assignment against Gibson. Pitching on two days' rest, Lolich outdueled Gibson 4–1 in St. Louis to clinch the championship for Detroit.

Lolich was born righthanded, but when he was a toddler a motorcycle fell on him and broke his left shoulder. A doctor recommended he throw lefthanded to straighten it out, and he continued to do so. As a boy Lolich pitched his Babe Ruth League team to two national championship finals, although he lost both.

The Tigers signed him in 1959. On Opening Day, 1962, Lolich was hit in the eye by a line drive while pitching for the Denver Bears and temporarily lost his sight. Afraid of being hit again, Lolich quit but returned later in the season.

In 1963 Lolich reached the major leagues. After a rookie year spent alternating between starting and the bullpen, he joined the regular rotation in 1964 and went 18–9, the first of 11 consecutive years in which he won at least 14 games. In 1967 his six shutouts led the league, and in 1969 he won 19 games and was selected to his first All-Star Game. He seemed to reach a new level in 1971, however, when he led the league with 25 wins, 308 strikeouts, and 29 complete games. The following season he had 22 wins and appeared in his second consecutive All-Star Game.

Having suffered through years of jibes about his weight, in 1972 Lolich explained, "I guess you could say I'm the redemption of the fat man. A guy will be watching me on TV and see that I don't look in any better shape than he is. 'Hey Maude,' he'll holler. 'Get a load of this guy and he's a 20-game winner.'"

After the 1975 season the Tigers traded Lolich to the Mets for outfielder Rusty Staub. He had one poor year and then sat out all of the 1977 season to become a free agent. Lolich signed with San Diego but was then moved to the bullpen; he retired after going 2–3 over two seasons. He later operated the Mickey Lolich Donut and Pastry Shop in Lake Orion, Michigan.

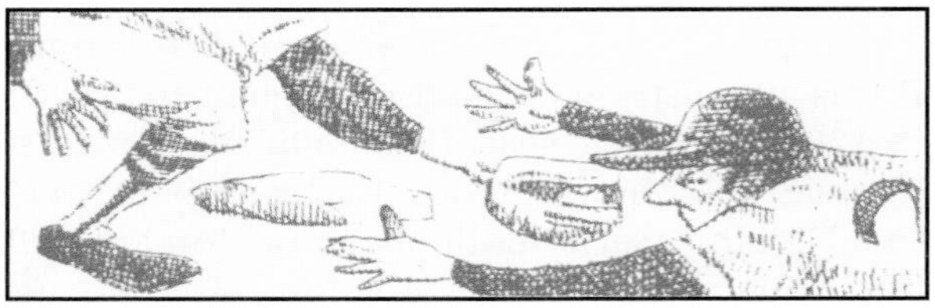

Sherm Lollar

Lollar, John Sherman **C**

1946–63 B:8/23/1924, Durham, AR D:9/24/1977, Springfield, MO Deb:4/20/1946, CLE AL BR/TR 6'1", 185

G	AB	R	H	HR	RBI	OBP	SLG	AVG
1752	5351	623	1415	155	808	.359	.402	.264

When he gave the eulogy at Sherm Lollar's funeral, Bill Veeck pointed out that everyone assembled had recognized Lollar's worth before he himself did. Veeck had traded Lollar away from the first two major league teams he owned, and only when he inherited Lollar on his third ballclub did the owner finally begin to appreciate the value of the veteran catcher.

There was nothing flashy about Lollar. A quiet, thoughtful man and a painfully slow baserunner, his strengths were excellent defensive skills, modest power, and an exceptional ability to handle pitchers. According to Al Lopez, who managed him in Chicago and who had been an outstanding catcher in his day, "Sherm's success was that the pitchers liked him personally—and they respected him. That's a great thing to have going for a catcher. It's tough to be pitching and have to worry about what a catcher's gonna call. If a catcher's got a reputation of being a rockhead, the pitcher's gonna have to worry that much more."

As a young man, Lollar worked as a muleskinner around Baxter Springs, Kansas, and it gave him an appreciation for hard work performed without complaint. He began playing baseball at Pittsburg (Kansas) State Teachers College and debuted professionally with Baltimore of the International League in 1943. He won the IL batting title in 1945 with a .364 mark and was called up to Veeck's Cleveland Indians the next year.

The Indians' regular catcher was Jim Hegan, probably baseball's best defensive catcher at the time, and Lollar saw little action, appearing in only 28 games. Before the 1947 season he was dealt to the New York Yankees for Gene Bearden. In New York, Lollar sat on the bench for two seasons while Yogi Berra became the star catcher. In 1949 he was sent to the St. Louis Browns in a multi-player swap.

Immediately installed as the Browns' regular catcher, Lollar hit .261 his first year and improved that to .280 the next. That second year he was selected to the All-Star Game despite having little chance to show off his pitcher-handling skills with the weak St. Louis staff. By then Veeck owned the Browns. He believed that the Yankees' Clint Courtney would add speed and hitting to the club, so he sent Jim McDonald to New York for Courtney and packed off Lollar and two other Browns to Chicago for five unwanted White Sox.

Although Lollar was the regular catcher for the White Sox from 1952 through 1954, manager Paul Richards always seemed on the verge of replacing him with a bigger bat or a faster runner. Matt Batts, Red Wilson, and Carl Sawatski all tried to displace Lollar but failed. In 1954 Lollar was again named to the All-Star Game, yet only when Marty Marion became manager in 1955 was his job made secure. Years later, Marion spoke of Lollar as his "assistant manager." He added, "You'd walk out to the mound and you'd look in Sherm's eyes and you knew whether the pitcher had anything or not. I made a lot of my decisions on Sherm's comments—and his looks."

Lollar was selected to the All-Star Game six times between 1954 and 1960. From 1956 through 1959, he had at least 70 RBIs each year. He also led AL catchers in fielding five times, finishing with a .992 career fielding mark.

It is ironic that the slow-footed Lollar finally began to achieve recognition after he joined the "Go-Go" White Sox, at the time the most fleet-footed team in the majors. After several second-place finishes, the White Sox finished first in 1959 and ended a streak of four straight Yankee pennants. Lollar had his best year, hitting 22 homers and guiding the White Sox pitchers to the league's lowest ERA.

The Los Angeles Dodgers then defeated the Sox in the World Series, four games to two. More than any other play, Chicago fans remember Lollar's being thrown out at home while trying to score from first with what would have been the tying run in a 4–3 loss in Game 2. In Game 4 he hit a three-run homer to tie the score, but the Dodgers rallied to win. Chicago won Game 5, 1–0, as Lollar chased home the only run by hitting into a double play.

Lollar retired after serving as a backup in 1963. He coached with Baltimore and Oakland from 1964 through 1968, and then became a manager in the high minors. He was thought to be in line for a major league job when he was felled by cancer in 1977.

Ernie Lombardi

Lombardi, Ernesto Natali **C**

1931–47 B:4/6/1908, Oakland, CA D:9/26/1977, Santa Cruz, CA Deb:4/15/1931, BRO NL BR/TR 6'3", 230

G	AB	R	H	HR	RBI	OBP	SLG	AVG
1853	5855	601	1792	190	990	.358	.460	.306

Ernie Lombardi fit the catcher stereotype—big and slow—but his measured manner behind the plate and on the baselines disappeared when he came to bat. The righthander hit ferocious line drives that struck fear into opposing fielders. He twice led the National League in batting, hitting .306 for his career.

Nicknamed "Schnozz" for his most prominent facial feature, Lombardi broke in with Brooklyn in 1931 and was traded to the Cincinnati Reds the following year. The league quickly learned to play infielders on the outfield grass because Lombardi could never beat out a grounder, and the distance gave the fielders more time to react to his wicked line drives. The big catcher once confessed, "Pee Wee Reese was in the league three years before I realized he wasn't an outfielder." Pitchers did not have the luxury of playing deep against Lombardi, and in 1937 he lined a ball back at the Chicago Cubs' Larry French that broke three of the pitcher's fingers.

Capable of getting very hot at the plate, Lombardi hit .303 hit first year as a full-time player, and then in 1935 began a streak of four consecutive years over .330. On May 8, 1935, he hit a double in each of four consecutive innings off four different pitchers. And on May 9, 1937, he tallied six hits in six at bats.

Lombardi was selected to the first of five consecutive All-Star Games in 1936. Two years later he led the league with a .342 batting average while producing career highs with 60 runs, 30 doubles, and 95 RBIs. That same year he caught both of Johnny Vander Meer's consecutive no-hitters.

The lingering memory of his defensive abilities is the "Lombardi Swoon" in the 10th inning of Game 4 of the 1939 World Series, when the New York Yankees' Charlie Keller scored on Joe DiMaggio's hit. Keller knocked Lombardi senseless when he crossed home plate, and the catcher lay sprawled and semiconscious as DiMaggio circled the bases with another run. "It was an awfully hot day in Cincinnati and I was feeling dizzy...When Keller came in he spun me around at the plate and I couldn't get up," Lombardi later explained.

Following a poor 1941 season, Cincinnati general manager Warren Giles sold Lombardi to Boston. Lombardi had feuded publicly with Giles over salary, calling Giles "the old goat." Lombardi made his former boss look bad the next year by hitting .330 and going back to the All-Star Game. Nevertheless, the next year Boston traded Lombardi to the Giants, where a .305 season led to his seventh and final All-Star appearance. He retired following the 1947 season.

Lombardi spent seven years as a press box attendant in San Francisco, and later had a job in a gas station. He died in 1977 at the age of 69. Giles, an influential Hall of Fame member, successfully lobbied against admitting Lombardi to Cooperstown, but the Veterans Committee elected the catcher posthumously in 1986—after Giles died.

Jim Lonborg

Lonborg, James Reynold **P**

1965–79 B:4/16/1942, Santa Maria, CA Deb:4/23/1965, BOS AL BR/TR 6'5", 210

W	L	PCT	G	SH	IP	BB	SO	ERA
157	137	.534	425	15	2464^{1}	823	1475	3.86

A brilliant performer for the 1967 Boston Red Sox "Impossible Dream" pennant winner, Jim Lonborg had an up-and-down career, spending seven years at Fenway Park before starring for the Philadelphia Phillies division winners a decade later. He then retired to a career in dentistry.

Lonborg received his degree in biology from Stanford University and then signed with the Red Sox in 1964. He split his only minor league season between Red Sox farm teams in the Carolina and Pacific Coast leagues, then joined Boston's rotation in 1965. After a shaky 9–17 freshman year, Lonborg shuttled between the bullpen and the starting rotation in 1966, when the Red Sox finished in ninth place.

The hard-throwing righthander won back his starting spot in 1967 and became the ace for a Red Sox team that shocked everyone by winning the pennant. Lonborg earned his only All-Star berth, tied Detroit's Earl Wilson for the AL lead with 22 wins, and struck out a circuit-leading 246 batters. He was second in the AL with 15 complete games and 273⅓ innings pitched, and won the Cy Young Award with 18 out of 20 first-place votes.

Lonborg won the big games for the Sox in a crazy four-way pennant race. On the regular season's final day, with the Red Sox and Twins dead even and Detroit one-half game behind and playing a doubleheader, Lonborg faced Minnesota's 20-game winner, Dean Chance, at Fenway Park.

He fell behind early on a pair of unearned runs. Leading off the fifth inning, Lonborg—13-for-99 on the season—bunted up the third base line for a single to start Boston's winning rally. The scoreboard, meanwhile, showed Detroit winning its first game. Lonborg went all the way for a 5–3 win and was carried off the field by adoring fans. "I was scared before the game," Lonborg said. "I was terrified afterward." Detroit lost the nightcap, handing the Red Sox the pennant.

On three days' rest, Lonborg started Game 2 of the World Series against St. Louis and threatened to make more history. He retired the first 19 Cardinals until walking Curt Flood on a 3–2 pitch in the seventh. He kept his no-hitter alive until Julian Javier doubled with two outs in the eighth. Lonborg's one-hit masterpiece, 5–0, evened the Series at one game apiece.

In Game 5, with the Sox down three games to one, Lonborg outpitched future teammate Steve Carlton, shutting out the Cardinals through eight and clinging to a 1–0 lead until the Sox scored twice in the top of the ninth. A homer by Roger Maris with two outs in the bottom of the ninth ended Lonborg's 17-inning World Series scoreless string, but he still earned a 3–1, three-hit victory. Red Sox manager Dick Williams brought Lonborg back on two days' rest for Game 7, but the Cardinals routed him for seven runs in six innings, including a home run by opposing starter Bob Gibson.

That winter Lonborg tore up his knee in a skiing accident and was shelved until late May. Arm woes followed, and he suffered through two losing seasons, eventually returning to the minors for portions of 1970 and 1971. At that point he shifted from power-pitcher to soft-tosser. After a 10–7 mark in 1971 the Red Sox included him in a 10-player deal that sent him to the Brewers. Lonborg won 14 games with Milwaukee the next season.

On October 31, 1972, Lonborg was part of another big trade, this time to Philadelphia. After winning 13 games his first year with the Phillies, he went 17–13 in 1974. That same season he slugged his third and final home run, a grand slam off Montreal righthander Chuck Taylor. In 1976 Lonborg went 18–10 to help propel the Phillies to the playoffs. He then started Game 2 of the 1976 NLCS against defending world champion Cincinnati. Lonborg had a 2–0 lead and had held the Reds hitless through five innings, but Philadelphia eventually lost the game and the series.

Arm troubles kept Lonborg out until May 25, 1977, but his 11–4 mark helped the Phillies return to the playoffs, where they met Los Angeles. Lonborg again started Game 2 and pitched even with Don Sutton through four innings. But he yielded a grand slam to Dusty Baker in the fifth, and the Dodgers rolled to a 7–1 win and won the series shortly thereafter.

Lonborg's arm woes continued and finally shut him down after he struggled through four games in 1979. The former fireballer, who led the American League in hit batsmen in 1967 and 1971, retired from drilling hitters to drill teeth.

Dale Long

Long, Richard Dale **1B**

1951, 1955–63 B:2/6/1926, Springfield, MO D:1/27/1991, Palm Coast, FL Deb:4/21/1951, PIT NL BL/TL 6'4", 210

G	AB	R	H	HR	RBI	OBP	SLG	AVG
1013	3020	384	805	132	467	.345	.464	.267

Dale Long spent 11 years in the minors as a power-hitting first baseman before he made it to the majors to stay. Then, in just eight games in 1956, he turned the baseball world on its ear. Long homered in eight consecutive games that May, shattering by two the old record belonging to Ken Williams and Lou Gehrig. Not until Don Mattingly in 1987 and Ken Griffey, Jr., in 1993 would anyone match the feat (and against watered-down pitching in smaller ballparks).

Long proved he was major league caliber in 1953 and 1954, when he played for the PCL's Hollywood Stars. Although his home park, Gilmore Field, was tough on lefthanded hitters, he slugged 35 homers in 1953, the most ever by a lefty there, and drove in 135 runs on his way to becoming league Most Valuable Player. He followed up with a 23-homer season in 1954 and moved to the Pirates the following year.

As a rookie in 1955 he hit 16 homers while batting .291. He also shared the league lead in triples (13) with Willie Mays. It wasn't Long's speed that got him those extra bases but pure power, supplying some advance warning of what was to come the next year.

In 1956 Long burst out of the starting gate with a rush and already had seven home runs when he hit a long homer off Cub Jim Davis on May 19. In the next day's doubleheader against the Braves, he slugged one off Ray Crone in the first game and another off Warren Spahn in the second.

His fourth homer in the streak, hit off Cardinals pitcher Herm Wehmeier, rattled a girder on the second deck of Forbes Field's right field. The next night Cardinals hurler Lindy McDaniel served up a pitch that Long belted over the 436-foot marker in right-center field. In the 47 years of Forbes Field history to that date, no one had ever hit a ball out of the park.

Homer number six was hit off Curt Simmons in Philadelphia. Before the next game, the team was boarding the bus to leave for the park when someone noticed that Long was not with them. Pittsburgh pitcher Nellie King ran out and lay down in front of the bus. "We're not leaving without our meal ticket," he said.

Manager Bobby Bragan moved his slugger from fourth to third in the order to give him a possible extra at bat if needed. The Phillies started junkballer Stu Miller in an attempt to thwart the powerful Pirates. Long rattled the top of the right-field fence with a double in his first at bat, but his next two trips to the plate produced line drives that were caught. In Long's last chance Ben Flowers threw him a 2–2 knuckleball that he hit over the light tower in right field. General manager Joe L. Brown called Long to congratulate him and notify him of a $2,500 raise, to $16,500. *Life* magazine did a five-page spread on the event, and Long got the ultimate accolade, appearing on the Ed Sullivan Show (pocketing an extra $500).

Pitcher Roy Face recalled how hot Long was during the streak. "When we were on the road, we'd have a half-hour batting practice and if Dale wanted to take the whole half hour we'd just stand around and watch him, he looked so good swinging."

The final game at Philadelphia was rained out, so 32,221 Pirates fans, the largest Forbes Field crowd in six years, saw Long swat his eighth homer in eight consecutive games, this one off the Dodgers' Carl Erskine. After the blast, fans stood and cheered until the slugger stepped out of the dugout to acknowledge their ovation. It was possibly the first "curtain call" homer in baseball history. The next night Don Newcombe ended the streak, but the amazing young Pirates were in first place, largely because of Long's batting feats.

Two weeks later, hitting .384 with 16 homers and 43 RBIs, Long fouled two consecutive pitches off his ankle. He was hurt but wouldn't leave the lineup. He proceeded to go 1 for 50, and the Pirates' dreams of glory were gone. Long finished the season at .263, with 27 homers and 91 RBIs.

Long didn't like the fact that Pirates general manager Brown was happy to praise a player going well, but cool toward a player in a slump. He told Brown so, and their relationship grew edgy. After a slow April in 1957, Long and Lee Walls were dealt to the Cubs at the beginning of May, for Gene Baker and Dee Fondy.

Long put up consecutive years with 20-plus home runs and batting averages of .305 and .271. Manager Bob Scheffing used him as a catcher in two games in 1958, the first time a lefty had gone behind the plate since Tom Doran caught two games for the 1906 Boston Americans. But Long was 33 when the 1959 season began; the rest of his career would be spent primarily as a pinch hitter with the Giants, expansion Senators, and Yankees.

He tried his hand as a minor league umpire for several years after his playing career ended in 1963, but gave it up and became a salesman, and an upstate New York sportcaster. In 1982 Commissioner Bowie Kuhn hired Long to travel the country overseeing minor league operations.

Herman Long

Long, Herman C. **SS**

1889–1904 B:4/13/1866, Chicago, IL D:9/17/1909, Denver, CO Deb:4/17/1889, KC AA BL/TR

5'8½", 160

G	AB	R	H	HR	RBI	OBP	SLG	AVG
1874	7675	1456	2128	91	1056	.335	.383	.277

In 1889 shortstop Herman Long made 117 errors. Today he would never have the chance to make so many without being booted back to the minors, but the game was different in 1889, when Long's numerous miscues didn't even lead the league. In more than 16 major league seasons he accumulated an astonishing 1,070 errors at shortstop alone, plus another six when he filled in at other positions. Add his minor league bobbles and he probably made more errors than any other man in baseball history.

Yet Long was regarded as one of the best shortstops of his day, and many authorities place him at the top of the list. Although he made scads of errors, he also covered more ground than any of his counterparts. Many of his misses came on balls that other shortstops could only watch go by from afar. Long was spectacularly acrobatic as he pursued batted balls, cutting off some hits with moves more likely to be seen at the circus. He ranks second all-time in total chances per game. The outstanding plays that occasionally resulted from his attempts made the extra errors worthwhile.

Fielders of the 1890s labored under atrocious conditions. Gloves were rudimentary pieces of leather that offered minimal hand protection. The often-lopsided baseballs bounced in unpredictable ways. Many diamonds were not much more than converted rock quarries. The field in Boston, where Long played half his games, was particularly hazardous. And hard-hearted scorekeepers of the day ruled that any touching of the ball that did not produce an out was an error.

Born to German immigrants, Long became a professional in 1887 with Arkansas City of the Kansas State League. Two years later he played shortstop and hit .275 with Kansas City of the American Association. When the National League's Boston Beaneaters hired Frank Selee in 1890 as manager, he paid Kansas City $6,200 for Long's contract. A tremendous judge of talent, Selee also acquired outfielder-second baseman Bobby Lowe, first baseman and leadoff hitter Tommy Tucker, and pitcher Kid Nichols. With Hugh Duffy and Tommy McCarthy and a few veterans, Selee's Beaneaters won three consecutive pennants starting in 1891.

Long was famous for making almost unbelievable plays. One day he couldn't quite reach a ball with his glove, so he stuck out his foot, deflected the ball into the air with his toe, caught it, and threw the runner out. And unlike most shortstops even in the 1890s, he hit with power. He slugged nine homers in 1891, fourth highest in the league, and his 129 runs scored placed second. In 1892 he was second in the league with 33 doubles. And in 1893 he led the NL with 149 runs scored.

One of those runs may have won the pennant for Boston. Pittsburgh was making a determined run for the title, but Long felled catcher Connie Mack with a broken leg in a collision at home plate. Pittsburgh fans insisted there was no play at the plate. Long argued Mack had illegally blocked his way, and that the catcher bore the broken leg to prove it. With Mack out of commission, Pittsburgh finished five games back.

Selee's Beaneaters played rugged but smart baseball. They pioneered the hit-and-run play, stole signs, and innovated other defensive tactics. Right fielder Tommy McCarthy regularly let fly balls drop and then turned double plays. But by 1894 the Baltimore Orioles were playing equally smart baseball and outdoing Boston in dirty tricks.

It helped that Boston was growing old and that the Orioles were the best-hitting team in the league. Boston fell in the standings as the Orioles swept to pennants from 1894 through 1896. But Long had three of his best seasons during those years, hitting over .300 each year. In 1896 he had his best season at bat, hitting .345 with 101 RBIs and 106 runs scored.

The Beaneaters were back in top form by 1897. Their infield combination of newcomer Fred Tenney at first, Bobby Lowe at second, future Hall of Famer Jimmy Collins at third, and Long at shortstop is often cited as the 19th century's best. Long hit .322 in 1897, and the Beaneaters won another pennant. The following year, as Boston won its fifth title of the decade, Long's batting average fell to .265, but he batted in 99 runs and scored an equal number.

Long posted his second 100-RBI season in 1899. But Brooklyn had put together a super team, adding most of the old Baltimore stars to their own, and Boston was simply outmanned. Although Long led the league with 12 home runs the next season, he was starting to slip. Ironically, as his range decreased at shortstop he became more sure-handed. In 1901 and 1902 he led the league's shortstops in fielding percentage.

Like so many other stars, Long jumped to the new American League in 1903. But he could no longer hit as he could in his younger days. After playing a single game with Mack's Philadelphia Athletics in 1904, he was released. Long managed in the minors through 1905, but he contracted tuberculosis, moved to Colorado for his health, and died there in 1909.

Ed Lopat

Lopat, Edmund Walter **P**

1944–55 M(1963–64, 90–124) B:6/21/1918, New York, NY D:6/15/1992, Darien, CT Deb:4/30/1944, CHI AL BL/TL 5'10", 185

W	L	PCT	G	SH	IP	BB	SO	ERA
166	112	.597	340	27	2439[1]	650	859	3.21

Ed Lopat was a key member of the New York Yankees juggernaut that won consecutive world championships from 1949 through 1953. The offerings of this lefthanded junkballer contrasted nicely with the fastballs of righthanders Vic Raschi and Allie Reynolds.

Lopat began his professional career in 1937 as a first baseman for the Class D Pennsylvania State Association's Greensburg Green Sox. Although he soon turned to pitching, he progressed slowly through the minors, due in part to his own personality. Extremely high-strung, he worried constantly about his performance and exploded into tantrums when things went wrong. His wife and physicians eventually helped him to control his anxiety, and Lopat became known for the calmness and consistency that earned him the nickname "Steady Eddie."

After seven years in the minors, Lopat won a spot with the Chicago White Sox in 1944. In four seasons with the Sox, he proved to be one of their most effective pitchers, fashioning a 50–49 record with the second-division team.

Unable to throw the fastball past a hitter consistently, Lopat survived because of good control and a variety of "junk"—curveballs, screwballs, sliders, and knuckleballs—all delivered at various speeds from several different motions. These junk pitches were deceptive, upsetting batters' timing and producing popups and easy grounders.

"My main purpose," said Lopat, "was to make a hitter hit off-stride. I couldn't overpower hitters, so I had to operate from a different angle. Being in the minors so long gave me a wider field of knowledge." Boston's Ted Williams said Lopat threw off his coordination every time he faced him, and Tommy Henrich, later Lopat's teammate on the Yankees, said that a batter facing Lopat "could never get set at home plate." Some batters complained that after facing Lopat, their timing remained off for several games.

The 1947 season was Lopat's best with the Sox. He finished 16–13, with a 2.81 ERA and a career-high 109 strikeouts. Traded to the Yankees the following February for three players, in his first season with New York he went 17–11 (including a 4–0, 11-hit shutout on July 17), but the Yankees finished third behind the Indians and the Red Sox.

In 1949 the Yanks embarked on the most successful run in the history of baseball, winning five consecutive pennants and five consecutive World Series. Raschi, Reynolds, and Lopat were the mainstays of New York's pitching staff. In those five seasons Raschi posted a 92–48 record, Reynolds was 83–41, while Lopat was a sparkling 80–36.

Lopat had mixed success in the 1949 and 1950 World Series. He was 1–0 in the 1949 Series, but his 6.35 ERA indicated it wasn't easy for him. In 1950 his ERA was 2.25, but he didn't receive a decision in two appearances.

In 1951 Lopat went 21–9 and pitched in his only All-Star Game. In the 1951 World Series he won Game 2 on a five-hitter, 3–1, then allowed only five hits in Game 5, which the Yankees won, 13–1. The next year Lopat experienced shoulder trouble and won only 10 games, but he bounced back in 1953 with an outstanding season. He led the American League with a 2.42 ERA, won 16 games, and topped the circuit in winning percentage, at .800. He picked up the victory in Game 2 of the 1953 World Series against the Dodgers, thanks to a two-run, eighth-inning homer by Mickey Mantle.

Lopat's greatest success came against Cleveland, New York's chief rival for several seasons. Once Lopat took the mound, the free-swinging Indians were all but finished. Cleveland tried a number of different lineups and raised the mound because they knew Lopat preferred a low hill, but nothing worked. One time the Cleveland organization even held a "special night" in Lopat's honor, when fans were invited to bring charms to help the Indians win. One fan even ran to the mound and threw a black cat at Lopat.

Lopat pitched for the Yankees into the 1955 season and was a leader on and off the field. In his later years he served as the mentor of young Whitey Ford. On July 30, 1955, he was traded to Baltimore, where he retired at season's end. He managed Richmond of the International League from 1956 through 1958, coached with the Yankees, and managed Kansas City in 1963 and 1964. Later, he worked as a scout for Montreal.

Davey Lopes

Lopes, David Earl **2B–OF**

1972–87 B:5/3/1945, East Providence, RI
Deb:9/22/1972, LA NL BR/TR 5'9", 170

G	AB	R	H	HR	RBI	OBP	SLG	AVG
1812	6354	1023	1671	155	614	.351	.388	.263

Davey Lopes was the second baseman for the major league's longest-running infield of all time. He combined power with quickness on the bases as few at his position ever have. His 1979 mark of 28 home runs is one of the better figures for a second baseman. Lopes also was one of the most effective basestealers ever, succeeding in 83 percent of his attempts and setting major league records with 47 steals at age 39 and 25 thefts at age 40.

One of 12 children, Lopes was an all-Rhode Island baseball and basketball player in high school. Undrafted, he attended Iowa Wesleyan College and transferred to Washburn University in Topeka, Kansas, winning All-America honors in baseball and basketball. Drafted in the 28th round by the San Francisco Giants in June 1967, he continued in school to receive a degree in education and taught during off-seasons.

The Dodgers selected Lopes in the secondary phase of the January 1968 draft. He signed, but because of school and military commitments played only parts of 1968 and 1969 in the Class A Florida State League, stealing 58 bases in 69 attempts. "I knew my speed was my ticket to the big leagues," he said later. An outfielder during his first two seasons, he began learning second base in 1971 from Class AAA manager Tommy Lasorda.

Lopes debuted with the Dodgers in September 1972 at age 27. He became the regular starter the next year, and the infield of Steve Garvey, Lopes, Bill Russell, and Ron Cey played together through 1981, a record nine-season run. Lopes' unexpected power helped make him an unusual leadoff hitter for the Dodgers; his 26 leadoff homers rank him high on the all-time list.

In only his second full year, Lopes gave a preview of his unusual pairing of abilities. On August 20, 1974, he hit three home runs in one game at Wrigley Field, adding a double and single for 15 total bases. Four days later he tied the major league single-game record for steals, with five against St. Louis. He finished the season with 59 steals.

Lopes had four hits, scored four times, drove in three runs, and stole three bases in his first postseason action, the Dodgers' four-game 1974 NLCS win over Pittsburgh. He went 2-for-18 but stole two bases and scored twice in the five-game World Series loss to Oakland.

In 1975 Lopes broke a 70-year-old major league record with 38 consecutive successful stolen base attempts. He led the NL with a career-high 77 steals in 89 tries that year and led it again with 63 steals in 1976.

In 1977 Lopes batted .283 and was the hero of NLCS Game 3 against the Philadelphia Phillies. Trailing 5–3 in the ninth with two outs, the Dodgers had a run in and a runner on third when Lopes hit a shot off the glove of Mike Schmidt at third. The ball ricocheted to shortstop Larry Bowa, but Lopes beat the play at first to knock in the tying run. He advanced to second on a wild pickoff attempt and scored the winning run on Bill Russell's single. In the World Series against the New York Yankees, Lopes had the Dodgers' only two steals and keyed their Game 5 win with a leadoff triple, but Los Angeles lost in six games.

Lopes earned his first of four straight All-Star berths in 1978. That year he batted.278 with 17 homers, won a Gold Glove, and stole 45 bases in 49 tries. He had three hits in each of the first two games of the NLCS rematch with the Phillies, driving in five runs and scoring three with a double, a triple, and two homers. In the World Series rematch with the Yankees, he homered twice, with five RBIs in the opener. In Game 6 he hit a leadoff homer, then singled, stole second, and scored in the third, but the Yankees took the Series again.

The next year Lopes set career highs with 28 homers, 73 RBIs, 97 walks, and 109 runs. In 1980 he received more votes for the All-Star Game than any other National Leaguer, and in 1981 he stole five bases in the Dodgers' five-game playoff win over the Montreal Expos. In another World Series meeting with the Yankees, his leadoff double sparked a three-run first inning in Los Angeles' 5–4 win in Game 3. Lopes then scored twice, stole two bases, and beat out an infield hit to drive in the winning run as the Dodgers evened the Series at two games apiece.

After making three errors in a Game 5 victory, Lopes started the Dodgers' winning rally in Game 6 with a single, and he scored twice as Los Angeles won the world championship. He led Series participants with six runs and four steals, giving him 10 lifetime swipes in the World Series, tying him for third on the all-time list.

On February 8, 1982, the Dodgers broke up the infield, dealing Lopes to Oakland for minor league second baseman Lance Hudson. That season, Lopes and outfielder Rickey Henderson set a major league record by combining for 158 steals (Henderson stole 130, Lopes 28). On June 15, 1983, Lopes drove in a career-high seven runs against Toronto with five hits, including a grand slam.

After two years as an A's regular, Lopes was traded to the Cubs on July 15, 1984, in a deal that sent pitcher Chuck Rainey and outfielder Damon Farmer to Oakland. The next year, as a 39-year-old part-timer, Lopes hit .284 and stole 47 bases in 51 tries. After being traded to Houston for pitcher Frank DiPino on July 21, 1986, he stole 25 bases in 33 tries at age 40 and made his final playoff appearance as a pinch hitter for the Astros.

Lopes retired after the 1987 season. His 557 career steals came in just 671 attempts. "A good base stealer should get seven out of ten," he said. "I tried to get eight out of 11."

Lopes served four years as a dugout and first-base coach with the Texas Rangers under Bobby Valentine and then joined the staff of another former Dodger, Orioles manager Johnny Oates, in 1992. After the 1993 season, Lopes got his first managerial experience in the Arizona Fall League. He coached for San Diego from 1995 through 1999. After years of interviews for managing jobs, he finally landed one on November 4, 1999, becoming manager of the Milwaukee Brewers.

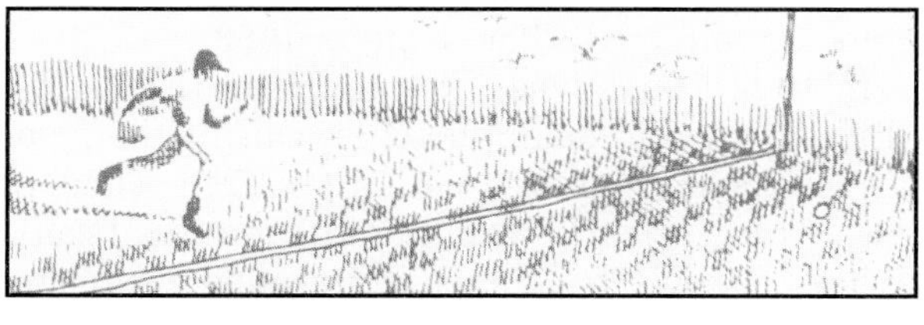

Al Lopez

Lopez, Alfonso Ramon **C**

1928, 1930–47 M(1951–69, 1,410–1,004) B:8/20/1908, Tampa, FL Deb:9/27/1928, BRO NL BR/TR 5'11", 165

G	AB	R	H	HR	RBI	OBP	SLG	AVG
1950	5916	613	1547	51	652	.326	.337	.261

One of the most successful and revered managers ever, Al Lopez also held the career mark for games caught for four decades. Lopez's 1954 Indians and his 1959 White Sox were the only teams to interrupt the Yankees' string of American League dominance from 1949 through 1964, and during his first nine years as a manager he finished no lower than second place.

As the son of Spanish immigrants who came to Tampa's Ybor City section from Madrid to work in the area's cigar factories, Lopez also worked in the factories during school vacations. Many scouts dismissed him as a catching prospect because he carried only 165 pounds on his 5'11" frame. But while the Washington Senators were training in Tampa in 1925, manager Bucky Harris let Lopez catch batting practice and warm up pitchers, including Walter Johnson. That taste of the big leagues also won Lopez an opportunity to catch for Tampa's team in the Florida State League.

He played there two years, was promoted to Jacksonville in the Southeastern League, and was purchased by the Dodgers in 1928 for $10,000. Dodgers manager Wilbert Robertson, a former catcher, was impressed after Lopez collected a couple of hits off Dazzy Vance in an exhibition game. He also liked the youngster's catching ability; Lopez had a good glove and strong arm, but his biggest asset was his ability to handle pitchers with his gentle, soothing personality. Lopez was persuasive but also comforting, the same qualities that helped him succeed as a manager.

The Dodgers farmed Lopez to the Class B South Atlantic League's Macon Peaches in 1928, and brought him to the majors late that September. After a year with the Southern League's Atlanta Crackers, Lopez came to Brooklyn for good in 1930.

In his first full season in the majors, Lopez hit .309 and knocked in 57 runs, both career highs. Although he twice more hit over .300, he was selected to the 1934 and 1941 All-Star Games mainly on the strength of his fielding. The Dodgers sent him to the Boston Bees in December 1935; with Boston he twice reached a career-best eight homers. In June 1940 he was traded to the Pirates, with whom he played until 1946. Prior to the 1947 season, Lopez was traded to Cleveland, where he played his final year.

Lopez led NL catchers in fielding four times and tied the league record by allowing no passed balls in 114 games in 1941. In 1946 he broke the career games-caught record of Rick Ferrell and retired with a career total of 1,918 games behind the plate, including a record 1,861 in the National League. Bob Boone broke Lopez's major league mark in 1987, and Gary Carter topped his National League mark in 1991.

After finishing his playing career, Lopez accepted a managing job at Indianapolis, Cleveland's top farm club. He won the pennant in 1948 and finished second the next two years. In 1951 he took over as manager of the Indians after Lou Boudreau was traded to Boston. In Cleveland, Lopez began his decade-long rivalry with former mentor Casey Stengel.

In the 1951 race, Lopez's Indians had the best pitching in the league, tied New York for the league lead in home runs, and briefly overtook the Yankees in mid-September before finishing five games out. They led the league in homers again in 1952 and would through 1955, featuring sluggers Larry Doby, Al Rosen, and Luke Easter. The Yankees took an early lead in 1953 and were never challenged, but Lopez turned the tables in 1954, directing the Indians to an American League-record 111 wins. That team featured the great pitching staff of Mike Garcia, Early Wynn, Bob Lemon, and Bob Feller—all but Garcia were elected to the Hall of Fame. (Another future Hall of Famer, Hal Newhouser, was finishing up his career in the bullpen.)

In the early 1950s Lopez developed the bullpen duo of Ray Narleski and Don Mossi. Lopez and Leo Durocher of the New York Giants, his opponent in the 1954 World Series, pioneered the use of two late-inning specialists. Lopez primarily went by the book, but Durocher—with two righthanders, one a knuckleballer—had to rely on hunches. In the Series the Giants upset the heavily favored Indians in four games, thanks to the bat of pinch hitter Dusty Rhodes and the glove of center fielder Willie Mays.

After two more second-place finishes, Lopez moved to the Chicago White Sox. In Chicago his light-hitting personnel and the spacious ballpark made home runs scarce, so he changed tactics. Yet his success continued. Lopez's White Sox, with Luis Aparicio and Jim Rivera, became the first team in the 1950s and the first American League team since 1945 to steal 100 bases. He juggled a lot of live arms and finished second to the Yankees before winning the pennant in 1959. In the World Series they ran into a hot reliever, Larry Sherry of the Dodgers, and lost in six games.

A series of wrongheaded trades left the Sox full of holes after that pennant-winning season, and in 1960 Lopez finished third for the first time in his career. He posted three more second-place finishes in 1963, 1964 (by only one game), and 1965, before retiring. He returned to the White Sox as a favor to ownership in 1968, replacing the fiery Eddie Stanky, who had burned out in the middle of the season. Lopez stayed on a few weeks of 1969, posting the only losing records of his managerial tenure.

Lopez proved that John McGraw's managerial heritage could prosper in kinder, gentler hands, without bluster, self-promotion, and all that yelling. The use of the running game and percentage use of relievers, as well as motivating players through something other than fear, were elements of Lopez's style that became standard in baseball during the 1960s. Most importantly, Lopez managed according to his personnel, recognizing their abilities and limitations. He was elected to the Hall of Fame in 1977.

Aurelio Lopez

Lopez, Aurelio Alejandro (Pena) **P**

1974, 1978–87 B:9/21/1948, Tecamachalco Puebla, Mexico D:9/22/1992, Matehuala, Mexico Deb:9/1/1974, KC AL BR/TR 6', 220

W	L	PCT	G	SV	IP	BB	SO	ERA
62	36	.633	459	93	910	367	635	3.56

For seven years with the Detroit Tigers, Aurelio Lopez was one of the most successful relief pitchers in baseball. For a good part of that time, he was the setup man for Tigers relief ace Willie Hernandez, but he was quite a talent himself, three times winning 10 or more games in relief.

Lopez signed with Choapas of the Mexican Southeast League in March 1967. The following year he moved up to the Mexican League's Mexico City Reds and then spent a year with Minatitlan of the Mexican Southeast League, where he pitched a no-hitter. He returned to the Reds in 1970, where he would stay until 1974. That season he led the circuit with 60 appearances, and the Kansas City Royals purchased his contract.

Ineffective with Kansas City, he was sold back to Mexico City in March 1975 and led the Mexican League in appearances each year from 1975 through 1977. Selected as the 1977 Mexican League MVP, in October of that year Lopez was sold to the Cardinals. St. Louis traded him in December 1978 to Detroit.

In Detroit, Lopez finally found the success that he had achieved in Mexico. In his first year there he went 10–5 with 21 saves and a 2.41 ERA. In 1980 he led the American League in relief wins, going 13–6 with another 21 saves. Lopez was selected to the All-Star Game in 1983.

In 1984 Lopez was a key figure in the Tigers' drive to a world championship. During the regular season he went 10–1 with a 2.94 ERA. Then, in the World Series, he won the fifth and final game against San Diego. Granted free agency in November 1985, he signed with Houston, where he spent his final two years in the majors. Lopez died in a 1992 automobile accident in central Mexico.

Hector Lopez

Lopez, Hector Headley (Swainson) OF-3B-2B
1955–66 B:7/9/1929, Colon, Panama Deb:5/12/1955, KC AL BR/TR 5'11", 182

G	AB	R	H	HR	RBI	OBP	SLG	AVG
1450	4644	623	1251	136	591	.333	.415	.269

Panama native Hector Lopez had two careers in his 12 years in the major leagues. His first was as a third baseman with the second-division Kansas City A's. The second was as an outfielder with the pennant-winning New York Yankees.

Lopez was not Gold Glove material at either position. From 1955 to 1958, he led AL third basemen in errors. Acquired by New York in 1959 with Ralph Terry in exchange for Johnny Kucks, Tom Sturdivant, and Jerry Lumpe, Lopez was simply hid in left field by the Yankees.

Lopez had been a starter from just about day one in the majors, and he hit .290 his rookie year. In his sophomore season he showed excellent power, hitting 27 doubles and 18 home runs, while driving in 69 runs. "Everything I learned about hitting I learned from Lou Boudreau," Lopez said of his manager at Kansas City. "He gave me the points."

Despite solid numbers in each of his first four years, Lopez was deemed expendable and was sent to the Yankees in 1959. He finished that year with career highs of 22 homers and 93 RBIs. Perhaps the highlight of his career was the last game of the 1961 World Series, when he drove in five runs with a homer and a triple.

Leaving the major leagues in 1966, Lopez played in the minors for two years. He then managed Buffalo in the International League and scouted before retiring from baseball. Later he worked as a recreation specialist for the Long Island, New York town of Hempstead.

Javy Lopez

Lopez, Javier (Torres) C
1992–* B:11/5/70, Ponce, Puerto Rico Deb:9/18/92 ATL NL BR/TR 6'3", 185

G	AB	R	H	HR	RBI	OBP	SLG	AVG
656	2280	283	662	119	378	.341	.503	.290

Outside of Mike Piazza and Ivan Rodriguez, few catchers active in the 1990s swung the bat as well as Javy Lopez. In 1998, his best season, the Puerto Rican backstop hit personal peaks with 34 homers, 106 RBIs, 73 runs scored, and 139 hits. He hit a team-best .336 with runners in scoring position, led major-league catchers with a .995 fielding percentage, and topped the National League by nailing 33.8 percent of the runners who tried to steal against him.

Lopez was on his way to a stellar 1999 season when he suffered a midseason knee injury that required surgical repair in midseason. Despite a heroic fill-in effort by backup catcher Eddie Perez, the Braves sorely missed Lopez's bat during the four-game World Series sweep by the Yankees.

Lopez turned pro when the Braves signed him as a nondrafted free agent on November 6, 1987. He got his first taste of big-league pitching five years later.

Twice an All-Star during six full seasons in the majors, Lopez hit a home run in his first All-Star at bat—as a pinch hitter in the 1997 game at Cleveland's Jacobs Field. He collected seven postseason homers, four of them during five different NL Championship Series. Lopez was Most Valuable Player of the 1996 NLCS, when he destroyed the St. Louis Cardinals by hitting .542 (13-for-24) with five doubles, two homers, and six RBIs in seven games.

Bobby Lowe

Lowe, Robert Lincoln 2B-OF-3B
1890–1907 M(1904, 30–44) B:7/10/1868, Pittsburgh, PA D:12/8/1951, Detroit, MI Deb:4/19/1890, BOS NL BR/TR 5'10", 150

G	AB	R	H	HR	RBI	OBP	SLG	AVG
1818	7065	1131	1929	71	984	.325	.360	.273

On May 30, 1894, in Boston, Bobby Lowe made baseball history by becoming the first man to hit four home runs in a single game. The feat has been accomplished only 11 times since, by sluggers such as Lou Gehrig, Willie Mays, Rocky Colavito, Chuck Klein, and Mike Schmidt. It's natural to assume that Lowe, too, was a feared power hitter, but in fact he was Boston's leadoff man. In 18 major league seasons he hit only 71 homers, and almost half of them were packed into two atypical seasons. Far from being a muscular slugger, Lowe was a slender 5 feet 10 inches and 150 pounds, certainly the smallest of the four-homer hitters.

Two weeks before Lowe's big day for the Boston Beaneaters, a fire broke out during a game with Baltimore that destroyed the team's regular ballpark, the South End Grounds. Until the park was rebuilt, the team played at the Congress Street Grounds, where the left-field fence was only 250 feet from home plate.

On May 30 Boston played a morning-afternoon Memorial Day doubleheader with the Cincinnati Reds. Lowe was 0-for-6 in the morning game and made another out leading off the second game against Elton Chamberlain. But in the third inning he drove a ball over the left-field fence for a home run, igniting a Boston rally. On his second trip to the plate that inning, Lowe popped another ball over the fence, this time with a teammate aboard. Boston manager Frank Selee was heard to shout, "Two home runs in one inning! That must be a record!"

When Lowe came up in the fifth inning with no one on, Reds left fielder Bug Holliday backed up all the way to the fence, but Lowe hit another pitch over it to become one of only seven players, at the time, to hit three home runs in one game. Chamberlain was still on the mound when Lowe came up in the sixth inning with two men on base. Lowe's first three homers had been hit off curveballs. Chamberlain thought Lowe would never expect another one. Wrong! Lowe clouted number four.

The crowd showered him with $160 in silver coins at home plate. The *Boston Globe* reported that all four homers were "line drives far over the fence...good for four bases on open prairie," which is not quite the same as saying that all or any of them would have cleared the fence at the old South End Grounds. Lowe wasn't through for the day, however, for in the eighth inning he whacked a single. His 17 total bases in one game remained a major league record until Joe Adcock hit four homers and a double in 1954.

Lowe idolized the great catcher Charlie Bennett and hoped to play catcher himself, but that was the only position he never played in the major leagues. He turned professional with Eau Claire of the Northwest League in 1887 as a shortstop-outfielder. Later Boston purchased his contract for the bargain price of $700 from Milwaukee of the Western Association. When Frank Selee took over the team in 1890, Lowe became the manager's favorite. In his first three seasons he was a "regular" utility man, usually playing left field but often moving to wherever he was needed. Versatility was his strong point, but he was a good hitter as well. On June 11, 1891, he went 6-for-6 with a double and a home run.

In 1893 Selee made Lowe Boston's regular second baseman. Through the rest of the decade he teamed with shortstop Herman Long to form perhaps the best middle infield combination of the time. The two men complemented each other well; Long was spectacular but erratic, while Lowe was the epitome of steadiness. Long was once described as playing shortstop like a man on a trapeze. If that was true, then Lowe was his net.

Lowe's move to second base coincided with a sudden outburst of power. He hit 14 home runs in 1893, and with the help of the short fence at the Congress Street Grounds, 17 in 1894. He had never hit more than six homers in a season before, and he never hit more than seven in any season thereafter. That 1894 season was his best offensively; he batted .346 with career highs in doubles, triples, RBIs, and runs—158 of the last, ninth-most in National League history. In 1895 Lowe's production fell off, but on May 3 he established a major league record by scoring six runs in a game, a mark still tied for the best ever.

A team player, Lowe rarely complained, and he was chosen over the club's greater stars to be team captain. When the Beaneaters won pennants in 1891 and 1892, Lowe was paid $1,800. In 1893 he received a $200 raise, but even during the pennant years of 1897 and 1898 he received only $3,000 a season.

In 1902 Lowe rejoined Selee with the Chicago Cubs, preceding Johnny Evers at second base. On April 20, 1904, Lowe was sold to Pittsburgh; Detroit acquired him 10 days later. He replaced Ed Barrow as manager halfway through the 1904 season, posting a 30–44 record. Lowe returned to player-only duty in 1905, and finished his career by appearing in 17 games with Detroit's pennant-winning team in 1907. Upon retiring, Lowe settled in Detroit and spent many years with its Department of Public Works.

John Lowenstein

Lowenstein, John Lee **OF–DH**

1970–85 B:1/27/1947, Wolf Point, MT Deb:9/2/1970, CLE AL BL/TR 6', 175

G	AB	R	H	HR	RBI	OBP	SLG	AVG
1368	3476	510	881	116	441	.340	.403	.253

John Lowenstein languished as a weak-hitting utility man and outfielder with the Cleveland Indians from 1970 through 1977. After a season with Texas, the Rangers waived him, and he appeared on his way out of the majors. Instead, Earl Weaver's Baltimore Orioles picked him up, and he began a second career that featured him as a key figure in Baltimore's World Series champions.

In his first eight full years in the majors, only once did Lowenstein bat as high as .250, and only once did he have more than eight home runs. But in Weaver's platoon outfield featuring Al Bumbry and Gary Roenicke, Lowenstein found a more regular offensive role and his hitting improved. In 1979 he hit .254 with 11 home runs; the next year his average was up to .311.

The 1982 season was Lowenstein's career year. He hit .320 with 24 home runs, 66 RBIs, and 69 runs scored, all career highs. He was also errorless in the outfield, leading the league in fielding percentage with a perfect 1.000 mark. The next year he was again a major contributor as the Orioles won the World Series. Lowenstein hit

.281 during the regular season with 15 homers and 60 RBIs. However, his playing time and his average both dropped off during the next two seasons, and he retired after the 1985 season.

Peanuts Lowrey

Lowrey, Harry Lee **OF–3B**

1942–43, 1945–55 B:8/27/1918, Culver City, CA D:7/2/1986, Inglewood, CA Deb:4/14/1942, CHI NL BR/TR 5'8½", 170

G	AB	R	H	HR	RBI	OBP	SLG	AVG
1401	4317	564	1177	37	479	.336	.362	.273

A versatile gloveman who could play the outfield as well as third and second base, Peanuts Lowrey had a long and solid career for four National League teams, spending most of it with the Chicago Cubs and the St. Louis Cardinals. He played a key role on the 1945 NL champion Cubs, batting .283 with 89 RBIs.

Lowrey first joined the Cubs in 1942 and became a regular the next year, batting .292 with 25 doubles and a dozen triples. He missed the entire 1944 season because of military service, but came back in the Cubs' championship year. A skilled contact hitter, he struck out only 27 times in 523 at bats. Although the Cubs lost the World Series to the Detroit Tigers in seven games, Lowrey went 9-for-29 for a .310 average.

The 1946 season saw Lowrey selected to his only All-Star Game. After several more excellent seasons, he was traded to Cincinnati in 1949 and then on to St. Louis the next year. With the Cardinals he hit .303 in 1951, striking out only 12 times in 370 at bats. After four-plus years with the Cardinals, he completed his career with the Philadelphia Phillies in 1955.

Pat Luby

Luby, John Perkins **P**

1890–92, 1895 B:6/1869, Charleston, SC D:4/24/1899, Charleston, SC Deb:6/16/1890, CHI NL TR 6', 185

W	L	PCT	G	SV	IP	BB	SO	ERA
40	41	.494	106	2	797^{1}	311	215	3.88

Pat Luby had a brief career in which he only once won as many games as he lost. But in 1890, his rookie season, he won 17 consecutive games for Cap Anson's Chicago White Stockings, a mark never surpassed by a rookie.

In 1890 the talent in the National League was severely depleted by widespread defections to the Players' League. In such an environment Luby was able to make his mark, going 20–9 with 26 complete games and a 3.19 ERA. His 17th consecutive win for the second place White Sox, on October 3, was a 3–2 victory over Amos Rusie, then in his first year with the New York Giants. Only Tim Keefe of the Giants with 19 in 1888 and Old Hoss Radbourn of Providence with 18 in 1884 had previously won more consecutive games in a single season.

Luby never posted a winning season after the Players' League collapsed and conditions returned to normal in the majors. In 1891 his ERA soared to 4.76 and his record dropped to 8–11. He was out of the majors after finishing 11–16 the following season. Luby returned to the big leagues in 1895 for a brief stint with the Louisville Colonels, but went 1–5 with a 6.81 ERA.

For a pitcher, Luby was also a danger at the plate. In the course of his major league career, he batted .235 with seven homers and 70 RBIs in 430 at bats.

Red Lucas

Lucas, Charles Frederick **P**

1923–24, 1926–38 B:4/28/1902, Columbia, TN D:7/9/1986, Nashville, TN Deb:4/19/1923, NY NL BL/TR 5'9½", 170

W	L	PCT	G	SH	IP	BB	SO	ERA
157	135	.538	396	22	2542	455	602	3.72

G	AB	R	H	HR	RBI	OBP	SLG	AVG
907	1439	155	404	3	190	.340	.347	.281

The main argument for the designated-hitter rule is that pitchers can't hit. People who make that argument must never have heard of Red Lucas. Lucas pitched in the big leagues for 15 seasons, mostly for the Cincinnati Reds and the Pittsburgh Pirates, but he was also an excellent—and frequent—hitter coming off the bench.

Lucas' total of 114 lifetime pinch hits was the major league record until it was broken a quarter of a century later by Jerry Lynch. In fact, his hitting was so good that at one point in his career the Boston Braves tried to switch him to second base. He compiled a .281 lifetime batting average and, unlike most pitchers, walked almost as many times as he struck out.

But it was as a pitcher that Lucas earned most of his salary. He started out with Nashville and Rome in 1920, and went 20–18 for Nashville in 1922. The following year he got a trial with the Giants. They sent him to San Antonio, where he was 18–9.

In 1926 the Reds brought Lucas up to stay. He displayed excellent control and three times led the National League in complete games. In 1927 Lucas went 18–11, and, on July 27 that year, he gave up only one hit and one walk in facing the minimum 27 batters against Brooklyn.

Perhaps Lucas' best season was 1929, when he went 19–12, led the league in complete games, and pitched 270 innings. After slipping a couple of years, he moved on to Pittsburgh for the 1934 season. There his best campaign was 1936, when he went 15–4 with a 3.18 ERA. Lucas retired following the 1938 season, but later pitched and managed for the Montreal Royals.

Ron Luciano

Luciano, Ronald M.

Umpire(1968–80) B:6/28/1937, Endicott, NY D:1/18/1995, Endicott, NY Deb:1968, AL 6'2", 240

A poll of the Major League Baseball Players Association in 1974 rated only two umpires as "excellent," and Ron Luciano was one of them. Just don't try to tell that to Earl Weaver, his longtime nemesis. While Luciano was umpiring for the International League, he tossed Weaver (who was managing Rochester) from the first four games in which they both participated. After Luciano had ejected Weaver eight times in the majors, the American League adjusted its schedule so that his crew would not officiate at Weaver's Orioles games.

Luciano stumbled into the umpiring profession. An All-America football lineman at Syracuse University, he signed to play professional football but kept getting injured. According to Luciano's autobiography, at the time he was desperate for a job. He pestered Spike Briggs, who owned both the football Lions and the baseball Tigers, about a scouting job in football.

Briggs finally offered Luciano the post of general manager of the Tigers' Lakeland, Florida, minor league team. "I had no idea what the general manager of a baseball team did," Luciano later admitted. He arrived in Florida a few weeks early to learn what his new job would entail and spotted an advertisement for a baseball school in Daytona Beach—Al Somers' Umpiring School. Soon Luciano was hooked on umpiring.

His natural gregariousness ran counter to the traditional notion of an umpire's behavior. He often engaged batters, fielders, and fans in conversation at inappropriate times during ballgames. "I did talk too much on the field. If I had kept quiet and concentrated on my job, I would have been a better umpire. But I wouldn't have enjoyed myself as much. I was simply having a good time and I wasn't afraid to show it," Luciano said.

One of his favorite ploys was the multiple call. Instead of simply calling a batter out, he'd bellow, "Out-out-out-out-out-out-out!" Luciano's record for the number of outs shouted on one call was 16, according to fellow umpire Bill Haller.

In 1972, while umpiring at first base, Luciano leaped toward a bat that had slipped out of the hands of the Yankees' Bobby Murcer and gave it a stunning "Foul-foul-foul-foul-foul!" call. He was fined $200 for conduct unbecoming an umpire. Sometimes he would take out an imaginary pistol and "shoot" a player out at first. Once Freddie Patek begged Luciano not to shoot him. Luciano obliged, but he pulled the pin out of an imaginary hand grenade and blasted Patek instead.

Retiring after 11 years as a major league umpire, Luciano joined NBC as a commentator for *The Game of the Week* for two years and co-authored three books of humorous baseball anecdotes. But his life ended in tragedy. On January 18, 1995, Luciano's body was discovered by a hunting friend in the garage of his home in Endicott, New York. The following day, police classified his death as a suicide from carbon monoxide poisoning.

Fred Luderus

Luderus, Frederick William **1B**

1909–20 B:9/12/1885, Milwaukee, WI D:1/4/1961, Milwaukee, WI Deb:9/23/1909, CHI NL BL/TR 5'11½", 185

G	AB	R	H	HR	RBI	OBP	SLG	AVG
1346	4851	570	1344	84	642	.340	.403	.277

Fred Luderus is not usually mentioned among the iron men of baseball history, but he did briefly hold the record for consecutive games played. He was also a key figure in the Philadelphia Phillies reaching the World Series in 1915.

Luderus made stops in Sault Ste. Marie, Winnipeg, and Freeport before reaching the majors with the Chicago Cubs in 1909. The next year he was traded to the Phillies. He hit for power early in his career, swatting a total of 56 home runs from 1911 through 1914 during the Dead Ball Era. His most productive season was 1911, when he hit .301 with 16 home runs, 24 doubles, and 99 RBIs.

In 1915 Luderus cut down on his swing. But even though he hit only seven homers that year, he had a career-high .315 batting average and 36 doubles. In that year's World Series against the Red Sox he was a bright light in Philadelphia's defeat, driving in six runs and batting an impressive .438.

Between 1916 and 1919 Luderus set a record of 533 consecutive games played. On September 24, 1919, the day of the 525th game of his streak, he was honored in Philadelphia with a "Fred Luderus Day." He was presented with a gold watch and a diamond stickpin between games of a doubleheader.

On August 22, 1918, Luderus collected a then-major league record for first basemen with seven assists in a game. A year later, on July 7, 1919, he was one of four Phillies who each stole two bases in a wild ninth inning against the Reds. After he retired, Luderus played and managed in the minor leagues at Toledo, Kansas City, Oklahoma City, Shreveport, and Omaha until 1928.

Dick Lundy

Lundy, Richard **SS-3B-2B**
Negro Leagues Player (1916–39) Manager
B:7/10/1898, Jacksonville FL D:1/5/1965, Jacksonville FL
BB/TR 5'11", 180

Dick "The King" Lundy very quietly compiled a record as one of the top shortstops in the Negro Leagues. John McGraw once said to him: "It's a shame you're a black boy. You could name your own price." Noted one sportswriter, "Lundy was very graceful; [there was] a nice rhythm to him. He was like [Pop] Lloyd. They were both long-armed guys. They covered a lot of ground. Lundy looked slow but he moved fast."

A switch hitter, Lundy's dexterity with a bat was equal to his deftness with a glove. He was a reliable .300 hitter who could also provide power, as evidenced by his 1923 season when he led the Eastern Colored League with 13 homers.

Having attended both Florida Baptist Academy and Cookman Institute, Lundy began his professional career in 1915, playing third base for his hometown team, the Duval Giants of Jacksonville, Florida. The team moved north to Atlantic City in 1916, becoming the Bacharach Giants, and Lundy moved north as well, although he soon jumped to another new club, the Hilldale Giants of Philadelphia. In 1921 he was back with the Bacharachs, however, after a court ruling invalidated the claims of Hilldale and the New York Bacharach Giants on Lundy, who had signed contracts with all three teams in 1920.

That season Lundy hit .484 and quickly established himself as the best shortstop in black baseball. In fact, when the great Pop Lloyd became the Bacharachs' player-manager in 1924, he stationed himself at second as a nod to Lundy's supremacy at short. In 1926 Lundy replaced Lloyd as the Giants' manager and led the team to pennants in 1926 and 1927. Playing against the Negro National League's Chicago American Giants in the 1926 black World Series, Lundy hit .325 and stole six bases in a losing cause.

The Bacharach Giants and the Baltimore Black Sox traded managers in 1929, and Lundy joined Oliver Marcelle, Frank Warfield, and Jud Wilson in Baltimore's "million-dollar infield." Despite being spiked by Lloyd and missing several games, he led the Black Sox to the Negro American League pennant, hitting .336 and stealing 16 bases.

In 1933 Lundy became manager of the Philadelphia Stars and, though past his prime, played in the Negro Leagues' inaugural East-West Game. His last years as an active player were spent with the Newark Eagles, where he was mentor to a pair of fledgling stars, Willie Wells and Ray Dandridge.

Although Negro League statistics are not complete, Lundy is credited with a career batting average of .330 over his three decades with nearly a dozen teams. He also batted .341 over eight seasons in the Cuban winter league, and .344 in exhibition games against major league opponents. After leaving baseball Lundy worked as a redcap in the Jacksonville, Florida railroad station. He died in 1965 after a long illness.

Dolf Luque

Luque, Adolfo Domingo de Guzman **P**
1914–15, 1918–35 B:8/4/1890, Havana, Cuba
D:7/3/1957, Havana, Cuba Deb:5/20/1914, BOS NL
BR/TR 5'7", 160

W	L	PCT	G	SV	IP	BB	SO	ERA
194	179	.520	550	28	3220[1]	918	1130	3.24

Dolf Luque was one of the finest major league players ever to come out of Cuba. "The Pride of Havana," as he was known, spent 20 years in the National League with four different clubs.

Luque had a fine breaking ball. Pitching for Long Branch of the New York–New Jersey League in 1913, he was 22–5, a performance that earned him a shot at the majors the following year. He had a brief appearance in 1914 with Boston's "Miracle" Braves, a team that moved from last place to first between July 18 and August 25. He then spent most of the following several years in the minors before moving on to the Cincinnati Reds in 1918, carving out a 6–3 record.

In 1919, as an occasional starter and frequent reliever, Luque went 10–3 with a 2.63 ERA, launching a streak of 10 consecutive seasons with 10 or more victories. He appeared in relief in Games 3 and 7 of the 1919 World Series against the Chicago White Sox without yielding a run.

Luque joined the Reds' regular rotation in 1920 and responded with a 13–9 record while limiting hitters to a league-low .225 batting average. Over the next two years he compiled losing records, but bounced back for his best season in 1923. That year he went 27–8 to lead the league in victories and winning percentage (.771); he also tossed six shutouts, and posted a 1.93 ERA. Teammates Pete Donohue and Eppa Rixey joined Luque as 20-game winners.

He finished below .500 in each of the next three seasons. However, wins and losses don't always reflect a pitcher's value, and Luque's case is an example. In 1925 he went 16–18 despite leading the NL with a 2.63 ERA. Opponents batted only .239 against him, and he had four shutouts.

In 1929 Luque slipped to a career-low five wins against 16 defeats and was traded to Brooklyn before the start of the 1930 season. In his two seasons with the Dodgers he won 21 games against

14 defeats, and then moved on to the Giants for the final four years of his career.

The highlight of Luque's stay in New York was undoubtedly his 1933 season. Appearing only in relief, he went 8–2 with a 2.69 ERA and four saves. He then made only one appearance in the World Series, but it came late in the fifth and final game. "Papa," as he was called at this stage of his career, entered in the sixth inning with the score tied, 3–3, and runners on first and third. He retired Luke Sewell on a grounder to short to end the inning, then held Washington scoreless into extra innings. Mel Ott's homer gave the Giants a 4–3 lead in the top of the 10th, and Luque retired the side in the bottom of the inning for the victory.

Luque finished his career in 1935. He later coached for the Giants and managed in Latin America. During a stint in the Mexican League he taught Sal Maglie the curveball that would confound hitters for a decade. In all, Luque had 40 years of service to baseball.

Greg Luzinski

Luzinski, Gregory Michael **OF–DH**

1970–84 B:11/22/1950, Chicago, IL Deb:9/9/1970, PHI AL BR/TR 6'1", 225

G	AB	R	H	HR	RBI	OBP	SLG	AVG
1821	6505	880	1795	307	1128	.366	.478	.276

Muscular, 225-pound Greg Luzinski had a swing so compact that it was said he could have hit a home run inside a telephone booth. The frugality of his swing meant that he could wait longer on pitches than most power hitters. A star football player in high school, Luzinski brought his gridiron intensity to the plate.

Danny Murtaugh scouted Luzinski when the slugger was still in high school. Murtaugh, who figured "the Bull" was too muscle-bound to hit well (a popular concept before scientific weight training), said to no one in particular, "I guess the boy can't hit the ball too hard." "My gracious," said a priest standing next to Murtaugh, "he hits them on the roof of that building." He indicated a structure near where they were standing, 350 to 370 feet from the plate and a couple of stories high. "Since he was a priest," Murtaugh recalled, "I knew he was telling the truth."

Luzinski signed with the Philadelphia Phillies at age 17 and played in Huron, Raleigh-Durham, Reading, and Eugene before making it to the majors in 1970 at age 19. After limited appearances for two years as a first baseman, he became a regular outfielder with the Phillies in 1972. That year Luzinski hit .281 with 18 home runs, 33 doubles, and 68 RBIs. The next year, he really turned it on, hitting .285 with 29 homers and 97 RBIs, although he did have a huge strikeout rate, going down 135 times during the year.

After an injury-plagued 1974 season, Luzinski began a four-year run of being selected to the All-Star Game each season. The first year, 1975, he hit .300 with 34 home runs, 85 runs scored, and a league-leading 120 RBIs. Two years later he had his best year, setting career highs with a .309 batting average, 39 home runs, 99 runs, 130 RBIs, and a .594 slugging average. But he also led the league in strikeouts, fanning 140 times. Luzinski ultimately retired with one of the worst strikeout ratios in major league history.

Led by Luzinski and Mike Schmidt, the Phillies won the NL East from 1976 through 1978, but were beaten in the NLCS each year. In 1976 the Reds swept them in three games although Luzinski hit .273 with two doubles, a homer, and three RBIs. Two years later in the NLCS he hit .375 with two home runs, but Los Angeles prevailed in four games.

Luzinski had his poorest season with the Phillies in 1980, hitting only .228 with 19 homers, but the Phillies picked up their game as a team. They won the World Series in six games against Kansas City, despite Luzinski going hitless and striking out five times in nine at bats.

On March 30, 1981, Luzinski was sold to the White Sox and became Chicago's designated hitter. He hit 21 homers his first season with the White Sox, and in 1982 he batted .292 with 18 home runs and 102 RBIs, his highest total since 1977. In 1983 the Sox were runaway winners of the AL West, and Luzinski played a key role. He hit 32 homers, knocked in 95 runs, and was among the league leaders with a .502 slugging average. Three of his homers that season cleared the Comiskey Park roof.

On June 8 and 9, 1984, Luzinski became one of only eight players in American League history to hit grand slams in consecutive games. Later that season he drove in at least one run in 10 consecutive games. Nevertheless, he finished the year hitting only .238 with 13 homers and 58 RBIs. He retired at season's end.

Sparky Lyle

Lyle, Albert Walter **P**

1967–82 B:7/22/1944, DuBois, PA Deb:7/4/1967, BOS AL BL/TL 6'1", 192

W	L	PCT	G	SV	IP	BB	SO	ERA
99	76	.566	899	238	1390^{1}	481	873	2.88

Sparky Lyle of the New York Yankees helped put the bullpen on the map in 1977, when he became the first American League reliever to capture a Cy Young Award. The puckish Lyle, who fit in nicely with what he termed George Steinbrenner's "Bronx Zoo," once asked the rhetorical question, "Why pitch nine innings when you can get real famous pitching two?"

Although most of the league records he set have since been broken in the era of the relief specialist, Lyle still ranks among the all-time leaders with 238 career saves. His dominance is show by the fact that between 1967 and 1980 Lyle's 231 saves were more than anyone else in the league, with Rollie Fingers second at 136.

Lyle was also one of baseball's best practical jokers. He cut manager Bill Virdon's director's chair in half with a hacksaw, scared a sleeping Phil Rizzuto awake on an airplane with a Wolfman mask, and hung pitcher Mike Kekich's waterbed on top of the scoreboard at Milwaukee's County Stadium. Once he had a casket delivered to the Yankees' clubhouse, where it sat for some time until Virdon called a team meeting. Then the lid creaked open and Lyle sat upright, intoning in a Bela Lugosi accent: "How do you pitch to Brooks Robinson?"

Dubbed "Sparky" by his father for his boundless energy, Lyle signed with the Baltimore Orioles in June 1964 after striking out 31 batters in a 17-inning game. He pitched with Bluefield in the Appalachian League and Fox Cities in the Midwest League. Left unprotected in the November 1964 draft, he became Red Sox property and was converted to relief work at Winston-Salem in the Carolina League.

The 1965 season was frustrating for Lyle, who spent 15 days on the disabled list even though he wasn't injured. Helping the team by pretending to be hurt damaged his ego, and he was "the lowest I've ever been in my entire life." But at spring training in Ocala, Florida, he met Ted Williams, who told him to add to his repertoire the toughest pitch to hit in baseball—the slider. Williams said, "It was the only pitch I couldn't hit consistently even when I knew it was coming."

Sent to Pittsfield in the Eastern League, Lyle pondered how to throw the pitch. "For three quarters of the season," he said, "the slider was on my mind constantly. I was always practicing, experimenting with different ways of holding the ball, different ways of releasing it. I never got any help from anybody."

No sooner did Lyle perfect the pitch than he was sent to Toronto in 1967. The club went bankrupt and his paycheck bounced, but the Red Sox made good on it and brought him up to Fenway. He pitched well that year, as Boston won its first pennant in 21 campaigns; he didn't pitch in the World Series, however, because he injured his arm with two weeks to go in the season.

Lyle went 6–1 and 8–3 for the Red Sox the next two years, but in March 1972 he was traded to the Yankees for first baseman Danny Cater. Lyle said, "Ralph Houk was managing the Yankees and he let me have the ball. I got the work I needed." That first year with New York, Lyle won nine games, led the league with 35 saves, recorded an ERA of 1.93, and was *The Sporting News* AL Fireman of the Year. The next year he was selected to the first of his three All-Star Games.

In 1976 Lyle again led the AL with 23 saves, but that was just a warm up for his best year, 1977. That season he led the league with 72 games pitched while going 13–5 with 26 saves and a 2.17 ERA. Even though 13 of the 28 voters left Lyle off the top of their lists, he captured his historic Cy Young Award.

Then, inexplicably, Steinbrenner signed Pittsburgh's Goose Gossage, the dominant reliever in the National League, to a six-year, $2.75 million contract, and acquired another free-agent stopper, righthander Rawly Eastwick. To Steinbrenner, stockpiling arms made sense. To Lyle, it meant nobody would get enough work. He and Steinbrenner feuded through the 1978 season, when Lyle went 9–3, and at season's end the pitcher went to Texas in a 10-player transaction.

Lyle was sold to the Philadelphia Phillies in September 1980 and the next year he went 9–6. But in August 1982 he was sold again, this time to the Chicago White Sox, who released him in October.

In 1990 Lyle wrote a novel (with David Fisher), *The Year I Owned the Yankees*. In 1998–99 he managed the Somerset Patriots in the independent North Atlantic League.

Jerry Lynch

Lynch, Gerald Thomas **OF**

1954–66 B:7/17/1930, Bay City, MI Deb:4/15/1954, PIT NL BL/TR 6'1", 189

G	AB	R	H	HR	RBI	OBP	SLG	AVG
1184	2879	364	798	115	470	.331	.463	.277

Jerry Lynch was an excellent left-handed pinch hitter for the Cincinnati Reds in the early 1960s. A defensive liability in the outfield, in desperation Lynch once borrowed shortstop Alex Grammas' glove and explained, "Maybe the glove will think I'm Alex and act accordingly." It didn't.

Lynch started his career at age 19 with Greenville in the Class C Cotton States League in 1950. In 1951 and 1952 he served in the military, returning in 1953 to play for the Norfolk Tars. He led the Class B Piedmont League with 541 at bats, 180 hits, 33 doubles, 22 triples, 133 RBIs, and a .333 batting average and was drafted by the Pittsburgh Pirates in November 1953.

In his three years with the Pirates, Lynch was a part-time outfielder and a pinch hitter. His success was variable, as he hit .239 his first year, jumped to .284 his second, but then dropped to

.158 his third year. After he spent much of that 1956 season on the disabled list, the Pirates dropped him, and the Reds drafted him in December of 1956.

Throughout his next seven years with the Reds, Lynch was again a part-time outfielder. He had two excellent years: 1958, when he hit .312 with 16 homers and 68 RBIs, and 1961, when he batted .315 in helping the Reds to the World Series. That latter year he went 19-for-47 for a .404 batting average as a pinch hitter, and slammed back-to-back pinch-homers on April 23 and 26.

Traded back to the Pirates in 1963 Lynch finished his career there three years later. In his career Lynch pinch-hit 18 homers (second to Cliff Johnson on the all-time list through 1999) and collected 116 pinch hits (the fifth highest all-time total) in 447 at bats. In 1964 he went into partnership with former Pirate teammate Dick Groat and operated the Champion Lakes golf course in Ligonier, Pennsylvania. Lynch later retired to Georgia.

Fred Lynn

Lynn, Fredric Michael **OF**
1974–90 B:2/3/1952, Chicago, IL Deb:9/5/1974, BOS AL BL/TL 6'1", 190

G	AB	R	H	HR	RBI	OBP	SLG	AVG
1969	6925	1063	1960	306	1111	.364	.484	.283

The first rookie to win the Most Valuable Player Award, Fred Lynn found his own opening performance a tough act to follow. Lynn's hang-loose, beachboy personality didn't fit his go-for-broke playing style. Frequently injured, at times his desire was questioned, but no one ever questioned his ability. He was a nine-time All-Star who hit 20 home runs 10 times in his career.

Raised in Southern California, Lynn played basketball, football, and baseball at El Monte High School. The Yankees drafted him as a pitcher in the third round of the June 1970 draft, but Lynn accepted a football scholarship to the University of Southern California, switching exclusively to baseball after his freshman year. He played center field on three College World Series winners in three years at USC, winning All-America honors in 1972 and 1973.

Although scouts loved Lynn's talent, they were far less enthusiastic about his personality, and that affected some evaluations. He lasted until the second round of the June 1973 draft, when the Red Sox chose him and signed him for a reported $40,000 bonus. Lynn made his minor league debut at Double-A Bristol, batting .259 with six home runs and 36 RBIs in 53 games. In 1974 at Triple-A Pawtucket, he batted .282 with 21 home runs and 68 RBIs, winning a September promotion to the Red Sox and hitting .419 in 15 big league games. Fenway Park taught Lynn, previously a dead-pull-hitter, that he could be successful going to all fields, and his adjustment to take advantage of the Green Monster in left was a key factor in his success.

The 1975 season was owned by Lynn and rookie teammate Jim Rice. Lynn missed unanimous selection as American League Rookie of the Year by a half-vote, split with Rice, who finished third in the MVP voting. They were perhaps the finest pair of rookies ever: Rice in left field, Lynn in center, leading the Red Sox to the AL East title. Lynn set a rookie record with a league-leading 47 doubles, while also topping the AL with 103 runs scored and becoming the first rookie to lead the league in slugging percentage, at .566. He finished second in batting (.331), third with 105 RBIs, fourth with 299 total bases, and hit 21 homers. On June 18, 1975, at Detroit, Lynn slugged three home runs, a triple, and a single to tie the league's single-game record for total bases. He also drove in 10 runs in the game, one less than the league record.

That year Lynn was named to his first of nine straight All-Star teams and won his first of four Gold Gloves. In a key game against the New York Yankees and Catfish Hunter on August 1, he reached on an error with two outs in the ninth of a scoreless tie, stole second, scored on a single, then made a game-saving tumbling catch on the warning track in left-center. He could seemingly do it all.

In the playoffs against the Oakland Athletics, the defending three-time world champions, Lynn doubled and knocked in two runs in the opener, singled to chase Vida Blue in a 6–3 come-from-behind win in Game 2, then singled and scored in Game 3. He batted .364 in the three-game sweep.

Against the Cincinnati Reds in the 1975 World Series, Lynn had two hits in the opener, made a great diving catch in Game 2, and threw out Ken Griffey trying for a triple in Boston's one-run victory in Game 5. In Game 6 he hit a three-run homer in the first inning. Hitless with two walks in a Game 7 loss, Lynn finished the Series with a .280 mark and five RBIs, giving him a .306 average with eight RBIs for the postseason.

A string of six nagging injuries began in 1976, keeping Lynn out of 30 games and leaving teammates questioning his courage. He was also one of three key Red Sox players who did not sign a contract, awaiting the new rules for the free agent era. Lynn admitted the contract situation took the fun out of baseball, but he still hit .314 and stole a career-best 14 bases. Named on the most ballots for the American League All-Star squad, he hit the first of his four All-Star Game homers.

In 1977 Lynn missed the first 27 games of the season after injuring his left ankle in spring training. On June 17 he and Rick Burleson achieved a baseball rarity; they led off a game against New York with back-to-back homers off Catfish Hunter. Lynn finished the season hitting .260 with 18 homers and 76 RBIs.

The following season Lynn played 150 games for the only time in his career and joined Rice and Dwight Evans to form the best outfield in baseball. Boston and New York finished in a tie at the end of the regular season, and in the AL East playoff game with the Yankees, Lynn had a single and an RBI. But, in his most important at bat, with two on and two out in the sixth, he smashed a liner toward the right-field corner off Ron Guidry. It looked like a sure double, but Lou Piniella made the catch and stifled the rally, allowing Bucky Dent's homer to give the Yankees a 3–2 lead they never relinquished.

After adding 20 pounds of muscle with weights during the off-season, Lynn set career highs in 1979 with 39 homers, 122 RBIs, 116 runs, 82 extra-base hits, 338 total bases, and 82 walks. He led the league in batting (.333) and slugging (.637). The next year he batted .301, hit for the cycle on May 13, and went 12-for-12 in stolen base attempts, but missed the final 37 games after breaking a toe by fouling a pitch off his right foot.

On January 23, 1981, with one year remaining on his contract, the Red Sox traded Lynn and pitcher Steve Renko to the California Angels for outfielder Joe Rudi and pitchers Frank Tanana and Jim Dorsey. To celebrate his long-rumored homecoming, Lynn signed a four-year contract. On May 8 he injured his left knee breaking up a double play; he was out until the strike settlement, reinjured the knee in August on another takeout slide, and, after trying to play through the pain, had surgery in September. He finished the year with a .219 batting average.

In 1982 Lynn cracked a rib running into a wall in September and missed a week. But he still batted .329 with 15 homers and 64 RBIs in the 61 second-half games and helped the Angels win the AL West. He was brilliant in the playoffs, winning the ALCS MVP Award despite his team's loss to the Milwaukee Brewers. In five games Lynn had a Championship Series record .611 average and a record-tying 11 hits, with five RBIs and five runs scored. His career .517 playoff batting average ranks first among players with 25 or more at bats.

More injuries shelved Lynn for 45 games in 1983. The next season he was moved to right field, and then shifted back to center. In early September he had at least one RBI in 10 straight games, and finished the season with 23 homers and 79 RBIs.

Signed to a five-year contract by the Baltimore Orioles, Lynn missed 31 games in 1985 because of torn ankle ligaments and a strained back. He still managed to belt 23 homers, surpassing 20 for the fourth consecutive year, a mark he would increase to seven years in a row. In 1986 he homered in four straight games between bouts with laryngitis, a strained wrist, a sprained ankle, and an injured shoulder.

In 1988 Lynn forced a change in baseball's rules. The Orioles traded him to Detroit on the August 31 deadline, but air-travel mishaps prevented him from reaching the Tigers before the midnight reporting deadline, making him ineligible for the playoffs. Commissioner Peter Ueberroth reinstated his postseason eligibility and relaxed the reporting rule. Lynn had a pinch-hit grand slam against the Orioles on September 25, but Detroit missed the playoffs.

Lynn played 117 games with Detroit in 1989, signing with the San Diego Padres at season's end. He played part-time in 1990 and found no takers in the free agent market.

Denny Lyons

Lyons, Dennis Patrick Aloysius **3B**

1885–97 B:3/12/1866, Cincinnati, OH D:1/2/1929, West Covington, KY Deb:9/18/1885, PRO NL BR/TR 5'10", 185

G	AB	R	H	HR	RBI	OBP	SLG	AVG
1121	4294	932	1333	62	755	.407	.443	.310

Denny Lyons was a righthanded hitter with speed who batted .310 for his career, with a .407 on-base percentage. In 1887, when a base on balls was considered a hit, Lyons compiled a 52-game "hitting" streak.

After spending most of 1885 with Columbus of the Southern League, Lyons played four games for Providence's National League team. He returned to the minors in 1886 and played with Atlanta, from whom the Philadelphia Athletics of the American Association purchased him.

In 1887, his first full year, Lyons had an excellent season. On April 26, 1887, he went 6-for-6, including two doubles and a triple, in an 18–17 win. On September 3 he rapped five doubles in a game. In between, Lyons forged the 52-game hitting streak, which was preserved twice with a walk but finally broken on August 29. Lyons ended the season with 43 doubles, 14 triples, 128 runs, 102 RBIs, and a .367 batting average. He also stole 73 bases and set a major league record for putouts at third base.

Two years later Lyons had another excellent year, batting .329 with 135 runs and 82 RBIs. The year after that he hit .354 and led the American Association in on base percentage and slugging average. However, he developed a reputation for drinking and was often fined and suspended.

In 1891 Lyons played with St. Louis of the

American Association. The next year he jumped to the National League Giants. On May 18, 1892, he collected the only hit off John McMahon and drove in the only run of the game to defeat the Orioles. Lyons averaged .257 for that season, but then rebounded to two .300-plus years while playing for Pittsburgh in 1893 and 1894. After a year with the St. Louis Browns, where he was hobbled by a knee injury, Lyons concluded his major league career with a second stint with the Pirates. His game seriously deteriorated in 1897 when Amos Rusie broke two of his fingers with a fastball on May 17.

After leaving the majors, Lyons played with Omaha and St. Joseph of the Western League, Wheeling in the Inter-State League, and Beaumont of the South Texas League.

Ted Lyons

Lyons, Theodore Amar **P**

1923–42, 1946 M(1946–48, 185–245) B:12/28/1900, Lake Charles, LA D:7/25/1986, Sulphur, LA Deb:7/2/1923, CHI AL BB/TR 5'11", 200

W	L	PCT	G	SH	IP	BB	SO	ERA
260	230	.531	594	27	4161	1121	1073	3.67

In the years just before World War II, Sunday was the best day for Chicago White Sox fans to go to Comiskey Park, for that was the day Ted Lyons pitched. In 1939 Chicago manager Jimmy Dykes began starting his 38-year-old star on Sundays, giving him extra rest through the week. Lyons lost his first Sunday assignment, then won eight in a row, all complete games. These regular Sunday starts continued through 1942. During those four seasons Lyons pitched 85 times and posted a 52–30 record with 72 complete games.

Lyons was a good high school student who was elected class president, planned to attend law school, played on the basketball team, and played infield. At Baylor University, baseball coach Frank Bridges converted him into a pitcher, and in 1923 Lyons pitched Baylor to the Southwest Conference championship.

The White Sox trained in Waco—the home of Baylor—and as a publicity stunt one day Lyons pitched to veteran catcher Ray Schalk. Schalk immediately told Chicago manager Kid Gleason to sign Lyons to a contract. The youngster never made it to law school.

Lyons turned down an offer from the Philadelphia Athletics and accepted Chicago's offer of $300 a month and a $1,000 bonus. He bought a Model T Ford and joined the White Sox in St. Louis in July 1923. He never played an inning of minor league baseball. In the first major league game he ever attended, Lyons appeared in relief.

He possessed an excellent fastball and soon added a fine curve. Lyons pitched as much with his head as with his arm, once explaining, "A pitch that the batter misses in the spring, he may hit out of the park in midseason. I figure I have to change my style of pitching against certain batters two or three times a year."

Never a strikeout artist, Lyons had good control, which improved nearly every year. In 1939 he tossed 42 consecutive innings without allowing a base on balls. As a result, he pitched fast games. One time he threw a complete game in only an hour and 18 minutes.

After a year split between starting and relief, Lyons made it to the regular rotation for the White Sox in 1925 and became a star. While pitching for a fifth-place team, he led the American League with 21 wins and five shutouts. In September he was pitching a perfect game until Bobby Veach of the Washington Senators singled with two outs in the ninth inning to break it up.

In 1926 Lyons won 18 games, including a 6–0 no-hitter against the Boston Red Sox on August 21. The following year, he tied Waite Hoyt of the pennant-winning Yankees for most wins, 22, while leading the AL with 30 complete games and 307⅔ innings pitched.

Lyons lost 20 games in 1929 despite some heroic efforts. On May 24 he pitched 21 innings, the third-most in league history, in a 6–5 loss to Detroit. He yielded 24 hits in the game, walked two, and struck out four. The next year he rebounded with 22 wins, leading the league with 29 complete games and 297⅔ innings pitched.

Known as one of baseball's nice guys, Lyons was nevertheless a fiery competitor. Once, when former teammate Moe Berg singled to beat him, Lyons chased him off the field and smacked him with his glove. "A fine friend you are!" Lyons shouted. He often helped himself win games: he was a very good fielder and, for a pitcher, a good hitter. He is one of only 17 American League pitchers ever to win 20 games and hit .300 in the same year, and his 364 lifetime hits rank 11th all-time among pitchers.

Lyons liked to joke about his hitting prowess, telling tall tales about the time he "knocked a hot dog out of the bun in a fan's hands and the mustard didn't even splatter." He also joked that during an exhibition at Joliet prison, his line drives tore such enormous holes in the walls that "the warden stopped the game, fearful of a prison break."

In his first seven complete major league seasons, Lyons won 124 games. Then, on a damp night in Houston during spring training, he tried to break off a curve and injured his shoulder. He struggled through the 1931 season, winning only four games. His fastball was gone.

A determined Lyons turned to a knuckleball and other junk pitches. He earned a starting position and won 31 games from 1932 through 1934, although he also lost 49. The White Sox were, as usual, mired deep in the second division, but Lyons could no longer overcome their shoddy play. Not until Dykes had the idea of using him only on Sundays did he again become a winning pitcher. In 1939, the first year of the plan—when he went 14–6 with a 2.76 ERA—he was selected to his only All-Star Game.

On September 15, 1940, the *Chicago Tribune* sponsored Ted Lyons Day and invited readers to send in a dime toward a gift. The paper collected enough dimes to buy Lyons a new car. The 1942 season was Lyons' 20th in a White Sox uniform. At age 41 he posted another 14–6 mark with a league-leading, career-best 2.10 ERA. He seemed poised to tie Walter Johnson's record for the most years spent by a pitcher with one team, but decided he had something more important to do: Lyons enlisted as a private in the Marines. He served for three years and saw combat in the South Pacific.

Returning to the White Sox in 1946, Lyons tied Johnson's record. However, despite a 2.32 ERA and five complete games in as many starts, he won only one game. When he was named White Sox manager early that season, he retired as a pitcher with a career record of 260–230. Had he played on a contending team, he most likely would have won 300 games.

Lyons completed a remarkable 356 games in 484 starts, and his career ERA of 3.67 is impressive, considering the era in which he pitched. Only six players—Brooks Robinson, Carl Yastrzemski, Cap Anson, Stan Musial, Al Kaline, and Mel Ott—had longer careers with one team. Only two players—Phil Niekro and Gaylord Perry—played more seasons without appearing in a World Series.

Lyons managed Chicago through the 1948 season. He was criticized for being too nice, but the White Sox had barely enough talent to be mediocre. He coached for Detroit from 1949 through 1953 and for Brooklyn in 1954. From 1955 through 1966 he scouted for the White Sox, then retired to manage a rice plantation in Louisiana with his sister.

The White Sox retired his uniform number 16. Lyons was named to the Hall of Fame in 1955.

Danny MacFayden

MacFayden, Daniel Knowles **P**

1926–41, 1943 B:6/10/1905, North Truro, MA D:8/26/1972, Brunswick, ME Deb: 8/25/1926, BOS AL BR/TR 5'11", 170

W	L	PCT	G	SH	IP	BB	SO	ERA
132	159	.454	465	18	2706	872	797	3.96

A slender, bespectacled New Englander, pitcher Danny MacFayden began his career close to home with the Boston Red Sox and returned to have his best years with the Boston Braves. He first gained attention as a high schooler in 1924, striking out 32 batters in a 17-inning game. Early in his career, however, MacFayden enjoyed his most success as a hitter. He batted near .300 in his first two years. On the mound he posted losing records in six of his first seven seasons.

In 1929 MacFayden's 10–18 record obscured a 3.62 ERA and league-best four shutouts. Not typically a strikeout pitcher, he once fanned New York Yankees Hall of Famers Babe Ruth, Lou Gehrig, and Tony Lazzeri in order with the bases loaded, a feat he later rated "the best single piece of pitching I ever did in my life." MacFayden learned to harness his fine curveball later in his career, and won 45 games for the Braves between 1936 and 1938.

Connie Mack

Mack, Cornelius Alexander **C–1B**

1886–96 M(1894–96, 1901–50, 3,731–3,948) B:12/22/1862, East Brookfield, MA D:2/8/1956, Philadelphia, PA Deb:9/11/1886, WAS NL BR/TR 6'1", 150

G	AB	R	H	HR	RBI	OBP	SLG	AVG
723	2695	391	659	5	265	.305	.300	.245

It is often said that baseball managers are hired to be fired. Many managers have even been dismissed from a first-place team or one that had just earned a pennant. But for 50 years Philadelphia Athletics manager Connie Mack didn't have to worry about where he would work the next season. Whether he won a pennant, as he did nine times, or finished last, as he did on 17 occasions, he knew the boss would have him back, because Mack also owned the team.

In later years many believed Cornelius Alexander McGillicuddy had adopted the name "Mack" as a kindness to newspaper typesetters, but Mack himself told writer Fred Lieb, "Except when we voted, our people always called themselves Mack." Mack's father, a Civil War veteran, worked in the cotton mills and shoe factories around Brookfield, Massachusetts. When he died, his son left school and worked in a shoe factory to help support the family. He also played ball with some local teams.

In 1884 Mack joined Meriden of the Connecticut State League. He spent 1885 with Hartford of the North East Connecticut State League and played one game with Newark in the Eastern League. In 1886 with Hartford, Mack caught 69 games and hit .248. In September the National League Washington Nationals acquired him. He hit .361 in 10 games and earned the starting catcher's job for the following season.

Mack's career as a major league catcher is often described as undistinguished, but this perception stems largely from his mediocre batting average. The 6-foot 1-inch, 150-pound string bean was never a strong hitter, compiling a .245 average in 11 seasons. But the most important part of a catcher's grueling and dangerous job was not hitting but throwing out base stealers.

Protective equipment was nearly nonexistent in the 1880s. Shin guards had not yet been invented, and the mitt, mask, and chest protector offered little real protection. In Mack's day a catcher stood several feet behind the plate when the bases were empty, but once a runner reached first, the catcher moved forward and became an easy target for foul tips. Bunting was a major part of the game, and the catcher was constantly racing out to either field a bunt or call which base an infielder should throw to.

Because of the dangerous and exhausting nature of their job, catchers were not expected to play in every game, and those who caught more than half of their team's games were seldom able to concentrate on their batting. Even Buck Ewing, the greatest catcher of the day and a career .303 hitter, seldom caught as many as half the season's games. King Kelly, another excellent hitter, usually caught only the most important games.

While Mack wasn't a Ewing or a Kelly with a bat in his hands, he was generally considered a strong defensive player, very smart and very tricky. He learned to brush players' bats with his glove, and he apologized with such sincerity that the batters often believed the interference was accidental. A caught foul tip was an out, and on swinging strikes Mack often mimicked the sound of a foul tip, thereby retiring many batters who never touched the ball.

After catching for Washington through 1889, Mack joined Buffalo of the Players' League. He invested some of his own money in the team, which may explain his appearance in a career-high 123 games. When the Players' League folded after one season, Mack joined Pittsburgh in 1891, the same year the team became known as the "Pirates" for its tricky maneuvers to acquire players. In 1892 he led all

National League catchers in fielding average.

Pittsburgh made a strong run for the pennant in 1893. The turning point of the season took place during a game with eventual champion Boston. With Herman Long of the Beaneaters on third, the runner on first took off for second. Mack threw to the base and then blocked the plate against the incoming Long. The return throw was slightly off mark and left Mack in an awkward position. Long slammed into him, fracturing the catcher's ankle. Mack missed most of the rest of the season, and Pittsburgh finished second. The injury cost him most of his speed and agility, and he played for only three more seasons, as a part-timer.

When the Pirates tumbled in the standings in 1894, Mack was named manager late in the season. The team had few good hitters, so one of his first moves was to freeze the baseballs in the clubhouse icebox before each game, thereby deadening them. Mack posted a winning record as the Pirates skipper in 1895 and 1896 but was fired after a dispute with an interfering owner.

Mack became manager of the Milwaukee team of the Western League in 1897 through his friendship with league president Ban Johnson. In 1900 the league changed its name to the American League, and in 1901 Johnson proclaimed that it would compete directly with the National League. Sporting goods manufacturer Ben Shibe was granted a franchise in Philadelphia. Mack became manager and owner of 25 percent of the club. He called the team the Athletics, after a Philadelphia team of the old American Association during the 1880s. When John McGraw said that a team in Philadelphia would be "a white elephant," or heavy money loser, a confident Mack took the white elephant as the team's symbol.

Known as the "Tall Tactician," Mack always managed in his street clothes. Another of his idiosyncrasies was his practice of moving his players around on the field by waving his scorecard. To the public he seemed like a fatherly, and later grandfatherly, figure. But Mack could make hard decisions. His players most admired his honesty.

Mack led the A's to their first pennant in 1902, largely behind pitchers Rube Waddell and Eddie Plank. Pitching, Mack often said, was 75 percent of baseball. Strong pitching always marked his winning teams, and Mack developed a reputation for turning young pitchers into stars. Both Plank and Chief Bender went directly from the college campus to the majors under Mack's guidance, and his patience with the talented but highly eccentric Waddell made possible the pitcher's greatest seasons.

In 1905 Mack won another pennant, but in the World Series, the second between the American and National Leagues, the Athletics were the victims of pitching. Although Bender shut out McGraw's Giants in one game, New York's Christy Mathewson threw three shutouts against Philadelphia, and Joe McGinnity tossed a fourth to give the Giants the Series. Waddell was unable to pitch in the Series due to an injury.

Mack rebuilt the Athletics during the next few years. In 1910 he developed his best team to date and won pennants in 1910, 1911, 1913, and 1914. Plank and Bender were still outstanding. Jack Coombs, another former college star, was the staff ace until an illness all but ended his career in 1913. The team also featured the "$100,000 Infield" of Stuffy McInnis, Eddie Collins, Jack Barry, and Frank Baker. The Athletics won the World Series in 1910, 1911, and 1913, twice defeating McGraw's Giants. Although they were heavily favored in 1914, the lightly regarded "Miracle" Boston Braves swept the A's in four games.

Despite being a success in the standings, the Athletics struggled financially. Attendance dropped dramatically in 1914 as Philadelphia fans took the club's success for granted. Meanwhile, the outlaw Federal League was offering huge contracts to NL and AL stars and Mack could not compete. Before the 1914 World Series he told Plank and Bender, both of whom had been loyal to Mack for years, to accept the more lucrative Federal League offers for the following season. The outbreak of war in Europe also cast the future of Organized Baseball in doubt. Many believed the United States would become involved and that baseball would be suspended.

Mack decided to sell off most of his stars, maintaining that the A's nucleus of young, inexpensive players could keep the team in contention. He was wrong. In 1915 Philadelphia nosedived to last and stayed there for seven seasons.

Beginning in 1922 Mack slowly brought the team back into contention. One player at a time, he added future Hall of Famers Mickey Cochrane, Lefty Grove, Al Simmons, and Jimmie Foxx to his existing stable of stars that included Jimmy Dykes, Bing Miller, George Earnshaw, Mule Haas, Rube Walberg, and Max Bishop. After finishing second in both 1927 and 1928, the Athletics won the pennant in 1929.

Mack surprised the Chicago Cubs in the World Series by starting veteran righthanded sidearm pitcher Howard Ehmke. Once a star hurler, by 1929 Ehmke was thought to be washed up and appeared infrequently for the A's. But Mack believed that Ehmke's sidearm deliveries coming out of the white-shirted background at Wrigley Field would baffle the Cubs.

Ehmke won the game, 3–1, striking out 14, a Series record that lasted 23 years. The A's trailed, 8–0, in the bottom of the seventh inning of Game 4, then rallied for 10 runs to win. They won the Series in Game 5 when, behind 2–0, they scored three runs in the bottom of the ninth. After the season Mack received the Edward W. Bok Award as the individual who had rendered the greatest service to Philadelphia.

Mack's star-studded A's won a second world championship in 1930 and a pennant in 1931, but the St. Louis Cardinals upset them in the World Series. By then the Depression held America in its grip. With the highest-paid team in baseball, Mack had no choice but to once again sell his stars. By 1935 the Athletics were back in the cellar.

During the next dozen years the team finished last nine times and never got out of the second division. Mack was still able to find and develop some good young players, but he was often forced to sell them before they reached stardom. There was one solace during those losing years, though—in 1937 Mack was inducted into the Baseball Hall of Fame.

In 1948 Mack managed his last first-division team, a veteran crew that edged into fourth place. By then he was 85 years old, and subordinates did most of the real managing. After the 1950 season, when the A's again finished last, Mack stepped down. In 53 seasons he had won 3,731 games and lost 3,948, both all-time records. Mack died in 1956 at age 93. By then, Shibe Park had been rechristened in his name, but his beloved A's had moved to Kansas City under new ownership.

Biz Mackey

Mackey, Raleigh **C-SS-3B-2B-1B-OF**
Negro League Player (1920–47) Manager B:7/27/1897, Eagle Pass, TX D:1959, Los Angeles, CA BB/TR 6', 240

Although the catcher Josh Gibson is often recalled as the Negro Leagues' greatest player, he was not known as a great defensive catcher. Fans of the time recognized Raleigh "Biz" Mackey as the real master behind the plate in the Negro Leagues.

Not that Mackey couldn't hit, too. He was a switch hitter who averaged .318 during his 20-season career. Nor was he limited to playing catcher; he occasionally filled needs at other positions, including shortstop. But it was his exceptional skill with a mitt, his magnificent throwing, and his uncanny handling of pitchers that won Mackey lasting fame.

He began his career in 1918, playing for two years with the San Antonio Black Aces, a fast local club. He often pitched and was said to have good speed and an overhand drop. When the team broke up in 1920, several of its top players, including Mackey, were sold to the Indianapolis ABCs. Though he weighed about 240 pounds, Mackey was extremely nimble. He amazed crowds by gunning runners down at second without shifting from his catcher's squat.

In 1922, his last season with the ABCs, Mackey hit .352. When the Eastern clubs raided the Midwestern teams of their stars, he joined the powerful Philadelphia Hilldales. His new club already featured star catcher Louis Santop, so Mackey played elsewhere initially, usually shortstop. The Hilldales won three straight pennants, as Mackey took over more and more of the catching duties.

A heavy drinker, he was accused on occasion of showing up for a game drunk, but apparently his performance did not suffer. He played for the Baltimore Elite Giants and the Philadelphia Stars during the 1930s and was chosen to play in the Negro League All-Star Game four times. When the black stars played barnstorming white players, Mackey more than held his own, batting .326 in 14 games.

As a player-manager in the 1940s, he helped groom such stars as Monte Irvin, Larry Doby, and Don Newcombe. His 1946 Newark Eagles won the pennant and the Negro League World Series, beating Satchel Paige and the Kansas City Monarchs.

One of his admirers was a young catcher named Roy Campanella, whom Mackey took under his wing. A 1941 fan vote placed the two men first and second as catcher for the East-West game, with Mackey first. Campanella always credited Mackey with teaching him how to catch. When Campanella was given a "night" in Los Angeles in 1959, he invited Mackey to join him.

Larry MacPhail

MacPhail, Leland Stanford
Executive B:3/3/1890, Cass City, MI D:10/1/1975, Miami, FL

Larry MacPhail was one of baseball's great pioneers. He was a primary force behind the introduction of night baseball, regular radio broadcasts of games, teams traveling by plane, batting helmets, the ballpark organ, and baseball's pension plan, among other things. In the course of 85 years, he also fathered several baseball dynasties, beat cancer twice, survived a heart attack, and posthumously entered the Hall of Fame in 1978.

Born into a prosperous banking family in Cass City, Michigan, Larry MacPhail was accepted at the U.S. Naval Academy at age 16 but turned down the appointment to attend Beloit College, the University of Michigan, and George Washington University. Emerging with a law degree in 1910, he began practicing in Chicago and opened his career with a record of 0–200 representing the Union Pacific Railroad against Midwestern shippers in suits stemming from the famous 1906 San Francisco earthquake.

When the United States entered World War I, the 28-year-old MacPhail enlisted in the Army as a private, rose to the rank of captain in command of an artillery battery, and, after the armistice, was at the center of a plot to kidnap Germany's exiled Kaiser Wilhelm. The adventurers got into the castle where the Kaiser was staying but almost became prisoners themselves. They captured only an ashtray—a monogrammed monstrosity featuring a pipe-puffing wolf, which MacPhail's son Lee still possesses—then survived being court-martialed. General John Pershing, commander of the American forces in Europe, called the stunt crazy but added, "I'd have given a year's pay to have been with those boys in Holland."

After the war MacPhail refereed Big Ten football and skidded through a series of ventures with uneven results until 1930, when he obtained an option to buy the impoverished Columbus franchise in the American Association. He brokered the sale of the club to Branch Rickey's St. Louis Cardinals farm system and won a sinecure as club president.

Lee MacPhail remembers his father taking the family to a professional football game one night in Portsmouth, Ohio. "He said to us, 'Look, you can even read a newspaper.' He thought it was very exciting." Larry MacPhail convinced the Cardinals to include lights in the new park they were building for his team. But Cards management subsequently bounced him for trying to get Columbus the best possible team regardless of the needs of the Cardinals system.

Within a year of his firing, MacPhail was in the majors. A bank had taken over the Cincinnati Reds from owner Sidney Weil, who coincidentally was Columbus' previous owner. MacPhail convinced local radio and manufacturing magnate Powell Crosley Jr. to take an option on the club. The two men persuaded National League owners to allow the Reds to play seven night games at home, one against each opponent. President Franklin D. Roosevelt flipped a switch at the White House to turn on the lights for Major League Baseball's first night game on May 24, 1935.

Crosley bought the Reds in June 1936, but within six months, MacPhail, who hadn't helped his cause by slugging a police sergeant in a hotel elevator, was again out of a job. Nonetheless, when the Reds won pennants in 1939 and 1940, MacPhail was hailed as the architect of their success even though he was no longer on the scene.

In 1938 he took over as general manager of the Dodgers, brought Red Barber to Brooklyn as his baseball voice, and got the bank that owned the team to install lights at Ebbets Field. Brooklyn's first night game, on June 15, 1938, was Johnny Vander Meer's second straight no-hitter.

MacPhail improved the Dodgers on the field by acquiring Leo Durocher to play short and then promoting him to manager. It was a highly flammable but winning combination. MacPhail regularly fired Durocher after midnight and rehired him by noon.

After adding to the team Pee Wee Reese and Joe Medwick, whose 1940 beaning led to MacPhail's interest in batting helmets, the general manager traded for Billy Herman. The Dodgers won their first pennant since 1920. "It's not the first lights, air travel, or radio when people talk about my grandfather," Andy MacPhail said. "First, it's the Dodgers, and how he turned them from doormats to contenders."

After the 1942 season MacPhail reentered the armed forces with the rank of lieutenant colonel and served in Washington as a special assistant to the secretary of war. He tried to form a syndicate to buy his own team, looking at the Phillies and Giants, but he ended up with an even bigger, less likely prize—the Yankees. Owner Jacob Ruppert had died in 1939, and his heirs were trying to peddle the club.

While still in the service, MacPhail had formed an ownership syndicate featuring John Hertz, a Chicago taxi fleet owner, which won favor from the Ruppert estate and its bankers. But Commissioner Kenesaw Mountain Landis disqualified Hertz because of his ties to horse racing. Meanwhile, the bank invited MacPhail to finalize the deal. It assumed he still had Hertz's financing because MacPhail neglected to mention Landis' veto.

Lee MacPhail recalled his father's deal. "He bought the team for $3 million, even though he didn't have a penny, really. As he often did, he went to '21' for a drink to try to figure out what to do." At the bar, MacPhail met Dan Topping, who had been MacPhail's tenant as owner of the Brooklyn Tigers football team and had also expressed interest in buying a baseball team with MacPhail. Topping and builder Del Webb, who was recommended by Bing Crosby, put up the money for the club and gave MacPhail a one-third interest for little or no cash plus a 10-year contract to run the club.

MacPhail installed lights at Yankee Stadium and built Organized Baseball's first stadium club restaurant. During an evening of furious drinking, he nearly overthrew the baseball universe when he talked Tom Yawkey into swapping Ted Williams for Joe DiMaggio, a deal Yawkey backed out of the next morning by asking that Yogi Berra also be part of the deal.

In 1947, under new manager Bucky Harris, the Yankees won their first pennant since 1943 and beat the Dodgers in a fabulous full-length World

Series. It featured Bill Bevens' near-no hitter, Al Gionfriddo's one-handed catch of Joe DiMaggio's drive, and Joe Page's five innings of shutout relief in the finale—after Harris asked MacPhail about bringing in Page or Allie Reynolds. In the delirious Yankees clubhouse, MacPhail tearfully announced his resignation.

The announcement shocked observers, and most expected him to rescind it the next day. But events at a Series celebration in Manhattan's Biltmore Hotel made MacPhail's resignation permanent. In the so-called "battle of the Biltmore," MacPhail drunkenly fought with everyone in sight. The next day, Webb and Topping bought him out for a reported $1.5 million. According to grandson Andy MacPhail, "Quitting on the heels of the world championship was something he always regretted."

Out of baseball for good, the elder MacPhail bought a farm north of Baltimore and Maryland's Bowie Race Track. He raised Black Angus cattle, bred racehorses, and ran the track. Financial troubles eventually led to a forced sale of the farm.

Lee MacPhail

MacPhail, Leland Stanford Jr.

AL President (1974–84) Executive B:10/25/1917, Nashville, TN

Leland "Lee" MacPhail Jr., son of prominent baseball executive Leland "Larry" MacPhail, followed in his father's footsteps to become one of the most powerful and respected men in the major leagues. MacPhail's early work experience came in the front offices of minor league clubs. After service in World War II he worked for his father, who co-owned the Yankees, as an executive in the club's minor league system. Promoted to director of player personnel in 1948, he helped build the most dominating team ever seen in baseball, a Yankee club that during the next 10 years went to nine World Series and won seven of them.

In 1958 Baltimore hired MacPhail as general manager, and under his direction the Orioles developed young stars such as pitcher Milt Pappas, second baseman Davey Johnson, and third sacker Brooks Robinson. The club also acquired shortstop Luis Aparicio and first baseman Jim Gentile. Before taking a job as top assistant to Commissioner of Baseball William Eckert in 1965, MacPhail was also responsible for the deal that sent Pappas and two others to the Reds for Frank Robinson. In 1966 it was essentially a MacPhail-built Orioles that won the first world championship in club history.

In October 1966 MacPhail took over as Yankees general manager. After George Steinbrenner bought the team, the junior MacPhail assumed the most senior role in the American League, that of league president. During his decade in charge he developed a reputation as a conservative and reasonable leader in a time of skyrocketing player salaries and AL expansion.

After resigning the American League presidency in 1984 he became president of the major league Player Relations Committee, representing owners in negotiations with the players' union. MacPhail's son, Andy MacPhail, has continued the family tradition, serving as vice president and general manager of both the Minnesota Twins and Chicago Cubs. Lee MacPhail was elected to the Hall of Fame in 1998.

Gary Maddox

Maddox, Gary Lee **OF**

1972–86 B:9/1/1949, Cincinnati, OH Deb:4/25/1972, SF NL BR/TR 6'3", 184

G	AB	R	H	HR	RBI	OBP	SLG	AVG
1749	6331	777	1802	117	754	.323	.413	.285

Ironically, Garry Maddox, one of the greatest defensive center fielders in history, is remembered in Philadelphia for the one he dropped. The Phillies center fielder had such great range, however, that Mets announcer Ralph Kiner once said, "two-thirds of the earth is covered by water, the other one-third is covered by Garry Maddox."

But in the 10th inning of the fourth and deciding game of the 1978 NLCS against the Dodgers, Maddox dropped a routine fly ball off the bat of Ron Cey. After Cey reached base on Maddox's muff, Los Angeles shortstop Bill Russell singled him in with the winning run. The headline in one Philadelphia paper read: "The Day Garry Maddox Dropped a Pennant."

"I can't say the sun was in my eyes or anything like that," Maddox explained. "I just missed the ball. I don't know how I missed it. It's that simple. The ball was right in my glove. It was not a tough play, just a routine line drive. I don't know whether I closed my glove too late or whether the ball hit my heel. I just missed it. All I know is I missed it."

The Giants drafted the 18-year-old Garry Lee Maddox out of Harbor College in the second round of the 1968 amateur draft. After playing a season of minor league ball he spent a year in the armed services in Vietnam.

In 1972 Maddox came up to the big club, where he had a mentor in Willie Mays. Mays, who also counseled a number of other young black outfielders including Bobby Bonds and Garry Matthews, gave Maddox a fielding glove that he used for many years.

In May 1975 the Giants traded Maddox to the Phillies for first baseman Willie Montanez. With Philadelphia, Maddox won Gold Gloves for eight straight seasons and helped the club claim six division flags. His offensive contributions are notable as well. He hit .330 in 1976 and stole more than 20 bases for six consecutive seasons.

In 1980 he doubled in outfielder-first baseman Del Unser with the winning run in the 10th inning of the final game of the NLCS. The Phillies went on to beat the Royals in the World Series.

Maddox's only other World Series appearance came in 1983 against Baltimore. His eighth-inning solo home run snapped a 1–1 tie in Game 1, but that was the only game Philadelphia won. The 34-year-old Maddox appeared in only 77 games the following season, though on June 10 he tied a major league record for outfielders by recording 12 putouts in a game.

Greg Maddux

Maddux, Gregory Alan **P**

1986–* B:4/14/1966, San Angelo, TX Deb:9/3/1986, CHI NL BR/TR 6', 170

W	L	PCT	G	SH	IP	BB	SO	ERA
221	126	.637	436	28	3068^2	691	2160	2.81

It is hard to imagine that Greg Maddux ever had a problem with major league hitters, yet the Atlanta Braves righthander, who won four Cy Young Awards before his 30th birthday, was hit hard his first two seasons. In 1986 and 1987 he went a combined 8–18 with the Chicago Cubs and had an ERA over 5.00.

After posting four solid seasons with the Cubs, recognition finally came to Maddux in 1992, when he pitched in the All-Star Game, led the league in wins with 20, and earned his first Cy Young award. His timing could not have been better, as he became a highly coveted free agent that winter. Maddux spurned the New York Yankees and their extra $6 million to come to Atlanta, where the Braves had appeared in back-to-back World Series.

Maddux won his second straight Cy Young Award with a 20–10 record, 267 strikeouts, and 2.36 ERA in his first year as a Brave. He was on pace to better those numbers in 1994 when the baseball strike ended his season with 16 wins and a minuscule 1.56 ERA. He bettered that the following year with a 19–2 season, 1.63 ERA, and 10 complete games to lead the league in each category. He then pitched a two-hitter against the Cleveland Indians in his first-ever World Series start. "He doesn't seem dominating," Cleveland's Jim Thome said, "then you look up on the scoreboard and you've got one hit and it's the eighth inning." Indeed, Maddux has never had an overpowering fastball, but his combination of pinpoint control with exceptional movement has baffled hitters for more than a decade. He's also been a model of efficiency, throwing a lot of innings with remarkably low pitch counts. "There's no secrets," Maddux said. "To pitch, you have to do two things. You have to locate your fastball and change speeds. That's all you have to do. If you can do those two things, you can pitch"

The Cy Young streak ended at four in 1996. Teammate John Smoltz had a Maddux-like year while Maddux's 15 wins seemed almost ordinary by his standards. Still, he was second in both innings (245) and ERA (2.72). He also won one game in each of the team's three postseason series, although he was the hard-luck loser in the Yankees' 3–2 World Series clinching victory in Game 6.

Maddux bounced back with a 19–4 season in 1997 as he led the NL with an .826 won-lost percentage and a ratio of only .77 walks per nine innings of work. His 2.20 ERA trailed only Pedro Martinez's 1.90. The following year he won 18 games and surpassed 200 strikeouts for the first time. Maddux showed signs of wear in 1999, as his ERA reached 3.57—still quite good in the high offensive environment of the late 1990s, but Maddux's first season over 3.00 since he joined Atlanta. Although he surrendered a career-worst 258 hits, he had enough support from teammates to post a 19–9 record. He also captured his 10th consecutive Gold Glove Award for outstanding fielding, second all-time among pitchers to Jim Kaat's 14.

Bill Madlock

Madlock, Bill **3B–2B**

1973–87 B:1/2/1951, Memphis, TN Deb:9/7/1973, TEX AL BR/TR 5'11", 185

G	AB	R	H	HR	RBI	OBP	SLG	AVG
1806	6594	920	2008	163	860	.369	.442	.305

The powerful, compact swing of Bill Madlock was a wonder to behold. He slashed line drives for 15 seasons in the majors, won four batting titles (two each with two different teams, a record), and was a key performer on three different division champions.

Madlock is one of those players for whom stat lines tell less than half the real story. On good teams he was a competent and productive participant. But when things turned sour, he could be moody, surly, selfish, and a negative clubhouse influence.

Despite his football-player physique, "Mad Dog" moniker, and the impression he gave as a hard-nosed player with powerful takeout slides at second, Madlock was more interested in winning batting championships than in being an everyday performer. He routinely sat out games rather than face tough pitchers.

But Pittsburgh fans loved him when he showed

up on June 28, 1979, after being acquired from San Francisco. Having Madlock to play third base allowed the Bucs to move Phil Garner back to his natural position at second, and the Pirate infield solidified.

A .261 hitter in San Francisco with a well-established reputation for surliness, Madlock belted the ball at a .328 clip and helped propel the Pirates' 1979 world championship win. He hit .375 in the World Series against the Orioles.

On May 1, 1980, Madlock argued a call with umpire Jerry Crawford. Holding his glove in his right hand, Mad Dog used it to emphasize his point—right in Crawford's face. Crawford lost control and accused Madlock of hitting him in the face with his glove; Madlock won one of the largest fines ($5,000) and longest suspensions (15 days) ever for a player. When he returned to play, he commented, "Baseball, hot dogs, apple pie, and violence."

When team captain Willie Stargell left the Pirates in the early 1980s, his jovial yet solid leadership was deeply missed, especially since many team members were then discovering the allure of cocaine. Manager Chuck Tanner looked for someone to assume a leadership role. He gave the captain title to Madlock.

Although Madlock was not directly involved in drug use, he didn't use his influence as a captain to discourage its proliferation throughout the clubhouse. In 1985, when the team was at its nadir and the "baseball drug trials" were taking place at a Pittsburgh courthouse, Madlock resigned his captaincy and announced a week later, "I'm sick of watching us play." By that time Madlock was carrying an additional 40 pounds on his 5-foot-11 frame. When asked about his physical condition, he replied, "They didn't encourage us to take care of ourselves, so I just let myself go."

The team was in turmoil, had been listed for sale, and had no prospective buyers. The owners brought back former general manager Joe L. Brown to do some housecleaning. Within a month the biggest clubhouse gripers and lazy on-field performers—George Hendrick, John Candelaria, and Bill Madlock—were gone. Madlock was sent to the Dodgers for Sid Bream, R.J. Reynolds, and Cecil Espy.

On a team with a chance to win, the hard-hitting Bill Madlock of old reappeared. During five weeks as a Dodger he hit .360, stole seven bases, and drove in 15 runs. He hit .333 with three home runs in the Dodgers' ill-fated loss to the Cardinals in the 1985 NLCS.

A .280 hitter the next year for Los Angeles, his average slumped to .180 by 1987, when the Dodgers released him on May 29. Six days later he signed with Detroit. The Tigers were in fifth place with a 25–24 record, and once again Madlock played a key role in winning a division flag.

Primarily a designated hitter, Madlock knocked in 50 runs in 87 games, batting .279 for Detroit that year, his last in the major leagues. Writer Bill James pointed out that Madlock "has been traded in midseason three times in his career and in each case his new team has gone on to win a division title. Think 'Mad Dog' hasn't had something to do with that?" Madlock ended his baseball career after playing for one year in Japan.

Dave Magadan

Magadan, David Joseph **3B–1B**

1986–* B:9/30/1962, Tampa, FL Deb:9/7/1986, NY NL
BL/TR 6'3", 200

G	AB	R	H	HR	RBI	OBP	SLG	AVG
1396	3899	491	1129	39	462	.396	.379	.290

Patience at the plate has defined Dave Magadan since he reached the majors with the New York Mets in 1986. Magadan rarely swings at a bad pitch. The result has been high walk rates and high batting averages—but, despite his size, too few extra-base hits and RBIs to become a star or even a consistent starter at the power-hitting positions of first or third base.

Magadan, a .525 hitter as a junior at the University of Alabama and the 1983 Golden Spikes Award winner, had the game-winning hit in his first major league start on September 7, 1986, the night the Mets clinched the National League East title. He was the heir apparent to Keith Hernandez as the Mets first baseman. In 1990 he batted a career-best .328 and led the NL with a .425 on-base percentage, yet lost his full-time job the following season; by 1993 he had left New York to embark on a journeyman player's tour of the major leagues: Florida, Seattle (where he played for his cousin Lou Piniella), Florida again, Houston, the Chicago Cubs, Oakland, and San Diego.

Although a painfully slow runner and merely adequate in the field, Magadan proved valuable to ballclubs whether he was in the lineup every day or once a week. "I reserve the word 'great' for a few players," said Oakland general manager Billy Beane, who employed Magadan in 1997 and 1998, "but Mags is an outstanding hitter, great plate discipline, and a good guy in the clubhouse."

Sherry Magee

Magee, Sherwood Robert **OF-1B**

1904–19 U(1928) B:8/6/1884, Clarendon, PA
D:3/13/1929, Philadelphia, PA Deb:6/29/1904, PHI NL
BR/TR 5'11", 179

G	AB	R	H	HR	RBI	OBP	SLG	AVG
2087	7441	1112	2169	83	1176	.364	.427	.291

Outfielder Sherwood Robert "Sherry" Magee was one of the best players in the National League during the deadball era. During his long career he excelled defensively while accumulating more than 2,000 hits and leading the league in batting once and in RBIs four times.

He is sometimes confused with infielder Lee Magee, who was suspended from baseball for life in 1919 for betting against his own team, and that may contribute to Sherry Magee's relative obscurity today. However, a more likely reason for his anonymity was that Sherry Magee did not play for a pennant winner until his last major league season, and then only as a substitute.

Magee joined the Philadelphia Phillies in 1904 and put in 11 solid seasons as their left fielder. His best season was 1910, when he led the National League in runs, RBIs, batting average, on-base percentage, and slugging average. After a strong 1914 season in which he led the league in hits, doubles, RBIs, and slugging, Magee expected to be named manager. When he wasn't, he demanded a trade. Ironically, in 1915 he was sent to Boston, the 1914 champions, just in time to miss the Phillies' first pennant.

Magee's fierce temper caused his five-week suspension in 1911 for knocking out umpire Bill Finneran while arguing over a called third strike. Surprisingly, Magee turned to umpiring himself after his playing days ended, but he spent only one year as a National League arbiter before dying of pneumonia in the spring of 1929.

Sal Maglie

Maglie, Salvatore Anthony **P**

1945, 1950–58 B:4/26/1917, Niagara Falls, NY
D:12/28/1992, Niagara Falls, NY Deb:8/9/1945, NY NL
BR/TR 6'2", 180

W	L	PCT	G	SH	IP	BB	SO	ERA
119	62	.657	303	25	1723	562	862	3.15

When it comes to choosing baseball's most intimidating pitchers, the name Sal "the Barber" Maglie always makes the list. He looked the part. With his dour expression and heavy beard, his picture seemed to belong on a post office wall instead of a baseball card. And he didn't get his nickname because he always looked like he needed a shave, either. It referred to the close shaves he gave hitters with the baseball.

"When I joined the Giants from Jersey City in 1945," Maglie recalled, "Mel Ott told me, 'If you want to make money, you got to beat the Dodgers. Pitch high and tight and low and away.'" Maglie seemed to prefer high and tight.

Maglie worked as a pipefitter until signing a $275-a-month contract with Buffalo in 1938 at the advanced age of 21. He stayed with the Bisons through 1940, then moved on to Jamestown. With Elmira in 1941 he won 20 games and led the Eastern League in innings pitched. The Giants drafted him in November of that year and assigned him to Jersey City.

He didn't pitch in the war years of 1943 and 1944, instead taking a defense-related job back home in Niagara Falls. But he returned to Jersey City in 1945 and made his major league debut later that season as a 28-year-old rookie, going 5–4 with three shutouts and a 2.35 ERA in 84 innings. He didn't pitch in the majors again until 1950.

That's because Maglie was one of the first players to defect to Jorge Pasquel's rebel Mexican League in 1946. The wealthy Pasquel previously had staffed the circuit with a combination of local and Caribbean players and stars from the Negro Leagues. In 1946 he went after major league talent, hitting the Giants particularly hard. Maglie, Ace Adams, Adrian Zabala, George Hausmann, Roy Zimmerman, Nap Reyes, Harry Feldman, and Danny and Al Gardella all headed south.

Conditions were harsh, and before long all wanted to return home. "The buses were driven by madmen," Maglie recalled. "They used to push those old wrecks as hard as they could on those narrow, winding roads in the mountains."

As it turned out, they could go home, but they couldn't play there. All of the so-called "Mexican Jumping Beans" faced a blacklist upon their return. For a while Maglie operated a Niagara Falls gas station. In 1949 he pitched for Drummondville in Quebec's outlaw Provincial League, going 18–6. Joining Maglie in that league were fellow outcasts Adrian Zabala, Roy Zimmerman, Harry Feldman, Danny Gardella, Fred Martin, Max Lanier, and Alex Carrasquel.

Commissioner Happy Chandler reinstated Maglie and the others in November 1949. When he had joined the Mexican League, Maglie had not been a notable figure. But upon returning to the Giants he immediately established himself as one of the National League's premier pitchers.

Maglie began the season in the bullpen, pitched well and finally got a chance to start when Giants manager Leo Durocher decided to make some changes in the rotation in the second half of the season.

Years later Durocher explained his decision to put Maglie in the rotation: "If a guy has 10 suits and somebody steals nine of them, and the guy has to go out that night, well, he's got to wear that one remaining suit. There we were in a lousy (nine-game) losing streak and I had to have a pitcher. I had Maglie and nobody else, so Maglie was it."

Maglie was an immediate success. He pitched an 11-inning victory over St. Louis in his first start and had a league-leading five shutouts in only 16 starts as he compiled an 18–4 record. The secret to his success was a willingness to pitch inside, not to mention one of the great curveballs of his time, a pitch that was all the more effective against righthanded batters who worried about being hit.

"When I'm pitching," Maglie explained, "I figure that the plate is mine, and I don't like anybody getting too close to it. I gotta throw at 'em. Hell, it's my bread and butter."

He was even better in 1951 when the Giants won the pennant with their dramatic stretch run against the Dodgers. He went 23–6 to lead the National League in wins and pitched a whopping 298 innings. Maglie would spend seven more years in the majors but he was never the same. That 298-inning season had put too much strain on his arm.

He was 18–8 in 216 innings in 1952 and then went 8–9 in only 145 innings the next season. He rebounded with a 14–6 record for the 1954 world champions but was waived to Cleveland on July 31, 1955. He was 38 years old.

Maglie was only a spare part to Cleveland Manager Al Lopez, and on May 15, 1956, the pitcher was sold—to Brooklyn. He had pitched well against Brooklyn in a midseason exhibition game in Jersey City, so the Dodgers figured they might as well take a shot for $1,000.

For many Dodgers fans, having Maglie on their side was tough to swallow. As a Giant, he had been evil incarnate. Now he was one of their own. "Even though the Dodgers fought me hard when I was with the Giants," Maglie said, "I don't carry a grudge with the players, because that's their job. And when I got to the Dodgers, they were pretty good. In fact, Carl Furillo became one of my best friends on the club."

At age 39 Maglie went 13–5 for the Dodgers, including the only no-hitter of his career, as he helped the Dodgers win their last pennant in Brooklyn. Don Drysdale remembered charting pitches for Maglie's first start with the Dodgers. "He threw 111 pitches," Drysdale claimed, "and 89 were curves, and of the 89 curves, 85 were strikes." Drysdale also learned a lot about intimidation from the old master, information Drysdale would put to good use.

Maglie pitched his no-hitter against the Phillies on September 25, 1956. Exactly three weeks later he was the victim of a no-hitter—a perfect game. While Don Larsen was making history in Game 5 of the World Series for the Yankees, Maglie was pitching a complete-game five-hitter, allowing only two runs. He had already beaten the Yankees in the Series opener on a complete-game nine-hitter.

The Barber went 6–6 in 19 games for the Dodgers in 1957 before being sold to the Yankees as September pitching insurance; he posted a 2–0 record in six games. After going 3–7 in 17 games for the Yankees and Cards in 1958, he finally retired.

Maglie scouted for the Cardinals in 1959 and was a pitching coach for the Red Sox and Seattle Pilots. In 1987 he suffered a stroke and never recovered, dying of pneumonia in a Niagara Falls nursing home in 1992. Niagara Falls' ballpark was named Sal Maglie Stadium in his honor.

Rick Mahler

Mahler, Richard Keith **P**

1979–91 B:8/5/1953, Austin, TX Deb:4/20/1979, ATL NL
BR/TR 6'1", 202

W	L	PCT	G	SH	IP	BB	SO	ERA
96	111	.464	392	9	1951[1]	606	952	3.99

Before the Atlanta Braves put together the best pitching staff in the 1990s, Rick Mahler held down the fort during the 1980s. A career losing pitcher with a lifetime 3.99 ERA, the righthander wasn't flashy, but he consistently provided 200-plus innings per year.

"You have to admire him," Braves teammate Dave Campbell once commented. "He doesn't have all that much natural ability, and he's had a lot more downs than ups in his career. But he's made himself a good big league pitcher."

Mahler, whose brother Mickey pitched in eight major league seasons, was signed as a free agent by the Braves in June 1975. He played with Kingsport, Greenwood, Savannah, and Richmond before coming to Atlanta in 1979.

A fine batter for a pitcher, Mahler got a hit in his first major league at bat against Chicago on May 5, and went on to hit for a career average of .179. Victories didn't come as easily early on, however. He appeared in 17 games as a reliever in his first two seasons, but did not receive a decision.

Mahler broke into Atlanta's starting rotation at the end of 1981 and pitched a shutout on Opening Day 1982. On September 5, 1982, he had a no-hitter going until Montreal's Al Oliver sent a Mahler pitch into the bleachers. Mahler went 9–10 for the division-champion Braves that season and pitched in relief against the St. Louis Cardinals in the Championship Series.

An excellent fielder with good control on a staff that was pitching-thin, Mahler was allowed to go farther in games than most pitchers. As a result, he led the National League in runs allowed three times, in hits allowed four times, and in losses once, with 18 in 1986.

His best season was 1984 when he went 13–10, with a 3.12 ERA. Mahler pitched two more Opening Day shutouts, in 1986 and 1987. After the 1988 season, he declared free agency and signed with the Reds. He retired after spending time pitching for both Montreal and Atlanta in 1991.

Hank Majeski

Majeski, Henry **3B**

1939–55 B:12/13/1916, Staten Island, NY D:8/9/1991, Staten Island, NY, Deb:5/17/1939, BO NL BR/TR 5'9", 180

G	AB	R	H	HR	RBI	OBP	SLG	AVG
1069	3421	404	956	57	501	.342	.398	.279

In the late 1940s Hank Majeski was perhaps the best defensive third baseman in the American League, setting a major league record in 1948 with a .988 fielding percentage. On August 27, 1948 he recorded six doubles in a doubleheader, establishing a major league record.

Majeski led the I-I-I League in batting in 1937 with a .345 mark and led the International League in hits (198), RBIs (121) and average (.345) in 1942. World War II interrupted his career; he served as a Storekeeper First Class on the USS Pontchartrain.

Majeski was a much-traveled player. Originally the property of the Braves he was sold to the Yankees in September 1942. In June 1946 New York sold him to the Athletics, who in turn traded him to the White Sox in December 1949 for pitcher Ed Klieman. The White Sox sent Majeski back to Philadelphia in June 1951 for shortstop Kermit Wahl. The A's sold him to Cleveland in June 1952. For the Indians he pinch-homered in the 1954 World Series.

After retiring as a player, Majeski coached at Wagner College, scouted for several major league teams, was a batting instructor for the Houston Astros and served as coach for minor league teams such as Oneonta in the New York-Penn League.

"I never could have met finer people anywhere," said Majeski just before his death, regarding his experiences in baseball.

Dave Malarcher

Malarcher, David Julius **3B-2B-SS-OF-C-P**

Negro League Player (1916–34) Manager B:10/18/1894, Whitehall, LA D:5/11/1982, Chicago, IL BB/TR 5'7", 148

"Gentleman Dave" Malarcher was a well-educated and soft-spoken man who also happened to be one of the best ballplayers of his day. The son of sharecroppers who were former slaves, he grew up in rural Louisiana and attended college in New Orleans, where he became captain of his school's baseball team and later played semi-pro ball.

His first professional experience as a player came with the Negro League Indianapolis ABCs in 1916. After military service in France in World War I, he returned to baseball. In 1920 he joined Rube Foster's Chicago American Giants. A switch-hitting speedster, Malarcher exhibited an excellent baseball mind and soon became regarded as the best black third baseman in the game.

He studied the game under Foster and neither drank, smoked, nor argued with umpires. Malarcher's prodigious hitting, scoring, and base stealing led the Giants to consecutive Black World Series championships in 1926 and 1927. Foster made him manager of the club in 1928; Malarcher again led the Giants to the Negro League championship series, but this time they lost.

After two years away from the game, Malarcher returned to the Giants and managed them to additional championships. Later in life he parlayed his handsome baseball salary into real estate and became a prolific published writer and poet.

Pat Malone

Malone, Perce Leigh **P**

1928–37 B:9/25/1902, Altoona, PA D:5/13/1943, Altoona, PA Deb:4/12/1928, CHI NL BL/TR 6', 200

W	L	PCT	G	SV	IP	BB	SO	ERA
134	92	.593	357	26	1915	705	1024	3.74

Cubs sidearmer Pat Malone led the National League in 1929 in wins, strikeouts, and shutouts, and the following year he did the same in victories and complete games. Pierce Leigh "Pat" Malone was a railway fireman at 16 and lied about his age to get into the Army. He started his baseball career with Knoxville in 1921 and was purchased by the Giants but never played for them. He returned to the minors with Waterbury, Toledo, Shreveport, Des Moines, and Minneapolis, before joining the Cubs.

The high-living Malone lost his first seven rookie decisions but managed to finish that 1928 season with a record of 18–13. He was well known for playing pranks on teammates. Among other nocturnal stunts, Malone would trap pigeons off hotel ledges. On one occasion he placed them under the sheets—startling his sleeping roommate, Percy Lee Jones.

After seven seasons with the Cubs, Malone was traded to the Cardinals in October 1934. Before he ever played a game with St. Louis, he clashed with Branch Rickey. Upset with his new boss's salary offer, he snapped, "You made a mistake and sent me the batboy's contract." Rickey solved these sorts of problems in the easiest way. In March, Malone was sold to the Yankees for $15,000. His insubordination may have paid off, as Malone joined a team overflowing with talent. Led by Lou Gehrig, Joe DiMaggio, and Bill Dickey, New York ran away with the 1936 pennant.

Unable to break into a starting rotation that included Lefty Gomez and Red Ruffing, Malone found success in the Yankees bullpen. He led the AL in relief wins and saves in 1936. That fall, he saved Game 3 in the World Series but lost Game 5 when he yielded a sacrifice fly in the 10th inning.

Malone pitched one more season with the Yankees, then spent several years pitching for minor league teams in Baltimore, Minneapolis, and Chattanooga. In retirement he was a farmer and operated a restaurant in Altoona, where he died at the age of 40.

Jim Maloney

Maloney, James William **P**

1960–71 B:6/2/1940, Fresno, CA Deb:7/27/1960, CIN NL BL/TR 6'2", 207

W	L	PCT	G	SH	IP	BB	SO	ERA
134	84	.615	302	30	1849	810	1605	3.19

Cincinnati's fireballing James William Maloney was among the toughest pitchers of the 1960s. He achieved a number of feats that landed him in the record books, including two officially recognized no-hitters. The first, on August 19, 1965, was a 1–0, 10-inning victory over the Cubs. Maloney struck out 12 and walked 10. The second was an April 30, 1969 10–0, 13-strikeout laugher over Houston. Ironically, the following evening Houston's Don Wilson no-hit the Reds and struck out 15.

However, there was also a third no-hitter: On June 14, 1965 Maloney pitched 10-innings of no-hit ball versus the Mets at old Crosley Field. But Maloney and the Reds lost 1–0 in the 11th on a Johnny Lewis home run.

On May 21, 1963 Maloney struck out eight consecutive Milwaukee Braves including Hank Aaron and Eddie Mathews. Two years later, on June 14, 1965, Maloney fanned 18 Mets in an 11-inning game. After retiring as a player Maloney managed Fresno of the California League and operated an auto dealership.

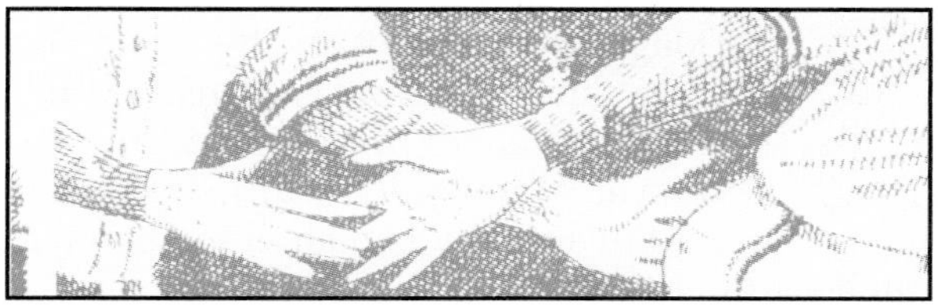

Frank Malzone

Malzone, Frank James **3B**

1955–66 B:2/28/1930, Bronx, NY Deb:9/17/1955, BOS AL BR/TR 5'10", 180

G	AB	R	H	HR	RBI	OBP	SLG	AVG
1441	5428	647	1486	133	728	.318	.399	.274

It was Boston third baseman Frank Malzone's misfortune to be one of the better players in the American League when the Red Sox were one of the worst teams in baseball. Outside of Boston, he is hardly remembered today. As a Sox regular from 1957 through 1965, he made the AL All-Star team six times. A fine defensive player, he batted .274 during his 12-year major league career, knocked in 79 or more runs six times, and hit 133 home runs.

When Frank James Malzone was growing up in the Bronx, his sister formed a neighborhood baseball team on which she was catcher and team captain; Malzone played right field. He went on to lead Samuel Gompers High School to the 1947 city championship. He then signed with the Red Sox in January 1948 for $150 a month. Although he played well during his first few seasons in the minors, he wasn't considered a prospect.

Playing for Scranton in 1950, Malzone shattered his ankle sliding into second base and missed the entire season. He recovered, then spent two years in the Army. Following his release, he continued to perform well. In 1955, while playing for Louisville, he was named the Most Valuable Player of the American Association and was called up by the Red Sox late in the season. In a doubleheader against Baltimore, his first big league start, he banged out six consecutive singles.

Shortly before Christmas that year, Malzone's infant daughter died. Although he held the regular third base job in 1956, Malzone was still distraught and batted only .165 in 27 games. Sent down to San Francisco of the Pacific Coast League, he rebounded to hit .297.

In 1957 Malzone was the AL's best third baseman, leading the circuit in fielding percentage and hitting .292, with a career-high 103 RBIs. In a game against Washington he recorded a then AL-record 10 assists. On May 22, 1957, Malzone, Gene Mauch, Ted Williams, and Dick Gernert tied a since-broken AL record by hitting four homers in an inning.

When fans selected Baltimore's George Kell as the AL starting third baseman in the All-Star Game, Manager Casey Stengel moaned, "Malzone's the hottest thing in our league, and I can't start him," and Kell concurred.

That season the Boston press wanted Malzone to be considered for the Rookie of the Year Award. At the time, it was unclear if he was still considered a rookie, due to his 103 at bats in 1956. The Baseball Writers Association finally appointed a special four-person committee to study the question; the group ruled that Malzone no longer qualified.

During the next few seasons, as the Red Sox went from bad to worse, Malzone continued to shine. He made the All-Star team each season through 1960, then again in 1963 and 1964. In 1965, at age 35, the righthanded hitter was forced to share his third base duties with lefthanded-hitting rookie Dalton Jones, and Malzone slumped to .239.

The Red Sox were in the midst of a youth movement, and Malzone didn't figure in their plans. At season's end Boston shipped him to the California Angels. He retired in 1966, after hitting .206 in only 155 at bats for the Angels that year. Malzone later worked for the Red Sox in a variety of positions, including advance scout.

Gus Mancuso

Mancuso, August Rodney **C**

1928, 1930–45 B:12/5/1905, Galveston, TX D:10/26/1984, Houston, TX Deb:4/30/1928, STL NL BR/TR 5'10", 185

G	AB	R	H	HR	RBI	OBP	SLG	AVG
1460	4505	386	1194	53	543	.328	.351	.265

A good catcher can hang around baseball for a long time, and Gus Mancuso was good enough to play 17 major league seasons. A good backstop need not even hit that well to get a job, but Mancuso finished with a lifetime .265 average. A reliable receiver who could handle difficult deliveries, he knew how to get the most out of the man on the mound. Those skills helped Mancuso reach five World Series with two different organizations.

August Rodney Mancuso got his first look at the big leagues in 1928 with the Cardinals, when he appeared in 11 games. But he didn't really stick until 1930, when he received some playing time while first-string catcher Jimmy Wilson was out of the lineup.

That year Mancuso hit .366 with a career-high .551 slugging average as the Cardinals nosed out the Cubs by two games to win the NL pennant. Mancuso played in only two World Series games that year, but he got two hits in seven at bats.

The 1931 season brought another Series appearance for Mancuso, but he remained a reserve. He hit .262 during the season and again appeared in only two games of the Fall Classic.

In 1932 the Cardinals tumbled to seventh place and used Mancuso as the bargaining chip with which to rebuild their squad. They sent Mancuso and pitcher Ray Starr to the Giants for pitchers Bill Walker and Jim Mooney, outfielder Ethan Allen, and catcher Bob O'Farrell. The trade helped both clubs. Mancuso went on to play in three World Series for the Giants, while Walker went 12–4 in 1934 to help the "Gas House Gang" win the world championship.

With the Giants, Mancuso finally became a first-string catcher, and he played in at least 122 games for four straight years. He batted .264, .245, .298, and .301 during those seasons, averaging 55 RBIs per campaign. His best year at the plate was 1936 when he hit .301, with a career-high nine homers and 63 RBIs. Blessed with an exceptional eye, Mancuso walked more than he struck out in all but two of his big league seasons, and he fanned only 264 times during his entire career.

More important than his hitting, Mancuso proficiently handled a Giants pitching staff that included Carl Hubbell, Hal Schumacher, and Freddie Fitzsimmons. The results could be seen when New York went to three World Series in a span of five years, beating Washington in one and losing to the Yankees twice. In all, Mancuso played in 18 Series games, hitting .173.

In 1937, partly because of a broken finger, Mancuso began to lose playing time, and in 1938 he saw action in only 52 games for the Giants. Normally that pattern would suggest a career winding down, but Mancuso still had enough major league skills to keep teams trading for him.

Following the 1938 season, New York sent him to the Chicago Cubs. After one season at Wrigley Field, Mancuso was on the move again, this time to Brooklyn. In 1941 he returned for his second stint with the Cardinals, playing in 106 games and batting .229. The following season St. Louis dealt him to the Giants for the second time, this time for cash.

In 1943 the 37-year-old Mancuso played in 94 games for the Giants, hitting .198 in 252 at bats. Two years later the Phillies picked him up and he finished his career in 1945 with a 70-game stint in Philadelphia. After his playing career ended, Mancuso managed in the minor leagues, and in 1950 he was a coach the Reds. He was also a broadcaster in both the major and minor leagues.

Les Mann

Mann, Leslie **OF**

1913–28 B:11/18/1893, Lincoln, NE D:1/14/1962, Pasadena, CA Deb:4/30/1913, BOS NL BR/TR 5'9", 172

G	AB	R	H	HR	RBI	OBP	SLG	AVG
1498	4716	677	1332	44	503	.332	.398	.282

It was to St. Louis outfielder Les Mann that Giants pitcher "Shufflin' Phil" Douglas wrote in 1922, offering to lose a key game to Mann's Cardinals. Mindful of the fate of Black Sox third baseman Buck Weaver, Mann quickly turned Douglas in, a move that eventually banished the boozing pitcher from the game.

Leslie "Major" Mann began professionally with Class D Nebraska City in 1910. He then moved on to Seattle, and played briefly in 1913 with Buffalo. He performed with the 1914 "Miracle" Braves, jumping to the Federal League in 1915. With the Chicago Whales he paced the Feds in triples that season.

Mann returned to the National League in 1916 as the Whales merged with the Cubs. As a Cubbie in 1918 he was part of a threatened World Series players strike that quickly fizzled. Traded back to the Braves in August 1919, Mann was waived in November 1920 to the Cardinals. There he was often used as a pinch runner, much to the amusement of Rogers Hornsby, who would tell him: "You're not a ballplayer, you're just a track man."

Released to the Reds in 1923 and once again to the Braves in 1924 he was waived to the Giants in July 1927. After retiring as a player, Mann, an active worker in the YMCA movement, helped found the National Amateur Baseball Association. Under his auspices an exhibition of baseball was held at the 1936 Olympics in Berlin.

Rick Manning

Manning, Richard Eugene **OF**

1975–87 B:9/2/1954, Niagara Falls, NY Deb:5/23/1975, CLE AL BL/TR 6'1", 180

G	AB	R	H	HR	RBI	OBP	SLG	AVG
1555	5248	664	1349	56	458	.319	.341	.257

Excellent defensive center fielder Rick Manning seemed headed for great things when he first arrived with Cleveland in the mid-1970s, but declining prowess with the bat dimmed his career. Richard Eugene Manning signed with Cleveland for a reported $65,000 bonus in 1972 and led the California league in triples and runs scored in 1973. In 1976, Manning's sophomore season, he led AL outfielders in fielding range and was awarded a Gold Glove. As late as 1982 Brooks Robinson said Manning "might be the best center fielder in the league, an outstanding all around defensive player."

Never a power hitter, his batting average dropped as he failed to make better use of his speed. Being with second-division Cleveland did little to help, and he lobbied for a trade, finally going to Milwaukee in June 1983.

On May 15, 1977 Manning struck out five times in a single game. On June 11, 1983 Manning, newly arrived in Milwaukee, recorded 12 center field putouts in a 15-inning contest.

Manning is married to the former Mrs. Dennis Eckersley.

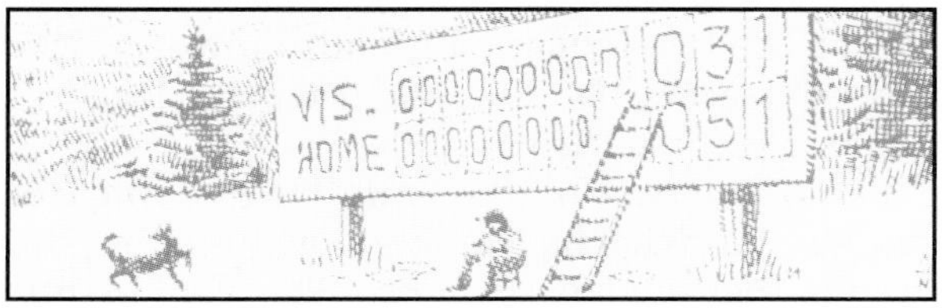

Felix Mantilla

Mantilla, Felix **2B-SS-OF-3B**

1956–66 B:7/29/1934, Isabela, Puerto Rico Deb:6/21/1956, MIL NL BR/TR 6', 160

G	AB	R	H	HR	RBI	OBP	SLG	AVG
969	2707	360	707	89	330	.331	.403	.261

Felix Mantilla was a part of baseball history on May 26, 1959. Pittsburgh's Harvey Haddix had pitched 12 innings of perfect baseball against Milwaukee. Mantilla, a utility infielder, led off the 13th and reached first base on third baseman Don Hoak's throwing error. Following an intentional walk, Joe Adcock homered to right field to win the game.

But there are other memories of Mantilla. Mets fans remember him for his annoying habit of breaking the wrong way on groundballs for the 1962 team that lost 120 games. Red Sox partisans recall him as a power-hitting third baseman who slugged 30 homers in 1964.

Originally a Milwaukee product, Mantilla (born Felix Mantilla Lamela) was a utility infielder on the Braves' pennant winners of 1957 and 1958. The Mets selected him in the October 1961 expansion draft. At the close of the 1962 season, they traded him to Boston for pitcher Tracy Stallard (who had surrendered Roger Maris' 61st homer), infielder Pumpsie Green, and shortstop Al Moran.

Mantilla's three years in Beantown were his best in the majors. He hit .315 in 1963, smacked 30 round-trippers in 1964, and drove in a career-high 92 runs in 1965. In April 1966 he was traded to the Astros for shortstop Eddie Kasko, who eventually became the Red Sox manager. Mantilla retired at the end of the 1966 season after hitting only .219.

Mickey Mantle

Mantle, Mickey Charles **OF-1B**

1951–68 B:10/20/1931, Spavinaw, OK D:8/13/1995, Dallas, TX Deb:4/17/1951, NY AL BB/TR 5'11", 198

G	AB	R	H	HR	RBI	OBP	SLG	AVG
2401	8102	1677	2415	536	1509	.423	.557	.298

Mickey Mantle once remarked, "I could never be a manager. All I have is natural ability." And what ability he had. Mantle's awesome power and speed made him a rightful heir to the legacy of Babe Ruth, Lou Gehrig, and Joe DiMaggio. By the time he retired in 1968, after 18 big league seasons, Mantle ranked among the all-time leaders in home runs and home run percentage, had played in 12 World Series, and had won three Most Valuable Player Awards, two back-to-back.

Mickey Charles Mantle was the son of Oklahoma lead and zinc miner Mutt Mantle. "I always wished my dad could be somebody else than a miner," Mantle once said. "I knew it was killing him. He was underground eight hours a day. Every time he took a breath, the dust and dampness went into his lungs."

Mutt Mantle named his boy after legendary catcher Gordon "Mickey" Cochrane and started him switch-hitting at age 5. "He believed that any kid could develop into a switch hitter if you taught him early enough," recalled Mantle. Mutt would pitch to young Mantle from one side, and Mickey's grandfather would lob the ball to him from the other.

Mantle played football and baseball for Commerce High School, earning the nickname "the Commerce Comet." During one football practice he was kicked in the left shin, and not only did his ankle swell to twice its normal size, but he also developed a 104-degree fever. He eventually developed osteomyelitis (inflammation of the bone marrow) and was threatened with amputation. But at Oklahoma City's Crippled Childrens Hospital, Mantle received penicillin injections every three hours around the clock, and his condition improved almost immediately.

When he recovered, New York Yankees scout Tom Greenwade signed him to a $400-a-month contract. When Mutt Mantle hinted his son could make as much working in the mines and playing ball on Sundays, Greenwade threw in a $1,100 bonus. Greenwade knew at the time he was getting someone special. "The first time I saw Mantle I knew how Paul Krichell felt when he first saw Lou Gehrig. He knew that as a scout he'd never have another moment like it."

Mantle was sent to Independence of the Class D K-O-M League, where he batted .313. He played shortstop and committed 47 errors in only 89 games. His next destination was Joplin in the Class C Western Association, where he hit a league-leading .383 with 26 homers and 136 runs batted in.

"He should lead the league in everything," Yankees manager Casey Stengel said of Mantle before the 1951 season. "With his combination of speed and power he should win the triple batting crown every year. In fact, he should do everything he wants to do."

One thing Mantle couldn't do, however, was play shortstop. He had made 55 errors at Joplin. With Phil Rizzuto still firmly in control of the position in New York, Mantle needed to find another role. He had the speed and range to play center field, but an aging Joe DiMaggio still owned the position, and any attempt to move New York's hero could cause a riot. Stengel tried Mantle in right field.

Mantle went north with the Yankees in 1951 and started on Opening Day. He impressed observers with a 450-foot homer off Randy Gumpert on May 1, but, overall, he had trouble adjusting to big league pitching. The Yankees finally realized that Mantle required more minor league seasoning and shipped him down to Kansas City.

Mantle's hitting slump continued. He called home and told his father, "I don't think I can play baseball any more." The next day Mutt Mantle arrived in Kansas City and started packing his son's belongings into a suitcase.

"What are you doing?" asked Mickey.

"Packing," his father answered. "You're going home. You're going to work in the mine, that's what we'll do. You can go back down there."

That was enough to jolt Mantle out of his slump. During his 40-game stay at Kansas City, he batted .361, hit 11 homers, drove in 50 runs, and was back in Yankee Stadium by the close of August.

In Game 2 of that year's World Series, Mantle tripped over an exposed drainpipe in Yankee Stadium's right-center field. He tore cartilage in his knee and missed the rest of the Series. The day after the injury, Mutt Mantle, a spectator at the World Series, was taken ill. By the next summer he was dead of Hodgkin's Disease, the same malady that had killed Mutt's father.

Mickey Mantle soon developed into a star, but he was still a small-town boy in the big city. He shared an apartment above the Stage Delicatessen with Hank Bauer and Johnny Hopp, and in his first year gained 25 pounds from eating corned beef, cheesecake, and matzo ball soup. He eventually became fast friends with Whitey Ford and Billy Martin—and with that duo, his diet was often more liquid than solid. "Everybody who roomed with Mickey said he took five years off their career," quipped Ford.

In 1957 a fight broke out at New York's Copacabana nightclub involving Mantle and Martin. In an effort to protect Mantle from further trouble the Yankees traded Martin to the Kansas City Athletics. The two remained friends, however. "We used to tease each other about whose liver was going to go first," said Mantle.

Part of the reason for Mantle's high living was his suspicion that he would follow his father and grandfather to an early grave. At age 46 Mantle lamented, "If I knew I was going to live this long, I would have taken better care of myself."

Mantle specialized in monster home runs. One of his most famous was a 565-foot blast at Washington's Griffith Stadium in 1953. "I never saw a ball hit so far. You could have cut it up into 15 singles," marveled Yankees pitcher Bob Kuzava. On May 13, 1955, Mantle hit three homers into the distant Yankee Stadium bleachers. Each cleared the 461-foot sign. On May 23, 1963, he struck the park's right field facade. It was estimated that—had it kept sailing—the ball would have traveled 602 feet.

Many of Mantle's pokes were scored as outs in Yankee Stadium's appropriately named "Death Valley," the deep left-center field portion of the park. Mantle hit 266 homers at home, four fewer than he blasted on the road.

Mantle was perhaps at his finest in the mid-1950s. In 1956 he won the American League Triple Crown with 52 homers, 130 RBIs, and a .353 batting average. He hit three more home runs in the World Series, won the AL Most Valuable Player Award. *The Sporting News* named him Major League Player of the Year.

In 1957 Mantle again won the MVP Award. In the 1957 World Series, Milwaukee second baseman Red Schoendienst came down on Mantle's right shoulder. The injury would hamper Mantle for years, although he would win another MVP Award in 1962, along with a Gold Glove.

In 1961 Mantle and teammate Roger Maris were both in pursuit of Babe Ruth's 60-home run single-season record. In September, Mantle developed a cold he couldn't shake and announcer Mel Allen recommended an East Side physician who could fix him right up—"the best there is." The doctor, garbed in a bloodstained smock, injected Mantle with some mysterious substance that immediately put him into a dizzied, feverish state.

Mantle missed several crucial games and had to have the area where he had been injected cut open and lanced. In the end he played eight fewer games and had 76 fewer at bats than Maris, who had eclipsed Ruth's record by a single homer. The doctor even had the nerve to send Mantle a bill. "I never did pay it," said Mantle. "I wanted to sue. A few years later he stopped practicing."

Even though that malady went away, injuries continued to haunt Mantle. Playing in Baltimore in June 1963, he broke his ankle and was out of the lineup for two months. His first at bat after returning to active duty was a pinch-hit, game-tying homer with two outs in the ninth inning.

But Mantle's best days were over. His damaged shoulder caused him great pain, and in the mid-1960s he had difficulty throwing and even batting from the left side. He played first base the final two years of his career.

During spring training in 1969 Mantle announced his retirement. "I can't play any more," he stated. "I can't hit the ball when I need to. I can't steal second when I need to. I can't go from first to third when I need to. I can't score from second when I need to. I have to quit."

After his retirement Mantle became involved in a number of ventures including a popular restaurant on New York's Park Avenue South. He also announced for a while on NBC's *Saturday Game of the Week*. He was inducted into the Hall of Fame in 1974, his first year of eligibility. When Mantle and Willie Mays worked as public relations representatives for Bally's Park Place Casino in Atlantic City, Commissioner Bowie Kuhn banned them from baseball. Both were reinstated in 1985.

In later years the once-shy Mantle emerged as a raconteur and may, in fact, have been even more popular than he was while playing. In one of his stories St. Peter met him at the Pearly Gates. "Sorry, Mickey," St. Peter said, "because of the way you lived on earth, you can't come in. But, before you leave, would you please autograph these baseballs for Him?"

After a 1993 stay in the Betty Ford Center in California, Mantle also emerged in the unlikely role of clean-living spokesman. He appeared on TV programs to talk about his experiences and to warn kids about drug and alcohol abuse. The transformation was apparently too late for Mantle himself. In 1994 he received a liver transplant at Baylor University Hospital in Dallas. Around the same time, he formed the Mickey Mantle Foundation to raise awareness of the importance of becoming an organ donor.

Ironically, it was during the successful transplant surgery that doctors discovered an inoperable cancer lesion. Mickey Mantle died August 13, 1995 at the age of 63. Bob Costas, who carried the Mick's baseball card in his wallet as an adult in tribute, gave a moving eulogy in New York.

Heinie Manush

Manush, Henry Emmett **OF**

1923–39 B:7/20/1901, Tuscumbia, AL D:5/12/1971, Sarasota, FL Deb:4/20/1923, DET AL BL/TL 6'1", 200

G	AB	R	H	HR	RBI	OBP	SLG	AVG
2008	7654	1287	2524	110	1183	.377	.479	.330

As the Babe Ruth era was dawning, as bigger and stronger players were swinging for the fences instead of poking bloops and chopping liners, Henry Emmett "Heinie" Manush made his way into the Detroit Tiger lineup. In 1921, his first year in the minors, Manush led his league with nine round-trippers. The next season he slugged 20 homers and 20 triples. Detroit's manager Ty

Cobb, the greatest hitter of the "slash-and-poke era," counseled Manush against swinging for the longball. "Choke up on the bat, hit line drives," Cobb told Manush.

Manush listened and learned so well that during his 17 major league seasons Manush batted .330. Six times he ranked among the league's top five hitters. Six times he rapped more than 40 doubles, leading the league twice. Three more times he topped 30 doubles, and in eight years he hit more than 10 triples, including years of 20, 18, and 17.

A lefthanded batter and thrower, Manush platooned in the Tigers outfield with the aging Bobby Veach in 1923, his first major league season. The team was loaded with offensive power. Manush batted .334, Veach .321. At age 36, Cobb still had enough fire to ring up a .340 average. Harry Heilmann batted .403. Warming the bench was porky 25-year-old Bob Fothergill, who hit .315.

In 1924 Cobb gave Manush almost 30 more outfield appearances, but Manush fell victim to the sophomore jinx, and his average tumbled to .289. The next season he batted only 277 times, since Al Wingo took over in left field and batted .370.

But Wingo couldn't maintain his average, and Manush moved back into the lineup full time in 1926. He responded with a .378 average and career-high 14 home runs. Manush began the final day's doubleheader a few points behind Ruth, Fothergill, and Heilmann in the batting race. But Manush went 6-for-9 and finished the season six points ahead of the Babe.

After the 1926 season George Moriarty replaced Cobb (soon implicated in a gambling scandal) as manager, quitting his job as an umpire to take the position. Manush, a Cobb devotee, didn't get along with Moriarty, and his average slumped to .298 although he cracked 18 triples, second in the league.

Manush wanted out, and he got his wish in December 1927 when he was dealt to the St. Louis Browns along with Lu Blue for Chick Galloway, Elam Vangilder, and Harry Rice.

Manush liked Sportsman's Park; its spacious outfield was perfect for his line drive power. He repeated his .378 average of two years earlier, played in every game, was second in the league in at bats, and led the AL with 241 hits. On top of that, he cracked 47 doubles, 20 triples, and 13 homers. But Washington's Goose Goslin, with nearly 150 fewer plate appearances than Manush, took the batting title in his final at bat of the year.

Manush finished third in the 1929 batting race with a .355 mark, leading the league again in doubles, with 45. On June 13, 1930, the Browns and the Washington Nats pulled off a blockbuster trade, exchanging Manush and Alvin "General" Crowder for none other than Goslin. Manush, batting .328 at the time of the trade, hit .362 for his new team to finish at .350, a tie for seventh best in the league.

Manush's average fell to .307 in 1931, but rebounded to .342 in 1932, and his .336 average in 1933 was only three points behind league-leader Jimmie Foxx. He hit safely in 33 consecutive games that year, and his 221 hits and 17 triples topped the league.

That season Manush made his only World Series appearances, but it was not a pleasant Series for the Senators. Bill Terry's Giants trounced them in five games. Manush managed only two singles in 20 plate appearances. Worse yet, in Game 4 he became only the second player to be ejected from a World Series. In the sixth inning Manush grounded into the hole between first and second, but Giants second baseman Hughie Critz made a great play and threw to Carl Hubbell at first for the out. Manush and the other Senators started carping at umpire Charlie Moran.

Suddenly Manush grabbed Moran's bow tie, stretched it out as far as the elastic band would allow, and let it snap back. Manush tried to take his place in the outfield to start the seventh inning, but Moran told him to get out. At first Manush wouldn't leave the field, but his teammates escorted him off. Commissioner Kenesaw Mountain Landis ruled that from that day on no one could be ejected from a Series game without his approval, and the rule stayed as long as Landis did.

Manush finished third in the American League batting race in 1934 behind Lou Gehrig and Charlie Gehringer. The Senators thought he was washed up at age 35 after he hit only .273, his lowest average ever, and they shipped him to the Red Sox.

After Manush hit a meager .291 in 82 games with Boston, the Dodgers picked him up in 1937. He batted .333 in 132 games in what turned out to be his final full season. His major league career ended in Pittsburgh in 1939.

Manush managed in the minors for six more years, and he scouted and coached for the Red Sox and Senators. During his minor league tenure at Rocky Mount, N.C., he instructed a young Johnny Pesky on the art of hitting line drives. Pesky said that Manush altered his stance, repositioned him in the batter's box, and made him a .300 hitter. In 1964 the Veterans Committee voted Manush into the Hall of Fame.

Rabbit Maranville

Maranville, Walter James Vincent SS-2B

1912–33, 1935 M(1925, 23–30) B:11/11/1891, Springfield, MA D:1/5/1954, New York, NY Deb:9/10/1912, BOS NL BR/TR 5'5", 155

G	AB	R	H	HR	RBI	OBP	SLG	AVG
2670	10078	1255	2605	28	884	.318	.340	.258

Rabbit Maranville was a defensive genius. He was also a perennial "league leader" in jokes and pranks, a natural clown who might have had more fun as a baseball player, both on and off the field, than anybody who ever played the game. Always a fan favorite, the shortstop had sure hands that snatched up balls. He was the kind of guy you wanted to have on your ballclub—until you tired of his waggish behavior. That's why he played for five different National League teams during his 23-year career.

For several years after his election to the Hall of Fame it was common for baseball fans who had never seen him play to laugh at the choice. After all, Maranville was a lifetime .258 hitter with 28 home runs.

Bill James responded to these charges in his *Historical Baseball Abstract*: "After hitting .266 in 1920 with one home run, Maranville was traded for three players and $15,000, and the fans were outraged. The perception that he was an extraordinarily valuable defensive player, whether accurate or not, was the perception of his own time, not something that was created after the fact."

Maranville set major league career records at shortstop in several categories including most chances, most putouts, most assists, and most years leading the league in putouts. Among NL shortstops, he holds the record for most years with 500 or more assists and most years leading the league in assists. For the record, he led the league in fielding percentage four times, putouts six times, assists four times, and chances per game three times.

In 1924, Maranville's 13th season in the majors, Glenn Wright was brought in to play short for the Pirates. Maranville, who had never played a major league game at second base, moved to second; during that season, Maranville led the league in fielding percentage, total chances (with a record 933), and double plays.

In 1914, his second full season in the majors, Maranville was an important addition to baseball history. His new double-play partner at second base was the "Crab," the legendary Johnny Evers, who was the centerpiece of the Cubs' "Tinker to Evers to Chance" double-play combination.

With the 33-year-old Evers and the 23-year-old Maranville anchoring the defense, the Boston Braves did something remarkable: 11½ games out and in last place on July 16, they won the pennant by 10½ games and swept Connie Mack's powerful A's in the World Series. Maranville hit only .246 during the season, but he batted .308 with three RBIs during the Series.

The Rabbit kept things lively with the Pirates, Cubs, Dodgers, and Cards before rejoining the Braves for the last six years of his career. One time, during a beanball brawl with the Cubs, the diminutive Maranville tried several times to get into the action but kept getting pushed away. Frustrated, he went to the first base coach's box and began to shadowbox. As he described it, "I got so excited that I gave myself an uppercut and knocked myself out." Turning their attention to Maranville's antics, the fans ignored the fight on the field. The next morning Commissioner Kenesaw Mountain Landis called Maranville to his office to compliment him for preventing a riot.

While Maranville played for the Pirates he sang tenor in a barbershop quartet with Charlie Grimm, Possum Whitted, and Cotton Tierney. The quartet would sing at the mention of beer. Imitating the flappers of the day, the four liked to take batting practice with their socks rolled down.

After a late-season collapse cost the Pirates the 1921 pennant, Bucs Manager Bill "Deacon" McKechnie decided to room with Maranville and his roommate, Moses "Chief" Yellowhorse, during the 1922 season, in hopes of keeping the pair under control.

During the first night of the experiment McKechnie went out for a movie, came home about 10 p.m., and heard both men snoring away. He might have thought his babysitting job was going to be easy. What happened, of course, was that the two wild men had gone out early and had drunk their fill. McKechnie began to undress and opened a closet door, whereupon a flock of pigeons flew out in his face. Emitting a startled roar, he awakened Maranville, who commented, "Hey, Bill, don't open that other closet. You just let out the Chief's pigeons. Mine are over there."

Other tales abound. A thirsty Jim Thorpe once hung the shortstop out of a hotel window by his ankles while demanding a drink. Maranville once stole second by diving between the legs of startled umpire Hank O'Day. And once, while demonstrating a hook slide in a vaudeville act, his vigorous effort took him all the way across the stage into the orchestra pit, over the shoulder of the first violinist, and into a large bass drum.

When Leo Durocher's family moved to Springfield, Massachusetts, Leo's father bragged so much about his son to Maranville that the shortstop had to meet Leo, then a teenager. Maranville, noticing Durocher's small size, gave him lessons on how a small player had to behave. He also gave

Durocher his first baseball glove and even cut out the leather in the pocket for him. He became Durocher's idol.

Maranville tried his hand at managing the Cubs in 1925, but he was no disciplinarian and lasted only 53 games. After the Dodgers released him in 1926 the Cards picked him up and sent him to the minors. The next year he spoke these immortal words: "The national consumption of alcoholic beverages took a sharp downturn after May 24, 1927. That's the day I quit drinking."

After he was brought back to the majors in 1928 he filled a big hole for the Cards at shortstop, and he played 112 games and formed a sensational double-play combination with Frankie Frisch. But Babe Ruth's Yankees swept them in the 1928 World Series.

Maranville was back with the Braves in 1929. Late in the 1933 season the 42-year-old was trying to swipe home as part of a double steal when he shattered two bones in his left leg. The injury kept him out of baseball for the entire season, and he played in only 23 games the next year, his last in the big leagues.

As a 44-year-old player-manager for minor league Elmira in 1936, he hit .323. He also managed in Montreal, Albany, and Springfield, and retired from the game in 1941. He later ran baseball clinics for the Hearst newspapers. Maranville was inducted into the Baseball Hall of Fame in 1954.

Firpo Marberry

Marberry, Fredrick **P**

1923–36 U(1935) B:11/30/1898, Streetman, TX D:6/30/1976, Mexia, TX Deb:8/11/1923, WAS AL BR/TR 6'1", 190

W	L	PCT	G	SV	IP	BB	SO	ERA
148	88	.627	551	101	2067¹	686	822	3.63

Fredrick "Firpo" Marberry was baseball's first great relief pitcher. Although previously a few players had achieved acknowledged success as a closer, no one was as successful as Marberry. Even after he retired, it was years before another reliever matched his fame.

Marberry played little baseball as a youth because farm chores took precedence. When he finally played ball, it was as a third baseman. He became a pitcher when he was 21 years old, and then his blistering fastball quickly gained him a reputation as the region's top young pitcher.

He first pitched professionally in 1922, with Mexia of the Texas-Oklahoma League. Before the year was out he advanced to Little Rock of the Southern Association. In 1923 Washington Senators owner Clark Griffith purchased his contract.

Upon his arrival in Washington, the 6-foot-1, 190-pound righthander was nicknamed "Firpo" due to his resemblance to Luis Firpo, the Argentinean heavyweight who once knocked boxer Jack Dempsey out of the ring before being KO'd himself. Marberry did not particularly care for the epithet, but it stuck.

Although he went 4–0 with the Senators, Marberry was a one-pitch hurler. His fastball overpowered batters for a few innings, but as Marberry tired, he was shelled.

Washington Manager Bucky Harris used him as a spot starter early in the 1924 season, but as the year wore on Marberry saw increasing duty in the bullpen. The results were excellent. He led the AL with 50 appearances, 35 in relief. Although the concept of the "save" was years away, modern research now credits him with a league-leading 15, the best ever at the time.

That season Washington won its first pennant. Ace Walter Johnson won the AL Most Valuable Player, but George Sisler, the St. Louis Browns' manager and star first baseman, pointed out that Marberry was the only important addition to a roster that had finished fourth in 1923.

In the World Series against the New York Giants, Marberry started and lost Game 3, but he picked up two saves in two relief appearances and allowed only one unearned run in three innings in the final game to keep the Senators within striking distance. They tied the score in the eighth and won in the 12th.

In 1925 Marberry's 55 appearances, all in relief, again led the league. In addition, he saved a league-high 15 games and won eight, leading the Senators to a second pennant win. Washington lost the World Series to Pittsburgh, however, and Manager Harris was widely criticized for underutilizing Marberry, who appeared in only two games for a total of 2⅓ innings.

Although the Senators failed to repeat in 1926, Marberry had perhaps his best year as a reliever. In 64 appearances, again the league high, he saved 22 games, a new record. He won three games as a starter and nine in relief.

In spite of his success in the bullpen, Marberry preferred to start. He improved his curve and learned to change speeds, although his fastball remained his "out" pitch. Harris began using him in more starting assignments, less frequently in relief. Yet in 1929 and 1932 Marberry still managed to lead the league in saves, with 11 and 13,

respectively. In 1929 he won 19 games for the Senators, 16 of them as a starter. The following season he won 15 games, including 11 straight.

In December 1932 Washington traded Marberry to Detroit for lefty Earl Whitehill. Used mainly as a starter with the Tigers, Marberry compiled a 16–11 mark, but he missed out on Washington's third and final pennant.

In 1934 Detroit took the American League flag as Marberry contributed a 15–5 season. He appeared twice in relief in the Series, including one outing in which he gave up four runs in two-thirds of an inning, as the Tigers lost to St. Louis.

After only five games in 1935, Marberry lost his touch. The pitcher was immediately hired as an American League arbiter, but he quit just as quickly because he didn't like the isolation of umpiring. When a comeback attempt in 1936 failed, he returned to Texas. There he found success in the wholesale gas distribution business, but an auto accident injury in 1949 limited his activity. Later, he owned and ran a recreation center.

Marberry compiled a career record of 53–37 in relief. He was the first professional ballplayer to relieve in 50 games in a season, the first to relieve 300 times, and the first to record 100 saves. His record 22 saves in 1926 stood until 1947.

Phil Marchildon

Marchildon, Phillip Joseph P

1940–50 B:10/25/1913, Penetanguishene, Ontario, Canada D:1/10/1997, Toronto, Ontario, Canada Deb:9/22/1940, PHI AL BR/TR 5'11", 175

W	L	PCT	G	SH	IP	BB	SO	ERA
68	75	.476	185	6	1214[1]	684	481	3.93

Righthander Phil Marchildon pitched valiantly for bad Philadelphia Athletics teams in the 1940s. His most famous moment came in July 1945 when he returned from nearly a year in German captivity to appear before a practically full house at Shibe Park.

"Fidgety Phil" began his baseball career pitching for mining teams in remote northern Ontario. He later tried out for and signed with the Toronto Maple Leafs. The Leafs farmed him out to Cornwall of the Class C Canadian-American League in 1939. Remarkably, it was not until his signing that the 25-year-old Marchildon heard that there were such organizations as the American or National Leagues.

It was not until he reached the majors at age 27 that anyone bothered to inform him that his mechanics were all wrong; he was throwing across his body. Debuting with the Athletics in 1940, he was shelled in two starts. The following season he was 10–15 and walked 118 batters in 204 innings. In fact, in each of his nine years in the majors he walked more men than he struck out.

In 1942 he posted a 17–14 mark despite leading the league in walks. That was his last year in the American League before he joined the Royal Canadian Air Force. In August 1944 his Halifax bomber was shot down over the North Sea near Denmark. In captivity he dropped nearly 40 pounds.

Marchildon made an emotional yet unsuccessful return in 1946. He tied teammates Dick Fowler and Lou Knerr for the league lead in losses and paced the AL in walks in 1947. On June 24, 1948, he walked 10 batters in one game against St. Louis.

After pitching one game for the Red Sox in 1950, Marchildon retired. In 1983 the Canadian Baseball Hall of Fame made him one of its first five inductees. His autobiography was published in Canada in 1993.

Juan Marichal

Marichal, Juan Antonio P

1960–75 B:10/20/1937, Laguna Verde, Dominican Republic Deb:7/19/1960, SF NL BR/TR 6', 185

W	L	PCT	G	SH	IP	BB	SO	ERA
243	142	.631	471	52	3507[1]	709	2303	2.89

First the leg...the glove...the hand...the pitch. Like a cobra mesmerizing a mongoose, Juan Marichal hypnotized hitters with a striptease-like delivery that made his pitches difficult to follow, much less hit. Working from a no-windup delivery, Marichal threw a fastball, a late-breaking slider that looked like a fastball, and a screwball that positively unhinged lefthanded hitters. Moreover, he delivered them overhand, sidearm, and submarine-style, giving the batter a lot to think about. Pittsburgh outfielder Roberto Clemente said, "It doesn't matter what he throws; when he's got it, he beats you."

Marichal won more than 20 games in six out of seven consecutive seasons for San Francisco, pitched 300 or more innings four times, and won 24 out of 25 decisions at Candlestick Park against the Dodgers. He also tied a record by pitching in eight All-Star Games, two of which he won in 1962 and 1964. In 1965 he won the Arch Ward Trophy as the Game's Most Valuable Player.

Success came naturally to Marichal. "The Dominican Dandy" (full name Juan Antonio Marichal y Sanchez) claimed that he had a good curve by age 10 and that he was working on his screwball by the time he was 15. He led his leagues in both wins and innings pitched in his first two full professional seasons, and his major league debut was a smashing success, a one-hit shutout against the Phillies. To prove it was no fluke, he followed it with another masterful outing, a four-hitter against the Pirates.

After putting together a 6–2 record in his rookie year, he went 13–10, 18–11, then won fewer than

21 games only once over the next seven years. During that stretch he led the league in wins, complete games, shutouts, and innings pitched twice each. In the 1960s, Marichal won 191 games, 27 more than the runner-up, St. Louis hurler Bob Gibson. In fact, Marichal won more games than Gibson in every year of that decade, yet he never won a Cy Young Award. The award was only given out to one pitcher in all of baseball until 1967, plus Sandy Koufax gobbled up three awards in four years.

In 1962 Marichal was called on to pitch the deciding game in the three-game playoff series with the Dodgers. He pitched into the eighth inning, leaving with the Giants behind, although they won in the ninth. Starting Game 4 of the World Series, he had allowed only two hits in four scoreless innings when a Whitey Ford pitch smashed his finger while he was trying to bunt. The injury forced him to leave the game, and he wasn't able to pitch again in the Series.

In June 1963 Marichal pitched the first no-hitter by a Giants pitcher since Carl Hubbell did it in 1929. Then, two weeks later, Marichal and Milwaukee moundsman Warren Spahn battled for 16 innings in one of the greatest pitching matchups of all time. Marichal and the Giants won, 1–0, on a Willie Mays home run.

On August 22, 1965, the Dodgers were playing the Giants. The pennant chase was heating up; so were tempers. Marichal threw two knockdown pitches in the early innings and Dodgers catcher John Roseboro called for Koufax to retaliate when Marichal came to the plate. Koufax's inside deliveries didn't upset Marichal; what set him off was the way Roseboro fired the ball back to Koufax, right past his ear. The Giants pitcher went berserk and clubbed Roseboro over the head with his bat, opening a gash. It took the umpires and both teams to wrest the bat away from Marichal.

For his outrageous actions he was suspended for nine days and fined $1,750. Many felt the penalties were much too lenient. Marichal, 19–9 at the time of the incident, missed two starts and was only 3–4 in his final seven decisions. The Giants lost the pennant to the Dodgers by two games.

Marichal's 1965 and 1966 seasons were two of the best ever by a pitcher. The on-base averages of hitters facing him those years were .240 and .230, statistics that rank Marichal in the all-time best. He slumped in 1967 to 14–10 but then came back to nearly double that win total the following year. His 26 wins led the NL in "the Year of the Pitcher." In 1969 he won his first ERA title.

In 1970 he had a severe reaction to a penicillin injection, which led to chronic arthritis and severe back pain, nearly ending his career. He came back, pitching without his patented fastball but with enough guile and control to win 18 games for the division-winning Giants. He pitched a complete game in Game 3 of the National League Championship Series but lost to Pirate hurler Bob Johnson, 2–1.

Marichal's back problems intensified in 1972, and he had his first losing season ever, managing to win only 6 times while losing 16. After off-season back surgery he went 11–15 and was sold to the Red Sox for the 1974 season, where he was 5–1 in spot starts. He gave his career one final try as a Dodger, although it took special pleading by Roseboro to persuade fans to overlook the 1965 incident. Marichal did not win Hall of Fame selection in his first two years of eligibility. He finally was selected after Roseboro again stood up for him and campaigned for his election, an act for which Marichal thanked him in his induction speech.

Marty Marion

Marion, Martin Whiteford **SS**

1940–50, 1952–53 M(1951–56, 356–372) B:12/1/1917, Richburg, SC Deb:4/16/1940, STL NL BR/TR 6'2", 170

G	AB	R	H	HR	RBI	OBP	SLG	AVG
1572	5506	602	1448	36	624	.323	.345	.263

Called "a regular floating ghost" by Yankees catcher Bill Dickey for his smooth style, lanky Marty Marion was an exceptionally talented shortstop for the Cardinals in the 1940s, the best fielder at his position of his time. Martin Whiteford Marion's slick style may have been a genetic gift—he was a descendant of Sir Francis Marion, the legendary, cunning "Swamp Fox" of the American Revolutionary War. Marty Marion was the recipient of two highly descriptive nicknames: "Slats," for his long legs and skinny torso, and "Octopus," for his long arms and ability to snatch up ground balls.

Marion was named to seven consecutive National League All-Star teams and started in five All-Star Games. During his tenure as part of St. Louis' solid defense up the middle along with center fielder Terry Moore and catcher Walker Cooper, the Cards won three World Series in four tries. In his peak years, from 1941 through 1949, the Cards either won the NL flag or finished second each season, finishing more than five games back only once.

Marion was severely injured in a childhood accident. After tumbling to the bottom of a 20-foot embankment, he spent more than half a year in a body cast. On crutches for a year after the cast was removed, his right leg was rendered permanently shorter, giving him a trick knee that could pop out of place at any time. The knee kept him out of the military during World War II and also probably shortened his baseball career.

After four seasons in the minors Marion became a Cardinal in 1940, quickly taking over the shortstop job. In 1942 Marion's Cardinals captured the pennant by winning 106 games, the most by a National League team since the 110 victories by the 1909 Pirates. The Dodgers won 104 games to finish second. Marion led the league that year with 38 doubles, the only time he topped the league in an offensive category. Batting eighth, he wasn't in the lineup for his offense.

The Cardinals looked overmatched as they began the 1942 World Series against the vaunted Yankees. In Game 1 they didn't manage a hit off Red Ruffing until Moore singled with two out in the eighth. The Yankees were coasting with a 7–0 lead when Marion came to bat in the last of the ninth with two men on and two out. He tripled to right, driving in St. Louis' first runs. Before the dust settled the Cardinals had scored twice more. Although they lost that game, 7–4, their postseason jitters had passed, and they went on to win the next four games, handing Joe McCarthy his only Series defeat with the Yankees.

In the third inning of a scoreless Game 3 Marion bunted and was thrown out, but McCarthy argued that the bunt was fielded in foul territory. The umpires agreed, giving Marion a second chance. This time he beat out the bunt and the Cards went on to score the only run they'd need, eventually winning, 2–0. Marion had only two hits in the Series, but he took part in three double plays and had 16 assists.

In 1943 the Yanks and the Cards met again in the World Series, and, once more, the Yanks could not get Slats out. His .357 average and .714 slugging average led all players. Marion's homer in Game 2 was one of few Cardinal highlights as the Yankees toppled St. Louis in five games.

In 1944 Marion batted .267 with 26 doubles, two triples, and six home runs. He scored 50 runs and knocked in 63. Although many players in the league posted better stats, Marion was voted NL Most Valuable Player that year by one point over Bill Nicholson, who hit 33 home runs. Obviously Marion, the league fielding-percentage leader, was being rewarded for his exceptional defense, joining Bob O'Farrell and Roger Peckinpaugh as one of the few MVPs honored almost solely for their glove work.

The Cardinals outdistanced the Pirates by more than 14 games in 1944 and took on the crosstown rival Browns, in St. Louis' only intracity World Series. The Series featured three one-run games, and the Cardinals finally prevailed in six. Marion led all fielders with 22 assists.

Knocked from the top in 1945 by the Cubs, the Cards finished in a tie with Brooklyn for the league title in 1946. Marion had two RBIs in the second game of the playoffs as the Cards swept the best-of-three series from the Dodgers. In the World Series they faced the Red Sox.

Cardinals manager Eddie Dyer employed a version of "the Williams Shift" against Sox slugger Ted Williams. Marion stayed at short, but third baseman Whitey Kurowski moved behind second. The frustrated Williams actually bunted to third for a base hit in Game 3. (Boston newspapers screamed "TED BUNTS!") Marion's two-base throwing error in Game 5 helped give the Sox a 3–2 Series lead, but his two hits and an RBI pushed St. Louis to a Series-tying 4–1 win in Game 6. The Cards won the Series in Game 7 as Enos Slaughter scored from first on Harry Walker's hit.

The 1946 season proved significant for another reason: the first rumblings of unionization in baseball were heard. Although owners managed to quash union activities, Marion was active in convincing them to contribute funds for the players' benefit. At his instigation a pension plan was established. In 1950 he and Fred Hutchinson barged into an owners' meeting to demand that the players have some say in the administration of their pension funds.

In 1950 Marion hit the first and only grand slam of his career, but the Cardinals finished in the second division for the first time since 1938. The following season Marion replaced Eddie Dyer as manager. A back injury kept him from playing, but he brought the team back to third place. The next year the Cards brought in Eddie Stanky to manage and released Marion.

In 1952 he served as a playing coach for the Browns under Rogers Hornsby. When the abusive Hornsby alienated everyone after 48 games, Marion replaced him. The Browns finished seventh, and when they fell back to eighth in 1953 he was fired. With nine games left in the 1954 season, Marion replaced Paul Richards at the White Sox helm, and he directed them to three third-place finishes.

Marion eventually moved into minor league management. He owned the Houston franchise in the Texas League, and later returned to St. Louis to manage the Cardinals' Stadium Club for 18 years.

Roger Maris

Maris, Roger Eugene **OF**

1957–68 B:9/10/1934, Hibbing, MN D:12/14/1985, Houston, TX Deb:4/16/1957, CLE AL BL/TR 6', 204

G	AB	R	H	HR	RBI	OBP	SLG	AVG
1463	5101	826	1325	275	851	.348	.476	.260

No record ever hung around a player's neck more like an albatross than Roger Maris' 61 homers in 1961. As late as the 1980 All-Star Game he fumed, "They acted as though I was doing something wrong, poisoning the record books or something. Do you know what I have to show for 61 home runs? Nothing. Exactly nothing."

In surpassing Babe Ruth's supposedly unsurpassable record, Maris faced the hostility of the baseball public on several fronts. First, although he had been the 1960 American League Most Valuable Player, he was basically a .269 hitter, still an unknown quantity unworthy of dethroning America's greatest sports hero. That he played the game with a ferocious intensity and that he was a brilliant right fielder and an exceptional baserunner, well, that was irrelevant.

Second, for most of the season Maris wasn't the only batter chasing the ghost of the Babe. His teammate Mickey Mantle, the successor to Ruth, to Lou Gehrig, and to Joe DiMaggio, was the people's choice. It was Mantle who hit 500-foot home runs that thrilled fans. It was Mantle who garnered support as the season-long chase headed toward September.

Maris? He was merely efficient, a lefthanded hitter who had just the swing to take advantage of that friendly porch in Yankee Stadium's right field. He rarely hit a homer more than 400 feet. His charisma quotient was almost nonexistent.

That 1961 season was the first year of expansion and the first year of the 162-game season. With the addition of two teams to the American League, many hitters had their greatest seasons, such as Norm Cash, who somehow hit .361. Expansion also meant an expanded schedule. Ruth had set his record in 1927 in a 154-game season. So for many people, Maris' feat would be tainted if he needed more than 154 games to break Ruth's record. Commissioner Ford Frick even announced that if Maris took more than 154 games to break the record it would go into the record books as a separate accomplishment from Ruth's—with an asterisk, so to speak.

"As a ballplayer, I would be delighted to do it again," Maris once remarked. "As an individual, I doubt if I could possibly go through it again. They even asked for my autograph at mass."

As always, Maris was being honest. He once said about playing baseball for living, "It's a business. If I could make more money down in the zinc mines, I'd be mining zinc." Could anyone have been more un-Ruthian?

Roger Eugene Maris was born in Hibbing, Minnesota. His family moved to Fargo, North Dakota, where he was an All-State halfback and was courted by University of Oklahoma football coach Bud Wilkinson. Maris left the Oklahoma campus after one look at the entrance examination.

A star in American Legion ball, Maris' next stop was a tryout with the Cleveland Indians under the supervision of Hank Greenberg, who once hit 58 home runs. "Have your father phone me as soon as you get home," Greenberg told Maris. Instead, Maris stopped off at Wrigley Field to see what the Cubs would offer him. The answer was exactly nothing. "Go home," the Cubs told him. "You'll never make it."

So Maris signed with Cleveland for a $5,000 bonus with another $10,000 promised if he made the majors. As soon as he arrived at the Indians' minor league camp he showed a stubborn streak that was an integral part of his personality. He refused to accept assignment to any Class D team and said he would accept a Class C assignment only if he were sent to the Indians' team in Fargo.

"We never let a boy play in his hometown," Cleveland farm director Mike McNally told him. "It subjects him to too much pressure."

"Not me," replied Maris. "I'm going to Fargo. That's definite. Now it's up to you to decide whether I go there just to live on my own or whether I go there to play ball for Cleveland."

He went to Fargo and hit .325 with only nine homers. Nevertheless he delivered another ultimatum: "Move me up to Class B, or I quit." The Indians sent him to Keokuk in the Class B 3-I League where his manager, Jo-Jo White, gave him some valuable advice. "Look, boy," White told him, "you're not a singles hitter. You're big and you've got power. Pull that ball to right field and see what happens."

Maris continued to alienate the Indians when he refused general manager Frank Lane's request for him to play winter ball. "Not me," Maris said. "I've been away from my wife and family too long. I'm going home."

Stubborn or not, Maris made it to the big leagues in 1957 at age 22. For a while he led the American League in homers and RBIs. Then he broke three ribs in a headfirst slide and ended up hitting .235, with 14 homers and 51 RBIs.

In June 1958 the Indians traded Maris and two others to Kansas City for Vic Power and Woodie Held. Maris, despite a .240 average, had 28 homers and 80 RBIs. The following year he was off to another good start when an appendix operation caused him to miss 45 games. Then came the trade that changed his life: in the off-season he was traded to the Yankees with Kent Hadley and Joe DeMaestri.

Maris was unusually tractable on his arrival in the Bronx. "I'd rather play right," he announced, "but I'm willing to play where the manager thinks I'll help the most." In his first game in pinstripes, Maris singled, doubled, and smacked two home runs. His MVP numbers included a league-leading 112 RBIs and 39 home runs, only one behind league-leader Mantle, although Maris missed 18 games with injuries.

In 1961 he stayed healthy and played 161 games, a career high. As he and Mantle made their charge at Ruth's home run record, the Yankees even considered switching Maris, who batted third, and Mantle, who batted fourth, to give Mantle a better shot at the record. If the switch had been made, Maris almost certainly would not have broken the record. Consider this: Maris did not receive one intentional walk in 1961. After all, who would walk Maris to get to Mantle?

The pressure to beat Ruth became so intense for Maris that clumps of his hair fell out. "I never wanted all this hoopla," Maris said. "All I wanted is to be a good ballplayer, hit 25 or 30 homers, drive in around a hundred runs, hit .280, and help my club win pennants. I just wanted to be one of the guys, an average player having a good season."

Mantle fell back in the middle of September when he suffered a hip injury. Maris kept it up and went into the season's 154th game in Baltimore with 58 homers. He gave it his best shot that night. He hit No. 59 and then hit a long foul on his second-to-last at bat. Alas, in his last at bat, against Hoyt Wilhelm, he hit a checked-swing grounder.

"Maybe I'm not a great man, but I damn well want to break the record," he said. He finally did it on the last day of the season against the Boston's Tracy Stallard. Fittingly it went about 340 feet into Yankee Stadium's right field porch.

Maris made back-to-back MVP honors, driving in a league-leading 142 runs. But 1961 was his last great season. He fell to 33 homers and 100 RBIs in 1962 as the Yankees won their third straight pennant, and then he was hit by a string of injuries during the next four seasons as the Yankees dynasty crumbled.

New York traded him to the Cardinals after he hit only .233, with 13 homers and 43 RBIs, in 1966. He left an angry man. The Yankees had questioned his courage for complaining constantly about a sore hand. It was only after the trade that he found out he'd played most of the season with a broken bone in his hand, which the Yankees doctors hadn't been able to diagnose.

Maris lasted two years with the Cards. Injuries had diminished his skills, but he was a useful member of two pennant-winning teams. A grateful Gussie Busch set him up with a lucrative beer distributorship after he retired.

Roger Maris died in December 1985 of lymphatic cancer. He was only 51. Babe Ruth's record of 60 home runs had lasted 34 years. Maris' record lasted 37 years—until both Mark McGwire and Sammy Sosa surpassed it in 1998.

Rube Marquard

Marquard, Richard William **P**

1908–25 B:10/9/1889, Cleveland, OH D:6/1/1980, Baltimore, MD Deb:9/25/1908, NY NL BB/TL 6'3", 180

W	L	PCT	G	SH	IP	BB	SO	ERA
201	177	.532	536	30	3306^2	858	1593	3.08

In his first big league start, in 1908, Rube Marquard hit the first batter, walked the next two, and then gave up a grand slam homer to Cincinnati catcher Hans Lobert. Since the New York Giants had paid a then-record $11,000 for his services, Marquard quickly became known as "the $11,000 Lemon." One day, however, he would be known as a Hall of Famer.

Richard William Marquard began his professional ballplaying career with Canton of the Central League in 1907, and the next year he played with Indianapolis of the American Association, which had optioned him to Canton the previous season. Marquard pitched brilliantly for Indianapolis in 1908, going 14–6, with six shutouts and a 1.58 ERA.

That year he intimidated another hot rookie, "Smokey Joe" Wood of Kansas City, by saying, "If I was you I wouldn't warm up now... I'm gonna beat you." Marquard delivered on his promise, winning, 2–1. When a local sportswriter noted his resemblance to lefthander Rube Waddell, Marquard became known as Rube for the rest of his career.

That fall, with several big league scouts in attendance, he pitched a perfect game, and the bidding for his services grew fast and furious. Cleveland, for whom Marquard had worked as a batboy, went to $10,500 before the Giants won the auction by bidding $11,000, the highest sum paid for a player up to that time.

The $11,000 Lemon went 5–13 in 1909 and registered a 4.46 ERA the following year. No one, not even Marquard's roommate, moundsman Christy Mathewson, could figure out exactly what had happened to the promising young fireballer.

However, in 1911 Marquard won his first three starts. By the time he had won 10 straight, Marquard had become "the $11,000 Beauty." Before his streak ended, he was credited with 19 straight wins, although he also won an uncredited 20th in relief of Jeff Tesreau. Marquard shares the major league record for consecutive wins with righthander Tim Keefe, although Keefe pitched from 50 feet away in 1888 and was credited with one win after pitching only the first inning.

Buoyed by his streak, Marquard finished 24–7 to lead the league in won-lost percentage (.774) and strikeouts (237). He still holds the major league record for most victories by a 21-year-old. In 1912 he tied the Cubs' Larry Cheney for most wins, with 26, and helped pitch the Giants to a second straight pennant. In Game 3 of the World Series against Boston, Marquard again hooked up with Joe Wood, once more beating him by a 2–1 score, then allowing only two unearned runs in Game 6 to win, 5–2.

That fall Marquard and his wife, singer Blossom Seeley, were the toast of vaudeville. They co-wrote a song entitled "The Marquard Glide," part of which went:

Stood up through all the knocks,
Had it on those "Red Sox"
You can bet all your rocks
On Reuben! Reuben!

Rube glided to 23 more wins in 1913, when two other Giants hurlers—Mathewson (25) and Jeff Tesreau (22)—also won more than 20 games. In one contest the following year Marquard went all the way to beat Pittsburgh's Babe Adams, 2–1, in 21 innings.

However the following season Marquard became one of the few major league pitchers to win 20 games one season and lose 20 the next. His record was 12–22 and the Giants failed to win the pennant for the first time since 1910. In 1915 he no-hit the Dodgers and Nap Rucker, 1–0, but that August the Giants waived Marquard to Brooklyn.

Marquard helped the Robins win the pennant in 1916, with a 13–6 record and a career-low 1.58 ERA. But he lost two games to Boston in that year's World Series. In 1917, his last great season, he went 19–12.

Two months after he lost the opening game of the 1920 World Series on two unearned runs, Brooklyn traded Marquard to the Reds. His major league career ended four years later with the Braves. He then coached in the minors and in 1931 umpired in the Eastern League before finally leaving baseball. The Veterans Committee elected him to the Hall of Fame in 1971.

Mike Marshall

Marshall, Michael Grant **P**

1967, 1969–81 B:1/15/1943, Adrian, MI Deb:5/31/1967, DET AL, BR/TR 5'10", 180

W	L	PCT	G	SV	IP	BB	SO	ERA
97	112	.464	723	188	1386²	514	880	3.14

The first reliever to win the Cy Young Award, Mike Marshall is best remembered for his iron-man work from the bullpen and for being a somewhat surly, extraordinarily intelligent "flake." He did things his way, did them well, and really didn't care what anyone else thought.

When Michael Grant Marshall was 11, a train struck a car he was riding in; the driver—his uncle—was killed, and Marshall's back was badly injured. The boy eventually recovered to become a three-sport star at local Adrian High School, but the injury sparked his deep interest in the mechanics of the human body.

After graduation in 1961, Marshall was offered a modest bonus from the Philadelphia Phillies and a baseball scholarship to Michigan State University. He claimed that MSU reneged on its scholarship offer, so he signed with the Phillies, but he later enrolled at MSU.

Marshall began his professional career as a shortstop. Although he hit well, his fielding was often atrocious. In three of his four seasons as a minor league infielder, he led the league in errors. Purchased by Detroit in 1962, Marshall's bothersome back forced him to abandon the infield and become a pitcher.

He progressed relatively quickly through the Tigers farm system and spent much of the 1967 season with Detroit. That year he pitched 59 innings, with an ERA of only 1.98, but the club returned him to the minors. Drafted by the expansion Seattle Pilots, Marshall pitched poorly in 1969 before the team sold him to Houston, which eventually traded him to the Expos in 1970.

He blossomed in Montreal. In 1971 the righthander developed a screwball, which finally gave him a weapon to use against lefthanded batters. The next season Marshall became one of the best relievers in baseball, appearing in a league-leading 65 games and collecting 14 wins and 18 saves, with an ERA of 1.78.

All the while, Marshall continued to attend college during the off-season. He quarterbacked an intramural football team that twice won the college championship, and in the classroom he specialized in physical education. He became obsessed with kinesiology, the study of the principles of mechanics and anatomy as they relate to human movement.

Marshall developed his own theories of pitching. He adopted a bizarre pickoff move to second base, twisting his body toward first and slinging the ball to second, and he believed he pitched best if he could work four or five times per week. In 1973 Marshall appeared in 92 games for the Expos, pitching 179 innings, and leading the National League with 31 saves.

Traded to the Dodgers for outfielder Willie Davis the following year, he responded with one of the more remarkable seasons a relief pitcher has ever had. He set a major league record by appearing in 106 games and pitching 208 relief innings. Between June 18 and July 3 he pitched in 13 consecutive games. Marshall won 15 games, saved 21, was named Cy Young Award winner, and helped the Dodgers win the pennant. In the 1974 World Series he appeared in all five games and gave up only a single run in nine innings as the Dodgers lost to Oakland.

Knee surgery and an injury to his ribcage hampered his performance during the next several seasons. He was traded to Atlanta and then Texas, where his troublesome back gave out. Marshall underwent surgery after the 1977 season and temporarily retired before Minnesota Manager Gene Mauch convinced him to try a comeback.

In 1978 Marshall earned his doctorate and returned to form on the mound, saving 21 games. He then declared free agency and signed a four-year, $1.2 million contract with the Twins. He saved another 32 games in 1979, though his 14 relief losses tied an AL record.

The following season physical ailments felled him again, and he appeared in only 18 games. He retired in 1981 after appearing in only 20 games for the New York Mets. He has since worked in academics, developing physical education programs for children.

Billy Martin

Martin, Alfred Manuel **2B–SS**

1950–53,1955–61 M(1969, 1971-83, 1985, 1988, 1,253–1,013) B:5/16/1928, Berkeley, CA D:12/25/1989, Johnson City, NY Deb:4/18/1950, NY AL BR/TR 5'11½", 165

G	AB	R	H	HR	RBI	OBP	SLG	AVG
1021	3419	425	877	64	333	.301	.369	.257

Alfred Manuel "Billy" Martin battled his way through life. As a player, coach, and manager, Billy Martin hustled on ballfields and traded punches with everyone from a marshmallow salesman to his own pitchers. He served five separate stints as Yankees manager under volatile club owner George Steinbrenner.

"He's the kind of guy you'd like to kill if he's playing for the other team," Cleveland general manager Frank Lane said in 1959, "but you'd like 10 of him on your side."

As a player, Martin's defining on-the-field moment came during Game 7 of the 1952 World Series. With the Yankees up 4–2 in the seventh inning, the Dodgers had the bases loaded and two out. Jackie Robinson hit a wind-blown infield popup in the vicinity of first baseman Joe Collins. Collins, however, seemed to lose sight of the ball, and neither he nor pitcher Bob Kuzava nor third baseman Gil McDougald went after it. Martin darted in and caught the ball at knee-level, snuffing out the Dodgers rally.

In 1953 Martin won the World Series' Most Valuable Player Award after the six-game victory over the Dodgers. For the Series he batted .500, with 12 hits, two homers, and eight RBIs.

Martin's defining off-the-field moment got him banished from the Yankees. At the Copacabana nightclub in May 1957 to celebrate teammate Mickey Mantle's birthday, Martin was involved in a fight in which a Bronx delicatessen owner suffered a concussion and a fractured jaw. Despite manager Casey Stengel's affection for Martin, whom he had managed at Oakland in 1948 and insisted that New York acquire, Martin was held responsible for the affair. He was traded to Kansas City, breaking up the triumvirate of Mantle, Martin, and Whitey Ford.

Martin's playing career ended after the 1961 season. He subsequently served an apprenticeship as a coach, scout, and minor league manager. He then began a major league managing career that consistently saw him lift teams in the standings, and yet annoy ownership so much that he was fired time and again.

He won 97 games and a division title with the Twins as a rookie manager in 1969. The next year he was gone. In 1971 he raised the Tigers from fifth to second, and then to first in 1973. He was terminated at season's end. In 1974 he brought the Rangers from sixth to second but was fired in midseason 1975. He brought Oakland from sixth to second in 1980 and during the 1981 split season also delivered a first-half pennant. But he was gone at the end of the 1982 season.

In 1975, when Steinbrenner engaged him as Yankees manager, Martin's odyssey as keeper of the Bronx Zoo began. The New York skipper captured a pennant for Steinbrenner in 1976 and a world championship in 1977.

Martin's tenure as Yankees manager, however, was marked by numerous clashes with the owner, five hirings and five firings, and battles with stars Thurman Munson and Reggie Jackson. One altercation with Jackson was broadcast on national television. "If you approach Billy Martin right, he's okay," said Yankees ace Ron Guidry at the time. "I avoid him altogether."

As a manager, Martin became involved in several highly publicized brawls, including an August 1969 flattening of pitcher Dave Boswell outside a Detroit bar. In September 1974, "Billy the Kid" punched 64-year-old Texas Rangers traveling secretary Burt Hawkins because of a disagreement about whether the Rangers wives should organize a club or not. And in October 1979 in Bloomington, Minnesota, he went one round with marshmallow salesman Joseph N. Cooper. "Lots of people look up to Billy Martin," former Yankees pitcher Jim Bouton once observed. "That's because he just knocked them down."

A poll of 600 former players conducted in 1987 rated Martin the eighth-best manager of all time—behind Stengel, Joe McCarthy, Walter Alston, John McGraw, Connie Mack, Earl Weaver, and Al Lopez and ahead of such contemporaries as Whitey Herzog, Sparky Anderson, and Tommy Lasorda.

Billy Martin died on Christmas Day, 1989, in a car crash near his home in Johnson City, New York. He was 61 years old.

Pepper Martin

Martin, John Leonard Roosevelt OF–3B
1928, 1930–40, 1944 B:2/29/1904, Temple, OK D:3/5/1965, McAlester, OK Deb:4/16/1928, STL NL BR/TR 5'8", 170

G	AB	R	H	HR	RBI	OBP	SLG	AVG
1189	4117	754	1227	59	501	.358	.443	.298

No one ever played baseball harder than John Leonard Roosevelt "Pepper" Martin. Though he was seldom graceful, he was fast—very fast—which made his reckless style an even sharper weapon. After seeing him play football, a sportswriter nicknamed him "the Wild Horse of the Osage." Martin explained his speed simply. "Well, I grew up in Oklahoma and out there, once you start running there ain't nothing to stop you."

Martin had a solid career, batting .298 lifetime, scoring more than 120 runs three times, and leading the National League in stolen bases three times. But it was the way he made his grand entrance—with an astounding performance in the 1931 World Series—that earned him a place in baseball history.

The Philadelphia A's were playing in their third consecutive World Series in 1931, and the team of Mickey Cochrane, Lefty Grove, Al Simmons, Jimmie Foxx, and George Earnshaw had humiliated the Cubs in the 1929 Fall Classic and had topped the Cardinals in 1930.

The difference between 1930 and 1931 was that the 1930 Cardinals didn't have Pepper Martin. After six years in the minors, Martin had simply hustled his way into the Cards center field position, prompting outfielder Taylor Douthit's trade early in the season.

Martin tore the potent A's apart in the Series. He batted .500, scored five runs, stole five bases, had 12 hits and four doubles—all tops in the Series. Commissioner Kenesaw Landis said to a friend, "Did you ever see anything like that Martin's performance? Why, there were times when I thought he would steal Mickey's [Cochrane] underwear."

The Series started with a ho-hum win for A's fans. Lefty Grove beat the Cards, 5–2, although he allowed an unusual 12 hits, three by Martin. Martin also swiped second base when the A's weren't paying attention: they were arguing over the call on outfielder Chick Hafey's steal of third.

Game 2 was all Martin: he had a double and a single, swiped two bases, and scored the only two runs of the game. He hit a double and scored two runs in Game 3 as the Cardinals beat Grove, 5–2. The Cards lost Game 4, 3–0, with only two hits off George Earnshaw. Martin had both of them, one a double, and stole another base.

Martin took center stage again in Game 5. He drove in the Cards' first run with a fly ball to the left-field wall in the first inning, then beat out a bunt to open the fourth, hit a two-run homer in the sixth, and singled to drive in a run in the eighth. He drove in four of the Cardinals' five runs as they won, 5–1. At that point Martin was hitting a remarkable .667, with 12 hits in five games. No one before or since has had more hits in a Series. The A's tightened their belts and kept Martin hitless the rest of the Series, but they couldn't keep him out of the action.

After losing Game 6, the Cardinals stormed back in Game 7. Martin walked and stole second to keep a two-run rally alive in the first inning. When the A's threatened in the ninth, Martin made the final catch of a sinking line drive with two on and two out. Martin's domination of the Series against a superior team was complete.

After the Series Martin went hunting back home. While sleeping in the tall grass one night, he suffered a nasty insect bite, and the result was an unpleasant, relentless skin infection. He got into just 85 games in 1932, playing some with a broken finger that no one knew about until a throw to first left a trail of bandage. When asked about it, he said, "It was just a small bone."

Moved to third base full time in 1933 to make outfield room for Joe Medwick, Martin stumbled, stammered, took balls off his chest, and threw wildly. His frustration showed in his batting average and behavior. In the final game of an early-season Cardinals homestand, Martin flung his bat into the dugout after a strikeout, chased it, and gave the bat rack a mighty boot, causing the whole pile to go flying. One landed in the lap of Mrs. Sam Breadon, wife of the Cardinals' owner. Martin was heavily booed; it was the low point of his career.

But the Cards were beginning a road trip, so manager Gabby Street decided to keep Martin at third. By the time they returned home, he was learning the position (although still playing like a wild man), and his batting eye was back. He finished the season at .316, leading the league with 122 runs scored. The Cards improved their record by 10 games, largely due to the addition of a loose-limbed Arkansas pitcher named Dizzy Dean.

As a third baseman, Martin's brutal style of play assured that his body would always be banged up. With his back aching in a game against Boston, he told the Braves they'd better not bunt. When the first batter disobeyed, Martin fired the ball at him, not the first baseman. After he hit the second bunter between the shoulder blades with a flaming toss, the bunt was dropped from the Braves' playbook for the day.

In 1934 the "Gas House Gang"—the wacky, fun-loving, hard-charging Cardinals—made their mark, and Martin was their leader. He played guitar in the Gang's Mudcat Band and kept the Cardinals loose by dropping water balloons on sportswriters, attaching smoke bombs to the spark plugs of fancy cars, and releasing sneezing powder in hotel lobbies. Playing an exhibition game once in fading light, he had trouble locating a line drive—until he pulled a flashlight out of his pocket.

That season Martin led the National League in stolen bases for the second consecutive year. With Dizzy and Paul Dean combining for 39 wins, first baseman Ripper Collins belting 35 home runs, and young Medwick hitting 18 triples, the Gang outlasted the Giants and made it to the World Series, this time against the Tigers.

Martin was in the middle of the action once again in the Fall Classic. He drove in a run and scored one as the Cardinals overpowered the Tigers, 8–3, in Game 1. He scored one run in a 12-inning, 3–2 Game 2 loss. And with a double and triple in Game 3, he scored half the team's runs in a 4–1 win.

Martin's poor hands at third resulted in three errors in Game 4, but he contributed three singles and two stolen bases as the Cardinals took Games 6 and 7. They were once again champions of the world. Martin's 11-hit total tied three other players for the Series high.

After 1936 Martin's playing time was reduced to fewer than 100 games a year. His batting averages stayed consistently close to .300, but his base stealing ability had left him. In 1940 he batted .316, then returned to the minors for several years as a player-manager. When World War II depleted the Cardinals' roster, Martin came back, played in 40 games in 1944, and retired.

He coached for the Cubs in 1956. A prosperous cattle rancher, he served as director of the Oklahoma State Penitentiary for a time. He was managing the Tulsa Oilers in 1965 when he died of a heart attack.

Dennis Martinez

Martinez, Jose Dennis (Emilia) **P**

1976–98 B:5/14/1955, Granada, Nicaragua
Deb:9/14/1976,BAL AL BR/TR 6'1", 185

W	L	PCT	G	SH	IP	BB	SO	ERA
245	193	.559	692	30	3999[2]	1165	2149	3.70

After seven full seasons of major league baseball, Dennis Martinez was a world champion, an 89-game winner, and a 28-year-old alcoholic. But Martinez not only battled back from his disease, he pitched 15 more years to become the winningest Latin American pitcher in major league history. After age 35 he made the All-Star team four times, won an ERA title, tossed a perfect game, and pitched in a World Series. He was a grandfather by the time he pitched his final game at age 43.

Martinez was just 21 when he became the first Nicaraguan-born pitcher in the major leagues. After a year as a spot starter with the Baltimore Orioles, he joined one of the best starting rotations in baseball. By 1982 he had five seasons with 14 or more wins, but alcoholism began taking its toll. Although the Orioles won the 1983 World Series, Martinez did not make a postseason appearance. Just two years removed from leading the American League in wins, Martinez was 7–16 with a team that won 98 regular season games. He sought help after the season.

Martinez pitched parts of three more seasons in Baltimore, but his second career did not really start until he was traded to Montreal in June 1986. In all but two of his eight seasons with the Expos, Martinez's ERA was 3.18 or below, reaching a major league low 2.39 in 1991. He led the National League that year with nine complete games and five shutouts, highlighted by a perfect game at Dodger Stadium on July 28, 1991. Martinez won in double digits seven times and hurled 220 innings or more six straight years with the Expos.

Martinez signed with the Cleveland Indians as a 38-year-old free agent before the 1994 season. "The reason we signed Dennis," Cleveland general manager John Hart said, "was that if we ever got to the postseason, this was a guy we could trust with a big game."

Martinez, who had the won the game that clinched the team's first pennant in 48 years, started Game 6 of the 1995 World Series with the Indians facing elimination. He allowed nine baserunners but no runs through 4⅔ innings. A home run surrendered by his replacement, Jim Poole, was the difference in a 1–0 game.

At age 40 Martinez finished first in a popularity poll in his native Nicaragua, and he was urged to run for president. He chose pitching over politics, but retained the nickname "El Presidente." After another year in Cleveland and a 1–5 start with the Seattle Mariners, Martinez retired in June 1997. He pitched briefly that winter in Puerto Rico, and the Braves were impressed enough to invite him to spring training. On August 12, 1998, he earned his 244th career victory to pass Juan Marichal for the most wins by a Latin pitcher. Martinez made his final major league appearances in that year's Championship Series. He won once and allowed no runs in four games.

Edgar Martinez

Martinez, Edgar **DH–3B**

1987–* B:1/2/1963, New York, NY D:9/12/1987, SEA AL BR/TR 5'11", 175

G	AB	R	H	HR	RBI	OBP	SLG	AVG
1387	4876	880	1558	198	780	.429	.523	.320

He wasn't the best defensive third baseman, and a knee injury early injury robbed him of whatever speed he had, but Edgar Martinez was one of the best hitters of his era. When, as a designated hitter, Martinez led the American League with a .356 average in 1995, he became the first righthanded hitter since Joe DiMaggio to notch two American League batting titles. His first had come in 1992 when he led the league with a .343 average.

Martinez never went more than eight at bats without a hit in 1995. He led the league with a .479 on-base percentage and a .433 average against lefties; he tied Albert Belle for most runs scored (121) and most doubles (52). The next year he became the first player to hit 50 doubles in consecutive seasons since Joe Medwick of the Cardinals in 1936 and 1937.

In Seattle's first-ever trip to the playoffs in 1995, Martinez showed he could hit in October as well. He mauled the New York Yankees with a .571 average that included 12 hits and 10 RBIs as the Mariners took the series in five games. In Game 4 Martinez set a postseason record with seven RBIs, the result of a three-run homer and a grand slam as the Mariners tied the series. He then delivered the final blow, a two-run, game- and series-winning double off Jack McDowell in Game 5.

With a .337 batting average in 1999, Martinez's .320 career mark placed him third among active players. The Mariners signed the quiet but steady performer to a contract extension following the season.

Pedro Martinez

Martinez, Pedro, Jaime **P**

1992–* B:10/25/1971, Manoguayabo, Dominican Republic Deb:9/24/1992, LA NL BR/TR 5'11", 170

W	L	PCT	G	SH	IP	BB	SO	ERA
107	50	.682	249	11	1359[1]	410	1534	2.83

Pedro Martinez stepped to the mound as the American League's starting pitcher in the 1999 All-Star Game at Fenway Park, a rare honor for a pitcher from the hometown team. The Boston Red Sox hurler struck out the first four batters—an All-Star Game record—and five of the six he faced to earn Most Valuable Player honors. He walked off the mound laying claim to being baseball's most dominant pitcher.

Early in his career, he was simply known as the younger brother of all-star Ramon Martinez. Despite a successful minor league career as a starting pitcher, he joined the Los Angeles Dodgers as a reliever. His fastball, clocked in the mid-90s, was always overpowering, but critics doubted that the slightly-built pitcher was strong enough to throw 200 innings each season. In 1993 he won 10 games out of the bullpen, yet that winter Los Angeles traded him to Montreal for second baseman Delino DeShields.

The Expos made Martinez a starter, but he quickly developed a reputation as a headhunter. There were 11 hit batsman, 12 ejections, and three fights in his 23 starts in 1994. He had a perfect game against Cincinnati broken up in the eighth inning when he hit Reggie Sanders with a pitch—and Sanders charged the mound. Martinez learned to control his emotions just as he learned to control opposing hitters. He won 11 games in 1994, and 14 the following year. On June 3, 1995, he pitched nine perfect innings in a scoreless game in San Diego; he left the game after giving up a leadoff hit in the 10th inning. In 1996 he surpassed 200 innings and 200 strikeouts for the first time.

The breakthrough came in 1997. He used his fastball, knee-buckling curve, and nearly unhittable changeup to win the National League Cy Young Award. He won 17 games, struck out 305 batters, and led the league with a 1.90 ERA and .184 opponents' batting average. Unable to afford their new star, the Expos traded Martinez to Boston, where he continued to excel. Martinez won 19 games and struck out 251 for Boston in 1998.

Martinez only got better in 1999. Despite missing some time due to injuries, including his two starts following his All-Star Game performance, Martinez won 23 games. He struck out 313, fanning 10 or more batters 19 times. In Game 1 of the Division Series, however, it appeared his season might be over when he had to leave in the fourth inning with a strained back muscle. Cleveland came back to win that game as well as Game 2, but the Red Sox won both games at Fenway to force a final encounter. Game 5 was tied 8-8 when Martinez made a surprising relief appearance. He held the Indians hitless over the final six innings, and Boston emerged with the series victory. Martinez then earned Boston's lone victory in the Championship Series, allowing just two hits in seven innings of a 13–1 victory over the Yankees.

Martinez easily won his second Cy Young Award in November. He lost a controversial vote for the Most Valuable Player to Texas catcher Ivan Rodriguez. The pitcher had more first-place votes than Rodriguez, but he was not named on two ballots.

Ramon Martinez

Martinez, Ramon Jaime **P**

1988–* B:3/22/1968, Santo Domingo, Dominican Republic Deb:8/13/1988, LA NL BR/TR 6'4", 165

W	L	PCT	G	SH	IP	BB	SO	ERA
125	78	.616	270	20	1752^{1}	712	1329	3.44

Ramon Martinez is more than just Pedro's older brother. He enjoyed an excellent career in his own right. At the age of 16, he was already pitching at Dodger Stadium. Granted, it was with the Dominican Republic baseball team in the 1984 Olympics, but by the end of the year, the Dodgers had signed Martinez.

Martinez made his major league debut at 20, and was in the big leagues to stay a year later. In his first full season in the major leagues in 1990, Martinez fashioned a 20–6 record, a 2.97 ERA, 12 complete games, 223 strikeouts in 234 innings. He finished second in the Cy Young voting that year to Pittsburgh's Doug Drabek.

Martinez not only became the youngest Dodger to win 20 games since 21-year-old Ralph Branca in 1947, he also tied a club record with 18 strikeouts in a 6–0 shutout of the Braves (Sandy Koufax fanned 18 twice). Martinez threw more pitches than anyone in the league during the season and pitched a hitless inning in the All-Star game at Wrigley Field.

He followed with 17 wins and four shutouts in 1991. Winning 41 of his first 59 big league decisions, Martinez looked to become the next great Dodgers' starting pitcher, but he struggled around the .500 mark the next four seasons. Dodger fans were starting to grumble when he took the hill against Florida on July 14, 1995. In his previous outing at Dodger Stadium, Martinez was booed off the mound after he gave up 10 runs to the Rockies. On this night, however, he retired the first 23 batters and finished with a no-hitter, the seventh pitched at Dodger Stadium.

"I feel like a giant out there," he said after the game. "I wanted to let people know that I can still pitch. I think people had forgotten about me."

He ended the year with a 17–7 record, prompting the Dodgers to re-sign Martinez. He responded with a 15–6 season, but then suffered a small rotator tear in 1997. He dipped to a 10-5 mark, but seemed back in form when he jumped off to a 7–3 start in 1998, only to see his season end with additional rotator cuff surgery. That October, when the Dodgers did not offer a contract to Martinez, he signed with the Red Sox, joining brother Pedro.

Although he spent most of the 1999 season on the DL, Martinez provided valuable support for his brother's Cy Young Award season that propelled Boston to the playoffs. Despite pitching in only 10 minor league rehab appearances and four big league games, Ramon started Game 3 of the Division Series against Cleveland. Although he did not earn the victory, the Red Sox rallied to win the game, and eventually the series. Martinez also started Game 2 of the Championship Series at Yankee Stadium and pitched well, holding a 2–1 lead in the seventh when Chuck Knoblauch doubled off him with two outs to drive in the tying run. Reliever Rheal Cormier later allowed the game-winning hit to Paul O'Neill.

Tino Martinez

Martinez, Constantino **1B**

1990–* B:12/7/1967, Tampa, FL Deb:8/20/1990, SEA AL BL/TR 6'2", 210

G	AB	R	H	HR	RBI	OBP	SLG	AVG
1157	4205	615	1156	213	798	.352	.486	.275

Tino Martinez was the New York Yankees' quiet, steady man of the late 1990s—a latter-day Chris Chambliss, but better at knocking in runs. His reliable glove at first base and productive bat helped the Yankees win three World Series in four years. He knocked in 486 runs in that span, an average of 122 per season, while embodying the selfless, team-first attitude that manager Joe Torre instilled in his players.

Before he was driving in runs for the Yankees or the Seattle Mariners, with whom he began his career, Martinez was leading the United States baseball team to a Gold medal at the 1988 Summer Olympics in Seoul. The Florida native attended the University of Tampa, where, in addition to being academic All-America, he was a Division-II All-America three times. He set school records in batting, home runs, and RBIs.

After spending a year at Double A Williamsport and two at Triple A Calgary, Martinez got a chance to play regularly in Seattle in 1992. He missed part of 1993 with an injury, then became Seattle's regular first baseman for the 1994 strike-shortened season. The following season he established himself with 31 home runs, 111 RBIs, and a .293 average. In that year's Divisional Series against the Yankees he had five RBIs to help the Mariners to a five-game victory. He hit just .136 against Cleveland, however, and the Mariners lost the American League Championship Series in six games.

In December of 1995 he was traded to the Yankees, inheriting the unenviable task of replacing fan favorite Don Mattingly at first base. Despite a slow start, Martinez eventually proved his worth, making a vital contribution to the team's 1996 World Championship season. Martinez reached his pinnacle with 44 homers, 141 RBIs, and .296 average in 1997. He followed that by leading the club in home runs in both 1998 and 1999, as New York notched two more World Series titles.

Tippy Martinez

Martinez, Felix Anthony **P**

1974–88 B:5/31/1950, La Junta, CO Deb:8/9/1974, NY AL BL/TL 5'10", 180

W	L	PCT	G	SV	IP	BB	SO	ERA
55	42	.567	546	115	834	425	632	3.45

Orioles reliever Tippy Martinez chipped in with two saves as Baltimore defeated the Phillies 4–1 in the 1983 World Series—capping a year in which he won the final game of the ALCS with four shutout innings against the White Sox. Selected by Washington in the 35th round of the June 1969 free-agent draft, Felix Anthony "Tippy" Martinez instead elected to attend Colorado State University. In July 1972, however, he signed as a free agent with the Yankees, spending the remainder of that season with Oneonta and Kinston. With the latter, he paced the Carolina League with 15 saves and 17 wild pitches in 1973. Martinez also played with the International League's Syracuse Chiefs before joining New York.

Martinez, along with Scott McGregor and Rick Dempsey, were part of a 10-player trade between New York and Baltimore in June 1976. His best years were spent with the Orioles pitching in the bullpen beside such relievers as Don Stanhouse, Tim Stoddard, and Sammy Stewart.

Phil Masi

Masi, Philip Samuel **C**

1939–52 B:1/6/1917, Chicago, IL D:3/29/1990, Mt. Prospect, IL Deb:4/23/1939, BOS NL BR/TR 5'10", 180

G	AB	R	H	HR	RBI	OBP	SLG	AVG
1229	3468	420	917	47	417	.344	.370	.264

In Game 1 of the 1948 World Series, the Braves' Phil Masi pinch-ran for fellow catcher Bill Salkeld as Johnny Sain and Cleveland's Bob Feller took a scoreless tie into the eighth inning. Feller attempted to pick Masi off, throwing to Lou Boudreau. It appeared that Masi had been picked off, but umpire Bill Stewart called Masi safe. Subsequent photos confirmed Masi should have been out. "Ten years later, Stewart told me he blew the call," noted Feller.

Later in the inning, right fielder Tommy Holmes proceeded to single beyond the reach of third baseman Kenny Keltner, scoring Masi with the game's only run. Feller, who threw only 85 pitches, became the first pitcher to lose a World Series nine-inning two-hitter.

Philip Samuel Masi, an excellent fielding catcher, started with Wausau and Eau Claire of the Northern League in 1936 and also appeared with Springfield in the Class C Middle Atlantic League before reaching the Braves. Traded to Pittsburgh in June 1949, he was sold to the White Sox in February 1950, where he played three seasons before retiring.

Bobby Mathews

Mathews, Robert T. **P-OF**

1871–87 B:11/21/1851, Baltimore, MD D:4/17/1898, Baltimore, MD Deb:5/4/1871, KEK NA BR/TR 5'5½", 140

W	L	PCT	G	SH	IP	BB	SO	ERA
166	136	.550	323	10	2734^{1}	336	1199	3.00

G	AB	R	H	HR	RBI	OBP	SLG	AVG
367	1390	158	267	1	73	.222	.217	.192

On May 5, 1871, the first game of the first professional league, the National Association, was played. The winning pitcher was the Fort Wayne Kekiongas' Bobby Mathews, a short but powerful 20-year-old who used his recently invented spitball to toss a 2–0 shutout at the Forest City team from Cleveland.

Bobby Mathews went on to become one of the most durable pitchers of professional baseball's early days, playing for five years in each of three different circuits: the National Association, the National League, and the American Association. He also became the only player ever to win 50 games in each of three major leagues. In addition to his 166 wins in the NL and AA, he had a 131–112 mark and a 2.68 ERA in 255 NA games.

He started 65 games for the Mutuals of New York in 1874, threw 62 complete games, and won 42 of them. He also pitched three straight 30-win seasons for the Philadelphia Athletics from 1883 through 1885. In addition to the spitball, Mathews was credited with developing the first legal pitch to break away from the batter, which he called his "out" pitch.

Eddie Mathews

Mathews, Edwin Lee **3B**

1952–68 M(1972–74, 149–161) B:10/13/1931, Texarkana, TX Deb:4/15/1952, BOS NL BL/TR 6'1", 200

G	AB	R	H	HR	RBI	OBP	SLG	AVG
2391	8537	1509	2315	512	1453	.378	.509	.271

Once upon a time Eddie Mathews was the greatest power-hitting third baseman in baseball history. And even after Philadelphia's Mike Schmidt came along, 512 homers and 1,453 RBIs secured Mathews a place in baseball's pantheon. When Mathews was just coming up with the Braves, Paul Waner said it best: "There's nothing I can teach that boy about swinging a bat. He's perfect." Ty Cobb agreed. "I've only known three or four perfect swings in my time. This lad has one of them."

Texas-born Edwin Lee Mathews grew up in Santa Barbara, California, and was a good enough football player to be offered scholarships to USC, UCLA, and several other schools. Mathews rejected them all for two reasons: one, he hated studying, and two, he was determined to play baseball.

No problem. All but two major league clubs were scouting him, and he had numerous offers. The largest offer came from the Dodgers—a $10,000 bonus and another $20,000 for his family. But there was a catch. At that time, bonus baby rules mandated that any free agent signed for $6,000 or more would have to spend two years in the majors right off the bat—with no chance to start down in the minors.

Neither Mathews nor his father saw any point in that. They scanned the list of proposals and saw that the club with the oldest third baseman was the Boston Braves. Bob Elliott, the 1947 MVP, was 32. Mathews was not eligible to sign with any team until the day after his high school class graduated. So at 12:01 A.M. on June 19, 1949, he signed with Braves scout Johnny Moore for $5,999.

Mathews joined the Braves in Chicago and found out that he had made the right choice in deciding to go to the minors. "I couldn't touch the ball, not even in batting practice," he recalled. The Braves assigned him to High Point-Thomasville in the Class D Carolina State League where he hit .363 with 17 homers in just 43 games. His fielding, however, was simply atrocious.

But the talent was there, and other clubs were aware of it. During the off-season, Brooklyn's Branch Rickey approached Boston owner Lou Perini about a trade involving some other players in the Braves organization. Rickey said he'd make the deal if Perini threw in "some Class D player like…er…what is that boy's name?…Oh, yes, Mathews." Perini passed.

Boston promoted Mathews to Atlanta of the Southern Association in 1950. Mathews started slowly but finished with 32 homers and 106 RBIs. At season's end he was promoted to Milwaukee in the American Association, and in his first at bat there, the 19-year-old hit a grand slam.

Mathews faced the military draft, however, so he enrolled in the Navy after the season. But only a few weeks after Mathews enlisted, his father was diagnosed with tuberculosis, and Mathews received a dependency discharge.

He got his chance after one more year in the minors. Elliott had staged a holdout in 1952 and was traded to the Giants on April 8. Again Mathews started slowly with his bat and his fielding was still deficient. To make matters worse he failed to get along with Boston's combative sportswriting community. The personable Elliott had been one of their favorites, but they were lucky to get a grunt out of Mathews. Said one writer: "The Braves traded away Bob Elliott, who averaged nearly 100 RBIs a season for five years, to make room for a mere babe who belongs back in the baseball nursery."

The slugger turned it around that season even though he led the National League in strikeouts, with 115. His first homer came off lefty Ken Heintzelman at Philadelphia's Shibe Park, and by the end of the season he'd hit 25, then a record for rookies. The last three came at Ebbets Field on the next-to-last day of the season, which made him the first rookie ever to hit three homers in a single game.

That was the Braves' last season in Boston and Mathews did not have fond memories of his year there. "About the only people who seemed to be interested in the Braves," he said, "were the 50 or so gamblers who always congregated in the first-base section of the stands."

In Milwaukee the introverted and often sullen Mathews found an entirely different atmosphere. Baseball was the biggest thing to hit Wisconsin since bratwurst. Fans showered the players with adulation. A thousand eyes saw everything they did. They could not go anywhere without attracting attention. To Mathews in particular it was not an ideal situation. In that first year in Milwaukee, he led the league with a career-high 47 homers and drove in a career-high 135 runs. It was also the first of his three straight 40-homer, 100-RBI seasons.

Still there were a number of unpleasant off-field incidents in those first years in Milwaukee. In May 1954 following a Sunday doubleheader, Mathews stopped over at the home of pitcher Bob Buhl, his roommate on the road. At about 2 A.M. he headed home and, realizing that he was past curfew, put the pedal to the metal. A police car passed him going in the opposite direction but quickly made a U-turn and started after Mathews.

Mathews ducked into an alley and shut off his lights. The cop found him anyway, and the incident made headlines. The story might have blown over when the judge fined Mathews $50 plus $4.15 court costs, but as he was leaving the courthouse a photographer approached him. "You shoot that picture," Mathews snapped, "and I'll break your arm."

Even at Mathews' wedding there was trouble with inquiring photographers. "If this wasn't my wedding day, buddy," the groom snarled, "I'd break your neck."

In 1955 Mathews was aboard the Braves' train for spring training when he came to blows with a fellow passenger. No charges were filed, but a year later Mathews and the Braves were sued. They settled out of court.

These and other incidents were all sidelights to the real Eddie Mathews story of the 1950s. From

his rookie season of 1952 through 1959 Mathews led all major leaguers with 299 home runs. It wasn't a home run, however, that provided him with his greatest moment in baseball. In 1957 Milwaukee won its only World Series, beating the Yankees in seven games. Mathews pulled out Game 4 with a 10th-inning homer off Bob Grim, and his dribbler of an infield single drove in the only run in Game 5.

But what mattered most to him was his backhand stab of Bill Skowron's bases-loaded one-hopper for the last out of Game 7. "That play ranked right up there with breaking the 500 home run barrier," Mathews said. "I'd made better plays, but that big one in the spotlight stamped me the way I wanted to be remembered."

In 1962 Mathews tore ligaments and tendons in his shoulder while swinging against the Houston Colt .45s' Turk Farrell. "The injury was slow to heal," Mathews said, "and even after it did, I became a defensive hitter and developed some bad batting habits."

Only 31 when he hurt his shoulder, after that his career started heading downhill, and he hit only 23 homers in both 1963 and 1964. He had one more high quality season left in 1965. He hit 32 homers with 95 RBIs in the Braves' last year in Milwaukee. Mathews moved with the Braves to Atlanta and hit only 16 homers with 53 RBIs in 1966. He was traded to Houston after the season, and the Astros traded him to Detroit in August 1967. He retired after only 52 at bats with the Tigers in 1968.

A coach for the Braves in 1971 and 1972, he replaced Luman Harris as Atlanta manager in August 1972 but was fired after 99 games in 1974. In 1978 Mathews was elected to the Hall of Fame. "The Hall of Fame is something I never thought about when I was playing," Mathews said. "But this is it for me. I don't know what else there is to do after being elected."

Christy Mathewson

Mathewson, Christopher **P**

1900–16 M(1916–18, 164–176) B:8/12/1880, Factoryville, PA D:10/7/1925, Saranac Lake, NY Deb:7/17/1900, NY NL BR/TR 6'1½", 195

W	L	PCT	G	SH	IP	BB	SO	ERA
373	188	.665	635	79	4780^{2}	844	2502	2.13

In a sport dominated by ruffians, Christy Mathewson exuded a sense of nobility. Not only was he a great pitcher—the co-holder of the National League record for career victories, with 373, and the league record-holder for most victories in a season, with 37—but also he was a gentleman, a man of moral convictions who inspired an entire generation of fans.

"Mathewson was the greatest pitcher who ever lived," said Connie Mack, who managed the rival-league Philadelphia Athletics through a record setting half-century of baseball. "He had knowledge, judgment, perfect control, and form. It was wonderful to watch him pitch when he wasn't pitching against you."

Mathewson won 30 or more games in a season on four separate occasions. For 12 consecutive years he captured a minimum of 22 victories. In the 1905 World Series against the Athletics he pitched three complete-game shutouts. In 1908 he walked an average of less than one player per game. From June 13 through July 18, 1913, he pitched 68 consecutive innings without surrendering a single base on balls.

Christopher Mathewson began pitching at age 13 for his hometown team in Factoryville, Pennsylvania. Previously, he had been the team's mascot and batboy, but his strong throwing arm attracted the club's attention. When the regular pitcher became ill Mathewson was given a tryout. At a warm-up game in the town square, he struck out the first batter and better than half the players he faced in the contest.

"You'll do, son," the team captain said at the game's conclusion, and Mathewson started the next official game. The slightly arm-weary youngster won the contest, 19–17, and even homered, batting cross-handed.

At Bucknell College Mathewson continued to star as a pitcher but also made a name for himself in football. He was known as "Gun Boots" because of his skill in dropkicking. Signed to a professional baseball contract with Taunton, Massachusetts, of the New England League for $90 per month, he never received the full amount of pay he had been promised. His professional debut came on July 21, 1899, in a 6–5 loss to Manchester. Mathewson went on to compile a 5–2 record.

It was at Taunton that Mathewson added a new pitch to his arsenal, learning the delivery from a lefthanded teammate. "Williams pitched this ball with the same motion that he threw his out-curve," noted Mathewson, "but turned his hand over and snapped his wrist as he let the ball go. He never could tell where it was going, so it was of no use to him in a game. It was a freak delivery. It fascinated me."

The next year Mathewson signed with Norfolk of the Virginia League for $80 a month. When manager John Smith saw Mathewson's performance in a football game against Pennsylvania, he crossed out "$80" on the contract and wrote in "$90."

Mathewson was 20–2 by late July, when he was sold to the Giants for $2,000. Smith had offers for Mathewson from both the Phillies and the Giants and gave the pitcher his choice. Mathewson, believing the Giants were more in need of good pitching, opted for New York.

In New York, manager George Davis christened Mathewson's trick pitch the "fadeaway." Despite his innovation, Mathewson proved ineffective in 1900, going 0–3 with a 5.08 ERA, and returned to Norfolk at season's end. The Cincinnati Reds proceeded to draft Mathewson off the Norfolk roster, but the Giants had second thoughts about handing the talented righthander back. They traded washed-up fireballer Amos Rusie for him on December 15, 1900. Rusie, who had already accumulated 245 big league victories, would not win another game. The deal was one of baseball's greatest steals.

In 1901 Mathewson went 20–17 for the seventh-place Giants. In 1902, however, he fell to 14–17. Early in the season New York manager Horace Fogel tried Mathewson at first base. Later that year John McGraw jumped over from the upstart American League's Baltimore franchise to manage the Giants. Fogel was still advising Giants owner Andrew Freedman and now had the brilliant idea of trying Mathewson at shortstop.

"You can get rid of Fogel," McGraw roared. "Anybody who doesn't know any more about baseball than that doesn't have a right to the ballpark. Trying to make a first baseman out of Mathewson! There's a kid with as fine a pitching motion as I ever saw and as much stuff as any young fellow to come up in years. He'll pitch from now on." And so he did.

Mathewson had a wide variety of pitches, including a fastball, curve, and the aforementioned fadeaway. Although the fadeaway was his most famous pitch, he never would say which of his offerings was the best. "Anybody's best pitch is the one the batters ain't hitting that day," he observed. "And it doesn't take long to find out. If they start hitting my fastball, they don't see it anymore that afternoon. If they start getting a hold of my curveball, I just put it away for the day. When they start hitting both of them on the same day, that's when they put me away."

As successful as he was, Mathewson was, to some extent, a hard-luck pitcher. Bad things often happened to the Giants when Mathewson took the mound in big games. It was Mathewson who was pitching against the Cubs on September 23, 1908, when first baseman Fred Merkle pulled his famed "Merkle Boner" play, forgetting to touch second base when Al Bridwell drove in what appeared to be the winning run. Merkle headed into the clubhouse to join the celebration but was called out by umpire Hank O'Day. The game ended in a deadlock.

That tie had to be replayed on October 8, 1908. With the pennant at stake, "Big Six" Mathewson was once again on the mound. He sailed along until the third inning, when center fielder Cy Seymour, stubbornly ignoring Mathewson's entreaties to play deeper, saw a Joe Tinker fly ball sail over his head for a triple. Four runs scored that inning, and the Giants lost the game, 4–2, as well as the flag.

Mathewson was the victim again in the 1912 World Series when Fred Snodgrass committed his "$30,000 Muff" in center field, then catcher Chief Meyers and Merkle let an easy foul pop drop between them. Mathewson lost another heartbreaker as the Red Sox won the game and the Series.

If Mathewson had one flaw, it was his lack of concentration when he had a big lead. "Matty was a great one for loafing when the pressure was off, when we were way ahead," teammate Larry Doyle said. "He was only great when he had to be. In tight ball games, he was darn near impossible to hit. But when the score was lopsided, Matty didn't seem to care a whit about his reputation and he'd toss in plenty of fat ones."

In 1914 Mathewson started to wear out. He finished with a record of 24–13, but in the second half of the season he began to complain of pains in his left side. In 1915 Mathewson suffered his first losing season since 1902, and by 1916 he was being used out of the bullpen. On July 20, 1916, McGraw traded Mathewson to the Reds along with two other future Hall of Famers, outfielder Edd Roush and third baseman Bill McKechnie, for Reds manager Buck Herzog and outfielder Red Killefer, a career .248 hitter.

Although the deal was made to allow Mathewson to manage Cincinnati, Reds fans were probably relieved to get him off the Giants' mound. For New York, Mathewson's record against the Reds was 64–18, with 22 wins in a row at one point.

Mathewson's last pitching performance, his only one for the Reds, was a specially contrived matchup against another aging hurler, the Cubs' Mordecai "Three Finger" Brown. In the second game of a Labor Day doubleheader, Mathewson outlasted Brown, 10–8.

After several decades the significance of this game became apparent. The annals showed that when Mathewson retired he had accumulated 372 victories, a National League record. Grover Cleveland Alexander subsequently won 373, erasing the Big Six's mark. But a statistician later discovered that a May 1902 Mathewson 4–2 victory over Pittsburgh had been erroneously entered in the record books as a loss. Mathewson's slice of history had been restored.

Mathewson managed Cincinnati until midseason 1918, when he joined the armed services and served as a captain on the Western Front, where he was hit by a whiff of poison gas. In 1919 he returned to baseball as a coach for the Giants, but two years later was diagnosed as having tuberculosis in both lungs.

He was sent to Saranac Lake, New York, for treatment, where one of his lungs collapsed. Baseball was his medicine. "When a fellow cannot read, or write, or talk, and can only move his fingers and forearms, it requires some resourcefulness to keep his mind off his troubles. I started working out a baseball game, figuring every chance and studying how it should be played mechanically so as to offer the same chances as are offered on a ballfield. It interested me and kept my mind engaged."

In 1922 Mathewson returned home, and his spirit was too strong to merely survive. In 1923 he accepted the role of president of Judge Emil Fuch's Boston Braves. It was a challenge Mathewson never should have taken. In 1925 the strain caused him to collapse. He returned to Saranac Lake and died there on October 7. In 1936 he was among the first five players to be enshrined in the Hall of Fame.

Jon Matlack

Matlack, Jonathan Trumpbour **P**

1971–83 B:1/19/1950, West Chester, PA
Deb:7/11/1971, NY NL BL/TL 6'3", 205

W	L	PCT	G	SH	IP	BB	SO	ERA
125	126	.498	361	30	2363	638	1516	3.18

Control pitcher Jon Matlack, a 22-year-old lefthander on a power-pitching New York Mets staff, won the 1972 Rookie of the Year Award with a 2.32 earned run average. His ERA, the fourth-lowest mark in the National League, was lower than the averages of established teammates Tom Seaver and Jerry Koosman.

Watching Koosman and Seaver pitch in his first spring training camp in 1968 had set Matlack back; he tried to throw harder and lost his excellent curveball in the process. "It took me three years to get that pitch back," he said. Armed once again with his curve, Matlack was 15–10 in 1972. "The whole year was just amazing," he remembered. "I never pictured myself being able to do so much in my first full season."

Bitten by bad luck in 1973, Matlack finished at 14–16 with a 3.20 ERA. But he threw a two-hit shutout against the Reds in Game 2 of the NLCS, and compiled a 2.16 ERA in the World Series despite a 1–2 record. Matlack lost Game 1 of the Fall Classic to Oakland, 2–1, then combined with Ray Sadecki on a five-hitter in Game 4 to tie the Series, 2–2. He started Game 7 but left the game after yielding two-run homers to Reggie Jackson and Bert Campaneris. The Athletics won the game and the Series.

The next few years followed a similar pattern—Matlack pitched well, but he got little offensive support. In 1974 he posted a losing record despite a 2.41 ERA and a league-leading seven shutouts. Two years later Jonathan Trumpbour Matlack had the best season of his career, winning a career-high 17 games and leading the National League with six shutouts.

Following a disastrous 1977 season, in which he was 7–15 with a 4.21 ERA, he was shipped to Texas in a four-team trade involving the Mets, Rangers, Pittsburgh Pirates, and Atlanta Braves. He bounced back with a 15–13 record and a personal-best 2.27 ERA before injuring his elbow. Matlack spent the next season rehabilitating from surgery, and although he came back to pitch four more years, his effectiveness was never the same. He later served as a pitching coach in the Chicago White Sox and Tigers organizations.

Gary Matthews

Mathews, Gary Nathaniel **OF**

1972–87 B:7/5/1950, San Fernando, CA Deb:9/6/1972, SF NL BR/TR 6'3", 190

G	AB	R	H	HR	RBI	OBP	SLG	AVG
2033	7147	1083	2011	234	978	.367	.439	.281

Outfielder Gary Matthews earned the nickname "Sarge" for his take-charge attitude and competitive spirit. Batting coach Billy DeMars once said that when Matthews is in the batter's box "he looks like he's going to kill you."

The Giants selected the 17-year-old Matthews in the first round of the June 1968 draft, hoping he would join Bobby Bonds and Garry Maddox in a new-generation San Francisco outfield. For several years, before the Giants traded Maddox and Bonds away and Matthews became a free agent, the trio was the best in the league. In 1973, his first complete big league season, Matthews hit .300 with 10 triples and won the NL Rookie of the Year Award. Remarkably consistent, he never batted below .278 in any the next nine years.

In 1976 Matthews slugged 20 homers and drove in 84 runs. During the off-season Braves owner Ted Turner swayed the outfielder into signing a five-year contract by greeting him with a billboard reading "Welcome Gary Matthews" when Sarge arrived in Atlanta for negotiations. Turner would later be suspended from baseball for a year for tampering with Matthews while he was still under contract. "If I had it to do all over again, knowing what I know about Ted,

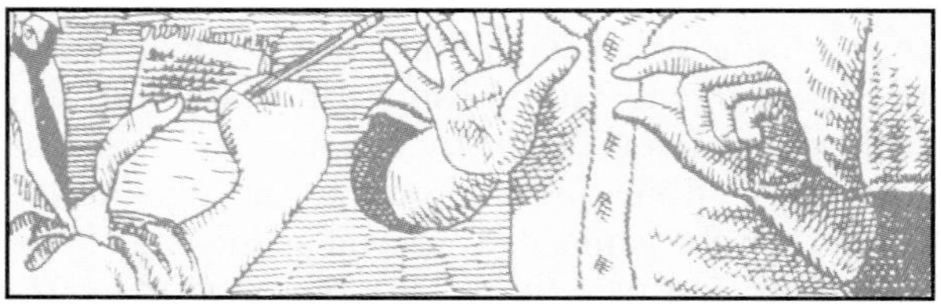

surely I wouldn't have made that decision," Matthews said later.

Matthews' best year was 1979, when he batted .304, with 27 home runs, 34 doubles, and 90 RBIs. He made the All-Star squad, hit three round-trippers on September 25, and joined teammates Dale Murphy and Bob Horner in the 20-homer club. But poor pitching decimated the Braves. Phil Niekro was the only pitcher to post a winning record—and he lost a league-leading 20 games. Atlanta finished in the NL West basement, 24 games back of Cincinnati.

On March 25, 1981, Matthews was traded to Philadelphia for pitcher Bob Walk. He hit .301 during the strike-shortened season, and the Phillies met Montreal in the NL East playoffs. Matthews recorded three hits in Game 3 and hit a solo homer in Game 4, both Phillies victories. However, the Expos won Game 5 to take the Series, despite Matthews' .400 average.

Although he slumped to a .258 batting average and 10 homers in 1983, Matthews won MVP honors in the NLCS with a .429 batting average and three home runs. He hit another homer in Philadelphia's five-game loss to the Orioles in the World Series. Phillies manager Dallas Green remarked, "He's into the game all the time. He's talking about baseball all the time. He's a lot like Pete Rose, really. He's a gamer."

Nevertheless, on March 26, 1984, Matthews went to Chicago in a five-player deal. That season he batted .291, drove in 82 runs, and led the league with 103 bases on balls, as the Cubs advanced to the NLCS. Matthews hit two home runs in Game 1 against San Diego, but batted just .200 for the Series, won by the Padres in five games.

His skills then began to fade. In July 1987 he was traded to Seattle for a minor leaguer. After hitting only .235 for the Mariners, Matthews retired. Matthews was later a minor league hitting coordinator for the Chicago Cubs and a coach for the Blue Jays.

Don Mattingly

Mattingly, Donald Arthur **1B**

1982–95 B:4/20/1961, Evansville, IN Deb: 9/8/1982, NY AL BL/TL 6', 175

G	AB	R	H	HR	RBI	OBP	SLG	AVG
1785	7003	1007	2153	222	1099	.363	.471	.307

In 1986 *The New York Times* conducted a poll of major leaguers, asking them to name the best player in the game. The Yankees first baseman Don Mattingly, who had won the American League's Most Valuable Player award in 1985, was the overwhelming choice of his peers. Indeed, at that point in his career, Mattingly's eventual place in the Yankees pantheon, alongside such fabled players as Lou Gehrig, Babe Ruth, and Joe DiMaggio, seemed assured. But a back injury in 1990 robbed him of his power, and the remainder of his career was only an echo of his former thunder.

Mattingly, known in the Bronx as "Donnie Baseball" or "Hit Man," was one of the most popular players ever to wear a Yankees uniform. He won the AL batting title in his first full season with the team, 1984, with a .343 average, while also leading the league in hits (207) and doubles (44). He claimed his first of nine Gold Glove awards that season, beginning a four-year stretch of leading the league in fielding percentage.

In his MVP season of 1985, the affable, moustached Mattingly slugged 35 homers, knocked in a league-leading 145 runs while scoring 107, and collected 211 hits, 86 of them for extra bases. The following year he continued to batter AL pitchers with his formidable combination of high-average hitting and power, lofting 31 home runs to go with a .352 batting average. Mattingly's 238 hits that year set a Yankees record, and his 53 doubles broke by one the club mark set by Gehrig in 1927. He also provided one of baseball's rarest spectacles, appearing in three games that season as a lefthanded third baseman.

On July 18, 1987, Mattingly tied a record that had endured since 1956 when he homered off Jose Guzman of the Texas Rangers. It was the eighth consecutive game in which he had homered, duplicating the mark established by Dale Long (and later equaled by Ken Griffey, Jr.). In all, Mattingly hit 10 homers over the eight-game span. On September 29 of that year, he homered with the bases full off Boston's Bruce Hurst, setting a major league single-season standard with six grand slams.

His power production tailed off a bit in 1988, yet Mattingly made headlines of another kind with his scathing criticism of the atmosphere created on the Yankees by owner George Steinbrenner. In 1989 he had his final season in the sun, hitting 23 homers and driving in 113 runs while batting .303. After the injury, though, he never again topped 17 homers or 86 RBIs, and managed to bat .300 only one more time, in the strike-shortened season of 1994.

After 1,785 career games, Mattingly made his first trip to the postseason in 1995, when the Yankees took on the Seattle Mariners in the Division Series. The Yanks lost in five, but Mattingly was glorious in defeat, assailing Seattle pitching for 10 hits (five of them for extra bases), six RBIs, and a .417 batting average. It was the last hurrah for the man who served as the Yankees' 10th captain. After sitting out the team's 1996 world championship season, Mattingly formally announced his retirement in January 1997. The Yankees retired his No. 23 later that year.

Gene Mauch

Mauch, Gene William **2B–SS**
1944–57 M(1960–82, 1985–87, 1,902–2,037)
B:11/18/1925, Salina, KS Deb:4/18/1944, BRO NL
BR/TR 5'10", 165

G	AB	R	H	HR	RBI	OBP	SLG	AVG
304	737	93	176	5	62	.335	.312	.239

In the history of baseball, only Connie Mack, John McGraw, and Bucky Harris managed longer in the big leagues than Gene Mauch's 26 years. But while Mack's teams visited the World Series seven times, McGraw's Giants nine, and Harris' teams three, Gene William Mauch never was able to take the Phillies, Expos, Twins, or Angels to the Fall Classic.

Three times Mauch came close, once by a single pitch. His 1964 Phils had a 5½-game lead with only 11 to play, but they came apart. Completely. As pitching, hitting, fielding, and baserunning disappeared, Mauch tried to control the damage by using only his best pitchers, Jim Bunning and Chris Short, sending them each out three times on only two days' rest. The plan didn't work. The Phils dropped 10 in a row to finish third to earn a spot in baseball infamy as "The Phabulous Pholding Phillies." Mauch described it tersely, "It was like watching someone drown."

In 1982, Mauch's Angels won the AL West by three games. And they handily took the first two games at home in that year's best-of-five ALCS. But Milwaukee won Games 3 and 4 and overturned a 3–1 Angel lead in Game 5 to move to the World Series. Mauch resigned as Angel field manager afterwards and moved to the front office as director of player personnel.

He returned to the dugout in 1985, and in the 1986 ALCS (now best-of-seven), Mauch's Angels won Games 1, 3 and 4. They took a 5–2 lead into the top of the ninth in Game 5, but the Red Sox pecked back for two runs. Angels ace reliever Donnie Moore was pitching to Dave Henderson with a 1–2 count, one on, and two out. One more strike and the Angels (and Mauch) would have their first-ever taste of World Series play. Three pitches later Henderson sent a Moore pitch crashing into the left-field seats. The Angels rallied to tie in the last of the ninth, but lost the game in the 11th. Then they dropped the two final games in Boston.

Mauch left managing for good after the next season's last-place finish. Throughout his career, he was known for tactical thinking and attention to detail. Scorers had to pay attention when working a game Mauch managed, as he would bring up pinch hitter after pinch hitter. "Most one-run games are lost, not won," he said.

Mauch was named NL Manager of the Year three times, including twice with the Phillies, and once when his Expos, only five years old, won 79 games.

Mauch enjoyed the challenge of trying to build a good team out of a bad one, but when he quit Minnesota in 1980 he announced he wouldn't manage a team unless it had a chance to win, which was why he joined the Angels the following season.

"If it's true you learn from adversity," Mauch once said, "then I must be the smartest SOB in the world."

Dal Maxvill

Maxvill, Charles Dallan **SS–2B**
1962–75 B:2/18/1939, Granite City, IL Deb:6/10/1962, STL NL BR/TR 5'11", 160

G	AB	R	H	HR	RBI	OBP	SLG	AVG
1423	3443	302	748	6	252	.295	.259	.217

A smart middle infielder who went on to become a Cardinals general manager, Dal Maxvill was an anemic .217 hitter. Charles Dallan "Dal" Maxvill earned a B.S. degree in electrical engineering from Washington University in St. Louis and started his baseball career with Winnipeg of the Northern League in 1960. He later played in Charleston, Tulsa, Jacksonville, and Indianapolis before reaching the majors with the Cardinals in 1962.

He hit .200 in the 1964 World Series against the Yankees, returned to the World Series in 1967 and hit .158, and, a year later set a Series record for ineptitude by going 0-for-22 in the 1968 Fall Classic.

Fortunately, Maxvill starred in the field. He won the Gold Glove at shortstop in 1968 and led NL shortstops in fielding percentage in 1970. At the same time his hitting reached an all-time low. He set NL records for fewest at bats, hits, doubles, long hits, batting average, and slugging average for players who appeared in 150 or more games.

In 1971 he once again led National League shortstops in fielding, and he was traded to Oakland in time to play in the 1972 World Series. He moved to Pittsburgh the next season but returned to the Athletics in 1974 in time to play in one more Series. He later coached for the A's, the Mets, the Braves, and the Cardinals before being named St. Louis general manager in February 1985, where he was instrumental in putting together the great defensive Cardinal team that won pennants that year and again in 1987.

Carlos May

May, Carlos **OF–DH–1B**

1968–77 B:5/17/1948, Birmingham, AL Deb:9/6/1968, CHI AL BL/TR 6', 215

G	AB	R	H	HR	RBI	OBP	SLG	AVG
1165	4120	545	1127	90	536	.360	.392	.274

Chicago White Sox outfielder Carlos May, younger brother of Lee May, captured *The Sporting News* AL Rookie of the Year Award in 1969, but his career nearly ended that August. He was stationed at Camp Pendleton with the Marines when a mortar misfired and almost cost him his right thumb. Skin graft surgery, however, restored its use.

May, who attended Southern University, started his professional career with the Gulf Coast League's Sarasota White Sox in 1966. He also played with Winter Haven, Appleton, and Lynchburg, leading the Carolina League with a .330 average in 1968. He saw brief action with the White Sox in 1968, then played 100 games in the outfield for the big league club in 1969. That season he batted .281, with 18 home runs and 68 RBIs.

May started 141 games in the outfield in 1970, hitting .285 with 28 doubles and 12 homers. The following season he was shifted from the outfield to first base, and he led AL first sackers with 19 errors in 1971. A year later he returned to the outfield, tied for the league lead in assists, and hit a career-best .308.

In 1973 May was the White Sox's designated hitter for 75 games, played the outfield for 70 games, and made two appearances at first base. That season he established career highs in homers, with 20, and RBIs, with 96. But he hit only eight round-trippers in each of the next two seasons and was traded to the Yankees in May 1976 for pitcher Ken Brett and outfielder Rich Coggins. May played in four games of the 1976 World Series against Cincinnati but went hitless in nine at bats.

In September 1977 May was sold to the Angels. He batted .333 in 11 games for the Halos but retired at season's end. He later worked for the U. S. Postal Service in Chicago. Carlos and Lee May combined to hit 444 home runs, tying them with the Boyer brothers for the third-best sibling total in major league history. Only the Aarons and DiMaggios hit more.

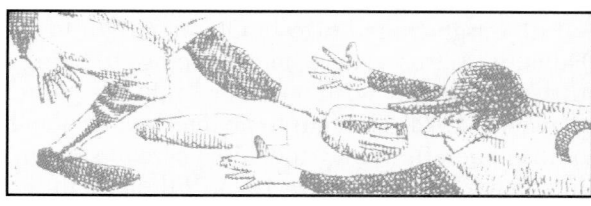

Dave May

May, David La France **OF**

1967–78 B:12/23/1943, New Castle, DE Deb:7/28/1967, BAL AL BL/TR 5'10½", 186

G	AB	R	H	HR	RBI	OBP	SLG	AVG
1252	3670	462	920	96	422	.320	.375	.251

Lefthanded-hitting outfielder Dave May reached his potential with the 1973 Milwaukee Brewers when he hit 25 home runs and batted .303. He was traded to the Atlanta Braves after the 1974 season to bring an aging Hank Aaron back to Milwaukee.

David La France May signed with San Francisco in 1962 and played with Salem of the Appalachian League that season. Drafted by the Orioles, he played in Stockton, Fox-Cities, Tri-City, and Rochester before coming to Baltimore in 1967.

The Orioles used May sparingly in three seasons. He received one at bat in the 1969 ALCS and one in the World Series. In June 1970 Baltimore traded him to the Brewers. Playing regularly in the majors for the first time at age 27, May responded by hitting .277 with 16 home runs in 1971. His numbers dropped off in 1972, but he came back in 1973 to post career highs in batting average, home runs, and RBIs. That season he also assembled a career-best 24-game hitting streak.

After a disappointing 1974 season in which he batted .226, May was traded to the Atlanta Braves for Aaron. In 1975 May hit 12 home runs in only 203 at bats with a career-high .493 slugging average. Prior to the 1977 season he was dealt, along with four other players and $250,000, to Texas for Jeff Burroughs. May's last season in the majors was 1978, which he split between Milwaukee and Pittsburgh.

A career .251 hitter, May hit 96 home runs in 12 seasons. He later became a sales representative for a cable television franchise in New Castle, Delaware. His son, Derrick—an outfielder—played for the Cubs, Marlins, Astros, Phillies and Expos.

Lee May

May, Lee Andrew **1B–DH**

1965–82 B:3/23/1943, Birmingham, AL Deb:9/1/1965, CIN NL BR/TR 6'3", 205

G	AB	R	H	HR	RBI	OBP	SLG	AVG
2071	7609	959	2031	354	1244	.315	.459	.267

Lee May was a consistent home run hitter and RBI producer for Cincinnati, Houston, and Baltimore in the late 1960s and the 1970s. He hit a lifetime 354 home runs and drove in 90 or more runs eight times during a big league career that spanned 18 seasons. However, bad luck with trades kept him from being a part of a world championship team.

Lee Andrew May's younger brother, Carlos, was also a big leaguer, in a career spent mostly with the White Sox. Lee May was a fine athlete, but when he was growing up, Major League Baseball had not yet come to the South. "I never had any ambition to be a big leaguer," he once said. "I liked to play baseball just to keep active. But I had no dreams. I had no hero, no team I rooted for. I just loved playing."

He attended Birmingham's Parker High School, where he played football as well as baseball. After Lee's summer baseball coach tipped off a connection at the Reds about the athlete, the big league club showed interest. Although May's grandmother had wanted him to go to college—he had already been offered a football scholarship to the University of Nebraska—the Reds sold her on baseball and signed May for $12,000.

Starting out with Tampa of the Florida State League in 1961, May batted .260 in 26 games. He began playing winter ball after that season and would eventually play five winters—three in Venezuela and two in Puerto Rico. He returned to Tampa in 1962 and again hit .260. In 1963 he batted .263 with Rocky Mount of the Carolina League and led league first basemen in errors, with 23.

May's breakthrough season came in 1964 with Macon of the Southern League. That season, he lived in garages "or any place people would rent to me," he recalled. "blacks couldn't room in the same place as white players. Restaurants wouldn't serve me." As his future manager, Sparky Anderson, once said, "Make Lee May mad, and he is an altogether different hitter, a 100 percent better hitter." That season May batted .303 and led the Southern League with 110 RBIs.

In 1965 May batted .321 with San Diego and had 34 home runs and 103 RBIs. In 1966 he hit .310 with Buffalo. In both of those seasons, he was called up for a taste of the big leagues. In 1967 he made the Reds' roster to stay. In 127 games he batted .265, with 12 homers and 57 RBIs. *The Sporting News* named him its NL Rookie of the Year.

In 1968 May arrived as a home run hitter. When he hit 22 homers that season, he began a string of 11 straight seasons with 20 or more round-trippers, including three in a row with more than 30: 38 in 1969, 34 in 1970, and a career-high 39 in 1971. The 1969 season was also his most productive RBI season, as he drove in 110 runs.

In three straight contests in May 1969, May hit two homers per game. In 1970 he helped the Reds to the World Series, where in his first Fall Classic he batted .389, with a team-best eight RBIs. Cincinnati lost in five games to the Orioles.

In November 1971 May went to Houston in a deal that brought second baseman Joe Morgan, outfielder Cesar Geronimo, and pitcher Jack Billingham to Cincinnati and helped create the dominant Big Red Machine. With the Astros, May contributed 29 homers and 98 RBIs in 1972, and 28 homers and 105 RBIs in 1973. In June 1973 he hit three homers in a game against the Padres.

On April 29, 1974, May hit two homers in one inning, but his production that season fell off to 24 homers and 85 RBIs. He was traded to Baltimore in December in a four-player deal that brought third baseman Enos Cabell to Houston. With Baltimore, May continued his 20-plus home run production and, in 1976, led the AL in RBIs, with 109. He became one of only a handful of players to have 100-RBI seasons in both leagues.

Then, inexplicably, May's playing time began to decrease. In 1979 the Orioles reached the postseason and defeated California in the ALCS. May saw very little action in the World Series, and the Orioles lost to the Pirates in seven games.

In October 1980 May became a free agent and signed with the Royals. He saw limited action during two seasons with Kansas City and went to the ALCS with the Royals in 1981, primarily as a spectator, as he watched them lose to Oakland. Released following the 1982 season, he later served as Royals batting coach.

Milt May

May, Milton Scott **C**

1970–84 B:8/1/1950, Gary, IN Deb:9/8/1970, PIT NL, BL/TR 6', 190

G	AB	R	H	HR	RBI	OBP	SLG	AVG
1192	3693	313	971	77	443	.321	.371	.263

The son of Philadelphia Phillies third baseman and longtime minor league manager Pinky May, Milt May seemed to have been born in a baseball uniform and catcher's gear. The slow-footed catcher had an intricate knowledge of the game. "You don't need a manager for a player like May," Duke Snider said in 1984. "He knows how to play the game, and he will do anything he can to win."

The Pittsburgh Pirates signed Milton Scott May as an infielder in 1968 and converted him to catching. He played in Bradenton, Gastonia, and Columbus in the minors and was named to Gulf Coast Rookie, Western Carolinas, and International League All-Star teams. The 20-year-old left-handed hitter came to Pittsburgh at the end of the 1970 season. As a backup to Manny Sanguillen, May singled in the winning run in Game 4 of the 1971 World Series.

Pittsburgh traded him in October 1973 to the Houston Astros, where he came close to being a full-time player with a career-high 127 games played in 1974. Thought to be the slowest player of his generation, May took six years to steal his first major league base, in 1975. "I thought they'd stop the game and give me second base," May quipped.

On May 4, 1975, May drove in baseball's 1,000,000th run when he plated Bob Watson on a three-run homer in San Francisco. Traded to the Detroit Tigers in December 1975, he broke his ankle six games into the 1976 season and was out for the rest of the year.

Sold to the Chicago White Sox in May 1979, May signed with the Giants as a free agent after the season. In 1981 May had his best season, hitting .310, the highest batting average ever compiled by a Giants catcher. Traded to the Pirates in August 1983, he retired after the 1984 season, and was vice president of a bank in Bradenton in 1985 before being named a Pirates advance scout in 1986.

In 1987 he was a roving catching and hitting instructor in the Pirates system and later became Pirates batting coach. He followed manager Jim Leyland to the Florida Marlins and made the bizarre switch from hitting coach to pitching coach when Leyland was hired by the Colorado Rockies for the 1999 season.

Rudy May

May, Rudolph **P**

1965–83 B:7/18/1944, Coffeyville, KS Deb:4/18/1965, CAL AL BL/TL 6'3", 207

W	L	PCT	G	SH	IP	BB	SO	ERA
152	156	.494	535	24	2622	958	1760	3.46

Rudy May threw an exceptional curveball that he delivered at different speeds, a rising fastball, a sinking fastball, and a changeup. Despite a respectable 3.46 lifetime ERA, the left-hander had a mediocre 152–156 record during his 16-year career. That's mostly the result of spending half his career with a weak Angels club in the early 1970s. May suffered 36 shutout defeats, accounting for nearly 25 percent of his losses. After leaving the Angels, his record was a much healthier 101–80.

A deliberate worker, May wore wire-rimmed glasses. He often paused on the mound, removed the glasses, took a handkerchief from his back pocket, and deliberately wiped the perspiration off the lenses between pitches.

The Twins signed Rudolph May in 1962, and he started his career with Bismarck-Mandan in the Northern League in 1963, leading the league with 25 wild pitches. Drafted by the White Sox in December 1963, he played with Tidewater and Indianapolis before being swapped to the Phillies in October 1964. Two months later he was traded to the Angels for zany pitcher Bo Belinsky.

In his 1965 major league debut, May started and allowed only one hit—a seventh-inning single to pinch hitter Jake Wood—but was removed in the ninth inning. He walked 78 batters in 124 innings that year, and on June 3 he showed everyone why he was a pitcher and not a position player by striking out twice in the same inning. Sent back to the minors, he returned to the Angels in 1969.

May twice struck out 13 batters in 1971, and he fanned 16 Minnesota Twins on August 10, 1972. He was 12–11 with a 2.94 ERA in 1972 and appeared ready for a breakthrough season. But in 1973 he lost a career-high 17 games. During one September contest against Oakland he walked 11 batters. Midway through the next season May was sold to the Yankees.

The mid-to-late 1970s were May's most productive years. He went 8–4 for New York in 1974, then followed with a 14–12 mark the next season. On June 15, 1976, he was involved in a 10-player deal with the Orioles. A 15-game winner in 1976, he went 18–14 in 1977, with 11 complete games and four shutouts.

In December 1977 May was traded to Montreal. He struggled in 1978 but flourished when moved to the bullpen the following season. In 1979 May was 10–3 with a 2.31 ERA. He then became a free agent and returned to the Yankees. New York won the AL East in 1980 and May played a key role; he was 15–5 and led the league with a 2.46 ERA. He started Game 2 of the ALCS but lost, 3–2, to the Royals.

An injury-prone player, May was on the disabled list for parts of 1971, 1974, 1978, 1980, 1982, 1983, and all of 1984.

John Mayberry

Mayberry, John Claiborn **1B–DH**

1968–82 B:2/18/1949, Detroit, MI Deb:9/10/1968, HOU NL BL/TL 6'3", 220

G	AB	R	H	HR	RBI	OBP	SLG	AVG
1620	5447	733	1379	255	879	.363	.439	.253

Known for his prodigious home runs into the right field bleachers, John Mayberry was a two-time All-Star whose best season came with the Royals in 1975. That year Mayberry established career highs in batting (.291), slugging (.547), doubles (38), home runs (34), runs scored (95), and RBIs (106), and he also led the league in home run ratio and bases on balls.

The Astros made the 18-year-old John Claiborn Mayberry their No. 1 draft pick in June of 1967, but he appeared in only 105 games for Houston in four seasons. On December2, 1971, the 220-pound first baseman was traded to Kansas City for pitchers Lance Clemons and Jim York, who won a combined 10 games during their brief careers with the Astros.

Mayberry, meanwhile, drove in 100 or more runs in three of his first four seasons in Kansas

City, and he played in two ALCS with the Royals. Ironically, Mayberry's least productive seasons in Missouri were in 1976 and 1977, the two years the Royals won the AL West. He hit .232 and .230 those seasons and was even worse in the playoffs, batting .222 in the 1976 ALCS and .167 the following postseason.

Criticized for sitting out the last game of the 1977 ALCS with a toothache, he was sold to the Blue Jays only days before the 1978 season started. Mayberry hit 20 or more homers in three of his four seasons in Toronto, and he often supplied the clutch hit. During one 14-month stretch he broke up three no-hitters.

The gregarious Mayberry was appreciated in Toronto, and manager Bobby Mattick named him team captain in 1981. Opposing player Bobby Grich once said, "Big John is so nice and easygoing you don't suspect anything when he asks you to take your foot off the bag to kick the dust away—until he tags you." Traded to the Yankees in May 1982, Mayberry retired at the end of the season with a total of 255 home runs.

Carl Mays

Mays, Carl William **P**

1915–29 B:11/12/1891, Liberty, KY D:4/4/1971, El Cajon, CA Deb:4/15/1915, BOS AL BL/TR 5'11½", 195

W	L	PCT	G	SV	IP	BB	SO	ERA
208	126	.623	490	31	3021^{1}	734	862	2.92

In the space of two years, Carl Mays, the surly pitcher with the submarine delivery, set in motion two events that forever changed the nature and structure of the game. One involved quitting his team in a snarling fit; the other resulted from throwing a pitch that killed a batter.

Mays, once described as having "the disposition of someone with a permanent toothache," was an excellent pitcher and a tough competitor. As a rookie he provoked a fight with Ty Cobb by throwing at him. He won 18 games or more seven times in the first dozen years of his 15-year major league career. On August 30, 1918, Mays pitched and won both games of a doubleheader to clinch the flag for Boston. In the World Series he started and won two games and allowed only 10 hits in a pair of complete-game victories.

That was to be the last Red Sox team to win a championship. In 1919 Mays was an abysmal 5–11, despite a 2.47 ERA. The team was playing poorly behind him, and he suspected (probably with good reason) that it was because they didn't like him. In the second inning of a July 19 game, the inept Sox were losing, 4–0, when catcher Wally Schang tried to throw out a base stealer at second. Mays, looking the other way, didn't see the ball, and it hit him in the back of the head. He finished the inning, then left the game and announced that he had gone fishing. He told management that he was battling an injury and facing personal problems and that he wanted to be traded.

The Yankees opened their purses and bought him for $40,000. When American League President Ban Johnson heard the news, he was irate; he didn't relish the idea of a player deciding when he could leave his team. He immediately suspended Mays for an indefinite period, at least until he returned to the Red Sox. But Yankees owner Jacob Ruppert wanted the pitcher. He obtained temporary injunctions that enabled Mays to pitch for him and finally took the case to the New York State Supreme Court, where he won a permanent injunction to prevent Johnson from interfering in his affairs.

Ruppert and two other owners became known as the "Insurrectionists" who tried to loosen Johnson's dictatorial grip on the game. When the Black Sox scandal hit in 1920 the weakened Johnson lost his job, and Judge Kenesaw Landis became baseball's first commissioner, establishing a new force for controlling the game that didn't change for 70 years.

During a pennant race that year, with the Yankees, White Sox, and Indians contending, Mays got the starting assignment for the August 16 game with Cleveland. It was a muggy, drizzly day in New York, but the rain stopped in the fourth inning with the Indians up, 3–0.

Ray Chapman, the popular Cleveland shortstop, stepped in against Mays to leadoff the fifth. Chapman froze for Mays' first pitch, which was thrown in his characteristic submarine style. The pitch hit Chapman on the left temple. Babe Ruth, in left field, heard the shattering sound as Chapman fell to the ground. The ball rolled toward third, and Mays picked it up and threw to first. Chapman got up, tried to walk, and fell again. He died the next day, his skull crushed on one side and fractured on the other.

The outrage directed at Mays was enormous. His deceptive delivery and willingness to throw inside had earned him the league lead in hit batsmen in 1917, and he ranked second in 1918 and 1919. He denied throwing at Chapman and expressed regret over the incident, but some teams swore they would never play against him again.

The sad death of Ray Chapman led to a major change in the rules of the game. After that, umpires were encouraged to keep only new, white balls in the game and to throw out those that had been darkened by dirt and grass. It was the single most dramatic difference between the dead-ball, poke-and-run game of the teens and the explosive home run era of the 1920s.

The antipathy expressed by fans and major league players gave the scowling Mays even more reason to grumble, but his performance wasn't hampered by the noise. In 1921 he led the majors with 27 wins and appeared in enough relief stints to be credited with seven saves. He won one game but took two tough losses in the Giants' victory over the Yankees in the 1921 World Series.

The Giants took the Series again in 1922, but Mays' scraps with manager Miller Huggins put him in the doghouse. He started and lost Game 4 of the Series, 4–3, and by the next year he and Huggins were constantly at each other's throats. Mays was allowed to pitch in only 23 games. On July 17 of that year, Huggins let Mays stay in a game in which he allowed 20 hits and 13 runs. Mays was sold to Cincinnati that December.

National Leaguers were as fooled by the submarine delivery as their American League counterparts had been. Mays won 20 games with Cincinnati in 1924 and 19 in 1926. His major league career ended as a Giants reliever in 1929. Later he worked as a scout for the Indians, the A's, and the Braves.

Willie Mays

Mays, Willie Howard **OF**

1951–52, 1954–73 Negro League Player (1948–50)
B:5/6/1931, Westfield, AL Deb:5/25/1951, NY NL BR/TR
5'11", 180

G	AB	R	H	HR	RBI	OBP	SLG	AVG
2992	10881	2062	3283	660	1903	.387	.557	.302

Willie Mays could do everything: hit for average, hit for power, run, field, and throw. There were better outfielders, players with better arms, batters with higher averages and more homers, and faster runners who stole more bases. But no one could do all those things at Mays' skill level. On top of that, "Say Hey" added a dash of showmanship and childlike delight that made him a fan favorite for 22 years.

In 1970 he explained how he felt about the game. "I like to play happy. Baseball is a fun game...and I love it." And when baseball was no longer fun, Mays got out. "When the game began to be a job, that bothered me. That's why I quit, when it began to be work. In baseball, at a certain age, you have to get out. You can't go back. There is nothing to go back to."

Mays' lifetime stats only hint at his greatness. When he retired, no one except Babe Ruth had hit more home runs. Mays played in at least 150 games in a season 13 times, a major league record. He holds the National League record for most games with two or more homers, at 63. He hit 22 extra-inning home runs in his career; Ruth is second with 16. Mays also won a batting title, finished second three times, and third twice. He led the National League in home runs four times, twice hitting more than 50.

Mays was the league's Most Valuable Player twice, at age 23 and again at age 34. He had 300 or more total bases in 13 consecutive seasons. Only Lou Gehrig equaled that feat, and only Hank Aaron exceeded it. Mays finished his career 10th all time in hits and slugging average, seventh in RBIs, sixth in games played, fifth in runs scored, fourth in extra-base hits, and third in total bases. *The Sporting News* named him Player of the Decade for the 1960s.

Defensively, he's in a league of his own. Mays is the all-time leader in outfield putouts and total chances, but numbers don't even begin to tell the story. Harry Hooper, who played next to Tris Speaker in the Red Sox outfield for six years, said that Mays was the best outfielder ever. In 1951 Mays caught a drive by Rocky Nelson in Pittsburgh's Forbes Field with his bare hand, and did the same thing to Roberto Clemente a few years later in the same park. In 1952 Mays knocked himself unconscious catching a ball hit by Dodger Bobby Morgan.

In the 1954 World Series Mays made a play that has gone down in baseball history as simply "the Catch." In Game 1 at the Polo Grounds, the score was tied, 2–2, in the eighth inning when two Indians reached base. Cleveland slugger Vic Wertz, who already had a triple and two singles in the game, belted a long flyball to deep center field. Mays sprinted away with his back to home plate, turned at the last second, and snagged the ball over his shoulder at a dead run more than 440 feet from home. He then spun in one motion and let fly a perfect throw that allowed only one baserunner to tag up and advance. The score stayed tied.

The incredible throw following the remarkable catch brought this quote from sportswriter Tommy Holmes: "It's doubtful there has ever been a more enthusiastic thrower than Willie Mays, who acts as if the possession of a baseball were a crime punishable by imprisonment."

In the top of the 10th inning of the same game, Wertz led off with a line drive to left-center field that looked certain to reach the wall for a potential inside-the-park home run. Mays sped over to cut it off and held Wertz to a double. Mays later said he thought that play was even better than the Catch. The Indians had never seen anything like it. The two plays demoralized them, and Cleveland, which had won 111 regular-season games, was swept in the Series.

For years, when baseball's best players met in the All-Star Game, Mays made it his personal show, demonstrating his incredible talents to the nation and intimidating the American Leaguers in the process. Mays was an All-Star every year after he returned from the service in 1954, playing 24 games in 20 years. (From 1959 through 1962 the leagues played two games each year.) He set the all-time All-Star records for at bats, hits, runs, extra-base hits, triples, and stolen bases.

At the 1955 All-Star Game Mays had two hits that rallied the National League to a 6–5 victory. In the

1956 Midsummer Classic he hit a two-run homer. In the 1957 contest he had two hits, including a key triple. In the first 1959 game his ninth-inning triple drove in the winning run. In the first 1960 game he led off with a triple and added a double and a single. In the second game that year, he slugged a homer among his three hits.

In the first 1961 All-Star Game Mays drove in the tying run with a double in the last of the 10th inning; he scored the winning run moments later. In 1963 he drove in two runs, scored two, swiped two bases, and made a superb grab in center. In 1965 he homered, walked twice, and scored the winning run. In 1968 his daredevil baserunning in the first inning led to the game's only run.

At age 17, Willie Howard Mays had signed his first professional contract, with the Birmingham Black Barons of the Negro National League. While at Birmingham, Mays benefited from the tutelage of Piper Davis. In his first year as a Baron, Mays' team won the league pennant in the final game when the youngster beat out an infield hit with the bases loaded and two out in the 11th inning.

Sold to the New York Giants in 1950 for $15,000, Mays was assigned to the team's Trenton farm club. At about this time a Giants scout had passed up the young Hank Aaron; it is intriguing to speculate about what fireworks might have occurred had the two greatest home run hitters in National League history been teammates. Interstate League pitching didn't faze Mays. He batted .353 and began 1951 playing for Minneapolis of the American Association. After 35 games he was hitting .477. The Giants called him up.

Mays struggled in his first two dozen plate appearances, failing to get a hit. Giants manager Leo Durocher saw the youngster weeping in the clubhouse and comforted him. "You're my center fielder as long as I'm the manager because you're the best center fielder I've ever seen," Durocher told him. The next game Mays homered off Warren Spahn, the first of 660 round-trippers he would clout during his career. Spahn later said, "I'll never forgive myself. We might have gotten rid of Willie forever if I'd only struck him out."

During the rest of his rookie season, Mays supplied occasional power and superb defense as the Giants stormed back to win the pennant. When Bobby Thomson hit his legendary home run, Mays was in the on-deck circle. Mays was voted National League Rookie of the Year.

He was called into the service after only 34 games

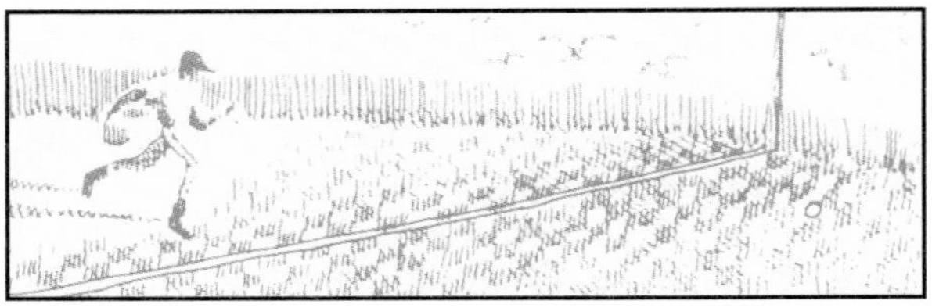

in 1952 and did not return until 1954. When he did come back, he lit up New York like a Roman candle. He led all National League hitters that year with a .345 average and 13 triples. He tied for third in home runs, with 41, drove in 110 runs, and scored 119. The Giants won the pennant by five games and swept the Indians in the World Series, thanks in part to "the Catch."

In 1955 Mays slugged a league-leading 51 home runs and 13 triples and also swiped 24 bases. It seemed that not a year went by without his leading the league in some category: triples in 1954, 1955, and 1957; home runs in 1954, 1962, 1965, and 1966; runs in 1958 and 1961; hits in 1960; slugging percentage in 1954, 1955, 1957, 1964, and 1965; and on-base percentage and walks in 1971.

On the streets of New York, Mays was considered a hometown hero. He would stop to play stickball with kids in Harlem, and his gleeful greeting, "Say hey," became his nickname. Durocher said "he lit up a room when he came in. He was a joy to be around." The Giants packed up and followed the Dodgers to the West Coast in 1958, where Mays didn't receive the same adulation.

Nevertheless, he continued to shine. He led the league with 49 home runs in 1962 and drove in 27 more runs than any teammate as San Francisco tied Los Angeles for the NL pennant. Mays clubbed two homers in the first game of the playoff, and in the final game his bases-loaded line drive off the body of Dodgers reliever Ed Roebuck ignited the winning rally. San Francisco moved on to the World Series, which they lost to the Yankees in seven taut games. In the bottom of the ninth of Game 7, with two outs and Matty Alou on first, Mays cracked a double to right. But a super throw from Roger Maris held Alou at third and the Giants fell, 1–0.

In 1963 Mays homered in the last of the 16th to give Juan Marichal a complete-game, 1–0 victory over Warren Spahn, who had also gone the distance. In 1971 the 40-year-old Mays walked a league-best 112 times as Giants won their division, but the Pirates prevailed in the NLCS.

In May 1972 the Giants traded Mays to the Mets for pitcher Charlie Williams and $50,000. The Mets were trying to recapture some of the old Big Apple magic. In his first game as a Met, Mays homered against San Francisco to give his new team a 5–4 win over his old. In his next game he walked and scored on a triple when he knocked the ball out of the catcher's glove, and the Mets won, 2–1. Two days later he slugged a two-run homer for another one-run Mets win. He reached base during his first 20 games in a Mets uniform.

By April 1973 he was hurting. He had fluid drained from both knees, and an aching right shoulder forced him to the bench. He played in only 66 games that season, but the Mets held on to win the NL East with the worst-ever winning percentage for a division or league champion. In Game 2 of that year's World Series, Mays delivered a 12th-inning single to put his club ahead to stay. It was his last major league hit. On his farewell night in Shea Stadium a sign read, "We who are about to cry salute you."

After Mays was hired in 1979 as a greeter and public relations personality for Bally's Casino in Atlantic City, Commissioner Bowie Kuhn suspended him from official involvement in Major League Baseball. Kuhn's successor, Peter Ueberroth, lifted the ban in 1985.

One testimony to Mays' legacy is the number of today's superstars who want to wear his uniform No. 24 as a tribute. They include outfielders Barry Bonds (while at Pittsburgh), Ken Griffey, Jr., and Rickey Henderson. Mays was named to the Baseball Hall of Fame in 1979, his first year of eligibility.

Bill Mazeroski

Mazeroski, William Stanley **2B**

1956–72 B:9/5/1936, Wheeling, WV Deb:7/7/1956, PIT NL BR/TR 5'11½", 183

G	AB	R	H	HR	RBI	OBP	SLG	AVG
2163	7755	769	2016	138	853	.302	.367	.260

Bill Mazeroski's place in baseball history is built on two nearly opposing factors. One, the stuff of high drama, happened in an instant; the other developed over a 17-year career. One involved a bat; the other, a glove. Unfortunately, Maz's one brief, shining moment at bat overshadowed his far more brilliant career afield.

Mazeroski's October 1960 home run over the left-field wall at Forbes Field brought a smashing end to a World Series marked with bizarre plays and unexpected events. The Pirates, who hadn't won a Series in 35 years, clawed and sputtered their way against the legendary New York Yankees.

The Pirates won four games in that Series by scores of 6–4, 5–2, 3–2, and 10–9; the Yankees wins were 16–3, 10–0, and 12–0. For the Series, the Pirates were outscored 55–27, outhit 91–60, and outhomered 10–4. Yet at 3:36 P.M. on October 13, Mazeroski turned on a high Ralph Terry fastball to decide the outcome of the Fall Classic. As a result, Mickey Mantle cried for hours, and New York manager Casey Stengel was fired.

Mazeroski's clout marked the stunning end to one of the wildest seventh games in Series history. It was only the third World Series game to end on a home run, and it was the only Series determined by a longball on the final pitch until 1993, when Toronto won the Series on Joe Carter's ninth-inning homer. Ironically, Mazeroski's homer overshadowed his remarkable and long-lived career as a second baseman.

Most fans unknowingly place Mazeroski in the category of an Al Weis or a Buddy Biancalana, journeymen players who each had one big Series hit. But Mazeroski's real claim to fame should be his long-term defensive excellence.

In fact, he might be called the all-time greatest defensive player at any position. Mazeroski holds more defensive titles than any other player, ever, and his major league records as a second baseman include most lifetime double plays, most double plays in a season, and nine years leading his league in assists. Author Bill James agrees that Mazeroski's defensive stats are the most impressive of any player at any position. And author Charles Faber, in his book, *Baseball Ratings*, awards points for percentage, assists, chances, and range factor to all players with 10 years' experience: Mazeroski leads every player from every era, regardless of position.

Maz's National League records include leading the league in chances eight times and in assists five consecutive years. He also led the NL in fielding percentage three times and was the Gold Glove second baseman eight times, competing with the likes of Julian Javier, Don Blasingame, Johnny Temple, Frank Bolling, Ken Hubbs, and Tony Taylor.

His work on the double play—a lightning-fast sidestep and quick throw to first—earned him the nickname "No Touch" because he never seemed to touch the ball; he simply redirected it to first. In Mazeroski's first of six All-Star Games, he received the ultimate compliment. During fielding practice, players on both teams, hardened major leaguers, stopped to watch Mazeroski field and throw. It was a tribute, the equivalent of stopping to watch Ted Williams hit.

Signed before his 18th birthday as part of general manager Branch Rickey's extensive talent searches, William Stanley Mazeroski hit .293 at Williamsport and .306 at Hollywood. The Pirates promoted him in July 1957. During Maz's first year, reporters got tired of hearing a Bucs official brag about what a fine person the youngster was—clean-cut, clean-living. A sportswriter interjected, "Right now the Pirates would be better off with a juvenile delinquent who could hit."

But Mazeroski batted .283 and .275 in his first two full major league seasons, and he hit 19 homers the second year. In 1962 he drove in 81 runs to lead the team—batting eighth all year—and his 138 career homers and lifetime .260 average compare favorably with such glove wizards as Ozzie Smith and Walter "Rabbit" Maranville.

Unlike players who broke in a new glove every year, Mazeroski used only three or four gloves during his entire 17-year career. After someone once referred to his battered mitt as a "pancake," his teammates put butter and maple syrup on it and tried to carve it up with a knife and fork. Maz repaired it and kept using it. Once Roberto

Clemente tried to get Maz to change to a new glove by giving his old one away. As Mazeroski related the story, "It was sitting in the dugout. It used to come apart a lot and it had leather patches all over it. Clemente picked it up and threw it to a kid in the stands. The kid took one look at it and threw it back."

A broken bone in his foot kept Mazeroski from All-Star status in 1965 for only the second time in eight years. In 1967, despite having pulled muscles in both his legs early in the season, Mazeroski set the National League record for games played in a season, with 163.

Mazeroski retired from active play in 1972, but he remained with the Pirates as a coach in 1973, coached at Seattle in 1979 and 1980, and has frequently been hired to work on infield play with promising prospects, such as former Expo Tim Wallach.

After Mazeroski retired, Kansas City second baseman Frank White, an eight-time Gold Glover, commented to sportswriter Jim Kaplan: "Bill Mazeroski has the fastest hands I've ever seen." Kaplan felt obliged to ask, "Where did you see him play, on film?" White answered, "No, I'm talking about his hands right now. I've seen him fooling around with the ball. He has the quickest hands I've ever seen."

After retiring from baseball Mazeroski owned and operated a golf course not far from Pittsburgh and lent his name to a baseball annual. A foray into local politics ended with a primary defeat in 1991.

Lee Mazzilli

Mazzilli, Lee Louis **OF–1B**

1976–89 B:3/25/1955, New York, NY Deb:9/7/1976, NY NL BB/TR 6'1", 185

G	AB	R	H	HR	RBI	OBP	SLG	AVG
1475	4124	571	1068	93	460	.361	.385	.259

The New York Mets made Lee Mazzilli their first local, top draft pick and billed him as the city's next great center fielder. As it turned out, Mazzilli made his biggest contribution to the Mets' revival from their late-1970s doldrums when he was traded to the Texas Rangers for pitchers Ron Darling and Walt Terrell. Mazzilli returned home to help the Mets win titles in 1986 and 1988 as a key bench player.

Reared in Brooklyn, the son of welterweight boxer Libero Mazzilli, Lee Louis Mazzilli was an eight-time speed skating champion in his age group and a high school all-American in baseball. The attractive young athlete was the Mets' first-round draft pick in June 1973, the 14th choice overall.

In his first two pro seasons, Mazzilli stole 46 and 49 bases, respectively, including a purported pro-record seven in a seven-inning California League game on June 8, 1975, for the Visalia Mets at San Jose. In 1976 he was a Texas League All-Star, leading the league with 111 walks and finishing second with 28 steals.

He made his Mets debut that September and set teenybopper hearts athrob. He impressed other Mets rooters with both a three-run pinch-hit homer off Darold Knowles in his second big league plate appearance and a two-out, two-run, ninth-inning blast off Pittsburgh's Kent Tekulve that sank Pirate pennant hopes. Mazzilli became the Mets' center fielder and leadoff hitter in 1977 after the club traded away pitcher Tom Seaver and outfielder-first baseman Dave Kingman.

In 1978 "the Italian Stallion," as Mazzilli was called in the wake of the popular Rocky films, began alternating between the top and the middle of the batting order, and on September 3 he became the first Met to homer from both sides of the plate in the same game. (The ambidextrous Mazzilli had given up lefthanded throwing as a pro and had a sub-par arm in the outfield.)

It was difficult to find the right role for Mazzilli, a highly disciplined hitter who exceeded 22 steals only twice and never exceeded 16 home runs during his 14-year career. His best year by far came in 1979, when he placed 10th in the National League batting race, at .303, and fourth in the league in on-base percentage, with .397. In addition, his 79 RBIs, 34 doubles, 93 walks, and 19-game hitting streak marks were all career highs.

Selected to the All-Star team that season, he tied the game with an opposite-field pinch-hit homer off Jim Kern in the eighth, then walked with the bases loaded to force in the winning run against crosstown rival Ron Guidry in the ninth. Mazzilli also scored five times, a league record.

In 1980 he shuttled between first base and center field, setting a career-high mark with 41 steals in 56 tries, but the late-season arrival of Mookie Wilson closed him out of center field. A spring 1981 trade for Kingman ended the first base option, sending Mazzilli to left. Slowed by back and elbow problems, he had a dismal year. On April 1, 1982, the Mets sent him to Texas for two hurlers who would start the franchise on the road to recovery.

In Texas, Mazzilli was plagued by shoulder and wrist problems, spending nearly six weeks on the disabled list in May and June. After he recovered the Rangers sent him back to New York on August 8, acquiring shortstop Bucky Dent from the Yankees in return. That winter the Bronx Bombers dealt Mazzilli to Pittsburgh for four minor leaguers, pitcher Tim Burke the lone notable, and Mazzilli began a second career as a bench player.

A switch hitter with a good eye, he developed into formidable weapon. In 1985 Mazzilli topped the league with 72 pinch-hit appearances, reaching base 31 times for a .437 pinch on-base percentage. But the rebuilding Pirates released him on July 23, 1986, and Mazzilli signed a minor league contract with the Mets a week later. After six games with Tidewater, he returned to New York as the Mets coasted to the NL East title.

During the 1986 postseason Mazzilli pinch hit nine times in the Mets' 13 contests, collecting three hits. One came during his league playoff-record five pinch-hit appearances against Houston, the others, in the World Series against the Boston Red Sox.

After failing in his first two opportunities, Mazzilli led off the eighth inning of Game 6 of the World Series with the Mets down 3–2, six outs away from elimination, singling to right off Calvin Schiraldi. He then scored the tying the run on teammate Gary Carter's sacrifice fly. In Game 7 Mazzilli pinch hit in the sixth, with one out and the Mets down 3–0, igniting a game-tying rally with a single. The Mets went on to win the crown.

Mazzilli tied for the league lead with 17 pinch hits in 1987, batting .309 in that role. In the 1988 playoffs he went 1-for-2, was hit by a pitch, and stole a base in three pinch-hit appearances against the Los Angeles Dodgers.

At the end of July 1989 the Mets put Mazzilli on waivers, and the Toronto Blue Jays claimed him for their pennant drive. A day later, the Jays acquired Wilson, who had taken Mazzilli's spot in the Mets' outfield at the start of the decade. As a pinch hitter, Mazzilli went 4-for-7, with four RBIs, and hit his sixth career pinch homer for the Jays down the stretch. However, he took an 0-for-8 collar in the Jays' playoff loss to the Oakland Athletics, making two starts as a designated hitter and pinch hitting in his final major league contest. He finished with 75 regular-season pinch hits in 332 at bats, a .226 average.

After retiring, Mazzilli worked as a broadcaster and an actor, hoping to cash in on his matinee idol looks. Although he took diction lessons to obscure his regional dialect, his first speaking part called for Brooklynese. In 1999 he was managing the Eastern League's Norwich Navigators. He was hired as first-base coach for the Yankees after the 1999 season

Jimmy McAleer

McAleer, James Robert **OF**

1889–1907 M(1901–11, 735–889) B:7/10/1864, Youngstown, OH Deb:4/24/1889, CLE NL BR/TR 6', 175

G	AB	R	H	HR	RBI	OBP	SLG	AVG
1020	3977	619	1007	11	469	.322	.310	.253

Jimmy "Loafer" McAleer excelled as a defensive outfielder for the Cleveland Spiders. Franklin Lewis wrote that he was "perhaps the most graceful outfielder known to the game with exception of Tris Speaker." But it was as an organizer, manager and owner in the American League that he made his mark.

James Robert McAleer was a key component in Ban Johnson's scheme to elevate the upstart American League to a major league. In 1901 McAleer came out of retirement in Youngstown, Ohio, to serve as the first manager of the league's Cleveland franchise, but also would help Johnson raid the St. Louis Cardinals of such talent as Jesse Burkett and Bobby Wallace. In 1902 he replaced Hugh Duffy as manager of the new St. Louis Browns franchise. In 1910–11 he managed Washington.

On September 16, 1911, McAleer, John I. Taylor and Secretary of the American League Robert McRoy became owners of the Boston Red Sox. During the 1912 World Series McAleer's ticket-selling practices caused much controversy among the team's Royal Rooters, as did his subsequent firing of manager Jake Stahl. In 1914 Ban Johnson forced McAleer to sell out to Joseph Lannin. Ill with cancer, McAleer shot himself in April 1931.

Dick McAuliffe

McAuliffe, Richard John **2B-SS-3B**

1960–75 B:11/29/1939, Hartford, CT Deb:9/17/1960, DET AL BL/TR 5'11", 176

G	AB	R	H	HR	RBI	OBP	SLG	AVG
1763	6185	888	1530	197	697	.344	.403	.247

A stalwart in the Tigers infield of the 1960s, Dick McAuliffe consistently posted high on-base percentages and hit between 10 and 20 homers per season. The lefthanded hitter held his bat parallel to the ground, waist-high, with his front foot dangling in the air.

Richard John McAuliffe played with Erie, Valdosta, Augusta, Knoxville, and Durham before arriving in Detroit in 1960. During his first three major league seasons he was used at shortstop, third base, and second base, but in 1963 he became the Tigers' regular shortstop. He hit a career-high 24 homers in 1964, and was selected to the AL All-Star team in 1965. However, later that season McAuliffe slid hard into a base and broke his wrist.

The Tigers inserted Ray Oyler at shortstop in 1967 and moved the 27-year-old McAuliffe to second base, where he again made the All-Star team. Only a .247 career hitter, McAuliffe twice managed to walk more than 100 times in a season. He led the league with 95 runs scored in 1968 and went through the entire season without grounding into a double play. Later that season he was suspended for five days for charging pitcher Tommy John.

Detroit won the 1968 pennant and met the St. Louis Cardinals in the World Series. Although he hit only .222 in the Series, McAuliffe scored five runs, drove in three more, walked four times, and homered in Game 3. He played a flawless second base, and the Tigers won the world championship in seven games.

In April 1969 McAuliffe led off two consecutive games with home runs, one of only 11 players in AL history to accomplish the feat. He homered in Game 4 of the 1972 ALCS, won by Oakland in five games. On October 23, 1973, he was traded to Boston for outfielder Ben Oglivie. He later owned coin-operated laundries in apartment complexes in West Simsbury, Connecticut.

Bake McBride

McBride, Arnold Ray **OF**

1973–83 B:2/3/1949, Fulton, MO Deb:7/26/1973, STL NL BL/TR 6'2", 190

G	AB	R	H	HR	RBI	OBP	SLG	AVG
1071	3853	548	1153	63	430	.348	.420	.299

Cardinals outfielder Arnold Ray "Bake" McBride captured the National League Rookie of the Year honors in 1974. McBride, whose father (also nicknamed Bake) pitched for the Kansas City Monarchs, graduated from Westminster College in his native Fulton, Missouri. Selected by the Cardinals in the 37th round of the June 1970 free agent draft, McBride played in the minors with Sarasota, Modesto, Arkansas, and Tulsa before arriving in the big leagues in 1973.

He hit .300 or better his first five years in the majors and was traded to the Phillies in a June 1977 five-player deal. On September 8, 1978, McBride tied the modern National League record for putouts in a game by a right fielder when he collected 10. That year he led league outfielders in fielding percentage.

McBride won Game 1 of the 1980 World Series with a three-run homer. He singled in the tying run and scored the winning run in Game 2. He batted .304 in the Series as the Phillies won the first world championship in their 98-season existence. It was McBride's last healthy season, however. He finished his career in 1983 as a member of the Cleveland Indians.

Dick McBride

McBride, James Dixon **P**

1871–76 M(1871–75, 161–85) B:1845, Philadelphia, PA D:10/10/1916, Philadelphia, PA Deb:5/20/1871, PHI NA TR 5'9", 150

W	L	PCT	G	SH	IP	BB	SO	ERA
0	4	.000	4	0	33	5	2	2.73

The Philadelphia Athletics' James Dickson "Dick" McBride was the first manager to capture a major league pennant when his 1871 club took the only National Association flag not won by the Boston Red Stockings. Although 1871 was the first league season for the Athletics, it was McBride's 10th campaign with the club, an operation that dated back to 1860. From 1864 through 1868, the team had gone 178–11. In 1870 McBride had thrown 625 innings for the A's. Known for his nasty temper and ready supply of sarcasm, McBride was only 26 as the 1871 season began. That year he would lead the National Association in won-lost percentage. He had a .668 winning percentage as a pitcher (149–74) in the NA. As a manager he led the Athletics to a 161–85 record.

In 1873 McBride paced the NA with three shutouts. The following year he held league batters to a circuit-best .241 average. When the Red Stockings and Athletics toured England in 1874 playing both baseball and cricket, McBride was an especially valuable addition to the expedition. He was described by Cal McVey as one of the "really expert cricketers" from America. When the National League formed in 1876 he joined Boston, but he lost his only four starts in the NL.

Joe McCarthy

McCarthy, Joseph Vincent

Manager (1926–46, 1948–50, 2,125–1,333)
B:4/21/1887, Philadelphia, PA D:1/13/1978, Buffalo, NY

He was a bush leaguer, and his early critics never let him forget it. But Joe McCarthy soon proved that a fellow with no major league playing experience could be as big league as anyone when it came to managing pennant winners.

In 24 big league seasons McCarthy captured nine pennants, and to this day he holds the records for most world championship teams managed, with seven, shared with Casey Stengel; best regular-season career won-lost percentage, at .615; and best career World Series won-lost percentage, at .698. He was also the first manager to win pennants in both the American and National leagues. In fact, his teams won with such regularity that his critics came up with a new label for him: "push-button manager."

McCarthy grew up in Germantown, a suburb of Philadelphia, and idolized Athletics manager Connie Mack. McCarthy left Niagara University to sign a contract with Wilmington of the Class B Tri-State League in 1907. He hit only .175 with Wilmington but by 1908 had advanced all the way up to Toledo of the American Association. Along the way, the infielder batted over .300 with Franklin in 1907 and with Wilkes-Barre in 1913.

He is sometimes confused with Joseph N. McCarthy, who had a brief big league career with the New York Highlanders and St. Louis Cardinals in 1906 and 1907, but this Joe McCarthy came along a few years later and never made the majors. He came closest while playing with Buffalo in 1915, when team president Ed Barrow was working on a deal to sell him to the Yankees (the former Highlanders). Instead McCarthy jumped to Brooklyn of the outlaw Federal League. The Yankees deal fell through, but so did McCarthy's chances with Brooklyn, for the Federal League collapsed before the start of the 1916 season.

McCarthy landed his first managerial job in 1913, with Wilkes-Barre. He did not manage again until 1919, when he took over Louisville of the American Association. With Louisville, McCarthy won pennants in 1921 and 1925. General manager William Veeck, Sr. of the last-place Cubs hired McCarthy to manage the ballclub in 1926.

In Chicago, McCarthy immediately came under fire as a "busher," unfit to manage a big league club. But he quickly established his authority by packing free-living, hard-drinking pitching legend Grover Cleveland Alexander off to the Cardinals. "All baseball knew then that McCarthy was managing the Cubs in fact as well as in name," noted sportswriter Warren Brown.

Cubs ownership also took notice. "Congratulations. I've been looking for a manager with enough nerve to do that," William Wrigley wired McCarthy.

Another of McCarthy's early moves was to acquire slugger Hack Wilson, who had been left unprotected at Toledo of the American Association by the Giants in 1925. McCarthy recommended to Veeck that Chicago draft Wilson. For $5,000 the future Hall of Famer became a Cub.

McCarthy delivered immediate improvement to the Cubs and brought them a pennant in 1929, but he was bested by his old idol Mack in the World Series. He finished second in the National League in 1930, but that was no longer good enough. Rogers Hornsby replaced him with only four days left in the season.

As luck would have it, the Yankees' managerial post had opened up, and McCarthy got the job. "[Yankees president] Colonel Ruppert was a wonderful man to work for," said McCarthy. "He never bothered me. He let me run the team."

The only orders McCarthy received from the millionaire brewer came at the close of each year's World Series: "Do it again next year."

"And generally we did. You've got to follow orders, right?" said McCarthy.

Just as McCarthy had faced a disciplinary problem with "Old Pete" Alexander in Chicago, he had another one in New York with Babe Ruth. The two men simply did not get along and barely spoke to each other. One of the problems was that Ruth, now winding down his playing career,

thought he should be Yankees manager. The slugger was told: "You can't manage yourself, how can you manage others?" Finally Ruth, like Alexander, was sent elsewhere.

McCarthy won a world championship in 1932 against his old team, the Cubs, and he followed that up with three second-place finishes. All the while, "Marse Joe" instilled his pride and his own brand of discipline in the Yankees. "So I eat, drink and sleep baseball 24 hours a day," he said. "What's wrong with that? The idea of this game is to win and keep winning."

From 1936 through 1943 McCarthy's Yankees did win, taking seven pennants and six world championships. In 1946 Larry MacPhail, flamboyant and mercurial, acquired the Yankees. Predictably, he and McCarthy clashed. The manager, pleading ill health, quit in midseason.

By 1948 he was managing Tom Yawkey's Boston Red Sox. A big question, of course, was how McCarthy and Ted Williams would interact. McCarthy immediately defused the situation. "A manager who cannot get along with a .400 hitter ought to have his head examined," said Marse Joe.

In 1948 and 1949 McCarthy suffered two agonizing disappointments, losing the 1948 pennant to Cleveland in a playoff and dropping the 1949 pennant to New York on the last day of the season. In both years some questionable decisions by McCarthy regarding Red Sox pitching played a key role in Boston's downfall. Halfway through the 1950 season McCarthy, in fourth place and worn out, stepped down as Sox manager.

McCarthy wasn't a fiery, combative manager who harangued umpires, as Leo Durocher and Earl Weaver were. "I learned early on that you couldn't do your ballclub much good if you weren't there," he observed.

However, in one incident McCarthy seemingly acted out of character. Yankees catcher Art Jorgens appeared to have tagged a runner in plenty of time, but umpire Bill McGowan called the runner safe. Jorgens turned around and touched McGowan and was promptly ejected. McCarthy ran out and wanted to know why his catcher was gone and was told it was because Jorgens had pushed McGowan. "Why, he just gave you a little push like that," McCarthy said, and he provided McGowan with an illustration.

"Isn't that enough?" responded McGowan.

McCarthy went through his question and demonstration again. McGowan didn't make much of it, but the crowd by now was going crazy, thinking McCarthy was shoving the umpire around.

Finally, McGowan caught on and told McCarthy, "Don't do that again." McCarthy just winked and walked away—still in the game.

In 1957 McCarthy was elected by the Veterans Committee to the Hall of Fame.

Tommy McCarthy

McCarty, Thomas Francis Michael **OF**

1884–96 M(1890, 4–1) B:7/24/1863, Boston, MA D:8/5/1922, Boston, MA Deb:7/10/1884, BOS UA BR/TR 5'7", 170

G	AB	R	H	HR	RBI	OBP	SLG	AVG
1275	5128	1069	1496	44	735	.364	.376	.292

Although Tommy McCarthy is a member of the Hall of Fame, many baseball scholars consider his selection one of the biggest mistakes the Veterans (then Old-Timers') Committee has made. McCarthy made it through a solid 13-year stint in three different major leagues, but did not enjoy a standout career.

McCarthy broke in with the Union Association in 1884 and made a few appearances with Philadelphia in the National League in 1886 and 1887, but he did not really establish himself until he joined the American Association's St. Louis Browns in 1888. He helped the Browns win the '88 pennant and gained a reputation as an outstanding defensive player. He was also a swift baserunner, stealing 93 bases in 1888 and leading the AA in stolen bases in 1890.

McCarthy moved to Boston and the National League in 1892, and helped Boston win NL pennants his first two years there. In Boston, he was also recognized for his fine defensive performance. He and Hugh Duffy, who played in the same Boston outfield from 1892 though 1895, were called "the Heavenly Twins" for their artistry in corralling flyballs. McCarthy was particularly known for trapping short flies in right field and turning them into double plays. He possessed not only great speed but also a fine throwing arm.

McCarthy's offensive performance was far more erratic. He did hit over .340 three times and drove in over 100 runs twice, but his offensive production was poor in other seasons. He concluded his above-average but unspectacular career with Brooklyn in 1896.

Tim McCarver

McCarver, James Timothy **C–1B**

1959–80 B:10/16/1941, Memphis, TN Deb:9/10/1959, STL NL BL/TR 6'1", 195

G	AB	R	H	HR	RBI	OBP	SLG	AVG
1909	5529	590	1501	97	645	.340	.388	.271

Tim McCarver has had three careers in baseball. First he was the brash catcher and co-captain of the St. Louis Cardinals pennant winners of the 1960s. In the late 1970s he became Steve Carlton's personal receiver and quipped that he and Carlton "would be buried 60 feet, 6 inches apart." After hanging up his shin guards McCarver moved to the broadcasting booth, ladling southern charm over portions of analysis, candor, and wit.

The son of a policeman, McCarver was raised in a blue collar neighborhood of Memphis, Tennessee, and played baseball, football, and basketball at Christian Brothers High School. Dozens of colleges were interested in him as an offensive lineman. McCarver chose the immediate payoff of baseball, signing with the St. Louis Cardinals on June 15, 1959, for a $75,000 bonus. After tearing up the Class D Midwest League, batting .360 in 65 games, he was promoted to Rochester, where he batted .357. He finished the 1959 season with St. Louis, playing in eight games at age 17.

McCarver didn't become a Cardinals regular until 1963. He starred in the team's 1964 World Series win over the New York Yankees, leading all regulars with a .478 average, catching all seven games, and getting at least one hit in every game. In the opener McCarver tripled, doubled, and scored the go-ahead run in the Redbirds' 9–5 comeback win. In Game 5 McCarver's third hit of the day was a game-winning, three-run homer in the top of the 10th. In the finale McCarver stole home on the back end of a double steal in the fourth inning and knocked in the sixth run of the Cardinals' 7–5 victory with a sacrifice fly. (McCarver said later that this World Series was easy, with little expected of him; under pressure in the 1967 Series, he hit just .125.)

A solid but unspectacular hitter and a smart receiver, McCarver had very good speed for a catcher and became the only backstop to lead a major league in triples, collecting 13 three-baggers in 1966. He was selected to the NL All-Star squad, singled to lead off the 10th inning, and scored the winning run in the 1966 contest before the home crowd at Busch Stadium.

Off to a blistering start in 1967, McCarver set career highs with 14 homers, 69 RBIs, and a .295 average, and finished second in Most Valuable Player voting to teammate Orlando Cepeda. His regular season numbers dropped in 1968, but McCarver glittered in the World Series against the Detroit Tigers, delivering a decisive three-run homer in Game 3, and tripling in each of the Cardinals' two other victories.

McCarver's greatest contributions to the Cardinals' pennant wins may have been in the clubhouse. Funny and in his own words, "fresh as hell," McCarver helped keep the team loose. At the start of one spring training, he handed out cards to answer routine inquiries from reporters.

Management acknowledged what the St. Louis players had already declared by naming McCarver co-captain with Curt Flood. McCarver and Flood were further linked in a seven-player swap with the Philadelphia Phillies, featuring first baseman Richie Allen, immediately after the 1969 season. Flood made the deal famous by refusing to report and suing baseball over the reserve clause.

After losing most of 1970 with an injury in his first season as a Phillie, McCarver caught Rick Wise's no-hitter on June 23, 1971. In June 1972 the Phillies traded McCarver to Montreal for catcher John Bateman, and McCarver caught a second no-hitter unfurled by Bill Stoneman in the season finale.

That winter the Cardinals reacquired him for outfielder Jorge Roque. McCarver played first base and caught, his days as a regular at an end. Sold to the Boston Red Sox on August 31, 1974, McCarver played a total of 23 games before being released in June 1975 to begin his second career.

After winning 27 games for the last-place Phillies in 1972, Steve Carlton had fallen into mediocrity. The Phils signed McCarver as Carlton's guru, with Bob Boone handling the rest of the staff. Carlton returned to form and the Phillies won three straight NL East titles beginning in 1976. McCarver also collected most of his 82 career pinch hits as a Phillie. By agreement, McCarver retired after the 1979 season and began his broadcasting career. He was reactivated in September 1980 and played in six games to qualify as a four-decade player, doubling in his final major league at bat.

As a broadcaster with the Phillies, Mets, and Yankees, as well as in network telecasts, McCarver won praise for his preparation, his situational thinking ("first-guessing, not second-guessing," he emphasized), and his repartee, although some critics said he talked too much, dwelled on minutiae, and cracked too many bad jokes. During the 1992 NLCS McCarver was an announcer for CBS. Atlanta Braves outfielder Deion Sanders, who also played football at the time for the Atlanta Falcons, joined the Falcons' afternoon game in Tampa Bay on Sunday, October 11, then traveled to Pittsburgh for Game 5 that night.

CBS cooperated fully in the stunt, providing coverage of Sanders' journey between two events it happened to be telecasting. However, Braves officials contended Sanders had violated an agreement with them by playing for the Falcons, and, based on that contention, McCarver criticized Sanders on the telecast. In the Braves' clubhouse celebration after winning the pennant, Sanders repeatedly doused McCarver with ice water to express his displeasure.

One of McCarver's high school classmates was Avron Fogelman, who became the owner of the Southern League Memphis Chicks and later a part-owner of the Kansas City Royals. Fogelman had the Chicks' home rechristened Memphis McCarver Memorial Stadium. McCarver said the "memorial" was for his arm, which never was an asset.

Bob McClure

McClure, Robert Craig **P**

1975–93 B:4/29/1952, Oakland, CA Deb:8/13/1975, KAN AL BR/TL 5'11", 170

W	L	PCT	G	SV	IP	BB	SO	ERA
68	57	.544	698	52	1158²	497	701	3.81

Bob McClure was known for a sweeping curveball, an intimidating pickoff move, and an offbeat sense of humor. His main attribute, though, was being lefthanded. Near the end of McClure's 19-year, seven-team career, Bob Uecker said of him, "If he was righthanded, he'd have been digging ditches ten years ago."

An injury to Milwaukee Brewers Rollie Fingers late in the 1982 season made McClure the closer in the Milwaukee bullpen in the World Series. McClure, a starter for most of the season, took the loss in relief in Game 2, but rebounded to save Games 4 and 5 against the St. Louis Cardinals. When the Cardinals rallied in the sixth inning of Game 7, McClure was called upon to face St. Louis first baseman Keith Hernandez, who had been his teammate in both Little League and high school. Hernandez delivered a two-run single that proved to be the Cardinals' margin of victory.

Although McClure never returned to the World Series, he pitched another 11 seasons. His long experience of waiting in the bullpen gave him the insight to write a book about "rotting"—the art of doing nothing.

Frank McCormick

McCormick, Frank Andrew **1B**

1934–48 B:6/9/1911, New York, NY D:11/21/1982, Manhassett, NY Deb:9/11/193, CIN NL BR/TR 6'4", 205

G	AB	R	H	HR	RBI	OBP	SLG	AVG
1534	5723	722	1711	128	951	.348	.434	.299

Frank McCormick grew up in Yorkville, the same Manhattan neighborhood that produced Lou Gehrig, McCormick's childhood idol. A solid-hitting first baseman for the Cincinnati Reds for most of his career, McCormick was a lifetime .299 hitter.

The durable McCormick, nicknamed "Buck," once played in 652 consecutive games, and he struck out rarely, only 189 times in 5,723 at bats. A pillar of the Reds' back-to-back pennant-winning teams of 1939 and 1940, he was the NL's Most Valuable Player in 1940.

Frank Andrew McCormick was playing semipro ball in Washington Heights, New York, in 1932 when he received a tryout with the Giants. He failed. "Son," said a scout, "if you have a good job, keep it." Undaunted, he wrote several letters to

Reds general manager Larry MacPhail, asking for a tryout. Invited to a tryout camp in Beckley, West Virginia, he had to borrow $50 from an uncle to make the trip. When McCormick arrived and saw a glut of outfielders, he said he was an infielder.

McCormick was signed and joined Beckley, a team in the Class C Mid-Atlantic League. In 1934 he batted .347, with 91 RBIs, in 120 games and was asked to join the Reds for a trial. Asked if he thought he could hit Brooklyn's Emil Leonard, McCormick said, "I can hit any pitcher." And he did, getting a hard hit through the infield. Later, however, he admitted, "I was so scared when I faced Leonard, my knees knocked together."

Returned to the minors, McCormick bounced around for a few years in Toronto, Nashville, Dayton, Decatur, Durham, and Syracuse. In Durham in 1936 he hit .381, with 211 hits, 49 doubles, and 138 RBIs, leading the league in each category. In 1938 he came up to the majors to stay. "The big league is where the men play," he said, "and now to find myself a part of it, well, the only comparable thrill I can recall is the first time I stepped into a pair of long pants. You know in my neighborhood, you had to be pretty well grown, 15 or 16 years old, before they allowed you that privilege."

McCormick showed he belonged right away. He led the league in hits his first three full seasons, collecting more than 200 in each of the first two campaigns. In 1939 he led the league in RBIs, with 128, and in 1940 he knocked in 127 runs, led league first basemen in fielding percentage, and topped the NL in doubles, with 44. He was named MVP that year. "There are a lot of honors in baseball, like being in an Opening Day lineup, playing in the All-Star Game, the World Series," he said. "But getting that MVP Award is a special thing. That's in a class by itself."

The Reds went to the World Series in both 1939 and 1940. In 1939 McCormick batted .400 as the Yankees swept Cincinnati. In the next year's Fall Classic he batted only .214, but the Reds took Detroit in seven games. Sold to the Phillies in 1945, McCormick went through 1,325 chances without an error from April 16, 1945, to September 23, 1946. He was released in May 1947 and signed by the Boston Braves, who released him in October 1948.

McCormick managed in the minors from 1949 to 1951 with Quebec of the Canadian-American League, Lima of the Ohio-Indiana League, and Bradford of the PONY League; he won a pennant with Quebec. He scouted and coached for the Reds and was part of their TV and radio crew from 1958 through the mid-1960s. In 1975 McCormick joined the Yankees' front office and was their director of group sales from 1978 until his death from cancer in 1982.

Jim McCormick

McCormick, James **P**

1878–87 M(1879–80, 1882, 74–96) B:1856, Glasgow, Scotland D:3/10/1918, Paterson, NJ Deb:5/20/1878, IND NL BR/TR 5'10½", 215

W	L	PCT	G	SH	IP	BB	SO	ERA
265	214	.553	492	33	4275^2	749	1704	2.43

Jim McCormick won 265 games during only 10 seasons from 1878 through 1887. The righthander led the National League in wins twice and finished his career with a 2.43 ERA. Adrian "Cap" Anson called Jim McCormick "one of the best men that ever sent a ball whizzing across the plate. He was a great big fellow with a florid complexion and blue eyes, and was utterly devoid of fear, nothing that came in his direction being too hot for him to handle."

Scottish-born James McCormick started his professional career with the Buckeye club of the International Association, and in 1878 he pitched for the National League's Indianapolis Browns. The team folded after just one season, and McCormick signed a contract to pitch for and manage the league's Cleveland Blues.

He won 20 games but lost a league-leading 40 in 1879. The following season McCormick turned it all around. He started 74 of the team's 84 games, completed 72, and won 45 with a 1.85 ERA. Although he stopped managing four games into the 1882 season, he still led the league in innings pitched, with 595⅔, and victories, with 36. The following season his .700 winning percentage and 1.84 ERA were league bests.

McCormick's numbers could have been even more incredible had he played for a winning ballclub. From 1880 through 1883 Cleveland finished higher than fourth place only once. McCormick suffered 43 shutout defeats during his career, including 10 in 1880 and eight in 1882.

Midway through the 1884 season McCormick jumped to the outlaw Cincinnati Reds of the Union Association with teammates Jack Glasscock and Fatty Briody. McCormick, who received $2,500 from Cincinnati, finished the season 21–3 with a league-leading 1.54 ERA. The Union Association folded after the season and McCormick, Glasscock, and Briody were only allowed to return to the NL after paying $1,000 in fines.

McCormick played with Providence and Chicago in 1885, finishing the season with a 21–7 record. During one stretch he won 14 straight games. He won three of five decisions in the 1885 World Series against the American Association St. Louis Browns.

In 1886 McCormick won his first 16 games en route to a 31–11 season. But he developed a sore arm and lost his only decision in the 1886 World Series against the Browns. He was traded to Pittsburgh and went 13–23 in 1887. The club attempted to cut McCormick's salary and he retired rather than take the cut.

Mike McCormick

McCormick, Michael Francis **P**

1956–71 B:9/29/1938, Pasadena, CA Deb:9/3/1956, NY NL BL/TL 6'2", 195

W	L	PCT	G	SH	IP	BB	SO	ERA
134	128	.511	484	23	2380¹	795	1321	3.73

Mike McCormick won the National League Cy Young Award in 1967. Why he did not have more years like 1967 and why he managed only a 134–128 lifetime record are mysteries. McCormick seemed to have all the tools; he was a hard-throwing left-hander with good control.

When he was in high school, all 16 major league clubs sought Michael Francis McCormick. He had assembled a 49–4 record in American Legion ball, including four no-hitters and one game in which he struck out 26 batters. He signed with the New York Giants for an estimated $50,000 bonus, pitched his first major league game for the Giants in 1956 at age 17, and cracked their starting rotation in 1958.

McCormick had some good luck on June 12, 1959, when he pitched a five-inning, rain-shortened no-hitter against the Phillies. He had actually given up a hit to Richie Ashburn in the sixth inning, but the rain came crashing down and the inning was never finished.

In 1960 McCormick led the National League with a 2.70 ERA, but he finished with a mediocre 15–12 record. That was his last winning season for the Giants. In 1961 he allowed a league-leading 33 home runs, and he was traded to Baltimore after the 1962 season in a six-player transaction. Only 6–10 in two seasons with the Orioles, in April 1965 McCormick went to Washington for a minor league pitcher and $20,000.

In 1966 McCormick went 11–14 for the Senators, his sixth straight non-winning season. At age 28 he seemed washed up. The Giants, now in San Francisco, traded journeyman pitcher Bob Priddy and Cap Peterson, a career .230 hitter, to the Senators in December 1966 to acquire McCormick.

The following season McCormick led the league in wins, with 22, and posted a 2.85 ERA. He won the Cy Young Award, and was named *The Sporting News* NL Pitcher of the Year and Comeback Pitcher of the Year. McCormick credited his curveball and screwball for his improvement.

But he turned out to be a one-year wonder. After going 23–23 during the 1968 and 1969 seasons, McCormick had a slow start in 1970 and was traded to the New York Yankees in July. It was clear that time was running out on the pitcher who collected antique clocks as a hobby. He pitched briefly for the Royals in 1971 and was released.

Barney McCosky

McCosky, William Barney **OF**

1939–53 B:4/11/1917, Coal Run, PA D:11/6/1996, Venice Beach, FL Deb:4/18/1939, DET AL BL/TR 6'1", 184

G	AB	R	H	HR	RBI	OBP	SLG	AVG
1170	4172	664	1301	24	397	.386	.414	.312

Barney McCosky lost three seasons to military service during World War II. Then, while still in his prime, a back injury cost him another full season and much of his ability. Nevertheless, when healthy, he was one of the best players in the American League. He could run, field, throw, and hit for average. While he lacked consistent home run power, he regularly whistled line drives into the outfield for doubles and triples.

Born William Barney McCosky to Irish and Lithuanian parents, he first played professionally with Charleston, South Carolina, in 1936, hitting .400 to lead the Mid-Atlantic League. In each of the next two seasons, with Beaumont of the Texas League, he hit better than .300.

In 1939 McCosky won the center field job with the Detroit Tigers and batted leadoff. Had there been a Rookie of the Year honor at the time, he would have been a contender. In 147 games he hit .311, scored 120 runs, and led all AL outfielders in putouts. His 190 hits ranked fourth in the league, and his 14 triples ranked second.

Most observers gave the Tigers little chance in the 1940 pennant race, but a shift of hulking first baseman Hank Greenberg to left field allowed slugger Rudy York to play first and improved the Tigers' chances. The two men hit 74 home runs and drove in 284 between them, but their defense suffered. Center fielder McCosky was forced to cover not only his own territory but much of left. Despite doing more than his share on the field, he responded with his best season at bat, hitting .340 and scoring 123 runs. He tied for the league lead in base hits, with 200, and led the circuit in triples, with 19.

The Tigers and the Indians waged a furious battle as the Yankees surged into contention at the end of the season. In a season-ending must-win game, unheralded Detroit pitcher Floyd Giebell outpitched Cleveland ace Bob Feller, and the Tigers won the pennant. Detroit then lost to the

Cincinnati Reds in an exciting seven-game World Series. McCosky hit .304 and tied for the Series' lead in runs scored.

He followed that performance with two more strong seasons for the Tigers, hitting .324 and .293. In 1943 he entered the service, missing the Tigers' 1945 pennant win and their defeat of the Chicago Cubs in the World Series.

McCosky returned to Detroit in 1946 and resumed duty in center field, but he started slowly. He hit only .198 in 25 games, and on May 18 the Tigers traded him to the Philadelphia Athletics for third baseman George Kell. Although Kell went on to a Hall of Fame career in Detroit, Philadelphia received a valuable player in McCosky. He got back on track and hit .354 for the remainder of the season with the Athletics, and .328 and .326 the next two seasons. The A's, perennial cellar dwellers, managed to finish fourth in 1948 and were considered long-shot contenders in 1949.

McCosky had injured himself after the 1948 season, displacing a vertebra in his back. He was out for the next year and voluntarily retired at age 32. He returned to action in 1950 but wasn't the same player. In 66 games he hit .240. He spent another three seasons in the majors, primarily as a pinch hitter. After hitting only .190 for Cleveland in 21 at bats in 1953, he retired again, this time permanently. Despite the subpar seasons following his injury, McCosky still compiled a .312 lifetime batting average.

Willie McCovey

McCovey, Willie Lee **1B–OF**

1959–80 B:1/10/1938, Mobile, AL Deb:7/30/1959, SF NL BL/TL 6'4", 210

G	AB	R	H	HR	RBI	OBP	SLG	AVG
2588	8197	1229	2211	521	1555	.377	.515	.270

When Willie "Stretch" McCovey was inducted into the Hall of Fame in 1986, Commissioner Peter Ueberroth noted, "Never has a more imposing figure stepped to the plate." At 6 feet 4 inches and 210 pounds, McCovey possessed a coiled and menacing lefthanded stance. He produced mammoth numbers during a 22-year career that climaxed with his enshrinement in the Hall of Fame in his first year of eligibility. His 521 home runs are the most by a lefthanded slugger in National League history. During the 1960s he led the NL three times in home runs and twice in runs batted in. In 1969 he was voted the NL Most Valuable Player after a season in which he batted .320 and led the league in eight offensive categories.

McCovey homered every 15.73 at bats, which is more often than players such as Lou Gehrig, Hank Aaron, Willie Mays, Frank Robinson, and Reggie Jackson. His 18 career grand slams are second only to Gehrig's 23. From 1959 to 1971, McCovey and Mays combined for 800 homers, to rank as the second-best long-ball duo in National League history. His No. 44 is one of eight numbers that have been retired by the Giants organization.

Giants scout Alex Pompez signed Willie Lee McCovey as a free agent in 1955. McCovey began his professional career with Sandersville, where he led Georgia State League led the league in RBIs. In 1959 he was batting .372 at Phoenix and leading the Pacific Coast League in homers with 29, when San Francisco called him up.

McCovey broke into the majors with a flourish on July 30, 1959, at San Francisco's Seals Stadium. He slugged two triples and two singles in a 4-for-4 debut against Philadelphia Phillies hurler Robin Roberts, a future Hall of Famer himself. Although he played in only 52 games his first season, McCovey batted .354 with 13 home runs and 38 RBIs, and had a 23-game hitting streak. He was voted NL Rookie of the Year.

His sophomore slump was severe. Despite beginning the season with seven homers in his first 15 games, his average dropped by more than 100 points to .238. He even spent time back in the minor leagues. Once he returned to the big leagues, he was there to stay. Until 1965 McCovey platooned in left field because Orlando Cepeda, the 1958 Rookie of the Year, was entrenched at first base. In the *Bill James Historical Abstract*, James notes that McCovey was "probably the only truly great player to have been platooned for several years at the start of his career."

From 1959 through 1964, McCovey received at least 365 at bats only once, in 1963. That year he led the league with 44 homers and drove in 102 runs. Even as a platoon player, McCovey demonstrated All-Star potential. On June 12, 1960, he belted the first of his three major league pinch-hit grand slams. On September 22, 1963, and April 22, 1964, he hit three consecutive home runs in a game.

In the Giants' pennant-winning year of 1962, McCovey belted 20 home runs in only 229 at bats. In Game 2 of the 1962 World Series against the Yankees, McCovey hit a tremendous seventh-inning home run off Ralph Terry, and the Giants won, 2–0. The Series eventually went seven games, ending in dramatic fashion. With two on and two outs in the ninth, and New York leading, 1–0, McCovey lined a 1–1 pitch from Terry directly at Yankees second baseman Bobby Richardson. That ended McCovey's first and last World Series.

In 1965, with Cepeda injured and traded shortly thereafter, McCovey took over at first base. McCovey remained there through 1973. Although he hit .300 only one more time, during his Most Valuable Player season of 1969, he became a feared and productive power hitter, leading the league in slugging percentage for three consecutive seasons from 1968 through 1970. In 1969 and 1970 McCovey smashed 84 home runs and drove in 252 runs, despite walking 258 times.

McCovey was a six-time NL All-Star, and he made history in the 1969 All-Star Game. He became the fourth player in All-Star competition to hit two home runs in a game. He also drove in three runs and won the Arch Ward Memorial Award as MVP.

Although he led the Giants with 39 homers and 126 RBIs in 1970, McCovey's multiple injuries took a toll. He suffered from a chronic knee condition, blurred vision, and shoulder and hip problems. In 1971 he submitted to surgery on his ailing left knee, and appeared in only 105 games. The following season he suffered a spiral fracture of his right arm in a collision with John Jeter of San Diego and was out of action for six weeks.

McCovey battled back to hit 29 home runs in 1973, but on October 25 the Giants traded him to the Padres with Bernie Williams for Mike Caldwell. In two and a half seasons with San Diego, McCovey hit 52 homers, including a pinch-hit grand slam on May 30, 1975. Sold to Oakland in August 1976, he opted for free agency at season's end.

In 1977 the Giants invited McCovey to spring training as a nonroster player. He made the club, and that season led the Giants with 28 home runs, 86 RBIs, and 15 game-winning hits. *The Sporting News* and United Press International named him Comeback Player of the Year. One of his biggest thrills of the season came on September 18—Willie McCovey Day at Candlestick Park. After going 0-for-3, he smashed a long two-out single to left-center in the ninth to score Derrel Thomas with the game-winning run.

McCovey appeared in just 108 games in 1978, but he hit his 500th career home run off Jamie Easterly on July 1 at Atlanta. On June 9, 1979, he hit career home run No. 512 off Pittsburgh's Grant Jackson, breaking Mel Ott's record for the most home runs by a lefthanded hitter in the National League. He got his 521st and final home run on May 3, 1980, a 385-foot shot off Montreal's Scott Sanderson, which moved McCovey into a tie on the all-time list with his boyhood idol Ted Williams.

Although considered the most popular San Francisco Giant ever, McCovey is probably best remembered for making the last out of Game 7 of the 1962 World Series—one of the most famous and dramatic confrontations in World Series history. Charles Schulz immortalized Bobby Richardson's heartbreaking catch of McCovey's line drive toward right field in one of his "Peanuts" comic strips.

"I'd like to be remembered as the guy who hit a line drive over Bobby Richardson's head," McCovey joked when learning of his Hall of Fame induction. But McCovey did have one consoling memory after the Series ended. That night, he was attending a performance of the Duke Ellington orchestra at a San Francisco nightclub. When the band spotted him, they dedicated a song to him with a special title, "You Hit It Good and That Ain't Bad."

After retiring as a player, McCovey was hired as vice president of sales for a wholesale linen firm in Napa, California. He also served as a special assistant to the president and general manager of the Giants, and has appeared at San Francisco's spring training camps to provide tips and inspirational advice to veterans and rookies alike. Each season he presents the Willie Mac Award, which was established in his name in 1980 and given to the Giants player who best exemplifies the spirit and leadership consistently shown by McCovey throughout his 22-year career.

Lindy McDaniel

McDaniel, Lyndall Dale **P**

1955–75 B:12/13/1935, Hollis, OK Deb:9/2/1955, STL NL BR/TR 6'3", 195

W	L	PCT	G	SV	IP	BB	SO	ERA
141	119	.542	987	172	2139[1]	623	1361	3.45

Lindy McDaniel's screwball was one of the best. The righthanded reliever led the National League in saves three times on the way to a 141–119 career record with 172 saves. Despite his stellar 20-year career, McDaniel never played for a pennant winner. Known for his glove as well as for his screwball, he once pitched a streak of 225 games without making an error.

Lyndall Dale McDaniel was from a family of pitching brothers that included Von McDaniel and minor league pitcher Kerry Don McDaniel. Salutatorian of his high school class, McDaniel attended the University of Oklahoma before transferring to Abilene Christian College.

Lindy signed with St. Louis for a $50,000 bonus in 1955 and had to stay on the Cardinals' roster because of the bonus rule in effect at the time. He was 15–9 as a starter in 1957. After McDaniel had a poor start in 1958 the Cardinals made him a reliever again. He led the league in saves in 1959 and 1960.

Traded to the Cubs after the 1962 season, he led the league in saves for Chicago. He won the Relief Pitcher of the Year Award again in 1963 despite surrendering three grand slams. He also threw three wild pitches in one inning on September 27.

In December 1965 Chicago traded McDaniel to San Francisco, who passed him along to the New York Yankees in July 1968. That August he retired 32 consecutive batters. He achieved his career high with 29 saves in 1970. McDaniel ended his career with Kansas City in 1975.

An avid Christian who circulated a monthly newsletter titled "Pitching for the Master," he became an ordained minister in the Church of Christ, and after leaving the game he ran a religious bookstore in Kansas City, Missouri.

Mickey McDermott

McDermott, Maurice Joseph **P**

1948–61 B:8/29/1928, Poughkeepsie, NY
Deb:4/24/1948, BOS AL BL/TL 6'2", 170

W	L	PCT	G	SV	IP	BB	SO	ERA
69	69	.500	291	14	1316^{2}	838	757	3.91

For years Maurice Joseph "Mickey" McDermott seemed on the verge of becoming a great pitcher for the Boston Red Sox. After the spindly lefthander had his one (and as it turned out, only) outstanding season, he was traded away. His problems were extreme wildness and, by his own admission, too much love for the fast lane. He was an excellent singer who performed at several Boston night spots and in the Catskills with Eddie Fisher. All told, he had a rollicking time, and although his career record was a disappointing 69–69, he had few regrets.

Brought up to stay with the Sox in 1949, McDermott spent three years as an unreliable though occasionally brilliant starter-reliever. In 1950, despite a 5.19 ERA and 124 walks in 130 innings, he had a winning 7–3 record. In 1953 he finally seemed to be on his way. Although he still walked more batters than he struck out, he went 18–10 with a very respectable 3.01 ERA. But before the next season rolled around he was dealt to Washington for Jackie Jensen. The deal was extremely unpopular at the time in Boston, but the fans were appeased when Jensen became a major star and McDermott struggled for two years with the Senators.

He wound down his career with short stints with the Yankees, A's, Tigers, and the Cardinals. A career .252 hitter, he often pinch hit, and the A's even tried him as a first baseman for a couple of games. He retired after the 1961 season.

Gil McDougald

McDougald, Gilbert James **2B-3B-SS**

1951–60 B:5/19/1928, San Francisco, CA
Deb:4/20/1951, NY AL BR/TR 6'1", 180

G	AB	R	H	HR	RBI	OBP	SLG	AVG
1336	4676	697	1291	112	576	.358	.410	.276

New York Yankees infielder Gil McDougald is best known for hitting the line drive that ended pitcher Herb Score's career. However, McDougald was a quality, multitalented player who was chosen the AL's 1951 Rookie of the Year. Because of the strong talent he was competing against in those days, versatility helped him. When Gilbert James McDougald reported to the Yankees in spring 1951, he was only a second baseman. Manager Casey Stengel asked him to give third a try, and McDougald was soon shuttling between third and second as an integral part of Stengel's complex platoon system. Five years later teammate Phil Rizzuto retired, and McDougald added another position to his resume: shortstop.

Signed by Yankees scout Joe Devine, McDougald maintained a close relationship with him as he moved up the Yankees chain. "They [old-time scouts] treated you more like family, and if you had problems they would talk to you, and they would talk to your manager, and they would try to help you out," said McDougald.

McDougald spent three seasons in the minors and never hit less than .336. During his rookie season with the Yanks he hit .306, with 14 homers, 63 RBIs, and 14 stolen bases. On May 3, 1951, he tied an AL record with six RBIs in one inning. Then he began hitting with a foot-in-the-bucket batting stance, and it worked for him until 1955, when he was caught in a slump. Stengel then ordered him to adopt a less power-oriented approach to hitting.

Said McDougald of his new stance, "I wasn't hitting the ball hard, but everything was dropping in. With the old stance, I thought I was hitting the ball harder, but the defense was bunching me, and I was trying to hit through too many players."

He hit a career-best .311 in 1956. The following season he led the league in triples. But on May 7, 1957, McDougald's liner back to the mound struck Score in an eye. Although the Cleveland moundsman made a partial comeback the following season and pitched a full season the next, McDougald's hit essentially made the unhittable hurler hittable. Virtually every fan is aware of that incident, but few know that McDougald himself was similarly injured.

During batting practice at Yankee Stadium in 1958 he was struck in the head by a line drive off the bat of Kansas City's Bob Cerv. It is thought that the force of the impact drove part of McDougald's eardrum into his skull, leading to progressive hearing loss.

McDougald's sixth-inning, pinch-hit single in the 1958 All-Star Game gave the American League a 4–3 victory. Ironically, McDougald had not been voted to the All-Star squad and did not want to attend. But Stengel called the shots and McDougald went.

In World Series competition McDougald became the first rookie to hit a Series grand slam, in Game 5 of the 1951 Fall Classic. However, he hit only .200 and made four errors at third base in the 1952 matchup. He belted two homers in the

1953 Series, but undoubtedly his best Fall Classic performance came in 1958, when the Yankees beat the Braves in seven games.

New York lost three of the first four games to the Braves. In Game 5 at Yankee Stadium, McDougald homered in the third and the Yanks cruised to a 7–0 victory. The two teams returned to Milwaukee, and in Game 6 McDougald's 10th-inning home run snapped a 2–2 tie. New York won the world championship the next day. McDougald batted .321, with five runs scored and four RBIs in the Series.

To this day McDougald still ranks among the World Series leaders in games (53), at bats (190), hits (45), home runs (7), runs scored (23), RBIs (24), bases on balls (20), and strikeouts (29). Yet it was the defensive portion of the game that gave McDougald the greatest satisfaction.

"Defense was fun," said McDougald. "My greatest thrill in baseball was when a pitcher came up to me and told me that I'd made a helluva play. Bobby Shantz, who in my opinion was the best fielding pitcher ever, must have been used to having an infield that didn't get many balls, because when I made a play for him, he was so ecstatic, I thought he must be kidding."

Following the 1960 season McDougald retired. Both the expansion Senators and Angels made overtures to lure him back into the game, but he remained inactive. After leaving the big leagues, McDougald coached baseball at Fordham University for seven seasons and served as a part-owner of a maintenance company based in New Jersey.

Jack McDowell

McDowell, Jack Burns **P**

1987–99 B:1/16/1966, Van Nuys, CA Deb:9/15/1987, CHI AL BR/TR 6'5", 180

W	L	PCT	G	SH	IP	BB	SO	ERA
127	87	.593	277	13	1889	606	1313	3.85

Jack McDowell capped off a stellar four-year span by winning the 1993 American League Cy Young Award and leading the White Sox to the AL West title. Much was expected from McDowell from the start. He was the fifth overall pick of the 1987 draft after leading Stanford University to the College World Series championship. By September he was pitching for the Chicago White Sox.

"Black Jack" won 73 games in the first four seasons of the 1990s. In 1992 he won 20 games for the first time, posting career bests in ERA (3.17) and innings pitched (260⅔). He finished second to Oakland's Dennis Eckersley in the Cy Young voting. The following year he won the Cy Young with a 22–10 record despite a mediocre first half during which the White Sox offense had to frequently rescue him. In 1994 he again pitched well but poor run support dragged his record down to 10-9 in the strike-shortened season.

By the time the strike was finally settled in 1995, the three-time All-Star was a New York Yankee. Despite winning 15 games and helping the Yankees earn their first postseason berth in 15 seasons, things did not go well for McDowell in New York. In the second game of an August doubleheader, after allowing nine runs in just over four innings, McDowell responded to the jeering of the hometown crowd with an obscene gesture as he walked into the dugout. Fined and reprimanded by club management, McDowell also gained the enmity of the local media and fans that seemed to affect his performance on the mound. In the Division Series he got a no-decision in Game 3, and made his first career relief appearance two nights later, surrendering the series-ending hit to Edgar Martinez.

McDowell, who had never had an ERA over 4.00 in his career before, gave up in excess of five runs a game in the next four seasons. He spent two years each with Cleveland and Anaheim, but injuries severely limited his effectiveness. The Angels placed him on waivers after he lost his only four starts in 1999.

Roger McDowell

McDowell, Roger Alan **P**

1985–96 B:12/21/1960, Cincinnati, OH Deb:4/11/1985, NY NL BR/TR 6'1", 182

W	L	PCT	G	SV	IP	BB	SO	ERA
70	70	.500	723	159	1050	410	524	3.30

In 1992 Roger McDowell's reputation as one of the biggest pranksters in baseball earned him a guest shot, along with Keith Hernandez, on a special one-hour *Seinfeld* episode entitled "The Boyfriend." But on the mound the relief pitcher was no joke. McDowell could keep the ball down—and in the ballpark.

McDowell arrived in New York as a starting pitcher in 1985. When he failed to last more than five innings in two tries he was moved to the bullpen and never started again. He tied for the team lead in saves with 17 in 1985 while compiling a 6–5 record in 62 games with a 2.83 ERA. He was also gaining a reputation for his antics in the bullpen and clubhouse. Even though McDowell was known to give a "hot foot" to an unsuspecting teammate, there was some method to his madness. "You're always under pressure," McDowell said of his closer role. "You have to have a different type of personality."

McDowell was one of the main reasons the Mets ran away with the National League East in 1986.

He won 14 games in relief to set a club record and eclipsed another Mets mark with 75 appearances. His 128 innings led all NL relievers, and his 22 saves outnumbered teammate Jesse Orosco by one. In the postseason he hurled five scoreless innings in the pennant-clinching sixth game of the Championship Series against Houston. He pitched in five World Series games against Boston and got the win in Game 7.

A hernia put McDowell on the disabled list at the start of the 1987 season. Despite a career-high 25 saves, McDowell allowed seven home runs in 88 innings and had a bloated 4.16 ERA. In 1988, he lowered his ERA to 2.63 and earned 15 saves in a setup role for Randy Myers, the team's new closer. McDowell did not pitch well in the NLCS, however. He had a 4.50 ERA in four games and took the loss in Game 4, which changed the momentum in the Dodgers' favor as the Mets lost in seven games.

McDowell turned things around in 1989, but he did it in a Phillies uniform. Sent to Philadelphia with Lenny Dykstra in June, McDowell allowed just seven earned runs in 44 innings with the Phillies and finished the year with a career-low 1.96 ERA. He remained in Philadelphia until the 1991 trading deadline when he was sent west to Los Angeles. He was a workhorse in the Dodgers bullpen until the baseball strike ended the 1994 season.

When baseball resumed play in 1995, McDowell was in Texas, where he put together a 7–4 record in 64 games. In December he signed on with a new ballclub, the Orioles, which had a familiar cast of characters. Davey Johnson, his manager with the Mets, and former New York teammates Orosco and Myers were already in Baltimore. McDowell finished his career by appearing in 41 games in 1996.

Sam McDowell

McDowell, Samuel Edward Thomas **P**
1961–75 B:9/21/1942, Pittsburgh, PA Deb:9/15/1961, CLE AL BL/TL 6'5", 218

W	L	PCT	G	SH	IP	BB	SO	ERA
141	134	.513	425	23	2492^{1}	1312	2453	3.17

For six years in the late 1960s, "Sudden Sam" McDowell was one of the game's dominant pitchers. At 6 feet 5 inches he was big and strong, and he boasted an intimidating fastball, a tricky curve, and an elusive change up. From 1965 through 1970 he averaged 275 strikeouts a year, more than one an inning, earning him the nickname, "the American League Sandy Koufax."

With his classic over-the-top delivery reminiscent of Koufax and Warren Spahn, he averaged less than seven hits allowed per nine innings during his career. But his skills disappeared abruptly. Three years after he led the AL with 304 strikeouts and 305 innings pitched in 1970, he was 6–10 in 135 innings with two teams. Two years later he was reduced to 34 innings of mop-up work in his final major league season.

McDowell was always trying to outdo himself. In his first big league appearance, he was sailing along with a three-hit shutout (five strikeouts, five walks) in the seventh inning when he threw a pitch so hard he fractured two of his ribs. McDowell was often criticized for trying to outsmart hitters when he didn't need to. He admitted as much himself. "It's not fun throwing fastballs to guys who can't hit them. The real challenge is getting them out on stuff they can hit," he once said.

Raised by a demanding, sports-obsessed father, Samuel Edward Thomas McDowell couldn't deal with the pressure of professional competition, and eventually became an alcoholic. In recovery, he became a consultant to numerous major league teams, assisting players with similar problems.

"Baseball is the greatest and worst thing that ever happened to me," he once said. "Not because people asked too much of me, but because I asked too much of myself. As it turned out, my talent was a curse. The curse was the way I handled it and didn't handle it.... I was the biggest, most hopeless, and most violent drunk in baseball."

Major league hurler Dick Radatz recalled, "We thought he was just stupid. It turned out he was never sober." But Radatz added, "I was always in awe of the arm that McDowell had, despite the drinking problem. He had one of the best arms of all time, a command of all the pitches, but he always wanted to trick people with his changeup or something else." The alcoholism also affected McDowell's personality. He constantly griped at umpires, and his teammates didn't like him.

In 1960 McDowell was signed straight out of Central Catholic High School in Pittsburgh to a Cleveland contract for a $75,000 bonus. He was not yet 18 years old. In addition to his baseball skills he also excelled at basketball, football, swimming, tennis, and track. In his first year in the minors he fanned 100 batters in 105 innings. In 1961, with Salt Lake City of the Pacific Coast League, he struck out 156 but walked 152. That performance earned him a trip to the majors—where he promptly broke his ribs.

During the next three years he made brief visits to the majors, until 1964 when he put together an 11–6 record and an impressive 177 strikeouts in 173 innings. The next season he was absolutely overpowering. He recorded a league-leading 2.18 ERA and struck out 325 men, the fourth-best season strikeout total ever, in only 273 innings. McDowell had become only the third AL pitcher ever to pass the 300-K mark. The league batted only .185 against him, a league low. Unfortunately, there was only one Cy Young Award given in 1965, and it went to Sandy Koufax.

In 1966 a sore arm reduced McDowell's innings pitched by 80. But he still put together back-to-back one-hitters, only the fourth time that has been accomplished this century, and led the AL in strikeouts and shutouts. In 1967 Jim Lonborg fanned 10 more men than McDowell to keep him from winning his third consecutive strikeout crown. That year Indians pitchers sent 1,189 batters down on strikes, setting a major league record later broken by Houston.

During the "Year of the Pitcher" in 1968, McDowell brought his ERA down by two runs per game, to 1.81. On May 1 McDowell struck out 16 Oakland A's. On July 12, again against Oakland, he fanned 15 batters. For the second straight year the Indians led the league in batters fanned. In fact, the 1968 Cleveland staff is the only pitching crew in history to strike out more batters than it allowed hits to. The Tribe finished in third place, their best showing in nearly 10 years.

The following season was more of the same for the talented, if erratic, fireballer. With a league-leading 279 strikeouts and four shutouts, he won more games than he ever had before, with 18. But his team didn't fare as well as they had the previous year. McDowell was the only pitcher with more than six decisions to post a winning record, and the Indians lost 99 times, finishing 46½ games behind Baltimore.

McDowell had his first and only 20-win season in 1970, leading the AL both in innings pitched and strikeouts. On May 6 he fanned 15 Chicago White Sox. Exactly two months later he struck out 15 Washington Senators. His 304 strikeouts were 74 more than runner-up Mickey Lolich's total, and *The Sporting News* named him Pitcher of the Year.

McDowell wanted a large salary increase for 1971. Alvin Dark, then both the Cleveland field and general manager, balked at the $100,000 salary McDowell wanted. Together they worked out a complicated pact based largely on incentives for specific performance levels; if McDowell reached the stated performance goals he could earn as much as $92,000. But Commissioner Bowie Kuhn voided the contract because at the time performance bonuses were against the rules. Kuhn fined Cleveland $5,000 for the mistake. McDowell was outraged; he left the team and demanded that he be declared a free agent. The Indians suspended him.

He returned after a few days and signed a new contract, but spent most of the summer sulking. His stats dropped precipitously: from 304 to 192 strikeouts, from 305 to 215 innings pitched, and an ERA increase of nearly half a run. He again led the league in walks, but with 22 more than the previous season, and in 91 fewer innings. His 153 free passes were 32 more than the AL's next-wildest pitcher that year.

The Indians and McDowell were ready to part company. In November 1971 McDowell was sent to San Francisco along with Frank Duffy for Gaylord Perry. Perry was four years older than McDowell, but the deal was a steal for the Indians. Perry's 24 victories the next year were more than McDowell would win in the remaining four years of his career.

A 1972 10-win season in San Francisco wasn't impressive enough to keep McDowell from being sold to the Yankees the following June, where he went 5–8 in 1973 and 1–6 in 1974, after moving to the bullpen. The Yanks released him, and his hometown Pirates picked him up for the 1975 season, during which he appeared in only 14 games, finishing 2–1.

During his career, the pitcher that Reggie Jackson called "Instant Heat" struck out 10 or more batters 74 times. He averaged 8.86 strikeouts per game.

Terris McDuffie

McDuffie, Terris **P–OF**

Negro League Player 1930–45 B:7/22/1910, Mobile, AL D:New York, NY BR/TR 6'1", 200

In 1945 Newark Eagles pitcher Terris "the Great" McDuffie and New York Cubans ace Dave "Showboat" Thomas tried out for Brooklyn general manager Branch Rickey. Both players were past their prime, however, and had been brought to the Dodgers' Bear Mountain spring training camp by sportswriter Joe Bostic of the newspaper, *People's Voice*.

Rickey, whose real Negro League interests lay elsewhere, watched for 45 minutes and was unimpressed. That they arrived unannounced and were accompanied by a photographer from the Communist *Daily Worker* did little to improve Rickey's disposition. Rickey signed Jackie Robinson later that year.

McDuffie began as an outfielder with the Birmingham Black Barons in 1930, leading the circuit with 18 stolen bases. He soon switched to pitching and in 1937, with the Newark Eagles, he led the Negro League in wins, complete games, and shutouts. In 1938 he went the route in all 27 games he started.

During the next seven seasons he pitched for the New York Black Yankees, the Philadelphia Stars, and the Homestead Grays. In 1941 he was 27–5 for the pennant-winning Grays and was the winning pitcher in that season's East-West All-Star Game. His last season in the Negro League was 1945, the same year as his unsuccessful tryout with the Dodgers.

McDuffie also pitched winter ball in Puerto Rico and Cuba. Once, while working for Dolf

Luque at Almendares in Cuba, McDuffie refused to pitch on just two days' rest. Luque reached into his desk drawer, pulled out a revolver, and asked again. "Gimme the ball," responded a nervous McDuffie, who proceeded to pitch a two-hitter.

Dan McGann

McGann, Dennis Lawrence **1B**
1896–1908 B:7/15/1871, Shelbyville, KY D:12/13/1910, Louisville, KY Deb:8/8/1896, BOS NL BB/TR 6', 190

G	AB	R	H	HR	RBI	OBP	SLG	AVG
1436	5222	842	1482	42	727	.364	.381	.284

Solid defensive first baseman Dan McGann teamed with player-manager John McGraw in Baltimore, St. Louis, and New York. Unfortunately, he is most remembered for his tragic end—a mysterious suicide best understood in terms of similar occurrences in his family's history.

Young Dennis Lawrence McGann made his professional debut with Shelbyville of the Bluegrass League in 1891, then moved on to that circuit's Harrodsville franchise, and later to Lexington and Maysville of the Kentucky League. With Lynchburg of the Virginia State League in 1895 he batted only .251, but the next season he hit a solid .345 in 42 games, a performance that secured his purchase by the Boston Beaneaters that August.

With Toronto in 1897 he led the Eastern League in triples, with 22, while batting .354. During the next few years he bounced from Baltimore to Brooklyn (both clubs were held by the same ownership), then to Washington and St. Louis before becoming part of the Baltimore Orioles in the newly formed American League.

In July 1902 Baltimore Manager John McGraw was eager to return to the National League. He, McGann, pitcher Joe "Iron Man" McGinnity, and utility man Roger Bresnahan jumped to the New York Giants. McGann, best noted as a fine glove man who five times led National League first basemen in fielding percentage, was also fast, stealing 20 or more bases eight times in his career. On May 27, 1904, he became the first player to steal five bases in a game—a feat not equaled in the senior circuit until the Dodgers' Davey Lopes did so on August 24, 1974, and not surpassed until Atlanta's Otis Nixon stole six on June 6, 1991.

In 1905 McGann batted .299, with 14 triples, as the Giants won the pennant. In the 1905 World Series he batted only .235 and struck out seven times, but in Game 3 he drove in four runs on three hits. The Giants defeated the A's in five games. In December 1907 McGann was traded back to the Boston club in an eight-player deal. His hitting fell off, and soon he was out of the major leagues. In 1909 and 1910 he played with Milwaukee of the American Association, where he continued to struggle at the plate, although he did manage to lead the league in putouts and fielding average in 1909.

After the 1910 season McGann expected to be traded to Louisville. Because that club was near his home of Shelbyville, Kentucky, this should have cheered the first baseman. However, on the night of December 13, 1910, while staying at Louisville's Besler's Hotel, McGann shot himself in the heart with a revolver. His suicide came as a great shock. McGann's health was good, and for a ballplayer of his era he was in exceedingly sound financial condition. McGann had accumulated a fair amount of real estate in Shelbyville and was thought to be worth $40,000. He had recently made bank deposits of $9,000 and $2,500, and was carrying a promissory note worth $1,000 when he died.

In McGann's family, though, there was a pattern of suicide and violence, and it was said "these thoughts...upset his mind." Slightly more than a year earlier one of McGann's brothers had taken his life; the previous New Year's Eve another brother had died as the result of infection following an accidental shooting; and 22 years prior McGann's sister had committed suicide following the death of their mother.

The local coroner ruled the cause of McGann's death to be suicide, but his two surviving sisters thought it murder. A diamond ring worth $800, which witnesses had noticed McGann wearing when he was last seen alive, was missing, although a diamond pin and $37 in cash in addition to the $1,000 note were still on the body when it was found.

Willie McGee

McGee, Willie Dean **OF**
1982–99 B:11/2/1958, San Francisco, CA Deb:5/10/1982, STL NL BB/TR 6'1", 175

G	AB	R	H	HR	RBI	OBP	SLG	AVG
2201	7469	1010	2254	79	856	.335	.396	.295

In the winter of 1981, the Yankees had a surplus of veteran outfielders that included Oscar Gamble, Jerry Mumphrey, and Dave Winfield, but desperately needed a lefthanded reliever. So New York sent a minor league prospect named Willie McGee to the Cardinals for journeyman reliever Bob Sykes, who would never pitch a game in pinstripes.

The trade would become one of the best in the history of the St. Louis franchise. The pigeon-toed McGee looked awkward and lacked power—a concern of the Yankees—but fit right into the Cardinals' need for speed and line-drive hitting at cavernous Busch Stadium. In 1982 the switch-hitting rookie center fielder batted .296, stole 24 bases, and played a solid center field as St. Louis made the postseason for the first time since the championship teams of the 1960s.

He batted .308 in that year's Championship Series sweep of the Atlanta Braves. In Game 3 of the '82 World Series he homered twice and made two leaping catches to give St. Louis a 6-2 victory over the Milwaukee Brewers. As the camera closed in on McGee's face late in the game, announcer Howard Cosell bellowed, "He looks like 'E.T.'" The inappropriate comparison of the outfielder to the alien from that year's biggest movie notwithstanding, the Cardinals won the Series in seven games.

With his explosive speed and slashing hitting style, McGee blossomed in 1985. He led the league with 18 triples, 216 hits, and a .353 batting average, capturing the Most Valuable Player Award as the Cardinals again won the pennant. McGee reached career highs with 11 home runs and 105 RBIs two years later, helping St. Louis to its third pennant in his six years as a full-time player.

In 1990 McGee won his second National League batting title, but he won it while playing in the American League. When the Cardinals fell out of contention, they decided to trade McGee, an impending free agent, to Oakland just prior to the waiver deadline of September 1. Although McGee already had enough plate appearances to qualify for the batting championship, he had to hope that no other NL batter would surpass his .335 mark. When no one did, McGee became the first player in history to win a batting crown in one league after being traded to the other league.

Although the A's made the World Series for the third straight year, McGee opted for free agency and moved across the Bay to the Giants. McGee spent four mostly productive seasons in San Francisco before signing a minor league contract with Boston. In 1996 he returned to the Cardinals, where he had remained a fan favorite, and batted better than .300 in a semi-regular role over the next two seasons. After hitting a career-low .251 as a reserve player in 1999, the 41-year-old McGee announced his retirement.

Joe McGinnity

McGinnity, Joseph Jerome **P**

1899–1908 B:3/19/1871, Rock Island, IL D:11/14/1929, Brooklyn, NY Deb:4/18/1899, BAL NL BR/TR 5'11", 206

W	L	PCT	G	SH	IP	BB	SO	ERA
246	142	.634	465	32	3441^{1}	812	1068	2.66

One might think that a fellow who pitched and won three doubleheaders in a month and answered to the name "Iron Man" got his nickname from his durability on the mound. But that wasn't the case with Iron Man Joe McGinnity. Actually, McGinnity's moniker came from an interview he gave after joining the Brooklyn Superbas in 1900. Asked by a reporter what he did during the off-season, McGinnity replied, "I work in my father-in-law's iron foundry in Oklahoma. I'm an iron man."

On April 20, 1893, Joseph Jerome McGinnity (known as "McGinty" during his minor league career) pitched his first professional game for the Montgomery Colts of the Southern League. He won, 10–2. *Sporting Life* wrote: "To judge by his work he is a jewel of the first water. He is a wonder and pitches a lightning ball." Nonetheless, McGinnity was only 10–19 that season.

McGinnity went on to pitch for Kansas City of the Western League in 1894 and continued his losing ways. From 1895 through 1897 no professional team would have him, so he pitched semipro ball in Decatur, Illinois. There he developed an underhand delivery and found that the ball curved sharply upward. This "upshoot," which he named "Old Sal," gave him new effectiveness.

In 1898 he returned to professional competition with Peoria of the Western Association. Appropriately enough, an "iron man" performance helped get him get into the majors. It was a 21-inning victory that caused a local resident to recommend him to Brooklyn Superbas owner Charles Ebbets. Ebbets bought McGinnity's contract, but because Brooklyn was then involved in a syndicate scheme with Baltimore, McGinnity was sent to the Orioles. There, under manager John McGraw, he led the National League with 28 victories.

Transferred back to Brooklyn the following year after Baltimore left the league, McGinnity led the NL in innings pitched for the first of four times. He won a league-high 29 games, including a 10-game victory streak. By winning five times in a stretch of six games, McGinnity helped nail down a pennant for Brooklyn. In appreciation of his efforts he was given the Superbas' championship trophy.

The following year was the American League's first season, and McGinnity jumped back to the now-American League Orioles, where McGraw was managing. That year he won 26 games and had a league-leading 39 complete games.

By July 1902, however, McGraw had tired of working under Ban Johnson, the new league's president. He jumped to the New York Giants and brought along as much Baltimore talent as he could. McGinnity was his prize catch.

The next year, 1903, was McGinnity's first 30-game season and the year in which he set the modern record with 434 innings pitched. His 44 complete games that year are the third-highest single-season total of all time, and he also became one of only two pitchers in major league history to win and lose 20 games in a season in both the

National League and American League. (He had been 26–20 for Baltimore in 1901.) McGinnity also pulled off the greatest feat of his career, pitching three doubleheaders in the span of a single month.

On August 1, 1903, he defeated Boston, 4–1 and 5–2. In each game he surrendered only six hits and walked one. On August 8 at the Polo Grounds he faced Brooklyn and beat them, 6–1 and 4–3. In that day's first contest McGinnity stole home with the game's first run. (He'd steal home again during the 1904 season.) And on August 31 he defeated Philadelphia, 4–1 and 9–2. In the second game he struck out nine and walked only one.

During the 1904 season McGinnity won 14 straight games. It took nine innings of no-hit ball by Cubs hurler Bob Wicker on June 11 to end McGinnity's skein. Although Wicker allowed one hit in the 10th inning, the Cubs beat McGinnity, 1–0, in the 12th. In the 1905 World Series, McGinnity lost to the Athletics' Albert "Chief" Bender, 3–0, in Game 2, but defeated Eddie Plank, 1–0, on a five-hitter in Game 4. New York won in five games.

McGinnity played a peripheral role in the famed "Merkle Boner" play. In that crucial September 23, 1908, game against the Cubs, the Giants' Fred Merkle failed to touch second base as the winning run scored on a hit by Al Bridwell. Cubs second baseman Johnny Evers retrieved the ball from the crowd and forced Merkle out at second. While all this was going on, McGinnity was coaching third. Realizing what had happened, he tried to wrestle the ball away from some Chicago players to prevent the force from occurring. He later maintained that the Cubs had substituted a new ball for the game ball. "I don't know where Evers got the ball that he used to claim the force-out, but it wasn't the ball that Bridwell hit because I flung that one out of sight," McGinnity claimed.

Although that was McGinnity's last major league season, he went on to enjoy an impressive minor league career. He won more than 200 games after being sent down, starting with league-leading totals of 29 and 30 victories with Newark in 1909 and 1910. As late as 1923, McGinnity won 15 games and pitched 268 innings for Dubuque of the Class D Mississippi Valley League. That season he was 54 years old, and, in addition to still pitching, he also managed the club to a pennant.

McGinnity finally returned to the majors as third base coach under Brooklyn manager Wilbert Robinson. McGinnity was not exactly subtle at third. He kept his hands buried deep within his Brooklyn sweater, and when he caught a signal from Robinson he went into a startling array of gestures. "Every time I give Joe a sign, it's like ringing a fire alarm. I don't know if any players are gettin' the sign, but I know everybody in the park is, including the peanut vendor," said Robinson.

McGinnity later was an assistant baseball coach at Williams College. He died of cancer in 1929 and was elected to the Hall of Fame by the Old Timer's Committee in 1946.

Lynn McGlothen

McGlothen, Lynn Everatt **P**

1972–82 B:3/27/1950, Monroe, LA D:8/14/1984, Dubach, LA Deb:6/25/1972, BOS AL BL/TR 6'2", 195

W	L	PCT	G	SH	IP	BB	SO	ERA
86	93	.480	318	13	1497[2]	572	939	3.98

A 6-foot 2-inch righthander with a powerful fastball, Lynn McGlothen was a good pitcher on mediocre teams. He won 44 games in three seasons with the Cardinals, and earned a spot on the All-Star team in 1974. Pitching for the Cardinals against the Reds on August 19, 1975, McGlothen entered his name in baseball history by striking out the side on nine pitches.

McGlothen was no stranger to athletic success, having been a Louisiana high school tennis champion for three years. He arrived in the major leagues with Boston in 1972 and went to St. Louis two years later. He won 16 games with a 2.69 ERA in his first season with the Cardinals.

Beset by shoulder problems in 1977, he missed nearly the entire season but returned to win 13 games for the Cubs in 1979. He won another 12 for Chicago the following year, but that was the last flash of brilliance left in his arm. McGlothen ended his career with the Yankees in 1982, pitching only four games. He died two years later at age 34 in a fire in Dubach, Louisiana.

Bill McGowan

William A. McGowan

Umpire 1925–54 B:1/18/1896, Wilmington, DE D:12/9/1954, Silver Spring, MD

Umpire Bill McGowan made his most famous call on April 26, 1931, after Lou Gehrig hit a ball into the stands. Baserunner Lyn Lary, unsure whether the ball was out of the park, slowed down, and Gehrig passed him on the basepaths. Quite properly, McGowan called Gehrig out. The lost home run left Gehrig in a tie for the league home run crown at the end of the season. It is ironic that McGowan, who was renowned for never shrinking from a tough call, making hundreds of them during his career, should be remembered for the simple enforcement of a well-known rule.

McGowan spent the 1912 season playing semi-professionally as a second baseman, an experience that convinced him to take up umpiring. At age 19 he became a professional umpire in a Class C league. After 10 years of hard work, he joined the American League.

McGowan was vigorous, aggressive, sharp-tongued, and unusually demonstrative in his gestures. Early in his career he was disdainfully nicknamed "Big Shot," but as appreciation for his ability grew, he was called "No. 1" and ranked by players and managers as the best in conducting a game. A *Sporting News* poll of players in 1935 named him the AL's Outstanding Umpire.

He was chosen as one of the arbiters for the first All-Star Game, in 1933, and during his career umpired four All-Star Games and eight World Series. In 1948 he was also selected as umpire-in-chief for the first playoff in AL history. McGowan is often credited with umpiring 2,541 consecutive games, but he apparently missed two games in 1931 because of diabetes.

McGowan rarely ejected players for arguing, but he didn't duck a rhubarb. One observer accurately noted, "He never ran away but knew when to walk." His occasionally short temper twice led to brief suspensions. Some of his supporters believe his run-ins with members of the press long delayed his election to the Hall of Fame, a tribute finally awarded in 1992.

McGowan opened the country's second school for umpires in 1939 and stayed active as an American League umpire until diabetes forced his retirement in 1954. In recognition of his superior status, the league doubled his pension. He died later that year.

John McGraw

McGraw, John Joseph **3B-SS-OF**

1891–1906 M(1899–1932, 2,763–1,948) B:4/7/1873, Truxton, NY D:2/25/1934, New Rochelle, NY Deb:8/26/1891, BAL NL BL/TR 5'7", 155

G	AB	R	H	HR	RBI	OBP	SLG	AVG
1099	3924	1024	1309	13	462	.466	.410	.334

"There has been only one manager and his name is John McGraw," Connie Mack once observed. That quote alone gives baseball fans a good indication of McGraw's place in baseball history. But not only was he one of the national pastime's most respected and feared tacticians, McGraw was also a scrappy infielder with a lifetime .334 average on one of baseball's greatest teams.

John Joseph McGraw's mother and four of his siblings died in a diphtheria epidemic, and he was sent to live with relatives. He still came under his father's supervision, however, which was no help to his baseball career. His father hated the game and walloped young McGraw once for breaking some church windows beyond right-center field. To protect his hide, McGraw became skilled at hitting to the opposite field.

McGraw pitched for local teams before signing a $40-a-month contract with Olean, New York, of the New York and Pennsylvania League in 1890. Converted into a third baseman by manager Albert Kenney, McGraw then bounced around the minor leagues before impressing Billy Barnie of the American Association Orioles in August 1891.

That Baltimore team was perhaps the toughest squad of all time, and the young McGraw soon emerged as the toughest and meanest Oriole. In those days rookies were as welcome on a club as a case of typhoid, and McGraw's arrival wasn't greeted with huzzahs. The diminutive rookie was jeered as a "batboy," and one day found himself literally shoved off the team bench. The brash McGraw proceeded to punch out his tormentors in full view of the Orioles' bewildered fans.

That incident gained him acceptance from his teammates. Soon McGraw was trying out new tricks. In those days only one umpire called each game, and McGraw developed such tactics as grabbing an opponent's belt as the player rounded third, causing runners to play with their belts loosened, or just physically blocking a runner from the base.

He also was a master at fouling off balls, waiting until he got just the right pitch to hit. "There wasn't any of them that could foul 'em off harder than McGraw," teammate "Wee Willie" Keeler said. "He could slam 'em out on a line so fast that even the umpire couldn't tell he was doing it on purpose." In spring training of 1930, a rapidly aging McGraw purposely fouled off 26 straight pitches.

If McGraw couldn't get on base that way, he had other options. He might, for example, just lean over the pitch and allow himself to be hit by it. Years later on seeing the introduction of batting helmets, Casey Stengel would remark, "If we'd had them when I was playing, John McGraw would have insisted that we go up to the plate and get hit in the head."

The Orioles captured three straight National League pennants from 1894 through 1896. In 1899 McGraw became the Orioles' player-manager, but when that franchise was lopped off from the National League in 1900 he was sold along with two other players to St. Louis for $15,000. He hated the idea of playing in that city and refused to report until the reserve clause was stricken from his contract. He played in only 99 games, but still hit .344.

In 1901 he became manager of Ban Johnson's American League entry in Baltimore. McGraw and Johnson were an odd combination. Johnson had pledged that one of the main tenets of the new league would be respect for umpires.

McGraw was the premier umpire-baiter in the land. Throughout 1901 and 1902 McGraw and Johnson clashed. Finally in July 1902 McGraw was suspended indefinitely.

In retaliation, McGraw conspired to deliver the Baltimore franchise to the forces of the National League. As part of the bargain he was named manager of the New York Giants. "McGraw was one of the hardest men in the league to control and now that he has left I cannot see how the American League has lost anything," Ban Johnson said at the time.

McGraw immediately began a housecleaning of the New York franchise. One of his first moves was to return promising young Christy Mathewson to full-time pitching duty. A McGraw predecessor, Horace Fogel, had attempted to shift Mathewson to the infield.

The Giants were a last-place club when McGraw arrived in 1902. By 1904 they were league champions. Although peace had been declared between the National and American leagues, and a World Series had been played in 1903, McGraw and Giants owner John T. Brush so hated Ban Johnson and his upstart circuit that they refused to take part in any postseason play that year.

In 1905, however, they relented, and it was a wise choice. Christy Mathewson pitched three shutouts against the A's, and the Giants became world champions. McGraw won pennants again in 1911, 1912, 1913, and 1917, but lost the World Series each year. "Not that this record reflects upon the system I have maintained as a manager, for frankly, I am not willing to concede that it does," McGraw wrote in *Baseball Magazine* in 1919.

McGraw's teams played "scientific" baseball, manufacturing runs instead of swinging for the fences. He was a teacher first and a manager second. "The Little Napoleon," said spitballer Burleigh Grimes, who pitched for McGraw's Giants in 1927, "taught me more about pitching in the first 15 minutes than I had learned in 11 previous seasons."

One of McGraw's methods was to sign as many college players as possible. McGraw, who had attended St. Bonaventure University, once said, "The difference is simply this—the college boy, or anyone else with even a partially trained mind, immediately tries to find his faults; the unschooled fellow usually tries to hide his. The moment a man locates his faults he can quickly correct them. The man who thinks he is keeping his mistakes under cover will never advance a single step until he sees the light."

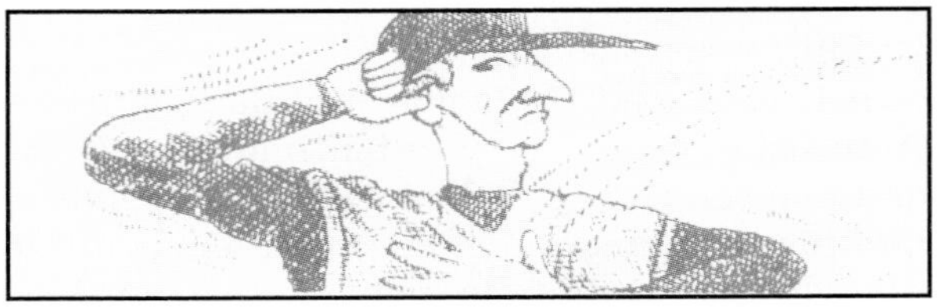

McGraw had his share of disappointments in the game. His club lost the 1908 pennant in heartbreaking fashion on the famed "Merkle Boner," in which Fred Merkle forgot to touch second base. In the 1912 World Series he had victory snatched away from him on Fred Snodgrass' "$30,000 Muff." He saw his young favorites, pitcher Christy Mathewson and outfielder Ross Youngs, die early. His trusted coach, Cozy Dolan, was banished from the game for an attempted fix.

One of McGraw's lowest moments came in June 1917 when he made a smart aleck remark to umpire Bill "Lord" Byron. The previous day, Reds catcher Tommy Clarke had given Byron some lip. The next day McGraw shouted to Clarke, "I don't know what you said, Tom, but whatever it was, it goes double for me." Byron countered, yelling that McGraw was "run out of Baltimore." Those were fighting words to McGraw, and he proceeded to punch Byron in the face. The two men rolled around until players from both the Giants and Reds pulled them apart.

National League president John K. Tener fined McGraw $500, the biggest fine in baseball history to that point, and suspended him for 16 days. A raging McGraw charged that Tener was under the thumb of the Phillies and was out to get the Giants. Called on the carpet by the league owners, McGraw turned tail and ran, denying "any intimation or utterance that might be construed to in any way reflect upon the ability, honesty, and integrity of the president of the league." McGraw escaped banishment from the league, but was hit with another $1,000 in fines.

McGraw truly relished his role of Little Napoleon, the baseball genius who directed each move and countermove on the diamond. One of his favorite activities was to call every pitch thrown by Giants hurlers. "I signaled for every ball that was pitched to Ruth during the last World Series," he said in 1923.

McGraw was at his cockiest in a crucial 1921 series against the Pirates. With the bases loaded, George "Highpockets" Kelly came to the plate for New York. Kelly worked the count to three balls and no strikes, and traditionally McGraw never allowed batters to hit on 3–0. Now determined to outflank the opposition, he flashed a sign for Kelly to swing away. Kelly did a double take but followed orders and delivered a grand slam. "McGraw comes strutting in [saying] if my brains hold out, we'll win it," Kelly recalled. The Giants swept the five-game series from Pittsburgh and won the pennant by four games.

McGraw captured world championships in 1921 and 1922, but lost the World Series in both 1923 and 1924. In the late 1920s and early 1930s he became increasingly irascible. "He could be very unfair at times," said longtime Giants third baseman Freddy Lindstrom. Often McGraw would not even bother to show up at the ballpark. Finally in 1932 he called first baseman Bill Terry into his office to turn over the manager's responsibilities to him. McGraw resigned on June 4, the same day Yankees legend Lou Gehrig hit four home runs in a single game.

McGraw died of cancer and uremia on February 25, 1934. He was elected to the Hall of Fame posthumously.

Tug McGraw

McGraw, Frank Edwin **P**

1965–84 B:8/30/1944, Martinez, CA Deb: 8/26/1891, NY NL BR/TL 6', 185

W	L	PCT	G	SV	IP	BB	SO	ERA
96	92	.511	824	180	1514²	582	1109	3.14

Relief pitcher Tug McGraw coined the 1973 Mets battle cry of "You gotta believe!" Whether he was sincere or not is a different story, but whatever his motive, it certainly worked. So did McGraw's screwball. During 19 seasons in the majors, McGraw emerged as one of the finest relief specialists of his era, blending tough pitching with whimsical humor. One of the all-time leaders in saves, relief wins, and strikeouts per nine innings, he appeared in one division playoff series and six NLCS and won two World Series rings.

Frank Edwin "Tug" McGraw came from a humble background. He recalled picking out secondhand shoes as a child for 50 cents a pair at the local St. Vincent DePaul Society. But he did have one advantage in life, an older brother, Hank, who was a fine athlete and provided a sports role model for young McGraw. "I think it was trying to grow up as good as Hank that gave me such a strong desire to compete," observed McGraw.

Upon graduating from high school Hank McGraw, a catcher, received a $15,000 Mets signing bonus, but when his younger brother graduated the scouts showed little interest. On Hank's recommendation, Tug enrolled at Vallejo Junior College. After graduating, there still wasn't any demand for his services, so McGraw (again at his brother's urging) took matters into his own hands and phoned Mets area scout Roy Partee. Partee was only moderately interested, and finally McGraw said he would sign for whatever the Mets would offer. Partee came up with $7,000. "I really think Partee supplied a good recommendation, because he knew I needed the money," said McGraw. The first thing McGraw did with his bonus was buy a convertible.

McGraw spent 1964, his first year in the minors, at Cocoa and Auburn and in the Florida Instructional League. During the off-season the talent-poor Mets flabbergasted McGraw by placing him on their 40-man roster. He appeared in 37 games with the Mets in 1965, going 2–7 with one save, and later in his career he had the honor of being the last active major leaguer to have been managed by Casey Stengel. One early career highlight was an August 26, 1965, victory over Sandy Koufax, the first over the lefthander in Mets history.

McGraw puzzled Mets management. On his first road trip he forgot his cap. This infuriated pitcher-coach Warren Spahn, who threatened to fine McGraw if he ever did it again. "So the next trip I remembered my hat but forgot my shoes," recalled McGraw. More significantly, the Mets didn't like the new pitch he was working on: the screwball.

In 1966 McGraw was used as a starter and his record was only 2–9. He made four starts in 1967, going 0–3, then was sent to Jacksonville. "It was a good move, because in all honesty I hadn't had enough time in the minors yet," admitted McGraw. "It was down there that I started throwing the screwgie [screwball], and I learned a lot about it." McGraw went 10–9 at Jacksonville with a league-leading 1.99 ERA.

At Jacksonville, McGraw also acquired his second trademark: his frantic banging of his glove against his leg. It started as a greeting to his wife Phyllis. "I started doing it every game whether she was there or not," he explained. "The fans came to expect it. It was a great big slap if I had gotten out of a big jam, a smaller slap if maybe I only got a singles hitter out. If I got hit hard I still gave a big slap, just to show the fans I would be back tomorrow."

In 1968 McGraw reported back to the Mets. There was a new manager in New York, Gil Hodges, but he didn't like the screwball either. Down went McGraw to the minors again. This time he got with the program, threw all curveballs—and hurt his arm doing it.

By 1969 he was back with the parent club, and his new pitch gained acceptance. That was the year of the "Miracle Mets," and McGraw, along with Ron Taylor and Cal Koonce, provided the relief work that helped make the miracle possible. McGraw was 9–3 with a 2.24 ERA and 12 saves. After sweeping the Braves in the NLCS, the Mets knocked off the heavily favored Orioles in five games in the Fall Classic. McGraw, who had notched a save in Game 2 of the NLCS, did not pitch in the World Series.

McGraw soon built a reputation as a free-spirited, highly quotable ballplayer. Once, when asked if he preferred Astro Turf to grass, he responded, "I don't know. I never smoked Astro Turf."

McGraw's best two seasons were 1971 and 1972. In 1971 he set career highs with 11 wins (against only four losses), a 1.70 ERA, and 109 strikeouts in 111 innings pitched. He was even better performance in 1972, going 8–6 with a 1.70 ERA and saving a career-high 27 games. He was even credited with the victory in that season's All-Star Game, as he yielded only one hit and struck out four in working the final four innings.

During the early months of the following season McGraw was simply horrible—and so were the Mets. Finally, Mets board chairman M. Donald Grant came into the New York clubhouse to deliver a pep talk, telling the players if they only believed they could win, they would.

McGraw went berserk, jumping around the room and grabbing his teammates, yelling, "He's right! He's right! Just believe. You gotta believe." He repeated the phrase over and over again. Some—including Grant—thought the exuberant McGraw was mocking the chairman. In any case, "You gotta believe" became a Mets mantra as New York came from last place on August 30 to win the race, despite posting the lowest winning percentage of any pennant winner in baseball history.

McGraw finished the season with 25 saves, then hurled five scoreless innings and picked up a save in the Mets' five-game win over the Reds in the NLCS. He pitched two scoreless innings in a 2–1 loss to the A's in Game 1 of the World Series. He blew a save in Game 2, but picked up the victory when the Mets scored four runs in the 12th inning. In Game 3 McGraw pitched two scoreless innings, but the Mets lost, 3–2, in 11 innings. New York evened the Series with a 6–1 win in Game 4, and Jerry Koosman and McGraw combined on a three-hit, 2–0 shutout in Game 5.

New York needed only one win in the final two games at Oakland to secure their second World Series title in five years. It was not to be, but it wasn't McGraw's fault. He pitched in five of the seven Series games, going 1–0 with a 2.63 ERA and one save.

McGraw was only 6–11 with three saves in 1974. That December, in a trade that shocked Mets fans, he was sent to Philadelphia. "I had this growth on my back," explained McGraw. "I think they thought I had cancer. They wanted to get rid of me before I died. I went to Philadelphia, had the growth removed without any problems, and had 10 pretty good years there."

McGraw continued to be a free spirit. After getting a raise to $75,000 one year, the fireman commented, "Ninety percent I'll spend on good times, women and Irish whiskey. The other 10 percent I'll waste."

McGraw got the key outs in the 1980 World Series. In the ninth inning of Game 5 he struck out Kansas City's Jose Cardenal with the bases loaded to preserve a 4–3 Philadelphia victory. In Game 6, the last of the Series, McGraw escaped from bases-loaded situations in both the eighth and ninth innings to provide long-suffering Phillies fans with their first World Series victory.

After leaving baseball McGraw worked for Philadelphia television station WPVI, invested in real estate, served as a spokesman for a bank, and ran a counseling office. But no matter what he did, McGraw always put his own spin on things. One time he observed, "Kids should practice autographing baseballs. This is a skill that's often overlooked in Little League." His son is country-western singing star Tim McGraw.

Scott McGregor

McGregor, Scott Houston **P**

1976–88 B:1/18/1954, Inglewood, CA Deb:9/19/1976, BAL AL BB/TL 6'1", 190

W	L	PCT	G	SH	IP	BB	SO	ERA
138	108	.561	356	23	2140²	518	904	3.99

Scott McGregor had a winning record every season from 1978 through 1984. The No. 1 pick of the Yankees in the 1972 draft, Scott Houston McGregor was part of a 10-player swap with the Orioles on June 15, 1976. He and Mike Flanagan became stalwarts of the Orioles' pitching staff, along with Jim Palmer.

McGregor's only 20-win season came in 1980, and he won his 20th game on the final day of the season. That helped erase some of the memories of the 1979 World Series, when the Orioles blew a 3–1 lead in games to the Pirates. McGregor had given up the Game 7 homer by Willie Stargell that gave Pittsburgh its world championship.

McGregor suffered arm injuries in 1982, falling to 14–12, but he rebounded well in 1983. He was 18–7, leading Baltimore starters in wins, with a .720 winning percentage, 36 starts, 12 complete games, and 260 innings pitched. McGregor also won the fifth and final game of the World Series, a five-hit, 5–0 shutout that ended the Phillies' season. He retired following the 1988 season, having won only two games since 1986.

Fred McGriff

McGriff, Frederick Stanley **1B–DH**

1986–* B:10/31/1963, Tampa, FL Deb:5/17/1986, TOR AL BL/TL 6'3", 215

G	AB	R	H	HR	RBI	OBP	SLG	AVG
1897	6786	1094	1946	390	1192	.384	.517	.287

Fred McGriff became one of a select group of players to lead both leagues in home runs—then gained the most attention in his career by anchoring the middle of a potent Atlanta Braves lineup for more than four seasons. He also hit for average and played a solid first base.

McGriff was selected by the New York Yankees in the 23rd round of the 1981 draft after setting numerous records at Jefferson High School in Tampa—marks which would eventually be broken by future Yankee Tino Martinez. In 1982 the Yankees traded McGriff to the Blue Jays, where he honed his trademark swing through nearly five more minor league seasons. He released his top hand, just as former Chicago White Sox hitting coach Walt Hriniak taught his students, but, upon contact, McGriff twirled the bat through the air with a unique flourish.

Used mostly as a designated hitter, McGriff showed signs of greatness in his 1987 rookie season with the Toronto Blue Jays when he hit 20 home runs in a span of 107 games, including a monstrous shot off Rick Rhoden into the 13th row of the upper deck at Yankee Stadium. It was estimated to have traveled 480 feet, which, at the time, was the longest home run at the Stadium since it had been refurbished in 1976.

In 1988 McGriff became the Jays' regular first baseman. That season he started a streak of seven consecutive seasons with 30 or more home runs, becoming just the ninth player to achieve that feat. He led the American League with 36 home runs in 1989. On December 5, 1990, McGriff and Tony Fernandez were sent to San Diego in an historic deal for Joe Carter and Roberto Alomar.

McGriff crushed 31 home runs for the Padres in 1991, and then led the NL with 35 in 1992. With the Padres on their way to a 100-loss season in 1993, McGriff was traded to Atlanta in a cost-cutting move in July. He ignited a 51–17 run that took the Braves to the division title. Playing in his first World Series in 1995, McGriff chipped in with two home runs as Atlanta conquered Cleveland.

He just missed his eighth straight 30-homer season in 1996. He hit 28 home runs, and batted .295 with 107 RBIs and 37 doubles. When the Braves fell behind three games to one in the NLCS, McGriff was hitting just .077; he drove in seven runs over the last three games as the Braves outscored the Cardinals 32-1 to win the pennant. McGriff batted .300 and homered twice in the World Series, but the Braves lost to the Yankees in six games.

After another solid year in Atlanta, he was traded to Tampa, his hometown. Surrounded by expansion-team talent, he hit .284 with 81 RBIs for the Devil Rays in 1998. He had one of his best seasons at age 35 in 1999, batting .310 with 32 home runs and 104 RBIs.

Deacon McGuire

McGuire, James Thomas **C-1B**

1884–1912 M(1898–1911, 210–287) B:11/18/1863, Youngstown, OH D:10/31/1936, Albion, MI Deb:6/21/1884, TOL AA BR/TR 6'1", 185

G	AB	R	H	HR	RBI	OBP	SLG	AVG
1781	6290	770	1748	45	840	.341	.372	.278

James "Deacon" McGuire's record of playing in 26 seasons stood until Tommy John tied it and Nolan Ryan then surpassed it. However, McGuire's last three seasons consisted of only one or two token appearances for clubs he was managing. Considerably more impressive are the 1,611 major league games that he caught during that time. He appeared in 85 or more games over 11 seasons during an era when catchers wore little protection. In 1904 at the age of 40 he caught in 97 games for a New York Highlanders team that was nosed out of the pennant on the last day of the season.

Deacon, a common nickname during the Victorian era for any ballplayer whose smoking, drinking, cursing, and churchgoing habits deviated from the norm, began his major league days in 1884 with Toledo of the American Association. He later became Washington's regular backstop, hitting over .300 five times between 1891 and 1899.

He managed Washington for part of the 1898 season, and Boston for most of 1907 and 1908. Late in 1909 he succeeded Nap Lajoie as Cleveland's manager, a job Lajoie was anxious to lose, and remained through the first 17 games of 1911. McGuire was consistent at the helm, never once managing a team to a winning record.

Mark McGwire

McGwire, Mark David **1B**

1986–* B:10/1/1963, Pomona, CA Deb:8/22/1986, OAK AL BR/TR 6'5", 225

G	AB	R	H	HR	RBI	OBP	SLG	AVG
1688	5652	1059	1498	522	1277	.398	.587	.265

There are sluggers whose power compels fans to stay in their seats so they don't miss an at bat. Mark McGwire's power compels fans to get to the park several hours early so they can watch him take batting practice. His tape measure homers thrill even those who are rooting for the opposing team.

McGwire—like another great slugger, Babe Ruth—was originally a pitcher. The Montreal Expos drafted the 17-year-old hurler in the eighth round of the 1981 draft, offering $8,500 to the high school senior, but McGwire opted for the University of Southern California.

He soon stopped pitching to concentrate on hitting—and hitting with power. He improved each season, but his junior year was the most spectacular: McGwire set the Pac-10 Conference record with 32 home runs, was named College Player of the Year by *The Sporting News*, and played for the 1984 U.S. Olympic team. The Oakland Athletics chose McGwire with the 10th overall pick of the draft, and had a cleanup hitter for the next decade as a result. In his first six major league seasons McGwire played for four division winners, three straight pennant winners, and one world champion.

When Jose Canseco was the most feared hitter in the American League in the late 1980s, the imposing presence of the 6-foot 5-inch McGwire in the on-deck circle forced managers to pitch to Canseco. McGwire set a rookie record 49 homers in 1987, and hit more than 30 home runs in each of the next there seasons. But in 1991, McGwire struggled, hitting only .201 with 22 home runs.

The following season proved to be a turning point for McGwire. He posted 42 home runs and 104 RBIs as he finished fourth in the American League Most Valuable Player balloting. "In 1992, I started using my mind when it came to baseball," McGwire said. "For the first time in my life, I sat back and really watched the game. I began to realize that I could only play on my physical ability for so long. It took me six years to realize that there is so much mental preparation that goes into this game."

Unfortunately, it was his physical condition that would hamper him in the following years. Painful heel and back injuries scuttled most of the 1993 and 1994 seasons. A strike-shortened season and two separate stints on the disabled list limited McGwire to just 104 games in 1995, but in his 317 at bats he put on one of the most prodigious power displays in major league history. He had more home runs than singles (39 to 35), and hit the most homers of anyone in history with so few at bats. Only Hank Aaron, who hit 40 homers in 392 at bats for the 1973 Braves, had ever come close.

McGwire's health permitted him to play 130 games in 1996, and he tied the record he set the season before with one home run every 8.13 at bats. He not only became the 14th player in history to surpass 50 home runs in a season, he was the first to do it in less than 600 plate appearances. Along the way he also reached the 300 home run plateau, which only Ruth had achieved in fewer at bats. Even more surprising was McGwire's career-high .312 average and 104 runs scored.

While his achievements rivaled Ruth for the speed in which they were accomplished, the name that now began to be associated with McGwire was Maris—and the number 61. When McGwire hit 11 homers in April of 1997, and Seattle slugger Ken Griffey Jr. topped him that month with 13, it became clear that the race to break Maris' single season home run record was on.

The A's had reacquired Jose Canseco in an attempt to reunite the "Bash Brothers," but a revitalized offense couldn't compensate for their horrendous pitching. As Oakland quickly sank into last place in the AL West, McGwire provided the few highlights of the A's 1997 season: a ninth-inning blast that spoiled the world championship flag raising at Yankee Stadium, an April 30 homer that dented the scoreboard at Jacobs Field, and a home run that led the Athletics past the Giants in the first-ever regular season game between the two Bay Area teams in interleague play.

McGwire hit 34 home runs through the first four months of the season. Despite his success on the field, it was clear that McGwire's days in Oakland were numbered. He would be a free-agent at the end of the 1997 season, and the rebuilding Athletics were unlikely to pay a 34-year-old slugger the kind of money he could earn elsewhere.

The Athletics worked out a trade with the St. Louis Cardinals in July 1997. McGwire, as a player with 10 years service time and five years with the same club, had the right to refuse any trade, but he reluctantly agreed to the deal. At least in St. Louis, he would be reunited with his first major league manager, Tony La Russa. It took a little time for McGwire to adjust to the National League; he homered only once in his first 10 days as a Cardinal, but soon started launching balls to new heights in St. Louis. The ovations at Busch Stadium were frequent, genuine, and never ending. Speculation before the trade had pointed to the divorced McGwire going to Anaheim at seasons end because it was near his son Matthew. In September his son came to St. Louis and gave the town his endorsement.

Hours after McGwire signed a three-year deal with the Cardinals on September 16, he responded to the huge ovation with a 517-foot home run. His 53rd homer the next day against Rodney Myers of the Cubs marked the highest total reached by any slugger since Maris in 1961. Myers quipped, "His bat looks like a toothpick."

McGwire finished the season with 58 home runs; only Ruth and Maris had hit more in a single season. At the same time, McGwire became the first player to homer in 17 different parks in a season, the first to hit 20 or more homers with two different teams in the same season, and the only man in history to hit more home runs than any other player in the majors yet still not qualify as the home run champion in either league.

In 1998 all eyes were on McGwire. Could he pick

up where he left off and set a new single season record? By June both McGwire and Sammy Sosa of the Cubs had broken the record for homers by the end of that month. The nation was swept up in the mania of the home run chase, as McGwire and Sosa engaged in a friendly race towards the record. At the end of August, both had 55 homers, just one shy of Hack Wilson's National League record—and within easy striking distance of Maris. McGwire homered twice on September 1 to surpass Wilson. On September 5 he hit his 60th to tie Ruth. Two days later he tied Maris. The next night, against Cubs pitcher Steve Trachsel, McGwire, known for his long, towering blasts, collected number 62 for the record by hitting a line drive just over the left field wall, his shortest—but biggest—home run of the year. Sosa and McGwire embraced on the field as a national television audience applauded. But there was still a lot of season—and a lot of Sosa—left.

On September 25, the season's final Friday, Sosa hit number 66 to move ahead of McGwire. "Big Mac" responded 45 minutes later with number 66 of his own. Then he poured it on in the last two games—67, 68, 69, 70. His final home run ball, one of the few that was not returned to him in exchange for souvenirs or tickets, fetched $3 million for the fan who caught it.

McGwire performed under media scrutiny rarely seen in sports. During one of his countless meetings with the media, a reporter spotted a bottle of a powdered supplement in his locker. McGwire said he took the supplement, androstenedione, in an effort to prevent the injuries that limited him to just 178 games from 1993 to 1995. The supplement, banned by a few sports leagues but legal in baseball, led to yet more stories on McGwire. He stopped using the androstenedione after the 1998 season.

In 1999 McGwire again surpassed the 60 home run mark and came close to his own record, topping out at 65. He extended his own record with his fourth straight 50-homer season. He also drove in an NL-best 147 runs, and ended the season with 522 career home runs to climb into the top 10 all-time.

Stuffy McInnis

McInnis, John Phalen **1B–SS**

1909–27 M(1927, 51–103) B:9/19/1890, Gloucester, MA D:2/16/1960, Ipswich, MA Deb:4/12/1909, PHI AL BR/TR 5'9½", 162

G	AB	R	H	HR	RBI	OBP	SLG	AVG
2128	7822	872	2405	20	1062	.343	.381	.307

The shouts of "that's the stuff, kid!" whenever John Phalen McInnis made a good play as a boy in the suburban Boston leagues eventually earned him the nickname "Stuffy." He started as a shortstop with the Philadelphia A's in 1909, but in 1911 Connie Mack switched him to first base to replace the aging Harry Davis. The move was a surprise, as the 5-foot-9 McInnis was hardly a towering target. But his sure hands, quickness, and general agility made him a key part of Mack's "$100,000 Infield," and McInnis helped the team win pennants in 1911, 1913, and 1914.

In 1918 he had the good fortune to become a regular with the Boston Red Sox champs, and in 1925 when he subbed with the Pittsburgh Pirates they won the pennant. Every team he played with during October won the World Series except the 1914 A's.

A line-drive pull-hitter who occasionally slapped the ball to right, McInnis hit over .290 during all but one of the 14 seasons that he spent as a major league regular. Although he batted in more than 1,000 runs during his career, he was best known for his defense: he led AL first basemen in fielding percentage six times. In 1921 with the Red Sox he made one error all season to compile an American League record fielding percentage of .9993. From May 31, 1921, to June 2, 1922, he handled a string of 1,700 consecutive errorless chances in 167 games. In 1927 he tried managing the Phillies but later quit to coach at Harvard and Amherst.

Ed McKean

McKean, Edwin John **SS**

1887–99 B:6/6/1864, Grafton, OH D:8/16/1919, Cleveland, OH Deb:4/16/1887, CLE AA BR/TR 5'9", 160

G	AB	R	H	HR	RBI	OBP	SLG	AVG
1654	6890	1227	2083	67	1124	.364	.417	.302

Ed McKean stayed close to home for most of his professional baseball career. The native Ohioan began his professional career in Youngstown, and played for two other minor league teams before finally making the major leagues with Cleveland's American Association franchise in 1887.

The Cleveland Blues (aka the Spiders) switched from the American Association to the National League in 1889. McKean's all-out effort, combined with his willingness to stand up to umpires, earned him the team's captaincy in 1891. The following summer the Spiders won the second half title of the league's split season, landing them a berth in the Temple Cup series. Although Cleveland lost to Boston, the recent additions of Jesse Burkett and Cy Young made the Spiders a perennial contender throughout the 1890s.

McKean was regarded as only an average defensive shortstop, but a dangerous batsman. From 1893 to 1896 he hit no lower than .310 and reached the 100-run and 100-RBI plateau each season. In 1895 McKean helped the Spiders upset the Baltimore Orioles in the Temple Cup. McKean batted over .300 in Cleveland's five-game victory. The Spiders claimed another berth in the Temple Cup the following year, but lost the series in four consecutive games.

An aging McKean fell into decline the next few seasons. In 1899 he was one of several players transferred from Cleveland to St. Louis—Frank and Stanley Robison owned both teams. The result was a fifth-place finish for St. Louis and a record-worst 20–134 for the Spiders in 1899. It was also McKean's final season. He retired after batting a career-low .260, then worked as a minor league manager at several different stops.

Bill McKechnie

McKechnie, William Boyd **3B-2B-SS**

1907, 1910–18, 1920 M(1915, 1922–26, 1928–46, 1,896–1,723) B:8/7/1886, Wilkinsburg, PA D:10/29/1965, Bradenton, FL Deb:9/8/1907, PIT NL BB/TR 5'10", 160

G	AB	R	H	HR	RBI	OBP	SLG	AVG
846	2843	319	713	8	240	.301	.313	.251

When Bill McKechnie was hired to manage the Pittsburgh Pirates in 1922, he was warned that the club included some real characters, such as shortstop Rabbit Maranville and his roommate, pitcher "Chief" Yellowhorse. To halt their incessant partying, McKechnie decided to become their third roomie. The Pirates soon made their first road trip under McKechnie to New York. After checking in at the hotel, McKechnie went out for dinner. Upon his return, he was surprised to find Maranville and Yellowhorse already in bed. This job may not be so tough, he thought. But when he opened a closet to hang up his coat, 20 pigeons exploded into the room.

As the shocked manager stood amid the cooing, flapping birds, Maranville sat up in bed and whispered, "You just let out the Chief's pigeons, Bill. Don't open the other closet. Mine are in there." Fortunately, patience was one of McKechnie's virtues. In more than a quarter century as a big league manager, it was tested many times.

William Boyd McKechnie was born into a devout Methodist-Episcopal family near Pittsburgh in 1886. His upbringing, his conservative lifestyle, and the fact that he sang for 25 years in a Methodist choir earned him the nickname "Deacon." He began playing baseball professionally in 1906 in Washington, Pennsylvania. During the next four years he played the infield for teams in Wheeling, West Virginia, and Canton, Ohio.

The Pittsburgh Pirates gave him a three-game trial in 1907, and from 1910 through 1912 he was their utility man. The switch hitter never hit better than .247 for the Pirates, but he was a good fielder and was considered an intelligent player.

Late in the 1912 season he was sent down to St. Paul of the American Association. He spent 1913 with St. Paul, the Boston Braves, and the New York Highlanders. When Highlanders manager Frank Chance was asked why he spent so much time off the field with McKechnie, he answered, "Because he knows more baseball than all the rest of my team put together."

McKechnie jumped to Indianapolis of the upstart Federal League in 1914, where he played third base and hit an uncharacteristic .304. The franchise moved to Newark in 1915, and McKechnie was named manager early in the season. He compiled a 54–45 record and moved the team up in the standings, but the league disbanded after season's end.

In 1916 McKechnie signed with the Giants, where he made baseball history on May 30 by tying the major league record for most times caught stealing in a game with three failed attempts. He was soon traded to Cincinnati in a deal that sent Christy Mathewson to the Reds as manager. After two years as a utility infielder, McKechnie was sold to Pittsburgh. In 1918, a year in which many baseball stars were either in the service or engaged in defense-related industries, McKechnie was the Pirates' regular third baseman. He retired in 1919 but came back as a reserve in 1920 before finishing his playing career with Minneapolis of the American Association in 1921.

When he took over as manager of the Pirates in 1922, they were in fifth place and going nowhere. McKechnie's mixture of patient understanding, firm-but-fair discipline, and solid baseball strategy helped lift the team to a tie for third. Two more third-place finishes followed in 1923 and 1924, but the Pirates won a few more games each season. In 1925 they won the National League pennant.

That team included three Hall of Famers—third baseman Pie Traynor and outfielders Max Carey and Kiki Cuyler. Pittsburgh faced defending world champion Washington in the World Series. With a pitching staff that included Walter Johnson and Stan Coveleski, the Senators were slight favorites to win. They started strong, taking three of the first four games, but Pittsburgh came back to win the last three games and claim their first title since 1909.

Although the Pirates added Paul Waner, another great hitter, to their lineup in 1926, they fell back to third place. Many of Pittsburgh's problems stemmed from the hiring of blunt-spoken Fred Clarke as McKechnie's adviser. His caustic comments provoked a small revolt among the players, and McKechnie was fired after the season.

McKechnie joined the St. Louis coaching staff in 1927. The Cards had won the 1926 pennant under Rogers Hornsby, who had then been traded to the New York Giants for Frankie Frisch. When new manager Bob O'Farrell failed to bring the Cardinals another pennant he was fired, and McKechnie was installed as manager for 1928.

The Cardinals roster included such hitters as Frisch, Chick Hafey, and Jim Bottomley, but they didn't gel until veteran Rabbit Maranville plugged a hole at shortstop. The Giants and Cubs finished strong, but the Cardinals won the 1928 race to give McKechnie his second pennant in four years. In the World Series the Redbirds squared off against a New York Yankees team that boasted Babe Ruth, Lou Gehrig, Tony Lazzeri, and other fearsome sluggers. It was no contest; New York won in a four-game sweep.

Cardinals ownership overreacted and demoted McKechnie to manager of their Rochester farm club. Crushed, he ran for the office of tax collector in Wilkinsburg, Pennsylvania, vowing to give up baseball if he won. He lost. Midway through the 1929 season Cardinals owner Sam Breadon realized his mistake and brought McKechnie back. Although the Cardinals posted a winning record, they still finished fourth.

McKechnie accepted a position as the Boston Braves' manager in 1930 and remained there through 1937. He took the perennially last-place Braves and, with very little talent on hand, turned them into a respectable ballclub.

In 1933 and 1934 the team actually posted a winning record and finished fourth, the franchise's only first-division finishes between 1921 and 1946. Particularly adept at handling pitchers, McKechnie turned aging minor league hurlers Lou Fette and Jim Turner into 20-game winners in 1937. The Braves finished fifth with a 79–73 record and McKechnie earned Manager of the Year honors.

In 1938 he took over as manager of the Cincinnati Reds, who had finished last in 1937. Two years later they won the pennant. McKechnie's Reds featured solid defense and the pitching of Bucky Walters, a converted infielder, and Paul Derringer, a righthander who'd had a losing record before McKechnie took over. The two men became stars under him. The 1939 team lost to the Yankees in the World Series but in 1940 defeated favored Detroit in seven games.

Johnny Vander Meer, who threw two consecutive no-hitters under McKechnie, summed up his manager's strengths: "I can sincerely say that I was proud to play for him. He was one of the greatest individuals I have ever met in my life, either on the field or off. Ballplayers never feared McKechnie; they respected him.

"He had a remarkable ability for evoking respect; a great handler of men. He was the most outstanding defensive manager I ever saw. We were not noted as a heavy-hitting team, so all his skills and insights were directed toward defense, from handling his pitchers to positioning his men in the field. He was so skillful at doing these things that we never had to score too many runs to win. McKechnie knew how to hold on to a one- or two-run lead better than any other manager."

The Reds stayed in contention for several more seasons, but by 1945 most of their better players were gone. When the club finished sixth in 1946, McKechnie was let go. McKechnie turned down several managerial offers to sign as a coach with the Cleveland Indians. As Lou Boudreau's right-hand man from 1946 through 1949, McKechnie was given much of the credit for developing Bob Lemon into a winning pitcher and Larry Doby into an outstanding center fielder. His sage advice and steady personality were of great help to Boudreau in 1948 when Cleveland won the pennant and World Series.

After coaching for Boudreau at Boston in 1952 and 1953, McKechnie retired to Bradenton, Florida. In 1962, three years before his death, he was elected to the Hall of Fame.

Jack McKeon

McKeon, John Aloysius

Manager (1973–75, 1977–78, 1988–90, 1997–*, 658–656) Executive B:11/23/1930, South Amboy, NJ

Jack McKeon earned the nickname "Trader Jack" while serving as the general manager of the San Diego Padres. His willingness to make blockbuster trades helped the Padres to their first World Series appearance in 1984. In a baseball career spanning more than 50 years, however, McKeon worked primarily as a field manager.

McKeon started as a catcher in the Pirates minor league organization in 1949. By 1955 he was serving as a player-manager for Fayetteville. In 17 seasons as a minor league manager, McKeon compiled a record of 1146–1123, earning Manager of the Year awards four separate times. His first major league job came with the Kansas City Royals in 1973. The young team finished in second place during his first season, but they regressed the following year. He was fired in July of 1975.

For parts of 1977 and 1978, McKeon managed the Oakland A's. Under team owner Charles O. Finely, he also served as an assistant general manager, scout and coach. In 1979 he was named general manager of the San Diego Padres. When the team got off to a slow start in 1988, McKeon fired manager Larry Bowa and named himself as Bowa's replacement. The team improved dramatically under his leadership, narrowly missing a division title in 1989.

After serving in the Cincinnati Reds front office for several years, McKeon was once again called upon to return to the field and resurrect a struggling team. The Reds had a stronger finish once he assumed control in 1997, and improved in 1998. The team won 96 games in 1999, but lost its bid for the Wild Card spot in the playoffs to the New York Mets in a one-game playoff.

Denny McLain

McLain, Dennis Dale **P**

1963–72 B:3/29/1944, Chicago, IL Deb:9/21/1963, DET AL BR/TR 6'1", 185

W	L	PCT	G	SH	IP	BB	SO	ERA
131	91	.590	280	29	1886	548	1282	3.39

In 1968 Denny McLain became the only pitcher in the second half of the 20th century to win 30 games in one season, and he led Detroit to the American League pennant and world championship. Five years later, arm injuries and a gambling problem pushed him into bankruptcy and out of baseball.

Dennis Dale McLain signed with the White Sox for $17,000 in 1962. In his first professional game, the hard-throwing righthander pitched a no-hitter for Harlan of the Appalachian League. McLain was one of three young bonus pitchers in the White Sox organization, but only two of them could be protected on the major league roster. In spring training of 1963, the White Sox matched McLain against fellow bonus baby Bruce Howard in an exhibition game. When Howard won, 2–1, McLain was left unprotected. The Detroit Tigers quickly drafted him.

McLain spent most of the 1963 season with Knoxville in the Sally League and then was called up to Detroit at the end of the season, pitching three games and winning twice. A few days later, he eloped with Sharyn Boudreau, daughter of Hall of Famer Lou Boudreau. McLain opened the 1964 season with Syracuse but was soon called back up to Detroit. He appeared in 19 games, going 4–5, but struck out 70 batters in only 100 innings.

In 1965 he developed a curveball and changeup and worked his way into the Tigers starting rotation. He made 29 starts, completing 13 of them, and went 16–6, striking out 192 in 220 innings, including 14 in 6⅔ innings of relief against the Red Sox on June 15. During that game he tied what was then an AL record by striking out seven consecutive batters.

McLain won 20 games in 1966, but his ERA skyrocketed to 3.92. Although his fastball was first-rate, his other pitches were substandard. In 1967 Tigers pitching coach Johnny Sain taught him to throw a sidearm slider. Starting slowly the next year, McLain developed confidence in the slider, won his first game on April 21, and finished the season with 17 victories.

McLain was ill-equipped to deal with the sudden onslaught of fame. He was both brash and immature, yet his instant success led him to believe that life was all too easy. In the go-go late 1960s, he lived a sort of twisted, mod lifestyle, reaping the benefits of early fame without a clue to its true meaning and significance.

The city of Detroit fell in love with McLain in 1968. He made the sportswriters' lives easy with his off-the-cuff quips. He drank a case of Pepsi a day and bragged that his success was because of his off-season bowling. At the All-Star break he was 16–2. By late August he was famous. Between pitching starts, McLain appeared on the *Today* show, *The Ed Sullivan Show*, the *Smothers Brothers Comedy Hour*, and a host of other programs. He was featured in *Life* and *Time* as he briefly became baseball's poster boy for the younger generation.

When he won on September 14, beating Oakland, he became the first pitcher to win 30 games since 1934, when Dizzy Dean won 30 for the Cardinals. Detroit won the AL pennant by 12 games. McLain finished 31–6, striking out 280 in 336 innings, and pitching 28 complete games with an ERA of 1.96. He won both the Cy Young Award and the Most Valuable Player Award in the Year of the Pitcher.

The Tigers met St. Louis in the World Series. Cardinals pitcher Bob Gibson had put up numbers similar to McLain's that year. Although Gibson won only 22 games, his ERA was a gaudy 1.12. The two pitchers faced each other twice in the Series, and Gibson won each time, 4–0 in Game 1 and 10–1 in Game 3. But the Tigers' Mickey Lolich picked up the slack. Although McLain finally collected a victory in Game 6, Lolich won three times, beating Gibson in Game 7 to give Detroit the world championship.

McLain followed up in 1969 with another fine season, winning 24 games with a 2.80 ERA, and leading the AL in games started, with 41, and innings pitched, with 325. McLain shared the Cy Young Award with Baltimore's Mike Cuellar.

Then the bottom fell out. He was pitching too much and living too fast. Before the 1970 season, a story appeared *in Sports Illustrated* that linked McLain to gamblers, and Commissioner Bowie Kuhn suspended him for half the season. McLain was forced into bankruptcy. Shortly after his return to play, the Tigers suspended him for a week after he dumped a bucket of water on a sportswriter. Kuhn subsequently suspended him again for carrying a gun. He finished the year at 3–5.

He was traded to the Washington Senators in a deal that Washington manager Ted Williams didn't endorse. McLain and Williams detested each other. Although McLain managed to pitch 217 innings in 1971, the results were disastrous.

He lost a league-high 22 games, his ERA was 4.27, and his arm was starting to fail him. Too many cortisone shots had taken their toll. Washington dumped him on Oakland, for whom he appeared in only five games in 1972 before being sent to the minor leagues. In late July he was traded to the Braves for Orlando Cepeda.

McLain's career with the Braves didn't last long. He went 3–5 in 15 games and was released. He attempted a comeback in 1973, appearing for Des Moines in the American Association and Shreveport of the Texas League, but his arm had lost its magic. McLain was out of baseball by age 30.

He went into television and radio work in Detroit, ran nightclubs, and then worked for the Class AAA Memphis Blues. When the team went under, McLain filed for bankruptcy again. His house burned to the ground in 1978, destroying all his baseball awards. They were replaced on Denny McLain Day at Tiger Stadium in 1982, but McLain's personal nightmare was just beginning. In 1985 he was convicted of extortion, racketeering, and drug possession. A decade later he went to prison again.

Although many fans consider McLain a one-year wonder, his career numbers aren't that shabby. During his career he yielded an average of 10.47 baserunners per nine innings, a better ratio than Hall of Famers Dizzy Dean, Whitey Ford, Bob Gibson, Carl Hubbell, Robin Roberts, and Warren Spahn.

Cal McLish

McLish, Calvin Coolidge Julius Caesar Tuskahoma **P**

1944–64 B:12/1/1925, Anadarko, OK Deb:5/13/1944, BRO NL BB/TR 6'1", 200

W	L	PCT	G	SV	IP	BB	SO	ERA
92	92	.500	352	6	1609	552	713	4.01

Cal McLish may have had the longest name in major league baseball history: Calvin Coolidge Julius Caesar Tuskahoma McLish. Better known as "Buster," McLish was a bust during his first six seasons with the Brooklyn Dodgers, Pittsburgh Pirates and Chicago Cubs.

Bumbling along with an 8–21 record, working mostly as a relief pitcher, McLish was shipped to the minor leagues after a dismal 4–10, 4.45 ERA campaign for the Cubs in 1951. His hopes and dreams shattered, McLish vanished into the obscurity of the bush leagues and five years passed before he resurfaced in Cleveland with the Indians.

Still working out of the bullpen, the righthanded McLish appeared in 37 games in 1956 and finished with a 2–4 record and an earned run average just under 5.00. There seemed no end to his losing ways. Then without warning, McLish won nine games the next season with a 2.74 ERA. He had suddenly become one of the best relievers in the game.

In 1958, with Early Wynn gone to the Chicago White Sox and Mike Garcia hurting with a sore arm, McLish moved into the Indians' starting rotation and established himself as the staff ace. He finished at 16–8 with a 2.99 ERA. In 1959 he was 19–8 with 113 strikeouts as the Indians finished second to the White Sox. His two-year run with the Tribe put McLish among baseball's pitching elite.

Following the season, however, McLish was traded with Billy Martin and Gordy Coleman to Cincinnati for Johnny Temple. McLish struggled for the Reds, going 4–14 and was quickly dealt to the White Sox. He closed out his seesaw, 15-year career with two strong seasons (11–5, 13–11) with the Philadelphia Phillies before a sore arm forced him to retire in 1964.

Don McMahon

McMahon, Donald John **P**

1957–74 B:1/4/1930, Brooklyn, NY D:7/22/1987, Los Angeles, CA Deb:6/30/1957, MIL NL BR/TR 6'2", 222

W	L	PCT	G	SV	IP	BB	SO	ERA
90	68	.570	874	153	1310²	579	1003	2.96

Don McMahon generated little fanfare during his many years as a relief pitcher, but when he stopped pitching, only Hoyt Wilhelm, Lindy McDaniel, and Cy Young had appeared in more major league games. McMahon pitched in 874 games and posted 153 saves. In 1959 he led the National League in saves, with 15.

Donald John McMahon began his career as a third baseman in the Milwaukee organization, but his strong arm convinced the management to convert him to pitching. Originally a starter, he was a 20-game winner for Owensboro of the Kitty League in 1954. But a poor performance (2–13, 5.01 ERA) at Toledo in 1955 prompted Atlanta Crackers manager Whitlow Wyatt to turn him into a reliever the following year.

McMahon, who pitched for seven teams in an 18-year big league career, always seemed to be on the trading block. In 1966 the Indians traded McMahon and pitcher Lee Stange to the Red Sox for former relief ace Dick "the Monster" Radatz. The following year Boston sent McMahon to Chicago for infielder Jerry Adair. In 1968 the White Sox sent him to the Tigers, who in turn sold him to the Giants, where he ended up as a pitcher-coach.

McMahon coached for the Giants, the Twins, and the Indians. At the time of his death in July 1987 he was a special assignment scout for the Dodgers. He collapsed while pitching batting practice at Dodger Stadium and died soon after.

Sadie McMahon

McMahon, John Joseph **P**

1889–97 B:9/19/1867, Wilmington, DE D:2/20/1954, Delaware City, DE Deb:7/5/1889, PHI AA BR/TR 5'9½", 165

W	L	PCT	G	SH	IP	BB	SO	ERA
173	127	.577	321	14	2634	945	967	3.51

John Joseph "Sadie" McMahon led the American Association in wins in 1890 and 1891. Although the origin of "Sadie" as a nickname is unknown, McMahon also shared in a second nickname. He and his catcher, Wilbert Robinson, were so rotund they became known collectively as "the Dumpling Battery."

The righthander pitched in the Philadelphia area and was signed by the Philadelphia Athletics in 1889, when he was 21 years old. McMahon put together a 36–21 1890 season with two clubs. That incarnation of the Athletics disbanded on September 17, 1890, and McMahon, along with Curt Welch and Wilbert Robinson, was sold to the Orioles.

In 1891 McMahon went 35–24 and led the American Association with five shutouts. During the 1890 and 1891 seasons McMahon paced the league in innings pitched with a total of 1,012. On June 25, 1891, McMahon became the first pitcher in major league history to surrender back-to-back homers—to Tom Brown and Bill Joyce of the Boston Red Stockings—at the start of game.

He moved with the Baltimore club to the National League in 1892 and nearly pitched a no-hitter on July 18, 1892. The Giants' Denny Doyle got the only hit off McMahon. Unfortunately, it knocked in a run, and McMahon lost the game, 1–0. Fined near the end of the season for heavy drinking, McMahon got into an argument with manager Ned Hanlon and was suspended for the rest of the season.

McMahon injured his shoulder in 1894 and would never again be the workhorse of the pitching staff. Nevertheless, he started 15 games in 1895, compiling a 10–4 record and a 2.94 ERA—the second best of his career—and the Orioles went to the World Series. McMahon was 0–2 with a 5.94 ERA as the Cleveland Spiders defeated the Orioles, four games to one.

In 1896 McMahon suffered from a stomach ailment while his shoulder problems worsened. He finished his major league career with Brooklyn in 1897. McMahon had a 173–127 career record over nine seasons.

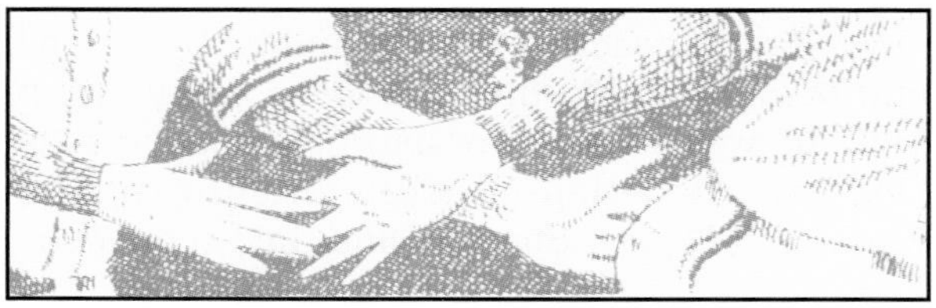

After being released by Brooklyn he moved to Delaware City, where he pitched for local teams and scouted for the Giants from 1911 through 1925.

Marty McManus

McManus, Martin Joseph **2B-3B-1B**

1920–34 M(1932–33, 95–153) B:3/14/1900, Chicago, IL D:2/18/1966, St. Louis, MO Deb:9/26/1920, STL AL BR/TR 5'10½", 160

G	AB	R	H	HR	RBI	OBP	SLG	AVG
1831	6660	1008	1926	120	996	.357	.430	.289

Martin Joseph "Marty" McManus played infield in the 1920s for some of the American League's poorest teams. He became the regular second baseman for the St. Louis Browns in 1921, a period when the usually dreadful Brownies contended for the pennant. In 1922, when St. Louis came within a game of winning the pennant, he hit .312 and drove in 109 runs. He hit better than .300 during the next two seasons as the Browns sank in the league standings.

In 1927 he was traded to Detroit, another second-division club, where he played third base. In 1929 he hit a personal high of 18 home runs. Although never a stylist with a glove, he led AL third sackers in fielding average in 1930. That same season, he topped the league with 23 stolen bases and hit .320. Swapped to the lowly Boston Red Sox in 1931, McManus was given the thankless task of managing the team in the years before Tom Yawkey arrived. In slightly less than two seasons, he won 95 games but lost 153. McManus finished his career with the Boston Braves in 1934, hitting .276. McManus served as a minor league manager for many years after leaving the majors.

Roy McMillan

McMillan, Roy David **SS**

1951–66 M(1972, 1975, 27–28) B:7/17/1930, Bonham, TX D:11/2/1997, Bonham, TX Deb:4/17/1951, CIN NL BR/TR 5'11", 170

G	AB	R	H	HR	RBI	OBP	SLG	AVG
2093	6752	739	1639	68	594	.316	.321	.243

The best-fielding shortstop of the early 1950s, Roy McMillan set a (since-broken) National League record for shortstops in 1954 when he turned 129 double plays. In 1953 and 1954 McMillan and second baseman Johnny Temple led the majors in twin killings.

Roy David McMillan had been a softball player while attending Texas A&M University in 1947, but he played well enough to be offered a professional hardball contract. He started with

Ballinger in the Longhorn League in 1947. Although he hit .275, McMillan had trouble with off-speed pitching. "I never saw a curveball before," he explained.

He went on to play at Tyler, Tulsa, and Columbia before breaking in with Cincinnati in 1951. In 1952 he was the Reds' starting shortstop, and during a four-year stretch he played in 598 consecutive games.

The righthanded batter and fielder was a career .243 hitter with little power, but he made up for his hitting in the field. He led NL shortstops in fielding percentage four times, in putouts three times, in assists four times, and in double plays for four consecutive seasons from 1953 through 1956.

"Roy McMillan was the only one I saw who could go in the hole twice in one game and throw out Richie Ashburn, and nobody could do that. No bat, but in the field he was superb," Cincinnati first baseman Joe Adcock said.

Although he was only 26, McMillan's range fell off precipitously in 1957. The bespectacled shortstop was traded to Milwaukee for pitchers Juan Pizarro and Joey Jay after the 1960 season. Braves manager Bobby Bragan benched him in favor of Denis Menke in 1964 and McMillan was traded to the Mets that May. On Memorial Day 1964, during the 14th inning of a 23-inning contest against the Giants, McMillan snagged a liner to start a triple play.

He retired in 1966 and became a coach in the Mets minor league system and later coached in New York. He was an interim manager for Atlanta in 1972 and for the Mets in 1975. "He's respected. There's more going on in his mind than coming out of his mouth," noted infielder Joe Torre.

Ken McMullen

McMullen, Kenneth Lee **3B–1B**

1962–77 B:6/1/1942, Oxnard, CA Deb:9/17/1962, LA NL BR/TR 6'3", 195

G	AB	R	H	HR	RBI	OBP	SLG	AVG
1583	5131	568	1273	156	606	.318	.383	.248

Signed by the Los Angeles Dodgers for a reported $60,000 bonus in 1960, Ken McMullen proved to be a distinct disappointment for that club. But after he was traded to Washington, along with slugging Dodgers first baseman Frank Howard, in 1965, McMullen blossomed into a slick-fielding major league third baseman with an occasional touch of power.

With the Senators, McMullen led AL third basemen in double plays, with 38, in 1967, and in total chances per game in 1967, 1968, 1969, and 1970. He had a record-tying 11 assists in a game in 1966. However, he played in the shadow of a slick-fielding third baseman Brooks Robinson of Baltimore. As a hitter, McMullen slugged 20 home runs in a season twice.

In April 1970 Washington traded McMullen to the Angels for outfielder Rick Reichardt and third baseman Aurelio Rodriguez. McMullen returned to the Dodgers in a November 1972 deal that sent Frank Robinson from Los Angeles to Anaheim.

With Oakland in 1976, McMullen led the AL in pinch hits with 9 hits in 31 chances. He retired after spending the 1977 season with the Milwaukee Brewers.

Fred McMullin

McMullin, Frederick William **3B**

1914, 1916–20 B:10/13/1891, Scammon, KS D:11/21/1952, Los Angeles, CA Deb:8/27/1914, DET AL BR/TR 5'11", 170

G	AB	R	H	HR	RBI	OBP	SLG	AVG
304	914	120	234	1	70	.333	.302	.256

When most people mention "Black Sox," Joe Jackson is usually the first name that comes to mind; Fred McMullin is the last. McMullin batted just twice in the infamous 1919 World Series, but, like Jackson, he was banned from the game for life because of the Chicago White Sox intentional loss of the Series to the Cincinnati Reds.

A good defensive infielder, McMullin went from the Pacific Coast League to the American League in 1914. He batted once for the Detroit Tigers, struck out, and was sent back to the PCL. The Chicago White Sox purchased his contract from the Los Angeles Angels in 1916. He hit .257 in 68 games.

McMullin played in every game of the 1917 World Series. Swede Risberg, Chicago's regular shortstop, hit so poorly down the stretch that McMullin was put in at third base and Buck Weaver moved to shortstop. McMullin's hitting proved to be little better (.125 in 24 at bats) and unnecessary as the White Sox defeated the New York Giants.

McMullin and Risberg alternated in the lineup over the next two years. McMullin was playing third base on a regular basis when he was injured in August of 1919. Risberg returned to shortstop and Weaver switched back to third. Late in the season McMullin overheard Risberg and first baseman Chick Gandil talking about a "fix" of the upcoming World Series with the Cincinnati Reds. McMullin demanded to be let in on the conspiracy. Fearing that he would reveal the plot publicly, McMullin was included. He went 1-for-2 in the Series.

When news of the scandal eventually broke, McMullin and seven teammates were suspended for the final week of the 1920 season. Although a jury acquitted the "Black Sox" in 1921, the players received far less lenient treatment from new baseball commissioner, Judge Kenesaw Mountain Landis. He banned McMullin and the other Black Sox from baseball for the rest of their lives.

Ironically, McMullin went into law enforcement following the ban. He worked in the Los Angeles office of the U.S. Marshal.

Dave McNally

McNally, David Arthur **P**

1962–75 B:10/31/1942, Billings, MT Deb:9/26/1962, BAL AL BR/TL 5'11", 190

W	L	PCT	G	SH	IP	BB	SO	ERA
184	119	.607	424	33	2730	826	1512	3.24

Dave McNally was one of the best left-handed pitchers in the major leagues during the late 1960s and early 1970s. He won 20 or more games in a season four consecutive years, 1968 through 1971, including an American League record-tying 15 games in a row to start the 1969 season.

But it wasn't on the pitcher's mound that McNally made his greatest contribution to baseball. His biggest victory came in a courtroom, where he and another pitcher, Andy Messersmith, won the battle against baseball's reserve clause, thus ushering in the new era of free agency. McNally's decision to challenge the reserve system, which bound players to their teams for life, came at the end of his career, between the end of the 1975 season and the beginning of the 1976 campaign. "I had no vision of what was going to happen," said McNally. "If someone had said that if we won the class action suit, in five years guys would be making a million dollars a year, I would have laughed at them. None of the owners envisioned it either. If they had, you can bet they would have taken a different approach."

Actually, McNally never benefited from the advent of free agency. A shoulder injury had ended his career with the Montreal Expos at the end of the 1975 season. He decided to challenge the reserve clause because he felt Montreal had reneged on certain promises made to him when the Expos obtained him from the Baltimore Orioles.

"The main reason I challenged the reserve clause was what happened to me in Montreal," McNally said. "Another thing that kept me going was what happened to younger players. A lot of them were being held in reserve instead of being let go to places where they could further their careers. We had a lot of young players in the Baltimore organization who couldn't break into our staff, but they couldn't do anything about it because they were locked up by the Orioles."

Messersmith, who was seeking a no-trade clause from the Los Angeles Dodgers, and McNally decided not to sign their contracts for the 1975 season. That didn't bother management, who simply renewed the players' contracts at their 1974 salaries. Owners felt immune from any legal challenge.

Three years earlier, outfielder Curt Flood had challenged baseball's reserve clause after being traded from the St. Louis Cardinals to the Philadelphia Phillies. Flood lost his case when the U.S. Supreme Court upheld the reserve clause and baseball's immunity from antitrust legislation.

But in December 1975 the two pitchers and the Major League Players Association took their case before arbitrator Peter Seitz, who declared McNally and Messersmith free agents and not bound to their old contracts. They were free to sell their services to the highest bidder. At the time, no one foresaw the impact of Seitz's decision. Commissioner Bowie Kuhn fired the arbitrator and denounced the ruling as "destructive to baseball."

Messersmith made the most of his newfound freedom, signing a five-year, $1.5-million contract with the Atlanta Braves. McNally, who had won close to 200 games for the Orioles, retired after the season and returned to his hometown of Billings, Montana, to open a car dealership.

"The time had come to leave baseball," he said. "If I had been a few years younger, I might have benefited from the case. But that was OK. I made good money in my day, and I made my point."

McNally made several strong points during his years as one of the mainstays of the Orioles pitching staff. From 1962 through 1974 he went 181–113 for the Orioles and helped pitch them to five AL East crowns and four World Series appearances.

McNally grew up never knowing his father, who was killed in World War II when Dave was just a toddler. At an early age, McNally showed special talent as a pitcher. He excelled for the high school and American Legion teams, and the Orioles signed him to a contract after he graduated from high school.

He reached the big leagues in 1962, and on September 26 hurled a 3–0 shutout against Kansas City in his first major league start. McNally became a member of the starting rotation in 1963, and he went 13–6 when the Orioles won the AL pennant in 1966. He started Game 1 of the World Series against the Los Angeles Dodgers but received a no-decision. In Game 4 he beat Don Drysdale on a four-hit shutout, as the Orioles completed an improbable four-game sweep.

McNally won 20 games for the first time two years later, posting a 22–10 record and logging 273 innings. He went 20–7 the following season, including 15 consecutive victories to start the season, as the Orioles won the AL East. In Game 2 of the ALCS against Minnesota, McNally struck out 10 batters in an 11-inning shutout. The Orioles lost to the Mets in the World Series, as McNally started two games (going 0–1) and hit a homer in Game 5.

A year later he posted a league-leading 24 victories as Baltimore repeated as AL champions. He notched a complete-game victory in Game 3 of the World Series, and the Orioles beat the Cincinnati Reds in five games.

In 1971 McNally led the league in winning percentage (21–5, .808), and the Orioles made their third consecutive appearance in the World Series. Baltimore became only the second staff in major league history to have four 20-game winners: McNally; Jim Palmer, 20–9; Pat Dobson, 20–8; and Mike Cuellar, 20–9. McNally won two games in the Series, but the Pittsburgh Pirates beat the Orioles in seven games.

McNally became the league's first $100,000-a-year pitcher in 1972, but he was never the same pitcher again. He had hurt his arm in the middle of the 1971 season and missed 38 days. He came back too soon and tore three muscles in his shoulder. That injury began to take its toll in 1972, and McNally slumped to 13–17, although he posted a 2.95 ERA. He went 17–17 in 1973 as the Orioles won the AL East title. In 1974 he went 16–10 to help the Orioles repeat as AL East champions.

The relationship between McNally and Orioles management became strained in the winter of 1974 when the lefthander won a salary arbitration case. McNally was hurt by some of the things management had said about his performance, and he requested a trade following the 1974 season.

The Orioles obliged by sending him to Montreal, along with outfielder Rich Coggins and minor league pitcher Bill Kirkpatrick, for outfielder Ken Singleton and pitcher Mike Torrez. It turned out to be one of the best trades the Orioles ever made as Singleton became an All-Star player and Torrez won 20 games in 1975.

McNally lasted only a few months before deciding he'd had enough. But before he left to go into the automobile business, he instructed Marvin Miller, executive director of the Players Association, to place his name next to Messersmith's in the test case against baseball's reserve clause. It gave him a prominent place in baseball history.

John McNamara

McNamara, John Francis

Manager (1969–70, 1974–77, 1979–88, 1990–91, 1996, 1,167–1,242) B:6/4/1932, Sacramento, CA

John McNamara was the 1986 American League Manager of the Year. But McNamara's failure to remove immobile first baseman Bill Buckner from Game 6 of that year's World Series, a decision blamed by many for the Red Sox's ultimate loss to the New York Mets, is his strongest legacy.

McNamara never reached the majors as a player, serving as a catcher at such minor league stops as Fresno, Houston, Lynchburg, Lewiston, Sacramento, Albuquerque, Tulsa, and Amarillo. Three times he led his leagues in assists and fielding percentage and twice in putouts. Along the way he earned a release from the Cardinals system in April 1955.

He began managing in 1959 with Lewiston of the Northwest League and also piloted Birmingham, Dallas, and Mobile before becoming an Oakland coach in 1968. Hired to replace Hank Bauer as A's manager in September 1969, McNamara was fired at the close of the 1970 season for being "too nice."

The low-key McNamara captured a division championship with Cincinnati in 1979 and a pennant with Boston in 1986. Fired by the Red Sox in mid-1988, he was replaced by Joe Morgan. McNamara also managed at San Diego and Cleveland.

Bid McPhee

McPhee, John Alexander **2B**

1882–99 M(1901–02, 79–124) B:11/1/1859, Massena, NY D:1/3/1943, San Diego, CA Deb:5/2/1882, CIN NL BR/TR 5'8", 152

G	AB	R	H	HR	RBI	OBP	SLG	AVG
2135	8291	1678	2250	53	1067	.355	.372	.271

Cincinnati's Bid McPhee was the finest second baseman of the 19th century. Although others, such as Fred "Sure-Shot" Dunlap, Bobby Lowe, and the National League's first batting champion, Ross Barnes, were occasionally more spectacular, no player was as consistent as McPhee. Some called him "King Bid."

The fourth among five children of a saddlemaker, John Alexander McPhee caused little trouble as a child. When McPhee was 6, his family moved to Illinois, where he started playing baseball. It's ironic that McPhee, the son of a man who made his living with leather, avoided using a glove long after their use became common.

His nickname, "Bid," or "Biddy" in its original form, is usually bestowed upon someone for being small, yet McPhee grew to 5 feet 8 inches and 152 pounds, not particularly undersized for a player of his era. In 1877 he went to Davenport, Iowa, to clerk in a commission house and play for the local team. He caught and played the outfield before discovering his true calling at second base. McPhee quit baseball for a time and concentrated on his job, but the lure of the diamond was too strong. In 1880 McPhee joined an independent team in Akron.

In 1882 the new American Association was formed, and the Cincinnati Reds were among its charter members. Cincinnati had been a charter member of the National League, competing in that circuit from 1876. But the club had been forced out in 1880 for refusing to sign a pledge banning Sunday baseball and for selling whiskey on park grounds. After a year without league play, Cincinnati fans were eager for major league ball. The less puritanical American Association allowed whiskey on the grounds and games on Sunday. It charged only 25 cents admission—half of the other league's rate. McPhee joined the new Reds and immediately became their regular second baseman. Although he hit only .228 in 1882, he led the league's second basemen in putouts, double plays, and fielding average. Star pitcher Will White won 40 games, and the Reds completed the 80-game schedule in first place with a winning percentage of .688, still a team record. At the end of the season, Cincinnati played a pair of games against Chicago's National League champions, with each team recording a shutout victory.

Although some baseball experts have since suggested that these two games constitute the first World Series, at the time they were considered strictly exhibitions. The National League disputed the AA's major league status and would not allow National League teams to play teams from the new league. To circumvent the rule, Chicago released all its players at the end of the season, and then played Cincinnati as a team of "independents." Eventually, the two leagues made peace, and NL and AA teams played in a postseason series beginning in 1884. But the Reds never made it that far again with McPhee.

During the next few years McPhee's eye at the plate improved. He developed a knack for drawing bases on balls and was occasionally used as a leadoff man. In 1887, the first and only year bases on balls counted as hits, McPhee batted .355, but only .289 by today's standards. In 1884 he scored more than 100 runs for the first time; he repeated the feat nine times.

McPhee hit an astonishing number of triples for a player who lacked much power. In 1887 he led the American Association with 19. Three years later he hit 22. In one 1890 game he smacked three triples off pitcher Amos Rusie. In 1886 he circled the bases seven times for inside-the-park home runs, and he led the league in homers.

McPhee stole 568 bases during his career, but that figure is misleading. No stolen base records were kept during the association's first four seasons. Its totals from 1886 through 1898, and those for the National League, include other baserunning feats such as going from first to third on a single or advancing an extra base on an out. These calculations resulted in some spectacular numbers. When McPhee "stole" 95 bases in 1887, he finished only fifth in the league. Four other players were credited with more than 100 thefts. Although McPhee excelled on the basepaths, he was hardly the Rickey Henderson of his day.

As proficient and consistent as McPhee was on offense, his defense made him a star. In David Faulkner's book on the history of defense, *Nine Sides of the Diamond*, the author notes that only a decade or so before McPhee began playing professionally, second basemen usually played on or near the bag. Because of the efforts of McPhee and a few others, the position evolved in the 1880s. Second basemen positioned themselves to their left, ranging toward first.

McPhee was not the first to make this move, but records indicate that he covered more ground than most second basemen and certainly had better hands. In 18 major league seasons, he led his league's second basemen in putouts eight times, in assists six times, in double plays 11 times, and in fielding percentage eight times.

Modern fans tend to look only at batting records. Fielding records are usually ignored and often mistrusted. Outstanding fielders are often remembered only through anecdotes. When the last eyewitness passes from the scene, great fielders are often forgotten. This is the case with McPhee. His name is unknown to most fans today.

Yet there are other reasons for his obscurity. McPhee played his entire career with Cincinnati, a team that won only one pennant in a race that took place in the American Association's first season. In addition, his personality did not lend itself to lasting fame. He was quiet and didn't drink or brawl. He played hard but was never thrown out of a game, a fact he was fiercely proud of. When the game was over, McPhee went home to his wife and children. The next day he'd show up on time for the game.

Cincinnati fans and management knew they had a star at second base. In 1887, after major league owners decided to cap player salaries at $2,000, the ink on the agreement was barely dry when they began paying some stars more than the cap. McPhee, for example, received a contract for $2,000 from the Reds, but he also received an informal letter promising him $2,300.

In 1890 Cincinnati left the American Association and rejoined the National League. In 1893, when the pitching distance was increased to more than 60 feet, McPhee's hitting showed substantial improvement. From 1894 through 1897, he batted over .299 each season.

By 1896 nearly all players wore gloves on defense. McPhee was a noticeable holdout, steadfastly playing barehanded. Each spring he soaked his hands in brine to toughen them for the season, ignoring suggestions that he put on a glove. Although he continued to field well, McPhee was no longer the best in the league. Finally, on Opening Day 1896, hampered by a sore finger, McPhee gave in and donned a leather glove. The results were exceptional. Once more he led the league in fielding average, and his mark of .978 set a record that lasted 23 years.

In 1897 McPhee suffered an ankle injury that limited him to 81 games and kept him out of action for three months. For a while, it looked as if his career was over. Cincinnati fans and sportswriters held a benefit and raised $3,500 for McPhee. He recovered, though, and played two more seasons before retiring as a player.

In 1901 he returned to manage the Reds; they finished last. In 1902 they showed some improvement, but McPhee quit after only 65 games amid rumors that former Baltimore Oriole Joe Kelley was about to replace him.

McPhee later moved to Los Angeles, where he scouted for the Reds for several years. He died in 1943 in San Diego. Fifty-seven years later, in March 2000, he was elected to the Hall of Fame.

Hal McRae

McRae, Harold Abraham **DH–OF**

1968, 1970–87 M(1991–94, 286–277) B:7/10/1945, Avon Park, FL Deb:7/11/1968, CIN NL BR/TR 5'11", 180

G	AB	R	H	HR	RBI	OBP	SLG	AVG
2084	7218	940	2091	191	1097	.355	.454	.290

Hal McRae played in four World Series, eight League Championship Series, and three All-Star Games. A career .290 hitter, he led the American League in doubles twice and in RBIs once. But his on-field abilities may have been exceeded by his leadership skills. "He's the one who taught us how to play this game," said second baseman Frank White, a teammate of McRae's in Kansas City. "I look up to him."

A three-sport (baseball, basketball, and football) high school star in Sebring, Florida, McRae later played baseball at Florida A&M. The Reds selected him in the sixth round of the June 1965 free-agent draft and sent him to Tampa in the Florida State League. The 20-year-old McRae batted only .154 in 22 games that season.

During the next four years McRae played for Peninsula, Buffalo, Knoxville, and Indianapolis—usually as a second baseman—before reaching the Reds in late 1968. Prior to the 1969 season, McRae appeared in the Puerto Rican Winter League. During one game, while sliding into home plate, he broke his leg in four places. "That cost me most of the 1969 season, and I never could run quite as well after that," he said. "The next few years I played some outfield, but most of the time I pinch-hit against lefthanders."

Hobbled as he was, McRae still found the Reds experience rewarding. "During the three years Pete Rose and I were teammates on the Cincinnati Reds, I learned the value of thinking aggressively," said McRae. "Although Rose and I sometimes talked hitting, Pete didn't really teach me what I now know—he showed me! I saw all those things worked for Pete because he was so aggressive, so I tried to make them work for me, and I think I've done a pretty good job."

Although he never appeared in more than 99 games in any of his three seasons with the Reds, McRae still managed to produce. In the 1970 World Series he batted .455 with two doubles and three RBIs. On July 27, 1971, he had four extra-base hits in a game. On June 1, 1972, he blasted a pinch-hit grand slam off Houston's Jerry Reuss. He pinch hit in the ninth inning of Game 5 of the 1972 NLCS against Pittsburgh, and as McRae batted, a Bob Moose fastball headed for the backstop. Cincinnati pinch-runner George Foster scampered home from third with the pennant-winning run.

In November 1972 McRae was traded to Kansas City ("one of the best breaks of my career") with pitcher Wayne Simpson for pitcher Roger Nelson and outfielder Richie Scheinblum. After a horrible first year in the new league, McRae in virtual desperation turned to Royals hitting coach Charlie Lau. "He turned my career around," said McRae. "I got my confidence back. The mind is a powerful thing. It can work for or against you."

McRae became one of the AL's premier designated hitters, although he was never entirely comfortable with being such a one-dimensional player. "It's hard to feel a part of the club," he admitted. "If you're not hitting, you're like a field-goal kicker who's not making field goals."

McRae batted .310 with 88 RBIs the next season, and he tied the major league record on August 27 when he had six extra-base hits in a doubleheader. After a .306 showing in 1975, he and teammate George Brett engaged in a sizzling race for the AL batting crown in 1976. On the last day of the season Brett won the title, .3333 to .3321, as Twins left fielder Steve Brye played deep on Brett's at bat and let an easy flyball drop for an inside-the-park home run. McRae charged it was racism; others hinted it was revenge for McRae's aggressive style of play.

Even before joining Kansas City, McRae was noted for his aggressiveness in breaking up double plays—including a celebrated slam into Yankee second baseman Willie Randolph in the 1977 ALCS. "Over the years I feel McRae has played dirty," charged Seattle's Glenn Abbott, "but he plays to win, and that's what it's all about."

McRae hit 21 homers, scored 104 runs, and led the league with a career-high 54 doubles in 1977, as the Royals won the AL West and faced the Yankees in the playoffs. He homered in Game 1, and he doubled twice and scored twice in Game 3, both Royals victories. But New York won Games 2, 4, and 5 to win the Series. McRae batted .444 in the five games and established an ALCS record with six runs in a five-game Series.

In 1980 Kansas City swept New York in the ALCS and met the Philadelphia Phillies in the World Series. McRae batted .375 and stroked two doubles, but the Royals lost the Series in six games. McRae made his final appearance in the All-Star Game in 1982, when he hit .308, launched a career-high 27 homers, and led the league with 46 doubles and a league-leading 133 RBIs. He hit .311 the following year. In 1985 he finally played on a world champion, as the Royals rallied to beat St. Louis in a thrilling seven-game World Series. He served as a player-coach for Kansas City in 1987.

In 1988 and 1989 he served as a hitting instructor in the Pirates organization. In 1989 McRae was also inducted into the Royals Hall of Fame and went back on the active list as a player-coach for the Bradenton Explorers of the abortive Florida Senior League. He batted only .171 in 13 games, then spent the next two years as the Expos' hitting coach.

On May 24, 1991, he replaced John Wathan as manager of the Royals, in the process becoming the fourth major leaguer (after Connie Mack, Yogi Berra, and Cal Ripken, Sr.) to manage his own son. Outfielder Brian McRae was already with the Royals when his father was appointed pilot.

McRae's most noted moment as Kansas City manager came on April 26, 1993, when he exploded in spectacular fashion against reporters in the Royals' clubhouse. First-year Royals pitcher David Cone, who had been signed as a free agent after spending most the last few seasons in a turbulent Mets clubhouse, told reporters: "I just want to thank everyone for making me feel at home." McRae became a Phillies coach in 1997.

Kevin McReynolds

McReynolds, Walter Kevin **OF**

1983–94 B:10/16/1959, Little Rock, AR Deb:6/2/1983, SD NL BR/TR 6'1", 210

G	AB	R	H	HR	RBI	OBP	SLG	AVG
1502	5423	727	1439	211	807	.331	.447	.265

Although Kevin McReynolds was a reliable slugger and a dependable left fielder, it was the price that the New York Mets paid to acquire him that troubled the fans and the press during his tenure at Shea Stadium. The Mets traded five players in the deal for McReynolds, including the popular Kevin Mitchell, a jack-of-all-trades as a rookie with the 1986 world champion Mets who would go on to hit 47 home runs in 1989 and win the Most Valuable Player Award that same year.

The Mets paid this price because the expectations for McReynolds were so high. The University of Arkansas slugger was on the cover of the first ever issue of Baseball America in 1981. He was the Minor League Player of the Year in 1983, and in 1984 he helped the Padres gain their first postseason berth in franchise history. He averaged 20 home runs and 82 RBI in three full seasons in San Diego, and he was one of the most coveted players in the National League when the blockbuster trade brought him to New York.

In his first season with the Mets, McReynolds posted career highs in home runs, doubles, and hits, and he was 14-for-15 in stolen base attempts. The following year, McReynolds batted a career-high .288 and knocked in 99 runs as the Mets won the NL East flag for the second time in three years. McReynolds' casual style in left field and on the basepaths lulled opposing baserunners and infielders into a false sense of security, thus enabling him to lead the league with 18 outfield assists and be perfect in 21 stolen base attempts. McReynolds finished third in National League MVP voting.

McReynolds' two run home run, sacrifice fly, and 4-for-4 performance in Game 6 of the 1988 NL Championship Series kept the Mets alive. However, New York lost the next night, and the Dodgers took the pennant, and ultimately, the World Series.

McReynolds remained a model of consistency with seasons that nearly mirrored each other in 1989 and 1990. He averaged 148 games, 144 hits, 23 home runs, and 84 RBIs for a team that finished second both years. The team dipped to fifth place in 1991, and McReynolds missed the 20-home run mark for the first time in six years. He was the fifth toughest batter to strike out, but he had more fly ball outs than anyone else in baseball.

On December 6, 1991, McReynolds was traded to Kansas City along with Gregg Jefferies and Keith Miller in return for Bret Saberhagen and Bill Pecota. In 1992 McReynolds landed on the disabled list for the first time in his career; the following year he found himself on the bench for the first time.

The man who replaced McReynolds in New York, Vince Coleman, fared little better; they were traded for each other after the 1993 season. McReynolds' second tour with the Mets was brief and injury-plagued, but he was perfect in the field and batted .303 with runners in scoring position. When the baseball strike arrived in August 1994, McReynolds retired at age 34.

Cal McVey

McVey, Calvin Alexander **1B-C-3B**

1871–79 M(1873, 1878–79, 91–64) B:8/30/1850, Montrose, IA D:8/20/1926, San Francisco, CA Deb:5/5/1871, BOS NA BR/TR 5'9", 170

G	AB	R	H	HR	RBI	OBP	SLG	AVG
265	1199	227	393	3	172	.340	.407	.328

Calvin McVey, a husky 16-year-old from Indianapolis, won a spot on the local university baseball team in 1867. By the next year young Cal was pounding out hits for two of the best local amateur clubs. His reputation spread at least as far as Cincinnati, where Harry Wright was assembling baseball's first completely professional team. Wright offered McVey the princely sum of $800 to play right field for the Red Stockings, and the youngster gladly accepted.

Throughout the 1869 season the Red Stockings toured the country from coast to coast, playing and defeating everyone who dared oppose them. Their tour was an important step toward the establishment of the first professional baseball league, the National Association, in 1871. Although he was one of the lower-paid team members, McVey proved to be one of its best hitters and was able to play nearly any position.

McVey followed Harry Wright to Boston, where the canny leader established a new Red Stockings team in the National Association. In the circuit's first season McVey batted a resounding .431 and led the league in hits. Wright's Red Stockings won the second league pennant in 1872 as McVey split time between catching and playing the outfield.

He accepted an offer to manage the Lord Baltimores club the next year and brought them in third behind Boston. The pressures of managing affected the 22-year-old skipper not a whit as he batted .380 while playing every position on the field except pitcher.

After his term as manager McVey returned to Boston and helped produce two more NA pennants. In 1874 he led the league in hits and runs scored, and in 1875 his 33 doubles and .506 slugging average were league bests. That same year the versatile McVey made his first attempts at pitching, starting two games and relieving in another. He came away with one victory against no defeats.

Meanwhile, Chicago White Stockings owner William Hulbert decided to improve his club at the expense of Boston's team. He convinced four Red Stockings stars—pitcher Al Spalding, second baseman Ross Barnes, catcher Deacon White, and McVey—to change the color of their hose for monetary considerations. He also recruited another star hitter, Adrian "Cap" Anson, from Philadelphia.

When word of the jumpers' intentions leaked out before the end of the 1875 season, the four stars were brutally booed by Boston crowds, an odd situation since the team was running away with its fourth straight pennant. The National Association folded at the end of the season, and Hulbert organized the National League to begin play in 1876.

Bolstered by the "Big Four," the White Stockings romped to the first National League pennant. McVey's contribution was a .347 batting average, slightly under the .361 he'd averaged during his five years in the NA. That season he also made 11 appearances on the mound, going 5–1 with a 1.52 ERA. After another year in Chicago McVey again tried managing, taking over the Cincinnati franchise. His team finished second in 1878 but McVey batted "only".306. The following season was his last with the Reds and his last in the major leagues.

McVey was not yet 30 and still one of baseball's top hitters when he gave up his major league career to move to California, a section of the country he'd first seen during the Red Stockings' tour 10 years earlier. He spent the next decade playing and managing for West Coast teams, later losing everything in the San Francisco earthquake of 1906. He was still in San Francisco when he died 20 years later.

Lee Meadows

Meadows, Henry Lee **P**

1915–29 B:7/12/1894, Oxford, NC D:1/29/1963, Daytona Beach, FL Deb:4/19/1915, STL NL BL/TR 5'9", 190

W	L	PCT	G	SH	IP	BB	SO	ERA
188	180	.511	490	25	3160^2	956	1063	3.37

Henry Lee "Specs" Meadows was the first modern major leaguer to wear glasses on the field, but he might have been happier during his first eight major league seasons had he been unable to see the scoreboard. Widely recognized as one of the National League's better pitchers, the nearsighted righthander labored for some of the circuit's weakest teams. Meadows lost 13 games by a score of 1–0. That record ranks as a model of futility behind only those of Walter Johnson and Jim Bunning.

After winning 40 games during two seasons with Durham of the North Carolina League, Meadows came to the majors in 1915 with the St. Louis Cardinals, a perennial tail-ender. The next season he led the league in losses with a 12–23 mark for the last-place Cards despite an excellent 2.58 ERA.

In 1919 he again led in losses with 10 each for the Cardinals and the Phillies, who acquired him in midseason. He managed a 16–14 record with the last-place Phils of 1920, but two more losing seasons followed. Several teams tried to acquire him, but Phillies owner William F. Baker was adamant about Meadows staying in Philadelphia, saying, "Meadows will have whiskers down to his knees before I trade him."

In 1923 Pittsburgh's Barney Dreyfuss waved Cotton Tierney, Whitey Glazner, and $50,000 under Baker's nose for the rights to Meadows. Baker made an agonizing reappraisal, and Meadows became a Pirate. He was an immediate success at Forbes Field, winning 16 games for the Bucs during his first Pittsburgh season. In 1925 the Pirates unseated the New York Giants as pennant winners with a powerful lineup that included Kiki Cuyler, Pie Traynor, and Max Carey. Meadows led the pitching staff with a 19–10 record. He pitched the opening game of the World Series, but lost to Walter Johnson, 4–1.

Although the Pirates slipped to third in 1926, Meadows had his only 20-win season that year to tie for the league lead with a 20–9 mark. In 1927, Pittsburgh was back on top, and Meadows finished 19–10. The Pirates' World Series opponents were the 1927 Yankees. Sometimes cited as the greatest team of all time, the Bronx Bombers destroyed the Pirates in four straight games. Meadows pitched Game 3, and after giving up two runs in the first, he held the Yanks scoreless for the next five frames. But in the seventh inning New York erupted for six runs to put the game out of reach.

It was the last important game that Meadows pitched, although he was only 33. A sore arm in 1928 limited him to only four appearances and effectively ended his career. He compiled 88 wins in a Pirates uniform, for a lifetime total of 188–180.

Doc Medich

Medich, George Francis **P**

1972–82 B:12/9/1948, Aliquippa, PA Deb:9/5/1972, NY AL BR/TR 6'5", 227

W	L	PCT	G	SH	IP	BB	SO	ERA
124	105	.541	312	16	1996[1]	624	955	3.78

Righthander George "Doc" Medich, the American League's 1981 shutout leader, entered medical school the day after his major league debut. His medical training came in handy one day in 1978 when he saved the life of a fan at Baltimore's Memorial Stadium by performing heart massage.

The Yankees signed Medich after selecting him in the 29th round of the June 1970 free agent draft. He performed with Oneonta, Manchester, Kinston, and West Haven before reaching New York. In 1972 the Pittsburgh-area native led the Eastern League in won-lost percentage, while posting a 1.44 ERA.

Medich's career season came when he registered 19 wins with the 1974 Yankees. In December 1975 he was traded to Pittsburgh in the transaction that sent Willie Randolph and two other players to New York.

Medich changed teams repeatedly in 1977. Eligible for free agency at the end of 1976, he signed with Oakland and stayed there for most of the following season. But in September he was sold to the Mariners, and less than two weeks later he was waived to the Mets. Granted free agency again, Medich signed with Texas that November of 1977, and he stayed with the Rangers until mid-1982, when he was traded to Milwaukee for the final stop of his career. After retiring, Medich, who had earned a degree in chemistry from the University of Pennsylvania and a medical degree from the University of Pittsburgh, practiced sports medicine in Pittsburgh.

Joe Medwick

Medwick, Joseph Michael **OF**

1932–48 B:11/24/1911, Carteret, NJ D:3/21/1975, St. Petersburg, FL Deb:9/2/1932, STL NL BR/TR 5'10", 187

G	AB	R	H	HR	RBI	OBP	SLG	AVG
1984	7635	1198	2471	205	1383	.362	.505	.324

Joe "Ducky" Medwick is most often remembered for his hits—on and off the field. When Medwick hit, he hit hard. Sometimes he hit the baseball; sometimes he slugged one of his teammates or another player. One day it all caught up with him when a pitcher gained revenge for a Medwick insult with a beanball that helped turn Medwick from a legitimate superstar into just another pretty good player.

But what a hitter he was before that beaning. Medwick led the National League in RBIs for three straight seasons. In 1937, in the middle of that streak, he won the Triple Crown and the Most Valuable Player Award, and he also led the league in hits, runs, doubles, slugging, and fielding average.

Born to Hungarian immigrant parents, Medwick grew up in New Jersey. During high school he starred in baseball, basketball, and football and was flooded with offers of football scholarships, including one from Notre Dame.

He chose baseball and was signed by Cardinals scout Charley "Pop" Kelchner. But Medwick wanted to keep his academic options open. So when St. Louis assigned him to Scottsdale in the Class C Middle Atlantic League in 1930, he played under the assumed name of Mickey King. In 75 games he batted .419 with 22 homers and 100 RBIs, and he decided his future lay in baseball.

With Houston in 1931 Medwick led the Texas League with 19 homers and 126 RBIs. The next season he batted .354 for Houston and collected an amazing 52 outfield assists. The Cardinals brought him up at season's end, and after hitting .349 in 26 games, he quickly established himself as one of the league's best hitters.

He had 18 homers and 98 RBIs in 1933, his first full season in the majors, and in 1934 he drove in 106 runs, the first of six straight 100-RBI seasons. He also led the league with a career-high 18 triples; he would record eight double-figure seasons of triples in his career.

In 1936 he won his first RBI title with 138, and among his league-leading 223 hits were 64 doubles, still an NL record. In his 1937 Triple Crown season he set career highs in batting average, with .374, and in slugging, at .641, and he had 237 hits, 31 homers, and 154 RBIs.

He was a bad-ball hitter, a free swinger who made contact and disdained walks. He struck out 83 times in 1934 and 59 times in 1935, but he never struck out more than 50 times in another season. "I think he shouldn't be allowed to carry a bat to the plate," pitcher Dutch Leonard once joked. "Make him use his fists to swing. Then he'd only hit singles."

About those fists. Sometimes he hit his own teammates with them. He flattened Rip Collins and Tex Carleton, and he threatened the Dean brothers. "It ain't fair," Dizzy complained. "Jes' as you're workin' up a head of steam and gittin' to the fightin' stage, Joe bops you and it's over. That ain't no way to fight."

Medwick himself had a pretty jaded outlook: "I have two good friends in the world, the buckerinos and the base hits. If I get the base hits, I will get the buckerinos."

Medwick's wildest moment in baseball, of course, was in Detroit, in Game 7 of the 1934 World Series against the Tigers. In the sixth inning Medwick tripled off the center-field fence for his 11th hit of the Series. As he slid into third, Tigers third baseman Marv Owen spiked him, either accidentally or deliberately. While on the ground Medwick began kicking at Owen and eventually punches were thrown. Umpire Bill Klem broke up the struggle and neither player was ejected. Medwick even offered to shake hands with Owen but he was refused.

In the bottom of the sixth Medwick jogged out to his position in left field and was met by a barrage of fruit and bottles from Detroit fans, already in a foul mood with their team getting beat 9–0. "I watched the crowd and Medwick, and the pelting missiles through my field glasses, and it was a terrifying sight," wrote *New York Daily News* reporter Paul Gallico. "Every face in the crowd, women and men, was distorted with rage. Mouths were torn open, eyes glistened and shone in the sun. All fists were clenched."

The fusillade continued, and then the chant went up: "Take him out! Take him out!" The scene continued for a long time. Somehow the crowd was working a loaves-and-fishes miracle with their produce. It appeared they would never run out of ammunition.

Finally Commissioner Kenesaw Mountain Landis summoned the umpiring crew, Medwick, and Cardinals manager Frankie Frisch to his box. In an unprecedented move, he ordered Medwick removed from the game rather than forfeiting the game to St. Louis. Medwick's removal didn't really matter—the final score was 11–0—but it did cost Medwick a chance to tie or break the 12-hit Series record.

Medwick followed his Triple Crown season with two more solid years. So it was surprising when on June 12, 1940, the Cardinals sent the 28-year-old Medwick and another player to the Dodgers for $125,000 and four players. Although Medwick's 117 RBIs had been good enough for second place in the National League in 1939, his 14 home runs had been a career low.

Six days after the trade, Medwick was beaned. That morning Medwick, Dodgers manager Leo Durocher, and Cardinals pitcher Bob Bowman had exchanged words in the elevator of Manhattan's New Yorker Hotel. Bowman was to start for the Cardinals that day, and according to Durocher he had shouted, "I'll take care of both of you guys! Wait and see!"

They didn't have to wait long. After the first three Dodgers hit line drives, Bowman hit Medwick in the temple with a fastball. Medwick was knocked unconscious with a severe concussion. As Medwick was carried off the field, the angry Durocher was restrained from going after Bowman. And while Durocher screamed that Bowman had done it on purpose, Dodgers general manager Larry MacPhail stood in front of the visitors' dugout, challenging the entire Cardinals bench. Police escorted Bowman off the field and back to his hotel. MacPhail tried to get him banned for life. The Brooklyn District Attorney's office probed the case but took no action.

Although Medwick still hit .305 for the rest of his career and averaged 85 RBIs a season from 1940 through 1944, he was no longer a hitter that pitchers feared. He totaled 21 homers between 1942 and 1944. In July 1943 he was sold to the Giants, and in June 1945 he was traded to the Braves. They released him just before spring training the next year. He hung around as a spare part for three more seasons—a year with the Dodgers and two with the Cardinals—before retiring with a .324 career batting average and 1,383 RBIs.

Medwick managed Miami Beach in the Class B Florida International League in 1949, Raleigh in the Class B Carolina League in 1951, and Tampa back in the Florida International League in 1952 before dropping out of baseball to go into business in St. Louis. In 1966 Bing Devine brought Medwick back to the Cardinals as their minor league batting instructor.

During a visit to Italy, Medwick was part of a papal audience. When each visitor was asked to state his occupation, Medwick responded, "Your Holiness, I'm Joe Medwick. I, too, used to be a Cardinal." The Veterans Committee elected him to the Hall of Fame in 1968.

Jouett Meekin

Meekin, George Jouett **P**

1891–1900 B:2/21/1867, New Albany, IN D:12/14/1944, New Albany, IN Deb:6/13/1891, LOU AA BR/TR 6'1", 180

W	L	PCT	G	SH	IP	BB	SO	ERA
153	133	.535	324	9	26031	1058	900	4.07

Jouett Meekin began his career as a semi-pro catcher, but changed positions one day when his team's pitcher didn't show up. He reached the major leagues in 1891, struggling to a 30-51 record with Louisville and Washington over the next three seasons. The New York Giants saw something they liked, however, and gave the Senators the princely sum of $7,500 for Meekin and catcher Duke Farrell before the 1894 season.

New York had bought themselves a world championship. By September the Giants had a two-man rotation: Meekin and Amos Rusie. The two combined for 69 of the team's 88 victories. Jouett led the National League in winning percentage, finishing 33–9, then added two Temple Cup wins in a four-game sweep of the Baltimore Orioles. Meekin's contributions were not restricted to pitching, either. He hit three triples in one game, and twice turned defeats into victories by smashing late-inning home runs.

Meekin never quite duplicated his success of 1894, but he went 62–36 over the next three seasons; he also batted close to .300 each year. By 1898 he was a sub-.500 pitcher (16–18). He quickly lost his effectiveness, and was washed up by the turn of the century. He later umpired in the minors, and spent 27 years as a fireman in his hometown.

Sam Mele

Mele, Sabath Anthony **OF-1B**

1947–56 M(1961–67, 524–436) B:1/21/1923, Astoria, NY Deb:4/15/1947, BOS AL BR/TR 6'1", 187

G	AB	R	H	HR	RBI	OBP	SLG	AVG
1046	3437	406	916	80	544	.329	.408	.267

The Boston Red Sox discovered Sam Mele, a gifted, natural athlete, on the baseball diamonds of Queens Park, just around the corner from his Astoria, New York, home. Mele broke into the big leagues with a flourish. A college basketball hotshot at New York University and the nephew of longtime Boston favorite Tony Cuccinello, Sabath Anthony "Sam" Mele made his Red Sox debut April 15, 1947, starting in the outfield alongside Ted Williams and Dom DiMaggio. A righthanded batter, Mele hit .302 with 12 home runs and 73 runs batted in during his surprising rookie season.

Traded to the Washington Senators in 1949, Mele led the American League in doubles with 36 and drove in a career-best 94 runs for the Senators in 1951. Mele's skills were much sought after as he bounced between Washington, Chicago, Baltimore, Boston, Cincinnati, and finally Cleveland, where he finished his 10-year career as a player in 1956.

Mele became even better known as a major league manager. He took over the Minnesota Twins from Cookie Lavagetto during the 1961 season and four years later went on to lead the club to the AL pennant with a 102–60 record. Only a three-hit shutout by Sandy Koufax of the Los Angeles Dodgers in Game 7 prevented Mele and the Twins from winning the world championship. In seven years as manager of the Twins, Mele had a 524–436 record.

Bill Melton

Melton, William Edwin **3B-DH**

1968–77 B:7/7/1945, Gulfport, MS Deb:5/4/1968 CHI AL BR/TR 6'2", 200

G	AB	R	H	HR	RBI	OBP	SLG	AVG
1144	3971	496	1004	160	591	.340	.419	.253

William Edwin "Bill" Melton led the American League with 33 home runs in 1971, and he did it the hard way. Bill Melton played his home games in cavernous Comiskey Park, becoming the first White Sox player to win a home run crown. He overcame the shame of striking out in 10 consecutive at bats in three games in 1970, the first AL batter to do so. He needed three home runs in less than 18 hours at Comiskey to beat out Reggie Jackson and Norm Cash for the 1971 title.

Melton slugged two homers off Milwaukee Brewers righthander Jim Slaton to forge a three-way tie on Wednesday night, September 29. Jackson and Cash had finished their seasons while Melton still had a Thursday afternoon contest. As he had on Wednesday, manager Chuck Tanner batted his slugger leadoff. In his second at bat against righty Bill Parsons, Melton belted the tiebreaker three rows deep into the left field stands and jumped on home plate with both feet after rounding the bases. Tanner doused him with champagne in the clubhouse. Melton expressed his disbelief at capturing the home run title and praised the Brewer pitchers for giving him a chance.

Melton, who was named to the 1971 All-Star team, collected 89 homers in his first three seasons as a regular. However, back trouble curtailed the righthanded pull-hitter's career. He suffered a herniated disk, which caused him to miss much of the 1972 season.

Melton returned in 1973 to hit 20 homers with a career-best .277 batting average. He hit 21 more homers in 1974. But when his production fell in 1975, the Sox traded him with pitcher Steve Dunning to the California Angels for first baseman Jim Spencer and outfielder Morris Nettles at the Winter Meetings. Melton left Chicago as the Sox's all-time leading home run hitter with 154, collected in the equivalent of six and a half seasons. He hit six more long balls as a part-timer with California but was homerless in 1977 following another winter trade to Cleveland.

Cliff Melton

Melton, Clifford George **P**

1937–44 B:1/3/1912, Brevard, NC D:7/28/1986, Baltimore, MD Deb:4/25/1937, NY NL BL/TL 6'5½", 203

W	L	PCT	G	SV	IP	BB	SO	ERA
86	80	.518	272	16	1453^{2}	431	660	3.42

Cliff "Mountain Music" Melton went 20–9 in his rookie season to help win a pennant for the Giants in 1937. Over 6'5", Clifford George Melton came from the Black Mountains of North Carolina and he enjoyed singing mountain ballads. He was also a man with a formidable temper and he tended to inspire nicknames. Among them were "the Towering Cliff of the Black Mountains" and "Mickey Mouse."

The lefthander started with Asheville of the Piedmont League in 1931 and played with Erie of the Central League in 1932. From 1932 through 1935 he pitched in Baltimore. Melton tried out with the Yankees in 1935 but flopped. Then the Giants bought Melton's contract, and he became a major leaguer in 1937 at age 25. He struck out 13 Boston Braves in his first major league game on April 25.

Used as a starter and a reliever, Melton excelled. He won 20 games and led the league in saves, with seven. In the 1937 World Series against the Yankees, Melton lost Game 2 to Red Ruffing and Game 5 to Lefty Gomez—who singled in the go-ahead run.

The Giants continued to use Melton to relieve and to start. He developed bone chips in his elbow, however, and he was operated on in August 1942. Bothered by arm troubles after that, he was demoted to Jersey City in 1944, ending his major league career.

José Méndez

Méndez, José Baez **P–SS**

Negro Leagues, 1908–26 B:3/19/1887, Cardenas, Matanzas, Cuba D:10/31/1928, Havana, Cuba BR/TR 5'8", 160

Baseball's troubadour of the tropics, Jose Méndez was an outstanding Cuban pitcher in the early 20th century. His success against touring major league clubs made him a national hero.

"Méndez carved out one of the most remarkable legends of Caribbean baseball's wealthy lore," noted Peter Bjarkman in Smoke: *The Romance and Lore of Cuban Baseball*. "His record against touring North American professional competition (including a number of visiting minor-league clubs) during 1908 and 1909 was a sterling 44 wins and 2 losses."

In 1908 Méndez beat the Cincinnati Reds three times, without allowing a run in 25 innings. He won games against Eddie Plank in 1910 and Christy Mathewson in 1911. In 1912 he defeated both Mathewson and Brooklyn's Nap Rucker within a three-day span. In 1911 he also faced the Negro League's Smoky Joe Williams in a legendary duel. For nine innings Williams didn't allow a hit; Méndez allowed only two. Méndez won the game after 10, by a 1-0 score.

His fastball was so blinding that Méndez once killed a teammate while pitching batting practice. In the summers, Méndez played with such teams as the U.S. multiracial All Nations club, the forerunner of the Kansas City Monarchs. He was the Monarchs' first manager and led them to pennants in 1923, 1924, and 1925. Late in his career, he put himself in to pitch the final game of the 1924 Black World Series and won, 5–0. Musically talented, Méndez played the cornet for dances after games and later traveled the Caribbean, playing the guitar and teaching baseball. He died of bronchopneumonia at age 41. Méndez was elected to the Cuban Baseball Hall of Fame in 1939.

Mario Mendoza

Mendoza, Mario **SS**

1974–82 B:12/26/1950, Chihuahua, Mexico Deb:4/26/1974, PIT NL BR/TR 5'11", 187

G	AB	R	H	HR	RBI	OBP	SLG	AVG
686	1337	106	287	4	101	.247	.262	.215

Major league ballplayers remember 1979 as the season the "Mendoza Line" was born. Named in honor of the spindly, weak-hitting shortstop from Chihuahua, Mexico, the Mendoza Line would become a mark of futility feared by all batters flirting with a .200 season batting average.

Mario Mendoza, in fact, failed to crack the .200 mark five times in his nine-year career. In his only year as an everyday shortstop he batted .198 for Seattle in 1978. He appeared in 148 games, came to bat 373 times, managed only 74 hits, and struck out 62 times.

After hitting a career-high .245 for the Mariners in 1980, Mendoza was dealt to the Texas Rangers. Following two unproductive seasons, Mendoza called it quits, retiring with a .215 lifetime average. He later managed in the Anaheim Angels farm system.

Denis Menke

Menke, Denis John **SS-3B-2B-1B**
1962–74 B:7/21/1940, Algona, IA Deb:4/14/1962, MIL NL BR/TR 6'5½", 190

G	AB	R	H	HR	RBI	OBP	SLG	AVG
1598	5071	605	1270	101	606	.346	.370	.250

Denis Menke's specialty was versatility. He could play any infield position reliably and was never an embarrassment at the plate. Signed as a $125,000 bonus baby, Denis John Menke batted .336 in his third professional season with Yakima of the Northwest League, hitting 28 homers and driving in 103 runs. After 50 appearances in 1962, Milwaukee brought him up for good in 1963, and he played 146 games all over the infield. Given the shortstop job the following year, he responded with a .283 average and 20 home runs.

Swapped to Houston after the 1967 season, Menke played a year at second, then moved to short when Joe Morgan arrived. An All-Star in both 1969 and 1970, he finished the latter season with a .304 average and 13 homers.

Menke was one of four Astros sent with Morgan to Cincinnati in November of 1971. As a third baseman, he did his usual workmanlike job as the Reds won the NL pennant. Menke belted a home run off Catfish Hunter in the Reds' Game 5 victory of the 1972 World Series.

Menke was 32 years old when the "Big Red Machine" won a second consecutive NL West title, and his age was showing. Although he played in 139 games in 1973, he batted only 241 times, with a .191 average. He returned to Houston the following season and retired after appearing in only 30 games as a pinch hitter.

Fred Merkle

Merkle, Frederick Charles **1B**
1907–26 B:12/20/1888, Watertown, WI D:3/2/1956, Daytona Beach, FL Deb:9/21/1907, NY NL BR/TR 6'1", 190

G	AB	R	H	HR	RBI	OBP	SLG	AVG
1638	5782	720	1580	60	733	.331	.383	.273

Poor Fred Merkle. One little mistake overshadowed a long and fruitful career. His baserunning blunder haunted him for the rest of his life, to the point that he refused to grant interviews. To this day, the "Merkle Boner" is the only thing most fans know about him.

Merkle was a rangy first baseman with unusual speed for a big man. He'd played halfback for a Toledo semipro football team in 1906, but baseball was his game. In September 1907, when he was only 19, the Giants bought Merkle for $2,500 and brought him to New York for a late-season trial.

Although Merkle hit only .255 in 15 games, Giants manager John McGraw was impressed enough to keep the first baseman on the New York roster. Merkle was used primarily as a pinch hitter in 1908 because regular first baseman Fred Tenney was an iron man. Tenney missed only one game all season—against the Chicago Cubs at the Polo Grounds on September 23.

The Cubs entered that game just percentage points behind the Giants. The score was tied, 1–1, as the contest entered the last half of the ninth. With two out, Merkle singled off Jack Pfiester, sending New York's Moose McCormick to third. Up stepped shortstop Al Bridwell, who singled to center, apparently scoring McCormick with the winning run.

However, three weeks earlier the Cubs had been involved in a similar situation at Pittsburgh. When the game-winning hit was made, Cubs second baseman Johnny Evers noticed that the runner on first hadn't bothered to touch second but, instead, had turned toward the clubhouse.

This was standard practice at the time, but, as Evers knew, the rules stated that the runner must touch second. Evers had called for the ball against the Pirates, but when he stepped on second for an apparent forceout, umpire Hank O'Day refused to call the runner out, claiming he hadn't seen the play. Pittsburgh was awarded the victory.

Ironically, O'Day was one of the two umpires at the Polo Grounds on September 23. When Bridwell singled for the Giants, Evers again began screaming for the ball. Once more the runner, this time Merkle, had headed for the clubhouse instead of advancing to second.

Joe McGinnity, the burly Giants pitcher who had been coaching at third base, sensed something was amiss. He wrestled with some Cubs players for the ball and by his account, threw it as far as he could. The Giants later said it had landed in the stands, but after some frenzy in the outfield, a baseball came bounding in to Evers. This time O'Day was ready to make the call, declaring Merkle out at second and disallowing the run. The game was called due to darkness and went into the books as a tie.

National League president Harry Pulliam turned down several Giants appeals, and when Chicago and New York finished the season in a dead heat atop the standings, the tie game had to be made up. The Cubs won it and advanced to the World Series.

The New York writers tarred and feathered Merkle in print, although his only crime was having the stupidity to do what hundreds of other runners had done for years. The favorite adjective, though not the nastiest, was "Bonehead," unfair since Merkle was actually a very intelligent young man. He and Bucknell graduate Christy Mathewson played bridge in the clubhouse when most players were lucky to make it through a game of rummy.

Shocked by the reaction to his baserunning miscue, Merkle wanted to quit baseball, but McGraw never blamed him and convinced him to return. Merkle stood up to a torrent of boos in 1909, became the regular first baseman the next year, and set a major league record on May 13, 1911, when he drove home six runs in one inning.

Merkle helped the Giants win pennants in 1911, 1912, and 1913. He hit a game-winning sacrifice fly in Game 5 of the 1911 World Series, scored five runs and drove in three in the 1912 Fall Classic, and homered in Game 4 of the 1913 Series. However, New York lost all three Series.

Traded to Brooklyn in 1916, Merkle went to his fourth World Series that season with the Dodgers. In August 1917 he was sold to Chicago and was the regular first baseman with the pennant-winning Cubs in 1918. He signed on with the Yankees in 1925, then coached for Miller Huggins in 1926. When the Yanks lost to Pete Alexander and the Cardinals that year, it marked Merkle's sixth Fall Classic without a win.

Merkle batted a respectable .273 and stole 272 bases, including 11 thefts of home, during his 16-year career. All told, it was a fine career except for one game, one inning, and one play.

Sam Mertes

Mertes, Samuel Blair **OF-2B**

1896–1906 B:8/6/1872, San Francisco, CA D:3/11/1945, San Francisco, CA Deb:6/30/1896, PHI NL BR/TR 5'10", 185

G	AB	R	H	HR	RBI	OBP	SLG	AVG
1190	4405	695	1227	40	721	.346	.398	.279

Sam Mertes stole 396 bases during his 10-year major league career, and he played in the first American League game in 1901. But the versatile fielder had his best year with the Giants when he led the National League in doubles and RBIs in 1903, whacking 32 two-baggers and knocking in 104 runs.

Nicknamed "Sandow" after a famous circus strongman, Samuel Blair Mertes began his big league career in 1896 with Philadelphia and moved to Chicago the next year. On July 4, 1898, Mertes stole home against Cy Young to tie the score in the eighth inning, then drove in the winning run in the ninth.

In 1901 Mertes jumped to the crosstown White Sox in the new American League and played in that circuit's first game on April 24, going 2-for-4. On May 9 the righthanded batter broke up a no-hitter in the 10th inning against Cleveland's Earl Moore.

An outfielder by trade, in 1902 Mertes played every position, including pitcher. He signed conflicting contracts with the White Sox and the Giants for 1903. The senior and junior circuits had an arbitration committee decide the case, and Mertes was awarded to the Giants.

On October 4, 1904, Mertes hit for the cycle in a 7–3 Giants loss to the Cardinals. Traded to the Cardinals in July 1906, he finished his major league career that season.

Andy Messersmith

Messersmith, John Alexander **P**

1968–79 B:8/6/1945, Toms River, NJ Deb:7/4/1968, BAL AL BR/TR 6'1", 200

W	L	PCT	G	SH	IP	BB	SO	ERA
130	99	.568	344	27	2230^{1}	831	1625	2.86

Wielding one of the best changeups of the expansion era, Andy Messersmith is most famous for throwing baseball owners a curve. Messersmith and longtime Orioles pitcher Dave McNally refused to sign contracts for the 1975 season, setting the stage for arbitrator Peter Seitz's landmark ruling that struck down the reserve clause and initiated the free-agent era.

The California Angels' top pick in the secondary phase of the June 1966 draft, Messersmith reached the majors 25 months later and allowed just 44 hits in 81⅓ innings, working mostly out of the bullpen. In 1969 and 1970, mainly as a starter, he won a total of 27 games and each season led the AL in opponents' batting average.

In 1971 he won 20 games for an Angels club that finished 10 games under .500 and was named to his first All-Star team—but did not pitch. Arm injuries sent Messersmith to the first losing record of his career in 1972. That November 28 the Angels sent him, along with third baseman Ken McMullen, to the Los Angeles Dodgers.

Messersmith returned to form, winning 14 games in 1973, and then reentered the 20-win club in 1974. With an 11–2 record at the break, Messersmith was tabbed to start the All-Star Game for the National League and was less than thrilled. "Putting a lot of emphasis on this game is wrong," Messersmith argued. "I think it can be taken too seriously." He pitched a less than stellar three innings, allowing both American League runs in the National League's 7–2 win.

He finished the regular season at 20–6 for a league-best .769 winning percentage, allowing the fewest baserunners per game and limiting hitters to the league's lowest on-base percentage for the NL West-winning Dodgers. Messersmith also won his first of two straight Gold Gloves and struck out a career-high 221 batters, one of his three 200-whiff seasons. He finished second in the Cy Young voting to teammate Mike Marshall, who appeared in a record 106 games.

In the playoffs, Messersmith threw seven strong innings against the Pittsburgh Pirates in Game 2. With the score tied, 2–2, he was removed for a pinch hitter in the top of the eighth, and the Dodgers rallied for three runs to make him a winner.

Messersmith pitched the World Series opener against the Oakland Athletics and yielded a homer to Reggie Jackson, an RBI double to opposing pitcher Ken Holtzman in his first at bat of the season, and a third run thanks to a wild throw by third baseman Ron Cey, in a 3–2 loss. In Game 4 Holtzman touched Messersmith for a homer in the third inning, but Messersmith took a 2–1 lead to the bottom of the sixth. Then walks and his own error on a pickoff attempt opened the door to a four-run rally that gave Oakland the victory, and the A's went on to win their third straight World Series.

After that season, Messersmith, who had been shocked by his trade the previous winter, asked for a no-trade clause. The Dodgers refused, and

Messersmith played the season under a renewed contract that included an increase from his 1974 salary of $90,000. Messersmith was aware that the Major League Baseball Players Association (MLBPA) did not believe a renewed contract was valid for more than one year, but the owners contended that each renewal carried an additional one-year renewal clause, effectively binding the player to his team for life.

In August 1975 Messersmith spoke to MLBPA executive director Marvin Miller. Messersmith wanted to file a grievance asking for free agency, as Catfish Hunter had done the previous fall, if he was unsigned by season's end. However, he remained willing to sign if the Dodgers would give him a no-trade clause. Late in the season, according to then-Commissioner Bowie Kuhn, the Dodgers were prepared to give Messersmith his no-trade clause. But the Player Relations Committee urged him to press the issue in arbitration. Meanwhile, the union discovered that lefthander Dave McNally, who had retired in June, also had not signed a 1975 contract. He agreed to file a grievance, ensuring the reserve clause showdown each side wanted.

In the midst of this tumult, Messersmith had another stellar season and was named to his third All-Star team, leading the league with 321⅓ innings pitched, 40 starts, 19 complete games, and seven shutouts, all career bests. His 2.29 ERA was Messersmith's lowest for a full season, and he even relieved twice with one save.

Arbitrator Peter Seitz, who had declared Hunter a free agent, started hearing the Messersmith and McNally cases on November 21, 1975. After testimony, he urged both sides to negotiate a settlement, but the owners refused. On December 23 Seitz ruled that one year meant one year, declaring Messersmith and McNally free agents.

Because of the ruling, players of all the clubs found themselves locked out of spring training by owners in 1976. Kuhn acted in time to get Major League Baseball's 100th season underway, but Messersmith, now unemployed, asked Miller, "What do I do next?" Rumors circulated that Messersmith had a sore arm, but the Dodgers team doctor issued a public statement testifying to his soundness.

The Yankees, who earlier had bagged Hunter, believed they had reached an agreement to sign Messersmith, but Kuhn invalidated that claim. Atlanta Braves owner Ted Turner won the ensuing bidding war, signing Messersmith to a $1.75-million multiyear deal on April 10, 1976, several days after the season began.

Despite missing spring training, Messersmith logged 207⅓ innings and finished 11–11 with a 3.04 ERA while pitching for a substandard Braves team playing in a hitter's park. He then missed most of 1977 with injuries. Messersmith's most notable experience during his Braves tenure came when Turner put nicknames on the backs of his team's uniforms. Turner decided No. 17 Messersmith's nickname would be "Channel" because Channel 17 identified Turner's Atlanta television station. Kuhn subsequently ruled that only real names could appear on uniform backs.

The Braves sold messersmith to the Yankees at the 1977 winter Meetings. He pitched well during spring training in 1978 before falling and injuring his shoulder while covering first base. He was ineffective in six outings, signed with the Dodgers for 1979, and was released after winning just two of 11 starts.

In his autobiography, MLBPA chief Miller pointed out the irony of Messersmith's situation. The righthander finished his career with the Dodgers, which was both what he'd wanted all along and what the Dodgers had refused to guarantee through a no-trade clause.

Although he made his greatest impact off the field, Messersmith left his mark on the record book during his 12 years in the majors. This changeup specialist is tied with J. R. Richard for the third-lowest career opponents' batting average, trailing two other flame-throwers, Nolan Ryan and Sandy Koufax. Messersmith also ranks among the all-time leaders in opponents' on-base percentage, strikeouts per nine innings, and adjusted ERA.

Bob Meusel

Meusel, Robert William **OF**

1920–30 B:7/19/1896, San Jose, CA D:11/28/1977, Downey, CA Deb:4/14/1920, NY AL BR/TR 6'3", 190

G	AB	R	H	HR	RBI	OBP	SLG	AVG
1407	5475	826	1693	156	1067	.356	.497	.309

Bob Meusel was a slugging outfielder who played for perhaps the greatest team of all time—the 1927 Yankees. Overshadowed by some of his teammates, especially Babe Ruth and Lou Gehrig, he was nonetheless a key contributor to "Murderers Row." He won a home run title, hit 40 or more doubles in five different seasons including his rookie campaign, and also delivered five 100-RBI seasons. Fleet of foot, "Long Bob" stole 142 bases in his career.

His name is scattered throughout the baseball annals. He is one of only two major leaguers to hit for the cycle three times in his career. On September 5, 1921, he tied a major league record with four assists by an outfielder in a game. In 1923 Yankee outfielders Meusel, Ruth, and Whitey Witt each batted .300. On May 16, 1927, Meusel stole second, third, and home in one game. During that season, Meusel, Ruth, Gehrig, and Tony Lazzeri each drove in 100 runs.

He did all of this with a nonchalance that led critics to complain that he did not work hard enough. In fact, it was not uncommon for him to be referred to in print as "Languid Bob." But his fellow ballplayers understood his ability, and they rated him just below Ruth and Gehrig.

Robert William Meusel was the younger brother of major leaguer Emil Frederick "Irish" Meusel. The two brothers hit a combined .309 during their major league careers, fourth-best among siblings. They also combined for 262 home runs.

Bob Meusel played minor league ball on the West Coast before joining the Yankees in 1920. The Yankees were on the verge of dominating the American League, and they finished third with 95 victories, their most ever to that point. Meusel hit .328 with 83 RBIs and 58 extra-base hits.

In 1921 the Yankees won their first pennant; Meusel, playing right field, hit 24 homers and drove in 135 runs. The Yankees met the Giants in a Subway Series, and the Meusel brothers found themselves playing on opposite teams. Irish, who played left field for the Giants, outplayed Bob by hitting .345 and driving in a Series-high seven runs. The Giants won the world championship in eight games.

The following season Bob Meusel played only 121 games as a result of being suspended (along with Ruth) by Commissioner Kenesaw Mountain Landis for an unauthorized barnstorming tour. Even so, Meusel batted .319 with 16 homers and 84 RBIs. The Yankees won their second straight flag and headed for another World Series against the Giants. With Irish Meusel again leading all players with seven RBIs, the Giants beat the Yankees, four games to one.

In 1923 Bob Meusel hit over .300 for the fourth time in as many major league seasons, and this time the Yankees downed the Giants in the World Series. Irish hit a homer in Game 2, but Ruth belted three round-trippers and Bob Meusel drove in a Series-high eight runs.

With Ruth sidelined by illness, the Yankees skidded to seventh place in 1925, even though Meusel led the league with 33 homers and 138 RBIs. In 1926 Meusel was a spectator to a controversial play that helped the St. Louis Cardinals clinch a seven-game triumph over the Yankees in the World Series. With St. Louis leading, 3–2, and two outs in the bottom of the ninth of Game 7, Meusel was up when Ruth tried to steal second base. Ruth was out, ending the Series.

The following year no such mistakes were made. The Yankees put together a team by which all others are measured. Meusel delivered career highs with 47 doubles and a .337 average. In the World Series the Yankees demolished the Pirates in four games, despite Meusel's .118 average.

Meusel's production started to slide in 1928, as he hit below .300 for only the second time in his career. But he did steal home in Game 3 of the World Series as the Yankees scored their second straight sweep, this one over the Cardinals. A year later, in what would prove to be his last season with the Yankees, he hit .261 in 100 games. Shortly after the season ended, the Cincinnati Reds acquired him. He hit .289 with 62 RBIs for the Reds in his final major league campaign.

Irish Meusel

Meusel, Emil Frederick **OF**

1914–27 B:6/9/1893, Oakland, CA D:3/1/1963, Long Beach, CA Deb:10/1/1914, WAS AL BR/TR 5'11½", 178

G	AB	R	H	HR	RBI	OBP	SLG	AVG
1289	4900	701	1521	106	819	.348	.464	.310

The New York Giants won four consecutive pennants from 1921 through 1924, and no player was more responsible for the ballclub accomplishing that feat than Irish Meusel. After joining New York in the middle of the 1921 season, this hard-hitting outfielder proved himself one of the better players in the National League, quite a feat considering that Hall of Famers Frankie Frisch and George Kelly were among his teammates.

The older brother of Bob Meusel, who spent 11 years in the majors, Irish played for four teams during a career that also lasted 11 years. He topped the 100-RBI mark for four straight years during his stay in New York, and he was a clutch performer in the World Series, driving in 17 runs in 23 games.

Although capable of hitting the longball, Meusel was an all-around ballplayer. Twice he reached double figures in doubles, triples, homers, and stolen bases in a season. Four times he posted a slugging average over .500. During his entire major league career, Meusel struck out only 199 times and never more than 33 times in a season. His arm was not among the best, but he was skilled and versatile enough to make some infield appearances.

Emil Frederick "Irish" Meusel got his first taste of major league ball with Washington at the end of the 1914 season, batting twice without a hit. He returned to the majors in 1918 and became a regular left fielder for Philadelphia's National League team. That season he batted .279 with 62 RBIs.

In 1919 Meusel batted .305, beginning a streak of six seasons above the .300 mark. But it also marked the first of three straight years Philadelphia finished in the cellar. Whether these dismal finishes had anything to do with Meusel's departure from Philadelphia is not known. What is known is that manager Bill Donovan suspended him for indifferent play in July 1921.

Shortly after that episode, Meusel was sent to the Giants for outfielder Curtis Walker, catcher Butch Henline, pitcher Jesse Winters, and $30,000 cash. Giants manager John McGraw made the deal, and it proved to be a brilliant one. During Meusel's first five years with the ballclub the Giants finished first four times and second once.

Playing 62 games for the Giants, Meusel finished the 1921 campaign with a .343 average and 14 homers. He went on to become the dominant player in the World Series, driving in seven runs as the Giants defeated the Yankees in the first Subway Series. He drove in three runs in Game 3 to lead the Giants to a 13–5 rout, then hit a two-run homer in Game 6 to help square the Series at three victories apiece. The Giants were world champions two days later.

Meusel enjoyed his statistically strongest season in 1922. He scored 100 runs for the first time in the majors and amassed career highs with 204 hits, 17 triples, and 132 RBIs. Six Giants batted at least .300 that season, and for the second straight year Irish met brother Bob in the World Series. Once again Irish drove in seven runs, including two in a 3–2 win over the Yankees in the opener, and the Giants engineered a four-game sweep.

Meusel would play in two more World Series, losing to the Yankees in 1923 and to the Washington Senators in 1924. In the meantime, he led the National League with 125 RBIs in 1923 and batted .310 in 1924. The following season he batted .328 with a career-high 21 homers and 111 RBIs. During the four-year period of 1922 through 1925, he averaged 117 RBIs.

In 1926 Meusel slipped badly, finishing with just 65 RBIs. The Giants fell to fifth place that season, and the following year McGraw was replaced as manager by Rogers Hornsby. But Meusel wasn't around to see it happen. In 1927 he wrapped up his career with a one-year stint in Brooklyn, where he hit .243.

The Meusel brothers hit a combined .309 during their major league careers, fourth best among siblings. They also combined for 262 home runs. Irish Meusel served as coach for the Giants in 1930, but he never had a big league managing job.

Levi Meyerle

Meryerle, Levi Samuel **3B–2B**

1876–84 B:7/1845, Philadelphia, PA D:11/4/1921, Philadelphia, PA Deb:5/20/1871, PHI NA BR/TR 6'1", 177

G	AB	R	H	HR	RBI	OBP	SLG	AVG
85	374	57	123	0	49	.334	.436	.329

The Sporting News' Alfred H. Spink described Levi Meyerle in the 1880s as "a very fair fielder," but he must have seen "Long Levi" on one of his better days. At a time of rough-hewn infields, gloveless hands, and heartless scorekeepers, fielding percentages in the .800s were the norm. Meyerle had a percentage in the .700s and once—in his greatest offensive season—fielded a truly horrific .654.

During five seasons in the National Association from 1871 through 1875, he made 260 errors in 222 games. By comparison, the 1992 Dodgers, perhaps the most butterfingered collection of fumblers to inhabit the major leagues in the past 50 years, committed 174 errors in 162 games as a team.

Meyerle spent four of his five NA seasons with Philadelphia, but in 1874 he played for Chicago. Early in the season, he committed six errors in one game against his old Philadelphia teammates. Chicago fans accused him of deliberately helping his former team, but as the season wore on they saw that Meyerle didn't have to try to make errors. They just came.

What made Levi Samuel Meyerle such a bad fielder? First of all, he was unusually tall at 6 feet 1 inch, and that put him a little further away from the trajectory of any bad hop. Second, he was wafer-thin, which made a second line of defense such as knocking the ball down with his chest unlikely. Third, he was slow, causing him to reach for balls that others might easily have stopped. Fourth, he had a tendency to get flustered in pressure situations. And finally, managers kept moving him from position to position in hopes of finding one he could play or else one that might serve as a safe haven where few balls were hit.

But despite horrendous fielding, he continued to be gainfully employed because the man could flat out hit. In the National Association's first season, he played all but two of champion Philadelphia's 28 games and came away with a breathtaking batting average of .492, not only leading the league but setting a standard that has not been approached by any subsequent hitter in any major league. Four years later, while with Chicago, he hit .403 for his second league batting title. In his other National Association years, Meyerle contented himself with hitting in the healthy .300s.

Once the National League was formed, Meyerle continued at a plush .300 clip for two more seasons, but a severely sprained ankle in 1877 made it difficult for him to run at all. He dropped out of the majors and played independent ball for several years. In 1884 he tried a comeback with Philadelphia's Union Association team, but after three games, multiple errors and only one hit, he packed it in for good.

Chief Meyers

Meyers, John Tortes **C**

1909–17 B:7/29/1880, Riverside, CA D:7/25/1971, San Bernardino, CA Deb:4/16/1909, NY NL BR/TR 5'11", 194

G	AB	R	H	HR	RBI	OBP	SLG	AVG
992	2834	276	826	14	363	.367	.378	.291

Like just about every other ballplayer of Native American descent in the early 20th century, star catcher John Tortes Meyers was called "Chief." After attending Dartmouth, he reached the major leagues at age 28 with the New York Giants in 1909. Appearing in 90 games as a rookie, he caught over 100 games in each of the next six seasons, at the time an unusually heavy schedule for a catcher.

The Giants won three straight pennants, from 1911 through 1913, as Meyers had his three best seasons, hitting .332, .358, and .312. Although New York lost all three World Series, Meyers hit .300 in the 1911 Fall Classic and .357 in the 1912 Series. The wear and tear of catching so many games then took its toll on his bat. Traded to Brooklyn in 1916, he helped the Robins win a pennant but hit only .247. He retired as a player after nine seasons with a .291 career batting average for 992 games.

In 1920, while managing in a semipro game, he was booed. Disgusted, he quit baseball. Meyers later worked for the U.S. Department of the Interior.

Cass Michaels

Michaels, Casimir Eugene **2B–SS–3B**

1943–54 B:3/4/1926, Detroit, MI D:11/12/1982, Grosse Pointe, MI Deb:8/19/1943, CHI AL BR/TR 5'11", 175

G	AB	R	H	HR	RBI	OBP	SLG	AVG
1288	4367	508	1142	53	501	.349	.353	.262

Infielder Cass Michaels, who three times led the American League in errors, ended his career at just age 28 after a 1954 beaning. The half-German, half-Polish Michaels came up to the White Sox as a 17-year-old third baseman named Casimer Eugene Kwietnewski, but found writers and fans had trouble with that name, so he later appealed for help in coming up with a more "American" moniker. "Cass Michaels" was the result.

Sent down to Little Rock in the Southern Association for more seasoning in 1944, he responded by hitting .356 in 54 games before being brought back to Chicago. By 1945 he was playing shortstop for the White Sox, but when Luke Appling returned from the service, Michaels (who had led AL shortstops in errors in 1945) shifted to second base. In 1949 he led circuit shortstops in games played, assists, and double plays.

In 1950 Michaels held out for a $3,000 raise, but general manager Frank Lane refused to grant it unless Michaels shed 15 pounds. That May, Lane included Michaels in a five-player trade with Washington. Two years later, he was traded to the Browns. In August 1952 he was waived to the Phillies but was sold back to the White Sox in December 1953 for his final season.

Clyde Milan

Milan, Jesse Clyde **OF**

1907–22 B:3/25/1887, Linden, TN D:3/3/1953, Orlando, FL Deb:8/19/1907, WAS AL BL/TR 5'9", 168

G	AB	R	H	HR	RBI	OBP	SLG	AVG
1982	7359	1004	2100	17	617	.353	.353	.285

In 1907 Washington Senators manager Clark Griffith sent a scout to look at outfielder Jesse Clyde Milan. The scout returned with not only Milan, who went by "Clyde," but a pitcher named Walter Johnson; the scout had surely made one of the most successful scouting trips of all time. Johnson and Milan ended up rooming together as fellow Senators for 15 years, until Milan became the club's player-manager in 1922. Both were quiet, gentle men. In fact, Milan lasted only one year as the Senators' skipper because he was considered too easygoing.

Griffith always considered Milan the best center fielder in Senators history. Extremely fast, he earned the nickname "Deerfoot." In 1912 he stole a league-record 88 bases to break Ty Cobb's stranglehold on the American League stolen base championship. The following season he stole 75 bases, again leading the lead. Milan would go on to steal 495 bases in his career.

A lefthanded batter, Milan had little power and hit only 17 home runs in 16 seasons. He also failed to hit for average early in his career, batting only .239 and .200 in his first two seasons with regular playing time. Eventually, he learned to use his speed and hit over .300 four times on his way to a career mark of .285. When his playing days were over, Milan had a long career as a minor league manager, then rejoined the Senators as a coach in 1937. He died in spring training in 1953.

Felix Millan

Millan, Felix Bernado (Martinez) **2B**

1966–77 B:8/21/1943, Yabucoa, Puerto Rico Deb:6/2/1966, ATL NL BR/TR 5'11", 172

G	AB	R	H	HR	RBI	OBP	SLG	AVG
1480	5791	699	1617	22	403	.324	.343	.279

Felix Millan concentrated on making contact at the plate, using a distinctive batting stance and choking up higher on the bat than any player in the modern era. Where Millan really earned his plaudits, though, was with an outstanding glove at second base. His 1969 Gold Glove winning performance helped the Braves capture the National League West.

Despite the Braves' fall from contention after 1969, Millan remained a defensive standout. In 1970 his batting average climbed to .310, and he was virtually impossible to strike out. That year he was named to the All-Star team a second time but was replaced after he suffered an injury. He continued his fine play in 1971 and returned to the All-Star Game.

After hitting .257 for Atlanta in 1972 and earning his second Gold Glove, he was traded to the New York Mets for two young pitchers, both of whom flopped in Atlanta. In 1973 the second sacker's dependable play and contact hitting helped the Mets to their second World Series appearance in their short history.

Millan stayed with New York and continued his consistent play as the Mets everyday second baseman for several years. In 1975 he became the first player in Mets history to play all 162 games in a season, and established a team record for hits (191) that stood until Lance Johnson broke it in 1996.

In mid-1977, however, Millan damaged his shoulder when Ed Ott slammed him into the Astro Turf in a brief and one-sided brawl at Three Rivers Stadium. That injury ended his major league career, though he went on to play for several years in Japan.

When he retired, his career average of 23.9 at bats per strikeout put him in the top 30 of all time, between legendary hitters Arky Vaughan and Mickey Cochrane.

Bing Miller

Miller, Edmund John **OF**

1921–36 B:8/30/1894, Vinton, IA D:5/7/1966, Philadelphia, PA Deb:4/16/1921, WAS AL BR/TR 6', 185

G	AB	R	H	HR	RBI	OBP	SLG	AVG
1820	6212	946	1936	116	990	.359	.461	.311

Edmund John "Bing" Miller was one of the stars of Connie Mack's great Philadelphia Athletics teams of 1929, 1930, and 1931. Overshadowed by such teammates as future Hall of Famers Al Simmons, Jimmie Foxx, Mickey Cochrane, and Lefty Grove, he hit .312 lifetime and annually posted respectable RBI totals even though he usually batted sixth.

Miller, whose younger brother, Ralph, played briefly with the Phillies and Senators in the early 1920s, signed his first minor league contract in 1914, but it was not until 1920, when he hit .322 with Little Rock of the Southern Association, that major league clubs took an interest.

Both Pittsburgh and Washington claimed him, and in his first major decision as commissioner,

Judge Kenesaw Mountain Landis awarded Miller to the Senators. Miller, long in the tooth for a rookie at age 27, hit a respectable .288 in 1921 before becoming part of a three-team trade that landed him in Philadelphia.

Under Mack's patient tutelage, Miller blossomed in 1922, hitting .336 with 90 RBIs. He followed with three more strong seasons, including a .342 batting average in 1924. Then, on June 15, 1926, Mack made a major blunder. He dealt Miller to the St. Louis Browns straight up for Baby Doll Jacobson, who was traded again that same day to Boston with two other players for pitcher Howard Ehmke and outfielder Tom Jenkins. Although Ehmke was a serviceable pitcher, Jenkins was a bust, and no one Mack put in right field hit with Miller's authority.

Recognizing his error, Mack reacquired Miller from the Browns after the 1927 season in exchange for pitching prospect Sam Gray. Although Gray won 20 games in his first year with the Browns, Mack had no cause to regret the deal. Miller, happy to be back with the A's, batted .329 with 85 RBIs in 1928. Six Athletics hit at least .300 that year, but Philadelphia finished second, three games behind the Yankees.

In 1929 Mack had a star at every position on one of baseball's greatest teams. His outfield boasted three excellent fielders and three .300 hitters. In left Al Simmons hit .365 with 34 homers and a league-leading 157 RBIs; Mule Haas in center batted .313 with 16 home runs and 82 RBIs; and Miller in right hit .335 with eight homers, 93 RBIs, and a career-best 29-game hitting streak.

Not surprisingly, Philadelphia rolled to its first pennant since 1914, outdistancing the Yankees by 18 games. Miller batted .368 in the World Series against the Chicago Cubs, coming through with a game-winning single in Game 1 and a Series-winning double in the bottom of the ninth of Game 5.

The Athletics continued to terrorize AL pitchers in 1930. Miller's batting average dropped to .303, but he knocked in 100 runs for the first and only time in his career. The 1931 A's won 107 games, the best record of their three-year pennant streak, but the Cardinals upset them in the World Series.

In 1932 Miller, at age 37, became a part-time pinch hitter and replacement outfielder, a role he filled ably for three more years with the Athletics and two more with the Red Sox. He even led the American League in pinch hits in 1934 and 1935.

But he detested called third strikes. When he found himself taking a few too many in 1936, he decided it was time to quit, retiring with 1,936 career hits.

The affable Miller, nicknamed after a comic strip character called George Washington Bings, coached for four different AL teams from 1937 through 1953, much of the time under his close friend, Jimmie Dykes. Miller died of a heart attack after a 1966 traffic accident. At the time, he was wearing a diamond tie clasp with the inscription "1930 World Champions."

Bob L. Miller

Miller, Robert Lane **P**

1957–74 B:2/18/1939, St. Louis, MO Deb:6/26/1957, STL NL BR/TR 6'1", 182

W	L	PCT	G	SV	IP	BB	SO	ERA
69	81	.460	694	51	1551[1]	608	895	3.37

Pitcher Robert L. "Bob" Miller, a righthander, was a teammate of hurler Robert G. "Bob" Miller, a southpaw, on the 1962 New York Mets. To avoid confusion, the expansion club roomed both hurlers together. "That way, if somebody calls for Bob Miller, he's bound to get the right one," explained team traveling secretary, Lou Niss.

Robert L. Miller's career was significantly more substantial than his roommate's. Signed in 1957 to St. Louis for a $20,000 bonus, he spent all of that year on the Cards' roster before being optioned to Rochester and Houston. After three years of limited usage by the Cardinals, he was left exposed in the expansion draft and taken by the Mets. He had a miserable 1962 with the Mets, going 1–12 for the awful expansion team, and was then mercifully traded to the Los Angeles Dodgers in the off-season. In 1964 he led the National League with 74 appearances for Los Angeles. In November 1967 he was traded along with Ron Perranoski and John Roseboro to the Twins. Almost two years later Miller started and lost Game 3 of the 1969 ALCS. Minnesota dealt him to Cleveland that December, and the following June the Indians sent him to the White Sox. He was sold again, this time across town to the Cubs in September. The Chicago club released him the following May.

Beginning another round of musical clubs, Miller was then signed by the Padres, who released him to Pittsburgh in August 1971. He played 52 games with the Pirates and then began the 1973 season with San Diego, who sold him to the Mets in September. Released by the Mets in October 1974, he was invited to the Padres' training camp the following spring but failed to make the club.

During his 17-year major league career Miller accumulated a 69–81 record, with a 3.37 ERA. Miller later coached for the Blue Jays and the Giants, and he also worked in the San Francisco front office.

Eddie Miller

Miller, Edward Robert **SS**

1936–50 B:11/26/1916, Pittsburgh, PA Deb:9/9/1936, CIN NL BR/TR 5'9", 180

G	AB	R	H	HR	RBI	OBP	SLG	AVG
1510	5337	539	1270	97	640	.290	.352	.238

During the course of his professional baseball career, Eddie Miller was traded for a number of ballplayers who, for various reasons, are much more familiar to us today. They include catcher Willard Hershberger, outfielder Vince DiMaggio, and shortstop Eddie Joost. Interestingly, Miller was a much better ballplayer than any of them. It was his fate never to play on a pennant-winning team and to never receive the public acclaim of many lesser players. But in the late 1930s and early 1940s Miller may have been the best fielding shortstop in baseball.

Edward Robert Miller went by "Eddie," but he was also dubbed "Eppie," a reference to his Pennsylvania Dutch background. In 1934 he tried out for the Pirates and appeared in a few exhibition games before being sent to play shortstop for Springfield in the Class C Mid-Atlantic League. That season he led the circuit in fielding percentage and was second in putouts and assists. He played for Wilmington and Toronto in 1935, and with Toronto in 1936 he led the league in putouts and double plays.

In both 1936 and 1937 he appeared briefly with Cincinnati before being assigned to Newark in exchange for Willard Hershberger. Acquired by Kansas City of the American Association in 1938, Miller starred, supplementing his fine glovework by hitting .290 with 14 home runs and 80 RBIs, as he helped lead the Royals to victory in the Little World Series.

After the season, the Reds traded Miller to the Boston Braves for DiMaggio, four other players, and cash. The move was a departure for the penny-pinching Braves, who usually sent players such as Miller in the other direction in exchange for cash. But club owner Bob Quinn was in the middle of a youth movement and thought Miller was the best young shortstop in the game.

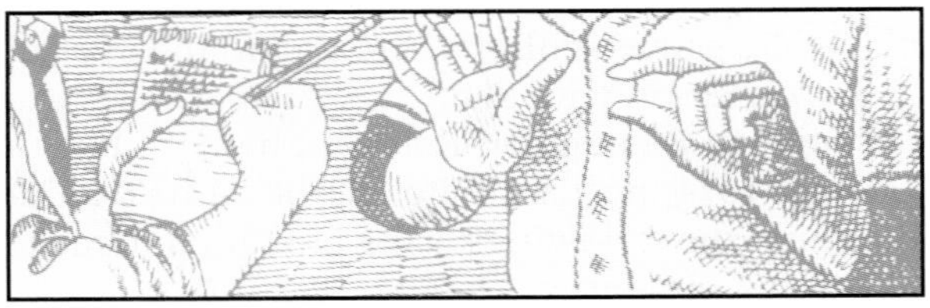

Quinn wasn't far off. Miller played part-time in 1939 and became a regular in 1940. He hit 14 home runs and knocked in 75, both second best on the club. He also led all National League shortstops in fielding percentage, was named to the All-Star team, and received 38 points in voting for the Most Valuable Player Award.

Although Miller slumped somewhat at the plate the next two seasons, he continued as the league's best shortstop, leading in fielding percentage and retaining his All-Star spot. But in December 1942 the Braves received an offer they couldn't refuse. For $25,000, Eddie Joost, and Nate Andrews, they shipped Miller back to Cincinnati.

Miller hit only .224 with the Reds in 1943 but knocked in 71 runs. He teamed with second baseman Lonnie Frey to form the league's best middle infield combination, as the two men turned 233 double plays. Miller continued to struggle at the plate through 1946, but his glove made him a perennial All-Star.

Oddly enough, Miller slumped while the pitching staffs were decimated by the war, yet he had his best year at the plate after the war ended. In 1947 he hit 19 home runs, knocked in 87, and led the National League with 38 doubles. But Miller was now more than 30 years old. After the season the Reds traded him to the Phillies for young outfielder Johnny Wyrostek and cash. Splitting his time between shortstop and second, Miller spent two seasons under manager Eddie Sawyer and was then waived to St. Louis, where he finished his career in 1950. He led all National League shortstops in fielding percentage a total of five times and made the All-Star team seven times, despite a career batting average of only .238.

Hack Miller

Miller, Lawrence H. **OF**

1916–25 B:1/1/1894, New York, NY D:9/17/1971, Oakland, CA Deb:9/22/1916, BRO NL BR/TR 5'9", 195

G	AB	R	H	HR	RBI	OBP	SLG	AVG
349	1200	164	387	38	205	.361	.490	.322

Lawrence H. "Hack" Miller could never live up to his legend. A star in the minor leagues, he was the son of a circus strongman and was billed as the strongest man to ever play major league baseball. Miller hit .333 with Wausau in 1914. He led the Northern League in hits in 1915 and 1916. In 1920 with Oakland, Miller led the Pacific Coast League in hits. The following season he led the Pacific Coast League in hits and batting with a .347 average.

Miller was 26 when he finally played a full season in the majors with the Cubs in 1922. He hit .352 with a .511 slugging average. The next year he hit 20 homers but faded out of the majors by

1926. After leaving the big leagues, Miller played for Oakland, Houston, Danville, Topeka, and North Platte.

Marvin Miller

Players Association Executive 1965–84 B:4/14/1917, Brooklyn, NY

Few men have affected baseball's history more than Marvin Miller. The Players Association executive director for 18 years, Miller led his union in a revolution that forever changed the balance of power between players and owners. "The players have so much power that they should get one more thing done," manager Paul Richards, Miller's bitter adversary, once said. "They should get Marvin Miller inducted into Cooperstown. That man has taken over."

Richards, of course, was being sarcastic. But the irony is that Miller might well be inducted into the Hall of Fame one day. Baseball's establishment failed to see the players' perspective—that Miller only taught the players how to fight and how to win.

Miller grew up a staunch Dodgers fan. During World War II he served with the War Labor Board and after the war he worked for the U.S. Reconciliation Service of the Labor Department, the International Association of Machinists, and the United Auto Workers before joining the United Steelworkers of America as a staff economist in 1950. Eventually he became their chief economist and a confidant of union presidents Philip Murray and I.W. Abel.

In 1965 Miller weighed job offers from Harvard and the Carnegie Endowment for World Peace. He also considered staying with the union and ultimately running for its presidency. While he was considering his options, representatives from the Players Association, seeking to replace Judge Robert Cannon, asked to meet with him.

Originally major league owners had seen the Players Association as a harmless company union. They even offered to fund its operation. But once Miller took over, all bets were off. After almost 100 years of absolute power the owners were not prepared to cede control. But the shrewd Miller was to turn the owners' arrogance back upon them to devastating effect.

Quickly he took a traditionally antiunion work force and rallied it behind him. "He was able to do it because he was honest and everything he said was the actual truth," Brooks Robinson contended. Miller was also among the smartest men in baseball. He combined a brilliant mind with an uncanny ability to lay out his position in such a logical manner that it seemed impossible to disagree with him.

In 1969 a strike threatened, but it was averted when management conceded to Miller by increasing the pension fund and the minimum major league salary and recognizing the right of players to employ agents. But in 1972 the Players Association staged the first general work stoppage in baseball history, delaying the start of the season for 13 days and forcing the cancellation of 86 regular-season games. The players wanted a 17-percent raise in pension benefits to keep pace with the cost of living since enactment of the last Basic Agreement in 1969 and $500,000 to cover increased health care benefits. The negotiations stalled.

On March 9 the White Sox became the first club to authorize the union's Executive Board to strike. Through mid-March a strike was unanimously supported. Not until four negative votes were cast by the Red Sox on March 16 did anyone break rank. The final vote was 663–10 in favor of strike authorization, with two abstentions.

Dick Young of the *New York Daily News*, the most influential sports columnist in the country, led the antiunion movement among the media, a movement that split along generational lines. "Ballplayers are no match for him," Young wrote of Miller. "He has a steel trap mind wrapped in a melting butter voice. He runs the players through a high-pressure spray the way an auto goes through a car wash, and that's how they come out, brainwashed. With few exceptions, they follow him blindly, like zombies."

The way the players saw it, Young was as blind as the owners. He refused to acknowledge that times were changing. Miller played devil's advocate with his union whenever a strike was near. He wanted to make sure union members understood the consequences of their actions. Finally a strike was authorized by an Executive Board vote of 47–0 with only the Dodgers' Wes Parker abstaining. Rick Reichardt, the player representative for the White Sox, characterized Miller's behavior during the vote as "very conservative," adding, "the whole tone of the meeting was very professional. He wasn't an instigator."

The strike began on April 1, five days before the start of the regular season. A storm of fan protest greeted the move. The players eventually won an increased management contribution of $490,000 to their benefits plan, plus a transfer of $400,000 in surplus pension funds to improve retirement benefits and maintain their health benefits.

"The real issues were never a question of pension or money," Miller said. "They were more of a question of human dignity." Lost amid the dollar figures in the newspaper stories was a very important concession that had been granted to labor—the right to arbitrate grievances. In just a few years that right would turn baseball on its head.

Coming hard on the heels of baseball's first strike was the U.S. Supreme Court's June 19 ruling in the Curt Flood case. Flood had challenged Major League Baseball's reserve clause, which effectively bound a player to his team in perpetuity. By a 5–3 majority, the high court reaffirmed the game's antitrust exemption that kept the reserve clause intact. Yet changes definitely were coming. In 1973 the players won the right to salary arbitration, a huge step for the union.

Then in December of that year arbitrator Peter Seitz voided Catfish Hunter's Oakland contract due to owner Charles Finley's failure to comply with its terms. By itself the decision hardly affected free agency, but the frenzied bidding war that erupted for Hunter's services presaged what would soon come.

The Yankees signed Hunter, one of baseball's best pitchers, to a multiyear deal worth more than $3 million. That opened a lot of eyes, especially on the players' side. They began to understand what they would be worth on the open market.

In December 1975 Seitz let the other shoe drop when he overturned the reserve clause in the Dave McNally and Andy Messersmith cases. The way the owners had always interpreted it, the reserve clause allowed them to perpetually renew a contract and thus bound a player to a team for as long as the team wished. In effect, the players contended, they were wage slaves no matter how well paid they were.

Seitz ruled that the option year in every contract was just that: one option year that could not be renewed perpetually. Miller was not entirely surprised. In one of Seitz's rulings involving the National Basketball Association, the arbitrator had cited a 1969 California Court of Appeals decision. It had given Rick Barry the right to sign with an American Basketball Association team after playing out his option year with the San Francisco Warriors. The NBA's option clause was an exact duplicate of Organized Baseball's. After Seitz's ruling, the players and owners worked out a new Basic Agreement that gave players the right to free agency after six years, a requirement still in effect.

Miller faced one more great battle. In 1980 owners wanted to institute compensation for teams losing free agents. Players adamantly opposed the owners' plan since it would severely damaged the players' negotiating leverage. The first midseason strike in baseball history was barely averted. But a year later on June 11, 1981, with the issue still unresolved, the players struck.

Again public sympathy was hardly with the players, who were now earning a minimum salary of $32,000 a year and an average wage of $193,000. The strike cost the players $28 million in lost wages, and the clubs each lost anywhere from $1.6 million to $7.6 million in revenues. In many cases the losses were offset by the owners' $50 million in strike insurance, which had been purchased at a cost of $2.2 million. Miller, who was making $160,000 a year, did not accept his salary for the duration of the strike.

The strike was settled on July 31, with one-third of the season lost, in a settlement that included complex compensation formulas. Eventually the owners had the compensation formulas scrapped because the union had insisted that all teams, not just those signing free agents, had to submit players to the compensation pool. This did not sit well with teams that opted out of the market but still lost a player.

Throughout the years Miller's chief antagonist was Bowie Kuhn, baseball's commissioner from 1969 to 1984. He considered Miller an "old-fashioned, 19th-century trade unionist who hated management generally, and the management of baseball specifically." For his part Miller said of Kuhn, "To paraphrase Voltaire on God, if Bowie Kuhn had never existed, we would have had to invent him."

When Miller retired in 1984 Reggie Jackson said, "Marvin Miller took on the establishment and whipped them. We never would have been free agents without him."

Stu Miller

Miller, Stuart Leonard **P**

1952–68 B:12/26/1927, Northampton, MA
Deb:8/12/1952, STL NL BR/TR 5'11½", 165

W	L	PCT	G	SV	IP	BB	SO	ERA
105	103	.505	704	154	1694	600	1164	3.24

Stu Miller is perhaps best remembered for the time the wind appeared to blow him off the mound in Candlestick Park during the 1961 All-Star Game. But his entire career represented a victory for the weak. The pallid righthander, whom Cardinals manager Eddie Stanky nicknamed "the Stenographer" for his lack of athleticism, used an assortment of slow and slower pitches to win 105 games and save 154.

On July 11, 1961, Miller was pitching for the National League in the ninth inning of that year's first All-Star Game in San Francisco. With the tying run on second, the afternoon wind rolled in just as the slight righthander was readying to pitch to Detroit's Rocky Colavito. Witnesses report that Miller was blown off the mound and was called for a balk.

"I know I balked," Miller explained. "All of a sudden the wind pushed my shoulder forward. My feet didn't move, so I didn't get blown off the mound as the story goes. Each time it gets told, I get blown farther off the mound. Then [umpire Stan] Landes moved the runners up. I went in and talked with Landes. He was sympathetic. But he told me, 'What can I do? It's the rule.'"

The balk allowed the tying run to score on Ken Boyer's error later in the inning. Miller and the National League won the game in the 10th inning on Roberto Clemente's game-winning single. After the game Landes was asked if Miller should have been pardoned because the gust was "an act of God." The umpire replied, "If it was an act of God, I blessed him. I gave him the final sacraments. But he still balked."

Stuart Leonard Miller stood nearly six feet tall but weighed only 165 pounds. "After high school I was in the navy two years. When I got out of the service, the Cards had 23 farm clubs; they needed players because the rosters had been depleted in World War II," explained Miller. "I didn't want to go to college, so when a scout asked me if I wanted to sign, I said 'why not?'"

He started with Salisbury in 1949 and led the Eastern Shore League in losses. The next year he led the PONY League in losses. In 1952 while he was at Columbus, his manager, Johnny Keane, boldly predicted that despite his physique Miller would win in the majors.

Miller proved Keane right on August 12, 1952, tossing a 1–0 shutout against Chicago in his major league debut. He recorded a 6–3 record with a 2.05 ERA as a starter for the Cardinals, but St. Louis skipper Eddie Stanky remained unimpressed. It appeared that Stanky's assessment was better than Keane's two years later when Miller was sent down to the minors after two seasons of ERAs well above 5.00.

Miller was traded along with Harvey Haddix to the Phillies in 1956 and then to the New York Giants prior to the 1957 season. In the Giants' first year in San Francisco in 1958, Miller, now splitting his time between starting and relieving, led the league with a 2.47 ERA. In 1961, being used only in relief, Miller had a 14–5 record, with a league-leading 17 saves, and won *The Sporting News* Fireman of the Year honors.

After appearing in his only World Series in 1962, Miller was traded to Baltimore. He had developed such impressively slow junk that he earned the sarcastic nickname "the Bullet" in the Baltimore clubhouse. In 1963 he led the AL with 27 saves and again won the Fireman of the Year Award. On April 30, 1967, Steve Barber and Miller combined to no-hit the Tigers—and lost the game, 2–1. Ten walks by Barber and two Baltimore errors led to both Detroit runs.

After five years in Baltimore, Miller finished his major league career with Atlanta at age 40 in 1968. He later operated a liquor store in San Carlos, California.

Jocko Milligan

Milligan, John **C-1B**

1884–93 B:8/8/1861, Philadelphia, PA D: 8/29/1923, Philadelphia, PA Deb:5/1/1884, PHI AA BR/TR 6', 192

G	AB	R	H	HR	RBI	OBP	SLG	AVG
772	2964	440	848	49	497	.341	.433	.286

Jocko Milligan was one of the best catchers of his era. As a rookie, he led all American Association catchers in fielding percentage. In four of the next six years, he topped all other AA catchers in double plays. Milligan also filled in at first base throughout his career.

He could handle the bat, too. Milligan topped .300 three times, with a high of .366 for the 1889 St. Louis Browns. Two years later, in 1891, he led the AA in doubles, finished second in home runs and slugging average, and fourth in RBIs.

Milligan began his major league career in his hometown of Philadelphia. After four years with the Athletics he moved to St. Louis, helping the Browns to the 1888 World Series. He batted .400 in an eight-game loss to the National League's New York Giants. Milligan returned to Philadelphia in the 1890 Players League, then stayed with the team another year after it was absorbed by the AA. Milligan finished his career with two years in the NL, playing with Washington, Baltimore, and New York.

Don Mincher

Mincher, Donald Ray **1B**

1960–72 B:6/24/1938, Huntsville, AL Deb:4/18/1960, WAS AL BL/TR 6'3", 213

G	AB	R	H	HR	RBI	OBP	SLG	AVG
1400	4026	530	1003	200	643	.351	.450	.249

First baseman Don Mincher homered in his first World Series at bat in the 1965 Fall Classic, hitting one deep to the right field bleachers off Don Drysdale. It was his only Series four-bagger in a 13-year career that yielded 200 regular-season circuit clouts.

Donald Ray Mincher began his pro career by turning down a University of Alabama football scholarship to sign with the White Sox, starting with Duluth-Superior of the Northern League in 1956. After playing at Davenport and Charleston, in April 1960 he was traded along with catcher

Earl Battey and $150,000 to the Senators for Roy Sievers.

The next season he was in Minnesota, beginning a six-year stint with the club. On June 9, 1966, the power-hitting Mincher was one of five Twins to homer in a single inning. In December that year the team sent him to California in a deal that brought pitcher Dean Chance to Minnesota.

In April 1968 Mincher was beaned by Cleveland's Sam McDowell, and that October he was selected by the Seattle Pilots in the American League expansion draft. That year he was immortalized in Jim Bouton's *Ball Four.* In January 1970 he was traded to Oakland, where he led AL first basemen in errors. The A's dealt him to Washington in May 1971, but after beginning the 1972 season with Texas, he was returned to Oakland. As a pinch hitter in that fall's World Series he went 1-for-3.

Mincher was placed on the voluntarily retired list in December 1972. He later operated a sporting goods store and served as general manager for Huntsville of the Southern League.

Minnie Minoso

Minoso, Saturnino Orestes Armas **OF–3B**
1949, 1951–64, 1976, 1980 B:11/29/1922, Havana, Cuba Deb:4/19/1949, CLE AL BR/TR 5'10", 175

G	AB	R	H	HR	RBI	OBP	SLG	AVG
1835	6579	1136	1963	186	1023	.391	.451	.298

Some baseball players' enthusiasm for the game is so palpable that they become immediate favorites of the fans. Such was the case with Saturnino Orestes Armas "Minnie" Minoso, the first dark-skinned Latin to play in the country and the first black to wear a White Sox uniform. In the 1950s he provided fans with some of the decade's most exciting baseball. Three decades later he was still stepping up to the plate for the Sox.

"I don't believe there is a player in the game today who can give you the thrill he can," White Sox owner Bill Veeck once said. "Without him in the lineup, it's just another ballgame." Minoso was as productive as he was exciting. He hit better than .300 in eight of his first 10 seasons, drove in 100-plus runs four times, and stole bases by the bushel.

Minoso, who grew up in Cuba's Matanzas Province, left school at age 14 to work in the region's sugar fields. He helped form a plantation baseball team, eventually becoming its manager. His skills sent him to Havana, where he secured a position on a semipro team sponsored by the Cuban Mining Company. In 1945 winter league play in Cuba, he was named Rookie of the Year.

In 1946 he signed with Alex Pompez's New York Cubans for $150 a month plus a boat ticket to Key West and train fare to New York. On the recommendation of Abe Saperstein, the Harlem Globetrotters' owner who was also a part-time scout for the Indians, Cleveland purchased the 25-year old Minoso in 1948 and assigned him to Dayton in the Class A Central League. He made it to Cleveland the next year, but he lasted only nine games. Sent down to San Diego, he had back-to-back 20-homer seasons; he drove in 115 runs in 1950.

He moved up to the majors as a 28-year-old rookie, but on April 30, 1951, he was part of a three-way trade with the Indians, White Sox, and Philadelphia Athletics. That trade cost the White Sox Gus Zernial, who went on to lead the American League in homers and RBIs that year for the A's. The deal, though, eventually turned out to be a steal for the White Sox. Minoso made an immediate impression on Chicago fans when he homered in his first at bat. He hit .326 that season and led the league in stolen bases and triples. That was a hint of things to come: Minoso would lead the AL in triples and steals three times each.

"That day, I never forget," Minoso said about his first game with Chicago. "It helped that I finally know I have a regular position." The position was left field. He had been a third baseman in the minors, and not a very good one. In 1951 he began his conversion to the outfield. Even though he outpointed the Yankees' Gil McDougald in 15 of 16 offensive categories, superior fielder McDougald beat him out in the Baseball Writers Association voting for American League Rookie of the Year. Minoso, however, did win *The Sporting News* Rookie of the Year honors.

When he came up to the majors, his English was limited. Once he was asked, "Don't you think it's going to be hard to play major league baseball if you can't speak English?" He responded: "Ball, bat, glove—she no speak English."

Besides hitting triples and stealing bases, Minoso was especially good at something else: getting hit by the baseball. He set an AL career record—since broken—by being hit 189 times. He still holds the career record for number of years leading the league in being hit by pitches, with 10. Not that it worried him. "No, I was not scared," he said, "because in baseball, I was never scared of nothing."

His fearlessness did cost him once. In May 1955 he suffered a hairline skull fracture after being beaned by Yankees righthander Bob Grim. Although he was playing again in only a couple of weeks, the injury did affect him. After back-to-back 100-RBI seasons at .313 and .320, Minoso hit .288 that year with 70 RBIs.

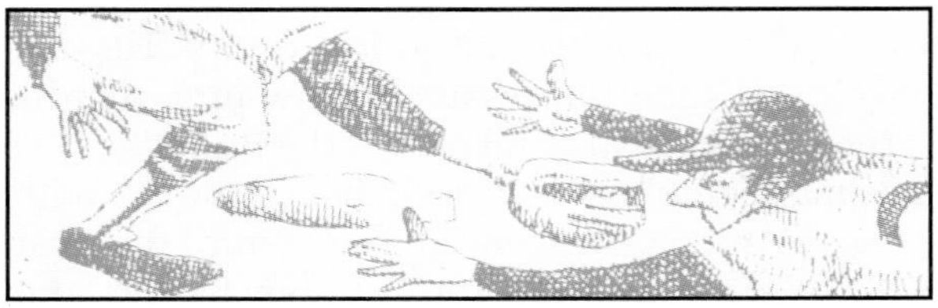

In December 1957, after hitting .310 with 103 RBIs, Minoso was traded to Cleveland in a deal that sent Early Wynn and Al Smith to Chicago. Minoso was heartbroken. "I feel like the whole world was over for me," he later said. "Like my city...had put me out."

The deal proved to be one of the keys to the 1959 White Sox winning their first pennant in 40 years. Even though Minoso wasn't part of it, White Sox owner Veeck presented him with a championship ring. Soon after that, Veeck reacquired Minoso in a seven-player trade. Minoso responded in 1960 by leading the AL in hits, with 184, and by finishing second to Roger Maris in RBIs. He was 37.

Father Time was catching up with Minoso. He fell to 82 RBIs in 1961, his last season as a regular, and he was traded to the Cardinals in November. He hung on for three more seasons before retiring in 1964—sort of. On September 11, 1976, Veeck, who was again running the White Sox, reactivated the 53-year-old Minoso so he could become a four-decade major leaguer. For once in his baseball career Minoso was nervous.

"It's been many years since I face pitching like this," he said. "I hope [the fans] forgive me." That day he went hitless against the Angels' Frank Tanana. But the next afternoon he faced 25-year-old Sid Monge, who had been only 20 days old when Minoso first appeared in the American League. Minnie took the first pitch and singled to left.

In September 1980 Veeck asked the 58-year-old Minoso to suit up again. He went 0-for-4 as a pinch hitter to join Nick Altrock as a five-decade player. On June 30, 1993, at 70 years old, Minoso became the first professional player to perform in six separate decades when he came to bat for the St. Paul Saints of the independent Northern League. Fittingly, Veeck's son Mike operated St. Paul.

Late in the 1993 season, after the White Sox had clinched the AL West title, the team announced that Minoso was going to be activated to bat in one game and become a six-decade American League player, but the acting commissioner, Bud Selig, nixed the plan.

Greg Minton

Minton, Gregory Brian **P**

1975–90 B:7/29/1951, Lubbock, TX Deb:9/7/1975, SF NL BB/TR 6'2", 190

W	L	PCT	G	SV	IP	BB	SO	ERA
59	65	.476	710	150	1130^2	483	479	3.10

Sinkerball hurler Greg Minton pitched 269⅓ innings without surrendering a home run during a stretch between the 1977 season and 1982. He also led the National League in games finished in relief in both 1981 and 1982. Gregory Brian Minton, who attended San Diego Mesa College, was chosen by Kansas City in the third round of the January 1970 free-agent draft. After pitching at Billings and Waterloo, he was traded to the Giants' organization in April 1973 for catcher Fran Healy. He performed at San Jose, Phoenix, Amarillo, and Fresno before reaching the majors with San Francisco in 1975.

During a 16-year major league career, the first 10 with the Giants, he was on the disabled list for parts of four seasons and made the All-Star team once, in 1982. In that Midsummer Classic, Minton pitched two-thirds of an inning, issuing one walk and striking out none.

Minton underwent elbow surgery before the 1987 season, and the Giants released him that May. He then signed with California, where he spent parts of two seasons on the disabled list before retiring in 1990.

Clarence Mitchell

Mitchell, Clarence Elmer **P**

1911–32 B:2/22/1891, Franklin, NE D:11/6/1963, Grand Island, NE Deb:9/7/1975, DET AL BL/TL 5'11½", 190

W	L	PCT	G	SH	IP	BB	SO	ERA
125	139	.473	390	12	2217	624	543	4.12

Brooklyn spitballer Clarence Mitchell came up to bat with two on and none out in the fifth inning of Game 5 of the 1920 World Series. Facing righthander Jim Bagby, he lined to Cleveland second baseman Bill Wambsganss. The result was the only unassisted triple play in World Series competition as Wambsganss caught runners Pete Kilduff and Otto Miller off base. Three innings later Mitchell hit into a double play.

Mitchell's career began with Franklin of the Class D Interstate League in 1909. He saw action with Red Cloud, Saginaw, Providence, and Denver of the Western League. He came up to Detroit in 1911 and then returned to the minors. In 1915 he won 22 games for Denver.

Brought up to Cincinnati the following year, he went 11–10 in 29 games for the Reds. In February 1918 the club sold Mitchell to Brooklyn. When the spitball was outlawed Mitchell was the only National League southpaw allowed to continue its use.

Mitchell was a good performer at the plate and was often used as pinch hitter or at first base. During his career he batted .252 in 1,287 at bats, with seven homers and 133 RBIs. He was traded to the Phils in February 1923, then to St. Louis in midseason 1928, but he had two of his most productive seasons at the end of his career with the New York Giants following a trade in May 1930. In 1931, at age 40, he recorded a career-high 13 wins for New York.

Dale Mitchell

Mitchell, Loren Dale **OF**

1946–56 B:8/23/1921, Colony, OK D:1/5/1987, Tulsa, OK Deb:9/15/1946, CLE AL BL/TL 6'1", 195

G	AB	R	H	HR	RBI	OBP	SLG	AVG
1127	3984	555	1244	41	403	.368	.416	.312

Dale Mitchell, the eighth-toughest man to strike out in major league history, is best remembered for a strikeout. It came in his next-to-last major league at bat, as a Brooklyn Dodgers, concluding an 11-year career in which all but two and a half months were spent with the Cleveland Indians.

Mitchell pinch-hit for Sal Maglie in Game 5 of the 1956 World Series and was called out on a 1–2 pitch by umpire Babe Pinelli, working his last major league game behind the plate. Mitchell's strikeout was the final out of Don Larsen's perfect game.

Mitchell contended to his death, and films seem to confirm, that the pitch was outside. In fairness to Pinelli, he'd seen a lot more strikeouts up close than Mitchell, who fanned only 119 times in 3,984 regular-season at bats, or once in every 33.5 at bats. In post-1942 records, Mitchell also owns the fourth- and sixth-best single-season marks for avoiding the whiff, fanning once in every 58.2 at bats in 1949 and once in every 56.8 at bats in 1952.

A lefthanded leadoff man and left fielder, Loren Dale Mitchell came up with the Indians in September 1946 and hit .432. A pure contact hitter, Mitchell walked nearly three times as often as he struck out during his 11-year career, yet never more than 67 times in a season. He hit singles, 973 of them among his 1,244 hits, and reached double figures in homers only twice, with a career high 13 in 1953.

During his official rookie year Mitchell batted .316, fifth best in the American League and the first of six .300 marks in his first seven years in the big leagues. For the 1948 world champion Indians, Mitchell reached career highs with 204 hits, a .336 batting average, 30 doubles, a 21-game hitting streak (which he matched in 1951), and 13 steals. He finished his career with 45 steals but was caught stealing 47 times.

He went 1-for-5 in the Tribe's pennant playoff game against the Boston Red Sox in 1948. In the World Series against the Boston Braves he went hitless in his first six at bats before singling to lead off the fifth inning of Game 2. He eventually scored on Lou Boudreau's single that knocked out Warren Spahn in Cleveland's 4–1 win, which evened the Series.

Cleveland won Game 3, 2–0, and after the Braves scored three runs in the top of the first in Game 4 against Bob Feller, Mitchell did the unlikely. He led off the bottom of the first with a home run, igniting a Cleveland comeback that eventually put the Indians up, 5–4. However, Feller and the bullpen collapsed, and Boston won by a count of 11–5.

In Game 6 Mitchell led off the third with an opposite-field double and scored on another Boudreau hit, giving the Tribe a 1–0 lead. With Cleveland ahead, 4–3, and the tying run on third in the eighth, Bob Kennedy and his better arm replaced Mitchell in left, even though Mitchell had led AL outfielders in fielding percentage in 1948 and 1949. Cleveland held on to win the game and the Series.

In 1949 Mitchell had his best all-around season, leading the American League with 203 hits and 23 triples. His .317 batting average and 274 total bases ranked fourth best in the league, and he had his best year as a base thief, with 10 steals in 13 attempts. In the All-Star Game, as a late-inning replacement for Ted Williams in left, Mitchell knocked in the final run with a double in the AL's 11–7 win.

In the 1952 All-Star Game, Mitchell was one of three starters from the Indians, but he went hitless in his only at bat of the rain-shortened contest. He finished the 1952 season batting .323, second to Philadelphia's Ferris Fain in the batting race, and hit .300 in 1953, his final year as a regular.

Al Smith replaced Mitchell as the Tribe's leadoff hitter and left fielder in 1954, and Cleveland won 111 games. Mitchell played only seven times in the field and went 14-for-44 as a pinch hitter, a .318 clip. Mitchell made three pinch-hit appearances in the World Series against the New York Giants that season. In the opener he drew a walk batting for Hank Majeski, who had been announced for Dave Philley, right after Willie Mays caught Vic Wertz's 460-foot drive.

Mitchell led the American League in pinch-hit at bats in 1955, going 13-for-45 for a .289 average, and he played eight games at first base and three in the outfield. After Mitchell went 3-for-22 as a pinch hitter and 4-for-30 overall in 1956, the Indians sold him to Brooklyn on July 29. He went 7-for-24 with the Dodgers and appeared in his third World Series. Mitchell failed to deliver in four pinch-hit appearances that series, including his famous strikeout, and he grounded out to short in his final major league at bat leading off the sixth inning of Game 7.

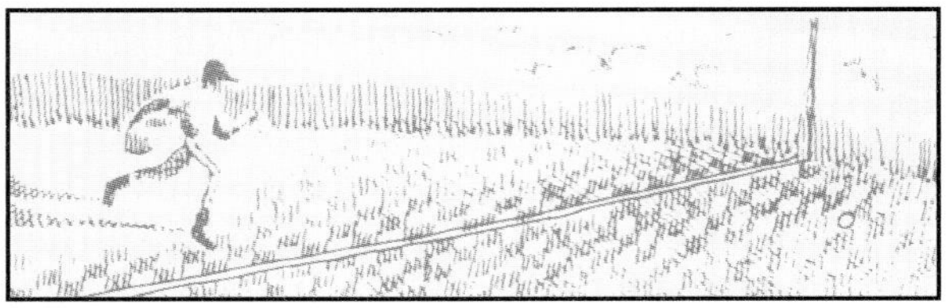

Kevin Mitchell

Mitchell, Kevin Darnell **OF-3B**

1984–94, 1996-98 B:1/13/1962, San Diego, CA Deb:9/4/1984, NY NL BR/TR 5'11", 210

G	AB	R	H	HR	RBI	OBP	SLG	AVG
1223	4134	630	1173	234	760	.363	.520	.284

A gang member as a youth, Kevin Mitchell survived several gunshot wounds to pursue a career in baseball. Mitchell rose from unheralded prospect to key contributor in the Mets' world championship season of 1986. The rookie slugger hit well while filling in at six different positions, including shortstop. His presence helped lead to the release of veteran outfielder George Foster late in the season.

Mitchell batted .250 in both the Championship Series and World Series. His two-out single in the bottom of the 10th inning of Game 6 of the World Series kept New York alive against Boston. He scored the tying run in the Mets' miraculous comeback on a wild pitch by Bob Stanley.

Despite his versatility and lively bat, the Mets decided to packaged Mitchell in a trade to San Diego for Kevin McReynolds. Playing in his hometown distracted Mitchell, and his tenure with the Padres lasted only 62 games. He was traded to San Francisco where he became the everyday third baseman. He did not reach his peak, however, until 1989, when he started wearing contact lenses. Now playing left field, Mitchell led the league with 47 home runs and 125 RBIs, earning the 1989 Most Valuable Player Award. He batted .353 with two home runs during the Championship Series, launching the Giants into the World Series. Mitchell also garnered attention that season when he misjudged a flyball in the left field corner but recovered in time to catch it with his bare hand.

Mitchell seemed destined for greatness, but increasing weight and a series of injuries hampered his performance. Bothered by a wrist injury in 1990, Mitchell's power numbers declined. They fell even further the next season, when he played in only 113 games. Mitchell also started to foster a reputation as a troublemaker, based on his chronic lateness and several off-the-field incidents.

The Giants, concerned about the character of Mitchell's friends and the amount of time he spent on the disabled list, traded him to Seattle for Billy Swift and two other pitchers. The Mariners expected Mitchell to produce huge numbers in the Kingdome, but a pulled stomach muscle and a broken bone in his foot limited him to 90 games and only nine home runs. The Mariners then traded him to the Reds, where he hit .341 and .326 with great power but limited plate appearances in two injury-filled seasons.

Mitchell spent the final years of his career trying to find and keep a job. After a disastrous attempt to play in Japan in 1995, Mitchell had brief stints with the Red Sox, the Reds, the Indians, and the Athletics over the next three years, but his injuries and personal troubles prevented him from sticking anywhere. He was forced into retirement after the Athletics let him go in 1998.

Mike Mitchell

Mitchell, Michael Francis **OF**

1907–14 B:12/12/1879, Springfield, OH D:7/16/1961, Phoenix, AZ Deb:4/11/1907, CIN NL BR/TR 6'1", 185

G	AB	R	H	HR	RBI	OBP	SLG	AVG
1124	4095	514	1138	27	514	.340	.380	.278

Mike Mitchell was an excellent outfielder who twice led the National League in triples. As a 27-year-old rookie with Cincinnati, in 1907, Mitchell set a record of 39 outfield assists that wasn't broken until Chuck Klein made 44 assists in 1930. In 1909 the righthanded hitter led the league with 17 triples and batted .310. Mitchell led the league again with 18 triples in 1910. The following season he hit for the cycle on August 11, 1911.

The Reds traded Mitchell to the Cubs as part of an eight-player deal that made Joe Tinker the Reds' player-manager on December 15, 1912. The Cubs waived him to Pittsburgh on July 29, 1913, and the Pirates waived Mitchell to Washington on July 20, 1914, where he finished his career at the end of the season. An artist with a fungo bat, Mitchell set a record by hitting a fungo more than 413 feet on September 11, 1907.

Johnny Mize

Mize, John Robert **1B**

1936–53 B:1/7/1913, Demorest, GA D:6/2/1993, Demorest, GA Deb:4/16/1936, STL NL BL/TR 6'2", 215

G	AB	R	H	HR	RBI	OBP	SLG	AVG
1884	6443	1118	2011	359	1337	.397	.562	.312

While his name is not often mentioned in any discussion of baseball's greatest sluggers, an examination of Johnny Mize's record reveals that Mize was a power hitter to be feared. He was, in fact, the rarest of hitters, a genuine home run threat who hit for a high average and seldom struck out. As writer Bill James has commented, "That doesn't leave out too much."

A.W. Laird's statistical analysis rates Mize as the fifth-best first baseman of all time, behind Lou Gehrig, Bill Terry, Jimmie Foxx, and George Sisler. He is the only man to hit 50 home runs in a season while fanning fewer than 50 times, and he hit three homers in a game six times. He also homered at least once in all 15 of the major league ballparks in use during his career.

After being signed to a pro contract with the Cardinals by Frank Rickey, Branch Rickey's brother, John Robert Mize was a star in the minor leagues. The Reds offered the Cards $55,000 for him, but he tore a hip muscle, and Cincinnati returned him to St. Louis. Then he tore a muscle in his other hip. He was ready to quit baseball, but he persevered and made it to the Cardinals in 1936 after surgery on both hips. After hitting .336 in six minor league seasons, Mize responded with an outstanding rookie performance as he slugged 19 home runs, hit .329, and drove in 93 runs.

He was nothing less than excellent in his next five years in St. Louis. With Enos Slaughter and Terry Moore in the same lineup the Cards scored a lot of runs, but their pitching wasn't good enough to carry them higher than second place. Mize drove in 100 runs or more every year; hit between .314 and .364; won a batting title, a doubles title, a triples title, two home run titles, and three slugging titles; and twice finished second in MVP voting. Teammate Joe Orengo christened Mize "the Big Cat" for the way he handled bad hops at first base. Stan Musial later used the nickname to describe Mize's graceful batting stance and the ease with which he casually avoided brush-back pitches.

Mize related a wonderful story about his contract negotiations with Branch Rickey in Donald Honig's *Baseball When the Grass Was Real*. "In 1939," Mize said, "I led the league in hitting with .349. Naturally after a year like that you look forward to talking contract. But when I sat down with Rickey, he said, 'Well, your home run production stayed pretty much the same.'

"So the next year I hit 43 home runs, which is still the Cardinal club record [since broken, of course, by Mark McGwire], and led the league in runs batted in. But my batting average went down. When I went in to talk contract this time, he said, 'Well, your batting average wasn't so good. Would you be willing to take a cut?' I led the league in hitting, then I led the league in home runs and runs batted in, and he wanted to know if I'd take a cut!" Mize asked to be traded instead.

The second phase of his career began a year later, when Mize got his wish and was traded to the Giants before the 1942 season for three players and $50,000. The Giants wanted him, but Mize was dismayed at having to play in the Polo Grounds. As a straightaway hitter, he felt that the park's distant center field fence and right field power alley would hurt him. "It's the worst place I could have been traded to," Mize said. But he was smart enough to adapt his hitting style to the park.

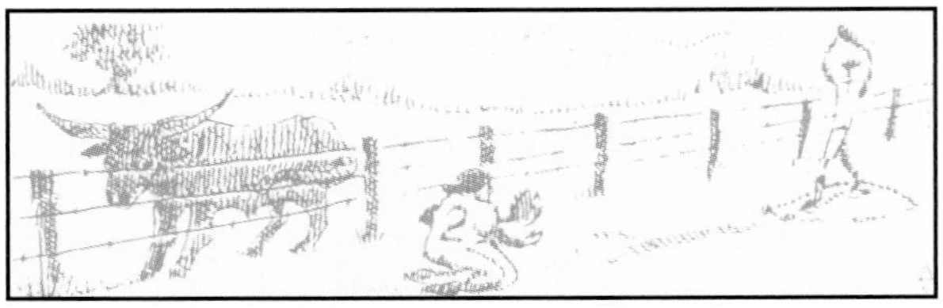

It was as a Giant that most people remember Mize. He led the league in RBIs and slugging percentage his first year there and then spent three years in the Navy. Toward the end of his tenure in the service Mize realized that military chow had added a few pounds to his already bulky frame, so he devised a unique approach to reconditioning. Stationed on a Pacific island, Mize entered a tin hut with its doors and windows sealed at high noon each day and put himself through a rigorous set of exercises. It paid off.

He returned to the Giants in 1946, but a Joe Page pitch in an exhibition game broke a bone in Mize's hand, and he saw action in only 101 games. Still, he hit .337 and slugged .576. The following year he belted 51 home runs to become the only National League lefty to ever hit 50 or more homers in a season. Unfortunately, he garnered only a tie for the league lead as Ralph Kiner of Pittsburgh also belted 51 round-trippers. But Mize captured league titles in RBIs and runs scored, and the Giants set the record for most home runs by a team in a season.

In 1948 Mize slugged 40 homers to again tie Kiner for the league lead, and he knocked in 125 runs, but his average fell below .302 for the first time. That same year Leo Durocher arrived as the Giants' manager, and he felt the team was overloaded with power hitters who couldn't run. When owner Horace Stoneham asked him to evaluate the talent, Durocher sent a four-word report: "Back up the truck."

Durocher cut Mize's playing time in 1949, and the Big Cat had his worst year ever. Meanwhile the Yankees, in their first year under Casey Stengel, had a hole at first base they couldn't fill. When they learned they could get Mize for only $40,000, they jumped at the deal.

Stengel called his new acquisition "a slugger who hits like a leadoff man." But just six days after becoming a Yankee, Mize separated his shoulder while diving to tag first base before the runner on a bunt play, and for the rest of the season he saw limited playing time. He did, however, have enough time to pinch-hit a single in the ninth inning of Game 3 of the 1949 World Series that won the game for New York.

For the next four years Mize served the Yanks well, providing power off the bench and occasionally starting. He led the league in pinch hits in 1951, 1952, and 1953. The 1952 World Series was the crowning achievement of his career. After making only one appearance in the first three games—a pinch-hit home run in a Yanks defeat in Game 3—he was installed at first in place of Joe Collins, who didn't have a hit in 11 at bats.

His home run in Game 4 provided all the runs Allie Reynolds needed as he threw a four-hit shutout. The Big Cat's three-run homer was centerpiece of a five-run Yanks fifth in Game 5, and it marked the first time a player had ever homered in three consecutive Series games. In Game 7, Mize's single brought home the first run in the Yankees' 4–2 victory. He finished with three home runs and six RBIs while batting an even .400.

Even in 1953, his final season, Mize was an important cog in Stengel's lineup as the Yankees cruised to their fifth consecutive championship. In May he reached base in seven consecutive pinch-hit appearances with five hits. His 19 pinch hits for the season is only one fewer than the league record; overall, he drove in 179 runs in a Yankee uniform with only 230 hits. He finished his career with 359 home runs, won or tied for home run leadership four times, and led his league in RBIs three times.

In Mize's later years, New York sportswriter Dan Parker penned a famous ode in which he paid tribute to the aging superstar:

Your arm is gone, your legs likewise.
But not your eyes, Mize, not your eyes

The Veterans Committee elected Mize into the Baseball Hall of Fame in 1981

Vinegar Bend Mizell

Mizell, Wilmer David **P**

1952–62 B:8/13/1930, Leakesville, MS D:2/21/1999, Kerville, TX Deb:4/22/1952, STL NL BR/TL 6'3½", 205

W	L	PCT	G	SH	IP	BB	SO	ERA
90	88	.506	268	15	1528²	680	918	3.85

Wilmer David Mizell hailed from the small Alabama town of Vinegar Bend, 85 miles northeast of Mobile, and gave the hamlet lasting fame when the press dubbed him "Vinegar Bend." In 1948 Mizell attended a two-day tryout camp in Biloxi, Miss. The last pitcher to work on the first day, Mizell struck out three batters on nine pitches. "The next day this giant storm came through," he said later, "and the camp had to be canceled. If I hadn't squeezed in there at the end, I'd never have made it to the Cardinals." Based on the tryout, Mizell was signed to a minor league by St. Louis for $175 per month.

Called up in 1952, he was an effective starting pitcher for St. Louis but he had his best season with Pittsburgh in 1960. Traded to the Pirates that May, he went 13–5 for Pittsburgh and helped propel them to the National League pennant, though he pitched poorly in the World Series against New York.

After completing his baseball career in 1962, Mizell lived in North Carolina where he worked for the Pepsi-Cola Co. in sales management and public relations. He entered politics shortly afterward, successfully running for Davidson County (North Carolina) commissioner. In 1966, Mizell, a Republican, was elected to Congress. He served in the House of Representatives until he was unseated in the post-Watergate election of 1974.

President Gerald Ford appointed him assistant secretary of commerce for economic development. In the early 1980s, President Ronald Reagan named him assistant secretary of agriculture for governmental and public affairs. Later, President George Bush made Mizell both deputy assistant secretary for intergovernmental affairs in the Department of Veterans Affairs, and executive director of the President's Council on Physical Fitness and Sports. Hospitalized after a severe heart attack, Mizell died February 21, 1999, in Kerrville, Texas.

Randy Moffitt

Moffitt, Randall James **P**

1972–83 B:10/13/1948, Long Beach, CA Deb:6/11/1972, SF NL BR/TR 6'3", 190

W	L	PCT	G	SV	IP	BB	SO	ERA
43	52	.453	534	96	781¹	286	455	3.65

Most relievers have to limit their arsenal for the sake of consistency. Not Randy Moffitt. He threw his pitches from a variety of angles. The son of Brewers scout Bill Moffitt and the brother of tennis great Billie Jean King, Randall James Moffitt was selected by San Francisco in the first round of the January 1970 draft after three excellent seasons at California State College at Long Beach. The righthander started with Fresno of the California League in 1970 and had a 1.60 ERA. He played with Phoenix in the Pacific Coast League from 1971 to 1972 where the Giants converted him to a reliever.

Moffitt was second in the National League with 15 saves in 1974. In 1980 he came down with a mysterious stomach ailment and missed almost all of the next two seasons. Doctors eventually discovered that the ailment was caused by a rare fungus, which they burned off; it was only the third known case of the disorder. The Giants released him in August 1981.

The Astros signed Moffitt to a minor league contract with Tucson and promoted him to Houston at the end of the season. Granted free agency in November 1982, he signed with the Blue Jays where he had a 6–2 record with 10 saves in 1983.

George Mogridge

Mogridge, George Anthony **P**

1911–27 B:2/18/1889, Rochester, NY D:3/4/1962, Rochester, NY Deb:8/17/1911, CHI AL BL/TL 6'2", 165

W	L	PCT	G	SH	IP	BB	SO	ERA
132	133	.498	398	20	2265^{2}	565	678	3.23

George Mogridge was a tall, thin lefty who won 132 games over 15 years, most of them for the New York Yankees and Washington Senators. He made it to the majors in 1911 for a cup of coffee with the White Sox. Chicago sold him to the Yankees in 1915, and on April 24, 1917, he pitched the team's first-ever no-hitter, beating the Boston Red Sox, 2–1.

Mogridge went 16–13 with a 2.18 ERA in 1918 and led the American League with 45 games and seven saves (and seven losses in relief). He also started 19 times, completing 13 games. He was traded to the Senators in January 1921. As a result, he missed being a part of five pennant winners in New York, but he was a key contributor to Washington's only world champion in 1924.

He won 16 games that season on a staff that included Walter Johnson and Tom Zachary, with workhorse Firpo Marberry coming out of the bullpen. His .593 winning percentage was his best as a starter. Washington won its first pennant by two games over the Yankees.

After starting and winning Game 4 of the World Series, Mogridge was the centerpiece of a Game 7 ploy by Bucky Harris, the Senators' 27-year-old rookie manager. Harris started righty Curly Ogden against the New York Giants but replaced him with the 35-year-old southpaw after two batters. Mogridge pitched shutout ball through the fifth inning on two days' rest. The Senators won the deciding game in 12 innings

Mogridge sometimes doctored pitches with resin, one of the substances banned after the beaning death of Ray Chapman in 1920, but he was able to get away with concealing resin on the underside of his cap bill.

He won 18 games in each of his first two seasons with the Senators. A late season trade to the St. Louis Browns in 1925 denied Mogridge a second pennant in Washington. He pitched his final two seasons with the Boston Braves.

Paul Molitor

Molitor, Paul Leo **DH–3B–2B**

1978–98 B: 8/22/1956, St. Paul, MN Deb: 4/7/1978, MIL AL BR/TR 6'0", 185

G	AB	R	H	HR	RBI	OBP	SLG	AVG
2683	10835	1782	3319	234	1307	.372	.448	.306

Paul Molitor quietly retired in 1998 with the eighth-highest hit total in major league history. A consummate line drive man, Molitor was a designated hitter for so long it's easy to forget that he was the starting second baseman in the 1980 All-Star Game. He played third base, second base, first base, and even some outfield, but his real position was hitter. He finished a 21-season career with 3,319 hits, including 605 doubles. In addition, he walked 1,094 times and stole 504 bases. His career totals of 234 home runs and 1,307 RBIs are remarkable for a player who only once hit over 20 home runs.

His numbers could have been even higher had he not been dogged by injuries throughout his career. (Managers figured out in the latter half of his career that by writing DH next to his name they stood a better chance of keeping him off the DL.) A ribcage muscle pull in 1980, torn ligaments in his ankle in 1981, ligament damage to his elbow in 1984, various injuries in 1986, a strained hamstring in 1987, two broken fingers in 1990, and assorted other ills cost him nearly 500 games. Molitor was on the disabled list 10 times with the Brewers from 1980 to 1990. In that time, however, he still managed to hit .300 or better five times, stole 30 or more bases five times, and scored 100 or more runs three times.

Despite playing his career in relatively small markets—Milwaukee, Toronto, and Minnesota—Molitor saw his share of the spotlight. He was the first player to have five hits in a World Series game in 1982, his 39-game hitting streak in 1987 was the fourth-longest in AL history, he made the All-Star team six times, and, although he never won a batting title, he finished behind John Olerud and ahead of Roberto Alomar in 1993 to make the Toronto Blue Jays the first team to have the top three hitters in a batting race.

Molitor became a Blue Jay as a free agent in 1993 following 15 seasons in Milwaukee. The 37-year-old star reached career highs in home runs (22) and runs batted in (111) to go along with a .332 average. He finished second in the Most Valuable Player voting for the season.

In the 1993 World Series, however, Molitor earned Most Valuable Players honors as he batted .500, leading the Blue Jays to a six-game victory over the Philadelphia Phillies. When the games shifted to the National League park and forced the teams to drop the DH, Molitor picked up a glove.

He displaced regular first baseman John Olerud, only the second time in major league history that a league-batting champion was benched in the World Series. Molitor played flawlessly in the field at first base and third base and was nearly perfect at the plate as well.

Molitor had 12 hits in 24 at bats with two doubles, two triples, two home runs, and eight RBIs. He tied the World Series record with 10 runs scored. His two-run triple in the first inning of Game 3 sent the Jays to a 10–3 laugher at Veterans Stadium, he led an 18-hit onslaught in Toronto's 15–14 win in Game 4, and his home run and triple staked the Blue Jays to a 5–1 lead in Game 6. After the Phillies staged a late rally to take the lead, Molitor singled to bring Joe Carter to the plate against reliever Mitch Williams in the ninth inning. With Toronto trailing, 6–5, Carter belted a three-run blast to left-center; Molitor crossed the plate with the winning run.

Molitor played two more seasons in Toronto before returning to his native Minnesota. In 1996, at age 40, he batted .341 and led the AL with 225 hits for the Twins. He became the first player in history to hit a triple for his 3,000th hit. He remained one of the toughest outs in the Minnesota lineup until he retired after the 1998 season. Manager Tom Kelly hired Molitor as a Twins coach after the 1999 season.

Bill Monbouquette

Monbouquette, William Charles **P**

1958–68 B:8/11/1936, Medford, MA Deb:7/18/1958, BOS AL BR/TR 5'11", 195

W	L	PCT	G	SH	IP	BB	SO	ERA
114	112	.504	343	18	1961²	462	1122	3.68

There may not be many bright memories of the Red Sox of the early 1960s, but an unmistakable flash of excellence came from the right arm of Bill Monbouquette. He began his career with Boston in 1958 and two seasons later ran off a streak of four straight years in which he won at least 14 games. Monbouquette's best season was 1963, when he went 20–10 with a 3.81 ERA-despite leading AL pitchers by allowing 258 hits. He allowed the same number of hits the following year while going 13–14 and once again led AL pitchers in that category.

Lacking an overpowering fastball, Monbouquette relied on control and speed changes in becoming an All-Star in 1960, 1962, and 1963. In 1960 he took the loss for the AL, allowing three home runs in two innings. A year later Monbouquette made history by striking out 17 Senators in a nine-inning game. He also threw a no-hitter against the White Sox on August 1, 1962, and nearly had another one against the Twins in September 1964, but it was thwarted by shortstop Zoilo Versalles' home run.

Monbouquette went on to pitch for the Yankees and the Giants. He left baseball after the 1968 season and later served as a major league and minor league coach.

Rick Monday

Monday, Robert James **OF–1B**

1966–84 B:11/20/1945, Batesville, AR Deb:9/3/1966, KC AL BL/TL 6'3", 200

G	AB	R	H	HR	RBI	OBP	SLG	AVG
1986	6136	950	1619	241	775	.362	.443	.264

Rick Monday was the first player selected in baseball's first amateur draft in 1965. Plucked by the Kansas City Athletics from Arizona State University for $104,000, outfielder Monday went on to enjoy a productive 19-year major league career. Although never quite as good as the A's had hoped he would be, Monday was nevertheless a talented and valuable competitor who played an important role on several successful clubs.

Monday grew up in Santa Monica, California. He was courted by Tommy Lasorda, then a Dodgers scout, but opted for a scholarship to Arizona State University. A center fielder for ASU, Monday led his team to the NCAA championship and in 1965 was named the College Player of the Year.

He spent only a season and a half in the minors before becoming a regular with the A's in 1967. During his rookie season, the Athletics' last in Kansas City, Monday hit 14 homers and drove in 58 runs. He also struck out more than 100 times for the first of eight seasons. Monday was selected to the AL All-Star team in 1968, and in 1969 he tied Lou Gehrig's league record by collecting RBIs in 10 consecutive games.

But Monday was no superstar. He struck out too much, especially for a guy who didn't hit more than 18 homers in any of his first six seasons in the majors. After the 1971 season he was traded to the Cubs for pitcher Ken Holtzman.

In the friendly confines of Wrigley Field, Monday finally began to display the power the A's had expected of him. On May 16, 1972, he hit three consecutive home runs. In five seasons with the Cubs he hit 20 or more home runs three times, with a career-high 32 in 1976. But his performance continued to be marred by a high number of strikeouts and a relatively small number of RBIs.

On April 25, 1976, the Cubs faced the Dodgers in Los Angeles. After walking out to center field in the bottom of the fourth, Monday noticed two young men racing across the field, one of them holding something under his arm. As the man unfurled his bundle, Monday noticed it was an

American flag. As he later recalled, "I saw they had a can of something and were pouring it over the flag. That's when I started to move."

Before the men could set the flag on fire Monday swept in as if it were a sinking line drive and snatched it away. "I figured they couldn't do any damage to the flag if they had no flag." As he ran off, security personnel moved in and arrested the intruders. The crowd gave Monday a standing ovation and burst out with "God Bless America." Monday became a hero. The Illinois legislature proclaimed a statewide "Rick Monday Day," and he was named grand marshal of the Flag Day parade in Chicago.

Nonetheless, after the season Monday was traded along with pitcher Mike Garman to the Dodgers for first baseman Bill Buckner, infielder Ivan DeJesus, and a minor league pitcher. With Los Angeles, Monday became a valuable role player. In Game 5 of the 1981 NLCS against Montreal, Monday's dramatic ninth-inning home run off Steve Rogers won the pennant for the Dodgers.

Monday played for the Dodgers through 1984, and was a particular favorite of manager Tommy Lasorda. Late in Monday's career Lasorda said of Monday and teammate Manny Mota, "They're so old they were waiters at the Last Supper."

Monday retired with 241 home runs—and 1,513 strikeouts. He later became a broadvaster.

Raul Mondesi

Mondesi, Raul Ramon **OF**

1993–* B:3/12/1971, San Cristobal, Dominican Republic Deb:7/19/1993, LA NL BR/TR 5'11", 202

G	AB	R	H	HR	RBI	OBP	SLG	AVG
916	3487	543	1004	163	518	.336	.504	.288

Raul Mondesi had one of the best arms in baseball and was an emerging star in Los Angeles, but his temper eventually tarnished his career as a Dodger. In his second season with the Dodgers, he even got the fans involved.

In the ninth inning of a 1995 game against St. Louis, Mondesi was ejected after arguing a strikeout call. Manager Tommy Lasorda suffered the same fate, and the Dodger Stadium fans, who had thrown souvenir balls on the field before the incident, tossed their remaining souvenirs in protest. The umpires forfeited the game to the Cardinals.

Mondesi overcame a poverty-stricken childhood in the Dominican Republic to become a major

league baseball player. His father died when Monday was only 7 and his mother raised her six children with the meager wages she earned from a laundry. Mondesi dropped out of school after the sixth grade. He learned to play baseball with a milk carton for a glove, a sock stuffed with paper for a ball and a limb from a guava tree as a bat. The first time the Dodgers saw the 17-year-old Mondesi play in 1988, however, they offered him a contract on the spot.

Mondesi made rapid progress with the Dodgers, moving from Class A Bakersfield to Class AAA Albuquerque in 1991. Evidence of a moody disposition then began to emerge. When the Dodgers recalled the more experienced Tom Goodwin to fill a temporary spot the following season, Mondesi responded by going AWOL. Instead of finishing the year in Los Angeles, he ended 1992 at Class AA San Antonio.

Mondesi was married over the winter and became a more mature ballplayer in 1993. He started the year in Albuquerque, and ended it in L.A. In 1994 Mondesi was the Dodgers right fielder, batting .306 with his 16 home runs and 16 outfield assists. He was the unanimous NL Rookie of the Year choice in 1994 and won Gold Gloves in 1995 and 1997.

He was named an All-Star in 1995, collecting 26 home runs, 88 RBIs, and a team high 91 runs scored. Mondesi had one of his best seasons in 1996. He led the Dodgers with 40 doubles and 98 runs scored. The following year he became the first Los Angeles player to hit 30 home runs and steal 30 bases. He racked up 191 hits and batted .310. After he signed a contract worth nearly $10 million per year, he slipped to .279 with 30 homers in 1998.

The 1999 season proved difficult for Mondesi, as well as the Dodgers, long reputed to have a divided clubhouse. Mondesi became the focal point of the team's lack of cohesion. During one game, he sat in the bullpen between innings, and in Montreal he unleashed a screaming fit against his general manager and manager. In the off-season the Dodgers traded Mondesi to Toronto for Shawn Green.

Don Money

Money, Donald Wayne **3B-2B-DH-SS-1B**

1968–83 B:6/7/1947, Washington, DC Deb:4/10/1968, PHI NL BR/TR 6'1", 190

G	AB	R	H	HR	RBI	OBP	SLG	AVG
1720	6215	798	1623	176	729	.330	.406	.261

Sure-handed third baseman Don Money established himself as a record-setting glove man in both major leagues. With the Phillies in 1972 he compiled a since-broken National League-record .978 fielding average. With Milwaukee in 1974 he established major league standards with only five errors in a season and a .989 fielding percentage. That year he also set big league marks with 88 consecutive errorless games and 261 consecutive errorless chances, a string that stretched from September 1973 to July 1974. No wonder his nickname was "Brooks," after legendary Oriole third sacker Brooks Robinson.

In June 1965 Syd Thrift, then a Pirates scout, signed Money as an amateur free agent. Originally a shortstop, Money led the Appalachian and Carolina Leagues in putouts, double plays, and assists at that position. He did not hit well until the 1967 season at Raleigh, when he batted .310, led the Carolina League in doubles, and was named its Most Valuable Player.

In December 1967 Pittsburgh traded Money and three other players to the Phillies in a transaction that sent pitcher Jim Bunning to the Pirates. Money played four games with Philadelphia in 1968 before being brought up to stay in 1969. He hit only .229 as a rookie, playing 126 games at shortstop. The next year he was shifted to third base to make room at short for Larry Bowa. That season Money batted a career-high .295 with 14 homers and 66 RBIs.

Money batted only .223 and .222 the next two seasons but performed ably at third base for the Phillies. After rookie third baseman and future Hall of Famer Mike Schmidt arrived in the majors, Money was traded in October 1972 to the Brewers as a part of a seven-player deal that brought pitcher Jim Lonborg to Philadelphia. In both 1976 and 1978 he played in the All-Star Game. In 1974 he was named to the squad but did not play. He was also selected in 1977 but was replaced because of an injury.

Money hit well in the clutch, particularly when coming off the bench. He was a pull-hitter who favored inside pitches, but he could be retired with breaking balls low and outside. From a closed, upright stance, he hit deep in the box. During his career Money collected 10 leadoff homers.

On April 10, 1976, Money experienced one of the stranger disappointments of his career. With the Brewers trailing the Yankees, 9–6, in the bottom of the ninth, Money stepped up to bat and hit the ball into the seats for what he thought was a game-winning grand slam. Neither Money nor Yankees pitcher Dave Pagan had realized that first baseman Chris Chambliss had called time. First base umpire Jim McKean made Money start all over again. He delivered an anticlimactic sacrifice fly.

In 1977 Money had his best power season, slamming 25 homers and driving in 83 runs. That season he was shifted to second base, and on June 24, 1977, he tied a major league record for second basemen with 12 assists in a nine-inning game.

In the strike-shortened 1981 season Money helped the Brewers to an American League East second-half title. In 1982 he batted .284 and hit 16 homers as the Brewers won the pennant. Money batted .231 in the seven-game World Series loss to the Cardinals.

Toward the end of his Brewers career Money filled in at second base, shortstop, and first base and as designated hitter. He did not appreciate players who put their own interests above those of the team. Money once commented about fellow Brewer George Scott, "He's an 'I' man. He's all for himself.... One time he held a team meeting and rapped the guys for not getting on base enough so he could drive in runs."

On April 11, 1980, Money and Cecil Cooper each hit grand slams in the same inning, only the fourth time ever that two teammates had accomplished the feat. After leaving the Brewers in 1983, Money played in Japan with the Kintetsu Buffalos. In 1999 he managed the Brewers' Class A Beloit Snappers of the Midwest League.

Willie Montanez

Montanez, Guillermo (Naranjo) **1B–OF**
1966–82 B:4/1/1948, Catano, Puerto Rico
Deb:4/12/1966, CAL AL BL/TL 6'1", 193

G	AB	R	H	HR	RBI	OBP	SLG	AVG
1632	5843	645	1604	139	802	.331	.402	.275

Willie Montanez was a colorful, almost legendary, character known for his hitting, fielding, charisma—and temper. No wonder Montanez was traded nine times in a 14-year career; many teams felt Montanez's energy was too much for one clubhouse to handle.

Still, there was no one who disputed his athletic skill. Originally signed by the Cardinals in 1965, Guillermo Montanez y Naranjo went to the Phillies in April 1970 as compensation for Curt Flood, who failed to report the previous October. As a rookie center fielder in 1971, Montanez stunned the National League by hitting 30 home runs—eight short of the major league rookie record set in 1930 by Wally Berger—and collecting 99 RBIs. The following year Montanez led the league with 39 doubles and 22 outfield assists.

The Phillies converted Montanez to first base in 1973, and by 1975 he led the league in assists. Montanez defended his assist crown with the Giants and Braves in 1976 and the Mets in 1978. He was error-prone, however, and led the league in that category in 1976. His flashy "snatch-catch" on popups did not make anyone feel sorry for him.

Montanez also left his mark as a hitter, three times batting over .300. He joined a small group of hitters in 1975 by driving in 101 runs with fewer than 15 home runs. In 1999 he was a Phillies scout, based in Caguas, Puerto Rico.

John Montefusco

Montefusco, John Joseph **P**

1974–86 B:5/25/1950, Long Branch, NJ Deb:9/3/1974, SF NL BR/TR 6'1", 180

W	L	PCT	G	SH	IP	BB	SO	ERA
90	83	.520	298	11	1652^{1}	513	1081	3.54

Outspoken and talented, Giants pitcher John Montefusco won 15 games as a rookie, including four shutouts. He also recorded 215 strikeouts that year, second only to Tom Seaver, and led the National League in strikeouts per game, averaging 7.94. His ERA was only 2.88. His efforts earned him league Rookie of the Year honors. "The Count of Montefusco," as he called himself, gave San Francisco fans a reason for hope. He talked a big game and he lived up to it. With Montefusco on the mound, the team climbed from fifth place to third.

The following year the Count pitched two scoreless innings against the AL All-Stars. His 16 wins that season included a no-hitter against the Atlanta Braves. He also increased his shutout total to a league-leading six and lowered his ERA to 2.84. Although the Giants finished a lackluster fourth, Montefusco was again among the league's toughest pitchers.

In 1977 Montefusco suffered an injury and dropped to 7–12. He recovered to post a winning season again in 1978, but arm problems continued to plague him. He mustered only three wins in 22 starts in 1979 and only four in 1980 as the Giants tried to revitalize him in a relief role. He fought with club manager Dave Bristol and was sent to the Braves.

Montefusco recorded only two wins and a save in nine starts and 17 relief appearances in Atlanta. He signed with San Diego in 1982 and went 10–11 as a regular in the rotation. The next year, with Dick Williams at the Padres' helm, the Count was shipped to the New York Yankees. He won five of his six starts for the Yankees, and fans began to wonder if his comeback was finally for real. It wasn't. He won only five more games for the Yankees in the next three years and retired from baseball after the 1986 season.

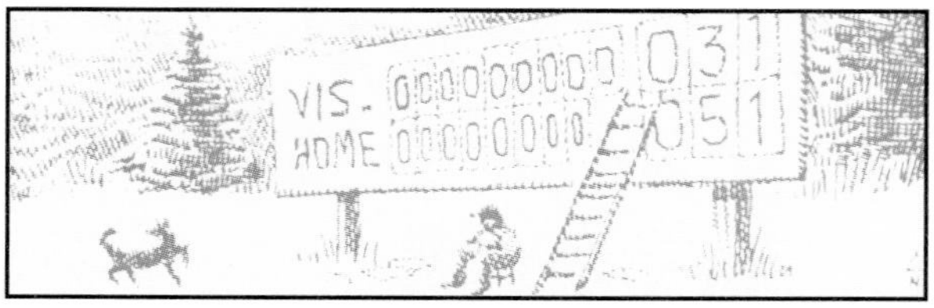

Jeff Montgomery

Montgomery, Jeffrey Thomas **P**

1987–99 B:1/7/1962, Wellston, OH Deb:8/1/1987, CIN NL BR/TR 5'11", 180

W	L	PCT	G	SV	IP	BB	SO	ERA
46	52	.469	700	304	868	296	733	3.27

Jeff Montgomery used location and guile to earn 304 saves for the Kansas City Royals. He did not have a blazing fastball or an unconventional pitching style like the sidearm delivery of his predecessor in Kansas City, Dan Quisenberry; Montgomery got outs by keeping hitters guessing. Only once did Montgomery strike out better than one batter per inning (50 in $44\frac{2}{3}$ in 1994). As his fastball slowed, Montgomery increasingly relied on a variety of curveballs, sliders, and changeups to remain effective.

Montgomery first emerged as a closer with a 7–3 record, 18 saves, and a 1.37 ERA for the Royals in 1989. Nevertheless, the team signed free agent stopper Mark Davis after the season. When Davis faltered in 1990, Montgomery resumed the closer's role and finished with 24 saves. He increased his total in each of the following three years. In 1993 Montgomery took the Rolaids Relief Man Award with a career-high 45 saves, which he achieved along with a 2.27 ERA and a .206 opponents' batting average. He had at least 24 saves in five of the next six seasons.

Wally Moon

Moon, Wallace Wade **OF-1B**

1954–65 B:4/3/1930, Bay, AR. Deb:4/13/1954, STL NL BL/TR 6', 175

G	AB	R	H	HR	RBI	OBP	SLG	AVG
1457	4843	737	1399	142	661	.374	.445	.289

Wally Moon and the Los Angeles Memorial Coliseum were a match made in heaven. The Dodgers outfielder used his unusual inside-out, lefthanded swing to punch hits off and over the 42-foot screen that stood only 251 feet from the plate. His "Moon Shots" were legendary even before he became a Dodger. In 1954, at age 24, Moon replaced Enos Slaughter in the St. Louis Cardinals' outfield. In his first major league at bat Moon hit a mammoth home run over the right-field pavilion in old Busch Stadium; the ball ultimately landed on Grand Boulevard. He hit .304 that season and won the Rookie of the Year Award.

During each of the next three seasons Moon hit at least .295 with 20 or more home runs. In 1957 Moon clouted 24 homers and put together two hitting streaks of at least 20 games. But he slumped in 1958, batting only .238 with seven homers and 38 RBIs.

The Dodgers had recently moved from Brooklyn to Los Angeles, where they played in the Memorial Coliseum, a facility erected for the 1932 Olympics. Because the distance from home plate to the outfield wall down the left field line was only 251 feet, a 42-foot screen was constructed to help prevent cheap home runs. Gambling that Moon's inside-out swing would give him an advantage in their makeshift ballpark, the Dodgers traded outfielder Gino Cimoli to the Cardinals for him in December 1958.

Moon shone bright in the Dodgers constellation, frustrating opposing pitchers by knocking their deliveries off or over the left field screen. In 1959 his .302 average, .396 on-base percentage, .495 slugging average, 19 home runs, and league-leading 11 triples helped the Dodgers win a surprise world championship.

He also contributed by informing his roommate, a struggling lefthanded pitcher named Sandy Koufax, that he had been tipping off his pitches with his delivery. On August 31, 1959, Koufax tied the major league record with 18 strikeouts in a nine-inning game. Moon won the game for his roommate, 5–2, with a dramatic ninth-inning, three-run blast.

Moon hit a home run in the 1959 World Series and followed up with two more productive seasons. In 1961 he hit .328 with a .505 slugging average, 89 walks, and a league-leading .438 on-base percentage. Opposing pitchers often opted to walk Moon rather than pitch to him in the Coliseum with runners on base.

In 1962 the Dodgers moved out of the Memorial Coliseum. Moon had so successfully adapted his swing to the friendly left field screen that he found it difficult to adjust to the Dodgers' new ballpark. He became a part-time player, and in the Dodgers' 1965 World Series victory he was used only as a pinch hitter. Moon retired after that season with 142 lifetime homers. He later became the baseball coach at John Brown University.

Charlie Moore

Moore Charles William **C–OF**

1973–87 B:6/21/1953, Birmingham, AL Deb:9/8/1973, MIL AL BR/TR 5'11", 180

G	AB	R	H	HR	RBI	OBP	SLG	AVG
1334	4033	456	1052	36	408	.321	.355	.261

Platooned at catcher for much of his lengthy career with the Milwaukee Brewers, Charlie Moore spent two seasons in everyday duty with the club as an outfielder. His regular season statistics were nothing special, but when the Brewers ended a lengthy postseason drought by winning the American League East in 1982, Moore suddenly displayed a red-hot bat. In the five-game Championship Series victory against the California Angels, he batted a team-high .462. Facing the St. Louis Cardinals in the World Series, Moore delivered with nine hits in 26 at bats for a .346 average. It was not enough, however, as St. Louis won the world championship in seven games.

Moore's heroic playoff performance won him another chance at a full-time job in right field the following season. He batted .284, but homered just twice in 529 at bats. He returned to an everyday role behind the plate in 1985. Moore finished his career with Toronto in 1987.

Donnie Moore

Donnie Ray Moore **P**

1975, 1977-88 B:2/13/1954, Lubbock, TX D:7/18/1989, Anaheim, CA Deb:9/14/1975, CHI NL BL/TR 6', 185

W	L	PCT	G	SV	IP	BB	SO	ERA
43	40	.518	416	89	655	186	416	3.67

It seemed that Donnie Moore had always come through for the California Angels. He had achieved 68 saves over the previous three seasons, plus another just days earlier as the Angels had forged ahead in the American League Championship Series against Boston. In the top of the ninth inning of Game 5, the journeyman turned relief ace was one out away from pitching the Angels into the 1986 World Series. The Angels never got there.

With two outs, a runner on first and his team clinging to a 5–4 lead, Moore had been summoned from the bullpen to face Red Sox reserve outfielder Dave Henderson. Moore was trying to get by on guile, rather than power; he had received a cortisone injection to his rib cage the previous night. Years later, teammate Doug DeCinces recalled his shock and disbelief when manager Gene Mauch, who had inexplicably lifted ace Mike Witt moments earlier, called upon his hurting closer to enter the game.

The injury, and the treatment, had taken a larger toll than either Moore or Mauch realized. Henderson turned on Moore's feeble 2–2 forkball for a two-run homer and gave the Sox a 6–5 lead. The Angels tied it in the bottom of the ninth, but Moore was still pitching in the 11th when Henderson's sacrifice fly gave the Red Sox the lead again—for good. Boston won the series in seven games.

Moore's life, already marred by heavy drinking and bursts of violent anger, went into a spiral after the ALCS. Injuries limited him to 14 appearances in 1987, and the California fans reminded him of his October failure every time he took the mound at home. The team released him in 1988 after a series of poor outings. Moore signed a minor league contract with Kansas City's AAA affiliate, but he was released again in June 1989.

Off the field, his marriage crumbled and bankruptcy loomed. On July 18, 1989, Moore shot his estranged wife, then killed himself with a gunshot to the head as his 10-year-old son watched in horror.

"All those people that booed him, I wonder how they feel," Tonya Moore, who survived three bullet wounds from her husband, asked in Mike Sowell's book, *One Pitch Away*. "Can they live with theirself, knowing each and every day that Donnie Moore might be dead because they didn't have enough courage to give him a hand?"

Jo-Jo Moore

Moore, Joseph Gregg **OF**

1930–41 B:12/25/1908, Gause, TX BL/TR
Deb:9/17/1930, NY NL BL/TR 5'11", 155

G	AB	R	H	HR	RBI	OBP	SLG	AVG
1335	5427	809	1615	79	513	.344	.408	.298

Jo-Jo Moore's slender build led to nicknames such as "Thin Man" and "The Gause Ghost." It also hurt his standing with the New York Giants. Manager John McGraw considered Moore too frail to compete in the National League, so the outfielder bounced back and forth between New York and the minor leagues. Moore only became the everyday left fielder when player-manager Bill Terry took over for the ill McGraw. Moore would help Terry's Giants win three National League pennants and a world championship.

Joseph Greg Moore attended Texas A&M and started out in the West Texas League in 1929. The Giants bought his contract from San Antonio after the 1930 season, and he played with Bridgeport, Newark, and Jersey City before coming up to the Giants to stay. Summoned from the minor leagues in 1932, Moore hit .305 in his first extended major league duty in 1932. The following year he helped New York win the World Series. The Giants also reached the Series in 1936 and 1937, but lost to the New York Yankees each time. Moore batted .391 in the 1937 championship; his nine hits tied a record for a five-game Series.

As the leadoff man, Moore didn't like to draw walks or take pitches; he was notorious for hitting the first pitch, so much so that many pitchers had standing orders to start him off with a pitch outside the strike zone. His speed and hustle from the left side of the plate aided his batting average and made him extremely difficult to double up on the bases. Moore hit .300 or better five times in his first seven full seasons, put together a 20-game hitting streak in 1932, and bettered it in 1934 with a 23-game skein.

When his hitting tailed off, the Giants tried to cut Moore's salary. Rather than accept less money, the six-time All-Star played two seasons for Indianapolis of the American Association. He later returned to his hometown of Gause, Texas, to run his farm and ranch.

Mike Moore

Moore, Michael Wayne **P**

1982–95 B:11/26/1959, Eakly, OK Deb:4/11/1982, SEA AL BR/TR 6'4", 205

W	L	PCT	ERA	G	SH	IP	BB	SO
161	176	.478	4.39	450	16	2831^{2}	1156	1667

Selected by the Seattle Mariners with the first overall pick in the 1981 amateur draft, Mike Moore came to the majors bearing the weight of high expectations. After experiencing rookie growing pains in 1982 with a 7–14 record, Moore showed improvement over the next two seasons, and seemed to break through in 1985, going 17–10 with a 3.46 ERA. But as Moore lost 47 games over the next three years, Seattle management soured on its one-time phenom and traded Moore to the division rival Oakland A's.

Moore quickly established himself as a mainstay in Tony LaRussa's Oakland rotation behind aces Dave Stewart and Bob Welch. He posted career bests in 1989 with 19 wins and a 2.61 ERA, and earned an All-Star berth as Oakland repeated as division champions. Moore tossed seven shutout innings in an ALCS victory over Toronto, and then posted a 2–0 record with a 2.08 ERA in two World Series starts against the Giants. The 1989 season began a streak of six seasons in which he won at least 11 games. After falling to 5–15 with the Tigers in 1995, Moore retired.

Terry Moore

Moore, Terry Bludord **OF**

1935–48 M(1954, 35–42) B:5/27/1912, Vernon, AL D:3/29/1995, Collinsville, IL Deb:4/16/1935, STL NL BR/TR 5'11", 195

G	AB	R	H	HR	RBI	OBP	SLG	AVG
1298	4700	719	1318	80	513	.340	.399	.280

In the years just before World War II, Terry Moore of the St. Louis Cardinals defined center field play in the National League. Whippet-fast, with a strong and accurate arm, he emulated Tris Speaker by playing so shallow that he turned would-be singles into outs. He also had Speaker's ability to break with the crack of the bat and outrun almost anything hit over his head.

Leo Durocher, then managing the Dodgers, was seldom lavish in complimenting opponents. But of the Cardinals' center fielder he said, "I don't see how they can rank anybody better than Moore. If a ball is in the air, he'll get it. Nobody can do better than that." No one appreciated Moore more than his own manager, Billy Southworth, who said, "To get an idea of Terry's worth, you should add to his batting average the base hits he cuts off every year."

Terry Bluford Moore grew up in St. Louis idolizing Chick Hafey, the Cards' center fielder of an earlier era. After a few years in the St. Louis farm system, Moore won the Cardinals' center field job as a rookie in 1935. The team had won the World Series the year before, putting young Moore squarely on the spot. He delivered.

There was never any question that he could catch anything hit in his direction, but he displayed a surprisingly dangerous bat as well. In one game he had four extra-base hits; in an early September contest he went 6-for-6. However, a week later he broke his leg sliding into second base. Without him, the Cardinals fell out of the league lead.

Because he was always chasing after flyballs and diving into bases, Moore was hampered by injuries throughout his career. In 1938 he lost nearly half a season after crashing into a concrete wall at Sportsman's Park. But he came back better than ever, earning the first of his four straight All-Star Game appearances in 1939.

Moore had large hands, but he wore perhaps the tiniest glove in the league—the fingers were only about three inches long. When he got his glove on the ball, though, it stayed there. Although he regarded his hitting as second in importance to his defense, he lifted his offensive output in 1939 by batting .295 with 17 home runs. The next year he repeated his home run total and batted over .300 for the only time in his career.

After a few so-so seasons, the Cardinals challenged for the pennant in 1941. They led the Dodgers during the summer, then fell back due to a rash of injuries. One of the most serious was a beaning that sidelined Moore with a concussion. While he was out of the lineup, Brooklyn steamed past St. Louis, and the Redbirds finished 2½ games back.

Named team captain in 1942, he also became a tutor. Rookie Stan Musial was slated for left field, and while he had all the talent in the world, "Stan the Man" remained a little raw on defense. Under Moore's guidance, Musial emerged as a solid defensive outfielder. The Cards' outfield—Musial, Moore, and Enos Slaughter—was the envy of the league.

The Dodgers held a 10½-game lead over the Cardinals in mid-August 1942. But St. Louis stayed healthy and won 43 of its final 51 games to win the pennant. They ambushed the favored Yankees in the World Series, winning in five games. Moore contributed a .294 batting average and his usual impeccable fielding.

He spent the next three years in the Army, and when he returned in 1946, he admitted, "I was a much better player before I went into the service than when I came out." Injuries limited him to only 91 appearances in 1946, and he hit only .263. Yet Moore still helped the Cards win another pennant. He was injected with painkillers before every game of the World Series against the Boston Red Sox, and despite a .148 batting average, when the seventh game ended he had his second world championship ring.

Although the Cardinals couldn't repeat as champions in 1947, Moore had a strong year, hitting .283. During one stretch he recorded nine consecutive hits, one shy of the major league record. In 1948, however, he slowed perceptibly and retired. He then served as a Cardinals coach and briefly managed the Phillies in 1954.

Bob Moose

Moose, Robert Ralph **P**

1967–76 B:10/9/1947, Export, PA D:10/9/1976, Martins Ferry, OH Deb: 9/19/1967, PIT NL BR/TR 6', 200

W	L	PCT	G	SV	IP	BB	SO	ERA
76	71	.517	289	19	1304^{1}	387	827	3.50

At age 21, Bob Moose was one of the most promising pitchers in the majors. He was dead just seven years later. Moose spent his entire major league career in Pittsburgh, a few miles from his hometown. He debuted as a teenager in 1967, posted a 2.73 ERA as a rookie the following year, and went 14–3—including a no-hitter against the eventual world champion New York Mets—in 1969.

He continued pitching between stints with the Marine Reserves. He had his busiest season in 1972, hurling 226 innings with a 13–10 record and 2.91 ERA, but it ended disastrously: Moose's wild pitch in the final game of the Championship Series gave Cincinnati the pennant.

Moose battled through a string of physical woes, including elbow problems and knee surgery. In 1974, he suffered a life-threatening blood clot in his pitching arm, necessitating two operations. He returned late the next season and made a key contribution to Pittsburgh's stretch drive, landing the Pirates in the postseason for the fifth time in six years.

Moose became the bullpen ace in 1976, leading the team in saves. Six days after the season ended, on his 29th birthday, Moose was en route to a party when he was killed in a car crash.

Jose Morales

Morales, Jose Manuel (Hernandez) DH-PH

1973–84 B:12/30/1944, Frederiksted, Virgin Islands Deb:8/13/1973, OAK AL BR/TR 6', 195

G	AB	R	H	HR	RBI	OBP	SLG	AVG
733	1305	126	375	26	207	.336	.408	.287

In 1976 Montreal's Jose Morales set a major league single-season record with 25 pinch hits. Originally a catcher who led four different minor leagues in errors, Morales was almost exclusively a pinch hitter and designated hitter in the majors. He finished his career with 123 pinch hits and 12 pinch-hit homers, ranking among the majors' top 10 in both categories.

Giants scout Pedro Zorilla signed Morales, a native of the Virgin Islands, in 1964. He was later drafted by Oakland and then sold to Montreal. He made his major league debut at age 28, but appeared in only 25 games for the Expos in 1974. The following season he batted .301 and led the National League with 15 pinch hits.

Morales saw action in 104 games in 1976, but 78 of his 158 at bats came as a pinch hitter. He batted a career-high .316 and late in the season broke the major league record with his 25th pinch hit. That eclipsed the previous mark of 24, set by St. Louis' Vic Davalillo in 1970 and Baltimore's Dave Philley in 1961. (John Vander Wal broke Morales' mark in 1995.)

Just days before the 1978 season was to begin, Morales was sold to Minnesota. In two of his three seasons with the Twins, Morales received more than 200 at bats. He hit better than .300 both of those seasons and twice led the AL in pinch hits. At the end of the 1980 season he signed with Baltimore as a free agent, but he played just one season with the Orioles. On April 28, 1982, Morales was traded to the Los Angeles Dodgers for third baseman Leo Hernandez.

Morales saw his only postseason action in 1983, when the Dodgers played the Phillies in the NLCS. He was hitless in two pinch-hit at bats, and the Dodgers were defeated in four games. Morales retired at age 39 after the 1984 season and went on to become a respected batting coach.

Pat Moran

Moran, Patrick Joseph C

1901–14 M (1915-1923, 748-586, .561) B:2/7/1876, Fitchburg, MA D:3/7/1924, Orlando, FL Deb:5/15/01, BOS NL BR/TR 5'10", 180

G	AB	R	H	HR	RBI	OBP	SLG	AVG
818	2634	198	618	18	262	.283	.312	.235

In 1915, his initial year managing the team, Pat Moran led the Philadelphia Phillies to the first National League pennant in their history. Four years later, he did the same in Cincinnati. The Reds won the 1919 World Series against the Chicago White Sox, but eight "Black Sox" were later banned from baseball for having fixed the Series.

A versatile athlete, Moran started his pro baseball career in 1897. He reached the National League with Boston in 1901. He quickly became the best defensive catcher in the NL. Moran twice led the league in both fielding and in double plays. His total of 214 assists (in just 107 games) in 1903 established a major league record.

A weak hitter, he later doubled as a pitching coach for the Phils. When the team's managerial position opened, his teammates talked the front office into giving the job to Moran. The Phils jumped from sixth place to first in his rookie year at the helm. After three more years with the club, Moran quit following a squabble with management. He got his next job as a result of miscommunication between management and manager.

Christy Mathewson, who had managed the Reds the previous three seasons, was in Europe recuperating from exposure to poison gas in the closing days of World War I. Owner Gary Herrmann sent several wires, but never heard from Mathewson. Moran, already signed as a coach with the New York Giants, was hired to replace Mathewson. Cincinnati improved by 22 games en route to the pennant. The underdog Reds defeated the White Sox in eight games in the best-of-nine World Series. A year later, eight members of the White Sox were indicted on charges of throwing the Series. Although a jury acquitted them, the "Black Sox" were banned from baseball for life. The decision likewise tainted Cincinnati's victory.

The Reds dipped in the standing the two years after the World Series, but Cincinnati rebounded for consecutive second-place finishes in 1922 and 1923. Moran's life ended abruptly when he died of Bright's disease in spring training 1924.

Keith Moreland

Moreland, Bobby Keith **OF-3B-1B-C-DH**
1978–89 B:5/2/1954, Dallas, TX Deb:10/1/1978, PHI NL BR/TR 6', 200

G	AB	R	H	HR	RBI	OBP	SLG	AVG
1306	4581	511	1279	121	674	.339	.411	.279

In six seasons with the Cubs, Keith Moreland came to epitomize the team. A powerful line-drive hitter with a lead glove, Moreland, like the Cubs, could score runs but also give them back in the field. "After you learn all the angles in this park, you could probably become a good pool player," Moreland said about playing the outfield in Wrigley Field. "On any given day, those lovely ivy-covered walls can bring you to your knees."

The 21-year-old Bobby Keith Moreland signed with the Phillies in 1975 and led Carolina League third basemen in errors in 1976. The Phillies gave up on Moreland at third base and made him a catcher. He led both the American Association and the Eastern League in passed balls the following season.

Moreland was promoted to Philadelphia at the end of 1978 and used as a back-up utility man and pinch hitter for three years. The righthanded hitter batted .333 in the 1980 World Series and .462 in the Division Playoffs of 1981. He was traded to the Cubs in December 1981.

Moreland became a nomadic regular with Chicago. He played third base one day, catcher the next and in the outfield the day after. Sportswriter Nick Peters put it bluntly when he wrote that "the guy can hit, but where to hide him?"

Playing several positions made a poor fielder into an even worse fielder. Moreland became the butt of jokes and even the subject of a song; "A Dying Cub Fan's Last Request," by Steve Goodman. In the song a dying Cub fan requests a funeral at Wrigley Field in which the Cubbies take the field and "have Keith Moreland drop a routine fly."

Moreland said he was upset about being included in the song because he would be remembered long after he left the game. Meanwhile, he batted over .300 twice and hit double-figures in home runs for six straight seasons from 1982 through 1987. In 1984 Moreland hit .279 with 80 RBIs to help win the NL East. He batted .333 in the NLCS.

In 1987 the Cubs moved Moreland full-time to third base, but that experiment only lasted one season. He was traded to San Diego in February 1988 and the Padres sent him to the Tigers in October 1988. In the middle of the 1989 season Moreland moved on to Baltimore and finally found his position, closing out his career as a designated hitter.

Omar Moreno

Moreno, Omar Renan (Quintero) **OF**
1975–86 B:10/24/1952, Puerto Armuelles, Panama Deb:9/06/1975, PIT NL BL/TL 6'2", 180

G	AB	R	H	HR	RBI	OBP	SLG	AVG
1382	4992	699	1257	37	386	.308	.343	.252

Born Omar Renan Moreno y Quintero in Panama, the talented outfielder was considered among the fastest men in the game during the late 1970s. Omar Moreno became a regular in the Pittsburgh Pirates' outfield in 1977. Batting leadoff, he hit safely occasionally and struck out often. But when he did get on, he often swiped additional bases and usually scored.

Moreno led the National League in thefts in 1978 and again in 1979, when he also scored 110 times—second only to Keith Hernandez of the Cardinals. He also provided enough defensive skill and hitting power to help the Pirates to the 1979 world championship.

In 1980 Moreno led the league in triples, with 13, and stole 96 bases. It was one fewer than league-leader Ron LeFlore's 97, but Moreno's mark still tied Ty Cobb's best base-stealing season. Moreno continued to survive on occasional contact and excessive speed until his Pirate contract expired at the end of 1982.

He signed with Houston and in August 1983 was dealt to the Yankees, where he saw regular action despite his declining speed. He finished his career as a utility outfielder for the Royals and the Braves.

Joe Morgan

Morgan, Joe Leonard **2B**
1963–84 B:9/19/1943, Bonham, TX Deb:9/21/1963, HOU NL BL/TR 5'7", 160

G	AB	R	H	HR	RBI	OBP	SLG	AVG
2649	9277	1650	2517	268	1133	.395	.427	.271

When the Big Red Machine was operating in the 1970s, Joe Morgan was its generator. And the generator was always running, even during the off-season. Morgan set up a gym in his garage, where he punched a speed bag, used handgrips and wrist rollers, and worked out every day before he got to his most serious training—dominoes. "In dominoes you have to concentrate on little things that happen and be able to remember them later," he explained. "When I make a mistake on the field, I put that mistake in the back of my head. When the same situation presents itself, I don't make the same mistake again."

Morgan made few mistakes on the field. On a Cincinnati team laden with All-Stars, Morgan was arguably the best between 1972 and 1977. During that six-year period he played in at least 141 games a season. He also walked more than 100 times each year and averaged 60 stolen bases, turning many of those walks into "doubles." Successful in nearly four out of every five steal attempts during his career, he stole 689 bases to rank among the all-time leaders.

Despite his 5-foot 7-inch, 150-pound frame, Morgan had plenty of pop in his bat. From 1972 to 1977 he averaged 21 homers and 84 RBIs, generally batting second in the Reds lineup. In the field, he won Gold Gloves every year from 1973 through 1977. He was named National League Most Valuable Player in both 1975 and 1976, the first back-to-back MVP winner since Ernie Banks in 1958 and 1959.

Morgan was an All-Star eight times, and helped his teammates win six division titles, four pennants, and two world championships. He was a first-year selection to the Hall of Fame in 1990.

Yet a fan who saw Joe Morgan on the field for the first time might have burst out laughing. Morgan wore a glove so small that spectators might have suspected that he bought his equipment in a toy store. At bat, the tiny second baseman would stride seriously to the plate and then, with a stony expression on his face, would flap his left arm up and down as he waited for the pitch.

But to see Morgan every day was to watch the most sincere athlete of his time. The consummate team player, "Little Joe" never led the league in batting average, RBIs, or home runs but consistently delivered key hits and plays in the clutch.

Scouts had ignored Joe Leonard Morgan at his Oakland high school. After he graduated, he went on to Oakland City College and Cal State-Hayward, where Houston scout Bill Wight recognized his talents. "He was small, and there wasn't much he could do about that," Wight would later say. "But I liked his aggressiveness. He was self-assured without being cocky." In the minors Morgan developed his distinctive arm flap before each pitch. His idol, Nellie Fox, had suggested the idea to him as a timing mechanism and as a reminder to keep his left shoulder up.

In 1964 at age 21, Morgan was named the Texas League MVP. In 1965 the lefthanded-hitting Morgan made it to the big leagues permanently—and, in the process, forced Nellie Fox to the bench. He recorded six hits in a 12-inning game on July 8, led the National League in walks, and won *The Sporting News* Rookie of the Year Award. In 1968 injuries limited him to only 10 games, but from 1969 through 1977 he stole at least 40 bases and scored at least 87 runs each season.

Despite twice being named to the All-Star team in Houston and showing enormous potential, Morgan was traded to the Reds in November 1971. Cincinnati also received Jack Billingham, a future 19-game winner, and Cesar Geronimo, a future .300 hitter, in the deal.

Harry Walker, the Houston manager, had labeled Morgan a troublemaker. "Anyone was a troublemaker who was smarter than Harry Walker," Morgan later explained, "and that didn't take much." Still, the front office had gotten the wrong impression.

The only trouble Morgan caused under Reds manager Sparky Anderson was for opposing teams. Anderson respected his second baseman's intelligence so much that he never relayed him a "take" sign in all their years together. From 1972 through 1976 Morgan led the league in on-base percentage four times, and averaged 22 homers and 62 stolen bases. More importantly for Morgan, the team won four division titles, three pennants, and two World Series.

In 1975 Morgan was named the NL MVP and got the game-winning hit with two out in the bottom of the ninth inning of the seventh game of the 1975 World Series against Boston. The Red Sox intentionally walked Pete Rose to face Morgan, who blooped a single to center to drive in Ken Griffey, Sr. with the winning tally.

Morgan's 1976 MVP season was a career best. He batted .320, hit 27 homers, drove in 111 runs and scored 113, stole 60 bases, and walked 114 times. It marked the third time in four years he hit at least 20 homers and stole more than 50 bases in the same season. During one 10-game stretch Morgan had at least one RBI in each game.

The Phillies decided to pitch around him in the 1976 NLCS, and Morgan went 0-for-7 but still scored two runs. The Yankees' decision to pitch to him in the Series was a big mistake. Morgan homered in the first inning of the opener, tripled, singled, and stole a base in Game 2, doubled in a run in Game 3, and walked, stole a base, and scored the first run of Game 4 as the Reds swept New York.

In 1977 he set a record for second basemen, making only five errors and handling 715 chances, but he tailed off a bit offensively in 1978 and 1979. Little Joe went to the NLCS again with the Reds in 1979, but the Pirates swept Cincy; Morgan went hitless.

On January 31, 1980, Morgan signed with the Astros as a free agent, and he helped his original team win the division title. The following season he went to play for Giants manager Frank Robinson, an old friend from Oakland. In 1982 the

Dodgers trailed the Braves by a game entering the final day of the season. San Francisco was hosting Los Angeles, and Morgan hit a dramatic home run to eliminate the Dodgers.

In 1983 Morgan was reunited with former colleagues Pete Rose and Tony Perez in Philadelphia, and he hit 16 homers, knocked in 59 runs, and scored 72 to help the "Wheeze Kid" Phillies win the pennant. Morgan homered twice in a losing cause as the Orioles won the Series.

Morgan made his 1984 farewell with Oakland memorable by replacing Rogers Hornsby as the most prolific home run-hitting second baseman of all time, with 268 (Ryne Sandberg later passed him). He then became a noted broadcaster for the Athletics, ABC, ESPN, and NBC.

Even though he was small, there was little Morgan couldn't do on a baseball field. He stole close to 700 bases, slammed 268 homers, and drew 1,865 walks. Morgan was named to nine National League All-Star teams. Despite having led all second basemen in errors in his rookie season, Morgan went on to lead second basemen in fielding percentage three times and won five Gold Gloves.

In his Hall of Fame acceptance speech, Morgan said, "I take my vote as a salute to the little guy, the one who doesn't hit 500 home runs. I was one of the guys that did all they could to win. I'm proud of my stats, but I don't think I ever got one for Joe Morgan. If I stole a base, it was to help us win a game, and I like to think that's what makes me a little special."

Mike Morgan

Morgan, Michael Thomas **P**

1978–79, 1982–83, 1985–* B:10/8/1959, Tulane, CA Deb:6/11/1978, OAK AL BR/TR 6'2", 215

W	L	PCT	G	SH	IP	BB	SO	ERA
134	180	.427	477	10	2598²	872	1310	4.19

Mike Morgan made his first major league start only a week after his high school graduation; he lost—something he got used to during his well-traveled major league career. Morgan was 18 years old when Oakland made him the fourth pick overall in the 1978 draft. He pitched a complete game in his professional debut, a 3–0 loss to Baltimore, but he was pounded in his next two starts and was quickly shipped to the minors.

Morgan spent most of the next three seasons in the minor leagues before being traded to the New York Yankees. That began his long and winding road through 11 organizations in the 19 years he's spent in the major leagues, not including two separate stints with the Cubs. In 1999 he became the first pitcher of the century to appear for 11 major league teams.

The peripatetic pitcher was in his 11th season when he posted his first winning record in the majors. He went 14–10 with the Dodgers in 1991, and appeared in his only All-Star Game. He followed with a 16–8 season for the Cubs in 1992, finishing third in the National League in wins and sixth in ERA.

When Morgan went a combined 12–25 over the next two seasons, many figured his career was finally over. But the Cardinals, Reds, Twins, Cubs, and Rangers all thought he could still pitch. After 21 professional seasons, he finally made his postseason debut in 1998 with the Cubs. His fourth winning season came in 1999, when he was 13–10 for Texas despite a 6.24 ERA.

George Moriarty

Moriarty, Goerge Joseph **3B-1B-OF**

1903–04, 1906–16 M(1927–28, 150–157) U(1917–26, 1929–40) B:6/7/1884, Chicago, IL D:4/8/1964, Miami, FL Deb:9/27/1903, CHI NL BR/TR 6', 185

G	AB	R	H	HR	RBI	OBP	SLG	AVG
1076	3671	372	920	5	376	.303	.312	.251

Umpire George Moriarty once called Jimmy Dykes out on strikes, much to Dykes' chagrin. The smoldering batter then turned to the arbiter and asked innocently enough, "How do you spell your name?" Moriarty obliged, and Dykes responded: "That's what I thought. Only one 'i.'"

Moriarty did more in baseball than serve as Dykes' straight man. A speedy player in his day who stole home 11 times, Moriarty began professionally with the Cubs, and then spent time with Little Rock and Toledo before making it back to the majors with the Highlanders. Sold to Detroit in January 1909, he became team captain. Moriarty finished his major league career with the White Sox and served as player-manager at Memphis for part of 1916.

In 1926 and 1927 he managed the Tigers, stepping down from a job as an American League umpire to take the post. After two seasons he returned to umpiring. In 1932 Moriarty dared the entire White Sox team to fight him. When pitcher Milt Gaston stepped forward, Moriarty flattened him with one punch—but broke his hand in the process.

In the 1935 World Series, after some blistering repartee, Moriarty ran Charlie Grimm and two others off the Cubs' bench. When a report was filed with Commissioner Kenesaw Landis, he fined all concerned—including Moriarty—$200 each.

After retiring as an umpire, Moriarty served the American League in a public relations capacity. He later scouted for Detroit, signing Harvey Kuenn, Billy Hoeft, and Bill Tuttle.

Ed Morris

Morris, Edward **P**

1884–90 B: 8/29/1862, Brooklyn, NY D: 4/12/1937, Pittsburgh, PA Deb: 5/1/1884, COL AA BB/TL 5'6", 165

W	L	PCT	G	SH	IP	BB	SO	ERA
171	122	.584	311	29	2678	498	1217	2.82

Ed "Cannonball" Morris won 114 games in his first three seasons in the American Association from 1884 to 1886. He had a league-best .723 winning percentage as a rookie, and threw a no-hitter is his first month with the Columbus Buckeyes. The AA dropped the Ohio club the following year, but the 34-game winner and nine teammates were sent to Pittsburgh to help the struggling Alleghenys.

Morris won 39 games and Pittsburgh jumped seven places in the standings from the previous year. He led the league in games, complete games, shutouts, strikeouts, and lowest opponents' batting average. He led the league with 41 wins and 12 shutouts in 1886. Pittsburgh jumped to the National League the following year, but things did not bounce Cannonball's way. On the field, a new rule prohibited his explosive leaping delivery; off the field, his drinking led to a suspension and ineffective pitching. In 1888, though, Morris worked on his motion and tried to keep out of trouble, and the result was far more positive—a 29–23 record and an NL-best 54 complete games in 1888.

Morris completed 217 of his 219 starts over a four-year span, including all 126 starts in 1885 and 1886. By 1889 a sore arm and other maladies limited him to a 6–13 record. He joined Pittsburgh's Players' League entry in 1890, and finished his career with an 8–7 mark. After retiring from baseball, Morris ran several businesses in the Pittsburgh area, and later worked for Allegheny County as a prison guard and highway superintendent.

Hal Morris

Morris, William Harold **1B**

1988–* B:4/9/1965, Fort Rucker, AL Deb:7/29/1988, NY AL BL/TL 6'4", 215

G	AB	R	H	HR	RBI	OBP	SLG	AVG
1147	3829	511	1169	73	499	.363	.435	.305

Hal Morris batted .300 three times in four years in the New York Yankees organization, yet he was traded to Cincinnati in December 1990. Less than a year later, he had a World Series ring.

Morris quickly made his mark as a rookie in 1990. He batted .340 in 309 at bats as the Reds won the NL West division. Morris then hit .417 in Cincinnati's Championship Series triumph, and drove in the eventual winning run as the Reds completed a World Series sweep of Oakland. In 1991 Morris battled for the National League batting title with Atlanta's Terry Pendleton until the season's final game; Pendleton won by a point, .319–.318.

Despite his consistent hitting and solid fielding, Morris never quite secured his hold on the team's first-base job. He lacked the power most teams expected from a first baseman; his best year was 16 homers and 80 RBIs in 1996. More importantly, his health was a constant concern; only twice in his first nine full seasons did Morris play more than 115 games. Shoulder surgery limited him to 96 games in 1997, as he batted .276 and hit just one homer.

The Reds declined to pick up his 1998 option, and Morris moved on to Kansas City—where his unconventional batting stance earned him the nickname "Happy Feet." Morris bounced back with a .309 average and appeared in 127 games at three different positions. Morris rejoined Cincinnati as a reserve in 1999.

Jack Morris

Morris, John Scott **P**

1977-94 B: 5/16/1955, St. Paul, MN Deb: 7/26/1977, DET AL BR/TR 6'3", 200

W	L	PCT	G	SH	IP	BB	SO	ERA
254	186	.577	549	28	3824	1390	2478	3.90

Jack Morris was the type of pitcher a manager wanted on the mound with everything on the line; he almost always came through—especially in October. He went to the World Series three times with three different teams, and won three world championships. He received the Babe Ruth Award in the World Series twice, and he was named the 1991 Series Most Valuable Player for his masterful 10-inning shutout in Game 7 against the Atlanta Braves.

Morris broke into the starting rotation of the Detroit Tigers in 1979. He won 17 games, marking the first of 14 double-digit victory seasons. He won 162 games during the 1980s, but the only time he led the American League in wins during that decade was in strike-shortened 1981 with 14 wins.

The Tigers got off to a stellar 35–5 start in 1984, including a no-hitter by Morris against the Chicago White Sox. Led by his 19 wins, Detroit captured the AL East title by 15 games. Morris

breezed to an 8–1 win in the Championship Series opener against the Kansas City Royals.

He surrendered a lead in the first inning of Game 1 of the World Series, but did not allow another run the rest of the way in a 3–2 complete-game victory. After the Tigers and San Diego Padres split the next two games, Morris pitched a complete game in Game 4 at Tiger Stadium. Detroit won its fourth world championship the next day.

The gruff Minnesota native joined the Twins as a free agent in 1991. He made the All-Star team for the fifth time, and helped the Twins become the first AL team to ever go from last place to first place in one season. Morris won twice as the Twins defeated the Toronto Blue Jays in the ALCS. He started three games in the World Series, allowing only three runs in 23 innings. He pitched out of a second-and-third, none out jam in the seventh inning of Game 7; he allowed only seven hits in 10 innings to win one of the greatest pitching duels to ever decide a Series.

The next day Morris declared free agency. He went to Toronto, where he led the AL with 21 wins. He didn't fare well in the postseason (0–3, 7.57 ERA), but still got his second consecutive championship ring. No longer a 200-inning workhorse, he pitched poorly for Toronto in 1993. He won 10 games for the Cleveland Indians before the strike ended the 1994 season. Morris tried to resurrect his career, even pitching for the independent St. Paul Saints, but he could not earn a return to the major leagues.

Lloyd Moseby

Moseby, Lloyd Anthony **OF**

1980–91 B:11/5/1959, Portland, AR Deb:5/24/1980, TOR AL BL/TR 6'3", 200

G	AB	R	H	HR	RBI	OBP	SLG	AVG
1588	5815	869	1494	169	737	.334	.414	.257

Lloyd Moseby was an impressive athlete with power, speed, and fielding ability who never quite reached stardom. The center fielder shared his fate with a Blue Jay outfield that included Jesse Barfield and George Bell and that many thought would be the best in baseball. Unfortunately, none met inflated expectations.

After his Little League coach cut him, Lloyd Anthony Moseby concentrated on basketball where he picked up the nickname "Shaker" because of his ability to elude defenders. He returned to baseball in high school and was good enough to be selected by the Blue Jays in the first round—the second choice overall—in June 1978.

Moseby played in Medicine Hat, Dunedin, and Syracuse before making the Blue Jays in 1980. Three years later he became the first Blue Jay to score 100 runs. He had a 21-game hitting streak, hit .315, stole 27 bases and was named to *The Sporting News* 1983 AL All-Star Team.

Moseby had another excellent season in 1984 leading the league with 15 triples, stealing 39 bases with 78 walks and 92 RBIs. He hit only .226 in the 1985 ALCS but tied for the team lead with four RBIs.

In the 1989 ALCS against Oakland, Moseby hit .313 with five walks. Afterward he signed with the Tigers as a free agent and played for two seasons in Detroit. He spent the 1992 season playing in Japan before retiring. In 1999 he coached for the Jays.

Wally Moses

Moses, Wallace **OF**

1935–51 B:10/8/1910, Uvalda, GA D:10/10/1990, Vidalia, GA Deb:4/17/1935, PHI AL BL/TL 5'10", 160

G	AB	R	H	HR	RBI	OBP	SLG	AVG
2012	7356	1124	2138	89	679	.364	.416	.291

Wallace "Wally" Moses finished his 17-year major league career with a .291 batting average, 174 stolen bases and 89 home runs. These are respectable numbers, but not numbers that qualify one for accolades like "great hitter," "a threat on the basepaths," or "power hitter." Yet, at some point in his career, Moses was all of these.

Moses started with Augusta in the Palmetto League in 1931, then played with Elmira, Monroe, Tyler, and Galveston before reaching Philadelphia in 1935. The outfielder broke his left arm running into a wall in August and was out for rest of the season.

In his seven seasons with the Athletics Moses proved to be a "great hitter," batting over .300 each season. And though he never hit as many as 10 homers in a season before or after, Moses certainly qualified as a "power hitter" in 1937 when he slammed 25 home runs and 86 extra-base-hits for a .550 slugging percentage.

Moses was to be traded to Detroit in December 1939, but the deal was canceled when Commissioner Kenesaw Mountain Landis declared Benny McCoy, who was to be traded for Moses, a free agent. Landis ordered free agency for a number of Tigers farm hands that the club had stockpiled. Two years later Moses was traded to the Chicago White Sox in December.

Though he never stole more than 21 bases in any other season Moses was certainly "a threat on the basepaths" in 1943 when he was second in the league with 56 swiped bases.

The White Sox traded Moses to the Red Sox in July 1946 in time for him to get a chance to play in his only World Series. He hit .417 in the Fall Classic and rapped four hits in one game. The Red Sox released Moses in November 1948 and he returned to the Athletics with whom he finished his career in 1951. He later became a successful batting coach.

Don Mossi

Mossi, Donald Louis **P**

1954–65 B:1/11/1929, St. Helena, CA Deb:4/17/1954, CLE AL BL/TL 6'1", 195

W	L	PCT	G	SV	IP	BB	SO	ERA
101	80	.558	460	50	1548	385	932	3.43

Rookie Don Mossi teamed with Ray Narleski to form a great bullpen tandem for the Cleveland Indians in the pennant-winning season of 1954. Donald Louis Mossi had started his pro career with Bakersfield of the California League in 1949 and 1950. He also pitched with Wilkes-Barre of the Eastern League, Wichita of the Western League, and Dallas and Tulsa of the Texas League.

In 1954 he was the starting pitcher on the day the Indians won their record-tying 110th game of the season. Mossi was 6–1 that season, with seven saves and an ERA of 1.94, and, although the Indians lost the World Series in four straight to the Giants, he was effective in the series, surrendering no runs in three appearances.

"The efficiency of their [Mossi's and Narleski's] work in the Indian bullpen was only overshadowed by their almost total lack of color and personality outside of it," wrote Brendan Boyd and Fred C. Harris in *The Great American Baseball Card Flipping, Trading and Bubble Gum Book.* As these writers put it, they looked like "two small-town undertakers who, having found the world at large a particularly cold and hardhearted place to do business in, have banded together in a separate and distrustful partnership for the purpose of self-preservation."

Traded as a pair, Narleski and Mossi were dealt to Detroit in November 1958. Mossi became a starter, winning 15 games in 1961, then later returned to relief. Sold to the White Sox in 1964, he finished his career with Kansas City in 1965.

An excellent fielder, Mossi had a lifetime .990 fielding average—a major league record for a pitcher that was later tied by Gary Nolan. After retiring from baseball Mossi installed Masonite in Ukiah, California.

Manny Mota

Mota, Manuel Rafael (Geronimo) **OF**

1962–82 B:2/18/1938, Santo Domingo, Dominican Republic Deb:4/16/1962, SF NL BR/TR 5'11", 168

G	AB	R	H	HR	RBI	OBP	SLG	AVG
1536	3779	496	1149	31	438	.358	.389	.304

The most accomplished pinch hitter in major league history, Manny Mota holds the record with 150 career pinch hits. "He could wake up on Christmas morning and rip a single into right field," quipped columnist Jim Murray.

Manuel Rafael Mota y Geronimo signed with the Giants in 1957. His bonus: $400, plus a plane ticket from his native Dominican Republic to the United States. Mota played with Michigan City, Danville, Phoenix, Springfield, Rio Grande Valley, Tacoma, and El Paso before hitting .176 for the Giants in 1962. In the off-season he was traded twice and ended up with Pittsburgh.

Mota played outfield, catcher, third base, and second base for the Pirates but did show any real fielding ability at any position. He was the Expos' first selection in the October 1968 expansion draft but was traded to the Dodgers with Maury Wills for Ron Fairly in June 1969.

As a pinch hitter and backup outfielder Mota hit over .300 for the Dodgers in five consecutive seasons from 1969 to 1973. The righthanded Mota hit .600 in three NLCS for the Dodgers but went hitless in three World Series. When he retired after the 1979 season, Mota was second on the all-time pinch-hit list behind Smoky Burgess. But when the Dodgers reactivated him on August 29, 1980, after Reggie Smith was injured, Mota recorded three pinch hits in seven at bats and passed Burgess' record.

Mota, a Dodgers coach, had one more at bat when he was activated at the end of 1982. He finished his career a .304 hitter and .297 as a pinch hitter (150-for-505). Mota continued his baseball career as a manager, working six seasons in the Dominican Winter League with Licey, Cambrioso, and Escogido and was named Manager of the Year in 1984 with Cambrioso.

Though his official birth date is February 18, 1938, it is said Mota is older, that he lied about his age when he was scouted. He had four sons in professional baseball and owned a restaurant in Santo Domingo called "Manny Mota's Dugout." He also operates the Manny Mota Youth League in the Dominican Republic.

Mike Mowrey

Mowrey, Harry Harlan **3B–SS**

1905–17 B:4/20/1884, Browns Mill, PA D:3/20/1947, Chambersburg, PA Deb:9/24/1905, CIN NL BR/TR 5'10", 180

G	AB	R	H	HR	RBI	OBP	SLG	AVG
1276	4291	485	1099	7	461	.334	.329	.256

Sometimes chemistry plays a big part in a player's success. The chemistry in St. Louis was just right for Cardinals third baseman Harry Harlan "Mike" Mowrey between 1910 and 1914. But playing with other clubs in the rest of his 13-year career, Mowrey struggled. The 20-year-old started his major league career with the Reds in 1905. The following season he hit .321 but in 1907 he suffered with a .252 average and played his way into being a part-timer Cincinnati.

Traded to the Cardinals on August 22, 1909, he became a much better player. He became known for the distinctive way he fielded a grounder. He would make no attempt to catch the ball but would flag it down with his glove and pick the ball off the dirt.

In 1910 Mowrey batted .282 and stole 21 bases. He topped the National League in double plays in 1912 and 1913 and saved the Cardinals many runs with his defensive play.

He was traded to Pittsburgh in an eight-player deal on December 12, 1913. Known as the "Five for Three Deal," Barney Dreyfuss had offered Miller Huggins a list of 12 Pirates to choose from in order to obtain Ed Konetchy, Bob Harmon, and Mowrey.

The Pirates were disappointed with the deal and finished seventh in 1914. A pulled tendon in his leg bothered Mowrey early in the 1914 season. He and Konetchy jumped to the Federal League Pittsburgh Rebels in 1915 where Mowrey led Federal League third basemen in fielding and assists in 1915.

Sold to the Brooklyn Dodgers as part of a Federal League settlement on February 10, 1916, he replaced Gus "Gee-Gee" Getz at third base for Brooklyn and led the NL in fielding percentage in 1916. In the eighth inning of Game 2 of the 1916 World Series, Mowrey was caught in a rundown between third and home. The game went on to be a legendary 14-inning duel between pitchers Babe Ruth and Sherry Smith, won by Boston, 2–1. Mowrey became something of the goat of the Series hitting only .176 with two errors.

After the 1916 season Mowrey and shortstop Ollie O'Mara held out and Charles Ebbets sent both to the minors. Mowrey finally signed a contract, spent the rest of 1917 back with Brooklyn, and retired at the end of the season.

Don Mueller

Mueller, Donald Frederick **OF**

1948–59 B:4/14/1927, St. Louis, MO Deb:8/2/1948, NY NL BL/TR 6', 185

G	AB	R	H	HR	RBI	OBP	SLG	AVG
1245	4364	499	1292	65	520	.324	.390	.296

Nicknamed "Mandrake the Magician" for his ability to poke hits through holes in the defense, New York Giants outfielder Don Mueller narrowly missed what should have been the two defining moments of his career. In the ninth inning of the final National League playoff game of 1951 Mueller delivered a key single but injured his ankle sliding into third base. He had to be replaced, and consequently missed scoring on Bobby Thomson's historic "Shot Heard 'Round the World" homer. Three years later he went into the last day of the season tied for the batting championship but lost to teammate Willie Mays by mere percentage points.

Mueller came from a baseball family. His father, Walter Mueller, played four seasons in the major leagues in the 1920s, and his brother was a minor leaguer with the Red Sox. Mueller grew up outside of St. Louis and played for Christian Brothers High School and on a Legion League team. Signed by Hall of Famer Mel Ott, Mueller arrived with the Giants in 1948 after stints in Jersey City and Jacksonville. The lefthanded-hitting, righthanded-throwing rookie was a poor outfielder and did not hit for power. But he was an exceptional contact hitter who batted .296 during his 12-year career and struck out only 146 times in 4,364 at bats.

In the deciding playoff game against the crosstown Dodgers on October 3, 1951, Alvin Dark led off the ninth with a single and Mueller singled him to second. After Monte Irvin popped out, Whitey Lockman ripped a double to left, scoring Dark and advancing Mueller to third. But Mueller injured his ankle sliding into third. As he was taken off the field Dodgers manager Chuck Dressen brought in pitcher Ralph Branca in relief. Branca promptly yielded Thomson's game-winning homer. Mueller remained out of the lineup for the World Series.

In 1953 Mueller hit .333. He entered the last day of the 1954 season tied with teammate Willie Mays for the NL batting title. Mays cut down his swing and stroked a series of singles to right field to win the crown. "It was a hard pill for me to swallow," admitted Mueller. "I got two hits in six times at bat, but Willie went 3-for-4. He finished on top with .3451. I was second with .3425. Willie fooled everybody. Robin Roberts was pitching for Philadelphia. All season Willie had been pulling the ball—he hit 41 home runs—but against Roberts he kept pushing the ball to right field."

Mays explained, "I did that against him all the time. Robin always kept the ball over the outside of the plate, so you had to forget about pulling it." Mays and Mueller were the last two National League teammates to finish first and second in a batting race in the 20th century. Mueller led the Giants with seven hits and batted .389 in the team's 1954 World Series sweep of Cleveland. But once again Mays stole the spotlight with his incredible over-the-shoulder catch in Game 1.

In 1955 Mueller batted .306 and put together a career-best 24-game hitting streak. But he slumped to .269 in 1956 and .258 in 1957. In March 1958 the Giants sold Mueller to the White Sox. In 1959 he left baseball and became a building inspector for an insurance company. He retired from the insurance business in 1983.

Terry Mulholland

Mulholland, Terence John **P**

1986–* B:3/9/1963, Uniontown, PA Deb: 6/8/1986, SF NL BR/TL 6'3", 206

W	L	PCT	G	SH	IP	BB	SO	ERA
103	115	.472	415	10	1990	514	1046	4.22

Broadcaster Bob Brenly called Terry Mulholland "the definition of the serviceable lefthander." His tendency to make return stops suggest that his employers value him as something more; Mulholland has had three stints with the San Francisco Giants and two each with the Philadelphia Phillies and Chicago Cubs, plus brief stops with the New York Yankees, Seattle Mariners, and Atlanta Braves.

Mulholland enjoyed his greatest success in his longest major league stay, with Philadelphia from 1989 to 1993. The lefty with the dazzling pickoff move threw a no-hitter against San Francisco on August 15, 1990. He won a career-high 16 games the following year, and earned the start in the 1993 All-Star Game. After leaving Philadelphia he endured four sub-.500 seasons before re-establishing himself with the Cubs in 1998. He contributed from the bullpen and the rotation as Chicago stole the Wild Card down the stretch. He did much the same for Atlanta in 1999.

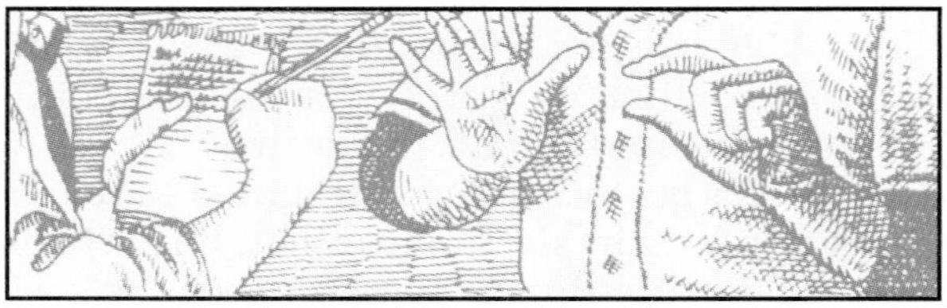

Tony Mullane

Mullane, Anthony John **P–OF**

1881–84, 1886–94 B:1/20/1859, Cork, Ireland D:4/25/1944, Chicago, IL Deb:8/27/1881, DET NL BB/TB 5'10½", 165

W	L	PCT	G	SH	IP	BB	SO	ERA
284	220	.563	555	30	4531[1]	1408	1803	3.05

G	AB	R	H	HR	RBI	OBP	SLG	AVG
784	2720	407	661	8	223	.307	.316	.243

One of the best pitchers of the 19th century, Tony Mullane was a showman both on and off the field. His stylish wardrobe, dark wavy hair, handsome features, and carefully waxed mustache made him a favorite with women and earned him the nickname "Count"—or, in a more disdainful form, "the Count of Macaroni." He was also called "the Apollo of the Box" because of his athletic build.

On the street, he looked like a leading man of the theater. Instead he was the leading figure, often on the losing end, in several battles with baseball club owners. He was as strong willed as he was physically strong, and his disputes cost him a chance to win 300 games, condemned him to a career of pitching for inferior teams, and may have kept him out of the Hall of Fame.

Irish-born Anthony John Mullane moved with his family to the United States, settling near Erie, Pennsylvania. As a young man, he was an all-around athlete, talented in boxing, skating, and baseball. He turned professional in 1880 as a righthanded pitcher with an independent team in Akron. Midway through the 1881 season, the National League's Detroit Wolverines offered Mullane a tryout, but he refused to appear until they tendered him a contract. The Wolverines then discovered that he had hurt his right arm and was pitching lefthanded. Mullane was not effective for the Wolverines, but his arm had recovered by the time he joined Louisville of the American Association in 1882.

Thereafter he usually pitched righthanded, but on occasion would switch arms, sometimes while a batter was at the plate. Three 19th-century pitchers are known to have thrown from both sides, but Larry Corcoran and Elton "Icebox" Chamberlain apparently tried the stunt only once (Greg A. Harris also "switch-pitched" once in 1995). Mullane did it fairly regularly. He wore no glove and could hide his choice until the last second. Of course the deception aided a devastating pickoff move. A versatile performer, Mullane often played the outfield when not on the mound, and played all four infield positions.

Mullane depended on his fastball but also threw a "drop," and he was often able to induce batters to swing at pitches off the plate. A master of intimidation, he hit so many batsmen that he was the main reason the AA passed a rule awarding first base to a hit batter.

In 1882 Mullane went 30–24 for Louisville and led the AA with 170 strikeouts. On September 11 against Cincinnati he pitched a no-hitter, the first recorded in league history. Pitching for the St. Louis Browns in 1883, he improved his record to 35–15 for the best winning percentage in the American Association.

When the Union Association announced that it intended to become a third major league in 1884, Mullane was a prime target for the new organization. He turned down the Browns' offer of $1,900 for the season and signed with the Unions for $2,500, violating the recently adopted—and legally untested—reserve clause. Despite a threat of blacklisting, he refused to return to the Browns. His rights were then shifted to Toledo of the AA in an attempt to prevent his playing with the Unions or helping one of the Browns' AA rivals.

Toledo, a new team, was unlikely to play any part in the pennant race. Mullane backed out of his UA contract when Toledo agreed to pay him $2,500 amid rumors that other AA teams were actually chipping in on the contract. Henry V. Lucas, the man behind the UA, obtained an injunction preventing Mullane from pitching in a game at St. Louis, but when Lucas tried to get the same ruling in Cincinnati, the judge threw the request out of court on the grounds that baseball was a sport and beneath the court's dignity.

Mullane won a career-high 37 games with Toledo in 1884. His catcher was Moses Fleetwood Walker, the first African-American to play Major League Baseball. Mullane resented having to pitch to a black receiver.

The Union Association collapsed after one season, as did Toledo of the AA. Mullane was sold back to St. Louis, but he signed instead with Cincinnati for $5,000, including a $2,000 advance. St. Louis owner Chris Von der Ahe charged Mullane with violating "baseball law" and brought him before the AA's directors. They suspended Mullane for a year and forced him to return $1,000 of Cincinnati's advance, yet he remained Reds property.

Mullane pitched for Cincinnati from 1886 through the middle of 1893. The team joined the National League in 1890 but seldom factored in pennant races. Mullane compiled an impressive record, twice topping 30 wins and winning more than 20 three other times. On September 20, 1888, he won both ends of a doubleheader against Philadelphia, 1–0 and 2–1.

On July 30, 1892, he pitched a 20-inning, 7–7 tie against Chicago. In midseason, the Reds abruptly slashed Mullane's salary from $4,200 to $3,500. When the pitcher protested, he was told his contract was "not worth the paper it is written on" and was handed a new one at the lower figure. He held out, but the Cincinnati owner preferred saving $700 to fielding a stronger team. By the following January, a desperate Mullane signed for only $2,100.

Cincinnati traded him to Baltimore in 1893, and he finished the season with 189 walks against only 95 strikeouts, one of the worst ratios in major league history. In late 1894 Baltimore passed Mullane on to Cleveland, but he was only 7–11 with a 6.59 ERA that season.

Mullane, who neither drank nor smoked, was firmly labeled a troublemaker. While he was not exactly booted out of the majors, his National League career ended as soon as his talents slipped to the average level. In 1895 he joined St. Paul of the respected Western League and won 60 games in three seasons. After a brief spell as an umpire, Mullane became a Chicago policeman and rose to the rank of detective. Despite his Catholic upbringing, he was married and divorced several times.

George Mullin

Mullin, George Joseph **P**

1902–15 B:7/4/1880, Toledo, OH D:1/7/1944, Wabash, IN Deb:5/4/1902, DET AL BR/TR 5'11" 188

W	L	PCT	G	SV	IP	BB	SO	ERA
228	196	.538	487	8	3686[2]	1238	1482	2.82

George Mullin was one of the greatest pitchers in Detroit Tigers history, though he could have been one of the great pitchers in Dodgers history instead—if only Brooklyn was located closer to Indiana. In 1901 the 21-year-old righthander found himself in the middle of the battle between the National League and the first-year American League. He created his own problem when he signed with both Brooklyn and Detroit. Mullin, who had played semi-pro baseball in Wabash, Indiana, and then married a girl from the town, chose Detroit because it was closer to his home.

"Wabash George" set the all-time Tigers mark in complete games and innings pitched. Only Hooks Dauss surpassed Mullin's total of 209 wins with the team. Mullin earned double-digit victory totals for 11 consecutive years. He won 20 or more games five times. In 1909 he reeled off 29 victories and sported a stingy 2.22 ERA.

On July 4, 1912, his 32nd birthday, he hurled a no-hitter against the St. Louis Browns in the second game of a doubleheader. No slouch at the plate, Mullin was used 101 times as a pinch hitter and had a career .262 batting average.

He pitched in three consecutive World Series. Although the Tigers lost each time, Mullin was 3-3 in seven career Series starts with a 1.86 ERA. He won twice in his final Series in 1909, including a shutout in Game 4, but Pittsburgh's Babe Adams pitched three complete-game victories as the Pirates won in seven games.

Mullin went to the Washington Senators in 1913. He moved back near his home with Indianapolis of the Federal League in 1914. The team moved to Newark the following year; Mullin went with them, but he was back in Wabash—for good—before the season ended.

Rance Mulliniks

Mulliniks, Steven Rance **3B-DH-SS**

1977–92 B:1/15/1956, Tulare, CA Deb:6/18/1977, CAL AL BL/TR 6', 170

G	AB	R	H	HR	RBI	OBP	SLG	AVG
1325	3569	445	972	73	435	.357	.407	.272

Toronto's Rance Mulliniks led American League third basemen in fielding percentage in 1984 and 1986 and tied for that honor in 1985. Mulliniks, the son of minor league pitcher Harvey Mulliniks, was selected by the Angels in the third round of the June 1974 free agent draft. With Salt Lake City in 1979 he batted .343 and led Pacific Coast League shortstops with a .968 fielding percentage. The Angels traded Mulliniks and Willie Mays Aikens in December 1979 to Kansas City. The Royals in turn dealt him to the Blue Jays in March 1982.

For five years Mulliniks was Toronto's everyday third baseman—at least every day that a righthander was starting. The lefthanded-hitting Mulliniks was murder against righties, but he sat against southpaws, usually replaced by Garth Iorg. When Kelly Gruber claimed the everyday job at third base in 1987, Mulliniks became the designated hitter.

In Toronto's first postseason series, the 1985 American League Championship Series, Mulliniks led the team with a .364 average and homered in a losing effort in Game 3. In the stretch that August and September he hit .351. He played in two more ALCS for Toronto, but his career ended shortly before the Blue Jays won the 1992 World Series. Milwaukee manager George Bamberger once said of Mulliniks: "We throw the guy everything we've got, and all he does is hang out ropes on us."

Joe Mulvey

Mulvey, Joseph H. **3B**

1883–95 B:10/27/1858, Providence, RI D:8/21/1928, Philadelphia, PA Deb:5/31/1883, PRO NL BR/TR 5'11½", 178

G	AB	R	H	HR	RBI	OBP	SLG	AVG
987	4063	598	1059	28	532	.287	.355	.261

Joseph H. Mulvey will not be remembered as a hero of baseball's labor wars by either side. He committed to jumping to the Players League in 1889 but then backed out. On December 18, 1889, the Brotherhood of Baseball Players expelled a number of players including Pebbly Jack Glasscock, John Clarkson, Kid Gleason, George Miller, Jake Beckley, Ed Delahanty and Joe Mulvey. Mulvey, Beckley, and Delahanty all returned to the Players League and were reinstated. But because of their erratic behavior they were known as "triple jumpers."

A third baseman that specialized in one-handed catches, Mulvey played four games with Providence before joining Philadelphia in 1883. In 1884 and 1885, he led the National League in both putouts and errors.

Mulvey played for Philadelphia in the American Association in 1891 and for the Phillies again in 1892. He ended his career with a season in Washington in 1893 and part of one in Brooklyn in 1895. Mulvey finished 1895 as a fill-in National League umpire.

Jerry Mumphrey

Mumphrey, Jerry Wayne **OF**

1974–88 B:9/9/1952, Tyler, TX Deb:9/10/1974, STL NL BB/TR 6'2", 185

G	AB	R	H	HR	RBI	OBP	SLG	AVG
1585	4993	660	1442	70	575	.351	.396	.289

Selected by the Cardinals in the fourth round of the June 1971 draft, Jerry Wayne Mumphrey played with Sarasota, Cedar Rapids, St. Petersburg (Arkansas), and Tulsa before coming to St. Louis in 1976. Traded twice after the 1979 season, the following season found the switch hitter in San Diego, where he stole 52 bases and was caught only five times. In April 1981 the Padres traded Mumphrey to the Yankees. After batting .307 for the season, he hit .500 in the ALCS against Oakland.

After pacing the National League in 1980 and the American League in 1981, Mumphrey gained the dubious distinction of leading two major leagues in errors at a position consecutively. But with the Yankees he began to exhibit exceptional range and became an excellent center fielder.

Mumphrey hit .300 again for the Yankees in 1982 but was hitting only .262 when the Yankees traded him to Houston for Omar Moreno in August 1983. Moreno did little for the Yankees, but Mumphrey hit .336 for Houston. The Astros traded Mumphrey to the Cubs after the 1985 season. He hit over .300 for the next two seasons with Chicago and recorded a .534 slugging percentage in 1987, but knee injuries had taken their toll and

Mumphrey could no longer play center field or steal bases. He retired in 1988 at age 36.

Red Munger

Munger, George David **P**

1943–56 B:10/4/1918, Houston, TX D:2/7/1998, Houston, TX Deb:5/1/1943, STL NL BR/TR 6'2", 200

W	L	PCT	G	SH	IP	BB	SO	ERA
77	56	.579	273	13	1228²	500	564	3.83

Cardinals righthander Red Munger was just hitting his stride at the All-Star break in 1944. The second year pitcher was 11–3 with a 1.34 ERA, on his way to what might have been one of the greatest seasons in baseball. But on the morning of the All-Star game he was inducted into the army. Munger returned after his tour of duty to have some good seasons but nothing approaching the season he was having when he was called to duty.

George David "Red" Munger played with New Iberia, Houston, Asheville, Sacramento, and Columbus before making the Cardinals in 1943 at age 24. He had a 9–5 record in his first season and saw teammate Howie Pollet be inducted into military service on the morning of the 1943 All-Star game.

Munger returned for the final six weeks of 1946. Pitching in his only World Series, Munger was backed by 20 Cardinals hits and beat the Red Sox 12–3 in Game 4. The following season Munger went 16–5 with six shutouts. Two years later he posted a 15–8 season.

On September 30, 1950, he and Gerry Staley each shut out the Cubs in a doubleheader. In 1951 Munger had a 4–6 record with a 5.32 ERA and was 0–1 with a 12.46 ERA when he was traded to Pittsburgh on May 3, 1952. He pitched poorly in Pittsburgh and was sent to the minor leagues. Not promoted again until 1956, he finished his major league career that year with Pittsburgh. After retiring Munger became an inspector for the Health Department in Houston.

Van Lingle Mungo

Mungo, Van Lingle **P**

1931–43, 1945 B:6/8/1911, Pageland, SC D:2/12/1985, Pageland, SC Deb:9/7/1931, BRO NL BR/TR 6'2", 185

W	L	PCT	G	SH	IP	BB	SO	ERA
120	115	.511	364	20	2113	868	1242	3.47

People who remember the 1970s far outnumber those who remember the 1930s. So if you play word association and say "Van Lingle Mungo," you're likely to make somebody think of a clever, jazzy, early '70s ditty by songwriter David Frishberg. It strung together names of players from the '30s and early '40s with Mungo's unusual name serving as the refrain. But few of today's fans know much besides the name of the fireballing righthander with the high leg kick.

Van Lingle Mungo—that really was his name—came to the Dodgers at the end of the 1931 season. One account called him "wild and mean." He would get visibly upset when his teammates made mistakes, and since he spent most of his career with poor Dodgers teams, that was a frequent occurrence. He tried to strike out as many batters as possible to minimize the chances for error, and as a result he led the National League in walks three times.

A heavy drinker who liked to carouse, once Mungo had to be smuggled out of Cuba to escape a machete-wielding husband. Apparently Mungo had been caught in bed with the man's wife, a nightclub singer.

Mungo was the Dodgers' durable ace for several seasons, going 81–71 between 1932 and 1936 and leading the NL in strikeouts in 1936 with 238—the most in the majors since Dazzy Vance fanned 262 for the 1924 Dodgers. After he hurt his arm in the 1937 All-Star Game he was never the same. This was the same All-Star Game that helped ruin Dizzy Dean's career. (Dean broke his toe in the game, tried to return too quickly and blew out his arm.)

Mungo became a junkballer. He was released by the Dodgers after 1941 and was signed by the Giants. Overall, he went only 13–25 between 1938 and 1943. He did not pitch in the majors in 1944, but the wartime player shortage provided him another chance in 1945. He went 14–7 for the Giants in 26 starts but that was his last gasp. He finished with a 120–115 career record.

Thurman Munson

Munson, Thurman Lee **C–DH**

1969–79 B:6/7/1947, Akron, OH D:8/2/1979, Canton, OH Deb:8/8/1969, NY AL BR/TR 5'11", 191

G	AB	R	H	HR	RBI	OBP	SLG	AVG
1423	5344	696	1558	113	701	.350	.410	.292

To those who spent any time around Thurman Munson, it was obvious that he was desperately insecure—as a player and as a person. He was never able to put the emotional scars of his childhood behind him, and he spent his entire career trying to get the respect he felt was his due.

The popularity of other catchers, such as Carlton Fisk, tormented Munson. Fisk was tall and ruggedly handsome. Munson may have been a superb athlete, but he was built like a fireplug. "Squatty Body" is what some Yankees called him. On one occasion, the Yankees daily press notes listed the AL assist leaders. For catchers, Fisk was listed with 27 and Munson with 25. Munson, incensed, wanted to know why he was being "shown up." He proceeded to drop three third strikes in the next game so that he could throw to first and take over the league lead in assists.

Akron-born Munson grew up in Canton; made All-State in baseball, basketball, and football; and went to Kent State on a football scholarship. But after the Yankees chose him as their first-round pick in the June 1968 draft, he dropped out of school and signed for $75,000. "I remember seeing a lot of horses back in Ohio," he once said. "Baseball just reminded me of a stallion running free. There was a freedom to the game."

He played only 99 games in the minors. And after batting .256 in 26 games in 1969, Munson took over as the Yankees' regular catcher in 1970. He was an instant success, winning the Rookie of the Year Award after hitting .302, and he quickly established himself as an excellent defensive catcher. His reflexes were exceptional, and his quick release on throws to second base was almost breathtaking.

After slumping to .251 in 1971, Munson batted .280 in 1972. His bust-out year was 1973: he hit .301 with 74 RBIs and a career-high 20 homers, and he won the first of his three Gold Gloves. He was still on reasonably good terms with the media at this point, but he knew that he could do better. "I'm a little too belligerent," he admitted. "I cuss and swear at people. I yell at umpires and maybe I'm a little too tough at home sometimes. I don't sign as many autographs as I should, and I haven't always been very good with the writers."

Then came 1974. Munson strained his forearm early in the season, but he never gave it time to heal and he never let on how serious the injury was. He just kept playing—catching 137 games—because the Yankees, for the first time since he joined the team, were in a pennant race. He hit only .261 with 60 RBIs. Worse yet, he committed 22 errors, almost all of them on throws, some of which curved embarrassingly into right-center. When the media tried to talk to him about his problem, he snubbed them or snarled at them.

His forearm healed during the winter, and he hit .318 with 102 RBIs in 1975, establishing himself as one of the game's best clutch hitters. He was also named the Yankees' first team captain since Lou Gehrig.

The Yankees breezed through the AL East in 1976 as Munson hit .302 with 17 homers and 105 RBIs. He easily won the AL Most Valuable Player Award, despite an informal team poll conducted by one of the Yankees beat writers that cited Mickey Rivers as team MVP. Munson hit .435 against the Royals in the ALCS, and the team made it back to the World Series for the first time in 12 years.

They were no match for the "Big Red Machine" and got swept in four games. Munson hit .529, but his nine hits were all singles and he didn't drive in a run. Meanwhile, Series MVP Johnny Bench hit .533 with two homers and six RBIs. In an interview after the final game Cincinnati manager Sparky Anderson was asked to compare Munson with the Reds catcher. "Don't ever embarrass a man by comparing him to Johnny Bench," was his answer. He didn't know that Munson had been brought to the room and was standing behind him.

Free agency became a reality that winter, and the Yankees' George Steinbrenner signed Reggie Jackson for $3 million. Munson fumed. Steinbrenner had broken a promise that Munson would always be the highest-paid Yankee. Munson was cool to Jackson at the start of spring training, but he was just starting to warm up to the outfielder when the latest issue of *Sport* hit the stands. "I'm the straw that stirs the drink," Jackson was quoted as saying. "It all comes back to me. Maybe I should say me and Munson. But he really doesn't enter into it. He can only stir it bad."

Munson was furious. For the rest of his career he rarely talked to the media. But he didn't let his anger affect his play. The Yankees won a second straight pennant as he hit .308 with 18 homers and 100 RBIs. He was the first major leaguer in 13 years—and only the second catcher—to hit .300 and drive in 100 runs for three straight seasons.

The Yankees won the 1977 World Series, but it was Jackson who was the hero with his memorable three-homer game against the Dodgers in Game 6. Indeed, Jackson was one of those special players who made everyone around him better, a feat Munson couldn't achieve.

The Yankees repeated as world champs in 1978 after one of the great stretch runs in baseball history. But 31-year-old Munson began showing the effects of nine years of catching every day. He hit .297 with only six homers and 71 RBIs. He still had one heroic moment left, however.

It came in the bottom of the eighth of Game 3 of the playoffs against the Royals. George Brett had just hit a two-run homer, his third homer of the game, to put the Royals on top, 5–4. Munson was up against Doug Bird with a runner on base. He hit a game-winning, 450-foot home run over Yankee Stadium's Death Valley in left-center.

He declined in 1979. In 97 games through August 1, he was hitting .288 with three homers

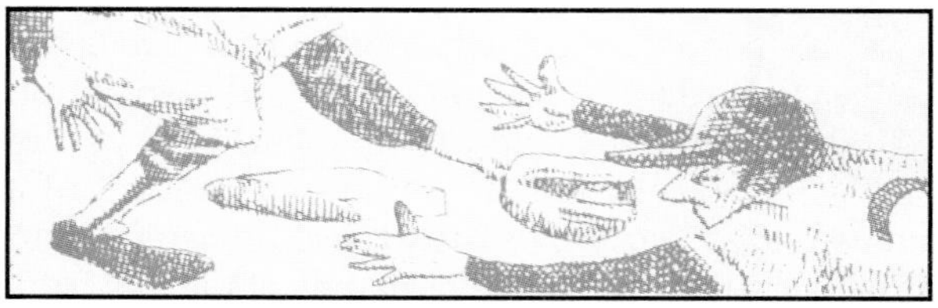

and 39 RBIs and talking retirement: his knees and shoulders ached constantly and he hated being away from his wife and three children. The burly catcher had found a way to spend more time with his family. Munson had gotten his pilot's license a few years earlier, and in 1979 he bought a twin-engine Cessna. He often flew home on his days off, and after the Yankees finished a road trip in Chicago the night of Wednesday, August 1, he flew home to spend Thursday with his family in Canton. He and Jackson had become friendly by then, and he invited Jackson to fly home with him and spend the next afternoon practicing takeoffs and landings at the Akron-Canton airport. But Jackson had to be back in New York the next day and declined.

At 3:02 p.m. on August 2, 1979, Munson's plane came down 1,000 feet short of the runway, where it crashed and burst into flames. The two passengers in the plane got out, but Munson was killed, probably because he wasn't wearing his shoulder harness. To this day, his locker in the Yankee Stadium clubhouse remains empty.

Masanori Murakami

Murakami, Masanori **P**

1964–65 B:5/6/1944, Otsuki, Japan Deb:9/1/1964, SF NL BL/TL 6', 180

W	L	PCT	G	SV	IP	BB	SO	ERA
5	1	.833	54	9	89^{1}	23	100	3.43

West met East when Japanese left-hander Masanori Murakami, the first Japanese import in American baseball, pitched for the San Francisco Giants in 1964–65. Murakami had belonged to the Nankai Hawks of Japan's Pacific League in 1964 and along with two other players was sent to play in the American minor leagues. Murakami, assigned to the Giants' Fresno farm team, pitched sufficiently well for San Francisco to exercise a $10,000 option on him and bring him up late in the season to the big club. Murakami signed another contract for 1965, but returned to Japan for the off-season and found himself under tremendous pressure to stay there.

In February 1965 the Nankai Hawks announced Murakami would play for them in 1965. In the subsequent wrangle Commissioner Ford Frick broke off baseball relations between the United States and Japan. Finally a compromise was reached, Murakami would pitch in America in 1965 but then return home.

In Japan Murakami was hampered by not being allowed to use the brushback pitch he had learned in the United States. His best season was 1968 when he was 18–4 with a 2.38 ERA, but otherwise he was mediocre and often heard the taunt of "Go Back to America" when he did poorly.

Bobby Murcer

Murcer, Bobby Ray **OF–DH**

1965–83 B:5/20/1946, Oklahoma City, OK Deb:9/8/1965, NY AL BL/TR 5'11", 180

G	AB	R	H	HR	RBI	OBP	SLG	AVG
1908	6730	972	1862	252	1043	.361	.445	.277

Like his idol Mickey Mantle, Bobby Murcer came out of Oklahoma and was signed as a shortstop by Tom Greenwade. When he took Mantle's place in the New York outfield in 1969 it was like a fairy tale come true. But Murcer's timing was all wrong; the Yankees dynasty had ended the year he signed, and in 1974 he was traded away just as George Steinbrenner began to rebuild the franchise.

Heartbroken when traded to the Giants in October 1974, Murcer had never wanted to play for another team. He spent 4½ years in self-imposed exile, pining for his pinstripes, but when he finally made it back to Yankee Stadium he was too late for New York's world championships in 1977 and 1978.

Murcer signed with the Yankees in 1964. After spending 1967 and 1968 in the army, he started 1969 as the Yanks' third baseman—and promptly committed 11 errors in 31 games. The Yankees moved Murcer to the outfield, where he hit .259 with 26 homers and 82 RBIs in his rookie season. On June 24, 1970, he tied an AL record by hitting four straight homers in a doubleheader. In 1971 he became an AL All-Star for the first of five straight seasons. That year he hit .331, belted 25 homers, and drove in 94 runs.

That was the peak of Murcer's career. He drove in between 88 and 96 runs from 1971 through 1977 but never again reached 100. In 1972 he slugged 30 home runs and led the American League with 102 runs scored, but he never hit 30 homers again. In 1973 Murcer topped .300 for the last time. Then came the trauma of 1974. That year the Yankees moved temporarily to Shea Stadium while Yankee Stadium was being renovated. Murcer, who hit 252 homers in his career, hit only 10 in 1974, daunted by the swirling winds and deeper fences of the Mets' home park.

Then came his move to right field. In 1970 and 1973 Murcer had led league outfielders in assists and in 1972 had won a Gold Glove. But when the Yankees obtained brilliant center fielder Elliott Maddox prior to the 1974 season, manager Bill Virdon wasted little time moving Murcer from center to right. Murcer publicly sulked. He continued to think of himself as Mantle's successor and thought center field belonged to him.

On October 22, 1974, Murcer went to the Giants in a blockbuster deal for Bobby Bonds. He put in two solid seasons in San Francisco but in

February 1977 was sent to Chicago for Bill Madlock. Although he recorded eight straight hits during one stretch in 1978, Murcer connected for only nine homers and 64 RBIs.

When he made it back into pinstripes on June 26, 1979, he was 33 years old and slipping. The Yankees, meanwhile, were going nowhere. On August 2 Murcer's close friend, Thurman Munson, was killed in a plane crash. Four days later, only hours after an emotional funeral in Canton, Ohio, Murcer enjoyed his greatest moment as a Yankee. He hit a three-run homer in the seventh inning and a game-winning, two-run single in the bottom of the ninth as the Yankees beat the Orioles, 5–4, on national TV.

In 1981 Murcer finally appeared in a World Series but went 0-for-3 as a pinch hitter as the Yankees lost to the Dodgers. He retired in June 1983. He became a Yankees broadcaster and part owner of the Triple-A franchise in his hometown of Oklahoma City.

Dale Murphy

Murphy, Dale Bryan **OF-1B-C**
1976–93 B:3/12/1956, Portland, OR Deb:9/13/1976, ATL NL BR/TR 6'5", 215

G	AB	R	H	HR	RBI	OBP	SLG	AVG
2180	7960	1197	2111	398	1266	.348	.469	.265

A complete player during his prime, Dale Murphy ranked among the premier sluggers of the 1980s and was the winner of back-to-back National League Most Valuable Player Awards in 1982 and 1983. He won five Gold Glove awards, belted at least 20 home runs for eight consecutive seasons, and, like many of the game's great sluggers, was one of the top strikeout victims of all time.

A devout Morman, Murphy was an all-city and all-state catcher at Woodrow Wilson High School in Portland, Oregon. The Braves selected him with the fifth pick in the first round of the June 1974 draft. Murphy batted .254 with five home runs and 31 RBIs in the Appalachian League that summer. In 1975 he hit .228 with five homers, and 48 RBIs in the Class A Western Carolinas League, playing first base in addition to catcher. His play won him a spot on the league's All-Star team.

Murphy moved up to Double-A Savannah in 1976, hitting 12 home runs, knocking in 55 runs, and batting .267 in 104 games. Late in the season he was promoted to Triple-A Richmond, where he hit four homers in 50 at bats while catching and playing the outfield. That earned him a call-up by the Braves, and he went 2-for-4 with two RBIs in his big league debut, September 13, 1976, at Dodger Stadium.

Murphy spent a full season at Richmond in 1977, putting together the kind of year the Braves had hoped for, with 22 homers, a league-leading 90 RBIs, 249 total bases, 33 doubles, and a .305 batting average. Exciting behind the plate, too, the lean 6'5" Murphy led the circuit in putouts, double plays, and passed balls. He earned his second September promotion to Atlanta, batting .316 in 18 games, and the Braves figured they had the next Johnny Bench.

On Opening Day 1978, though, Murphy was the Braves' starting first baseman, and he caught just 21 games that season. He batted only .226 and led the National League in strikeouts as well as in errors at first, but he did manage to hit 23 homers and 79 RBIs. In 1979 Murphy opened the season at catcher, but again logged most of his playing time at first base. Although he played 47 fewer games than he did in 1978, he still hit 21 home runs—including a three-homer game May 18—with 57 RBIs.

That season convinced Braves manager Bobby Cox that Murphy had a future in the major leagues—but not as a catcher. "He was so big, and he had such a powerful throwing arm, it was hard to get it organized to make a good throw," Cox recalled. "That's the only reason he was converted. He became a great outfielder, not a good one."

Opening 1980 in his third position in three years, Murphy played left field and made the All-Star team. He again led the league in strikeouts, but his long swing also yielded 33 homers, third in the league, mostly to the opposite field. Murphy and Bob Horner became a devastating one-two punch, combining for 479 homers during their nine seasons together.

The 1981 Opening Day lineup had Murphy in center field, where he showed good speed, fine instincts, and a strong arm. He won five straight Gold Gloves starting in 1982 while shifting between left and center. After slumping in the strike-shortened 1981 campaign, Murphy became a star in 1982. He played in every game, as he would for four straight seasons, a streak that ran to 740 games.

In 1982 Murphy tied for the NL lead with 109 RBIs, was league runner-up with 36 homers and 113 runs, ranked third with 303 total bases, fourth with 93 walks, batted .281, and stole 23 bases in 34 tries. He was elected to start the All-Star Game by the fans for the first of five straight seasons.

The Braves, under .500 during each half of the 1981 campaign, won 13 straight games to start 1982 and held on to take the NL West flag. But Murphy had just three singles in the playoffs against St. Louis as the Braves scratched out only five runs and were swept in three games. In the league MVP vote, Murphy won comfortably over Cardinals outfielder Lonnie Smith.

In 1983 Murphy became the league's fourth back-to-back MVP winner, and at 27, the youngest player to win the award in consecutive seasons. He batted a career-high .302, led the NL with a career-high 121 RBIs and a .540 slugging percentage, and finished second with 131 runs scored, 318 total bases, and 36 homers. Murphy also stole 30 bases in 34 tries, becoming the sixth player in major league history, and the first National League player since Bobby Bonds 10 years earlier, with 30 homers and 30 steals in the same season. The Braves finished second in the division, a showing they would not equal or surpass during the rest of Murphy's tenure as a Brave.

As the Braves fell in the standings, Murphy kept hitting. He became Atlanta's lone bright light in the basement. Involved with numerous charities in the midst of baseball's scandals and greed, he maintained his All-American hero image. In 1984 Murphy led the National League with a .547 slugging percentage and 303 total bases, and tied Mike Schmidt for the home run lead with 36. He finished ninth in MVP voting.

Murphy won the home run title outright in 1985 with 37 and knocked in 111 runs, his fourth straight season with at least 36 homers and 100 RBIs. He also led the circuit with 118 runs and 90 walks, reached double figures in stolen bases for the fifth consecutive season, and batted .300 for the second and final time, despite tying for the National League lead with 141 strikeouts.

In 1986 Murphy dramatically extended his consecutive-game streak. On April 29 he cut his hand bracing himself against the fence after making a catch. The cut required nine stitches, and it was expected to keep him out of action for at least a week. But the next night, he came off the bench to homer. He extended the streak two more months before taking a day off July 9 and ending a run that had begun September 27, 1981. Murphy's run of 30-homer, 100-RBI seasons also came to an end in 1986. He had 29 homers, 83 RBIs, and batted .265—his lowest mark since 1981.

Murphy switched to right field in 1987 and his offense rebounded with career highs of 44 homers and 115 walks, as he batted .295. But in 1988 Murphy's output fell again. Although he showed up on the leader board in power categories, he batted only .226 and was no longer a dominant offensive player.

He had arthroscopic surgery on his right knee after the season and returned to center field, but his numbers fell further in 1989. One of the season's few highlights came during a July 27 win over the San Francisco Giants. Murphy hit two home runs in the sixth inning. His six RBIs in the inning tied a league record.

Despite the poor finish, Murphy was the second leading home run hitter of the 1980s with 308, was second in RBIs with 929, and ranked fifth with 1,553 hits. He played in 1,537 of his teams' 1,557 games. At 34, Murphy was still one of the most popular players in the game, and his fans and colleagues hoped he would return to his previous heights. The Braves cashed in his remaining trade value, sending him to the Philadelphia Phillies on August 3, 1990, with pitcher Tommy Greene for pitcher Jeff Parrett and others. Ironically, the Braves won their first of three straight NL West titles the season following the trade of their signature player.

Murphy played regularly for the Phillies in 1991. Though he didn't advertise his Mormon faith and rarely took offense to vile locker-room banter, his presence did lead some of his earthier teammates to watch their language in the clubhouse. He had knee surgery again in 1992 and played just 18 games, leaving him two home runs short of the 400-mark.

The Phillies re-signed him for 1993, but had no room on their roster and traded him to the expansion Colorado Rockies. There he played just 26 games before retiring in late May after batting .143 with no homers, leaving his career total at 398.

Murphy finished having hit exactly one homer per every 20 at bats. His 31 career multihomer games rank him higher than Billy Williams, Gil Hodges, Hack Wilson, and Carl Yastrzemski.

Danny Murphy

Murphy, Daniel Francis **2B–OF**

1900–15 B:8/11/1876, Philadelphia, PA D:11/22/1955, Jersey City, NJ Deb:9/17/1900, NY NL BR/TR 5'9", 175

G	AB	R	H	HR	RBI	OBP	SLG	AVG
1496	5399	705	1563	44	702	.336	.405	.289

The Philadelphia Athletics' dynasty of 1910 to 1914 was known for its "$100,000 Infield." The A's probably wouldn't have won as many championships without Danny Murphy, a fine infielder in his own right, patrolling the outfield behind them.

After eight years in the minor leagues and a couple of cups of coffee with the New York Giants, Murphy made his debut with the A's on July 8, 1902. It was a memorable day: he went 6-for-6, including a grand slam. Over the next six years, Murphy became one of the AL's top second baseman.

In 1908 the A's asked Murphy to move to right field; future Hall of Famer Eddie Collins took over at second base. Murphy became a fine outfielder, leading the American League in fielding in 1909 and assists in 1911. He starred in the 1910 and 1911 World Series, batting a combined .326 with 10 runs, six doubles, and 12 RBIs in 11 games.

Murphy was named captain of the A's in 1912. He also suffered a broken kneecap that year, an injury that ended his career as a regular. He managed in the minors for four years, then scouted and coached for the A's and Phillies for another six.

Dwayne Murphy

Murphy, Dwayne Keith **OF**

1978–89 B:3/18/1955, Merced, CA Deb:4/8/1978, OAK AL BL/TR 6'1", 185

G	AB	R	H	HR	RBI	OBP	SLG	AVG
1360	4347	648	1069	166	609	.359	.402	.246

Overshadowed in Oakland's outfield by Rickey Henderson and Tony Armas, Dwayne Murphy nonetheless made a name for himself with his tremendous range in the outfield. As a result, he captured six straight Gold Glove Awards between 1980 and 1985 and lead all AL outfielders in total chances in 1980, 1982, and 1984.

A product of California's San Joaquin Valley, Dwayne Keith Murphy was selected by the A's in the 15th round of the June 1973 free agent draft. His minor league career included stops at Lewiston, Burlington, Modesto, Chattanooga, Tucson, and Vancouver.

Murphy led the AL with 22 sacrifice hits in 1980, and batted .545 in the 1981 special division series against Kansas City. That year he led the league in game-winning RBIs with 15 and was named to *The Sporting News* AL All-Star team. He also contributed to the A's with his patience at the plate, finishing in the top five in the league in walks three straight years from 1980 through 1982.

Later in his career, Murphy, already hampered by chronic foot problems, injured his back in 1986 and did rehabilitation assignments in the minors during both 1986 and 1987. Granted free agency in November 1987, he was signed by the independent Fresno club of the California League in May 1988. Back in the San Joaquin Valley, he hit just .206 in 13 games and was released in early June. The Tigers signed him, sent him to Toledo, and brought him up in midseason. He finished his career with Philadelphia in 1989.

Jack Murphy

Murphy, Jack Raymond Jr.

Sportswriter B:2/5/33, Tulsa, OK D:9/25/80, San Diego, CA

From 1981 to 1996, Qualcomm Stadium, the home of the San Diego Padres, had a less impersonal name. It was called Jack Murphy Stadium, or simply "The Murph," in honor of the man who led the campaign to bring major league baseball to San Diego.

Witty and prolific, Jack Murphy enjoyed a 30-year career as a sportswriter for the *San Diego Union*, and made a name for himself writing features and profiles for *the New York Times Magazine, The New Yorker, Newsweek,* and other national publications. Red Smith, one of his drinking buddies, shared the opinion of many that Murphy was at his best extolling the glories of hunting and fishing, but he was a boxing buff and an engaging commentator on horse racing and team sports as well. He joined the *Union* following two stints with the *Tulsa World* (before and after World War II, in which he served with the U.S. Marines), the *Fort Worth Star-Telegram,* and the *Daily Oklahoman* in Oklahoma City. A passion for sports ran in Murphy's family; his younger brother, Bob, enjoyed a long career calling games for the New York Mets.

A highly visible Democrat in a predominantly Republican city and county, Murphy was nonetheless able, through his newspaper columns, to rally bipartisan support to bring professional football and baseball to San Diego in the 1960s. The Padres played their first game at San Diego Stadium on April 8, 1969; in 1981, the ballpark was rechristened in memory of Murphy, who had died after a three-month battle with cancer the previous year.

Johnny Murphy

Murphy, John Joseph **P**

1932–43, 1946–47 B:7/14/1908, New York, NY D:1/14/1970, New York, NY Deb:5/19/1932, NY AL BR/TR 6'2", 190

W	L	PCT	G	SV	IP	BB	SO	ERA
93	53	.637	415	107	1045	444	378	3.50

John "Grandma" Murphy owned a spate of relief records until bullpen specialists of a later era broke them: 12 relief wins in both 1937 and 1943, 107 career saves, and 73 career relief wins. Johnny Murphy was given his nickname by teammate Pat Malone because of his incessant complaining about meals and accommodations. After graduating from Fordham University in 1929, he was signed by Yankees scout Paul Krichell and performed for Albany, St. Paul, and Newark, before settling in at New York. Originally a spot starter, Murphy became the foremost relief specialist of his era, four times leading the league in saves. In six World Series he complied an ERA of 1.10.

He voluntarily retired in April 1944 and performed war work during the 1944 and 1945 seasons. In 1946 he returned to New York, but was released the following April—at which point he signed with the Red Sox.

Murphy then spent 15 years as Boston's farm director but was dismissed in 1961 as part of an overall front office shake-up. He served the fledgling Mets in a variety of capacities including chief scout, vice president (1964–67), and general manager in December 1967. He is given a lot of credit for putting together the "Miracle" Mets of 1969.

Eddie Murray

Murray, Eddie Clarence **1B–DH**

1977–97 B:2/24/1956, Los Angeles, CA Deb:4/7/1977, BAL AL BB/TR 6'2", 200

G	AB	R	H	HR	RBI	OBP	SLG	AVG
3026	11336	1627	3255	504	1917	.363	.476	.287

Eddie Murray was never spectacular, but he was always productive and ended his career with numbers that placed him among the game's great players. When he retired in 1997, Murray was among the all-time leaders in home runs and RBIs, although he had led the league in those categories only once—in the strike-shortened 1981 season. He never had 200 hits in a season, yet retired 11th on the all-time hit list. When he walked off the field for the last time, only Pete Rose, Hank Aaron, Carl Yastrzemski, and Ty Cobb had played in more games or had more at bats than Murray.

Murray let his playing do his talking during his career; his relationship with the media was silent at best and quite acrimonious at worst. Whenever he joined a new team he was usually quickly labeled a negative influence in the clubhouse by the press. Murray, however, was also a ballplayer that many teammates looked up to, so the harsh climate that always existed between him and the press often extended itself to the dynamic between his teams and reporters. Murray was also often at odds with management over various issues. Many who played beside Murray now praise him for the leadership he gave his teams, but during his career he was perceived by most non-players who dealt with him as more trouble than inspiration.

The Baltimore Orioles first baseman was the American League Rookie of the Year in 1977, an All-Star in his sophomore season, and the cleanup hitter for the AL champions in 1979. Murray began a run of six straight years of finishing in the top 10 of the AL Most Valuable Player voting in 1980, including two second-place finishes, though he never won the award. Murray helped clinched his only world championship with a pair of home runs in Game 5 against the Phillies in 1983.

He continued to pile up productive numbers. By Murray's 11th season he was the Orioles' all-time home run king. When the 1980s ended he was baseball's leading RBI man of the decade (996). Traded to the Dodgers, Murray batted a career-high .330 in his native Los Angeles in 1990. He left the Dodgers as a free agent after the 1991 season and joined the New York Mets.

The Mets had assembled a roster of high-priced talent that included Bobby Bonilla, Howard Johnson, Vince Coleman, and Willie Randolph, but Murray was the only one who played reasonably well. He led the 1992 team in nearly every category and he tied a career-high with 37 doubles. Murray also hit his 400th career home run that season, and passed former Met Keith Hernandez as the all-time leader in assists by a first baseman.

In 1993 he reached the 100-RBI plateau for the first time since 1985, and he again led the team in most major offensive categories, but the Mets endured their worst season since 1966. Murray left New York after the season to join the Indians, but hit just .254 with Cleveland in the strike shortened 1994. In 1995, however, he exploded for one last great season, batting .323, helping to lead the Indians to the division title. On June 30, he became the 20th player to reach 3,000 hits in a career. He batted .385 in the Division Series, and while he had only two hits in the World Series, his 11th-inning single drove in the winning run in Game 3.

His poor hitting during the first half of 1996 knocked him out of the Indians' plans, however, so Cleveland traded Murray back to his original major league team, the Orioles. Murray was cheered as he marked his triumphant return to Baltimore with a home run in his first game back with the team. Later that season, Murray passed Hank Aaron with his 20th consecutive year with at least 75 RBIs. And on September 7 he joined Aaron and Willie Mays as the only players with 500 home runs and 3,000 hits. He followed those achievements by hitting .400 in the Division Series and batting .267 with a home run in the ALCS for the Orioles.

Murray signed with his fifth team, the Anaheim Angels, as a free agent following the 1996 season. He was traded back to the Dodgers late in the season, where, after appearing in only nine games, he retired at the age of 41. He returned to Baltimore again, as a coach in 1998.

Red Murray

Murray, John Joseph **OF**

1906–17 B:3/4/1884, Arnot, PA D:12/4/1958, Sayre, PA Deb:6/16/1906, STL NL BR/TR 5'10½", 190

G	AB	R	H	HR	RBI	OBP	SLG	AVG
1264	4334	555	1170	37	579	.323	.379	.270

Cardinals outfielder John Joseph "Red" Murray led the National League in homers in 1909. With teammate Josh Devore, he combined power with speed to steal 100 bases in 1910. He finished second in the NL in thefts each year from 1908 to 1910.

On December 12, 1908, Murray was traded with Bugs Raymond and Admiral Schlei to the New

York Giants for Roger Bresnahan, who would become manager in St. Louis. Murray played for three Giants pennant winners. He went 0-for-21 in the 1911 World Series against the Philadelphia Athletics, but he batted .323 in the following year's Series against the Boston Red Sox and .250 in a rematch with the A's in 1913; the Giants lost each year.

In 1912 Murray led National League outfielders in fielding. That season he made a celebrated catch at Forbes Field that was often called the best in the history of that park. It saved a rain-soaked victory for Christy Mathewson. At the riotous conclusion of an August 30, 1913, game at Baker Bowl, one fan waved a pistol in Murray's face until a policeman intervened. The Giants released Murray in midseason 1915. The Cubs picked him up. In 1917 he returned to the Giants briefly to finish his major league career.

Danny Murtaugh

Murtaugh, Daniel Edward **2B**

1941–43, 1946–51 M(1957–64, 1967, 1970–71, 1973–76, 1,115–950) B:10/8/1917, Chester, PA D:12/2/1976, Chester, PA Deb:7/6/1941, PHI N BR/TR 5'9", 165

G	AB	R	H	HR	RBI	OBP	SLG	AVG
767	2599	263	661	8	219	.331	.317	.254

Danny Murtaugh was the man that Pittsburgh's front office kept bringing out of retirement to manage the Pirates. It was as if no other manager ever really understood the Bucs the way the man with the boxer's face and ready wit did. Murtaugh always downplayed his ability with self-deprecating humor. While other managers raged or raved, he sat in a rocking chair in the clubhouse with a large cigar that replaced the mouthful of tobacco that he had always sported on the field. He regaled visitors with stories, putting up a pretense of half-awake incompetence that couldn't have been further from the truth.

Pitcher Steve Blass remembered that every year, after the final spring roster cuts, Murtaugh held the same clubhouse meeting and delivered—word for word—the same speech. "Fellows," he would say, "this is it, 25 of you guys, me and the coaches, we're going north now. Blow everyone away if you can. Don't expect me to outmanage anybody. If you keep me close in the eighth inning, I'll lose it every time."

Despite his facade of ineptitude, Murtaugh won two pennants and three division titles during four tours of duty with the Bucs, and three of his teams finished second. He finished with a lifetime record of 1,115–950, an outstanding .540 winning percentage. Twice he led the underdog Pirates to seven-game World Series victories.

Certainly his skill as a player had nothing to do with his managerial excellence. Aside from leading the National League with 18 stolen bases in 1941, his rookie season, Murtaugh's nine-year major league career was totally undistinguished. A second baseman, he played for three different teams—the Phillies, Braves, and Pirates—and hit only eight homers in 2,599 at bats.

After retiring as a player in 1951, he became the manager at New Orleans, where he met Joe L. Brown, a rising star in the Pirates' front office. When Brown became Pittsburgh's general manager, he brought Murtaugh to the big league club as a third base coach.

In August 1957 the abrasive Bobby Bragan ruffled Brown's feathers for the final time. Brown installed his old buddy as manager on an interim basis. The team played .500 ball under Murtaugh, better than it had done for a full season in eight years, so he was given a one-year contract. The team surprised all of baseball in 1958 by climbing to second place behind the Braves.

The Pirates, the laughingstock of baseball during the 1950s, won 23 games in their final at bat in 1960, and Murtaugh's Bucs claimed Pittsburgh's first pennant in 33 years. The Yankees scored twice as many runs as the Pirates in the World Series, yet lost on Bill Mazeroski's shot over the left-field wall at Forbes Field in Game 7.

After an 80–82 finish in 1964, Murtaugh retired, citing health problems, and became a special-assignment scout for the team. When the brash Harry Walker was fired as the Bucs' manager in mid-1967, Murtaugh was coaxed back to settle the club down for the final half of the season. Larry Shepard took the reigns in 1968 and 1969, and Murtaugh returned to scouting duties until the 1970 season. During a discussion regarding who should fill Shepard's not-so-large shoes, Murtaugh mentioned that his doctor had given him a clean bill of health. Brown hired him on the spot.

The unflappable Murtaugh led new stars such as Blass, Manny Sanguillen, Richie Hebner, and Al Oliver to a division championship in 1970 before the Reds swept them in the National League Championship Series. The 1971 team performed even better, disposing of the Giants in the playoffs and defeating the supposedly unbeatable Orioles in the World Series. But Murtaugh was hospitalized during the season and missed 22 games because of various illnesses. He retired again six weeks after the Series.

In 1973 the Irishman came back to manage and led the Bucs to division championships in 1974 and 1975. In 1976 Pittsburgh put together a late-season drive to finish second, but it was clear that the Pirates' run was over. After the season both Brown and Murtaugh retired, and the former manager died of a stroke three months later. Shortly thereafter the Pirates retired Murtaugh's uniform number, 40.

When asked about the art of managing, Murtaugh once said, "I'd like to have that fellow who hits a home run every time at bat, who strikes out every opposing batter when he's pitching, who throws strikes to any base or the plate when he's playing outfield, and who always is thinking two innings ahead about just what he'll do to baffle the other team....The only trouble is to get him to put down his cup of beer and come down out of the stands and do those things."

Stan Musial

Musial, Stanley Frank **OF-1B**

1941–63 B:11/21/1920, Donora, PA Deb:9/17/1941, STL NL BL/TL 6', 175

G	AB	R	H	HR	RBI	OBP	SLG	AVG
3026	10972	1949	3630	475	1951	.418	.559	.331

Los Angeles Dodgers manager Tommy Lasorda once said, "They talk about Stan Musial being a great guy. What I want to know is, who wouldn't be a great guy with over 3,600 hits?" Therein lies the problem with Stan Musial. Mild-mannered and unassuming, Musial is usually defined in comparison to others. Although he is the statistical equal of both Joe DiMaggio and Ted Williams, he lacked DiMaggio's grace, Williams' intense personality, and the media presence of both. As a result, Musial has suffered in comparison. There is no question, however, that he was one of the greatest players of his generation.

Musial was born in Donora, Pennsylvania, a hardscrabble mill town 28 miles east of Pittsburgh. As a teenager he started playing semipro baseball and basketball with nearby mill teams. During his junior year of high school Musial starred as a pitcher for the Donora High team, striking out 17 batters in his first appearance on the mound. In the summer of 1937, before Musial's senior year, scout Andrew French of St. Louis' Class D farm club in Monessen, Pennsylvania, signed the youth to a contract valued at $65 a month.

As was common at the time, the Cardinals did not file the contract until the following summer, allowing Musial to play high school basketball that winter. He thought the Cards had forgotten about him, however, and entertained feelers from the Indians and Yankees and attended tryouts held by the Pirates. Finally, in June, he received notice from the Cardinals to report to their minor league club in Williamson, West Virginia.

Working primarily as a pitcher, Musial struggled through two seasons in Class D Williamson. One Cardinals official even recommended his release, but in 1940 Musial went 18–4 for Daytona Beach of the Florida State League and hit .311, splitting his time between the outfield and the pitcher's mound. The Cardinals didn't know that late in the 1940 season Musial had taken a tumble making a shoestring catch in the outfield, injuring his right shoulder.

During one of the first days of spring training in 1941, the problem with Musial's arm became obvious after he gave up long home runs to Terry Moore and Johnny Mize. At the Cardinals organizational meeting later that spring Musial was again nearly released, before Ossie Varek, who'd scouted him in high school, offered to give him a chance in the outfield at Class C Springfield of the Western Association.

Musial blossomed at Springfield, batting .379 and smacking a league-best 26 home runs in 87 games before he was called up to the Triple-A Rochester to help the Red Wings make the playoffs. He continued to hit well for Rochester and received a surprise call-up to St. Louis at season's end.

In only 47 at bats Musial batted .426 and proved he could run and throw well enough to play in the outfield at the big league level. Although he slumped in spring training the following year, manager Billy Southworth took a chance and installed Musial as the Cardinals' regular left fielder. Musial responded by hitting .315 in 1942 and helping the team win 43 of its last 52 games to earn the pennant by two games over Brooklyn.

St. Louis faced New York in the World Series. Pitcher Johnny Beazley won two games, and the Cards dumped the Yankees in five games. Musial hit only .222 but made several fine plays in the field.

St. Louis repeated as National League champs by 18 games in 1943, paced by Musial's league-best .357 batting average, 48 doubles, and 20 triples. This time the Yankees prevailed in a five-game World Series; Musial hit .278. The Cards won the National League championship again in 1944 and beat the crosstown Browns in the first and only all-St. Louis Series. Musial was named NL Most Valuable Player that year, and led all players in the World Series with seven hits.

Musial was drafted into the navy in January 1945 and assigned to ship repair in Pearl Harbor. He managed to spend as much time playing baseball as he did repairing ships before being mustered out in time for the 1946 season. The Cardinals won their fourth pennant in five seasons under new manager Eddie Dyer in 1946. Musial had his best season to date, winning his second MVP Award and leading the league in runs, hits, doubles, and triples with a .365 batting average. During one three-game stretch he registered 12 hits. In midseason he replaced a slumping Dick Sisler and accepted a transfer to first base.

Musial also turned down an offer of $175,000 from the Mexican League. During one series in Brooklyn, whenever he came to the plate the Dodgers fans began chanting, "Here comes the man. Here comes the man." St. Louis sportswriter Bob Broeg wrote a column about the incident, and Musial was dubbed "Stan the Man" for the remainder of his career.

The Cardinals faced the Red Sox in the 1946 World Series. Although the press salivated over the showdown between Musial and the Red Sox's Ted Williams, arguably the two best hitters in the game, both disappointed. Williams, hampered by a sore elbow, hit only .200, and Musial was only marginally better, batting .222 in St. Louis' seven-game win. The Series was the last for both players.

Like Williams, Musial played much of the next two decades for teams that fell short in the pennant race. Despite this, his individual numbers got even better. From 1946 through 1955 Musial missed only 17 games. He developed into a home run threat, hitting a career-high 39 home runs in 1948, when he won his third and last MVP Award. That season his .373 batting average was 43 points better than his closest competitor. He also won the RBI title and was second in homers.

On July 24, 1949, Musial hit for the cycle, and on May 2, 1954, against the New York Giants in St. Louis, he hit a major league-record five home runs in a doubleheader, the last against knuckleballer Hoyt Wilhelm. He boomed 20 home runs in the first 50 games of the season before tailing off to finish with 35. In 1955 his 12th-inning home run in the All-Star Game gave the National League a 6–5 victory.

On May 13, 1958, Musial doubled off Chicago righthander Moe Drabowsky for his 3,000th career hit. But in 1959 when Musial slumped to only .255, many followers thought it was time for him to retire. He played on, refusing to accept part-time duty, and in 1962, at age 41, he hit .330 in 433 at bats, his best performance since 1954 and the third-highest average for a player over age 40. During the 1962 season Musial also tied a league record for most home runs in consecutive at bats with four.

After seeing his average slip to .255 again in 1963, Musial retired, having doubled off Cincinnati's Jim Maloney for his final, 3,630th career hit as a Cardinal. Teammate Joe Garagiola once said that the only way to get Musial out was to "walk him. Then pick him off first base." Musial's odd batting stance served him well in his 22 major league seasons. After appearing in 24 All-Star Games, Musial retired as the major league leader in total bases and the National League leader in hits, games played, and runs. He finished with a .331 lifetime batting average, 475 home runs, and 1,951 RBIs.

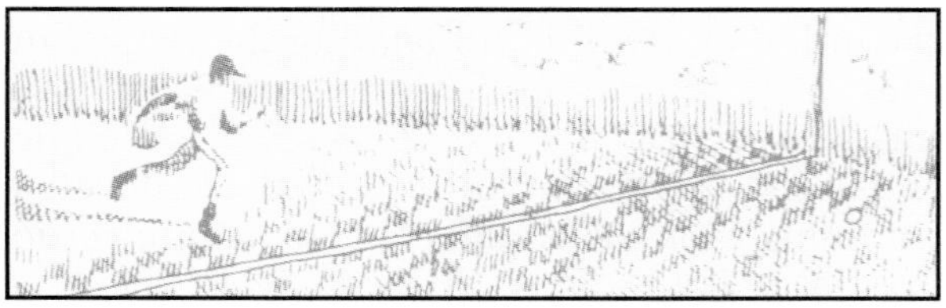

Musial later opened a successful restaurant in St. Louis, Stan and Biggie's, and worked for the Cardinals in the front office. His uniform number, 6, was retired by the St. Louis organization, and in 1969 Musial was elected to the Hall of Fame. In 1998 the Society for American Baseball Research (SABR) bestowed on Musial only its fourth Hero of Baseball Award.

Mike Mussina

Mussina, Michael Cole **P**

1991–* B:12/8/68, Williamsport, PA Deb:8/4/91, BAL AL
BR/TR 6'2", 185

W	L	PCT	G	SH	IP	BB	SO	ERA
136	66	.673	254	14	1772	421	1325	3.50

Beating Mike Mussina has not been an easy task for his opponents. With an 18–7 season in 1999, the big righthander upped his career winning percentage to .673, second only to Pedro Martinez among active pitchers with more than 100 wins. In nine years with the Baltimore Orioles, Mussina has had only two seasons in which he endured double-digit losses.

The proverbial "All-American" kid, Mussina, was born in Williamsport, Pennsylvania, the home of the Little League World Series. By age 4 he was already throwing a ball against a wall in his basement in imitation of the great pitchers of his youth. The Orioles drafted him in the first round out of Stanford University, where he earned a degree in economics. (His senior thesis was titled, "The Economics of Signing out of High School as Opposed to College.") Mussina went 25–12 at Stanford; 14–4 in a very brief minor league career; and after an abbreviated rookie season in 1991, he fashioned four straight All-Star seasons. His 19 wins tied Atlanta's Greg Maddux for the most wins in the majors in 1995. A fine fielding pitcher, Mussina won his fourth Gold Glove Award in 1999.

Mussina added a cut fastball to his repertoire in the middle of a 1992 game with men on base. That gave him six pitches, all delivered with dazzling control. "The one thing about Mike is, he has the ability to repeat his mechanics time in and time out in any given situation," said Ed Sprague, Sr., the Orioles scout who signed Mussina. "That's why he can put the ball wherever he wants. That's why he's so consistent."

In the 1997 American League Division Series, Mussina dominated the Mariners, winning two of

Baltimore's three games and striking out 16. Although the Orioles were clipped by the Indians in the Championship Series, it was no fault of Mussina's. He performed heroically, striking out an ALCS record 15 batters in Game 3, but wasn't around for the bizarre denouement when Cleveland won on a botched suicide-squeeze in the 12th inning. He struck out another 10 Indians in the sixth and final game, but Baltimore couldn't score for him, stranding 14 baserunners and losing in 11.

The best illustration of Mussina's work ethic took place during the 1993 All-Star Game in Baltimore. American League manager Cito Gaston spent the ninth inning hearing it from the crowd at Camden Yards as Mussina warmed up fruitlessly in the bullpen while Toronto's Duane Ward retired the side in order. Gaston had not ordered Mussina to warm up; the third-year pitcher decided to do it on his own so he could get in some work between starts. With Gaston managing the All-Star Game again the following year, Mussina pitched a scoreless fifth inning.

Jim Mutrie

Mutrie, James J.

Manager (1883–91, 658–419) B:6/13/1851, Chelsea, MA D:1/24/1938, New York, NY

Some regard him as little more than a figurehead, but Jim Mutrie was a key figure in bringing major league baseball to New York City and in making it a success. Moreover, among major league managers with more than 1,000 games, his .611 winning percentage ranks second only to Joe McCarthy's .615.

Like McCarthy, James J. Mutrie never played in the major leagues. He played both baseball and cricket as a youth. After several years with amateur teams around Chelsea, he joined the Androscoggin club of Lewiston, Maine, in 1875. The next year he played shortstop and served as field captain for the independent Fall River, Massachusetts, club, and in 1877 he became its manager. Although he was a good leader and a fair fielder, Mutrie was a poor hitter, batting only .167 in 1877. After hitting .186 the next season with New Bedford he retired to the sidelines.

Mutrie organized and managed a team in Brockton, Massachusetts, but it failed in 1880. Undaunted, he moved to New York City and convinced local businessman John B. Day to sponsor a team. With the help of Day and the Manhattan Polo Club, Mutrie leased the Polo Grounds in upper Manhattan. Most of his players were brought in from a recently defunct team in Rochester. From 1880 through 1882 Mutrie's New York Metropolitans won 201 games, lost 136, and tied seven, taking on both professional and amateur teams.

In October 1882, again with the backing of Day, Mutrie entered the Mets in the American Association, which had just completed its first season. Two months later Day put a second team, the Gothams, in the established National League. Most of the Gotham players came from the failed National League franchise in Troy, New York, which Day had purchased.

Thanks to Mutrie's leadership skills and Tim Keefe's pitching, the Mets finished fourth their first year in the AA and then won the 1884 pennant. Mutrie arranged a series of postseason games, now regarded by some as the first World Series, against the NL champion Providence Grays. Charley "Old Hoss" Radbourn, who had pitched the Grays to the pennant, continued his mastery and won three straight games.

The older National League was more prestigious than the American Association. In addition, the NL charged 50 cents for admission while the AA collected only 25 cents. Realizing that there was more money to be made in the National League, Day transferred Mets stars Keefe and Dude Esterbrook to the Gothams. But according to the rules of the day, when Keefe's and Esterbrook's contracts expired with the Mets there was a 10-day period during which any other AA team could sign them before the Gothams had a chance.

To forestall this possibility Mutrie took the two stars on a trip to Bermuda. The American Association owners were outraged and passed a resolution barring Mutrie from further employment in their league. The punishment became moot when he took over as manager of the National League Gothams in 1885.

The flamboyant Mutrie, nicknamed "Truthful Jim," was popular with his players, the press, and fans. He cut an impressive figure with his trademark stovepipe hat and handlebar mustache. As manager he made out the lineup card but left most game strategy to his field captains, the usual procedure at the time. His function was similar to that of today's general manager and road secretary. The Gothams were a strong team and had an unusual number of tall players. Mutrie took to calling them his "giants," and the name soon stuck.

With such stars as Keefe, Mickey Welch, Buck Ewing, John Montgomery Ward, Roger Connor, and Jim O'Rourke, all future Hall of Famers, the Giants won the 1888 and 1889 pennants and World Series. But the 1890 war with the Players' League destroyed the team. Most of the Giants were deeply involved in the Brotherhood—Ward was its president—and 13 Giants jumped to the new league in protest of the National League owners' proposed salary restrictions. Although the PL collapsed after only one year, Day lost control of the Giants in the fallout. After New York finished third in 1891, the new club owners voted Mutrie out as manager.

After leaving baseball Mutrie ran several businesses, including a hotel in Elmira and a newsstand on Staten Island. He suffered from health and financial difficulties until the mid-1920s, when Giants owner Charles Stoneham and manager John McGraw gave him a pension.

Buddy Myer

Myer, Charles Solomon **2B-SS-3B**

1925–41 B:3/16/1904, Ellisville, MS D:10/31/1974, Baton Rouge, LA Deb:9/26/1925, WAS AL BL/TR 5'10½", 163

G	AB	R	H	HR	RBI	OBP	SLG	AVG
1923	7038	1174	2131	38	850	.389	.406	.303

Lifetime .303 hitter Charles "Buddy" Myer led the American League in batting with a .349 average in 1935. After a rocky major league start at third base, he twice led AL second basemen in fielding percentage. Myer, who graduated from Mississippi A&M in 1925, attended spring training that year with Cleveland. When the Indians tried to send him to Dallas of the Texas League for seasoning, Myer did not like the terms of his proposed contract and refused to report. Not having signed a contract, he was free to take his services elsewhere and so he signed instead with New Orleans. After batting .336 there in 99 games, Myer's contract was purchased late in the season by Washington for $25,000.

Myer, who had played in just four regular season major league games, played in three Fall Classic contests in 1925. This was thanks to the fact that Pirates pitcher Vic Aldridge had beaned regular Senators third baseman Ossie Bluege in Game 2.

In 1926 Myer replaced Roger Peckinpaugh as the Senators' shortstop, but fielding deficiencies led him to be traded to the Red Sox in May 1927. In 1928 Myer, who once beat out 60 bunts in a season, led the AL in stolen bases.

Clark Griffith called his trading of Myer "the dumbest deal I ever made" and in December 1928 sent five players to Boston to retrieve him. In 1935 when he led the league in batting, Myer edged out Cleveland's Joe Vosmik for the lead on the last day of the season.

Randy Myers

Myers, Randall Kirk **P**

1985–98,* B:9/16/62, Vancouver, WA Deb:10/6/85, NY NL BL/TL 6'1", 215"

W	L	PCT	G	SV	IP	BB	SO	ERA
44	63	.411	728	347	884[2]	396	884	3.19

Randy Myers followed in the tradition of hard-throwing pitchers who have come through the New York Mets farm system. Briefly up with the team in the mid-1980s, it was not until 1987 that he showed an ability to get batters out on a consistent basis. Myers struck out 92 in 75 innings, and held lefthanded batters to a .175 average. His penchant for wearing camouflage fatigues and reading weapons magazines in the clubhouse only fortified his reputation as a fierce competitor.

The development of the young southpaw led the Mets to trade Jesse Orosco prior to the 1988 season. Myers didn't disappoint. He finished with a 7–3 record, a 1.72 ERA, and was 26-for-29 in save situations (second best in the league). Opponents batted .190 against him overall and an amazing .108 at Shea Stadium. He went 2–0 with a 0.00 ERA in three appearances in the National League Championship Series, although the Mets lost to the Dodgers in seven games.

Randall K. Myers—announcer Tim McCarver liked to accentuate the "K"—had another stellar season in 1989. He fashioned a streak of 22 scoreless innings, racked up 88 strikeouts, and earned 24 saves. He held opponents to a .192 average at Shea, which gave batters a lifetime .171 opponents average at home (the lowest home game average in 15 years). But that home changed for Myers on December 6, 1989, when the Mets sent him to Cincinnati with Kip Gross in exchange for John Franco and Don Brown.

Myers saved 31 games, made the All-Star team, and won the World Series with the Reds in 1990. He was the ringleader of the "Nasty Boys" in the Cincinnati bullpen, and shared Most Valuable Player honors with teammate Rob Dibble in the NLCS. He saved the clinching game in the Reds' shocking sweep of the A's in the World Series.

In 1991, Myers split time in the rotation and the bullpen before he was shipped to the Padres. He regained his form in San Diego and saved 38 games, but he moved to Chicago the following year and found a place in the record books.

Myers set an NL record with 53 saves for the Cubs in 1993. He appeared in 73 games, a career high, and walked away with the Rolaids Relief Man of the Year Award. Myers made the All-Star team the next two years and totaled 112 saves in a Cubs uniform, including a league-high 38 in 1995. The most lasting impression of him at Wrigley Field, however, occurred when a fan came out the stands to trade punches with the reliever after a late-inning home run.

In 1996 Myers signed with Baltimore as a free agent and surpassed 30 saves with his fourth team. He had two saves in Baltimore's victory over the Indians in the Division Series. He appeared in three ALCS games, but the game-winning home run he surrendered to Bernie Williams of the Yankees in the 11th inning of Game 1 marked the first run he had allowed in 16⅓ career postseason innings.

Signed by the Blue Jays to a big free agent deal starting in 1998, Myers had 23 saves prior to the '98 All-Star break to establish a team mark, but the Blue Jays nevertheless were disappointed enough with his overall pitching to dump his salary on San Diego in midseason for two minor leaguers, and Myers finished with a combined 4–7 record with a 4.92 ERA. In 1999 Myers had surgery that sidelined him for the season. With 347 career saves, he was second only to John Franco (416) among active pitchers at the end of the 1900s.

Charles Nagy

Nagy, Charles Harrison **P**

1990–* B:5/5/1967, Bridgeport, CT Deb:6/29/1990, CLE AL BL/TR 6'3" 200

W	L	PCT	G	SH	IP	BB	SO	ERA
121	86	.585	268	6	1766^{1}	529	1143	4.20

Throughout the 1990s, Charles Nagy was the most reliable starting pitcher for a Cleveland Indians team that consistently contended for the pennant. Following an injury-marred 1993 season, when he suffered a case of the shingles and hurt his right shoulder, Nagy didn't miss a start through the 1999 season.

A member of the 1988 U. S. Olympic baseball team that won the gold medal in Seoul, Korea, Nagy was selected by the Indians in the first round (17th pick overall) in the 1988 amateur draft. He was Carolina League Pitcher of the Year in 1989, and the Indians' Minor League Pitcher of the Year in 1990 after going 13–8 with a 2.52 ERA at Double-A Canton-Akron. The following year, he was part of the Tribe's rotation, starting 33 games and going 10–15.

Nagy established himself as Cleveland's ace in 1992. He won 17 games, including a one-hitter against the Baltimore Orioles on August 8, and earned a spot on the All-Star team. Over a two-year stretch in the mid-1990s Nagy was a combined 33–11, with his 16 victories in 1995 helping to lead Cleveland to the AL pennant. He won the deciding game in the Indians' three-game sweep of the Boston Red Sox in the 1995 Division Series.

Although he took the loss as the AL's starting pitcher in the 1996 All-Star Game, Nagy had no trouble winning during the season and finished with a league-best .722 winning percentage. Baltimore pounded him, however, in Game 1 of the 1996 Division Series. He struck out 12 in his next start, but the Indians lost the series in four games.

Nagy helped Cleveland reach the World Series in 1997. He held the Orioles scoreless for seven innings in Game 6 of the Championship Series; the Indians clinched the pennant with a 1–0 win in 11 innings. Called to face the Marlins in the 10th inning of Game 7 of the World Series—his first relief appearance since his rookie year—Nagy surrendered Edgar Renteria's Series-winning hit in the 11th inning.

Nagy notched his 100th career victory against the Seattle Mariners on August 25, 1998. He became a 17-game winner for the third time in 1999, despite a 4.95 ERA.

Billy Nash

Nash, William Mitchell **3B**

1884–98 M(1896, 62–68) B:6/24/1865, Richmond, VA D:11/15/1929, East Orange, NJ Deb:8/5/1884, RIC AA BR/TR 5'8½", 167

G	AB	R	H	HR	RBI	OBP	SLG	AVG
1549	5849	1072	1606	60	977	.366	.381	.275

Billy Nash played third base in Boston for 11 seasons and served as the Beaneaters' team captain. He has almost been forgotten, however, due to the hitting and innovative fielding achievements of his successor, Hall of Fame third baseman Jimmy Collins.

Nash made it to the big leagues with Richmond of the American Association in 1884. The next year he went to Boston, and the season after that he became a regular. Over the next decade he never hit less than .260, and he always drove in 75 or more runs. Nash's best year came in 1893, when he batted .291, hit 10 homers, and had 123 RBIs. That year he also led all National League third basemen in fielding average.

A leader on and off the field for Boston's pennant winners of 1891–93, Nash continued to produce even when the Beaneaters weren't playoff quality, driving in 108 runs in 1895. He left Boston in 1896 to become the Philadelphia Phillies' player-manager. Nash's team produced only a 62–68 record, but on a scouting trip to Fall River, Massachusetts, he scored big by returning with eventual Hall of Famer Nap Lajoie.

Denny Neagle

Neagle, Dennis Edward **P**

1991–99 B:9/13/1968, Gambrills, MD Deb:7/27/1991, MIN AL BL/TL 6'2", 217

W	L	PCT	G	SH	IP	BB	SO	ERA
90	60	.600	286	7	1311	378	998	3.82

One of baseball's more durable and reliable pitchers in the 1990s, Denny Neagle led the National League in wins (20 in 1997), starts (31 in 1995), and innings (209⅔) in 1995), and finished third in the NL's Cy Young Award voting in 1997. Without Neagle's performance in the final month, the 1999 Reds could not have tied the Mets for the Wild Card slot in the standings.

The first Red to win six straight starts since Tom Browning won eight straight in 1989, Neagle went undefeated from August 30 to September 25, 1999, before getting a no-decision at Milwaukee. His 5–0 showing and 2.00 ERA in September earned him his first NL Pitcher of the Month Award. He appeared in relief in the one-game playoff against the Mets, but the Reds lost.

Neagle landed in Cincinnati as part of a five-player trade in November 1998. Once the top starter for Pittsburgh, Neagle was handed that role again with the Reds, but lost it when he spent two early stints on the disabled list with shoulder problems. After getting his first win for Cincinnati on July 20, Neagle went 9–2 with a 3.11 ERA over his last 13 starts. The two-time All-Star topped a dozen wins in four of his eight previous seasons.

Drafted and signed by the Twins, Neagle was a 20-game winner in the minors. He reached the Twins in 1991, was traded to Pittsburgh a year later, and then spent two seasons in the bullpen before becoming a full-time starter in 1994. The best season of his career came in 1997 with pitching-rich Atlanta, where he went 20–5 on a team that boasted three Cy Young Award winners.

Greasy Neale

Neale, Alfred Earle **OF**

1916–22, 1924 B:11/5/1891, Parkersburg, WV D:11/2/1973, Lake Worth, FL Deb:4/12/1916, CIN NL BL/TR 6', 170

G	AB	R	H	HR	RBI	OBP	SLG	AVG
768	2661	319	688	8	200	.319	.332	.259

Although he always claimed that his abilities were limited, Greasy Neale was talented enough to play professionally in two sports. Early on he was best known as a fast outfielder with a reliable bat, and he spent eight seasons in the major leagues and starred in a World Series. But the year after he joined the Cincinnati Reds, he also began playing football with the Canton Bulldogs of the pre-NFL Ohio League.

Neale, who had earned his lifelong nickname in an argument with another youngster, had excelled at basketball, football, and baseball at West Virginia Wesleyan College. The Reds signed him after college, and in 1916, his first year in the majors, he batted .262. The next year he boosted that to .294. That, however, was the offensive high-water mark of his career. Neale's main value was as a wide-ranging outfielder and base-stealing threat.

In 1919 the longtime cellar-dwelling Reds won the NL pennant. In that year's World Series, they met the Chicago White Sox and defeated them in eight games. Only later was it revealed that eight of the White Sox players had conspired to throw the Series. Neale was a star for Cincinnati, batting .357 and leading the Reds with 10 hits. Traded to the Philadelphia Phillies in 1921, he returned to the Reds before the season ended. After three appearances in 1924 he left the majors, but not major team sports.

Neale had started coaching football even while he was still playing for the Reds, and he was a successful college football coach for a number of years. When millionaire Alexis Thompson succeeded Bert Bell as the owner of the Philadelphia Eagles in 1941, he hired Neale as his coach. The Eagles had been a perennial second-division club since they were founded in 1933, but Neale built them into a power. They were runners-up in their division in 1944, 1945, and 1946.

Then, in 1947, the Eagles won the NFL's Eastern Division. The next year they went one better, defeating the Chicago Cardinals, 7–0, for the championship. A year later they defeated the Los Angeles Rams in the title game, 14–0. Neale retired after the 1950 season. He was later elected to both the College Football Hall of Fame and the Pro Football Hall of Fame.

Art Nehf

Nehf, Arthur Neukom **P**

1915–29 B:7/31/1892, Terre Haute, IN D:12/18/1960, Phoenix, AZ Deb:8/13/1915, BOS NL BL/TL 5'9½", 176

W	L	PCT	G	SH	IP	BB	SO	ERA
184	120	.605	451	28	2707²	640	844	3.20

Had Art Nehf pitched during the television era, instead of from 1915 through 1929, he might have been elected to the Hall of Fame. In addition to being a winner, he had many of the qualities prized—and exploited by—today's media. He starred for a dynasty based in New York, carried a big price tag, and made several appearances in the World Series.

Nehf spent 15 years in the majors, breaking in with the Boston Braves and also playing for the New York Giants, Cincinnati Reds, and Chicago Cubs. He wasn't overpowering, but he worked with near-impeccable control. He walked only 640 batters during his career, and his personal high of 76 came in 1918, when he led the league with 28 complete games.

Nehf got his start with the Braves in 1915, one year after their miracle World Series championship. Within two years he was in the starting rotation, and in 1917 and 1918 he led the club in victories. On August 1, 1918, he pitched 21 innings in a 2–0 loss to Pittsburgh. In August 1919 Nehf was involved in a historic financial deal. After starting 8–9, he went to the Giants for four players and $55,000. At the time it was the largest sum ever paid for a baseball player.

In 1920 Nehf justified the Giants' expenditure, going 21–12. For the next four years, the Giants were the best team in the league, with Nehf as one of the key components of their success. In the 1921 World Series against the Yankees, he started the final game, defeating a future Hall of Famer, Waite Hoyt, in Game 8. In the ninth inning Nehf retired pinch hitter Babe Ruth on an infield grounder, and wrapped up the Series two outs later.

The next year's Series found Nehf once again pitching the clincher, this time outdueling Joe Bush, the Yankees' 26-game winner, in a 5–3 victory. In all, he split eight decisions while pitching in five World Series, but he compiled an ERA of only 2.16.

In 1925 Nehf went 11–9, and the Giants slipped to fifth place. On May 11, 1926, he was sold to Cincinnati, which in turn dealt him to the Cubs the following year. Nehf made his final World Series appearances with the Cubs in 1929, both in relief. In Game 4, he was one of the victims of the greatest comeback in World Series history.

Trailing Philadelphia two games to one, the Cubs had opened an 8–0 lead. In the seventh inning the A's rallied to knock out Chicago starter Charlie Root, and Nehf entered the game with an 8–4 lead and two men on base. Mule Haas hit a fly ball to center that was lost in the sun by Hack Wilson. By the time the ball was retrieved, Haas had a three-run homer. Nehf walked Mickey Cochrane and was replaced, and Philadelphia scored three more runs in the inning to win the game. Two days later the A's were world champions.

As it turned out, Cochrane was the final batter that Nehf faced in the big leagues. Upon leaving baseball, he worked as an engineer. He suffered a heart attack in 1932 and was never able to work again. At the time of his death in 1960, a wire account described Nehf as one of the best lefthanders in National League history.

Robb Nen

Nen, Robert Allen **P**

1993–98 B:11/28/1969, San Pedro, CA Deb:4/10/1993, TEX AL BR/TR 6'4", 200

W	L	PCT	G	SV	IP	BB	SO	ERA
31	32	.492	428	185	497^{2}	199	527	3.29

Robb Nen, the son of former major league first baseman Dick Nen, had the right pedigree to go from a 32nd-round draft pick to one of the best relief pitchers in baseball. He was a starter in the minor leagues with Texas, but was made into a full-time relief pitcher after being traded to the Florida Marlins in 1993.

Nen began the 1994 season as a setup pitcher in Florida's bullpen; he became the team's closer when season-ending injuries claimed two other pitchers. He wound up with 15 saves in 1994, saved 23 the next season (including 19 after the All-Star break), and became known as one of the top relievers in the game. He blew away enemy hitters with a 100 mph fastball and 90 mph slider.

He won nine and saved 35 in 1997 as the Marlins went on to win the World Series. Nen saved four games and won another in the postseason, allowing no runs in seven of his eight appearances. He was one of the first Marlins to be traded during the club's post-championship dismantling, going to the Giants for three minor leaguers. Nen continued his dominance in San Francisco, saving 40 games with a 1.52 ERA in an All-Star year in 1998. He saved 37 games for the Giants in 1999.

Graig Nettles

Nettles, Graig **3B**

1967–88 B:8/20/1944, San Diego, CA Deb:9/6/1967, MIN AL BL/TR 6', 186

G	AB	R	H	HR	RBI	OBP	SLG	AVG
2700	8986	1193	2225	390	1314	.332	.421	.248

A great glove, a powerful lefthanded stroke, and gritty durability were the key attributes of third baseman Graig Nettles' 22-year major league career, half of which was spent in the glamorous but intense pressure cooker of New York with George Steinbrenner's Yankees. The first six seasons of Nettles' career were divided between the Minnesota Twins and the Cleveland Indians.

Nettles was never a regular in Minnesota, where he played mainly outfield but some third base. He was traded after the 1969 season in the deal that sent Luis Tiant to Minnesota. In his three seasons as the regular third basemen with the Indians, Nettles became a major producer, hitting 71 homers and driving home 218 runs. It was enough to earn him a ticket to the Big Apple as part of a trade that sent prospects John Ellis, Jerry Kenney, Charlie Spikes, and Rusty Torres to Cleveland.

In New York Nettles quickly became a star, demonstrating his lightning reflexes at the hot corner and his ability to power baseballs into Yankee Stadium's short right field porch. He hit at least 20 home runs in each of his first seven years in New York. In 1975 Nettles was selected to the first of his six All-Star Game appearances. Strangely, he did not make the All-Star Game the next year, despite the fact that his 32 home runs led the American League and helped carry Billy Martin's Yankees to their first pennant in 12 years. But the Yanks suffered a humiliating sweep at the hands of the Cincinnati Reds in the World Series.

In 1977 Nettles belted 37 home runs, second in the league behind Boston's Jim Rice, and had 107 RBIs, both career highs, as the Yankees won the pennant and went on to defeat the Los Angeles Dodgers in six games for their first World Series title since 1962. The following season Nettles batted a career-high .276 as the Yankees won their third straight pennant. In the World Series rematch with the Dodgers, Nettles' spectacular play in the field in Game 3 lifted the Yankees and turned around the Series' which the Yankees had trailed 2–0. He made four terrific defensive plays to break the Dodgers' momentum as the Yankees took four straight to win their second consecutive championship.

In spring training 1984, after 11 years in New York, Nettles was traded to the San Diego Padres for pitchers Dennis Rasmussen and Darin Cloninger. Nettles hit at least one homer in six straight games in his first year in San Diego. He then appeared in all five games of the 1984 World Series loss to Detroit.

Nettles signed with the Braves in 1987, a season highlighted by his pinch-hit grand slam off Houston's Aurelio Lopez on May 21. He closed out his career with the Montreal Expos as a part-timer in 1988. Nettles' legacy includes 319 round-trippers as a third baseman, the most ever at that position in the American League.

Don Newcombe

Newcombe, Donald **P**

1949–51, 1954–60 B:6/14/1926, Madison, NJ
Deb:5/20/1949, BRO NL BL/TR 6'4", 225

W	L	PCT	G	SH	IP	BB	SO	ERA
149	90	.623	344	24	2154^{2}	490	1129	3.56

Don Newcombe was the first great African-American pitcher in the major leagues. The ace of the Dodgers' "Boys of Summer" staff, he was the only player ever to win Rookie of the Year, Cy Young, and Most Valuable Player awards.

Born in Staten Island, Newcombe grew up in New Jersey. Large for his age, he began pitching semipro ball at age 13. Five years later—with many regular players in the Armed Forces—he joined Effa Manley's Newark Eagles of the Negro National League. In October 1945 Newcombe pitched in an exhibition game at Ebbets Field. Despite coming out after two innings because his arm tightened up, he was asked by scout Clyde Sukeforth to report the next day to the Dodgers' office. There the righthander signed a contract for $375 a month plus a $1,500 bonus. He thought he was signing with the Brooklyn Brown Dodgers. But in 1946 Newcombe, Jackie Robinson, Roy Campanella, and pitcher Roy Partlow were assigned to train with the minor league Montreal Royals, a Dodgers farm club.

In part because few clubs in the Dodgers system would accept blacks, Newcombe and Campanella were assigned to Nashua of the Class B New England League. There he went 14–4 in 1946 and 19–6 the next year. "They liked me because I was so big and could throw the ball hard," said Newcombe, who was known as "Big Newk." "But I was always wild. I didn't know where the ball was going."

Promoted to Montreal in 1948, Newcombe went 17–6. He started 1949 with the Royals but then was quickly promoted to the Dodgers. Clobbered in his first appearance, he thought he was going back to Montreal, but manager Burt Shotton gave him some words of encouragement and a starting assignment. Newcombe rose to the occasion, shutting out Cincinnati, 3–0. He finished the season 17–8 and was named NL Rookie of the Year.

One of Newcombe's weaknesses was his failure to stay focused. He would lose concentration, get sloppy, and find himself in trouble. Robinson demanded more from him. If he saw Newcombe's attention wandering, he would say, "You should go to the clubhouse and take your uniform off and go home because you don't want to pitch. You've got no business in the big leagues, Newk. You ought to go home, because you are fooling around."

That fall Newcombe had his first World Series disappointment. He faced off against Yankees ace Allie Reynolds in the opener, and it turned out to be one of the great pitching duels in Series history. Newcombe lost, 1–0, when Tommy Henrich led off the bottom of the ninth with a home run.

Newcombe followed his big rookie season by going 19–11 in 1950 and 20–9 in 1951; he was selected to the NL All-Star squad in each of his first three years. But what everybody remembers from those two seasons was a home run he gave up and a game he couldn't finish. On the final day of the 1950 season, with the Dodgers trailing the Phillies by one game, Newcombe pitched nine strong innings against Philadelphia. But in the 10th Dick Sisler beat him with a three-run homer. Then, in the final contest of the 1951 season—the rubber match of a three-game playoff between the Dodgers and Giants—Newcombe took a 4–1 lead into the ninth, gave up three hits, and recorded only one out. He had to be relieved by Ralph Branca, who gave up Bobby Thomson's famous home run.

Newcombe spent 1952 and 1953 in the military. He struggled when he came back in 1954, going 9–8 with a 4.55 ERA. But he rebounded in the Dodgers' dream season of 1955 with a 20–5 record, despite being suspended by manager Walter Alston for refusing to pitch batting practice. Not until he apologized and pitched in relief was he allowed to start again.

In 1956 Newcombe had his greatest season, going 27–7 and becoming the first pitcher to win the Cy Young and the Most Valuable Player awards in the same season. But he failed again in the big finale when he started Game 7 of the World Series and didn't survive the third inning.

After 1956 it was all down hill for Newcombe. The Dodgers traded him to the Red Sox in June 1958, and in July 1960 he was sold to Cleveland. He was 31 and his big league career was over. Alcoholism had caught up with him. "In 1956 I was the best pitcher in baseball," he recalled. "Four years later, I was out of the major leagues. It must have been the drinking. When you're young, you can handle it, but the older you get, the more it bothers you."

When Newcombe returned to baseball in 1962, spending a year in Japan with the Chunichi Dragons, it was as a hitter, not a pitcher. One of the better hitting pitchers ever, he had a .271 career average in the major leagues, and set an NL record for pitchers with seven homers in 1955. He was still drinking heavily in Japan, however, and quickly wore out his welcome.

Back in the United States, Newcombe had difficulty holding jobs, and his behavior was increasingly erratic. His first marriage dissolved. He nearly killed himself and his second wife by driving into oncoming traffic. He nearly drowned his son in a swimming pool. Finally his wife took their children away. Newcombe got down on his knees and swore that he would never drink again, and he quit.

At the end of the 1990s, Newcombe was counseling players in the Dodgers organization about substance abuse. "I had friends who died young because nobody cared about them drinking," he told young players. "The Dodgers care. I care. You can come to me."

Hal Newhouser

Newhouser, Harold **P**

1939–55 B:5/20/1921, Detroit, MI D:11/10/1998, Bloomfield Hills, MI Deb:9/29/1939, DET AL BL/TL 6'2", 192

W	L	PCT	G	SH	IP	BB	SO	ERA
207	150	.580	488	33	2993	1249	1796	3.06

Hal Newhouser is the only pitcher who ever won back-to-back Most Valuable Player Awards. His dominance of the American League—going 29–9 with a 2.22 ERA in 1944 and 25–9 with a 1.81 ERA in 1945, while leading the league in strikeouts both years—is sometimes unfairly attributed to the shortage of quality players caused by World War II. But that doesn't give enough credit to Newhouser, a seasoned professional with an excellent slider who was kept out of the military by a heart condition.

When Newhouser was in high school, Detroit Tigers scout Wish Egan took a special interest in the hometown boy. Egan persuaded Newhouser to give up high school sports in favor of playing in the more challenging American Legion League. In 1938 Egan received permission to sign the 17-year-old and took a cash bonus of five $100 bills to the Newhouser home. He gave one to Newhouser and four to his father.

Later that day Egan's secretary called and said, "I have terrible news for you. Mickey Cochrane is out as manager and Del Baker is going to take his place." Egan calmly replied, "A couple of years from now, the Tigers will win pennants no matter who manages them because I just signed the greatest lefthanded pitcher I ever saw—a kid by the name of Hal Newhouser."

Egan convinced Tigers management to bring Newhouser to Detroit in September of 1939, despite the youngster's mixed results in the minors. In his initial four full years with the Tigers, Newhouser went a disappointing 34–51. But after Paul Richards helped him to develop a slider, Newhouser's improvement was staggering. In the following five seasons he went 118–46, pitched 25 shutouts, led the league three times in wins, and twice in strikeouts and ERA.

With the 1945 pennant, Egan's 1938 prediction came true. Then Newhouser pitched the Tigers to a world championship, winning two of his three World Series decisions against the Cubs. Hammered in the opener, he yielded seven runs in less than three innings, but came back to win Game 5 and the decisive Game 7.

Newhouser was selected to the All-Star Game seven consecutive times in the 1940s, but a sore shoulder took its toll on him by 1950. After several marginal seasons, the Tigers released the 32-year-old hurler in July of 1953. Newhouser signed on with Cleveland in 1954; the Indians used him judiciously in relief, and he went 7–2 for the pennant winners.

Newhouser retired in 1955, and tried his hand at coaching and scouting before becoming a banker. The Veterans Committee elected Newhouser to the Hall of Fame in 1992.

Bobo Newsom

Newsom, Louis Norman **P**

1929–30, 1932, 1934–48, 1952–53 B:8/11/1907, Hartsville, SC D:12/7/1962, Orlando, FL Deb:9/11/1929, BRO NL BR/TR 6'2", 220

W	L	PCT	G	SH	IP	BB	SO	ERA
211	222	.487	600	31	3759[1]	1732	2082	3.98

There may have been a more traveled, more injured, more quotable, or more entertaining pitcher than Bobo Newsom, but it is hard to think of one offhand. "He was as tough as shoe leather, as unlucky as an old maid, as colorful as a treeful of owls, and about the friendliest fellow you'd ever want to meet," one baseball writer said about Newsom. He could pitch, too.

Managers and owners were often willing to acquire this baseball nomad, but they just as often regretted it. Whether he was winning 20 or losing 20—he did each three times—Newsom would usually do something to infuriate the management.

Washington Senators owner Clark Griffith once instructed coach Earl Brucker never to let him sign Newsom again. "I know he'll meet me at the train," Griffith told Brucker in spring training, "and I know that if you don't stick by me every minute, I'll weaken and sign him up." He did.

Newsom spent 20 years in the majors and changed uniforms 15 times. He had five tours of duty with the Senators, three with the Browns, and two each with the A's and the Brooklyn Dodgers.

The Dodgers brought him up to the big leagues for the first time in 1929 for only three games. Newsom won 30 games the next season for the Los Angeles Angels of the Pacific Coast League, although he claimed it was actually 32. "Who ya gonna believe, Bobo," he challenged skeptics (using the name that he applied both to himself and to others), "the record book or the guy that done it?"

In 1932 Newsom was on his way to spring training with the Cubs when he drove over a 200-foot cliff, miraculously sustaining only a broken leg. While recuperating, he amused himself by writing letters to Cubs owner P.K. Wrigley, letting him know what a fine pitcher he had obtained. When Newsom finally got back on his feet, one of the first things he did was attend a mule auction, where one of the animals kicked him in the same leg, fracturing it once more.

Newsom finally landed a starting job in 1934 with the St. Louis Browns, and on September 18 of that year he pitched nine innings of no-hit baseball against the Red Sox. But he lost the game in the 10th on two walks and a bad-hop base hit. Years later, Newsom was asked if he had pitched any other no-hitters. "Just the one," he responded. "They don't grow in bunches like bananas, son."

The next year Newsom was traded midseason to Washington. In one game he got two strikes on the Indians' Earl Averill and shouted, "Now, Bobo, I'm gonna whiff you with an outside pitch!" Averill lined the pitch off Newsom's knee. Newsom managed to throw him out at first, however, and then proceeded to shake off the pain and pitch a complete game. "I got a piece of news for you," he informed the Senators' trainer after the contest. "Bobo thinks his laig is broke." It was, and Newsom was out for five weeks.

At the next year's season opener, with President Franklin Roosevelt in attendance, the Yankees' Ben Chapman laid down a bunt, which Washington third baseman Ossie Bluege fielded and fired toward first. The throw plunked Newsom squarely in the jaw, breaking it in two places. "When the president comes out to see ol' Bobo pitch, ol' Bobo ain't gonna let him down," Newsom said through clenched teeth. He refused to leave the game and pitched a 1–0, four-hit shutout.

After going 60–67 in his first four full seasons—with three different teams—Newsom had three straight 20-win seasons starting in 1938. His best year was 1940 when he went 21–5 for the Tigers, a season capped by a 13-game winning streak. He also pitched three scoreless innings in the All-Star Game, which he had been selected to for the third consecutive year. But it was against the Reds in the 1940 World Series that Newsom had his proudest moments.

The morning after Newsom beat Paul Derringer in Game 1, his father died of a heart attack in his Cincinnati hotel room. The Newsom family returned home to South Carolina, but Bobo stayed and dedicated his performance in Game 5 to his father. He pitched a three-hit shutout. Manager Del Baker sent Newsom out to pitch Game 7, and when Newsom was asked if he was going out to win another one for his father, he said, "Why, no. I think I'll win this one for myself." He didn't but he came close, giving up two runs in the seventh in a 2–1 loss.

In 1941 Newsom became the highest-paid pitcher in the game at $35,000 per year. But he proceeded to lead the league with 20 losses, against 12 wins. Detroit sold him to Washington the next March, but his stay at Griffith Stadium was brief. That August, Newsom was peddled to Brooklyn, where his presence nearly precipitated a player revolt and reduced manager Leo Durocher to begging Branch Rickey to unload the pitcher.

After playing for four teams during World War II, Newsom was back with a pennant winner in 1947. Sold on waivers to the Yankees in July, he won seven games and was voted a 75-percent World Series share. When he went out to order his world championship ring, he informed the jeweler, "Just make it three-quarter size, that's my measure in this town."

With that kind of irreverence, Newsom's tenure with the stuffy Yankees was short. He signed on with the Giants in 1948 but was released in midseason. He spent the next three years in the minors, but in 1952, at age 44, he made it back to the majors with the Senators. He lasted 10 games before being traded to Philadelphia.

Newsom finally retired in 1953 at 46. Lifetime he was 211–222, which made him only the second pitcher, after Jack Powell, to win 200 games and still have a losing record.

Kid Nichols

Nichols, Charles Augustus **P**

1890–1901, 1904–06 M(1904–05, 80–88) B:9/14/1869, Madison, WI D:4/11/1953, Kansas City, MO Deb:4/23/1890, BOS NL BB/TR 5'10½", 175

W	L	PCT	G	SH	IP	BB	SO	ERA
361	208	.634	620	48	5056^{1}	1268	1873	2.95

Amos Rusie, Cy Young, and Kid Nichols are generally held to have been the three greatest pitchers of the 19th century. Rusie was the premier strikeout artist of the time. Young continued to pitch for another decade and retired with untouchable career totals. But Nichols was the winningest pitcher of the 1890s, collecting 30 more victories than Young and 64 more than Rusie. Moreover, he was the only one of the three to pitch his team to a pennant during that decade, and he did it five times.

The slender righthander delivered a basic overhand fastball from a windup so simple it was almost nonexistent. "Many a pitcher uses an elaborate windup," he said in 1901, "and I have been repeatedly asked to adopt one. I have persistently refused. I don't approve of it because it interferes with the control of the ball. It's a useless exertion on the arm; and as far as confusing the batter is concerned, it doesn't always work." Although his fastball compared favorably with Rusie's, Nichols' real strength was his control. Batters knew a fastball was coming, but they had no idea where it would be placed.

Nichols first gained attention as a pitcher in 1886 while hurling for the Blue Avenue Club, an amateur team in Kansas City. In 1887 he turned professional with Kansas City of the Western League and won 21 games. He split the next season between Kansas City and Memphis, then pitched spectacularly in 1889 for Omaha of the Western Association, going 36–12. Frank Selee, his manager at Omaha, was hired to manage Boston's National League team in 1890, and he brought Nichols with him.

Selee faced a difficult task in Boston. Although the club had finished second in 1889, most of its best players had jumped to the Players' League in 1890. But Selee, an astute judge of talent, purchased first baseman Tommy Tucker from Baltimore, versatile Bobby Lowe from minor league Milwaukee, and shortstop Herman Long from Kansas City. Then he installed Nichols as ace of the pitching staff.

Nichols, nicknamed "Kid" because of his youth and his slender build, went 27–19 and posted a 2.23 earned run average. He completed all 47 of his starts and led the league with seven shutouts. In 1891 Selee's Beaneaters took the National League pennant, winning 23 of 30 September games to clinch the flag despite not having a .300 hitter. Nichols went 30–17 and even found time to lead the league with three saves. Because of interleague squabbles, no World Series was held between National League and AA winners, preventing what would have been an all-Boston affair.

The Beaneaters were even better in 1892. Outfielder Hugh Duffy added some heavy hitting, and Nichols improved his record to 35–16. That year the National League divided the season into halves, declaring that the winners of each would meet at season's end in a "World Series." Boston won the first half by a big margin and finished the year with the best overall record, but Cleveland collected the second-half crown. In the postseason series, Boston knocked off Cleveland without a loss. Nichols pitched the final game, defeating Young.

In 1893 the pitching distance was increased from 50 feet to 60 feet 6 inches, adversely affecting many pitchers. Nichols' strikeout total was cut in half, from 187 to 94, and his ERA went up by more than half a run. Yet the Kid remained one of the league's most effective hurlers, going 34–14. Boston coasted to its third straight pennant.

From 1894 through 1896, as injuries and age caught up with the Beaneaters, they finished well behind the Baltimore Orioles, but Nichols remained superb. He won 32 games in 1894, 26 in 1895, and a league-high 30 in 1896. Selee rebuilt the club in 1897, and the pennant race that season was a battle between the Beaneaters and Orioles. Boston took the pennant by two games, paced by Nichols' mark of 31–11.

Selee's Beaneaters won the pennant again in 1898. Nichols led the league in wins for the third straight year with a 31–12 record, the seventh time in eight years he had registered at least 30 victories. In 1899 the Beaneaters slumped, and so did Nichols. His slide continued in 1900, when he had his first losing season, going 13–16.

Boston's owners were notoriously cheap. When the American League declared itself a major league in 1901, many of the Beaneaters jumped to the new circuit for better wages. Nichols stuck it out and pitched well, earning 19 wins, but was released at the end of the season in a cost-cutting move. He became pitcher-manager of Kansas City of the Western League and won 48 games in two seasons.

In 1904 Nichols returned to the National League and won 21 games as St. Louis pitcher-manager. A pair of brothers, Frank and Stanley Robison, owned the Cardinals. Frank had hired Nichols, who didn't get along with Stanley; subsequently, Stanley fired Nichols as manager early in 1905.

The Cardinals kept Nichols as a pitcher, but when Stanley tried to humiliate him by ordering him to serve as gate attendant before a game, Nichols balked and was released. He won a few games for the Phillies and then retired.

In his career Nichols won 361 games, sixth best all-time, with an amazing 531 complete games in 561 starts. After retiring, Nichols and Cubs shortstop Joe Tinker opened a string of bowling alleys in Kansas City. Nichols became one of the finest bowlers in the area, winning a championship trophy at age 64. He also dabbled in real estate and the motion-picture business. In 1949, four years before his death at age 83, he was enshrined in the Hall of Fame.

Bill Nicholson

Nicholson, William Beck **OF**

1936, 1939–53 B:12/11/1914, Chestertown, MD D:3/8/1996, Chestertown, MD Deb:6/13/1936, PHI AL BL/TR 6', 205

G	AB	R	H	HR	RBI	OBP	SLG	AVG
1677	5546	837	1484	235	948	.365	.465	.268

For a five-year period at the beginning of the 1940s, Bill Nicholson was as dangerous a longball threat as there was in the National League. He earned the nickname "Swish" for the mighty cuts he would take as he limbered up outside the batter's box. His fans would chant, "Swish, Swish, Swish" each time he waved his bat in menacing fashion at an opposing pitcher. And as often as anyone during that time, when the powerful Nicholson connected, the ball traveled far into the seats.

Nicholson first reached the majors in 1936, when he had a brief stint with the Philadelphia A's. But he got his first serious look in 1939 when he joined the Chicago Cubs. His home run assault began the next year when he socked 25—second most in the league—knocked in 98 runs, batted .297, and was selected to his first of four All-Star Games. During the next two seasons Nicholson became one of the most feared batters in the National League, finishing third and fourth in home runs, with 26 and 21, respectively.

But Nicholson was just warming up. In 1943 he hit 29 homers and had 128 RBIs, both league highs, and batted a career-high .309. He lost out on the Most Valuable Player Award to Cardinals first baseman Stan Musial. The following year Nicholson hammered 33 homers, drove in 122 runs, and scored 116 runs, each tops in the NL. He never equaled those numbers during the remainder of his career, however, and he spent his last five seasons as a part-time player with the Philadelphia Phillies.

Joe Niekro

Niekro, Joseph Franklin **P**

1967–88 B:11/7/1944, Martins Ferry, OH Deb:4/16/1967, CHI NL BR/TR 6'1", 190

W	L	PCT	G	SH	IP	BB	SO	ERA
221	204	.520	702	29	3584	1262	1747	3.59

Although Joe Niekro always pitched in the shadow of his older brother, Phil, he still managed a 22-year career and was, for a time, one of the best pitchers in the major leagues. The Niekros had 539 major league victories, better than any other brother combination ever, and Joe contributed 221 wins to that total.

The brothers grew up in coal country, in the Appalachian foothills of eastern Ohio. Joe was five years younger than Phil, and, since he attended West Liberty State College before signing with the Chicago Cubs in 1966, his older brother beat him into professional baseball. At the time Joe signed, Phil was already into his third season as a reliever for the Braves.

Joe began his career with a standard fastball and curveball. He made the Cubs' starting rotation in 1967 and went 10–7. The following year he was 14–10, but he was traded to the expansion Padres early in the 1969 season. Joe struggled in San Diego with a poor team, finishing the year 8–18, and was traded to Detroit in December for pitchers Pat Dobson and Dave Campbell.

After one year in Detroit, Joe began to be used more regularly in relief than as a starter. He hurt his arm in 1972 and appeared in two games for Class AAA Toledo, in one of them pitching a no-hitter, before going down again with arm miseries. Although he came back in 1973 to pitch effectively for Toledo, Detroit gave up on him and he joined his brother Phil and the Braves in a waiver deal.

Although Joe spent only parts of two seasons in Atlanta, the experience changed his career. Under his brother's tutelage, he began throwing the knuckleball, which became his major weapon. Joe threw it harder than Phil and never abandoned his other pitches, which he could still throw effectively. In 1975 Joe was sold to the Houston Astros, and in 1976 he hit his first and only major league home run, coming, ironically, against his brother.

Joe pitched primarily in relief for two seasons before being added to the Astros' starting rotation in 1978. The next year it all came together: he led the league with 21 victories and five shutouts, was named to the All-Star Game, and finished second to Bruce Sutter in the Cy Young Award voting. In 1980 his 20 wins paced the Astros to their first division championship. In Game 3 of the NLCS against Philadelphia that year, Joe pitched 10 scoreless innings in an 11-inning, 1–0 Houston win. The Astros, however, lost the Series in five games. In the playoffs following the strike-shortened 1981 season, Niekro again pitched shutout ball, going eight innings in another 11-inning, 1–0 Astros win. But once again his team fell in five, this time to Los Angeles.

Niekro had three more excellent seasons with the Astros, notching 17 wins in 1982, 15 in 1983, and 16 in 1984. The following season, however, he was only 9–12 when he was dealt to the Yankees for pitcher Jim Deshaies and two players to be named later. In New York, Joe was reunited with Phil, but not for long—Phil signed with Cleveland prior to the 1986 season.

On May 23, 1987, Joe beat California, 3–0, to put the Niekro brothers in a tie with the Perrys, Jim and Gaylord, with 529 victories. Phil collected win 530 a week later. But the Yankees released Joe, and he signed with Minnesota, with whom he went on to pitch in the World Series. He returned to the Twins in 1988 but retired after only five appearances.

Phil Niekro

Niekro, Philip Henry **P**

1964–87 B:4/1/1939, Blaine, OH Deb:4/15/1964, MIL NL BR/TR 6'1", 180

W	L	PCT	G	SH	IP	BB	SO	ERA
318	274	.537	864	45	5404[1]	1809	3342	3.35

To opposing teams, pitcher Phil Niekro and his knuckleball must have seemed to be a permanent fixture of the game. Niekro pitched for two decades with the Braves, in Milwaukee and Atlanta, before spending four years in the American League. He won more than 300 games and lost more games than any other National League pitcher in the 20th century. Phil and Joe Niekro hold the record for most wins by a brother combination in major league history: 539.

The Niekros' father was a fastball pitcher in an industrial league in eastern Ohio. While playing catch when Phil was 10 or 11 years old, his father threw him a knuckleball as a joke. The knuckler eluded young Niekro, but it fascinated him and he wanted to learn how to throw it. By the time he reached high school, Phil had become so proficient with the pitch that his father could no longer catch it.

The Milwaukee Braves were sufficiently interested in Phil and his knuckleball to sign him for a $500 bonus. He made the rounds of minor league teams, and, according to writer Pat Jordan, who pitched with Niekro in 1959, "appeared only in the last innings of hopelessly lost games. He was inefficient because he could not throw his knuckleball over the plate, and preferred instead, to deal up one of his other pitches, all of which were deficient."

Mastery of the knuckleball came slowly but surely. After a brief appearance with the Braves in 1964, he made the major-league roster to stay in 1965 as a relief pitcher. In 1967 Niekro began to be used as an occasional starter, and he went 11–9 with nine saves and a league-leading 1.87 ERA.

Soon Niekro was ace of the Atlanta staff. In 1969 he won 23 games and was selected to his first All-Star Game, as the Braves captured the first NL West title. That year he struck out 193 against only 57 walks. He then lost in Game 1 of the first NLCS to Tom Seaver, as the Mets swept the Braves in three games. Niekro struggled in 1970, losing 18 games and seeing his ERA soar to 4.27. He developed a sore arm after two more successful seasons, and Atlanta manager Eddie Mathews moved him to the bullpen at the start of 1973.

Niekro eventually returned to the rotation, and on August 5, 1973, he no-hit the Padres, the first no-hitter for the Braves since 1961. In 1974 Niekro again won 20 games, tying for the league lead in victories. He also led the league with 18 complete games and 302 innings pitched.

In the following seasons, Niekro continued to be the ace of the staff, but the Braves became progressively weaker and weaker; thus, his 15 victories in 1975 and 17 in 1976 were very impressive. In 1977 Atlanta lost 101 games and finished in the NL West basement. Niekro went 16–20, but he led the league again in strikeouts, complete games, and innings. On July 29 he struck out Pittsburgh's Dave Parker, Bill Robinson, Rennie Stennett, and Omar Moreno in the sixth inning, becoming the ninth National Leaguer to fan four batters in one frame.

The Braves finished at the bottom in 1979, losing 94 and finishing 24 games behind first-place Cincinnati. But Niekro won 21 games, becoming the last player in the major leagues to win 20 for a last-place team. He also lost 20 games, to become the first pitcher since 1906 to win and lose at least 20 games in the same season. He pitched a whopping 342 innings that year, including a career-best 23 complete games, leading the league in both categories for the third consecutive year.

Always a strong fielder, Niekro won Gold Glove Awards in 1978, 1979, and 1980, and added two more in 1982 and 1983. His ups and downs on the mound continued in those years, however. In 1980 he went 15–18, then led the league in winning percentage in 1982, when he was 17–4 to lead the Braves to the NL West title.

The Braves released Niekro, 44, following the 1983 season. He signed with the Yankees and won 16 games in each of two seasons in the Bronx. He won his 300th game in 1985, leaving off the knuckleball until the last two pitches of the game.

Most of Niekro's final two seasons were spent with Cleveland and Toronto, although Atlanta resigned him on September 23, 1987, for one last appearance in a Braves uniform. He started a game and lasted until he loaded the bases in the fourth inning.

Niekro won 121 games after he turned 40, the most wins by anyone over that age in baseball history. In addition, he holds major league records for most wins at four specific ages—16 at age 45, 16 at age 46, 11 at age 47, and 7 at age 48. Thanks to the knuckleball, he also set a National League career record for wild pitches, with 200. At his retirement, he also held the dubious distinction of having the worst Opening Day record—0–7—of any pitcher in major-league history.

Phil Niekro might have won many more games had he pitched for a contending club. The Braves were perennial also-rans throughout the 1970s, and often afforded Niekro little or no run support. His 49 shutout losses are the third most in major league history, trailing only Nolan Ryan and Walter Johnson.

The Braves honored Niekro by retiring his uniform, No. 35. He went on to coach the Colorado Silver Bullets, an all-woman professional baseball team. On January 6, 1997, in his fifth year of eligibility, Niekro was elected to the Hall of Fame.

Bob Nieman

Nieman, Robert Charles **OF**

1951–62 B:1/26/1927, Cincinnati, OH D:3/10/1985, Corona, CA Deb:9/14/1951, STL AL BR/TR 5'11", 195

G	AB	R	H	HR	RBI	OBP	SLG	AVG
1113	3452	455	1018	125	544	.375	.474	.295

St. Louis Browns outfielder Bob Nieman began his major league career by homering in his first two at bats, on September 14, 1951, when he faced Mickey McDermott of the Boston Red Sox at Fenway Park. He never reached such dizzying heights again, but Nieman spent a productive decade in the big leagues.

Nieman, who had earned a journalism degree from Kent State, started in baseball with Muncie in 1948. He led the Class D Ohio–Indiana League with 186 hits, 45 doubles, 23 homers, 131 RBIs, and a .367 batting average. He also played with Tulsa, Charleston, Sunbury, Columbia, and Oklahoma City, and in 1951 he led the Texas League by batting .324.

In 1952 Nieman became a regular for the Browns, and he tied for the lead among American League outfielders in double plays. He also hit .289 with 18 home runs. Despite his production, he was traded in December 1953 to the Detroit Tigers. In his much-traveled career, Nieman later played for the Chicago White Sox, the Baltimore Orioles, the St. Louis Cardinals, the Cleveland Indians, and the San Francisco Giants. After leaving the majors, he starred with the Chunichi Dragons in Japan in 1963, batting .301. Nieman later served as a scout for the Indians, Dodgers, A's, White Sox, and Yankees.

Otis Nixon

Nixon, Otis Junior **OF**

1983–* B:1/9/1959, Columbus County, NC Deb:9/9/1983, NY AL BB/TR 6'2", 180

G	AB	R	H	HR	RBI	OBP	SLG	AVG
1709	5115	878	1379	11	318	.345	.314	.270

Although he turned 40 before the 1999 season started, Otis Nixon helped the Atlanta Braves reach the World Series for the first time since 1996 by serving as a pinch runner with base-stealing potential. With 26 stolen bases in 84 games, Nixon increased his career total to 620, 17th on the lifetime list.

Nixon had career highs in both steals (72) and batting average (.297) in 1991 during his first stint with the Braves, when he was obtained from Montreal in a four-player trade just prior to spring training of that year. The switch-hitter proved a perfect leadoff man for the Braves, who rose from worst in 1990 to first in 1991 after acquiring Nixon and signing seven free agents. But the Braves lost a seven-game World Series to the Minnesota Twins after Nixon was suspended for substance abuse in mid-September.

A spectacular defensive center fielder, Nixon made a leaping, over-the-fence catch of an Andy Van Slyke drive to preserve a 1–0 Atlanta win during the 1993 NL West pennant race with San Francisco. It is remembered in Atlanta team history simply as "The Catch."

Nixon stole at least 50 bases in a season four times, and moved around the major leagues as much as he motored around the basepaths. A first-round draft pick by the Yankees in 1979, he played for nine different teams in the major leagues.

Gary Nolan

Nolan, Gary Lynn **P**

1967–73, 1975–77 B:5/27/1948, Herlong, CA Deb:4/15/1967, CIN NL BR/TR 6'2½", 197

W	L	PCT	G	SH	IP	BB	SO	ERA
110	70	.611	250	14	1674^2	413	1039	3.08

When healthy, Gary Nolan was a finely tuned pitching machine. But he was injured frequently enough in his 10-year career to make him more a case of "what could have been" than "what was."

The Cincinnati Reds signed Nolan in 1966. He had great stuff, including a fastball clocked at 95 mph. After less than a season in the minors, Nolan made the big leagues in 1967. In his rookie year he struck out 15 San Francisco batters in one night game despite being lifted after seven innings. He finished the season 14–8 with 206 strikeouts.

However, arm problems set in during 1968, and Nolan's time was limited during the next two seasons. Fully recovered in 1970, he went 18–7 and then won Game 1 of the NLCS. Two years later, Nolan led the league in winning percentage with a 15–5 record but missed playing in the All-Star Game due to neck and shoulder problems. He pitched well in the NLCS and World Series despite continuing pain.

Nolan missed virtually all of 1973 and 1974 with arm and shoulder problems but posted back-to-back 15–9 seasons in 1975 and 1976. In the latter year, the Reds swept the Yankees in the World Series, with Nolan winning the final game 7–2.

Traded to the Angels for a minor league infielder in June 1977, Nolan ended his career that year at age 29. He had a career .990 fielding average, tying for the best in major league history among pitchers. He later worked for the MGM Hotel and Casino in Las Vegas.

Hideo Nomo

Nomo, Hideo **P**

1995–* B:8/31/1968, Osaka, Japan Deb:5/2/1995, LA NL BR/TR 6'2", 210

W	L	PCT	G	SH	IP	BB	SO	ERA
61	49	.555	151	5	960^2	427	1031	3.82

When the Los Angeles Dodgers offered Japanese pitcher Hideo Nomo a $2 million signing bonus in 1995, no one in the organization had seen him pitch in more than a year—with the exception of a two-minute highlight video. The gamble paid off for both the Dodgers and Nomo, who became the National League's Rookie of the Year that season, edging out Atlanta's Chipper Jones by 14 votes.

At the time of his signing, Nomo was only the second Japanese player to make the major leagues (preceded by Masanori Murakami with the San Francisco Giants in 1964–65) and the first to make the jump from a professional Japanese team. Los Angeles immediately fell in love with him, and "Nomomania" ensued as American and Japanese journalists and photographers chronicled his every move. The Dodgers even sent sushi vendors into the stands to peddle the delicacies for $5.25 a pop.

Nomo was more than hype. Like Fernando Valenzuela 14 years before, he overcame his inability to speak English to quickly establish himself as one of the best pitchers in the National League. For one month, at least, Nomo was the best pitcher in the game, winning NL Pitcher of the Month honors in June 1995 with a 6–0 record and a 0.89 ERA. He started the All-Star game and finished the year at 13–6 with a 2.54 ERA. Nomo led the league in strikeouts with 236 and had nearly two more strikeouts per nine innings (11.10) than runner-up John Smoltz of the Atlanta Braves.

That season batters hit just .182 against "The Tornado," a nickname Nomo picked up because of his twisting, quirky pitching motion. As a rookie he also allowed fewer runs per nine innings at home (1.73) than anyone in the NL. He tied for the league lead with three shutouts, but also had the most balks (five) and wild pitches (19). Nomo had 16 strikeouts against the Pirates—a league high in 1995—and also pitched a one-hitter against the Giants.

In 1996, Nomo turned in one of the most remarkable feats of the year on September 17. At Coors Field, where the Colorado Rockies batted .343 as a team and shattered their own record with 149 home runs in 81 games, Nomo pitched the 20th no-hitter in Dodgers history. Overall, he had a solid sophomore season, finishing second in the NL with 234 strikeouts and posting a 3.19 ERA. He suffered his worst outing of the season, however, in Game 3 of the Division Series, when he was knocked out in the fourth inning as Atlanta completed a sweep.

At the end of the 1997 season, Nomo underwent arthroscopic surgery on his right elbow. He was traded to the New York Mets midway through 1998 and endured his first losing season, going a combined 6–12 with a 4.92 ERA. Sent to the Brewers in '99, he rebounded with a 12–8 record. On September 8, the former ace of the Kintetsu Buffalos struck out his 1,000th batter in his 146th game. Only Roger Clemens and Dwight Gooden had reached that plateau in fewer appearances.

Fred Norman

Norman, Fredie Hubert **P**

1962–64, 1966–67, 1970–80 B:8/20/1942, San Antonio, TX Deb:9/21/1962, KC AL BB/TL 5'8", 160

W	L	PCT	G	SH	IP	BB	SO	ERA
104	103	.502	403	15	1939^2	815	1303	3.64

Fred Norman had been in the major leagues for more than a decade before he won at least 10 games in a season. Once having done it, however, he became a mainstay of the Cincinnati pitching rotation, and won at least 11 games for seven years in a row.

Norman signed with the Athletics in 1961 and played in Shreveport, Binghamton, and Lewiston before being brought up to Kansas City in 1962. He played parts of two seasons with the Athletics before being traded to the Cubs in December 1963. Between cups of coffee with Chicago, Norman played in Dallas-Fort Worth, Salt Lake City, and Wenatchee.

Traded to Los Angeles in April 1967, Norman did not see the majors again until 1970 when, pitching in relief, he went 2–0 for the Dodgers. However, his 5.23 ERA got him waived to the Cardinals in September. Norman was traded in June 1971 to San Diego, where, primarily as a starter, he recorded a 3–12 record. The 30-year-old pitcher hit bottom in 1973, going 1–7 with a 4.26 ERA before being traded to the Cincinnati Reds.

Pitching as a starter and reliever with a powerful Reds lineup behind him, Norman became a consistent winner. He went 12–4 for Cincinnati's world champions in 1975, beating the Pirates in Game 2 of the NLCS, and won another dozen as the Reds repeated in 1976.

After seven years as a successful starter, Norman was granted free agency in November 1979 and signed with the Expos the following month. He became one of the higher paid players in baseball, getting a $125,000 signing bonus and $450,000 for the first year of a three-year contract. He pitched only one season for the Expos, however, before becoming a minor league pitching instructor in the Montreal organization.

Mike Norris

Norris, Michael Kelvin **P**

1975–83, 1990 B:3/19/1955, San Francisco, CA Deb:4/10/1975, OAK AL BR/TR 6'2", 175

W	L	PCT	G	SH	IP	BB	SO	ERA
58	59	.496	201	7	1124¹	499	636	3.89

In 1980, when Billy Martin became the Oakland A's manager, he took a struggling Mike Norris and inspired the 25-year-old pitcher to a 22–9 record. The fireballing righthander narrowly missed winning that season's Cy Young Award. But many believe the toll Norris paid for pitching 284 innings that year was a sore arm that prevented him from being a dominant hurler ever again.

Norris was selected in the first round of the January 1973 draft by the A's and played minor league baseball with Burlington, Birmingham, Tucson, and Vancouver. Pitching his first major league game in 1975, Norris shut out the White Sox. He struggled for the next five seasons, however, winning only 12 times in that span.

In 1980 Martin took over, and he showed great confidence in a young pitching staff that included Norris, Steve McCatty, Matt Keough, Rick Langford, and Brian Kingman. Martin let the young hurlers pitch more innings than any other modern era manager would probably have allowed. The short-term result of Martin's aggressive managerial style was an AL West title in 1981.

During his great 1980 season, Norris had a 2.53 ERA and 180 strikeouts. He contributed a 12–9 record in the strike-shortened 1981 season, was selected to the All-Star Game, and pitched a shutout in Game 1 of the division playoffs against Kansas City. He also won the Gold Glove in both years.

One by one the young Oakland pitchers developed arm problems in 1982, and like the others, Norris' career faded. After being bounced from the majors for drug use, he pitched several years for the San Jose Bees in the California League.

Billy North

North, William Alex **OF**

1971–81 B:5/15/1948, Seattle, WA Deb:09/3/1971, CHI NL BB/TR 5'11", 185

G	AB	R	H	HR	RBI	OBP	SLG	AVG
1169	3900	640	1016	20	230	.366	.323	.261

Billy North matched blazing speed with an equally fiery attitude. An outstanding fielder and a solid hitter, he was a spark plug for the great Oakland teams of the mid-1980s.

North began his career with the Chicago Cubs, but became a regular in 1973, his first year in Oakland. He batted a career-high .285 and helped propel the A's to the World Series. The next year—as the A's steamed towards another World Series title—he led the American League with 54 stolen bases. He also managed to achieve something most outfielders only dream about: an unassisted double play. North also left no doubts about his tempestuousness. That year, he and teammate Reggie Jackson got into a celebrated brawl.

North again led the AL in steals with 75 in 1976. At the end of that season there was a mass exodus of free agents from Oakland. On Opening Day 1977, North was the only A's regular who had been there the year before. He was plagued by injuries that season and the next year was traded to Los Angeles. North returned to form with the Giants in 1979, when he stole 58 bases, the second best in the National League. A series of injuries limited his playing time over his last two years, and he was out of the game for good after 1981.

Jim Northrup

Northup, James Thomas **OF**

1964–75 B:11/24/1939, Breckenridge, MI
Deb:9/30/1964, DET AL BL/TR 6'3", 190

G	AB	R	H	HR	RBI	OBP	SLG	AVG
1392	4692	603	1254	153	610	.335	.429	.267

A stalwart in the Tigers' outfield in the 1960s, Jim Northrup didn't really make news until he hit four grand slams in 1968. On June 24 that year, the lefthanded batter hit two grand slams in the same game; he belted another five days later.

Northrup had been a star quarterback at Alma College. The NFL's Chicago Bears and the AFL's New York Titans both offered him contracts, but he signed with the Tigers for a $20,000 bonus in 1960. After playing minor league ball with Duluth-Superior, Decatur, Knoxville, and Syracuse, where he was named 1964 International League Rookie of the Year, the 24-year-old Northrup came to Detroit at the end of the 1964 season.

Northrup became a regular for the Tigers in 1966, but he didn't hit the headlines until Detroit's pennant year in 1968. The World Series was a pitchers' duel in which the Cardinals featured the overpowering Bob Gibson. But Northrup led the Tigers with eight RBIs and two home runs, including one off Gibson. The most important one, however, was a decisive third inning grand slam in Game 6 that helped knot the Series at three games apiece.

The next year Northrup had his best season, hitting .295 with 25 homers. The highlight came on August 29, when he went 6-for-6 against the A's, including a dramatic 13th-inning homer over the right-field roof of Tiger Stadium.

In August 1974 the Tigers traded Northrup to Montreal. A month later the Expos sold him to Baltimore. He retired after the 1975 season and became a manufacturer's representative in Troy, Michigan.

Jack Norworth

Songwriter B:1879, Philadelphia, PA D:9/1/1959, Laguna Beach, CA

"Take Me Out to the Ball Game" has been recorded by announcer Harry Caray, Braves pitcher Buzz Capra, and by a quartet made up of Ralph Branca, Roy Campanella, Tommy Henrich, and Phil Rizzuto. But vaudeville performer Jack Norworth, who had never been to a ball game, was the author of the ditty.

One day in 1908 Norworth was standing on a New York subway platform when he saw a sign that proclaimed, "Baseball Today—Polo Grounds." Inspired, he quickly wrote on a scrap of paper the words to a song that featured a feverish female fan named Kitty Casey (later changed to Nelly Kelly). When her beau offered to take her to Coney Island, she demanded, instead, "Take me out to the ball game."

Albert Von Tilzer added music, and an anonymous vaudevillian tried out the song on the public that summer, but with little success. Then, on October 24, after "Merkle's Boner" and a Tigers-Cubs World Series had made baseball even more popular nationally, song-and-dance man Billy Murray sang the song, which became a huge hit overnight and, over time, baseball's national anthem. What few people realize is that the song we sing today is merely the chorus. Two verses describe Nelly's passion for the game.

Spurred by his success, Norworth tried another baseball song, "Let's Get the Umpire's Goat," co-written with vaudeville star (and one of his five wives) Nora Bayes. Norworth once claimed he wrote "more than 3,000 songs, seven of them good." Among the other six gems were "Shine On Harvest Moon" and "Meet Me in Apple Blossom Time." In his later years Norworth became an avid baseball fan and was a patron of the Laguna Beach Little League.

Joe Nuxhall

Nuxhall, Joseph Henry **P**

1944, 1952–66 B:7/30/1928, Hamilton, OH
Deb:6/10/1944, CIN NL BL/TL 6'3", 219

W	L	PCT	G	SH	IP	BB	SO	ERA
135	117	.536	526	20	2302^{2}	776	1372	3.90

Service in the Armed Forces during World War II reduced the availability of many of those most fit for play in Major League Baseball. Hence, players not yet old enough for conscription, returning old-timers, and men not suited for military service replaced the established stars.

On June 10, 1944, the Cincinnati Reds were losing a 13–0 laugher, so they gave 15-year-old Joe Nuxhall a try on the mound. The frightened novice stayed only two-thirds of an inning and gave up five runs on five walks, two singles, and a wild pitch. He thus became the youngest player to play in a major league game in the 20th century. He also immediately went down to the Reds' minor league system.

Nuxhall did not see major league action again until 1952. Then he split his time between starting and relief for several years, until by 1955 he had become a tough-to-hit workhorse, winning 17 games and hurling more innings than any National League pitcher except Robin Roberts of the Phillies. He also led the league with five shutouts and was named to the All-Star Game.

The Reds were an average team without great support for their pitching, and Nuxhall made the All-Star Game again in 1956 despite finishing the year 13–11. However, the next three years he had an uninspiring record of 31–30. In 1960 Nuxhall was switched to a relief role to make way for younger Reds pitchers with stronger arms. The next year he was traded to the Kansas City A's, where his ERA climbed to 5.34. Ironically, the Reds won the National League pennant that year.

In 1962 the Los Angeles Angels selected Nuxhall in the expansion draft, but they quickly dealt him back to Cincinnati. Nuxhall responded with a 5–0 record as an occasional starter. In 1963 he was back in the Reds' starting rotation, going 15–8 with 14 complete games, and bringing his ERA back down to 2.61. After three more years on the mound in Cincinnati, he became a longtime broadcaster for the Reds.

Johnny Oates

Oates, Johnny Lane **C**

1970, 1972–81 M(1991–99, 715–638) B:1/21/1946, Sylva, NC Deb: 9/17/1970, BAL AL BL/TR 5'11", 188

G	AB	R	H	HR	RBI	OBP	SLG	AVG
593	1637	146	410	14	126	.311	.313	.250

Following the well-trod path of the cerebral catcher-turned-manager, Johnny Oates concluded his big-league playing career in 1981 and immediately began coaching in the minors. Ten years later, he earned his first managing job in the majors with the Baltimore Orioles, the team that drafted him in 1967. Oates led Baltimore to winning records in three of his four seasons as manager. Working for intrusive owner Peter Angelos, amid constant rumors of his dismissal, took a heavy emotional toll. "Baseball had me like this," Oates said years later, clenching a fist. After he was dismissed in 1994, "Everything got better."

Oates landed with the Texas Rangers. He guided Texas to a 74–70 record in 1995. A year later the Rangers ended the franchise's 35-year playoff drought. Oates shared Manager of the Year honors with Yankees skipper Joe Torre. Two more division titles in 1998 and 1999 added to his reputation as a premier manager. Three times, however, Texas was paired up with the Yankees in the Division Series—and three times the Rangers lost to the eventual world champions.

Pete O'Brien

O'Brien, Peter Michael **1B–DH**

1982–93 B:2/9/1958, Santa Monica, CA Deb: 9/3/1982, TEX AL BL/TL 6'1", 198

G	AB	R	H	HR	RBI	OBP	SLG	AVG
1567	5437	654	1421	169	736	.340	.409	.261

Pete O'Brien emerged as a promising power hitter and a great fielder for the Texas Rangers in the mid-1980s. Just as those Rangers teams never reached the postseason, O'Brien never made the leap from competent supporting player to leading man.

O'Brien struggled in 1983, his first full season, hitting just .237 with eight home runs. Manager Doug Rader stuck with him, though, and O'Brien responded by raising his average by 50 points and pounding 18 homers in 1984. He improved upon those numbers the next three seasons, but after his production declined somewhat in 1988, the Rangers sent him to Cleveland.

O'Brien signed a four-year, $7 million free agent contract with Seattle before the 1990 season. He proved a disappointment in his first season with the Mariners, landing on the disabled list for the first time in his career. He rebounded in 1991, boosting his power numbers and leading the American League with a .997 fielding percentage. But with hot prospect Tino Martinez pushing him for playing time, O'Brien's role shrank in 1992. He retired after his contract ran out the following season.

Jack O'Connor

O'Connor, John Joseph **C–OF–1B**

1887–1904, 1906–07, 1910 M(1910, 47–107) B:6/2/1869, St. Louis, MO D:11/14/1937, St. Louis, MO Deb:4/20/1887, CIN AA BR/TR 5'10", 170

G	AB	R	H	HR	RBI	OBP	SLG	AVG
1451	5380	713	1417	19	738	.307	.336	.263

"Rowdy Jack" O'Connor, a major leaguer for 21 years, spent the heart of his career with the Cleveland Spiders from 1892 through 1898. His rambunctious personality fit in perfectly with the aggressive Spiders, often described as a bunch of "thugs" and "hooligans." Led by the notorious Patsy Tebeau, the Spiders were even more vicious in their use of spikes, profanity, beanballs, and various other dirty tricks than were the more successful and celebrated Baltimore Orioles. Although O'Connor's longtime batterymate, Cy Young, was regarded as one of the league's true gentlemen, the behavior of other Spiders overshadowed his civility.

O'Connor's major league career began in 1887 in the old American Association. While playing with Columbus in 1889 and 1890, he led AA catchers in fielding average. The latter season he also hit .324, which would prove to be the best batting average of his career. With the collapse of the American Association after the 1891 season, O'Connor moved on to Cleveland. There he topped 50 RBIs six times in seven years and hit better than .280 five consecutive seasons.

O'Connor played with four other teams before leaving the majors in 1907. In 1910 he managed the St. Louis Browns into last place with a 47–107 record and came back for an appearance in one game.

O'Connor, also known as "Peach Pie," is best remembered for what happened in his final day as manager of the hapless Browns. Cleveland's Nap Lajoie entered the season-ending doubleheader trailing the despised Ty Cobb in the batting race by three points. Lajoie had eight hits in the doubleheader, including six bunts that went for hits because O'Connor "recommended" that rookie third baseman Red Corrigan play deep. Cobb still claimed the batting title, and a new Chalmers automobile, while O'Connor was subsequently fired.

Hank O'Day

O'Day, Henry Francis **P**

1884–90 M(1912, 1914, 153–154) U(1895, 1897–1911, 1913, 1915–37) B: 7/8/1862, Chicago, IL D: 7/2/35, Chicago, IL Deb: 5/2/1884, TOL AA TR 6', 180

W	L	PCT	G	SH	IP	BB	SO	ERA
73	110	.399	201	5	1651	578	663	3.74

Hank O'Day was a pitcher and a manager, but his most famous moment came as an umpire, when his call helped decide the heated pennant race between the New York Giants and Chicago Cubs in 1908. Ironically, O'Day had ties to both teams in his baseball career. As a late-season acquisition, he won nine of his 10 starts to help the Giants win the 1889 pennant. As a manager, he skippered the Cubs six years after his famous call helped Chicago win the pennant.

O'Day's pitching career was undistinguished. He didn't have a winning season until his final year. He lost 28 times in 40 starts as a rookie for Toledo of the American Association. He was a 20-game loser in the National League for Washington in both 1887 and 1888. When he wasn't pitching, O'Day occasionally filled in as a National League umpire.

He began the 1889 season with a 2–10 mark for the Nationals. In July he was sold to the Giants and went 9–1. O'Day posted two complete-game victories in the World Series to help the Giants defeat Brooklyn, six games to three. In 1890 he finally had a winning season, posting a 22–13 record for New York's entry in the short-lived Players' League.

O'Day became a full-time umpire in 1894. He umpired in the NL for 35 years; only Bill Klem, a 37-year veteran, served longer. O'Day's 10 World Series were also second to Klem.

In 1912 O'Day resigned to manage the Cincinnati Reds. After leading the Reds to a fourth-place finish, he returned to umpiring the following year. In 1914 he went back to the dugout and managed the Cubs to a fourth-place finish. Once again, he returned to umpiring and served until 1927.

O'Day was the only umpire who ever ejected manager Connie Mack. He worked the first modern day World Series in 1903, and he was the second base umpire when Bill Wambsganss turned an unassisted triple play in the 1920 World Series. O'Day's legacy, however, remains September 23, 1908, and Fred Merkle.

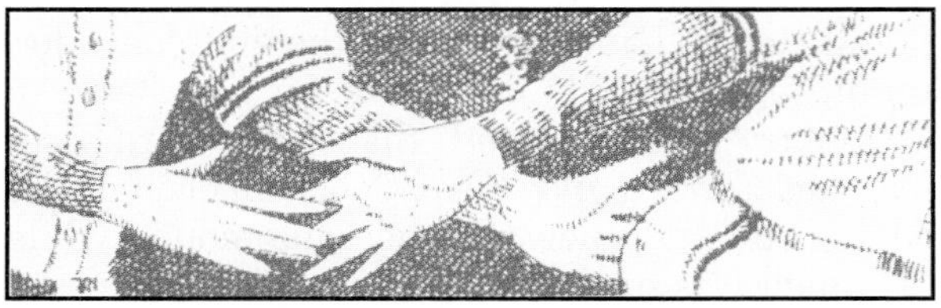

The Cubs and Giants were locked in a 1–1 tie at the Polo Grounds in the bottom of the ninth inning. With runners on first and third and two out, Al Bridwell's single appeared to drive in the winning run for the Giants. Running from first, Merkle headed for the Giants' clubhouse in center field—he never touched second. Chicago second baseman Johnny Evers produced a ball and argued that Merkle should be out on a force play. O'Day, working behind home plate, had been involved in an argument with Evers over a similar play in Pittsburgh three weeks earlier. He had let that play stand; this time he called the runner out. Because of "Merkle's Boner," the game was replayed after the season. The Cubs won the game and the pennant.

Blue Moon Odom

Odom, Johnny Lee **P**

1964–76 B:5/29/1945, Macon, GA Deb:9/5/1964, KC AL BR/TR 6', 185

W	L	PCT	G	SH	IP	BB	SO	ERA
84	85	.497	295	15	1509	788	857	3.70

After signing Johnny Lee Odom to a $75,000 bonus soon after his 1964 high school graduation (Odom was 42–2 with eight no-hitters), Kansas City A's owner Charlie Finley, ever the promoter, decided to call him "Blue Moon." Finley had already given the nickname "Catfish" to a North Carolina farmboy named Jimmy Hunter.

Odom spent parts of four seasons with the A's while they were still in Kansas City, but his career suddenly seemed to take off when the team moved to Oakland in 1968. That year he went 16–10 with a 2.45 ERA and was named to the All-Star team. He followed that with another All-Star appearance in 1969, when he went 15–6.

Bone chips in his elbow hampered Odom the next two years, but he bounced back in 1972, when he again went 15–6 and was a key member of the A's first World Series team. He went 2–0 in two starts without allowing a run in the ALCS. He kept it up in the World Series with a 1.59 ERA in two starts, but didn't have a victory to show for it. Odom lost Game 3, 1–0, and lasted into the fifth inning of Game 7 before Hunter relieved him.

Odom's fall to 5–12 in 1973 didn't keep the A's from a return trip to the Series, and his brawl with Rollie Fingers before the Series didn't prevent the A's from repeating as world champs, even though Fingers needed five stitches in his head. The next year Odom was used mainly in relief, where he went 1–5 with but a single save.

Odom pitched briefly with the Indians and Braves in 1975, and with the White Sox in 1976 he teamed up with Francisco Barrios to throw an unaesthetic no-hitter against his old teammates from Oakland. Always a wild man, Odom walked nine men in the five hitless innings he pitched. Barrios finished for him. It was the last game Odom would win in the majors.

Lefty O'Doul

O'Doul, Francis Joseph **OF**

1919–20, 1922–23, 1928–34 B:3/4/1897, San Francisco, CA D:12/7/1969, San Francisco, CA Deb:4/29/1919, NY AL BL/TL 6', 180

G	AB	R	H	HR	RBI	OBP	SLG	AVG
970	3264	624	1140	113	542	.413	.532	.349

They called Lefty O'Doul "The Man In The Green Suit" because he was given to wearing a bright green sport jacket day in and day out. They might have also called him the founder of Japanese baseball, one of the major leagues' best hitters, and "Mr. Pacific Coast League," because, in his lengthy and varied career, he was all of these things.

O'Doul started out as a pitcher. He was signed by the San Francisco Seals of the PCL in 1917, but farmed out to their Western League affiliate in Des Moines. Brought to the Seals in 1918, he went 13–9 and performed capably under such harsh conditions as playing same-day doubleheaders in two different cities.

In 1919 the Yankees brought O'Doul to New York, but he hurt his arm and was used primarily as a pinch hitter and outfielder before being returned to San Francisco in 1921. There he went 25–9 and batted .338. Recalled to the Yankees in 1922, O'Doul appeared in only eight games and was traded in October to the Red Sox. In one game against Cleveland (known as "The Indian Massacre"), he faced 16 batters and surrendered 13 runs in just one inning of work. Final score: 27–3.

In 1924 Boston sold his contract to the PCL's Salt Lake City Bees. Aided by that city's high altitude and by the park's small dimensions, O'Doul hit .392 and drove in 101 runs. The next year he collected 309 hits and 191 RBIs for the Bees. "Cripes, you could hit a ball with one hand, and it would fly out of that park," he recalled years later.

In 1927, back with San Francisco, O'Doul was named the Pacific Coast League's first-ever Most Valuable Player, winning a $1,000 cash prize. Following that season he was purchased by the Giants and practiced pulling the ball to take advantage of the Polo Grounds' short foul lines. Despite his hitting .319 in 1928, John McGraw gave up on O'Doul, sending him to Philadelphia in October. Obviously, his problems didn't stem from not being able to hit; it was his glove and his arm that created difficulties. A sportswriter for the *San Francisco Chronicle* once said: "He could run like a deer. Unfortunately, he threw like one too."

With the hapless Phillies in 1929, O'Doul banged out a league-leading .398 average and 32 home runs. With two games left to play, he had 247 hits, three short of Rogers Hornsby's National League record. The two contests were against the Giants, and John McGraw started two quality left-handers. However, O'Doul went 7-for-7 to set a new NL hit record with 254 (tied the next season by Bill Terry).

Slowed down by tonsillitis in 1930, O'Doul nonetheless managed a .383 batting average with 22 homers in that hitter's year. But in October he was traded to Brooklyn with Fresco Thompson for three other players and cash. He won his second batting title with the Dodgers in 1932, with a .368 average.

Then suddenly things went sour. In 1933 O'Doul went hitless in his first 27 at bats, and in June he was traded back to the Giants. Despite his sub-par season, he was named to the premiere All-Star Game. In the sixth inning of Game 2 of that fall's World Series against Washington, O'Doul was called on to pinch hit after an intentional walk to Mel Ott had loaded the bases. On a 1–2 count O'Doul singled in two runs for what the *Spalding Guide* called "the turning point of the game, and as it turned out, of the Series as well." What O'Doul didn't reveal until years later was that he had stepped across the plate as he batted—and should have been called out. When O'Doul left the major leagues following the 1934 season his lifetime batting average of .349 was exceeded only by Ty Cobb, Rogers Hornsby, and Joe Jackson.

Starting with the Seals in 1935 O'Doul began a long career of managing in the Pacific Coast League. He remained with San Francisco until 1951 (serving as vice president of the club from 1948 to 1951), winning pennants in 1935, 1946, and 1947. "That feller out there in Frisco is the best manager there is," said Casey Stengel. "Why isn't he up there in the majors where he belongs?"

At San Francisco O'Doul developed a reputation as one of baseball's premier batting instructors, helping such hitters as the DiMaggio brothers, Ted Williams, and Gene Woodling. He managed San Diego from 1952 to 1954, Oakland in 1955, Vancouver in 1956, and Seattle in 1947. With Vancouver, at age 59, O'Doul sent himself up as a pinch hitter and walloped a triple. How did he do it? There were two reasons, he said: "The first is clean living, and the second is to bat against a pitcher who's laughing so hard he can hardly throw the ball."

Starting in the early 1930s O'Doul made the first of more than 20 trips to Japan. There he assisted Matsutoro Shoriki in founding the first professional team, which he dubbed the Giants in honor of his last major league club. After Japan's defeat in World War II, O'Doul returned to the country to help restore baseball and the defeated nation's morale.

On leaving baseball in 1958, O'Doul founded a popular San Francisco restaurant. It remains a landmark on Geary Street just off Union Square. He died of a heart attack at age 72.

Joe Oeschger

Oeschger, Joseph Carl **P**

1914–25 B:5/24/1892, Chicago, IL D:7/28/1986, Rohnert Park, CA Deb:4/21/1914, PHI NL BR/TR 6', 190

W	L	PCT	G	SH	IP	BB	SO	ERA
82	116	.414	365	18	1818	651	535	3.81

Boston Braves righthander Joe Oeschger shares the record of pitching the longest major league game (by innings) ever, with his opponent in the contest, Brooklyn pitcher Leon Cadore. On May 1, 1920, Oeschger and Cadore each went the distance in a 26-inning marathon that was called on account of darkness. Oeschger allowed one run in the fourth; Cadore gave up one in the fifth. Cadore struck out seven, walked five, and surrendered 15 hits. Oeschger allowed just nine hits and four walks. Although neither team changed pitchers during the game, both changed catchers.

Oeschger received a degree in engineering from St. Mary's College in northern California. He began his 11-year major league career with Philadelphia in 1914. By 1917 he had become a regular starter, and that year he finished 15–14. The next season, however, his record dropped off to 6–18 and he went back to being an occasional player.

Obtained by Boston in 1919, Oeschger spent four and a half years there, riding a roller coaster of success. In 1921, he went 20–14 and led the NL in shutouts. The next year his ERA skyrocketed, and his record dropped to 6–21. Perhaps the highlight of his years in Boston came on September 8, 1921, when he became one of the few pitchers in major league history to record three strikeouts in an inning on just nine pitches.

On November 12, 1923, Oeschger was traded with Billy Southworth to Boston for three players, one of them Casey Stengel. He spent two more years in the majors.

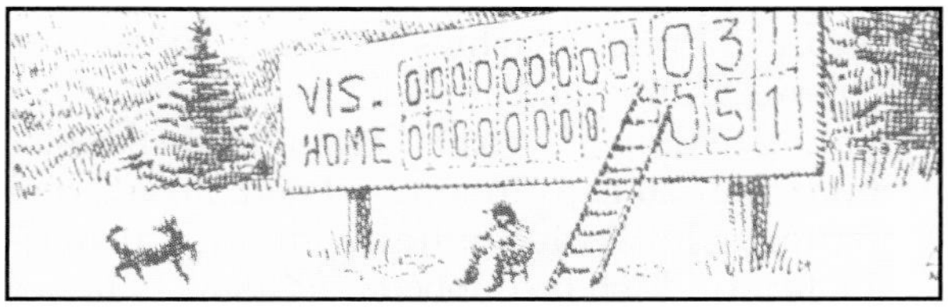

Bob O'Farrell

O'Farrell, Robert Arthur **C**

1915–35 M(1927, 1934, 122–121) B:10/19/1896, Waukegan, IL D:2/20/1988, Waukegan, IL Deb:9/5/1915, CHI NL BR/TR 5'9½", 180

G	AB	R	H	HR	RBI	OBP	SLG	AVG
1492	4101	517	1120	51	549	.360	.388	.273

Bob O'Farrell is often confused with two other longtime major league catchers: "Duke" Farrell, who played between 1888 and 1905, and Rick Ferrell, whose career lasted from 1929 to 1947. Although all three were fine players, O'Farrell, who played in the National League from 1915 to 1935, is the only one to have been selected his league's Most Valuable Player.

"Irish Bob" O'Farrell first played in the majors in September 1915, when the Cubs called him up at 18. He went 1-for-3 in two games, then made brief appearances with the big league club in 1916 and 1917. In 1918 the Cubs recalled O'Farrell to back up veteran Bill Killefer, and this time it was for keeps. Chicago won the pennant in O'Farrell's first full season in the majors. Two years later, when Killefer was sidelined with a broken finger, O'Farrell took over the starting spot.

After being a relatively light hitter his first several years, O'Farrell came into his own in 1922, hitting .324. The next year he batted .319 and had 84 RBIs. In 1924, however, the young Gabby Hartnett replaced O'Farrell. One of the greatest catchers of all time, Hartnett was four years younger than O'Farrell, who probably would have spent the rest of his career as a reserve if he had stayed with the Cubs.

Fortunately for O'Farrell, the St. Louis Cardinals traded for him early in the 1925 season. St. Louis was in last place when O'Farrell joined them, but Rogers Hornsby was soon named manager, and the team began to win. The Cardinals finished fourth, and Hornsby, who won the Triple Crown, was named league MVP.

In 1926 the Cardinals won the first pennant in franchise history in a close race with Cincinnati and Pittsburgh. O'Farrell caught 146 games, a brutal assignment in the St. Louis heat. Nevertheless, he hit .293, drove in 68 runs, and nursed a none-too-robust pitching staff to victory. O'Farrell hit .304 and caught all seven games of the World Series, including Pete Alexander's famous strikeout of Tony Lazzeri to preserve the final-game victory. For his all-around play and leadership, O'Farrell was selected league MVP.

Over the winter Hornsby's contract dispute with Cardinals owner Sam Breadon resulted in his being traded to the New York Giants. Outraged St. Louis fans called for Breadon's scalp. Bill Killefer, who had been Hornsby's first lieutenant, turned down the offer to succeed him. Breadon, feeling the heat, named the popular 30-year-old O'Farrell as player-manager of the 1927 Cards.

O'Farrell didn't have Hornsby's bat in his lineup, and he lost regular shortstop Tommy Thevenow for two-thirds of the season with a broken leg. But his greatest loss was himself: a sore arm limited him to 61 games. Despite these obstacles, he brought the Cardinals home only a game and a half behind the first-place Pirates. Yet it wasn't good enough for Breadon, who fired O'Farrell as a manager while retaining him as a player.

Early in 1928, the Cards traded O'Farrell to the Giants, for whom he shared catching duties with Shanty Hogan for five seasons. In 1933 he returned to the Cardinals, and the next year he signed on with Cincinnati as a playing manager. After 90 games and only 30 Cincinnati wins, O'Farrell was released. According to general manager Larry MacPhail, O'Farrell accepted defeat too easily. MacPhail said he'd go to the clubhouse after a loss and find the manager hauling out his golf clubs instead of haranguing the players. MacPhail's criticism stuck, and O'Farrell never managed another major league team. He retired after playing a few games with the Cardinals in 1935.

Jose Offerman

Offerman, Jose Antonio (Dono) SS-2B-1B

1990–* B:11/8/1968, San Pedro de Macoris, Dominican Republic Deb:8/19/1990, LA NL BB/TR 6', 165

G	AB	R	H	HR	RBI	OBP	SLG	AVG
1143	4145	610	1162	30	381	.368	.377	.280

A product of the infielder factory that is San Pedro de Macoris, Dominican Republic, Jose Offerman was proclaimed a defensive magician in the making when he broke in with Los Angeles. But his play soon told a different story: Offerman committed an astounding 42 errors in 1992, the most by a Dodgers shortstop in 51 years, and three times led the majors in errors. Worse yet, Offerman fell into disfavor with manager Tommy Lasorda during the 1994 season, and was briefly sent to the minors. An easy scapegoat in L.A. for an underachieving ballclub, Offerman was booed at Dodger Stadium even when he was introduced at the 1995 All-Star Game.

After the Dodgers traded Offerman to Kansas City the following winter, he responded with a .303 average while playing four different positions. Positioned exclusively at second base the next two seasons, he batted .297 and .315. He stole 45 bases and hit a league-topping 13 triples in 1998. As a free agent, Offerman then signed a four-year, $26 million contract with Boston that struck many as excessive, especially considering the Red Sox refusal to pay departing free agent slugger Mo Vaughn. Offerman silenced his critics by earning another All-Star selection—and this time was cheered heartily by the Fenway Park fans.

Ben Oglivie

Oglivie, Benjamin Ambrosio (Palmer) OF–DH

1971–86 B:2/11/1949, Colon, Panama Deb:9/4/1971, BOS AL BL/TL 6'2", 170

G	AB	R	H	HR	RBI	OBP	SLG	AVG
1754	5913	784	1615	235	901	.340	.450	.273

Ben Oglivie was so quiet and unassuming a player that for half his career he went unnoticed, moving from club to club, suffering from the knock that he was no more than a platoon player. He was regarded as a liability in the field and on the basepaths. Nicknamed "Spiderman," he gave the appearance that his arms and legs went in opposite directions as he chased a ball. And he'd barrel into bases when others might execute a graceful hook slide. Nothing looked natural with Oglivie, except his incredibly fluid swing, the whip-snap of his wrists, and the high follow-through that sent sizzling line drives at terrified first basemen.

Oglivie was raised in the Bronx. A seventh-round draft choice of the Boston Red Sox in 1968, he sent off few sparks as he moved through the minors. He made his Red Sox debut in 1971, and appeared in 94 games the next season. But in 1973 his batting average slumped to .218, and late that year the Red Sox traded him to the Tigers for fading second baseman Dick McAuliffe.

In Detroit, with its friendly right-field wall, Oglivie found his way into the lineup progressively more often, and his power numbers increased as his playing time did—from four homers in 1974, to nine in 1975, 15 in 1976, and 21 in 1977. Throughout his years with the Tigers, Oglivie was outwardly patient. An intelligent, bookish man who read philosophy, he attended four colleges and studied Zen Buddhism because, he said, it "merges into one with sports." He would let the game come to him.

In 1978 it did, with Oglivie's trade to Milwaukee for pitchers Jim Slaton and Rich Folkers. Although he was still rested against lefthanders, he had personal highs in almost every offensive category, including batting average (.303.) The following season teammate Larry Hisle blew out a shoulder. It was a break for Oglivie, who had to play every day. To everyone's surprise, he could hit lefthanded pitchers after all. He could also get to fly balls, throw out opposing baserunners, and drive in his own. On July 18, 1979, he hit three home runs in a game for the first of three times in his career, a day that helped propel him to a total of 29 homers by the end of the season.

The 1980 season saw it all come together for Oglivie. He hit .304, batted in 118 runs, led the American League with 41 homers, and was selected to the All-Star Game for the first of three times. The Brewers made the playoffs in the strike-shortened 1981 season, as they did in 1982, when Oglivie was again named to the All-Star Game. That year he hammered 34 home runs, and was one of four Brewers—the others being Robin Yount, Gorman Thomas, and Cecil Cooper—with at least 100 RBIs.

Oglivie finished the ALCS against the Angels with just two hits in 15 at bats. However, he hit a crucial homer in Game 5, as Milwaukee became the first team to win a pennant after trailing two games to none. In the World Series he homered in Game 7 to keep the Brewers close, but St. Louis overcame a 3–1 deficit to win the world championship.

Oglivie played four more seasons in the majors, but his power days were over. After a five-homer season in 1986, he took his Zen spirit to Japan. Playing for the Kintetsu Buffaloes, he launched 24 homers in 1987 and 22 more in 1988, batting .300 or better both years. In 1999 he coached for the South Atlantic League's Hickory Crawdads.

Sadaharu Oh

Japanese Player B:5/20/1940, Tokyo, Japan 5'11", 173

Sadaharu Oh, the most prolific home run hitter of all time, played his entire career for the Yomiuri (Tokyo) Giants in Japan. Oh combined an unorthodox, one-footed batting stance and a uniquely Eastern hitting philosophy to help him slam 868 home runs during a 22-year career.

Born in Tokyo in 1940 to a Japanese mother and a Chinese father, Oh faced the ravages of war and prejudice at an early age. When he was 5, he experienced the bombing of Tokyo. "I remember the fire—but as though it happened on another planet at another time," he recalled. "The sky was red. I had never seen such a color before, nor have I since. And it was night. Or so I thought. Actually, it was morning, but the smoke, my mother told me, was so thick it turned day into night."

Oh signed with the Giants in 1959, and his early struggles at the plate gave no indication of the heroics to come. A natural lefthanded hitter who had been forced to bat righthanded in high school, Oh was converted back into a lefty by the Giants, who also made him a first baseman. "My big weakness was that I had a 'hitch' in my swing," Oh said. "The hitch grew more, not less, pronounced with time, so that at the beginning of my first year as a pro it was very deeply ingrained."

In 1962 the Giants' batting coach, a distinguished swordsman named Hiroshi Arakawa, taught Oh to hit the way master swordsmen learn to battle. According to Arakawa there were seven steps to proper hitting form—fighting spirit, stance, grip, backswing, forward stride, downswing, and impact. As part of the training, Arakawa advised Oh to use the "flamingo" stance. This holistic approach, which included meditation, required absolute commitment. Oh practiced hitting in front of mirrors and took more than half an hour of batting practice before each game. Once, when Oh questioned this rigorous regimen, Arakawa told him, "Standing in this position, if you hitch, you will fall flat on your ass."

As a result of this training Oh strung together 19 straight 30-plus home run seasons, despite a yearly schedule of only 140 games. He won back-to-back Triple Crowns in 1973 and 1974, earned five batting championships, and led the Japanese Central League in RBIs 13 times and home runs 15 times. He hit four homers in a single game in 1963, set the Japanese single-season home run record with 55 in 1964, and was named Most Valuable Player nine times. After retiring in 1980 Oh managed the Tokyo Giants.

How Oh would have fared in American baseball is difficult to determine. The longer fences and stronger pitching may have cut down on his production. But most major leaguers who played against him during goodwill tours of Japan agree with Clete Boyer, who was the first American professional to be traded to a Japanese league. He said about Oh, "If he played in the U.S. he'd be a superstar. He'd probably lead the league in home runs and would hit with the best of them."

Bob Ojeda

Ojeda, Robert Michael **P**

1980–94 B:12/17/1957, Los Angeles, CA

Deb:7/13/1980, BOS AL BL/TL 6'1", 190

W	L	PCT	G	SH	IP	BB	SO	ERA
115	98	.540	351	16	1884[1]	676	1128	3.65

Although Bob Ojeda won 115 games in the major leagues, his solid 15-year career was overshadowed by tragedy. On March 22, 1993, a spring-training boating accident claimed the lives of Cleveland teammates Tim Crews and Steve Olin. Ojeda survived with scalp lacerations and other trauma, but following arthroscopic surgery on his left shoulder he would return to pitch in only 11 more ballgames before retiring.

Ojeda began his career in 1981 with the Red Sox. With six wins in 10 starts, he finished third in Rookie of the Year voting. Ojeda established his credentials with a strong finish to the 1983 season when he went 7–1 in his final eight starts, with a 1.83 ERA. Even though he tied for the American League lead in shutouts with five in 1984, he had an uninspiring 44–39 record in six seasons with Boston. When he was traded to the Mets after the 1985 season, many people felt the Red Sox had gotten the better of the deal.

That perception quickly changed as "Bobby O" emerged as one of the best pitchers in baseball in 1986, with an 18–5 record and a league-high .783 winning percentage. He finished second in the National League with a 2.57 ERA, tied for third in wins, and was fourth in the Cy Young voting. He won six straight from June 5 to July 28 as the Mets ran away with the NL East.

Ojeda was even better in the postseason. He won Game 2 of the Championship Series after the Mets dropped the opener. He started Game 6 at the Astrodome—the longest game in postseason history, which the Mets finally won in 16 innings to set up the World Series against Ojeda's old team.

The Mets again were down, this time by two games to none, before Ojeda made his first start in the Series. He had to be nearly perfect against the Red Sox at Fenway Park, and he was. The Mets staked him to a lead, and Ojeda cruised to a 7–1 win. He got the start in Game 6 and again it was an epic contest. Ojeda battled Roger Clemens before leaving the game with the score tied. The Mets came from behind to win with an unforgettable 10th-inning rally started against Calvin Schiraldi, the principal in the trade between these two clubs the previous year. Schiraldi took the loss again in Game 7.

Ojeda missed most of 1987 with an injury to his left elbow. His ERA dipped to 2.88 on five shutouts in 1988, but he finished with a 10–13 record. The Mets again pulled away from the pack in the NL East, and Ojeda figured to be a big part of their postseason plans. The day the Mets clinched the division title Ojeda accidentally severed the upper portion of his left middle finger with a pair of electric hedge clippers. After a nearly six-hour operation, there were questions whether he would pitch again; without him, the Mets would not win the pennant again in 1988.

Ojeda bounced back to finish the 1989 season with a 13–11 record, but spent much of 1990 in the bullpen. The Mets traded him to the Dodgers to bring Hubie Brooks back to New York. Ojeda finished his two years in Los Angeles with an 18–18 record. He moved on to Cleveland after the 1992 season, when the tragic boating accident occurred. Recovered from his injuries, he pitched twice as a reliever after rejoining the team on August 7, and made his first start against the Blue Jays. He was rocked for three runs to open the game, but settled down to throw five shutout innings. His last major-league win came at the expense of Clemens and the Red Sox.

Ojeda spent a short season with the Yankees in 1994. He was released on May 6 after two ineffective starts.

John Olerud

Olerud, John Garrett **1B**

1989–* B:8/5/1968, Seattle, WA Deb:9/3/1989, TOR AL BL/TL 6'5", 205

G	AB	R	H	HR	RBI	OBP	SLG	AVG
1396	4765	752	1434	172	762	.410	.481	.301

In the spring of 1997 Ted Williams was asked which current hitters he liked to watch. John Olerud was on his short list. At the time the answer was surprising. Olerud's career was spiraling downward. Toronto manager Cito Gaston was down on the former American League batting champion, and the Blue Jays had just practically given the low-key first baseman away to the New York Mets. But almost instantly Olerud was back on track, proving Teddy Ballgame's judgment to be astute.

The son of a minor league catcher, Olerud had never played a game in the minors. Despite suffering a brain aneurysm at Washington State, he went directly from college ball to the major leagues. Olerud's presence resulted in a blockbuster deal that sent first baseman Fred McGriff and shortstop Tony Fernandez to San Diego for Joe Carter and Roberto Alomar in 1990. Olerud was Toronto's first baseman on back-to-back world champions.

Olerud's career year with the Jays was 1993, when he led the American League with 54 doubles, a .473 on-base percentage, and a .363 batting average, in addition to going 2-for-2 in the All-Star Game and hitting a solid .348 in the ALCS. For the next three seasons, however, Olerud's average declined as Toronto attempted to extract more power from him.

In December 1996 the Jays traded him to the Mets for righthander Robert Person. So happy was Toronto to be rid of the lanky, laconic Olerud that they paid a hefty share of his salary in New York. Olerud turned his career around at Shea Stadium.

A painfully slow runner but a slick fielder, Olerud helped to stabilize both the Mets' infield and the batting order. In 1997 he drove in 102 runs. The following year he hit a team-record .354. In 1999 he set a team record with 125 walks as the Mets made the postseason for the first time since 1988.

With the Mets facing elimination in the eighth inning of Game 4 of the Championship Series against Atlanta, Olerud singled to drive in the tying and go-ahead runs. He homered in the first inning the next day as part of a wild, 15-inning victory. It turned out to be Olerud's final game at Shea. The free agent first baseman returned to his hometown team, the Seattle Mariners, so his parents could watch his son grow up.

Steve Olin

Olin, Steven Robert **P**

1989–92 B:10/4/1965, Portland, OR D:3/22/1993, Little Lake Nellie, FL Deb:7/19/1980, BR/TR 6'3", 185

W	L	PCT	G	SV	IP	BB	SO	ERA
16	19	.457	195	48	273	90	173	3.10

Pitching staffs have often been decimated by injuries, but no tragedy has shattered a pitching staff—or a team—so completely as the one that occurred on March 22, 1993. Cleveland Indians closer Steve Olin spent that day getting to know two new teammates; it was his last day alive.

On a rare off day in spring training, newly acquired pitchers Tim Crews and Bob Ojeda went boating with Olin on Little Lake Nellie, near the Indians' new spring training home in Winter Haven, Florida. In the dark, Crews, who had just moved to the area a month earlier, was unaware that the dock jutted out 185 feet into the water. At 39 miles an hour, passengers Olin and Bob Ojeda didn't see it coming, either.

Olin, 27, was killed instantly. The 31-year-old Crews—who it later was discovered had been drinking that night—died from head injuries. Ojeda had the top of his scalp ripped open, but survived. It was the most shocking tragedy in Cleveland Indians history since a pitch from Carl Mays killed Ray Chapman in 1920.

Olin had appeared almost exclusively in relief since he first arrived in the major leagues in 1989. When Mike Hargrove, who had managed Olin in the minor leagues, was selected as skipper in Cleveland, the 25-year-old hurler became the closer. Olin had 17 saves for an Indians team that won just 57 games. The following year he saved 29 games, and his 72 appearances were the third-highest total in the American League and the most ever by a Cleveland righthander. Despite less than two years of major league experience as a closer, Olin was third on the Indians' all-time list with 48 career saves when he was killed.

Tony Oliva

Oliva, Pedro (Lopez) **OF–DH**

1962–76 B:7/20/1940, Pinar del Rio, Cuba Deb:9/9/1962, MIN AL BL/TR 6'2", 190

G	AB	R	H	HR	RBI	OBP	SLG	AVG
1676	6301	870	1917	220	947	.356	.476	.304

Until a bum knee ruined his career, Tony Oliva was a true superstar. He could hit for average, he could hit with power, he could run, he could field, and, boy, could he throw.

Famed scout Joe Cambia signed the Cuban Oliva to a Minnesota Twins contract. His real name was Pedro Oliva y Lopez, but he entered the United States on his brother Tony's passport and was known as Tony from that day on. With Fidel Castro's rise to power, Oliva had been lucky to be able to leave Cuba at all. En route to the United States, he was stranded in Mexico City with visa problems for 11 days. When he finally arrived, he had only three days to convince the Twins of his value. His fielding was ragged and the team released him. A second look at his swing, however, got him a chance.

Assigned to Wytheville of the Class D Appalachian League, Oliva was seriously hampered by his inability to speak English. His manager wrote out two slips of paper for him. One said "ham and eggs"; the other, "fried chicken." Oliva subsisted on that diet for three months. Finally, he summoned enough courage to point to a candy bar he wanted. He got home, unwrapped it, bit into it, and nearly gagged. His "candy bar" was actually chewing tobacco.

At Wytheville, Oliva simply tore up the league. He hit .410 in 64 games, with 81 RBIs. Promoted to Charlotte of the Sally League in 1962, he hit .350 with 17 homers and 93 RBIs. The next year he moved up to Triple A and batted .304 with 23 homers for Dallas-Fort Worth.

Oliva wasn't considered a hot prospect when he began his rookie season in 1964. "Fair hitter, can make a good utility outfielder," summed up *Baseball Digest*. But he earned a starting job and then went on to lead the American League with a .323 batting average, 109 runs, 217 hits, and 43 doubles. He also homered 32 times. Oliva's hit total tied a major league rookie record, and his 374 total bases set the rookie record. Predictably, he was named AL Rookie of the Year.

The following year Oliva won a second straight batting title at .321, making him the first player to win the batting crown in his first two major league seasons. He was a key reason that Minnesota won the American League pennant, and *The Sporting News* named him AL Player of the Year. In 1966 he batted .307, led the league in hits for a third consecutive year, and won a Gold Glove for his play in right field.

"Watching Tony Oliva hit a baseball is like hearing Caruso sing, Paderewski play the piano, or Heifetz draw a string across a bow," wrote Phil Elderkin of the *Christian Science Monitor*. Actually, Oliva was the quintessential bad-ball hitter, collecting more than 50 walks in a season only once. "You pick out the pitches that appeal to you," he once explained. "It's the same as getting married. You pick out the girl who appeals to you."

Fielders couldn't second-guess Oliva because he hit the ball to all fields with power. After his rookie season he averaged 21 homers a year from 1965 through 1971. He had one of the quickest swings in the game. But Oliva had a major weakness. Twins trainer "Doc" Lentz remembered the first time he saw Oliva. "From the knee down his right leg was bent at a 45-degree angle. I remember thinking, 'Even if he makes the majors, he'll only last as long as those knees hold out.'"

In the end Oliva outlasted his knees, but it was a painful process that saw him endure seven operations. In 1966 and 1967 he underwent surgery for torn ligaments in his right knee. The next two years he led the league in both hits and doubles. But in July 1971 he dove for a fly ball hit by Oakland's Joe Rudi and tore the cartilage in his damaged knee. Hitting .375 at the time, he limped on until September as his average dropped to .337—still good enough for his third batting title. He also led the league in slugging percentage, but he would never be tops in an offensive category again.

In 1972 Oliva played only 10 games. He was in terrible pain even when off the field. His roommate, Rod Carew, recalled that when he was sleeping he would sometimes hear Oliva moaning and groaning. Carew would get up and wander all over the hotel trying to find ice to put on Oliva's knee. "I'd look at his leg," Carew said, "and I'd see scars and the way it was all racked up and I'd wonder how he could continue on." He was able to continue only because the American League instituted the designated hitter in 1973. That year Oliva batted .291 with 92 RBIs and hit the first homer ever by a DH. But his numbers declined steadily after that, and he retired in 1976.

After his playing days, Oliva served as the Twins' batting coach and was responsible for transforming Kirby Puckett from a singles hitter into a dangerous batting threat. Oliva was also a minor league hitting instructor with the Twins and served as a manager in the Mexican League.

Al Oliver

Oliver, Albert **OF–1B–DH**

1968–85 B:10/14/1946, Portsmouth, OH
Deb:9/23/1968, PIT NL BL/TL 6', 195

G	AB	R	H	HR	RBI	OBP	SLG	AVG
2368	9049	1189	2743	219	1326	.348	.451	.303

He got his nickname "Scoops" from someone with a sense of humor. In his first two years of minor-league play, Al Oliver committed 64 and 75 errors, respectively, at first base. But fielding was not what Oliver was about—he was a hitter, pure and simple. His hits were hard, slashing, line drives into the gaps. During Oliver's first few years with the Pirates, announcer Bob Prince was fond of saying that he was hitting .280, "but it's a hard .280."

After batting .315 at Columbus in 1968, Oliver was promoted to Pittsburgh and spent most of the 1969 season at first base. He hit .285 with 17 home runs, and tied for second in NL Rookie of the Year voting. Richie Hebner and Manny Sanguillen were also rookies in 1969. They joined Oliver, Willie Stargell, and Roberto Clemente to form the heart of the potent Pirates offense that became known as "the Lumber Company." This was the gang of which Jim Palmer said, "Some players see a fastball and their eyes light up and they say, 'Oh boy, a fastball.' The Pirates say, 'Oh boy, a baseball.'"

During the next two seasons Oliver was moved around in the field. He initially platooned at first base with Bob Robertson, then with Gene Clines in center field, but he felt management was not giving him a chance to settle into one position. He blamed the situation on race, prompting the local media to quickly label him a hothead and a troublemaker. Oliver was never as popular with the Pittsburgh fans as Sanguillen, Stargell, and Clemente.

Pittsburgh beat San Francisco in four games in the 1971 NLCS, and one of the big hits was Oliver's three-run homer in Game 4. However, his bat fell silent in the World Series against Baltimore. He batted only .211, although the Pirates were victorious in seven games.

In 1972 Oliver settled in as the regular center fielder, batting .312 to start a run in which he hit .300 or better in 11 of 13 seasons. He was also selected to his first of seven All-Star Games. He batted .321 in 1974 and .323 in 1976, but on December 8, 1977, he was traded to Texas, part of a four-team deal that involved the Pirates, Rangers, Mets, and Braves.

Oliver finished among the American League's top 10 batters in each of his four seasons with Texas, never hitting below .309. In 1980 he registered 209 hits and drove in 117 runs. During that season he tied a league record with four home runs (and six extra-base hits) in a doubleheader. However, the next year he was moved from the outfield to designated hitter, and his production dropped dramatically. On March 31, 1982, he was shipped to Montreal for Larry Parrish and Dave Hostetler.

The Expos installed Oliver at first base, and, at age 35, he had his career season. He led the National League with a .331 batting average and tied Dale Murphy for the RBI title with 109. He also led the league with 43 doubles and 204 hits, becoming the first major leaguer to have a 200-hit, 100-RBI season in both leagues.

Oliver led the league in doubles the next season, but that was his last as a full-time starter. In 1984 he split the season between the San Francisco Giants and the Philadelphia Phillies, and in 1985 it was the Los Angeles Dodgers and the Toronto Blue Jays. Oliver's last hurrah was in the 1985 ALCS, when he batted .375 and came through with two game-winning hits. But Toronto released him after the season, and, at the age of 39, he retired.

Gregg Olson

Olson, Greggory William **P**

1988–* B:10/11/1966, Scribner, NE Deb:9/2/1988, BAL AL BR/TR 6'4", 206

W	L	PCT	G	SV	IP	BB	SO	ERA
40	37	.519	581	217	629[2]	303	549	3.23

Gregg Olson, who played with Frank Thomas and Bo Jackson at Auburn University, was the fourth player taken in the 1988 June draft. Olson elected to play with the U.S. Olympic team, but he left the Olympic squad before the summer games to begin his professional career.

Although Olson set numerous school records as a starting pitcher at Auburn, he was immediately made into a professional closer. He saved five games in his first 16 minor league appearances, and was in Baltimore by September. While Olson threw hard, his out pitch was an old-fashioned, breathtaking hard curveball that completely befuddled opposing hitters. Starting the 1989 season as the Orioles' closer, he converted his first 15 save opportunities on the way to an American League rookie record 27 saves. He helped keep the O's in the division race until the final weekend of the season. Olson walked away with the AL Rookie of the Year Award.

Olson was one of the dominating relief pitchers in the game in the early 1990s, but elbow problems late in 1993 derailed his career. It would be five more years before he was again a major league closer. He bounced around with Atlanta, Cleveland, Kansas City, Detroit, Houston, and Minnesota before finally finding a home with the expansion Arizona Diamondbacks in 1998. Olson posted 30 saves in Arizona's inaugural season, then saved 14 and won nine more in 1999, as the D-backs gained a postseason berth in their second season of existence.

Walter O'Malley

O'Malley, Walter P.

Owner B:10/9/1903, Bronx, NY D:8/9/1979, Rochester, MN

Probably no man in baseball history has ever been so hated in a community as Walter O'Malley, who hijacked Brooklyn's beloved Dodgers and moved them to Los Angeles. When Brooklyn-born writers Jack Newfield and Pete Hamill once decided to list the three most despicable villains of the century, each wrote down Hitler, Stalin, and O'Malley.

O'Malley was born in the Bronx, attended Culver Military Academy, and earned an engineering degree from the University of Pennsylvania and a law degree from Fordham. He began to practice law in New York City in 1931, and in 1941 George McLaughlin, president of the Brooklyn Trust Company, which held the Dodgers' substantial loans, appointed O'Malley as the club's attorney.

Under club president Larry MacPhail, the once-pathetic Dodgers had become a competitive team, but their finances were still a mess. O'Malley stepped in to straighten them out and did a marvelous job. By 1944 the franchise was in the black. When stock held by the Ebbets and McKeever families was made available in 1945, O'Malley, general manager Branch Rickey, and John L. Smith, president of Pfizer Chemical Corporation, each ended up with 25 percent of the franchise.

Both Rickey and O'Malley were strong-willed men, and it is not surprising that they clashed on virtually every issue. Rickey had an encyclopedic knowledge of baseball on his side, but O'Malley had Smith. When Smith died, however, his widow decided to sell out. By prior agreement the stock had to be offered to both O'Malley and Rickey before it could go to any outsider.

Only O'Malley had the money to acquire the shares, but before Rickey left for the Pirates he rigged a scheme that jacked the price up to $1.05 million. O'Malley grudgingly paid because it gave him control of the franchise. He was able to purchase the Smith stock because the Dodgers were not his only financial undertaking. He owned the New York Subway Advertising Company, which had an estimated value of $7 million, and he was a partner in the Brooklyn Borough Gas Company. O'Malley's other holdings were part ownership of a $5-million building materials manufacturing company, partial ownership of a building block company, and six percent ownership of the Long Island Railroad.

Once O'Malley had control of the club, the "Rickey people" were pushed out. This didn't affect the Dodgers' team, which continued to dominate the National League. O'Malley was making good money, but he still wasn't making enough to be satisfied. Ebbets Field may have been cozy and lovable, but it could only hold 31,902 fans. O'Malley also felt that the neighborhood surrounding Ebbets Field was declining, a legacy of the middle-class exodus to the suburbs.

By 1956 O'Malley was working overtime on a plan to leave Ebbets Field, and he was planning on more than one level. First there was the local angle. He had the engineering firm of Clarke and Rapuano develop plans for a new ballpark on Atlantic Avenue near the Long Island Railroad Terminal. Wherever the Dodgers ended up, O'Malley was intent on building the first privately owned stadium in 30 years. The city fathers, not aware of how serious O'Malley was about moving the franchise, made two counterproposals. The first involved a site at Brooklyn's Parade Grounds. The second was outside of Brooklyn at Flushing Meadow in Queens, where Shea Stadium was later built. O'Malley wasn't interested.

At a banquet in 1956 Cubs owner P.K. Wrigley made a rare public appearance, and O'Malley took advantage of the opportunity to offer Wrigley a swap: the Cubs' Los Angeles Angels franchise for the Dodgers' Fort Worth Cats. The deal was consummated in February 1957, paving the way for the Dodgers' shift to Los Angeles.

In the meantime O'Malley had been in contact with Los Angeles officials. Early in the 1956 season Los Angeles County supervisor Kenneth Hahn had visited New York in an attempt to secure a team for Los Angeles. He had no thought whatsoever of cajoling the defending world champs into moving west. His real target was Calvin Griffith's Washington Senators. Instead O'Malley contacted Hahn and stunned him with the news that he intended to move the Dodgers to Los Angeles.

After the season O'Malley secretly visited Los Angeles and toured the city in a sheriff's department helicopter, looking for an acceptable stadium site. He found it in a place called Chavez Ravine a few minutes drive from the downtown area. O'Malley was understandably tight-lipped about his plans, but word eventually leaked out. On May 29, 1957, the National League gave approval for both the Dodgers and the Giants to move to the West Coast. Giants' owner Horace Stoneham was also eager to leave New York. The Polo Grounds was crumbling and the neighborhood around it was in irreversible decline.

On October 7 the Los Angeles City Council voted to swap Chavez Ravine for nearby Wrigley Field, which O'Malley had acquired in the franchise swap with the Cubs. The city agreed to spend $2 million to upgrade the area, and the county to sink $2.4 million into access roads. The next day O'Malley announced that the Brooklyn Dodgers were no more.

His team took temporary quarters at the huge Los Angeles Coliseum until Dodger Stadium, built with a $10-million advance from Union Oil of California, was completed in 1962. O'Malley made sure his franchise was as profitable as possible. There were no water fountains in Dodger Stadium until loud protests were made. Likewise there was no free television coverage of Dodgers home games at first. O'Malley hated to give away anything for free. But even with water fountains and free TV, the Dodgers prospered beyond his wildest dreams.

Because of his wealth, success, and brains he became organized baseball's most powerful owner. "It's just a lot of bunk to say I run baseball and am more powerful than the commissioner," O'Malley once argued. Yet it was an open secret that O'Malley had installed Bowie Kuhn as commissioner in 1969, and had then prevented Kuhn's unseating in 1975 during an owners' revolt. And it was also O'Malley who had Kuhn call off the owners' spring training lockout in 1976.

O'Malley died of cancer at the Mayo Clinic in Minnesota in 1979. His son Peter owned the Dodgers franchise until it was sold in 1997.

Buck O'Neil

O'Neil, John Jordan **1B–OF**
Negro League Player, M(1937–55), Manager
B:11/13/1911, Carrabelle, FL BR/TR 6'2", 190

If he had been born 40 years later, Buck O'Neil might have managed in the majors. But because he flourished during baseball's era of segregation, he was limited to managing in the Negro Leagues. From 1948 through 1955 he managed the Kansas City Monarchs to five pennants and a pair of Black World Series. In 1962 he broke a significant color barrier when the Cubs hired him as the majors' first black coach.

O'Neil, a righthanded-hitting first baseman, first played professionally for the Miami Giants and the Shreveport Acme Giants before making it to the Negro Leagues with the Memphis Red Sox in 1937. He moved to the Monarchs in 1938 and played in Kansas City for the next 13 years. Statistics from the Negro Leagues are sketchy, but what records there are show that O'Neil batted .345 in 1940 and, after returning from two years in the Navy, .350 in 1946 and .358 in 1947. He became the Monarchs' player-manager in 1948, and hit.330 the following year. He retired as a player after hitting .253 as a part-timer in 1950.

Prior to his tenure as a Cubs coach, O'Neil scouted for Chicago and was astute enough to sign two future Hall of Famers, Ernie Banks and Lou Brock. He also worked as a special scout for the Kansas City Royals. As of 2000, O'Neil had logged many years on the Baseball Hall of Fame's Veterans' Committee, and was chairman of the board of the Negro Leagues Museum in Kansas City, Missouri.

Paul O'Neill

O'Neill, Paul Andrew **OF**

1985–* B:2/25/1963, Columbus, OH Deb:9/3/1985, CIN NL BL/TL 6'4", 215

G	AB	R	H	HR	RBI	OBP	SLG	AVG
1774	6242	885	1809	242	1099	.372	.475	.290

His statistics were always impressive, but to truly appreciate Paul O'Neill you had to watch him on a day-to-day basis. He was a very good right fielder with one of the best arms in the game; he was a fine clutch hitter who batted between .300 and .359 in six of his seven years with the New York Yankees, winning one batting title. But most of all Paul O'Neill was a competitor.

O'Neill graduated Brookhaven High School in Columbus, Ohio. He was primarily a pitcher in high school, earning All-State honors in baseball and basketball. O'Neill grew up a Willie Mays fan, but claims the most dramatic moment he ever witnessed was Pete Rose's 4,192nd hit, which he saw from the Reds' bench in his rookie year.

In 1985 and 1986 O'Neill appeared in just eight games with the Reds, but his playing time increased over the next two seasons. He was Cincinnati's regular right fielder when the Reds won the World Series in 1990. In the National League Championship Series against Pittsburgh that year, O'Neill led the team with a .471 average and threw out a pair of runners. He was just 1-for-12, though, in the Series sweep of Oakland.

O'Neill had 28 homers and 91 RBIs the following year, and got to play in his first of five All-Star games as a reserve, but the Reds dropped to fifth place with a 74–88 record. In 1992 the team rebounded to win 90 games, but still finished eight games behind Atlanta. O'Neill's average dropped to .246 as he labored over the last two months with a sore wrist and hand caused by a checked swing. On November 3 he was traded to the New York Yankees.

If O'Neill had any shortcomings at the plate, American League pitchers didn't find them. Not only did he hit over .300 (after never reaching that mark before) for six straight years from 1993–1998, he slugged over .500 four times and over .600 in 1994, numbers he never approached in eight years with the Reds. In the strike-shortened 1994 campaign he led the AL in batting with a .359 mark.

During O'Neill's seven seasons with the club, the Yankees were in postseason play five times and would have been there in '94 if the strike hadn't cancelled the playoffs. O'Neill had fine Division Series against Seattle in 1995 (three homers, six RBIs, .333), Cleveland in 1997 (two homers, seven RBIs, 421), and Texas in 1998 (.364). But in four World Series he was just 10-for-58 (.172) with a homer and five RBIs.

Against the Braves in 1999 O'Neill had a crucial two-run single during the eighth inning of the Yankees' Game 1 victory. On the morning of the day the Yanks swept the Series, O'Neill's father, Chick, died. He had played minor league ball and taught his son how to play the game.

Steve O'Neill

O'Neill, Stephen Francis **C**

1911–25, 1927–28 M(1935–37, 1943–54, 1040–821) B:7/6/1891, Minooka, PA D:1/26/1962, Cleveland, OH Deb:9/18/1911, CLE AL BR/TR 5'10", 165

G	AB	R	H	HR	RBI	OBP	SLG	AVG
1590	4795	448	1259	13	537	.349	.337	.263

Steve O'Neill was a respected manager known for helping young pitchers, including 17-year-old Bob Feller. In a lengthy career, he compiled an impressive major league record and led Detroit to victory in the 1945 World Series.

O'Neill had three brothers—Mike, Jack, and Jim—who also played in the major leagues. He started his playing career with Elmira in 1910, and that year the Athletics acquired him, although he didn't see any action. The next year O'Neill played for Worcester in the New England League before being brought up to Cleveland at the tail end of the season.

For the next decade, O'Neill had a solid, if uninspiring career. His batting average peaked at .295 in 1913 and dipped as low as .148 in 1917. The Indians' championship 1920 season was the highlight of his playing career. O'Neill hit .321, reaching career highs with 157 hits, 63 runs, 39 doubles, and three homers. He went on to hit .333 in what would prove his only World Series as a player.

Traded to the Red Sox before the 1924 season, O'Neill was waived to the Yankees a year later. With his batting skills diminished, he rode the bench for the Yankees in 1925 and played part of 1926 with Reading and Toronto in the International League. He returned to the majors in a backup role with the St. Louis Browns in 1927 and 1928.

O'Neill served as player-manager at Toronto from 1929 to 1931, as player-coach with Toledo in 1932, and as player-manager at Toledo in 1933 and 1934.

He started 1935 as a coach for the Indians but took over as manager in the middle of the season, remaining until the end of the 1937 campaign. While managing the Tigers from 1943 to 1948, O'Neill developed an exceptional pitching staff, won a world championship (1945), and finished second three times. He later managed the Boston Red Sox and the Philadelphia Phillies.

Tip O'Neill

O'Neill, James Edward **OF–P**

1883–92 B:5/25/1858, Woodstock, Ontario D:12/31/1915, Montreal, Quebec Deb:5/5/1883, NY NL BR/TR 6'1½", 167

W	L	PCT	G	SH	IP	BB	SO	ERA
16	16	.500	36	0	289	115	91	3.39

G	AB	R	H	HR	RBI	OBP	SLG	AVG
1054	4255	880	1386	52	757	.392	.458	.326

There is an unfortunate tendency among baseball historians to ignore Tip O'Neill's remarkable 1887 season. During that year, for the first and only time, bases on balls were counted as hits. O'Neill's recorded batting average of .492 is generally thought of as an aberration made possible by a rules mistake. However, once the walks are removed, his batting mark for that year is still .435, the second highest ever recorded. Furthermore, he led the old American Association in runs, hits, doubles, triples, home runs, and RBIs.

O'Neill first reached the majors as a pitcher with the New York Gothams in 1883. The next year he went 11–4 with St. Louis of the American Association, but a sore arm caused him to give up pitching and turn to the outfield. From the start, hitting was his strong suit, and he hit .350 in 1885, helping St. Louis win the first of four straight American Association pennants.

In 1886 O'Neill had the lowest batting average of his five years as a regular St. Louis outfielder—"only" .328—but he led the league in RBIs. After his record year, he again led the American Association in batting in 1888, albeit with a less gaudy .335. He repeated that average in 1889 before joining Chicago of the Players' League and then finishing his career in 1892 with Cincinnati of the National League.

Jesse Orosco

Orosco, Jesse Russell **P**

1979, 1981–* B:4/21/57, Santa Barbara, CA Deb: 4/5/79, NY NL BR/TL 6'2", 185

W	L	PCT	G	SV	IP	BB	SO	ERA
84	75	.528	1090	141	1216	538	1103	3.03

Jesse Orosco had endured the hard times as much as any New York Met—last-place finishes in 1979, 1982, and 1983, plus fifth place in 1980 and 1981—so it was only fitting that he would be the man on the mound when the team finally won it all. And of all the images of the Mets' 1986 World Championship season, the most lasting is the image of Orosco on his knees with both fists in the air after the final out. Seconds later, he disappeared under a sea of teammates in front of the mound at Shea Stadium. Ironically, Orosco was the player to be named later in the 1979 trade for Jerry Koosman, who was the man on the mound when the Mets won their only other World Series in 1969.

Orosco went from rookie ball in the Twins organization in 1978 to the New York Mets the following season. In 1983, he turned in a career year with the Mets, reaching personal bests in wins (13) and ERA (1.47), and finishing third in Cy Young Award balloting. Orosco reeled off 27 ⅔ consecutive scoreless innings from July 22 to August 24, during which span he won nine straight games. He was named National League Player of the Month for his unbeatable August.

He had another terrific year for the Mets in 1984, winning 10 games in relief and recording a then-club record 31 saves. He made the All-Star squad for the second year running as the Mets improved to second place. The emergence of righthander Roger McDowell out of the bullpen dropped Orosco's save total to 17 in 1985, but the lefty continued to shine. He struck out six consecutive Pirates in two games on April 16 and 17 at Pittsburgh, and his late-inning work helped keep the Mets in the hunt for the National League East title until the last weekend of the season.

In 1986 Orosco passed Tug McGraw (85 saves) to become the club's all-time saves leader (a mark John Franco would later claim). Both Orosco and McDowell had 20-save seasons. In a July 22 game against Cincinnati, the two relievers were in the game at the same time from the fifth inning on. They moved from the mound to the outfield and back, depending on whether the batter was righthanded or lefthanded. Orosco even had a putout in the outfield.

Orosco was simply amazing in the 1986 postseason. He won three games against the Astros in the Championship Series, including the four-hour, 42-minute marathon in Game 6 at the Astrodome. Orosco pitched the final three innings of that 16-inning classic and allowed three runs, but he got the final out with the tying run at third for a 7–6 win and the pennant. In the World Series, he did not allow a run in 5⅔ innings, earned two saves, and contributed an RBI single. At 11:26 P.M. on October 27, he struck out Boston's Marty Barrett to bring the Mets their second world championship.

Although he earned his 100th career save in 1987, Orosco slumped and was traded to the Dodgers before the 1988 opener. He moved to the American League in 1989 and spent three years in Cleveland and three in Milwaukee before winding up in Baltimore. In 1996 with the Orioles he was reunited with former Mets manager Davey Johnson as well as Randy Myers and Roger McDowell, old bullpen pals at Shea. Orosco appeared in 66 games and put together a 3.40 ERA—remarkable considering he had a 27.00 ERA following a 16-run eighth-inning explosion by Texas on April 19.

The 39-year-old lefty pitched in all four games in Baltimore's 1996 Division Series victory over the Indians and he appeared four times in the five-game loss to the Yankees in the Championship Series. Despite a fine 6–3 season in 1997, Orosco saw limited action in his team's Division Series victory over the Mariners and its loss to Cleveland in ALCS.

On December 11, 1999, Orosco, the oldest active player in baseball, returned to the Mets in a straight-up swap for lefthander Chuck McElroy. Going into the 2000 season, he had appeared in 1090 games, 1086 of them in relief—both major league records.

Jim O'Rourke

O'Rourke, James Henry **OF-C-3B-1B**
1872–93, 1904 M(1881–93, 246–258) B:9/1/1850, Bridgeport, CT D:1/8/1919, Bridgeport, CT Deb:4/26/1872, MAN NA BR/TR 5'8", 185

G	AB	R	H	HR	RBI	OBP	SLG	AVG
1774	7435	1446	2304	50	1010	.355	.421	.310

Jim O'Rourke was a versatile, verbose, and excellent hitting 19th-century ballplayer. He played in more than 100 major league games at each of six different positions—his preferred left field slot, center field, right field, third base, first base, and catcher. In 14 of his 19 seasons he sported a batting average of above .300, while playing a lead role on eight different championship teams. And his tendency to make long-winded pronouncements earned him the nickname "Orator Jim."

O'Rourke's father died when Jim was young, and he became the family breadwinner, playing baseball only after completing his daily chores. When he was offered a professional contract, his mother would not allow him to sign until the team agreed to provide the family with a farm laborer to take over his duties.

His professional career began in 1872 as a shortstop for the Middletown Mansfields of the National Association. The next year O'Rourke joined the Boston Red Stockings, the pennant winners the year before. The Irish were not regarded highly in Boston at the time, so manager Harry Wright suggested that O'Rourke change his name. The player replied, "Mr. Wright, I would rather die than give up my father's name. A million dollars would not tempt me."

His fine play soon won over the Boston fans, and O'Rourke eventually became a local favorite. In his first season with the Red Stockings he hit .350, but his batting average dropped to .316 in 1874 and .291 in 1875, although he led the league in home runs both years with totals of five and six. The ball was far less lively than it is today, and teams played only half the number of games. O'Rourke's six homers in 1875 represented 14.2 percent of the 42 hit by the entire league.

The National League was formed in 1876, and the Red Stockings team was a charter member. The first NL game was played on April 22 of that year, when Philadelphia played host to Boston. Philadelphia pitcher Lon Knight retired the first two men he faced before O'Rourke cracked a single to left, the first hit in National League history. He went on to hit .327 in the league's inaugural season. In 1877 the Red Stockings won the pennant as O'Rourke hit .362, fourth best in the league, and led the circuit in runs scored and on-base percentage.

In 1879 George Wright, the Boston shortstop and younger brother of Harry, jumped to Providence to become the Grays' player-manager. O'Rourke was also unhappy in Boston because his employers taxed the players $20 per season for uniforms and 50 cents a day for travel maintenance. Although sympathetic fans chipped in to pay the fees, a disgruntled O'Rourke followed the younger Wright to Providence. The defections of Wright and O'Rourke led Boston owner Arthur H. Soden to propose the inclusion of a reserve clause in player contracts. Before 1879 players had been free at the end of the season to sign with any team they chose. O'Rourke followed the move with one of his best seasons, hitting .348. With the title at stake, Providence beat Boston in four of the last six games to capture the pennant and, remarkably, O'Rourke's sixth championship in seven seasons.

O'Rourke returned to Boston in 1880 and led the National League with six home runs. He became manager of the Buffalo Bisons in 1881, and in 1884 led the league with 162 hits and a .347 batting average. Dealt to the New York Giants in 1885, he led the league with 16 triples.

In 1888 and 1889 O'Rourke once again found himself on a pennant-winning team. The Giants included six future Hall of Famers: pitchers Tim Keefe and Mickey Welch, catcher Buck Ewing, first baseman Roger Connor, shortstop John Montgomery Ward, and O'Rourke. After winning each pennant the Giants went on to defeat the American Association champions in the World Series.

In 1890 O'Rourke and many other baseball stars jumped to the Players' League, a circuit created and run by the players in response to their grievances with the National League and American Association owners. At age 38 O'Rourke had one of his best seasons for the league's New York team, batting .360 with 115 RBIs. When the league collapsed after only one season, he returned to the Giants for two more years and retired as player-manager with Washington in 1893.

Eleven years later, at age 52, O'Rourke visited the Polo Grounds. Giants manager John McGraw let him catch New York's pennant-clinching win.

O'Rourke singled once in four trips to the plate.

O'Rourke's nickname, "Orator," was not given lightly. According to baseball historian Lee Allen, O'Rourke's "command of the English tongue was astonishing and bizarre." To cite merely one of his many baroque effusions: upon learning that Louis Sockalexis, a Penobscot Indian who played for Cleveland, had signed a contract containing a clause that he refrain from drinking, O'Rourke remarked, "I see that Sockalexis must forego frescoing his tonsils with the cardinal brush; it is so nominated in the contract of the aborigine."

After retiring as a player, O'Rourke worked one season as a National League umpire and managed Bridgeport in the Connecticut League from 1897 through 1908, taking over as league president from 1907 to 1913. On one occasion manager O'Rourke got into an argument with an umpire. His flowery rhetoric deserted him, and he let fly with some four-letter words. Suddenly realizing what he had done, he turned to the crowd and gravely announced that president O'Rourke was fining manager O'Rourke for using profanity.

One of Bridgeport's leading citizens, O'Rourke served on both the fire and the paving-and-street commissions. He also earned a law degree from Yale. On a frigid New Year's Day in 1919 he insisted on walking into Bridgeport to meet a client. He contracted pneumonia and died on January 8. In 1945 he was named to the Hall of Fame.

Dave Orr

Orr, David L. **1B**
1883–90 M(1887, 3–5) B:9/29/1859, New York, NY
D:6/2/1915, Richmond Hill, NY Deb:5/17/1883, NY AA
BR/TR 5'11", 250

G	AB	R	H	HR	RBI	OBP	SLG	AVG
791	3289	536	1125	37	627	.366	.502	.342

Big Dave Orr carried a big bat, as demonstrated by his lifetime slugging percentage of .502. He was also a big man, whose bulk may have been his undoing.

Orr began in baseball with the Alaskas club of Brooklyn, before joining the fledgling New York Giants in 1883. John B. Day, owner of both the Giants and the New York Metropolitans of the American Association, shifted Orr to the latter club.

The following season, Orr led the American Association with a .354 batting average and 162 hits. A strong finish (6-for-12) at the end of the 1885 season saw him almost repeat, as he finished at .342, one point behind Pete Browning for the batting crown. He also led the league in triples and slugging percentage. On June 12 of that year, he had his career day, going 6-for-6 and hitting for the cycle. In 1886 Orr hit .338; led the circuit in hits, triples and slugging; and became the first player to collect 300 total bases in one season.

Orr went to Brooklyn when the Mets franchise disbanded following the 1887 season. Newly named team captain, he feigned illness and spent August 2, 1888, at Coney Island. Outraged, Brooklyn owner Charles Byrne stripped him of his captaincy, and then sold him to Columbus in 1889. In 1890 Orr jumped to Brooklyn of the Players' League. He was enjoying perhaps his best season that year, when he suffered a stroke that paralyzed his left side. Some blamed his corpulence. Orr later served as press box attendant for the Federal League's Brooklyn Tip-Tops.

Joe Orsulak

Orsulak, Joseph Michael **OF**
1983–97 B: 5/31/1962, Glen Ridge, NJ
Deb: 9/1/1983, PIT BL/TL, 6'1", 196

G	AB	R	H	HR	RBI	OBP	SLG	AVG
1494	4293	559	1173	57	405	.327	.374	.273

Though he seldom hit for power, Joe Orsulak parlayed a strong arm and a respectable lefthanded bat into a major-league career that lasted 14 seasons. He led the American League with 22 outfield assists—a Baltimore club record—in 1991, despite missing 19 games. A contact hitter who did his best hitting against righthanded pitchers, Orsulak seldom struck out, walked, or made an error. In 1991, he batted .348 with a count of 0-2, the third-best mark in the league. He had decent speed, but after consecutive 24-steal seasons in 1985 and 1986, he never reached double figures again in that category.

Orsulak played for five different teams, spending four years with the Pittsburgh Pirates and five with the Orioles before joining the New York Mets, who signed him as a free agent, for three seasons. After a year with the Florida Marlins, he completed his career with the 1997 Montreal Expos.

Jorge Orta

Orta, Jorge (Nunez) **2B-DH-OF**
1972–86 B:11/26/1950, Mazatlan, Mexico
Deb:4/15/1972, CHI AL BL/TR 5'10", 175

G	AB	R	H	HR	RBI	OBP	SLG	AVG
1755	5829	733	1619	130	745	.338	.412	.278

A Mexican League hitting star, Jorge Orta seldom hit well enough in the majors to overcome his liabilities in the field. Mexican-born, but the son of Pedro Orta—who was known as "the Babe Ruth of Cuba"—Orta turned down a basketball scholarship to UCLA to play in the Mexican Center League in 1968. Three years later, he led the Mexican League with a .423 average for San Luis Potosi.

On the recommendation of Roland Hemond, the White Sox signed Orta in November 1971. He seemed competent at no position and hit only .202 for Chicago in 1972, but the team stuck with him. He became the regular second baseman the next year, and in 1974 he finished second in the American League with a .316 average, enjoying three five-hit games along the way. During the next five years Orta proved solid with the bat, but less so with the glove.

A free agent after the 1979 season, Orta signed with Cleveland. The Indians made him an outfielder in 1980 and he responded by hitting .291 and being selected to the All-Star Game. Two years later, however, the Indians traded him to Los Angeles. Orta had poor seasons with the Dodgers and Blue Jays before going to Kansas City in 1984. He was the lefthanded designated hitter for the Royals for three years, and retired after playing very little in 1987.

Orta was named to the Mexican Baseball Hall of Fame in 1976. In 1999 he coached for the Pacific Coast League's New Orleans Zephyrs.

Al Orth

Orth, Albert Lewis **P–OF**

1895–1909 B:9/5/1872, Tipton, IN D:10/8/1948, Lynchburg, VA Deb:8/15/1895, PHI NL BL/TR 6', 200

W	L	PCT	G	SH	IP	BB	SO	ERA
204	189	51.9	440	31	3354^{2}	661	948	3.37

G	AB	R	H	HR	RBI	OBP	SLG	AVG
602	1698	183	464	12	184	.298	.366	.273

Known as "the Curveless Wonder," Al Orth won 204 major league games despite relying on little more than an underhand fastball he threw at several speeds. He was also an excellent hitter for a pitcher, batting above .300 five times and being played in the outfield on occasion to take advantage of his bat.

Orth attended DePauw University in 1893 before playing baseball with Lynchburg in 1894 and 1895. Sold to the Philadelphia Phillies for $1,000 on August 13, 1895, he finished his abbreviated season with an 8–1 record. Orth won either 14 or 15 games in each of the next five years before breaking through as a 20-game winner in 1901, when he led the league with six shutouts.

After that season Orth jumped to Washington in the new American League. Two and a half years later he was traded to the New York Highlanders. Up to that point Orth had always had excellent control, averaging less than two walks per game in his career. He also threw from an unfamiliar underhand angle that confused batters. But he needed something more, and in 1904 his new Highlander teammate Jack Chesbro taught him the spitball. Orth finished the season 11–6, won 18 games the next season, and then, in 1906, led the league with 27 wins, 36 complete games, and 338⅔ innings pitched.

Orth won 14 and lost 21 the next year, but he made up for it, somewhat, by hitting .324. He was given less and less work, however, and he retired in 1909 after having played principally at second base. He managed Lynchburg and then served as an umpire in the Virginia League before officiating in the National League from 1912 to 1917. Orth served as a YMCA worker in France during World War I, following which he umpired in the Virginia League. He later coached at Washington and Lee University and at the Virginia Military Institute.

Claude Osteen

Osteen, Claude Wilson **P**

1957–75 B:8/9/1939, Caney Spring, TN Deb:7/6/1957, CIN NL BL/TL 5'11", 173

W	L	PCT	G	SH	IP	BB	SO	ERA
196	195	.501	541	40	3460^{1}	940	1612	3.30

Claude Osteen had the misfortune of pitching for the Los Angeles Dodgers when their staff included such luminaries as Sandy Koufax, Don Drysdale, Don Sutton, Tommy John, and Andy Messersmith. Osteen, though, did more than pull his own weight. He often outperformed his better-known teammates, winning 20 games twice and being named to three All-Star teams.

Osteen signed for a big bonus with the Cincinnati Reds straight out of high school in Tennessee. He made his major league debut in relief at age 17, but despite pitching well he was soon sent down. He excelled in the minors, however, and earned a regular place on the Reds' relief staff in 1960. But a 5.03 ERA resulted in another trip to the minors, and prior to the end of the 1961 season Osteen was dealt to the Washington Senators for pitcher Dave Sisler and cash.

In 1962 Osteen was thrown into the Senators' rotation and immediately proved an effective pitcher on a poor team. In late 1964, after going 15–13, he was traded to the Dodgers with infielder John Kennedy and $100,000 for slugger Frank Howard and several other players.

In 1965 he took his place in the Dodgers' rotation, which included Koufax, Drysdale, and Johnny Podres. Although his record was only 15–15, Osteen was superb, recording an ERA of 2.79. The Dodgers won the pennant, and Osteen was nearly unhittable in the World Series against Minnesota. He hurled seven scoreless innings to win Game 4 and yielded only a single run in a losing effort in Game 6. The Dodgers won in seven.

Osteen was a 17-game winner in 1966 as the Dodgers returned to the World Series, this time losing in four games to the Baltimore Orioles. He lost Game 3 to Wally Bunker, 1–0, but he outperformed both Koufax and Drysdale. In his three career World Series starts, Osteen's ERA was 0.86.

Koufax retired after the World Series loss, and Osteen paced the Dodgers' staff with 17 wins in 1967. His performance earned him his first trip to the All-Star Game. He won 20 games in both 1969 and 1972 for the Dodgers, and then won 16 in 1973 for his 10th consecutive season of 12 or more victories. Despite that, he was traded to the Houston Astros prior to the 1974 season in a deal that brought outfielder Jimmy Wynn to Los Angeles.

On August 15, 1974, Osteen was dealt to the Cardinals, who in turn sent him to the Cubs in 1975. In his final year he went 7–16 with a career-high 4.36 ERA. After retiring as a player, Osteen returned to the majors as a coach for St. Louis, Philadelphia, Texas, and Los Angeles.

Amos Otis

Otis, Amos Joseph **OF**

1967, 1969–84 B:4/26/1947, Mobile, AL Deb:9/6/1967, NY NL BR/TR 5'11", 166

G	AB	R	H	HR	RBI	OBP	SLG	AVG
1998	7299	1092	2020	193	1007	.347	.425	.277

An integral member of the division-winning Royals teams of the late 1970s, Amos Otis started his career in the Red Sox organization. Boston signed the 18-year-old Otis to a contract in 1965. The following year he was drafted off a minor league roster by the New York Mets and converted from a first baseman to an outfielder. Otis spent part of the 1967 and 1969 seasons with the Mets, but the club wanted him to play third base and he refused, so he spent most of the late '60s in the minors.

Prior to the 1970 season the Mets traded Otis to the Kansas City Royals for Joe Foy. In Kansas City he immediately became a starter and a fan favorite, although he was sometimes criticized for his casual attitude and one-handed catches. In his first year he led the league in doubles and became the first Royals player to participate in an All-Star Game, an honor he received five times. In the early 1970s, Otis twice hit .300 and once, in 1971, led the league with 52 stolen bases, including five in a single game against Milwaukee.

Otis put on his greatest performance in the 1980 World Series, when he hit .478 with three homers in a losing effort. Released after a contract dispute in 1983, he played his final season in Pittsburgh. He later served as a batting coach in the Padres' organization.

In 1986 Otis and pitcher Steve Busby were the first players inducted into the Royals' Hall of Fame. As of 1999 he still ranked among the club's top five players in most career offensive categories.

Jim O'Toole

O'Toole, James Jerome **P**

1958–67 B:1/10/1937, Chicago, IL Deb:9/26/1958, CIN NL BB/TL 6', 198

W	L	PCT	G	SH	IP	BB	SO	ERA
98	84	.538	270	18	1615^1	546	1039	3.57

Jim O'Toole was a promising lefthanded pitcher whose career was abbreviated by shoulder problems. He had excellent control and a strikeout pitch, but not durability.

Recruited from the University of Wisconsin, the 21-year-old O'Toole won *The Sporting News* Minor League Player of the Year Award in 1958 after winning 20 games and striking out 189 for Nashville. The next year he earned a position on the Reds' staff, and by 1960 he had become a member of the regular rotation.

In 1961 O'Toole won 13 of his last 15 decisions to help bring a National League pennant to Cincinnati. He finished the season 19–9 and was chosen to pitch the World Series opener for the Reds. In both of his Series appearances, however, O'Toole faced Whitey Ford, and both times he lost as the Reds were shut out.

O'Toole won at least 16 games in each of the next three seasons, and was selected to the All-Star Game in 1963. However, he developed a sore shoulder in 1965, which greatly reduced his effectiveness. He retired after the 1967 season, and later sold real estate and waste disposal contracts in Cincinnati. O'Toole was elected to the Reds' Hall of Fame in 1970.

Mel Ott

Ott, Melvin Thomas **OF-3B**

1926–47 M(1942–48, 464–530) B:3/2/1909, Gretna, LA D:11/21/1958, New Orleans, LA Deb:4/27/1926, NY NL BL/TR 5'9", 170

G	AB	R	H	HR	RBI	OBP	SLG	AVG
2730	9456	1859	2876	511	1860	.414	.533	.304

Mel Ott was one of the greatest players ever to wear a Giants uniform, and probably the most popular Giant of his time. The small, soft-spoken Louisiana native was a slugger who knew how to take advantage of the Polo Grounds' short porch in right field and a superb outfielder who played the corners of the wall expertly and erased many a runner from the basepaths.

The Broadway stars and other fans who frequented the right-field bleachers known as "Ottville" claimed Ott as their own. Legendary New York restaurateur Toots Shor was one of them. One time he was chatting with Sir Alexander Fleming, discoverer of penicillin, in his restaurant when he noticed Ott walk in. "Excuse me," Shor said to

Fleming. "Somebody important just came in."

Ott was one of the "nice guys" who inspired Dodgers manager Leo Durocher to utter his most memorable line. Early in the 1943 season Durocher was talking to reporters about Eddie Stanky. He told them that Stanky was snappish, tough, and a winner. As Durocher talked, Ott and his Giants took the field to warm up. Durocher emphasized his point: "Take a look at that Number Four there. A nicer guy never drew breath," he said of Ott. "Take a look at them. All nice guys. They'll finish last. Nice guys finish last."

But Ott was more than a nice guy; he was the center of his club's offense. The Giants were built on pitching and defense in his era, and Ott was the man who created the runs. From 1928 through 1945 he led the Giants in home runs every year on his way to becoming the first National League player to sock 500 homers. He topped the league in home runs six times. He also led the Giants in RBIs nine times, topping the 100 mark nine times in a 10-year period.

One reason for Ott's power numbers was his ability to make use of the 257-foot right field porch in the Polo Grounds. He hit 323 of his 511 home runs there, more than any other player has ever hit in one park.

Another reason for Ott's success was his keen batting eye. He is one of only five players to hit 40 homers in a season without striking out more than 40 times. Moreover, he led the league in bases on balls six times, and he was walked five times in a game on four occasions—twice as often as anyone else. Often pitched around, he set the National League record with 10 seasons of 100 or more walks. When he retired he held the league record for lifetime walks, a mark broken by Joe Morgan 35 years later.

Ott's batting style was dramatically different. As the pitch approached the plate he would step high with his forward (right) foot as he raised and lowered the bat vertically. As the ball neared the hitting zone he stepped forward with his right foot, shifting his weight for maximum leverage. By then his bat was low and almost horizontal, and he was in perfect hitting position to uncoil a smooth, level swing.

He brought that swing to the majors as a 17-year-old, having never played a day in the minors. He was too green to break into the Giants' lineup, but manager John McGraw was afraid that minor league skippers would try to alter the kid's unusual stroke. So Ott sat on the bench next to McGraw for two years and got an unsentimental education from the old master. When a player made a mistake, McGraw would turn to the youngster and say, "You wouldn't ever do that to me, would you, son?"

McGraw brought Ott along carefully, building his confidence. Ott had only 60 at bats his first season, but he batted .383. He was the youngest player in history to pinch-hit successfully and was 9-for-24 that season in that role. In 1927 he pinch-hit 46 times, more than anyone else in the league, and played 32 games in the outfield.

The following year Ott became a regular outfielder, and he responded by batting .322 with 18 homers and 77 RBIs. In 1929 he exploded with one of the best years a player so young has ever had. He hit .328, slugged 42 homers, drove in 151 runs, scored 138, and led the league with 113 walks. He also participated in 12 double plays, most ever for an outfielder.

This was just the start, as Ott sustained a remarkably productive and consistent performance over the next 15 years. In 1932 he led the league in home runs. The next year, although his production dropped off a notch, he helped power the Giants to the World Series for the first time since 1924. There, against the Washington Senators, Ott provided big hits in two of the Giants' four victories. In Game 1 he went 4-for-4 and drove in three runs. In Game 5 he homered into Griffith Stadium's center field bleachers to win the game, and the Series, for New York.

In 1934 Ott led the league in home runs and RBIs and was selected to the first of 11 consecutive All-Star Games. Two years later the Giants captured another flag, with Ott leading the league in home runs and slugging average and finishing in the top five in runs, total bases, RBIs, walks, and on-base percentage. But the Yankees, with Lou Gehrig and Joe DiMaggio, battered the Giants in six games to win the world championship.

The 1937 season was an instant replay. The Giants repeated as league champs, and Ott tied Joe Medwick for the home run title and led the league in walks. But the Yanks won the Series in five games. Ott won his third consecutive home run title in 1938, but the cracks were beginning to show on the team. During the next three seasons the Giants fell to fifth place, then sixth, and then fifth again. Bill Terry wanted out of the manager's job. Ott replaced him.

When Ott took the skipper's reins in 1942, he tried to emulate John McGraw and be something he wasn't—tough and nasty. He was still capable of hitting home runs (he led the league again in 1942) and walked more than 100 times. But as a rugged manager he was a flop. He began to berate his players and criticize them in public. He levied ridiculous fines. When pitcher Bill Voiselle gave up a homer on an 0–2 pitch, Ott slapped him with a $500 fine. Voiselle's salary was only $3,500.

After a while Ott abandoned his nasty act and reverted to his more natural, pleasant form. He basically quit playing after the 1945 season, and he hit his last home run in 1946. But the Giants were never a threat under his leadership. They finished last twice and fifth twice. In 1947 they won 20 more games than they had in 1946 and finished fourth, but owner Horace Stoneham had seen enough, and he replaced Ott with Durocher.

Ott moved into the Giants' front office, where he was second in command to Carl Hubbell in running the team's farm system. He took a job managing Oakland of the Pacific Coast League in 1951, the year he was inducted into the Baseball Hall of Fame. He lasted another season at Oakland's helm and then worked as a Tigers broadcaster for several years. He died in 1958 as a result of injuries he suffered in a car wreck.

Orval Overall

Overall, Orval **P**

1905–10, 1913 B:2/2/1881, Farmersville, CA D:7/14/1947, Fresno, CA Deb:4/16/1905, CIN NL BB/TR 6'2", 214

W	L	PCT	G	SH	IP	BB	SO	ERA
108	71	.603	218	30	1535^{1}	551	935	2.23

Orval Overall had a short but brilliant career with the Chicago Cubs in the first decade of the 20th century. Along with Mordecai "Three Finger" Brown, Ed Reulbach, and Jack Pfiester, the hard-throwing righthander was a valuable member of the National League's strongest pitching staff between 1906 and 1910, when Chicago won four pennants and two world championships. Standing 6-foot-2 and weighing 214 pounds, Overall was a power pitcher whose stock-in-trade was a mighty fastball.

Overall joined Cincinnati in 1905, compiling an 18–23 record with the fifth-place Reds. In June of the following year, the Cubs acquired him for slumping pitcher Bob Wicker and $2,000. Overall responded by going 12–3 on the team that won an all-time record 116 games in a season. He pitched only in relief in the World Series, as the "Hitless Wonder" White Sox upset the Cubs.

The next year Overall went 23–7, with a 1.68 ERA and a league-high eight shutouts. He pitched the first nine innings of the World Series opener, a 3–3 tie, then won Game 4 against the Tigers on a five-hitter. In 1908 he won two World Series games, including a three-hit shutout in the finale—the last victory by a pitcher for a Chicago Cubs world championship team in the 20th century.

Although the Cubs missed the pennant in 1909, Overall went 20–11 with a 1.42 ERA and led the league with nine shutouts and 205 strikeouts. In 1910 he developed a sore arm, but still managed to go 12–6. He was then knocked out by the Philadelphia A's in Game 1 of the World Series, his only appearance in that year's Fall Classic. That was it for Overall. An attempted comeback failed in 1913.

Marv Owen

Owen, Marvin James **3B**

1931, 1933–40 B:3/22/1906, Agnew, CA D:6/22/1991, Mountain View, CA Deb:4/16/1931, DET AL BR/TR 6'1", 175

G	AB	R	H	HR	RBI	OBP	SLG	AVG
1011	3782	473	1040	31	497	.339	.367	.275

Detroit third baseman Marv Owen was a central figure in one of the most controversial incidents in World Series history. In the sixth inning of Game 7 of the 1934 World Series, St. Louis outfielder Joe Medwick tripled and came sliding hard into third base in a contest that the Cardinals had already well-nigh won. Owen and Medwick mixed it up on the field, and a few minutes later Medwick was singled home. The score was 9–0, Cardinals.

When Medwick returned to his position in left at the Tigers' Navin Field, irate Detroit fans began showering him with garbage. Commissioner Kenesaw Mountain Landis ordered Medwick to leave the game. Getting Medwick tossed, however inadvertently, was probably Owen's biggest contribution to his team. A solid fielder not known for his hitting in the postseason, he was only 3-for-49 in the 1934 and 1935 World Series.

Owen began his big league career in 1931, with Detroit. His best regular season was 1934, when he hit .317, had 34 doubles, and drove in 96 runs. Prior to the 1938 season, he was traded to the White Sox. He retired following the 1940 season, which he spent with the Boston Red Sox.

Mickey Owen

Owen, Arnold Malcolm **C**

1937–45, 1949–51, 1954 B:4/4/1916, Nixa, MO Deb:5/2/1937, STL NL BR/TR 5'10", 190

G	AB	R	H	HR	RBI	OBP	SLG	AVG
1209	3649	338	929	14	378	.318	.322	.255

Catcher Mickey Owen's failure to catch a third strike in Game 4 of the 1941 World Series against the New York Yankees ranks as one of the most dramatic moments in baseball history—and one of the most heartbreaking for Brooklyn fans. Fireballing Hugh Casey was on the mound for Brooklyn, and it looked as if Leo Durocher's

Dodgers were about to knot the Series at two games apiece. They held a 4–3 lead with two outs in the top of the ninth, and Tommy Henrich represented the Yankees' last hope. The third-strike pitch (some said it was a spitter, although Owen denied it) scooted past the Dodgers' catcher. Henrich reached first base, and before the inning was over four runs had scored. Brooklyn lost the game, and the following day, the Series.

"I gave Casey the curveball sign, and he threw that big one, and it broke down like that, and I was looking for that smaller, quick one," Owen recalled. "I was late getting my glove down there and it went right by me. My fault."

Owen started his professional career in 1934 at Rogers-Bentonville of the Arkansas State League. The next year he joined the St. Louis Cardinals organization with Springfield of the Western Association, where he hit .310. Called up by the Cardinals in 1937, his hitting hovered around .260 in three full seasons.

On December 4, 1940, Owen was traded to the Dodgers for catcher Gus Mancuso, a minor league pitcher, and $65,000. He was selected to the All-Star Game in each of his first four years in Brooklyn. Owen served in the Navy late in World War II and, in April 1946, jumped to Jorge Pasquel's Mexican League. Pasquel was attempting to transform his circuit into a rival of Major League Baseball. He signed Owen for a $15,000 bonus plus $12,500 per year for each of five seasons.

Owen soon found the conditions and cuisine unacceptable and decided to return home. But he feared Pasquel's agents would prevent him from leaving Mexico. So Owen escaped by surreptitiously flying to Brownsville, Texas. Once back in the United States, however, he found himself blacklisted from the major leagues. He was not allowed to play professionally until Commissioner Happy Chandler lifted the ban on June 5, 1949. Owen then signed with the Chicago Cubs, for whom he played until 1951. He served as a player-coach with Kansas City of the American Association in 1952 and as a player-manager with Norfolk of the Piedmont League in 1953, before returning to the majors for one season with the Boston Red Sox in 1954.

Owen managed Jacksonville of the South Atlantic League in 1956 and scouted for the Orioles in 1958 and 1959. Returning home to Missouri in 1960, he established the Mickey Owen Baseball School for Boys and became involved in politics. Owen was elected sheriff of Greene County, Missouri, in 1964. In 1980 he mounted an unsuccessful campaign to become lieutenant governor of Missouri.

Spike Owen

Owen, Spike Dee **SS**

1983–95 B:4/19/1961, Cleburne, TX Deb:6/25/1983, SEA AL BB/TR 5'10" 170

G	AB	R	H	HR	RBI	OBP	SLG	AVG
1544	4930	587	1211	46	439	.326	.341	.246

Light-hitting Spike Owen's glove kept him in the major leagues for 13 seasons. Twice (1989, 1990) he led National League shortstops in fielding percentage. In 1986, with Seattle and Boston, he paced American League shortstops with 133 double plays and 767 total chances. Back in the NL in 1990, he set a since-broken league record for shortstops by playing 66 consecutive errorless games. But perhaps the most interesting thing about Spike Owen is his actual first name. It really is Spike.

Owen, whose brother Dave played short for the Cubs and the Royals, was a Seattle first round draft choice in June 1982. In 1986, the Red Sox, hoping to shore up their defense for the pennant drive, acquired Owen and outfielder Dave Henderson for infielder Rey Quinones, a player to be named later, and cash. Owen responded with some heavy hitting in the postseason, batting .429 in the ALCS against the Angels and .300 in the World Series against the Mets.

The Red Sox traded him to Montreal in December 1988. In Montreal Owen hit his defensive peak, but after the 1992 season he declared free agency and signed with the Yankees. He batted just .234 in New York and the team packed him off to the Angels, where he hit a surprising .310 in part-time service in 1994. The next year, though, he slipped to .229, and his term in the majors was up.

Tom Paciorek

Paciorek, Thomas Marian **OF–1B–DH**

1970–87 B:11/2/1946, Detroit, MI Deb:9/12/1970, LA NL BR/TR 6'4", 215

G	AB	R	H	HR	RBI	OBP	SLG	AVG
1392	4121	494	1162	86	503	.328	.415	.282

Tom Paciorek was once selected as the second best-looking player in baseball, behind Jim Palmer. But he had a lot more going for him than looks; despite spending virtually all of his career as either a backup or platooned, he was also a talented player.

Paciorek posted excellent minor league stats, topping the .300 mark five times. Playing for Albuquerque in 1972, he led the league in at bats, runs, hits, doubles, and homers, tallied 107 RBIs, and batted for a .307 average; he was named Minor League Player of the Year.

The Dodgers of the early 1970s were loaded with outfielders. Behind Willie Davis and Manny Mota, they had Willie Crawford, Von Joshua, Bill Buckner, and Lee Lacy. Paciorek just couldn't find a spot. So late in 1975 he was swapped to Atlanta along with Jimmy Wynn, Lacy, and Jerry Royster for Dusty Baker and Ed Goodson.

In 1976 Paciorek played outfield, first base, and third base for the Braves, appearing in more than 100 games for the first time in his career. He batted .290 and gave promise of bright things in the future. But the next year his average dipped to .239. The Braves released him in March 1978, re-signed him in April, then released him again in May.

Paciorek was picked up by Seattle, and moved regularly to the outfield. He suddenly came into his own, hitting .299 for the rest of that season. In his fourth year with the Mariners he hit .326 with 14 home runs and 28 doubles and was selected to play in the All-Star Game.

Traded to the White Sox for three players before the 1982 season, Paciorek hit .312 while playing almost exclusively at first base. The following year he played first and the outfield as the White Sox captured the American League West title. Paciorek contributed a .307 batting average and 32 doubles.

In 1985 he was traded to the Mets. He spent the next two years with Texas, retiring in 1987. He later went into broadcasting. Paciorek had two brothers, John and Jim, who also played in the major leagues. John holds a major league record as the only lifetime 1.000 batter with as many as three hits.

Andy Pafko

Pafko, Andrew **OF–3B**

1943–59 B:2/25/1921, Boyceville, WI Deb:9/24/1943, CHI NL BR/TR 6', 190

G	AB	R	H	HR	RBI	OBP	SLG	AVG
1852	6292	844	1796	213	976	.351	.449	.285

An All-Star outfielder who played in four World Series, Andy Pafko would have played in two more except that he had the misfortune to be on the losing side of two pennant playoffs eight years apart. "Handy Andy" reached the major leagues when he was 22. Called up to the Chicago Cubs from Los Angeles of the Pacific Coast League, he made his big league debut on September 24, 1943. He banged out a single and a double and drove in four runs as the Cubs beat the Philadelphia Phillies, 7–4, in a game called in the bottom of the fifth because of rain.

He became a regular in 1944, and was selected for his first All-Star Game the following year. That year the Cubs also won the pennant, as Pafko hit .298, drove in 110 runs, and led the league in fielding average. He scored three runs in Game 1 of the World Series against the Detroit Tigers, but hit .214 and drove in only two runs in the Chicago's seven-game loss.

After an injury-plagued 1946 season, Pafko rebounded in 1947 with the first of four consecutive All-Star appearances. He also topped .300 for the first time, hitting .302. The next season he had perhaps his best overall season, hitting .312 with 26 home runs and 101 RBIs.

He hit a career-high 36 homers in 1950, including three in one game on August 2. Pafko was acquired by the Brooklyn Dodgers in June 1951 to fortify left field. In 84 games for the Dodgers he hit .249, with 18 homers and 58 RBIs. He also made a spectacular catch in the final game of the season to help force a playoff. It was not quite enough. In the third contest of the playoff against the Giants, the forlorn Pafko, pressed against the left field wall in the Polo Grounds, watched as Bobby Thomson's famous homer sailed into the lower stands, winning the pennant for the Giants.

The next year the Dodgers took the pennant, but Pafko was dealt to Milwaukee after the season for $50,000 cash and second baseman Roy Hartsfield. Pafko found himself on a rising club in Milwaukee. His first year he hit .297, with 17 home runs and 72 RBIs, but his production dropped each successive year, and he play less and less. He appeared in the World Series two more times; he gained his only championship ring in 1957, and batted .333 the next year in a seven-game defeat.

In 1959 the Braves narrowly missed a third straight pennant and wound up tied with the Dodgers on the last weekend of the season. In the ensuing best-of-three playoff, the Dodgers took two games to advance to the World Series. That bitter end marked Pafko's final experience as a player. He stayed on as a coach for Milwaukee from 1960 through 1962.

Joe Page

Page, Joseph Francis **P**

1944–50, 1954 B:10/28/1917, Cherry Valley, PA D:4/21/1980, Latrobe, PA Deb:4/19/1944, NY AL BL/TL 6'2", 205

W	L	PCT	G	SV	IP	BB	SO	ERA
57	49	.538	285	76	790	421	519	3.53

The modern, well-paid relief specialist owes some thanks to Joe "Fireman" Page. With his overpowering fastball and ability to kill opposing rallies, Page lent pride and respectability to bullpen work by graphically demonstrating the value of a relief pitcher. A big, strong lefthander who today would be a "closer," Page was simply an ace reliever in his day. That a relief specialist was named to the All-Star Game three times in the 1940s shows what a vital component Page was for the Yankees.

Page was born in the coal country of Pennsylvania. The son of a miner, he was the oldest of seven children. At 18, he barely escaped losing his left leg after a car struck him. He spent nearly a year in the hospital and protected the injury with a shin guard well into his major league career.

He arrived in the majors in 1944 and opened with a 5–1 record, earning a spot on the American League All-Star team. But he injured his shoulder in a base-running mishap and finished the season with six straight defeats. For the next two years he split time between starting and relieving.

In 1947 Page's position on the roster was in jeopardy until the inning that may have saved his career. Manager Bucky Harris put Page into a game against the Red Sox. New York trailed by two runs, and Boston had two on and no outs. Outfielder Ted Williams reached on an error, loading the bases. Page threw three straight balls to Bobby Doerr, then struck him out and pulled through the inning unscathed. Of Page's 56 outings that year, 54 were in relief. He finished the year 14–8 with a league-leading 17 saves and a 2.48 ERA

The Yankees won the pennant, and Page appeared in four of the seven World Series games, going 1–1 with a save. In Game 7 he entered in the top of the fifth, right after the Yankees had taken a 3–2 lead. He nursed the one-run edge until his teammates could add some insurance. The Dodgers did not manage a hit off of him until the last inning, and the Yankees wrapped up the Series.

In 1948 Page led the league with 55 appearances and made the All-Star team for the third time. The following season Casey Stengel replaced Harris as manager, and Page enjoyed a spectacular year. He led the league with 60 appearances, carved out a 13–8 record, and saved a league-high 27 games. In fact, Page saved the Yankees' season in one of the most famous weekends in baseball history.

The Red Sox came to Yankee Stadium holding a one-game lead and needing to win only one of the final two games to secure the pennant. Boston took a 2–0 lead in the first game, knocking out Yankees starter Allie Reynolds. Page entered and walked in a pair of runs but settled down after that, shutting down the Red Sox until the Yankees came back for a 5–4 victory. New York won the pennant the next day.

Then, for the second time in three years, Page nailed down the World Series. After getting the win in Game 3, he entered Game 5 in the seventh inning with the Yankees leading and held the Dodgers scoreless the rest of the way for the title.

His workload began to take its toll. Unlike modern closers, Page averaged two innings per appearance, and regularly pitched three innings or more in relief. His record slid to 3–7 in 1950, and his career with the Yankees was over. He resurfaced in 1954 with the Pirates but pitched in only seven games, retiring at the end of the season. He died of heart failure on April 21, 1980, in Latrobe, Pennsylvania.

Satchel Paige

Paige, Leroy Robert **P**

1948–49, 1951–53, 1965 Negro League Player (1926-48, 1950) B:7/7/1906, Mobile, AL D:6/8/1982, Kansas City, MO Deb:7/9/1948, CLE AL BR/TR 6'3½", 180

W	L	PCT	G	SV	IP	BB	SO	ERA
28	31	.475	179	32	476	180	288	3.29

Baseball historians may debate whether Satchel Paige was the finest pitcher the Negro Leagues ever produced. There is certainly no question that he was the most celebrated. Whether the discussion centers on his fabulous control or the mystery of his age, Paige remains one of the most fascinating figures in baseball history. Yet when the 40-ish Paige came to the major leagues in 1948, *The Sporting News* publisher, J.G. Taylor Spink, was infuriated. "To bring in a pitching rookie of Paige's age is to demean the standards of baseball," Spink wrote. "I demeaned the big leagues considerable that year," Paige later replied. "I win six and lose one."

Paige was born in Mobile, Alabama, the seventh of 11 children. The official date is 1906, but 1903 and 1908 have also been suggested. He got his nickname from toting bags at the Mobile railroad station at the age of 7. He got his hesitation pitch from throwing rocks at other kids, fooling them into ducking too soon. He was a scrappy youth, and in school he was involved in numerous battles. He was sent to the Industrial School for Negro Children at Mount Meigs, Alabama, for truancy, breaking windows, and fighting. He was not released until he was 17. Even then his ability to throw a baseball attracted attention.

Paige signed on with a local black semipro team, the Mobile Tigers. In 1924 he won roughly 30 games and lost only one. He pitched with the Tigers until 1926, when the Negro Southern League's Chattanooga Black Lookouts offered him $50 a month to pitch for them. From the beginning, Paige amazed all observers with his fastball and control. He called his curve his "be ball," "because it be where I want it to be." Soon he was a celebrity in the world of southern black baseball. He had his own roadster, played guitar with Louis Armstrong's orchestra, and supped with Jelly Roll Morton. Although record keeping was lax at the time, it was estimated that he was winning 60 games a year and striking out 10 to 18 batters per contest.

In 1931 Paige went north to one of the finest black teams around, Gus Greenlee's Pittsburgh Crawfords. His salary was $200 a month. With the Crawfords, Paige teamed with Josh Gibson to form one of baseball's most impressive batteries. Gibson hit gargantuan home runs and Paige provided the pitching; in a three-year period, Paige won an estimated 105 games, while losing only 37.

Paige was constantly on the road. "One day I pitched a no-hitter for the Crawfords against the Homestead Grays" in Washington, he recalled later. "That was on July 4; I remember because somebody kept shooting off firecrackers every time I got another batter out. Those firecrackers were still popping when I ran out of the park, hopped in my car, and drove all night to Chicago. I got there just in time to beat Ted Trent and the Chicago American Giants, 1–0, in 12 innings. And the same day, somebody said I was supposed to be in Cleveland."

In 1942 Paige would have similar vexing travel plans. Scheduled to pitch in the Negro World Series for the Kansas City Monarchs, Paige was stopped for speeding and was delayed from getting to Shibe Park to pitch against the Grays. He didn't arrive until the third inning. The Grays were ahead, 4–3, and had a runner on first. Paige, with no time to loosen up, was inserted into the game. He proceeded to warm up by trying to pick the runner off first. Once he was loose, he pitched to the batter and handled the Grays easily for the rest of the game. The Monarchs came back to win, 9–5, for Paige's third win of the Series.

While in Pittsburgh, Paige met a young waitress at Greenlee's Crawford Grill. Her name was Janet Howard, and they later married. Family responsibilities gave Paige a desire to earn bigger salaries than Greenlee was paying (now up to $700 a month), so in 1934 he signed with a semipro team in Bismarck, North Dakota. When he arrived in Bismarck, Paige set out to prove that he was as good as his reputation. He set up a matchstick on a stick beside home plate and knocked it off in 13 of 20 tries. Then he let loose with his fastball. He was so fast and the ball moved in such a way that the Bismarck catcher would not warm him up without wearing shin guards and a chest protector.

Throughout the 1930s, Paige crisscrossed the country. In 1934 he also pitched for the Cuban House of David team, at one point even donning a false beard. To while away winters, he put together the Satchel Paige All-Stars. In one three-season span, the team won 128 games (including 40 against squads featuring big leaguers) and lost only 23.

Paige engaged major league opposition numerous times during his career. No batter who faced him ever downplayed his ability. "Paige was the best pitcher I ever saw," said Bob Feller. "I'm judging him on the way he overpowered or outwitted some of the best major league hitters of his day." Cardinals pitcher Dizzy Dean once remarked, "If me and Satch were together in St. Louis, we would clinch the pennant by July and go fishing from then until World Series time." In one 13-inning matchup in 1934, Paige bested Dean, 1–0, and struck out 17.

In 1935 Paige again pitched for Bismarck and the House of David, but he soon found himself on the road to the Dominican Republic. Dominican dictator Rafael L. Trujillo was recruiting a baseball team and sent an emissary to the United States with $30,000 and orders to recruit the best team he could find. He assembled a team featuring Paige, Gibson, and Cool Papa Bell. After arriving in Santo Domingo, the Negro Leaguers saw that this game was genuine hardball. Heavily armed soldiers ringed the ballparks. It was win—or else. "You could see Trujillo lining up his army. They began to look like a firing squad," said Paige. Against the Estrellas de Oriente team, the nervous Americans lost the first three games, then bore down and won the final four contests. "You never saw ol' Satch throw harder," Paige admitted.

When Greenlee sold the pitcher's contract to the Newark Eagles, Paige packed his bags and headed for Mexico. But while playing in Mexico in 1938, he seriously damaged his arm, and his pitching future seemed doubtful. J.L. Wilkinson of the Kansas City Monarchs bought Paige's contract from Newark, figuring he would use the hurler as a draw for a sort of junior varsity version of the club. Paige would play first and pitch occasionally. Wilkinson got one of the biggest bargains in baseball history. Soon Paige was better than ever, and he helped lead the Monarchs to

Negro American League titles each year from 1939 to 1942.

In 1946 Branch Rickey broke baseball's color barrier when he signed Jackie Robinson. "Somehow I'd always figured it would be me," said Paige. "Maybe it had happened too late, and everybody figured I was too old. Maybe that was why it was Jackie and not me."

Actually, Paige was too old—too old if he were anybody but Satchel Paige. He continued to pitch well against big leaguers in postseason exhibitions (particularly against one squad led by Bob Feller after the 1947 season) and in Negro League competition, but as the 1948 season opened he was still on the Monarchs' roster. Then colorful Cleveland Indians owner Bill Veeck decided to give Paige a chance. Despite cries that the Paige signing was just another Veeck publicity stunt, Paige went 6–1 for the Indians in 1948, giving major league audiences a hint at what a great hurler he still was. After Veeck sold the Indians in 1949, however, Paige was released and went back to barnstorming. But when Veeck acquired the St. Louis Browns, he brought Paige back to the big leagues.

In 1952 Paige was 12–10 for the Browns, and he gained a league-leading eight wins in relief, with 10 saves. The following season he saved 11 games although his record was only 3–9.

After leaving the majors, Paige continued to pitch. He barnstormed in 1954 and rejoined the Monarchs in 1955. In 1956 he signed up again with Veeck, who was operating the Miami Marlins in the International League. On August 7, 1956, more than 50,000 fans saw Paige pitch at the Orange Bowl. He finished the year 11–4 with a 1.86 ERA. He had two more excellent years before his relations with the Miami management deteriorated.

Paige briefly popped up again with Portland of the Pacific Coast League in 1961 and posted a 2.88 ERA. He later barnstormed with the Indianapolis Clowns. In 1965 Charles Finley brought him back for one more game in Kansas City, and he pitched three shutout innings against the Boston Red Sox. In 1968 it was discovered that Paige was only 158 major league days short of qualifying for a $7,000-a-year pension, and he was placed on the Atlanta Braves' roster as a coach.

The Committee on Negro Leagues inducted Paige to the Baseball Hall of Fame in 1971. Paige felt that he should have reached the Hall of Fame without the vote of a special committee, but he acknowledged that there were many other great Negro League players, who, unlike Josh Gibson or himself, would not be remembered. "There were many Satchels and many Joshes," he said.

Rafael Palmeiro

Palmeiro, Rafael (Corrales) **1B-OF-DH**

1986–* B:9/24/1964, Havana, Cuba Deb:9/8/1986, CHI NL BL/TL 6', 188

G	AB	R	H	HR	RBI	OBP	SLG	AVG
1940	7281	1157	2158	361	1227	.373	.513	.296

While Mark McGwire, Frank Thomas, and Mo Vaughn drew more attention during the 1990s, Rafael Palmeiro may have been the most consistent first baseman in baseball. He hit 20 or more home runs each year from 1991 to 1999, batted .300 or better six times during the decade, and drove in 100 or more runs five times in six years. He also led all major leaguers in games played in the 1990s, and was second to former Chicago Cubs teammate Mark Grace in hits and doubles during the decade. A three-time Gold Glove Award winner, Palmeiro was so respected at first base that in 1999 he was given the honor despite playing only 28 games at the position.

Despite his impressive credentials, Palmeiro was allowed to walk away as a free agent twice during the decade. Each time the split centered over the perception that the four-time All-Star was preoccupied with his numbers. In both cases, the team that let Palmeiro go soon came to regret its decision.

After the 1988 season the Texas Rangers acquired Palmeiro from the Cubs, where he had played his first three seasons. He batted .296 as a Ranger, but Texas let Palmeiro go following a bitter dispute in 1993. Palmeiro charged that Will Clark, a former college teammate at Mississippi State, had undercut his negotiations with the club to sign his own deal. Palmeiro landed with the Baltimore Orioles in 1994, and batted .319 with 23 homers and 76 RBIs before the season-ending strike intervened. He blasted 159 home runs over his next four seasons and drove in 100 runs each year.

Baltimore was negligent in starting negotiations in 1998 with Palmeiro. By the time the Orioles were ready to deal, he was talking to the Rangers. Palmeiro's family had never moved from Texas, and that consideration ultimately led him to reject a richer, last-minute hour offer from the Orioles. Comfortable in Arlington, Palmeiro put together a tremendous 1999 season, finishing with a .324 average, 47 homers and 148 RBIs, all career highs. Although injuries forced to spend most of the season as a designated hitter, he still played 158 games, the 10th time in his 14-year career he played in more than 150 games.

Dean Palmer

Palmer, Dean William **3B**
1989, 1991–* B:12/27/1968, Tallahassee, FL Deb:9/1/1989, TEX AL BR/TR 6'2", 195

G	AB	R	H	HR	RBI	OBP	SLG	AVG
1125	4064	624	1035	235	701	.328	.483	.255

A free-swinging power-hitting third baseman playing in a peak era for home runs, Dean Palmer was perfectly situated to take advantage of his talent. Palmer was a third-round pick by the Texas Rangers in 1986 as a 17-year-old. He blossomed into a power threat in 1989 in Double A, but failed in a brief tryout with the Rangers in September 1989. Palmer did not arrive in the majors for good until 1992.

Initially, Palmer struck out more than once per game and could not hit for average, yet his power numbers increased during each of his first three full seasons. On June 3, 1995, Palmer suffered a ruptured left biceps tendon. At the time, he was among the top 10 in the American League in batting, slugging, on-base percentage, runs, and home runs. Fortunately, surgery successfully reattached the tendon, and Palmer came back in 1996 to hit .280 with 38 home runs and 107 RBIs.

Traded to Kansas City during 1997, Palmer was an All-Star with the Royals the following season. He signed a five-year deal as a free agent with the Detroit Tigers, who expected him to be a cornerstone of their rebuilding plans. He had a solid first season in Motown with 38 home runs and 100 RBIs in 1999.

Jim Palmer

Palmer, James Alvin **P**
1965–67, 1969–84 B:10/15/1945, New York, NY Deb:4/17/1965, BAL AL BR/TR 6'3", 196

W	L	PCT	G	SH	IP	BB	SO	ERA
268	152	.638	558	53	3948	1311	2212	2.86

Of the 18 pitchers who have won 20 or more games eight times, only three played in the American League, and only Jim Palmer of the Baltimore Orioles began his career after World War II. Palmer strung together those 20-win campaigns from 1970 through 1978, overcoming arm injuries to average 288 innings per season.

The Orioles won seven titles during Palmer's 19-year tenure, five of them highlighted by the amusing Mutt-and-Jeff feud between the elegant, well-bred pitcher and his pugnacious manager, Earl Weaver. The youngest pitcher ever to throw a World Series shutout, Palmer also was the only pitcher to win World Series games in three decades. He won three Cy Young Awards, and drew the third-highest plurality among pitchers elected to Cooperstown.

"Looking at films of myself," Palmer once admitted, "I felt like maybe I ought to put more into this." His delivery was the antithesis of Nolan Ryan's drop-and-drive style. Palmer stood tall and paused in his delivery before releasing the ball from a uniquely high arm angle. Weaver tried to maximize Palmer's advantage by pitching him at home in day games whenever possible because a white house behind the Memorial Stadium fence effectively obscured his release point.

Through the 1970s Palmer mainly used a fastball, slider, and changeup, perfecting the curveball later in his career. He was fast but not overpowering, and threw a light ball that longtime catcher and coach Ellie Hendricks said had a hop at the end, whether Palmer was throwing 95 or 85 miles per hour. He was a rare hurler who successfully pitched high in the strike zone but did not possess devastating stuff. Baltimore's old ballpark, with its spacious center field and short foul lines, encouraged outfielders to bunch towards center, and Palmer probably led the league every year in flyouts down the middle.

Adopted by a wealthy family two days after his birth, Palmer split his first nine years between a Park Avenue apartment in New York City and a Westchester County estate. After his father's death in 1954, his mother married character actor Max Palmer. Following a brief stay in Beverly Hills, the family moved to Scottsdale, Arizona, where young Palmer became a star in baseball, football, and basketball.

He signed with the Orioles for a reported $60,000 bonus in August 1963, and went 11–3 with a 2.51 ERA in his first professional season with Aberdeen, South Dakota, of the Northern League. His rookie season included a no-hitter, but he also walked 130 batters in 129 innings. Despite his control problems, Palmer was promoted to Baltimore in 1965, part of the second tier of the so-called "Baby Bird" pitchers, which included Wally Bunker and Dave McNally.

Brought to the majors as a long relief specialist, Palmer joined the starting rotation in 1966, and his team-high 15 victories that season included the first of four pennant clinchers. In that year's World Series Game 2 the 20-year-old Palmer outdueled Sandy Koufax and shut out the Dodgers, 6–0. The Orioles cruised to a four-game sweep but Palmer developed a sore arm.

During the 1967 season Palmer went to the minors to try to recapture his form. At Rochester of the International League he had his first encounter with Weaver. In 1968 Palmer retreated all the way to Class A ball looking for answers. Surgery didn't seem to help. But that winter, pitching for Santurce in Puerto Rico, his arm "miraculously" bounced back. Palmer's recovery is one of the few cases of a young pitcher making a total recovery from a serious arm injury early in his career.

Returning in 1969 to the Orioles, now managed by Weaver, Palmer shut out the Washington Senators on the first Sunday of the season. After a month on the disabled list he beat Oakland on August 13 at Memorial Stadium with "the ugliest no-hitter ever," by Palmer's reckoning. He survived six walks and two errors to win, 8–0. He completed the season with a league-high .800 winning percentage at 16–4 for the AL champion Orioles. He lost Game 3 of the 1969 World Series against the Mets.

Completely healthy in 1970, Palmer pitched a league-leading 305 innings, tied for most shutouts with five, was named to the first of six AL All-Star teams, and began a run of four straight 20-win seasons. The Orioles again went to the World Series, this time winning in five games over Cincinnati. Palmer started and won Game 1.

With Palmer, McNally, Mike Cuellar, and new starter Pat Dobson, the Orioles featured a quartet of 20-game winners in 1971, a feat matched only by the 1920 Chicago White Sox. The Orioles had their third straight 100-win season and took the AL East title by a dozen games. For the third straight year the Orioles swept the AL Championship Series, this time over the A's. Palmer pitched the clincher for the third straight year.

Palmer started Game 2 of the World Series, allowing seven hits in eight innings as the Orioles ran away with an 11–3 win. In Game 6 he yielded two runs but held the Pirates in check as the Orioles tied the score. Palmer left for a pinch hitter after nine innings, and Baltimore won an inning later. The Pirates, however, won Game 7 behind Steve Blass' four-hitter.

Palmer registered 21 wins and a career-low 2.07 ERA in 1972, and upped the victory total to 22 in 1973, topping the American League with a 2.40 ERA and winning his first Cy Young Award. The Orioles took the AL East again, and Weaver chose Palmer for the playoff opener against Oakland. Palmer dispatched the defending world champions with a five-hit shutout, fanning 12 and extending the Orioles' ALCS winning streak to 10 games. His four playoff wins were unsurpassed by any pitcher until Dave Stewart collected his fifth ALCS win in 1990. The A's won three of the next four games to take the pennant.

The two teams met again in the following postseason. In Game 3 Vida Blue shut out the O's, 1–0, on just two hits, and Palmer was tagged for his only playoff loss. The A's captured the pennant in four games and took their third-straight World Series title.

Palmer had been hampered by elbow problems in 1974, but he came back to have his best season in 1975, setting career highs with 23 wins, 323 innings, and 10 shutouts—only the third time since 1914 that an American League pitcher reached double figures in that category. He won his second Cy Young Award, and also took the ERA crown for the second time in his career.

In 1976 Palmer won 22 games and became the league's first pitcher to win back-to-back Cy Young Awards outright. (Denny McLain won the Cy Young trophy in 1968 and tied with Mike Cuellar in 1969.) Palmer followed with a league-leading 20 wins in 1977 and 21 wins in 1978. In his sensational nine-year period, he was selected to the All-Star Game six times.

Palmer's career began to slow down after that, but his feuds with Weaver escalated. "Palmer would get into trouble with Earl because Earl thought Jim was trying to be the manager on the mound," recalled third baseman Brooks Robinson. "Earl used to say he'd move the defense six steps to the left so that, after Jim moved them three steps to the right, the outfielders would wind up where Earl wanted them. Palmer and Weaver were a pair of the two sharpest baseball minds I've ever been around," Robinson added, "and each thought he understood the game better than the other."

Palmer retired in 1984 after a poor start. He returned to baseball shortly after being inducted into the Hall of Fame in 1990. But after spring training in 1991 he gave up mound work, restricting his activities to pitches of a different kind—advertising for underwear and a money-lending organization. He continued to voice his opinions on baseball as an announcer for the Orioles.

Milt Pappas

Pappas, Milton Stephen **P**

1957–73 B:5/11/1939, Detroit, MI Deb:8/10/1957, BAL AL BR/TR 6'3", 190

W	L	PCT	G	SH	IP	BB	SO	ERA
209	164	.560	520	43	3186	858	1728	3.40

Milt Pappas is often used as evidence of the vagaries of the Hall of Fame voting. In 17 big league seasons Pappas went 209–164 with an ERA of 3.40. In contrast, Don Drysdale went 209–166 with a 2.95 ERA over 14 seasons. Drysdale was elected to the Hall of Fame, whereas Pappas has only even been on the ballot once, and then because of his own vociferous complaints. He received five of 432 possible votes.

Although Pappas was a very good pitcher, he was definitely not Hall of Fame material. Election to the Hall of Fame is often a popularity contest, and, as his campaign for the Hall of Fame demonstrated, Pappas was always most popular with himself.

Pappas was born Miltiades Stergios Papastegios in Detroit, where his parents, Greek immigrants, ran a grocery store. Pappas starred at Detroit's Cooley High School and signed with Baltimore in 1957. Fourteen major league teams were interested in him, but he was already figuring the odds. "Before I signed," he said later, "I averaged out the age of every pitching staff in the big leagues. Baltimore had the oldest staff, so I figured it was my best chance."

He was right; at 18 he went directly to the major leagues. He held New York scoreless for two innings in his debut, then sat on the bench for several weeks. One evening Pappas was out late; returning to his hotel at 2:30 AM, he tried to enter his room, but teammate Brooks Robinson was asleep inside with the only key. Pappas was forced to ask the hotel's assistant manager to let him in. Orioles manager Paul Richards found out, and Pappas was sent to Knoxville of the South Atlantic League.

He returned to Baltimore at the end of the year, was invited to spring training the following season, and made the team. The precocious young pitcher went 10–10, and it looked as if the Orioles had found a star. But while Pappas continued to pitch well, he also earned a reputation as a brash hothead and became one of the most disliked pitchers in the league. He talked back to veteran batters, complained to scorekeepers, and argued with his manager. Surprisingly, his biggest day in baseball was actually as a hitter. On August 27, 1961, he hit three homers in the same game.

Because Pappas had great potential, his behavior was tolerated. By age 24, with six full years in the big leagues already under his belt, he had compiled a record was 81–58, at the time one of the best in baseball history for pitchers under 25 years old. He headed a similarly precocious staff of "Baby Birds" that included such phenoms as Steve Barber, Wally Bunker, Jim Palmer, and Dave McNally. After winning 16 games in both 1963 and 1964, Pappas seemed to be on the verge of stardom.

He never quite became the pitcher everyone believed he could be. After the 1965 season, when the Orioles finished in third place and appeared poised to challenge for the pennant, he and outfielder Dick Simpson were traded for Frank Robinson. The deal has since gone down as one of the worst in the history of baseball. Robinson won the Triple Crown and led the Orioles to the world championship, while Pappas never pitched as well in Cincinnati as he had in Baltimore. In June 1968 he was traded to Atlanta, where he struggled. He won only 18 games in parts of three seasons and was shelled in his only postseason appearance, in the 1969 National League Championship Series.

In 1970 Pappas was traded to the Cubs, and he pitched as well as he ever had. In both 1971 and 1972 he won 17 games, leading the league with five shutouts in 1971. On September 2, 1972, he no-hit San Diego, yielding only one walk in an 8–0 victory. But in 1973 he slumped to 7–12 with a 4.28 ERA. More than 3,000 innings of pitching had taken their toll. Pappas retired at age 34.

Chan Ho Park

Park, Chan Ho **P**

1994–* B:6/30/1973, Kongju, South Korea

Deb:4/8/1994, LA NL BR/TR 6'2", 185

W	L	PCT	G	SH	IP	BB	SO	ERA
47	33	.587	151	0	723²	345	663	4.07

After pulling strings with the Korean government, the Dodgers signed Chan Ho Park in January 1994. He debuted for Los Angeles on April 8, becoming the first Korean to pitch in the major leagues. He was also the first National Leaguer since 1978 to skip the minor leagues, although he was later sent down to harness his control.

Fans may have snickered when he bowed to the umpire in his first major league at bat, but Park quickly gained respect in the league. He devastated hitters with a moving 94-mph fastball, a tight curve, and a sharp-breaking slider. While Park was successful in the bullpen in 1996, he was even more effective once he cracked the Dodgers' starting rotation. He won 14 games in 1997 and 15 games the following year. He was named NL Pitcher of the Month with a 4–0 mark and 1.05 ERA in July 1998.

The Korean government then threatened to call Park back home to fulfill his mandatory year of military service. After he helped his native Korea win the gold medal in the 1998 Asia Games in Thailand, however, an agreement was reached to exempt him from service. In Los Angeles, he continued to draw large numbers of Korean fans to his starts at Dodger Stadium. Park said he received 150 fan letters a week—100 of which came from his native country.

Dave Parker

Parker, David Gene **OF–DH**
1973–91 B:6/9/1951, Calhoun, MS Deb:7/12/1973, PIT NL BL/TR 6'5", 230

G	AB	R	H	HR	RBI	OBP	SLG	AVG
2466	9358	1272	2712	339	1493	.342	.471	.290

Dave Parker actually had two careers, both successful ones. The brash, cocky Parker, playing under the watchful eye of Willie Stargell in Pittsburgh, was often called the best player in the game in the late 1970s. After Parker joined Cincinnati in 1984, he became not just a potent offensive force but a team leader as well.

Despite his size and his power numbers at a Cincinnati high school, Parker wasn't taken until the 14th round of the 1970 baseball draft. He had rushed for 1,300 yards as a fullback his junior year of high school, but he tore up his knee in his first game as a senior. College football scholarship offers disappeared, and baseball wasn't too interested either.

But it wasn't just the injury that made scouts wary. Parker's noisy personality was already well known. Pirates scout Howie Haak said, "When the Reds heard we drafted him, they laughed at us."

Parker hit over .300 every full minor league season he played. Twice he led his league in total bases. And he was not just big and strong, he was fast. He could steal bases, knock the ball out of the park, and throw out runners with his powerful arm.

Promoted to the Pirates, his brashness was a perfect fit for the team. In a raucous, rude clubhouse, he learned quickly that he could be louder and cruder than anyone else. Led by Willie Stargell, the Pirates were a hard-hitting, outrageous team. And Dave Parker belonged. He made his first appearance in a Pirates uniform the year after Roberto Clemente died, and before long Pittsburgh sportswriters were trying to prove Parker was a better player than Clemente.

Clemente hadn't driven in more than 100 runs until he was 32 years old and never won a slugging title. Parker batted .308, hit 25 home runs, drove in 101 runs, led the league in slugging percentage, and finished tied for second in triples in 1975, his first year as a regular. Two years later he led the league with 215 hits, 44 doubles, and a .338 batting average. He was also the NL's top outfielder in putouts and assists. Parker had a tremendous arm and won three consecutive Gold Glove Awards.

The 1978 season was Parker's most glorious with the Pirates, although it wasn't without its bumps and bruises. In early July in the ninth inning of a game against the Mets, he tried to score the winning run on a short flyball. He was called out, and in a collision with catcher John Stearns, Parker broke his jaw. But that didn't keep him out of the lineup for long. He returned within two weeks, wearing a football face mask connected to his batting helmet. Playing like a man possessed, he almost single-handedly drove the team from 11½ games back on August 12 to within one-half game on September 5. Although the Pirates ultimately finished second, Parker had written his name in Pittsburgh baseball annals.

Parker's late-season heroics earned him his second consecutive batting title. He also led the league in slugging percentage, the only player to win both since Billy Williams in 1972. He hit 30 home runs and drove in 117. Parker received the NL Most Valuable Player Award; then he became the first player in baseball to sign a contract worth $900,000 a year.

In 1979 Parker's numbers fell off, but he still hit .310 and finished among the top five in the league in runs, doubles, and total bases. He won MVP honors at the All-Star Game, dazzling fans with his bat and arm. The Pirates won the NL East title, swept Cincinnati in the Championship Series, and toppled the Orioles in a sensational seven-game World Series. Parker batted .341 with six RBIs in the postseason.

Parker was at the top of the baseball world. But it all began to fall apart the next year. The old knee injury acted up, and he played the entire season with fluid in his knee. His batting average fell below .300 for the first time in five years, and his production dipped in every category. Then he was slow to come back from off-season knee surgery, and his weight ballooned. In the following years, although he continued to play with his old intensity, his body let him down. He began to experiment with cocaine.

The Pittsburgh fans turned on him. Their relationship with the imposing millionaire had always been tenuous; now it became outright venomous. The brashness and the gold chains had been tolerated when the team won, and Stargell would wink his approval. Suddenly, it was not all right anymore. On the day of the Three Rivers Stadium celebration to honor Stargell's long career and contributions, a disgruntled fan threw a nine-volt battery that barely missed Parker's head. Nobody in Pittsburgh seemed upset when the Pirates let Parker become a free agent after the 1983 season.

Cincinnati welcomed the hometown boy back with a large contract. Parker was back in shape, no longer toying with drugs, and his knee seemed healthy. He was appreciated in Cincinnati, and he performed. In 1984 he drove in 94 runs. Late that year the Reds brought back another hometown hero, Pete Rose, to be their player-manager. Rose and Parker, embattled superstars, became the best of friends.

In 1985 Parker, at age 34, led the NL in doubles, with 42, and RBIs, with 125. He led the league in total bases, batted .312 with 198 hits, and was second in the MVP balloting. He also spent several days testifying in Pittsburgh before the grand jury that was investigating cocaine use by major league players. Commissioner Peter Ueberroth suspended Parker, and several others, for one year in February 1986; his suspension was waived in favor of a $120,000 fine, which was 10 percent of his salary, and charitable work.

The episode didn't affect Parker's stroke. In 1986 he topped all NL hitters in total bases for the second straight season, was second with 116 RBIs, and tied for second in home runs, with 31. Parker's knee began to bother him again in 1987, but despite terrible swelling, he still played 153 games. Rose was feeling the pressure from management for finishing second again, and he tried to shift the blame to his huge superstar. Parker, who had been named team MVP three of his four years in Cincinnati, was dealt to Oakland in the off-season for Jose Rijo and Tim Birtsas.

The A's wanted Parker to be a leader in the clubhouse, and they also wanted his bat in the designated-hitter slot. Despite a thumb injury that sidelined him for seven weeks, he still hit 12 homers and 55 RBIs and the A's went to the World Series. When his thumb healed in 1989 he ripped 22 home runs and had 97 RBIs, more than famous slugging teammates Jose Canseco and Mark McGwire. Parker hit two home runs in the ALCS, and a double and a homer in the earthquake-interrupted World Series as the A's became world champs.

In 1990 Milwaukee signed Parker to a contract. Once again his role was to hit the longball and provide a positive clubhouse influence. He hit .289, with 21 homers and 92 RBIs. The next year he played for California and Toronto before retiring.

Wes Parker

Parker, Maurice Wesley **1B–OF**

1964–72 B:11/13/1939, Evanston, IL Deb:4/19/1964, LA NL BB/TL 6'1", 180

G	AB	R	H	HR	RBI	OBP	SLG	AVG
1288	4157	548	1110	64	470	.353	.375	.267

Wes Parker was a fine-fielding first baseman and often the best hitter on the Los Angeles Dodgers in the late 1960s and early 1970s. Although he probably would have batted no higher than sixth in the order for a club that was more productive offensively, he was well suited to batting second and often filled the number three or four slot for the weak-hitting Dodgers. A patient line drive hitter, he didn't have the power one expected from a first baseman. That didn't matter to the Dodgers, who appreciated his steady play and clutch hitting.

A native of Chicago, Parker attended Claremont Men's College and the University of Southern California. He signed with the Dodgers in 1963 and hit .305 for Santa Barbara of the California League before moving up to Albuquerque of the Texas League, where he hit .350 in only 23 games. After one year in the minors, Parker joined the Dodgers for good in 1964.

After splitting his time between first base and the outfield that season, Parker displaced Ron Fairly at first in 1965. He led the NL in sacrifice hits, with 19, and tied the NL record for highest fielding percentage by a first baseman. Behind Sandy Koufax's 26 wins and Don Drysdale's 23, the Dodgers won the pennant and beat Minnesota in the seven-game World Series. Parker hit .304 in the Series, contributing a home run in Game 4.

In 1965 and 1966 Parker teamed with Maury Wills, Jim Lefebvre, and Junior Gilliam to form the majors' only all-switch-hitting infield. On June 5, 1966, he hit home runs from each side of the plate. The Dodgers won another pennant that season but fell to Baltimore in four straight in the Series. The Orioles' pitching staff dramatically exposed a weakness on the Los Angeles team that haunted the Dodgers for much of the next decade. They simply couldn't hit. Although their pitching kept them competitive, their poor hitting prevented them from winning the pennant.

In 1967 Parker won the first of six consecutive Gold Gloves for his work at first base. At the plate, things turned around for him in 1969. Prior to that year, he had hit between .238 and .253 in each of his full seasons. In 1969 he jumped almost 40 points, hitting .278.

Batting in the heart of the order, Parker enjoyed his best season in 1970. He hit for the cycle on May 7, then achieved another baseball rarity by driving in more than 100 runs while hitting 10 or fewer homers. He hit .319, knocked in 111 runs, and led the NL with 47 doubles.

Parker hit .274 and .279 the next two seasons while maintaining his excellent play at first. But after the 1972 season the Dodgers released shortstop Maury Wills. Parker, a close friend of Wills, underwent a period of self-assessment and decided to retire only a week after his 33rd birthday. He said that he wished for "a more settled life" and longed to pursue other interests. "Major league baseball," he said, "is a game for single men in their twenties....If you're in it too long, you're trapped."

Parker led NL first basemen in fielding percentage six times. Through 1999 he was tied with four others for the highest career fielding percentage, with a mark of .996. He came out of retirement in 1974 to play in Japan, and hit .301

with 14 homers for Nankai. He then became a broadcaster and television actor, and has been a baseball trading card dealer since the 1970s.

Mel Parnell

Parnell, Melvin Lloyd **P**

1947–56 B:6/13/1922, New Orleans, LA Deb:4/20/1947, BOS AL BL/TL 6', 180

W	L	PCT	G	SH	IP	BB	SO	ERA
123	75	.621	289	20	1752^{2}	758	732	3.50

For a period of five years Mel Parnell was one of the dominant pitchers in all of baseball. He was a crafty lefthander best known for his wicked breaking balls.

Parnell first reached the major leagues with the Red Sox in 1947. The next year he moved into the starting rotation and went 15–8. But 1949 was the year he really dominated. That season Parnell went 25–7 with four shutouts, a 2.77 ERA, a league-leading 27 complete games, and an AL-high 295 innings. He was selected to the All-Star Game, but didn't get an opportunity to continue his magic in the postseason as the Red Sox lost a one-game lead to the Yankees over the final weekend of the season.

Although Parnell never quite matched that magnificent season, he continued as one of the better pitchers in the league through the early 1950s, recording two 18-victory seasons before going 21–8 in 1953. The next year he suffered a broken arm, and he was never able to regain his touch. He retired two years later.

Lance Parrish

Parrish, Lance Michael **C–DH**

1977–95 B:6/15/1956, Clairton, PA Deb:9/5/1977, DET AL BR/TR 6'3", 220

G	AB	R	H	HR	RBI	OBP	SLG	AVG
1988	7067	856	1782	324	1070	.315	.440	.252

Through hard work and determination, Detroit's Lance Parrish transformed himself from a poor defensive catcher and good hitter into an all-around star performer. In the process he was named to eight All-Star Games and earned four *Sporting News* AL Silver Slugger Awards and three Gold Glove Awards.

Parrish was the Tigers' first-round draft choice, and the 16th selection overall, in the June 1974 free-agent draft. With Bristol that year he played third and the outfield, batted only .213, and led Appalachian League batters with 92 strikeouts. Converted to catching with Lakeland of the Florida State League, he led the circuit with 31 passed balls. This unfortunate trend continued, as he paced the Southern League in passed balls in 1976 and the American Association in 1977. In both seasons, however, he also led in assists and fielding percentage.

Even when his batting skill helped Parrish make it to the majors, his defensive troubles continued, as he led the American League with 21 passed balls in 1979—his first full season in the majors—and with 17 in 1980. His disagreements with Detroit manager Sparky Anderson added to his troubles. Parrish wanted to bulk up, but Anderson held to more traditional views on the subject of weight training. When Parrish's muscles paid off with homers and RBIs, however, Anderson changed his tune. "He proved his point," Anderson said. "For me to criticize him now would be ignorant."

Parrish hit .276 in 1979 and then was selected to his first All-Star Game the next year, a season in which he batted .286, hit 24 home runs, and drove in 82 runs. He missed part of the season in 1981.

In 1982 the Tigers hired former Detroit catcher Bill Freehan to work with Parrish, and there were almost immediate results. His talents were showcased in the 1982 All-Star Game at Montreal's Olympic Stadium. Entering the game in the fourth inning as a replacement for Chicago's Carlton Fisk, Parrish proceeded to throw out three of the four NL runners who attempted to steal bases: Steve Sax, Al Oliver, and Ozzie Smith. Only Pittsburgh's Tony Pena made it to second base, and the call was so close that American League manager Billy Martin stormed out of the dugout to protest umpire John McSherry's decision. Parrish's hitting was impressive as well, as he hit .284 with 32 homers and 87 RBIs.

Parrish had even a better year in 1983, winning his first Gold Glove and attaining career highs with 80 runs, 42 doubles, and 114 RBIs. Despite Gold Gloves in 1984 and 1985, Parrish faced criticism for lack of leadership. "Everybody puts too much emphasis on leadership," he countered. "Everybody on this club is a professional athlete. Everybody is at times going to be the leader. When I have to say something, I'll say it. A pat on the back. That's as much help as is necessary."

In the mid-1980s former Baltimore luminary Brooks Robinson said, "All-Star catchers who average 99 RBIs and win Gold Gloves are hard to find. The Tigers are fortunate to have Lance. He is the best all-around catcher in the league. He does everything well behind the plate and has earned the confidence of the pitching staff."

Anderson had praise as well. "I think he's the best catcher in baseball," Sparky declared. "He'll have to improve, though, because I want to see him in the Hall of Fame. The fans here are gonna get spoiled. They're seeing a great one. I feel sorry for our next catcher."

Back problems hobbled Parrish in 1986, causing him to miss half the season. After five consecutive All-Star selections, he was granted free agency that November and signed with the Phillies. However, he failed to repeat the offensive performances that he had in Detroit, as his average dipped to .245 and then .215. After the 1988 season, he was traded to the California Angels, where he replaced catcher Bob Boone. Parrish had four seasons with the Angels and then brief stints with Seattle, Cleveland, Pittsburgh, and Toronto.

Parrish finished his career with 1,818 games caught and 324 homers. He retired with the third-highest home run total by a catcher, trailing only Carlton Fisk (376) and Johnny Bench (327). He later coached for the Tigers under Larry Parrish, who, incidentally, is no relation.

Larry Parrish

Parrish, Larry Alton **3B-OF-DH**
1974–88 M(1998–99, 82–104) B:11/10/1953, Winter Haven, FL Deb:9/6/1974, MON NL BR/TR 6'3", 215

G	AB	R	H	HR	RBI	OBP	SLG	AVG
1891	6792	850	1789	256	992	.321	.439	.263

For brief spells, Larry Parrish looked like one of the great pure power hitters the game has seen. From July 4 to July 10, 1982, the Texas Rangers' third baseman had one of the most impressive weeks in baseball history, connecting for three grand slam home runs. Three other times in his career Parrish hit three homers in a game—in 1977, 1978, and 1985.

Parrish signed with Montreal as an undrafted free agent in May 1972. He played in the Expos' system at Jamestown, West Palm Beach, and Quebec City. With West Palm Beach in 1973 he was voted the Florida State League's Most Valuable Player. Promoted to the Expos in 1974, the next year he became the regular third baseman. A competent hitter for five years, in 1979 Parrish suddenly became a star. He raised his career best batting average 30 points by hitting .307 and doubled his best former total of home runs, with 30. He also played in the All-Star Game, and was chosen Montreal's Player of the Year.

By the end of the 1981 season, Parrish was Montreal's career leader in a number of offensive categories. Nevertheless, in March 1982 he was traded with first baseman Dave Hostetler to Texas for outfielder Al Oliver. Parrish turned on the power for the Rangers, hitting at least 22 home runs and driving in 88 runs four times in a five-year span.

In 1987 Parrish made his second All-Star Game while hitting a career-high 32 home runs and driving in 100 runs. By the time he was released in July 1988, he was the Rangers' all-time career home run leader. The Boston Red Sox signed him shortly thereafter, but released him at season's end.

Late in the 1998 season Parrish replaced Buddy Bell as Detroit's manager. He piloted the team in its final year in Tiger Stadium in 1999, but at the end of the season he was abruptly fired and Phil Garner took his place.

Camilo Pascual

Pascual, Camilo Alberto (Lus) **P**
1954–71 B:1/20/1934, Havana, Cuba Deb:4/15/1954, WAS AL BR/TR 5'11", 185

W	L	PCT	G	SH	IP	BB	SO	ERA
174	170	.506	529	36	2930[2]	1069	2167	3.63

Camilo Pascual was famous for a sharp-breaking curveball that many historians and players rank alongside that of his contemporary Sandy Koufax as among the best of all time. Pascual could throw it where he wanted, and he proved it with two 15-strikeout games and a career with more than twice as many strikeouts as walks.

Pasqual spent the first seven years of his career with the old Washington Senators, becoming a starter in his third season in the majors. However, the Senators were a miserable team during that time, but he managed to go 17–10 and was named to the 1959 All-Star team. He repeated as an All-Star four of the next five years.

When the Senators moved to Minneapolis for the 1961 season, everything seemed to change. Pascual was 15–16 his first year there and then put together back-to-back 20-win seasons. He led the American League in strikeouts all three years, and twice led in shutouts and complete games.

Pascual went 9–3 as the Twins captured the pennant in 1965. He took the mound at Dodger Stadium in Game 3 of the World Series with the Twins already leading two games to none, but Claude Osteen blanked Minnesota and Los Angeles went on to win in seven games. Pasqual returned to Washington after the 1966 with the expansion Senators. His arm was hurting, and

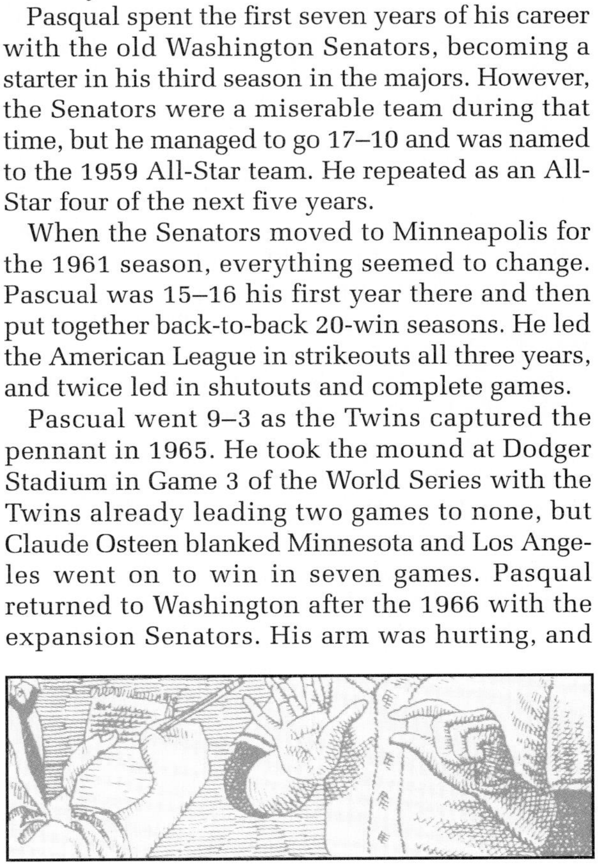

things were no different during his three seasons in the capital than they had been before. He struggled to a 27–27 mark in three years. Two years later he was gone from baseball.

Claude Passeau

Passeau, Claude William **P**
1935–47 B:4/9/1909, Wayensboro, MS Deb:9/29/1935, PIT NL BR/TR 6'3", 198

W	L	PCT	G	SH	IP	BB	SO	ERA
162	150	.519	444	26	2719^{2}	728	1104	3.32

Four-time All-Star Claude Passeau was an all-around athlete. He was an outstanding pitcher who could also hit for power and field flawlessly. He had a .192 career batting average with 15 home runs, and he once handled 273 consecutive chances without an error.

Passeau reached the majors with the Pittsburgh Pirates in 1935, but the next year joined the Philadelphia Phillies, for whom he both started and relieved, leading the National League in innings pitched in 1937. When the Phillies moved to their new home, Shibe Park, in 1938, Passeau became the first Phillies pitcher to win a game there.

Swapped by the last-place Phillies to the Cubs in May 1939 for Kirby Higbe and two others, Passeau led the league in strikeouts that year and became the bulwark of the wartime Cubs staff, pitching more than 220 innings and winning between 14 and 20 games during each of the next six seasons. In 1940 he won a career high 20 games, and the next year he was chosen to the first of five All-Star Games.

Passeau relied on a tailing fastball that resembled the modern slider. But neither that pitch nor any other one seemed to work for him in the 1941 All-Star Game, when he blew a two-run NL lead in the last of the ninth, allowing two singles, a walk, and a three-run homer by Ted Williams to lose the game, 7–5.

Passeau's final starring season was 1945. Playing for the last Cubs team to win an NL pennant in the 20th century, he went 17–9 with a career-best 2.46 ERA and led the league with five shutouts. In the World Series he hurled a masterpiece. In a one-hit shutout of the Tigers he allowed only two baserunners, a third-inning single to Rudy York and a walk to Bob Swift; his sacrifice fly drove in one of his team's three runs.

Freddie Patek

Patek, Frederick Joseph **SS**
1968–81 B:10/9/1944, Seguin, TX Deb:6/3/1968, PIT NL BR/TR 5'5", 148

G	AB	R	H	HR	RBI	OBP	SLG	AVG
1650	5530	736	1340	41	490	.311	.324	.242

At 5 feet 5 inches and less than 150 pounds, Freddie Patek was the smallest man in the majors when he played. He once said, "I'd rather be the smallest player in the majors than the tallest player in the minors." He may have been small, but he was a hard-working, hustling infielder who maximized his natural skills at every turn.

Patek could run. He stole 38 bases his first season in the minors and led the International League the following year with 42. When he reached the majors with the Pittsburgh Pirates in 1968, he kept it up, stealing 18 bases in only 61 games his first year. But his batting was weak enough that the Pirates swapped him to Kansas City for the 1971 season. Patek blossomed at Royals Stadium. He hit a career-high .267 with a league-leading 11 triples. He even hit for the cycle one game, and was second in the American League with 49 stolen bases.

He was never quite that successful again as a hitter, but he continued to make things happen. Four of the next five years he was in the top five in steals in the AL, leading the league with 53 in 1977. The three-time All-Star had 385 career steals.

Defensively Patek was exceptional. He led league shortstops in double plays three years in a row, 1971 through 1973, and in 1972 and 1973 he had the highest fielding rating in the league. By 1975 his defensive skills were slipping, but he was still a valuable member of the Royals' team that reached the postseason three years in a row. In both the 1976 and 1977 Championship Series, Patek was 7-for-18, for a .389 average. He drove in nine runs in the two series, and had a total of five doubles and a triple. Kansas City's frustration of losing to the Yankees in the ninth inning of the last game of the ALCS for two consecutive years was summed up by a famous photograph of Patek alone in the dugout with his head in his hands.

Patek ended his career as a utility player for California, but he did not go quietly. The diminutive shortstop launched three home runs in a 20–2 rout of the Red Sox at Fenway Park on June 20, 1980. He retired the following year.

Max Patkin

Patkin, Maxie

Baseball Clown B:1920 D:10/30/1999, Paoli, PA

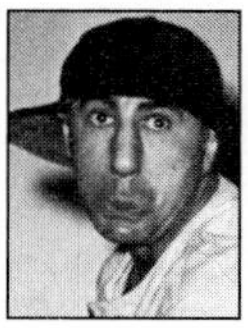

Max Patkin's 79 years were full of pranks and pratfalls and dedicated to getting the next laugh. He was known as "The Clown Prince of Baseball," and his act lasted more than 50 years. His props included a baggy 1930s-style uniform, a question mark sewn on the back of his jersey, a cap tilted sideways, a giraffe-like neck, and a face that could be contorted in a thousand shapes as if made of rubber.

By his own estimate, Patkin made more than 4,000 appearances. He crawled through Yogi Berra's legs, kissed Frank Howard before Hondo homered, and played himself in the movie *Bull Durham*. Once, back in the 1960s, he made a grotesque face at a couple in the front row and got a face full of beer for his trouble. "So I should care," Patkin shot back, "I get $500 for tonight." He would spit in his glove and tell people, "I bought it six years ago, with S & H green stamps."

He could be found all over the minor leagues. No major league team used Patkin regularly after the 1940s, not since Patkin was employed by one of baseball's greatest vaudevillian, Bill Veeck. Patkin described his own act as "corny," but added, "the fans liked it."

Patkin first became a fan of baseball while watching Jimmie Foxx play in Shibe Park in his native Philadelphia. Like many who eventually found work outside the game, he wanted to be a player. His pitching skills took him as far as the White Sox minor league system, but his break did not come as a result of his baseball talent. Pitching for a navy team in Hawaii during World War II, Patkin turned his rubbery neck to watch one of his serves fly out of sight, courtesy of Joe DiMaggio, then playing for the Army Air Force. Unrehearsed, Patkin began to chase DiMaggio around the bases, like a mime following his subject, imitating every pace of the Yankee Clipper's trot. The laughter it inspired had people calling for more. A diamond wannabe's star was on he rise.

Many people caught him mimicking the first baseman's warm-up tosses, or giving signs like a third-base coach to the strains of "Rock Around the Clock." He even mimicked the great baseball art of spitting, spewing water from his mouth after taking a long drink.

He was not the first to take clowning to ball fields—Al Schacht, a former pitcher and coach for the Washington Senators, was also known as "The Clown Prince"—but Patkin was certainly the most memorable. Any time the Phillie Phanatic, San Diego Chicken, or even Mr. Met cavorts on the field, the spirit of Max Patkin is never far away.

Gabe Paul

Paul, Gabriel

Executive B:1/4/1910, Rochester, NY D:4/26/1998, Tampa, FL

As general manager of the Indians and Reds, Gabe Paul was called "tight fisted," and as the Yankees general manager in the 1970s he earned the nickname "Dial-A-Deal." Paul helped make Cincinnati a pennant winner, and was instrumental in the Yankees' return to competitiveness in 1976 and successive World Series victories in 1977 and 1978.

Gabe Paul started out as a batboy in 1920, at the age of 10, for his hometown Rochester Red Wings of the International League. He conspired with manager George Stallings, who had run the "Miracle" Braves of 1914, to give the home team an edge. If the Red Wings led in the late innings, Stalling sent young Paul to a grocery store behind left field where baseballs were stored in an ice box. Deadened by the cold, the baseballs would be slipped into the umpire's supply for the visitor's final at bats.

He was earning $1.50 a week as a part-time sportswriter in 1928, when Warren Giles, then the new president of the Red Wings, hired him to file stories during the club's spring training in Louisiana. When Giles became Reds general manager, he took Paul along as publicity director. Paul became GM after Giles was named National League president.

Paul called on his publicity background to help Reds players land berths on the 1957 All-Star Game at a time when fan balloting determined the starters. He had local papers print the Reds' starting lineup every day, indicating where fans should place an "X," and had similar ballots distributed at Crosley Field. While the Reds finished fourth that year, they had seven players voted to start the All-Star game. Commissioner Ford Frick kept five Reds' starters but removed Gus Bell and Wally Post and replaced them with Willie Mays and Hank Aaron. The vote was taken from the fans the following year.

Paul's reputation as a tight-fisted GM was well earned. When pitcher Art Fowler came into his office asking for an increase from $11,000 to $12,000 in 1954, Paul got Fowler to sign for $9,000. Paul was handicapped by a shoestring budget, yet built Cincinnati into a contender with guile and shrewdness. He left the Reds the year before they won the pennant in 1961, but deserved credit for assembling the team. Paul engineered trades that brought pitcher Joey Jay and second baseman Don Blasingame.

After a brief stint with expansion Houston he went to New York to resurrect the Yankees. In

1972 Paul introduced owner Michael Burke to George Steinbrenner III after Burke had the choice of buying the team himself or finding a suitable partner. Early in 1973 it was announced that Steinbrenner and Burke had purchased the team for $10 million. At a price $3 million less than CBS had paid in 1965, the purchase was a bargain—but not for Burke. Following a brief power struggle, Burke, Lee MacPhail, and Ralph Houk were cast adrift and Steinbrenner took control; Paul emerged as general manager.

Paul's trades made the Yankees a contender for more than half a decade. Before the 1974 season, he acquired Lou Piniella for aging reliever Lindy McDaniel. Three weeks into the 1974 season, the Yankees sent Fritz Peterson, Tom Buskey, Steve Kline, and Fred Beene to the Indians for Chris Chambliss, Dick Tidrow, and Cecil Upshaw. On December 11, 1975, Paul traded Doc Medich to Pittsburgh for Willie Randolph, Dock Ellis, and Ken Brett. That same day he traded Bobby Bonds to California for Mickey Rivers and Ed Figueroa. Paul's best decision, however, might have been a trade he didn't make. In 1977 Steinbrenner was anxious to deal with the White Sox for Bucky Dent. Chicago wanted pitcher Ron Guidry, but Paul refused. Instead he included Oscar Gamble, Bob Polinsky, La Marr Hoyt, and $200,000. Guidry would enjoy one of the best seasons in recent memory, going 25–3 with a 1.74 ERA in 1978. In all, Paul's wheeling and dealing led to five division titles, four pennants, and two World Series victories between 1976 and 1981.

He resigned from the Yankees in 1978 and returned to the Indians, retiring after the 1984 season. He died at the age of 88 in 1998.

Joan Payson

Payson, Joan Whitney

Owner (1962–75) B:2/5/1903, New York, NY
D:10/4/1975, New York, NY

Joan Whitney Payson, the first owner of the New York Mets, truly loved the game of baseball—and had ample funds available to fulfill that love. All her money, however, couldn't make the original Mets any better.

One of her grandfathers, John Hay, had served as private secretary to Abraham Lincoln and as Secretary of State under Presidents McKinley and Roosevelt. Her other grandfather, William Collins Whitney, served as Secretary of the Navy under President Grover Cleveland. Her brother, John Hay "Jock" Whitney, owned the *New York Herald-Tribune,* served as Ambassador to the Court of St. James, and was national finance chairman of the Republican Party.

Joan Payson was active in both the world of art (her collection included Vincent Van Gogh's "Irises" that sold for $53.9 million in 1987) and the world of racing (her Greentree Stables produced the Horse of the Year in both 1949 and 1953 and she loved to give her mounts baseball names such as Hall of Fame, Shut Out, and Third League). In 1957 *Fortune* magazine estimated her personal worth between $100 million and $200 million.

Payson first attended baseball games as a child at the Polo Grounds. As an adult, she owned 10 percent of the New York Giants. She was the only stockholder to vote against the move to San Francisco.

When the National League voted to return to New York via expansion, Payson picked up a 30 percent share of the team from Mrs. Dorothy J. Killiam (a former Dodgers fan), who withdrew her support; as a result, Payson became the majority stockholder. Eventually she owned roughly 80 percent of the franchise.

Payson picked Mets as the team's name after dismissing other candidates such as Burros, Rebels, Jets, Continentals, Avengers, Skyliners, Skyscrapers, Bees, and Meadowlarks (it was close, though, between Mets and Meadowlarks). She helped land Casey Stengel as the team's first manager. She also lobbied to secure such veterans as Gil Hodges for the team. After that, however, she was content to sit in the stands and root for her team. Her only control of the team on the field was in the superstitions department; she crossed her fingers at key moments or turned her back on certain batters. Investment broker M. Donald Grant controlled everything else.

When the Mets first started play in 1962, Payson was off on a cruise to the Greek islands. She instructed her underlings to wire her each Mets score. Each day an account arrived of yet another loss. Finally, she wired home:

PLEASE TELL US ONLY WHEN METS WIN

Later she ruefully recalled, "That was about the last word I heard from America."

Some speculated that she invested in the Mets as a tax shelter. Instead, the more the team lost, the more money Payson made. Then in 1969 she got something she probably never dared dream of: a world championship.

After her death, her husband Charles Shipman Payson inherited the team. He had little interest in baseball and delegated even more control to Grant. Later her daughter, Lorinda de Roulet, and granddaughters Bebe and Whitney de Roulet briefly assumed management of the franchise. The team was sold to a group headed by Doubleday & Co. on February 21, 1980.

Dickey Pearce

Pearce, Richard J. **SS**

1871–77 M(1872, 1875, 49–35) U(1878, 1882) B:2/29/1836, Brooklyn, NY D:10/12/1908, Wareham, MA Deb:5/18/1871, NY NA BR/TR 5'3½", 161

G	AB	R	H	HR	RBI	OBP	SLG	AVG
33	131	13	26	0	14	.222	.206	.198

In baseball's early days the shortstop basically stood stock-still in the same place and waited for balls to be hit to him. The position was the "right field" of its day, not valued highly, and the players sent there were the ones deemed most likely to do damage defensively. Dickey Pearce changed all that. Although built like a tree stump at 5 feet 3 inches and 161 pounds, he saw no advantage to being rooted to one spot. The first shortstop to roam around, chasing flyballs into the short outfield, he positioned himself according to hitters' tendencies, playing closer to the bag when a double play was in order, and created the style of shortstop play fans are accustomed to today.

Although the statistics of his playing career are so meager that they can hardly be used to judge Pearce's abilities, he was considered the finest at his position in the decade of the 1870s, with his only real competition coming from Hall of Famer George Wright. Pearce and pitcher Jim Creighton may have been the first two players to be full professionals. And the Brooklyn Atlantics, the team Pearce played for throughout the 1860s, was one of the most potent aggregates of its era.

Pearce was one of the first true stars of the game. He broke into what was then big-time "base ball" in 1856. Newspaper reports of the era rate him highly for his playing skills, his intelligence, and his use of psychology. Journalists Henry Chadwick, Sam Crane, William Rankin, and A.H. Spink are just a few of the noted baseball commentators who praised him.

By 1858 Pearce was already an established star, playing shortstop in the Fashion Race Course All-Star Games between New York and Brooklyn, an early foreshadowing of the Dodgers–Giants rivalry. The three-game series, held at a site less than 300 yards from the present Shea Stadium, were the first at which admission was charged.

It has been claimed that Pearce "invented" the bunt in 1866. Whether he did or not, he was clearly one of the first masters of what was called "the tricky hit." However, bunting did not become a true part of baseball strategy until Tim Murnane introduced the bunting bat, which had one flat side, years later.

Despite his lack of speed, Pearce was a leadoff hitter for most of his career—the all-time king of the "fair-foul hit," a batted ball that landed fair and then skipped foul. According to the rules of the time, such a ball was still in play. At least one biographer speculates that the rule change in 1876, which eradicated the "fair-foul hit," was targeted at Pearce and Ross Barnes. But Pearce was 40 years old when the rule was passed, his career all but over.

When the Atlantics disbanded in 1870, Pearce joined the New York Mutuals of the new National Association for two years. As their player-manager in 1872, he led the Mutuals to a 34–20 record, good enough for third place in the league of about a dozen teams. Returning to a revivified Brooklyn Atlantics team in the Association for 1873 and 1874, he hit .300 and .298.

For unexplained reasons, he then abandoned his hometown team and joined St. Louis. He played for the Brown Stockings in 1875, the National Association's last year, and in 1876, the first year of the new National League. He also managed St. Louis to a creditable 39–29 record in 1875. He retired from the major leagues with a .198 average in just 33 National League games. In five National Association seasons, he batted .257; Pearce also twice led the NA in fielding percentage.

Pearce finished his career playing for various St. Louis teams, and at age 48 spent his final season as a player-manager of Quincy in the Northwestern League in 1884. He later umpired in the Northwestern League and also served as a National League umpire in 1878 and 1882. Pearce's connection with baseball concluded in 1890, when he served as a groundskeeper for the New York entry in the Players' League, which played in the park later christened the Polo Grounds.

In evaluating Pearce's career, historian Frank Phelps said, "The meager statistics of his time obscure Pearce's greatness. Besides his importance as a pioneer in developing better techniques, strategies, and mechanics of play, he was generally regarded for 20 years as the best all-round offensive and defensive shortstop in baseball, except during George Wright's very top seasons."

Monte Pearson

Pearson, Montgomery Marcellus

1932–41 B:9/2/1909, Oakland, CA D:1/271978, Fresno, CA Deb:4/22/1932, CLE AL BR/TR 6', 175

W	L	PCT	G	SH	IP	BB	SO	ERA
100	61	.621	224	5	1429^{2}	740	703	4.00

Monte Pearson frustrated managers by only pitching if he was in top physical condition. He missed numerous starts due to minor arm and body ailments. Every October, though, he was in perfect shape. He won a World Series game for the New York Yankees each year from 1936 to 1939.

Pearson began his career with the Cleveland

Indians in 1932. The following season he led the American League with a 2.33 ERA. In 1934 he racked up 18 wins. Pearson was then traded to the New York Yankees following a disappointing 1935 season.

He won a career-high 19 games in his first season with the Yankees, leading the AL with a .731 winning percentage and stingy .233 batting average against him. Pearson played on four consecutive world championship teams with the Yankees. He completed three of his four career Series starts and compiled a 1.01 ERA. Pearson's best World Series performance was his last: a two-hit shutout against the Cincinnati Reds in 1939.

On August 27, 1937, he pitched a no-hitter against the Indians in the second game of a doubleheader. Pearson was named to American League All-Star teams in 1936 and 1940. Not surprisingly, his manager kept the chronic complainer on the bench in each game.

Roger Peckinpaugh

Peckinpaugh, Roger Thorpe **SS**

1910, 1912–27 M(1914, 1928–33, 1941, 500–491)
B:2/5/1891, Wooster, OH D:11/17/1977, Cleveland, OH
Deb:9/15/1910, CLE AL BR/TR 5'10½", 165

G	AB	R	H	HR	RBI	OBP	SLG	AVG
2012	7233	1006	1876	48	739	.336	.335	.259

In 1925, his last year as a regular major league shortstop, Washington's Roger Peckinpaugh had a marvelous season, hitting .294, fielding his position exquisitely, and earning American League Most Valuable Player honors. Then, in the World Series, the steady veteran played one of the worst seven-game stretches imaginable. He hit adequately but made eight errors, including several at critical moments as the Senators lost in seven games. The joke went around that he was World Series MVP, too—for the Pirates!

Peckinpaugh has first reached the majors at age 19 with Cleveland. After a couple of years with the Indians, he became the New York Yankees' shortstop for nine seasons. At age 23 he even spent the last 20 games of the 1914 season as New York's manager, finishing with a 10–10 mark.

His best year with the Yankees was perhaps 1921, the team's first pennant season. He hit .288, scored 128 runs, and had 71 RBIs. Nevertheless, before the next season he was traded to Washington, were he combined with second baseman Bucky Harris to form an ace double-play combination. Peckinpaugh was one of the heroes of Washington's 1924 World Series victory over the Giants, leading the Senators with a .417 batting average.

Peckinpaugh was of the Honus Wagner school of shortstopping: broad-shouldered, big-chested, and bowlegged. Seldom slick and never graceful, he nonetheless covered the ground and got the job done. He retired in 1927 after a year with the Chicago White Sox. He later managed the Indians and served in their front office.

Barney Pelty

Pelty, Barney **P**

1903–12 B:9/10/1880, Farmington, MO D:5/24/1939, Farmington, MO Deb:8/20/1903, STL AL BR/TR
5'9", 175

W	L	PCT	G	SH	IP	BB	SO	ERA
92	117	.440	266	22	1908	532	693	2.63

For several years Barney Pelty was one of the better pitchers in baseball, but his lack of support while playing for the traditionally weak St. Louis Browns led to an ugly won-lost record. Despite a career 2.63 ERA, only twice in 10 years with the Browns did Pelty have a winning record.

Pelty joined the Browns in 1903 and became a regular starter the next year, when he went 15–18. In 1906 he had his best year, finishing second in the American League with a 1.59 ERA—the 17th-lowest ERA in the league's history. That season Pelty went 16–11 while holding batters to an AL-low .206 average.

The next year, pitching for Jimmy McAleer's sixth-place club, Pelty dropped to a 12–21 record. That tied Philadelphia Athletics hurler Al Orth for the American League lead in losses. He also hit a Browns club-record 17 batters. Pelty pitched less in the following years. Sold to Washington in June 1912, he finished his career with that club.

Alejandro Pena

Pena, Alejandro (Vasquez) **P**

1981–92, 1994–96 B:6/25/1959, Cambiaso, Dominican Republic Deb: 9/14/1981, LA NL BR/TR 6'1", 205

W	L	PCT	G	SV	IP	BB	SO	ERA
56	52	.519	503	74	1057^{2}	331	839	3.11

Alejandro Pena's performance during the 1991 stretch drive was the major factor in Atlanta's one-game margin of victory in the National League West. Acquired from the New York Mets in an August waiver deal, Pena filled a need created by closer Juan Berenguer's arm injury. Pena went 11-for-11 in save opportunities to go with a 2–0 record and 0.51 ERA. He also got the final three outs in the first combined no-hitter in National League history on September 11.

He continued to shine in the Championship Series, saving three of the Braves' four wins against Pittsburgh. The season ended in Minnesota with Pena on the mound in the 10th inning of Game 7 of the World Series; the 1–0 loss was his first in a Braves uniform. The hard-throwing Pena never again matched his 1991 form, but he reached double digits in saves five times.

As a starter, Pena led the NL with four shutouts and a 2.48 ERA in 1984. A shoulder injury the following year, however, prompted a move to the bullpen. Pena pitched for five first-place teams, including world champions in Los Angeles (1981, 1988) and Atlanta (1995). Kirk Gibson's famous home run in Game 1 of the 1988 World Series made Pena the winning pitcher. He pitched five innings of shutout relief in that Series as the Dodgers won in five games.

Tony Pena

Pena, Antonio Francisco (Padilla) **C**

1980–97 B:6/4/1957, Monte Cristi, Dominican Republic Deb:9/1/1980, PIT NL BR/TR 6', 181

G	AB	R	H	HR	RBI	OBP	SLG	AVG
1988	6489	667	1687	107	708	.311	.364	.260

A superb defensive catcher who had few peers at calling a game, Tony Pena was one of the premiere players at his position in the 1980s. Pena's signature move was stretching out one leg and setting up a target as low as possible; it helped him win four Gold Glove awards over his 18-year major league career.

A product of the Pittsburgh Pirates organization, Pena made the first of his five All-Star appearances in 1982. That campaign inaugurated a five-year stretch during which he played at least 138 games, hit at least 10 home runs, and batted .286 or better four times.

Pena moved on to St. Louis in a trade that included Andy Van Slyke in April of 1987. Hampered by injury in his first year in St. Louis, he batted just .214 in 116 games, but atoned with a spectacular postseason. He batted .381 in the seven-game victory over San Francisco in the Championship Series, then hit .409 with four RBIs and a stolen base in a seven-game World Series loss to the Minnesota Twins. Healthy again in 1988, he played in more than 140 games in both of his remaining two seasons with the Cards.

He signed with Boston as a free agent in 1990 and caught at least 126 games in each of his four seasons at Fenway, winning a Gold Glove in 1991. Pena's offensive numbers were in decline, however, and his days as a regular catcher were over. Pena was signed as a backup in Cleveland,

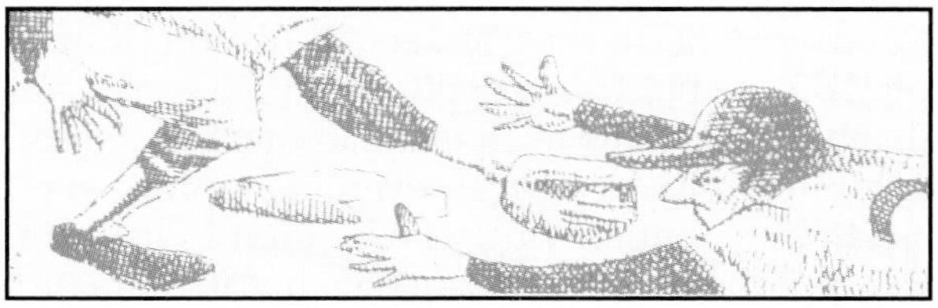

but filled in for injured Sandy Alomar, Jr. for much of 1995. In the Indians' Division Series opener against Boston, he stole the spotlight with a game-winning home run in the 13th inning. He finished his career by playing in the postseason in each of his final three seasons. He played his final major league game for Houston in the 1997 Division Series.

Terry Pendleton

Pendleton, Terry Lee **3B-DH**

1984–98 B:7/16/1960, Los Angeles, CA Deb:7/18/1984, STL NL BB/TR 5'9", 180

G	AB	R	H	HR	RBI	OBP	SLG	AVG
1893	7032	851	1897	140	946	.318	.391	.270

When the St. Louis Cardinals gave up on Terry Pendleton after seven seasons, the stocky third baseman signed as a free agent with Atlanta in 1991 and became the National League's Most Valuable Player. Then he almost did it again the next season.

While helping the Cardinals win NL pennants in 1985 and 1987, Pendleton averaged .259 with six home runs and 63 RBIs during his tenure in St. Louis. His inconsistency, however, was maddening to the Cards; he batted .324 as a rookie and .240 the next year. He hit just .230 in his last season in St. Louis. Predictably, he drew little interest on the free agent market in 1990. Last-place Atlanta signed him to a four-year contract that turned out to be the move that turned around a decade of losing.

In 1991 Pendleton led the league in batting average and hits, tied for first in total bases, and was third in slugging percentage. He became the first player to raise his average as many as 80 points and improve his home run total by 15 or more in one year. He also brought his experience with winning ballclubs to a perennial loser. The Braves rallied in the second half to take the division title, and then the pennant. In the World Series Pendleton batted .367 with two home runs in a losing effort. In the off-season he received the rare combination of MVP and Comeback Player of the Year award , as well as his third Gold Glove.

In 1992 Pendleton again led the league in hits. He had a career-high 105 RBIs and led the NL with 182 runs produced. He finished second to Pittsburgh's Barry Bonds in the MVP voting; the Braves, however, beat the Pirates in the NLCS in seven games for the second straight year. For the first time, Pendleton played in a World Series that didn't go seven games, but for the fourth time, his team lost.

Following two mediocre seasons in Atlanta, Pendleton again revived his career—this time as a Florida Marlin. He shook off nagging shoulder, back, and knee problems to play in all but 10 of Florida's games in 1995. He batted .290, including a .313 average over his last 102 games.

He was traded back to the Braves in August 1996. He played in his fifth World Series, and lost once more. Pendleton was a reserve in Cincinnati and Kansas City the next two years. He retired after the 1998 season.

Herb Pennock

Pennock, Herbert Jefferis **P**

1912–17, 1919–34 B:2/10/1894, Kennett Square, PA D:1/30/1948, New York, NY Deb:5/14/1912, PHI AL BB/TL 6', 160

W	L	PCT	G	SH	IP	BB	SO	ERA
241	162	.598	617	35	3571^{2}	916	1227	3.60

New York Yankees manager Miller Huggins called Herb Pennock the greatest lefthander in the history of baseball. "If you were to cut that bird's head open," Huggins said, "the weakness of every batter in the league would fall out." He won five World Series games without a loss and retired with 241 career wins.

Pennock signed with the Philadelphia Athletics out of Wenonnah Military Academy instead of going on to the University of Pennsylvania. He went directly to the major league club in 1912, but did not see extended action until two years later. In 1914 Pennock went 11–4 but failed to impress manager Connie Mack because he had no fastball and had trouble finding the plate.

Instead of inspiring fear in hitters, Pennock became the butt of their jokes. One Tigers outfielder said, "The only comforting thing about hitting against him is that you don't have to be afraid of getting hurt. Even if he hits you on the head with his fastball he won't knock your hat off." In fact he became more known for his off-the-field activities, being dubbed "the Knight of Kennett Square" because he raised thoroughbreds and hosted fox hunts in his home town of Kennett Square, Pennsylvania.

In 1915 Mack traded Pennock to the Red Sox, where he languished in the bullpen for two and a half years. "When I was struggling I pitched in games, in batting practice, before games, in morning games, and during the off-season. When I couldn't get anyone to catch me I'd throw against a stone wall or against a barn door....It wasn't always fun, but I kept on plugging away because it meant so much to me."

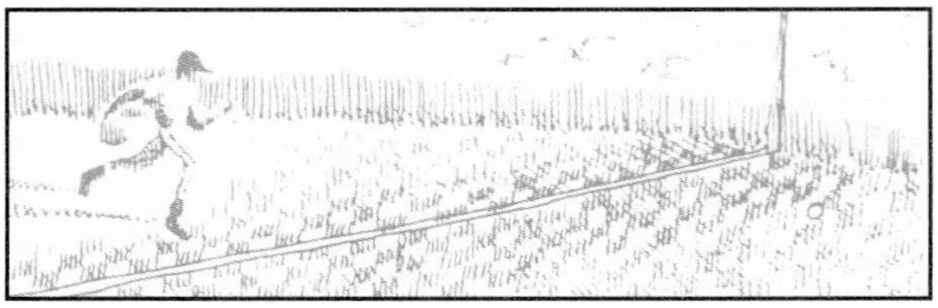

In 1919, after serving a year in the military, Pennock broke into the starting rotation with the Red Sox and found his control. His greatest day in a Red Sox uniform came in 1921 when he beat Bob Shawkey and the Yankees, 1–0, on the strength of his own inside-the-park home run.

After four solid years at Boston, he was traded to the Yankees. In New York with the bats of "Murderers Row" behind him, Pennock's record soared. He went 19–6 in his first year in New York, leading the league in winning percentage. Two of the next three years he won more than 20 games, and then he hit 19 again in 1927. Meanwhile, he became nearly unhittable in October. In Game 3 of the 1927 World Series Pennock retired the first 22 Pittsburgh batters before Pie Traynor singled to left. His lifetime ERA in World Series play was an enviable 1.95.

In 1928 Pennock developed a sore arm, which he attempted to cure through "bee sting therapy." He exposed his arm to a horde of bees, and it swelled painfully, showing no improvement. He later told reporters, "All I can say is that nature intended self-respecting bees to spend their time getting honey out of flowers and not go drilling into a pitcher's arm."

As a less frequent starter for the next five years, he still averaged almost 10 wins a season. When the Yankees released Pennock he returned to the Red Sox in 1934 and pitched in relief during his 22nd and final season.

He was a Red Sox coach from 1936 to 1940 and then supervisor of the team's farm system. In 1944 he became general manager for Philadelphia and helped put together the youthful pennant-winning Phillies team known as "the Whiz Kids." He died in 1948, the year he was inducted into the Hall of Fame.

Joe Pepitone

Pepitone, Joseph Anthony **1B–OF**

1962–73 B:10/9/1940, Brooklyn, NY Deb:4/10/1962, NY AL BL/TL 6'2", 200

G	AB	R	H	HR	RBI	OBP	SLG	AVG
1397	5097	606	1315	219	721	.303	.432	.258

Joe Pepitone was one of four promising rookies brought up by the Yankees in 1962 to help form the core of the next great Yankees dynasty. Right away he and rookie classmate Jim Bouton caught on to the Yankees' tradition of hard play off the field, and Pepitone added a zest and flamboyance to the team that had previously been exhibited only by proven team champions such as Mickey Mantle, Whitey Ford, and Billy Martin. By the time he left the Yankees in 1970, he had become one of the most visible symbols of a failing organization that featured aging and injury-plagued stars and unmanageable new players.

After Pepitone had played a year with limited action, the Yankees made room for him at first base in 1963 by trading popular power-hitter Moose Skowron. An instant crowd favorite because of his local roots and Italian descent, Pepitone responded to full-time play by hitting .271 with 27 home runs as the Yankees went to the 1963 World Series. In the Series, however, Pepitone hit a dismal .154 and made an error in Game 4 on a throw from Clete Boyer that allowed the winning Dodgers run to score. The Yankees were swept.

Pepitone hit 28 homers, drove in a career-high 100 RBIs, provided consistent fielding, and was selected to his second consecutive All-Star Game in 1964 in helping the Yankees squeak past the White Sox and back to the World Series. He again hit only .154 in the Series, but he hit a crucial grand slam in Game 6. The Cardinals, however, won in seven games.

By 1965 Pepitone's fielding had become reliable enough to earn him his first Gold Glove, but he was hitting only .247. In 1966 he won another Gold Glove and hit 31 homers, but as his attention shifted more and more to his celebrity status, his on-field performance leveled off. In his last six years with the Yankees, he did not hit above .255. He also failed to show up on game day a few times, allegedly because he was being pursued by various bookies. Before the 1970 season, the Yankees relocated him to Houston.

Midway through that season, the Astros shipped Pepitone to the Cubs, who were looking for the right veteran players to round out a promising squad. Pepitone hit .268 and had 26 homers for the full season, but the Cubs finished five games behind the Pirates. In 1971 Pepitone played nearly full-time in Chicago, and responded with the best average of his career at the plate, hitting .307. However, his power production dropped significantly. By 1972 the Cubs had demoted him to part-time status, and in mid-1973, they traded him to Atlanta for the last days of his major league career.

Pepitone signed a $140,000 contract with the Yakult Atoms in Japan. His flamboyant style soon clashed with Japanese life. He arrived with shoulder-length hair, complained about the food and high prices, missed games because of "headaches" from bumping his head on low hotel room doors, and hit .163 in 14 games while disco dancing into the wee hours. He finally flew home, leaving a large phone bill unpaid and the Japanese with a new noun, "pepitone," meaning a goof-off.

Always concerned with his appearance, Pepitone is credited by Jim Bouton in *Ball Four* as being the first player to style his hair with a blow-dryer in a major league clubhouse. Pepitone's own book, *Joe, You Coulda Made Us Proud*, tells the story of his struggle to play baseball while avoiding the perils of growing up in Brooklyn.

Eddie Perez

Perez, Eduardo **C**

1995–* B:5/4/1968, Cuidad Ojeda, Venezuela
Deb:9/10/1995, ATL NL BR/TR 6'1", 175

G	AB	R	H	HR	RBI	OBP	SLG	AVG
313	818	88	212	24	101	.311	.403	.259

Eddie Perez's main role on the Atlanta Braves teams of the late 1990s was to serve as personal catcher for staff ace Greg Maddux. In 1996 Maddux had a 1.89 ERA in the 16 games caught by Perez. Over the next two seasons, he was behind the plate for 63 of the pitcher's 67 starting assignments.

Perez was signed as a free agent by Braves scout Pedro Gonzalez in 1986. He was selected to the International League All-Star team in 1995, and got his first major league hit that season, a two-run homer off Cincinnati's Mike Jackson. Perez established himself in 1998, when he made the most of limited playing time by hitting .357 with runners in scoring position and .336 overall. He was the hero of Atlanta's Game 3 clincher against in the Cubs in the National League Division Series, hitting a grand slam off Rod Beck en route to a 6–2 victory. He also went 3-for-4 in the Championship Series, which Atlanta lost to San Diego.

During the 1999 season, Perez became Atlanta's regular catcher after Javy Lopez was lost for the season due to injury. He also became known as a hot head after he was suspended for four games and fined $1,000 for fighting. The incident occurred when Philadelphia's Paul Byrd, a former teammate, hit Perez with a pitch in the third inning, the second time in less than a week that Byrd had hit Perez. The next inning, as Byrd came to bat and attempted to apologize, Perez threw a punch, setting off a brawl. Byrd remained in the game and won, while Perez sat in the clubhouse.

Perez was an unlikely hero in the 1999 NLCS against the Mets. In Game 2 he hit a tie-breaking two-run homer to clinch a 4–3 victory. For the series, he hit .500 (10 for 20), with two homers and five RBIs. His clutch hitting throughout the series earned him NLCS Most Valuable Player honors.

Tony Perez

Perez, Atanasio (Rigal) **1B–3B**
1964–86 M(1993, 20–24) B:5/14/1942, Ciego De Avila, Cuba Deb:7/26/1964, CIN NL BR/TR 6'2", 205

G	AB	R	H	HR	RBI	OBP	SLG	AVG
2777	9778	1272	2732	379	1652	.344	.463	.279

Tony Perez went about his business quietly and efficiently. Perez and Johnny Bench were the leading run producers of Cincinnati's "Big Red Machine" that won back-to-back world championships in 1975 and 1976. For 10 consecutive years, Perez knocked in at least 90 RBIs; seven of those years he was selected to the All-Star Game.

Cuban-born Perez built up his muscles lifting sacks of sugar in a mill, a job he hated. In March 1960 he attended a tryout camp and was signed by Reds scout Tony Pacheco. The only bonus he received, Perez once said, was "$2.50 for my visa." That was enough. He took the first plane possible to the United States and started his professional baseball career with Geneva, in the New York–Penn League, as a second baseman.

The first few minor league seasons were difficult for Perez, who was only 17 when he came to the United States. "I couldn't speak English that well, and I had trouble understanding the manager sometimes," he said. "I went to the movies a lot, and that helped me learn the language." Perez had no trouble making his presence felt on the field, however. In 1961 he led the league with a .348 average, 160 hits, and 132 RBIs. He hit .292 with Rocky Mount in 1962 and .302 with Macon in 1963, won the Pacific Coast League's Most Valuable Player Award with San Diego in 1964, and came up to Cincinnati to stay in 1965.

After two years of splitting the job at first base, in 1967 Perez became the Reds' regular third baseman. He batted .290, with 26 home runs and 102 RBIs, and was named Most Valuable Player of the All-Star Game after he hit a 15th-inning home run to win the game for the National League. He also impressed defensively. "He is as good a fielding third baseman as there is in the league," said Maury Wills, who played shortstop for the Dodgers in the 1960s. "Tony has the most accurate throwing arm I have ever seen."

Perez had perhaps his two finest seasons back to back, in 1969 and 1970. In the former year, he hit .294 with 37 homers, 122 RBIs, and 103 runs. The next year he topped that, with a .317 batting average, 40 homers, 129 RBIs, and 107 runs. In 1970 he combined with Johnny Bench and Lee May to hit 119 home runs, the third-most by a trio of National League teammates in history.

His production dipped a bit after the 1970 season, but he was still one of the best in the league, hitting 20 or more homers each of the next five years, accounting for more than 100 RBIs three consecutive seasons, and three times during a six-year stretch robbing pitchers of no-hitters.

Known for needling his teammates, Perez was one of the inspirational leaders of the Big Red Machine, which included Bench, Pete Rose, Dave Concepcion, Joe Morgan, and Ken Griffey, Sr. "He could hand it out rougher than anyone, yet somehow he could do it without offending," said former Reds manager Sparky Anderson. "That team had a lot of leaders...But only when Perez left did I realize he was *the* leader. He did the most to keep all those leaders in harmony. Doggie could handle it all."

Perez was known as "Big Doggie" for his ability to drive in runs. "If the game lasts long enough, Tony will find a way to win it," said his former minor league skipper, Dave Bristol. "Tony has the perfect temperament for baseball. He's a big, easy-going guy, but he'll fight...he's a battler."

When it came to postseason play, Perez was either very good or very bad. He hit .333 in the 1970 National League Championship Series, but had only one hit in 18 at bats in the 1970 World Series. He batted just .200 in the 1972 NLCS and then hit .435 in the World Series. After a .091 performance in the 1973 NLCS, Perez rebounded to hit .417 in the 1975 NLCS. In the 1975 World Series against the Red Sox, Perez started 0-for-15, but in Game 5 he hit two home runs and drove in four runs to spur the Reds to victory. In Game 7, with the Reds trailing, 3–0, Perez homered over the "Green Monster" off Bill Lee. Cincinnati went on to win the game and the Series.

In December 1976 Perez was traded to Montreal, where the next year he hit .283 with 91 RBIs. The Reds were never the same again. "Losing Tony took so much chemistry away," said Reds president Bob Howsam. "He had more of an effect on our team—on and off the field—than I ever realized."

Granted free agency in November 1979, Perez signed with the Red Sox and had his last big year in 1980, hitting 25 homers and collecting 105 RBIs. On May 31 of that year Perez, Carlton Fisk, and Butch Hobson hit back-to-back-to-back homers in the sixth inning of a game against Milwaukee. In doing so, Perez entered the baseball annals as one of a select group of players to accomplish the feat in both leagues. On June 17, 1979, Perez, Gary Carter, and Ellis Valentine of the

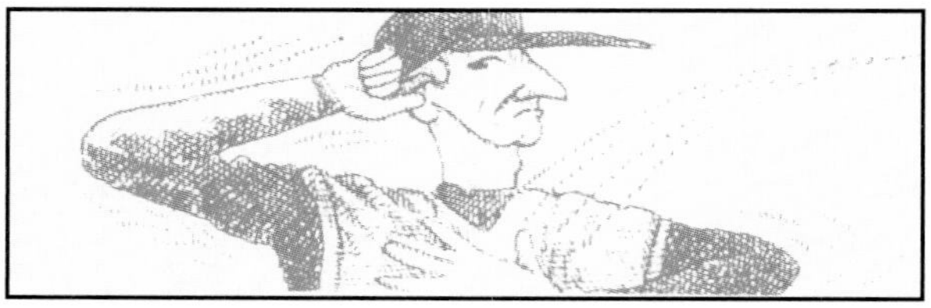

Expos had hit consecutive home runs in the fourth inning of a game.

His playing time and production fell off dramatically after 1980. Released in November 1982, he signed with the Phillies in January 1983. He was a contributor on the "Wheeze Kids," Philadelphia's aged club that captured the pennant. He returned to the Reds in 1984. He hit his last home run on October 4, 1986, the day before he retired. That homer tied him with Orlando Cepeda for the most career home runs, with 379, by a Latin player.

After he retired, Perez was a Reds coach until 1993, when embattled owner Marge Schott named him manager. However, he was fired by general manager Jim Bowden just 44 games into the season. Perez, who became a U.S. citizen in 1971, is the father of first baseman Eduardo Perez. His son Victor was a minor league outfielder.

Tony Perez was long considered a Hall of Fame caliber player, but getting into Cooperstown was no easy feat. He finished in the top four in vote-getters each year until he finally got the call for the Hall of Fame in January 2000.

Lou Perini

Perini, Louis R.

Owner (1945–62) B:1904 D:4/16/1972, West Palm Beach, FL

Braves owner Lou Perini was raised in the construction business and knew what it took to build things. He built a successful franchise twice, in two different cities. And when he moved the club from Boston to Milwaukee in 1953 he set off shock waves that changed baseball forever.

Perini, Guido Rugo, and Joe Maney were "the Three Steam Shovels," construction magnates who bought interests in the Braves in 1942. But the club was in constant financial trouble, and they tired of regularly having to cough up more cash to keep the team operating. So, with their wallets swollen from wartime construction projects, they bought out the other owners in 1944.

The Steam Shovels hired smart baseball men—John Quinn as general manager and Billy Southworth as field manager—and bought themselves a pennant in 1948. Although the Braves lost the World Series to Cleveland, they were highly profitable, drawing nearly 1.5 million fans. Perini, Rugo, and Maney sponsored innovations such as the "Brave Sketchbook," a collectible item similar to the yearbooks teams sell today. They hired Billy Sullivan, who later owned the National Football League's New England Patriots, to handle promotions and marketing, a position few teams filled. They produced and distributed a highlight film to help sell tickets, and they introduced numerous game-day promotions to fight for the hearts and minds of Boston fans. He also helped the start the Jimmy Fund, a children's cancer charity, which was later adopted by the Red Sox and remains one of the city's most popular charities.

But the Red Sox were putting on significant pressure for Boston's attendance dollar. The Braves' caliber of play and attendance began to fall, and Perini and two brothers bought out the other partners. In 1952 only 280,000 fans showed up to see the club in Boston.

Then St. Louis Browns owner Bill Veeck gave Perini an idea. Veeck was fighting the same battle in St. Louis that Perini was fighting in Boston—local competition from a dominant team. Veeck had previously owned the Milwaukee Brewers of the American Association, loved the town, and wanted to move the Browns there. But Perini, then owner of the minor league Brewers, wouldn't give his approval. Instead, deciding to forego another poor season in Boston, he moved the Braves to Wisconsin.

The shift was approved less than a month before the 1953 season was to begin. Fans in Boston complained bitterly, calling Perini a "carpetbagger." *The Sporting News*, however, praised Perini for his "courage and foresightedness." By moving to Milwaukee, Perini had executed the first switch of a major league team to another city since 1903, when the American League transferred the Baltimore franchise to New York, where the team became the Highlanders and, later, the Yankees.

Perini's move opened the floodgates. After no franchise moves in 50 years, within two years two other American League teams that had to compete with National League teams in the same city shifted locales: the Browns moved to Baltimore, where they became the Orioles, and the Philadelphia Athletics shifted to Kansas City. Three years after that Walter O'Malley and Horace Stoneham took the Dodgers and Giants out of New York, leaving Chicago as the only city represented by both leagues.

The Milwaukee Braves could not have been more successful. In 1953 they finished second and drew 1,826,397 fans. The next year 20-year-old Henry Aaron joined third baseman Eddie Mathews, shortstop Johnny Logan, pitcher Warren Spahn, catcher Del Crandall, and outfielder Bill Bruton to make the Braves a powerhouse.

They finished in third place in 1954, and 2,131,388 fans showed up to see them. In 1957 they beat the Yankees in the World Series. When Mickey Mantle referred to Milwaukee as a "bush league town," he was greeted at the station by thousands of fans waving "Welcome to Bushville" signs.

In 1958 the Yankees beat the Braves in a seven-game World Series, and in 1959 the Braves suffered another blow, losing a best-of-three playoff to the Dodgers. After finishing second in 1960, they stumbled to fourth and fifth the next two years. In November 1962, Perini sold all but 10 percent of the team's stock to a Chicago-based group—the LaSalle Corporation—for $6.2 million. He sold out completely before the Braves moved to Atlanta, ending his career in baseball.

Cy Perkins

Perkins, Ralph Foster **C**

1915, 1917–31, 1934 M(1937, 6–9) B:2/27/1896, Gloucester, MA D:10/2/1963, Philadelphia, PA Deb:9/25/1915, PHI AL BR/TR 5'10½", 158

G	AB	R	H	HR	RBI	OBP	SLG	AVG
1171	3604	329	933	30	409	.319	.352	.259

Catcher Cy Perkins wasn't a star hitter, but his receiving skills kept him a major league regular until finally moved aside by Hall of Famer Mickey Cochrane—to whom he imparted his wealth of experience. Perkins led the American League in assists three times, in games caught twice, and in putouts once.

Unexpectedly, Perkins' nickname Cy did not come from any resemblance to baseball immortal Cy Young. Rather it was a reference to a character by the name "Cy Perkins" found in a then-popular play, *The Old Homestead*.

Perkins paced Carolina League catchers in fielding percentage in both 1914 and 1915. After brief appearances in 1915 and 1917, he joined the Philadelphia Athletics full-time in 1918 and became the regular catcher the following year. For the next six years Perkins started for the Athletics, having his most productive year offensively in 1921, when he hit .288 with 12 home runs and 73 RBIs. On opening Day 1925 rookie Cochrane pinch-hit for him. "I knew right then I had lost my job as regular," said Perkins. He had, and he spent the next six years as Cochrane's backup, before being sold to the Yankees in December 1930. He played briefly for the Yankees in 1931 and then became a coach for them the next two years. He moved to Detroit, where he spent six years as a coach, having a cameo role as a player in one game in 1934 and temporarily serving as manager in 1937.

Perkins enlisted in the United States Navy in November 1942 and served until 1944. He later managed Hazleton and Burlington in the minors, and coached for the Philadelphia Phillies. With the Phillies he was especially noteworthy in the development of pitcher Curt Simmons.

Ron Perranoski

Perranoski, Ronald Peter **P**

1961–73 B:4/1/1936, Paterson, NJ Deb:4/14/1961, LA NL BL/TL 6', 192

W	L	PCT	G	SV	IP	BB	SO	ERA
79	74	.516	737	179	1174^{2}	468	687	2.79

Known for his poise on the mound, lefty Ron Perranoski was one of the first true relief specialists in the major leagues. He came up to the Dodgers in 1961 and pitched in 53 games, 52 of them in relief. That one start was the only one of his career, and he went on in the next 13 years to become one of the great relievers of his era.

Perranoski was a painfully thin child, at one point just 75 pounds and 5 feet 5 inches tall. Even after that he was described as "a real scarecrow." When he started playing baseball he was a first baseman—until he lost his glove. "My dad bought me a fielder's glove so I had to get another position," he recalled. "I tried pitching."

Given an experimental start with his high school's junior varsity, he threw a no-hitter. Later he pitched his team to the New Jersey state championship, recording 56 straight scoreless innings. Offered $4,000 by White Sox scout Dutch Deutsch, instead he went to Michigan State on a scholarship.

In 1958 Perranoski signed with the Cubs for $21,000 and pitched in the Chicago system for Fort Worth, Burlington, and San Antonio. In April 1960, just back from six months in the army, he was sent to the Dodgers along with $25,000 and two other players for aging Don Zimmer.

Perranoski was disappointed. He thought he had a better chance of making the majors with the Cubs. He struggled initially in Triple A Montreal, but things got better after a tip from a teammate solved the problem he was having with his curveball. Then he was sent to St. Paul for the American Association playoffs. When he got to Minnesota, he found out he was being made a reliever.

In those days the bullpen was not a status address. Pitchers almost always went there when they weren't good enough to start. But Perranoski did as he was told, even dropping plans to continue his education at Michigan State so he could perfect his new trade in the instructional league.

He was a quick study. Dodgers manager Walter Alston said, "I know he's got the right temperament for a relief pitcher. It's like ice water." The Mets' Tim Harkness agreed, remembering one time his club faced Perranoski. "He turned around and stuck his tongue out at me. What a cool SOB he is. He knew he was going to throw that big, damn curve in there."

Perranoski joined the Dodgers for the beginning of the 1961 season. In each of the next two years he led the National League in games pitched. His best season was 1963, when he went 16–3, leading the league in won-lost percentage, with a 1.67 ERA and 21 saves for the world champions. In 1965 Perranoski had a sore arm and got off to a bad start. He was rumored to be on the trading block, then was hampered by a pulled hamstring. But he finally got healthy and helped the Dodgers to another pennant, posting an 0.38 ERA in his last 47⅔ innings.

On September 12, 1966, Perranoski tied a league record for consecutive relief strikeouts when he fanned six straight Cardinals. After the following season, however, he was traded to Minnesota with Johnny Roseboro and Bob Miller for Mudcat Grant and Zoilo Versalles.

With the Twins Perranoski led the American League with 31 saves in 1969 and with 34 in 1970—then an AL record. That was his last big season. The relief specialist was still a relatively new species, and Perranoski, 34, had averaged 107 innings a year in his more than 10 years with the majors. His arm was cooked.

He pitched parts of two more seasons before retiring. Perranoski then served as the Dodgers' minor league pitching coach until becoming their major league pitching coach in 1981. He remained with the Dodgers through 1994. In 1997 he moved up the coast as the Giants' pitching coach.

Gaylord Perry

Perry, Gaylord Jackson **P**

1962–83 B:9/15/1938, Williamston, NC Deb:4/14/1962, SF NL BR/TR 6'4", 215

W	L	PCT	G	SH	IP	BB	SO	ERA
314	265	.542	777	53	5350¹	1379	3534	3.11

Rule 8.02 of the Official Baseball Rules specifically prohibits a pitcher from either defacing the baseball or applying any foreign substance to it. Section E states that "the umpire shall be the sole judge on whether any portion of this rule has been violated." Gaylord Perry openly flaunted this rule for most of his career and was seldom caught. Although the spitball was banned in 1920 and last thrown legally in 1934 by pitcher Burleigh Grimes, who was allowed to use the pitch until his retirement, Perry may have been baseball's most successful spitballer.

Perry grew up on a small tenant farm in eastern North Carolina. His father was a successful semi-pro pitcher and taught both Gaylord and his older brother, Jim, the ins and outs of pitching. Both boys were excellent pitchers and basketball players at Williamston High School, and both turned down scholarship offers to play college basketball in favor of professional baseball. Gaylord signed with the Giants for a then team-record $73,500 in 1958.

Although a friend of his father's had shown Perry how to throw a spitball while the youth was still in high school, the illegal pitch was not yet part of his repertoire; he depended on a good fastball, curve, and changeup. He moved quickly through the minors, and, after leading the Pacific Coast League with 16 wins for Tacoma in 1961, he was called up to the Giants. He bounced back and forth between San Francisco and Tacoma for several seasons, pitching well in Triple A but getting roughed up at the major league level.

That all changed in 1964. Disappointed with his performance and impatient with the development of his slider, Perry noticed veteran pitcher Bob Shaw throwing a curious pitch that came in thigh-high, then broke sharply down to the hitter's ankles. Perry asked Shaw to teach him the pitch. It was the spitball, and Perry's future life of crime was assured. Although Perry took several seasons to learn to control the pitch effectively, it made an immediate difference, and he pitched his way into the Giants' starting rotation in 1964.

The rules at the time made it easy to get away with using the spitball. Pitchers were allowed to put their fingers to their mouth on the mound. They were supposed to wipe them dry, but a phantom wipe was easy to learn. Some have since claimed that at least 25 percent of major league pitchers were using the pitch in the mid-1960s. Unlike a fastball, which is released with backspin, the spitball tumbles forward, making a sudden, sharp drop as it approaches the plate. Saliva on the first two fingers of the pitching hand allows the pitcher to squeeze the ball at the point of release and impart a forward spin.

Perry put it all together in 1966. With both his spitball and slider under control, he became an overnight sensation. He won 21 games and was the winning pitcher in the All-Star Game. On July 22 he struck out 15 Phillies. He finished the season with 201 strikeouts and walked only 40.

He was even better in 1967, lowering his ERA from 2.99 to 2.61. During one stretch he hurled 40 consecutive scoreless innings. But he lost 10 one-run decisions and finished the season with a 15–17 record. The spitball suddenly became a hot topic. As long as no one pitcher was too effective with it, few people complained; Perry's success was out of the ordinary. Before the 1968 season, Rule 8.02 was amended to forbid the pitcher to put his hand to his mouth.

Perry adapted. All winter he practiced throwing a similar pitch using grease instead of saliva. He stood before a mirror practicing the artful transfer of grease from his belt or another part of his uniform to his hands. In his first few spring outings Perry was shelled, but he mastered the new pitch just as the season began and resumed his winning ways. Everyone knew he was throwing the pitch, but no one could quite figure out how he loaded the ball. Perry became a master at decoying the batter and using the spitball as a psychological weapon. His pitching hand went to his cap and his neck, and then he'd adjust his belt, wipe his hand on his shirt, return to his cap, and appear to be delivering a speech in sign language before finally releasing the ball. By that time the batter was either overanxious or convinced Perry was throwing a spitter.

When asked about his success, Perry just smiled and gave the credit to his "super-slider." Nobody believed him, but nobody could catch him in the act either. Perry pitched a no-hitter against Bob Gibson and St. Louis on September 17, 1968.

In 1970 Perry won 23 games, led the National League in shutouts and innings pitched, and finished second in the Cy Young voting to Gibson. His brother, Jim, won 24 games for the Twins and won the American League's Cy Young Award. They were the first brothers to win 20 games apiece in the same season.

San Francisco traded Gaylord Perry to Cleveland in 1972, and he responded with the best season of his career, winning the Cy Young Award with a sparkling 1.92 ERA and leading the AL with 24 wins. The trade set a pattern for the remainder of his career. After several successful seasons, he'd be traded to a team that believed his presence would either help them to a pennant or put fans in the park. The club usually failed to match Perry's performance, and the pattern would be repeated.

The Perry brothers were united in Cleveland in 1974. Gaylord won 21 games, including 15 straight—one shy of the AL record—and Jim added 17 victories. But on May 20, 1975, Jim was traded to Oakland for Blue Moon Odom. Less than a month later Gaylord was dealt to Texas for Jim Bibby, Jackie Brown, Rick Waits, and $100,000.

After winning 15 games for the Rangers in both 1976 and 1977, Perry was traded to San Diego in January 1978. He won 21 games that season and his second Cy Young Award. The 40-year-old hurler was the first pitcher to win the Cy Young Award in both leagues. Selected to his fifth and final All-Star Game in 1979, at the end of that season Perry signed with Texas again. But the Rangers traded him at midseason to the Yankees. He then played with Atlanta in 1981, Seattle in 1982, and Kansas City in 1983. Perry won his 300th game with Seattle in 1982 and retired after the 1983 season with 314 wins.

One of the few negatives of Perry's career is that he never appeared in a World Series in 22 seasons. Only Phil Niekro played longer, 24 seasons, without appearing in a World Series. The 529 victories by the Perry brothers are second only to the Niekros' 539. The Perrys combined for more strikeouts (5,110) and shutouts (85) than any other brothers tandem.

Perry published an entertaining biography, *Me and the Spitter*, in 1974. After he retired, he returned to North Carolina and became a farmer. He was inducted into the Baseball Hall of Fame in 1991.

Jim Perry

Perry, James Evan **P**

1959–75 B:10/30/1935, Williamston, NC Deb:4/23/1959, CLE AL BB/TR 6'4", 200

W	L	PCT	G	SH	IP	BB	SO	ERA
215	174	.553	630	32	3285^{2}	998	1576	3.45

Although Jim Perry is best remembered as Hall of Fame pitcher Gaylord Perry's older brother, Jim paved the way for one of the game's most successful brother acts. He was the first in the family to make it to the major leagues and was an All-Star while Gaylord was still working on a new pitch, which turned out to be the spitball.

Jim Perry entered the American League in 1959 with the Cleveland Indians. He won 12 games with a 2.65 ERA, struck out 79 batters in 153 innings, and finished second place in the AL Rookie of the Year balloting. The following year he led the league with 18 wins, a .643 winning percentage, and four shutouts. In his third year, Perry was named to the All-Star Game.

Early in the 1963 season the Indians traded Perry to Minnesota. Two years later he went 12–7 as the Twins reached the World Series only to lose to Sandy Koufax and the Dodgers. For the next three years Perry split his time between starting and the bullpen.

In 1969 under manager Billy Martin, Perry became a regular starter, and he responded with a 20–6 record as the young Minnesota team went to the very first American League Championship Series. Perry pitched eight innings in the opener, but the Orioles won the game in 12 innings and swept the series.

The next year, as brother Gaylord recorded 23 wins in San Francisco and placed second in the Cy Young balloting, Jim Perry led the American League with 24 wins, while throwing four shutouts.

He also was voted his league's Cy Young Award. Also that season the Perrys became the first sibling pitchers to face each other in the All-Star Game.

Jim Perry had four more seasons winning at least 13 games. In 1974 he and Gaylord pitched together on the Indians, and Jim recorded 17 wins, with a 2.96 ERA. He retired following the 1975 season, after being traded to Oakland with Dick Bosman for Blue Moon Odom and cash.

Together, the Perrys struck out more batters—5,110—than any other pair of pitching brothers in the major leagues, tossed more shut outs, and won more games than any other siblings except Phil and Joe Niekro.

Johnny Pesky

Pesky, John Michael **SS-3B-2B**
1942, 1946–54 M(1963–64, 1980, 147–179)
B:9/27/1919, Portland, OR Deb:4/14/1942, BOS AL
BL/TR 5'9", 168

G	AB	R	H	HR	RBI	OBP	SLG	AVG
1270	4745	867	1455	17	404	.394	.386	.307

Although he has gone down in history as a World Series goat, Johnny Pesky has always insisted that he didn't hesitate in the famous play that decided the 1946 Series. With the Red Sox and Cardinals tied in the seventh game, 3–3, Enos Slaughter of St. Louis started the bottom of the eighth inning with a single. He was still on first with two out when Harry Walker lined a hit into left-center over shortstop Pesky's head. Outfielder Leon Culberson retrieved the ball and threw to Pesky, who glanced at Slaughter before throwing home—the famed hesitation.

"I knew Slaughter was going home," Pesky said more than 40 years later. Slaughter's dash beat the relay, which was slightly up the third-base line, to give the Cardinals a 4–3 lead. The Red Sox got their first two runners on base in the top of the ninth but failed to push a run across, so Pesky's hesitation has always been an issue.

Pesky joined the Red Sox in 1942, taking over at shortstop for player-manager Joe Cronin. He batted .331 as a rookie, and his 205 hits led the league. He was the runner-up to outfielder Ted Williams in the batting race, the fifth time American League teammates had finished one-two.

After spending the next three seasons in the military service, Pesky took up right where he left off. He led the AL with 208 hits in 1946 and with 207 in 1947, tying the major league record for consecutive seasons leading the league in hits. In Boston's pennant-winning 1946 season he finished third in the league with a .335 average. He also became the first American Leaguer to score six runs in a game. Also that season he collected 11 consecutive hits and he was named to his only All-Star team. Pesky returned for the 1947 season 30 pounds heavier after his off-season marriage. It didn't matter to his hitting, as he was again third in the batting race and had a 26-game hitting streak.

Shifted to third base in 1948 to make room for Vern Stephens, Pesky led major league third basemen in double plays, but he failed to hit .300 for the only time in his seven years as a regular. In 1949 he was back up to a .306 average, had a career-high 69 RBIs, drew 100 walks, and fanned only 19 times in 604 at bats. He moved back to shortstop in 1951, his last year before injuries ended his regular status.

Pesky was traded to the Detroit Tigers in 1952. On August 15 that year, playing shortstop behind pitcher Virgil Trucks at Yankee Stadium, Pesky couldn't get Phil Rizzuto's third-inning grounder out of his glove. The official scorer first called it a hit and then telephoned the Tiger dugout. When Pesky admitted he should have made the play, the call was changed to an error. Trucks held the Yankees hitless the rest of the way and was credited with his second no-hitter of the season.

Pesky finished his playing career in the major leagues in 1954. He managed in the Detroit system before rejoining the Red Sox as a minor league manager of their top farm club in 1961 and 1962. He managed Boston in 1963 and 1964.

After leaving the Red Sox, he coached for the Pittsburgh Pirates' organization, and then he returned to the Sox as a broadcaster in 1969. He stayed with Boston after that, coaching for 10 years, selling TV ads, working in the front office, instructing in the minors, and serving as manager after Don Zimmer's dismissal. In 1990 he took over the Pawtucket Red Sox at age 70.

Gary Peters

Peters, Gary Charles **P**
1959–72 B:4/21/1937, Grove City, PA Deb:9/10/1959, CHI AL BL/TL 6'2", 200

W	L	PCT	G	SH	IP	BB	SO	ERA
124	103	.546	359	23	2081	706	1420	3.25

Gary Peters won 19 games for the Chicago White Sox and led the American League with a 2.33 ERA as a rookie in 1963. When he led the league with 20 victories the following season, he seemed on his way to the Hall of Fame. He wasn't. Peters hurt his arm in 1965 and was never quite the same.

In 1956 the White Sox signed Peters out of high school in Grove City, Pennsylvania, and turned the first baseman into a pitcher. In his first minor league season, with Holdrege of the Nebraska State League, the lefthander went 10–5 and led the league in both games and innings pitched. Peters moved slowly and steadily through the Sox minor league system, winning in double figures at nearly every stop but earning a reputation as an oddball; obsessed with aerodynamics, he whittled boomerangs in his spare time.

Each year from 1959 through 1962 the White Sox called Peters up to Chicago late in the year to pitch a game or two, and each spring Peters found himself back in the minor leagues. On July 24, 1959, while pitching for Indianapolis of the American Association, he hurled a no-hitter against Minneapolis. But even that didn't get him an extended trip to the majors. Finally, in 1963, the reluctant White Sox put him in the starting rotation. It was make-or-break time for Peters.

He made it. Somehow Peters found it easier to set up major league hitters than those in the minor leagues. His good control helped keep runners off base, and Comiskey Park turned home runs into long outs. At one point he reeled off 11 consecutive wins, setting a team record. He was named AL Rookie of the Year, beating out teammate Pete Ward and Minnesota outfielder Jimmie Hall.

In 1964 Peters won 20 games, finished with a 2.50 ERA, and was selected to play in the All-Star Game. After pitching 273 innings he developed a sore arm. Trying to pitch through his arm problems in 1965, he struggled to only 10 wins.

Peters seemed to get a second wind in 1966. He won 12 games and again led the AL in ERA, at 1.98. The next year he was back up to 16 victories with an excellent 2.28 ERA and he was selected to his second All-Star Game. But his delicate arm couldn't take the strain of pitching 200-plus innings, and in the tight American League pennant race of 1967 the White Sox called on him again and again. He pitched 260 innings—and paid the price the following season.

In 1968, "the Year of the Pitcher," Peters' arm gave out and he slumped badly, winning only four games. Surprisingly, his bat kept him in the rotation, as the White Sox were easily the worst hitters in baseball. In the first two months of the season, none of their starters hit better than .200. On May 28 Peters—a career .222 hitter—batted sixth.

After one more disappointing season, the White Sox dealt Peters along with catcher–first baseman Don Pavletich to the Red Sox for infielder Syd O'Brien and a second player. Peters spent three seasons with Boston, going 16–11 in his first year but finishing his career in the bullpen. He retired in 1972.

Fritz Peterson

Peterson, Fritz Fred **P**

1966–76 B:2/8/42, Chicago, IL Deb:04/15/1966, NY AL
BB/TL 6', 200

W	L	PCT	G	SH	IP	BB	SO	ERA
133	131	.504	355	20	2218^{1}	426	1015	3.30

Although he was in a starting rotation for the New York Yankees or Cleveland Indians for 10 years, Fritz Peterson received more attention for happenings off the field. In 1973 Peterson and fellow Yankees' pitcher Mike Kekich shocked the baseball world when they admitted that in the off-season they had swapped dogs, children, and wives. "It wasn't a sex thing. It was not a cheap swap," contended Peterson.

Peterson had played semipro hockey before reaching the major leagues in baseball. In 1966 he joined the Yankees, and over the next four years was a solid, if uninspiring, pitcher. Then in 1970 he suddenly became successful, going 20–11 with a 2.90 ERA and being selected for the All-Star Game. Peterson won his 20th game of the last day of the season, with the victory saved by Lindy McDaniel. Peterson was so nervous about getting the win, he actually hid under manager Ralph Houk's desk until it was all over. Later he admitted: "I sure wanted that twentieth. Did you ever see a list of nineteen-game winners?"

Peterson won 17 games in 1972, but then it all unravelled in 1973, when his record dropped to 8–15. Peterson and his wife had been married since 1964. In 1972 Peterson and Kekich began discussing wife-swapping and soon followed up on the idea. When their "life-swap" became public, a furor erupted.

Peterson married the former Susan Kekich in 1974. He was traded to Cleveland that same year. (Mike Kekich had been traded to Cleveland a year earlier.) In 1975 Peterson went 14–8, but the next year his ERA soared to 5.55 and he was out of baseball by the end of the season. Peterson later worked in real estate and sold disability insurance to athletes.

Rico Petrocelli

Petrocelli, Americo Peter **SS-3B**
1963, 1965–76 B:6/27/1943, Brooklyn, NY
Deb:9/21/1963, BOS AL BR/TR 6', 185

G	AB	R	H	HR	RBI	OBP	SLG	AVG
1553	5390	653	1352	210	773	.336	.420	.251

Rico Petrocelli is best remembered as one of the few shortstops to hit with consistent power in the 1960s, but it helped that he played for the Boston Red Sox. The inviting "Green Monster" in Fenway Park's left field turned many of his otherwise routine flyballs into home runs. Petrocelli hit nearly two-thirds of his 210 career home runs at Fenway, and his batting average was more than 40 points higher at home than on the road.

The Red Sox signed Petrocelli in 1961 for a $40,000 bonus. In his first pro season at Winston-Salem of the Carolina League, he hit 17 home runs and knocked in 80 RBIs while leading league shortstops with 48 errors. He played in the minors for two more seasons, improving somewhat in the field and hitting for power, but often striking out and hitting for a low average. Nevertheless, he won Boston's starting shortstop job in 1965.

Along with the likes of slugger Tony Conigliaro, first baseman Tony Horton, and pitcher Jerry Stephenson, Petrocelli represented the first wave of a Red Sox youth movement that eventually resulted in the team's surprise pennant in 1967. In 1965 Petrocelli put up minimal numbers, batting .232 with 13 home runs and 33 RBIs.

With the arrival of manager Dick Williams in 1967, Petrocelli found a leader with whom he could communicate, and his performance improved almost immediately. He played a key role in the team's drive to the pennant, hitting 17 home runs, upping his average to .259, and being selected to play in the All-Star Game. In the field he was a steady, if not spectacular.

In 1969 everything came up roses for Petrocelli. He batted .297, a full 30 points higher than the second-highest average of his career. He also hit 40 home runs—a team record for a shortstop—drove in 97, and set career-highs for hits, runs, doubles, and walks.

His newfound power continued in the following seasons, as he hit 29 home runs in 1970 and 28 in 1971. But the Red Sox grew disenchanted with Petrocelli's fielding and in 1971 acquired shortstop Luis Aparicio. Petrocelli was moved to third, where his lack of range was less obvious, and he spent five seasons there as a regular. However, his offensive production dropped throughout the 1970s, and in 1976 he lost his starting spot and appeared in only 85 games.

Petrocelli's last hurrah came in the 1975 playoffs and World Series. He hit a key home run at Fenway in Game 2 of the Championship Series. He batted .308 in the Sox's seven-game loss to Cincinnati in the Series. He retired after the 1976 season.

Petrocelli remained in the Boston area and spent several years working for the Jimmy Fund, a children's cancer charity started by Boston Braves owner Lou Perini and adopted by the Red Sox when the Braves moved to Milwaukee. He then worked for the Red Sox organization as a hitting instructor and became manager of Triple A Pawtucket in 1992 before resigning to spend more time with his family.

Fred Pfeffer

Pfeffer, Nathaniel Frederick **2B-SS**
1882–97 M(1892, 33–42) B:3/17/1860, Louisville, KY
D:4/10/1932, Chicago, IL Deb:5/1/1882,TRO NL BR/TR
5'10½", 184

G	AB	R	H	HR	RBI	OBP	SLG	AVG
1670	6555	1094	1671	94	1019	.312	.369	.255

Although he featured two bursts of power-hitting, second baseman Fred Pfeffer, a key-element in Cap Anson's "Stonewall Infield," was best known as one of the premier fielders of his day. From 1884 to 1891 Pfeffer led his league in putouts; four times he paced it in assists and seven times in double plays.

Pfeffer joined Anson's White Stockings in 1883. The next year, having hit only one home run in each of his first two major league seasons, he hit 25 homers, second in the league only to teammate Ned Williamson. Those figures, however, were greatly inflated by the cozy right field corner of Chicago's Lakefront Park, which historians estimate at 230 to 270 feet from home plate. Prior to 1884 any ball hit over the right field wall was a double. In 1884 it counted as four bases.

Three years later, Pfeffer hit 16 homers for the only other season in which he reached double figures. He played for the White Stockings until he joined the Players' League in 1890. After that league folded, Pfeffer then came back for one year with the White Stockings, before playing four years in Louisville, and then finishing his career back in Chicago

After leaving the majors, Pfeffer tried his hand at a number of things: semipro ball, coaching at the University of Wisconsin, managing in the

Three-I League, saloon-keeping, and serving as press attendant at a Chicago racetrack.

Jeff Pfeffer

Pfeffer, Edward Joseph **P**

1911, 1913–24 B:3/4/1888, Seymour, IL D:8/15/1972, Chicago, IL Deb:04/16/1911, STL AL BR/TR 6'3", 210

W	L	PCT	G	SH	IP	BB	SO	ERA
158	112	.585	347	28	2407¹	592	836	2.77

Fastballer Jeff Pfeffer recorded two 20-win seasons and helped Brooklyn to win two of its early pennants. However, he was known just as much at the time as an intimidating thrower who regularly knocked down any batter who dared get too close to the plate.

Pfeffer's professional career started in 1909 in the Minnesota–Wisconsin League, but he did not reach the majors to stay until he made a brief appearance with St. Louis late in 1911. He joined Brooklyn in 1913 and became a star for the club the next year. In 1914, he went 23–12 with a 1.97 ERA. The next year he won 19 more games. He had his best season in 1916, when he helped propel Brooklyn to the World Series with a 25–11 record on a 1.92 ERA.

He spent most of the 1918 season in the Naval Reserve. Two years later he went 16–9 and Brooklyn was back in the World Series. In June 1921 Pfeffer was traded to the St. Louis Cardinals, and had two successful seasons. He went 9–3 to finish the 1921 season, and followed that up with a 19–12 record the next year. But in May 1924 he was waived to Pittsburgh. Pfeffer finished his career in the minors with San Francisco and Toledo. He umpired in the American Association from 1931 to 1933.

Pfeffer came to be called Jeff after older brother "Big Jeff" Pfeffer, who pitched for Boston and Chicago from 1905 to 1911. Big Jeff's name wasn't Jeff either—it was Francis Xavier—but he resembled heavyweight champion James J. Jeffries.

Dave Philley

Philley, David Earl **OF–1B**

1941, 1946–62 B:5/16/1920, Paris, TX Deb:9/6/1941, CHI AL BB/TR 6', 188

G	AB	R	H	HR	RBI	OBP	SLG	AVG
1904	6296	789	1700	84	729	.335	.377	.270

Dave Philley was a good everyday player, but he was more successful off the bench. Through 1999 Philley still owned a major league record with nine consecutive pinch hits and the American League record of 24 pinch hits in a season.

Philley became a switch hitter at age 10 after breaking an arm. While the broken arm was healing he had to hit from the opposite side of the plate and found he was good at it. Originally a catcher, Philley began his career with the Marshall club in 1940. He played for Monroe and Shreveport, fielded seven games for the White Sox in 1941, and served for half a season in St. Paul before joining the army in 1942.

He returned in 1946 and played for Milwaukee before being promoted to the White Sox as an outfielder. In four full seasons in Chicago, Philley established himself as a solid hitter with little power and a fielder with poor range but as having an exceptionally good throwing arm. He was traded to Philadelphia in April 1951, where, two years later, he had perhaps his best season, batting .303 with career highs in hits, runs, and doubles. Surprisingly, he was traded to Cleveland after that season. Philley explained, "At the end of the season [Athletics manager] Connie Mack told me he did not have the money to pay me what I deserved and allowed me to negotiate with Hank Greenberg, who was GM of the Indians."

In July 1955 Cleveland waived Philley to the Orioles, and in three of the next five years he played for more than one team during the season. Philley set his major league record for consecutive pinch hits at the end of the 1958 season. He added one more on opening day, 1959. He set the AL pinch-hit record in 1961 while playing for the Orioles.

Philley was a .299 career pinch hitter. Only a career .270 hitter, he explained his pinch-hitting success: "When I went up to pinch-hit I felt the pitcher was in a jam, not me. I made it a point to study pitchers, know what they threw to me, and what they threw to players who hit like I did. I was ready for them."

In 1962 Philley finished his career with Boston at age 42 and became a scout for the team. He later left baseball and became a cattle rancher in Texas.

Deacon Phillippe

Phillippe, Charles Louis **P**

1899–1911 B:5/23/1872, Rural Retreat, VA D:3/30/1952, Avalon, PA Deb:4/21/1899, LOU NL BR/TR 6'½", 180

W	L	PCT	G	SH	IP	BB	SO	ERA
189	109	.634	372	27	2607	363	929	2.59

In the rough-and-tumble world of baseball in the early years of the 20th century, any player who didn't drink, smoke, chew, or curse like a sailor was liable to be tagged with a nickname reflecting as much. Deacon Phillippe lived a clean life, and also his long face, sad eyes, and quiet demeanor reinforced this nickname.

He threw baseballs with the same discipline and control he exercised in his daily life. Phillippe was one of the greatest control artists ever: in 2,607 innings pitched he walked a scant 363 batters, and his career average of 1.25 walks per game was the best of any pitcher in the 20th century.

Phillippe began his pitching career with semi-pro clubs on the South Dakota plains. After he won 21 games for Minneapolis of the Western League in 1898 he was drafted by the Louisville Colonels of the National League, for whom he won 21 games in 1899, his rookie year.

Along with Washington, Cleveland, and Baltimore, the Colonels were dropped from the league for 1900, but team owner Barney Dreyfuss was allowed to merge his club with the Pittsburgh Pirates. By bringing in such stars as Honus Wagner, Fred Clarke, and Phillippe, Dreyfuss laid the groundwork for a team that would win three consecutive pennants from 1901 to 1903.

Phillippe won at least 20 games in each of his first five NL seasons. In his best year, 1903, the Pirates had lost two outstanding pitchers, Jack Chesbro and Jesse Tannehill, who had both jumped to the rival American League, but Phillippe helped fill the gap with his 25–9 record.

The two leagues made a tentative pact in 1903, and Dreyfuss challenged the Boston Pilgrims, winners of the AL pennant, to a best-of-nine World Series against his NL champion Pirates. Unfortunately, by the time the Series began, injuries and illness had decimated his pitching staff. Twenty-game winner Sam Leever had a sore arm, and 16-game winner Ed Doheny was suffering a nervous breakdown.

At first it seemed Phillippe might be able to do the job on his own. He won the opening game, 7–3, defeating Cy Young on six hits. After only one day's rest he pitched a four-hitter in 4–2 victory in Game 3. Then travel and a rainout allowed Phillippe two days' rest before he came back in Game 4 to scatter nine hits and win, 5–4.

But Pittsburgh could not get a victory from any of their other pitchers. After six games the Series was tied. Dreyfuss pushed Game 7 back a day, claiming that the weather was too cold, so that Phillippe could gain an extra day's rest. After three full days off, the still-weary Phillippe pitched his fourth complete game of the Series but lost, 7–3.

The Series moved back to Boston for the eighth game, with the Pilgrims needing only one victory to triumph. The game was rained out, giving Phillippe one more precious day of rest before he took the mound again. He pitched well in his fifth complete game of the Series—a record that will probably never be broken—but Boston touched him for three runs while Bill Dinneen shut out the Pirates for the second time.

A sore arm, perhaps the result of overwork in the World Series, limited Phillippe to a 10–10 mark in 1904, but he rebounded the following year for his sixth 20-win season. After another bout of arm trouble he won eight games for the pennant-winning Bucs of 1909 and went 14–2 in 1910. He left baseball in 1911 and then worked in a Pittsburgh steel mill and later became a court bailiff. In 1969 he was voted Pittsburgh's all-time righthanded pitcher.

Tony Phillips

Phillips, Keith Anthony **OF-2B-3B-SS-DH**
1982–* B:4/25/1959, Atlanta, GA Deb:5/10/1982, OAK AL BB/TR 5'10", 175

G	AB	R	H	HR	RBI	OBP	SLG	AVG
2161	7617	1300	2023	160	819	.377	.389	.266

Although Tony Phillips hated being called a utilityman, he was regarded as baseball's preeminent utility player of the 1980s and 1990s. He was also one of the game's best leadoff hitters.

Originally a second baseman in the Montreal Expos organization, Phillips came to the majors in 1982 as a shortstop with the Oakland Athletics. He became a full-time player in 1983, and over the years the A's used the talented athlete, a five-sport letterman in high school, all over the field. In 1988 Phillips played every position except pitcher and catcher for the pennant-winning Athletics, and in 1989 helped Oakland win a world championship.

It was only after leaving the A's, however, that Phillips showed just how dynamic a player he could be. Signing with Detroit as a free agent in 1990, he started at five different positions in his first year with the Tigers, and in 1991 he hit 17 home runs. The next year he led the majors in runs scored with 114, and in 1995, as a California Angel, he hit a career-high 27 homers.

Phillips also began to display a less admirable side to his personality. Always known as a competitive player, his fiery disposition became extreme. During one game in 1996, Phillips, then with the White Sox, changed into street clothes, went behind the grandstand, and punched a fan who had been heckling him. The low point came in August 1997, when he was arrested for cocaine possession in a seedy Anaheim motel.

Suspended and later released by the Angels, Phillips joined the Blue Jays the following spring. The New York Mets, searching for a leadoff hitter, traded for Phillips in July. Although he hit a game-winning home run against Atlanta on September 5, he was mostly ineffective in his 52 games with the club. In 1999 the 40-year-old Phillips returned to Oakland, where he became the driving force on a surprising contender. In August, however, he suffered a broken leg while sliding into second base, cutting short one of his most productive seasons.

Mike Piazza

Piazza, Michael Joseph **C**

1992–* B:9/4/1968, Norristown, PA Deb:9/1/1992, LA NL BR/TR 6'3", 197

G	AB	R	H	HR	RBI	OBP	SLG	AVG
981	3653	611	1200	240	768	.394	.575	.328

Mike Piazza put together offensive numbers like few other catchers in history, but he was only drafted because of a favor to a family friend. Vince, Mike's father, was a close friend of Tommy Lasorda, and the Los Angeles Dodgers skipper convinced his team to draft Piazza in the 62nd round of the 1988 draft. Lasorda arranged a private workout when Piazza was not offered a contract. Lasorda put his final imprint on Piazza's career by announcing that the young ballplayer would become a catcher.

As a boy, Piazza wanted to be a pitcher. He won a district title as one—he also played the field—and he knew how to toss a curveball. He disliked wearing the heavy catching equipment, and he told his pals he would never be a catcher. Naturally, the reverse occurred.

After Lasorda's decision, Piazza went to Campo Las Palmas in the Dominican Republic to learn his new craft. He was the first American student they had ever seen. Somewhere between there and the countless bus rides to and from Salem (Northwest League), Vero Beach (Florida State League), Bakersfield (California League), San Antonio (Texas League), Albuquerque (Pacific Coast League), plus a winter in Mexicali (Mexican League), Piazza figured out how to do his job.

Piazza was a unanimous choice for National League Rookie of the Year in 1993. Showing extraordinary opposite-field power, he batted .318 with 35 home runs and 112 RBIs. Strike-shortened seasons in 1994 and 1995 curtailed his power numbers slightly, but his batting average improved. He batted .346 in 1995 to finish second in the NL batting race.

In 1996, the first 162-game season since his rookie season, Piazza batted .336 with 36 home runs, 105 RBIs, and a .422 on base percentage. He was Most Valuable Player in the All-Star Game at Philadelphia's Veteran's Stadium, where he used to serve as batboy when the Dodgers came to town. He finished second to San Diego's Ken Caminiti for NL MVP.

In 1997 Piazza again finished second in the MVP race, this time to Larry Walker of the Colorado Rockies. Piazza beat out the rest of the NL for the inaugural CNN/SI and *Total Baseball* Ted Williams Award, measuring production based on a formula devised by *Total Baseball*. His 201 hits were the highest ever by a catcher.

After five extraordinary years in Los Angeles, Piazza became enmeshed in a salary dispute. The Dodgers traded him to Florida in a big-name, bigger-salary swap in May 1998; Piazza was sent to the Mets for three top prospects a week later. Despite a sometimes hostile reception in New York, the streaky Piazza finished the season batting .328. Speculation had him heading elsewhere as a free agent, but Piazza signed a seven-year contract as one of the game's top paid players.

In 1999 the Mets survived a thrilling stretch drive to edge into the playoffs as the Wild Card, thanks in part to Piazza's 40 home runs, 124 RBIs, and 100 runs scored. Hampered by a thumb problem, Piazza missed two playoff games against Arizona, and had to leave two Championship Series games early against Atlanta because of a slight concussion. He hit just .182 in the postseason, but he still managed 10 RBIs. He hit a game-tying home run in Game 6 of the NLCS; the exhausted and ailing catcher had to be removed shortly thereafter.

The wear and tear of catching every day has led many to wonder whether Piazza may one day switch to another position to add to his longevity. Piazza, whose appearance in New York forced the Mets to trade long-time catcher Todd Hundley in 1998, remains committed to catching. From 1995 to 1999 Piazza caught more games than any other National Leaguer at his position; only Ivan Rodriguez of Texas played more games at catcher in that span. Piazza won Silver Slugger Awards and appeared in the All-Star Game in each of his first seven full years in the major leagues.

Billy Pierce

Pierce, Walter William **P**

1945, 1948–64 B:4/2/1927, Detroit, MI Deb:6/1/1945, DET AL BL/TL 5'10", 160

W	L	PCT	G	SH	IP	BB	SO	ERA
211	169	.555	585	38	3306^{2}	1178	1999	3.27

Billy Pierce was selected to the All-Star game seven times, starting three times in four years and allowing just one run. Despite not being as familiar a name to current fans as southpaws Vida Blue, Carl Hubbell, or Lefty Grove, Pierce earned more career shutouts than the other three.

Named Most Valuable Player in *Esquire*'s 1944 All-American Boys game, Pierce won a four-year scholarship to study medicine at the University of Michigan. "There were several clubs I could have signed with," he said later, "but Detroit was my hometown."

By 1947, Pierce was playing in Buffalo under Paul Richards, a one-time regular customer at the Detroit drugstore owned by Pierce's father. Pierce was 14–8 for the International League Bisons but irritated Richards by spending his off-days scrimmaging with Detroit Red Wing bad boy Ted Lindsay.

Although 3–0 in his first extended action with the Tigers in 1948, and listed as one of five "untradables" on the club, Pierce went to the White Sox for Aaron Robinson in the first (and probably best) deal made by general manager Frank "Trader" Lane. According to Pierce, he found out about the trade while listening to his car radio.

Detroit later tried to call off the deal, but Lane knew what he had in Pierce. When Paul Richards took over as Chicago's manager in 1951 he worked with pitching coach Ray Berres to slow Pierce's delivery and sharpen his control. Pierce improved immediately and won 15, 15, and 18 games in Richards' first three years.

Pierce's pitching repertoire owed something to Ted Williams. Speaking with Lane, the Boston legend remarked, "That little guy you have, he's got to come up with a slider." Lane replied, "You tell him that." The next time Boston came to Comiskey, Williams came up in the ninth with two on, two out, and Pierce protecting a one-run lead. Williams popped up what he'd thought was a fastball to end the game. He told Lane, "I've got to learn to keep my mouth shut."

Pierce established his credentials as one of the best pitchers in the league in 1955, when he went 15–10 with a league-leading 1.97 ERA. The next year the ERA went up, but so did the win total, as he finished 20–9 with an AL high 21 complete games.

Pierce won 20 games for the second straight season in 1957 and just missed a perfect game when Senators pinch hitter Ed Fitzgerald doubled with two out in the ninth. In 1958 he won 17 games, led the league in complete games for the third year in a row, and was selected to his fourth consecutive All-Star Game.

Traded to the Giants in 1962, he contributed immediately. He went 16–6, shutting out the Dodgers in the first game of the best-of-three playoff, and three-hitting the Yankees in Game 6 of the World Series. Pierce retired after the 1964 season and went into sales with Continental Envelope,

in Evergreen Park, Illinois. Lane summed up Pierce's career with these words, "You didn't need a relief pitcher. If we were a run ahead going into the seventh or eighth, the ballgame was over."

Jimmy Piersall

Piersall, James Anthony **OF**

1950, 1952–67 B:11/14/1929, Waterbury, CT
Deb:9/7/1950, BOS AL BR/TR 6', 175

G	AB	R	H	HR	RBI	OBP	SLG	AVG
1734	5890	811	1604	104	591	.334	.386	.272

In the 1950s slick-fielding outfielder Jimmy Piersall's bout with mental illness made the nation's headlines and was eventually chronicled in the book *Fear Strikes Out* and a subsequent film adaptation starring Anthony Perkins. At a time when psychiatric disorders were rarely talked about, Piersall showed that they could indeed be conquered.

Piersall had faced pressure long before he began his pro baseball career. His father, a house painter, had already reached middle age by the time Jimmy came along, and during the Depression the Piersalls often had to resort to public assistance. From the beginning, father and son worked out together at baseball. Young Piersall particularly enjoyed catching the ball, and one day he exclaimed about how much fun a particularly difficult catch had been. "I don't want you thinking about fun. When you grow up I want you to become a slugger such as Jimmie Foxx," his father grumbled.

If Piersall could not become another Foxx, he could at least become a successful major leaguer. That was his father's dream, and the unrelenting drive to achieve it helped put Piersall on edge. "I would do anything to avoid his anger," Piersall later said. "He set down my rules, and I tried hard not to disobey them, for I lived in fear of his wrath."

More difficulty followed. When Piersall's mother was institutionalized, the uncertainty of her circumstances preyed on the boy's mind. Meanwhile, Piersall's father continued to push him toward a baseball career, steering him away from other sports. Once, when Piersall broke his right wrist in a YMCA playground touch football match, his father berated him for risking his whole career "for a lousy game of touch football," and threatened to knock him "right into the middle of next week." Just prior to this time Piersall started suffering from intense headaches.

He did manage to secure permission to play high school basketball. During a Connecticut state tournament he dislocated his jaw, and it had to be snapped back into place. Witnessing this, his father collapsed from a heart attack and was taken to a hospital.

Piersall had planned to attend Duke University to play under coach Jack Coombs. But with his father now ill, all plans changed. He accepted a three-year Red Sox bonus contract at $4,000 per year, plus a trip to Boston's Lahey Clinic for his father. Piersall was now sole supporter of his family.

That summer he played for Scranton, where he led the Eastern League in doubles, RBIs, and putouts, and impressed all observers with his marvelous work in center field. He spent the next two seasons at Louisville and was called up briefly in 1950. In 1951 he was sent back down to the minors, this time one step below Louisville, to Birmingham of the Southern Association. Piersall responded with a .346 average but seethed over the demotion.

That December he was leafing through *The Sporting News* and came across an item about the Red Sox and their new manager, Lou Boudreau: "One planned move is the converting of Jimmy Piersall, minor league outfielding sensation with Birmingham last season, into a shortstop....Boudreau will tutor Piersall personally at the special training session. The manager himself will decide whether or not the youngster has a future as a shortstop. 'If he does,' Boudreau said, 'I'll farm him out a year. I'd never take him up as a shortstop right off.'"

The news set Piersall off into a frenzy of speculation. He correctly deduced that he was in a no-win situation—if he couldn't make the switch he would disappoint Boston management, but if he did, his reward would be another season in the minors. He also imagined that Boudreau was trying to ruin him and couldn't get the idea out of his mind. He considered not reporting to camp. When he did arrive in Sarasota, something snapped within him. The already hyperactive Piersall became extremely aggressive, getting into fights with Yankees player Billy Martin and teammate Mickey McDermott.

The experiment at shortstop failed, and Piersall returned to center field. But he began acting bizarrely, doing the hula on the field, hitching a ride on the Red Sox bullpen car, and publicly mocking teammate Dom DiMaggio. Finally, Boston returned him to Birmingham. There his behavior worsened. He feverishly whispered instructions to teammates. He fired a ball at close range to his own pitcher and later got down on all fours to retrieve it. Eventually the Red Sox urged Piersall to obtain counseling. They flew him back to Massachusetts, where he received electroshock therapy. The treatment was successful, but Piersall could remember nothing of his outrageous behavior.

As he once recalled, "From the moment I walked into the lobby of the Sarasota-Terrace Hotel in Sarasota, Florida, to report to the Red Sox special training camp on the morning of January 15, 1952, until the moment I came to my senses in the violent room of the Westborough State Hospital in Massachusetts the following August, my mind is an absolute blank."

To find out what he had done during that time frame he reviewed scrapbooks kept by his wife. "This dreadful stage of [my life] was an open book to thousands of baseball fans all over the country. I couldn't let it remain closed to me," he said. Piersall returned to the major leagues and excelled with his glove. Casey Stengel termed him the "best defensive right fielder I have ever seen. Better even than Ross Youngs." Piersall led the American League three times in fielding percentage, twice in putouts, and once in double plays. He won Gold Gloves in 1958 and 1961.

Piersall's best season was probably 1956. He hit .293, led the American League with 40 doubles, and had career highs with 176 hits, 87 RBIs, and a .449 slugging percentage. He was selected to his second All-Star Game.

Piersall may have been calmer after his shock treatments, but he was never dull. He once hid behind Yankee Stadium's monuments, but his most publicized exploit came late in his career. After stints with the Indians and Senators, Piersall was dealt to the New York Mets in 1963, where Stengel was his new manager. At the Polo Grounds, Piersall hit his 100th career home run and proceeded to run around the bases backwards. "That way I can see where I've been. I always know where I'm going," he quipped.

Stengel was not amused by the stunt nor by Piersall's .194 batting average. "There's only room for one clown on this team," grumbled Stengel, who got rid of him. Piersall finished his playing career with the Angels and later became a broadcaster for the White Sox and the Rangers. In 1999 he was a roving instructor in the Cubs' system.

Lou Piniella

Piniella, Louis Victor **OF–DH**

1964, 1968–84 M(1986–88, 1990–*, 1019–949)
B:8/28/1943, Tampa, FL Deb:9/4/1964, BAL AL BR/TR
6'2", 198

G	AB	R	H	HR	RBI	OBP	SLG	AVG
1747	5867	651	1705	102	766	.336	.409	.291

Lou Piniella was a large, likable man whose hot temper always seemed to get him into trouble. In New York, not an easy town in which to be liked, he won awards in consecutive years as a fan and media favorite. He was both a solid, if unexceptional, player and a successful manager.

Piniella was a Catholic All-America in high school basketball. However, he chose to pursue baseball, and after high school graduation he spent seven years in the Baltimore, Washington, and Cleveland farm systems. Claimed by the Seattle Pilots in the 1969 expansion draft, he was swapped to the other expansion team, Kansas City, before the season began.

The muscular outfielder showed line drive power in his first full year, hitting 21 doubles, six triples, and 11 homers with a .282 average. He was voted American league Rookie of the Year, narrowly beating out pitchers Mike Nagy and Ken Tatum and outfielder Carlos May. For the next three years Piniella hit well and played adequate defense for Kansas City. He hit .301 with a career high 88 RBIs in 1970. Two years later his .312 average was second in the league behind Rod Carew's .318. He also led the league with 33 doubles and was selected to the All-Star Game.

After Piniella slumped to .250 in 1973, the Yankees came calling. They offered the Royals 38-year-old hurler Lindy McDaniel for Piniella and pitcher Ken Wright. Kansas City, remarkably, said yes. Piniella's on-field fiery attitude coupled with his pleasant demeanor off the field made him a true Yankee. In 11 years in pinstripes, he hit better than .300 five times. His arm became something to fear too: three times he nailed more than 10 baserunners in a season.

The New York club, long a legend, had been down for a dozen years. Two years after Piniella joined the Yankees they were coming back. From 1976 through 1981 the Yanks were in the postseason every year but one. In 1978 the team fought back from a 14-game deficit to the Red Sox, and the two clubs had to play a one-game playoff to determine the division champ.

Piniella was in right field in the last of the ninth, and the Yankees were up by a run. Boston, however, had Rick Burleson on first and one out. Jerry Remy lined a ball into right-center that Piniella lost in the afternoon sky. He charged in toward it, then stopped stock-still. He raised his arms in dismay for an instant before dropping them to his sides. "I was saying to myself, 'Don't panic. Don't wave your arms and let him know you've lost it,'" he recalled later. The ball bounced to his right and several feet in front of him. He was able to reach out and snag it before it got past him. Burleson had to stop at second. The next batter, Jim Rice, hit

a deep fly to Piniella, and Burleson was able to advance to third. Had Piniella not made the heads-up play, Burleson would have scored on the Rice fly. Carl Yastrzemski then popped up to end the game.

In five postseason appearances with New York, Piniella batted .313, with six doubles. In 1983 and 1984, his final two seasons for the Yankees, he was a part-time player while working as a batting coach. He kept his job after hanging up his spikes as a player, and, in 1985, when club owner George Steinbrenner fired skipper Billy Martin for the third time, Piniella took over as manager.

Under Piniella the Yankees finished second in 1986. Martin, who was working in the front office, kept up a constant stream of criticism of Piniella's managing. The team, decimated by injuries, fell to fourth in 1987. Steinbrenner rehired Martin to run the club in 1988 and made Piniella general manager, but paperwork wasn't Piniella's strong suit. He quit after a few months, moving to a position as special assignment scout and consultant. Against his better judgment, Piniella let Steinbrenner talk him into returning as manager when the owner again fired Martin 68 games into the season. Piniella's second tenure as manager was no better than his first.

Piniella took the manager's job in Cincinnati in 1990. His famous temper was most embarrassing that season when, during an argument with the umpires, he ripped a base off its moorings, flung it into the outfield, chased after it, and threw it again. Cincinnati hosted a city-wide base-tossing contest soon after. Nevertheless, the Reds held first place from Opening Day forward and won the NL West title. The Reds beat the Pittsburgh Pirates in six to take the pennant, and then swept the heavily favored Oakland Athletics in the World Series.

The Reds finished fifth in 1991 but returned to second in 1992. Piniella, constantly clashing with tempestuous owner Marge Schott, quit after the season. He joined the Seattle Mariners in 1993 and guided them through two improving seasons.

In 1995 Seattle caught up with the first-place California Angels and then won a one-game playoff for the first postseason berth in franchise history. Seattle lost the first two Division Series games at Yankee Stadium, but won the last three games. Piniella brought in Randy Johnson, the eventual 1995 Cy Young Award winner, into the game in the ninth inning on one day's rest. The Mariners rallied for two runs in the bottom of the 11th to win. Seattle, however, lost the Championship Series to Cleveland in six games.

Powered by league MVP Ken Griffey, Jr., the Mariners again won the AL West in 1997. Piniella's Mariners finished third in both 1998 and 1999.

Vada Pinson

Pinson, Vada Edward **OF**

1958–75 B:8/11/1938, Memphis, TN D:10/21/1995, Oakland, CA Deb:4/15/1958, CIN NL BL/TL 5'11", 181

G	AB	R	H	HR	RBI	OBP	SLG	AVG
2469	9645	1366	2757	256	1170	.330	.442	.286

By his first full season, at age 20, Vada Pinson was already a great ballplayer. He led the National League with 47 doubles and 131 runs scored, while hitting .316 with 20 homers and stealing 21 bases. After several more excellent years, the rest of his career was a slow and uneven downward spiral.

Pinson's family moved to Oakland when he was 7, and he later attended the same high school as outfielders Curt Flood and Frank Robinson. He signed with Cincinnati in 1957 and played with Wausau and Visalia before reaching the Reds in 1958. That spring he was the subject of a misunderstanding. Coach Jimmy Dykes mistakenly believed that he was Spanish and talked to Pinson in signs and broken English. Pinson finally said, "Mr. Dykes, if there is something you want me to do with my stance, please tell me;" Dykes almost fell over.

In Pinson's first major league game he hit a grand slam to beat Pittsburgh, 4–1, but he was demoted soon after. He returned in 1959 and had an exceptional rookie season. Pinson was only the fourth National League rookie to collect more than 200 hits, but he lost Rookie of the Year honors to San Francisco's Willie McCovey. That season Braves manager Fred Haney predicted, "For now...Hank Aaron. For the future, there's no doubt about it...Vada Pinson." Reds batting coach Wally Moses cautioned, "For Vada, the sky's the limit. But he'll have to get there himself. You can't put him there."

An excellent lefthanded fielder, Pinson led the league in outfield putouts each year from 1959 through 1961, winning a Gold Glove in 1961. He also scored more than 100 runs in each of his first four full seasons and stole more than 20 bases in his first five full years.

In his second season, Pinson again led the league in doubles, with 37. The next year he was even better, finishing second in the NL with a .343 batting average, while leading the league with 208 hits. However, he hit a disappointing .091 against the Yankees in the 1961 World Series.

In 1962, angered by a column by Cincinnati sportswriter Earl Lawson, he took a swing at the scribe. "I'm just glad Pinson gets more body into his swings with the bat than he does with his fist," Lawson joked. He swore out a warrant for Pinson's arrest, although he later dropped the charges.

Pinson had another great performance in 1963. He hit .313, with 22 homers, 27 stolen bases, a career-high 106 RBIs, and a league-leading 204 hits and 14 triples. After that season, however, he began to be hampered by a recurring hamstring pull. In 1964 he hit only .266, with eight stolen bases, and showed significantly less range in the outfield.

By 1966 it was clear that Pinson's legs were not up to his previous pace. After hitting.271 in 1968, with only five home runs, the Reds traded him to St. Louis. Pinson had another lackluster season there and was sent to Cleveland for outfielder Jose Cardenal.

Pinson temporarily revived in the American League and hit 24 homers in 1970. In 1971 he disappointed again and was shipped to California. After two mediocre seasons with the Angels, Pinson was traded to Kansas City, where he finished his career in 1975. After he retired Pinson became a batting instructor in the Mariners' system and later for the Tigers.

Wally Pipp

Pipp, Walter Clement **1B**

1913, 1915–28 B:2/17/1893, Chicago, IL D:1/11/1965, Grand Rapids, MI Deb:6/29/1913, DET AL BL/TL 6'1", 180

G	AB	R	H	HR	RBI	OBP	SLG	AVG
1872	6914	974	1941	90	997	.341	.408	.281

First baseman Wally Pipp carved himself a unique niche in New York Yankees history and baseball lore because of a game he didn't play. On June 2, 1925, complaining of a headache, Pipp decided to sit out a game. His replacement, Lou Gehrig, took over and held the job for a record-breaking 2,130 consecutive games. To this day, if a player takes a day off and his replacement has a good game, someone is bound to mention the name of Wally Pipp.

Pipp was a reliable and productive hitter and fielder, the Yankees' regular first baseman for 10 years. He led the American League in home runs in 1915 and 1916, when he had low batting averages. He then changed his emphasis, exchanging some of the power for percentage points, and he hit .329 in 1922. He was the first baseman on the Yankees' first three pennant winners.

Pipp actually had perhaps his best season the

year before Gehrig took over. He hit .295 while leading the league with 19 triples and driving in a career-high 114 runs. Traded to Cincinnati before the 1926 season, he played there three seasons before retiring.

George Pipgras

Pipgras, George William **P**

1923–24, 1927–35 U(1938–46) B:12/20/1899, Ida Grove, IA D:10/19/1986, Gainesville, FL Deb:6/9/1923, NY AL BR/TR 6'1½", 185

W	L	PCT	G	SH	IP	BB	SO	ERA
102	73	.583	276	16	1488¹	598	714	4.09

George Pipgras was one of those lucky pitchers who hurled for the New York Yankees during the heyday of Babe Ruth and Lou Gehrig. He possessed one of the better fastballs in the American League, but his career 4.09 ERA suggests that his won-loss record depended on the bats behind him.

Originally scouted and signed by the Chicago White Sox, Pipgras was released before he reached the majors because of wildness. The Yankees acquired his contract and kept him on their roster in 1923 and 1924, but he pitched only 48 innings in two seasons, walking 43 batters. Manager Miller Huggins predicted that Pipgras would become a good pitcher after two years in the minors and sent him down. He returned to the Yankees in 1927, earning a spot on the team that many consider the greatest of all time. Still wild, he was seldom used early in the season, but when lefthander Dutch Ruether missed a start, Pipgras took his place and won. He finished the season with a 10–3 record despite an ERA of 4.11. In the World Series against Pittsburgh, Pipgras was a surprise choice to start Game 2. He came through with a seven-hit, complete-game 6–2 victory, and the Yankees swept the Pirates in four games.

Pipgras had his best season in 1928. He led the American League with 24 victories and 300⅔ innings pitched, and his 3.38 ERA was the lowest of his career. The Yankees took their third consecutive pennant and again won the World Series in four games, with Pipgras defeating Grover Cleveland Alexander and the St. Louis Cardinals, 9–3, in Game 2.

Pipgras won 18 games in 1929 as the Yankees fell to second place. After a couple of mediocre years, he came back in 1932 with a strong 16–9 record, and the Yankees returned to the winner's circle. Once more they swept the Series in four games, defeating the Chicago Cubs. Pipgras started for New York in the third game when Babe Ruth delivered his "called shot," to the center field bleachers. Pipgras gave up nine hits and three walks in eight innings to receive credit for the 7–5 win.

Early in the 1933 season he was sold to the Boston Red Sox along with third baseman Billy Werber for $100,000. Pipgras was 9–8 for the Sox, but near the end of the season he broke his arm in a freak accident. Pitching against Detroit, he attempted to throw a curve and felt a bone crack in his arm. Although he tried to come back for two seasons, he pitched only eight more innings.

Pipgras was hunting with Tom Yawkey when the Red Sox owner suggested he take up a career as an umpire. Yawkey helped him find a place in the Eastern League, and by 1938 Pipgras was working in the American League.

He had a short fuse and was quick to eject players and managers whom he thought had stepped over the line. In one game between the St. Louis Browns and the Chicago White Sox he threw out 17 men. Pipgras himself had spent 17 seasons in the majors and minors without once being ejected from a game. Ironically, the former pitcher was generally considered a "batter's umpire," with a narrow strike zone. Pipgras retired from baseball after the 1946 season.

Juan Pizarro

Pizarro, Juan Ramon (Cordova) **P**

1957–74 B:2/7/1937, Santurce, Puerto Rico Deb:5/4/1957, MIL NL BL/TL 5'11", 190

W	L	PCT	G	SV	IP	BB	SO	ERA
131	105	.555	488	28	2034¹	888	1522	3.43

Juan Pizarro was a valuable starting pitcher for Al Lopez's White Sox of the early 1960s and was twice selected to the All-Star Game. But he spent half his career coming out of the bullpen, and he managed 10 wins in a season only twice other than his All-Star years.

Pizarro broke into the major leagues with Milwaukee in 1957 after going 23–6 for Jacksonville in the Southern League, where he had recorded 318 strikeouts in only 274 innings pitched. He could not crack the Braves' strong starting rotation of the late 1950s, and in the next four years he never won more than six games.

Traded to the Reds with pitcher Joey Jay for slick-fielding shortstop Roy McMillan in December 1960, Pizarro was sent to the White Sox the same day in a deal for third baseman Gene Freese. In Chicago Pizarro found the success that had eluded him in Milwaukee. He won 14 games his first season there and threw two two-hitters the next year. In 1963 he won 16 games with a 2.39 ERA and was selected to the All-Star Game. The next year he won 19 games and was chosen to the All-Star Game again.

Used largely in the bullpen after 1965, Pizarro bounced from team to team for the next decade before retiring following the 1974 season. Perhaps the highlight of that last 10 years was when he outpitched Tom Seaver, winning, 1–0, on the strength of his own home run.

Eddie Plank

Plank, Edward Stewart **P**

1901–17 B:8/31/1875, Gettysburg, PA D:2/24/1926, Gettysburg, PA Deb:5/13/1901, PHI AL BL/TL 5'11½", 175

W	L	PCT	G	SH	IP	BB	SO	ERA
326	194	.627	623	69	4495²	1072	2246	2.35

According to baseball lore, lefthanded pitchers are brash, eccentric, and free-spirited. They are allegedly unpredictable, their talent matched and often exceeded by their egos. Rube Waddell of the Philadelphia Athletics, who terrorized American League batters and created his own mythic persona at the beginning of the 20th century, was the prototype—a Roman candle that blazed brightly but all too soon went out.

His teammate, Eddie Plank, was just the opposite. Level-headed, reliable Plank left no humorous anecdotes. Compared with Waddell, he was dull, but Plank's career was ultimately more successful. He played tortoise to Waddell's hare, and the winner was the same in baseball as in fable. Plank was a great pitcher long after Waddell had become an entertaining memory.

Born in Gettysburg, Pennsylvania, Plank was nicknamed "Gettysburg Eddie." He attended Gettysburg Academy, worked part-time as a tour guide of the battlefield, and enrolled in Gettysburg College, where the baseball coach was former major league pitcher Frank Foreman. Plank had played little baseball up to that time, but Foreman convinced him to come out and pitch for the college team. When Plank graduated in 1901, Foreman recommended him to Connie Mack, who was about to launch the Philadelphia Athletics in the first year of the American League.

Plank never played in the minors. He made his first appearance for the A's in May 1901 and gave up three runs in four innings of relief. Five days later he won his first major league game. He improved as the season progressed, and finished at 17–13 with a 3.31 earned run average. His 28 complete games are among the most compiled by a major league rookie.

The A's won their first pennant in 1902 as Plank collected the first of his eight 20-win seasons. He threw a good fastball and a fair curve from a three-quarter motion, occasionally dropping to sidearm. His control was good, but Plank nibbled at the plate and lured hitters into swinging at pitches just outside the strike zone.

The deliberate Plank would stand on the mound and rub up the baseball, adjust his belt, step off the mound, knock dirt from his spikes, go back onto the mound and ask for a new sign, reposition his cap, pull up a sock, and finally throw a pitch low and outside. Then the show would start again. He would fiddle with his glove, rebutton his shirt, ask for a new ball, and on and on. Umpires often had to order him to pitch. The games he pitched lasted hours, and many fans refused to come to them because they knew they'd miss the last train home. His strategy was primarily psychological. If his fidgeting upset fans, it drove batters up the wall, driving them to distraction until they swung at a bad pitch.

In 1903 Plank won 23 games, while starting a league-leading 43. Remarkably, his 2.38 ERA was the first of 15 consecutive years that his earned run average would finish lower than 2.90. The next year he increased his win total to 26, a figure that he would match eight years later.

Plank was consistently superb during the regular season and consistently unlucky in World Series play. In 1910 he sat out the Series when Mack decided to use only righthanders in defeating the Chicago Cubs. Plank won Game 2 of the 1911 Series against the Giants with a five-hitter, 3–1, but lost Game 5 in relief when he gave up a run in the 10th inning. In 1913 Christy Mathewson beat him, 3–0, in Game 2, but Plank came back to win the final game, 3–1, over Mathewson on a brilliant two-hitter. The Braves swept the A's in four games in 1914, and Plank was a 1–0 loser in Game 2. Despite an outstanding 1.38 ERA in seven World Series appearances, Plank's record was only 2–5.

After the Athletics lost the 1914 World Series, Mack let most of his veterans go and decided to rebuild with younger players. His decision was based on economics. With war breaking out in Europe, baseball's future was uncertain. Of more immediate importance was a "war" at home against the upstart Federal League. Mack knew the Federal League had offered generous contracts to Plank and Bender. Rather than make them choose between loyalty and their bank accounts, Mack released them.

Plank won 21 games for the St. Louis team in the Federal League in 1915, but the league collapsed. He stayed in St. Louis to pitch for the Browns for two seasons, going 16–15 in 1916 and 5–6, despite a 1.79 ERA, in 1917. He then was traded to New York, but at age 42 opted to retire instead of suit up for the Yankees.

In 17 major league seasons, including his year in the Federal League, Plank won 327 games, a record for career victories by a lefthander until it was surpassed by Warren Spahn in 1961. Plank was no slouch with a bat either. Although his lifetime average was only .206, he recorded 331 hits to rank among the top 20 pitchers of all time. In addition, during a game on August 30, 1909, Plank became one of the few big league pitchers to steal home.

After he retired Plank returned to Gettysburg, where he farmed and operated an automobile agency. In 1926, at age 50, he died of a stroke. He was named to the Hall of Fame in 1946, the same year Waddell was enshrined.

Dan Plesac

Plesac, Daniel Thomas **P**

1986–* B:2/4/1962, Gary, IN Deb:4/11/1986, MIL AL BL/TL 6'5", 215

W	L	PCT	G	SV	IP	BB	SO	ERA
51	61	.455	822	154	917	323	850	3.67

Dan Plesac notched 100 saves and made three All-Star appearances for the Milwaukee Brewers in his first four major league seasons, handcuffing batters with a blazing fastball and sharp slider. Then his career almost came to an end through injury.

Plesac first noticed shoulder soreness late in 1989; it carried over into 1990. He signed a large contract, and felt obliged to pitch through the pain. His saves dipped, his ERA ballooned nearly two points, but he never went on the disabled list. Plesac lost his closer's job in 1991—he even started 10 games—then moved to the Chicago Cubs after the 1992 season. The following year he was finally diagnosed with chronic bursitis and tendonitis in the shoulder, caused by a severe deterioration of the muscles in the back of his shoulder.

Through years of strengthening exercises and some changes to his mechanics, Plesac managed to build himself back into an effective situational reliever. He filled that role in Pittsburgh, Toronto, and Arizona. He became a Diamondback following a midseason 1999 trade and wound up making the first postseason appearance of his career. In 1999 Plesac appeared in 50 or more games for the seventh consecutive year. "Because I got by on raw ability those first few years," he said, "when I started having arm problems I didn't know how to pitch...I had to make some adjustments."

Eric Plunk

Plunk, Eric Vaughn **P**

1986–* B:9/3/1963, Wilmington, CA Deb:5/12/1986, OAK AL BR/TR 6'5", 217

W	L	PCT	G	SV	IP	BB	SO	ERA
72	58	.554	714	35	1151	647	1081	3.82

Although a top prospect early in his career, Eric Plunk may best be known as the player twice traded for Rickey Henderson. A fourth-round pick of the New York Yankees in 1981, the hard-throwing young pitcher was traded to Oakland for Henderson following the 1984 season. Because extreme wildness (102 walks in 120 innings in 1986) prevented him from being successful as a starter, Plunk was converted into a reliever in 1987.

He was enjoying a good year in Oakland in 1989 when he was traded back to the Yankees, again in a package deal for Henderson. The Yankees tried him as a starter but eventually returned him to the bullpen, where he developed into a quality set-up pitcher despite his poor control.

Released by both New York and Toronto before the 1992 season began, Plunk signed with the Cleveland organization. Plunk won nine games in 1992, and saved 15 games the following season. His best attribute with the Indians was his durability. He pitched 50 or more games five times between 1992 and 1997; he pitched in 41 games during the strike-shortened 1994 season. He won his first postseason game in the 1997 Championship Series, then was traded to Milwaukee during the 1998 season.

Johnny Podres

Podres, John Joseph **P**

1953–55, 1957–67, 1969 B:9/30/1932, Witherbee, NY Deb:4/17/1953, BRO NL BL/TL 5'11", 192

W	L	PCT	G	SH	IP	BB	SO	ERA
148	116	.561	440	24	2265	743	1435	3.68

Johnny Podres was a lifelong Dodgers fan. Fittingly, Podres earned Brooklyn's only world championship, and he later helped the Dodgers win two more World Series after the club had relocated to Los Angeles.

Signed by Amsterdam, New York, restaurateur and part-time Dodgers scout Alex Isabel, Podres started with Newport News in the Piedmont League in 1951. He quickly moved to Hazard in the Mountain State League where he won 21 games and led the league in won-lost percentage, strikeouts and ERA. After going 5–5 with Montreal in 1952, Podres joined the Dodgers in 1953.

At the time fellow pitcher Clem Labine said of him, "He was a good kid, good-hearted. Anything you wanted you could have. But nothing concerned him except having a good time."

Podres went 9–4 as a rookie and then had his first taste of the World Series at Ebbets Field that fall. He started Game 5 against the Yankees when Mickey Mantle hit a grand slam into the upper deck of the left field stands to put the game away, the only World Series decision Podres would ever lose.

Two years later, he got revenge on the Bronx Bombers in an unforgettable way. Starting Game 3 at Brooklyn, Podres beat the Yankees, 8–3, after yielding another solo homer to Mantle. With the teams tied at three wins apiece, Podres was given the ball for Game 7 at Yankee Stadium. The first three innings were scoreless. Podres remarked, "When the game began, I had the Yankees looking for my changeup. I established early in the game that I was going to throw it, and then as the shadows in the fall in Yankee Stadium came on, I went to my fastball and hard curve. In the last four or five innings, I threw only one change, the last pitch of the game."

Podres gave up eight hits, and the Dodgers won, 2–0, to win the only championship of their 67 years in Brooklyn. Podres was named Most Valuable Player of the Series and Sportsman of the Year by *Sports Illustrated*.

Podres spent 1956 in the Navy, but returned the next year to lead the National League in ERA and shutouts. In 1959 Podres helped the Los Angeles Dodgers make it to the World Series by going 14–9. He then won Game 2, 4–3 and got a no-decision in Game 6, when the Dodgers went on to win to take their first championship in Los Angeles.

In 1961 he had perhaps his greatest year in the majors, finishing 18–5 to lead the NL in won-lost percentage. He won Game 2 of the 1963 World Series at Yankee Stadium. The Dodgers, who had beaten the Yankees just once in seven World Series while playing in Brooklyn, swept the Yanks in the first Series between Los Angeles and New York.

Podres was plagued by bone chips in his elbow after being hit by a pitch in 1964. He underwent surgery in June, and missed the rest of the season. Sold to Detroit in May 1966, he was out of baseball by 1968. He returned with the San Diego Padres in 1969, only to voluntarily retire that June.

Podres later worked as a pitching coach with the Padres, Boston Red Sox, Minnesota Twins, and Philadelphia Phillies.

Howie Pollet

Pollet, Howard Joseph **P**

1941–43, 1946–56 B:6/26/1921, New Orleans, LA D:8/8/1974, Houston, TX Deb:8/20/1941, STL NL BL/TL 6'1½", 175

W	L	PCT	G	SH	IP	BB	SO	ERA
131	116	.530	403	25	2107^{1}	745	934	3.51

Howie Pollet led the National League in ERA and was an All-Star both before and after World War II. He was in military service from age 22 to 25, and had two 20-win seasons for the Cardinals after the war.

Pollet had impressive credentials before joining the St. Louis Cardinals late in 1941. He had twice recorded 20 wins for Houston in the Texas League, including a no-hitter against Shreveport on April 25 of that year. He immediately got people's attention with five wins, six complete games, and a 1.93 ERA in nine outings.

Two years later Pollet had a streak of three shutouts and 28 consecutive scoreless innings before enlisting in the Army Air Corps in July. As it was, he finished the 1943 season 8–4 with a league-leading 1.75 ERA.

Returning to the Cardinals in 1946, Pollet took up right where he had left off, pacing the National League with 21 victories, 266 innings pitched and a 2.10 ERA. However, late in the season he hurt his arm, and he was never fully healthy in 1947. That winter he was operated on by Dr. Robert Hyland and his career gradually returned to normal.

In 1949 Pollet was back on track, going 20–9 and leading the league with five shutouts. His performance, however, quickly dropped off again. The Cardinals traded him to Pittsburgh after an 0–3 start in 1951 Pollet spent five more years with Pittsburgh, the Cubs, and the White Sox, but he never regained his former magic.

Luis Polonia

Polonia, Luis Andrew (Almonte) **OF**

1987–96, * B:10/12/1964 Santiago, Dominican Republic Deb:4/24/1987, OAK AL BL/TL 5'8", 152

G	AB	R	H	HR	RBI	OBP	SLG	AVG
1262	4496	680	1322	29	375	.346	.381	.294

Luis Polonia returned after two years out of the major leagues to excel as Detroit's leadoff hitter in 1999. In his first decade in the major leagues he had varying degrees of success with the Oakland Athletics, New York Yankees, California Angels, Baltimore Orioles, and Atlanta Braves. After the 1996 World Series with Atlanta, the 32-year-old outfielder with a hefty salary couldn't find a job. Only the Tampa Bay Devil Rays were interested, primarily because they needed to sign players for their fledgling organization.

The Devil Rays signed Polonia to a two-year contract in 1997, one year before they began play, and loaned him to the Mexico City Tigers. South of the border, he hit .377 in 1997 and a league-best .381 in 1998, attracting the attention of Detroit scout Ramon Pena, who had signed hot Tigers prospect Juan Encarnacion. The high number of curveballs in Mexico actually helped Polonia, who once had trouble handling breaking balls.

Detroit purchased Polonia's contract for $300,000 and brought him to 1999 spring training. He didn't stick but played well enough at Triple A to earn his another shot at the big leagues. He went 5-for-5 in his second game and filled the void in the Detroit leadoff spot, where six others had failed. Though he wasn't called up until May 28, Polonia hit .324 with 39 extra-base hits and 17 stolen bases in 87 games. He led the Tigers with a .526 slugging mark.

Early in his career with the Yankees, Polonia's

reputation was tarnished by an incident in Milwaukee when he was arrested for having sex with a 15-year-old girl in the team's hotel following a game with the Brewers. He later pleaded no contest, paid a fine, and served no jail time, but his services were no longer wanted in New York. Traded to California, Polonia stole 48 or more bases three straight seasons and established himself as a major league outfielder.

Darrell Porter

Porter, Darrell Ray **C–DH**

1971–87 B:1/17/1952, Joplin, MO Deb:9/2/1971, MIL AL BL/TR 6', 193

G	AB	R	H	HR	RBI	OBP	SLG	AVG
1782	5539	765	1369	188	826	.357	.409	.247

Darrell Porter was a fine defensive catcher and a powerful, if not always consistent, hitter. He had a long career highlighted by four years in Kansas City in the middle of it, when he and the Royals were at their peaks. He later battled back from substance abuse to lead the Cardinals to a world championship.

Porter came into the majors with the 1971 Milwaukee Brewers, and after two seasons on the bench took over as their regular catcher in 1973. He was selected to the All-Star Game the following year. Each of the next two years his performance dipped, however, as his batting average fell from .241 to .232 to.208.

Porter's biggest piece of luck was that he played for a franchise that hadn't climbed out of the American League cellar since its inception. Milwaukee management cleaned house following the 1976 season and Porter was sent to Kansas City. Although the Royals had come into existence in 1969, the same year as the Brewers (originally the Seattle Pilots), Kansas City was already a strong club and had won a division title that year. Early in the 1977 season Porter replaced Royals catcher Buck Martinez and went on to have his best year to that point. Porter batted .333 in the Championship Series, but the Royals lost to the Yankees.

In 1978 Porter hit .265 and drove in 78 runs. He was again selected to the All-Star Game and again hit well in the ALCS; the Royals, however, lost to the Yankees for the third straight year.

The next year he enjoyed his best season. He batted .291 and led league with 121 walks while scoring 101 runs and driving in 112, making him the only second catcher (after Mickey Cochrane) to surpass the century mark in bases on balls, runs scored, and RBIs in a single season. He also led the AL in slugging percentage.

Although the Royals rebounded in 1980, Porter was unhappy under new manager Jim Frey, and his performance dropped off. In the playoffs he batted just .100, although Kansas City finally beat the Yankees for the pennant. He struggled in the World Series and was benched in Game 4; Philadelphia beat the Royals in six games.

A free agent after the season, Porter signed with the St. Louis Cardinals, where he was reunited with former Royals manager Whitey Herzog. Porter admitted he had alcohol and substance abuse problems, and underwent rehabilitation. Although stroner emotionally, Porter seemed to seemed to have lost his old form as a player. His play hardly made up for the loss of Cardinals favorite Ted Simmons, whom he replaced.

In 1982 Porter batted just .231, but he was unstoppable in the postseason. In the NLCS he hit .556 with five walks; tied a record with three doubles; and scored at least once in each game. Suddenly he was again the offensive and defensive anchor of the team. He earned NLCS Most Valuable Player honors as the Cardinals swept Atlanta.

In Game 2 of the World Series against the Milwaukee Brewers, with his club down two runs, Porter smacked a sixth-inning, two-out double that scored two and tied the game, setting the Cardinals up for an eventual win. In Game 6 the Cardinals were down three games to two but pounded Milwaukee pitching to take the game easily. Porter hit a two-run homer. In the final contest, he knocked in a key insurance run to seal the Cardinals' victory. Porter was named World Series MVP and was hailed a hero in St. Louis.

Porter remained as the Cardinals' regular catcher until the 1985 season. In 1986 he joined the Texas Rangers. They used him behind the plate and as a designated hitter for two seasons, but with his power and his ability to get on base beginning to fail him, Porter retired after the 1987 campaign.

Mark Portugal

Portugal, Mark Steven **P**

1985–* B:10/30/1962, Los Angeles, CA Deb:8/14/1985, MIN AL BR/TR 6', 190

W	L	PCT	G	SH	IP	BB	SO	ERA
109	95	.534	346	4	1826^{1}	607	1134	4.03

Mark Portugal played only one season of high school baseball as a catcher-outfielder, but his arm looked good enough for the Minnesota Twins to sign him as a non-drafted free agent pitcher in 1980. He averaged 10 wins a season and made steady progress in his first four minor league seasons. He could not, however, duplicate that success at the major league level with the Twins.

After four years in Minnesota, the last season in relief, he was traded to Houston. Portugal was able to use his sinker and devastating changeup to his advantage at the pitcher-friendly Astrodome, but he also developed arm problems. He was disabled three times in four years in Houston, including twice in 1992. He rebounded in 1993 with his finest season: an 18–4 record, a league-leading .818 won-lost percentage, and a 12-game winning streak.

Portugal signed with San Francisco as a free agent, then was traded to Cincinnati during the 1995 season to help the Reds win the National League Central title. Portugal clashed openly with Reds skipper Ray Knight during most of 1996, and was in Philadelphia by 1997. The veteran righthander joined the Boston Red Sox in 1999. He nearly retired in June, and was released shortly before the Red Sox began postseason play.

Cum Posey

Posey, Cumberland Willis **OF**
Negro League Player (1911–28), Manager (1912–35) Owner (1911–46) B:6/20/1880, Homestead, PA D:3/28/1946, Pittsburgh, PA BR/TR 5'9", 145

Cum Posey's Homestead Grays wrote a record never approached by any other U.S. pro team in any sport—they won nine straight pennants from 1937 to 1945 with Josh Gibson, Buck Leonard, and Cool Papa Bell generating the power. Only the Tokyo Giants, with nine straight Japanese championships, can match them. Yet they may not have been the greatest Grays teams of all.

The 1926 club, starring Joe Williams, won 43 straight (mostly against white semipro teams). The 1930 Grays, with Williams, Gibson, and Oscar Charleston, won 11 out of 12 from the western champion Monarchs. And the 1931 club boasted a record of 136–17, again mostly against semipros. They even challenged the white major league Pirates to a winner-take-all series, but Pittsburgh simply refused.

Posey's father was a wealthy barge captain, his mother the first black to graduate from Ohio State. At various times Cum attended Penn State, Pittsburgh, and Duquesne universities, but failed to graduate from any of them. He was considered the best black basketball player in America in 1913 and also managed the Murdock Grays, a steel mill team. Eventually he founded the Loendi Big Five, which claimed the U.S. basketball championship of 1919. He gained control of the Homestead Grays in the early 1920s, played for the team until 1928, and managed it until 1935. His brother, Seward "See" Posey was instrumental in booking games and handling administrative responsibilities.

When the Depression struck, the Grays lost their stars to racketeer Gus Greenlee's well-bankrolled Pittsburgh Crawfords. Cum got his own racketeer, Sonnyman Jackson, and fought back, eventually driving Greenlee out of the league. In 1937 Posey bought Gibson back for $2,500, and the team went 152–11 to embark on their pennant streak.

The Grays shuttled between Pittsburgh and Washington by bus, playing two or three games a day, against both league and semipro competition. Rain could wipe out all profit for the week, until World War II brought prosperity at last. In 1945 Posey's Grays sometimes drew 30,000 fans to Griffith Stadium hours after the American League Senators had played there before 3,000. But when baseball was at last integrated after the war, the raids of major league clubs soon destroyed Cum's life investment. The Indians snatched Luke Easter for only $10,000. Posey moaned, "It's like coming into a man's store and stealing the merchandise right off the shelves."

Wally Post

Post, Walter Charles **OF**
1949, 1951–64 B:7/9/1929, St. Wendelin, OH D:1/6/1982, St. Henry, OH Deb:9/18/1949, CIN NL BR/TR 6'1", 203

G	AB	R	H	HR	RBI	OBP	SLG	AVG
1204	4007	594	1064	210	699	.325	.485	.266

Strikeout-prone slugger Wally Post was extremely popular with Cincinnati Reds fans—maybe a shade too popular. In the balloting for the 1957 All-Star Game, Cincinnati boosters absolutely stuffed the ballot boxes. A last-minute deluge of 500,000 ballots overwhelmed opponents at virtually every position.

With the exception of first baseman George Crowe, every member of the Reds' starting lineup gained a starting berth. Chosen for the game were catcher Ed Bailey, second baseman Johnny Temple, shortstop Roy McMillan, third baseman Don Hoak, right fielder Frank Robinson, center fielder Gus Bell, and left fielder Post. Since Cincinnati was destined to finish fourth that year, the preponderance of Reds hardly seemed appropriate. Commissioner Ford Frick took action, citing the "overbalance of Cincinnati votes," and removed Bell and Post from the team. Manager Walter Alston eventually reinstated Bell to the roster. Post was left behind to watch the game on television.

Post began his professional career in 1946 as a pitcher with Middletown of the Class D Ohio State League and then moved with the franchise to Muncie in 1947. He was 17–7 with a 3.33 ERA, but his .338 batting average attracted almost as much attention. After he went 8–11 in the South Atlantic League in 1948, he was made an outfielder for Charleston of the Central League. In 1953 he led the American Association with 120 RBIs.

After short visits to the majors in four different seasons, Post made the transition for good in

1954. After he delivered 18 homers and 83 RBIs, manager Birdy Tebbetts said, "The kid can do everything you'd ever want of a ballplayer: run, throw, steal a base, hit with all kinds of power."

The next year Post proved it, batting .309, hitting 40 home runs, scoring 116 runs, and driving in 109. Many of his homers were tape-measure jobs, a fact that added to his reputation and popularity. His slugging was tempered, however, by his many strikeouts. He fanned more than 100 times, as he did the next season, when he hit 36 homers and had 83 RBIs. In fact, Post's ratio of at bats to strikeouts was 4.92, a mark among the poorest in the game's history up to that point.

In December 1957 the Reds traded Post to the Phillies for pitcher Harvey Haddix. Two years later the Phillies returned him in a midseason deal. As a part-timer in 1961, Post produced a .585 slugging percentage, helping the Reds to their first pennant in 20 years. In Game 5 of the World Series, he connected off Yankees pitcher Bud Daley for a two-run homer. Although Cincinnati lost, Post had six hits in the Series and scored three runs.

Post had extremely limited playing time in 1963 and 1964, and he retired after playing only five games for Cleveland. He became a sales manager for the Minster Food Company in Minster, Ohio.

Pam Postema

Postema, Pam

Umpire B:1954

Pam Postema was the first woman to umpire in Triple A baseball. She called games in the Pacific Coast League, umpired some major league spring training games in 1988 and 1989, and officiated at the 1988 Hall of Fame game between the New York Yankees and the Atlanta Braves in Cooperstown. Many thought she would be promoted to the major leagues, but, despite generally high ratings as an umpire, she was released after the 1989 season. She subsequently sued the Triple A Alliance and the National and American Leagues.

Postema grew up on a farm in Willard, Ohio, where she played third base for a local team. In 1976 she applied to the Al Somers Umpiring School in Florida but was turned down because the school didn't have "proper facilities" for women. Postema wrote back, "I have strong kidneys. I don't have to go to the bathroom." Later she visited Somers personally and asked him to reconsider; Somers and partner Harry Wendlestedt relented.

Despite graduating with a high ranking, Postema was not offered a position in professional baseball immediately. Instead she umpired for schools and in semipro leagues until she was hired to work in the Gulf Coast Rookie League in 1977. Five years earlier Bernice Gera had become the first professional woman umpire, but she quit after one game because of abuse.

Postema worked her way up through Class A and AA baseball to the Pacific Coast League. Known for calling a consistent game behind the plate and for exercising tight control, she ejected many players and managers from games and once became so exasperated by the antics of the "Phillie Phanatic" mascot that she threatened to throw him out of a game.

Postema polarized many people's attitudes about the women's movement, and she was released with little explanation. When her suit against the two major leagues was settled, she went on to write a book about her experiences. Published in 1992, it is entitled, *You've Got to Have Balls to Make It in This League.*

Nels Potter

Potter, Nelson Thomas **P**

1936, 1938–41, 1943–49 B:8/23/1911 Mt. Morris, IL D:9/30/1990, Mt. Morris, IL Deb:4/25/1936, STL NL BL/TR 5'11", 180

W	L	PCT	G	SV	IP	BB	SO	ERA
92	97	.487	349	22	1686	582	747	3.99

Nels Potter was an ordinary pitcher who helped lead a downtrodden franchise to previously inconceivable heights: Potter pitched the St. Louis Browns into the World Series. Granted, it was in the middle of World War II, and the crosstown Cardinals ultimately defeated the Browns in the Series, but it was the club's only pennant in 53 seasons in St. Louis.

Earlier that season, on July 20, 1944, Potter had been ejected for putting his fingers to his mouth while pitching—the first major league pitcher to be so banished. The Browns were playing the New York Yankees that day, and the fuss had started with Browns manager Luke Sewell complaining about New York pitcher Hank Borowy going to his mouth. This was an odd strategy in view of Sewell's own pitcher's tendency to do the same thing.

Borowy promptly desisted, but Potter could not break his habit. Umpire Cal Hubbard warned him twice. Finally, Hubbard told Sewell that if he had to warn Potter again, the pitcher would be out. Potter made an exaggerated licking motion and was tossed.

Potter had been around long enough to know better. After pitching one inning for St. Louis in 1936, he had returned to the majors with the Philadelphia A's in 1938. That year he went 2–12 with a 6.47 ERA, but somehow he was still in the league the next year. After more than three years with the A's, he was traded to Boston in 1941. A knee injury kept Potter out of the service during World War II, but also helped keep him out of baseball in 1942.

He returned in 1943 with the Browns and looked to be a new player. That year he went 10–5 with a 2.78 ERA, more than four point lower than it had been in his previous year. The 1944 season was the big one for Potter. He went 19–7 as the Browns went to the World Series. There he was a true hard-luck story. He made two starts and surrendered only one earned run, but six Browns errors gave him an 0–1 record.

In 1945 Potter won 15 games, but neither he nor the Browns were able to recreate the magic of their pennant season. He landed with the Boston Braves late in the 1948 season and contributed to the team's first pennant since 1914. Potter, who had won five games with a 2.33 ERA in 18 games for Boston, started Game 5 of the World Series. Pitching in front of a then World Series record crowd of 86,288 in Cleveland, Potter did not survive the fourth inning. The Braves rallied to beat the Indians, but Cleveland won the Series the next day. Potter retired after the 1949 season.

Shirley Povich

Povich, Shirley Lewis

Sportswriter B:7/15/1905, Bar Harbor, ME D:6/4/1998, Washington, DC

Shirley Povich's byline first appeared in the *Washington Post* on August 5, 1924. It last appeared on Friday, June 5, 1998, the morning after he died at the age of 92. That first report was about the Washington Senators, written in the only year they won a World Series. His last column concerned Mark McGwire, who at that point had amassed 414 home runs. "To judge McGwire a better home run hitter than Ruth at a moment when McGwire is exactly 300 home runs short of Ruth's career output is, well, a stretch," he wrote. Even at 92, not much eluded him.

Povich saw it all. He supported his opinion on Ruth with another opinion from a pitcher he covered in the 1920s. "Walter Johnson once said when asked to compare the Babe's swats with those hammer blows of Lou Gehrig and Jimmie Foxx and Hank Greenberg, 'Lemme say this, those balls Ruth hit got smaller quicker than anybody else's.'" Said *Chicago Tribune* sports columnist Jerome Holtzman, "If it hadn't been for his friend Red Smith, Shirley would have been regarded as the best sports columnist in the country."

Povich's writing earned many distinctions. He won the Grantland Rice Award and was also cited for outstanding service as a World War II correspondent with the Marines in the Pacific in 1945. But nothing could compare with the dubious distinction of appearing in the very first volume of *Who's Who in American Women* in 1958. The editors had taken a paragraph on him from another volume, *Who's Who in America*, even though it stated that he was married to Ethyl. "The next year," he laughed, "they dropped me, like they used to do in the *New York Social Register* if you had a married a stripper—the snobs." Povich was the eighth of 10 children and was named for a grandmother, Sarah, or "Shirley," as it was loosely translated into Yiddish.

Povich grew up in Bar Harbor, Maine, and in 1924 was invited by *Post* publisher Edward McLean to come to Washington where he could start two jobs. One paid $20 a week for being McLean's caddie on his personal golf course; the other paid $12 for being a copy boy at the paper. His first task was to carry the golf bag of McLean's pal, Warren G. Harding, President of the United States. Povich started as a police reporter at the *Post*, and then rose to a position as sports reporter, while studying law at Georgetown University. In 1926, at age 21, he was named sports editor, the youngest sports editor of a metropolitan daily in the nation.

From there he covered some of the most noteworthy events in American sports history. He witnessed the Jack Dempsey-Gene Tunney "long count" heavyweight championship bout in 1927. He saw Ruth's mythic "called shot" in the 1932 World Series. "He didn't really call the shot," Povich mused. "He was pointing at the pitcher, Charlie Root, for quick-pitching him, and he was calling him names."

Povich's best attribute was a pointed, even surprising prose style. When Don Larsen pitched his perfect game on October 8, 1956, Povich wrote, "The million-to-one shot came in. Hell froze over. A month of Sundays hit the calendar. Don Larsen today pitched a no-hit, no-run, no-man-reach-first game in a World Series." That was but one example of his natural elegance. When Washington Redskins owner George Preston Marshall would not sign black players, Povich took him on. One Monday he wrote, "Jim Brown, born ineligible to play for the Redskins, integrated their end zone three times yesterday."

After attending a Washington Bullets basketball game in 1996, the 91-year-old Povich wrote, "They don't shoot baskets anymore; they stuff

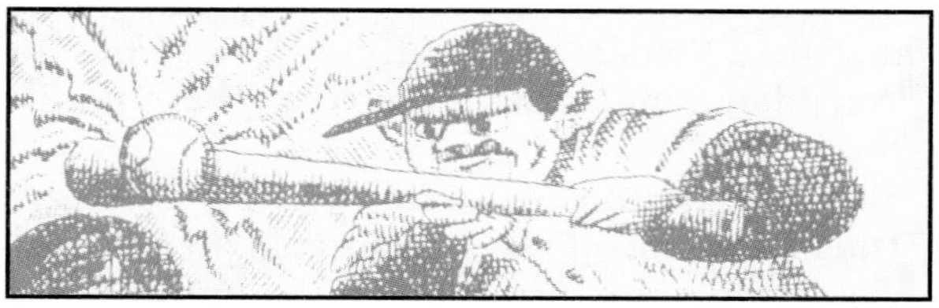

them, like taxidermists." By then, he had been "officially" retired for 23 years and one of his sons, Maury, had become a recognized journalist—albeit as a "tabloid television" personality. Shirley Povich went on writing and graced the pages of the *Post* with more than 15,000 columns over seven decades.

Boog Powell

Powell, John Wesley **1B–OF**

1961–77 B:8/17/1941, Lakeland, FL Deb:9/26/1961, BAL AL BL/TR 6'4", 240

G	AB	R	H	HR	RBI	OBP	SLG	AVG
2042	6681	889	1776	339	1187	.364	.462	.266

In a Baltimore lineup that featured righthanded sluggers Frank and Brooks Robinson, Boog Powell was just as imposing from the left side. The 6-foot 4-inch, 240-pound Powell was one of the great sluggers of the mid 1960s and early 1970s as the Orioles won four pennants and played in five Championship Series. His power hitting propelled him to American League Most Valuable Player status in 1970.

It was not his playing but his playfulness that earned Powell the nickname "Boog." Even as a child the blond-haired Powell was mischievous. His family called him "Boog," as in "What's that little bugger up to now?" using their colloquial pronunciation.

Powell joined the Orioles late in the 1961 season and became a regular outfielder the next year. It took him a little while to catch on to major league pitching. In his first year he hit only .243 with 15 home runs. The next year he increased that to .265 with 25 homers. And in 1964 he was up to .290 with 39 homers.

After a disappointing year, Powell returned to form in 1966 to help propel the Orioles to a World Series title. That year he had 34 homers and 109 RBIs. Three of the homers came in one game on August 15, all to the opposite field at Boston's Fenway Park. Earlier that season, he had tied an American League record with 11 RBIs in one game. Powell continued his performance in the World Series sweep of the Dodgers, leading the Orioles with a .357 batting average.

For four successive years, from 1968 to 1971, Powell was selected to the All-Star Game. His biggest years among those were the middle two. In 1969 he batted .304, hit 37 home runs, and drove in 121. On August 25 of that year, the slow-footed slugger even hit an inside-the-park home run against the Seattle Pilots.

When Powell won the MVP Award in 1970, he was the first AL first baseman so honored since Detroit's Hank Greenberg in 1940. Powell batted .297 with 35 homers and 114 RBIs as the Orioles went to the World Series for the third time in five years. Although Brooks Robinson stole the show with his glove, Powell homered twice and drove in five runs as the Orioles beat the Reds in five games.

In 1973 and 1974, Powell's power declined precipitously, and the Orioles traded him to Cleveland. He won Comeback Player of the Year honors in 1975 while playing for former teammate Frank Robinson, then the Indians' manager. But the following year Powell was hobbled by injuries. Released in March 1977, he signed with the Dodgers in time for the upcoming season.

Leaving baseball at the close of 1977, Powell went home to Key West, Florida, where he owned a marina. Later he reappeared in the public eye in the popular Miller Lite television commercials. When Baltimore's Oriole Park at Camden Yards opened in 1992, "Boog's Barbeque" stand on the premises became a popular attraction. The resilient and good-natured Powell later survived colon cancer.

Jack Powell

Powell, John Joseph **P**

1897–1912 B:7/9/1874, Bloomington, IL D:10/17/1944, Chicago, IL Deb:6/23/1897, CLE NL BR/TR 5'11", 195

W	L	PCT	G	SH	IP	BB	SO	ERA
245	254	.491	578	46	4389	1021	1621	2.97

Jack Powell and Bobo Newsom are the only two pitchers ever to win more than 200 games yet finish with losing records for their careers. Despite that mark, Ty Cobb considered the stocky, redheaded Powell to be one of the toughest righthanders he ever faced. Throwing a baffling spitball with an easy sidearm delivery, Powell pitched more than 300 innings in a season six times and more than 200 innings in nine others, mostly for second-division teams.

In June 1897 Powell joined the National League's Cleveland Spiders, where Cy Young was the reigning ace. The next year Powell won 23 games and tied for the NL lead with six shutouts. When the stars of the Cleveland team were transferred to St. Louis in 1899 (the same family owned both teams), Powell won 23 games for the Cardinals, while pitching a league-high 40 complete games.

In 1902 Powell jumped to the crosstown Browns of the year-old American League. He won 20 or more games for the third time. Two years later, he did it with yet another team: the New York Highlanders.

Powell preferred living in St. Louis, where he, his brother-in-law, and former batterymate Jack O'Connor ran a saloon. In mid-1905 he returned to the Browns, where he pitched for the next seven years. The Browns were such a weak team at that point that he went 13–14 in 1906 despite having a 1.77 ERA, and 7–11 four years later despite a 2.30 ERA. Overall, Powell had a 117–143 record in a decade with the Browns; in that time his ERA never rose above 3.30 in a season.

Vic Power

Power, Victor Pellot **1B-2B-3B-OF**
1954–65 B:11/1/1927, Arecibo, Puerto Rico
Deb:4/13/1954, PHI AL BR/TR 5'11", 195

G	AB	R	H	HR	RBI	OBP	SLG	AVG
1627	6046	765	1716	126	658	.317	.411	.284

Vic Power was one of the game's greatest fielding first basemen, as proven by his seven consecutive Gold Gloves. But his success was more than the Gold Gloves. The man had style with a capital "S." Until he came along there was an unwritten rule about fielding: catch the ball with two hands. Power's legacy to baseball is the one-handed catch.

Born Victor Pellot, Power originally wanted to be an artist. His ambitions changed at age 13, when his father died from tetanus after an industrial accident. He decided to be a lawyer so he could bring suit against his father's former employers. But in 1947 he dropped that idea and signed with Caguas of the Puerto Rican Winter League for $250 per month. The next winter his salary doubled, and he was able to afford a house in San Juan for his family.

In 1949 former Negro Leagues catcher Quincy Trouppe brought Power to Canada to play with Drummondville in Quebec's outlaw Provincial League, a circuit that featured many of the former Mexican League jumpers. He hit .341. In 1950 the Provincial League joined Organized Baseball, and Power batted .334, with 105 RBIs.

In Drummondville, he became Power. Pellot had unfortunate sexual connotations in French, so he took his mother's maiden name. Yankees scout Tom Greenwade, who had signed Mickey Mantle, traveled north to check out Power. While Greenwade watched, Power committed an error, and Greenwade reported that he was a poor fielder. However, the scout liked him as a hitter, and the Yankees paid $7,500 for him. When Power learned of the sale, he demanded a cut and received $500.

Power reached the high minors quickly. In 1951 he was sent to Syracuse, where he batted .291. With Kansas City in 1952 he batted .331 and led the Triple-A American Association with 40 doubles and 17 triples. Rumors circulated widely that Power would become the first black Yankee.

The Yankees, however, wanted a more tractable black man than Power, who was simply mystified by American racial mores and was forever either challenging them or running afoul of them. Once in spring training with the Yankees, the team bus passed through Georgia and halted for a rest room stop. "They called the sheriff," Power recalled. "He arrested me, and only after the Yankees begged him did he agree to a $500 bond. I never went back for the trial and I guess they're still looking for me.

"But things like that were always happening. I wasn't allowed to go to the white hotel. I stayed in the best house in the colored section, and that was usually a funeral parlor. I slept with dead people at night. Or let's say I tried to sleep. I was too scared most of the time. Puerto Ricans are a very superstitious people. Yet the worst thing about all this was that I had to compete with well-rested guys. Maybe that's why I didn't make the Yankees."

In Kansas City, Power compounded the Yankees' displeasure by keeping company with white women, hardly the image George Weiss, the conservative general manager of the Yankees, wished to project. He kept Power at Kansas City again in 1953, and the first baseman led the American Association with 217 hits, for a .349 average. At season's end, Power was finally placed on New York's 40-man roster.

Now it seemed certain that Power would finally make the Yankees. It was not to be. In December 1953, he was part of an 11-man trade with the Philadelphia Athletics. The first black Yankee turned out to be Power's Kansas City roommate, Elston Howard.

Power soon established himself as the slickest first baseman in baseball. He won a Gold Glove in each of the first seven years it was awarded to a first baseman. One statistic is telling: he led American League first basemen in assists six times, even though he was righthanded at a position that gives a lefty a huge edge.

It wasn't just that he was competent or even brilliant. He was flashy, and although he hated to hear it, he was a showboat—and probably the best-fielding first baseman between Hal Chase and Keith Hernandez. In an age when fielders were cautioned to make all catches with both hands, Power flagrantly used only one—and used it better than anyone else used two. "If the guy who invented the game wanted players to catch with two hands, he'd have put two gloves on 'em," he said. And when Power said it, somehow it made sense.

Power was also a good hitter. In 1955, the A's first year in Kansas City, he hit .319 with 34 doubles, 19 homers, and 91 runs. Three out of his four years in Kansas City he topped the .300 mark.

In June 1958 the Athletics traded Power and Woodie Held to Cleveland for Roger Maris and two other players. For the year he hit .312 with 37 doubles and an AL-leading 10 triples. With the Indians that year he stole home twice in one game. In the eighth inning he did it to tie the score. In the ninth he did it once more to win the game.

In April 1962 Power was traded to Minnesota, where he took young Tony Oliva under his wing. Oliva was impressionable; once, Power told him that Ted Williams credited shoveling snow for his great hitting ability. All winter Oliva kept busy shoveling out Power's sidewalk and driveway.

By 1964 Power's career was winding down, and in June he was sent to the Angels in a three-way trade involving Cleveland. Power amused himself singing Spanish songs with owner Gene Autry and indulging in less innocent amusements elsewhere. The Angels sold Power to the Philadelphia Phillies in September 1964, as Gene Mauch's club desperately tried to shore up its defense and win a pennant.

Power was sold back to the Angels in November. At season's end he had a chance to play in Japan but turned it down, thinking he would pursue a career in acting. His only role was as a bit player in a western. Power retired after the 1965 season and returned to Puerto Rico in 1967, where he managed an amateur team and ran instructional clinics for children. He also secured a government position involving sports and scouted for the Angels.

Del Pratt

Pratt, Derrill Burnham **2B**

1912–24 B:1/10/1888, Walhalla, SC D:9/30/1977, Texas City, TX Deb:4/11/1912, STL AL BR/TR 5'11", 175

G	AB	R	H	HR	RBI	OBP	SLG	AVG
1836	6826	856	1996	43	968	.345	.403	.292

Del Pratt spent most of his career playing second base for second-division clubs. Although considered a step below contemporary Eddie Collins at his position, Pratt hit for a high average, was a consistent run producer, stole 20 or more bases six times, and played in at least 100 games during every one of his 13 seasons. Defensively, he led American League second basemen in putouts five times.

Pratt came up with the St. Louis Browns in 1912 and made an impact immediately, hitting .302 as a rookie. Over the next few years his average slowly declined. That didn't stop him from leading the American League with 103 RBIs in 1916. The Browns were consistent losers in those years, but when owner Phil Ball accused them publicly of not putting forth their best efforts, Pratt and another player sued. They settled out of court, and in 1918 Pratt was traded to the Yankees for pitcher Urban Shocker.

In New York Pratt turned his batting around, going from .275 to .292 to .314 in his three years there. However, he fought with club management over the distribution of third-place money, so the Yankees traded him to Boston, where he was assured of seeing no first-division money at all. He did, however, prove his quality in Boston, hitting .324 in 1921, with 102 RBIs.

He followed that with three more years—the last two in Detroit—with batting averages above .300. He was only four hits shy of 2,000 when he retired.

Jerry Priddy

Priddy, Gerald Edward **2B**

1941–43, 1946–53 B:11/9/1919, Los Angeles, CA D:3/3/1980, North Hollywood, CA Deb:4/17/1941, NY AL BR/TR 5'11½", 180

G	AB	R	H	HR	RBI	OBP	SLG	AVG
1296	4720	612	1252	61	541	.353	.373	.265

Jerry Priddy and Phil Rizzuto came to New York in 1941 as a highly touted double-play combo that was supposed to fill the middle infield for the Yankees for years to come. Rizzuto lived up to his billing, but Priddy spent his 11-year career with four different teams, never really quite fulfilling the expectations of him.

The slick-fielding Priddy moved up quickly through the Yankees' farm system. In 1939, his third season in the minors, he was already in Triple A with the Kansas City Blues. He hit .333 with 24 homers and 107 RBIs, while leading the American Association in putouts and assists. The next year Priddy drove in 116 runs and batted .306, while Rizzuto hit .347 and was named *The Sporting News* Minor League Player of the Year.

Both performances earned them a shot with the Yankees, and Priddy and Rizzuto started 1941 as New York's middle infield. But neither began the season well, and both were benched by Yankees manager Joe McCarthy. Rizzuto ultimately straightened out and hit .307. Priddy, however, played only 56 games, hitting .213. He made things worse by alienating McCarthy, who had been his strong supporter when the season started. He was convinced the big leagues needed him and acted accordingly.

Priddy hit .280 in 59 games in 1942, but the Yankees decided he wasn't necessary, and they traded him to Washington. Apart from his personality, The Yankees realized that Priddy he was married with no children, and thus likely to be drafted. The 1943 Senators finished second, and Priddy made the most of his chance to play every day, hitting .271. But the Yankees were right: Priddy was drafted and spent the next two years playing service ball in Hawaii.

After he was discharged in January 1945, Priddy soon alienated Senators manager Ossie Bluege. When Priddy's average slipped to .214 in 1947, he was sent packing, sold for $25,000 to the St. Louis Browns. He had two of his best seasons with the Browns. In 1948 he hit .296, with a career-high 79 RBIs, and he led American League second basemen in putouts, assists, and double plays. He hit .290 in 1949, but the impoverished Browns sent him to Detroit after the season for $100,000 and journeyman pitcher Lou Kretlow.

Priddy had two solid seasons with the Tigers, leading the league in assists and double plays in both 1950 and 1951. His 150 double plays in 1950 were a 20th century AL record. But in 1952 he broke his leg sliding into second base, and a year later he was out of the majors.

Priddy subsequently managed in the minors, and then went on the PGA tour, sponsored by a wealthy manufacturer. Priddy's winnings on the golf course were few and far between, however. His best tournament finish was seven strokes off the lead in the 1960 Western Open. It netted him $230.

In 1973 Priddy was arrested during the U.S. Open at Pebble Beach. Charged with extortion, he was accused of phoning a steamship company and demanding $25,000 to keep a bomb from being set off aboard a cruise ship in the Pacific. Priddy was found guilty and received a nine-month sentence. He died in 1980 after suffering a heart attack at his North Hollywood home.

Bob Prince

Broadcaster B:1917, Los Angeles, CA D:6/10/1985, Pittsburgh, PA

Unlike many of his contemporaries, Bob Prince did not have a mellifluous voice. All he had was a rolling rasp, a home run call, and an unflagging passion for his work, which just happened to be calling the games of the Pittsburgh Pirates.

A native of Los Angeles, Prince began his broadcasting career in 1941 and joined the Pirates' booth in 1948. He had a tough act to follow—his predecessor, Rosey Rosewell, was a local institution who greeted every Pirates homer with "Hurry up, Aunt Minnie, raise the window," or "Open the window, Aunt Minnie, here it comes." At Forbes Field, or in the studio where Rosewell would re-create road games, the signature call was always accompanied by the sound effect of glass being shattered.

As Rosewell's successor, Prince proved even more idiosyncratic. He would eat an apple and read a book while calling a game. He would talk of dinners he had with Perry Como or Bing Crosby, and when he was through with these stories he'd recap: "Groat just grounded to short, Clemente and Stargell flew out; three outs." His audience loved it.

Prince could also get away with unrestrained rooting for the home team. If the Bucs were down a run in the ninth, he'd say, "All we need is a bloop and a blast." If the Pirates got the blast you were treated to a spirited rat-a-tat-tat: "Stargell swings and hits it deep to right, back-back-back-back, you can kiss it goodbye, over the roof, home run!" Such rapid fire commentary earned Prince his nickname, "The Gunner."

His tags for Pittsburgh players were equally colorful. Roberto Clemente was dubbed "Arriba" or "The Great One"; Bill Virdon was "The Quail"; Dave Parker, "The Cobra," and Willie Stargell "Willie The Starge."

Prince called the Pirates through their 1960 World Series dream win over the Yankees and their 1971 comeback against Baltimore. In 1951 he was in the booth and the guest of Russ Hodges on the day Bobby Thomson hit his "Shot Heard 'Round the World." After the blast, Hodges dashed to the locker room, located beyond the center field fence at the Polo Grounds. He threw the mike to Prince and asked him to take over. Prince uttered what would be his signature: "We had 'em all the way!"

Bob Costas once described Prince as "quirky, provincial and irreplaceable." But he was much more that that, as his firing in 1975 proved. Prince balked when Edward Wallis, regional vice president of Westinghouse Broadcasting started to give orders about how Prince should broadcast and who he should allow into his booth—namely Westinghouse guests and clients, who sauntered in and out during broadcasts and could often be heard rooting against Pittsburgh in the middle of Prince's narrative.

When the firing came, thousands of Pirates' fans marched on the downtown headquarters of Westinghouse. After the smoke had cleared the Pirates had a new voice in Milo Hamilton, who in 1974 had called Hank Aaron's 715th homer in Atlanta.

Price joined ABC for its launch of *Monday Night Baseball*. The combination of Warner Wolf, Bob Uecker, and Prince in one booth was destined to fail. With "network guys" talking in his ear, telling him to keep up the chatter, fearful of even a moment dead air, Prince was in shackles.

The Pirates decided to have Prince rejoin their radio team KDKA in 1985. He fought back tears in a press conference: "This is a very emotional

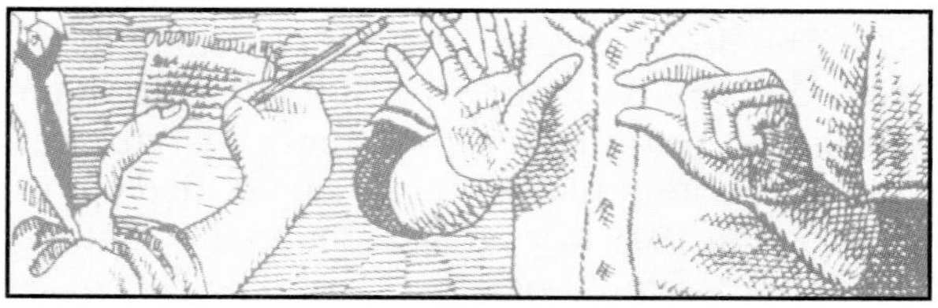

thing for me," he said. "I'm just delighted to be returning. Other than my family, you're giving me back the only thing I love in the world." But the sweet homecoming was undercut by Prince's declining health.

Doctors removed cancerous growths from his mouth in April. He was out of the hospital by early May, but he called only three games, becoming ill during a lengthy rain delay. He was readmitted to the hospital, this time for hydration and pneumonia in both lungs, and doctors decided to stop his radiation treatments. He died shortly thereafter. Pirates general manager Joe L. Brown proclaimed, "To many he was more than just the Voice of the Pirates; he was the Pirates. There is no doubt that he was one of the great sports announcers of all time."

In 1986 Prince received the Ford Frick Award from the Baseball Hall of Fame. Prince, who served as an announcer longer than anyone in club history, received the "Pride of the Pirates" Award, and was honored before Opening Day 1999.

Hub Pruett

Pruett, Hubert Shelby **P**

1922–24, 1927–28, 1930, 1932 B:9/1/1900, Malden, MO D:1/28/1982, Ladue, MO Deb:4/26/1922, STL AL BL/TL 5'10½", 165

W	L	PCT	G	SV	IP	BB	SO	ERA
29	48	.377	211	13	745	396	357	4.63

Lefthander Hub Pruett really had extraordinary success against just one batter—but that batter happened to Babe Ruth. Pruett, a medical student in the off-season, first faced Ruth as a rookie with the St. Louis Browns in May 1922. In two plate appearances, Ruth struck out and walked. Then in a June relief assignment Pruett fanned Ruth again. Two days later he started against the Yankees and struck out Ruth three more times, while also issuing another walk.

In a July game Ruth tapped back to Pruett, then struck out three straight times (the last with the bases full). By August, word was starting to get around. When the Yankees loaded the bases in one game and Ruth was coming to the plate, Pruett sauntered in from the bullpen. He struck Ruth out once more.

In his first 12 plate appearances Ruth struck out nine times against Pruett—and hit the ball exactly once. The secret to Pruett's success was a screwball used effectively on the inside part of the plate.

That first year was the highlight of Pruett's career. Used mostly as a reliever, he went 7–7 with a 2.33 ERA. But he was never so effective again. His ERA increased by two points the next year, and then went up from there.

After three years with the Browns, Pruett became a starter for one year with the Philadelphia Phillies. He was rocked regularly and often, finishing 7–17 with a 6.05 ERA. He finished his career in 1932, having pitched one year each with the New York Giants and the Boston Braves.

Despite their early meetings, Pruett and Ruth never really got acquainted until just before Ruth's death in 1948. "I want to thank you for putting me through med school. If it wasn't for you, no one would have heard of me," said Pruett.

Kirby Puckett

Puckett, Kirby **OF**

1984–95 B:3/14/1961, Chicago, IL Deb:5/8/1984, MIN AL BR/TR 5'8", 210

G	AB	R	H	HR	RBI	OBP	SLG	AVG
1783	7244	1071	2304	207	1085	.363	.477	.318

Kirby Puckett did not possess the prototypical athletic build of other superstars, but it did not prevent him from becoming one of the game's most popular players. He was loved in Minnesota and was considered baseball's goodwill ambassador everywhere else. He had played in 10 straight All-Star Games and seemed on his way to 3,000 hits when glaucoma abruptly ended his career.

Built like a fire plug, the 5-foot 8-inch, 210-pound Puckett made the unusual jump from Class A to the major leagues in 1984. He collected four hits in his debut with the Twins and became a fixture in the Minnesota lineup. He batted .296 as a rookie, but hit no home runs. When he clubbed only four home runs in 1985, the Twins questioned whether the squatty-bodied outfielder would ever hit with power.

Their fears came to an end the next season, when Puckett worked with former batting champion Tony Oliva and started kicking his left leg as part of his approach at the plate. The leg kick helped transform Puckett's offensive game. He powered 31 home runs while lifting his batting average 40 points. Puckett was an All-Star for the first time.

Some critics of Puckett felt he needed to shed a few pounds from his unusual frame, but the young star maintained his playing weight. In 1987 Puckett led the league in hits, continued to hit with power, and pushed Minnesota to the American League pennant. He batted .357 and scored five runs in the World Series, spearheading the Twins to the first world championship in franchise history.

Puckett led the AL again in hits each of the next two seasons, becoming only the third player after Ty Cobb and Oliva to lead the American League in hits for three straight years. Puckett also led the league in hitting with a .339 mark in 1989, becoming the first righthanded batter to lead the AL in batting over a full season since 1970. (Righthanded-swinging Carney Lansford led the league in hitting in strike-shortened 1981.) Puckett, an accomplished defensive center fielder, earned the first of his six Gold Glove awards in 1988.

In 1991 Puckett topped .300 for the fifth time in six years. He also helped the Twins return to postseason play. Puckett batted .429 against Toronto to win the Championship Series MVP Award. In Game 6 of the World Series Puckett made a game-saving catch against Ron Gant and then rocked a game-winning home run against Charlie Leibrandt in the 11th inning, setting the stage for the Twins' second world championship in five years.

Puckett became eligible for free agency after the 1992 season, but turned down the possibility of more lucrative offers from other clubs to remain in Minnesota, where he had become an icon. Jovial and always smiling, Puckett was constantly involved in numerous area charities. Even with the Twins slipping in the standings, Puckett remained a national figure; his home run and double earned All-Star MVP honors in 1993.

In 1994 Puckett switched to right field in an effort to save wear and tear on his legs. The move rejuvenated Puckett's bat. He drove in a league-leading 112 runs in only 108 games during the strike-shortened season. That year Puckett received the Branch Rickey Award in honor of his extensive community service.

Puckett was batting .314 and looking for his 100th RBI of the season when he faced Cleveland's Dennis Martinez on September 28, 1995. Puckett was hit on the left side of the face, causing a broken jaw and a deep cut inside his mouth. It turned out to be his final plate appearance in the major leagues.

He was diagnosed with glaucoma the following spring. The disease, unrelated to the errant pitch that ended his 1995 season, caused irreversible damage to the vision in his right eye and forced him to retire. Always concerned with others first, Puckett singled out the dour Martinez at his retirement press conference. "I just want to say I love you," he said. "He didn't do it on purpose. I was hanging out over the plate cheating."

As his teammates sat in the audience close to tears, Puckett told them, "Don't take it for granted. Tomorrow is not promised to any of us, so enjoy yourself."

Puckett enjoyed himself every day he took the baseball diamond. His departure left the game without its most congenial superstar. In 1997 Puckett became only the fifth player in franchise history to have his uniform number retired, joining Oliva, former teammate Kent Hrbek, and Hall of Famers Rod Carew and Harmon Killebrew.

Terry Puhl

Puhl, Terry Stephen **OF**

1977–91 B:7/8/1956, Melville, Saskatchewan, Canada
Deb:7/12/1977, HOU NL BL/TR 6'2", 200

G	AB	R	H	HR	RBI	OBP	SLG	AVG
1531	4855	676	1361	62	435	.351	.388	.280

Terry Puhl was proof that being solid and dependable can keep a player in the major leagues for a long time. Not a star to the public, Puhl nevertheless retired with the major league fielding record for outfielders with a career .9932 average. In 15 years he committed only 18 errors.

A native of Saskatchewan, Puhl started playing "Mosquito League" baseball when he was 6 years old, but he also enjoyed such other Canadian pastimes as curling, tobogganing, and hockey. "Starting in September, guys can barely wait to put their baseball gear away and put on skates," Puhl said. "They're all ready for hockey. It just isn't possible to play baseball around our town except from June until the end of August. There isn't any place to do any hitting, even if you love baseball. That's why when Canadians make it in professional baseball, they are usually pitchers. The short season doesn't affect a pitcher as much as a hitter."

Puhl started attending tryout camps at age 15, and Cincinnati showed some interest in signing him as a pitcher. Puhl eventually signed as an outfielder with the Astros in September 1973. The club sent him to Covington of the Appalachian League in 1974, beginning a minor league career that took him to Dubuque, Memphis, Charleston, and Columbus, Georgia.

In July 1977 Puhl finally made it to Houston. He immediately impressed with his superb batting eye, putting together a 17-game hitting streak and batting .301 for the half-season. The next year he was in the regular lineup from the start, and his .289 batting average, 32 stolen bases, and excellent overall play resulted in his selection to the All-Star Game, the only time of his career.

In 1979 Puhl hit .287, stole 30 bases, and played 152 games in right field without committing one error. His fielding was a sign of things to come. In the field he never had more than three errors in a season, and when he dropped a liner in 1984, everybody noticed. It was only the second flyball he had muffed in seven years.

Puhl was a classic streak hitter. One of the highlights of his career was the 1980 National League

Championship Series against Philadelphia. The Astros lost in five games, but Puhl led all regulars in the series with 10 hits and a .526 batting average. Houston, however, lost in five games.

His career began to decline in 1985 after he suffered a severe hamstring injury. An ankle injury the next spring further limited his mobility. Nevertheless, he continued to perform well for the Astros, recording a career-high .303 batting average in 1988.

After spending his entire professional career with the Astros, Puhl was cut loose following a 1990 season spent mostly on the disabled list. He signed as a free agent with the Mets for the next year and was cut in spring training. He then hooked up with Kansas City for 15 games before retiring.

Harry Pulliam

Pulliam, Harry C.

NL President (1903–09) B:1869, Kentucky D:7/25/1909, New York, NY

The National League helped kill Harry Pulliam. A quiet, nervous bachelor who lived in a room at the New York Athletic Club, Pulliam was described by writer Francis Richter as "a dreamer, a lover of solitude and nature, of books, of poetry, of music, and flowers." He was earnest and sincere, but, as NL president, he lacked the psychological armor to deal with either the ruthless, venal team owners or a pushy, critical press.

Pulliam received a law degree from the University of Virginia and then moved to Louisville to enter the newspaper business. Barney Dreyfuss, who owned the Louisville Colonels franchise in the National League, convinced Pulliam to join the team as road secretary. When Dreyfuss sold his Louisville franchise back to the league and took over the Pittsburgh Pirates in 1900, Pulliam went with him. His reputation for honesty and hard work led to his election as National League president in 1903.

Somewhat ominously, Pulliam was a compromise candidate from the start. The league was bitterly split over the presidency; half of the owners backed Albert G. Spalding and the other half supported New York Giants owner Andrew Freedman. From the moment he took office, Pulliam was sniped at from both sides. Adding to his problems, during his first four years he was also league secretary and treasurer.

After 1903 baseball was ruled by the National Commission: the presidents of the two leagues and a third owner who served as chairman. Ban Johnson controlled the American League with an iron fist, but Pulliam's National League was pulled in as many directions as there were owners. Moreover, Cincinnati's Garry Herrmann, the chairman of the commission, usually sided with his friend Johnson. Whenever a vote went against the National League, the owners criticized Pulliam for his perceived weakness.

In 1907 he turned over the positions of secretary and treasurer to John Heydler, but the pressures on Pulliam eased only temporarily. The following year he had the final say in what is arguably the most controversial game in league history.

On September 23, 1908, the Cubs and Giants were locked in a 1–1 tie at the Polo Grounds in the bottom of the ninth inning. With runners on first and third and two out, Al Bridwell's single appeared to drive in the winning run for the Giants. Running from first, Merkle headed for the Giants' clubhouse in center field—he never touched second. Cubs second baseman Johnny Evers produced a ball and argued that Merkle should be out on a force play. Umpire Hank O'Day, working behind home plate, had been involved in an argument with Evers over a similar play in Pittsburgh three weeks earlier. He had let that play stand; this time he called the runner out. With pandemonium on the field, the game could not be resumed that day.

The decision fell in Pulliam's lap and he backed the umpires. Because of "Merkle's Boner," the game was replayed after the Cubs and Giants ended the season in a tie. Chicago won the game and the pennant.

Pulliam's decision earned him vicious criticism from John McGraw and Giants owner John T. Brush. A ticket-scalping controversy brought him into conflict with Chicago owner Charles W. Murphy. Other powerful owners, including Herrmann and even Dreyfuss, weighed in against him in one dispute or another. Pulliam took it all to heart and believed that the league's future was entirely his responsibility. In February 1909 he suffered a nervous breakdown at a banquet for National League owners.

After a leave of absence, he returned to work in June, apparently in better spirits. On July 25, 1909, he rose from the dinner table at the New York Athletic Club, went up to his room, and killed himself with a revolver.

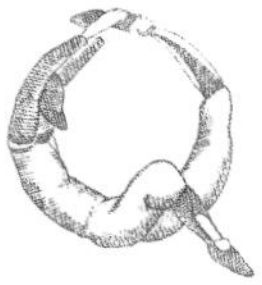

Joe Quinn

Quinn, Joseph J. **2B-1B-SS**

1884–86, 1888–1901 M (1895, 1899 23–132)
B:12/25/1864, Sydney, Australia D:11/12/1940,
St. Louis, MO Deb:4/26/1884, STL UA BR/TR 5'7", 158

G	AB	R	H	HR	RBI	OBP	SLG	AVG
1768	6879	891	1797	29	794	.302	.327	.261

Joe Quinn was much traveled in more ways than one. He was baseball's first Australian-born player, and, until Craig Shipley in 1986, its only player from that continent. He also played for nine teams in four major leagues in 17 years. Quinn got his start with the ill-fated Union Association of 1884, and, being a fine fielding second baseman, was one of the few players to go from that lackluster circuit to a successful career. He led the league in fielding percentage three times and appeared in World Series competition in 1892 and 1896.

Quinn also gained a reputation because, while visiting the offices of *The Sporting News* in September 1889, he spilled the beans regarding the plan to form the Players' League in 1890. In 1895 Quinn managed St. Louis for part of the season, and in 1899 he presided for most of the season over the Cleveland Spiders, a team that he led to a won-lost percentage of .103. In off-seasons Quinn served as an undertaker.

Jack Quinn

Quinn, John Picus **P**

1909–15, 1918–33 B:7/5/1883, Janesville, PA
D:4/17/1946 Pottsville, PA Deb:4/15/1909, NY AL
BR/TR 6', 196

W	L	PCT	G	SV	IP	BB	SO	ERA
247	218	.531	756	57	3920[1]	860	1329	3.29

Age did not seem to be a hindrance for Jack Quinn. At 48 and 49—in 1931 and again in 1932—he led the National League in saves, with 15 and eight, respectively. That latter year made him the oldest player ever to lead a league in a major statistic. And he also still holds the record as the oldest man ever—at 49—to win a major league game.

Originally John Quinn Picus, he rearranged his name to John Picus Quinn, but should not be confused with contemporary John "Pick" Quinn, a catcher who appeared in only one major league game, for the Phillies in 1911.

Quinn was promoted to the New York Highlanders in 1909 after finishing 1908 with a 14–0 record in Richmond. He both started and pitched out of the bullpen for New York, as he would do with nine different clubs in three major leagues during his 23-year career. On September 15, 1913, while with the Boston Braves, Quinn stole home. The next year he jumped to Baltimore of the new Federal League and had his best season: Quinn went 26–14 with a 2.60 ERA.

After two years out of the majors, Quinn joined the Chicago White Sox late in the 1918 season, before returning the next year to New York. In 1921 he had his first World Series appearance, taking a loss for the Yankees in the third game. When he returned to the World Series with the Philadelphia Athletics in 1929, his pitching was off again, although the Athletics were able to wipe out an eight-run deficit with 10 in the seventh to win, 10–8.

Quinn claimed his place in the baseball record books in his last decade in the major leagues, when he broke a number of age records. On June 27, 1930, at age 46, he became the oldest player to hit a homer. At 47 he became the oldest man ever to finish a World Series game. Until Phil Niekro arrived, Quinn held the major league record for most wins achieved after the age of 40, with a 109–97 mark.

Jamie Quirk

Quirk, James Patrick **C-3B-DH-OF**

1975–92 B:10/22/1954,Whittier, CA Deb:9/4/1975, KC AL BL/TR 6'4", 200

G	AB	R	H	HR	RBI	OBP	SLG	AVG
984	2266	193	544	43	247	.300	.347	.240

Considering he never really made it as a day-to-day player, Jamie Quirk played a remarkable 18 years in the majors, serving as a utility man primarily for Kansas City and Oakland. In high school Quirk excelled in both football and baseball. As a senior, he batted .410, but he also signed a letter of intent to play football for Notre Dame. Baseball won out when the Kansas City Royals selected him in the first round (18th choice overall) of the June 1972 draft. He started out as a shortstop in the minors with Billings, San Jose, Jacksonville, and Omaha.

Quirk reached the majors in 1975 and served as a utility man for the Royals. His first appearance was as a pinch hitter for George Brett. On September 20, 1975, as a pinch hitter, he hit his first homer, off Rollie Fingers. The Royals traded Quirk to the Milwaukee Brewers in December 1976. But he was traded back to

Kansas City in 1978 and was converted to catcher. The next year he hit a career-high .304. However, his batting average dropped each of the next four years.

Quirk had a turbulent year in 1984. In the preseason, St. Louis released him as a player and then named him as a coach. However, he returned to the playing ranks with the White Sox in May. In September Chicago sold him to Cleveland, but the Indians released him in October. In all of that time, he had played in only four games and had only three at bats, although his only hit was a home run.

In 1985 the Royals re-signed him, and he played there four more years despite fielding problems that saw him lead the American League with 31 passed balls in 1986. Yet Quirk was very effective at throwing out runners.

As a free agent in 1989 he had brief periods of play with the Yankees, the A's, and the Orioles. In 1990 he rejoined the A's and hit a solid .281. He remained with the A's until 1992, when he retired with a career .240 average. Quirk became a coach with the Royals in 1994.

Dan Quisenberry

Quisenberry, Daniel Raymond **P**

1979–90 B:2/7/1953, Santa Monica, CA D:9/30/98, Leawood, KS Deb:7/8/1979, KC AL BR/TR 6'2", 180

W	L	PCT	G	SV	IP	BB	SO	ERA
56	46	.549	674	244	1043^{1}	162	379	2.76

For a stretch of six years in the 1980s Dan Quisenberry was the best relief pitcher in the American League, leading the league in saves five times and in appearances three times. In that period "Quiz" was selected for three All-Star Games and helped the Kansas City Royals to four playoff appearances and a pair of World Series.

Not a closer in the traditional sense, Quisenberry was a submariner who did not have the stuff to overpower hitters. Instead, he relied on his sinker and got hitters to put the ball on the ground, then relied on his fielders to do the rest. He was kidded about his unorthodox delivery, and the fact that he needed flawless, if not spectacular, defense behind him. But for years the formula worked. Quisenberry possessed impeccable control, walking only 162 batters in his career, or less than one every four appearances.

Quisenberry broke into the majors in 1979, at the age of 26. He made 32 relief appearances as a rookie, going 3–2 with five saves. The next year he became the Royals' closer, saving a league-high 33 games. In his first World Series, Quisenberry went only 1–2 with a save, blowing leads in Games 2 and 5; Del Unser reaching him for key doubles both times. After the final game, a reporter asked, "What do you plan to do now that the Series is over?" Quisenberry replied, "I'm looking forward to putting on my glasses with the fake nose so I can walk around and be a normal person."

That was a normal comment for a man who was a regular at banquets, not only because he received many awards, but also because he could entertain an audience with clean, sly humor. He poked fun at himself, others, or anything else in the world, including baseball. Once, when mentioned in the same sentence as hard-throwing reliever Goose Gossage, Quisenberry said, "I don't feel comfortable being compared to a guy who throws harder than God."

Quisenberry led the league in saves from 1982 to 1985. His catcher during the glory years, John Wathan, was once asked why the Royals closer never wore down. His reply: "There's nobody there to get tired. It'd be like asking a broom if it was getting tired."

By late 1985, however, a little mystery had gone out of Quisenberry's pitches. At least Royals manager Dick Howser must have thought in Game 2 of the 1985 World Series against the St. Louis Cardinals. With Kansas City down by a game and trying to hold a two-run lead in the ninth inning, Howser stayed with starter Charlie Leibrandt as St. Louis scored a run and then loaded the bases. With Quisenberry in the bullpen and Leibrandt obviously tiring, Terry Pendleton hit a soft liner down the third-base line for a three-run double. Howser then brought in "Quiz," who recorded the final out of the inning, but the damage was done. Things turned out right for the Royals, however, as they won the Series in seven games, with Quisenberry picking up a win in Game 6.

However, he collected only 21 more saves with the Royals, and was let go during the 1988 season. St. Louis picked him up, and, although he went 2–0 for the Cards, he had a 6.16 ERA and no saves. Quiz turned in one more solid year, in 1989, although not in a closer's role.

Quisenberry retired after the 1990 season. He died in 1998 of a brain tumor at age 45.

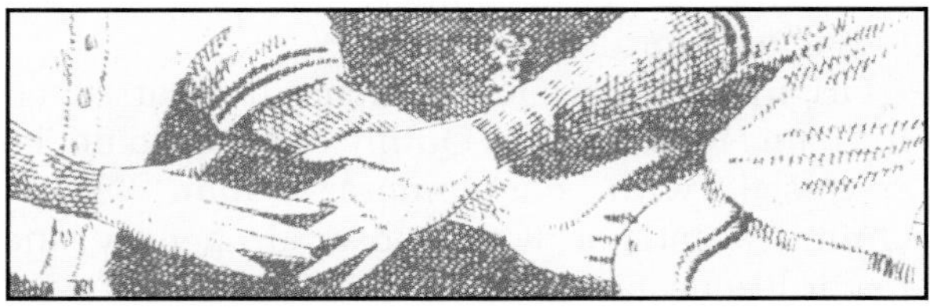

Dick Radatz

Radatz, Richard Raymond **P**

1962–67, 1969 B:4/2/1937, Detroit, MI Deb:4/10/1962, BOS AL BR/TR 6'5", 235

W	L	PCT	G	SV	IP	BB	SO	ERA
52	43	.547	381	122	693^{2}	296	745	3.13

Dick Radatz certainly was a horrifying sight for American League batters in the 1960s. At 6 feet 5 inches and 235 pounds "The Monster" led the league in saves in both 1962 and 1964, helping to create a new fashion in hulking, hard-throwing relief pitching. Radatz could not only throw hard, but he combined his fastball with a varied assortment of junk pitches. It was an effective mix, and in the 1963 All-Star Game he struck out five of the six batters he faced. In the following year's All-Star Game, however, Johnny Callison tagged him for the game-winning homer.

Signed by Boston in 1959, Radatz was groomed as a reliever at such stops as Raleigh, Minneapolis, and Seattle. With Raleigh in 1960 he struck out 133 in just 107 innings.

His best years with the Red Sox were 1963 and 1964. During that span he won 31 games and saved 54.

In the mid 1960s Radatz developed control problems and even consulted a hypnotist for help. In 1966 the Red Sox traded a declining Radatz to Cleveland for pitchers Don McMahon and Lee Stange. "That city [Boston] meant everything to me," said Radatz, "For years I couldn't understand why I was traded or get over the pain of it." Radatz was ineffective for the Indians and was sold to the Cubs, who sent him to Tacoma. After posting a 9.00 ERA, Radatz received his outright release in March 1968. He spent 1968 with the Toledo Mud Hens in the Detroit organization, not returning to the major leagues until 1969 when he split the season with Tigers and expansion Expos, the Tigers moving him to Montreal for cash. "I just went through the motions with the other clubs," Radatz confessed.

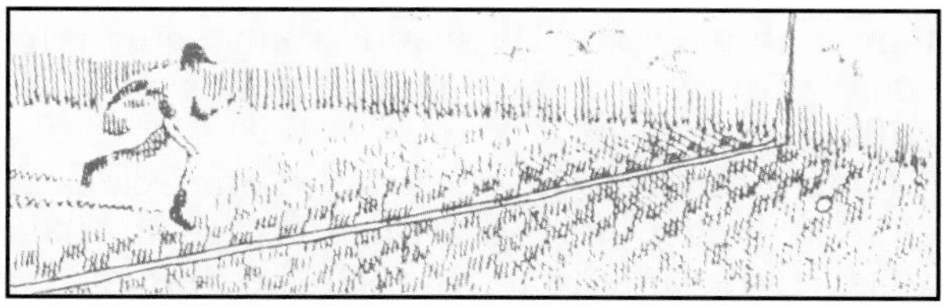

Charley Radbourn

Radbourn, Charles Gardner **P-OF**

1880–91 B:12/11/1854, Rochester, NY D:2/5/1897, Bloomington, IL Deb:5/5/1880, BUF NL BR/TR 5'9", 168

W	L	PCT	G	SH	IP	BB	SO	ERA
309	195	.613	528	35	4535^{1}	875	1830	2.67

Charley Radbourn was a great pitcher who was apparently difficult to like. The *Providence Journal-Bulletin* dubbed the hard-drinking player "Lord Radbourn" and called him "erratic, capricious, and ill-tempered." He also won a major league record 59 games in one season and often filled in at other positions when he wasn't pitching.

In 1880, his first season in the major leagues, an injured arm limited him to part-time infield duty for Buffalo. His arm recovered in 1881, and he won 25 games with the Providence Grays. He shared mound duty with John Montgomery Ward. In 1882 he finished 33–20, leading the league in shutouts and strikeouts. Outstanding again in 1883, he led in appearances and in victories, with 48, and ranked second in complete games, innings pitched, strikeouts, and earned run average.

Notably suspicious, even paranoid, it was his suspicious personality that brought about his great 1884 season. Early in the season he shared Providence pitching duties with 21-year-old Bill Sweeney, another righthander who was considered something of a phenomenon. Radbourn was apparently jealous of the youngster and disliked Sweeney.

At midseason, Old Hoss was suspended by his team. One account claims the suspension resulted from "improper conduct," and another claims he was suspended for cursing his catcher and firing a baseball at him so hard that it knocked him flat. Radbourn thought the catcher, who'd just dropped a third strike, deserved it.

Just after Radbourn's suspension, Sweeney jumped the Providence team and joined St. Louis of the outlaw Union Association. The Grays were left with only one pitcher—Radbourn. Thinking quickly, Radbourn offered to pitch the rest of the season for a small bonus and the right to become a free agent after the season ended. Providence management had no recourse but to agree, and the suspension was dropped.

Old Hoss didn't actually pitch every remaining game (several position players filled in), but he didn't miss many games, including a stretch from August 21 to September 15 that encompassed most of a 20-game Providence winning streak that won the team the pennant. His 678⅔ innings pitched for the season are only an inning and a third short of the record set by Cincinnati's Will White in 1879.

A three-game playoff series for the baseball world championship, which some consider the first World Series, was arranged that same year with the American Association champions, the New York Mets. Radbourn's mastery continued: he won all three games and allowed only three runs.

Radbourn's 59 wins in 1884 are six more than any other pitcher has collected in a season. Most of the wins included in his total were played in the season's second half. For all his efforts, including the postseason, he won 62 games and was paid $3,000.

He also managed to lead the National League in ERA that year. Of course, the rules of the day mandated that pitchers throw underhanded, a style Radbourn continued to use after overhand tosses were made legal because the underhanded pitches put less strain on his arm.

Even so, his big year took a toll on his arm. Some days, Old Hoss came to the park unable even to comb his hair with his right hand. He would apply hot towels to the arm for a couple of hours and then toss around an iron ball. Then he'd switch to a baseball and would throw it at ever-increasing distances until he could get it to the plate. He would pitch nine innings—usually more effectively than did his opponent.

Although he won more than 20 games in each of his next three seasons, pitching for Providence and then Boston, he lost almost as often as he won. His strikeout totals decreased sharply. By 1888 his arm seemed gone, but he came back to post a 20–11 mark in 1889 and go 27–12 with Boston's Players' League team in 1890.

Retiring after the 1891 season, Radbourn operated a combination pool hall and saloon in Bloomington, Indiana. He lost an eye in a hunting accident in 1894 and spent the last years of his life as a recluse in a back room of his saloon.

Rip Radcliff

Radcliff, Raymond Allen **OF**

1934–43 B:1/19/1906, Kiowa, OK D:5/23/1962, Enid, OK Deb:9/17/1934, CHI AL BL/TL 5'10", 170

G	AB	R	H	HR	RBI	OBP	SLG	AVG
1081	4074	598	1267	42	533	.362	.417	.311

Rip Radcliff hit .325 or better for four of five years in the late 1930s. The Chicago White Sox first noticed Radcliff when he led the Southeastern League with 15 homers and 116 RBIs and had a .369 average with Selma in 1930. He was acquired by Chicago that year, but was soon back in the minors.

By 1934 Radcliff made the White Sox lineup and in 1936 was chosen as an All-Star. In the All-Star Game Radcliff made a terrific catch off the bat of Joe Medwick. The next day, July 8, he felt so empowered that he went 6-for-7.

In December 1939 Radcliff was traded to the St. Louis Browns. He went on to lead the American League in hits with 200 and batted a career-best .342 in his first year with the Browns. He was then sold to the Tigers for $25,000 on May 5, 1941. In 1943, his last season in the major leagues, Radcliff led the American League with 44 pinch-hitting appearances. Radcliff later managed Greensboro of the Class C Carolina League to a last-place finish in 1948.

Alex Radcliffe

Radcliffe, Alexander **3B-SS-OF-P**

Negro League Player (1932–46) B:7/26/1905, Memphis, TN D:7/18/1983, BR/TR 6', 200

Negro Leaguer Alex Radcliffe brother of Ted "Double Duty" Radcliffe, earned a reputation of one of black baseball's finest third basemen as he led the Negro American League in homers in both 1944 and 1945. "Radcliffe in my estimation, became one of the truly great third basemen in baseball history," his manager, Dave Malarcher, said. According to Malarcher he was a "fast man, a powerful hitter, and one who possessed the mind," meaning that he was major league material.

Originally from Memphis, Radcliffe moved with his entire family to Chicago, living four blocks from the home of Rube Foster's American Giants. He began his career with that club in 1926. In 1937 the Radcliffes became the first brothers to appear together in East-West competition. Before 46,247 fans at the 1944 East-West Game, Alex Radcliffe, then with the Cincinnati Clowns, doubled, while his brother, catching for the Birmingham Black Barons, later homered to tie the score. He set East-West Game records with 11 games played (including seven straight) and 44 at bats, while batting .341.

Double Duty Radcliffe

Radcliffe, Theodore **C-P**

Negro League Player (1928–50) Manager B:7/7/1902, Mobile, AL, BB/TR, 5'10", 190

Ted "Double Duty" Radcliffe earned his nickname the hard way—by catching Satchel Paige in the first game of a Negro league doubleheader at Yankee Stadium in 1932 and in the second game pitching a 4–0 shutout. Writers Damon Runyon and Heywood Broun were in the stands. Runyon, in his next column, gave Radcliffe the sobriquet.

Radcliffe made Negro League All-Star Teams as either a pitcher or a catcher in 1937, 1938, 1939, 1941, 1943, and 1944. In 1934 he managed a white team that barnstormed across Canada. During that tour Jimmie Foxx was seriously beaned, reducing his effectiveness for the rest of his career.

"He didn't have that good curve ball, but he could beat you 2–1, 1–0," shortstop Jake Stephens said of Radcliffe, "Never got the recognition he should have received. In my book he was one of the greatest." In part, recognition for Radcliff has been hampered by a lack of statistics, but it is known that in 11 games against major leaguers he hit .389 (14-for-36). Double Duty Radcliffe's brother Alex also starred in the Negro Leagues.

Doug Rader

Rader, Douglas Lee **3B**

1967–77 M(1983–86, 1989–91, 388–417) B:7/30/1944, Chicago, IL Deb:7/31/1967, TEX NL BR/TR 6'3", 215

G	AB	R	H	HR	RBI	OBP	SLG	AVG
1465	5186	631	1302	155	722	.325	.403	.251

Doug Rader was a free-spirited, free-swinging third baseman who once said, "If I hadn't become a ballplayer, I would like to have been a pirate or a Tahitian warlord." He was good enough to hit 155 career home runs and dominate the National League at his position defensively for five years during the late 1960s and early 1970s. He had a reputation for having peculiar fun, such as driving a golf cart into a lake, and was eager to supply sportswriters with off-beat theories. For instance, he explained 1984's rabbit-ball stats by noting, "The old ones had Lee MacPhail's name. The new ones have Bobby Brown, and the fewer letters make them less wind-resistant."

Rader went on to manage in the big leagues, where he tried to install a loose atmosphere on his ballclubs. Unfortunately for Rader, the most fun comes from winning, and he was never able to get a taste of postseason play in his 11 seasons as a player, two stints as a coach, or five campaigns as a big league manager.

Nicknamed "The Red Rooster" for his red hair, and sometimes called "Foghorn Leghorn" after the cartoon character with the less-than-retiring personality, Rader spent most of his career with the Houston Astros. This may have cost him a few home runs, since the Astrodome was one of the toughest parks in which to hit the longball. In perhaps his key lifetime stat, Rader struck out 1,055 times, almost exactly twice as often as he walked (528). He never made an All-Star squad or led his team in a major offensive category, but he held Houston's third base job for seven years and appeared in at least 129 major league games eight years in a row.

Rader made his major league debut a day after his 23rd birthday. Playing primarily at first base, he batted .333 in 162 at bats and hit his first two major league home runs. During the 1968 season Rader took over third base from veteran Bob Aspromonte. From 1969 through 1975 Rader was the team's regular third baseman. He hit the first of his three Astrodome grand slams off Philadelphia's Luis Peraza on May 27 in the ninth inning, the only homer Peraza ever gave up in the majors. In 1970 Rader won the first of his five consecutive Gold Gloves and assembled a career-high 17-game hitting streak. On June 4 he reached Montreal's Dan McGinn for a first-inning grand slam. He also hit one off St. Louis pitcher Jerry Reuss on May 16, 1971.

After the 1975 season the Astros shipped Rader to San Diego, where he hit .257 as the team's third baseman in 1976. The Padres sold his contract to Toronto during the 1977 season, and that's where his career ended. Between the Padres and Blue Jays in 1977 Rader slammed 18 homers, at that point one of the highest home run totals ever by a player in his final season.

Rader was back in a major league uniform as a coach with the Padres in 1979, and then he went to the minors to gain some managerial experience. He piloted San Diego's Triple A team in Hawaii for three years and posted a winning record. But it was the Texas Rangers, not the Padres, who gave Rader his first chance to manage in the majors. They hired him on November 1, 1982, at which time he became the club's 12th manager in as many years. Rader brought some stability, but not success, to the position. He finished third in 1983 with a 77–85 mark, then last with a 69–92 record in 1984. He was fired when the Rangers got off to a 9–23 start in 1985.

A coach with the Chicago White Sox in 1986 and 1987, Rader got a second chance to manage when the Angels hired him in 1989. He won 91 games, the best mark of his career, but it was only good enough for third place. He was let go after leading California to an 80–82 mark in 1990. He later coached for the A's, Marlins, and Cubs.

Tim Raines

Raines, Timothy **OF**

1979–* B:9/16/1959, Sanford, FL Deb:9/11/1979, MON NL BB/TR 5'8", 178

G	AB	R	H	HR	RBI	OBP	SLG	AVG
2353	8694	1548	2561	168	964	.388	.427	.295

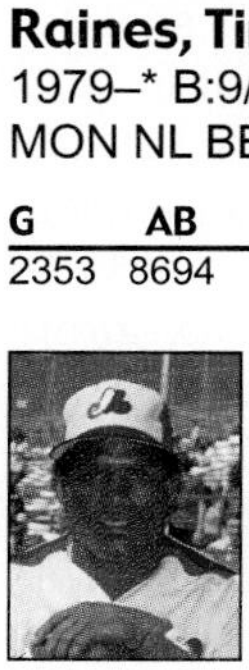

Tim Raines completed his 21st season in the major leagues in 1999. The man they call "Rock" because of his half-back-type build produced a solid career based almost entirely on his speed. At his peak, he was the National League equivalent of Rickey Henderson—batting for high averages, getting on base with walks, leading the league in stolen bases, and scoring runs.

Raines was a baseball and football star at Seminole High School in Florida when he was taken in the fifth round by the Montreal Expos in the June 1977 free agent draft. Two years later Raines made his major league debut as a September call-up, serving exclusively as a pinch runner. By 1981, after being named Minor League Player of the Year by Topps and *The Sporting News*, Raines was ready to play on a regular basis with the Expos.

Raines set a rookie record by stealing 71 bases, despite playing in just 88 games due to the player strike and a September injury. He finished second in the National League Rookie of the Year balloting to Fernando Valenzuela. While his average fell from .304 to .277 in 1982, he continued to dominate on the basepaths, leading the league with 78 steals. His next four years he stole 305 bases while his average steadily climbed. In 1986 he led the National League with a .334 average and a .415 on-base average. Through 1999 Raines stole 807 bases and was caught only 146 times, giving him the greatest-ever steal percentage, an .8469 percent success rate compared to runner-up Eric Davis' .8442.

A seven-time All-Star, Raines also played on the 1996 and 1998 world championship Yankees. In 1999, after signing with Oakland, Raines was diagnosed with lupus. He was forced to stop playing to seek treatment, but was feeling well enough to accept an invitation to spring training by the Yankees in 2000.

Manny Ramirez

Ramirez, Manuel Aristides(Onelcida) OF

1993–* B:5/30/1972, Brooklyn, NY Deb:9/2/1993, CLE AL BR/TR 6', 190

G	AB	R	H	HR	RBI	OBP	SLG	AVG
849	3031	573	932	198	682	.404	.576	.307

Manny Ramirez reached the majors at age 21 already an accomplished hitter, but fell short in other areas of the game. In 1995, his first full season, Ramirez hit .308 with 31 home runs and 107 RBIs as the Indians posted a 100–48 record. Although he contributed three postseason homers, his mental error proved costly to the Indians who ultimately lost a six-game World Series to Atlanta. With his team trailing in Game 2, Ramirez was picked off first base to defuse a potential rally.

His numbers improved the following year as Cleveland rolled to another division title. Ramirez batted .375 in an upset loss to the Baltimore Orioles in the Division Series. In 1997 Ramirez raised his batting average to a career-high .326. He hit two homers against Baltimore in the Championship Series, but his reputation suffered when he was again picked off first base in Game 3. Despite two homers and six RBIs in the World Series, he batted just .154 and committed an error in a seven-game loss to the Florida Marlins.

The perception of Ramirez as a distracted man-child was reinforced by many examples of absentmindedness and irresponsibility with money. In one instance Ramirez reportedly asked a clubhouse attendant to have his car washed and to pay with money in the glove compartment. When the attendant looked inside, he found $10,000 in cash.

After working with Indians team psychologist Charles Maher to improve his focus, Ramirez quieted critics with a monster 1998 season. He had 45 homers and 145 RBIs in 150 games, plus four postseason homers. He continued his barrage in 1999. He batted a career-high .333, and his league-leading 165 RBIs broke Hal Trosky's 63-year-old club record. His defense in right field also showed marked improvement. He received the *Total Baseball* Ted Williams Award as the league leader in production in 1999.

Pedro Ramos

Ramos, Pedro (Guerra) P

1955–70 B:4/28/1935, Pinar del Rio, Cuba Deb:4/11/1955, WAS AL BB/TR 6', 185

W	L	PCT	G	SV	IP	BB	SO	ERA
117	160	.422	582	55	23552	724	1305	4.08

One slice of Pedro Ramos' career shows the magic touch the Yankees had when it was their turn to win the pennant. They acquired Ramos for the 1964 stretch run, and the talented righthander from Cuba responded by pitching the best ball of his life. His efforts helped the Yankees win their fifth straight American League pennant. Ramos arrived too late to qualify for the World Series, but at least he got a glimpse of victory after years spent in the second division.

With a sizzling fastball, a cigar at the ready, and an outgoing personality, Ramos spent 15 years in the major leagues. During the course of his career, he served up a tape-measure home run to Mickey Mantle—whom he was constantly challenging to a footrace—and started an all-Cuban triple play.

Pedro Ramos y Guerra signed with the Senators for $150 per month and then was dumped without ceremony in a new country. Like many other Hispanic players who came to the United States, he faced a language barrier. But his fastball transcended a lot of problems, and just weeks short of his 20th birthday he found himself in the majors. Back then, however, pitching for the Washington Senators was not a lot of fun. From the time Ramos came aboard in 1955 through 1959, the Senators finished last in the American League four times and climbed as high as seventh once. Ramos wasn't much better and had trouble throwing strikes early in his career—he walked more batters than he struck out in 1956.

Even so, he recorded at least 10 wins from 1956 through 1960. The bad news? During three of those seasons he led the league in losses, and in two of them he yielded the most hits in the league. On May 30, 1956, Ramos served up one of Mantle's longest home runs. It came in the fifth inning of the first game of a doubleheader at Yankee Stadium. Mantle hit a 2–2 pitch that hit just below the top of the roof cornice in right field. No one has ever hit a fair ball out of Yankee Stadium, but Ramos' pitch was one of two that Mantle hit to the facade. It struck a point 370 feet from home plate, 117 feet off the ground, and rocketed off the roof hard enough to bounce back to the field.

Ramos started an all-Cuban triple play on July 23, 1960. It came in the third inning of a game against the Kansas City Athletics after Bill Tuttle and Jerry Lumpe opened with singles. With the runners moving on a full count, Whitey Herzog lined back to Ramos, who threw to Julio Becquer at first, doubling off Lumpe. Becquer fired to shortstop Jose Valdivielso to get Tuttle.

Ramos was on the mound for the old Senators in the last game they played before the franchise moved to Minnesota for the 1961 season. On that day, October 2, 1960, Ramos went the distance in a 2–1 loss to the Orioles' Milt Pappas. Ramos spent one year with the Twins, winning 11 and losing a league-leading 20.

Just before Opening Day in 1962, he was traded to Cleveland for first baseman Vic Power and left-handed pitcher Dick Stigman. In two-plus years with the Indians, Ramos won 26 games and lost 30, including a 9–8 mark in 1963, only his second season above .500. Ramos made more noise with his bat than his arm in Cleveland. On May 30, 1962, he hit two home runs, including a grand slam off Baltimore's Chuck Estrada. In the sixth inning of a game on July 3, 1963, Woodie Held, Ramos, Tito Francona, and Larry Brown hit consecutive homers, making the Indians the second team in major league history to hit four straight home runs. But Ramos was no Ruth; his lifetime batting average was .155, and in 1963 he fanned in eight straight at bats.

His best day on the mound may have been July 31, 1963, when he struck out 15 Los Angeles Angels. Yet in 1964 Ramos was dealt to the Yankees for $75,000 and two players to be named later (who turned out to be pitchers Ralph Terry and Bud Daley). Ramos was a workhorse for New York in that final month of the 1964 season, making 13 appearances. In an astonishing turn for someone who had often experienced control problems, Ramos struck out 21 batters in 22 innings and did not issue a single base on balls. The Yankees needed every bit of Ramos' excellence, because they beat out the White Sox by just one game.

Ramos spent two more full years with the Yankees, before he was traded to the Phillies prior to the 1967 season. He also played for Pittsburgh and Cincinnati before returning to the Senators in 1970. He made four appearances for Washington and called it quits. Ramos did some coaching in Latin America after his playing days, and he also was in the cigar business. He ran afoul of the law on drug and weapons charges and was sentenced to three years in prison. He later served as a major league scout.

Len Randle

Randle, Leonard Shenoff — 3B-2B-OF

1971–82 B:2/12/1949, Long Beach, CA Deb:6/16/1971, WAS AL BB/TR 5'10", 169

G	AB	R	H	HR	RBI	OBP	SLG	AVG
1138	3950	488	1016	27	322	.323	.335	.257

During the 1970s Len Randle had a rollercoaster career in the majors. Billy Martin once said of Randle, "He's one of the league's more exciting players. He has speed, talent, and combativeness. He makes things happen."

Randle was an educated baseball player. He attended Arizona State University and received a B.S. in political science before starting his baseball career. Drafted by the Cardinals in June 1967, he didn't sign and decided to finish school instead.

In 1970 Randle was the Washington Senators' top pick in the free agent draft. He started with Denver of the American Association and was soon brought up to the Senators. In 1972 the Senators became the new Texas Rangers. Randle played five seasons with the Rangers, including a .302 season as a regular in 1974. Then, after he hit just .224 in 1976, he lost his job at second to rookie

Bump Wills the following spring. Rangers manager Frank Lucchesi called him a "punk"—Randle punched him out. He was suspended, fined, and, not surprisingly, traded.

On April 27, 1977, he became a New York Met for cash and a player to be named later. He was one of the bright spots on a dreadful team, batting a career best .304 as New York's third baseman. Following a 71-point drop in his batting average, the Mets released Randle before the 1979 season. He spent time in the minor leagues with both the Giants and Pirates before he finished the season with the Yankees. Finally Randle became a free agent and eventually signed with Seattle in February 1981. It was as a Mariner that Randle pulled a stunt that has been fodder for highlight videos ever since: he got down on all fours and tried to blow a fair ball to the other side of the third-base foul line. His new tactic was disallowed.

Willie Randolph

Randolph, Willie Larry **2B**

1975–92 B:7/6/1954, Holly Hill, SC Deb:7/29/1975, PIT NL BR/TR 5'11", 166

G	AB	R	H	HR	RBI	OBP	SLG	AVG
2202	8018	1239	2210	54	687	.375	.351	.276

Of the savvy trades general manager Gabe Paul made to transform the Yankees into a powerhouse in the mid-1970s, perhaps the best was the one that sent pitcher Doc Medich to the Pirates for Dock Ellis and Willie Randolph. The desperate Bucs also threw Ken Brett into the deal. In his first year as a Yank, Ellis won 17 games and became comeback player of the year, but he was gone only a year later. Randolph settled in at second base on a team noted for raucous disharmony, added a refreshing amount of quiet fortitude, and was a productive, respected player for 13 seasons. On defense, the Yanks were always among the league leaders in double plays even though Randolph had to adjust to 31 different shortstops.

With the exception of poor offensive years in strike-shortened 1981 and an injury-prone 1988, Willie Larry Randolph's numbers for the Yanks were a masterpiece of consistency—averages between the high .270s and .294, around 20 doubles a year, on-base percentages in the .380s—year after year after year.

Randolph was a Yankees All-Star four times, and he played on teams that reached postseason

play five times and twice won world championships. His career stats as a Yankee place him high among the team's many legends.

When he became eligible for free agency after the 1988 season, the Yanks ignored him in favor of Steve Sax. Randolph repaid the favor by signing with the Dodgers; he proceeded to hit .282 and was named to the All-Star team. He played for Oakland in the 1990 World Series, finished his career with the Mets in 1992. He later returned to the Yankees, working in the front office and then becoming the team's third-base coach.

Bill Rariden

Rariden, William Angel **C**

1909–20 B:2/4/1888, Bedford, IN D:8/28/1942, Bedford, IN Deb:8/12/1909, BOS NL BR/TR 5'10", 168

G	AB	R	H	HR	RBI	OBP	SLG	AVG
982	2877	272	682	7	272	.320	.298	.237

In Game 6 of the 1917 Giants–White Sox World Series, New York catcher Bill Rariden played a key role in one of the most famous incidents in Series history. In the fourth inning, Chicago's Eddie Collins broke from third base on a ball Happy Felsch hit back to pitcher Rube Benton. Collins appeared to be caught off base, but suddenly rushed past Rariden, who had moved far up the line. With nobody covering the plate, Collins headed for home. Third baseman Heinie Zimmerman, who received most of the public's blame, had no choice but to chase Collins across home plate—since no one had bothered to cover that base. The White Sox went on to win the game and take the Series.

The light-hitting catcher was always on the periphery of significant moments. He left the Boston Braves before the 1914 season—the same year they won the pennant as the "Miracle" Braves—and jumped to the Indianapolis Hoosiers, who won the Federal League pennant. The next year he moved with the club to Newark. He led the Federal League in putouts, assists, and fielding range in both seasons of its existence.

When the Federal League folded, Rariden went to the New York Giants. He paced National League receivers in games caught and putouts in 1916 and in fielding percentage in 1918. Despite his gaffe in the 1917 World Series, he batted .385 against the White Sox.

In February 1919, Rariden was traded to the Reds for Hal Chase who had recently been embroiled in game-fixing allegations. Rariden played in that year's World Series against the White Sox and batted .211. His one world championship was tainted a year later when eight members of the White Sox were indicted for conspiring to fix the Series.

Vic Raschi

Raschi, Victor John Angelo **P**

1946–55 B:3/28/1919 West Springfield, MA
D:10/14/1988, Groveland, NY Deb:9/23/1946, NY AL
BR/TR 6'1", 205

W	L	PCT	G	SH	IP	BB	SO	ERA
132	66	.667	269	26	1819	727	944	3.72

Joe DiMaggio, Mickey Mantle, Yogi Berra, and Phil Rizzuto stole the headlines as the Yankees won five straight World Series from 1949 through 1953. But the Bombers would have been busts without the trio of Allie Reynolds, Eddie Lopat, and Vic Raschi, who combined for a 255–117 regular season record during that span.

As distinguished as Reynolds and Lopat were, neither could match what Raschi accomplished during those five years. The 6-foot 1-inch, 205-pound righthander went 92–40, averaging more than 18 wins per season. Raschi assembled three straight 21-victory campaigns, one of them in 1950 when he led the American League with a .724 winning percentage.

Raschi's excellence extended to the postseason, where he appeared in six World Series, all won by the Yankees, and compiled a 5–3 mark. The four-time All-Star still ranks as one of the best clutch pitchers in Yankees history.

Out of West Springfield, Massachusetts, and blessed with a right arm that could throw a ball seemingly with the speed of a bullet, he was nicknamed "The Springfield Rifle." Though primarily a fastball pitcher, he also threw a slider and a changeup. His control, while not outstanding, was good enough, and he was a very tough competitor who benefited from the instruction of Jim Turner, both in the minors and majors.

Scouted by the Yankees in his early teens, Raschi signed a contract that provided for his college education. He attended William and Mary, but dropped out at the behest of the Yankees, who wanted him to get some experience in the minor leagues. Raschi served as a physical trainer in the Air Force during World War II, then played in Portland and Newark before being promoted to the majors at the end of 1946.

In 1947 Raschi went 7–2 and the Yankees won the pennant. He made two World Series appearances as a reliever, but did not pick up a decision. The following year the Yankees fell to third, but Raschi led the team with 19 victories and made the All-Star team for the first time. Entering the All-Star Game in the fourth inning, he hurled three scoreless frames and singled home a pair of runs in the American League's 5–2 victory.

New York's five-year dynasty began in 1949, with Raschi again leading the team in wins. He had 21 of them, and the last one came on the final day of the regular season in a winner-take-all game against the Red Sox. In the World Series he split two decisions, losing a 1–0 duel to Brooklyn's Preacher Roe in Game 2, then wrapping up the Series with a workmanlike 10–5 victory in Game 5.

In 1950 Raschi assembled perhaps his best season, leading the league with a .724 winning percentage. He also turned in a World Series masterpiece in Game 1 against Philadelphia's Jim Konstanty, winning, 1–0.

Raschi went 21–10 and led the American League in starts and strikeouts in 1951. He took the mound in Game 6 of the World Series against the Dodgers, needing a victory to clinch another world championship. He allowed only one run in six innings, and the Yankees prevailed, 4–3.

The following season Raschi went 16–6, won 11 straight games during one stretch, recorded the lowest ERA of his career (2.78), and enjoyed his best World Series. Twice, after Brooklyn victories, he pulled the Yankees even. In Game 2 he beat Carl Erskine, 7–1, to tie the Series at one victory apiece. Then in Game 6, with the Yankees on the verge of elimination, he outpitched Billy Loes, 3–2, sending the Series to a seventh game, which was won by Reynolds.

Raschi's career as a Yankee ended in 1953, when he went 13–6 and refused to take a pay cut. New York sold him to the Cardinals, where he went 8–9 in 1954. He retired after splitting the 1955 campaign between the Cardinals and Kansas City Athletics. In his later years, Raschi lived in Geneseo, New York, where he operated a liquor store and did some high school coaching.

Johnny Ray

Ray, John Cornelius **2B**

1981–90 B:3/1/1957, Chouteau, OK Deb:9/2/1981,
PIT NL BB/TR 5'11", 185

G	AB	R	H	HR	RBI	OBP	SLG	AVG
1353	5188	604	1502	53	594	.336	.391	.290

For a time it appeared Johnny Ray was going to have a long and distinguished career as a National League second baseman. Instead, he was traded to California and eventually wound up in Japan.

Ray was a 12th-round pick of the Astros in the June 1979 draft. He did stints in the minors with Sarasota, Daytona Beach, Columbus, and Tucson. In 1981 he led the Pacific Coast League in doubles. In August he was traded to the Pirates. Ray revealed his worth in 1982 when he led the National League in putouts, assists, total chances—and errors. *The Sporting News* named him National League Rookie of the Year.

The speedy Ray became a doubles specialist. He

hit 30 or more in five straight seasons and tied for the league lead in doubles in 1983 and 1984. A good baserunner, he was particularly skilled in going from first to third or from second to home. As a batter he was very tough to strike out.

In 1985 Duke Snider said, "Johnny Ray is an All-Star as far as I am concerned. He's shown us everything a second baseman could have. He runs the bases well, throws well, hits well. He's turned into a very good player." In 1986 he made only five errors the entire season. However, with Jose Lind waiting in the wings, Ray was traded to the Angels in September 1987, as California made an unsuccessful run to win the division.

Ray made the American League All-Star team in 1988—the only time he received the honor. He spent much of 1989 and 1990 on the disabled list. In December 1990 he was released by the Angels and signed with the Yakult Swallows in Japan.

Bugs Raymond

Raymond, Arthur Lawrence **P**

1904–11 B:2/24/1882, Chicago, IL D:9/7/1912, Chicago, IL Deb:9/23/1904, DET AL BR/TR 5'10", 180

W	L	PCT	G	SH	IP	BB	SO	ERA
45	57	.441	136	9	854^2	282	401	2.49

When Bugs Raymond sat down in a restaurant for lunch one day, the waiter asked him how he threw his famous spitball. "I'll show you," said Raymond. He stood and picked up his water glass, wet two fingers, kicked his leg high into the air, and hurled the glass through a plate glass window. "That's how it's done," said Bugs. "Notice the break."

Although his major league career was relatively short, Raymond earned a lasting reputation as one of baseball's more humorous characters. He accumulated more anecdotes per innings pitched than almost anyone else. Although his stories are told for their humor, they add up to create a biography that is quite tragic. His nickname identified him as a nut case, but Raymond was actually an out-of-control drunk, baseball's ultimate alcoholic.

Stocky, righthanded spitballer Arthur Lawrence Raymond had a short trial with Detroit at the end of the 1904 season but didn't really find a place in the majors until he joined the Cardinals late in 1907. Already a confirmed alcoholic, the notion spread that he pitched better while intoxicated.

Apparently, some of his minor league managers had even encouraged him to drink. St. Louis manager John McCloskey, a kindly man, didn't go quite that far, but he let Bugs design his own wet training routine. He only asked the wayward pitcher to show up sober on the days he was scheduled to pitch. Even that regimen was too strict for a man with Raymond's thirst and temperament.

On one occasion McCloskey stewed in the clubhouse, waiting for Raymond's arrival. He telephoned to sayhe couldn't make his start that day because of a terrible toothache. McCloskey and ordered him to come to the ballpark, toothache or not. Raymond arrived just before game time with no sign of a toothache, but obviously a sheet or two to the wind. Without warming up, he defeated the pennant-bound Chicago Cubs, 3–1.

In 1908, despite a 2.03 ERA, Raymond went 15–25 for the last-place Cardinals. St. Louis was shut out 11 times when he pitched. After the season, he and two other players were traded to the New York Giants in the deal that sent Roger Bresnahan to St. Louis to become manager. In his first year with New York, Raymond went 18–12, though his ERA jumped to 2.47.

Unlike his previous managers, John McGraw tried to save Raymond from himself. McGraw tried to keep tabs on his pitcher through Raymond's roommates and once even sent the pitcher's own family on the road to keep an eye on him. But nothing kept Raymond from his appointed rounds with the bottle. One day he was scheduled to pitch the second game of a doubleheader, so during the first game McGraw locked him in the clubhouse with guards at the door. Raymond lowered a bucket out the window, and some of his admirers filled it with bottles.

During games Raymond would toss balls over the fence, and his drinking buddies would send back bottles of booze in return. McGraw then put guards outside the fence, but Raymond found a way around them. On one occasion McGraw handed him a baseball and sent him to the bullpen. Ball in hand, Raymond walked out of the Polo Grounds and over to Eighth Avenue, where he traded the ball for a drink. Even fines didn't phase him. Finally, McGraw sent Raymond's paycheck straight to his wife. When Raymond found out, he told McGraw sourly, "If my wife gets the money, let her pitch."

By 1910 Raymond was of little use to the Giants. After the season they sent him to dry out at a sanitarium in Illinois. When that didn't work, they released him in 1911. About a year later, McGraw got a letter from Raymond saying he was having a hard time of it. "I have my own troubles," McGraw wrote back. In September Raymond was kicked in the head during a drunken barroom brawl in Chicago. He died of a cerebral hemorrhage at age 30.

Al Reach

Reach, Alfred James **OF-2B**

1871–75 Owner (1883–1902) M(1890, 4–7)
B:5/25/1840, London, England D:1/14/1928, Atlantic City, NJ Deb:5/20/1871, PHI NA BL/TL 5'6", 155

Al Reach enriched the game of baseball, and baseball returned the favor. His rags-to-riches saga, a diamond version of the Horatio Alger story, is not without its twists and contradictions. One of baseball's earliest stars, for many years Reach was considered the first truly professional player. A lefthanded second baseman in the days when such oddities were not unknown, he was admired for his batting skills, although the available statistics indicate he was an easy out.

Reach's contributions to the game and the rewards he derived from it in retirement were completely out of proportion to his playing career. His corner cigar store became a million-dollar business, and despite lacking a formal education, Reach published one of the most influential baseball guides of the period.

He built the most modern ballpark of his era and lived to see it become an antiquated eyesore. American League baseballs bore his signature, yet he owned a National League team. And although English-born, Reach supported the Anglophobic notion that baseball originated in America.

Alfred James Reach was brought to America as an infant. While the boy was growing up in Brooklyn, his English father taught him how to play cricket; Reach preferred baseball.

Although he was small, standing only 5 feet 6 inches and weighing 150 pounds, he was quick, sure-handed, and a talented enough hitter to join one of Brooklyn's best clubs, the Eckfords, at age 15. The Eckfords were only nominally an amateur team; by the 1860s their better players were either rewarded with well-paying outside jobs or paid under the table.

Reach was one of the Eckford's better players. According to the rudimentary statistics compiled at the time, in nine games in 1861 he scored 20 runs and made 25 outs. In 1862 he turned down an offer, perhaps involving remuneration, to join a Baltimore team. But even if Reach received his first pay as early as 1861, Big Jim Creighton of the Brooklyn Excelsiors and several others preceded him as a professional by a year or two.

Nevertheless, Reach was an acknowledged star, and in 1862 and 1863 the Eckfords claimed to be U.S. baseball champions. In 1865 the Philadelphia Athletics made him an offer he couldn't refuse, paying him $25 a week "for expenses." At a time when a steak dinner cost 25 cents, such "expenses" were a sham that preserved an appearance of amateurism. Within a year three other Philadelphia players were accused of "professionalism," but Reach somehow avoided the charge.

Although he both batted and threw lefthanded, Reach usually played second base. Today no lefthanded player would be considered as a second baseman, but the only real drawback is a split-second pivot before throwing to first. Reach's other talents apparently compensated for the deficiency.

According to one set of records, in 1869 Reach had 242 hits, collecting 416 total bases in 46 games. But the Athletics' opponents were no match for them, and the team won many games by 30 or 40 runs. Competition apparently improved in 1870, when Reach managed only 75 hits in 37 games.

Professionalism in baseball was an accepted fact by 1871. The first professional league, the National Association, was formed, and Philadelphia won its first pennant with a 21–7 record. Reach hit .352 on a team that averaged .320. In the following years his batting average twice fell below .200, and in five National Association seasons he hit only .247. He managed the team to third place in both 1874 and 1875.

Reach retired after the 1875 season and opened a cigar store in Philadelphia. Sportsmen hung out in the shop, and Reach became a manufacturer and retailer of sporting goods.

He joined Benjamin Shibe, the inventor of the cork-center baseball, in business, and together the two men pioneered mass production sporting goods and mail order sales. In a nation suddenly gone mad for sports, the partners were soon worth their weight in golden baseballs.

In 1883 Reach began publishing *Reach's Official Baseball Guide*, an annual compilation of baseball statistics and essays that soon rivaled the Spalding guides in popularity. That same year Reach and Colonel John Rogers, a lawyer and politician, brought National League baseball back to Philadelphia. Reach called his new team the Phillies. They finished dead last in their first season with an atrocious 17–87 record.

Reach sold out to his major sporting goods competitor, A.G. Spalding & Bros., in 1891. Although Spalding now had a virtual monopoly, the company maintained the appearance of competition by retaining the Reach name. In later years Spalding manufactured the official National League baseball; Reach manufactured the official American League ball. Yet both were made in the same Philadelphia factory and were simply stamped with different names.

Under Reach, the Phillies built Baker Bowl, the league's finest park, an imposing structure seating 20,000 fans. When it burned down in 1894, Reach rebuilt it on the same spot, partially of steel, a first for baseball. He served as club president until 1902.

A millionaire several times over, Reach performed one final service for baseball. In 1907 he was named to the Mills Commission, a committee picked by Spalding to determine the national pastime's true origins and prove that they were American rather than English. The committee discovered a letter from an old man in Denver who distinctly remembered Abner Doubleday spontaneously conceiving baseball on a spring day in 1839 at Cooperstown, New York. Reach signed his name to the report endorsing this pipe dream, and for more than 30 years, in the face of overwhelming evidence to the contrary, it stood as the official version of baseball's beginning.

Jeff Reardon

Reardon, Jeffrey James **P**

1979–94 B:10/1/1955, Dalton, MA Deb:8/25/1979, NY NL BR/TR 6'1", 195

W	L	PCT	G	SV	IP	BB	SO	ERA
73	77	.487	880	367	1132¹	358	877	3.16

Jeff Reardon once held the record for career saves, yet he never saved a game until he became a major leaguer. Signed by the Mets, Reardon spent his minor league career at Lynchburg and Jackson as a starter. In 1977 the righthander led the Carolina League in shutouts. In 1978 he paced the Texas League with 17 wins and an .810 winning percentage. Not until the following year at Tidewater did the Mets convert him into a reliever.

Reardon teamed with fellow righthander Neal Allen to give the then-woeful Mets a solid bullpen. That ended in May 1981, when New York inexplicably traded Reardon to the Expos for damaged-goods outfielder Ellis Valentine—arguably one of the worst trades in Mets' history.

Reardon blossomed in Montreal. By 1985 he was leading the league with 41 saves and was named *The Sporting News* National League Fireman of the Year. In February 1987 the Expos traded Reardon to the Twins. Like the Mets, the Expos would regret dealing away Reardon.

He helped lead the Twins to the 1987 World Series. In his first year in the American League he was the leader in saves and earned American League Co-Fireman of the Year from *The Sporting News*. He posted a career-high 42 saves in 1988.

After the 1989 season, the western Massachusetts native declared free agency and signed with the Boston Red Sox. He broke Rollie Fingers' record of 341 saves as a member of the Red Sox in 1992. Later that season Boston traded him to the Braves. He reached the World Series, but allowed the game-winning hit in both of his Series appearances. He signed with Cincinnati as a free agent after the 1992 season. Reardon ended his 16-year major league career with the Yankees.

Dick Redding

Redding, Richard **P–OF–1B**

Negro League Player (1911–38) Manager B:1891, Atlanta, GA D:1948, Islip, NY BR/TR 6'4", 210

A towering righthander with an overpowering fastball, "Cannonball Dick" Redding was a star for the Negro League's Lincoln Giants before World War I. He and teammate "Smokey Joe" Williams formed what may have been the most dominating pitching tandem in baseball history. Those who saw him claim that Redding may have been the best ever. Outfielder Jesse Hubbard said, "Redding and Williams were better pitchers than Satchel Paige. Satchel didn't throw as hard as Dick Redding. You should have seen *him* turn the ball loose." Redding pioneered the no-windup delivery and the crowd-pleasing hesitation pitch long before Paige made the moves famous.

In his rookie season, 1911, Redding won 17 consecutive games. The following year, playing against a mix of Negro League and semi-pro competition, he posted a record of 43–12 and pitched several no-hitters, including a 17-strikeout perfect game against the Jersey City Skeeters. Another time he struck out 24 Minor League All-Stars in one game. Redding won 20 consecutive games for the Lincoln Stars in 1915 and led the 1917 Indianapolis ABC's to a championship.

After returning from combat in France in World War I, Redding was unable to recapture his success on the mound. He pitched for several teams in the Negro Leagues and Cuba, eventually leaving the field to become a manager. Redding was well liked, but was not particularly good at running a ballclub. He stayed in baseball until 1938, and died shortly after his retirement.

Rick Reed

Reed, Richard Allen **P**

1988–95, 1997–* B:8/16/1964, Huntington, WV
Deb:8/8/1988, PIT NL BR/TR 6', 205

W	L	PCT	G	SH	IP	BB	SO	ERA
49	40	.551	151	4	836^{1}	165	515	3.90

Rick Reed shuttled between the majors and minors for nine years before he was signed as a replacement player by Cincinnati in spring training of 1995. For taking the job in the wake of the 1994 players' strike, Reed was still ostracized by the players' union long after he had proved himself many times over on the field.

The Pittsburgh Pirates chose Reed in the 26th round of the 1986 amateur draft. Pitching for Triple-A Buffalo in 1991, his 14–4 season earned him recognition as the American Association's Most Valuable Pitcher. His first few years with the Pirates were lackluster, however, and Reed was traded to Kansas City. He pitched a seven-hit shutout for the Royals against the California Angels on September 30, 1992 in the same game that George Brett collected his 3,000th hit.

Reed bandied between the big leagues and their farm teams for several years. He took the job as a replacement player during the 1995 strike so he could buy a new car for his diabetic mother; her car had one door held down by a rope. After the strike was settled, he spent almost the next two years in the minor leagues.

He finally landed in the major leagues for good with the Mets in 1997, winning 13 games and posting a 2.89 ERA. In 1998 he was named to the National League All-Star squad after a great first half, finishing the year at 16–11. Although prone to the long ball his control was such that some called him "a poor man's Greg Maddux."

In a crucial game for the Mets on October 2, 1999, when the team was fighting for a postseason berth, Reed tossed a three-hit shutout with 12 strikeouts against the Pittsburgh Pirates. He won both his postseason starts for the Mets in 1999.

Ron Reed

Reed, Ronald Lee **P**

1966–84 B:11/2/1942, LaPorte, IN Deb:9/26/1966,
ATL NL BR/TR 6'6",215

W	L	PCT	G	SV	IP	BB	SO	ERA
146	140	.510	751	103	2477^{2}	633	1481	3.46

Before he played professional baseball, Ron Reed was already a star on the basketball court. At Notre Dame he averaged 18.9 points and 14.3 rebounds per game, twice leading the Fighting Irish to the NCAA tournament. Drafted by the National Basketball Association's Detroit Pistons, the 6-foot 6-inch forward was a key man off the bench as a rookie in 1965. Reed also wanted to play baseball, however, and for two years played both in the NBA and the Atlanta Braves farm system.

As Reed's playing time on the court diminished, he rose through Atlanta's farm system, reaching the big leagues at the end of the 1966 season. Leaving the Pistons to focus solely on baseball for the first time, he emerged as a dominant starting pitcher at Triple A Richmond in 1967. Reed paced the International League with 17 complete games and led his team to the pennant.

Reed won his first six starts in 1968, and became the first Atlanta rookie to make the All-Star team. Along with Phil Niekro, he anchored the Braves rotation that won a division title in 1969. After 11 seasons as a major league starter, Reed found himself in Philadelphia's bullpen in 1976. He helped complement Phillies' closer Tug McGraw as the team won six division titles over the next eight seasons. Reed earned a save in Game 2 of the 1980 World Series, and made three appearances in Philadelphia's 1983 Series loss to the Orioles.

Jimmie Reese

Reese, James Herman **2B**

1930–32 Coach (1973–94) B:10/1/1901, New York, NY
D:7/13/1994, Santa Ana, CA Deb:4/19/1930, NY AL
BL/TR 5'11½", 165

G	AB	R	H	HR	RBI	OBP	SLG	AVG
232	742	123	206	8	70	.324	.373	.278

Someone had to be the best fungo hitter in the world, and that someone happened to be long-lived Jimmie Reese, one-time roommate of Babe Ruth. Fungo hitting involves tossing a ball up in practice and hitting it to waiting fielders. No one could do it better than Reese—even when he was in his 80s.

James Herman Reese (originally James Herman Soloman) had not started out as fungo hitter, but as batboy for the Los Angeles Angels in 1917. He excelled as a slick-fielding second baseman with Oakland and Los Angeles in the Pacific Coast League where he often led the circuit in putouts and fielding percentage.

In 1930 he and Lyn Lary were sold to the Yankees for a then-record $125,000. In the majors Reese collected 15 pinch hits in 33 at bats for a .455 average.

He managed in the Pacific Coast League, Western International League, and for World War II service teams, scouted for the Boston Braves and Montreal Expos, and coached for a variety of minor league clubs.

Reese was 72 when he got his first job as a major league coach. He remained an Angels coach through the final year of his life in 1994. He was honorary captain for the American League All-Star Team in 1992.

Pee Wee Reese

Reese, Harold Henry **SS-3B**

1940–58 B:7/23/1918, Ekron, KY D:8/14/1999, Louisville, KY Deb:4/23/1940, BRO NL BR/TR 5'9", 175

G	AB	R	H	HR	RBI	OBP	SLG	AVG
2166	8058	1338	2170	126	885	.366	.377	.269

Pee Wee Reese had a knack for providing just what the Dodgers needed to win. At the right moment he would bunt to start a big inning, turn a tough double play, pay a timely mound visit to a faltering pitcher, hit a key single or even a home run, or steal a base to put an important run in scoring position—whatever it took.

In a golden age of shortstops such as Marty Marion, Phil Rizzuto, and Lou Boudreau, Reese often outshone and even outlasted them all. He played at least 140 games in every year from 1941 to 1956, except for a three-year stretch in military service. He consistently made more putouts, stole more bases, and scored more runs than any other shortstop in the league and helped the Dodgers win seven pennants in 16 seasons.

Harold Henry Reese grew up in Ekron, Kentucky, and earned his nickname as a kid because of his expertise at shooting marbles. His baseball career began in 1938 when he signed with the last-place Louisville Colonels of the American Association. In 1939 he spurred them to a pennant, leading the league in triples and stolen bases. At age 19 he was already showing enough leadership to be called "the Little Colonel."

Red Sox boss Tom Yawkey was impressed with Reese and planned to have him replace Joe Cronin at shortstop, but Cronin returned from a Louisville scouting trip with a negative evaluation of Reese. Many of Cronin's contemporaries thought that the veteran shortstop was afraid of losing his job, but his assessment led the Sox to sell Reese's contract to Brooklyn for $75,000.

Reese's major league career got off to a poor start. He broke a bone in his heel, and when he returned to play, Cincinnati pitcher Jake Mooty beaned him. Reese hit .272 in only 84 games that season. In 1941 he hit .229 and led the league with 47 errors, and in the World Series against the Yankees he hit .200 and made three errors. But by 1942 he was an All Star for the first of 10 consecutive years and led National League shortstops in both putouts and assists.

Military duty interrupted Reese's ballplaying. In the Navy he played on the same team as Yankee Phil Rizzuto. Their manager, Bill Dickey, played Rizzuto at third and gave Reese the shortstop job.

When Reese returned to Brooklyn in 1946 he quietly inspired his team. In perhaps his most important show of leadership, the Kentuckian welcomed Jackie Robinson to the Dodgers in 1947 with a friendly arm around his shoulder. The whole team rallied behind the newcomer, and Reese had the best hitting year of his career, batting .284 with a league-leading 104 walks.

The World Series that year against the Yankees was a seven-game affair in which Reese batted .304, drove in four runs, and stole three bases. With the Yanks up two games to none, Reese contributed a key single to a six-run second inning in Game 3 to keep the Dodgers alive. Facing elimination in Game 6, Reese chipped in with a double, two singles, two runs scored, and two RBIs as Brooklyn evened the Series. Despite his contribution Brooklyn went down in defeat in Game 7.

In 1949 Reese led the league in scoring, crossing the plate 132 times. The Dodgers won the pennant again that year, but the Yanks continued to dominate in the World Series, winning in five games as Reese's .316 average and team-leading six hits went for naught.

In 1952 he led the National League in stolen bases with 30. The Dodgers again won the flag and again fell to the Yankees in the World Series. Reese hit .345 in the Series, tying Mickey Mantle and Duke Snider for the most hits with 10. The Dodgers seemed to be making a comeback in the seventh inning of Game 7 when they loaded the bases with two out, but Yanks second baseman Billy Martin made a heads-up, running grab of a popup by Jackie Robinson to put an end to Brooklyn's hopes. Reese, who had been on first, had already crossed the plate when Martin caught the ball.

Reese was 37 years old when the 1955 season started, but he still scored 99 runs. The Dodgers won the National League flag by 13½ games, and when the Yankees won the first two World Series games at home history appeared to be repeating itself.

But the Dodgers knocked Bob Turley out of the box in the second inning of Game 3, and when the dust cleared Reese had driven in two runs and Roy Campanella three. A solo homer by Campanella, a two-run shot by Hodges, and a three-run blast by Snider gave the Dodgers a victory in Game 4. Roger Craig's 5–3 win in Game 5 put the Dodgers in a position to become world champs for the first time ever. But the first six Yankees up in Game 6 scored five runs against Karl Spooner, sending the Dodgers to Game 7.

Reese led off in the top of the sixth inning with a single and scored to give the Dodgers a 2–0 lead. In the bottom of the sixth, first-year Dodgers manager Walter Alston brought in Sandy Amoros to play left for defensive purposes. The Yankees were threatening with one out and two on when Berra lined a drive deep into the left-field corner. Amoros made a remarkable one-handed catch, then spun and threw to Reese, whose accurate relay easily doubled Gil McDougald off first. Johnny Podres stifled another Yankee threat in the eighth, and the Dodgers came home as world champions.

In 1957 the 38-year-old Reese played most of his games at third base, and Charlie Neal moved to short. Before the start of the next season Walter O'Malley moved his team to Los Angeles and the great era of New York City baseball came to an end. Reese played a few games for the West Coast version of the team, but he retired to become a coach for the 1959 season.

He teamed with Dizzy Dean as a popular play-by-play duo on NBC. He later returned to Louisville, where he had business interests, including an executive role with Hillerich & Bradsby, the manufacturers of the Louisville Slugger bat. Reese was elected to the Hall of Fame by the Veterans Committee in 1984. In 1997 the Society for American Baseball Research (SABR) awarded him its Hero of Baseball Award.

Phil Regan

Regan, Philip Raymond **P**

1960–72 M(1995, 71–73) B:4/6/1937, Otsego, MI
Deb:7/19/1960, DET AL BR/TR 6'3", 200

W	L	PCT	G	SV	IP	BB	SO	ERA
96	81	.542	551	92	1372[2]	447	743	3.84

Relief pitcher Phil Regan was called "the Vulture" for the way he picked up easy victories after Dodgers starters had done all the work. He was noted for the effective downward motion of one pitch—which he said was a slider but hitters insisted was a spitball.

As a freshman at Wayland High School in Michigan, Philip Raymond Regan wrote an essay on what he expected to be doing in 10 years: pitching for the Tigers. The righthander went a long way toward realizing that dream when he signed with Detroit in the spring of 1956. He played with Jamestown, Durham, Birmingham, Charleston, and Denver before reaching Detroit in 1960. He lost all four of his decisions that season, but rebounded to post winning records, mostly as a starter, from 1961 to 1963.

Regan went 5–10 in 1964 and was sent down to Syracuse in 1965. Traded to Los Angeles on December 15, 1965, for infielder Dick Tracewski, he turned his career around with the Dodgers, becoming one of baseball's most effective relievers. Along the way Regan changed his delivery, to one usually described as "herky-jerky."

In 1966 Regan went 14–1 with a league-leading 21 saves and a 1.62 ERA. His performance earned him *The Sporting News* National League Comeback Player of the Year Award. In the midst of the 1966 pennant race, Sandy Koufax had gone 11 innings in a 1–1 duel with Jim Bunning. Regan appeared in the 12th and got the win. In Koufax's next start, he pitched seven innings and left with the score, 1–1. Regan came in and again received the "W." In those 18 innings Koufax had struck out 26 and came away with nothing. Regan had two wins. To Koufax, Regan was a "vulture"—and the name stuck.

In the spring of 1968 Regan experienced an odd swelling in his joints. He could barely lift a coffee cup. A physician diagnosed him as having rheumatoid arthritis, and the prognosis was not good. Regan quickly read as much as he could about arthritis, a disease with many forms. He read about one type of rheumatoid arthritis—a rare one—that lasted only 30 days.

Within a month Regan and outfielder Jim Hickman (then in the minors) were traded to the Cubs for outfielder Ted Savage and pitcher Jim Ellis. Chicago ordered Regan to take a medical examination, and it revealed there was no longer anything wrong with him. He had the 30-day variety of rheumatoid arthritis and was never bothered by the disease again.

Regan and Hickman, both discards from the Dodgers, became key figures for the 1969 Cubs—almost a team of destiny. Regan pitched well early in that season, but tired down the stretch as the "Miracle" Mets caught the Cubs. The blame was often laid at manager Leo Durocher's feet for overworking Regan, who made 71 appearances.

At the time Regan didn't think that was a problem, but later reflected on it and gave the theory more credence. "I didn't feel tired in 1969," he commented. "But I may have lost that crispness. Your pitches aren't as good, but you don't know it."

Regan was often accused of employing a spitter while pitching for the Dodgers and the Cubs. In August 1968 Regan collided with Reds catcher Pat Corrales. Cincinnati pitcher George Culver claimed that after the play, he found a tube of Vaseline and several slippery elm tablets at home plate. National League president Warren Giles held a hearing, but afterwards league umpires were ordered to lay off Regan.

After being sold to the White Sox in June 1972, Regan retired from the game. He rejected an offer to pitch in Japan and went into business. But baseball lured him back. He coached at Grand Valley College in Michigan, scouted and coached for the Mariners, and also scouted for the Dodgers. After the 1994 season, Regan replaced Johnny Oates as Orioles manager and lasted one year. He filled out the lineup card the day Cal Ripken broke Lou Gehrig's streak for consecutive games played; that day he also filled out several more lineup cards, which he later auctioned off.

In 1997 he returned to the bench as the Cubs pitching coach. In 1998 Chicago's patched-together staff helped the Cubs win the National League Wild Card. In 1999 he was pitching coach for the Indians.

Jerry Reinsdorf

Reinsdorf, Jerry M.

Owner (1981–*) B:2/26/1936, Brooklyn, NY

Not long after Jerry Reinsdorf purchased the Chicago White Sox in January 1981, he threatened to move the team to Florida. Thus began the tenure of one of baseball's most controversial owners. He bought the team from legendary Bill Veeck, who was in his second stint as owner of the team.

One of the first things Reinsdorf did was to bring catcher Carlton Fisk to Chicago. He also allowed manager Tony La Russa to nurture his young and talented pitching staff. The result was a division title in 1983, the first postseason appearance by a Chicago baseball team since Veeck's "Go-Go Sox" took the 1959 pennant. The White Sox drew 2 million customers for the first time.

When Reinsdorf wanted a new ballpark to replace venerable Comiskey Park, built in 1910, he threatened to move the franchise to St. Petersburg, Florida. With a new stadium already underway in Florida, Illinois legislators gave in at the last moment and voted to build a new ballpark in Chicago. New Comiskey Park opened across the street from the old park in 1991. Unfortunately, Baltimore's Camden Yards opened just one year later, offering modern amenities while retaining the feel of an old ballpark. A little more than a year after it opened, Chicago's new stadium seemed cold and obsolete.

The White Sox still had life, though. Led by slugging first baseman Frank Thomas and a core of talented pitchers, the team rose from a decade of mediocrity to win the American League West in 1993, and looked ready to advance further in 1994. They never did, in large part because of the hard-line stance of their owner.

Two years after leading the successful push to oust baseball commissioner Fay Vincent, Reinsdorf urged his fellow owners to demand a salary cap similar to the one implemented in the National Basketball Association, where Reinsdorf owned the Chicago Bulls. Already viewed as the driving force behind the appointment of "interim" commissioner (and Milwaukee Brewers owner) Bud Selig, Reinsdorf quickly developed a contentious public rivalry with players' union head Donald Fehr , whom Reinsdorf said had "a pathological hatred of baseball owners."

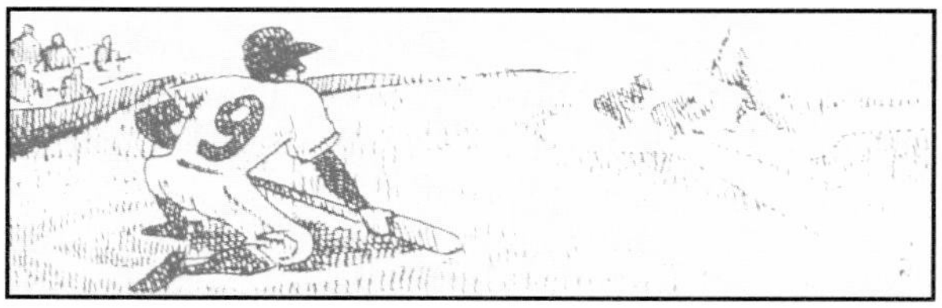

Their personal animosity helped fuel the nearly eight-month strike. A long-term deal was finally reached in November 1996—a deal that Reinsdorf strongly opposed even as he unwittingly contributed to its passage.

The proposal called for limited revenue sharing through a luxury tax imposed on the wealthiest teams. Twelve owners, led by Reinsdorf, initially rejected it. Two weeks later an identical agreement passed by a 26–4 vote. The difference? In between the two votes Reinsdorf signed free agent outfielder Albert Belle to a record five-year, $55 million contract that seemed to contradict the owner's call for fiscal restraint. He claimed the move was necessary to revive interest among White Sox fans. The following July, with his team just three and a half games out of first place, Reinsdorf effectively ended his team's season by trading three veteran pitchers for prospects, now arguing that his team could not compete, anyway. Almost on cue, the depleted Sox faded from the race.

Reinsdorf wore many hats: an attorney, a certified public accountant, a specialist in real estate securities, as well as a member of several boards, but in the public eye he seemed fitted with a black hat more often than not as one of the most cantankerous owners in professional sports.

Pete Reiser

Reiser, Harold Patrick **OF-3B**

1940–52 B:3/17/1919, St. Louis, MO D:10/25/1981, Palm Springs, CA Deb:7/23/1940, BRO NL BL/TR 5'11", 185

G	AB	R	H	HR	RBI	OBP	SLG	AVG
861	2662	473	786	58	368	.380	.450	.295

A batting champion in his first full season, Pete Reiser is one of baseball's great unfinished symphonies. Reckless play extinguished a star who experts say ranked among the very greatest in the game. "He had everything but luck," Brooklyn Dodgers manager Leo Durocher said. Durocher rated Willie Mays the greatest ballplayer he ever saw, adding, "Willie was, but Reiser could have been."

"Reiser out-hustled anyone," Dodgers teammate Pee Wee Reese said. "I don't know if he totally lacked peripheral vision or what, but when that ball was hit he had just one thing in his mind, catching it." After one 1947 crash into Ebbets Field's concrete wall, Reiser was given his last rites. Sportswriter Red Smith counted 11 times Reiser was carried off the field. Warning tracks and padded fences came about because of Reiser's mishaps.

Under 6 feet and 185 pounds, Harold Patrick "Pete" Reiser combined surprising extra-base power with blinding speed. In the Dodgers organization, "Reiser speed," like a Koufax fastball, remains a standard by which prospects are judged. Reiser ran a 100-yard dash in 9.8 seconds—wearing a baseball uniform and spikes.

A St. Louis native, Reiser originally signed with the Cardinals. With Commissioner Kenesaw Mountain Landis suspicious of the Cardinals' stockpile of talent, St. Louis general manager Branch Rickey asked Dodgers counterpart Larry MacPhail to shelter the prospect temporarily. However, after Reiser banged out 14 straight hits in spring training, Brooklyn couldn't let him go. "Pistol Pete" joined the Dodgers in July 1940, playing primarily at third base.

In 1941 Reiser became Brooklyn's center fielder and a member of the majors' only all-.300 hitting outfield with Dixie Walker and Ducky Medwick. Besides winning the batting crown by 24 points at .343, Reiser led the circuit in triples, runs, and slugging, tied for the doubles lead, and started in center field for the National League All Stars. He accomplished all of this despite two serious beanings and a head-first slam into the Ebbets Field wall.

The Dodgers won their first pennant in 21 years, and faced the Yankees in the World Series. Reiser was 0-for-9 with a walk until doubling to lead off the seventh inning of a scoreless Game 3, but the Dodgers failed to score him and lost, 2–1. In Game 4 Reiser's two-run homer in the fifth inning gave the Dodgers a 4–3 lead, but the Yankees rallied for four in the ninth after Mickey Owen missed a potential game-ending strike three. In Game 5 Reiser tripled in the first inning but was stranded, and knocked in the Dodgers' only run with a third-inning fly to right, as the Yankees won the game, 3–1, and the Series.

On July 2, 1942, in St. Louis, Reiser suffered one of his worst injuries. In the 12th inning of a scoreless tie, Reiser chased Enos Slaughter's shot to the center-field fence. Flying at full speed, Reiser caught the ball, hit the concrete wall, and the ball trickled out of his glove. Reiser instinctively threw to Reese, but Slaughter scored the winning run just ahead of the relay.

Reiser, who remembered nothing after making the throw, collapsed in the clubhouse and was rushed to the hospital. He had a concussion and separated left shoulder. The Dodgers had a double-digit lead in the pennant race, and Reiser admitted his play appeared foolhardy, but contended, "You slow up a half step, and it's the beginning of your last ballgame."

Reiser came back to start in the All-Star Game four days later, but was plagued by dizzy spells for the rest of his life. "They never asked me if I could, they only asked me if I would," Reiser said of playing hurt. The Dodgers lost their lead, and Reiser's average fell from .383 to .310 after he was injured.

But Reiser never changed his approach. He separated his right shoulder diving over a hedge and landing in a ditch making a catch playing for an Army team in 1943. (During his three years in the military, Reiser met Jackie Robinson at Fort Riley, Kansas, and would become a staunch supporter when Robinson integrated the majors.)

Back with the Dodgers in 1946, Reiser won his second league stolen base crown with 34, including a record seven steals of home, and was named to his final All-Star team. Late in the season, while attempting to make a diving catch, Reiser dislocated his left shoulder, broke his left ankle, and tore muscles in his left leg. His near-fatal collision with the Ebbets Field wall in 1947 reduced his playing time to 110 games, but he batted .309 and stole 14 bases, second in the league to teammate Robinson, as the Dodgers won the pennant and met the Yankees in the World Series again.

In Game 1 Reiser's first-inning hustle—reaching second when Robinson got trapped on his grounder to the mound—set up the Dodgers' first run, and his sixth-inning infield hit led to their second tally. However, Brooklyn lost the game, 5–3. Game 2 at Yankee Stadium was a nightmare for Reiser. Suffering from vertigo, he misplayed four balls in the Yankees' 10–3 win. Reiser was in the starting lineup for Game 3, was removed for a pinch hitter in the second inning, and did not start another Series game.

At only 28 years old, he never played regularly again. After he saw part-time duty in 1948, the Dodgers traded him to the Boston Braves for another fading outfielder, Mike McCormick. After two years in Boston, Reiser spent 1951 with the Pirates and 1952 with the Cleveland Indians. He then coached for the Los Angeles Dodgers from 1960 through 1964, worked under Durocher with the Chicago Cubs from 1966 through 1969, spent two seasons with the California Angels, and then returned to the Cubs for the 1971 and 1972 seasons.

Steve Renko

Renko, Steven **P**

1969–83 B:12/10/1944, Kansas City, KS
Deb:6/27/1969, MON NL BR/TR 6'5", 230

W	L	PCT	G	SH	IP	BB	SO	ERA
134	146	.479	451	9	2494	1010	1455	3.99

A star quarterback at the University of Kansas, Steven Renko was drafted by the Oakland Raiders but decided not to pursue a career in football. Renko was chosen by the Mets as a first baseman in the 10th round of the June 1965 draft. After he led Eastern League first basemen in errors, Renko was switched to pitcher. For Memphis on July 21, 1968 he no-hit Albuquerque. Although he pitched for seven Mets minor league teams, he never pitched for the club in New York. He was traded to Montreal in the June 1969 deal that sent Donn Clendenon to the Mets.

The expansion Expos just let him pitch, even though he remained wild. Renko struck out seven straight Mets on October 3, 1972, although he finished the season at 1–10. In 1971 he tossed two of his career one-hitters, and in 1974, he led the National League with 19 wild pitches, once uncorking three in an inning.

In May 1976 Renko was dealt to the Cubs, beginning a series of trades that took him to five more clubs before his release by the Kansas City Royals in October 1983. In 1999 he was coaching for the Southern League's Huntsville Stars.

Edgar Renteria

Renteria, Edgar Enrique **SS**

1996–* B:8/7/1976, Barranquilla, Colombia Deb:5/10/1996, FLA NL BR/TR 6'1", 172

G	AB	R	H	HR	RBI	OBP	SLG	AVG
547	2150	329	611	23	177	.343	.369	.284

After driving in the winning run in the bottom of the ninth of Game 1 of the 1997 National League Division Series, Florida Marlins shortstop Edgar Renteria proclaimed, "This is the happiest moment of my life." Little did he know that things would get even better. In Game 7 of the World Series the 22-year-old Renteria hit a two-out, bases-loaded, 11th-inning single to make world champions of the Marlins, a team only five years removed from its first National League game.

Just the fourth Colombian native to play in the majors, Renteria quickly established himself as a solid player and a hero to his countrymen. A star in the minors for four years, he was runner-up in National League Rookie of the Year voting in 1996. His 22-game hitting streak was the longest by a rookie since Jerome Walton hit in 30 straight games in 1989. On the strength of his postseason heroics in 1997, Renteria was voted Colombia's man of the year in an opinion poll and received the "San Carlos Cross of the Order of the Great Knight," his nation's highest honor.

In 1998, even after he watched the fire sale that dismantled the Marlins' championship club, the unflappable Renteria batted .282, stole 41 bases,

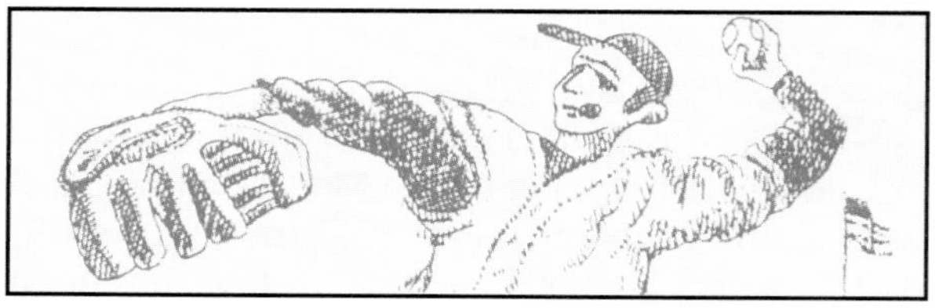

and earned All-Star honors. Traded to the Cardinals in 1999, he kept up his steady hitting, base stealing, and glove work.

Merv Rettenmund

Rettenmund, Mervin Weldon **OF**

1968–80 B:6/6/1943, Flint, MI Deb:4/14/1968, BAL AL BR/TR 5'10", 195

G	AB	R	H	HR	RBI	OBP	SLG	AVG
1023	2555	393	693	66	329	.383	.406	.271

Merv Rettenmund could have played professional football, having been drafted as a halfback out of Ball State by the Dallas Cowboys, but he chose baseball and signed with the Orioles. It turned out to be a smart move; he played in four World Series and six playoff series with three different clubs.

Rettenmund drew notice even before he reached the major leagues, hitting .331 with 22 home runs for Triple A Rochester and being named by *The Sporting News* as the Minor League Player of the Year. Rettenmund, an outfielder, didn't stop hitting upon reaching the American League. He led the Orioles for two straight years, batting .322 in 1970 and .318 in 1971. He never approached those numbers again, but he remained in Baltimore through the 1973 season.

Rettenmund was traded to the Reds in 1974 and used primarily as a platoon player and pinch hitter. By 1977 he had honed his skills as a pinch hitter, leading the National League by going 21-for-67 for the Padres. It was the eighth highest total for pinch hits in a single season. Rettenmund played three more seasons with the California Angels before retiring in 1980.

Ed Reulbach

Reulbach, Edwin Marvin **P**

1905–17 B:12/1/1882, Detroit, MI D:7/17/1961, Glens Falls, NY Deb:5/16/1905, CHI NL BR/TR 6'1", 190

W	L	PCT	G	SH	IP	BB	SO	ERA
182	106	.632	399	40	2632^{1}	892	1137	2.28

Ed Reulbach won 97 games in his first five seasons in the major leagues, and had an ERA of 2.03 or under in each of those seasons. His lifetime record included 40 shutouts. Despite his success, he never received a single vote for the Hall of Fame in his lifetime.

Reulbach was prepared if baseball didn't work out. He went to college at a time when few ballplayers took that route. He studied electrical engineering at Notre Dame and pre-med at the University of Vermont, playing independent and professional ball under assumed names between terms. He joined the Chicago Cubs in 1905, posting 18 wins, including nine in a row, with five shutouts and a 1.42 ERA.

"Big Ed" was even better as the Cubs won three straight pennants from 1906 to 1908. He led the National League in winning percentage all three years, setting a league record. In 1908 Reulbach hurled 44 straight scoreless innings, including two shutouts over Brooklyn in one day. He was also 2–0 in World Series competition, with a one-hitter over the White Sox in 1906. Reulbach fashioned winning streaks of 12 in 1906 and 14 in 1909.

After posting a 136–65 record in eight-plus seasons with the Cubs, Reulbach was dealt to the Dodgers in 1913. Released a year later, Reulbach latched on with the Federal League. Reulbach had his last hurrah, winning 21 games for Newark in 1915. After the league folded, Reulbach joined the Boston Braves in 1916.

He was active in players' rights movements, helping to organize the Base Ball Players' Fraternity, and serving as its first Secretary. He worked in the shipyards during World War I, then spent decades in various business ventures, including manufacturing, construction, and insurance. Reulbach died on the same day as Ty Cobb in 1961.

Rick Reuschel

Reuschel, Rickey Eugene **P**

1972–91 B:5/16/1949, Quincy, IL Deb:6/19/1972, CHI NL BR/TR 6'3", 235

W	L	PCT	G	SH	IP	BB	SO	ERA
214	191	.528	557	26	3548[1]	935	2015	3.37

Although he looked more like someone pitching at the annual Fourth of July picnic than a major league hurler, Rick Reuschel was one of baseball's more effective pitchers for nearly 20 years. An intense competitor, Reuschel could hit and field well despite his 6-foot 3-inch, 235-pound frame. He could even run—the climax of the 1986 Pirates highlight film showed Reuschel scoring a winning run from second base with a thunderous slide at home.

His large body didn't interfere with his pitching. The key to Rickey Eugene Reuschel's long-term success was an extraordinary economy of movement. Throwing effortlessly with almost no windup, Reuschel relied on superb control. He never walked more than 76 batters in a season even though he routinely pitched more than 200 innings. Bob Brenly, Reuschel's catcher toward the end of his career, said, "He doesn't get anybody out. They get themselves out."

Reuschel won 10 games in 1972, his first season with the Cubs, and didn't fall below that total for the next eight years. He was christened "Big Daddy" by teammate Mike Krukow early in his career, but he was actually the little brother of teammate Paul Reuschel. In August 1975 Rick and Paul became the first brothers to pitch a major league shutout together.

A month later Rick was the starter and loser in the most lopsided shutout defeat in history. In that 22–0 whitewash by the Pirates, Bucs second baseman Rennie Stennett became the only major leaguer in the 20th century to go 7-for-7 in a nine-inning game. Reuschel retired only one batter in the first inning, allowing eight earned runs.

Despite that devastating outing, he routinely started 35 to 38 games a year, averaged 14 wins for the less than awe-inspiring Cubbies. In 1977 he led Chicago to its only .500 season during that era. He finished 20–10 and recorded four shutouts. Swapped to the Yanks during the 1981 strike season, he won four games down the stretch to help them gain a share of the American League East.

A rotator-cuff tear put Reuschel on the shelf for the 1982 season, and his return from surgery was slow. He had two so-so years with the Cubs. The Pirates, desperate for pitching help of any kind, signed him as a free agent. Reuschel returned to form in grand style, compiling a 14–8 record accompanied by a 2.27 ERA that earned him Comeback Player of the Year honors. He was responsible for nearly 25 percent of the lowly Bucs' victory total.

The Pirates sent him to San Francisco late in 1987 in a move designed to cut their payroll, and Reuschel once again had a chance to pitch for a team in contention. He came through, putting together a 5–3 record that helped the Giants win a divisional championship. His combined Pirate–Giants stats that year included league-leading efforts in complete games and shutouts. He also won his second Gold Glove.

Remarkably, he had his two best seasons in the next two years, at the ages of 39 and 40. In 36 starts in 1988 he won 19 games. In 1989 he went 17–8 and started for the National League in the All-Star Game. He did not earn a decision in that game but he surrendered a massive home run by Bo Jackson to lead off the game for the American League.

Reuschel helped pitch the Giants to the pennant, earning the win in the clinching game in the Championship Series against his former Cubs teammates. In the World Series he surrendered a three-run homer by Oakland's Terry Steinbach and took the loss in Game 2. Reuschel pitched parts of two more years with San Francisco before finally calling it quits at age 42.

Jerry Reuss

Reuss, Jerry **P**

1969–90 B:6/19/1949, St. Louis, MO Deb:9/27/1969, STL NL BL/TL 6'5", 217

W	L	PCT	G	SH	IP	BB	SO	ERA
220	191	.535	628	39	3669^{2}	1127	1907	3.64

Jerry Reuss was a clown in the clubhouse but all business on the mound. Signed as a $30,000 bonus baby by the Cardinals in 1969, he quickly earned a reputation as a free spirit—holding out after going 1–0, 7–8, and 14–14, because teammate Steve Carlton was doing it. Carlton, however, had just come off a 20–9 season. Cards owner Auggie Busch ordered Reuss traded in 1972, and the Cards got Lance Clemons and Scipio Spinks for the talented pitcher, who the next year won 16 games for Houston.

In another one-sided deal, Reuss went next to the Pirates for catcher Milt May. After walking 101 in 1974, Reuss dramatically improved his control. A lively presence in the Bucs clubhouse, he had a waggish sense of humor, a bushy mustache, and long, shaggy blond hair. Reuss won 34 games in his first two years in Pittsburgh as the Pirates won consecutive division titles.

Dealt to the Dodgers after the 1978 season, he slumped. But an 18–6 year in 1980 earned him a spot on the All-Star team and the Comeback Player of the Year Award. He finished second to his old pal Steve Carlton in Cy Young voting and tossed a no-hitter in which only one batter reached base safely, on a shortstop error. In the strike-shortened 1981 season he won 10 games plus a 2–1 complete-game victory over Ron Guidry in Game 5 of the World Series. The win turned the tide for the Dodgers, who won the next game to become world champions.

Reuss pitched for Dodger division champs in 1983 and 1985 as well, but injuries hurt his effectiveness over the next two seasons. He put together another impressive comeback for the White Sox in 1988, winning 13 times for a team that won only 71 games. After earning a 9–9 record for the White Sox and Brewers in 1989, he returned to the Pirates in 1990. He pitched only seven innings for Pittsburgh before retiring.

Reuss was only the second pitcher in baseball history to win 200 games without recording a 20-win season; Milt Pappas was the first. Reuss became a baseball announcer for ESPN.

Allie Reynolds

Reynolds, Allie Pierce **P**

1942–54 B:2/10/1915, Bethany, OK D:12/26/1994, Stillwater, OK Deb:9/17/1942, CLE AL BR/TR 6', 195

W	L	PCT	G	SV	IP	BB	SO	ERA
182	107	.630	434	49	2492^{1}	1261	1423	3.30

Allie Reynolds, known as "Superchief" because of his partly Native American ancestry, had a commanding presence on the mound. At his best when the stakes were at their highest, Reynolds was a Yankee for eight seasons, and while he was there the Bronx Bombers went to the World Series six times.

The Oklahoma native attended the university now known as Oklahoma State on a track scholarship. He could run the 100-yard dash in 9.8 seconds, and he was also a star running back on the football team. Baseball? He wasn't interested until a knee injury his sophomore year kept him from running track, and he started pitching in the intramural league. Hank Iba, who coached baseball and basketball at the university, saw Reynolds play and asked him to pitch batting practice.

"I tried it because I didn't have anything else to do except piddle around with intramural ball," Reynolds said. "But it wasn't a good idea. I struck everybody out." He stopped piddling around with intramurals and joined the team as a pitcher. After he graduated, the football Giants offered Reynolds $100 a game. "I went to Mr. Iba for advice because I didn't know anything about professional sports and he told me, 'If I were you, I'd consider baseball before football.' It was a fine suggestion."

Reynolds signed with the Indians in 1939 for $1,000 and reported to Springfield in the Class C Middle Atlantic League. After going 18–7 with Wilkes-Barre in 1942 and leading the Eastern League in ERA and strikeouts, he was ready for the big time.

He was 11–12 in 1943 and led the American League in strikeouts with 151. He also walked 109 batters in 199 innings. He had a great fastball and a wicked curve, but he still had a lot to learn about pitching. He was 18–12 in 1945 against the aging veterans and secondary players who filled the majors during the last year of World War II. He also led the American League with 130 walks in 247 innings. But he got a cold dose of reality in 1946 when he fell to 11–15.

Then Reynolds' career took a dramatic turn. Yankees general manager Larry MacPhail was looking to dump aging Joe Gordon and the Indians needed a second baseman. They were offering a pitcher. The newly hired New York manager, Bucky Harris, asked seasoned Yankees outfielders Joe DiMaggio and Tommy Henrich for some advice. The message from both was the same: get Reynolds.

At this point, Reynolds was 30 years old and had only a 51–47 career record despite great stuff. He started slowly with the Yankees. Then he got some advice from 40-year-old Spud Chandler, in his last year in the majors. "Don't just throw the ball," Chandler told him. "Think about what you're doing. Change speeds. Set hitters up. Think, think, think." Reynolds listened. In 1947, his first year in pinstripes, he went 19–8 and led the American League in winning percentage with .704.

That season he also began to establish himself as one of the great World Series pitchers when he won Game 2 in New York's eventual seven-game victory over Brooklyn. Two years later, as the Yankees won the first of their unprecedented five straight World Series, he hooked up with Don Newcombe in Game 1 for one of the finest pitching duels in Series history. Reynolds prevailed, 1–0, when Henrich led off the bottom of the ninth with a home run. He finished with a two-hitter, and thought he could have had a no-hitter. The two hits came on a ball that was lost in the sun in Yankee Stadium left field and a groundball that somehow sneaked between his legs.

In Game 4, Reynolds got the save for Eddie Lopat, retiring all 10 Dodgers he faced. He was 7–2 with four saves and a 2.79 in six World Series. He often did double duty in his Yankee years. Casey Stengel once said about Reynolds, "[He was] the best pitcher at starting and relieving I've ever managed. In fact, I'd go further and tell you he's the best at the two things that I've ever seen. What I mean is, he's two pitchers rolled into one."

In 1951, Reynolds became only the second major leaguer, with Johnny Vander Meer, to pitch two no-hitters in the same season. The first was against Cleveland in midseason, a 1–0 game decided on Gene Woodling's home run in the eighth inning. As Reynolds came into the Yankees dugout after the eighth, he turned to Lopat and said, "Ed, do you think I can pitch a no-hitter?" Lopat, a superstitious man, was aghast. Not only did he not respond, he walked out of the dugout, and then out of the ballpark.

The second no-hitter came on September 28 in the middle of a wild pennant race against the Red Sox. This was an 8–0 laugher—until there were two out in the ninth. The batter was Ted Williams. He lifted a towering pop foul that Yogi Berra drifted under—and dropped. Williams then popped the next pitch to almost the same exact spot. This time Berra caught it.

Reynolds' last great season was 1952 when he went 20–8, his only 20-win season, with a league-leading 2.06 ERA. He also led the league in strikeouts with 160 and in shutouts with six while completing 24 of 29 starts. For good measure, he saved six games. But he injured his back the next year when the Yankee team bus was in an accident, and although he went 26–11 with 20 saves over the next two seasons, he was forced to retire after the 1954 season. Reynolds later served as head baseball coach at Oklahoma State.

Craig Reynolds

Reynolds, Gordon Craig **SS**

1975–89 B:12/27/1952, Houston, TX Deb:8/1/1975, PIT NL BL/TR, 6'1", 175

G	AB	R	H	HR	RBI	OBP	SLG	AVG
1491	4466	480	1142	42	377	.293	.345	.256

Though Craig Reynolds began his career with the Pittsburgh Pirates in 1975, he spent the bulk of his 15-year career with his hometown team, the Houston Astros. In between, he spent two seasons with the Seattle Mariners, where he was the starting shortstop for the first-year expansion club in 1977. It was Reynolds' first season as an everyday player.

A year later, Reynolds made the American League All-Star team for the first time when he hit a career-best .292. He became a National League All-Star in 1979, his first with the Astros. He appeared in each of Houston's first three playoff appearances, but never advanced to the World Series.

Reynolds reaped the rewards of artificial turf by leading the NL with 12 triples during the split season of 1981. Used primarily as an everyday shortstop, he showed his versatility late in his career by switching to a utility role in his last two seasons, playing all four infield positions as well as the outfield, plus two pitching appearances in blowout losses.

Shane Reynolds

Reynolds, Richard Shane **P**

1992–* B:3/26/1968, Bastrop, LA Deb:7/20/1992, HOU NL BR/TR 6'3", 210

W	L	PCT	G	SH	IP	BB	SO	ERA
79	61	.564	211	5	1234^{2}	251	1067	3.70

After Randy Johnson's dominance in the final two months of the 1998 season, the prospect of Shane Reynolds taking the mound for Opening Day 1999 must have been less than thrilling to many Houston Astros fans. Reynolds was not as flashy, but was just as consistent.

While Johnson racked up strikeouts and victories in his short stint with the Astros in 1998, Reynolds quietly set new career highs that season in wins (19) and strikeouts (209). Reynolds, who had been slowed by knee problems in 1997, showed his accustomed superlative control with just 53 walks in 233⅓ innings. He was at his best when he spotted his fastball and curve early in the count to get ahead of hitters, then went for the kill with his nasty split-finger fastball.

"Most guys that you project as [aces] are guys that throw real hard," Astros manager Larry Dierker said. "What it boils down to is making good pitches. Hitting the spots and having movement on your pitches is more important than running the radar gun up."

Reynolds went 16–14 in 1999, suffering through periods where teams feasted on his fastball. He rebounded at the end of the season, and picked up Houston's lone win in a four-game Division Series defeat by Atlanta.

Flint Rhem

Rhem, Charles Flint **P**

1924–28, 1930–36 B:1/24/1901, Rhems, SC D:7/30/1969, Columbia, SC Deb:9/6/1924, STL NL BR/TR 6'2", 180

W	L	PCT	G	SV	IP	BB	SO	ERA
105	97	.520	294	10	1725^{1}	529	534	4.20

Flint Rhem was a rawboned righthander with a fiery fastball and a thirst for the hard stuff. Although the fastball won him 105 major league games, his fondness for the bottle was what won him a lasting place in baseball lore.

Rhem joined the Cardinals in 1924 and put in two unremarkable seasons. In 1926 he suddenly became a star, tying for the league lead in victories with 20 as the Cardinals won their first pennant. But after that one brilliant season Flint Rhem became unreliable. Some blamed his erratic performance on his taste for Prohibition booze, and he was even sent back to the minors for a while in the hope that he would dry out.

In 1930 he was back in form as St. Louis prepared for a crucial, late-season series at Brooklyn. Rhem, scheduled to pitch the opener, showed up in the morning disheveled and reeking of alcohol. He claimed that he had been kidnapped, held in a room at gunpoint, and forced against his will to drink cup after cup of hard liquor. He was certain that the kidnappers were gamblers who planned to bet heavily on Brooklyn. Although no one believed Rhem's tale, no one could disprove it, and he escaped unpunished. When Rhem's pitching skills fell below the level of his alibis he was shuttled around to three other National League teams.

Rick Rhoden

Rhoden, Richard Alan **P**

1974–89 B:5/16/1953, Boynton Beach, FL Deb:7/5/1974, LA NL BR/TR 6'3", 195

W	L	PCT	G	SH	IP	BB	SO	ERA
151	125	.547	413	17	2593^{2}	801	1419	3.59

Rick Rhoden overcame numerous physical problems in childhood to become a major league pitcher. Rhoden contracted osteomyelitis, an infection of the bone and bone marrow that can kill the bone tissue, and was forced to wear a leg brace until he was 12. In addition, he had to have surgery to remove part of his left knee so that it wouldn't outgrow the right one. Then, after he had recovered, an accident involving a rusty pair of scissors led to another leg infection. On top of all that, after eight years as a professional pitcher, he had to undergo rotator cuff surgery.

Regardless of the numerous setbacks, Rhoden was a superior athlete who used his fastball and slider to pitch 16 years in the major leagues. As a minor leaguer he was unimpressive. In his final year in Triple A his record was 9–10 with a 4.40 ERA, but he still worked his way in the Dodgers rotation. In 1976 he went 12–3 and earned a spot on the All-Star team. He was the youngest member of a Los Angeles staff that included Burt Hooton, Tommy John, Don Sutton, and Charlie Hough.

The following season John led the staff with 20 wins, and Rhoden was second with 16. In that year's Championship Series, Rhoden was called in to quench Philadelphia's fire in Game 3 with his team trailing, 3–2. He held the Phillies scoreless for 4⅓ innings, and the Dodgers pulled out the victory. He lost Game 1 of the World Series in the 12th inning when a Willie Randolph double and a Paul Blair single drove in the winning run. Given another long relief stint in Game 4, he held the Yankees to one run in seven innings.

Rhoden helped the Dodgers reach the postseason again the following year. He pitched four innings in Game 4 of the NLCS, once again holding the Phillies close until the Dodgers pulled out the win that put them in the World Series. However, Rhoden was never used in the Series as the Dodgers lost to the Yankees for the second straight year.

He was dealt to the Pirates even-up for Jerry Reuss before the 1979 season, but Rhoden's shoulder was hurting. He appeared in just one game as a Pirate before being placed on the disabled list. He underwent surgery on his shoulder during the off-season. Sent to Portland for rehabilitation, he pitched a seven-inning no-hitter and was soon recalled to the big club. In 1980 he started 20 games for the Pirates; the next year he was the team's No. 1 starter, and he assembled a 9–4 record during the strike-shortened season.

For the next five years he was a model of consistency, leading the Pirates in starts and innings pitched every year, winning between 10 and 16 games. But Rhoden was a Pirate when it was no fun to be a Pirate; the team, embattled by drug problems and an unsurprising lack of fan support, fell from dominance to become the perennial last-place club. Rhoden wanted out, and got his wish in November 1986 when Syd Thrift dealt him to the Yankees, along with pitchers Cecilio Guante and Pat Clements, for three young pitchers: Doug Drabek, Brian Fisher, and Logan Easley. Thrift's postseason analysis of the deal: "Drabek, Fisher, and Easley won 23 games for the Pirates; Rhoden won 16, so we gained seven wins and saved $797,500."

Rhoden won 28 games in two New York seasons, impressive considering the Yankees finished in fourth place one season and fifth place the next. He was reunited with Tommy John in the Big Apple—in 1987 they combined to go 29–16. Sent back to the National League in 1989, Rhoden ended his career with Houston.

Rhoden was one of the best hitting pitchers of his time. He batted over .300 three times and showed power on occasion. He won the league Silver Slugger award for pitchers three years in a row. In 1982 he slugged a homer and a double in the same inning. In 1987 the Yankees actually used him as a designated hitter for one game. He was an excellent fielder, too, and made only six errors in 16 major league seasons.

Although he was never caught, he was frequently accused of doctoring the ball. While in Pittsburgh, Rhoden was overheard saying to his teammates in the bullpen, "When you pitch against Sutton, do anything you want to the ball. If they catch you, blame it on him." In 1987 umpires confronted him with two balls that had been scuffed in exactly the same spot—across the American League logo. In 1988 an umpire told a sportswriter that one ball he took from Rhoden looked as though it had been worked over with a chisel. Seattle's Jim Snyder described a Rhoden souvenir as "looking like it had an open cab door hanging off the side of it."

Dusty Rhodes

Rhodes, James Lamar **OF**

1952–59 B:5/13/1927, Mathews, AL Deb:7/15/1952, NY NL BL/TR 6', 180

G	AB	R	H	HR	RBI	OBP	SLG	AVG
576	1172	146	296	54	207	.329	.445	.253

An incorrigible free spirit off the field, Dusty Rhodes made a name for himself as one of the great clutch hitters in World Series history—much to the wonder of his New York Giants manager, Leo Durocher. A streaky lefthanded hitter with a stroke tailor-made for the old Polo Grounds with its short right-field porch, Rhodes became a World Series legend in 1954.

After hitting 15 homers during the year as a part-time outfielder and pinch hitter, he played a pivotal role in the Giants' four-game Series sweep of the Cleveland Indians. His pinch-hit homer off Bob Lemon with two on in the 10th inning won Game 1. The next day, he tied Game 2 with a pinch single off Early Wynn in the fifth, then homered off Wynn in the seventh for the final run of the 3–1 Giants win. Then in Game 3, he had a pinch-hit single that drove in two runs. For the entire Series, Rhodes was 4-for-6 with two homers and seven RBIs.

Rhodes remained with the Giants through 1957 and returned from the minors to play for them briefly in San Francisco in 1959. As a pinch hitter he was 55-for-260 including 15-for-45 in that magical 1954 season. It was also in 1954 that Rhodes had his greatest day—compiling two doubles, two triples, and two homers in a doubleheader on August 29. After his retirement he remained in the New York City area.

Grantland Rice

Rice, Grantland

Sportswriter B:11/1/1880, Murfreesboro, TN D:7/13/1954

Today, sportswriter Grantland Rice may be most associated with football—he coined the term "The Four Horsemen" to describe Notre Dame's legendary backfield—but he was also a highly skilled baseball writer. Like many sportswriters, Rice first aspired to be a ballplayer.

Rice played second base at Vanderbilt University, and in 1904 tried out with Atlanta of the Southern Association. He did not hit particularly well, but kept busy writing articles for the *Atlanta Constitution*. Also trying out for the team was future Brooklyn Dodgers great Nap Rucker. "One day," Rucker recalled, "the manager said to this boy, 'Why don't you quit and be a sports editor? You write better than you play second base?'" Rice took the advice.

While writing for the *Constitution,* Rice became instrumental in bringing attention to a young Ty Cobb after receiving a number of letters attesting to his play. Rice wrote in his column that "over in Alabama there's a young fellow named Cobb who seems to be showing an unusual amount of talent." Only years later when the two became friends did Rice learn that Cobb had written all those letters himself.

Rice later wrote for the *Cleveland News*, where he produced some interesting parodies of *Casey at the Bat*. He returned to Nashville before moving to New York in 1911. There the "poet of the press box" wrote for the *New York Evening Mail*, the *New York Tribune*, and the *New York Sun*. His column, "The Sport Light," became syndicated in 1930. "If you were singled out in 'Sport Light,' you were something special," noted writer Ken Sobol, "you were said to be on your way. You had that something extra."

Rice's 14 published works included *The Duffer's Handbook of Golf* (1926) and his autobiography, *The Tumult and the Shouting* (1954). His most famous misquoted words may have been that it didn't matter whether you "won or lost, but how you played the game." In 1966 he was a recipient of the J.G. Taylor Spink Award, which is displayed at the National Baseball Hall of Fame.

For the record his lead in the "Four Horsemen" story went like this: "Outlined against a blue-gray October sky, the Four Horsemen rode again. In dramatic lore they are known as Famine, Pestilence, Destruction and Death. But these are only aliases. Their real names are Stuhldreher, Miller, Crowley and Layden. They formed the crest of the South Bend Cyclone before which another Army football team was swept over the precipice at the Polo Grounds yesterday afternoon as 55,000 spectators peered down on the bewildering panorama spread on the green plain below."

Jim Rice

Rice, James Edward **OF–DH**

1974–89 B:3/8/1953, Anderson, SC Deb:8/19/1974, BOS AL BR/TR 6'2", 205

G	AB	R	H	HR	RBI	OBP	SLG	AVG
2089	8225	1249	2452	382	1451	.356	.502	.298

From the late 1970s to the mid-1980s Jim Rice was probably the American League's most dangerous batter. He collected more than 200 hits four times, drove in more than 100 runs five times, and finished his career with a lifetime .298 batting average and 382 home runs. Often misunderstood by the Boston press, Rice was nonetheless one of the best hitters in Red Sox history.

As a high schooler James Edward Rice, one of nine children, received football scholarship offers from Clemson University, the University of North Carolina, and the University of Nebraska. The Pirates, Angels, and Red Sox scouted him but some scouts thought Rice was lazy because he would lie down between innings. Boston scout Mace Brown knew the young prospect was only trying to conserve energy—Rice had a job after school loading boxes. The Red Sox drafted Rice in the 15th round and signed him for a $45,000 bonus.

He progressed slowly through the minor leagues, gaining confidence and skill at each step. In 1974 he won the International League Triple Crown, and was named the International League Rookie of the Year and Most Valuable Player; and *The Sporting News* named him its Minor League Player of the Year. He was ready for Boston.

Rice had a spectacular rookie season for the Red Sox in 1975, when he batted .309 with 22 homers and 102 RBIs. Unfortunately, his performance was overshadowed by Fred Lynn's Rookie of the Year and MVP season. That was the first of many times that Rice felt underappreciated by Boston fans and media, a feeling that may or may not have been justified. Still, it didn't seem to affect his relationship with Lynn. "Freddy and I got along well in those years," Rice once said. "There was no jealousy. We respected each other."

A pitch by Detroit's Vern Ruhle broke Rice's hand in September and he missed the memorable 1975 World Series, in which the Sox fell to the Reds in seven games. After a solid sophomore season, he exploded in 1977. That year he led the American League with 39 home runs and a .593 slugging average while batting .320 and driving in 114 runs. He hit three homers in a game on August 29.

In 1978 he won the AL Most Valuable Player Award. That season Rice batted .315 and led the league with 46 home runs, 139 RBIs, 213 hits, 15 triples, and a .600 slugging average. He was the last player in the 20th century to hit at least 40 home runs with at least 200 hits.

In 1979 Rice put up almost identical numbers. During this period Rice was considered the most dangerous hitter in the league. Baseball fans argued back and forth about whether the game's best player was Rice or Pittsburgh's Dave Parker. "I've never heard a bat louder than his," Ken Harrelson said of Rice. "You hear it going through the strike zone and the sound is unmistakable. It goes 'vump.' That's when he misses." Rice was amazingly strong. It was said that his bat once broke on a checked swing.

In 1982 Rice helped save the life of a 5-year-old boy who was struck by a foul ball. While everyone else was stunned at the sight of the bleeding boy, Rice jumped into the stands and carried him into the clubhouse and to an ambulance. Rice was nominated for an NAACP award for his quick thinking.

In 1983 Rice again led the league in home runs, with 39, and in RBIs, with 126, and he hit better than .300 for the sixth time in his career. But he never captured the imagination of the Boston public. He was perceived as surly. "I'm not a talkative guy, not a guy who parades himself around for the press. I do my job. I come in before games, have my cup of tea and go out and play. Then I go home," he once said.

"I understand a writer's got a job to do, and if he wants to talk about my performance or what happened on the field, fine. But then the questions start about what I think about other people, and I don't like to second-guess. I don't talk about the way things should be done. That's why you have an owner, a president, and a general manager."

Rice drove in 110 runs in 1986, the season the Red Sox next won the pennant. The Sox advanced past the Angels in a classic seven-game American League Championship Series. Rice hit two homers and drove in six runs against California, but batted only .161. In Boston's seven-game loss to the Mets in the World Series, Rice hit .333 and scored six runs, but failed to drive in a run.

Rice never had great speed. In 1984 he set a major league record by grounding into 36 double plays. He led the American League in that category in 1982, 1984, and 1985, and tied for the lead in 1983. He grounded into 315 double plays in his career, third most all-time. Following the 1987 season Rice underwent knee surgery, which further slowed him down. He moved from the outfield to predominantly designated hitter duty.

Rice's production declined dramatically following his knee problems. On one occasion manager Joe Morgan sent in Spike Owen to pinch hit for Rice, resulting in a shoving match between Rice and Morgan. In 1988 Boston reached the ALCS but lost in four straight games to the A's. Rice managed only two hits, one RBI, and a .154 batting average in the Series.

The Sox released Rice following the 1990 season. When he retired, the Red Sox announced a day to honor him and pitcher Bob Stanley. But Rice refused to participate. A Red Sox player who asked not to be identified understood why. "Rice gave Boston 15-plus years and hit more homers for the Sox than anyone but Ted Williams and Carl Yastrzemski," the player said. "And not only do they treat him like a utilityman, but they ask him to share a day with Bob Stanley—which is like asking Yaz to share his day with Mike Torrez."

Sam Rice

Rice, Edgar Charles **OF**

1915–34 B:2/20/1890, Morocco, IN D:10/13/1974, Rossmor, MD Deb:8/7/1915, WAS AL BL/TR 5'9", 150

G	AB	R	H	HR	RBI	OBP	SLG	AVG
2404	9269	1514	2987	34	1078	.374	.427	.322

Sam Rice made one of the most famous and controversial catches in World Series history. During Game 3 of the 1925 Series Rice was playing right field for the Washington Senators against Pittsburgh. Washington was leading, 4–3, in the eighth inning when Pirates catcher Earl Smith smashed a Firpo Marberry pitch to deep right-center field, where temporary stands had been erected to handle the overflow crowd at Griffith Stadium. Rice took off like a shot and arrived at the edge of the stands just as the ball descended. He leaped, stuck up his glove, tumbled into the crowd, and disappeared.

At least 10 seconds passed before he emerged, holding the ball high. Umpire Cy Rigler, who had run out from second base, signaled an out, and the Pirates went crazy. They even appealed the call to Commissioner Kenesaw Mountain Landis. All Rice would tell Landis (or anyone else) was, "The umpire said I caught the ball." More than 1,600 fans in the bleachers filed notarized affidavits describing what they saw, but the eyewitness reports were contradictory. The debate cooled only after the Pirates won the Series in seven games.

Over the years, Rice refused to elaborate on his initial statement. But he did send a letter to the Hall of Fame, stipulating that it could be opened only after his death. When he died in 1974, the letter confirmed the umpire's call: Rice provided a detailed description of the catch, ending with the assertion, "at no time did I lose possession of the ball."

In 1908 Rice married and moved to Illinois where he and his wife had two children. In 1912, however, his wife, both children, and his parents were killed in a tornado. Rice took off and wandered around the country. He worked at odd jobs and eventually joined the Navy. Before his family tragedy, he had failed at tryouts as a pitcher for several minor league teams. He continued to pitch in the Navy, and in 1914 he appeared for Petersburg of the Virginia League. The club owner was impressed and bought Rice's release from the service.

Near the end of the 1915 season Rice was sent to the Washington Senators to repay a debt owed by the Petersburg club. When Washington president-manager Clark Griffith announced the acquisition of a pitcher named Rice to the press, he was asked the newcomer's first name. Griffith had no idea, but without pausing he blurted out, "Sam." Forever after, the 5-foot 9-inch, 150-pound Edgar Charles Rice was known as Sam.

His career as a major league pitcher was short. After 39 innings, Rice was pronounced too wild. On the other hand, he was fast, had a strong arm, and had collected seven hits in nine pinch-hit at bats. Griffith, nicknamed "the Old Fox," made one of his craftier decisions and switched Rice to the outfield. Rice quickly mastered the position. In 1917, his first full season as a regular in the outfield, Rice hit .302. He missed most of the 1918 season while serving in the army, but when he returned in 1919 he hit .321 and embarked on a 14-season run as Washington's regular right fielder.

The great racehorse Man o' War was a sports sensation in 1919 and 1920. Rice's teammates began to call him "Man o' War" because of both his military service and his speed. In 1920 Rice hit in 29 consecutive games and led the American League with 63 stolen bases. In his career he stole 351 bases. Rice was also one of the more difficult hitters to strike out. In 1929 he fanned only nine times in 616 at bats. Overall, he struck out only once in every 33.7 at bats, the eighth-best ratio of all time.

His only weakness was a lack of power. Seventy-six percent of Rice's base hits were singles, and most of his rare extra-base hits resulted from speed rather than power. Of his 34 career home runs, 21 were inside the park. Rice, who threw righthanded but batted from the left side, stood straight up at the plate and slapped the ball into left field.

The Senators played in Griffith Stadium, where it was particularly hard to hit a home run, especially to left field, where the fence was more than 400 feet from the plate. But it was a good park for triples, and Rice cracked out 184 three-base hits. In 1923 he hit 18 to lead the league, and in nine other seasons he reached double figures. In 1923 Rice also achieved a baseball rarity—while playing right field in the sixth inning of a game against Cleveland, he turned an unassisted double play.

In 1924 the Senators won their first American League pennant. Rice led the league with 216 hits and batted .334. From late August to late September, as the Senators overtook the New York Yankees, he hit safely in 31 consecutive games. In an exciting seven-game World Series, Washington defeated the New York Giants to become world champions.

In 1925 Rice set the American League record with 182 singles and collected 227 total hits to bat .350. The Senators repeated as pennant winners but fell to the Pirates in the World Series. Rice had hit only .207 in the 1924 Series against the Giants, but he was spectacular in a losing effort in 1925. In addition to his famous catch he hit .364, scored five runs, and knocked in three. His 12 hits, all singles, led players from both teams. In 1926 he led the league in hits again with 216, giving him a three-year total of 669.

Rice remained Washington's regular right fielder through 1932, when he was 42 years old. Although he didn't lead the league in any offensive category after 1926, he batted at least .310 from 1928 through 1932 and put together a 28-game hitting streak in 1930. He helped the Senators win a third pennant as a part-timer in 1933, making him a part of all three Washington league championships.

He spent a final season with Cleveland, and then retired to his farm in Maryland, only 13 hits shy of 3,000. In later years he was often asked why he retired so close to the magic number. "You must remember," he'd explain, "there wasn't much emphasis on 3,000 hits when I quit. And to tell the truth, I didn't know how many hits I had."

Remarkably consistent, Rice scored at least 91 runs every season from 1922 through 1929 and finished with a total of 1,515. Although he batted leadoff for much of his career, he still amassed 1,078 RBIs. His lifetime batting average was .322, and he never batted below .293. Few players have hit better than .300 after the age of 40—Rice did it a record three times. In 1963 he was elected to the Hall of Fame.

J.R. Richard

Richard, James Rodney **P**

1971–80 B:3/7/1950, Vienna, LA Deb:9/5/1971,
HOU NL BR/TR 6'8", 222

W	L	PCT	G	SH	IP	BB	SO	ERA
107	71	.601	238	19	1606	770	1493	3.15

In 1980 Houston Astro J.R. Richard seemed on the verge of greatness. The huge righthander had just led the National League in ERA and was on track to record his second 20-win season. He could throw the ball through a wall, cranking his velocity up to 98 miles per hour. "I could probably be the greatest thing since Kellogg's Corn Flakes if I played in New York," he once observed, and he was probably right. Then came the stroke that tragically cut short a promising career. But the stroke also led him to take a different attitude toward life.

Reared in rural Louisiana, James Rodney Richard, who would grow to be 6-feet 8-inches, was a high school phenomenon. He attracted attention in football, basketball, and baseball. As a punter he averaged a rumored 67.5 yards per kick, and as a basketball player he scored 35 points per game. At least 103 schools offered him scholarships—some said it was more than 200.

As a baseball player, his arm was unbelievably powerful. Said one scout: "Every time [the catcher] would catch one of J.R.'s pitches it would knock him back about a foot, it seemed. It was unbelievable the arm the guy had." Houston signed him for a $100,000 bonus. When he reached the minors, he didn't know how to throw from the stretch. He never had to in high school, he said. No one had reached base against him.

In his first major league start, on September 15, 1971, he struck out 15 San Francisco Giants, but he had trouble staying with the Astros. He charged racism and threatened to quit baseball, but there were other reasons why Houston hesitated in putting him in the rotation. He was wild (three times he led the National League in walks), his fielding was atrocious, and he threw so hard at the beginning of a game that he tired too quickly.

But still there was his awesome speed. Richard's fastball was in the 98- to 100-mph range, and his slider was in the low 90s. "The most awesome creature I ever saw on a mound was J.R. Richard," said Sparky Anderson. "When everything was going right for him, there was no chance."

In 1978 Richard became the first National League righthander in the 20th century to record 300 strikeouts in a single season. He did it again in 1979, when he led the league with a 2.71 ERA. From 1976 through 1979 he averaged more than 18 wins per season. In 1980 he was nearly unhittable (he was 10–4 with a 1.89 ERA) but complained of fatigue. Some accused him of malingering—at least they did until July 30, 1980.

Richard was playing catch with former Astros utilityman Wilbur Howard when he suffered the stroke. He felt nauseated and weak and lay down on the field, as Howard kept repeating, "J.R., you all right?" A blood clot had formed in Richard's pitching shoulder and caused a blockage in a blood vessel near his rib cage. The clot then moved to Richard's brain, causing the stroke. The entire left side of Richard's body was paralyzed. Through surgery and therapy he regained the use of his arm and leg, but he was left with a facial paralysis that impaired his speech.

Richard attempted a comeback. He ran four miles a day and got his fastball back up to 90 mph; however, the effects of the stroke seriously hampered his already poor fielding ability. He pitched in Class A and also briefly in Class AAA. He started six games with Tucson of the Pacific Coast League in 1982, but was 0–2 with a 13.68 ERA. He uncorked 10 wild pitches in just 24⅓ innings pitched. Ultimately Richard accepted his misfortune philosophically. "I'm not bitter," he said. "It was God's decision." He called his switch in lifestyles, "The Big Trade."

After two bad marriages and a series of bad investments, Richards was broke. In 1994 he was homeless, the former strikeout king was found living under a bridge. He was taken in by the Now Testament Church in South Houston and later became a minister in the church and worked to establish baseball programs for kids. "I always knew God was on my side," Richards told *The Sporting News* in 1999. "I just wasn't on my own side."

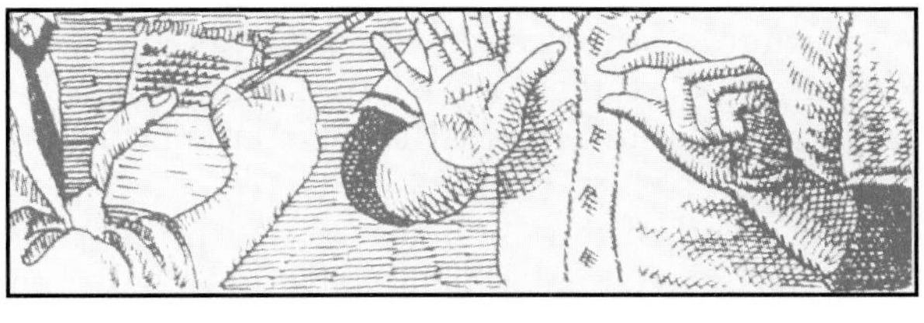

Paul Richards

Richards, Paul Rapier **C**
1932–35, 1943–46 M(1951–61, 1976, 923–901)
B:11/21/1908, Waxahachie, TX D:5/4/1986,
Waxahachie, TX Deb:4/17/1932, BRO NL BR/TR
6'1½", 180

G	AB	R	H	HR	RBI	OBP	SLG	AVG
523	1417	140	321	15	155	.305	.301	.227

Paul Richards is generally credited as one of the smartest men in baseball history—a catcher with an exceptional gift for handling pitchers, a great teacher, and a true innovator. Richards is credited, for example, with the invention of the "Iron Mike" pitching machine and the "Big Mitt" Gus Triandos used to catch Hoyt Wilhelm. Yet, for all his smarts, Richards never seemed to be around when his efforts at building teams paid off. By then, he'd already moved on to the next challenge.

The lanky Texan began his career as a weak-hitting third baseman and ambidextrous pitcher. From 1932 through 1935 he was a part-time catcher for Brooklyn, the Giants, and the A's. While playing under Giants manager Bill Terry, he studied how managers behaved and learned about pitching and catching from working with Carl Hubbell.

Sent back to the minors, Richards managed the Atlanta Crackers from 1938 through 1942. He returned to the big leagues during the war years to play for the Tigers, where he had his greatest moment of playing glory. His two doubles and four RBIs led the Tigers' to a 9–3 win in Game 7 to clinch the 1945 World Series.

He returned to the minors in 1947 and managed Buffalo and Seattle before landing his first major league managing assignment with Chicago. The White Sox hadn't been out of the second division in eight years, but in 1951 they finished fourth under Richards, with an 81–73 mark. They matched that record in 1952, and won 89 and 91 games the next two seasons—unfortunately without ever moving up in the standings.

Richards moved on to Baltimore, emphasizing solid pitching, defense, speed, and a strong bullpen. From a pitching staff called " the Kiddie Korps," he was a master at getting the most out of young arms and fragile egos. Pitchers like Billy O'Dell, Milt Pappas, and Jack Harshman prospered under his tutelage. The young Pappas was held to 70 pitches per game—since limiting a starter's pitch count was another Richards innovation.

Richards also moved Hoyt Wilhelm out of the bullpen, and he threw a no-hitter against the Yankees. In fact, by 1960 the Orioles were challenging the Yankees. But at that time Richards had become intrigued by the possibility of starting a team from scratch. In 1961 he went south as the first general manager for the Houston Colts .45s. He stayed through 1965, but his vision in building a system wasn't felt in Houston until after he left the club. When the Braves moved to Atlanta in 1966, Richards joined them for seven years as vice president of baseball operations. There he saw one of his teams come close to a championship, but the 1969 Braves lost to the Mets in the first National League Championship Series.

After several years of semi-retirement, he was approached by Bill Veeck in 1976 and asked to manage the White Sox. Although they won only 64 games for Richards in his one season at the helm, he stayed on as director of player development and helped build the team that won the American League West in 1983.

Richards' final baseball job was as a consultant for the Texas Rangers. He finished with a lifetime record as manager of 923–901, a .506 winning percentage, and died on the golf course in his hometown of Waxahachie, Texas.

Bobby Richardson

Richardson, Robert Clinton **2B-3B**
1955–66 B:8/19/1935, Sumter, SC Deb:8/5/1955,
NY AL BR/TR 5'9", 170

G	AB	R	H	HR	RBI	OBP	SLG	AVG
1412	5386	643	1432	34	390	.301	.335	.266

Yankees second baseman Bobby Richardson combined fine fielding and a reputation for clean living to become one of the American League's best second basemen of his day. Richardson became a Christian at age 14 and kept to his principles throughout his playing career. "Look at him. He doesn't drink, he doesn't smoke, he doesn't chew, he doesn't stay out late, and he still can't hit .250," commented a puzzled Casey Stengel.

Once, after striking out for the third time in a game, first baseman Moose Skowron came storming back to the Yankees bench, muttering obscenities. He walked past Richardson, caught himself, said "Sorry, Bobby," then continued on past him with another string of blasphemy. The Yankees bench exploded with laughter.

It was Richardson's fielding and not his virtue that kept him in the New York lineup. Gold Gloves, after all, count more to management than following the Golden Rule. Richardson was awarded that symbol of fielding excellence each year from 1961 through 1965. During that span he was also named second baseman on *The Sporting News* All-Star Team. He led the American League in double plays four times and in putouts twice. In 1961 Richardson turned a league-leading 136 double plays, a career high and one of the best totals in American League history.

Yet, when Richardson first came up with the Yankees, his hitting was so weak that he was twice sent back to the minors. Stengel kept after him to lay off first pitches and try for more walks. A .266 career hitter, Richardson posted a lifetime .305 average in World Series competition and had a particularly impressive Series in 1960, collecting 11 base hits and 12 RBIs. In Game 3 he set a Series record with six RBIs. One of his 11 hits came after getting the sign to bunt. He attempted to lay one down but fouled it off. This time the sign was "hit away." Richardson hoped to drive the ball to right to stay out of a double play. Instead, he hit a grand slam to left field. Richardson was the first player from the losing side to win a World Series Most Valuable Player Award.

After the 1960 World Series, Stengel was let go as Yankees manager. "I hated to see Casey leave," said Richardson. "He'd been more than fair to me through the years, giving me valuable advice and providing many opportunities to play when he really didn't have to."

Richardson's most famous moment came in the ninth inning of Game 7 of the 1962 World Series against the San Francisco Giants. The Yankees were ahead, 1–0, with two outs and runners on second and third. New York manager Ralph Houk and pitcher Ralph Terry decided to pitch to Willie McCovey. In the course of the Series, McCovey had hit two grounders to Richardson, who had bobbled both of them, just barely getting McCovey at first base in each case. "Don't fumble the ball or it will cost us $125,000," shortstop Tony Kubek said to Richardson. Seconds later, McCovey, on a 1–1 count, savagely lined one of Terry's fastballs just barely to Richardson's left. The second baseman snagged it to end the Series. In his final World Series in 1964, Richardson batted .406 and collected a Series-record 13 hits.

The singles-hitting Richardson did not attract as much attention as his power-hitting teammates. "A valuable contribution to the 'Keep Bobby Humble Department' were letters from fans asking me to secure Mickey Mantle's autograph for them," Richardson said.

At the end of the 1965 season, with the Yankee dynasty in tatters, Richardson and Kubek both wanted to retire but thought it would be bad for the club if they went out at the same time. Since Kubek had been injured a good part of 1965, he was the first to go, and Richardson left the following year.

After retiring as a player, Richardson coached baseball at the University of South Carolina. He became active in the Fellowship of Christian Athletes and delivered the benediction at the 1972 Republican Convention. He became president of Baseball Chapel.

Hardy Richardson

Richardson, Abram Harding **2B–OF–3B**

1879–92 B:4/21/1855, Clarksboro, NJ D:1/14/1931, Utica, NY Deb:5/1/1879, BUF NL BR/TR 5'9½", 170

G	AB	R	H	HR	RBI	OBP	SLG	AVG
1331	5642	1120	1688	70	822	.344	.435	.299

Abram Harding "Hardy" Richardson was a member of Buffalo's "Big Four," a quartet of strong players who starred for the team during its seven-year stay in the National League from 1879 to 1885. Dan Brouthers, Jim White, Jack Rowe, and Richardson kept Buffalo in contention most seasons, but they couldn't fill up the park. In 1886 Detroit paid $7,000 for the whole team just to get the Big Four. Richardson led the National League in hits and home runs in his first year with the Detroit Wolverines. In 1887 the Big Four paid off by bringing Detroit a pennant.

Although he preferred second base, "Old True Blue" Richardson played wherever he was needed, even pitching and catching on a few occasions. His strength was his bat. He compiled a .299 batting average over 14 seasons and, with Boston of the Players' League in 1890, he hit .326 and had a league-leading 146 RBIs. With Detroit in 1886, Richardson led the league in both homers and hits. On September 9 of that season he collected three triples in a single game—and also doubled.

Traded to Boston in 1889, he jumped to the Players' League in 1890 and led that ill-fated circuit in RBIs. From 1889 to 1891 he appeared with three different Boston clubs in three different leagues (the National League, Players' League, and American Association).

When not on the diamond, Richardson was a crack shot; he issued a $1,000 challenge to anyone who could outshoot him "on-the-wing." No one collected. The former slugger later operated a hotel in Utica and was employed at the Remington Typewriter Works at nearby Ilion, New York.

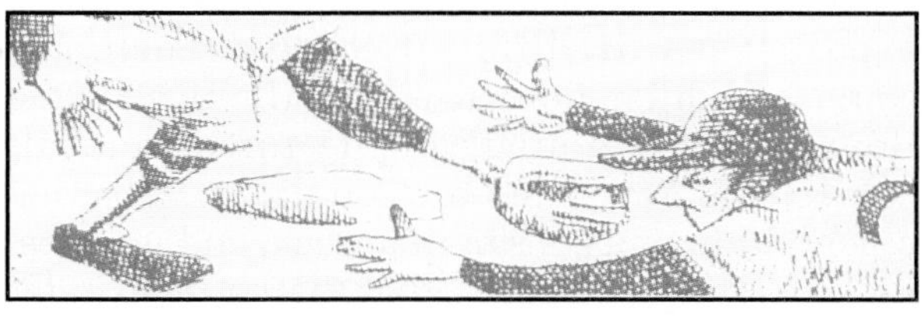

Lee Richmond

Richmond, J Lee **P–OF**

1879–83, 1886 B:5/5/1857, Sheffield, OH D:10/1/1929, Toledo, OH Deb:9/27/1879, BOS NL TL 5'10", 155

W	L	PCT	G	SH	IP	BB	SO	ERA
75	100	.429	191	8	1583	269	552	3.06

On June 12, 1880, Lee Richmond ensured the survival of his name in baseball annals. Whenever a major league pitcher achieves the rare feat of a perfect game, someone is sure to ask, "Who was the first to accomplish such a feat?" The answer is Lee Richmond, who was also the first lefthander to execute a no-hitter on a major league diamond.

Richmond performed his perfecto for Worcester in a game against Cleveland, then both members of the National League; he won by a razor-thin margin of 1–0. Although perfect on that June day, Richmond finished a six-year major league career with a losing record of 75–100.

Richmond first attracted attention while pitching for Oberlin College. In the fall of 1876 he enrolled at Brown University and, eligibility requirements being what they were at the time, went out for the baseball team the following spring. He was consigned to the outfield but soon returned to pitching.

During the winter of 1878–79 he worked out in the Brown gym perfecting his curveball. He learned to toss a sharp-breaking "downer" and, according to one source with a curious disregard for the laws of physics, a curve that broke upward. The work paid off when Richmond led Brown to the 1879 college championship. He signed with Worcester's then minor league club and pitched a no-hitter in his first game.

Richmond's success played a part in Worcester's decision to join the National League the following year, and gave their star lefty the opportunity to pitch the game that etched his name in baseball history. Unfortunately, Worcester's three-year stay in the league was not a happy one. After a fifth-place finish in 1880, they plunged to last and stayed there. Toiling behind one of the league's weakest batting attacks, Richmond was nevertheless credited with 79 percent of the team's total wins during three mostly dismal seasons.

Richmond used his baseball salary to pursue medical studies in the winter. After a few appearances for Providence in 1883, mostly as an outfielder, he retired to practice medicine in Ohio. Three years later, he made three undistinguished appearances for Cincinnati's American Association team in an aborted comeback, and then hung up his spikes for good.

Branch Rickey

Rickey, Wesley Branch **C**
1905–07, 1914 M(1913–15, 1919–25, 597–664)
Executive B:12/20/1881, Flat, OH D:12/9/1965,
Columbia, MO Deb:6/16/1905, STL AL BL/TR 5'9", 175

G	AB	R	H	HR	RBI	OBP	SLG	AVG
120	343	38	82	3	39	.304	.324	.239

Branch Rickey was a baseball genius, the greatest front-office man the game has ever known. He was also a sanctimonious, hypocritical cheapskate, a man who would play fast and loose with the rules and go back on his word when it suited him. That he was a successful general manager for 42 consecutive years, for the Browns, Cardinals, Dodgers, and Pirates, becomes almost irrelevant when compared to how much he did to shape the modern baseball landscape.

First, he literally invented the farm system in the early 1920s when he was with the Cardinals. Before that the minor leagues were composed of independent teams that survived by developing and then selling players to the majors.

Second, he integrated baseball. Over half a century later—a half century that has seen *Brown vs. Board of Education*, the Civil Rights Act, the Voting Rights Act, and Cassius Clay's transformation into Muhammad Ali—it's easy to underestimate the impact and significance of Rickey's decision to sign Jackie Robinson. Certainly, it was inevitable that baseball's color line was going to be broken. But when Rickey hired Robinson, America's armed forces were still segregated and African Americans were still being lynched in parts of the country. What Rickey did transcended the game and became a significant event in the history of the United States.

Finally, his plans to form a third major league in 1959 convinced the leaders of Major League Baseball that they had to expand. That was the beginning of a sports explosion in this country that continues to this day.

Raised on an Ohio farm, Wesley Branch Rickey coached and played semipro baseball and football to pay his way through Ohio Wesleyan College. A devout Methodist, he kept a promise to his mother that he would not play or work on Sundays. He wouldn't even travel on the Sabbath. Of course, later in his career his teams played on Sundays and he always called the ballpark to check on the day's receipts.

While at Ohio Wesleyan he also coached the baseball team. He had a black first baseman, Charles Thomas, who was refused admission to a South Bend hotel on a trip to play Notre Dame. Rickey finally persuaded hotel management to allow Thomas to share his room. In the room, according to Rickey, Thomas rubbed his hands together and cried to his 21-year-old coach, "Black skin, black skin. If only I could make it white." Years later, Rickey tearfully retold the story and said it was the genesis of his crusade to break the color barrier in the major leagues.

A catcher with a strong arm, Rickey began his professional career in 1903, and after impressing scouts while playing for Dallas he was purchased by the Reds late in the 1904 season. But Reds manager Joe Kelley released him when he learned that Rickey wouldn't play on Sundays.

Rickey went back to Dallas in 1905, was sold to the White Sox, and then was traded to the Browns. He told the Browns that he'd only play from June 15 to September 15 because he planned to pursue a law degree from Allegheny College and coach the school's baseball and football teams. And he wouldn't play on Sundays. The Browns agreed to his stipulations. However, he played only one game that season, going hitless in three at bats. Then he headed home to Ohio to tend to his seriously ill parents.

He returned to the Browns in 1906 and had his best season, hitting .284 in 201 at bats. But he got into a conflict with his manager, Jimmy McAleer, who warned Rickey he would withhold a portion of his salary if he left before the end of the season. Rickey stayed after college officials at Allegheny gave him a leave of absence, but he told Browns owner Bob Hedges that he would never play for McAleer again. Hedges obliged by selling Rickey to the New York Highlanders.

Rickey hurt his arm during the winter, which ultimately sabotaged his career. Because of the injury, he didn't report to New York until midseason. On June 28, 1907, in his first game for manager Clark Griffith, Rickey's arm was still sore, and the Senators stole a record 13 bases on him. He hit .182 in 137 at bats, and except for two cameo at bats in 1914 when he was managing the Browns, his playing career was over.

He began taking law classes at Michigan and in 1911 became the school's baseball coach. After he got his degree and went into practice he also agreed to do some scouting for the Browns. In 1913 Rickey became a full-time employee of the Browns as an executive assistant, and soon after that became their general manager. In the final weeks of the season Hedges gave him the manager's job as well, which Rickey kept through the 1915 season. True to his oath, he stayed home on Sundays, letting a coach handle the team.

Rickey's background in football led him to experiment with different coaching methods, some of which he'd tried at Michigan. The Browns' 1914 training camp featured handball courts to improve hand-eye coordination, batting cages, sliding pits, a running track, and lectures. Rickey strongly believed that there was a "right way" to play baseball, and that it could be taught.

He refined this approach with the Dodgers in the 1940s, converting an old military base in Vero Beach, Florida, into Dodgertown, a state-of-the-art spring training complex for organization-wide instruction. Rickey introduced the first "Iron Mike" pitching machines there, and he also had strings set up to outline the strike zone for pitching workouts. "Gentlemen, I do not know the game of baseball," Rickey, the grand thespian, would intone with his mellifluous voice at the start of one of his standard spring addresses, "but I intend to learn it."

His innovations didn't help the Brownies, but his legal background and Michigan connection did. George Sisler had signed a professional contract as an underage high schooler without parental consent, but he had not accepted any money. He then decided to enroll at Michigan. When the pro contract threatened his eligibility, Rickey advised the family to move to invalidate the agreement. Rickey was thus able to keep the star of his team, and the grateful young Sisler signed with Rickey's Browns when he graduated in 1915—after Rickey convinced club owner Bob Hedges to break a gentlemen's agreement that had earmarked Sisler for the Pirates.

By the time Sisler had become a star for the Browns, Hedges had sold the team to Phil Ball, and Rickey had moved across town to the bankrupt Cardinals as club president. After serving as a major in a World War I chemical warfare unit with Ty Cobb, Christy Mathewson, and Sisler, Rickey returned to the Cardinals as president and, saving a $10,000 salary, as field manager. After the club finished seventh in 1919 while teetering on the verge of bankruptcy, Sam Breadon bought 72 percent of the stock. Rickey owned the rest.

Breadon demoted Rickey to vice president but allowed him to continue as field manager. About that time Rickey developed his farm system plan—out of necessity. The Cardinals could not afford to compete with other teams to purchase top talent from independent minor league teams. His task was monumental. First, he developed a philosophy: he would look for speed and strong arms. Rickey believed those gifts were essential and that other baseball skills were teachable. But that was the easy part.

Rickey had to devise a method of acquiring teams. He had to establish a system of tracking and evaluating players in every organization in the majors. He had to hire a network of scouts and organize tryout camps. He also had to develop an organization-wide teaching system. It was a task perfectly suited to Rickey's energy and intellect, and one he was able to carry out even though he was still the field manager. When he was done, the Cardinals farm system included 33 teams. In contrast, each major league franchise today operates only five or six minor league teams.

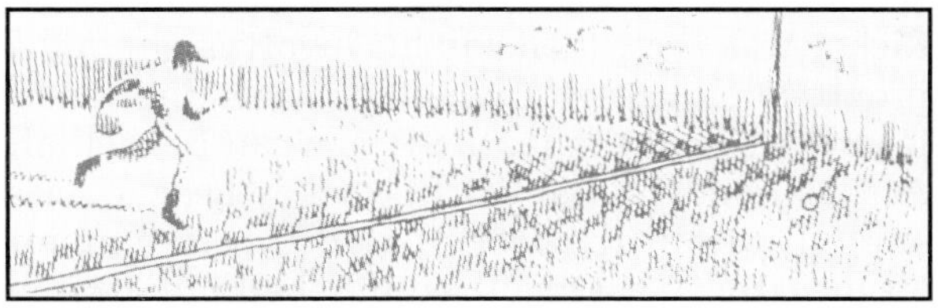

By 1925 the Cardinals were on the verge of becoming a force in the National League. (Starting in 1926 they would win five pennants in the next nine years.) Rickey wanted to stay on as manager. But 38 games into the season Breadon ordered second baseman Rogers Hornsby to take the job, and an angry Rickey sold his stock in the team to Hornsby. Rickey finished his managerial career with a 597–664 record, and never ended a season higher than third place.

Rickey was well suited to being a full-time executive. Although he never uttered a curse stronger than "Judas Priest" and did not drink alcohol, he was, for all his religious pretensions, a skilled manipulator of baseball's rules and people. He also had the gift to spot talent, and it didn't hurt that he was a shrewd trader. Rickey's motto: it's better to trade a player a year early instead of a year late.

He was also a cartoonist's dream, a living caricature with bushy eyebrows and big jowls. He wore wire-rimmed glasses, favored bow ties, and smoked enormous cigars. Then there was his rhetoric. He loved using $5 words, and could he ever turn a phrase. "Luck is the residue of design," his best known saying, remains in vogue decades later. He acquired his nickname, "the Mahatma," in the 1940s, when Gandhi became a player on the world stage. The nickname was somewhat tongue-in-cheek, but it also shows the respect given to the man who had such a significant impact on the game.

His tenure with the Cardinals proceeded smoothly until 1937, when Commissioner Kenesaw Mountain Landis investigated charges that Rickey was illegally signing and stashing players in his huge farm system. Landis ordered the release of 73 Cardinal farmhands from Rickey's "chain gang," and gave the players the right to sign with any team they wanted.

Rickey's parsimony became legendary. Johnny Mize actually believed that Rickey preferred to have his teams finish a close second so that he could cash in on a pennant-race gate without having to fork over pennant-winning raises to his players. Enos Slaughter once said that Rickey "would go to the vault to get change for a nickel." Eddie Stanky described one negotiation with Rickey, "I got a million dollars worth of advice and a very small increase." Pittsburgh's Ralph Kiner recalled Rickey denying his promise for a raise after Kiner had won the National League home run title. Said Rickey, "We finished last with you and we can finish last without you."

Dodgers outfielder George Shuba was negotiating with Rickey and wanted an increase to $23,000. During the meeting, Rickey was summoned to another office for a phone call. As he waited, Shuba noticed a contract with Jackie Robinson's name on it for $21,000. When Rickey returned, Shuba agreed to take $20,000. Later, he found out that the Robinson contract was a phony and that Rickey's phone call was a setup.

While he was nickel-and-diming his players, Rickey was becoming a rich man. He had a deal with the Cardinals and Dodgers that gave him a 10-percent commission on every player sale—talk about possible conflicts of interest. Bill Veeck told a more sinister Rickey story in the book, *Veeck As in Wreck*. It seems Rickey once agreed to a deal over the phone, then went back on his word, and denied that the phone conversation had ever taken place.

By 1942 Rickey's contract was up in St. Louis. He was fed up with Breadon, and vice versa. No one really knows if he was fired or if he quit, but he moved over to the Dodgers without missing a beat. Rickey protégé Larry MacPhail was leaving the Dodgers club after building it into a contender, so Brooklyn hired Rickey as president and general manager. He also bought 25 percent of the team.

Rickey could now move ahead with his plans to integrate baseball. By the end of World War II Rickey sensed the timing was right. He also knew it was a smart move. More and more teams were starting to copy his farm system, and he wanted, as always, to stay a step ahead of the competition. And unlike Veeck, who integrated the American League when he signed Larry Doby in 1947, Rickey never paid a Negro League team for a player, knowing Negro League owners would not want to be blamed for delaying the end of the color barrier.

Rickey's expansion machinations began in the spring of 1945, when he announced the formation of the Brooklyn Brown Dodgers to play in a new United States Baseball League and dispatched scouts to search the Negro Leagues for talent. However, the Brown Dodgers and USBL were a scam designed to hide Rickey's real purpose—the integration of the established major leagues. At first he intended to sign several black prospects, then he decided to sign only one. His scouts suggested pitcher Don Newcombe, but Rickey deemed the 19-year-old too young for the pioneer role, foreseeing the abuse the first African American major leaguer would encounter.

The second choice was Kansas City Monarchs shortstop Jackie Robinson, who was 26, a former army officer, and a four-sport star at UCLA. In their now-famous first meeting, Rickey warned Robinson of the trials he'd have to endure without being able to retaliate. An angry Robinson asked, "Do you want a player afraid to fight back?" Rickey replied, "I want a player with the guts not to fight back."

On October 23, 1945, with the approval of his Dodgers partners, Rickey signed Robinson. After a brilliant 1946 season in Montreal, Robinson joined the Dodgers in 1947 and was an immediate star. Rickey's Dodgers thus got the jump on the rest of baseball, signing such black stars as Newcombe, catcher Roy Campanella, pitcher Joe Black, and second baseman Jim "Junior" Gilliam. As a result, between 1947 and 1956 the Dodgers won seven pennants in 10 years.

Rickey, however, did not last long enough in Brooklyn to enjoy all the fruits of his labors. Walter O'Malley, one of Rickey's partners, wanted control of the team, and his first order of business was to engineer Rickey's ouster. Here, finally, was someone as intelligent and devious as Rickey.

O'Malley made his move after the 1950 season, when he led a boardroom coup that forced Rickey out. Rickey, however, cried all the way to the bank because a clause in his contract forced the Dodgers to match the highest bid for his stock if he was not rehired. Rickey produced a $1.25-million offer, more than double O'Malley's estimate of the stock's value. O'Malley went to his grave believing the offer was a phony.

Rickey moved on to Pittsburgh, laying the foundation for the 1960 Pirates team that won the World Series. His greatest coup with the Pirates was drafting Roberto Clemente from the Dodgers, who were trying to hide him in the minors by not playing him regularly.

Rickey's last venture was the Continental League, his response to the majors' repeated refusal to expand beyond 16 teams. One of his fellow "owners" was Joan Payson, who eventually acquired the expansion New York Mets franchise. Rickey was 77 by then, but his involvement in the proposed new league, which presaged the American Football League, the American Basketball Association, and the World Hockey League, was enough to put the fear of God into the major leagues. By 1961 Organized Baseball initiated an expansion program that has since nearly doubled the number of major league teams.

Rickey died in 1965, less than two weeks before his 84th birthday. He was inducted into the Hall of Fame in 1967.

Dave Righetti

Righetti, David Allan **P**

1979, 1981–95 B:11/28/1958, San Jose, CA Deb:9/16/1979, NY AL BL/TL 6'3", 198

W	L	PCT	G	SV	IP	BB	SO	ERA
82	79	.509	718	252	1403^2	591	1112	3.46

The Yankees traded Sparky Lyle, one of the greatest lefthanded relievers in club history, for a young southpaw who eventually became the Yanks' all-time saves leader. Dave Righetti came to New York in the deal that sent Lyle to Texas following the 1978 season.

In 1981 Righetti posted a 2.05 ERA in 15 starts, won American League Rookie of the Year honors, and won three games in the postseason. Although he pitched in the majors for 14 more years, his rookie year marked his only appearance in the postseason.

Righetti struggled with control at the start of 1982, prompting the Yankees to demote him to the minor leagues. He returned to New York later that year and finished with 11 wins. His rising fastball and bending curve helped Righetti win 14 of 22 decisions the following season. On July 4, 1983, his talents fully peaked when he became the first Yankee to pitch a no-hitter since Don Larsen in 1956.

No one realized it at the time, but Righetti's no-hitter represented the high point of his career as a starter. When the Yankees lost relief ace Rich Gossage after the season, manager Yogi Berra made a controversial decision and moved Righetti to the closer's role. "Rags" made a smooth transition to the bullpen, saving 60 games over the next two seasons.

In 1986 Righetti achieved All-Star status on his way to a major league-record 46 saves (Bobby Thigpen surpassed the mark in 1990). Righetti appeared in the All-Star Game again in 1987, but his ERA rose to 3.51 and his saves dropped to 31. His 224 saves as a Yankee easily surpassed both Gossage (151) and Lyle (141) on the club's all-time saves chart.

Righetti decided to move closer to home and signed with San Francisco after the 1990 season. He pitched well in his first year with the Giants, but slipped badly in 1992 and lost his closer's role. He was ineffective in situational relief, and bounced around with Oakland and Toronto in 1994. Righetti finished his career the way he started it; as a starter. He went 3–2 in nine starts for the Chicago White Sox in 1995.

Righetti returned to baseball in 1999 as a roving instructor with the Giants organization. After the season he was named the team's major league pitching coach.

Bill Rigney

Rigney, William Joseph **2B–3B–SS**

1946–53 M(1956–72, 1976, 1,239–1,321) B:1/29/1918, Alameda, CA Deb:4/16/1946, NY NL BR/TR 6'1", 178

G	AB	R	H	HR	RBI	OBP	SLG	AVG
654	1966	281	510	41	212	.334	.376	.259

A light-hitting utility infielder, manager with a losing record, scout, nomadic executive, and broadcaster, Bill Rigney has combined all the talents he had with lots of energy to be in baseball for more than half a century. He had other career options.

Rigney grew up in the San Francisco Bay Area, where his father had a successful tile business that Rigney could have perpetuated. He was too distracted by baseball. As a semi-pro player, he caught the attention of a New York Yankees scout. Rigney thought he would have a better chance signing with an independent operation, so he signed with the Oakland Oaks in 1938.

The Oaks farmed Rigney out to Spokane of the Western International League, where he batted .083 in 16 games. He also played at Vancouver-Bellingham and Topeka before reaching Oakland to stay in 1941.

Rigney's baseball career was interrupted by World War II. He signed up for Naval Aviation but had to struggle to pass the eye test. Rigney was nicknamed "Specs," and it took some pull by Oaks owner Brick Laws to get him in the navy. Following the war Rigney hooked up with the Giants as an infielder and played with them until 1953.

"I think the important thing about me was how much I wanted it," Rigney once said of his career as a player. "I played with a lot of intensity. Sometimes that can make up for any shortcomings a player might have in natural physical ability."

Moving between second base, third, and shortstop, Rigney hit a career-high 17 homers (including his only grand slam) in 1947 and made the All-Star Game in 1948—although he didn't get a chance to bat. In 1950 he was reduced to part-time action, and he batted .300 in 90 at bats in 1952. He played in the 1951 World Series and was 2-for-4 as a pinch hitter in the Giants' six-game loss to the Yankees.

"It was probably around 1952 or 1953 that I began thinking of managing," he said. "I wanted badly to stay in the game. I could see my playing career winding down." Rigney started his managing career with Minneapolis of the American Association in 1954. In 1955 he won a pennant with that team and *The Sporting News* named him its Minor League Manager of the Year.

The following season Rigney was hired to manage the Giants. He lasted until June 1960. With the team playing the best ball of his stewardship, Rigney was replaced by Tom Sheehan. Gene Autry immediately hired Rigney to be the first manager of the Angels. *The Sporting News* named him its Major League Manager of the Year in 1962 after he brought the second-year expansion club to a third-place finish. That was the highlight of his eight-plus seasons for Autry. Rigney was fired in May 1969.

Rigney took over as the manager of the Twins in 1970, replacing Billy Martin. The Twins won the American League West, but were swept by Baltimore in the Championship Series. During his two-plus years in Minnesota, Rigney often battled with Rod Carew over Carew's declining play at second base. (Carew wound up switching to first base in 1976.)

In the face of a losing record as a manager (he was 1,239–1,321, plus one tie), Rigney managed to keep his sense of humor. Bothered by the Twins' high team ERA one year, he said, "It's not big if you look at it from the standpoint of the national debt." Another time, he offered: "Of all the things we have in this game—hits and runs and stolen bases and home runs—the thing we have the most of is outs."

The Twins fell to fifth place in the West in 1971, and Rigney was swept out halfway through the 1972 season. He became an assistant to Charlie Finley in Oakland and did commentary on A's games on radio. He joined the Giants in 1976 to work with new owner Bob Lurie in reorganizing the franchise. He ended up replacing Wes Westrum as Giants manager that year and finished fourth in the National League West.

Rigney later served as a scout for the Padres, then joined Oakland following the 1982 season as a special assistant to A's president Roy Eisenhardt. He did A's TV in 1983 and 1984 and served as an analyst for Oakland games on *SportsChannel*. "There has never been a single day when I regretted going into baseball and not going into the tile business," he once said.

Jose Rijo

Rijo, Jose Antonio (Abreu) **P**

1984–95 B:5/13/1965, San Cristobol, Dominican Republic Deb:4/5/1984, NY AL BR/TR 6'2", 200

W	L	PCT	G	SH	IP	BB	SO	ERA
111	87	.561	332	4	1786	634	1556	3.16

Much was expected from Jose Rijo at an early age. The pitcher was signed by the New York Yankees when he was only 15, and made his major league debut at 19. After part of one season with the Yankees, he was packaged off to Oakland for Rickey Henderson. The Oakland Athletics then sent him to the Cincinnati Reds three years later for Dave Parker. It was with his third team that the young pitcher made his mark.

Rijo earned Most Valuable Player honors in Cincinnati's 1990 World Series sweep over the A's. He won twice with 14 strikeouts and an 0.59 ERA in the most stunning World Series sweep since 1954. His 7–0 victory in the opener ended Dave Stewart's six-game postseason winning streak. After two more unlikely victories by the Reds, Rijo and Stewart faced off again in Game 4. Oakland nicked Rijo for a run in the first inning, but he then retired 20 straight batters. Cincinnati rallied late to win the game, 2–1, and complete the sweep.

Rijo reeled off a 58–33 record from 1990 to 1993. Wild early in his career, he now struck out three batters for every walk. Rijo led the National League in winning percentage in 1991, and paced the league in strikeouts the next year. By the time he turned 30 in 1995 he had already spent a dozen seasons in the major leagues. He went on the disabled list in June, and despite several comeback attempts he never pitched again in the major leagues.

Jimmy Ring

Ring, James Joseph **P**

1917–28 B:2/15/1895, Brooklyn, NY D:7/6/1965, New York, NY Deb:4/13/1917, CIN NL BR/TR 6'1", 170

W	L	PCT	G	SV	IP	BB	SO	ERA
118	149	.442	389	11	2357[1]	953	833	4.13

Righthander Jimmy Ring was an innocent bystander when it came to the gambling scandals of the Black Sox era. In Game 4 of the fixed 1919 World Series Ring defeated Eddie Cicotte 2–0 on a three-hitter, surrendering hits to only Joe Jackson, Happy Felsch, and Chick Gandil. In five innings of relief in Game 6 he lost a 10-inning contest to Dickie Kerr.

In 1918 Ring, entering a game in relief for the Reds, was approached by first baseman Hal Chase who told him, "I've got some money on this game, kid. There's something in it for you if you lose." Ring paid him no mind, but lost anyway. The next morning, Chase silently passed him a $50 bill. Ring reported the incident to Reds manager Christy Mathewson who in turn reported it to National League president John Heydler. Heydler presided over a hearing and dismissed the case for lack of evidence because Mathewson had since left for France during the closing stages of World War I.

After winning 26 games with Utica in 1916 Ring was drafted by the Reds and was traded to the Phils for Eppa Rixey on November 22, 1920. After five years in Philadelphia he was sent to the

Giants. New York dispatched him to the Cardinals in December 1926 in one of the most famous trades of the 1920s: he and Frankie Frisch to St. Louis in exchange for Rogers Hornsby. Finishing his career with the Phillies, he pitched briefly for Toledo and Newark after leaving the majors.

Cal Ripken, Jr.

Ripken, Calvin Edwin, Jr. **SS–3B**
1981–* B:8/24/1960, Havre de Grace, MD
Deb:8/10/1981, BAL AL BR/TR 6'4", 225

G	AB	R	H	HR	RBI	OBP	SLG	AVG
2790	10765	1561	2991	402	1571	.347	.451	.278

Cal Ripken, Jr. will be forever remembered for "the streak." Ripken became the most durable player to ever put on a major league uniform on September 6, 1995, when he appeared in his 2,131st consecutive game. He surpassed Lou Gehrig's "unbreakable record" (according to Gehrig's plaque at Yankee Stadium) at a time when baseball was still suffering the repercussions of the 1994 baseball strike. The national Ripken watch, as he approached the magic number, helped heal some of the wounds felt by many fans. The ovation at Camden Yards on that historic night lasted more than 20 minutes.

The following season Ripken would also break the world record of 2,216 consecutive games, a number reached by Sachio Kinugasa a third baseman for the Hiroshima Carp of Japan's Central League. Ripken's streak would end at 2,632 on September 19, 1998 with no one in the ballpark aware of the game's significance. The next night, 30 minutes before the final Orioles home game of the year, Ripken unexpectedly asked Baltimore manager Ray Miller to take him out of the lineup. He wasn't hurt; he could have played; it was simply time to put an end to a personal accomplishment that had begun to overshadow team goals. Ryan Minor was his replacement.

Ripken was an Oriole practically from birth. He was born and raised in Maryland, the son of an Orioles minor league manager, Cal Sr., the taciturn founder of "the Oriole Way." Baltimore drafted the young Ripken out of high school in the second round of the 1978 amateur draft. Ripken broke into the major leagues shortly after the close of the 1981 players strike, debuting as a pinch runner on August 10 against Kansas City. Like Gehrig, once he stepped on the field, it was nearly impossible to get him off it.

In 1982 he was named American League Rookie of the Year after leading rookies in nearly every offensive category. He started the season at third base, but soon shifted to shortstop where he would play every game, and practically every inning, for the next 14 seasons before returning to third base in 1997. He wouldn't miss a game at third for almost two seasons.

In that span, Ripken became one of the game's best shortstops with both the bat and glove. Ripken won the AL MVP in 1983 as the leader of an Orioles team that won the World Series; in 1991 he won the award again because of his outstanding achievements (34 homers, 114 RBIs, .556 slugging average) on a sixth-place team. In between MVPs, his father was hired to manage the club, but Cal Sr. was dismissed in the midst of a 21-game losing streak to start the 1988 season.

Cal Jr. became one of baseball's most popular players: through 1999 he had appeared in 17 straight All-Star Games. He set a major league record (since broken) with 95 consecutive errorless games in 1990, and followed that with back-to-back Gold Glove Awards in 1991 and 1992. He also earned numerous honors for his work off the field as well, including the Bart Giamatti Caring Award (1989), Roberto Clemente Award (1992), and Lou Gehrig Award (1992).

In 1993 Ripken passed Ernie Banks as the all-time home run leader for shortstops. The following year he hit his 300th home run. On September 2, 1999, he became the 29th player to hit 400 home runs, but his season ended prematurely—with him just nine hits shy of 3,000—because of surgery to relieve pressure in his lower back. His .340 average in 332 at bats was the highest of his career, but it was the first time in 19 years that he failed to play in at least 99 percent of his team's games.

Swede Risberg

Risberg, Charles August **SS**
1917–20 B:10/13/1894, San Francisco, CA
D:10/13/1975, Red Bluff, CA Deb:4/11/1917, CHI AL
BR/TR 6', 175

G	AB	R	H	HR	RBI	OBP	SLG	AVG
476	1619	196	394	6	175	.311	.332	.243

The "Black Sox." The name still reverberates more than 80 years after a group of White Sox players conspired to fix the 1919 World Series. One of the villains in this sordid tale was Charles August "Swede" Risberg. The White Sox shortstop was a key conspirator in the fix, not only with his intentional, on-field mistakes but also with his threats of violence against teammate "Shoeless Joe" Jackson if he talked to the authorities.

Risberg, a masterful fielder but a weak hitter, was brought up to the White Sox from the Pacific Coast League in 1917 so that Buck Weaver could be shifted over to third. But Risberg's hitting was so anemic at .203 that manager Clarence "Pants" Rowland benched him for most of the World Series against the Giants. With Weaver moved over to short and Fred McMullin filling in at third, the Sox won.

At the start of 1918 Rowland announced that Risberg would have to bat much better than his previous season to win back his job. He did, hitting .256. Enlisting in the army that August, Risberg returned to the White Sox in 1919. But by June the new manager, Kid Gleason, had tired of Risberg's inconsistent hitting. Weaver once again moved to short, and McMullin took over at third. McMullin was injured in early August, however, and Risberg once again became a starter.

When McMullin recovered, Gleason decided to keep playing Risberg. But the move was only partially based on Risberg's talents. Gleason simply announced that Weaver was better at third than at short. So Risberg stayed at short, hitting a respectable .256, as the White Sox won the pennant and headed for the Series against the Reds. Noted the *Chicago Tribune*'s Irving Sanborn at the time, "Risberg and Weaver have been performing feats that have astonished the natives of the towns in which they played."

Risberg, however, was one of the first players that Chicago first baseman Chick Gandil approached about fixing the Series. On September 21, 1919, Risberg, Gandil, Weaver, and McMullin met with Eddie Cicotte, Lefty Williams, Oscar "Happy" Felsch, and Jackson to discuss the fix. Risberg, who received less than $3,000 in salary in 1919, agreed to go along with the conspiracy. Later he wired a friend, St. Louis second baseman Joe Gedeon, about it.

In the fourth inning of Game 1 of the Series, Risberg attracted suspicion by holding onto a relay throw long enough to prevent a double play. No error was scored. "He paused too long," Sanborn wrote, "and let [shortstop Larry] Kopf beat the play to first by a toenail. A double play would have retired the side scoreless." Instead the Reds scored five runs and put the game out of reach.

In the second inning of Game 6, with Dickie Kerr pitching, Risberg booted an easy grounder. In the fourth, on a grounder by second baseman Morrie Rath, Risberg threw to third, trying to nail pitcher Dutch Ruether. The shortstop hit Ruether in the back instead of throwing to first for the sure out. Ruether scored on the play, and Rath took second.

Gleason, like so many others, had his suspicions. After one of the losses he saw Cicotte and Risberg in the lobby of Cincinnati's Hotel Sinton. The two were inappropriately cheerful, even laughing.

Eventually the fix blew wide open, and all eight players were brought to trial in Chicago. In April, with the court date approaching, Risberg, Jackson, Felsch, Williams, and McMullin scheduled a barnstorming tour of Illinois, Indiana, and Wisconsin. But the reluctance of many local semipro teams to face them canceled their plans. In May they formed the South Side Stars and announced they would play every Sunday in Chicago. The city council's judiciary committee stepped in, however, and threatened to revoke the ballpark's license unless the five were booted from the team. They were.

A jury found all eight White Sox innocent, but newly installed Commissioner Kenesaw Mountain Landis banished them from the game for life. Almost a decade later Risberg alleged that many members of the Sox, including those he contemptuously termed the "white lilies," were involved in bribing the Tigers to throw four games in 1917 to help give Chicago the pennant. The charges were tossed out.

Risberg took up dairy farming in Minnesota after being banned from baseball. Later he moved to northern California, where he operated a tavern near the Oregon border. He died in 1975, the last surviving member of the eight Black Sox.

Jungle Jim Rivera

Rivera, Manuel Joseph **OF**

1952–61 B:7/22/1922, New York, NY Deb:4/15/1952, STL AL BL/TL 6', 196

G	AB	R	H	HR	RBI	OBP	SLG	AVG
1171	3552	503	911	83	422	.330	.402	.256

Jungle Jim Rivera, whose fine catch off Charlie Neal helped preserve a 1–0 White Sox victory in Game 5 of the 1959 World Series, spent more than four years in an army prison before reaching the American League. Manuel Joseph Rivera, who for some reason was called "Jim", had originally been charged with the rape of his commanding officer's daughter. When an examination proved her to be still a virgin he was then charged—and convicted—of attempted rape.

Through the efforts of Gainesville (Florida State League) owner Earl Mann, Rivera was released and began his professional career with that club in 1949. Rivera also played for Pensacola and Seattle before he was sold to the White Sox for $65,000 in 1952. When his former Seattle manager, Rogers Hornsby, signed as Browns manager, he urged owner Bill Veeck to secure Rivera's contract. Rivera went to St. Louis in an eight-player November 1951 deal, but returned to the White Sox the following July, where he led the American League in triples in 1953 and in stolen bases in 1955.

Renowned for his hustle, his fielding, and a hitch in his swing, Rivera was no shrinking violet. On Opening Day 1961 in Washington he received an autograph from President John Kennedy, only to chide the Chief Executive: "What's this? This is just a scribble! I can hardly make it out! You'll have to do better than this, John."

Mariano Rivera

Rivera, Mariano **P**

1995–* B:11/29/1969, Panama City, Panama Deb:5/23/1995, NY AL BR/TR 6'4", 170

W	L	PCT	G	SV	IP	BB	SO	ERA
26	13	.667	266	129	376²	119	337	2.58

After five years in baseball, Mariano Rivera was considered the best closer in the game. Not employing the theatrics of some relievers, Rivera was forever calm on the mound, almost casual, in situations of the highest pressure. The native of Panama capped his 1999 season with two saves and a win in the New York Yankees' World Series sweep of the Atlanta Braves, earning the Series Most Valuable Player Award. So dominant was Rivera that he didn't allow an earned run over the last three months of the 1999 season, from July through the postseason.

Rivera added 12⅓ scoreless innings, two wins and six saves to his postseason ledger in 1999. After the Series, teammate David Cone called Rivera "automatic."

The wiry righthander split his first season in 1995 between Triple A Columbus and the Yankees. Of his 19 major league appearances that year, nine were starts. Although he was generally unimpressive as a starter, posting a record of 5–3 with a 5.51 ERA, he gained notice in a July 4 start at Chicago in which he struck out 11 in eight innings. In three appearances in the 1995 Division Series against Seattle he struck out eight and allowed no runs in five innings; the highlight was three scoreless innings he tossed in the Yankees' 15-inning victory against the Mariners.

In 1996 Rivera finished 8–3 in a setup role for closer John Wetteland. In 107 innings he recorded 130 strikeouts, the most by a reliever in club history (Rich Gossage fanned 122 in 1978). Rivera also had a 26-inning scoreless streak. In the postseason he allowed just one run in 14⅓ innings.

Wetteland, the World Series MVP, was allowed to sign with Texas as a free agent for the 1997 season. Rivera posted 43 saves in his first season as closer. The eighth-inning home run he allowed to Cleveland's Sandy Alomar in Game 4 of the Division Series was only his second run allowed in postseason play. The blow, which cost the Yankees a shot at repeating as world champions, bothered Rivera greatly yet it only made him more determined to succeed.

In 1998 he was impeccable, tossing 13⅓ scoreless postseason innings as the Yankees swept San Diego in the World Series. Rivera's 1999 regular season was his best yet. He had a major league-leading 45 saves, while opponents hit a paltry .176 against him.

Mickey Rivers

Rivers, John Milton **OF–DH**

1970–84 B:10/31/1948, Miami, FL Deb:8/4/1970, CAL AL BL/TL 5'10", 165

G	AB	R	H	HR	RBI	OBP	SLG	AVG
1468	5629	785	1660	61	499	.329	.397	.295

Mickey Rivers was an original, a man-child who would throw away money by the fistful at the racetrack, sulk like a child when he was unhappy, and deliver incomprehensible monologues that would leave his listeners baffled. Yet he could be equally perceptive.

His legacy of bizarre stories goes back to his days at Miami Dade Community College. One day Rivers was missing just as a game was about to start. He was found halfway between the clubhouse and the park—asleep under a tree in full uniform. Another time, college teammate Bucky Dent looked around the outfield in the middle of the game and saw his center fielder vaulting the fence. He found out later that Rivers was trying to avoid some unfriendly people he had just seen arrive at the park.

It was at Miami Dade that the word "Gozzlehead" first entered baseball's vocabulary. According to Rivers, who called almost everybody "Goz" or "Gozzlehead," it came from his Miami neighborhood. Put politely, it implied a lack of physical beauty. Rivers sometimes used a variation: "Warplehead." On special occasions, he trotted out a third friendly insult: "Mailboxhead."

The Braves, impressed by Rivers' quick bat and sheer speed, signed him in 1969. He hit .307 in rookie league ball but was traded to the Angels for Bob Priddy and Hoyt Wilhelm as Atlanta looked for some September pitching insurance. Rivers spent three seasons shuttling between the minors and the big club and finally stuck in 1974. Given a chance to play regularly he hit .285, led the American League in triples—with 11 in only 118 games—and stole 30 bases.

His speed was blinding. Watching him fly around the bases for one of his three-baggers was a sight not easily forgotten. His walk to home plate was equally memorable. He would hobble from the on-deck circle, hunched like an old man, his bat dragging behind him, before finally settling into the lefthanded batter's box. Of course, the instant he hit the ball he would transform into a human jet engine. During his career he grounded into only 44 double plays—or once every 128 at bats, one of the best ratios in major league history.

Rivers had one flaw as a leadoff batter: he refused to take walks. A career .295 hitter, he walked only 266 times in 5,629 plate appearances. His career high was 43 bases on balls in 1975. That season he hit .284 and led the league in triples, with 13. He also topped the circuit with a career-high 70 steals, the most in the American League since Ty Cobb stole 96 in 1915.

That winter Yankees general manager Gabe Paul stole Rivers and pitcher Ed Figueroa in a trade for Bobby Bonds. Rivers was a revelation. He batted .312, stole 43 bases, drove in 67 runs, and was his teammates' overwhelming choice for club Most Valuable Player as the Yankees won their first pennant in 12 years. In addition Rivers finished third as the Most Valuable Player choice of the Baseball Writers Association of America.

The Reds swept the Yankees in the 1976 World Series, and Rivers batted only .167. The next season, when Reggie Jackson signed on, the Yankees became "the Bronx Zoo." Rivers fit right in with the new level of insanity in the clubhouse. He hit .326 with career highs in home runs (12) and RBIs (69) despite missing 24 games with an assortment of injuries.

His petulant side surfaced in the fifth game of the 1977 Championship Series in Kansas City. He sat in the trainer's room as the game was about to start, refusing to play because Paul would not give him yet another advance on his salary. Fran Healy, the reserve catcher who had acted as a negotiator all season to keep people from strangling each other, finally convinced Rivers to play. Rivers singled off Larry Gura in the ninth to bring in the winning run, and the Yankees won their second straight pennant.

Rivers batted just .222 in the 1977 World Series, but the Yankees won the Series anyway, in six games over the Dodgers. While he slumped badly in 1978, his mouth was in working order. The Yankees of that era would take turns insulting each other in the back of the bus; it was their way of letting off steam. But one day the repartee between Rivers and Jackson got out of hand, and Rivers crossed the line. "Reggie Manuel Jackson. Your first name's a white man's name, your middle name's a Spanish man's name, and your last name is a black man's name. You don't know who you are." Rivers' remark was ironic. He had confused Jackson's actual middle name, Martinez, with that of then Manager Billy Martin, with whom Jackson had recurring confrontations.

In the middle of another Rivers–Jackson "dialogue" on the road, a truck passed the bus. Jackson pointed to the truck and said, "That's you in 15 years, Rivers. A truck driver." Rivers replied, "Yeah, but I'll be a happy truck driver."

Rivers' greatest contribution to the Yankees' second straight world championship came in the 1978 playoff game with the Red Sox. He was on deck in the seventh inning when Bucky Dent fouled Mike Torrez's third pitch off his foot. As Dent got treatment from the trainer, Rivers noticed that Dent was using his batting practice bat, which was cracked. Rivers gave him one of his own, and Dent hit a home run on the next pitch.

Rivers then batted .455 in the ALCS (his career playoff average was .386) and .333 in the World Series, but his days in pinstripes were numbered. The Yankees were getting tired of his off-field antics and his moody ways. Although traded to the Rangers in an eight-player deal on August 1, 1979, he fully expected to return to the New York club. Or as he put it, "Me and George [Steinbrenner, then the club's owner] and Billy [Martin], we're two of a kind."

He followed with a terrific season in 1980, establishing career highs in batting average (.333), runs (96), hits (210), doubles (32), and on-base percentage (.355). He had two hitting streaks of at least 20 games. In 1981, his last year as a regular, Rivers batted .286. He was 32 years old, and his body was starting to betray him. He missed most of 1982 with injuries but rebounded to hit .300 in 1984, his final season. Rivers retired after the Rangers released him the following spring. He went on to work with children for the Dade County Recreation Department.

Eppa Rixey

Rixey, Eppa **P**

1912–17, 1919–33 B:5/3/1891, Culpeper, VA
D:2/28/1963, Cincinnati, OH Deb:6/21/1912, PHI NL
BR/TL 6'5", 210

W	L	PCT	G	SH	IP	BB	SO	ERA
266	251	.515	692	37	4494²	1082	1350	3.15

Until surpassed by Warren Spahn, Eppa Rixey held the National League record for victories by a lefthander, with 266. He held on to the 20th century National League record for career losses, with 251. Through 1999 his .515 winning percentage remained the worst of any starter in the Hall of Fame.

National League umpire Cy Rigler, who was spending the off-season studying law and coaching basketball and baseball there, discovered Rixey on the University of Virginia campus. Rixey was playing basketball on the school team when Rigler encouraged him to try his hand at pitching. The umpire was so impressed with Rixey's fastball that he predicted a future in professional baseball for the youth. "I plan to be a chemist," replied an uninterested Rixey. Rigler countered, "I'll make a deal with you. I'll arrange for the Phillies to give you a $2,000 bonus and we'll split it." Rixey did sign on with the Phils, but the National League had just adopted a rule barring umpires from serving as scouts, so the bonus was voided.

Rixey never pitched a day in the minors, although he took a detour before going to the Phillies in 1912. He wanted to finish up his undergraduate work, and he promised to stay in shape by working out in the school gymnasium. The Phils gave their consent, and Rixey did not report until June of that year. He finished his rookie season with a 10–10 record and a 2.50 ERA.

Philadelphia won the 1915 pennant behind the league-leading 31 wins by Grover Alexander. Rixey was 11–12 with a respectable 2.39 ERA. The Phillies lost three of the first four games of the World Series to Boston, but they carried a 4–2 lead into the eighth inning of Game 5. Rixey had entered the game in relief in the third inning and had not allowed a run. But he was tagged by Duffy Lewis for a two-run homer in the eighth that tied the game, and Harry Hooper greeted Rixey with a Series-winning home run in the ninth.

In 1916 Rixey rebounded with the first of four 20-win seasons. His ERA was a career-low 1.85, and he struck out a personal-best 134 batters. However, the following season he became one of the few pitchers to win 20 games one season and lose 20 the next. On February 22, 1921, the Phillies traded him to the Reds for pitcher Jimmy Ring and outfielder Greasy Neale. He won 20 games three times and had two 19-win seasons during his 13-year stay with the Reds.

A .191 career hitter, Rixey once collected a homer, two doubles, and two singles in the same game against Jesse Haines of the Cardinals. He excitedly phoned his fiancée in Cincinnati to tell her the news. "Goodness," she exclaimed. "Something dreadful is about to happen in St. Louis if you hit a home run." Her intuition was correct: the next day a tornado touched down there.

Rixey was a turtle on the basepaths. He'd spent a decade in the majors before he swiped his first base. Three years later he went after No. 2, teaming up with the equally lead-footed Bubbles Hargrave in a double-steal attempt. "Gabby Hartnett, the best thrower in the game, couldn't believe it," chortled Rixey. "He just stood there openmouthed and forgot to throw."

Rixey delivered winning records the first eight years he was with Cincinnati. In 1922 he won a league-leading 25 games, and he won at least 20 in 1923 and 1925. Toward the end of his career, Rixey was often used in relief. Once, after a tough day at the ballpark, Rixey's car was pulled over by a Cincinnati police officer, and Rixey was issued a speeding ticket. When Rixey appeared in court the judge found him guilty and fined him $10, but then suspended the fine.

Afterwards he explained his leniency. "It seemed to me," said the judge, "that Mr. Rixey deserved some consideration because he probably was preoccupied with worry over having been knocked out of the box yesterday afternoon, and wasn't really himself when he was driving last night."

Eppa was Rixey's real first name, but he was also known as "Jephtha;" the nickname was a creation of Cincinnati sportswriter Bill Phelon, who simply liked the sound of it. "It sounds," a tolerant Rixey mused, "like a cross between a Greek letter fraternity and a college yell."

After retiring from the game in 1933, Rixey went full-time into the insurance business he had started. His 21 seasons in the National League were a record until Steve Carlton surpassed him.

Rixey was a fan favorite. Writer Ira Smith once observed that "his good sportsmanship and fine traits of character [were the] main factors in his popularity." Rixey died in 1963, the same year he was named to the Hall of Fame.

Phil Rizzuto

Rizzuto, Philip Francis **SS**

1941–56 B:9/25/1917, Brooklyn, NY Deb:4/14/1941, NY AL BR/TR 5'6", 160

G	AB	R	H	HR	RBI	OBP	SLG	AVG
1661	5816	877	1588	38	563	.351	.355	.273

Phil Rizzuto's rank among the best shortstops in major league history was a matter of great debate, particularly because Rizzuto, unlike his longtime crosstown rival, Pee Wee Reese, had not been elected to the Hall of Fame. On February 25, 1994, Rizzuto was finally elected to Cooperstown.

"The Scooter" was an excellent fielding shortstop who had one sensational offensive year for one of the greatest ballclubs of all time—the Yankees of the late 1940s and early 1950s. Statistically, Rizzuto pales next to Reese, particularly in offensive categories. In Most Valuable Player voting, Rizzuto finished in the top 10 only three times, but he ranked first, second, and sixth. Reese made the list eight times, but never placed higher than fifth.

It seems that Rizzuto's two most important attributes—his glove and his leadership—are difficult strengths to evaluate. Opponent Ted Williams said that Rizzuto made the difference in the sensational Yankees–Red Sox late-season pennant races during those years. Joe DiMaggio said that Rizzuto "holds the team together." Yankees pitcher Vic Raschi said, "My best pitch is anything the batter grounds, lines, or pops up in the direction of Rizzuto." New York manager Casey Stengel, in his inimitable fashion, said, "What about this shortstop Rizzuto who's got nothing but daughters but throws out the lefthanded hitters in the double play?" *The Sporting News* had no doubt from 1949 through 1952—Rizzuto won its vote for top major league shortstop each year.

Defensively, Rizzuto was one of the best American League shortstops of his time. He led all American League shortstops in double plays three times. One year he and Joe Gordon set the league record for double plays by a keystone combo. He also was the league leader in total chances per game three times, in fielding percentage and putouts twice, and in assists once. He played errorless ball for 21 consecutive World Series games. Although not blessed with exceptional foot speed or a great arm, he had fast hands and more than compensated for his shortcomings with intelligent placement and a quick release.

He was born Fiero Francis Rizzuto, the son of a trolley car conductor. The diminutive shortstop tried out for New York's two National League clubs at age 16. Giants manager Bill Terry sent him home; Dodger skipper Casey Stengel said, "Go get a shoe box."

But after Rizzuto was named Minor League Player of the Year for Kansas City in 1940, the Yanks brought him up. His timing was excellent; Frankie Crosetti had been New York's shortstop for 10 years, but age was catching up to him. Rizzuto was the Yankees starter as a rookie and batted .307. After hitting only .111 in the 1941 World Series against the Dodgers, Rizzuto's bat came alive the following fall. He hit .381, with a homer, two runs, and two stolen bases. The Yankees won both Series.

But World War II was underway, and he entered the military. Both he and Pee Wee Reese found themselves on the same navy team. Manager Bill Dickey, who was Rizzuto's teammate in New York, made Rizzuto the third baseman; Reese stayed at short.

In 1946 Rizzuto returned to the Yankees and received a nasty beaning from Nels Potter of the Browns. For the rest of his career, Rizzuto suffered from dizzy spells. The Yankees easily won the 1947 pennant, and knocked off the Dodgers in seven games in the Series. Rizzuto batted .308 against Brooklyn, with three runs, two RBIs, and two stolen bases.

After a hot start in 1949, he was moved to leadoff from his customary eighth slot, hit .275, and finished second in league MVP voting. Although he hit only .167 in the World Series against Brooklyn, he played flawlessly at shortstop and scored a key run in Game 1. New York won the Series in five games.

In 1950 Rizzuto won the AL MVP Award as he batted a career-high .324 and finished second in the league with 200 hits. He walked 92 times and slugged .439, the only time he topped the .400 mark. He was perfect in the field in the Yankees' World Series sweep of the Phillies.

Rizzuto's average fell 50 points the next year, but in a vital September game against the charging Red Sox, Rizzuto did what he did best. He pulled off a masterful squeeze bunt to break a 1–1 tie in the ninth and bring home Joe DiMaggio with the winning run.

The World Series that year was tied at a game apiece when Eddie Stanky led off the Giants' fifth with a walk. He lit out for second base on a hit-and-run, and Yogi Berra made a great throw to nail him by a mile. But "the Brat" lived up to his name; he kicked the ball out of Rizzuto's glove and wound up at third. Four batters later Whitey Lockman homered, and the Yankees had to fight back to win the Series in six games. For decades the Stanky "kick" rankled Rizzuto, although he claimed the play got the Yankees fired up enough to turn the Series around.

By 1953 Rizzuto was slowing down. Andy Carey and Willie Miranda shared duties at short with Rizzuto for the Yankees that season. In addition, the sensitive Rizzuto was having more and more problems with Stengel. Knowing that Rizzuto couldn't take criticism to his face, it had been Casey's habit to direct the remarks meant for Rizzuto at Gil McDougald. McDougald later commented, "It took me five or so years to realize what Casey was doing. I don't think Rizzuto ever did." By 1955 the 37-year-old Scooter was down to 79 games at short, playing behind Billy Hunter.

In Game 7 of that year's World Series a poor play by Rizzuto hurt the Yankee cause severely. With two out, Rizzuto on at second, and Billy Martin at first in the third inning of a scoreless game, McDougald rapped a slow chopper down the third-base line. Dodgers third sacker Don Hoak had no chance of a play at first base, so he let the ball go, hoping it would roll foul. It didn't. Instead it hit Rizzuto as he was sliding into third. He was called out, the inning was over, and the Dodgers beat the Yankees in a World Series for the first time.

Rizzuto was released unceremoniously on Old Timer's Day in 1956. Yankees management called him into the front office and asked his advice on cutting a player. Rizzuto thought they were serious and offered some suggestions, but in fact they were letting him know the player to be cut was Rizzuto himself.

Kicked upstairs into the Yankee broadcast booth, Rizzuto's first accomplishment was to bring about a rapprochement between announcers Mel Allen and Red Barber. Both had been professionally cool to each other for years, but they united in their resentment against the appearance of the untrained former ballplayer. Outlasting both Allen and Barber, Rizzuto became a hit with the fans. "Holy Cow!" became his trademark.

Rizzuto's greatest strength as an announcer was his ability to amuse. According to Curt Smith, "He was his own best subject matter, and veering from play-by-play to discourse on allergies, and lightning, plane trips, and crumb cakes, the Scooter seemed utterly right at home." Even Barber had to admit, "Phil had the quickest reflexes, next to Jackie Robinson, I ever saw. He has a sparkling charm when he wishes to turn it on, and no matter the jam he gets in, he gets out of it by assuming a childlike innocence he can call upon instantly."

Some of Rizzuto's delightful on-the-air comments were put together in a book, *O Holy Cow! The Selected Verse of Phil Rizzuto*, in 1993. But Rizzuto could also be dull, and was often ridiculed for it. Once, a man who had died on the operating table miraculously recovered. Wondering what it must have been like to be temporarily dead, David Letterman commented, "It must have been like listening to Phil Rizzuto during a rain delay."

Over the years, those who advocated Rizzuto's enshrinement in the Hall of Fame pointed to his high placement in many World Series categories, both offensively and defensively. His detractors argued that this was simply because no shortstop ever played in as many World Series games as he did. They also pointed out that he hit more than .300 only twice in his 13-year career, and that he topped .280 only one other time. On the other hand, he was a superb bunter and excellent at hitting behind the runner. Also, for five consecutive years Rizzuto led the league in sacrifice hits.

For 15 years the Baseball Writers Association had passed over Rizzuto. After the 11th year of consideration by the Veterans Committee he was finally elected to the Hall of Fame in 1994. Throughout the years of being passed over, Rizzuto said that he didn't think he belonged in the Hall, either as a player or as a broadcaster. However, some reporters claimed that his failure to be elected bothered him "more than you think."

He was gravely affected by Mickey Mantle's death in 1995. He decided to stay with the team to announce a game rather than attend his friend's funeral; he regretted the decision and at age 77 retired as the team's broadcaster.

Always a popular figure in New York, he gained national attention away from the diamond for his running dialogue in Meat Loaf's hit song, "Paradise by the Dashboard Light."

Bip Roberts

Roberts, Leon Joseph **2B-OF-3B**

1986–98 B:10/27/1963, Berkeley, CA Deb:4/7/1986, SD NL BB/TR 5'7", 165

G	AB	R	H	HR	RBI	OBP	SLG	AVG
1202	4147	663	1220	30	352	.360	.380	.294

After a long minor league apprenticeship, undersized but versatile Bip Roberts arrived as a superior contact hitter and base-stealing threat atop the San Diego Padres lineup in 1989. Available for duty at second, third, or in the outfield, Roberts batted .309 with 46 steals in 1990. Injuries derailed him the following season—the first of 10 trips to the disabled list over the next eight seasons. His address changed nearly as frequently. He changed uniforms six times over the final seven years of his career.

Roberts was an All-Star in his first season in Cincinnati in 1992. He batted .323, stole 44 bases, and tied a National League record with 10 straight hits in September. An undiagnosed thumb injury and friction with batting coach Ray Knight, among others, ended his Cincinnati honeymoon. Roberts underwent reconstructive surgery on his thumb following the 1993 season.

He returned to the Padres and hit .320 the following season. After another injury-marred campaign in 1995, Roberts was traded to Kansas City for Wally Joyner. A late-season trade in 1997, this time to Cleveland, enabled Roberts to reach the postseason for the only time in his career. He finished the season over .300 for the sixth time in nine years. He split his final season with Detroit and Oakland.

Robin Roberts

Roberts, Robin Evan **P**

1948–66 B:9/30/1926, Springfield, IL Deb:6/18/1948, PHI NL BB/TR 6', 190

W	L	PCT	G	SH	IP	BB	SO	ERA
286	245	.539	676	45	4688^2	902	2357	3.41

Early in his career Robin Roberts acted on a suggestion from Phillies coach Benny Bengough, who felt the young righthander was rushing his pitches and should develop a prewindup routine to slow himself down. Roberts came up with a series of actions that he carried out with every pitch. He would hitch his belt, adjust his left trouser leg, tug his cap, wipe his brow, go into an easy windup, and—flash!—his fastball would be across the plate. Not only was this painstaking routine mesmerizing in itself, but it also made his fastball seem that much quicker and more surprising to batters. As Red Schoendienst described Roberts' delivery, "The ball seemed to skid across the strike zone as though it were on a piece of ice."

Bengough's suggestion no doubt helped Roberts achieve his 286 major league victories, but it was one of the very few times after Roberts reached the majors that he ever listened to anyone else's advice on the art of pitching. Hardheaded and confident, he did it his way.

Roberts was the son of a Welsh coal miner who had immigrated to the United States with his family in 1921 and settled in Springfield, Illinois. At an early age he became interested in sports and distinguished himself in basketball. Michigan State offered him a scholarship, but World War II intervened, and he spent 1944 and part of 1945 as an Army Air Force cadet. After being discharged he enrolled at Michigan State, where he eventually earned a bachelor of science degree in physical education.

At East Lansing, Michigan, Roberts began to show his ability as a pitcher, tossing a pair of no-hitters. One of them was against archrival Michigan, then coached by former major league pitcher Ray Fisher. During the summer Fisher managed a semipro team in Montpelier, Vermont, in a league made up mostly of college players who wanted to attract the attention of major league scouts. Roberts joined Fisher's team and within two years found himself pursued by six major league teams.

The choice came down to either the Boston Braves or the Philadelphia Phillies. Roberts agreed to work out for both at Wrigley Field in Chicago. The Phillies came first and after watching him pitch offered him a $25,000 signing bonus. At the time, the sum was more most major leaguers made in a season, but the young pitcher hesitated. The Braves had previously offered to treat his parents to an all-expenses-paid week's vacation in Chicago. Roberts called his father in Springfield and pointed out that he could easily pay for their trip out of his bonus money. The elder Roberts gave his blessing and Robin Roberts became a Phillie.

Roberts was joining one of the most consistently bad teams in baseball history. The club had not won a pennant since 1915 and had seldom finished in the first division. However, under team president Robert M. Carpenter, Jr., and general manager Herb Pennock, Philadelphia had been building a strong farm system since the end of World War II. Their many fine prospects were about to descend upon the major leagues.

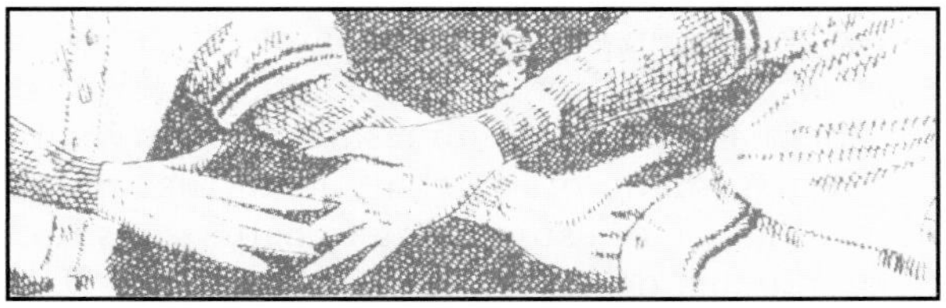

Much to Roberts' frustration, the Phillies sent him to Wilmington in 1948 to begin his career. He believed he was ready for major league competition from the start, and when he won nine of 10 decisions with an ERA hovering around 2.00 the Phillies promoted him to the big club. During the remainder of the season he won seven and lost nine for the sixth-place Phils.

In 1949 the Phillies advanced to third place. They acquired the nickname "the Whiz Kids" because of the number of fine young players arriving on their roster. Roberts split 30 decisions that year but established himself as the ace of the pitching staff.

The Brooklyn Dodgers were favored to win the 1950 pennant, but the Phillies got off to a fast start in what became a four-team race throughout the first half of the season. The Dodgers, Cardinals, Braves, and Phillies all took turns leading the league, but at midsummer Philadelphia began to pull ahead. Although center fielder Richie Ashburn was a .300 hitter and right fielder Del Ennis a strong home run threat, the Phillies were not among league team leaders in run scoring. The club's strength was its pitching. Roberts and Curt Simmons, another sensational "bonus baby," made a terrific righty–lefty starting tandem. Jim Konstanty, at age 33 hardly a Whiz Kid, provided steady relief with his bewildering palmball.

With 11 days left in the season the Phillies ' enjoyed a seemingly safe 7½-game lead over Brooklyn and Boston. Yet Philadelphia was in trouble. At the beginning of September, 17-game winner Simmons had been called into military service. Other pitchers had developed various ailments. Suddenly minus much of their pitching, the Phillies stopped winning and the Dodgers went on a tear.

Brooklyn and Philadelphia were scheduled to meet at Ebbets Field for their final two games of the season. The Phillies still needed one more victory to clinch the pennant, but Brooklyn took the first game handily. Both teams sent their aces to the mound for the finale: Don Newcombe for the Dodgers, Roberts for the Phillies. Each had won 19 games, but Roberts was starting for the third time in five days and making his sixth try for an elusive 20th victory.

The teams were tied 1–1 in the bottom of the ninth when Roberts seemed to fade, allowing a walk and two singles. Brooklyn's Cal Abrams was thrown out at the plate on the second hit, but that left runners on second and third with only one out. Roberts walked Jackie Robinson intentionally and then retired the next two Dodgers on a popup and a fly. In the top of the 10th inning, Phillies left fielder Dick Sisler, son of Hall of Famer George Sisler, hit a three-run homer. When Roberts stopped the Dodgers in the bottom of the

10th the Phillies had their first 20-game winner since 1917. More important, they had their first pennant in 35 years.

The powerful Yankees made short work of the Phillies in the World Series, sweeping them in four straight. Roberts started Game 2 and took a 1–1 tie into the 10th inning, only to be defeated by a Joe DiMaggio home run.

Despite the World Series loss, the future looked bright for the Whiz Kids, but they never reached such heights again. No one could blame Roberts. Beginning in 1950 he put together a string of six straight 20-win seasons. In 1952 he went 28–7, the most victories by a National Leaguer since 1935. *The Sporting News* named him Major League Player of the Year, an honor he earned again in 1955 when he was 23–14 for a fourth-place team.

Roberts had two natural weapons: a blazing fastball and remarkable, pinpoint control. Although seldom thought of as a strikeout artist, he led the league in that category in 1953 and 1954. He put his pitches just where he wanted them, yet his masterful control sometimes worked to his disadvantage. Batters, knowing there was little chance that they would be hit by a Roberts pitch, dug in and swung from the heels. Consequently he gave up home runs in record numbers. His 46 homers allowed in 1956 stood as the major league mark for many years. But because he walked batters so seldom—fewer than two free passes per game—most of the homers he served up cost him only single runs.

By the mid-1950s it was apparent that Roberts had started to slip. From 1950 through 1955 he never worked fewer than 304 innings. In five of those six seasons he led the league in innings pitched, and from 1952 through 1956 he led in complete games, but the heavy workload was taking a toll on his fastball. In 1956 he fell a victory short of 20 wins, but, more ominously, his ERA shot up to 4.45. The next year he collapsed completely, winning 10 and losing 22. Manager Mayo Smith urged him to develop another pitch, perhaps a slider. Roberts stubbornly refused to change his ways.

Three mediocre seasons followed, but in 1961 he won only a single game against 10 losses. His ERA shot up to 5.85. Finally the Phillies sold Roberts to Baltimore. His 234 victories in a Phillies uniform were a club record at the time and still represent the team best for righthanders. Roberts made something of a comeback with the

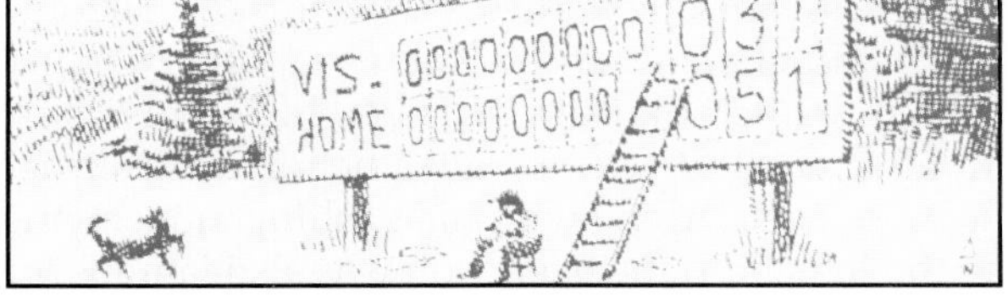

Orioles, using guile and his still-great control to register 42 victories in more than three seasons. He had his sights set on 300 wins when he was sent back to the National League in mid-1965, but after brief stints with the Astros and Cubs he was released only 14 wins shy of his goal. He tried a comeback with Reading of the Eastern League in 1967 at age 40, but arm trouble ended his career.

Roberts was baseball coach at the University of South Florida for a time before rejoining the Phillies organization as a minor league instructor. In 1976 he was named to the Hall of Fame.

Bob Robertson

Robertson, Robert Eugene **1B**

1967–79 B:10/2/1946, Frostburg, MD Deb:9/18/1967, PIT NL BR/TR 6'1", 210

G	AB	R	H	HR	RBI	OBP	SLG	AVG
829	2385	283	578	115	368	.334	.434	.242

In Pittsburgh they thought Bob Robertson was going to be the next Ralph Kiner. He tore through the minor leagues with an impressive display of power. He led the three different minor leagues in home runs from 1965 to 1969, and that included a full missed season with a kidney obstruction in 1968.

He slammed 27 homers and drove in 82 runs in his rookie year of 1970, but those were his major league high water marks. In the 1971 Championship Series he put on an awesome display. After the Pirates lost Game 1 to the Giants, Robertson blasted three home runs and a double for five RBIs at Candlestick Park the next day to even the series. He homered off Juan Marichal in his first at bat in Game 3 to help the Bucs to a 2–1 win. When the Pirates won their first pennant in 12 seasons the next day, Roberston's .438 average was perhaps the biggest reason. He smacked two home runs and drove in a team-best five runs as the Pirates won the World Series in seven games.

He never lived up to expectations in Pittsburgh, though. Roberto Clemente reportedly chastised him in the locker room for living the high life following the team's loss in the 1972 NLCS. Eventually Willie Stargell moved in from the outfield to replace the solid-fielding Robertson at first base. Although a less and less important member of Pittsburgh's famed "Lumber Company," Robertson still played in five postseasons as a Pirate.

After sitting out the 1977 season, the Pirates released Robertson. He signed with Seattle and was again released at season's end. Invited to Kansas City's spring camp, Robertson failed to make the Royals, but he managed to hook on with Toronto where he finished his career. After retiring he did public relations work for a grocery chain.

Charlie Robertson

Robertson, Charles Culbertson **P**

1919, 1922–28 B:1/31/1896, Dexter, TX D:8/23/1984, Fort Worth, TX Deb:5/13/1919, CHI AL BL/TR 6', 175

W	L	PCT	G	SH	IP	BB	SO	ERA
49	80	.380	166	6	1005	377	310	4.44

When Charlie Robertson was good, he was very, very good...then there was the rest of the time. In only his third major start he pitched the sixth perfect game in major league history, yet he never had a winning season.

After spending 1917 with Sherman in the Western Association, the White Sox purchased his contract. He spent the 1918 season in the Army Air Service. When he returned from World War I, he pitched one game before the Sox optioned him to Minneapolis in the American Association.

On April 30, 1922, he retired all 27 Detroit Tigers for a 2–0 victory. The perfecto was saved on a diving catch by left fielder Johnny Mostil. Ty Cobb thought Robertson was aided by illegal substances, and even asked the umpire to inspect Chicago first baseman's Earl Sheely glove. Tigers outfielder Harry Heilmann issued similar complaints. "It sounded like the squawk of a trimmed sucker," gloated the *Chicago Tribune*'s Irving Vaughn.

Arm problems plagued Robertson for the remainder of his career. His best season was his rookie year, when he finished with a 14–15 record. He fared no better in later stops with the St. Louis Browns and Boston Braves. After leaving the majors, Robertson, an Austin College graduate, coached college ball.

Bill Robinson

Robinson, William Henry **OF-1B**

1966–1969, 1972–83 B:6/26/1943, McKeesport, PA Deb:9/20/1966, ATL NL BR/TR 6'3", 205

G	AB	R	H	HR	RBI	OBP	SLG	AVG
1472	4364	536	1127	166	641	.303	.438	.258

The New York Yankees hoped that Bill Robinson would become the next Mickey Mantle when they acquired the outfielder from the Atlanta Braves in 1967. They were disappointed. He neither hit for power nor average in his three years with the Yankees. He was sent down to the minors where he toiled for two more seasons before a trade brought him to Philadelphia for another chance in the majors.

In his second year with the Phillies he looked poised to be a star, hitting .288 with 25 home runs, but Robinson regressed the following season and in April 1975 was traded to Pittsburgh where for a time he again flourished. In 1977 he had his career year, posting 26 homers and 104 RBIs with a .304 average. In 1975 and 1979 Robinson helped the Bucs to the postseason. In a three-day period in 1977 Robinson hit two grand slams.

His productivity began to decline, however, and in June 1982 he was returned to the Phillies where he played his final two seasons. Robinson later served as a Phillies minor league batting instructor and as a Mets coach. In February 1988 he managed the Caracas Lions to the Caribbean world championship. His son Bill played in the Mets and Angels system.

Brooks Robinson

Robinson, Brooks Calbert **3B**

1955–77 B:5/18/1937, Little Rock, AR Deb:9/17/1955, BAL AL BR/TR 6'1", 190

G	AB	R	H	HR	RBI	OBP	SLG	AVG
2896	10654	1232	2848	268	1357	.325	.401	.267

Baltimore probably has more men named Brooks than any other city. They were named, of course, after Brooks Robinson, the stellar Orioles third baseman. A fixture for 23 seasons, Robinson was a great fielder. One admirer said, "He plays third base like he came down from a higher league." Few people, if anybody, will dispute that Robinson is one of the greatest third basemen of all time. Mike Schmidt and George Brett, among others, were better hitters, but few at the hot corner matched Robinson's fielding prowess. Robinson's glove work belied the conventional wisdom of the time—that third base was an unimportant position defensively.

The first great player developed by the American League edition of the Orioles and the perfect hero for the great Orioles teams of the 1960s and early 1970s, he was dependable, efficient, and completely without pretension. Only Cal Ripken has approached Robinson's level of reverence among Orioles fans.

Robinson set virtually every major league career fielding record at third base, including highest fielding average, most games, most putouts, most assists, most chances, and most double plays. He also set major league records by leading the American League in assists eight times, games played eight times, and fielding average 11 times. He tied the league record by leading in chances eight times. Starting in 1960 he won 16 consecutive Gold Gloves, a figure matched only by pitcher Jim Kaat.

"Worst athlete I ever saw," former Orioles pitcher Jim Palmer said of Robinson. Then, Palmer added, while pointing to his body from his waist to his feet, "But I never saw a better athlete from here to here." Along with his flashing movements to the left and right, Robinson was also famous for charging bunts, picking them up barehanded, and flinging them to first in one smooth motion.

The Orioles discovered Brooks Calbert Robinson playing second base in a church league in Little Rock, Arkansas, and signed him with a $4,000 bonus after he finished high school in 1955. "He couldn't run, couldn't throw, and—when he first came up at 18, 19 years old—he couldn't hit," longtime opponent and broadcaster Tony Kubek recalled.

Robinson hit well at his first stop at York of the Piedmont League in 1955, batting .331 and earning a September promotion to Baltimore. His average dropped nearly 60 points at San Antonio of the Texas League, but his power numbers improved and he gained another late season call-up. He opened 1957 in Baltimore but was returned to San Antonio. After spending all of 1958 with the Birds, he made a final trip to the minors in early 1959, batting .331 for Vancouver with six homers and 32 RBIs in 42 games. Robinson returned to the Orioles for good on July 9, 1959.

Robinson developed into a good run producer and moderate power threat with the O's. He was third behind Roger Maris and Mickey Mantle in the 1960 AL Most Valuable Player voting. In 1964 the Orioles finished two games behind the first-place Yankees, and Robinson was voted American League MVP, setting career highs with a .318 batting average, 28 homers, and a league-leading 118 RBIs, along with his fifth-straight fielding-average crown. Robinson had his second, and last, 100-RBI season when the Orioles won the pennant in 1966. That season he finished second in the MVP balloting to Triple Crown winner and teammate Frank Robinson.

Brooks won MVP honors at the 1966 All-Star Game, collecting three hits, including a triple off Sandy Koufax, and scoring the AL's lone run in a 2–1, 10-inning loss. In 18 All-Star Games Robinson had a .289 average, three triples, and a homer, yet he played for a losing squad 15 times.

The addition of Frank Robinson in 1966 turned the Orioles from contenders into winners and their same-name stars helped propel the team to a World Series berth against Los Angeles. In the Series, Brooks homered off Don Drysdale in his first postseason plate appearance, right after Frank's two-run shot. But Brooks had only two more hits in the Orioles' four-game sweep, batting .214.

In 1969 Major League Baseball expanded and split into four different divisions, and the Orioles won the first AL East title with 109 wins. Robinson tattooed Minnesota Twins pitching for seven hits in 14 at bats in the Orioles' three-game Championship Series sweep. Facing the underdog New York Mets in the World Series, Robinson tied Game 2 with a seventh-inning single but grounded out in the bottom of the 10th with two on in the Oriole's 2–1 loss. Hitless in the next four games, he still contributed some drama in the ninth inning of Game 4. With the Orioles trailing, 1–0, and runners on first and third with one out, Brooks sliced a sinking line drive to right. Right fielder Ron Swoboda charged and made an improbable diving catch, turning a likely hit into a game-tying sacrifice fly. The Mets won the game on a botched bunt in the bottom of the 10th, then took Game 5 to win the world championship. Robinson hit only .053 in the Series, but his reputation as a World Series goat would end the following season.

In 1970 the Orioles repeated in the AL East, with 108 wins, and Robinson hit. 583 in their playoff rematch with Minnesota. After their ALCS sweep the Orioles advanced to the World Series, facing the Cincinnati Reds.

The 1970 World Series became known as "the Brooks Robinson Series." With Cincinnati's lineup of powerful righthanded batters and the Orioles pitching staff of predominantly lefthanded slowballers, Robinson knew he'd "have some business." It was the first Series that featured artificial turf, and Robinson loved the stuff. "Defensively, you almost feel invincible," he declared.

In Game 1 the Orioles fell behind, 3–0, after three innings. But in the sixth after Baltimore had tied the score, Robinson made the first of his memorable defensive plays. The Reds' Lee May led off with a one-hop shot down the third-base line that passed the bag and hooked into foul ground. Robinson crossed the line to make a lunging backhanded grab, spun 180 degrees, and made a throw that was "more like a turnaround jump shot in basketball," he recalled. But the one-hop throw nipped May.

The value of Robinson 's play went beyond mere artistry because the Reds got the next two runners on base but did not score. Robinson capped the performance with a seventh-inning home run off Gary Nolan, providing the winning margin in the Orioles' 4–3 victory.

In Game 2 Robinson robbed May again with a backhanded grab to start a double play in the third, keeping the Reds from expanding a 4–0 lead. Then, with the O's trailing 4–1 in the fifth, Paul Blair and Boog Powell each singled home a run, and Robinson knocked in the tying run with a single. He then scored behind Powell on Elrod Hendricks' double to give the Orioles a 6–4 lead. The Birds won, 6–5.

In Game 3 in Baltimore, with two runners on and none out in the first inning, Robinson leaped to snag Tony Perez's bouncer, tagged third, and relayed to first for a double play. Then he caught a liner off the bat of Johnny Bench for the third out of the inning. In the bottom of the inning Robinson staked Dave McNally to a lead with a two-out, two-run double. In the second inning Robinson made one of his patented charging plays on Tommy Helms' roller, and in the sixth Robinson made a full-length dive to his left to snag another Bench liner. In the bottom of the sixth Robinson doubled and scored on McNally's grand slam, turning the contest into a laugher.

Robinson led off the second inning of Game 4 with a home run to tie the game, 1–1, the start of a 4-for-4 afternoon. The Orioles, however, lost 6–5. Baltimore came back from a 3–0 first-inning deficit to win Game 5, 9–3. Robinson contributed a single, caught Bench's liner for the first out of the ninth, and threw out Pat Corrales for the last out of the Series.

Naturally, Robinson was chosen Series MVP. He had batted .429 with two homers, two doubles, five runs scored, a team-high six RBIs, and a Series-best nine hits—not to mention his glove work. The MVP Award included an automobile from *Sport* magazine, leading Bench to grumble, "If he wanted a car that badly, we'd have given him one."

Robinson had his last outstanding year at the plate in 1971, the Orioles' third straight 100-win season, which brought an AL East crown. In the playoff opener against the Oakland A's, the Orioles were trailing, 3–1, in the seventh against pitcher Vida Blue. Robinson singled to keep a rally going, and scored the tying run on Curt Motton's pinch double. The Orioles won, 5–3. In Game 2 Robinson hit the first of four homers off Catfish Hunter in the O's 5–1 win. In Game 3, with the score tied, 1–1, Robinson delivered a two-run single. The Orioles won their third straight pennant and ninth straight playoff game. Robinson led the Birds with four hits, batted .364, and tied for the team lead with three RBIs.

In the World Series against Pittsburgh Robinson collected a Series-best seven hits. The Orioles took the first two games. In Game 2 Robinson singled home the first run in an 11–3 rout, reaching base in all five trips with two more singles and a pair of walks. He scored twice and knocked in two runs. The Pirates took the next two games to tie the Series, and in Game 5 Robinson's error on a groundball allowed the Pirates to score their third run in a 4–0 win.

With the Series back in Baltimore for Game 6, Robinson had another single and drove Frank Robinson home with a sacrifice fly in the bottom of the 10th for a 3–2 O's victory. But in Game 7 Bucs hurler Steve Blass shut down the Birds, 2–1, on four hits to give Pittsburgh the championship. Robinson batted a team-leading .318 in his final World Series.

Robinson played for two more Orioles division winners in 1973 and 1974, but his declining offensive production carried over into the playoffs, where the Orioles lost in both years to Oakland. Despite his .083 average in the 1974 ALCS, his career playoff mark stands at .348, one of the best averages among participants with at least 50 at bats. In 1975, his final season as a regular, Robinson hit only .201. Because he was experiencing financial difficulties, he remained with the Orioles for two more seasons, backing up Doug DeCinces at third. Robinson's last home run, on April 19, 1977, came appropriately at Memorial Stadium—a game-winning, three-run, 10th-inning pinch-hit off Dave LaRoche.

He retired as a player on August 21, remaining in uniform as a coach. He then joined the Orioles television crew, and teamed with agent Ron Shapiro to form Shapiro Robinson Associates. The agency represents many of the current top players, including Cal Ripken (and had represented Kirby Puckett). Robinson was named to the Hall of Fame in 1983, his first year of eligibility.

Don Robinson

Robinson, Don Allen **P**

1978–92 B:6/8/1957, Ashland, KY Deb:4/10/1978, PIT NL BR/TR 6'4" 231

W	L	PCT	G	SV	IP	BB	SO	ERA
109	106	.507	524	57	1958[1]	643	1251	3.79

Don Robinson won *The Sporting News* National League Rookie of the Year honors in 1978 when he posted a 14–6 record with the Pittsburgh Pirates. He would never live up to that early promise, although he would pitch in the majors for 15 seasons.

Selected by the Pirates in the June 1975 free agent draft, Robinson toiled at Bradenton, Charleston, Shreveport, and Columbus before reaching Pittsburgh. After his sterling rookie season, elbow, shoulder, and assorted other problems would plague him for the rest of his career. Despite injuries in 1981 that limited him to only two starts and 16 appearances overall, he came back to post a career-high 15 wins in 1982 despite yielding a league-high 26 homers.

Robinson converted to relief work and overcame knee problems in 1986. In July 1987 the Pirates traded Robinson to San Francisco where he helped the Giants win division titles in 1987 and 1989. In 1987 he tied teammate Scott Garrelts for the league lead with 11 relief wins.

He turned free agent in October 1991 and

signed with California the following January. He finished his career later that season with Philadelphia. A career .231 hitter, Robinson was named to *The Sporting News* NL Silver Slugger Team in 1982, 1989, and 1990. At one point the Pirates even experimented with him in the outfield.

Frank Robinson

Robinson, Frank **OF-DH-1B**

1956–76 M(1975–77, 1981–84, 1988–91, 680–751)
B:8/31/1935, Beaumont, TX Deb:4/17/1956,
CIN NL BR/TR 6'1", 195

G	AB	R	H	HR	RBI	OBP	SLG	AVG
2808	10006	1829	2943	586	1812	.392	.537	.294

Few ballplayers have had as much impact on the game as Frank Robinson. He was the first—and through 1999 the only—player to win the Most Valuable Player Award in both leagues. He won the National League MVP with Cincinnati in 1961, and won the American League honor it his first season with Baltimore in 1966. In 1975 he brought the same fire and intensity to his job as the first African American manager in the major leagues. In 1982, his first year of eligibility, he was voted into the Baseball Hall of Fame, capturing 89 percent of the writers' ballots.

Robinson collected 586 career home runs. He cleared the fences in 33 different locations. But he was far more than just a slugger, finishing his career as a .294 hitter with 204 stolen bases in 281 attempts. Robinson also ranks third lifetime in most times hit by a pitch, with 204, a testimony to his aggressive style. Earl Weaver, who managed Robinson and the Orioles to three consecutive pennants from 1969 to 1971, marveled at Robinson's "death-defying stance...with his upper body and head over the plate. [He] dared pitchers to hit him."

Although Robinson played for five teams during his 21-year career, his main achievements came with the Cincinnati Reds from 1956 through 1965 and with the Baltimore Orioles from 1966 through 1972. He won the Reds' left field job in spring training of 1956, had a stellar season, and was voted National League Rookie of the Year. His 38 home runs tied Wally Berger's National League rookie record, and he led the league with 122 runs scored.

In 1957 Robinson batted .322 and was the one of seven Reds voted to the All-Star Game through a ballot-stuffing effort by the club and its fans. He remained in the starting lineup even after angry Commissioner Ford Frick removed two of Robinson's teammates. It was the first of 11 All-Star Game appearances for Robinson as a player.

An arm injury in 1958 caused Robinson's batting average to drop to .269, but he still won a Gold Glove. He rebounded with another solid season in 1959, posting 36 home runs, 125 RBIs, and a .311 batting average. In 1960 he led the league with a .595 slugging average, the first of three consecutive slugging titles.

In 1961 Robinson was voted league MVP as the Reds won their first pennant since 1940. He stole 22 bases in 25 attempts to lead the league in stolen base efficiency. In 1962 he put up even better numbers, with 39 home runs, 136 RBIs, and a .342 average. He missed winning the league batting and total bases titles when the Giants and Dodgers played a three-game postseason playoff, which enabled the Dodgers' Tommy Davis to win the batting title and the Giants' Willie Mays to capture the total-bases crown.

At the end of the 1965 season Cincinnati general manager William DeWitt traded Robinson to the Orioles for pitchers Milt Pappas and Jack Baldschun and outfielder Joe Simpson. DeWitt branded Robinson "an old 30," a phrase that would ultimately cost him his job. Robinson sparked the Orioles to four pennants and two World Series titles in the next six years.

In Robinson's first season in Baltimore he led the Orioles to a pennant and a World Series sweep of the Los Angeles Dodgers. He won the Triple Crown with 49 home runs, 122 RBIs, and a .316 average, and was named American League MVP. In early May he also became the first player ever to hit a home run out of Baltimore's Memorial Stadium, connecting off Indians righthander Luis Tiant. Robinson's drive went over the left-field grandstand into the parking lot beyond, measuring 451 feet on the fly and rolling to a stop 540 feet from home plate.

Robinson was batting .337 in late June 1967 when he sustained a serious head injury in a collision at second base. He missed a month of play and suffered from double vision for a year and a half afterward. In 1968, while still recovering from that injury, he had an attack of the mumps and suffered a muscle tear in his right shoulder. He hit only .268 with 15 homers.

In 1969 the Orioles began a run of three straight pennants, with Robinson belting 32 home runs, driving in 100 runs, and hitting .308. During that season, with the blessing of Weaver, Robinson instituted a postgame "kangaroo court" in which players and even the manager could be tried for minor baseball offenses. Wearing a mop-style wig, Robinson served as the judge in an exercise of baseball levity that loosened players' tensions and created camaraderie. The court was convened only after a Baltimore victory—the court was in session frequently.

Despite his success in the regular season, Robinson had his share of trouble in the postseason. In three AL Championship Series he batted only

.206 with two home runs and five RBIs. In five World Series he hit .250 with eight home runs and 14 RBIs. But he had a knack for making most of his hits count. In the 1966 Series sweep of the Dodgers he hit two home runs off ace righthander Don Drysdale, one of which was the only run scored in the Game 4 clincher. In the bottom of the ninth of Game 6 of the 1971 World Series, Robinson forced a Game 7 by scoring the winning run from third base on a short fly to the Pittsburgh outfield.

He was traded to the Los Angeles Dodgers for four players including Doyle Alexander after the 1971 season. Following his trade, the O's retired Robinson's No. 20, making him the first Baltimore player so honored. Robinson returned to the American League in 1973 with the California Angels and hit 30 home runs with 97 RBIs.

Traded to Cleveland in 1974, Robinson hit only .200 in 15 games, but was named the Indians' player-manager for the following season. On Opening Day 1975 Robinson became the first African American to manage in the major leagues. He also hit a home run in his first at bat to help register his first managerial victory.

In 1976 Robinson led the Indians to an 81–78 record, only their third winning season since 1959. But after a slow start in 1977, Robinson became the first African American manager to be fired. The following year he accepted the position as manager of the Orioles' International League affiliate in Rochester, New York. He then returned to Baltimore as a coach for the next two years.

In the middle of 1981 he was hired as skipper of the San Francisco Giants, where he stayed through the middle of 1984. His best record was 87–75 in 1982, good for a third-place finish in the NL West. Robinson resurfaced as manager of the Orioles after the Birds opened the 1988 season by going 0–6. Baltimore went on to lose a major league record 21 straight games at the start of the season. The Orioles rebounded with a strong second-place finish in 1989, staying in the race until the last weekend of the season. Robinson was rewarded with the AL Manager of the Year Award. After a mediocre 1990 season and a poor start the following year, Johnny Oates replaced him as manager. Robinson stayed on as assistant general manager in the Oriole front office.

Over time Robinson did mellow somewhat, but he remained an outspoken advocate of equal opportunity for African Americans in baseball. Four of the coaches on his managerial staff in Baltimore were black, but as he noted in his book, *Extra Innings*, African Americans filled only 21 of 180 major league coaching jobs as of 1987. When Robinson was fired, so ultimately were most of his coaches.

During Robinson's 32-minute 1982 Hall of Fame induction speech he thanked his school coach in Oakland, California, George Powles, for teaching him how to play the game of baseball and how to lose. Turning to Rachel Robinson, Frank Robinson paid homage to her late husband, Jackie Robinson, without whom, the inductee said, "I don't know if that door would have been opened again for a long, long time."

Jackie Robinson

Robinson, Jack Roosevelt **2B-1B-3B-OF**
1947–56 B:1/31/1919, Cairo, GA D:10/24/1972, Stamford, CT Deb:4/15/1947, BRO NL BR/TR 5'11", 204

G	AB	R	H	HR	RBI	OBP	SLG	AVG
1382	4877	947	1518	137	734	.410	.474	.311

One of baseball's most historic moments came in 1947 when Brooklyn's Jackie Robinson became the first African American player to compete in modern major league baseball. Instead of fanfare, Robinson was greeted with unprecedented hostility, pressure, and publicity, but he was buoyed by the knowledge that every one of his fellow African Americans was counting on him to succeed. The stakes were a lot higher than a pennant race or a batting title. "To do what he did has got to be the most tremendous thing I've ever seen in sports," said Brooklyn teammate Pee Wee Reese, whose gesture of acceptance turned the tide for Robinson the rookie.

Robinson had starred in baseball, football, track, and basketball at Pasadena Junior College and later at UCLA. Alongside Kenny Washington, he nearly took UCLA to the Rose Bowl. He was also All-America in basketball, and he broke a national record for the long jump previously set by his brother, Mack. When his athletic eligibility ended, Robinson left UCLA, got a job with the National Youth Administration, and played briefly with the Honolulu Bears football club.

After World War II broke out, Robinson was accepted at the Army's Officers Candidate School and was commissioned as a second lieutenant. At Fort Riley, Kansas, he was not allowed to play on either the football or baseball team. When the football team was being formed, Robinson was ordered to go home on leave. When the baseball team held tryouts, he was told to audition for the non-white team, only to discover that the team didn't exist. Later, after being sent to Fort Hood, Texas, Robinson was court-martialed for violating Jim Crow statutes. Although found innocent, in November 1944 he was given an honorable discharge.

In April 1945 Robinson signed a $450-a-month contract with the Negro American League's Kansas City Monarchs. But he didn't enjoy the barnstorming life and segregated facilities and didn't fit in with his less-educated teammates. Unknown to Robinson, Brooklyn general manager Branch Rickey was hatching a scheme to integrate the major leagues.

The first step of Rickey's master plan was the formation of the six-team United States Baseball League, a new African American circuit that included a franchise called the Brooklyn Brown Dodgers. This enabled Rickey to dispatch scouts to survey black talent without arousing suspicion.

Rickey's choice of Robinson as the first modern African American major leaguer was both surprising and apt. Robinson was neither the most talented nor the most famous Negro Leaguer, but his college education and experience as an officer weighed in his favor. He was also relatively young, and most of the best-known Negro League stars were well past their prime. Perhaps most importantly, Rickey knew he couldn't take a chance on a hard-living playboy, and Robinson was a man of modest social habits.

In April 1945, before Robinson heard from Rickey, he was given a tryout by the Boston Red Sox, who ironically were the last major league club to integrate. Robinson and fellow Negro Leaguers Sam Jethroe and Marvin Williams were each given a perfunctory trial and a quick brush-off.

On August 27, 1945, Rickey brought Robinson to the Dodgers' offices at 215 Montague Street in Brooklyn Heights. Robinson, who thought Rickey wanted him for the Brown Dodgers, was shocked to learn that the Brooklyn general manager wanted him to sign with the minor league Montreal Royals. But before any deal could be completed, Rickey needed to evaluate Robinson's ability to handle the pressure and abuse that, as a pioneer, he was certain to encounter.

To test Robinson, Rickey observed the ballplayer's responses to a series of hypothetical scenarios, including one in which a white player hurls offensive racial epithets at Robinson and then punches him in the face. Rickey took a mock swing at Robinson, and hollered, "What do you do now, Jackie? What do you do now?" Robinson replied, "I get it, Mr. Rickey. I've got another cheek. I turn the other cheek." That was the answer Rickey wanted to hear. On October 23 he announced that Robinson had signed a contract with Montreal.

Robinson's first appearance in Organized Baseball took place at Jersey City's Roosevelt Stadium on April 18, 1946. In front of a packed house, Robinson went 4-for-5 with a homer, four RBIs, four runs, and two stolen bases. In what was to become his trademark, he defiantly danced away from the base, unnerving Jersey City pitchers into committing two balks.

It was a good start, but the resistance that Rickey had feared soon followed. Syracuse fans taunted Robinson, there was a rumored protest by Baltimore players, and Robinson's two black teammates that year washed out. By the end of the season the exhausted Robinson was a nervous wreck. He was also the International League's batting champion at .349.

Robinson was clearly ready for the big leagues, but Rickey was still playing his cards close to his vest. He sent Robinson to Havana for Dodgers spring training in 1947, at the same time keeping him on the Montreal roster. Rickey was like a chess master, plotting every move and trying to anticipate every countermove.

One countermove he may not have anticipated was a revolt by some of the Dodgers. A number of players, including Dixie Walker, began circulating a petition to present to Rickey stating their opposition to playing with a black man. But Manager Leo Durocher woke the players up late one night for a team meeting and told them to take their petition and stuff it. Rickey arrived the next day and repeated the message. The mutiny was over before it started.

Rickey was not content, however, to have Robinson's teammates merely accept him; he wanted them to want Robinson. In an effort to win the players over, he scheduled seven exhibition games between Montreal and Brooklyn, during which Robinson's .625 batting performance opened a few eyes, to say the least. Still, Robinson's spot in the Dodgers lineup was not announced until five days before Opening Day. Ironically, the news was overshadowed by Durocher's suspension for consorting with gamblers.

On April 15, 1947, before 26,623 Ebbets Field fans, the majority of whom were African Americans, Robinson played his first major league game. The 28-year old went hitless that day and struggled for the first part of the season. The behavior of several other National League teams didn't help.

The Phillies, under manager Ben Chapman, were so hostile and vicious that they drove Eddie Stanky, a one-time opponent of Robinson, to publicly defend his teammate. In Cincinnati locals made death threats not only against Robinson but also against Reese, his teammate and supporter. A hush fell over the Cincinnati crowd as Reese walked over to Robinson and signaled his support by putting his arm around him. In May St. Louis management and National League president Ford Frick quashed a threatened strike by Cardinals

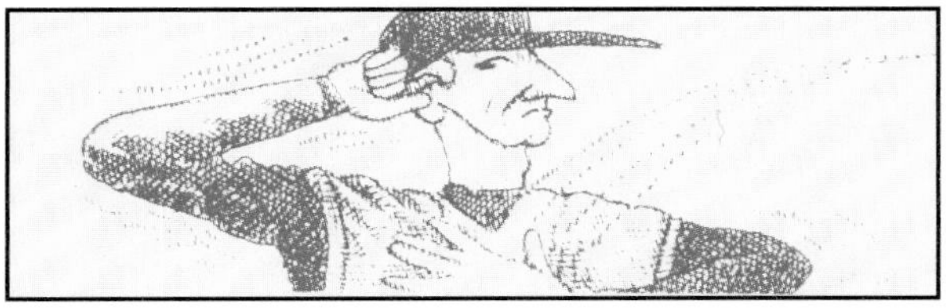

players.

"I do not care if half the league strikes," Frick said. "Those who do will encounter quick retribution. All will be suspended, and I don't care if it wrecks the National League for five years. This is the United States of America and one citizen has as much right to play as another. The National League will go down the line with Robinson, whatever the consequences."

In June Rickey brought up pitcher Dan Bankhead to room with Robinson. Meanwhile, Robinson had not only started hitting but also began to shake up the entire league with his brash baserunning, daring pitchers to pick him off. With Robinson leading the charge, the Dodgers won the pennant, and he captured both *The Sporting News* and the Baseball Writers Association Rookie of the Year honors. Even Walker, an early opponent of Robinson's signing, admitted, "He is everything Branch Rickey said he was when he came up from Montreal."

Robinson was the sparkplug of the great Dodgers teams of the 1950s. He batted .300 or better six straight years and led the league in 1949 with a .342 average, winning the Most Valuable Player Award in the process. He led league second basemen four times in double plays and twice in stolen bases. Remarkably, he also stole home 19 times. Red Schoendienst once said, "If it wasn't for him, the Dodgers would be in the second division."

The continued threats, verbal abuse, and pressure, however, eventually got to Robinson. Always a proud man, he often had to stifle his combative instincts in order to make Rickey's experiment succeed. "He always wanted to be right," pitcher Don Newcombe said. "That's one thing I didn't like about Jackie. He always wanted to be right, and you can't be right all the time. You have to be wrong sometime."

Robinson had been an "old" rookie—28 in 1947—and for the last few years of his career he was bothered by knee trouble and had problems with Dodgers management. In late 1956 his playing days ended in a swirl of confusion and controversy. He sold a story to *Look* magazine for $50,000 in which he announced his intention to retire. He did not, however, officially inform the Dodgers, and in December they traded him to the New York Giants for journeyman pitcher Dick Littlefield and $30,000.

The Giants offered Robinson $60,000 to stay on, and he considered the offer. But when Dodgers general manager Buzzie Bavasi claimed that the *Look* article had only been a ploy by Robinson to get a bigger contract, Robinson stubbornly decided to prove him wrong. He retired at age 37.

Out of baseball, Robinson busied himself with a variety of interests, including a position with a coffee company and the board chairmanship of Freedom National Bank.

Robinson grew increasingly ill with diabetes, suffered two heart attacks, and died from the second one at his Stamford, Connecticut, home in 1972. The Dodgers retired his No. 42, and in 1962 he was elected to the Hall of Fame in his first year of eligibility. In 1987 the National League Rookie of the Year Award was renamed for him. In 1997, in an unprecedented move, Acting Commissioner Bud Selig ordered that his No. 42 be retired by every major league team.

Wilbert Robinson

Robinson, Wilbert **C**

1886–1902 M(1902, 1914–31, 1,399–1,398)
B:6/29/1863, Bolton, MA D:8/8/1934, Atlanta, GA
Deb:4/19/1886, PHI AL BR/TR 5'8½", 215

G	AB	R	H	HR	RBI	OBP	SLG	AVG
1371	5075	637	1388	18	722	.316	.346	.273

Team captain of the three-time National League champion Baltimore Orioles, rotund catcher Wilbert Robinson enjoyed a solid career as a player, but he is best remembered for his years as a coach and manager. Robinson publicly split from longtime partner John McGraw and became manager of the Brooklyn Dodgers, fueling baseball's longest-running rivalry, winning two pennants, and turning the Dodgers into "Uncle Robby's Daffiness Boys." A skillful developer of pitchers, notably Rube Marquard, and Dazzy Vance, Robinson liked hard stuff—from hurlers and from bottles. He fostered lax discipline and outrageous escapades.

Robinson followed his brother, Fred, into professional baseball in 1886. In almost five seasons with Philadelphia of the American Association, Wilbert never hit better than .244. He joined Baltimore, at that time still a member of that same league, late in the 1890 season. At 5 feet 8½ inches and 215 pounds in his prime, Robinson never hit for much power, although he went 7-for-7 in a nine-inning game on June 10, 1892, a major league record matched by Rennie Stennett 83 years later. Robinson's 11 RBIs in that game were unsurpassed until Jim Bottomley drove in 12 in 1924.

A five-time .300 hitter, in 1894 Robinson batted .353 for the first of three straight pennant winners. He constantly talked baseball with teammates McGraw, Hughie Jennings, and Joe Kelley, refining the Orioles' aggressive hit-and-run style as well as their intimidation and cheating tactics. Robinson and McGraw also became partners in the Diamond Cafe in Baltimore, a billiards parlor. To increase business, they installed a bowling alley. They could afford only used pins, which they shaved down, inventing what is now called duckpin bowling.

When Baltimore manager Ned Hanlon and his top players moved to Brooklyn in 1899, McGraw and Robinson stayed behind, citing their obligations to the lucrative cafe. They held out again when the National League eliminated the Baltimore franchise and assigned the pair to Brooklyn. The Dodgers traded them to St. Louis, the National League post furthest from Baltimore, to punish their insolence. They agreed to report on condition that they become free agents at season's end. Robinson hit only .248 with St. Louis in 1900, and returned to Baltimore's new American League franchise in 1901.

In mid-1902 McGraw was hired to manage the New York Giants, and at the end of that season the Baltimore franchise moved to New York. Robinson, however, stayed in Baltimore to mind the saloon, eventually acquiring McGraw's share of the business, to avoid uprooting his family. He managed the Orioles for the last 83 games of 1902, and after the franchise was moved to New York, he caught for Baltimore's minor league team until a broken finger ended his playing career in 1904. In addition to running the saloon, Robinson worked in his father's butcher shop.

He occasionally assisted McGraw at Giants spring training and during the season. In 1911 Robinson became a full-time coach under McGraw, specifically assigned to help develop Richard "Rube" Marquard, an expensive purchase known as the "$11,000 Lemon" after three disappointing seasons. Working with Robinson, Marquard won 73 games during the next three seasons.

But tensions between the dictatorial McGraw and the easygoing, voluble Robinson culminated in Robinson's firing at a season-end party in 1913, after McGraw claimed that Robinson had failed to relay a sign that cost the Giants the World Series. The following season Marquard was only 12–22, but little did he know that he'd soon be reunited with Robinson.

Robinson signed on as manager of the Brooklyn Dodgers for 1914, and McGraw played up the managers' personal and professional rivalry in public for the rest of his tenure. In August 1915 Robinson purchased Marquard from the Giants, and Robinson managed the Dodgers to their first pennant of the century in 1916. The team reached the World Series again in 1920 but lost for the second time. During his 18 years in Brooklyn, Robinson became such a beloved figure that his team became known as the Robins and, by extension, "the Flock."

Both Dodgers pennant winners under Robinson boasted the league's best ERA, aided by Marquard in 1916 and by Burleigh Grimes in 1920. The Robins made their last legitimate pennant run in 1924 behind pitching ace Dazzy Vance, a late-blooming fireballer Robinson cultivated by giving him extra rest between starts. The Dodgers lost the flag to the Giants by 1½ games, and finished sixth in each of the next five seasons. In addition to his development of pitchers, Robinson was also mentor to three outstanding future managers—Casey Stengel, Al Lopez, and Paul Richards.

Winning or losing, the Robins were always entertaining. During spring training in 1917 Dodgers players befriended a local woman aviator, and soon flying was the talk of the camp. After hearing that Gabby Street had caught a ball dropped off the Washington Monument, an undoubtedly well-lubricated Robinson bragged that he could catch a ball dropped from an airplane, even though he was 54 and well above his playing weight.

On the appointed day, Stengel substituted a grapefruit for the baseball. Robinson circled unsteadily under the descending spheroid and actually got a glove on it before it splattered across his chest. Robinson felt the ooze, thought it was blood, and screamed that he was dying—until he tasted the juice. He later conceded that he probably would have been killed if a real baseball had been dropped from the plane.

With the jovial, cardigan-clad Uncle Robbie and the Daffy Dodgers, it was common to see players reading papers on the bench, missing and disobeying signs, and spending their off-hours drinking and playing cards to the detriment of their performance the next day. Robinson tried to discipline the team by instituting a Bonehead Club, with a schedule of heavy fines for inattentiveness. Robinson himself became the first paying member after submitting a laundry list instead of a lineup card at home plate. He soon abandoned the idea.

Babe Herman came on board in the late 1920s and quickly became a practicing member of the Daffiness Boys. A good hitter who was less proficient in other aspects of the game, Herman once slugged a ball off the wall with the bases loaded, and three Dodgers wound up on third base; Herman had doubled into a double play. After the incident it became standard practice in Brooklyn, upon hearing that the Dodgers had multiple men on base, to ask, "Which base?"

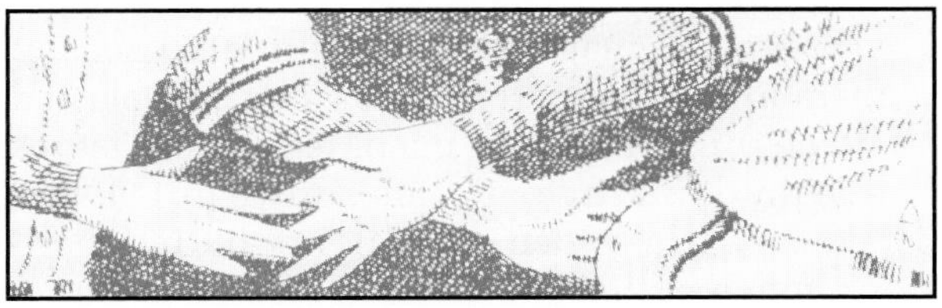

After Charles Ebbets died, Robinson became Dodgers president in 1926 as a compromise candidate between Ebbets' feuding heirs. One faction forced Robinson out in 1929, but he extracted a proviso allowing him to manage for two more years. He departed after the 1931 season with a big league managerial record of 1,399–1,398 in 19 seasons. After leaving the Dodgers at age 68, he served as president of the Atlanta Crackers of the Southern Association from 1933 until his death from a stroke the following year. In 1945 he was elected to the Hall of Fame.

Alex Rodriguez

Rodriguez, Alexander Emmanuel **SS**

1994–* B:7/27/1975 New York, NY Deb:7/8/1994, SEA AL BR/TR 6'3", 190

G	AB	R	H	HR	RBI	OBP	SLG	AVG
642	2572	493	791	148	463	.365	.551	.308

If Ernie Banks spoke the first word on what a power-hitting shortstop might accomplish, Alex Rodriguez might have the final say. Banks hit 40-plus home runs in four consecutive seasons, from 1957–1960, between the ages of 26 and 29. Rodriguez reached the 40-mark twice by age 24. Only Mel Ott, Tony Conigliaro, and Eddie Mathews reached 100 career home runs faster than the four-time All-Star shortstop.

The first player taken in the 1993 amateur draft, Rodriguez made his major league debut at age 18. In his first full season as a starter in 1996, Rodriguez established himself as a premier player. Playing in 146 games, he scored 141 runs, hit 54 doubles, 36 homers, and knocked in 123. He led the league in batting with a .358 mark, making him the first American League shortstop to lead the league in hitting since Lou Boudreau in 1944. He also slugged .631, three points higher than his more famous teammate Ken Griffey, Jr. He finished second to Texas slugger Juan Gonzalez in a very close ballot for American League Most Valuable Player. Rodriguez did, however, was the landslide choice as *The Sporting News* Major League Player of the Year.

His numbers dipped slightly in 1997, but he batted .300 for the second time. He returned with a vengeance in 1998, hitting .310 and knocking in 124 runs. His 42 home runs were the most ever by an American League shortstop; adding in his 46 stolen bases, he became the third member of the 40-40 club.

Although Rodriguez began the 1999 season with an injury that cost him 33 games, he blasted 42 home runs (to lead all major league shortstops for the third time in four years), drove in 111, and batted .285. In a golden age of power-hitting shortstops, much of the talk centered on Nomar Garciaparra and Derek Jeter in the Northeast, but Rodriguez was making a case for himself in the Northwest as the best of the lot.

Aurelio Rodriguez

Rodriguez, Aurelio (Ituarte) **3B**

1967–83 B:12/28/1947, Cananea, Sonora, Mexico Deb:9/1/1967, CAL AL BR/TR 5'10", 180

G	AB	R	H	HR	RBI	OBP	SLG	AVG
2017	6611	612	1570	124	648	.276	.351	.237

Aurelio Rodriguez had a 17-year career in the majors as a third baseman because of his exceptional fielding ability. Rodriguez's best season's batting average was .265. Although he hit 19 homers one season and 15 another, he was not considered a power hitter. Yet seven teams wanted his defense. He led American League third basemen in double plays and fielding percentage twice each. In 1976 he won a Gold Glove, the first time an American League third baseman other than Brooks Robinson had won the award since 1960.

Rodriguez started his career with the Angels in 1967. He went to Washington in 1970, but was sent to Detroit after the season in an eight-player deal that made Denny McLain a Senator. After nine years in Detroit, Rodriguez played his final four years with the Padres, the Yankees, the White Sox (twice), and the Orioles. His 1978 fielding percentage of .987 was the third best in major league history at the time. His 4,150 career assists stood as ninth on the all-time list among third baseman through the 1999 season.

Ivan Rodriguez

Rodriguez, Ivan (Torres) **C**

1991–* B:11/27/1971, Manati, Puerto Rico Deb:6/20/1991, TEX AL BR/TR 5'9", 205

G	AB	R	H	HR	RBI	OBP	SLG	AVG
1169	4443	649	1333	144	621	.340	.465	.300

Ivan Rodriguez set the standard for catchers in the 1990s, batting .300 with home run power and an ability to absolutely shut down opponents' running game. By the end of the 1999 season Rodriguez had thrown out 342 of the 725 attempts to steal. He nailed 42 of 80 runners in 1998, and topped that with 41 of 75 in 1999—an amazing 55 percent. Rodriguez won a Gold Glove in his first full season in 1992, and won the award every remaining year of the decade. His defensive abilities helped support a Texas pitching staff that was frequently below average.

Rodriguez made his major league debut with the Texas Rangers as a 19-year-old, taking over the starting catcher duties when he arrived in June of

1991. The following year he was named to the All-Star team, another honor that he would receive annually for the rest of the decade. Even that early in his career it was clear that he was an exceptionally talented ballplayer. Yankees manager Joe Torre, a former All-Star catcher himself, called Rodriguez "the best catcher I've ever seen. I'm talking about total package."

Rodriguez was nicknamed "Pudge" by his teammates, not so much for his physical appearance but to draw a comparison to another great catcher with the same tag, Hall of Famer Carlton Fisk. While many questioned whether Rodriguez was worthy of the compliment, he simply let his performance silence the critics. He raised his batting average in each of his first four seasons, and in 1996 hit 47 doubles, the most ever by a backstop. Among catchers, only Mickey Cochrane scored more runs in a single season. In 1996 he became the first American League catcher to surpass 190 hits in a season.

In 1999 Rodriguez took his offense to another level, setting an American League record for home runs by a catcher (35) and batting .332, the highest average for an AL backstop since Bill Dickey's .362 in 1936. The season culminated with Rodriguez being named the AL Most Valuable Player, edging out Boston pitcher Pedro Martinez for the honor in a very close vote.

No matter what he contributed with his bat, however, it was his defensive presence that set Rodriguez apart. Texas manager and former major league catcher, Johnny Oates said, "There are three ways to judge a catcher—quickness in getting rid of the ball, velocity in making the throw, and accuracy. No one I've ever seen has been able to do all three as well as Ivan Rodriguez."

What about Johnny Bench, who won 10 National League Gold Gloves in Cincinnati? "Bench didn't have the quickness that (Rodriguez) has," Oates said. "He had the great velocity. He threw runners out but he didn't pick runners off. I mean, Pudge can embarrass you with his quickness and his accuracy."

Preacher Roe

Roe, Elwin Charles **P**

1938, 1944–54 B:2/26/1915, Ash Flat, AR
Deb:8/22/1938, STL NL BR/TL 6'2", 170

W	L	PCT	G	SH	IP	BB	SO	ERA
127	84	.602	333	17	1914[1]	504	956	3.43

Elwin "Preacher" Roe startled the baseball world when he admitted in a July 4, 1955, *Sports Illustrated* article that he regularly employed a spitball during his glory days with the Brooklyn Dodgers. Actually, it was the fact that he admitted it that surprised folks; that he threw a wet one was pretty common knowledge. Hitters would often joke that they "just hit the dry side" of Roe's offerings.

Roe, who took his nickname from his early desire to be a minister, was reared in an extremely rural part of Arkansas. Roe's father, Dr. Charles Edward Roe, had played minor league ball with Memphis and Pine Bluff in 1917 and 1918 and wanted one of his six sons to be a major leaguer. Elwin was the answer to his dreams.

Elwin Charles Roe attended and played baseball for Harding College, a religious school, in Searcy, Arkansas, where he averaged 18 strikeouts a game. Five clubs sent scouts to check him out. "It was the Yankees and the Cardinals who made the best offers," recalled Roe, "but this part of the United States isn't Yankee country, if'n you get me. The Yankees was thought of as the best club in baseball, which no doubt they was, but down here we talked about the Cardinals."

Roe was signed to a $5,000 St. Louis contract by Branch Rickey's brother, Frank. The Cardinals promoted Roe to the big club immediately, but he made only one appearance and was shellacked. He then spent 1939 through 1943 in the minors with Rochester and Columbus. In 1943 Roe led the American Association in strikeouts with 136, and in 1944 he was the Pirates' Opening Day starting pitcher. He lost a two-hitter, 2–0.

Roe enjoyed two strong years for Pittsburgh. In 1945 he blazed his way to a league-leading 148 strikeouts. But then his fortunes took a downturn. Other talented players returned home from the war, and then Roe was injured in an off-season altercation with a referee at a high school basketball game. "He decked me. I got a skull fracture and a lacerated brain. The fracture ran 8 inches long," recalled Roe. Worse, his left arm was damaged in the altercation.

The 1947 season was a disaster for Roe. He went 4–15 with a 5.25 ERA, and walked more batters than he struck out. On December 8, 1947, he was traded to Brooklyn along with Billy Cox and Gene Mauch for Dixie Walker, Hal Gregg, and Vic Lombardi. At this point Roe added a spitball to his repertoire. It was enough to transform his career. Twice—in 1949 and 1951—he led the National League in won-lost percentage.

In Game 2 of the 1949 World Series, Roe was hit in the right forefinger by Johnny Lindell's fourth-inning smash back to the box. Roe made the play, but it took two tiny holes drilled in his fingernail to relieve the swelling. He pitched the rest of the game in intense pain. Nonetheless, Roe beat New York, 1–0, surrendering just six hits and no walks.

Roe's career year was 1951. He went 22–3, and his .880 winning percentage is among the best in league history. Twice he had winning streaks of 10 games. It appeared as if the Dodgers were on their way to another pennant. By August 12 Brooklyn had a 13½-game lead over the second-place Giants. But the Giants rallied to force a best-of-three playoff and won the pennant on Bobby Thomson's "Shot Heard 'Round the World."

In 1952 Roe went 11–2, and in Game 3 of the 1952 Series he outdueled Eddie Lopat, 5–3. Said Casey Stengel: "I tell ya, it's impossible to outsmart him. He's a smart operator all right; just about the smartest pitcher around today."

Of course, Roe's effectiveness depended on the spitter. Reds manager Luke Sewell once complained: "Without his spitter he wouldn't be half as effective, and you can quote me." When Roe finally confessed for *Sports Illustrated*, his former teammates still played dumb. "He never threw one against me in batting practice so I take it he never threw one in the game," quipped Pee Wee Reese. Roe himself later said he allowed the article to be printed in an attempt to get the spitter legalized. After retiring from baseball, Roe owned and operated "Preacher Roe's Supermarket" in West Plains, Missouri.

Bullet Joe Rogan

Rogan, Wilbur

Negro League Player (1917–38) Manager B:1889 D:1967

Pitching great Satchel Paige said that Bullet Joe Rogan was the only hurler he knew who both pitched and batted cleanup. Many who saw them both rated Rogan and Paige as equals on the mound. But, as Paige said, Rogan could hit, too. Bullet Joe was tiny, and he swung a very heavy bat. Standing deep in the batter's box, he became an expert at getting to low pitches and hitting them long distances. His lifetime average in recorded Negro Leagues games is .339, 10th best ever.

At the other end of the pitch, Rogan had mastery of more deliveries than his catchers had fingers (and toes). With no windup, he threw three curves, a drop, a forkball, a palmball, and a spitter. They said his hard curve was faster than most guys' heaters. In 11 Negro League seasons he compiled a 111–43 mark for a .721 winning percentage, the highest in Negro League history, and added an 8–4 record in postseason play.

Rogan was 30 years old when Casey Stengel, then a Pittsburgh outfielder, "discovered" him, or so the story goes. Rogan had been in the army for nine years and was the star of the 25th Infantry Wreckers. Stengel was barnstorming in the Southwest when he saw Rogan, and he recommended the player to the owner of the Monarchs in Stengel's hometown of Kansas City.

Rogan's best season in the Negro Leagues was 1924—at age 35. He went 15–5 on the mound, playing in a total of 50 games, as an outfielder and second baseman when he wasn't pitching. He hit .411. In the first Black World Series that year he was the Kansas City star against the Hilldale club of Philadelphia. He pitched four games, with two wins, one loss, and a tie. For the six games he didn't pitch he played center and batted .325 for the Series.

When Rogan became manager of the Monarchs two years later, "he wanted to run the club like they did it in the army," one player complained. He continued at the helm through 1938 and did some umpiring after he hung up his spikes. In his final game against white major leaguers, in 1937, Rogan batted against Mace Brown, Lon Warneke, and a young Bob Feller. Rogan had three hits and stole a base. He was 48 years old.

Billy Rogell

Rogell, William George **SS–3B**

1925–40 B:11/24/1904, Springfield, IL Deb:4/14/1925, BOS AL BB/TR 5'10½", 163

G	AB	R	H	HR	RBI	OBP	SLG	AVG
1482	5149	755	1375	42	609	.351	.370	.267

Slick-fielding shortstop Billy Rogell teamed with Hall of Famer Charlie Gehringer to form a smooth keystone combination for the American League champion Detroit Tigers of 1934 and 1935. Although not noted for his batting, Rogell had extra-base power, and he collected more than 20 doubles in seven consecutive seasons. In 1934 he had 100 RBIs as part of the best run-producing infield in history.

Rogell began his professional baseball career in 1923 with Coffeyville, Kansas, in the Southwestern League, but he was released after only six weeks and moved in with his sister in Chicago for the rest of the season. He played with Salina of the Southwestern League the next year, where he hit .317, and was purchased by the Red Sox. "I got 300 bucks a month my first year in the big leagues in '25. That spring I hit about .390, and manager Lee Fohl kept me," Rogell said.

However, he washed out in Boston as the Red Sox tried to convert the switch hitter into a pure righthanded hitter. "They just screwed me up for a couple of years," complained Rogell. He was released at the end of the 1928 season. In 1929 he signed with St. Paul of the American Association and played next to third baseman Ben Chapman. After Rogell hit .336 and drove in 90 runs, five big league clubs, the Pirates, Phillies, White Sox, Tigers, and Yankees, were after him. He selected Detroit.

With the Tigers Rogell led American League shortstops in fielding three straight years; in double plays twice; and in putouts, assists, and fielding range once each. The 1934 Tigers set the all-time RBI record for an infield, with 462. Rogell collected 100, Gehringer had 127, first baseman Hank Greenberg drove in 139, and third baseman Marv Owen had 96.

Rogell played on a fractured ankle in the 1934 World Series against St. Louis, but he still managed to deliver four RBIs in Game 4. In the fourth inning of that game, it was Rogell's throw that hit pinch runner Dizzy Dean square in the head, leading to newspaper headlines that read, "X-Ray of Dean's Head Shows Nothing." The always-competitive Rogell commented: "If I'd have known his head was there, I would have thrown the ball harder."

Rogell was primarily a leadoff hitter, but unlike the leadoff batters of later years, he did not steal many bases. "They didn't want me to steal," he explained. "I had Gehringer and Cochrane and Greenberg hitting behind me. We did a lot of hitting and running."

The Tigers returned to the World Series in 1935 and were seven-game winners over the Cubs. From 1936 through 1938, Rogell was incredibly consistent—he batted between .274 and .276, scored between 85 and 88 runs, and hit between 64 and 71 RBIs. But after the 1938 season, Rogell injured his arm playing handball. Detroit general manager Jack Zeller traded him to the Cubs in December 1939 for Dick Bartell in a deal described as "one worn-out shortstop for another."

Rogell arrived at the Cubs' spring training camp at Catalina Island and soon became embroiled in an argument over the merits of the 1935 Tigers versus the 1935 Cubs. "You don't belong here," manager Gabby Hartnett finally shouted. Rogell demanded his release. The Cubs refused, so he sat on the Chicago bench for most of the 1940 season and batted only .136 in 33 games.

His major league playing days were over, and Rogell managed and played in the minors until he fractured his shoulder in an automobile accident. He then returned to Detroit and served for many years (until age 77) on the Detroit City Council. "I think I did a lot for that city," said Rogell. "I was chairman of the committee that built that big airport there. Also the roads and bridges committee."

Rogell was a vocal critic of modern ballplaying—including the practice of ballplayers selling autographs. Said Rogell: "I had a company in Pennsylvania offer me $3 for each signature and I told them to go to hell. I don't sell my signature to anybody."

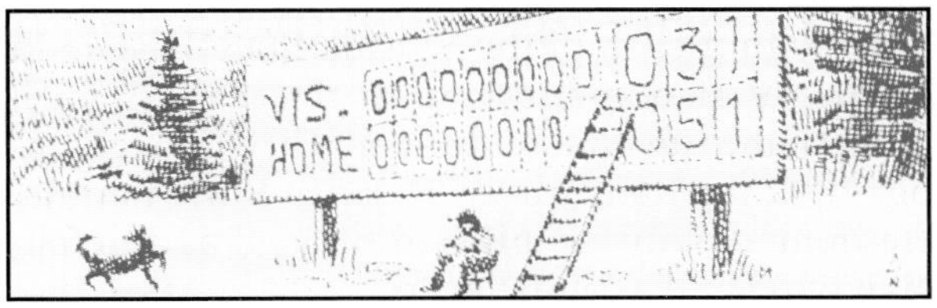

Kenny Rogers

Rogers, Kenneth Scott **P**

1989–* B:11/10/1964, Savannah, GA Deb: 4/6/1989, TEX AL BL/TL 6'1", 205

W	L	PCT	G	SV	IP	BB	SO	ERA
114	78	.594	502	28	1701^{1}	651	1114	4.05

On July 29, 1994, Kenny Rogers pitched a perfect game for the Texas Rangers against the California Angels, only the 12th such gem of the century up to that point. New York fans may be forgiven for wishing that just a fraction of that perfection could have been channeled into his postseason appearances with the Yankees and the Mets.

Rogers did not play organized baseball until his senior year at Plant City High School in Florida. There he played almost exclusively as an outfielder, hitting .375 and earning the team's defensive player of the year award. The Rangers signed Rogers based on his arm strength. He kicked around the minor leagues without distinction for seven years, playing in Sarasota, Burlington, Daytona Beach, Tulsa, Salem, and Charlotte. Rogers compiled a record of 22–38 over those years, and the only sign that he might be major league material was that he averaged a strikeout per inning in two seasons.

Rogers landed in the major leagues as a relief pitcher. He excelled in that role for four years in Texas, including an American League-best 81 appearances in 1992. The following year, however, he was made into a starting pitcher. Rogers thrived in the new role. He won 16 games in 1993, and went 17–7 in 1995—appearing in the All-Star Game for the only time in his career. He was tempted by the big bucks and big lights of New York, and signed with the Yankees as a free agent.

His overall 18–15 record as a Yankee was not so bad, but his 1996 postseason was horrendous. He did not last past the third inning in any of his three postseason starts, surrendering 15 hits, six walks, and 11 runs in seven innings. Although the Yanks rallied to win each of his starts on their way to a world championship, he was still reviled in the Bronx.

Rogers was traded to Oakland and won 16 games in 1998, with the Yanks footing most of his salary. He returned to New York midway through the 1999 season, but this time to the Mets. He went 5–1 down the stretch to help the club to a Wild Card spot.

The postseason was a different story. The October bugaboo that tormented Rogers in 1996 came back to haunt him in 1999. Rogers took three of the Mets' five postseason losses. Opponents batted .348 against him, and in 12 innings he walked nine batters, including Atlanta's Andruw Jones with the bases loaded to bring in the run that ended the Championship Series. In 19 career postseason innings Rogers had an ERA of 9.47. Undaunted, he returned to Texas as a free agent in 2000.

Steve Rogers

Rogers, Stephen Douglas **P**

1973–85 B:10/26/1949, Jefferson City, MO
Deb:7/18/1973, MON NL BR/TR 6'1", 182

W	L	PCT	G	SH	IP	BB	SO	ERA
158	152	.510	399	37	2837^2	876	1621	3.17

Longtime Expos righthander Steve Rogers never lived up to the expectations that followed his sparkling debut. But he pitched 13 seasons in Montreal, was an All-Star five times, won 158 games, and holds most Montreal career pitching records. Drafted by the Yankees in the 60th round of the June 1967 amateur draft, Rogers elected to attend college at the University of Tulsa, where he obtained a degree in petroleum engineering. In June 1971 the Expos took him in the secondary phase of the amateur draft.

Rogers' rookie ERA of 1.54 in 134 innings was the fourth lowest by a National League freshman since 1900. He was named *The Sporting News* 1973 Rookie Pitcher of the Year. But in two of his next three seasons he led the league in losses. Regardless, Rogers was the best the struggling Expos had. In 1974 he was named to the All-Star team, earning 37 decision in 38 starts that season—including 22 losses.

On June 8, 1978, Rogers narrowly missed a no-hitter against the Dodgers; the one hit he surrendered was a home run by Reggie Smith. He went 13–10 that season with a 2.47 ERA. The following year he won 13 again and led the league with five shutouts.

As a pitcher, Rogers combined his 90-mph fastball with sharp breaking curveballs. "Rogers is the epitome of the thinking man's pitcher," said announcer and former ballplayer Ralph Kiner. "He exploits a batter's patience and won't give in to the hitter when behind in the count. He is very consistent." A decent fielder, Rogers also helped himself with a sneaky pickoff move and good bunting skills.

Rogers' Expos came closest to a pennant during the 1981 strike-shortened season. Montreal captured the second-half title before battling the defending world champion Phillies in the special division playoff that was created that year. Rogers opened the series by beating Steve Carlton and the Phillies, 3–1. He then took the deciding fifth contest by blanking Carlton on only six hits. Rogers knocked in a pair of runs on two hits, as he notched his fourth shutout in his last 12 starts. Opposing manager Dallas Green gave Rogers plenty of credit: "We wanted Lefty [Carlton] to pitch like Rogers and our team to play like their team. It just didn't happen."

Montreal faced the Dodgers in the Championship Series. Rogers hurled a seven-hit victory in Game 3, giving the Expos a 2–1 lead in the Series. In Game 5 manager Jim Fanning brought Rogers into the contest in the ninth inning with the score tied. It was only the third relief appearance of Rogers' big league career. With two outs in the ninth, Los Angeles' Rick Monday homered off Rogers to give the Dodgers a 2–1 win and the pennant.

"This wasn't supposed to be the last chapter of a book written for a sixth grader," Rogers said at the time. "One pitch different and I could have written a fairy tale ending. Only this was reality."

Rogers overcame his disappointment to lead the league in ERA in 1982, when he won 19 games. He had the honor of starting the first All-Star Game played in Canada. He pitched three innings and got the win for the National League at Olympic Stadium.

He went 17–12 and led the league again with five shutouts in 1983, but in 1984 Rogers suffered from serious arm problems and noticed Montreal fans had turned on him. "They're booing me at home on the introductions. They're not doing that to anyone else," he observed. He left the game in 1985.

Cookie Rojas

Rojas, Octavio Victor (Rivas) **2B-OF**

1962–77 M(1988, 1996, 76–79) B:3/6/1939, Havana, Cuba Deb:4/10/1962, CIN NL BR/TR 5'10", 170

G	AB	R	H	HR	RBI	OBP	SLG	AVG
1822	6309	714	1660	54	593	.309	.337	.263

Although Cookie Rojas played all nine positions in his career, plus designated hitter, he was an All-Star five times as a second baseman. Phillies fans voted him the team's best second baseman in a 1969 contest. A pitcher's best friend, Rojas kept runners off the bases with diving grabs and gutsy throws in double-play situations. He earned his reputation for courage and preached determination: "No matter how down you are or how tired you are, you gotta go out and play to win. That's the tag you want to get—the tag of a winner."

Octavio Victor Rojas' parents wanted him to be doctor, but he chose baseball. He started with West Palm Beach of the Florida State League in 1956. He also spent time in the minors with Savannah, Havana, and Jersey City. In November 1962 the Reds traded Rojas to Philadelphia. He immediately established himself as a defensive whiz and a fan favorite.

In 1965 Rojas was selected to the All-Star team. He led the National League in putouts in 1967, and in 1968 led league second basemen in fielding percentage and double plays. Sent to St. Louis in the infamous Curt Flood deal in October 1969, Rojas was shuffled off to Kansas City a year later. Rojas enjoyed a tremendous resurgence with the young Royals. He led the American League in fielding in both 1971 and 1974. He represented the Royals in each All-Star Game from 1971 to 1974, and stayed with the club long enough to play a part on the first two division winners in team history in 1976 and 1977.

Rojas went into coaching immediately upon his retirement. He joined the Cubs in 1978 and later spent 10 years as a scout and special assistant. In 1988 he replaced Gene Mauch as manager of the Angels when Mauch resigned due to poor health. He later coached for the Florida Marlins and the New York Mets. In Game 4 of the 1999 Division Series Rojas got into a heated shoving match with the umpiring crew on a ball that down the line late in a close game. The Mets won the game and the series, but Rojas was suspended for most of the Championship Series.

Scott Rolen

Rolen, Scott Bruce **3B**

1996–* B:4/4/1975, Evansville, IN Deb:8/1/1996, PHI NL BR/TR 6'4", 210

G	AB	R	H	HR	RBI	OBP	SLG	AVG
465	1713	297	479	82	297	.380	.500	.280

Scott Rolen burst on the scene in 1997 as the unanimous choice for National League Rookie of the Year. He led NL rookies in nine major offensive categories, and he led the league's third basemen in total chances and putouts. A talented baserunner, Rolen tied for the club lead with 16 steals; only Chipper Jones of the Braves had more stolen bases among major league third basemen that year.

Rolen had been named "Mr. Baseball" as the best high school baseball player in Indiana, but most teams felt that he would go to college and play basketball. Although the Angels and Red Sox were both very interested, both passed on him in the first round of the 1992 draft. The Phillies took Rolen in the second round and signed him for a $240,000 bonus.

He flew through every level of the farm system in less than four years, and made his debut with the Phillies on August 1, 1996. He quickly accumulated 130 at bats, the maximum allowable to still qualify as a rookie, but his season ended there: Steve Trachsel of the Cubs broke his right arm with a pitch on September 7. At the end of his stellar 1997 season Florida's Antonio Alfonseca hit Rolen with a pitch; teammate Curt Schilling, just one K away from becoming just the second National League pitcher to reach 320 strikeouts, was ejected from his final start for hitting John Wehner in retaliation.

In 1998 Rolen exploded for 110 RBIs and scored 120 runs. In the field, his agility and strong arm resulted in a Gold Glove Award. Rolen blasted 26 home runs and had 77 RBIs in just 112 games when he was forced to sit out the rest of the 1999 season with a lower back injury.

Red Rolfe

Rolfe, Robert Abial **3B**

1931–42 M(1949–52, 278–256) B:10/17/1908, Penacook, NH D:7/8/1969, Guilford, NH Deb:6/29/1931, NY AL BL/TR 5'11½", 170

G	AB	R	H	HR	RBI	OBP	SLG	AVG
1175	4827	942	1394	69	497	.360	.413	.289

Some players are much greater than their statistics show—you had to see Yankees third baseman Red Rolfe to fully appreciate his accomplishments. He was the third baseman on six pennant winners, batting ahead of the likes of Joe DiMaggio, Lou Gehrig, and Bill Dickey.

"The luckiest thing I ever did was sign with the Yankees. When you're with really great players, they pull you along," said the modest third baseman. But opponents felt the Yankees were lucky to have Rolfe. Philadelphia Athletics manager Connie Mack said, "You know, they talk about all the other fellas on that team, but I notice the man who hurts us when it counts is that third baseman. There is a real team player. You might get him out three times, but then he'll come up where it means the ballgame, and sure as anything, he's going to knock those runs in. Or, if the Yankees need that one big play in the field, they usually get it at third base."

Robert Abial "Red" Rolfe played shortstop at Dartmouth University, where he graduated in 1931 with a degree in English. "I really wanted to be a newspaperman," he explained. "While I was still a Yankee, I wrote a baseball column which had too much inside dope, I'm afraid, for president Ed Barrow told me to cease and desist."

Yankees scout "White Ties" McCann signed Rolfe for a large bonus, and manager Joe McCarthy let Rolfe pinch run for New York in a 1931 game. Rolfe was then farmed out to Albany and Newark for the next three years. He came back to New York in 1934 and was gradually converted into a third baseman.

Rolfe led the league with 15 triples and hit .319 in 1936. On June 11, 1936, he hit three homers and a double in one game. That year six Yankees batted at least .300, and Rolfe went to the first of his six World Series. He hit .400 with five runs and four RBIs to help his team defeat the crosstown Giants, four games to two.

Selected to *The Sporting News* All-Star teams from 1937 through 1939, Rolfe led the American League in runs, hits, and doubles in 1939. He was often at his best in the World Series—he batted better than .300 in the 1936, 1937, 1941, and 1942 World Series. Following bouts with ulcers and other ailments, Rolfe retired after the 1942 season at age 35. Joe McCarthy said of his No. 2 hitter, "Rolfe was a real ballplayer, sick or well."

Rolfe coached baseball at Yale from 1943 through 1947, and in 1947 he also coached for the Toronto Huskies of the Basketball Association of America. He spent that summer coaching for the Yankees, and later that year became supervisor of scouting for the Tigers. He ascended to farm director in 1948. In 1949 he was named manager of the Tigers and immediately turned the team into contenders.

"I had to crack the whip when I took over in Detroit. Putting it bluntly, I inherited a complacent ballclub. Few players were in the habit of going all out," Rolfe remembered. He also helped George Kell lift his average by recommending he change his stance. The team won 95 games in 1950 but finished second to the Yankees. Rolfe was named Manager of the Year, but the Tigers finished last in 1952, and Rolfe was fired.

In 1954 he became Dartmouth's athletic director and remained at the college until 1967. Just before his death in 1969, Dartmouth renamed its varsity ballfield Red Rolfe Field. That same year the Yankees named Rolfe the team's all-time third baseman.

Rich Rollins

Rollins, Richard John **3B**
1961–70 B:4/16/1938, Mount Pleasant, PA
Deb:6/16/1961, MIN AL BR/TR 5'10", 185

G	AB	R	H	HR	RBI	OBP	SLG	AVG
1002	3303	419	887	77	399	.330	.388	.269

Rich Rollins was a hard-hitting third baseman with occasional power but little mobility. Rollins signed out of Kent State University where he earned a B.S. in education. He bloomed as a second baseman with Wilson of the Carolina League, hitting .341 in 62 games. "I was never a star athlete in high school, and I wasn't a star in college," he said. "When I started to play in the minors, people discouraged me at everything I did. I just kept on going."

In the first game of a doubleheader Rollins hit two homers. A local merchant had agreed to give $300 to anyone who hit three homers in a single day. His Wilson teammates suggested he go to opposing catcher Norm Kampshor of Greensboro and offer to split the prize with him if Kampshor would tell him what pitches were coming. Rollins said, "Not only did he tell me what was coming, but after awhile he starting asking me what I'd like to have thrown. And I'd say fastball, or change, and I'd get it." Nonetheless he hit only one double in four at bats. The pitcher was Jim Bouton.

Rollins spent 1961 with Syracuse and Charlotte and reached Minnesota at the end of the Twins' first season in Minnesota. Although the rookie led American League third basemen in errors in 1962, Rollins was the AL All-Star third baseman in the two games played that year; he went 2-for-5 in All-Star competition.

In 1964 he tied for the American League lead in triples and again led AL third baseman in errors. On June 9, 1965, he was one of five Twins to homer in the seventh inning against the Kansas City Athletics. Although he played most of the 1965 season at third base for the Twins, Harmon Killebrew, who moved over from first, replaced him in the World Series. Rollins appeared only as a pinch hitter in Minnesota's seven-game loss to the Dodgers.

He was selected by the Seattle Pilots in the expansion draft in October 1968 and retired in 1970 after playing briefly for the Indians. He became director of group sales for the Cleveland Cavaliers of the National Basketball Association.

Eddie Rommel

Rommel, Edwin Americus **P**
1920–32 U(1938–59) B:9/13/1897, Baltimore, MD
Deb:4/19/1920, PHI AL BR/TR 6'2", 197

W	L	PCT	G	SV	IP	BB	SO	ERA
171	119	.590	500	29	2556[1]	724	599	3.54

While working as a steamfitter's helper on a ship in World War I, Eddie Rommel scalded his hand terribly. He started experimenting with a knuckleball during his recovery. He perfected the pitch with Baltimore, and by 1920 he was throwing it in the major leagues for the Philadelphia Athletics. Rommel used his new pitch judiciously.

In his famed book, *The Hot Stove League*, author Lee Allen recalled the game in which Rommel outdueled Cleveland's George Uhle without throwing a single knuckleball, "but the batters were always expecting and were kept off stride." The result was a remarkably efficient 56-minute victory for Rommel.

In 1922 Ed Rommel had one of the finest seasons of all time—27–13 for the seventh-place A's, a feat comparable to Steve Carlton's 27–10 mark with the last-place Philadelphia Phillies of 1972.

The next year Rommel led the league in losses and was 18–19 with the sixth-place A's.

In five roller coaster years, from 1921 to 1925, Ed and his knuckler led the league in victories and losses twice each. As the team's best pitcher, he was often called on to put out late-inning rallies on days when he didn't start. He led the American League in appearances in 1922 and 1923.

By the time the next A's championship team developed, Rommel was past his prime. Nevertheless, he was 28–11 during the pennant-winning seasons of 1929 to 1931. He later became an outstanding umpire. He served as an American League arbiter from 1938 to 1959.

Jim Rooker

Rooker, James Philip **P**

1968–80 B:9/23/1942, Lakeview, OR Deb:6/30/1968, DET AL BR/TL 6', 201

W	L	PCT	G	SH	IP	BB	SO	ERA
103	109	.486	319	15	1810^{1}	703	976	3.46

Jim Rooker began his baseball career as an outfielder. It was not until 1964 at Duluth-Superior in the Northern League that he started pitching—and not until 1968 that he reached the majors. The Tigers, who had signed Rooker in 1960, returned him to the minors after just two games. In September he was sold him to the Yankees, and was allowed to be selected by the Kansas City Royals in that October's American League expansion draft.

Rooker got a chance to pitch in Kansas City, but little support; in fact, he often had to provide his own. On July 7, 1969, Rooker became the first Royal to homer twice in a single game. On June 17, 1970, he collected five RBIs in one game. His pitching record improved, from 4–16 as a rookie to 10–15 in 1970, yet he was soon spending more and more time at Omaha in the American Association. In October 1972 he was sent to Pittsburgh in exchange for reliever Gene Garber.

Rooker thrived in the National League. Each year from 1973 through 1977 he earned victories in double digits, including a career-high 15 in 1976. He then played a key role in Pittsburgh's 1979 World Series victory. When Bruce Kison was knocked out of the box in the first inning of Game 1, Rooker entered and held Baltimore scoreless through the fourth inning. The Orioles won the game, but Rooker's performance him the Game 5 start. With the Pirates on the verge of elimination, Rooker allowed just one run in five innings. Pittsburgh rallied to win the game, and the Bucs won the next two games to take the world championship.

Released after the 1980 season, Rooker served as a Pirates broadcaster from 1981 through 1993. When the Pirates took a lopsided lead early on Philadelphia one night, Rooker quipped that he would walk back to Pittsburgh if the Bucs lost the game. The Phillies rallied to win, and Rooker later made that walk, raising money for charity. The story became, of all things, the subject of a beer commercial

Charlie Root

Root, Charles Henry **P**

1923–41 B:3/17/1899, Middletown, OH D:11/5/1970, Hollister, CA Deb:4/18/1923, STL AL BR/TR 5'10½", 190

W	L	PCT	G	SV	IP	BB	SO	ERA
201	160	.557	632	40	3197^{1}	889	1459	3.59

Babe Ruth points to the center field bleachers in the 1932 World Series to signal where he will homer—and then does as he promised. So goes the legend. But did it happen that way? The pitcher was Charlie Root and he said no.

One fact cannot be argued—there was bad blood between the Yankees and the Cubs. Mark Koenig, a former Yankee, had joined the Cubs in midseason of 1932 and was pivotal in their pennant drive, yet his fellow Cubs voted him only half a World Series share. The Yankees were incensed by Chicago's treatment of their old teammate. Ruth led the attack and called the Cubs players "tight" and "cheapskates."

The press picked up Ruth's remarks, goading Cubs fans into a fury. In the fourth inning of Game 3, Ruth came to bat against Root. The crowd was throwing lemons at the Babe and booing furiously. Root threw a strike, and Ruth held one finger aloft, indicating strike one. The Babe raised two fingers after Root pitched his second strike.

With one strike to go, either Ruth held up his bat to indicate he had a single strike left or he pointed to the center field bleachers to signal where he would send Root's next offering. (It depends on what you want to believe.) Ruth then told catcher Gabby Hartnett, "It only takes one to hit it," and proceeded to wallop the ball deep into the center field bleachers. Some claim it was the farthest ball ever hit at Wrigley Field.

Root, on the other hand, always vehemently denied that Ruth called his shot. "He didn't point," swore Root. "If he had, I'd have knocked him on his fanny. I'd have loosened him up. I took my pitching too seriously to have anybody facing me do that."

The Cubs had picked up Root after he had posted back-to-back 20-win seasons for Los Angeles of the Pacific Coast League in 1924 and 1925. His 26 wins for the Cubs in 1927 led the league and earned him a place on *The Sporting News* All-Star team.

Root was a fine pitcher. He won at least 13 games 10 times in his career, led the league in winning percentage in 1929, and was tops in shutouts in 1940. However, if the Babe had to pick a pitcher on whom to call a World Series shot, Root was a likely suspect. Although Root won more than 200 regular season games, he was 0–3 with a 6.75 ERA for four different Series.

Root's major league career ended in 1941. The following season he compiled an 11–14 record for the Hollywood Stars in the Pacific Coast League. In 1943 he was named pitcher-manager of the Stars, and he went 15–5 with a 3.09 ERA. He stayed with Hollywood in 1944, and in 1945 and 1946 he went on to manage Columbus of the American Association. After several minor league stops, he coached for the Cubs from 1951 to 1953 and again in 1960, and for the Milwaukee Braves in 1956 and 1957. In 1969 Root was named the Cubs all-time righthanded pitcher. He died the following year.

Pete Rose

Rose, Peter Edward, Sr. **OF-1B-2B-3B**
1963–86 M(1984–89, 412–373) B:4/14/1941, Cincinnati, OH Deb:4/8/1963, CIN NL BB/TR 5'11", 200

G	AB	R	H	HR	RBI	OBP	SLG	AVG
3562	14053	2165	4256	160	1314	.377	.409	.303

Pete Rose, baseball's "Charlie Hustle," never did anything halfway in his entire life. His all-consuming passion for playing serious baseball is legendary. "I'd walk through hell in a gasoline suit to keep playing baseball," he once said. Rose set the all-time record for games played, with 3,562, and hits, with 4,256, and he compiled the National League's longest 20th century hitting streak: 44 games. Rose popularized the headfirst slide and would run to first base even on a walk. He was a superstar, but his federal conviction for tax evasion and his banishment from Organized Baseball for allegedly betting on games have made him *persona non grata* at the Baseball Hall of Fame.

When Rose came to the Cincinnati Reds in 1963, he won National League Rookie of the Year honors and established a reputation as a hard-driving, arrogant player. His nickname, Charlie Hustle, was not originally a compliment.

One of the defining moments of Rose 's career came during the 1970 All-Star Game at Oakland. In the 12th inning Rose came barreling into home plate with the winning run. He hit catcher Ray Fosse hard at the plate; the impact separated Fosse's shoulder, and the injury eventually brought Fosse's career to a premature end.

In 1973 Rose was shifted from second base to left field. The following season was probably his finest, as he led the league in batting for the third time, collected a career-high 230 hits, and was chosen Most Valuable Player. His Reds won the NL West but dropped the National League Championship Series to the upstart Mets. In the playoffs, the husky Rose became embroiled in a brawl with the much lighter New York shortstop Bud Harrelson. Rose had slid hard into Harrelson while trying to break up a double play. Words were exchanged, and then blows.

Outraged Shea Stadium fans showered Rose with debris. When a liquor bottle sailed down at Rose, Reds manager Sparky Anderson pulled his team off the field until order was restored.

"Me sliding hard into Harrelson trying to break up a double play was baseball, the way it's supposed to be played," Rose later explained without apology. "I'm no damn little girl out there. I'm supposed to give the fans their money's worth, and play hard, and try to bust up double plays—and shortstops."

In 1975 Rose switched to third base to make room for newcomer Ken Griffey, Sr. Rose was named MVP of that year's World Series after he collected 10 hits and batted .370 in the seven-game classic against the Boston Red Sox. In 1978 Rose thrilled the baseball world by recording the longest modern hitting streak in the league and posing a strong challenge to Joe DiMaggio's 1941 major league mark. At age 37, Rose was far older than 26-year-old DiMaggio, who had hit in 56 straight games, and 28-year-old Tommy Holmes, who set the old 20th century National League mark of 37 straight. "I told the writers I didn't want a car for the streak, or anything like that," Rose joked. "Just give me a bottle of Geritol and a jar of Grecian Formula. I was having fun."

Rose eventually hit in 44 straight games. Atlanta pitcher Gene Garber broke his streak on August 1, 1978. Rose got four hits the following night, but he was still angry at Garber's nibbling on the corners of the plate in the ninth inning the night before: "I honestly think that in that last at bat Garber didn't throw me a single strike," he said.

It was a banner year for Charlie Hustle. Not only had he compiled his record streak, but on May 5 he had become the youngest player ever to garner 3,000 hits. He became a free agent at season's end and signed an $805,000 contract with the Phillies, more than twice what the Reds had offered him.

The Phils moved Rose to first base, and he helped carry them to their first-ever world championship in 1980. Yet he was clearly slowing down, and in 1983 Philadelphia released him. "We hate to lose Pete," said Phils president Bill Giles, "but I want to be frank. His bat speed is slowing down." Rose's agent, Reuven Katz, secured a $500,000 contract from Montreal. "Not bad for a 43-year-old singles hitter with no bat speed," chortled Katz.

With Montreal he was no longer effective, but he was seriously closing in on Ty Cobb's all-time record for hits. In August 1984 Rose was traded back to Cincinnati and named playing manager. "I got to the point [in 1985] where I knew I was going to break the record," said Rose. "All I had to do was what I had always done: see the ball, hit the ball, and it would come. See the ball, hit the ball, and don't get hurt. I'm pretty good at all three."

Although research showed that Cobb had 4,189 hits, Major League Baseball ruled that his figure of 4,191 was the "official" mark. Rose had technically already broken Cobb's hit mark when he came to the plate on September 11, 1985, but try telling that to the packed house at Riverfront Stadium.

Rose faced San Diego's Eric Show and took the first pitch; he fouled off his second pitch, and took another. At 8:01 P.M. Rose lined Show's next offering into left field for hit No. 4,192. Cincinnati fans went wild. Fireworks erupted and overhead a Goodyear blimp flashed the news. A red Corvette with the license plate "PR 4192" was driven onto the field. The cheering went on for a full seven minutes.

"I started crying," said Rose, "and Tommy Helms, the coach, put an arm around me and motioned for my son, Petey, the batboy. I hugged my son and then I cried real hard."

Despite a series of disappointing second-place finishes and a 1988 shoving match with umpire Dave Pallone that resulted in a 30-day suspension, Rose retained his managerial post with owner Marge Schott's Reds. However, trouble was heading his way.

Rumors of Rose's gambling problems began circulating publicly in March 1989. Long known as an avid bettor on dog and horse racing, Rose was accused of violating Major League Baseball's Rule 21, which bars wagering on any contest in which a person has a duty to perform. The penalty: ineligibility.

At first, Rose laughed off the charges: "I'd be willing to bet you, if I were a betting man, that I have never bet on baseball." But the allegations would not go away. Trial attorney John M. Dowd completed an official 225-page report on May 9. It contained material that would shortly lead to Rose's downfall. Although Commissioner A. Bartlett Giamatti stressed that the report was highly confidential (and even copyrighted it), it was released to the press by court officials on June 26.

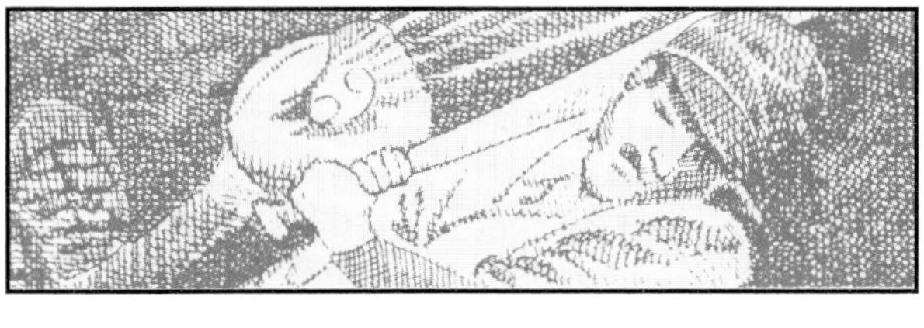

Based largely on the corroborated testimony of two Rose associates, Ron Peters and Paul Janszen, the report said that Rose was a compulsive gambler and that in 1985, 1986, and 1987 Rose had bet on baseball games. Copies of Rose's own records indicated that from May 17 to July 3, 1987, he had wagered $852,600 on 390 games, including 52 involving the Reds. Rose stayed true to his competitive nature: all bets on Cincinnati were to win.

On June 19 Rose counterattacked, charging in a Hamilton County, Ohio, common pleas court that Giamatti's investigation was hardly "fair and impartial." Rose asked the court to prevent the commissioner from judging the case. Cincinnati Judge Norbert Nadel issued a landmark ruling, granting Rose a two-week restraining order on Giamatti, but a federal judge quickly questioned Nadel's jurisdiction. On August 17 a three-judge federal panel agreed that any case involving Rose and the commissioner belonged before federal jurists, not in a local Cincinnati court—a severe blow to Rose's hometown defense strategy. Rose now sought to negotiate a settlement with Giamatti.

On August 24, 1989, the agreement was consummated. It declared the Cincinnati manager "permanently ineligible." In the agreement Rose admitted that he had been treated fairly in the official investigation and promised that he would not seek to reverse its results "in court or otherwise." The agreement specifically gave Rose the right to apply for reinstatement under Rule 15(c). But despite a provision that the commissioner "would not make any formal findings" on Rose's alleged gambling, Rose was banned from the game. Minutes later Giamatti told the press, "Yes, I have concluded that [Rose] bet on baseball." Giamatti died of a heart attack just a week after the announcement.

Rose's troubles mounted. On April 20, 1990, he pleaded guilty to felony counts of concealing income on his 1985 and 1987 tax returns. Judge S. Arthur Spiegel sentenced Rose to two five-month terms to be served concurrently, with no possibility of parole. After his release Rose would have to spend an additional three months in a halfway house. Following that, he would have to perform 1,000 hours of community service, including at least 20 hours per week with boys' clubs and inner-city schools in Cincinnati. A $50,000 fine, plus the cost of his confinement and supervision, was imposed. Spiegel also ordered Rose to seek counseling for his gambling addiction.

Rose began his sentence on August 8, 1990, at a federal facility in Marion, Illinois. He was assigned to the prison machine shop, working for 11 cents per day. During Rose's incarceration, two enterprising reporters sneaked into the prison and conducted an interview with him that was published in the *National Enquirer*. "I made mistakes and I'm very sorry for them," Rose told them. "But I'm paying for them every day."

Speculation quickly arose as to whether Rose, although ineligible to participate in Organized Baseball, was eligible for election to the Baseball Hall of Fame. That issue was settled, at least temporarily, in February 1991 when the Hall adopted a rule stating that "any player on Baseball's ineligible list shall not be an eligible candidate."

"The matter of Pete Rose is now closed," Giamatti said in announcing Rose's banishment from baseball. "It will be debated and discussed. Let no one think it did not hurt baseball."

Despite the ban, Rose has returned to minor league fields as a motivational speaker and sometime coach. He signed a "special services" contract with the Sacramento Steelheads of the independent Western Baseball League in 1999, and performed duties that included limited coaching in spring training and throwing out the first ball of the season. In July 1999 a "Pete Rose Museum" opened in Cooperstown, just one block from the Hall of Fame. A vote by the fans put Pete Rose back on the field for the first time in a decade in 1999; Rose was voted to the "All-Century Team" in a credit card promotion. He basked in the applause before Game 2 of the World Series, but a pointed post-ceremony interview with NBC reporter Jim Gray marred the moment. Despite the support of fans, Commissioner Bud Selig remained firm that the ban would not be lifted in the near future.

Johnny Roseboro

Roseboro, John Junior **C**

1957–70 B:5/13/1933, Ashland, OH Deb:6/14/1957, BRO NL BL/TR 5'11½", 190

G	AB	R	H	HR	RBI	OBP	SLG	AVG
1585	4847	512	1206	104	548	.329	.371	.249

On August 22, 1965, at Candlestick Park, Giants batter Juan Marichal attacked Dodgers catcher John Roseboro, whacking his head with the bat. Marichal was suspended for the vicious assault, which shocked the public. It began as a brush-back pitch war when San Francisco pitcher Marichal threw at Los Angeles batters Maury Wills and Ron Fairly. Dodgers starter Sandy Koufax tried to retaliate against Willie Mays. The catcher also took action. While Marichal was at bat, Roseboro whizzed a return throw to the mound close to the batter's head.

Marichal claimed that Roseboro's throw had nicked his ear. Roseboro denied it. "Why did you do that?" screamed Marichal. Then Marichal hit Roseboro three times in the head with his bat. Roseboro got up to retaliate. He swung several times at the pitcher. As the fight unfolded, Marichal and Giants leadoff batter Tito Fuentes (also holding a bat) both stood over a defenseless Roseboro, his protective mask torn off.

Koufax and Giants third base coach Charlie Fox attempted to break up the fight. Both benches spilled onto the field. Marichal ran toward his dugout, and the bloodied Roseboro took off after him. Giants outfielder Willie Mays yelled, "Stop fighting! Your eye is out." That hardly reassured Roseboro.

Marichal then began taunting Roseboro, and then Dodgers coach Danny Ozark attacked Marichal. "I went after Marichal because he was making fun of someone he had hurt unfairly," Ozark later said. Roseboro was a shocking sight. "I thought the bat had knocked Roseboro's left eye out," said Dodger manager Walter Alston. "There was nothing but blood where his eye had been."

National League president Warren Giles suspended Marichal for nine days and eight playing dates and fined him $1,750. He also barred the pitcher from accompanying his club on its final trip to Los Angeles on September 6–7, 1965; Marichal actually missed only one start. "Of course I had provoked the incident," Roseboro later admitted. "But I don't think anything I did justified Marichal hitting me on the head with his bat."

Roseboro debuted with the Dodgers in 1957, their last year in Brooklyn. The following season he was the Dodgers' starting catcher, and he caught at least 100 games for 11 of the next 12 years. Roseboro was behind the plate for two of Koufax's four no-hitters—on June 30, 1962, against the Mets, and on May 31, 1963, against the Giants.

A career .249 hitter, he established career highs with 18 homers and 59 RBIs in 1961. But he had little success with the bat in the postseason. He hit .219 in four World Series, striking out 12 times in 70 at bats. His postseason highlight was a three-run homer in Game 1 of the 1963 Series.

Although Roseboro eventually recovered fully from the Marichal attack, he was traded along with pitchers Ron Perranoski and Bob Miller to the Twins in November 1967 for shortstop Zoilo Versalles and pitcher Mudcat Grant. After helping the Twins to the 1969 American League West championship, Roseboro, who was 1-for-5 in a losing cause in the Championship Series, was released. He was signed by Washington that December. At the time, Roseboro was promised consideration if the Senators' managing job became open. In midseason he was again released, but he was kept on until year's end, technically as a coach.

From 1971 to 1974 he served as Angels' bullpen coach. After leaving California he fell on hard times. "Before I hocked my guns, I considered sticking someone or someplace up," he confessed.

"I was an honest man but I was desperate.... A lot of men have been humbled. I was." Roseboro eventually went into the insurance business and later wrote an autobiography entitled *Glory Days with the Dodgers and Other Days with Others.*

Al Rosen

Rosen, Albert Leonard **3B**
1947–56 B:2/29/1924, Spartanburg, SC Deb:9/10/1947, CLE AL BR/TR 5'10½", 180

G	AB	R	H	HR	RBI	OBP	SLG	AVG
1044	3725	603	1063	192	717	.386	.495	.285

After Al Rosen spent several seasons waiting to crack the Cleveland Indians lineup, he became the dominant power-hitting third baseman in the game. He left the field at age 32 under unusual circumstances and then returned 20 years later to become a success in the front offices of the Yankees, Astros, and Giants.

His nickname, "Flip," had been given to Rosen for his softball pitching style. Flip was no pushover. A noted tough guy, he spent time as an amateur boxer and had his nose broken 11 times. Rosen attended college both before and after his military stint in the navy during World War II. He signed a contract with the Indians, but his reputation as a poor fielder kept him in the minors, particularly with smooth glove man and fan favorite Ken Keltner entrenched at third. In 1949 the 32-year-old Keltner hit only .232, and he was released. The Indians gave the job to Rosen in 1950.

Rosen, 26 at the time, broke in with a bang. His 37 homers led the American League and set a league rookie record that stood until Mark McGwire broke it 37 years later. Rosen scored 100 runs and drove in 116. His totals dropped off to 24 homers and 102 RBIs the following season, but no other third baseman in the game supplied anywhere near as much offense.

In 1952 Rosen led the league in RBIs with 105, swatted 28 homers, and scored 101 runs. Those were nothing compared to his 1953 numbers. Not only were Rosen's 115 runs scored and .613 slugging average league bests, but he also led the league with 43 home runs and 145 RBIs. He lost the batting title to Washington's Mickey Vernon by one point. Needing a hit in his final at bat to win the Triple Crown, Rosen chopped a roller to third base and was out by half a step.

Nevertheless, Rosen set single-season records for third basemen in RBIs and total bases. He was a unanimous choice for Most Valuable Player. Rosen's confidence at the plate extended into the field. A mediocre defender when he arrived at the majors, he led league third basemen in assists in 1950, and in assists, double plays, and total chances per game in 1953.

Chosen as his league's third baseman for the All-Star Game in 1954, he put on a show for his hometown fans in Cleveland's Municipal Stadium, slugging two homers and adding a single for five RBIs. And although he broke a finger during the season, he still managed 102 RBIs and 24 home runs.

The Indians won a league-record 111 games and the pennant in 1954, but Rosen and the rest of his teammates barely had a chance to enjoy being in the World Series. The New York Giants engineered a four-game sweep, as Cleveland was outscored, 20–9 in the Series. Rosen had just three hits, all singles, in 12 at bats.

An off-season auto accident landed Rosen in the hospital with whiplash, and the injury dogged him during the 1955 season. Meanwhile, he and club management were at odds over his salary. When his performance didn't match his previous season's numbers, Indian fans started booing Rosen. A disgusted Rosen quit after the next season. He had a successful business as a stockbroker, so he didn't need the money. But it was a disappointing way for a tough guy like Rosen to leave the game.

Almost two decades later in 1978, after volatile owner George Steinbrenner forced Gabe Paul out as Yankees president, he hired Rosen as Paul's replacement. That November, acting on a tip from a scout, Rosen went after Texas farmhand Dave Righetti and landed him, though it took a complicated 10-player-plus-cash swap to pull it off. Righetti became a key man on the New York pitching staff for 10 years, and Rosen quickly developed a reputation as a tough negotiator.

Steinbrenner's constant meddling didn't sit well with Rosen, however, and he quit the team during the 1979 All-Star break. He sent a note to Steinbrenner, saying, "I'll always love you as a friend. I just can't work for you." Bally's Hotel and Casino in Atlantic City offered him a position, and he accepted.

While at Bally's, Al Rosen hired Willie Mays as a greeter and public relations man. Commissioner Bowie Kuhn promptly notified Mays that he could not work as a scout and coach for the Mets if he also worked for a casino. Kuhn applied the same sanctions to Mickey Mantle four years later. The Mays–Mantle bans were two of Kuhn's least popular moves.

Baseball beckoned again in 1980 when mercurial Houston owner John McMullen fired popular general manager Tal Smith and replaced him with Rosen. As Astros general manager for six years, Rosen helped build a young team that was always close but seldom on top.

Houston won the second half of the split season of 1981 but dropped the first round of postseason play to Los Angeles. A tumble to fifth in 1982 was followed by third- and second-place finishes the next two years. Among Rosen's more valuable acquisitions in Houston were Dickie Thon, Ray Knight, and Mike LaCoss, along with the sly theft of Mike Scott from the Mets for Danny Heep.

Giants owner Bob Lurie lured Rosen away from Houston in 1985. Rosen saw to it that Roger Craig was named manager, and they brought the Giants back from mediocrity to National League champions. Rosen landed Kevin Mitchell, Dave Dravecky, and Craig Lefferts in the same deal to provide punch and pitching. The rise of talented youngsters Will Clark and Robby Thompson through the farm system solidified the infield. The Giants returned to the World Series in 1987 for the first time in 16 years and then repeated in 1989.

Allan Roth

Roth, Allan

Statistician B:Montreal, Quebec, Canada D:3/ 4/1992, Los Angeles, CA

Before computers, *Total Baseball*, rotisserie leagues, sabermetrics (or even the Society for American Baseball Research) there was Allan Roth. Hired by Brooklyn in 1947, Roth was baseball's first full-time statistician, and the system of recording data he developed decades ago continues to shape the way we look at and think about the game.

Something of a prodigy, the Montreal-born Abraham (he later legally changed it to Allan) Roth was only 3 when he amused relatives by counting backwards from a hundred—by twos. He was not entirely cerebral, however. One year, at Strathcona Academy, he scored all his football team's touchdowns.

As a teenager Roth experimented with baseball statistics, working first with International League and then major league data. Accepted to McGill University and even provided with a scholarship, he was unable to attend because of family financial difficulties. His brother Max was already in the school, and Roth had to find employment to help support the family.

In 1940 Roth, now a salesman, began writing to *The Sporting News* and to Dodgers general manager Larry MacPhail concerning the results of his studies, putting together myriad statistical situations, most of which we would take for granted today, but which he was often presenting for the first time.

He kept writing to the Dodgers. In September 1941 he submitted a pitch-by-pitch analysis of that fall's World Series. The following month he was hired by National Hockey League president Frank Calder to assemble statistical analysis for the league. Roth responded by inventing the system of charting every pass.

Roth continued to press Brooklyn for a job as team statistician. MacPhail's replacement, Branch Rickey, was interested in the idea, but since Roth was a Canadian citizen (and an epileptic besides) getting him across the border to work was no easy task. Roth busied himself with articles for *The Standard* and with more work on hockey—but preferred baseball. "I had always thought that baseball was a better field than hockey," said Roth, "Basically, baseball is a percentage game. I thought that everything in the game should be tabulated and developed a number of theories which Rickey went for."

Finally, in 1947 Roth was allowed to work in the United States, and was immediately hired by Rickey as baseball's first statistician. Roth soon introduced a whole series of new statistics, recording everything from bunts to possible RBIs—all, of course, for the exclusive and very secretive use of the Dodgers. A milestone article appeared in *Life* magazine in 1954 that detailed Roth's theories. Also featuring Branch Rickey, it was headlined "A New Formula Explodes Baseball's Myths."

Typical of Roth's work in the 1950s was this analysis: "Close, low-scoring games follow a definite pattern. Eleven men usually get on base in the first eight innings on hits, walks, and errors. Going into the ninth inning 24 men have been retired, making a total of 35 who have gone to bat. The first man up in the ninth, therefore, completes the fourth complete swing through the batting order and then come the top two men. In tight games, hitters below the second slot seldom get five chances to hit."

Not everyone on the Dodgers appreciated Roth's work. Charlie Dressen was one who did not, but Walter Alston did. "It was rumored that Alston never made a move without checking with Allan first," said Vin Scully.

Roth also edited *Who's Who In Baseball*. In 1964 he left the Dodgers to become statistician for NBC's *Game of the Week*. He continued to publish material and to make it available to major league clubs. In the early 1980s he left NBC to handle baseball analysis for ABC. Roth's health had long been in decline when he died of a heart attack in Los Angeles on March 4, 1992. The Los Angeles chapter of the Society of American Baseball Research has been named in his honor. His papers may be found in the Amateur Athletic Foundation archives in Los Angeles.

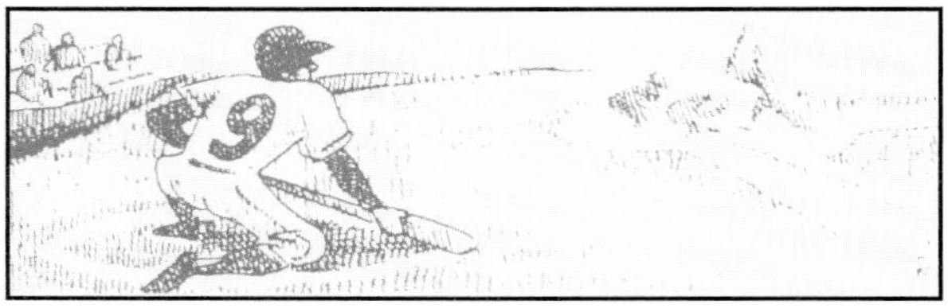

Edd Roush

Roush, Edd J **OF**

1913–29, 1931 B:5/8/1893, Oakland City, IN
D:3/21/1988, Bradenton, FL Deb:8/20/191, CHI AL
BL/TL 5'11", 170

G	AB	R	H	HR	RBI	OBP	SLG	AVG
1967	7363	1099	2376	68	981	.369	.446	.323

At age 15 Edd Roush got a chance to play for the town baseball team when one of the regulars didn't show up for a game. He got a couple of hits and became a regular himself. Two years later Roush discovered that some of the players were receiving $5 per game under the table. Believing that he was one of the team's better players, he asked for his share—and was turned down. So he went some 12 miles down the road and signed with archrival Princeton. "And don't think that didn't cause quite a ruckus," he later told writer Lawrence Ritter. "Especially when Princeton came over to play Oakland City at Oakland City, with me in the Princeton outfield."

How fitting that Roush should have begun his baseball career with a dispute over money. It was a first step toward his becoming what Cincinnati manager Pat Moran called "the great individualist in the game." Edd J Roush was as unique as the extra "d" in his first name. It wasn't short for Edward, Edwin, or anything else. His middle initial also stood alone, without a period. Roush's grandfathers were named Joe and Jim, so the "J" was a tactful compromise made by his parents. However, they never passed that particular quality along to their son Edd.

In later years a story circulated that Roush was a natural righthanded thrower but had hurt his arm as a boy and was forced to learn to throw lefty. The truth is that he had indeed thrown righthanded as a kid, but only because there was no lefthander's glove available. Truly ambidextrous, he felt he threw farther with his left arm. In 1912, when he signed his first professional contract with Evansville of the Kitty League, Roush finally bought a lefthander's glove. His father, a dairy farmer and former semipro player, was enthusiastic about his son's prospects. "I didn't expect to make it all the way to the big leagues," Edd admitted later, "but I just had to get away from them damn cows."

In 1913 he was hitting .314 for Evansville when he was purchased by the Chicago White Sox. After a nine-game tryout he was optioned to Lincoln, Nebraska. When Indianapolis of the new Federal League offered him $225 a month for 1914, almost twice what he would have made at Lincoln, he jumped. He hit .325 as a part-timer for Indianapolis and then hit .298 playing regularly for Newark. When the Federal League collapsed, Roush, outfielder Benny Kauff, and infielder Bill McKechnie were sold to the New York Giants.

Roush took an immediate dislike to Giants manager John McGraw and the way he berated his players. One day McGraw picked up Roush's bat, which at 48 ounces was the heaviest in the majors. "Don't ever let me catch you using that bat again," he ordered. Roush responded, "This is the first damn league I ever played in where the manager picked the bat for you."

"What league did you ever hit .300 in?" sneered McGraw. "Every league I ever played in," Roush said, exaggerating only slightly. "And I'd do it in this league, too, if I'd play regularly." A short time later Roush was traded to Cincinnati in an unusual deal. The Giants received infielder Buck Herzog and outfielder Wade Killefer for Roush, McKechnie, and Christy Mathewson; all three players the Giants traded eventually made it to the Hall of Famers. Mathewson became Cincinnati's manager. The Reds really wanted Kauff, who had been the Federal League's biggest star, but McGraw, in a huge miscalculation, talked them into taking Roush instead.

Installed as a center fielder, Roush was soon regarded as the National League's premier player at the position and became the Reds' most popular player. He continued to swing his heavy bat. Not that it gave the 5'11", 170-pound lefthanded hitter home run power—he hit only 68 homers in his career. Although his bat weighed four ounces more than the monster used by Babe Ruth, it was short, with much of the weight in the extra-thick handle. The bat enabled Roush to bunt, to get good wood on inside pitches, or to slap outside pitches into left field. One year he reportedly slapped seven hits, including a triple, on pitchouts. Roush claimed he never broke a bat. He started each season with six, and the only ones he'd lose were those he gave away to fans.

In 1917, his first full season with the Reds, he led the National League in hitting, at .341. He missed the 1918 title by .002, but in 1919 he won his second championship with a .321 mark as Cincinnati surprised everyone by winning the National League pennant. They won the World Series over Chicago in eight games, but shortly thereafter the baseball world was shocked to learn that eight members of the White Sox had been bribed by gamblers to throw the Series. Roush always maintained that the Reds were a vastly

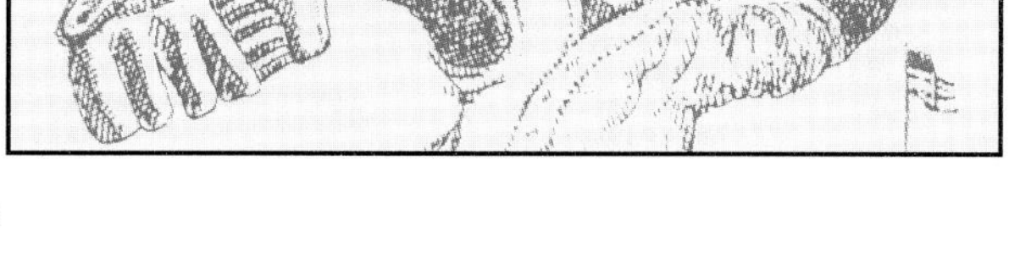

underrated team and that they would have won even if the games had been played fairly. Roush did his part in the Series, scoring six runs and driving in seven.

Roush considered spring training both a waste of time and a likely opportunity to become injured on some of the rough fields the teams used for exhibition games as they traveled north. Even when offered a satisfactory contract, he held out until the season was ready to start. Because he always kept himself in tip-top shape, he was able to step right into the lineup. In a serious holdout over money in 1923, he didn't sign until July 23. When he returned, he banged out three hits in his first game and went on to hit .352 for the rest of the season.

From 1917 through 1926 his lowest batting average was his league-leading .321 in 1919. On August 23, 1919, he stroked two doubles in one inning. In 1920 and 1924 he assembled 27-game hitting streaks. In 1923 he led the league with 41 doubles, and the following season he led the league in triples with 21.

Meanwhile, Roush played center field brilliantly. Teammate Heinie Groh said enthusiastically, "Why, Eddie used to take care of the whole outfield, not just center field. He was far and away the best outfielder I ever saw." When the Reds' regular left fielder was sidelined for part of the 1919 season, Roush suggested to manager Pat Moran that he put pitcher Rube Bressler, a good hitter, in left. Roush promised to position Bressler for each batter. At the end of two weeks, Bressler said, "There's nothing to this outfielding. We're right in front of every line drive. What I can't understand is why we have to move around so much."

Almost from the day he traded Roush, McGraw tried to get him back. At last, in 1927 he swung a deal that made Roush a Giant again. But Roush refused to report, even as the Giants repeatedly increased their offer. Finally, McGraw confronted him in person. "Don't you want to play for me?" he asked. "Hell no!" said Roush.

He finally accepted a three-year deal for $70,000 after McGraw promised not to direct any of his harangues toward him. Three years later, after he'd hit .324, the Giants tried to cut his salary by $7,500. Roush held out for the entire 1930 season. McGraw finally gave up and released him. Roush played with Cincinnati in 1931 and then retired. Having saved his money and invested shrewdly, Roush had a comfortable retirement, traveling and doing whatever he pleased. In 1962 he was named to the Hall of Fame.

Jack Rowe

Rowe, John Charles **SS–C–OF**

1879–90 M(1890, 5–14) B:12/8/1856, Hamburg, PA D:4/25/1911, St. Louis, MO Deb:9/6/1879, BUF NL BL/TR 5'8", 170

G	AB	R	H	HR	RBI	OBP	SLG	AVG
1044	4386	764	1256	28	644	.323	.392	.286

Jack Rowe was a talented shortstop and catcher, and one of the Buffalo Bison's "Big Four" hitters—along with Dan Brouthers, Deacon White, and Hardy Richardson—of the 1880s. But Rowe and White are best remembered for their refusal to be sold to Pittsburgh, which led to the establishment of the Players' League in 1890.

At age 22 John Charles Rowe joined the new National League Buffalo Bisons in 1879. The left-handed hitter led the league in triples with 11 in 1881 when he hit .333 with a .480 on-base percentage. A review in the *New York Clipper* read, "He is a sure catch, a swift and accurate thrower, and faces pluckily the swiftest and wildest pitching. He also excels in batting, and being an earnest and hard-working player, is one of the most useful men of the Buffalo team."

In August 1885, Detroit, who would finish 38–74, purchased the entire Buffalo franchise for $7,000 in order to get its best players. On September 17, 1885, the "Big Four" were to play for Detroit, but National League president Nick Young ordered umpire Bob Ferguson to forfeit the game to New York. The players were forced to play the rest of season with Buffalo. Buffalo was left without a National League team in 1886 and the Big Four played for the Detroit Wolverines. They won the pennant in 1887 when Rowe hit .318.

After the 1888 season Wolverines owner Frederick Stearns sold White and Rowe to Pittsburgh. Rather than play for Pittsburgh, Rowe and White purchased control of Buffalo's International League team and intended to play there. Pittsburgh owner Bill Nimick said that Rowe and White would "play for Pittsburgh or they will play for nobody." The Pittsburgh owner was said to have passed word that any player competing with or against Rowe and White faced expulsion.

As a result, the two players sat out the first half of 1889 and finally reported to Pittsburgh. But the incident brought resolve to the players' union, which arranged to start the Players' League in 1890. Rowe and White were part owners of the new Buffalo Bisons and played for themselves in the short-lived Players' League in 1890. Rowe played in the minor leagues from 1891 through 1893 and later managed. After that he operated a cigar store in Buffalo.

Schoolboy Rowe

Rowe, Lynwood Thomas **P**

1933–43, 1946–49 B:1/11/1910, Waco, TX D:1/8/1961, El Dorado, AR Deb:4/15/1933, DET AL BR/TR 6'4½", 210

W	L	PCT	G	SH	IP	BB	SO	ERA
158	101	.610	382	22	2219^{1}	558	913	3.87

One day in September 1934 Detroit pitcher Schoolboy Rowe was being interviewed on the radio following a 2–0 victory over Washington. His fiancée, Edna Mae Skinner, was present, and Rowe suddenly blurted out, "How'm I doin' Edna?" That remark got a lot of attention, particularly from the Dean brothers in the upcoming World Series, but throughout his 15-year career Rowe did very well indeed.

Lynwood Thomas Rowe, reared in El Dorado, Arkansas, was nicknamed "Schoolboy" after a heckler at a church league game shouted, "Don't let that schoolboy strike you out!" Rowe was 15 at the time. Rowe signed a professional contract with Fort Smith of the Western Association while still in high school, but he refused to report for duty and was content to play five seasons of semi-pro ball instead. Eventually he enrolled at the University of Texas. After two weeks there he was informed that, due to the playing contract he had signed years ago, he was athletically ineligible.

Discouraged by his inability to play in college, in 1932 Rowe finally reported for minor league duty. By then Fort Smith had sold Rowe's contract to Evansville, which in turn had peddled it to the Tigers' Texas League farm club at Beaumont. While playing on the team with future great Hank Greenberg, Rowe went 19–7 with a league-leading 2.34 ERA.

On April 15, 1933, Rowe made his first major league start for the Tigers, shutting out the White Sox, 3–0. Later that year he hurt his arm fielding a bunt and was out for part of the season. Rowe was slow coming around in the spring of 1934 and Mickey Cochrane, the new Tigers manager, put the word out that Rowe was headed back to Beaumont unless he quickly recuperated. Rowe was soon taking his regular turn for what became his best season in the majors.

Beginning on June 15 Rowe won 16 straight games (tying the American League record) before being beaten by the Yankees in late August. He finished 24–8 as Detroit won it first pennant since 1909. For the opener of the World Series against the Cardinals, however, Cochrane bypassed his ace for Alvin "General" Crowder, who lost to St. Louis and Dizzy Dean, 8–3. "Mickey used good gumption," said Dean. "You see, he knew if I was at my best, nobody could beat me. So he saved Schoolboy Rowe for another game instead of puttin' him against me like I would have admired to have him done."

The next day Rowe won, 3–2, in 12 innings, shutting out the Cardinals after the fourth inning and retiring 22 straight batters during one stretch. In Game 6, with the Tigers one victory from a world championship, Rowe was beaten, 4–3, by Paul Dean, who drove in the winning run with a seventh-inning single. The Tigers were blown out, 11–0, the next day.

Rowe won 19 games in each of the next two seasons and was a workhorse. From 1934 through 1936 he averaged 262 innings a year. The Tigers met the Cubs in the 1935 World Series, and Rowe lost the first game, 3–0. He pitched four innings of relief to record the win in Game 3, but he dropped a 3–1 decision in Game 5. Detroit won Game 6, as Rowe took part in his only world championship in his 15-year career.

Then his arm went bad. He was 1–4 in 1937 when he worked only 31 innings, and he was 0–2 the next season, pitching only four innings. He had one more memorable season: in 1940 he went 16–3 for the pennant-winning Tigers. His .842 won-lost percentage led the league, and the Tigers were confident entering the World Series against the Reds.

However, the Series was a nightmare for Rowe. He allowed four runs in 3⅓ innings in a Game 2 loss and was then chased with four hits and two runs in a third of an inning of Game 6. The Tigers blew a three-games-to-one lead and lost the Series. Rowe's ERA in his two starts was a whopping 17.18.

In 1941 he was only 8–6, and on April 30, 1942, he was sold to the Dodgers. His arm still hurt, and he ended up in Triple-A Montreal after nine appearances with Brooklyn. The Phillies bought him from the Dodgers the next spring, and, surprisingly, he went 14–8 with a 2.94 ERA in 199 innings.

His next stop was two years with the navy. By 1946 he was back with the Phillies. He went 35–24 as a spot starter during the next three seasons but retired after getting only six starts and going 3–7 in 1949. Rowe pitched well considering his arm troubles. His career record was 158–101, and his winning percentage was an excellent .610.

Rowe was also an excellent hitter for a pitcher, and he was often used as a pinch hitter. He led the National League in pinch hitting in 1943 when he went 15-for-49, for a .306 average. On May 2, 1943, he hit a pinch-hit grand slam off Boston's Al Javery, one of only five pitchers to pinch hit a homer with the bases loaded. He had a .263 career batting average with 18 homers and 153 RBIs in 909 at bats.

Rowe was a large man. At 6 feet 4½ inches and 210 pounds, he hit the first ball ever into the Polo

Grounds center field bleachers, although he did it in batting practice. And when he pinch hit for Warren Spahn in the 1947 All-Star Game, he became the first player to appear in the Midsummer Classic for both leagues.

Bama Rowell

Rowell, Carvel William **2B–OF**

1939–48 B:1/13/1916, Citronelle, AL Deb:9/4/1939, BOS NL BL/TR 5'11", 185

G	AB	R	H	HR	RBI	OBP	SLG	AVG
574	1901	200	523	19	217	.316	.382	.275

On May 30, 1946, presaging Roy Hobbs in Bernard Malamud's *The Natural*, the Braves' Bama Rowell smashed the Ebbets Field scoreboard clock with a homer, showering shards of glass upon right fielder Dixie Walker. It took an hour for the timepiece to stop functioning—and 41 years for Rowell to collect the Bulova watch promised to anyone who hit the stadium clock.

Carvel William Rowell began in 1937 with Cordele in the Georgia-Florida League; he hit for a .241 average. He split 1938 between Winston-Salem of the Piedmont League and Dayton of the Middle Atlantic League. With Hartford in 1939 he averaged .297, with 72 RBIs, and led the Eastern League in stolen bases. That same year he was brought up to Boston. In an August 14, 1940, doubleheader Rowell accepted 25 out of 26 chances. On September 25, 1941 he committed three errors in the third inning. That season he led the National League in miscues.

Rowell entered the army in December 1941. Discharged in October 1945, he returned to baseball. In March 1948 the Braves sent Rowell, first baseman Ray Sanders, and $40,000 to Brooklyn for Eddie Stanky. When the Dodgers sent Sanders back to Boston, the Braves recompensed Brooklyn with another $100,000. Rowell was waived a month later to Philadelphia, where he ended his career.

Pants Rowland

Rowland, Clarence Henry

Manager (1915–18, 339–247) U(1923–27) Executive B:2/12/1879, Platteville, WI D:5/17/1969, Chicago, IL

Pants Rowland managed the White Sox to a world championship—before they went crooked. He was an obscure choice to become a major league manager, but he led Chicago to three consecutive winning seasons, culminating in its 1917 World Series title.

Rowland never played in the major leagues, his professional career limited to catching in the minors. His nickname of Pants dated from his playing days. He showed up one day wearing his brother's trousers, which were several sizes too large. Ironically, Pants later became known as a sharp dresser, often attired in stylish cream-colored trousers.

His minor league managing career included service with the Dubuque Dubs (Class B Three-I League) in 1908, the Grays Harbor Grays (Class B Northwestern League) in 1909, and the Jacksonville Jacks (Class D Northern Association) in 1910. From 1911 through 1914 he returned to the Three-I League, managing Peoria. Chicago White Sox owner Charles Comiskey hired Rowland to replace Jimmy Callahan on December 17, 1914.

The White Sox improved steadily under Rowland, finally winning the 1917 American League pennant. In the World Series they faced John McGraw's New York Giants. The Sox won their second—and last—World Series of the 20th century in six games. The lasting image of the Series was Giants third baseman Heinie Zimmerman chasing Chicago's Eddie Collins across an unoccupied home plate.

The White Sox had a losing season in the war-shortened 1918 season, and Rowland was back in the minors in 1919—managing the Milwaukee Brewers to a last-place finish in the American Association. He returned to the majors as an American League umpire from 1923 through 1927. In midseason of 1928 he replaced James Hamilton as manager of the Southern Association's Nashville Vols. In 1931 he took the helm of the International League's Reading Keys, remaining with them when they relocated to Albany, New York, on August 6, 1932.

His second tour of minor league managing was at a higher level—but no more successful—than his first. Rowland scouted for the Cubs from 1933 through 1941, after which he became president of the Pacific Coast League. He remained in that post until 1954, when he became Cubs vice president, a post he held until his death in 1969.

Nap Rucker

Rucker, George **P**

1907–16 B:9/30/1884, Crabapple, GA D:12/19/1970, Alpharetta, GA Deb:4/15/1907, BRO NL BR/TL 5'11", 190

W	L	PCT	G	SH	IP	BB	SO	ERA
134	134	.500	336	38	2375¹	701	1217	2.42

Nap Rucker was Brooklyn's first great southpaw. Although his tenure with the club was relatively brief and he was saddled with poor support, some said he was the franchise's best left-hander until Sandy Koufax came along.

George Rucker, as he was named at birth, pitched briefly for Atlanta of the Southern Association in 1904. Also trying out for the team was a second baseman from Tennessee who wasn't hitting well, but who kept busy writing articles for the *Atlanta Constitution*.

Recalled Rucker, "One day the manager said to this boy, 'Why don't you quit and be a sports editor? You write better than you play second base?'" The player, Grantland Rice, took the advice. "And he became a great one, didn't he?" Rucker said.

It was Rice, in fact, who had discovered Rucker and recommended him to Atlanta manager Abner Powell. Rice also gave him the name Napoleon. Rice, however, couldn't keep Rucker from being sent to Augusta in the Sally League because of control problems. With Augusta the following season, Rucker pitched a no-hitter and roomed with Ty Cobb.

Even then Cobb was possessed by demons. Rucker and Cobb had developed a routine where Cobb would return home first after games and bathe. Rucker would saunter in at his leisure. One day, Rucker was knocked out of a game and got home first. He was in the tub when Cobb arrived. An infuriated Cobb burst into the room and literally tried to strangle Rucker. Rucker held him off and asked, "Are you crazy, Ty?" Cobb answered, "You don't understand, Nap. I've just got to be first—all the time."

Other Augusta teammates included Eddie Cicotte, Clyde Engle, and Ducky Holmes, all future major leaguers. Rucker was 13–11 for Augusta in 1905. The following season he went 27–9, led the league in victories, and was drafted by Brooklyn for $500.

Rucker was one of the first pitchers to have his pitching speed measured scientifically. On October 6, 1912, Rucker traveled to the Remington Arms Plant in Bridgeport, Connecticut. He was clocked at 113 feet per second (roughly 77 miles per hour). Walter Johnson was later measured on similar equipment at 122 feet per second (83 miles per hour).

On September 5, 1908, in the second game of a doubleheader, Rucker no-hit the Boston Braves, 6–0, striking out 14 and walking none. Three Brooklyn errors separated Rucker from a perfect game. On July 24, 1909, Rucker struck out 16 batters in a game against the Pirates. In 1912 he was part of another memorable contest, against Rube Marquard of the Giants.

"Rube had run his streak of wins to 18. He was after 19," Rucker recalled. "Well, I pitched my head off. I wanted to win. My wife was there in the stands. Charlie Ebbets was there. It was a low-score, low-hit game, and I should have won. But I didn't, and only a few days later [Jimmy] Lavender of the Cubs stepped in and ended Marquard's streak."

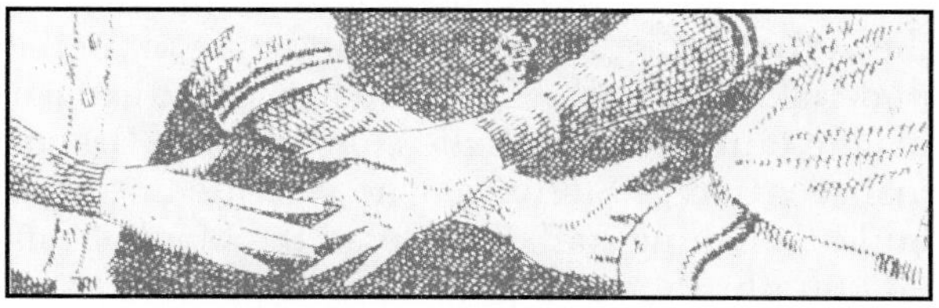

This was not Rucker's only hard-luck loss. During the course of his career he lost 10 games by a score of 1–0. A 2–0 loss on April 15, 1915 came on a no-hitter by Marquard. "I never pitched on a championship team until 1916 and then I was about through," said Rucker. "I wanted to quit before they gave it to me. I could have done minor league pitching but I couldn't have worked often enough."

Rucker, whose one 20-win season (22–18) in 1911 was followed by a 20-loss season (18–21) in 1912, finished his career with a 134–134 record. He appeared in one World Series, pitching two scoreless innings in the 1916 Series, won by Boston in five games.

After retiring, Rucker scouted for Brooklyn in the South. He also took up farming, having bought his first farm with his share from the 1916 World Series. He later became mayor of Roswell, Georgia, and longtime water commissioner for that town.

Joe Rudi

Rudi, Joseph Oden **OF–1B**

1967–82 B:9/7/1946, Modesto, CA Deb:4/11/1967, KC AL BR/TR 6'2", 200

G	AB	R	H	HR	RBI	OBP	SLG	AVG
1547	5556	684	1468	179	810	.314	.427	.264

One of the quieter stars of the Oakland A's dynasty of the 1970s, outfielder Joe Rudi shone brightest in Game 2 of the 1972 World Series when he homered and fielded his way onto a page of postseason history. With the A's leading the Reds, 1–0, in the third inning, Rudi went to work offensively, launching a solo homer off Cincinnati's Ross Grimsley. The score remained 2–0 entering the ninth inning. Tony Perez led off with a single for the Reds, and Denis Menke followed with a deep drive to left field. Rudi thought it was a home run, but charged after it anyway. As he neared the fence, he jumped.

"It might have been two feet below the top of the fence," said Rudi. "If it had been a couple of inches higher I don't think I could have caught it, because I stretched as high as I could and caught it right on the edge of my glove."

Cincinnati got one run in that inning, but probably would have tied the game had it not been for Rudi's spectacular, leaping backhanded catch. Oakland won the game, 2–1, and took the Series in seven games.

A three-time All-Star, Rudi won Gold Gloves in 1974, 1975, and 1976. He was also named to *The*

Sporting News American League All-Star Fielding Team those years. In 1972, 1974, and 1976 Rudi was selected to *The Sporting News* AL All-Star Team.

Managers and coaches praised Rudi's commitment and work habits. "Joe is probably the most dedicated person I've ever met," said batting guru Charlie Lau. "He never stops looking, thinking, and experimenting. He's 'hungry' if you want to call it that." A's manager Dick Williams declared, "A manager would like to have 25 Joe Rudis on his ballclub."

Originally signed by the Cleveland organization, Rudi was traded on December 1, 1965, to the Kansas City Athletics for outfielder Jim Landis and pitcher Jim Rittwage. Rudi first appeared in an A's uniform in 1967, the team's last season in Kansas City. But he wasn't a permanent starter until 1971, when Oakland won the first of five consecutive division titles. He hit a career-high .305 in 1972, when he led the league with 181 hits and nine triples. Two years later he batted .293, led the league in doubles, and established career highs in home runs, with 22, and in RBIs, with 99.

In 38 postseason games, Rudi never committed an error. In Game 5 of the 1974 World Series, Rudi's seventh-inning solo homer off Dodgers ace reliever Mike Marshall snapped a 2–2 tie and propelled the A's to their third straight world championship. Oakland's dynasty came to an abrupt end the following season when Boston engineered a three-game sweep of the A's in the Championship Series.

Oakland owner Charlie Finley attempted to break up his team in June 1976, selling Rudi and pitcher Rollie Fingers to the Red Sox for $2 million. But Commissioner Bowie Kuhn voided the deal. In 1976 Rudi played out his option with Oakland and signed a five-year, $2,090,000 contract with the Angels. At the time only Reggie Jackson's $3 million deal with the Yankees was more lucrative.

Rudi, however, spent most of 1977 on the disabled list, on which he later had two more stints. In four seasons with the Angels he never hit better than .264. He was traded to Boston in January 1981, along with pitchers Frank Tanana and Jim Dorsey, for outfielder Fred Lynn and pitcher Steve Renko.

When his five-year contract expired after the 1981 season, he returned to Oakland as a free agent. He hit .212 in 71 games and retired at season's end. Rudi finished his career with a lifetime .264 average and 12 career grand slams.

"Let me tell you something about hitting," Rudi told the *Christian Science Monitor* in 1977. "When you're going good, it doesn't make any difference who the pitcher is, whether it's a night game or a day game, or where the ballpark is located. I don't take a lot of theories up to the plate with me. I look for what I think is a good pitch and then I swing at it. If there is more to hitting than I just told you, I don't know about it."

Dick Rudolph

Rudolph, Richard **P**

1910–27 B:8/25/1887, New York, NY D:10/20/1949, Bronx, NY Deb:9/30/1910, NY NL BR/TR 5'9½", 160

W	L	PCT	G	SH	IP	BB	SO	ERA
121	108	.528	279	27	2049	402	786	2.66

Dick Rudolph won 26 games in 1914 and helped lead the "Miracle" Braves to an unexpected world championship. One of the best control pitchers in major league history, Rudolph averaged just 1.77 walks per nine innings pitched. As a result, he yielded just 10.42 baserunners per nine innings, a better ratio than future Hall of Famers Carl Hubbell, Robin Roberts, Jim Palmer, and Bob Gibson, all winners of at least 250 games.

Rudolph got his start with Bronx, New York, semipro teams and was a fairly successful pitcher at Fordham University, where he once defeated the Yale Elis, 3–2, at the Polo Grounds. He dropped out of college in 1906 to sign with the Newark Indians of the Eastern (International) League.

Newark soon dropped him, but Rudolph caught on with the Toronto Maple Leafs. There, he won 20 games three times and 18 games twice between 1907 and 1913. But he could not escape from the minors. Rudolph received two brief trials with the Giants, but could not make the talented club. In his major league debut in 1910, he surrendered 16 hits in losing to the Phillies, 8–2.

Rudolph threw a spitter, but it was his curveball and control that got him by. The spitter was generally used to set up and confuse hitters. "The best that could be said about [Rudolph's spitter] is that it was wet," catcher Hank Gowdy once quipped.

Rudolph's frustration only grew in 1912, when the International League voted a salary limit of $400 per month. In April 1913 Rudolph jumped the club, vowing to quit baseball and go into the undertaking business if he were not sold to a major league club. To the rescue came Boston Braves manager George Stallings, who was attempting to build a pitching staff. He offered the Maple Leafs $4,000 plus another pitcher and a player to be named later. Rudolph, however, balked, saying that he wanted a guarantee he would pitch in the majors. "I never will play in a minor league again," he said, "and I will not stand to be traded back to the bushes by your club."

Stallings reassured him, and in 1913 Rudolph put together a 14–13 record for the fifth-place Braves. In 1914 the Braves were in last place as late as July 18. Then they got hot, as Rudolph won 12 straight during one stretch. Boston climbed to second place on August 12 and passed the slumping Giants for good on September 8. They eventually won the pennant by a whopping 10½ games.

Stallings picked Rudolph to pitch Game 1 of the World Series against the heavily favored Philadelphia Athletics. Cubs manager Hank O'Day predicted the A's would win four straight. Detroit skipper Hughie Jennings thought the odds should be 10–1 in favor of Philadelphia. Philadelphia pitcher Chief Bender told his manager, Connie Mack, "We don't need to scout this bush league outfit."

Sure enough, the Series was a rout, with the Braves doing the routing. In Game 1 Boston knocked Bender out in the sixth. For his part, Rudolph was masterful. He struck out eight and allowed just five hits; the only run he surrendered was unearned on an error by right fielder Herbie Moran.

The Braves won Games 2 and 3, and Rudolph had some good personal news, becoming a father in the meantime. In Game 4 Rudolph bested the A's, 3–1, on seven hits and seven strikeouts for the first sweep in World Series history. (There had been a tie in the 1907 Fall Classic.)

The following season Rudolph won 22 games, but the Braves finished in second place. He went 19–12 with a career-low 2.16 ERA in 1916.

Rudolph was one of those allowed to continue using the spitter after 1919 (spitters had been disallowed for players who didn't use it as a standard in their repertoires).

Rudolph coached for the Braves from 1921 to 1927, making occasional appearances on the mound. In midseason 1924 he stepped in for Dave Bancroft as Braves manager, but was replaced by Bancroft after going just 11–27. Rudolph later managed for Portland of the New England League and Waterbury of the Eastern League. He also coached freshman baseball at Fordham. The business Rudolph eventually went into was undertaking.

Muddy Ruel

Ruel, Herold Dominic **C**

1915, 1917–34 M(1947, 59–95) B:2/20/1896, St. Louis, MO Deb:5/29/1915, STL AL BR/TR 5'9", 150

G	AB	R	H	HR	RBI	OBP	SLG	AVG
1468	4514	494	1242	4	534	.365	.332	.275

Muddy Ruel's greatest stroke of luck came on another catcher's misfortune. In Game 7 of the 1924 World Series there was one out in the bottom of the 12th. Ruel was up for the Senators against the Giants' Jack Bentley, and Bentley induced him to hit a soft pop foul in back of the plate. Veteran catcher Hank Gowdy threw off his mask and promptly tripped right over it, and Ruel had a second life. He made the most of it by hitting a double. Two batters later he scored the winning run on Earl McNeely's lucky-bounce hit over Freddy Lindstrom's head.

Ruel played with the St. Louis Browns, New York Giants, and Boston Braves before he arrived in Washington in 1923. He batted .300 in three of his first five years with the Senators and the club won back-to-back pennants in 1924 and 1925.

He obtained a law degree and later worked in Commissioner Happy Chandler's office. Following that he was farm director at Detroit.

Herold Dominic Ruel obtained his nickname from falling into a mud puddle as child and getting covered from head to toe in the stuff. His father commented "Look at Muddy over there." The mud washed off—the name stuck.

Dutch Ruether

Ruether, Walter Henry **P**

1917–27 B:9/13/1893, Alameda, CA D:5/16/1970, Phoenix, AZ Deb:4/13/1917, CHI NL BL/TL 6'1½", 180

W	L	PCT	G	SV	IP	BB	SO	ERA
137	95	.591	309	18	2124^{2}	739	708	3.50

Eddie Cicotte gained fame for losing the first game of the 1919 World Series, but few fans know the pitcher who won that contest. Walter Henry "Dutch" Ruether not only captured Game 1 but also batted .667 in the 1919 Series. In the fourth inning he tripled to the fence in left-center field, scoring both Greasy Neale and Ivey Wingo. He singled in the sixth, then tripled to deep center in the eighth, scoring Neale again; in Game 7 he pinch hit. Overall for the Series he drove in four runs.

Ruether batted .258 lifetime, with seven home runs and 111 RBIs in 969 at bats. He was often used as a pinch hitter, collecting 34 pinch hits.

Frank Graham said: "He never cared much for training rules but he knew how to pitch, and he never really got out of hand. He was a big southpaw with plenty of stuff and plenty of...moxie."

On August 27, 1926, he was traded from the Senators to the Yankees. He lost Game 3 of that fall's World Series to Pop Haines. He started 1927 as New York's fourth starter but was injured and lost his job to George Pipgras.

In 1928 Ruether was 29–7 for the San Francisco Seals and was voted by sportswriters to the Pacific Coast League All-Star team. He led the league in wins and percentage and hit .316 in 72 games. Ruether later managed Seattle in the Pacific Coast League. He also scouted for the Cubs and Giants.

Red Ruffing

Ruffing, Charles Herbert **P**

1924–47 B:5/3/1904, Granville, IL D:2/17/1986, Mayfield Heights, OH Deb:5/31/1924, BOS AL BR/TR 6'1½", 205

W	L	PCT	G	SH	IP	BB	SO	ERA
273	225	.548	624	45	4344	1541	1987	3.80

Red Ruffing overcame two kinds of pain to become a Hall of Fame hurler: physical pain and the sting of performing for a last-place club. Throughout his career Ruffing pitched with four toes missing from his left foot, and for most of his playing days he suffered from adhesions in his throwing shoulder. He was also afflicted with having to play on one of the worst ballclubs in history, the Red Sox of the 1920s. But he persevered to reach the Hall of Fame. Hall of Fame backstop Bill Dickey once said, "If I were asked to choose the best pitcher I've ever caught, I would have to say Ruffing."

Ruffing attended school until age 15, when he went to work mining coal in Nokomis, Illinois. Ruffing's father also worked in the mines and managed the company baseball team, where Ruffing played first base and the outfield until an accident occurred below ground. His left foot got caught between two mining cars, costing him four toes.

For a year the hobbled Ruffing gave up baseball. When he returned, he took up pitching for his father's team. "The foot bothered me the rest of my career and I had to land on the side of my left foot in my follow-through," the soft-spoken Ruffing said.

Shortly after his return to baseball, Ruffing's team was scheduled to play against a team loaded with heavy hitters. When Ruffing's fellow pitchers suddenly developed sore arms, he was pressed into service and performed creditably, losing a 10-inning, 3–2 game because his left fielder muffed a flyball. In his next start he struck out 16 batters.

Ruffing's impressive work soon caught the attention of the manager of the local semipro team, who asked him how much he was earning for his mound work. "My dad doesn't pay any of his players," Ruffing responded. When he was offered $75 to pitch three games in the coming week, Ruffing thought to himself, "My dad just lost a pitcher."

In 1923 Ruffing signed his first pro contract with Danville of the Three-I League. He played for Dover of the Eastern Shore League in 1924, and displayed the wildness (89 walks and only 88 strikeouts) that would plague him during the early portion of his career. Despite posting losing records with both clubs, Ruffing was acquired by the Red Sox and was soon pitching in Fenway Park.

In those days the Red Sox were a pitiful franchise, having been gutted of their best players by owner Harry Frazee to cover his financial problems. In each of Ruffing's first three full major league seasons he walked more batters than he struck out. From 1925 through 1929 he ranked third in the American League in bases on balls. For two straight years he led the league in losses. In fact, from 1925 through 1929 he lost a major league-high 93 games. During one pitiful stretch in 1929 he lost 12 consecutive games.

No one could have won with that Red Sox ballclub, but Boston decided they could improve matters by moving Ruffing off the mound. Ruffing had hit .314 with two homers in 1928 and .307 with a pair of home runs in 1929, and the Sox seriously considered converting him into an outfielder—bad foot and all. One day, however, Yankees manager Miller Huggins came up to Ruffing and advised him, "You never will be more than a fair outfielder, and you could be a great pitcher....I'm going after you."

Huggins died not long afterward, but the Yankees organization shared his high opinion of Ruffing. In May 1930 New York acquired the pitcher for outfielder Cedric Durst and $50,000. The turnaround was immediate. For Boston, Ruffing had been 39–96. For the rest of his career, he was 234–129. With the Yankees he won 20 or more games four straight times and led the American League in strikeouts in 1932. In World Series competition he was nearly unbeatable, starting five Series openers and winning six straight decisions at one point.

Ruffing believed in the value of conditioning and in the significance of control—interesting choices considering his own handicap and his early propensity to issue bases on balls. "There are two important things to remember," he once

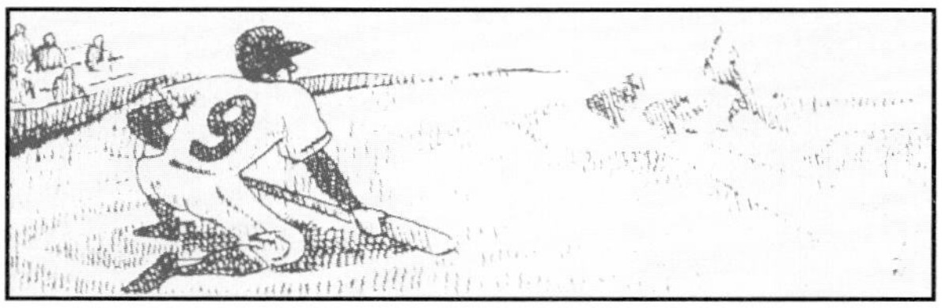

said. "Keep in shape and know where each pitch is going. It pays off. I knew where my pitches were going because I worked on control continuously. I never had a curveball. If I threw a curve at a batter he'd laugh. But by being able to pitch the ball hard and where I wanted, I became successful. Ask Hank Greenberg. I struck him out a few times."

In 1930 Ruffing went 15–5 for the Yankees and hit .364 with 17 runs, eight doubles, two triples, four home runs, and 22 RBIs. On September 18 he hit two home runs in one game, a feat he would repeat on June 17, 1936. After winning 16 games in 1931 and 18 games in 1932, Ruffing struggled on the mound in 1933. He did, however, hit a grand slam Boston's Bob Weiland.

Ruffing rebounded to win 19 games in 1934 and 16 in 1935, and in 1936 he started his streak of four 20-win seasons. In the 1938 World Series, Ruffing was 2–0 with a 1.50 ERA, and his 8–3 complete-game victory in Game 4 gave the Yankees a four-game sweep of the Cubs and their third consecutive world championship.

Ruffing won more than 20 games and batted better than .300 in 1939. He is one of the few pitchers in major league history to do both. In 1942 he went 14–7, posting his ninth straight winning season. In Game 1 of the 1942 World Series, Ruffing came close to immortality but ended up in the showers. He issued two first-inning walks, then pitched flawless baseball. In the sixth inning, he turned to a fellow Yankee and said, "You guys don't have to be so damned quiet. I know I've got a no-hitter, and if I get through the eighth I'll keep it."

He couldn't. With two outs in the bottom of that inning, Terry Moore got the first hit off Ruffing, and then the lefthander unraveled. In the ninth the Cardinals scored four runs and chased Ruffing, but he still recorded a 7–4 victory.

Ruffing spent the next two years in the service. The 38-year-old had a severely damaged left foot, a wife, two children, and was the sole supporter of his family and mother-in-law—and was still drafted. "The last doctor I saw was an army doctor," Ruffing said. "He put on his report that what I could do on the outside I could do on the inside. He would have drafted any ballplayer. So that's how I got in."

Ruffing returned to the Yankees in July 1945 and went 7–3 with a 2.89 ERA. He started the 1946 season 5–1 with a 1.77 ERA, but then suffered a broken kneecap. Released by the Yankees that September, he finished his career with the White Sox in 1947.

Ruffing made 536 major league starts, compiling a career record of 273–225. He was 7–2 with a 2.63 ERA in World Series action. A career .269 hitter, he drove in more runs than any pitcher in major league history, and his 36 lifetime homers rank third among pitchers, behind only Wes Ferrell and Bob Lemon. In 1962 Ruffing became the first pitching coach of the expansion New York Mets.

Elected to the Hall of Fame in 1967, Ruffing suffered a stroke in 1973 that confined him to a wheelchair. He continued to attend induction ceremonies in Cooperstown for most of the rest of his life.

Pete Runnels

Runnels, James Edward **1B-2B-SS**

1951–64 M(1966, 8–8) B:1/28/1928, Lufkin, TX D:5/20/1991, Pasadena, TX Deb:7/1/1951, WAS AL BL/TR 6', 170

G	AB	R	H	HR	RBI	OBP	SLG	AVG
1799	6373	876	1854	49	630	.376	.378	.291

When most people think of the left field wall at Fenway Park, they think of righthanded sluggers like Walt Dropo or Dick Stuart sending flyball after flyball over the friendly "Green Monster." Possibly they think of middle infielders like Rico Petrocelli or Felix Mantilla, who became sluggers of a sort because they happened to be playing in a ballpark that helped righthanded pull-hitters, even if they weren't especially muscular.

But there were others who benefited from "the Wall," like lefthanded spray hitter Pete Runnels. Think of him as a poor man's Wade Boggs, a player with little power (his career high in homers was 10) who could slap hit after hit off that inviting wall.

Runnels came to the Red Sox after spending seven years with the Senators, where he hit better than .300 only once. After seven years at Griffith Stadium, with its spacious outfield and smaller foul territory, Runnels immediately took to his new surroundings. Runnels did not bat lower than .314 in his five seasons in Boston and won two batting titles.

Texas native James Edward "Pete" Runnels entered the Marines after high school and then enrolled in Rice University after his discharged in 1948. He left after one semester to sign with the Cardinals, despite St. Louis manager Eddie Dyer's advise that he stay in school.

In 1949, his first year as a professional, with Chickasaw in the Class D Sooner State League, he led the league in batting average (.372), hits, and doubles. After he hit .330 with Texarkana in the Class B Big State League, the Senators bought him for $12,500. His next stop was Chattanooga, where he hit .356. That earned him a promotion to the Senators in 1951, and he batted .278 in 78 games as a shortstop.

During the next 13 seasons Runnels was tried

at all four infield positions; he was very ordinary at each. He led American League second basemen in fielding in 1960, but he was also second-to-last in chances per game, which tells you all you need to know about his range. The next season he led league first basemen in fielding—and finished last in chances per game.

His best season in Washington was 1956, when he hit .310 with eight homers and a career-high 76 RBIs. But the Senators soured on him after he slumped to .230 in 1957. He came to the Red Sox in a January 1958 trade for Norm Zauchin and Albie Pearson. Boston had found a No. 2 hitter for its power-hitting club. Runnels hit .322 in 1958 and finished second to teammate Ted Williams in the batting race. Runnels scored a career-high 103 runs.

He finished third in the batting race in 1959 at .314, and he finally won the crown in 1960 when he hit .320. "I was the lightest champion since Billy Goodman 11 years before, and I must have been the sickest of all time," observed Runnels, who stood an even 6 feet and weighed only 170 pounds. "I had stomach ulcers and was on a strict diet the last month of the season."

Despite his lofty average, he wasn't very productive. He drove in only 35 runs in 528 at bats in 1960 and was only a semiregular in 1961, batting .317 in 360 at bats. Chuck Schilling, an excellent glove man, had taken over at second, and Vic Wertz had a very productive year as a part-time first baseman.

Wertz was gone the next year and Runnels became the everyday first baseman, hitting a career-high .326 to win his second batting title at the rather advanced age of 35. He played in the All-Star Game for the third time in four years.

It was his last year in Boston. The National League had expanded to Houston and Runnels wanted to play closer to home.

"The people in Boston were just tremendous," said Runnels. "Fenway was a great park to hit in and the Red Sox were a great organization [but] I went to Mr. Yawkey and told him I'd like to be nearer home and he said, 'I hate to see you go, but I'll help you,' and he did. He was just the finest man."

The Astros got him in a trade for Roman Mejias, but Runnels was all but washed up. He hit only .253 in 124 games in 1963 and was released on May 19, 1964, after batting .196 in 22 games. Runnels returned to Boston as a coach, and managed the last 16 games of the 1966 season (going 8–8) after Billy Herman was fired. Runnels opened a sporting goods store in Pasadena, Texas. He later operated Camp Champions, a coed summer camp in Marble Falls, Texas. He died of a stroke in 1991.

Jacob Ruppert

Ruppert, Jacob

Owner (1915–1939) B:8/5/1867, New York, NY D:1/13/1939, New York, NY

A high-living, big-spending son of a brewery magnate, Jacob Ruppert was no stranger to the elite of New York society. In fact, he had served as a four-term U.S. congressman from the "silk stocking" district of Manhattan. He went from silk stockings to sweat socks courtesy of Giants manager John McGraw. In 1915 McGraw introduced Ruppert to millionaire engineer and contractor Colonel Tillinghast L'Hommedieu Huston and suggested that the two of them buy the downtrodden New York Yankees.

Having paid $460,000 for the Yanks, Ruppert chose people to run his team and didn't interfere with them. Behind Huston's back, he hired Miller Huggins to manage the team. Huston's dislike of Huggins eventually caused the dissolution of Huston's partnership with Ruppert.

Ruppert obtained Babe Ruth from the Red Sox in 1919 and shortly thereafter, hired Red Sox manager Ed Barrow as the team's business manager. With the Huggins–Ruth–Barrow threesome in place, the Yankees won a rash of pennants and became the dominant team in the American League.

When pitcher Carl Mays jumped the Red Sox in 1919, Ruppert signed him. American League president Ban Johnson tried to suspend Mays, but Ruppert wouldn't stand for it. In the first direct assault on Johnson's power, Ruppert sued and won a temporary restraining order that overruled the suspension. This move split league owners into two factions. Comiskey of Chicago and Frazee of Boston joined Ruppert and Huston in confronting Johnson and became known as "the Insurrectionists." Later, Ruppert and Huston filed a $500,000 suit against Johnson and the league, claiming that the president was trying to run them out of baseball. Mays became a Yankee, and the Insurrectionists were largely responsible for Johnson's eventual ouster. Ruppert's power led him to play a key role in the downfall of the three-man National Commission that oversaw the game. Commissioner Kenesaw Mountain Landis replaced the tribunal.

He was called Colonel Ruppert because of his rank in the seventh regiment of the National Guard. He looked after his own interests, building Yankee Stadium to house his star Babe Ruth.

It cost $2.5 million but was well worth the investment. The Yankees consistently outdrew New York's two National League teams and won the World Series seven times from the new stadium opened until Ruppert's death in 1939.

Ruppert had two ideas that became part of baseball legend. He was the first owner to give all his players regular numbers, although the Indians had briefly worn them in June 1916. He also designed the Yankees' distinctive uniform to hide Babe Ruth's increasing girth. The pinstripes came to symbolize a baseball dynasty.

Bob Rush

Rush, Robert Ransom **P**

1948–60 B:12/21/1925, Battle Creek, MI Deb:4/22/1948, CHI NL BR/TR 6'4", 205

W	L	PCT	G	SH	IP	BB	SO	ERA
127	152	.455	417	16	2410²	789	1244	3.65

The National League in the 1950s seemed full of big, beefy righthanded pitchers named Bob who threw overhand and were expected to deliver plenty of innings. The Pirates had Bob Friend, the Braves had Bob Buhl, and the Cubs had Bob Rush.

From 1949 through 1956 Rush led Chicago in starts and innings pitched five times and was second once. He won nine games or more every year. Yet, like many solid pitchers on poor teams, he took a lot of losses: 18 in 1949, 20 in 1950.

In 1952 both the Cubs and Rush got hot. Rush turned in an ERA of 2.70, lower by a run than his previous best season. He finished at 17–13 as the Cubs finished .500 for the first time since 1946. He also cracked 28 hits and knocked home 15 runs, for a .292 average. Rush appeared in that season's All-Star Game. The second National League pitcher, he was cuffed around for four hits in two innings, but rain abbreviated the game to five innings, and Rush got the win.

After going 6–16 in 1957, his worst won-lost performance, Rush and two other Cubs were sent to the Milwaukee Braves for Taylor Phillips and Sammy Taylor. On the more talented Braves team, Rush was the third pitcher behind Warren Spahn and Lew Burdette, and with 20 starts he sported a 10–6 record. The Braves won the pennant. In that year's World Series, Rush started and lost Game 3 when Don Larsen and Ryne Duren combined to shut out the Braves.

In 1959, Rush, in relief, took the loss in the second playoff game against the Dodgers, which sent Los Angeles to the World Series. During the 1960 season, the Braves sent Rush to the White Sox where he closed out his 13-year career.

Amos Rusie

Rusie, Amos Wilson **P**

1889–95, 1897–98, 1901 B:5/30/1871, Mooresville, IN D:12/6/1942, Seattle, WA Deb:5/9/1889, IND NL BR/TR 6'1", 200

W	L	PCT	G	SH	IP	BB	SO	ERA
246	174	.586	463	30	3778²	1707	1950	3.07

Many candidates have been proposed as the fastest pitcher of all time, including Nolan Ryan, Sandy Koufax, Bob Feller, Lefty Grove, Walter Johnson, and minor leaguer Steve Dalkowski. Yet Connie Mack, who in 50 years of managing the Philadelphia Athletics observed nearly every important pitcher since the 1890s, insisted that Amos Rusie was the fastest of them all. Longtime Giants manager John McGraw agreed. One piece of compelling evidence supports their claim: in 1893 the pitching distance was moved back from 50 feet to 60 feet 6 inches to give batters a chance against Rusie's overpowering fastball.

Rusie started his career modestly enough as an outfielder on a semipro team in Indianapolis. One day the regular pitcher was having no luck and a teammate suggested that Rusie replace him. As soon as the substitute pitcher uncorked his first fastball, his days in the outfield were over. While pitching exhibition games for an Indianapolis semipro outfit called the "Sturm Avenue Never Sweats," Rusie shut out both Boston and Washington of the National League. Rusie, who had quit school at an early age to work in a factory, had found a new occupation.

In 1889 at age 18 he joined Indianapolis of the National League. Although he finished only 12–10, gave up 246 hits in 225 innings, and walked 116, everyone who saw his fastball knew that Rusie was a potential star. The NL desperately needed stars in 1890. An owners' plan to rank the players according to ability and pay them fixed salaries based on their ranking backfired. The Brotherhood of Professional Base Ball Players, originally a benevolent association, organized its own Players' League in protest. Many National League and American Association stars jumped to the new league.

The New York Giants were particularly hard hit. National League champions in both 1888 and 1889, they had featured many of baseball's best-known players. Almost all of them had now joined the Players' League. When the Indianapolis team folded after the 1889 season, the National League, recognizing the importance of a strong franchise in New York, engineered the transfer of several of the best Indianapolis players, including Rusie, to New York.

The 1890 season was one of the most disagreeable in baseball history. Fans were disgusted by the interleague arguing and by players jumping from team to team. Most clubs in all three leagues lost money. The Players' League collapsed after one season. The American Association hung on like a ghost for one more year, then disappeared. The National League survived, but at great cost to the owners.

One of the season's few bright spots was Rusie's emergence as a star pitcher. His record with the sixth-place Giants was only 29–34, but his league-leading 341 strikeouts excited the fans. When the stars returned to the National League in 1891, Rusie kept pace and again led the league in strikeouts, with 337. His record improved to 33–20, and on July 31 he no-hit Brooklyn, 6–0, one of his league-best six shutouts. In 1892 Rusie collected his second 30-win season with a 32–31 mark, and his 288 strikeouts were second in the league. But he was as wild as he was fast. In his first three seasons in New York he gave up more than 260 walks each year. His wildness, combined with his speed, terrified batters.

The 6-foot 1-inch, 200-pound Rusie was an imposing figure. Giants catcher Dick Buckley once admitted to putting a sheet of lead in his glove to enable him to catch Rusie's fastball. Chicago Cubs outfielder Jimmy Ryan said, "Words fail really to describe the speed with which Rusie sent the ball. He was a man of great height, great width, prodigious muscular strength and the ability to put every ounce of his weight and sinew on every pitch. The distance was shorter then. Rusie had the whole box to move around in, instead of being chained to a slab; and the giant simply drove the ball at you with the force of a cannon. It was like a white streak tearing past you."

When Rusie first arrived in New York he had been only 19 years old and green as grass. New York went wild over the youngster from Indiana and nicknamed him "The Hoosier Thunderbolt." The big town had certainly seen baseball All-Stars before. Tim Keefe, Buck Ewing, and Roger Connor of the championship 1888 and 1889 clubs were idolized by many fans, but their followings were nothing compared to Rusie's. His name appeared in a Mr. Dooley story and in a Weber-and-Fields vaudeville skit. A hotel bar named a drink in his honor. A paperbound book, *Secrets of Amos Rusie, the World's Greatest Pitcher, How He Obtained His Incredible Speed on Balls*, sold for 25 cents. Actress Lillian Russell, the era's preeminent sex symbol, asked to be introduced to Rusie.

Ironically, when Rusie's success caused the pitching distance to be increased in 1893, the greater distance may have actually made him a better pitcher. His curveball, almost as quick as his fastball, was more effective at the new distance. He won 33, 36, and 23 games during the next three seasons, and each year he led the league in shutouts. His strikeout numbers fell to around 200 but still led the league all three years.

Despite Rusie's talent and popularity, the Giants were in financial trouble. They released him near the end of the 1892 season so they could save half a month's salary. New York planned to sign him again later and thought the other teams had agreed not to pick him up in the meantime; management was wrong. The Chicago Cubs signed Rusie for $6,500 plus a $2,000 bonus. New York had to pay dearly to buy back his contract, then tried to count the bonus against his salary.

That was only the beginning of Rusie's problems with Giants management. In 1895 Tammany Hall politician Andrew Freedman bought the team. Within a year his shady maneuvers, arbitrary manner, and nasty temper made him baseball's most detested owner. In his first year the Giants went through three managers, the third being an actor friend of Freedman's. The team plummeted from second place to ninth.

Freedman decided that Rusie was overpaid and wanted to get some of the money back. He fined the pitcher for a series of offenses that Rusie denied. After the season, Freedman refused to rescind the fines and offered him a contract for only $2,500. Rusie held out for the entire season, then sued Freedman for $5,000. Partly because of the suit, partly because Rusie was a good drawing card, and partly because some of the owners were decent men, the league paid him the money.

Rusie returned to the Giants in 1897 and won 48 games during the next two seasons. But late in 1898 something popped in his shoulder as he made a pickoff throw to first. His arm went dead. He was only 27 years old. He rested the arm for two years, hoping it would heal. He planned a comeback and became part of one of the most one-sided deals in history.

In 1900 the Giants had let young Christy Mathewson go back to Norfolk after an unimpressive New York debut; the Cincinnati Reds proceeded to draft Mathewson off the minor league team's roster. The Giants traded the once great Rusie for the future great Mathewson. Rusie tried to come back with the Reds, but after three games he knew it was no use. He retired after 10 seasons with a record of 245–174, 1,934 strikeouts, and 1,704 walks. Of his 427 starts, he completed 392.

Rusie returned to Indiana, worked in a paper and pulp mill, and did some freshwater pearling.

From 1911 to 1921 he was a steamfitter in Seattle. Then John McGraw offered him a job as superintendent of the Polo Grounds. Rusie worked for McGraw until 1929 and then returned to Seattle and died there in 1942. In 1977 he was named to the Hall of Fame.

Bill Russell

Russell, William Ellis **SS–OF**

1969–86 M(1996–98, 173–149) B:10/21/1948 Pittsburg, KS Deb:4/7/1969, LA NL BR/TR 6', 175

G	AB	R	H	HR	RBI	OBP	SLG	AVG
2181	7318	796	1926	46	627	.312	.338	.263

No infield played together longer than the Dodgers quartet of Steve Garvey, Davey Lopes, Bill Russell and Ron Cey. For eight years, 1974 through 1981, they held down the fort, and four times during that period the Dodgers advanced to the World Series. They lost to Oakland in the 1974 Series, and to the Yankees in both 1977 and 1978, thanks largely to Reggie Jackson. In the 1981 World Series, the Dodgers finally beat the Yankees, four games to two.

Of the four players in the Dodgers infield, Russell lasted the longest. He remained a Dodger uniform from the time he was signed by the club in 1966 until he was fired as the team's manager in the middle of the 1998 season. He retired in 1986 having played in more games than any Los Angeles Dodger; Zack Wheat played in 2,322 games when the team was located in Brooklyn.

Russell was a team player, specializing in the little things that endear players to managers: bunting, stealing, hitting behind runners. He usually hit in the .270s (although injuries held him to .206 in 84 games in 1975). A converted outfielder, he was a solid glove man at shortstop.

In the 1974 National League Championship Series, Russell had seven singles to set a record for one-base hits in a four-game series. In the 1978 NLCS he batted .412, and his two-out single in the bottom of the 10th in Game 4 provided the victory that put the Dodgers in the World Series.

A pitch shattered his right index finger in 1980, and he was never able to throw as well. Russell stayed with the team in a part-time capacity through 1986, then became a Dodgers coach for five years until taking a managerial job in the Dodgers minor league system. He managed the Dodgers from 1996 through part of the 1998 season, compiling a 173–149 record. In 1999 he was managing the Southern League's Orlando Rays, a Devil Rays farm team.

Babe Ruth

Ruth, George Herman **OF–P–1B**

1914–35 B:2/6/1895, Baltimore, MD D:8/16/1948, New York, NY Deb:7/11/1914, BOS AL BL/TL 6'2", 215

G	AB	R	H	HR	RBI	OBP	SLG	AVG
2503	8399	2174	2873	714	2213	.474	.690	.342

W	L	PCT	G	SH	IP	BB	SO	ERA
94	46	.671	163	17	1221^{1}	441	488	2.28

Babe Ruth was not only the greatest baseball player who ever lived, but he was also the most flamboyant. His unique personality made him one of the most recognizable names and faces in American history. In the 1920s his name appeared in print more often than anyone except the president of the United States. In World War II, when American soldiers shouted "To hell with the Emperor!" at their Japanese counterparts, the Japanese hollered back, "To hell with Babe Ruth!"

Ruth was a presence of mythic proportions. While he was changing baseball and its economics forever, he was also defining a uniquely American kind of folk hero: a larger-than-life athlete with even larger appetites, an intense love of children, and an irrepressible sense of fun.

At age 7 George Herman Ruth was already too much for his parents to handle. After being classified as incorrigible, he was shipped off to St. Mary's Industrial School for Boys, a reform school run by Catholic brothers several miles from the Ruth home in Baltimore. One of the brothers, a 6-foot 6-inch, 250-pound giant named Matthias, was the school's disciplinarian. He took a special liking to Ruth and became his father figure and coach, working with the youngster for hours on hitting, fielding, and pitching. Ruth later called Brother Matthias the greatest man he'd ever known.

In 1914 Jack Dunn, owner of the minor league Baltimore Orioles, signed the 19-year-old Ruth to a contract as a pitcher. Dunn had to become Ruth's legal guardian in order to do so. The Ruth deal was for $100 a month for six months. As the youngster walked to the pitcher's mound with Dunn on the first day of spring training, someone hollered, "Look at Dunnie and his new babe." One of the most famous nicknames in history was born.

Ruth immediately established himself as a

major talent. Dunn doubled his pay to $1,200 in May and upped that by $600 more in June. By early July Ruth's record was 14–6. But because of competition from the upstart Federal League, Dunn was losing money. On July 8, after a game for which only 17 people paid to see his team play, Dunn sold Ruth, pitcher Ernie Shore, and catcher Ben Egan to the Boston Red Sox for $8,500.

The Sox signed Ruth to a 2½-year contract worth $3,500 a season. Ruth made his major league pitching debut on July 11, beating Cleveland, 4–3. After three decisions the Sox sent him back to the minors, where he compiled an 8–3 record for Providence and hit his first professional home run to win a 1–0 game. He was called back up to the big league team the next season.

During the next three years Ruth became the best lefthanded pitcher in baseball. He won 18 games in 1915, 23 in 1916, and 24 in 1917. In 1915 the American League batted .212 against him; only teammate Dutch Leonard was tougher to hit. In 1916 the opposition hit only .201 against him, lowest in the league. He also led the American League with nine shutouts and a 1.75 ERA. Only two pitchers had more wins or strikeouts. In 1917 Ruth spun 35 complete games in 38 starts to lead the league.

In 1915 the Red Sox won their third World Series in as many tries, although Ruth didn't pitch in the five games and batted only once, grounding out. In 1916 the Sox faced Brooklyn in the Series, and Ruth opposed Sherry Smith in Game 2 for one of the greatest pitching duels in Series history. Brooklyn scored in the first, Boston scored in the third, and the game stayed tied at 1–1 until the bottom of the 14th inning when Boston won. Both pitchers went the distance in the longest World Series game played in the 20th century.

The Red Sox finished second in the American League in 1917, but they returned to the Series in 1918 and won again. Ruth pitched a six-hit shutout in Game 1, and when the Cubs scored in the eighth inning of Game 4 they broke Ruth's string of 29⅔ consecutive scoreless Series innings. That record lasted until Whitey Ford topped it in 1961.

Ruth's pitching frightened batters, and his manners and personal habits frightened everyone else. Simply stated, he was crude. Never having been schooled in etiquette and reveling in his immense salary and status, Ruth ate more, drank more, belched more, and swore more than anyone else in baseball. Ugly nicknames surfaced, but no one dared speak them to his face. At 6 feet 2 inches and nearly 200 pounds, he was the biggest and strongest guy on the team.

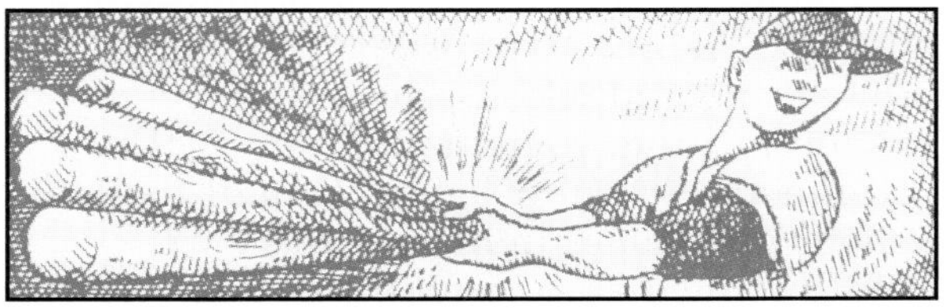

During the 1918 season Sox center fielder Harry Hooper advised manager Ed Barrow to move Ruth to the outfield full time. Hooper saw the value of having the big man's bat in the lineup every day. In Ruth's first 361 major league at bats he had hit almost .300 and had slugged an astonishing nine home runs. A dozen home runs was all it usually took to lead the league at the time.

Barrow's compromise was to have Ruth pitch in 20 games, play the outfield in 59, and cover first base in 13 more. Ruth hit 11 homers in only 317 at bats to lead the league, and tied for fifth with 11 triples. His homers were already legendary, and he liked the attention he got as a slugger. The experiment was ruled a success. Ruth moved to the outfield for 111 games in 1919 and made only 17 appearances on the mound. That year he exploded for 29 home runs, setting a new major league record; he homered in every American League park. He scored 103 runs and drove in 114, both league-leading totals, and also led the league in on-base and slugging percentages.

But even Ruth's homers couldn't lift the Red Sox above sixth. In the off-season Sox owner Harry Frazee, needing money to invest in a hot new play on Broadway, sold Ruth to the Yankees for $125,000 and a $300,000 loan.

When Ruth arrived in New York the Yankees had never won a pennant in their history. But with the help of former Red Sox players Ruth, Ernie Shore, Carl Mays, Joe Bush, Duffy Lewis, and Wally Schang, among others, the Yankees grew into the greatest dynasty in baseball history. The Red Sox, who had been world champions three times in the eight years Ruth played on the team, did not win another World Series in the 20th century. As a result, Boston's inability to capture a championship has often been attributed to "the Curse of the Bambino."

In 1920 the Yankees finished third, three games back, in a roaring pennant race. Ruth hit a mind-boggling 54 home runs that season, scored 158 runs, and drove in 137. He batted .376, 54 points higher than he ever had before, and slugged an incredible .847, still a single-season record. The Polo Grounds was much more accommodating to lefthanded longball hitters than Fenway Park, and the new Yankee fell in love with the place.

In September 1920 a Carl Mays pitch struck Cleveland shortstop Ray Chapman on the head, and he died several days later. About the same time the facts concerning the 1919 World Series "Black Sox Scandal" were made public. Both events altered baseball forever. In response to Chapman's death, baseball changed its rules for 1921. Scuffed, dirty, and battered balls were removed from play, and pitchers were no longer allowed to damage or tamper with the ball to gain an edge.

Ruth took advantage of the white, undoctored baseballs to rip 59 homers, drive in 171 runs, and score 177 times. The Yankees won the pennant for the first of three straight seasons. Still only 26 years old, Ruth hit his 137th career homer, surpassing the previous lifetime record of Roger Connor.

Ruth ushered in a new era of power in baseball, winning back the fans that had been soured by the Black Sox Scandal. He capitalized on his fame, planning a postseason barnstorming tour featuring himself and some other stars. But Commissioner Kenesaw Mountain Landis, trying to establish the World Series as the definitive postseason event, warned Ruth against his plans.

Several of the players who had signed up for the tour backed out, but Ruth and teammate Bob Meusel were defiant. Landis suspended both for the first six weeks of the 1922 season. Ruth returned in a surly mood, squabbled with umpires, and was suspended three times before the season ended. Appearing in fewer than 100 games, Ruth hit "only" 35 homers and drove in 99 runs. It was the first season since 1917 that he had not led the league in home runs. He would fail to lead the league only once more in the next nine years.

In 1923 the Yankees opened their glorious new park, Yankee Stadium, and sportswriter Fred Lieb was quick to dub it "The House that Ruth Built." On Opening Day, in front of a then-record 74,200 fans, Ruth provided the Yankees' margin of victory with a three-run homer. Babe liked his new digs. He led the league in runs, homers, RBIs, walks, and slugging and on-base averages, just as he had in 1920 and 1921. More importantly, in 1923 the Yankees claimed their first world championship, beating the Giants in the Series after losing the two previous years.

In 1925 Ruth appeared at training camp in awful shape. He'd spent weeks in Arkansas taking baths and exercising during the day, but had been burning the candle all night. After collapsing several times on the train ride back north he was operated on for an "intestinal abscess."

Amid speculation about the cause of Ruth's illness, one sportswriter conjured up a story that Ruth had simply eaten too many hot dogs and had drunk too much soda pop. As a result, the slugger's malady became known as "The Bellyache Heard 'Round the World." But given Ruth's cast-iron stomach, the explanation seemed unlikely. Ruth didn't leave the hospital for seven weeks and didn't play in a game for the Yanks until June 1.

After Ruth returned to the game Yankees manager Miller Huggins finally had to put his foot down about Ruth's carousing. He suspended Ruth and fined him $5,000, 10 percent of his annual salary. Ruth had to apologize to be reinstated. At first he refused and tried to have Huggins fired, but management backed the field boss.

The Yankees finished in seventh place, and many felt Ruth's career was over at age 31. But in 1926 the Babe went back to the gym and showed up for spring training weighing a lithe 212 pounds. In addition, the Yanks found a new first baseman, Lou Gehrig, and he and Ruth set off on a seven-year tear the likes of which the sport had never seen—and probably will never see again. During that span the Ruth–Gehrig duo averaged 84 homers and 303 RBIs a year. In 1927 Ruth slugged 60 home runs, a feat that was among his proudest achievements. ("Let's see someone top that," he boasted; it took 34 years.) Gehrig, meanwhile, finished second to the Babe in AL home runs each season from 1927 to 1931.

The Yanks won pennants in 1926, 1927, 1928, and 1932. They swept the World Series in three of those seasons, with Ruth batting .400, .625, and .333 and slugging .800, 1.375, and .733 in postseason play.

The 1932 World Series was a nasty one. Players from the Cubs and Yankees traded one insult after another. Putting on a show in batting practice before Game 3, Ruth hollered his opinion of Wrigley Field to the Cubs saying, "I'd play for half my salary to hit in this dump all year."

The Yankees were down, 4–3, in the fifth inning of that game when Ruth came to bat against Cubs pitcher Charlie Root. When Ruth took strike one, he held up one finger to indicate he knew the count. He repeated the gesture on the second strike. With one strike to go,

Ruth held up his bat to indicate he had a single strike left or he pointed to the center field bleachers to signal where he would send Root's next offering. Ruth then told catcher Gabby Hartnett, "It only takes one to hit it," and proceeded to wallop the ball deep into the center field bleachers.

Some who were at the game say that Ruth "called his shot," announcing he would hit a home run on the next pitch to center field. Others refused to believe this, including pitcher Root, who stated he would have put that pitch in Ruth's ear if the Babe had done such a thing. Regardless of the facts, the called shot became a part of baseball lore. Of the Babe's countless clouts from exhibitions to World Series games, it is arguably his most famous.

In 1933, with Ruth aging and Gehrig slumping, the Yankees fell to second place. Ruth seldom played an entire game that season or the next, as he was now being removed for defensive reasons in the late innings. His playing career was winding down, and Ruth wanted to become the manager of the Yankees. They suggested he manage their Newark Bears International League farm club to get some experience. He refused. The Tigers were considering making Ruth their manager, but, in typical fashion, Ruth failed to show up for a meeting with Detroit owner Frank Navin.

After the 1934 season Ruth led a group of Americans who toured Japan. The Japanese were amazed by the power and antics of the superstar. But the Yankees didn't sign him for 1935. The Boston Braves offered Ruth what they described as a three-level position: player, assistant manager, and vice president. The last two were a sham. Boston was only trying to beef up attendance by having the overweight, aging legend around.

By this time Ruth wasn't a pretty sight. Elbie Fletcher, a Braves rookie that year, said, "We were all awed by his presence. He still had that marvelous swing, and what a beautiful follow-through! But he was 40 years old. He couldn't run, he could hardly bend down for a ball, and of course he couldn't hit the way he used to. It was sad watching those great skills fade away. To see it happening to Babe Ruth, to see Babe Ruth struggling on a ballfield, well, that's when you realize we're all mortal and nothing lasts forever."

On May 25, 1935, in Pittsburgh, Ruth homered in his first two trips to the plate, singled in his third appearance, and in the seventh inning hit a ball over the right field roof of Forbes Field. It was his final major league home run, and it was, typically, a monster shot. Some consider his blast the longest ball ever hit at Forbes Field. He played in only a handful of games after that before retiring.

Ruth spent the final 13 years of his life waiting for the call to become a manager, but it never came. The closest he got was a position as a coach with the Brooklyn Dodgers in 1938. But when the club's managerial post opened the next year Leo Durocher got it, and Ruth wasn't rehired.

Until he developed throat cancer in 1946 Babe lived a comfortable life, cashing in on the investments his business manager, Christy Walsh, had made for him. Ruth was also active in the Ford Junior Legion baseball program. When he died in 1948, thousands paid their respects to the great slugger as his body lay in state at Yankee Stadium.

He died as the owner of 56 major league batting records, plus 10 AL marks. His record of 60 home runs in a single season was not surpassed until Roger Maris hit 61 in 1961. Ruth's lifetime 714 home run mark was not touched until Henry Aaron broke it in 1974 after nearly 3,000 more at bats than Ruth had needed to accomplish the feat. Ruth's average of one home run for every 11.76 at bats was for long the best in major league history—and may one day (as Mark McGwire plays through his career) be the best again.

Ruth's legacy went beyond baseball statistics. Because Ruth was well paid by the end of his career, he helped increase salaries for all players. In 1914, as a rookie in Baltimore, he earned $600, and by 1930 he was up to $80,000. When someone pointed out to Ruth that he was earning $5,000 more than President Herbert Hoover's annual salary, Ruth is said to have replied, "So what? I had a better year than he did."

Dick Ruthven

Ruthven, Richard David **P**

1973–86 B:3/27/1951, Sacramento, CA Deb:4/17/1973, PHI NL BR/TR 6'3", 190

W	L	PCT	G	SH	IP	BB	SO	ERA
123	127	.492	355	17	2109	767	1145	4.14

Dick Ruthven began his professional career at the major league level. The Phillies were in need of pitching help and thrust the 22-year-old college All-America on the mound in 1973. He held his own on a staff that featured Steve Carlton and a mixture of middle-of-the-road veterans. In December 1975 the Phils sent Ruthven to the White Sox with righthander Roy Thomas and infielder Alan Bannister for southpaw Jim Kaat and shortstop Mike Buskey. The Sox then turned around and shipped Ruthven to the Braves.

Ruthven emerged as the second man on Atlanta's staff behind Phil Niekro. Ruthven made the All Star team in 1976, but lost a league-high 17 games. In June 1978 the Braves sent him back to the Phillies for righthanded reliever Gene Garber.

In Ruthven's absence, the Phillies had become a playoff contender. In 1980 he won a career-high 17 games, and earned the win in relief in wild Game 5 of the Championship Series with Houston. In a game that featured late heroics from both sides, Ruthven nailed down the final out that put Philadelphia in the World Series for the first time in 30 years. He then pitched nine solid innings in Game 4 of the World Series; Philadelphia lost the game in the 10th, but won their first-ever world championship in six games.

In May 1983 Ruthven was traded to the Cubs for lefthanded relief pitcher Willie Hernandez. In Chicago his career quickly unraveled, as he went 10–17 in three seasons before being released in 1986.

Jimmy Ryan

Ryan, James Edward **OF**

1885–1900, 1902–03 B:2/11/1863, Clinton, MA
D:10/26/1923, Chicago, IL Deb: 10/8/1885, CHI NL
BR/TL 5'9", 162

G	AB	R	H	HR	RBI	OBP	SLG	AVG
2012	8164	1642	2502	118	1093	.374	.444	.306

Jimmy Ryan was one of baseball's better offensive performers of the 1890s. He went from Holy Cross College to the Eastern League in 1885. He played both the outfield and shortstop, an oddity considering that he threw lefthanded. Later that season, the Chicago White Stockings purchased his contract.

In 1886 manager Cap Anson began playing Ryan regularly in right field. Ryan batted over .300 and contributed to Chicago's second consecutive National League pennant. The following year Ryan moved to center field, a transition made easier by his terrific foot speed. From 1888 to 1890 Ryan batted .307 with a minimum of 30 stolen bases each season. In 1888 he put together one of his finest seasons, leading the NL in hits, home runs, doubles, and total bases.

In 1890 the lure of a better contract from the Players' League sent Ryan to Chicago's entry in the new league. Although he batted .340, the Players' League folded after one season. Ryan returned to Anson's club, where he played all three outfield positions. Ryan reached a career high with a .361 batting average in 1894. He did not bat below .300 for the rest of the decade.

Although Ryan's hitting and power made him a dangerous leadoff man, he was not well liked by Anson; the manager felt Ryan had tried to undermine his authority. In 1900 Ryan's average fell by 24 points, resulting in his release. Ryan decided to continue his career in the minor leagues, joining St. Paul as player-manager.

His success with the bat in the Western League resulted in a return ticket to the major leagues. He joined Washington in 1902 and batted .320 in 120 games. Ryan slumped to .249 in his final major league campaign, but still reached 100 hits for the 17th consecutive season as a big league player. He accumulated impressive totals in several categories, including stolen bases (418).

After managing briefly in the minors, Ryan left baseball completely. He remained in Chicago, where he worked in the assessor's office before becoming a deputy sheriff. He died suddenly from heart failure in 1923.

Nolan Ryan

Ryan, Lynn Nolan **P**

1966, 1968–93 B:1/31/1947, Refugio, TX
Deb:9/11/1966, NY NL BR/TR 6'2", 195

W	L	PCT	G	SH	IP	BB	SO	ERA
324	292	.526	807	61	5386	2795	5714	3.19

Major league baseball's all-time strikeout leader, with 5,714, Nolan Ryan hurled a record seven no-hitters during his remarkable 27-year career. A physical marvel, he was still throwing fastballs more than 90 miles per hour in his final year, at age 46. "When I was eight years old I knew I could throw a ball past batters," Ryan once said. But it was not until late in his career that Ryan learned how to hit a catcher's glove. The righthander walked a major league record 2,795 batters and lost 292 games, the third most in major league history, despite having one of the best fastballs (regularly clocked at more than 100 mph in his prime) and one of the best curveballs ever.

Although the Alvin, Texas, native once struck out 19 players in a seven-inning high school game, he was not chosen until the 10th round of the June 1965 draft, when the New York Mets decided to take a chance on him. In 1965 Ryan topped the Appalachian League in hit batsmen. In 1966, his first full year in the minor leagues, he struck out 272 batters in 183 innings at Greenville of the Western Carolina League and led the league in wins with 17. Not surprisingly, he was named WCL Pitcher of the Year. Later in the year he was promoted to Williamsport of the

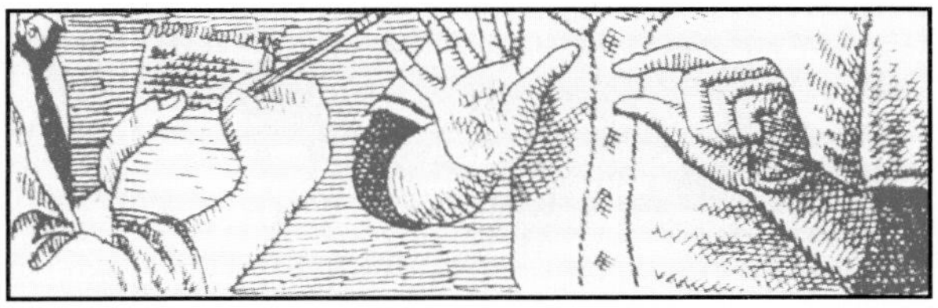

Eastern League. In one game he struck out 21 Pawtucket batters in 9⅓ innings.

Ryan made two appearances with the Mets in 1966, going 0–1 with a 15.00 ERA. He spent the first six months of 1967 in the army reserves, returned with tendonitis in his right elbow, and spent the rest of the year in the minors. In 1968, Ryan's first full season with New York, he struck out 133 batters in 134 innings, including a then-club record 14 Reds on May 18. The following season Ryan went 6–3 with a 3.53 ERA and recorded the first official save in Mets history. He pitched seven innings in relief in Game 3 of the Championship Series to clinch the Mets' first pennant. Ryan appeared in his only World Series that year, pitching 2⅓ innings of scoreless relief to earn a save in Game 3; Tommie Agee bailed him out of a bases-loaded jam with his second fantastic catch of the game.

In 1970 and 1971 Ryan struggled with his control. He walked 97 batters in 132 innings while going 7–11 in 1970, and walked 116 in 152 innings in 1971, when he went 10–14.

On December 10, 1971, the Mets traded Ryan, whose career record up to that point was only 29–38, to the California Angels along with three other players for Jim Fregosi. It was arguably the best trade in Angels history.

Remarkably, Ryan considered quitting baseball before his career in California even got started. Ryan, who had struggled in spring training, was upset with the baseball labor situation. "That was the year of the first [players'] strike and if it had gone on another week I would have quit and gone back to Alvin. And once I would have done that, I wouldn't have come back. I would have gotten a job as a laborer, and that would have been it," Ryan said later.

In eight years with the Angels, Ryan led the league in strikeouts seven times, five times recording more than 300 strikeouts. In 1973 he fanned a major league record 383. He retired as the franchise's all-time leader in wins, starts, and innings, but was later passed by Chuck Finley in those departments. Through 1999 no one was close to Ryan's 40 shutouts, 156 complete games, and 2,416 strikeouts as an Angel. He was also the only Angel with multiple no-hitters.

"The Ryan Express" pitched two no-hitters in 1973. On May 15 at Kansas City, Ryan fanned 12 Royals, including at least one in every inning except the fifth. Exactly two months later, Ryan no-hit the Tigers in Detroit, becoming the fifth man in major league history to throw two no-hitters in a season. He finished that gem with 17 strikeouts.

Ryan tossed his third no-hitter on September 24, 1974, at Anaheim, when he struck out 15 and survived eight walks to beat the Twins, 4–0. He went 22–16 that season with a 2.89 ERA and a league-leading 367 strikeouts. Only four other American League pitchers had won 20 games on a last-place team; it was also Ryan's only career 20-win season.

Hampered by arm trouble in 1975, Ryan won only 14 games but tied Sandy Koufax for the most career no-hitters when he shut down the Orioles on June 1. During the next four seasons Ryan's overall record with the Angels was a mediocre 62–61. He was bothered by injuries, and in three of those four seasons led the league in bases on balls.

In November 1979 the Astros signed free agent Ryan to a $4.5 million, four-year contract. Ryan was more than happy to return home and pitch. "At one point I was called by an old friend from the Angels who wanted to know what it would take to get me to stay," Ryan recalled. "I basically told him it would take [general manager] Buzzie Bavasi's leaving. I didn't want to play for the man or be associated with him."

While with the Angels, Ryan's strikeout ratio had been consistently better than one per inning, but he had also averaged more than four walks per game. In his first six years with Houston he harnessed his stuff, reduced both his strikeouts and walks, and suddenly became a winning pitcher. In 1980 and 1981 Ryan led the Astros to three postseason appearances. He finished the strike-shortened 1981 season with a league-best 1.69 ERA. He pitched a record fifth no-hitter against the Dodgers on September 26, 1981. In that year's special NL West Division Championship Series, Ryan was 1–1 with a 1.80 ERA, but he lost Game 5 to Los Angeles, 4–0.

On April 27, 1983, Ryan struck out Montreal's Brad Mills to break Walter Johnson's career strikeout record of 3,509. In 1986 Ryan once again began to strike out more than one batter an inning, but he kept his walks down.

After a 12–8 campaign in 1986 and another appearance in the NLCS, in 1987 Ryan had one of the most unlucky seasons in the annals of pitching. He struck out 270 batters in 211 innings with a league-leading 2.76 ERA. Yet, inexplicably, his record for the season was a disappointing 8–16. As a result, he became the first pitcher not to win the Cy Young Award after leading the league in strikeouts and ERA.

Ryan led the league in strikeouts again in 1988 despite missing the last two weeks of the season because of a hamstring injury. After the season the Astros offered him a contract with a 20-percent salary cut. On December 7, 1988, Ryan signed as a free agent with the Texas Rangers. In Arlington Ryan went from great pitcher to baseball legend.

In his first season with the Rangers, at age 42, Ryan led the majors in strikeouts and ranked among American League leaders in innings, ERA, and wins. He pitched a pair of one-hit complete games and carried five different no-hitters into the eighth inning or later, losing two in the ninth. On August 22 Ryan fanned Oakland's Rickey Henderson for his 5,000th strikeout.

Ryan's adherence to a grueling physical fitness routine paid off in a career longer than any other power pitcher's. In 1990, at age 43, he became the oldest pitcher to throw a no-hitter by beating Oakland, 5–0, on June 11. The following month he became the 20th pitcher to win 300 games and the fourth-oldest to accomplish that feat. In 1991 Ryan ranked third in the league with 203 strikeouts, compiled the league's fifth-best ERA, and tied for the seventh-highest winning percentage. As the major leagues' oldest player at age 44, Ryan pitched his seventh no-hitter on May 1. He recorded his 5,500th strikeout on September 30.

Although Ryan was still capable of throwing hard, his stamina began to give out in 1991 and a series of nagging injuries reduced his playing time in his final two years. On September 22, 1993, Ryan faced only six Mariners batters before hurting his right elbow and leaving the last major league game of his great career.

His major league record 5,714 strikeouts exceed Steve Carlton's second-place total by an amazing 1,578. During his career Ryan struck out 49 Most Valuable Players and 21 Hall of Famers. His strikeout victims included Hank Aaron, Roberto Clemente, Bobby Bonds, Barry Bonds, Ken Griffey, Sr., and Ken Griffey, Jr.

Popular nationwide for his amazing feats, Ryan is a regional hero in his native Texas, where he owns three cattle ranches. He wrote an autobiography titled *Throwing Heat.* He was elected to the Hall of Fame in 1999, his first year of eligibility. Later that year he was selected for baseball's All-Century Team; he received more votes from fans than any other pitcher.

Bret Saberhagen

Saberhagen, Bret William **P**

1984–95, 1997–* B: 4/11/1964, Chicago Heights, IL
Deb: 4/4/1984, KC AL BR/TR 6'1", 195

W	L	PCT	G	SH	IP	BB	SO	ERA
166	115	.591	396	16	2547^{2}	471	1705	3.33

Bret Saberhagen, just 21 years old, stared down the St. Louis Cardinals and helped the Kansas City Royals win the 1985 World Series. Saberhagen put together a 20–6 record, 3.48 ERA, 158 strikeouts, and just 38 walks in his first full season as a starter in the major leagues. He was less than spectacular, however, in the American League Championship Series. He failed to make it out of the fifth inning in either of his starts against the Toronto Blue Jays. The Royals still battled back from a three-games-to-one deficit to knock off Toronto.

By the time he took the mound in Game 3 of the World Series, Kansas City had already lost two home games. Saberhagen allowed only one run on six hits in a complete-game victory in St. Louis. The Royals lost the following night to trail three games to one, but they rallied to take the next two games and force a seventh game. Saberhagen pitched a five-hit shutout and even scored a run in Kansas City's 11–0 rout in Game 7. He walked away with Most Valuable Player honors for the Series. He was named the American League Cy Young Award winner less than a month later.

Saberhagen began an odd pattern of having a great season in odd numbered years, and struggling in even-numbered years. He was 7–12 in 1986, but his 18–10 record the following season earned him Comeback Player of the Year at the age of 23. He dipped below .500 in 1988, and rebounded the next season as the league leader in wins, ERA, complete games, and innings to snatch his second Cy Young trophy.

He went to the New York Mets in a blockbuster trade in 1992, but injuries and an unfortunate joke marred his time with the Mets. A 1993 bleach-spraying incident with reporters gained more notoriety than did Saberhagen's feat of achieving more wins (14) than walks (13) in 177 ⅓ innings in 1994.

The Colorado Rockies, hoping that his postseason experience would rub off on the third-year club, traded for Saberhagen in July 1995. He posted a 6.28 ERA in Denver, and lasted just four innings in his only playoff start. Shoulder injuries forced him to miss almost all of the next two years.

In 1998, however, Saberhagen re-emerged with the Boston Red Sox. He made 31 starts—his highest total in a decade—and won 15 games. He also received his second career Comeback Player of the Year Award. Despite three trips to the disabled list in 1999, Saberhagen won 10 games to help Boston reach the postseason for the second consecutive season.

Chris Sabo

Sabo, Christopher Andrew **3B**

1988–96 B:1/19/1962, Detroit, MI Deb:4/4/1988, CIN NL BR/TR, 6', 185

G	AB	R	H	HR	RBI	OBP	SLG	AVG
911	3354	494	898	116	426	.329	.445	.268

Although his career lasted only nine seasons, Chris Sabo made the All-Star team three times and twice led National League third basemen in fielding percentage. His quick hands and clutch hits made him an integral part of Cincinnati's infield.

A second-round selection in the June 1983 amateur draft, Sabo enjoyed an excellent rookie season five years later. He named NL Rookie of the Year in 1988, when he his .271 and stole a career-best 46 base. Capitalizing on hitting tips from Lou Piniella, then Cincinnati's manager, Sabo reached his offensive peak in 1991 with a .301 average, 26 home runs, and 88 RBIs.

As a key member of the 1990 Reds, Sabo batted .563 with two home runs against Oakland in the World Series as Cincinnati pulled off a shocking sweep of the favored A's. He was an NL All-Star in 1988, 1990, and 1991, starting at third for the NL in both 1990 and 1991.

Known for his hustling style of play, Sabo was also the first major leaguer to wear goggles. A fan favorite, he spent his first six seasons with the Reds before moving to the Orioles in 1994. He then played for the White Sox and Cardinals before returning to Cincinnati for his final season in 1996.

Ray Sadecki

Sadecki, Raymond Michael **P**

1960–77 B:12/26/1940, Kansas City, KS
Deb:5/19/1960, STL NL BL/TL 5'11", 180

W	L	PCT	G	SH	IP	BB	SO	ERA
135	131	.508	563	20	2500^{2}	922	1614	3.78

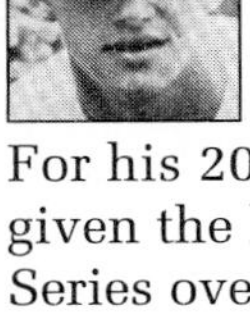

Raymond Michael Sadecki's promise earned him a large signing bonus from the Cardinals in the late 1950s. He rose to the top of the St. Louis pitching staff by 1964, his fifth year with the team. For his 20-win performance that season he was given the honor of starting Game 1 of the World Series over teammate Bob Gibson, who had won only 19 games. He faced aging "Chairman of the Board" Whitey Ford, but Sadecki got the first of his club's four World Series wins.

In 1965 Sadecki had a terrible year, but so did the entire St. Louis club. From world champions the previous season the club dropped to seventh place. As St. Louis players were sent elsewhere, Ray Sadecki was exchanged for a gem of a San Francisco first baseman named Orlando Cepeda. With the struggling Giants, Sadecki struggled too, but he also had some of his best seasons. One such year was 1968—although he won only 12 and lost 18, he finished the season with more than 200 strikeouts, a 2.91 ERA, and six shutouts. When his ERA climbed to 4.23 the next year, he was sent to the Mets.

Sadecki came to the Mets in 1970 as a fifth man in a four-man rotation, but his arm was tiring. By 1973 he was almost completely converted into a middle reliever, and with the additional rest his ERA was down in a respectable range for the third year in a row. His efforts helped the Mets to the National League crown, and in the World Series he recorded a save. Oakland knocked off New York in seven games.

In 1975 he went back to St. Louis and then floated around both leagues, playing for the Braves, the Royals, the Brewers, and the Mets again. He retired after the 1977 season with 135 big league wins.

Johnny Sain

Sain, John Franklin **P**

1942–55 B:9/25/1917, Havana, AR Deb:4/24/1942, BOS NL BR/TR 6'2", 200

W	L	PCT	G	SV	IP	BB	SO	ERA
139	116	.545	412	51	2125^{2}	619	910	3.49

Of all the jobs in major league baseball, pitching coach is one of the most difficult to evaluate. Pitchers will credit a coach with this or that "tip," but how much difference can the coach really make? Does the coach make the pitcher, or does the pitching staff make the coach? Like ballplayers, pitching coaches come in all sizes and strategies. There is the intense analyst (Mel Harder), the one-pitch instructor (Roger Craig with his split-finger fastball), the simplifier-motivator (Ray Miller), and the favorite uncle (George Bamberger).

Johnny Sain defied categories. No other coach succeeded with so many pitchers using so many different styles. He coached a number of hurlers who had never won 20 games in a season until he joined their team. And they would never win 20 again after he left. The pitchers included Whitey Ford, Ralph Terry, and Jim Bouton of the Yankees; Mudcat Grant and Jim Kaat of the Twins; Earl Wilson and Denny McLain of the Tigers; and Wilbur Wood and Stan Bahnsen of the White Sox. Dave Boswell and Jim Perry of Minnesota applied Sain's teachings and won 20 soon after he was gone, and Detroit's Mickey Lolich won 20 shortly after Sain left and gave the coach credit.

Although teaching the slider was one of Sain's specialties (learning the pitch rejuvenated Whitey Ford's career and helped McLain and Kaat), he taught much more. For one thing, he didn't believe that running was the key to good pitching, which endeared him to most hurlers immediately. He also was one of the first to have the next day's pitcher chart the hitters. He rarely visited the mound to talk to a pitcher and seldom spoke to one during the game, unless the pitcher asked a question. Sain believed in preparation and focus, so he spent his time getting pitchers ready and did not disturb them once they were on the mound.

"Pitching coaches don't change pitchers," Sain said. "We just stimulate their thinking." He stressed rehearsal and practice to make the correct moves automatic—part of the subconscious mind, as he described it. When he first met a pitcher, he would hit fungoes and watch how the pitcher threw the ball back to him. "That will generally be his natural way of throwing and the way he should pitch," Sain said.

Bouton called him "the greatest pitching coach who ever lived." In fact, one time when the Yankees wouldn't give Sain a $2,500 raise, causing him to quit, Bouton called and said he would have paid the $2,500 to keep Sain on the team. Mickey Lolich put it this way: "Johnny Sain loves pitchers. Maybe he doesn't love baseball so much, but he loves pitchers. Only he understands them."

Sain moved a lot and had a chance to work with plenty of different pitchers. He started as a coach with the Kansas City Athletics and worked with six other teams over the next three decades: 1961–63, New York Yankees; 1965–66, Minnesota Twins; 1967–69, Detroit Tigers; 1970, California Angels; 1971–75, Chicago White Sox; 1977 and 1985–86, Atlanta. Five of the teams he coached won pennants, although he frequently clashed with managers.

Like all experts, Sain believed completely in his way of doing things. Yankees manager Ralph Houk feared Sain was after his job. Old-school Detroit manager Mayo Smith couldn't figure out Sain's way of thinking. One day Sain had other business to attend to, and Smith made the pitchers run. When Sain returned, he asked Smith, "Are we going to go with what made this staff lead the league in complete games last year, or with what hasn't worked here in 25 years?" When Smith traded Dick Radatz, Sain's pet pupil, to Montreal, Sain quit.

As a pitcher himself, Sain believed in letting the batter hit the ball. He won 20 games four times, but three of those years he was also league leader in hits allowed. His father taught him the curve when he was a boy. He used the curve and slider to get to the majors in 1942, and in his first game he retired all nine men he faced. "I noticed they started taking me seriously," he said. But after 40 appearances Sain was drafted into the armed services and joined the navy.

Returning to the big leagues as a 28-year-old, he was eager to learn. He credited Casey Stengel and Billy Southworth, his first two managers in Boston, as major influences. An intelligent player, Sain knew how to help himself with the bat, both as a hitter and as a bunter. In his 11 years, he struck out only 20 times. In 1946 he barely missed no-hitting the Reds when a ninth-inning pop fly fell among a crowd of Braves. He finished that season 20–14, and his 24 complete games were the most by any National League pitcher.

The following year he and Warren Spahn became the workhorses of the Boston staff: each won 21 games, and no other Braves pitcher won 12. Sain also demonstrated his all-around skills as a .347 hitter.

In 1948 Spahn and Sain joined forces to pitch the Braves to the World Series, although the legendary refrain of "Spahn and Sain and pray for rain" was not entirely accurate. Vern Bickford also had a great year, going 11–5, and Bill Voiselle won 13 games. Sain led the league in wins, with 24, complete games, with 28, and innings pitched (Spahn was third). Sain also led the league in sacrifice hits, becoming the first pitcher to ever do so.

Sain was at the plate for the most controversial play of the 1948 World Series against Cleveland. In Game 1 Sain and Bob Feller had both been nearly unhittable into the eighth inning, allowing a total of four hits between them. With pinch runner Phil Masi on second in the last of the eighth, Feller spun and fired to Lou Boudreau, apparently picking Masi off, but the runner was called safe. The next batter, Tommy Holmes, singled in Masi with the game's only run. Cleveland came back to win the Series in six games.

In 1949 the veteran Braves collapsed under the weight of their age (only two of the 1948 regulars were under 31), and Sain fell to 10–17. Sain won 20 again in 1950, but a shoulder injury hampered his effectiveness the following year. On August 30, 1951, Sain, with a 5–13 record, was sent to the Yankees for $50,000. New York also threw in the erratic young arm of Lew Burdette.

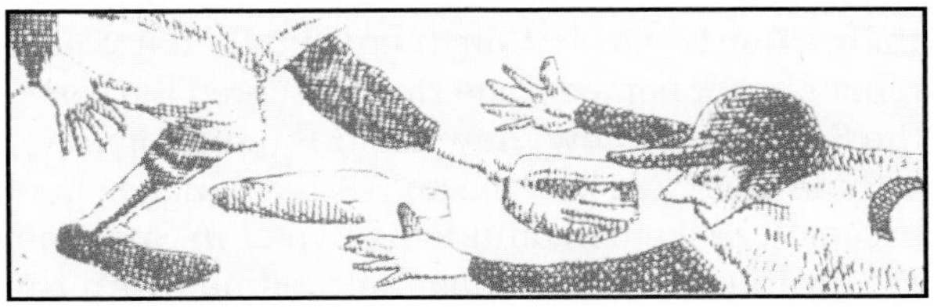

Sain appeared in only seven games for the Yanks at the tail end of the season, but his 2–1 record was deemed important enough by his teammates to earn him a full World Series share. Sain became a vital cog for Casey Stengel's creatively managed team. He won 11 games in 1952 and 14 in 1953 as a swingman. Stengel even used him as a pinch hitter. Once Sain batted for Joe Collins, who already had two hits in the game, and drove a liner over Minnie Minoso's head in left field to drive in the winning run.

Between the 1951 and 1952 seasons Sain's shoulder problem persisted, so he tried a new X-ray therapy. The experimental treatment worked so well for Sain that he became an advocate for it. At Sain's urging, Eddie Lopat tried it, too. Later, Whitey Ford subjected himself to the treatment—five times. Mel Stottlemyre had it done six times.

Sain made a career-high 45 appearances in 1954, all in relief, and he led the league with 22 saves. He and Enos Slaughter were traded to the Kansas City A's in May 1955, and Sain finished his playing career that year. In 1959 he started an even more successful career as a thinking man's pitching coach.

Slim Sallee

Sallee, Harry Franklin **P**

1908-21 B:2/3/1885, Higginsport, OH D:3/23/1950, Higginsport, OH Deb:4/16/1908 STL NL BL/TL 6'3", 180

W	L	PCT	G	SV	IP	BB	SO	ERA
174	143	.549	476	36	2821^{2}	573	836	2.56

Slim Sallee was a talented pitcher with an affinity for the bottle. Teams gave up on him three times, but he helped his new team win a pennant each time. A junkballer with impeccable control, Sallee had more wins (21) than walks (20) for the 1919 pennant-winning Cincinnati Reds.

"Scatter" started his career away from the pennant hunt. He won 68 games from 1911 to 1914 even though the St. Louis Cardinals finished in the first division just once in that span. After Sallee recorded a 3.15 ERA as a rookie in 1908, his ERA did not reach 3.00 again for a full season until 1920. He also pitched frequently out of the bullpen; he led the National League in saves three times.

In the midst of another poor season by the Cardinals, Sallee was sold to the New York Giants in July 1916. He helped the Giants capture the National League pennant in 1917 by going 18–7 with a sparkling 2.17 ERA. After an 8–8 season, the Giants lost their patience with Sallee. The Reds grabbed the southpaw off waivers in March 1919. Sallee had a 2.06 ERA and led the staff with a 21–7 record. He pitched twice in the best-of-nine World Series against the heavily-favored Chicago White Sox. Sallee hurled a complete-game victory over Lefty Williams in Game 2. He lost Game 7 to Eddie Cicotte, but the Reds won the tainted Series the next day. Almost a year after the Series was over eight members of the "Black Sox" were indicted for attempted to fix the Series.

When the Reds lost patience with Sallee, the Giants claimed him off waivers in September 1920. Although Sallee went 6–4 in relief for the NL champions in his final season, he did not pitch in the 1921 World Series.

Tim Salmon

Salmon, Timothy James **OF–DH**

1992–* B:8/24/1968, Long Beach, CA Deb:8/21/1992, CAL AL BR/TR 6'3", 220

G	AB	R	H	HR	RBI	OBP	SLG	AVG
955	3483	608	1015	196	660	.397	.524	.291

Three years before he was named American League Rookie of the Year, Tim Salmon's baseball career was nearly ended by an errant pitch. Salmon took a pitch flush on the jaw while playing for Class A Palm Springs in 1990. Although he required the services of a plastic surgeon, he was back in uniform three months after the injury.

Far from being intimidated by the incident, Salmon gained a new sense of appreciation for the opportunity to play baseball—and a new approach to his craft. "I recognized that I had to take my at bats more seriously," he said years later. "Sometimes you get so caught up in your swing, your stance...you're focused on everything except the ball. I figured out this is a dangerous game, that I need to focus on seeing the ball and hitting the ball."

Salmon earned a late-season call-up to the Angels in 1992, and was named the AL's top rookie a year later with a .283 average, 31 home runs, and 95 RBIs. In 1995 he batted .330 with 34 homers and 105 RBIs. He followed that with 129 RBIs in 1997. Foot and wrist injuries hampered him in 1998 and 1999, but he remained one of the team's main power threats.

Juan Samuel

Samuel, Juan Milton **2B–OF**

1983–98 B:12/9/1960, San Pedro de Macoris, Dominican Republic Deb:8/24/1983, PHI NL BR/TR, 5'11", 175

G	AB	R	H	HR	RBI	OBP	SLG	AVG
1720	6081	873	1578	161	703	.317	.420	.259

Juan Samuel came to the Philadelphia Phillies as a hitter boasting power and speed, capable of batting first or third in the lineup, but he left the game as a utility player who never seemed to have reach his potential. In 1984, his first full season, Samuel was named National League Rookie Player of the Year by *The Sporting News* and made the first of two trips to the All-Star Game. From the leadoff spot, he set an NL record with 701 at bats while hitting .272 with 15 home runs, 69 runs batted in, and 72 stolen bases—a rookie record bested by Vince Coleman the following year. Samuel also led the league with 168 strikeouts and hurt the defense with 33 errors at second base.

Despite being the only man to reach double digits in doubles, triples, homers, and steals in each of his first four seasons, Samuel proved ill suited to the leadoff spot. He continued to strike out at an alarming rate and failed to develop the discipline necessary to draw walks, negating his speed. His career on-base percentage was only .317.

Frustrated with his development at second base, the Phillies finally moved Samuel to the outfield, only to watch his offense suffer. Philadelphia sent him to the Mets in 1989 in a midseason trade that would lay the foundation of the Philadelphia team that won the pennant four years later. It brought the Phils Lenny Dykstra, soon to be the league's top leadoff man, and reliever Roger McDowell. Samuel never even played a full season in New York.

The Mets tried him as a leadoff hitter and center fielder, but Samuel was disappointing in both roles and traded after the 1989 season. He made the All-Star team with the Dodgers in a resurgent 1991 season, then embarked on a journeyman's career. From 1992 to 1995 he played for the Reds, Tigers, and Royals (twice). He spent his final three seasons with the Blue Jays.

Ryne Sandberg

Sandberg, Ryne Dee **2B–3B**

1981–94, 1996–97 B:9/18/1959, Spokane, WA Deb:9/2/1981, PHI NL BR/TR 6'2", 180

G	AB	R	H	HR	RBI	OBP	SLG	AVG
2164	8385	1318	2386	282	1061	.347	.452	.285

Ryne Sandberg not only had incredible power for a second baseman, he was also one of the steadiest fielders to ever play the position. He retired in 1997 with the most home runs (277) by a second baseman, and the highest fielding average (.989) of anyone that played more than 800 games at the position.

From birth, Sandberg seemed destined to play baseball. His parents were watching a New York Yankees game while trying to agree on a name for their soon-to-arrive fourth child; when a young relief pitcher named Ryne Duren entered the game, the Sandbergs knew they found the right name.

Ryne Sandberg became an All-State high school baseball, basketball, and football star in Spokane, Washington. *Parade* magazine named him the starting quarterback on its All-America team. Nebraska and Oklahoma recruited him as a college quarterback, but Sandberg chose baseball instead.

The Philadelphia Phillies selected Sandberg in the 20th round of the 1978 draft. He was a slick-fielding shortstop in the minor leagues, leading his league in assists and double plays three times. He appeared in 13 games for the Phillies in September 1981. The Phillies projected Sandberg as a third baseman, and the youngster had little chance of unseating All-Star Mike Schmidt.

In January 1982 the Phillies traded Sandberg and shortstop Larry Bowa to Chicago for shortstop Ivan DeJesus. Sandberg's scouting report in the *Chicago Tribune* read, "good speed but a light bat." That summation seemed prophetic when the 22-year-old rookie third baseman managed only one hit in his first 32 trips to the plate. Overcoming the slow start, he finished with a .271 batting average; Sandberg also led the team in stolen bases (32) and runs scored (103).

Over the winter the Cubs signed third baseman Ron Cey, causing Sandberg to move to second base. Intentional or not, the switch proved brilliant. In 1983 Sandberg began a record nine-year run as the Gold Glove winner at second base. He played four full seasons without a throwing error.

In 1984, his third season in the majors, Sandberg and the Cubs enjoyed a fairy tale year. He batted a career-high .314, stole 32 bases, led the majors with 114 runs scored, and tied for the major league lead with 19 triples. He also continued his steady play in the field. He had a 61-game errorless streak, committing just six errors all season. He made the first of 10 consecutive trips to the All-Star Game. Sandberg's heroics propelled the Cubs into the postseason for the first time since 1945. He was named National League Most Valuable Player, becoming the first Cub to win the award since Hall of Fame shortstop Ernie Banks in 1959—the year Ryne Sandberg was born.

"Ryno" credited Cubs manager Jim Frey for his breakthrough season. "I didn't feel that I belonged, that I was good enough to play," Sandberg said. "Jim Frey gave me confidence." At the start of the 1984 season, Frey told his insecure second baseman to just relax and start swinging for the fences.

The home runs came. He hit 26 in 1985, 30 in 1989, and a league-leading 40 in 1990. He became the first second baseman to lead the National League in homers since Rogers Hornsby in 1925. That season Sandberg also set a record with 123 consecutive errorless games. All the while he was an outstanding baserunner; he stole 20 or more bases nine times (344 for his career), and scored 100 or more runs six times

In 1993 Sandberg batted .300 for the third time in four years, but the following season started slowly. He endured a 1-for-28 slump early in the season and by mid-June was hitting .238, some 50 points below his major league average

On June 13, 1994, the 34-year-old Sandberg announced he was retiring because, "I am certainly not the type of person who can ask the Cubs organization and the Chicago Cubs fans to pay my salary when I am not happy with my mental approach and my performance." After skipping the 1994 strike and the abbreviated 1995 season, Sandberg found that he missed baseball.

He returned to the Cubs in 1996 and quickly regained his power stroke, hitting 25 home runs and driving in 92 runs. While his range was not what it once was, he still committed just six errors in 1,234 innings. By the end of the 1997 season, however, he was no longer able to produce at a level he expected of himself. He bowed out amid a thunderous ovation at Wrigley Field.

Deion Sanders

Sanders, Deion Luwynn **OF**

1989–95, 1997, * B:8/9/1967, Ft. Myers, FL
Deb:5/31/1989, NY AL BL/TL 6'1", 195

G	AB	R	H	HR	RBI	OBP	SLG	AVG
609	2048	302	545	38	164	.324	.398	.266

When he put his mind to it, Deion Sanders was a good baseball player; the problem was, his mind turned to football every September. He was a two-sport player for eight seasons until the risk of injury led him to play football exclusively.

The Kansas City Royals drafted Sanders out of high school, but he opted for Florida State. He was a three-sport star at FSU: track and field (he qualified for the 1988 Olympic trials as a sprinter), baseball (he played center field for the College World Series runner-up in 1986), and football (he played on four bowl-game winners). He was a football All-America twice and won the Jim Thorpe Award as the nation's best defensive back.

The New York Yankees signed Sanders as a 30th-round choice in 1988. The next year "Prime Time" (a name he gave himself) was drafted by the Atlanta Falcons to play football. In September 1989 he became the first player to hit a home run and score a touchdown as a professional in the same week. He later became the first person to play in both a Super Bowl and a World Series. In postseason play he twice won Super Bowl rings, and batted .533 in his lone World Series with the Atlanta Braves in 1992.

His only 100-game season in baseball was 1997, when he stole a career-best 56 bases for the Cincinnati Reds. He concentrated solely on football after that season, but he decided to give baseball another shot in spring training 2000.

Scott Sanderson

Sanderson, Scott Douglas **P**

1978–96 B:7/22/1956, Dearborn, MI Deb:8/6/1978, MON NL BR/TR 6'5", 200

W	L	PCT	G	SH	IP	BB	SO	ERA
163	143	.533	472	14	2561^{2}	625	1611	3.84

Scott Sanderson suffered through back, elbow, shoulder, thumb, and knee injuries, yet lasted 19 seasons with seven teams. After beginning his career as a power pitcher and would-be ace of Montreal's staff, Sanderson evolved into a finesse pitcher who managed to give his employers a high number of quality starts each season. In his first five years with the Expos, Sanderson intimidated batters with his size, 95-mph fastball, and aggressive style. In 1980, when he mixed in his slow curve and slider, he racked up a 16 wins and a 3.11 ERA.

Traded to the Cubs in 1983, Sanderson suffered a series of injuries. After he underwent major back surgery in 1989, his fastball all but vanished, and his career was in jeopardy. Sanderson, though, learned a new pitch, the forkball, and—despite delaying games with his deliberate style—he kept hitters off balance with a change of speed and excellent control. Although his best season with Chicago was an 11–9 record in 1989, he was a contributing member of the staff as the Cubs won the National League East in both 1984 and 1989. Sanderson and Rick Sutcliffe were the first major leaguers since World War II to pitch for the Cubs in two separate postseasons.

Sanderson moved on to Oakland in 1990, and responded with his most successful season. He won 17 games for the Athletics, and pitched in his only World Series. He then joined the Yankees in 1991, winning 16 games and earning his only invitation to the All-Star Game. Continually playing through pain and plagued by the home run ball, he pitched for the Angels, Giants, and White Sox over his final four seasons.

Jack Sanford

Sanford, John Stanley **P**

1956–67 B:5/18/1929, Wellesley Hills, MA D:3/7/2000, Beckley, WV Deb:9/16/1956, PHI NL BR/TR 6', 190

W	L	PCT	G	SH	IP	BB	SO	ERA
137	101	.576	388	14	2049^{1}	737	1182	3.69

Strikeout artist Jack Sanford developed into a 24-game winner and the ace of the San Francisco Giants' 1962 pennant-winning club. He accomplished this only five years after bursting onto the scene in 1957 as National League Rookie of the Year. Sanford began his ball career with a tryout for the Boston Braves. He wasn't signed, but later he hooked up with the Phillies. He had an undistinguished seven-year stint in the minor leagues, including a 1–6 mark with a 7.06 ERA at one stop and a 2–9 slate with a 7.28 ERA at another.

After spending 1955 and virtually all of 1956 in the service, Sanford beat out Phillies teammate Ed Bouchee for Rookie of the Year honors the following season. He was 19–8 and led the league in strikeouts as well as wild pitches. He fell off to 10–13 in 1958, was traded to the Giants in 1959, and bounced back to win 15 games for San Francisco that season. In April he one-hit the Cardinals, allowing only Stan Musial's pinch-hit seventh-inning single. In 1960 Sanford won only 12 games, but six were shutouts—the best mark in the league.

After that season the Giants launched a program to remake the 31-year-old pitcher. "Jack Sanford was a fastball pitcher," recalled his manager, Alvin Dark. "The average hitter's favorite pitch is a fastball over the plate, thigh-high to armpits. He can handle that. In the spring of 1961 [we] made Sanford throw a slider or a curve on the first pitch to every hitter he faced, even if it meant getting behind. I wanted him to be able to get those pitches over when the hitter was thinking fastball." The strategy worked. In 1962 Sanford won 24 while losing only seven. He had 16 straight victories and finished second to Dodgers hurler Don Drysdale for the Cy Young Award.

In that fall's World Series against the Yankees, Sanford won Game 2 with a three-hit shutout. In Game 5 he struck out 10 but lost to Ralph Terry and then lost to Terry again, 1–0, in Game 7. After the Series, the Yankees admitted they had underestimated Sanford. "We were told he was a six-or seven-inning pitcher," Mickey Mantle said. "We figured if we kept it close, Sanford would lose his stuff by the eighth." Yankees manager Ralph Houk said, "We were wrong about Sanford. He's one heck of a pitcher." Said Sanford, who suffered from a bad cold during the Series, "When you pitch a Series shutout against the Yankees, you can't complain about anything. I just kept blowing my nose and pitching strikes."

In 1964 Sanford suffered an injury to his right shoulder, and the resulting problems continued into 1965. That July he underwent surgery to correct circulatory problems in the shoulder. Sold to the Angels in 1965, he was 13–7 for California in 1966 and led the American League in relief wins.

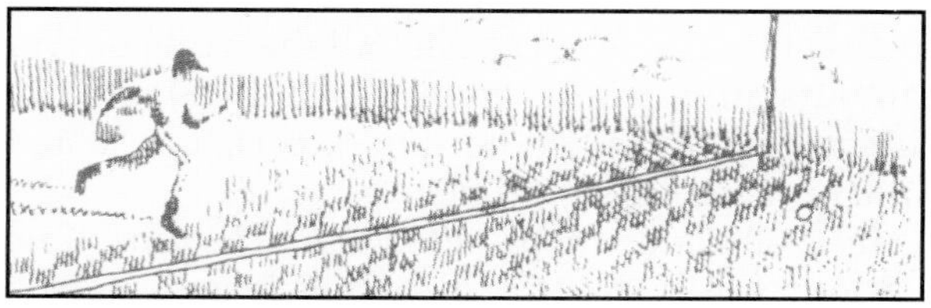

Sent to Kansas City in 1967, he retired at season's end. Sanford became a golf pro at a West Palm Beach, Florida, country club. He later scouted for the Orioles.

Manny Sanguillen

Sanguillen, Manuel De Jesus (Magan) C
1967–80 B:3/21/1944, Colon, Panama Deb:7/23/1967, PIT NL BR/TR 6', 193

G	AB	R	H	HR	RBI	OBP	SLG	AVG
1448	5062	566	1500	65	585	.329	.398	.296

A Panamanian with a contagious smile, Manny Sanguillen overcame defensive inadequacies to become a respected catcher. He could also hit, and his lifetime .296 average is among the highest among all catchers. He avoided the walk and sprayed line drives like his teammate and idol, Roberto Clemente.

Sanguillen's infectious optimism was the perfect foil to Clemente's brooding intensity. In an ill-advised move, Pirates manager Bill Virdon tried to make Sanguillen his right fielder in 1973, to replace Clemente, who had died in a plane crash the previous New Year's Eve. Manny Sanguillen was the only member of the Pirates family who did not attend Clemente's funeral. Instead he dove in the waters where Clemente's plane went down, searching for his friend.

Sanguillen came to the big leagues along with Richie Hebner and Al Oliver—a threesome that played important roles in the great Pirates teams of the 1970s. The Pirates won five division titles with Sanguillen as their catcher. After the 1976 season, he was traded to Oakland with $100,000 for manager Chuck Tanner. The Pirates let Sanguillen stay on the West Coast for only one year—they brought him back in 1977, and he was the third-string catcher on Pittsburgh's world championship team in 1979. He won Game 2 of that World Series with a two-out, ninth-inning pinch single.

Benito Santiago

Santiago, Benito (Rivera) C
1986–* B:3/9/1965, Ponce, Puerto Rico Deb:9/14/1986, SD NL BR/TR 6'1", 182

G	AB	R	H	HR	RBI	OBP	SLG	AVG
1467	5145	569	1340	170	677	.308	.415	.260

Benito Santiago was one of baseball's best catchers in the late 1980s; by the late 1990s he was one of baseball's best traveled backstops. Santiago was selected to the National League All-Star team each season from 1989 to 1992. Later, he donned the catching gear for five clubs from 1994 to 1999. Wherever he suited up, few baserunners dared challenge the catcher who became renowned for throwing out runners while kneeling.

Santiago earned National League Rookie of the Year honors with the San Diego Padres in 1987. He batted .300 with 18 home runs, 21 steals, and a rookie-record 34-game hitting streak. He won three straight Gold Gloves from 1988 to 1990. His work behind the plate allowed San Diego to deal away another fine young catcher, Sandy Alomar, Jr., in 1989. Santiago's offensive output subsequently declined, however, and the Padres let him leave as a free agent after 1992.

He spent two seasons with the expansion Florida Marlins before moving on to Cincinnati in 1995, where he batted .286 and helped the Reds to the NL Central crown. Santiago slugged a career-high 30 homers—including four consecutive home runs over a two-day span—for the last-place Phillies in 1996. Santiago signed a two-year deal with Toronto, but struggled in the American League; he slumped in 1997 and missed nearly all of 1998 following an off-season car accident. He returned to the National League with the Chicago Cubs in 1999.

Ron Santo

Santo, Ronald Edward 3B
1960–74 B:2/25/1940, Seattle, WA Deb:6/26/1960, CHI NL BR/TR 6', 190

G	AB	R	H	HR	RBI	OBP	SLG	AVG
2243	8143	1138	2254	342	1331	.366	.464	.277

Ron Santo was often called the National League's version of Brooks Robinson. He won five Gold Gloves, compared with Robinson's 16, but Santo more than made up for it in the hitting department—and Santo often had to carry his team as well. The Cubs slugger was a durable player who played with a disability he kept hidden until he retired: diabetes.

Santo missed only 23 of a possible 1,595 games from 1961 through 1970. He established a major league record by leading the league nine times in total chances. He shares the National League record for most years leading the league in assists, with seven, and in double plays, with six. Offensively, in 15 big league seasons Santo batted .277, with 342 home runs and 1,331 RBIs. His numbers compare favorably with those of other notable third baseman, including Robinson, Freddie Lindstrom, Eddie Mathews, Mike Schmidt, and Pie Traynor.

Diagnosed with diabetes just before becoming a big leaguer, Santo kept his handicap to himself. "I was always careful not to give myself a shot of insulin in the locker room in front of anybody," he once said. "I always did it in private." He let few in on his secret and begged newsmen not to report it. "[Diabetes was] one reason I played so hard," Santo theorized. "I keep thinking my career could end any day. I never really wanted out of the lineup. The diabetes thing was hanging over my head."

On one occasion, Santo was in the on-deck circle when he felt a reaction coming on. Billy Williams kept fouling off pitch after pitch as Santo, unable to sneak back into the dugout for a much-needed candy bar, grew increasingly weaker. By the time he reached the plate he was barely able to swing the bat. Even though the bases were loaded, he thought to himself, "Just swing and get out of there."

"So I swing," he later recalled, "and would you believe it, it's a bases-loaded home run. I really sped around those bases to get back to those candy bars in a hurry." It was one of five grand slams Santo hit during his career.

Santo grew up in Seattle, in an ethnic neighborhood called "Garlic Gulch." After graduating from Franklin High School, he was recruited by all 16 major league teams. Sensing that the Cubs offered a quick route to the majors, he turned down an $80,000 offer by Cleveland to sign with Chicago for only $20,000. Besides, Santo explained, "even when I was a kid... I'd dream about playing for the Cubs."

In the minors, Santo needed work defensively. "In his first year as a pro," wrote Jim Brosnan, "Ron Santo threw so many baseballs over first and into the stands at San Antonio that the team's general manager, Marvin Milkes, declared he was going to sell those first base seats at a premium since the fans who sat there were pretty sure to get a free baseball during the game."

Santo led the Texas League with 153 putouts, but also committed a circuit-pacing 53 errors and ended the season with a horrendous .884 fielding average. His .327 batting average, however, gave the Cubs reason for hope. Santo had hopes of making the Cubs in the spring of 1960. He had been hitting and fielding well and had been getting assurances from manager Charlie Grimm. But on April 8, 1960, the Cubs acquired Don Zimmer from Los Angeles, and Santo was sent back to Houston of the American Association. He hit .268 there and was recalled in midseason.

In 1961 Santo was brought up to stay. But that was the era of owner P.K. Wrigley's experimental College of Coaches, in which numerous Chicago coaches would take turns at managing the Cubs during the course of a season. "It was terrible," complained

Santo. "Every two weeks a different coach. One day you're stealing bases, the next day you're hitting home runs." The idea was abandoned after it produced no visible improvement in the Cubs' record.

In the 1960s Santo not only performed well offensively, hitting 30 or more home runs in four straight seasons, but he also won five Gold Gloves and led the National League a record-setting eight times in total chances.

"Was Brooks Robinson a better fielder than Ron Santo?" asked Hall of Fame outfielder Billy Williams. "I played left field behind Santo all those years, and I'm telling you that sucker was quick. I saw him make plays that nobody else could have made. He was out there every day, hurt or not; he had marvelous instincts; and he could hit."

The 1969 season was the year that Cubs fans' pennant hopes were dashed by the late-season surge of the "Miracle" Mets. Santo played well but was involved in two controversies that helped sink the Cubs' chances. First, he angered opponents around the league by jumping up and clicking his heels after key base hits and Cubs victories. The second conflict involved reclusive center fielder Don Young. Young's two errors were pivotal in an embarrassing July 8 loss to the Mets, and Santo was quoted in the media as criticizing Young. Some felt Santo helped destroy Young's career, although Young later absolved him of any blame.

Santo spent his last year in the majors with the White Sox, where he clashed with Sox superstar Dick Allen. Santo criticized Allen's erratic work habits. Allen said, "Santo thought himself a Chicago institution because he had played all those years with the Cubs. He thought he should be the team leader automatically."

Both men were soon gone. Allen walked off the team on September 14, 1974. Santo, even though he had another year left in his contract, decided to retire at season's end and forfeited $120,000 in salary.

After leaving the game, Santo lost money in a Chicago pizzeria venture, but later profited in the crude oil business, on real estate investments, and as an owner of four Kentucky Fried Chicken franchises. His greatest success came as a one-third owner of the Unipoint Corporation, which operates Union 76 truck stops and has more than 900 employees. Santo joined the Cubs as a WGN radio color commentator in 1990.

Santo still suffers the effects of diabetes. He has been diagnosed with retinopathy, which has impaired his vision. Further deterioration of his sight has been slowed by laser treatments three times a week. "If I had been diagnosed for retinopathy [in 1979]," Santo says now, putting a positive spin on matters, "I'd have been legally blind within three years and totally blind within five." He was hospitalized after suffering a heart attack on June 21, 1999, but he later returned to the Cubs broadcast booth.

Hank Sauer

Sauer, Henry John **OF**

1941–59 B:3/17/1917, Philadelphia, PA Deb:9/9/1941, 9/17/1941, CIN NL BR/TR 6'4", 199

G	AB	R	H	HR	RBI	OBP	SLG	AVG
1399	4796	709	1278	288	876	.347	.496	.266

Hank Sauer's selection as National League Most Valuable Player in 1952 set off a firestorm of controversy. True, he tied for the league lead in homers, with 37, and paced the circuit in RBIs, with 121. Yet his defensive skills were lacking, and most importantly, he played for the fifth-place Cubs. It was the first time a player from a second-division club had won an MVP Award. "Anybody who must know the difference between a bunt and a punt must be completely flabbergasted," said one annoyed critic. Sauer edged out the Philadelphia favorite, pitcher Robin Roberts. Several Brooklyn candidates—Joe Black, Jackie Robinson, Pee Wee Reese, Roy Campanella, and Duke Snider—cancelled each other out in the voting. Even Sauer was speechless. "Yeah, I'm surprised," he said on recovering his composure. "But I can tell you this, I'm sure tickled pink. I thought maybe the other guy, Roberts, would win it."

Cubs manager Phil Cavarretta defended the choice: "I wouldn't trade Sauer for both Roberts and Black. I can't tell you how many games he won for us with his bat....He catches any flyball he gets close to, saved games for us with his throwing, and played when I thought he couldn't even swing a bat. I don't know how a guy could be more valuable than that."

Sauer began his professional career as a first baseman in the Yankees farm system after famed New York scout Paul Krichell, the man who discovered Lou Gehrig, signed him. Sauer started with Butler of the Class D Pennsylvania State Association in 1937. The following year he led that circuit with 135 hits, 29 doubles, and a .351 average. He also paced it with 26 errors. He continued to hit the ball hard in the minors but failed to make the grade in several trials with the Cincinnati Reds. The nearly two years he spent in the Coast Guard during World War II also impeded his progress.

In 1946 Sauer had a respectable year with the International League's Syracuse Chiefs, hitting 21 homers and collecting 90 RBIs while batting .282. The next season he received valuable advice from Chiefs manager Jewel Ens. Ens, who thought that Sauer was "getting around too fast," made him employ some 40-ounce Chick Hafey bats. The effect was immediate. Sauer responded with 50 homers—not easy to do in Syracuse's mammoth MacArthur Stadium. He also amassed a league-leading 141 RBIs and averaged .336—only three points behind batting champion Nippy Jones. *The Sporting News* named him Minor League Player of the Year.

Brought back to Cincinnati in 1948, Sauer established a since-surpassed season home run record of 35 for the club. But he also struck out often and was slow in the field. Management decided to ship him to the Cubs in a June 1949 trade.

Sauer hit 11 homers in his first month in Chicago but cemented his reputation as a slow-footed outfielder. The *Chicago Tribune*'s Bob Logan once described center fielder Frankie Baumholtz, stuck between Sauer in left and the notoriously slow Ralph Kiner in right, as "the only Cubs outfielder to play left, right, and center at the same time at Wrigley Field."

Sauer twice hit three home runs in a single game. Both times he accomplished the feat against the Phillies' Curt Simmons. It was the first time any pitcher had twice been victimized by the same batter for three homers in a game. Sauer hit six pinch-hit home runs during his career, and he had two or more homers in a single game 31 times. He hit more than 30 home runs in a season six times, topping the list with 41 in 1954.

Sauer was traded to the Cardinals in March 1956. With the Giants in 1957, after two poor seasons, he collected 26 home runs and 76 RBIs and was selected National League Comeback Player of the Year.

Sauer's philosophy of hitting was simple: "You have a round ball and a round bat, and you try to hit it square." He coached for the Giants in 1959 and scouted and served as a special instructor for the organization through 1984. In the 1970s his son Hank Sauer Jr. was signed by San Francisco but never reached the majors.

Steve Sax

Sax, Stephen Louis **2B**

1981–94 B:1/29/1960, Sacramento, CA Deb:8/18/1981, LA NL BR/TR 5'11", 185

G	AB	R	H	HR	RBI	OBP	SLG	AVG
1769	6940	913	1949	54	550	.336	.358	.281

As the lone rookie in the lineup of the defending world champion Los Angeles Dodgers, second baseman Steve Sax quickly established himself as one of the game's bright young stars. In his first full season in 1982, Sax was named to the All-Star team, then earned National League Rookie of the Year honors with a .282 batting average and 49 stolen bases. Sax posted nearly identical numbers the following year. Offense was never the problem.

Sax was a defensive liability, seemingly unable to make routine throws to first base. Manager

Tommy Lasorda tried levity to fix the situation. In a practical joke lifted from *The Godfather*, Sax found a pig's head in his hotel bed with a note demanding better defensive play. It ultimately took hours of extra work with Dodgers coach Monty Basgall to overcome the problem. "I made that old guy go out there at 3 o'clock every day, even in Atlanta when it was 90 degrees and the humidity was 85," Sax said.

Sax was traded to the New York Yankees prior to the 1989 season. He showed his improved form by leading the league in fielding percentage. He made two All-Star trips in his three seasons in the Bronx; he appeared in a total of five All-Star games. He remained a base stealing threat throughout his 14-year career, which included stops with the Chicago White Sox and Oakland A's. Sax had 444 career stolen bases, with nine 30-steal seasons.

Al Schacht

Schacht, Alexander **P**

1919–21 B:11/11/1892, Bronx, NY D:7/14/1984, Waterbury, CT Deb:9/18/1919, WAS AL BR/TR 5'11", 142

W	L	PCT	G	SV	IP	BB	SO	ERA
14	10	.583	53	2	197	61	38	4.48

Christy Mathewson taught him the screwball, and, perhaps inevitably, Al Schacht became one. Long before teams had mascots like the San Diego Chicken, there was Schacht, the "Clown Prince of Baseball," who got laughs at ballparks like no one else until the original Mets. Costumed in a baseball uniform, layered with a top hat and tails, Schacht toured ballparks alone and in combination with Nick Altrock, doing schtick like "the nearsighted pitcher," "the seeing-eye umpire," and "me and my shadow."

Destined to be in baseball, Schacht was born on the site of what was to become Yankee Stadium and spent a good chunk of his childhood watching the New York Giants play at the Polo Grounds right across the river. Befriended by Mathewson, he occasionally threw batting practice to the team and developed a considerable bug for the game.

He pitched his high school team to a city championship and in 1912 played minor league and semipro ball, and ended the season playing for Cleveland in the outlaw United States League. But it wasn't until after he came back from serving in the armed forces in World War I that the comedian became serious about pitching.

In 1919 he pitched well for Jersey City, going 19–17 with 10 shutouts for a seventh-place team that was only 56–93. After each shutout he would mail to Washington manager Clark Griffith a newspaper clipping about his performance and a note saying "why don't you get wise to yourself and get this fellow?" The letters were signed "Just a Fan." Griffith appeared at Schacht's last shutout and bought his contract.

Schacht went 2–0 that season and had a good start going in 1920 before he injured his shoulder in a collision at second base. But he came back later that season and won Griffith's undying gratitude. Walter Johnson had just pitched the first no-hitter of his career up in Boston, and Griffith Stadium was jammed for Johnson's next start. When it was announced that the scheduled hurler had a sore arm, fans were enraged and threatened to tear the place apart.

Al Schacht volunteered to pitch. "I never heard such booing in my life," he said, recalling the moment he stepped out of the dugout. "Then came the cushions, a shower of them." But Schacht beat the Yankees, 4–3, striking out Babe Ruth three times, twice with the bases loaded.

Schacht was never really the same after that, and his major league playing career ended after 1921. He and former pitcher Nick Altrock became a comedy team and both were paid $1,000 to perform at the World Series in 1921. Although they were partners for a dozen years, they didn't speak for the last eight because of a remark Altrock made about Schacht's Jewish heritage.

The Clown Prince was a Senators coach for years until manager Joe Cronin was traded to Boston. Schacht went with him and, three years later, opened a successful New York restaurant that became his stage—except when he entertained during the World Series.

Schacht once said that he loved to buy top hats for the act because haberdashers made perfect straight men. "Those hat guys thought I was nuts," he explained. "I'd go in and buy a hat, pay twenty-five or thirty dollars for it, and tell them never mind about wrapping it up. I'd put it on a chair and sit on it to get it in shape."

Schacht retired from comedy in the 1960s. He died in 1984.

Germany Schaefer

Schaefer, Herman A. **2B-1B-3B-SS**

1901–18 B:2/4/1877, Chicago, IL D:5/16/1919, Saranac Lake, NY Deb:10/05/1901, CHI AL BR/TR 5'9", 175

G	AB	R	H	HR	RBI	OBP	SLG	AVG
1150	3784	497	972	9	308	.319	.320	.257

There really was a player who stole first base. The problem was that he was on second base when the play started. Infielder Herman A. "Germany" Schaefer had already established a reputation as one of the game's most outlandish characters when he executed that stunt sometime between 1906 and 1908. Oddly enough, there was method in his madness. Schaefer, then with Detroit, was playing against Cleveland. He was on first, and teammate Davy Jones was the runner on third. Schaefer proceeded to steal second. Standing on that bag, he shouted to Jones, "Let's try it again!" With that he headed straight for first, hoping to draw a throw from the catcher that would allow Jones to steal home.

The catcher, however, simply stood there dumbfounded at what Schaefer was attempting. Jones didn't move either. In fact, everyone was too startled to move. An argument ensued regarding the legality of what had just occurred. There didn't seem to be any rule against it, so the matter stood. When play resumed, Schaefer took off again—this time in the right direction—for second base. The catcher threw to second, Jones broke for the plate, and both runners were safe. Mission accomplished.

Another time Schaefer pulled off an equally flamboyant stunt. The Tigers were playing the White Sox and were losing, 2–1, with one on and two out in the bottom of the ninth inning. Schaefer, who had sliced his thumb while opening a beer bottle, was coaching at third. Suddenly, he was called on to pinch hit. He grabbed a bat and stepped to the plate, grandly announcing, "Ladies and gentlemen, permit me to introduce to you Germany Schaefer, the world champion batsman who will now give you a demonstration of his batting ability."

With that, the small crowd booed Schaefer mercilessly. He then proceeded to wallop a game-winning home run over the fence. Circling the bases, Schaefer slid wildly into first, yelling, "Schaefer leads at the quarter by a half." Then he stood up and when he got to second slid again, hollering, "At the half, it's Schaefer by a head." At third he announced, "Schaefer leads by a mile." Arriving at home he slid once more, dusted himself off, and announced to the patrons, "This, ladies and gentlemen, concludes this afternoon's performance."

Schaefer began his career on Chicago area semi-pro teams. In 1898 he signed on with Sioux Falls before moving on to Kansas City and St. Paul, reaching the majors with the Cubs in 1901. Following his two-year stay with Chicago, he played with Milwaukee of the American Association until returning to the majors with Detroit in 1905.

Never a great hitter, his versatility and good humor kept him in the majors for many years. Prior to the 1907 World Series between Schaefer's Tigers and the Chicago Cubs, Schaefer lobbied to have receipts from a tie game go towards the players' share of the gate. When the first game of the Series ended in a 12-inning tie, Schaefer's gambit considerably enriched his fellow players.

When he was too old to play, Schaefer teamed for several years with former White Sox pitcher Nick Altrock in a comedy coaching routine for Washington. (Altrock was also Al Schacht's comedy partner.) Schaefer later scouted for the New York Giants. He was invited to join the 1917 White Sox–Giants world tour, and his performances along the way added to the popularity of the enterprise. At one point Schaefer went into vaudeville with Detroit shortstop Charley O'Leary, but they were given the hook when their teammates pelted the duo with an assortment of fresh produce.

After the United States declared war on Germany in April 1917, Schaefer requested that he no longer be referred to as "Germany." Instead he asked to be called "Dutch." In 1919 Schaefer, who had been in ill health, had a heart attack and died while aboard a train near Saranac Lake, New York.

Ray Schalk

Schalk, Raymond William **C**

1912–29 M(1927–28, 102–125) B:8/12/1892, Harvey, IL D:5/19/1970, Chicago, IL Deb:8/11/1912, CHI AL BR/TR 5'9", 165

G	AB	R	H	HR	RBI	OBP	SLG	AVG
1762	5306	579	1345	11	594	.340	.316	.253

Everything Ray Schalk did was against type. An almost puny catcher who stole 176 bases, he was a squeaky-clean member of the Chicago "Black Sox," who were accused of fixing the 1919 World Series. When Schalk, a Chicago native, broke in with the White Sox at age 20 in 1912, he looked even younger. Opponents taunted the boy-sized man, "Hey, sonny, where's your mama?" and "Raymond, you got your diapers on?" When Schalk arrived at the ballpark one day, a policeman told him, "No kids allowed here, sonny! Move on." Schalk responded, "But I'm a player." The cop reached for him and said, "And I'm the president of the United States." Schalk kept protesting as the cop first told him to beat it then finally agreed to show him around the dugout. But his teammates pretended not to know him.

Eventually he was known as a Hall of Famer. An all-around fine catcher with an excellent arm and soft hands, Schalk was a field general who inspired his pitchers. He caught a record four no-hitters, one each by Jim Scott, Joe Benz, Ed Cicotte, and Charlie Robertson, including Robertson's perfect game. And Schalk was all over the field on defense.

Nicknamed "Cracker," Schalk would sometimes shoot out of the catcher's box and often made putouts at third base himself. On a few occasions he covered second base. "One day a ball was hit over the infield and in front of the center fielder," he recalled. "I had a hunch it would fall safely, so I ran out over the pitcher's mound and when the ball dropped in I yelled to Eddie Collins, who threw the ball to me in time to tag the runner as he slid in. We worked the play two or three times more." He was the first catcher to make a putout at all four bases.

During the 1919 World Series, some reports say, Schalk suspected a fix was on and got into a clubhouse fight with Lefty Williams and Swede Risberg. Schalk denied that the incident happened. "There never was such a fight. I don't know who started that story....As a matter of fact, I did challenge Risberg verbally early in the Series, but it was the same kind of criticism that many players give their teammates for bad plays in the heat of battle. I told Risberg what I thought of some of his plays, but I did not charge him at the time with trying to toss the game."

Schalk rarely talked about the scandal and turned down many offers to write his account of it. He replaced Collins as White Sox manager in 1927. Although Schalk remained on the roster he seldom played himself. He resigned as manager after a July 4 doubleheader in 1928. Making $25,000 a year as a catcher-manager, he wanted to stay on as a catcher and said he would take $15,000. Charles Comiskey, known for his frugal ways, offered him only $6,000. Schalk threatened to sue the White Sox but never followed through.

Retiring fully after an 18-year playing career, Schalk coached for the White Sox for two years before managing in the minors for a decade, mostly in Buffalo. He coached sporadically later and operated a Chicago bowling alley. He was elected to the Hall of Fame in 1955.

Wally Schang

Schang, Walter Henry **C–OF**

1913–31 B:8/22/1889, South Wales, NY D:3/6/1965, St. Louis, MO Deb:5/9/1913 PHI AL BB/TR 5'10", 180

G	AB	R	H	HR	RBI	OBP	SLG	AVG
1842	5307	769	1506	59	710	.393	.401	.284

Walter Henry Schang's career began in 1913, when he took over behind the plate for Connie Mack's two-time world champion Philadelphia Athletics. With his baserunning skills and good hitting, he fit right into an A's team laden with talent and intelligence. Before Schang played in his 100th major league game, he had already hit .357 and belted one home run in the 1913 World Series. He instantly made a name for himself among such illustrious teammates as Eddie Collins, Frank "Home Run" Baker, and Jack "Stuffy" McInnis. The club won its third American League pennant in four seasons.

Schang was an excellent defensive catcher, and in 1915 he set an American League record when he gunned down six attempted steals in a single game. After the 1917 season, Connie Mack unloaded almost his entire squad of starters in the face of diminishing gate receipts. He sold Schang and batterymate Herb Pennock to the Boston Red Sox. In 1918 Schang again caught for a world champion team. As the Red Sox defeated the Cubs in the World Series, Schang led all Boston batters with a .444 postseason average. He also provided reliable guidance for a Red Sox pitching staff that included Babe Ruth and Carl Mays. In 1919 he had the first of his six .300-plus seasons.

In 1920 Schang and batterymate Waite Hoyt were traded from the Red Sox to the New York Yankees. The two were the latest in a series of players sold to the Yanks by Red Sox owner Harry Frazee. With new talent that also included Babe Ruth, Herb Pennock, Carl Mays, Ernie Shore, and Hubert "Dutch" Leonard, the Yankees made it to their first World Series in 1921. Although New York lost the best-of-nine championship, Schang's hitting was second only to Babe Ruth's among position players. With Schang behind the plate and a pitching staff good enough to keep Babe Ruth in the outfield, the Yankees continued to win American League flags. In 1923 they took their first of 25 World Series championships in the 20th century.

Before the 1926 season New York sold Schang to the St. Louis Browns, where he played as well as ever both offensively and defensively. In 1930, his 18th year in the league, Schang returned to Connie Mack's Athletics as a backup catcher and offered leadership and advice to young Mickey Cochrane as the A's took another world championship. Schang spent a final 30 games with the Detroit Tigers in 1931 before retiring.

Curt Schilling

Schilling, Curtis Montague **P**

1988–99 B:11/14/1966, Anchorage, AK Deb:9/7/1988, BAL AL BR/TR 6'4", 215

W	L	PCT	G	SH	IP	BB	SO	ERA
99	83	.544	326	13	1691^{2}	454	1571	3.38

In an age when pitchers rarely finished their starts, Curt Schilling was a throwback to a time before pitch counts and closers. In his first 12 years in the major leagues, Schilling, a former reliever, completed more than one out of every four career starts. An avid memorabilia collector, as well as military historian, he was aware of the names behind every record he broke.

Coming up through the minor leagues, Schilling was not treated like a phenom; he was trade bait. Boston, Baltimore, and Houston each traded him by the time he was 25. He arrived in Philadelphia in a trade with the Astros for Jason Grimsley in 1992. After 16 relief appearances for the Phillies, he started a game against Houston and won. He never returned to the bullpen.

Schilling pitched back-to-back shutouts in July. In September he pitched a one-hitter. In all, he completed 10 of his 26 starts, including four shutouts. He won 16 games the following year, but his greatest moments came in October. In the Championship Series Schilling struck out 19 Atlanta Braves in 16 innings over two starts, including the first five batters he faced in Game 1. He did not get a decision in either start—both Philadelphia wins—yet he was named the NLCS Most Valuable Player. He then went 1–1 in Philadelphia's six-game loss to the Toronto Blue Jays, throwing a five-hit shutout in Game 5.

Schilling spent much of the next two years on the disabled list. He opened the 1996 season on the DL, but returned in May to lead the National League in complete games. Schilling signed a long-term contract with the Phillies to open the 1997 season and responded with the best year of his career. He won a career-high 17 games and became a strikeout machine. He fanned 319—and walked just 58—to break Steve Carlton's club strikeout mark. He broke J.R. Richard's league record for strikeouts by a righthander in his final start, only to ejected from the game a few innings later. He hit Florida's John Wehner with a pitch because rookie third baseman Scott Rolen had been drilled immediately after a home run. "We're supposed to play the game as a team," Schilling said, "and that's what we did."

After a surprising first half to the season, the Phils fell apart in August 1998, but not because of Schilling. He led the NL in starts, complete games, innings, and strikeouts. He reached 300 strikeouts in his final start, making him just the fifth pitcher to reach that mark in back-to-back seasons. Schilling got off to a sensational start in 1999. Although he earned his first All-Star Game start, lingering shoulder problems limited him to just 30⅓ innings after the break. Without Schilling to anchor the rotation (15 wins) and rest the bullpen (eight complete games), the Phils stumbled again in the second half. He underwent shoulder surgery after the season.

Mike Schmidt

Schmidt, Michael Jack **3B–1B**

1972–89 B:9/27/1949, Dayton, OH Deb:9/12/1972, PHI NL BR/TR 6'2", 203

G	AB	R	H	HR	RBI	OBP	SLG	AVG
2404	8352	1506	2234	548	1595	.384	.527	.267

Mike Schmidt was a great slugger, a record-setting fielder, a three-time National League Most Valuable Player, and the finest Philadelphia Phillie ever, according to a 1983 vote by Philadelphia fans. Schmidt hit 548 homers. Only Babe Ruth, Harmon Killebrew, Jimmie Foxx, and Mickey Mantle scaled the 500-home run peak in fewer at bats.

He led the National League in home runs a record eight times; only Ruth led his league more often. He slugged 30 or more home runs in a season 13 times, a figure surpassed only by Hank Aaron, and reached 35 homers 11 times, more often than anyone but Ruth. Schmidt and Ralph Kiner are the only players to homer in four consecutive at bats on two different occasions. Schmidt hit 509 of his home runs as a third baseman, including 48 in 1980, both records for the position. Schmidt was no slouch with the glove, either. He won 10 Gold Gloves, more than any third baseman except Brooks Robinson, and his 2,212 games at third base rank third all time.

Schmidt received All-America honors as a shortstop, as well as a bachelor's degree in business administration, at Ohio University. The Phillies selected him in the second round of the June 1971 draft. In his first and only full minor league season Schmidt was selected as the Pacific Coast League's All-Star second baseman and earned a late-season promotion to Philadelphia.

In 1973 Schmidt shared duties at third base with Cesar Tovar but was overmatched at the plate. He batted .196, the lowest average among major league regulars, and struck out 136 times in 367 at bats. But Schmidt told *Sport* magazine that while playing winter ball in Puerto Rico he'd "found a swing that made things happen." He explained, "I was standing at the plate nice and relaxed, and that sucker went off my bat a mile."

Schmidt led the league with 36 homers in 1974, the first of three straight home run titles. He also had the first of nine 100-RBI seasons and won his first of five league slugging titles. Schmidt batted .282 that year, his best average of the 1970s, despite 138 strikeouts. Among his hits that season was perhaps the longest single ever, a drive off a speaker suspended from the roof of the Astrodome. Schmidt also drew 106 walks for the first of his seven 100-walk seasons, stole 23 bases (he had a career-best 29 the following year), and received the first of 12 All-Star selections.

Schmidt had one of his greatest days on April 17, 1976, at Wrigley Field, when he became the 10th major leaguer to hit four home runs in four consecutive at bats. The Phillies erased a 13–2 deficit and won, 18–16, on his 10th-inning homer. Schmidt finished the contest with eight RBIs and 17 total bases, one shy of the major league record. He went on to tie Willie Stargell's record with 11 home runs in April and won his third straight home run title that season.

Beginning in 1976 the Phillies won three straight NL East crowns but were defeated in the National League Championship Series each time. Schmidt received much of the blame from Philadelphia fans, who have been known to boo Santa Claus as well as the best third baseman ever.

In the 1976 playoffs against the Cincinnati Reds, Schmidt made a key error in Game 1, trying to tag a runner at third instead of taking a routine out at first. Schmidt tied for the team lead by batting .308 in the series, but the Big Red Machine swept the Phillies.

In the 1977 playoff opener against the Los Angeles Dodgers, Schmidt reached on an error and scored one run, then singled in the winning run in the ninth for a 7–5 Phillies win. But he went 0-for-11 the rest of the way. The Dodgers won the next three games to advance to the World Series.

In a 1978 playoff rematch with the Dodgers, Schmidt's error in the opener helped create a four-run inning, erasing a 1–0 Phillies lead. The Philadelphia pitchers served up four Dodgers homers in the 9–5 loss. Phillies manager Danny Ozark batted Schmidt in the leadoff spot in Game 2. He got a single, but the Phils were shut out. In Game 3, batting sixth, Schmidt doubled and scored in the Phillies' 9–4 win, forcing Game 4. Leading off again, he doubled in the first as the Phillies loaded the bases but failed to score. They lost in 10 innings.

During the 1978 season Schmidt had made a key change at the plate. Always a selective hitter, he started looking for pitches he could drive to any field instead of trying to pull every pitch. "He changed his whole approach to hitting late in his career, which made him an even better hitter," said broadcaster and Hall of Famer Richie Ashburn, who saw Schmidt play as many games as anyone.

In 1979 Schmidt hit 45 home runs, including four in a row over two games in July. He also led the league with 120 walks. In 1980 Schmidt won the home run crown with 48 and the RBI title with 121, the first of four times in seven seasons that he would lead the league in both categories in the same season. He batted .286, his best career mark to that point, and, at age 31, won his first MVP Award. It was also his final year playing with Greg Luzinski, with whom he combined for 503 home runs in nine years, to that point the sixth-best home run total by two teammates in league history.

In 1980 the Phillies finally won the pennant, but it took four extra-inning games against the Astros in the NLCS to do it. After winning Game 1 of the World Series against Kansas City, the Phillies were down, 4–2, in Game 2 when a Schmidt double sparked a rally in the eighth inning. They won the game, 6–4. In Game 3 Schmidt slugged his first postseason homer in a losing cause. He beat out a bunt in Game 4 and knocked in a run with a sacrifice fly in another loss. In Game 5 Schmidt's two-run homer put the Phillies on the board. Then, with Philadelphia down 3–2 in the ninth, Schmidt singled to ignite the rally that won the game. In Game 6 he singled in the Phillies' first two runs in the third inning. The team went on to win, 4–1, for the first world title in franchise history. Schmidt batted .381, scored six times, knocked in seven runs, and won Series MVP honors. Finally, Philadelphia's fickle fans treated him like the hero he was.

In the strike-shortened 1981 season Schmidt led the majors with 31 homers and 91 RBIs in 102 games. He batted a career-high .316, led the league in both slugging and on-base percentage, and won his second straight MVP Award. The Phillies came out on top in the first half of that year's split season, but lost to the Montreal Expos in the division playoff.

Schmidt missed two weeks of the 1982 season with a fractured rib and fell two home runs short of the league crown. In 1983 he led the league with 40 homers and also had the league's best on-base percentage for the third straight year. The Phillies' "Wheeze Kids," with veteran imports Pete Rose, Tony Perez, Joe Morgan, and Gary Matthews, won the NL East and met the Dodgers in the playoffs.

In the NLCS Schmidt's first-inning homer off Jerry Reuss was the only run of Game 1. Schmidt went on to bat .467, best among the Phillies regulars, as the team advanced to the World Series against the Orioles. Schmidt was hitless in the first three games of the Series before blooping a broken-bat single to keep a rally going. But it was his only hit and his only time on base. He went 1-for-20 with six strikeouts as the Orioles beat the Phillies in five games.

In 1984 Schmidt won the home run and RBI titles and his ninth straight Gold Glove. Moved to first base in 1985, he returned to third in 1986, his third MVP season, when he again won the home run and RBI titles. He also won the slugging title, his 10th Gold Glove, and led league third basemen in fielding percentage for the only time in his career.

Schmidt suffered his most serious injury in 1987, a torn right rotator cuff. He missed more than 50 games and broke his string of nine consecutive seasons with 30 or more homers. He rehabilitated the shoulder during the winter and came back for the 1988 season at age 39, but retired on May 29 in a tearful ceremony.

Schmidt and the Phillies never came to terms on a job for him in the front office. They reconciled sufficiently for him to deliver the first pitch of the Phillies' first home game of the 1993 World Series, the team's first postseason appearance since his retirement.

Before the ceremonial toss Schmidt admitted, "When I watch films of myself, I wish I had more fun playing. I wish I enjoyed myself more. But I was consumed with the pressure of trying to perform at a high level."

On January 10, 1995, Schmidt was voted into the Baseball Hall of Fame. Schmidt, appearing on the Hall of Fame ballot for the first time, received 444 of the 460 votes cast and easily surpassed the magic number of 345 (75 percent) needed for election. Schmidt became the 26th player to win election on his first ballot.

Red Schoendienst

Schoendienst, Albert Fred **2B-OF-SS-3B**
1945–63 M(1965–76, 1980, 1990, 1,041–955)
B:2/2/1923, Germantown, IL Deb:4/17/1945, STL NL
BB/TR 6', 170

G	AB	R	H	HR	RBI	OBP	SLG	AVG
2216	8479	1223	2449	84	773	.338	.387	.289

Baseball fans reveal their age when they describe Red Schoendienst. For the young, Schoendienst is an older coach. For the middle-aged, he is a manager. For the elderly, Schoendienst is a second baseman. So it goes with a man who stays in a major league uniform for over half a century, playing in 10 All-Star Games and appearing in 2,216 games as a player, 2,100 as a manager, and well over 2,000 more as a coach.

Best known for his glove, Schoendienst led National League second basemen in double plays twice, putouts and assists three times, and fielding percentage six times. He led the league in pinch hitting in 1962, going 22-for-72, and hit .300 or better seven times.

In 1942 Albert Fred Schoendienst hitchhiked from Illinois to St. Louis for an open tryout with the Cardinals. Though 500 hopefuls attended, scout Joe Mathes chose Schoendienst and drove him home to get his father's signature on a contract. Schoendienst senior was painting a bridge when Mathes presented his offer but was able to negotiate a bonus—a ham sandwich and a glass of milk.

The switch hitter led the International League in batting with a .337 mark. He was the first 20-year-old to achieve that distinction since Wee Willie Keeler in 1892. After strains of tuberculosis were found in Schoendienst's lungs, he was not allowed to serve in the armed forces. He came up with the Cardinals in 1945 and led the league in stolen bases with 26 Only one other time (in 1946) during his 19-year career did reach double figures in steals.

In 1949 he hit .297, led National League second basemen in assists, putouts, and fielding percentage, and accepted 268 chances before making his first error. In 1950 he won the All-Star Game at Comiskey Park with a 14th-inning homer, and he had a streak of 320 errorless chances. Traded to the Giants in 1956 and to Milwaukee in 1957, he played on two pennant-winning Braves teams before going back to St. Louis and ending his career there in 1963.

He coached for the Cardinals until after the 1964 season, when he replaced Johnny Keane as manager. Schoendienst managed the Cards for 12 years, winning two pennants and a world championship in 1967. His laid back style on a team full of veteran stars could be summed up by his address to his team in 1968: "Run everything out and be in by twelve." The Cards won the pennant again that year.

After the 1976 season he returned to coaching. Schoendienst filled in as interim manager of the Cards in 1980 and again in 1990. He was inducted into the Hall of Fame in 1989.

Dick Schofield

Schofield, John Richard **SS-2B**
1953–71 B:1/7/1935, Springfield, IL Deb:7/3/1953, STL NL BB/TR 5'9", 163

G	AB	R	H	HR	RBI	OBP	SLG	AVG
1321	3083	394	699	21	211	.319	.297	.227

Dick Schofield was a fine-fielding shortstop and infielder who played for seven different teams during the course of his 19-year major league career, including three separate stints with the Cardinals. But in only three of those seasons was Schofield a major league regular. The problem wasn't his glove, it was his bat. Schofield hit his weight—sometimes—but then he weighed only 163 pounds.

John Richard "Dick" Schofield was one of many high-priced "bonus babies" of the 1950s, forced by the rules of the time to endure several seasons on a major league roster when he probably would have benefited more from playing time in the minors. Like many other bonus babies, Schofield never really recovered from the experience.

In 1953 the St. Louis Cardinals signed him out of high school in Springfield, Illinois, for a reported $40,000. During the next two seasons he appeared in only 76 games and came to bat only 46 times. In 1955 he was sent to Omaha of the American Association, and in two seasons there he both hit and fielded well. In 1957 he returned to the Cardinals but struggled with big league pitching.

In 1958 he was traded to Pittsburgh in exchange for outfielder Gene Freese and shortstop Johnny

O'Brien. Schofield's initial role in Pittsburgh was to back up shortstop Dick Groat. He did his job but still didn't hit.

In 1960 the Pirates challenged for the National League pennant. On September 6, Groat, in the midst of a career year that later earned him a batting title and the NL Most Valuable Player Award, came to bat against Milwaukee pitcher Lew Burdette. Burdette threw inside, and the ball struck Groat's hand as he raised it protectively. Groat's wrist was broken.

Light-hitting Schofield stepped in and enjoyed the best month of his career. He hit .403 in 21 games. Groat returned just before the season ended as the Pirates went on to win the pennant and surprise New York in the Series. Schofield returned to the bench with a season average of .333, a career high, which he duplicated in three Series at bats that year.

Finally, in 1963, his 10th season in the major leagues, Schofield became the Pirates' regular shortstop, a position he held through 1964. Teamed with second baseman Bill Mazeroski, Schofield earned well-deserved kudos for his glove work and even managed to hit a respectable .246. In May 1965 he was traded to the San Francisco Giants for shortstop Jose Pagan. Schofield went on to lead the league in fielding percentage for that position.

By 1966 Schofield had resumed his role as a backup infielder. During the next several seasons he was traded almost annually for a succession of increasingly forgettable talent. Everybody wanted Schofield, but once they had him it seemed he immediately became expendable.

In May 1966 the Giants sold him to the Yankees. In September the Dodgers acquired him in exchange for pitcher Thad Tillotson and cash. The Dodgers released him in 1967, and Schofield signed with the Cardinals. After the Cardinals won the pennant, Schofield was dealt to the Red Sox for pitcher Gary Waslewski. Boston let him go in 1971, and the Milwaukee Brewers picked him up. They promptly traded him back to the Cardinals, along with two other players, for Ted Kubiak and a minor league pitcher

During his major league career Schofield hit only .227, the 17th worst for batters with 1,500 or more at bats (he had 3,083). He hit a mere 21 home runs. Despite his weak batting Schofield was used over 300 times as a pinch hitter. He retired after the 1971 season.

Schofield later became a member of the Illinois Youth Commission. His son, Richard Craig Schofield, became a fine-fielding major league shortstop—although he batted just three points higher than his dad over his 14-year career. While usual thought of as baseball "father," the elder Schofield was also a baseball "son."

"I guess I always wanted to be a ballplayer," he said. "Dad [John Schofield, Sr.] played in the Eastern League and at San Antonio." Schofield obtained his nickname "Ducky" from his father, who derived it from a type of fowl common around Philadelphia. Said Schofield: "When I started with St. Louis in 1953, my dad met some of the Cardinal players. When they found that 'Ducky' was his nickname they started calling me that."

Marge Schott

Owner(1985–99)

Marge Schott dined with the president, schmoozed with the pope, and became the first woman to accept baseball's championship trophy. Sadly, however, she will be known mostly for her ethnic slurs, targeting African Americans, Jews, Asians, Italians, and homosexuals—as well as working mothers.

A sixth-generation Cincinnatian, Schott inherited her husband's local business empire when he died in 1968. She became an astute businesswoman herself, becoming the first woman ever to own a major metropolitan-area General Motors dealership. She became a limited partner of the Reds in 1981 before taking controlling interest of the team four years later.

Living alone in her big house with her St. Bernard, Schottzie, Schott adopted the Reds as her family. She took Schottzie to the ballpark, where a pooper scooper was at the ready. Though notoriously tight with the buck, she took pride in keeping ticket prices affordable. Schott lunched with President George Bush and met Pope John Paul II, offering him his very own Reds jacket. In 1990 her club stunned the baseball world with a sweep of mighty Oakland in the World Series.

In 1993, however, Schott was suspended from baseball for one year for slurs against outfielder Eric Davis. She uttered other racial slurs, once saying that "only fruits wear earrings." When umpire John McSherry died on Opening Day 1996, the sold-out game was postponed. Schott's take on the situation was: "I feel cheated." Two weeks later she approached umpire Harry Wendelstedt before a game, and he turned his back to her.

Her worst moments came during extended interviews. In a 1996 interview with ESPN, she stated that "Hitler was good at the beginning" and that "he just went too far." Owners forced her to give up day-to-day operation of the team through the 1998 season. Muzzled by her fellow owners, banned from the stadium, and forbidden to be part of running her team, Schott finally sold the Reds in 1999.

Ossee Schreckengost

Schreckengost, Ossee Freeman **C-1B**

1897–1908 B:4/11/1875, New Bethlehem, PA D:7/9/1914, Philadelphia, PA Deb:9/08/1897, LOU NL BR/TR 5'10", 180

G	AB	R	H	HR	RBI	OBP	SLG	AVG
895	3057	304	829	9	338	.297	.345	.271

Dubbed by Connie Mack as "the Harpo Marx of his time," catcher Ossee Freeman Schreckengost roomed with Rube Waddell and had it written into the pitcher's 1904 contract that the colorful Waddell could not eat crackers in bed. Said Schreckengost: "His munching keeps me up all night, and I can't sleep with all those crumbs on my sheets."

It was never dull rooming with Waddell. Once a drunken Waddell jumped out of his hotel window after betting he could fly. When he woke up in the hospital he berated Schreckengost: "Why didn't you stop me? I coulda been killed." Schreckengost responded, "What? And lose the hundred dollars I bet against you?"

Originally in the National League, Schreckengost jumped to Boston on the founding of the American League in 1901, was sold to Cleveland that October, and moved to the Athletics in June 1902.

Schreckengost, one of the last catchers not to use shin guards, was far ahead of his time in another regard; he was one of the first catchers to catch one-handed. A good defensive catcher who excelled at handling pitchers, Schreckengost led the league in putouts six straight years. He also led twice in percentage, errors, and fielding range, and once in games caught, double plays, and assists.

Sold to the White Sox in May 1908, Schreckengost was behind the plate during the monumental pitching duel between Big Ed Walsh and Cleveland's Addie Joss on October 2, 1908 (Joss threw a no-hitter; Walsh lost, 1–0). In that game, Schreckengost ruptured a tendon in his right forefinger trying to snag one of Walsh's spitters and committed a passed ball that cost the White Sox the game.

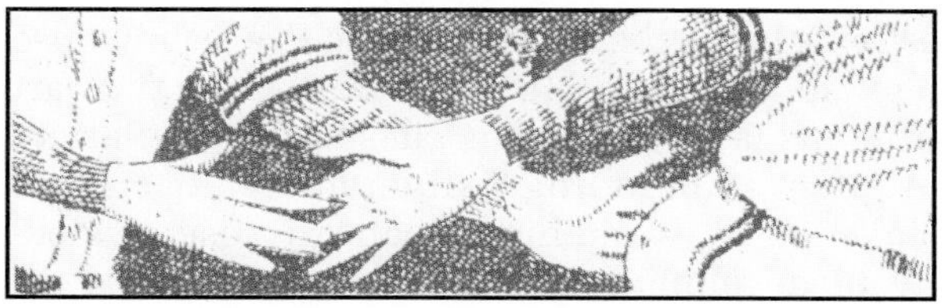

Frank Schulte

Schulte, Frank M. **OF**

1904–18 B:9/17/1882, Cohocton, NY D:10/2/1949, Oakland, CA Deb:9/21/1904, CHI NL BL/TR 5'11", 170

G	AB	R	H	HR	RBI	OBP	SLG	AVG
1806	6533	906	1766	92	792	.332	.395	.270

Outfielder Frank "Wildfire" Schulte was a power-hitting, solid-fielding member of the Chicago Cubs who helped them to four National League pennants. He led the league in home runs in 1910 and 1911, and in RBIs in 1911. That season, he was awarded a Chalmers automobile as league Most Valuable Player, the first year an official MVP Award was given to a player in each league. (Ty Cobb won in the American League.)

Frank M. Schulte began his career by playing semipro ball in such places as Blossburg, Pennsylvania, and Waverly, New York. In 1902 he signed with Syracuse of the New York State League, where he remained until the Cubs purchased his contract in August 1904.

The 1911 season was quite remarkable for Schulte. He became the first player to hit four grand slams in a season and also the first player to collect at least 20 doubles, triples, homers, and stolen bases in a single season—a feat not duplicated until Willie Mays did it in 1957. On July 20 Schulte hit for the cycle, and on August 15 he collected a home run and a double in the same inning. Schulte was also a daring baserunner and stole home 22 times during the course of his career, an accomplishment that places him fifth on the all-time list.

In July 1916 Schulte was traded to Pittsburgh. Later in the year he broke two ribs in "a friendly wrestling bout" with pitcher Duster Mails and was out for the rest of the season. Schulte was sold on waivers to the Phillies in June 1917, released by Philadelphia at the end of the season, and signed by Washington in December 1917.

Schulte got his nickname because of his admiration for the actress Lillian Russell. One time Schulte's Cubs were in Vicksburg at the same time Russell was in town with her play *Wildfire*. She gave a party for Schulte and his teammates. In appreciation, Schulte, who owned race horses, named one of his trotters "Wildfire." Before long he too was known by the name.

One of Schulte's idiosyncrasies was his belief that finding a hairpin guaranteed him a base hit. If either prong of the lucky pin was bent, Schulte believed the hit would go in that direction.

Schulte also had a penchant for bats that were unusually thin-handled for his era—he would break about 50 of them in a season. They weighed approximately 40 ounces, and although many players would inspect a Schulte model before ordering new bats, they would invariably dismiss the style as a "twig."

When he left the majors, Schulte managed Binghamton of the International League from the start of the 1919 season until July 23 of that year. He then returned to the playing ranks and spent further time in the minors with Toronto, Syracuse, Atlanta, and Oakland before retiring in 1922.

In early 1930 Schulte was hospitalized in Brooklyn with paralysis but recovered. He died in 1949.

Fred Schulte

Schulte, Fred William **OF**

1927–37 B:1/13/1901, Belvidere, IL D:5/20/1983 Belvidere, IL Deb:4/15/1927, STL AL BR/TR 6'1", 183

G	AB	R	H	HR	RBI	OBP	SLG	AVG
1179	4259	686	1241	47	593	.362	.408	.291

For most of his career, outfielder Fred Schulte was best known as a defensive star. But in the 1933 World Series he led Washington with a .333 batting average and four RBIs, and in Game 5 he hit a three-run homer into Griffith Stadium's distant left-field pavilion.

Schulte's minor league highlight came in 1924 with the pennant-winning Waterloo Hawks of the Class D Mississippi Valley League. That season he hit a league-leading .368 and also led the circuit with 167 hits. Purchased by the St. Louis Browns, he was optioned to the American Association's Milwaukee Brewers. With Milwaukee in 1926 he batted .347, with 13 homers and 104 RBIs. The following season he batted .317 in 60 games for the Browns, and he cracked the starting outfield in 1928. In 1929 Schulte led American League outfielders in fielding percentage, committing only two errors all season.

Two of Schulte's most productive major league seasons were 1931 and 1932. In each season "Fritz" hit nine homers and scored at least 100 runs. But on December 14, 1932, Schulte was traded to Washington in a six-player deal. In 1933 he batted .295, drove in a career-high 87 runs, and paced American League outfielders in putouts. He then continued his hot hitting in the World Series.

Waived to Pittsburgh in January 1936, Schulte later managed and coached in the minors. From 1947 through 1964 he did some scouting for the Cincinnati Reds, Chicago White Sox, and Milwaukee Braves.

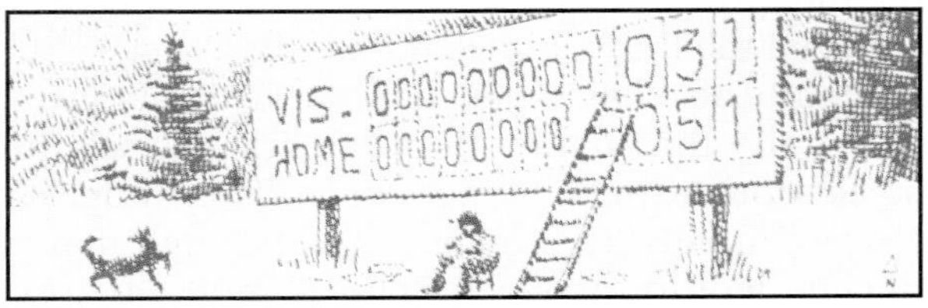

Hal Schumacher

Schumacher, Harold Henry **P**

1931–42, 1946 B:11/23/1910, Hinckley, NY D:4/21/1993, Cooperstown, NY Deb:4/15/1931, NY NL BR/TR 6', 190

W	L	PCT	G	SH	IP	BB	SO	ERA
158	121	.566	391	27	2482^{1}	902	906	3.36

"Prince Hal" Schumacher was a worthy complement to "King Carl" Hubbell in the New York Giants' pitching rotation of the 1930s and early 1940s. Together, from 1931 to 1942, they formed the third-best lefty–righty combination in National League history, with 358 victories and only 237 losses. Only the duos of Warren Spahn and Lew Burdette and Hooks Wiltse and Christy Mathewson did better in the senior circuit.

Harold Henry Schumacher grew up playing ball in Dolgeville, New York. His high school principal in 1928 secured a scholarship for him to attend St. Lawrence University, where he starred in basketball, played fullback and halfback on the football team, and excelled on the mound.

In 1931 manager John McGraw signed Schumacher to play for the Giants and announced to reporters, "Say, boys, I've got the best-looking young pitcher out there I've seen in years. He's got plenty of stuff and he isn't too green. He may come up with something real soon."

Schumacher spent most of that season on the New York bench, but for five weeks he was optioned to Bridgeport of the Eastern League. He remained with the Giants' organization in 1932. When he had signed with New York, Schumacher had dropped out of college, but he had decided to use his baseball earnings to finish his education. On June 12, 1933, Schumacher was to receive his St. Lawrence diploma. Not only was he able to attend the ceremony (it was an off-day on the National League schedule), but the entire Giants team came up with him by train. And not only did they attend, but they also played the St. Lawrence team on the diamond, defeating them 12–4 before an estimated 9,000 fans. It was filmed for the Pathé newsreels, and announcer Graham McNamee broadcast it on NBC radio.

Schumacher featured what is known as a "heavy" fastball, one that thuds into a catcher's mitt. "I know that every young pitcher who shows a fastball is compared to Dazzy Vance," claimed Giants teammate Freddie Lindstrom. "But honestly, Schumacher's the first one I've seen whose fast one actually skips like the Dazzler." Apart from his fastball, Schumacher featured a variety of pitches, including a slider and an overhand sinker. Later, when his fastball was losing velocity, he developed a palmball.

In 1933 Schumacher helped pitch the Giants to a world championship. In 1934 he paced the New York staff in victories, with 23 wins. And between May 19 and July 15, 1935, he won 11 straight games—the longest National League streak of the season.

In Game 5 of the 1936 World Series, Schumacher defeated the Yankees in 10 innings, 5–4. He faced his biggest test in the third inning, when he walked Tony Lazzeri and Red Ruffing and then unleashed a wild pitch that advanced both runners. Frank Crosetti reached on shortstop Dick Bartell's low throw as Lazzeri scored. Red Rolfe bunted for a base hit, and the bases were loaded. He bore down and proceeded to strike out both Joe DiMaggio and Lou Gehrig, and he retired Bill Dickey on a flyball to right to escape without further damage.

At the plate Schumacher performed acceptably for a pitcher. He boasted a modest .202 lifetime average, but he hit for power, collecting 15 career home runs. In 1934 he batted .239, with six homers and 19 runs scored. He also hit two homers in one game that season.

Schumacher gave his teammates a scare during one game played on a brutally hot afternoon in St. Louis. He passed out from the heat in the sixth inning, and no heartbeat was detected, but he was packed in ice and revived.

During World War II, Schumacher spent the seasons from 1942 through 1945 as an officer on an aircraft carrier before returning to pitch for the Giants in 1946. After retiring from baseball with a 158–121 lifetime mark, Schumacher became executive vice president with the Adirondack Bat Company in his hometown of Dolgeville. He remained with them until 1968, after which he spent some time working with the Little League organization in Williamsport, Pennsylvania.

Herb Score

Score, Herbert Jude **P**

1955–62 B:6/7/1933, Rosedale, NY Deb:4/15/1955, CLE AL BL/TL 6'2", 185

W	L	PCT	G	SH	IP	BB	SO	ERA
55	46	.545	150	11	858[1]	573	837	3.36

Herb Score was one of baseball's might-have-beens. The Cleveland Indian lefthander was seemingly on his way to the Hall of Fame—until a line drive off the bat of Yankee Gil McDougald ruined his career in 1957.

Score was a high school sensation. Scouts from 14 of the 16 major league clubs were camping on his doorstep. Four clubs promised to top his best offer. Score received a concrete offer of $80,000 from one club, but he signed with Cleveland for $60,000. He made that decision based on the friendship he had established with Cy Slapnicka, the scout who also had signed pitcher Bob Feller.

The Indians sent Score to their Indianapolis club in 1952, but he pitched wildly, and they demoted him to Reading in 1953. The next year Score returned to Indianapolis and set the American Association on fire, leading in innings pitched at 251, with 22 wins, a league-record 330 strikeouts, 140 walks, and a 2.62 ERA. *The Sporting News* named him Minor League Player of the Year.

As a rookie with Cleveland in 1955 he went 16–10, with a league-leading 245 strikeouts in 227⅓ innings, an American League rookie record. It was also the highest strikeout total by a big leaguer since Feller set the top major league mark of 348 in 1946. Sixteen of Score's strikeouts came against the Red Sox on May 1, including nine in the first three innings. Score's 2.85 ERA was also the fourth best in the league. To no one's surprise, the Baseball Writers Association of America elected him AL Rookie of the Year.

Score was even better in 1956. He went 20–9 and led the league with five shutouts and 263 strikeouts. He struck out 15 Senators on May 19 and started in the All-Star Game. He was 23 years old.

"He made perfect seem second-rate," teammate Rocky Colavito said. "He had a burning desire to excel. In warm-ups he didn't jog, he ran. In playing catch along the sidelines, he didn't lob, he threw. Even after he won a game, he talked to me for hours about how he might have played better. He wouldn't accept an average performance."

Score started 1957 strongly, and Red Sox owner Tom Yawkey offered Cleveland $1 million in cash for him. The Indians turned it down. On May 7 Score faced the Yankees at Cleveland's Municipal Stadium. He retired leadoff batter Hank Bauer. McDougald was next and he lined one back through the box. Score could see it coming straight at his eye, but there was nothing he could do. He bled profusely and his teammates stuffed a towel around his mouth and nose. "Hey, get the towel out, you're going to choke me!" he shouted. "I was conscious the whole time and lucid and calm. I think I was the calmest one there," he recalled.

When they got him back to the clubhouse, Score realized he couldn't see anything out of his damaged eye. "Do I still have an eye?" he asked the team physician. He did, but he had to spend eight days in a Cleveland hospital, motionless, in total darkness.

When he came back he was never the same. He hung on for six years, trying to reclaim his brilliance. Instead, he won 19 games and lost 27. "You know, people think what happened to me that night cost me my career," Score said years later. "But they're wrong. That had nothing to do with my losing my effectiveness. The following spring I was pitching as well as I ever did. Then I was pitching in Washington. In the third or fourth inning my arm started to bother me. I didn't say anything. I figured it would work out. These are the mistakes you make when you're young."

In 1960 Score was traded to the White Sox for pitcher Barry Latman. Chicago asked him to go down to the San Diego farm club. He complied, but he was still ineffective. His last stop was Indianapolis, where the results were the same. "Some people asked me why I went back to the minor leagues," Score said. "They felt I was humiliating myself. But I never felt humiliated. There was no disgrace in what I was doing. The disgrace would have been in not trying." Score retired as a player in 1962 and broadcast Cleveland baseball for over 30 years.

Everett Scott

Scott, Lewis Everett **SS**

1914–26 B:11/19/1892, Bluffton, IN D:11/2/1960, Fort Wayne, IN Deb: 04/14/1914, BOS AL BR/TR 5'8", 148

G	AB	R	H	HR	RBI	OBP	SLG	AVG
1654	5837	552	1455	20	551	.281	.315	.249

Every fan knows that Lou Gehrig played in 2,130 consecutive games, but few today remember the player whose streak Gehrig broke. It was Lewis Everett "Deacon" Scott, the Luis Aparicio of his day. Scott led American League shortstops in fielding percentage from 1916 to 1923. He also led league shortstops twice each in putouts, assists, and double plays.

Scott broke in with the Red Sox in 1914, played in the 1915 World Series without distinction, and started his streak on June 20, 1916, at Fenway Park. From 1914 through 1918 Scott never hit better than .241 in any season. But he appeared in three World Series during those five years, each of them won by the Red Sox.

On December 21, 1921, Scott and pitchers Sad Sam Jones and Joe Bush were traded to the Yankees in exchange for four players and $50,000, as owner Harry Frazee began dismantling the Red Sox. Scott replaced Babe Ruth as Yankees captain in 1922, as Ruth lasted just six days with the title.

By 1925 Scott's streak stood at 1,307 games. On May 6 manager Miller Huggins benched Scott for Pee Wee Wanninger, noticing that Scott was slowing down because of bad knees. Ironically, on June 1, Gehrig pinch-hit for Wanninger to begin his own consecutive games streak and, of course, later became the captain of the Yankees.

Scott, meanwhile, was sold to Washington on June 17. He played with the Chicago White Sox and Cincinnati Reds in 1926 before retiring at the end of the season.

George Scott

Scott, George Charles **1B–3B–DH**

1966–79 B:3/23/1944, Greenville, MS Deb:4/12/1966, BOS AL BR/TR 6'2", 215

G	AB	R	H	HR	RBI	OBP	SLG	AVG
2034	7433	957	1992	271	1051	.335	.435	.268

George Scott was built like an overweight linebacker and wore a batting helmet in the field, but his work around first base was positively graceful. From 1967 through 1976 he won eight Gold Gloves. The two years he didn't win the Gold Glove he had an excuse—he was splitting time between first and third base.

Scott, who picked up the nickname "Boomer" because he could hit the baseball a great distance, signed with the Red Sox in 1962 as a third baseman, but he made it to the majors in 1966 as a first baseman. As a rookie he hit .245, with 27 homers and 90 RBIs and a league-leading 152 strikeouts. He became just the second rookie first baseman to start the All-Star Game.

The next year he hit .303 for the pennant-winning 1967 Red Sox, with 19 homers and 82 RBIs (and 119 strikeouts). He also won his first Gold Glove. And then came 1968—Scott had as bad a year as a player can have. He hit .171, with three homers and 25 RBIs, in 350 at bats. He won his second Gold Glove, but that hardly compensated for his offensive numbers.

Being overweight didn't help. Scott always had problems with his weight, and later in his career he ballooned up to 250 pounds, but his big problem was a severe case of "Fenwayitis." Given the short distance to the Fenway Park's "Green Monster" in left field, the righthanded slugger started trying to pull balls over the wall, which completely threw off his swing. "He got so bad he was pulling off the ball every time he swung," said Dick Williams, his manager then. "His swing was messed up for a couple of years." According to Williams, Boston general manager Dick O'Connell came up with a novel strategy to get Scott to stop trying to pull the ball.

"He made a deal with George," Williams said. "For every hit he got from the shortstop position to the right field line, Dick would give him $20, and in those days $20 meant something. And every hit George got from the shortstop position to the left field line, George had to give Dick $10."

In 1969 Scott platooned at two different positions: against righthanders he played third base and Dalton Jones played first base, and against righthanders Scott played first and rookie Syd O'Brien handled third. In 1970 he hit .296, with 16 homers and 63 RBIs, again moving between first and third. He was still striking out frequently—he fanned 1,418 times in 7,433 career at bats—but ever so slowly he was beginning to put his swing back in order.

His career really took off after he was traded to the Brewers in October 1971 in a 10-player deal that brought outfielder Tommy Harper to the Red Sox. The next season Scott hit 20 homers and drove in 88 runs for Milwaukee, and in 1973 he batted a career-best .306, with 24 homers and 107 RBIs.

Two years later he led the league in homers and RBIs, but in 1977 he was traded back to the Red Sox in a deal that sent first baseman Cecil Cooper to the Brewers. Scott had his last hurrah that year when he hit 33 homers and drove in 95 runs. He also made the All-Star team for the third and final time.

He was 33 years old, however, and his weight problems were catching up to him. He retired in 1979 after hitting only six homers in 346 at bats that season. Scott continued to play in Mexico and went on to manage there. He later returned to Boston, where he spent part of his time coaching baseball for Roxbury Community College. He went on to manage the Massachusetts Mad Dogs of the independent Northeastern and Northern leagues.

Jim Scott

Scott, James **P**

1909–17 U(1930–31) B:4/23/1888, Deadwood, SD D:4/7/1957, Jacumba, CA Deb:4/25/1909, CHI AL BR/TR 6'1", 235

W	L	PCT	G	SH	IP	BB	SO	ERA
107	113	.486	317	26	1892	609	945	2.30

Despite pitching a no-hitter and winning 20 games, Jim Scott's life remains something of a mystery. Former teammate Doc White claimed that Scott, who threw the spitball and screwball, invented the mud ball. And some say that "Death Valley Jim" founded his own religious cult. His nickname was after "Death Valley Scotty," a fabled character of the pioneer West.

In 1913 the righthander led the American League in both starts and losses and was a rare 20-game winner and loser. On June 22 of that year he struck out 15 Browns. Scott, who in his career had two one-hitters, pitched nine hitless innings against Washington on May 14, 1914; the Senators had two hits in the 10th to win the game, 1–0. The first hit was a single by Chick Gandil who was then knocked in by Howard Shanks.

Scott was 7–0 against the Philadelphia Athletics in 1915, including a 5–0 shutout on August 29 that he lasted just 68 minutes. It was one of his league-leading seven shutouts that season. Scott pitched for the White Sox in 1917, but the picture gets muddy after that.

He reportedly served in France in World War I. Then in the 1920s he supposedly founded a religious cult in Southern California. He reappeared in baseball as an umpire, serving as an arbiter at the minor league level and for the National League in 1930 and 1931.

Mike Scott

Scott, Michael Warren **P**

1979–91 B:4/26/1955, Santa Monica, CA Deb:4/18/1979, NY NL BR/TR 6'3", 215

W	L	PCT	G	SH	IP	BB	SO	ERA
124	108	.534	347	22	2068^{2}	627	1469	3.54

From 1979 through 1984 Mike Scott was merely another pitcher barely clinging to a major league job. He had an excellent fastball, a very mediocre breaking ball, and no changeup to speak of. His career record was a dismal 29–44. "I was a guy who just kind of hung on, sometimes as the 10th guy on a 10-man pitching staff," he said. "I never knew from one game to the next whether I'd be looking for a new line of work." Then he met former Tigers pitching coach Roger Craig and the split-finger fastball. Two years later, he was the National League's Cy Young Award winner.

Scott began his pro career as a second-round selection of the Mets and was first assigned to Jackson of the Texas League in 1976. From 1977 to 1980 he spent parts of every year with Tidewater of the International League. With the bottom-dwelling Mets of the early 1980s, Scott continued to pitch unimpressively. His best victory total was seven in 1982 when he compiled a 5.14 ERA. New York gave up on Scott after that season, dealing him to Houston for outfielder Danny Heep. Scott had a modicum of success in 1983, going 10–6, but in 1984 he fell to 5–11.

It was Astros third baseman Enos Cabell who first suggested that Scott try a split-finger fastball. Cabell had spent two seasons in Detroit and recalled the success pitching coach Roger Craig had in teaching the pitch. "You know that split-fingered fastball Bruce Sutter throws?" Cabell said to Scott. "Craig taught that to Jack Morris and converted him into a 20-game winner."

The Astros approached Craig, who was between positions, and he agreed that if Scott were to come out to his San Diego home that winter he would work with him on the delivery. "The split-fingered fastball is a very difficult pitch to throw," Craig once said. "Sometimes I can tell a guy after he's thrown four pitches to forget it and try something else. The first time Scott threw it, I knew he was going to master it."

The turnaround was almost immediate. "The first time I threw it in spring training, I knew it was going to work," Scott said. "Guys were swinging at balls in the dirt that day." Now he had an off-speed pitch to complement his fastball, and what an off-speed pitch it was—it literally exploded downward. As a result, in 1985 he went 18–8. "Having the split-finger made all the difference," Scott said. "It didn't matter that I had a 90-mph fastball and pretty good control. If the hitters in this league know what's coming, they'll hit it."

Scott's won 18 games again in 1986, and his other stats zoomed off the chart. He led the NL in ERA and innings pitched. The 31-year-old pitcher also led the league with 306 strikeouts; at the time, only two other pitchers over age 30 had recorded 300 or more strikeouts—and both had done in the 1800s. (Sandy Koufax, Nolan Ryan, and Mickey Lolich had all done it at age 30, and Ryan later struck out 301 in 1989 at age 42.)

The increase in strikeouts was unprecedented. Scott's previous high had been 137 just the previous season. The year before he added the splitter, he fanned 83. Even in the minors his best had been only 93.

Scott saved his best for last in 1986. On September 25 he clinched the NL West title for Houston by pitching a 2–0 no-hitter against San Francisco. Against the Mets in the National League Championship Series, Scott compiled an 0.50 ERA, won two games, and struck out 19 in 18 innings. He had the Mets so baffled that during his 3–1 win in Game 4, the Mets collected balls looking for scuff marks as proof for the umpire. The underlying feeling among fans and the media was that if New York had to face Scott in a do-or-die Game 7, the result was practically a foregone conclusion. The Mets won Games 5 and 6 in extra innings to clinch the pennant, but Scott was named the NLCS Most Valuable Player.

Scott won not only the National League Cy Young Award in 1986, but he also was named *The Sporting News* National League Pitcher of the Year. The belief persisted that Scott's success was due not so much to the splitter but to his doctoring of the ball, and doubters dubbed him "Mike Scuff." He denied the charge and was backed up by at least one National League arbiter. "I've been in this league 25 years and I'll stake all my experience, all my career, on the fact that Scott doesn't doctor the baseball," umpire Doug Harvey contended in 1987.

Scott was effective, if not brilliant, in the next two years, for a combined 30–21, and he managed his only 20-win season in 1989, when he was 20–10. But arm problems caught up to him and he was out of baseball two years later.

Vin Scully

Broadcaster B:11/29/1927

Vin Scully brought Dodgers baseball to three generations of Dodgers fans. He first called the games with Red Barber in Brooklyn and later was one of baseball's last solo acts in the broadcast booth in Los Angeles. His voice remains one of the most distinctive in broadcasting history.

"When I was growing up, everybody wanted to be a nurse, doctor, lawyer. Not me. I wanted to be a sportscaster," said Scully. He attended Fordham Prep, graduated from Fordham University, played center field on the school team, and oversaw the school radio station.

After he served two years in the navy, Scully joined WTOP in Washington in February 1950. Later that same year he began broadcasting Dodgers games with Barber and Connie Desmond, replacing Ernie Harwell, who had been hired by the New York Giants.

In 1954, when he was only 26 years old, Scully became the Dodgers' No. 1 announcer after Barber went to the Yankees. Writer Harold Rosenthal said, "Dodger boss Walter O'Malley had taken an instant liking to Vin. He was an outgoing kind of guy. So there was no question that Scully would get the top job, even though he was just a kid."

When the Dodgers went west in 1958, Scully went with them and educated a generation of fans. He has been named the nation's outstanding sportscaster four times, and in 1987 he received the Ronald Reagan Media Award from the United States Sports Academy.

More than just an announcer, Scully has become a celebrity in his own right. In 1976 Dodgers fans voted him the Most Memorable Personality in Los Angeles baseball history. In 1982 he had his star placed on Hollywood's Walk of Fame.

Tom Seaver

Seaver, George Thomas **P**

1967–86 B:11/17/1944, Fresno, CA Deb:4/13/1967, NY NL BR/TR 6'1", 206

W	L	PCT	G	SH	IP	BB	SO	ERA
311	205	.603	656	61	4782^{2}	1390	3640	2.86

Nicknamed "The Franchise" because of his value to the Mets in the late 1960s and early 1970s, Tom Seaver is one of only a few players who, by example, have turned a struggling team into a winner. The stocky, muscular, Seaver harnessed considerable power from a leg drive that was so hard his right knee pounded the mound as he released the ball. He won three Cy

Young Awards, led the league in wins and ERA three times each, and struck out 3,640 batters en route to compiling a 311–205 record during 20 seasons.

The son of former Walker Cup golfer Charles Seaver, "Tom Terrific" attended the University of Southern California. The Braves originally signed him in February 1966 for $40,000 plus $11,000 in other considerations, but Commissioner William D. Eckert voided his contract because USC's season had already started when Seaver signed.

Eckert ruled that any club wishing to match the Braves' figure could bid on Seaver. The names of three bidding teams—the Mets, the Phillies, and the Indians—were put into a hat, and New York, the team Seaver wanted to play for, won.

In 1966 Seaver was assigned to Jacksonville of the International League, where it soon became apparent that he was more than a power pitcher. Jacksonville manager Solly Hemus said, "He has so much poise. Tom reminds me of Bob Gibson out on the mound. He's in command all the time, and the kid is only 21 years old. Tom Seaver has a 35-year-old head on top of a 21-year-old body. Usually we get a 35-year-old arm attached to a 21-year-old head."

In 1967 Seaver, at age 23, won the National League Rookie of the Year Award when he went 16–13 with a 2.76 ERA for a dismal Mets team. "When I came to the Mets there was an aura of defeatism on the team, a feeling of 'let's get it over with.' I could not accept that," Seaver said.

By 1969 a staff of young pitchers that included Nolan Ryan, Jerry Koosman, Gary Gentry, and Seaver took the "Miracle" Mets to the world championship. Seaver was 25–7 with a 2.21 ERA that year. Fittingly, Seaver started and won the first postseason game in Mets history, which was also the first ever National League Championship Series game. The Mets swept the Braves in three games to take the pennant. He went 1–1 with a 3.00 ERA to help defeat the favored Orioles four games to one in the World Series.

"If the Mets can win the World Series, the United States can get out of Vietnam," Seaver said at the time. He and his wife placed an ad in *The New York Times* on December 31, 1969, which said, "On the eve of 1970, please join us in a prayer for peace. Tom and Nancy Seaver."

Seaver won the 1969 Cy Young Award, was named *The Sporting News* Pitcher of the Year, and narrowly lost the Most Valuable Player Award to Willie McCovey. He became the second player to win both a Rookie of the Year Award and a Cy Young Award. Don Newcombe had been the first.

On April 22, 1970, Seaver struck out 19 San Diego, including the last 10 batters in the game for a 2–1 Mets win. The 10 consecutive strikeouts broke an 86-year-old record, and Seaver's mark remained unmatched through the end of the 20th century. San Diego pitching coach Johnny Podres, who had once struck out eight consecutive batters, said, "[Seaver] was fantastic, outstanding. There was no doubt in my mind he would break the record. He had perfect rhythm. As hard as he was throwing, he was still hitting the spots. If you didn't swing, it was still a strike."

During his first 10½ seasons Seaver won 189 games and lost 110 for the Mets and collected three Cy Young Awards. His lowest ERA during that stretch came in 1971 when he recorded a 1.76 mark. He was 1–1 with a 1.62 ERA in the 1973 NLCS against the Reds, which New York won in five games. The Mets, whose 83 wins were the lowest ever for a National League champion, lost to Oakland in seven games.

In 1975 he sparkled with a 22–9 record, a 2.38 ERA, and a league-leading 243 strikeouts. In 1976 Seaver once again led the National League in strikeouts, his ninth straight season with at least 200 strikeouts. But trouble was brewing in paradise.

Seaver, a proud man, feuded with Mets general manager M. Donald Grant on a variety of issues. The final straw came when *New York Daily News* columnist Dick Young, a Grant ally, wrote that "Nolan Ryan is getting more money than Tom Seaver and that galls Tom because Nancy Seaver and Ruth Ryan are very friendly and Tom Seaver long has treated Ryan like a little brother."

Seaver demanded a trade and Grant was happy to comply. In what is remembered in New York as "the Midnight Massacre," Grant traded Seaver and Dave Kingman in separate deals on June 15. Seaver went to Cincinnati for second baseman Doug Flynn, pitcher Pat Zachry, and outfielders Steve Henderson and Dan Norman.

In an emotional press conference after the trade, Seaver broke down in tears and could not continue. Columnist Red Smith wrote that "Tom Seaver has been one of the finest pitchers in the game....He is his own man, thoughtful, perceptive, and unafraid to speak his mind. Because of this, M. Donald Grant and his sycophants put Seaver away as a troublemaker. They mistake dignity for arrogance."

Seaver pitched in Cincinnati until 1982, twice leading the league in winning percentage. On June 16, 1978, he notched the only no-hitter of his major league career, beating St. Louis, 4–0. In the strike-shortened 1981 season Seaver went

14–2 with a 2.55 ERA. But the following season he was only 5–13, the first losing season of his career. On December 15, 1982, Seaver was traded back to the Mets.

He was welcomed back with open arms by Mets fans, but the team, which had not finished above fifth since Seaver left, offered little support. He struggled to a 9–14 mark and in January 1984 the White Sox claimed him in the compensation draft after losing free agent Dennis Lamp to the Blue Jays.

Seaver was livid and threatened to retire rather than pitch for the White Sox. He finally relented and pitched two solid seasons for Chicago, winning 15 games in 1984 and 16 in 1985. Ironically he won his 300th game in New York—at Yankee Stadium—as a member of the White Sox. On June 29, 1986, Seaver, sporting a 2–6 record, was traded to the Red Sox where he went 5–7. The Red Sox faced the Mets in that year's World Series and Seaver was in visitor's dugout at Shea Stadium when the Mets won in seven games. Seaver was injured and did not pitch in the Series; in fact, he did not pitch again.

He tried to come back with the Mets as a free agent in 1987, but injuries kept him from a third tour of duty in New York. The Mets retired Seaver's No. 41 in 1992.

Seaver began a career in broadcasting in 1975, when he did work for Channel 2 in New York. He also worked during the postseason for ABC and NBC from 1976 to 1982, and for CBS Radio as well. He later broadcast for the Yankees and in 1999 became a Mets broadcaster. He has also written several books on pitching. Seaver was named to the Hall of Fame in 1992, his first year of eligibility.

Pat Seerey

Seerey, James Patrick **OF**

1943–49 B:3/17/1923, Wilburton, OK D:4/28/1986, Jennings, MO Deb:6/09/1943, CLE AL BR/TR 5'10", 200

G	AB	R	H	HR	RBI	OBP	SLG	AVG
561	1815	236	406	86	261	.321	.412	.224

Several well-known players—including Willie Mays, Lou Gehrig, Gil Hodges, and Mike Schmidt—hit four home runs in a single game. So did Pat Seerey.

Seerey started his professional career in 1941 with Appleton, where he batted .330 and led the Wisconsin State League with 31 homers and 117 RBIs. He enjoyed more success for Cedar Rapids in 1942, topping the 3-I League with 33 homers. Seerey reached the majors with sheer power alone. "Pat's theory was just to hit the ball," explained Hank Greenberg. "He didn't do any thinking at all. He had a slight hitch in his swing. When the ball was thrown around the letters of the uniform, he would get under it and usually strike out or pop up."

An all-or-nothing hitter, Seerey led the American League in strikeouts in his first three full seasons in the majors. But he also had a three-homer performance for Cleveland on July 13, 1945, when he drove in eight runs. Bob Feller returned from the service in 1945, and Seerey's two-run homer gave "Rapid Robert" a victory in his first game back.

A defensive liability, Seerey rates a footnote afield. On September 13, 1946, as the Indians used the "Williams Shift," Ted Williams collected his only inside-the-park home run when he punched a ball over Seerey's head in left field.

Seerey belted a career-high 26 homers in 1946, but the following season he batted only .171 with 11 round-trippers. He played 10 games for Cleveland in 1948 before he was traded to the White Sox in June. Six weeks later, on July 18, he hit four homers in a game against the Philadelphia Athletics. The first three came in consecutive innings off Carl Scheib, the fourth in the 11th inning off Lou Brissie, as Chicago won the game, 12–11.

Although he slugged 19 homers in 1948, he also struck out a league-leading 102 times in only 363 at bats. He was released in 1949, his career over at the ripe age of 26.

David Segui

Segui, David Vincent **1B**

1990–* B:7/19/1966, Kansas City, KS Deb: 5/8/1990, BAL AL BB/TL 6'1", 202

G	AB	R	H	HR	RBI	OBP	SLG	AVG
1113	3603	498	1028	102	487	.355	.435	.285

David Segui was born into a baseball family. His father Diego pitched for seven major league teams, and was the only player to play for both the Seattle Pilots and Seattle Mariners. David was drafted in the 18th round of the 1987 June draft by Baltimore out of Louisiana Tech.

He did not hit for big power during most of his career, which is why both the Orioles and the Mets tried unsuccessfully to make him into an outfielder. He never hit more than 12 home runs until 1997, his sixth full year in the majors. That year he smacked 21 homers and batted a career-best .307 for the Expos. He signed as a free agent with Seattle, where he had another solid season in 1998 despite playing with a bad knee for the final two months. He was traded to Toronto in midseason 1999 for two young pitchers.

Segui's good reputation with the glove helped keep him in the lineup even though he lacked the power normally expected from a first baseman. He committed only 34 errors in 965 games at first base. Through 1999 he had the third-best career fielding percentage among first basemen, behind only Steve Garvey and Don Mattingly.

Diego Segui

Segui, Diego Pablo (Gonzalez) **P**

1962–75, 1977 B:8/17/1937, Holguin, Cuba
Deb:4/12/1962, KC AL BR/TR 6', 190

W	L	PCT	G	SV	IP	BB	SO	ERA
92	111	.453	639	71	1807^{2}	786	1298	3.81

At times in his career Diego Segui was both a reliable starting pitcher and an effective reliever, but the putrid teams he played for kept the Cuban righthander from winning with any consistency. Although he actually had a .500 record or better eight times, he also led the AL in losses in 1964, one of five seasons his winning percentage was .320 or worse. Mickey Mantle once called him one of the American League's most underrated players.

Segui first made the majors with the 1962 Kansas City Athletics. A slow-working practitioner of the forkball (which some said was wet), he had two impressive seasons before his luck ran out. He went 19–43 with the A's and Washington Senators between 1964 and 1967; his teams finished last three times in that span.

By age 30, Segui was out of the majors, and just short of a pension. With two sons (including future big leaguer David) to support, Diego worked his way back to the A's bullpen—now located in Oakland. Segui went 12–6 with 12 saves for the hapless 1969 Seattle Pilots. He was voted the team's Most Valuable Player. The Pilots relocated to Milwaukee, and Segui returned to Oakland. He led the AL with a 2.56 ERA in 1970, and helped the A's win a divisional title the following year.

After two years apiece in St. Louis and Boston, Segui wound up with the expansion Seattle Mariners in 1977. He was the team's Opening Day starter, making him the only man to play for both Seattle clubs. He lost the opener and six more decisions before he was released. He returned to the minors where, at age 40, he pitched a perfect game.

Peter Seitz

Seitz, Peter

Professional Arbitrator B:5/17/1905, D:10/17/1983, New York, NY

Peter Seitz never swung a bat or pitched an inning during a major league game, yet his impact on Organized Baseball was as great as Babe Ruth's. He made his mark on the game in 1975 when he laid the groundwork for baseball's current system of free agency as an arbitrator for the major league clubs and the Major League Baseball Players Association (MLBPA). He was also permanent arbitrator for the National Basketball Association and the National Basketball Players Association.

Although Seitz's rulings as an arbitrator covered a broad range of labor and management problems, it was his role in both professional baseball and basketball that attracted national attention. His rulings in the cases of pitchers Andy Messersmith of the Los Angeles Dodgers and Dave McNally of the Montreal Expos revolutionized the way major league clubs signed their players.

Messersmith and McNally requested free agent status after pitching in the 1975 season without signing new contracts. Messersmith was looking for a no-trade clause in his new contract, and McNally was upset about the Expos' reneging on certain promises they had made to him, so both refused to sign their 1975 contracts.

For nearly 100 years Organized Baseball had lived by a reserve clause that bound players to their clubs for their entire professional careers unless they were traded, sold, or released. Messersmith and McNally challenged the legality of the automatic renewal clause in the standard contract.

They played a full year without signing contracts, then demanded their freedom. Their appeal was heard by three officials: John Gaherin, who represented the owners; Marvin Miller, the economist who was executive director of the MLBPA; and Seitz, a professional arbitrator from New York who served as an impartial judge. (A year earlier Seitz had ruled that Catfish Hunter's contract was void; Hunter then took his services to the highest bidder.

In a 70-page opinion, Seitz cast the deciding vote that ruled Messersmith and McNally free agents. "It was represented to me," Seitz said, "that any decision sustaining Messersmith and McNally would have dire results, wreak great harm to the reserve system and do serious damage to the sport of baseball and would encourage many other players to elect and become free agents.

"The panel's sole duty is to interpret and apply agreements and understandings of the parties. If any of the expressed apprehensions and fears are soundly based, I am confident that the dislocations and damage to the reserve system can be avoided or minimized through good-faith collective bargaining between the parties." Following his decision, Seitz was immediately fired by baseball's owners, who called his action detrimental to the game.

Seitz, a lawyer, held other important positions as an arbitrator. In 1965 and 1966 he was a public member of the American Arbitration Association's labor-management panel that studied collective bargaining procedures in New York City and made recommendations that provided the basis for the Office of Collective Bargaining and the city's current labor law. He was also a public member of the National Wage Stabilization Board, counsel and assistant to the director of the Federal Mediation and Conciliation Service, and director for industrial relations for the Defense Department.

Kevin Seitzer

Seitzer, Kevin Lee **3B-1B-DH**

1986–97 B:3/26/1962, Springfield, IL Deb:9/3/1986, KC AL BR/TR 5'11", 190

G	AB	R	H	HR	RBI	OBP	SLG	AVG
1439	5278	739	1557	74	613	.378	.404	.295

Kevin Seitzer pounded out six .300 seasons, despite several personal and physical hardships over his career. He began his career as George Brett's replacement at third base; a move that was, no doubt, made easier by the fact that Brett simply moved to first base.

Seitzer batted .323 in 96 at bats as a September call-up for the Royals in 1986. Seitzer hit .323 again in 1987 and actually led the league with 207 hits. On August 2 he went 6-for-6 with two home runs and seven RBIs against the Red Sox. He played in the All-Star Game, and he would have been the AL Rookie of the Year if not for Mark McGwire's 49 home runs.

Seitzer, an excellent breaking-ball hitter, used the whole field and did not strike out much. Away from the park, however, he suffered from a drinking problem and a troubled marriage. He became a born-again Christian in 1989, which he said helped turn his life around.

Seitzer's average dipped to the upper .200s for several seasons. Because of his lack of speed and power, his mediocrity at third base, and his bad knees beginning in 1991, he bounced to Milwaukee, to Oakland, and again to the Brewers. He rebounded to bat .314 in 1994. He suffered multiple facial fractures when hit by a pitch from Melido Perez in August; Seitzer returned two games later wearing a helmet with a facemask.

He hit .311 in an All-Star season with Milwaukee in 1995, and batted .326 the following yea. He was traded to Cleveland in deal for Jeromy Burnitz late in the season, and played in the postseason for the first time. His final at bat came the following year in the World Series.

Kip Selbach

Selbach, Albert Karl **OF**

1894–1906 B:3/24/1872, Columbus, OH D:2/17/1956, Columbus, OH Deb:4/24/1894, WAS NL BR/TR 5'7", 190

G	AB	R	H	HR	RBI	OBP	SLG	AVG
1610	6158	1064	1803	44	779	.376	.411	.293

Until the latter days of his career, outfielder Kip Selbach seemed condemned to play for teams that wallowed at the bottom of league standings. Beginning in 1894, Selbach spent five years on Washington's hapless National League team, went to sixth-place Cincinnati in 1899, and moved on to last-place New York a year later. A jump to the American League in 1902 landed him with Baltimore, another last-place club, followed by a year and a half with the tail-end Washington Senators.

A righthanded batter who usually hit around .300, Selbach stole 20 or more bases nine times, led the National League in triples in 1895 with 22, and was solid defensively. Nevertheless, he was sometimes the target of critics who blamed him for his teams' shortcomings. When he made three errors in an inning during a 1904 game, AL president Ban Johnson suspended him for indifferent play.

Shortly afterward he was traded to Boston, where he found himself for once with a contender. Although his hitting had fallen off, Selbach was able to help the team to the 1904 American League pennant. He later said the highlight of his career was catching the final out in the game that made Boston the champion. The highlight was tempered by the fact that the National League champion New York Giants refused to play in the World Series. Two years later, when he played his final major league game, Boston had dropped all the way to last in the standings.

Frank Selee

Selee, Frank Gibson

Manager (1890–1905, 1,284–862) B:10/26/1859, Amherst, NY D:7/5/1909, Denver, CO

Ned Hanlon of the battling Baltimore Orioles may have been more famous, but soft-spoken Frank Selee is widely regarded as the premier manager of the 1890s and early 1900s. Selee built powerhouse teams in both Boston and Chicago.

The mustachioed, sad-looking Selee possesses the fourth best won-lost record (.598) in major league history among managers with at least 1,000 games; only Jim Mutrie, Charles Comiskey, and Joe McCarthy had better managerial records. Selee won five pennants in his 16-year big league career—and would certainly have won more had his life not been cut short by tuberculosis.

The son of a Methodist minister, Selee lived for a time in Truro on Cape Cod, but spent most of his youth in Melrose, Massachusetts. Never much of the player, his pro career appears to consist of a few games for Waltham and Haverhill of the Massachusetts State League in 1884. He managed Haverhill in 1885–86 and won pennants with Oshkosh (76–41, .649) of the Northwest League in 1887 and with the Omaha Omahogs (83–38, .686) of the Western Association in 1899.

When Selee replaced Jim Hart as Boston Beaneaters manager in 1890, the team was suffering badly from defections to the rival Players' League. Selee brought in talent such as pitcher Kid Nichols and second baseman Bobby Lowe from the Western Association and managed to bring the team in fifth.

The next year he captured his first National League pennant, as the Beaneaters went 87–51, beating out Cap Anson's Chicago White Stockings by 3½ games. Selee's Beaneaters repeated in 1892, posting an impressive 102–48 record, outpacing Cleveland by 8½ games. In the postseason Boston again vanquished Cleveland five games to none (with one tie). In 1893 the Beaneaters won again, recording an 86–43 mark.

Boston did not win another pennant, however, until 1897 when Kid Nichols won 30 games and the team was 93–39. The team was led by third baseman Jimmy Collins (who Selee had stuck with when he previously struggled) and first baseman Fred Tenney (who he had converted from catching). In the postseason Baltimore defeated Boston 4–1 in Temple Cup competition. Nichols "slipped" to 29 wins in 1898, but the club went 102–47 and won another pennant.

Selee won those pennants by being a sharp judge of talent who drilled his players in the fundamentals. Some credit him with devising the hit-and-run play. But he was no martinet. He treated his players with respect and gave them a great deal of leeway in how they played the game. "He didn't bother with a lot of signals," said Bobby Lowe, "but let his players figure out their own plays. He didn't blame them if they took a chance that failed. He believed in place-hitting, sacrifice-hitting, and stealing bases. He was wonderful with young players."

Selee never made more than $3,500 per season, managing the Beaneaters. To supplement his income he (along with former Philadelphia first baseman Sid Farrar—father of opera singer Geraldine Farrar) he operated a haberdashery in Melrose.

"If I make things pleasant for the players, they reciprocate," Selee once revealed, "I want them to be temperate and live properly. I do not believe that men who are engaged in such exhilarating exercise should be kept in strait jackets all the time, but I expect them to be in condition to play. I do not want a man who cannot appreciate such treatment."

When Ban Johnson founded the American League, Beaneaters ownership refused to financially compete and lost talent to the new league. The club tumbled in the standings, and ownership made Selee the fall guy, replacing him as manager with Al Buckenberger.

Jim Hart, now owner of the Cubs, saw Selee was available and in 1902 hired him to take over his rather dispirited franchise. Selee never won a pennant with Chicago but created a team that would later become a National League powerhouse. He converted Frank Chance from a catcher to first baseman, Johnny Evers from a shortstop to a second baseman, and Joe Tinker from a third baseman to a shortstop. Selee's Cubs were on the verge on becoming a dynasty when tuberculosis struck, forcing him to retire during the 1905 season. Chance took over as player-manager. "Selee built the team that won three straight pennants in Chicago," said Fred Tenney, "and Chance got all the credit."

Selee managed the Pueblo Indians of the Class A Western League in 1906 but finished last. In 1907 he failed to finish out the season at Pueblo. He died in Denver in 1909. He was elected to the Hall of Fame in 1999.

Bud Selig

Selig, Allan H.

Owner (1970-98) Commissioner (1992–*) B:7/30/1934, Milwaukee, WI

Bud Selig grew up watching the minor league Milwaukee Brewers; at 35 he became owner of a major league team and named it the Brewers; and at 58 he became overseer of every team in baseball. Selig led a group of dissatisfied owners that forced the ouster of baseball commissioner Fay Vincent in September 1992. Selig replaced Vincent on an interim basis. After nearly six years of "searching" for a permanent commissioner, the owners unanimously elected Selig.

It seemed an unlikely climax for a former automobile executive from Wisconsin. Selig changed his allegiance from the Chicago Cubs to the Braves when the franchise moved from Boston to Milwaukee in 1953. He was a major stockholder in the team by the early 1960s. When the Braves moved on to Atlanta, Selig organized a group of local investors intent on bringing another franchise to Milwaukee. After several disappointments, their efforts bore fruit when a bankruptcy court awarded the Seattle Pilots to Selig's group on April 1, 1970. A week later the re-christened Brewers played their first game at County Stadium.

Selig's Brewers won just one pennant in his 28 years in charge, but his fellow owners valued him nonetheless. With the collective bargaining agreement due to expire in 1994, he rallied the owners behind a proposal calling for revenue-sharing and a salary cap—a concept the players union flatly rejected. On August 12, with Tony Gwynn chasing .400 and the New York Yankees and Montreal Expos having dream seasons, play was suspended. A month later, to the shock of fans worldwide, Selig announced the cancellation of the World Series.

Over eight months of ensuing negotiations, everyone from children to presidents tried and failed to move the parties toward compromise. In February the owners invited "replacement players"—the retired, the marginal, and others—to fill training camps and start preparing for the season. Finally, on March 31, a federal judge issued an injunction against the owners, and the real players returned to work (with a reduced 144-game schedule). A new four-year contract was later signed.

After the strike, baseball tried new directions: another round of playoffs, interleague play, limited revenue sharing, and more expansion. Some ideas proved popular and successful; for example, the universal retirement of Jackie Robinson's number, and games in Mexico and other locations. Other attempts, such as the Baseball Network and Selig's failed push for radical realignment of the leagues, did not work. In 1998, however, the Brewers, under the stewardship of his daughter, Wendy Selig-Prieb, became the first team ever to switch from the American League to the National League. That same season, young fans found renewed excitement in the game after years of flagging interest; that can be attributed more to the likes of Mark McGwire and Sammy Sosa than anything that occurred in the commissioner's office. Regardless, that office became more powerful in 1999.

Baseball became centralized in the commissioner's office. Owners unanimously approved a consolidation of scheduling, discipline, and umpiring in September 1999; this came just weeks after a showdown between umpires and the commissioner's office led to the loss of 22 umpires. The jobs of both league presidents—positions that predated the role of commissioner in Organized Baseball—were essentially eradicated.

In the first days of the 21st century Selig received even more power. The owners voted to give Selig the unprecedented authority to do what he sees fit to improve the game, including the ability to fine clubs up to $2 million. Selig announced that all Internet rights for baseball's 30 franchises were placed under the umbrella of Major League Baseball, with all revenue to be shared equally. It remained unclear how this would work over time, but optimists felt it was a step towards addressing baseball's most pressing issue: the growing discrepancy between teams from small and large markets. The resolution of that problem will likely be the defining achievement—or failure—of Selig's tenure.

George Selkirk

Selkirk, George Alexander **OF**

1934–42 B:1/4/1908, Huntsville, Ontario, Canada D:1/19/1987, Ft. Lauderdale, FL Deb:8/12/1934, NY AL BL/TR 6'1", 182

G	AB	R	H	HR	RBI	OBP	SLG	AVG
846	2790	503	810	108	576	.400	.483	.290

It is reported that when George Selkirk first stepped up to bat wearing Babe Ruth's No. 3 on his uniform, the fans at Yankee Stadium booed him. No one could be expected to fill Babe Ruth's shoes, of course. From Selkirk's point of view, he had spent eight years in the minors before the Yankees figured they could use him. Moreover, his nickname, "Twinkletoes," bestowed for his style of running on the balls of his feet, certainly lacked the oomph of "the Sultan of Swat."

But without much fanfare, the Canadian-born George Alexander Selkirk served as a dependable fielder and hitter who drove in more than 100 runs twice in five full seasons as a Yankee. He was a key figure on the overpowering Joe McCarthy-era Yankees. In nine seasons in pinstripes, Selkirk cashed six World Series checks and was twice an All-Star.

At 6-foot 1-inch and 182 pounds, Selkirk had muscles on top of muscles. He could wrestle Lou Gehrig and hold his own. Selkirk had power, if not of Ruthian dimensions. In his best year, 1939, he homered 21 times and drove in 101 runs. He also hit 18 homers twice and 19 once.

Selkirk drove in 107 runs, belted 18 homers, and batted .308 in 1936. He then hit two homers and a triple to drive in three runs in New York's World Series triumph. He started the Yankees eighth-inning rally in Game 1 with a single, and although he was thrown out at home on an infield grounder, another Yank scored and the men from the Bronx won, 2–1. Selkirk's single to left drove in the first score for the Yankees in Game 4, and they never lost the lead. He had four hits in the final two games for a Series average of .333.

Although he played in only 78 games in 1937 because of a broken collarbone, he again had an impact on the World Series. He knocked in six runs and scored five, both more than any other player. He drove in two runs in Game 1 as the Yankees exploded for seven runs in the sixth inning to turn a 1–0 deficit into a rout. Selkirk had three RBIs in Game 2 in another Yankees romp.

In the 1938 World Series, Selkirk brought home the first run of Game 1 with a bobbled infield bouncer, and the Series was, for all intents, over. Despite his great year at the plate in 1939, Selkirk managed only two hits in 12 at bats in that year's Series sweep.

By 1940 notable New York outfielder-first baseman Tommy Henrich crowded the 32-year-old Selkirk out of his full-time job. Selkirk played in only 118 games that year, 70 the next, and 42 in 1942, pinch-hitting three times in the 1941 and 1942 Series.

Selkirk continued his professional career as a minor league manager in the Yankees system. He moved into the front office, first as a director of player personnel for the Kansas City A's, and then as general manager and vice president of the Washington Senators. He later scouted for the Yankees.

Andy Seminick

Seminick, Andrew Wasil **C**

1943–57 B:9/12/1920, Pierce, WV Deb:9/14/1943, PHI NL BR/TR 5'11", 187

G	AB	R	H	HR	RBI	OBP	SLG	AVG
1304	3921	495	953	164	556	.347	.417	.243

Tough-as-nails Andy Seminick led National League catchers in errors five times and suffered many a disappointment on his way to the majors. But as "Grandpa Whiz" on the 1950 Philadelphia "Whiz Kids" team, he helped the Phillies capture their first pennant in 35 years.

His father was a Russian-born coal miner who suffered through periods of unemployment during the Great Depression. Seminick later quit high school to become a collier. He also played baseball as many nights as he could. In 1940, after trying out with some Pittsburgh farm clubs, he was offered a contract with London of the Class D PONY League. But he was handed his release after batting .156 and committing seven errors in only 19 games.

The always soft-spoken Seminick wouldn't give up. He moved to Detroit, played with the Carp Coal Company's semipro team, and badgered the Tigers for a tryout. Finally, a letter from the ballclub arrived, special delivery. "It was from Wish Egan, the chief scout of the Tigers," recalled Seminick. "He told me not to come out anymore."

The Giants similarly instructed Seminick to forget it, but the next spring he made his way down to Tallahassee, Florida, where he signed with the Southern Association's Knoxville Smokies. They assigned him to Elizabethton of the Appalachian League. Seminick managed to stick with Elizabethton and then was promoted to Knoxville. Due to World War II, many big league players were forced to join the service. A bum knee kept him out of the military and the one-time Class D castoff soon found himself in the majors.

Seminick arrived in Philadelphia via a circuitous route. Milwaukee Brewers owner Bill Veeck was somehow aware that the Phils coveted Seminick. Veeck quickly bought him from Knoxville for $15,000. Within a couple of days, he turned around and sold him to Philadelphia for $35,000. Seminick still had plenty of rough edges, and coach Cy Perkins, a former catcher, tried to smooth them out. During the late 1940s Seminick played under Phillies manager Ben Chapman, who tongue-lashed him mercilessly. "I don't know how Seminick stood the abuse Chapman gave him," recalled one teammate.

In 1948 rookie manager Eddie Sawyer fostered a more positive attitude on the Philadelphia club, and Seminick responded. On June 2, 1949, he hit two homers in a single inning. Six weeks later he pounded a homer and a double in the same inning. From September 1949 through July 1950 he slugged three grand slams.

In 1950 Sawyer's psychology paid off for the team at large as the Phillies captured their first pennant since 1915. The youthful club's members, known as "the Whiz Kids," edged out Brooklyn for the pennant. Seminick had career bests of 24 home runs and 68 RBIs in both 1949 and 1950.

On September 27, 1950, Seminick severely damaged his ankle in a home plate collision with the Giants' Monte Irvin. Seminick played through the World Series, which the Yankees swept in four games, but for eight weeks afterward the ankle had to be immobilized in a cast.

Giants manager Leo Durocher said of Seminick: "The more I thought about it afterward, the more I said to myself, 'Here's a real man!' He'll break your back if he has to while the game is on, and he expects you to do the same. When it's all over, he'll shake your hand. That's the way it should be. He's my kind of ballplayer."

On December 10, 1951, Seminick was dealt to Cincinnati in a seven-player trade that brought Smoky Burgess to the Phillies. He played three seasons with the Reds, hitting two grand slams in 1952 and 19 homers in 1953. On April 30, 1955, Seminick was traded back to the Phillies for, among others, Smoky Burgess. Seminick retired in 1957.

Seminick served for many years as the Phils' bullpen coach. He also managed in the Philadelphia farm system in such places as Elmira, Des Moines, Williamsport, Miami, Chattanooga, Macon, and Reading. In a 1969 vote of Phillies fans, Seminick was voted the club's all-time catcher.

Hank Severeid

Severeid, Henry Levai **C**

1911–26 B:6/1/1891, Story City, IA D:12/17/1968, San Antonio, TX Deb:5/15/1911, CIN NL BR/TR 6', 175

G	AB	R	H	HR	RBI	OBP	SLG	AVG
1390	4312	408	1245	17	539	.342	.367	.289

Hank Severeid was unusually durable, catching 1,225 games in the majors and another 1,132 in the minors for a total of 2,357. In 1937 he made his final appearance behind the plate, catching both games of a season-ending doubleheader in the Texas League—at age 46.

From 1911 through 1913 Severeid played a total of 95 games for Cincinnati, but he hit poorly. The St. Louis Browns brought him back to the majors in 1915. He remained their regular backstop for the next 10 years, catching at least 100 games in every season except his first and the 1918 season, when he spent part of the year in military service.

Although he lacked longball power, the 175-pound righthanded batter became a reliable hitter and in 1921 hit a career-high .324. The Browns came close but never won a pennant during Severeid's tenure; St. Louis fell one game short in 1922 despite George Sisler's .420 batting average. Severeid hit 99 points less, but for the second year in a row he had a career-high 78 RBIs.

Dealt to Washington in 1925, he served as the backup catcher for the pennant-winning Senators. The following year he performed in the same capacity for the American League champion Yankees. Severeid hit .280 in eight World Series games. After leaving the majors he batted over .300 for five consecutive seasons in the Pacific Coast League.

Joe Sewell

Sewell, Joseph Wheeler **SS–3B**

1920–33 B:10/9/1898, Titus, AL D:3/6/1990, Mobile, AL Deb:9/10/1920, CLE AL BL/TR 5'6½", 155

G	AB	R	H	HR	RBI	OBP	SLG	AVG
1903	7132	1141	2226	49	1055	.391	.413	.312

Shortstop Joe Sewell was a smooth fielder and a lifetime .312 hitter. He was also, without question, the hardest man in the history of the game to strike out. Even considering the standards of his day, his bat control was remarkable, and by contemporary standards his strikeout ratio is unbelievable. Sewell fanned only once in every 62.6 at bats. Second on the all-time list is Lloyd Waner at 44.9. One of the very best of the post-expansion era was Felix Millan at 23.9.

His ability to make contact resulted in seasons when Sewell fanned only three or four times. In one year, during which Sewell struck out only four times, three of them occurred on called strikes. In only one case did Sewell swing and miss. And at least one of the called third strikes was highly questionable.

"The ball was right at the bill of my cap," recalled Sewell. "[Umpire Bill McGowan] said, 'Strike three, you're out. Oh my God, I missed it, Joe.' But I didn't say a word. I just walked back to the bench. And the next day he came out and apologized and I said, 'Bill, don't worry about it. You were honest about it.'"

Sewell felt there were three key factors in batting: knowing the strike zone, making allowances for the umpire behind the plate, and keeping your eye on the ball. "I hit the ball just about every time I swung at it," he contended late in life. "I could see a ball leave my bat. A lot of people don't believe that's possible. But it sure is.

"All you have to do is watch it. It doesn't disappear when you put the bat on it. I watched a big league game not long ago and I saw some boys striking at balls that I swear they missed by a foot. They couldn't have been looking at those balls. You just know they couldn't."

Alabama-born Joseph Wheeler Sewell, named for a Confederate cavalry officer, was the son of a country doctor. The elder Sewell encouraged sons Joe, Luke, and Tommy to attend the University of Alabama. All did, and all became major league ballplayers. Luke, an American League catcher for 20 seasons, shared the major league record for the most career no-hitters caught, with three. Tommy had only one at bat in the majors, with the Cubs during the 1927 season.

"When I came to the University it was the best break I ever had in my life," contended Joe Sewell. "We had a football coach who came in here from Cleveland named Zinn Scott. He also wrote for the *Cleveland Plain Dealer*. He recommended me and Luke and Riggs Stephenson to the Cleveland Indians. There were seven of us from our baseball team that went off to the major leagues and made it."

After graduating from Alabama in 1920, Sewell signed with the New Orleans Pelicans of the Southern Association. He had only been there for 92 pro games and was hitting .289 when he was ordered to report to the Cleveland Indians.

The Indians were battling the Yankees and the White Sox for the pennant and desperately needed a shortstop. The popular and talented Ray Chapman had been killed by a Carl Mays pitch on

August 16, 1920, and had been replaced by light-hitting Harry Lunte. Lunte soon pulled a hamstring and was out of action.

That's when the Indians called on the inexperienced Sewell. It would have been easy for him to fail. He was called upon during the pressure of a tremendous pennant race, and he was filling in under the most tragic of circumstances. For one game, he sat on the Cleveland bench and thought, "I ain't supposed to be here."

Then manager Tris Speaker inserted him into the lineup against the Philadelphia Athletics. The first time up, Sewell lined a hard-hit ball to center, but it was caught. In his second at bat he hit a pitch over third and into the left-field corner where it rattled around and enabled Sewell to reach third base. "Boy, I went around those bases just like I was flying. Not even my toes seemed to touch the ground. When I got to third base I said to myself, 'Shucks, this ain't so tough up here.' And, from that day on, I was never nervous again."

In 1920 Sewell hit .329 as Cleveland captured the pennant. In the World Series, however, he hit only .174 and committed six errors at short. Despite Sewell's poor performance, the Indians won the Series, defeating the Dodgers in seven games in a best-of-nine series.

For a man of his size, Sewell was a remarkably durable player. He had run up a streak of "460 or so consecutive games" when he was spiked by St. Louis Browns pitcher Elam Van Gilder and missed the next game. He then proceeded to put together another streak of 1,103 straight contests. "And I must have played almost a month with [my] shoe cut open before I was back to normal. But I played," said Sewell, who finally was put out of action again by the flu.

Sewell hit at least .315 each season from 1923 through 1929. Converted to a third baseman in the late 1920s, Sewell was released by Cleveland in January 1931 and signed with the Yankees. In the 1932 World Series against the Cubs he hit .333. That was the Series that featured Babe Ruth's fabled "Called Shot" home run off pitcher Charlie Root. "Do I believe he really called it?" asked Sewell. "Yes sir. I was there. I saw it. I don't care what anybody says. He did it. He probably couldn't have done it again for a thousand years, but he did it that time."

After hanging up his spikes, Sewell coached for the Yankees in 1934 and 1935, then scouted for Cleveland for 11 seasons and the Mets for a year. He coached baseball at the University of Alabama for six seasons and captured both the Southeastern Conference championship and Coach of the Year honors in 1968. He also worked for a Tuscaloosa dairy and for a time owned a hardware store. Sewell was inducted into the Hall of Fame in 1977.

Luke Sewell

Sewell, James Luther **C**

1921–39, 1942 M(1941–46, 1949–52, 606–644)
B:1/5/1901, Titus, AL D:5/14/1987, Akron, OH
Deb:6/30/1921, CLE AL BR/TR 5'9", 160

G	AB	R	H	HR	RBI	OBP	SLG	AVG
1630	5383	653	1393	20	696	.323	.341	.259

Luke Sewell accomplished something that no other man in the history of baseball was ever able to do: he managed the St. Louis Browns to a pennant. The stocky Alabaman took over as the Browns' skipper early in the 1941 season, and the club finished a surprising third in 1942. In 1944 a deep pitching staff, clutch hitting, and wartime call-ups that put many of baseball's best players in military service combined to get the Browns into the World Series. They lost to their crosstown rivals, the Cardinals. In 1945 the Browns returned to their usual form. Sewell was fired in 1946 and had little luck in a later term with Cincinnati.

Apart from his managerial achievement, James Luther "Luke" Sewell is best known as the younger brother of Hall of Famer Joe Sewell. A third brother, Tommy, had one at bat with the Cubs in 1927. Never the hitter his brother Joe was, Luke Sewell averaged .259, with a high of .294 in 1927. He did, however, share Joe's keen batting eye, striking out only once in every 17.5 at bats.

Starting in 1921 he caught more than 100 games in nine different seasons. He spent his first 12 years as a player with Cleveland, where veteran catcher Steve O'Neill taught him. Later he replaced O'Neill. In 1933 the Indians dealt him to Washington, where he caught 141 games for the pennant-winning Senators.

After playing for two years in Washington, Sewell spent four years in Chicago with the White Sox. He ended his major league career playing 16 games with Cleveland in 1939 and then six games as player-manager for St. Louis in 1942.

Rip Sewell

Sewell, Truett Banks **P**

1932–49 B:5/11/1907, Decatur, AL D:9/3/1989, Plant City, FL Deb:6/14/1932, DET AL BL/TR 6'1", 180

W	L	PCT	G	SH	IP	BB	SO	ERA
143	97	.596	390	20	2119^{1}	748	636	3.48

"By the grace of God, by being shot, I became a better pitcher," Rip Sewell said in describing how he came to develop one of baseball's most astounding pitches, the blooper or "eephus" ball. Sewell created the famous pitch during his 12-year tenure with the Pittsburgh Pirates, but his professional career began with Detroit. After his brief stint with the 1932 Tigers, a fistfight with teammate Hank Greenberg kept him off the 1933 team. So Sewell, a native of Alabama and a distant cousin of ballplayers Joe Sewell and Luke Sewell, spent seven years in the minors before the Pirates claimed him late in 1938.

At age 31 he wasn't expected to contribute much to the team, but he surprised everyone by winning 10 games in 1939 and leading the staff with 52 appearances. The following year he did even better, winning 16 games and finishing third in the league in ERA as the Pirates improved to a fourth-place finish under new manager Frankie Frisch.

Sewell's record plummeted in 1941 when he led the league in losses with 17. That year, while he was hunting in Ocala National Forest, another hunter mistook him for game and shot him with a double-barreled shotgun at close range. "Tore holes in me as big as marbles," Sewell recalled. "One of them smashed up the big toe which I pitched off of. I had to learn how to walk all over again." Not to mention pitch. He had to walk and throw while holding his right big toe up in the air. Pitching under such a handicap led him to invent the blooper pitch.

The first time he tried the pitch, in an exhibition game, he fanned Tiger bonus baby Dick Wakefield, and the crowd went crazy. Everyone asked him what he called the pitch, but he hadn't yet given it a name. Bucs outfielder Maurice Van Robays suggested the term "eephus," saying, "Eephus ain't nothin', and that's a nothin' pitch."

The eephus ball's regular-season debut was even more dramatic. Sewell led the Cubs, 1–0, in the ninth inning with the bases loaded, two out, and a 3–2 count on Cub hitter Dom Dallessandro. Sewell let go of the ball, which flew out of his hand with a backspin like a shot put then arced 25 feet in the air before crossing the plate on its way down for strike three. At first Dallessandro "stood there like a soldier," Sewell recounted. Then the batter said, "If this was a rifle, I'd shoot you right between the eyes."

The eephus, used mostly for effect, made the old-timer's fastball look even faster. According to sportswriter and historian Fred Lieb, "It was the fancy of the fans, and every time Rip was scheduled to pitch, it was good for another 3,000 to 5,000 fans, at home or on the road." The pitch helped Sewell lead the National League with 21 wins and 25 complete games in 1943 and 21 more wins the following year.

One batter who wasn't fooled by the blooper was Ted Williams. Williams saw Sewell before the 1946 All-Star Game and said, "You're not going to throw that pitch to me, are you?" Sewell swore that he would. When Williams came to bat in the bottom of the eighth with the American League already leading, 8–0, the Boston star shook his head from side to side, letting Sewell know that he didn't want any bloopers pitched to him. In response Sewell announced out loud that a blooper was on the way. Williams fouled off one blooper, watched another for a ball, then took a surprise fastball for a strike. On the next pitch Williams leaped up in the batter's box to swing from his heels at the eephus. Sewell later swore that was the only time a batter connected with the pitch for a home run.

In 1946 Sewell found himself at the center of a controversy. Robert Murphy, a union organizer from Boston, felt that baseball players should have formal bargaining powers similar to those of workers' guilds. He decided to begin his recruiting with the Pirates because Pittsburgh had been a strong labor town for years.

Sewell was the leader of the players opposed to the union, and his widely quoted comment showed what a devoted organization man he was: "First the players wanted a hamburger, and the owners gave them a hamburger. Then the players wanted a filet mignon, and they gave them a filet mignon. Then they wanted the whole damn cow, and now that they got the cow they want a pasture to put him in. You just can't satisfy them." Commissioner Happy Chandler rewarded Sewell's obedience by giving him a new watch.

But not even the eephus pitch could stave off advancing age. Sewell spent several years in the bullpen before retiring from the game in 1949 at age 42.

Cy Seymour

Seymour, James Bentley **OF–P**

1896–1910, 1913 B:12/9/1872, Albany, NY D:9/20/1919, New York, NY Deb:4/22/1896, NY NL BL/TL 6', 200

G	AB	R	H	HR	RBI	OBP	SLG	AVG
1528	5682	737	1723	52	799	.347	.405	.303

W	L	PCT	G	SH	IP	BB	SO	ERA
61	56	.521	140	6	1029	655	584	3.76

Lefthander James Bentley "Cy" Seymour received his nickname (short for "Cyclone") as a tribute to his fastball, and he led the National League in strikeouts in 1898. His arm soon deadened, but he was a strong enough hitter to lead the National League in 1905 in batting, RBIs, hits, doubles and triples. His stubbornness also helped lose the 1908 pennant for the New York Giants.

In the October 8 Cubs–Giants playoff game, Joe Tinker was facing Christy Mathewson in the third inning. Seymour was playing shallow, and he refused to move, although both Mathewson and Turkey Mike Donlin signaled for him to go back. Tinker hit the ball deep into left center, and Seymour immediately saw his mistake as he raced back. He leaped for the ball, just missing a catch that would have been easy had he been 10 feet back. The misplay led to four Chicago runs in the inning and gave the Cubs a 4–2 victory and the National League pennant.

Seymour had jumped to the American League's Baltimore Orioles after his arm went dead in 1901. He then moved on to Cincinnati and had his best year with the Reds in 1905. The Giants got him back in the middle of the 1906 season. Seymour drove in 92 runs for the Giants in 1908, but it was his last season as an everyday player. He played with the Giants until 1910, then returned in 1913 for a final season with the Boston Braves.

Orator Shaffer

Shaffer, George **OF**

1874–75, 1877–86, 1890 B:1852, Philadelphia, PA D:Not known Deb:5/23/1874, HAR NA BL/TR 5'9", 165

G	AB	R	H	HR	RBI	OBP	SLG	AVG
842	3442	584	974	10	308	.328	.369	.283

Most outfielders are known for their gloves or their bats. George "Orator" Shaffer is best remembered for his mouth. Although reference guides say he was nicknamed for his "oratorical abilities," author Larry Names is a bit more blunt. He says of Shaffer, "The man couldn't keep his mouth shut for more than half a minute."

Mouth and all, Shaffer started his major league career in the National Association in 1874. He played for the Hartford Dark Blues, New York Mutuals, and one of the three National Association teams in Philadelphia, before joining the Louisville National League club of 1877 that folded because of a gambling scandal. After a stint with Indianapolis, he joined the NL Chicago White Stockings, where he batted .304 in 1879.

The excitement did not stop when Shaffer left the diamond. It turned out that he and Chicago teammates Joe Quest and Silver Flint hadn't paid all their bills in Indianapolis. When the White Stockings passed through Indianapolis in 1879 on the way back to Chicago from Cincinnati, police boarded the train looking for the trio. Flint and Shaffer escaped by hiding in the train's baggage car, but Quest was apprehended and dragged off the train. Cap Anson finally got him back by paying his $55 in debts.

Shaffer was released at the end of the 1879 season because the White Stockings were out of the pennant race and Albert Spalding wanted to cut his high salary. After a few years in Cleveland and a short stay in Buffalo, Shaffer jumped to the St. Louis Maroons of Henry Lucas' Union Association in 1884. That season he led the league in doubles and finished second in the circuit in batting average, slugging average, on-base percentage, hits, runs, and total bases to teammate Fred "Sure Shot" Dunlap.

Shaffer was reinstated along with three other players to the National League on April 17, 1885, only after paying a $500 fine for violating the reserve rule. His hitting dropped off substantially when he returned to the National League with the St. Louis club, also owned by Lucas.

In 1890, his last season in professional baseball, Shaffer led American Association outfielders in fielding and played with his younger brother, Taylor Shaffer, on the Philadelphia Athletics. During his career Orator led NL outfielders in games played three times, in assists four times, and in errors once.

Mike Shannon

Shannon, Thomas Michael **3B–OF**

1962–70 B:7/5/1939, St. Louis, MO Deb:9/11/1962, STL NL BR/TR 6'3", 195

G	AB	R	H	HR	RBI	OBP	SLG	AVG
882	2780	313	710	68	367	.313	.387	.255

Mike "Moonman" Shannon was not a power hitter, but when his Cardinals teammates needed it, he could hit a ball into lunar orbit. He was also a native of St. Louis, and his clutch hitting made him a hometown favorite. He contributed much to the team's success during the 1960s.

Shannon served as a utility outfielder for the Redbirds from 1962 through 1964, but he started all seven games of the 1964 World Series. He began the St. Louis hit parade with a Game 1 homer off Whitey Ford. Shannon led the Cards with six runs scored in the Series victory over the Yankees.

In 1967, after the Cardinals acquired Roger Maris from the Yankees, Shannon was moved to third base. He performed admirably at his new position, and with Maris' added slugging power the Cardinals were back on top of the National League that year. In Game 3 of the 1967 World Series, Shannon belted a crucial homer, and again the Cardinals took the championship in seven games. In 1968 the Cards lost to the Tigers in the Series despite a home run and four RBIs by Shannon.

Shannon was still the Cards' regular third baseman when he became ill with nephritis, a rare kidney disease. He was forced to retire in 1970. Shannon joined Jack Buck in the Cardinals radio booth in 1972, the start of a three-decade run as one of baseball's most successful broadcast teams.

Bobby Shantz

Shantz, Robert Clayton **P**

1949–64 B:9/26/1925, Pottstown, PA Deb:5/1/1949, PHI AL BR/TL 5'6", 142

W	L	PCT	G	SV	IP	BB	SO	ERA
119	99	.546	537	48	1935[2]	643	1072	3.38

Bobby Shantz was a lefthanded pitcher with a natural curveball who might have been one of the best of his generation if not for an arm injury. In 1952 he won 11 straight games and had a 24–7 record with a 2.48 ERA for the Philadelphia Athletics. He injured his arm in 1953 and eventually became a steady relief pitcher for several clubs.

Of Pennsylvania Dutch descent, Shantz formed his own team, the Saratoga Pee Wees, when he was only 8 years old. "I owned the ball, so naturally I was the pitcher," he later explained. In high school he played center field. When he graduated in June 1942 he was only 4'11" and weighed 110 pounds. Rejected by the military because of his size, Shantz took a job in a shipyard and joined a sandlot team, the Homesburg Ramblers, where he discovered he had a natural curve. Meanwhile, he had grown to an even 5 feet tall (he eventually reached 5½ feet) and was accepted into the army. Discharged in 1947, Shantz pitched in the semi-professional Eastern Pennsylvania League. He attracted enough attention by defeating Phillies' bonus baby Curt Simmons to convince the A's to sign him.

In 1948 Shantz was 18–7 with Lincoln of the Western League and led the league in wins and strikeouts. He started the 1949 season with Philadelphia. On May 6 he relieved Carl Scheib in the third inning and pitched nine innings of no-hit ball against Detroit. He eventually yielded two hits and a run in the 13th inning, but still won, 5–4.

After going 18–10 in 1951, Shantz won 11 straight in 1952. One of the victories was a 12–0 drubbing of the Yankees in which Shantz also executed a successful squeeze bunt, pulled off a hit-and-run single, and doubled. "Everything went right," Shantz said of 1952. "Groundballs and line drives went right at someone. It was one of those lucky years." The A's, in the midst of a horrendous stretch as a franchise, even finished four games over .500.

In the 1952 All-Star Game Shantz struck out Jackie Robinson, Whitey Lockman, and Stan Musial. "I only pitched one inning that day. I got Robinson and Musial on curveballs. I don't remember what I struck out Lockman with. I couldn't wait to pitch some more. Instead, we had to sit in the clubhouse for an hour, and then the rain kept coming. Then the umps called it off."

Boston's Walt Masterson broke Shantz's wrist with a pitch in September 1952. Shantz developed shoulder pain the following spring. "The doctor said it was from favoring my wrist. From that point on I could never snap my curve the way I had," Shantz said.

He pitched a dozen more years for several clubs, accepting 50 cortisone shots to dull the pain along the way. In 1957, with the Yankees, Shantz was 11–5 with a league leading 2.45 ERA. He started Game 2 of the World Series against Milwaukee, but lost, 4–2, to Lew Burdette. He also made relief appearances in Games 4 and 7. The Braves won the Series in seven games.

Shantz won eight straight Gold Gloves from 1957, the first year the award was given, through 1964. "I had to be a good fielder," he explained, "I nearly got killed a few times."

Shantz's last World Series performance came in the middle innings of Game 7 of the 1960 Series, won by the Pirates on Bill Mazeroski's dramatic home run in the bottom of the ninth. The following year Shantz was a Pirate. Over the next three years he would also pitch in Houston, St. Louis, and Cincinnati.

After the 1964 season Shantz left baseball and bought a bowling alley with former catcher Joe Astroth. He later operated an ice cream parlor.

Bob Shaw

Shaw, Robert John **P**

1957–67 B:6/29/1933, Bronx, NY Deb:8/11/1957, DET AL BR/TR 6'2", 195

W	L	PCT	G	SV	IP	BB	SO	ERA
108	98	.524	430	32	1778	511	880	3.52

Like many players before him, Bob Shaw suffered from a fear of flying, but he obtained his own pilot's license to conquer his fear. He also preceded the fitness craze by several decades, doing daily calisthenics and running from hole to hole while playing a round of golf. However, his pitching method made him a target for umpires and opponents alike.

Umpires called a major league-record five balks on Shaw on May 4, 1963, when he was pitching for the Braves against the Cubs. Three of the balks came in the third inning, which tied a major league record. The last came during the ninth inning and allowed the winning run to score in a 3–2 Cubs victory.

This was a time when National League arbiters were under orders to enforce the balk rule. By April 26 umpires had called 69 balks in 73 games in the NL, as opposed to only two in 63 American

League contests. Shaw said, "In six seasons before that I had maybe one balk called on me. But when they decided to enforce this one-second stop, it was hard to adjust." That season Shaw set a since-broken major league record with eight balks.

Later in his career opponents were up in arms again, alleging that Shaw threw a spitball. On July 25, 1966, Cubs manager Leo Durocher had umpires check the ball 12 times in one game. "The only time they complain about my throwing a spitter is when I'm winning," contended Shaw. "When I'm losing they leave me alone."

Educated at the St. Lawrence and Adelphi schools, Shaw excelled at basketball and played with Kimball Union, the top prep school team in New England. He signed with the Tigers' organization in 1953, pitching for Jamestown, Durham, Augusta, Syracuse, Charleston, and Toronto. In 1958, during his first spring training with Detroit, he jumped the club when management wanted to return him to the minors. "I wanted no part of that, and I went home," said Shaw. "I had just had a big winter season in Cuba and thought I should get a major league chance."

In June 1958 the Tigers traded him with infielder Ray Boone to the White Sox for pitcher Bill Fischer and outfielder-first baseman Tito Francona. The following season Shaw went 18–6 and led the American League in won-lost percentage to help pitch Chicago to its first pennant in 40 years. On October 6, in Game 5 of the World Series, Shaw beat Sandy Koufax, 1–0, at the Los Angeles Coliseum before the largest crowd in baseball history—92,706.

In spring 1961 Shaw held out for more money, appearing in 14 games before being traded that June to Kansas City in an eight-player deal. The Athletics subsequently traded him to Milwaukee in December. He won 15 games with a 2.80 ERA for the Braves in 1962 and represented the club in the All-Star Game, pitching two scoreless innings.

In December 1963 he was sent to San Francisco in a seven-player transaction. The next season he won 16 games for the Giants, including a one-hitter against the Phils on June 25 that was marred only by outfielder Wes Covington's home run.

"I've been handicapped with late starts. In 1959, when I won 18 games for the White Sox, and again last year, when I won 16 for the Giants, I didn't get my first start until six weeks after the season began," Shaw observed in 1961. "In my book those were 20-game years, even though I didn't win that many."

Shaw again held out for more money in 1966. He got off to a bad start, and in June the Giants sold him to the New York Mets, where the controversy regarding his alleged use of a spitball swirled around him—despite his denials. "If they don't believe me, it's okay. The more they complain the better I like it," Shaw contended.

He was released and grabbed by Durocher's Cubs in June 1967; Chicago released him outright that September. After his playing days were over, he managed in the Florida State League, scouted for the A's and the Yankees, served as a minor league pitching instructor for the Dodgers, and coached for the Brewers.

Bob Shawkey

Shawkey, James Robert **P**

1913–27 M(1930, 86–68) B:12/4/1890, Sigel, PA
D:12/31/1980, Syracuse, NY Deb:7/16/1913, PHI AL
BR/TR 5'11", 168

W	L	PCT	G	SH	IP	BB	SO	ERA
196	150	.566	488	33	2937	1018	1360	3.09

Bob Shawkey played under two of the greatest managers of all time and helped both of them win pennants. He came up with the Philadelphia Athletics during Connie Mack's half-century reign and finished his career with the New York Yankees under future Hall of Fame skipper Miller Huggins. Shawkey went on to follow them into the major league managing fraternity but could match neither their success nor their longevity.

Then again, neither Mack nor Huggins matched what Shawkey accomplished as a player. Shawkey won 196 games and averaged 32 appearances per year despite missing almost an entire campaign to military service. Shawkey finished with a career ERA of 3.09. Four times he collected at least 20 wins in a season, including a career-high 24 in 1916. He had the honor of starting the first game played at Yankee Stadium and beat Boston pitcher Howard Ehmke, 4–1, as Babe Ruth hit a home run.

Shawkey made his professional debut in 1911 for Harrisburg of the Tri-State League. Two years later he came to Connie Mack's club in midseason and found himself among future Hall of Famers Frank "Home Run" Baker, Eddie Collins, Chief Bender, Eddie Plank, and Herb Pennock. Shawkey fir right in; he put together a 6–5 record and 2.34 ERA in 18 appearances.

In 1914 Shawkey assumed a larger role, going 16–8. His record placed him third in victories on a well-balanced Philadelphia staff that featured six others with at least 10 wins. He recorded 18 complete games and a career-best five shutouts.

That year the A's finished 8? games ahead of the second-place Red Sox and were favored in the World Series. But they encountered the "Miracle" Braves, who had rallied from last place and never lost their momentum. With Boston leading, three games to none, Shawkey started Game 4. He allowed three runs in five innings before being removed in favor of Herb Pennock. The Braves went on to win, 3–1, sweeping the Series.

The next year Mack broke up his club for financial reasons and sent Shawkey to the Yankees for $18,000. Shawkey celebrated his first full season in New York with 24 wins, a 2.21 ERA, and a league-leading eight saves. But he slipped to 13–15 in 1917, then missed almost all of 1918 after enlisting in the navy and serving as a yeoman.

When he returned from the service, Shawkey embarked on a superb six-season run, winning at least 16 games each year. He posted 20 victories in both 1919 and 1920. On September 27, 1919, he struck out a career-high 15, and during one stretch in 1920 he won 11 consecutive games. His 2.45 ERA in 1920 was a league low.

Shawkey went 18–12 in 1921 to help the team win the pennant. In the World Series he made one start and one relief appearance, neither one of them very effective, as the Yanks lost the best-of-nine Series to the New York Giants.

In 1922 Shawkey reached the 20-win plateau again. This time he had a solid performance in the Series. After allowing three runs in the top of the first inning of Game 2, he settled down and went the distance in a 3–3, 10-inning tie; it was the only game the Giants didn't lose. The following year he won 16 and lost 11, then picked up his only World Series victory in Game 4 by scattering 12 hits over $7\frac{2}{3}$ innings in an 8–4 victory over the Giants. The Yankees won in six games for Shawkey's only world championship in five World Series.

In 1924 the Yankees didn't win the pennant, but Shawkey compiled his second straight 16–11 mark, completing a stretch in which he went 110–81. He slid to 6–14 in 1925, then battled a damaged foot in 1926, although he did manage to pitch in three games of a seven-game loss to the Cardinals in the World Series. He appeared in 19 games for the 1927 Yankees, then spent a year in the minors with Montreal, before calling it a career.

In 1929 Shawkey was offered a job as pitching coach under Huggins, and he did such a good job that Huggins recommended him as a possible successor for the managerial post. Art Fletcher, the assistant manager, was Huggins' first choice, but upon Huggins' death on September 29, 1929, Fletcher declined the offer. When the job was made available to Shawkey, he took it. He guided the Yankees to an 86–68 record in 1930, good for third place. But the following season the club replaced him with Joe McCarthy, ending Shawkey's major league managing career.

William Shea

Shea, William Alfred

League Organizer B:6/21/1907, Brooklyn, NY
D:10/2/1991, New York, NY

With many stadiums now bearing a corporation's name, some may ask, "What business is Shea in?" New York's Shea Stadium is not named after a company; it is named after the man responsible for returning National League baseball to the city.

When both the Dodgers and Giants left New York after the 1957 season, mayor Robert F. Wagner asked politically-connected attorney William Shea to head a committee to return the National League to New York. Shea was the ideal man for the job. He had played baseball at George Washington High School, football at NYU, and both football and basketball at Georgetown. Later he served as a legal counsel for the Brooklyn Trust Company (along with Walter O'Malley).

Shea's father-in-law was the biggest bookmaker at New York City area tracks in the 1920s, when bookmaking was still legal. In the 1940s Shea owned the American Football League's Long Island Indians, a Washington Redskins farm team. He later became a partner with Ted Collins in the National Football League's short-lived Boston Yanks.

When Wagner first approached Shea about obtaining a new team for New York, Shea thought his task would be an easy one. "We'll just have to steal a team from another city," he told the mayor, "the same way Los Angeles and San Francisco moved in on us. Either that, or get some sort of expansion."

Easier said than done. First, Shea approached Cincinnati owner Powel Crosley about hijacking the Reds, offering him a lease on a new ballpark to be built in Flushing Meadows, Queens. Crosley said no. So did Pittsburgh's John Galbreath and Philadelphia's Bob Carpenter.

At that point Shea shifted strategy. He would lobby the NL to expand to 10 teams. He later admitted he was "silly enough to think that the National League owed New York something. Here we supported two teams for all those years. Well, the National League didn't feel that way at all. They didn't feel anything. They couldn't have cared less."

On July 27, 1959, at New York's Biltmore Hotel, Shea unveiled another strategy: a new major league. The Continental League would feature teams in New York, Houston, Minneapolis-St. Paul, Toronto, and Denver. Two more franchises would be named later. Play would begin in 1961.

On August 18, 1959, Shea named Branch Rickey as president of the new league. Soon the American League began to talk of expansion. Within a year, the NL was also considering the idea. By August 1960 major league expansion was virtually assured, and Shea and Rickey pulled the plug on the Continental League. The National League voted to return to New York on October 17, 1960.

Some thought that New York's new ballpark should be named for Rickey. Rickey thought otherwise. "The first one to agree with me about a third league was Shea," he wrote to the city council. "By George, he leaped into action. He was like a turkey in a tobacco patch, not caring if he knocked down the stalks to get the worm....He brought back the National League to New York. The responsibility for the result is his and his alone."

Jimmy Sheckard

Sheckard, Samuel James Tildon **OF**

1897–1913 B:11/23/1878, Upper Chanceford, PA
D:1/15/1947, Lancaster, PA Deb:9/14/1897, BRO NL
BL/TR 5'9", 175

G	AB	R	H	HR	RBI	OBP	SLG	AVG
2122	7605	1296	2084	56	813	.375	.378	.274

Before the 1906 World Series, Chicago Cubs outfielder Jimmy Sheckard boasted that he would hit .400 against the pitching of the White Sox, the Cubs' opponents. Instead, he went 0-for-21 and didn't hit a ball out of the infield. His embarrassing performance was one factor in the White Sox's six-game victory, one of the greatest upsets in Series history.

Though never a great hitter, Sheckard, who batted lefthanded and threw righthanded, was far better than his Series performance indicates. He spent 17 seasons in the majors, compiled some fairly good career statistics, and played on five pennant winners. He was a fine defensive performer and one of the best baserunners of his day. Luckily, he was able to show his abilities in several more World Series.

One of the few Pennsylvania Dutch to play in the majors, Sheckard became a professional ballplayer with Portsmouth of the Virginia State League in 1896. The next year, when he hit .370 with Brockton to lead the New England League, the Brooklyn Dodgers acquired him and tried him at shortstop for 13 games, just long enough that it was clear he belonged in the outfield.

Although Sheckard hit .277 in 105 games in 1898, he was cast off to Baltimore in 1899 when the Orioles' owners bought a controlling interest in the Brooklyn club and amalgamated the two teams to Brooklyn's advantage. When Sheckard hit .295, scored 104 runs, and led the league with 77 stolen bases for the Orioles, Brooklyn took him back. In 1900 Sheckard hit .300 as a substitute for the remarkable outfield of Willie Keeler, Fielder Jones, and Joe Kelley.

In 1901 Jones jumped to the new American League. Sheckard replaced him and had the best season of his career, batting .353, with 116 runs scored and 104 RBIs. He led the NL with 19 triples and a .536 slugging average and hit a career-high 11 home runs. On September 23 and 24, 1901, Sheckard hit grand slams in consecutive games. Through 1999 only three other National League players had ever accomplished the feat.

In 1902 Sheckard jumped to the American League but returned to Brooklyn after only four games. In 1903 he hit .332, led the league with nine homers, and tied Frank Chance of the Cubs for the lead in stolen bases, with 67. That season he had his last .300 average, but Sheckard was not alone in the general malaise that overcame hitters at this time. The dead ball and the perfection of trick pitches sent batting averages plummeting in both leagues.

In 1906 Sheckard was traded to the Cubs for four players. He was one of the final pieces in the assemblage of one of baseball's great teams, which included infielders Joe Tinker, Johnny Evers, and Chance. Before being upset in the 1906 World Series, the Cubs won a record 116 games. They bounced back from their loss to the White Sox to win pennants again in 1907, 1908, and 1910.

Sheckard hit .238 in the Cubs' World Series victories over Detroit in both 1907 and 1908. In 1910, when the Cubs lost to Philadelphia, he drove in the winning run in the only game Chicago won. Although Sheckard's batting percentage was average to poor through these years, he was extremely adept at reaching base on walks. In 1908, when his average dipped to .231, his on-base percentage was .336.

Ironically, when the Cubs slipped from first place, Sheckard became even more talented at drawing bases on balls. In 1911 he collected 147 free passes, a record that stood for more than 30 years. He also led the league in runs scored that season, with 121, and was the league leader in walks in 1912, with 122.

Sold to the Cardinals in 1913, he finished his major league career with the Reds later that season. In 1914 he served as player-manager of Cleveland's entry in the American Association, and in 1917 he coached for the Cubs. Leaving baseball, he ran into hard luck, and his modest savings were wiped out by the stock market crash. He worked at various laboring jobs until 1947, when he was struck and killed by a car.

Earl Sheely

Sheely, Earl Homer **1B**

1921–31 B:2/12/1893, Bushnell, IL D:9/16/52, Seattle, WA Deb:4/14/1921, CHI AL BR/TR 6'3½", 195

G	AB	R	H	HR	RBI	OBP	SLG	AVG
1234	4471	572	1340	48	747	.383	.399	.300

While little-known today, White Sox first baseman Earl "Whitey" Sheely combined defense and clutch hitting to make himself a valuable addition to some otherwise lackluster White Sox teams in the club's post-Black Sox Era. On May 20–21, 1926 Sheely set a major league record with seven extra-base hits (six doubles and a home run) in two consecutive games.

Sheely began in baseball in 1912 and—with a brief stop in Los Angeles—spent 1916 through 1920 with Salt Lake City in the Pacific Coast League, reaching the White Sox only after Chick Gandil had left the club in the wake of the Black Sox scandal.

A tough batter to strike out, he tied for the second-best career clutch-hitting rating in the history of the game and in his day was among the American League's best fielding first basemen. Three times he led the AL in putouts and double plays and twice in assists and fielding average.

On returning to the Pacific Coast League in 1930 he posted a .403 average, 289 hits and 180 RBIs for San Francisco, all league-leading totals. Sheely scouted for the Red Sox from 1936 to 1943, managed the Sacramento Solons from 1943 to 1945 and in 1948 became general manager of the Seattle club in the Pacific Coast League.

Gary Sheffield

Sheffield, Gary Antonio **OF-3B**

1988–* B:11/18/1968, Tampa, FL Deb:9/3/1988, MIL AL BR/TR 5'11", 190

G	AB	R	H	HR	RBI	OBP	SLG	AVG
1308	4645	779	1345	236	807	.397	.501	.290

Gary Sheffield never lacked confidence. The nephew of All-Star pitcher Dwight Gooden, Sheffield earned Minor League co-Player of the Year from *The Sporting News* in 1988. As a 20-year-old rookie he remarked, "I should have been here years ago." In four seasons with the Milwaukee Brewers, however, his best campaign was a .294, 10-homer year in 1990. Sheffield alienated teammates, fans, and the media—a recurring theme for the eventual five-time All-Star.

Hopelessly at odds with Brewers management, Sheffield was traded to the San Diego Padres in 1992. He responded with a near-Triple Crown performance. He batted a league-high .330 with 33 home runs and 100 RBIs. *The Sporting News* named him NL Comeback Player of the Year. When San Diego dropped in the standings the following year, Sheffield's play suffered. The Padres, eager to shed the soon-to-be free agent, traded Sheffield to Florida in June 1993.

After two injury-marred seasons, Sheffield erupted again in 1996. He established career highs with 42 home runs, 120 RBIs, and 142 walks; he also led the National League with a .469 on-base percentage. After the season the Marlins signed Sheffield to a six-year, $61 million contract, then surrounded him with new high-priced teammates.

Although Sheffield struggled in 1997, Florida won the National League Wild Card. He batted .556, plus five walks, in a three-game sweep of the San Francisco Giants in the Division Series. Sheffield scored six runs in the Championship Series as the Marlins upset the Atlanta Braves. In the World Series he batted .292 with a homer and five RBIs, plus a game-saving catch in Game 3, to help Florida defeat Cleveland in seven games. Not long after the celebration ended, however, owner Wayne Huizenga started breaking up the world champions. In May 1998 Sheffield was traded to the Los Angeles Dodgers in a blockbuster seven-player deal. Sheffield batted .300 in each of his first two seasons as a Dodger.

Bert Shepard

Shepard, Bert Robert **P**

1945 B:6/28/1920, Dana, IN Deb:8/4/1945, WAS AL BL/TL 5'11", 185

W	L	PCT	G	SV	IP	BB	SO	ERA
0	0	–	1	0	5^{1}	1	2	1.69

He showed what one could do with will power—and one leg. A rather undistinguished minor leaguer, Bert Shepard was shot down in May 1944 in aerial combat over France during World War II, and lost his right leg. He was captured by the Germans, then liberated from Stalag IX-C in October 1944.

Bert Shepard was fitted with a wooden limb and worked at playing ball while still in captivity. Taken to Walter Reed Hospital, he met Undersecretary of War Robert Patterson who, impressed by Shepard's resolve to play again professionally, brought him to the attention of Washington Senators owner Clark Griffith.

He was signed first as a coach, but when he got a chance to pitch against Brooklyn in a July exhibition, he held the Dodgers to five singles in four innings. On August 4, 1945, Shepard took the mound in relief at Griffith Stadium for his only major league appearance. With the bases loaded he struck out the first man he faced, Catfish Metkovich, and allowed Boston just one run in 5⅓ innings.

Later Shepard pitched briefly with a White Sox farm club at Longview (East Texas League) and was signed by the A's for Anaheim (California League), but was released quickly both times. His best stint in the minors came in 1941 as a pitcher-first baseman with Bisbee (Arizona-Texas League).

Bob Sheppard

Public Address Announcer

Joe DiMaggio's final year in baseball was Bob Sheppard's first season as public address announcer at Yankee Stadium. Half a century later his resonant voice still reverberated throughout the stadium: "The center fielder...number 51...Bernie Williams...number 51."

Sheppard played first base and quarterback at St. John's University. He later served as PA announcer for both sports, and, fittingly, served as a speech teacher at his alma mater. He spent 44 years as announcer for the New York Giants football team at the Polo Grounds, Yankee Stadium, and Giants Stadium. He also handled Army football, both the New York Yankees and Brooklyn Dodgers of the All-America Football Conference, and the New York Titans of the American Football League.

Baseball was Sheppard's signature sport. From his small one-man booth in the press box at Yankee Stadium, American League players knew they weren't really in the big leagues until Sheppard's rich and subtle voice announced their name.

Bill Sherdel

Sherdel, William Henry **P**

1918–32 B:8/15/1896, McSherrystown, PA D:11/14/1968, McSherrystown, PA Deb:4/22/1918, STL NL BL/TL 5'10", 160

W	L	PCT	G	SV	IP	BB	SO	ERA
165	146	.531	514	26	2709^{1}	661	839	3.72

A prototypical crafty lefthander, Bill Sherdel relied on good control, an assortment of pitches, and guile during a 15-season career spent mostly with the St. Louis Cardinals. As both a starter and reliever he chalked up double-digit figures in victories eight times and won 21 games in 1928.

A blithe spirit who was known to whistle or sing to himself on the mound, Sherdel came up to the Cards in 1918 and helped transform the team from a perennial tail-ender into a contender. In 1925 he led the National League in won-lost percentage at .714 during his 15–6 season. The next year he was 16–12 as the Cardinals won their first pennant. He started the first World Series game in franchise history, but he was outpitched by Herb Pennock of the Yankees, 2–1. Pennock beat Sherdel again in Game 5, 3–2, but the Cardinals won the Series in seven games.

In 1928, when the Redbirds won their second flag, Sherdel had his best season with a 21–10 mark. He also saved five games that season to lead the league, the third time he topped the National League in that category. He lost both his starts in the Yankees' four games sweep; giving him an 0–4 mark in Series competition despite a respectable 3.26 ERA.

Larry Sherry

Sherry, Lawrence **P**

1958–68 B:7/25/1935, Los Angeles, CA Deb:4/17/1958, LA NL BR/TR 6'2", 204

W	L	PCT	G	SV	IP	BB	SO	ERA
53	44	.546	416	82	799^{1}	374	606	3.67

Without Larry Sherry the Los Angeles Dodgers probably could not have reached, must less won, the 1959 World Series. Summoned from the minors during the season, Sherry proved to be the key reliever the Dodgers needed down the stretch as they captured the National League pennant. He went on to win Most Valuable Player honors for the World Series as Los Angeles defeated the Chicago White Sox in six games. Sherry never again pitched in a World Series, but he was fortunate just to be able to walk.

He was born with clubfeet. Sherry needed operations and braces to even give him a chance at a life in sports. He certainly had nothing wrong with his arm, and he had size going for him, too. He would grow to be 6 feet 2 inches and weigh 204 pounds. Sherry played baseball at Fairfield High School in Los Angeles, where his coach saw him as a player with a strong arm who was too big for the infield. The coach suggested that Sherry try pitching, and the rest became World Series history.

First, however, Sherry had to reach the big leagues, and he did so in 1958 after six years of working in the minors. In his first look at the majors, he showed he had a lot to learn. He pitched in only five games, allowing 10 hits and seven walks in 4⅓ innings for a 12.46 ERA. Surprisingly, Dodgers manager Walter Alston was impressed with his stuff.

Sherry sharpened his control and developed a slider in winter ball. He came back with some strong work for St. Paul of the American Association and was called up during the 1959 season. Working as both a starter and a reliever, Sherry was as tough to hit as almost anyone in the league. He allowed only 75 hits in 94 ⅓ innings and compiled a 2.19 ERA. In one relief appearance against the Cardinals, he entered in the first inning and went the rest of the way to give the Dodgers a victory.

That season the Dodgers and the Milwaukee Braves wound up in a first-place tie and met for a best-of-three series to settle the National League pennant. In the first game, Sherry entered in the second inning when Alston gave an early hook to Danny McDevitt. With one out, one run in, and two men on base, Sherry got opposing pitcher Carlton Willey to hit a grounder to shortstop Maury Wills, who bobbled it to load the bases. Bobby Avila then grounded into a force play, producing a run that gave Milwaukee a 2–1 lead. Sherry held off the Braves the rest of the way, allowing only four hits in 7 ⅔ innings. Los Angeles wound up with a 3–2 victory and wrapped up the pennant in the next game.

Sherry's effectiveness extended through the World Series against the Chicago White Sox. He appeared in four games, winning two and saving two. In Game 6 he relieved Johnny Podres in the fourth inning with one on. He allowed a single and a walk to load the bases but shut down the Sox at that point. Los Angeles won the game, 9–3, to take the Series. By winning the Series MVP Award, Sherry became a national celebrity, making appearances at department stores and banquets and on *The Ed Sullivan Show.*

In 1960 Sherry had a league-leading 13 relief victories. He remained with the Dodgers through 1963, then was sent to Detroit. Despite a foot injury, he went 7–5 with 11 saves for the Tigers in 1964. He delivered an 8–5 season with a career-high 20 saves in 1966 but didn't have much left in his arm.

He was sent from Detroit to Houston during the 1967 season, then finished his playing career with the California Angels in 1968. Sherry had two stints as a major league coach, one with Pittsburgh and the other with California.

Sherry was the youngest of four brothers, including Norm, who made it to the majors as a catcher and became Larry's batterymate on the Dodgers from 1959 to 1962. Norm and Larry Sherry formed the major league's last brother battery of the 20th century.

Billy Shindle

Shindle, William **3B–SS**

1886–98 B:12/5/1860, Gloucester, NJ D:6/3/1936, Lakeland, NJ Deb:10/5/1886, DET NL BR/TR 5'8½", 155

G	AB	R	H	HR	RBI	OBP	SLG	AVG
1422	5807	992	1561	31	758	.323	.357	.269

Shortstop Billy Shindle of the Philadelphia Quakers of the 1890 Players' League set the all-time record for errors in a season by a shortstop when he committed 119. Despite his staggering number of errors, Shindle actually led Players' League shortstops in double plays in 1890. On September 26, 1890, Shindle registered 12 assists in a nine-inning game. It stood as the major league record for shortstops, until Washington's Danny Richardson recorded 13 on June 30, 1892.

Fortunately for Shindle, the 1890 season was his only year as a regular shortstop. Four times he led his league's third basemen in assists, three times in putouts, twice in double plays and errors, and once in fielding percentage. He had his bad days as well.

Shindle set a National League record with seven errors in a doubleheader on April 23, 1892; he erred twice in the first game and five times in the second. In that second game, Shindle's miscues contributed to a 19–9 Baltimore loss.

Shindle's redeeming quality was the fact that he was a good hitter. He drove in 90 or more runs three times and scored at least 90 runs six times. On August 26, 1890 Shindle went 6-for-6, collecting two doubles, a triple, and three singles. He was thought of so highly that Brooklyn traded future Hall of Famers Wee Willie Keeler and Dan Brouthers for Shindle and George Treadway in January 1894.

Urban Shocker

Shocker, Urban James **P**

1916–28 B:8/22/1890, Cleveland, OH D:9/9/1928, Denver, CO Deb:4/24/1916, NY AL BR/TR 5'10", 170

W	L	PCT	G	SH	IP	BB	SO	ERA
187	117	.615	412	28	2681^{2}	657	983	3.17

The New York Yankees' dynasty might have begun a year earlier than it did had the ballclub not traded Urban Shocker in the winter of 1918. Shocker blossomed into a 20-game winner in 1920, a total that might have helped make up the three games that separated the Yankees from first place that season. And Shocker seemed to do some of his best work against the team that traded him.

Shocker, one of the great spitballers, went on to win at least 20 games in four straight campaigns. He returned to the Yankees in time to play for their World Series teams of 1926 and 1927. Smart and competitive, he finished with a 187–117 record, for a .615 winning percentage that ranks among the best of all time. His life was all too brief, however, and one year after he won 18 games for the 1927 Yankees, he died.

Born Urbain Jacques Schockor in Cleveland on August 22, 1890, he grew up in Detroit. He began his career as a catcher in the Michigan and Canada environs. The righthander's background as a receiver made him a skillful hitter and fielder in the majors.

The Yankees spotted him pitching in Ottawa of the Canada League and purchased his contract for $750 in 1915. He made his major league debut in 1916, going 4–3 with a 2.62 ERA. The following season he split time between the Yankees and the minors, finishing the season with an 8–5 record for the big league team.

In January 1918 Yankees manager Miller Huggins included Shocker in a five-player deal with the St. Louis Browns for pitcher Eddie Plank, infielder Del Pratt, and $15,000. Plank, at the end of his Hall of Fame career, retired and never reported to the Yankees. Pratt was a capable second baseman who hit .275, .292, and .314 in his three seasons in New York. Shocker, meanwhile, became a Yankees nemesis.

In 1921 Shocker turned in what was probably his best year. He led the American League with 27 victories, lost only 12 games, and compiled a 3.55 ERA. He also won 20 games the next two seasons, and led the AL in strikeouts in 1922. On September 6, 1924, Shocker's last season in St. Louis, he pitched two complete-game victories over the White Sox in a doubleheader.

Shocker was a somewhat controversial figure in an era when ballplayers didn't have the support of a strong union. He and the Browns got into a dispute over the club's policy on taking wives on road trips. That led to a suspension. Also, Shocker was said to have had trouble getting along with managers Lee Fohl and George Sisler.

A December 1924 transaction that sent Joe Bush to St. Louis returned Shocker to the Yankees. Even though Shocker pitched and won the season opener against Washington, 1925 was not a good year for either him or the Yankees. The ballclub finished seventh in an eight-team league, and Shocker, at 12–12, failed to post a winning record for the only time in his career.

In 1926 Shocker went 19–11 to help the Yankees win the pennant. He started Game 2 of the World Series against the Cardinals and allowed five runs in seven innings to take the loss. He pitched in relief in New York's 10–2 defeat in Game 6, and the Cardinals won the Series the next day.

Shocker was 18–6 for the 1927 Yankees but did not appear in their four-game World Series sweep of Pittsburgh. Shocker's career, and his life, ended in 1928. The year began with a contract dispute, but Shocker finally reported and pitched in one game. He then retired to Denver, where he had hoped to spend time in a radio shop and in aviation. After pitching in a semipro tournament, he developed pneumonia. After a long bout with illness, he died on September 9 at age 38.

Ernie Shore

Shore, Ernest Grady **P**

1912–20 B:3/24/1891, East Bend, NC D:9/24/1980, Winston-Salem, NC Deb:6/20/1912, NY NL BR/TR 6'4", 220

W	L	PCT	G	SH	IP	BB	SO	ERA
65	43	.602	160	9	979^{1}	270	309	2.47

Ernie Shore's baseball career will forever be tied to that of Babe Ruth. Shore was Ruth's teammate with Baltimore of the International League, and he was purchased by the Red Sox in the same deal that brought Ruth to the big leagues. He was Ruth's roommate in Boston, then was sold to New York in a deal that foreshadowed Ruth's eventual transfer. And Shore became famous, not for pitching a perfect game, but for pitching a perfect game in relief of Ruth.

Like Ruth, Ernest Grady Shore was one of Baltimore owner Jack Dunn's many valuable young players. He joined the minor league Orioles directly from Guilford College in his native North Carolina in June 1914. On July 8 Shore was packaged with Ruth and catcher Ben Egan and sold to Boston for about $25,000. In his first appearance, Shore pitched a two-hitter to beat Cleveland, 2–1.

Ruth's behavior nearly drove Shore back to North Carolina. Shortly after joining Boston, Shore told manager Bill Carrigan that he was returning home. When asked why, he responded, "I can't live with that man Ruth." When Carrigan inquired further, Shore said, "There's a place where friendship stops. I told him he was using my toothbrush, and he said, 'That's all right. I'm not particular.'" The story, probably apocryphal, nonetheless points out Shore's problem with Ruth. No matter what Shore did, Ruth was always right there, larger than life, and drawing all the attention.

The 23-year-old Shore, three years older than Ruth, was more experienced, however. The Red Sox sent Ruth to minor league Providence a few weeks after the trade while Shore was immediately installed in the Red Sox rotation. He finished the season 10–4, with a sparkling ERA of 1.89.

He was even better in 1915, when he went 19–8 with an ERA of only 1.64 as the Red Sox won the pennant; Ruth was 18–8 with an ERA nearly a full run higher. Regardless, the press sang Ruth's praises and all but ignored Shore. Carrigan knew better and started Shore in Game 1 of the World Series against the Phillies. Shore pitched well but lost to Grover Cleveland Alexander, 3–1. He came back to beat Philadelphia, 2–1, in Game 4 as the Red Sox won in five games. Ruth made a single Series appearance as a pinch hitter and failed to reach base.

Ruth won 23 games in 1916, and Shore fell off to 16 as the Sox won another pennant. Yet Shore again outperformed Ruth in the Series, winning two games in Boston's five-game victory. In Game 5 Shore held Brooklyn hitless for 4 ⅓ innings and then scattered three singles as Boston wrapped up the Series.

On June 23, 1917, Boston faced Washington at Fenway Park. Ruth walked leadoff hitter Ray Morgan on four pitches, complaining mightily to plate umpire Brick Owens after each pitch. When Ruth punched Owens in the face after ball four, Ruth was ejected from the game.

In came Shore, who was allowed only eight warm-up tosses. On his first pitch, Morgan tried to steal second and was thrown out. Shore retired the next 26 batters and was credited with a perfect game, only the fourth in major league history at the time. (Years later Major League Baseball declared that it was not a perfect game.) Ruth was suspended for 10 days—and still received most of the headlines.

Shore joined the service and missed the 1918 season. Red Sox owner Harry Frazee, in need of some cash to finance his theatrical productions, sold Shore, pitcher Dutch Leonard, and outfielder Duffy Lewis to the Yankees for $15,000, the first sale in what would later be called "the Rape of the Red Sox." But Shore again received second billing, as most fans believe the pillaging began with the sale of Ruth in 1920.

Shore hurt his arm late in the 1917 season and never pitched as well in New York as he had in Boston. After two disappointing seasons, he retired in 1920. Asked once by an interviewer if he resented Ruth, Shore politely replied, "He was the best-hearted fellow who ever lived." Shore later became a sheriff in North Carolina.

Chris Short

Short, Christopher Joseph **P**

1959–73 B:9/19/1937, Milford, DE D:8/1/1991, Wilmington, DE Deb:4/19/1959, PHI NL BR/TL 6'4", 205

W	L	PCT	G	SH	IP	BB	SO	ERA
135	132	.506	501	24	2325	806	1629	3.43

It took Chris Short the first third of his career to come up with the third pitch he needed to be a great pitcher. He spent the final third of his playing career coping with chronic back pain. In between, the 6-foot 4-inch lefthander went 83–54 for the Philadelphia Phillies.

In 1957 Short signed with Philadelphia out of the University of Delaware and debuted with the Phillies in 1959. Teammates sarcastically nicknamed him "Style" after he showed up the first day with an extra suit rolled up in a plastic bag. He had few high points, stylistic or otherwise, until near the end of the 1963 season.

On September 13, 1963, Short struck out 14 batters in a win over the Dodgers, and five days later he beat the Mets in New York, 5–1, to record the last win at the soon-to-be-bulldozed Polo Grounds.

"I saw Chris go through the whole transition from being a thrower to a pitcher," Cardinals outfielder Lou Brock said. "When he started out, we as hitters would wait for him to throw either a fastball or a nickel slider. Then, all of a sudden he came up with a vicious curve. He gave me problems. He knew how to pitch and threw a lot of low-run games."

Short was an All-Star in 1964, the year the Phillies almost won the pennant. He made the All-Star team again in 1967 but pitched in only two games in 1969 as he recovered from corrective back surgery. Pitching in pain, Short won only 20 games over his last four seasons and pitched briefly for the Brewers before retiring.

Later an insurance agent in Wilmington, Delaware, Short suffered a brain aneurysm and fell into a coma in 1988. He never regained consciousness. Phils pitcher Art Mahaffey organized the Chris Short All-Star Golf Classic and raised $115,000 for the pitcher's family.

Burt Shotton

Shotton, Burton Edwin **OF**

1909, 1911–23 M(1928–34, 1947–50, 697–764)
B:10/18/1884, Brownhelm, OH D:7/29/1962, Lake Wales, FL Deb:9/13/1909, STL AL BL/TR 5'11", 175

G	AB	R	H	HR	RBI	OBP	SLG	AVG
1387	4945	746	1338	9	290	.365	.333	.271

When Brooklyn Dodgers manager Leo Durocher was suspended for the 1947 season, Barney Shotton was the man Branch Rickey tapped to fill in. The 62-year-old Shotton came out of retirement to lead the Dodgers to the NL pennant. He stepped aside when Durocher's suspension ended, only to return when the volatile Durocher resigned midway through the 1948 season. Shotton led the Dodgers to a second pennant in 1949.

Despite his success, "Barney" Shotton was not embraced in Brooklyn. He was a favorite of Rickey's, but disliked by the players, writers and fans. Soft-spoken and easygoing, he managed in street clothes, wearing a bowtie under a blue windbreaker. Sportswriter Dick Young mockingly called him "KOBS"—Kindly Old Burt Shotton. When Walter O'Malley assumed control of the team in 1950, Shotton was unceremoniously dumped.

In his previous major league incarnation, Shotton was the starting centerfielder for the St. Louis Browns from 1911-1917. The fleet left-hander spent a year with the Washington Senators before returning to St. Louis, where he spent the last five years of his career as a reserve with the Cardinals. After retiring as a player in 1923, he spent the next several years as a Cardinals' coach before taking the managerial reins for the Philadelphia Phillies in 1928. In Shotton's six seasons at the helm, the Phillies posted only one winning season, a fourth place finish in 1932. Barney spent time as a major league coach with Cincinnati and Cleveland, and managed minor league teams in Syracuse, Rochester, and Columbus. He died in 1962 at the age of 77.

Eric Show

Show, Eric Vaughn **P**

1981–91 B:5/19/1956, Riverside, CA D:3/16/1994, Dulzura, CA Deb:9/2/1981, SD NL BR/TR 6'1", 185

W	L	PCT	G	SH	IP	BB	SO	ERA
101	89	.532	332	11	1655	610	971	3.66

Although he was an effective starting pitcher for most of his 11-year major league career, Eric Show will be remembered for one pitch. On September 11, 1985, the San Diego righthander threw a fastball to Cincinnati. Reds player-manager Pete Rose, who lined it into left field for a single—the 4,192nd hit in Rose's career to make him baseball's all-time hit king. (Previous research had shown that Cobb actually had 4,190 career hits, so technically Rose had already broken Cobb's record when he came to bat against Show that night; Major League Baseball ignored the findings, so Show's pitch was destined for the highlight reel.)

Show had moved into San Diego's rotation full-time in 1983 and won 15 games. A year later, he went 15–9 with a 3.40 ERA, as the Padres won the National League West and advanced to the first World Series in team history. In 1985 Show lowered his ERA to 3.09, but his record dropped to 12–11 and the Padres fell to third place.

With the exception of a 16-win season in 1988, Show struggled with injuries and ineffectiveness for the remainder of his career. Sadly, he fared little better in his life after baseball. He died on March 16, 1994, from an overdose of heroin and cocaine.

Norm Siebern

Siebern, Norman Leroy **1B–OF**

1956–68 B:7/26/1933, St. Louis, MO Deb:6/15/1956, NY AL BL/TR 6'3", 205

G	AB	R	H	HR	RBI	OBP	SLG	AVG
1406	4481	662	1217	132	636	.372	.423	.272

Promising Yankees outfielder Norm Siebern became the goat of Game 4 of the 1958 World Series when his two misplays helped ensure a 3–0 loss to the Milwaukee Braves. Ironically, Siebern won a Gold Glove Award that year.

In the sixth inning Siebern allowed a flyball by Red Schoendienst's to fall for a triple. In the seventh he misplayed a bloop by Warren Spahn into a run-scoring single. Both plays were caused by playing in Yankee Stadium's difficult left field, its "sun field."

In 1957 Siebern had been named *The Sporting News* Minor League Player of the Year as he paced the American Association in average, runs, hits, doubles and triples. The following year he was a regular in New York, batting .300 for the eventual world champions. In December 1959, Siebern went to the Kansas City Athletics in the deal that sent Roger Maris to New York.

He went on to become a three-time All-Star as a first baseman. He best year was 1962 when he established career highs with 25 home runs, 117 RBIs, 114 runs scored, and a .308 average.

After retiring, Siebern scouted in 1969 for Atlanta and part-time for the Royals for five seasons. He also operated insurance agencies in Independence, Missouri, and Naples, Florida.

Dick Siebert

Siebert, Richard Walther **1B**

1932–45 B:2/19/1912, Fall River, MA Deb:9/7/1932, BRO NL BL/TL 6', 170

G	AB	R	H	HR	RBI	OBP	SLG	AVG
1035	3917	439	1104	32	482	.332	.379	.282

Dick Siebert enjoyed moderate success as a singles- and doubles-hitting first baseman, but saw his greatest moments as a college baseball coach. Starting in the minors in 1929, Siebert sat out the 1931 season and played briefly with the Dodgers and the Cardinals before finding a home with Connie Mack's Philadelphia Athletics. During the offseason, he began preparing for a fulltime coaching career by coaching basketball at Concordia Junior College. He led American League first basemen in assists in 1945.

After retiring as a player, Siebert coached baseball at the University of Minnesota, his alma mater. He spent 31 seasons with the Gophers, winning the College World Series in 1956, 1960, and 1964. He was twice named College Coach of the Year and in 1978 was named Lefty Grove Award winner in recognition for furthering the cause of college baseball.

Siebert's son Paul pitched for the Astros and Mets. He was involved in a controversial trade that saw slugger Dave Kingman leave New York for San Diego.

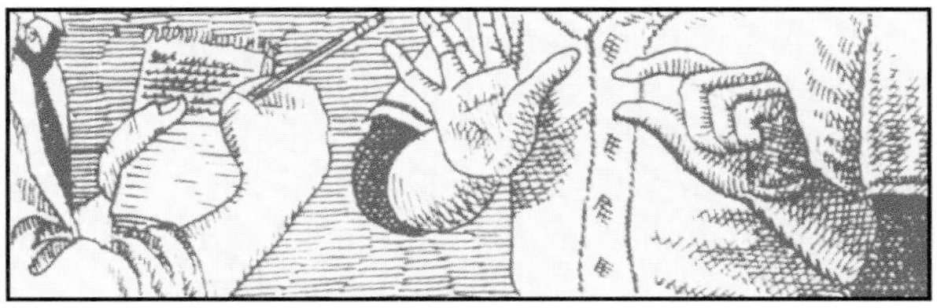

Ruben Sierra

Sierra, Ruben Angel (Garcia) **OF–DH**

1986–* B:10/6/1965, Rio Piedras, Puerto Rico
Deb:6/1/1986, TEX AL BB/TR, 6'1", 200

G	AB	R	H	HR	RBI	OBP	SLG	AVG
1662	6409	887	1723	239	1047	.322	.451	.269

Ruben Sierra was more of a shooting star than a superstar. A slugging switch hitter with a powerful outfield arm, he joined the Texas Rangers in 1986 when he was only 20 and immediately became an everyday player. In his second season hit a career-high 30 home runs to go with 109 RBIs. Two years later he led the American League with 119 RBIs, another career best, and made the All-Star team for the first of four times. Sierra would never again, however, match that level of production.

Sierra's 1989 statistics (.306 average, 29 home runs, 101 runs scored, and 119 RBIs) made him a Most Valuable Player candidate; he finished a close second in the American League voting to Milwaukee's Robin Yount. Sierra was accused of being moody, not hustling, and providing indifferent outfield play. More and more he was used as a designated hitter.

Texas sent Sierra to Oakland in August 1992 in a blockbuster trade involving Jose Canseco. Sierra lasted nearly three seasons, posting modest numbers with the A's, before moving to the Yankees, where he was ill-suited to a big market environment. Sierra's decline was swift. In his final three seasons he wore the uniform of the Yankees, Tigers, Blue Jays, Reds, and White Sox. He was only 32 when he dropped below the major league level in 1998.

Roy Sievers

Sievers, Roy Edward **1B–OF**

1949–65 B:11/18/1926, St. Louis, MO Deb:4/21/1949, STL AL BR/TR 6'1", 195

G	AB	R	H	HR	RBI	OBP	SLG	AVG
1887	6387	945	1703	318	1147	.357	.475	.267

In the 1950s Roy "Squirrel" Sievers, performing for the lowly Browns and Senators, overcame a career-threatening injury to become one of the American League's premier sluggers. Casey Stengel once said that Sievers had "the sweetest righthanded swing in the league." It was sweet enough to produce 318 career home runs.

Sievers was raised in St. Louis, only a few blocks from Sportsman's Park, home to both the Cardinals and the Browns. Cardinals scout Walter Shannon kept an eye on Sievers, but the youngster signed instead with Jack Fournier of the Browns, thinking he stood a better chance of making the majors with that threadbare club than with the talent-rich Redbirds. Seaver's only bonus was a pair of spikes. He later learned that the Cardinals would have given him $10,000.

Before reporting to the minors Sievers spent two years in the military, playing service ball in Kentucky. Discharged in February 1947, Sievers reported to Hannibal, where he led the Class C Central Association in runs, hits, homers, and RBIs. In 1948 he faltered in the Eastern League and was demoted to the 3-I League, where he batted .309.

A torrid spring the following year earned him a promotion to St. Louis. Sievers became the Browns' first (and last) Rookie of the Year. He hit .306 with 16 homers and 91 RBIs in 1948, but the Browns couldn't leave well enough alone. Coaches in the organization tinkered with his batting style in an effort to get him to hit more to right field; the result was a terrible sophomore season, including a 68-point drop in his batting average. "After that," Sievers recalled, "I said I was going back to my own way of hitting and I never let anyone change me again."

Purely mechanical problems gave way to physical problems in 1951. Sievers had been farmed out to San Diego, and while diving for a ball in the outfield he dislocated his shoulder. Limited to 31 games in 1951 and only 11 games in 1952, his future looked bleak. But Browns owner Bill Veeck was convinced that Sievers could come back. Even though Veeck had a wooden leg, he spent long hours hitting grounders to Sievers so that the player could work on his throwing. Finally, Veeck sent him to Dr. George Bennett of Johns Hopkins. Bennett didn't want to operate, but Veeck pleaded. The result was a minor medical miracle. Sievers was able to play 92 games in 1953.

Veeck was forced out of the American League after that season, however, and the new Browns ownership traded Sievers to Washington for journeyman outfielder Gil Coan. It was a big blunder. In 1954 Sievers hit 24 homers with 102 RBIs despite a .232 batting average. Until Tony Armas hit .218 with 107 RBIs in 1983, it was the lowest batting average ever by a 100-RBI man.

Sievers quickly established himself as one of the league's best run producers. He had four 100-plus RBI seasons in the five years from 1954 through 1958. The only player in the league with more RBIs during that span was Jackie Jensen.

One of Sievers' biggest fans was then-Vice President Richard Nixon. Nixon once said, "Roy Sievers is a boy who symbolizes great character, sportsmanship, and guts." In fact, when Nixon returned from debating Nikita Khrushchev in Moscow, he sent word that he wanted Sievers to meet him at the airport. While assorted dignitaries waited for the future President, Nixon was busy talking baseball with Squirrel.

In 1957 Sievers led the league with 42 homers and 114 RBIs, both career highs. During one stretch he hit homers in six consecutive games. He beat out Ted Williams and Mickey Mantle for the home run crown. Outperforming two future Hall of Famers meant a great deal to Sievers; years later he told Williams, "Ted, you deprived me of my Triple Crown." Williams was confused until Sievers reminded him that he had hit .301 that year (another career high), and that Williams had nipped him in the batting race by a mere 87 points.

After that remarkable year Sievers wanted a 100-percent raise, which would take him up to approximately $34,000. He had to settle for an 80-percent increase from Washington owner Calvin Griffith. After the next season, when Sievers hit 39 homers with 108 RBIs, Griffith wanted to cut Sievers' salary by 10 percent. "Calvin, you've got to be kidding," responded Sievers. Griffith insisted that a cut was in order because Sievers hadn't led the league in anything.

A lot of clubs wanted to pry Sievers loose from Griffith, but the White Sox were the most persistent. In 1959 Bill Veeck, now with Chicago, made his first proposal to land Sievers. "It was fantastic," said White Sox manager Al Lopez. "Something like $250,000, plus Washington could've picked four or five players from a list of about 10 players. I wouldn't have given the money for him, let alone the players."

Sievers slumped badly in 1959, and Veeck got him for a slightly cheaper price in April 1960: Earl Battey, Don Mincher, and $150,000. Lopez still wasn't crazy about having Sievers. Until first baseman Ted Kluszewski slumped, the manager kept his expensive acquisition on the bench. That season was the closest Sievers came to a World Series as the White Sox finished third. Sievers did his job, though, with 28 homers, 93 RBIs, and a career-best 21-game hitting streak. After nearly identical numbers the next year, Sievers was traded to the Phillies. He was 35 years old, but he still averaged 20 homers and 81 RBIs the next two seasons.

On May 26, 1963, Sievers made baseball history. He hit a pinch-hit grand slam off Cincinnati hurler Bill Henry two years after having performed the feat with the White Sox. He retired as one of only three players to hit pinch-hit grand slams in both leagues.

Sold to the expansion Washington Senators in July 1964, he batted .180 for the season. He was given his unconditional release after 21 at bats in 1965. In his career he had 27 multihomer games and hit 10 grand slams.

Sievers coached for the Reds in 1966. He then managed in the Mets' system for two years with Williamsport of the Eastern League, and later piloted Oakland's Burlington team of the Midwest League. After leaving baseball he worked for the Yellow Freight Company in St. Louis until retiring in 1986.

Sievers has been a hit in numerous old-timer's games, clad in a replica St. Louis Browns uniform. In fact, he has received many offers to buy the uniform, which was a gift from Bing Devine. "It's nice to know collectors think so much of it, but the fact is, so do I," said Sievers. "This uniform is something I'll keep the rest of my life."

Al Simmons

Simmons, Aloysius Harry **OF**

1924–41, 1943–44 B:5/22/1902, Milwaukee, WI D:5/26/1956, Milwaukee, WI Deb:4/15/1924, PHI AL BR/TR 5'11", 190

G	AB	R	H	HR	RBI	OBP	SLG	AVG
2215	8759	1507	2927	307	1827	.380	.535	.334

"I hate pitchers," Al Simmons once said. "Those guys are trying to take the meat and potatoes right off my plate, the bread and butter out of my mouth." Said Yankees outfielder Tommy Henrich, "When Al Simmons would grab hold of a bat and dig in, he'd squeeze the handle of that doggone thing and throw the barrel of that bat toward the pitcher in his warm-up swings, and he would look so bloomin' mad—in batting practice. What a smasher he was. He's got to be the most vicious man I ever saw at home plate. Oh, but he was one angry man when he strode up to bat. He hated that pitcher with a vengeance and showed it."

He briefly attended Stevens Point Teachers College, and played semipro baseball for a team in Juneau, Wisconsin, before signing in 1922 to play professionally with the Milwaukee Brewers of the American Association. Born Aloys Syzmanski, he changed his name to Simmons, which he found in a newspaper ad for a hardware store.

In 19 games for the Brewers he hit only .222, and was farmed out to Aberdeen of the South Dakota League, where he hit .365. The next year he moved up to Shreveport of the Texas League, hit .360, then returned to Milwaukee for the final 24 games of the season, hitting .398. Owner Connie Mack of the Philadelphia Athletics bought his contract for the 1924 season for $50,000.

Simmons had an unusual batting stance. His left foot was pointed straight down the third-base line, and as the pitch was delivered he strode toward third. He appeared to be pulling off the pitch, what was traditionally called "stepping into the bucket." The bucket was the water bucket on the bench. Consequently he was called "Bucketfoot Al," much to his displeasure.

Simmons later explained, "Although my left foot stabbed out toward third base, the rest of me, from the belt up, especially my wrists, arms, and shoulders, was swinging in a proper line over the plate. A fellow's got to hit the way that comes naturally to him." He added, "Hitters are born, not made."

Mack told his players, "Let that young man alone. If he can hit like [he hit at Milwaukee], it's all right with me if he stands on his head at the plate." Criticism all but disappeared when Simmons hit .308 with 102 RBIs as a rookie. That was just a hint at his potential. He drove in 100 runs in each of his first 11 seasons and batted .300 each of those seasons as well.

In his sophomore season Simmons cracked out 253 hits, the fourth-highest total ever, and hit .387. He scored 122 runs and drove in 129. He finished second in the American League in slugging average with a .599 mark.

After nearly a decade in the second division, usually in last place, Mack was rebuilding his Athletics in the mid-1920s. Infielder Jimmy Dykes, pitcher Eddie Rommel, catcher Cy Perkins, and outfielder Bing Miller were already in Philadelphia when Simmons and second baseman Max Bishop arrived in 1924. In 1925 Mack added catcher Mickey Cochrane and pitcher Lefty Grove. The team jumped to second place in the American League.

In a few more years all the pieces of the puzzle were in place. Jimmie Foxx came to the team in 1926 but didn't have a position until Mack installed him at first base in 1929. Foxx and Simmons then formed a one-two batting punch that rivaled the New York Yankees' duo of Babe Ruth and Lou Gehrig.

Mack rejuvenated the A's by recruiting talented youngsters, but he also hired some veterans in their final seasons. Outfielders Ty Cobb, Tris Speaker, and Zack Wheat all played for Philadelphia in the late 1920s. Although Cobb was generally detested, Simmons got along with him well. Simmons never had trouble with anyone who could help make him a better hitter. But Simmons' single-minded attention to his own hitting made him unpopular with many teammates.

In 1927 Simmons hit for the highest batting average of his career, with .392, but a groin injury limited him to only 106 games. Nevertheless, he knocked in 108 runs. The next year illness restricted him to 119 games, but he hit .351 with 107 RBIs. Later, when his career was over and he was only 73 hits shy of 3,000, Simmons considered whether there might have been occasions

when he could have played despite illness or injury.

Simmons stayed healthy in 1929. He hit .365 with 34 home runs, 114 runs scored, and a league-leading 157 RBIs. *The Sporting News* named him league Most Valuable Player, and the Athletics moved past the Yankees to capture their first pennant since 1914.

Philadelphia then beat the powerful Chicago Cubs in a five-game World Series in which Simmons hit .300. In Game 4 the A's were trailing, 8–0, in the seventh inning when Simmons led off with a home run. Philadelphia eventually scored 10 runs in the inning, the greatest rally in World Series history.

In 1930 Simmons won the league batting title with a .381 mark. He led the league with 152 runs, hitting 36 home runs and collecting 165 RBIs. Out of curiosity, Washington Senators owner Clark Griffith checked Simmons' season record and discovered that 14 of his home runs were hit in the eighth or ninth inning.

Simmons also led league outfielders in fielding in 1930. Although his powerful bat garnered all the attention, he was also one of the best defensive outfielders of his day, sure-handed and blessed with an excellent arm. When Lefty Grove lost his bid for a league-record 17th straight win because of a substitute left fielder's misplay, he was enraged at Simmons for being out of the lineup.

The Athletics took their second straight pennant in 1930. In the World Series the St. Louis Cardinals took them to six games before the A's triumphed. Simmons hit .364, including home runs in both the first and final games.

Simmons held out for a salary increase in 1931. At the beginning of the season Mack announced that Simmons would not be in the Opening Day lineup. Mack took a cab to Shibe Park that morning. As he reached for his wallet, the cabbie told him, "If you can't afford Al Simmons, you can't afford me either." A few hours later Simmons signed a three-year contract. On the first pitch to him that day, Simmons homered.

Simmons hit .390 in 1931 to win his second consecutive batting championship. He added 105 runs scored, 128 RBIs, and 22 homers as the Athletics won their third pennant in a row. They disappointed in the Series, however. Behind the inspired play of Pepper Martin, St. Louis defeated Philadelphia in seven games. Simmons hit .333 with eight RBIs and for the third straight Series, two home runs.

Philadelphia fell to second place in 1932, 13 games behind the Yankees. After so much success, the A's seemed to lack their earlier spark. Simmons said later, "When I finally decided I had it made, I was never again the ballplayer I was when I was hungry." His batting average slipped to .322, but he still hit 35 home runs, with 151 RBIs, 144 runs scored, and a league-leading 216 hits.

The Depression destroyed the A's. Connie Mack could no longer afford to pay high salaries without an influx of cash. As the 1932 season ended, he sold Simmons, Jimmy Dykes, and outfielder Mule Haas to the Chicago White Sox for $150,000.

White Sox fans expected Simmons to continue hitting in the .360 to .380 range. But he no longer had the terrifying Jimmie Foxx batting behind him, nor was Comiskey Park as friendly toward hitters as Shibe had been. Still, he was named to play in the inaugural All-Star Game and batted .331 for the season with 119 RBIs. His 14 home runs, however, were his lowest total since his rookie year.

During the winter of 1933 and 1934 the Sox moved Comiskey's home plate 10 feet closer to the fences. The move was intended to help Simmons, but he increased his home run total by only four. In reality, he never was a true home run hitter like Foxx, who hit towering shots. Most of Simmons' homers were line drives.

Although chosen for the All-Star Game for the third straight season in 1935, Simmons had a poor year. His RBIs dropped to 79, his first major league season he did not top 100. His batting average fell to .267. Sold that December to Detroit for $75,000, he rebounded to hit .327 with 112 RBIs, his 12th and final time over the 100 mark.

During the next several years he played for Washington, the Boston Braves, Cincinnati, the Boston Red Sox, and eventually the Athletics again. Simmons finally retired after playing only four games in 1944. Following his retirement Simmons coached for the Athletics and Cleveland. He was elected to the Hall of Fame in 1953, three years before his death from a heart attack.

Curt Simmons

Simmons, Curtis Thomas **P**

1947–67 B:5/19/1929, Egypt, PA Deb:9/28/1947, PHI NL BL/TL 6', 187

W	L	PCT	G	SH	IP	BB	SO	ERA
193	183	.513	569	36	3348[1]	1063	1697	3.54

Curt Simmons of the Phillies, like Johnny Antonelli of the Braves, survived the pressures of being a postwar bonus baby to establish a fine record as a National League pitcher. The left-handed Simmons was originally a right fielder, but one day in 1943 the 13-year-old was brought in to mop up a game for his hometown team of the Cement Boro League. He performed well but still remained an outfielder. Invited to play on a local American Legion team, Simmons was pressed into pitching service in the district championship game. He struck out 11 to win the game.

He still didn't want to pitch, because it cut down on his at bats, but resigned himself to his new role. Along the way he learned to throw a curve, and before he knew it the scouts were eager to check him out as he pitched his high school to three district championships, recorded three no-hitters, and averaged 17 strikeouts per contest.

On June 2, 1947, the day Simmons was to graduate from high school, Philadelphia general manager Herb Pennock brought the entire Phillies club to town. Simmons faced them and surrendered only five hits while striking out 12. Four hours later he graduated, and the Phillies signed him to a $65,000 bonus.

Sent to Wilmington of the Class B Inter-State League, he went 13–5 and struck out 197 in 147 innings. The Phillies brought him up for the last game of the 1947 season, and he recorded a complete-game five-hitter against the Giants.

In 1948 and 1949 Simmons floundered. He lost a combined 22 games and his ERA approached 5.00 both seasons. On September 6, 1948, he walked 12 batters in only seven innings of work.

"Simmons had a great arm; he could really fire," recalled Phillies manager Eddie Sawyer. "His problem was that he had received too much well-meaning advice. He had been overcoached more than any pitcher I ever saw. Everybody and his brother had tried to straighten him out because he appeared to be doing everything you're not supposed to do—he had that herky-jerky motion and he threw across his body, among other things."

Finally, Sawyer took Simmons aside and told him to simply go back to what had made him great in high school. "He smiled and did just as asked," said Sawyer. "It took him a while to shake off all the bad advice he'd gotten....But he was happy; he was getting squared away."

In 1950 Simmons showed great improvement, winning 17 games as an integral member of the Phils' pennant-winning "Whiz Kids." However, he wasn't there to help them win it at the end. With only a few weeks left in the season he was called into the Army Reserve. Even without Simmons, the Phillies held the Yankees to 11 runs in four games, but New York allowed just five runs in sweeping Philadelphia.

The tandem of Simmons and Hall of Famer Robin Roberts was statistically the seventh-best lefty–righty pitching combo in major league history. From 1948 through 1960 they combined for 347 victories against only 299 defeats.

Simmons is credited with a famous observation about Hank Aaron: "Henry Aaron is the only ballplayer I have ever seen who goes to sleep at the plate. But trying to sneak a fastball past him is like trying to sneak the sunrise past a rooster." Yet Simmons was one of the few pitchers who enjoyed any success against Aaron.

"Over the years, Curt Simmons was the toughest," Aaron admitted. "Things usually even out in baseball. One year, a pitcher can give you a lot of trouble but the next year you catch up with him. But Simmons gave me the most problems."

Simmons won 15 games in 1956 and 12 the following season. But he lost 14 games in 1958, then injured his arm and appeared in only seven games in 1959. In May 1960 the Phillies unconditionally released the sore-armed righthander. He signed with the Cardinals and showed signs of new life, winning 15 games and even stealing home on September 1, 1963.

Ironically, in 1964 the Phillies used their only two dependable pitchers, Chris Short and Jim Bunning, continuously down the stretch and burned out both; Philadelphia lost 10 straight in the final weeks of the season. Simmons won 18 games and helped the Cardinals sneak in and steal the pennant. In the 1964 World Series Simmons pitched well in Game 3, getting a no-decision in a 2–1 Cardinal loss. But he surrendered back-to-back homers to Roger Maris and Mickey Mantle and took the loss in Game 6. The Cardinals, behind Bob Gibson, won the Series in seven games.

It was his last productive season. Simmons bounced around with the Cardinals, Cubs, and Angels over the next four seasons. After retiring, Simmons became the owner-manager of a golf course near Ambler, Pennsylvania

Ted Simmons

Simmons, Ted Lyle **C-DH-1B**

1968–88 B: 8/9/1949, Highland Park, MI
Deb:9/21/1968, STL NL BB/TR 6', 200

G	AB	R	H	HR	RBI	OBP	SLG	AVG
2456	8680	1074	2472	248	1389	.352	.437	.285

Ted Simmons was one of baseball's most durable and best-hitting catchers. A switch hitter, he hit .300 or better seven times and drove in 90 or more runs eight times. In 1983 he put on a tremendous display of clutch hitting by driving in 108 runs while hitting only 13 homers. Twice in his career he belted pinch-hit grand slams. Five times he performed in All-Star Games; three other times he was selected but did not play.

Simmons, an all-state football star at Southfield High School in Michigan, received scholarship offers from Michigan, Purdue, Michigan State, and Colorado. He was the Cardinals' first selection (10th overall) in the June 1967 free-agent draft, signing with them for a $50,000 bonus. In 1968 St. Louis assigned him to Modesto, where he led the circuit with a .331 average and 117 RBIs and was chosen as both the California League's Most Valuable Player and Rookie of the Year. With Tulsa in 1969 he hit .317 and drove in 88 runs.

The lefthanded Simmons was taught to switch-hit by his older brothers. He did not feel comfortable with it, however, until he reached the majors. Simmons recalled, "I almost quit [switch-hitting]. But [Cardinals managers] Kenny Boyer and Red Schoendienst saw something in my swing and told me that I'd eventually come out of it if I stayed with it." He did. Three times in his career Simmons hit homers from both sides of the plate in a game. And not only could Simmons switch-hit, but he could also switch-catch. "I could play first base either righthanded or lefthanded," he once boasted.

Simmons was extremely frustrated in St. Louis. During his 10 full seasons with the Cardinals, the team finished second three times, third three times, fourth two times, and fifth twice. "Winning. That's what I want," he said. "That's all there is. You can't think like, 'Maybe I'll go to Cincinnati and do it there.' I can't go to the front office and say, 'Hey, you gotta get better players.' It's tough enough just being a player. I just have to keep playing and worry about myself."

Simmons in turn was often the target of fan frustration in St. Louis. Once, when he was asked about Cardinals fans, he answered, "Too many of them don't know what's going on." Despite the boo birds, Simmons was a powerful offensive force for the Cardinals, and as a hitter he was often rated ahead of fellow receiver Johnny Bench.

In 1973 and 1975 Simmons caught more than 150 games. In 1975 he also recorded 188 hits as a catcher, just shy of Yogi Berra's 1950 catcher's record of 191. On April 16, 1978, Simmons caught Bob Forsch's no-hitter against the Phillies. Seven years earlier he had been on the receiving end of Bob Gibson's no-hit gem against the Pirates.

Like Simmons, St. Louis manager–general manager Whitey Herzog was thinking about winning. Otherwise the two had little in common, and they were constantly feuding. After Herzog acquired catcher Darrell Porter as a free agent, he engineered a series of major transactions that ultimately brought Bruce Sutter and a world championship to the Cardinals.

Simmons was dealt to Milwaukee and, although he had some trouble adjusting to American League pitching, helped the Brewers to a second-half championship in the strike-shortened 1981 season. In 1982 Simmons hit 23 homers and drove in 97 runs as the Brewers won the pennant. That same year, Herzog's Cardinals won the National League flag. In the World Series, Simmons hit two homers and the Brew Crew entered Game 6 ahead, three games to two. But the Cardinals won two straight to become world champions.

At the close of the 1983 season Simmons was granted free agency, but he re-signed with the Brewers. With his catching skills rapidly eroding, Simmons found himself switched to designated hitter and first baseman. In March 1986 he was traded to the Braves, where he finished his career as a member of the club's "Bomb Squad" of utility players.

Although a superb hitter, Simmons was not a good defensive catcher. His 182 career passed balls set a modern record, and he led the National League in that department three times. "The decision to make a catcher out of him can be questioned," baseball historian Bill James once observed, noting not only that he lacked a good throwing arm but also that he might have achieved 3,000 hits had he played another position.

Still, Simmons did have one strength as a catcher: he was an excellent handler of pitchers. "To me, he's a real good defensive catcher," commented Cardinals pitcher Clay Carroll. "He knows what he's doing back there. I don't have to shake him off that much. When I'm not throwing right, he comes out right away and lets me know about it. And he reminds me what to do in certain situations. I really have confidence in him. All he does is give the sign and I throw it."

Simmons, who majored in speech and in radio and television in college, was a somewhat erudite player. "He didn't sound like a baseball player. He said things like 'Nevertheless,' and 'If, in fact,'" Dan Quisenberry said. In October 1988 Simmons became director of player development for the Cardinals. In February 1992 he replaced Larry Doughty as Pittsburgh's general manager. It was not an enviable position to be in. Under orders to cut costs, Simmons slashed the division champion Pirates' payroll from $35 million to $24 million, but lopped off much talent in the process.

In early June 1993, Simmons, a heavy smoker, suffered a heart attack and underwent emergency balloon angioplasty. On June 19, 1993, he resigned as general manager. "After talking this over with my wife, we decided that it looks like the Pirates have put themselves in pretty good shape," Simmons explained. "Maybe it's time to do that for myself." He returned to the front office with the San Diego Padres in 1999.

Bill Singer

Singer, William Robert **P**

1964–77 B:4/24/1944, Los Angeles, CA Deb:9/24/1964, LA NL BR/TR 6'4", 200

W	L	PCT	G	SH	IP	BB	SO	ERA
118	127	.482	322	24	2174	781	1515	3.39

Righthander Bill Singer teamed with Nolan Ryan on the 1973 Angels to fan 624 opponents, setting a record as the highest strikeout total notched by two teammates. He twice won 20 games. Nicknamed "the Singer Throwing Machine," he received a $50,000 signing bonus from the Dodgers in 1961.

In the minors he performed with Reno, Albuquerque, and Spokane, leading the Pacific Coast League with 17 complete games in 1965. He tossed a no-hitter against Dallas on April 23, 1964.

In 1969, Singer's third full season in the majors, he won 20 games for the Dodgers and recorded a career-low 2.34 ERA. Sidelined by hepatitis for the first half of 1970, he came back to no-hit the Phillies on July 20, 1970 as he struck out 10 and walked none. The only baserunner was Oscar Gamble, who reached on a hit-by-pitch. At season's end, though, Singer was back on the disabled list, this time with a broken finger.

Traded with Frank Robinson to California in November 1972, he was reached for three runs in two innings in the 1973 All-Star Game. He went on to win 20 games and strike out 241, good for third in the league; teammate Ryan set a 20th century mark with 383.

Singer, however, only had one more season with more than 10 wins. He was traded to Texas in December 1975 and to the Twins with three other players and $250,000 for Bert Blyleven in June 1976. The Blue Jays took him in the November 1976 expansion draft. He retired after the 1977 season.

Ken Singleton

Singleton, Kenneth Wayne **OF–DH**

1970–84 B:6/10/1947, New York, NY Deb:6/24/1970, NY NL BB/TR 6'4", 213

G	AB	R	H	HR	RBI	OBP	SLG	AVG
2082	7189	985	2029	246	1065	.391	.436	.282

Ken Singleton was a rare commodity—a switch hitter with power. Singleton was born in New York City, grew up in Mount Vernon, just north of the city, and was drafted by the New York Mets in the third round of the January 1969 amateur draft. But he was traded before he had a chance to be a star in New York.

Ken Singleton made it to the majors in just over a year, hitting .263 in 198 at bats in 1970, the year after the "Miracle" Mets had won the world championship. The next season he went to bat 298 times and, though he hit just .245, showed promise with 13 homers and 46 RBIs. That turned out to be his last year in New York.

The Mets, in need of an established outfielder, sent the 24-year-old Singleton to the Expos with Tim Foli and Mike Jorgensen for Rusty Staub. Singleton had his first great season while playing at Jarry Park in Montreal. In 1973 he batted .302 with 23 homers and 103 RBIs as the Expos' right fielder. That season he also registered a career-high 20 assists. Singleton had below-average speed but a howitzer for an arm.

He slumped to nine homers and 74 RBIs in

1974, and the Expos made the same mistake as the Mets. In fact, they came up with one of the more lopsided deals in the history of the game.

On December 4, 1974, Montreal sent Singleton and Mike Torrez to the Orioles for Dave McNally, Rich Coggins, and Bill Kirkpatrick. Kirkpatrick never appeared in the majors, Coggins was out of the majors in two years, and McNally's arm blew out permanently after 77 innings in Montreal.

Torrez, meanwhile, won 20 games for the Orioles in 1975, while Singleton spent the next 10 years as a key member of Orioles' teams that perennially challenged for the division title. Singleton's best seasons were 1979 and 1980. He hit .295 with 35 homers and 111 RBIs for the 1979 team won the American League pennant. Although Baltimore lost the World Series to the Pirates in seven games, Singleton hit .357. The next year he hit .304 and drove in 104 runs as the Orioles won 100 games yet finished second to the Yankees in the American League East.

In 1981 Singleton recorded 10 consecutive hits, the most in the American League since 1952. Two years later, at age 36, he became the Orioles' designated hitter. He was now one of the two or three slowest runners in the league, and one of the easiest to double up. He retired with a share of the major league record for most 150-game seasons (four) without stealing a base.

Singleton chipped in with 18 homers and 84 RBIs in 1983 as the Orioles won their first World Series since 1970, beating the Phillies in five games. But since this Series was played without a DH, Singleton spent most of the time watching. He batted twice, walking once and striking out once.

That was his last hurrah. He produced only six homers and 36 RBIs in 1984 and retired. Singleton made a second career as a broadcaster with the Expos and Yankees.

Dick Sisler

Sisler, Richard Allan **1B–OF**

1946–53 M(1964–65, 121–94) B:11/2/1920, St. Louis, MO D:11/20/98, Nashville, TN Deb:4/16/1946, STL NL BL/TR 6'2", 205

G	AB	R	H	HR	RBI	OBP	SLG	AVG
799	2606	302	720	55	360	.336	.406	.276

It wasn't easy following in the footsteps of a Hall of Fame father who had a career .340 average and was twice American League batting champion with gaudy averages of .407 and .420. But Dick Sisler, son of St. Louis Browns first baseman George Sisler, tried anyway. All things considered, he didn't do a bad job. Just ask the Philadelphia Phillies' Whiz Kids.

Bigger than his father at 6 feet 2 inches, 205 pounds, Dick Sisler was an outfielder-first baseman with power who put up rather ordinary numbers throughout his brief but historic major league career. For the most part, he was a Sisler in name only. But on October 1, 1950, at Ebbets Field in Brooklyn, all that changed with one mighty swing of his bat. Playing on the final day of the season, the Phillies and Dodgers were locked in a 1–1 tie in the top of the 10th inning with the pennant on the line. Brooklyn fans were heckling the Phils when Sisler stepped to the plate with two runners on base. With pressure weighing on his broad shoulders, Sisler found the legendary Sisler swing and crushed a home run to give the Phillies their first National League flag in 35 years.

In the World Series against the New York Yankees, Sisler went 1-for-17 as the Phillies were swept in four straight. Three years later he returned to the minors as a player and manager until he became a coach for Cincinnati. In 1964 Sisler replaced the ill Fred Hutchinson as Cincinnati's manager. He led the Reds to an 89–73 season in 1965. He later coached for the Mets, Yankees, Padres, and Cardinals.

George Sisler

Sisler, George Harold **1B**

1915–22, 1924–30 M(1924–26, 218–241) B:3 /24/1893, Manchester, OH D:3/26/1973, Richmond Heights, MO Deb:6/28/1915, STL AL BL/TL 5'11", 170

G	AB	R	H	HR	RBI	OBP	SLG	AVG
2055	8267	1284	2812	102	1175	.379	.468	.340

George Sisler twice hit .400, set a single-season record for hits, stole bases with abandon, and in his rookie season outdueled one of the greatest pitchers ever, before being struck by a career-threatening illness. Sisler's relative anonymity among baseball fans isn't because of his numbers. A career .340 hitter, he led the league in average and hits twice, and was the American League's top base stealer four times. But "Gorgeous George" lacked those intangibles that transform mere talent into the stuff of legends. "He lacked the fiery flamboyance of Ty Cobb and the boisterous brilliance of Babe Ruth," Hall of Fame second baseman Eddie Collins said. "George was a great first baseman and a great hitter, but he was too quiet and clean-living to win headlines."

Sisler attended Central High School in Akron, Ohio, and later enrolled in the University of Michigan engineering program. He also tried out for the baseball team. Managing the squad was Branch Rickey, who had just given up his failing law practice. When the freshman Sisler showed up to audition for the varsity, Rickey tolerantly let him toss the ball around with the big kids for a day. "The workout was unforgettable," Rickey recalled. "He pitched batting practice and, for the next 20 minutes, created no end of varsity embarrassment. His speed and control made him unhittable. All his moves were guided by perfection of reflexes, which made him quick, graceful, accurate—the foundation of athletic greatness. It was all there."

Still Rickey kept Sisler with the freshmen. When Sisler got a starting assignment in an intrasquad game, the headline in the school newspaper, *The Michigan Daily*, read, "Unearth 'Find' in Interclass Game; Sisler, Freshman Engineer, Twirls for Seven Innings and Strikes Out 20 Men." In that game Sisler threw so hard that his catcher had trouble holding onto the ball. Sisler's 20th strikeout victim reached first base on a passed ball, and proceeded to second and third in the same fashion. The baserunner finally attempted to score on still another muff by the catcher, but Sisler tagged him out at the plate to end the game.

Not surprisingly, Sisler began to attract professional attention. Although still a minor, he had signed a professional contract with Akron in the Class C Ohio-Pennsylvania League. If that contract were valid, Sisler's athletic eligibility at Ann Arbor would be in jeopardy. When Rickey appeared before organized baseball's governing body, the National Commission, to argue Sisler's case, he contended, "You must not force recognition of this illegal contract. If you do, you will forever alienate parents and colleges and even high schools. For who is going to trust you, if you cajole minors into signing contracts and then declare them suspended—as you have tried to suspend Sisler—when they change their minds?" Neither of Sisler's parents had agreed to the contract, and he had not accepted any payment. The National Commission ruled, 2–1, in Sisler's favor.

In Sisler's freshman season he pitched 57 innings, allowing just 20 hits and striking out 84. At the same time he hit .442. During his varsity college career Sisler batted .404 and struck out 232 in 153 innings. But before he graduated on June 10, 1915, he discovered that no team except the Pirates was interested in acquiring his services. Apparently a "gentleman's agreement" existed between the major league clubs to allow Pittsburgh, which had previously purchased Sisler's contract from Columbus, to retain him despite the National Commission ruling. Rickey, now with the Browns, talked St. Louis ownership into signing the prospect.

Sisler went immediately to the majors, and in 1915 split his time between the outfield, first base, and the pitcher's mound. One of his pitching assignments, the one he referred to as his most memorable day in baseball, involved a duel against the great Walter Johnson. Johnson had been Sisler's boyhood hero. When Johnson had recorded his 55⅔-inning scoreless streak, Sisler said he was as proud as though he'd done it himself.

On the subject of facing his hero, Sisler said, "I'll never forget that one. We knew Johnson would be on the mound, but Rickey hadn't told us who would do our hurling. That night, Branch came into my room and told me I would pitch. I didn't want to sleep. The next day, I was going to pitch against Walter Johnson—and I beat him." Sisler prevailed in the mound duel, 2–1. After the game was over he nearly apologized to "the Big Train" for defeating him.

However, as good a pitcher as Sisler was, his future, like that of another lefthander, Ruth, was not on the mound. By 1918 "Gorgeous George" was already considered one of the best first basemen in the game. Sisler, it was written, "has dazzling ability of the Cobbesque type. He is just as fast, showy, and sensational, very nearly if not quite as good as a natural hitter, as fast in speed of foot, an even better fielder, and gifted with a versatility Cobb himself might envy."

By 1920 he had defeated Cobb for a batting championship, hitting .407, and Sisler established the all-time major league record of 257 hits in a season. "I always considered the 1920 season my best," he said. Even better than 1922, when he hit .420 and paced the circuit in hits and runs. That year he hit in 41 consecutive games and won the American League Most Valuable Player Award. "He single-handedly led us down to the wire in the pennant race that year," Branch Rickey said. "Why, he only struck out 14 times in 586 at bats. We should have won the pennant, but the Yankees edged us out."

Sisler did damage not only with his bat. He also led the league in stolen bases four times. As a fielder he was considered the best in the business, an unmatched genius with the glove. Seven times he topped league first basemen in assists and fielding average, six times in putouts, and three times in double plays.

Although considered one of the game's gentlemen, Sisler also displayed flashes of temper. Once, after pitcher Bob Groom criticized him mercilessly for failing to snag a high throw, Sisler stormed over to Groom and with one punch sent him to the dugout floor. On another occasion Sisler hit umpire George Hildebrand with his glove, drawing a brief suspension.

Although Sisler compiled a lifetime .340 average and batted .3997 from 1920 through 1922, he

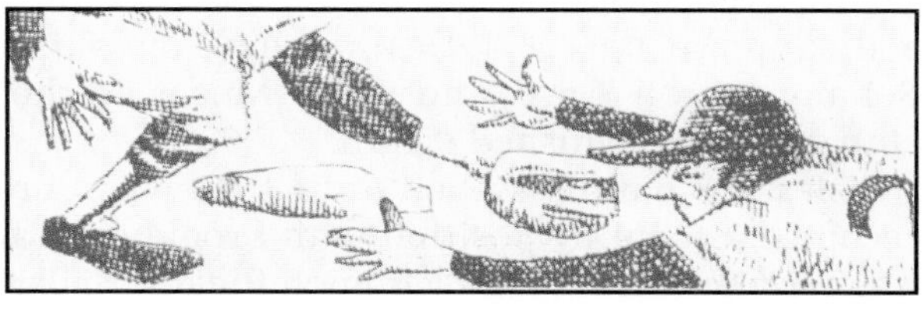

might have been even better if he had not suffered from serious eye problems. In January 1923 Sisler came down with an attack of the flu that badly aggravated his sinuses, which in turn left him with a serious case of double vision. Consequently he sat out the entire 1923 season.

"All season long I suffered," Sisler said. "I felt sorry for the fans, for my teammates, for everyone, except for myself. I planned to get back into uniform for 1924. I just had to meet a ball with a good swing again, and then run. The doctors all said I'd never play again, but when you're desperate, when you're fighting for something that actually keeps you alive—well the human will is all you need."

When he returned to action in the spring of 1924 he still saw two balls at the plate but worked his way through it, hitting better than .300 in six of his last seven seasons. But he was not the George Sisler of old. "When he came back, we soon learned something," said the Yankees' Bob Shawkey. "And this shows how mean it was in those days. When he was up at the plate, he could watch you for only so long, and then he'd have to look down to get his eyes focused again. So we'd keep him waiting up there until he'd have to look down, and then pitch. He was never the same hitter after that."

In January 1922 Sisler had returned to St. Louis from managing the Vernon club in the California Winter League. He said, "It gave me an insight into baseball from the manager's point of view. Perhaps an idea of how managers may be expected to react to a given situation will improve my playing. However, I have no ambitions to be a manager."

Yet at the beginning of the 1924 season he replaced Jimmy Austin as Browns manager, a position he held through 1926. "I never should have accepted the role in the first place," Sisler later confessed. "I simply wasn't ready to manage. I was only 31, and it was too early in my career."

In December 1927 Sisler was sold to Washington for $25,000 but hit so poorly that his market value plummeted to just $7,500 the following May when he went to the Braves. Boston released Sisler at the end of the 1930 season, but he signed on with Rochester of the International League where he batted .303 in 159 games and led the league in assists.

In 1932 he became player-manager of the Texas League's Shreveport Oilers. The club moved to Tyler, Texas, in May when their park burned. That's where he ended his playing career, batting a disappointing .287. Despite having Wally Schang, Aaron Ward, and Wally Moses on the club, the Oilers finished eighth.

Sisler was out of baseball until 1943 when he accepted a scouting position with Brooklyn and was reunited with mentor Branch Rickey. Sisler managed Newport News of the Piedmont League in 1945 and scouted again for Brooklyn from 1946 through 1950. When Rickey moved over to Pittsburgh, Sisler went with him, remaining as a Pirates scout until 1956. He then worked as their batting instructor through 1961, before again returning to the Pirates scouting ranks. He was elected to the Hall of Fame in 1939.

Ted Sizemore

Sizemore, Theodore Crawford **2B**

1969–80 B:4/15/1945, Gadsden, AL Deb:4/7/1969, LA NL BR/TR 5'10", 165

G	AB	R	H	HR	RBI	OBP	SLG	AVG
1411	5011	577	1311	23	430	.327	.321	.262

Drafted in the 40th round in 1966 and nicknamed "the Runt" by teammate Don Drysdale, Ted Sizemore beat the odds and won the National League Rookie of the Year Award in 1969. Named to Detroit All-City teams in basketball, football, and baseball, Theodore Crawford Sizemore chose to go to the University of Michigan, where in 1965 he was the Big Ten All-Star catcher. Unable to break into the Dodgers lineup as a catcher because of veterans Tom Haller and Jeff Torborg, Sizemore switched positions in spring training. Manager Walter Alston needed a second baseman.

Although Sizemore was a success at second, the Dodgers traded him after the 1970 season to St. Louis for Dick Allen. St. Louis teammate Lou Brock credited Sizemore with unselfishly helping him to break the career stolen base record by taking pitches when Brock was stealing. Brock had his most productive seasons in the five years that Sizemore, a patient hitter, followed him in the lineup. Sizemore played with four other clubs, including the pennant-winning Phillies teams of 1977 and 1978. In 1978 he hit .385 in the Championship Series. He retired in 1980 to become vice president of Rawlings Sporting Goods.

Bill Skowron

Skowron, William Joseph **1B**

1954–67 B:12/18/1930, Chicago, IL Deb:4/13/1954, NY AL BR/TR 5'11", 195

G	AB	R	H	HR	RBI	OBP	SLG	AVG
1658	5547	681	1566	211	888	.335	.459	.282

Bill Skowron played a solid first base and provided another big bat for Casey Stengel's Yankees dynasty of the 1940s and 1950s. His greatest moment came in the 1958 World Series. Against Milwaukee that postseason, Skowron drove in the winning run in Game 6 and hit a three-run homer in Game 7. When Skowron became a World Series hero, fans learned that Skowron's nickname "Moose" was not a reference to his considerable size. Instead it was a contraction of "Mussolini," the name with which his grandfather had dubbed him as a small child.

In 1951 Skowron signed with the Yankees for a $25,000 bonus. He spent that season with the Binghamton Triplets and the Norfolk Tars. At Norfolk he led the Class B Piedmont League with a .334 average. Promoted to Triple A Kansas City in 1952, he hit .341 and led the league with 31 homers and 134 RBIs. *The Sporting News* named him Minor League Player of the Year. The Yankees organization was determined, however, that Skowron remain at Kansas City in 1953. He wasn't brought up to New York until the following season.

Skowron batted over .300 in his first four seasons with the Yankees, from 1954 through 1957. From 1960 through 1962, he hit more than 20 home runs three seasons in a row. Traded to the Dodgers in November 1962 for pitcher Stan Williams, Skowron came back to haunt the Yankees. In the 1963 World Series against the New Yorkers, he had five hits, including a solo homer.

Skowron was sold to Washington in December 1963, and then traded to the White Sox in July 1964. After retiring, Skowron started the Mackle Brothers Company in Florida. In 1977 he returned to his native Chicago to work for a printing firm.

Jimmy Slagle

Slagle, James Franklin **OF**

1899–1908 B:7/11/1873, Worthville, PA D:5/10/1956, Chicago, IL Deb:4/17/1899, WAS NL BL/TR 5'7", 144

G	AB	R	H	HR	RBI	OBP	SLG	AVG
1298	4996	779	1340	2	344	.352	.317	.268

Jimmy Slagle was not much of a hitter, but he was one of the fastest players in the first years of the 20th century. James Franklin Slagle sported a variety of nicknames and they were all about speed and small stature. Jimmy stood only 5 feet 7 inches tall and weighed 144 pounds. Known as "Rabbit," "Shorty," and "the Human Mosquito," he stole six bases for the Cubs in the 1907 World Series against Detroit, a record for a five-game Series. He also became the first player to record two steals in one inning of a Series contest.

Slagle made his major league debut for the National League's Washington Senators in 1899. He was sold to the Philadelphia Phillies the following January, who traded him to the Boston Beaneaters in 1901. The following season he joined the Cubs. Slagle's best years in Chicago were 1902 and 1903. He hit .315 with 40 stolen bases in 1902, then batted .298 with a career-high 104 runs scored the following season. In 1903 Slagle and Frank Chance combined for 100 stolen bases, joining Brooklyn's Jimmy Sheckard and Sammy Strang as the first National League teammates to swipe at least 100.

The Chance-managed Cubs dominated the National League in 1907, winning 107 games and finishing 16 games ahead of second-place Pittsburgh. Slagle almost won Game 1 of the World Series for the Cubs with his daring baserunning. The score was tied, 3–3, in the 10th inning and Slagle was on third after stealing that base. With Harry Steinfeldt at bat, Detroit catcher Boss Schmidt failed to handle one of starter Wild Bill Donovan's pitches. Slagle came tearing in toward the plate and would have scored, except that umpire Hank O'Day called him out due to Steinfeldt's interference on Schmidt. The game ended as a tie, but the Cubs took the next four games to win the Series. Slagle retired at the end of the 1908 season, a lifetime .268 hitter.

Jim Slaton

Slaton, James Michael **P**

1971–86 B:6/19/1950, Long Beach, CA Deb:4/14/1971, MIL AL BR/TR 6', 185

W	L	PCT	G	SH	IP	BB	SO	ERA
151	158	.489	496	22	2683²	1004	1191	4.03

Righthander Jim Slaton spent most of his major league career with the Brewers, arriving the year after the team made its debut in Milwaukee. He endured losing seasons for six straight years as the Brewers foundered, and was on hand for the team's two postseason appearances.

Slaton, who attended Antelope Valley Junior College, was a 14th round choice of the Seattle Pilots in the 1969 amateur draft. By the time he made the majors in 1971 the Pilots had become the Brewers. Demoted to Evansville in 1972 he pitched a 5–0 no-hitter against Wichita. He was Milwaukee's workhorse, starting at least 30 games and pitching 200 or more innings each year from 1972 to 1977. He was Milwaukee's representative on the 1977 All-Star team.

Traded to Detroit in December 1977 he recorded a career-high 17 victories in his lone year with the Tigers. On gaining his free agency he returned to Milwaukee in November 1978. After winning 15 games in 1979, Slaton developed rotator cuff problems the following year. He was forced to make a transition from starter to reliever.

He pitched in four of the five games in Milwaukee's loss to the Yankees in the 1981 Division Playoff. The following year he won 10 games as the Brewers won the American League East. He picked up a save in Game 4 of the Championship Series and earned the win in the fourth game of the 1982 World Series. In 1983 Slaton compiled 14 wins in relief, a Brewers club record.

Good at keeping runners close to the base, Slaton was also a better than average fielding pitcher. Once Slaton was asked if he thought the ball was getting livelier. "Only when I'm pitching," he answered. In 1999 he was coaching for the Pacific Coast League's Tacoma Raniers.

Enos Slaughter

Slaughter, Enos Bradsher **OF**

1938–59 B:4/27/1916, Roxboro, NC Deb:4/19/1938, STL NL BL/TR 5'9", 192

G	AB	R	H	HR	RBI	OBP	SLG	AVG
2380	7946	1247	2383	169	1304	.382	.453	.300

Outfielder Enos "Country" Slaughter never stopped hustling, whether he was dashing for the plate in the 1946 World Series or limping to first base with a broken foot at age 43 with the Milwaukee Braves. During his career, Slaughter batted .300 and ran out every hit—and every out.

Slaughter got his start at a Cardinals tryout in Greensboro, North Carolina, in the fall of 1934. At the urging of *Durham Morning Herald* sportswriter Fred Haney, St. Louis invited Slaughter, who hailed from Roxboro, North Carolina, to test his luck, but made it clear that if he failed, he was responsible for his own transportation home. He didn't have to worry about the return fare.

For a fellow who made his reputation by running, Slaughter initially was not very fast afoot. In fact, he ran flat-footed, as the Cardinals' Billy Southworth pointed out to him one day in 1935. Southworth urged Slaughter to run on the balls of his feet. Slaughter practiced virtually nonstop for the next four days. By the end of those four days he had cut four steps off his run to first base.

Slaughter spent the next season at Columbus of the Class B South Atlantic League. In one game, manager Eddie Dyer spied him moping toward the dugout, lost in thought about his own poor performance. "Son, if you're tired, we'll try to get you some help," said Dyer. The words hit Slaughter like a slap in the face. He recalled, "I suddenly realized people don't care how sorry I felt for myself. That's when I started running." He never stopped.

In 1937 Slaughter paced the American Association in batting with a .382 mark and gained a nickname from Columbus Redbirds manager Burt Shotton: "Country." Slaughter was promoted to St. Louis in 1938 but received only $400 a month for the honor. "We didn't make no money with the Cards. They all said we was hungry ballplayers," Slaughter said.

In 1939 he received a raise to $600 a month, and did everything he could to earn it. On New Year's Day Slaughter and his father had gone hunting for rabbits. Both contracted tularemia from the infected carcasses. His father was dead in three days. Against a physician's orders, an ailing Slaughter still reported to spring training and that season led the National League in doubles, putouts, assists, and double plays.

Even a fractured collarbone failed to slow Slaughter down for long. In 1941, to avoid a collision with center fielder Terry Moore, he ran into a concrete wall. Before the bone could set, he was back in uniform. Swinging at one pitch caused his wound to rip open and blood spurted out. He wasn't exaggerating when he later said, "I'll never quit. They'll have to tear my uniform off me."

Slaughter considered the 1942 Cardinals "by far the best team I ever played on. We had everything, we just felt we could beat anybody." That season he was second in the National League in batting, at .318, and led the league with 17 triples and 188 hits. In Game 2 of the 1942 World Series, Slaughter's ninth-inning throw to nail Tuck Stainback at third helped defeat New York, 4–3. The Cardinals beat the Yankees in five games, handing Joe McCarthy his only Series loss as New York manager.

Slaughter went into the service in 1942, and did not come out until the 1946 season. In between, he played service ball to entertain the troops, including a game on recently captured Iwo Jima. In 1946 Slaughter helped spark the Cardinals to another pennant. He hit .300 for the fifth straight year, slammed a career-high 18 home runs, and led the league with a career-high 130 RBIs. In that year's World Series against the Red Sox he let all of America know just what kind of a ballplayer he was.

Slaughter went 4-for-6 and scored four runs in Game 4. In the sixth inning of that game, with the bases loaded and one out, Boston's Hal Wagner ripped a pitch off George Munger. Slaughter raced back and caught it as Rudy York tagged and headed for home. "The throw was so impossibly far that it wouldn't even be attempted. But Slaughter, who never gave up on anything, threw York out at the plate," noted *The New York Times*.

Then in Game 5 Slaughter was hit on the right elbow by a pitch from Joe Dobson. He was in intense pain, but wouldn't give Dobson the satisfaction of knowing that. Ignoring his pain, he stole second, and despite the formation of a potentially dangerous blood clot, was determined to play the rest of the Series. Slaughter vowed, "The fellers need me. No matter what you say, I'm playin'."

Slaughter's injury turned out to be a broken elbow, but prior to Game 6 he got his elbow patched and then singled in a run in the Cards' third-inning winning rally. In the eighth inning of Game 7 Slaughter stole the World Series with his daring baserunning. With the score tied, 3–3, Slaughter led off the inning with a single, but the next two batters were retired and Slaughter held his base. Then, with left fielder Harry Walker at bat, Slaughter was in motion. "I feel I caught the infield by surprise. I was just stealing second," admitted Slaughter. As Slaughter took off, Walker hit a ball into center.

It dropped for a hit. Center fielder Leon Culberson, who had just been inserted to replace an injured Dom DiMaggio, picked the ball up and fired it to the cutoff man, shortstop Johnny Pesky. Pesky paused for only a second to see if Walker would attempt to try for second. All the while, Slaughter—wildly running through coach Mike Gonzalez's stop signal—was tearing around third, heading for home. Slaughter came in with what turned out to be the winning run. His heroics have been described as "the biggest steal since Jimmy Valentine quit cracking safes."

In 1947 Slaughter's average fell below .300, to .294, for the first time since his rookie season, but he still scored 100 runs for the third straight year and batted in 86. On June 29 he drove in 10 runs in a doubleheader, the third-best total in National League history. In 1950 and 1952 Slaughter hit fewer than 15 home runs and drove in more than 100 runs. No other major leaguer has accomplished the feat more than once.

In April 1954 the time finally came for Slaughter to leave the Cardinals. He was traded to the Yankees for Bill Virdon, Mel Wright, and a minor league outfielder. In letting the 37-year-old Slaughter go, St. Louis owner August A. Busch praised him as "one of the greatest players" in Cardinals history. Slaughter sat in front of his locker and wept openly. "I never felt as bad when my father died as when I was released [sic] by the Cardinals," Slaughter said.

The magazine *Soviet Sport* even took notice, attacking "flesh peddling in disregard of the player's wishes and rights...a typical example of beer and beizbol. The beizbol bosses care nothing about sport or their athletes, but only about profits."

On September 9, 1954, Slaughter had New York's only hit against Baltimore's Joe Coleman. It marked the third time in Slaughter's career that he had robbed a pitcher of a no-hitter. Traded to Kansas City along with Johnny Sain in May 1955, a year later he was waived back to the Yankees.

Slaughter was a key factor in manager Casey Stengel's platoon system. In 1956, at age 40, he hit .350 and homered in the World Series. "He's old but he still glues his meat together after he gets hurt," Stengel said.

Primarily used as a pinch hitter in 1957 and 1958, Slaughter made his final World Series appearances those seasons. New York was beaten by Milwaukee in the 1957 Series, but came back to beat the Braves the following season. In September 1959 the Yankees sent Slaughter to the Braves, who were in contention for the National League pennant. Hobbled by a broken foot, Slaughter wasn't sure he could really help his new club. "If you can swing the bat, we can get a runner for you," said Milwaukee's John McHale. That was all Slaughter needed to hear to give it one last try.

He retired at the end of the season with 2,383 career hits, 1,247 runs, and 1,304 RBIs. The Veterans Committee inducted Slaughter into the Baseball Hall of Fame in 1985.

Roy Smalley

Smalley, Roy Frederick, Jr. **SS-DH-3B**

1975–87 B:10/25/1952, Los Angeles, CA
Deb:4/30/1975, TEX AL BB/TR 6'1", 185

G	AB	R	H	HR	RBI	OBP	SLG	AVG
1653	5657	745	1454	163	694	.348	.395	.257

It happens so often. A player is on his way to an outstanding career until his body gets in the way. For Roy Smalley, the son of major league shortstop Roy Smalley, Sr., and the nephew of big league manager Gene Mauch, the problem was his lower back. The medical term was spondytitis, and it robbed Smalley of most of his range at shortstop and affected his hitting as well, though he was able to stay in the majors until he was 34.

Smalley Jr. played for two NCAA champs at Southern California, where he majored in philosophy. He was soft-spoken and intelligent, the antithesis of the macho athlete, but he could play. The Rangers' first-round pick in the January 1974 draft, he signed for a $100,000 bonus and made it to the majors in 1975.

He was traded to the Twins in June 1976 in the deal that sent Bert Blyleven to Texas, which meant Smalley's manager was his Uncle Gene. Smalley hit .259 that season and .231 in 1977 with six homers and 56 RBIs while leading American League shortstops in total chances, double plays, and chances per game.

No one was prepared for what happened in 1978. That he led all major league shortstops in total chances and American League shortstops in double plays was no shocker, but the 19 homers and 77 RBIs certainly were. He was even better in 1979, when he was the league's starting shortstop in the All-Star Game. Smalley hit 24 homers and drove in 95 runs while leading the majors in total chances and his league in double plays and chances per game. His 144 twin-killings were a league record for shortstops, broken the next season by Rick Burleson.

He was the total package now—a shortstop with range and power. But his back began to bother him in 1980, when his production slipped to 12 homers and 63 RBIs. His condition worsened during the 1981 strike-shortened season, as he played in only 56 of the Twins' 110 games.

In April 1982 he was traded to the Yankees for pitchers Ron Davis and Paul Boris and shortstop Greg Gagne. That season Smalley hit 20 homers with 67 RBIs, but he played only 93 games at short and his range was quickly disappearing. When the White Sox decided they needed a shortstop to help chase the Royals in the middle of the 1984 season, they decided Smalley was the answer. They were wrong. Not only that, one of the players they sent to the Yankees was future Cy Young Award winner Doug Drabek.

Chicago sent Smalley back to the Twins in February 1985, but by that point he was restricted almost exclusively to designated hitter. He hit .246 with 20 homers in 1986, including switch-hit round-trippers in the same game on May 16. His last season was 1987, when Minnesota defeated St. Louis in the World Series. By then Gagne was the regular shortstop, but Smalley made four pinch-hit at bats in the Series, stroking a double and walking twice.

John Smiley

Smiley, John Patrick **P**

1986–97 B:3/17/1965, Phoenixville, PA Deb: 9/1/1986, PIT NL BL/TL 6'4", 200

W	L	PCT	G	SH	IP	BB	SO	ERA
126	103	.550	361	8	1907[2]	496	1284	3.80

Smiley became Pittsburgh's top lefty as the Pirates won back-to-back National League East titles in 1990 and 1991. Smiley, a 12th-round June pick by the Pirates out of high school in 1983, had first landed in the majors in September 1986. He pitched 75 games in relief through 1987, but. his career took off when he was placed in Pittsburgh's rotation in 1988.

He posted a 20–8 record in 1991, tying for the NL lead in wins and winning percentage. Smiley did not fare well in that October's Championship Series, however, losing his two starts while allowing eight runs in less than three innings of work. He was traded to Minnesota following that season for salary reasons; the Pirates got young lefthander Denny Neagle in return. After only one summer in Minneapolis, Smiley signed with Cincinnati as a free agent.

Although he slumped in 1993, Smiley won 36 games for the Reds over the next three seasons. He made his second All-Star team in 1995, and helped Cincinnati win the NL Central title. He was traded to Cleveland in July 1997, but he never got a chance to pitch in the postseason for the eventual American League champions. He broke the humerus bone in his left arm while warming up for a start against Kansas City less than two months after he was acquired from the Reds. The gruesome injury robbed him of the rest of that year and all of 1998 and 1999. Smiley's injury was identical to the injury that ended the careers of Tom Browning and Dave Dravecky.

Al Smith

Smith, Alphonse Eugene **OF–3B**

1953–64 Negro League Player (1946–48) B:2/7/1928, Kirkwood, MO Deb:7/10/1953, CLE AL BR/TR 6'1", 191

G	AB	R	H	HR	RBI	OBP	SLG	AVG
1517	5357	843	1458	164	676	.360	.429	.272

One of baseball's enduring images is that of a fan pouring beer on an outfielder's head. The date was October 2, 1959. The place was Comiskey Park in Chicago. The outfielder was Al Smith of the White Sox. In the top of the seventh inning of Game 2 of the World Series, a fan tried to catch a two-run homer hit by Charlie Neal of the Dodgers and accidentally dumped a cup of beer on Smith. "At first I was angry. I thought somebody had thrown beer at me," the outfielder recalled.

As a high school star in St. Louis, Smith scored 10 touchdowns in one game and was a Golden Gloves boxing champion. He originally signed with the Negro League Cleveland Buckeyes and then moved to Wilkes-Barre of the Eastern League in 1948. In 1949 he led the league with 17 triples. Smith moved up to San Diego in 1950 and Indianapolis in 1952, finally reaching the big leagues with the Indians in 1953.

In 1954 Smith made an auspicious World Series debut, hitting Johnny Antonelli's first pitch in Game 2 over the left-field roof at the Polo Grounds, but the New York Giants swept the Indians. In 1955 Smith led the American League with 123 runs scored and hit .306. His batting average tailed off during the next two years, and in December 1957 he was traded to the White Sox along with Early Wynn for Minnie Minoso and Fred Hatfield.

Minoso was a star in Chicago, and local fans loudly denounced the transaction. Nearly two years later, on August 26, 1959, Sox owner Bill Veeck Jr. held an Al Smith Night in an effort to heal the rift caused by the trade. Anyone named Smith, Schmidt, or Smythe was admitted free and given a button reading "I'm a Smith and I'm for Al." Overcome with emotion, Smith hit into two double plays and dropped a flyball that cost a run as Chicago lost to the Red Sox. He hit just .237 in Chicago's pennant-winning season and didn't hit much better in the World Series as the White Sox lost to the Dodgers in six games.

Smith batted a career-best .315 in 1960 and made his second appearance in the All-Star game. In 1963 Smith was traded along with Luis Aparicio to Baltimore. He went back to Cleveland in December of that year and ended his career with the Red Sox. He later worked as a district supervisor of parks in Chicago.

Dave Smith

Smith, David Stanley **P**

1980–92 B:1/21/1955, Richmond, CA Deb:4/11/1980, HOU NL BR/TR 6'1", 195

W	L	PCT	G	SV	IP	BB	SO	ERA
53	53	.500	609	216	809^{1}	283	548	2.67

Mike Scott was one of the main reasons the Astros had a good shot at beating the Mets in the 1986 National League Championship Series; Houston reliever Dave Smith was one of the main reasons the Astros didn't win. Smith blew two ninth-inning save opportunities in his only two appearances in the series. He took the loss in Game 3 when the Mets' Lenny Dykstra connected for a two-run, game-winning homer with one out in the bottom of the ninth. With the Astros leading Game 6 in the top of the ninth and with Scott, already 2–0 in the series, prepared to pitch a seventh game, Smith allowed the Mets to rally once again. New York tied Game 6 and eventually clinched the pennant in 16 innings.

Despite his difficult 1986 NLCS, Smith was one of the most effective relievers in Astros history. In fact, Smith had pitched well in his previous postseason appearances with Houston in 1980 and 1981. He defeated Tug McGraw in Game 3 of the 1980 NLCS as Dennis Walling's sacrifice fly drove in the game's only run in the 11th inning. Smith, who had been drafted by the Astros out of San Diego State University in 1976, became the franchise leader in saves and appearances.

Smith never won a game with another team. He signed with the Cubs as a free agent and went 0–6 in his lone full season with the Cubs in 1991. He was named pitching coach of the Padres in 1999.

Elmer Smith

Smith, Elmer Ellsworth **OF–P**

1886–89, 1892–1901 B:3/23/1868, Pittsburgh, PA D:11/3/1945, Pittsburgh, PA Deb:9/10/1886, CIN NL BL/TL 5'11", 178

G	AB	R	H	HR	RBI	OBP	SLG	AVG
1234	4684	912	1454	37	663	.398	.434	.310

W	L	PCT	G	SH	IP	BB	SO	ERA
75	57	.568	149	9	1210^{1}	422	525	3.35

When Babe Ruth and Smokey Joe Wood converted from successful major league pitchers to successful major league outfielders, they had Elmer Ellsworth Smith to use as a model. As a 19-year-old in 1887, Smith won 34 games with Cincinnati and led the American Association with a 2.94 ERA. But by the following spring he had developed a sore arm.

On July 4, 1888, Smith was just 5–9, though he finished strongly to end the year at 22–17. The following year, however, Smith again had arm problems, and by 1890 he was in the minors with Kansas City. Smith's arm recovered in K.C., and he went 23–9. He also batted .331. After a .314 season in 1891, Smith returned to the majors with Pittsburgh, this time as an outfielder.

A speedy player, Smith swung a 54-ounce bat and featured a strong arm. He batted .300 or better for the Pirates from 1893 through 1898, including a career-best .356 in 1894. On August 1, 1894, he stroked three doubles and a triple in the same game.

In 1898 Smith signed with the Cincinnati Reds. He hit .342 and assembled a 30-game hitting streak, but his average tailed off the next season to .298. Smith spent the last two years of his career with Cincinnati, the New York Giants, Pittsburgh Pirates, and Boston Beaneaters.

Frank Smith

Smith, Frank Elmer **P**

1904–15 B:10/28/1879, Philadelphia, PA Deb:4/22/1904, CHI AL BR/TR 5'10½", 194

W	L	PCT	G	SH	IP	BB	SO	ERA
139	111	.556	354	27	2273	676	1051	2.59

Lightning struck not once but twice for White Sox righthander Frank Smith when he pitched no-hitters against the Detroit Tigers on September 6, 1905 and the Philadelphia Athletics on September 20, 1908. During that 1908 season, stung by owner Charles Comiskey's accusations of drunkenness, Smith left the club to practice his off-season profession of piano moving. Reporters then ridiculed him with the nicknames of "Piano Mover" and "Piano Legs," which may have been improvements over his previous nickname, "Nig."

Born Frank Elmer Schmidt, he attended Grove City College. In the minors he played for Raleigh in 1901 and Atlanta and Birmingham in 1902. He arrived in the major leagues with the White Sox in 1904 and won 16 games as a rookie. He improved to 19 wins in 1905, and went on to win 20 games twice. In 1909 he led the American League in strikeouts, but the White Sox traded him to the Red Sox the following year. The Red Sox sold him to Cincinnati for $5,000 in May

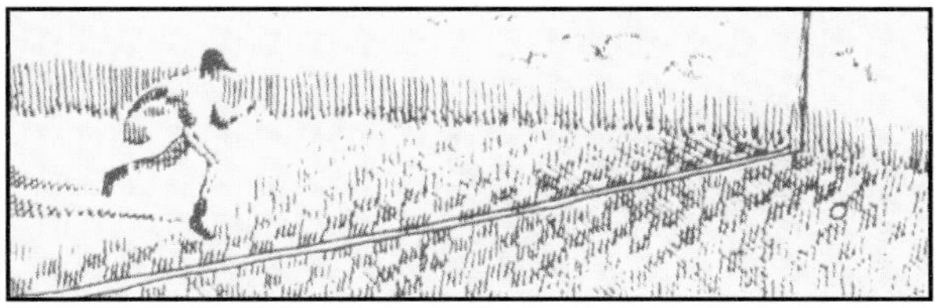

1911, but he spent most of 1912 and all of 1913 with Montreal before jumping to Baltimore of the Federal League in 1914. The Terrapins traded him to the Brooklyn Brookfeds in June 1915.

Germany Smith

Smith, George J. **SS**

1884–98 B:4/21/1863, Pittsburgh, PA D:12/1/1927, Altoona, PA Deb:4/17/1884, ALT UA BR/TR 6', 175

G	AB	R	H	HR	RBI	OBP	SLG	AVG
1710	6552	907	1592	47	797	.289	.332	.243

If you were told that the slickest-fielding shortstop in baseball history was named Smith, you might assume that Ozzie Smith was the topic of discussion. And although "the Wizard of Oz" was a perennial Gold Glove winner, his numbers don't match those of 19th-century star Germany Smith.

George J. "Germany" Smith, who was born in Pittsburgh but was of German ancestry, not only holds the career record for assists per game at shortstop, with 3.70, but he is the record-holder for all fielders regardless of position. In the category of most assists-per-game in a season, Germany Smith's 4.21 in 1885 is tops and his 4.04 mark in 1892 is eighth. Today's observers, however, might focus more on Smith's fielding percentage (a lifetime .902) and the number of errors he committed (94 in 1888 alone). Yet in Smith's era, a fielding average under .900 could lead a major league, as his .886 mark did in 1887.

Smith began his professional career in 1884 with the Union Association's Altoona Mountain Citys. Later that season the National League's Cleveland Blues acquired him. In 1885 he signed with the Brooklyn Bridegrooms and appeared in 108 games, starting a 13 season-string with at least 100 games played. On June 29, 1889, he nearly set a National League record for shortstops with 12 assists in one game. Smith played in both the 1889 and 1890 "World Series" with the Bridegrooms, although the club represented different leagues each year—the American Association in 1889 and the National League in 1890.

When John Montgomery Ward arrived as shortstop-manager in 1891, Smith was sent packing to Cincinnati. Like Ozzie, Germany had some of his best seasons at the plate in his later years. He batted .300 for the only time in his career in 1895, scored more than 70 runs in 1894 and 1895, and drove in more than 70 runs in 1894, 1895, and 1896. In 1897 Smith returned to Brooklyn, and a year later he finished his career with the National League team in St. Louis—as would Ozzie a century later.

Lee Smith

Smith, Lee Arthur **P**

1980–97 B:12/4/1957, Shreveport, LA Deb:9/1/1980, CHI NL BR/TR 6'6", 225

W	L	PCT	G	SV	IP	BB	SO	ERA
71	92	.436	1022	478	1289^{1}	486	125	3.03

Lee Smith wasn't expected to replace ace reliever Bruce Sutter, the 1979 Cy Young Award winner, it just worked out that way. Then Smith surpassed Sutter. In fact, he surpassed every reliever in baseball history. Smith, who had just one save in his first two major league seasons, retired as the all-time saves leader with 478.

Sutter went to the rival St. Louis Cardinals as a free agent in 1981. The Cubs tried to fill in with Dick Tidrow; the result was the National League's worst record. The next year Smith took over as the closer. He appeared in 72 games, chalking up 17 saves. In 1983 Smith improved to a league-leading 29 saves in 32 opportunities; he had an impeccable 1.65 ERA, and held opposing hitters to a league-low .175 batting average. He was named to the All-Star team for the first of seven times in his career.

Smith was instrumental in the Cubs' drive to win the National League East title in 1984. His 33 saves marked the first of nine times he saved 30 or more games in a season. He saved Game 2 of the NL Championship Series against the San Diego Padres, but surrendered a bottom-of-the-ninth home run by Steve Garvey that won Game 4 and tied the NLCS. The Padres won the pennant the next day.

Less than four years after becoming a closer, Smith saved his 100th career game on July 9, 1985. A little more than a year later he broke Sutter's club record with his 134th save. In 1987 he became the first NL reliever to record 30 or more saves in four consecutive seasons. He threw three scoreless innings to earn the victory in the 13-inning All-Star Game. Smith finished the season poorly, and he was traded to the Boston Red Sox for pitchers Al Nipper and Calvin Schiraldi.

Smith saved 44 games over two years with the Red Sox. When Massachusetts native Jeff Reardon arrived at Fenway Park in 1990, Smith's days in Boston were numbered. (he got revenge by later breaking Reardon's all-time save record.) Traded to the Cardinals for Tom Brunansky in May, Smith racked up 27 saves in St. Louis. He followed that with seasons of 47, 43, and 43 saves. He set the club mark for saves with 160, and he established a major league mark by not making an error from 1982 to 1992.

He returned to the American League at the end of the 1993 season with the New York Yankees. He moved to Baltimore as a free agent the following year. He led the AL in saves and earned his fourth Fireman of the Year Award. He joined the California Angels the following year, and saved 37 games. When young fireballer Troy Percival emerged as the team's stopper in 1996, Smith was sent to Cincinnati. He finished his career with the Montreal Expos in 1997.

Mayo Smith

Smith, Edward Mayo **OF**

1945 M(1955–59, 1967–70, 662–612) B:1/17/1915, New London, MO D:11/24/1977, Boynton Beach, FL Deb:6/24/1945, PHI AL BL/TR 6', 183

G	AB	R	H	HR	RBI	OBP	SLG	AVG
73	203	18	43	0	11	.333	.236	.212

Although Mayo Smith got just one chance to play in the major leagues, a second chance at managing brought him a world championship. He had only 73 games as an outfielder with the Philadelphia Athletics to show for 20 years in the minor leagues. He persevered, becoming a successful minor league manager with teams in Amsterdam, Birmingham, and Norfolk.

Smith became a major league manager in 1955, guiding the Philadelphia Phillies to fourth place, followed by consecutive fifth-place finishes. The Phils were mired in eighth place when he was fired midway through 1958. He managed the Cincinnati Reds the following year, again being dismissed in midseason. "It was humiliating," said the usually jovial Smith.

He served as a super scout with the New York Yankees until 1967, when the Detroit Tigers gave Smith another chance to manage. Detroit remained in a memorable four-team pennant race until the final day of the season. The Tigers finished in a tie for second, just one game back. Despite falling short, Smith finally had the players needed to win. In 1968 the Tigers led the American League in runs, home runs, fielding, and boasted a 31-game winner in Denny McLain. Detroit won the pennant by 12 games.

Smith faced a quandary heading into the World Series. Al Kaline had missed a large stretch of the season, giving Mickey Stanley a chance to excel. Now that Kaline was healthy, how would Smith fit four outfielders into three slots? The manager made a bold move. He shifted Stanley to shortstop, replacing the weak-hitting Ray Oyler. Stanley fielded flawlessly, yet the Tigers still trailed the St. Louis Cardinals three games to one. He pitched Mickey Lolich twice in the last three games; the Tigers beat St. Louis four games to three.

Smith was named Manager of the Year by *The Sporting News*. He managed the Tigers for two more seasons before retiring. Smith suffered a stroke on November 22, 1977. He lapsed into a coma and died two days later at the age of 62.

Ozzie Smith

Smith, Osborne Earl **SS**

1978–96 B:12/26/1954, Mobile, AL Deb:4/7/1978, SD NL BR/TR 5'11", 150

G	AB	R	H	HR	RBI	OBP	SLG	AVG
2573	9396	1257	2460	28	793	.339	.328	.262

Ozzie Smith was in a class by himself at shortstop. Thomas Boswell of the *Washington Post* once wrote of him, "Instead of '1' his number should be '8,' but turned sideways because the possibilities he brings to his position are almost infinite."

The National League's career leader in Gold Gloves and arguably the best-fielding shortstop of all time, Smith also made himself into an above-average hitter and high-average base-stealer. It was Smith's glove, however, that made him a legend. He not only got to balls that other players could not even reach, he turned them into double plays; in fact, Smith retired having taken part in more twin-killings than any shortstop in history. He also rarely missed games. Only Luis Aparicio played more games at the position than Smith.

"The Wizard of Oz" was adored in St. Louis, where he did a backflip on his way to his position before each game. Smith became one of baseball's most popular players; he was picked for the All-Star team 15 times in his 19-year career.

Smith attended Locke High School in Los Angeles with Eddie Murray, and was selected by the Padres in the fourth round of the 1977 free agent draft. After winning two Gold Gloves in San Diego and setting a record for assists with 621 in 1980, Smith was traded to the Cardinals for shortstop Garry Templeton after the 1981 season. In his first year as a Cardinal, St. Louis won its first world championship in 15 years. Smith led the league's shortstops in fielding for the first of a record seven times. He also hit two home runs, doubling his four-year output in San Diego.

Learning to fit his talents to the spacious dimensions and artificial turf at Busch Stadium, the switch-hitting Smith became an expert bunter and hit-and-run specialist. He improved his batting average to .276 by 1985, when the Cardinals won their division again. Smith blossomed in the Championship Series against the Dodgers. With the score and the series tied, 2–2, in Game 5, he homered in the bottom of the ninth to win the game. It was the only lefthanded home run of his career. Smith batted .435 in the Cardinals' six-game victory and earned NLCS Most Valuable Player honors. The Cardinals stumbled in the World Series, however, as Smith batted just .087 and the team hit only .185. The Royals won in seven games.

In 1987, for the fifth time in Smith's six years in St. Louis, the Cardinals led the league in team fielding. They won another pennant but lost a seven-game Series to the Twins. That year, Smith finally reached the .300 mark, won his accustomed Gold Glove, and finished second to Andre Dawson in Most Valuable Player voting.

In 1991 he set a record for NL shortstops, committing just eight errors in 150 games, and won his 13th consecutive Gold Glove in 1992 to break a tie with Willie Mays and Roberto Clemente for most in the National League. He also amassed 580 stolen bases and was major league baseball's career leader in assists for shortstops.

After retiring as a player, the affable Smith replaced the late Mel Allen as host on the long-running television show *This Week in Baseball.* It was fitting because Smith's countless acrobatic plays on the highlight-based program had helped make the show a hit.

Red Smith

Smith, Walter Wellesley

Sportswriter B:9/25/1905, Green Bay, WI D:1/15/1982, Stamford, CT

There will never be agreement on who was baseball's greatest hitter or pitcher, but few could dispute that Red Smith was the game's greatest reporter of the 20th century. Smith's contemporary, Roger Kahn, once said of him, "Red Smith was a serious man, but never heavy. He wreathed himself, as he wreathed his writing, in wit and grace, courtesy and kindness." Even people outside of baseball knew how good Smith was. Chicago Bears owner-coach George Halas once said, "To know Red Smith was to know greatness."

Walter Wellesley Smith graduated from Notre Dame in 1927 and became a general assignment reporter for the *Milwaukee Sentinel* that same year. In 1928 he moved to the *St. Louis Star* as a copyreader. When the entire sports department was fired, Smith took over. In 1936 he became a columnist for the *Philadelphia Record.* Sports editor Stanley Woodward, who thought Smith was "the best newspaper writer in the country," recruited Smith for the *New York Herald Tribune.* Woodward added, "In [Smith] the best attributes of the 'gee whiz' and the 'aw nuts' schools are mingled."

Smith's first "Views of Sport" column appeared in the *Herald Tribune* on September 24, 1945. The *Trib* became his greatest showcase. During his tenure the column was syndicated and appeared in approximately 500 papers. When in 1966 the *Tribune* was absorbed into the consolidated *World Journal Tribune,* Smith went along. In 1971 he joined *The New York Times* and stayed until his death on January 15, 1982.

He earned a Pulitzer Prize in 1976 and also won the Grantland Rice Memorial Award. His books included *Out of the Red, Views of Sport, Red Smith on Fishing, Red Smith's Sports Annual, The Best of Red Smith, Strawberries in the Wintertime,* and *To Absent Friends.*

Reggie Smith

Smith, Carl Reginald **OF–1B**

1966–82 B:4/2/1945, Shreveport, LA Deb:9/18/1966, BOS AL BB/TR 6', 195

G	AB	R	H	HR	RBI	OBP	SLG	AVG
1987	7033	1123	2020	314	1092	.370	.489	.287

Outfielder Reggie Smith was one of the premier switch hitters in major league history, the first to record 100 or more homers in each league. With Boston he homered from both sides of the plate in a single game four times, and he repeated the feat twice with the St. Louis Cardinals. Later he became part of a 30-homer quartet in Los Angeles.

As a high school student in California, Smith was all-state in both baseball and football. Although the Dodgers gave him a tryout, the Twins signed him as a free agent in June 1963. Originally a shortstop (he led Appalachian League shortstops in errors in 1963), he was grabbed for $8,000 in the December 1963 minor league draft by Boston and eventually converted into an outfielder.

After leading the International League in batting in 1966, Smith was promoted to the Red Sox and soon established himself as a quality outfielder. In 1968 he won a Gold Glove and led the American League in putouts. In 1970 he tied for the league lead in assists. That year he was named to *The Sporting News* AL All-Star Team.

Smith struggled at the plate in his first full season in the majors, batting .246 with a career-high 95 strikeouts. But he made up for his low average by hitting 15 homers and 24 doubles. Smith homered in Game 3 of the 1967 World Series against the Cardinals and then went deep again in Game 6. But Bob Gibson held the Sox to only three hits in Game 7, giving the Cardinals the world championship.

The following season Smith led the league with 37 doubles. He batted .303 the next season, drilled 30 homers and a league-leading 33 doubles in 1971. With Boston, however, Smith became enmeshed in a series of controversies, including a fight with Bill "Spaceman" Lee during a game. In 1971 Billy Conigliaro accused Smith and Carl Yastrzemski of conspiring to get his brother, Tony, traded to the Angels. The following year Carlton Fisk gave a speech in which he alleged that the Red Sox were looking to Yaz and Smith for leadership but "hadn't seen it yet."

In 1973 Smith tore ligaments in his knee. Club management told him he was ready to play again, but Smith refused, producing medical testimony that he had not fully recovered. Accusations of malingering dogged him. Smith thought part of his problem in Boston was racial. "They don't want a black star," he charged. "I know one thing. As far as I'm concerned they had one, and they didn't appreciate him. Nothing is going to change my mind about that."

Smith refused to attend meetings of the Red Sox booster club "because they didn't have one black member." He was quoted as saying that the Red Sox would not sell good seats to blacks. He denied making the latter charge.

In October 1973 the Red Sox traded Smith and pitcher Ken Tatum to the Cardinals for pitcher Rick Wise and outfielder Bernie Carbo. Smith responded positively to the move. "I wasn't having fun anymore, and I'm having fun again," he remarked. Despite injuring a thigh muscle in mid-June, Smith went on to have his only 100-RBI season in 1974. He also batted .309 as each of the Cardinals starting outfielders—Bake McBride at .309, Lou Brock at .306—hit above .300. On May 22, 1976, Smith hit three homers in a game against Philadelphia. But in June Smith was traded to Los Angeles for catcher Joe Ferguson, outfielder Bob Detherage, and minor league infielder Fred Tisdale.

The deal turned out to be a steal for the Dodgers. Smith helped them win pennants in 1977, 1978, and 1981. He hit a total of six home runs in World Series competition. In 1977 the Dodgers became the first team to feature four players with 30 or more homers when Smith, Steve Garvey, Dusty Baker, and Ron Cey all accomplished it. Smith described hitting homers on that team as "easy." He said, "Because of our team, we just went up to contact the ball hard for base hits. And because of our hitters, we saw a lot of fastballs."

In his final four major league seasons, knee, neck, and ankle problems beset the seven-time All-Star. Granted free agency in November 1981, he signed with the Giants. At the time, his total of 18 homers in 1982 was the second-highest for a final season in National League history. After leaving the majors Smith played in Japan with the Yomiuri Giants. He hit 45 home runs over 186 games in 1983 and 1984.

He became a minor league hitting instructor for the Dodgers in 1989 and later became the organization's minor league field coordinator. Smith served as first base coach and hitting instructor in Los Angeles from 1995 to 1998. He is the owner/operator of Reggie Smith Baseball Centers in Encino, California.

Sherry Smith

Smith, Sherrod Malone **P**

1911–27 B:2/18/1891, Monticello, GA D:9/12/1949, Reidsville, GA Deb:5/11/1911, PIT NL BR/TL 6'1", 170

W	L	PCT	G	SV	IP	BB	SO	ERA
114	118	.491	373	21	2052[2]	440	428	3.32

Arguably, the greatest pitching duel in World Series history took place on October 9, 1916, between one southpaw who became a household name and another who didn't. On the winning side was Boston's Babe Ruth, who would soon become the greatest home run hitter in major league history. On the losing side was Brooklyn's virtually forgotten Sherry Smith.

It was Game 2 of the Series, and Brooklyn had lost the opener. The Dodgers drew first blood against Ruth, scoring a first-inning tally on center fielder Hy Myers' inside-the-park home run, which skipped past center fielder Tilly Walker. Boston evened the score in the third when Ruth hit a grounder to second that drove in Everett Scott from third. After that both pitchers bore down, hurling inning after inning of scoreless ball. In the eighth inning Brooklyn had an excellent chance to score against Ruth, but third baseman Mike Mowrey got caught in a rundown between third and home.

The stalemate continued until the bottom of the 14th, when Smith walked leadoff batter Dick Hoblitzel—Hoblitzel's fourth walk of the game. He was sacrificed to second and was then taken out for pinch runner Mike McNally. Pinch hitter Del Gainer then singled in the winning run.

That Smith's downfall had been a base on balls was ironic, because he was one of the best control pitchers in history, averaging less than two walks per nine innings of work. Smith's daughter once told an interviewer, "They say Daddy learned how to pitch by throwing balls of cotton at rabbits in the cotton fields. I used to say 'Daddy, how about that story?' And he'd just laugh—he was a man of very few words, but knowing him it was probably true."

Smith was also incredibly skilled at holding runners on base. It is said that only two bases were ever stolen off him. "He was the only pitcher I ever saw who could completely conceal his intentions from the runner," said the great baserunner, Max Carey. Smith, observed American League umpire George Moriarty, had "a miracle move. For years [runners] tried timing it, but to no avail." Amazingly, he never committed a balk.

The loss to Ruth aside, Smith had a good year in 1916—he even stole home on April 19. The one negative during that season occurred when Brooklyn manager Wilbert Robinson was demonstrating how the old Orioles used to bunt. "See? That's the way. Once you learn how to do it, you never forget it," Robinson said after successfully laying a few down off Walter "Duster" Mails. Properly inspired, Smith, who was pitching that afternoon, picked up a bat and said, "Wait a minute. Let me try it." On the first pitch Mails hit Smith right between the eyes. Smith had to be carried off the field.

Smith didn't have another winning season until 1920, when he was 11–9 with a career-low 1.85 ERA. On May 3, 1920, he engaged in another marathon performance, again losing, 2–1. He pitched 18⅓ innings against Boston, giving up 13 hits while striking out three and walking five.

In Game 3 of the 1920 World Series he defeated the Indians, 2–1. He experienced some control trouble in the first inning but settled down and, backed by Brooklyn's much-maligned "$100 Infield," pitched a three-hitter. In Game 6 he opposed Mails, who had gone a perfect 7–0 for Cleveland that season. The Indians prevailed, 1–0, then won the Series the next day.

On September 18, 1922, Smith, who was once described as "strong as a horse and tireless as a Missouri mule," went to Cleveland on waivers. In five seasons with the Tribe he went 44–48. He retired at the end of the 1927 season. Smith went on to manage the Macon Peaches of the Class B Southeastern League in 1932. The league disbanded in late May.

He later pursued a career in law enforcement, first at the federal prison in Reidsville, Georgia, then with the Madison, Georgia, Police Department. He was Chief of Police when he died at home of a heart attack in September 1949.

John Smoltz

Smoltz, John Andrew **P**

1988–* B:5/15/1967, Detroit, MI Deb:7/23/1988, ATL NL
BR/TR 6'3", 210

W	L	PCT	G	SH	IP	BB	SO	ERA
157	113	.581	356	14	2414¹	774	2098	3.35

In 1987 the Tigers traded Detroit native John Smoltz to the Atlanta Braves for Doyle Alexander and went to the playoffs exactly once in the ensuing 13 seasons. The Braves, with Smoltz an integral part of their rotation, made the playoffs eight times during the 1990s. Alexander's career in Detroit was over in 1989, the same year Smoltz's was just beginning.

In his first two seasons with the Braves, Smoltz won 12 and 14 games, respectively, with a team that lost 97 both years. In 1991, seemingly overnight, Atlanta's entire pitching staff became as good as any in baseball. The team's starting four—Smoltz, Tom Glavine, Steve Avery, and Charlie Leibrandt—won 67 games, two more victories than the entire team had in either 1989 or 1990. The Braves rallied the final week of the season to beat the Dodgers for the National League West title.

Smoltz won twice in the Championship Series against the Pittsburgh Pirates, pitching a complete game six-hitter in the deciding seventh game at Three Rivers Stadium to give the Braves their first pennant since the team moved to Atlanta in 1966. He pitched equally well in the World Series, allowing the Minnesota Twins only two runs in 14 innings. But he ran into another hot pitcher, Jack Morris, in the seventh game. Smoltz matched Morris zero for zero for eight innings before the Twins prevailed, 1-0, in 10 innings for the world championship.

The Braves won the division by eight games to set up an NLCS rematch with Pittsburgh. This time Smoltz pitched three times in the playoffs, beating the Pirates and Doug Drabek in Games 1 and 4 and again getting the nod in the deciding seventh game. He allowed only two runs, but Drabek kept the Braves scoreless until a miraculous ninth-inning rally gave Atlanta its second consecutive pennant. Smoltz was named NLCS Most Valuable Player.

He won once against Toronto in the World Series, and was denied another victory when reliever Jeff Reardon surrendered a two-run homer to Ed Sprague in the ninth inning of Game 2. The Braves lost in six games.

Smoltz hooked up in another World Series duel in 1996 with Andy Pettitte of the Yankees in the last game ever played at Fulton County Stadium. Smoltz allowed only an unearned run as New York won the game, 1-0, and went on to beat the Braves in six. It was a frustrating end to a nearly perfect 1996 season by Smoltz. He led the major leagues in wins (24) and strikeouts (276), and led the National League in innings pitched (253). He easily won the Cy Young Award, joining teammates Greg Maddux and Glavine as winners of the trophy.

It cost the Braves $31 million for four years to keep Smoltz as a free agent after the 1996 season, but the Braves never really considered life without Smoltz. In 1997 he won 15 games, led the league with 215 strikeouts, and recorded a career-best 2.85 ERA.

In 1998 Smoltz had another Cy Young caliber season, going 17-3 for a league-leading .850 percentage with a 2.90 ERA; Atlanta's Glavine took the award. In the Division Series, he frustrated the Cubs on five hits, but gave up 13 hits and six runs in two starts against San Diego as the Padres bumped the Braves in the NLCS.

By 1999 Smoltz had long ago cemented his reputation as a big-game pitcher, but he managed to pitch through elbow pain as the Braves won their eighth consecutive division title. Pitching at different angles to take the strain off his elbow, Smoltz still managed to win 11 games, and his 3.19 ERA was second only to Kevin Millwood on the Atlanta staff. In his first career relief appearance, he saved the win for Millwood in Game 2 of the NLCS against the Mets. He turned in a noble effort in Game 4 of the World Series, losing 4–1 to Roger Clemens and the sweeping New York Yankees.

Duke Snider

Snider, Edwin Donald **OF**

1947–64 B:9/19/1926, Los Angeles, CA Deb:4/17/1947, BRO NL BL/TR 6', 190

G	AB	R	H	HR	RBI	OBP	SLG	AVG
2143	7161	1259	2116	407	1333	.381	.540	.295

Edwin Donald "Duke" Snider was immortalized in Terry Cashman's song, "Talkin' Baseball," with its chorus of "Willie, Mickey, and the Duke"—referring to the All-Star trio of Snider, Willie Mays, and Mickey Mantle. During the 1950s, when all three players patrolled center field for New York teams, Snider hit more home runs (326) and drove in more runs (1,031) than anyone in the game.

Life in the major leagues was a constant battle for the temperamental Snider. Raised in California, he was given the nickname "Duke" by his hard-driving father because of his regal bearing at age 5. Snider's superior attitude later found expression in his relentless sulking and brooding, and he would frequently explode with rage when he struck out or when his hotel room wasn't satisfactory.

At age 17 Snider batted as a Dodger in a 1944 exhibition game against the U.S. Military Academy and clouted a monumental three-run homer. Branch Rickey marveled at the "steel springs" in the young ballplayer's legs, but Snider soon found the routines of calisthenics beneath him and began to pout. Rickey, a shrewd amateur psychologist, told him to take off his uniform and go home. Snider apologized and asked for a second chance. Sent to the minors, he led the Piedmont League with 25 assists.

After spending all of 1945 and part of 1946 in the military, Snider made the Dodgers roster for 1947. When his boyhood hero, Pete Reiser, knocked himself out of the lineup after running into Ebbets Field's center field fence on June 4, Snider was his replacement. He struck out 24 times in 83 at bats and was returned to the minors. His .316 average in St. Paul and .327 mark for Montreal in 1948 earned him another shot at the big club.

In 1949 Hall of Famer George Sisler tutored Snider. Sisler's task, Rickey explained, was "to help Snider establish a relationship with the strike zone." Snider had to stand at the plate with his bat ready, but was not allowed to swing at pitches. He had to call balls and strikes and check with Sisler to see if the calls were correct. Snider eventually learned well enough to collect 971 walks in the big leagues. With the injured Reiser now at first base, Snider became the Dodgers' regular center fielder in 1949, belted 23 homers, and sent 92 runs home while scoring 100 himself. The lefthander was a strategic addition to a Dodgers lineup dominated by righthanders.

Although the Dodgers scored 130 more runs than any other National League team that year, the pennant race came down to the wire. Needing a win on the final day of the season, they blew a 5–0 lead and were tied, 7–7, in the top of the 10th. Snider delivered a run-scoring single to bring the pennant back to Brooklyn.

He didn't fare so well in the World Series against the Yankees, managing only three hits in 21 at bats and striking out an embarrassing eight times in the five games to set a record that wouldn't be broken until 1984 by Carmelo Martinez. Yankee Joe DiMaggio explained, "He was trying to kill the ball."

In 1950 Snider batted .321, led the league in hits, and collected more than 30 home runs and 100 RBIs for the first time in his career. Once again the Dodgers needed a final-day victory to reach the postseason, and once again Snider came through, with a single to center. But Richie Ashburn made a perfect throw home to nail Cal Abrams, and the Dodgers lost to the Whiz Kids in the 10th.

Snider was benched for his casual attitude in August of 1952. The punishment apparently had an impact, for he returned to hit over .400 in the last two months of the season, finishing at .303 as the Dodgers scampered to the pennant. In that year's feverish Series against the Yankees, Snider became only the third player to hit four homers in a Series. Babe Ruth and Lou Gehrig were the others. His eight RBIs led both teams and his sixth-inning homer won Game 1 for Brooklyn. He singled home the tying run in the seventh inning of Game 5 and doubled in the winning run in the top of the 11th, but the Dodgers lost the Series in seven games.

Brooklyn put on a power show in 1953. Snider belted 42 homers, the first of five years in a row that he would hit 40 or more round-trippers (tying the league record). Meanwhile, Roy Campanella hit 41, Gil Hodges another 31, and the team homered at least once in 24 straight games—one game shy of the 1941 Yankees' all-time record. Brooklyn scored 217 more runs than any other team in the league and won the flag by 13 games. Although the Bums batted .300 in the World Series, with Snider contributing .320, the Yankees won in six games.

Despite Snider's .341 average, the team finished second in 1954 to Leo Durocher's Giants. Snider sulked. Teammate Carl Erskine said of him, "No one agonized more over not doing well." In the middle of the 1955 season, a slumping Snider exploded in the clubhouse after being booed by the Brooklyn crowd. "They're the lousiest fans in baseball," he roared at the reporters, who printed his quote the next day. After apologizing, Snider finished with 42 homers and league-leading totals of 136 RBIs and 126 runs scored.

After seven heartbreaking Series defeats, "next year" finally arrived in Brooklyn when the Dodgers took the 1955 Fall Classic from the Yanks in seven games. Snider led all Dodgers regulars with his .320 average, and his four home runs made him the first player to hit four homers in two different World Series.

He won his first home run title in 1956 with 43 and led the National League in walks, slugging, and on-base percentage. Also he raised eyebrows when an article entitled "I Play Baseball for Money, Not for Fun" was published in *Collier's*. Based on notes taken by high-profile sportswriter-editor Roger Kahn several years earlier, the story quoted Snider saying, "I feel that I'd be just as happy if I never played another baseball game again."

Rumors that owner Walter O'Malley planned to move the Dodgers to the West Coast were rife in 1957. When the official announcement was made on October 8, Brooklyn fans denounced O'Malley as the devil in disguise. The 31-year-old Snider knew his career would be changed forever. He later said, "When they tore down Ebbets Field, they tore down a little piece of me."

In their first year in California the Dodgers played in the Los Angeles Coliseum, a football stadium. The right-field foul pole was 301 feet from home, as opposed to 297 in Brooklyn, but the distance rapidly receded to 390 where the wall met the fence and ballooned out to 440 in right center. Suffering from a bad knee, Snider played in only 106 games, and his home run total dropped from 40 to 15, although he managed a .312 average.

The following season the fence was moved in and Snider responded with 23 home runs, the last time he topped 20. Winning the first two games of a best-of-three playoff series for the National League crown, the Dodgers eliminated the Braves. Then they beat up on the "Go-Go" White Sox in the World Series. Snider strained his knee and was removed from Games 1 and 2 for defensive purposes. He didn't start again until Game 6, when his two-run third-inning homer gave the Dodgers the lead for keeps. His knee plagued him throughout 1960, and he broke an elbow in 1961. When he was able to play, Snider platooned with Ron Fairly.

In April 1963 the New York Mets purchased Snider, hoping that the former New Yorker's nostalgic value would help boost attendance. They also hoped that Snider could work with some of their younger hitters. But when Snider tried to offer advice to Ed Kranepool, the young player snapped back, "You ain't doing so hot yourself." Nevertheless, Snider was the only Met selected for the 1963 All-Star Game. He had one last chance in 1964, as a Giant, and batted .210 in 91 games.

Snider stayed in the game as a scout and minor league manager, working for the Dodgers and Padres and managing teams in Spokane and Kennewick, Washington, and Alexandria, Louisiana. After two years as the Expos' batting instructor, he joined their announcing team. He later came back to the Dodgers to broadcast games on cable TV.

Fred Snodgrass

Snodgrass, Frederick Carlisle **OF–1B**

1908–16 B:10/19/1887, Ventura, CA D:4/5/1974, Ventura, CA Deb:6/4/1908, NY NL BR/TR 5'11½", 175

G	AB	R	H	HR	RBI	OBP	SLG	AVG
923	3101	453	852	11	351	.367	.359	.275

Fred Snodgrass is remembered today as the "goat" of the 1912 World Series, the man whose "$30,000 muff" cost the New York Giants the victory. One historian even stated, inaccurately, that his dropping of a flyball "allowed the tying and winning runs to score." It only demonstrates how time tends to distort memory.

In truth, Snodgrass made a simple error not unlike similar errors made by every outfielder at one time or another. His error did not lose the Series. It did not even allow a run to score. It allowed the potential tying run to reach base. Had the Giants gone on to play sound baseball, the error would have proved harmless and been forgotten. Instead, someone had to be blamed for the loss, and Snodgrass seemed the most obvious choice. For more than 60 years he lived with that charge.

Giants manager John McGraw, indulging his passion for horse racing during an off-season trip to the West Coast, discovered Snodgrass catching for a semipro team and offered him a contract. Snodgrass played a few games for the Giants in 1908 and was on the bench the day of the most famous Giants "boner," made by Fred Merkle, whose failure to touch second base on a game-winning hit inevitably cost New York the pennant. In later years, Snodgrass defended Merkle as a victim of circumstance almost as readily as he defended himself.

In 1909 Snodgrass, called "Snow" by his teammates, was switched to the outfield. In 1910 he became the Giants' regular center fielder and hit .321, the only time in his career he surpassed .300. But his most important attribute was his speed.

Although many Giants disliked McGraw for his profane and sarcastic tongue, Snodgrass simply believed that McGraw was a fair man who rightly blasted his men for mental lapses but never criticized a player for a physical error. Snodgrass would soon see his beliefs confirmed.

The Giants won the 1911 National League pennant by 7½ games over the defending champion Cubs. Snodgrass hit .294 and stole 51 bases that season, but his bat was nowhere to be found in the Series. New York lost the World Series to Philadelphia in six games as the brilliant pitching of Chief Bender, Jack Coombs, and Eddie Plank held the Giants to a team batting average of only .175. Snodgrass managed only two hits in 19 at bats.

In 1912 the Giants won 103 games and easily outdistanced the Cubs and Pirates. McGraw had assembled one of the fastest teams ever: his speedsters stole 319 bases, led by Snodgrass' 43. New York's pitching staff led the National League in earned run average. Rookie Jeff Tesreau topped all league hurlers with a 1.96 mark. Christy Mathewson and Rube Marquard were both 20-game winners.

Their American League opponents were also a dominating club. The Boston Red Sox had won 105 games and boasted the great outfield of Duffy Lewis, Tris Speaker, and Harry Hooper. Their pitching staff was led by Smokey Joe Wood, who had a 34–5 record and 1.91 ERA.

McGraw started Tesreau in the opening game, but Wood beat him, 4–3. The next day at Boston, Mathewson pitched brilliantly, but five New York errors allowed four unearned runs to score, and the game ended in a tie after 11 innings. Marquard evened the Series with a 2–1 seven-hitter, but Wood came back to scatter nine hits in a 3–1 win to put Boston in front. When Hugh Bedient outpitched Mathewson to win Game 5, 2–1, the Giants' backs were to the wall. But Marquard won his second start in Game 6, and, after the Boston fans rioted before the seventh game, New York hammered Wood for six runs in the first inning. Snodgrass' double knocked in the first two Giants runs.

On October 18 the teams met in Boston for the deciding game. Mathewson started for the Giants, Bedient for the Red Sox. New York pushed across a run in the third inning and seemed to have another in the fifth when Larry Doyle smashed a long drive to right center. But Hooper made a remarkable catch just as the ball was about to clear the fence. Boston tied the game in the seventh inning when Olaf Henriksen, batting for Bedient, doubled home Jake Stahl.

Wood came in to relieve, and the game went into extra innings. In the top of the 10th New York's Moose McCormick cracked his fourth double of the Series and came home on Merkle's single. The final New York out came on Chief Meyers' hot grounder back to the box, which Wood fielded with his bare hand.

Wood, an excellent hitter, was due to lead off Boston's end of the 10th, but his hand was swollen from Meyers' drive. Clyde Engle was called on to pinch-hit. Mathewson, still pitching, induced Engle to hit a high, lazy fly to center. Snodgrass moved under the ball—and dropped it. By the time he recovered, Engle was on second. Nevertheless, the Giants were still ahead, 2–1, with their ace on the mound.

Hooper then smashed a line drive to deep left center, which he figured would be a sure triple. But Snodgrass outran the ball to make what he always insisted was the best catch of his life. Engle tagged and went to third. Mathewson, one of the great control artists of all time, then walked Red Sox second baseman Steve Yerkes, a .252 hitter.

Tris Speaker followed with an easy foul fly down the first base line. Merkle, Mathewson, and catcher Chief Meyers converged. Either Mathewson or Merkle could have made the catch, but both had shied away. Meyers made a game try, but the ball fell just out of his reach in foul territory. Hooper, watching the play from the nearby Boston bench, always insisted that Merkle backed off because Mathewson called for Meyers to make the play.

Given a reprieve, Speaker singled to right, scoring Engle with the tying run. Yerkes went to third, and Speaker reached second on the throw back in. Duffy Lewis was intentionally walked to set up a force play, but Larry Gardner hit a long sacrifice fly to right to bring in Yerkes with the winning run.

In the finger-pointing that followed, Mathewson, a New York icon, escaped blame even though he had tired badly and may have called for the wrong man on Speaker's foul. The cause of the defeat was somehow credited to Snodgrass. McGraw knew better. The following year, he gave Snodgrass a $1,000 raise, and Snodgrass

responded with one of his best seasons, hitting .291 as the Giants won their third pennant in a row. But they also lost their third consecutive World Series, falling victim to the Philadelphia Athletics' superior pitching. Snodgrass hit .333 in the Series.

Sold to the Boston Braves in August 1915, Snodgrass played for one more season, then left the majors. In nine seasons he averaged .275, scored 453 runs, and stole 215 bases. Ironically, defense was his strong suit. Yet when he died in 1974, the headlines of several obituaries identified him as the man who had made the famous muff in the 1912 World Series.

J.T. Snow

Snow, Jack Thomas **1B**

1992–* B: 2/26/1968, Long Beach, CA Deb: 9/20/1992, NY AL BB/TL 6'2", 202

G	AB	R	H	HR	RBI	OBP	SLG	AVG
951	3311	471	870	132	537	.350	.434	.263

Son of former longtime National Football League wide receiver Jack Snow, J.T. Snow starred in baseball at the University of Arizona. The New York Yankees took him in the fifth round of the 1989 June draft. He made his debut with New York late in 1992 after being named the International League Most Valuable Player that year, but he was traded to the Angels in a multiplayer deal for Jim Abbott before the 1993 season. Snow spent four seasons with the Angels before being traded to the Giants for Allen Watson and a minor leaguer after the 1996 season.

Snow displayed a consistent bat with below average-to-mediocre power for a first baseman. His best season was 1997, his first year in San Francisco, when he set career highs in most offensive categories. J.T. was expected to miss a good portion of that season after being hit in the face by a Randy Johnson pitch early in spring training, but he came back quickly and started at first base on Opening Day. He changed from switch-hitting to batting left-handed late in 1998.

Snow was one of the best defensive first basemen in baseball. He won five consecutive Gold Gloves from 1995 through 1999, and committed only 36 errors in his eight major league seasons. He made only one miscue in 1135 chances in 1998.

Hank Soar

Soar, Albert Henry

Umpire (1950–73) B:8/17/1914, Alton, RI 6'2", 218

Long-time American League umpire Hank Soar participated in three professional sports—baseball, football and basketball. Albert Henry Soar attended Providence College for three years, where he was named Little All-America in football. He quit that school, however, to play semi-pro baseball. Soon he was back on the gridiron, with the Boston Shamrocks in 1936 and the New York Giants from 1937 to 1946. In the Giants' 1938 National Football League title game against the Green Bay Packers, Soar caught a 23-yard touchdown pass from Ed Danowski for the margin of victory.

In 1947 Soar coached the Providence Steam Rollers of the Basketball Association of America to a 2–17 record. He was a backfield coach with Rhode Island State College from 1947 to 1949. Umpiring a World War II exhibition game, Soar impressed Connie Mack and he began umpiring professionally in 1947 with the New England League. He was promoted to the American Association in May 1949 and to the American League in 1950, where he served until 1973.

"Hank Soar was rated the best umpire on the bases four or five years in a row in a poll conducted by *The Sporting News*," former AL umpire Bill Kinnamon pointed out in John Skipper's book, *Umpires*. "They've stopped doing it now because it caused some hard feelings—but Hank was good on the bases. He just seemed to have a knack for it."

Chief Sockalexis

Sockalexis, Louis M. **OF**

1897–99 B:10/24/1871, Old Town, ME D:12/24/1913, Burlington, ME Deb:4/22/1897, CLE NL BL/TR 5'11", 185

G	AB	R	H	HR	RBI	OBP	SLG	AVG
94	367	54	115	3	55	.355	.414	.313

It took Louis M. Sockalexis, an American Indian ballplayer from Maine, only 94 big league games and 367 at bats to become a baseball legend—so famous that almost 20 years after his brief, fleeting career the Cleveland baseball team was named the Indians in his honor. A superb athlete, Sockalexis was so fast that he was once timed in full baseball gear at 10 seconds in the 100-yard dash. He had an exceptional throwing arm, "one of the first great arms in baseball," according to historian Bill Curran. And he could hit with power such as people in the Dead Ball Era of baseball had never seen before.

Sockalexis inspired tall tales. It was said that he once hit a baseball 600 feet, a highly unlikely feat considering the balls of mush of his time. It was also said that he threw a ball from Oak Hill on Indian

Island (the Penobscot reservation in Old Town, Maine, where Sockalexis grew up) that hit the smokestack of the Jordan Lumber Mill. That would have been a neat trick—the two spots are more than three-quarters of a mile apart.

Someone once claimed that Sockalexis was a direct descendant of Sitting Bull. It has also been said that Gilbert Patten, who wrote boys' baseball novels under the pen name of Burt L. Standish, based his famous Frank Merriwell character on Sockalexis.

Sockalexis' incredibly short career was brought to an end by alcoholism. He spent much of his final years as a panhandler, begging for pennies to buy one more glass of whiskey. A report in 1900, only one year after he had left Major League Baseball, tells of a disheveled Sockalexis, with his toes poking through the holes in his worn-out shoes, being tossed in jail for 30 days for vagrancy.

By the time he was 20 years old Sockalexis was already a New England legend on the baseball and football fields. Mike "Doc" Powers, captain of the woeful Holy Cross baseball team and a future big league catcher, spotted Sockalexis in 1894 during a Maine barnstorming tour. He arranged for Sockalexis to join the school as a "special" student since he hadn't finished high school. Sockalexis single-handedly put Holy Cross on the baseball map. His feats immediately grew into legend. He stole six bases in one game, two for himself and four more as designated runner for an injured Holy Cross teammate.

Sockalexis was at Holy Cross in 1895 and 1896. When Powers transferred to Notre Dame, his protégé followed. But it was at Notre Dame that Sockalexis first ran afoul of the bottle. He was there only one month before being expelled for public drunkenness. The Cleveland Spiders snapped him up for the majors for $1,500.

He was an immediate smash. In six exhibition games he had 10 assists. *Sporting Life* described his physique in glowing terms: "A massive man with gigantic bones and bulging muscles." Although Sockalexis was about 5-foot-11 and 185 pounds, he was huge for his time. As writer Luke Salisbury described him, "He was as big as the football linemen of his day and faster than the backs."

Early in his rookie season he made a remarkable catch to save a game. Soon after, a sensational throw sent tongues wagging and writers to their dictionaries in search of new adjectives. But although Sockalexis was not the first American Indian to play major league baseball, he was certainly the first to be treated like one. Opposing fans went crazy. They took to wearing Indian headdresses and screaming war whoops every time Sockalexis came to bat.

The stolid, college-educated Sockalexis claimed the fan rudeness didn't bother him. In his first appearance in New York, against acclaimed fireballer Amos Rusie, the war whoops were silenced when he smashed a line drive homer. In Cleveland his exploits were greeted with uproarious cheers.

In the four games before July 4, 1897, Sockalexis was 11-for-21. Only twice that season had he gone without a hit in two consecutive games. His batting average was .335. But the Fourth of July celebration was too much for him. The facts blur here, but Sockalexis missed several games afterward. It was clear he had gone on a drinking tear and had hurt his ankle; some say it happened when he tried to sneak out of a second-floor hotel room where he was being guarded by teammates trying to keep him from drinking anymore. A newspaper of the time referred to "a tryst with a pale-faced maiden and a dalliance with the grape."

Whatever the cause, he was hurt. When he returned he went 9-for-18, but his fielding was atrocious. He might have been drunk, or just severely hung over, but everyone noticed it. The *Cleveland Plain Dealer* of July 13, under the headline "A Wooden Indian," commented, "Sockalexis acted as if he had disposed of too many mint juleps previous to the game.... Sockalexis...was directly responsible for all but one of Boston's runs. A lame foot is the Indian's excuse, but a Turkish bath and a good rest might be an excellent remedy."

Sporting Life opined, "Too much popularity has ruined Sockalexis by all accounts. It is no longer a secret that Cleveland management can no longer control (him)." Manager Patsy Tebeau had had enough; from July 25 to September 12 Sockalexis played only once. In his final game that year he made two errors, although he finished the season with a .338 average, three homers, 42 RBIs in 66 games, and 16 stolen bases. He was part of one of baseball's first .300-hitting outfields, along with Jesse Burkett, who batted .383, and Ollie Pickering, who hit .352.

When playing every day, it was easier for Sockalexis to control his drinking. But sitting on the bench was a different story. The team put up with him for only 21 games in 1898 and 7 more in 1899 before they let him go. Out of baseball by 1903, he worked as a laborer when he wasn't on a binge throughout New England. He died in 1913.

The Cleveland team employed several nicknames throughout the years prior to the arrival of Sockalexis and after his departure. The one that stuck the longest was "Naps," in honor of the team's player-manager, Napoleon Lajoie. After Lajoie was released in 1914, a Cleveland newspaper held a contest to rename the team. The win-

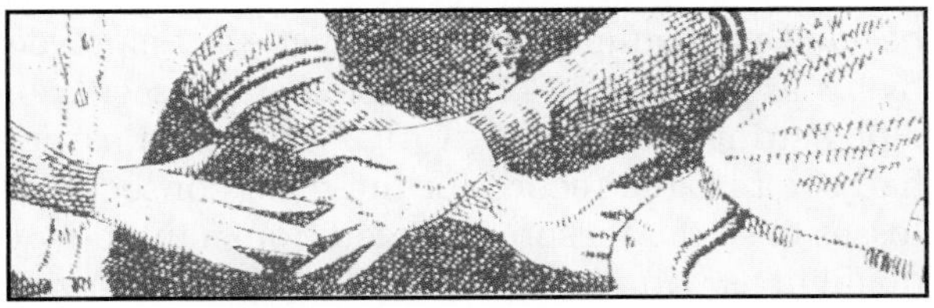

ning entry was "Indians." The fan that sent it in explained that it would be a testament to the game's first American Indian, Louis "Chief" Sockalexis.

Author Jay Feldman says that Sockalexis "ranks among the truly tragic figures of baseball history." Luke Salisbury used the Sockalexis story as the basis of his novel, *The Cleveland Indian: The Legend of King Saturday.*

Sammy Sosa

Sosa, Samuel Peralta **OF**

1989–* B:11/12/1968, San Pedro de Macoris, Dominican Republic Deb:6/16/1989, TEX AL BR/TR 6', 185

G	AB	R	H	HR	RBI	OBP	SLG	AVG
1409	5289	841	1413	336	941	.326	.510	.267

Until the 1998 season many baseball fans outside of Chicago would have had trouble identifying Sammy Sosa. But after his historic duel with Mark McGwire in pursuit of the single-season home run record, the personable outfielder became a celebrity in the United States and a folk hero in his native country, the Dominican Republic.

"Slammin' Sammy" was already a very good player, hitting 30 homers and batting in over 100 runs each year from 1995 to 1997. He exhibited a cannon arm and good speed. On the other hand, he struck out too often, ran bases erratically, and made mistakes in the field. The Cubs hoped for more. In 1998 they got it.

Sosa became a more patient hitter, raising his batting average and power numbers. Sosa exploded for 20 home runs in June, the most ever hit in a month. As he battled all season with McGwire for the most coveted record in baseball, Sosa seemed to delight in his rival's accomplishments. His unfeigned generosity, along with a bubbly enthusiasm for the home run chase, endeared Sosa not only to fans but to many who had only a passing interest in the game. It transformed Wrigley Field, already one of baseball's most beloved parks, into a standing-room-only shrine to Sosa.

By season's end, Sosa became the second player to surpass Roger Maris' single season record, but his 66 home runs still left him just shy of McGwire's 70. He did, however, lead the majors with 158 RBIs, the fourth-highest total ever by a National Leaguer and the most in the NL since Cub Hack Wilson's record-setting 191 and Chuck Klein's 170, both in 1930. More important, Sosa became a consummate team player—as displayed by his league-best 134 runs scored and career-high .308 batting average. The Cubs, who a year earlier had set a league record for the most consecutive losses to start a season, emerged from a three-way dogfight as winner of the NL Wild Card. Sosa was the overwhelming choice over McGwire for 1998 National League Most Valuable Player.

Following the season, Sosa put his newfound celebrity to good use by raising money for hurricane victims in the Dominican Republic. When he returned to his country on October 21, thousands of people turned out in the rain to welcome him. To commemorate the havoc Sammy wrought on National League pitching, Dominican President Leonel Fernandez dubbed him "Hurricane Sosa," and awarded him the nation's top medal. Sosa also had a grand parade in his honor in New York.

Sosa's numbers were down, but only slightly, in 1999. He again shadowed McGwire in the home run derby, this time slugging 63 and driving in 141 runs. Sosa and McGwire became the first two players to ever reach 60 homers in back-to-back seasons.

Mario Soto

Soto, Mario Melvin **P**

1977–88 B:7/12/1956, Bani, Dominican Republic Deb:7/21/1977, CIN NL BR/TR 6', 185

W	L	PCT	G	SH	IP	BB	SO	ERA
100	92	.521	297	13	1730¹	657	1449	3.47

In Game 3 of the 1979 National League Championship Series, with a total of three big league wins under his belt, third-year Reds pitcher Mario Soto pitched two innings of no-hit ball in relief against the Pittsburgh Pirates. Unfortunately, the Pirates had already taken a six-run lead over the Reds and led the Series two games to none. Although he would soon become one of the toughest pitchers of his day, it was the last postseason action Soto would see. The Pirates completed their sweep of Cincinnati that day and went on to capture the World Series.

In 1980 the righthanded fireballer worked as a reliever, but when it became clear how tough he was to hit, the Reds made him a starter. Although he pitched only 190 innings that season, he struck out 182 batters to finish third on the strikeout list and allowed the fewest hits per game in the National League. His opponents' batted a minuscule .187 that year. Despite Soto's effort, the Reds were losing the key players of their most celebrated championship era to free agency, and the team sunk to third for the first time since 1971.

Dark years lay ahead for Cincinnati. Soto, however, was brilliant. In 1981 he again finished third on the strikeout list. In 1982 he made his first of three consecutive All-Star teams and whiffed a Reds-record 274 opponents, trailing only Steve Carlton's 286. Soto's ratio of strikeouts per game was best in the league, with an average of 9.57 whiffs per nine innings.

He was nearly as good the following year, striking out 242 and climbing to second in Cy Young Award balloting, and he was still smoking in 1984 and 1985. Although he never won more than 18 games in a season, the fiery righthander consistently ranked near the top of the league, beside Carlton, Ryan, Seaver, Phil and Joe Niekro, and later Fernando Valenzuela and Dwight Gooden. From 1981 through 1985 he struck out more batters than anyone else in the major leagues.

On May 12, 1984, Soto was one out away from a no-hitter when Cardinals outfielder George Hendrick homered to tie the game. The Reds rallied for a run in the bottom of the ninth to give him a 2–1 victory. Less than three weeks later, Soto's fiery personality spilled over on the field in an ugly incident in Chicago.

On May 27 third base umpire Steve Ripley signaled that Ron Cey's long fly down the line was a three-run homer. Soto went ballistic. He shoved Ripley and incited a 32-minute melee. He grabbed a bat and went after a Wrigley Field vendor who had thrown a bag of ice at him. Although the umpires later reversed Ripley's call, Soto was ejected. NL president Chub Feeney suspended him for five days. Soto was suspended for five more days when he got into a fight with Claudell Washington in June.

Soto injured his throwing arm in 1986, just as the Reds were becoming contenders again. He attempted a comeback in 1987 but was released for good in mid-1988. He retired second on the Reds' all-time strikeout list, with 1,449 batters whiffed in 1,730 ⅓ innings. His career mark of 7.54 strikeouts per nine innings ranks among the top figures in baseball history.

Billy Southworth

Southworth, William Harrison **OF**

1913–29 M(1929, 1940–51, 1,044–704) B:3/9/1893, Harvard, NE D:11/15/1969, Columbus, OH Deb:8/4/1913, CLE AL BL/TR 5'9", 170

G	AB	R	H	HR	RBI	OBP	SLG	AVG
1192	4359	661	1296	52	561	.359	.415	.297

Billy Southworth had a very successful career, both as a player and manager. He was a career .297 hitter and a career .597 skipper. He managed four pennant-winning seasons with the Cardinals and Braves, and he retired with the fifth best lifetime winning percentage among managers.

Southworth, a lefty-hitting outfielder who could run, debuted with the Indians in 1915, hitting .220 in 60 games. He resurfaced with the Pirates in 1918 and moved into the starting lineup the following season. Traded to the Braves in 1921, he hit .308 with 79 RBIs. Injuries limited him to 43 games in 1922, but he returned the following season to hit .319 with 78 RBIs. He moved to the Giants in 1924 and had his best season in 1926 for the Giants and Cards, with career highs in average (.320), home runs (16) and RBIs (99).

Southworth began his managing career in the Cardinals' system in 1928 with Rochester, winning the pennant and returning to the majors in 1929 as the Cards' player-manager. His players considered him a strict taskmaster and resisted the changes he wanted to make. He lasted 88 games (43–45) before returning to Rochester, where he won three more pennants.

Southworth got another chance with St. Louis when Ray Blades was fired early in 1940. He moved the Cards from sixth to third that year, finished second in 1941, and then won three straight pennants. The Cards won the 1942 and 1944 World Series.

After finishing second in 1945, Southworth moved to the Boston Braves for $50,000. He won a pennant in 1948, behind the arms of Warren Spahn and Johnny Sain. When asked during the season what his plans were for the rotation, Southworth replied, "Spahn, Sain, and pray for rain." The Braves, making their first World Series appearance since 1914, lost to the Indians in six games.

A heavy drinker, Southworth suffered what was officially described as a nervous breakdown in 1949. He guided the club to consecutive fourth-place finishes before he quit in the middle of the 1951 season.

Warren Spahn

Spahn, Warren Edward **P**

1942–65 B:4/23/1921, Buffalo, NY Deb:4/19/1942, BOS NL BL/TL 6', 175

W	L	PCT	G	SH	IP	BB	SO	ERA
363	245	.597	750	63	5243^{2}	1434	2583	3.09

Lefthander Warren Spahn was so good for so long that it's amazing he ever questioned his qualifications for the Hall of Fame—but he did. The winningest lefthander in major league history, Spahn won 20 games 13 different times, a mark equaled only by Christy Mathewson. He recorded 63 shutouts, the National League record for a lefthander, and produced a lifetime ERA of 3.09.

A consummate competitor, Spahn once observed, "When I'm pitching I feel I'm down to the essentials. Two men, with one challenge between them, and what better challenge than between pitcher and hitter?"

Spahn started his baseball career playing first base for the junior squad of Buffalo's Lake City Athletic Club while his father held down third base for the senior team. Later, both father and son performed in the same infield. Spahn wanted to play first base for his South Park High School team, but since the incumbent had already been named all-city, Spahn thought it best to switch to the mound.

In 1940 he signed with the Boston Braves and was assigned to Bradford of the Class D PONY League. No bonus was involved. If there had been a bonus, the Braves might have thought they had wasted their money. Twice that first year Spahn injured his arm, and he worked only 66 innings. But the next year Spahn graduated to Evansville of the Class B 3-I League, where he led the league with 19 wins, a .760 won-lost percentage, and a 1.83 ERA.

Spahn started the 1942 season with the big league club, and saw Braves pitcher Jim Tobin hit two home runs on Opening Day. Spahn concluded that he wanted to be that type of pitcher. Boston manager Casey Stengel had other ideas for Spahn, however. When the rookie refused to throw a brushback pitch at Brooklyn shortstop Pee Wee Reese, Stengel demoted Spahn to Hartford of the Eastern League. There Spahn went 17–12 with a 1.96 ERA. "It was the worst mistake I ever made," Stengel later admitted.

Spahn didn't return to Boston in 1943. Drafted into the army and assigned to the 176th Combat Engineers Battalion. Spahn fought in the Battle of the Bulge and participated in the taking of the key Rhine crossing bridge at Remagen, Germany. Several in his company were lost when the bridge finally collapsed. He received a Bronze Star, as well as a Purple Heart for being hit with shrapnel.

Spahn's bravery won him a battlefield commission, but the rare honor also cost him six more months in the army and an additional three months out of his baseball career. He spent the extended time in Germany with the Army of Occupation, replacing a fellow officer who had been killed.

Many have speculated about how many more games Spahn might have won in the majors had he not spent more than three seasons in the army, but Spahn approached the topic philosophically. "People say that my absence from the big leagues may have cost me a chance to win 400 games," he reflected. "But I don't know about that. I matured a lot in three years, and I think I was better equipped to handle major league hitters at 25 than I was at 22. Also, I pitched until I was 44. Maybe I wouldn't have been able to do that otherwise."

Spahn returned to Boston in July 1946 and was faced with two tasks: winning a spot in the Boston

rotation and marrying his fiancée, Lorene Southard. Braves manager Billy Southworth wanted Spahn to put off the ceremony until the season's end, and even offered to be best man, but Spahn wouldn't wait.

He and Lorene were married August 10, 1946, a Saturday. Spahn got the day off. The game was rained out anyway and was made up the following day as part of a Sunday doubleheader. Spahn was called in to relieve in one game and lost on a Sid Gordon homer.

Spahn quickly emerged as one of the top pitchers in the league. In 1947 he won 21 games and led the National League in ERA. In 1948 he was a key member of the Braves' "Spahn and Sain and Pray For Rain" pitching staff. Some have pointed out that the duo's won-lost percentage was actually lower than the team's as a whole, .591 as compared with .595. This, however, fails to take into account the tremendous success the two pitchers enjoyed down the stretch.

On Labor Day Spahn and Sain opposed the Dodgers in a doubleheader. Spahn, who had gotten off to a very slow start that year, won the first game on a five-hitter, 2–1, pitching 14 innings. In the second game Sain shut out Brooklyn, 4–0. No games were scheduled for the following two days, and then it did indeed rain. Spahn and Sain won the next two games, followed by a day off, and Boston's two other starters split a doubleheader. Sain and Spahn then defeated Chicago on September 14 and 15. The team had another day off. Then the two staff aces took the mound again and won a pair of games against Pittsburgh.

Exhausted from this stretch drive, Spahn started and lost Game 2 of the World Series. He won Game 5 in relief, but surrendered a run in two innings of relief as Cleveland won Game 6 and the Series.

In 1951 Spahn surrendered the first base hit to a slumping young prospect named Willie Mays. "He was something like 0-for-21 the first time I saw him. His first major league hit was a home run off me—and I'll never forgive myself. We might have gotten rid of Willie forever if I'd only struck him out," Spahn said.

Although not remembered as a strikeout artist, Spahn led the National League in that category from 1949 through 1952. On June 14, 1952, he struck out 18 batters in a 15-inning contest against Chicago. After the Braves moved to Milwaukee in 1953 he helped the club win two more pennants and a world championship. He won the Cy Young Award in 1957, and beat the Yankees twice in the 1958 World Series.

Spahn was a true craftsman on the mound, much more a pitcher than a thrower. "A pitcher needs two pitches—one they're looking for and one to cross 'em up," he once observed. Batters could take a "comfortable" 0-for-4 against Spahn.

Hitters would get around enough to hit the ball, but not well enough to do any real damage. They would be only slightly off. "Hitting is timing. Pitching is upsetting timing," Spahn theorized.

Spahn did not record any no-hitters until late in his career; he cemented his reputation as an ageless wonder by pitching two of them after his 39th birthday. At Milwaukee's County Stadium, he no-hit the Phillies for his 20th win of the 1960 season, the 11th time he had reached that number. He struck out 15 batters, his career high for nine innings.

The following year Spahn did it again. He no-hit San Francisco, 1–0, just five days after his 40th birthday. "It was so easy, it was pathetic," commented Spahn. "Everything went my way and they kept guessing wrong. But let's face it, I was just plain lucky. I walked a man twice to start an inning—a cardinal sin with a one-run lead—not once, but twice, and got away with it." Of course, what Spahn didn't mention is that after both walks he took care of the runners personally by starting double plays. Later that season Spahn notched his 300th career victory, defeating the Cubs, 2–1, on a six-hitter.

Spahn, one of baseball's better hitting pitchers, hit 35 lifetime home runs, the National League record for a hurler and fourth-best on the all-time list. In 1958 he became one of the few pitchers to bat .300 and record 20 wins in the same season.

Toward the end of his career Spahn was sent to the last-place Mets, where he briefly served as a pitcher-coach under Casey Stengel. Spahn once quipped, "I'm probably the only guy who worked with Stengel before and after he was a genius." Spahn and fellow Mets player-coach Yogi Berra teamed up for a historic battery. "I don't think we're the oldest battery, but we're certainly the ugliest," remarked Berra. At about that time Stan Musial said, "I don't think Spahn will ever get into the Hall of Fame. He'll never stop pitching." But he did retire from playing, in 1965, after going 3–4 for the San Francisco Giants.

After leaving the majors Spahn coached for the Mexico City Tigers and also pitched a few games in Mexico. Some criticized Spahn for continuing to pitch at his age. "I don't care what the public thinks," said Spahn. "I'm pitching because I enjoy pitching."

He served as a pitching coach first for the Cleveland Indians and later in Japan with the Hiroshima Toyo Carp from 1973 to 1978, before retiring to his ranch in Hartshorne, Oklahoma. Following the death of his wife he returned to the game for two seasons as a minor league pitching instructor in the Angels organization.

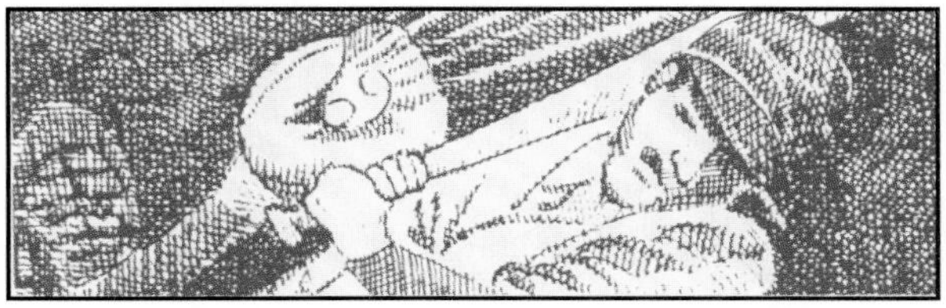

Despite his many achievements, Spahn actually questioned whether he would be welcomed in Cooperstown. "It will be a great honor if I'm voted in, but it's something a player should never expect will happen," said Spahn. He was elected to the Hall of Fame in 1973, his first year of eligibility.

Albert Spalding

Spalding, Albert Goodwill **P-1B**

1871–1878 M(1876–77, 78–47) Owner (1882–91)
B:9/2/1850, Byron, IL D:9/9/1915, San Diego, CA
Deb:5/5/1871, BOS NA BR/TR 6'1", 170

W	L	PCT	G	SH	IP	BB	SO	ERA
48	12	.800	65	8	539^{2}	26	41	1.78

G	AB	R	H	HR	RBI	OBP	SLG	AVG
127	550	83	158	0	79	.299	.355	.287

In 1899 a *New York Times* reporter described Al Spalding in the following manner: "His face is that of a Greek hero, his manner that of a Church of England Bishop...and he is the father of the greatest sport the world has ever known." Baseball has more than enough "fathers," among them Alexander Cartwright, Harry Wright, and Henry Chadwick—but in the late 19th century, Spalding was the most respected name in baseball. When Spalding talked, baseball people listened.

Small wonder, for Spalding did it all. He was a star player, a pennant-winning manager, and the president of the most successful club of his era. And through his sporting goods company, the largest in the world, his name was on the baseball itself. At a time when every American who read Horatio Alger harbored the dream of becoming a captain of industry, Spalding was proof that it was indeed possible to rise from humble beginnings to become wealthy, honored, and influential. That he made his ascent by means of America's national game was icing on the cake.

Born in Byron, Illinois, Albert Goodwill Spalding grew up in nearby Rockford. When he was 12 a baseball from a sandlot game rolled to his feet. He picked it up and returned it with such a strong and accurate throw that he was asked to join the game. With that, his life's work had begun. Three years later the young righthander defeated Forest City, Rockford's adult team, and was asked to pitch for them. Fortunately, the school principal was a baseball fan and allowed young Albert to be excused from classes to practice with the team.

In 1867 George Wright's Washington Nationals toured the Midwest, pummeling the locals. On their way to Chicago they stopped off in Rockford for a little exercise and were shocked to be beaten by the 16-year-old farm boy, 29–23. Today, 23 runs scored on a pitcher may not appear impressive, but few of the runs scored off Spalding were earned; they were the result of cow-pasture ballfields and barehanded fielding.

The feat was shocking enough to make headlines back East and was underlined the next day when the Nationals beat Chicago's best team, the Excelsiors, 49–4. Spalding was quickly hired by a Chicago grocery store owner at $40 a week, about 10 times what he could have made in Rockford. Of course, groceries had nothing to do with Spalding's "real" job. He had been hired to pitch for the Excelsiors, a supposedly amateur team.

When the grocer went bankrupt Spalding returned to Rockford, sadder but richer, and added to his reputation as the best pitcher in the Midwest. In 1871 Harry Wright put together a team in Boston to compete in the National Association, baseball's first league. The team featured Harry's brother, George, and several other players from the famous professional Cincinnati Red Stockings of 1869 and 1870. Wright offered Spalding $1,500 to join them.

In their first season Wright's Boston Red Stockings played only 31 games. Spalding won more games than any pitcher in the league and finished 19–10, but the team finished second to Philadelphia. From then on, however, the Red Stockings dominated the league, winning four consecutive pennants, each more easily than the last. In one four-year period Spalding went 185–43, culminated by a 54–5 mark in 1875. By then he was not only the most famous pitcher in America, but he was also one of the richest.

In an era when few pitchers recorded a high number of strikeouts, Spalding was no different. In 1873 he struck out only 31 batters in 497 innings. The pitcher's job was to keep the batter so off-balance that he would hit easy grounders and soft flies. Before delivering the ball, Spalding stood facing the batter with his feet splayed like a ballet dancer. He brought the ball up to his chin in both hands, then stepped forward and fired the ball underhanded, as required. Although he never learned to throw a curve, he had a good fastball, an even better change of pace, and good control.

During the 1875 season William Hulbert, president of the Chicago White Stockings, began secret negotiations with Spalding and three other Boston stars to persuade them to jump to his team the following year. Although players were allowed to move after the season, they could only do so if not contracted to another club. Hulbert's interference was against National Association rules, but that wasn't a problem for Hulbert, who had much larger plans than simply improving his ballclub. He intended to form an entire new league, one he hoped to make tighter, stronger, and more lucrative.

Hulbert recruited Spalding , listening to his suggestions about how to create a new and improved circuit. Spalding was intrigued by the idea of returning to Illinois and thrilled by a new challenge. The fact that Hulbert offered him more money than he could make in Boston was also a factor.

Hulbert's National League played its first season in 1876. To no one's surprise, the Chicago White Stockings won the first league pennant behind pitcher and manager A.G. Spalding. He compiled a 47–12 record with a 1.75 ERA. In the few games he didn't pitch, Spalding played outfield or first base and hit .312.

The following season the strain of pitching hundreds of innings took its toll, and Spalding won only one game, giving him 48 wins in the National League, on top of the 204 wins he had in the National Association. The 1877 season was his only year as a pitcher that he did not lead his league in victories. He spent the rest of the season playing first base. In 1878 he played one game before retiring. Only 28, Spalding was off to bigger, brighter, and richer things.

In 1877 he formed A.G. Spalding & Bros. Company to manufacture and sell sporting goods. He offered to pay the National League one dollar for every ball it used if it agreed to use only the baseballs he manufactured. The scheme crushed his competition and made Spalding the exclusive provider of the official major league baseball. For every dollar he gave the league, he took in thousands more in nationwide sales. He cemented his position as an industry leader by publishing *Spalding's Official Baseball Guide*, an annual compendium of official league statistics and other baseball comment.

Spalding's motto was "Everything is possible to him who dares." He proved that it was even more possible if one had an "in" with the National League, a measure of intelligence, and a ruthless desire to crush the competition. Within a few years Spalding had a virtual monopoly of the sporting goods industry. While other former players, notably Al Reach and George Wright, started their own sporting goods companies, they were eventually swallowed up by Spalding.

It is worth noting that, starting in 1901, the new American League used a Reach baseball while the National League continued to use the Spalding. But by then Spalding owned Reach's company. All the baseballs in both leagues were manufac-

tured in the same factory and simply had different names stamped on the horsehide.

Spalding had a keen eye for promotion. While still in Boston he helped Harry Wright organize a baseball exhibition trip to England to convince the British to abandon cricket in favor of baseball. The Brits didn't agree, but Spalding still thought it was a good idea. In 1888 he organized a two-team tour to 14 countries, introducing the game to anyone they found. He sold little equipment, but did return with some smashing pictures of ballplayers climbing the pyramids.

In 1882 Spalding became president of the Chicago White Stockings, his old team. They won the pennant, their third in a row, and also took flags in 1885 and 1886. When the players revolted against the arbitrary rule of the team owners in 1890 and formed the Players' League, Spalding became head of the National League's war committee. Although the Players' League managed to convince most of the National League stars to join the new league and PL games outdrew those of the National League, Spalding was determined to fight the upstart organization head on. He scheduled games on the same dates in cities where both leagues operated, cajoled and bribed players into returning to the National League, initiated lawsuits, gained the support of the press by threatening to withdraw advertising, found players for teams, and convinced the upstart league's investors that he would never quit. The National League actually lost more money than its competitor, but the newcomers gave up and collapsed after a single season.

Following the 1891 season Spalding let others run the White Stockings, although he retained his financial interest. A few years later a block of owners tried to turn baseball into a monopoly through interlocking ownership. Spalding led the opposition, and eventually the drastic plan was defeated.

On a larger canvas, he helped organize the Chicago World's Fair in 1893 and was a U.S. commissioner to the Olympic Games in 1901, for which he received the French Legion of Honor. In 1910 he ran and lost in a campaign for a seat in the Senate representing California.

Spalding always maintained that baseball was American in origin, whereas the famous writer Henry Chadwick, who edited *Spalding's Guide*, insisted that the game was descended from the English game of rounders. In 1905 Spalding put together a blue-ribbon panel—consisting of men who already agreed with him—to investigate the origins of baseball. He produced a letter from an old man in Denver who claimed to have been present at Cooperstown, New York, in 1839 when Abner Doubleday spontaneously invented the game. With that, Doubleday, who became a Civil War hero, was crowned as the inventor of the national pastime. Research has since shown that Doubleday no more invented baseball than he did the bass drum, but Spalding had successfully convinced the public that baseball was native to America.

He died in 1915, never knowing that Chadwick was right, that a Hall of Fame would be established in Cooperstown, or that in 1939 he would be elected to it.

Tully Sparks

Sparks, Thomas Frank **P**

1897, 1899, 1901–10 B:12/12/1874, Etna, GA D:7/15/1937, Anniston, AL Deb:9/15/1897, PHI NL BR/TR

W	L	PCT	G	SH	IP	BB	SO	ERA
121	137	.469	313	19	2335^{2}	629	778	2.79

By the time he turned 30, Tully Sparks had toiled for the Phillies, Pirates, Brewers, Giants, and Pilgrims, with a 44–74 record to show for it. This was more a reflection on his teams than his performance.

Things began to turn around for Sparks in 1905. That year he went 14–11 with a 2.18 ERA, and his Phillies improved by 31 games, vaulting from eighth to fourth. The Phils remained near the middle of the pack for the rest of his career. In 1906 Sparks was 19–16 with a 2.16 ERA for a sub-.500 team. He set career highs in complete games, innings, shutouts, and strikeouts that year.

In 1907 he went 22–8, 2.00 ERA, earning 27 percent of his team's victories for the second straight season. The following year he logged a 16 wins and a 2.60 ERA. Only six NL pitchers topped his 71 wins in that span.

Things then went swiftly downhill. Sparks won only six more games before his big league career ended in 1910. He finished with a sub-.500 record despite a creditable 2.79 ERA.

Tris Speaker

Speaker, Tristram E. **OF**

1907–28 M(1919–26, 617–520) B:4/4/1888, Hubbard, TX D:12/8/1958, Lake Whitney, TX Deb:9/14/1907, BOS AL BL/TL 5'11½", 193

G	AB	R	H	HR	RBI	OBP	SLG	AVG
2789	10195	1882	3514	117	1529	.428	.500	.345

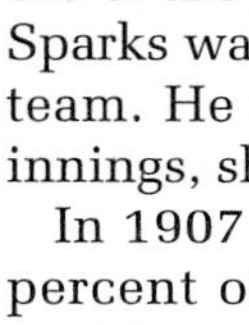

Tris Speaker played unusually shallow in center field, so shallow that he recorded 448 assists, more than any other outfielder in baseball history. In 1909 and 1912 he set the American League record with 35 assists in a season. In 1918 he played so close to second base that he made two unassisted double plays. On countless other occasions he turned probable hits into routine outs.

Some now consider Speaker's defensive mastery a by-product of the Dead Ball Era, when fly-balls to deep center field were rare. They argue that Speaker could risk the chance of one or two balls a week sailing over his head because of the number of soft drives he'd catch by playing so shallow, a luxury that modern outfielders can't afford. Even Speaker, some say, would have to play much deeper today.

But the evidence is to the contrary. Speaker played the last nine years of his 22-year major league career after the lively ball was introduced in 1920. He continued to play within spitting distance of second base, and he continued to get away with it. His secret was a seemingly prescient ability to get a jump on a batted ball.

Joe Sewell, who patrolled shortstop for Speaker's Cleveland Indians starting in 1920, said, "I played seven years with him right behind me in shallow center field. You know how an infielder gets down for the pitch? Well, you'd get down and the ball would be hit—a shot. You'd turn, and in all that time I never did see him turn. He'd be turned and gone with his back to the plate, the ball, the infield, and when he'd turn around again, there would be the ball."

Perhaps the single greatest proof of his mastery of the outfield is that Speaker is remembered for his fielding even though he was one of the greatest hitters in baseball history. His career marks include a .345 batting average, fifth best overall, as well as 3,514 hits, 1,882 runs scored, 1,529 RBIs, and 434 stolen bases.

An outstanding high school athlete, Tristram E. Speaker worked as a telegraph linesman and cowpuncher before joining Cleburne of the North Texas League in 1906 as a lefthanded pitcher for $50 a month. He saw little action and less success on the mound. After the young recruit lost six consecutive starts, Cleburne lost its regular right fielder to injury. Speaker told the manager he could play the position and soon became an outfielder. He batted only .268 his first year but hit .314 with Houston the following season.

When Pittsburgh owner Barney Dreyfuss heard about the young hitter he was intrigued, until he learned that Speaker smoked cigarettes. The Boston Red Sox showed more interest, bringing him up for seven games in September but writing him off when he batted only .158. The Red Sox didn't send him a contract for 1908, so Speaker paid his own way to Marlin, Texas, where the New York Giants were training, and offered his

services to manager John McGraw. Unimpressed, McGraw said there was a "No Vacancy" sign on his outfield and didn't even give him a tryout.

Speaker moved on to the Red Sox training camp in Little Rock, Arkansas. Although not welcomed with open arms, he was allowed to train with the team. When it was time to head north the Red Sox gave Speaker to the Little Rock ballclub in payment for the use of the facilities, retaining an option to buy him back at a nominal sum. After the youngster hit .350 to lead the Southern Association, Boston exercised its option, but Speaker hit only .220 in 31 games at the end of the season.

During this period Cy Young, the great pitcher, turned Speaker into a great outfielder. "Cy used to hit fungoes to me every day when I joined the Red Sox," Speaker later explained. "He always tried to hit the ball just one step beyond me so that I couldn't catch it unless I hustled. I watched him, and in a few days I knew just by the way he swung whether the ball would go to my right or left. Then I figured that if I could do that with a fungo hitter, I could do it in a ball game. I asked our pitchers how they pitched to each batter. I also studied the batter and when he started his swing, I knew if he would hit to my left or right and I was on my way."

Speaker won the center field job in 1909 and hit .309. Nearly six feet tall and a solid 193 pounds, the lefthanded hitter sprayed the ball to all fields. Never a big home run hitter, of the four times he reached double figures in homers, three came in the 1920s after the lively ball arrived. His specialty was the line drive, and when coupled with his speed, a single often became a double or triple. His 222 career three-base hits are the sixth-highest total ever; his 792 doubles are an all-time record. Speaker led the AL in two-base hits eight times, topping 50 on five different occasions.

Speaker picked up the nickname "Spoke" from some dugout wag with an affinity for the past tense. But Speaker acted more like his other namesake, "the Grey Eagle," on the ballfield, even when pushing 40. He played in 100 or more games for 19 consecutive seasons and hit better than .300 in all but one.

When the Red Sox won the pennant in 1912, they did it behind the strength of Smokey Joe Wood's arm and one of the best outfields ever assembled. Wood, Speaker's roommate, went 34–6. Flanking Speaker was left fielder Duffy Lewis, who drove in 109 runs, and right fielder Harry Hooper, who scored 98.

That year Speaker won the Chalmers Award, a forerunner of the Most Valuable Player Award. He hit .383, scored 136 runs and drove in 90, led the league in doubles, with 53, and in home runs, with 10, and stole 52 bases. He finished off a good year's work by hitting .300 to lead the Red Sox to a World Series victory over the New York Giants. In 1915 Boston finished first again; Speaker hit .322 for the season and .294 in the Sox's World Series win over Philadelphia.

Speaker was an incorrigible practical joker, and practical jokes are seldom funny to their victims. One time he pulled off Duffy Lewis' cap and showed the crowd Lewis' glistening bald pate. Lewis, who had shaved his head because of the heat and was worried that the fuzz wouldn't return, was not amused. He threw a bat against Speaker's shins, and the center fielder didn't walk much for a couple of days.

The Federal League was formed in 1914 and tried to lure established stars away from the majors with big salaries. Naturally, Speaker was high on the new league's list. To keep him happy in Fenway Park, the Red Sox increased his wages to $18,000 a year, one of the highest salaries in baseball.

But when the Feds went belly up after the 1915 season, Red Sox owner Joe Lannin saw no reason to pay a king's ransom for a center fielder whose only other option was to return to Texas and punch cows. He tried to cut Speaker's salary by half. Speaker proposed that Lannin take a flying leap. When neither side budged, Lannin traded Speaker to Cleveland in April 1916 for pitcher Sad Sam Jones, third baseman Fred Thomas, and $50,000.

The Red Sox still managed to win the 1916 pennant. Speaker won the American League batting crown with a .386 average and led the league with 211 hits, 41 doubles, a .470 on-base percentage, and a .502 slugging average.

He continued to star for the Indians. In 1919 Speaker replaced Lee Fohl as manager. Although the team began winning under him, his own performance suffered, and Speaker finished with a .296 average, the only time he ever hit below .300 while playing regularly.

In 1920 he was brilliant. He coaxed outstanding years out of his pitchers, platooned half his lineup, and when star shortstop Ray Chapman was killed by a pitched ball Speaker plugged in rookie Joe Sewell. Speaker was also fortunate to have a superb center fielder named Speaker, who hit .388 with 107 RBIs. Cleveland won its first American League pennant by edging the Yankees and White Sox, who had eight players indicted because of the Black Sox scandal in the closing days of the season. Then, in a World Series that produced the first Series grand slam, the first Series home run by a pitcher, and the first unassisted triple play in a Series, the Tribe downed Brooklyn to become world champions.

Speaker continued to manage Cleveland through 1926. Although he didn't win another pennant, he had only two losing seasons. Several of his best seasons with a bat came during this period. In 1923 at age 35 he hit .380 with a career-high 130 RBIs. In 1925 he recorded a career-best .389 average.

Following the 1926 season a disgruntled former teammate accused Speaker and Ty Cobb of fixing a game back in 1919, the year of the Black Sox threw the World Series. Commissioner Kenesaw Mountain Landis investigated and gave both men a clean bill of health; but in the meantime Speaker and Cobb, Detroit's player-manager, were released by their clubs. Speaker signed with Washington and hit .327 in 1927. He finished his career the next year as a sub on Connie Mack's Philadelphia Athletics; Cobb also finished his career on Mack's bench in Philadelphia.

Speaker managed for a couple of seasons in the minors, and then became a broadcaster in Kansas City. After World War II he coached for Cleveland. His special project was Larry Doby, who played second base in the Negro Leagues. With Speaker's help, Doby became one of the top center fielders in the American League.

Speaker was elected to the Hall of Fame in 1937. His plaque states that he was "the greatest center fielder of his day." Many would change the last three words to "ever."

Chris Speier

Speier, Chris Edward **SS-3B-2B**

1971–89 B:6/28/1950, Alameda, CA Deb:4/7/1971, SF NL BR/TR 6'1", 182

G	AB	R	H	HR	RBI	OBP	SLG	AVG
2260	7156	770	1759	112	720	.329	.349	.246

Shortstop Chris Speier reached stardom early in his career, being named to the All-Star team from 1972 to 1974. Speier, who had just turned 24 when the 1974 All-Star Game was played, was never again selected to represent his league. He did, however, perform in the majors for 15 more seasons.

Selected in the 11th round by the Washington Senators in the June 1968 free agent draft, Speier remained at the University of Santa Barbara. He signed with the Giants when selected in January 1970. He reached the majors after just one season at Amarillo, where he led Texas League shortstops in putouts and assists.

Speier led National League shortstops in assists in 1972 and in fielding in 1975. Traded to the Expos for shortstop Tim Foli in April 1977, he hit for the cycle for Montreal on July 20, 1978. (He repeated the feat 10 years later with the Giants on July 9, 1988.) He batted .400 in the Divisional Series caused by the 1981 split-season. He played in all 10 Expos postseason games that year.

On September 22, 1982 he drove in eight runs against the Phils. Speier was traded to St. Louis in July 1984, and just a month later was sent to Minnesota. In April 1985 he signed with the Cubs as a free agent. He returned to the Giants the following year. In 1987 he hit two grand slams within the space of five games. That year he won the club's Willie Mac Trophy for inspirational play. In 1999 he was managing the Pacific Coast league's Tucson's Sidewinders.

Jim Spencer

Spencer, James Lloyd **1B–DH**

1968–82 B:7/30/1947, Hanover, PA Deb:9/7/1968, CAL AL BL/TL 6'2", 195

G	AB	R	H	HR	RBI	OBP	SLG	AVG
1553	4908	541	1227	146	599	.310	.387	.250

Jim Spencer was a promising young rookie in 1968 when the California Angels installed him as their regular at first base. An excellent defensive infielder, he had occasional home run power that the Angels hoped would blossom into big league slugging ability. It eventually did, but like many other talented Angels of his era, Spencer had his best years with another team.

Spencer took the first of his two Gold Gloves in 1970. The next year he hit 18 home runs but posted a disappointing .237 batting average. Despite leading the league in fielding percentage two straight years, the Angels tried to convert him to the outfield in 1972. The next year the Angels sent Spencer to the Texas Rangers for first baseman Mike Epstein.

In Texas Spencer improved his hitting to the .270 range, allowing the Rangers to sometimes utilize him as a designated hitter. He stayed with the team until December 1975, when he was traded to the Chicago White Sox. With the South Siders, Spencer won his second Gold Glove and led the American League in fielding average for the fourth time in 1977. When he became a free agent in 1978, the financially beleaguered Sox couldn't afford to keep him, and he signed with the Yankees as a free agent.

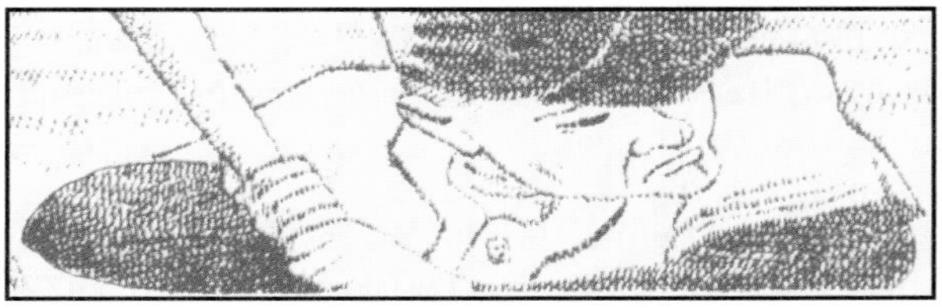

Spencer served in a utility role for the Yankees during their 1978 world championship season, acting as both designated hitter and first baseman. He saw regular action as the club's DH in 1979, and in 1980 he backed up Bob Watson at first and Eric Soderholm as designated hitter. Picked up by the Oakland A's in 1981 as a backup first baseman, Spencer played in that year's postseason as the A's lost the Championship series to the Yankees. He stayed with the A's in a reserve role for 1982 and then retired.

J.G. Taylor Spink

Editor B:12/6/1888, St. Louis, MO D:12/7/1962, Clayton, MO

From the perspective of today's baseball milieu, where everyone from players to batboys views journalists as the enemy, it's hard to grasp the prestige J.G. Taylor Spink enjoyed—and the power he wielded—as editor of *The Sporting News* from 1914 through 1962. Spink was not only the hard-working, profane, sentimental editor of baseball's most important publication; he was the self-appointed guardian of the sport, and moved in the game's most powerful inner circles.

Spink's uncle, Alfred H. Spink, founded *The Sporting News* in 1886. When he brought his brother Charles (Taylor's father) into the business, Charles dumped all sports coverage that didn't deal with baseball and in doing so created the magazine that became known as "The Baseball Bible" for many years. When Charles died in 1914, Taylor took over the editorial reins and built *The Sporting News* into a successful worldwide empire. After Taylor passed away in 1962, his son, C.C. Johnson Spink, guided the publication for 15 years until it was sold.

As soon as Taylor assumed editorial responsibility, he let the world know where he stood. His father had supported challenges to the baseball establishment, including the Brotherhood, the American League (the first National Agreement, which ended the war between the American and National leagues, was written by *TSN* editor Joe Flanner), and the Federal League; Taylor Spink was of a more conservative stripe.

In his editorials he railed against the Federal League, greatly pleasing his mentor, American League president Ban Johnson. (Taylor Spink's son was named after Johnson.) When efforts to resolve the baseball war failed, it was Spink who got Johnson to sit down with Phil Ball of the St. Louis Feds and work out the agreement that ended the last threat to two-league baseball for nearly 50 years.

Four years later, when Johnson felt the Yankees should hire manager Miller Huggins away from

St. Louis, he feared reprisals from the other league. Johnson enlisted Spink to feel Huggins out and ultimately persuade him to become the Yanks field general. And it was Spink who gave the diminutive Huggins the famous sartorial advice before a meeting with New York owner Jake Ruppert: "And lose that damned cloth cap; Ruppert thinks you're a jockey already!"

Driven by Spink's powerful ego and thirst for hard work, *The Sporting News* flourished. He expanded coverage to include the box scores of all major and minor league games—all the way down to D Class ball (although he made the minor leagues pay for the privilege). He created a network of more than 300 stringers to make certain that every tidbit of baseball news in the whole country would be available to his readers. When World War I reduced subscriptions, Spink conjured up a scheme to get the publication into the soldiers' hands free of charge. A generation of American men became avid *Sporting News* readers.

When the major leagues dropped their official Player of the Year awards because of silly rules and politicking, *The Sporting News* and Spink stepped in to fill the void. Spink also initiated a Rookie of the Year Award a season before the Baseball Writers Association did. At the urging of writer Jerome Holtzman, Spink also created the first annual award for relief pitchers.

Spink's editorials were feisty defenses of the baseball establishment, although he occasionally spoke out against poor playing conditions in the minors and other less-than-vital issues. When Babe Ruth fell ill early in 1925, the unsympathetic Spink sniped, "The king has become the jester."

Spink's correspondents were quick to inform him of scuttlebutt. When information about player gambling came his way, he notified league officials. Spink took behavior that might damage the game as a personal affront. Accordingly he was asked by the major leagues to aid in the investigation of the "Black Sox" scandal.

But the one man Spink could not cotton to was Commissioner Kenesaw Mountain Landis. Probably because of Spink's devotion to Ban Johnson, who in Spink's view had been usurped by Landis, Spink spouted off against the Judge in print at every opportunity. Once, he called the estimable commissioner "an erratic and irresponsible despot." Landis, no slouch when it came to invective himself, referred to Spink as a "swine."

In 1947 Spink published *Judge Landis and 25 Years of Baseball*, on the whole an intelligent and evenhanded history of the tumultuous era of baseball under the Judge's reign. But the book also contained a 15-page reprint of an article by Stanley Frank that can only be called an adoring homage to Spink, whom Frank christened in the article as "Mr. Baseball." Frank wrote, "Spink's gripes are the fan's gripes. Hearing him talk about baseball, you can't doubt his authenticity or sincerity as a spokesman." Many suspect that the book was actually written by longtime *TSN* correspondent Fred Lieb.

In his later years Spink testified in favor of baseball retaining its antitrust exemption, and poetically boasted that baseball players were more than just athletes. "Men in baseball represent a symbol," he declared. He shouted down opponents of the reserve clause as "Communistic."

Spink also supported amateur baseball and was a founding board member of the American Baseball Congress. In the year of his death Spink was honored by the Hall of Fame for his exceptional journalistic contributions to the game. The J.G. Taylor Spink Award is now given annually to outstanding baseball journalists.

Paul Splittorff

Splittorff, Paul William **P**

1970–84 B:10/8/1946, Evansville, IN Deb:9/23/1970, KC AL BL/TL 6'3", 210

W	L	PCT	G	SH	IP	BB	SO	ERA
166	143	.537	429	17	2554^{2}	780	1057	3.81

The first 20-game-winning pitcher in Kansas City Royals' history, Paul Splittorff remains among the club's leader in every major pitching category. Although he never again matched his 1973 total of 20 wins, Splittorff was one of the team's most reliable starters. He helped the Royals become one of the most successful new franchises of the expansion era.

From 1976 through 1978 Kansas City took three consecutive division crowns, but each year they lost the American League flag to the Yankees. Splittorff won a game in both the 1976 and 1977 American League Championship Series.

In 1977 he won 16 games and posted the best winning percentage in the league. He won 19 games the following year. In 1980, when Kansas City finally took its first pennant, he started Game 3 of the ALCS, in which the Royal rallied to finally beat the Yankees for the pennant. Although he posted only two wins in seven postseason mound appearances, he never recorded a loss.

Karl Spooner

Spooner, Karl Benjamin **P**

1954–55 B:6/23/1931, Oriskany Falls, NY D:4/10/1984, Vero Beach, FL Deb:9/22/1954, BRO NL BR/TL 6', 185

W	L	PCT	G	SH	IP	BB	SO	ERA
10	6	.625	31	3	116^{2}	47	105	3.09

Karl Spooner's major league debut for Brooklyn late in 1954 was simply brilliant. He beat the pennant-winning Giants in back-to-back shutouts, striking out 27 batters. This remarkable performance made him a celebrity and led to an appearance on *The Ed Sullivan Show*.

But that was it for the fastballing Karl Benjamin Spooner. In spring training the following year, pitcher Johnny Podres was shelled in the second inning, and Dodgers manager Walter Alston replaced him with Spooner. "I just wasn't ready," he recalled later. "What else can I say? I felt something pop as soon as I got out there."

First diagnosed with tendonitis, Spooner actually had torn his rotator cuff. Racked with pain, he nonetheless pitched effectively in 1955, including an appearance in Game 2 of the World Series when he struck out six Yankees in three innings. In Game 6, however, he was knocked out in the first inning. That was his last major league appearance. Spooner returned to the minor leagues in 1956 and waited in vain for his arm to recover.

Chick Stahl

Stahl, Charles Sylvester **OF**

1897–1906 M(1906, 14–26) B:1/10/1873, Avila, IN D:3/28/1907, West Baden, IN Deb:4/19/1897, BOS NL BL/TL 5'10", 160

G	AB	R	H	HR	RBI	OBP	SLG	AVG
1304	5069	858	1546	36	622	.369	.416	.305

Chick Stahl was a star outfielder for the Boston Beaneaters of the National League and the Boston American League franchise that won the first World Series in 1903. Charles Sylvester Stahl came up as a rookie for the Beaneaters in 1897 and hit .354. Four years later he jumped to the Boston Somersets in the new American League (they became the Pilgrims in 1903 and the Red Sox in 1907). Through 1902 he was a career .323 hitter. Injuries limited him to 77 games in 1903, but he batted .303 with three triples in the World Series as the Pilgrims upset the Pirates.

Late in the 1906 season Stahl took over in Boston as player-manager, replacing his best friend, future Hall of Famer Jimmy Collins. The club was 14–26 under Stahl, and finished last by 45½ games. But the collapse of the Red Sox was the least of Stahl's problems in the spring of 1907.

He was married to Julia Harmon of Roxbury, Massachusetts, and was having an affair with a woman named Lulu Ortman, who had twice tried to shoot him after he refused to marry her. When another woman told Stahl that she was pregnant by him, he was unable to bear the strain. He committed suicide on March 28, 1907, in the West Baden Hotel in West Baden, Indiana, by swallowing carbolic acid. Stahl was 34.

Jake Stahl

Stahl, Garland **1B–OF**

1903–10, 1912–13 M(1905–06, 1912–13, 263–270) B:4/13/1879, Elkhart, IL D:9/18/1922, Monrovia, CA Deb:4/20/1903, BOS AL BR/TR 6'2", 195

G	AB	R	H	HR	RBI	OBP	SLG	AVG
981	3425	405	894	31	437	.323	.382	.261

Jake Stahl had left baseball behind and was working in a bank when American League president Ban Johnson induced him to manage the 1912 Red Sox. He delivered a world championship, but the aftermath of the triumph was bitter controversy.

Stahl's 1912 club won 105 games—best in the American League until topped by the 1927 Yankees—and won the pennant by 14 games. During the Series, Red Sox president Jimmy McAleer forced Stahl to pitch Bucky O'Brien (instead of Smokey Joe Wood) in Game 6. Some say McAleer was attempting to unnecessarily prolong the Series—and extend his profits.

O'Brien indeed lost, but Wood started and lost the next day. The Red Sox won the Series on a two-run rally in the 10th inning of Game 8 on an inning prolonged by two miscues by the New York Giants, including the famous "Snodgrass muff"—a dropped flyball by dependable outfielder Fred Snodgrass.

In 1913 player-manager Stahl hurt his ankle and couldn't play first. The team no longer performed with the vigor it had in 1912, and McAleer suspected him of attempting to wrest control of the team. In a stormy session at a Chicago hotel dining room, Stahl was fired and never managed again.

Before managing and banking, Stahl had entered the majors with Boston in 1903 and was sold to Washington in January 1904, where he became player-manager in 1905. In March 1907, Stahl was sold to the White Sox, but refused to report and was instead sold to the New York Highlanders. In July 1908 the Red Sox re-acquired Stahl. Even though he led American League batters with 10 home runs in 1910, he retired at season's end. When he returned to the club as player-manager in 1912, he was induced in part by a share of stock in the club.

Gerry Staley

Staley, Gerald Lee **P**

1947–61 B:8/21/1920, Brush Prairie, WA
Deb:4/20/1947, STL NL BR/TR 6', 195

W	L	PCT	G	SV	IP	BB	SO	ERA
134	111	.547	640	61	1981^{2}	529	727	3.70

"Go-Go" White Sox reliever Gerry Staley nailed down Chicago's 1959 pennant by inducing Cleveland's Vic Power to hit to shortstop Luis Aparicio for a bases-loaded double play. It was the first White Sox pennant in 40 years.

Staley had been a successful starter during the early part of his major league career, mostly with the Cardinals. His best season was 1953, when he posted an 18–9 record and was named to the National League All-Star squad. But when his record slipped in 1954 he was sent packing. In May 1956 the Yankees released Staley to the White Sox on waivers, and manager Marty Marion converted him into a reliever. "I'd played with Marty, and Marty knew what I could and I couldn't do," Staley said.

The righthander sometimes threw a knuckleball but relied mainly on a slider. Staley and his roommate, Turk Lown, together formed the steady bullpen that helped the Sox win the 1959 pennant. Staley pitched in four games in the Series, picking up a save and a loss as the Los Angeles Dodgers beat Chicago in six games.

The following year he won 13 games out of bullpen and was named to his third All-Star team. That was it for Staley. He pitched ineffectively for three different teams in 1961 and left the majors after the season. He later coached at Portland and became superintendent for parks and recreation in Clark County, Washington.

Harry Staley

Staley, Henry Eli **P**

1888–95 B:11/3/1866, Jacksonville, IL. D:1/12/1910, Battle Creek, MI Deb:6/23/1888, PIT NL BR/TR 5'10", 175

W	L	PCT	G	SH	IP	BB	SO	ERA
136	119	.533	283	10	2269	601	746	3.80

An 1890 *Sporting Life* portrait of Harry Staley was accompanied by the caption, "the hated pitcher of the Pittsburgh Players' League Club." One can only assume this was written from the standpoint of the opposing batsmen of the league, who managed only a .290 on-base percentage against him, lowest in the circuit.

Staley's career started in the National League with Pittsburgh at age 22. He was 12–12 as a rookie and 21–26 in his first full season. Jumping to the Players' League for its one season, Staley went 21–25. He returned to the Pirates in 1891 and was promptly shipped to Boston. Staley won 20 games in 30 starts, and again recorded the lowest opposition on-base percentage at .290.

In 1892 Staley again won 20 games and added another win in Boston's "World Series" sweep of Cleveland. It was downhill from there, as Staley slipped to 18–10 and 12–10 in the first two seasons the pitching distance was moved to 60 feet 6 inches. He finished his career in St. Louis. Of his 136 career wins, 106 came in a five-year span. Staley died at age 43 of complications from surgery.

George Stallings

Stallings, George Tweedy **C–1B**

1890, 1897–98 M(1897–98, 1901, 1909–10, 1913–1920, 879–898) B:11/17/1867, Augusta, GA D:5/13/1929, Haddock, GA Deb:5/22/1890, BRO NL BR/TR 6'1", 187

G	AB	R	H	HR	RBI	OBP	SLG	AVG
7	20	3	2	0	0	.182	.150	.100

George Tweedy Stallings was called "the Miracle Man" after managing the Boston Braves from last place in the middle of the 1914 season to a world championship. This spectacular feat of leadership crowned his career. As late as July 15 the Braves were in last place—a position they had occupied on merit from 1909 through 1912. But in 1914 they were not really out of the race, never falling more than 11½ games behind. In mid-July, Stallings modified his usual caustic and profane personality into a softer, more positive style. He told his team they could not lose, and, surprisingly, they began to win.

Stallings himself described the team as, "one .300 hitter, the worst outfield that ever flirted with sudden death, three pitchers, and a good working combination around second base." While it was true that outfielder Joe Connolly was the only regular to top .300, Stallings, one of the first managers to platoon successfully, achieved excellent results by shuffling his six outfielders. The pitching load was carried by Dick Rudolph at 27–10, Seattle Bill James at 26–7, and Lefty Tyler at 16–14. The double-play combination of veteran Johnny Evers and young Rabbit Maranville performed brilliantly and kept the whole team motivated.

By August, the Braves caught the New York Giants for first place, and after weeks of exchanging the lead, Boston finally clinched the pennant. They were heavy underdogs in the World Series against the returning champion Philadelphia Athletics, but won four straight games to complete "the miracle."

Stallings was a graduate of Virginia Military Institute and later a student at the College of Physicians and Surgeons in Baltimore. A catcher and first baseman, his entire major league playing career consisted of four games with Brooklyn in 1890 and three games when he was manager of the Philadelphia Phillies in 1897–98, his first major league managerial job. It eventually evaporated in a player revolt. One of the players told the press, "We are fed up with the way Stallings has been riding us, and we decided we had enough of him and would regard him as our manager no longer. For weeks he's been handling us like a lot of cattle."

Stallings was a cultured southern gentleman off the field but an unspeakably profane monomaniac in the dugout. Some considered his use of vicious invective even more devastating than John McGraw's. His superstitions were famous. He could not abide peanut shells or pieces of torn paper, and opponents drove him into a rage by littering deliberately in front of the dugout. When something good occurred for his team, he would freeze in his position until his luck changed, believing that by doing this he could prolong the good luck. One day he was just leaning over to pick up a piece of paper when one of his Braves got a hit. He held that position through a 10-hit rally and then was carried from the field.

The Detroit Tigers' first manager in 1901, Stallings first received wide acclaim after taking the New York Highlanders to second place in 1910. However, Hal Chase undermined him to the team owner, and Stallings resigned. He became Braves manager in 1913 and the club finished fifth, a remarkable accomplishment in itself. The Braves finished second and third in the seasons after the "miracle" year and then dropped to the second division. Stallings was a fine manager, but the team lacked first-rate players. He retired in 1920.

On his deathbed in 1929, Stallings was supposedly asked what ruined his heart. He sighed and said, "Oh, those bases on balls!" Then he groaned and turned his face to the wall.

Eddie Stanky

Stanky, Edward Raymond **2B–SS**

1943–53 M(1952–55, 1966, 1977, 879–898)
B:9/3/1916, Philadelphia, PA D:6/6/1999, Daphne, AL
Deb:4/21/1943, CHI NL BR/TR 5'8", 170

G	AB	R	H	HR	RBI	OBP	SLG	AVG
1259	4301	811	1154	29	364	.410	.348	.268

Branch Rickey once said that Eddie Stanky "can't hit, he can't run, he can't field, he can't throw. He can't do a goddamn thing—but beat you." The fiery little infielder with a knack for drawing walks was nicknamed "the Brat." He went to the World Series with three different teams and, according to many accounts, made life miserable for opponents and teammates alike.

Although Edward Raymond Stanky hit only .243 during his senior year at Northeast High School in Philadelphia, he was signed by the Athletics and sent to Greenville of the East Dixie League. After a few months he wanted to come home and wired his mother for train fare. She refused to send her son the money and told him not to come back home because she didn't want quitters in the family. Stanky cried for hours but resolved not to quit.

He played for several teams without distinction. Macon manager Milt Stock made Stanky his leadoff hitter and influenced Stanky to be more patient at the plate. Stanky married Stock's daughter, Dickie, but his own father-in-law traded him to Milwaukee. In his new surroundings, with his new wife, Stanky hit .342, led the American Association in doubles and runs scored, and won the Most Valuable Player Award.

Stanky got his big break in 1943. The righthanded hitter had lost the hearing in his left ear after three separate beanings and was excused from service duty. Charlie Grimm, his manager in Milwaukee, took over the Cubs and promoted the 26-year-old second baseman to the big leagues. Stanky played 142 games for the Cubs in 1943, hitting .245 with 15 doubles, 92 runs, 92 walks, and 47 RBIs. In 510 at bats he didn't hit a single home run.

The Cubs traded Stanky to the Dodgers in June 1944. In three full seasons in Brooklyn Stanky led the league in walks twice, in on-base percentage once, and in runs scored once. In both 1945 and 1946 he had more walks than hits. He repeated the feat in 1951, and is the only player in major league history to record more hits than walks in three separate seasons. The Dodgers went to the World Series in 1947, but lost to the Yankees in seven games.

When Jackie Robinson broke baseball's color barrier in 1947, Stanky objected, but he defended Robinson on the field. The Dodgers moved Robinson to second base and traded Stanky to the Boston Braves before the 1948 season.

Although he spent two months on the disabled list with a broken ankle suffered in a collision with Brooklyn catcher Bruce Edwards, Stanky helped the Braves win a pennant in 1948. He hit a career-high .320 during the season, then walked seven times in the World Series for a .524 on-base percentage. Cleveland beat Boston in six games.

There was dissension in the Braves clubhouse in 1949, and some felt that Stanky's outspoken manner had contributed to manager Billy Southworth's eventual breakdown. Despite hitting .285 that year, Stanky was traded to the New York Giants after the season, where he was reunited with manager Leo Durocher, his former skipper with the Dodgers.

Stanky and Durocher had seemed to inspire each other in Brooklyn, and it happened again in New York. In 1950 Stanky hit .300 with eight homers and 115 runs and led the league with 144 walks and a .460 on-base percentage. On June 22 and August 30, Stanky walked twice in the same inning. Although other players have also drawn two bases on balls in the same inning, no player except Stanky has done it twice in the same season.

In 1951 Stanky slammed a career-high 14 homers and was part of "The Miracle of Coogan's Bluff." After Bobby Thomson hit his dramatic three-run homer to win the National League pennant, Stanky celebrated by hopping on Durocher's back in the third base coaching box. But Stanky was disappointed in his third World Series in as many tries, as the Yankees beat the Giants in six games.

Traded to the Cardinals in December 1951, he became their playing manager. The team finished third in 1952, and Stanky won *The Sporting News* Manager of the Year honors. He retired as a player after the 1953 season with a career .268 batting average.

Stanky was far from popular with his players. "I never felt as bad when my father died as I did when I was released by the Cardinals," confided Enos Slaughter. "The Cards were all fine people, except one. That was Eddie Stanky." Stanky was fired in May 1955.

He managed in the minor leagues in 1956 and coached for Cleveland in 1957 and 1958. Stanky was assistant to the general manager in St. Louis from 1959 through 1964 and served as the Mets' farm director in 1965. Named White Sox manager in 1966, he finished fourth that season. Chicago won 89 games in 1967, but Stanky made derogatory remarks about Boston's Carl Yastrzemski during the 1967 pennant race that have been credited by some with lighting a fire under Yastrzemski and helping the Red Sox to a pennant. He was fired again in 1968. Stanky then coached at the University of South Alabama, racking up 14 winning seasons, transforming the Jaguars into a power, and sending 40 players to the pro ranks.

He interrupted his tenure at South Alabama with a return to the majors in 1977, when he replaced Frank Lucchesi as Rangers' manager. In one of the briefest managerial tenures of all time, the usually tenacious Stanky won his first game in Texas and abruptly returned to Alabama. He said he was not up to the task. His wife later explained that Stanky had been homesick and his father was ill. Stanky himself underwent open heart surgery in 1980. He retired in 1983, without a single losing season at Southern Alabama. He died of heart failure on June 6, 1999 at his home in Daphne, Alabama.

Bob Stanley

Stanley, Robert William **P**

1977–89 B:11/10/1954, Portland, ME Deb:04/16/1977, BOS AL BR/TR 6'4", 215

W	L	PCT	G	SV	IP	BB	SO	ERA
115	97	.542	637	132	1707	471	693	3.64

Resilient Bob Stanley was an all-around hurler. Long relief, short relief, spot starter—whatever was needed, Stanley and his seemingly indestructible right arm provided it. He endured all the highs and lows of the Red Sox from 1977 to 1989: he recorded one of the highest winning percentages in major league history in 1978, and he delivered the wild pitch that allowed the Mets to tie Game 6 of the 1986 World Series.

Stanley was Boston's first pick in the secondary phase of the January 1974 draft and was a starter during his three years in the minors. As a rookie in 1977 Stanley was 8–7 in 41 games, including 13 starts. His career took off in 1978, when he went 15–2 with a 2.60 ERA and 10 saves in 53 games, 50 of them in relief. His .882 winning percentage that year was the eighth highest of the 20th century.

When the Red Sox needed a starter in 1979, Stanley responded by going 16–12 with four shutouts in 40 games, 30 of them starts. But after posting a 10–8 record in 52 games (with 17 starts) in 1980, he had only two starts in the next six seasons. Not an exceptional closer—when he recorded a career-high 33 saves in 1983 he also blew 14 opportunities—he was often the best the Red Sox had, and he was always willing to go the extra mile. For example, in 1982 he pitched a remarkable 168⅓ innings in 48 relief appearances, or close to four innings per appearance.

In 1985 he started pitching more often but facing fewer hitters. That following year he earned a place in the annals of Boston World Series infamy. The Red Sox were only one strike away from winning their first World Series since 1918. But then, with a 2–2 count on Mookie Wilson, Stanley wild-pitched the tying run home, even though many people thought catcher Rich Gedman should have been charged with a passed ball. Wilson poked Stanley's 3–2 sinker through Bill Buckner's legs, and Ray Knight scored the winning run. The Mets went on to take Game 7 and the world championship.

In 1987 Stanley moved back into the rotation for 20 starts but went 4–15 with a 5.01 ERA. He was put on the disabled list for the first time in his career with a sore shoulder. He spent two more seasons as a spare part in the Boston bullpen and retired in 1989 with a 115–97 record, a team-record 132 saves, and the Red Sox career record for appearances, with 637.

Mickey Stanley

Stanley, Mitchell Jack **OF–1B**

1964–77 B:7/20/1942, Grand Rapids, MI
Deb:9/13/1964, DET AL BR/TR 6'1", 195

G	AB	R	H	HR	RBI	OBP	SLG	AVG
1516	5022	641	1243	117	500	.300	.377	.248

One of the great defensive outfielders of the modern era, Mickey Stanley made no errors in both 1968 and 1970 while playing in more than 140 games each year. He won Gold Glove Awards in both of those seasons and also in 1969 and 1973. During his 15-year career he recorded errorless streaks of 164 and 220 games. Yet this great defensive outfielder is best remembered as a World Series shortstop.

Stanley was the focal point of an unusual managerial strategy in the 1968 World Series. Tigers manager Mayo Smith, looking to add a bat to his lineup to counter Cardinals pitching—and also as a sentimental gesture toward Al Kaline, who had never appeared in a Series in his 15 years with Detroit—moved Stanley to shortstop and installed Kaline in the outfield for the Series.

The move paid off: Stanley made no important errors while Kaline batted .379 and drove in eight runs to help the Tigers win their first world championship since 1945. Regular shortstop Ray Oyler, whose anemic .135 average had helped Smith decide to pull the daring move with Stanley, finished each of Detroit's four Series victories as a defensive replacement while Stanley moved back to the outfield.

Mike Stanley

Stanley, Robert Michael **C–DH–1B**

1986–* B:6/25/1963 Ft. Lauderdale, FL Deb:6/24/1986,
TEX AL BR/TR 6'1", 185

G	AB	R	H	HR	RBI	OBP	SLG	AVG
1377	3940	592	1071	173	656	.376	.460	.272

Through six seasons of part-time catching duty with the Texas Rangers, Mike Stanley's major accomplishment was to catch Nolan Ryan's seventh and final no-hitter in 1991. Joining the New York Yankees, Stanley finally earned an everyday role in 1993 and came through with a .305 average and 26 home runs. He earned an All-Star selection in 1995, and hit three home runs against Cleveland in the first game of an August doubleheader. He then batted .313 with a homer in New York's riveting loss to Seattle in the Division Series.

The Yankees wanted a better receiver behind the plate, and so did Boston; the Red Sox signed Stanley and played him at first base and as a designated hitter. The Yankees got Stanley back in a trade for the stretch run. He went 3-for-4 off the bench in New York's 1997 Division Series loss to Cleveland.

Stanley signed with Toronto in 1998, but a midsummer trade sent him back to Boston. He finished 1998 with a career-high 29 homers. Stanley, now a first baseman, added 19 homers and 72 RBIs for the Sox in 1999 as he reached the postseason for the fourth time.

Willie Stargell

Stargell, Wilver Dornel **OF–1B**

1962–82 B:3/6/1940, Earlsboro, OK Deb:9/16/1962,
PIT NL BL/TL 6'2½", 225

G	AB	R	H	HR	RBI	OBP	SLG	AVG
2360	7927	1195	2232	475	1540	.363	.529	.282

Willie Stargell was at the center of the Pittsburgh Pirates offense for nearly 20 years. It was his class, decency, ebullience, and leadership that had the greatest influence on his team's performance. His most famous saying was, "The umpire says 'Play ball,' not 'Work ball.'" After Roberto Clemente's tragic death in 1972, Stargell reluctantly assumed the role of team leader. Before long he relished it.

Stargell played the game with a combination of professional intensity and childlike joy. His silly pregame catches with Manny Sanguillen were worth the price of admission. During one game later in Stargell's career, he was given the steal sign. When it became obvious he was going to be called out by yards, he signaled for a time out.

Wilver Stargell has lived his life with the poise and dignity of one who has witnessed human behavior at its worst and has decided to rise above it. While playing in Texas and New Mexico at age 18 he became disillusioned by the racism surrounding him. He nearly quit the game after a rabid fan held a shotgun to his head and threatened to kill him if he got a hit that night. After a dispiriting performance in the 1971 World Series Willie told writer Roger Angell, who followed baseball for *The New Yorker*, "There's a time in a man's life when he has to decide if he's going to be a man."

In his rookie season in 1963 Stargell hit .243 with 11 homers in 304 at bats. Splitting his play between the outfield and first base in 1964, he batted 421 times and belted 21 homers, including the first home run ever hit at Shea Stadium.

He won the regular left field job the next year, and he responded with 27 homers and the first of five 100-RBI seasons. He averaged 27 homers in cavernous Forbes Field during the next five seasons, including seven shots over the 86-foot high stands in right field. In the park's 61-year history that feat was accomplished only 18 times.

When the Pirates moved to Three Rivers Stadium in June 1970 Stargell finally had a park suited to his power game. He hit the first Pirates homer there and finished the season with 31. In one game that season he tied a major league record with five extra-base hits. The Pirates won their division, although they were swept by the Reds in the National League Championship Series.

The next season Stargell took full advantage of his new home. He hit a career-high 48 homers to lead the National League while batting .295, with 125 RBIs for the NL East champs. His record-setting 11 home runs in April included two three-homer games. Stargell also led the league with 154 strikeouts, and finished his career with 1,936—the all-time leader until Reggie Jackson passed him.

The Bucs won the NLCS as well as the World Series, as Clemente put on a clinic. Stargell, however, had just five hits and only one RBI in the Series after going 0-for-14 in the NLCS.

About this time Stargell opened a fried chicken restaurant in Pittsburgh's Hill District. As a promotional idea, the chicken was free for anyone who was waiting in line to order when Stargell hit a home run. Pirates broadcaster Bob Prince began to call for him to homer with the words, "Come on, Wilver. Let's spread some chicken on the Hill."

Stargell assembled a .293 average, 33 homers, and 112 RBIs as the Pirates again won the NL East in 1972. But Stargell and his teammates were forced to swallow a bitter pill that winter. Clemente died in a plane crash on New Year's Eve 1972, while trying to deliver relief supplies to Nicaraguan earthquake victims. Clemente's proud, almost regal, style of play had been the heart of the Pirates for years. Adding to the team's problems was the replacement of Danny Murtaugh, their easygoing manager, by the intense Bill Virdon.

Stargell rose to the occasion. In a year when no team seemed to want to win the NL East (the Mets finally prevailed with an 82–79 record), he almost single-handedly yanked the Bucs into the playoffs. Despite being moved back to the outfield, then returned to first base, he hit .299 and led the league in slugging, doubles, homers (44), and RBIs (119). But Pete Rose hit .338 that year with 230 hits for the division-champion Reds, and Stargell finished second in the MVP voting again.

Stargell averaged 25 homers and 93 RBIs in the next two seasons as the Pirates won their division but lost the NLCS to the Dodgers and the Reds. Then came 1976 and 1977, nightmare years for Stargell. In 1976 his wife, Delores, was diagnosed with a blood clot on her brain; a distracted Stargell hit .257 with 65 RBIs. The next year he tried to break up a fight on the field and ended up with a pinched nerve in his left elbow that ended his season and his streak of 13 consecutive years of hitting at least 20 homers.

The 1978 season was a turnaround for both the Pirates and also Stargell. He hit .295 with 28 homers and 97 RBIs and won the NL Comeback Player of the Year Award. The Pirates chased the Phillies down to the wire before finishing 1½ games back.

The Bucs picked up in 1979 where they had left off the year before. They won one clutch game after another to hold off the Expos and clinched the division on the last day of the season. In a key September series a wild throw by Stargell cost the Bucs a game. "I saw the deep man," Stargell joked. "He was wide open, but I overthrew him."

The next day Stargell slugged a monstrous home run to all but clinch the pennant. He had only 424 at bats that season—he was, after all, 39—but his 32 homers and 82 RBIs were good enough for him to be named National League co-MVP, with Keith Hernandez of the Cardinals. It was the first time the award had ever ended in a tie and Stargell was the oldest man ever to be named MVP.

Then came the 1979 NLCS and World Series. Just as Clemente took charge in 1971, Stargell rose to the occasion this time. He hit .455 in the NLCS. His heroics against the Reds included a three-run homer in the 11th inning to win Game 1, a double and a single in the 3–2 Game 2 victory, and a homer, a double, and three RBIs in Game 3.

In the World Series the Pirates had to fight back from a 3–1 deficit to force a seventh game with the Orioles. Trailing 1–0 in the sixth inning, Stargell hit a game-winning, two-run homer off Scott McGregor. He hit .400 for the Series with three homers, seven RBIs, and four doubles, setting a Series record with 25 total bases. He also achieved a rare triple coup by being named MVP of the NLCS and of World Series to go with his regular-season MVP award. In addition he was *The Sporting News* Man of the Year and the *Sports Illustrated* Co-Sportsman of the Year, with local Steelers quarterback Terry Bradshaw.

He won all these honors for more than just his superb play. Stargell's leadership was the one ingredient the Pirates could not have done without. When a player had a personal problem, he went to Stargell. The team adopted Sister Sledge's disco hit "We Are Family" as their anthem, and for one year, at least, it all made sense. The small gold stars he

awarded to teammates for spirited play even made the Bucs' stovepipe hats look stylish.

Stargell was a true father figure. In the eighth inning of Game 7 of the Series, with the Bucs up 2–1 and two Orioles on base, Stargell walked to the mound to speak to reliever Kent Tekulve. At bat was Terry Crowley, whose double off Tekulve had cost the Bucs Game 4. "Teke," Stargell said, "show the people why you're the best in the National League. And if you don't think you can do that, you play first and I'll pitch." Crowley grounded out.

After the glory of 1979 Stargell's body began to slow down. The slugger retired in 1982, and on September 6, 1982, the team and the city honored him with a day at Three Rivers—an outpouring of affection for the man they called "Pops." But in the afternoon a fan with a different view of the team threw batteries at Dave Parker. The contrast on that one day illustrated that the Pirates' glory years were gone, to be followed by almost a decade of dismal performances and drug use. The team that had won six division titles in the 1970s simply fell apart.

During the abysmal 1985 season, a year of drug trials, bad play, and the inability of the Galbreath family to sell the team, Pirates management tried to resurrect some of the better times. They brought back legendary announcer Bob Prince, whose firing 10 years earlier had cost the team both attendance and prestige, and hired Stargell to coach first base. It didn't help. When the new owners dumped manager Chuck Tanner, he took Stargell with him as a coach to Atlanta. A longtime civic leader and founder of the Stargell Foundation to fight sickle-cell anemia, he continued his philanthropic efforts after he left baseball.

When Stargell retired he was the Pirates' career leader in home runs (475), RBIs (1,540), and eight other categories, and despite all the strikeouts, he finished with a .282 batting average. He hit the first four balls into the right field upper deck at Three Rivers Stadium, and was the only person in the 20th century to have hit two fair balls out of Dodger Stadium. As Dodgers hurler Don Sutton once said, "He doesn't just hit pitchers. He takes away their dignity."

Chuck Tanner said, "Having Willie Stargell on your ballclub is like having a diamond ring on your finger." Roger Angell simply described him as "the most admired and admirable player of his time." Stargell was inducted into the Hall of Fame in 1988, his first year of eligibility.

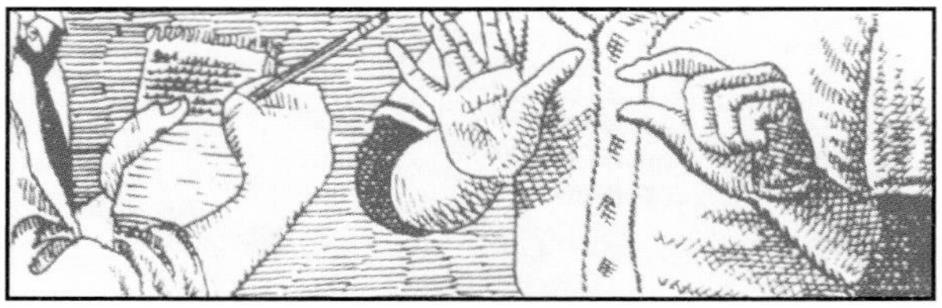

Joe Start

Start, Joseph **1B**

1871–86 B:10/14/1842, New York, NY D:3/27/1927, Providence, RI Deb:5/18/1871, MUT NA BL/TL 5'9", 165

G	AB	R	H	HR	RBI	OBP	SLG	AVG
798	3433	590	1031	7	357	.330	.370	.300

In an era when putouts on even the simplest plays could not always be taken for granted, durable first baseman Joe Start earned the nickname "Old Reliable" for his sure-handed approach to the game. He may also have been the first to play away from first base, although Charles Comiskey is often credited with that innovation. Start ranks high in putouts per game and total chances per game. Playing without a glove, "Rocks" was better than most in holding on to even the most errant throws.

Start began his career prior to the founding of the first professional league. He played with the Enterprise club in 1860–1861, and the Atlantics from 1862 to 1870, helping them to undefeated seasons in 1864 and 1865. He turned professional around 1867. In 1871 the Atlantics returned to amateur status and Start shifted over to the New York Mutuals, then in the new National Association.

When the National League replaced the NA, Start played a year each in New York and Hartford before settling in with the Providence Grays for seven years. He finished with a season in Washington. Start returned to the Providence area and operated a hotel.

Jigger Statz

Statz, Arnold John **OF**

1919–20, 1922, 1927–28 B:10/20/1897, Waukegan, IL D:3/16/1988, Corona Del Mar, CA Deb:7/30/1919, NY NL BR/TR 5'7½", 150

G	AB	R	H	HR	RBI	OBP	SLG	AVG
683	2585	376	737	17	215	.337	.373	.285

Veteran minor leaguer Jigger Statz spent his entire 18-season bush league career with just one club, the Pacific Coast League's Los Angeles Angels. In the course of that career he set a number of minor league and PCL records, most of which will probably never be broken. His 18 seasons with Los Angeles are the minor league record for years with one club. He holds career PCL records for games (2,790), runs (1,996), hits (3,356) doubles (595) and triples (137). He is fourth on the all-time minor league list for runs scored and sixth in hits.

Statz actually began his career in the majors, joining John McGraw's New York Giants in midseason 1919, fresh out of Holy Cross College. He played with three other major league clubs, but whenever he went to the minors it was to Los Angeles. Statz was an excellent baserunner and on September 16, 1934, stole six bases. He led the Pacific Coast League in stolen bases in 1931 (45), 1935 (53), and 1936 (43). In 1932 Statz, who had a lifetime .315 average with Los Angeles, won the first-ever Pacific Coast League Most Valuable Player Award as he hit .347 and scored a league-leading 153 runs.

In 1934 Statz was part of one of the PCL's finest clubs. The Angels went 137–50 for a .733 won-lost percentage. Statz hit .324 and stole a career high 61 bases. His teammate, right fielder Frank Demaree, won the Triple Crown with 45 home runs, 173 RBIs, and a .383 average. The pitching staff featured three 20-game winners and four others pitchers with over 13 victories.

Statz was also an exceptional fielder and would cut a hole in the palm of his glove so as to obtain a better feel. Any time another Los Angeles outfielder would fail to make a play, frustrated Angels' fans would yell, "Jigger would have had it." He was player-manager of Los Angeles from 1940 through 1942. Arnold John Statz got his nickname from the use of a golf iron called a "jigger." He was reputed to be baseball's best golfer.

Rusty Staub

Staub, Daniel Joseph **OF-DH-1B**

1963–85 B:4/1/1944, New Orleans, LA Deb:4/9/1963, HOU NL BL/TR 6'2", 200

G	AB	R	H	HR	RBI	OBP	SLG	AVG
2951	9720	1189	2716	292	1466	.366	.431	.279

Rusty Staub was a redheaded teen sensation with the expansion Houston Colt .45s, a cultural icon with the Montreal Expos, a blue-collar RBI man with the Detroit Tigers, and a man-about-town with the New York Mets. He played 23 big league seasons and was the first player to collect 500 or more hits with four different clubs—Houston, Montreal, Detroit, and New York.

Daniel Joseph Staub came across his nickname very early. "I wanted to name him Daniel so I could call him Danny for short," said his mother. "But one of the nurses nicknamed him Rusty for the red fuzz he had all over his head, and it stuck." When Rusty was 3 years old, his father gave him a baseball bat and told him to "swing it."

As a teenager, Staub helped Crescent City Post win the American Legion Championship, defeating the Billings, Montana, club led by a pitcher named Dave McNally. Sixteen big league clubs scouted Staub—even Ted Williams came down to talk to him. He eventually signed with the Houston Colt .45s on September 11, 1961, for $100,000.

Sent to Durham of the Carolina League, Staub batted .293 with 23 home runs. He led Carolina League first basemen in putouts and assists (and errors), and was named league Most Valuable Player. By the following year, 1963, he was a regular with the second-season Houston club at age 19. Staub hit his first major league home run on June 3, 1963, off Don Drysdale at Colt Stadium. But the rookie batted only .224, with six homers and 45 RBIs in 513 at bats. After he failed to improve his numbers during the first half of 1964, he was demoted to Oklahoma City. "It might have been the end of the world," Staub recalled. "I bit my lip all the way to the airport."

At Oklahoma City, Staub batted .314, with 20 homers and 45 RBIs in 71 games. That earned him a ticket back to Houston. "I had to decide what kind of hitter I was going to be," Staub later said. "Now I go up to bat with the idea of hitting the ball where it's pitched and hitting it on a line or on the ground. I tell myself to stay back and wait until I see the pitch. When I do I attack it. Snap! One reflex action—the same every time."

Staub, who would later become a restaurateur, began to develop his cooking skills while playing instructional ball in Scottsdale, Arizona. He and his roommates didn't have enough money to eat in restaurants all the time. "So I wrote a letter to my mother," he said, "and she sent me recipes and cooking hints."

Back in Houston, Staub got his batting average and run production up, batting .333 with 74 RBIs and a league-leading 44 doubles in 1967. In January 1969 the Colts traded him to Montreal for Donn Clendenon and Jesus Alou. Clendenon, however, refused to report, and the deal wasn't completed until April when Montreal sent pitchers Jack Billingham and Skip Guinn, along with $100,000, to Houston.

Staub became a star in Montreal. Nicknamed "le Grande Orange," he was now a mature 25-year-old. His home run production, which had never topped 14 in Houston, reached 29 in 1969 and 30 in 1970. On August 1, 1970, he hit four homers in a doubleheader. After he batted .311, with 19 homers and 97 RBIs, in 1971, the Expos traded him to the Mets at the start of the 1972 season for Ken Singleton, Tim Foli, and Mike Jorgenson.

A big part of the Mets' 1973 league championship season, Staub hit .279 with 15 homers and 76 RBIs. Playing with an injured shoulder he batted only .200 in the Mets' five-game victory over the Reds in the Championship Series, but contributed three homers and five RBIs. In the World Series he hit .423, led both clubs with 11 hits, and tied Reggie Jackson for most RBIs, with six. But the Mets lost in seven games.

In 1975 Staub set a Mets record by driving in 105 runs, a mark not broken until Howard Johnson knocked in 117 runs in 1991. After that season the Mets made a regrettable deal, sending Staub to Detroit for Mickey Lolich. Staub continued in an RBI groove for the Tigers. He drove in 96 in 1976, 101 in 1977, and 121 in 1978. He was named designated hitter on *The Sporting News* AL All-Star team in 1978.

Detroit sold Staub back to Montreal in July 1979 and then traded him to Texas for two infielders before the 1980 season. He became a free agent after the 1980 season and signed again with the Mets. Staub had opened Rusty's Restaurant in New York City in March 1977, so he was more than happy to return to the Big Apple.

Staub spent his last five seasons with the Mets as a part-time player and pinch hitter extraordinaire. In 1983 he collected a club-record 24 pinch hits, one shy of the major league record. They included eight in a row, one short of the big league mark. He became the 11th player to record 100 career pinch hits. When he finished his playing days in 1985, he had 2,716 career hits.

Staub began a long-running broadcasting career with the Mets in 1986. "Sure, I'll miss playing, but I think I'm ready for this," he said. "Let's face it, I've already had three last seasons." In 1986 Staub and Bud Harrelson were the first players inducted into the New York Mets Hall of Fame. In 1992 the Montreal Expos retired his uniform No. 10.

Turkey Stearnes

Stearnes, Norman Thomas **OF-1B**
Negro Leagues Player (1923–42) B:5/8/1901, Nashville, TN D:9/41979, Detroit, MI BL/TL 6', 175

According to Satchel Paige, Turkey Stearnes was "one of the greatest hitters we ever had. He was as good as anybody who ever played ball." Fellow Hall of Famer Cool Papa Bell once declared, "If they don't put Turkey Stearnes in the Hall of Fame, they shouldn't put anybody in. In March 2000 the Veterans Committee finally heeded the words of Papa Bell and elected Turkey Stearnes to the Hall of Fame.

A slugger who batted from the left side, Norman Thomas Stearnes picked up his nickname as a kid because of the unusual way he ran. Stearnes batted from an uncommonly open stance with his right heel twisted and his big toe up. He played for five teams from 1923 to 1940 and smacked 181 career homers in 903 games, finishing with a .352 career average.

Stearnes began with the Detroit Stars in 1923 and spent seven years with the club, hitting .365 as a rookie, .375 in 1926, and .378 in 1929. He also averaged 18 homers a year in seasons that ranged from 60 to 88 games. His high was 1928, when he smacked 24 in 82 games.

When the Stars encountered financial difficulty in 1931, Stearnes moved on and eventually ended up playing for the Chicago American Giants for four years. He helped the Giants to the pennant in two of those years. Stearnes' last four years on a major Negro League team were spent with the Kansas City Monarchs, and once again he was able to contribute towards pennants, which the Monarchs captured in both 1940 and 1941. In his 30s Stearnes was still good enough to play in four of the first five East-West Games, black baseball's biggest attraction.

John Stearns

Stearns, John Hardin **C**
1974–84 B:8/21/1951, Denver, CO Deb:9/22/1974, PHI NL BR/TR 6', 185

G	AB	R	H	HR	RBI	OBP	SLG	AVG
810	2681	334	696	46	312	.345	.375	.260

John Stearns, the second pick in the country in the 1973 draft, arrived in New York as an unknown player in a trade involving one of the most popular Mets. Tug McGraw, whose 1973 rallying cry, "Ya Gotta Believe," helped launch the Mets to an unlikely pennant, was sent to the Phillies with two other players in December 1974 for Del Unser, Mac Scarce, and Stearns. McGraw helped the Phillies go to the playoffs six times and win the 1980 World Series. Stearns was a four-time All-Star in New York, but injuries ended his career just as the Mets were about to turn the corner.

"Dude" Stearns was All-Big Eight in baseball and football at the University of Colorado. He always played catcher as if he were part of a goal-line stand. With Pittsburgh Pirates locomotive Dave Parker chugging towards home for the tying run in the ninth inning, the 6-foot 5-inch runner slammed into the 185-pound catcher. Stearns went out to shake the winning pitcher's hand; Parker went on the disabled list with a broken cheekbone.

Stearns had pop with the bat as well. He had 24 or more doubles in each of the five years he played at least 98 games. His most surprising asset was his speed: Stearns broke a 75-year-old record for catchers with 25 stolen bases in 1978. His NL record for catchers lasted for 20 years until surpassed by Pittsburgh's Jason Kendall.

Stearns signed a five-year contract in 1979, and responded with a career-high 131 hits. Stearns already had 25 doubles on July 26, 1980, when a foul tip broke his right index finger. Injuries kept him on the bench for most of the next four years. Stearns retired in spring training of 1986 with Texas.

He started a second career as a coach with the Houston Astros, Milwaukee Brewers, New York Yankees, Cincinnati Reds, and Baltimore Orioles. He also was a broadcaster for ESPN in 1992. He rejoined the Mets as an advance scout in 1999 and was named to the coaching staff in 2000.

Terry Steinbach

Steinbach, Terry Lee **C**

1986–99 B:3/2/1962, New Ulm, MN Deb:9/12/1986, OAK AL BR/TR 6'1", 195

G	AB	R	H	HR	RBI	OBP	SLG	AVG
1546	5369	638	1453	162	745	.329	.420	.271

Catcher Terry Steinbach was often overlooked on an Oakland Athletics team that featured sluggers Mark McGwire and Jose Canseco and ace pitchers Dave Stewart, Bob Welch, and Dennis Eckersley. Steinbach nonetheless won respect for defensive prowess, unmatched toughness, and timely hitting. While one-time roommate McGwire and others worked in the spotlight, Steinbach quietly earned three All-Star selections. When critics claimed he was an unworthy choice to start the 1988 All-Star Game, Steinbach homered and was named the game's Most Valuable Player.

In 1989 when Oakland won its only championship in three straight World Series appearances, Steinbach's seven RBIs paced all hitters during the four-game sweep. In 1996 he finally took center stage with 35 home runs and 100 RBIs. The 34 blasts he hit as a catcher set an American League record for catchers. Despite his newfound pop, he remained one of league's best callers of pitches. Occasionally pitchers from other teams watched videos of A's games for insight on how to face certain hitters.

A free agent after the season, he turned down much bigger offers from the A's, Blue Jays, and Cubs to return to his native Minnesota and suit up for the Twins. Through three seasons full of nagging injuries, he helped guide a young pitching staff through the big league learning curve. The former World Series star earned respect bordering on awe from teammates and baseball people for his tenacity and leadership. He retired after the 1999 season.

George Steinbrenner

Steinbrenner, George M.

Owner (1973–*) B:7/4/1930, Cleveland, OH

Since 1973 George Steinbrenner, the brash, bullying owner of the Yankees, has sided firmly with the long tradition of meddling management who can't keep their hands off the baseball team. And, true to his character, he has meddled more than anyone else. Everything Steinbrenner does he does to excess.

Steinbrenner put together a money-generating empire that begins and ends with the Yankees' coveted logo. Steinbrenner's tactics, however unnerving, have borne fruit. His Yanks of the late 1970s and early 1980s won five division titles in a six-year span. The juggernaut clubs of the late 1990s were not dissimilar from the other Yankees teams that dominated baseball throughout the 20th century.

During his incorrigible and irrepressible tenure in baseball, Steinbrenner has hired some of the savviest players around, and sooner or later humiliated them off the payroll (usually followed by an acerbic exchange in the papers). One of the first owners to take full advantage of the free agent system, he built a team that won back-to-back world championships in 1977 and 1978. Then he threw good money after bad on highly untalented, but expensive, free agents, and his team fell into chaos. The once-proud Yankees became known as the "Bronx Zoo." The 1980s marked the first decade the Yankees hadn't won a World Series since the 1910s, but the franchise rebounded in the 1990s, culminating in an American League-record 111 regular-season wins in 1998 season and a repeat World Series sweep in 1999.

Steinbrenner was the leader of 15 limited partners who bought the Yankees from CBS for $10 million, $3.2 million less than the network had paid nine years earlier. "I won't be active in day-to-day club operations at all," he said at the time. It wasn't long before one partner commented, "Nothing is more limited than being a limited partner of George's."

When Don Baylor was asked why he said he would reject an offer by Steinbrenner to manage the Yanks, he replied, "I came into this game sane, and I want to leave it sane." No Steinbrenner relationship was ever more typical than his mercurial connection with the scrappy Billy Martin, a man he hired five times and fired five times. It was Martin who said of Reggie Jackson and Steinbrenner, "They deserve each other. One's a born liar, the other's convicted."

In 1974, Steinbrenner pleaded guilty to charges of making illegal campaign contributions to Richard Nixon. Commissioner Bowie Kuhn suspended him for two years, then reinstated him after 15 months. In 1990, investigations by the commissioner's office indicated that Steinbrenner had paid a small-time gambler $40,000 to "dig up dirt" on Dave Winfield so that Steinbrenner could back out of his contractual agreement to contribute to Winfield's educational foundation. Commissioner Fay Vincent banned Steinbrenner from the game. Less than three years later, in one of his last acts as commissioner before he got fired, Vincent reinstated the man they called "The Boss."

Back in baseball again in 1993, Steinbrenner lectured the press at spring training with predictions on the season and then made headlines during the regular schedule by threatening to move the Yankees to New Jersey unless the city built him a new stadium in a better part of town. The Yankees remained in the Bronx through the end of the decade, but he brought the Garden State a little closer to Yankee Stadium when he created the YankeeNets in 1999.

Steinbrenner sought the merger between the Yankees and the National Basketball Association franchise when sale talks with Cablevision System Corporation collapsed after the 1998 World Series. By merging, the two teams will have much greater leverage in negotiations for their next broadcast contracts in the lucrative New York cable television market. The Yankees' $486 million, 12-year contract with Cablevision's MSG Network is set to expire after the 2000 season and the Nets' contract with Fox Sports New York, another Cablevision unit, runs out after the 2001–2002 season. As always, Steinbrenner likes to have the chips in front of him.

Harry Steinfeldt

Steinfeldt, Harry M. **3B-2B**
1898–1911 B:9/29/1877, St. Louis, MO D:8/17/1914, Bellevue, KY Deb:4/22/1898, CIN NL BR/TR 5'9½", 180

G	AB	R	H	HR	RBI	OBP	SLG	AVG
1646	5896	758	1576	27	762	.330	.360	.267

Harry Steinfeldt is the answer to one of baseball's most famous trivia questions: Who played third base in the famous Tinker-to-Evers-to-Chance infield? But Steinfeldt was no trivial performer. He made a significant contribution to the success of one of baseball's most famous teams.

He originally planned to be an actor. But he performed so well in a baseball game played by his theatrical troupe that he decided to give it a whirl. In 1898 he joined the Cincinnati Reds and remained their regular third baseman for eight seasons.

Steinfeldt had an unusually strong arm and was sure-handed in the field. A righthanded batter, he hit with some power, and although he usually hit around .250, he was occasionally much better. In 1903 he batted .312 with 83 RBIs and led the National League in doubles. The 1906 season, his first year with the Cubs, also turned out to be his finest year. He hit .327, led the league with 176 hits and 83 RBIs, and topped league third basemen in fielding percentage. He led in fielding percentage again in 1907 and 1910. Steinfeldt helped the Cubs to four pennants and two world championships from 1906 through 1910.

He is the only member of that Cubs infield not in the Hall of Fame: first baseman-manager Frank Chance, second baseman Johnny Evers, and shortstop Joe Tinker were all inducted in 1946. Steinfeldt received one vote for the Hall of Fame on three occasions.

Casey Stengel

Stengel, Charles Dillon **OF**
1912–25 M(1934–43, 1949–60, 1962–65, 1,905–1,842) B:7/30/1890, Kansas City, MO D:9/29/1975, Glendale, CA Deb:9/17/1912, BRO NL BL/TL 5'11", 175

G	AB	R	H	HR	RBI	OBP	SLG	AVG
1277	4288	575	1219	60	535	.356	.410	.284

Casey Stengel, who knew how to tell a story, sometimes started one like this: "Now take Ty Cobb, who is dead at the present time." Or he sometimes said, "There comes a time in everyone's life, and I've had plenty of them." Stengel left behind too many stories, too many laughs, too many outrageous stunts, and too many run-on sentences that started at Point A and meandered through the rest of the alphabet. His version of the English language even developed a name—Stengelese.

From 1910, when he signed his first pro contract, until 1965, when a broken hip forced him to retire as the Mets' manager, "the Ol' Perfessor," was consumed by baseball. He had no hobbies. All that mattered to him was the game and his wife, Edna.

Born in 1890 in Kansas City, Charles Dillon Stengel's nickname Casey was derived from the initials of his hometown—K.C. He began playing semipro ball when he was still in high school. In 1910 he was shipped to Kankakee, a Class C team, for his first pro season. Less than three years later, he was playing for the Brooklyn Dodgers. Besides his gift of gab, he had decent power, above-average speed, and was a good lefthanded hitter.

He spent the winter after his first two years in the minors studying dentistry at Kansas City's Western Dental College and undoubtedly would have become a dentist if he had washed out of baseball. Stengel was the kind of student who stuck a cigar in the corner of a corpse's mouth in anatomy class. He also established his reputation as a clown par excellence in the minors. At Montgomery, his last stop before the majors, he noticed a manhole in right field, and while everyone's attention was elsewhere one day, he pried off the cover and hid under it. When a batter hit a fly ball to right, he popped out and nonchalantly caught the ball.

Arriving in Brooklyn, Stengel came up with a novel solution to some hazing. Tradition prevented rookies from getting batting practice swings, so he handed out business cards as an introduction and requested that he be allowed to take his turn. On July 17, 1912, Stengel made his major league debut and singled four times. He stayed with Brooklyn through 1917, hitting .316 in 1914 and driving in a career-high 73 runs in 1917.

In January 1918 he was traded to the Pirates. In his first game back at Ebbets Field, the home fans booed him unmercifully. Undaunted, he found a sparrow, tucked it under his cap just before his next at bat.

When the crowd let loose with another round of boos, he doffed his cap, and the boos turned to waves of laughter.

After two years in Pittsburgh and a year and a half in Philadelphia, Stengel landed in New York with the Giants. John McGraw, the team's irascible manager, became his greatest influence. McGraw already had the status of a legend, and from him Stengel learned about the virtues of platooning. He came to hate being platooned by McGraw just as much as the Yankees would hate being platooned by Stengel 30 years later. Stengel also learned from McGraw how to motivate players—by sarcasm, by fear, or by stroking—and how important it was to be flexible, in game strategy or in planning the club roster during the off-season.

Stengel, whose playing career was winding down in the mid-1920s, had his greatest moments on the field in the 1923 World Series against the Yankees, as the Giants lost their bid to become the first team to win three straight Series. Stengel won Game 1 with an inside-the-park home run with two outs in the ninth—the first Series homer in new Yankee Stadium. Then he won Game 3 with a seventh-inning homer off Sad Sam Jones that broke a scoreless tie.

Following the Series, New York traded Stengel to the Boston Braves. He hit .280 in 1924 but played only 12 games in 1925. He left the majors to become a player-manager and club president for Worcester of the Eastern League. He managed in the minors until 1934, when he was named manager of the Dodgers. The best of his three years there was his first, when Brooklyn won 71 games. When he was fired, or as Stengel might have phrased it, "discharged," he hooked up with the Boston Braves and managed them for six years through 1943.

The Braves were another poor team, finishing in seventh place four times and recording a winning record only once. Stengel missed the first 47 games of the 1943 season in Boston, having suffered a broken leg when a taxicab hit him. A local columnist indicated the level of esteem he had for the manager when he wrote, "The man who did the most for baseball in Boston was the motorist who ran down Stengel and kept him away from the Braves for two months." The club discharged Stengel at the end of the season.

Stengel was now age 53 and without a job for the first time in 33 years. Early the following season, the Cubs hired Charlie Grimm as their manager. Grimm, who owned a piece of the Triple-A Milwaukee Brewers, had been managing that club. He promptly hired Stengel as his replacement in Wisconsin. Bill Veeck, the Brewers' principal owner, was somewhere in the South Pacific fighting in World War II, and the move was made without his knowledge. When Veeck found out, he was livid; he considered Stengel a talentless clown.

For once, Veeck was wrong. Stengel led the Brewers to a pennant, and for good measure, the team set an attendance record. After being named Minor League Manager of the Year with the Oakland Oaks in 1948, Stengel got his big break. Yankees general manager George Weiss had first met Stengel in 1916, and they had become friends while they both worked in the Eastern League. Weiss always thought Stengel was a first-rate manager and had tried to convince Lee MacPhail to hire Stengel as New York's manager in 1947. When MacPhail sold his interest in the Yankees, Weiss took over the front office and one year later he hired Stengel to manage the team.

New York fans were shocked to hear that the Yankees had hired Stengel because the club was the most pompous and staid operation in baseball. Stengel told some reporters after he was hired, "I didn't get the job through friendship. The Yankees represent an investment of millions of dollars. They don't hand out jobs like this just because they like your company. I know I can make people laugh and some of you think I'm a damn fool, [but] I got the job because the people here think I can produce for them." He did indeed. His teams won 10 pennants and seven World Series in 12 years, including an unprecedented five straight World Series in Stengel's first five seasons on the job—the greatest run by any manager in the game's history.

His best year was probably that first one. The 1949 Yankees were devastated by an incredible run of injuries. Joe DiMaggio, who had a bum heel, didn't play his first game until June 28. Stengel juggled his lineup and somehow got the Yanks home by one game after they beat the Red Sox in the last two games of the season at Yankee Stadium. A humble Stengel said, "I couldn't have done it without my players."

Stengel's eye for talent was exceptional. He insisted that Yogi Berra be force-fed into the lineup as the everyday catcher, and let him learn the subtleties of the position on the job. Stengel's pre-spring training instructional school for Yankee minor leaguers was the genesis of the Instructional League. His ability to platoon the right players at the right time was uncanny. He would make moves that baffled people, going against the percentage time and time again, yet he was almost always right. The lessons he learned from McGraw were finally paying off.

In *Stengel: His Life and Times*, biographer Robert Creamer wrote that Stengel "had the kind of understanding of a situation that is often described as intuitive—immediate comprehension of a problem

and its solution without recourse to orderly, reasoned analysis—but that is probably just rapid-fire, computer-speed deduction derived from long experience. The best chess players occasionally play this way, making moves they can't immediately explain or justify; Stengel did the same in baseball."

He also kept having a good time. After Bill Veeck installed the first exploding scoreboard in Comiskey Park, Stengel smuggled in firecrackers for the Yankees' next visit to Chicago. When Yankee Clete Boyer hit the team's first homer that day, Stengel and his players set the fireworks off on the dugout steps, and he danced a jig.

After the Yankees lost the 1960 World Series to the Pirates in seven games, Yankees owners Del Webb and Dan Topping discharged Stengel and Weiss. Stengel was 70 years old, and the Yankees had Ralph Houk ready to step in. Houk was a favorite of the players and Stengel was certainly not. He had a cruel streak that surfaced at times, and his sarcastic comments had devastated many a player.

The Yankees held a press conference to announce that Stengel was leaving the team, claiming he was retiring. He put everyone straight: "They paid me off in full and told me my services are not desired any longer by this club." Later that day Stengel said, "I'll never make the mistake of being 70 again."

After sitting out the 1961 season, he was back in 1962 with the expansion Mets, hired by his old buddy, George Weiss. The 1962 Mets were the worst team in baseball history. They went 40–120 and played some of the most bizarre baseball ever witnessed. They won only 51 and 53 games the next two seasons, but despite their failures on the field, they were a phenomenal success off the field.

Everywhere he went, Stengel sold the "Amazing Mets" and the game of baseball. He talked about "the Youth of America," who would one day turn the Mets into champions. He talked about "the New Breed" of Mets fans who flocked to the Polo Grounds and then to Shea Stadium. He talked before the games, he talked after the games, he talked in bars, he talked in airports, he talked in hotels, he talked anywhere he could find a person willing to listen. If he fell asleep on the bench every so often, what did it matter? He was in his mid-70s and his most important work was being done off the field.

Stengel managed his last game on July 24, 1965, though he didn't bow out quietly. That night at Toots Shor's restaurant he attended a party to honor the invitees for the next day's Old Timer's Game. He fell, breaking his left hip. A few weeks later, Stengel retired officially after 3,766 games, 1,905 wins, and 1,842 losses as a manager. He won 10 pennants, which tied him with his mentor, John McGraw, for the most in major league history.

The next year Stengel was elected to the Hall of Fame, and both the Mets and Yankees retired his uniform No. 37. Stengel died at his Glendale, California, home on September 29, 1975. But his Stengelese will live forever. Asked one time why he never visited Montreal, Stengel answered, "Because then there'd be two languages I couldn't speak—French and English."

Rennie Stennett

Stennett, Renaldo Antonio (Porte) 2B

1971–81 B:4/5/1951, Colon, Panama Deb:7/10/1971, PIT NL BR/TR 5'11", 175

G	AB	R	H	HR	RBI	OBP	SLG	AVG
1237	4521	500	1239	41	432	.308	.359	.274

On September 16, 1975, Pittsburgh second baseman Rennie Stennett became the first player in the 20th century to collect seven hits in a nine-inning contest. In that contest the Pirates beat the Cubs by the incredible margin of 22–0. His 7-for-7 day matched the record set by Wilbert Robinson in 1892.

The Pirates signed Stennett as a free agent in February 1969. He started as an outfielder with Gastonia of the Western Carolinas League and led the league in assists. He also put in stints at Salem, Columbus, and Charleston before reaching Pittsburgh, where he beat out Dave Cash for the second base job.

Stennett went on to lead National League second basemen in putouts twice and in total chances once. At one point he played 59 straight errorless games at second. Pirates general manager Joe E. Brown once said of Stennett, "There hasn't been a player in baseball, not even Pete Rose, who hustled more than Rennie Stennett."

But Stennett batted only .196 in four National League Championship Series appearances with the Pirates and lost the second base job to Phil Garner. In November 1979 he became a free agent and signed with the Giants.

Vern Stephens

Stephens, Vernon Decatur SS–3B

1941–55 B:10/23/1920, McAlister, NM D:11/3/1968, Long Beach, CA Deb:9/13/1941, STL AL BR/TR 5'10", 185

G	AB	R	H	HR	RBI	OBP	SLG	AVG
1720	6497	1001	1859	247	1174	.355	.460	.286

Vern Stephens, a power-hitting shortstop, batted behind Ted Williams in Boston for several years, and together they were an imposing slugging duo. At 5 feet 10 inches and 185 pounds, Stephens was no monster, but he was able to utilize Fenway Park's Green Monster to compile some impressive numbers.

Sports were a priority in his family when Vernon Decatur Stephens was growing up, but 100-pound Vern, or "Junior," was too small to make his high school teams. He built himself up with a regimen of bodybuilding and swimming and was a star in American Legion baseball by the age of 16.

Signed by the St. Louis Browns, Stephens showed power in the minor leagues. A testy knee and allergies kept the 21-year-old Stephens out of military service, and when St. Louis shortstop Johnny Berardino went off to war, Stephens took over. In 1942 the rookie batted .294, belted 14 homers, and drove in 92 runs, second most on the team. The perennial second-division Browns jumped to third place in the American League. Manager Luke Sewell said he "never saw anyone develop as quickly" as Stephens did.

In 1943 Stephens increased his home run output to 22 and was named to his first of eight All-Star teams. The following year he led all American League batters in RBIs, with 109, making him only the second Brown to ever do so. He finished third in the Most Valuable Player voting behind Detroit hurlers Hal Newhouser and Dizzy Trout.

After leading the league in home runs in 1945, with 24, Stephens was one of several major leaguers enticed by large contracts to join Jorge Pasquel's Mexican League. The deal Stephens signed was a lush one: five years at $25,000, plus a $15,000 signing bonus. Reacting to the owners' fear that such contracts would lead to more player defections, Commissioner Happy Chandler declared that any player who signed with Pasquel would be suspended from the majors for five years.

Stephens had played two games in Mexico when a contingent—including his father, a minor league umpire, and Browns scout Jake Fournier—arrived to talk him into returning. Stephens disguised himself in his father's clothes and a floppy old hat to make his return across the border in a cab. Stephens returned most of the bonus money he had received from Pasquel, and Chandler did not punish him.

Stephens hit .307 in 1946, but his power numbers slipped to only 14 homers and 64 RBIs. After a similar offensive performance in 1947, the Browns dealt Stephens to Boston. The Red Sox figured Stephens' power stroke would be potent in Fenway, and they were right. Stephens was a perfect fit for the team and the park.

Batting in a lineup that included Dom DiMaggio, Bobby Doerr, Johnny Pesky, and of course, Ted Williams, Stephens clubbed 29 homers and drove in 137 runs in 1948, leading the team in both categories. The Sox scored 50 more runs than anyone else in baseball, although they lost a one-game playoff for the league championship to the Indians.

In 1949 Stephens and Williams were one of the greatest one-two punches in baseball history. Williams led the American League with 43 home runs, 39 doubles, and 162 walks. Stephens hit 39 homers and tied Williams for the league lead with 159 RBIs. Their combined totals of 82 homers and 318 RBIs elicited memories of Ruth and Gehrig. But the Red Sox once again were stifled in their pennant hopes, losing to the Yankees on the last two days of the season.

Stephens continued his power surge in 1950 with 30 homers and 144 RBIs, the latter tying teammate Walt Dropo for the league lead. He hit an even .300 in 1951, but his home run (17) and RBI (78) totals plummeted. His old knee injury was wearing him down, and he was forced to move to third base.

Stephens stayed in the majors through 1955, spending time with Baltimore, the Chicago White Sox, and the Browns, but he never again hit more than eight homers in a season again.

Riggs Stephenson

Stephenson, Jackson Riggs **OF–2B**

1921–34 B:1/5/1898, Akron, AL D:11/15/1985, Tuscaloosa, AL Deb:4/13/1921, CLE AL BR/TR 5'10", 185

G	AB	R	H	HR	RBI	OBP	SLG	AVG
1310	4508	714	1515	63	773	.407	.473	.336

His first name was Jackson, which is why he went by his middle name. But Riggs Stephenson's more appropriate moniker was "Old Hoss," because he was a batting horse. A football star at the University of Alabama (where he also played baseball with his lifelong friend and teammate Joe Sewell), Stephenson damaged his right shoulder on the gridiron and, as a result, never threw well again. In 1921 he came directly from college to the majors and spent four years with the Indians trying to play second base. But making the pivot throw was beyond his capabilities.

The disabled shoulder, however, did not impair his hitting. Stephenson batted .330, .339, .319, and .371 during his first four years with the Tribe. Cleveland manager Tris Speaker decided Stephenson should become an outfielder, and he optioned him to Kansas City in the American Association in 1925 to learn the position. Stephenson threw out 14 runners in 118 games while batting .325.

When Joe McCarthy was hired to manage the Chicago Cubs for the 1926 season, he went looking for hitters. The first one he grabbed was Hack Wilson, an unprotected Giants farmhand. Next was Stephenson, whom he pried loose for two players who would never play another inning of major league ball. With Wilson leading the league in home runs and Stephenson batting .338, the Cubs leaped from last place to fourth.

In 1927 Stephenson cracked a National League-leading 46 doubles, hit .344, and scored 101 runs. Wilson was the league's top home run hitter in the league again, but the Cubs finished fourth once more. McCarthy needed another piece in his puzzle, and he found it in Pittsburgh. Outfielder Kiki Cuyler had run afoul of manager Donie Bush, and the Cubs stole him in a deal for two players after the 1927 season.

The outfield trio of Cuyler, Wilson, and Stephenson clicked in 1928. Cuyler led the league in stolen bases, Wilson led it in home runs, and Stephenson batted .324. They combined for 289 RBIs and 57 home runs. The Cubs ended the season just four games out of first place. The following season the three Cubs put together one of the greatest offensive performances by any outfield. Stephenson hit .362, drove in 110 runs, and added 17 homers. Between the three of them they collected 371 RBIs; Wilson had the lowest average of the trio at .345.

It was the first outfield in the league's history to have three men with more than 100 RBIs each. For good measure, Rogers Hornsby also contributed 149 RBIs. The Cubs scored 982 runs—more than any team had ever scored before in a single season—and they breezed to the pennant. In the World Series against Connie Mack's Philadelphia Athletics, Stephenson sported a .316 average and drove in three runs, but the Cubs went down in five games.

The 1930 season marked the beginning of the hitting explosion in baseball. Five teams scored more than 950 runs, among them the Cubs, who tacked on 988. Hack Wilson knocked in a major league-record 190. Stephenson batted .367 but drove in just 68 runs, probably because there was no one left on base by the time he batted. The Cubs, however, fell two games short of the Cardinals for the pennant.

A broken ankle in 1931 reduced Stephenson's playing time to 80 games, and the Cubs finished third, 17 games out. During the 1932 season the volatile Hornsby was ousted as manager in favor of the genial Charlie Grimm. The Cubs, in second place at the time, played nearly .650 baseball the rest of the way and won the pennant again. Stephenson's 49 doubles and .324 average led the team.

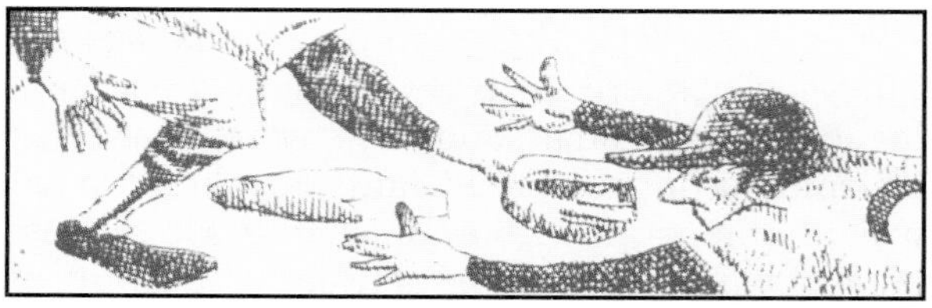

Unfortunately for Chicago, its Series opponent was the New York Yankees of Babe Ruth and Lou Gehrig. The Bronx Bombers scored nearly twice as many runs as the Cubs did, sweeping the Series, which is best remembered for Ruth's purported "called shot." Stephenson hit a club-best .444 in the Series, giving him a lifetime .378 average in nine Series games.

The 1933 season was the 35-year-old Stephenson's last full one in the major leagues. Playing in 97 games, he rapped out a .329 average. In 1934 he appeared in only 38 games (23 as a pinch hitter) and batted .216 in 74 at bats—only the second time in a 14-year major league career that he hit below .300.

Sent to the minors, Stephenson's batting skills were still potent enough for Triple A. He swatted .355 for Indianapolis in 1935 and .343 as a player-manager for Birmingham in 1936. He continued to manage in the minors for three more seasons.

Bill Stern

Broadcaster B:7/1/1907, Rochester, NY D:11/19/1979, Rye, NY

Some of the greatest stories in baseball history never really happened. They were merely figments of the imagination of Bill Stern, one of baseball's premier announcers and storytellers in the early days of radio. Stern was known for his insatiable appetite for creating drama—often when there really wasn't any. One of his most famous tales depicted Abraham Lincoln on his deathbed pleading with Abner Doubleday not to let baseball die.

Stern broke into show business as a stage manager at Radio City Music Hall in New York. In 1934 he got his start in broadcasting by doing a two-minute play-by-play of a college football game with Graham McNamee. Soon afterwards NBC assigned him to broadcast the Army-Illinois football game by himself. He told all his relatives to write or wire NBC to say what a terrific job he had done. Unfortunately, they didn't wait until the game had been played. When Stern's boss got the wires, he fired Stern without ceremony.

In 1934 the self-promoting announcer broadcast some games in the Southwest, but an auto accident landed him in the hospital and his leg had to be amputated. His old boss visited and promised Stern a job if he recovered. Stern was soon made director of sports programming at NBC, a post he held for 15 years.

During the late 1940s Stern published collections of his fanciful football and baseball tales, which became best-sellers despite their obvious historical flaws. In the film *Pride of the Yankees* he appeared as himself. In 1952 he joined ABC.

There, his ongoing battle with alcoholism resulted in his being pulled off the air during a broadcast. He later worked for the Mutual Broadcasting System before dying of a heart attack in 1971.

Harry M. Stevens

Stevens, Harry Mozely

Baseball Pioneer B:1856, London, England D:5/3/1934, New York, NY

It is hard to visualize a baseball game without picturing fans munching on hot dogs or perusing a scorecard. And the man who gave us these staples of the American ballpark was an Englishman, Harry Mozely Stevens. Harry Payne Whitney once noted that Stevens "parlayed a bag of peanuts into a million dollars." The peanuts part wasn't entirely accurate, but the million dollars was conservative.

The London-born Stevens had moved to America from Derby, England, only five years before he attended his first baseball game. It was in Columbus, Ohio, in the 1880s, and Stevens had been going door-to-door along that city's 70th Street selling copies of *The Life of General Logan*, the biography of a Civil War hero and Ohio politician.

Selling door-to-door was not Stevens' first job in America. To support his wife and children, he had worked in a steel mill in Niles, Ohio, before it was closed by labor troubles. Now, tired from pounding the pavement, he approached Columbus' Recreation Park as an American Association contest was about to begin.

Partly just to rest, Stevens bought a ticket and went in. The game confused him and he couldn't figure out who the players on the home-team Columbus Discoverers were—let alone the identities of the visitors. To solve the problem, Harry Stevens invented the scorecard. It's true that rosters had previously been distributed to fans, but never in combination with a mechanism for scoring the game. Stevens combined both and sold advertising to pay for the printing bills. For $700 he obtained the rights to sell the cards for a nickel apiece at the park. Clad in a bright red jacket he moved through the stands, occasionally quoting the classics, in order to peddle his wares. The idea caught on immediately. Soon the immigrant was selling scorecards out of parks in Pittsburgh, Wheeling, Milwaukee, and Toledo and obtaining concession rights to boot.

In 1894 "Scorecard Harry" hit the big time, securing permission to sell in New York's Polo Grounds. A few years later, after noting that his standard fare (he'd branched out from scorecards) was not selling in colder weather, he devised the idea of slapping a frankfurter into what was then called a piano roll. The result was the hot dog.

In 1911 the Polo Grounds caught fire and sustained severe damage. Giants owner John T. Brush, then in the last years of his life, was in no position to rebuild on his own. Stevens extended him the cash. Stevens was not only a businessman, however, he was also a fan. "Not a club owner, he would gladly have been one, and especially of his beloved Giants whom he had seen and been a part of in their days of need and their other days of prosperity," noted the 1935 *Spalding's Guide*. "In the course of his business, Mr. Stevens witnessed thousands of baseball games, and Babe Ruth and Christy Mathewson were his heroes, but his greatest thrill came on that day when his boy, Joe, playing on the Yale team at the Polo Grounds, came up with the bases loaded in the ninth inning and delivered the hit that defeated Princeton and won the intercollegiate championship."

Stevens held the concession privileges to more than just ballparks. In 1901 he was asked to cater a party onboard the yacht of a fellow named Knapp. Knapp was secretary of the Jockey Club and invited millionaire horseman William C. Whitney to the affair. Whitney was looking for a concessionaire for the Saratoga Race Track. Stevens got the job, and Harry M. Stevens Incorporated moved into the Sport of Kings.

In later years the firm did business at the Belmont, Aqueduct, Hialeah, Tropical Park, and Gulfstream racetracks, as well as at the Roosevelt and Yonkers harness tracks. To keep busy in the winter, Stevens also branched out to Madison Square Garden. Stevens died on May 3, 1934, in his apartment in New York's Murray Hill Hotel.

Bill Stewart

Umpire (1933–54) B:9/20/1895, Fitchburg, MA D:2/18/1964, Jamaica Plain, MA

National League umpire Bill Stewart is best remembered for his 1948 controversial call. In the eighth inning of a scoreless duel in Game 1 of the World Series, Bob Feller threw to shortstop Lou Boudreau, attempting to pickoff pinch runner Phil Masi. It appeared Masi was out, but Stewart called "safe." Masi would then score the game's only run and Feller lost despite a two-hitter. A decade later Stewart admitted to Feller that he blew the call.

Stewart began in professional ball as an outfielder-pitcher in 1913, performing at such stops as Worcester, Chambersburg, Harrisburg, Montreal, Richmond, Louisville, St. Joseph, Syracuse, Nashua, and Waterbury. In June 1917 he was the first International League player to volunteer for military service. He appeared on the 1919 White Sox roster, but due to an injury, never appeared in any games.

Stewart scouted for the Red Sox, coached at Boston University, and managed semipro and minor league teams. He began umpiring in the old Eastern League in 1930 and also worked in the New York–Pennsylvania and International leagues. In August 1933 he became a National League umpire. He worked in 715 consecutive games until he was felled by an appendicitis attack in September 1938s. Stewart, who called Johnny Vander Meer's second consecutive no-hitter in 1938, officiated in four World Series and four All-Star Games.

He spent nine years as a National Hockey League referee. In 1937 and 1938 he was named manager-coach of the Chicago Black Hawks and became the first American-born coach to capture the Stanley Cup. He also coached hockey at Massachusetts Institute of Technology and the Milton Academy.

Dave Stewart

Stewart, David Keith **P**

1978, 1981–95 B:2/19/1957 Oakland, CA Deb: 9/22/1978, LA NL BR/TR 6'2", 200

W	L	PCT	G	SV	IP	BB	SO	ERA
168	129	.566	523	19	2629^{2}	1034	1741	3.95

Dave Stewart was a big game pitcher. As a starter he was undefeated in the American League Championship Series, and was twice named ALCS Most Valuable Player. For good measure, he was World Series MVP as well. He played in the postseason six times in his career, including five out of six seasons from 1988 to 1993. All this October success, however, began with losses in his first two postseason games—as a reliever.

An All-America selection in baseball and football in high school, Stewart was drafted by the Dodgers as an 18-year-old out of Merritt Junior College in 1975. After six years in the minor leagues, the Dodgers brought him up as a reliever in 1981. In the divisional playoffs necessitated by the strike, Stewart was called on in two big spots; he failed both times. He allowed a game-ending two-run home run to Alan Ashby of the Houston Astros in Game 1. He was charged with the only run scored by either team in Game 2, for his second loss in as many days. His ERA for the series, which the Dodgers rallied to win, was 40.50. He did not pitch again until the World Series; he allowed no runs in two games as the Dodgers beat the New York Yankees.

That was Stewart's career highlight for the next six years. After limited success in Los Angeles, he moved on to the Texas Rangers, where he failed to capitalize on a chance to be a starting pitcher. With the Philadelphia Phillies he used exclusively in relief, seeing only 16 innings of work over two seasons. He had an unspectacular 30–35 career record when he was released by the Phillies in May 1986. Stewart seemed washed up at 29.

"Stew" hooked on with his hometown Oakland Athletics and got another chance in the starting rotation; within a year became the league's most consistent pitcher. From 1987 to 1990 he won 20 games each season; he led the AL in starts three times, in complete games and innings twice apiece, and once each in wins and shutouts. On June 29, 1990, he threw a no-hitter against the Toronto Blue Jays; Fernando Valenzuela of the Los Angeles Dodgers tossed a no-hitter the same night. It marked the first time since 1898 that two major league pitchers threw separate no-hitters in one day.

Despite his accomplishments, Stewart made only one All-Star team, and never finished higher than second in the Cy Young balloting. He won his awards in the postseason.

He was 8–0 with a 2.03 ERA in 10 Championship Series starts. His teams played in the ALCS five times, and won the pennant four times. In the World Series his record was a lackluster 2–4 with a 3.32 ERA, but he dominated the 1989 Series.

Stewart tossed a 5–0 complete-game shutout in Game 1 of the World Series against the San Francisco Giants. Oakland won Game 2 of the "Bay Series" the next day, but a tragic earthquake postponed Game 3 for 10 days. The Oakland native spent much of that time trying to help survivors cope with the tragedy. (He later received the Bart Giamatti Award for exceptional community service from the Baseball Assistance Team.)

When October 27 arrived and Stewart had the ball in his hands, it was business as usual. He allowed just three runs in seven innings to win Game 3 of an eventual sweep. In 16 World Series innings he struck out 14 Giants and had a 1.69 ERA to earn MVP honors

After his final 20-win season, Stewart won 23 games and lost 21 over a two-year span. He went to Toronto as a free agent in 1993. He won only 12 regular season games for the Blue Jays, but again dominated the ALCS. He beat the Chicago White Sox twice to earn MVP honors.

After his first losing year in a decade, Stewart returned to Oakland in 1995 and retired midway through the season. He started his front office career as a special assistant to Oakland general manager Sandy Alderson in 1996. He took a similar job with San Diego the following year, but

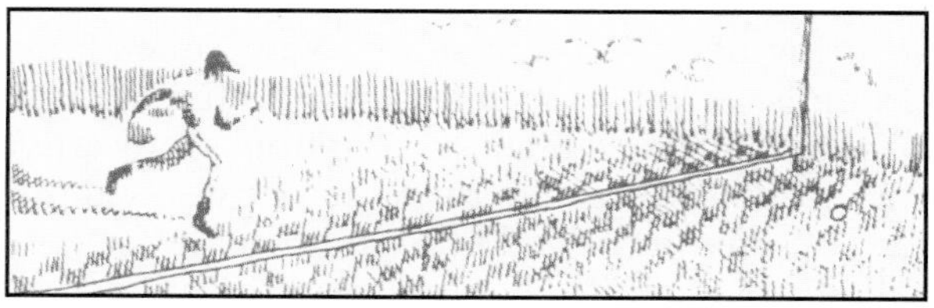

when the Padres needed a top-notch pitching coach, he returned to the dugout. The Padres won 98 games and the National League pennant, while their ERA of 3.63 was more than a full run better than it had been the year before. Stewart returned to the front office with Toronto as assistant general manager in 1999.

Dave Stieb

Stieb, David Andrew **P**

1979–93, 1998 B:7/22/1957, Santa Ana, CA
Deb:6/29/1979, TOR AL BR/TR 6'1", 195

W	L	PCT	G	SH	IP	BB	SO	ERA
176	137	.562	443	30	2895^{1}	1034	1669	3.44

Dave Stieb was supposed to have been an outfielder. He was a good defensive player and had big league hitting potential when, in 1978, someone in the Toronto Blue Jays' farm system also noticed he had an amazing throwing arm. He came up to the Blue Jays as a hurler midway through the following season, starting 18 games and winning eight. He went on to a 14-year pitching career as a Blue Jay.

When he left the team in 1992 he was the winningest and most outspoken pitcher in the young history of baseball's second Canadian franchise. It was a history that went from miserable to remarkable, and it was built around Stieb.

At first he toiled long and hard as the ace pitcher for a hapless expansion club that never seemed to really be expanding. He was good enough to achieve personal recognition immediately, pitching in five All-Star Games during his first seven seasons. It took all seven of those seasons, however, for the rest of the Blue Jays to contend.

In 1982 Stieb's 19 complete games topped the league, as did his five shutouts. In 1983 he was again among the league leaders in complete games and shutouts, and he ranked third in strikeouts. His five-year cumulative winning percentage was .520, and he never threw more than 17 wins. His effort was among the Blue Jays' best in Toronto's rise to fourth place.

In 1984, despite his unimpressive win totals, it was clear that Dave Stieb was the top pitcher in the game. He struck out 198 batters—only six fewer than league-leader Mark Langston—and posted a 2.83 ERA. He allowed the fewest hits per game of any American League pitcher and limited opponents to a .221 batting average, also the best in the league. Still, he won only 16 games, and the Blue Jays finished 15 games behind the eventual world champion Tigers. Stieb and the Jays, who had another top pitcher named Doyle Alexander, had captured second place.

In 1985 Toronto captured its first division championship. Along the way, Stieb hurled the lowest ERA in the league and finished near the top of many pitching categories for the fourth consecutive year. He almost hurled a no-hitter in August but gave up a home run in the ninth to nix the effort. Had the best-of-five ALCS not been expanded to seven games in 1985, the Blue Jays might have captured the pennant that year and Dave Stieb might have been a hero.

He threw eight shutout innings in Game 1 and allowed just one run in Game 4, a contest that also went to Toronto, and the club took a three-games-to-one lead. But the more experienced Royals came back for two more wins, and Stieb was called in to put them away before the hometown crowd in Game 7. In the sixth inning he loaded the bases with two walks and a hit batsman. Four runs eventually scored. Demoralized, the Jays couldn't mount a comeback.

The next year was his worst to that point, and the Blue Jays slipped to fourth. The following season a reborn Stieb began to regain his form. By 1988 he was back on top, hurling in his sixth All-Star Game, and as tough to hit as ever. Although he had been the workhorse of the team all decade, he was seeing less action. He complained publicly that he was being benched so the team wouldn't have to pay him bonuses under a clause activated by the number of innings he pitched.

Stieb took a no-hitter to 8 ⅔ innings in back-to-back games in September; both times he surrendered hits in the ninth. He was the first pitcher ever to lose back-to-back near-no-hitters. The Jays, who had been back in contention, finished the year in a slump. Neither they nor Stieb alone were able to win the big games.

In August 1989 Stieb seemed jinxed again. He retired 26 consecutive Yankee batters before giving up a double and losing a perfect game. Nevertheless, his numbers were as solid as ever, and the Blue Jays clinched the AL East. In the playoffs Stieb posted losses in both of his starts against a formidable Oakland team. The Jays, who suddenly couldn't seem to hit, went down in five games.

In 1990 Stieb posted a career-high 18 wins and the second best ERA of his career, 2.93. He was an All-Star again, for the seventh time, and he finally earned his no-hitter. The following year a completely revamped Toronto team again captured the division, but this time the Jays did it mostly without the help of an injured Stieb. In 1992, when the Blue Jays celebrated their finest hour by finally winning the world championship they had

approached so many times, Stieb, who for so long had been their No. 1 pitcher, was unable to contribute. In 1993 he was picked up by the division title-bound Chicago White Sox. Stieb was ineffective in limited action and was unused in the postseason. He did not play in the major leagues again until 1998. His comeback entailed 19 appearances, including three starts, and his 175th career win as a Blue Jay.

Snuffy Stirnweiss

Stirnweiss, George Henry **2B**

1943–52 B:10/26/1918, New York, NY Deb:4/22/1943, NY AL BR/TR 5'8½", 175

G	AB	R	H	HR	RBI	OBP	SLG	AVG
1028	3695	604	989	29	281	.362	.371	.268

Snuffy Stirnweiss brings back memories of war-time baseball, when the game's best players were in military service. The absence of so many sluggers allowed Stirnweiss to lead the league in hitting in 1945 with a .309 mark, the third lowest ever for an American League batting champion.

Stirnweiss was the best player on the Yankees in 1945, when Joe DiMaggio, Phil Rizzuto, and other key players were away. Babe Ruth praised him, in the Bambino's own unpretentious style: "That sawed-off runt playing second base is the only ballplayer who could have gotten a uniform when the Yankees had a real ball club," Ruth said.

Stirnweiss, who earned his nickname because he suffered from a lifelong sinus condition, first made headlines when he stole an International League record 73 bases in 1942 for Newark, the Yankees' top farm team. He was nearly sold to the Dodgers late in that season. New York general manager Ed Barrow, who was feuding with Dodgers management, changed his mind—perhaps recognizing Snuffy's skills or perhaps just to spite Brooklyn.

Given an $8,000 contract for 1943, Stirnweiss was brought up to the big club, but not as a second baseman. Joe Gordon was coming off a season in which he was named Most Valuable Player, and there was no way a rookie was going to replace him. Stirnweiss was switched to shortstop with disappointing results, hitting just .219 in 83 games. Joe McCarthy had Stirnweiss sit next to him in the dugout, and the Yankees manager, who had taking a liking to the scrappy, hustling infielder, imparted his baseball wisdom to the rookie on a daily basis.

When Gordon went into the service before the 1944 season, Stirnweiss seized the second base job. (Snuffy was rejected for service because of gastric ulcers, which had plagued him since college). As the club's leadoff hitter, he led the AL in runs (125), hits (205), triples (16), and stolen bases (55), the first of consecutive years in which he led both leagues in steals. By midseason, McCarthy was calling him "the best second baseman in the game today."

Stirnweiss got off to a solid start in 1945 and was hitting .333 by the end of April, but he dropped off and McCarthy gave up on an ill-fated experiment to bat him third. Stirnweiss was all the team could brag about that year, since by August the Yanks had faded and wound up finishing fourth.

The race for the batting title was more thrilling, with Stirnweiss battling Chicago White Sox third baseman Tony Cuccinello and Boston Red Sox outfielder Johnny Lazor. Only eight players in the league topped .300 and several of them, Lazor included, didn't reach the minimum number of plate appearances to be considered for the batting crown. Though hitting just .297 on September 15, Snuffy went on a roll with a series of multi-hit games. Cuccinello ended his season with a 1-for-3 day on September 25, and then sat on the sidelines as Chicago's last three games were rained out. Stirnweiss had three hits on September 29, designated Snuffy Stirnweiss Day at Yankee Stadium, to raise his average to .306. In the season finale he had three more hits, inching him to .309 and giving him the crown. He also posted AL bests in hits (195), runs (107), triples (22), slugging (.476), stolen bases (33), putouts by a second baseman (432), and double plays (119). It adds up to make Snuffy's greatest year one of the top five individual seasons ever by a Yankee.

In 1946, with the war over and Gordon back with the team, Stirnweiss was moved to third base. His average declined by 58 points, and he would never again hit over .256. By 1949 his legs were giving him trouble and he had become a part-time player. The next year he was traded to the St. Louis Browns, and he finished out his career in Cleveland in 1950 and 1951.

After his baseball career was over, he became a banker and a foreign freight agent, and also served as the director of a sandlot baseball program run by *New York Journal-American*. On September 15, 1958, he caught a commuter train in Red Bank, New Jersey, for the ride into New York, where he had a noon business meeting. In Elizabeth, New Jersey, the train—the engineer was apparently incapacitated—ran several signals and plunged off an open drawbridge into a river. Stirnweiss was one of more than three dozen people who were killed. He left a wife and six children.

Jack Stivetts

Stivetts, John Elmer **P–OF**

1889–99 B:3/31/1868, Ashland, PA D:4/18/1930, Ashland, PA Deb:6/26/1889, STL AA BR/TR 6'2", 185

W	L	PCT	G	SH	IP	BB	SO	ERA
203	132	.606	388	14	2887[2]	1155	1223	3.74

G	AB	R	H	HR	RBI	OBP	SLG	AVG
601	1992	348	593	35	357	.344	.439	.298

Had he not been such an effective pitcher, John Elmer "Happy Jack" Stivetts, a strapping 6-foot 2-inch hard thrower from Pennsylvania's anthracite coal district, might have had a big league career as an outfielder. He played nearly 200 games in the field and hit .300 or better four times. On three different occasions he blasted two home runs in a game.

He joined St. Louis of the American Association in 1889 and won 60 games for the Browns in 1890–91, but a run-in with the irascible owner Chris Von der Ahe prompted Stivetts to jump to Boston of the National League. Stivetts enjoyed his most productive season with his new team.

Fireballer Stivetts and control artist Kid Nichols provided Boston with baseball's best one-two pitching combination in 1892. The Beaneaters took the pennant as Stivetts contributed both with his arm and his bat. While filling in as a left fielder, Stivetts homered in the 12th inning to win a 1–0 game over Brooklyn. The next day he no-hit the same team, 11–0, and wound up the season with 35 wins.

When the pitching distance was moved back in 1893, Happy Jack slumped, as did many other hurlers. He bounced back with three strong seasons in the mid-1890s before an arm injury finished his career.

Milt Stock

Stock, Milton Joseph **3B–2B–SS**

1913–26 B:7/11/1893, Chicago, IL D:7/16/1977, Fairhope, AL Deb:9/29/1913, NY NL BR/TR 5'8", 154

G	AB	R	H	HR	RBI	OBP	SLG	AVG
1628	6249	839	1806	22	696	.339	.361	.289

In late June and early July of 1925 Brooklyn third baseman Milt Stock collected a record 16 hits in one four-game period. Stock started with the Fond du Lac Mudhens of the Class D Wisconsin-Illinois League in 1911. That October he was drafted by the New York Giants but was released to Buffalo in April 1912. In 1913 he played for Mobile.

Stock was brought up to the Polo Grounds the following year. In January 1915 the Giants traded him to the Phils. Philadelphia in turn sent him to the Cardinals as part of a six-player deal in January 1919. Stock recorded four straight .300 seasons with St. Louis. In 1924 he was traded to Brooklyn. He played an entire doubleheader at second base without making a putout on August 19, 1925.

Stock served as player-manager with Mobile from 1926 through 1928 and with Dallas in 1929. He managed at Knoxville, Beckley, Monessen, Macon, and Portsmouth. At Macon he managed Eddie Stanky, who eventually became his son-in-law. Stock later traded Stanky.

Stock returned to the majors as a coach for the Cubs and then shifted over to Brooklyn. It was Stock who waved Cal Abrams home in the deciding last play of the 1950 season. When the Phils' Richie Ashburn threw out Abrams at the plate, the pennant was lost. Stock was fired a few days later. He later coached with the Pirates.

George Stone

Stone, George Robert **OF**

1903, 1905–10 B:9/3/1877, Lost Nation, IA D:1/3/1945, Clinton, IA Deb:4/20/1903, BOS AL BL/TL 5'9", 175

G	AB	R	H	HR	RBI	OBP	SLG	AVG
848	3271	426	984	23	268	.360	.396	.301

George Stone once said that for every year he played baseball, it left him one year behind in starting a business and establishing a life for himself. The quiet and philosophical outfielder felt that the only people that controlled the business of baseball were the owners. Stone later established himself in the baseball business by owning a team in Lincoln, Nebraska. He eventually became a minor league president.

Other than a brief two-game trial with Boston in 1903, Stone spent the rest of his career with the St. Louis Browns, after an early season stint with Boston in 1903. Stone batted .296 as a rookie and led the American League with 187 hits. The following season he batted .358 to edge baseball great Nap Lajoie for the batting title. He also led the league in slugging and on-base percentage, becoming the first American Leaguer other than Lajoie (1901 and 1904) to lead in all three categories in one season.

Stone was also a very nimble baserunner. He stole 20 or more bases in five of his seven seasons. He stole 132 bases for his career.

John Stone

Stone, John Thomas **OF**

1928–38 B:10/10/1905, Lynchburg, TN D:11/30/1955, Shelbyville, TN Deb:8/31/1928, DET AL BL/TR 6'1", 178

G	AB	R	H	HR	RBI	OBP	SLG	AVG
1200	4494	739	1391	77	707	.376	.467	.310

American League outfielder John Stone recorded a .310 career average and topped the .300 mark seven times during his 11-year career. He put together two impressive hitting streaks and was traded straight up for a Hall of Famer.

Stone starred in baseball and football at Marysville College and graduated with a bachelor's degree in 1928. He turned professional with Evansville of the Class B 3-I League that year and batted .354 before being called up by the Detroit Tigers during the season. After two years of part-time duty he became a Detroit regular in 1930 and promptly hit in 34 straight games.

In 1931 Stone again went on a streak, hitting in 23 straight games and posting a .327 average for the season. On May 30, 1933, he tied a major league record by collecting six extra-base hits in a doubleheader, including four doubles and two homers. It is a measure of Stone's stature that he was traded to Washington for Hall of Fame outfielder Goose Goslin on December 20, 1933.

"Rocky" Stone hit .315 his first year in Washington and on June 16, 1935, he got eight hits in a doubleheader against the Browns—two triples, two doubles, and four singles. In 1936 he batted a career-high .341. After one more good year and a subpar season, Stone was forced to retire because of illness.

Steve Stone

Stone, Steven Michael **P**

1971–81 B:7/14/1947, Euclid, OH Deb:4/8/1971, SF NL BR/TR 5'10", 175

W	L	PCT	G	SH	IP	BB	SO	ERA
107	93	.535	320	7	1788^{1}	716	1065	3.97

Steve Stone was a journeyman pitcher who had one remarkable year and then pitched his final major league game the following season. Stone, who had been Thurman Munson's batterymate at Kent State, had an excellent curve and a mediocre fastball. From 1971 through 1979 he pitched for the Giants, the White Sox, and the Cubs, compiling an unremarkable 78–79 record with a 4.06 ERA. In one incredible season Stone went 25–7 for the Orioles and won the 1980 American League Cy Young Award.

"I found out this year how to win and one of the keys is don't play on a sixth-place club," Stone explained. So why did he log a mediocre 11–7 season the previous year when the Orioles won the pennant? Probably because he was still absorbing the teachings of Ray Miller, the Orioles' outstanding pitching coach. As Stone said, "Miller helped me mechanically by getting me to speed up my time between pitches and limiting my pitch selection early in a game."

He also had help from a self-described witch. Stone had been consulting with Ruth Revzen for several years, but she was prophetic in the spring of that year. In June he had a 5.01 ERA, yet he had a respectable 6–3 record by benefit of a good bullpen and a high-scoring offense. In John Holway's book, *The Baseball Astrologer*, Stone said that Revzen assured him his season would turn around and he would pitch in the All-Star Game. He won his next five games and was named as the All-Star starter. With Revzen making a rare appearance in the stands at Dodger Stadium, Stone threw three perfect innings in the game, the first time that had happened since 1966.

Stone eventually won 10 starts in a row and went 19–4 after June 8. He led the major leagues with a .781 won-lost percentage. Sadly, there was no encore to Stone's stellar season. After a career-high 251 innings in 1980, Stone's shoulder blew out. At age 34 his baseball career was over. Two years later he started a new career as a color analyst for the Cubs on WGN TV, where he became the perfect foil for irrepressible partner Harry Carey. A bon vivant and restaurateur Stone went into the restaurant business as a partner in a chain of eateries called Lettuce Entertain You.

Horace Stoneham

Stoneham, Horace C.

Owner (1936–76) B: 4/27/1903, Newark, NJ D:1/7/1990, Scottsdale, AZ

Horace Stoneham was one of baseball's most colorful owners during his 40-year tenure with the Giants. He snatched his archrival's manager, apologized to Minneapolis fans for the midseason promotion of Willie Mays, and was a part of two of the greatest upset victories in baseball history. Stoneham, however, will forever be remembered for moving the New York Giants to San Francisco.

The Fordham graduate joined Giants as a team executive under the ownership of his father Charles in 1929. He assumed the club presidency when his father died in January 1936. At 32 he became the youngest major league owner in baseball history. Stoneham's first decision was one of his best: retaining Bill Terry as manager. The Giants won back-to-back pennants in Stoneham's first two seasons as owner. The club went into a slow decline that hit bottom with a last-place finish in 1946.

Perhaps Stoneham's most stunning move was hiring manager Leo Durocher from the hated Brooklyn Dodgers in midseason 1948. Three years later the rebuilt Giants rebounded from a 13½-game deficit in August to earn a first-place tie with the Dodgers on the last day of the season. New York won the best-of-three playoff on Bobby Thomson's "Shot heard 'round the World" on October 3, 1951.

The Giants won the pennant again in 1954 after Willie Mays—a 1951 midseason call-up from Minneapolis—returned from military service. The Cleveland Indians won a then-American League record 111 regular season games, but couldn't win a game against the Giants in the World Series. New York's shocking sweep resulted in Stoneham's only world championship.

Both the team and attendance declined in succeeding seasons. Stoneham lost a battle for a new ballpark, and after the 1957 season moved his team west when Brooklyn owner Walter O'Malley convinced him both clubs would prosper in California.

Giants' attendance doubled from 1957 (650,000) to 1958 (1,272,000). The Giants moved from Seals Stadium to Candlestick Park in 1960, but the swirling winds made life uncomfortable for players and fans. The Giants won their final pennant for Stoneham in 1962.

Attendance began to drop—especially after the Kansas City Athletics moved to Oakland in 1968. Stoneham tried to move the Giants again, this time to Toronto. Mayor George Moscone held up the sale until a local buyer could be found to meet the purchase price. Stoneham sold the team to real estate magnate Bob Lurie on March 2, 1976.

Bill Stoneman

Stoneman, William Hambly **P**

1967–74 B:4/7/1944 Oak Park, IL Deb:7/16/1967, CHI NL BR/TR 5'10", 170

W	L	PCT	G	SH	IP	BB	SO	ERA
54	85	.388	245	15	1236^1	602	934	4.08

In their inaugural season of 1969, the Montreal Expos posted a woeful record of 52–110. Bill Stoneman provided one of the few highlights.

A little-known pitcher acquired from the Cubs, Bill Stoneman had made just two starts in 46 appearances over the course of two seasons in Chicago. When manager Gene Mauch installed Stoneman in Montreal's rotation, the righthander responded with the first great moment in franchise history. Stoneman threw a no-hitter in the 10th game in team history, a 7–0 triumph over Philadelphia on April 17.

Stoneman remained with Montreal through the 1973 season. He went 17–16 for his only winning season in 1971, completing 20 games. A year later, Stoneman earned a spot on the National League All-Star team, as well as a second no-hitter, a 7–0 win over the Mets on October 2. Stoneman served in the Montreal front office from 1984 until 1999, when he hired as general manager of the Angels.

Mel Stottlemyre

Stottlemyre, Melvin Leon, Sr. **P**

1964–74 B:11/13/1941, Hazelton, MO Deb:8/12/1964, NY AL BR/TR 6'2", 190

W	L	PCT	G	SH	IP	BB	SO	ERA
164	139	.541	360	40	2661^1	809	1257	2.97

With his nasty sinker and confident demeanor, Mel Stottlemyre was the ace of the Yankees for nine years. He won 20 games or more three times and led the league in complete games twice and innings pitched once. Unfortunately, the bulk of his career occurred when the Yankees weren't the team we think of today as the mighty Yankees.

After his rookie year his team finished second (a full 15 games out of first), and then slid to fifth, sixth, ninth, and 10th over the next four years. When the league was split into two divisions, the Yankees finished fourth three times in the American League East. Yet Stottlemyre's ultimate status may have less to do with his pitching performances than with his ability as a highly regarded pitching coach and father of a promising young hurler, Todd Stottlemyre.

Mel Stottlemyre led the International League with an nifty 1.42 ERA for Richmond in 1964. In August he was promoted to New York, where his sinker baffled American League hitters. He went 9–3 down the stretch with an ERA of 2.06. In the World Series that year he seven-hit the Cardinals for a victory over Bob Gibson in Game 2, and he left Game 5 after allowing just one earned run in seven innings. The Yankees tied the game in the ninth but lost in the 10th. He was the loser in Game 7, lasting only four innings.

Given Whitey Ford's slot in the rotation during 1965 spring training, Stottlemyre tumbled into a controversy. Mickey Mantle told a reporter in jest that he was upset about his old pal Whitey losing his job—Mantle promised to loaf in the outfield until the situation was rectified. The sportswriter missed the joke, and everyone in the Yankees organization was sorely embarrassed.

Stottlemyre continued toward stardom with his 20-win season and league leads in complete games, with 18, and innings pitched, with 291. His low sinker, thrown with excellent control, was the pitch he relied on. In nine years of pitching more than 250 innings, he never walked 100 batters in a season.

Stottlemyre was a thinking man's pitcher, always looking for the edge. He noticed that Boston's Carl Yastrzemski talked to himself when at the plate. Stottlemyre read the hitter's lips. "If he was saying, 'Be quick, be quick,' I'd throw him a changeup. If he was saying, 'Stay back, stay back,' I'd throw a fastball," Stottlemyre explained.

The next year he achieved a dubious distinction as one of a handful of pitchers to win 20 games one year and lose 20 the next. That figure is often the mark of a durable starter on a bad team, which is definitely what the 10th-place Yankees were in 1966. Fortunately, Stottlemyre could provide some offense himself: in 1964 he had a five-hit game, and he clubbed an inside-the-park home run the following season.

After winning 16 games in 1971, Stottlemyre's ERA jumped nearly half a run the following year. He bulled through a 16–16 mark in 1973, but in 1974, with a rotator cuff tear, he struggled to a meager 6–7 record. He never pitched again.

The Seattle Mariners hired him as their pitching coach in 1977. Working with young pitchers such as Glenn Abbott and Rick Honeycutt, he saw the team's ERA improve every year he was with the club. Davey Johnson hired him to coach the young Met pitchers in 1984. Stottlemyre received credit for helping Dwight Gooden become more than just a thrower as a rookie in 1984 and later for helping him salvage his career following a drug suspension a dozen years later. Stottlemyre remained with the Mets through the 1993 season. He worked with the Astros for two years before returning to New York as pitching coach of the Yankees in 1996. Stottlemyre, who had struggled with bad teams at Yankee Stadium as a pitcher, reaped the benefits of the team's wealth with three world championships over the next four years.

Todd Stottlemyre

Stottlemyre, Todd Vernon **P**

1988–* B:5/20/1965, Sunnyside, WA Deb:4/6/1988, TOR AL BL/TR 6'3", 195

W	L	PCT	G	SH	IP	BB	SO	ERA
129	113	.533	349	6	2076	773	1499	4.22

As a Toronto Blue Jays farmhand, Todd Stottlemyre boasted a mid-90s fastball, a nasty slider, and a fine pedigree: his father was former Yankees ace and four-time All-Star Mel Stottlemyre. Occasional control lapses and ensuing big innings frequently proved Todd's undoing; in seven seasons with Toronto his record was just 69–70. His problems were especially apparent in October: in four postseason starts through 1993, Stottlemyre was 0–3 with a 10.26 ERA.

Stottlemyre finally started to silence the doubters when he moved to Oakland in 1995. Under manager Tony La Russa, Stottlemyre showed newfound maturity and achieved better results: he went 14–7 with a career-high 205 strikeouts. Stottlemyre followed former La Russa and pitching coach Dave Duncan to St. Louis in 1996. Stottlemyre again posted 14 wins and added two more victories in the postseason.

After another successful year and a half with the Cardinals, Stottlemyre helped Texas reach the playoffs following a midseason trade in 1998. The following year he joined Arizona's crack rotation behind Randy Johnson. Despite a partially torn rotator cuff that sidelined him for three months, Stottlemyre proved his grit in the 1999 Division Series by registering Arizona's only win over the New York Mets.

George Stovall

Stovall, George Thomas **1B**

1904–15 M(1911–15, 313–376) B:11/23/1878, Independence, MO D:11/5/1951, Burlington, IA Deb:7/4/1904, CLE AL BR/TR 6'2", 180

G	AB	R	H	HR	RBI	OBP	SLG	AVG
1414	5222	547	1382	15	564	.292	.339	.265

First baseman George Stovall's nickname, "Firebrand," was derived from his terrible temper and tendency towards agitation. Whether it was brawling, fomenting a player strike, or helping to organize a new major league, Stovall was always ready to stir things up.

On one occasion, Cleveland player-manager Napoleon Lajoie dropped Stovall down a few pegs in the batting order. Stovall, as might be expected, thought little of the idea. One evening in a Philadelphia hotel lobby, he smashed Lajoie over the head with a nearby chair. Only the intervention of other players kept Stovall from continuing the beating.

Oddly enough, Lajoie took no disciplinary action. "George didn't mean anything by it," Lajoie later recalled. "Besides, he was a good ballplayer, and we needed him." In the 1906 season, however, Stovall was suspended by Lajoie after accusing his manager of hiring outside spies to report on Cleveland players.

Stovall may have lost that one, but he managed to make American League president Ban Johnson back down, something achieved by few players. In the spring of 1911, Hall of Fame pitcher Addie Joss died of spinal meningitis. On the day of Joss' funeral, his Cleveland teammates were scheduled to play in Detroit. Led by Stovall, the club decided to strike if necessary in order to attend his funeral. "If you fellows will stick with me, we'll force the Detroit club to cancel this opening game," Stovall told his fellow players.

At first, Johnson was inclined to order the recalcitrant players to perform as scheduled. But faced with their unanimous opposition (even manager Jim McGuire backed them), Johnson gave way. The entire Cleveland team, as well as representatives of the Tigers, came to Toledo for the services. Later, an All-Star Game was organized in Cleveland to benefit the Joss family.

One of the reasons management put up with someone like Stovall is that he was an exceptional fielder. From 1908 to 1911 he led AL first basemen in fielding percentage. Three times he paced that league in assists and double plays. Additionally, in 1915 he led the Federal League in assists. With the Browns on August 7, 1912, Stovall tied a (since-broken) major league record with seven assists at first base in one game.

Stovall was named captain of the Naps in 1909 and playing manager in the middle of the 1911 season. He took the club from seventh to third, but he was traded to the Browns in December when Harry Davis took over. With St. Louis he again became a player-manager. However, he was in constant hot water with Browns owner Robert Hedges over such issues as Stovall's refusal to audition college students and his spitting tobacco juice in an umpire's eye.

Stovall argued for Hedges to grant him his release and said that no man "ought to be bartered like a broken down plow horse." Under ordinary circumstances Hedges would have had the upper hand, but something very significant was brewing, and Stovall would become the first player to take advantage of it.

In 1913 an outlaw minor league, the Federal League, had operated in the Midwest. Now, under the leadership of "Fighting Jim" Gilmore, the Feds would attempt to assume major league status, moving into major league territories, and signing major league players. Stovall was the first player to violate the reserve clause and sign with the Feds, going to its Kansas City franchise. Aside from playing for the new circuit, Stovall was also instrumental in helping it sign other players from the established leagues. In 1915 he was named player-manager of the Kansas City Packers.

Stovall retired at the end of that season. His brother, Jesse, pitched two major league seasons, one with the Indians in 1903 and one with the Tigers in 1904.

George Stovall later became the president of the Association of Professional Ballplayers. Chartered in Los Angeles in 1924, the APB was a charitable group for destitute ballplayers. Stovall then scouted for Pittsburgh from 1935 to 1940.

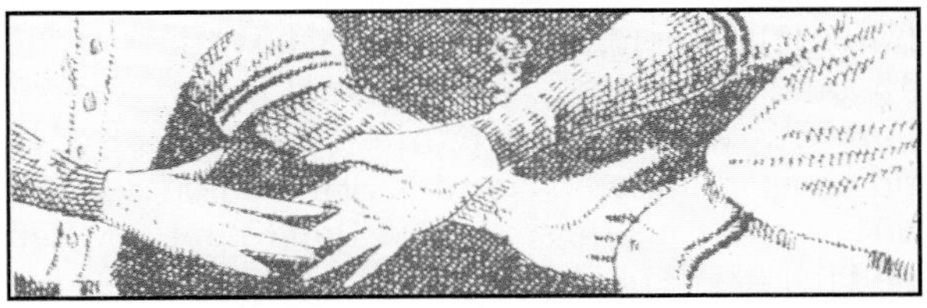

George Stovey

Stovey, George Washington

19th-Century Pitcher (1886–96) B:1866 D:3/22/1936, Williamsport, PA BL/TL

Lefthander George Washington Stovey was the game's first great African-American pitcher and an unwilling participant in one of the key incidents that fully segregated the game in the 19th century. The light-skinned lefthander was the last African-American to be allowed to pitch in Organized Baseball for 60 years.

Stovey began pitching with Jersey City in the Eastern League in 1886, where opposition batters collected just a .167 average against him. Said *Sporting Life*: "If the team would support him they would make a far better showing. His manner in covering first from the box is wonderful."

On July 19, 1887, Stovey and the Newark Little Giants of the International League were scheduled to play an exhibition against Cap Anson's Chicago White Stockings. The battery featured Stovey and catcher Fleet Walker, who in 1884 had been the first African-American to play in the major leagues as a member of the American Association's Toledo Blue Stockings. Anson went into a rage and forced Walker and Stovey out of the game.

At about the same time, major league owners passed a resolution banning black players because of the objections of white players, and the long period of segregation in Organized Baseball began. The resolution was later modified, merely proving that rules need not be written to be effective.

Stovey finished the year with 34 wins for Newark and also filled in as an outfielder. Regardless, he was released at season's end. Stovey had 60 wins in parts of six seasons in Organized Baseball. He later pitched for all-black teams.

Harry Stovey

Stovey, Harry Duffield **OF-1B**

1880–93 M(1881, 1885, 63–75) B:12/20/1856, Philadelphia, PA Deb:5/1/1880, WOR NL BR/TR 5'11½", 175

G	AB	R	H	HR	RBI	OBP	SLG	AVG
1486	6138	1492	1771	122	908	.361	.461	.289

Harry Stovey was one of the best players of the 1880s. He was a league leader in home runs five times, RBIs once, triples and runs scored four times, doubles once, slugging percentage three times, and stolen bases twice. Yet he played under the name of "Stovey" so his mother

would not know he was a ballplayer. His real name was Harry Duffield Stowe.

He began professionally with the Athletics in 1877 and played with New Bedford both before and after that team joined the International Association. At New Bedford he served under Frank Bancroft. When Bancroft switched to Worcester in National League Stovey went with him.

Stovey hit two triples in one inning—and three in the game on August 18, 1884. He hit for the cycle on May 15, 1888, and drove in eight runs in a game in 1892. A good fielder and baserunner, Stovey jumped to the Players' League in 1890 and was the leader in stolen bases in that league's only season of existence. He had previously led the American Association in thefts. After leaving baseball Stovey became a New Bedford police officer.

Sammy Strang

Strang, Samuel Nicklin **3B–2B**

1896, 1900–08 B:12/16/1876, Chattanooga, TN D:3/13/1932, Chattanooga, TN Deb:7/10/1896, LOU NL BB/TR 5'8", 160

G	AB	R	H	HR	RBI	OBP	SLG	AVG
903	2933	479	790	16	253	.377	.343	.269

It is sometimes contended that Sammy Strang's "coming through in the pinch" led to the term "pinch hitter." Strang's skills as a regular did not keep him one place for any length of time. In 1901 Strang jumped from the New York Giants to the Chicago White Sox in the new American League—and then jumped back to the Chicago Cubs, for whom he had played in 1900. The Cubs traded him back to the Giants in February 1902. In March 1903 New York peddled him to Brooklyn, but he was sold back once more to the Polo Grounds in February 1905. That year he led the National League with eight pinch hits.

A fiery player, in 1907 he was ejected from four games, a total surpassed on the Giants only by manager John McGraw. He was known as the "The Dixie Thrush," but in March 1908 Strang reverted to using his former name, Strang Nicklin. (Actually his given name was Samuel Strang Nicklin.) "I have decided to use my real name," he told associates. "Not long ago I was thinking I would like to meet some of my old friends whom I knew in my college days. They didn't connect Sammy Strang with Strang Nicklin, and a lot of them don't know that I am playing ball. If there is anything coming to me in my career I want it credited to my family name."

Strang Nicklin, however, was not the ballplayer Sammy Strang had been. McGraw became disgusted with his poor play and sold him to Baltimore in the Eastern League on June 9, 1908.

Monty Stratton

Stratton, Monty Franklin Pierce **P**

1934–38 B:5/21/1912, Celeste, TX D:9/29/1982, Greenville, TX Deb:6/2/1934, CHI AL BR/TR 6'5", 180

W	L	PCT	G	SH	IP	BB	SO	ERA
36	23	.610	70	5	487^{1}	149	196	3.71

In the late 1930s Monty Stratton had just established himself as a first-rate starting pitcher for the White Sox when a hunting accident cost him his right leg and his career. The story of that personal tragedy was told in the popular motion picture *The Stratton Story*, starring Jimmy Stewart. The 1949 film exaggerated the success of Stratton's comeback but won the Academy Award for best original screenplay for screenwriter Douglas Morrow.

An All-Star pitcher in 1937, when he was 15–5, Stratton had gone 15–9 in 1938 but lost his leg that November after accidentally shooting himself with a revolver while hunting rabbits. A benefit game in 1939 at Comiskey Park netted him $28,000.

In 1946 Stratton, nicknamed "Gander" after his tall, lanky build, attempted a comeback. He signed a contract with Sherman of the Class C East Texas League and went 18–8 with a 4.16 ERA and a respectable .974 fielding average. He struck out 108 and walked only 43 in 218 innings.

Darryl Strawberry

Strawberry, Darryl Eugene **OF–DH**

1983–* B:3/12/1962, Los Angeles, CA Deb:5/6/1983, NY NL BL/TL 6'6", 200

G	AB	R	H	HR	RBI	OBP	SLG	AVG
1583	5418	898	1401	335	1000	.360	.505	.259

At the start of his career, Darryl Strawberry's potential seemed boundless. The top pick in the country out of Crenshaw High School in Los Angeles in 1980, he raced through the Mets' minor league system. He arrived in New York in May 1983, and slugged 26 homer runs to handily win the National League Rookie of the Year Award. He would become the most prolific slugger in Mets history, but injuries, legal problems, and drug abuse were to prevent Strawberry from establishing himself among baseball's elite.

In 1984 the Mets finished second in the National League East and never finished lower than that again during Strawberry's tenure at Shea Stadium. In 1985 the Mets were 32 games over .500 with him in the lineup, but only five games over in the 43 games he missed with a hand injury. A year later Strawberry showed the kind of explosive postseason force he could be. He had been 0-for-10 against Houston southpaw Bob Knepper when he faced him in Game 3 of the National League

Championship Series with two runners on and the Mets down by three; he homered and the Mets went on to win. In Game 5 Nolan Ryan stopped the Mets for nine innings on two hits, but one of those hits was a Strawberry home run, and the Mets won it in 12 innings, 2–1. Although Strawberry batted just .208 in the World Series, he belted an 0–2 pitch from Al Nipper over the right field fence for a key insurance run in Game 7.

Strawberry hit 39 home runs in each of the next two seasons. Strawberry's commitment to the club was questioned when he confessed during the 1988 NLCS that his dream was to play in Los Angeles with his old friend Eric Davis, who was with Cincinnati at the time. The following spring Strawberry got into a fight with teammate Keith Hernandez before the team photo shoot. In the last year of his contract in 1990, Strawberry hit 37 homers and drove in 108 runs, then sat out several crucial games down the stretch with back spasms when the Mets had a chance to catch Pittsburgh.

In just eight seasons, "Straw" set Mets career records for home runs, RBIs, extra base hits, and runs. He finished second in the Most Valuable Player voting in 1988, was selected to start the All-Star Game five times, had more 100-RBI seasons than any Mets player in history, and was a member of the exclusive 30-home run, 30-stolen bases club. Yet his seemingly daily mood changes made back-page news in New York's tabloids and his personal problems drained his concentration. The Mets made only a token offer to sign him as a free agent.

A $23.5 million, five-year contract brought Strawberry home to Los Angeles. In 1991, he hit 28 home runs and drove in 99 runs for the second-place Dodgers, but he played only 75 more games with the team over the next two years due to back problems.

Strawberry started the 1994 season at the Betty Ford Clinic for a drug problem, then signed with the Giants after Los Angeles released him. The year ended with a tax evasion indictment, and the 1995 season began with a drug suspension. Still, he finished the year in the postseason when the Yankees picked him up for the stretch run.

After the Yanks released Strawberry, he played his way back into the game with the St. Paul Saints of the independent Northern League. The Yankees brought him back on July 4, 1996, and he hit 11 home runs in the second half of the season.

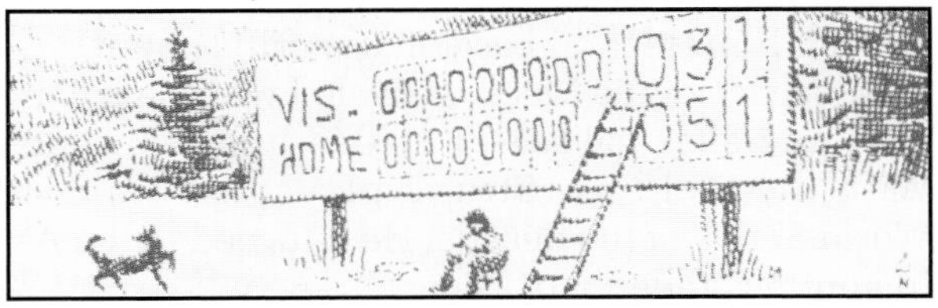

Strawberry hit three homers in a game against the White Sox on August 8, and won another game in the bottom of the ninth with his 300th career home run. He was hitless in the Division Series and batted just .188 in the World Series, but tormented Baltimore in the ALCS with three home runs and a .417 average.

Strawberry's 1997 season was all but lost to a knee injury. The 37-year-old slugger again resurrected his career in 1998, hitting 24 homers in 101 games before a diagnosis of colon cancer ended his season on October 1. Strawberry's efforts to overcome his disease were widely lauded and he regained much of the popularity he had squandered earlier in his career. The Yankees wore his number 39 on the back of their caps throughout the playoffs. While recovering from surgery, however, he was arrested on drug and solicitation charges in Florida. Once again his career was in jeopardy and his reputation in tatters. Nevertheless, Strawberry returned to the Yankees for the end of the 1999 season, contributing to their second consecutive world championship. In December 1999 the Yankees picked up a $750,000 option for 2000 on the troubled slugger; a month later he failed another drug test and was suspended for one year.

Gabby Street

Street, Charles Evard **C**

1904–05, 1908–12, 1931 M(1929–33, 1938, 365–332)
B:9/30/1882 Huntsville, AL D:2/6/1951, Joplin, MO
Deb:9/13/1904, CIN NL BR/TR 5'11", 180

G	AB	R	H	HR	RBI	OBP	SLG	AVG
504	1501	98	312	2	105	.273	.256	.208

Gabby Street was known as "Walter Johnson's catcher," yet he gained his greatest acclaim for catching a baseball dropped from the top of the Washington Monument. Later he was fired as manager of the St. Louis Cardinals after producing back-to-back pennants. Always a gifted talker, Gabby became an entertaining announcer with the Cards, sharing the booth with a young Harry Carey.

Street played for South Kentucky College. He started his professional career with Hopkinsville in the Kitty League in 1890, playing for the princely sum of $60 per month. Sold to Terre Haute in the Central League and then to Cincinnati, he made his big league debut in 1904.

He bounced around, going from Cincinnati to the Boston Braves and back to Cincinnati in 1905. The next two seasons he played with the San Francisco Seals of the Pacific Coast League. In 1908 he was sold to Washington and returned to the major leagues. With the Senators, Street became known as Walter Johnson's catcher, even though he played for Washington just four years, and the last two on a part-time basis. Street's best batting average during those four years was .222.

In *Walter Johnson: Baseball's Big Train*, author Henry W. Thomas wrote that Johnson credited his success to Street for helping him maintain his concentration. Plus Street was not afraid to take the blame if one of his calls for a pitch ended up costing Washington the game.

"What a catcher he was," Johnson said, "a big fellow, a perfect target, a great arm, spry as a cat back of the plate, always talking, full of pep and fight. Gabby was always jabbering and never let a pitcher take his mind off the game. When we got in a tight spot Gabby was right there to talk it over with me. He never let me forget a batter's weakness."

The young Johnson won 14 and 13 games in Street's first two seasons, then 25 in each of Street's last two seasons in Washington. By then, "the Big Train" was up to speed and Street was out of town.

During his stay with Washington, Street settled a bet between two sportsmen by catching a ball tossed from the top of the Washington monument on the morning of August 21, 1908. Although reported to be "considerably jarred by the impact," he pocketed a $500 prize and then caught Johnson's 3–1 victory over Detroit that later that day.

Street was traded to the New York Highlanders in December 1911. From there he returned to the minors. When the United States entered World War I, Street enlisted, saw action in Europe, and left with the rank of sergeant. He was later called "Old Sarge."

Back in baseball as a manager in 1930, Street brought the Cardinals a pennant in his first year at the helm. They were defeated by the Philadelphia Athletics in six games in the World Series but repeated as pennant-winners in 1931. In a rematch with the A's, the Cards won in seven games. Nevertheless, St. Louis owner Sam Breadon fired Street in July 1933. The Cards had won only 11 of their last 33 games and were drawing less than 1,000 fans per contest. Street, seemingly unable to control the emerging Gas House Gang, particularly Dizzy Dean, was replaced by Frankie Frisch.

Street dropped out of baseball and then returned to manage the St. Louis Browns to a seventh-place finish in 1938. He managed in the minors before returning to St. Louis as a Cardinals broadcaster until his death in 1951. "He was a great talent, so charming, so colorful," Harry Caray said. "He could go on the air, be himself, and be a hit."

Cub Stricker

Stricker, John A. **2B**

1882–88 B:2/15/1860, Philadelphia, PA Deb:5/2/1882, PHI AA BR/TR 5'3", 138

G	AB	R	H	HR	RBI	OBP	SLG	AVG
1196	4635	790	1106	12	411	.306	.294	.239

At just 5 feet 3 inches and 138 pounds, second baseman Cub Stricker was one of smallest men to ever play major league baseball. He was also one of the better fielding second baseman in the game's history.

John A. Stricker (originally Streaker) played amateur ball before joining the American Association in 1882. In the course of his big league career he led circuit second basemen in putouts and errors three times; games played and assists twice; and in double plays once. Through 1999 he remained seventh in chances accepted and total chances per game; fifth in putouts per game; and sixth in putouts per contest.

When the Brotherhood of Professional Baseball Players plotted to launch their own circuit, in 1889 they assigned Stricker to watch the gate at the Cleveland ballpark so as to ascertain what attendance they could expect. When the Players' League formed, Stricker was named to its Board of Directors, representing the Cleveland club along with its owner, Albert L. Johnson. He later returned to the National League and managed St. Louis for part of the 1892 season.

Amos Strunk

Strunk, Amos Aaron **OF**

1908–24 B:1/22/1889, Philadelphia, PA D:7/22/1979, Llanerch, PA Deb:9/24/1908, PHI AL BL/TL 5'11½", 175

G	AB	R	H	HR	RBI	OBP	SLG	AVG
1512	4999	696	1418	15	530	.359	.374	.284

One of the finest defensive outfielders of all time, Amos Strunk began his major league career with his hometown Philadelphia Athletics at age 18. He became a regular in 1912, and batted .294 over the next six years. The injury-prone Strunk was better known for his defense, however, using his speed and sure hands to good effect. He also used his speed on the bases; he had 185 steals and mastered the "double-squeeze"—scoring from second base on a sacrifice bunt.

Manager Connie Mack quarreled with Strunk in 1917 and after the season traded him to Boston. With the Red Sox, Strunk played in his fifth World Series of the decade. He returned to the A's in another trade in 1919.

Strunk went to the Chicago White Sox on waivers in 1920. He batted a career-high .332 with the Sox in 1921, and was the American League's top pinch hitter two years later. In 1924 Strunk signed once again with the A's, where he finished his career. Strunk then spent a half-century as an insurance broker before dying at age 90.

Dick Stuart

Stuart, Richard Lee **1B**
1958–69 B:11/7/1932, San Francisco, CA
Deb:7/10/1958, PIT NL BR/TR 6'4", 212

G	AB	R	H	HR	RBI	OBP	SLG	AVG
1112	3997	506	1055	228	743	.319	.489	.264

He could hit, when he wasn't striking out. In fact, Dick Stuart hit more than 20 home runs six times in his short career. But he will forever be remembered as "Dr. Strangeglove."

No matter what Stuart could do with a bat, it was always overshadowed by his incredible—but, nonetheless, always cheerful—ineptitude with his glove. "He's a Williams-type player. He bats like Ted and fields like Esther," said one sportswriter. And Stuart himself noted, "One night in Pittsburgh, 30,000 fans gave me a standing ovation when I caught a hotdog wrapper on the fly."

Signed for a $10,000 bonus by the Pirates as an outfielder, Stuart spent 1951 at Modesto of the California League, where he batted just .229 with four homers. Nonetheless, he was given a slight raise. With typical modesty he wrote back, "Your contract isn't much but I'm signing. Your .229 hitter in 1951 is your .332 hitter in 1952."

He wasn't far off. For Billings in 1952 he led the Pioneer League with 31 homers and 121 RBIs, while batting .313. He spent 1953 and 1954 in the military, and when he came out he was promptly cut from the New Orleans roster—for insisting on taking batting practice with only clean balls. He then spent a few games with the Mexico City Tigers, returned to Billings, and, despite playing only 101 games there, again led the Pioneer League in homers with 32.

Stuart's most famous year was 1956. In 141 games for the Lincoln Chiefs of the Western League, he smashed 66 homers while driving in a league-leading 158 runs. At Puebla one of his homers traveled 610 feet on the fly. Stuart's already-large ego went into overdrive. While still in the minors he exclaimed, "I like to walk down the street and hear them say, 'Jesus, there goes Dick Stuart.' I like to see my name in the paper, especially in the headlines. I crave it. I deserve them headlines."

His performance earned him a chance to make the Pirates in 1957, but he struck out too much and fielded abysmally. Bobby Bragan called him "one of the worst outfielders I've ever seen." Soon the versatile Stuart would become one of the worst first basemen anyone had ever seen.

In 1957 Stuart hit 45 homers playing in three different minor leagues. The following season he hit 31 home runs in 80 games for Salt Lake City in the Pacific Coast League before the Pirates called him up in midseason. He hit 16 homers in only 67 games as a rookie and then averaged 28 over the next three years. In 1960 he played on his lone world championship ballclub. He batted .150 against the Yankees as the Pirates won the World Series in seven games.

Then came his best all-around year, 1961, when he hit a career-high .301 with 35 homers and 117 RBIs, and a league-leading 121 strikeouts. One analyst reported that had the shorter left field still been at Forbes Field in 1961, Stuart would have hit 62 homers.

"Dr. Strangeglove" lived up to all phases of his reputation. He was a regular first baseman for seven of his 10 years in the big leagues, and he led his league in errors each of those seven years, including an astounding 29 one season. If ever a player needed the designated hitter rule, it was Dick Stuart—unfortunately his fielding and decreasing productivity forced him out of the game four years before the DH debuted in a game.

In November 1962 Stuart was traded to the Red Sox, where he continued to butcher balls at first base. "Stuart's car should have one of those low-number license plates," joked Dick Radatz. "It should be E-3." His teammates were not amused by Stuart's lack of team spirit, nor by his undermining of manager Johnny Pesky.

Of course, Stuart also continued to hit home runs. Fenway Park was made for his righthanded power. He finished second in the American League in 1963 with a career-high 42 round-trippers and led the league with 118 RBIs. Despite—or perhaps because of—his fielding, he was immensely popular in Boston, hosting a highly-rated Sunday night local television show. Red Sox attendance increased by 210,000 during his first season with the club.

Even though he hit 33 homers and drove in 114 runs the following year, he continued to strike out at an alarming rate. Stuart struck out about once every four at bats, which is not uncommon these days but was unheard of then.

Stuart's attitude soon wore out his welcome with management. Sportswriter Al Hirshberg

wrote, "Dick Stuart insults waitresses and stewardesses, heads for the nearest bar, and ignores training." In December 1964 he was traded to Philadelphia for sore-armed pitcher Dennis Bennett. Stuart had one good year left, hitting 28 homers with 95 RBIs in 1965. The following February he was traded to the Mets, and later in the season he signed with the Dodgers. He hit only seven homers in 69 games that season, and he was hitless in two at bats of the 1966 World Series.

Taking a sabbatical from American baseball, Stuart signed with Japan's Taiyo Whales in 1967 and hit .280 with 33 homers and 79 RBIs. The next year he hit .217 with 16 homers and 40 RBIs, and it was sayonara, Strangeglove-san.

"After being the only American player on a team in Hiroshima, nothing bothers me anymore," said Stuart on his return to the States. He hit .157 with one homer in 51 at bats with the Angels in 1969 and then retired. He later became a securities analyst.

Tom Sturdivant

Sturdivant, Thomas Vigil **P**

1955–64 B:4/28/1930, Gordon, KS Deb:4/14/1955, NY AL BL/TR 6'1", 186

W	L	PCT	G	SV	IP	BB	SO	ERA
59	51	.536	335	17	1137	449	704	3.74

The 1956 and 1957 seasons were righthander Tom Sturdivant's heyday. In both seasons he won 16 games for the Yankees. In Game 4 of the 1956 World Series he defeated Brooklyn, 6–2, with a complete game. In 1957 he led the American League with a .727 won-lost percentage.

In 1958 Sturdivant developed a sore arm and never won more than nine games in a season again. But he did get to see the country. In May 1959 he was traded to Kansas City. In December 1959 the Athletics sent Sturdivant to the Red Sox. The Red Sox let him go in the December 1960 American League expansion draft, and the Washington Senators picked him up. In June 1961 Sturdivant went to Pittsburgh in exchange for knuckleballer Tom Cheney. He spent part of that season with Columbus of the International League.

Sturdivant, who started in the minors as an infielder, was nicknamed "Snake" because of his outstanding curveball. He retired after the 1964 season and became an executive with the Rollins Trucking Company in Oklahoma City.

George Suggs

Suggs, George Franklin **P**

1908–15 B:7/7/1882, Kinston, NC D:4/4/1949, Kinston, NC Deb:4/21/1908, DET AL BR/TR 5'7½ ", 168

W	L	PCT	G	SV	IP	BB	SO	ERA
99	91	.521	245	17	1652	355	588	3.11

George Suggs had a number of fine seasons in the major leagues, twice winning 20 games, but the righthander made the mistake of having a bad year in the Federal League in 1915. The league folded after the season and the best of the players were combined with existing teams in the American and National leagues. Suggs was 35 and coming off an 11–17 season, and he signed with Raleigh of the Class D Carolina State League. He never made it back to the major leagues.

Suggs started with Greensboro in 1904 and played with Jacksonville and Memphis before coming to the Tigers for part of 1908. The Tigers farmed him out to Mobile. But Otto Jordan of the opposing Atlanta team (part of the Reds' farm system) said, "Suggs is 100 percent too strong for the Southern league. He can make his mark anywhere. He is a wonder and if worked often enough will win a big majority of his games in any company." As a result the Reds bought Suggs' contract.

Suggs went 20–12 with a 2.40 ERA in 1910. He recorded two more winning seasons in Cincinnati and was offered a $3,600 salary for 1913. He insisted on $4,200 and wrote to Reds owner Garry Herrmann, "I have always been ready to work, in turn or out, and have kept in condition every day in the season. I am now in as good condition as ever in my life and am confidant that I can give the club good service this season." Herrmann complied but Suggs went 8–15 in 1913. He jumped to the new Federal League in 1914 and won 24 games for the Baltimore Terrapins.

Gus Suhr

Suhr, August Richard **1B**

1930–40 B:1/3/1906, San Francisco, CA Deb:4/15/1930, PIT NL BL/TR 6', 180

G	AB	R	H	HR	RBI	OBP	SLG	AVG
1435	5176	714	1446	84	818	.368	.428	.279

He held the National League record for most consecutive games played—but Gus Suhr ended his streak to attend his mother's funeral. Signed by San Francisco in the Pacific Coast League in 1925, Suhr played for the Seals through 1929, with the exception of most of 1925 when he was optioned to the Three-I League. In 1929 he hit .381 and registered 51 homers and

177 RBI. He was aided that year by playing in every inning of 202 games. With the exception of games played, none of those were league-leading totals, but he did score a circuit-pacing 196 runs.

A slick-fielding first baseman, Suhr played in a then-league record 822 straight games from September 11, 1931 to June 4, 1937. On April 29, 1930 he walked six times in a single game. He is one of the few rookies to drive in over 100 runs in a season, but his 107 RBIs in 1930 were topped that same year by Wally Berger's record 119. In 1938 he led National League first basemen in putouts and double plays (he had previously led the league in double plays in 1930). In July 1939 Suhr was traded to the Phillies. He played his final major league game the following year.

Clyde Sukeforth

Sukeforth, Clyde Leroy **C**

1926–34, 1945 M (1947, 2–0) B:11/30/1901, Washington, ME Deb:5/23/1926, CIN NL BL/TR 5'10", 155

G	AB	R	H	HR	RBI	OBP	SLG	AVG
486	1237	122	326	2	96	.319	.331	.264

Clyde Sukeforth is the scout who recommended that the Brooklyn Dodgers sign Jackie Robinson—before he even had a chance to see him play. Sukeforth had been sent to scout Robinson when he was a young shortstop playing for the Kansas City Monarchs in the Negro Leagues. Because of a shoulder injury Robinson was out of the lineup, but after talking with him Sukeforth was so impressed with the young player's intelligence and character that he gave his full endorsement. A few days later Brooklyn's Branch Rickey signed Robinson to a minor league contract.

Sukeforth enjoyed a modest career as a major league catcher, then managed in the minors before going to work for Rickey. He was actually the Dodgers manager when Robinson made his major league debut in 1947. Sukeforth replaced Leo Durocher, who had been suspended for the season for consorting with gamblers. After two games Burt Shotton then took over and guided Brooklyn to the pennant.

When Rickey left the Dodgers to join the Pirates, Sukeforth followed. In 1954 Rickey asked Sukeforth to scout Joe Black, the former Dodgers pitcher who had been dispatched to the minor leagues. As with Robinson in 1945, Black never did perform in front of Sukeforth. He did, however, spot a raw but rifle-armed outfielder. Sukeforth told Rickey to draft Roberto Clemente after the season. Having played a part in the signing of two of the game's most influential players, Sukeforth eventually settled into retirement in the small town of Waldoboro, Maine, just a few miles from his birthplace.

Billy Sullivan

Sullivan, William Joseph, Sr. **C**

1899–1916 M(1909, 78–74) B:2/1/1875, Oakland, WI D:1/28/1965, Newberg, OR Deb:9/13/1899, BOS NL BR/TR 5'9", 155

G	AB	R	H	HR	RBI	OBP	SLG	AVG
1147	3647	363	777	21	378	.254	.281	.213

Billy Sullivan always hit his weight, though he weighed only 155 pounds. With more than 2,000 at bats, Sullivan wasn't the worst hitter of all time. In fact, his lifetime average of .213 is robust compared to the .170 posted by Bill Bergen. He was, aptly, a member of the worst-hitting champs in history, the Chicago White Sox of 1906—"the Hitless Wonders." Their catcher was truly hitless in the Series, going 0-for-21 with nine strikeouts.

Sullivan did not stay in the major leagues for 16 years because he was a great hitter. In that World Series he helped navigate the young Sox staff through a Cubs lineup that won a record 116 games during the season; the Cubs hit just .196 (the Sox batted .198).

His career began in 1899 with Boston. He jumped to White Sox and caught the first American League game on April 24, 1901. It was a career day, because Sullivan collected two hits and scored a run. Sullivan batted under .200 five times, but he led the American League in fielding percentage four times.

He managed the Sox in 1909, and owner Charles Comiskey promised both Sullivan and Big Ed Walsh lifetime employment; then, he let both of them go. Sullivan was released on the next-to-last day of spring training in 1914. "Where am I to go?" Sullivan asked. "I can still play." He played one more game, for the Tigers in 1916.

His son, William Joseph Sullivan, Jr., also called "Bill," caught in the majors, too (some people say Charles Comiskey paid for his college education). In 1940 the Sullivans became the first father-son catching duo in World Series history. Unlike his dad he hit safely in the Series, but he wasn't far removed—Bill Jr. batted just .154 as his Tigers fell in seven games.

Frank Sullivan

Sullivan, Franklin Leal **P**

1953–63 B:1/23/1930, Hollywood, CA Deb:7/31/1953, BOS AL BR/TR 6'6½", 215

W	L	PCT	G	SV	IP	BB	SO	ERA
97	100	.492	351	18	1732	559	959	3.60

Frank Sullivan was a two-time All-Star who tied for the American League lead with 18 victories in 1955. A durable starter, he also led the AL in innings pitched in 1955 and pitched 200 or more innings for four straight years. He later converted to a reliever, but with much less success—as evidenced by his 3–16 record with the putrid 1961 Phillies.

Sullivan began his professional career with San Jose in the California League in 1948 and quickly found himself with a rough crowd. He roomed with three grizzled veterans who made him go out and get beer for them. Often they would kick him out of his lodgings and make him sleep in the street. Not surprisingly, he didn't pitch well at San Jose.

His next stop was Oroville of the Class D Far West League, where in one game he walked three men in each inning but still pitched a shutout. He spent the 1951 and 1952 seasons in the military. Sullivan reached the rank of sergeant in the army while serving in Korea.

In 1953 Sullivan had just been married when he was called into his manager's office. He thought he was going to be chewed out for getting hitched in midseason, instead Sullivan was told he was being promoted to the Red Sox. In his first major league appearance he entered a game in relief against Detroit with the bases loaded and none out. Nobody scored, but Sullivan admitted, "It was a lot tougher than Korea."

At 6 feet 6½ inches tall, Sullivan was the tallest pitcher in the American League when he was traded for Gene Conley, the tallest pitcher in the National League, in December 1960. Sullivan spent his last year in the majors, 1963, with Minnesota. After his retirement he worked as a golf pro in Kauai.

Billy Sunday

Sunday, William Ashley **OF**

1883–90 B:11/19/1862, Ames, IA D:11/6/1935, Chicago, IL Deb:5/22/1883, CHI NL BL/TR 5'10", 160

G	AB	R	H	HR	RBI	OBP	SLG	AVG
499	2007	339	498	12	170	.300	.317	.248

Billy Sunday was drunk. Not falling-down drunk, but drunk enough, and so were his White Stockings teammates, King Kelly, Ned Williamson, and Silver Flint. They sat on the curb at the intersection of State and Madison streets in Chicago and listened as a "gospel wagon" pulled up close by and began a service.

Quietly Sunday began to weep as he recalled the Methodist hymns his mother sang back home in Ames, Iowa. Suddenly he stood and headed for the nearby Pacific Garden Mission. "Goodbye boys," he told his friends. "I'm through. I'm going to Jesus Christ. We've come to a parting of the ways." The outfielder was about to set off on a path that would make him the world's most famous evangelist of his time.

Sunday had not had an easy youth. His father was killed in the Civil War just weeks after Billy's birth, and his mother eventually had to send her children to homes for impoverished soldiers' orphans. As a teenager, Sunday worked in a hotel and on a farm before moving to Marshalltown, Iowa, where he found a job in a furniture store and a place on the town baseball team.

Marshalltown was the home of White Stockings manager Cap Anson. He watched young Sunday play and said he "ran like a scared deer." Anson brought him up to Chicago in 1883.

Far from the greatest ballplayer in the world, Sunday may have been the 19th century's fastest. He needed all the speed he could muster because his hitting was undistinguished and, at least early in his career, his fielding was erratic. His lifetime fielding average was just .883, and in 43 games in 1884 his average was an atrocious .663. Yet in 1888 he improved sufficiently to lead the league in putouts. That season he also became the first major league outfielder to record an unassisted double play. At the close of his career, his fielding was spectacular.

Sunday was credited with 84 stolen bases in 1890, his last season. Reports said that he could round the bases in 14 seconds flat. He once stole second, third, and home on consecutive pitches. In 1887 the *Boston Herald* rated him, along with King Kelly and John Montgomery Ward, among the league's best baserunners.

One time Sunday and Arlie Latham agreed to race one another in a 100-yard dash. The betting by teammates was fierce—some reports say $75,000—and Sunday decided he didn't want to participate in something that involved gambling. Anson took him aside and reminded him that his teammates had their life savings bet on him. Sunday relented and beat the speedy Latham by 10 feet.

While in Chicago, Sunday attended Northwestern University during the off-season and coached football and baseball there. He did not immediately retire from the game upon finding religion, although he did refrain from playing on the Sabbath and from cards, gambling, alcohol, and the theater. His teammates, while not exactly flocking to his banner, extended him their respect. "Bill, religion ain't my long suit, but if ever old Mike can help you, just let me know, for I won't knock you," promised Kelly.

A story Sunday liked to tell on the gospel trail involved a game in which Chicago and Detroit were battling for the National League championship. Detroit had runners on second and third, with two out. Charlie Bennett was at the plate for Detroit and launched a line drive toward some temporary seats set up for the overflow crowd.

Sunday said, "I ran, and as I ran I made a prayer. 'God, if you ever helped mortal man, help me to get that ball, and you haven't very much time to make up your mind, either.' I jumped and shoved out my left hand and the ball stuck. I jumped up with the ball in my hand. Up came Tom Johnson. Tom used to be mayor of Cleveland. 'Here is $10, Bill. Buy yourself the best hat in Chicago. That catch won me $1,500.' An old Methodist minister later asked me, 'Why, William, you didn't take the $10, did you?' I said, 'You bet your life I did.'"

In the spring of 1891, the 28-year-old Sunday announced that he was leaving his $3,500-a-year baseball career and going to work for the Chicago YMCA for $83 a month. "I heard the Lord ask me to play ball for Him, so I signed up," said Sunday. He put the same energy into his preaching that he put into his famous catch.

In 1917 he hit New York City for a series of revivals that resulted in more than 98,000 conversions. Estimates suggest that in his lifetime Sunday preached to 85 million people and converted a million of them. When he died in 1935, *The New York Times* called him "the greatest high-pressure and mass-conversion Christian evangelist that America has ever known."

Jim Sundberg

Sundberg, James Howard **C**

1974–89 B:5/18/1951, Galesburg, IL Deb:4/4/1974, TEX AL BR/TR 6', 195

G	AB	R	H	HR	RBI	OBP	SLG	AVG
1962	6021	621	1493	95	624	.328	.348	.248

In a 16-year career, Jim Sundberg appeared in 1,962 games, 1,927 behind the plate. Only three major leaguers—Carlton Fisk, Bob Boone, and Gary Carter—caught more games. Sundberg led the American League in total chances six times, in putouts six times, in assists six times, in fielding percentage six times, and in double plays four times.

His .995 fielding percentage in 1979 established a league record. He won six Gold Glove Awards; when he retired only Cincinnati's Johnny Bench had won more at the position. On top of it all, Sundberg was tough to steal on, some seasons nailing more than 50 percent of all potential basestealers. He eventually became a pretty fair hitter.

Sundberg, a star catcher at the University of Iowa, was drafted first by the Oakland A's and later by the Texas Rangers, but he opted not to sign with either team. In 1973, after being drafted by the Rangers for a second time, he finally signed. Sundberg played only 91 games in Double A before becoming the regular catcher in Texas in 1974.

Although no one questioned his defensive ability, his bat was another matter. Sundberg struggled in his first three seasons; in 1975, when he caught a career-high 155 games, he batted a just .199. Two years later he broke out to hit .291. In 1978 he had a career-best 22-game hitting streak and made the All-Star team.

A beaning by a Don Aase fastball nearly ended his career in 1979, but Sundberg was as resilient as he was talented. In six of his first seven seasons he caught at least 140 games. He went on to establish a league record for catchers during the 1979 season by committing only four errors. On another occasion he was out of the Rangers' lineup following a hemorrhoid operation. The team expected him to miss at least three or four games, but Sundberg was out of the lineup for only seven innings.

After starring in Texas, where he caught pitchers as varied in style as Charlie Hough, Ferguson Jenkins, Gaylord Perry, and Jon Matlack, Sundberg was sent to Milwaukee in December 1983 for catcher Ned Yost and minor league pitcher Don Scarpetta. It was a lopsided trade. Sundberg made the All-Star team in 1984, while Yost was soon in the minor leagues, and Scarpetta never pitched an inning in the majors. In January 1985 Sundberg was traded to Kansas City in a six-player, four-team deal involving the Royals, Brewers, Rangers, and New York Mets.

Sundberg helped Kansas City win the American League West title in 1985, then had several key hits in the ALCS against Toronto. In Game 7 Sundberg's bases-loaded triple broke open a 2–1 game. He finished the series with a homer, three runs scored, and six RBIs. He then caught every inning in the Royals' seven-game victory over St. Louis in the World Series. His six runs scored in the Series led all participants.

After one more year in Kansas City, Sundberg was dealt to the Chicago Cubs for outfielder Thad Bosley and pitcher Dave Humpert. Sundberg spent a year and a half with the Cubs before returning to Texas in 1988. He caught 73 games in 1989 and retired at season's end.

B.J. Surhoff

Surhoff, William James **C-OF-3B**

1987-99 B:8/4/64, Bronx, NY Deb:4/8/87, MIL AL BL/TR 6'1", 200

G	AB	R	H	HR	RBI	OBP	SLG	AVG
1716	6195	809	1738	146	893	.335	.415	.281

Before the Milwaukee Brewers drafted him in 1985, B.J. Surhoff had already made a name for himself in the amateur ranks. He starred for the University of North Carolina, where he set a school record with a .392 batting average. He was a key player on the United States 1983 Pan American team as well as the 1984 Olympic team. *The Sporting News* honored him as its College Player of the Year in 1985.

After just one full season in the minors, Surhoff became Milwaukee's starting catcher. He was steady if unspectacular behind the plate for the Brewers for six seasons. In 1993 Surhoff stopped catching and played most of his games at third base and in the outfield. His batting average rose from .252 during his last year as a catcher to .320 just three years later.

Rejuvenated, Surhoff left Milwaukee as a free agent and signed with the Baltimore Orioles. It was there, in cozy Camden Yards, that he found his power stroke. In Milwaukee, Surhoff had only once hit more than seven home runs; in Baltimore, he became a slugger, stroking 20 or more homers in three of his first four seasons. The 1999 season was his finest, as Surhoff played in his first All-Star Game and posted career highs with 28 home runs and 107 RBIs.

Surhoff grew up in athletic family in Rye, New York. His brother Rick pitched for the Phillies and Rangers, and his father Dick played in the National Basketball Association for the New York Knicks and Milwaukee Hawks in the 1950s.

Rick Sutcliffe

Sutcliffe, Richard Lee **P**

1976, 1978–94 B:6/21/1956, Independence, MO Deb:9/26/1976, LA NL BL/TR 6'7", 215

W	L	PCT	G	SH	IP	BB	SO	ERA
171	139	.552	457	18	2697[2]	1081	1679	4.08

Rick Sutcliffe came to Chicago in one of the greatest midseason trades in Cubs history. A fifth-place team just a year earlier, the Cubs got off to a great start in 1984, but desperately needed a staff ace to hold off the equally surprising New York Mets. Sutcliffe, unhappy and laboring below the .500 mark with the Cleveland Indians, was available. Acquired in June, he turned out to be the difference for the Cubs in a tight race in the National League East in 1984.

Sutcliffe had pitched in the NL for parts of five years with the Los Angeles Dodgers, including a 17–10 record as the 1979 Rookie of the Year. When he returned to the league in 1984, however, it was as if he had arrived from another planet. The 6-foot-7-inch, red-bearded righthander hurtled towards home plate with a motion that hid the ball from view until just before his release. He struck out 155 batters in 150 innings with the Cubs on his way to a remarkable 16–1 record. He became just the fourth pitcher to win 20 games in a season while pitching in both the AL and NL. Sutcliffe unanimously won the NL Cy Young Award, even though he pitched in just 20 games with the Cubs.

On September 24 Sutcliffe did something that hadn't been done in 40 seasons: he pitched the Cubs into the postseason. Sutcliffe two-hit the Pirates to clinch the NL East title. In the Championship Series opener at Wrigley Field, he shut down the San Diego Padres and hit a home run against Eric Show in a 13–0 blowout. A Padres rally off Sutcliffe in the seventh inning of Game 5—aided by Leon Durham's error—cost the Cubs the pennant.

Injuries and ineffectiveness over the next two years kept Sutcliffe from approaching his 1984 success. He bounced back with a league-high 18 wins in 1987 and won 16 games in 1989 to help the Cubs reach the postseason again. Shoulder injuries limited him to just six wins over his last two years as a Cub. The Baltimore Orioles signed Sutcliffe as a free agent on December 19, 1991.

Sutcliffe was impressive enough in spring training to earn the start in the inaugural game at Oriole Park at Camden Yards. Sutcliffe, at 36 the oldest Opening Day pitcher in Orioles history, notched a 2–0 shutout against Cleveland. After 14 starts he was tied for the major league lead with nine wins. Although he was not as sharp the rest of the season, his 16–15 record still earned him AL Comeback Player of the Year honors.

After a second season in Baltimore, the Missouri native made his final stop with the St. Louis Cardinals in 1994. Upon retirement, he served as a minor league pitching instructor. He also worked as a broadcaster.

Bruce Sutter

Sutter, Howard Bruce **P**

1976–88 B:1/8/1953, Lancaster, PA Deb:5/9/1976, CHI NL BR/TR 6'2", 190

W	L	PCT	G	SV	IP	BB	SO	ERA
68	71	.489	661	300	1042^{1}	309	861	2.83

The first practitioner of what came to be called "the pitch of the 1980s," the split-finger fastball, Bruce Sutter was for nine years the dominant closer in the National League. He was a Cy Young Award winner—only the second reliever to be so honored—a four-time winner of the Fireman of the Year Award, and a five-time save leader, who had at least 21 saves every one of those years.

When he retired in 1988, he was the National League leader in career saves, with 300. Whitey Herzog, who managed Sutter in St. Louis, said, "Sutter's nine years were probably the top nine years in the history of the game."

The split-fingered fastball, also known as the "splitter" because of its resemblance to the "spitter" or spitball, was slightly different from the old, familiar forkball that pitchers had been throwing since onetime Phillie Bert Hall first tried it in 1908. "Tiny" Bonham, Roy Face, and Lindy McDaniel all used the forkball, but the action on their pitch was more like a sinking changeup.

Howard Bruce Sutter was blessed with exceptionally large hands—his fingers were "a full joint longer than normal," according to historian Martin Quigley—and a limber wrist that enabled him to throw the pitch harder. Sutter's splitter was much more deceiving to batters because it spun quickly enough to look like a fastball.

Hub Kittle, a longtime pitching coach, described Sutter's pitch: "As he comes over and down with very fast arm action, just like his fastball, the ball squirts out with sinker spin from his thumb. The ball comes in looking like a straight fastball with a velocity around 85 miles an hour. As it gets to the plate, it just seems to sit, like an airplane coming in for a landing."

One of the key advantages of the splitter is that it works equally well on lefthanded and righthanded hitters. As a result, clubs with Sutter pitching for them didn't need a lefty–righty bullpen tandem; he could handle both. Interestingly, Roger Craig, the pitching coach and manager given credit for popularizing the splitter, learned it from Sutter.

Part of the reason for Sutter's success with the split-finger fastball was his exceptional control of it. He routinely walked a third as many men as he struck out, and he did not throw a wild pitch after 1984. Opponents batted only .223 against him in a career shortened by 11 operations, including elbow and knee surgery.

Sutter's professional career started after he realized that playing for Old Dominion was no ticket to the big leagues. He began playing semipro ball, and the Cubs signed him in 1971. During 1972, his first season in the minors, he injured his elbow. He described the injury as "popping the joint." Afraid to tell anyone, he went home after the season and paid a doctor to repair the damage. But when he went to spring training in 1973, he was fearful about what a curveball might do to his arm. He tried to get by without one, but after the Cubs pitching coach, Fred Martin, noticed Sutter's exceptionally long fingers, he suggested that Sutter try the forkball as an alternative.

Although Sutter took three minor league seasons to perfect the pitch, the Cubs could not ignore his ERA in two of those seasons: 1.35 and 2.15. He made the majors early in 1976. At age 23 he earned 10 saves in 52 appearances and took charge of the Cubs bullpen.

He began the 1977 season on fire. By midseason he had 26 saves and had pitched 75 innings. A pulled muscle, however, kept him from appearing in the All-Star Game, and he could manage only five saves the rest of the season. His final total was still only four behind Rollie Fingers for the league lead.

Sutter notched 27 saves in 1978 for the fifth-place Cubs, and in 1979 he won the Cy Young Award when he spun a 2.23 ERA to accompany his 37 saves. After the season he applied for salary arbitration, one of the first stars to do so. Sutter asked for $700,000; the Cubs offered half that. The arbitrator, required to choose one figure or the other, went with Sutter. The decision sent shock waves throughout major league baseball. As a result a player with a handful of experience could compare his stats to someone with a proven portfolio, even someone who had signed a rich free-agent contract. Richard Wagner, conservative owner of the Reds, called the Sutter decision "an atom bomb for our industry."

After he led the league in saves again in 1980 and was chosen for the All-Star Game for the fourth straight year, Whitey Herzog and the Cardinals went after him. Sutter became a Cardinal in exchange for three players and was the cornerstone of their bullpen for four years, leading the league in saves for three of those years.

The Cardinals won the NL East in 1982. Sutter was the winning pitcher in Game 2 of the NLCS and saved Game 3 as the Cards swept the Braves. He won Game 2 and saved Games 3 and 7 of the World Series, striking out six Brewers in the 7⅔ innings he pitched. He retired all six batters he faced in Game 7 to give St. Louis its first world championship since 1967.

Even with Sutter continuing his mastery of NL hitters, the Cards did not finish closer than 11 games from first during the next two seasons. And Sutter, whose 45 saves had tied the major league record for a season, chose to try free agency. Not surprisingly, the relief ace became the richest player in baseball at the time. The Atlanta Braves signed him for six years at $10 million. But the intelligent Sutter wasn't seeking instant riches. The contract paid him just $750,000 a year for the six years, with the remaining money invested in an insurance plan from which Sutter could receive more than $1 million a year for 30 years, beginning in 1991.

Sutter saved 23 games for the Braves in 1985, but a shoulder problem, the last in a succession of injuries that contributed to shortening his career, kept him out of action for nearly two years. He threw only 18 innings in 1986 and none at all in 1987. In 1988 Sutter returned and was able to pile up 12 saves for the Braves by All-Star time. But his arm wearied. He collected only two more saves before the end of the season, and then he left the game for good.

Mule Suttles

Suttles, George **1B–OF**

Negro Leagues Player (1918–44) Manager, Umpire B:3/2/1901, Brockton, LA D:1968, Newark, NJ BR/TR 6'6", 215

Prior to the premier of Josh Gibson, power-hitting first baseman Mule Suttles was often known as the "Black Babe Ruth." With second baseman Dick Seay, shortstop Willie Wells and third baseman Ray Dandridge comprised the so-called "million-dollar infield"—the conjecture being that's what they'd have been worth had they been white.

Suttles, a former coal miner, was a huge man—6 feet 6 inches and 230 pounds. In 1925, in just 87 games, he led the Negro National League in homers (26), triples (19), and average (.418); he even stole 11 bases. It was estimated that once in Havana's Tropical Park he hit a home run close to 600 feet. He was especially potent in East-West Game competition, batting .412 and slugging .883 in five contests. In 1933 he hit the first homer in East-West Game history. His 11th-inning home run won the 1935 contest.

In the field the enormous Suttles was adequate. "He wasn't graceful, but anything they threw he could handle," former teammate Double Duty Radcliffe said. Suttles played into his 40s, but reassured teammates he was still up to it. "Don't worry about the Mule going blind, just load the wagon and give me the lines," he would say.

Don Sutton

Sutton, Donald Howard **P**

1966–88 B:4/2/1945, Clio, AL Deb:4/14/1966, LA NL BR/TR 6'1", 185

W	L	PCT	G	SH	IP	BB	SO	ERA
324	256	.559	774	58	5282^{1}	1343	3574	3.26

Don Sutton is the only pitcher to win 300 games despite recording only one 20-win season. He pitched 200 or more innings in each of his first 21 seasons, except for the 1981 strike-shortened year. He was also a clutch performer in several postseason performances. "When I pitch during the regular season, it's work," he once said. "To me it's a routine thing, like going to the office or walking into a factory. You have a job to do and you go out and try to do it. But the playoffs, the World Series, and things like the All-Star Game are just plain fun."

Sutton was a sharecropper's son on a farm near Pensacola, Florida. His schoolteacher, Henry Roper, showed the youngster how to throw a baseball when he was 10 years old. Recalling his mentor, Sutton said, "The guy...taught me to pitch the way I do now—the same philosophy—and I was immediately able to throw strikes. I've pitched basically the same way for as long as I can remember, with a fastball, curve, slider, and changeup."

The Los Angeles Dodgers signed Sutton as a free agent in September 1964 for $7,500. In 1965 he was assigned to Santa Barbara in the California League. He got off to a quick start there with an 8–1 record, a 1.50 ERA, and 101 strikeouts in 84 innings. At midseason, he was promoted to Triple-A Albuquerque in the Texas League. He was 15–6 with a 2.78 ERA, and won Texas League Player of the Year honors.

In 1966 he went to spring training with the big club. The Dodgers' top pitchers, Sandy Koufax and Don Drysdale, were contract holdouts that spring, and Sutton got a long look. "[Dodgers manager Walter] Alston was forced to pitch Bill Singer and me about 40 innings," Sutton recalled. "I stayed busy that spring and I made the club."

Sutton won 12 and lost 12 and contributed 226 innings as the fourth starter on a club that won the NL pennant and then lost the World Series to the Orioles in four straight games. His 209 strikeouts were the most by an National League rookie since Grover Cleveland Alexander's 227 in 1911. Sutton and Koufax combined for 526 strikeouts, the third most by a duo in league history.

During the next three seasons, Sutton suffered through the Dodgers' decline and pitched under .500 for second-division Los Angeles ballclubs. Then from 1970 through 1976, he won 125 games, culminating with his only 20-win season. He completed at least 10 games in each of those seasons,

including a career-high 18 in 1972. In 1972 he also led the league in shutouts with nine.

In 1974 he pitched the Dodgers to an NL West title, then won two games in their four-game victory over the Pirates in the Championship Series. Sutton gave up just one earned run to win the opener with a four-hit shutout and then combined with Mike Marshall on a three-hitter for the clincher. In the World Series, Sutton started two games and recorded the Dodgers' lone win, in Game 2, as they fell to Oakland in five games.

Following his 20-win season in 1976, Sutton dropped off to 14–8 in 1977. But he was named Most Valuable Player in the All-Star Game, and the Dodgers again won the NL West. Sutton pitched a complete-game win in Los Angeles' four-game victory over the Phillies in the NLCS. In the World Series against the Yankees, Sutton started the opener and took a no-decision in the Dodger loss. He came back in Game 5, with the Yankees up three games to one, and pitched a complete-game victory. New York wrapped up the Series in Game 6 as Reggie Jackson hit three consecutive home runs in his defining World Series' performance.

On the surface the 1978 season was nearly identical: Sutton won 15 games, the Dodgers beat the Phillies in four games in the NLCS, and then lost to the Yankees in six. Yet two incidents that season established his reputation as an iconoclast.

That season Sutton and Dodger Steve Garvey scuffled in the Shea Stadium visitors' clubhouse, apparently over comments regarding Garvey and teammate Reggie Smith. "All you hear about on our team is Steve Garvey, the All-American boy. Well, the best person on this team for the last two years—and we all know it—is Reggie Smith," Sutton said later. "Reggie Smith doesn't go out and publicize himself....Reggie's not a facade or a Madison Avenue image. He's a real person."

Sutton also came under suspicion for doctoring the baseball that year. Ejected from a game for defacing a ball, he threatened to sue the National League. Over the years, Sutton would use that suspicion as a psychological tool in his war with batters. When reporters asked if he scuffed up the ball, he would reply, "Never on Sunday." When they asked if he used foreign substances on the ball, he answered, "Vaseline is made right here in the USA."

"Sutton has set up such a fine example of defiance that someday I expect to see a pitcher walk out to the mound with a utility belt on—you know, file, chisel, screwdriver, glue," said longtime pitching coach Ray Miller. "He'll throw a ball to the plate with bolts attached to it."

Sutton was 13–5 for the Dodgers in 1980 and won the NL ERA title with a 2.21 mark. He became a free agent following the season and signed with the Houston Astros. Pitching on the same staff as Nolan Ryan, Sutton seemed the antithesis of "The Ryan Express." Sutton told manager Bill Virdon that he preferred to be relieved in the sixth or seventh inning if he could get a win. Back in 1975 he had said, "I'm the most loyal player money can buy."

On August 30, 1982, Sutton was traded to the Milwaukee Brewers for three players to be named later, as the Brewers pushed for the American League East pennant. Sutton paid dividends: he was 4–1 in seven starts and defeated Jim Palmer and the Orioles in the division clincher on the final day of the regular season. He started and won Game 3 in the Brewers' five-game ALCS victory over California. In the World Series Sutton earned a no-decision in Game 2, then, with a chance to clinch the Series in Game 6, Sutton was bombed, 13–1. St. Louis won in seven games.

Sutton's record fell to 8–13 in 1983, but he bounced back to go 14–12 in 1984. He was traded to Oakland in December 1984, then to California in September 1985. He won 15 games between the two teams that season, re-signed with California as a free agent, and won 15 games the next season, at age 41. In June 1986 he defeated the Texas Rangers, 5–1, to notch his 300th victory.

Sutton returned to the Dodgers for the 1988 season and then retired to become a broadcaster. He finished his career as the Dodgers' all-time strikeout leader, topping Sandy Koufax. A humble Sutton said, "Comparing me with Sandy Koufax is like comparing Earl Scheib with Michelangelo." However, former Astros teammate Nolan Ryan once said of Sutton, who had five career one-hitters and nine two-hitters, "He may have been the best finesse pitcher I ever saw."

Sutton's name is scattered throughout baseball's annals. He struck out 3,574 batters and had 30 games with 10 or more strikeouts. He hurled 58 shutouts, and recorded 44 wins after age 40. His career yield of 10.29 baserunners per nine innings compares favorably with Hall of Famers Catfish Hunter's 10.21, Ferguson Jenkins' 10.28, and Don Drysdale's 10.33.

Yet some critics questioned Sutton's merits for the Hall of Fame. Sutton's 256 losses are the eighth most in major league history. He won 20 games just once, never led the league in victories, and was named to only four All-Star teams. However, only 11 men in 117 years of major league baseball have won more games. Sutton won 324 games; Hall of Famers Koufax and Drysdale won 374 games—combined. Sutton finally won election to Cooperstown in 1998, on his fifth try.

Ezra Sutton

Sutton, Ezra Ballou **3B-SS**

1871–88 B:9/17/1850, Palmyra, NY D:6/20/1907, Braintree, MA Deb:5/4/1871, CLE NA BR/TR 5'8½", 153

G	AB	R	H	HR	RBI	OBP	SLG	AVG
1031	4281	739	1231	21	518	.315	.381	.288

Ezra Sutton, one of the great third basemen of the 19th century, participated in a number of historic firsts for the infant national pastime. He played in the first National Association game (Cleveland at Fort Wayne on May 4, 1871) and made the first error. He hit the first professional league home run on May 8, 1871 (as well as the second later that same day). On June 14, 1876, he and teammate George Hall became the first players to record three triples in a National League contest.

When William Hulbert was putting together his Chicago White Stockings club for 1876 (the machinations surrounding which eventually led to the National League), Sutton was one of two players he illegally signed from the Athletics. Sutton, however, reneged on the deal and stayed with Philadelphia.

On August 27, 1887, Sutton scored six runs in a single game. After leaving baseball, Sutton's life took a horrible downturn. His sawmill business failed, he became paralyzed for life in 1890, and in 1906 his wife died after a lamp exploded and set her afire. Sutton died a year later.

Bill Swift

Swift, William Charles **P**

1985-86, 1988-98 10/27/1961, Portland, ME Deb: 6/7/1985, SEA AL BR/TR 6', 180

W	L	PCT	G	SV	IP	BB	SO	ERA
94	78	.547	403	27	1599^2	507	767	3.95

The 14th of 15 children, Bill Swift was All-America at the University of Maine and pitched for the 1984 U.S. Olympic team. He was the second player picked in the 1984 June draft. One year later he was in the majors with Seattle after just seven starts in Double A. He pitched in 52 games, 38 of them starts, in his first two years with the Mariners.

Bill Swift depended on an excellent heavy sinker and two breaking pitches, but injuries cost him appearances and effectiveness throughout his career. He made only five minor league appearances in 1987 before his season ended because of elbow problems that lingered throughout the rest of his career. He made a comeback as a reliever. In 1991 he had a 1.99 ERA and 17 saves in 71 appearances. After the season he was traded to San Francisco with Mike Jackson and Dave Burba in exchange for Kevin Mitchell and Mike Remlinger.

Swift returned to a starting role and had two very good years with the Giants. In 1992 he went 10–2 with a 2.08 ERA, the lowest for a National League starter in seven seasons. He won 21 games the next season as the Giants nearly won the NL West. Swift signed with the Colorado Rockies as a free agent for 1995, but recurring elbow problems limited him to part-time duty for three years. Resurfacing with Seattle in 1998, Swift made 26 starts before he was pulled from the rotation late in the year. His career ended when Seattle released him before the start of the 1999 season.

Greg Swindell

Swindell, Forrest Gregory **P**

1986–* B:1/2/1965, Fort Worth, TX Deb: 8/21/1986, CLE AL BR/TL 6'3", 225

W	L	PCT	G	SH	IP	BB	SO	ERA
119	108	.524	502	12	2070^2	468	1413	3.82

Greg Swindell was the second overall player taken in the June 1986 draft after a stellar career at the University of Texas. Swindell went 43–8 in his three years with the Longhorns, earned three All-America selections, and was the youngest player on the 1984 U.S. Olympic team. He made only three minor league starts prior to his major league debut with Cleveland.

He was 8–10 in his first two seasons with the Indians, including a 15-strikeout game in 1987. He became one of American League's top left-handers in 1988, winning 18 while hurling four shutouts and 12 complete games. He won 13 games in 1989, and made his only All-Star appearance. The hard-thrower was the ace of Cleveland's rotation until his trade to the Cincinnati Reds for Jack Armstrong and two other pitchers after the 1991 season.

Swindell won 12 games with a 2.70 ERA with the Reds in 1992, but he disliked playing in Cincinnati. He signed a lucrative free agent deal with the Houston Astros in the off-season. Swindell and fellow Texan Doug Drabek, who had also returned to his home state as a big-money free agent, were double-barrel busts in Houston.

His velocity gone, Swindell became an effective middle reliever with the Indians, Minnesota Twins, Boston Red Sox, and Arizona Diamondbacks. He had just one blown save and a 2.51 ERA in 63 games in 1999 to help the Diamondbacks reach the postseason in just their second year of existence.

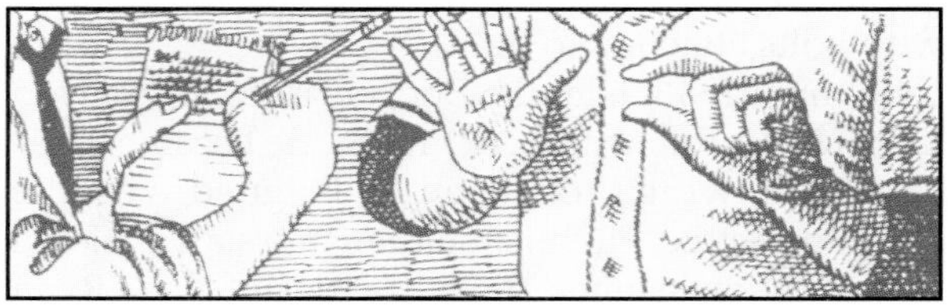

Ron Swoboda

Swoboda, Ronald Alan **OF**

1965–73 B:6/30/1944, Baltimore, MD Deb:4/12/1965, NY NL BR/TR 6'2", 205

G	AB	R	H	HR	RBI	OBP	SLG	AVG
928	2581	285	624	73	344	.325	.379	.242

When Ron Swoboda first arrived in New York in 1965 as a 20-year-old rookie, Mets manager Casey Stengel exclaimed, "Amazing strength. Amazing power. He can grind the dust out of the bat. He will be great, super, wonderful. Now if only he can learn to catch a flyball."

Swoboda eventually turned Stengel's evaluation on its head. He never matched the initial outburst he exhibited in his first half-season, when he hit most of his 19 home runs. In Game 4 of the 1969 World Series, however, he made a circus catch of Brooks Robinson's line drive in the ninth inning. A run scored on the diving catch to tie the game, but the Mets won in 10 innings.

While everyone remembers his catch, few remember that "Rocky" batted .400 in the Series. He had two hits in Game 5 and doubled home Cleon Jones with the run that broke a 3–3 tie in the eighth inning, allowing the Mets to win the world championship.

Swoboda had been a key contributor to the Mets' incredible 38–11 finish to overtake the Cubs for the 1969 National League East title. On September 15, 1969, when Steve Carlton struck out 19 Mets, it was Swoboda's two homers that gave New York a 4–3 victory.

After half a season with the Expos and over three years with the Yankees, Swoboda retired following the 1973 season. He later became a broadcaster in New York, Phoenix, and New Orleans.

Pat Tabler

Tabler, Patrick Sean **1B-DH-OF**

1981–92 B:2/2/1958, Hamilton, OH Deb:8/21/1981, CHI NL BR/TR 6'2", 200

G	AB	R	H	HR	RBI	OBP	SLG	AVG
1202	3911	454	1101	47	512	.348	.379	.282

Pat Tabler excelled at delivering with the bases loaded. Over the course of his career, the righthanded batter hit nearly .500 with all bases occupied. At first it seemed like a statistical fluke, but the years rolled by and Tabler kept doing the job. In 1983 he hit .579 and drove in 25 runs in 19 bases-loaded at bats. The next year he hit .556 with 15 RBIs in nine at bats, and the year after that he went .857 with the bases loaded.

Tabler was named Cincinnati's high school Most Valuable Player and Player of the Year. He was the Yankees first-round selection in the June 1976 draft. He played in Oneonta, Fort Lauderdale, West Haven, Nashville, and Columbus before being traded in 1981 to the Cubs for Bill Caudill and Jay Howell. After playing parts of the 1981 and 1982 seasons with the Cubs, Tabler was traded twice in the off-season and ended up with Cleveland, where he hit .291.

In 1986 the 28-year-old hit .326 overall, fourth-best in the American League. His 51-point gain over 1985 was highest in the league as Tabler stepped into a breach created by Cory Snyder's ankle injury. Alternating as Cleveland's first baseman and designated hitter, Tabler batted .307 and reached career bests in most offensive categories. Traded to Kansas City in the middle of 1988, Tabler later played with the Mets and Blue Jays.

Only average in the field, Tabler was an excellent hitter who liked to hit against power pitchers. As the years passed, Tabler, lacking substantial power and speed, was increasingly used as a pinch hitter. He played for the 1991 AL Eastern Division champion Toronto Ble Jays, and ended his career with two pinch-hit appearances for Toronto's 1992 World Series winners.

Jim Tabor

Tabor, James **3B**

1938–1947 B:11/5/1916, New Hope, AL D:8/22/1953, Sacramento, CA Deb:8/2/1938, BOS AL BR/TR 6'2", 175

G	AB	R	H	HR	RBI	OBP	SLG	AVG
1005	3788	473	1021	104	598	.322	.418	.270

Jim "Rawhide" Tabor was all or nothing in the field. He led the American League third baseman five straight times in errors, but he also led the American League in putouts and assists once each and in double plays twice. The main reason Tabor was in the lineup because he could hit. As a rookie he collected four homers in a doubleheader against the Philadelphia Athletics on July 4, 1939. Three were in the second game, and two of those were grand slams. He drove in a grand total of 11 runs in the twin bill.

He was not afraid to let his feelings be known. Tabor, who attended the University of Alabama before signing with the Red Sox, caught minor league teammate Ted Williams lollygagging in the outfield. When Williams allowed a ball go all the way to wall, Tabor slammed him against a locker after the game. "If you ever do that again, I'll shove you in that goddamn locker and kill you." Another story about Tabor, when he was playing for the Sox, has Lefty Grove walking over to berate the third baseman after an error. "You're hired to pitch," said Grove, "I'm here to play third base. Get out there and pitch."

In 1941 Red Sox manager Joe Cronin suspended Tabor for missing an exhibition game. Tabor was a hard drinker, but, said teammate Tony Lupien, "He hustled. He was tough."

He entered the army on October 23, 1944 and was discharged on December 14, 1945. Sold to the Phillies in January 1946, he led the National League in fielding double plays that year.

Frank Tanana

Tanana, Frank Daryl **P**

1973–93 B:7/3/1953 Detroit, MI Deb:9/9/1973, CAL AL BL/TL, 6'3", 195

W	L	PCT	G	SH	IP	BB	SO	ERA
240	236	.504	638	34	4188^{1}	1255	2773	3.66

A successful transition from hard thrower to finesse pitcher allowed left-hander Frank Tanana to forge a 21-year major league career. Although he never won 20 games in a season he was a consistent enough performer to post an impressive 240-win total by the time he retired.

Tanana broke in with the California Angels in 1973. He split four decisions that season, then won at least 14 games for the next five seasons. He led the American League with 269 strikeouts in 1975; it marked the only time between 1972 and 1979 that Angels teammate Nolan Ryan didn't lead the league. Tanana paced the AL with seven shutouts and a 2.54 earned run average in 1977.

Tanana won at least 12 games in a season a dozen times. He had his best winning percentage (.655) in 1976, when he went a career-best 19–10 for the Angels. It was the second of three straight seasons in which he struck out more than 200 hitters.

Five years after breaking in at age 20, however, Tanana's fastball was spent. Slowed by a sore shoulder, he made only 17 starts in 1979. The Angels traded him to the Boston Red Sox after the 1980 season. He left California ranking second to Nolan Ryan on the all-time Angel list in wins, starts, complete games, strikeouts, innings, and shutouts.

The highlight of Tanana's post-California tenure came with the Tigers in 1987. The Detroit native defeated the Toronto Blue Jays on the last day of the season, 1–0, to win the American League East title for the AL Championship Series. After seven-and-a-half years in Detroit, he spent his final season in New York with the Mets and Yankees in 1993.

Jesse Tannehill

Tannehill, Jesse Niles **P**

1894–1909, 1911 B:7/14/1874, Dayton, KY D:9/22/1956, Dayton, KY Deb:6/17/1894, CIN NL BB/TL 5'8", 150

W	L	PCT	G	SH	IP	BB	SO	ERA
197	117	.627	358	34	2750^1	477	940	2.79

Jesse Tannehill was an excellent hitting pitcher, a lifetime .256 hitter who often pinch-hit or played the outfield, and the first pitcher to win 20 games and hit .300 in the same season. On at least one occasion, Tannehill may have been too accomplished for his own good. In 1904, pitcher Vic Willis remembered Tannehill as, "the fellow who dislocated his shoulder hitting fungo flies before a game we played in Pittsburgh a few years ago. They had to give him ether to put his arm back in place."

An excellent control pitcher who allowed few base runners, Tannehill debuted with Cincinnati in 1894 and returned to the majors with Pittsburgh, going 9–9 in 1897. The next year he soared to 25–13, and he went 24–14 in 1899. In 1900 he had the second-best won-lost percentage in the National League, going 20–6 and hitting .336. On September 20, 1900, he demonstrated even more versatility by stealing home.

He led the league in ERA in 1901 and jumped to the New York Highlanders in 1903. After a 15–15 season for New York, he was traded to Boston for Long Tom Hughes in December. Tannehill had the last laugh. He no-hit the White Sox on August 17, 1904, beating Ed Walsh, 6–0. (Jesse's brother Lee went 0-for-3.) In July 1908 he was traded to Washington and in 1911 ended back where he'd started, in Cincinnati.

Lee Tannehill

Tannehill, Lee Ford **3B- SS**

1903–12 B:10/26/1880, Dayton, KY D:2/16/1938, Live Oak, FL Deb:4/22/1903, CHI AL BR/TR 5'11", 170

G	AB	R	H	HR	RBI	OBP	SLG	AVG
1090	3778	331	833	3	346	.269	.273	.220

Lee Tannehill was one of the best fielders in the early years of the American League. He led American League third basemen in assists four times, in double plays twice, and in errors once. When he shifted over to shortstop, his range was equal to any player in the league and he was the first player at his position to make two unassisted double plays in a season. But, unlike his brother Jesse, who was a good hitting pitcher for 15 years, Lee was not much of a threat offensively. The most damage Lee ever did with a bat came in 1905, when a bat slipped out of his hand and broke teammate Gus Dundon's jaw.

Although he fit right in with the "Hitless Wonder" White Sox of 1906, Tannehill was yanked from the World Series after he batted .111 in the first three games. His replacement, George Davis, batted .308 and the White Sox shocked the Cubs in six games.

Tannehill had just three career home runs but he did hit the first homer ever in Comiskey Park at the park's opening on July 31, 1910. It was a ground-rule homer that bounded through an iron gate in left field in the fourth inning. An inning later Ty Cobb homered to virtually the same spot to aid in Detroit's 6–5 win.

On August 4, 1911, Tannehill turned two unassisted double plays against Washington. Although his .254 average in 1911 was a career high, he was released after playing just four games the following year.

Chuck Tanner

Tanner, Charles William **OF**

1955–62 M(1970–1988, 1,352–1,381) B:7/4/1929, New Castle, PA Deb:4/12/1955, MIL NL BL/TL 6', 185

G	AB	R	H	HR	RBI	OBP	SLG	AVG
396	885	98	231	21	105	.325	.388	.261

A local columnist once called Chuck Tanner "Pittsburgh's cockeyed optimist." That might have been an understatement. He managed in the big leagues for 17 full seasons and parts of two others, and wherever he went, he smiled—all the time. He told his players how wonderful they were, how lucky they all were to be alive, how lucky they were to be able to make a living playing baseball. Pessimism was not permitted. Frowns were discouraged.

Tanner grew up during the Great Depression and lived with his family in a tiny house without electricity or running water. Luckily, Chuck's father had both steady work in a steel mill and a sunny outlook that he passed on to his son. "You know," Chuck Tanner once said, "I always thought we were just as happy and had as much as anybody."

An outfielder, Tanner signed with the Boston Braves out of high school and spent nine years in the minors. He made it to the majors in 1955, and on the first pitch he saw as a major leaguer he delivered a pinch-hit home run off the Reds' Gerry Staley. That was the highlight of his career as a player. He spent four full seasons and parts of four others in the majors and finished with a .261 average and 21 homers. After his last year as a player, 1962, he worked for 26 years as a manager. He was fired only once, in 1988 from Atlanta, his last job.

Roland Hemond gave Tanner his first managing job, in the Angels system, and when Hemond became general manager of the White Sox late in the 1970 season he quickly hired Tanner. His 1971 team went 79–83, a 23-game improvement over the previous season's mark. With Dick Allen on board in 1972, the White Sox went 87–67 and made a run at the eventual world champion Oakland A's, finishing in second place by 5½ games.

Tanner gave Allen lots of room. When Allen was late to the park, Tanner let it go. He told Allen again and again how great he was, how important he was to the team, and Allen responded with a Most Valuable Player season. Tanner also turned Wilbur Wood into a starter and a 20-game winner. He worked with Jim Kaat on a no-windup delivery after Kaat was traded to Chicago in 1973 and resuscitated his career.

Tanner spent three more years in Chicago but never matched that 1972 season. When Charlie Finley beckoned in 1976, Tanner moved to Oakland. Free agency was about to become a reality and Finley traded holdout Reggie Jackson to Baltimore just before the start of the season. Without Reggie's bat, Tanner had to rely on foot speed, so he had the A's run and run and run. When they were through running, they were in second place, 2½ games behind the Royals, and they were the new American League record holders for stolen bases in a season with 341—the most steals since the 1911 New York Giants set the major league record with 347.

There was another remarkable aspect to that season: Tanner's relationship with Finley. "You've read all the stories about Finley calling his managers at all hours," Tanner once said. "Well, he rarely called me. I guess it's because I shocked him by calling him. He told me he never had a manager who called him."

Tanner soon realized that the A's were going to be split up, and he had a chance for his dream job—going back home to manage the Pirates. So Finley let him go, in exchange for Manny Sanguillen and $100,000. Tanner managed the Pirates from 1977 through 1985 and his "We Are Fa-mi-ly" team won the 1979 World Series after three straight second-place finishes in the National League East.

That championship season was hectic. The clubhouse was often a madhouse, players' wives danced on the top of the dugout, and the pennant race went down to the last weekend. Through all of it, Tanner kept smiling and kept believing. Reliever Kent Tekulve remembered Tanner's mother dying during the Series. The Pirates were down, three games to one, and Tanner said, "My mother went upstairs to get us some help." The Bucs overcame the deficit and beat the Orioles with a game-winning home run by Willie Stargell in the sixth inning of the seventh game.

The Pirates never came close again after that season, and in 1985 Tanner presided over an aging team that was mired in a drug scandal. In a total collapse, the Bucs finished last with a 57–104 record. It was time to move. Tanner's last stop was Atlanta. With the Braves organization, the smiles didn't work. Bobby Cox, the general manager at the time, was rebuilding a crumbling franchise from scratch and Tanner was supposed to be the caretaker. Tanner was fired after 39 games (and only 12 wins) in his third season. He went home to New Castle, retiring with a record of 1,352–1,381. His son Bruce pitched for the White Sox in 1985.

Danny Tartabull

Tartabull, Danilo (Mora) **OF–DH**
1984–1997,* B:10/30/1962, San Juan, Puerto Rico
Deb:9/7/1984, SEA AL BR/TR 6'1", 205

G	AB	R	H	HR	RBI	OBP	SLG	AVG
1406	5011	756	1366	262	925	.371	.496	.273

Unlike his father Jose, who hit two home runs in nine seasons, Danny Tartabull was a feared slugger in the American League. Tartabull had five 100-RBI seasons and three 30-homer campaigns.

The converted shortstop broke into the 1986 Seattle lineup as an outfielder. Tartabull's best season in Seattle resulted in 25 home runs and 96 RBIs in 1986. Those numbers improved following a trade to Kansas City a year later. Tartabull hit a career-best .309 and set a club record with three grand slams in 1988. He blossomed into an All-Star in 1991 under the tutelage of Royals manager Hal McRae. McRae got him to start hitting the ball up the middle; Tartabull responded with a personal best of .316 batting average and a league-best .593 slugging percentage.

He was lured to the Yankees for the 1992 season with a large multi-year contract. Tartabull had 31 homers and 102 RBIs in 1993, but his 156 strikeouts were one shy of his career worst. When his production fell in 1994, the Yankee Stadium boo-birds made Tartabull their favorite target.

The Yankees traded him to Oakland late in the 1985 season. After driving in 102 runs combined in 1994 and 1995, Tartabull took off with the White Sox in 1996. He had 101 RBIs on just 120 hits, including 27 home runs. Philadelphia signed the resurgent slugger as a free agent, but an injured foot ended his Phillies career after just three games. The Padres, in need of a power bat, brought a healthy Tartabull to training camp in 2000.

Frank Taveras

Taveras, Franklin Crisostomo (Fabian) SS

1971–82 B:12/24/1949, Las Matas De Santa Cruz, Dominican Republic Deb:9/25/1971, PIT NL BR/TR 6', 168

G	AB	R	H	HR	RBI	OBP	SLG	AVG
1150	4043	503	1029	2	214	.302	.313	.255

Shortstop Frank Taveras could run. He couldn't hit very well and was maddeningly erratic in the field, but during his 11-year career he stole 300 bases in 1,150 games. Taveras spent his first full five seasons in the majors with the Pirates. He became the Bucs' regular shortstop in 1974, and the highlight of his career was leading the National League in stolen bases, with 70, in 1977.

Although his lifetime average was .255, respectable for a shortstop, he had a grand total of two homers—one every 2,022 at bats. As for clutch hitting, he drove in 214 runs, or one every 19 at bats.

Taveras was traded to the hapless Mets early in the 1979 season and, despite his flaws, was one of the team's better players. Mistaking Taveras for a team leader, Mets owner Lorinda deRoulet, the daughter of the late Joan Payson, gave him a five-year contract extension. He was out of baseball in 1982, long before the contract was up.

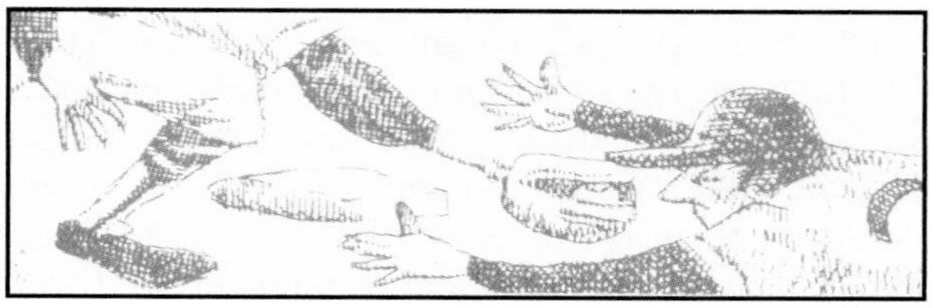

Dummy Taylor

Taylor, Luther Haden P

1900–08 B:2/21/1875, Oskaloosa, KN D:8/22/1958, Jacksonville, IL Deb:8/27/1900, NY NL BR/TR 6'1", 160

W	L	PCT	G	SH	IP	BB	SO	ERA
116	106	.523	274	21	1916^{1}	551	767	2.75

Deaf pitcher Luther "Dummy" Taylor was more than just a curiosity on John McGraw's Giants. He was a quality starter who won 21 games for New York in 1904. The gangly Taylor taught many of the Giants—including McGraw—how to use sign language. One day Taylor was vehemently expressing to McGraw what he thought of umpire Jimmy Johnstone. Suddenly Johnstone thumbed Taylor right out of the game. Taylor expressed shock. McGraw demanded "What for?" Then Johnstone proceeded to duplicate all of Taylor's signs. "For that. And I wouldn't take that from him even if he pulled off his shoes and said it with his toes," Johnstone concluded.

The righthander started his career with the Giants in 1900 and led the league with 45 appearances in 1901. He pitched briefly for the Indians at the beginning of the 1902 season but returned to New York during the season. Taylor left the Giants in 1908 after compiling a career 116–106 record with a 2.75 ERA. He played in the minors for five more years and then umpired in the Midwest. Taylor later joined the staff of the Illinois School for the Deaf.

In 2000, more than 40 years after his death, Taylor became a protagonist in a novel: *Havana Heat*. Author Darryl Brock picked up Taylor's story in 1911, when he went with the Giants on an exhibition trip to Havana. Although fictional, Brock's characters included many members of the Giants and the renowned Cuban national team of that era.

Jack Taylor

Taylor, John W. P

1898–1907 B:1/14/1874, New Straitsville, OH D:3/4/1938, Columbus, OH Deb:9/25/1898, CHI NL BR/TR 5'10", 170

W	L	PCT	G	SH	IP	BB	SO	ERA
152	139	.522	310	19	2617	582	657	2.66

Jack Taylor won 20 games four times and earned 152 wins during his career, but his claim to fame was an uncanny ability to finish what he started. On June 20, 1901, he pitched a complete game. Through his next 186 starts—more than five years' worth—he pitched a complete game every time he started. One game went 19 innings; another went 18—he finished them both. On another occasion, he pitched both ends of a doubleheader. Fifteen times he relieved other, less stouthearted hurlers, and each time finished the game.

Taylor was not a particularly imposing physical specimen. At 5 feet 10 inches and 170 pounds, he was average or a little less for a pitcher of his day. Finally, on August 9, 1906, he was relieved in a game.

Although he pitched only 10 years in the National League, two of them partial seasons, Taylor had six seasons of over 300 innings and completed 278 of his 286 starts. For all his finishing up what he started, he led the league only once in complete games, with 39 in 1904.

Ron Taylor

Taylor, Ronald Wesley **P**

1962–72 B:12/13/1937, Toronto, Ontario, Canada
Deb:4/1/1962, CLE AL BR/TR 6'1", 195

W	L	PCT	G	SV	IP	BB	SO	ERA
45	43	.511	491	72	800	209	464	3.93

Ron Taylor was a quality relief pitcher for the Mets in their 1969 "Miracle" year, but another miracle occurred in 1972 when the 34-year old righthander applied to a Toronto medical school and started on the path that would make him a successful physician. "I must have suffered some brain damage hanging around [Jerry] Koosman but I decided to try it," he recalled. "I had to present letters of recommendation and one of the most important came from [Mets executive] Donald Grant. He really went to bat for me."

The son of a Welsh immigrant to Canada, Taylor earned an engineering degree, reporting late to spring training for four years as he finished course work. Originally signed by Cleveland for a $4,000 bonus, he pitched in the World Series for both the Cardinals and Mets. He never allowed a run in 10 ⅓ career postseason innings

Always an intellectual, Taylor amused and baffled teammates with such observations as "I just found out what's driving me crazy—it's baseball." and "Doubleheader tomorrow, barring nuclear holocaust."

On the mound he was all business. He came to spring training in 1967 as a nonroster player and proceeded to lead New York in both appearances and saves for four consecutive years The only Met with postseason experience entering the 1969 season, Taylor provided veteran leadership in a bullpen that included the enigmatic Tug McGraw. He picked up a win and a save in New York's three-game sweep of the Braves in the National League Championship Series. He then saved Game 2 of the World Series.

He finished his career with the Padres in 1972. His medical career later brought him back to baseball as team physician for the Blue Jays.

Perhaps nostalgic for his days as a Miracle Met, Taylor muses: "Sometimes I dream of coming back as a pitcher and not making it."

Tony Taylor

Taylor, Antonio Nemesio (Sanchez) **2B**

1958–76 B:12/19/1935, Central Alara, Cuba
Deb:4/15/1958, CHI NL BR/TR 5'9", 179

G	AB	R	H	HR	RBI	OBP	SLG	AVG
2195	7680	1005	2007	75	598	.322	.352	.261

Tony Taylor established himself as reasonably good offensive second baseman in the 1960s, although his lack of range made him a defensive liability. Taylor began his career with Texas City-Thibodeux as a third baseman-shortstop in 1954 and led the Evangeline League in triples with 12. The following year he paced the Northern League in both triples and stolen bases. After stops in Danville and Dallas, he was drafted by the Chicago Cubs and converted to a second baseman.

The Cubs traded Taylor along with pitcher Cal Neeman to the Phillies for pitcher Don Cardwell and first baseman Ed Bouchee in May 1960. That year he made the All-Star team and got a hit in his only at bat. In 1964 he set a National League record for the fewest assists by a second baseman in 150 or more games when he registered just 358.

In June 1971 Taylor was traded to the Tigers for minor league pitchers Mike Fremuth and Carl Kavanaugh. With the Tigers he was a skilled pinch hitter and helped them to an American League East title. In December 1973 he was unconditionally released by the Tigers and re-joined the Phillies.

He played parts of 15 seasons with Philadelphia. His six steals of home is good for second place in Phillies history. He later had two tours as a coach for the Phillies and coached with the Marlins in 1999.

Birdie Tebbetts

Tebbetts, George Robert **C**

1936–52 M(1954–58, 1961–66, 748–705)
B:11/10/1912, Burlington, VT D:3/24/1999, Manatee, FL
Deb:9/16/1936, DET AL BR/TR 5'11½", 170

G	AB	R	H	HR	RBI	OBP	SLG	AVG
1162	3704	357	1000	38	469	.341	.358	.270

George Robert "Birdie" Tebbetts had to wait his turn to crack the Detroit Tigers' starting lineup. In the mid-1930s the catching position was occupied by the likes of Mickey Cochrane, Ray Hayworth, and Rudy York.

Finally getting a chance in 1939, Tebbetts batted .261 with 53 RBIs in 106 games, as the Tigers finished fifth behind the powerhouse New York Yankees. In 1940, with Tebbetts batting .296 and working with such pitching greats as Bobo Newsom and Schoolboy Rowe, the Tigers defeated the Cleveland Indians by a single game to win the American League pennant. However, they lost the World Series to Cincinnati in seven games, as Tebbetts took an 0-for-11 collar in the four games he saw action. Birdie spent three years in the service and returned to the Tigers' starting lineup in 1946. Traded to the Boston Red Sox in 1947, he later finished his career with the Cleveland Indians.

Tebbetts went on to manage the Cincinnati Reds, the Milwaukee Braves, and the Indians over an 11-year period. His best team was the 1956 Reds, who won 91 games yet finished in third place—Brooklyn won the pennant by a game over Milwaukee, with Cincinnati two games back. He led the Indians to 87 wins in 1965, a total the franchise did not reach again for 30 years.

Patsy Tebeau

Tebeau, Oliver Wendell **1B-3B**

1887, 1889–1900 M(1890–1900, 726–583)
B:12/5/1864, St. Louis, MO D:5/15/1918, St. Louis, MO
Deb:9/20/1887, CHI AL BR/TR 5'8", 163

G	AB	R	H	HR	RBI	OBP	SLG	AVG
1167	4618	671	1291	27	735	.332	.364	.280

Patsy Tebeau was a player-manager who led the Cleveland Spiders to three postseason appearances during the 1890s, including a championship in 1895. In a 13-year major league career he batted .280 and achieved a .556 winning percentage as a manager.

Tebeau began his professional career in 1886 with St. Joseph of the Western League, where he batted .294 as a second baseman. Switched to third base the following year with Denver, he hit .424 in 95 games. The White Stockings were interested enough to bring him up to the majors that year, but Tebeau was a flop, hitting only .162 in 20 games for Chicago.

He spent 1888 with Minneapolis and Omaha of the Western Association, then Cleveland purchased him and he joined the Spiders in 1889. That season he batted .282, with eight home runs, 76 RBIs, and 26 stolen bases.

In 1890 Tebeau jumped to the Cleveland franchise of the Players' League. He batted .300, scored 86 runs, and finished the season as the team's skipper as well as its third baseman. He returned to the Spiders the following year, hit .261 in only 61 games, and became manager midway through the season.

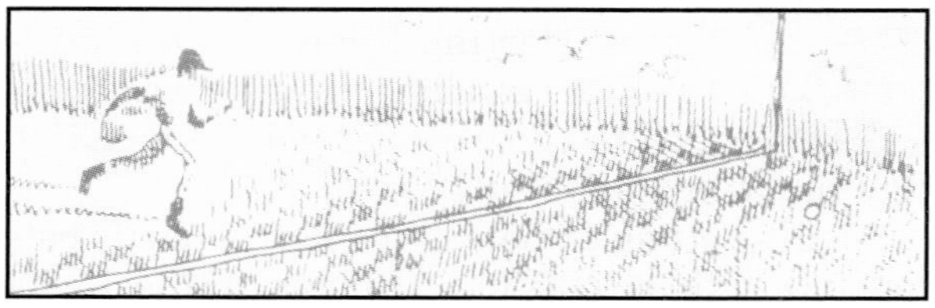

Tebeau was known as a tough, aggressive leader. "Show me a team of fighters and I'll show you a team that has a chance," he once said. But apparently he was also a modest man. He managed Cleveland to the National League pennant in 1892, but before they met the Boston Beaneaters in the annual World's Series, he conceded, "We are not claiming to be equal to the big task of beating the Bostons, but we will do our best." Their best, alas, wasn't good enough. The Spiders managed one tie, and the Beaneaters won the other five games.

In 1895 Tebeau and Cleveland returned to the World Series. This time the Spiders beat the Baltimore Orioles, four games to one, on pitcher Cy Young's three victories. In the 1896 Series rematch against Baltimore, Tebeau injured his back swinging the bat in Game 1 and was out for the remainder of Series. He watched from the bench, wrapped in a heavy winter overcoat.

After the back injury Tebeau was never the same player. In 1899 Cleveland's ownership stripped the Spiders of its talent and sent it to St. Louis, which the Robison brothers also owned. Tebeau was included in the move. He guided St. Louis to 84 wins but it was only good for fifth place. He was fired in 1900 in midseason.

After his playing days he opened a saloon. In 1918 he committed suicide, shooting himself with a revolver he had tied to his right wrist. He was 53 years old. Tebeau was the brother of major league player George "White Wings" Tebeau, who owned clubs in Denver, Louisville, and Kansas City and reportedly became a millionaire from his investments.

Kent Tekulve

Tekulve, Kenton Charles **P**

1974–89 B:3/5/1947, Cincinnati, OH Deb:5/20/1974, PIT NL BR/TR 6'4", 180

W	L	PCT	G	SV	IP	BB	SO	ERA
94	90	.511	1050	184	1436^{1}	491	779	2.85

If baseball had ever held an Ichabod Crane look-alike contest, Kent Tekulve would have been the hands-down winner. He stood 6 feet 4 inches tall and supposedly weighed 180 pounds. A sportswriter once wrote that Tekulve "looks like the poster child for an anti-scurvy campaign." Another likened him to a "plucked chicken," and still another said he was "as thin as the center field foul pole."

But from behind his dark glasses, Tekulve used his deadly sidearm delivery to make him one of the most durable and effective relievers of his time. He lasted 16 years in the majors, from 1974 through 1989—most of them with the Pirates. He never started a major league game, but he was at the end of many games in his 16-year career. The gangly reliever got the last out of Game 7 of the 1979 World Series against the Orioles; it was Tekulve's fifth appearance of the Series.

He led the majors in games pitched four times and appeared in 90 or more games three times. Tekulve finished with a career 2.85 ERA and had back-to-back 31-save seasons in 1978 and 1979. By the time he was done slinging from the side, held the major league record for relievers: 1,050 games. That mark was surpassed by Jesse Orosco in 1999.

Tekulve had few opportunities to swing a bat, a painful fact made obvious by his hitting record. He was 10-for-121 in his career, an .083 mark—one of the worst batting averages in major league history. Traded to the Phillies early in the 1985 season, Tekulve stayed with them through 1988 and finished with the Reds in 1989.

Johnny Temple

Temple, John Ellis **2B**

1952–64 B:8/8/1928, Lexington, NC D:1/9/1994, Anderson, SC Deb:4/15/1952, CIN NL BR/TR 5'11", 175

G	AB	R	H	HR	RBI	OBP	SLG	AVG
1420	5218	720	1484	22	395	.365	.351	.284

When Johnny Temple first came up to the major leagues, one sportswriter described the second baseman as "a throwback to the old-time, hell-bent for leather, tobacco-chewing players of the Ty Cobb era." That throwback became a four-time All Star, a steady fielder and an effective contact hitter who finished with a .284 career batting average and only 338 strikeouts in 5,218 at bats.

From 1954 through 1959 Temple was the Cincinnati Reds' regular second baseman. During the last four full seasons of his career he moved to Cleveland, to Baltimore, and to Houston. In 1964 he returned to Cincinnati to serve as a player-coach. After being dismissed as by the Reds, Temple engaged in a knock-down-drag-out brawl with fellow coach Reggie Otero. Temple later told reporters: "Twelve years ago I walked into Crosley Field a top-notch professional ballplayer. I'm going out like a bum—beat up, nothing to do and nowhere to go. I'm through in the game."

His troubles, however, were just beginning. Temple lost a sizable fortune in bad investments and tax liens, struggled with alcoholism, and was fired from a state job for filing improper expense vouchers. In November 1977 he was arrested in connection with the theft of heavy equipment and charged with grand larceny.

Garry Templeton

Templeton, Garry Lewis **SS**

1976–91 B:3/24/1956, Lockney, TX Deb:8/9/1976, STL NL BB/TR 5'11", 190

G	AB	R	H	HR	RBI	OBP	SLG	AVG
2079	7721	893	2096	70	728	.306	.369	.271

A switch-hitting speedster, Garry Templeton was a good hitter and an excellent fielder. At age 21, in his first full season of 1977, he became the youngest major leaguer ever to tally 200 hits in a season. He also led the league with 18 triples and batted .322, good for second in the National League. The epitome of the speedy and powerful shortstop, he was an easy choice for that year's All-Star team.

In 1979 Templeton became the first switch hitter to pound 100 hits from each side of the plate—although at the end of the season he took at bats solely from the right side to give him more chances to set the record. He led the National League with 211 hits and 19 triples, ranking him league-best in triples for the third straight year. In the field he was solid. Chosen as an alternate for the All-Star Game, he refused to go unless he was named a starter, saying, "If I ain't startin', I ain't departin'." He stayed home.

In 1980 Templeton became increasingly unhappy in St. Louis under new skipper Whitey Herzog. By the strike-split 1981 season the Cards were back in contention, and Templeton was in the hot seat with Herzog and St. Louis fans. He made clear his desire to be traded during a late-season game, when he expressed his discontent to a hometown fan with an obscene hand gesture.

The Cardinals swapped Templeton for a young and equally promising shortstop named Ozzie Smith, who was outgrowing the San Diego Padres' price range. Smith was not as powerful a hitter, but he was a better fielder and had already earned his second Gold Glove. The two seemed virtually interchangeable. In San Diego, Templeton continued to play steady ball. Although his former St. Louis teammates went to the World Series in 1982, he helped the Padres make it there in 1984. Templeton made the All-Star team again in 1985, avoiding controversy by being elected a starter along with four of his San Diego teammates.

As the decade of the 1980s continued, Templeton stayed steady in the field, but his hitting gradually declined. Smith's hitting just got better, and as he piled up Gold Glove after Gold Glove, the Cardinals continued to repeat their pennant-winning ways. Neither Templeton nor the Padres matched their earlier success. Templeton spent the last half of the 1991 season with the New York Mets and then retired. In 1999 he was managing the Eastern League's Erie Seawolves.

Gene Tenace

Tenace, Fury Gene **C-1B**
1969–83 M(1991, 19–14) B:10/10/1946, Russellton, PA
Deb:5/29/1969, OAK AL BR/TR 6', 190

G	AB	R	H	HR	RBI	OBP	SLG	AVG
1555	4390	653	1060	201	674	.391	.429	.241

In the early 1970s the Oakland A's fielded a team of colorful figures noted for unusual green and gold uniforms, swashbuckling mustaches, and clubhouse brawling. Oakland's Gene Tenace was invisible as a backup catcher and utility player—he came into full view in the World Series.

Fury Gene Tenace's only hit in the 1972 American League Championship Series was a single in the fifth game, but it drove in the run that paved the way for the A's to win the pennant. In the World Series Tenace came to bat in the second inning of Game 1 with two outs and a runner on first. Tenace blasted a pitch from Reds hurler Gary Nolan—a two-run homer. Once more Tenace homered off Nolan in the fifth inning, and the A's won, 3–2, as the quiet catcher drove in all their runs and he became the first player to homer in his first two Series at bats.

Tenace hit another home run in Game 4, singled to keep alive a ninth-inning rally, and scored the winning run. His three-run homer in Game 5 put the A's ahead to stay, and he drove in two of the A's three runs in their 3–2 Game 7 victory. All in all, he hit four homers, drove in nine runs, and batted .348. Appropriately, he won the Series Most Valuable Player Award.

That Series performance earned him the starting catcher job with the A's for the 1973 season. For the next four years he was a significant contributor in the offensive lineup, slugging 22 homers or more every year and walking more than 100 times three years in a row. But his offense was curious: he seldom doubled and wasn't much of a singles hitter. In 1974 he established a dubious record of hitting only 58 singles, the fewest number by a player who participated in 150 games or more. That small number belied his 26 homers and league-leading 110 walks.

Like most of the key players of the three-time world champion A's, Tenace flew the coop when free agency became legal. Tenace was signed by Ray Kroc in 1977 to play for the San Diego Padres for five years for $1.81 million. He became the fourth-richest player in the game at the time.

Although Kroc knew he had signed a World Series hero, he apparently hadn't realized that this same player was only a lifetime .245 hitter. After Tenace hit .233 and .224 in his first two years in San Diego, Kroc was taking major heat for spending so much for so little.

Tenace wasn't hitting for average, but he was still getting walked a lot—125 times to lead the National League in 1977, followed by 101, 105, and 92 walks during the following three seasons in San Diego. It wasn't good enough for the Padres. Tenace was swapped to the Cardinals in December 1980 in the 11-man megatrade that included Rollie Fingers, Terry Kennedy, Bob Shirley, and Steve Swisher.

He was touted as a possible managerial candidate during his later years. The Pirates all but announced he would succeed Chuck Tanner as their field boss when they obtained him in 1983. When the year ended though, Tanner was still the manager and Tenace had retired. He served as a coach for the Astros for two years before moving to the Blue Jays from 1990 through 1997. He got to manage in 1991, but only as a fill-in while Cito Gaston recovered from a back injury.

Fred Tenney

Tenney, Frederick **1B-C-OF**
1894–1911 M(1905–07, 1911, 202–402) B:11/26/1871, Georgetown, MA D:7/3/1952, Boston, MA
Deb:6/16/1894, BOS NL BL/TL 5'9", 155

G	AB	R	H	HR	RBI	OBP	SLG	AVG
1994	7595	1278	2231	22	688	.371	.358	.294

A lefthanded catcher at Brown University, Fred Tenney became one of baseball's greatest first basemen. Tenney went straight from Brown in 1894 to the Boston Beaneaters of the National League, and then straight to the bench for the better part of three seasons. He could hit well enough, averaging over .300 in limited opportunities, but he had no place to go in the field. Aside from the ingrained prejudice against southpaw backstops, Tenney just wasn't a major league catcher, and an attempt to make him an outfielder only revealed a second position he could not play adequately.

At last, in 1897, manager Frank Selee tried him at first base. The results were amazing. The man who couldn't catch or play the outfield quickly became the slickest first sacker in the league. Along with second baseman Bobby Lowe, shortstop Herman Long, and third baseman Jimmy Collins, Tenney gave the Beaneaters an airtight inner defense that paced the team to consecutive pennants in 1897 and 1898. His speed on the bases and bat control made him an ideal No. 2 hitter, and he batted well over .300 in both championship years.

Unfortunately, Selee moved on to Chicago, while some of the Beaneaters stars grew old, and several defected to the American League. The Beaneaters owners, renowned for their ability to squeeze their dimes, refused to spend any for adequate replacements, and the team made a beeline for the basement.

In 1905 Tenney was named manager of the hopeless squad, and the owners promised him a bonus if they made a profit; he earned it by, among other things, scrambling into the stands for foul balls. Tenney then brokered the sale of the team to the Dovey brothers in 1907 and wound up with a share of it.

Unfortunately, he and the Doveys seldom saw eye to eye. At the end of the season he was fired as manager and sent over to the New York Giants as a player. Tenney led the league in runs scored in 1908 but was injured late in the season. It was his absence from the lineup in a crucial September game that allowed young Fred Merkle to make the baserunning blunder for which he became famous.

After another injury-plagued season with the Giants, Tenney played for Lowell of the New England League and took one last shot as player-manager in Boston. He could still field and hit, but an eighth-place finish led to his retirement from baseball.

Walt Terrell

Terrell, Charles Walter **P**

1982–92 B:5/11/1958, Jeffersonville, IN Deb:9/8/1982, NY NL BL/TR 6'2", 205

W	L	PCT	G	SH	IP	BB	SO	ERA
111	124	.472	321	14	1986[2]	748	929	3.33

Walt Terrell was a reliable righthander who got his big league break from the New York Mets in 1982. Although he lost each of his three starts that year, the following season he pitched reliably, winning eight and losing eight. He also showed some hitting power, slugging two home runs in one game in 1983.

Terrell had come to New York along with Ron Darling in a trade with Texas for Lee Mazzilli. After the 1984 season the Mets traded the promising Terrell to the Detroit Tigers for infielder Howard Johnson. While Johnson helped the Mets reach the World Series, Terrell was developing into a fine pitcher. He posted three straight winning seasons with Detroit, including a 17-victory campaign in 1987 when the Tigers took the American League East flag.

At the beginning of the 1988 season, the Tigers' second-most reliable starter was on the disabled list. Terrell had slipped and fallen on some ice before reporting to spring training and had injured his ankle. He did not pitch at all in the preseason and was still a question mark when the season opened. Although he eventually recovered enough to hurl 206 innings that year, he posted a 7–16 record.

In October 1988 Terrell was dealt to the San Diego Padres, who were rebuilding their pitching staff and were expected to have a good year. However, Terrell went 5–13 in 19 starts, and the Padres sent him to the Yankees. He won six games for New York but his ERA ballooned to 5.20. In 1990 tbe Pirates signed him but he finished the season back with the Tigers, where he remained until 1992.

Adonis Terry

Terry, William H. **P–OF**

1884–97 B:8/7/1864, Westfield, MA. D:2/24/1915, Milwaukee WI Deb:5/1/1884, BRO NL BR/TR 5'11½", 168

W	L	PCT	G	SH	IP	BB	SO	ERA
197	196	.501	440	17	3514[1]	1298	1553	3.74

G	AB	R	H	HR	RBI	OBP	SLG	AVG
667	2389	314	594	15	287	.295	.344	.249

At nearly six feet tall, William H. Terry was a great hunk of a man whose handsome features were said to bring more women to the ballpark in the 19th century than Ladies Day. His nickname said it all—"Adonis."

Although the gorgeous righthander was primarily a pitcher, he was a good all-around player who spent over 200 games in the field. He compiled a career .249 batting average, seldom batting ninth even when appearing as a pitcher.

Terry was first and foremost a pitcher. He joined Brooklyn's American Association team in 1884 and went 25–52 in his first two seasons with a second-division team. He tossed no-hitters against St. Louis in 1886 and Louisville in 1888. As the team improved, so did his record. Terry won 22 games in 1889 as Brooklyn won the AA pennant.

The following season, when Brooklyn entered the National League and some of the league's best players absconded to the Players' League, he finished 26–16, and Brooklyn won another pennant. In 1895 he went 21–14 for Chicago.

Bill Terry

Terry, William Harold **1B**

1923–36 M(1932–1941, 823–661) B:10/30/1898, Atlanta, GA D:1/9/1989, Jacksonville, FL. Deb:9/24/1923, NY NL BL/TL 6'1", 200

G	AB	R	H	HR	RBI	OBP	SLG	AVG
1721	6428	1120	2193	154	1078	.393	.506	.341

First baseman Bill Terry, the last National Leaguer to hit .400, earned a reputation as a stubborn, unsentimental man who long before the era of free agency played the game for the money that was to be made from it. "I'm giving this game the best years of my life," Terry contended. "I'd make any other business pay for that. Why should baseball, because it's a game, be treated any different?"

Terry's early life was marred by hardship and helped provide him with the cold edge that later rattled so many people. His parents separated when he was quite young, and to survive he had to begin work at age 13 unloading freight cars. When he was 15 the St. Louis Browns promised him a tryout, but while waiting to travel to spring training he was given his release.

Terry began his professional career in 1915 pitching with Newnan of the Class D Georgia-Alabama League, moving up to Shreveport of the Texas League for 1916 and 1917. While he posted respectable statistics, even recording a no-hitter in June 1915, Terry was in severe financial difficulties. At one point he was forced to hock his wife's wedding band in order to buy food.

When he was sold to Kid Elberfeld's Southern Association club at Little Rock, he refused to report and instead took employment with the Standard Oil Company, where he served as player-manager for the firm's crack baseball team, the Polarines. The pay was lucrative, reaching as high as $300 per week.

By this time Terry had shifted over to first base, and it was no secret how good he was. Manager John McGraw saw him perform and was determined to have him for the Giants. He invited Terry to his quarters at Memphis' Peabody Hotel and attempted to sell him on the idea of playing for New York—or at least for their farm club at Toledo. "For how much?" was Terry's instant response.

McGraw was incredulous that anyone would even think twice about joining the Giants, let alone express such mercenary thoughts. "Excuse me if I don't fall all over myself, but the Giants don't mean a thing to me unless you can make it worth my while," Terry shot back. "I'm doing all right here. I have a nice home and I'm in no hurry to leave it or the job. If I can make much more money going to New York, I'll go."

It took three weeks for the two men to come to terms. Terry signed for $5,000 a year with the stipulation that he was the property of the Giants and not of any minor league team, although he would be sent to Toledo for seasoning. Terry hit .336 for Toledo in 1922 and .377 in 1923 and even managed the Mud Hens for part of the 1923 season.

While Terry would later lead the National League in assists and putouts five times, when he first came up to the Polo Grounds he still needed work on his fielding. His main weaknesses were in turning first-to-second-to-first double plays and in throwing home, but hard work soon overcame these problems. In 1924 he was platooned with future Hall of Famer George "Highpockets" Kelly, and in 1925 Terry became a regular.

His batting soon established him as the premier first baseman in the National League. "Terry is essentially a line-drive hitter," observed one New York writer. "His favorite hit is a sizzling single or two-bagger. Such hits travel with amazing velocity and are difficult to handle. A home run to Terry is merely an accident. He didn't hit the ball any harder, but he hit it at a greater elevation."

Wrangles about money continued with McGraw. Once, weary of an impasse regarding salary, McGraw informed Terry he could negotiate a trade for himself to another club. Terry shot back, "Make your own deals. I have enough trouble playing first base."

Terry's great season was 1930, when he batted .401 and the entire National League hit .303; even a .400 average was no guarantee of winning the batting crown. As late as August 1, Terry's .396 average was only the fifth best in the league.

In 1931 Terry hit .349, losing the league batting championship by an eyelash (.3489 to .3486) to St. Louis outfielder Chick Hafey. McGraw threatened Terry with a $3,000 pay cut. The two by now were barely speaking. "You've been blaming other people for the mistakes you've been making for 20 years," Terry told the increasingly irascible McGraw. On June 3, 1932, Terry was called into McGraw's office. "I was expected to be notified I was traded," he later admitted. "I don't want anybody hearing this," McGraw said in low tones. "Bill, you don't have to answer this now. Wait a while if you like. But how would you like to manage the Giants?"

Terry didn't hesitate. "Mac, there's no need for me to wait. I'll take it now," he replied. The following year Terry transformed the foundering club he had inherited into world champions with a Series win over Joe Cronin's Washington Senators.

In 1934 Terry made the biggest gaffe of his career. Before the new season opened, the laconic, usually humorless Terry was asked what he thought about the also-ran Brooklyn Dodgers' chances in the race. "Is Brooklyn still in the league?" he joked.

The quip inspired Casey Stengel's Dodgers to take a late-season two-game series against the Giants and hand St. Louis the pennant. Stengel later told Terry he had considered visiting him in the New York clubhouse after the second game to cheer him up. "It's a good thing you didn't. You would have been thrown out on your ass," responded Terry.

Terry's Giants rebounded to win pennants in 1936 and 1937, but each year they lost the World Series to the Yankees. At the close of the 1941 season Mel Ott replaced Terry as manager.

Terry stayed with the Giants for another season as a $30,000-a-year farm director but then quit to return home. "I intend to devote myself to the cotton business and watch baseball from the outside," said Terry. "I'm not worried about the game. No business in the world has ever made more money with poorer management. It can survive anything."

Because Terry's relationship with the members of the Baseball Writers Association of America was not the best, he was not selected for the Baseball Hall of Fame until 1954. He received votes from the BBWAA in 15 different seasons, and he eventually gained entrance to Cooperstown by just six votes. He did, however, manage to gain more votes than Joe DiMaggio, who had to wait another year before he was elected to the Hall of Fame. In 1955 Terry unsuccessfully attempted to purchase the Giants.

Ralph Terry

Terry, Ralph Willard **P**

1956–67 B:1/9/1936, Big Cabin, OK Deb:8/6/1956, NY AL BR/TR 6'3", 195

W	L	PCT	G	SH	IP	BB	SO	ERA
107	99	.519	338	20	1849^{1}	446	1000	3.62

It was Yankees righthander Ralph Terry who delivered the 1–0 pitch that Bill Mazeroski dramatically hit out of Forbes Field to win the 1960 World Series. Two years later it was Terry who delivered the pitch that Willie McCovey hit right at Bobby Richardson to end the World Series.

Terry was signed originally by the Yankees but was traded with Billy Martin to Kansas City in June 1957. The Yankees retrieved Terry from their "farm" in May 1959, and he eventually appeared in five straight World Series for New York. He lost twice in the 1960 Series, culminating with Mazeroski's famous blow. In the 1962 Series, he was shut out in Game 2 but came back to win Game 5. A three-day rain delay allowed him to start again in Game 7. He was brilliant, tossing a four-hitter and got the 1–0 win when McCovey lined out.

In 1962 he led the American League with 23 wins and 299 innings pitched. That same season, he gave up a league-high 40 homers. The following season he tied for the American League lead in complete games.

In October 1964, Terry was sent to Cleveland to complete a deal for reliever Pedro Ramos, who helped the Yankees to their last pennant for a decade. Terry was traded back to Kansas City in April 1966 and in August of that year was sold to the Mets. After retiring from baseball, Terry became a golf pro in Kansas.

Jeff Tesreau

Tesreau, Charles Monroe **P**

1912–18 B:3/5/1889, Silver Mine, MO D:9/24/1946, Hanover, NH Deb:4/12/1912, NY NL BR/TR 6'2", 218

W	L	PCT	G	SH	IP	BB	SO	ERA
115	72	.615	247	27	1679	572	880	2.43

Pitcher Charles Monroe "Jeff" Tesreau spent a short, but interesting, seven-year career with the New York Giants. Tesreau was given the nickname "Jeff" after Jeff Tesreau, a famous heavyweight boxer. In 1912 he was purchased from Toronto and became an immediate hit in New York. Tesreau was the first modern rookie to pitch a no-hitter, leaving the Phillies hitless on September 6. That same year he led the National League in ERA and won 17 games, most of them in the second half of season. One victory—under today's scoring rules—actually went to Rube Marquard since Marquard relieved Tesreau before the winning run scored.

Tesreau was John McGraw's surprise choice to start Game 1 of the 1912 World Series. He pitched three times against Smokey Joe Wood of the Red Sox. He lost Games 1 and 4 but won Game 7—it was not the deciding game because an earlier tie forced the Series to go eight games. He collected two hits in his victory and batted .375 for the Series.

In Game 1 of the 1913 World Series he gave up no hits in two innings of relief; in Game 3 he was beaten by Bullet Joe Bush. Tesreau led the National League in shutouts in 1914 and relieved for an inning in the 1917 World Series. He ended his career with Giants in 1918. After retiring from baseball, Tesreau coached at Dartmouth. He became popular in Hanover, New Hampshire, and was urged to run for public office. But because he used his nickname from the sports world wouldn't resonate with the voters, Jeff was disqualified—a local ordinance specified that a candidate's legal name must go on the ballot.

Mickey Tettleton

Tettleton, Mickey Lee **C–DH**

1984–97 B:9/16/1960, Oklahoma City, OK Deb:6/30/1984, OAK AL BB/TR 6'2", 212

G	AB	R	H	HR	RBI	OBP	SLG	AVG
1485	4698	711	1132	245	732	.372	.449	.241

A switch-hitting catcher with power, Mickey Tettleton was a patient hitter and consistent run producer. Reaching the majors with the Oakland A's in 1984, Tettleton proved he could hit home runs—but little else. Traded to the Orioles in 1988, he raised his average to .261 and hit 11

home runs in 283 at bats, impressing Baltimore enough to win the everyday job a year later. Tettleton made the most of his opportunity, slugging 26 home runs as Baltimore rebounded from a 107-loss campaign to finish two games off the division pace. The secret to his success, he revealed in a tongue-in-cheek article, was the cereal Fruit Loops.

After slumping to a .223 average in 1990, Tettleton was traded to Detroit. He responded with 31 home runs in 1991, the first of three straight seasons in which Tettleton topped 30 homers. He was on pace to do it again in 1994, but the players' strike ended the season in mid-August. When play resumed nearly nine months later, Tettleton had signed with the Texas Rangers as a free agent. With defensive stalwart Ivan Rodriguez behind the plate for Texas, Tettleton saw time as a designated hitter and in the outfield. He delivered 32 home runs and a .510 slugging average. He retired in 1997.

Tim Teufel

Teufel, Timothy Shawn **2B**

1983-93 B:7/7/1958, Greenwich, CT Deb:9/3/1983, MIN AL BR/TR 6'0", 175

G	AB	R	H	HR	RBI	OBP	SLG	AVG
1073	3112	415	789	86	379	.338	.404	.254

As one half of a second-base platoon for the New York Mets in the late 1980s, Tim Teufel played a key supporting role on one of the dominant teams of the period. Although he grew up in upscale Greenwich, Connecticut, fans enjoyed his blue-collar work ethic on the field, as well as the "Teufel Shuffle, the ritual that prepared him for an at bat.

As a rookie for Minnesota in 1984, Teufel showed unusual pop for a second baseman, clubbing 14 home runs and finishing fourth in the Rookie of the Year voting. Traded to New York before the 1986 campaign, the righthanded-hitting Teufel was platooned with Wally Backman by Mets skipper Davey Johnson.

Teufel's error in Game 1 of the 1986 World Series allowed Boston's Jim Rice to score the game's only run. He rebounded, however to bat .444 with one home run in the Series as New York took the title in seven games. In 1987 he hit 14 homers in just 299 at bats. Teufel played three more years in New York before being traded to San Diego, where he played his final three seasons. He raised capital for different investment companies, but he returned to baseball and the Mets as a scout in 1998.

Bob Tewksbury

Tewksbury, Robert Alan **P**

1986–98 B:11/30/1960, Concord, NH Deb:4/11/1986, NY AL BR/TR 6'4", 200

W	L	PCT	G	SH	IP	BB	SO	ERA
110	102	.519	302	7	1807	292	812	3.92

In 1992 and 1993, Bob Tewksbury walked 40 men in 446 ⅔ innings—or 0.8 per game. No starter since Red Lucas in the 1930s had thrown with greater precision. With a fastball timed in the low-80s, even in his prime, Tewksbury relied on control. He liked to work quickly, nipping the corners with his curve, slider, and changeup, occasionally tempting hitters with the fastball just off the plate. He struck out few but induced many to hit ground balls.

Not drafted until the 19th round in 1981, Tewksbury spent most of the decade either in the minors or on the disabled list. He had a solid rookie season with the Yankees in 1986, going 9–5 with a 3.31 ERA, then shuttled between Triple-A affiliates and the Yankees, Cubs, and Cardinals before establishing himself in St. Louis in 1990. In one of the best efforts of his career, Tewksbury threw a one-hitter for the Cards on August 17, 1990, allowing only one man to reach base.

He won 16 games in 1992, led the National League with a .762 winning percentage, finished second with a 2.16 ERA, and pitched in the All-Star Game. After a career-best 17 wins the following year, his ERA began to rise precipitously. He managed to hang on for five more seasons with St. Louis, Texas, San Diego, and Minnesota before retiring. His lifetime walks-per-game ratio of 1.45 stood as the greatest mark since the Dead Ball Era.

Ernest Lawrence Thayer

Thayer, Ernest Lawrence

Journalist, Poet B:8/14/1863, Lawrence, MA D:8/21/1940, Santa Barbara, CA

On June 3, 1888, a poem appeared on page four of *The San Francisco Examiner* under the byline "Phin" that has become perhaps the most famous verse ever written in America. Subtitled "A Ballad of the Republic, Sung in the Year 1888," the piece is better known simply as "Casey at the Bat."

Ernest Lawrence Thayer, the author, was a regular contributor to *The Examiner* and ran the poem as a bit of doggerel for his humor column. By the time it was published, Thayer had left San Francisco and returned home to Worcester, Massachusetts, to run a family-owned textile mill.

One summer afternoon in August 1889 after an exhibition game, members of the New York Giants and the Chicago White Stockings went to a vaudeville show at Wallack's Theater in New York. Notified that ballplayers were in the audience, the actor DeWolf Hopper quickly memorized Thayer's poem from a newspaper clipping.

Players such as Adrian "Cap" Anson and William "Buck" Ewing reacted wildly to the poem, and Casey, a new American folk hero, was born in the public imagination. Hopper began a long career giving stirring recitals of this remarkable piece of baseball Americana and, by his own count, delivered it more than 10,000 times.

The poem has been made into a film at least five times, including once as a sensational Warner Brothers cartoon. It has been parodied so often that in 1967 Martin Gardner felt compelled to anthologize every caricature, continuation, and extension of the original poem in a book titled *The Annotated Casey at the Bat.*

Awareness of Thayer's verse is so great—virtually everyone has seen or heard at least part of the poem—that it is easy to miss its essential qualities of humor and grace. In the 1988 *SABR* (Society for American Baseball Research) *Review of Books*, historian and critic Glenn Stout dug back into the original to uncover its remarkably clean style, delicate wit, and altogether American baseball ending.

Here it is, exactly as it appeared in 1888, the poem that brought American baseball to verse and that has lived a rich and full life for more than a century since.

Casey at the Bat:
A Ballad of the Republic, Sung in the Year 1888

The outlook wasn't brilliant for the Mudville nine that day;
The score stood four to two with but one inning more to play.
And then when Cooney died at first, and Barrows did the same,
A sickly silence fell upon the patrons of the game.
A struggling few got up to go in deep despair. The rest
Clung to that hope which springs eternal in the human breast;
They thought if only Casey could get a whack at that—
We'd put up even money now with Casey at the bat.
But Flynn preceded Casey, as did also Jimmy Blake,
And the former was a lulu and the later was a cake;
So upon that stricken multitude grim melancholy sat,
For there seemed but little chance of Casey's getting to the bat.
But Flynn let drive a single, to the wonderment of all,
And Blake, the much despised, tore the cover off the ball;
And when the dust had lifted, and the men saw what had occurred,
There was Jimmy safe at second and Flynn a-hugging third.
Then from 5,000 throats and more there rose a lusty yell;

It rumbled through the valley, it rattled in the dell;
It knocked upon the mountain and recoiled upon the flat,
For Casey, mighty Casey, was advancing to the bat.
There was ease in Casey's manner as he stepped into his place;
There was pride in Casey's bearing and a smile on Casey's face.
And when, responding to the cheers, he lightly doffed his hat,
No stranger in the crowd could doubt 'twas Casey at the bat.
Ten thousand eyes were on him as he rubbed his hands with dirt;
Five thousand tongues applauded when he wiped them on his shirt.
Then while the writhing pitcher ground the ball into his hip,
Defiance gleamed in Casey's eye, a sneer curled Casey's lip.
And now the leather-covered sphere came hurtling through the air,
And Casey stood a-watching it in haughty grandeur there.
Close by the sturdy batsman the ball unheeded sped—
"That ain't my style," said Casey. "Strike one," the umpire said.
From the benches, black with people, there went up a muffled roar,
Like the beating of the storm waves on a stern and distant shore.
"Kill him! Kill him!" shouted someone in the stand;
And it's likely they'd have killed him had not Casey raised his hand.
With a smile of Christian charity great Casey's visage shone;
He stilled the rising tumult, he bade the game go on.
He signaled to the pitcher, and once more the spheroid flew;
But Casey still ignored it, and the umpire said, "Strike two."

"Fraud!" cried the maddened thousands, and echo answered "Fraud!"
But one scornful look from Casey and the audience was awed.
They saw his face grow stern and cold, they saw his muscles strain,
And they knew that Casey wouldn't let that ball go by again.
The sneer is gone from Casey's lip, his teeth are clenched in hate;
He pounds with cruel violence his bat upon the plate.
And now the pitcher holds the ball, and now he lets it go,
And now the air is shattered by the force of Casey's blow.
Oh! somewhere in this favored land the sun is shining bright;
The band is playing somewhere, and somewhere hearts are light,
And somewhere men are laughing, and somewhere children shout;
But there is no joy in Mudville—mighty Casey has struck out.

Unlike his hero, Thayer didn't strike out, but he did try to distance himself from his creation. After others tried to claim authorship, Thayer grudgingly came forward, said he had created Casey, but refused to take a penny for his efforts. Accordingly, with no copyright claims, the poem has been reprinted, plagiarized, and performed on stage, screen, and radio. An opera, *The Mighty Casey*, written by Pulitzer Prize–winner William Schuman, was performed in Cooperstown, New York, in 1991.

Tommy Thevenow

Thevenow, Thomas Joseph **SS-3B-2B**
1924–38 B:9/6/1903, Madison, Ind. D:7/29/1957, Madison, IN Deb:9/4/1924, STL NL BR/TR 5'10", 155

G	AB	R	H	HR	RBI	OBP	SLG	AVG
1229	4164	380	1030	2	456	.285	.294	.247

Tommy Thevenow got his chance in 1926 and made the most of it as the everyday shortstop for the world champion Cardinals. Although he played 12 more seasons in the majors, his career was unfortunately plagued by injuries. He was able to repeat his excellent 1926 performance only one time.

In 1924 and 1925 Thevenow served as the Cardinals' backup shortstop. But in 1926 he played in every one of his team's 156 games, hit .256 with 63 RBIs, and led National League shortstops in putouts, assists, total chances, and chances per game—he was also second in double plays. In the Cards' World Series upset of the Yankees, Thevenow hit a team-leading .417, with four RBIs.

He held out the following season. When he returned he severely broke his ankle; the accident left him with a limp and ruined his career. The next two seasons he hit .194 and .205 as a part-timer and then was traded to the Phillies.

Thevenow had one more big season left in 1930. He played every game for the Phillies and batted a career-high .286. He led the league in putouts, assists, total chances, and double plays and was second in chances per game. He never came close to this feat again. Later he broke his jaw, finger, and leg in an auto accident.

For the next five years Thevenow was a utility infielder for the Pirates. In 1936 he played for the Reds and in 1937 with the Braves. He finished back in Pittsburgh in 1938.

Bobby Thigpen

Thigpen, Robert Thomas **P**
1986–94 B:7/17/1963, Tallahassee, FL Deb:6/6/1986, CHI AL BR/TR 6'3", 195

W	L	PCT	G	SV	IP	BB	SO	ERA
31	36	.463	448	201	568^{2}	238	376	3.43

Reliever Bobby Thigpen enjoyed one truly remarkable season in an otherwise modest career. In 1990 with the Chicago White Sox he set the major league record with 57 saves, playing a hand in 65 percent of the team's victories. In his league-leading 77 appearances, he worked 88 innings with 70 strikeouts and a 1.83 ERA. He also made his only All-Star appearance, finished fifth in the American League Most Valuable Player balloting and fourth in the Cy Young.

In his first four seasons, Thigpen enjoyed some success, although his ERA climbed each year. He was among the American League leaders in saves with identical totals of 34 in the two seasons before his career year. In 1990 he was unhittable. Although the White Sox finished second to Oakland, Thigpen helped make sure the team's final year at 80-year-old Comiskey Park was a memorable one.

Thigpen was back in 1991 at the new Comiskey Park, but the magic was not there. In 1991, however, he returned to his former level of performance. His saves dropped to 30 and his ERA increased to 3.49. The following year he saved only 22 as his ERA swelled to 4.75.

Philadelphia and Seattle both tried to revive Thigpen's career but with no success. He failed to

save a game for either club. In the four seasons that followed his remarkable 57-save season, he saved a total of just 53 games.

Derrel Thomas

Thomas, Derrel Osbon **2B-OF-SS-3B**

1971–85 B:1/14/1951, Los Angeles, CA Deb:9/14/1971, HOU NL BB/TR 6', 160

G	AB	R	H	HR	RBI	OBP	SLG	AVG
1597	4677	585	1163	43	370	.319	.322	.249

A man of many talents, in the course of his major league career Derrel Thomas not only performed at every infield and outfield position but caught five games for the Dodgers in 1980 and one in 1985. He used his speed not only in getting back on balls in the outfield, but also in baserunning and bunting.

A broken leg bone suffered in the 1982 season slowed him down, however. Derrel Thomas also had lengthy stints on the disabled list in 1976, 1978 and 1983. A bit of a hot dog, the switch-hitting Thomas was known for his hard slides into second basemen. With the Los Angeles Dodgers, he was proud to wear No. 30, the uniform of his childhood idol, Maury Wills. "He has the worth of three good players with all he can do," praised announcer Tim McCarver in 1984, "He is the Dodgers' best center fielder."

He played three different positions for the Dodgers in the 1981 World Series. Thomas played in all four games of the 1983 National League Championship Series and led all Los Angeles regulars with a .444 average.

Frank Thomas

Thomas, Frank Edward **1B-DH**

1990–* B:5/27/1968, Columbus, GA Deb:8/2/1990, CHI AL BR/TR 6'5", 257

G	AB	R	H	HR	RBI	OBP	SLG	AVG
1371	4892	968	1564	301	1040	.446	.573	.320

Frank Thomas was called "The Big Hurt." Opposing pitchers knew why. The two-time American League Most Valuable Player became the first player in history to hit .300 with 20 home runs, 100 RBIs, 100 walks, and 100 runs scored in seven consecutive seasons. Remarkably, two of those years were shortened because of the players' strike.

The start of his career compared favorably with some of baseball all-time greats. He hit more homers over a comparable stretch than Ted Williams (not counting the two years Williams spent in military service in World War II), and also topped Williams' six-year run of driving in 100 runs and walking 100 times. Fittingly, Thomas was the first American League winner of the Ted Williams Award. The honor, presented by CNN/Sports Illustrated and *Total Baseball*, measured production based on a formula combining on-base average and slugging average to measure the most productive hitters. Thomas finished the 1997 season with an adjusted production of .467.

Thomas played football and basketball as well as baseball at Columbus High School in Georgia, and was a good enough football player to earn a scholarship to play tight end at Auburn University. As a freshman baseball player at Auburn, Thomas and Albert Belle, then a junior at Louisiana State University, both set school records with 21 home runs in 1987 in the Southeast Conference. (Thomas and Belle, who would become major league teammates in 1997 and 1998, each set school records with 49 career home runs.) The White Sox chose Thomas with the seventh overall pick in the 1989 draft.

A year later, after only 180 minor league games, Thomas was playing for the Sox. He batted .330 in 191 at bats in 1990, the highest average by a White Sox hitter with at least 200 plate appearances since 1942. In his first full season in 1991 he hit 32 home runs while batting .318. Pitchers around the American League quickly took notice and shied away from the powerful young hitter. He walked an incredible 138 times to lead the American League. His resulting .454 on-base percentage also lead the league.

Thomas then began a string of seasons that in another era would have earned him Triple Crown honors. In 1993 he posted 41 home runs, 128 RBIs and a .317 average and was named the American League MVP. He was a repeat winner the next year, this time hitting 38 home runs, with 101 runs batted in and a .353 average in a strike-shortened season. In the 1993 American League Championship Series, although the Sox lost to the eventual world champion Toronto Blue Jays in six games, Thomas hit .353 with a record 10 walks.

In 1997 Thomas added his first batting title, .347, to his list of accomplishments. He had such a commanding lead in the race that even though he went hitless in his last 10 at bats of the season, he still won the title by 17 points over Edgar Martinez. Thomas also finished with 35 home runs despite a poor start that saw him go without a homer for almost the first month of the season. Slowed by an injured right foot that eventually required surgery in September, his power num-

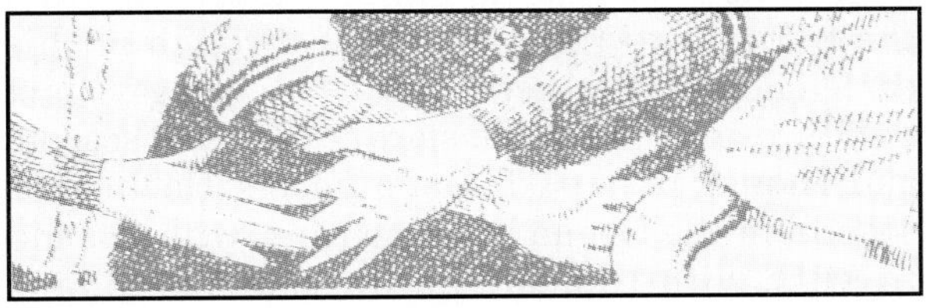

bers dropped off in 1999. He failed to drive in 100 runs for the first time since 1990, although he batted over .300 for the ninth time in 10 seasons.

Frank Thomas

Thomas, Frank Joseph **OF–1B–3B**

1951–66 B:6/11/1929, Pittsburgh, PA Deb:8/17/1951, PIT NL BR/TR 6'3", 205

G	AB	R	H	HR	RBI	OBP	SLG	AVG
1766	6285	792	1671	286	962	.323	.454	.266

Pittsburgh fans take hometown ballplayers to heart in a way that most metropolitan fans do not. From his first full season in 1953 Pittsburgh native and Pirates slugger Frank Thomas won the hearts of the locals. The muscular Thomas belted 30 home runs that year to help fans stop mourning the trade of traded slugger Ralph Kiner. And because Thomas was of Eastern European heritage, he was "one of us" to thousands of Pittsburgh blue-collar workers who shared his Eastern European ancestry.

Despite the promise he showed in his rookie season, Frank Joseph Thomas ultimately proved to be only a pale imitation of Kiner. Unlike Kiner, Thomas couldn't hit for average. His highest seasonal mark was a decidedly unheroic .298. And where Kiner's prodigious home runs seemed to pierce the clouds, a typical Thomas home run was a line drive down the line in left field, just inside fair territory. Thomas' pull-hitting approach served him well in spacious Forbes Field, with its 365-foot left-field line.

As a young man Thomas entered a Catholic seminary to study for the priesthood, but he traded a life of prayer for the life of a player. He signed with Pittsburgh in 1947 and came up to the majors in 1951. While the big league Bucs were stumbling to a dismal 112-loss season, Thomas lit up the scoreboard in New Orleans, where he hit 35 homers and drove in 131 runs to lead the Southern Association. As a full-time Pirate in 1953 Thomas drove in 102 runs and belted 30 home runs.

"Greenberg Gardens," the short left-field fence in Forbes Field that had been erected to enhance Hank Greenberg's slugging and helped make Kiner a star, was removed after the 1953 season. Thomas' numbers fell with it. However, his five seasons of 23 or more home runs from 1954 through 1958 were enough to keep him a fan favorite.

Although Thomas had bounced around from the outfield to third and first throughout his career, Pirates manager Danny Murtaugh gave him the third-base job at the start of the 1958 season, and Thomas put up All-Star numbers. He finished second in the league in home runs, with 35, and in RBIs, with 109, and he slugged .528 to rank fourth. Although he was almost 30 years old he seemed to be at his peak.

On January 30, 1959, Thomas was sent to Cincinnati to begin a trek around the National League during which he changed teams eight times in as many years. He hit only 12 homers for the Reds in 1959 because of a thumb injury and was acquired by the Cubs for the 1960 season. His 21 homers that year were offset by his poor average and low RBI total, so the Cubs dealt him to Milwaukee early in the 1961 season.

Happy to be in the company of the Braves' sluggers, Thomas returned to form and belted 25 home runs. On June 8 of that year the Braves hit four consecutive home runs: after Eddie Mathews, Hank Aaron, and Joe Adcock unloaded, Thomas followed suit.

The brand-new New York Mets purchased Thomas from the Braves for $125,000. As the 32-year-old "bonus baby" of the Mets, Thomas was the main rain producer during their initial season. The Polo Grounds, with its short porch in left, was tailor-made for his pull-hitting swing. In August of that year he had three consecutive two-homer games, and he hit 34 home runs with 94 RBIs for the season batting cleanup. His franchise home run mark stood until Dave Kingman broke it in 1975.

Manager Casey Stengel eventually tired of Thomas' exaggerated swing, and since Thomas would not change his style he played less and less. His home run total fell to 15 in 1963. By August 1964 he had played in only 60 games, so the Phillies picked him up for two minor leaguers and cash to help them hold down first place. Thomas hit seven homers in only 39 games for the Phils, but he broke his thumb sliding and wasn't available when the Phillies went into their famous swoon and lost the pennant.

An ugly racial incident that occurred while Thomas was with the Phils in 1965 is, sadly, the most memorable event of his career. He had always enjoyed the banter and horseplay of major league clubhouses. When offered a "power handshake" by a black teammate, Thomas would grab the player's thumb, bend it back painfully, and then laugh hysterically.

Quiet Wes Covington was a frequent target of Thomas' racist remarks. When teammate Dick Allen objected to the way Thomas was treating Covington during batting practice on July 3, Allen and Thomas squared off and Allen threw a left hook to Thomas' jaw. "He knew it was coming," Allen said later. "I was looking for a fair one, Philadelphia-style." Thomas responded by hitting Allen on the left shoulder with a bat. It took five men to restrain Allen from retaliating.

Allen at the time was at the beginning of what became an excellent career (although some claim that the Thomas incident led to his legendary moodiness). In the ensuing game Allen had three hits and Thomas belted a pinch-hit homer. After the homer Allen shook Thomas' hand, but Phils management, worried about damage to their budding superstar and nervous about racial tensions in a city that had seen major rioting the previous summer, released Thomas immediately after the game.

One-time teammate Richie Ashburn explained Thomas' behavior in this way: "He didn't get the tag 'Big Donkey' because of his smarts. A lot of guys in baseball could give the needle, but Thomas never knew when to quit. His timing was always just off."

That year Thomas signed with Houston, and he was then dealt to Milwaukee. After the Braves released him he batted five times for the Cubs the following season before leaving the game. A comeback attempt with Tacoma of the Pacific Coast League resulted in only one homer in 79 at bats.

Gorman Thomas

Thomas, Gorman James **OF–DH**

1973–86 B:12/12/1950, Charleston, SC Deb:4/6/1973, MIL AL BR/TR 6'2", 210

G	AB	R	H	HR	RBI	OBP	SLG	AVG
1435	4677	681	1051	268	782	.328	.448	.225

A bit rough around the edges, outfielder Gorman Thomas was nonetheless a fan favorite in Milwaukee with his power hitting and demolition derby style of defense. "The fans come to see me strike out, hit a home run, or run into a fence," he once noted. "I try to accommodate them at least one way every game."

He wasn't kidding about the strikeouts. Not only did Thomas twice lead the American League in whiffs, he also paced the Midwest League, Texas League, and Pacific Coast League in strikeouts during a climb to the majors. Thomas was the first player ever selected by the Seattle Pilots in the June 1969 draft, but did not play for a Seattle ballclub for another 15 years. That's because the insolvent Pilots became the Milwaukee Brewers in 1970.

Of course, Thomas also led the Texas and Pacific Coast leagues in home runs, and he led the American League with 45 in 1979, while striking out a league-leading 175 times (including five times in a nine-inning game, tying a major league record). Thomas and Brewers teammate Ben Oglivie combined for more than 70 homers that year, as they would for two of the next three seasons.

Thomas tied for the home run title with 39 in 1982 while fanning 143 times, as the Brewers won the AL East. Milwaukee beat the California Angels in five games to win the pennant, but Thomas had only one hit in the Series, a Game 1 two-run homer. In the World Series against the Cardinals he struck out seven times in 26 at bats and hit only .115 in the seven-game Series.

When he wasn't crashing into fences, Thomas was an excellent center fielder with a strong arm. "Stormin' Gorman" was a favorite of Brewers fans because of his hustle and his obvious delight in playing a kid's game for a living. Good natured, honest, and able to laugh at himself, he was also a favorite of baseball writers. Thomas wore his thick hair almost to his shoulders, sported an oversized Fu Manchu mustache, and usually needed a shave—leading Chicago sportswriter Bob Verdi to write: "He's got the kind of face, if he came into your home with your daughter, you'd disown them both."

His career began to fade when he developed rotator cuff problems, and he was traded to Cleveland in the middle of the 1983 season. Dealt to the Seattle Mariners after the season, Thomas batted .157 in just 108 at bats in 1984. He rebounded to hit 32 homers with 87 RBIs in 1985 and belted three homers in a game at the Kingdome on April 11. But that was his last gasp. He retired after hitting .187 in 315 at bats in 1986.

His lifetime batting average was only .225, one of the lowest in major league history among players with at least 2,500 at bats. He struck out a whopping 1,339 times in 4,677 at bats, or once every 3.49 at bats, one of worst ratios of all time. On the other hand, Thomas swatted 268 home runs, and his home run ratio of 17.45 compared favorably with contemporary Reggie Jackson's 17.52.

Roy Thomas

Thomas, Roy Allen **OF**

1899–1911 B:3/24/1874, Norristown, PA D:11/20/1959, Norristown, PA Deb:4/14/1899, PHI NL BL/TL 5'11", 150

G	AB	R	H	HR	RBI	OBP	SLG	AVG
1470	5296	1011	1537	7	299	.413	.333	.290

Roy Thomas was a lefthanded slap hitter with absolutely no power, the very caricature of a leadoff hitter. Despite terrific speed, in a career stretching from 1899 through 1911 he hit only 100 doubles, 53 triples, and seven home runs in 1,470 games. However, he was the National League's champion "walking man," leading the league in bases on balls in seven of his first nine seasons. His on-base average was over .400 in each of his first seven seasons, and he led the league in that category in 1902 and 1903. His career on-base average of .413 was 123 points above his .290 batting average. He also knew what to do when he was on base; he had 244 career steals.

His ability to foul off pitches until he wrangled a walk is often cited as one reason for creation of the foul-strike rule. In his first three years with the Philadelphia Phillies, when such strong hitters as Ed Delahanty, Nap Lajoie, and Elmer Flick batted behind him, Thomas scored over 100 runs each season, including a league high of 132 in 1900. After the Phillies sluggers jumped to the American League, his number of runs scored dropped, but Thomas still collected 1,011 for his career. A crackerjack center fielder, he led league outfielders in putouts from 1903 through 1905, in assists in 1905, and in fielding average in 1906.

Jim Thome

Thome, James Howard **3B–1B**

1991–* B:8/27/1970, Peoria, IL Deb:9/4/1991, CLE AL BL/TR 6'4", 220

G	AB	R	H	HR	RBI	OBP	SLG	AVG
916	3077	609	883	196	579	.415	.547	.287

Jim Thome followed an unlikely path to become one of baseball's most productive hitters. Because no four-year colleges seriously recruited the skinny high school standout from Peoria, Illinois, Thome opted for junior college. In June 1989, after just one season, he became Cleveland's 13th-round draft pick.

As he filled out to a brawny 225 pounds and developed a home run stroke, Thome rose quickly through the minors. He received a late-season call-up to the Indians in 1991, just his third year in professional baseball. Injuries hindered him the following season, but he dominated Triple A pitching in 1993, and by August of that year was in the big leagues to stay.

Thome displayed a powerful bat, leading American League third basemen with 20 home runs in 1994. He also endeared himself to Indians fans with his gritty throwback play, complete with high socks and pine-tar-covered batting helmet. In 1995 he was a key member of a potent Cleveland lineup, posting a .314 average and 25 homers. For an encore, he hit .311 with 38 home runs in 1996.

When the Tribe asked him to switch to first base, he did so without complaint. His 40 home runs in 1997 helped lead the Indians to their second AL pennant in three years and earned him his first All-Star selection. A broken hand slowed Thome the next season, yet he produced 30 home runs and made his second consecutive All-Star appearance.

Even when he slumped slightly in early 1999, Thome remained popular. The rabid Cleveland fans helped to elect him to his first All-Star Game start. He regained his form to help the Indians become the first club since the 1950 Boston Red Sox to score 1,000 or more runs in a season. Thome drove in 108 of those runs, scored 101 times, and walked 127 times, the third time in four years he surpassed the 100 mark in each of those categories. His potent bat and hard-nosed play were major reasons why the Indians won the AL Central every year from 1995 through 1999. Once in the postseason, Thome proved even more dangerous: he had 16 home runs and 35 RBIs in his first 50 career postseason games.

Jason Thompson

Thomson, Jason Dolph **1B**

1976–86 B:7/6/1954, Hollywood, CA Deb:4/23/1976, DET AL BL/TL 6'3", 210

G	AB	R	H	HR	RBI	OBP	SLG	AVG
1418	4802	640	1253	208	782	.369	.438	.261

Jason Thompson was a 100–100–100 man—with the Pirates in 1982. The power-hitting first baseman drove in 101 runs, walked 101 times, and struck out 107 times. His 11-year career, which was cut short by knee problems when he was only 32, had its share of unusual moments. He was an intensely private person who went out of his way to hide his emotions, both on and off the field. He did that so well that many people accused him of indifference. It was a bum rap; he was usually playing in pain.

The Tigers drafted Thomson out of California State University-Northridge, in the fifth round of the June 1975 amateur draft. In the majors a year later, Thomson hit .218 with 17 homers as a rookie. He exploded in 1977 with 31 homers and 105 RBIs. Two of his home runs cleared the right-field roof of Tiger Stadium.

When the Tigers realized they were eventually going to lose Thompson to free agency, they traded him to California in the middle of the 1980 season for outfielder Al Cowens. Between the two teams Thompson batted .288, with 21 homers and 90 RBIs. In spring training 1981 the Angels tried to sell Thompson to George Steinbrenner's Yankees for a seven-figure amount. But Commissioner Bowie Kuhn voided the deal because it exceeded the cash purchase ceiling he had set in the wake of Charlie Finley's unsuccessful attempt to sell Vida Blue to the Yankees, and Rollie Fingers and Joe Rudi to the Red Sox in the middle of the 1976 season.

So on April 1, 1981, the Angels traded Thompson to the Pirates for catcher Ed Ott and pitcher Mickey Mahler. A year later Thompson had his 100–100–100 season. He also hit 31 homers in 1982, becoming only the eighth player to hit 30 or more home runs in both leagues.

Thompson never came close to those numbers again. His knees were getting worse and the Pirates traded him to the Expos for two nondescript minor leaguers just before the start of the 1986 season. After 30 games Thompson was batting .196 and had not hit a home run. He was released and never played in another major league game.

Robby Thompson

Thompson, Robert Randall **2B**

1986–96 B:5/10/1962, West Palm Beach, FL
Deb:4/8/1986, SF NL BR/TR 5'11", 170

G	AB	R	H	HR	RBI	OBP	SLG	AVG
1304	4612	671	1187	119	458	.331	.403	.257

Robby Thompson was a good fielder who turned into a reliable hitter for the San Francisco Giants. As the pivot man in the team's league-leading 183 double plays, he was a key member of the 1987 National League West champions. In the Championship Series he stole two bases, added a home run and a triple, but the Giants lost to the St. Louis Cardinals in seven games.

In the minor leagues, Thompson had been an unimpressive .257 hitter in three seasons. He proved to be a different player in a major league uniform. He doubled off Nolan Ryan in his debut, and finished his rookie year batting .271. He even set a major league record—for being caught stealing four times in one game.

When the Giants reached the postseason again in 1989. Thompson batted .278 and homered in back-to-back games as the Giants beat the Chicago Cubs in five games. Thompson hit just .091 as Oakland swept San Francisco in the earthquake-interrupted 1989 World Series.

In 1993 Thompson earned a Gold Glove for his play at second base and batted .312—41 points higher than his previous career best—and had career highs in hits, doubles, and RBIs. He was named to the All-Star team for the second time, but for the second time injury kept him from playing. Even with a broken cheekbone—the result of an errant pitch by San Diego's Trevor Hoffman—Thompson returned to the lineup just eight days later to play in the season finale. Despite winning 103 the Giants missed the postseason by one game. In three more years with the Giants, injuries kept Thompson from building on his All-Star production of 1993. He joined the Indians in 1997, but injuries forced him to retire before he could play a game in Cleveland.

Sam Thompson

Thompson, Samuel Luther **OF**

1885–98, 1906 B:3/5/1860, Danville, IN D:11/7/1922, Detroit, MI Deb:7/2/1885, DET NL BL/TL 6'2", 207

G	AB	R	H	HR	RBI	OBP	SLG	AVG
1407	5984	1256	1979	127	1299	.384	.504	.331

According to a report published in the *Spalding Guide* of the 1890s, "Big Sam" Thompson belonged "to that rutty class of batsmen who think of nothing else when they go to the bat but gaining the applause of the groundlings by the novice's hit to the outfield for a homer, one of the least difficult hits known to batting in baseball as it needs only muscle and not brains to do it."

Without question, the "groundlings" loved Thompson. But he was often denigrated in the press as just a big dumb slugger, a hitter of "stupid" home runs instead of more "intelligent" singles. The media seemed not to notice that Thompson collected enough hits of all kinds—home runs, triples, doubles, and singles—to rank as one of the best batsmen of the day. Similarly, they overlooked his sure work in the outfield, his excellent arm, and that he drove more runs home than anyone else at the time.

Admittedly, RBI totals were an informal statistic during the 19th century, but someone should have noticed that Thompson's presence in the lineup usually resulted in a high number of runs crossing the plate. Not until much later did researchers discover by examining fading box scores that Sam Thompson was the best RBI man ever.

Many players were nicknamed "Big" in the 19th century, but Sam Thompson was one who deserved the title. He stood 6 feet 2 inches and weighed 207 pounds, a Goliath in his time. Trained as a carpenter, Thompson played baseball on neighborhood sandlots. In 1883 Indianapolis minor league manager Dan O'Leary visited Danville looking for this player who, residents said, "never does anything but hit home runs."

O'Leary's team was scheduled to play an exhibition game against the Detroit Wolverines of the National League and he thought Thompson might be of some help. O'Leary found him fixing a roof and asked him to play. Thompson said he was making $2.50 a day as a carpenter, and that he'd play only if he was paid the same wage.

Thompson played a few games professionally with Evansville of the Northwest League in 1884, then moved up to Indianapolis of the Western League in 1885. When Indianapolis manager Bill Watkins was hired as the Detroit skipper, he took Thompson along as a sub. At age 25, Thompson was old for a rookie.

According to legend, Thompson got his first chance to play when the regular left fielder sustained an injury. But Detroit had no uniform to fit Thompson. He finally appeared on the field looking like a grown man in a little boy's costume, and the crowd laughed when he came up to bat. Naturally, he slammed a drive deep into the outfield. As he passed first base, Thompson's cuffs slipped above his knees. When he rounded second, his pants split up the back. In that sorry condition, he slid into third with his first major league hit. The crowd roared, and from that moment on Thompson was one of Detroit's most popular players.

Thompson was modest and given to self-deprecating humor. In later years he said that his home runs were only bunts compared to the blasts of Babe Ruth. Others pointed out that Ruth had set his home run records with a far livelier baseball than the heavy orb that Thompson swung at. Despite the dead ball, nearly one third of Thompson's hits were for extra bases.

The first time Thompson faced Boston he noticed that second baseman Jack Burdock was playing him shallow. The catcher, aware of Thompson's power, called to the second sacker to move back, but the cocky Burdock replied, "Nobody can knock 'em through Birdie." Thompson smashed the next pitch straight at the second baseman, who avoided decapitation by dropping flat on the ground.

Thompson threw and batted lefthanded and possessed an unusual batting stance. He began in an extreme crouch and, then, as the ball approached the plate, he uncoiled and leaped into the pitch, swinging from his heels. The style seemed likely to result in many strikeouts, yet only once in Thompson's career did he fan as many as 31 times in a season.

From the moment they entered the National League the Detroit Wolverines were also-rans. In 1886 they took steps to change their fate. League member Buffalo was in financial trouble, so Detroit bought the team, acquiring stars Dan Brouthers, Hardy Richardson, Jack Rowe, and Deacon White for $7,000. Led by the four new players and by Thompson, who hit .310 in his second season, the Wolverines jumped to second place with a .707 winning percentage.

The next year Detroit won the pennant, scoring 969 runs in 127 games. The four players from Buffalo again starred, but Thompson was the team's most valuable player. He led the league with 203 hits, 23 triples, 166 RBIs, a .372 batting average, and a slugging average of .571. The St. Louis Browns, American Association champions for the third straight year, challenged the Wolverines to an extended best-of-15-games World Series, played in 10 different cities: St. Louis, Detroit, Pittsburgh, Brooklyn, New York, Philadelphia, Boston, Washington, Baltimore, and Chicago.

Although Brouthers was able to play only one game because of an ankle injury, Detroit won 10 games to become world champions. Thompson led all hitters with a .362 batting average and became the first to hit two home runs in postseason play. His running catch in Game 7 preserved a Detroit win.

The team was the toast of Detroit in 1888. Some believe they enjoyed far too many toasts, which was why they tumbled to fifth place. But Thompson had a sore arm that limited him to only 56 games. After the season the Wolverines disbanded and sold their stars to other league teams. Thompson went to the Philadelphia Phillies.

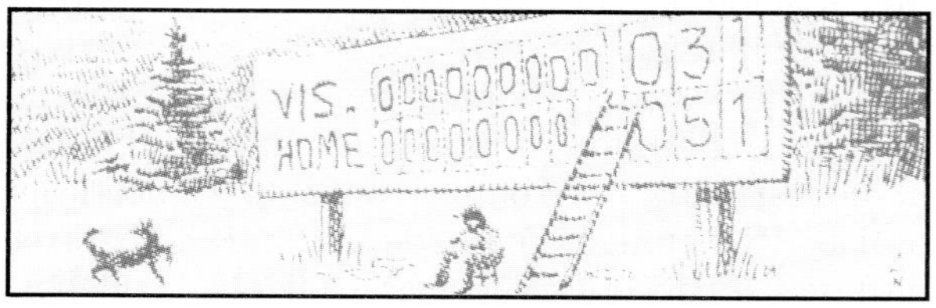

In 1889 Thompson's arm, one of the strongest in the league, was back at full strength. Many believe that Thompson was the first outfielder to throw all the way to home plate on one bounce. Yet for such a big man he was surprisingly fast in the outfield. On a number of occasions he fearlessly crashed into the fence, and always seemed to come out of such encounters in better condition than the fence. He led league outfielders in fielding in 1894 and 1896.

In his first year in Philadelphia Thompson led the league with a career-high 20 home runs, an astounding number for that era. In 1890 he paced the league with 172 hits and 41 doubles. When the pitching distance was increased to more than 60 feet in 1893, his batting average soared. Thompson hit .370 with 126 RBIs. His 222 hits and 37 doubles topped the league.

In 1894 the Phillies' three outfielders all hit better than .400. Left fielder Ed Delahanty batted .407, and Thompson and center fielder Billy Hamilton were close behind at .404. Although limited to only 99 games by an injury, Thompson drove in 141 runs, second in the league. If the Phillies had any pitching, they would have been sensational. They didn't, so they finished fourth.

In 1895 Thompson had his best overall season. He batted .392, recorded 211 hits, scored 131 runs, and hit 45 doubles, 21 triples, and a league-leading 18 home runs. His 165 RBIs topped the league, as did his .654 slugging average. The Phillies climbed to third.

Thompson's batting average declined to .298 in 1896 because of a bad back, although the slugger still managed to crack a dozen homers and drive in 100 runs. The next season his back problems worsened. He played in only three games in 1897 and 14 in 1898 before calling it quits. Returning to Detroit, Thompson became involved in politics and real estate. When his back felt better he played ball for the Detroit Athletic Club, which sometimes drew more fans than the new American League Tigers.

At the end of the 1906 season the Tigers were decimated by injuries. As Chicago and New York fought each other for the pennant, Detroit had several key games remaining with the White Sox. Thompson was cajoled out of retirement to bolster the team. The Tigers were initially criticized in New York for "handing" the pennant to Chicago by playing a 46-year-old in their outfield. Although the White Sox did win their games with the Tigers, Thompson acquitted himself well. Playing in the final eight games, he fielded flawlessly, drove in three runs, scored four, and batted .226. Those figures were hardly up to his old standards, but under the circumstances, they weren't bad. After his second and final retirement he remained close to the game, serving as an unofficial adviser to Tigers executive Frank Navin. Thompson died in 1922 of heart disease.

In 1,407 major league games Thompson had delivered 1,979 hits and compiled a career batting average of .331. His career home run total of 127 is one of the highest of the 19th century. He scored 1,256 runs and knocked in 1,299 for an average of .923 per game; through 1999 it remained the best ever for any player with more than 10 years in the majors. Lou Gehrig, at .922, is second, and Hank Greenberg's .915 ranks him third. In 1974 the Veterans Committee elected Thompson to the Hall of Fame.

Bobby Thomson

Thomson, Robert Brown **OF–3B**

1946–60 B:10/25/1923, Glasgow, Scotland
Deb:9/9/1946, NY NL BR/TR 6'2", 185

G	AB	R	H	HR	RBI	OBP	SLG	AVG
1779	6305	903	1705	264	1026	.333	.462	.270

The most dramatic end to a regular season took place on October 3, 1951, when the Giants' Bobby Thomson delivered a three-run homer off Dodgers pitcher Ralph Branca to give New York the pennant. It was rightfully dubbed "the Shot Heard 'Round the World."

Thomson had homered against Branca only two days before, and one quarter of his season's 31 home runs to that point had come against Dodgers pitching. "Bobby," called out Giants manager Leo Durocher as Thomson headed for the plate that day, "remember the pitch he threw you Monday? Well, he's not going to throw you that one again." Then he added quietly, "Bobby, if you ever hit one, hit it now."

Thomson recalled the at bat: "I took the first one down the middle, a ball I should have swung at. I waited again. Branca's pitch came in high and inside, and I got a fleeting glimpse of it. I guess I saw it better than that! I was quick with my hands. After I hit it, I watched it go. At first I was sure it was a home run. Then I saw the ball start to sink when I got halfway to first. I look again, and I realized it was disappearing into the stands. Then I knew we were all right. I jumped and skipped around the bases like I was half-nuts. 'Gee whiz,' I kept saying, 'gee whiz!' I guess you could call me an accidental hero."

Born in Glasgow, Scotland, Thomson, "the Staten Island Scot" signed a Giants contract in 1942. He played in the minors at Bristol, Rocky Mount, and Jersey City, with three years out for military service during World War II. His first full season was 1947, the year the Giants as a team hit a record 221 home runs. Thomson hit 29 of them.

In 1949, with Thomson in left field, the entire New York outfield hit better than.300. That year Thomson batted .309, with 27 homers and 109 RBIs. "By that time," he said, "there were people who thought I was the fastest man in the National League." In 1952 he topped the league in triples, with 14, while hitting 24 homers and driving in 108 runs.

In February 1954 the Giants traded Thomson to Milwaukee for four players and $50,000. In spring training the Braves were playing an exhibition game against the Yankees. Thomson was on first base. Right before the game he had told broadcaster Mel Allen how lucky he was to have escaped any injuries during his career thus far.

Then Thomson took off for second, "trying to break up a double play," he recalled. "Well, I stayed up too long and, when I tried to get out of the way of Woodie Held's throw, I did a kind of half slide and broke my ankle." The triple fracture was complicated by Thomson's allergic reaction to the chemical that held the surgical tape on his leg. The Braves replaced him in the lineup with a rookie named Hank Aaron.

Thomson rebounded with a 20-homer season for Milwaukee in 1956. On May 30, 1956, Thomson, Aaron, and Eddie Mathews hit back-to-back-to-back homers. Thomson finished the day with four homers, split between two games of a doubleheader. Four Braves—Thomson, Aaron, Mathews, and Joe Adcock—hit at least 20 homers that season, and three Milwaukee hurlers—Warren Spahn, Lew Burdette, and Bob Buhl—won at least 18 games. But the Braves finished one game back of Brooklyn in the National League standings.

Milwaukee won the pennant the next two seasons, but Thomson wasn't a part of the celebration. In June 1957 he was traded back to the Giants for future Hall of Fame second baseman Red Schoendienst. The following April New York dealt Thomson to the Cubs. Still a potent hitter, he hit 21 homers in 1958. He split his final year between the Red Sox and Baltimore, then entered the business world in northern New Jersey.

Decades later, Thomson felt no less strongly about his "Shot Heard 'Round the World." He conceded, "I'd be a liar if I don't admit I'll cherish that moment till the day I die."

Dickie Thon

Thon, Richard William **SS**

1979–93 B:6/20/1958, South Bend IN Deb:5/22/1979, CAL AL BR/TR 5'11", 175

G	AB	R	H	HR	RBI	OBP	SLG	AVG
1387	4449	496	1176	71	435	.319	.374	.264

As Cal Ripken and Robin Yount led a wave of young, hard-hitting shortstops in the American League, Houston's Dickie Thon appeared on the verge of duplicating their efforts in the National League. Thon began to show promise in the 1982 season with a league-high 10 triples and a career-best 37 stolen bases. The following season, Thon added another dimension to his game, slugging 20 home runs and earning a spot on the NL All-Star team with a .286 average and 34 steals.

Thon was off to another fine start in the first week of the 1984 season when his career was derailed. Facing the New York Mets, Thon was struck in the head by a high fastball from Mike Torrez. The Houston shortstop fell to the ground bleeding, his season suddenly over.

Contending with headaches, blurred vision, and nausea, Thon was unable to return to action until midway through the 1985 season. The injury continued to hamper Thon through two more seasons of part-time play with the Astros. He did not return to an everyday role until 1989, when he hit .271 with 15 homers for Philadelphia. After two more seasons with the Phillies and another two in the American League with Texas and Milwaukee, Thon retired at age 35.

Andy Thornton

Thornton, Andre **1B–DH**

1973–79, 1981–87 B:8/13/1949, Tuskegee, AL Deb:7/28/1973, CHI NL BR/TR 6'2", 205

G	AB	R	H	HR	RBI	OBP	SLG	AVG
1565	5291	792	1342	253	895	.364	.452	.254

Hard-hitting first baseman Andy Thornton was in both the Braves and Phillies organizations before he made the majors, and didn't really settle into a spot with the Cubs or Expos either. But on December 10, 1976, Cleveland made one the best steals in club history, obtaining Thornton from Montreal for Jackie Brown.

The proud but unassuming Thornton was a deeply religious man who engendered respect on the field with his powerful bat, and off the field with his sincere devotion to Christian beliefs. Twice Thornton slugged more than 30 homers and drove in more in 100 runs in a Cleveland uniform. Twice more he passed the 90 mark in RBIs. In 1982 he became the second Indian to draw 100 walks and drive in 100 runs (Al Rosen was the first in 1950).

During his 11 years in Cleveland, he led the Tribe in home runs seven times, including four seasons in a row. Only a succession of injuries—he missed the entire 1980 season and almost half of 1981—kept him from becoming the all-time Indian home run leader. He finished his career with 214 homers as an Indian, just 14 behind Hal Trosky.

Jim Thorpe

Thorpe, James Francis **OF**

1913–19 B:5/28/1887, Prague, OK D:3/28/1953, Long Beach, CA Deb:4/14/1913, NY NL BR/TR 6'1", 185

G	AB	R	H	HR	RBI	OBP	SLG	AVG
289	698	91	176	7	82	.286	.362	.252

Professional baseball originally was the undoing of football and track-and-field star Jim Thorpe. Yet, when all seemed lost, it was baseball that provided him with a means of earning a living.

Thorpe became a national figure as an All-America running back at Carlisle Indian School, but he became a worldwide figure when he won both the decathlon and the pentathlon at the 1912 Olympics in Stockholm, a feat that has never been duplicated. "Sir, you are the greatest athlete in the world," the King of Sweden told Thorpe as he presented him with his medals. Thorpe replied, "Thanks, King."

Soon afterward Thorpe's world came crashing down around him. Newspapers reported that he had violated his amateur standing by playing baseball for $60 a month in the summers of 1909 and 1910 for Rocky Mount and Fayetteville of the Class D Eastern Carolina League.

Such practices were not unusual back then. Each summer scores of college athletes played minor league ball—but almost always under assumed names. Thorpe naively performed under his own name, and because of that he was stripped of his Olympic medals. "I did not play for money," Thorpe wrote to James E. Sullivan, president of the American Athletic Union. "I was not very wise in the ways of the world and did not realize this was wrong....I was doing what many other college men had done, except they did not use their own names."

In February 1913 manager John McGraw signed Thorpe to a three-year, $5,000-per-annum New York Giants contract, largely as a publicity stunt, but with some hope that Thorpe could help his team. When asked how he expected Thorpe to make the transition to the big leagues, McGraw responded, "All I know is that he is the one all the sports fans in the country want to see. I've got all the players I need to win, and Thorpe isn't going to hurt us at the gate."

Later that month Thorpe reported to the Giants' camp at Marlin, Texas, where McGraw tried him out at first base before shifting him to the outfield. Following a 1913 season that saw him hit only .143 in 19 games, the newly married Thorpe participated in a baseball tour overseas, bringing along his wife. A conflict erupted between Thorpe and McGraw on the tour when the manager did not deem Thorpe's behavior appropriate for a married man. He even lectured his new player on the dangers of drinking and card playing. Throughout his major league career Thorpe would prove to be a disciplinary problem.

Thorpe never really developed as a ballplayer and spent most of the 1914 season with Milwaukee of the American Association. In 1915 McGraw sent him down to Harrisburg, and in 1916 he was back in Milwaukee. Thorpe was sold to Cincinnati in 1917, just in time to participate in two no-hitters by Reds pitcher Fred Toney. On May 2, 1917, his slow roller in the 10th inning brought in the only run of the double no-hitter between Toney and Chicago's Hippo Vaughn; Larry Kopf, who had begun the inning with the first hit of the day by either team, crossed the plate on the play. Cincinnati released Thorpe late in the season, and he was re-signed by McGraw. He batted .237 in a career-high 308 at bats that year with two teams.

After a squabble about playing time, Thorpe was traded to the Boston Braves for pitcher Pat Ragan in May 1919. He hit .327 in 60 games for the Braves that year, his last season in the majors. He was 33 years old.

Of course, it was in professional football that Thorpe made his real mark. Starting with the Canton Bulldogs in 1915, he also performed for Toledo, Rock Island, and New York. In addition, Thorpe appeared as a bit player in several Hollywood films, including the James Cagney classic, *White Heat.* (He's one of the message-passers in the famous scene in the prison mess hall in which Cagney goes berserk.) Burt Lancaster played Thorpe in a 1951 movie about his life: *Jim Thorpe, All-American.* Shortly before his death, Thorpe even tried to develop a nightclub act.

In 1950 Thorpe was named the greatest athlete of the half century. Thirteen years later he was elected to the Pro Football Hall of Fame. In 1982 the International Olympic Committee restored to Thorpe the medals it had stripped from him nearly seven decades earlier.

Marv Throneberry

Throneberry, Marvin Eugene **1B-OF**

1955, 1958–63 B:9/2/1933, Collierville, TN
D:6/23/1994, Fisherville, TN Deb:9/25/1955, NY AL
BL/TL 6', 197

G	AB	R	H	HR	RBI	OBP	SLG	AVG
480	1186	143	281	53	170	.313	.416	.237

The 1962 Mets were the laughingstock of baseball, and Marv Throneberry was their star clown. The first player the Mets picked up in the major league draft was catcher Hobie Landrith, who caught only 23 games before being swapped to the Orioles for first baseman Throneberry. The Marv Throneberry saga began on June 17, 1962. In the top of the first, the clumsy first baseman got in the way of a runner in the middle of a rundown and was called for interference. Then in the bottom of the inning, he slugged a triple, but Cubs first baseman Ernie Banks pointed out to the umpire that Throneberry had missed the bag at first. The umpire called him out on the appeal.

Manager Casey Stengel started to protest, but first base coach Cookie Lavagetto stopped him, saying, "Don't argue too hard, Case. The guy missed second too." Throneberry's fielding faux-pas cost the team four runs and his baserunning blunder at least one more. The Mets lost 8–7.

Several weeks later Throneberry hit a ninth-inning, three-run homer to turn what would have been a 14th straight Met defeat into a victory. A star was born. The fans fell in love with Throneberry and nicknamed him "Marvelous Marv." Before long Throneberry took advantage of his status, using his self-effacing, good-old-boy humor to good effect. He told sportswriters before a Sunday doubleheader, "I've got good news for you guys today. I'm only playing one game." When the club celebrated Stengel's 72nd birthday that July, Throneberry complained that he hadn't gotten his piece of cake. Casey commented, "We were gonna give you a piece, Marv. But we were afraid you'd drop it."

Throneberry was actually part of a brother act. Faye Thronberry was his more sure-handed than his younger sibling, but the outfielder batted .236—one point lower than Marvelous Marv. Marv's first appearance in the majors was in a single game with the Yankees in 1955. Back in the minors with Triple-A club in Denver, he clouted more than 40 home runs in each of the next two seasons. As a Yankee in 1958 and 1959 he continued to show promise as a power-hitter. After the 1959 season he was traded to Kansas City, where he batted .250 with 11 home runs in 1960. By June of the following year he was playing in Baltimore, where he batted only 105 times before becoming a Met.

Throneberry slugged 16 homers, drove in 49 runs, hit .244, and provided some comic relief for the Mets during their atrocious inaugural year. He got into a salary squabble with management before 1963, and the Mets released him. His final words to sportswriters as he left the clubhouse on his way to Buffalo were, "I ain't done yet."

As a ballplayer he was finished, but Marvelous Marv resurfaced in the 1970s when a beer company cast him in a series of commercials that used former athletes, coaches, and umpires. Throneberry appeared in several of the spots and coined a famous new personal theme line: "I still don't know why they asked me to do this commercial."

Sloppy Thurston

Thurston, Hollis John **P**

1923–33 B:6/2/1899, Fremont, NE D:9/14/1973, Los Angeles, CA Deb:4/19/1923, STL AL BR/TR 5'11", 165

W	L	PCT	G	SV	IP	BB	SO	ERA
89	86	.509	288	13	1542^2	369	306	4.24

Hollis John Thurston, a curveballing righthander who first appeared in the majors in 1923, was nicknamed "Sloppy" because he was so meticulous about his appearance and dressed the part of the Jazz Age dandy. Far from being a cosmopolitan, Thurston had come to the big leagues from rural Fremont, Nebraska.

He came up with the St. Louis Browns in 1923, was sold to the Chicago White Sox a month into the season and went 7–8 in 46 games as a rookie. He had his career season in 1924, going 20–14 for the last-place team, leading the American League in complete games (28 in 36 starts) and hits (330 in 291 innings).

Arm woes prevented Thurston from approaching those numbers again. He was 10–14 with a 6.17 ERA in 1925 and was traded to the Senators in 1927, going 13–13 despite allowing 254 hits in 205 ⅔ innings. He returned to the minors when more arm problems surfaced, but he returned to the majors with Brooklyn in 1930, going 33–29 over the next four years and finishing with an 89–86 career record.

Despite his average career, Thurston's name appears in the record books. In the first game of a doubleheader against the New York Giants on July 29, 1932, he allowed six home runs, a major league record he shares with four other pitchers. Thurston became a scout after he retired and signed Ralph Kiner for the Pirates.

Luis Tiant

Tiant, Luis Clemente (Vega) **P**

1964–1982 B:11/23/1940, Marianao, Cuba Deb:7/19/1964, CLE AL BR/TR 5'11", 190

W	L	PCT	G	SH	IP	BB	SO	ERA
229	172	.571	573	49	3486^1	1104	2416	3.30

Luis Tiant, probably most famous for his pirouette pitching motion and his postgame cigars, was an outstanding hurler for the Cleveland Indians and the Boston Red Sox during the 1960s and 1970s. "Tiant is the Fred Astaire of baseball," Reggie Jackson once said. Broadcaster Curt Gowdy added that Tiant's pitches seemed to come "from everywhere except between his legs." Tiant won 229 games during his big league career, posted four 20-win seasons, and led the American League in shutouts and ERA twice each.

Tiant was the son of Luis Eleuterio Tiant, a great Cuban pitcher who could not play in the major leagues because he was black. "When I was 17," the younger Tiant once said, "I told my mother and father I wanted to be a ballplayer. My father said no because he felt there was no place in baseball for a black man. But my mother finally got him to let me try."

Tiant failed a tryout with the Havana Sugar Kings of the International League. In February 1959 former All-Star Bobby Avila signed him to the Mexico City Tigers of the Mexican League. After the 1961 season, the Indians purchased Tiant's contract from Mexico City for $35,000. In the minors Tiant pitched for Jacksonville of the International League, Charleston of the Eastern League, Burlington of the Carolina League, and Portland of the Pacific Coast League. In 1963 he pitched a no-hitter for Burlington. In 1964 he went 15–1 for Portland and was the PCL Player of the Year.

During the 1964 season the Indians called up Tiant. He started 16 games for Cleveland, and won 10 of them. He also pitched three shutouts and posted a 2.83 ERA. In 1966 he pitched four consecutive shutouts and led the American League with five for the season. In 1968 he won 21 games and led the league with a 1.60 ERA, but Detroit hurler Denny McLain's 31 wins overshadowed Tiant's remarkable performance. Even in the "Year of the Pitcher" Tiant's .168 opponents' batting average was phenomenal. It was the lowest mark ever recorded as was his 5.30 hits per game (four years later Nolan Ryan allowed just 5.26 hits per game).

That year the Cleveland starter began using his famous herky-jerky pitching motion. "The first time I do it was against California," recalled Tiant, who spoke Spanish as his first language and developed some unique speech patterns as he learned English. "I forget who was batting, but I know it bother him....The motion depends on how I feel, how I think the batter is thinking. Sometimes I do nothing but throw the ball. You can't use the motions too much or they will get used to it."

Tiant had been a regular in winter ball, but after his 1968 season the Indians ordered him to take the winter off. That strategy backfired and Tiant lost his sharpness in the 1969 season. He led the league in defeats, with 20, and Cleveland traded him during the off-season to Minnesota in a six-player deal that brought Graig Nettles to the Indians.

In 1970 Tiant was off to a 6–0 start for the Twins when he fractured a shoulder blade. "The doctor

tell me he only saw it happen before with a javelin thrower," Tiant said. "But the doctor tell me that rest will heal it." The Twins, however, couldn't wait and after his poor performance during spring training in 1971, they gave Tiant his release. "It was the most forlorn experience I ever had in baseball," recalled the club's public relations director, Tom Mee. "One by one, everyone on the team walked over to Luis and shook his hand before getting on the bus. Then we left him there, practically in tears, standing by himself in the hotel lobby. It was awful."

In April the Braves signed Tiant to a minor league contract and then released him in May. The Red Sox signed him and sent him to Louisville of the International League. Only 20 days later he was called up to Boston. He was only 1–7 for the Red Sox that season, but in 1972 he went 15–6 with six shutouts and a league-leading 1.91 ERA and was named Comeback Player of the Year by *The Sporting News*.

Tiant won 20 games or more for the Sox three times during the next four years. In the Red Sox's pennant-winning 1975 season, he defeated the Oakland A's on a three-hitter in Game 1 of the Championship Series. Tiant then became on of the stars of one of the most entertaining World Series ever played.

In the opener of the 1975 World Series his single started the rally that broke open a scoreless game. He allowed only five hits in a 6–0 shutout. He tossed another complete-game victory in Game 4. After four days of rain he started historic Game 6. He trailed 6–3 entering the bottom of the eighth inning, but Bernie Carbo, pinch-hitting for Tiant, launched a three-run homer that tied the game. Boston won the unforgettable contest in the 12th inning on Carlton Fisk's home run that nearly went foul.

That year he finally got together with his father, whom he had not seen since 1961. In 1976 Tiant won 21 games for the Red Sox, but he got into a contract squabble with the new team ownership over a verbal agreement that the late owner Tom Yawkey had made with him guaranteeing his salary for 1977. In December his parents died within three days of each other.

After a 13–8 season in 1978, Tiant became a free agent and signed with the Yankees. He won 13 games for New York. Tiant even starred in a commercial for Yankee Franks that ended with the tag line, "It's great to be with a wiener."

He finished his career seeing limited action in Pittsburgh in 1981 and in California in 1982. Tiant moved to Canton, Massachusetts, where he worked for Northeastern University as part of Project Teamwork, a program sponsored by Reebok International Limited in which athletes speak to high school students to urge them to stay in school.

Dick Tidrow

Tidrow, Richard William **P**

1972–84 B:5/14/1947, San Francisco, CA
Deb:4/18/1972, CLE AL BR/TR 6'4", 213

W	L	PCT	G	SV	IP	BB	SO	ERA
100	94	.515	620	55	1746²	579	975	3.68

Dick Tidrow was named *The Sporting News* Rookie Pitcher of the Year in 1972 when he went 14–15 in 39 games with Cleveland, but his best years came later when he played as a relief specialist. Swapped to the Yankees with Chris Chambliss in early 1974, Tidrow started in 29 games that year. For the next three years he became one of New York's busiest relievers.

Tidrow earned the nickname "Dirt" because of his no-nonsense playing style: he got the job done without antics or fanfare. As Sparky Lyle's setup man he was a major contributor to the Yankees' pennant wins in 1976 and 1977.

Injuries to Catfish Hunter and Don Gullett forced Tidrow into the starting rotation in 1978, where he managed only a 7–11 record. Minutes after Tidrow posted a bad outing against the Tigers in May 1979, general manager Al Rosen got a phone call from owner George Steinbrenner, who ordered him to "get rid of Tidrow." The pitcher was dealt to the Cubs.

Back in his usual role as setup man, this time for Bruce Sutter, Tidrow performed well, appearing in 263 games in the next four seasons, including a league-leading 84 appearances in 1980. He pitched in nearly half of his team's games during the strike-shortened 1981 season. Tidrow finished his career with 50 appearances for the 1983 White Sox and 11 for the 1984 Mets. Tidrow later joined the front office with the Giants, serving as scouting director before becoming a vice president.

Mike Tiernan

Tiernan, Michael Johnson **OF**

1887–99 B:1/21/1867, Trenton, NJ D:11/9/1918, New York, NY Deb:4/30/1887, NY NL BL/TL 5'11", 165

G	AB	R	H	HR	RBI	OBP	SLG	AVG
1476	5906	1313	1834	106	851	.392	.463	.311

"Silent Mike" Tiernan was one of those players who let his bat do his talking for him. Reluctant to boast of his accomplishments or even to dispute an umpire's call, Tiernan twice led the National League in home runs and once in slugging percentage and hits.

Tiernan, who was born across the street from the Trenton State Prison in New Jersey, was originally a pitcher. He earned a reputation as a strikeout artist with Trenton and Jersey City in the Eastern League. Acquired by the New York

Giants, he refused to sign, however, unless he was converted to the outfield. The Giants agreed and never had any cause to regret it.

On June 15, 1887 Tiernan scored six runs in a 29–1 pasting of the Phillies. On that day he had two triples, three singles and a walk. On August 25, 1888, he hit for the cycle.

After retiring from the game, Tiernan operated a restaurant in New York City. He died of tuberculosis.

Joe Tinker

Tinker, Joseph **SS**

1902–16 M(1913–1916, 304–308) B:7/27/1880, Muscotah, KS. D:7/27/1948, Orlando, FL. Deb:4/17/1902, CHI NL BR/TR 5'9", 175

G	AB	R	H	HR	RBI	OBP	SLG	AVG
1804	6434	774	1687	31	782	.308	.353	.262

"Tinker to Evers to Chance" is the refrain of the poem by newspaperman Franklin P. Adams, about the Chicago Cubs' double-play combination of the 1900s. The verse, titled "Baseball's Sad Lexicon," immortalized shortstop Joe Tinker, keystoner Johnny Evers, and first baseman Frank Chance. For his part, Tinker was far from a natural. But during a 15-year career, from 1902 through 1916, he was one of the best defensive shortstops of his time; he could also handle a bat and was an excellent baserunner.

The 14-year-old Tinker was an apprentice to a paperhanger when he started his baseball career as a semiprofessional. In 1898 his Coffeyville, Kansas, team played an exhibition against the Kansas City Blues, and manager Bill Hulen recommended him to Denver of the Western League. In addition to Denver, Tinker played for Great Falls–Helena and Portland, where he committed 61 errors, a high total even in those days, and had an .851 fielding percentage.

He came up to the Cubs in 1902 and hit a respectable .282 during his first two seasons, but he also committed 141 errors during that span. After two years Tinker had honed his fielding skills, and in 1905 he led all National League shortstops in double plays.

During his next eight years with Chicago, Tinker led National League shortstops four times in fielding percentage, three times in fielding runs, and twice each in assists and putouts. Not coincidentally, the Cubs won four pennants in the five seasons from 1906 through 1910.

Although Tinker was only a .262 career hitter, he was excellent on both ends of the hit-and-run play. As a hitter he could guide the ball through an opening in the infield at the last moment, and his 336 career stolen bases are a testament to his speed and excellent instincts on the basepaths.

During the 1908 pennant race the righthanded batter was credited with several big hits against the Giants. New York and Chicago had ended the regular season in a tie, and a playoff was necessary to decide the winner. Tinker won the game with a double over the head of center fielder Cy Seymour, who had ignored pitcher Christy Mathewson's request to play deeper against Tinker.

Despite the ballclub's success, life was not paradise on the Chicago team. A petty disagreement about a cab ride caused a rift between Tinker and Evers, and they refused to even speak to each other for many years.

In December 1912 the Cubs traded Tinker to Cincinnati. One year later Cincinnati sold him to Brooklyn club owner Charles Ebbets for $15,000, with $10,000 to be paid to Tinker. Two days after the deal, the Reds' board of directors challenged club owner Garry Herrmann's right to sell Tinker. "What kind of monkey business is that? What is Herrmann, the president of the club or the office boy?" Ebbets snapped.

In stepped Cubs owner Charles Webb Murphy, who publicly expressed an interest in getting Tinker back, angering Ebbets even further. The Cincinnati directors finally confirmed the original deal, but by the time Brooklyn manager Wilbert Robinson arrived in Chicago to present Tinker with the $10,000—and Robinson was authorized to go even higher if necessary—he learned that Tinker was in Indianapolis, signing with the Federal League.

In 1914 and 1915 Tinker managed and played for the Federal League's Chicago Whales. He also recruited Washington ace Walter Johnson to pitch in the league. Johnson was to receive $17,500 for each of three years and a $6,000 advance. Senators owner Clark Griffith upped the ante, however, and Johnson quickly—and probably illegally—jumped back to the Senators.

When the Federal League folded, Whales owner Charles Weeghman gained control of the Cubs and merged the two teams, and Tinker took over managing Chicago for one season. Tinker retired from the majors after the 1916 season.

The following two years he acted as manager and president of the American Association's Columbus franchise, playing briefly for the team in 1917. While there he pulled a stunt that helped lead to the abolition of the spitball. Although pitchers usually doctored a ball inconspicuously, at the time the pitch was legal.

Tinker's batters could not hit the spitball, so he sent one of his own hurlers to the mound with a large file, and the Columbus pitcher very publicly hacked away at the ball, causing much controversy. At season's end the pitch was abolished in the American Association and shortly thereafter in the majors.

Following his stint with Columbus, Tinker managed in Orlando and Jersey City and later scouted for the Cubs. When the nation's economy collapsed in 1929 he was financially ruined because his money was in Florida real estate. The next year, however, Tinker opened a billiards parlor in Orlando, and when Prohibition was repealed, he opened the city's first bar. Orlando's Tinker Field is named in his honor.

In 1946 the Veterans Committee named Tinker to the Hall of Fame along with Evers and Chance. The next year Tinker required a leg amputation, and after being hospitalized for a respiratory ailment the following year, he died on his 68th birthday.

Jack Tobin

Tobin, John Thomas **OF**

1914–27 B:5/4/1892, St. Louis, MO D:12/10/1969, St. Louis, MO Deb:4/16/1914, STL FL BL/TL 5'8", 142

G	AB	R	H	HR	RBI	OBP	SLG	AVG
1619	6174	936	1906	64	581	.364	.420	.309

St. Louis native Jack Tobin spent most of his career playing in his hometown. He joined the St. Louis Terriers of the Federal League team in 1914 and the following year led the league with 184 base hits. When the league folded, he moved to the St. Louis Browns. As their regular right fielder from 1918 through 1924, he joined Ken Williams and Baby Doll Jacobson in a potent, .300-hitting outfield.

Tobin led off for the Browns and garnered over 200 hits for four straight seasons, from 1920 through 1924, with a high of 236 in 1921, when he batted a career-best .352. He scored more than 120 runs in both 1921 and 1922, when the Browns came within a game of winning the pennant. The 142-pound Tobin, who batted and threw left-handed, exhibited surprising power in 1921 when he led the American League with 18 triples. In both 1922 and 1923 he hit 13 home runs.

In 13 seasons Tobin batted .309 and scored 936 runs. He was a coach for the Browns from 1949 through 1951 and later scouted for the team.

Phil Todt

Todt, Philip Julius **1B**

1924–31 B:8/9/1901, St. Louis, MO D:11/15/1973, St. Louis, MO Deb:4/25/1924, BOS AL BL/TL 6', 175

G	AB	R	H	HR	RBI	OBP	SLG	AVG
957	3415	372	880	57	453	.305	.395	.258

In the aftermath of owner Harry Frazee's firesale of the Red Sox, first baseman Phil Todt was one of the few bright spots on the club. Todt led the American League in fielding percentage with a .997 mark in 1928 and in putouts, assists and errors in 1926. His totals that year—chances accepted and putouts—are among the highest in history. That year he received five votes for AL Most Valuable Player. He is among the lifetime leaders in chances accepted per game.

"In the field we had one outstanding player, Phil Todt, our first baseman," recalled Red Sox outfielder Walter Shaner, "He was a smooth fielder, but he swung up around his shoulders every time, and he only hit if they threw it there."

After almost seven years as a regular with last-place Boston, he joined the pennant-winning Philadelphia Athletics in 1931. He walked in his only World Series appearance in the A's seven-game loss to the Cardinals; it was his last game as a major leaguer. Todt went to the minor leagues the following year and remained with St. Paul in the American Association through 1937. He managed St. Paul in 1933 and 1937. In 1939 he managed Crookston of the Northern League.

Considering the fact that the Red Sox finished last in his final seven years in Boston, it seems appropriate that the word "Todt" is German for "death." Following his retirement he operated a flower shop in St. Louis, no doubt specializing in funerals.

Bobby Tolan

Tolan, Robert **OF–1B**

1965–71 B:11/19/1945, Los Angeles Deb:9/3/1965, STL NL BL/TL 5'11", 170

G	AB	R	H	HR	RBI	OBP	SLG	AVG
1282	4238	572	1121	86	497	.317	.382	.265

Cincinnati Reds outfielder Bobby Tolan paced all National Leaguers in stolen bases with 57 in 1970. He played in four World Series with two different clubs and teamed with Pete Rose to form one of the best 1–2 punches in the major leagues during the early 1970s.

The nephew of Eddie Tolan, who won two gold medals in the 1932 Olympics, Bobby Tolan signed originally with the Pirates and was sent to Reno of the California League in 1963. Drafted by the Cardinals in December 1963, he played in the St. Louis chain at Tulsa and Jacksonville and eventually became a backup outfielder in St. Louis. He made brief appearances in the 1967 and 1968 World Series before being traded with pitcher Wayne Granger to Cincinnati for outfielder Vada Pinson in October 1968.

Tolan made an immediate impact in Cincinnati, batting No. 2 in the Reds' lineup behind Rose. In 1969 he tied for the National League lead in putouts and hit a career-high 21 homers. The following season he was selected to *The Sporting News* NL All-Star Team. From 1965 through 1981 Rose and Tolan were the league's only teammates to lead off a game with consecutive home runs—

and they did it three times, including April 7, 1969, off future Hall of Famer Don Drysdale.

Not only did Tolan lead the league in stolen bases in 1970, he established career highs in batting average (.316), slugging average (.475), doubles (34), runs scored (112), and bases on balls (94). All three Reds outfielders—Tolan, Rose, and Bernie Carbo—batted at least .300 that season, and Tolan was one of six Cincinnati players to hit at least 15 homers. The Reds ran away from the pack in the NL West.

In Game 2 of the Championship Series against Pittsburgh Tolan homered and scored all three Cincinnati runs. He then drove in the game-winning run in the eighth inning of Game 3, leading the Reds to a sweep. Baltimore defeated Cincinnati in the World Series, although Tolan hit another homer, in Game 2.

In January 1971 Tolan tore his Achilles tendon playing basketball and missed the entire season. In 1972, however, he led the league in putouts and was named *The Sporting News* Comeback Player of the Year. The following season Tolan was having problems with Reds management, and on November 9, 1973, he was traded to San Diego.

Tolan injured his knee in July 1974 and was on the disabled list until September. Released by the Padres in February 1976, he was signed by Philadelphia in March. He had three at bats in the 1976 NLCS but was released by the Phillies in May 1977. Tolan hooked on with the Pirates that June, and, granted free agency in October, he played in Japan with the Nankai Hawks in 1978. Tolan's major league career ended in 1979 after 22 games with the Padres. He later managed Beaumont in the Texas League and coached in the major leagues.

Jeff Torborg

Torborg, Jeffrey Allen **C**

1964–73 M(1977–79, 1989–1993, 492–551)
B:11/26/1941, Plainfield, NJ Deb:5/10/1964, LA NL
BR/TR 6'½", 195

G	AB	R	H	HR	RBI	OBP	SLG	AVG
574	1391	78	297	8	101	.270	.265	.214

Jeff Torborg once observed about catchers: "There must be some reason why we're the only ones facing the other way." During the darker days of his managing career, this one-time Manager of the Year might have been questioning his decision to manage a baseball team, as well.

Torborg set an NCAA record by batting .537 at Rutgers University. He became the Dodgers' first $100,000 bonus baby, signing with that club at the urging of Ozzie Nelson, a fellow Rutgers alumnus. Never a great major league hitter, Torborg was a defensive whiz who caught Sandy Koufax's perfect game on September 9, 1965, and no-hitters by Bill Singer on July 20, 1970, and Nolan Ryan on May 15, 1973.

Torborg's playing career ended in 1973 with the Angels. A career .214 hitter, he hit just eight lifetime homers. In midseason 1977 the 35-year-old Torborg replaced Frank Robinson as manager of the Cleveland Indians. The Tribe finished fifth that season, sixth in 1978, and 95 games into the 1979 season Torborg was fired and replaced by Dave Garcia.

In 1990 Torborg, a Yankees coach for most of the 1980s, guided a young White Sox team to a surprising second-place finish in the American League West. He was named Manager of the Year by AP, UPI, *The Sporting News*, and the Baseball Writers Association.

In October 1991 Torborg signed a four-year contract to manage the Mets. But during his short tenure the franchise collapsed in a heap of losses and controversy. Dallas Green replaced Torborg in midseason 1993. Torborg took his insights to the broadcast booth.

Earl Torgeson

Torgeson, Earl **1B**

1947–61 B:1/1/1924, Snohomish, WA D:11/8/1990, Everett, WA Deb:4/15/1947, BOS NL BL/TL 6'3", 180

G	AB	R	H	HR	RBI	OBP	SLG	AVG
1668	4969	848	1318	149	740	.387	.417	.265

Earl Torgeson was not the first "the Earl of Snohomish," nor was he even the best. Cleveland's Earl Averill, who also hailed from Snohomish, Washington, was a six-time All-Star for the Indians in the 1930s. Torgeson was dependable hitter in the 1950s. This "Earl of Snohomish," however, seemed to be more interested in the Marquis of Queensberry's sport, as the bespectacled first baseman was better known for his brawling than his batting. Once, when he was in the minor leagues, he not only hurled the opposing second baseman's glove into the stands, but also he hurled the second baseman there, too.

His major league bouts included a memorable match with Warren Spahn in 1953. "I had a real good headlock on him," Torgeson recalled. "It was a retaliation thing. I felt I had to act. If someone was making me a target I couldn't sit still."

Torgeson came up with the Boston Braves in 1947. The following year he led all regulars with a .389 average in the World Series, but the Braves fell to the Indians in six games. He injured his shoulder in 1949 and missed most of the season. Although the injury hampered him for the rest of his career he managed to play in the major leagues for another 12 years. In 1950 he led the National League in runs scored.

Boston traded him to the Phils in February 1953 as part of a four-club exchange. In 1955 he was sold to the Tigers. He appeared in the 1959 World Series for the White Sox and finished his career as a player-coach for the Yankees in 1961.

Torgeson was later elected county commissioner from Snohomish. He was indicted for illegally using his office for political gain, but was not convicted.

Frank Torre

Torre, Frank **1B**

1956–60, 1962–63 B:12/30/1931, Brooklyn, NY
Deb:4/20/1956, MIL NL BL/TL 6'3", 205

G	AB	R	H	HR	RBI	OBP	SLG	AVG
714	1482	150	404	13	179	.352	.372	.273

Sure-handed first baseman Frank Torre twice led the National League in fielding. But it was his bat and baserunning that put his name in the baseball annals. On September 2, 1957, Torre tied a 20th century record by scoring six runs in a single game.

Signed by the Boston Braves' organization in 1951, Torre hit .300 or better in three of his four minor league seasons. By the time he reached the major leagues in 1956 the team was located in Milwaukee. In 1957 he took over for slugger Joe Adcock at first base after the first baseman broke his leg. In that year's World Series Torre homered twice. His bat was still so suspect, however, that even after delivering a homer in Game 4 he was replaced by a pinch hitter in the ninth inning.

The following season Torre batted .309, hit six homers, and drove in 55 runs. The Braves won the pennant again but lost to the Yankees in the World Series. Torre hit only .176 in the seven-game Series. In 1960 the Braves tired of Torre's weak offense and demoted him to the minors. Playing at Louisville, he hit .282 that year and .307 in 1961. The Phillies purchased his contract in December 1961, but Torre played only two more seasons in the majors before retiring.

After leaving baseball, Torre, the older brother of Joe Torre, became an executive with the Rawlings Sporting Goods Company. Frank Torre was in the hospital awaiting a heart transplant as brother Joe, managing the Yankees, faced Atlanta in the 1998 World Series. Joe underwent successful transplant surgery on the eve of Game 6, as the series stood 3–2 in favor of the Yankees. The next day, the Yanks won.

Joe Torre

Torre, Joseph Paul **C-1B-3B**

1960–77 M(1977–84, 1990–*, 1273–1236)
B:7/18/1940, Brooklyn, NY Deb:9/25/1960, MIL NL
BR/TR 6'2", 212

G	AB	R	H	HR	RBI	OBP	SLG	AVG
2209	7874	996	2342	252	1185	.367	.452	.297

After conquering a weight problem, Joe Torre won the National League Most Valuable Player award and added the word "svelte" to hundreds of sportswriters' vocabularies. But Torre took a lot longer to conquer his "wait" problem. He set a record with 4,272 games as a big league player and manager with out ever participating in a World Series. Then in 1996, his first season at the helm of the New York Yankees, he guided the club to a world championship. Two years later he did it again, picking up an American League record 114 wins on the way to the 1998 Series win. For an encore, Torre guided the Yankees to their 25th World Series championship in 1999.

Joseph Paul Torre grew up in Brooklyn, where he played third base at St. Francis Prep. He was the product of a baseball family. His father scouted for the Milwaukee Braves and later for the Baltimore Orioles, and Joe's older brother, Frank, played first base for the Braves. It was no surprise that Joe signed with Milwaukee in 1959.

With Eddie Mathews occupying third base, the Braves converted Torre into a catcher. His bat, however, was his ticket to the majors. In 1960, his first season of pro ball, Torre won the Class A Northern League batting title, hitting .344. Late that season he was promoted to Milwaukee and singled off Harvey Haddix in his first major league at bat.

Torre spent barely a month of 1961 at Milwaukee's Triple-A club, batting .342 to earn a permanent promotion to the Braves. He played 113 games in 1961, filling in when regular catcher Del Crandall was injured. In 1962 he and Crandall shared catching duties, and the next year Torre began playing first base when he wasn't behind the plate, in order to get his bat in the lineup. That season he even made two outfield appearances. Torre was selected to the National League All-Star team for five straight seasons, starting in 1963, and he had four more consecutive selections, starting in 1970.

When Crandall was traded to San Francisco in an eight-player deal that brought Felipe Alou to Milwaukee for the 1964 season, Torre became the Braves' regular catcher. He led National League receivers with a .995 fielding average and flowered as a power hitter, with 36 doubles, 20 homers, 109 RBIs, and a .321 batting average. He also led the league in grounding into double plays, a dubious distinction he'd achieve again in 1965, 1967, and 1968. He finished fifth in the league's 1964 MVP voting and received a smattering of votes the next two years.

In 1965 Torre slammed 27 homers. He was one of a league-record six 20-home run hitters on the Braves, an arsenal matched only by the 1961 Yankees, 1964 Twins, and 1986 Tigers. He also won his only Gold Glove and hit a two-run homer in the first inning of the All-Star Game.

The Braves moved to Atlanta in 1966 and led the league in home runs for the second straight season. Torre batted .315 and was one of the team's three 30-home run hitters, socking a career-high 36. He suffered a broken cheekbone in April 1968, missing three weeks, which caused a drop in his power numbers. But he led the league's catchers in fielding percentage for the second time.

On St. Patrick's Day 1969, the Braves traded Torre to St. Louis for first baseman Orlando Cepeda, the league's 1967 MVP and a team leader for the back-to-back National League champion Cardinals. Torre replaced Cepeda at first base, fielded better, outhit him by 32 points, and knocked in 13 more runs. But the Braves scrambled from behind to win the inaugural NL West flag while the favored Cardinals were never in the NL East race.

The next winter the Cards made another big swap, trading catcher Tim McCarver and center fielder Curt Flood to Philadelphia in a seven-player deal that included Richie Allen as their principal acquisition. The Cardinals had 20-year-old catcher Ted Simmons on the way, but without Torre to play behind the plate in 1970, they probably wouldn't have made the deal.

As it turned out, Flood refused to report to the Phillies, and the Cardinals sent Willie Montanez and Cal Browning to the Phils to complete the deal. Flood's subsequent lawsuit began the downfall of the reserve clause, and the Cardinal plans went back to the drawing board after third baseman Mike Shannon was forced to retire due to kidney disease.

Torre began the 1970 season catching and made the All-Star team at that position. But when Shannon left the lineup, Torre shifted to third base, a position he hadn't played since high school. He finished with yet another banner year at the plate, setting career highs with a .325 average, second-best in the league, and 203 hits, including 57 for extra bases. He also knocked in 100 runs, his best power output in four years. The Cardinals decided that Torre would be their regular third baseman.

To prepare for the new assignment, Torre put himself on the popular Stillman water diet: lots of protein, no carbohydrates, and eight glasses of water a day. He dropped more than 20 pounds before spring training and had his best season in the majors. He led both leagues with 230 hits, 137 RBIs, 352 total bases, and a .363 average, winning the National League MVP over Willie Stargell. Torre clouted 24 homers that season but never again hit more than 13 or knocked in more than 81 runs in any of his six remaining major league seasons.

After playing mainly at third base in 1972, he shifted across the diamond to first base for the next two years. Hitting for the cycle on June 27, 1973, was the highlight of those years. During the 1974 World Series the New York Mets continued their habit of collecting longtime players for their troublesome third base position. They acquired Torre for veteran pitcher Ray Sadecki and youngster Tommy Moore.

The Mets soon learned that Torre had slowed down. In his first year in New York, Torre grounded into a league-record four double plays in a nine-inning game, tying the major league mark first set 30 years earlier by Goose Goslin. During his career, Torre hit into 284 double plays, ninth on the all-time list.

Torre batted .306 as a semiregular in 1976, playing first more often than third. But he was no longer a power threat. On May 31, 1977, the Mets fired manager Joe Frazier and appointed Torre, who remained on the roster as a player until June 18.

Skipper Torre approved of the unpopular deal sending Tom Seaver to Cincinnati. The Mets played slightly better under Torre but finished last, as they would the next two seasons. In 1980 the Mets contended for first place as late as July, but the team collapsed in the second half and finished with 95 losses—although the club avoided the cellar. New York came within four games of .500 in the second half of 1981, yet Torre was fired by Mets general manager Frank Cashen after the season.

In 1982 Torre replaced Bobby Cox in Atlanta, and with the blossoming of Dale Murphy and a healthy Bob Horner, the Braves started the season 13–0 and won the NL West title. In the playoffs against the St. Louis Cardinals, rain erased Phil Niekro's 1–0 lead in the opener. The Braves lost the replay and the next two. They were NL West runners-up the next two seasons, and Torre was fired.

Torre then became a broadcaster for the California Angels but was frequently mentioned for vacant managing jobs. He took over the last-place St. Louis team on August 1, 1990, giving him the distinction of managing all three teams for which he played. He led the Cards to a surprising second-place finish in 1991, and the 1992 team held first place briefly in May before falling to second.

In 1993 the Cards appeared poised to challenge the Phillies for the NL East flag. They began a late July series in Philadelphia four games behind but dropped three straight and faded to third.

The weak-hitting Cards slipped to fourth in 1995. Torre was fired as the season wound down. He landed in the Bronx, continuing a tradition of Yankees skippers (Casey Stengel, Yogi Berra, Dallas Green) who also managed the Mets. The Yankees held off Baltimore for the team's first division title since 1981. New York then defeated Texas in four games in the Division Series. Thanks to an 11-year-old boy whose over-the-wall catch of a Derek Jeter flyball, controversially credited as a homer, the Yankees went on to win the Championship Series in five games over the Orioles. Although they looked outclassed as they lost the first two games of the World Series to the Atlanta Braves at home, the Yanks rebounded with four straight wins. The victory was especially sweet for Torre, not just because he had waited so long, but also because brother Frank received a long-awaited heart transplant the day before Game 6.

After Cleveland eliminated the Wild Card Yankees from the postseason in 1997, New York bounced back to dominate the 1998 baseball season, sweeping the outmatched San Diego Padres in the World Series. Torre missed the raising of the championship banner on Opening Day 1999; he was recovering from successful surgery for prostate cancer in March. He returned to work in May and guided the Yankees to their third world championship in four years.

Mike Torrez

Torrez, Michael Augustine **P**

1967–84 B:8/28/1946, Topeka, KA Deb:9/10/1967, STL NL BR/TR 6'5", 220

W	L	PCT	G	SH	IP	BB	SO	ERA
185	160	.536	494	15	3044	1371	1404	3.96

Pitcher Mike Torrez took the mound for seven different teams in his 18-year major league career and won at least 10 games per season for each of them. No other pitcher ever enjoyed such widespread success.

Torrez pitched for the Cardinals, Expos, Orioles, Athletics, Yankees, Red Sox, and Mets. In the prime of his career, from 1974 to 1979, he pitched for five different clubs and won at least 15 games every season, a significant achievement since he usually lacked offensive support. He caught a popup for the final out of the Yankees' World Series triumph in 1977, and then the next year he delivered the pitch that Bucky Dent hit over the "Green Monster" to help send the Yankees on their way to another world championship.

Torrez's wildness may have contributed to his frequently being traded. The fastballing 6-foot-5-inch hurler led his league in walks three times and regularly gave 80 to 90 free passes a year. Torrez was rarely the principal starter, and although he had more than a dozen complete games seven times, he was a good—but never a great—pitcher. Consequently he was often trade bait for teams in search of another quality starter.

In 1970, his first full season in the majors, Torrez went 10–4 as a Cardinals swingman. Moved into the rotation the following season, he fell to 8–10, with an ERA of over 4.00. Dealt to the Expos, Torrez won 15 games twice in three years before being sent to Baltimore.

Orioles manager Earl Weaver, master of the pitching staff, studied Torrez's technique and decided that the big righty needed a slow curve to set up his other pitches. Weaver instructed his pitching coach, George Bamberger, to teach Torrez the pitch. Torrez responded with his best season ever, 20–9, leading the American League in winning percentage.

With the advent of free agency, Oakland boss Charlie Finley decided to dispose of some high-priced talent. Reggie Jackson and Ken Holtzman went to Baltimore for Torrez and Don Baylor in 1976. Torrez posted a 16–12 record for Oakland before moving on to the Yankees, whose star hurlers Jim "Catfish" Hunter and Don Gullett were both down with injuries. New York gave Oakland three players for Torrez, and the Yanks got their money's worth.

Torrez filled the gap perfectly. He won 14 games as a Yankee to help New York beat out Weaver's Orioles for the division title. In the final game of the Championship Series Torrez relieved Ron Guidry in the third inning with the Yanks down, 3–1, and held the Royals scoreless into the eighth, giving New York a chance to come back with four runs in the last two innings for the win. In the World Series Torrez started and completed two games with victories. He was the pitcher during Reggie Jackson's three-homer onslaught in Game 6 that locked up the world championship for New York.

At the peak of his career Torrez became a free agent, and the Red Sox made him a rich man with a seven-year pact totaling $2.5 million. Starting more often than anyone else on the Boston staff, he had a typical year and went 16–13 with 15 complete games. He will forever be remembered for his final start that season.

In 1978 the Red Sox folded and let the Yankees tie them for the flag. Torrez started the one-game playoff and held a 2–0 lead into the seventh inning. With two men on and an 0–2 count, Bucky Dent fouled a pitch off his foot. As the Yankees trainer examined Dent, Torrez became impatient. He hung the next pitch and Dent cemented his name in Red Sox lore by lofting an infamous pop-fly, three-run homer to left field. The Yanks went on to the ALCS and ultimately captured the World Series

After three more up-and-down seasons with Boston, Torrez was sent to the Mets before the 1983 season for a minor league third baseman. Torrez won 10 and lost 17 on a staff that featured Tom Seaver in his return season in New York—the Mets didn't do much for him either, as Seaver went 9–14 with an ERA that was a run per game lower than Torrez's mark.

Torrez was the Mets' Opening Day starter in 1984. He gave up six runs in less than two innings to end a streak of 13 years in which the Mets had won on Opening Day. In his next start Torrez threw a fastball that struck Houston's Dickie Thon in the head. The pitch shattered the bones around his eye and nearly ended the batter's career. That year, after being traded to Oakland, Torrez pitched two innings and then retired from baseball.

Cristobal Torriente

Torriente, Cristobal **OF**

Negro League Player (1914–32) B:1895, Cuba D:1938, New York, NY

Many authorities place Cristobal Torriente, known as the "Cuban Strongman," in the all-time All-Negro Leagues outfield. In 1919 Torriente, Hall of Famer Oscar Charleston, and speedster Jimmy Lyons patrolled the grass for the Chicago American Giants, making perhaps the best outfield trio ever among black teams.

Torriente was called "the Babe Ruth of Cuba," and in 1920 he and the Babe faced each other in Havana. Ruth went 0-for-4 against Cuban pitching. Torriente, on the other hand, hit three homers, two off first baseman Highpockets Kelly and one off Ruth himself. Two home runs were usually good enough to lead the league for an entire season in the cavernous parks on the island, making Torriente's feat the more remarkable.

Torriente wore bracelets, which he shook before going to bat, and a red bandana around his neck, for his Cuban club, the Rojos, or Reds. He was Cuban batting champion three times, stolen base champ four times, and triples and home run champ five times each. In 1919–20 he led in every batting department. Torriente's highest averages were .401 in Cuba, 1915–16, and .402 in the U.S. in 1920. He led the Negro League in 1923 with .389.

Torri pitched occasionally and even played a lefthanded second base. He was also a notorious playboy, and died an alcoholic at an early age.

Cesar Tovar

Tovar, Cesar Leonardo **OF-2B-3B**

1965–76 B:7/3/1940, Caracas, Venezuela
Deb:4/12/1965, MIN AL BR/TR 5'9", 155

G	AB	R	H	HR	RBI	OBP	SLG	AVG
1488	5569	834	1546	46	435	.337	.368	.278

At various times Cesar Tovar led the American League in doubles, triples, and hits, he was a regular for most of his career, and he had 226 career steals, but Tovar's legacy was playing all nine positions in a game. On September 22, 1968, the versatile Tovar spent an inning at each position in a game against the Kansas City A's. Fittingly, the first batter he faced as a pitcher was Bert Campaneris, who originally accomplished the feat of playing all nine positions on September 8, 1965, against the Angels. While on the mound, Tovar managed to strike out Reggie Jackson.

Tovar also shares the major league record for breaking up no-hitters. He had the lone safety in five one-hitters—against Dave McNally, Mike Cuellar, Catfish Hunter, Barry Moore, and Dick Bosman.

Born Cesar Leonard Perez, he led the New York–Pennsylvania, Carolina, and Pacific Coast leagues in runs scored and stolen bases. The Twins acquired him from the Cincinnati Reds in December 1964, and he made his major league debut in 1965. Two years later he led the American League in at bats. On May 18, 1969, Tovar and teammate Rod Carew both stole home in the same inning.

Tovar played in two American League Championship Series with the Twins. In the 1969 ALCS he batted only .077 in Minnesota's three-game loss to the Baltimore Orioles. He hit .300 for the first time in 1970 and led the league in doubles and triples. Once again, however, the Orioles swept the Twins in the postseason; Tovar hit .385 in the ALCS.

In 1971 Tovar batted .311 and recorded a league-leading 204 hits. He hit for the cycle on September 19, 1972, and that year he led the American League in hit-by-pitches. Traded to the Philadelphia Phillies after the 1972 season, in December 1973 he was sold to the Rangers. Midway through the 1975 season Oakland acquired Tovar, and he went one-for-two in that year's ALCS.

Tovar's last season in the majors was 1976, which he split between the A's and Yankees. After retiring as a player, Tovar scouted in his native Venezuela.

Alan Trammell

Trammell, Alan Stuart **SS**

1977–96 B:2/21/1958, Garden Grove, CA
Deb:9/9/1977, DET AL BR/TR 6', 175

G	AB	R	H	HR	RBI	OBP	SLG	AVG
2293	8288	1231	2365	185	1003	.354	.415	.285

Only Ty Cobb and Al Kaline played more years in Detroit than Alan Trammell. At a time when the shortstop position was becoming more offense-oriented, Trammell held his own against the likes of Cal Ripken and Robin Yount. Trammell won the Gold Glove Award four times, the Silver Slugger Award three times, and was a six-time All-Star. His main attribute, though, was stability.

Selected in the second round by the Tigers in 1976, Trammell made his major league debut on September 9, 1977. To his left was second baseman Lou Whitaker, also making his debut. They would play together in an American League record 1,918 games. The Tigers suffered four straight losing seasons, then enjoyed 11 consecutive winning seasons, including a world championship.

As Detroit rolled to a record 35–5 start in 1984, many thought that Trammell might follow Yount and Ripken as the third shortstop in a row to be named the league's Most Valuable Player. Although Willie Hernandez would edge him out as MVP for the season, Trammell received an trophy of his own in October.

Following a .314 regular season, Trammell batted .364 against the Kansas City Royals in a sweep of the American League Championship Series. Then in his first World Series at bat, he singled to drive in a run against the San Diego Padres. He had two hits in each of the first three games of the Series. In crucial Game 4 at Tiger Stadium, he homered twice with Whitaker on base to give Detroit a three games to one lead. The Tigers won the World Series the next day, and Trammell earned Series MVP honors with a .450 average, two home runs, six RBIs, and five runs scored.

His best season was 1987. Trammell posted career highs with a .343 average, 205 hits, 109 runs, 28 home runs, and 105 RBIs. He finished second to George Bell in the MVP voting, but his Tigers overtook Bell's Blue Jays on the final day of the season for the AL East title.

Although Trammell suffered several injuries over the final decade of his career, he still finished near the top in most offensive categories in Tigers history. When he retired in 1996, his .977 fielding average was higher than that of any shortstop in the Hall of Fame. He spent two years in the Tigers front office before returning to the field as the team's hitting instructor in 1999. Although a fan favorite in Detroit, Trammell was not retained when the Tigers changed managers after the 1999 season. After 24 seasons in the Tigers organization, Trammell joined the Padres as a coach.

Cecil Travis

Travis, Cecil Howell **SS–3B**

1933–47 B:8/8/1913, Riverdale, GA Deb:5/16/1933,
WAS AL BL/TR 6'1½", 185

G	AB	R	H	HR	RBI	OBP	SLG	AVG
1328	4914	665	1544	27	657	.370	.416	.314

Cecil Travis reached the apex of his career in 1941. The Senators' left-handed-hitting shortstop led the American League with 218 hits, recorded a .520 slugging percentage, and hit for a .359 average—second only to Ted Williams. He also established himself as a better-than-average fielder. But when the United States joined World War II, Travis was drafted and served from 1942 to 1944. When he returned from the war, he was not the same athlete.

"My problem when I got back to baseball was my timing," he explained. "I could never seem to get it back the way it was after laying out so long. I saw I wasn't helping the ballclub, so I just gave it up."

Travis, youngest of 10 children, was raised on a 200-acre Georgia farm. He became interested in baseball in high school and played semipro ball in Fayetteville, Arkansas. He attended an Atlanta baseball school that was run by retired major league shortstop Kid Elberfeld. After Elberfeld talked Joe Engel of the Chattanooga Lookouts into signing the 16-year-old, Travis hit .424 for Chattanooga in 13 games in 1931. In the off-season Washington acquired his contract, but he spent 1932 in Chattanooga, where he batted .356 and collected 203 hits.

Travis started the 1933 season at third base with Washington because Senators regular Ossie Bluege was injured. The lefthanded hitter showed his opposite-field stroke immediately, and hammered five hits to left in his first game. When Bluege healed, Travis went back to the minors.

After Travis got back to the majors again, Cleveland pitcher Thornton Lee beaned him on June 5, 1934. Travis was hospitalized for 12 days. Two days after being discharged he returned to the Senators' lineup and faced Lee again, tripling to right-center on the first pitch. In 1935 he excelled as a third basemen, but was switched back to shortstop the following year.

In eight of his first nine seasons Travis batted better than .300. Although he missed part of the 1939 season after he came down with influenza that made him a "walking skeleton," he still managed to hit .292. Travis retired from the major leagues in 1947 and scouted for Washington until 1948.

Pie Traynor

Traynor, Harold Joseph **3B**

1920–37 M(1934–39, 457–406) B:11/11/1899, Framingham, MA D:3/16/1972, Pittsburgh, PA Deb:9/15/1920, PIT NL BR/TR 6', 170

G	AB	R	H	HR	RBI	OBP	SLG	AVG
1941	7559	1183	2416	58	1273	.362	.435	.320

When Major League Baseball announced its all-time team during the centennial celebration in 1969, Pie Traynor was the third baseman. Since that time, several players have surpassed many of his fielding stats, and his production on offense has been called into question by revisionist historians. But longtime New York Giants manager John McGraw, himself a former third sacker, called Traynor "the greatest team player of his time."

No nicer person ever wore a baseball uniform. The man who got his nickname from his favorite dessert was a quietly polite gentleman who during his later years became a fixture around Pittsburgh, always willing to stop and talk baseball with anyone who recognized him.

For some reason, Traynor's performance at shortstop as a teenager in the Boston area didn't attract the attention of either of the two major league clubs there. Instead, he joined the big leagues by way of the Pirates. Pittsburgh owner Barney Dreyfuss signed him during the 1920 season when he was playing for Portsmouth of the Virginia League. Traynor appeared in 17 games for the Bucs that year before the club sent him to Birmingham for seasoning. In his only season there he hit .336 and belted 13 triples.

In 1922 Traynor took over the third base job in Pittsburgh. Fielding whiz Rabbit Maranville was his shortstop. Traynor hit .282, but a dozen of his 161 hits were three-baggers. Helped by the spaciousness of Forbes Field, he swatted fewer than 10 triples only twice during the 13 full seasons he played.

In 1923 his 19 three-base hits led the National League. Although Traynor was not a fast runner, he slugged long line drives into the gaps and stretched doubles into triples with savvy base running. He seldom struck out, but he was notoriously impatient at the plate: only twice during his 17-year career did he walk more than 50 times in a season.

Traynor had a powerful throwing arm, although he could be wild at times. But with his quick release, he was excellent at charging bunts and slow-chopped hits, and he was a legend at stopping balls hit down the third-base line. More than once a wire-service story read "(So and so) hit a double down the third-base line but Traynor threw him out."

When shortstop Glenn Wright joined the Pirates in 1924, he and Traynor formed a tandem on their side of the infield that frustrated many a righthanded pull-hitter. Catcher Al Lopez said that getting a ball past them was practically impossible.

Traynor led league third basemen in putouts seven times, tying the records of Ron Santo and Willie Jones for most league leads. Traynor also topped in assists in 1923, 1925, and 1933 and in fielding average in 1925. He shares the NL single-game record for most double plays initiated by a third baseman, with four, and holds the league record for lifetime putouts. But he also leads in lifetime errors.

In 1925 Traynor was one of four Bucs to drive home more than 100 runs, and that season the Pirates returned to the World Series after a 16-year absence. Pittsburgh's Series opponents were the Senators of pitching ace Walter Johnson, and Traynor was one of the Series' stars.

In a 4–1 opening defeat, Traynor homered off Johnson for the only Bucs run. In Game 2 his leadoff triple in the second inning became Pittsburgh's first run. In addition, Traynor drove in runs in each of the last three Series games. His triple in Game 7 tied the contest for the Pirates in the seventh inning, but Washington outfielder Joe Harris and keystoner Bucky Harris teamed up to throw Traynor out as he tried to extend his three-bagger into a homer. In the rain-soaked eighth inning, the Bucs beat the Nats on Kiki Cuyler's bases-loaded double. For the Series, Traynor took part in a pair of twin killings, led all fielders with 24 assists, and batted .346.

From 1925 through 1930 Traynor averaged .340, including seasons of .356 and .366. In the 1927 Series, Babe Ruth's Yanks swept the Bucs, but Traynor achieved a touch of glory: his single broke up Herb Pennock's no-hit attempt in the eighth inning of Game 3.

As Traynor aged into his 30s, his batting averages dropped into the low .300s. Still he was named the league's third baseman for both the premiere All-Star Game in 1933 and the Midsummer Classic of 1934, when he became the Pirates' playing manager. However, in a game that year against the Phillies he overslid home, and as he reached back to touch the plate, the Philadelphia catcher fell on his right arm. Traynor's playing career was virtually over. He played in only 62 games after that season.

Under Traynor's pleasant demeanor, the Pirates finished fourth in both 1935 and 1936. In 1937 they climbed to third, and they led the league for most of 1938, until the Cubs made a fierce charge for first. Chicago catcher-manager Gabby Hartnett's famous "Home Run in the Gloamin'" off one of baseball's first relief specialists, Mace

Brown, capped the Chicago's effort. The Pirates finished second.

In 1939 the Bucs tumbled into sixth, and Traynor was fired. A national sportswriter blasted Bucs ownership, saying that Traynor was merely a scapegoat for poor front-office management.

After his ouster, Traynor took a job as a sports commentator on a Pittsburgh radio station. He also became a part-time scout and instructor for the Pirates, and each spring training Traynor tutored some new Bucs third baseman. In 1948 the Veterans Committee inducted him into the Hall of Fame. He remained a scout for the Pirates until his death in 1972.

Tom Tresh

Tresh, Thomas Michael **OF-SS**

1961–69 B:9/20/1937, Detroit, MI Deb:9/3/1961, NY AL BB/TR 6', 191

G	AB	R	H	HR	RBI	OBP	SLG	AVG
1192	4251	595	1041	153	530	.337	.411	.245

In 1962 New York Yankees shortstop Tom Tresh captured the Baseball Writers Association and *The Sporting News* American League Rookie of the Year awards while Tony Kubek was in the service. His performance led him to be heralded as "the next Mickey Mantle."

Thomas Michael Tresh wore No. 15, just like his father, Mike Tresh, did with the White Sox. Tom started his professional career with St. Petersburg in 1958, leading Florida State League shortstops in fielding. In 1961 he was named International League Rookie of the Year. During his rookie season Tresh played 111 games at shortstop and 43 in the outfield. He batted a career-high .286, hit 20 homers, drove in 93 runs, and scored 94 more. Selected as the shortstop on *The Sporting News* AL All-Star Team, he won Game 5 of the 1962 World Series with an eighth-inning, three-run homer. In Game 7 he robbed Willie Mays of a base hit to help preserve New York's 1–0 victory. His .321 Series average topped all Yankees.

Tresh's World Series hot streak continued the following year as he collected a two-run homer in Game 1 off Sandy Koufax. In three World Series he posted a .277 average, with four homers and 13 RBIs.

Three times Tresh switch-hit homers in the same game. The only other player to accomplish the feat between 1941 and 1966 was Mantle. On June 6, 1965, Tresh, long converted to the outfield, hit four homers in a Yankee Stadium doubleheader against the White Sox. That year he also won the AL Gold Glove Award. In 1966 he belted a career-high 27 homers and led the league in sacrifice flies.

Tresh hurt his knee in an exhibition game the following spring and underwent surgery. He batted only .219 in 1967 and .195 in 1968. Traded to Detroit on June 14, 1969 for outfielder Ron Woods, he retired at season's end. Tresh later served as assistant placement director at Central Michigan University.

Gus Triandos

Triandos, Gus **C-1B**

1953–65 B:7/30/1930, San Francisco, CA Deb:8/13/1953, NY AL BR/TR 6'3", 215

G	AB	R	H	HR	RBI	OBP	SLG	AVG
1206	3907	389	954	167	608	.324	.413	.244

Power-hitting, slow-footed Baltimore catcher Gus Triandos was having trouble catching Hoyt Wilhelm's dancing knuckleballs. Pitch after pitch bounded past the lumbering backstop. Then the Orioles' general manager designed an especially large catcher's mitt for Triandos, one so big that it prompted a 1965 rule limiting the size of catchers' mitts.

"I think catching Hoyt Wilhelm and his knucklers ruined my career," said Triandos. "The more I caught him the worse I got. I was always worried that one of the pitches would get by me and runs would score. Maybe I was too anxious about screwing up. In any case, I let it get to me. There was a great deal of uncomfortableness. I never enjoyed catching. It tears you apart. I guess I was too clumsy and slow to do anything else."

Triandos stole only one base during his 1,206-game career that began with manager Casey Stengel's New York Yankees in 1953. "I was overmatched on the Yankees," said Triandos. "The park was too tough on righthanders. And I was always so damn slow. Stengel didn't like guys like me. I would have showed him if I was there longer. Anyway, who was going to replace Yogi? He's the most durable catcher who ever lived."

Since Triandos was surplus, New York general manager George Weiss made him a key figure in the biggest trade ever, an 18-player deal between the Yankees and the newly relocated Baltimore Orioles in late 1954. In fact, it was such a large trade that only the first part of it was announced on November 18; the other announcement had to wait until December 3.

Among New York players traded to Baltimore were pitchers Harry Byrd, Jim McDonald, and Bill Miller; catcher Hal Smith; second baseman Don Leppert; third baseman Kal Segrist; shortstop Willy Miranda; outfielder Gene Woodling; and Triandos. Orioles dealt to the Yankees included pitchers Mike Blyzka, Don Larsen, and Bob Turley; catcher Darrell Johnson; first baseman Dick Kryhoski; shortstop Billy Hunter; and outfielders Jim Fridley and Ted del Guercio.

Triandos twice caught no-hitters, one with the Orioles and the second with Philadelphia. The first was pitcher Hoyt Wilhelm's win over the New York Yankees on September 20, 1958. The second was Jim Bunning's perfect game against the Mets at Shea Stadium on Father's Day, 1964. In the ninth inning Bunning called Triandos to the mound. "He calls me out and says I should tell him a joke or something, just to give him a breather," recalled Triandos. "I couldn't think of anything. I just laughed at him."

Triandos was asked after the Bunning no-hitter if it had been easier to catch than the Wilhelm game. "Are you kidding?" exclaimed Triandos. "Did you ever try to catch a knuckler?" In the middle of the 1965 season Triandos was traded to Houston. He retired after that season.

Manny Trillo

Trillo, Jesus Manuel Marcano **2B–3B**

1973–89 B:12/25/1950, Caripito, Venezuela
Deb:6/28/1973, OAK AL BR/TR 6'1", 164

G	AB	R	H	HR	RBI	OBP	SLG	AVG
1780	5950	598	1562	61	571	.318	.345	.263

Manny Trillo once said, "The best thing about baseball is that you can do something about yesterday tomorrow." During his 17-year career Trillo had many successful tomorrows, playing in four All-Star Games and helping the Phillies win the first world championship in franchise history in 1980.

Signed by the Phillies as a free agent in January 1968, Trillo was sent to Huron of the Northern League. In 1969 he was drafted by Oakland after playing at Spartanburg of the Western Carolinas League. He later played at Birmingham, Iowa, and Tucson before reaching Oakland in 1973.

After playing in only 38 games in two years for the A's, he was traded with two other players to the Cubs for future Hall of Famer Billy Williams. In Chicago Trillo became a consistent second baseman, appearing in at least 150 games from 1975 through 1978 and fielding everything to come his way. In 1977 he hit a respectable .280 and followed that up with a .261 mark in 1978.

Nevertheless, in February 1979 he was traded to the Phillies in an eight-player transaction, and the following season he won the first of three Gold Gloves. In 1980 Trillo batted .292 and established career highs in doubles, with 25, and triples, with nine. He hit .381 in the National League Championship Series and teamed with Larry Bowa to shut down the Astros on defense. Although he tapered off at the plate in the World Series, hitting only .217, his defense was first-rate as the Phils beat the Royals in six games.

Trillo had a career year afield in 1982, going 89 straight errorless games and leading the league in fielding percentage. He not only was adept at getting to balls, but his quick whip-like throw to first belied the old wives tale that second baseman don't have strong arms.

After the 1982 season he was traded to Cleveland with four other players for Von Hayes. In 1983 Trillo became the first player to start successive All-Star games for different leagues.

Traded to Montreal in August 1983, he became a free agent in November 1983 and signed with San Francisco. By then a part-timer, Trillo returned to the Cubs in 1986. He finished his career with Cincinnati in 1989.

Hal Trosky

Trosky, Harold Arthur, Sr. **1B**

1933–41, 1944, 1946 B:11/11/1912, Norway, IA
D:6/18/1979, Cedar Rapids, IA Deb:9/11/1933, CLE AL
BL/TR 6'2", 207

G	AB	R	H	HR	RBI	OBP	SLG	AVG
1347	5161	835	1561	228	1012	.371	.522	.302

Hal Trosky wanted to be a pitcher, but it didn't work out. Instead, he became a first baseman and led the American League in putouts twice and assists, fielding range, and double plays once. A lifetime .302 hitter, he drove in more than 100 runs in six straight seasons.

Born Harold Arthur Troyavesky, he started his professional career with Cedar Rapids and Dubuque of the Mississippi Valley League in 1931, did some pitching, and batted .302. He also played with Quincy of the 3–I League, Burlington of the Mississippi Valley League, and Toledo of the American Association, hitting .300 wherever he played.

Brought up to Cleveland in the waning moments of the 1933 season, he became the Indians' starting first baseman in 1934 and enjoyed one of the finest rookie campaigns in major league history. He hit three homers in a game on May 30, 1934, and finished the season with a .330 batting average, 35 home runs, and 142 RBIs. Only two rookies in American League history—Mark McGwire and Al Rosen—have hit more homers, and Ted Williams and Walt Dropo are the league's only rookies to drive in more runs in a season.

In 1936 Trosky led the league with 162 RBIs and had a 28-game hitting streak. He also belted 42 home runs and batted .343, joining a short

list of major leaguers who have hit 40 homers and registered 200 base hits in the same season. The only other American Leaguers to accomplish it are Babe Ruth, Jimmie Foxx, Lou Gehrig, Joe DiMaggio, Al Rosen, Hank Greenberg, and Jim Rice.

Four years later Trosky was one of the "Crybaby" Indians who demanded that Cleveland owner Alva Bradley remove manager Ossie Vitt. Pitcher Mel Harder was the first player to complain to Bradley, but Trosky phoned Bradley shortly thereafter and said, "I just want to tell you that I'm 100 percent in favor of the story you're now hearing. Those are my sentiments without reservation."

The 1940 season was Trosky's last productive campaign. He batted .295, hit 25 homers, and drove in 93 runs. After appearing in only 89 games he announced his retirement after the 1941 season because of migraine headaches. Trosky returned to farming in Iowa, decided he wanted to return as a player, and his contract was sold to the Chicago White Sox in November 1943. He hit 10 homers in 1944, sat out again in 1945, then returned in 1946 to slug the last two of his 228 lifetime round-trippers.

Trosky later scouted for the White Sox. His son, Hal Trosky Jr., achieved what his father never could—he became a major league pitcher, although he had a short career. Trosky Jr. made two appearances for the White Sox in 1958, going 1–0 with a 6.00 ERA. He never pitched in another big league game.

Dizzy Trout

Trout, Paul Howard **P**

1939–52, 1957 B:6/29/1915, Sandcut, IN D:2/28/1972, Harvey, IL Deb: 4/25/1939, DET AL BR/TR 6'2½", 195

W	L	PCT	G	SV	IP	BB	SO	ERA
170	161	.514	521	35	2725^{2}	1046	1256	3.23

Dizzy Trout dominated the American League for two years during World War II. About the only pitcher who had more success during that span was teammate Hal Newhouser, who won 80 games and two Most Valuable Player Awards between 1944 and 1946. Together, Newhouser and Trout were a deadly lefty-righty combination in the American League.

Trout began his baseball career in Terre Haute, Indiana, in 1935. A man with a booming voice and an irreverent manner, Paul Trout was nicknamed Dizzy by a local newspaper. "I figured that by acting a little screwy I could draw extra customers for the club, furnish copy for the newspapers, and make more money for myself," Trout explained years later.

By 1938 he had worked his way up to spring training with Detroit. He arrived on his motorcycle and circled the field a few times before dismounting and reporting to manager Mickey Cochrane. "That's very nice, Dizzy," Cochrane said. "Now you can keep on going to Toledo." After a year with the Ohio farm team Trout returned to Detroit, but it wasn't until 1943 that he distinguished himself, with a 20–12 record and five shutouts for the Tigers.

Wartime call-ups decimated major league rosters, and the Tigers leaned heavily on Trout in 1944. That year he pitched 33 complete games and 352 innings, finishing the season at 27–14. His 2.12 ERA led the league, as did his 51 pitching runs and seven shutouts. He also contributed offensively, hitting .271, with five home runs and 24 RBIs.

In 1945 Trout won only 18 games, but again he was given the load to carry in September. He pitched six games in nine days, September 8–16, to help the Tigers win the pennant. "In those days you didn't worry about sore arms or three days' rest," Trout explained. "You just kept burning them in and hoping the plate umpire had 20–20 vision."

During the World Series that year Trout pitched a five-hitter. His numbers gradually dropped off from there, possibly due to the buildup of innings, to the return of the war veterans, or to the time he bet someone he could lift a 365-pound barrel and ruined his back.

Trout once struck out Boston slugger Ted Williams with two on and two out to nail down a 2–1 win, and then he asked Williams to autograph the ball. "As Dad told it Ted just sort of glared at him, but signed it anyway and tossed it back to him," said his son, major league lefthander Steve Trout.

"The next week, as fate would have it," Trout continued, "Dad's pitching against the Red Sox again, this time in Boston. And wouldn't you know, the circumstances are almost identical. It's the late innings, Dad's winning the game 2–1, and Williams comes up again with two out and two on. Only this time, he hits a tremendous home run deep into the right field seats. As he's trotting around the bases, he looks over his shoulder at my dad and says, 'I'll sign that SOB, too, if you can find it.'"

Dizzy Trout retired from baseball in 1952, but after an impressive pitching performance in an old-timer's game in 1957 he was signed by the Orioles and played in two big league games that year. He went on to be a colorful broad-

caster in Detroit. Chicago owner Bill Veeck hired him in 1959 to serve as a public spokesman for the White Sox. Trout died of cancer in 1972.

Virgil Trucks

Trucks, Virgil Oliver **P**

1941–58 B:4/26/1917, Birmingham, AL Deb:9/27/1941, DET AL BR/TR 5'11", 198

W	L	PCT	G	SH	IP	BB	SO	ERA
177	135	.567	517	33	2682^{1}	1088	1534	3.39

For Virgil Trucks, the 1952 season was decidedly mixed. The Tigers righthander pitched two no-hitters that year, but he ended the season with a 5–19 record—by far the worst of his career.

Nicknamed "Fire" for his blazing fastball, he had a storied minor league career. In 1938, at age 19, he went 25–6 for the Andalusia club and led the Alabama–Florida League in ERA, with 1.25. He also set a strikeout record for the circuit, with 418 in only 273 innings.

Trucks was an immediate success in his rookie year, going 14–8 in 1942 and followed with a 16–10 sophomore season. He then joined the navy and did not return to the Tigers until the last weeks of the 1945 season, just in time to win the second game of the World Series from the Cubs, 4–1.

In 1946 Trucks picked up where he had left off. A consistent winner, he had only two losing seasons during his 17-year career: In 1947 when he went 10–12, and five years later when 40 percent of his wins were no-hitters. In 1952 Trucks became one of only three hurlers, along with Johnny Vander Meer and Allie Reynolds, to pitch two no-hitters in the same year. Later Sandy Koufax and Nolan Ryan would also accomplish the feat.

Trucks pitched his first no-hitter against the Senators in Detroit on May 15, 1952. He won, 1–0, on teammate Vic Wertz's two-out, ninth-inning homer off Washington moundsman Bob Porterfield. In Trucks' next start on May 21 against Philadelphia he almost had another no-hitter. He gave up only two hits after the seventh inning and won, 5–1.

His second no-hitter came on August 25 at Yankee Stadium—also a 1–0 victory. Trucks retired the last 20 hitters in order. The game was tainted by a scoring irregularity, however. Yankees shortstop Phil Rizzuto had led off the third inning with a grounder to Johnny Pesky at third base. Pesky bobbled it and recovered, throwing to first baseman Walt Dropo. But Rizzuto beat out the relay. Official scorer John Drebinger of the *New York Times* first called it an error, but he quickly reversed his decision over his fellow reporters' objections.

By the fifth inning, as the journalists persisted and as Trucks hadn't given up any clean hits, Drebinger began to question his own judgment. In the seventh he phoned Pesky. "It was my fault," Pesky told the scorer. "I booted the ball. I had it in my glove but it squirted loose just as I reached to take it out." The totals on the scoreboard changed and the crowd of 13,442 roared its approval.

Trucks retired the Yankees in order in the eighth, and then in the ninth he struck out the leadoff batter, Mickey Mantle. Joe Collins then lashed a liner to outfielder Johnny Groth, which Groth hauled in, and Hank Bauer hit a vicious ball to rookie second baseman Al Federoff. Federoff's knees buckled, but he held onto the ball and threw to Dropo for the last out.

Traded after the season, Trucks played for five other major league teams, including Detroit again in 1956, before retiring in 1958 with a 177–135 lifetime record. He later coached for the Pirates, scouted for the Atlanta Braves, and was named director of the Recreation Department in Leeds, Alabama.

Tommy Tucker

Tucker, Thomas Joseph **1B**

1887–99 B:10/28/1863, Holyoke, MA D:10/22/1935, Montague, MA Deb:4/16/1887, BAL NL BB/TR 5'11", 165

G	AB	R	H	HR	RBI	OBP	SLG	AVG
1687	6479	1084	1882	42	848	.364	.373	.290

Tommy Tucker, first baseman for Boston's National League champions of 1891 through 1893, set the batting average record for a switch hitter. As part of an excellent infield that included Billy Nash at third, Herman Long at shortstop, and Joe Quinn or Bobby Lowe at second, Tucker led league first basemen twice in fielding percentage. However, his range, never exceptional, lessened considerably toward the end of his 13-year career.

Although Tucker never batted over .279 in the minors, he became a respectable major league hitter, topping .300 four times and finishing with a .290 lifetime average. He lacked power, but early in his career he was a dangerous runner, stealing 85 bases as a rookie in 1887. With Baltimore of the American Association in 1889, he produced 196 base hits to bat an uncharacteristic .372. Both figures led the league, and that batting average remained unchallenged by an switch hitter through the close of the 20th century.

John Tudor

Tudor, John Thomas **P**

1979–90 B:2/2/1954, Schenectady, NY Deb:8/16/1979, BOS AL BL/TL 6', 185

W	L	PCT	G	SH	IP	BB	SO	ERA
117	72	.619	281	16	1797	475	988	3.12

He was the rarest of creatures: a left-hander who could win consistently at Fenway Park. But the tall, cool south-paw John Tudor had his greatest years as a St. Louis Cardinal.

Tudor earned a bachelor of science degree in criminal justice from Georgia Southern University. Drafted by the Mets in June 1975, he did not sign. Instead, the Red Sox drafted him in the secondary round of the January 1976 draft. He signed with Boston and began in the minors with Winston-Salem. On June 28, 1977, he hurled a seven-inning no-hitter for Pawtucket against Reading.

After being used as a spot starter and reliever for several years in Boston, Tudor became a steady winner in 1982, when he was 13–10, and 1983, when he went 13–12. Traded to the Pirates in December 1983 for Mike Easler, he lasted only one season before he was dealt to the Cardinals in December 1984. After a 1–7 record to start the season, Tudor put together an amazing stretch in which he won 20 of his final 21 decisions. He led the National League in shutouts in 1985 to help the Cardinals win their second pennant in four seasons.

He lost Game 1 of the Championship Series to the Dodgers but won Game 4. In the World Series (called the "I-70 Series" after the freeway that crosses Missouri between Kansas City and St. Louis), he won Games 1 and 4 against the Royals. However, Tudor lost his cool and was hammered in Game 7. Afterward he punched an electric fan in the clubhouse and cut his hand fairly badly. Nevertheless, he was the 1985 St. Louis Baseball Writers Association Man of the Year (with Willie McGee and Tom Herr), and the lefthanded pitcher on *The Sporting News* National League All-Star Team. Tudor would have won the Cy Young Award, too, except Dwight Gooden walked away with it after leading the league in wins, strikeouts, and ERA for New York.

On April 19, 1987, Mets catcher Barry Lyons ran into the Cards' dugout chasing a foul pop and landed on Tudor, breaking the pitcher's right kneecap. Tudor recovered to win Game 3 in the 1987 World Series but still needed arthroscopic knee surgery in December.

The Cards traded him to the Dodgers for Pedro Guerrero in August 1988, but Tudor was injured much of 1989. He worked on rehabilitation at Bakersfield and Vero Beach. Made a free agent in November 1989, he re-signed with St. Louis the following month. In 1990 he went 12–4 to earn *The Sporting News* Comeback Player of the Year, but Tudor retired at season's end.

Bob Turley

Turley, Robert Lee **P**

1951–63 B:9/19/1930, Troy, IL Deb:9/29/1951, STL AL BR/TR 6'2", 215

W	L	PCT	G	SH	IP	BB	SO	ERA
101	85	.543	310	24	1712^{2}	1068	1265	3.64

Pitcher Bob Turley won the Cy Young Award in 1958 when he was, quite simply, the best pitcher in baseball. A quiet, religious man, he won quite a few ballgames by stealing the opponents' signs. He told Peter Golenbock, "I simply had the ability to pick up signs from opposing pitchers. I picked up a tremendous amount of them and relayed them to Mickey Mantle....I called a tremendous amount of home runs for Mickey."

The Yankees thought they had signed Turley out of high school, but instead they had mistakenly signed his uncle, who was just two years older. The younger Turley signed with the Browns and started with Belleville of the Illinois State League in 1948. He moved to Aberdeen in 1949 and led the Northern League with 23 wins and 205 strikeouts.

After stops at San Antonio and Wichita, Turley pitched one game for the St. Louis Browns and spent 1952 and most of 1953 in the military. He starred with the Orioles in 1954, their maiden season, leading the league in strikeouts, with 185.

Turley went to the Yankees as part of a 18-player deal completed in December 1954. He won his first seven games as a Yankee but got bombed in Game 3 of the World Series against the Dodgers. He also lost Game 6 of the 1956 World Series to the Dodgers' Clem Labine, 1–0, in 10 innings.

In 1958 Turley came into his own. He led the American League in wins, won-lost percentage and walks, won the Cy Young Award, and then starred in the World Series. Although knocked out in the first inning of Game 2, he started and won Game 5, picked up a save in Game 6, pitched 6 ⅔ innings of relief to win Game 7, and was World Series Most Valuable Player.

He suffered from bone chips in 1960, was on the disabled list for a month in 1961, and was sold to the Angels on a conditional basis in October 1962. He retired after the 1963 season and said, "I'd like to be remembered as a guy who gave everything he had, a guy who was well-liked and respected by both his teammates and opponents, and a guy who didn't sully the game with controversy." Turley entered the securities business in Dunwoody, Georgia, and later relocated to Marco Island, Florida.

Ted Turner

Turner, Robert Edward

Owner (1976–*) M(1977, 0–1) B:11/19/1938, Cincinnati OH

After Hank Aaron left the Braves in 1974 the Atlanta team had little to cheer about. Even so, when local media mogul Ted Turner and his investor group plunked down around $12 million on a fifth-place Atlanta franchise in January 1976, they considered the purchase a bargain.

Another Turner-run business, Turner Communications, had recently been granted the rights to beam its local television programming via satellite to cable television service providers across the United States. The regular spectacle of the Braves performing was exactly what Turner needed to give his local station a national audience base and realize his dream of a cable television service that provided viewing to millions instead of only a few remote households.

Sports pundits wondered aloud about who got the worse deal when the Braves fell to sixth in Turner's first year, and Turner himself sparked more media interest than the players. He started his inaugural year by rankling fellow owners with his signing of Andy Messersmith. The Dodgers ace and Orioles pitcher Dave McNally had finally won free agency for players through a legal challenge to Organized Baseball's reserve clause. While other owners reeled from the stunning legal decision, Turner penned Messersmith to a multi-year deal worth more than $1 million, a huge salary increase for a player considered one of the top pitchers in the league.

In midseason Turner unveiled plans for a new television "SuperStation," WTBS TV-17, to be broadcast via satellite from Atlanta, with Braves games at the core of its programming day. The maverick owner then gave Messersmith uniform No. 17 and the nickname "Channel." When Messersmith's new moniker was sewn above his uniform number, "Channel 17" became the anchor of the Braves rotation.

National League president Charles "Chub" Feeney chastised the brash millionaire for his cheap advertising ploy, but it worked. Turner gained national exposure for his team and his television network, and attendance at Atlanta–Fulton County Stadium picked up. Players realized the implications of Messersmith's signing when the real bidding began in the fall. By establishing the market price, Turner had gotten a relatively good deal even though Messersmith finished the year at 11–11.

Turner tried to finesse baseball's free agency market again the following year by agreeing to a deal with San Francisco outfielder Gary Matthews before Matthews' existing contract with the Giants had expired. Already looked upon by Commissioner Bowie Kuhn and the other club owners as an undesirable, Turner was suspended for a year and was fined on charges of contract tampering. He fought the decision in court and remained in control of the team.

On May 11, 1977, with the Braves already in a long losing streak, Turner further complicated the controversy when he appointed himself field manager of the failing Braves. He fired manager Dave Bristol and stepped into the dugout himself, in full uniform. Turner did not claim baseball expertise. He presented his move as an attempt to get closer to his investment to see what the managerial job entailed before choosing Bristol's replacement.

The next day, National League management disallowed the move, and Bristol was reinstated. Later in the year Turner's legal appeal to his suspension was overruled, and his sentence began. After Bristol finished the 1977 season the Braves hired Yankees coach Bobby Cox as manager to help rebuild the team. Away from the game, however, Turner, "the Mouth of the South," was becoming a star.

His sporting pursuits turned back to yachting during his year away from baseball. As captain of the America's Cup yacht, *Courageous*, the dapper Turner created national interest in a sport that had been ignored for more than a century.

After he was reinstated with the Braves he continued to concentrate on his growing media empire but did not shirk the financial obligations of his baseball team. With Cox selecting players, Turner invested heavily in promising talent. The strategy did not pay off in the standings, and Cox left the team for Toronto after the 1981 season.

The talent Turner and Cox had assembled jelled the next year under new skipper Joe Torre. The Braves started 1982 with 13 straight wins for the best start in league history. Midway into the season they looked as if they had the pennant already clinched. Instead they slumped in the worst imaginable way, losing 19 of 21 games.

Baseball fans in households with cable television—now roughly one-third of all American homes—watched as the Braves plummeted, and the Giants and Dodgers gained ground. The three-way pennant race went down to the last week and then the last day, as the Braves led the Dodgers by a game. Inexperienced and cracking under the pressure, the Braves lost their final contest. When the Dodgers did the same, Atlanta was nevertheless handed the division flag.

The Braves' success that season reinforced Turner's growing influence as a national media king and proved that the boisterous southern businessman could not only sway public opinion but could also run a baseball team. Turner was becoming one of the era's earliest and most visible symbols of success.

After their 1982 triumph—and subsequent sweep at the hands of the Cardinals in the National League Championship Series—the Braves slowly sank back down in the standings. In 1985 Turner rehired Cox away from the Blue Jays as general manager, put Chuck Tanner in the dugout, and quietly set to work building his team again. Despite amassing the most promising talent available, the Braves finished last or second-to-last in every season from 1985 through 1990. Away from the game, Turner spent the decade pioneering new cable stations and formats, taking the Braves and the Cable News Network (CNN) as far as South America and involving himself in land, agriculture, and other investments.

By 1991 cable television had spread to every corner of the United States. More than half of all American homes now subscribed. Suddenly Turner's baseball plans were developing as nicely as his other business ventures. The Braves climbed back to the top of the National League, becoming the first NL team to go from worst to first in a single season.

Although he had long ago lost his status as America's most celebrated millionaire to Donald Trump, Turner was back in the spotlight again. Once the nation's most eligible bachelor, Turner wooed and married controversial movie star Jane Fonda and the pair were often seen together at games rooting for his Braves. Although the club lost the 1991 World Series to the Twins, the Atlanta organization had a strong young team featuring the best pitching staff Turner's money could buy.

In the winter of 1991, the United States became involved in the Persian Gulf War, and Turner's CNN broadcast live pictures of war into American homes. The station became America's favorite news source literally overnight.

Atlanta was back on top of the National League in 1992, but the Braves lost the World Series to the Toronto Blue Jays. The Braves continued winning throughout the decade. Atlanta won the division title in every completed season from 1991 to 1999, not even missing a beat when the franchise was switched from the NL West to NL East. The Braves won the World Series in 1995, but lost twice to the Yankees—in 1996 and 1999.

As the Braves prospered, Turner seemed to mellow, looking more settled in his box seat than did the loud and ambitious young man who once took over the team himself. During the 1993 playoffs, cameras even caught him dozing off once.

Terry Turner

Turner, Terrence Lamont **SS-3B-2B**
1901, 1904–19 B:2/28/1881, Sandy Lake, PA D:7/18/1960, Cleveland, OH Deb:8/25/1901, PIT NL BR/TR 5'8", 149

G	AB	R	H	HR	RBI	OBP	SLG	AVG
1659	5921	699	1499	8	528	.308	.318	.253

Known as "Cotton Top" because of his blonde hair, Terry Turner claimed that sliding feet first hurt his ankles—and so pioneered the use of the headfirst slide. Turner practiced his technique on the bases; he stole 256 bases over 17 seasons.

Turner was a slick fielder when he broke in with the Pirates in 1901, but he soon went down to the minors. In 1904 he returned to the majors with the Cleveland Indians and became a regular his rookie year. In 1906 he led American League shortstops in games played, assists, double plays, range, and fielding percentage; in 1907 he led in fielding percentage and double plays.

Turner gradually moved to third base. He led American League third basemen in fielding percentage in 1912 and 1914 and in double plays in 1913. In January 1919 he was waived to the Philadelphia Athletics where he was a part-timer for a year and then retired.

Lefty Tyler

Tyler, George Albert **P**
1910–21 B:12/14/1889, Derry, NH D:9/29/1953, Lowell, MA Deb:9/20/1910, BOS NL BL/TL 6', 175

W	L	PCT	G	SH	IP	BB	SO	ERA
127	116	.523	323	30	2230	829	1003	2.95

New Englander Lefty Tyler was a major part of the "Miracle" Braves in 1914, and a workhorse in Boston for seven years. More than 80 years and two franchise shifts later, he is still one of the winningest lefthanders in Braves history.

After playing college, semi-pro, and minor league

ball, Tyler debuted for Boston in 1910 at age 20. Using his "cross-fire delivery," he led the National League in complete games in 1913. In 1914, when the Braves rallied from last place on July 18 to win the pennant, Tyler posted his first winning season (with his brother Fred catching six games for the team). Lefty had one start in the shocking World Series sweep of the Philadelphia Athletics, pitching 10 innings in an eventual 12-inning win in Game 3.

Tyler had 30 career shutouts, 10 of them by a 1–0 margin. He beat the New York Giants to end their record 26-game winning streak in 1916. Two years later he pitched a 21-inning victory with only one walk and one run allowed.

Tyler was traded to the Cubs in 1918 and enjoyed his best season, going 19–8 with a league-leading eight shutouts and a 2.00 ERA. He added a victory in Chicago's World Series loss to the Boston Red Sox.

When Tyler turned up lame in 1919, Cubs' owner Bill Veeck, Sr. sent him to the Mayo Clinic to determine the problem. "Bad teeth" was the diagnosis, but removing them didn't seem to help much. His career was over at age 31. Tyler umpired in the minor leagues for several years. He later toiled in such diverse occupations as a power company employee and a shoe-cutter.

Peter Ueberroth

Ueberroth, Peter V.

Commissioner (1984–89) B:9/2/1937, Evanston, IL

Peter Ueberroth was hired as organized baseball's sixth commissioner to restore financial sanity to the game. Through clever marketing, improved licensing agreements, large television contracts, and corporate sponsorships, he made great strides in that direction. Unfortunately, he misread the ability of the players' union to get what it wanted, and the owners had to turn over all the profits they had reaped under Ueberroth's regime—and more. And when he left the job after five years in office, Ueberroth handed his successor, Bart Giamatti, one of the hottest potatoes baseball had ever handled: the Pete Rose gambling controversy.

Ueberroth made his fortune with a travel agency he started with $5,000. When he sold the enterprise it was the second largest business of its kind in North America. But he achieved fame with his performance as commissioner of the 1984 Olympic Games in Los Angeles. He used slick marketing, bent the arms of corporate sponsors, and enlisted thousands of unpaid volunteers to help the Olympics turn $215 million in profit.

Ueberroth had first caught the attention of major league owners in 1982 when he delivered a presentation to them about the drug-testing procedures for the Olympics. They were impressed enough to offer him the job of commissioner in 1983 and to ask then-Commissioner Bowie Kuhn to remain in office until Ueberroth's stint with the Olympic Games ended. Ueberroth was elected to the post in March 1984 and assumed office on October 1 of that year.

He had seen how brutally the club owners and the press had treated Kuhn, so Ueberroth did not take the job until several changes had been made in the organization. He would be the chief executive officer of Major League Baseball, all administrative departments would report directly to him, he could be rehired by a simple majority of owners' votes, and the maximum limit on fines he could issue was raised from $5,000 to $250,000. These ideas, suggested by Kuhn, were vital to Ueberroth's accepting the position.

During his first week on the job, Ueberroth had to deal with a strike by the umpires. The large settlement he offered struck some fear into the more financially conservative owners. During negotiations with the players' union, the commissioner ordered the owners to open their books to show the players the complete economic picture. After they looked at the numbers, the players' union started asking more questions, and the immense losses originally stated were reduced by half or more. The players went on strike, but Ueberroth helped settle the issue in only two days. One of the players' largest concerns was that owners would work in collusion to hold down free-agent signings, so they requested and received contract language to prevent such actions. That clause proved to be the undoing of Ueberroth's legacy of profit for owners.

Six months into his term, Ueberroth demonstrated his grasp of public relations when he reinstated Willie Mays and Mickey Mantle, both of whom Kuhn had banned from major league employment because of their positions with a gambling casino. Yankees owner George Steinbrenner, no fan of Kuhn, said, "Peter Ueberroth is the greatest thing since chocolate ice cream. I'm a Ueberroth man."

Another early Ueberroth pronouncement ended the postseason designated-hitter conflict. Introduced by the American League in 1973, the designated hitter had been used in the World Series in alternating years since 1976. In every other year in the Series, the American League teams couldn't use the valuable designated-hitter weapon, and their pitchers were forced to bat, something they did poorly. Ueberroth ruled that the designated hitter would be used every year, but only in American League parks.

During Ueberroth's second year as commissioner, a Philadelphia caterer was put on trial in Pittsburgh for drug trafficking. The parade of witnesses included many active players, and a large number openly testified to drug use. Organized baseball received a giant, cocaine-smeared black eye. Thus, early in 1986 Ueberroth suspended seven players for drug use, among them Dave Parker, Joaquin Andujar, Lonnie Smith, and Keith Hernandez. They were required to sit out a year unless they paid fines equal to one tenth of their annual salaries, performed 200 hours of community anti-drug work, and agreed to submit to random drug testing for the rest of their playing careers. In all, Ueberroth fined or suspended 21 different players for involvement with drugs. His anti-drug stance touched some owners, too. He fined the Texas Rangers $250,000 for bringing up pitcher Steve Howe before he had proven he could stay clean.

In early 1987 some clumsy words from the mouth of Dodgers scout Al Campanis during a television interview threw harsh light on baseball's lack of sensitivity when it came to hiring blacks to fill management positions. Ueberroth appointed a blue-ribbon committee to deal with the problem, but the move seemed more public posturing than effective action.

Regardless of whether Ueberroth could sell the players on drug testing or the owners on hiring blacks, he could sell corporations on supporting baseball. During his term, corporate sponsorships kicked in millions to the sport's coffers. From mounting losses when he took the job, Ueberroth substantially increased the game's income through merchandising and licensing. During the first three years of Ueberroth's tenure, baseball realized a $206 million profit.

His biggest financial coup was selling the right to air major league games to CBS for $1.08 billion for a four-year period starting in 1990. ESPN also kicked in $400 million for the same period. Baseball owners were rolling in money.

Then the Major League Baseball Players Association (MLBPA) filed a grievance, claiming that the owners had done exactly what they had promised not to—they had colluded in the signing of free agents. Ueberroth had taken the extraordinary step of having lawyers present at all owners' meetings just to make sure they said nothing that could be construed as collusion, and those running the MLBPA saw this as proof they intended to do just that.

When the owners saw each other's books, they realized that throwing vast sums at average players was a bad idea, and free agent signing slowed. That was proof enough for the arbitrator hearing the case. Three times the union filed collusion charges; three times it won its case. In total, Major League Baseball had to return $280 million to the free agents who hadn't been signed. Ueberroth's crown as financial savior of professional baseball developed a major crack. He decided not to seek a second term.

In early 1989 Ueberroth called Pete Rose on the carpet for alleged gambling activities. When Rose denied that he gambled or that he owed large sums of money to bookies, Ueberroth and future Commissioner Giamatti weren't persuaded. Before his term expired, Ueberroth hired John Dowd, a Washington, D.C., trial lawyer and onetime director of a federal task force on organized crime, to start the investigation that would ultimately result in Rose's banishment from the game. Ueberroth turned over the reigns to Giamatti on April 1, 1989.

Ueberroth later served as managing director of The Contrarian Group, a business management company headquartered in Newport Beach, California. In 1998 United States Water Polo, Inc., the national governing body for the sport, awarded Ueberroth, a star water polo player at San Jose State, its first Duke Paoa Kahanamoku Award.

Bob Uecker

Uecker, Robert George **C**

1962–67 B:1/26/1935, Milwaukee, WI Deb:4/13/1962, MIL NL BR/TR 6'1", 190

G	AB	R	H	HR	RBI	OBP	SLG	AVG
297	731	65	146	14	74	.295	.287	.200

Light-hitting, little-used journeyman catcher Bob Uecker outdid Joe Garagiola at his own game by cashing in on a less than mediocre career, becoming in his own way—or at least in his own mind—"Mr. Baseball." Uecker had been a decent sandlot pitcher in Milwaukee and attracted some attention from a Braves scout, but his baseball career did not begin until he enlisted in the Army at age 19. Stationed in Missouri, he talked himself onto the Fort Leonard Wood team by claiming to have played for Marquette University, which actually did not have a baseball team. In fact, Uecker had never been to college.

In the Army Uecker became a catcher, and the Braves scouted him again. This time they offered him a $3,000 bonus. "For the signing ceremony," noted Uecker, "the Braves' officials took us to one of the city's swankiest restaurants. My dad was so nervous he rolled down the window and the hamburgers fell off his tray."

Uecker went to the minors for $250 a month at Eau Claire in the Class C Northern League. His start was unimpressive: a .171 average with 17 RBIs. Nonetheless, he became the first homegrown Milwaukee product to play for the Braves. Of course, as Uecker blithely pointed out: "I was also the first Milwaukeean sent to the minors and the first traded."

The Braves traded Uecker to the St. Louis Cardinals when Tim McCarver was injured, and he played (occasionally) for the world champions. That year, two students at Drury College in Missouri noted that, from Opening Day until July 2, the Cardinals had not won a game in which Uecker had played. Such consistency demanded recognition, and the result was the Bob Uecker Fan Club, which eventually reached 500 members and featured the slogan: "Bob Uecker is a Great American." Uecker finished his career playing for Philadelphia and the Braves, who had moved to Atlanta.

In 1971, Milwaukee owner Bud Selig retained Uecker as a member of the Brewers' broadcasting crew, a position he still held through the 1999 season. He was named Wisconsin Sportscaster of the Year five times and was inducted into the Wisconsin Performing Artists Hall of Fame in 1993 and into the Wisconsin Broadcaster's Association Hall of Fame in 1994.

Uecker made comic appearances at an Atlanta nightclub with jazz trumpeter Al Hirt, which led to the first of numerous appearances on NBC's *Tonight Show*. His rising profile helped place him as a regular from 1976 to 1982 on ABC's *Monday Night Baseball*. His self-mocking style also gained him popularity in commercials for the Miller Beer Company, which in turn won him a starring role in the ABC sitcom *Mr. Belvedere*. Uecker also hosted two syndicated TV shows, *Bob Uecker's Wacky World of Sports* and *Bob Uecker's War of the Stars*. He authored a book, *Catcher in the Wry*, a humorous look back at Uecker's experiences as a player.

George Uhle

Uhle, George Ernest **P**

1919–34, 1936 B:9/18/1898, Cleveland, OH D:2/26/1985, Lakewood, OH Deb:4/30/1919, CLE AL BR/TR 6', 190

W	L	PCT	G	SV	IP	BB	SO	ERA
200	166	.546	513	25	3119^{2}	966	1135	3.99

George "The Bull" Uhle was not only a durable pitcher who won 200 games and twice led the American League in complete games, innings pitched, and victories, he was also a fine hitter who boasted a lifetime .289 average. In one game, on April 28, 1921, the pitcher had six RBIs.

Uhle's most lasting contribution to the game, however, may be the invention of the slider (although discovery of that pitch is usually credited to George Blaeholder of the St. Louis Browns). "It was a sailing fastball, and that's how come I named it the slider," Uhle said. "The real slider is a sailing fastball."

Uhle began his professional career with Cleveland in the year before that club's world championship season of 1920. His only World Series experience came in that season, when the 22-year-old shut out Brooklyn over two relief appearances. His best season was in 1923, when he went 26–16 (five more wins the American League's runner-up), and batted .361. In December 1928 the Indians traded Uhle to Detroit for two players. On May 13 the next year he pitched 20 innings against the White Sox, staying in the game until he was removed for a pinch runner.

In April 1933 Uhle was sold to the Giants, who released him in June, when he signed with the New York Yankees. Cut loose by the Yankees in midseason 1934, he went to the minors, pitching in his first minor league game with Toledo. He returned to the majors in 1936, with Cleveland again, going 0–1 in seven games. Uhle later coached for several major league clubs and managed Buffalo in the International League.

Frank Umont

Umont, Frank William

Umpire (1954–73) B:11/21/1917, Staten Island, NY D:6/20/1991, Fort Lauderdale, FL 5'11", 218

Not many people who knew American League umpire Frank Umont's background gave him a hard time behind the plate. Although he never played college football, Umont nonetheless played guard and tackle for the National Football League's New York Giants in 1944 and 1945.

The 220-pound Umont began his umpiring career in the Class D Western Carolina League in 1950, then worked in the Piedmont League during 1951–52 and in the American Association in 1953. He reached the American League in 1954.

Umont's most famous confrontation came in 1969, when he ejected the Orioles' fiery manager Earl Weaver for smoking in the Baltimore dugout. The next day Weaver sauntered out to home plate to deliver his lineup card to Umont. Dangling from his lip was a candy cigarette. Before Umont could make any comments, Weaver ate the candy. "He thinks he's a big league manager," Umont said. "He wants respect, but if he acts like a child, he is not going to get it." Umont worked in four All-Star Games, one AL Championship Series, and four World Series.

Del Unser

Unser, Delbert Bernard **OF–1B**

1968–82 B:12/9/1944, Decatur, IL Deb:4/10/1968, WAS AL BL/TL 6'1", 180

G	AB	R	H	HR	RBI	OBP	SLG	AVG
1799	5215	617	1344	87	481	.321	.358	.258

Del Unser was one of the best defensive outfielders in baseball from the late 1960s through the 1970s. Despite hitting only .230 and .231 in two years in the minors, the Senators promoted him to the big leagues in 1968 for his glove. True to form, he batted .230 for manager Jim Lemon and hit only one homer, but his defense was good enough to win him the American League Rookie of the Year Award from *The Sporting News*.

Knowing that as a defensive specialist his playing time might be limited, Unser worked hard to improve his offense. His batting average leapt 56 points in 1969, when he led the league with eight triples. In 1972 he went to Cleveland, and the following year to the Phillies. In Philadelphia he chalked up his best offensive numbers yet, hitting .289 and .264.

Before the 1975 season, the New York Mets traded Tug McGraw and two other players for

Unser, Mac Scarce, and John Stearns. Unser soon became a Shea Stadium favorite because of his quality defense. He also hit well that year, collecting a .294 average.

In the middle of the 1976 season, in one of the worst deals in Mets history, Unser and infielder Wayne Garrett were sent to the Expos for Jim Dwyer and Pepe Mangual. Unser hit a 12 home runs and compiled a .273 average in his first full season in Montreal, but in 1978, with his famous defensive skills starting to diminish, he played almost twice as many games at first base as in the outfield and slumped terribly at the plate, finishing with a dismal .196 average.

Sent back to Philadelphia in 1979, he found a new role as a pinch hitter, once homering in three consecutive pinch-hit at bats to tie a senior circuit record. Unser was a key man off the bench for Dallas Green's 1980 world champion Phillies. A .316 pinch hitter, his clutch performance in Game 5 of the National League Championship Series helped his team to the World Series. Unser had been 0-for-3 coming into the game but made a key pinch hit during a five-run Phillies rally in the top of the eighth that put them ahead. Unser stayed in the game as a right fielder, delivered another big hit, and scored the winning run in the top of the 10th. Unser continued to come through during the World Series. In Game 2 his eighth-inning pinch double got the Phils rolling to four runs that inning and a 6–4 victory. Unser doubled again as a pinch hitter in Game 5, scoring Mike Schmidt and tying the game 3–3. Then Unser scored the winning run. The Phils won the Series the next day.

It was Unser's last hurrah. After collecting only nine hits in 59 at bats in 1981, he began the 1982 season by going 0-for-14 and then retired. In 1999 he was a scout for Philadelphia.

Willie Upshaw

Upshaw, Willie Clay **1B–DH**

1978, 1980–88 B:4/27/1957, Blanco, TX Deb:4/9/1978, TOR AL BL/TL 6', 185

G	AB	R	H	HR	RBI	OBP	SLG	AVG
1264	4203	596	1103	123	528	.337	.419	.262

For a couple of years Willie Upshaw looked like he was going to have a terrific career. Then opposing pitchers figured out the weaknesses Upshaw couldn't overcome, and his success diminished.

A first cousin of Pro Football Hall of Famer Gene Upshaw, Willie signed with the New York Yankees in 1975 as a fifth-round draft choice. Two years later, he was taken by the Toronto Blue Jays in the expansion draft.

As a drafted player, Upshaw had to spend all of 1978 with the Blue Jays. He hit .237, then spent 1979 and most of 1980 in the minors. He hit only .171 for Toronto in 1981, so when he hit .267 with 21 homers and 75 RBIs in 1982, he was one of the game's major surprises. And when, the next year, he hit .306 with 27 homers and 104 RBIs, he looked like a star in the making.

American League pitchers soon discovered his vulnerability to inside fastballs. A mechanical hitter whose swing was anything but smooth, his bat just was not quick enough to turn on those pitches. Upshaw's batting average and RBIs fell each year for the rest of his major league career.

Toronto sold Upshaw to Cleveland in March 1988. He hit .245 with 50 RBIs for the Indians that season, his last as a player in the majors. He spent 1989 and 1990 with Fukuoka in Japan and then retired. Upshaw spent 1991 and 1992 as a minor league batting instructor for the Blue Jays and was the Rangers' batting coach in 1993. Upshaw later had success as manager of the Bridgeport Bluefish of the independent Atlantic League.

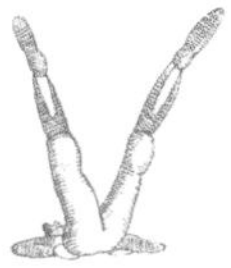

Mike Vail

Vail, Michael Lewis **OF**

1975–84 B:11/10/1951, San Francisco, CA Deb:8/18/1975, NY NL BR/TR, 6', 185

G	AB	R	H	HR	RBI	OBP	SLG	AVG
665	1604	146	447	34	219	.315	.400	.279

Mike Vail showed early promise as an outfielder with the New York Mets but never became more than a role player in the major leagues. Promoted to the Mets in August 1975, he hit in 23 straight games (from August 22 to September 15) and tied the National League rookie record set by Joe Rapp and Richie Ashburn. On the down side, Vail struck out seven times in a doubleheader on September 26.

Vail graduated from DeAnza Junior College, where former major leaguer Ed Bressoud coached him. Drafted by the Cardinals in June 1970, Vail developed into an above-average hitter under the tutelage of Joe Medwick, who was serving as a St. Louis minor league instructor.

The Cardinals didn't include Vail in their plans and traded him to the Mets in December 1974. Vail became International League Player of the Year with Tidewater in 1975. He led the league in batting with a .342 average and nine triples. In his last minor league appearance he had a 19-game hitting streak broken.

In the offseason of his rookie year with the Mets, Vail dislocated his right foot and damaged his Achilles tendon playing basketball at Old Dominion College. He didn't play again until June 15 and lost most of what little speed he had.

The Mets had counted on Vail to be part of their future, but he batted 85 points lower in 1976 than he had in his rookie season

Waived to Cleveland in March 1978, Vail spent part of the season with Portland of the Pacific Coast League. Then he was shuffled along to the Chicago Cubs and four other National League teams. Although he remained a consistent hitter, his defensive skills deteriorated over the course of his career. He retired in 1984 after 10 seasons in the major leagues.

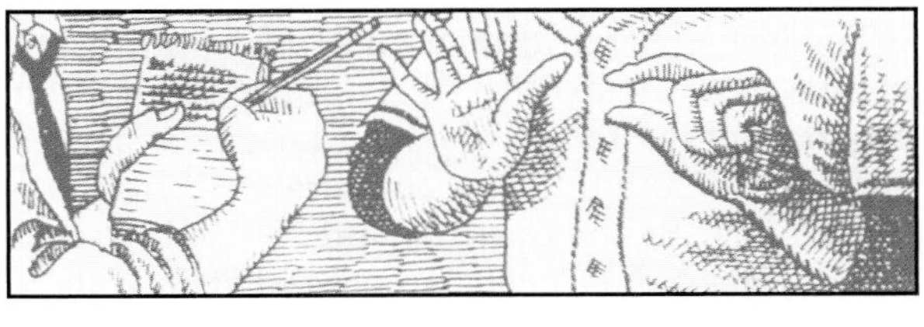

John Valentin

Valentin, John William **SS-3B**

1992–* B:2/18/1967, Mineola, NY Deb:7/27/1992, BOS AL BR/TR, 6', 185

G	AB	R	H	HR	RBI	OBP	SLG	AVG
961	3613	582	1022	118	521	.366	.463	.283

John Valentin was part of a powerful Seton Hall University lineup that included future All-Stars Mo Vaughn and Craig Biggio. Valentin and Vaughn continued to team together in Boston's minor league system, before they were reunited in the Red Sox infield. Valentin quickly established himself as the club's hardest-hitting shortstop since Rico Petrocelli. Valentin batted .316 in 1994, then put up a .298 average with 27 homers and 102 RBIs a year later.

Valentin balked when the team asked him to switch positions to accommodate rookie shortstop Nomar Garciaparra. Ultimately, Valentin moved to second base, then to third when Tim Naehring was hurt in midseason. He adjusted well at both positions, and batted .306 with a league-high 47 doubles. Garciaparra, meanwhile, was named the American League Rookie of the Year.

Valentin signed a long-term deal with Boston after the 1997 season, but he bristled when close friend and team leader Vaughn left via free agency a year later. Vaughn's absence and some nagging injuries hampered Valentin during the 1999 season, but he atoned in large measure with a stunning eruption in Game 4 of the Division Series against Cleveland. He blasted two homers and tied a record with seven RBIs.

Bobby Valentine

Valentine, Robert John **SS-OF**

1969–79 M(1985–92, 1996–*, 866–838) B:5/13/1950, Stamford, CT Deb:9/2/1969, LA NL BR/TR, 5'10", 189

G	AB	R	H	HR	RBI	OBP	SLG	AVG
639	1698	176	441	12	157	.319	.326	.260

After managing 1,704 major league games without a playoff appearance, the most since divisional play began in 1969, Bobby Valentine broke through with the Mets in 1999. His club defeated the Arizona Diamondbacks in the Division Series before succumbing to the Atlanta Braves, although five of the six games were decided by one run. It had been a tumultuous ride all season for Valentine—but nothing new for the charismatic, and sometimes controversial, manager.

Bobby Valentine had been a Connecticut high school football star who declined numerous college scholarships to pursue a baseball career.

Drafted in the first round of the June 1968 free agent draft by the Los Angeles Dodgers, Valentine quickly made a mark. In 1970 he led the Pacific Coast League with a .340 batting average, 122 runs, 211 hits, 324 total bases, 39 doubles, 16 triples, and 10 sacrifice flies. He was the league's Player of the Year.

A series of injuries would derail Valentine's promising career. First he fractured a cheekbone from a pitched ball in the PCL playoffs. Following a trade to the California Angels, he broke his right leg in two places when he ran into a wall at Anaheim Stadium in May 1973. The injury almost ended his career. In June 1974 he separated a shoulder.

Dealt to the San Diego Padres in September 1975, he spent most of 1976 at Hawaii before going to the Mets in June 1977 in a deal for Dave Kingman. Released by the New York Mets in March 1979, Valentine ended his playing career with the Mariners.

After working as a minor league instructor for the Padres and the Mets, Valentine became third-base coach for the Mets in November 1982. On May 16, 1985, Valentine replaced Doug Rader as manager of the Texas Rangers. In 1986 Valentine was named UPI American League Manager of the Year, but he never brought the Rangers a title and was fired in 1992.

In 1994 he became manager of the Mets Class AAA farm team in Norfolk. The following year he became the first American manager in Japan. Valentine piloted the Chiba Lotte Marines in the Pacific League to a 69–58–3 mark, the franchise's best record. He returned to Norfolk in 1996 and had the team at a 76–57 mark on August 26 when he replaced Dallas Green as Mets manager.

As he helped the Mets end a six-season losing drought, the spotlight increasingly turned on Valentine—and the manager always seemed to say something that would keep the focus on him. A painful five-game losing streak at the end of the 1998 season kept Valentine's team from making the postseason.

A difficult stretch in June 1999 led to the firing of two of his coaches, yet Valentine survived and rallied his team as it battled the Atlanta Braves for the Eastern Division title. A seven-game losing streak in the final two weeks seemed to doom the Mets' chances and likely result in Valentine's removal. Once again he engineered a turnaround. Although they were fortunate that Cincinnati lost several key games at the end, the Mets won their final three to force a one-game playoff, then defeated the Reds to win the Wild Card. And one more time Bobby Valentine had found a way to overcome adversity.

Ellis Valentine

Valentine, Ellis Clarence **OF**

1975–85 B:7/30/1954, Helena, AR Deb:9/3/1975, MON NL BR/TR, 6'4", 207

G	AB	R	H	HR	RBI	OBP	SLG	AVG
894	3166	380	881	123	474	.319	.458	.278

Few players showed as much promise as Ellis Valentine. He could field, hit for average, and hit with power. In the late 1970s Valentine—along with Expos teammates Andre Dawson and Warren Cromartie—were touted as the best outfield in baseball.

But announcer Tim McCarver voiced the feelings of many when he said, "One wonders about Ellis. There are those with far less talent doing much better. Is it motivation? Desire? I can't answer that."

The Expos drafted Valentine in June 1972 and he spent time in the minors with Cocoa, West Palm Beach, Quebec City, Memphis, and Denver. In 1975 he led the International League in hits, runs, and total bases and broke into the majors with a bang, hitting .364 in 12 games for Montreal.

In 1977 he hit two rare inside-the-park homers at Olympic Stadium and wowed fans with his arm. In 1978 he won a Gold Glove and led the league in assists. But then, on May 30, 1980, a Roy Thomas pitch hit him in the face. Valentine was out of the lineup for 40 days and was never the same again.

He was traded to the New York Mets in May 1981 for Jeff Reardon and another player. In November 1982 Valentine became a free agent and signed with the Angels. He ended his career with the Rangers in 1985.

Fernando Valenzuela

Valenzuela, Fernando (Anguamea) **P**

1980–91, 1993–97 11/1/1960, Navajoa, Mexico Deb:9/15/1980, LA NL, BL/TL 5'11", 195

W	L	PCT	G	SH	IP	BB	SO	ERA
173	153	.531	453	31	2930	1151	2074	3.54

Fernando Valenzuela wasn't just the first pitcher to win the Cy Young and Rookie of the Year awards; he created "Fernandomania." Built like a bull on its hind legs, the moon-faced Mexican southpaw rolled his eyes skyward as he delivered his trademark screwball.

The last of 12 children born to a farming family about 250 miles south of Arizona, Valenzuela began pitching in the Mexican League at age 17. He learned how to throw the screwball from former Dodger Bobby Castillo, and he used his new pitch to lead the Central League in strikeouts in

1978. He started the following season with Yucatan, but scout Mike Brito engineered his sale to the Dodgers on July 6. After just 30 minor league starts, Valenzuela was promoted to the Dodgers on September 10, 1980. He did not allow an earned run in 10 relief appearances.

Valenzuela became the emergency starter on Opening Day 1981 when Jerry Reuss came up lame. Valenzuela hurled a 2–0 five-hit shutout over the Houston Astros. He won his first eight starts, with an astonishing ERA of 0.50. He completed seven of those starts, and threw five shutouts in his first seven outings, including 36 straight scoreless innings. That was just part of Fernandomania. Valenzuela had an air of mystery. He spoke through an interpreter. His age was disputed. He also gave the Dodgers a long-sought hero for the local Mexican market.

Valenzuela led the National League with eight shutouts, tying the rookie record set by Ewell Russell of the 1913 Chicago White Sox. Valenzuela was the first rookie to lead the National League in strikeouts; he also topped the league in complete games and innings. After winning Rookie of the Year honors, he won the Cy Young Award by the margin of one second-place vote over Tom Seaver.

In the divisional playoffs necessitated by the strike, Valenzuela allowed just two runs in 16 innings against the Astros. He lost to Montreal's Ray Burris in Game 2 of the Championship Series, but they met in pennant-deciding Game 5. Valenzuela allowed one run in the first inning, drove in the tying run in the fifth, and then got the win when Rick Monday homered in the top of the ninth. After the Dodgers dropped the first two games of the World Series to the New York Yankees, Valenzuela survived nine hits and seven walks for a 5–4 complete-game victory in Game 3. The Dodgers won the Series in six games.

Valenzuela made 255 consecutive starts without missing a turn from Opening Day 1981 through July 1988. He also won the first $1 million salary in arbitration following the 1982 season.

Despite his shape, Valenzuela was a good all-around athlete. He collected 187 career hits, and won two Silver bats as the league's best-hitting pitcher. Winner of a Gold Glove in 1986, Valenzuela also appeared in the outfield and at first base in several extra-inning games during his career.

Valenzuela started the 1985 season by not allowing a run for 41 consecutive innings. He finished the year with a 17–10 mark and a career-low 2.45 ERA as the Dodgers won the NL West title for the third time in his five seasons. Valenzuela beat the St. Louis Cardinals in Game 1 of the NLCS. He walked a playoff-record eight batters in Game 5, but maintained a 2–2 tie through eight innings. Reliever Tom Niedenfuer allowed Ozzie Smith's game-winning home run in the ninth inning. St. Louis won the pennant in six games.

In 1986 Valenzuela led the league with 21 wins and topped the majors with 20 complete games. His 242 strikeouts were second to Houston's Mike Scott; Valenzuela also finished second to Scott in the NL Cy Young vote. In 1987 he tied for the league lead with 12 complete games, giving him 96 in seven seasons as a starter. His massive workload resulted in a stretched anterior capsule in his pitching shoulder the following season.

Valenzuela returned to the rotation in 1989. The following year he topped 200 innings for the seventh time in nine seasons. On June 29 he threw a no-hitter against the Cardinals at Dodger Stadium; Oakland's Dave Stewart no-hit Toronto the same night. It marked the first time since 1898 that two major league pitchers threw separate no-hitters on the same day.

Valenzuela was released in spring training 1991. He signed with the Angels, making 12 minor league starts, then two dismal efforts for California. He was released again.

Valenzuela returned to Mexico and pitched effectively in the summer and winter leagues in 1992, rebuilding his arm strength. He made the Baltimore Orioles out of spring training in 1993, and he found new life as a fifth starter. Featuring a cut fastball with his screwball, Valenzuela was AL pitcher of the month in July with a 3–0 record and 1.56 ERA. He finished the season with an 8-10 mark and a 4.94 ERA. He returned to Mexico in 1994, with a brief stop in Philadelphia.

The San Diego Padres gave Valenzuela a try in 1995. He went 8–3 in 29 games, and won 13 games the following year. One of his proudest moments occurred on August 16, 1996, when he pitched the first major league game ever played on Mexican soil. Valenzuela defeated the Mets, much to the delight of the fans in Monterrey. After a rough start in 1997, he was traded to the Cardinals. Valenzuela, with a 2–12 mark, was released for a final time in July.

Elmer Valo

Valo, Elmer William **OF**

1940–43, 1946–61 B:3/5/1921, Ribnik, Czechoslovakia D:7/19/1998, Palmerton, PA Deb:9/22/1940, PHI AL BL/TL, 5'11", 190

G	AB	R	H	HR	RBI	OBP	SLG	AVG
1806	5029	768	1420	58	601	.399	.391	.282

One of only a handful of Czech-born major leaguers, Elmer Valo was certainly the most famous, and no doubt the only one from Ribnik. He began his professional career with Federalsburg of the Eastern Shore League in 1939. At Wilmington in 1940 he led the Interstate League with a .364

batting average, 159 hits, 31 doubles, and 16 triples. Elmer William Valo came up to the majors with the Philadelphia Athletics at the end of that season and later moved with the franchise to Kansas City. He logged a total of 20 seasons in the big leagues, missing 1944 and 1945 due to military service.

Valo was noted for his aggressive style of play, particularly in challenging outfield fences. He also had some notable achievements as a hitter. He topped .300 five times as a regular, attaining a career-best .364 in 1955. On May 1, 1949, he hit two bases-loaded triples in a game, and on August 2, 1950, he hit for the cycle. Toward the end of his career Valo became a pinch-hitting specialist, going 90 for 386, as well as drawing 91 walks.

"If ever there was a guy who'd give you 120 percent, it was Valo," former White Sox general manager Frank "Trader" Lane said. "What a hard-working son of a gun he was and what a good ballplayer he was."

Valo left the majors after the 1961 season with a career .282 average. He later coached for Cleveland and scouted for the Phillies.

Dazzy Vance

Vance, Clarence Arthur **P**

1915–35 B:3/4/1891, Orient, IA D:2/16/1961, Homosassa Springs , FL Deb:4/16/1915, PIT NL BR/TR, 6'2", 200

W	L	PCT	G	SH	IP	BB	SO	ERA
197	140	.585	442	29	2966^{2}	840	2045	3.24

Dazzy Vance was the prototypical late bloomer. After playing for a decade in the minor leagues and failing in three trials with major league clubs, he burst on the scene in 1922 at age 31 and became the top pitcher in the National League. Clarence Arthur Vance was born in the farm community of Orient, Iowa. Inevitably, he was called "the Orient Express," but he acquired his more famous nickname, "Dazzy," while still a youngster. One of Vance's neighbors owned a rifle of which he was inordinately proud. Whenever the neighbor showed it off, he'd crow, "Ain't it a dazzy?" Vance adopted the expression and soon his schoolmates hung the nickname on him for good.

Vance turned professional in 1912 with Red Cloud of the Nebraska State League. Two seasons passed before he posted a winning record. The righthander had unusually long arms and could throw the ball with terrific speed, but lacked control. In 1914 Vance appeared to harness his talent as he went 17–4 for Hastings of the NSL during the first part of the season, then finished with a 9–8 mark for St. Joseph of the stronger Western League. He struck out 302 batters during the season.

Pittsburgh gave Vance a look at the majors in 1915, but in less than three innings he walked five, gave up three hits, and was sent back to St. Joseph. He won 17 games in 1915 but struggled with his control, walking 110 men and hitting 25 in 264 innings. Late in the season the New York Yankees called him up. Although he went 0–3 and still had trouble throwing the ball over the plate, the Yankees believed he had potential. The next spring, however, Vance developed an inflamed elbow; the glands that secreted liquid to lubricate the joint had dried up. A doctor said that the injury would take five years to heal completely.

Vance returned to the minor leagues and pitched for a number of teams, including Columbus, Toledo, Memphis, Rochester, Sacramento, and New Orleans. The Yankees brought him back for a two-game trial in 1918, but he was shelled. He pitched sparingly, trying to nurse his elbow back to health. As his condition slowly improved, Vance cautiously increased his playing time. He learned to control his pitches and developed a curve. His fastball didn't really return until 1921, five years after he hurt his arm—right on schedule.

His manager at New Orleans discovered that Vance needed an extra day of rest in order to pitch effectively. Most pitchers at the time worked every fourth day, but when Vance did so, he was clobbered. Pitching every fifth day instead, he won 21 games for the Pelicans. Nevertheless, no major league club was enticed by a 30-year-old, sore-armed pitcher who'd already flunked three major league trials. The Brooklyn Dodgers acquired Vance only because of an interest in New Orleans catcher Hank DeBerry. The Pelicans refused to sell DeBerry unless the Dodgers also took Vance, and Brooklyn reluctantly agreed.

The Brooklyn team was often called the Robins, in honor of veteran manager Wilbert Robinson. "Uncle Robbie," as he was often called, was known for his enormous patience, especially with washed-up pitchers. His knack for squeezing a few extra seasons out of aging arms had helped Brooklyn win surprise pennants in 1916 and 1920. Vance turned out to be Robinson's most successful reclamation project.

As a 31-year-old rookie, Vance went 18–12 for the 1922 Robins and led the National League in strikeouts. His five shutouts tied for the league lead. Vance won 18 games in 1923, including 10 straight during one stretch, then had his greatest season in 1924. He finished 28–6, leading the league in wins, complete games, strikeouts, and earned run average. His 2.16 ERA was nearly half a run less than that of his nearest competitor. During one stretch he won 15 consecutive games, and on August 1 Vance struck out seven straight Cubs. On September 14 Vance hurled a "perfect" third inning against Chicago, striking out the side on nine pitches.

Brooklyn finished a surprising second that season, only a game and a half behind the pennant-winning Giants. Although Rogers Hornsby hit .424 in 1924, the highest batting average of the 20th century, Vance was named the league's Most Valuable Player.

He again led the league in victories in 1925, going 22–9, but Brooklyn fell to seventh place. On July 20 Vance struck out a career-high 17 batters in a 10-inning game against St. Louis. On September 13 he tossed a no-hitter against the Phillies, 10–1.

Vance's long arms and high leg kick produced a blinding fastball and a sharp-breaking curve. Vance also pitched with intelligence. He wore a long-sleeve undershirt with a tattered right sleeve to distract the hitter. The first time he faced Braves outfielder Wally Berger he struck him out on three straight fastballs. His next time at the plate, Berger fanned on three consecutive curves. "What kind of pitching is that?" he complained. "You learn how to strike me out one way and then you ignore what you've learned to strike me out another way!" Vance smiled and remarked, "The unexpected pitch is still the best pitch anyone can throw."

On another occasion, as he started to throw to the plate, he saw Sparky Adams break from third. Rather than allow Adams to score, Vance plunked the batter in the ribs and Adams had to return to third. The run never scored.

The Robins of the 1920s were dubbed the "Daffiness Boys" due to their occasional bizarre behavior and erratic play. Vance was one of the three runners who ended up on third base when Babe Herman allegedly "tripled into a triple play." (In fact, he only doubled into a double play.) Vance was the only one of the three runners who was actually entitled to the base.

Despite his reputation as a free spirit, Vance was deadly serious when he pitched and extremely successful as a ballplayer. After his MVP year he signed a three-year contract worth $47,500 per season. In the late 1920s he was the highest-paid pitcher in the league. Although the Robins gave him little run support, Vance continued to post winning records. In 1927 his record was only 16–15, but his ERA was just 2.70, and he led the league with 25 complete games. On June 17 he struck out 15 batters in a nine-inning game for the third time in his career.

In 1928 Vance won 22 games and led the league with a 2.09 ERA and 200 strikeouts. It was his seventh consecutive season leading the league in strikeouts, and he also posted a league-high four shutouts.

After 188 major league wins, all with Brooklyn, Vance was traded to St. Louis after the 1932 season. He hung on for three more years as a relief pitcher—with the Cardinals, the Reds, and then Brooklyn again—in search of win number 200. Although he won only nine more games, he did get a chance to pitch in the World Series, throwing an inning and a third of shutout ball for the Cardinals against Detroit in Game 4 of the 1934 Series.

Vance retired in 1935 with a record of 197–140. On 33 occasions he struck out at least 10 batters in a game. After retiring, Vance managed his extensive real estate holdings in Florida. He was elected to the Hall of Fame in 1955.

Johnny Vander Meer

Vander Meer, John Samuel **P**

1937–51 B:11/2/1914, Prospect Park, NJ D:10/6/1997, Tampa, FL Deb:4/22/1937, CIN NL BB/TL, 6'1", 190

W	L	PCT	G	SH	IP	BB	SO	ERA
119	121	.496	346	29	2104²	1132	1294	3.44

Johnny Vander Meer was the archetypal wild lefthanded pitcher. From 1941 to 1943 he won more games than any other lefty in baseball, led the National League in strikeouts all three seasons, and finished first or second in most walks surrendered. But what he accomplished in two games in June 1938 earned him a place in baseball history. Vander Meer pitched a no-hitter against the Braves on June 11, then repeated the feat four days later, beating the Dodgers. "Double No Hit" and "the Dutch Master" became his nicknames.

In the June 11 game, Vander Meer's fastball was exceptionally lively, according to his catcher, Ernie Lombardi. Although it wasn't as fast as it had been on previous occasions, it was tailing, and Braves hitters couldn't do a thing with it. Only five batters hit fly ball outs. Vander Meer walked three, but Lombardi picked off two of them, so Vander Meer didn't have to throw from the stretch very often. The Reds won the game, 3–0.

The June 15 contest was the first night game ever at Ebbets Field. Nearly 40,000 fans showed up, including a large contingent from Vander Meer's New Jersey neighborhood. In the somewhat dim lighting of the evening, the Dodgers stayed loose because Vander Meer was very wild. His fastball was steaming, but he pushed the count to 3–2 against many hitters. In the seventh inning, his curve, which had been useless early on, started to find the plate at the same time that his fastball began to lose gas.

But in the ninth, with a 6–0 lead and one out, Vander Meer's control deserted him entirely. He loaded the bases on walks. A hard Ernie Koy hopper to third was turned into a forceout at home to keep the run from scoring. Leo Durocher, who recently had been acquired by Brooklyn, was called on to pinch hit.

Although he couldn't get around on a Vandy hummer, Durocher still slugged a pitch foul into the upper deck in right field to bring the count to one ball and two strikes. The next pitch nicked the outside corner of the plate for a game-ending strikeout—or so Vander Meer and Lombardi thought. But diminutive umpire Bill Stewart was having trouble seeing around the huge Lombardi. He called the pitch a ball. Durocher then swatted a sinking line drive that Harry Craft nabbed in center to end the game and preserve the no-hitter. Stewart later admitted he was grateful Durocher's ball was caught; he knew he had blown the call on the next-to-last pitch. Vander Meer made more than $10,000 in endorsements for his achievement.

Interestingly, in the game before the first no-hitter, Vander Meer had not allowed a hit for six innings when a batter hit a "bleeder" into center in the ninth. In his next start after the second no-hitter, a special guest was in the audience. Cy Young, 70 years old and the holder of the record for consecutive no-hit innings with 24, came to Cincinnati to see the game. Vander Meer allowed a hit in the fourth to end his string at 21. His two no-hitters made 1938 the only year between 1917 and 1944 that a National League pitcher logged multiple no-hitters.

Ironically, the two teams Vander Meer defeated in his no-hitters were the two teams that owned his rights before the Reds. Neither could find a use for the wild lefty with the slashing fastball. Vander Meer had been a Dodgers farmhand before being traded to the Braves system. The Braves sent him to Durham for the 1936 season, where he was 19–6, fanned 295, and was named Minor League Player of the Year by *The Sporting News*. The Reds picked him up from there, and he made his major league debut for them in 1937.

Vander Meer finished his two no-hit season with a 15–10 record, including 10 straight victories during one stretch. The following year he returned to the mound after a rain delay, slipped, and tore muscles in his shoulders. He was disabled for most of 1939 and had to return to the minors in 1940 for rehabilitation. He came back strong in 1941, winning 16 and leading the league in strikeouts. Vander Meer added 18 wins in 1942 and 15 more in 1943, leading the league in strikeouts both years. In 1943 Vander Meer also topped the league's hurlers with 162 walks and became the league's first pitcher in 22 years to steal home.

After serving in the Navy during World War II, he returned to pitch 15 innings of the longest scoreless tie in major league history, 19 innings, on September 11, 1946. Vander Meer's arm woes resurfaced, and he won only 44 more games in his career through 1951. His 17 wins for the Reds in 1948 once again paced the staff, but he also led the league in bases on balls for the second time. On April 21, 1948, he walked 12 men in a game against St. Louis.

Vander Meer accepted his wildness. "As far as I was concerned, I was out there to pitch 11 innings," he once said. "Because my nine was the equivalent of someone else's 11."

Vander Meer later managed in the minor leagues at every level, and even returned to pitch one more no-hitter, for Tulsa in the Texas League. His opposing manager that day was Harry Craft, the man whose catch off Durocher had preserved his second no-hitter.

John Vander Wal

Vander Wal, John Henry **OF–1B**

1991–* B:4/29/1966, Grand Rapids, MI Deb:9/6/1991, MON NL BL/TL, 6' 2", 190

G	AB	R	H	HR	RBI	OBP	SLG	AVG
849	1318	160	333	37	197	.341	.407	.253

More might have been expected out of a third-round draft pick, but John Vander Wal put together a good career as a pinch-hitting specialist. He broke in with the Montreal Expos, and soon became manager Felipe Alou's ace in the hole. With Moises Alou, Marquis Grissom, and Larry Walker in the outfield, there wasn't much room for Vander Wal to play on an everyday basis, so Alou utilized Vander Wal in double switches and as a late-inning weapon off the bench.

Vander Wal was sold to Colorado in 1994 and led the National League in pinch hits. In 1995 he set a major league record with 28 pinch hits, breaking the old mark of 25, set by Montreal's Jose Morales in 1976. Vander Wal also led the major leagues with four pinch-hit home runs. His late-inning heroics helped the Rockies to a postseason appearance in just their third year of existence.

Vander Wal helped the San Diego Padres to their second-ever World Series following an August 1998 trade. He went 6-for-15 with a double, a triple, a homer, and four RBIs in the 1998 postseason. Vander Wal surpassed 100 career pinch hits in 1999, joining the all-time top 10 in that category.

George Van Haltren

Van Haltren, George Edward Martin **OF–P**

1887–1903 M(1892, 1–10) B:3/30/1866, St. Louis, MO D:9/29/1945, Oakland, CA Deb:6/27/1887, CHI AL BL/TL, 5'11", 170

W	L	PCT	G	SH	IP	BB	SO	ERA
40	31	.563	93	5	689[1]	244	281	4.05

G	AB	R	H	HR	RBI	OBP	SLG	AVG
1984	8021	1639	2532	69	1014	.385	.417	.316

George "Rip" Van Haltren began his career in the late 1880s as a lefthanded pitcher. Like Babe Ruth a generation later, he evolved into a hard-hitting outfielder. Unlike Ruth, who was outstanding on the mound, George Edward Martin Van Haltren was never a star pitcher. In his best season, for Brooklyn of the Players' League in 1890, he won 15 games, but that was the last year in which he pitched more than a few games a season. Also unlike Ruth, Van Haltren was not a power hitter. In 17 seasons he never reached double figures in home runs.

Nevertheless he was a consistent .300 hitter, topping that figure 12 times and finishing with a .316 career mark. Van Haltren's 2,532 career base hits are all the more impressive considering that teams played only 130-game seasons through much of his career. He scored 1,639 runs, with 11 seasons of more than 100, and twice exceeded 100 RBIs on his way to a career total of 1,014. Curiously, he led his league in a major offensive category only twice: in 1896 he led in triples with 23, and in 1900 he tied for the stolen base lead with 45.

Van Haltren's best years were with the New York Giants from 1894 through 1903; in each of his first eight seasons with New York he hit over .300. Unfortunately for Van Haltren, the Giants of that era were also-rans; otherwise he might be better remembered today.

Andy Van Slyke

Van Slyke, Andrew James **OF–1B**

1983–95 B:12/21/1960, Utica, NY Deb:6/17/1983, STL NL BL/TR, 6'2", 192

G	AB	R	H	HR	RBI	OBP	SLG	AVG
1658	5711	835	1562	164	792	.352	.443	.274

Andy Van Slyke was one of the best defensive center fielders of the late 1980s and early 1990s. He had 245 steals in 304 attempts for a remarkable 80.6 stolen base average; he was even faster with a quip to reporters who followed him in search of a good quote. "Slick" usually gave it to them.

An All-America in baseball and state honoree in basketball at New Hartford High School in upstate New York, Van Slyke was chosen by the St. Louis Cardinals in the first round of the June 1979 draft. Van Slyke signed, but did not play pro ball in 1979 because of a hand injury sustained in his final high school game. Injuries slowed his progress in the minor leagues, but he exploded at Louisville with 41 RBIs and a .368 average in his first 54 games of 1983. He arrived in the major leagues as a result of the controversial trade that sent former batting champion Keith Hernandez to the New York Mets on June 15, 1983. The Cardinals insisted they made the trade to create a spot for Van Slyke; still, the team couldn't figure out where to play the rookie.

He played outfield, third base, and first base during his first two years in St. Louis. In 1985 Van Slyke became the regular right fielder. He showed off his arm with 13 assists and four outfield double plays. He was one of five Cardinals with 30 or more steals, and he was also second on the team with 13 home runs. He remained virtually helpless against lefthanded pitching, however. Platooned with late-season acquisition Cesar Cedeno, Van Slyke went a combined 2-for-22 in the Championship Series and World Series.

His career took a turn for the better on April 1, 1987. The Cardinals traded Van Slyke, catcher Mike LaValliere, and pitcher Mike Dunne to Pittsburgh for catcher Tony Pena. Van Slyke initially complained that he'd just gotten grass to grow at his St. Louis home, but his career blossomed with the rebuilding Pirates. Manager Jim Leyland moved him to center field, an ideal setting to display his arm and range. He was a three-time All-Star at the position.

In 1988 Van Slyke hit 25 home runs, drove in 100 runs, and led the National League with 15 triples. In June he had a streak of 11 straight games with at least one RBI, the longest in the majors since 1942 and longest in the NL since 1929. Van Slyke won his first of five straight Gold Glove Awards.

With Van Slyke, Bobby Bonilla, and Barry Bonds, the Pirates had the league's best outfield. Pittsburgh won the NL East title each season from 1990 to 1992; they lost each year in the NLCS. Van Slyke was a .190 hitter in the postseason; Bonilla (.250) and Bonds (.191) weren't much better for Pittsburgh.

Van Slyke had his best all-around season in 1992. He led the NL with 199 hits and 45 doubles, topped the majors with 65 multi-hit games, and finished second in the batting race at .324. Van Slyke also turned the first unassisted double play by a major league outfielder since 1974.

He broke his collarbone crashing into an outfield fence on June 15, 1993. In his limited playing time, he had a second straight .300 season. Van Slyke, whom the Pirates had kept while Bonilla, Bonds, and Doug Drabek became free agents during the early 1990s, became an ex-Pirate in 1995. Injuries limited Van Slyke to just 17 games as a Baltimore Oriole; a .159 average got him traded to Philadelphia. He retired after the season.

Arky Vaughan

Vaughn, Joseph Floyd **SS–3B–OF**

1932–48 B:3/9/1912, Clifty, AR D:8/30/1952, Eagleville, CA Deb:4/17/1932, PIT NL BL/TR, 5'10½", 175

G	AB	R	H	HR	RBI	OBP	SLG	AVG
1817	6622	1173	2103	96	926	.406	.453	.318

Shortstop Arky Vaughan was one of the National League's premier hitters in the 1930s. Never a flamboyant player, he left baseball at an early age and died young, virtually forgotten until his election to the Hall of Fame in 1985.

Floyd Ellis Vaughan was born in the rural village of Clifty, Arkansas, although his family moved to California just a few months later. They lived in the far northern part of the state—the farm community of Ukiah—then later near in the oil fields area surrounding Fullerton, near Los Angeles. In the late 1930s Vaughan converted to Catholicism and changed his name from Floyd Ellis Vaughan to Joseph Floyd Vaughan. Baseball nicknames expert James Skipper notes that Vaughan is the only Arkansas-born player to be nicknamed Arky, and that he received the nickname well before he reached the major leagues—at age 4.

In high school at Fullerton, Vaughan starred in several sports, and in 1930 the Yankees heard about him. Scout "Vinegar Bill" Essick scheduled a trip to observe Vaughan but detoured on the way to survey another prospect in Long Beach. At the same time, Pirates scout Art Griggs was visiting Fullerton to check out catcher Willard Hershberger. Once he got there, he forgot all about the receiver—and signed Vaughan. Oddly enough, when Essick arrived and found that Vaughan was no longer available, he made the most of his trip by signing Hershberger.

In 1931 Pittsburgh sent Vaughan to the Wichita Aviators in the Class A Western League where he hit .338 with 21 homers and 81 RBIs. He also led the circuit in runs scored with 145 while splitting his playing time between shortstop and third base. In the playoffs that year, Vaughan hit .444 against the Des Moines Demons.

The Yankees, in the meantime, were still eyeing Vaughan. Their general manager, Ed Barrow, called the Pirates and offered $40,000 for the prospect. "If he's worth $40,000 to Barrow, he must be worth as much to us. No, I'll keep Vaughan," decided Pirates owner Barney Dreyfuss.

Newly-appointed manager George "Moon" Gibson installed Vaughan at shortstop in 1932—a bold move because Vaughan had only one year of professional experience. No one second-guessed the decision, however, as Vaughan hit .318. The Pirates, who had come in fifth in 1931, battled for the 1932 pennant, eventually finishing second.

Playing in spacious Forbes Field, he paced the league in triples three times. He led all major leaguers in that category from 1932 to 1941. In that span he also placed fifth in batting average and doubles, and 11th in slugging percentage. In 1935 he led the league in batting, with .385, and in slugging, with .607. In three seasons he led the National League in walks.

Not surprisingly, Vaughan had some monster individual performances. On May 1, 1933, he and teammate Earl Grace hit grand slams in the same game. The following month Vaughan hit for the cycle. On July 19, 1939, he again hit for the cycle, one of just a handful of players to accomplish that feat twice.

In 1940 Frankie Frisch took over the Pirates. He and Vaughan did not get along, and on December 12, 1941, Vaughan was traded to Brooklyn for four players. "Many of the (Pirate) faithful shook their heads," wrote Fred Leib. "They didn't want to see Arky get away."

Because Vaughan had a large family and was in no danger of being drafted he became a prized commodity to a sport losing players to World War II, yet he announced plans to leave the Dodgers in 1943—to tend to his ranch in California. Branch Rickey coaxed him back, and, despite bad knees, Vaughan hit .305 and led the league in runs scored and stolen bases in 1943. From 1944 through 1946, Vaughan did spend his summers at his ranch. In 1947 the Dodgers coaxed him out of retirement, and he hit .325 in 64 games. He doubled and walked in three plate appearances in the 1947 World Series.

After slumping to a career-worst .244 in 1948, he was unconditionally released by the Dodgers. He retired with a .318 career average, including 12 seasons of hitting at least .300. He was one of the toughest players in the game to double up, averaging a double play every 87.5 at bats. Vaughan signed on with the Pacific Coast League's San Francisco Seals in 1949, and hit .288 in 97 games before retiring from the game.

On the morning of August 30, 1952, Vaughan, now farming in Northern California, finished his chores. He and companion Bill Wimer visited one of the nearby lakes. While the two were fishing, their rowboat overturned. Both men drowned when Vaughan attempted to save Wimer, who could not swim.

Greg Vaughn

Vaughn, Gregory Lamont **OF**

1989–* B:7/3/1965, Sacramento, CA Deb:8/10/1989, MIL AL BR/TR, 6', 193

G	AB	R	H	HR	RBI	OBP	SLG	AVG
1377	4869	824	1197	292	882	.340	.479	.246

Overshadowed by his better-known cousin, first baseman Mo Vaughn, Greg Vaughn eventually emerged as a devastating power hitter. Through his first six seasons in Milwaukee, the righthanded hitter was classified as a low-average slugger who produced just enough longball pop to offset his frequent strikeouts. In 1996 he exploded for 31 home runs and a .280 average in his first 102 games of the season. The Brewers, unwilling to re-sign the soon-to-be free agent, traded him to San Diego. Although he batted just .206 after the trade, Vaughn added 10 homers in 43 games as the Padres won the National League West title.

Vaughn re-signed over the winter but batted just .216 in 1997, battling for at bats in an overcrowded outfield that included Tony Gwynn, Rickey Henderson, and Steve Finley. After Henderson's departure, and a few adjustments to his batting stance, Vaughn roared back in 1998. He slammed a team-record 50 homers and drove in 119 runs to lead San Diego to the National League pennant. When the season ended, Vaughn again found himself too expensive for his employer; the Padres traded him to Cincinnati. As a Red, he struggled through the first half but ended the season on a tear, belting 16 of his 45 homers after September 1. After the season he landed in Tampa Bay as a free agent.

Hippo Vaughn

Vaughn, James Leslie **P**

1908–21 B:4/9/1888, Weatherford, TX D:5/29/1966, Chicago, IL Deb:6/19/1908, NY AL BB/TL, 6'4", 215

W	L	PCT	G	SH	IP	BB	SO	ERA
178	137	.565	390	41	2730	817	1416	2.49

On May 2, 1917, at Chicago's Weeghman Park, Hippo Vaughn of the Cubs and Fred Toney of the Reds settled into perhaps the greatest pitching duel of all time. For nine innings the two athletes pitched no-hit ball—the only time that has happend in major league history.

Only 2,500 fans occupied the future Wrigley Field on that cold, windy day. Toney allowed just one runner, Cy Williams, on a fifth-inning walk. Vaughn twice walked Heinie Groh, but on both occasions he was erased on a double play. Cincinnati's Greasy Neale reached on an error but was caught stealing.

In the 10th inning, with one out, Reds shortstop Larry Kopf singled off Vaughn and advanced to third when Williams dropped Hal Chase's flyball. Kopf then scored when Jim Thorpe bounced a ball back to Vaughn that went for a hit. In losing, Vaughn struck out 10 while walking two. Toney struck out three while also walking two.

Less than two months later, Vaughn defeated Pittsburgh in both ends of a doubleheader, 4–1 and 5–1. He said that he could have pitched a tripleheader if needed. On August 9 he capped his unusual year by stealing home.

In 1918 Vaughn's league-leading 22 victories, 148 strikeouts, and 1.74 ERA won him a pitching triple crown. His 290⅓ innings pitched also led the circuit. In 1919 he went 21–14 and again led the league in innings pitched and strikeouts.

During the 1918 World Series, against Boston, Vaughn pitched three complete games and recorded a 1.00 ERA. He lost the opener to Babe Ruth, 1–0, pitching a five-hitter and striking out six. In Game 3 Vaughn lost to Carl Mays, 2–1; both men pitched seven-hitters. In Game 5 Vaughn defeated Sad Sam Jones, 3–0, shutting out Boston on five hits.

Vaughn began his career with the New York Highlanders, the team that later became the Yankees. As a minor leaguer he had pitched two no-hitters, including a 17-inning gem in 1909. In 1910, his rookie season in the majors, Vaughn posted five shutouts and an ERA of only 1.83, both marks among the best freshman totals in history. Two years later, however. the Highlanders waived him to Washington. The following season he joined the Cubs, where he remained through 1921. During the course of his 13-year career, Vaughn won 178 games while losing 136, and 10 of his wins were 1–0 victories.

His nickname, "Hippo", came from either the lumbering way he ran or his immense bulk. Some sources say that the 6'4" southpaw weighed close to 300 pounds at the close of his career.

Mo Vaughn

Vaughn, Maurice Samuel **1B**

1991–* B:12/15/1967, Norwalk, CT Deb:6/27/1991, BOS AL BL/TR, 6'1", 230

G	AB	R	H	HR	RBI	OBP	SLG	AVG
1185	4352	691	1312	263	860	.393	.538	.301

In November 1995 newspaper headlines across the nation screamed out, almost in unison, "Mo Valuable Player." The news of Mo Vaughn as American League Most Valuable Player was somewhat controversial, however. Vaughn's numbers were good, some would even say great, but his statistics paled in comparison to those put up by Albert Belle of the Indians or even Edgar Martinez of the Mariners. Belle was the first player in history to hit 50 home runs and 50 doubles in the same season and Martinez hit 56 points higher than Vaughn, his on base percentage was 91 points higher, and he had almost 50 more walks.

Jose Canseco, who batted behind Vaughn in the Boston lineup, put it in perspective. "I thought it would come down here between he and Albert [Belle], but this was the right choice because it's not necessarily the bigger stats, it's who helped the team win more," said Canseco, the 1988 AL MVP. "Mo was the most valuable."

He tied Belle for the AL lead in RBIs, slugged 39 home runs, compiled a .575 slugging percentage, batted .300, and scored 98 runs. The moody Belle and the quiet Martinez—personalities probably had some effect on the voting by the baseball writers—helped their respective teams end long playoff droughts in 1995, but the Red Sox looked more like a last-place team than a division champion when the season started. Vaughn let his teammates follow his lead.

Vaughn led by example from the time he first starting playing baseball at 10 in Norwalk, Connecticut. He obliterated the competition at Trinity Pawling Prep, then did the same at Seton Hall

University. Playing on the same team as future major league stars John Valentin and Craig Biggio, Vaughn slugged a school-record 28 home runs as a freshman. He was later voted Big East Player of the Decade. The Red Sox selected him with the 23rd overall pick in 1989.

He was in the minors for just two seasons until he was called up to Boston, but he was sent back to Triple A in May 1992. After a little more than month in Pawtucket, Vaughn returned to the major leagues for good. He batted .300 or better each season from 1994 to 1998. His career-best .337 average in 1998 fell two points shy of the AL batting title.

Mo Vaughn, the cousin of major leaguer Greg Vaughn, was beloved in Boston both for his work at Fenway Park and his sincere efforts away from the field. He promised, and delivered, a home run for 11-year-old leukemia patient Jason Leader in 1993. Vaughn remained in constant contact with the boy for the last 15 months of his life. He was a pallbearer and delivered a touching eulogy at Leader's funeral. He also started the Mo Vaughn Youth Development Program, and was active in the day-to-day operations of the facility in Dorchester, Massachusetts.

Even after he missed two games in the middle of the 1995 pennant race as the result of a barroom scuffle, Vaughn, who received a black eye defending his girlfriend, received a standing ovation from the Fenway faithful when he came to the plate. "People in Boston love Mo Vaughn," former Red Sox teammate Andre Dawson said in 1995. "Whatever happens—even if he slumps a little next year—people are still going to love him."

They'll love him, that is, until he comes to Fenway wearing another uniform. After a long and bitter feud with Boston general manager Dan Duquette, Vaughn brought his leadership skills and big bat to Anaheim after the 1998 season. In his first trip to Boston, the fans at Fenway greeted Vaughn in a manner usually reserved for Yankees. Despite being hobbled since the first day of the 1999 season with a leg injury, Vaughn still managed to reach 30 home runs and 100 RBIs for the fifth time.

Bobby Veach

Veach, Robert Hayes **OF**

1912–25 B:6/29/1888, Island, KY D:8/7/1945, Detroit, MI Deb:8/6/1912, DET AL BL/TR, 5'11", 160

G	AB	R	H	HR	RBI	OBP	SLG	AVG
1821	6656	953	2063	64	1166	.370	.442	.310

A fine outfielder with an excellent arm and a career .310 average, Bobby Veach led the American League in RBIs three times in the 1910s. His explosive bat complemented the abilities of Tigers teammate Ty Cobb.

Veach played in Peoria, Kankakee, and Indianapolis before coming up to Detroit in 1912 at age 24. In 1915 Veach led the league in doubles, with 40, and RBIs, with 112. His best season came in 1919, when the lefthanded hitter led the league in hits, doubles, and triples and batted .355, with a .519 slugging average. On September 17, 1920, he made six hits and hit for the cycle in a 12-inning game.

Although Veach possessed good speed, which helped him in the outfield, he was reckless on the basepaths. For every successful steal he made, he was thrown out almost as often. Before the 1924 season the Tigers sold him to the Red Sox, who in May 1925 traded him to the Yankees. That year Veach came between manager Miller Huggins and Babe Ruth. Huggins was tired of Ruth's carousing and sent Veach up to pinch hit for the Babe on August 9, to teach the slugger a lesson.

Despite hitting .353 for the Yankees, Veach was waived to Washington later that season. Pinch-hitting on September 19, Veach broke up White Sox hurler Ted Lyons' no-hit bid with two out in the ninth inning. He played in his only World Series as a pinch hitter with Washington that fall. In 1926 Veach was back in the minors. He died in 1945 after suffering for many years from abdominal problems.

Bob Veale

Veale, Robert Andrew **P**

1962–74 B:10/28/1935, Birmingham, AL Deb:4/16/1962, PIT NL BB/TL, 6'6", 212

W	L	PCT	G	SV	IP	BB	SO	ERA
120	95	.558	397	21	1926	858	1703	3.07

Standing 6 feet 6 inches, throwing hard—and wild—Bob Veale was frightening to bat against. Seven years in a row he walked more than 90 men. To make matters worse for National League hitters, the hefty lefthander didn't see very well, a fact reinforced as he constantly removed his thick glasses to wipe off the sweat. Not surprisingly, he had a lot of strikeouts to go with the walks.

In 1964 he became only the third Pirate to lead the league in strikeouts, fanning 250. He was one of the league's best strikeouts pitchers over the next two years as well. In a 12-inning game in 1964 that took nearly three hours because of rain delays, Veale's frequent cool-down and warm-up periods didn't hurt him as he struck out 16 Phillies.

Veale won at least 16 games per season from 1964 through 1967. But as the Pirates struggled to field a pennant contender, he couldn't break the .500 mark the following three years, and was finally relegated to the bullpen. He managed six bullpen victories without a loss for the 1971 Bucs, but his ERA was a horrendous 6.99. He had one appearance for two-thirds of an inning in the 1971 World Series. Sent to the Red Sox in 1973, Veale saved 11 games that year for Boston.

Bill Veeck Jr.

Veek, William Louis, Jr.

Owner (1946–49, 1951–53, 1959–61, 1976–80)
B:2/9/1914, Chicago, IL D:1/2/1987, Chicago, IL

Bill Veeck was baseball's promotional genius and, perhaps, its only populist owner. His many memorable innovations included planting the ivy at Wrigley Field in Chicago, inventing the exploding scoreboard, letting fans manage his teams, putting a shower in the bleachers, integrating the American League by signing Larry Doby and Satchel Paige, opening a day-care center in Cleveland Stadium, and, most memorable of all, sending a midget to the plate as a pinch hitter. Veeck also brought pennants to two teams that had gone a combined 68 years without any.

During his stints as owner of the Cleveland Indians, the Chicago White Sox (twice), the St. Louis Browns, and two minor league teams, Veeck practiced his belief that any team that relied solely on true baseball fans for its patronage would "go out of business by Mother's Day." With this in mind, Veeck became the game's P.T. Barnum, a characterization he hated. He preferred to be called a hustler, and literally wrote the book on the art: *The Hustler's Handbook*.

Veeck was driven to be different, and his drive to succeed changed the face of baseball. Associates swear that his mind worked twice as fast as everyone else's, and he exploited that advantage throughout his career. Veeck never wore ties, not even to his weddings, and he was known in Chicago as "Sportshirt Bill." It was great public relations for his common-man image—and great relief for a man with chronic skin irritation and asthma.

The unconventional Veeck couldn't resist knocking the baseball establishment. "My dad would walk into a room, look for the three biggest stuffed shirts, pull out a verbal pin, and go at them," recalled Veeck's son Mike, who would himself run minor league clubs. The New York Yankees were Veeck's favorite target, particularly their humorless, portly general manager, George Weiss, architect a final Yankees dynasty. Veeck addressed him as "Old Pus Bag" and stomped on Weiss' fedora at one memorable league meeting.

But even Veeck's image as baseball's great maverick outsider was a hustle. Professing utter disdain for the baseball establishment, Veeck was in fact born into it. His father, William Louis Veeck, Sr., was a *Chicago American* columnist, man-about-town, and relentless critic of the Cubs. In 1918 Cubs owner William Wrigley challenged the older Veeck, "If you're so smart, why don't you see if you can do a better job?" Veeck accepted, becoming the Cubs' vice president and treasurer, and a year later, team president.

At age 11 Bill Veeck took his first job in baseball as a Wrigley Field vendor and office boy. "I'm the only human being ever raised at a ballpark," Veeck loved to say. Much later, several of his nine children could say the same thing, as Veeck and his second wife Mary Frances resided in an apartment at Sportsman's Park while he owned the Browns. The young Veeck left Wrigley Field to attend two of the nation's most prestigious prep schools, Andover and the Ranch School in Los Alamos, New Mexico. The tall, solidly built, sandy-haired teen obtained a diploma from neither, although he entered Kenyon College in 1932 and played football there.

Veeck left school to work for the Chicago Cubs in 1933 after his father died. During an unusual second-generation collaboration with club owner and chewing gum heir William Wrigley, Veeck ran tryouts, wrote advertisements, and kept books when he wasn't attending night school, studying business, accounting, and engineering at Northwestern University. In 1940 he was named club treasurer and assistant secretary, but he was convinced that he would rise no further.

The Cubs always held a special place in his heart, and many who knew Veeck contended that he dreamed to his final days of owning the team. He spent his final seasons with the Cubs establishment at the ballpark in the Wrigley Field bleachers, between the ivy he'd planted in 1938 and the scoreboard he'd built. He left the organization when the Cubs began selling bleacher seats in advance, a practice Veeck decried as an affront to regular fans. When Veeck left the Cubs in 1941 he cited conflicts between "baseball men" and "gum men."

At age 27, with former Cub Charlie Grimm as a partner, Veeck bought the Milwaukee Brewers of the American Association and unleashed his promotional talents. Every Brewers game became an unpredictable event as Veeck staged most of his promotions unannounced. A visit to the ballpark meant live music, surprise giveaways of everything from live lobsters and guinea pigs to nails, plus a chance to talk directly to Veeck as he mingled with spectators. "I think people look at it as quaint, Dad sitting in the stands," Mike Veeck once said. "It was just his way of doing market research."

Complaints from graveyard-shift workers who couldn't attend night games prompted Bill Veeck to stage 8:30 A.M. starts. At the first morning game Veeck himself served fans coffee and corn flakes, attracting national attention. Veeck also spruced up the ballpark, making it as clean and comfortable as possible. To help his team on the field, Veeck wasn't above doctoring the infield, moving fences between seasons—or even between innings—or staging a timely lighting-system failure.

Following a three-year stint in the Marines that cost Veeck his right leg (his medical record lists 36 lifetime operations) he sold the Brewers. The story that in 1943 Veeck schemed to buy the Phillies, intending to stock the National League team with black stars, is now highly suspect. In 1946 Veeck purchased the American League's Cleveland Indians as part of a 10-member syndicate that included celebrity and one-time Cleveland resident Bob Hope.

In the Indians he saw a team that was nearly profitable without really trying, and he had plenty of ideas to try. Longtime Veeck associate Rudie Schaffer said, "Back before Bill stirred up the pot, the biggest promotion in the major leagues was to open the gates and say we're playing at three." Aside from promotions, Veeck also took some practical steps, such as getting Indians games broadcast on radio by giving away the rights, moving the team from decaying League Park to larger Municipal/Cleveland Stadium, and hiring public relations man Bob Fishel to help promote the team.

Veeck was an instant hit in Cleveland, carousing with the city's elite until the wee hours, then heading for an all-night truck stop to swap stories and hand out tickets. When Cleveland got too quiet he flew to New York's Copacabana Club after night games to listen to jazz and play charades, catching the first morning flight home. Roland Hemond, White Sox general manager under Veeck, said, "Working five years with Bill was like working ten years with anybody else because you slept so little, but every minute was to be treasured."

The Indians' 1948 world championship, the Tribe's first since 1920, was Veeck's finest moment. That year the team drew an unprecedented 2,620,627 fans—a record that stood for three decades—and won their one-game pennant playoff against the Boston Red Sox. Pitching for Cleveland was Gene Bearden, a rookie knuckleballer acquired from the hated Yankees on the recommendation of Casey Stengel, formerly one of Veeck's managers in Milwaukee. Bearden also won his only World Series start and saved the finale of the Tribe's six-game Series win over the Boston Braves. "Lost in a lot of the showmanship was a tremendously sound baseball mind," Mike Veeck commented.

In 1949 Veeck sold the Indians, partly to offset the financial fallout from the end of his first marriage and partly because he needed a new challenge. He found it with the St. Louis Browns, a team whose 1944 wartime pennant was the only bright spot in a half-century of futility. In 1935 the Browns drew only 80,972 fans for the season, fewer than Veeck's Indians had drawn in a single game. Veeck bought the Browns in 1951, but he was never able to match his Cleveland success on the field or at the gate.

The Browns did provide the setting for what became Veeck 's most famous stunt: he sent 3-foot 7-inch, 65-pound Eddie Gaedel to bat on August 19, 1951. Veeck claimed he had not read Ring Lardner's short story, "You Could Look It Up," in which a pinch-hitting midget is induced to swing at a fat pitch and grounds out. Veeck warned Gaedel, "I've got a man up in the stands with a high-powered rifle, and if you swing at any pitch, he'll fire."

"For a minute, I felt like Babe Ruth," Gaedel said, after drawing a walk. Veeck contended that putting Gaedel in the batting order, like his other stunts, was "a practical idea, too." He planned to use Gaedel again, with the bases loaded, but American League president Will Harridge was outraged and barred midgets from Major League Baseball.

As Browns owner, Veeck tormented his Sportsman's Park tenants, the Cardinals. He painted the park brown, festooned it with Browns memorabilia and barred Cardinals officials from the owner's box. To further provoke the Cards, Veeck hired Redbirds immortal Rogers Hornsby as Browns manager and later replaced him with another Cardinals legend, Marty Marion. Veeck also took on another former Card, Dizzy Dean, as his broadcaster.

Veeck doubled the Browns' attendance to more than 500,000 in 1952, his first full season running the team. But by the time Anheuser-Busch bought the Cardinals in February 1953 Veeck was already trying to move the Browns to Los Angeles, Milwaukee, Baltimore, or Florida. Veeck expected to secure approval for the move to Baltimore at a March 1953 league meeting, and he sold Sportsman's Park to Busch for $800,000, with an additional $300,000 payment to follow if Veeck moved the Browns out of town. The league's other owners, however, refused Veeck's request, forcing him to stay in St. Louis. He finally won approval to move the franchise after the 1953 season but only on the condition that he sell the team.

Veeck retreated to his Lazy Vee ranch in New Mexico, got involved in efforts to bring Major League Baseball to Los Angeles and San Fran-

cisco, ran a minor league franchise in Miami in 1956, became a telecaster, and was rebuffed in his efforts to buy the Philadelphia Athletics, Detroit Tigers, and even the Ringling Brothers Circus. He also did public relations work in Cleveland, at one point dropping the Cleveland Indians' account when they failed to follow his advice.

Finally in March 1959, he succeeded in purchasing a majority stake in the White Sox, rescuing the American League franchise from an ugly row among Comiskey family heirs. Aided by the midseason acquisition of slugger Ted Kluszewski, the White Sox won the pennant in 1959, their first in 40 years, but lost to the Dodgers in the World Series.

The Sox also set a Chicago attendance record with 1.4 million admissions, then drew 1.6 million in 1960 (both since surpassed). Veeck put players' names on the backs of the Sox road uniforms and spruced up Comiskey Park by adding many of the unique touches that made the old place lovable. He painted the stadium exterior white and built the exploding scoreboard, a 130-foot monstrosity towering beyond center field that featured fireworks, sound effects, and 10 electronic pinwheels triggered by White Sox home runs. In response, Stengel's Yankees once lit sparklers to celebrate one of their homers.

In an effort to push his power-poor team to a 1960 repeat, Veeck engineered a series of shortsighted trades, giving up outfielder Johnny Callison, first baseman Don Mincher, and catcher Earl Battey. Veeck's failing health may have accounted for his poor judgment. In June 1961 he sold the Sox and moved to Maryland's Eastern Shore, suffering from reduced blood flow to the brain and a chronic cough.

He recovered his health, wrote the autobiography *Veeck—As in Wreck* with Ed Linn, and plotted his return to baseball. He ran the Suffolk Downs race track near Boston from 1968 to 1970, increasing attendance and attracting a broader audience through unprecedented promotions. In 1970 Veeck testified for Curt Flood in Flood's suit over Organized Baseball's standard reserve clause.

Veeck finally got back into baseball when he bought the White Sox again, in December 1975—over the objections of many owners—to prevent the team from leaving Chicago. Two weeks later the reserve clause was voided, making it difficult for the thinly capitalized Veeck to operate.

GM Roland Hemond and Veeck devised a "rent-a-player" scheme, scooping up players in their final year before free agency or signing those who couldn't get long-term contracts, such as players battling back from injuries. This strategy transformed the dull White Sox into the exciting "South Side Hit Men" of 1977. The rebuilt team, featuring outfielders Oscar Gamble and Richie Zisk, collected 90 victories, set new franchise home run and attendance records, and won Veeck another Executive of the Year Award.

Veeck's innovations with his final major league team included planting a public address microphone in the broadcast booth to catch Harry Caray's rendition of "Take Me Out to the Ballgame," beginning a tradition that Caray would later take with him to the Cubs. A less successful musical promotion, "Disco Demolition Night," resulted in a White Sox forfeit after fans stormed the field between games of a doubleheader as record albums were thrown on a bonfire. Failing health and finances forced Veeck to sell the club in 1980.

When Veeck died in 1986, Minnie Minoso attended his funeral wearing a White Sox uniform. Veeck was elected to the Hall of Fame in 1991.

Bill Veeck Sr.

Veeck, William Louis, Sr.

Executive B:1/20/1878, Booneville, IN D:10/5/1933, Chicago, IL

He presided over a successful baseball team for 15 years; yet, if not for his son, Bill Veeck, Sr., might be all but forgotten by baseball historians. He started the Veeck family in a baseball obsession that has spanned three generations.

The elder Bill Veeck began his career in journalism. He worked his way up from printer's devil to reporter at the *Louisville Courier Journal*. He moved to Chicago, where he covered baseball—under the pen-name "Bill Bailey"—for the *Inter-Ocean*, *Chronicle*, and *Evening American*. Noted for his candid style, Veeck leveled criticism at Cubs management in one column. Owner Phil Wrigley offered Veeck a front-office job with the Cubs, if he thought he could do better. Veeck accepted, becoming vice president of the team in 1918. He was named president the following year.

The team was mediocre during Veeck's first seven years at the helm, but was a perennial contender during the last eight. From 1926 to 1933, the Cubs won two pennants and finished in the first division each year.

Though not characterized by flamboyance, Veeck's reign was not without controversy, unconventional ideas, or historical note. He clashed with manager Rogers Hornsby, who accused him of being a "backseat driver." With the Depression crippling attendance, Veeck proposed the outrageous idea of interleague play. He gave his son, Bill, Jr., his first job in baseball: hot dog vendor. (Grandson Mike Veeck later brought the family touch to several major and minor league teams.)

Veeck, Sr. died suddenly of leukemia after the 1933 season. During the final World Series game that year, flags at Griffith Stadium flew at half-mast in his memory.

"His passing is not only a great personal shock to me, but an irreparable loss to the National League and baseball," NL president John Heydler said. "He has been a powerful leader in our councils for years and one on whom we could depend in any action for the benefit of baseball. His background, his personality, and his far-sightedness equipped him particularly for excellent leadership."

Robin Ventura

Ventura, Robin Mark **3B**

1989–* B:7/14/1967, Santa Maria, CA Deb:9/12/1989, CHI AL BL/TR, 6'1", 198

G	AB	R	H	HR	RBI	OBP	SLG	AVG
1415	5130	746	1421	203	861	.370	.450	.277

When the Chicago White Sox signed Robin Ventura in 1988, they had to go all the way back to Eddie Collins to find a player with such impressive college credentials. After three years at Oklahoma State University, Ventura was voted College Player of the Decade by *Baseball America* and was also the publication's third baseman on the All-Time College All-Star Team. Ventura had a 58-game hitting streak as a sophomore and set the OSU record for hits despite being drafted in the first round after his junior year.

The lefthanded hitting Ventura continued to garner accolades when he spent the summer of 1988 playing for the U.S. Olympic baseball team, batting .409 to help lead the Americans to the gold medal in Seoul. After one year at Double A Birmingham, he was playing with the White Sox. He won the starting job at third base in 1990, leading all American League rookies with 150 games played. Ventura spent most of the season in the second spot in the batting order. He batted .249, suffering through a horrible 0-for-41 stretch that saw him go without a hit for 16 games.

Ventura raised his average more than 30 points the following year, and topped 20 home runs and 100 RBIs. He was AL Player of the Month in July with a .357 average, 12 home runs (two of them ending games), and 33 RBIs. He also won the first of five Gold Gloves for the White Sox; he later added a sixth with the New York Mets.

Ventura had two hits in the 1992 All-Star Game in San Diego on his 25th birthday. The following year, however, he charged the mound after being struck by a pitch from 46-year-old Nolan Ryan. The normally affable Ventura was suspended for two games and criticized throughout the league for the incident. He finished the season as the first AL third baseman in 15 years to exceed 90 RBIs for three consecutive years.

On September 4, 1995, he became just the eighth player in history to hit two grand slams in one game and the first to do it since Frank Robinson in 1970. On May 20, 1999, after signing as a free agent with the Mets, Ventura became the first player in history to hit grand slams in both ends of a doubleheader.

Ventura had a stellar 1999 season in New York, emerging as a team leader and quickly becoming one of the best third basemen in Mets history. He smacked 32 homers, knocked in 120 runs, and his slick defense galvanized an already stellar infield. His most memorable moment of 1999, however, was his "grand slam" in the 15th inning that won Game 5 of the NLCS against the Braves. With the winning run having crossed the plate, Ventura was mobbed by his teammates at second base, with the result that his homer was officially scored a single; New York tabloids dubbed it "the grand slam single."

Mickey Vernon

Vernon, James Barton **1B**

1939–43, 1946–60 M(1961–63, 135–227) B:4/22/1918, Marcus Hook, PA Deb:7/8/1939, WAS AL BL/TL, 6'2", 180

G	AB	R	H	HR	RBI	OBP	SLG	AVG
2409	8731	1196	2495	172	1311	.359	.428	.286

James Barton "Mickey" Vernon was one of President Dwight D. Eisenhower's favorite ballplayers, which pretty well sums up Vernon's playing style: never flashy, always dependable. Vernon quietly set a number of fielding records while playing more games at first base than any other player in the 20th century.

Vernon accomplished the rare feat of playing in each of four decades, made possible by his eight at bats in 1960 while a player-coach for the Pirates. He holds the major league record for lifetime double plays by a first baseman and leads all American League first basemen in career putouts, assists, and chances. In one 23-inning game in 1943 he participated in a record 10 double plays.

As a batter Vernon had his ups and downs. Writer Bill James called him "the most inconsistent player ever to play the game." After three unspectacular years with the Senators from 1941 through 1943 he went into the navy, where he worked on his batting eye on the Norfolk base team.

When he returned to the majors in 1946 he won the batting title by spraying the ball more and worrying less about homers, and he also led the league in doubles. Vernon won his second batting crown in 1953, when he was 35, yet in the half-decade between those titles he never hit .300. The year after his .353 title in 1946 his average fell 88 points, and the following year it dropped 23 more.

In 1949 Washington traded Vernon and Early Wynn to Cleveland for three players. Vernon responded favorably to the shorter fences at Municipal Stadium with a .291 average and 18 homers. He also led the league in both putouts and assists for the first time. But the Indians gave up on him after he started the 1950 season with a meager .189 average in 90 at bats and returned him to the Senators for pitcher Dick Weik. In his final 90 games of the season Vernon batted .306.

He batted .293 with 87 RBIs for Washington in 1951, then slumped by 42 points in 1952. In 1953 he came roaring back. Both Vernon and Cleveland's Al Rosen were having banner years: Rosen led the league in homers and RBIs, Vernon paced the circuit in doubles, and their averages were only fractions apart (Vernon .336, Rosen .333) as the final day of the season began. Rosen went 3-for-5 that day, ending his season at .336. Vernon went 2-for-4 to take the title at .337.

When his teammates realized that Vernon might have to bat again in the ninth they took steps to ensure that he would win the title. Mickey Grasso doubled with two out in the eighth but wandered far enough from second to make sure he got picked off. In the ninth, Kite Thomas led off with a single and tried unsuccessfully to stretch it into a double; his effort was described as "leisurely." The next batter, Eddie Yost—known for his incredible batting eye—swinging on a third strike over his head. Pete Runnels struck out, too, on an "excuse me" half-swing. The eminently likable Vernon didn't have to bat and captured his somewhat tainted title.

The following year Vernon's average fell by 47 points. He edged over the .300 mark in 1955 and hit .310 for the Red Sox in 1956, returned to Cleveland for the 1958 season, and was traded to Milwaukee for Humberto Robinson. Released after the 1959 season, he worked for the Pirates as a hitting coach in 1960, reuniting him with his pal Danny Murtaugh, Pittsburgh's manager. They had played American Legion ball together in the 1930s.

Vernon remained in baseball for 18 more years as a coach and manager. He coached the Pirates in 1960 and 1964, the Cardinals in 1965, Montreal in 1977 and 1978, and the Yankees in 1982. He managed the expansion Senators to last-place finishes in 1961, 1962, and 1963. He was a minor league batting instructor for the Royals and Dodgers as well as a Yankees scout. Vernon managed in the minors at Vancouver, Richmond, and Manchester, New Hampshire. In 1969, at the celebration of professional baseball's centennial, he was voted the all-time first baseman of the Washington Senators.

Zoilo Versalles

Versalles, Zoilo Casanova (Rodriguez) SS-3B
1959–69, 1971 B:12/18/1939, Veldado, Cuba
D:6/9/1995, Bloomington, MN Deb:8/1/1959, WAS AL
BR/TR, 5'10", 150

G	AB	R	H	HR	RBI	OBP	SLG	AVG
1400	5141	650	1246	95	471	.292	.367	.242

Zoilo Versalles was considered "moody" early in his career. But he steadily improved his game to become a strong defensive player and one of the premier offensive shortstops of his era. His career peaked with a spectacular year in 1965 as he led his team to the World Series and won the American League Most Valuable Player Award.

After appearing in brief major league stints in 1959 and 1960, Versalles, nicknamed "Zorro," was installed at shortstop for the relocated Twins in their inaugural season in Minnesota. Versalles demonstrated immediately that he could hit.

He put together a .280 average, with 25 doubles and five triples. After a slump in 1962 he was named to the All-Star team in 1963, finishing the season with 31 doubles, a league-leading 13 triples, and 10 homers. He also won a Gold Glove, breaking Luis Aparicio's five-year lock on the award. The next year he provided even more power, racking up 33 doubles, a league-tying 10 triples, and 20 home runs.

Versalles' 1965 season ranked among the greatest offensive seasons that any shortstop had put together to that point. Versalles led the league in total bases, at bats, doubles, triples, and runs scored. He also slugged 19 homers. Versalles won his second Gold Glove that year and was named MVP by more than 100 points over teammate Tony Oliva. In the World Series, Versalles' team took the Los Angeles Dodgers, led by Hall of Fame pitchers Sandy Koufax and Don Drysdale, to seven games before losing.

Back problems began to bother Versalles in 1966. He never again hit more than 20 doubles, seven triples, or seven home runs in a season. After tours with the Dodgers, Cleveland, and Washington, Versalles spent a year in the Mexican League before closing out his career with Atlanta in 1971.

Fay Vincent

Vincent, Francis T., Jr.
Commissioner (1989–92) B:5/29/1938, Waterbury, CT

Fay Vincent was one of the members of the old boy network that came to baseball with his friend Bart Giamatti. Vincent became commissioner after Giamatti's death and held the office until he resigned in 1992, forced out by club owners.

The son of a former Yale college baseball captain who played in a semipro game the day Vincent was born, Fay grew up as a fan—and a lousy player. Upon becoming commissioner, Vincent joked, "The most surprised guy in the United States is the guy who coached me in American Legion. He's thinking, 'The kid couldn't hit, field or throw, and look where he is now.'"

Vincent attended Williams College, where he received a rough initiation. Locked in his room as the result of a prank, he attempted to escape across an icy ledge, fell, and broke his back. During his recovery—bedridden and immobilized in a body cast—baseball games on the radio were one of his greatest pleasures. Later in life he could not stay on his feet for long periods, walking only with the aid of a cane and enjoying a commissioner's perquisite of riding onto baseball fields in a golf cart.

After college Vincent attended Yale Law School. He became a specialist in corporate finance law, working for the Securities and Exchange Commission. A chubby, balding, family man with thick glasses, Vincent came to mind when Williams College alumnus Henry Allen needed an outsider to clean up Columbia Pictures in the wake of an embezzlement scandal. Hardly the Hollywood type, Vincent nonetheless succeeded at Columbia, and when Coca-Cola acquired the studio, he became head of the parent company's entertainment division. Vincent subsequently engineered Coca-Cola acquisitions, making the corporation the world's largest supplier of television programs.

Coca-Cola moved Vincent into international sales, but he was ready for a change when his best friend, Giamatti, called in 1989. Giamatti wanted a strong businessman by his side, inventing the deputy commissioner post for Vincent. "We expected this to be less intense than our previous jobs," Vincent recalled. "It wasn't."

Vincent's first baseball assignment involved a scandal. He was Giamatti's point man in the negotiations that resulted in Pete Rose's banishment from the game. With that controversial matter settled, Vincent and his boss flew together to their summer homes for Labor Day weekend to relax. When Giamatti suffered a fatal heart attack on September 1, the club owners quickly approved Vincent to complete Giamatti's five-year term.

Six weeks after burying his friend, a new tragedy confronted Vincent. Minutes before the start of World Series Game 3 at Candlestick Park, a powerful earthquake rocked the San Francisco Bay Area. More than 60 people died and property damage ran into the billions. Vincent helped keep what he called "our modest little sporting event" in context as the Bay Area dug out from the disaster. Resisting calls to postpone the Series, Vincent agreed twice to delay its resumption. His calm presence in the aftermath of the quake earned high grades and helped win him his spurs as the Commissioner.

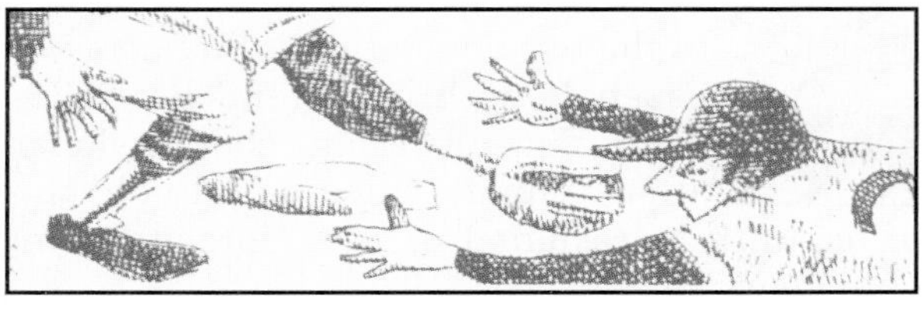

Vincent took to heart the clause that empowered him to act "in the best interests of baseball." But some critics said he failed to realize that his bosses—the owners—no longer believed there were significant baseball interests beyond the ones affecting their own teams. Vincent took his responsibilities to the game seriously. The owners and the players' union also took their economic interests seriously and resented what they perceived to be Vincent's interference.

When owners locked out players during spring training in 1990 after the expiration of their Basic Agreement, Vincent held a press conference, proposing an end to the lockout in exchange for a no-strike pledge from players for the 1990 season. The position made sense to fans, who wanted to see the games played, but it was not acceptable to players or club owners.

In August 1990 Vincent permanently banned New York Yankees owner George Steinbrenner, another Williams College alumnus, after finding that Steinbrenner had paid admitted-gambler Howie Spira $40,000 for unsavory information about Yankees outfielder Dave Winfield, who was engaged in a contractual conflict with the club owner. Steinbrenner, like Rose, denied any wrongdoing. Unlike the Rose banning, however, this settlement came with virtual assurance that Steinbrenner would be reinstated after two years. He was also allowed to retain his Yankees ownership and to appoint his son-in-law to run the team.

Vincent helped big league owners cut subsidies to the minor leagues and assert greater control over them. Vincent also provided the fig leaf for owners' failed efforts to revise the draft to allow teams to retain rights to high school players for five years. Vincent said baseball should not compete against colleges, but the real intent of the rule was to prevent million-dollar bonuses to high schoolers. Vincent also supported the owners on expansion, fending off criticism during the tortuous five-year process that finally resulted in a decision in 1991. When the league fought over splitting the financial windfall from the deal, Vincent issued a compromise decision pleasing neither side.

Though he generally spoke with a lawyer's caution, he could be surprisingly frank. After CBS and ESPN cited major losses on their baseball deals, Vincent asked, "Where would ESPN be without baseball? There are only so many tractor pulls and billiard matches you can televise."

In early 1992 Vincent publicly opposed a bid by the Japanese owners of Nintendo to purchase the Seattle Mariners. Nintendo's lead man in the project, Minoru Arakawa, was a Seattle resident, which would have been a first for a Mariners owner. But Vincent cited a policy against investment from outside North America, a policy that deputy commissioner Stephen Greenberg was forced to admit did not exist. With Seattle's Congressional delegation threatening action if the franchise moved to St. Petersburg, Florida, Vincent eventually supported the Nintendo bid.

Vincent's end began in a swirl of controversy during June 1992. The owners demonstrated their commitment to cut Vincent out of labor negotiations by hiring Richard Ravitch to head the Player Relations Committee—at a higher salary than the commissioner was paid. Vincent agreed to his exclusion from labor negotiations and then told newspapers he had withstood a palace coup and remained in total control of the game.

Another controversy loomed after Vincent learned that Yankees manager Buck Showalter and general manager Gene Michael had voiced mild support for pitcher Steve Howe, who had requested a grievance hearing to protest his permanent suspension from baseball after another drug offense. Vincent summoned both Showalter and Michael to his office for a scolding at 11 A.M., only two hours before the team's game that afternoon. Then in July, Vincent ordered a realignment for 1993, moving the Cubs and Cardinals from the NL East to the NL West. The Cubs opposed it. They sued in a Chicago court and overturned the order.

The owners invited Vincent to an emergency meeting on September 3, 1992, to debate the role of the commissioner. After he refused to attend, 18 clubs voted to ask for his resignation. Vincent vowed to stay on, but on September 7, he took the owners' suggestion and stepped down. The New York Mets, Vincent supporters to the bitter end, let the former commissioner throw out the first ball on Opening Day 1993. After refusing an offer to become the Mets top business executive, Vincent later joined the team's board of directors.

Critics contended that Vincent's departure removed the final pretense that baseball was anything more than another business, and that his behavior probably ended any possibility of Organized Baseball ever again appointing a commissioner with real power. Milwaukee Brewers owner Bud Selig replaced Vincent on an interim basis; seven seasons later Selig was officially named to the post.

Frank Viola

Viola, Frank John **P**

1982–96 B:4/19/1960, Hempstead, NY Deb:6/6/1982, MIN AL BL/TL, 6'4", 209

W	L	PCT	G	SH	IP	BB	SO	ERA
176	150	.540	421	16	2836^{1}	864	1844	3.73

Frank Viola was a Cy Young winner, a World Series Most Valuable Player, the starting pitcher in the 1988 All-Star Game, and one of the game's premier southpaws with the Minnesota Twins. He went from a shell-shocked rookie at the brand-new Hubert H. Humphrey Metrodome in 1982 to the toast of the Twin Cities five years later. He won two of his three starts against the Cardinals in the 1987 World Series, including Game 7. Viola won the Cy Young Award the following year with a 24–7 record and 2.64 ERA.

He was not indispensable, though. When Viola slumped to an 8–12 record in his first 24 starts of 1989, he was sent to the Mets on the July 31 trading deadline for five pitchers: Rick Aguilera, David West, Kevin Tapani, Tim Drummond, and Jack Savage.

Despite the five-for-one discrepancy in numbers, it initially looked like the Mets had gotten the better of the deal. Viola, a native of East Meadow, New York, and a phenom at St. John's University, seemed to fit in well at Shea Stadium. He shut out the Dodgers and Orel Hershiser on August 28, the first regular-season matchup of defending Cy Young Award winners.

He started the 1990 season with a 4–0 record and an ERA of 1.32; the season ended with his 20th victory. Viola led the National League with 249⅔ innings pitched, tied for the league lead with 35 starts, and finished fourth with a 2.67 ERA. He placed third in the NL Cy Young voting behind Doug Drabek and Ramon Martinez.

An infected fingernail and a tumor on his pitching hand threw Viola off balance in 1991. He appeared in the All-Star Game for the third time, but he ended the season in a 1–10 slump. To make matters worse, the pitchers the Mets had sent to the Twins for Viola helped Minnesota to a world championship. Viola's short stay in New York ended in December when he signed with the Red Sox as a free agent.

Viola surpassed 34 starts and 200 innings with Boston in 1992 for the 10th straight year. He also came within a ninth-inning single of a no-hitter in Toronto. The 1993 season started well, but he missed a start for the first time in May and underwent elbow surgery in September.

His only win of 1994 came in a rematch of an NCAA Tournament duel of 13 years earlier, against Yale alum and former Mets teammate Ron

Darling. Once again Viola came out on the winning end of a 1–0 score. Shortly thereafter he tore the muscles and tendons in his pitching arm against Seattle and underwent "Tommy John" (tendon transplant) surgery. He retired in 1996 following failed comeback attempts in Cincinnati and Toronto.

Bill Virdon

Virdon, William Charles **OF**

1955–68 M(1972–84, 995–921) B:6/9/1931, Hazel Park, MI Deb:4/12/1955, STL NL BL/TR, 6', 175

G	AB	R	H	HR	RBI	OBP	SLG	AVG
1583	5980	735	1596	91	502	.318	.379	.267

As an outfielder for the Pittsburgh Pirates, Bill Virdon was a defensive marvel. He knew where to position himself and was speedy enough to intercept the flight of sure hits. Signed to a Yankee contract in 1950, he spent four years in the New York farm system, unable to earn a spot in an outfield stocked with players the caliber of Mickey Mantle and Hank Bauer. A throw-in as part of the trade to St. Louis that made Enos Slaughter a Yankee, Virdon batted .333 in 1954 to lead the International League and added 22 home runs and 98 RBIs. When the Cardinals brought him up in 1955 his .281 average and 17 homers earned him National League Rookie of the Year honors.

Virdon was traded to the Pirates in May 1956. It was one of Pittsburgh general manager Joe L. Brown's first deals, and one of his best. Virdon rapped out a .334 average for the Pirates that year, hitting .319 overall for the season. Although he would never hit that well again, he proved a steady leadoff batter and superb center fielder for the next nine years.

At the plate he teamed up with Dick Groat to form a slick hit-and-run combo, and in the outfield he and superstar right fielder Roberto Clemente formed a bastion of defense. Virdon led the National League in outfield double plays in 1959 and won a Gold Glove in 1962.

When the Pirates met the supposedly invincible Yankees in the 1960 World Series, Virdon almost single-handedly won two games with his glove. In the fourth inning of Game 1, with Pittsburgh fighting to maintain a 3–1 lead with two on and nobody out, Virdon made an acrobatic catch at the wall, snagging a booming Yogi Berra flyball. The Pirates held on to win. In Game 4 the Pirates were leading 3–2 in the seventh at Yankee Stadium when Bob Cerv slugged a ball to the right-center wall with two men on and one out. Virdon timed his leap perfectly to make the catch; the Pirates held on to win and even the Series.

The quiet, bespectacled Virdon had always been a serious student of the game, so it was no surprise when he was hired to manage Williamsport of the Eastern League after his playing career ended (for the first time) in 1965. He managed Jacksonville of the International League in 1967 before returning to the Pirates as a player-coach under manager Larry Shepard. When neither Shepard nor his successor Alex Grammas proved to be what the Pirates needed, Danny Murtaugh returned to the helm and made Virdon his right-hand man, and the Pirates won the pennant and the Series.

Virdon took over as manager, and many thought that his 1972 Pirates were even stronger than the world champions of the previous year. They won the NL East by 11 games, but Virdon's ace reliever, Dave Giusti, couldn't hold a 3–2 lead in the ninth inning of the fifth and final game of the Championship Series, and the Bucs lost to the Cincinnati Reds on a wild pitch by Bob Moose.

After Clemente was killed on New Year's Eve, the Pirates never regrouped in 1973. Virdon tried shuffling the lineup and platooning players, which only irritated the already frustrated Bucs, and major blowups with Richie Hebner and Dock Ellis made front-page headlines in Pittsburgh. Virdon was fired with 26 games remaining in the season; Murtaugh replaced Virdon.

New owner George Steinbrenner hired Virdon to manage the Yankees in 1974, and Virdon took them to second place after three straight fourth-place finishes. In 1975 the Yanks were in third place when Texas fired manager Billy Martin. Steinbrenner and Martin met, and Virdon was sent packing. Virdon never won a game in Yankee Stadium. During his tenure the Yanks played in Shea Stadium while the old park was being renovated.

Houston hired Virdon immediately, and he helped build a strong team in his seven-plus seasons with the club. Unlike the established Pirates, the Astros were more amenable to Virdon's managerial moves. Using all 25 of his players, he led them to third-place finishes in 1976 and 1977. They finished second in 1979 and in 1980 won the first division title in franchise history.

Once again Virdon's team couldn't hold a lead in the final game of the NLCS. Ahead 5–2 in the eighth, Virdon removed Nolan Ryan, and two relievers later the Phillies had scored five times. Houston's two-run comeback in the last of the eighth came to naught when the Phils scored in the 11th to win, 8–7.

Virdon's Astros won the second half NL West title in the unique format of the 1981 strike year, but lost again in the first round of the expanded playoffs. The Dodgers took three straight games after Houston had won the first two. With the

Astros mired in fifth place in 1982, Virdon was fired with 51 games to go in the season.

He brought Montreal to a third-place finish in his next managerial assignment in 1983, but the Expos were a fifth-place team when he was dismissed late in August 1984. Virdon returned to Pittsburgh as a hitting instructor and bench coach under Jim Leyland. He rejoined the Astros in 1997 as a coach under manager Larry Dierker.

Ossie Vitt

Vitt, Oscar Joseph **2B–3B**

1912–21 M(1938–40, 262–198) B:1/4/1890, San Francisco, CA D:1/31/1963, Oakland, CA Deb:4/11/1912, DET AL BR/TR ,5'10", 150

G	AB	R	H	HR	RBI	OBP	SLG	AVG
1065	3760	560	894	4	295	.322	.295	.238

Ossie Vitt was a weak-hitting, slick-fielding third baseman who had a 10-year career with the Tigers and Red Sox from 1912 through 1921, playing alongside Hall of Famers Ty Cobb and Sam Crawford. It was as a manager that Vitt received notoriety—and an ignominious ending.

He had achieved some fame as a minor league skipper when he got a chance to pilot the 1937 Newark Bears, a team many people said was second only to their parent Yankees in all of baseball. With players such as Charlie Keller, George McQuinn, Babe Dahlgren, Willard Hershberger, and Joe Gordon, the Bears won the pennant by 25½ games and earned Vitt a major league managing job with Cleveland.

The Indians finished a respectable third for him in 1938 and 1939, but they were no real challenge to the Yankees juggernaut. In 1940, however, the Yankees stumbled badly after four straight World Series triumphs, and the Indians were in the pennant race until the last weekend of a tumultuous season. Vitt's abrasive style was too much for the players, who launched an unsuccessful coup in midseason that turned them into the laughingstock of the game.

The year began promisingly, with Bob Feller throwing an Opening Day no-hitter against the White Sox, but before long the players were grumbling about Vitt. After Mel Harder hung on for a close win in relief, Vitt greeted him with: "It's about time you win one with all the money you're making."

Behind the players' backs he was even worse. As Ted Williams and the Red Sox were beating up on Feller one day, Vitt stomped up and down the dugout, screaming, "Look at him! He's supposed to be my ace! How can I win a pennant with that kind of pitching?" He was talking about the man who would lead the American League in wins, complete games, innings, and strikeouts.

On June 13 first baseman Hal Trosky led a group of 10 players to a meeting with owner Alva Bradley. They claimed the Indians could not win the pennant with Vitt in charge. While Bradley promised to look into their complaints, he felt that giving them power over the manager was a bad idea, and said so. He also cautioned against letting word of the meeting become public. Unfortunately, someone didn't listen to him. The next day Gordon Cobbledick ran a front-page story in the *Cleveland Plain Dealer,* accusing the players of being "Crybabies." The nickname stuck. All around the league, especially in Detroit—the team they were battling for the pennant—the Indians were subjected to an unheard-of level of fan abuse. They were routinely pelted with verbal abuse, baby bottles, lollipops, and diapers.

Efforts by the team to put up a unified front behind Vitt, such as signing a published letter agreeing to support him, didn't do much good. At one point, after Vitt had called for a pitching change, Trosky charged the mound and persuaded him to leave the first hurler in.

Vitt's demeanor softened somewhat, but he didn't have the skills to bring his team back together. On the final weekend, with three games to play against the Tigers, the Indians needed a sweep to tie for first. Feller started the first game against no-name Floyd Giebell and pitched well, but a home run by Rudy York sealed Cleveland's fate. They lost the game and the pennant. Vitt's team finished second, only one game out of first, but his major league managerial career was over.

Omar Vizquel

Vizquel, Omar Enrique (Gonzalez) **SS**

1989–* B:4/24/1967, Caracas, Venezuela Deb:4/3/1989, SEA AL BB/TR, 5'9", 165

G	AB	R	H	HR	RBI	OBP	SLG	AVG
1464	5196	734	1429	34	449	.340	.350	.275

A unique defensive stylist whose range and dramatic flair reminded many of Ozzie Smith, Omar Vizquel honed his craft on the rough-hewn ballfields of Venezuela. As a youth Vizquel developed his knack for barehanding grounders, as he did on the final out of Chris Bosio's no-hitter on April 22, 1993. Harold Reynolds, a former Seattle teammate turned broadcaster, said of Vizquel, "For a pitcher, all they have to do is get the ball on the ground and they know he's going to come up with it."

Like Ozzie, Omar improved his offense as his career progressed. Following a trade to Cleveland after the 1993 season, Vizquel emerged as a baserunning threat. He stole 186 bases from 1995 to 1999. After hitting higher than .273 just once in his first seven seasons, he batted .280 or better every season from 1996 through 1999. He also grabbed his share of postseason glory.

In 1997 Vizquel hit .500 with four steals to lead the Indians to a Division Series upset of the New York Yankees. After a miserable 1-for-25 performance in Cleveland's Championship Series victory, Vizquel stole five bases and scored five runs as the Tribe fell to Florida in the World Series. Vizquel was back at it the next year in the ALCS against the Yankees, batting .440 with four steals in a losing effort. He did not commit an error in his first 46 postseason games.

In 1999 Vizquel finally was paired with a second baseman whose defensive gifts matched his own: eight-time Gold Glove Award winner Roberto Alomar. The tandem provided brilliance afield, but Vizquel also turned in a career year at the plate with a .333 average, 66 RBIs, and 42 steals. Vizquel won his seventh consecutive Gold Glove.

Bill Voiselle

Voiselle, William Symmes **P**

1942–50 B:1/29/1919, Greenwood, SC Deb:9/1/1942, NY NL BR/TR, 6'4", 200

W	L	PCT	G	SH	IP	BB	SO	ERA
74	84	.468	245	13	1373^{1}	588	645	3.83

Bill Voiselle wore his address on the back of his uniform. His number was 96, which was also the name of his hometown in South Carolina. In 1944, with the Giants' pitching staff decimated by military service, Voiselle received 41 starts. He made the most of them, compiling a 21–16 record and leading the National League in strikeouts and innings pitched. His 25 complete games ranked third in the league.

"Big Bill" started 35 times the next season, but with less impressive results: he finished the season at 14–14. In June 1947 the Giants sent Voiselle to the Boston Braves. The next season, his 13 wins helped the Braves make a surprise World Series appearance. Voiselle pitched in the rotation after Warren Spahn and Johnny Sain—when the Braves supposedly prayed for rain. By 1950 he was out of baseball after an 0–4 season for the Cubs.

Chris Von der Ahe

Von der Ahe, Christian Fredrick Wilhelm

Owner (1882–98) M(1895–97, 3–14) B:11/7/1851, Hille, Germany D:6/7/1913, St. Louis, MO

Chris Von der Ahe lived a life that was both comic opera and high tragedy. Easily the most colorful baseball owner of the 19th century, Von der Ahe never really understood the game, yet he produced one of the greatest teams of the era. His promotional gall foreshadowed the antics of Bill Veeck, while his meddlesome interference on the field brings to mind George Steinbrenner.

Little is known about Von der Ahe's early life. He was born in Germany, and came to the United States in 1867. By 1870 he was in New York; he later moved to St. Louis, where he worked as a grocery clerk and eventually opened a tavern on the western edge of the city. Von der Ahe bought real estate and increased his earnings as a landlord. His saloon was near a field known as Sportsman's Park, where large crowds attended amateur baseball games and then headed to the tavern.

St. Louis was a charter member of the National League in 1876 but dropped out after the 1877 season. Alfred H. Spink backed the Browns, a local independent team named after the old National League club. In 1881 he contacted O.P. Taylor in Cincinnati and suggested that he organize a team to play an exhibition game against the Browns. Cincinnati had also dropped out of the league because of a league ban on Sunday games. The exhibition drew a huge crowd to Sportsman's Park.

Von der Ahe, who held the concession rights, was impressed. Later that fall, Spink and Taylor met with representatives of other cities and formed a new major league, the American Association. Its members included St. Louis, Cincinnati, Baltimore, Louisville, Philadelphia, and Pittsburgh. The new league allowed the sale of beer and liquor at the games and charged only 25 cents for admission compared to the 50 cents the National League charged.

Spink asked Von der Ahe to help sell 180 shares of the new St. Louis team, but instead Von der Ahe bought the shares himself. By his own admission, Von der Ahe knew nothing about baseball, so Spink hired the players, including young Charlie Comiskey, a first baseman from Dubuque. Comiskey was only a fair hitter but a fine fielder. More important, he was an astute judge of talent himself and a strong leader who before long was serving as both captain and manager of the team. In 1885 Comiskey's Browns won the American Association championship and tied the National League's Chicago White Stockings in their "World Series."

The two teams both won championships the next season and met in the 1886 World Series; the Browns defeated the White Stockings in what turned out to be the high point of the American Association's existence. The Browns won two more flags, in 1887 and 1888, but were bested by the National League in the World Series. Their streak of four pennants in a row was not matched until John McGraw's New York Giants of 1921 through 1924.

These were halcyon years for the Browns and Von der Ahe. In his thick, German accent, Von der Ahe referred to himself as "Der Poss President." Wearing a silk hat and walking his two greyhounds, Snoozer and Schnauzer, the chubby leader personally led his players onto the field. Later he would ceremoniously cart the day's receipts to the bank in a wheelbarrow. After the game much of the crowd retired to Von der Ahe's tavern, where the owner often bought drinks for the house. "Money," he said, "dot ist to schpend."

Von der Ahe built a newer and grander ballpark to house his team, declaring the new Sportsman's Park to be "der piggest diamond" in the Midwest. Comiskey tactfully informed him that all baseball diamonds were the same size. Then, declared Von der Ahe, it was "der piggest infield" in the Midwest.

Comiskey's greatest contribution to the team's success was his ability to deal with Der Poss President. Von der Ahe was full of ideas to improve the show, and Comiskey kept him within bounds. Comiskey joined the Players' League in 1890, and although he returned to the Browns in 1891, he left for good the following year. Without Comiskey to reign him in, Von der Ahe careened toward disaster.

When the American Association collapsed after the 1891 season, Von der Ahe's Browns were one of four AA teams grudgingly admitted into what became a 12-team National League. In search of another Comiskey, Von der Ahe ran through 12 managers from 1894 through 1896. In 1895 alone, eight different men were in charge. Von der Ahe himself even took over as manager for one game in 1895, two in 1896, and 14 in 1897, compiling a record of 3–14.

As the fortunes of the Browns plummeted, Von der Ahe put his money into promotions instead of ballplayers. Determined to make Sportsman's Park "the Coney Island of the West," he brought in a Wild West show with real Indians, hired at $12 per person, and put a racetrack around the field. Although the league was outraged at such stunts, Von der Ahe pressed on. Only declining crowds and increasing debt got his attention. Upset by rainouts, he once asked the league to distribute rainouts more equally.

Meanwhile, his personal life was in total disarray. In 1897 he was placed in the Allegheny County Jail over a $2,500 debt to the Pittsburgh Pirates. The National League agreed to pay the debt if Von der Ahe got out of Organized Baseball. The Browns were eventually sold at auction.

In 1899 Von der Ahe filed for bankruptcy. He retained ownership of the tavern, but business was poor. In 1908 Comiskey, by then owner of the Chicago White Sox, arranged a benefit game between the two St. Louis teams, which helped Von der Ahe live out his remaining years with some dignity. He died in 1913 of dropsy and cirrhosis of the liver. At his funeral, Comiskey praised Von der Ahe as "the grandest figure baseball has ever known."

Joe Vosmik

Vosmik, Joseph Franklin **OF**

1930–44 B:4/4/1910, Cleveland, OH D:1/27/1962, Cleveland, OH Deb:9/13/1930, CLE AL BR/TR, 6', 185

G	AB	R	H	HR	RBI	OBP	SLG	AVG
1414	5472	818	1682	65	874	.369	.438	.307

Joe Vosmik's skills began to erode when he was only 29, but he had already had quite a run. Vosmik, a left fielder, hit better than .300 in six of his first eight seasons—twice bettering .340—while averaging 91 RBIs.

Born in Cleveland in 1910, Vosmik signed with his hometown Indians in 1929. According to one account, Cleveland general manager Billy Evans needed to sign one more kid at a tryout camp and asked his wife's opinion. Allegedly she chose "the good-looking blond boy."

Vosmik hit .381 and .397 during his two seasons in the minors and took over left field for the Indians in 1931, batting .320 with a career-high 117 RBIs while striking out only 30 times in 591 at bats. Vosmik never did strike out much—only 272 times in 5,472 at bats, or once every 20 at bats.

He batted .312 with a career-high 10 homers and 97 RBIs the next season before slumping badly in 1933. After batting .341 in 104 games in 1934, he had his career season in 1935. Vosmik led the American League in hits (216), doubles (47), and triples (20) while driving in 110 runs and finishing one point behind Senators second baseman Buddy Myer in the batting race.

After Vosmik's average dropped to .287 in 1936, he was traded to the St. Louis Browns. He hit .325 the next season, with 93 RBIs. Sent to the Red Sox in 1938 he batted .324, with a league-leading 201 hits.

The decline began in 1939, when he hit .276. Promptly sold to Brooklyn, Vosmik played one season as a regular, was released by the Dodgers in 1941 and resurfaced during World War II for 36 at bats, and seven hits, as a Senator in 1944.

Pete Vuckovich

Vuckovich, Peter Dennis **P**

1975–83, 1985–86 B:10/27/1952, Johnstown, PA Deb:8/3/1975, CHI AL BR/TR, 6'4", 220

W	L	PCT	G	SV	IP	BB	SO	ERA
93	69	.574	286	10	1455¹	545	882	3.66

Milwaukee's Pete Vuckovich was voted the American League Cy Young Award in 1982, but the hard-throwing 6-foot 4-inch righthander may have sacrificed his career to win it. The Brewers were in a pennant race, and Vuckovich took cortisone shots in the shoulder to enabled him to pitch through nagging shoulder pain. In 1983, at age 30, he was diagnosed with a torn rotator cuff. He retired in 1986 with a career 93–69 record. Vuckovich's motivation was simple. "I really hate hitters," he said. "They're goofy. They're trying to get me, to ruin my career, so I hate them."

An all-state athlete in three sports at Pennsylvania's Conemaugh Valley High School, Vuckovich went on to Clarion State College and played four years of American Legion Baseball before the White Sox selected him in the third round of the June 1974 draft. He played with Appleton, Knoxville, and Denver before coming to the White Sox in 1975. Drafted by the Blue Jays in the second round of the 1976 expansion draft, he pitched the Blue Jays first shutout, beating Jim Palmer and the Orioles on June 23, 1977. Vuckovich was traded to St. Louis after the season and recorded a 39–31 record and a 3.20 ERA over three seasons with the club.

Vuckovich came to the Brewers in a seven-player deal after the 1980 season. In the strike-shortened 1981 season, Vuckovich tied for the most major league wins with a 14–4 record. He added another win in Game 4 of the division playoff against the Yankees.

Vuckovich went 18–6 and helped the Brewers to the World Series in his Cy Young year in 1982. But by the time the postseason arrived his arm injury had weakened the pitcher and he went 0–2. After resting for much of the 1983 season, Vuckovich had major surgery on his right shoulder on April 3, 1984. He returned to the Brewers for parts of the 1985 and 1986 season with limited success, but the pain kept returning. He retired, and later did some broadcasting for the Brewers. He joined the Pittsburgh Pirates as pitching coach in 1997.

Rube Waddell

Waddell, George Edward **P**

1897–1910 B:10/13/1876, Bradford, PA D:4/1/1914, San Antonio, TX Deb:9/8/1897, LOU NL BR/TL 6'1½", 196

W	L	PCT	G	SH	IP	BB	SO	ERA
193	143	.574	407	50	2961[1]	803	2316	2.16

If it's true that lefthanders—particularly lefthanded pitchers—are zanier than righthanders, then George Edward "Rube" Waddell was the lefty of all lefties. Historian Lee Allen described Waddell's 1903 season: "He began that year sleeping in a firehouse in Camden, New Jersey, and ended it tending bar in a saloon in Wheeling, West Virginia. In between those events he won 22 games for the Philadelphia Athletics, played left end for the Business Men's Rugby Football Club of Grand Rapids, Michigan, toured the nation in a melodrama called *The Stain of Guilt*, courted, married and became separated from May Wynne Skinner of Lynn, Massachusetts, saved a woman from drowning, accidentally shot a friend through the hand, and was bitten by a lion."

On one occasion after being fined $100 by one of his distraught managers, Waddell asked why. The manager replied that it "was for that disgraceful hotel episode in Detroit." Waddell answered, "You're a liar. There ain't no Hotel Episode in Detroit."

A muscular six-footer with a wicked overhand delivery of a blazing fastball and an excellent curve, Waddell was a strikeout pitcher in an era when most batters choked up and slapped at the ball. He led his league in strikeouts seven times, six consecutively. He ranks among the top 30 in strikeouts per game, but he's the only hurler on that list to have pitched prior to 1950. When he struck out 302 batters in 1903, no other pitcher in the American League fanned even 200. Waddell's 349 strikeouts in 1904 was baseball's all-time record until Sandy Koufax broke it 61 years later.

As tough as he was on the mound, Waddell was even tougher to deal with personally. His childlike love of fire engines enticed him away from games to chase them. And he regularly would pitch, win, and then disappear, often going fishing until it was his turn to pitch again. He might be found tending bar or playing marbles with kids. And he loved to lead parades.

One teammate recalled Waddell dunking his left arm in a barrel of ice water before a game. "I've got so much speed today," Waddell had said, "I'll probably burn up the catcher's glove if I don't cool it off."

By age 18 Waddell was already a semipro star in Butler, Pennsylvania. He came from a poor family and preferred fishing to schooling, so the $500 contract he signed in 1896 with Louisville of the National League must have seemed like a million dollars to him. But he jumped the team after pitching only two games because manager Fred Clarke fined him $50 for excessive drinking. He went to Detroit of the Western League, but he packed up after only nine appearances to play semipro ball in Canada.

Upon returning to the Western League with Columbus-Grand Rapids in 1899, he won 27 games, and Louisville decided to give him another chance. Waddell was 7–2 in nine starts, and his eccentricities and awesome talent made him a big draw—both during and after the season. Come November he worked as an alligator wrestler in Florida.

After the 1899 season Louisville owner Barney Dreyfuss got word of the National League's plan to shut down his team, so he bought into the Pirates and "traded" most of his Louisville team to Pittsburgh. Waddell joined Honus Wagner, Fred Clarke, and others on the Pirates. During his first year in Pittsburgh he went only 8–13, but he led the league with a 2.37 ERA. He left the team in July and went to play for Connie Mack in Milwaukee of the Western (soon to be American) League.

Of all his managers, only Mack was able to handle the overgrown child. Instead of giving Waddell a paycheck, which would be gone in hours, Mack paid the pitcher in $10 or $15 installments, as he needed the cash.

In Milwaukee Mack recognized how he could get the most from his talented but twisted pitcher. Waddell had just finished pitching a 17-inning game, won by his own triple. Mack and the opposing manager agreed to limit the second game of that day's doubleheader to five innings. Mack made Waddell an offer: "You can take off and go fishing for the next three days if you'll pitch the second game." Waddell threw a five-inning shutout. When it appeared that Waddell might have straightened himself out with a 10–3 record, the Pirates demanded his return.

But he was still the same old Rube. After Waddell lost two starts for Pittsburgh in 1901, player-manager Clarke told Dreyfuss he'd had enough of the screwy lefty. "Sell him, release him, drop him off the Monongahela Bridge; do anything with him you like, so long as you get him off my ball team," Clarke said. Dreyfuss concurred, and Waddell was sold to the Orphans.

Waddell was 13–15 for Chicago in 1901, and was suspended for the final month of the season for erratic behavior; he spent the time playing semipro ball in Wisconsin. He latched on with a group of barnstorming big leaguers after the season, and after they made a trip to the West Coast, Waddell didn't want to leave. He began the 1902 season with Los Angeles, and by the middle of the season he was 12–8 and batting .283. Mack sent two Pinkerton agents to bring him back to the Philadelphia A's, who had bought his contract from Chicago.

Waddell pouted through his first game with the Athletics and lost. But the patient Mack didn't give up on him. Waddell won 10 straight games in July and finished the season 24–7. His league-leading 210 strikeouts were 50 more than Cy Young's mark.

For the next several years Waddell, Eddie Plank, and Chief Bender formed the meanest rotation in baseball. Waddell led the league in strikeouts every year from 1902 through 1907, and in the last five of those seasons he fanned more hitters than anyone else in the game. On July 2, 1902, he became the first man to strike out the side on nine pitches. In 1904 Young beat him, 3–0, by pitching a perfect game. The next season Waddell returned the favor, besting Young in a 20-inning pitchers' duel. Waddell took the ball from that game and used it to get drinks—in at least 20 different bars.

When the Mackmen won the American League flag in 1905, Waddell was the ace of the A's staff and appeared in a league-leading 46 games. He won 27 of those, against only 10 losses, despite missing the last month of the season. It seems that Waddell had ridiculed teammate Andy Coakley's new straw hat, and the two pitchers scuffled during a train trip. Coakley fell on Waddell's left arm, injuring it. As a result, Waddell did not pitch in the World Series.

When someone reported that gamblers had gotten to Waddell to keep him out of the Series, Mack was outraged. "Ridiculous!" he snorted. "Money means nothing to him." Respected writer Joe Vila claimed, "Wiser men had him holed up in a lush Manhattan apartment with a group of Broadway showgirls, his expenses paid by a New York betting crowd." The Athletics lost the Series in five games—every game a shutout. By now even Mack was about to run out of patience with the unpredictable southpaw. After compiling a 34–30 record the next two seasons, Waddell was sold for $5,000 to the St. Louis Browns.

In his first appearance against his old teammates in 1908, Waddell struck out 16 batters, setting a new single-game strikeout mark. The crowds still loved him: 28,000 Philadelphia fans turned out to Columbia Park to watch him pitch in one game. After a 19–14 season, the Browns were worried about what kind of trouble Waddell might cause before spring training. So they hired him as a hunter for the off-season. He stayed out of trouble and kept the Browns' front office personnel supplied with duck and venison.

The next season Jimmy Austin and his New York teammates were riding in their carriage to a game when they saw rival pitcher Waddell step out of a saloon, a large glass of beer in hand. He toasted them and waved as they passed. Somehow he made it to the game on time, and he pitched well enough for the first three innings. But with two on in the fourth, Austin homered. The rankled Waddell glared at Austin all the way around the bases, but the 360-degree turn made him dizzy and he fell down.

After Waddell won 11 and lost 14 in 1909, St. Louis released him early in 1910. He pitched for Newark of the Eastern League and then went to Minneapolis to play for Joe Cantillon's Millers in the American Association. According to historian Bill James, the Millers were the best minor league team of their era. Waddell was 20–6 his first season there and 12–6 the next. He and Cantillon became close friends, and Waddell stayed with Joe and his family after the 1912 season.

That winter a dike broke not far from the Cantillon home, and Waddell went to offer help. He stood in deep, icy water for hours, piling sandbags to block the rushing stream. He caught a miserable cold and never recovered. After he pitched poorly for a Northern League team in 1913, Cantillon had Waddell sent to a San Antonio tuberculosis sanitarium, where he died in 1914. He was elected to the Hall of Fame in 1946.

Heinie Wagner

Wagner, Charles F. **SS-2B**

1902–18 M(1930, 52–102) B:9/23/1880, New York, NY D:3/20/1943, New Rochelle, NY Deb:7/1/1902, NY NL BR/TR 5'9", 183

G	AB	R	H	HR	RBI	OBP	SLG	AVG
983	3333	402	834	10	343	.319	.326	.250

Charles F. "Heinie" Wagner was a popular shortstop for the Boston Red Sox just after the turn of the century. One of his major duties was to make sure Babe Ruth, the team's best pitcher at the time, stayed out of trouble. Manager Bill Carrigan assigned Wagner to room with Ruth in order to keep an eye on the fun-loving pitcher. When Ruth jumped the club in July 1918, Wagner tracked him down in Baltimore and brought him back.

Wagner had an astute baseball mind. Along with Harry Hooper and Everett Scott, he advised Ed Barrow, who had taken over as Boston's manager in 1918, on various moves, including the switching of Ruth from the pitcher's mound to the outfield.

In the field Wagner was one of the better shortstops of his era. He often would use his big feet to knock down hard-hit grounders, and he twice led American League shortstops in total chances per game. The fans adored Wagner, and they presented him with a loving cup after the Red Sox won the 1912 pennant. He was the team's regular shortstop from 1908 to 1913 and he compiled a lifetime batting average of .250 for 12 big-league seasons.

Wagner served as Red Sox manager for one season, replacing Carrigan (who'd come back to Boston for a second term at the helm) in 1930. The Red Sox finished dead last under Wagner and he was replaced the following season.

Honus Wagner

Wagner, John Peter **SS-OF-1B-3B**

1897–1917 M(1917, 1–4) B:2/24/1874, Chartiers, PA D:12/6/1955, Carnegie, PA Deb:7/19/1897, LOU NL BR/TR 5'11", 200

G	AB	R	H	HR	RBI	OBP	SLG	AVG
2792	10430	1736	3415	101	1732	.391	.466	.327

If a knowledgeable baseball fan in 1910 had been asked to name Major League Baseball's all-time All-Star team, the shortstop would undoubtedly have been Honus Wagner. Ask a knowledgeable fan today the same question and their choice at shortstop would be the same. Every other player of Wagner's era has since been surpassed in overall excellence at his position. Only Wagner remains.

When the first five men were elected to the Hall of Fame in 1936, Wagner joined Babe Ruth and Ty Cobb as the first three position players to be immortalized. There probably has never been a more genuine, honest, decent, and beloved ballplayer than Honus Wagner. Despite his awesome talents he was always modest and friendly, throughout his playing career and afterwards.

The reason for Wagner's longevity as baseball's best shortstop is simple. No other shortstop has ever combined offensive and defensive excellence the way he did. Ungainly in appearance, he was a superb fielder, with large, strong hands and a wicked arm. Longtime manager John McGraw once said, "The only way to get a ball past Honus is to hit it eight feet over his head."

Despite his legendary bowed legs, Wagner was extraordinarily fast on the base paths, leading his league in stolen bases five times. Three times he stole second, third, and home in a single inning. As a hitter, he ranks among the top 20 of all time in six different categories.

Although Wagner was supremely well coordinated, his appearance belied his grace. At 5-foot-11 and a stocky 200 pounds, he sported a barrel chest and long arms with thick-fingered hands. A versatile athlete, he frequently toured as a barnstorming basketball player with his brothers during the off-season, causing Pirates ownership much distress. He was so bowlegged, one wit said, that a beer barrel could be rolled between his legs. Another said Wagner could tie his shoes without bending over. Stories abound of Wagner grabbing a grounder and heaving it to first along with a fistful of dirt and grass he had snatched up at the same time.

John Peter Wagner's nickname was a variation on the German "Hans" or "Johannes." He grew up in Mansfield, Pennsylvania, later renamed Carnegie. Now part of greater Pittsburgh, it was in those days an hour by carriage from the city. The Pirates offered Wagner a contract in 1894, but they wanted to send him to Kansas City, which sounded too far away for the home-minded Honus. He signed with Steubenville instead, and played with four other minor league teams before Barney Dreyfuss obtained him in 1897 for his National League Louisville Colonels. Wagner was primarily an outfielder and third baseman for Louisville during his three years there.

Wagner came to the Pittsburgh Pirates in 1900, in the largest trade in baseball history up to that time. Dreyfuss, having heard that his Louisville team was about to be dropped from the National League, sent 14 players to Pittsburgh for $25,000 and four Pittsburgh players. Dreyfuss then purchased the Pittsburgh team. Traded to Pittsburgh along with Wagner were future Hall of Famers Fred Clarke and Rube Waddell.

Playing right field, third base, second base, first base, and even pitching (he hurled three scoreless innings) during the 1900 season, Wagner won his first batting title and led the league in triples, doubles, and slugging average. In 1901 at age 17, he became Pittsburgh's regular shortstop after Horace "Bones" Ely jumped to Ban Johnson's upstart American League. That year the Pirates won the first of three consecutive league championships. In 1903 they played Boston in the first World Series of the modern era, losing five games to three because of a decimated pitching staff.

From 1903 through 1909 Wagner led the National League in hitting seven times and finished second once. He won four slugging titles and led the league in on-base percentage four times, stolen bases three times, RBIs twice, triples twice, doubles five times, and hits and runs once each. In 1908 Wagner was only two home runs shy of a Triple Crown. *Total Baseball*'s Total Player Rating ranks him first every year from 1903 through 1909. Wagner's decade ranks with the performances of Rogers Hornsby and Ruth during the 1920s as the greatest offensive 10-year spans in Major League Baseball history.

He drove in six runs in the 1909 World Series against the Tigers of Ty Cobb, the first time that two batting champions faced each other in a Series. Wagner hit .333, Cobb .231, and the Pirates sent Detroit down to their third consecutive Series defeat.

Wagner played eight more years after 1909, although Pittsburgh never tasted a pennant again. He won another batting title in 1911 and drove in 102 runs to top all NL hitters in 1912 at age 38, but his days of league leadership were over.

The first player to have his name engraved on a Louisville Slugger bat, Wagner was also the first player to amass 3,000 hits, although many still credit Cap Anson. During his career he won eight batting titles, led the league in doubles eight times, and finished with more triples than any other player in the league. He led the league in extra-base hits seven times, sharing the major league record with Stan Musial and Ruth.

He ranks among the all-time top 15 in four categories: hits (seventh with 3,415), doubles (eighth with 640), stolen bases (10th with 722), and at-bats (13th with 10,430). He is also in the top 20 in games played, total bases, runs batted in, and runs. Wagner has the highest lifetime batting average of any shortstop, at .327, and only one other shortstop stole more bases. He is ranked ninth among all players lifetime in *Total Baseball's* Total Player Rating.

These achievements are all the more impressive against the fearsome hurlers Wagner faced in his day. His lifetime average against Christy Mathewson was .324 in 327 at bats; against Kid Nichols it was .352 in 105 plate appearances. Against Cy Young, Wagner hit .343 in 70 at bats. In 135 contests against Nap Rucker he hit .356.

Bill James states that Wagner "was the greatest athlete in baseball," and adds, "Acknowledging that there may have been one or two whose talents were greater, there is no one who has ever played the game that I would be more anxious to have on a baseball team." Among the legendary baseball people who called Wagner the greatest player ever were Ed Barrow, Sam Crawford, Bill Klem, John McGraw, and Branch Rickey.

A crowd pleaser on the field, Wagner was also an extremely well-liked person off the field. While Cobb was a snarling spitfire and Nap Lajoie a perfect patrician, Wagner was a man of the people, humble, forthright, and friendly. He always had a sly grin under his huge nose, and he was adored wherever he went. As early as his third year in professional baseball, fans were throwing "Wagner Days" for him and naming their children after him.

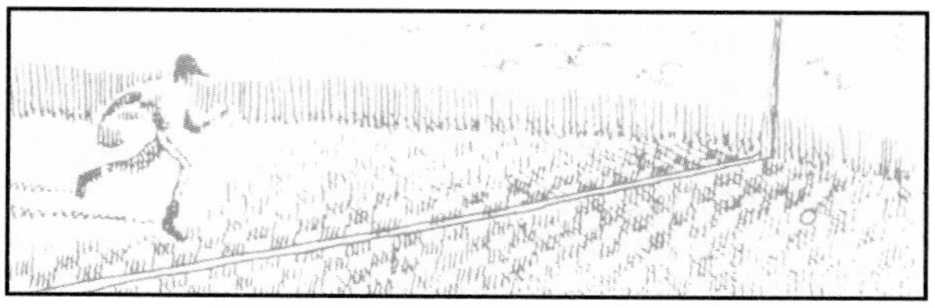

Pittsburgh had days honoring him in 1902, 1903, 1908, and 1909. In his last season, 1917, these tributes were held all over the league. According to historian Lee Allen, "Everywhere the Pirates went there were 'days' for Wagner. Occasionally, grateful fans would present him with something as valuable as a silver service, but he would usually be 'honored' with a dozen roses, which he would modestly accept and lavishly praise before the batboy could find a way to dispose of them."

Once when a cigarette company put out baseball cards, Wagner sent back the check he had received and asked that the cards with his picture be destroyed. He didn't think encouraging children to smoke was a good idea. By doing so he inadvertently created the most valuable baseball card of all time.

In an era of roughneck baseball, Wagner was as tough as they came, but he never picked a fight or continued one. He was never one to bait umpires. The Pirates made him their manager in 1917, but Wagner lasted only five games; being the boss was not his style. For the next 16 years he tried a variety of jobs: coaching at Carnegie Tech (now Carnegie-Mellon), serving as doorman for the Pennsylvania State Legislature, and even operating a sporting goods store, which retains his name to this day, on Forbes Avenue in downtown Pittsburgh.

He also still swung the bat. The tale is told that he hit a dramatic home run to win a semipro game at age 52. On June 9, 1933, the Pirates honored him with another "Honus Wagner Day." The parade through Pittsburgh lasted two hours and featured 800 automobiles. Wagner played in the old timer's game that day, handling seven chances perfectly. His baseball instinct still intact at age 59, he snagged a grounder with men on first and second and fired to third to force the runner. Later in the game he threw out a runner at home. After the game he received $1,500 cash and three slabs of ham and bacon. When he was handed the check, he apologized for his team's losing the game.

The Pirates brought him back as a coach, and he stayed with them for the next 18 years. But Wagner's coaching duties were less important than his role as baseball sage and beloved old uncle. He always had a story to tell. The "Wagner Encyclopedia" of baseball tall tales has added much to baseball legend and lore, and has driven many a researcher crazy trying to sift the truth from the fiction.

One story has it that a rookie pitcher circa 1910 entered a game with the bases loaded and asked

Cubs third baseman Heinie Zimmerman how to pitch to Wagner. Zimmerman answered, "Whatever you do, don't pitch him tight. Keep the ball outside." When the rookie did as he was advised, Wagner rapped a bases-clearing double down the right-field line. "I thought you said he couldn't hit the outside pitch," the youngster said to Zimmerman. "I didn't say that," Zimmerman replied. "I just said don't pitch him inside—I've got a wife and two kids back home."

Wagner related a story that he once picked up a rabbit that was running across the infield and threw it to first, whereupon the umpire called the runner out "by a hare." He also claimed that he threw a dog to second when the critter picked up the ball and Wagner couldn't get it away from him.

He loved to tell the yarn about his tough introduction to the big leagues. In his first game, he said, he slugged a sure triple against Baltimore, but Orioles first baseman "Dirty Jack" Doyle gave him the hip, Hughie Jennings forced him wide at second, and John McGraw blocked him off third and then knocked the wind out of him with a tough tag on the stomach. Manager Fred Clarke, coaching at third, "cussed out the newcomer" Wagner for his naiveté.

Two other stories relate how Wagner responded his next time up. In the first version, he beat out a bunt to John McGraw and ran over Doyle, causing McGraw's throw to go astray, and Wagner wound up on third. In the second version—the one Wagner preferred to tell—he belted a deep drive to center, and on his way around the bases he dumped Doyle on his behind, left Jennings in the dirt at second, and trampled all over McGraw's feet coming into third. McGraw was enraged. The tickled Clarke sauntered over from the coach's box and said, "Nice day, ain't it, Muggsy?"

In a game in St. Louis, Wagner reportedly went to the plate against a fireballing righty who had baffled the Bucs. Wagner took two called strikes and then "reached out barehanded, grabbed the next fastball and threw it back." He asked, "Is that your changeup?" Although Wagner fanned on the next pitch, the rattled hurler walked the next five Pirates and Pittsburgh won.

Another story, which has since been verified, concerns an early experiment in night baseball in Wilmington, Delaware, in 1894. Visibility was poor, and the fans, unhappy with the performance, got nasty. The players then quit taking the game seriously, angering the fans even more. At one point a pitcher inserted a firecracker into a baseball and delivered it to Wagner, who gave it a good crack. When the ball exploded, the fans decided enough was enough. They rushed the box office for refunds, but by then the owners and local backers had divvied up the receipts and hightailed it out of there.

One of the most famous Wagner stories involves Ty Cobb in the 1909 World Series. Many writers have repeated the tale of how Cobb taunted Wagner as soon as Cobb got to first base in the Series opener, calling him offensive names, and announcing that he would steal second on the first pitch. The story goes on that Wagner took the throw and tagged Cobb out on the mouth, loosening his teeth (in some versions), knocking several out (in others), and bloodying Cobb's lip enough to require several stitches (in yet others).

But that particular tall tale is a confabulation. Wagner never tagged Cobb out at second in the entire Series. Cobb stole second only once, his third time up in Game 1. In truth, Cobb had great respect for Wagner, and in his own autobiography says, "Spike Honus Wagner? It would have taken quite a foolhardy man."

Arthritis in his famous bowlegs finally forced Wagner out of uniform in 1951. Four years later the Pirates unveiled a huge bronze statue of the old shortstop sculpted by Frank Vittor in Schenley Park outside Forbes Field. In 1972 the statue was moved to its present site outside Gate C at Three Rivers Stadium. The words in the statue dedication program summed up Wagner's character: "He played with the confidence born of exceptional natural talents and abilities and a consuming love of the game… Fighting heart and intense competitive spirit… and yet he maintained a sense of humor… a fine gentleman."

One final image of Honus Wagner comes from former Pirates owner Bill Benswanger, the son-in-law of Barney Dreyfuss, who brought Wagner back to coach. "I chanced to see Honus lumbering down the sidewalk ahead of me, the setting sun shining through the arch in his marvelously bowed legs."

Leon Wagner

Wagner, Leon Lamar **OF**

1958–69 B:5/13/1934, Chattanooga, TN
Deb:6/22/1958, SF NL BL/TR 6'1", 195

G	AB	R	H	HR	RBI	OBP	SLG	AVG
1352	4426	636	1202	211	669	.343	.455	.272

Expansion gave him a chance, and Leon "Daddy Wags" Wagner grabbed it with both hands. For five years in the 1960s Wagner was one of the game's better sluggers. "Wags always thought he was the greatest hitter in baseball," said Phillies general manager Lee Thomas, a teammate of Wagner's on the 1961 Angels. "He didn't care a lot about defense. He felt he was paid to hit the ball out of the park and that's what he tried to do just about every at bat. And he had great power."

Leon Lamar Wagner signed with the Giants in 1954. He made it to the majors in the second half of the 1958 season and hit .317 with 13 homers and 35 RBIs in 74 games. After slumping to .225 with five homers in 1959, he was traded to the Cardinals after the season. Hitting only .214 in 39 games with St. Louis, he spent most of 1960 in the minors.

Wagner was 26 years old by then and going nowhere. But the American League had recently expanded, and the new California Angels franchise picked him up along with two other players and some cash in exchange for Al Cicotte, a pitcher whose career was on the skids. The deal turned out to be highway robbery. In 1961 Wagner hit .280 with 28 homers and 79 RBIs as the Angels stayed in contention until August and won a startling 70 games, which remained the record for an expansion club through 1999. He was even better in 1962, hitting 37 homers and driving in 107 runs, both career highs.

After hitting .291 with 26 homers and 90 RBIs in 1963, Wagner was traded to the Indians for Barry Latman and Joe Adcock. He responded by upping his totals to 31 homers and 100 RBIs in 1964, and hitting a career-best .294 for a full season in 1965. Over the five-year span from 1961–65, Wagner averaged 30 homers and 91 RBIs.

He started to slip in 1966, and continued to slide the next season, with only 15 homers and 54 RBIs. After two more years—with the Indians, White Sox, and Giants—Wagner was through. He finished his career with 211 home runs in only 4,426 at-bats.

A great talker and a fan favorite, Wagner opened a clothing store with the wonderful name "Get Your Clothes at Daddy Wags." "He was a character, but a nice character," Thomas said of him. "He liked to have fun."

Eddie Waitkus

Waitkus, Edward Stephen **1B**
1941–55 B:9/4/1919, Cambridge, MA D:9/15/1972, Jamaica Plain, MA Deb:4/15/1941, CHI NL BL/TL
6'1", 175

G	AB	R	H	HR	RBI	OBP	SLG	AVG
1140	4254	528	1214	24	373	.344	.374	.285

A slick fielder at first base and a solid hitter, Eddie Waitkus played for 11 seasons in the major leagues and finished with a lifetime .285 average. But he's best known for an incident later echoed in Bernard Malamud's *The Natural* and its film adaptation.

Edward Stephen Waitkus had his most successful years as a Cub from 1946 through 1948, when he hit .304, .292, and .295. After an off-season trade to the Phillies for Walter "Monk" Dubiel and Emil "Dutch" Leonard, Waitkus was hitting .306 in the middle of June. Then an adoring female fan shot him in the chest.

Ruth Ann Steinhagen was a 19-year-old Chicagoan whose zealous devotion to the handsome Waitkus bordered on the bizarre. She couldn't talk about anything else, and she claimed she even dreamed about him. She constructed a shrine to Waitkus in her bedroom, decorated with newspaper photos of the first baseman. She even learned Lithuanian because of Eddie's background. "As time went on," she admitted, "I just became nuttier and nuttier about the guy, and I knew I would never get to know him in a normal way... and if I can't have him nobody else can. And then I decided I would kill him."

Steinhagen bought a used rifle, checked into the Chicago hotel where the Phils were staying, and left a message that she wanted to see Waitkus. Receiving the message about midnight, the affable bachelor thought he'd check it out. When he arrived at her room, she took the rifle out of a closet and shot him in the chest.

Questioned soon afterward, Steinhagen said, "I admire him now more than ever before. He showed so much courage as he lay there on the floor. The way he looked up at me and kept smiling." In the hospital, Waitkus said to reporters, "I don't know what got into that silly honey. Why pick on a nice guy like me?" In court, Steinhagen was declared deranged.

Despite undergoing four operations, Waitkus made a remarkable recovery. He played all 154 games the next year and batted .284 in the lead-off spot. The Phillies won the pennant for the first time since 1915. And although the Yanks swept them in the World Series, Waitkus always said that his 1950 Series appearance was the thrill of his baseball life.

Waitkus continued his solid hitting and smooth play in Philadelphia through 1953. He was then was traded to Baltimore, but returned to the Phillies in 1955 to play his final 33 major league games.

The mental hospital released Steinhagen around the same time, and Waitkus feared for his life, though she never came near him again. But in retrospect, Ruth Ann Steinhagen may have gotten her wish to kill Eddie Waitkus. After his death from cancer in 1972, doctors surmised that the bullet wound and subsequent operations may have opened the door to the disease that ultimately took his life.

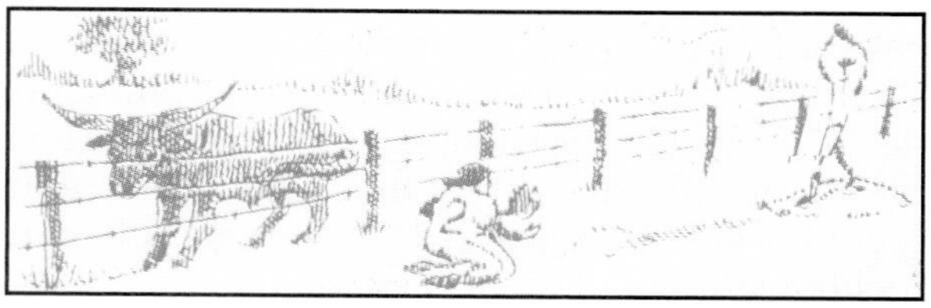

Dick Wakefield

Wakefield, Richard Cummings **OF**

1941–52 B:5/6/1921, Chicago, IL D:8/26/1985, Wayne County, MI Deb:6/26/1941, DET AL BL/TR 6'4", 210

G	AB	R	H	HR	RBI	OBP	SLG	AVG
638	2132	334	625	56	315	.396	.447	.293

In 1941 $52,000 was quite a sum of money, but the Tigers evidently felt that young prospect Richard Cummings Wakefield was worth it. They signed him for a $52,000 bonus out of the University of Michigan, making him one of baseball's very first bonus babies. For a couple of years it looked as though the Tigers had made a good investment, but Dick Wakefield eventually drifted out of the game. In the opinion of most people, it was because baseball didn't mean very much to him.

At the end of 1941 Wakefield made it to the Tigers for seven at bats and then spent all of the next year in the minors. Recalled to Detroit in 1943, he hit .316 and led the American League with 200 hits and 38 doubles. Although World War II had depleted the majors' talent, the 6-foot-4, 210-pound Wakefield was considered a player with a big future.

He was even better the next season, hitting .355 with 12 homers and 53 RBIs in 78 games before being called into the military. But when he came back to the Tigers in 1946 he was not the same player. He hit .268 with 59 RBIs in 111 games that year, and in 1947 his numbers were .283 with 51 RBIs in 112 games. The following season he dropped to .276, and in 1949 his career nosedived when he hit an anemic .206 in 59 games.

Wakefield was traded to the Yankees and played three games for them in 1950. He was out of the majors for good after playing three games for the Giants in 1952, retiring with a .293 career batting average. He was only 31 years old.

Tim Wakefield

Wakefield, Timothy Stephen **P**

1992–93, 1995–* B:8/2/1966, Melbourne, FL Deb:7/31/1992, PIT NL BR/TR 6'2", 204

W	L	PCT	G	SH	IP	BB	SO	ERA
79	67	.541	216	6	1184^{2}	506	770	4.34

After washing out as an infielder, Tim Wakefield started throwing the knuckleball in the minor leagues. The Pittsburgh Pirates drafted him as a first baseman out of Florida Tech in 1988, but he hit just .189 in his first professional season. He was converted to pitcher in midseason 1989, and was baffling big leaguers just three years later.

In 13 starts, Wakefield notched an 8–1 record with a 2.15 ERA to help Pittsburgh win its third consecutive division title in 1992. He tossed two complete-game victories in a four-day span against the Atlanta Braves in the Championship Series. Unfortunately, he was unable to repeat that initial success. Following a sophomore season in which he went 6–11, Wakefield was sent to the minors; he led the American Association in hits, walks, runs allowed, and losses. He was released in April 1995, but was signed immediately by the Boston Red Sox.

Wakefield caught lightning in a bottle a second time, winning 16 games and posting a 2.95 ERA as Boston's ace. He helped the Red Sox win a division title and earned Comeback Player of the Year honors from *The Sporting News*. For the next three seasons, the veteran knuckleballer's performance in the Red Sox rotation was as erratic as his mainstay pitch. In 1999, however, Wakefield performed yeoman service for Boston in a surprising role. Called upon to work in relief by manager Jimy Williams after closer Tom Gordon was injured, Wakefield saved 15 games in 18 opportunities.

Rube Walberg

Walberg, George Elvin **P**

1923–37 B:7/27/1896, Pine City, MN D:10/27/1978, Tempe, AZ Deb:4/29/1923, NY NL BL/TL 6'1½", 190

W	L	PCT	G	SV	IP	BB	SO	ERA
155	141	.524	544	32	2644	1031	1085	4.16

George Elvin "Rube" Walberg was a tall, strong lefthander who was part of one of the most dominating pitching rotations in history. As a member of Connie Mack's Athletics for nine seasons, he worked on a staff that included Lefty Grove, Howard Ehmke, George Earnshaw, Eddie Rommel, and Jack Quinn. That staff won four American League earned run titles, in 1926, 1928, 1929, and 1931. And, with the great hitting of Jimmie Foxx, Mickey Cochrane, and Al Simmons, the A's won consecutive pennants from 1929 through 1931.

Walberg pitched long before the days when every team required a relief specialist. For his era, only hurlers Wilcy Moore of the Red Sox and Firpo Marberry of the Senators could be considered true bullpen aces. Walberg was used as both a starter and a reliever, starting 307 games during his career and relieving in 237.

With a lifetime record of 155–141, Walberg was not a Hall of Fame pitcher. His strengths were his

fastball and his ability to change speeds. Two things held him back: wildness, and an occasional lapse of concentration. In seven seasons during his career he walked more batters than he struck out. And while his teammate Grove was a study in high-voltage intensity, Walberg often had a casual approach to the game.

Once, early in his career, Walberg was loafing through a game when his catcher, Cochrane, walked to the mound, grabbed the young pitcher's shoulders, spun him around and delivered a swift kick to the hurler's posterior. Walberg got the message, but his change in attitude wasn't permanent. Years later, Cochrane on occasion still had to dispense verbal reminders to Walberg.

From 1927 through 1932, the glory years of the Athletics, Walberg won 101 games. However, he seldom fit into the postseason pitching plans of manager Mack. Fearful of the potent righthanded bats on the 1929 Cubs, Mack kept lefties Grove and Walberg on the bench, relying on Ehmke and Earnshaw. Walberg pitched in only two games of the World Series that year, both in relief, for a total of 6 ⅓ innings, although he did get the win in Game 5, the deciding contest.

The Philadelphia club didn't need Walberg's help in the following season's Fall Classic, either. Walberg started Game 3 against the Cardinals but couldn't last through the fifth inning and took the loss as the Athletics went on to win the championship. And in the 1931 Series loss to St. Louis he pitched only three innings in two relief appearances.

Jack Dunn, owner of Baltimore's International League team, originally signed Walberg. Dunn knew talent; he had also signed Babe Ruth and Lefty Grove. The Giants acquired Walberg from Dunn, but Walberg's attitude didn't please manager John McGraw, and Mack picked him up on waivers in 1923.

Already 28 years old at the start of the 1924 season, Walberg appeared in only six contests for Philadelphia that season, but by the next year he was starting 20 games and relieving in 33 more. He stayed a vital part of the Athletics' staff until 1933, when he had only his second losing season in a Philadelphia uniform, going 9–13.

That December, Mack completed the dismantling of his championship team, sending Walberg, Grove, and second baseman Max Bishop to the Red Sox. Walberg continued to serve as a swingman in Boston and remained there for four years, but he never won more than six games per year. He played his final season at the age of 41. After retirement Walberg tried his hand at a number of business ventures, from real estate to restaurants to golf courses.

Curt Walker

Walker, William Curtis **OF**

1919–30 B:7/3/1896, Beeville, TX D:12/9/1955, Beeville, TX Deb:9/17/1919, NY AL BL/TR 5'9½", 170

G	AB	R	H	HR	RBI	OBP	SLG	AVG
1359	4858	718	1475	64	688	.374	.440	.304

Curt Walker, nicknamed "Honey" because he came from Beeville, Texas, had a sweet swing that produced a lifetime batting average of .304 over 12 major league seasons. He began his big league career with the New York Yankees in 1919 and then jumped over to the National League New York Giants for the 1920 season. The Giants traded him along with two other players and $30,000 for Irish Meusel to the Philadelphia Phillies in July of 1921.

Walker became the Phillies' regular right fielder in 1922 and established himself as one of the best hitters in the league by batting .337 and knocking in 89 runs in 148 games. He was traded to the Cincinnati Reds in May of 1924 and was the team's regular right fielder for seven years.

In 1925, Walker led NL outfielders in fielding percentage, and in 1926 he achieved a rare feat at the plate by hitting two triples in one inning. In 1930, he scored five runs in a game. Upon his retirement from baseball in 1931 he was elected justice of the peace in his hometown of Beeville.

Dixie Walker

Walker, Fred **OF**

1931–49 B:9/24/1910, Villa Rica, GA D:5/17/1982, Birmingham, AL Deb:4/28/1931, NY AL BL/TR 6'1", 175

G	AB	R	H	HR	RBI	OBP	SLG	AVG
1905	6740	1037	2064	105	1023	.383	.437	.306

Fred "Dixie" Walker had a father, uncle, and brother who all played in the major leagues. Dixie and his brother "Harry the Hat" Walker are the only siblings to both win batting titles—Dixie in 1944, Harry in 1947. Together they compiled a lifetime batting average of .303. They were one of only six brother duos to bat a combined .300 or better lifetime.

After five years in the minors Walker was called up to the Yankees in 1933. Although the Yanks prematurely touted him as the next Babe Ruth, Walker responded with a creditable 15 homers.

That season he was involved in one of the wackiest plays in baseball history when, in a game against the Senators, the hustling right fielder nearly overtook Lou Gehrig on the base path, and both were tagged out as they slid into home only inches apart. After the game, rookie Washington manager Joe Cronin said, "That day, I realized anything could happen... This could be the year that Washington wins the pennant." They did, indeed.

Walker's zeal on the playing field also caused him some pain. He ripped a shoulder muscle when he collided with a wall and saw limited action until he was sold to the White Sox in 1936. In 1937 he drove in 95 runs, hit .302, and led the American League in triples with 16, but his shoulder was still a mess. Doctors tried a delicate operation that involved drilling holes in the bone and pulling the muscles through in order to keep them taut. Walker then tore loose cartilage in his knee. Sent to the Tigers in a six-player deal before the 1938 season, he managed to hit .308, but with almost no power his RBI total dropped to only 43.

The Tigers gave up on Walker during the 1939 season and released him. Dodgers general manager Larry MacPhail snatched him up—bad shoulder, torn cartilage, and all—for the waiver price, and Walker started a brand-new, highly successful eight-year career in Brooklyn.

Walker soon became one of the most popular players in Dodgers history. One reason Brooklyn fans took to him so quickly was the way he performed against the club's archenemy, the Giants. In 1940 Walker hit .436 against the team from Manhattan. There was only one full season in which he hit less than .300 in a Dodgers uniform, and he became known, in Brooklynese, as "the People's Cherce."

When he won the National League batting title in 1944, detractors pointed out that he had won it during the war years, when many stars were in the service. Walker reminded them that Stan Musial was 10 points behind him. In 1945 Walker hit .300 and scored 102 runs, while belting a career-high 42 doubles and a league-leading 124 RBIs.

As the league's first player representative, Walker spoke out in favor of contributing post-season and All-Star television profits to the players' pension package, and Commissioner Happy Chandler agreed with him. However, player reps in those days were mindful of the hands that fed them, and Walker obligingly supported the reserve clause when testifying before the U.S. Senate committee investigating baseball's antitrust exemption.

In 1947 owner Branch Rickey announced in spring training that Negro Leagues star Jackie Robinson would be joining the Dodgers. Walker challenged Rickey's decision by persuading other players to sign a petition stating that they would refuse to play if Robinson was on the roster. A late-night appeal by manager Leo Durocher quelled the revolt, but Walker did write to Rickey and ask to be traded. Rickey complied a year later, but it should be said of Walker that he was civil and helpful to Robinson while they were teammates.

Rickey's deal was one of the best the Dodgers ever pulled off. For the 37-year-old Walker and two other players the Dodgers got Preacher Roe, Billy Cox, and Gene Mauch from the Pirates. Walker continued to hit well after moving to Pittsburgh, and his .316 average helped the Bucs jump from the cellar to fourth place. In 1949 he led the National League in pinch hits, with 13. After that season he retired, a lifetime .306 hitter.

Walker spent nearly 28 years as a minor league manager and as a coach for the Cards, the Braves, and the Dodgers. One of his prize pupils was Steve Garvey. Looking back on his career, Walker conceded in a 1972 interview that Jackie Robinson was a great ballplayer.

Fleet Walker

Walker, Moses Fleetwood **C**

1884 B:10/7/1856, Mt. Pleasant, OH D:5/11/1924, Cleveland, OH Deb:5/1/1884, TOL AA BR/TR

G	AB	R	H	HR	RBI	OBP	SLG	AVG
42	152	23	40	0	—	.325	.316	.263

As most baseball history buffs know, Jackie Robinson was not the first black baseball player to reach the major leagues. That honor belongs to Moses Fleetwood Walker, a catcher with the 1884 Toledo team of the American Association.

His brother, Welday Walker, also played five games as an outfielder with the same club that year, but it is Moses, known as "Fleet," who is recognized as the first black to play in the majors, in part because he played regularly, sharing the catching duties with another rookie—James "Deacon" McGuire. Both Walker and McGuire were known primarily for their defense, although Walker out-hit McGuire during that season by nearly 80 points. McGuire went on to play 25 more years, the longest career of any player until Nolan Ryan, while Walker had only that one season in the majors.

The son of a physician, Walker attended and played baseball for both Oberlin College and the University of Michigan before turning professional with Toledo's Northwestern League team in 1883. When Toledo joined the American Association the next year, Walker was in the majors.

During this period Jim Crowism was rampant in America, and Walker had problems in some cities. He was forced to sit out a game in Louisville when a white player from the home team refused to play on the same field with him, and he was benched for an exhibition game in

Richmond, Virginia, when the Toledo manager received a letter threatening an attack if Walker played.

When Cap Anson brought his Chicago White Stockings to Toledo for an exhibition game, he threatened to pull his team off the field if Walker played. The Toledo manager called his bluff, and rather than go home without being paid for the trip, Anson backed down.

Toledo went under after the 1884 season, and Walker joined Cleveland of the Western League. He and other black players were not legally banned from Organized Baseball at that point; in fact, there were as many as 50 blacks in the minor leagues at one time or another.

By 1887, Walker was with Newark of the International League, where he and George Stovey formed baseball's first black battery. Newark booked a July exhibition game in Chicago, and Anson had a chance for revenge on his own turf. He went into a rage and forced Walker and Stovey out of the game.

At about the same time, major league owners passed a resolution banning black players because of the objections of white players, and the long period of segregation in Organized Baseball began. The resolution was later modified, merely proving that rules need not be written to be effective.

After two seasons with Syracuse, Walker retired to Ohio, where he operated a newspaper and an opera house and became an advocate of black emigration to Africa as a response to American racism.

Gee Walker

Walker, Gerald Holmes **OF**

1931–45 B:3/19/1908, Gulfport, MS D:3/20/1981, Whitfield, MS Deb:4/14/1931, DET AL BR/TR 5'11", 188

G	AB	R	H	HR	RBI	OBP	SLG	AVG
1784	6771	954	1991	124	997	.331	.430	.294

Gerald Holmes "Gee" Walker, a fast runner and solid hitter, was extremely erratic in the field and on the basepaths. Although not really a power hitter, he knocked in more than 75 runs in a season six times, twice exceeding 100 RBIs in a year.

Walker broke into the big leagues with the 1931 Detroit Tigers and spent seven seasons with the team, including trips to the World Series in 1934 and 1935. His reputation as a careless runner solidified in 1934, when manager Mickey Cochrane suspended him for 10 games for getting picked off base twice in the same game.

That same year, Walker was picked off first base in Game 2 of the World Series after he had delivered a ninth inning pinch single that knocked home the tying run. Walker was thoughtlessly arguing with St. Louis bench jockeys when pitcher Bill Walker (no relation) threw over to first base and caught him off guard.

In 1937, Walker was traded to the Chicago White Sox in a six-player deal and he spent two seasons with them before being sold to the Brooklyn Dodgers. Before seeing play, he went to the Washington Senators in a December trade. After a season with the Senators, during which he hit .294 and knocked in 96 runs, Walker was dealt to the Red Sox, who immediately sent him to Cleveland. He played one season for the Indians before being sold to the Cincinnati Reds, for whom he played his final four big-league campaigns. Walker sold real estate in Mississippi and Florida upon his retirement from baseball and was later named to the Mississippi Sports Hall of Fame.

Harry Walker

Walker, Harry William **OF**

1940–55 M(1955, 1965–72, 630–604) B:10/22/1916, Pascagoula, MS Deb:9/25/1940, STL NL BL/TR 6'2", 190

G	AB	R	H	HR	RBI	OBP	SLG	AVG
807	2651	385	786	10	214	.358	.383	.296

"Harry the Hat" Walker came from a baseball family. His father pitched in the majors for four seasons, his uncle played big league ball, and his brother Dixie was a major leaguer for 18 years. Walker and his sibling are one of six brother sets with a combined lifetime average of better than .300.

The Walkers are also the only two brothers in baseball history to both win batting titles. Dixie won his in 1944, when Harry was in the Army earning a Bronze Star and a Purple Heart in Germany. Harry Walker won his title three years later under odd circumstances. Because he had been traded during the season, his win represented the only time a player had led the league in hitting while appearing on two different teams in the same league.

"Harry the Hat," whose nickname derived from his habit of constantly tugging on his cap between pitches, began his big league career in 1940 with St. Louis. He did two things exceptionally well: hitting and talking. As a batter, he exceeded the .300 mark four times during seven seasons from 1942 through 1950, including his league-leading .363 in 1947. His most famous hit occurred during Game 7 of the 1946 World Series against the Red Sox. Cards teammate Enos Slaughter was running from first when Walker cracked a hit into left. The fleet-footed Slaughter ran through the third base coach's stop sign to score the run that decided the Series.

When Walker practiced his other skill—gabbing—which was most of the time, hitting was his favorite subject. As a manager he often drove his players to distraction with extended soliloquies on the art of batsmanship. During his final managerial job one of Walker's players expressed concern about Walker's health. "I don't know. Harry's a born .300 talker, but he's only talking about .280 this year," he said.

Walker's last full season as a player was 1949. From 1951 through 1954 he managed in the minors, and in midseason 1955 he took over the Cards' managerial post for the remaining 118 games. He piloted minor league teams following the 1955 season and from 1959 through 1962 had a stint as a coach for St. Louis, after which he went back to managing in the minors. In 1965 he was hired to manage the Pirates.

As Pittsburgh's skipper, he encouraged outfielder Matty Alou to use a bigger bat and to swing down on the ball in order to take advantage of his speed. Alou's batting average jumped a remarkable 111 points and he won the National League batting title. Walker had a similar effect on Roberto Clemente. As soon as Walker arrived in Pittsburgh he treated Clemente as the team's leader and star, giving the outfielder the respect he had always craved but had never really received. Clemente's career took a dramatic upturn.

After finishing sixth the previous year, the Bucs under Walker finished third twice, and in 1966 they were in the chase until the final weeks of the season. But Walker's inability to handle pitchers caused clubhouse strife. The Pirates replaced him with Danny Murtaugh 84 games into the 1967 season. Walker then went to Houston as batting coach. In 1968 he took over for Grady Hatton as Astros manager 61 games into the campaign.

Walker's loud carping about hitting was even more of a problem in Houston than it had been in Pittsburgh. Outfielders Bob Watson and Cesar Cedeno both seemed to improve at the plate, but Houston players as a whole had trouble dealing with Walker. In 1972, with the team in second place, they openly revolted. Walker was fired in midseason and Leo Durocher took his job. After the season the Astros voted to give Durocher a full Series share and to give Walker nothing, but Durocher made them reconsider.

Walker's last job in baseball was as a special batting instructor for the Cardinals in 1973. In an 11-year playing career he averaged .296 in 2,651 at bats. He made the All-Star team in 1943.

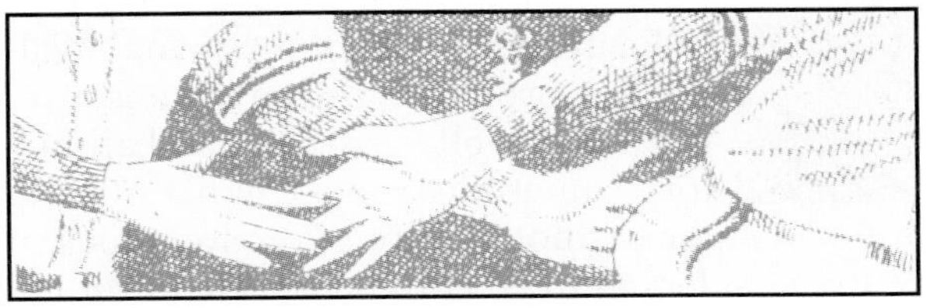

Larry Walker

Walker, Larry Kenneth Robert **OF**

1989–* B:12/1/66, Maple Ridge, British Columbia, Canada Deb:8/16/1989, MON NL BL/TL, 6'3", 215

G	AB	R	H	HR	RBI	OBP	SLG	AVG
1298	4592	886	1431	262	855	.393	.567	.312

Larry Walker got his first major league hit in his first major league game, off San Francisco's Mike LaCoss on August 16, 1989. By the end of the 1999 season he had added 1430 more hits, during a decade that saw him blossom into one of the game's great stars. After moving to the Colorado Rockies in 1995 from the Montreal Expos, Walker's batting averages soared as high as Coors Stadium, with home run and RBI totals to match. He won back-to-back batting crowns in 1998 (.363) and 1999 (.379); those marks, plus his .366 in 1997, made Walker the first player since Al Simmons (1929–31) to hit over .360 in three straight seasons.

As a rookie with the Expos in 1990, Walker tied Andre Dawson's club record with 19 first-year home runs. He also tied for the National League lead in outfield assists (12), and in 1991 tied a major league record with two outfield assists in one inning against St. Louis. Walker appeared in his first All-Star Game in 1992. He also placed fifth in the National League Most Valuable Player balloting, won his first Silver Slugger Award, and captured the first of two consecutive Gold Gloves. His 16 outfield assists led the league—he even nailed two runners at first base on apparent singles.

The Canadian native was one of several All-Star caliber players to leave the Expos when the players' strike ended the 1994 season. Signed by the Colorado Rockies as a free agent, the thin air in Denver had an immediate impact on Walker. He ranked second in the NL in home runs, total bases, slugging percentage, and extra-base hits in 1995, helping the Rockies reach the playoffs for the first time. A broken collarbone curtailed his 1996 season, yet he still managed to set an NL record with extra-base hits in six consecutive at bats (two doubles, three triples, one homer) against Pittsburgh on May 21 and 22.

Walker's golden year was 1997. He was named the National League's MVP in a landslide vote after leading the league with 49 home runs and driving in 130. His power display was not due to a Coors Field advantage, as 29 of his home runs were hit on the road. Walker's .720 slugging percentage was the fifth highest in NL history, and his 409 total bases were the most in the majors since Stan Musial's 429 in 1948. He came within four hits of winning the NL's first Triple Crown since Joe Medwick in 1937.

Walker was criticized for sitting out against former minor league buddy and nasty lefthander

Randy Johnson during interleague play in June 1997. A few weeks later Walker faced Johnson in the first inning of the All-Star Game. Johnson flew the first pitch over Walker's head. Without blinking, Walker stepped across home plate, put his batting helmet on backwards, and stood in as a righthanded hitter against "the Big Unit." The humorous exchange ended with Walker earning a walk.

After another banner year in 1998, Walker's 1999 season was cut short by a knee injury. Even so, he qualified for his second consecutive batting title, topping Arizona's Luis Gonzalez by a whopping 43 points. He won his fifth Gold Glove (and third in a row) and appeared in his fourth All-Star Game.

Rube Walker

Walker, Albert Bluford **C**

1948–58 B:5/16/1926, Lenoir, NC D:12/12/1992, Morganton, NC Deb:4/20/1948, CHI NL BL/TR 6'1", 185

G	AB	R	H	HR	RBI	OBP	SLG	AVG
608	1585	114	360	35	192	.296	.341	.227

Rube Walker's tenure as a major league player was unremarkable. In 11 years as a backup catcher, Walker fielded well but hit only .227 and never had more than 213 at bats in a season. It was as a pitching coach for the Mets that he made his name and left a legacy—the five-day rotation.

As a child, Albert Bluford Walker got his nickname because he spent a lot of time hanging around the ballpark with a player called "Rube." Walker started in pro ball in 1943 with Erwin of the Appalachian League and made it to the Cubs in 1948, hitting .275 in 79 games.

On June 15, 1951, Walker was traded to the Dodgers. He became a footnote in baseball history as the man who called the Ralph Branca pitch that the Giants' Bobby Thomson hit for that year's pennant-winning home run. Walker was behind the plate in that game because Brooklyn's regular catcher, Roy Campanella, was out with a hurt knee.

Walker spent the rest of his career with the Dodgers. In 1958, his last year in the majors, he served as player-coach. He managed in the minors for the next six seasons and in 1965 became Gil Hodges' pitching coach with the Senators. After three seasons Walker followed Hodges to the Mets. The Mets' system had produced a bumper crop of fine young pitchers, including Tom Seaver, Jerry Koosman, Nolan Ryan, Gary Gentry, and Tug McGraw. Walker and Hodges decided to establish a five-day rotation to ensure that their young power pitchers weren't overworked. At the time, the four-day rotation was still the norm. But after the Mets won the World Series in 1969, the rest of the majors adopted the five-man rotation.

Walker stayed with the Mets through 1981 as pitching coach for managers Hodges, Yogi Berra, Joe Frazier, and Joe Torre. Later Walker joined Torre in Atlanta for three years, retiring after Torre's firing in 1984.

"Rube's biggest strength was his concern for the long-term physical well-being of his pitching staff," said Seaver. The careers of Walker's protégés support this: Seaver pitched until he was 41 years old, Koosman until he was 42, McGraw until he was 40, and Ryan until 46.

Tilly Walker

Walker, Clarence William **OF**

1911–23 B:9/4/1887, Telford, TN D:9/20/1959, Unicoi, TN Deb:4/12/1911, WAS AL BR/TR 5'11", 165

G	AB	R	H	HR	RBI	OBP	SLG	AVG
1421	5067	696	1423	118	679	.339	.427	.281

Clarence William "Tilly" Walker was a late bloomer. A power-hitting outfielder, he had his first big season at age 30, when he tied Babe Ruth for the American League home run title. Walker started in the majors in 1911 with the Senators, was sold to the St. Louis Browns after the next season, and hit .298 in 1914, his first year as a regular. His six homers tied for third in the league. After a mediocre season in 1915, he was sold to Boston, where he continued to struggle for two years.

His career turned around after a trade to the A's in 1918. His 11 homers that season tied Babe Ruth for the league lead. Two years later, he hit 17 homers, third best in the league, as the lively ball era dawned. Walker followed with his best seasons, hitting .304 with 23 homers and a career-best 101 RBIs in 1921. The following season, at age 35, he blasted 37 homers, second in the league, and 99 RBIs. But when Connie Mack decided that home runs were a passing fad and decided to move back the fences and emphasize speed in 1924, Walker's run was over. He played in only 52 games and hit two homers that season, his last in the majors. He spent the next six seasons in the minors before retiring.

Bobby Wallace

Wallace, Roderick John **SS–3B**

1894–1918 M(1911–12, 1937, 62–154) B:11/4/1873, Pittsburgh, PA D:11/3/1960, Torrance, CA Deb:9/15/1894, CLE NL BR/TR 5'8", 170

G	AB	R	H	HR	RBI	OBP	SLG	AVG
2383	8618	1057	2309	34	1121	.332	.358	.268

Of all the players enshrined in the Hall of Fame, Roderick John "Bobby" Wallace is probably the most obscure. Even fans well versed in baseball history sometimes have trouble placing him. His name is not on any of the long lists of batting leaders in the record books. He never led his league in a single offensive category, and his career batting average is one of the lowest among position players in the Hall of Fame. He was not a World Series hero, and he never played for a pennant-winning team.

Neither is his biography festooned with amusing anecdotes. Wallace was in no way a "character" himself, and he apparently spent little time hanging out with those who were. He was, according to contemporary accounts, a very good fielding shortstop, but the statistics are equivocal. Although he led American League shortstops in fielding percentage two times, he also led in errors twice. He spent 25 years in the major leagues, a very long career, but during nine of those seasons he played only part-time.

Nevertheless, in 1911 when Ty Cobb, Tris Speaker, and Nap Lajoie were the toast of the AL, Pittsburgh Pirates owner Barney Dreyfuss said, "The best player in the American League, the only man I would get if I could, plays on a tail-end team, and few people pay any attention to him. I mean Bobby Wallace of St. Louis. I wish I had him." At the time, Wallace was 37 and coming off a season in which he hit only .258. But Dreyfuss was a reliable judge of shortstops. On his own team was a fellow named Honus Wagner.

As a youngster, Wallace worked in his brother-in-law's feed store in Millvale, Pennsylvania, and pitched for a semipro team in nearby Franklin for $45 a month. One day early in 1894 he went into Pittsburgh to try out with the Pirates but was turned away by manager Connie Mack as "too small." (Eventually, Wallace grew to 5-foot-8 and 170 pounds, nearly average for a player of his day.) After Mack's refusal, Wallace went back to Franklin and the prospect of a life in the feed store. In September, however, he received a wire from George "Patsy" Tebeau of the Cleveland Spiders, who was desperate for a pitcher.

On September 15, 1894, Wallace made his major league debut against Boston. He was shelled, giving up 14 hits in six innings. A few days later he defeated the Philadelphia Phillies, and before the season ended he earned a second win. The next year he was a regular starter, going 12–14 as the Spiders finished second to the Baltimore Orioles. At the time, the National League was the only major circuit, and at the end of the season, the first-place and second-place teams played for the Temple Cup in an attempt to elicit some postseason enthusiasm from the fans. That year the Orioles took little interest in the contest and were easy victims of the Spiders. Wallace sat on the bench throughout the five-game series.

On July 21, 1896, Zeke Wilson and Wallace tossed back-to-back shutouts in a doubleheader against Washington. As the season ended, the Orioles and Spiders had once again finished first and second. The Orioles, stung by criticism of their lackadaisical play the year before, disposed of the Spiders in four straight one-sided contests. Wallace lost the second game, 7–2.

That appearance, save a two-inning stint in 1902, ended his pitching career. In 1897 Tebeau moved Wallace to third base to replace aging Chippy McGarr. Wallace responded with the best offensive year of his career, batting .335, scoring 99 runs, and driving in 112. On July 14 he hit the only grand slam of his major league career.

He continued to hit well in 1898, prompting Tebeau to make another switch. Shortstop Ed McKean was fading, and Wallace was moved over in 1899. As Wallace said later, "I knew I had found my niche."

The Spiders made a switch of their own in 1899. The Robison brothers, who owned the Cleveland franchise, contrived to purchase the bankrupt St. Louis club. Dissatisfied with the attendance in Cleveland, they moved the Spiders' best players to St. Louis. The new St. Louis club, nicknamed the "Perfectos," expected to contend for the pennant. But despite the presence of such stars as Cy Young, Jesse Burkett, Tebeau, and Wallace, the team never jelled in its new surroundings.

The National League froze player salaries at a maximum $2,500, so in 1901 Wallace accepted an offer to jump to the American League. He was told he would be paid one of the top salaries in the new league but soon learned that others were receiving a great deal more. He angrily abrogated his contract before ever playing a game and returned to St. Louis, where he hit .324, the second-highest average of his career. On May 4 of that season he had 12 assists as shortstop in one game.

In 1902 the American League withdrew its weak Milwaukee franchise and established a team in St. Louis—the Browns—to confront the established NL Cardinals. To woo fans, the Browns offered Wallace a $6,500 advance and a five-year, no-trade contract for $32,500, likely making him the highest-paid player in baseball. He signed, and with Wallace at shortstop, the Browns finished second. Without him, the Cardinals won 20 fewer games than the previous season.

That was the Browns' high point for years to come. Wallace remained their regular shortstop through 1912 and stayed on in a substitute role for four more seasons, but only once did the team climb as high as fourth place. Wallace led AL

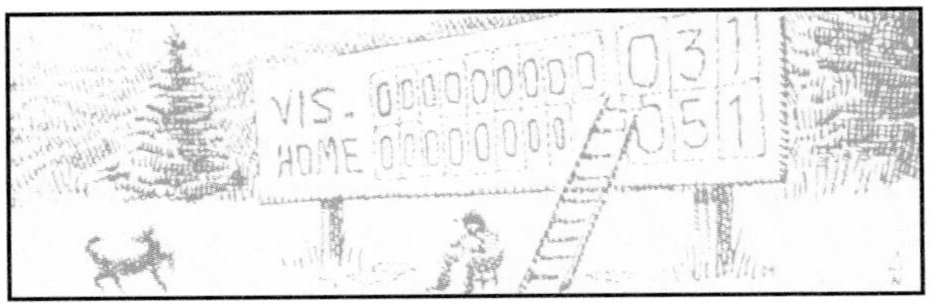

shortstops in fielding in 1905 and 1908, but he hit poorly. In no full season after 1905 did he hit above .258. In 1911, against his better judgment, he agreed to try his hand as the Browns' manager. Early the next season, with the team still mired in eighth place, he was replaced as skipper, although he continued to play shortstop.

In 1912 Wallace missed part of the season with a broken hand, and in 1914 he was seriously burned in an accident. He became an American League umpire in 1915 but quit and returned to the Browns before the season ended. He tried managing at Wichita of the Western League in 1917, but after being released in June, he signed back with the Cardinals. He played only 32 games in 1918, and then retired as a player.

Although Wallace's career batting average was only .268, his cumulative statistics are fairly impressive: he collected 2,309 hits, scored 1,057 runs, knocked in 1,121 runs, and stole 201 bases. Wallace later managed in the minors, coached for Cincinnati, and worked as a scout for the Reds for 33 years. In 1953, seven years before his death, he was named to the Hall of Fame.

Tim Wallach

Wallach, Timothy Charles **3B**
1980–96 B:9/14/1957, Huntington Park, CA
Deb:9/6/1980, MON NL BR/TR, 6'3", 200

G	AB	R	H	HR	RBI	OBP	SLG	AVG
2212	8099	908	2085	260	1125	.319	.416	.257

Tim Wallach homered in his first plate appearance as a pro and duplicated the feat in his first major league at bat. During a 17-year career in the majors, he led the league in doubles twice and won three Gold Gloves at third base. He topped 20 homers five times.

Wallach spent his first 13 seasons with the Montreal Expos, where he became team captain and played in five All-Star games. He set club records for career hits, doubles, and RBIs. Although Wallach never made it to the World Series, he helped three teams finish first: the Expos in 1981 and the Los Angeles Dodgers in 1995 and 1996.

A Southern Californian, Wallach jumped at the chance to complete his career in Los Angeles. With the Expos anxious to cut costs and age from their roster, he was traded to the Dodgers in November 1992. Although Wallach hit 23 homers in 113 games for the 1994 Dodgers, he did not deliver the offense the club had expected. He joined the California Angels in 1996, but was released by the last-place team in midseason. The Dodgers picked him up again and Wallach was the team's third baseman through the Division Series. He retired after the season.

Denny Walling

Walling, Dennis Martin **OF-3B-1B**
1975–92 B:4/17/1954, Neptune, NJ Deb:9/7/1975, OAK AL BL/TR 6'1", 185

G	AB	R	H	HR	RBI	OBP	SLG	AVG
1271	2945	372	799	49	380	.341	.390	.271

Dennis Martin "Denny" Walling was a valuable utility player for the Houston Astros from 1977 to 1988. The Oakland Athletics selected the college All-American in the secondary phase of the 1975 draft but traded him to Houston in 1977. He started out as an outfielder but also saw duty at first base with the Astros from 1980 through 1982. In 1983 the club gave him a trial at third. Initially, he was a poor defensive third baseman, but through hard work he became better than average at the position. His versatility at three positions enabled him to become a valuable part of the team.

Walling still holds the Astros' all-time record for pinch hits. His most dramatic hit for Houston was a home run that clinched the 1986 National League West title on the same day that his teammate Mike Scott pitched a no-hitter.

Walling was traded to St. Louis for pitcher Bob Forsch in August 1988. He spent a few seasons with the Cardinals before becoming a free agent and signing with the Texas Rangers. He later returned to the Astros to finish his career. In 1999 he was a roving instructor in the Baltimore Orioles system.

Ed Walsh

Walsh, Edward Augustine **P**
1904–17 M(1924, 1–2) B:5/14/1881, Plains, PA
D:5/26/1959, Pompano Beach, FL Deb:5/7/1904,
CHI AL BR/TR 6'1", 193

W	L	PCT	G	SH	IP	BB	SO	ERA
195	126	.607	430	57	2964^{1}	617	1736	1.82

"Big Ed" Walsh never lacked self-confidence. One sportswriter described him as "the only man I ever saw who could strut standing still." Walsh had an unbounded faith in his pitching ability, and most of the time it was warranted.

The youngest of 13 children of an Irish immigrant coal miner, Edward Augustine Walsh worked in the mines and developed strong shoulders and arms on his 6-foot-1, 193-pound frame. After playing baseball for a local semipro team, he turned professional and began pitching for Wilkes-Barre of the Pennsylvania State League in 1902. Walsh appeared in only four games and collected one win before moving up to Meriden of the Connecticut League, where he went 15–5. In 1903 the righthander won 11 for Meriden and nine for Newark of the Eastern League.

His 20 wins got the attention of Chicago White Sox owner Charles Comiskey, whose interest grew when he learned that Walsh threw only fastballs and wasn't considered a red-hot prospect. Walsh was available for only $750. When given the choice between an expensive, highly touted prospect and an affordable sleeper, Comiskey always voted with his wallet.

At White Sox training camp in 1904 Walsh roomed with Elmer Stricklett, a minor league pitcher who threw a spitball and was willing to pass on his knowledge to anyone interested. He told Walsh to spit between the seams of the baseball, grip it with his fingers between the seams, and throw it like a fastball. The resulting pitch had the speed of a fastball but no rotation, which caused it to break like a knuckleball.

Stricklett later pitched for a couple of weak Brooklyn teams, but he never had the opportunity to work for a contender. Another Stricklett pupil, "Happy" Jack Chesbro of the New York Highlanders, flourished with the spitball and won 41 games in 1904, the 20th-century record. Chesbro had already experimented with a spitter, but under Stricklett's tutelage he gained command of the pitch.

Walsh liked the new pitch but, like Chesbro, he couldn't control it initially. For two years he struggled by with just a fastball. Walsh won 14 games during limited pitching opportunities in 1904 and 1905, but in 1906 he finally got his spitter under control.

The 1906 Chicago White Sox are legendary. The dead ball had depressed offensive production everywhere, but few teams were as affected as Chicago. American League teams combined for a meager .249 batting average, and the White Sox's average of .230 was lowest in the league. Five Chicago regulars batted lower than .250. Only Boston in the National League, loser of 102 games, had worse hitting. But the White Sox won the pennant and earned the nickname "the Hitless Wonders."

The White Sox didn't compensate for their lack of hitting with power; their seven home runs were last in the league, as was their slugging average of .286. Yet they were not totally inept offensively. Using speed, walks, and timely, if infrequent, base hits, they scored more runs than five of the league's other teams.

The strength of the White Sox was good defense and great pitching. Righthander Frank Owen won 22 games. Nick Altrock won 20, and fellow lefty Doc White won 18. Walsh, with his new spitball, was 17–13, and he led the league with 10 shutouts and compiled a sparkling 1.88 ERA. Still, the Sox were in fourth place as late as August, but they surged into first place during a 19-game winning streak to take the pennant by three games over the Highlanders.

The Sox faced the Chicago Cubs in the only all-Chicago World Series. The Tinker-to-Evers-to-Chance Cubs had slaughtered their National League foes on the way to an all-time record 116 victories; the Series looked like a mismatch. Yet the Sox still had some momentum after their furious September finish, while the Cubs had coasted in with a big lead for the last month of the season.

Altrock outdueled "Three Finger" Brown, 2–1, in the opener. The Cubs' Ed Reulbach evened the score, one-hitting the Sox the following day. Walsh pitched Game 3. The spitball had rarely been seen in the NL, and the Cubs struck out 12 times and registered only two hits while losing, 3–0. But the Cubs came back as Brown tossed a two-hitter to edge Altrock, 1–0, in Game 4.

In the crucial fifth game, White Sox manager Fielder Jones called on Walsh. Walsh wasn't at his best, but neither was the White Sox defense. They made six errors and allowed four unearned runs to score. Walsh gave up two earned runs himself but left in the seventh inning with an 8–6 lead. After being held to just 11 hits in the first four games, the Pale Hose uncharacteristically exploded for 12 hits in Game 5. Doc White pitched three shutout innings in relief, and the Sox held on for a 3–2 lead in the Series.

The following day the White Sox crushed Brown and Orval Overall for 14 hits to win, 8–3, and become world champions. In six games Sox batters had hit only .198, but Walsh, White, Altrock, and Owen held the Cubs to a .196 clip.

Owner Comiskey was so pleased with the upset that he threw an extra $15,000 into the World Series pot to be divided among his players. The move was atypical for the tightfisted Comiskey; after thinking it over, he decided to count the "bonus" against the players' 1907 salary. Although the White Sox players were upset by the owner's move, they still fought for the 1907 pennant until the last week of the season before succumbing to Detroit.

That year Walsh went 24–18. The team's poor hitting cost him, as he was shut out eight times. He completed a league-leading 37 of his 46 starts, led all pitchers with 422 ⅓ innings pitched, and posted a league-leading 1.60 earned run average. He also relieved in 10 games and, under modern rules, earned four saves.

In 1908 Walsh had one of the best seasons in major league history. He led the league with 40 victories, 66 appearances, 42 complete games, 464 innings pitched (the modern record), 269 strikeouts, 11 shutouts, and six saves. His ERA was a skimpy 1.42. Detroit, Cleveland, and Chicago fought to the end for the pennant, and Walsh pitched seven of the last nine games.

On September 27 he beat Boston, 3–0. Two days later he pitched a doubleheader against the Bosox and won, 5–1 and 2–0. On October 2 he pitched brilliantly in a losing effort against Cleveland, striking out 15 and allowing only a single unearned run while the Indians' Addie Joss twirled a perfect game. Three days later Walsh held the Tigers to a single run to record his 40th victory. But the Sox finished third, a game and a half behind pennant-winning Detroit.

When Walsh slipped to 15–11 in 1909, critics speculated that he had been overworked the previous two seasons. That may have been true, but there was another reason for his ineffectiveness. Cleveland shortstop Neal Ball had noticed that, although Walsh went to his mouth before every pitch, he threw the spitter only when he also pulled the bill of his cap. Word got around, and until it got back to Walsh, hitters could tell whether he was going to throw a fastball or spitball. Despite his off year, Walsh still led the league with eight shutouts and lowered his ERA to 1.41.

In 1910 Walsh went a misleading 18–20; he paced the league with a career-low 1.27 ERA. The White Sox compiled a miserable .211 team batting average and committed 314 errors. Comiskey finally got Walsh some support in 1911, and the pitcher posted consecutive 27-win seasons. On August 27, 1911, he beat Boston, 5–0, on a no-hitter. At the end of the 1912 season the White Sox and Cubs played a series of exhibitions in Chicago. Walsh, pitching nearly every day, hurled four complete games and relieved twice. The next spring his arm was shot.

He struggled through another four seasons, never pitching more than 100 innings. In 1916 he asked Comiskey for a year off to rest his arm. Instead, he was released. A comeback attempt with the Boston Braves ended after 18 innings. At a farewell dinner he told the audience, "I won't say it is the happiest moment of my life because it isn't. The happiest moments of my life were spent playing baseball."

Walsh managed in the minors in 1920, umpired in the AL in 1922, and coached baseball at Notre Dame in 1926. During most of the 1920s he was a White Sox coach. His son, Edward Arthur Walsh, pitched for the Sox from 1928 through 1932 but compiled a mediocre 11–24 record. Walsh retired in Connecticut until arthritis forced him to move to Florida in 1957. He died two years later at age 78.

Although Walsh spent 14 seasons in the majors, most of his career statistics were accumulated in the seven seasons from 1906 through 1912. He finished with a record of 195–126, with 57 shutouts, and a 1.82 ERA, the lowest career ERA for any pitcher with more than 1,000 innings. He was also a superior fielder, a fair hitter, and the first American League pitcher to steal home twice. He was elected to the Hall of Fame in 1946.

Bucky Walters

Walters, William Henry **P–3B**

1931–50 M(1948–49, 81–123) B:4/19/1909, Philadelphia, PA D:4/20/1991, Abington, PA Deb:9/18/1931, BOS NL BR/TR 6'1", 180

W	L	PCT	G	SH	IP	BB	SO	ERA
198	160	.553	428	42	3104^2	1121	1107	3.30

G	AB	R	H	HR	RBI	OBP	SLG	AVG
715	1966	227	477	23	234	.286	.344	.243

Bucky Walters started his professional career as a pitcher but failed miserably. He then detoured into a lengthy stint at third base. When a ballclub desperate for pitching switched him back to the mound, they created a Most Valuable Player and provided the National League with its dominant pitcher during World War II.

Growing up, William Henry Walters played sandlot ball around the Philadelphia area and was offered a contract to play with Montgomery in the Class B Southeastern League. His grandmother scraped up $10 to buy him a suitcase, and off he went. He washed out at Montgomery, however, and was sent to High Point in the Class C Piedmont League. Walters was a pitcher then but a poor one, going just 5–6 with a 5.29 ERA, 20 strikeouts, and 40 walks. He could hit, though, batting an even .300, and he was soon converted to an infielder.

Walters started the following year with Portland of the New England League. When the circuit folded in late June, he hooked up with Williamsport and hit .326 in 1931, leading to his acquisition by the Boston Braves. In two partial seasons with Boston, Walters hit .211 and .187. He was sold outright to the San Francisco Missions, for whom he hit .376 in 91 games in 1933 before the Red Sox purchased him.

Walters hit a grand slam for the Sox on May 13, 1934, but overall he was a disappointment. Twenty-three games into the 1934 season, with his average barely above .200, he was sold on waivers to Gerry Nugent's Phillies. Philadelphia was not a prosperous club under normal circumstances, and during the Depression things were worse. Recalled Walters: "The Phillies would make a western trip just praying they wouldn't get rained out in Chicago on Saturday or Sunday so they'd have enough money to get home."

Dividing his time between the Red Sox and the Phillies in 1934, Walters hit eight homers (a career high) and drove in 56 runs. But Phils player-manager Jimmie Wilson thought he could use Walters to bolster his rather pitiful staff, often shell-shocked from having to pitch in the Baker Bowl. Twice Wilson pitched him in 1934, and the results were excellent, but Walters didn't want to return to the mound.

In the spring, however, Wilson told coach Hans Lobert to convince Walters that pitching was his ticket to fame and fortune. Also, the Phils had just acquired third baseman Johnny Vergez, who might take Walters' job anyway. Finally Walters relented, saying, "I'll give pitching a try, but there's one thing I want understood before I do. If I don't make it as a pitcher, I want another chance at third."

Wilson agreed and then sweetened the deal by offering Walters $100 for every game he won during the season. His first victory was a 2–1 squeaker over the world champion Cardinals. Another early win was a 1–0 decision over Chicago, in which Walters drove in Wilson with the winning run.

In 1935 Walters was 9–9, and although he lost a league-leading 21 games the following season, he led the National League with four shutouts. In 1937 he led the league in games started, and on September 29 he hit the second grand slam of his career. Walters was now a valuable commodity for the Phillies president, who often had to sell players to pay his bills. As the 1938 trading deadline approached, Reds general manager Warren Giles made an offer the impoverished Nugent could not easily refuse: two players plus $50,000 for the pitcher.

The acquisition of Walters, just 4–8 at the time, did not make headlines in Cincinnati, where the double no-hit activities of Johnny Vander Meer were about to monopolize the news. In fact, during Vander Meer's second no-hitter, Walters was ordered to warm up in the Reds bullpen, leading to a storm of boos from the Ebbets Field fans, who uncharacteristically were pulling for an opponent that night.

But soon Walters was in the spotlight. For the remainder of 1938 he was 11–6 with Cincinnati, giving him a winning record for the season. The next year saw him win 27 games to help propel Cincinnati to its first pennant in 20 years. Walters captured the pitching Triple Crown, leading the

National League in victories, ERA, and strikeouts. He also batted .325 to join a short list of pitchers to win 20 games and hit .300 in the same season. Walters won the league's Most Valuable Player Award and was named *The Sporting News* All-Around Player of 1939.

In the World Series that year he lost Game 2 as a starter and Game 4 as a reliever as the Yankees swept the Reds. Not that he got very much in the way of offensive or defensive support. In Game 2 Cincinnati was no-hit for seven and a third innings and finished with just two hits. In Game 4 the Reds committed three errors in the 10th inning, allowing the Yankees to score three runs and win the Series. However, Walters would soon get a chance to redeem himself.

Following the 1939 season Walters received a raise to $22,000, the most money he'd ever make in the big leagues. He earned it in 1940, leading the league in victories and ERA, and the Reds repeated as pennant winners. In the Series that year the Reds faced catching problems. Most devastating, Willard Hershberger had committed suicide in August. Ernie Lombardi was temporarily sidelined from a badly twisted ankle. By default the job of catching in the Fall Classic went to Walters' old friend Wilson, now a coach under Cincinnati manager Bill McKechnie The 40-year-old Wilson hit .353 against Detroit in the Series.

Walters started Game 2 and was a mess. His first eight pitches were balls. Wilson walked slowly out to the mound and said, "Now look, just calm down. You're throwing too hard. Just be yourself. Let them hit the ball." Walters took the advice. Charlie Gehringer smashed a single into right, but after that Walters settled down and pitched a complete-game victory.

Cincinnati trailed in the Series, three games to two, when Walters took the mound for Game 6. He hurled a five-hit shutout and contributed a homer to his cause. The Reds scored two runs in the seventh inning of Game 7 and held on for the win, 2–1, for their first world championship since the tainted Series of 1919.

Walters had another big year in 1944, when he led the league with 23 victories. From 1939 through 1944 he was perhaps the most powerful pitcher in baseball. His total of 121 victories during that stretch was 20 more than his closest competitor, Mort Cooper. Walters also ranked first in ERA, with 2.67, among all pitchers with more than 1,000 innings pitched. Never a control pitcher, Walters relied on a sinking fastball and sweeping curveball for his effectiveness. Remarkably, 42 of his 198 lifetime victories were shutouts.

On May 20, 1945, Walters hit two of his 11 major league home runs. But on July 31 he injured his arm in a 2–0 shutout against the Cardinals. He was unable to finish the game and worked in only two more contests the rest of season. He came back in 1946 to go 10–7 and achieve a baseball rarity by stealing home in a game on April 20. His ERA of 2.46 was under 3.00 for the eighth time in nine years. But despite an 8–8 record the following season, his ERA ballooned to 5.75.

Still on the Reds' active roster, Walters replaced Johnny Neun as club manager in early August 1948. Although Walters is often credited with the development of Ewell Blackwell, the new skipper could only get the team as high as seventh and was let go with three games remaining in the 1949 season.

In 1952 Walters became the last manager in Milwaukee minor league history, replacing interim manager Red Smith in June. Walters took the club to a first-place finish, and then became a Milwaukee Braves coach in 1953.

Bill Wambsganss

Wambsganss, William Adolph **2B-SS**

1914–26 B:3/19/1894, Cleveland, OH D:12/8/1985, Lakewood, OH Deb:8/4/1914, CLE AL BR/TR 5'11", 175

G	AB	R	H	HR	RBI	OBP	SLG	AVG
1491	5237	710	1359	7	520	.328	.327	.259

In 1920 Cleveland second baseman Bill Wambsganss secured a place in baseball history by pulling off one of the most spectacular plays ever—an unassisted triple play in the World Series. The feat had never been done before, and through 1999 it hadn't been done since.

As a young man William Adolph Wambsganss, the son of a Lutheran minister, was preparing to follow in his father's footsteps by entering a theological seminary in St. Louis. He was simply not cut out for the job, however, because he was absolutely terrified of public speaking. As he later recalled, "Unfortunately, nobody there was willing to take the bull by the horns and say right out that this kid just wouldn't make a good minister. So I went through. It's a joke, but I did."

It is said that the Creator works in mysterious ways. At the seminary was another student who had played professional baseball. In 1913 the manager of the Cedar Rapids club wrote to him, asking if he knew of any good shortstops. He recommended Wambsganss.

Wambsganss played for Cedar Rapids that season and part of the next, and in August 1914 he was sold to the Cleveland Indians. At Cleveland he was converted into a second baseman and combined with shortstop Ray Chapman for a smooth keystone combo.

Despite Chapman's death from a beaning during the 1920 season, the Indians won the American League pennant and played the Brooklyn Robins in the World Series that fall. With the Series knotted at two games apiece, the teams squared off for Game 5 on Sunday, October 10. The Indians broke through in the first inning, scoring four runs on right fielder Elmer Smith's grand slam, the first in Series history. In the fourth inning Cleveland starter Jim Bagby made it 7–0 when he smacked a three-run homer into the center field bleachers, the first World Series homer ever by a pitcher.

In the fifth inning Brooklyn second baseman Pete Kilduff led off with a single against Bagby, followed by another single from catcher Otto Miller. The Robins had runners on first and second with none out. Next up was Clarence Mitchell, a good-hitting pitcher who had relieved starter Burleigh Grimes. Brooklyn manager Wilbert Robinson signaled for a hit-and-run.

Kilduff and Miller took off, and Mitchell sent a screaming line drive in the direction of second base. Wambsganss hadn't been near the bag when the pitch was thrown, but he ran frantically and dove for the ball, coming up with a beautiful one-handed grab for the first out. By now Kilduff had almost reached third, and it took little effort for Wambsganss to scramble to his feet and touch second for a double play. In the next moment, Wambsganss seemed about to throw the ball to first for an easy third out, but Cleveland shortstop Joe Sewell yelled, "Tag him! Tag him!"

"You see," Sewell recalled, "Bill had run to the bag, made sure he touched it, but hadn't yet looked toward first base. He had his arm cocked to throw, but when he looked around there was Otto Miller, running right toward him. Bill just went up to him and touched him on the chest with the ball, just as easy as saying hello. I think that was the first that Otto Miller realized the ball had been caught. When Bill touched him, Miller stopped in his tracks with the most dumbfounded look on his face."

The 26,884 fans at Cleveland's League Park weren't quite sure what they had witnessed. "So there was dead silence for a few seconds," recalled Wambsganss. "Then as I approached the dugout, it began to dawn on them what they had just seen, and the cheering started and got quickly louder and louder and louder. By the time I got back to the bench it was bedlam, straw hats flying onto the field, people yelling themselves hoarse, my teammates pounding me on the back."

Wambsganss died in 1985 at the age of 91. In 13 years in the big leagues he amassed 1,359 hits in 1,491 games and recorded 3,411 putouts and 4,262 assists, but he will always be remembered as the man who pulled off the unassisted triple play in the 1920 World Series.

Lloyd Waner

Waner, Lloyd James **OF**

1927–45 B:3/16/1906, Harrah, OK D:7/22/1982, Oklahoma City, OK Deb:4/12/1927, PIT NL BL/TR 5'9", 150

G	AB	R	H	HR	RBI	OBP	SLG	AVG
1993	7772	1201	2459	27	598	.353	.393	.316

Lloyd James Waner was the younger and smaller of the Waner brothers, the best-hitting sibling combo that ever played the game. Lloyd had an 18-year career; big brother Paul played in 20 big league seasons. For 13 of those years they played next to each other in the Pittsburgh Pirates outfield. Together, Lloyd and Paul banged out 5,611 hits—517 more than the three Alou brothers, 753 more than the three DiMaggios, and 1,394 more than the five Delahantys. The Waners were the second set of brothers to be inducted into the Hall of Fame, following 19th-century pioneers George and Harry Wright.

Born almost three years apart in Harrah, Oklahoma, the Waner boys were very close growing up. They spent as much time as they could playing baseball, learning to hit corncobs with broomsticks. Their father, a former professional ballplayer himself, encouraged them. Paul once commented, however, "Our sister Alma was the best hitter in the family."

Paul was Lloyd's first hitting coach, instructing him to hit down on the ball and to go for line drives rather than power. That was good advice, since neither of them was taller than 5-foot-9, nor weighed more than 150 pounds. Although Paul produced more extra-base hits (including four times as many homers) than his brother did during their major league careers, the two had similar batting styles, keeping the bat at rest on their shoulders until the pitcher began his delivery.

Lloyd's batting success came in part from his exceptional eye. He holds the major league record for fewest strikeouts by an outfielder with more than 500 at bats—only eight, in 1933. In 1941 Lloyd didn't fan for 77 consecutive games. He struck out 20 times only once after his rookie year, and in 18 seasons whiffed only 173 times. His ratio of one strikeout per 44.9 at bats is the second best in major league history. The younger Waner also preferred to put the bat on the ball rather than walk; he never took more than 40 free passes in a season.

Lloyd Waner was one of baseball's first speedsters. After his arrival scouts began to pay more attention to foot speed than they had in the past. His quickness made him an outstanding center fielder as well. He led the National League in putouts four times, including 1931 when he tracked down 515 fly balls, the 10th-highest total ever. His 18 putouts in a 1935 doubleheader are also a record.

Signed to a contract with San Francisco of the Pacific Coast League, Lloyd sat on the bench for the 1925 season and watched his brother Paul hit .401. Lloyd was upset because the team had backed out of its verbal commitment to a $1,500 signing bonus, and on the advice of a Pirates scout he asked for his release early in the 1926 season. The Seals obliged, and on brother Paul's recommendation the Pirates put the younger Waner under contract. He hit .345 for Columbia of the Sally League, and was named league Most Valuable Player.

While Lloyd was tearing up the South Atlantic League, Paul was making his major league debut, hitting .336 with a league-leading 22 triples in 1926. Lloyd reported to spring training in 1927 with his brother, hoping to win a reserve outfielder position. The Bucs outfield seemed complete with brother Paul, speedy Kiki Cuyler, and slugging Clyde Barnhart. But Barnhart showed up grotesquely overweight. All the steam baths in Paso Robles, California, couldn't get him into reasonable condition, so Lloyd won the starting job.

His first year was one to remember. He set the major league rookie record with 223 hits; 198 of them were singles, equaling Wee Willie Keeler's mark from the 19th century. Waner hit .355 and led the league in runs scored with 133. Big brother Paul led the league with a .380 average, 131 RBIs, 18 triples, and 237 hits. The two Waners combined for 460 hits and 247 runs, and on September 4 hit home runs in the same inning.

During one exceptionally productive stretch for the two of them in Brooklyn that summer, a Brooklynite was heard to holler, "Every time I look up there's that little poyson [person] on thoid [third] and that big poyson on foist [first]." The Waners were christened "Big Poison" and "Little Poison" in the newspapers.

In 1927 the Bucs edged out the Cards for the National League flag. A story is told that before the World Series, the Waners watched Babe Ruth and Lou Gehrig take batting practice. The younger said to the older, "Gee, they're pretty big guys, aren't they?" The dumbfounded Pirates were then swept by the powerful Yanks.

But Lloyd later said that the story wasn't true, denying that he and his brother ever watched the Yankees warm up. He added, "I don't think Paul ever saw anything on a ballfield that would scare him." The facts bear him out. The Yankees did not squash the Pirates in the Series. Although the New Yorkers won in four games, two of them

were decided by one run, and the final game was lost on a ninth-inning wild pitch. And the Poisons outhit Ruth and Gehrig, .367 to .357. Lloyd hit .400; his six hits included a double and a triple.

The two brothers went on a national vaudeville tour following the Series, earning $2,000 a week. Paul noodled on the saxophone, Lloyd pretended to play violin ("Every so often we'd hit the same notes as the orchestra," he recalled), and they told baseball jokes. The fans loved them, and they were offered an additional 10-week tour, but the brothers realized their futures were on the diamond, not on the stage, and quit to begin training for the next season.

Lloyd had more than 220 hits in each of the next two years, and led the league with 20 triples in 1929, marking the third consecutive year that a player named Waner was the league's triples champ. On June 9, 1929, the Waner brothers hit home runs in the same game. Six days later Lloyd had six hits in a 14-inning contest. Little Poison missed most of the 1930 season with appendicitis but still hit .362. In 1931 he returned with a .314 average and league-leading 214 hits.

During the next six years, while the Pirates bounced between second and fifth, Lloyd's average twice fell below .285. But starting in 1935 he hit .309 or better four years in a row, including a .313 showing in 1938, the year the Pirates lost the pennant late in the season on Gabby Hartnett's famous "Homer in the Gloaming." Lloyd had a 22-game hitting streak that season (his career best was a 23-gamer in 1935), and on September 15 the Waners hit homers in the same inning.

By 1939 Bucs management was looking to make room for some up-and-coming outfield talent, namely Maurice Van Robays and Johnny Rizzo. Waner played in only 92 outfield games that year and 42 the next. Swapped to the Boston Braves, then to Cincinnati a month later, he batted .292 for the season. When the Reds released him he caught on with the Phillies, but when they traded him to Brooklyn after the 1942 season he decided to hang up his spikes.

But these were the war years. At age 37, Lloyd had to find a job in a defense plant or risk being drafted. Branch Rickey asked him to join the Dodgers in 1944, and he did, hitting .286 in 15 games. Late in the season he rejoined the Pirates, where his career ended in 1945.

He retired with 2,459 hits and a career batting average of .316. He then scouted for the Pirates for the next four years and for Baltimore in 1955. In 1967, 15 years after his brother Paul was elected to the Hall of Fame, Lloyd Waner joined him in Cooperstown.

Paul Waner

Waner, Paul Glee **OF**

1926–45 B:4/16/1903, Harrah, OK D:8/29/1965, Sarasota, FL Deb:4/13/1926, PIT NL BL/TL 5'8½", 153

G	AB	R	H	HR	RBI	OBP	SLG	AVG
2549	9459	1627	3152	113	1309	.404	.473	.333

Paul Glee Waner was bigger than his younger brother, Lloyd, but not by much—both were about 5-foot-9 and weighed approximately 150 pounds. Growing up together in Oklahoma, they were constant companions and best friends. They played in same Pittsburgh Pirates outfield for 14 years, and together they formed the best-hitting brother act in baseball history, combining for 5,611 hits.

Paul's hitting philosophy was to keep the bat still, on the shoulder, until the pitch was thrown. He advised, "Be relaxed, don't wave the bat, don't clench it. Be ready to hit down with the barrel of the bat. Just swing it and let the weight drive the ball. Let the pitcher move first. Then, as he draws his arm back, you draw the bat back and you are ready. If a pitcher sees you fiddling with the bat, he'll stall until your arms are tired before you even get a chance to hit."

His philosophy worked. Waner ranks 10th in career doubles and triples and 13th in lifetime hits. Eight times he registered more than 200 hits in a season; only Pete Rose and Ty Cobb achieved that mark more often. He was the seventh player in baseball history to reach the 3,000-hit mark. And after Waner passed 3,000 in 1942, it would be 15 years until another hitter (Stan Musial) would get there.

Waner liked to hit down the lines, to spread out the fielders and make it more likely for hits to drop. He felt that a hit to straightaway left would be either a single or an out, but the same hit down the line would be either a double or a foul ball, and if it was foul, you were still hitting.

Like Lloyd, the older Waner had an exceptional batting eye. During one game in September 1931 he drew five bases on balls. Both Lloyd and Paul had six-hit games in their careers, although Paul's had a little more flash. Late in his rookie season he had been moved to second in the lineup after usually batting third. He was enjoying a cigarette when the manager hollered to him to get up and hit. He stubbed out his butt, grabbed the first bat he could find, and delivered a hit. The next five times he picked up the nearest bat in reach, and hit safely each time—six hits with six different bats. "It's not the bat; it's the batter," he told his teammates. His trick didn't work the next day.

Casey Stengel said Paul Waner was the best right fielder he ever saw in the National League. "He had to be graceful," Casey said, "because he could slide without breaking the bottle on his hip." Waner was said to be a heavy drinker. One writer claimed he "hit doubles and triples during games and drank them after."

It's hard to imagine a man playing drunk or hungover that often and still averaging .333 over 20 years. It seems more likely, as brother Lloyd put it, that "Paul thought you played better when you were relaxed and drinking was a good way to relax."

"They didn't watch over you then the way they do now," teammate Ace Adams said. At any rate, when Pirates manager Pie Traynor felt a soberer Waner would be more valuable to his 1938 team, Paul stopped drinking. But when his batting average plummeted to .240s, Traynor took him out for a drink. Waner was able to finish at .280, the only sub-.300 average of his first 14 years in the majors.

Waner started his professional career by spending three years in the Pacific Coast League playing for San Francisco. After batting .369 and .356, he heard some wag crack, "You'll probably have to hit .400 to get to the majors." So he did, delivering a .401 mark and 75 doubles in 174 games to lead the league. Detroit manager Ty Cobb wanted him, but tightfisted Tigers owner Frank Navin wouldn't come up with the $40,000 the Seals wanted. Pittsburgh owner Barney Dreyfuss did, giving them $100,000 for Waner and Hal Rhyne, although Rhyne was considered the better prospect at the time.

All was not well with the Pirates in 1926. That was the year of the "A-B-C Incident," in which three disgruntled stars were given their walking papers within days of each other. Waner was the team's bright spot. He hit a league-leading 22 triples, the third-most all-time by a National League rookie, and swatted 35 doubles, the first of nine straight seasons with at least 30. His .336 average was second in the league to Eugene "Bubbles" Hargrave's .353, although Bubbles batted only 326 times. By modern rules, Waner was the batting champ.

In 1927 Lloyd joined Paul in the Pirates outfield and the two tore up the league. From June 3 through June 19 Paul had extra-base hits in 14 consecutive games, still the major league record through 1999. During that stretch he also drove in a run in each of 12 straight games, the second longest streak in league history. He led the league with 237 hits, a .380 average, 17 triples, and 131 RBIs. Lloyd, meanwhile, slapped 223 hits—198 of them singles—and led the league with 133 runs. That was the year the Waners acquired their nicknames, Big Poison (Paul) and Little Poison (Lloyd), thanks to a vociferous Brooklyn fan's pronunciation of "person."

The Yankees took the Pirates in four games in the 1927 World Series, but the Waner brothers outhit Babe Ruth and Lou Gehrig in the Series by 10 points. Buoyed by their success, Paul and Lloyd embarked on a successful vaudeville tour.

The Pirates were not serious contenders in the pennant chase for the next 10 years, but the Waners continued to swat line drives. Paul was the top hitter in the league again in 1934 and 1936. He ripped 50 doubles in 1928 and 62 in 1932 to lead the NL, and he scored more runs than anyone else in the league in 1928 and 1934. On May 20, 1932, Paul tied a major league record with four doubles in one game.

The Pirates lost the NL flag in the final days of 1938. After playing in only 89 games and batting .290 in 1940, the 37-year-old Waner was released. He latched on with Brooklyn and then moved to the Boston Braves to play under Stengel. Waner was slowing down and so was his bat speed, but he still appeared in 106 games that year. In June 1942 he recorded his 2,999th hit, and when a Pittsburgh official scorer tried to award him No. 3,000 on a poorly handled infield bouncer, Waner waved him off. The scorer changed his ruling to an error, and Big Poison had a clean hit two days later off Pittsburgh's Rip Sewell. Waner's quest for No. 3,000 was one of the first statistical milestones to receive national press attention; historian Bill James hypothesized that the recent opening of the Hall of Fame had made baseball fans more aware of such benchmarks.

Waner batted .311 in 1943 but had little left in his legs. Because of a succession of injuries, Stengel had to play him in center field during a midsummer game. Waner chased after a triple to right-center, then, still panting, had to track down a ball slugged to left-center. When the next batter blooped a shallow fly toward him, Waner charged in, fell down, and just lay there. He couldn't find the energy to get up. He spent 1944 in a Dodgers' uniform, filling in as best he could while many players were in the military, and finished his playing career with the Yankees in 1945.

His knowledge of hitting was highly regarded, and he wrote a book on the subject. During 1947 spring training Ted Williams sought out Waner to ask him about hitting against the "Williams Shift," a strategy employed by opposing managers against the slugger. And Tommy Holmes, who held the National League record for the longest consecutive-game hitting streak until Pete Rose broke it, admitted he learned a lot from Waner.

Paul Waner was elected to the Hall of Fame in 1952. Signed on as a hitting coach by the Milwaukee Braves in 1957, he filled the same post

with the Cardinals in 1958 and 1959 and with the Phillies in 1960. The Phils brought him back in 1965 to work with their young hitters, and he died that August. Two years later brother Lloyd joined Paul in the Hall of Fame.

Hall of Fame pitcher Burleigh Grimes once remarked, "I saw a lot of good hitters but I never saw a better one than Paul Waner. I once threw a sidearm spitter right into his belly and he hit it into the upper deck. I may have got Waner out but I never fooled him."

Arch Ward

Journalist, Baseball Pioneer B:12/27/1896 D:7/9/1955

Arch Ward's first job was as the first sports publicity director ever to be hired by his alma mater, Notre Dame. After one year there he moved to the *Rockford Star* to write sports. Five years later he was in the big leagues of sports journalism: sportswriter and (later) sports editor of the *Chicago Tribune*.

In 1933, Ward hit upon the idea of having a baseball game between stars from both leagues, as a sporting way to complement the World's Fair in Chicago that year. He saw that July 6 was an open date for all major league clubs, so he began to push the idea in his columns. In addition to promoting the city and the Fair, Ward felt it could serve a charitable cause as well: raising funds for the "Professional Ball Players of America." This was during the worst of the Depression, and Ward figured some former players who were financially strapped would benefit. Many owners disliked the idea, and when they finally agreed to it, they firmly stipulated it would be a one-time event.

As history has demonstrated, the game was a smash. John McGraw came out of retirement to manage the National League. Babe Ruth, even though he was 38 years old, was the star, with both a two-run homer and a critical running catch. Seventeen eventual Hall of Famers played for the 47,595 fans who flocked to Comiskey Park. Of the $52,000 raised, $45,000 was donated to former players in need of financial assistance.

The next year New York said it deserved a chance to host such a game. In that contest Carl Hubbell performed his feat of fanning Ruth, Lou Gehrig, Jimmie Foxx, Al Simmons, and Joe Cronin in a row, and from then on nothing except World War II could stop the annual All-Star Game. (They even played two All-Star Games a year from 1959 through 1962.)

In 1934 Ward conjured up another All-Star idea: the College All-Stars against the champions of the NFL. That one didn't last as long. Ward remained as *Tribune* sports editor through 1950.

Duane Ward

Ward, Roy Duane **P**

1986–93, 1995 B:5/28/1964, Park View, NM
Deb:4/12/1986, ATL NL BR/TR, 6'4", 210

W	L	PCT	G	SV	IP	BB	SO	ERA
32	37	.464	462	121	666^{2}	286	679	3.28

Success came slowly to Duane Ward, but the end of his career came suddenly. After saving 45 games to help the Toronto Blue Jays win their second straight world championship in 1993, he arrived in spring training several months later with a tender shoulder. At first, it was simply thought to be soreness. After the season began it was called a cartilage tear. Eventually Ward was diagnosed with a torn rotator cuff that ended both his season and—following a brief comeback attempt in 1995—his career.

A heavy workload may have contributed to Ward's downfall. He pitched more than 100 innings and topped 60 outings for five straight years from 1988 to 1992. Not coincidentally, the Blue Jays won three division titles in that span. Ward mixed a heavy sinking fastball with an explosive, late-breaking slider that many felt was the best in the game. He kept the ball in the park and averaged four strikeouts for each walk. In 1991, when he appeared a league-leading 81 times, he fanned 132 batters in 107 ⅓ innings.

Ward came to Toronto in 1986 via Atlanta, where he had been a starter for five years in the minor leagues. With the Blue Jays he worked out of the bullpen and in 1988 became the top set-up man for closer Tom Henke in 1988. Ward became so effective that the Blue Jays kept him and sent Henke to the Texas Rangers after the 1992 World Series. Ward won or saved 47 of Toronto's 95 wins in 1993. His final victory in a major league uniform came on October 23, 1993—the night Joe Carter's three-run home run in the bottom of the ninth inning beat the Phillies for the world championship.

Gary Ward

Ward, Gary Lamell **OF-DH-1B**

1979–90 B:12/6/1953, Los Angeles, CA Deb:9/3/1979, MIN AL BR/TR 6'2", 202

G	AB	R	H	HR	RBI	OBP	SLG	AVG
1287	4479	594	1236	130	597	.330	.425	.276

One wonders what kind of career Gary Ward might have had if family problems and physical ailments hadn't interrupted it while he was still in his early 30s. He was one of the American League's most exciting players during a four-year stretch from 1982 to 1985.

Signed by the Minnesota Twins in August 1972, Gary Lamell Ward reached the major leagues in

1979 and became the Twins regular left fielder in the strike-shortened 1981 season. That same year *Baseball Digest* named him AL Rookie of the Year after he hit .264 with 29 RBIs in 85 games. A year later he was an established star, hitting .289 with 28 homers and 91 RBIs, as well as recording 13 outfield assists. For that performance, Ward was named Twins Player of the Year. In 1983, he led American League outfielders with 24 assists—the highest total since Stan Spence had 29 for Washington in 1944—and also hit 19 homers while driving in 88 runs. But the Twins traded Ward to the Texas Rangers over the winter of 1983.

Ward started slowly with the Rangers, but came on strong over the last two months of the season and finished at .284 with 21 homers and 79 RBIs. He posted similar numbers the next year, but his career started a downward spiral beginning in 1986. Although he hit .316 in 105 games, he left the team on four separate occasions due to family emergencies, and in 1986 he missed most of September after surgery to remove a blockage in his abdomen. Ward became a free agent in 1986 and signed a three-year contract with the Yankees, but he was no longer the forceful player he had been. He ended his career with Detroit in 1990.

John Ward

Ward, John Montgomery **SS-2B-P-OF**

1878–94 M(1880–94, 412–320) B:3/3/1860, Bellefonte, PA D:3/4/1925, Augusta, GA Deb:7/15/1878, PRO NL BL/TR 5'9", 165

G	AB	R	H	HR	RBI	OBP	SLG	AVG
1825	7647	1408	2104	26	867	.314	.341	.275

W	L	PCT	G	SH	IP	BB	SO	ERA
164	102	.617	292	24	2461^2	253	920	2.10

If John Montgomery "Monte" Ward wasn't the most important person in Major League Baseball during the late 19th century, he certainly was the most interesting. Few others had such a leading role in shaping baseball history. His career as a star player, winning manager, labor organizer, and club owner placed him at the center of many of the period's most significant events, both on and off the field.

A gifted student athlete, Ward attended Pennsylvania State College and won acclaim as a pitcher on the baseball team. He pitched an exhibition game for the independent Philadelphia Athletics in 1877, and although he lost, 5–0, he accepted a professional contract from a team in Wisconsin for $20 a week and a $75 bonus. His hometown newspaper editorialized, "There is no reason why a baseball pitcher should not become eventually a great man, but the chances for Monte's sake, we are sorry to say, are against it, and trust he will pause and reconsider."

Ward proved the critics wrong. In 1878, his rookie season, he was the star righthanded pitcher for Providence of the National League, winning 22 games and leading the league with a 1.51 ERA. On August 9 he pitched and won two games in one day.

The great George Wright and "Orator Jim" O'Rourke joined the Providence team in 1879. With a better defense behind him and a stronger offense, Ward pitched the Grays to the pennant. He won a league-leading 47 games and lost only 17. His .734 winning percentage and 239 strikeouts also led the National League. In 1880 he won 40 games and threw a league-leading nine shutouts. On June 17 of that year, he threw the second perfect game and third no-hitter in league history, a 5–0 win over Buffalo.

But Ward was only 20 years old, and the strain on his arm proved too great. After pitching 587 innings in 1879 and 595 in 1880, he battled a sore arm during the next three seasons, pitching fewer innings each year. Yet when he was able to throw, he continued to be successful. On August 17, 1882, he won an 18-inning game, 1–0. But by 1884 his arm was shot, and he appeared in his final nine games as a hurler. In seven seasons Ward won 161 games against 101 losses.

Although finished as a pitcher, Ward was hardly washed up as a player. Even as early as 1879, when he was at his best as a hurler, Ward played outfield or third base on the days he wasn't on the mound. A righthanded thrower, he was a fair lefthanded batter, particularly adept at bunting and hitting behind a runner. Ward was an excellent baserunner and fast in the field. Furthermore, he was an exceptional leader. In 1880, though younger than most of his teammates, he even filled in as manager for part of the season.

After his arm went bad, Ward spent more time as a position player. In 1883 the New York Gothams acquired his contract, and during most of the 1884 season he was New York's regular center fielder. He hit .253 and scored 98 runs. According to some reports, he threw lefthanded to rest his ailing right arm.

Although he never returned to the mound, his arm recovered enough to allow him to become the Gothams' regular shortstop in 1885. Ward was instantly one of the top players at the position. In 1885 and 1887 he led NL shortstops in putouts, and in 1887 he also led the league in fielding percentage.

Ward was credited with a league-leading 111 stolen bases in 1887. However, according to the rules of the day, runners were awarded "steals" whenever they took an extra base on a hit or an out. There's no way to determine how many of Ward's steals would count under today's rules.

The Giants of the late 1880s were a star-studded team whose roster included six players who would one day grace the Hall of Fame: pitchers Tim Keefe and Mickey Welch; catcher Buck Ewing; first baseman Roger Connor; outfielder "Orator" Jim O'Rourke, and shortstop Ward. An article that appeared in 1912 in the *New York Journal* stated that, "New York fans considered [Ward] the most dashing, daring and winning player in a pinch the club ever had. He was, too, the hero of more close games that were won—pulled out of the fire by individual excellence, grit and ginger—than any other Giant, old or new."

In both 1888 and 1889 the Giants won the National League pennant, and much of the credit went to their dashing shortstop. He turned in clutch performances in the two "World Series" against American Association champions that followed the Giants' pennant wins. In 1888, when New York defeated the St. Louis Browns in 10 games, Ward hit .379.

The following year, as New York won in nine games, he was even better, hitting .417, scoring 10 runs, and stealing 10 bases. The Giants trailed in the Series three games to two going into the sixth game. Hank O'Day shut out New York for eight innings and St. Louis led, 1–0, but in the bottom of the ninth Ward singled and then stole second and third. He scored to tie the game on Connor's single. Then, in the 11th inning, he drove in the winning run. The Giants went on to win the next three games and the Series.

While enjoying a full career on the field, Ward also remained busy off the field, earning a law degree from Columbia University. In 1885 the Brotherhood of Professional Base Ball Players was formed to protect and benefit the players collectively and individually, to promote a high standard of conduct, and to foster and encourage the interests of baseball. Ward was elected president. Some team owners feared any sort of player organization, but most at least paid lip service to the aims of the Brotherhood.

In the next few years the owners began to push the players into a corner. In 1887 Ward published an article criticizing several practices the players found unfair, including the reserve clause in contracts, which bound a player to a particular club forever. He pointed out that "the law of the land" did not govern the game of baseball.

After the 1888 season Albert Spalding led a group of stars on a globe-trotting tour to introduce baseball and open new markets for his sporting goods. While Ward and other stars were out of the country, the owners pushed through a rule to categorize the players and pay them according to rank. Since the owners determined the categories, the new system first lowered, and then froze, player salaries.

For more than a year Ward tried to negotiate, but the owners refused to recognize the Brotherhood. Finally, the situation reached an impasse. In 1890 the players, under Ward, revolted, solicited financial backers, and formed the Players' League. Most star players in both the National League and the American Association jumped to the new league.

During the 1890 season the three major leagues competed in many of the same cities. All three lost money, and the backers of the Players' League lost heart, even though their attendance was the best of the three. After only one year the new league collapsed. A year later the mortally wounded American Association also went under, and the National League absorbed four of its teams.

Ward was shortstop and manager of the Players' League's Brooklyn team, which finished second. In the settlement after the season, the club's backer and Ward each gained stock in the Brooklyn National League club. Ward assumed the player-manager position with Brooklyn, a team that soon became popularly known as "Ward's Wonders." He moved the club up to third in the standings in 1892, when he led the league with 80 stolen bases.

That same year Ward won 20 shares of New York Giants stock on a bet with one of their stockholders on where the Giants would finish. Today, such a conflict of interest, not to mention betting on standings, would be prohibited by Organized Baseball. It was common in the 1890s for owners to own shares in other teams, and occasionally players and managers did the same. In fact, half the owners in the league held Giants stock.

The team, however, was going rapidly downhill. Because the National League needed a strong draw in New York, both to protect its stock holdings and to ensure a large visitor's share of the take, the other club owners worked out a deal. Ward resigned as Brooklyn manager and became the Giants' skipper. In 1893 New York finished fifth in the 12-team National League, and in 1894 Ward pushed them to second.

In an effort to establish a profitable postseason series similar to the prototypical World Series of the 1880s, the National League instituted the Temple Cup in 1894, with the division winner playing the second-place finisher in a best-of-seven series. The Baltimore Orioles won the pennant that year but didn't take the Temple Cup very seriously. Ward's Giants ambushed the Orioles and swept them in four straight games. Ward himself hit .294 and led his team in RBIs.

At age 34 Ward was at the pinnacle of the baseball world, a successful player-manager of a championship team. He chose that moment to retire. His successful law practice was growing, but he resigned primarily due to his inability to get along with Andrew Freedman, the Tammany Hall politician who had taken over the Giants. Ward was hardly alone; few men could work for Freedman for long. By the time he sold his control of the Giants in 1903, Freedman had fired or otherwise lost a dozen managers and driven the Giants to the lowest point in their history.

Ward became a leading corporate lawyer in New York but continued to be involved in baseball. He represented Amos Rusie when the famous pitcher sued Freedman for money he was owed. The case was eventually settled out of court to Rusie's benefit. In 1909 Ward was a leading, though eventually unsuccessful, candidate to become NL president. In 1911 and 1912 he was president and part owner of the Boston Braves, and in 1913 he was business manager of the Brooklyn team in the Federal League.

Ward was the founder and first president of the Long Island Golf Association. He wrote several books and numerous magazine articles on baseball. He died in 1925, and nearly 40 years later, in 1964, he was named to the Hall of Fame.

Pete Ward

Ward, Peter Thomas **3B-1B-OF**

1962–70 B:7/26/1939, Montreal, Quebec, Canada Deb:9/21/1962, BAL AL BL/TR 6'1", 200

G	AB	R	H	HR	RBI	OBP	SLG	AVG
973	3060	345	776	98	427	.342	.405	.254

The son of National Hockey League star Jimmy Ward, Pete Ward was a quality third baseman for the Chicago White Sox during the 1960s. He overcame an unorthodox stance to become a decent hitter. "I got a real silly stance," he once confessed. "Fundamentally I got a bad swing."

Originally signed by Baltimore in 1958, Ward led the 3-I League in batting with a .345 mark in 1960, and two seasons later paced the International League in doubles. Traded to Chicago in a January 1963 transaction that sent Luis Aparicio to the Orioles, on Opening Day Ward began his big-league career with a bang by commencing an 18-game hitting streak. He finished his inaugural season with a .295 average, 22 homers, and 84 RBIs, a performance that earned his selection as *The Sporting News* AL Rookie of the Year.

Injuries, however, curtailed what might have been a very promising career. In 1965 Ward hurt his neck in an auto accident, and in 1966 he suffered a back injury. He ranked as the AL's best pinch hitter in 1969, but retired after playing 66 games for the Yankees in 1970. After leaving baseball he operated an Oregon travel agency.

Lon Warneke

Warneke, Lonnie **P**

1930–45 B:3/28/1909, Mt. Ida, AR D:6/23/1976, Hot Springs, AR Deb:4/18/1930, CHI NL BR/TR 6'2", 185

W	L	PCT	G	SH	IP	BB	SO	ERA
192	121	.613	445	30	2782^{1}	739	1140	3.18

St. Louis sportswriter J. Roy Stockton dubbed Lon Warneke "the Arkansas Hummingbird" after what Stockton termed his "darting form of delivery." That delivery was good enough to earn the big righthander the National League lead in victories three times and in shutouts twice.

Yet Lonnie Warneke might never have made it to the major leagues had it not been for catcher Zack Taylor's advice. Taylor counseled Warneke to watch the plate instead of his feet, noting that Warneke "keeps lookin' at his dogs instead of the hitter." Once that flaw was corrected, there was no stopping Warneke.

In high school Warneke's diamond experience was limited to first base. He became a pitcher by throwing batting practice for Houston of the Texas League. Signed by the Cardinals, Warneke was so unimpressive that they quickly dropped him. But he caught on with Alexandria of the Cotton States League, and Cleveland sent a scout to look at him. That day it rained, and to amuse himself Warneke pantomimed rowing over to second base. The scout had no sense of humor and reported, "He's a screwball. Forget him."

The Cubs, however, paid $10,000 to take a chance on Warneke. In 1931, his first full major league season, he reportedly went out and purchased 12 suits of clothes. But he still wasn't rich enough to consider the off-season a vacation—that winter he delivered telegrams for Western Union.

In 1932 Warneke arrived. That year he led the senior circuit in victories, won-lost percentage, shutouts, and ERA, and was named to *The Sporting News* Major League All-Star team. His Cubs faced the Yankees in that year's World Series.

Before taking the mound in Game 2 Warnecke made contradictory statements to journalists. First he said, "Maybe I'll beat 'em and maybe I won't. I ain't worryin'. Why should you?" But to a passing photographer he warned, "I never pitch for any pictures when I'm going to pitch. Superstitious, hell! I just think it's unlucky." Perhaps he was photographed on the sly. Warneke lost 5–2 to Lefty Gomez.

In 1934 Warneke started the season in grand style, hurling back-to-back one-hitters on the road.

On Opening Day he held Cincinnati batters helpless for 8 ⅓ innings before Adam Comorosky singled. In his second start he gave up only a fifth-inning double to the Cardinals' James "Ripper" Collins.

In the 1935 World Series Warneke four-hit the Tigers in Game 1 and surrendered only three hits in Game 5 before leaving with a sore shoulder after six shutout innings. "I don't give a damn if it's the World Series. Your arm is more important than any ballgame," yelled manager Charlie Grimm to Warneke when he yanked the unhappy pitcher.

In October 1936 Warneke went to the Cardinals in a deal that sent Ripper Collins to the Cubs. Warneke fit right in with the freewheeling Redbirds, even joining teammate Pepper Martin's clubhouse combo, the Mudcat Band. On August 30, 1941, Warneke no-hit the Reds, 2–0, surrendering only one walk and striking out two; his team committed two errors. In June 1942 the three-time 20-game winner was sold back to the Cubs. He spent 1944 and most of the following year in the service.

In 1946, with the help of Cubs owner P.K. Wrigley, Warneke obtained a position umpiring in the Pacific Coast League. In 1949 he was promoted to the National League. The next challenge he met was obtaining the proper garb. "I tried every place to get a blue serge suit. But I'm doggoned, they just aren't to be had," he complained. Warneke became the only man to both pitch in and umpire a World Series.

After retiring as an arbiter Warneke spent 10 years as a judge in Mount Ida, Arkansas, where he had always spent his winters. "Heck, I can live a whole winter down home for $50. I can't live a week up [North] for that," he once remarked.

Claudell Washington

Washington, Claudell **OF**
1974–90 B:8/31/1954, Los Angeles, CA Deb:7/5/1974, OAK AL BL/TL 6', 190

G	AB	R	H	HR	RBI	OBP	SLG	AVG
1912	6787	926	1884	164	824	.328	.420	.278

Claudell Washington was one of those rare gems discovered playing sandlot baseball. He had never played baseball in high school, but after seeing him in action in the sandlots of Berkeley, California, the Oakland Athletics took a chance with him. He ended up playing 15 years in the majors.

A lefthanded hitter, Washington compiled a lifetime batting average of .278 and hit 164 home runs. He hit three homers in a game for the Chicago White Sox on July 14, 1979, against the Detroit Tigers, and duplicated that feat with the Mets on June 22, 1980, against the Dodgers. Previously, only Babe Ruth and Johnny Mize had ever hit three homers in a game in each league.

Signed in July 1972, just one month shy of his 18th birthday, Washington spent two years in the minors at Coos Bay, Burlington, and Birmingham before joining the A's midway through the 1974 season. He immediately showed he belonged in the majors by hitting .285 in 73 games. Washington first attracted national attention in the 1974 World Series when he helped the A's defeat the Dodgers in five games. Playing all three positions in the outfield, he had four hits in seven at bats for a .571 average.

Washington played three seasons for the A's then started a vagabond career that included stops with the Rangers, White Sox, Mets, Braves, and Yankees. His best season came with Atlanta in 1982 when he knocked in 80 runs and scored 94.

Herb Washington

Washington, Herbert Lee **Pinch Runner**
1974–75 B:11/16/1951, Belzoni, MS Deb:4/4/1974, OAK AL BR/TR, 6', 170

G	AB	R	H	HR	RBI	OBP	SLG	AVG
105	0	33	0	0	0	—	—	—

Herb Washington never batted, never fielded, and was resented by his Oakland A's teammates for taking up a roster spot. A world-class sprinter at Michigan State University, Washington was to be another of Oakland owner Charlie O. Finley's baseball innovations: the designated runner. Unlike the designated hitter, however, Washington could only be used once per game.

Oakland had already employed outfielder Allan Lewis almost exclusively to pinch-run for parts of six seasons. "The Panamanian Express" was discontinued after the 1973 season. Much to the annoyance of his players, Finley signed Washington during spring training in 1974. Unlike Lewis, who batted .207 and played the field occasionally, Washington had not played baseball since his junior year in high school. He was used as a pinch runner 92 times as Oakland won its third straight world championship. Washington stole 29 bases, but the "world's fastest human" was also caught 16 times; he was 31 of 48 in his career.

Washington retired early in the 1975 season. "They wanted to send me to the minors, and I just wasn't interested," he said. "I could still run on the

pro track circuit." He left Oakland with a World Series ring, a hefty sum of cash, and the distinction of holding a singular place in baseball lore.

U. L. Washington

Washington, U. L. **SS–2B**

1977–87 B:10/27/1953, Stringtown, OK Deb:9/6/1977, KAN AL BB/TR, 5'11", 175

G	AB	R	H	HR	RBI	OBP	SLG	AVG
907	2797	358	703	27	255	.315	.343	.251

U.L. Washington knew what to do when he arrived in Kansas City. As a product of the player development program known as the Royals Baseball Academy, he was taught how to get on base by using the fast surface and deep power alleys at Royals Stadium. Considering Washington had the likes of Amos Otis, Hal McRae, and George Brett waiting to drive him in, the program was based on a sound theory.

Washington was best known for his speed and defense (as well as the toothpick always lodged in his mouth), but he also made things happen with his bat. He launched the first two home runs of his career in memorable fashion, going deep from both sides of the plate against Oakland on September 21, 1979. In his first playoff action in 1980, Washington drove in the eventual game-winning run in Game 2 and scored the winner in Game 3 as Kansas City swept the New York Yankees in the American League Championship Series.

He produced his best offensive season in 1982, batting .286 with 10 home runs, and followed with a career-high 40 stolen bases in 1983. Injuries and ineffectiveness cost him his everyday job the following year, and he was traded to Montreal before the 1985 season. Later that year a convicted drug dealer fingered Washington as one of several Royals who regularly used cocaine in the early 1980s. After retiring in 1987, he began a successful minor league coaching career with Pittsburgh and Kansas City.

John Wathan

Wathan, John David **C–1B**

1976–85 M(1987–92, 326–320) B:10/4/49, Cedar Rapids, IA Deb:5/26/1976, KC AL BR/TR, 6'2", 205

G	AB	R	H	HR	RBI	OBP	SLG	AVG
860	2505	305	656	21	261	.320	.343	.262

John Wathan was a big catcher without much power, but he made up for it with good speed on the basepaths. During his 10 years as a Kansas City Royal he was effective as a backup catcher or a platoon player, but struggled when he was asked to play a larger role.

Wathan spent three years at the University of San Diego, starring in both baseball and basketball. He was Kansas City's first selection in the January 1971 draft. His first four years in the minors were rocky, but in 1975 he led his Omaha club in hitting and played in the American Association All-Star Game. The following year he broke into the big leagues.

Wathan's 36 stolen bases in 1982 were the most ever for a catcher. He was below average defensively, however, and opposing runners didn't hesitate to steal on him. In his decade with Kansas City, he made seven trips to the postseason, with his best showing a .300 average in the Royals' 1981 loss to Oakland in the AL West Division Playoff.

After retiring in 1985, Wathan spent a year and a half as a Royals coach before assuming the managerial duties in August 1987. He inherited a talented team that he led to a third-place finish in 1988 and second in 1989. The Royals slipped to sixth place in 1990 and Wathan was fired after a 15–22 start the following year. He served as an interim manager with the Angels in 1992 after Buck Rodgers was injured in the team's bus accident, and later was a coach with the Boston Red Sox.

Bob Watson

Watson, Robert Jose **1B–OF**

1966–84 B:4/10/1946, Los Angeles, CA Deb:9/9/1966, HOU NL BR/TR 6'2", 205

G	AB	R	H	HR	RBI	OBP	SLG	AVG
1832	6185	802	1826	184	989	.367	.447	.295

Bob Watson was an intelligent, quiet, dependable hitter and outfielder who posted a career .295 batting average. He was the first African-American ever to serve as general manager for a major league team, and he is also the answer to two obscure trivia questions. Who is the only man to hit for the cycle in both leagues? Watson did it for Houston in 1977 and for the Red Sox in 1979. Who scored Major League Baseball's one-millionth run? Watson, on May 4, 1975.

The story of the one-millionth run is a curious one. Publicity surrounding the approaching event was substantial, and statistics experts had their calculators and clocks ready. Everybody knew that it would happen on that day, and every player was eager for the chance to go down in history. John Montefusco was pitching for the Giants. Watson was on second for the Astros with two out and Jose Cruz on first.

When Milt May hit the ball out of the park, Watson scampered home as fast as he could to be sure he'd be the one-millionth scorer. But Cruz stopped between first and second to watch the ball and relish the moment. May, in the slightly dazed home run trot of a man who hardly ever homers, almost ran into the dawdling Cruz. Umpire John McSherry ruled that May had not passed Cruz. If May hadn't come to his senses in time Watson's run would have been nullified, and run number one million would instead have been scored seven seconds later in Milwaukee.

Raised by his grandparents near the Watts district of Los Angeles, Robert Jose Watson played baseball for Fremont High School along with fellow future big leaguers Willie Crawford and Bobby Tolan. Although signed by the Astros as a catcher, the 6-foot-2, 205-pound Bobby "Bull" Watson had pretty much hung up his catcher's gear by his third minor league season. After flopping in a 45-game stint with Houston in 1968, he made the big club in 1970 and batted .272 while driving in 61 runs.

Playing right field as part of a highly talented outfield that included Jimmy Wynn and Cesar Cedeno, Watson hit .312 with 16 home runs in both 1972 and 1973, driving in 86 and 94 runs, respectively. When Lee May was traded before the 1975 season, Watson became Houston's first baseman. In 1975 he hit .324, and in both 1976 and 1977 he drove in more than 100 runs. Watson's .289 batting average in 1978 was the same as in 1977, but his RBI total fell to 79. After a slow start in 1979 the Astros swapped him to the Red Sox.

Watson found new life in Boston, hitting .337 with 53 RBIs and 13 homers in 84 games. After the season he declared free agency and was signed by the Yankees. As New York's regular first baseman he batted .307, drove in 68 runs, and again hit 13 homers.

In that year's ALCS Watson hit .500, including three doubles and a triple, but the Kansas City Royals beat the Yankees. A groin injury hobbled Watson for most of 1981, but he had recovered enough by that year's World Series against the Dodgers to play a significant role. He belted a three-run homer in Game 1 and drove in two runs in Game 2, but Los Angeles pitchers eventually got the better of him, holding him to only one hit in his last dozen at bats. Watson finished at .318 for the Series, with seven RBIs.

In April 1982 the Braves brought Watson back to the National League. The following season he batted .309 for Atlanta in 65 games, including a .407 average as a pinch hitter. He retired as a player after the 1984 season. While in Atlanta Watson suggested to Braves leadoff hitter Brett Butler that he could use his running speed to greater advantage if he learned to bunt; Butler took Watson's advice and became one of the best bunters for hits in the game.

From 1986 through 1988 Watson was a key member of Tony La Russa's coaching staff for the A's. La Russa assigned Watson the task of watching the person in the dugout who was suspected of giving signs for pitchouts; Watson would relay the information to first base coach Rene Lachemann.

Watson broke a long-standing barrier when he was named the Houtson Astros' general manager following the 1993 season, making him the first African-American to hold that title in the majors. Seven months later he was diagnosed with prostate cancer. In 1995 he replaced Gene Michael as Yankees general manager. The Yankees won the World Series in 1996, but the 51-year-old Watson, confessing he was "burned out," retired from the Yankees in February 1998, being replaced by his 30-year-old assistant Brian Cashman.

Buck Weaver

Weaver, George Daniel **SS-3B**

1912–20 B:8/18/1890, Pottstown, PA D:1/31/1956, Chicago, IL Deb:4/11/1912, CHI AL BB/TR 5'11", 170

G	AB	R	H	HR	RBI	OBP	SLG	AVG
1254	4809	623	1308	21	420	.307	.355	.272

Third baseman Buck Weaver was one of eight players who were banned for life from Major League Baseball for their involvement in the 1919 "Black Sox" scandal. In baseball's most disgraceful episode, several Chicago White Sox players allegedly accepted payoffs from gamblers to throw the 1919 World Series.

Weaver's story may be the most tragic of them all. Despite being asked to take part in the fix, he accepted no money. In fact, it was clear to the other conspirators that Weaver's intense dedication to the game would make it impossible for him to perform at less than his full ability. By any estimation Weaver played a great Series. He hit .324, with four doubles and a triple among his 11 hits, and he fielded 27 chances without an error. Weaver's crime was that he had known about the scandal but had not informed anyone about it. As Commissioner Judge Kenesaw Mountain Landis phrased it in his banishment statement, "No player that sits in a conference where the ways and means of throwing games are planned and discussed and does not promptly tell his club about it, will ever play professional baseball."

In his day Weaver was considered one of the best third basemen in his league. His strategy of playing shallow made it especially tough for dead-ball master bunters to hit against the White Sox. In fact, baseball great Ty Cobb refused to bunt while Weaver was stationed at third.

George Daniel Weaver broke into baseball as a shortstop, but his poor fielding earned him the nickname "Error-A-Day." Shortly after his first season, while chopping lumber with his friend Ossie Vitt, Weaver noticed that he was more likely to hit his mark in the wood when he swung from the left rather than from the right. He became a switch hitter and raised his batting average 48 points.

Weaver was a valuable link in the potent White Sox lineup of the time, banging doubles and triples and hitting .284 and .296 for the 1917 and 1919 Chicago pennant winners. In 1920, his final year before expulsion, he posted a career-best .331 average with 34 doubles and eight triples.

When the "Black Sox" trial was set for a day in June 1921 in Chicago, Weaver at first requested a separate trial, but he was refused. He deliberately distanced himself from his former teammates, sitting apart from their defense table. It seemed clear to him that he had done nothing wrong.

According to historian Harold Seymour, Judge Hugo Friend "had already decided before instructing the jury that there was so little evidence against Weaver, Happy Felsch, and gambler Carl Zork that he would not allow a verdict against them to stand." In addition, Weaver had heard that John McGraw of the Giants was eager to sign him as soon as the trial was over. When "not guilty" verdicts were announced for all eight teammates, Weaver and Swede Risberg danced around the courtroom. But the following day, despite the verdict, Landis decided to ban all eight players from baseball forever. Weaver's life was shattered.

A petition signed by 14,000 Chicagoans in one day did nothing to change Landis' mind. Five months later Weaver appealed to Landis personally to change his ruling. The Commissioner never bothered to notify Weaver of his decision. Instead Landis simply released a statement to the press, saying, "Birds of a feather flock together. Men associating with gamblers and crooks could expect no leniency."

Weaver applied to Landis several more times for reinstatement, even obtaining a good word on his behalf from Judge Friend, but to no avail. He reapplied to Landis' successors, Happy Chandler and Ford Frick, with the same negative results. He later became a Chicago pharmacist. From 1921 through 1934 he played on a succession of semipro and outlaw teams.

Earl Weaver

Weaver, Earl Sidney
Manager (1968–86, 1,480–1,060) B:8/14/1930, St. Louis, MO BR/TR 5'7", 160

Earl Weaver was a baseball strategist of the first order. He was also combative, opinionated, disciplined, raucous, and possessed of an insatiable desire to win. As a player Weaver never made it out of the minors, but he took to managing like a duck to water. In 11 years of minor league managing his teams won three pennants and never finished below fourth. In his last two years at Triple-A Rochester his teams finished only one game back because of losses on the final day of the season.

Weaver developed what has become known as "the Baltimore Way." In 1961 he was given responsibility for organizing all workouts for Baltimore farmhands below Triple A. He devised a system of fundamental practice techniques used throughout the organization. For the first time, a player moving from level to level could count on a familiar style of practice and play.

Weaver's system played a large part in Baltimore's success after he took over the big club. When a writer accused Weaver of being a "pushbutton manager," Orioles general manager Harry Dalton replied with a snort, "Pushbutton manager? He built the machine and installed all the buttons."

Weaver's managerial philosophy was based on knowing what each player could do and getting the player to do it at the right time. He demonstrated a knack for finding appropriate roles for journeyman players. By platooning John Lowenstein with Gary Roenicke in left field he created an excellent run-producing duo. "A manager's job is to select the best players for what he wants done," Weaver explained. "They're not all great players, but they can all do something."

He said his philosophy boiled down to "pitching, defense, and the three-run homer." As facile as that sounds, Weaver was implying that one-run strategies were self-limiting in the big-inning game of baseball. He explained, "I have nothing against the bunt—in its place. But most of the time that place is in the bottom of a long-forgotten closet." He hated the hit-and-run play even more, and didn't even have a sign for it.

To ensure good performance on the mound Weaver hired some of the game's best pitching coaches—George Bamberger and Ray Miller. Weaver studied player and pitcher performance like no one ever had before. Extensive charts told him what each batter did against each pitcher in every situation. Much of the situational strategy taken for granted in today's game resulted from Weaver's innovations. In addition, he kept in touch personally with each of his players in an effort to discover what motivated them.

Apart from victories, Weaver's most notable successes came with his hurlers. By using his own powers of insight and putting his pitching coaches to work to execute his ideas, he built sensational mound staffs. His teams led in complete games nearly every season. And he let his pitchers call their own games, figuring they knew best what was working.

In his 17 years as Baltimore manager, Weaver's pitchers won six Cy Young Awards. When Weaver saw Mike Cuellar devouring big league hitters with a screwball in winter ball in Puerto Rico, he realized that pitching wasn't the lefty's problem in the majors; the problem was the language difference. Weaver obtained a bilingual catcher, Ellie Hendricks, and paired him with Cuellar. Cuellar won a Cy Young Award in Baltimore.

Weaver, who pioneered the use of the radar gun in the majors, knew how to handle relievers, too. One of his rules was that no pitcher warmed up in the bullpen for more than three consecutive games.

Weaver was promoted from minor league manager to major league coach for the 1968 season. Baltimore manager Hank Bauer suspected that Weaver was the heir apparent for his job, and he was right. Halfway through the season Weaver took over. The team played .585-ball under his direction, and the third-place Orioles moved up to second.

In 1969 Weaver's Orioles won 109 games and went to the World Series, but were defeated by the surprising Mets. Baltimore won it all in 1970. The following season the Orioles lost the Series to Pittsburgh, then won division championships in 1973 and 1974. Weaver's O's finished in second place for the next three years, slipped to fourth in 1978, and then returned to the 100-win plateau and the World Series in 1979. But the Pirates again denied Weaver and his team the world championship. The Birds finished in second place in 1980 and in both halves of the strike-split 1981 season. After losing the AL East on the last day of the 1982 season, Weaver retired.

The next season, under Joe Altobelli, the Orioles won their first world championship since 1970, defeating Philadelphia. But in 1984 Baltimore tumbled all the way to fifth. When 1985 promised to be more of the same, Weaver was coaxed out of retirement, but he couldn't make much difference. In 1986 he had his first losing season ever and retired for good.

Weaver's fiery personality earned him numerous enemies among American League umpires. His antics, including faking a heart attack and tearing second base off its moorings and refusing to give it back, bordered on the childish. He turned the bill of his cap around whenever he argued with an umpire in order to get as close to the arbiter's face as possible. Weaver was tossed from nearly 100 games and was suspended six times for questionable behavior. His most publicized battles were with Ron Luciano, a large, fun-loving arbiter who had thrown Weaver out of games the first four times they crossed paths in Class AAA and couldn't seem to stop when he got to the bigs. Three times Weaver was ejected from both games of a doubleheader, twice before the second game even started.

In his 17 seasons at Baltimore's helm Weaver won six AL East titles, four pennants, and one World Series. Only Yankees manager Joe McCarthy posted more 100-win seasons.

Earl Webb

Webb, William Earl **OF**

1925, 1927–28, 1930–33 B:9/17/1897, Bon Air, TN D:5/23/1965, Jamestown, TN Deb:8/13/1925, NY NL BL/TR, 6'1", 185

G	AB	R	H	HR	RBI	OBP	SLG	AVG
650	2161	326	661	56	333	.381	.478	.306

Earl Webb was the quintessential "one-year wonder." His major-league record 67 doubles in 1931 was more than twice his previous or subsequent career best.

The son of a coal miner, Webb quit school at age 12 to work as a "trapper," opening and closing mine shafts for five cents an hour. On Sundays Webb walked eight miles to pitch for a local town team in Ravenscroft, Tennessee. A scout noticed Webb's impressive right arm and offered him a contract in 1921. At first, Webb said no, but his father convinced him to give up the mines.

He debuted in the Mississippi State League as a pitcher, but he also played outfield. In 1924 Webb gave up pitching entirely. By his own admission, he was a poor fielder. "I have seen some mighty bad outfielders," Webb once said, "but none of them had anything on me."

Webb played sporadically for the New York Giants and Chicago Cubs. He batted .301 for the Cubs in 1927, but was shipped to the Pacific Coast League when he slumped the following year. His breakthrough occurred when the Boston Red Sox purchased his contract.

In 1930 Webb batted .323 with 16 home runs and also improved on his defense. The following year he batted a career-best .333 to go with his record 67 doubles. Some Boston writers criticized Webb for sometimes stopping at second base when he could have continued running; he had only three triples among his 196 hits that season.

When Webb had only nine doubles through 52 games in 1932, the Red Sox traded him to Detroit. His numbers continued to dwindle, both with the Tigers and with the Chicago White Sox in 1933. At age 36, just two years removed from his astonishing 1931 season, he was out of the major leagues for good. He died of a heart attack in 1965 at age 67.

Mitch Webster

Webster, Mitchell Dean **OF**

1983–95 B:5/16/1959, Larned, KS Deb:9/2/1983, TOR AL BB/TL 6'1", 185

G	AB	R	H	HR	RBI	OBP	SLG	AVG
1265	3419	504	900	70	342	.332	.401	.263

An intense switch hitter, Mitch Webster spent seven years in the Los Angeles Dodgers' and Toronto Blue Jays' farm systems, getting only a handful of at-bats in the majors. Despite some good minor league performances—a batting title in 1979 and All-Star Most Valuable Player Award in 1984—the major league opportunity didn't manifest until he caught the eye of the Montreal Expos, who acquired him in 1985. In September of that year, he tied a club record by homering in four consecutive games.

Although Webster didn't hit a lot of home runs, he had some spectacular moments in an otherwise ordinary career. On July 6, 1986, he had five hits in a game against Atlanta. His performance was overshadowed by that of the Braves' Bob Horner, who became the 11th player in big-league history to hit four homers in one game.

Webster never drew enough walks to be a successful leadoff hitter. He was never particularly effective as a base-stealer, and his defense was only adequate. Yet Webster kept his career alive by transforming himself into one of the better pinch hitters in the National League. He filled that role for five years with the Los Angeles Dodgers, retiring after the 1995 season.

Al Weis

Weis, Albert John **2B–SS**

1962–71 B:4/2/1938, Franklin Square, NY Deb:9/15/1962, CHI AL BB/TR 6', 170

G	AB	R	H	HR	RBI	OBP	SLG	AVG
800	1578	195	346	7	115	.279	.275	.219

Al Weis' name belongs with those of Al Gionfriddo, Cookie Lavagetto, and Dusty Rhodes: players whose careers were otherwise colorless, but who starred at crucial moments in the white-hot pressure of the World Series. In December of 1967, the Mets obtained Tommy Agee from the White Sox. Slender infielder Weis was included in the deal, as a utility man. Weis had hit .296 one year for Chicago, but his lifetime total was just three homers when he became a Met.

During the 1969 season, Weis belted two critical homers to help win back-to-back July games against the league-leading Cubs. But he saved his best for the World Series. The Mets had lost Game 1 and were locked in a 1–1 duel in the ninth in Game 2 when Weis came to bat with men on first and third and two out. He slapped a single to left to drive in the winning run. In Game 5, the Orioles had a comfortable 3–0 lead before the Mets scored twice in the sixth. Weis then led off the seventh with a home run to tie the game. The Mets scored twice in the eighth and won their first World Series.

Weis appeared in only 75 games the following year. He was out of baseball before the 1971 season was over.

George Weiss

Weiss, George

Executive (1932–71) B:6/23/1895, New Haven, CT D:8/13/1972, Greenwich, CT

To George Weiss—the first Yankees farm director, then the team's general manager—goes much of the credit for creating the Yankees dominance from the 1930s through the 1960s. He was named Major League Executive of the Year four times.

Weiss began by promoting Sunday exhibition games against major league clubs in his native New Haven. In 1920 he purchased that city's Eastern League franchise. In 1929 Weiss moved up to Baltimore in the International League and on December 31, 1932, Col. Jacob Ruppert hired him to create and oversee a Yankees farm system.

Weiss presided over a far-flung empire of farm clubs, which regularly fed the best talent to New York. In 1948 he was promoted to the post of general manager. One of his first acts was to hire Casey Stengel as Yankees manager. Both were fired after the 1960 World Series, and both subsequently were hired to preside over the expansion New York Mets. Weiss retired in December 1971. Said rival general manager Frank "Trader" Lane: "I never made a single deal with him. He was too smart."

Walt Weiss

Weiss, Walter William **SS**

1987–* B:11/28/1963, Tuxedo, NY Deb:7/12/1987, OAK AL BB/TR 6', 175

G	AB	R	H	HR	RBI	OBP	SLG	AVG
1415	4494	594	1157	25	368	.354	.326	.257

Walt Weiss spoke softly but carried a big glove. The switch-hitting shortstop, in the majors primarily for his defense, helped seven teams reach postseason play during his 13-year career. He was American League Rookie of the Year in 1988, his first full season with the Oakland Athletics; a decade later he was starting shortstop for the National League All-Stars in 1998 while playing for the Atlanta Braves. In between he also played for the Florida Marlins and Colorado Rockies.

In 1997, displaced by the younger and faster Neifi Perez in Denver, Weiss signed a three-year contract to play for the Braves, where incumbent shortstop Jeff Blauser was also a free agent. He got off to a great start in 1998 but was slowed by physical problems and his son's midseason bout with *E. coli* bacteria. Weiss received a heartfelt ovation for his son's successful recovery at the 1998 All-Star Game at Coors Field. He finished that season with a .280 average, 20 points above his career mark.

Weiss struggled at the plate, however, during the 1999 season. When his replacement, Jose Hernandez, also struggled, Weiss returned to the regular lineup for the postseason. His remarkable diving stop and throw to the plate with the bases loaded in the 10th inning preserved a tie in Division Series Game 3 at the Astrodome. Atlanta went on to win that game and take the series in four games.

In was not the first time he had shone in the postseason. Weiss had a great American League Championship Series for Oakland in 1988, abusing Red Sox pitching for a .333 average with two doubles in Oakland's four-game sweep. Not a power hitter, he made a reputation as a contact hitter and excellent bunter.

Bob Welch

Welch, Robert Lynn **P**

1978–94 B:11/3/1956, Detroit, MI Deb:6/20/1978, LA NL BR/TR, 6'3", 190

W	L	PCT	G	SH	IP	BB	SO	ERA
211	146	.591	506	28	3092	1034	1969	3.47

Bob Welch's two greatest achievements seemed as if they were lifetimes apart. In 1978 as a brash 21-year-old he outdueled Reggie Jackson in one of the most memorable at bats in World Series history. Twelve years later, he won 27 games and a Cy Young Award. Through it all he waged a personal battle with alcoholism.

A dominant fireballer at Eastern Michigan University, Welch breezed through the minors and joined the Dodgers in June 1978. He went 7–4 with a 2.02 ERA as a swingman that summer, then wound up on the hill in the bottom of the ninth inning of Game 2 of the World Series. Los Angeles led the Yankees, 4–3, with two on and two out. The batter was Jackson, who had slugged four homers in his last two Series games. After eight tense pitches that filled the count, Welch challenged Jackson with high heat. The result was a swing and a miss. "The kid beat me," Jackson said later.

Over the next 12 years, Welch proved one of the most reliable pitchers in baseball. He became a full-time starter in 1980, appearing in the All-Star Game that year. He won in double digits in five of six years, with the exception of the 1981 strike season. He was traded to Oakland after the 1987 season, and pitched against the Dodgers in the World Series the following October. He started in the Athletics' only win in the five-game upset by Los Angeles.

Welch won 17 games for the second straight year in 1989, and he won his first postseason game since 1978. Throwing an over-the-top 90-mph fastball, Welch painted the corners and was afraid of no one. By 1990 he had perfected a new pitch—the split-finger fastball. Supported by Oakland's "Bash Brothers" offense and relief ace Dennis Eckersley, he went 27–6, receiving a decision in all but two of his starts. From 1969 to 1999, only Steve Carlton (with Philadelphia in 1972) matched Welch's 27 wins. Over his final four seasons, however, Welch suffered back, shoulder, and elbow injuries. He still gutted out his 200th victory in 1993.

His consistency was even more remarkable considering his troubles with alcohol. At a time when such candor was rare among athletes, Welch went public with his drinking problem and subsequent rehabilitation. He recounted his struggles in the book *Five O'Clock Comes Early.*

Mickey Welch

Welch, Michael Francis **P**

1880–92 B:7/4/1859, Brooklyn, NY D:7/30/1941, Concord, NH Deb:5/1/1880, TRO NL BR/TR 5'8", 160

W	L	PCT	G	SH	IP	BB	SO	ERA
307	210	.594	564	41	4802	1297	1850	2.71

"Smiling Mickey" Welch spent his career in the shadow of Tim Keefe. The two righthanders were teammates for most of their years in the major leagues, and in most of those seasons Keefe was regarded as the ace of the pitching staff. Welch readily admitted that Keefe was the better pitcher of the two and in his old age ranked him as the greatest pitcher of the 1880s. Still, if Welch was not the greatest of his time, he was undoubtedly one of the greatest.

Michael Francis Welch started playing baseball on the streets and sandlots. He turned professional in 1877 when he joined the Poughkeepsie Volunteers, a semipro club. Two seasons with Auburn and Holyoke of the National Association followed. In 1880 he went to play for the Troy Trojans, then a member of the National League, where he became an instant sensation.

Although he stood only 5-foot-8 and weighed 160 pounds, Welch was known for his durability. He finished his rookie season at 34–30, all of them complete games. His fastball and curveball were little better than average, but he also threw a screwball, a rarity at the time.

Keefe joined the Haymakers in August 1880 and went only 6–6. In his second year, however, he established himself as the staff ace, and Welch slipped to number two in the rotation. Welch started "only" 40 games in 1881, again completing every one, and finished 21–18. On July 4 he celebrated his 22nd birthday by pitching two complete-game victories against Buffalo. He was not relieved until his second start in 1882, having begun his major league career with a remarkable 105 complete games in as many starts.

The 1883 season was Troy's last in the league. When John B. Day was granted both a National League and an American Association franchise in New York City, he bought the Haymakers for $7,000. Day divided the roster between his two teams. Welch joined the National League Gothams while Keefe pitched for the American Association Metropolitans. The teams played on adjoining fields separated by a canvas fence. When both teams were at home, fans high in the bleachers at one park were able to watch both games.

In 1883 and 1884 Welch won a total of 64 games for the Gothams and pitched almost 1,000 innings. He also played 38 games as an outfielder in 1883, hitting three homers, five triples, and 12 doubles. But his best work was done on the mound. On August 28, 1884, he set a major league record with nine consecutive strikeouts. The record wasn't broken until Tom Seaver fanned 10 straight in 1970.

At the same time, Keefe won 77 games and pitched the Mets to the 1884 AA pennant. But the Metropolitans were losing money. Their tickets cost only 25 cents, while the Gothams charged 50 cents. The Mets would have to double the Gothams' attendance to bring in the same amount of money, which was highly unlikely. In an effort to boost admissions, Day shifted outfielder and .314 hitter "Dude" Esterbrook, manager Jim Mutrie, and Keefe to the Gothams. The move nearly precipitated a war between the two leagues.

With the arrival of Keefe, Welch once again became his team's second pitcher. If he was upset at what amounted to a demotion, he never let on. His sanguine personality led him to be nicknamed "Smiling Mickey" by a newspaper cartoonist. According to Welch's 1941 obituary, "Smiling Mickey's paycheck never exceeded $4,000 a year and he earned the money. Mutrie had him playing center field on the days he wasn't pitching and he also had to be at the park an hour ahead of time to watch the turnstile."

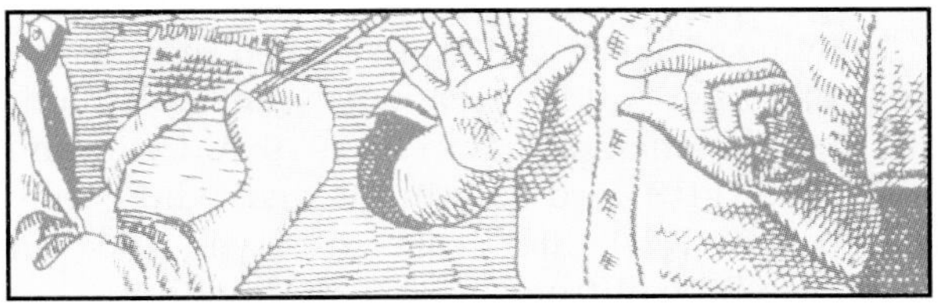

The 1885 season was Welch's best. He went 44–11, won 12 more games than Keefe, and finished with the best winning percentage in the league—the only time he ever led the NL in any category except bases on balls. During one stretch he won 17 consecutive games.

Although Welch and Keefe formed the best pitching combination in the league, the team didn't win a pennant until 1888. That year the Gothams (now called the Giants) defeated the AA champion St. Louis Browns in a so-called World Series as Keefe won four games and Welch split two decisions. The Giants repeated as NL champions in 1889 and defeated Brooklyn in the Series. Surprisingly, neither Welch nor Keefe won a Series game that year. But "Cannonball" Crane and Hank O'Day, the Giants third and fourth pitchers, won six games between them.

The Brotherhood War disrupted the 1890 season. The owners had devised a plan to rank players according to their ability, with a maximum salary of $2,500. For many players, including Welch, it meant a drastic salary cut. The Brotherhood of Professional Base Ball Players, formed in 1885 as a benevolent organization, decided to fight and set up its own Players' League to compete against the established major leagues. Most stars jumped to the new league. The 1890 season was a complete disaster for the National League and the American Association as nearly every team lost money.

Despite being one of the founders of the Brotherhood, Welch elected to stick with the Giants. He won only 17 games as his career neared its end. His 15th win was the 300th victory of his career, and Welch joined Jim Galvin and Keefe as members of the exclusive club.

The Players' League dissolved after its first year, and the severely wounded American Association struggled through one more season before it, too, folded. The National League took years to recover.

In 1891 Welch won only five games, and in 1892 friction developed between Smiling Mickey and manager Pat Powers. After only one start, Welch's contract was transferred to the Giants' minor league club at Troy. Mickey reported in mid-June, won 17 games, and then retired. His major league record was 308–209, with 525 complete games in 549 starts.

Welch moved to Holyoke, Massachusetts, where he served as steward of the Elks Club. In 1912 John McGraw offered him a job as one of the custodians of the Polo Grounds. For many years Welch stood watch at the entrance to the bleachers, reminiscing with fans and always smiling. In 1973 he was named to the Hall of Fame.

David Wells

Wells, David Lee **P**

1987–* B:5/20/1963, Torrance, CA Deb:6/30/1987, TOR AL BL/TL, 6'4", 225

W	L	PCT	G	SV	IP	BB	SO	ERA
141	99	.587	444	13	2077	507	1410	4.05

In 1997 at age 34, David Wells finally arrived to post the best years of his career. Wells, who looked like a refugee from a beer and softball league, was 34–14 in his two years with the New York Yankees. In the decade before coming to New York, the stocky lefthander had pitched 200 innings and won 15 games in a year just once. Nevertheless, the Yankees signed Wells as a free agent on December 17, 1996.

Wells requested the uniform number worn by his idol, Babe Ruth. When he was informed that No. 3 was retired and never to be worn again by a Yankee, he did the next best thing, asking for and getting No. 33. His adulation for Ruth was such that he bought a Yankees cap once worn by the Bambino for $35,000. He wasn't permitted to wear it, though, since it wasn't the same as the caps worn by his teammates.

Wells finished 16–10 in 1997 and won a Divisional Series playoff game against Cleveland, before New York was eliminated three games to two. Early the next season Wells gave indications that he could pitch even better for the Yankees. On "Beanie Baby Day" at Yankee Stadium on May 17, 1998, Wells zipped through a hapless Minnesota Twins lineup to pitch the 13th perfect game in baseball history. It was the first perfect game in the Bronx since Don Larsen threw his masterpiece in the 1956 World Series. Ironically, Wells had attended the same San Diego high school as Larsen. His gem left the Yankees with a 31–9 record in a season that would see them rewrite the American League record book with the incredible mark of 114–48. Wells finished his career year at 18–4, then notched four of the Yankees' 11 postseason wins against Texas, Cleveland, and San Diego to raise his lifetime October record to 8–1.

On February 18, 1999, Wells was dealt with Homer Bush and Graeme Lloyd to Toronto for Roger Clemens. The trade was controversial, since Wells was instrumental in New York's success, seemed to genuinely enjoy being a Yankee, and was beloved by the media and fans. But Clemens was coming off consecutive Cy Young Awards—and consecutive pitcher's "Triple Crown" years—in Toronto. Pitching for the second-place Blue Jays, Wells finished 17–10, bringing his three-year record to 51–24. He was among the league leaders in innings pitched.

Willie Wells

Wells, Willie James

Negro League Player (1924–49) B:8/10/1905, Austin, TX D:1/22/1989, Austin, TX BR/TR 5'8", 160

Although his arm was not strong, legendary shortstop Willie Wells knew how to position himself, and he boasted a speedy release on his accurate throws. As one opponent put it, "Everyone thought they could beat it out. 'He just got me by a step that time. If I run a little harder, I'll beat him.' But they never did. It would be the same way the next time. It was always just by a step."

Wells was one of the four great shortstops of the Negro Leagues. Wherever he played, his teams were winners. He was the shortstop for the St. Louis Stars when they won consecutive league championships in 1928, 1929, and 1930. He provided the same spark for the Chicago American Giants in 1933. When he joined the Newark Eagles with his longtime pal Mule Suttles ("the Damon and Pythias of black baseball," Cum Posey called them), they formed half of what became known as the black "Million Dollar Infield," joining Dick Seay at second and the hard-nosed Ray Dandridge at third.

In the early part of his career Wells was also an exceptional hitter, winning batting titles in 1929 (.368) and 1930 (.404). Statistics from the Negro Leagues are incomplete, but he's credited with a lifetime batting average of .334. Against white major leaguers Wells rang up a .392 average in recorded games. He could also hit for power, as demonstrated by his 27 home runs in 88 games in 1926, the Negro National League single-season record.

As a kid, Wells idolized Negro Leagues catching giant Biz Mackey and followed the star around, hoping to get a free pass into the park. Later, Wells played with his boyhood hero. Eight times Wells was chosen to participate in the classic Negro Leagues All-Star Game, the annual East-West contest. In those games he compiled a .281 average against the best in Negro baseball.

Known as "the Devil," Wells played several seasons of winter ball in Cuba, where he led Almendares to the championship in 1939 and won the league's MVP award, and in Mexico, where they called him "El Diablo." He also played a season in Puerto Rico, hitting .378 with Aquadilla.

Pitchers loved throwing inside to the fiery Wells, and he was one of the first players to wear a batting helmet in self-defense. He became a well-respected manager, known for his ability to instruct young players in the finer points of baseball. After retiring from the game, he worked in a New York City deli for 13 years before moving back to Austin, Texas in 1973 to care for his aging mother. He was elected to the Hall of Fame in 1997, eight years after he died of congestive heart failure.

Billy Werber

Werber, William Murray **3B**

1930–42 B:6/20/1908, Berwyn, MD Deb:6/25/1930, NY AL BR/TR 5'10", 170

G	AB	R	H	HR	RBI	OBP	SLG	AVG
1295	5024	875	1363	78	539	.364	.392	.271

Billy Werber played 10 seasons for the Yankees, Red Sox, A's, Reds, and Giants between 1933 and 1942. A career .271 hitter, he was an excellent third baseman and effective leadoff man who hit an occasional home run and drew more than a few walks. He was also one of the fastest players in the game, leading the American League in stolen bases three times. Unfortunately, his exploits on the field were overshadowed by his racist outbursts.

A graduate of Duke University, William Murray Werber liked to flaunt his education. He once corrected a teammate who, calling for a ball, yelled, "I got it." Werber insisted that the proper usage was "I have it." It was this attitude that led the great columnist Red Smith to consider Werber his "least favorite player."

But what Werber did on the diamond is far less significant than what he did off the field. Born in 1908 in Berwyn, Maryland, his college degree did not keep Werber from advocating segregated baseball.

In April 1945 Vito Marcantonio, the American Labor Party congressman from East Harlem in Manhattan, introduced a resolution in Congress calling for an investigation of baseball's color barrier. A few days later Werber sent the congressman a letter. Didn't Marcantonio know, Werber asked, that the movement to admit black players was partly Communist-inspired? Or that "Negroes do not like the whites, nor are the whites ready to accept the blacks as social equals"?

According to Werber, white players would not play with blacks, nor would they "eat at the same table, use the same showers and toilet facilities, or sleep in the same Pullmans." Why, Werber wrote, should white players be deliberately agitated for "the sake of tryouts of three or four black players who might or might not be able to make good?" He added, "A dog and a cat will not naturally bed down together and we accuse neither of being undemocratic... they are most happy and content when playing among their own kind."

After he left baseball Werber went into the family life insurance business, retiring in 1972. Two years later, after Bowie Kuhn publicly called for Major League Baseball to hire its first black manager, Werber wrote a letter to the editor that was published in *The New York Times*. In the letter he sarcastically called for baseball to push for 25 percent of its managers to be black since 25 percent of its players were black. In 1978 Werber self-published a book about his career titled *Circling the Bases*.

Vic Wertz

Wertz, Victor Woodrow **OF–1B**

1947–63 B:2/9/1925, York, PA D:7/7/1983, Detroit, MI Deb:4/15/1947, DET AL BL/TR 6', 186

G	AB	R	H	HR	RBI	OBP	SLG	AVG
1862	6099	867	1692	266	1178	.366	.469	.277

"I look at it this way," Vic Wertz once said. "If it had been a home run or a triple, would people have remembered it? Not likely." Wertz was talking about the play that has gone down in baseball legend as simply "the Catch"—the towering fly ball that he powered well over 400 feet in Game 1 of the 1954 World Series, only to see it snagged by Willie Mays in a breathtaking act of defensive artistry. Mays then made an equally sensational throw to allow only a single-base advance by one of the two base runners.

Wertz had already reached Giants pitcher Sal Maglie for three hits, including a two-run triple in the first inning that had given Cleveland the lead. But when he came to bat in the eighth with Larry Doby and Al Rosen on base, Leo Durocher replaced Maglie with lefty Don Liddle. When asked about the catch afterwards, Durocher said it was routine. "Routine!" the reporters protested. "Routine for Willie Mays, I mean," Leo replied.

New York won the game in the last of the ninth on Dusty Rhodes' pinch homer, and the Giants went on to sweep the Indians. Wertz hit .500 in that Series, twice the average of any other Cleveland regular, and led both teams with eight hits. It was his only postseason appearance during his 17-year career.

Victor Woodrow Wertz first played professional baseball at age 17, hitting .239 for Winston-Salem of the Piedmont League. With Buffalo in 1946 he hit .301, slugged 19 homers, and drove in 91 runs. Greatly impressed, the Tigers promoted the powerful young lefthanded hitter, and in his rookie year he banged 22 doubles, the first of eight times in his career that he would reach that mark. In 1949 Wertz was installed as the Tigers' regular left fielder and became an All-Star, collecting 20 homers, 133 RBIs, and a .304 average for the season.

He drove in 123 runs in 1950 and 94 in 1951, but in August 1952 the Tigers sent Wertz, Dick Littlefield, and two others to the St. Louis Browns for Ned Garver and three additional players. Wertz hit 23 homers that season for the two teams. He added 19 the following year for the Browns, but was swapped to Cleveland on June 1, 1954, and had his World Series moment with the Indians that fall.

After three years of split duty in the outfield and at first base, Wertz was installed as Cleveland's permanent first baseman in 1955. In August of that year he suffered a non-paralytic form of polio, but he made a remarkably quick recovery and in 1956 had the best home run year of his career, slamming 32 while driving in 106 runs. He continued his power surge in 1957 with 28 homers and 105 RBIs.

A leg injury kept Wertz out of all but 25 games in 1958, and the Indians swapped him and Gary Geiger to the Red Sox in December for Jimmy Piersall. At age 35 in 1960, Wertz hit 19 homers with 103 RBIs, the fifth 100-plus RBI season of his career.

Late in the 1961 season Wertz was waived to the Tigers. The next year he hit .324 for Detroit in 74 games, including a league-leading 17 pinch hits, but his power stroke was gone—only five of his hits had left the park. When the Tigers cut him in early 1963 he played 35 games with the Minnesota Twins before retiring.

Wertz became a successful operator of a beer distributorship in Detroit, and also scouted for the Tigers for several years. According to historian Bill James, along "with Hodges and Kluszewski, Wertz ranks as [one of] the best first basemen of the 1950s."

Sam West

West, Samuel Filmore **OF**

1927–42 B:10/5/1904, Longview, TX D:11/23/1985, Lubbock, TX Deb:4/17/1927, WAS AL BL/TL 5'11", 165

G	AB	R	H	HR	RBI	OBP	SLG	AVG
1753	6148	934	1838	75	838	.371	.425	.299

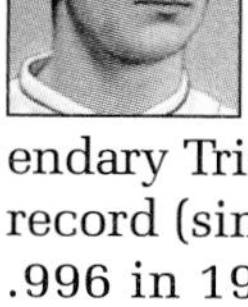

One of the smoothest fielding outfielders of his era, Sammy West starred for the Washington Senators and St. Louis Browns from 1928 to 1937. Tutored on outfield defense by the legendary Tris Speaker, West set an American League record (since broken) for fielding percentage with .996 in 1928. He led AL outfielders in fielding percentage, putouts, and double plays twice and tied for the league lead in assists once. An accomplished hitter as well, he compiled a .299 average for 16 major-league seasons. He hit .300 or better 10 times, reaching a career high of .333 for Washington in 1931.

Samuel Filmore West began his big league career with the Senators in 1927. He spent six seasons in Clark Griffith Park before being traded to the Browns in 1932 in a deal that sent future Hall of Famer Leon "Goose" Goslin to Washington. West played with St. Louis until a 1938 trade sent him traded back to the Senators, who released him in 1942. The White Sox signed him in March of that year, and finished the season in Chicago. At that point West entered the Army and saw action in World War II. Discharged in June of 1945, he returned to baseball as a coach for the Senators.

Wes Westrum

Westrum, Wesley Noreen **C**

1947–57 M(1965–75, 260–366) B:11/28/1922, Clearbrook, MN Deb:9/17/1947, NY NL BR/TR 5'11", 185

G	AB	R	H	HR	RBI	OBP	SLG	AVG
919	2322	302	503	96	315	.357	.373	.217

Wes Westrum was a part-time catcher for the New York Giants in 1948 and 1949, sharing time behind the plate with Walker Cooper and Ray Mueller. When he finally became the regular in 1950, he responded with an excellent year: 23 home runs, 71 RBIs, and a .999 fielding percentage. In one game in June of that year he slugged three homers and added a triple against the Reds. He also led the league in assists and double plays by a backstop.

Westrum was more than a durable catcher with power, however. He was a student of the game, knowledgeable enough to coach and manage in the big leagues for 17 years after his playing career ended. One of Westrum's most famous quotes was on the subject of baseball. "It's like church," he said. "Many attend, but few understand."

As a player, Wesley Noreen Westrum set an International League record in 1949 when he clouted five grand slams, despite appearing in only 51 games that year. He would later hit five grand slams in the bigs, including a vital one that won a critical game in July 1951 and moved the onrushing Giants into second place.

Westrum started all three games of the playoffs against the Dodgers that year, but he was absent when teammate Bobby Thomson hit his famous "Shot Heard 'Round the World," a three-run, ninth-inning homer that clinched the division title for New York. The catcher—one of seven future managers, incidentally, on the rosters of those two teams—had been removed for a pinch hitter in the eighth.

In 1955 Westrum had an embarrassing experience in a game against Brooklyn. The Dodgers' Sandy Amoros had swung and missed on a strike three, but his hefty swing brought the bat all the way around, beaning Westrum. The dazed catcher couldn't recover in time to find the ball and keep Amoros from reaching first. Shortly thereafter a rule change was made to prevent similar occurrences.

Westrum moved with the Giants to San Francisco as a coach. But thanks to a chance encounter at a Cleveland bar, he later returned to New York as a coach and, eventually, manager of the Mets. As Jack Lang, a longtime New York sportswriter, tells the story, he and Mets skipper Casey Stengel were enjoying each other's company and having a few drinks during the 1963 All-Star break in Cleveland. The two closed the press lounge at one in the morning and were heading back to their hotel when they saw a dim neon sign with one word on it: "Bar." Stengel suggested they stop for one more.

Sitting at the far end of the tavern's bar was Westrum, whom Stengel knew from his years with the Giants. The former catcher and "the Ol' Perfessor" began to talk baseball, and they talked the night away. Stengel had never realized how much Westrum knew about the game. After that season the Mets and Giants pulled off an unheard-of swap: a coach for a coach. Mets coach Cookie Lavagetto was interested in being closer to his home in Oakland, California, and Stengel wanted Westrum at his side.

The two men got along famously, and on occasion Westrum even rivaled Stengel in malapropisms. After listening to an hour-long diatribe in Stengelese, Westrum turned to a friend and said, "Boy, after they made him they threw away the molding."

When Stengel broke his hip in 1965 he named Westrum to be his interim replacement, even though Yogi Berra, who already had managerial experience, was also a Mets coach. The "interim" proved to be permanent. Westrum kept the job for the 1966 season, but the spirit of Stengel lingered. After a tensely fought spring training game that year, Westrum was heard to say, "Whew! That was a real cliff dweller."

That year, for the first time in their history, the Mets did not lose 100 games. They won 66 and

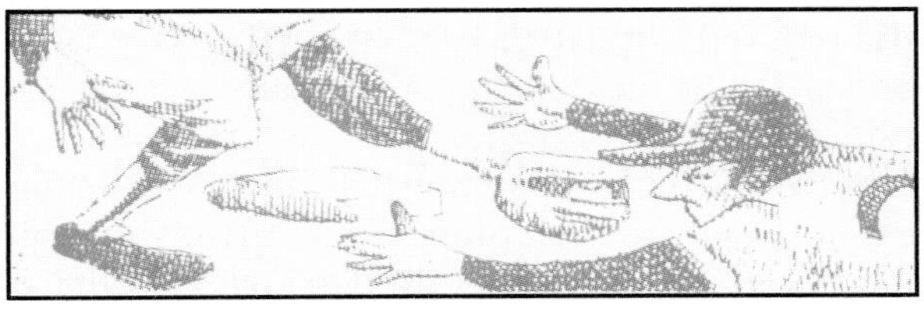

moved out of the cellar, where they had been since their premiere season. The team's apparent progress was a fluke, however. Although rookie Tom Seaver was showing flashes of brilliance the next year, the Mets were flirting with another 100-loss season when Westrum quit in late September. He was frustrated, both with the team he had been given and with the lack of respect he received from fans, the media, and the front office. Of his tenure as Mets manager, Westrum said, "I had one foot in the grave and the other on a banana peel."

Westrum returned to San Francisco to coach the Giants and was hired as manager when Charlie Fox was fired in the middle of the 1974 season. Under Westrum the Giants moved from fifth to third, but when the team was sold in the off-season, new management was chosen.

John Wetteland

Wetteland, John Karl **P**

1989–* B:8/21/1966, San Mateo, CA Deb:5/31/1989, LA NL BR/TR, 6'2", 195

W	L	PCT	G	SV	IP	BB	SO	ERA
42	40	.512	556	296	705	228	751	2.82

Despite a blazing fastball that tantalized scouts and coaches, John Wetteland was nearly released by the Los Angeles Dodgers after losing 10 straight minor league decisions in 1987. His manager, Kevin Kennedy, persuaded the organization to give Wetteland more time. He eventually made it through the minors, reaching Los Angeles in 1989.

During parts of three seasons with the Dodgers, Wetteland's erratic habits and bizarre pronouncements earned him the nickname "Cosmic Cow" and the disapproval of manager Tommy Lasorda. He was traded twice within a month in the 1991 off-season and landed in Montreal. Kennedy, by then a coach with the Expos, convinced manager Felipe Alou to let Wetteland try closing.

By then, thanks to marriage and a newly discovered spirituality, Wetteland was at peace with himself and surprised baseball observers by posting 37 saves. He saved 43 the next year and 25 more in 1994, but the strike ended both the Expos' World Series hopes and Wetteland's career in Canada. Montreal traded Wetteland to the New York Yankees shortly after the strike was resolved.

Following an up-and-down first season in New York, Wetteland had 43 saves—tops in the league—in 1996 to anchor one of the great bullpens in baseball history. He capped his dream season with seven saves in the 1996 postseason. Wetteland saved all four Yankees' World Series wins to earn Most Valuable Player honors. He signed a lucrative free-agent contract with the

Texas Rangers after the season, and then posted 116 saves for Texas from 1997–99.

Gus Weyhing

Weyhing, August **P**

1887–1901 B:9/29/1866, Louisville, KY D:9/4/1955, Louisville, KY Deb:5/2/1887, PHI AA BR/TR 5'10", 145

W	L	PCT	G	SH	IP	BB	SO	ERA
264	232	.532	538	28	4324[1]	1566	1665	3.89

Lanky righthander Gus Weyhing won at least 30 games a year from 1889 to 1892, earning the nicknames "Cannonball" and "Rubber-Winged Gus." From the start of his major league career, Weyhing won 23 or more games a year for seven consecutive seasons. Part of the reason for his success was a lack of shyness in pitching tight to hitters, plunking 286 of them in his career.

August Weyhing began pitching professionally in 1885 with Richmond in the Virginia League. He would have become a major leaguer even sooner than he did but the Charleston club of the Southern League refused to part with his services, even raising his salary to $75 a month to keep him in the minors. He left Charleston, however, in July 1886, feigning a sore arm, and in the off-season signed with the Philadelphia Athletics of the American Association.

With Philadelphia on July 31, 1888, Weyhing pitched a no-hitter against the Kansas City Cowboys, beating them by a score of 4–0. Only two runners reached base and both were caught stealing. Nine years after he was through as a player, Weyhing had one of the shortest managing careers on record, being fired after the opening day of the 1910 Western Association season.

Zack Wheat

Wheat, Zachary Davis **OF**

1909–27 B:5/23/1888, Hamilton, MO D:3/11/1972, Sedalia, MO Deb:9/11/1909, BRO NL BL/TR 5'10", 170

G	AB	R	H	HR	RBI	OBP	SLG	AVG
2410	9106	1289	2884	132	1248	.367	.450	.317

Zack Wheat was a line drive hitter, but under the right circumstances he could put a ball into the stands. New York Giants manager John McGraw figured those circumstances existed whenever Wheat and the Dodgers visited the Polo Grounds. McGraw knew the lefthanded-hitting Wheat handled curveballs as well as any hitter in the league. He also was well aware that the distance down the right-field foul line was less than 260 feet. McGraw was convinced that Wheat would jerk any breaking ball down the line for a homer and ordered his pitchers not to throw Wheat a curveball.

One day Giants pitcher Jess Barnes whipped two quick strikes past the Brooklyn left fielder. For some reason, Wheat knew the next pitch would be a curve. "I hit the ball way back in the upper deck," he said later. "I knew it was a homer when the ball was hit. As I was running to first base I could hear McGraw shouting, 'Barnes, you blankety-blank pinhead, that'll cost you $500!'"

Zachary Davis Wheat was born in Missouri in 1888, when the passions of the Civil War still ran high. His name was a declaration of neutrality by the Wheat family: his first name honored United States President Zachary Taylor; his middle name honored Confederate President Jefferson Davis. Nonetheless, his last name resulted in the inevitable nickname "Buck."

Wheat played semipro baseball in Kansas and then signed with Shreveport of the Texas League in 1908. He hit only .268 and moved on to Mobile of the Southern League in 1909. Although his batting average fell to .246, he was signed by a Dodgers scout, prompting Brooklyn president Charles Ebbets to grumble: "That's the trouble around here. We have too many .246-hitting outfielders." The scout promised that the rookie would hit, and in the remaining 26 games of the season Wheat batted .304 for the Dodgers.

From September 1909 through 1926, Wheat was the regular Dodgers left fielder. For years, a sign on the outfield wall at Ebbets Field proclaimed: "Zack Wheat caught 300 flies last year; Tanglefoot flypaper caught 10 million." The only change from season to season was the number of Wheat's putouts. He hit .300 or better in 14 seasons and roamed the outfield with speed and sure hands. In 1917 *Baseball Magazine* said, "Tris Speaker may be the greatest outfielder in the world, but Zack Wheat is the easiest, most graceful of all outfielders." His only weakness was his delicate ankles, and he suffered numerous sprains.

In the early 1920s a New York newspaper asked its readers to select the city's most popular player. At the same time that Babe Ruth was rewriting home run records for the Yankees and Frankie Frisch was leading the Giants to four straight pennants, the paper's readers chose Zack Wheat.

When Wheat first joined the team, Brooklyn was mired in the second division. The Dodgers won the pennant in 1916 and again in 1920 under manager Wilbert Robinson; both times Brooklyn lost the World Series, first to Boston in five games and then to Cleveland in a wild seven games that included the only unassisted triple play in Series history. Wheat hit only .211 during the 1916 Series, but he hit .333 and led all batters with nine hits in the 1920 Series.

Between the two pennant seasons, Wheat won his only batting championship in 1918, although it required an executive ruling to make it official.

The ground rules for eligibility for the title were unclear, and the season had been shortened because of World War I. Wheat finished at .335 in 105 games and Billy Southworth of Pittsburgh hit .341 in only 64 games, while Edd Roush of Cincinnati hit .333 in 113 games. National League president John Heydler declared Wheat the winner of the title.

Once described as "165 pounds of scrap iron, rawhide, and guts," Wheat was quiet and soft-spoken off the field. On the field he often argued an umpire's calls, but he always knew when to stop and was never thrown out of a game. He was a smart ballplayer, but one day in Brooklyn he missed a bunt sign on two consecutive pitches. In exasperation, manager Robinson pantomimed a bunt, witnessed by everyone in the park. To foil the play, the opposing pitcher delivered a high, inside fastball; Wheat stepped back and knocked it over the fence.

Despite his offensive prowess, Wheat's personal favorite baseball moment was a fine defensive play. On May 1, 1920, the Dodgers and Boston Braves were tied, 1–1, in a 26-inning marathon, the longest game by innings in major league history. At one point the Braves had runners on first and third with two out when the batter singled to left. Every other outfielder would have fruitlessly thrown home, but Wheat grabbed the ball on the bounce, fired it to second, and got the forceout before the man on third crossed the plate.

Late in the 1926 season, Wheat hit his last National League home run. As he rounded first base, he pulled a muscle so severely that he was forced to stop and sit down at second base. Rabbit Maranville came out to run for him but was waved away. Wheat rose after a few minutes and walked the remaining 180 feet to home plate.

Brooklyn released Wheat after the 1926 season. He signed for one year with Connie Mack's Philadelphia Athletics and showed he still had something left by hitting .324. He then played 82 games for Minneapolis of the American Association in 1928 and retired.

Wheat had four hitting streaks that stretched at least 20 games, including a career-best 29-gamer in 1916. After leaving baseball, he served on the Kansas City, Missouri police force until 1936, when an accident in a patrol car forced him to quit. Later he ran a fishing camp. He was named to the Hall of Fame in 1959. When he died in 1972, at age 83, Casey Stengel, who played with him in the Brooklyn outfield, said, "Zack Wheat was the only great ballplayer who was never booed."

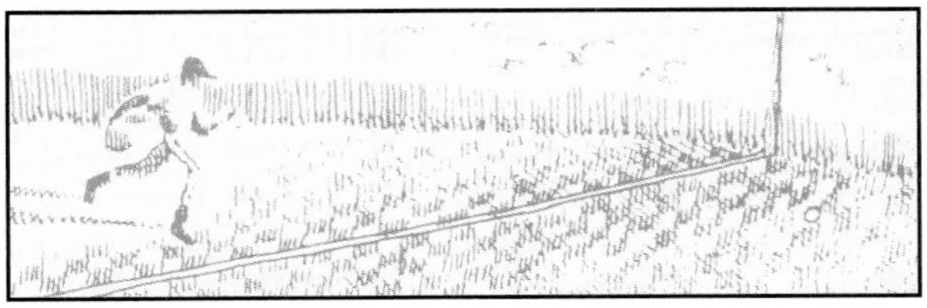

Lou Whitaker

Whitaker, Louis Rodman **2B**

1977–95 B:5/12/1957, Brooklyn, NY Deb:9/9/1977, DET AL BL/TR, 5'11", 160

G	AB	R	H	HR	RBI	OBP	SLG	AVG
2390	8570	1386	2369	244	1084	.366	.426	.276

Lou Whitaker enjoyed his share of individual glory. His 2,308 games as Tigers second baseman was 102 more than Hall of Famer Charlie Gehringer, who, like Whitaker, spent his entire 19-year career in Detroit. He joined Hall of Famer Joe Morgan as only the second player to log 2,000 games at second with 2,000 hits and 200 home runs. Nevertheless, Whitaker will best be remembered for teaming up with shortstop Alan Trammell for an American League record 1,918 games.

Born in Brooklyn but raised in Martinsville, Virginia, Whitaker was selected by the Tigers in the fifth round of the June 1975 draft. He was a third baseman his first two seasons in the minor leagues, then converted to second base. In September 1977 he and Trammell debuted in the same game.

"Sweet Lou" batted 285 with 61 walks to win the 1978 AL Rookie of the Year honors. After hitting a total of 12 home runs in his first four seasons, Whitaker smacked 15 homers and batted .286 in 1983. The next year he won the first of three straight Gold Gloves and was selected to the All-Star team for the first of five consecutive seasons. He also set career highs with 206 hits and a .320 average. Batting one and two in the order, Whitaker and Trammell (.319) became the first AL double play duo in 34 years to bat .300.

Whitaker's hot bat in April—a 10-game hitting streak, .442 batting average, and 13 runs scored—helped Detroit forge a 35–5 start in 1984. The Tigers won the pennant with ease. Whitaker doubled and scored in the first inning of the World Series opener, on his way to leading all players with six runs scored. He also led both teams with 18 assists and handled 33 chances without an error. The Tigers defeated the San Diego Padres in five games.

Whitaker topped the 20-home run plateau for the first time in 1985; he also cleared Tiger Stadium's right field roof. The following year he was part of an infield in which every player had 20 or more home runs, and one of six Tigers with 20 homers. In 1987 Whitaker had career highs with 110 runs and 38 doubles, each third-best in the league, as the Tigers came from behind to win the AL East on the season's final weekend. Whitaker hit his first postseason home run in Game 2 of the Championship Series, but the Minnesota Twins took the pennant in five games.

In 1989, aided by an off-season conditioning program and a slightly restructured batting style, Whitaker reached career highs with 28 homers, 85 RBIs, and 89 walks. Although his fielding range decreased, his batting eye remained keen. He batted .290 or better in each of his final three seasons, including a career-best .415 on-base percentage at age 36 in 1993. He retired in 1995.

Bill White

White, William De Kova **1B–OF**

1956–69 NL President(1989–94) B:1/28/1934, Lakewood, FL Deb:5/7/1956, NY NL BL/TL 6', 195

G	AB	R	H	HR	RBI	OBP	SLG	AVG
1673	5972	843	1706	202	870	.353	.455	.286

Born the son of a sharecropper in the Florida panhandle, Bill White was a pioneer in opening doors for blacks in baseball—in the Carolina League in the early 1950s, later as a broadcaster, and still later as the National League's first black president. The Gold Glove first baseman was a five-time All-Star with the St. Louis Cardinals and a fighter for civil rights throughout his careers as player and executive.

White was a child when his family moved to northern Ohio, where his father became a steelworker and his mother a clerk with the Air Force. "I was an only child," said White, "and pretty well taken care of, never wanted for anything and never had to work."

A natural leader, White was elected president of both his junior and senior classes in high school. His mother hoped he would attend Florida A&M and become either a teacher "or someone's secretary." White, however, wished to become a doctor and attended Hiram College, a progressive school that admitted only students in the top third of their graduating class.

He had no ambition to play pro ball of any sort. But in 1952 White was presented with a lucrative offer from Giants scout Tony Ravich, a former big league catcher and minor league manager. Ravich took White to Forbes Field to audition for the Giants. White was so impressive that Giants manager Leo Durocher shouted to Ravich, "Get him out of here fast. If [Pirates president] Branch Rickey sees this kid, he'll get him."

White debuted in the New York Giants system in 1953 with Danville of the Class B Carolina League. Segregation still ruled, and he was the only black on the team. He had asked to be sent to St. Cloud, Minnesota, of the Class C Northern League to avoid any trouble, but New York management refused. "I had constant trouble with baiters in Burlington-Graham, North Carolina," he recalled. "The more the fans gave it to me, the harder I hit the ball, so they eventually decided to leave me alone, which was a victory over bigotry."

Promoted to Sioux City of the Class A Western League in 1954, White tied for the league lead in hits and led the league in homers, putouts, and stolen bases, while batting .319. He hit .295 with Dallas in the Texas League in 1955 but was not happy about returning to the South. "Perhaps the Giants weren't sensitive to the problems I faced in the Carolina League," he said.

White spent only 20 games at Minneapolis in 1956 before being promoted to New York, and on June 7 he homered in his first major league at bat. Despite spending part of the year in the American Association, he led National League first basemen in both putouts and assists. White spent all of the 1957 season and most of 1958 in the Army, stationed at Fort Knox, Kentucky. After a racial incident, he quit the post's baseball team.

By the time White returned to the Giants, they had moved to San Francisco and installed young Orlando Cepeda at first base. In March 1959 White was traded, along with third baseman Ray Jablonski, to St. Louis for pitchers Sam Jones and Don Choate.

In St. Louis a first baseman named Stan Musial blocked White's career path. White bided his time, playing the outfield until Musial retired. A career .286-hitter, White was not always the most adroit fielder. One collision with the ivy-covered walls at Wrigley Field left him with 28 stitches over his left eyebrow.

White persevered and was a National League All-Star in 1959, 1960, 1961, 1963, and 1964. Once moved back to first base, he won Gold Gloves each year from 1960 through 1966. He was just as active off the field. In 1961 White led the fight to persuade the Cardinals to abandon segregated facilities in St. Petersburg, Florida.

In October 1965 the Cardinals traded White, catcher Bob Uecker, and veteran shortstop Dick Groat to Philadelphia for pitcher Art Mahaffey, outfielder Alex Johnson, and catcher Pat Corrales. With Philadelphia in 1966, White continued a six-year streak of hitting 20 or more home runs, which he had begun in St. Louis. He also drove in more than 100 runs for the fourth time.

White had begun his broadcasting career while still with the Cardinals, doing a five-minute radio show each Saturday on KMOX. After retiring from baseball, he landed a job with Philadelphia's WFIL-TV, an ABC affiliate, doing a brief segment on the evening news program. But that didn't last long. "I got tired of working three minutes a day," he remarked, "and putting in 12 hours to do that."

Making it known that he wished to move on, he was approached by New York Yankees president

Mike Burke, and in January 1971 signed a year's contract to broadcast Yankees games. "My first year I was terrible," White confessed. "I had no style. The second year I was a little less terrible."

White, who teamed with Phil Rizzuto in the Yankee booth for 17 years, worked hard at perfecting a style. "Bill would tape-record his segment of every game on radio and on his way back—he had a two-hour commute to his home—he would listen to it on his car stereo," said fellow Yankees broadcaster Frank Messer. "That was something that, to be honest with you, I never did even when I first started."

White, who at one time was part of the broadcast team that covered Monday night baseball for ABC, was offered the post of Yankees general manager but turned it down. He believed he was not yet ready for such a position. He changed his mind in February 1989, when at the urging of Commissioner A. Bartlett Giamatti he was appointed National League president—the first African-American to hold a major league's presidency.

"If I didn't think I could do this job, I would have been foolish just to take it for historical significance," White said at the time. Added Braves vice president Henry Aaron: "I don't think they could have found anyone more qualified for this position."

Deacon White

White, James Laurie **C-3B-OF-1B**

1871–90 M(1872, 1879, 9–11) B:12/7/1847, Caton, NY D:7/7/1939, Aurora, IL Deb:5/4/1871, CLE NA BL/TR 5'11", 175

G	AB	R	H	HR	RBI	OBP	SLG	AVG
1299	5335	849	1619	18	756	.344	.382	.303

In the beginning there was Deacon White, the first batter in major league history when he led off on May 4, 1871, against the Fort Wayne Kekiongas. He made both the first hit and the first extra-base hit (a double), and hit into the first double play. White, who also caught the game, went 3-for-4 as his Cleveland Forest City club lost, 2–0.

James Laurie White was nicknamed "Deacon" because he was a superintendent in a Sunday school in his native Caton, New York. He was a religious man who did not smoke, drink, or gamble. White started a local Caton team in 1866 after being introduced to the game by a soldier returning from the American Civil War. "I was immediately hooked on the new game," he said. The following year he played with a club in Corning, New York. In 1869 he played for the Forest City team, and in 1871 when the club became a member of the National Association, the first major league, he remained.

Generally thought of as the best catcher of the 1870s, White exerted a great deal of influence on the game. He fought to legalize the curveball and taught the pitch to his brother, Will White, who went on to become a three-time 40-game winner. White was also responsible for several equipment advances. "In those days the catcher stood far behind the batter," he later explained. "He caught the ball barehanded on the first bounce. I got the idea of using a glove, made a mask for my face, and stood right behind the batter. That caused a sensation, too. Al Spalding liked the idea of the mask so well that he started a company to make them."

A .303 career hitter, from 1873 through 1875 White was part of Boston's "Big Four" hitters, along with Spalding, Cal McVey, and Ross Barnes. In 1876, however, White jumped to the nascent National League. He played for Chicago, Boston, and Cincinnati before moving to the Buffalo Bisons in 1881. He covered third base for the Bisons and became part of their "Big Four," along with Jack Rowe, Hardy Richardson, and Dan Brouthers.

In 1885 the Detroit Wolverines bought the entire Buffalo team for $7,000 in order to obtain the Big Four. The Wolverines' president, Fred Stearns, liquidated the Buffalo franchise the following year, and in 1887 Detroit won the world championship. After the 1888 season, Detroit sold the contracts of Rowe and White to the Pittsburgh Allegheny organization, but instead of reporting, the players bought shares in the Buffalo team of the Eastern Association. The management of both the Wolverine and the Allegheny clubs insisted that the athletes play for Pittsburgh and, it is said, sent word that any player taking the field with or against them would be blacklisted from the National League.

Detroit president Fred Stearns claimed that the reserve clause in the players' contracts prevented them from playing for another team. "White may have been elected president of the Buffalo club or president of the United States, but that won't enable him to play ball in Buffalo," Stearns contended. "He'll play ball in Pittsburgh or get off the earth."

Rowe and White sat out half a season and threatened to test the reserve clause in court, but eventually reported to Pittsburgh. However, the incident caused so much consternation among players that they created a Players' League in 1890, and White and Rowe played for and became part owners of the new Buffalo Bisons. The club was a poor collection of veterans. The *Cincinnati Inquirer* called them "the Home for respectable old men." The league folded after one season.

Despite his many contributions to baseball, as of 1999 White had not been elected to the Hall of Fame. He batted .303 in 5,335 at bats in his 15-year career.

Devon White

White, Devon Markes **OF**

1985–* B:12/29/1962, Kingston, Jamaica Deb:9/2/1985, CAL AL BB/TR, 6'2", 182

G	AB	R	H	HR	RBI	OBP	SLG	AVG
1768	6796	1047	1784	190	786	.320	.418	.263

An exceptional defensive centerfielder with speed and pop, Devon White made the most of his first chance to play regularly. In 1987 White slammed 24 home runs, stole 32 bases, and scored 103 runs for the California Angels. He won two Gold Gloves over the next three seasons, but fought with Angels manager Doug Rader. He was an All-Star in 1989, then demoted to the minor leagues a year later.

White was traded to Toronto, where he thrived under the more relaxed approach of Blue Jays manager Cito Gaston. Showing greater selectivity at the plate, White hit a career-best .282 and stole 37 bases in 41 tries. He also won his third Gold Glove, starting a run of five straight. As the Jays became annual playoff participants, White rose to the occasion: he had an American League record .392 batting average in 74 Championship Series at bats. He batted .260 for Toronto in the World Series as the Blue Jays won back-to-back championships in 1992 and 1993. In Game 4 of the 1993 Series against Philadelphia, with the Phils ahead 14–11 in the eighth, he capped a come-from-behind rally with a hit off Mitch Williams to give Toronto a 15–14 victory and a 3–1 Series lead.

White signed with the Florida Marlins as a free agent after the 1995 season. He played a key role in Florida's 1997 world championship, including a grand slam in the clinching game of the Division Series. He moved to expansion Arizona when the Marlins were dismantled after the World Series. White was the first All-Star in Diamondbacks history, hitting 22 homers and stealing 22 bases in his one season in the desert. He signed a three-year deal with the Los Angeles Dodgers prior to the 1999 season.

Doc White

White, Guy Harris **P**

1901–13 B:4/9/1879, Washington, DC D:2/19/1969, Silver Spring, MD Deb:4/22/1901, PHI NL BL/TL, 6'1", 150

W	L	PCT	G	SH	IP	BB	SO	ERA
189	156	.548	427	45	3041	670	1384	2.39

A fine pitcher as well as a good hitter, Doc White set a record for most consecutive shutouts. No one paid much attention to his record, however, until it was about to be broken.

White, whose real name was Guy, came by his nickname legitimately. After graduating from Georgetown University he practiced dentistry in his native Washington, D.C. between 1902 and 1906. A man of many talents, he also became an accomplished singer and businessman.

White gained notice as a pitcher at Georgetown when he struck out the first nine Holy Cross batters in one game. After a summer of independent ball, he went straight from college to the big leagues, landing with the Philadelphia Phillies in 1901. He joined the Chicago White Sox two years later. White became one of the best lefthanders of his era, ranking fourth in victories among southpaws by the time he retired.

His breakthrough year was 1906, when he posted an 18–6 record and a league-best 1.52 ERA. In the heat of the pennant race, White reeled off five straight shutouts in September, allowing just 18 hits in 45 innings. He capped off the year by pitching three games in the World Series for the "Hitless Wonders." He lost Game 2, but came back to save Game 5. He won Game 6 to complete a stunning upset over the cross-town Cubs.

White strung together 65 straight innings without allowing a base on balls in 1907, and led the AL with 27 wins. He never again won 20, although he had win totals in double-digits the next four years. A solid hitter and fielder, he even played second base in 1906. In 1909 he appeared in more games in the outfield than on the mound.

White spent seven years in the minors serving in managerial and executive capacities. He later embarked on a long teaching and coaching career in scholastic sports. When Don Drysdale recorded five straight shutouts in 1968, people scurried to the record books to find that the mark had been set by White 64 years earlier; they also discovered that Doc was still alive at 89. The day before Drysdale notched his record sixth straight shutout, White sent him a telegram: "It will be a great satisfaction to me to have someone who is a credit to the game break my record." White died that winter.

Frank White

White, Frank **2B-SS**

1973–90 B:9/4/1950, Greenville, MS Deb:6/12/1973, KC AL BR/TR 5'11", 170

G	AB	R	H	HR	RBI	OBP	SLG	AVG
2324	7859	912	2006	160	886	.295	.383	.255

Frank White was the best defensive second baseman of his era. A graduate of the Kansas City Royals' Baseball Academy, Frank spent his entire 18-year major league career (1973 to 1990) with the Royals. He compiled a respectable .255 lifetime batting average, but his glove brought him his greatest fame. White won eight Gold Gloves for defensive excellence, including six in a row, and led American League second basemen in fielding percentage three times. In 1977, he played 62 straight games without making an error.

Although not known as a power hitter, White hit 20 or more homers in a season two times and reached double figures in homers 13 times. He also stole 20 or more bases in a season three times.

White's greatest moment came when he was awarded the Most Valuable Player trophy for the 1980 AL Championship Series. He earned it by hitting .545 in the Royals three-game sweep of the New York Yankees for the league pennant. The Royals lost the World Series to the Philadelphia Phillies that year, but five Octobers later they were back in the Fall Classic, this time against the St. Louis Cardinals. It was White's home run off Joaquin Andujar in Game 3 that sparked Kansas City to its eventual triumph over the Cards.

In 1986, White was voted the Royals Player of the Year, hitting .272 with 22 home runs and 84 RBIs. He coached for Boston from 1994–1996, and was hired to coach by Kansas City in 1997. As of 1999, he was still serving the Royals in that capacity.

Roy White

White, Roy Hilton **OF–DH**

1965–79 B:12/27/1943, Los Angeles, CA Deb:9/7/1965, NY AL BB/TR 5'10", 172

G	AB	R	H	HR	RBI	OBP	SLG	AVG
1881	6650	964	1803	160	758	.363	.404	.271

When Bill Virdon took over as Yankees manager in 1974, he was not especially impressed with Roy White. White had been an excellent outfielder for some mediocre Yankees teams, but Virdon thought White had seen his best days and began platooning him. White never said a word. He just waited for a chance to prove Virdon wrong.

White got his chance in 1975, and Virdon was impressed enough to say publicly that White was a better player than he had originally thought. White, Virdon said, was one of those players who do all the little things, and it had taken the manager a while to appreciate how good a player White really was. That assessment was typical of White's career.

Roy Hilton White played baseball at Compton High in Los Angeles with such future major leaguers as Reggie Smith, Dock Ellis, Don Wilson, Bobby Tolan, and Dave Nelson. A fleet-footed switch hitter, he signed with the Yankees in 1962 as an infielder and hit .225 in 115 games as a rookie in 1966. By then he was being converted into an outfielder, although he had to be positioned in left because of his weak arm.

White split the next season between Class AAA and the big club, hitting .224 in 70 games with New York. His breakout year was 1970, when he posted career highs with a .296 average, 22 homers, 94 RBIs, and 109 runs while stealing 24 bases and walking 95 times. In 1972 he led the American League with 99 walks. White even became the Yankees' cleanup hitter, although he was only 5-foot-10 and 160 pounds.

After hitting .292 with 19 homers, 84 RBIs, and an American League record 17 sacrifice flies in 1971, White saw his numbers slip the next three seasons. He rebounded to hit .290 in 556 at bats with a career-best 32 doubles in 1975. He was batting second in the lineup now, a far better spot for him. He led the league in runs with 104 and swiped 31 bases, a career high, as the Yankees waltzed to the 1976 AL pennant. His numbers trailed off in 1977, however, but he still helped the Yankees to win their first World Series in 15 years.

In 1978, at age 34, White went on the disabled list for the first time with a hamstring injury. He played only 103 games that season, but he was an important contributor down the stretch in the Yankees' memorable pennant race against the Red Sox. He hit .313 in the ALCS against the Royals, including the game-winning homer in the clinching Game 4.

White batted .333 against the Dodgers as the Yankees repeated in the Series. It was to be his last hurrah. In 1979, his final season in the majors, he hit .215 in only 205 at bats. He then spent three seasons with the Tokyo Giants, becoming one of the most popular major leaguers to ever play in Japan.

Sammy White

White, Samuel Charles **C**

1951–62 B:7/7/1928, Wenatchee, WA D:8/5/1991, Princeville, HI Deb:9/26/1951, BOS AL BR/TR 6'3", 195

G	AB	R	H	HR	RBI	OBP	SLG	AVG
1043	3502	324	916	66	421	.307	.377	.262

Samuel Charles White first attracted national attention as a basketball player. He was an All-American at the University of Washington and had a tryout with the Minneapolis Lakers. A native of Wenatchee, Washington, White also excelled at baseball and was signed by the Boston Red Sox in 1949. He made it to the majors in 1951 and by the following season had become the club's primary catcher. White served the Red Sox as their starting catcher for six seasons and earned a reputation as one of the best defensive backstops in the major leagues.

"He steals more strikes from umpires than anyone else," New York Yankees manager Casey Stengel once said of White, alluding to the catcher's ability to "frame" a pitch. "I'm not being critical. I'm just bowing to his skills."

On June 11, 1962, White hit a ninth-inning grand slam off the legendary Satchel Paige at

Boston's Fenway Park. After he got halfway past third base, White crawled the rest of the way to home, then kissed the plate. A year later he became the only modern player to score three runs in an inning as the Red Sox erupted for 17 runs in the seventh and beat the Detroit Tigers, 23–3.

White was traded to Cleveland in March 1960, but he refused to report and the deal was canceled. Sold to Milwaukee in June 1961, he would up his big league career with the Philadelphia Phillies in 1962. Upon his retirement from baseball, White became a golf pro in Hawaii.

Sol White

White, Soloman **2B-3B-OF**

Negro League Player (1887–1912, 1920–26) Manager, Writer B:6/12/1868, Bellaire, OH D:8/1955, New York, NY BR/TR 5'9", 170

One of black baseball's true founding fathers, Sol White's life spanned the time between the segregation of professional baseball in the 1880s and Jackie Robinson's debut with the Dodgers in 1947. As a player, manager, and writer, he was candid and articulate in his advocacy for integrated baseball.

"King Solomon" played for integrated minor league teams from 1887 through 1895, was a star second baseman (and played every position but pitcher) for several Negro Leagues powerhouses, and helped found and manage one of the top African-American teams of the first decade of the century. Perhaps even more importantly, in 1907 White wrote the only history of the early years of Negro League ball, *Sol White's Official Base Ball Guide*. Although incomplete and biased toward Eastern clubs, it is an invaluable source of information for Negro Leagues historians. Sadly, when White tried to publish an updated version of the book later in his life, he could not raise the necessary funds.

White was born only three years after the end of the Civil War in Bellaire, Ohio, a small town across the Ohio River from Wheeling, West Virginia. He grew up to be a fast runner and a feared hitter. Although he is listed at 170 pounds, photos make him look considerably thinner. He played for the integrated Ohio State League team in Wheeling in 1887 and batted .381, but was cut when the league drew the color line in 1888.

He later played for integrated teams in Trenton, New Jersey; York, Pennsylvania, and Fort Wayne, Indiana. White never batted less than .333, and his lifetime average in the integrated minors was an impressive .360. But by 1895 integration in professional baseball was no longer a possibility, thanks to Adrian "Cap" Anson and other opponents of racial harmony.

White then began a long career as a Negro Leagues player and manager. From 1887 through 1901—while simultaneously enrolled at Wilberforce University until 1890—he played for seven different teams: the Pittsburgh Keystones, New York Gorhams, Cuban Giants, Philadelphia Big Gorhams, Page Fence Giants, Cuban X Giants, and Chicago Columbia Giants. White's proficiency at second base forced the legendary Frank Grant to move over to shortstop with the Big Gorhams. The team played more than 100 games one season and lost only four.

Historian John Holway explains White's nomadic tendencies this way: "Almost every team he played on claimed the black world championship, and each time...the loser promptly stole White and won the flag itself the following year."

In 1902 White paired up with Philadelphia sportswriter H. Walter Schlichter to found the Philadelphia Giants, which White managed from 1904 through 1907. The Giants attracted the best black players in the game and became the dominant force in Negro Leagues baseball. The records indicate that from 1902 through 1906 they played 680 games and won 507 of them. In 1904, the year after Boston and Pittsburgh met in the first modern-day World Series, White's Philadelphia team played the Cuban X Giants in the first Negro Leagues "World Series." The Cubans took the title in seven games.

The following year White and his Giants were nearly unbeatable, winning 134 and losing only 21. The team they challenged to another "World Series" didn't bother to show up for the games. In 1906 the Giants went 108–31. They offered to play the winner of the Cubs-White Sox World Series, "and thus decide who can play baseball best, the white or black Americans." They received no answer to their invitation.

In 1910 White moved on to the Brooklyn Royal Giants, possibly over a pay dispute with Schlichter, and spent 1911 managing the New York Lincoln Giants. He left the game after managing the Boston Giants the following year. He was back in 1920, however, when he went to work in the front office of the new Columbus team of the Negro National League. Four years later White returned to managing with the Cleveland Browns, and he also piloted the Newark Stars of the Eastern Colored League in 1926.

In addition, White served for years as a regular columnist for the *New York Amsterdam News*. In

his book, White notes with pride that fewer and fewer African-American teams needed clowns and bizarre showmanship to attract crowds. He also paints an honest picture of the difficulty of life as a Negro Leaguer, pointing out that the average major leaguer made $2,000 in 1906, while the average black netted only $466.

He wrote, "The colored players are not only barred from playing on white clubs, but at times games are canceled for no other reason than objections being raised by a Southern ballplayer, who refuses to play against a colored ballclub. These men from the South who object to playing are, as a rule, fine ballplayers, and rather than lose their services, the managers will not book a colored team."

White discussed possible changes in racial policy in his writing on accommodations. "The colored ballplayer suffers great inconvenience at times, while traveling. All hotels are generally filled from the cellar to the garret when they strike a town. It is a common occurrence for them to arrive in a city late at night and walk around for several hours before getting a place to lodge.

"The situation is far different in this respect than it was years ago. At one time the colored teams were accommodated in some of the best hotels in the country. The cause of this change is no doubt due to the condition of things from a racial standpoint. With the color question uppermost in the minds of the people at the present time, such proceedings on the part of hotel-keepers may be expected and will be difficult to remedy."

Nevertheless, White added, "Baseball is a legitimate profession. It should be taken seriously by the colored player. An honest effort of his great ability will open the avenue in the near future wherein he may walk hand in hand with the opposite race in the greatest of all American games—baseball."

Will White

White, William Henry **P**
1877–86 M(1884, 44–27) B:10/11/1854, Canton, NY
D:8/31/1911, Port Carling, Ontario, Canada
Deb:7/20/1877, BOS NL BB/TR 5'9½", 175

W	L	PCT	G	SH	IP	BB	SO	ERA
229	166	.580	403	36	3542^{2}	496	1041	2.28

The White brothers were second only to the Wright brothers among sibling baseball stars of the 19th century. Deacon White was a versatile slugger from 1871 through 1890. His brother Will, the first major league player to wear glasses on the field, was an exceptional righthanded pitcher.

William Henry White pitched his first major league games in 1877 for Boston, where he formed a brother battery with Deacon for a few games. From 1878 through 1880, they both played for Cincinnati. In 1879, Will pitched 680 innings and 75 complete games, both league-leading marks, while compiling a 43–31 record. When Cincinnati lost its National League franchise in 1881, White pitched several games for Detroit.

When the American Association was formed in 1882 and Cincinnati became a charter member, White joined the club and stayed through the remainder of his career. He led the AA with 40 wins, 52 complete games, eight shutouts, and 480 innings pitched in 1882. The following year, he topped all hurlers with 43 wins, six shutouts, and a 2.09 ERA. White's seven shutouts led the league in that category for the third straight year in 1884 as he finished 34–18. After leaving baseball, "Whoop-La" White became a successful businessman in Buffalo.

Burgess Whitehead

Whitehead, Burgess Urquhart **2B–3B**
1933–37, 1939–41, 1946 B:6/29/1910, Tarboro, NC
D:11/25/1993, Windsor, NC Deb:4/30/1933, STL NL
BR/TR, 5'10½", 160

G	AB	R	H	HR	RBI	OBP	SLG	AVG
924	3316	415	883	17	245	.304	.331	.266

Burgess Whitehead was a Phi Beta Kappa at the University of North Carolina before turning pro. He joined the "Gashouse Gang" Cardinals, serving as a valuable utility man and earning the nickname "The Gazelle" for his speed and grace afield. St. Louis vice president Branch Rickey deemed Whitehead too frail to play every day, however, and traded him to the New York Giants for four players after the 1935 season.

Whitehead proved Rickey wrong—then proved him right. He played every game for the Giants in 1936 and 1937, helping them to the National League pennant both years. He then suffered a physical and mental breakdown the following year, and missed the entire season. Whitehead returned in 1939, but was ineffective and flighty. He incurred two suspensions for training violations.

Whitehead made a comeback in 1940, batting .282 in 133 games. After slipping to .228 the next year, he was demoted to the minors, and then sold to Pittsburgh. Whitehead joined the Army Air Corps in 1942, and returned for a final stint with the 1946 Pirates. He later ran a prosperous feed and livestock business in North Carolina, and also

served as an assistant golf pro. He was inducted into the North Carolina Sports Hall of Fame in 1981.

Earl Whitehill

Whitehill, Earl Oliver **P**

1923–39 B:2/7/1900, Cedar Rapids, IA D:10/22/1954, Omaha, NE Deb:9/15/1923, DET AL BL/TL 5'9½", 174

W	L	PCT	G	SH	IP	BB	SO	ERA
218	185	.541	541	16	3564²	1431	1350	4.36

Southpaw Earl Whitehill started out as a soccer player, but had to give it up after an injury. Soccer's loss was baseball's gain; Whitehill went on to enjoy a 17-year major league career, pitching mostly for Detroit and Washington in the 1920s and 1930s.

In his first minor league season, with Columbia of the South Atlantic League, Whitehill went 20–10. He would have only one other 20-win season, with the Senators in 1933, although he was a consistent double-digit winner for 13 consecutive seasons.

Whitehill was known for his fiery temper. In the minors, at Birmingham of the Southern Association, probably in response to taunts, he once went into the grandstand and challenged all comers. In the majors in 1933 he was once so incensed by umpire Brick Owens' call on a Lou Gehrig home run that he threw Owens' whiskbroom over the grandstand.

Whitehill made his major league debut when Detroit manager Ty Cobb inserted him into an 8–0 Tigers romp in the seventh inning. He contributed to a 9–8 Tiger defeat. He settled down to win 17 games for Detroit in 1924, his first full season in the majors.

In 1930 Whitehill had a no-hitter going against the New York Yankees until the eighth inning, when the opposing pitcher, Roy Sherid, singled for the only hit of the game. Once, while barnstorming, Whitehill did pitch a no-hitter, calling in the outfield in the ninth inning—and getting away with it.

In December 1932 Detroit traded Whitehill to the Senators. He helped them win the pennant the following season, and in the World Series he shut out the New York Giants in Game 3 for Washington's only victory. His 22 wins that year made him the Senators' last 20-game winner until Bob Porterfield two decades later.

Following the 1936 season Whitehill was traded to Cleveland in a three-way deal also involving the White Sox. The Senators' owner, Clark Griffith, said he had made the deal "to get rid of Whitehill's $12,000 salary and his dynamic disposition." Whitehill finished his career in the National League with the Cubs in 1939.

During his playing days, Whitehill attained some measure of celebrity when he married Violet Linda Oliver, best known as the model on the Sun Maid Raisins box. After he retired, he coached for the Indians, the Phillies, and the Buffalo Bisons, and was a sales representative for Spalding Sporting Goods.

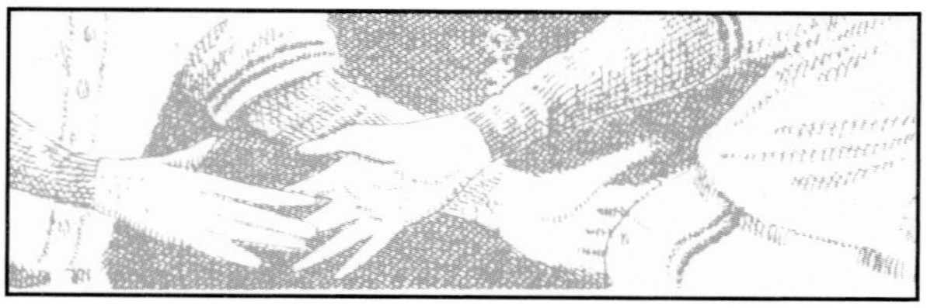

Mark Whiten

Whiten, Mark Anthony **OF**

1990–* B:11/25/1966, Pensacola, FL Deb:7/12/1990, TOR AL BB/TR, 6'3", 215

G	AB	R	H	HR	RBI	OBP	SLG	AVG
934	3097	463	802	105	422	.342	.415	.259

Mark Whiten turned in one of the greatest single-game performances in baseball history on September 7, 1993. As the St. Louis Cardinals faced the Cincinnati Reds in a doubleheader, Whiten followed an unremarkable performance in the first game with a four-homer, 12-RBI eruption in the nightcap. Both marks tied major league records.

Although capable of tape-measure home runs and laser strike throws from the outfield, Whiten never became a star or even stayed with one club long enough to become a regular. He changed teams eight times between 1991 and 1998. When he showed that he couldn't consistently hit breaking balls, pitchers rarely challenged him with a fastball. More often than not, Whiten would get himself out.

As if to complement his record-tying performance in 1993, Whiten enjoyed his best season that year with the Cardinals, hitting 25 home runs and driving in 99 runs. He also earned recognition from National League managers as possessing the best outfield arm.

Fred Whitfield

Whitefield, Fred Dwight **1B**

1962–70 B:1/7/1938, Vandiver, AL Deb:5/27/1962, STL NL BL/TL 6'1", 190

G	AB	R	H	HR	RBI	OBP	SLG	AVG
817	2284	242	578	108	356	.301	.443	.253

A power-hitting first baseman, Fred Whitfield played nine seasons in the major leagues and distinguished himself briefly in the mid-1960s as a home run hitter. His days in the limelight were brief, lasting only two seasons, but he played well enough to earn a berth on *The Sporting News* American League All-Star team in 1965.

Whitfield started his professional baseball career with Keokuk in the Midwest League in 1958. He led the Carolina League in RBIs (118) and doubles (29), while batting .309. Released by both the Pittsburgh Pirates and Baltimore Orioles organizations, he eventually signed on with the St. Louis Cardinals in 1962. Whitfield played 73 games for the Cards that season and hit .266 with eight homers and 34 RBIs. That was good enough to earn him a berth on the Topps Rookie All-Star team.

The Cardinals traded him to the Cleveland Indians in 1962, and by 1965 Whitfield had become the Indians' regular first baseman. In 1965 he had his best season, hitting .293 with 26 homers and 90 RBIs in 132 games. Ten of his home runs came against the New York Yankees. Whitfield enjoyed another good campaign in 1966 with 27 homers and 78 RBIs in 137 games. By 1967, however, he had lost his everyday job and was out of baseball by 1970.

Jim Whitney

Whitney, James Evans **P–OF**

1881–90 B:11/10/1857, Conklin, NY D:5/21/1891, Binghamton, NY Deb:5/2/1881, BOS NL BL/TR, 6'2", 172

G	AB	R	H	HR	RBI	OBP	SLG	AVG
550	2144	316	559	18	280	.313	.375	.261

W	L	PCT	G	SH	IP	BB	SO	ERA
191	204	.484	413	26	3496[1]	411	1571	2.97

Jim Whitney was one of the best double-duty players of all time. In the early 1880s he often served as his team's ace pitcher and cleanup batter. Nicknamed "Grasshopper Jim" because of his bony frame, he bounced around the minor leagues for two years before landing in Boston in 1881.

As a rookie Whitney led National League pitchers in games, complete games, and innings, and his 31–33 record for the sixth-place Red Stockings made him the NL leader in both wins and losses. Overcoming early wildness, he became one of the best control pitchers in baseball history. Between 1882 and 1885, Whitney struck out 995 batters while walking just 140 in 1,711 innings—an average of 0.74 walks per nine innings. He earned 37 of his team's 63 wins in 1883 as Boston won the pennant.

When not pitching, Whitney usually played outfield or first base. In 1882 he was among the league's top five in batting and slugging average, and in 1883 he became the first major leaguer to score six runs in a game. One of his 18 career home runs was judged the longest ever hit in Detroit to that point.

From 1886 to 1890, Whitney moved from Boston to Kansas City to Washington to Indianapolis to Philadelphia, losing more games than he won. After being hit in the chest by a batted ball, Whitney developed tuberculosis. He died at age 33.

Pinky Whitney

Whitney, Arthur Carter **3B–2B**

1928–39 B:1/2/1905, San Antonio, TX D:9/1/1987, Center, TX Deb:4/11/1928, PHI NL BR/TR 5'10", 165

G	AB	R	H	HR	RBI	OBP	SLG	AVG
1539	5765	696	1701	93	927	.343	.415	.295

Pinky Whitney's career was a two-part affair. From 1928 through 1932 he was a big star for the Phillies, a terrific hitter and RBI man, and a brilliant third baseman. In Part II, from 1933 through 1939, Whitney was just a decent player.

Arthur Carter Whitney got his nickname from his brother, who thought he resembled a bat-wielding cartoon character named Pinky Thompson. He got his chance in 1928 after the Phillies acquired him in a minor league draft, and he batted .301 with 103 RBIs.

In 1929 Whitney hit .327 with 115 RBIs and 200 hits (the Phillies that year were the only team to ever have four 200-hit players). He also posted career highs in doubles (43) and triples (14). Additionally, he led National League third basemen in putouts, assists, total chances, double plays, and chances per game, and just missed leading the league in fielding percentage. The following season he led the league in putouts, assists, total chances, and double plays, and finished second in fielding percentage by one point.

The hitter's year of 1930 also saw Whitney reach career highs in average (.342) and hits (207) while driving in 117 runs. Throughout his first five years, he batted .312 and averaged 103 RBIs, while leading the league or finishing near the top in most fielding categories.

The Phillies sent Whitney to the Braves in June 1933. (He was traded back to the Phils in April 1936.) Between 1933 and 1937 Whitney batted .278, averaged 70 RBIs, and led the league in chances per game twice and in double plays, assists, and fielding percentage once. He batted a career-best .341 for the Phillies in 1937. He retired after hitting .187 in 34 games in 1939.

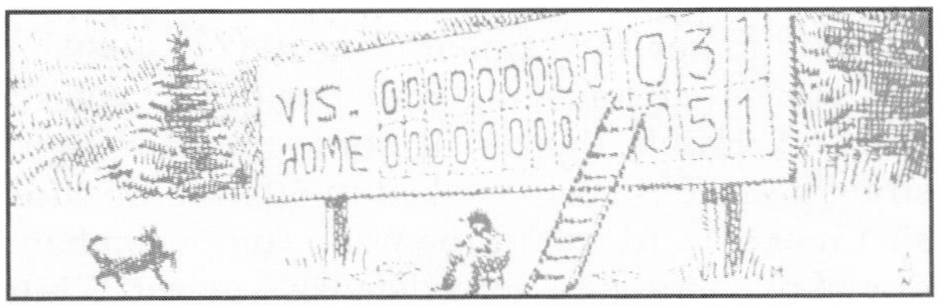

Ed Whitson

Whitson, Eddie Lee **P**

1977–91 B:5/19/1955, Johnson City, TN Deb:9/4/1977, PIT NL BR/TR, 6'3", 195

W	L	PCT	G	SH	IP	BB	SO	ERA
126	123	.506	452	12	2240^1	698	1266	3.79

The "Bronx Zoo" had few tenants less happy than Ed Whitson. The Yankees pitcher of the mid-1980s became the poster boy for players who couldn't handle the critical media and more demonstratively critical fans in New York.

Whitson began his career with the Pirates, followed by stints in San Francisco and Cleveland. He found his niche in San Diego, helping the Padres reach the World Series in 1984. When it came time to make a choice as a free agent that winter, he signed a long-term deal with the Yankees. He chose poorly.

After starting the 1985 season 0–6, Whitson was followed home to New Jersey by carloads of hostile fans. He later received death threats. Whitson fought with manager Billy Martin at a Baltimore bar, breaking Martin's arm; the manager subsequently blasted Whitson as "a crazed kook."

Lou Piniella, who replaced Martin in 1986, refused to pitch Whitson at Yankee Stadium. Ineffective on the mound, often disabled, shuttled between the rotation and bullpen, Whitson finally announced, "I want like hell to get out of New York." The Yanks traded him back to San Diego during the 1986 season. Ironically, Whitson was 5–2 as a Yankee and only 1–7 with San Diego that year.

In a less threatening environment, Whitson subsequently returned to his winning ways, posting between 10 and 16 victories each season between 1987 and 1990. He retired as a Padre in 1991.

Ernie Whitt

Whitt, Leo Ernest **C**

1976–21 B:6/13/1952, Detroit, MI Deb:9/12/1976, BOS AL BL/TR 6'2", 200

G	AB	R	H	HR	RBI	OBP	SLG	AVG
1328	3774	447	938	134	534	.327	.410	.249

Ernie Whitt was acquired by the Toronto Blue Jays off the roster of the Boston Red Sox in the 1976 expansion draft. It turned out to be one of the best moves the Blue Jays ever made. Although often platooned Whitt became a mainstay of Toronto's catching corps and was the team's number one catcher from 1982 to 1989.

A steady, if unspectacular performer, Whitt reached double figures in home runs for eight straight seasons and knocked in 50 or more runs six times. A hard worker, he was a competent handler of pitchers and a good defensive player. Whitt played on two AL East championship teams during his years with the Blue Jays, and was named to *The Sporting News'* AL All-Star team in 1988. Traded to Atlanta the next year, he finished his career with Baltimore in 1991. He remained a popular figure in the Toronto area after retiring from baseball, and coached for the Blue Jays in 1999.

Possum Whitted

Whitted, George Bostic **OF–3B**

1912–22 B:2/4/1890, Durham, NC D:10/16/1962, Wilmington, NC Deb:9/16/1912, STL NL BR/TR 5'8½", 168

G	AB	R	H	HR	RBI	OBP	SLG	AVG
1025	3630	440	978	23	451	.313	.361	.269

George Bostic "Possum" Whitted was a versatile player for five National League teams. Primarily an outfielder, he also filled in at all four infield positions. He got his nickname as a kid, because he often hunted possums.

After breaking in with the Browns in 1912, Whitted hit .220 in 123 games as a jack-of-all-trades in 1913. Traded to Boston in June 1914, he contributed to the amazing dash of "the Miracle Braves" to the World Series. He batted .261 for Boston while playing five positions, but managed only .214 during the Braves' four-game sweep of the Philadelphia A's.

Whitted made the 1915 World Series as well, this time as a Philadelphia Phillie. He hit .281 in 128 games for the Phils, most of them in the outfield, and was 1-for-15 in the five-game Series loss to the Red Sox.

Staying put as an everyday outfielder the next two seasons, Whitted batted .281 with 68 RBIs in 1916 and .280 with 70 RBIs and a career-best 29 stolen bases the following year. He was traded to the Pirates for Casey Stengel in August 1919 and was sold to the Dodgers in March 1922. He batted only once for Brooklyn that season, his last in the majors. After his playing days, Possum returned to his boyhood love and raised hunting dogs.

Alan Wiggins

Wiggins, Alan Anthony **2B–OF**

1981–87 B:2/17/1958, Los Angeles, CA D:1/6/1991, Los Angeles, CA Deb:9/4/1981, SD NL BB/TR 6'2", 160

G	AB	R	H	HR	RBI	OBP	SLG	AVG
631	2247	346	581	5	118	.331	.309	.259

Second baseman Alan Wiggins' career—and ultimately his life—was cut short by recurrent drug problems. He became the first major leaguer to die after contracting the AIDS virus.

After attending Pasadena City College, Alan Anthony Wiggins was an Angels' first-round draft (seventh pick overall) in the January 1977 free agent draft. Released after playing with Idaho Falls and Quad Cities, he then signed with the Dodgers' system and was sent to Lodi, where he stole 120 bases. Spotted by the Padres' Jack McKeon while twice stealing second, third and home in the same game, Wiggins was drafted for $25,000 by San Diego in December 1980.

Brought to the majors, Wiggins appeared in 15 ganes for the Padres in 1981. The following year he was arrested for cocaine possession and suspended for 30 days. In 1983 Wiggins faced a similar drug-related suspension, but in 1984 he helped lead the Padres to their first National League flag. On May 17 of that year he tied a since-broken league record with five stolen bases in one game. In 10 postseason games he bunted successfully four times. At that point he received a four-year, $2.5 million San Diego contract.

The following season, however, Wiggins checked into a drug rehab center. The frustrated Padres traded him to Baltimore that June. By 1989 his drug problems had driven Wiggins out of the major leagues. In November 1990 he was admitted to Los Angeles' Cedars-Sinai Hospital. Six weeks later, shrunken to just 70 pounds by AIDS, Wiggins—age 32—was dead.

Milt Wilcox

Wilcox, Milton Edward **P**

1970–86 B:4/20/1950, Honolulu, HI Deb:9/5/1970, CIN NL BR/TR 6'2", 185

W	L	PCT	G	SH	IP	BB	SO	ERA
119	113	.513	394	10	2016[2]	770	1137	4.07

Although best remembered as a member of the Tigers' starting rotation, Milt Wilcox nailed down a pennant for Cincinnati with a 3–2 relief victory over Pittsburgh in the 1970 NLCS. His victory completed a sweep of the Pirates by the Reds, who went on to lose the World Series to the Baltimore Orioles.

Selected by the Reds in the second round of the June 1968 free-agent draft, the Hawaiian-born Wilcox played for Tampa, Sarasota, and Indianapolis before reaching Cincinnati. With Indianapolis in 1970, he no-hit Evansville on July 4, led the league with five shutouts, and was named American Association Pitcher of the Year.

In December 1971, the Reds traded Wilcox to Cleveland, where his 1973 and 1974 seasons were disrupted by stints on the disabled list and with the military. Traded to the Cubs in February 1975, he was sent down to Wichita in 1976. In July of that year he was sold to the Tigers, who kept him on their Evansville farm club for the remainder of the season.

Wilcox played with Detroit for the next nine seasons. In 1984 he enjoyed his best campaign, posting a record of 17–8, then winning Game 3 of the ALCS and Game 3 of the World Series. Released in December 1985 (after having been on the disabled list since June), he was signed by Calgary of the Mariners' organization. Wilcox was given a spot on the Seattle staff in 1986, but was released by the team that June.

Hoyt Wilhelm

Wilhelm, James Hoyt **P**

1952–72 B:7/26/1923, Huntersville, NC Deb:4/19/1952, NY NL BR/TR 6', 195

W	L	PCT	G	SV	IP	BB	SO	ERA
143	122	.540	1070	227	2254[1]	778	1610	2.52

Hoyt Wilhelm, who didn't make it to the majors until he was almost 29 years old and then pitched until he was almost 49, is the most famous knuckleballer in baseball history. Although a starter for a few seasons in Baltimore, he also happens to be the first pitcher used primarily in relief to make it into the Hall of Fame.

Wilhelm was one of 11 children of an impoverished North Carolina tenant farmer, but he never had to sneak away from his chores to play baseball. His father could see that his son had talent, and encouraged the youngster to perfect his skills. Unlike most knuckleballers, who use the pitch only as a last resort, Wilhelm was always interested in the knuckler, and he wore the fuzz off a tennis ball as a kid when he practiced getting the grip just right.

"It takes no effort at all to pitch a knuckleball," Wilhelm said in a 1954 interview. "No windup is necessary. It's so simple that very little warm-up in the bullpen is required. That's why I can pitch so often without being overworked. I learned the knuckler myself. Fooled around with it in high school. I used to read about Freddie Fitzsimmons and Dutch Leonard, but nobody showed me anything. I developed it myself."

Ben Brown, his coach at Cornelius High School, allowed Wilhelm to use the trick pitch. "He did a lot to instill confidence in me," Wilhelm recalled. "When I pitched I didn't throw it to the middle of the plate. I picked a zone and tried to throw the ball in there."

After graduating from high school Wilhelm signed with Mooresville in the Class D North Carolina State League. "They cut me," he said. "I went home, got a friend to catch me, kept me throwing the pitch. Two weeks later, they called me back."

Originally a starter, he went 10–3 with a 4.25 ERA in 1942, and then was drafted into the Army. Missing the next three seasons, Wilhelm fought at the Battle of the Bulge and received a Purple Heart. He returned to Mooresville in 1946 and spent the next two seasons there, going 21–8 and 20–7. Wilhelm later speculated about why he didn't escape the minors until 1952: "[The] only thing I can say is maybe [it was] because I was a knuckleball pitcher. Nobody thought too much of me."

At age 28 he finally became a major leaguer—and a reliever. Leo Durocher, the Giants manager, thought all knuckleballers should be relievers. "I really liked Durocher," said Wilhelm decades afterward. "He was the guy who gave me my first chance to play in the big leagues." But part of the credit for Wilhelm's success in the bullpen goes to former knuckleballer Fitzsimmons, then a Giants coach. He suggested that Wilhelm stop throwing sidearm and adopt a three-quarter delivery.

Wilhelm was 15–3 with 11 saves in 1952 and became the first rookie to lead the National League in ERA, with 2.43, and winning percentage, with .833. He pitched in a league-high 71 games, setting a since-broken rookie record, and worked a whopping 159 ⅓ innings. But perhaps the most remarkable event of his season came on April 23, the day he won his first game. In his first major league at bat he homered to the opposite field off Boston's Dick Hoover. Wilhelm had 431 more at bats in his career and never hit another homer. In fact, his .088 career batting average is one of the worst among pitchers with at least 100 at bats.

The only disappointment of Wilhelm's first season came when the Rookie of the Year voting was announced. Wilhelm finished second to Brooklyn reliever Joe Black, who was 15–4 with 15 saves in 142 innings for the pennant-winning Dodgers.

Of course, Wilhelm's fluttering deliveries made life difficult for his catchers. With Wilhelm pitching in the eighth inning on September 10, 1954, Ray Katt set a modern record with four passed balls. But the good came with the bad. In the 1954 World Series, Wilhelm did not allow a run in two appearances and retired the last five batters in Game 3 to earn a save as the Giants swept the Indians in four games.

But after 1954 Wilhelm slumped. He didn't save a single game in 1955 and his ERA ballooned to 3.83 in 1956. "Hoyt began to worry and try different things and the more he changed, the worse he got," said Wes Westrum, the only Giants backstop who could really handle him.

On February 26, 1957, the Giants traded Wilhelm to the Cardinals for utility man Whitey Lockman. "At first it shook me a little bit," Wilhelm recalled. "Then I figured as long as I was in the big leagues it didn't really matter, what the heck." Considering what lay before him, that was an indispensable attitude to have.

In September 1957 St. Louis sold Wilhelm to Cleveland, where manager Bobby Bragan gave him his first major league start on May 4, 1958. Wilhelm was ineffective and was released that August. He was 35, an age when baseball careers are usually ending. But Wilhelm was just beginning.

The AL Orioles, managed by Paul Richards, were his next stop. Richards, who was known for rejuvenating older pitchers, decided to use Wilhelm as both a starter and reliever. On September 20, 1958, in only his third start for the Orioles, Wilhelm no-hit the Yankees. He threw only 99 pitches—87 of them knucklers—as Baltimore defeated New York, 1–0, on catcher Gus Triandos' homer.

In 1959 Wilhelm won his first nine starts, but finished the season at just 15–11. Still, he led the league with a 2.19 ERA, becoming the first pitcher to have led both leagues in that category. By then Richards had designed a special 41-inch catcher's mitt for Triandos to handle Wilhelm's knuckleballs. But Triandos was traded after the 1962 season, and there was no catcher left on the Orioles who could even remotely handle Wilhelm. He was traded to the White Sox in January 1963 in a deal that brought shortstop Luis Aparicio to Baltimore.

Wilhelm saved 21 games his first season in Chicago. In 1965, as he was saving 20 games and pitching 144 innings as a 42-year-old, J.C. Martin was scrambling after 33 passed balls to set a league record.

"I remember once, when I was with the White Sox riding a bus in spring training, some rookie catcher said he'd catch me without a mask," said Wilhelm. "Couple of days later, I was warming up to throw batting practice and he was catching me. After about three pitches, I had it warmed up pretty good. [I] threw one that landed in his eye, just like you'd placed it there. By the time I got to him, his eye was swollen shut. After that, he used the mask."

In October 1968 the Kansas City Royals selected Wilhelm in the expansion draft, but that December he was traded to California. In September 1969 he was waived to Atlanta, and with some clutch pitching down the stretch, helped the Braves to an NL West title.

Wilhelm moved on to the Cubs in September 1970, and that November he was traded back to Atlanta. But the Braves barely used him and gave him his unconditional release on June 29, 1971. Convinced that he could still pitch, Wilhelm agreed to go to the Dodgers' Class AAA affiliate in Spokane. He was four weeks shy of his 48th birthday when he made it back to the majors, but he never won a game for Los Angeles. He got his final release one month short of his 49th birthday.

At the end of his career, Wilhelm's 1,070 game appearances topped all other major league pitchers. The Baseball Writers Association voted him into the Hall of Fame in 1985. "I guess what took Wilhelm so long to make it was because he wasn't a friendly guy," Detroit sportswriter Joe Falls wrote. "At least he wasn't very accommodating to the writers. I tried to interview him just once, and he looked at me as if I were some sort of a creep. I never tried again."

Ted Wilks

Wilks, Theodore **P**

1944–53 B:11/13/1915, Fulton, NY Deb:4/25/1944, STL NL BR/TR 5'9½", 178

W	L	PCT	G	SV	IP	BB	SO	ERA
59	30	.663	385	46	913	283	403	3.26

Given a chance by World War II manpower shortages, 28-year-old Cardinals rookie Theodore Wilks responded with a great season in 1944. He went 17–4 and led the National League in won-lost percentage (.810). After losing his initial major league decision, he peeled off 11 straight wins from July 2 to September 2. In that fall's World Series against the Browns he saved the deciding Game 6.

From 1938 to 1943 the Polish-American Wilks had pitched in the minors, with stops at Rochester, Houston, and Columbus. He was 20–10 with the Houston Buffs in 1941.

In 1945 Wilks came down with a sore arm. Bone chips were removed from his elbow, and he was shelved for the remainder of the season. Relying on control, he was converted to bullpen work in 1946 and his 8–0 record tied him for the season's best winning streak. His string continued as he went 4–0 in 1947.

Nicknamed "Cork" by Cards catcher Joe Garagiola for his effectiveness as a stopper, in 1949 Wilks paced the NL in appearances and saves. With Garagiola he was traded to Pittsburgh in June 1951. That year he led the league in relief wins, appearances, and saves. The following August Wilks was dealt to Cleveland. Released just two months short of qualifying for a major league pension, Wilks pitched for three more seasons in the minors before retiring. The righthander later served as a court bailiff in Houston.

Ed Willett

Willett, Robert Edgar **P**

1906–15 B:3/7/1884, Norfolk, VA D:5/10/1934, Wellington, KS Deb:9/5/1906, DET AL BR/TR 6', 183

W	L	PCT	G	SH	IP	BB	SO	ERA
102	100	.505	274	12	1773^{1}	565	600	3.08

Ed Willett was one of the pitching mainstays of the Ty Cobb-era Detroit Tigers of the early 1900s. Willett joined the Tigers in 1906 and became a regular member of the rotation two years later. A regular for six seasons, he logged more than 220 innings in five of those campaigns. He won 21 games for Detroit's 1909 American League pennant-winning team. Used only in relief in the World Series, Willett did not allow a run in seven-and-two-thirds innings as the Tigers lost to Pittsburgh in seven games.

Willett won in double figures in all six of his seasons as a starting pitcher for the Tigers. Although not a very good hitter, he did distinguish himself at the plate on June 30, 1912, when he hit two home runs in one game. In 1914 Willett became the first member of the Tigers to jump to the newly formed Federal League. He joined the St. Louis team but was ineffective and released in the middle of the 1915 season.

Bernie Williams

Williams, Bernabe (Figueroa) **OF**

1991–* B:9/13/1968, San Juan, Puerto Rico Deb:7/7/1991, NY AL BB/TR, 6'2", 205

G	AB	R	H	HR	RBI	OBP	SLG	AVG
1096	4269	754	1298	151	681	.391	.487	.304

Bernie Williams was never regarded as the best centerfielder to ever play for the New York Yankees (think Joe DiMaggio and Mickey Mantle), and he was never considered the best centerfielder of his day (think Ken Griffey, Jr.). In his own quiet way, however, the multi-talented switch hitter became a star of a very high magnitude. Among his credentials were a batting title, three Gold Gloves, and three World Series rings.

Williams was born in Puerto Rico, where in Little League and Babe Ruth baseball he played against Juan Gonzalez and Ivan Rodriguez. At the age of 15 he displayed his athletic potential by winning four gold medals at an international track meet; he was ranked among the top 400-meter runners in the world for his age group. Drafted by the Yankees in 1985 he spent seven years in the minors before sticking with the big club in 1993.

Williams played a steady center field, boasting excellent range and a good arm, but his offensive potential remained largely untapped for his first five seasons as a major leaguer. In 1996 he began to hit with power on a more consistent basis (29 home runs and 102 RBIs) while maintaining a high average (.305). He became the ideal number-three hitter in the Yankees lineup. Williams also proved to be a clutch performer in the postseason as New York won its first World Series title in a generation. He was named MVP of the 1996 AL Championship Series.

A first-time All-Star in 1997, Williams continued to improve his game. He raised his average to .328 while hitting 21 home runs in only 129 games. He also won his first Gold Glove. The quiet slugger, whose loudest moments in the clubhouse came when he played classical guitar music for teammates, became embroiled in contentious and prolonged salary negotiations. The haggling did not, however, diminish his play.

Williams won the 1998 American League batting title with an average of .339, and once again the Yankees became world champions. In the victorious clubhouse his joy was subdued, however, as there seemed a very strong possibility that Williams had played his last game with the team.

Williams became a free agent in October 1998 and began negotiating with other clubs as well as with the Yankees. A deal with the Red Sox seemed imminent, and the Yankees already were searching for a replacement, when Williams instructed his agent to give New York one last chance. The result was a seven-year deal that kept the centerfielder in pinstripes.

Clearly more relaxed, Williams enjoyed another solid year in 1999. He led the Yankees with 100 walks and a .435 on-base percentage and followed his batting title with a .342 mark and a .536 slugging average. He won a third consecutive Gold Glove. In October he also collected another World Series ring, as the Yankees won their third title in four years.

Billy Williams

Williams, Billy Leo **OF–DH**

1959–76 B:6/15/1938, Whistler, AL Deb:8/6/1959, CHI NL BL/TR 6'1", 175

G	AB	R	H	HR	RBI	OBP	SLG	AVG
2488	9350	1410	2711	426	1475	.364	.492	.290

He never won a home run title, appeared in a World Series, or was chosen Most Valuable Player. Yet Billy Leo Williams was a consistently good ballplayer who, throughout an outstanding major league career from 1959 through 1976 that eventually landed him in the Hall of Fame, spent most of the time in the shadows of his more famous teammates on the Chicago Cubs. Two of those Cubbie teammates, shortstop-first baseman Ernie Banks and righthanded pitcher Ferguson Jenkins, also became Hall of Famers. And third baseman and cleanup hitter Ron Santo also diverted attention from Williams simply because of his more flamboyant personality.

Yet day after day, year after year, Williams put up productive numbers, performed admirably in the outfield, and played virtually every game. He finished his career with a .290 lifetime batting average, 426 home runs, and 1,475 RBIs. He was Rookie of the Year in 1961 and an All-Star six times, and in 1972 he won the National League batting title with a .333 average. Leo Durocher, his former manager, had this to say about him: "In spring training I said, 'Well, this year I'm going to give him a rest.'... But every time I made out my lineup card, I had to put him in there. It would have been like scratching Whirlaway and Seabiscuit from a big race."

Williams grew up in Mobile, Alabama, where the slightly older Hank Aaron was an idol and first baseman Willie McCovey was a friendly rival. He won his only high school letter as a defensive end and was offered a football scholarship to Louisiana's Grambling State University. Instead he played third base for the semipro Mobile Black Bears. One day, with a scout for the Cubs in attendance, Williams performed especially well and was offered a deal. "There was no money involved," he recalled. "My father got a cigar and I got a ticket to Ponca City [Oklahoma]."

In 1959, while battling homesickness at San Antonio, Williams had the good fortune to be tutored by Rogers Hornsby, the Hall of Fame second baseman and three-time .400-hitter. Hornsby accurately predicted stardom for his pupil, taking Williams under his wing and teaching him the strike zone. A few weeks later "the Rajah" told the Cubs' front office, "Get that kid Williams up there as fast as you can; he's wasting his time here."

After brief appearances with the Cubs in 1959 and 1960, Williams got a start in left field on June 15, 1961, his 23rd birthday. He hit a grand slam to beat San Francisco and never left the starting lineup again. At season's end he was named the Baseball Writers Association of America's Rookie of the Year.

Williams finished his rookie campaign with a .278 batting average, with 25 home runs and 86 RBIs. It was the first of 13 straight seasons in which he would hit more than 20 homers and drive in no fewer than 84 runs.

From September 1963 through September 1970 Williams played in 1,117 consecutive games, establishing a National League record that lasted until San Diego first baseman Steve Garvey surpassed it in 1983. Williams broke Stan Musial's previous record in style on September 29, 1969, Billy Williams Day at Wrigley Field, going 5-for-9 as the Cubs swept a doubleheader from the Cardinals.

As with so many other aspects of his career, Williams' achievement that year was obscured by the Cubs' losing the NL East to the Mets after building a large lead through most of the season. Although the team tired and slumped at the end, Williams hit .304 in September; he was the lone Cub regular to bat better than .300 during the stretch drive.

In 1970 Williams led the league in hits, with 205, and in runs scored, with 137, and finished second to Cincinnati's Johnny Bench with 42 home runs and 129 RBIs. In 1972 he won his only batting and slugging titles with .333 and .606 averages, respectively. Beyond that he smashed 37 homers and drove in 122 runs, again second to Bench, who edged Williams in the league MVP voting that year.

A steady performer, Williams was occasionally spectacular. In 1968 he hit for the cycle, smacked three homers in one game, and tied a major league record by hitting two more home runs in the next game—five consecutive homers in all. In 1972 he went 8-for-8 in a doubleheader. In the 1975 ALCS against the Red Sox, however, Williams was 0-for-8 in two games as a designated hitter for Oakland.

In Rick Phelan's *Our Chicago Cubs*, Williams said that his greatest hit was the home run he smacked on Opening Day, 1970, in the bottom of the 13th inning off the Cardinals' Bob Gibson, giving Ferguson Jenkins the victory. Three years later Williams became the highest-paid player in Cubs history when he signed for $150,000. It was a testament to his skill, although Williams acknowledged his lack of showmanship in his biography: "People say I'm not an exciting ballplayer. I go out there and catch the ball and hit the ball and play the game like it should be played."

Williams had to wait until 1987, his sixth year of eligibility, before the BBWAA finally voted him into the Hall of Fame. He had fallen only four votes short in 1986, missing a chance to be immortalized alongside his old Mobile, Alabama rival, McCovey. Bitter at the narrow margin of defeat, he was delighted at his election the following year. "It's like an Oscar to an actor, a Pulitzer Prize to a writer, a Nobel Prize to a scientist," he said.

At the induction ceremony at Cooperstown, Williams paid tribute to his late mother and his father, a onetime ballplayer "who unloaded banana boats to put food on the table." Working as a batting coach for the Cubs at the time of his induction (which coincided with the 40th anniversary of Jackie Robinson's integration of the big leagues), Williams took the occasion to urge baseball officials to accelerate the hiring of African-Americans on all levels, from third base coaches to managers to "yes, even owners."

Cy Williams

Williams, Fred **OF**

1912–30 B:12/21/1887, Wadena, IN D:4/23/1974, Eagle River, WI Deb:7/18/1912, CHI NL BL/TL
6'2", 180

G	AB	R	H	HR	RBI	OBP	SLG	AVG
2002	6780	1024	1981	251	1005	.365	.470	.292

When baseball fans refer to the "Williams Shift," they mean the right-field-oriented defense deployed by Lou Boudreau against Red Sox slugger Ted Williams in the 1940s. But few fans know that National League managers routinely placed five of their fielders to the right side of second base more than 20 years earlier to counter a different slugging outfielder named Williams.

Fred "Cy" Williams was such an effective left-handed pull-hitter that he almost never hit a ball to left field. Although Cy never rivaled Ted in batting average or home runs, the earlier Williams was nevertheless one of the most fearsome power hitters of his day, leading the league or tying for the lead in home runs four times while compiling a .470 lifetime slugging average.

Williams first attracted attention as an athlete at Notre Dame, where he played football (with Knute Rockne), excelled at track, and starred on the baseball team while studying architecture. The Chicago Cubs were so impressed that, after seeing him in an exhibition game, they signed him immediately after his graduation in 1912 and brought him directly to the majors.

After subbing for three years Williams became a regular outfielder in 1915 and slammed 13 home runs; the following year his 12 homers tied for the league lead. He slumped in 1917 and was traded to the Philadelphia Phillies for 36-year-old Dode Paskert in one of the worst deals ever made by a franchise famous for giveaways.

If ever a ballpark were designed for a single player, Philadelphia's Baker Bowl was made for Williams. It was only 281 feet to the fence down the right field line—perfect for a pull-hitter like Williams. The introduction of the "lively ball" in 1920 completed the picture. That season Williams led the league with 15 homers and lifted his batting average above .300 for the first time.

Williams topped .300 in five of his next six seasons while improving his home run numbers. In 1923 his 41 homers tied him with Babe Ruth for the major league lead. He won his fourth league home run title with 30 in 1927 at the age of 39. When Williams left the majors after the 1930 season, his total of 251 career homers was the National League record for a lefthanded batter, and he had collected 1,005 RBIs in 19 seasons.

Despite Williams' slugging, the Phillies never finished better than seventh during his years as a regular. The absence of other strong batters in their lineup may explain why he only had one season, 1923, with over 100 RBIs. After retiring from baseball, Williams became a successful architect in Wisconsin.

Dick Williams

Williams, Richard Hirschfeld **OF-3B-1B**

1951–64 M(1967–69, 1971–88 1,571–1,451) B:5/7/1929, St. Louis, MO Deb:6/10/1951, BRO NL BR/TR 6', 190

G	AB	R	H	HR	RBI	OBP	SLG	AVG
1023	2959	358	768	70	331	.315	.392	.260

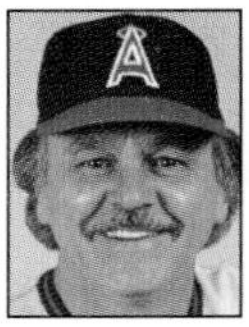

Throughout his career as a player and a manager, Dick Williams was known, rightfully, as a tough guy. When his brusque demeanor wasn't a problem for his players, he won. When they began to whine about it, he lost. Williams managed six different teams, three of which he took to the World Series, while a fourth fell one pitch short. Only Hall of Fame skipper Bill McKechnie had equal success with three teams. Williams was not a pitcher's manager, but he hired smart pitching coaches and usually got enough from his staff to win.

As a player, Williams spent 13 years with five teams, kept around because he would do anything to win—play any position, take on any assignment, from bench jockey to sign-stealer. He became a do-anything player because his skills were not enough to make him a star.

Richard Hirschfeld Williams started his major league career with Brooklyn in 1951. He made his only World Series appearance as a player in the 1953 Fall Classic, going 1-for-2 in the Dodgers' six-game loss to the Yankees. In 1956 he was waived to Baltimore, and later that season he hit his first career grand slam. During the next eight years Williams moved from Baltimore to Cleveland, back to Baltimore, then to Kansas City, back to Baltimore, and finally to Boston. He played 456 games in the outfield, 257 at third base, 188 at first base, and 20 at second base. His best season at the plate was 1959 when he set career highs in homers (16) and RBIs (75).

Williams finished his playing career in 1964 with the Red Sox. He went to Toronto to manage Boston's International League team, and he won pennants and the IL-American Association championship both years. Hired in 1967 at age 38 to manage the Red Sox, who had finished ninth the previous year, Williams made it clear from day one that he was in charge. The country club attitude that had prevailed in Boston for years was wiped away in an instant. Williams eliminated the position of team captain ("There's only one boss here," he said), which irked captain Carl Yastrzemski until Yaz realized that not having the extra responsibility would make it easier to focus on playing. Yaz had the best year of his career, and the Sox performed a miracle to win the American League flag in one of the closest races ever.

But Williams' ugly side showed through, too. He said that trying to talk to George "Boomer" Scott was "like trying to talk to cement." The Sox lost the World Series when ace Jim Lonborg had to pitch Game 7 on just two days' rest, and Williams left him in an inning too long. Williams said afterward, "I suffered not only the pain of losing but the far worse pain of wondering if I'd done enough." For the rest of his career, fans and the media would accuse him of overmanaging.

The Red Sox couldn't repeat the magic, and with players complaining that he was too tough on them Williams was replaced as manager late in the 1969 season. He joined Gene Mauch's coaching staff in Montreal. Under Mauch he learned to give situational signs to his third base coach two or three pitches ahead of time, to deter opposition sign-stealers.

Hired to manage the Oakland A's in 1971, Williams was blessed with a team loaded with talent and united in dislike of its owner, Charlie Finley. The A's won the AL West during Williams' first year, then won two consecutive World Series in 1972 and 1973. Among Williams' most vital changes were the conversion of Rollie Fingers into a reliever and the use of a lefty-righty tandem as setup men. In the 1972 Series, Williams made a superb call to outfox the Reds. With men on first and third in the eighth inning, Fingers threw a 2-2 pitch to Reds slugger Johnny Bench that got past the catcher. The runner on first moved to second. Williams came out and appeared to instruct his pitcher to intentionally walk Bench; really, he told Fingers to throw a strike. The catcher stood with his right arm extended as if Bench would be walked, and Fingers sneaked a slider over for strike three.

Williams was often second-guessed, however. During the 1973 World Series Mike Andrews, who had played the keystone position for Williams' 1967 Red Sox, was inserted as the A's second baseman for defensive purposes in the ninth inning of Game 2. He made two errors that led to three Mets runs in the 12th inning. Disgusted by the debacle, A's owner Finley trumped up a story about Andrews being injured, forced the team doctor to compose a letter putting him on the disabled list, and then made Andrews sign it. Commissioner Bowie Kuhn stopped the charade, and Williams announced to his players the next day that he would not be back to manage the A's in 1974; he had had enough of Finley's abrasive meddling.

Hired to manage the California Angels halfway through the 1974 season, Williams lasted through 1975 and 96 games into 1976 before being ousted. His Angels teams finished last in the AL West in both 1974 and 1975.

In 1977 Williams moved to Montreal, where he had a better crop of young talent. The Expos moved up from sixth the year before he arrived to fifth, and then to fourth. In 1979 they were only two games behind the division-winning Pirates; in 1980, they were only one behind first-place Philadelphia.

Williams managed Montreal to a first-place finish in the second half of the strike-shortened 1981 season, and the Expos toppled the Dodgers to advance to the NLCS. But Williams made a decision that cost him the pennant. With the score tied, 1–1, in the ninth inning of the final game, he brought in his ace starter, Steve Rogers, in relief. Rogers had pitched a complete game three days earlier, and Rick Monday swatted a homer off him that kept Williams from his third World Series.

He returned to the Fall Classic three years later, however, as manager of the San Diego Padres. The Padres, who had finished at exactly .500 in Williams' first two seasons there, were an interesting amalgam of old and new stars, among them Steve Garvey, Tony Gwynn, Goose Gossage, and Kevin McReynolds.

Williams' most daring change in 1984—moving Alan Wiggins from the outfield to second base in order to get Carmelo Martinez's bat into the lineup—was a huge success. After losing the first two NLCS games to the Cubs in Chicago, San Diego responded with a three-game sweep at home to win the Series. Interestingly, when Williams faced Detroit Tigers manager Sparky Anderson in the World Series, one of them was assured of becoming the first manager to win the Series for teams in both leagues. The honor went to Anderson.

The next season Wiggins suffered a relapse into drug usage, and Williams took the blame when the team fell to third. He moved to Seattle, hoping to once again mold a young and talented crew into pennant winners. But "the second day after I took the job, I knew I'd made a mistake," Williams said. The owner was a tightwad, and the general manager and Williams didn't see eye to eye. In addition, the manager's tough tactics no longer sat well with contemporary players. After he was fired 56 games into the 1988 season, Williams explained, "I didn't want to baby-sit millionaires who run to their agents, who run to the owners, and that is the situation now."

Lifetime as a manager Williams was 1,571–1,451, a winning percentage of .520. His teams were 9–9 in pennant competition and 12–14 in the World Series.

Earl Williams

Williams, Earl Craig **C–1B**

1970–77 B:7/14/1948, Newark, NJ Deb:9/13/1970, ATL NL BR/TR 6'3" 220

G	AB	R	H	HR	RBI	OBP	SLG	AVG
889	3058	361	756	138	457	.321	.424	.247

If Earl Williams had taken baseball a little more seriously, he might have become a superstar. Possessed of great talent and tremendous power as a hitter, he marched to the beat of his own drummer and never acquired the self-discipline it takes to become a great player.

Williams had a sensational debut season with the Atlanta Braves in 1971, socking 33 homers with 87 RBIs to earn Rookie of the Year honors. He kept it up the following year, hitting 28 homers and knocking in 87 runs, but unfortunately he was often late for games, practices, and buses. The Braves traded him to Baltimore in November 1972 in a deal that sent second baseman Davey Johnson to Atlanta.

Williams did reasonably well in his first season with the Orioles, hitting 22 homers and driving in 83 runs, but he slumped badly in 1974 and was traded back to Atlanta in 1975. After 61 games the Braves sold him to Montreal. He was claimed on waivers by Oakland in March 1977 and was released after the season.

That winter Williams' mother took out an ad in *The New York Times* saying her son was looking for work as a ballplayer. The Expos offered him a tryout, but he never showed up. In 1980 he played in the Mexican League with Campeche but batted only .200 in 47 games.

Jimmy Williams

Williams, James Thomas **2B–3B**

1899–1909 B:12/20/1876, St. Louis, MO D:1/16/1965, St. Petersburg, FL Deb:4/15/1899, PIT NL BR/TR 5'9" 175

G	AB	R	H	HR	RBI	OBP	SLG	AVG
1456	5481	781	1507	49	796	.337	.396	.275

Jimmy Williams had one of the greatest rookie seasons in baseball history. Breaking in with the Pittsburgh Pirates in 1899, he posted a .355 batting average, nine homers (a career high), and 116 RBIs. He also led the National League in triples with 27 and scored a career-best 126 runs.

He would score more than 100 runs in a season only once more in his career and would never again reach the 100-RBI mark.

He never had another season quite like it, but Williams continued to be one of the better all-around players in the major leagues for nearly a decade. A third baseman with Pittsburgh, he jumped to the American League with Baltimore in 1901 and switched to second base, where he became one of the best defensive players in the league. He twice led AL second basemen in fielding percentage, assists, and double plays.

Nicknamed "Buttons" because of his small stature, Williams twice led the league with 21 triples, in 1901 and 1902. He moved from Baltimore to the New York Highlanders in 1903 and then to the St. Louis Browns in 1908. The following year, after having eked out a .195 batting average in 110 games, his career was over.

Ken Williams

Williams, Kenneth Roy **OF**

1915–29 B:6/28/1890, Grants Pass, OR D:1/22/1959, Grants Pass, OR Deb:7/14/1915, CIN NL BL/TR 6', 170

G	AB	R	H	HR	RBI	OBP	SLG	AVG
1397	4862	860	1552	196	913	.393	.530	.319

Slugging outfielder Ken Williams was the first American Leaguer other than Babe Ruth to top 30 home runs in a season. He accomplished the feat in 1922, the year Ruth missed the first six weeks of the season because Commissioner Kenesaw Mountain Landis didn't take to the Babe's off-season barnstorming tours. Williams led the league with 39 homers and 155 RBIs that year. From 1918 through 1931, Williams and the Babe's teammate Bob Meusel were the only players other than Ruth to win the AL home run crown.

In 1922 Williams became the first player in junior circuit history to homer three times in one game and the first to hit a home run twice in one inning. He homered in six straight games in late July and early August, setting a major league record that wouldn't be broken for 34 years. Playing for the St. Louis Browns, Williams batted .332, hit 11 triples, and assembled a career-best 28-game hitting streak. With his 37 steals, he became the first player to bat .300, hit more than 30 homers, and steal more than 30 bases in the same season. No one would do it again until Willie Mays in 1957.

Williams excelled at playing at home: he hit 32 of his 39 dingers that year in St. Louis' Sportsman's Park. But throughout his entire career, Williams' achievements would take second billing to Ruth's or teammate George Sisler's. For example, during Williams' awesome 1922 season, Sisler—who was voted the AL's Most Valuable Player—batted .420, propelled by a 41-game hitting streak. Even more remarkably in some ways, Williams' Brownies finished a scant one game behind the powerful Yankees in 1922. It was the closest the Browns had come to a pennant in the club's 21-year history, and it was the closest they would come for another 22 years, when they finally won the flag in the talent-depleted war year of 1944.

It took a while for the lefthanded-hitting, righthanded-throwing Oregonian to stick in the majors. Williams was unimpressive in parts of two seasons with Cincinnati, but in his fifth year of professional ball he hit 24 homers to lead the Pacific Coast League. The Browns beckoned, but after only two games in 1918, Williams was called off to military duty. Returning in 1919, he began a streak of batting better than .300 in 10 of the next 11 years.

After hitting 10 home runs in 1920, Williams allegedly began to imitate Ruth's swing during batting practice, and he liked the results. He preceded his league-leading 1922 performance with 24 homers and 117 RBIs, and he followed it with 29 round-trippers and a career-high .357 average in 1923.

A fractured ankle reduced Williams' playing time (and homers, to 18) in 1924. A beaning knocked him out of some of the 1925 season, but he still managed to lead the AL in slugging percentage, with a .613 mark. That season he also finished with more RBIs than games played, the second time in his career he had accomplished the feat. The only other players to do it twice are all in the Hall of Fame: Ruth, Lou Gehrig, Hank Greenberg, Al Simmons, Jimmie Foxx, and Joe DiMaggio.

For some reason, Ty Cobb, then the manager of the Tigers, took a special dislike (as opposed to Cobb's generic universal dislike) to the tall outfielder. By all accounts, Williams was a pleasant enough person, but once, after he had bunted for a hit against the Tigers, Cobb kept Detroit keystoner Charlie Gehringer "after school" for the sole purpose of screaming at him about misplaying Williams' bunt.

After slipping to 17 homers in both 1926 and 1927, Williams was sold by the Browns for $10,000 to the Red Sox. However, he hit only 11 homers in his two seasons there. He was released to the Yankees for the 1930 season but was unable to agree on a contract. Apparently, he wanted pay comparable to Ruth's. The Yankees let him go

before he ever played a game for them, and he finished up back in Portland, where he hit .350 and .276 in his final professional seasons.

Lefty Williams

Williams, Claude Preston **P**

1913–20 B:3/9/1893, Aurora, MO D:11/4/1959, Laguna Beach, CA Deb:9/17/1913, DET AL BR/TL 5'9", 160

W	L	PCT	G	SH	IP	BB	SO	ERA
82	48	.631	189	10	1186	347	515	3.13

When the plot to throw the 1919 World Series was hatched by White Sox players Chick Gandil and Ed Cicotte in anger over the tightwad antics of their owner, Charles Comiskey, the two conspirators knew they could not lose the Series on their own. Cicotte would pitch, at most, three games. They needed another pitcher and enlisted Claude Preston "Lefty" Williams.

Williams' complicity can be credited to the effective salesmanship of Cicotte and Gandil. Williams was only 26 years old, and as the winner of 23 games that season, he seemed to be on his way to a long and productive baseball career. A taciturn southerner who pitched like an artist, he used precision control to set up hitters with tactical perfection. But he was well aware that, at $3,000 a year, he was underpaid compared to other pitchers with similar skills and statistics.

White Sox manager Kid Gleason had dismissed the rumors that swirled around his club as the Fall Classic between Chicago and Cincinnati began. But after Cicotte's 9–1 loss in the Series opener, Gleason told catcher Ray Schalk to watch Williams carefully in the second game. After three well-pitched innings, Williams walked two of the first three men to face him in the fourth. Schalk was livid. Apparently Williams was crossing him up, not throwing what the catcher signaled. After a run-producing single, Schalk threw out a potential base stealer, but Williams walked another batter. Never before had he issued three passes in one inning. Prior to the Series, he had walked only 58 batters in nearly 300 innings.

The next batter tripled, and the Sox were down 3–0. They lost the game, 4–2, although the White Sox had 10 hits to the Reds' four. Williams had walked six batters. After the game Schalk grabbed Williams under the grandstand, pummeling him until teammates pulled them apart.

After Cicotte lost Game 4, Gandil gave Williams two envelopes, each one containing $5,000. Williams kept one and delivered the other, as instructed, to outfielder Joe Jackson.

Under Schalk's fierce eyes, Williams pitched well in Game 5, but his outfield played miserably. Jackson and Happy Felsch misplayed fly balls in the sixth inning that led to four runs for the Reds.

With the Reds leading the best-of-nine Series four games to one, Dickie Kerr took his second Series victory for the Sox in Game 6. Then Cicotte, angry because the gamblers had stopped paying off, pitched and won Game 7. The other Black Sox players felt the same way; they had been double-crossed, and now they were determined to win the Series.

In a bizarre event straight out of baseball's gummiest fiction, on the night before Game 8, Williams and his wife were returning to their hotel after dinner when the pitcher spotted a man in a bowler hat smoking a cigar. Eliot Asinof, describing the scene in his book *Eight Men Out*, wrote that the stranger "wanted to have a word with Williams in private, and a nod indicated to Lefty's wife that she should excuse herself. The man went right to the point. He bluntly told Williams he was to lose the next game... No, it wasn't a question of money anymore. Williams was not going to get paid another dime! He was going to lose that ball game or something was going to happen to him. Maybe something might happen to his wife, too... Williams was not to last even one inning!"

Williams responded to the threat. Throwing nothing but fastballs over catcher Schalk's protests, he retired only one batter. Four runs scored, and despite a four-run comeback in the last of the eighth, the Sox lost the game and the Series.

Prior to the 1920 season Comiskey held World Series paychecks for Williams and the other suspected members of the fix as the club owner tried to decide what action would be appropriate. Williams had another typical season in 1920, sporting a 22–14 record in 299 innings.

In June 1921 a Chicago court acquitted all of the alleged conspirators, but the new Commissioner, Kenesaw Mountain Landis, suspended them from Organized Baseball for life. Williams remained in Chicago, operating a poolroom for years before moving to California to run a plant nursery business. From 1921–22 and 1926–27, he pitched for a variety of outlaw semipro clubs.

Matt Williams

Williams, Matthew Derrick **3B**

1987–* B:11/28/1965, Bishop, CA Deb:4/11/1987, SF NL BR/TR, 6'2", 210

G	AB	R	H	HR	RBI	OBP	SLG	AVG
1560	5872	850	1575	334	1050	.319	.496	.268

By age 29, Matt Williams had slugged more home runs (225) than any third basemen in the Baseball Hall of Fame—Mike Schmidt included—had amassed at a similar point in their careers. In 1994 he was on pace to tie the single season home run mark of Roger Maris, hitting 43

in only 112 games for the San Francisco Giants before the strike halted the season. His 35-homer, 142-RBI season in 1999 led the Arizona Diamondbacks to the postseason in the franchise's second year of existence.

Williams split three seasons between San Francisco and Triple-A Phoenix from 1987 to 1989. In that time he struck out 181 times in 693 at bats while batting just .197 with the Giants. Despite a .202 regular season average in 1989, he batted .300 with two home runs and nine RBIs in the National League Championship Series against the Cubs. He hit another homer and started all four games of the earthquake-interrupted World Series against Oakland, which the A's won in four games.

Williams led the NL in RBIs in his first 100-game season in 1990. His strikeouts remained high over the next several years, but his batting average was .267 or better in nine of his next 10 seasons.

He was having a great year in 1996 when his season ended prematurely because of a shoulder injury. The Giants traded Williams to the Indians in November, and he was a major contributor to Cleveland's 1997 pennant-winning season. In the Tribe's World Series loss to the Florida Marlins, Williams hit .385 and had a home run in the team's Game 4 victory. Sent back to the NL in 1999, his big bat carried Arizona to a division title.

One of the smoothest-fielders among his contemporaries at third base, Williams won his fourth Gold Glove Award in 1996. He once attributed his defensive play to a drill he was introduced to at the University of Nevada-Las Vegas, where infielders were forced to field ground balls in practice with a ping-pong paddle strapped to their glove hand.

Mitch Williams

Williams, Mitchell Steven **P**

1986–95, 1997 B:11/17/1964, Santa Ana, CA
Deb:4/9/1986, TEX AL BL/TL, 6'4", 205

W	L	PCT	G	SV	IP	BB	SO	ERA
45	58	.437	619	192	691^{1}	544	660	3.65

"I pitch like my hair's on fire," reliever Mitch Williams once said. Indeed, he reveled in his tightrope-walking ways, christening his Texas home "The 3 and 2 Ranch." With an unorthodox delivery that literally propelled him off the mound, Williams deterred hitters from digging in against him—but his lack of control often made it unnecessary to do so. For his career, Williams held hitters to a .216 average, but walked over seven batters per nine innings.

Traded from Texas to the Cubs in 1989 and then to Philadelphia two years later, Williams posted impressive save totals that belied his many near-disasters. In 1993 the Phillies rose from years of futility to win the NL East, and Williams notched a team-record 43 saves. In the National League Championship Series, he gained two wins—both after squandering leads inherited from ace Curt Schilling, who hid under a towel in the dugout during the ordeal—and also had two saves as the Phils dispatched favored Atlanta. After saving Game 2 of the World Series against Toronto, the pitcher known as "Wild Thing" entered Game 4 with Philadelphia ahead 14–11 in the eighth and surrendered two-out hits to Rickey Henderson and Devon White to give Toronto a 15–14 victory and a 3–1 Series lead.

Exhausted physically and emotionally, Williams had a chance at redemption in Game 6 in Toronto, when the Phillies rallied to take a 6–5 lead into the bottom of the ninth. With his velocity well below normal, Williams issued a leadoff walk to Henderson. After an out and a single, he faced Joe Carter. The result was the first come-from-behind, Series-clinching home run in history, as Carter pounded a slider over the wall to give the Blue Jays the title.

Smokey Joe Williams

Williams, Joseph

Negro League Player (1905–32) B:4/61886, Seguin, TX
D:3/12/1946, New York, NY BR/TR 6'4", 190

In the eastern states they called Joseph Williams "Smokey Joe"; out west he was known as "Cyclone." Either way, this righthanded fireballer was the greatest pitcher in black baseball for the first half of the 20th century. He was voted so by a select group of Negro Leagues experts in a 1952 *Pittsburgh Courier* poll—beating out Satchel Paige by a single vote.

A large man, Williams was extremely soft-spoken, more a loner than a socializer. His perennial trademark was a big cigar, clamped between his teeth every second that he wasn't pitching. He threw with almost no windup and with a smooth motion, but he was remarkably fast. Even at age 50 he could sneak a fastball past a hitter.

Williams' earliest years in baseball (when he was *really* fast, they say) were in his native Texas with the San Antonio Broncos between 1905 and 1909. In three years there his record was reported to be 80–20. (Accurate statistics for the

early years of black baseball are difficult to obtain.) He pitched and beat Rube Foster in San Antonio and Foster immediately signed him to his Chicago Giants.

Williams, an African-American who was also part Comanche, became an immediate success in the Negro National League. According to one expert, his best year was probably 1914, when he won 12 and lost two in Negro League play and sported a record of 41–3 in outside games. In 1924 he fanned 24 Brooklyn Bushwicks, a powerful semipro team. In 1930 he fanned 27 Kansas City Monarchs while pitching a 12-inning contest for the Homestead Grays. The "record" may be a little tainted, however.

The game was played at night, under the Monarchs' traveling light fixtures. Visibility was poor. In addition, Williams' mound opponent, Chet Brewer, was working the ball over with an emery board, so Williams retaliated, using sandpaper to even the score. Brewer struck out 19 himself. Williams' catcher that night was 18-year-old Josh Gibson, pressed into service for the Grays because other backstops were afraid to try to catch Williams in the dim light. Williams was somewhere between 44 and 50 years old at the time.

When Homestead's Cum Posey signed Williams in 1925, it was the club's first step toward becoming one of the great Negro Leagues teams of all time. The records, whether reported or accurate, still indicate that Williams lost only five games in his six years with the Grays. He was more famous than any black player of the era, with the possible exception of Rube Foster.

Williams' performances against major league teams are legendary. Verified records indicate he had a 22–7 career mark (with one tie) against them. It's important to note that two of those losses came when he was already closer to 50 years of age than 40, and another two were by 1–0 margins. The first four times Williams faced white teams, he tossed three shutouts. He blanked major leaguers nine more times before he was through.

In 1912 Williams shut out the NL champion New York Giants. In 1915 he topped Grover Cleveland Alexander and the Phillies with a 10-strikeout, 1–0 three-hitter. Although there are no official records, many testify to a performance in 1917 against the Giants during which he fanned 20 and allowed no hits but lost the game, 1–0, on an error. It was after this game that a Giants player gave Williams the nickname "Smokey," either a reference to major league hurler Smokey Joe Wood or a description of Williams' speed.

On another occasion Williams bested Walter Johnson 1–0. He also defeated Hooks Wiltse, Rube Marquard, Waite Hoyt, Rube Walberg, and Jack Quinn. During his career, in addition to the Broncos, the Chicago Giants, and the Grays, he pitched for the Austin Leland Giants, the New York Lincoln Giants, the Chicago American Giants, the Brooklyn Royal Giants, and the Detroit Wolves. In 1999 the Veterans Committee elected Williams to the Baseball Hall of Fame.

Stan Williams

Williams, Stanley Wilson **P**

1958–72 B:9/14/1936, Enfield, NH Deb:5/17/1958, LA NL BR/TR 6'5", 230

W	L	PCT	G	SV	IP	BB	SO	ERA
109	94	.537	482	43	1764^1	748	1305	3.48

A big, strapping righthander with a blazing fastball, Stanley Wilson Williams pitched 14 seasons in the major leagues and compiled a record of 109–94. He had his best years for the Los Angeles Dodgers, winning in double figures for three straight seasons from 1960 to 1962.

Williams joined the Dodgers in 1958, and the following year won Game 2 of the National League playoff against the Milwaukee Braves to give Los Angeles the pennant. Three years later, however, he walked in San Francisco's pennant-winning run in the decisive third game of a playoff between the Dodgers and the Giants.

Williams was traded to the New York Yankees in November of 1962 for first baseman Bill Skowron and spent two years with the Yanks before being sold to Cleveland in March of 1965. He got into only 19 games for the Indians over a two-year period because of an injury but bounced back to win 13 games for the Tribe in 1968.

He was moved to the Minnesota Twins along with Luis Tiant in December of 1969 in a trade that sent third baseman Graig Nettles to the Indians. Williams was made a relief pitcher in 1970 and pitched six scoreless innings in the ALCS. He was traded to the St. Louis Cardinals in September 1971 and finished his career with the Boston Red Sox in 1972. He later coached for the Red Sox, White Sox, Yankees, Reds, Cubs, and Mariners.

Ted Williams

Williams, Theodore Samuel **OF**

1939–60 M(1969–72, 273–364) B:8/30/1918, San Diego, CA Deb:4/20/1939, BOS AL BL/TR 6'3", 205

G	AB	R	H	HR	RBI	OBP	SLG	AVG
2292	7706	1798	2654	521	1839	.483	.634	.344

Ted Williams' one goal in life, he once said, was "to walk down the street and have people say, 'There goes the greatest hitter who ever lived.'" In a 23-year career that included two stints in the military, Williams came very close to achieving his goal. If he's *not* the greatest hitter who ever lived, he is certainly near the top of the list.

Williams' parents didn't get along, and the youngster was left alone much of the time when he was growing up in San Diego. He spent his days hunting and fishing or playing ball at nearby North Park. Hour after hour he and his friends played baseball. By the time he entered Herbert Hoover High School, Williams had swung at thousands of pitches. Hitting, for him, was an obsession.

Williams excelled at Hoover as both a pitcher and an outfielder. His high school eligibility ended before he graduated, and Yankees scout Bill Essick tried to sign Williams in the summer of 1936. But Ted's mother, May, refused to sign the contract and moved the boy out of town before he completed high school. Then the San Diego Padres joined the Pacific Coast League, and owner Bill Lane convinced May Williams to let her son play for his team. For $150 a month, 17-year-old Ted Williams became a professional ballplayer.

All arms, legs, and enthusiasm, the gangly Williams hit .271 in 42 games during the remainder of the 1936 season. Red Sox general manager Eddie Collins came to San Diego on a scouting trip late in the season, spotted Williams' sweet swing, and was intrigued. After "the Kid" put up big numbers for San Diego in 1937, homering in every PCL park and batting .349, the Red Sox purchased him for $25,000.

Williams played for the Minneapolis Millers of the American Association in 1938. Rogers Hornsby, who worked briefly for the Millers as a batting instructor, told Williams to always "get a good ball to hit." Williams won the AA Triple Crown, hitting .366 with 43 home runs and 142 RBIs. He also distracted his teammates with his immature antics and brazen self-confidence. Millers manager Donie Bush threatened to quit if Williams stayed on the team. Owner Mike Kelley replied that Williams was hitting .360; if Bush chose to leave, so be it. The manager stayed.

Williams arrived in Boston for spring training in 1939 and picked up where he'd left off in Minneapolis—on and off the field. Incensed at missing a pop foul in an exhibition game, he picked up the ball and hurled it out of the park. Manager Joe Cronin fined him $50. Williams brashly responded, "I'll pay you $50 for every one I throw out if you'll pay me $50 for every one I'll hit out."

The Boston fans and the press fell in love with the cocky right fielder, dubbing him "the Splendid Splinter." Williams responded by lifting his

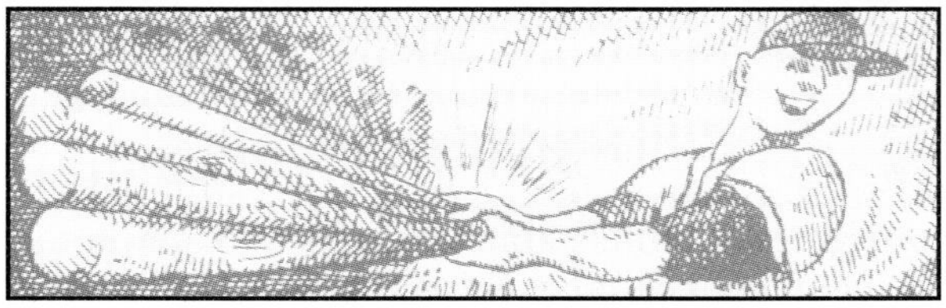

cap by its button and tipping it grandly. He finished his rookie year with a .327 average, 31 home runs, and 145 RBIs. Seven of the home runs landed in the right field bleachers at Fenway Park, where only five other players had previously homered.

The Red Sox built bullpens in right field before the 1940 season, cutting the distance to the fence. The area was dubbed "Williamsburg." Williams was switched to left field to save his eyes from the sun and had another fine season, hitting .344, but his power numbers dropped. He did lead the league with 134 runs, beginning a stretch of five consecutive seasons in which he topped the AL in that category.

Some fans and members of the press carped that he didn't work hard enough. They desperately wanted an American League pennant, and it was becoming clear that not even Williams could carry the Red Sox past the Yankees. A disgruntled Williams claimed he'd rather be a fireman. When the crowd responded with boos, Williams blasted them. He squared off with the press and the Fenway fans for the remainder of his career, refusing to blink or back off. He didn't understand how they could turn against him, and he vowed never again to tip his cap.

But the animosity between Williams and the media never affected his hitting; in fact, he tried to silence the critics with his bat. In 1941 he was at his best. He chipped a bone in his ankle during spring training and got off to a slow start, pinch-hitting and making one premature start before returning for good in late April. But once he got going he didn't stop.

On May 15 Williams began the longest hitting streak of his career, batting .488 in 23 games to raise his average to .430. Ironically, his feat was obscured by the performance of Joe DiMaggio, who had started his record-setting hitting streak on the same day. At the All-Star break Williams was hitting .405 with 16 home runs and 62 RBIs. DiMaggio had surpassed Willie Keeler's 44-game hitting streak and was about to make history. Williams even got into the act, relaying any news about DiMaggio from the scoreboard operator at Fenway Park to Joe's brother, Dom DiMaggio, in center field.

At the All-Star Game in Detroit Williams briefly snatched the spotlight away from DiMaggio when his ninth-inning, three-run homer gave the American League a 7–5 win. DiMaggio's streak stopped at 56 games, but Williams continued to hit and entered a season-ending doubleheader in Philadelphia batting .39955. It was speculated that he might sit out the final day, but instead Williams had six hits in the twin bill and finished at .406—the last man to hit .400 in the 20th century.

On December 7, 1941, the Japanese bombed Pearl

Harbor. In late May of 1942 Williams responded to public pressure and enlisted in the Navy air corps. Trained as a pilot, he spent three and a half seasons in the military, primarily training other pilots, before returning to baseball in 1946.

That year the Red Sox assembled their best team in years and won the pennant. At the All-Star Game Williams delighted the crowd in Fenway Park by blasting Rip Sewell's odd pitch, called an "eephus," into the bleachers. That season also saw him increasingly challenged by the "Boudreau Shift," when Cleveland manager Lou Boudreau crowded six of his fielders on the right side of second base and dared Williams to pull the ball. (Actually, Boudreau's old manager Roger Peckinpaugh had first sprung the shift against Williams in 1941.)

The Red Sox met the St. Louis Cardinals in the 1946 World Series. Williams had been plunked on the elbow by a pitch just before the Series and hit only .200 against the Cards, as Boston lost in seven games. It was little consolation that Williams was selected the AL's Most Valuable Player.

The next few seasons were repeats of 1946. Williams put up big numbers and the Red Sox fell short. The team finished third in 1947 and Williams won the Triple Crown, but DiMaggio was voted MVP by the Baseball Writers Association. Williams always blamed Boston writer Mel Webb for leaving him completely off the ballot, thereby costing him the award, but Webb didn't even have a vote that year—a writer in the Midwest had left Williams off the ballot instead. He collected only three first-place votes; had any of the 20 other writers who voted for Williams picked him even one place higher, he would have won the award.

The Red Sox finished the 1948 season tied with Cleveland but lost a playoff. In 1949 they led New York by one game with only two games remaining, but were beaten twice by the Yankees and finished a game back. In 1950 Williams crashed into the fence chasing down a drive by Ralph Kiner and broke his elbow. And in 1951 the favored Red Sox slumped in September and finished third.

When Williams was called back into the service because of the military action in Korea, the Red Sox held Ted Williams Day on April 30, 1952. For at least one day Williams' troubles with the press and the fans were forgotten. Most people thought it would be his final big league game, and the 34-year-old star homered off Dizzy Trout for his 324th home run.

Williams was a pilot in the Marines' air wing in Korea. He flew 39 missions, crash-landed once after taking flak, and survived several other close calls. He returned to the Red Sox lineup on August 6, 1953. After the two-year layoff and without the benefit of spring training, he hit .407 in 91 at bats and smacked 13 home runs.

Although not quite the player he had been before his stint in Korea—he never again collecting 100 RBIs—Williams remained a productive hitter. He briefly retired in 1955, and then returned to hit .356 with a .703 slugging average, his highest marks in either category since 1951.

Yet Williams' battles with the press and fans continued. He spit at the crowd, flipped them the bird, threw a bat into the stands, and did just about everything he could to irritate people. When the Red Sox were no longer contenders, however, the fans warmed to Williams, and he enjoyed his greatest popularity since his rookie year. In 1957 at age 40, Williams flirted with the .400 mark once again, finishing at .388. In 1958 he hit .328 to win his sixth, and last, batting crown.

Williams slumped badly in 1959, battling a neck injury all year and hitting only .254. But he bounced back in 1960 to hit .316 with 29 home runs, the last of which provided the most memorable moment of his career.

A few days before the end of the season Williams indicated his intention to retire. At his final home game the Red Sox held a modest ceremony and made a simple announcement to the crowd of just over 13,000. Williams came to the plate in the eighth inning against Jack Fisher of the Orioles. With the count 1-and-1, Williams drove the ball on a long, low line over the right-field fence for his 521st and last home run. He didn't look up, didn't smile, and didn't tip his cap, not even after Red Sox manager Pinky Higgins sent him out to right field in the top of the ninth, only to be replaced by Carroll Hardy.

"Teddy Ballgame" retired with a host of records. He won two MVP awards, six batting titles, led the American League in home runs and RBIs five times, and finished with a career batting average of .344. He was walked more times than anyone other than Babe Ruth, and at the end of the 20th century he had the highest walk percentage, or walks per plate appearances, than anyone in baseball history. After retiring Williams spent most of his time enjoying his second-favorite sport, fishing, and appeared in spring training as a batting instructor for the Red Sox. He was the first person to be elected to both the baseball and the fishing halls of fame.

When he was elected to the Baseball Hall of Fame in 1966 Williams surprised everyone by giv-

ing a memorable speech that contained a plea to include players from the Negro Leagues in the shrine. In 1969 he became manager of the Washington Senators, led them from the cellar to fourth place, and was named Manager of the Year. When the club moved to Texas in 1972 Williams lost interest in the job and retired.

Williams continued to spend much of his time fishing. He occasionally appeared at spring training, and became involved with his own brand of baseball cards, earning more in a weekend signing autographs than he ever did playing a season of baseball. He even opened his own Ted Williams Museum and "Hitters Hall of Fame." In 1997 the Society for American Baseball Research bestowed on him its Hero of Baseball Award. The following year Williams began a crusade to enshrine Black Sox outfielder Shoeless Joe Jackson in the Hall of Fame. "He's served his sentence," wrote Williams, "and it's time for Baseball to acknowledge his debt is paid."

On Ted Williams Day at Fenway Park in the summer of 1991 Williams finally made peace with the fans and press of the city of Boston. He tipped his cap.

Ned Williamson

Williamson, Edward Nagle **3B-SS**

1878–90 B:10/24/1857, Philadelphia, PA D:3/3/1894, Willow Springs, AR Deb:5/1/1878, IND NL BR/TR 5'11", 210

G	AB	R	H	HR	RBI	OBP	SLG	AVG
1201	4553	809	1159	64	667	.332	.384	.255

A teammate of Cap Anson's on the 1880s Chicago White Stockings, Ned Williamson was a member of the famed "Stone Wall Infield" that included Anson, Tom Burns, and Fred Pfeffer. The infield played together as a unit for seven seasons, and the White Stockings won two pennants during that time.

One of the best defensive players of his era, Williamson led league third basemen in fielding percentage and double plays five times and in assists six times. He also led all shortstops in each of five categories—games played, assists, putouts, errors, and double plays—on one occasion.

The versatile Williamson played all four infield positions, caught, and even pitched occasionally during his 13-year career. He led the majors in doubles with a then-record 49 in 1883 and topped the National League in home runs with 27 in 1884—an astounding total for that era.

Williamson, though, was helped that year by a change in the rules at Chicago's Lake Front Park. Previously, any ball hit over the cozy right-field fence was a ground-rule double. In 1884 the rule was changed to make such hits home runs. Williamson, a righthanded hitter, could easily reach the fence in right (it was only 196 feet from the plate) and took advantage of it. His home run total stood as the single-season record until Babe Ruth broke it by hitting 29 in 1919.

Vic Willis

Willis, Victor Gazaway **P**

1898–1910 B:4/12/1876, Cecil Corners, MD D:8/3/1947 Elkton, MD Deb:4/20/1898, BOS NL BR/TR 6'2" 185

W	L	PCT	G	SH	IP	BB	SO	ERA
249	205	.548	513	50	3996	1212	1651	2.63

In 1902 Vic Willis established a modern record by pitching 45 complete games. The durable righthander threw 300 or more innings in each of eight seasons as he put his excellent curveball to maximum advantage.

Victor Gazaway Willis began his baseball career in 1895 with Harrisburg of the Pennsylvania State League. In 1896 and 1897 he pitched for Syracuse of the Eastern (now International) League, going 10–6 and 21–16. In 1898 he came up to the big leagues with the National League Boston Beaneaters.

On August 7, 1899, Willis pitched a no-hitter against Washington, defeating Bill Dinneen, 7–1. He struck out five and walked four as three errors were made behind him. Willis finished the year at 27–8, pitching a league-high five shutouts and posting a 2.50 ERA. In 1902, when he set the 20th century record for complete games, he failed to go the distance in only two of his 47 decisions. The workhorse won 27 and lost 20 for the Beaneaters, leading the NL with 410 innings pitched, 225 strikeouts, and three shutouts.

Willis' 29 losses in 1905 remains the modern record. That year's Boston staff also featured three other 20-game losers; Willis managed to escape the scene of the crime via a December 1905 trade to Pittsburgh. The Pirates saw him as the potential key to wresting the National League pennant away from John McGraw's Giants, with whom Pittsburgh was engaged in a particularly bitter and personal feud. That strategy finally paid off in 1909, when Willis went 22–11 and Pittsburgh bested the Tigers in the World Series. It was his fourth consecutive 20-win season for the Pirates.

Willis left the majors after going 9–12 for the St. Louis Cardinals in 1910. He had chalked up eight 20-win seasons on the way to a 249–205 record with a 2.63 ERA. Although he recorded 50 career

shutouts, he was also on the losing end of 37 blankings. Considered for many years to be one of the finest pitchers from baseball's early era not in the Hall of Fame, he was finally elected to the Cooperstown shrine in 1995.

Maury Wills

Wills, Maurice Morning **SS-3B**

1959–72 M(1980–81, 26–56) B:10/2/1932, Washington, D.C. Deb:6/6/1959, LA NL BB/TR 5'11", 170

G	AB	R	H	HR	RBI	OBP	SLG	AVG
1942	7588	1067	2134	20	458	.331	.331	.281

No one would ever confuse the short and slight Maury Wills with the enormous Babe Ruth, but Wills in his own way shook up baseball in the 1960s much as Ruth had done in the early 1920s. The Babe had ushered in a new era in baseball by single-handedly making the home run a dominant offensive weapon. For his part, Wills reinvented the stolen base; without him the exciting careers of superstars such as Lou Brock and Rickey Henderson would not have been possible. For teams at the dawn of the 21st century, speed is a prerequisite if they hope to be competitive.

It's hard to imagine how slow 1950s players were. The hit-and-run play was rare, bunting was uncommon, and base stealing was a lost art. The only notable base stealer of the era was Luis Aparicio of the "Go-Go" White Sox. Dominant players of the 1950s, especially in the National League, were often slugging first basemen and outfielders. Although Willie Mays, Mickey Mantle, and Hank Aaron were more than capable of stealing bases, they put their emphasis on the long ball.

Wills' 50 stolen bases in 1960, his first full season as the Dodgers' shortstop, were more than any National League player had stolen in a season since Max Carey's 51 in 1923. When Wills stole 104 bases in 1962, he broke the major league record of 96 that Ty Cobb had set in the dead-ball days of 1915. Perhaps more impressive, Wills' 104 thefts were more than any *team* had stolen in any of the first seven years of the 1950s.

Wills was no overnight sensation. His minor league career lasted more than eight seasons, during which he played every position—including pitcher and catcher—at one point or another. He hit over .280 a few times, but the major leagues weren't interested. At one point the Dodgers even lent him to the Tigers; the Tigers gave him back.

Wills might have languished indefinitely in the minors were it not for the intervention of two mentors. Bobby Bragan, his manager in Spokane in 1958, saw the infielder take two lefthanded "joke" swings in batting practice and recommended that Wills try switch-hitting. For the first time in years, Wills had something to strive for. While playing winter ball that season he begged people to throw to him so he could practice the lefthanded stroke. He was hitting .313 early in the 1959 season when the Dodgers brought him up. In Los Angeles Wills hit .260, but he was struggling early in the 1960 season when Dodgers coach Pete Reiser made him a special project.

Reiser and Wills worked together for two hours every day. The first 90 minutes were devoted to batting school, the last half-hour to mental attitude. "He taught me to believe in myself," Wills said. He finished the season with a .295 average and a league-leading 50 steals, the first of six years in a row that he would outsteal everyone else in the NL.

In 1961 Wills' average and stolen base total dropped off, although his 35 swipes were still enough to lead the league. The next year Wills exploded, forever redefining the concept of speed as an offensive weapon. He broke Cobb's 47-year-old record while batting .299 with a league-leading 10 triples. Cobb had stolen 96 bases in 156 games; in the same number of games Wills had stolen 97. Even more remarkably, he was caught stealing only 13 times, while American League catchers had nailed Cobb 38 times in 1915.

As a measure of Wills' offensive value, the 1962 Dodgers had approximately the same team batting and slugging averages as they had in 1961, yet they scored 107 more runs and won 13 more games. Wills' 104 stolen bases exceeded the combined total of his teammates, who together accounted for 94 thefts.

Dodger Stadium groundskeepers hardened the infield dirt to ensure that Wills got a good jump. The other teams retaliated. When the Giants hosted the Dodgers for Game 1 of the league playoff series that year, Wills found a swamp around first base. The Dodgers lost. In Game 2, this time in Los Angeles, Wills stole a base and scored a run in an 8–7 Dodgers victory. In Game 3 he hit safely four times and stole three more bases (numbers 102, 103, and 104), but the Giants scored four times in the top of the ninth to win the playoff. Wills was named Most Valuable Player, despite having battled for a losing cause.

He injured his foot on Opening Day, 1963, and didn't fully recover until 1965. With his foot fully healed he was off and running, with five steals in his first two games; by season's end he had 94 thefts. The Dodgers won the pennant, and Wills stole three bases and hit .367 in the World Series, including a record-tying four-hit game.

Wills began the 1966 season as a tired 33-year-old. Having never possessed great speed, he relied instead on his careful study of pitchers' moves and on taking a long lead to get the edge. Many years of diving back to first on attempted pickoffs had worn him down. For the first time since 1959 Wills was not the league's stolen base leader. The Dodgers took the flag again, but they were humiliated in a four-game World Series sweep by the Orioles.

Traded after the season to Pittsburgh for Gene Michael and Bob Bailey, Wills hit .302 and .278 the next two seasons. He was left unprotected in the expansion draft, however, and claimed by Montreal. The Dodgers later reacquired him, along with Manny Mota, for Ron Fairly and Paul Popovich.

Wills played regularly in 1970 and 1971, but age had slowed him down. Despite appearing in 149 games in 1971, he stole only 15 bases. The following season Bill Russell replaced him as the Dodgers' shortstop. The 1972 season was Wills' last as a major leaguer, and he went on to broadcast games, manage winter league ball, and work as a Dodgers minor league instructor.

Wills became the majors' second black manager when Seattle hired him to replace Darrell Johnson in 1980. He took over a sixth-place team, pronounced them "Maury Wills' Mariners," and proclaimed that he would teach them how to steal a pennant. But Maury never really got the Mariners to listen. He had severe discipline problems with the team, and sometimes he himself didn't seem to be paying attention. Once he submitted a lineup card showing two players at the same position.

Early in the 1981 season Oakland manager Billy Martin noticed something strange about the batters' boxes in Seattle, and asked umpire Bill Kunkel to measure them. Sure enough, they were a foot too long. Wills had ordered his groundskeepers to extend the boxes toward the pitching mound to give his hitters an advantage against the A's curveballs.

Wills was fined $500 and suspended for two days. "That's not cheating," he said, probably remembering the infields in Los Angeles and San Francisco, "just a little gamesmanship." Not long after, he was fired, bringing his baseball career to an abrupt end.

Walt Wilmot

Wilmont, Walter Robert **OF**

1888–98 B:10/18/1863, Plover, WI D:2/1/1929, Chicago, IL Deb:4/20/1888, WAS NL BB/TR

G	AB	R	H	HR	RBI	OBP	SLG	AVG
960	3981	725	1098	58	594	.337	.404	.276

On August 22, 1891, Walt Wilmot set three all-time records for drawing bases on balls. The Chicago outfielder walked six times in a doubleheader that day, a mark later equaled by Mel Ott (twice), Johnny Mize, Clay Dalrymple, Cleon Jones, and Jack Clark.

Remarkably, Wilmot's free passes all came in one game of the twin bill, giving him the National League record for most bases on balls in a single game. Two American Leaguers, Jimmie Foxx and Andre Thornton, duplicated that feat in the 20th century.

In the sixth inning of that game Wilmot walked twice, making him the first man in National League history to do so. And in the sixth inning of the doubleheader's other contest Wilmot struck out twice.

In 1889 Wilmot led the league in triples, with 19. In 1890 his 13 homers paced the talent-drained National League. Wilmot posted career bests in 1894 with a .330 average, 130 RBIs, and 45 doubles. He left the majors after the 1898 season with a lifetime .276 average.

Chief Wilson

Wilson, John Owen **OF**

1908–16 B:8/21/1883, Austin, TX D:2/22/1954, Bertram, TX Deb:4/15/1908, PIT NL BL/TR 6'2", 185

G	AB	R	H	HR	RBI	OBP	SLG	AVG
1280	4624	520	1246	59	571	.311	.391	.269

Outfielder Owen "Chief" Wilson accumulated one of baseball's most unlikely records in 1912—36 triples in a single season. It is unlikely for several reasons. First, Wilson never recorded more than 14 triples in any other season. In fact, he never registered more than 34 doubles. Second, the number is far above the second-highest modern total for three-base hits in a season—26 by Joe Jackson in 1912, Sam Crawford in 1914, and Kiki Cuyler in 1925. It also exceeds the 19th-century record of 31 set by Heinie Reitz in 1894.

Lastly, although minor leaguers have exceeded most other major league records at some point in time, Wilson's mark even surpasses the minor league record for triples, 32, set by Jack Cross of London in the Class B Michigan-Ontario League in 1925.

Setting the finer points of historical precedent aside, Wilson, a line-drive hitter, collected 24 of his 36 triples in Forbes Field. Although he may have had a home field advantage for three-base hits in the spacious ballpark, in 1912 he still outpointed Honus Wagner, the second-best triples hitter on the team that year, by 16 three-baggers. In another category, 31 of Wilson's 59 career home runs were inside-the-park jobs.

Wilson began his minor league career with Austin in the Texas League in 1905 and switched over to Fort Worth in midseason. Halfway through 1907 he was sent to Des Moines in the Western League, where he hit .323 and earned a promotion to Pittsburgh.

On July 3, 1910, Wilson hit for the cycle. On July 24, 1911, he collected three triples in one game, tying the modern record. He twice led NL outfielders in fielding percentage. In 1914 he recorded a league-leading 34 outfield assists.

In December 1913 Wilson was sent to the St. Louis Cardinals in an eight-player trade. He finished his professional career with San Antonio of the Texas League in 1917.

Don Wilson

Wilson, Donald Edward **P**

1966–74 B:2/12/1945, Monroe, LA D:1/5/1975, Houston, TX Deb:9/29/1966, HOU NL BR/TR 6'3" 205

W	L	PCT	G	SH	IP	BB	SO	ERA
104	92	.531	266	20	1748^1	640	1283	3.15

One of a handful of pitchers to have thrown more than one major league no-hitter, Don Wilson tossed two no-hitters and might have had a third if his manager hadn't pulled him for a pinch hitter. Wilson, who spent all nine of his major league seasons with the Houston Astros, pitched his first no-hitter against Atlanta on June 18, 1967, at the Astrodome. He struck out 15, and Houston won 2–0.

His second no-hitter came on May 1, 1969, against the Reds at Crosley Field. In that game he went to full counts on the first three batters in the eighth and ninth innings. He struck out 13 and walked six. Wilson had another shot at a no-hitter on September 4, 1974. He had not allowed a hit over eight innings but was losing, 2–1, and was lifted for a pinch hitter by manager Preston Gomez.

Although he pitched for poor teams for most of his career, Wilson was remarkably steady. He won in double figures in all but his rookie season and posted a career 3.15 ERA. Wilson committed suicide on January 5, 1975. His uniform No. 40 was retired by the club after his death.

Earl Wilson

Wilson, Robert Earl **P**

1959–70 B:10/2/1934, Ponchatoula, LA Deb:7/28/1959, BOS AL BR/TR 6'3", 216

W	L	PCT	G	SH	IP	BB	SO	ERA
121	109	.526	338	13	2051^2	796	1452	3.69

Earl Wilson played only 11 games as a catcher, the position for which he had been signed, for Bisbee-Douglas of the Arizona-Texas League in 1953. He was a powerful hitter, but with his great arm and 216 pounds of muscles on a 6-foot, 3-inch frame, management wisely decided his place was on the pitching mound, not behind the plate.

The fastball was Wilson's strong suit, not control. In a six-year minor league career, he averaged almost 7.5 walks per nine innings. When the Boston Red Sox gave him his first try in 1959, he allowed only 21 hits in 23⅔ innings, but he issued 31 free passes. He eventually curbed his wildness and used his blazing heat and powerful bat to remain in the majors for 11 seasons.

From Louisiana's bayou country, Robert Earl Wilson was actually the first African-American player signed by the Red Sox. However, a stint in the Marines moved him behind Pumpsie Green in integrating the Boston team. He made it to the majors for good in 1962, when he went 12–8 with a 3.90 ERA. He threw a no-hitter against Bo Belinsky of the Angels in Fenway Park on June 26 of that year.

Wilson's control had improved, but not by much. In 191 innings in 1962, he walked 111 batters. Only three other American League hurlers gave up more. In 1963 not only did he lead the league with 105 walks, but threw 21 wild pitches. And although he cut his walks down dramatically, he couldn't get his record above .500 in 1963, 1964, or 1965.

The best thing that happened to Wilson was his trade to Detroit in June 1966. He was dealt to the Tigers, along with outfielder Joe Christopher, for outfielder Don Demeter and pitcher Julio Navarro. For the Tigers he went 13–6 and improved his earned run average by nearly 1.5 runs over his last season in Boston.

The next year he was able to work with legendary pitching coach Johnny Sain. Wilson responded with a career year, winning 22 games to tie Boston's Jim Lonborg for the league lead. The Tigers scrapped with the Red Sox in one of the game's most exciting pennant races. With 10 games to go in the season, Wilson was brought in relief for the first time that year to try to thwart a Red Sox rally and prevent a disastrous sweep. He uncorked a wild pitch that put the Sox ahead, and the Tigers never really got back in the race.

In 1968 the Tigers won the pennant. Wilson was the number-two starter behind Denny McLain. McLain won 31 games, Mickey Lolich won 17, and Wilson added 13 in the last season before Championship Series play.

Wilson started Game 3 of the World Series, but after having walked his sixth man, he was removed by manager Mayo Smith with two on, one out, and the Tigers ahead, 2–1, in the fifth inning. Tim McCarver promptly homered off reliever Pat Dobson, and the Tigers lost the game. But thanks to Lolich's three victories, Detroit won the Series in seven games.

The Tigers finished second in the AL East in 1969, and Wilson contributed a typical season: 35 starts, a 3.31 ERA, and a 12–10 record. Traded to San Diego after 18 appearances and a 4–6 record in 1970, he finished his career going 1–6 in the senior circuit.

As a hitter, Wilson topped the .200 mark five times and slugged 35 home runs. Among pitchers, only Wes Ferrell, Bob Lemon, and Red Ruffing hit more. However, it took Ferrell nearly 1,200 at bats to hit his; Wilson accomplished the feat in only 740 at bats. He belted two round-trippers in one game on August 16, 1965, the 17th anniversary of Babe Ruth's death, and he whacked a grand slam off Boston's Dan Osinski in 1966. He had seven-homer seasons in 1966 and 1968, hit six long balls in 1965, and five in 1964.

Glenn Wilson

Wilson, Glenn Dwight **OF**

1982–93 B:12/22/1958, Baytown, TX Deb:4/15/1982, DET AL BR/TR 6'1", 190

G	AB	R	H	HR	RBI	OBP	SLG	AVG
1201	4151	451	1098	98	521	.309	.398	.265

A college All-American at Sam Houston University, Glenn Dwight Wilson was a first-round draft choice of the Detroit Tigers in June 1980. He played nine years in the major leagues from 1982 through 1990, compiling a lifetime .265 average.

Wilson debuted with the Tigers in 1982 and started in right field for them in 1983. He was traded to the Philadelphia Phillies for relief pitcher Willie Hernandez in 1984. (Hernandez ended up winning the American League Cy Young and Most Valuable Player awards while leading the Tigers to a world championship.) Wilson started for four seasons in the Phillies' outfield. He knocked in 102 runs for the Phillies in 1985 and led National League outfielders in assists and errors twice. He also has the unenviable total of 27 career stolen bases in 52 career attempts.

Wilson was traded to Seattle in 1987 and the following year was dealt to Pittsburgh. In May of 1989 the Pirates traded him to Houston for catcher Alan Ashby, but Ashby vetoed the trade and then was released by the club. Three months later Wilson was sent to the Astros, with whom he finished his career in 1990.

Hack Wilson

Wilson, Lewis Robert **OF**

1923–34 B:4/26/1900, Ellwood City, PA D:11/23/1948, Baltimore, MD Deb:9/29/1923, NY NL BR/TR 5'6", 190

G	AB	R	H	HR	RBI	OBP	SLG	AVG
1348	4760	884	1461	244	1062	.395	.545	.307

In Chicago, the line "Hack Wilson is a low-ball hitter and highball drinker" used to get a lot of laughs. Later, when Lewis Robert "Hack" Wilson died young and penniless, it didn't seem so funny. Strictly speaking, it wasn't true in either case. Wilson liked high fastballs, and when he was on his game he could knock any pitch into orbit. And when he was out on the town, he never confined himself to highballs.

In a sense, Wilson's career mirrored America of the 1920s and 1930s. He rollicked through the Roaring 20s with a carefree, live-for-today attitude, but when the bleak tomorrow arrived in the 1930s, he suffered. One day Cubs manager Joe McCarthy tried to teach Wilson a lesson. "If I drop a worm in a glass of water, it swims around," he told Wilson. "If I drop it in a glass of whiskey, the worm dies. What does that prove?"

"If you drink whiskey, you'll never get worms," Wilson responded.

Physically, he was a sight to behold, a hybrid of Danny DeVito and Arnold Schwarzenegger. Wilson stood only 5-feet 6-inches and weighed at least 190 pounds. He had massive shoulders, a barrel-shaped chest, and a protruding stomach, and his neck measured 18 inches around. His short arms were larger than some guys' legs, and his short legs had a greater girth than most waists. Supporting all this bulk was a delicate pair of size-six feet.

No one in his right mind tried to mess around with Wilson. When a card game in the Giants' clubhouse erupted into an argument, he kayoed a teammate with one punch. In Cincinnati one day he laid out Reds pitcher Ray Kolp during a game and put another Reds hurler, Pete Donohue, down for the count later that evening at the train station. For a time Wilson considered becoming a professional boxer, but Commissioner Kenesaw Mountain Landis nixed the idea.

Wilson was a surprisingly able outfielder, even though two of the most infamous incidents of his career centered on fielding misadventures. In the 1929 World Series he somehow lost two balls in the sun during the same inning, helping the Philadelphia Athletics score 10 runs against his Cubs. Later, with Brooklyn, he was snoozing away in right field as the Dodgers changed pitchers at the Baker Bowl. In disgust, the hurler coming off the mound turned and fired the ball into the nether regions of right field, where it reverberated off the tin-plated wall. Thinking he'd slept into the next at bat, the suddenly awake Wilson played the carom perfectly and pegged it on a line to second base, then wondered why everyone convulsed in laughter. "Best throw he made all year," manager Casey Stengel is purported to have said.

Wilson quit school in the sixth grade and worked as a printer's apprentice, an ironworker in a locomotive factory, and a shipyard laborer, among other jobs. He eventually made his way into baseball, joining Martinsburg of the Blue Ridge League as a catcher in 1921. In 1922 he hit 30 home runs in 84 games to win a promotion to Portsmouth of the Virginia League, where he was switched to the outfield.

When he led the league in triples, home runs, RBIs, and batting average, the Giants brought him up to the majors. New York's clubhouse man despaired of finding a uniform to fit Wilson's odd dimensions. Finally manager John McGraw tossed the outfielder one from his own locker. "Don't disgrace that uniform," he growled. "A great player once wore it. Me!"

"A great player will wear it now," Wilson deadpanned.

He reportedly acquired the nickname "Hack" while he was with the Giants, because of his resemblance to the famous wrestler and strongman George Hackenschmidt. Others insisted he was named after Hack Miller, a Cubs outfielder reputed to be the strongest man in baseball. Still others noted his resemblance to a taxicab, and a few thought the name came from the way Wilson had played the outfield before he had mastered the niceties of his position.

Wilson was a fair player with the Giants, but his brawling, drinking, and happy-go-lucky attitude annoyed McGraw, who believed the world was best faced with clenched teeth. When Wilson started slowly in 1925, New York optioned him to Toledo. Then, through what McGraw always insisted was a clerical error, the Giants failed to renew their option on Wilson, and he was drafted by the Cubs.

The big-shouldered Wilson took to the City of Big Shoulders. In 1926 he led the National League with 21 homers while batting .321 with 109 RBIs. The next year he tied Philadelphia's Cy Williams for the homer lead, with 30, and upped his RBIs to 129. In 1928 he and St. Louis' Jim Bottomley shared the home run crown, with 31.

A large part of Wilson's success was due to the careful handling of Joe McCarthy. The Cubs' skipper knew when to pat him on the back and when to bawl him out. He could not prevent Wilson from drinking, but did manage to slow him down. He also protected Wilson from the wrath of owner Phil Wrigley, a strong prohibitionist.

Wilson's numbers improved each season. In 1929 he hit 39 home runs and just missed the home run title, but he led the league in RBIs with 159, batted .345, and helped the Cubs win their first pennant since 1918. He was criticized after losing the two flyballs in the sun during the Cubs' World Series loss to the Athletics. But McCarthy rebuilt the slugger's ego by the 1930 season, and Wilson had one of the most remarkable offensive seasons on record. He hit .356, set the league record for home runs with 56 (broken by Mark McGwire and fellow Cub Sammy Sosa in 1998), and knocked in 190 runners for a major league record. As with Joe DiMaggio's 56-game hitting streak, Wilson's RBI record appears likely to last forever.

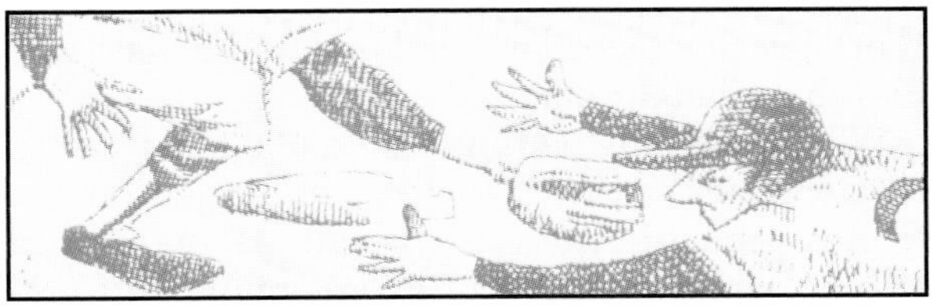

McCarthy left the Cubs to manage the Yankees after the 1930 season. His replacement was the blunt and brusque Rogers Hornsby, who had none of McCarthy's interpersonal skills. Under Hornsby's unrelenting criticism Wilson curled up like the worm in the glass of whiskey. In 1931 he hit only 13 homers with 61 RBIs and a .261 batting average.

Chicago dealt him to the Cardinals, who passed him on to Brooklyn before he had played an inning. He had a fair season with the Dodgers in 1932, knocking in 123 runs, but then his skills progressively deteriorated. By 1935 Wilson was back in the minor leagues, trying unsuccessfully to make a comeback with the International League's Albany Senators.

Upon leaving baseball Wilson took a succession of menial jobs, even presenting himself as an example of the evil consequences of alcoholism on radio. Many players have better totals, but few have come close to matching his best seasons. After a long campaign, his admirers finally convinced the Veterans Committee to name Wilson to the Hall of Fame in 1979.

Jim Wilson

Wilson, James Alger **P**

1945–58 B:2/20/1922, San Diego, CA D:9/2/1986, Newport Beach, CA Deb:4/18/1945, BOS AL BR/TR 6'1½", 200

W	L	PCT	G	SH	IP	BB	SO	ERA
86	89	.491	257	19	1539	608	692	4.01

Jim Wilson survived a skull fracture during 1945, his rookie season, to become an All-Star pitcher in two leagues. In August of that year, Wilson was pitching for the Boston Red Sox against Detroit when a line drive off the bat of Hank Greenberg hit him squarely in the head. The ball was hit so hard it fractured his skull and put a dent in it a quarter of an inch deep.

Out of action for a long time, Wilson did not pitch regularly in the majors again until 1951 with the Boston Braves. His comeback reached its peak in 1954 when he made the All-Star team and also no-hit the Philadelphia Phillies.

The Braves sold him to Baltimore in April of 1955 and Wilson made the AL All-Star team with the Orioles. Traded to the Chicago White Sox in 1956, he won 15 games for them in 1957 while leading the American League with five shutouts.

After retiring as a player Wilson became vice president of the Milwaukee Brewers and later director of Major League Baseball's Central Scouting Bureau.

Jimmie Wilson

Wilson, James **C**

1923–40 M(1934–38, 1941–43, 493–735) B:7/23/1900, Philadelphia, PA D:5/31/1947, Bradenton, FL Deb:4/17/1923, PHIL NL BR/TR 6'1½", 200

G	AB	R	H	HR	RBI	OBP	SLG	AVG
1525	4778	580	1358	32	621	.336	.370	.284

One of the top National League catchers during the 1920s and early 1930s, James "Ace" Wilson began his career with the Philadelphia Phillies but was traded to St. Louis in 1928 and helped the Cardinals to three pennants. Wilson led the league's catchers in double plays and putouts twice and in assists and games caught once. He played 18 seasons in the majors and compiled a lifetime .284 average.

Wilson also managed in the major leagues, serving five years as playing manager of the Phillies (1934 to 1938) and three seasons as manager of the Chicago Cubs (1941 to 1943). His teams never finished higher than fifth, but during his tour of duty with the Phillies he did help convert Bucky Walters from an infielder into a pitcher. Walters went on to become a star pitcher for the Cincinnati Reds.

Wilson batted over .300 four times and played on World Series teams with the Cardinals in 1928, 1930, and 1931, and memorably with the Reds in 1940. Forced to play all six games in the 1940 Fall Classic because of an injury to Ernie Lombardi, the 40-year-old Wilson became a star, batting .353 and leading the Reds to a seven-game victory over the Detroit Tigers.

Mookie Wilson

Wilson, William Hayward **OF**

1980–91 B:2/9/1956, Bamberg, SC Deb:9/2/1980, NY NL BB/TR 5'10",170

G	AB	R	H	HR	RBI	OBP	SLG	AVG
1403	5094	731	1397	67	438	.315	.386	.274

In Game 6 of the 1986 World Series Mookie Wilson's 10th-inning grounder went through Bill Buckner's legs, giving the New York Mets a dramatic come-from-behind victory over the Boston Red Sox. With the Mets trailing, 5–4 and down to their final strike, Wilson fouled off pitch after pitch. Then Red Sox reliever Bob Stanley threw a pitch that catcher Rich Gedman should have been able to handle, but didn't. As Gedman scrambled after the ball, Kevin Mitchell scored from third, and Ray Knight moved into scoring position at second.

Wilson fouled off two more pitches, and then hit a slow grounder to Buckner at first. The ball squiggled through, and Knight came tearing around third to score the winning run. The Mets went on to win the world championship, and Buckner became the Series goat.

William Hayward "Mookie" Wilson, a speedy base runner and a center fielder with good range, came to the major leagues with the Mets in 1980. He became a Shea Stadium favorite, and crowds loved to greet him with a loud "Moooo." But the switch hitter had several major flaws as a player—a weak arm, a tendency to strike out, and a very low on-base percentage for a leadoff hitter. With the arrival of Lenny Dykstra in 1985 Wilson found himself platooned by manager Davey Johnson. His best season was 1987, when he hit .299 in 124 games.

In 1989 the 33-year-old Wilson was traded to the Blue Jays. He later coached first base for the Mets. He stepson Preston debuted in the majors in 1998.

Willie Wilson

Wilson, Willie James **OF**

1976–94 B:7/9/1955, Montgomery, AL Deb:9/4/1976, KC AL BB/TR, 6'3", 195

G	AB	R	H	HR	RBI	OBP	SLG	AVG
2154	7731	1169	2207	41	585	.328	.376	.285

In the late 1970s and throughout the 1980s, Willie Wilson turned Royals Stadium into his personal racetrack. He hit five inside-the-park home runs in 1979, and finished his career with a total of 13. Only Roberto Clemente had more triples than Wilson's 147 between World War II and the end of the 20th century. Wilson also excelled at stealing bases, totaling 668 for his career, including 11 consecutive years of 30 or more.

In 1974 Wilson turned down a football scholarship from the University of Maryland, confident he could make it as a switch-hitting baseball player. In his rookie year of 1978, he defied the odds by stealing 46 bases in just 198 at bats. He hit .315 with a league-high 83 steals in 1979, then took his game to an even higher level in 1980.

The free-swinging slash hitter set a record with 705 at bats while rapping 230 hits, the second-highest total in the AL in 44 years. He also paced the league with 133 runs and 15 triples. His finest season ended on a sour note, however, with a World Series record 12 strikeouts in a six-game loss to Philadelphia.

Wilson won the batting title in 1982, his first of two All-Star seasons. In 1985 he legged out 21 triples—most in the majors since 1949—and in October atoned for his World Series slump the previous year by batting .367 as the Royals beat St. Louis in seven games to win a world championship.

Boasting great range in center field, Wilson played 148 consecutive errorless games in 1987. His remaining seasons, however, were uneventful, as age and nagging injuries took their toll. Discarded by the Royals after 1990, he played out the string with the A's and Cubs.

In October 1983, Wilson was one of four Royals who admitted they had attempted to possess cocaine; he served a brief prison sentence. The incident blemished an otherwise brilliant career.

Hooks Wiltse

Wiltse, George Leroy **P**

1904–15 B:9/7/1880, Hamilton, NY D:1/21/1959, Long Beach, NY Deb:4/21/1904, NY NL BR/TL 6', 185

W	L	PCT	G	SV	IP	BB	SO	ERA
139	90	.607	357	33	2112^{1}	498	965	2.47

Between 1904 and 1914 lefthander George Leroy "Hooks" Wiltse combined with his Giants teammate Christy Mathewson for 435 wins, making them the second-best lefty-righty duo in history. The southpaw pitched some memorable games, including a no-hitter against the Phillies in the first game of a July 4, 1908 doubleheader. It took Wiltse 10 innings to record a 1–0 victory that day, but it could have been a perfect game. With two outs in the bottom of the ninth, umpire Cy Rigler failed to call a third strike on the batter. Later Rigler admitted he easily could have rung him up. Wiltse then hit the batter, but he retired everyone else. He struck out six in the contest.

Wiltse struck out four batters in an inning on May 15, 1906. He had already disposed of Jim Delahanty and Tommy Corcoran when Admiral Schlei swung, missed, and reached first base when the ball got away from the catcher. Wiltse fanned Chick Fraser to complete the inning; he recorded seven straight whiffs that day. In 1904 Wiltse recorded 12 consecutive victories. In 1908 he went 23–14, and in 1909 he was 20–11.

Some think that Wiltse obtained his nickname from his good curveball. Actually, he gained the moniker from his habit of skillfully "hooking" batted balls on the mound. "That's hooking them, George!" catcher Frank Bowerman would call out. However, Wiltse's brother Lewis was known as "Snake," because of his curve.

In Game 2 of the 1913 World Series Wiltse, who loved to field, was sent in to play first base when Fred Merkle and Fred Snodgrass went down with injuries. Wiltse helped preserve Mathewson's 3–0 blanking of the A's with several fine plays.

Wiltse pitched in New York for 11 years, on four pennant-winners and one world championship team. He spent his last year with Brooklyn of the Federal League.

Bobby Wine

Wine, Robert Paul Sr. **SS**

1960–72 M(1985, 16–25) B:9/17/1938, New York, NY Deb:9/20/1960, PHI NL BR/TR 6'1", 187

G	AB	R	H	HR	RBI	OBP	SLG	AVG
1164	3172	249	682	30	268	.265	.286	.215

Weak-hitting shortstop Bobby Wine won a Gold Glove in 1963, but his lack of offensive skills kept him from getting more playing time. His .215 lifetime average is the third worst for players with 3,000 or more at bats. In 1970, however, he turned a record-setting 137 double plays at short.

Wine began in the Phillies system with Johnson City of the Appalachian League in 1957. He actually hit over .300 in his first two minor league seasons, while twice leading the minors in putouts, assists, and errors.

In 1966 Wine lost most of the season to a wrenched back. In May 1968 he underwent surgery for a ruptured spinal disk and was out for the remainder of the season. In April 1969 he was sent to the Expos as a replacement for Larry Jackson, who had been picked from the Phillies in the expansion draft but who had chosen to retire.

Wine briefly served as an interim manager for the Braves, and he also coached for the Phils, Braves, and Mets, in addition to scouting. His son, Robbie (Robert Paul Jr.), was the Astros' first-round draft pick in the 1983 amateur draft. Robbie Wine appeared in 23 games for Houston in 1986 and 1987.

Dave Winfield

Winfield, David Mark **OF**

1973–88, 1990–95 B:10/3/1951, St. Paul, MN Deb:6/19/1973, SD NL BR/TR 6'6" 220

G	AB	R	H	HR	RBI	OBP	SLG	AVG
2973	11003	1669	3110	465	1833	.355	.475	.283

A talented, durable player, Dave Winfield posted Hall of Fame-level offensive statistics and also won seven Gold Gloves. He is perhaps most famous, however, for his fractious relationship with controversial Yankees owner George Steinbrenner. Their feud put Steinbrenner on baseball's "permanently" ineligible list, although only temporarily.

Winfield was both a star pitcher and basketball player at the University of Minnesota. With the Golden Gophers he not only posted a 13–1 record, he batted .400 into the bargain. He was named MVP of the 1973 College World Series and sought after not only by baseball's San Diego Padres, but also by the NBA's Atlanta Hawks (a fifth round pick), the ABA's Utah Stars (sixth round), and the NFL's Minnesota Vikings (15th round). Although only the fourth pick of the Padres in the June 1973 amateur draft, Winfield went immediately from the campus to the majors, singling off Jerry Reuss in his first at bat and hitting safely in his first six games.

Winfield became the star on the second-division Padres, and as free agency approached, he delivered a 34-homer, 118-RBI season for San Diego in 1979 and won Gold Gloves in 1979 and 1980. Larger and more prosperous franchises set their sights on Winfield, and he was ready to cash in.

Some thought *too* eager. "Frankly speaking," said Padres broadcaster Jerry Coleman, "I think Dave was afraid of getting hurt. He had a life contract staring him in the face, and he didn't want to get hurt."

The bidding came down to the Mets, Yankees, Braves and Astros. The Mets offered $1.5 million a year for five seasons. The Yankees countered with a $1 million signing bonus, 10 years at $1.4 million per year and a cost-of-living clause. All told, it could be worth $23 million. A 50-percent buy-out clause for the last two years was included.

As part of the agreement Steinbrenner personally agreed to contribute or cause to be contributed $300,000 to the David M. Winfield Foundation each year for the decade. That agreement would eventually become a key bone of contention between Winfield and Steinbrenner.

Not everyone thought Steinbrenner had made a wise investment. "For a guy six-foot-eight," observed Billy Martin, then managing the A's, "he's got the softest bat I've ever seen, and for George Steinbrenner to give him 23 million, he must be losing his horsefeathers."

Winfield's first year with the Yankees was good but not spectacular. The next season, 1982, he delivered 37 homers—his career high—and knocked in 106 runs, his first of five consecutive years topping the 100-RBI mark. No Yankee had accomplished that since Joe DiMaggio had strung together seven straight 100-RBI seasons from 1936–42.

On August 4, 1983 came the celebrated "Seagull Incident." While playing center field in Toronto Winfield attempted to scare a gull off the field by throwing a ball near it. The ball took a short bounce off the artificial turf at Exposition Stadium and killed the bird.

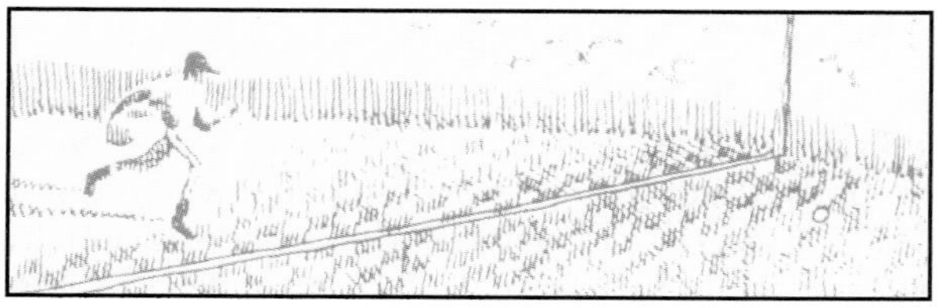

"They said he hit the gull on purpose," said Billy Martin, now his manager. "They wouldn't say that if they'd seen the throws he'd been making all year. First time he hit the cutoff man all year." Authorities in Toronto weren't laughing. Toronto police booked Winfield on a charge of cruelty to animals, held him for 90 minutes and released him on $500 bail. Charges were dropped the following day, but in the spring training edition of *Yankee* magazine Winfield appeared on the cover—with seagulls flying around his head.

Dissension had arisen quickly between Steinbrenner and Winfield, first sparked by the owner's miscalculations over the cost-of-living provisions of Winfield's contract. Steinbrenner called Winfield "the most selfish athlete I've ever known" and tagged him "Mr. May" in contrast to Reggie Jackson's title of "Mr. October." "He's a good player," said Steinbrenner, "but not a superstar, not the way Reggie Jackson was. He can't carry the ball club and rise to the moment the way Reggie did here. Dave's a good ballplayer and an athlete. He's just not a superstar."

Still, few players in the majors were as productive as Winfield between 1982 and 1986. In addition to his RBI numbers he scored more than 100 runs in 1984 and 1985, and on the last day of the 1984 season, after a spirited race, he lost the American League batting title to teammate Don Mattingly (.343 to .340). Winfield won Gold Glove Awards in 1982, 1983, 1984, 1985, and 1987.

In 1989 Winfield and Steinbrenner launched lawsuits against each other in regard to payments to the Winfield Foundation. Winfield alleged that Steinbrenner had failed to make $450,000 in payments to the entity. Steinbrenner countersued, alleged that Winfield, himself, had failed to make $300,000 in contractually committed donations to the foundation. The controversy was settled out of court. Winfield agreed to pay $230,000 into his foundation and to reimburse it for $30,000 in "inappropriately expended" funds.

On December 2, 1986, Steinbrenner received a call from a Winfield associate, gambler Howard Spira. An unpaid, low-level employee of the Winfield Foundation from 1981 to 1984, Spira had also worked for Top Hat, a firm Winfield agent Al Frohman had formed to generate endorsement income. Spira indicated to Steinbrenner that he had incriminating information on Winfield. "I'm anxious to hear what you have to say," the Yankees owner replied.

Spira and Steinbrenner met in Tampa in December 1986 and April 1987. Spira flew to Florida at Steinbrenner's expense. He alleged that the Foundation had misused funds, that Winfield and Frohman had invented false death threats as an alibi for Winfield's 1-for-22 performance in the 1981 World Series, and that Winfield had lent

Spira $15,000 and then two weeks later threatened to kill him if it were not repaid (in the amount of $18,500). Spira claimed that Winfield held a gun to his head to compel payment.

On January 9, 1990 Steinbrenner paid Spira $40,000 for the information, but soon Spira demanded $110,000 more. On March 2, Spira told Steinbrenner that unless he received the money he was "going to make everything I've gone through public." Steinbrenner called in the FBI, alleging extortion. The FBI raided Spira's apartment, seizing tapes Spira had made of conversations with Steinbrenner. On March 23 a Tampa grand jury indicted Spira on eight counts of attempted extortion against Steinbrenner and for making threats against both Steinbrenner and Winfield.

Steinbrenner provided various reasons for the payment to Spira, one of which was "I did it out of the goodness of my heart. No other reason." (Spira's mother had cancer.) Another of his justifications: "You don't know what it's like when you've got a guy out there calling and threatening to kill people in your family." Steinbrenner alternately claimed it was to protect Yankees manager Lou Piniella from Spira making public his gambling habits.

Commissioner Fay Vincent found Steinbrenner's actions to be "not in the interests of baseball," constituting "a pattern that borders on the bizarre." Shortly thereafter, Spira was convicted of extortion. On July 30, 1990, Steinbrenner and Vincent signed an agreement placing the Yankees' owner on the "permanently ineligible list." Although Steinbrenner retained ownership of the team he was not to "consult upon or participate in major financial and business decisions of the New York Yankees."

In the midst of this turmoil, Winfield was having on-field problems. He had missed the entire 1989 season due to a herniated disk, which resulted in a total blockage of the spinal canal and intense pressure on the spinal nerves. The once Gold Glove fielder started the 1990 season as the Yankees designated hitter. It appeared, however, that he was washed up. New York manager Bucky Dent began platooning him, and on May 11 Winfield was traded to the Angels for once-promising righthander Mike Witt. Despite the promise of finally being free of Steinbrenner, Winfield—as a 10-and-5 player (10 years in the majors and five years with one club)—vetoed the trade. The Yankees countered by pointing out that Winfield (now on the last year of his 10-year contract) had in December 1980 agreed to accept a trade to any of seven clubs (Angels, Royals, A's, Blue Jays, Dodgers, and Mets).

Nothing happened until a May 14, 1990 meeting between Winfield and Steinbrenner, in which Steinbrenner agreed that if an arbitrator found that Winfield should remain with the Yankees it would be in the capacity of a full-time player. The next day, however, the club turned over $100,000 in incentive bonuses to Winfield and the commissioner announced that Winfield would join California.

Still, Winfield did not report. A Players Association grievance procedure was scheduled for May 16, but was supplanted by a negotiating session in which the Angels agreed to extend Winfield's contract through 1991—at a salary of $3.1 million. Even that agreement generated new controversy, as the Angels accused Steinbrenner of "tampering in its grandest form" by helping Winfield secure additional compensation from California. They sought $2 million in damages. Ultimately, they were awarded $250,000.

Winfield showed he was not through. In 1990 he led American League outfielders in fielding percentage and paced the Angels in RBIs, runs, and slugging percentage. He was named *The Sporting News* Comeback Player of the Year.

On April 13, 1991, he hit three homers in one game against Minnesota. On June 24, 1991 versus Kansas City he hit for the cycle, becoming the oldest player to accomplish that feat. He signed with Toronto after the season's conclusion. In 1992 he became the oldest player to record 100-or-more RBIs in a season, helped by a record 32 RBIs in August. His two-run double in the 11th inning of Game 6 of the 1992 World Series gave the Blue Jays a 4–3 win over Atlanta and the world championship.

Dropped by the Blue Jays immediately following their victory, on December 18, 1992 Winfield signed a two-year contract with the Twins. With Minnesota in 1993 he achieved one of the most coveted milestones for a hitter, getting his 3,000th career hit on September 26 off Dennis Eckersley (he finished with 3,110). Winfield spent 1995, his final year as a player, as a designated hitter for the Cleveland Indians.

Rick Wise

Wise, Richard Charles **P**

1964–82 B:9/13/1945, Jackson, MI Deb:4/18/1964, PHI NL BR/TR 6'2", 195

W	L	PCT	G	SH	IP	BB	SO	ERA
188	181	.509	506	30	3127	804	1647	3.69

Rick Wise enjoyed a long career as a quality starter in both major leagues, but his reputation suffered by dint of being constantly compared to Steve Carlton. In February 1972 the Cardinals obtained Wise from the Phillies in an even exchange for the future Hall of Famer. Carlton went 329–244 in his career; Wise went just 188–181.

A righthander, Richard Charles Wise was a bonus baby with the Phillies and pitched his first major league game in 1964 at age 18. A good hitting pitcher, he slammed 15 homers in his career, including six in his best season, 1971. On June 23, 1971, Wise pitched a no-hitter against the Reds and hit two homers, making him the first pitcher ever to homer in his own no-hitter. He finished that season with a 17–14 record and a 2.88 ERA. Carlton, for whom he was traded the next year, went 20–9.

Wise pitched the win for the National League in the 1973 All-Star Game. After that season the Cardinals traded him to the Red Sox, and his 19 wins helped Boston to a World Series. He won the final game of the ALCS, defeating Oakland, 5–3. After getting a no-decision in Game 3 of the Series, Wise relieved Dick Drago in the 12th inning of the dramatic Game 6 and got the win when Carlton Fisk homered in the bottom of the inning.

In 1978 Boston traded Wise to Cleveland in a deal that brought Dennis Eckersley to the Red Sox. Two years later Wise signed as a free agent with the Padres, where he finished his career in 1982.

Bobby Witt

Witt, Robert Andrew **P**

1986–* B:5/11/1964, Arlington, MA Deb:4/10/1986, TEX AL BR/TR, 6'2", 205

W	L	PCT	G	SH	IP	BB	SO	ERA
138	155	.471	409	11	2406^{1}	1344	1918	4.82

Bobby Witt made his major league debut less than a year after the Texas Rangers had selected him as the third overall pick in the 1985 draft. The 22-year-old with the golden arm just reared back and fired—and the results showed it. Witt led the American League in walks in three of his first four seasons.

Witt also enjoyed stretches of brilliance. After Texas briefly sent him to the minors in 1988, he returned to reel off nine straight complete games, winning six and averaging nearly a strikeout an inning. In 1990 everything came together. Witt went 17–10 with a 3.36 ERA and 221 strikeouts, but a rotator cuff tear and subsequent elbow surgery slowed his velocity, and his control problems lingered.

It was not until a 1992 trade to Oakland and extended work with A's pitching coach Dave Duncan that Witt made the transition from thrower to pitcher. He won 14 games for Oakland in 1993, and following a trade back to Texas notched 16 victories for the Rangers in 1996. When Witt was traded to the St. Louis Cardinals in mid-1998, he was second all-time in victories and strikeouts among Texas pitchers.

Mike Witt

Witt, Michael Atwater **P**

1981–91, 1993 B:7/20/1960, Fullerton, CA Deb:4/11/1981, CAL AL BR/TR 6'7", 192

W	L	PCT	G	SH	IP	BB	SO	ERA
117	116	.502	341	11	2108^{1}	713	1373	3.83

Mike Witt's lively fastball and vicious curve made him one of the American League's most successful pitchers during the mid-1980s. As ace of the California Angels rotation, Witt won at least 15 games in each season between 1984 and 1987. He pitched at least 220 innings per season between 1984 and 1989. And he pitched the 13th perfect game in major league history, a 1–0 gem over Texas on the final day of the 1984 season.

Not coincidentally, Witt's best season was his team's best season. His 18–10 record, 2.84 ERA and 208 strikeouts, all career highs, led the Angels to the 1986 AL West title. He added a complete-game win over Boston in the Championship Series. Witt would have won the series-clinching Game 5 as well, if California's bullpen held up; the Red Sox captured the series in seven games.

Witt's wins decreased in each of the next three seasons as his ERA rose. The Angels traded him to the Yankees for Dave Winfield midway through 1990. Witt pitched well for New York down the stretch, but he blew out his elbow in his second start of 1991. After a two-year battle to resume his career, he retired in 1993.

Mark Wohlers

Wohlers, Mark Edward **P**

1991–* B:1/23/1970, Holyoke, MA Deb:8/17/1991, ATL NL BR/TR, 6'4", 207

W	L	PCT	G	SV	IP	BB	SO	ERA
31	22	.585	388	112	386^{1}	204	437	3.73

Mark Wohlers was just 20 years old when he helped the Atlanta Braves reach the postseason in 1991. He pitched two innings of a combined no-hitter with Kent Mercker and Alejandro Pena on September 11. In October he made five appearances in the Championship Series and World Series without allowing a run. Still, the Braves searched in vain for a closer while Wohlers bounced back and forth between Triple-A Richmond and Atlanta for three seasons.

Wohlers finally stuck in the big leagues as a set-up man in 1994. He earned the job as closer the following year. He put together a career-best 2.09 ERA while saving 25 games in 65 appearances. The hard-throwing reliever—often timed at 100 mph—had 90 strikeouts in 64⅔ innings. He saved a club-record 39 games in 1996, pitched in the All-Star Game, and reached triple digits in strikeouts for the only time in his career. But disaster struck in the fourth game of the World Series, when he yielded a game-tying, three-run, eighth-inning homer to the Yankees' Jim Leyritz, wiping out a potential edge of three games to one for the Braves.

After Atlanta lost the Series, Wohlers began to fade. He earned 33 saves but posted a 3.50 ERA in 1997; he also experienced frequent bouts of control trouble. A year later he endured two stints on the disabled list, marital problems that ended in divorce, and his mother's heart attack. Though he managed eight saves early in the season, Wohlers had none after straining an oblique muscle in May. Unable to throw strikes even when assigned to minor league teams, he was eventually placed on the disabled list for "an inability to pitch."

Wohlers surprised everyone by making the Braves out of 1999 spring training, but was so wild in two appearances that Atlanta traded him to the Reds in mid-April. He spent most of the year on the disabled list, first with an anxiety disorder and then with a torn elbow ligament that required "Tommy John" surgery on July 6. With a one-year layoff likely, the Reds released Wohlers. His sudden and mysterious inability to get the ball anywhere near the plate brought comparisons to Pirates pitcher Steve Blass, who became bafflingly wild less than a year after winning 19 games in 1972.

Jimmy Wolf

Wolf, William Van Winkle **OF**

1882–92 M(1889, 14–51) B:5/12/1862, Louisville, KY D:5/16/1903, Louisville, KY Deb:5/2/1882, LOU AA BR/TR 5'9", 190

G	AB	R	H	HR	RBI	OBP	SLG	AVG
1198	4968	779	1440	18	593	.327	.387	.290

One of the great stars of the 19th century's American Association, Jimmy "Chicken" Wolf participated in all 10 seasons of that league's existence starting in 1882. He holds most of the early league's career offensive records—most games (1,195), most hits (1,438), most doubles (213), most triples (109), and most total bases (1,923).

William Van Winkle Wolf was known to most as "Jimmy" before he got the nickname "Chicken." No coward, Wolf disobeyed Louisville manager John Dyler's orders to not eat a large meal of chicken stew before a game. Wolf subsequently made several errors in the contest, so player Pete Browning christened him "Chicken" in honor of the meal.

A fine defensive player, Wolf filled in at every position including pitcher and catcher but mainly played in the outfield. He was a career .290-hitter, and he led the AA with a .363 average in 1890. In the 1890 World Series against the National League Brooklyn Bridegrooms he batted .360 with eight RBIs. After the AA folded in 1891 Wolf played three games in 1892 with St. Louis of the National League.

Shortly after retiring from the game, Wolf was working as a Louisville fireman when he severely injured his head in an on-the-job accident. He was confined to the Lakeland Insane Asylum until his death in 1903 at age 41.

George Wood

Wood, George A. **OF**

1880–92 B:11/9/1858, Boston, MA D:4/4/1924, Harrisburg, PA Deb:5/1/1880, WOR NL BL/TR 5'10½", 175

G	AB	R	H	HR	RBI	OBP	SLG	AVG
1280	5371	965	1467	68	601	.329	.403	.273

They referred to George A. Wood by the nickname "Dandy" because "he cut a fine figure." During the late 19th century he was a well-rounded player with one of the strongest arms in baseball. Wood played from 1880 to 1892 and was used at every position except catcher. He posted a lifetime batting average of .273 and hit 68 home runs in his 13 seasons, which was a high number for the Dead Ball Era.

Wood was one of the best outfielders of his day, twice leading the league in double plays and games played, and once each in assists and putouts. He also led the league in errors on two occasions.

Wood spent most of his career with Detroit and Philadelphia of the National League, although his best season came in 1890 with Philadelphia of the Players' League when he hit .289 with nine homers and 102 RBIs. After retiring as an active player, he umpired in the New England League and was appointed marshal of the Pennsylvania Public Service Commission by Gov. John K. Tener, himself a former big leaguer.

Smokey Joe Wood

Wood, Howard Ellsworth **P–OF**

1908–22 B:10/25/1889, Kansas City, MO D:7/27/1985, West Haven, CT Deb:8/24/1908, BOS AL BR/TR 5'11", 180

W	L	PCT	G	SH	IP	BB	SO	ERA
117	57	.672	225	28	1434^{1}	421	989	2.03

G	AB	R	H	HR	RBI	OBP	SLG	AVG
696	1952	266	553	23	325	.357	.411	.283

Joe Wood was called "Smokey Joe" because of the amazing speed of his fastball. Once, in 1912, the great Walter Johnson was asked about his young rival. "Can I throw harder than Joe Wood?" Johnson replied, mulling the question. "Listen, my friend, no man alive can throw harder than Smokey Joe Wood."

That same year the 22-year-old Wood enjoyed one of the finest seasons any pitcher ever had, going 34–5. Ten of those victories were shutouts, and 16 of them were consecutive. As it turned out, that was the high-water mark of Smokey Joe's pitching career.

Born Howard Ellsworth Wood, he grew up on the Kansas prairie and in rough Colorado mining towns. Wood's father, an attorney, panned for gold in the Klondike. "But wherever I was I played baseball," Wood recalled. "That's all I lived for. When I sat up on the front seat of that covered wagon next to my father, I was wearing a baseball glove. That showed anybody who was interested where I wanted to go."

Wood got his start in baseball in September 1906 with one of the Bloomer Girls teams, composed of both men and women players. After performing with the club, he was offered a job in the team's infield for the rest of the season. It was not what he expected baseball to be like, but he took the job.

In January 1907 Wood signed a $90-a-month contract with Cedar Rapids of the 3-I League. Before it came time for him to report, however, Cedar Rapids owner Belden Hill sent him to Hutchinson of the Western Association. "He didn't sell me," said Wood. "He just gave me away." Wood struck out more than 200 batters for Hutchinson and was sold to the American Association's Kansas City Blues. In mid-1908 John I. Taylor's Boston Red Sox acquired him for $7,000.

Wood started slowly, and for a while his claim to fame was merely being Tris Speaker's roommate. But in 1911 he won 23 games for fifth-place Boston, including a July 29 no-hitter against the Browns in which he struck out 12 and walked only two. Shortly thereafter, sportswriter Paul Shannon dubbed the young fastballer "Smokey Joe" in the *Boston Post.*

That year was nothing, however, compared to his epic 1912 season, when Wood also posted the fifth-best won-lost percentage (.872) in American League history. "I've seen some pretty fair pitching," contended teammate Harry Hooper, "but I've never seen anything like Smokey Joe Wood in 1912."

That same season Walter Johnson recorded a league-record 16 straight victories for the Senators, a streak that ended in late August. Wood soon threatened the mark. He had begun a streak of his own on July 8 and by early September had 13 consecutive wins. On Friday, September 5, a head-to-head matchup between the two pitchers took place at Fenway Park, as Boston manager Jake Stahl moved Wood up a day in the rotation.

Thirty thousand fans packed the place to see if Johnson could stave off his challenger. "So thickly were the public massed, and so impossible was it for the squadron of police to keep them back, that the players' pits were abandoned, the contestants bringing their war clubs out almost to the baselines," noted sportswriter Manville Webb Jr.

The game was scoreless until the sixth inning, when Speaker doubled down the third-base line. Then Duffy Lewis lifted a high fly to right that Washington outfielder Danny Moeller got his glove on but couldn't hold. Speaker scored on the play, and that was all Wood needed to defeat Johnson, 1–0. "That was probably the most exciting game I ever played in or saw," Hooper said.

Wood went on to notch two more victories, tying Johnson, but then losing his try for a record 17th straight win on unearned late-inning runs. That September, Wood even received two menacing letters, threatening him with death. Unlike high-profile individuals in today's security-conscious society, Wood and his teammates "laughed them off."

In the 1912 World Series that October, the Red Sox faced the Giants, and feelings ran high. In New York, Wood had to draw the blinds down in his cab to keep from being pelted with rocks by unruly Giants fans. Wood started three games in the Series, each time against spitballer Jeff Tesreau.

In Game 1, Wood ended a ninth-inning Giants rally by fanning Art Fletcher and Doc Crandall, getting his 10th and 11th strikeouts. Of his strikeout of Fletcher, Wood said, "I threw so hard I thought my arm would fly right off my body." In Game 4, Wood beat Tesreau again, batting in the third run in a 3–1 victory and striking out eight.

An eighth matchup was required as Game 2 had been a tie, and Game 8 went into extra innings. Boston batted in the bottom of 10th, down 2–1. Wood, due up first, was removed for a pinch hitter. Ordinarily, he would have hit, but in the top of the inning his pitching hand had been hit by a line drive and was badly swollen. Aided by Fred Snodgrass' muff of a routine fly ball, the Red Sox rallied and made Wood a three-game winner in the Series.

The year 1912 was a great one for Wood, but it was also nerve-racking. "The tension on Joe was just terrific all that season," recalled Hooper. "I still remember talking to him before one of the Series games and suddenly realized that he couldn't speak. Couldn't say a word. The strain had started to get too much for him."

The following year things got to him physically as well. In a game against the Tigers, Wood reached down to field a groundball, slipped on the wet grass, and broke his thumb. It was in a cast for three weeks, and Wood wasn't the same after it healed. "I never pitched again without a terrific amount of pain in my right shoulder. Never again," he said.

Sore arm and all, Wood won the ERA crown in 1915, but that was his last year on the mound. In 1916, unable to pitch at all, he retreated to his Pennsylvania farm until it occurred to him that he was still a ballplayer if no longer an able pitcher.

The Red Sox allowed him to make a deal for himself, and in February 1917, Cleveland purchased him for $15,000. There he was reunited with Speaker and began the process of converting to the outfield. He had always been a good hitter (on July 4, 1913, he recorded two doubles in the same inning), and in 1918, given a chance because of wartime call-ups, he became an outfielder.

Wood knew he would make it back, thanks in part to a marvelous day he had at the Polo Grounds on May 24, 1918. During the 19-inning game he homered to left in the seventh, saved the game with an extraordinary catch in the ninth, and threw a man out at second in the 12th. In the last inning he won the game for the Indians with another homer to left.

In 1923 Wood was offered the position of baseball coach at Yale University at the same salary he had been getting at Cleveland. He remained at Yale until 1942.

Wilbur Wood

Wood, Wilbur Forrester **P**

1961–78 B:10/22/1941, Cambridge, MA

Deb:6/30/1961, BOS AL BR/TL 6', 180

W	L	PCT	G	SV	IP	BB	SO	ERA
164	156	.512	651	57	2684	724	1411	3.24

During the 1970s White Sox knuckleballer Wilbur Wood moved from setting records in the bullpen to pulling an "Iron Man" act in the Chicago rotation. In a single season he won and lost 20 games, started both ends of a doubleheader, and piled up phenomenal innings-pitched totals.

In 1960 the Red Sox signed Wilbur Forrester Wood for a $30,000 bonus. "They offered me the most money so, yeah, they were my favorite team," he said. One of a number of high-priced Boston prospects of that era, he performed at Waterloo, Raleigh, and Winston-Salem before making his first Red Sox appearance.

Wood pitched well enough in the minors, but in Boston he was never able to duplicate his success. However, even then—before developing his knuckleball—he was displaying signs of the stamina that would later serve him so well. With York in 1962 he led the Eastern League in starts and innings pitched. With Seattle in 1964 he paced the Pacific Coast League in complete games.

Boston sold Wood to the Pirates in September 1964. The Pirates in turn traded him to the White Sox in October 1966. In Chicago, Wood met Hoyt Wilhelm, who instructed him in the use of the knuckleball. In view of his limited major league success with a standard repertoire, Wood felt he had little to lose.

"The first thing Wilhelm did after I approached him for help was ask how long I had been monkeying with the knuckler," Wood said. "When I told him I had been using it on and off since junior high in Belmont, Massachusetts, he was satisfied."

Before long Wood was effectively using the knuckler, and in 1968 he set an American League record (since broken) for most games pitched, 88. "That was just being in the right spot at the right time," recalled Wood. "Hoyt's arm was bothering him at the beginning of the year. And Bob Locker's arm was bothering him at the beginning of the year. And so I got a chance and I got off to a pretty good start." That season he was named AL Fireman of the Year.

In 1971 manager Chuck Tanner and pitching coach Johnny Sain took over the team, and with the emergence of young reliever Terry Forster, Wood was relegated to the nether regions of the Sox's bullpen. However, when starting pitcher Joe Horlen injured his knee, Tanner asked Wood if he would mind replacing him, and soon Wood was established as a starter—with his knuckleball making it possible. Fourteen of Wood's 22 victories that season came on only two days' rest.

The following year Wood accelerated his workhorse act. His 49 starts were only two short of Jack Chesbro's modern record, and his 376 ⅔ innings pitched were the most since Grover Cleveland Alexander's 387 in 1917. During the 1972 season Wood issued fewer than two walks per nine innings and worked 10 games without giving up one base on balls. At one point Wood went through a string of nine contests without surrendering more than one walk per game.

"Obviously, the knuckleball makes Wilbur effective," pointed out the Orioles' Paul Blair, "but what makes him even more effective is the fact that he throws it over for strikes. It never goes the same way, but it is always in the strike zone." *The Sporting News* named Wood its 1972 AL Pitcher of the Year.

The same year, Tanner toyed with the idea of using Wood to start both games of a twin bill. "Later, we actually announced Wilbur would pitch both games of a doubleheader in Boston if he won the first, but he didn't," recalled Tanner. "We'll never announce it again or even talk with Wilbur about it in advance. But someday after winning one, we'll just let him go out and work the second if he wants to. I'm sure he could do it."

As good a pitcher as Wood was, he was a terrible hitter. His lifetime average was .084, with a .090 slugging average. Starting in the majors in 1961, he didn't collect his first hit until 1967. In 1972 he had his best year for average, batting .136, but he struck out 65 times, the record for a pitcher in a season. The next year the AL introduced the designated hitter.

Wood's accomplishment of a 20-victory and 20-loss season in 1973 put him in select company (his actual record was 24–20). The feat had only been accomplished eight times previously in the century and not since Senators ace Walter Johnson went 25–20 in 1916. In 1979 fellow knuckleballer Joe Niekro was added to the list.

In 1973 Tanner made good on his promise to use Wood in two games of a doubleheader. First, on May 28 Wood pitched six innings to gain a victory, completing a suspended game against Cleveland. Fifteen minutes later he came out to start the regularly scheduled game, which he won, 4–0. Finally, on July 20 at Yankee Stadium, Wood started both games of a doubleheader. He lost, 12–2 and 7–0.

By 1975 Wood, growing increasingly pudgier, seemed to be losing his effectiveness. He might have reversed the trend, but in May 1976 a smash off the bat of Detroit's Ron LeFlore hit him in the kneecap, leaving Wood in agony and out for the rest of the season. Ironically, that September, LeFlore himself was hospitalized with a ruptured tendon in his right knee.

Wood pitched for two more seasons but never really came all the way back, particularly in terms of control. "I think I was trying to be a little cautious with the knee," he explained. "Psychologically, it worked against me a little bit, because I think I was trying to put the ball in a given area—which you really can't do. I was trying to protect myself a little bit… I think that's probably what helped increase my walks."

In August 1978 Wood was dropped from the rotation, and he accused owner Bill Veeck of ordering the move. Wood vetoed trades to Milwaukee and Pittsburgh when each club refused to extend him a contract through 1979. After leaving baseball, he operated a fish store outside Boston. "I can't kick at all," he said. "Baseball was good to me."

Hal Woodeshick

Woodeshick, Harold Joseph **P**

1956–67 B:8/24/1932, Wilkes-Barre, PA Deb:9/14/1956, DET AL BR/TL 6'3", 200

W	L	PCT	G	SV	IP	BB	SO	ERA
44	62	.415	427	61	847^{1}	389	484	3.56

A competent pitcher who enjoyed only modest success as a starter, Hal Woodeshick became a quality reliever in the last five years of his career. Starting out with the Detroit Tigers, he pitched for three American League teams from 1956 to 1961, when his contract was sold to the Houston Colt .45s. It was with Houston that Woodeshick became a solid reliever. Used as a starter in 1962, he was switched to the bullpen in 1963 and responded by posting a 1.97 ERA with 10 saves in 55 relief appearances.

In 1964 Woodeshick led the National League in saves with 23, and then was traded to St. Louis midway through the following season. Although he was stuck behind Joe Hoerner and Nelson Briles in the Cardinals' bullpen he still managed to save 15 games and make 51 appearances.

Woodeshick pitched for the Cardinals for two more years and appeared in the 1967 World Series, pitching one scoreless inning in Game 6. His appearance helped the Cardinals set a record for most pitchers used in a World Series game, with eight. It was also his last appearance on the mound.

Gene Woodling

Woodling, Eugene Richard **OF**

1943–62 B:8/16/1922, Akron, Ohio Deb:9/23/1943, CLE AL BL/TR 5'9½", 195

G	AB	R	H	HR	RBI	OBP	SLG	AVG
1796	5587	830	1585	147	830	.388	.431	.284

New York Yankees Gene Woodling and Hank Bauer shared left field under manager Casey Stengel's platoon system in the 1950s. The strategy resulted in complaints from both men, but nearly every autumn they each received a World Series ring.

A four-time minor league batting champion, Woodling led the American League with a .429 on base percentage in 1953. Nevertheless, after the 1954 season the Yankees traded him to Baltimore in a record 17-player deal. He went on to play for Cleveland, Baltimore again, and Washington before he was sold in 1962 to Stengel's dismal expansion Mets.

"He gave me hell all those years about wanting to play," Stengel said. "Now he can play all he wants." Woodling retired at season's end after 17 years in the majors.

As if playing with the Yankees of the 1950s weren't luck enough for any man, Woodling also struck oil on his Ohio farm. Even though he became instantly rich, he kept scouting part-time for the Indians and providing investment know-how for his former teammates.

"My advice for ballplayers is simple," Woodling said. "Buy land. Why? Because ballplayers aren't qualified to go into the business world. If they go into land, no one will steal it from them."

Todd Worrell

Worrell, Todd Roland **P**
1985–89, 1992–97 B:9/28/1959, Arcadia, CA
Deb:8/28/1985, STL NL BR/TR, 6'5", 222

W	L	PCT	G	SV	IP	BB	SO	ERA
50	52	.490	617	256	693^{2}	247	628	3.09

Todd Worrell's 36 saves in 1986 established a record for the most saves by a rookie. He also won the National League Rookie of the Year Award, even though he had tied a World Series record the previous fall.

Worrell worked 21 innings in 17 games for the St. Louis Cardinals in 1985, posting three wins and five saves. He earned the win in Game 6 of the NL Championship Series against the Los Angeles Dodgers, then worked in the World Series against the Kansas City Royals and tied a Series mark with six straight strikeouts in Game 5. Despite the late season workload, Worrell was technically still a rookie the following year.

He continued to post impressive numbers. Worrell saved at least two games against every National League team in 1986. He saved 33 games the following year and appeared in his second World Series. He was an All-Star in 1988, becoming the first pitcher to top 30 saves in each of his first three seasons. In his first four full seasons, he pitched in 264 games.

And then suddenly, Worrell couldn't throw the ball at all. He didn't pitch in the major leagues from Labor Day 1989 to spring training 1992.

Two elbow operations and arthroscopic shoulder surgery forced him to start all over. Worrell, who had been a closer since his first day in the major leagues, returned in 1992 as a set-up man for new Cardinals closer Lee Smith. Worrell saved only three games, but he broke Bruce Sutter's club record with his 128th career save in September. Three months later, he signed with the Dodgers as a free agent.

Worrell worked his way back into the closer's role in Los Angeles. He was named to the All-Star team and helped the Dodgers reach the playoffs in both 1995 and 1996. He saved 35 games in 1997, giving him 256 for his career in just over eight years as an everyday closer. Despite interest from several teams, Worrell announced his retirement in December 1997.

Al Worthington

Worthington, Allan Fulton **P**
1953–54, 1956–60, 1963–69 B:2/5/1929, Birmingham, AL
Deb:7/6/1953, NY NL BR/TR 6'2", 205

W	L	PCT	G	SV	IP	BB	SO	ERA
75	82	.478	602	110	1246^{2}	527	834	3.39

Giants righthander Al "Red" Worthington began his major league career by tossing 6–0 shutouts in his first two starts. In his debut on July 6, 1953 he two-hit the Phillies. Five days later, he four-hit Brooklyn. Nonetheless, he never lived up to his early promise, and several times he was demoted to the minors.

Worthington, who relied on a slider, pitched at Nashville and Minneapolis prior to reaching the Giants in 1953. At Nashville he paced the Southern Association with 152 strikeouts and 140 walks. Back with Minneapolis in 1955, his 19 wins led the American Association.

Back in the big leagues in 1958, Worthington enjoyed his finest season, going 11–7 for San Francisco. The Giants, however, traded him to the Red Sox in March 1960, and he was released to Minneapolis that May. That September the White Sox acquired him and placed him on their Indianapolis roster. Continuing his stellar pitching in the minors, he tossed a no-hitter against Hawaii on August 26, 1961, and led the American Association with a .789 won-lost percentage in 1962.

Acquired by the Twins in 1964, Worthington began his longest unbroken stretch in the majors, sticking with the club until his retirement in 1969. Pitching for the Twins, he recorded a career-high 21 saves in 1965, going 10–7 and contributing to Minnesota's first pennant. In the World Series against the Dodgers, he was unscored upon in four innings of work. Worthington paced the American League with 18 saves in 1968.

Worthington, who had attended Howard College and received his bachelor's degree from Samford College, later did a stint as Twins pitching coach. He also coached at Lynchburg Baptist College at Lynchburg, Virginia.

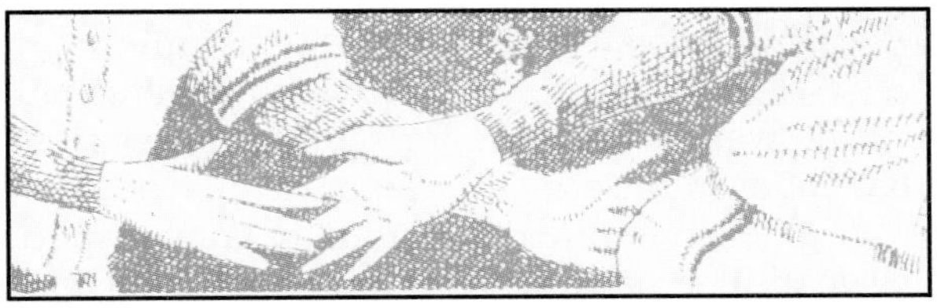

Clyde Wright

Wright, Clyde **P**

1966–75 B:2/20/1941, Jefferson City, TN
Deb:6/15/1966, CAL AL BR/TL 6'1", 185

W	L	PCT	G	SH	IP	BB	SO	ERA
100	111	.474	329	9	1728^{2}	550	667	3.50

Clyde Wright won a combined 20 games in his first four years in the major leagues. He then left the majors, came back with a new pitch, and won 22 games in 1970.

A spot starter in his first tour with the Angels, Wright was waived after a disastrous 1969 season, in which he posted a record of 1–8. He went off to winter ball, hoping to find himself. What he found was a pitch he could master—a screwball. The Angels welcomed him back to Anaheim and put him atop the rotation. In 1970 Wright earned the AL Comeback Player of the Year Award: he went 22–12 with a 2.83 ERA, pitched in the All-Star Game, and even threw a no-hitter against the A's on July 3. Trainer Freddie Frederico gave him a nickname, "Skeeter," because "You can't call a major leaguer Clyde."

Wright's screwball continued to bedevil batters in 1971 and 1972, winning 34 total games. The next two years, however, he lost a combined 39 games. Following a forgettable 9–20 season with the Milwaukee Brewers in 1974, Wright finished his career with Texas.

Clyde groomed his son, Jaret, to be a major league pitcher. Although the father never reached the postseason—and only played on two teams that finished over .500—his son emerged as a postseason hero for Cleveland in 1997. Jaret Wright beat the Yankees twice in the 1997 Division Series, and later won a World Series game. He left Game 7 of the Series with a lead, but Florida rallied against the Indians' bullpen to win the world championship.

George Wright

Wright, George **SS**

1871–82 M(1879, 59–25) B:1/28/1847, Yonkers, NY
D:8/21/1937, Boston, MA Deb:5/5/1871, BOS NA
BR/TR 5'9½", 150

G	AB	R	H	HR	RBI	OBP	SLG	AVG
329	1494	264	383	2	132	.277	.323	.256

During the late 1860s and early 1870s George Wright was undoubtedly the best baseball player in the country. He played on the earliest championship teams and even managed one himself, and he was responsible for several innovations that changed the way the game was played.

Wright also founded a nationally known sporting goods company and was important in advancing several other sports in America. The year he died, he was elected to the Hall of Fame. Nevertheless, in actual contributions to the game of baseball, Wright ranks well behind his older brother, Harry.

George Wright learned cricket from his father. The game was played regularly at Elysian Fields in Hoboken, New Jersey, where baseball was played as well, so Wright grew up playing both sports. While still in his early teens, Wright he the New York Gothams' junior baseball club. By age 15 he was a member of the senior club and soon became the regular shortstop.

At about the same time Wright also became an assistant pro with the St. George Cricket Club. He then moved to Philadelphia and in 1865, the year the Civil War ended, was both a pro for the Philadelphia Cricket Club and shortstop for the Philadelphia Olympians.

At the time, baseball was supposed to be an amateur sport, although many players were paid under the table. Wright's amateur status was not affected by his job with the cricket club because it was considered a teaching position. In 1866, however, Wright returned to New York to play baseball with the Gothams. He then jumped in midseason to the Unions of Morrisania, an almost certain sign that some inducement was involved. In addition to secret payments, many players were offered jobs that required little effort for good pay.

The following year Wright was the captain of the Washington Nationals. He was listed on the roster as a government clerk, but the address of his office was a public park. He was back with the Unions in 1868.

By this time Wright was regarded as one of the best players in the country. Many thought him superior to Dickey Pearce, who had virtually invented the position of shortstop. Wright, however, demonstrated far greater physical skills than Pearce. He was much faster and his stronger arm allowed him to play deeper, thereby increasing his range. And although Pearce's fans admired his ability to position himself correctly for different batters, Wright also possessed that skill. At bat, there was simply no comparison. Pearce was a clever "hit 'em where they ain't" type of hitter, but Wright, despite standing only 5-foot-9 and weighing only 150 pounds, was a feared slugger.

His talents at the plate, however, were secondary to his fielding. Wright had remarkably soft hands and perfected a style of catching the ball with his elbows bent to cushion the shock. He supposedly pulled off the first hidden ball trick, starting a tradition of early players who tucked a baseball away in their uniforms or in tall grass for use as needed, and often trapped short flies to create double plays.

In 1904, more than 20 years after Wright had retired, a story in *The Sporting News* recalled, "Whenever he would pull off one of those grand, unexpected plays that were so dazzlingly surprising as to dumbfound his opponents, his prominent teeth would gleam and glisten in an array of white molars that would put our own Teddy Roosevelt and his famed dentistry far in the shadow." And in 1911, when Honus Wagner was at the height of his career playing the same position as Wright, the *New York Journal*'s Sam Crane called Wright "the best shortstop ever."

In 1869 Harry Wright, who had moved to Cincinnati, was given the task of putting together the first openly professional team. His first call was for his younger brother. George Wright was paid $1,400 for the season, $200 more than Harry paid himself for managing and playing center field. Many years later, the shortstop insisted he was paid $2,000, but his statement conflicts with all the published records.

Whatever he was paid, Wright was worth it. The Cincinnati Red Stockings toured from coast to coast, defeating all comers. Precisely how many games they played is in dispute because some games against lesser town teams were apparently not counted in the official record. One source credits Wright with a .629 batting average with 49 home runs in 57 games, while another claims he hit .518 with 59 homers in 52 games.

To be fair, much of the opposition was second rate. The Red Stockings often won by such scores as 53–9 and 48–12, and many games were played on fields with no outfield fences. Whenever he hit the ball over an outfielder or between fielders, the speedy Wright could circle the bases.

The Red Stockings were not the first completely professional team, of course; they were merely the first to admit it. Their undefeated record, though, helped make professionalism respectable. When they lost a few games on their 1870 tour, interest in the team waned, but many cities responded with the desire to field their own professional teams.

The year 1871 saw the formation of the first professional league, the National Association. Harry Wright moved on to Boston and organized a new Red Stockings team, and George tagged along as the star shortstop. Although Boston narrowly missed the first National Association pennant, the club followed with four straight flags, each won more easily than the last.

National Association teams played on enclosed fields and faced much better pitching than the 1869 Cincinnati team had. In five seasons, 262 games, Wright hit only eight home runs, but he batted .353 and collected 65 doubles and 39 triples. Boston's continued success destroyed interest in the league's pennant races, but the National Association faced a number of other problems. In 1876 a much stronger circuit, the National League, was formed. Harry Wright's Red Stockings were charter members, but they lost the initial pennant to the Chicago White Stockings, a team that had coaxed away four of Boston's stars.

Again the competition was improved, and George Wright's days as a great slugger were over. In seven National League seasons, he batted only .256. He remained a superior fielder, however, and helped Boston win pennants in 1877 and 1878. The next year, after a dispute with the Boston owners, he jumped to the Providence Grays as player-manager. In his only season at the helm, Wright was a rousing success. The Grays finished five games ahead of brother Harry's Red Stockings and won the league pennant, George's seventh in eight years.

In 1871 Wright opened a sporting goods business in Boston, taking on Henry A. Ditson as a partner in 1879. Although he returned to the Red Stockings in 1880 and was active through 1882, Wright played very little, as Wright & Ditson was becoming a major sporting goods concern. Through his business, Wright played a large part in popularizing tennis and Canadian ice hockey in the United States. He also introduced golf to Boston and laid out the city's first course.

Wright's interest in baseball remained strong, and he served on the commission that wrongly identified Abner Doubleday as the game's inventor. Eventually the National League issued him pass No. 1, and he was a frequent guest at major league games. In 1937, he was inducted into the Hall of Fame as one of the game's pioneers.

Glenn Wright

Wright, Forest Glenn **SS**

1924–35 B:2/6/1901, Archie, MO D:4/6/1984, Olathe, KS Deb:4/15/1924, PIT NL BR/TR 5'11", 170

G	AB	R	H	HR	RBI	OBP	SLG	AVG
1119	4153	584	1219	94	723	.328	.447	.294

Although given the nickname "Buckshot" for his scattergun-throwing arm, Glenn Wright set a record in his rookie season for assists by a shortstop (601) that wasn't touched until Ozzie Smith broke it 56 years later. He was only the fifth ballplayer to turn an unassisted triple play when he performed the feat on May 7, 1925, in a game against the Cardinals in Pittsburgh.

The addition of Forest Glenn Wright to the Pirates in 1924 helped the team to win a world championship in 1925 and a pennant in 1927. In addition to his defensive spark, he was a surprisingly powerful hitter for a shortstop, with an 18-homer season as a Pirate and a 22-homer year with the Brooklyn Dodgers. He drove in more than 100 runs three times as a Buc and once as a Dodger.

The Pirates traded Wright to the Dodgers before the 1929 season for southpaw pitcher Jesse Petty and second baseman Harry Riconda, but Wright crushed his right shoulder while playing handball in the off-season, and his famous arm was never the same again. He retired after hardly playing a season with the Chicago White Sox in 1935.

Wright is a member of the American Association Hall of Fame for his superb play with the Kansas City Blues in 1922 and 1923, which included his performance in a best-of-nine victory in the 1923 Junior World Series over Jack Dunn's legendary Orioles.

Harry Wright

Wright, William Henry **OF**

1871–77 M(1871–93, 1,225–885) B:1/10/1835, Sheffield, England D:10/3/1895, Atlantic City, NJ Deb:5/5/1871, BOS NL BR/TR 5'9½", 157

G	AB	R	H	HR	RBI	OBP	SLG	AVG
2	7	0	0	0	0	.000	.000	.000

Upon his death in 1895, William Henry "Harry" Wright was saluted by legendary baseball writer and promoter Henry Chadwick, who proclaimed, "There is no doubt that Harry Wright was the father of professional base ball playing." A pioneer who was instrumental in the game's evolution from loose affiliations of genteel sporting clubs to organized leagues of professional teams, Wright helped keep the game clean and later became a legendary manager. His brother, George, was the superior ballplayer, but Harry was the brains of the duo.

Wright instituted dozens of innovations, including the backup system, whereby fielders back up each other and pitchers back up bases; he also introduced pregame batting practice, and the drill of hitting fungo flyballs to outfielders before a game. He invented hand signals and was the first to reposition his defensive players to suit the style of the batsman. He introduced the double steal and the original hidden ball trick, in which players concealed an extra ball to be produced if the game ball escaped them at an inconvenient moment. In 1870 Wright's catcher became the first player to wear a glove; five years later he helped originate the facemask for catchers.

Wright even influenced how the players looked. He abandoned the old practice of tying the pants at the cuffs so they wouldn't interfere with running, which gave the players a pantaloon look. Instead, he put his men in flannel knickers, and the brightly colored socks his Cincinnati team wore led to the nickname of Red Stockings. Of course, not all his innovations took hold. For example, he frequently had his team take the field by marching nine abreast to first before running, with each peeling out of formation, to take their positions.

Not surprisingly, Wright was an early student of statistics. He devised his own detailed box scores and pored over them in search of ways to improve his team's chances. In fact, so much time spent studying the notes may have caused him to temporarily lose his sight for a year in 1890.

But perhaps Wright's most significant contribution to the early game was his total dedication to fairness and good sportsmanship. According to historian David Voigt, Wright "believed the British standards of sportsmanship should dominate organized baseball." One of Wright's teams went down to defeat in one of baseball's most dramatic losses because of his belief in absolute fairness.

In 1870, after Cincinnati had won about 60 consecutive games, the ballclub faced the Brooklyn Excelsiors, the most powerful team in the East. After nine innings the score was tied, 7–7, and both clubs were ready to call it a day, in the custom of the time. But Wright insisted the game be played to a finish. His team lost in the 11th inning, ending the most storied winning streak in baseball history and establishing the East Coast teams as forces to be reckoned with.

The *Cincinnati Enquirer* said of Wright, "He is a base ball Edison. He eats base ball, breathes base ball, thinks base ball, and incorporates base ball in his prayers." Wright understood the business side of the game, too. In the earliest days of baseball the captain did what the field manager does today. The manager acted as general manager, accountant, and traveling secretary. Devising a schedule was a demanding task at that time because formal leagues did not exist. As early as 1869 Wright wrote to a friend about his scheduling frustrations: "Base ball is business now, Nick, and I am trying to arrange our games to make them successful and make them pay, irrespective of my feelings, and to the best of my ability."

The story of baseball's Wright brothers began in England, where Harry was born in Sheffield. George came along 12 years later in Yonkers, New York. The St. George Cricket Club in New York City hired their immigrant father, a star cricket player, in the early 1850s. In America, both boys took after their father, becoming quality cricketers. By age 19 Harry was a professional bowler, the cricket equivalent of the pitcher, for St. George's famous Dragonslayers.

But both Wrights also saw the fun of the new "base ball" game being played around the city. They didn't expect to make a living at it; Harry learned the jeweler's trade. But before long both were collecting a salary by playing ball for Alexander Cartwright's Knickerbockers. Harry accepted an offer to be a player and instructor for the Cincinnati Cricket Club in 1865 while his brother, still a teenager, stayed in New York. But even in the wilds of Cincinnati, Harry still played baseball. In 1867 he hit seven home runs in a game against a team from Holt, Kentucky.

In 1869 the town fathers of Cincinnati decided that having a baseball team would be good for their growing city. So they hired Harry Wright as manager and told him to acquire quality players. Although the 1869 Red Stockings may not have been the first team to field paid players, the ballplayers were the first "to make no bones about their professionalism," according to historian Mark Alvarez.

Harry signed his young brother George and several other excellent players. The team playing for Cincinnati in 1869 had only one player from the city on its roster. In 1870 the Red Stockings began a triumphant national tour during which they won every one of their 60 games.

By the time the National Association was formed in 1871, Wright had become an important figure. He took most of the talented Red Stockings with him to Boston, and although his team finished third in the National Association's first year, it won the pennant the next four seasons. Playing in the outfield and occasionally pitching, Wright batted .274 and had a 4–4 mound record in the NA.

But the Association was a rough-and-tumble organization, loose in structure and lacking central power. The threat of gamblers fixing games was omnipresent. The league's first champions, the Philadelphia Athletics, had their pennant displayed in their favorite saloon. That kind of behavior didn't sit well with Wright.

When businessman William Hulbert decided a new league was necessary, he consulted Wright on structure, rules, and franchise locations. Wright was the secretary at the first meeting of the National League when it was organized in late 1875.

Hulbert signed "the Big Four" of Wright's team—pitcher Ross Barnes and versatile position players Al Spalding, Cal McVey, and Deacon White—to his Chicago ballclub. The White Stockings went on to win the first National League crown. Wright's Boston Red Stockings finished fourth, and the manager even made a token field appearance. Wright was 0-for-3 in 1876, and finished his National League career 0-for-7 with two strikeouts.

Wright bounced back in 1877 and 1878, taking the league flag both times behind stars such as his brother George, "Orator" Jim O'Rourke, and ace hurler Tommy Bond, who won 40 games to lead the league both years. George moved to Providence for the 1879 season and his team took the crown while Harry's dropped to second.

Notorious Boston owner Arthur Soden fired Wright after a sixth-place finish and some player grumbling in 1880. He moved to Providence as manager for two years, and then finished his managerial career in 1893 after a decade at the helm for Philadelphia. Wright was appointed director of league umpires after he left managing, but the post was largely honorary.

Wright's all-time record as a manager was 1,225 wins, 825 losses. But numbers don't do the man justice. With his immaculate chin whiskers and ever-professional demeanor, Wright was a unique figure in the game of that era. Baseball at the time was still a rough game; umpires often took their lives into their hands when they made calls that were unpalatable to the home crowd. But according to historian Harold Seymour, "about the only manager who didn't go after umpires was old Harry Wright."

When a young hopeful wrote to Harry Wright asking what was necessary to become a professional ballplayer, the old cricketer replied that a good ballplayer must be "a sure catch, a good thrower, strong and accurate; a reliable batter and good runner; all to be brought out, if in you, by steady and persevering practise [sic]." Wright also cautioned against tobacco and intoxicating drink and recommended that the youth "eat hearty—roast beef rare will do." In 1953, nearly 58 years after his death, Wright was inducted into the Hall of Fame.

Taffy Wright

Wright, Taft Shedron **OF**

1938–49 B:8/10/1911, Tabor City, NC D:10/22/1981, Orlando, FL Deb:4/18/1938, WAS AL BL/TR 5'10", 180

G	AB	R	H	HR	RBI	OBP	SLG	AVG
1029	3583	465	1115	38	553	.376	.423	.311

Outfielder Taffy Wright wasn't much of a fielder, but he knew what to do with his bat. In 1938, his first major league season, he hit a league-leading .350 for the Senators. Thirteen years later, however, Major League Baseball took back his batting title. Wright had appeared in exactly 100 games that season, often as a pinch hitter, and he received only 263 official at bats. In those days a player had to appear in 100 games to be eligible for the batting crown, but in 1951, when the rules were revised, Wright's title was revoked in favor of Jimmie Foxx's .349 average in 149 games and 565 at bats.

The lefthanded-hitting Wright hit better than .300 five more times during his nine-year career, but he never won another batting crown. Nor did he ever appear in a World Series, which is probably why his name often draws blank stares from baseball fans.

Wright batted .309 during his sophomore season, but on December 8, 1939, he was traded with pitcher Pete Appleton to the White Sox for outfielder Gee Walker. Wright continued to hit well in his new surroundings. In 1940 he batted .337 with 88 RBIs. On July 3, 1940, he provided his own fireworks a day early by blasting a pinch-hit grand slam off Detroit's Lynn Nelson.

The following season Wright hit .322, belted a career-best 10 homers, and entered the baseball annals by driving in at least one run for 13 consecutive games, an American League record. He had a total of 22 RBIs during that stretch from May 4 to May 20, and finished the season with a career-high 97 RBIs.

In 1942 he had collected 100 hits in 300 at bats when he received his notice to join the service. During World War II Wright played as much baseball as possible, appearing for the Air Force team at Hickham Field in Honolulu. He returned to the White Sox after the war and hit .324 in 1947. The following season, when he hit the last of his three career grand slams, his average dipped to .279. On November 15, 1948, Wright was sold to the Philadelphia Athletics. His career ended after 59 games for the A's in 1949.

Phil Wrigley

Wrigley, Phillip K.

Owner (1932–77) B:12/5/1894 D:4/12/1977, Elkhorn, WI

From today's cynical perspective, baseball's early days might seem naive or romantic—teams were owned by families; sons rose through the ranks before succeeding their fathers; and fairness and decency were supposedly the rule. While speaking about the old guard of owners, former Commissioner Bowie Kuhn once said, "I think of those men as persons who loved and cared about the game and who would support what was best for the game overall, even if that was adverse to their club's interests...They would grumble and fight with city hall, they were highly opinionated, but the thought of bucking central administration on a matter critical to the game was anathema to them."

No family ever loved the game more than the Wrigleys of Chicago. From 1916 to 1981 they were responsible for the Cubs and their fans, and they treated both with dignity and humanity. William Wrigley, who had made a fortune selling chewing gum, became a minority stockholder in the Cubs in 1916. Within five years, he was the sole owner. His son, Philip, took over in 1932 and retained control of the team until his death in 1977. Four years later, his family sold the team.

Phil Wrigley, unlike his colorful and gregarious father, was shy, even backward. He studiously avoided the limelight and even refused to go to Cubs games for many years rather than be bothered by fans and photographers. However, no matter where he was, he listened to the game on radio or watched it on television, and no matter what he was doing, he stood up during the seventh-inning stretch. Many people misinterpreted Wrigley's aversion to publicity as indifference to his team, but nothing could be further from the truth.

Wrigley was active in philanthropic and charitable organizations, and he was generous to a fault. After he fired Charlie Grimm as manager, he kept him on the payroll for the rest of his life. When Wrigley heard that former Cubs star Hack Wilson had died destitute, he took over all funeral arrangements. The Commissioner's office called and offered to pay half. Wrigley said, "I never went to a half funeral." The Cubs picked up the entire tab, including a monument to the departed slugger.

When "the Mad Russian," Lou Novikoff, a former Cubs outfielder, fell on hard times, Wrigley supported him. When new Commissioner Kuhn investigated manager Leo Durocher for alleged gambling activity, Wrigley did more than just stand by his manager; he offered to pay Durocher's legal expenses. Honesty was second nature to Wrigley; he scrupulously docked his salary from the gum company for the time he spent working on Cubs business.

He cared about his players, and he cared about the fans, some of the most loyal in the history of the game. For years he would not permit more than 14,000 tickets to be sold before any game; the remaining 22,000 had to be available for fans to walk up that afternoon and buy them. He tore down the revenue-producing ads on the park's outfield walls and replaced them with more aesthetically pleasing ivy. Despite his dour countenance, Wrigley was accessible and friendly. Anyone could drop by his office.

The Cubs owner was most famous for refusing to install lights in Wrigley Field. As late as 1953 he said, "The future of major league baseball is in the daytime."

Wrigley did more than just take over his father's chewing gum and baseball businesses and count the cash. He was a dedicated innovator in both business and baseball, and demonstrated the same concerns for his employees in both endeavors. When he was barely out of his teens, he toured the world and established the gum company's first overseas manufacturing operation, in Australia. During the Great Depression he guaranteed his employees that they would not lose their jobs, and he gave them all a raise.

Although he stood firm for the tradition of day baseball, Wrigley was ahead of his time in many other aspects of the game. He devised a baseball school long before Kansas City did. He instituted a scientific research study to analyze players' reflexes and other motor skills that was viewed as so outlandish that the press hooted him out of doing it. He initiated loudspeakers in the park, so the fans could hear player lineup changes and other information. The scoreboard at Wrigley Field was the first to flash balls and strikes, and to indicate whether a close play had been ruled a hit or an error. He was the first to seed the path between the pitcher's mound and home plate with grass.

One of Wrigley's more unusual ideas received a great deal of belated attention as a vehicle for a Hollywood movie—the All-American Girls' Professional Baseball League (AAGBL). Started with four teams in 1943, the league lasted six years with some degree of financial success. It was celebrated in the 1992 Columbia Pictures film *A League of Their Own,* in which Garry Marshall played a character based on Wrigley.

Not all of Wrigley's ideas were so successful, though. In 1932 he hired a swami to sit behind home plate and hex the opposition. Although this would be viewed as a publicity stunt today, Wrigley was actually careful to keep it quiet. Nonetheless, it didn't work. He hired Lou Boudreau out of the broadcasting booth to manage the club, and when that wasn't successful, he instituted a "college of coaches" concept, in which the team had a rotating system of head coaches rather than a single manager. When that proved to be a disaster, Wrigley had the good sense to hire Leo Durocher to take charge, and the Cubs had their best season in 25 years.

Wrigley was not afraid to speak up against the wishes of the other owners. He didn't approve of Major League Baseball's monopoly over the minor leagues and told Congress so. When the first stirrings of a players' union were heard in 1946, Wrigley was one of the owners on a special committee to develop a pension plan and other player benefits. However, Wrigley's father had been a bigger spender on player salaries than his son proved to be. When William Wrigley purchased Rogers Hornsby, a Chicago sportswriter wondered if the price of gum would go up.

When the younger Wrigley took over the team, the Cubs were the toast of the National League, winning pennants in 1932, 1935, 1938, and 1945. But despite their pennants, the Cubs always found a way to lose the big one. As historian Art Ahrens points out, "Even in their halcyon days, the Cubs displayed an embarrassing penchant for falling apart in the World Series." They never once won a Series under the Wrigley aegis.

Wrigley also owned the Los Angeles Angels of the Pacific Coast League, who played in the West Coast's version of Wrigley Field. When Walter O'Malley wanted to move his Brooklyn Dodgers to Los Angeles, Wrigley took in payment the entire Dodgers Fort Worth Class AAA team.

Wrigley was happiest when tinkering in his garage with some mechanical device. When his son, William, once bought a new sports car, Phil Wrigley snatched the auto from him and immediately took the engine apart and rebuilt it for maximum precision and power.

Four years after Wrigley's death, his family sold the Cubs for $20.5 million. Ironically, the longest-standing owners of one of the game's most beloved franchises thereby helped usher in what some call a new age of greed. The purchaser, the Chicago Tribune Corporation, also owned superstation WGN. Many critics believe that, to the new owners, baseball is merely another moneymaking product, an annual sitcom or "dramedy."

By contrast, although he was cordial and helpful to the print media throughout his long life, Phil Wrigley would not give radio or TV interviews. He said, "It's the difference between information and show business."

Whit Wyatt

Wyatt, John Whitlow **P**

1929–45 B:9/27/1907, Kensington, GA D:7/16/1999, Carrollton, GA Deb:9/16/1929, DET AL BR/TR 6'1", 185

W	L	PCT	G	SH	IP	BB	SO	ERA
106	95	.527	360	17	1761	642	872	3.79

Most pitchers are either stars or has-beens by the age of 31, but Whitlow Wyatt managed to beat the odds as a late bloomer in the big leagues. In 1929 he won 22 games for Evansville in the 3-I League, but he struggled for the next eight years in the American League, never fulfilling the promise he'd shown in Evansville. By 1938 he was back in the minors with Milwaukee of the American Association. After Wyatt led the AA in wins, strikeouts, and ERA, Brooklyn decided to risk $40,000 and give the 31-year-old righthander one more chance.

This time Wyatt was an immediate success, and he improved yearly due to his excellent control, rising fastball, and tricky slider. The hard-nosed Wyatt, once called "the meanest guy I ever saw" by Joe DiMaggio, had no qualms about knocking down batters. According to Wyatt, Dodgers manager Leo Durocher would leave $200 or $300 in the hurler's locker whenever he flattened a hitter or two.

Named to the National League All-Star squad four times, Wyatt pitched shutout ball in both the 1940 and 1941 All-Star Games. His 22–10 record in 1941 tied him with teammate Kirby Higbe for the most wins in the majors. The Dodgers won their first pennant since 1920 that season and Wyatt split two decisions in the World Series, throwing a pair of complete games. He followed with season records of 19–7 and 14–5 before age finally caught up with him.

In 1954 Wyatt managed the Southern Association's Atlanta Crackers to a pennant and a seven-game win over Houston in the Dixie Series. He died at age 91 of complications from pneumonia.

Butch Wynegar

Wynegar, Harald Delano **C**

1976–88 B:3/14/1956, York, PA Deb:4/9/1976, MIN AL BB/TR 6', 194

G	AB	R	H	HR	RBI	OBP	SLG	AVG
1301	4330	498	1102	65	506	.351	.347	.255

For a five-year period, Harold Delano "Butch" Wynegar was one of the best catchers in the American League, until injuries began to erode his talents. Wynegar was only 20 years old when he joined the Minnesota Twins as their starting catcher in 1976. For five seasons he was a bulwark behind the plate, catching 135 or more games each year.

He earned a spot on the 1976 All-Star team, the youngest player at that time to ever appear in the contest. A solid hitter in the .255–.270 range, Wynegar also excelled behind the plate and led the league's catchers in double plays in 1980. He began to experience injuries in 1981, and the Twins traded him to the Yankees in May 1982. He played for the Yankees until 1986 when mental stress forced the club to put him on the restricted list. The Yankees traded Wynegar to California in 1986, but foot problems prevented him from playing much. After appearing in only 27 games in 1988, he retired.

Early Wynn

Wynn, Early **P**

1939, 1941–44, 1946–63 B:1/6/1920, Hartford, AL D:4/4/1999 Venice, FL Deb:9/13/1939, WAS AL BB/TR 6', 200

W	L	PCT	G	SH	IP	BB	SO	ERA
300	244	.551	691	49	4564	1775	2334	3.54

Mickey Mantle once said that pitcher Early Wynn was "so mean he'd knock you down in the dugout." The overpowering righthander had five 20-win seasons and 300 career victories, and has a plaque in the Hall of Fame.

Opposing hitters remember Wynn for the way he established himself with inside fastballs. Once when Ted Williams refused Wynn's invitation to go fishing in the Everglades, Wynn said, "Admit it. You're afraid to go into the Everglades with me." Williams replied, "No hitter ever would go into the Everglades with a pitcher like you. His body might never be found."

Wynn would have won even more games had he not pitched six full seasons and parts of two others for the weak-hitting Washington Senators. He suffered 45 shutout defeats—many of them with the Senators—accounting for nearly one-fifth of his career 244 losses. As it was, some of his best run-support came from his own bat. The switch-hitting Wynn compiled a .214 batting average with 17 homers and 173 RBIs. Called upon to pinch-hit 90 times in his career, he is one of only five pitchers to stroke a pinch-hit grand slam, turning the trick against Detroit's Johnny Gorsica on September 15, 1946.

In 1936, at age 16, Wynn tried out with the Senators in Florida and impressed Clyde Milan, who signed him. He played for Sanford and Charlotte before breaking in with Washington late in 1939. Wynn made three appearances with the Senators that season and five more in 1942, when he went 3–1 with a 1.58 ERA.

Washington finished in second place in the American League in 1943, and Wynn won 18 games with a 2.91 ERA. But the following season Washington was terrible, losing 90 games and finishing in the cellar. The Senators led the league in errors and were next-to-last in home runs, affording Wynn little offensive support. Despite a respectable ERA of 3.38, Wynn lost a league-leading 17 games, including 11 straight.

Wynn spent all of 1945 in the armed services and returned for part of the 1946 season. The next year he won 17 games, but he finished 8–19 in 1948 and was traded with Mickey Vernon to Cleveland in December for three players. Wynn said Cleveland pitching coach Mel Harder made him a consistent winner. "He showed me how to improve my grip and delivery of the curveball and also encouraged me to throw a knuckleball," Wynn recalled.

Nicknamed "Gus" (short for "Gloomy Gus"), Wynn had his first big year as an Indian in 1950, going 18–8 and leading the league with a 3.20 ERA. He was one of three Indians to win 20 games in 1951, joining Bob Feller (22) and Mike Garcia (20). The Tribe remained in the pennant race until the final two weeks, before finishing second, five games behind the Yankees.

Cleveland got off to a blazing start in 1952, while the Yankees were just 18–17 by the end of May. When Labor Day arrived, New York was 2½ games behind Cleveland, but was faced with 18 of its last 21 games on the road. The Indians, meanwhile, had 20 of their last 22 at home. The two clubs met in mid-September before more than 73,000 fans and the Yankees beat Garcia, 7–1. Cleveland finished the season two games back, despite Wynn's 23 victories. The Indians finished second again in 1953 and Wynn, who went 17–12 with a 3.93 ERA, was offered a 25-percent pay cut.

In 1954 Wynn and teammate Bob Lemon topped the league with 23 victories apiece, and the Indians ran away with the pennant, winning 111 games. After Lemon lost the World Series opener against the Giants in a game remembered for the great catch made by Willie Mays off a drive by Vic Wertz, Wynn started Game 2. He had a 1–0 lead entering the bottom of the fifth, but New York scored twice in the inning and added an insurance run in the seventh. Wynn allowed only four hits in seven innings, but was the tough-luck loser. The Giants went on to sweep the Indians in four games.

In 1955 rookie Herb Score made his major league debut for the Tribe, going 16–10 with a league-leading 245 strikeouts. Wynn won 17 games and Lemon added 18 victories, but the Indians finished three games back of the Yankees. Wynn, Score, and Lemon each won 20 games in 1956, but New York cruised to its seventh pennant in eight years. During one game, a line drive off the bat of Jose Valdivielso hit Wynn in the jaw. He refused to come out of the game immediately. When he finally did leave, he required 16 stitches and lost seven lower teeth.

The following season was a nightmare for both Wynn and the Indians. Despite leading the league in strikeouts, Wynn posted a 14–17 record, and his 4.31 ERA was his highest since 1948. On May 7 a line drive by New York's Gil McDougald struck Score in the eye. The injury all but ended his career. Cleveland finished in sixth place, and on December 4 Wynn was traded to the White Sox along with Al Smith for Minnie Minoso and Fred Hatfield.

Wynn led the American League in strikeouts again in 1958, and he picked up the win in the All-Star Game, ironically on a pinch-hit single by McDougald. In 1959, at age 39, Wynn had his greatest season. He led the league in starts and innings pitched (for the third time), won 22 games, started the first 1959 All-Star Game, was named Cy Young Award winner, and pitched the "Go-Go" Sox to the pennant. Wynn shut out the Dodgers in the Series opener, 11–0, but was ineffective in Game 4,as the White Sox committed three miscues in one inning. Facing a must-win situation in Game 6, Wynn was bombed in three innings, and Los Angeles breezed to a 9–3 win and a world championship.

When the 1962 season started, Wynn had 292 career wins. He went 7–15, leaving him one victory short of 300. Unsigned by the Sox the next season, he was picked up in June by the Indians. He lasted only five innings against Kansas City on July 13, but he posted his 300th win. "I never slept the night before," Wynn recalled. "The gout was killing me. ...It was so nice to win 300 though. I felt I had it coming to me after pitching so well for so long and losing so many tough ones."

Wynn, who pitched in four decades, was the major league's all-time leader in walks until Nolan Ryan surpassed him. He later became a pitching coach with the Indians and Twins and a manager in the Twins' farm system. After retiring from coaching, Wynn became a broadcaster for the Toronto Blue Jays and the Chicago White Sox. He was named to the Hall of Fame in 1972. He died in 1999 at a Florida nursing home at age 79, following a stroke.

Jimmy Wynn

Wynn, James Sherman **OF**

1963–77 B:3/12/1942, Hamilton, OH Deb:7/10/1963, HOU NL BR/TR 5'9", 170

G	AB	R	H	HR	RBI	OBP	SLG	AVG
1920	6653	1105	1665	291	964	.369	.436	.250

Jim Wynn packed a lot of power into a relatively small frame. At 5-feet 9-inches and 170 pounds he didn't have the physique usually associated with a power hitter, but he belted 291 homers during a 15-year major league career. His power at the plate earned Wynn the nickname "the Toy Cannon." In a career that lasted from 1963 to 1977, he hit 20 or more homers in a season eight times and surpassed 30 homers in a year three times.

Wynn spent most of his career with the Houston Astros, playing 11 seasons for the club after being drafted in 1962. His best season with Houston came in 1967 when he hit 37 home runs, drove in 107, and scored 102 while playing in 158 games. It earned him a spot on *The Sporting News* NL All-Star team. In 1969 Wynn led the league in walks with 148 (while striking out 142 times), and did it again in with Atlanta, drawing 127 passes in 1976.

A fine base runner and solid outfielder, Wynn twice led the National League in putouts and once in assists. He also stole 225 bases during his career, reaching a high of 43 in his first full season (1965).

Traded to the Los Angeles Dodgers in 1974, Wynn was a key factor in helping them win the pennant, slugging 32 homers and knocking in 108 runs. He played two seasons for the Dodgers before being dealt to the Braves. Sold to the Yankees in November of 1976, Wynn was used sparingly. He finished his career with the Milwaukee Brewers later that year.

Carl Yastrzemski

Yastrzemski, Carl Michael **OF-1B-DH**
1961–83 B:8/22/1939, Southampton, NY
Deb:4/11/1961, BOS AL BL/TR 5'11", 182

G	AB	R	H	HR	RBI	OBP	SLG	AVG
3308	11988	1816	3419	452	1844	.382	.462	.285

Carl Yastrzemski had a tough task in 1961: replacing Boston Red Sox legend Ted Williams in Fenway Park's left field. After a slow start, he succeeded admirably, winning a rare Triple Crown in the Red Sox's "Impossible Dream" season of 1967, collecting 400 home runs and 3,000 hits, and ultimately gaining induction into the Hall of Fame, in 1989.

Yastrzemski grew up on a Long Island potato farm. A shortstop when he signed with Boston in 1958, Yaz received a reported $100,000 bonus. The Red Sox soon moved him to second base. With Raleigh in the Carolina League he posted a league-leading .377 batting average in 1959 but also led the entire circuit in errors, with 45. The next season Boston promoted him to Minneapolis in the American Association and shifted him to the outfield. In Minneapolis he hit .339, led the league in hits with 193, and was slated to replace the retired Williams on Opening Day 1961.

In his first big league at bat, Yastrzemski singled off Kansas City's Ray Herbert, but he soon struggled. "I remember…I was a scared rookie, hitting .220 after the first three months of my baseball season, doubting my ability," said Yaz when being inducted into the Baseball Hall of Fame. "A man was fishing up in New Brunswick. I said, 'Can we get a hold of him? I need help. I don't think I can play in the big leagues.' He flew into Boston, worked with me for three days, helped me mentally and gave me confidence that I could play in the big leagues. I hit .300 for the rest of the season. I'd like to thank Ted Williams."

One piece of advice Williams gave Yaz was "Don't ever let anyone monkey with your swing." He raised the bat as if reaching for something on a high shelf, but as the pitch arrived he was able to pull the ball with the best in the game.

Yaz batted .266 as a rookie, and two years later he led the American League with a .321 average, 183 hits, 40 doubles, and 95 walks. He struggled the next season, but in 1965 rebounded to bat .312 and lead the league with 45 doubles and a .536 slugging average. On May 14 he hit for the cycle for the only time in his career.

Yastrzemski's biggest season was 1967. The Red Sox had finished in ninth place the previous year, and neither Yastrzemski nor the Sox were off to a good start that season. On May 14 Boston was tied for eighth place, with an 11–14 record. Yastrzemski was at .260 with just two home runs. In June White Sox manager Eddie Stanky publicly commented that Yastrzemski was an All-Star "from the neck down."

The next day against Chicago, Yastrzemski went 6-for-9 in a doubleheader. In his last at bat, Yastrzemski homered. As he motored around the bases he tipped his cap to Stanky. Yaz was on his way to one of the best all-around seasons in baseball history.

As the season drew to a close, Yaz faced pressure on two fronts—nailing down his Triple Crown, particularly by staving off Minnesota's Harmon Killebrew for the home run title, and by outlasting the Twins and the Tigers to help the Red Sox win their first pennant since 1946.

Minnesota entered the final weekend one game up on Boston and Detroit. The Twins were in Boston for the last two games of the season, while the Tigers had back-to-back doubleheaders left with the Angels. The Red Sox needed to win both games, with the Tigers doing no better than a split with the Angels. Yastrzemski was in reasonably good shape for the batting and RBI titles, but he was tied with Killebrew at 43 homers apiece. With four Twins games left to Yastrzemski's two for Boston, Killebrew had the edge.

On Saturday all went well for Boston. The Sox rallied for a 6–4 victory, and the Tigers split with the Angels. Killebrew homered, but so did Yaz, who collected three hits and four RBIs. On Sunday Boston was behind, 2–0, in the fifth when Yastrzemski came up to bat with the bases full. Yaz lined a two-run single to center to tie the game. The Red Sox got three more that inning and won the game. Yaz went 4-for-4. He didn't homer, but neither did Killebrew. Yastrzemski had won his Triple Crown with a .326 average, 121 RBIs, and 44 homers.

"The moment the game was over I sprinted for the dugout," Yastrzemski said. "The fans were pouring onto the field, if they'd caught me they'd have torn my uniform into shreds for souvenirs. As it was I got pawed all over."

The Tigers won the first game of the doubleheader Sunday, to close to within a half-game of the Red Sox, but as all of Boston tuned in on radio, the Angels won the second game, 8–5. The Impossible Dream was reality; the Sox were on their way to the World Series.

The Cardinals and Red Sox split the first six games of the Series. Yastrzemski homered twice in Game 2 in a 5–0 Boston victory, and fourth-inning home runs in Game 6 by Yaz, Reggie Smith, and Rico Petrocelli set a Series record and in the end propelled the Red Sox to an 8–4 victory. Boston ace Jim Lonborg took the mound for Boston in Game 7, but Bob Gibson opposed him. Gibson, who had already won twice in the Series, allowed only three hits, struck out 10, and hit a home run as the Cardinals prevailed, 7–2. Yastrzemski hit .400 in the Series, but Lou Brock outshone him, batting .414, with 12 hits, eight runs and a Series-record seven stolen bases.

Yastrzemski worked hard at his game and took endless batting practice. "Yaz did it all the time," said Red Sox outfielder Joe Lahoud. "We'd be on the road, and he'd call, 'C'mon, we're going out to the ballpark.' I'd say, 'Christ, it's only one o'clock. The game's at seven.' He lived, breathed, ate, slept baseball. If he went 0–for–4, he couldn't live with it. He could live with himself if he went 1-for-3. He was happy if he went 2–for–4. That's the way the man suffered."

Yaz led the league in batting for the last time in 1968 with the lowest average ever to lead a major league: .301. In 1969 he hit 40 homers and drove in 111 runs, and the following season he led the league in slugging, and runs while adding 40 home runs.

In 1975 Yastrzemski belted a three-run homer in the All-Star Game, but slumped to .269 with just 14 homers. Nonetheless, the Red Sox won the AL East thanks to stellar performances by rookies Fred Lynn and Jim Rice. Oakland was favored to win its fourth straight pennant, but Boston engineered a surprising sweep of the Championship Series, as Yaz hit .455. In Game 3 he cracked two hits and made two defensive gems to lead the Red Sox into the World Series. Yastrzemski hit a respectable .310 in the Series against Cincinnati, with four RBIs and seven runs scored. But once again the Sox were done in seven games. Cincinnati beat Boston in the finale, 4–3, as Yaz popped up for the final out.

On May 19, 1976, Yaz hit three home runs in one game and finished the season with 21 round-trippers and 102 RBIs. The following season Yastrzemski, Rice, and Butch Hobson each drove in at least 100 runs, but Boston finished in a tie for second place, three games behind the Yankees.

One of Yastrzemski's biggest disappointments came during the 1978 season. The Red Sox and Yankees finished in a first-place tie in the AL East, setting up a one-game playoff. Boston had a 2–0 lead in the seventh, but Bucky Dent's three-run homer put New York on top. With two outs in the ninth and Goose Gossage pitching for New York, Yastrzemski came up with two men on. "The pitch came in, on the inside, just at the knees," Yaz recalled. "My pitch. I swung, but just as I got the bat out, the ball exploded on me, coming in quicker than I had thought. I tried to turn on it, but I got underneath the ball." The game was over and so was Boston's season.

Possibly Yastrzemski's greatest achievement was to collect 400 homers and 3,000 hits, joining Stan Musial, Willie Mays, and Hank Aaron in the record books. "I'm very pleased and very proud of my accomplishments, but I'm most proud of that," Yaz commented. "Not [Ted] Williams, not [Lou] Gehrig, not [Joe] DiMaggio did that. They were Cadillacs and I'm a Chevrolet."

Yaz recorded his 3,000th hit on September 12, 1979, off New York's Jim Beattie. He confessed to feeling immense strain once he got closer to the milestone: "The 3,000-hitting thing was the first time I let individual pressure get to me. I was uptight about it. When I saw the hit going through, I had a sigh of relief more than anything."

Yastrzemski retired after the 1983 season with 3,419 hits, including 452 home runs. He hit better than .300 six times. His uniform No. 8 was retired by the Red Sox. "I was lucky enough to have the talent to play baseball," Yastrzemski said. "That's how I treated my career. I didn't think I was anybody special, anybody different."

Tom Yawkey

Yawkey, Thomas Austin

Owner (1933–76) B:2/21/1903, Austin, TX D:7/9/1976, Boston, MA

Some may scoff at Tom Yawkey, the millionaire sportsman whose millions could not buy a world championship for the Boston Red Sox and whose generosity left him branded as "paternalistic." But in 1980 Yawkey, solely on the strength of his character as Boston owner, was inducted into the Baseball Hall of Fame. No one else has ever made the grade simply by being an owner—not Jacob Ruppert, not Walter O'Malley, not John T. Brush.

Thomas Yawkey was not originally Tom Yawkey; he was born Thomas Yawkey Austin. His uncle, William Hoover Yawkey, had owned the Detroit Tigers. William Yawkey was fabulously wealthy, with money from interests in mining, logging, and oil. Thomas' father died when he was very young, and his wealthy uncle took in young

Tom and his mother. After Tom's mother died in 1917, William Yawkey and his wife formally adopted Thomas Yawkey Austin and changed his name to Thomas Austin Yawkey.

Hall of Famer Eddie Collins, then a Philadelphia A's coach, suggested in 1933 that Tom Yawkey buy the Red Sox. Yawkey had attended Collins' old prep school, the Irving School in Tarrytown, New York, where he had been runner-up for that institution's prestigious Edward T. Collins Medal for best scholar-athlete. Ty Cobb introduced Yawkey to Collins and the two discovered that besides baseball and their alma mater, they had something else in common: hunting. Yawkey invited Collins down to his palatial 50,000-acre South Carolina retreat, and the two became fast friends.

In what Collins later described as a "purely idle conversational subject," he one day remarked to Yawkey that the impoverished Red Sox franchise was for sale. Bob Quinn and his associates desperately needed to unload the club. Yawkey was interested—but only if Collins would run it for him. Collins at first refused, but when A's boss Connie Mack urged him to take advantage of the opportunity, he relented.

Yawkey at the time was just coming into his inheritance. Some have said it was more than $40 million. Others have estimated it at far less, but in any case, he received it on February 21, 1933, on his 30th birthday. Four days later he was owner of the Red Sox.

At the time, the Red Sox were a substandard club, still not recovered from Harry Frazee's gutting of the franchise more than a decade before. "It would be the height of folly to dump a lot of money into the thing all at once in the hope of quick and salutary results. Even if you wanted to do that, where would you go for players?" Yawkey was quoted as saying.

His patience didn't last long. In May 1933 he bought catcher Rick Ferrell from the St. Louis Browns. A few days later he purchased George Pipgras and Bill Werber from the Yankees for $100,000. Then came a buying spree in Philadelphia. From the Athletics in December 1933, he obtained Lefty Grove, Rube Walberg, and Max Bishop for two players and $125,000. In December 1935 he acquired Jimmie Foxx for a journeyman pitcher and $150,000. And from the Washington Senators in October 1934 he obtained Clark Griffith's son-in-law, shortstop-manager Joe Cronin, for an infielder and $250,000.

The infusion of such talent did not deliver a pennant. Next, Yawkey turned to creating a farm system and engaged former umpire and Indians general manager Billy Evans to handle the task. Evans was a shrewd baseball man, and he acquired the Louisville franchise to obtain shortstop prospect Pee Wee Reese. Friction arose when Cronin used his influence to get Reese sold to Brooklyn, and Evans was eased out of Boston.

One successful product of the Red Sox organization was outfielder Ted Williams, whom Boston purchased from San Diego of the Pacific Coast League. With talent like Williams and Bobby Doerr, Yawkey finally won his first pennant in 1946. Still, Yawkey kept buying players like Junior Stephens and Ellis Kinder for stacks of cash.

Yawkey, however, did not win a second pennant until 1967, when the Red Sox rose from ninth one season to first the next. "This is the greatest day of my life. They went from the bottom to the top and I'm proud of these fellows," Yawkey said on October 1, 1967, the day that Boston clinched.

A third pennant followed in 1975 with rookies Fred Lynn and Jim Rice leading the way. But in each of the three World Series that Yawkey's Red Sox played, Boston lost in seven excruciating games.

Despite his millions, Yawkey never enjoyed high society. He preferred the company of old friends such as Vin Orlando, the Red Sox clubhouse attendant, and Tommy McCarthy, the club press steward. Yawkey also liked working out with Red Sox players. Even in his 60s, he often shagged flies or took batting practice at Fenway Park.

Yawkey received a flood of criticism for his slowness in integrating the club. In 1959 the Red Sox used their first black player, Pumpsie Green; they were the last major league team to integrate, 12 years after the coming of Jackie Robinson. Yawkey denied any charges of racism: "I don't care what a man's race is. He can be black, white, Indian, Chinese, just so long as he plays baseball to the best of his ability."

One source estimated that Yawkey lost $20 million on the Red Sox over the years, but he hardly frittered his fortune away as he was still worth $200 million at the time of his death. "Perhaps some people think I have wasted my life," commented Yawkey. "I can't help that. I was always taught to help others, that those of us fortunate enough to be born with material abundance should do what we can for those who are not. I do what I can."

When Ted Williams heard that Yawkey had died of leukemia on July 9, 1976, he said, "I feel so badly, I don't know what to say. He had a heart

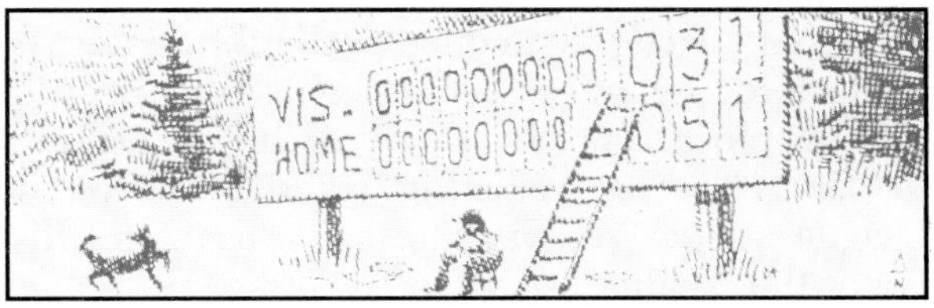

as big as a watermelon. I loved the man from the bottom of my heart. He was unselfish, fair, sincere, and honest."

In addition to transforming the Red Sox from one of baseball's weakest clubs to among the healthiest while creating a New England institution, Yawkey rebuilt Fenway Park into a charming and cozy landmark. Fenway's address, as all Red Sox fans know, is 4 Yawkey Way. Upon her husband's death, Jean R. Yawkey served as the majority owner and general partner of the Red Sox. She remained in that role until she died in 1993.

Steve Yeager

Yeager, Stephen Wayne **C**

1972–86 B:11/24/1948, Huntington, WV Deb:8/2/1972, LA NL BR/TR 6', 190

G	AB	R	H	HR	RBI	OBP	SLG	AVG
1269	3584	357	816	102	410	.300	.355	.228

Catcher Steve Yeager earned a share of the 1981 World Series Most Valuable Player honors primarily because his homer in the seventh inning off the Yankees' Ron Guidry gave the Dodgers a 2–1 Game 5 win. But his most lasting contribution to the game during his 15-year career was introducing the catcher's neck-protector flap in 1976. A freak accident led to his innovation. While kneeling in the on-deck circle, he was hit in the neck by the barrel of a shattered bat. He had seven wood splinters removed and realized his injury could have been even more serious.

Yeager, the nephew of famous test pilot Chuck Yeager, was chosen by the Dodgers in the fourth round of the June 1967 free-agent draft and caught at Ogden, Dubuque, Daytona Beach, Bakersfield, and Albuquerque before reaching the majors in 1972. Described by Lou Brock as "the best throwing arm in baseball," Yeager earned a reputation as an intelligent caller of pitches. Four times he led National League catchers in fielding range while leading the Dodgers to six division championships. Although he batted just .178 in those six NLCS, he hit a cumulative .298 in four World Series. His career batting average was .228.

In a 19-inning game on August 8, 1972, Yeager tied a league record with 22 putouts and broke another record with 24 chances accepted. Yeager, who once posed for a *Playgirl* centerfold, signed as a free agent with Seattle in November 1986, his last year in the majors. In 1999 he was coaching for the California League's Lake Elsinore Storm a Class A affiliate of the Anaheim Angels

Rudy York

York, Preston Rudolph **1B–C**

1934, 1937–48 M(1959, 0–1) B:8/17/1913, Ragland, AL D:2/5/1970, Rome, GA Deb:8/22/1934, DET AL BR/TR 6'1", 209

G	AB	R	H	HR	RBI	OBP	SLG	AVG
1603	5891	876	1621	277	1152	.362	.483	.275

Rudy York set an American League record in 1942 with 146 assists and then broke it the following year by recording 149. In 1944 he established a major league record with 163 double plays. Although all the marks have since been surpassed, the numbers indicate that Rudy York was an adequate first baseman. Nevertheless, one sportswriter quipped he was "part Indian and part first baseman." While Red Smith observed: "No matter where York was stationed in the field, he always played the same position—at bat." The criticisms no doubt stemmed from the fact that it took York far longer to find a regular position than it took him to locate his batting eye.

At least the "part Indian" idea was true. Said York: "They say in that record book that I'm Indian-Irish, but there's durn little Irish in me. I'm a Cherokee Indian, and I'm proud of it. Of course when I was in the big leagues, that didn't help me out much. Any time an Indian puts on a baseball uniform he's twice as interesting a character as the other fellow."

The son of an Alabama millworker, York left school in the third grade to help support four other children in the family. By the time he was 13 he was playing on the mill team. Colonel Bob Allen of Knoxville of the Southern Association signed York at 17, but kept the boy on the bench and released him after one month. Detroit scout Eddie Goosetree gave York a second chance. At Shreveport, where the Tigers first sent him, he played second base. Then at Beaumont he played third base, first base, catcher, and the outfield. In 1935 he led the circuit in homers, with 32, and RBIs, with 117, and was named Texas League Most Valuable Player.

In the spring of 1936 the Tigers tried York out at third base but soon optioned him to Milwaukee. "I had my greatest season [in Milwaukee], was voted the Most Valuable Player, and went back to Detroit to stay," he said of his situation. "But I was still a man without a position."

Hank Greenberg blocked his progress at first and Mickey Cochrane was in his way behind the plate. In May 1937 Cochrane was beaned and put out of action, but York still did not play on a regular basis. Finally on August 4, after the Tigers lost six straight, York was installed at catcher. He homered that day, hit three more at a series in spacious Griffith Stadium, and by the last day of the month had 16 homers for August, needing just one more to tie Babe Ruth's record for most home runs in a month. On August 31 York collected two homers off Washington Senators hurles Pete Appleton. He not only broke Ruth's record, but the seven RBIs he collected that day gave him 49 for the month—one more than the previous record set by Lou Gehrig in August 1935. York finished his rookie season with 35 homers and 103 RBIs. "August always was my month," York said. "I could hit anything they'd throw at me in August, golf ball or tennis ball."

The Tigers still didn't know where to play York. In 1938 he hit 33 homers (including four grand slams) and drove in 127 runs, while appearing in 116 games behind the plate, 14 in the outfield, and one at first base. That season York and Greenberg combined for 91 homers. York batted .307 in 1939, but played in only 102 games, 67 behind the plate.

Finally, in 1940 the Tigers gave Greenberg a $20,000 bonus to move to left field. That season York set career highs with a batting average of .316, a slugging average of .583, 186 hits, 46 doubles, 134 RBIs, and 105 runs scored. Detroit won the American League pennant and met Cincinnati in the World Series. York's two-run homer in the seventh inning of Game 3 lifted the Tigers to a 7-4 victory, but the Reds won the World Series in seven games.

York homered off Mort Cooper in the 1942 All-Star Game. In 1943 he led the American League with 34 homers and 118 RBIs. But when his production slipped, Tigers fans turned on him. He batted only .179 in the 1945 World Series and was sent to the Red Sox in January 1946 for infielder Eddie Lake.

He helped Boston win the pennant with his sixth season of more than 100 RBIs. On July 27, 1946, York belted two grand slams in a single game. In Game 1 of that fall's World Series, his 10th-inning home run off Cardinals starter Howie Pollet gave the Sox a 2–1 win. In Game 3 his first-inning, three-run homer off Murry Dickson broke the game open. But Enos Slaughter's mad dash from first base in Game 7 scored the winning run and gave the Cardinals the Series.

Boston traded York to the Chicago White Sox in June 1947 for first baseman Jake Jones. York hit only .233 between the two teams and was released at the end of the season. His playing career ended in 1948 after 31 games with the Philadelphia Athletics. York was a Red Sox coach from 1959 through 1962. He served as an interim manager in 1959, going 0–1 in between managers Pinky Higgins and Billy Jurges.

A career .275 hitter, York blasted 277 home runs, including 12 grand slams. York estimated that he made $250,000 from baseball. "But I never saved any," he admitted. "When I started making money it burned a hole in my pocket. I'd never had any money when I was a kid, and I wanted to spend it for things I'd always wanted." After leaving baseball, York was employed as a firefighter for the State of Georgia.

Tom York

York, Thomas Jefferson **OF**

1871–85 M(1878, 1881, 56–37) U(1886) B:7/13/1851, Brooklyn, NY D:12/17/1936, New York, NY Deb:5/9/1871, TRO NL BL 5'9", 165

G	AB	R	H	HR	RBI	OBP	SLG	AVG
690	2733	467	741	10	315	.317	.387	.271

In an era when many players were as rough as sailors, outfielder Tom York was renowned as a gentleman both on and off the field. An 1880s article in the *New York Clipper* lauded him as "hard-working and reliable" as well as "affable and courteous." He was also an excellent all-around player who helped his team both at bat and in the field.

A lefthanded-hitting Brooklyn native, York began his career at age 19 with Troy in the first season of the National Association. During the next four seasons he played for three different teams, averaging .280 and performing admirably in the outfield, where he displayed excellent judgment, good speed, sure hands, and a strong arm.

When the National League formed in 1876 York played for Hartford, but moved to Providence in 1878, where he stayed for five years. In his first season with the Grays he led the new league in triples with 10. He batted over .300 three times, and even served as team captain.

York retired as a player after the 1885 season. He tried his hand at umpiring the following year but quit in midseason. "I would rather live on a dollar a day than stand the blackguarding which every umpire is subject to," he said. He eventually returned to baseball as a press box guard in Yankee Stadium. His death in 1936 left only three surviving players from the National League's first year.

Eddie Yost

Yost, Edward Frederick Joseph **3B**

1944, 1946–62 M(1963, 0–1) B:10/13/1926, Brooklyn, NY Deb:8/16/1944, WAS AL BR/TR 5'10", 170

G	AB	R	H	HR	RBI	OBP	SLG	AVG
2109	7346	1215	1863	139	683	.395	.371	.254

Eddie Yost had such a legendary batting eye that it was said he could draw a walk in a pepper game. Nicknamed "the Walking Man," he drew 1,614 free passes during his 18 years as a big leaguer. Through 1999, only seven men had received more free passes. It wasn't because teams were afraid to pitch to Yost, either. His lifetime average was only .254, and he hit just 139 home runs. Yost led the American League in walks six times, breaking 150 and 140 once each. In fact, every year from 1946 through 1960, the league leader in bases on balls was either Ted Williams, Mickey Mantle, or Yost.

While he was never a true power-hitter, playing most of his career in cavernous Griffith Stadium with its 407-foot left-field wall, it is generally overlooked that the righthanded Yost ranks behind only Rickey Henderson, Bobby Bonds, and Paul Molitor in leadoff home runs with 28. He had six leadoff dingers in 1959 alone.

Yost went directly from New York University to the Washington Senators. He played only seven games in 1944 and missed most of the next two seasons due to military service. In 1947 he became the Senators' regular third baseman.

Yost's two best years as a batter (not a walker) were 1950, when he hit .295, and 1951, when he batted .283 and socked a league-leading 36 doubles. In 1950 he combined for 310 hits and walks, more than either Babe Ruth or Lou Gehrig had mustered in 1928. Ruth had 308, Gehrig 305.

Yost played 838 straight games from July 6, 1949, until he was sidelined with tonsillitis in 1955. In 1956 he managed to accumulate 119 hits—and 151 bases on balls; he's one of only seven major leaguers to record more walks than hits in a season. In 1959 and 1960 when he led the league in walks, he also had the American League's best on-base percentage.

Given his power and eye, Yost would have been the ideal leadoff man except for his lack of speed. Playing 14 full seasons and parts of four others, he collected just 72 stolen bases. While speed was not part of his makeup, defense most definitely was. Yost led major league third basemen in putouts for a record eight times. His lifetime total of 2,356 putouts was just 16 shy of Jimmy Collins' record total; Brooks Robinson later passed them both.

Yost played the majority of his career as a Senator. He also spent two years as a Tiger, and was selected by the Los Angeles Angels in the 1961 expansion draft. He finished his career in 1962. In 1963 Yost got his name into the record books as a big league manager. He replaced Washington favorite Mickey Vernon as the Senators manager for just one game (a loss) and was in turn replaced by Gil Hodges.

Nevertheless, his intelligent approach to the game earned him jobs as a third base coach for the Angels, Senators, Mets, and Red Sox. He spent 23 years as a major league coach, mostly manning the third-base box.

Anthony Young

Young, Anthony Wayne **P**

1991–96 B:11/19/1966, Houston, TX Deb: 8/5/1991, NY NL BR/TR 6'2", 210

W	L	PCT	G	SV	IP	BB	SO	ERA
15	48	.238	181	20	460	167	245	3.89

Anthony Young had the attitude of a winner and the hard luck of one of baseball's greatest losers. During a nightmarish stretch in 1992 and 1993 in which Young lost a record 27 straight decisions for the New York Mets, the only thing seemingly more certain than another "L" next to Young's name in the box score was a quote from the righthander that things would turn around. Bounced between the rotation and the bullpen, Young went 2–14 in 1992, but preferred to stress his 15 saves. Incredibly, his record worsened to 1–16 a year later despite a 3.77 ERA.

Young's lone victory, a 5–4 triumph over the Marlins on July 28, was a morbid highlight for a last-place Mets team that lost 103 games. Young's win over Florida was his first since April 19, 1992—a span of 465 days. Even then the Mets had to score twice in their final at bat to keep him from taking another loss. The grateful pitcher was mobbed by his teammates.

Young was traded to the Cubs following the 1993 season. After struggling with injuries through two unremarkable seasons in Chicago and one more in Houston, he retired with a career 3.89 ERA, but also a .238 winning percentage.

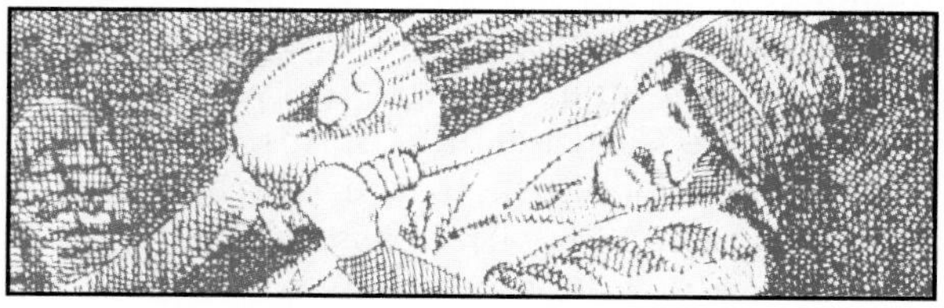

Cy Young

Young, Denton True **P**

1890–1911 M(1907, 3–3) B:3/29/1867, Gilmore, OH D:11/4/1955, Newcomerstown, OH Deb:8/6/1890, CLE NL BR/TR 6'2", 210

W	L	PCT	G	SH	IP	BB	SO	ERA
511	316	.618	906	76	7356	1217	2803	2.63

One question that never can be answered is, How many Cy Youngs would Cy Young have won if there had been a Cy Young Award when he pitched?0 Various historians and statisticians have given estimates of four to six, but such assertions are based solely on numbers and ignore the human factor. Because Cy Young was well liked, he might have been voted the award a couple of times even when he wasn't statistically the best pitcher in his league.

Young is significant not only because of how many seasons he was the best pitcher in the league but also because of his consistency over a long career. While other pitchers came and went, Young turned in one very good year after another. In several single seasons he was probably the best pitcher in baseball, but for nearly two decades he was always one of the best. He won 30 or more games five times, 25 or more 12 times, and 20 or more 15 times.

When Young first arrived in the major leagues John Clarkson, Tim Keefe, and Old Hoss Radbourn were still star pitchers. When he retired, Walter Johnson and Christy Mathewson were well into their careers. Amos Rusie and Kid Nichols were among Young's contemporaries, yet Young was still pitching years after they retired. By the time he called it quits after 22 seasons Young had compiled a record that will never be matched, and for this reason his name is on the modern award signifying pitching excellence.

Young was born on an Ohio farm in 1867. In his prime he stood 6 feet 2 inches and weighed 210 pounds. He always credited his durability to hard work on the farm as a youth. Yet most ballplayers of his era came from a similar background. In 1889, when Young was still called "Dent," he played third base for the Tuscarawas County semipro team in Ohio. The next year he turned professional as a pitcher with Canton of the Tri-State League.

Young was 15–15 in August when the National League Cleveland Spiders acquired him. In one version of the deal, the Canton manager owed a debt to Cleveland, which he repaid with Young. In another, the Cleveland manager bought Young for $300 and a suit of clothes for the Canton manager. Still other reports set the sale price at $500, with the new suit going to Young, who had arrived in Cleveland looking like a country bumpkin. Once the deal—whatever it was—was done, the burly right-hander went 9–6 for the seventh-place Spiders.

He picked up the nickname "Cy" early in his career. Some say the name was short for "Cyclone," because of the speed of his pitches. A more common suggestion is that "Cy" was a common name for a rube.

A story in *Sporting Life* appears to support both contentions. "As the players came from the clubhouse for practice an uncouth figure that brought a titter from the stands shambled along behind them. It was Denton T. Young, the new 'phenom.' Darius Green, the Pied Piper and other noted characters of fact and fiction had nothing on Young for weirdness of appearance. The baseball knickerbockers he wore had been made for a man many inches shorter and served the recruit little better than a bluff. His jersey shirt stretched across his massive body like a drumhead, and his arms dangled through its sleeves almost to the shoulder. He dragged himself across the field bashfully, every angle of his great frame exaggerated and emphasized, and the stands tittered again. The great (Cap) Anson saw Young. 'Is that the phenom?' he asked with a sneer."

As the story goes, the Chicago players all laughed when they saw Young. *Sporting Life* continued, "The gaunt figure lost its uncouthness as he warmed to his work, and the ball shot to the catcher's thin glove with a crack that betokened even greater speed than the flash of the sphere in the sunlight... The game began and the Chicago batters strode to the plate arrogant and confident. One after the other they threw down their bats and returned to the bench puzzled and baffled...Young grew even more effective as the innings passed and Chicago left the field beaten and blind with rage. Then the crowd which had laughed at the unique figure of the new pitcher arose in a mass and gave him an ovation." After the game Anson offered Cleveland $1,000 for the young pitcher. He was laughed out of town.

Cleveland raised the phenom's salary from $300 to $1,400 in 1891. Young came through with a 27–22 record in 423 innings pitched. He was still a bit wild and walked 140 batters, but in the next decade his control improved steadily. When the pitching distance was moved back to 60-plus feet in 1893, many pitchers experienced control problems. Not Young. Eventually he became one of baseball's "control artists," walking only slightly more than one batter per game. According to historian

Lee Allen, "There have been faster pitchers ... but his control was so unerring and he was so tireless that he just kept throwing as if he were systematically chopping down a tree."

The old American Association went under after the 1891 season. Hoping to create a postseason moneymaker, the National League divided the 1892 season into two halves, with the winner of the first half meeting the second-half winner in a so-called "World Series." Boston won the opening half, and Cleveland took the second part of the season behind Young. He finished 36–11, leading the league with a .766 winning percentage, nine shutouts, and an earned run average of 1.93. Young opened the postseason by pitching an 11-inning scoreless tie against Boston's Jack Stivetts, but Boston won the next five games to take the Series.

Often praised for his sportsmanship, Young was considered one of the National League's gentlemen during the 1890s. Perhaps he stood out because his Spiders teammates were generally regarded as a bunch of thugs. The Baltimore Orioles, who won pennants from 1894 through 1896, are better known today for their notorious behavior. But according to Lee Allen, "the Spiders could hold their own with the Orioles when it came to umpire-baiting, tricky play, and general cussedness. Their field captain and manager, Patsy Tebeau, was the prototype of hooligans, and his players cheerfully followed his example."

The great hitter Jesse Burkett, one of the Spider outfielders, ranked second only to Tebeau in his ability to intimidate an opponent with fists, spikes, or brutal profanity. When the Orioles and Spiders faced each other there was likely to be blood on the field and blue air above it.

In 1895 the Spiders and Orioles faced off in "the Temple Cup Series," another National League attempt to create a postseason draw. The Orioles didn't take the contest seriously and lost to the Spiders in five games. Young, a 35-game winner in the regular season, won three of the five postseason games. When the two teams met the next year in another Temple Cup series, the Orioles, stung by criticism of their 1895 performance, swept the Spiders in four games.

On September 18, 1897, Young pitched a 6–0 no-hitter against Cincinnati. That was a fleeting success. Despite his pitching, Burkett's hitting, and Tebeau's reign of terror, the Spiders began to slip. Attendance fell, and Cleveland owners Frank and Stanley Robison acquired the St. Louis franchise as well. In 1899 they moved their best players, including Young, to St. Louis and left Cleveland with the dregs. Young hated the heat in St. Louis. Nor was he particularly fond of the $2,400 cap the National League had placed on salaries.

When Ban Johnson offered him $3,000 to pitch for Boston in the new American League, Young jumped. His first three years in Boston were three of his very best. Young led the new league in victories all three seasons while compiling a 93–30 mark.

By the time Boston won the pennant in 1903, relations with the National League had improved to the point that a real World Series was staged between Boston and Pittsburgh. In the best-of-nine affair Young's teammate Bill Dinneen emerged as Boston's pitching star with three wins, including the final game. Young lost the opening game, then pitched seven innings of relief in another Boston loss in Game 3. He pulled double duty in that contest, taking tickets before the game when Boston's overflow crowd swamped the gates. He came back to beat Pittsburgh, 11–2 and 7–3, in Games 5 and 7.

Young helped pitch Boston to another pennant in 1904, but the National League champion New York Giants refused to take part in a World Series. His 26 wins included a league-leading 10 shutouts. In one early-season stretch he threw 44 consecutive scoreless innings. During the streak, on May 5 against Philadelphia, he tossed a 3–0 perfect game.

When Boston slipped to fourth place the following year, Young suffered the first losing season of his career. Still, he completed 32 of 33 starts, lowered his ERA to 1.82, and struck out a personal-best 208 batters. In 1906, however, Young did not meet his usual standards. His record dropped to 13–21, and his ERA ballooned to 3.19. Some people wondered if Young, by then 39 years old, was nearing the end of his career.

In 1907, the year Boston's team was renamed the Red Sox, manager Chick Stahl committed suicide during spring training. Young was named to take over, even though he did not want the job,. Young told team owner John I. Taylor that he would run the club only until someone else could be found. He went 3–3 to open the season before Taylor produced a replacement. Young gladly resumed his pitching duties and won 22 games with a 1.99 ERA for the seventh-place Red Sox.

On June 30, 1908, at age 41, he pitched his third no-hitter, an 8-0 win over New York, and went on to compile his last 20-win season. On August 13 the *Boston Post* sponsored Cy Young Day, and a team of all-stars played the Red Sox that afternoon. A crowd of 20,000 jammed the Huntington Avenue Grounds, and another 10,000 fans were turned away. Young received a leather traveling bag from the umpires, a silver cup from the players, numerous floral tributes, and $6,000. The great pitcher was so overcome with emotion that he couldn't speak.

In 1909 Young was sold to Cleveland for $12,500, and he went 19–15. In 1911 he split his final season between Cleveland and the Boston Braves, winning seven games. His arm was still sound, but Young complained that he was too fat to field bunts.

In 1937 Young was the third pitcher named to the Hall of Fame, after Walter Johnson and Christy Mathewson. He retired to his farm in Ohio but lost a fortune in the stock market and was forced to board with neighbors. He remained active until his final years. The aging Young often sat in his favorite armchair, looking out over the familiar Ohio landscape, proud of his victory total. He once told a visitor, "Far as I can see, these modern pitchers aren't going to catch me." Young died in 1955. The next year the award bearing his name was given for the first time.

Young compiled an astonishing record. He won 511 games and lost 316, more wins and losses than any other pitcher. He also set records for most starts, complete games, and innings. In 1993 he was given permanent recognition in Boston when Northeastern University erected a statue of him approximately where the pitcher's mound at the Huntington Avenue Grounds once was.

Dick Young

Sportswriter B:1918 D:8/31/1987, Bronx, NY

A highly opinionated, irascible writer for the *New York Daily News* and later *The New York Post*, Dick Young was living proof of the postulate that the style is the man. He was 19 when he started writing for the *Daily News* in 1937 and left for the *Post* 45 years later. Throughout his career he had a style highly unsuitable for those with thin skin. Star ballplayers and managers, general managers and camera crews—he took them all on. He possessed a suffer-no-fools brand of vitriol, but even his enemies would not dispute that he was one of a kind.

There was the time Young found out that Burt Shotton, selected by Branch Rickey to manage the Dodgers after Durocher was suspended in 1947 for consorting with gamblers, had a rather juvenile system of keeping a score book. Shotton used an "F" for fly and "O" for out, hardly the scientific way of doing things. "With that goofy score book," Young opined, "no wonder the old bastard is always one out behind the other manager."

His acerbic tongue was again in evidence a few years later. Upon taking the managerial reins of the Giants, Leo "The Lip" Durocher uttered the classic comment on his congenial predecessor at the Polo Grounds, Mel Ott. "Nice guys finish last," said Durocher (Ott's club was actually fourth when Durocher took over). "Right," said Young when the 1949 season ended. "And not so nice guys finish fifth."

Young could also wax romantic and go with the moment, and he could take umbrage in a players' behalf. Once, while talking to Louis Effrat of *The New York Times,* the topic of Jackie Robinson's salary came up. Robinson, who was hitting .363 at the time, was making a respectable $19,000 in 1949. "Jackie's got to get a raise," Young said. Then he remembered Robinson's difficulty in finding hotel accommodations in Cincinnati and St. Louis. "He leads the league," Young said, "in everything but hotel reservations."

In 1956 and 1957, when rumors swirled that the Dodgers were leaving for Los Angeles, the club played some of its games in Jersey City. After one such game Young began his story, "Inching their way westward ..." He insisted that Walter O'Malley told him he wanted to leave Ebbets Field "because the area is getting full of blacks and spics." O'Malley denied having said any such thing. When beat writer Roger Kahn pressed Young, he said, "Oh, yeah. O'Malley also said the trouble with Brooklyn was that the place had too many blacks and spics and Jews."

Young railed against "new" developments in sports like high salaries and drug use. He was also a testy opponent of television and its increasing encroachment on the space once reserved for sportswriters. When a TV crew plowed into the clubhouse one day, he brawled with the technicians. He routinely came out against high-priced players. Young used his column to attack Tom Seaver as a spoiled ingrate when the Mets star was involved in a contract dispute. (Seaver later did an amusing "as-told-to" piece for *Harpers*, titled "How I Lost My Job Through the *Daily News*.") Ten years later when Dwight Gooden returned to the Mets after undergoing treatment for drug abuse, Young's column sported the headline "Stand Up and Boo."

In 1980 Young signed, but did not honor, a four-year deal with the *News*, saying that the paper could not guarantee his $131,000 salary over the last two years of the contract. At the time, the *News* was up for sale. The $1.5 million breach-of-contract suit against him was later dismissed.

Young was a president of the Baseball Writers Association of America. In 1978 he received the J. G. Taylor Spink Award "for meritorious contributions to baseball writings." He died in August 1987 of complications resulting from intestinal surgery several months earlier.

Eric Young

Young, Eric Orlando **2B-OF**
1992–* B:5/18/1967, New Brunswick, NJ Deb:7/30/1992, LA NL BR/TR 5'9", 180

G	AB	R	H	HR	RBI	OBP	SLG	AVG
935	3314	566	959	43	338	.372	.395	.289

Eric Young, who in 1993 became the first batter in Colorado Rockies history, found new life in the high altitude of Denver. Former Rockies teammate Dante Bichette called Young "the most exciting player I've ever played with." Young led the National League in triples in 1995, and was the league's top basestealer a year later.

He was selected from the Los Angeles Dodgers in the expansion draft of November 1992. Young batted .269 with 42 steals in 1993, but manager Don Baylor wanted more. After a stint in the outfield, injuries elsewhere forced Young back into action at second midway through the 1995 season. He immediately provided an offensive spark, finishing the year with a .317 average and 35 steals as the Rockies reached the playoffs in only their third year of play. He batted .438 in a four-game loss to Atlanta in the Division Series.

In 1996 he batted .324 and even drove in 74 runs. When his numbers dipped in 1997, however, Young and Baylor again clashed. Colorado traded Young back to the Dodgers after the All-Star break. Though his 292 career steals and patience at the plate remained assets, a questionable glove and a large contract were his downfall in Los Angeles. Despite their earlier transgressions, Young was reunited with new Cubs manager Baylor in a 1999 off-season trade in Chicago.

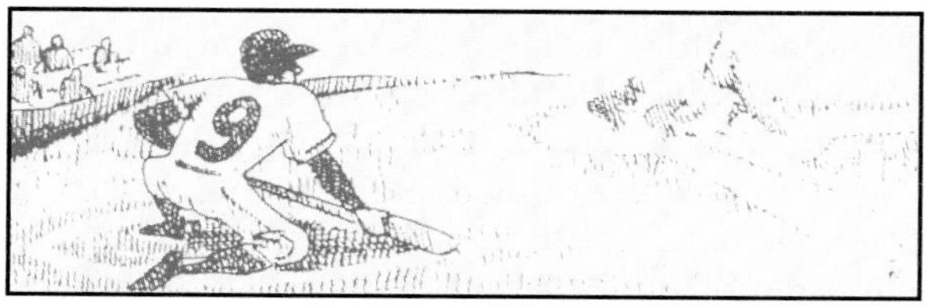

Irv Young

Young, Irving Melrose **P**
1905–08, 1910–11 B:7/21/1877, Columbia Falls, ME D:1/14/1935, Brewer, ME Deb:4/14/1905, BOS AL BL/TL 5'10", 170

W	L	PCT	G	SH	IP	BB	SO	ERA
63	95	.399	209	21	1384²	316	560	3.11

He was known as "Young Cy" or "Little Cy," but there was no comparing Irv Young to the immortal Cy Young. Cy Young was a winner; Irv Young, alas, was mostly a loser. Young had the dubious achievement of losing 20 or more games in three straight years from 1905 through 1907 with the National League's Boston Doves. His best chance to win with the poor-hitting Braves was to keep the other team from scoring at all; of his 63 career wins, 21 were shutouts.

He won 20 games in his rookie year, which would have been a remarkable feat if he hadn't also lost 21 that season. He was one of three 20-game losers on the Boston team, joining Vic Willis, who lost 29 games, and Chick Fraser, who dropped 21. Young set rookie records, however, with 41 complete games and 378 innings pitched.

In 1906 Young lost 25 games and was joined in the 20-loss column by three other pitchers—Vive Lindaman with 23 loses, Big Jeff Pfeffer with 22, and Gus Dorner with 25. Young did manage to lead the league in complete games and innings pitched for the second year in a row. He also pitched a one-hitter against Brooklyn. Even though Young lost 23 games in 1907, Pittsburgh expressed interest in acquiring him. In June 1908 Boston traded him to the Pirates for two pitchers. He returned to the minors, after finishing the season with Pittsburgh but came back to the White Sox for the 1910 and 1911 seasons.

Joel Youngblood

Youngblood, Joel Randolph **OF-3B-2B**
1976–89 B:8/28/1951, Houston, TX Deb:4/13/1976, CIN NL BR/TR 6', 180

G	AB	R	H	HR	RBI	OBP	SLG	AVG
1408	3659	453	969	80	422	.332	.392	.265

On August 4, 1982, Joel Youngblood became the first major leaguer to collect hits for two different clubs in two different cities on the same day. He began the day as a Met and singled in an afternoon contest against the Cubs at Wrigley Field. During the game, he was told that he had been traded to Montreal. Youngblood flew to Philadelphia, where the Expos were playing a night game, arriving in time to pinch-hit a single off Steve Carlton.

The righthanded hitter was a second-round draft choice in June 1970. Youngblood came to the majors with the Reds in 1976 but was traded to the Cardinals before the 1977 season. In June 1977 he was sent to the Mets.

He was an outfielder with a strong arm, but managers often tried to work him into the lineup as part of the infield. New York Mets manager Joe Torre attempted to make a third baseman out of him. With San Francisco in 1983 he was tried at second. Neither experiment worked.

Youngblood had his best years in New York, where he hit 37 doubles and 16 home runs in 1979. In 1981, before a knee injury cut short his season, he was hitting .350 and was named to the NL All-Star team. After finishing 1982 with the Expos, Youngblood moved on to the Giants. In 1989 he ended his playing career where it began in 1976, in Cincinnati. He later served as a major league coach with the Reds and Brewers.

Ross Youngs

Youngs, Ross Middlebrook **OF**

1917–26 B:4/10/1897, Shiner, TX D:10/22/1927, San Antonio, TX Deb:9/25/1917, NY NL BL/TR 5'8", 162

G	AB	R	H	HR	RBI	OBP	SLG	AVG
1211	4627	812	1491	42	592	.399	.441	.322

"I'm going to give you a kid who is going to be great player," Giants manager John McGraw informed Rochester manager Mickey Doolan in 1917. "Take good care of him because if anything happens to him, I'll hold you personally responsible." The player in question was a 20-year-old outfielder named Ross Youngs, a McGraw favorite and an eventual Hall of Famer, whose brilliant career was cut short by a fatal kidney ailment.

"Pep" Youngs helped McGraw win four straight pennants from 1921 to 1924. In the seventh inning of Game 7 of the 1921 World Series, Youngs hit a triple and a double to ignite a seven-run Giants rally—the first player to collect two hits in a single World Series inning.

Youngs had been a star halfback at West Texas Military Academy. He got off to a rocky start in baseball when Austin of the Texas League released him after a brief 1914 trial. In 1915 he played in the Middle Texas and Central Texas leagues, but both leagues disbanded in midseason.

In 1916 at Sherman of the Western League, Youngs led the circuit in hits and runs, plus a .362 batting average. Scout Dick Kinsella spotted him and recommended him to McGraw. At Rochester, under Doolan, Youngs batted .346 and was called up to New York at the end of the season.

Although not a power hitter, Youngs hit for average, had great speed, and featured a powerful throwing arm. He hit better than .300 in seven of his eight full seasons in the majors, including a career-best .356 in 1924. He stole home 10 times, once hit three triples in a game, and hit for the cycle on April 29, 1922.

Youngs' Giants defeated the Yankees in the 1921 and 1922 World Series. He hit .375 in the 1922 Series, and he batted .348 when the Yanks gained revenge on the Giants the following year. An allegation of wrongdoing that involved Youngs and several other members of McGraw's team tainted the Giants' 1924 pennant. Late in the pennant race, it was reported that Giants infielder Jimmy O'Connell had approached Phillies shortstop Heinie Sand with the offer: "I'll give you a hundred dollars if you don't bear down too hard." O'Connell admitted the incident and said he had been put up to it by coach Patrick "Cozy" Dolan, Youngs, second baseman Frankie Frisch, and first baseman George "Highpockets" Kelly. All but Dolan denied the charges and were exonerated by the newly installed commissioner of baseball, Kenesaw Mountain Landis. O'Connell and Dolan were banned for life.

In June 1926 Youngs—leading the club in batting—had to be hospitalized due to what was publicly described as an "intestinal disorder." It was, however, a severe urinary tract infection, the result of an earlier infection that passed from his throat to his kidneys. Youngs returned to the team in the middle of August but was under a nurse's care. He finished the season at .306, was bedridden for all of 1927, and died that October.

"He was the greatest outfielder I ever saw," said McGraw. "He could do everything that a baseball player should do and do it better than most players. As an outfielder, he had no superiors. And he was the easiest man I ever had to handle. In all his years with the Giants he never caused one moment's trouble for myself or the club. On top of that, a gamer player than Youngs never played ball."

McGraw kept pictures of Youngs and Christy Mathewson above his desk. Youngs was elected to the Baseball Hall of Fame in 1972.

Robin Yount

Yount, Robin R **SS-OF-DH**

1974–93 B:9/16/1955, Danville, IL Deb:4/5/1974, MIL AL BR/TR 6', 170

G	AB	R	H	HR	RBI	OBP	SLG	AVG
2856	11008	1632	3142	251	1406	.346	.430	.285

In his last trip around the bases at Milwaukee's County Stadium, Robin Yount reprised one of the most memorable scenes of his 20-year career: he made the circuit on a motorcycle. Presented with a new Harley-Davidson by the Milwaukee Brewers, for whom he had played his entire career, Yount acknowledged the thunderous ovation from the 47,000 fans present by circling the stands, waving, and slapping high fives. The ride recalled the ceremony that followed the Brewers' appearance in the 1982 World Series (which they lost to the Cardinals in seven games), in which Yount—that year's American League Most Valuable Player—zoomed across the diamond on his Harley, shaking his fist to the roar of the crowd. The image epitomized Yount's jubilant approach to the game of baseball, and to life.

One of only three men in major league history ever to be named MVP at two different positions, Yount was an exuberant athlete who once considered giving up baseball for professional golf and whose passion for motor sports rivaled his love of the national pastime. His dedication to the game, his all-around ability, and his loyalty to the often-mediocre Milwaukee Brewers franchise combined to make him a throwback to an earlier age.

"No one plays like Robin," teammate B.J. Surhoff declared in a 1990 *Sports Illustrated* profile that followed Yount's second MVP season. "He runs out every ground ball to the pitcher as hard as he can. He is the best baserunner in baseball, he plays hitters perfectly, he's an incredible clutch hitter, he gives himself for the team at all personal costs. When you play with him, you realize that he plays the game on the edge."

Yount once told *Sports Illustrated,* "Living on the edge is the only way to play—baseball or whatever."

During a storybook career at Taft High in Woodland Hills, California, Yount learned about the world of pro baseball from his brother Larry, a pitcher who lasted eight years in the Houston Astros' farm system. Robin arrived in the big leagues in 1974 after playing only a single season in the minors. At age 18, he was the youngest player in the major leagues.

Legend has it that when immortal slugger Henry Aaron joined the Brewers in 1975, the intrepid teenager was among the first to greet him. "Hello, Mr. Aaron," Yount reportedly said. "I'm Robin Yount." Yount gave little indication those first couple of seasons that his uniform number would one day take its place beside those of Aaron and Rollie Fingers on display at County Stadium. Instead, he looked like a light-hitting shortstop. In 1976 he became the youngest major leaguer ever to play in 161 games. That same year he led American League shortstops in double plays.

He showed some improvement at the plate in his first three seasons, but 1977 was a breakthrough year for "the Kid," as he was tagged by his older teammates. Yount hit .288 that year, bettering his previous season's average by 36 points. Meanwhile, the young franchise continued to struggle in the AL East. The Brewers won only 67 games in 1977 and endured their second straight sixth-place finish, 33 games out. Under new manager George Bamberger, however, the Brewers reversed their fortunes the following year, launching the ascent that eventually took them to the 1982 World Series.

Interestingly enough, it was before that season that Yount left spring training to consider a different career—as a pro golfer. A scratch golfer who once shot two over par at Pebble Beach, Yount had a legitimate shot at the PGA Tour. Mulling his options (and riding dirt bikes in the Arizona mountains), he didn't return to the team until May. Phil Yount later said that this was the only time he'd stepped into his youngest son's life with advice. Robin returned to baseball with renewed purpose, and he also had a new double play partner in Paul Molitor; the two would be teammates for the next 15 seasons.

In 1978 he set then career highs for batting average, RBIs, triples, and home runs, barely missing his first .300 season. Yount led the rejuvenated Brewers to a 93–69 record, fourth best in the majors, and a third-place finish in the AL East. The 1980 season was the first of his three All-Star seasons. He collected 49 doubles and 82 extra-base hits to lead the league, and he picked up his 1,000th hit. He also racked up 317 total bases—the third-highest total ever by a shortstop. His 23 homers matched his combined total for the previous four seasons. Although the Brewers could manage only a third-place finish in their division, the roster that would carry them to the pinnacle the next two seasons was in place.

The Brewers racked up the best record in the league in the second half of the strike-shortened 1981 season, only to fall to the New York Yankees in the division playoffs. In the five-game series with New York, Yount batted .316—which proved to be only a tune-up for his remarkable 1982 campaign.

Yount put together perhaps the best season ever by an American League shortstop to that point. He led the majors in slugging (.578), hits (210), doubles (46), and total bases (367). He finished second in the majors in batting at .331. He drove in 114 runs and hit 12 triples. He led league shortstops in assists and became the first AL shortstop to lead the league in slugging and total bases. Yount also became the first AL shortstop to hit over .300 with at least 20 homers and 100 RBIs.

Milwaukee finished with the best record in baseball at 95–67. In the season-ending showdown with the Baltimore Orioles, Yount cemented his reputation as a clutch hitter. By winning the first three contests of their four-game homestand with the Brewers, Baltimore had tied for the division lead. In the game to determine the division champion, the Orioles started future Hall of Famer Jim Palmer. Yount touched him for a homer in the top of the first and homered again in the third as Milwaukee took the AL East title.

Facing the California Angels in the Championship Series, the Brewers became the first team to capture the pennant after being down two games. Yount hit .414 in the "Suds Series" against St. Louis, including a home run to help win Game 5, but the Brewers came up short in Game 7.

Yount collected a plethora of postseason honors that year, including AL MVP, *The Sporting News* Player of the Year, and his first Gold Glove Award. Although he maintained his high level of play during the next several years, injuries, inconsistency, and managerial changes (four managers in four years) led to a series of fifth- and sixth-place finishes for the Brewers. Yount received more fan votes than any other player in 1983 All-Star balloting, but, ironically, it was his last appearance in the All-Star Game. The following year he began to suffer from the shoulder problems that would eventually drive him out of the infield.

After the 1984 season, in which he scored over 100 runs for the third year in a row and narrowly missed his third consecutive .300 year, he underwent surgery to repair tendon and bone damage in his right shoulder. In 1985, while playing in the outfield for the first time in his career, his shoulder problems worsened. He underwent shoulder surgery for the second time in less than 12 months. Few would have predicted that he would have eight more productive major league seasons.

Following the surgery, Yount put together four consecutive .300 seasons, culminating in his second MVP year in 1989. His .997 fielding percentage in center field led the majors in 1986, making him the first player to lead the American League in fielding in both the outfield and the infield.

Yount began to pass milestones on the road to Cooperstown. He notched his 2,000th hit on September 6, 1986, at age 30, becoming the seventh-youngest player ever to reach that plateau. He hit for the cycle on June 12, 1988, and collected his 1,000th career RBI on August 27. He reached the 2,500-hit plateau on July 2, 1989, and after the season he captured his second MVP Award as the only player to appear on every ballot cast.

Only three players in major league history have been named MVP at two different positions: Stan Musial and Hank Greenberg, and Robin Yount—all Hall of Famers. It's worth noting that both Musial and Greenberg played outfield and first base—the latter being a much less demanding position than shortstop. In the next four years the Kid—then in his mid-30s—never achieved the same preeminence at the plate, but his top-notch fielding, heads-up base running, and competitive fire remained formidable. In July 1991, however, Yount developed a severe case of kidney stones and was placed on the disabled list for only the second time in his long career.

The 1992 season saw Yount achieve a number of important career milestones: 10,000 at bats (the 15th player in history), run number 1,500, and, in the final month of the season, his 3,000th career hit—a single off Cleveland's Jose Mesa at County Stadium. Only the 17th major leaguer to reach the 3,000-hit plateau, Yount was the third youngest to do so, behind immortals Ty Cobb and Henry Aaron.

Throughout 1993—his 20th season in the majors—Yount was rumored to be considering

retirement, and after a so-so campaign in which he hit .258, the decision became less difficult. On February 11, 1994, he made it official.

"I've never really looked forward to this day, but it's here," Yount told an overflow crowd at a press conference in the Brewers' clubhouse. Typically, he had passed up the remaining year of his contract—which called for him to make $3.2 million in 1994—because he could no longer dedicate himself fully to off-season training.

Teammate and friend B. J. Surhoff pointed out to *Sports Illustrated's* Peter Gammons that throughout his career, Robin Yount had always led by example. "Robin's the greatest leader there is," Surhoff said. "Someday some of the guys will wake up and realize that they played with the perfect baseball player, the ultimate warrior, and didn't appreciate it." Yount was voted into the Hall of Fame in his first year of eligibility in 1999.

Tom Zachary

Zachary, Jonathon Thompson Walton **P**

1918–36 B:5/7/1896, Graham, NC D:1/24/1969, Burlington, NC Deb:7/11/1918, PHI AL BL/TL 6'1", 187

W	L	PCT	G	SH	IP	BB	SO	ERA
186	191	.493	533	24	3126^{1}	914	720	3.73

Tom Zachary surrendered Babe Ruth's 60th home run on the last day of the 1927 season, enabling the Babe to break his own record of 59. A year later pitcher and slugger were teammates, and Zachary would annoy the Babe by stubbornly insisting that the historic ball had gone foul.

Zachary was introduced to professional baseball in an unusual way. While still a student at Guilford College in 1918, Zachary was about to travel to France to serve in a Quaker-organized Red Cross unit during World War I. He was in Philadelphia and, to pass the time, went over to see Athletics manager Connie Mack. Mack signed the southpaw. "Reckon I bragged on myself a lot, and pitchers were scarce that year," Zachary later reflected.

Zachary, realizing that he was still in college and hoping to maintain his collegiate eligibility, pitched under an assumed name, Zack Walton. He won two games before he shipped overseas. "Got knocked out of both but it's in the book as two wins," he said.

The next year, Senators owner Clark Griffith signed Zachary. "I just got tired of waiting for Mr. Mack to make up his mind about money when I got back," Zachary explained. "So I signed up with Griff."

In 1920 Zachary joined the Senators' staff. He won at least 15 games in each of the next three seasons, including a career-best 18 in 1921. In 1924 he went 15–9 and helped pitch Washington into the World Series against the New York Giants. The Senators lost Game 1, but Zachary tied the Series with a victory the next day. In Game 6, with the Senators needing a win to stay alive, Zachary hurled a complete-game six-hitter. Washington went on to win Game 7 in 12 thrilling innings.

Zachary led the American League in games started in 1925, but his record fell to 12–15. He made just one relief appearance in the 1925 World Series, which the Senators lost to the Pittsburgh Pirates in seven games. The following February he was dispatched to the St. Louis Browns in a deal which sent "Bullet Joe" Bush to Washington. The Senators reclaimed Zachary on waivers in July 1927. He was in the midst of his third straight losing season when he pitched to Ruth on September 30, 1927.

In Ruth's first three plate appearances against Zachary that day, he walked and singled twice. The Babe came to bat in the eighth inning, with the score tied, 2–2, and Mark Koenig on third with one out. Zachary's first offering was a fastball, which Ruth took for strike one. The second was a screwball, which was high for ball one. The next pitch was a low, inside fastball that Ruth stepped away from slightly as he swung. The ball headed for the right field foul line, and the only question was whether it would stay fair. When it did, the 10,000 fans in attendance went wild.

Zachary shouted to umpire Bill Dinneen that the ball was foul, but Dinneen thought otherwise. "He tossed his glove to the ground, muttered to himself, turned to his mates for consolation and got everything but that," the *New York Times*' James Carolan wrote. "There is no denying that Zachary was putting everything he had on the ball."

Less than a year later, on August 23, 1928, Zachary was sold on waivers to the Yankees. The Senators—and most observers—thought that Zachary's career was over. They were wrong. He pitched Game 3 of that year's World Series, getting a complete-game, 7–3 victory over Jesse Haines of the Cardinals.

In 1929 Zachary had a perfect year, winning 12 and losing none to set the major league record for most victories in an undefeated season. Zachary then moved on waivers to the Boston Braves and Brooklyn Dodgers, and in 1936 wound up with the Philadelphia Phillies. "Always said if I ever got stuck in that Baker Bowl, it would be time to quit," said Zachary. And he did.

Geoff Zahn

Zahn, Geoffrey Clayton **P**

1973–85 B:12/19/1945, Baltimore, MD Deb:9/2/1973, LA NL BL/TL 6'1", 180

W	L	PCT	G	SH	IP	BB	SO	ERA
111	109	.505	304	20	1849	526	705	3.74

"Some night," observed Bob Lemon, "Zahn's going to deliver the ball, and by the time it gets there, he's going to find out the batter has been waived out of the league or traded." The left-handed Zahn did not throw hard, so he was never considered a top prospect. He was drafted by the White Sox, Red Sox, and Tigers while at the University of Michigan but waited until he had his degree to sign with the Dodgers in January 1968. Los Angeles traded him to the Cubs in May 1975 for pitcher Burt Hooton. Chicago released him in January 1977 and he joined Minnesota that March.

Zahn went 14–14, with a 3.03 ERA, in 1978 and 13–7 in 1979. After the 1980 season he became a free agent and signed with the Angels. In 1982 he won 18 games with the Western Division champions and finished sixth in the voting for the American League Cy Young Award. He started Game 3 of the American League Championship Series with a chance to sweep the Brewers. Zahn was chased by Milwaukee in the fourth inning—the Brewers won the next two games as well to steal the pennant.

Zahn had shoulder problems in 1983. But he came back in 1984 to win 13 games with a 3.12 ERA, and led the league with five shutouts. Recurring shoulder miseries in 1985 ended his career at age 40.

Todd Zeile

Zeile, Todd Edward **3B-C**

1989–* B:9/9/1965, Van Nuys, CA Deb:8/18/1989, STL NL BR/TR 6'1", 190

G	AB	R	H	HR	RBI	OBP	SLG	AVG
1473	5344	722	1430	183	805	.351	.430	.268

Todd Zeile was billed as a potential franchise cornerstone during his ascent through the minor leagues. The St. Louis Cardinals liked the young catcher so much that they let All-Star backstop Tony Pena go to Boston as a free agent, but Zeile struggled through a trying rookie season in 1990. His hitting improved following a move to third base. Zeile drove in 103 runs in 1993, then blasted 19 homers in 113 games the following season. A contract dispute with Cardinals management led to a midseason trade to the Chicago Cubs in 1995.

Zeile suited up for five more teams over the next three seasons. He signed with Philadelphia in 1996, and was sent to Baltimore in August. The Orioles traded him to his hometown Dodgers that winter, and he hit a career-high 31 homers for Los Angeles in 1997. The following May, he was exiled to the cost-cutting Marlins with Mike Piazza for four players. He hung around with last-place Florida until August, when a trade to Texas put him in the postseason. Through three teams, he topped 90 RBIs for the third straight season. Zeile spent all of 1999 with Texas, but after the season he was on the move again—this time by his own choice. The free agent spurned the Rangers' offer and moved to New York to become a first baseman with the Mets.

Gus Zernial

Zernial, Gus Edward **OF**

1949–59 B:6/27/1923, Beaumont, TX Deb:4/19/1949, CHI AL BR/TR 6'2½", 210

G	AB	R	H	HR	RBI	OBP	SLG	AVG
1234	4131	572	1093	237	776	.331	.486	.265

Ozark Ike was a popular comic strip in the 1950s. The hero was an easy-going, home run hitter with a knack for saving his team with prodigious blasts. When Gus Zernial began knocking balls out of American League parks, "Ozark Ike" seemed a fitting nickname even though he was from Texas. From 1951 to 1957, playing for the A's in Philadelphia and Kansas City, he recorded 191 homers, second only to Mickey Mantle's 207 in the American League. Among all major leaguers in that span he was seventh, ranking ahead of future Hall of Famers Willie Mays, Roy Campanella, and Ted Williams.

Gus led the AL with 33 homers and 129 RBIs in 1951. He posted three straight 100-plus RBI seasons from 1951 through 1953. In 1953 he powered a career-high 42 home runs, including a pinch-hit grand slam.

The outfielder bounced around in his early years in professional baseball. He signed with the Cardinals in 1941 but spent 1942 to 1945 in the Navy. On his return, he became the property of the Atlanta Crackers, who assigned him to Burlington, where he hit .330 and was drafted by the Cleveland organization. The Indians tried to farm him out to Baltimore (still in the International League), but he failed to clear waivers and was claimed by the White Sox.

He broke in with the White Sox in 1949, and he hit 29 home runs for Chicago in 1950. But in April 1951, the Sox sent Zernial to Philadelphia in a three-team trade that gained Minnie Minoso for Chicago. In Philadelphia (and later in Kansas City), the home runs kept coming. But though "Ozark Ike" the comic strip character made numerous game-saving catches, Gus was less than a gazelle in the field. His enthusiastic pursuit of in the outfield flyballs twice led to broken collarbones.

As Zernial's career wore down, manager Lou Boudreau platooned him in Kansas City. Later, he was a bench player in Detroit, knocking 15 pinch hits in 1958. Zernial was out of baseball by the end of the 1959 season.

"From the time I was a youngster," Zernial said, "baseball was always magic for me.... It was a childhood dream come true. I wouldn't change that for anything in the world."

Chief Zimmer

Zimmer, Charles Louis **C**

1884–1903 M(1903, 49–86) U(1904) B:11/23/1860, Marietta, OH D:8/22/1949, Cleveland, OH Deb:7/18/1884, DET NL BR/TR 6', 190

G	AB	R	H	HR	RBI	OBP	SLG	AVG
1280	4546	617	1224	26	625	.339	.369	.269

Chief Zimmer revolutionized the art of catching when in 1887 he became the first catcher to station himself directly behind home plate for every play. Previously, receivers had retreated from the plate when runners were on base. Zimmer stood (or squatted) his ground and refused to move back.

A fine defensive catcher, Zimmer consistently led the National League in putouts, assists, and double plays. Despite his nickname, he was not a Native American. In 1886 he captained a team called the Poughkeepsie Indians and was addressed as "Chief" as a result.

He was colorful. He used a raw steak in his mitt to lessen the pain of receiving fastballs. Legend has it that he hit the home run in Boston that traveled farther than any home run in history. The ball supposedly landed in a car of the Boston–Albany Railroad and went all the way to Fall River.

Zimmer started his major league career with brief stays in Detroit in 1884 and New York in 1886. He settled with Cleveland, where he caught for Cy Young for many seasons. He appeared in three postseason series for Cleveland and hit .333 in the 1895 Temple Cup series against Baltimore. He moved to Louisville in 1899.

When Barney Dreyfuss purchased the Louisville club after the 1899 season and merged it with the Pirates, Zimmer was one of the players he took along to Pittsburgh. In January 1903 he was sold to the Phillies on waivers so he could become their player-manager. Zimmer umpired the following year in the National League.

Don Zimmer

Zimmer, Donald William **3B-2B-SS**

1954–65 M(1972–73, 1976–82, 1988–91, 1999, 906–873) B:1/17/1931, Cincinnati, OH Deb:7/2/1954, BRO NL BR/TR 5'9", 177

G	AB	R	H	HR	RBI	OBP	SLG	AVG
1095	3283	353	773	91	352	.291	.372	.235

Longtime major league player, manager, and coach Don Zimmer has been described in many ways during a half century in baseball. Boston lefthander Bill Lee categorized him as a "gerbil." Zimmer himself said: "I'm just a .235 hitter with a metal plate in his head." And in 1962, when Casey Stengel was asked if Zimmer was the heart of the expansion Mets, he replied, "Why he's beyond that. He's the perdotius quotient of the qualificatilus. He's the lower intestine."

Truly, Zimmer was all of these things—and more. A promising playing career was nearly ended on July 7, 1953, when Zimmer (then in the American Association) was plunked in the head by a Jim Kirk fastball. He was near death, unconscious for nearly two weeks, unable to speak for eight, and emerged 44 pounds lighter. Installed into his skull were four "buttons...like tapered corkscrews in a bottle."

In 1956 with Brooklyn, Don suffered another injury when he was struck by a Hal Jeffcoat pitch and collected a broken cheekbone. Despite his injuries, Zim spent a dozen years in the major leagues as a valuable utility man with occasional power. He was the first third baseman in Mets history; his 0–for–34 stretch during his brief career with the club helped christen an endless parade of mediocre Mets at the position. After concluding his major league career in 1965, he played for Toei in the Japanese Pacific League, where he hit .188 in 87 games.

Zimmer managed in the minors at Knoxville, Buffalo, Indianapolis, and Key West before becoming a major league coach with Montreal in 1971. His first managerial position came in April 1972, when he replaced Preston Gomez as Padres manager.

Zimmer managed the infamous 1978 Boston Red Sox. His club blew a 14-game lead to the New York Yankees, then ended the season with eight straight wins to force a one-game playoff for the American League East title. The Yankees won the 163rd game of the season with a thrilling, 5–4 decision at Fenway Park. When Zimmer managed the Chicago Cubs to the playoffs in 1989, he was named Associated Press Manager of the Year.

He coached for seven different teams, including three stints with the New York Yankees. The opinionated "Popeye" walked away from the Colorado Rockies midway through the 1995 season, but he was hired by Joe Torre to be his bench coach with the Yankees in 1996. With Torre and Zimmer sitting side by side in the dugout, the Yankees won three world championships in four years. Zimmer even filled in as manager for the first two months of the 1999 season while Torre underwent cancer treatment; Zim guided the Yanks to a 21–15 mark in his first stint as a skipper since 1991. He is the father of Tom Zimmer, a minor league player and manager and longtime Giants scout.

Heinie Zimmerman

Zimmerman, Henry **3B-2B**
1907–19 B:2/9/1887, New York, NY D:3/14/1969, New York, NY Deb:9/8/1907,CHI NL BR/TR 5'11½", 176

G	AB	R	H	HR	RBI	OBP	SLG	AVG
1456	5304	695	1566	58	796	.331	.419	.295

Heinie Zimmerman was a strong hitter but, as his league-leading 39 errors in 1914 suggests, a below-average fielder. He was also a bit below average in the honesty department. In 1919 he and teammate Hal Chase were banned from baseball for attempting to entice their New York Giants teammates to throw games.

A righthanded hitter, Zimmerman started his major league career with the Cubs in 1907, played in parts of 10 seasons in Chicago, and went to two World Series. In 1912 he led the league with a .372 average, 14 home runs, and 69 extra-base hits for a league-leading .571 slugging percentage. The 103 RBIs he was originally credited with were enough to claim the Triple Crown; some 50 years later, however, researchers at Information Concepts, Inc., the group that compiled *The Baseball Encyclopedia*, downgraded Zimmerman's total to 99. Honus Wagner was the belated RBI champion of 1912.

The native New Yorker went home to the Giants during the 1916 season and led the league with 83 RBIs. In 1917 Zimmerman again led the league in RBIs, with 102. He wore the goat horns in the 1917 World Series after he "chased" White Sox baserunner Eddie Collins across home plate in the fourth inning of the sixth and final contest. The play occurred when Oscar "Happy" Felsch hit one back to pitcher Rube Benton. Collins, who had been at third, was caught in a rundown on his way home. Somehow, with Zimmerman holding the ball, Collins slipped past catcher Bill Rariden and headed for home. Neither Benton nor first baseman Walter Holke were backing up the play, and the lumbering Zimmerman had no choice but to chase the speedy Collins across the plate. As Zimmerman pointed out, the only person he could throw the ball to was umpire Bill Klem. The Giants lost the game, 4–2.

Two years later Zimmerman and Chase tried to induce teammates to throw the final game of the 1919 season; it turned out to be the final game of both players' careers. Zimmerman became a steamfitter following his expulsion from baseball.

Richie Zisk

Zisk, Richard Walter **OF-DH**
1971–83 B:2/6/1949, Brooklyn, NY Deb:9/8/1971, PIT NL BR/TR 6'1", 208

G	AB	R	H	HR	RBI	OBP	SLG	AVG
1453	5144	681	1477	207	792	.355	.466	.287

Richie Zisk replaced Roberto Clemente in right field for the Pirates less than a season after Clemente's tragic death. Selected by the Pirates in the June 1967 draft, Zisk led the Appalachian, Carolina, and International leagues in homers, and also paced the International League in RBIs. At age 18 he was Appalachian League Player of the Year in 1967. Zisk was ready for a shot as an everyday player in the major leagues, the question was where he would fit on a veteran-filled contender known as the "Pittsburgh Lumber Co."

Zisk played briefly for the Pirates in 1971 and 1972. When Clemente was killed in a plane crash on December 31, 1972, catcher Manny Sanguillen initially replaced the Hall of Famer in right field. Sanguillen soon moved back behind the plate. Zisk took over in right field, batting .324 in 333 at bats. In May 1974 he collected RBIs in 10 consecutive games, knocking in 19 runs during that span and finishing the season with 100 RBIs. Rifle-armed Dave Parker displaced Zisk to left field the following year, and Willie Stargell moved from the outfield to first base. The Pirates won division championships in 1974 and 1975, and Zisk hit .400 in Championship Series play.

Zisk, however, was unhappy with the Pirates and complained about being "buried alive in Pittsburgh." In December 1976 the Pirates traded Zisk, along with pitcher Silvio Martinez, to the White Sox for pitchers Terry Forster and Rich Gossage. With the Sox in 1977, Zisk had career highs with 30 home runs and 101 RBIs.

Granted free agency that November, he signed with Texas, where he played for three years. The Rangers sent Zisk to Seattle in an 11-player trade in December 1980. The two-time All-Star was exclusively a designated hitter with the Mariners, and hit .311 with 16 homers in only 357 at bats in the strike-shortened 1981 season. Zisk homered in five straight games during the season and won AL Comeback Player of the Year honors. Yet as the Mariners finished in the second division, Zisk was still not happy. "The only thing we led baseball in," he said, "was team meetings."

Injuries forced Zisk to retire after the 1983 season. He later joined the Indians as a minor league hitting instructor. He served as the Cubs organization's instruction coordinator for three years. After two years away from the game, he returned as hitting coach with Florida State League's Daytona Cubs.

Notes on Contributors

Notes on Contributors

Paul Adomites was born and raised in Pittsburgh and lives there now, although he has also lived in Oregon, Florida, and New York. He served as publications director for the Society of American Baseball Research from 1987 to 1990. He founded *The SABR Review of Books*, has contributed to *Total Baseball*, and has written on such diverse topics as ethnic cooking and the history of technology.

David Aretha has edited more than 30 sports books for Publications International, Ltd., including *20th Century Baseball Chronicle*, *The Best of Baseball*, and *Sluggers! History's Heaviest Hitters*. He has authored five sports books for kids, and he writes player profiles for Topps baseball and basketball cards (about 3,000, since 1997).

Jeff Campbell is chairman of the Society of American Baseball Research (SABR) Music and Poetry Committee and executive producer of the *Diamond Cuts* series of baseball song compilations. He is a reporter for *Total Baseball Daily* and was a contributor to the *Total Baseball Catalog*.

Bob Carroll, a former high school teacher, is a freelance writer and illustrator living in North Huntingdon, Pennsylvania. He is the founder and executive director of the Professional Football Researchers Association (PFRA). His baseball books include *Baseball Between the Lines*, *The Whole Baseball Catalog* (with David Pietrusza and Lloyd Johnson), *The Dodgers Trivia Book*, and *The Major League Way to Play Baseball*. He has contributed to *Total Baseball* and authored a regular column for *Old Tyme Baseball News*. Among his football credits are *Total Football*, *The Hidden Game of Football* (with Pete Palmer and John Thorn), and *When the Grass Was Real*. He regularly provides cartoons for *Pro Football Weekly*. His hobbies are listening to classical music, cleaning the Augean stables, and writing threatening letters.

Eliot Cohen founded *Major League Monthly*, a forum for baseball opinion and research, in 1985. A graduate of Yale and Stanford, Cohen has also edited the annual *Who's Who in Baseball* and covered New York teams for United Press International. His book reviews have appeared in publications ranging from *The New York Times* to the *SABR Review of Books*. Formerly a city planner in his native New York and a U.S. diplomat in Tanzania, Cohen wrote on consumer issues, urban planning, and international relations before specializing in baseball. He is now an editor for *Bloomberg Business News* in Hong Kong.

Neil Cohen toiled for much of his professional career at *Sport* magazine, where he held positions of editor and managing editor. Following that, he was unlucky enough to be present at the demise of *The National Sports Daily*, where he served as senior editor. He then turned his attention to explaining sports to children as an associate editor at *Sports Illustrated for Kids*.

Bill Deane is a freelance baseball researcher and writer stationed near Cooperstown, New York, where he spent eight years as Senior Research Assistant for the National Baseball Library & Archive. He has authored six books and nearly 200 articles for such publications as *Total Baseball*, *Baseball America*, and *USA Today Baseball Weekly*, and was a recipient of the 1989 SABR-Macmillan Baseball Research Award. Deane resides in Fly Creek, New York, with his wife Pam and daughter Sarah.

Jed Donahue is a book editor for a publishing house whose list has included Minnie Minoso's autobiography, *Extra Innings: My Life in Baseball*, and the Chicago White Sox yearbook. He also works as a freelance writer. A graduate of Georgetown University, he worked for three years under syndicated columnist and baseball enthusiast George Will. He lives in Washington, D.C.

David Fischer, a native of Philadelphia, worked for three years as the lead baseball and football producer for NBC Sports Online. His journalism and fiction have appeared in print and online in a variety of locations since 1995. He currently lives in Takoma Park, Maryland, where he is pursuing his master's degree in public policy, working on a novel, and scanning the agate type daily in hopes that the Phillies will bolster their pitching. He contributed to *Total Football*, and its spinoffs *Total Cowboys, Total Steelers, Total Quarterbacks*, and *Total Super Bowl*.

Greg Gallo has served with the *New York Post* since 1977 and has been sports editor since 1994. He previously worked at *The National Star*.

Michael Gershman was best known among baseball fans for *Diamonds: The Evolution of the Ballpark*, which won the 1993 CASEY Award and also received that year's SABR-Macmillan Award. He was also familiar to collectors for his series of *Baseball Card Engagement Books* and *Baseball Stadium Postcard Albums*. He was co-editor of *Total Baseball* and *Total Football* and co-founder of Total Sports. Michael Gershman passed away on January 4, 2000, during the preparation of this book.

Gary Gillette is a nationally known baseball author, analyst, and editor. He worked on the *Baseball Weekly 2000 Insider* recently published by Total/*Sports Illustrated*, and is currently working on another TSI book, *The Hidden Game of Baseball*, an updated and revised edition of the baseball classic. He has been a contributor to *Total Baseball*. Gillette was a vice president of Total Sports, Inc. from 1997-1999. Online, he served as the executive editor of *Total Baseball Daily* from 1996-1999, as the editor of The Baseball Workshop OnLine on America On Line in 1996, and as a contributor to AT&T Interchange and *Sports Illustrated* on-line in 1996. The author and editor of many baseball books, Gillette's credits include: *Baseball Weekly 1999 Insider; The Spy: Baseball '98; The Scouting Report: 1995* and *1996; The Great American Baseball Stat Book 1992, 1993,* and *1994;* and *1992 Fantasy League Baseball*. Other baseball books Gillette has contributed to include the annual *Baseball Weekly Almanacs 1992-99, The Great American Baseball Stat Books 1986-87,* and *The 1990 Baseball Annual*. Gillette also works as a legal expert witness on baseball-related litigation and as a consultant on salary arbitration. From 1992-97, Gillette was the president and owner of The Baseball Workshop.

Henry Hecht has served as a baseball beat writer for the *New York Post*.

Mikhail Horowitz is a senior editor at Total Sports. He is the author of *Big League Poets* (City Lights, 1978), a wry collection of collages and captions illuminating the baseball careers of immortal bards. His poem, "Pearly Babe," was featured in 1999 on the Los Angeles Dodgers' website, where you could click to hear it read by Vin Scully.

Bob Klapisch covers baseball for *The Bergen Record* and *The Sporting News*. A former columnist for the *New York Daily News*, he is the author of *High and Tight: The Rise and Fall of Dwight Gooden and Darryl Strawberry* and co-author of *The Worst Team Money Could Buy*, which chronicled the collapse of the New York Mets. Klapisch lives in New Jersey.

Sean Lahman is a senior editor for Total Sports and co-editor of the most recent edition of *Total Baseball*. He is a member of SABR and founder of the Baseball Archive web site. Lahman has published articles in journals and reference works, and has been a contributor to annuals such as *Great American Baseball Stat Book, The Big Bad Baseball Annual, The Rotisserie Baseball Analyst*, and *Baseball Preview*. He attended the University of Cincinnati and lives in Woodstock, New York with his wife Heather and their three children.

Lee Lowenfish is the author of *The Imperfect Diamond: A History of Baseball's Labor Wars*, co-author (with Tom Seaver) of *The Art of Pitching*, author of *The Professional Baseball Athletic Trainers' Fitness Book*, contributor to *The New York Times, The New York Daily News*, and *Newsday*, and has taught sports history at the University of Maryland and other colleges.

Bill Madden majored in journalism at the University of South Carolina and launched his sportswriting career at United Press International in New York in 1970. From 1980 to 1988, Madden was the New York Yankees beat writer for the *The Daily News*. He became that publication's national baseball correspondent in 1989. In 1990 he collaborated on the best-selling book, *Damned Yankees*. In his years at *The Daily News* he was responsible for breaking numerous baseball stories, including the National League's surprise election of Bill White as its president in February 1989. In addition to writing for *The Daily News*, Madden has also contributed to numerous publications including *Total Baseball* and a semiweekly sports collecting column for *The Sporting News*.

Bruce Markusen graduated from Hamilton College in 1987 with a B.A in English-Writing and began a seven-year stint at WIBX Radio in Utica, New York. He hosted a nightly sports-talk show, anchored daily afternoon sports updates, and eventually graduated to the position of sports director. Markusen joined the staff of the National Baseball Hall of Fame Library as a Senior Researcher in March 1995. He has conducted numerous audio-visual interviews for the Hall of Fame's archives and narrated several Hall of Fame video productions. Markusen's *Baseball's Last Dynasty: Charlie Finley's Oakland A's*, won the Seymour Award from the Society for American Baseball Research as the best baseball book of 1998. His second book, *Roberto Clemente: The Great One*, was also published in 1998. Markusen has written for *Baseball Digest*, *Elysian Fields Quarterly*, and *Oldtyme Baseball News*.

Fred McMane is the author of such books as *Hakeem Olajuwon*, *Scottie Pippen*, *Superstars of Men's Track and Field*, *Winning Women: Eight Great Athletes and Their Unbeatable Stories* (with Cathrine Wolf), *My Hero* (with Cathrine Wolf), *Track and Field Basics*, and *The Worst Day I Ever Had*.

David Pietrusza, former president of the Society for American Baseball Research (SABR) and editor-in-chief of Total Sports, is the author of *Judge and Jury: The Life and Times of Judge Kenesaw Mountain Landis*, winner of the 1998 CASEY Award. He is also the author of *Lights On!: The Wild Century-Long Saga of Night Baseball* (a finalist for the 1997 CASEY Award), *Minor Miracles: The Legend and Lure of Minor League Baseball*, *Major Leagues*, and *Baseball's Canadian-American League*. He co-edited *Total Baseball*, *The Total Baseball Catalog*, *Total Mets*, *Total Braves*, and *Total Indians*. He served as managing editor of the first edition of *Total Football: The Official Encyclopedia of the NFL*, and edited seven books on football. Pietrusza served as producer for the documentary *Local Heroes* for PBS-station WMHT and as a consultant for the Baseball Online segment of the PBS LearningLink system. He has appeared on ABC-TV, ESPN, and National Public Radio and written for numerous publications including *USA Today Baseball Weekly* and *Baseball America*. A former member of the Amsterdam (New York) City Council, Pietrusza serves as Public Information Officer for the New York State Governor's Office of Regulatory Reform.

Beau Riffenburgh was formerly editor-in-chief for Total Sports. He was on the public relations staff of the Los Angeles Lakers before serving eight years as an associate editor and senior writer for NFL Properties, where he was the author of *The Official NFL Encyclopedia*, *Running Wild*, and *Great Ones*. He has written 15 books and contributed to many more. He has spent 11 years in Cambridge, England, where he is a lecturer in the History Faculty at the University of Cambridge and is editor of *Polar Record*, the world's oldest journal of polar research. In Britain he also coached "American football" for eight years at the university level, posting an overall record of 68–12–2 and winning three national titles.

Dan Schlossberg is baseball editor of *Legends Sports Memorabilia* and the *Encyclopedia Americana Annual*; senior editor of *Bill Mazeroski's Baseball*; and a regular contributor to *Street & Smith's Official Baseball Yearbook*, *Sports Collectors Digest*, and numerous team and in-flight periodicals. His byline has also appeared in *Baseball Digest*, *The Sporting News*, and The Official World Series and All-Star programs. The former Associated Press (AP) sportswriter has also written baseball card backs for Donruss, Fleer, Pinnacle, Topps, and Upper Deck and covered the All-Star Game, playoffs, World Series, winter meetings, and spring training for newspapers, magazines, and wire services. He is a frequent public speaker on baseball. Schlossberg's books include *The Baseball Catalog Millennium Edition*, *The Baseball Book of Why*, *The Baseball IQ Challenge*, *Baseball Stars of 1985, 1986,* and *1987*, *Pitching*, *Barons of the Bullpen*, *BasebalLaffs*, and *Hammerin' Hank: the Henry Aaron Story*. He was a contributor to *Total Braves*, the *1992-97 Baseball Almanac*, and *Players of Cooperstown: Baseball's Hall of Fame*, and *The Wit & Wisdom of Baseball*. He resides in Fair Lawn, New Jersey.

Ken Shouler taught philosophy for 18 years in the City University of New York before joining Total Sports, where he is now senior editor of reference. His books include *The Experts Pick Basketball's Best 50 Players in the Last 50 Years* (1997) and *The Real 100 Best Baseball Players of All-Time and Why* (1998). He also freelanced for a number of magazines, including *Sport*, *Inside Sports*, *Biography*, *Billiards Digest*, and *Street and Smith's*, *Peterson's* and *Athlon's* annuals. Shouler was project editor for *Home Run: My Life in Pictures* by Hank Aaron (1999). He was one of the panelists selected by Major League Baseball to pick the "All-Century Team" and appeared in MLB's All-Century video. He is currently project editor for *Total Billiards: The World Encyclopedia of Cue Sports* and *Total Basketball*. The ghostwriter of two political autobiographies (he wouldn't even tell *us* who they were for), Shouler also writes regularly for *Cigar*

Aficionado and lives in Harrison, New York, with his wife, Rose Marie.

Matthew Silverman is associate publisher in charge of reference at Total Sports. He served as managing editor for the sixth edition of *Total Baseball* and the second edition of *Total Football.* He has edited seven offshoots of *Total Football,* including *Total Packers, Total Steelers, Total Cowboys,* and *Total Super Bowl.* He also contributed to Total Baseball Daily on www.totalbaseball.com and co-edited *Total Mets.* Formerly a junior editor for *Variety* in New York, he worked for three New England newspapers before joining Total Sports. He resides in High Falls, New York, with his wife, Debbie, and daughter, Jan.

Glenn Stout is co-author with Dick Johnson of *Ted Williams a Portrait in Words and Pictures, DiMaggio: An Illustrated Life,* and *Jackie Robinson: Between the Baselines.* He is co-editor of *The Best American Sports Writing of the Century* and *of The Best American Sports Writing* annual series.

Mike Tully has contributed to such works as *Players of Cooperstown, Baseball's Hall of Fame,* the 1992, 1994 and 1995 *Baseball Almanacs,* and the 1996–97 *Hockey Almanac.*

Photo Credits

Name	Source	page
Aaron, Henry	Transcendental Graphics	1
Aase, Don	Transcendental Graphics	4
Abbott, Jim	Major League Baseball	4
Adair, Jerry	Transcendental Graphics	5
Adams, Babe	Transcendental Graphics	5
Adams, Dr. D. L.	Paula Mirabile Baker	6
Adams, Sparky	Transcendental Graphics	8
Adcock, Joe	Transcendental Graphics	8
Agee, Tommie	Transcendental Graphics	9
Aguilera, Rick	Major League Baseball	9
Aikens, Willie Mays	Transcendental Graphics	10
Aker, Jack	Transcendental Graphics	10
Aldridge, Vic	Transcendental Graphics	11
Alexander, Dale	Transcendental Graphics	11
Alexander, Doyle	Transcendental Graphics	12
Alexander, Grover Cleveland	Transcendental Graphics	12
Allen, Dick	Transcendental Graphics	13
Allen, Ethan	Transcendental Graphics	15
Allen, Johnny	Transcendental Graphics	15
Allen, Mel	Transcendental Graphics	16
Allen, Newt	Transcendental Graphics	17
Alley, Gene	Transcendental Graphics	17
Allison, Bob	Transcendental Graphics	18
Alomar, Roberto	Major League Baseball	18
Alomar, Sandy, Jr.	Major League Baseball	19
Alomar, Sandy, Sr.	Transcendental Graphics	20
Alou, Felipe	Major League Baseball	20
Alou, Jesus	Transcendental Graphics	21
Alou, Matty	Transcendental Graphics	22
Alou, Moises	Major League Baseball	22
Alston, Walter	Transcendental Graphics	23
Altobelli, Joe	Photo File	24
Altrock, Nick	Transcendental Graphics	25
Ames, Red	Transcendental Graphics	25
Amoros, Sandy	Transcendental Graphics	26
Andersen, Larry	Photo File	26
Anderson, Brady	Major League Baseball	27
Anderson, John	Transcendental Graphics	27
Anderson, Sparky	Transcendental Graphics	27
Andujar, Joaquin	Transcendental Graphics	29
Anson, Cap	Transcendental Graphics	29
Antonelli, Johnny	Transcendental Graphics	31
Aparicio, Luis	Transcendental Graphics	32
Appier, Kevin	Major League Baseball	33
Appling, Luke	Transcendental Graphics	33
Archer, Jimmy	Transcendental Graphics	34
Arlett, Buzz	Transcendental Graphics	35
Armas, Tony	Transcendental Graphics	36
Arroyo, Luis	Transcendental Graphics	36
Ashburn, Richie	Transcendental Graphics	36
Ashby, Alan	Transcendental Graphics	38
Ashford, Emmett	Transcendental Graphics	38
Assenmacher, Paul	Major League Baseball	38
Autry, Gene	Transcendental Graphics	39
Averill, Earl	Transcendental Graphics	40
Avery, Steve	Major League Baseball	41
Avila, Bobby	Transcendental Graphics	42
Babich, Johnny	Transcendental Graphics	43
Backman, Wally	Transcendental Graphics	43
Badgro, Red	Transcendental Graphics	44
Baerga, Carlos	Major League Baseball	44
Bagby, Jim	Transcendental Graphics	44
Bagwell, Jeff	Major League Baseball	45
Bahnsen, Stan	Transcendental Graphics	45
Bailey, Bob	Transcendental Graphics	46
Bailor, Bob	Photo File	46
Baines, Harold	Transcendental Graphics	47
Baker, Dusty	Transcendental Graphics	47
Baker, Frank	Transcendental Graphics	48
Baldwin, Lady	Transcendental Graphics	49
Baldwin, Mark	Transcendental Graphics	50
Ball, Phil	Transcendental Graphics	50
Bamberger, George	Photo File	50
Bancroft, Dave	Transcendental Graphics	51
Bancroft, Frank	Photo File	52
Bando, Sal	Transcendental Graphics	52
Bankhead, Dan	Photo File	53
Bankhead, Sam	Transcendental Graphics	53
Banks, Ernie	Transcendental Graphics	54
Bannister, Floyd	Transcendental Graphics	55
Barber, Red	Transcendental Graphics	55
Barber, Steve	Transcendental Graphics	56
Barfield, Jesse	Transcendental Graphics	57
Barker, Len	Transcendental Graphics	58
Barlick, Al	Transcendental Graphics	58
Barnes, Jesse	Transcendental Graphics	59
Barnes, Ross	Transcendental Graphics	59
Barney, Rex	Transcendental Graphics	60
Barr, Jim	Transcendental Graphics	60
Barrett, Marty	Transcendental Graphics	60
Barrow, Ed	Transcendental Graphics	61
Barry, Jack	Transcendental Graphics	62
Bartell, Dick	Transcendental Graphics	63
Bass, Kevin	Photo File	64
Battey, Earl	Transcendental Graphics	64
Bauer, Hank	Transcendental Graphics	64
Baumholtz, Frankie	Transcendental Graphics	65
Bavasi, Buzzie	Transcendental Graphics	66
Baylor, Don	Transcendental Graphics	66
Beaumont, Ginger	Transcendental Graphics	67
Beck, Boom-Boom	Transcendental Graphics	68
Beck, Rod	Major League Baseball	69
Beckert, Glenn	Transcendental Graphics	69
Beckley, Jake	Transcendental Graphics	69
Beckwith, John	John Holway	70
Bedrosian, Steve	Photo File	71
Belanger, Mark	Transcendental Graphics	71
Belcher, Tim	Major League Baseball	72
Belinsky, Bo	Transcendental Graphics	72
Bell, Buddy	Transcendental Graphics	73
Bell, Cool Papa	Transcendental Graphics	74
Bell, Gary	Transcendental Graphics	75
Bell, George	Photo File	75
Bell, Gus	Transcendental Graphics	76
Bell, Jay	Major League Baseball	76
Belle, Albert	Major League Baseball	77
Bench, Johnny	Transcendental Graphics	77
Bender, Chief	Transcendental Graphics	79
Benes, Andy	Major League Baseball	80
Beniquez, Juan	Transcendental Graphics	80
Bennett, Charlie	Transcendental Graphics	81
Bentley, Jack	Transcendental Graphics	81
Benton, Rube	Transcendental Graphics	82
Berg, Moe	Transcendental Graphics	82
Berger, Wally	Transcendental Graphics	83
Bernhard, Bill	Transcendental Graphics	84
Berra, Yogi	Transcendental Graphics	84
Bescher, Bob	Transcendental Graphics	86
Bevacqua, Kurt	Transcendental Graphics	86
Bibby, Jim	Transcendental Graphics	86
Bichette, Dante	Major League Baseball	87
Bierbauer, Lou	Transcendental Graphics	87
Bigbee, Carson	Transcendental Graphics	88
Biggio, Craig	Major League Baseball	88
Bilko, Steve	Photo File	89
Billingham, Jack	Transcendental Graphics	89
Bishop, Max	Transcendental Graphics	89
Black, Bud	Photo File	90
Black, Joe	Transcendental Graphics	90
Blackburne, Lena	Transcendental Graphics	91
Blackwell, Ewell	Transcendental Graphics	91
Blaeholder, George	Transcendental Graphics	92
Blair, Paul	Photo File	93
Blake, Sheriff	Transcendental Graphics	93
Blanchard, Johnny	Transcendental Graphics	94
Blass, Steve	Transcendental Graphics	94
Blattner, Buddy	Transcendental Graphics	95
Blauser, Jeff	Major League Baseball	95
Blefary, Curt	Transcendental Graphics	96
Blomberg, Ron	Transcendental Graphics	96
Blue, Lu	Transcendental Graphics	97
Blue, Vida	Transcendental Graphics	97
Bluege, Ossie	Transcendental Graphics	98
Blyleven, Bert	Transcendental Graphics	98
Bochte, Bruce	Transcendental Graphics	99
Bochy, Bruce	Major League Baseball	100
Boddicker, Mike	Transcendental Graphics	100
Bodie, Ping	Transcendental Graphics	100
Boggs, Wade	Transcendental Graphics	101
Bond, Tommy	Transcendental Graphics	102
Bonds, Barry	Transcendental Graphics	102
Bonds, Bobby	Transcendental Graphics	103
Bonilla, Bobby	Major League Baseball	104
Bonura, Zeke	Transcendental Graphics	105
Boone, Bob	Transcendental Graphics	105
Boone, Bret	Major League Baseball	106
Boone, Ike	Transcendental Graphics	107

Name	Source	page
Clemente, Roberto	Transcendental Graphics	209
Clements, Jack	Transcendental Graphics	212
Clendenon, Donn	Transcendental Graphics	212
Clift, Harlond	Transcendental Graphics	213
Cloninger, Tony	Transcendental Graphics	213
Cobb, Ty	Transcendental Graphics	213
Cochrane, Mickey	Transcendental Graphics	218
Colavito, Rocky	Transcendental Graphics	220
Colbert, Nate	Transcendental Graphics	221
Coleman, Jerry	Photo File	221
Coleman, Joe	Transcendental Graphics	222
Coleman, Vince	Photo File	222
Collins, Dave	Photo File	223
Collins, Eddie	Transcendental Graphics	223
Collins, Jimmy	Transcendental Graphics	224
Collins, Rip	Transcendental Graphics	225
Collins, Shano	Transcendental Graphics	225
Combs, Earl	Transcendental Graphics	226
Comiskey, Charles	Transcendental Graphics	227
Concepcion, Dave	Transcendental Graphics	228
Cone, David	Major League Baseball	229
Conigliaro, Tony	Transcendental Graphics	230
Conine, Jeff	Major League Baseball	231
Conlan, Jocko	Transcendental Graphics	231
Conley, Gene	Transcendental Graphics	232
Connoly, Tom	Transcendental Graphics	232
Connor, Roger	Transcendental Graphics	233
Connors, Chuck	Transcendental Graphics	234
Conroy, Wid	Transcendental Graphics	234
Cooley, Duff	Transcendental Graphics	234
Coombs, Jack	Transcendental Graphics	235
Cooney, Johnny	Photo File	235
Cooper, Cecil	Transcendental Graphics	236
Cooper, Mort	Photo File	236
Cooper, Walker	Transcendental Graphics	237
Cooper, Wilbur	Photo File	238
Corcoran, Larry	Transcendental Graphics	238
Corcoran, Tommy	Transcendental Graphics	239
Corkhill, Pop	Transcendental Graphics	239
Courtney, Clint	Photo File	239
Coveleski, Harry	Transcendental Graphics	240
Coveleski, Stan	Transcendental Graphics	240
Covington, Wes	Transcendental Graphics	241
Cox, Billy	Photo File	242
Cox, Bobby	Transcendental Graphics	242
Cox, Danny	Transcendental Graphics	242
Coyle, Harry	National Baseball Hall of Fame Library, Cooperstown, NY	243
Craig, Roger	Transcendental Graphics	243
Cramer, Doc	Transcendental Graphics	244
Crandall, Del	Transcendental Graphics	244
Crandall, Doc	Transcendental Graphics	244
Crane, Ed	Transcendental Graphics	245
Cravath, Gavvy	Transcendental Graphics	245
Crawford, Sam	Transcendental Graphics	246
Creighton, Jim	Transcendental Graphics	247
Criger, Lou	Transcendental Graphics	248
Critz, Hughie	Transcendental Graphics	248
Cromartie, Warren	Transcendental Graphics	249
Cronin, Joe	Transcendental Graphics	249
Crosetti, Frank	Transcendental Graphics	250
Cross, Lave	Transcendental Graphics	251
Cross, Monte	Transcendental Graphics	251
Crowder, Alvin	Transcendental Graphics	252
Crowe, George	Transcendental Graphics	252
Crowley, Terry	Major League Baseball	253
Crutchfield, Jimmy	Transcendental Graphics	253
Cruz, Jose	Major League Baseball	253
Cruz, Julio	Photo File	254
Cuccinello, Tony	Transcendental Graphics	254
Cuellar, Mike	Photo File	254
Cullenbine, Roy	Transcendental Graphics	255
Cummings, Candy	Transcendental Graphics	255
Cunningham, Joe	Transcendental Graphics	256
Cuppy, Nig	Transcendental Graphics	256
Cutshaw, George	Transcendental Graphics	256
Cuyler, Kiki	Transcendental Graphics	257
Dahlen, Bill	Transcendental Graphics	259
Dahlgren, Babe	Transcendental Graphics	259
Daily, Hugh	Transcendental Graphics	260
Dalkowski, Steve	National Baseball Library	260
Dalrymple, Abner	Transcendental Graphics	260
Daly, Tom	Transcendental Graphics	261
Dandridge, Ray	Transcendental Graphics	261
Danforth, Dave	Transcendental Graphics	262
Danning, Harry	Transcendental Graphics	262
Dark, Alvin	Transcendental Graphics	262
Darling, Ron	Photo File	263
Darwin, Danny	Photo File	264
Daubert, Jake	Transcendental Graphics	264
Dauer, Rich	Major League Baseball	265
Daulton, Darren	Photo File	265
Dauss, Hooks	Transcendental Graphics	266
Davalillo, Vic	Transcendental Graphics	266
Davenport, Jim	Transcendental Graphics	266
Davis, Alvin	Photo File	266
Davis, Chili	Major League Baseball	267
Davis, Curt	Transcendental Graphics	267
Davis, Eric	Major League Baseball	267
Davis, George	Transcendental Graphics	268
Davis, Glenn	Photo File	269
Davis, Harry	Transcendental Graphics	269
Davis, Jody	Transcendental Graphics	270
Davis, Mark	Photo File	270
Davis, Piper	Transcendental Graphics	270
Davis, Storm	Photo File	271
Davis, Tommy	Transcendental Graphics	271
Davis, Willie	Transcendental Graphics	272
Dawson, Andre	Transcendental Graphics	273
Day, John B.	Transcendental Graphics	273
Day, Leon	Transcendental Graphics	274
Dean, Dizzy	Transcendental Graphics	274
Dean, Paul	Transcendental Graphics	276
DeCinces, Doug	Photo File	276
Dedeaux, Rod	Transcendental Graphics	277
Deer, Rob	Topps	277
DeJesus, Ivan	Transcendental Graphics	278
Delahanty, Ed	Transcendental Graphics	278
Delahanty, Jim	Transcendental Graphics	279
Delgado, Carlos	Major League Baseball	279
Demaree, Al	Transcendental Graphics	279
Demaree, Frank	Transcendental Graphics	280
Demeter, Don	Transcendental Graphics	280
DeMontreville, Gene	Transcendental Graphics	280
DeMoss, Bingo	Transcendental Graphics	281
Dempsey, Rick	Transcendental Graphics	281
Denny, Jerry	Transcendental Graphics	281
Denny, John	Transcendental Graphics	282
Dent, Bucky	Transcendental Graphics	282
Dernier, Bob	Transcendental Graphics	283
Derringer, Paul	Transcendental Graphics	283
DeShields, Delino	Major League Baseball	284
Devereux, Mike	Photo File	284
Devlin, Art	Transcendental Graphics	284
Devlin, Jim	National Baseball Library Library, Cooperstown, NY	285
Devore, Josh	Transcendental Graphics	285
Dials, Lou	Transcendental Graphics	285
Diaz, Bo	Transcendental Graphics	286
Dibble, Rob	Photo File	286
Dickey, Bill	Transcendental Graphics	286
Dickson, Murry	Transcendental Graphics	287
Dierker, Larry	Major League Baseball	288
Dihigo, Martin	Transcendental Graphics	289
DiMaggio, Dom	Transcendental Graphics	289
DiMaggio, Joe	Transcendental Graphics	290
DiMaggio, Vince	Transcendental Graphics	291
Dinneen, Bill	Transcendental Graphics	292
Doak, Bill	Transcendental Graphics	292
Dobson, Joe	Transcendental Graphics	293
Dobson, Pat	Transcendental Graphics	293
Doby, Larry	Transcendental Graphics	293
Doerr, Bobby	Transcendental Graphics	294
Donahue, Red	Transcendental Graphics	294
Donaldson, John	Transcendental Graphics	295
Donlin, Mike	Transcendental Graphics	295
Donohue, Pete	Transcendental Graphics	296
Donovan, Bill	Transcendental Graphics	297
Donovan, Dick	Transcendental Graphics	297
Donovan, Patsy	Transcendental Graphics	298
Dooin, Red	Transcendental Graphics	298
Doolan, Mickey	Transcendental Graphics	298
Doran, Bill	Photo File	299
Dotson, Richard	Transcendental Graphics	299
Doubleday, Abner	Transcendental Graphics	300
Dougherty, Patsy	Transcendental Graphics	301
Douglas, Phil	Transcendental Graphics	301
Douthit, Taylor	Transcendental Graphics	302
Dowd, Tommy	Transcendental Graphics	303
Downing, Al	Transcendental Graphics	303
Downing, Brian	Transcendental Graphics	304
Doyle, Jack	Transcendental Graphics	304
Doyle, Larry	Transcendental Graphics	305
Drabek, Doug	Photo File	305
Drabowsky, Moe	Transcendental Graphics	305
Dravecky, Dave	Transcendental Graphics	306

Name	Source	page
Dressen, Chuck	Transcendental Graphics	307
Drew, J.D.	Major League Baseball	308
Dreyfuss, Barney	Transcendental Graphics	308
Driessen, Dan	Transcendental Graphics	309
Dropo, Walt	Transcendental Graphics	309
Drysdale, Don	Transcendental Graphics	310
Duffy, Hugh	Transcendental Graphics	311
Dugan, Joe	Transcendental Graphics	312
Duncan, Dave	Transcendental Graphics	312
Dunlap, Fred	Transcendental Graphics	313
Dunn, Jack	Transcendental Graphics	313
Dunston, Shawon	Major League Baseball	314
Duren, Ryne	Transcendental Graphics	315
Durham, Leon	Transcendental Graphics	316
Durocher, Leo	Transcendental Graphics	316
Dwyer, Frank	Transcendental Graphics	319
Dwyer, Jim	Transcendental Graphics	320
Dyer, Eddie	Transcendental Graphics	320
Dykes, Jimmie	Transcendental Graphics	320
Dykstra, Lenny	Transcendental Graphics	321
Earnshaw, George	Transcendental Graphics	323
Easler, Mike	Transcendental Graphics	323
Easter, Luke	Transcendental Graphics	323
Eastwick, Rawly	Transcendental Graphics	324
Ebbets, Charles	Transcendental Graphics	324
Eckersley, Dennis	Photo File	325
Eckert, William	Transcendental Graphics	326
Eckhardt, Ox	Transcendental Graphics	327
Edmonds, Jim	Major League Baseball	327
Edwards, Johnny	Transcendental Graphics	327
Egan, Wish	National Baseball Library Library, Cooperstown, NY	328
Ehmke, Howard	Photo File	328
Eichhorn, Mark	Photo File	329
Eisenreich, Jim	Photo File	329
Elberfeld, Kid	Transcendental Graphics	329
Elliott, Bob	Transcendental Graphics	330
Ellis, Dock	Transcendental Graphics	330
Ellsworth, Dick	Transcendental Graphics	331
Emslie, Bob	Transcendental Graphics	332
Engel, Joe	Transcendental Graphics	332
Engle, Clyde	Transcendental Graphics	332
English, Woody	Transcendental Graphics	333
Ennis, Del	Transcendental Graphics	333
Epstein, Mike	Photo File	333
Erickson, Scott	Major League Baseball	334
Erskine, Carl	Transcendental Graphics	334
Esasky, Nick	Photo File	335
Essegian, Chuck	Photo File	335
Etchebarren, Andy	Transcendental Graphics	335
Etten, Nick	Transcendental Graphics	336
Evans, Billy	Transcendental Graphics	336
Evans, Darrell	Photo File	337
Evans, Dwight	Transcendental Graphics	337
Evers, Hoot	Transcendental Graphics	338
Evers, Johnny	Transcendental Graphics	338
Ewing, Buck	Transcendental Graphics	339
Faber, Red	Transcendental Graphics	341
Face, Roy	Transcendental Graphics	341
Fain, Ferris	Transcendental Graphics	342
Fairly, Ron	Transcendental Graphics	342
Falk, Bibb	Transcendental Graphics	342
Falkenberg, Cy	Transcendental Graphics	343
Farrell, Duke	Transcendental Graphics	343
Fassero, Jeff	Major League Baseball	343
Faust, Charlie	Transcendental Graphics	344
Feeney, Chub	Transcendental Graphics	345
Fehr, Donald	USA Today Baseball Weekly	345
Feller, Bob	Transcendental Graphics	346
Felsch, Happy	Transcendental Graphics	348
Ferguson, Bob	Transcendental Graphics	349
Ferguson, Charlie	Transcendental Graphics,	349
Ferguson, Joe	Transcendental Graphics	350
Fernandez, Alex	Major League Baseball	350
Fernandez, Sid	Transcendental Graphics	350
Fernandez, Tony	Major League Baseball	351
Ferrell, Rick	Transcendental Graphics	352
Ferrell, Wes	Transcendental Graphics	352
Ferriss, Dave	National Baseball Hall of Fame Library, Cooperstown, NY	353
Fetzer, John	Transcendental Graphics	354
Fidrych, Mark	Transcendental Graphics	354
Fielder, Cecil	Major League Baseball	355
Figeuroa, Ed	Transcendental Graphics	355
Fingers, Rollie	Transcendental Graphics	355
Finley, Charlie	Transcendental Graphics	356
Finley, Chuck	Major League Baseball	357
Finley, Steve	Major League Baseball	358

Name	Source	page
Finney, Lou	Transcendental Graphics	358
Fisher, Eddie	Transcendental Graphics	358
Fisher, Jack	Transcendental Graphics	359
Fisher, Ray	Transcendental Graphics	359
Fisk, Carlton	Transcendental Graphics	359
Fitzsimmons, Freddie	Transcendental Graphics	360
Flack, Max	Transcendental Graphics	361
Flanagan, Mike	Photo File	361
Fletcher, Art	Transcendental Graphics	362
Fletcher, Scott	Photo File	362
Flick, Elmer	Transcendental Graphics	362
Flint, Silver	Transcendental Graphics	364
Flood, Curt	Transcendental Graphics	364
Foli, Tim	Transcendental Graphics	366
Fonseca, Lew	Transcendental Graphics	366
Force, Davy	Transcendental Graphics	367
Ford, Dan	Transcendental Graphics	368
Ford, Hod	Photo File	368
Ford, Whitey	Transcendental Graphics	369
Forsch, Bob	Transcendental Graphics	370
Forsch, Ken	Transcendental Graphics	370
Forster, Terry	Transcendental Graphics	370
Fossas, Tony	Major League Baseball	371
Fosse, Ray	Transcendental Graphics	371
Foster, Bill	Photo File	371
Foster, George	Transcendental Graphics	372
Foster, Rube	Transcendental Graphics	373
Fothergill, Fatty	Photo File	374
Fournier, Jack	Transcendental Graphics	374
Foutz, Dave	Transcendental Graphics	375
Fowler, Bud	Transcendental Graphics	375
Fox, Nellie	Transcendental Graphics	376
Fox, Pete	Transcendental Graphics	376
Foxx, Jimmie	Transcendental Graphics	376
Franco, John	Major League Baseball	378
Franco, Julio	Major League Baseball	379
Francona, Tito	Transcendental Graphics	379
Frankhouse, Fred	Transcendental Graphics	379
Fraser, Chick	Transcendental Graphics	380
Frazee, Harry	Transcendental Graphics	380
Freehan, Bill	Transcendental Graphics	382
Freeman, Buck	Transcendental Graphics	381
Fregosi, Jim	Transcendental Graphics	382
French, Larry	Transcendental Graphics	382
Frey, Lonny	Transcendental Graphics	383
Frick, Ford	Transcendental Graphics	383
Friend, Bob	Transcendental Graphics	384
Frisch, Frank	Transcendental Graphics	384
Fryman, Travis	Major League Baseball	385
Fryman, Woodie	Transcendental Graphics	386
Fullerton, Hugh	Transcendental Graphics	386
Furillo, Carl	Transcendental Graphics	386
Gaedel, Eddie	Transcendental Graphics	389
Gaetti, Gary	Major League Baseball	389
Gagne, Greg	Photo File	390
Galan, Augie	Transcendental Graphics	390
Galarraga, Andres	Major League Baseball	390
Galehouse, Denny	Transcendental Graphics	391
Galvin, Pud	Transcendental Graphics	391
Gamble, Oscar	Transcendental Graphics	392
Gandil, Chick	Transcendental Graphics	392
Gant, Ron	Major League Baseball	393
Gantner, Jim	Transcendental Graphics	394
Garagiola, Joe	Transcendental Graphics	394
Garber, Gene	Photo File	395
Garcia, Mike	Transcendental Graphics	395
Garciaparra, Nomar	Major League Baseball	396
Gardella, Danny	Transcendental Graphics	397
Gardner, Larry	Transcendental Graphics	397
Garms, Debs	Transcendental Graphics	398
Garner, Phil	Transcendental Graphics	398
Garr, Ralph	Transcendental Graphics	399
Garrett, Wayne	Transcendental Graphics	399
Garver, Ned	Transcendental Graphics	400
Garvey, Steve	Photo File	400
Gaston, Cito	Topps	401
Gedman, Rich	Photo File	402
Gehrig, Lou	Transcendental Graphics	402
Gehringer, Charlie	Transcendental Graphics	404
Gentile, Jim	Transcendental Graphics	405
Gerhardt, Joe	Transcendental Graphics	406
Geronimo, Cesar	Photo File	406
Getzien, Charlie	Transcendental Graphics	406
Giamatti, Bart	Transcendental Graphics	407
Gibson, Bob	Transcendental Graphics	408
Gibson, Josh	Transcendental Graphics	410
Gibson, Kirk	Photo File	411
Giles, Warren	Transcendental Graphics	412

Name	Source	page
Gilkey, Bernard	Major League Baseball	412
Gilliam, Junior	Photo File	413
Gilmore, Fighting Jim	Transcendental Graphics	414
Gionfriddo, Al	Transcendental Graphics	414
Giusti, Dave	Transcendental Graphics	415
Gladden, Dan	Photo File	415
Glasscock, Jack	Transcendental Graphics	416
Glavine, Tom	Major League Baseball	416
Gleason, Kid	Transcendental Graphics	417
Goltz, Dave	Transcendental Graphics	418
Gomez, Lefty	Transcendental Graphics	418
Gonzalez, Juan	Major League Baseball	419
Gooden, Dwight	Major League Baseball	419
Goodman, Billy	Transcendental Graphics	420
Goodman, Ival	Transcendental Graphics	421
Gordon, Joe	Transcendental Graphics	421
Gordon, Sid	Transcendental Graphics	422
Gordon, Tom	Major League Baseball	423
Gore, George	Transcendental Graphics	423
Goslin, Goose	Transcendental Graphics	424
Gossage, Rich	Photo File	425
Gowdy, Curt	Transcendental Graphics	425
Gowdy, Hank	Transcendental Graphics	426
Grace, Mark	Transcendental Graphics	427
Graney, Jack	Transcendental Graphics	427
Grant, Charles	Transcendental Graphics	428
Grant, Eddie	Transcendental Graphics	428
Grant, Frank	Transcendental Graphics	429
Grant, Mudcat	Transcendental Graphics	429
Grantham, George	Transcendental Graphics	430
Gray, Pete	Transcendental Graphics	430
Green, Dallas	Transcendental Graphics	431
Green, Dick	Transcendental Graphics	431
Greenberg, Hank	Transcendental Graphics	432
Greenlee, Gus	Transcendental Graphics	434
Greenwell, Mike	Photo File	435
Greer, Rusty	Major League Baseball	435
Grich, Bobby	Photo File	435
Griffey, Ken Jr.	Major League Baseball	436
Griffey, Ken Sr.	Transcendental Graphics	437
Griffin, Mike	Transcendental Graphics	438
Griffith, Clark	Transcendental Graphics	438
Grimes, Burleigh	Transcendental Graphics	440
Grimm, Charlie	Transcendental Graphics	441
Grimsley, Ross	Transcendental Graphics	442
Grissom, Marquis	Major League Baseball	442
Groat, Dick	Transcendental Graphics	443
Groh, Heinie	Transcendental Graphics	444
Gromek, Steve	Transcendental Graphics	444
Gross, Kevin	Photo File	445
Grote, Jerry	Transcendental Graphics	445
Grove, Lefty	Transcendental Graphics	445
Gruber, Kelly	Photo File	447
Gubicza, Mark	Photo File	447
Guerrero, Pedro	Transcendental Graphics	448
Guerrero, Vladimir	Major League Baseball	448
Guidry, Ron	Transcendental Graphics	449
Guillen, Ozzie	Major League Baseball	450
Gullett, Don	Transcendental Graphics	450
Gullickson, Bill	Photo File	451
Gumbert, Harry	Transcendental Graphics	451
Gura, Larry	Transcendental Graphics	452
Gustafson, Cliff	University of Texas	452
Gwynn, Tony	Major League Baseball	452
Haas, Mule	Transcendental Graphics	455
Hack, Stan	Transcendental Graphics	455
Haddix, Harvey	Transcendental Graphics	456
Hadley, Bump	Transcendental Graphics	457
Hafey, Chick	Transcendental Graphics	458
Hahn, Noodles	Transcendental Graphics	459
Haines, Jesse	Transcendental Graphics	460
Hairston, Jerry	Transcendental Graphics	461
Hall, Dick	Transcendental Graphics	461
Hallahan, Bill	Transcendental Graphics	461
Haller, Tom	Transcendental Graphics	462
Hamilton, Billy	Transcendental Graphics	462
Hamilton, Milo	Photo File	463
Hamilton, Steve	Transcendental Graphics	463
Hamner, Granny	Transcendental Graphics	463
Haney, Fred	Transcendental Graphics	464
Hanlon, Ned	Transcendental Graphics	464
Hansen, Ron	Transcendental Graphics	466
Harder, Mel	Transcendental Graphics	466
Hardy, Carroll	Transcendental Graphics	467
Hargrave, Bubbles	Transcendental Graphics	467
Hargrove, Mike	Transcendental Graphics	468
Harnisch, Pete	Major League Baseball	468
Harper, Tommy	Transcendental Graphics	469
Harrah, Toby	Transcendental Graphics	469
Harrelson, Bud	Transcendental Graphics	470
Harrelson, Ken	Transcendental Graphics	471
Harridge, Will	Transcendental Graphics	471
Harris, Bucky	Transcendental Graphics	472
Harris, Greg A.	Transcendental Graphics	473
Hart, Jim Ray	Transcendental Graphics	473
Hartnett, Gabby	Transcendental Graphics	474
Hartung, Clint	Transcendental Graphics	475
Harvey, Bryan	Photo File	476
Harvey, Doug	National Baseball Hall of Fame Library, Cooperstown NY	476
Harwell, Ernie	Transcendental Graphics	476
Hassey, Ron	Transcendental Graphics	477
Hatcher, Billy	Major League Baseball	478
Hatcher, Mickey	Transcendental Graphics	478
Hauser, Joe	Transcendental Graphics	479
Hawley, Pink	Transcendental Graphics	479
Hayes, Charlie	Major League Baseball	479
Hayes, Von	Transcendental Graphics	480
Hazle, Hurricane	Transcendental Graphics	480
Heath, Jeff	Transcendental Graphics	480
Heathcote, Cliff	Photo File	481
Hebner, Richie	Transcendental Graphics	481
Hecker, Guy	Transcendental Graphics	481
Hegan, Jim	Transcendental Graphics	482
Heilmann, Harry	Transcendental Graphics	482
Held, Woodie	Transcendental Graphics	484
Helmsley, Rollie	Transcendental Graphics	484
Henderson, Dave	Photo File	484
Henderson, Ken	Transcendental Graphics	485
Henderson, Rickey	Transcendental Graphics	485
Henderson, Steve	Transcendental Graphics	486
Hendrick, George	Transcendental Graphics	486
Hendrix, Claude	Photo File	487
Henke, Tom	Photo File	487
Henrich, Tommy	Transcendental Graphics	488
Henry, Bill	Transcendental Graphics	488
Hentgen, Pat	Major League Baseball	489
Herman, Babe	Transcendental Graphics	489
Herman, Billy	Transcendental Graphics	490
Hernandez, Keith	Transcendental Graphics	491
Hernandez, Livian	Major League Baseball	493
Hernandez, Orlando	Transcendental Graphics	493
Hernandez, Roberto	Major League Baseball	493
Hernandez, Willie	Photo File	494
Herndon, Larry	Transcendental Graphics	495
Herr, Tom	Transcendental Graphics	495
Herrmann, Garry	Transcendental Graphics	496
Hershiser, Orel	Transcendental Graphics	496
Herzog, Buck	Transcendental Graphics	497
Herzog, Whitey	Transcendental Graphics	498
Heydler, John	Transcendental Graphics	499
Hickman, Jim	Transcendental Graphics	499
Higbe, Kirby	Transcendental Graphics	500
Higgins, Pinky	Transcendental Graphics	500
Higham, Dick	Transcendental Graphics	500
Hill, Pete	Transcendental Graphics	501
Hiller, John	Transcendental Graphics	501
Hines, Paul	Transcendental Graphics	501
Hisle, Larry	Transcendental Graphics	502
Hoak, Don	Transcendental Graphics	502
Hobson, Butch	Transcendental Graphics	503
Hodges, Gil	Transcendental Graphics	503
Hodges, Russ	Transcendental Graphics	504
Hoerner, Joe	Transcendental Graphics	505
Hoffman, Trevor	Major League Baseball	505
Hofheinz, Roy	Transcendental Graphics	505
Holke, Walter	Transcendental Graphics	506
Holland, Al	Photo File	506
Hollins, Dave	Major League Baseball	507
Hollocher, Charlie	Transcendental Graphics	507
Holmes, Ducky	Transcendental Graphics	507
Holmes, Tommy	Transcendental Graphics	508
Holtzman, Jerome	Jerome Holtzman	509
Holtzman, Ken	Transcendental Graphics	509
Honeycutt, Rick	Photo File	510
Hooper, Harry	Transcendental Graphics	511
Hooton, Burt	Transcendental Graphics	512
Hopp, Johnny	Transcendental Graphics	513
Horlen, Joel	Transcendental Graphics	513
Horner, Bob	Transcendental Graphics	514
Hornsby, Rogers	Transcendental Graphics	515
Hornung, Joe	Transcendental Graphics	517
Horton, Willie	Transcendental Graphics	517
Hotaling, Pete	Transcendental Graphics	518
Hough, Charlie	Transcendental Graphics	518
Houk, Ralph	Transcendental Graphics	519

Name	Source	page
Howard, Elston	Transcendental Graphics	520
Howard, Frank	Transcendental Graphics	521
Howe, Art	Major League Baseball	521
Howe, Steve	Transcendental Graphics	522
Howell, Harry	Transcendental Graphics	522
Howell, Jay	Photo File	522
Howser, Dick	Transcendental Graphics	523
Hoy, Dummy	Transcendental Graphics	524
Hoyt, LaMarr	Transcendental Graphics	524
Hoyt, Waite	Transcendental Graphics	525
Hrabosky, Al	Transcendental Graphics	526
Hrbek, Kent	Transcendental Graphics	526
Hriniak, Walt	Transcendental Graphics	527
Hubbard, Cal	Transcendental Graphics	528
Hubbard, Glenn	Transcendental Graphics	528
Hubbell, Carl	Transcendental Graphics	529
Hubbs, Ken	Transcendental Graphics	530
Hudlin, Willis	Transcendental Graphics	530
Huggins, Miller	Transcendental Graphics	531
Hughes, Long Tom	Transcendental Graphics	533
Hughson, Tex	Transcendental Graphics	533
Hulbert, William	Transcendental Graphics	533
Hundley, Randy	Transcendental Graphics	535
Hundley, Todd	Major League Baseball	536
Hunt, Ron	Transcendental Graphics	537
Hunter, Catfish	Transcendental Graphics	538
Hurst, Bruce	Photo File	539
Hutchinson, Fred	Transcendental Graphics	540
Hutchison, Bill	National Baseball Hall of Fame Library, Cooperstown NY	542
Incaviglia, Pete	Major League Baseball	543
Iorg, Garth	Photo File	543
Irvin, Monte	Transcendental Graphics	543
Isbell, Frank	Transcendental Graphics	544
Ivie, Mike	Photo File	545
Jackson, Bo	Transcendental Graphics	547
Jackson, Grant	Transcendental Graphics	547
Jackson, Joe	Transcendental Graphics	547
Jackson, Larry	Transcendental Graphics	549
Jackson, Mike	Major League Baseball	549
Jackson, Randy	Transcendental Graphics	549
Jackson, Reggie	Transcendental Graphics	550
Jackson, Travis	Transcendental Graphics	552
Jacobson, Baby Doll	Transcendental Graphics	552
Jacoby, Brook	Photo File	553
James, Seattle Bill	Transcendental Graphics	553
Janowicz, Vic	Transcendental Graphics	553
Jansen, Larry	Transcendental Graphics	554
Javier, Julian	Transcendental Graphics	554
Javier, Stan	Major League Baseball	554
Jay, Joey	Transcendental Graphics	554
Jeffcoat, Hal	Transcendental Graphics	555
Jefferies, Gregg	Major League Baseball	556
Jenkins, Fergie	Transcendental Graphics	556
Jennings, Hughie	Transcendental Graphics	557
Jensen, Jackie	Transcendental Graphics	559
Jethroe, Sam	Transcendental Graphics	559
Jeter, Derek	Major League Baseball	560
John, Tommy	Transcendental Graphics	560
Johnson, Alex	Transcendental Graphics	561
Johnson, Ban	Transcendental Graphics	562
Johnson, Bob	Transcendental Graphics	563
Johnson, Charles	Major League Baseball	564
Johnson, Cliff	Transcendental Graphics	564
Johnson, Darrell	Transcendental Graphics	564
Johnson, Davey	Major League Baseball	565
Johnson, Deron	Transcendental Graphics	566
Johnson, Howard	Transcendental Graphics	566
Johnson, Judy	National Baseball Hall of Fame Library, Cooperstown NY	567
Johnson, Lance	Major League Baseball	568
Johnson, Lou	Transcendental Graphics	568
Johnson, Randy	Major League Baseball	568
Johnson, Walter	Transcendental Graphics	569
Johnston, Jimmy	Photo File	571
Johnstone, Jay	Transcendental Graphics	571
Jones, Charley	Transcendental Graphics	571
Jones, Chipper	Major League Baseball	571
Jones, Cleon	Transcendental Graphics	572
Jones, Davy	Transcendental Graphics	572
Jones, Doug	Major League Baseball	573
Jones, Fielder	Transcendental Graphics	573
Jones, Mack	Transcendental Graphics	574
Jones, Nippy	Photo File	574
Jones, Randy	Transcendental Graphics	574
Jones, Ruppert	Photo File	575
Jones, Sad Sam	Transcendental Graphics	575
Jones, Willie	Transcendental Graphics	576

Name	Source	page
Joost, Eddie	Transcendental Graphics	576
Jordan, Brian	Major League Baseball	577
Joss, Addie	Transcendental Graphics	577
Joyce, Bill	Transcendental Graphics	578
Joyner, Wally	Transcendental Graphics	579
Judge, Joe	Transcendental Graphics	579
Jurges, Billy	Transcendental Graphics	579
Justice, David	Major League Baseball	580
Kaat, Jim	Transcendental Graphics	583
Kaline, Al	Transcendental Graphics	583
Kamm, Willie	Transcendental Graphics	585
Karros, Eric	Major League Baseball	585
Kauff, Benny	Transcendental Graphics	586
Kauffmann, Ewing	National Baseball Hall of Fame Library, Cooperstown NY	586
Keane, Johnny	Transcendental Graphics	587
Keefe, Tim	Transcendental Graphics	587
Keeler, Willie	Transcendental Graphics	588
Kell, George	Transcendental Graphics	590
Keller, Charlie	Transcendental Graphics	591
Kelley, Joe	Transcendental Graphics	592
Kellner, Alex	Transcendental Graphics	594
Kelly, George	Transcendental Graphics	594
Kelly, King	Transcendental Graphics	595
Kelly, Pat	Transcendental Graphics	597
Kelly, Tom	Major League Baseball	598
Keltner, Ken	Transcendental Graphics	598
Kemp, Steve	Transcendental Graphics	599
Kendall, Jason	Major League Baseball	599
Kennedy, Bob	Transcendental Graphics	600
Kennedy, Brickyard	Transcendental Graphics	600
Kennedy, Terry	Photo File	600
Kent, Jeff	Major League Baseball	601
Kern, Jim	Transcendental Graphics	601
Kerr, Buddy	Transcendental Graphics	602
Kerr, Dickie	Transcendental Graphics	602
Kessinger, Don	Transcendental Graphics	603
Key, Jimmy	Photo File	603
Killebrew, Harmon	Transcendental Graphics	604
Killefer, Bill	Transcendental Graphics	605
Killen, Frank	Transcendental Graphics	606
Killian, Ed	Transcendental Graphics	606
Kilroy, Matt	Transcendental Graphics	606
Kinder, Ellis	Transcendental Graphics	607
Kiner, Ralph	Transcendental Graphics	607
King, Jeff	Major League Baseball	609
King, Silver	Transcendental Graphics	609
Kingman, Dave	Transcendental Graphics	609
Kirke, Jay	Transcendental Graphics	610
Kison, Bruce	Transcendental Graphics	610
Kitson, Frank	Transcendental Graphics	611
Kittle, Ron	Transcendental Graphics	611
Klein, Chuck	Transcendental Graphics	612
Klem, Bill	Transcendental Graphics	613
Klesko, Ryan	Major League Baseball	614
Kline, Ron	Transcendental Graphics	614
Kling, Johnny	Transcendental Graphics	615
Kluszewski, Ted	Transcendental Graphics	615
Knepper, Bob	Photo File	616
Knight, Ray	Transcendental Graphics	616
Knoblauch, Chuck	Major League Baseball	617
Knoop, Bobby	Transcendental Graphics	617
Knowles, Darold	Photo File	618
Koenig, Mark	Transcendental Graphics	618
Konetchy, Ed	Transcendental Graphics	619
Konstanty, Jim	Transcendental Graphics	619
Koosman, Jerry	Transcendental Graphics	620
Koufax, Sandy	Transcendental Graphics	620
Kranepool, Ed	Transcendental Graphics	623
Krausse, Lew	Transcendental Graphics	623
Kreevich, Mike	Transcendental Graphics	624
Kremer, Ray	Photo File	624
Kress, Red	Transcendental Graphics	624
Kroc, Ray	Transcendental Graphics	625
Kruk, John	Photo File	625
Krukow, Mike	Photo File	626
Kubek, Tony	Transcendental Graphics	626
Kuenn, Harvey	Transcendental Graphics	627
Kuhel, Joe	Transcendental Graphics	627
Kuhn, Bowie	Transcendental Graphics	628
Labine, Clem	Transcendental Graphics	631
Lacy, Lee	Transcendental Graphics	631
Lajoie, Napoleon	Transcendental Graphics	632
Lamp, Dennis	Transcendental Graphics	634
Landis, Jim	Transcendental Graphics	634
Landis, Kenesaw Mountain	Transcendental Graphics	635
Lane, Frank	Transcendental Graphics	637

Name	Source	page
Lange, Bill	Transcendental Graphics	637
Langford, Rick	Photo File	638
Langston, Mark	Major League Baseball	638
Lanier, Hal	Transcendental Graphics	639
Lanier, Max	Transcendental Graphics	639
Lankford, Ray	Major League Baseball	640
Lansford, Carney	Photo File	640
LaPorte, Frank	Transcendental Graphics	640
Lardner, Ring	Transcendental Graphics	641
Larkin, Barry	Major League Baseball	641
Larkin, Gene	Photo File	642
Larkin, Henry	Transcendental Graphics	642
Larkin, Terry	Transcendental Graphics	642
Larsen, Don	Transcendental Graphics	643
La Russa, Tony	Transcendental Graphics	643
Lary, Frank	Transcendental Graphics	645
Lary, Lyn	Transcendental Graphics	645
Lasorda, Tommy	Transcendental Graphics	646
Latham, Arlie	Transcendental Graphics	647
Lau, Charlie	Transcendental Graphics	647
Lavaetto, Cookie	Transcendental Graphics	648
Lavelle, Gary	Photo File	649
Law, Vern	Transcendental Graphics	649
Lazzeri, Tony	Transcendental Graphics	650
Leach, Tommy	Transcendental Graphics	651
Lee, Big Bill	Transcendental Graphics	652
Lee, Bill	Transcendental Graphics	653
Lee, Thornton	Transcendental Graphics	654
Leever, Sam	Transcendental Graphics	654
LeFlore, Ron	Transcendental Graphics	655
Leibrandt, Charlie	Topps	655
Leifield, Lefty	Transcendental Graphics	656
Leiter, Al	Major League Baseball	656
Leland, Frank	Transcendental Graphics	657
Lemon, Bob	Transcendental Graphics	657
Lemon, Chet	Transcendental Graphics	658
Lemon, Jim	Transcendental Graphics	659
Leonard, Buck	Transcendental Graphics	659
Leonard, Dennis	Transcendental Graphics	660
Leonard, Dutch (Emil)	Transcendental Graphics	660
Leonard, Dutch (Hubert)	Transcendental Graphics	661
Leonard, Jeffrey	Transcendental Graphics	661
Lewis, Buddy	Transcendental Graphics	662
Lewis, Duffy	Transcendental Graphics	662
Leyland, Jim	Major League Baseball	662
Leyritz, Jim	Major League Baseball	664
Lezcano, Sixto	Transcendental Graphics	664
Linares, Omar	Transcendental Graphics	665
Lindblad, Paul	Photo File	665
Lindstrom, Freddie	Transcendental Graphics	665
Linz, Phil	Transcendental Graphics	667
Litwhiler, Danny	Transcendental Graphics	667
Lloyd, Pop	Transcendental Graphics	667
Lobert, Hans	Transcendental Graphics	668
Lofton, Kenny	Major League Baseball	668
Logan, Johnny	Transcendental Graphics	669
Lolich, Mickey	Transcendental Graphics	670
Lollar, Sherm	Transcendental Graphics	671
Lombardi, Ernie	Transcendental Graphics	671
Lonborg, Jim	Transcendental Graphics	672
Long, Dale	Transcendental Graphics	673
Long, Herman	Transcendental Graphics	674
Lopat, Eddie	Transcendental Graphics	675
Lopes, Davey	Transcendental Graphics	676
Lopez, Al	Transcendental Graphics	677
Lopez, Aurelio	National Baseball Hall of Fame Library, Cooperstown NY	678
Lopez, Hector	Transcendental Graphics	679
Lopez, Javy	Major League Baseball	679
Lowe, Bobby	Transcendental Graphics	679
Lowenstein, John	Photo File	680
Lowrey, Peanuts	Transcendental Graphics	681
Luby, John	Transcendental Graphics	681
Lucas, Red	Transcendental Graphics	681
Luciano, Ron	Photo File	682
Luderus, Fred	Transcendental Graphics	682
Lundy, Dick	Transcendental Graphics	683
Luque, Dolf	Transcendental Graphics	683
Luzinski, Greg	Transcendental Graphics	684
Lyle, Sparky	Transcendental Graphics	684
Lynch, Jerry	Transcendental Graphics	685
Lynn, Fred	Transcendental Graphics	686
Lyons, Denny	Transcendental Graphics	687
Lyons, Ted	Transcendental Graphics	688
MacFayden, Danny	Transcendental Graphics	691
Mack, Connie	Transcendental Graphics	691
Mackey, Biz	Transcendental Graphics	693
MacPhail, Larry	Transcendental Graphics	693

Name	Source	page
MacPhail, Lee	Transcendental Graphics	695
Maddox, Garry	Transcendental Graphics	695
Maddux, Greg	Major League Baseball	696
Madlock, Bill	Transcendental Graphics	696
Magadan, Dave	Major League Baseball	697
Magee, Sherry	Transcendental Graphics	698
Maglie, Sal	Transcendental Graphics	698
Mahler, Rick	Photo File	699
Majeski, Hank	Transcendental Graphics	700
Malarcher, Dave	Transcendental Graphics	700
Malone, Pat	Transcendental Graphics	700
Maloney, Jim	Transcendental Graphics	701
Malzone, Frankie	Transcendental Graphics	701
Mancuso, Gus	Transcendental Graphics	702
Mann, Les	Transcendental Graphics	702
Manning, Rick	Transcendental Graphics	703
Mantilla, Felix	Transcendental Graphics	703
Mantle, Mickey	Transcendental Graphics	703
Manush, Heinie	Transcendental Graphics	705
Maranville, Rabbit	Transcendental Graphics	707
Marberry, Firpo	Transcendental Graphics	708
Marchildon, Phil	Photo File	709
Marichal, Juan	Transcendental Graphics	709
Marion, Marty	Transcendental Graphics	710
Maris, Roger	Transcendental Graphics	711
Marquard, Rube	Transcendental Graphics	713
Marshall, Mike	Transcendental Graphics	714
Martin, Billy	Transcendental Graphics	715
Martin, Pepper	Transcendental Graphics	716
Martinez, Dennis	Photo File	717
Martinez, Edgar	Major League Baseball	718
Martinez, Pedro	Major League Baseball	718
Martinez, Ramon	Major League Baseball	719
Martinez, Tino	Major League Baseball	719
Martinez, Tippy	Photo File	720
Masi, Phil	Photo File	720
Mathews, Bobby	Transcendental Graphics	720
Mathews, Eddie	Transcendental Graphics	720
Mathewson, Christy	Transcendental Graphics	722
Matlack, Jon	Transcendental Graphics	724
Matthews, Gary	Transcendental Graphics	724
Mattingly, Don	Photo File	725
Mauch, Gene	Transcendental Graphics	726
Maxvill, Dal	Transcendental Graphics	726
May, Carlos	Transcendental Graphics	727
May, Dave	Transcendental Graphics	727
May, Lee	Transcendental Graphics	727
May, Milt	Transcendental Graphics	728
May, Rudy	Transcendental Graphics	729
Mayberry, John	Transcendental Graphics	729
Mays, Carl	Transcendental Graphics	730
Mays, Willie	Transcendental Graphics	731
Mazeroski, Bill	Transcendental Graphics	733
Mazzilli, Lee	Transcendental Graphics	734
McAleer, Jimmy	Transcendental Graphics	735
McAuliffe, Dick	Transcendental Graphics	735
McBride, Bake	Transcendental Graphics	736
McBride, Dick	Transcendental Graphics	736
McCarthy, Joe	Transcendental Graphics	736
McCarthy, Tommy	Transcendental Graphics	738
McCarver, Tim	Transcendental Graphics	738
McClure, Bob	Transcendental Graphics	739
McCormick, Frank	Transcendental Graphics	739
McCormick, Jim	Transcendental Graphics	740
McCormick, Mike	Transcendental Graphics	741
McCosky, Barney	Transcendental Graphics	741
McCovey, Willie	Transcendental Graphics	742
McDaniel, Lindy	Transcendental Graphics	743
McDermott, Mickey	Transcendental Graphics	744
McDougald, Gil	Transcendental Graphics	744
McDowell, Jack	Major League Baseball	745
McDowell, Roger	Transcendental Graphics	745
McDowell, Sam	Transcendental Graphics	746
McDuffie, Terris	Transcendental Graphics	747
McGann, Dan	Transcendental Graphics	748
McGee, Willie	Transcendental Graphics	748
McGinnity, Joe	Transcendental Graphics	749
McGlothlen, Lynn	Transcendental Graphics	750
McGowan, Bill	Transcendental Graphics	750
McGraw, John	Transcendental Graphics	751
McGraw, Tug	Transcendental Graphics	753
McGregor, Scott	Photo File	754
McGriff, Fred	Major League Baseball	754
McGuire, Deacon	Transcendental Graphics	755
McGwire, Mark	Major League Baseball	755
McInnis, Stuffy	Transcendental Graphics	757
McKean, Ed	Transcendental Graphics	757
McKechnie, Bill	Transcendental Graphics	758

Name	Source	page
Ruffing, Red	Transcendental Graphics	980
Runnels, Pete	Transcendental Graphics	981
Ruppert, Jacob	Transcendental Graphics	982
Russell, Bill	Transcendental Graphics	985
Rush, Bob	Transcendental Graphics	983
Rusie, Amos	Transcendental Graphics	983
Ruth, Babe	Transcendental Graphics	985
Ruthven, Dick	Transcendental Graphics	988
Ryan, Jimmy	Transcendental Graphics	989
Ryan, Nolan	Transcendental Graphics	989
Saberhagen, Bret	Transcendental Graphics	993
Sabo, Chris	Photo File	993
Sadecki, Ray	Transcendental Graphics	993
Sain, Johnny	Transcendental Graphics	994
Sallee, Slim	Transcendental Graphics	995
Salmon, Tim	Major League Baseball	996
Samuel, Juan	Transcendental Graphics	996
Sandberg, Ryne	Transcendental Graphics	996
Sanders, Deion	Photo File	997
Sanderson, Scott	Transcendental Graphics	998
Sanford, Jack	Transcendental Graphics	998
Sanguillen, Manny	Transcendental Graphics	999
Santiago, Benito	Major League Baseball	999
Santo, Ron	Transcendental Graphics	999
Sauer, Hank	Transcendental Graphics	1001
Sax, Steve	Transcendental Graphics	1001
Schacht, Al	Transcendental Graphics	1002
Schaefer, Germany	Transcendental Graphics	1002
Schalk, Ray	Transcendental Graphics	1003
Schang, Wally	Transcendental Graphics	1004
Schilling, Curt	Major League Baseball	1004
Schmidt, Mike	Transcendental Graphics	1005
Schoendienst, Red	Transcendental Graphics	1007
Schofield, Dick	Photo File	1007
Schott, Marge	National Baseball Hall of Fame Library, Cooperstown, NY	1008
Schreckengost, Ossee	Transcendental Graphics	1009
Schulte, Frank	Transcendental Graphics	1009
Schulte, Fred	Transcendental Graphics	1010
Schumacher, Hal	Transcendental Graphics	1010
Score, Herb	Transcendental Graphics	1011
Scott, Everett	Transcendental Graphics	1012
Scott, George	Photo File	1012
Scott, Jim	Transcendental Graphics	1013
Scott, Mike	Transcendental Graphics	1013
Scully, Vin	Transcendental Graphics	1014
Seaver, Tom	Transcendental Graphics	1014
Seerey, Pat	Transcendental Graphics	1016
Segui, David	Photo File	1016
Segui, Diego	Transcendental Graphics	1017
Seitz, Peter	Corbis	1017
Seitzer, Kevin	Photo File	1018
Selbach, Kip	Transcendental Graphics	1018
Selee, Frank	Transcendental Graphics	1018
Selig, Bud	Transcendental Graphics	1019
Selkirk, George	Transcendental Graphics	1020
Seminick, Andy	Transcendental Graphics	1021
Severeid, Hank	Transcendental Graphics	1022
Sewell, Joe	Transcendental Graphics	1022
Sewell, Luke	Transcendental Graphics	1023
Sewell, Rip	Transcendental Graphics	1023
Seymour, Cy	Transcendental Graphics	1024
Shaffer, Orator	Transcendental Graphics	1025
Shannon, Mike	Transcendental Graphics	1025
Shantz, Bobby	Transcendental Graphics	1026
Shaw, Bob	Transcendental Graphics	1026
Shawkey, Bob	Transcendental Graphics	1027
Shea, William	Transcendental Graphics	1028
Sheckard, Jimmy	Transcendental Graphics	1029
Sheely, Earl	Transcendental Graphics	1030
Sheffield, Gary	Major League Baseball	1030
Shepard, Bert	Transcendental Graphics	1030
Sheppard, Bob	National Baseball Hall of Fame Library, Cooperstown, NY	1031
Sherdell, Bill	Transcendental Graphics	1031
Sherry, Larry	Transcendental Graphics	1031
Shindle, Billy	Transcendental Graphics	1031
Shocker, Urban	Transcendental Graphics	1032
Shore, Ernie	Transcendental Graphics	1033
Short, Chris	Transcendental Graphics	1034
Shotton, Burt	Transcendental Graphics	1034
Show, Eric	Transcendental Graphics	1035
Siebern, Norm	Transcendental Graphics	1035
Siebert, Dick	Transcendental Graphics	1035
Sierra, Ruben	Photo File	1036
Sievers, Roy	Transcendental Graphics	1036
Simmons, Al	Transcendental Graphics	1037
Simmons, Curt	Transcendental Graphics	1039

Name	Source	page
Simmons, Ted	Transcendental Graphics	1040
Singer, Bill	Transcendental Graphics	1041
Singleton, Ken	Transcendental Graphics	1041
Sisler, Dick	Transcendental Graphics	1042
Sisler, George	Transcendental Graphics	1042
Sizemore, Ted	Photo File	1044
Skowron, Bill	Transcendental Graphics	1044
Slagle, Jimmy	National Baseball Hall of Fame Library, Cooperstown, NY	1045
Slaton, Jim	Transcendental Graphics	1045
Slaughter, Enos	Transcendental Graphics	1046
Smalley, Roy	Transcendental Graphics	1047
Smiley, John	Major League Baseball	1048
Smith, Al	Transcendental Graphics	1048
Smith, Dave	National Baseball Hall of Fame Library, Cooperstown, NY	1049
Smith, Elmer	Transcendental Graphics	1049
Smith, Frank	Transcendental Graphics	1049
Smith, Germany	Transcendental Graphics	1050
Smith, Lee	Transcendental Graphics	1050
Smith, Mayo	Transcendental Graphics	1051
Smith, Ozzie	Transcendental Graphics	1051
Smith, Red	Transcendental Graphics	1052
Smith, Reggie	Transcendental Graphics	1052
Smith, Sherry	Transcendental Graphics	1053
Smoltz, John	Major League Baseball	1054
Snider, Duke	Transcendental Graphics	1055
Snodgrass, Fred	Transcendental Graphics	1056
Snow, J.T.	Major League Baseball	1058
Soar, Hank	Transcendental Graphics	1058
Sockalexis, Chief	Transcendental Graphics	1058
Sosa, Sammy	Major League Baseball	1060
Soto, Mario	Transcendental Graphics	1060
Southworth, Billy	Transcendental Graphics	1061
Spahn, Warren	Transcendental Graphics	1061
Spalding, Albert	Transcendental Graphics	1063
Sparks, Tully	Transcendental Graphics	1065
Speaker, Tris	Transcendental Graphics	1065
Speier, Chris	Transcendental Graphics	1067
Spencer, Jim	Transcendental Graphics	1068
Spink, J.G. Taylor	National Baseball Hall of Fame Library, Cooperstown, NY	1068
Splittorff, Paul	Transcendental Graphics	1069
Spooner, Karl	Transcendental Graphics	1070
Stahl, Chick	Transcendental Graphics	1070
Stahl, Jake	Transcendental Graphics	1070
Staley, Gerry	Transcendental Graphics	1071
Staley, Harry	Transcendental Graphics	1071
Stallings, George	Transcendental Graphics	1071
Stanky, Eddie	Transcendental Graphics	1072
Stanley, Bob	Photo File	1073
Stanley, Mickey	Transcendental Graphics	1074
Stanley, Mike	Major League Baseball	1074
Stargell, Willie	Transcendental Graphics	1074
Start, Joe	Transcendental Graphics	1076
Statz, Jigger	Transcendental Graphics	1076
Staub, Rusty	Transcendental Graphics	1077
Stearnes, Turkey	Phil Dixon Collection	1078
Stearns, John	Photo File	1078
Steinbach, Terry	Major League Baseball	1079
Steinbrenner, George	Transcendental Graphics	1080
Steinfeldt, Harry	Transcendental Graphics	1080
Stengel, Casey	Transcendental Graphics	1080
Stennett, Rennie	Transcendental Graphics	1082
Stephens, Vern	Transcendental Graphics	1082
Stephenson, Riggs	Transcendental Graphics	1083
Stern, Bill	Transcendental Graphics	1084
Stevens, Harry M.	Transcendental Graphics	1085
Stewart, Bill	Transcendental Graphics	1085
Stewart, Dave	Transcendental Graphics	1086
Stieb, Dave	Transcendental Graphics	1087
Stirnweiss, Snuffy	Transcendental Graphics	1088
Stivetts, Jack	Transcendental Graphics	1089
Stock, Milt	Photo File	1089
Stone, George	Transcendental Graphics	1089
Stone, John	Transcendental Graphics	1090
Stone, Steve	Transcendental Graphics	1090
Stoneham, Horace	Transcendental Graphics	1090
Stoneman, Bill	Transcendental Graphics	1091
Stottlemyre, Mel	Transcendental Graphics	1091
Stottlemyre, Todd	Major League Baseball	1092
Stovall, George	Transcendental Graphics	1093
Stovey, George	Noir Tech Collectibles	1093
Stovey, Harry	Transcendental Graphics	1093
Strang, Sammy	Transcendental Graphics	1094
Stratton, Monty	Transcendental Graphics	1094
Strawberry, Darryl	Transcendental Graphics	1094
Street, Gabby	Transcendental Graphics	1095